...There's No Place Like The History Place

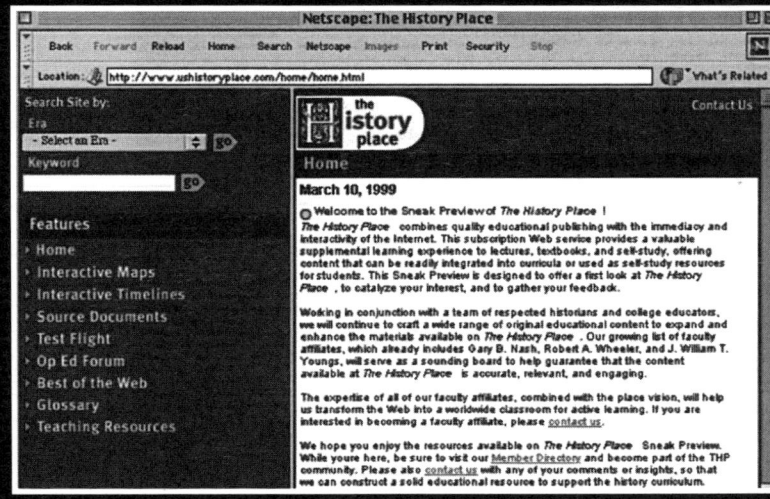

http://www.ushistoryplace.com

Welcome to The History Place, a new online resource for students and instructors of the United States History survey. The pedagogical mission of The History Place is to introduce the lessons of the past using the innovative technological tools of today. The History Place features a variety of learning tools and references designed to make study easier, more engaging, and more rewarding.

The History Place is developed by Peregrine Publishers in partnership with a growing number of historians and writers, including Gary Nash of UCLA, Saul Cornell of the Ohio State University, and John Nicols and Jim Mohr of the University of Oregon.

Congratulations!

With your purchase of *America and Its Peoples, Fourth Edition*, Addison Wesley Longman is pleased to provide you with a twelve-month subscription to The History Place, a unique Web resource for history students. At The History Place, you'll find a continually enriched learning resource that includes interactive maps, timelines, and other learning activities; a rich collection of source documents; the powerful TestFlight testing tool for self-assessment; and much more.

To explore this valuable teaching and learning resource:

1. Go to www.awl.com/martin
2. Click on The History Place login icon
3. Follow the instructions to register your subscription using the following access code:

WSMV-LEAPT-CREEL-TIGON-SUINT-PRIES

4. During the registration process, you will choose a personal user ID and password for use in logging into the site. Once your subscription is confirmed, you can begin using The History Place immediately.

Your pre-assigned access code can be used only once to establish your subscription, which is not transferable and is limited to twelve months from the date of activation. If you purchased a used textbook, this access code may have already been used. However, you can find information on how to purchase a subscription on The History Place registration page.

The History Place is a registered trademark of Pearson Education, Inc.

America
and Its Peoples

4TH EDITION

AMERICA
and Its Peoples

A Mosaic in the Making

James Kirby Martin
University of Houston

Randy Roberts
Purdue University

Steven Mintz
University of Houston

Linda O. McMurry
North Carolina State University

James H. Jones
University of Arkansas

Longman

New York   Boston   San Francisco
London   Toronto   Sydney   Tokyo   Singapore   Madrid
Mexico City   Munich   Paris   Cape Town   Hong Kong   Montreal

FOR OUR STUDENTS

Publisher: Priscilla McGeehon
Senior Acquisitions Editor: Jay O'Callaghan
Director of Development: Lisa Pinto
Development Manager: Betty Slack
Executive Marketing Manager: Sue Westmoreland
Supplements Editor: Jennifer Ackerman
Production Manager: Patti Brecht
Project Coordination, Text Design, and Electronic Page Makeup: Nesbitt Graphics, Inc.
Cover Designer/Manager: John Callahan
Cover Art: Collage by Michael Staats using the following images: Harriet Beecher Stowe, Harriet Beecher Stowe Center; Chief Joseph, Montana Historical Society; Mark Twain © Bettman/Corbis; Queen Liliuokalani © Corbis; Telegraph © Bettman/Corbis; Teddy Roosevelt © Fulton Getty/Liaison Agency; Steamboats © Hulton Getty/Liaison Agency; Abraham Lincoln, Library of Congress; Ulysses S. Grant, Library of Congress.
Maps: Mapping Specialists, Ltd.
Collage Art: Michael Staats
Photographer, Collage Art: Keith Tishken
Photo Researcher: Pearson Image Resource Center
Senior Print Buyer: Dennis J. Para
Printer and Binder: Quebecor World Taunton
Timeline Printer: Edison Lithographing and Printing Corp.
Cover Printer: The Lehigh Press, Inc.

For permission to use copyrighted material, grateful acknowledgment is made to the copyright holders on pages C-1–C-4, which are hereby made part of this copyright page.

Library of Congress Cataloging-in-Publication Data
America and its peoples : a mosaic in the making / James Kirby Martin ... [et al.].—4th ed.
    p. cm.
  Includes bibliographical references and index.
  ISBN 0-321-07985-X (v. 1)—ISBN 0-321-07984-1 (v.2)—ISBN 0-321-07910-8
  (single vol. edition)
    1. United States—History.   I. Martin, James Kirby

E178.1.A4886 2000
973—dc21   00-040122

Copyright © 2001 by James Kirby Martin, Randy Roberts, Steven Mintz, Linda O. McMurry, and James H. Jones

All rights reserved. No part of this book may be used or reproduced, stored in a retrieval system, or transmitted, in any form or by any means, electronic, mechanical, photocopying, recording, or otherwise, without the prior written permission of the publisher. Printed in the United States.

Please visit our website at http://www.awl.com/martin

ISBN 0-321-07910-8 (single volume)
ISBN 0-321-07985-X (volume 1)
ISBN 0-321-07984-1 (volume 2)

2345678910—QWT—030201

BRIEF *Contents*

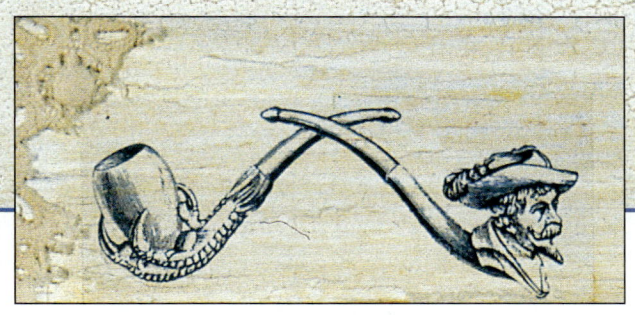

Detailed Contents vii
Maps xxi
Tables and Figures xxiii
Preface xxv
About the Authors xxxi

1 THE PEOPLING AND UNPEOPLING OF AMERICA 3
2 PLANTATIONS AND CITIES UPON A HILL, 1620–1700 35
3 PROVINCIAL AMERICA IN UPHEAVAL, 1660–1760 65
4 BREAKING THE BONDS OF EMPIRE, 1760–1775 99
5 THE TIMES THAT TRIED MANY SOULS, 1775–1783 127
6 SECURING THE REPUBLIC AND ITS IDEALS, 1776–1789 159
7 THE FORMATIVE DECADE, 1790–1800 189
8 THE JEFFERSONIANS IN POWER, 1800–1815 211
9 NATIONALISM, ECONOMIC GROWTH, AND THE ROOTS OF SECTIONAL CONFLICT 1815–1824 233
10 POWER AND POLITICS IN JACKSON'S AMERICA 257
11 AMERICA'S FIRST AGE OF REFORM 283
12 THE DIVIDED NORTH, THE DIVIDED SOUTH 319
13 CULTURES COLLIDE IN THE FAR WEST 353
14 THE HOUSE DIVIDED 383

15 A NATION SHATTERED BY CIVIL WAR, 1860–1865 409
16 THE NATION RECONSTRUCTED: NORTH, SOUTH, AND THE WEST, 1865–1877 445
17 EMERGENCE AS AN ECONOMIC POWER 479
18 THE RISE OF AN URBAN SOCIETY AND CITY PEOPLE 515
19 END-OF-THE-CENTURY CRISIS 549
20 IMPERIAL AMERICA, 1870–1900 579
21 THE PROGRESSIVE STRUGGLE, 1900–1917 605
22 THE UNITED STATES AND WORLD WAR I 639
23 MODERN TIMES, 1920–1929 671
24 THE AGE OF ROOSEVELT 699
25 THE END OF ISOLATION: AMERICA FACES THE WORLD, 1920–1945 727
26 WAGING PEACE AND WAR 763
27 IKE'S AMERICA 791
28 POWER SHIFTS: THE EMERGENCE OF THE SOUTH AND WEST 819
29 VIETNAM AND THE CRISIS OF AUTHORITY 845
30 THE STRUGGLE FOR A JUST SOCIETY 875
31 AMERICA IN OUR TIME 911

Appendix A-1
Glossary G-1
Credits C-1
Index I-1

DETAILED Contents

Maps xxi
Tables and Figures xxiii
Preface xxv
About the Authors xxxi

1 THE PEOPLING AND UNPEOPLING OF AMERICA 3
"A special instrument sent of God"

THE FIRST DISCOVERY OF AMERICA 5
A Diversity of Cultures • The Myth of the "Virgin" Land • Eastern Indians on the Eve of Contact

PREPARING EUROPE FOR WESTWARD EXPANSION 10
Changing Population Pressures • Crusades, Commerce, and the New Learning • Nation-States Support the First Explorations

EXPLORERS, CONQUERORS, AND THE MAKING OF NEW SPAIN 16
Conquistadores Overrun Native Americans • Constructing the Spanish Empire • Success Breeds Envy and Contempt

CHALLENGERS FOR NORTH AMERICA: FRANCE AND ENGLAND 20
The Protestant Reformation Stirs Deep Tensions • Defying the Supremacy of Spain • England Prepares for Westward Expansion

JOINING IN THE INVASION OF AMERICA 24
The Roanoke Disaster • Merchant Capitalists Sponsor the Founding of Virginia • Struggling Jamestown Survives • Dutch and French Adventurers

CONCLUSION 30

CHRONOLOGY OF KEY EVENTS 29
SUGGESTIONS FOR FURTHER READING 30
INTERNET RESOURCES 32
KEY TERMS 32
REVIEW QUESTIONS 33

THE AMERICAN MOSAIC:
Indian Scalping and European War Dogs 12

THE PEOPLE SPEAK:
Powhatan Pleads for Peace and Harmony (1609) 28

2 PLANTATIONS AND CITIES UPON A HILL, 1620–1700 35
"Slaves excepted"

FROM SETTLEMENTS TO SOCIETIES IN THE SOUTH 37
Searching for Laborers • To Be Like English Subjects at Home • Crushing Powhatan's Confederacy • A Model for Other Royal Colonies • Proprietary Maryland and the Carolinas

RELIGIOUS DISSENTERS COLONIZE NEW ENGLAND 42
The Rise of Puritan Dissenters at Home • Godly Mission to New England • Testing the Limits of Toleration • "Hivings Out" Provoke Bloody Indian Relations

FAMILIES, INDIVIDUALS, AND COMMUNITIES: SURVIVING IN EARLY AMERICA   49

Life and Death, North and South • Roles for Men, Women, and Children

COMMERCIAL VALUES AND THE RISE OF CHATTEL SLAVERY   55

Declension in New England • Stabilizing Life in the Chesapeake Region • The Beginnings of American Slavery • Shifting to Slavery in Maryland and Virginia • The World the Slaves Made

CONCLUSION   60
CHRONOLOGY OF KEY EVENTS   61
SUGGESTIONS FOR FURTHER READING   60
INTERNET RESOURCES   63
KEY TERMS   63
REVIEW QUESTIONS   63

THE AMERICAN MOSAIC:
Childbirth in Early America   52

THE PEOPLE SPEAK:
William Bradford's History of Plymouth Plantation   45

3 PROVINCIAL AMERICA IN UPHEAVAL, 1660–1760   65

"Stripped and scourged and run the gauntlet"

DESIGNING ENGLAND'S NORTH AMERICAN EMPIRE   67

To Benefit the Parent Nation • Seizing Dutch New Netherland • Proprietary Difficulties in New York and New Jersey • Planting William Penn's "Holy Experiment"

DEFYING THE IMPERIAL WILL: PROVINCIAL CONVULSIONS AND REBELLIONS   73

Bacon's Bloody Rebellion in Virginia • The Glorious Revolution Spills into America • New England's Witchcraft Hysteria • Settling Anglo-American Differences

MATURING COLONIAL SOCIETIES IN UNSETTLED TIMES   78

An Exploding Population Base • The "Europeanizing" of America • Intellectual and Religious Awakening • International Wars Beset America • Showdown: The Great War for the Empire • Allies as Enemies: Making War on the Cherokees

CONCLUSION   95
CHRONOLOGY OF KEY EVENTS   94
Suggestions for Further Reading   95
INTERNET RESOURCES   97
KEY TERMS   97
REVIEW QUESTIONS   97

THE AMERICAN MOSAIC:
Colonial Pastimes   84

THE PEOPLE SPEAK:
Olaudah Equiano on His Ship Passage as a Slave to America   80

4 BREAKING THE BONDS OF EMPIRE, 1760–1775   99

"Truly the man of the revolution"

PROVOKING AN IMPERIAL CRISIS   101

A Legacy of War-Related Problems • Getting Tough with the Americans • Parliament Endorses Direct Taxes

"LIBERTY, PROPERTY, AND NO STAMPS"   106

Emerging Patterns of Resistance • Protest Takes a Violent Turn • Resistance Spreads Across the Landscape • Parliament Retreats

A SECOND CRISIS: THE TOWNSHEND DUTIES   111

Formulating a New Taxation Scheme • Mustering Further American Resistance • A "Bloody Massacre" in Boston • Parliament Backs Down Again

THE RUPTURING OF IMPERIAL RELATIONS   117

The Necessity of Vigilance • The Tea Crisis of 1773 • Parliament Adopts the Coercive Acts • Hurling Back the Challenge: The First Continental Congress

CONCLUSION   123
CHRONOLOGY OF KEY EVENTS   122
SUGGESTIONS FOR FURTHER READING   123
INTERNET RESOURCES   125
KEY TERMS   125
REVIEW QUESTIONS   125

THE AMERICAN MOSAIC:
Those Hated Customs Informers   112

THE PEOPLE SPEAK:
Dr. Joseph Warren's Boston Massacre Oration (1772)   118

5 THE TIMES THAT TRIED MANY SOULS, 1775–1783   127
"Starve, dissolve, or disperse"

RECONCILIATION OR INDEPENDENCE   129
The Shooting War Starts • Moderates Versus Radicals in Congress • The Expanding Martial Conflict • Lord Dunmore's Proclamation of Emancipation • Resolving the Independence Question

WITHOUT VISIBLE ALLIES: THE WAR IN THE NORTH   140
Britain's Massive Military Buildup • The Campaign for New York • Saving the Cause at Trenton • The Real Continentals

RESCUING THE PATRIOTS: TOWARD GLOBAL CONFLICT   146
France Offers Covert Assistance • The British Seize Philadelphia • Capturing Burgoyne's Army at Saratoga

THE WORLD TURNED UPSIDE DOWN   149
Revamping British Strategy • The Tide of War Turns at Last • Franco-American Triumph at Yorktown • A Most Generous Peace Settlement

CONCLUSION   155
CHRONOLOGY OF KEY EVENTS   154
SUGGESTIONS FOR FURTHER READING   155
INTERNET RESOURCES   157
KEY TERMS   157
REVIEW QUESTIONS   157

THE AMERICAN MOSAIC:
The Battle of Bunker Hill   136

THE PEOPLE SPEAK:
Thomas Paine's *American Crisis I* (December 1776)   145

MAP ESSAY:
Lexington and Concord: The Shot Heard 'Round the World   134

6 SECURING THE REPUBLIC AND ITS IDEALS, 1776–1789   159
"Others may never feel tyrannic sway"

ESTABLISHING NEW REPUBLICAN GOVERNMENTS   161
People Victorious: The New State Governments • The Articles of Confederation

CRISES OF THE CONFEDERATION   164
Struggle to Ratify the Articles • Turmoil over Financing the War • Threatened Military Coup: The Newburgh Conspiracy • Drifting Toward Disunion • Daniel Shays's Rebellion

HUMAN RIGHTS AND SOCIAL CHANGE   170
In Pursuit of Religious Freedom • The Propertyless Poor and the West • Women Appeal for Fundamental Liberties • The Dilemma of Race and Racism

SECOND NEW BEGINNING, NEW NATIONAL GOVERNMENT   179
The Framers of the Constitution • A Document Constructed by Compromises • The Ratification Struggle

CONCLUSION 184
CHRONOLOGY OF KEY EVENTS 184
SUGGESTIONS FOR FURTHER READING 185
INTERNET RESOURCES 186
KEY TERMS 187
REVIEW QUESTIONS 187

THE AMERICAN MOSAIC:
Birth Control in the Early Republic 176

THE PEOPLE SPEAK:
Abigail Adams Exhorts Her Husband to "Remember the Ladies" (1776) 173

7 THE FORMATIVE DECADE, 1790–1800 189

An "outrageous and wretched scandalmonger"

THE ROOTS OF AMERICAN ECONOMIC GROWTH 191

IMPLEMENTING THE CONSTITUTION 192
Establishing the Machinery of Government • Defining the Presidency • Alexander Hamilton's Financial Program

THE BIRTH OF POLITICAL PARTIES 195
World Events and Political Polarization • 1793 and 1794: Years of Crisis • Washington Retires

A NEW PRESIDENT AND NEW CHALLENGES 202
The Presidency of John Adams • A New National Capital • The Quasi War with France • The Alien and Sedition Acts

THE REVOLUTION OF 1800 205

CONCLUSION 206
CHRONOLOGY OF KEY EVENTS 207
SUGGESTIONS FOR FURTHER READING 208
INTERNET RESOURCES 209
KEY TERMS 209
REVIEW QUESTIONS 209

THE AMERICAN MOSAIC:
Yellow Fever in Philadelphia: Pills and Politics 198

THE PEOPLE SPEAK:
Gabriel's Revolt 205

8 THE JEFFERSONIANS IN POWER, 1800–1815 211

"A dangerous man"

JEFFERSON TAKES COMMAND 213
Who Was Thomas Jefferson? • Jefferson's Goal: To Restore Republican Government • Reforming the Federal Government • War on the Judiciary • International Conflict • Disunionist Conspiracies

THE AMERICAN EAGLE CHALLENGES THE FRENCH TIGER AND THE BRITISH SHARK 220
"Dambargo" • A Second War of Independence • Early Defeats • The Tide Turns • The War's Significance

CONCLUSION 229
CHRONOLOGY OF KEY EVENTS 228
SUGGESTIONS FOR FURTHER READING 229
INTERNET RESOURCES 230
KEY TERMS 230
REVIEW QUESTIONS 230

THE AMERICAN MOSAIC:
The Shawnee Prophet Tenskwatawa and His Warrior Brother Tecumseh 224

THE PEOPLE SPEAK:
Religion in the Early Republic 214

9 NATIONALISM, ECONOMIC GROWTH, AND THE ROOTS OF SECTIONAL CONFLICT, 1815–1824 233

"No smoking, drinking, or swearing"

THE GROWTH OF AMERICAN NATIONALISM 235
Neo-Hamiltonianism • Strengthening American Finances • Protecting American Industry • Conquering Space • Judicial Nationalism • Defending American Interests in Foreign Affairs

THE GROWTH OF THE AMERICAN ECONOMY 241
Accelerating Transportation • Speeding Communications • Transforming American Law •

Resistance to Technological Innovation • Early Industrialization • The Growth of Cities

THE GROWTH OF POLITICAL FACTIONALISM AND SECTIONALISM 248

The Panic of 1819 • The Missouri Crisis

CONCLUSION 252
CHRONOLOGY OF KEY EVENTS 252
SUGGESTIONS FOR FURTHER READING 253
INTERNET RESOURCES 254
KEY TERMS 255
REVIEW QUESTIONS 255

THE AMERICAN MOSAIC:
Denmark Vesey and the Slave Conspiracy of 1822 250

THE PEOPLE SPEAK:
Growing Up Female in the Early Republic 235

10 POWER AND POLITICS IN JACKSON'S AMERICA 257

The "people's" candidate

POLITICAL DEMOCRATIZATION 259

The Expansion of Voting Rights • Popular Attacks on Privilege

THE REBIRTH OF PARTIES 261

Birth of the Second Party System • The Presidency of John Quincy Adams • The "American System" and the "Tariff of Abominations" • The Election of 1828

ANDREW JACKSON: THE POLITICS OF EGALITARIANISM 266

Expanding the Powers of the Presidency • Clearing the Land of Indians • Sectional Disputes over Public Lands and Nullification • The Bank War • The Jacksonian Court • Jackson's Legacy

RISE OF A POLITICAL OPPOSITION 277

A Party Formed by Coalition • Who Were the Whigs?

CONCLUSION 279
CHRONOLOGY OF KEY EVENTS 278
SUGGESTIONS FOR FURTHER READING 279
INTERNET RESOURCES 281
KEY TERMS 281
REVIEW QUESTIONS 281

THE AMERICAN MOSAIC:
The Cholera Epidemic of 1832: Sinners and Saints 262

THE PEOPLE SPEAK:
The Cherokee Nation Protests Against Jackson's Removal Policy (1836) 271

11 AMERICA'S FIRST AGE OF REFORM 283

"And a'n't I a woman?"

SOURCES OF THE REFORM IMPULSE 284

Social Problems on the Rise • A New Moral Sensibility • The Second Great Awakening • Religious Diversity

MORAL REFORM 289

SOCIAL REFORM 290

The Problem of Crime in a Free Society • The Struggle for Public Schools • Asylums for Society's Outcasts

RADICAL REFORM 293

Early Antislavery Efforts • The Rise of Abolitionist Sentiment in the North • Abolitionist Arguments and Public Reaction • Division Within the Antislavery Movement • The Birth of Feminism • Catalyst for Women's Rights • Utopian Communities

ARTISTIC AND CULTURAL FERMENT 301

American Transcendentalism • A Literary Renaissance • Ethnic Voices • American Art

AMERICAN POPULAR CULTURE 308

The Popular Novel • Forms of Popular Entertainment

CONCLUSION 313

CHRONOLOGY OF KEY EVENTS 312

SUGGESTIONS FOR FURTHER READING 313

INTERNET RESOURCES 316

KEY TERMS 317

REVIEW QUESTIONS 317

THE AMERICAN MOSAIC:
 Gouging Fights and Backcountry Honor 286

THE PEOPLE SPEAK:
 Women's Rights: Seneca Falls Declaration and Resolutions (1848) 300

12 THE DIVIDED NORTH, THE DIVIDED SOUTH 319

"Some other means of cultivating their estates"

A DIVIDED CULTURE 320

THE EMERGENCE OF A NEW INDUSTRIAL ORDER IN THE NORTH 321

The Transformation of the Rural Countryside • The Disruption of the Artisan System of Labor • The Introduction of the Factory System • Labor Protests • The Movement for a Ten-Hour Day • The Laboring Poor • Immigration Begins • The Divided North

SOUTHERN DISTINCTIVENESS 331

The Plantation Legend • The Old South: Images and Realities • Impact of Slavery on the Southern Economy • Growth of a Distinctive Southern Identity • The Decline of Antislavery Sentiment in the South • "Reforming" Slavery from Within • Southern Nationalism • Southern Radicalism

SLAVERY 339

The Legal Status of Slaves • Slave Labor • Material Conditions of Slave Life • Slave Family Life • Slave Cultural Expression • Slave Resistance • Free African Americans

CONCLUSION 346

CHRONOLOGY OF KEY EVENTS 347

SUGGESTIONS FOR FURTHER READING 347

INTERNET RESOURCES 350

KEY TERMS 350

REVIEW QUESTIONS 350

THE AMERICAN MOSAIC:
 Policing the Pre–Civil War City 332

THE PEOPLE SPEAK:
 Slave Resistance 345

13 CULTURES COLLIDE IN THE FAR WEST 353

"Vampires, in the guise of men"

THE HISPANIC AND NATIVE AMERICAN WEST 355

Spanish America • The Mission System • Impact of Mexican Independence • Native Americans • Impact of Contact

THE SURGE WESTWARD 358

Opening the West • Pathfinders • Mountain Men • Trailblazing • Settling the Far West • Life on the Trail

MANIFEST DESTINY 362

Gone to Texas • The Texas Question • Webster-Ashburton Treaty • Oregon • The Mormon Frontier

WAR WITH MEXICO 370

Why War? • The War • War Fever and Antiwar Protests • Peace • The Fate of Mexican Americans • The War's Significance • Political Crisis of the 1840s • The Gold Rush

CONCLUSION 379

CHRONOLOGY OF KEY EVENTS 378

SUGGESTIONS FOR FURTHER READING 379

INTERNET RESOURCES 381

Key Terms 381
Review Questions 381

THE AMERICAN MOSAIC:
Tejanos at the Alamo 366

THE PEOPLE SPEAK:
Mexican Americans Defend Their Land and Rights (1859) 375

14 THE HOUSE DIVIDED 383

The "slave power" conspiracy

THE CRISIS OF 1850 385

The South's Dilemma • The Compromise of 1850: The Illusion of Sectional Peace • The Fugitive Slave Law

DISINTEGRATION OF THE PARTY SYSTEM 391

The Know Nothings • Young America • The Kansas-Nebraska Act • Revival of the Slavery Issue

THE GATHERING STORM 398

"Bleeding Kansas" and "Bleeding Sumner" • The Election of 1856 • The Supreme Court Speaks • The Lecompton Constitution: "A Swindle and a Fraud"

CRISIS OF THE UNION 401

The Lincoln-Douglas Debates • Harpers Ferry

Conclusion 406
Chronology of Key Events 405
Suggestions for Further Reading 406
Internet Resources 407
Key Terms 407
Review Questions 407

THE AMERICAN MOSAIC:
Physicians and Planters, Prescription for Slave Medical Care 392

THE PEOPLE SPEAK:
John Brown Defends His Raid on Harpers Ferry (1859) 404

15 A NATION SHATTERED BY CIVIL WAR, 1860–1865 409

"We will make our stand"

FROM SECESSION TO FULL-SCALE WAR 411

Electing a New President • Secession Rends the Union • Lincoln Takes Command • An Accounting of Resources

"FORWARD TO RICHMOND!" AND "ON TO WASHINGTON!" 418

Planning the Union Offensive • Yankee Reverses and Rebel Victories in the East • Federal Breakthrough in the West

TO AND FROM EMANCIPATION: THE WAR ON THE HOME FRONT 424

An Abundance of Confederate Shortages • Directing the Northern War Effort • Issuing the Emancipation Proclamation • Emancipation Tests Northern Resolve

BREAKING CONFEDERATE RESISTANCE, 1863–1865 431

The Tide Turns: Gettysburg and Vicksburg • Crushing Blows from Grant and Sherman • Total War Forces Surrender

Conclusion 439
Chronology of Key Events 439
Suggestions for Further Reading 440
Internet Resources 442
Key Terms 442
Review Questions 442

THE AMERICAN MOSAIC:
Pickett's Charge at Gettysburg 432

THE PEOPLE SPEAK:
Frederick Douglass Calls upon African Americans to Take Up Arms Against the Confederacy (1863) 430

MAP ESSAY:
Antietam: "We Will Make Our Stand" 422

16 THE NATION RECONSTRUCTED: NORTH, SOUTH, AND THE WEST, 1865–1877 445

"I'd like tuh see any man put me outer dis house"

POSTWAR CONDITIONS AND ISSUES 447

The War's Impact on Individuals • Unresolved Issues

PRESIDENTIAL RECONSTRUCTION 451

Lincoln's Plan • Johnson's Plan • Black Codes in the South

CONGRESSIONAL RECONSTRUCTION 454

"Radical" Reconstruction • Black Suffrage

RECONSTRUCTION IN THE SOUTH 460

Carpetbaggers, Scalawags, and Black Republicans • Character of Republican Rule • Black and White Economic and Social Adaptation • Violent White Resistance

RECONSTRUCTION IN THE NORTH AND WEST 465

Northern Shifts in Attitudes • Western Expansion, Racism, and Native Americans • Final Retreat from Reconstruction

CONCLUSION 473

CHRONOLOGY OF KEY EVENTS 474

SUGGESTIONS FOR FURTHER READING 475

INTERNET RESOURCES 476

KEY TERMS 476

REVIEW QUESTIONS 477

THE AMERICAN MOSAIC:
Day of Jubilo: Slaves Confront Emancipation 448

THE PEOPLE SPEAK:
Testimony Against the Klan 466

17 EMERGENCE AS AN ECONOMIC POWER 479

"I want to congratulate you on being the richest man in the world"

AMERICA: LAND OF PLENTY 481

Mineral and Geographic Possibilities • Technological Change • An Expanding Railroad Network

CREATING A FAVORABLE CLIMATE: THE ROLE OF IDEOLOGY, POLITICS, AND FINANCE 484

Social Darwinism and the Gospel of Wealth • Laissez-faire in Theory and Practice • Corporations and Capital Formation

THE RISE OF BIG BUSINESS 489

Controlling Competition • New Managerial Styles and an Expanding Middle Class • Mass Marketing, Assembly Lines, and Mass Production • The Power of Bigness

VARIETIES OF ECONOMIC CHANGE IN THE WEST AND SOUTH 494

Western Expansion and Exploitation • The Changing Nature of Farming • The New South

WORKING IN INDUSTRIAL AMERICA 502

The Conditions of Work • Worker Discontent • Early Labor Violence • Unorganized and Organized Labor

CONCLUSION 509

CHRONOLOGY OF KEY EVENTS 509

SUGGESTIONS FOR FURTHER READING 510

INTERNET RESOURCES 512

KEY TERMS 513

REVIEW QUESTIONS 513

THE AMERICAN MOSAIC:
The Wild West 496

THE PEOPLE SPEAK:
The Gospel of Wealth 485

18 THE RISE OF AN URBAN SOCIETY AND CITY PEOPLE 515

"Murder with a hatchet"

THE NEW IMMIGRANTS 517

"Birds of Passage" • In Search of a New Home

NATIVISM: THE ANTI-IMMIGRANT REACTION 520

Sources of Conflict • Closing the Golden Door

NEW CITIES AND NEW PROBLEMS 523

City Technology • The Segregated City • The Problems of Growth • From Private City to Public City

CITY CULTURE 530

Night Life and Day Life • From the Genteel Tradition to Realism and Naturalism • Describing the Urban Jungle • Painting Urban Reality • The Sounds of the City

ENTERTAINING THE MULTITUDES 534

Of Fields and Cities • "I Can Lick Any Sonofabitch in the House" • The Excluded Americans

- From Central Park to Coney Island • The Magic of the Flickering Image • The Agony of Painless Escape

CONCLUSION 543

CHRONOLOGY OF KEY EVENTS 543

SUGGESTIONS FOR FURTHER READING 544

INTERNET RESOURCES 546

KEY TERMS 547

REVIEW QUESTIONS 547

THE AMERICAN MOSAIC:
College Football Wars 538

THE PEOPLE SPEAK:
How the Other Half Lives 529

19 END-OF-THE-CENTURY CRISIS 549

"You shall not crucify mankind upon a cross of gold"

EQUILIBRIUM AND INERTIA: THE NATIONAL POLITICAL SCENE 552

Divided Power: The Parties and the Federal Government • Subtle Differences: The Bases of Party Loyalty • The Business of Politics: Party Organization • The Struggle for Inclusion: Women and Politics

STYLE OVER SUBSTANCE: GOVERNMENT IN THE GILDED AGE, 1877–1892 556

Hayes and the "Money Question" • Garfield, Arthur, and the Patronage Issue • Cleveland, the Railroads, and Tariffs • Harrison and Big Business • Legislative Activity on Minority Rights and Social Issues

REVOLT OF THE WEST AND SOUTH 562

Grievances: Real and Imagined • The Farmers Organize • The Agrarian Agenda • Emergence of the Populist Party

DEPRESSION AND TURBULENCE IN THE 1890S 567

The Roots and Results of the Depression • Expressions of Worker Discontent • Deteriorating Race Relations • The Tide Turns: The Election of 1896

CONCLUSION 575

CHRONOLOGY OF KEY EVENTS 574

SUGGESTIONS FOR FURTHER READING 575

INTERNET RESOURCES 576

KEY TERMS 577

REVIEW QUESTIONS 577

THE AMERICAN MOSAIC:
"Rise, Brothers!": The Black Response to Jim Crow 572

THE PEOPLE SPEAK:
Lynch Law in America 571

20 IMPERIAL AMERICA, 1870–1900 579

"A colossus of ignorance"

CONGRESSIONAL CONTROL AND THE REDUCTION OF AMERICAN POWER 581

Trimming the State Department • Reducing the Military • Seward's Dream

THE SPIRIT OF AMERICAN GREATNESS 582

American Exceptionalism • Sense of Duty • Search for Markets • The New Navy • Large Policy

THE EMERGENCE OF AGGRESSION IN AMERICAN FOREIGN POLICY 586

Confronting the Germans in Samoa • Teaching Chile a Lesson • Plucking the Hawaiian Pear • Facing Down the British

THE WAR FOR EMPIRE 589

The Spirit of the 1890s • The Cuban Revolution • The Yellow Press • The Spanish-American War • Freeing Cuba • The Imperial Debate • The War to Crush Filipino Independence • Keeping the Doors Open

CONCLUSION 601

CHRONOLOGY OF KEY EVENTS 601

SUGGESTIONS FOR FURTHER READING 602

INTERNET RESOURCES 603

KEY TERMS 603

REVIEW QUESTIONS 603

THE AMERICAN MOSAIC:
Theodore Roosevelt and the Rough Riders 596

THE PEOPLE SPEAK:
March of the Flag 583

21 THE PROGRESSIVE STRUGGLE, 1900–1917   605

"We object to being called here to meet a criminal"

THE PROGRESSIVE IMPULSE   607
America in 1901 • Voices for Change • The Muckrakers

PROGRESSIVES IN ACTION   611
The Drive to Organize • Urban Beginnings • Reform Reaches the State Level

PROGRESSIVISM MOVES TO THE NATIONAL LEVEL   621
Roosevelt and New Attitudes Toward Government Power • Taft and Quiet Progressivism • Wilson and Moral Progressivism

PROGRESSIVISM IN THE INTERNATIONAL ARENA   628
Big Stick Diplomacy • Dollar Diplomacy • Missionary Diplomacy

PROGRESSIVE ACCOMPLISHMENTS, PROGRESSIVE FAILURES   631
The Impact of Legislation • Winners and Losers

CONCLUSION   635
CHRONOLOGY OF KEY EVENTS   634
SUGGESTIONS FOR FURTHER READING   635
INTERNET RESOURCES   637
KEY TERMS   637
REVIEW QUESTIONS   637

THE AMERICAN MOSAIC:
The White Plague   612

THE PEOPLE SPEAK:
An Account of the Proceedings of the Trial of Susan B. Anthony   617

22 THE UNITED STATES AND WORLD WAR I   639

"The intellectual hero of World War I"

THE ROAD TO WAR   641
The Guns of August • American Neutrality • Allied Violations of Neutrality • Submarine Warfare • Preparedness Campaign • The Election of 1916 • The End of Neutrality

AMERICAN INDUSTRY GOES TO WAR   651
Voluntarism • "Hooverizing" • Peace with Labor • Financing the War

THE AMERICAN PUBLIC GOES TO WAR   653
Selling the War • Political Repression • Wartime Reform • African Americans and the Great Migration

THE WAR FRONT   658
The War at Sea • Raising an Army • The Defeat of Germany

SOCIAL UNREST AFTER THE WAR   659
Mounting Racial Tension • Labor Unrest and the Red Scare

THE TREATY OF VERSAILLES   661
The Fourteen Points • Discord Among the Victors • The Struggle for Ratification • The Election of 1920

CONCLUSION   666
CHRONOLOGY OF KEY EVENTS   666
SUGGESTIONS FOR FURTHER READING   667
INTERNET RESOURCES   668
KEY TERMS   668
REVIEW QUESTIONS   669

THE AMERICAN MOSAIC:
The First Day of the Somme   644

THE PEOPLE SPEAK:
Woodrow Wilson, Address to Congress (1917)   650

23 MODERN TIMES, 1920–1929   671

"Biological duty"

THE EMERGENCE OF MODERN AMERICA   673
Urban Growth • The Rise of a Consumer Economy

THE FORMATION OF MODERN AMERICAN CULTURE   677
Mass Entertainment • Spectator Sports • Low-Brow and Middle-Brow Culture • The Avant-Garde • The Sex Debate

THE CLASH OF CULTURES   681
The New Woman • Prohibition • The Scopes

Trial • Xenophobia and Restricting Immigration • The Ku Klux Klan • African-American Protests • The Harlem Renaissance

THE REPUBLICAN RESTORATION 689

Handsome Harding • Silent Cal • The Twilight of Progressivism • The Election of 1928

THE GREAT CRASH 691

Speculative Manias • The Market Crashes • Why It Happened

CONCLUSION 694

CHRONOLOGY OF KEY EVENTS 694

SUGGESTIONS FOR FURTHER READING 695

INTERNET RESOURCES 697

KEY TERMS 697

REVIEW QUESTIONS 697

THE AMERICAN MOSAIC:
The Sexual Revolution of the Early 1900s 682

THE PEOPLE SPEAK:
Margaret Sanger, "Happiness in Marriage" (1926) 674

24 THE AGE OF ROOSEVELT 699
"Shakespeare in overalls"

THE GREAT DEPRESSION IN GLOBAL PERSPECTIVE 700

THE HUMAN TOLL 701

The Dispossessed • Private and Public Charity

PRESIDENT HERBERT HOOVER RESPONDS 704

Conservative Responses • Government Loans

FRANKLIN ROOSEVELT AND THE FIRST NEW DEAL 705

The Election of 1932 • The First 100 Days • The New Dealers • The Farmers' Plight • The National Recovery Administration • Jobs Programs • Roosevelt's Critics

THE SECOND NEW DEAL 712

The Wagner Act • Social Security • The Election of 1936

THE NEW DEAL, WOMEN, AND MINORITY GROUPS 715

Women • African Americans • Mexican Americans • Native Americans

THE NEW DEAL IN DECLINE 717

Court Packing • The Depression of 1937

POPULAR CULTURE DURING THE GREAT DEPRESSION 720

Artistic and Literary Endeavors • Hollywood During the Great Depression

CONCLUSION 721

CHRONOLOGY OF KEY EVENTS 722

SUGGESTIONS FOR FURTHER READING 723

INTERNET RESOURCES 725

KEY TERMS 725

REVIEW QUESTIONS 725

THE AMERICAN MOSAIC:
The Tuskegee Syphilis Study 718

THE PEOPLE SPEAK:
Francis Perkins, "The Social Security Act" (1935) 714

25 THE END OF ISOLATION: AMERICA FACES THE WORLD, 1920–1945 727
The "final solution to the Jewish problem"

DIPLOMACY BETWEEN THE WARS 729

American Diplomacy During the 1920s • United States Policy Toward Latin America • The Isolationist Mirage

The Coming of World War II 731
Conflict in the Pacific • Italy • Germany • The American Response to Hitler • War Begins • "The Arsenal of Democracy" • A Collision Course in the Pacific • Pearl Harbor

America Mobilizes for War 737
Mobilizing the Economy • Taming Inflation • Election of 1944 • Molding Public Opinion

Social Changes During the War 740
Women • African Americans • Mexican Americans • Fear of Enemy Aliens • Internment of Japanese Americans

The War in Europe 745
The Grand Alliance • Early Axis Victories • Stemming the German Tide • Liberating Europe • The Yalta Conference

The War in the Pacific 750
Island Hopping • The Dawn of the Atomic Age • The Manhattan Project • Hiroshima and Nagasaki

The Road to War 757
Conclusion 757
Chronology of Key Events 758
Suggestions for Further Reading 759
Internet Resources 761
Key Terms 761
Review Questions 761

THE AMERICAN MOSAIC:
Hiroshima and Nagasaki 752

THE PEOPLE SPEAK:
That Day at Hiroshima 754

MAP ESSAY:
Landings on D-Day: The Longest Day 748

26 WAGING PEACE AND WAR 763
"I am not and never have been..."

Containing the Russian Bear 765
Origins of the Cold War • A World Divided • Tough Talk • The Marshall Plan: "Saving Western Europe"

The Containment Policy 770
Berlin Test • Troubling Times • The Korean War

The Cold War at Home 776
Adjusting to Peace • Confronting the Demands of Labor • Failure of the Fair Deal • Searching for the Enemy Within • The Rise and Fall of Joseph McCarthy

The Paranoid Style 781
HUAC Goes to Hollywood • "What's Wrong with Our Kids Today?"

Conclusion 785
Chronology of Key Events 786
Suggestions for Further Reading 786
Internet Resources 788
Key Terms 789
Review Questions 789

THE AMERICAN MOSAIC:
The Kefauver Crime Committee 782

THE PEOPLE SPEAK:
NSC-68 774

27 IKE'S AMERICA 791
"What else could we do?"

Quiet Changes 793
"I Like Ike" • "Dynamic Conservatism" • A Country on Wheels • Ike, Dulles, and the World • A New Face in Moscow • 1956: The Dangerous Year • The Troubled Second Term •

Sputnik and Sputtering Rockets • Third-World Challenges • Not with a Bang, But a Whimper

WE SHALL OVERCOME 803
Taking Jim Crow to Court • A Failure of Leadership • The Word from Montgomery

THE SOUNDS OF CHANGE 810
Father Knows Best • The Other Side of the Coin • The Meaning of Elvis • A Different Beat

CONCLUSION 814

CHRONOLOGY OF KEY EVENTS 815

SUGGESTIONS FOR FURTHER READING 815

INTERNET RESOURCES 817

KEY TERMS 817

REVIEW QUESTIONS 817

THE AMERICAN MOSAIC:
Integration in Sports 804

THE PEOPLE SPEAK:
Images and Illusions 812

28 POWER SHIFTS: THE EMERGENCE OF THE SOUTH AND WEST 819
"The genuine article"

THE EMERGENCE OF THE SOUTHERN RIM 822
From the Long Hot Summer to the Sunbelt • A Shift in Race Relations • The Business of the South Is Business

THE MYTH AND REALITY OF THE WEST 825
Packaging the West • Washington and the West • From Extraction to Diversification • The Problems and Benefits of Growth

POLITICS WESTERN STYLE 834
An Aberration or an Omen? • Shifting Party Loyalties • The Politics of Liberation

CONCLUSION 839

CHRONOLOGY OF KEY EVENTS 840

SUGGESTIONS FOR FURTHER READING 841

INTERNET RESOURCES 842

KEY TERMS 842

REVIEW QUESTIONS 843

THE AMERICAN MOSAIC:
AIDS: A Modern Plague 832

THE PEOPLE SPEAK:
The Conscience of a Conservative 835

29 VIETNAM AND THE CRISIS OF AUTHORITY 845
"Uncle Ho"

THE ILLUSION OF GREATNESS 847
Television's President • The "Macho" Presidency • Something Short of Camelot • *Cuba Libre* Revisited

VIETNAM: AMERICA'S LONGEST WAR 851
A Small Corner of a Bigger Picture • Kennedy's Testing Ground • Texas Tough in the Gulf of Tonkin • Lyndon's War • To Tet and Beyond • The Politics of a Divided Nation

THE TORTUOUS PATH TOWARD PEACE 862
Outsiders on the Inside • Vietnamization: The Idea and the Process • A "Decent Interval" • The Legacy of the War

CHRONOLOGY OF KEY EVENTS 870

CONCLUSION 871

SUGGESTIONS FOR FURTHER READING 871

INTERNET RESOURCES 873

KEY TERMS 873

REVIEW QUESTIONS 873

THE AMERICAN MOSAIC:
My Lai and the Question of War Ethics 868

THE PEOPLE SPEAK:
Bloods 860

MAP ESSAY:
Logistics in a Guerrilla War: The Longest War 858

30 THE STRUGGLE FOR A JUST SOCIETY 875
The "endless discontents" of a "scold"

THE STRUGGLE FOR RACIAL JUSTICE 877
Freedom Now • To the Heart of Dixie • "Bombingham" • Kennedy Finally Acts • The

March on Washington • The Civil Rights Act of 1964 • Voting Rights • Black Nationalism and Black Power • The Civil Rights Movement Moves North • The Great Society and the Drive for Equality • White Backlash • The Struggle Continues

THE YOUTH REVOLT 890

The New Left • The Making and Unmaking of a Counterculture

LIBERATION MOVEMENTS 892

Women's Liberation • Sources of Discontent • Feminism Reborn • Radical Feminism • The Growth of Feminist Ideology • The Supreme Court and Sex Discrimination • The Equal Rights Amendment • Impact of the Women's Liberation Movement • ¡Viva La Rasa! • The Native-American Power Movement • Gay and Lesbian Liberation • The Earth First

CONCLUSION 904

CHRONOLOGY OF KEY EVENTS 905

SUGGESTIONS FOR FURTHER READING 906

INTERNET RESOURCES 908

KEY TERMS 908

REVIEW QUESTIONS 908

THE AMERICAN MOSAIC:
César Chávez and La Causa 900

THE PEOPLE SPEAK:
Rev. Martin Luther King, Jr., Letter from Birmingham City Jail 881

31 AMERICA IN OUR TIME 911

"Dirty tricks"

CRISIS OF POLITICAL LEADERSHIP 914

Restraining the Imperial Presidency • New-Style Presidents

WRENCHING ECONOMIC TRANSFORMATIONS 915

The Age of Inflation • Oil Embargo • Foreign Competition and Deindustrialization • Whipping Stagflation

A NEW AMERICAN ROLE IN THE WORLD 917

Détente • Foreign Policy Triumphs • No Island of Stability

THE REAGAN REVOLUTION 920

Reaganomics • The Reagan Doctrine • A Remarkable Ideological Turnaround • The Reagan Revolution in Perspective

THE BUSH PRESIDENCY 923

A Kinder, Gentler Nation • Economic and Foreign Policy • Collapse of Communism • The Persian Gulf War • Enter Bill Clinton

THE CLINTON PRESIDENCY 930

"It's the Economy, Stupid" • Foreign Policy

CONCLUSION 935

SUGGESTIONS FOR FURTHER READING 935

CHRONOLOGY OF KEY EVENTS 936

INTERNET RESOURCES 938

KEY TERMS 939

REVIEW QUESTIONS 939

THE AMERICAN MOSAIC:
The End of Two Eras 926

THE PEOPLE SPEAK:
The Starr Report and the White House Rebuttal 932

MAP ESSAY:
The First Crisis of the Post-Cold War Era: The Persian Gulf War 928

APPENDIX

THE DECLARATION OF INDEPENDENCE A-2

THE CONSTITUTION OF THE UNITED STATES OF AMERICA A-4

AMENDMENTS TO THE CONSTITUTION A-9

PRESIDENTIAL ELECTIONS A-14

VICE PRESIDENTS AND CABINET MEMBERS BY ADMINISTRATION A-17

SUPREME COURT JUSTICES A-25

ADMISSION OF STATES TO THE UNION A-27

TERRITORIAL EXPANSION OF THE U.S. A-28

U.S. POPULATION, 1790–1990 A-29

ETHNIC DIVERSITY OF THE U.S., 1990 A-30

Glossary   G-1

Credits   C-1

Index   I-1

MAPS

Endpapers: The United States; The World

Page
- 6 Routes of the First Americans
- 7 The Aztecs, Mayas, and Incas
- 10 The Atlantic Community, Late 1400s
- 11 Vinland
- 17 Voyages of Exploration
- 25 Roanoke Island
- 25 Conflicting Land Claims
- 26 Powhatan's Confederacy
- 41 Chesapeake Settlements, 1650
- 42 Barbadian Connection
- 49 New England Colonies, 1650
- 50 Population Comparison of New England and Chesapeake, Mid-1600s
- 58 West African Kingdoms, Late 1400s
- 59 African Slave Trade
- 69 Iroquois Nations
- 71 Middle Colonies, 1685
- 77 Colonial Trade Routes, 1750
- 82 Distribution of Immigrant Groups and the Great Wagon Road, Mid-1700s
- 83 Western European Migration
- 93 Significant Battles of the French and Indian War, 1756–1763
- 102 North America, 1763
- 103 Pontiac's Rebellion
- 104 Colonial Products in the Mid-1700s
- 120 Quebec Act of 1774
- 134 **Map Essay** Lexington and Concord: The Shot Heard 'Round the World
- 142 Northern Theater of War, 1775–1778
- 151 Southern Theater of War, 1780–1781
- 166 Western Land Claims Ceded by the States
- 171 Wilderness Road
- 172 First Territorial Survey
- 175 Slave Concentration, 1790
- 201 British Posts and Indian Battles
- 217 Barbary States
- 219 The Louisiana Purchase and Route of Lewis and Clark
- 223 The War of 1812
- 227 Indian Land Cessions
- 238 The United States in 1819
- 247 1810 Population Density
- 247 1820 Population Density
- 247 1830 Population Density
- 249 Missouri Compromise
- 260 Extension of Male Suffrage
- 266 Election of 1828
- 270 Trail of Tears (Indian Removal)
- 271 Black Hawk War
- 323 Agriculture and Industry, 1850
- 325 Cotton Textile Industry
- 356 California Missions
- 358 Donner Party
- 361 Western Trails
- 364 Texas Revolution
- 368 Oregon Country, Pacific Northwest Boundary Dispute
- 373 Mexican-American War
- 386 Slave Concentration, 1820
- 387 Slave Concentration, 1860/The Cotton Kingdom

xxi

xxii Maps

Page

Page	
397	Compromise of 1850/Kansas-Nebraska Act
397	Gains and Losses in the Congressional Election of 1854
398	Bleeding Kansas
412	Election of 1860
413	Secession
420	Civil War, 1861–1862
422	**Map Essay** Antietam: "We Will Make Our Stand"
435	Civil War, 1863–1865
456	Reconstruction and Redemption
469	Indian Battles and Reservations
472	Election of 1876
499	Rise of Tenancy
506	The Great Railroad Strike, 1877
518	Immigration, 1880–1889 and 1900–1909
594	Spanish-American War, Cuban Theater
598	American Empire
626	Election of 1912
628	Panama Canal
630	American Interventions in the Caribbean
642	European Alliances and Battlefronts
659	United States Participation on the Western Front
663	American Military Forces in Russia, 1918
664	Europe After World War I
673	Growth of Chicago
676	African-American Population, 1910 and 1950
707	Electoral Shift, 1928 and 1932
733	Axis Takeovers in Europe, 1936–1939

Page

Page	
744	Location of Nazi Concentration and Death Camps
744	Location of Internment Camps for Japanese Americans
747	World War II, European Theater
748	**Map Essay** Landings on D-Day: The Longest Day
750	World War II, Pacific Theater
768	Europe After World War II
775	Korean War
796	United States Interstate Highway System
825	Migration to the Sunbelt, 1970–1981
830	Damming Western Waters
837	Election of 1964
837	Election of 1968
838	Population Shifts, 1980–1986
851	Vietnam and Southeast Asia
856	Vietnam Conflict, 1964–1975
858	**Map Essay** Logistics in a Guerrilla War: The Longest War
919	Conflict in the Middle East and Europe
922	U.S. Involvement in Central America and the Caribbean
929	**Map Essay** The First Crisis of the Post–Cold War Era: The Persian Gulf War

Appendix

A-27	Admission of States to the Union
A-28	Territorial Expansion of the U.S.
A-30	Ethnic Diversity of the U.S., 1990

TABLES and Figures

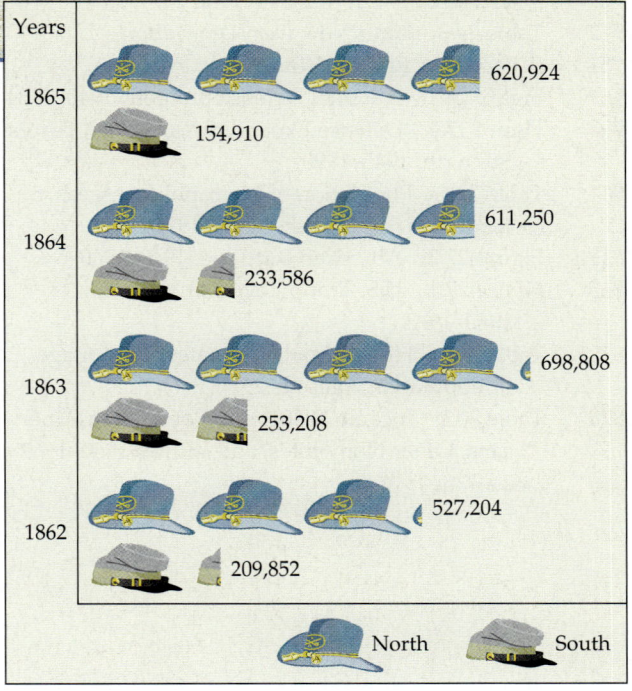

Page		
21	Figure 1.1	The Tudor Monarchy of England
41	Figure 2.1	The Stuart Monarchy of England
78	Table 3.1	Colonial Population Growth, 1660–1780
79	Figure 3.1	Slave Importation Estimates, 1701–1775
91	Table 3.2	The Imperial Wars, 1689–1763
114	Table 4.1	Estimated Population of Colonial Port Towns Compared to London, England (1775)
130	(Chap. 5)	Road to War, 1763–1776: War for American Independence
162	Table 6.1	Personal Wealth and Occupations of Approximately 900 Representatives Elected to Prewar and Postwar Assemblies (Expressed in Percentages)
163	Table 6.2	Family and Personal Wealth of Approximately 450 Executive Officials in Late Colonial and Early Revolutionary Governments (Expressed in Percentages)
183	Table 6.3	Ratification of the Constitution of 1787
206	Table 7.1	Election of 1800
222	(Chap. 8)	Road to War: War of 1812
264	Table 10.1	Election of 1824
267	Figure 10.1	Voter Population and Turnout, 1824–1860
327	Figure 12.1	Total Immigration, 1841–1860
329	Figure 12.2	Immigration by Country of Origin, 1840–1860
331	Figure 12.3	Slaveowning Population, 1850
334	Figure 12.4	Southern White Population, 1860
335	Figure 12.5	Railroad Growth, 1840–1860
370	(Chap. 13)	Road to War: Events Leading to the Mexican-American War
415	Figure 15.1	Resources, North and South
416	(Chap. 15)	Road to War: Civil War
419	Figure 15.2	Comparative Troop Strength, North and South

Page		
427	Table 15.1	Previous Occupations of Sampled White Union and Confederate Soldiers
437	Table 15.2	Incidence of Disease Among Union Soldiers
438	Figure 15.3	The Human Cost of War
455	Table 16.1	Reconstruction Amendments, 1865–1870
484	Figure 17.1	Railroad Construction, 1861–1920
488	Figure 17.2	Index of U.S. Manufacturing Production, 1864–1914
491	Figure 17.3	Iron, Steel, and Coal Production 1870–1900
524	Figure 18.1	Urban and Rural Population, 1870–1920
555	Figure 19.1	Voter Participation in Presidential Elections, 1876–1920
563	Figure 19.2	Price Indexes for Consumer and Farm Products, 1865–1913
624	Table 21.1	Progressive Era Legislation and Amendments
649	(Chap. 22)	Road to War: World War I
653	Figure 22.1	Labor Union Membership, 1897–1920
662	Table 22.1	Woodrow Wilson's Fourteen Points, 1918: Success and Failure in Implementation
684	Figure 23.1	Women in the Workforce, 1900–1940
702	Figure 24.1	Unemployment, 1929–1942

xxiii

Page

Page	
703	Table 24.1 Depression Shopping List, 1932–1934
707	Figure 24.2 Bank Failures, 1929–1933
707	Table 24.2 Legislation Enacted During the First Hundred Days, March 9–June 16, 1933
712	Table 24.3 Later New Deal Legislation
757	(Chap. 25) Road to War: World War II
769	Figure 26.1 National Defense Budgets, 1940–1964
797	Figure 27.1 Defense Expenditures, Armed Forces Strength, 1945–1990
811	Table 27.1 Population of Metropolitan Areas, by Region, Size, and Race, 1950–1970
811	Figure 27.2 American Birthrate, 1940–1960
865	Figure 29.1 U.S. Troop Levels in Vietnam, 1960–1972
877	Table 30.1 High School Graduates (Percentage of Population Ages 25–29)
878	Table 30.2 Income Distribution of African Americans, Other Nonwhites, and Whites 1960, 1969
878	Figure 30.1 Unemployment, 1950–1970
885	Table 30.3 Black Voter Registration Before and After the Voting Rights Act of 1965
887	Figure 30.2 Federal Spending on Social Programs, Excluding Social Security
888	Figure 30.3 Federal Aid to Education, 1964–1970
893	Figure 30.4 Women in the Workforce, 1950–1985
894	Figure 30.5 American Birthrate, 1960–1985
897	Table 30.4 Percentage of Females in Selected Occupations
898	Table 30.5 Ratio of Divorces to Marriages, 1890–1987
917	Figure 31.1 Consumer Price Index, 1960–1990
921	Figure 31.2 Budget Deficits, 1940–1990

Appendix

A-29	U.S. Population, 1790–1990, Urban and Rural
A-29	U.S. Population, 1790–1990, White and Nonwhite

PREFACE

Americans are of two minds about history. Popular history fascinates them. Many of Hollywood's most popular films—from *Birth of a Nation* to *Titanic*—draw on history for their themes, characters, and drama. Nothing underscores this fascination with history better than the point that more Americans visit historical sites and museums like Colonial Williamsburg or the Smithsonian Institution on an annual basis than attend major league baseball games.

Academic history is much less popular, however. At colleges and universities, the number of history majors and enrollment in history courses has fallen at an alarming rate. At the high-school level, history requirements have increasingly been replaced by courses in social studies. A recent poll found that high school students consider history the least relevant subject that they study.

We have designed *America and Its Peoples* to convey American history's excitement and drama. The story that we tell is fraught with conflict, suspense, and controversy, and we have sought to recapture this excitement by writing a book built around vivid character sketches, colorful anecdotes, a strong narrative pulse, and a wide-angle view that allows us to examine such subjects as crime, disease, the family and sexuality, and sports.

A history textbook, in our view, need not be dull, humorless, or lifeless. Rather, it should bring the past back to life in all of its complexity, underscoring history's relevance to our daily lives. The issues addressed in this book—colonialism, revolution, the origins of racial prejudice, the costs and benefits of industrialization and urbanization—are anything but trivial. They remain very much a part of the human story today.

Nor do we think that a textbook should insulate readers from controversy. One of history's greatest benefits is that it allows us to "second guess" the decisions and choices made in the past, to reassess the meaning of past events, and to reevaluate real-life heroes and villains. History, we believe, is the ideal laboratory for critical thinking. By engaging the past, we can assess the roles of individuals and of social forces in producing historical transformations, and learn to evaluate conflicting interpretations of people and events. This textbook demonstrates that history is an arena of debate and contention as exciting as any other.

Each generation must produce a history that addresses the concerns of its own time. In writing *America and Its Peoples*, we have sought to fashion a history of the United States that speaks to the realities of a changing America. Today, the United States is the most ethnically diverse nation in the world. Over the past four centuries, 45 million people arrived in America from Africa, Asia, and Europe. In *America and Its Peoples* we recount the histories of the diverse ethnic, religious, and racial groups that have come to make up our society. We underscore the pivotal role that ethnicity, race, and religion have played in our nation's social, cultural, and political development. From its earliest settlement, America has been a multicultural society, and by placing ethnicity, race, gender, and class at the very heart of our narrative, we have sought to present a new perspective on how our multifaceted culture and politics functioned through time.

Contemporary American society perceives itself as beset by unprecedented problems—of ethnic and racial tension, economic stagnation and inequality, crime, family upheaval, and environmental degradation. In *America and Its Peoples*, we have made a special point of uncovering the historical roots of the problems confronting American society today. One of history's values is that it can show how previous generations confronted the controversial issues of their times, allowing us to assess their achievements as well as their failures.

Americans are an optimistic, forward-looking people who, in the course of everyday life, care little about the past. More than two centuries ago, Thomas Jefferson gave pointed expression to this attitude when he declared that "the earth belongs to the living and not the dead." But as the famous novelist William Faulkner once observed, "the past is never dead. It's not even past." We are convinced that the very worst forms of bigotry, fanaticism, and racism are ultimately grounded in historical ignorance and mythology. History reminds us that our values, our identities, and our most pressing social problems are rooted in our historical experience. Thus, in writing this book, we have not simply sought to create an encyclopedic compendium of names, dates, events, and concepts; we have conceived of United States history as a dramatic story: a story involving contention, struggle, compromise, and, above all, conflicting visions of the nation's dominant values.

Today, many Americans are wary about the future and uneasy about the state of their society. In *America and Its Peoples* we have written a textbook that emphasizes historical contingency—the idea that different decisions and choices in the past would have created a very different world today. Ours is a history that emphasizes the importance of personal choice and collective action; a history that stresses peoples' capacity to shape their own destiny. We believe that this is an inspiring historical lesson with profound implications for the nation's future.

FEATURES

Written by scholars who regularly teach the introductory U.S. history survey, *America and Its Peoples* is an exceptionally readable textbook that brings history to life through the stories of the women and men who shaped our history as a people. Highly sensitive to students' needs and interests, the authors place ethnicity, race, and gender at the core of the historical narrative, not as adjunct information. Carefully balancing cultural, diplomatic, economic, military, political, religious, and social history, the authors pay special attention to the clash of ideas and peoples that has shaped American history. Thoroughly revised and totally up-to-date, the fourth edition contains comprehensive coverage of the Clinton presidency.

America and Its Peoples is a textbook that students will genuinely enjoy reading. It thoroughly treats the history of all Americans, including extensive coverage of women, African Americans, Asian Americans, Hispanic Americans, and Native Americans. It offers exceptionally complete coverage of the areas that were originally colonized by Spain, to meet the special needs of students who live in the Sunbelt. An example of this coverage is the unique chapter (28) on the West and the South in the twentieth century, which examines the growing importance of these areas in our nation's recent history.

Concisely and vividly written, the textbook contains a wealth of special features designed to stimulate student interest in history and reinforce student learning.

NEW TO THIS EDITION

- *"The People Speak"* These excerpts from primary sources introduce students to critical documents in American history and allow them to hear the past speak in its own voice. Introductory headnotes provide the historical context for each document. One "People Speak" excerpt appears in each chapter.
- *Key Terms* In each chapter, 10 to 15 key terms are highlighted in boldface type to alert students to the principal concepts, events, and individuals discussed in the chapter. A page-referenced list of the key terms at the end of each chapter offers students the opportunity to review the main ideas and persons covered in the chapter.
- *Glossary* A thorough glossary at the end of the book provides definitions for each key terms and succinct identification of each key concept, individual, and event. Each glossary term is page referenced so that students can easily locate discussion of the term in its historical context.
- *Review Questions* End-of-the-chapter review questions allow students to examine how well they have absorbed the chapter content and invite them to think critically about the issues discussed in the chapter. The review questions can be used to spark class discussions or for written assignments.
- *Internet Resources* At the end of each chapter, guides to history resources on the World Wide Web direct students to sources of additional information that can be easily accessed online.
- *Comparative Chronology* A fold-out, illustrated timeline provides a thorough and accessible chronological reference guide for U.S. history. The timeline notes key events and trends in political, diplomatic, social, economic, and cultural history.

In addition to these new features, *America and Its Peoples*, Fourth Edition, includes a number of other components and pedagogical aids designed to engage students' interest and enhance their learning:

- Pictorial chapter-opening collages address students' capacity for visual learning by presenting images of the people, places, and events students will encounter in the chapter.
- Chapter-opening outlines help students organize their study by identifying the main topics and subtopics discussed in the chapter.

- Vignettes at the beginning of each chapter grab students' attention with a fascinating story of an individual or an event. The final paragraphs of the vignette succinctly introduce chapter themes and link the vignette to the chapter narrative.
- "The American Mosaic" essays, one in each chapter, offer an in-depth examination of some aspect of such high interest topics as crime, medicine, sports and other leisure-time activities, the experience of combat, and the reshaping of private life.
- Five full-page watercolor battlefield maps offer close examination of key battles in America's wars. An essay accompanying each battlefield map describes the battle in detail and explores its historical significance.
- "Road to War" tables summarize the key events that led up to the declaration of each of America's wars, providing students with a specialized chronology for these pivotal events in U.S. history.

SUPPLEMENTS

A comprehensive and up-to-date supplements package accompanies *America and Its Peoples*.

FOR QUALIFIED ADOPTERS

The History Place Web Site—Martin Special Edition (*www.awl.com/martin*) This special edition of *The History Place* combines quality educational publishing with the immediacy and interactivity of the Internet. The Web site contains a continually updated source of maps, timelines, and other interactive learning activities. It also houses a rich collection of primary documents, news, and online quizzes that correspond to the text's organization. A free subscription to *The History Place—Martin Special Edition* is included with every new copy of the student text.

Martin Online (*www.awl.com/martin*) Instructors can take advantage of the online course companion that supports this text. The instructor section of the Web site includes the instructor's manual, teaching links, animated maps, thematic timelines, narrated photo essays, and visual downloads. Additionally, instructors can take advantage of Syllabus Builder, our comprehensive course management system.

Instructor's Manual This extensive resource by Mark Newman of the University of Illinois, Chicago, begins with essays on teaching history through maps, film, and primary sources. Each chapter contains a synopsis, sample discussion questions, lecture supplements, and instructional flowcharts. The manual includes a reproducible set of map exercises by James Conrad of Nichols College, designed to teach basic geographical literacy.

Test Bank Written by Ken Weatherbie and Brian Hart of Del Mar College, the test bank contains multiple choice, true/false, and essay test items. The questions are keyed to topic, difficulty level, cognitive type, and relevant text page.

Computerized TestGen EQ Computerized Testing System This flexible, easy-to-use computer test bank includes all the test items in the printed test bank. Available on dual platform CD-ROM and floppy disks, the software allows you to edit existing questions and add your own items. Tests can be printed in several different formats and can include graphs and tables.

Text Map Transparencies A set of 40 four-color transparencies from the maps and figures in *America and Its Peoples*.

Comprehensive American History Transparency Set This vast collection of American history transparencies is a necessary teaching aid. It includes over 200 maps covering social trends, wars, elections, immigrations, and demographics. Included is a set of reproducible map exercises.

Discovering American History Through Maps and Views Transparency Set Created by Gerald Danzer of the University of Illinois at Chicago, the recipient of the AHA's 1990 James Harvey Robinson Prize for his work in the development of map transparencies, this set of 140 four-color acetates is a unique instructional tool. It contains an introduction on teaching history through maps and a detailed commentary on each transparency. The collection includes cartographic and pictorial maps, views and photos, urban plans, building diagrams, and works of art.

Discovering American History Through Film Created by Randy Roberts of Purdue University, this guide provides instructors with a creative and practical tool for stimulating class discussions. The sections include "American Films: A Historian's Perspective," and a listing of "Films for Specific Periods in American History." The narrative film explains the connection between each film and the topics being studied.

Video Lecture Launchers Prepared by Mark Newman of the University of Illinois at Chicago, these video lecture launchers (each two to five minutes in duration) cover key issues in American history from 1877 to the present. The launchers are accompanied by an instructor's manual.

American Impressions: A CD-ROM for American History This unique, groundbreaking product for the U.S. Survey course is organized in a thematic framework that allows in-depth coverage of each topic. Hundreds of photos, maps, art, graphics, and historical film clips are organized into narrated vignettes and interactive activities to create a tool for both professors and students. Topics include "When Three Cultures Meet," "The Constitution," "Labor and Reform," and "Democracy and Diversity." It is available on Windows or Macintosh floppy disks.

This Is America Immigration Video Produced by the Museum of Immigration, this video tells the story of immigrant America. By showing the personal stories and accomplishments of immigrants, it explores the contributions of millions of immigrants to America.

FOR STUDENTS

The History Place Web Site—Martin Special Edition *(www.ushistoryplace.com/martin)* This special edition of *The History Place* combines quality educational publishing with the immediacy and interactivity of the Internet. The Web site contains a continually updated source of maps, timelines, and other interactive learning activities. It also houses a rich collection of primary documents, news, and online quizzes that correspond to the text's organization. A free subscription to *The History Place—Martin Special Edition* is included with every new copy of the student text.

Martin Online *(www.awl.com/martin)* The online course companion provides a wealth of resources for students using *America and Its Peoples*. Students will find chapter summaries, practice test questions, interactive web exercises, animated maps, primary sources, thematic timelines, and more.

Interactive Edition CD-ROM for *America and Its Peoples* This unique CD-ROM takes students beyond the printed page, offering them a complete multimedia learning experience. It contains the full text of the book on CD-ROM, with contextually placed media icons—audio, video, photos, figures, Web links, practice tests, primary sources, and more—that link students to additional content directly related to key concepts in the text. Free when packaged with the text.

StudyWizard Computerized Tutorial Prepared by Ron Petrin of Oklahoma State University, this interactive program helps students learn major facts and concepts through drill and practice exercises and diagnostic feedback. Available on dual-platform CD-ROM and floppy disks, StudyWizard provides immediate correct answers and the text page number on which the material is discussed.

Study Guide Designed to provide students with a comprehensive review of the text material and to encourage application and critical analysis of the material, this guide was prepared by Eddie Weller of San Jacinto College. Each chapter contains a chapter overview, learning objectives, important glossary terms, and multiple choice and essay questions.

Everything You Need to Know About Your History Course Written by Sandra Mathews-Lamb of Nebraska Wesleyan University for first-year university students, this guide provides invaluable tips on how to study, use a textbook, write a good paper, take notes, read a map, graph, or bar chart, and review primary and secondary sources.

Longman American History Atlas This four-color historical atlas includes 69 maps designed especially for this volume. This valuable reference tool is available shrink-wrapped with the text at a low cost.

Mapping American History: Student Activities Written by Gerald Danzer of the University of Illinois at Chicago, this free map workbook for students features exercises designed to teach how to interpret and analyze cartographic materials as historical documents. The instructor is entitled to a free copy of the workbook for each copy of *America and Its Peoples* purchased from Longman.

Mapping America: A Guide to Historical Geography, Second Edition Written by Ken Weatherbie of Del Mar College, this free two-volume workbook contains 35 exercises correlated to the text that review basic American historical geography and ask students to interpret the role geography has played in American history.

America Through the Eyes of Its People, Second Edition This single-volume collection of primary documents reflects the rich and varied tapestry of American life. The revised edition includes more social history and enhanced pedagogy. It is available shrink-wrapped with *America and Its Peoples* at no charge.

Sources of the African-American Past Edited by Roy Finkenbine of the University of Detroit at Mercy, this collection of primary sources covers the themes in the African American experience from the West African background to the present. Balanced between political and social history, it offers a vivid snapshot of the lives of African Americans in different historical periods, and includes documents representing women and different regions of the United States. Available at a minimum cost when bundled with the text.

Women and the National Experience Edited by Ellen Skinner of Pace University, this primary source reader contains both classic and unusual documents describing the history of women in the United States. The documents provide dramatic evidence that outspoken women attained a public voice and participated in the development of national events and policies long before they could vote. Chronologically organized and balanced between social and political history, this reader offers a striking picture of the lives of women across American history. Available at a minimum cost when bundled with the text.

Reading the American West Edited by Mitchel Roth of Sam Houston State University, this primary source reader uses letters, diary excerpts, speeches, interviews, and newspaper articles to let students experience how historians research and how history is written. Every document is accompanied by a contextual headnote and study questions. The book is divided into chapters with extensive introductions. Available at a minimum cost when bundled with the text.

Library of American Biography Series Edited by Oscar Handlin of Harvard University, each of these interpretive biographies focuses on a figure whose actions and ideas significantly influenced the course of American history and national life. At the same time, each biography relates the life of its subject to the broader themes and developments of the era. Brief and inexpensive, they are ideal for any U.S. History course. New editions include *Abigail Adams: An American Woman*, Second Edition by Charles W. Akers; *Andrew Carnegie and the Rise of Big Business*, Second Edition by Harold C. Livesay; and *Eleanor Roosevelt: A Personal and Public Life,* Second Edition by J. William T. Youngs.

A Short Guide to Writing About History Written by Richard Marius of Harvard University, this short guide introduces students to the pleasures of historical research and discovery while teaching them how to write cogent history papers. Focusing on more than just the conventions of good writing, this supplement shows students first how to think about history, and then how to organize their thoughts into coherent essays.

Learning to Think Critically: Films and Myths About American History In this guide, Randy Roberts and Robert May of Purdue University use well-know films such as *Gone With the Wind* and *Casablanca* to explore some common myths about America and its past. Many widely held assumptions of out country's past originate from, or are perpetuated by, popular films. Which are true? How can a student of history approach documents, sources, and textbooks with a critical and discerning eye? This short handbook scrutinizes some popular beliefs to help students develop a method of inquiry to approach the subject of history.

ACKNOWLEDGMENTS

Any textbook project is very much a team effort. Here we acknowledge with gratitude the assistance of the many talented historians who have served as reviewers and whose valuable critiques have greatly strengthened the final product.

Elizabeth Reilly Ansnes, San Jose State University; James Banks, Cuyahoga Community College; Robert A. Becker, Louisiana State University; Surendra Bhana, University of Kansas; Ballard Campbell, Northeastern University; Raymond W. Champagne, Jr., University of Scranton; Paul G. E. Clemens, Rutgers University; Kenton Clymer, University of Texas, El Paso; Roy E. Finkenbine, University of Detroit; Mark S. Foster, University of Colorado, Denver; J. David Hoeveler, University of Wisconsin, Milwaukee; Melissa M. Hovsepian, University of St. Thomas, Texas; Deborah M. Jones, Bristol Community College; Kathleen Kennedy, Western Washington University; Sterling J. Kernek, Western Illinois University; Stuart E. Knee, College of Charleston; Lee Bruce Kress, Rowan University; Thomas Lewis, Mount Senario College; Terrence Lindell, Wartburg College; James McCaffery, University of Houston, Downtown; M. Catherine Miller, Texas Tech University; Daniel Nelson, University of Akron; Mark Newell, Ramapo College; Peter L. Petersen, West Texas A&M University; Jon H. Roberts, University of Wisconsin, Stevens Point; David P. Shriver, Cuyhoga Community College; Jason H. Silverman, Winthrop University; Jason Tetzloff, Defiance College; Gary E. Thompson, Tulsa Junior College; Eddie Weller, San Jacinto College South; Larry Wilson, San Jacinto College Central.

Each author has received invaluable assistance from friends, colleagues, and family. James Kirby Martin thanks Don R. Gerlach, Joseph T. Glatthaar, Irene Guenther, Karen Guenther, Katie Harrison, J. Kent McGaughy, David M. Oshinsky, Cathy Patterson, Jeffrey T. Sammons, Halt T. Shelton, and Karen Martin, whose talents as an editor and critic are too often overlooked. Randy Roberts thanks Terry Bilhartz, Aram Goudsouzian, James S. Olson, and Joan Randall. Steven Mintz thanks Susan Kellogg for her encouragement, support, and counsel. Linda O. McMurry thanks Joseph P. Hobbs, John David Smith, Richard McMurry, and William C. Harris. James H. Jones thanks Laura Auwers, James S. Olson, Terry Rugeley, Kimberley Weathers, and especially Linda S. Auwers, who contributed both ideas and criticisms. All of the authors thank Gerard F. McCauley, whose infectious enthusiasm for this project has never wavered. And above all else, we wish to thank our students to whom we have dedicated this book.

The Authors

ABOUT the Authors

James Kirby Martin holds the rank of Distinguished University Professor of History at the University of Houston. His areas of special interest include early American history, including the era of the American Revolution, American military history through the years of the Civil War, and the history of such social-behavioral issues as drinking and smoking in America. He is the author, co-author, or editor of eleven books, including *Men in Rebellion* (1973), *In the Course of Human Events* (1979), *A Respectable Army: the Military Origins of the Republic* (1982), and *Drinking in America* (1982, revised edition 1987). His most recent book, *Benedict Arnold, Revolutionary Hero: An American Warrior Reconsidered* (1997) was the recipient of the Homer D. Babbidge, Jr. Award and was named by the *Los Angeles Times* to its list of the best 100 books published that year. Martin serves as general editor of the *American Social Experience* series, New York University Press. His many interests also include the study of ordinary persons and the ways in which their lives have shaped the course of American historical development. His capacity to present these lives in meaningful historical contexts helps explain why his students consistently rank him among the very best teachers in the department.

Randy Roberts earned his Ph.D. degree from Louisiana State University. His areas of special interest include modern U.S. history and the history of sports and films in America. He is a faculty member at Purdue University, where he has won both the Murphy Award for outstanding teaching and the Society of Professional Journalists Teacher of the Year award. The books on which he is author or co-author include *Jack Dempsey: The Manassa Mauler* (1979, expanded edition, 1984), *Papa Jack: Jack Johnson and the Era of White Hopes* (1983), *Heavy Justice:* The State of Indiana *v.* Michael G. Tyson (1994), *My Lai: A Brief History with Documents* (1998), *John Wayne: American* (1995), *Where the Domino Fell: America in Vietnam, 1945–1990* (1990, revised edition 1996), and *Winning Is the Only Thing: Sports in America Since 1945* (1989). Roberts serves as the co-editor of the Sports and Society series, University of Illinois Press, and is on the editorial board of the *Journal of Sports History*.

Steven Mintz earned his Ph.D. degree at Yale University. One of the nation's leading authorities on the history of the family as well as a noted expert on slavery, social reform, and the history of film, Mintz is Professor of History, John and Rebecca Moores University Scholar, and Associate Dean at the University of Houston. His books include *The Boisterous Sea of Liberty* (with David Brion Davis, 1998), *Moralists & Modernizers: America's Pre-Civil War Reformers* (1995), *Domestic Revolutions: A Social History of American Family Life* (with Susan Kellogg, 1989), and *A Prison of Expectations: The Family in Victorian Culture* (1983). A pioneer in the integration of new computer and communication technologies in teaching and research, he moderates a scholarly discussion list on the history of slavery. Each summer, he team-teaches a seminar on "The Origins and Nature of New World Slavery" for high school teachers and National Park Service rangers at Yale University.

About the Authors

Linda O. McMurry is a member of the Department of History at North Carolina State University. Earning her Ph.D. degree from Auburn University, she specializes in African-American history. Her interest in personal perspectives and experiences of history has led her to write three biographies of African Americans: *To Keep the Waters Troubled: The Life of Ida B. Wells* (1998), *Recorder of the Black Experience: A Biography of Monroe Nathan Work* (1985), and *George Washington Carver: Scientist and Symbol* (1981). Both the Wells and Carver biographies are listed in the *New York Review of Books Readers' Catalog* of the best books in print. A recipient of a Rockefeller Foundation Humanities fellowship, McMurry has been active as a consultant and lecturer on topics relating to the black experience in America, appearing on such programs as NPR's "Morning Edition" and C-SPAN's "Booknotes." Although she enjoys research and writing, teaching has always been the top priority to McMurry, and she seeks to bring history alive for her students. She was pleased to win the top research award for her college in 1999, but was even more thrilled to win the college's top teaching award that same year.

James H. Jones earned his Ph.D. degree at Indiana University. His areas of specialization include modern U.S. history, the history of medical ethics and medicine, and the history of sexual behavior. The Distinguished Alumni Professor at the University of Arkansas, Jones is also on the advisory board of the Arkansas Center for Oral and Visual History. He has been a senior fellow of the National Endowment for the Humanities, a Kennedy fellow at Harvard University, a senior research fellow at the Kennedy Institute of Ethics, Georgetown University, and a Rockefeller fellow at the University of Texas Medical Branch, Galveston. His published works include *Bad Blood: The Tuskegee Syphilis Experiment, A Tragedy of Race and Medicine* (1981) revised edition (1993), which was named to the *New York Times Book Review* list of best books of 1981 and received the Arthur Viseltear prize for the Best Book in Public Health History. His most recent publication *Alfred C. Kinsey: A Public/Private Life* (1997) was a finalist for both the Pulitzer Prize in biography and for the Penn Center Award.

America
and Its Peoples

1

THE PEOPLING AND UNPEOPLING OF AMERICA

THE FIRST DISCOVERY OF AMERICA
A Diversity of Cultures
The Myth of the "Virgin" Land
Eastern Indians on the Eve of Contact

PREPARING EUROPE FOR WESTWARD EXPANSION
Changing Population Pressures
Crusades, Commerce, and the New Learning
Nation-States Support the First Explorations

EXPLORERS, CONQUERORS, AND THE MAKING OF NEW SPAIN
Conquistadores Overrun Native Americans
Constructing the Spanish Empire
Success Breeds Envy and Contempt

CHALLENGERS FOR NORTH AMERICA: FRANCE AND ENGLAND
The Protestant Reformation Stirs Deep Tensions
Defying the Supremacy of Spain
England Prepares for Westward Expansion

JOINING IN THE INVASION OF AMERICA
The Roanoke Disaster
Merchant Capitalists Sponsor the Founding of Virginia
Struggling Jamestown Survives
Dutch and French Adventurers

"A special instrument sent of God"

The Pilgrims called him Squanto, a corruption of his given name, Tisquantum. Each Thanksgiving Americans remember him as the valued native friend who saved the suffering Pilgrims from starvation. Few know the other ways in which Tisquantum's life reflected the disastrous collision of human beings that occurred in the wake of Christopher Columbus's first voyage of discovery to America in 1492. European explorers believed they had stumbled upon two empty continents, which they referred to as the "new world." In actuality, the new world was both very old and the home of millions of people. These Native Americans experienced chaos and death when they came into contact with the Europeans. A little more than 100 years after Columbus, at the time of the Pilgrims, the American Indian population had declined by as much as 90 percent. The tragic story of Tisquantum and his tribe, the Patuxets of eastern Massachusetts, vividly portrays what happened.

Born about 1590, Tisquantum acquired the values of his Algonquian-speaking elders before experiencing much contact with adventurers from overseas. Tribal fathers taught him that personal dignity came from respecting the bounties of nature and serving one's clan and village, not from acquiring material possessions. He also learned the importance of physical and mental endurance. To be accepted as an adult, he spent a harrowing winter surviving alone in the wilderness. When he returned the next spring, his Patuxet fathers fed him poisonous herbs for days on end, which he unflinchingly ate—and survived by forced vomiting. Having demonstrated his fortitude, tribal members declared him a man.

Tisquantum is best remembered for the assistance he gave the Pilgrims in providing for the necessities of life, but his own life—and death—illustrate the tensions and problems created by contact between Native American and European cultures.

Living among 2000 souls in the Patuxet's principal village, located on the very spot where the Pilgrims settled in 1620, Tisquantum may well have foreseen trouble ahead when fair-skinned Europeans started visiting the region. First there were fishermen; then in 1605 the French explorer, Samuel de Champlain, stopped at Plymouth Bay. More fatefully, Captain John Smith, late of the Virginia colony, passed through in 1614. Smith's party treated the Patuxets with respect, but they viewed the natives as little more than wild beasts, to be exploited if necessary. Before sailing away, Smith ordered one of his lieutenants, Captain Thomas Hunt, to stay behind with a crew of mariners and gather up a rich harvest of fish. After completing his assignment, Hunt lured 20 Indians, among them Tisquantum, on board his vessel and, without warning, set his course for the slave market in Malaga, Spain.

Somehow Tisquantum avoided a lifetime of slavery. By 1617 he was in England, where he devoted himself to mastering the English tongue. One of his sponsors, Captain Thomas Dermer, who had been with Smith in 1614, asked Tisquantum to serve as an interpreter and guide for yet another New England expedition. Eager to return home, the native readily agreed and sailed back to America in 1619.

When Dermer's party put in at Plymouth Bay, a shocked Tisquantum discovered that nothing remained of his once-thriving village, except overgrown fields and rotting human bones. As if swept away by some unnamed force, the Patuxets had disappeared from the face of the earth. Trained to hide his emotions, Tisquantum grieved privately. Soon he learned about a disastrous epidemic. Thousands of natives had died in the Cape Cod vicinity of diseases heretofore unknown in New England—in this case probably chicken pox carried there from Europe by fishermen and explorers. When these microparasites struck, the native populace, lacking antibodies, had no way of fending them off.

Tisquantum soon left Dermer's party and went in search of possible survivors. He was living with the Pokanoket Indians when the Pilgrims stepped ashore in December 1620 at the site of his old village. The Pilgrims endured a terrible winter in which half their numbers died. Then in the early spring of 1621 a lone Indian, Samoset, appeared in Plymouth Colony. He spoke halting English and told of another who had actually lived in England. Within a week Tisquantum arrived and agreed to stay and help the Pilgrims produce the necessities of life.

Tisquantum taught them how to grow Indian corn (maize), a crop unknown in Europe, and how to catch great quantities of fish. His efforts resulted in an abundance of food, celebrated in the first Thanksgiving feast during the fall of 1621. To future Pilgrim Governor William Bradford, Squanto "was a special instrument sent of God for their good beyond their expectation."

The story does not have a pleasant ending. Contact with the English had changed Tisquantum, and he adopted some of their practices. In violation of his childhood training, he started to serve himself. As Bradford recorded, Squanto told neighboring Indian tribes that the Pilgrims would make war on them unless they gave him gifts. Further, he would unleash the plague, which the English "kept . . . buried in the ground, and could send it among whom they would." By the summer of 1622 Squanto had become a problem for the Pilgrims, who were eager for peace. Then he fell sick, "bleeding much at the nose," and died within a few days as yet another victim of some European disease.

As demonstrated by Tisquantum's life, white-Indian contacts did not point toward a fusing of Native American and European customs, values, and ideals. Rather, the westward movement of peoples destroyed Indian societies and replaced them with European-based communities. The history of the Americas (and of the United States) cannot be fully appreciated without considering the reasons that thousands of Europeans crossed the Atlantic Ocean and sought dominance over the American continents and their native peoples. Three groups in particular, the Spanish, French, and English, succeeded in this life-and-death struggle that changed forever the course of human history.

THE FIRST DISCOVERY OF AMERICA

The world was a much colder place 75,000 years ago. A great ice age, known as the Wisconsin glaciation, had begun. Year after year, water being drawn from the oceans formed into mighty ice caps, which in turn spread over vast reaches of land. This process dramatically lowered ocean levels. In the area of the Bering Straits, where today 56 miles of ocean separate Siberia from Alaska, a land bridge emerged. At times this link between Asia and America, *Beringia*, may have been 1000 miles wide. Most experts believe it provided the pathway used by early humans to enter a new world.

These people, known as Paleo-Indians, were nomads and predators. With stone-tipped spears, they hunted mastodons, woolly mammoths, giant beavers, giant sloths, and bighorn bison, as well as many smaller animals. The mammals led prehistoric men and women to America up to 30,000 or more years ago. For generations, these humans roamed Alaska in small bands, gathering seeds and berries when not hunting the big game or attacking and killing one another.

Eventually, corridors opened through the Rocky Mountains as the ice started to recede. The migratory cycle began anew. Animals and humans trekked southward and eastward, reaching the bottom of South America and the east coast of North America by about 8000 B.C. This long journey covered thousands of miles and took several centuries to complete. In the process Paleo-Indians had become Native Americans.

A Diversity of Cultures

As these first Americans fanned out over two continents, they improved their weapons. They flaked and crafted such hard quartz stones as flint into sharper spear points, which allowed them to slaughter the big game more easily. Also, with the passing of time, the atmosphere began to warm as the ice age came to an end. Mammoths, mastodons, and other giant mammals did not survive the warming climate and needless overkilling.

The first Americans now faced a serious food crisis. Their solution was ingenious. Beginning in Central America between roughly 8000 and 5000 B.C., groups of humans started cultivating plant life as an alternative food source. They soon mastered the basic techniques of agriculture. They raked the earth with stone hoes and planted seeds that produced crops as varied as maize, potatoes, squashes, pumpkins, and tomatoes.

This agricultural revolution profoundly affected Native American life. Those who engaged in farming were no longer as nomadic. They constructed villages and ordered their religious beliefs around such elements of nature as the sun and rain. With dependable food supplies, they had more children, resulting in a population explosion. Work roles became differentiated by gender. Men still hunted and fished for game, but they also prepared the fields for crops. When not caring for children, women did the planting, weeding, and harvesting.

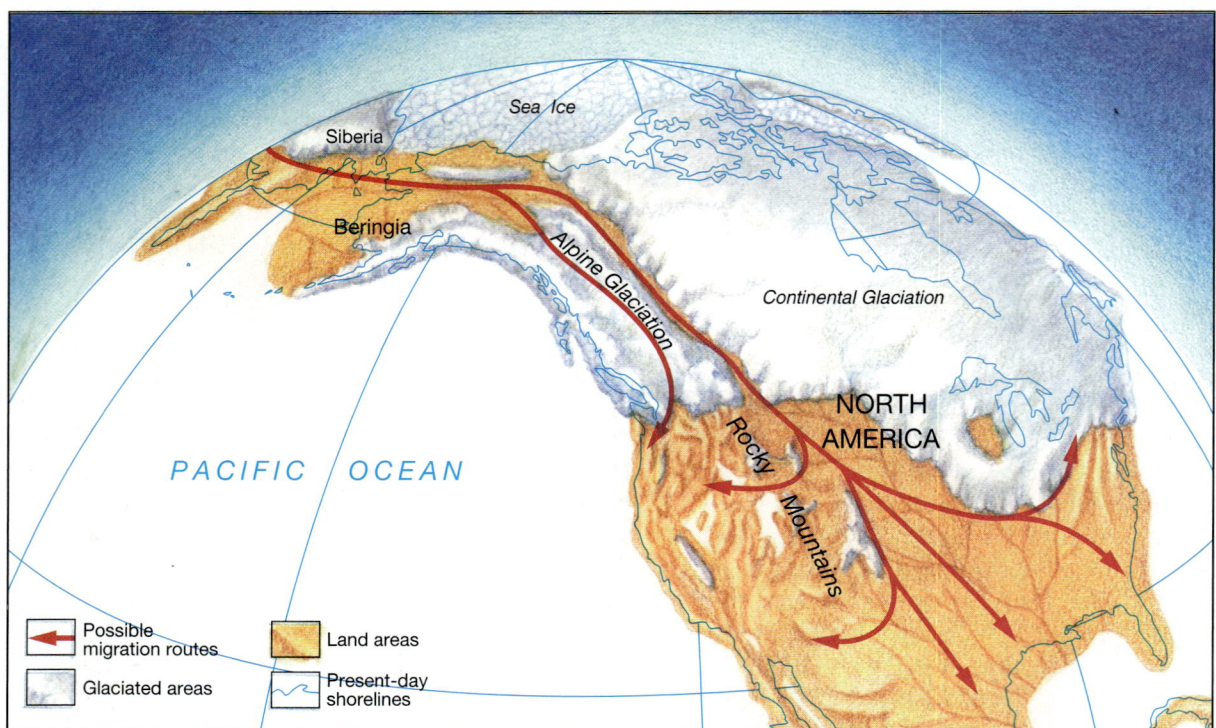

Routes of the First Americans

The Paleo-Indians migrated across the land bridge that once linked Asia and America. They then journeyed southward and eastward in populating North and South America.

Ultimately, out of these agriculturally oriented cultures evolved complex Native American societies, the most sophisticated of which appeared in Central America and the Ohio and Mississippi river valleys. Emerging before A.D. 300, the Mayas of Mexico and Guatemala based their civilization on abundant agricultural production. They also built elaborate cities and temples. Their craft workers produced jewelry of gold, silver, and other precious metals, and their merchants developed extensive trading networks. Their intellectuals devised forms of hieroglyphic writing, mathematical systems, and several calendars, one of which was the most accurate in the world at that time.

Powerful nobles and priests ruled over ordinary inhabitants in the highly stratified Maya social order. However, no strong central government existed, and warfare eventually broke out among the principal population centers. This internal strife so weakened the Mayas that after A.D. 1000 warlike peoples from the north began to overrun and conquer them. First came the Toltecs, then the Aztecs. The Aztecs called their principal city Tenochtitlán (the site of present-day Mexico City). At its zenith just before the Spanish conquistadores appeared in 1519, Tenochtitlán had a population of 300,000, making it one of the largest cities in the world at that time. The Aztecs imitated many aspects of Maya culture, and they brutally extracted tribute, both in wealth and lives, from subject tribes. Their priests reveled in human sacrifice, since Huitzilopochtli, the Aztec war god, voraciously craved human hearts. At one temple dedication, Aztec priests sacrificed some 20,000 subject peoples. Not surprisingly, these tribes hated their oppressors. Many later cooperated with the Spanish in destroying the Aztecs.

Other mighty civilizations also emerged, such as the Incas of Peru, who came into prominence after A.D. 1100. Settling in the Andes Mountains, the Incas developed a sophisticated food supply network. They trained all young males as warriors to protect the empire and their kings, whom they thought of as gods and to whom all riches belonged. The Incas were even wealthier than the Aztecs, and they particularly prized gold and silver, which they mined in huge quantities—and which made them a special target for Spanish conquerors.

In North America the Mound Builders (Adena and Hopewell peoples) appeared in the Ohio River valley around 1000 B.C. and lasted until A.D. 700.

The Aztecs, Mayas, and Incas

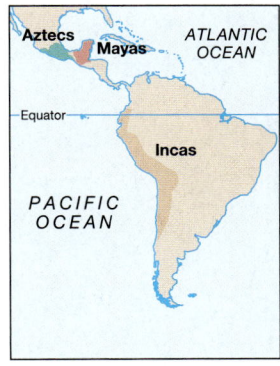

The Aztecs, Mayas, and Incas evolved from simple agriculturally based groups to become politically and socially complex civilizations.

Tlaloc (right), the Aztec rain god, represented fertility and emphasized the importance of water and moisture as a basis for agricultural prosperity. The mural below depicts the many facets of Maya civilization, which involved extensive agricultural production, far-reaching trading networks, complex architectural designs in urban centers, and the crafting of jewelry from rare metals.

These natives hunted and gathered food, but they obtained most of their diet from agriculture. They also raised such crops as tobacco for ceremonial functions. Their merchants traded far and wide. Fascinated with death, they built elaborate burial sites, such as the Great Serpent Mound in Ohio. In time they gave way to the Temple Mound Builders (Mississippian peoples), who were even more sedentary and agriculturally minded. They too were great traders, and they constructed large cities, including a huge site near Cahokia, Illinois, where as many as 75,000 people lived amid 85 large temple mounds.

For unknown reasons the Mississippian culture broke apart before European contact. Remnant groups may have included the Choctaws and Creeks of Mississippi and Alabama, as well as the Natchez Indians. In the rigidly stratified Natchez society the Great Sun was the all-powerful chief, and he ruled over nobles and commoners, the latter bearing the unpleasant name of "stinkards." As with their Mississippian forebears, when eminent individuals died, others gave up their lives so that central figures would have company as they passed into eternity. All but exterminated by the French in the 1730s, the Natchez were the last of the Mound Builders in North America.

The snake-shaped Great Serpent Mound, located in southern Ohio, is one of the lasting legacies of the Adena and Hopewell cultures. The mound is about 20 feet wide; uncoiled, its length would be more than 1300 feet.

The Myth of the "Virgin" Land

Beginning with the agricultural revolution, population in the Americas increased rapidly. Estimates vary widely. One authority has claimed a native populace of up to 120 million persons by the 1490s, whereas other experts suggest a figure of 50 to 80 million, with 5 to 8 million of these people inhabiting North America. Europe's population, by comparison, was roughly 75 million at the time of Columbus, which underscores the mistaken impression of European explorers that America was a "virgin" or "vacant" land.

Over several centuries the Native American populace developed as many as 2200 different languages, some 550 to 650 of which were in use in Central and North America at the time of Columbian contact. So many languages implied immense cultural diversity. Although sophisticated civilizations of enormous wealth did exist, most natives belonged to small, less complex groups in which families formed into clans—and clans into tribes.

Developing lifestyles to fit their environments, native groups varied greatly. Tribes in Oregon and Washington, such as the Chinooks, did some farming, but fishing for salmon was their primary means of subsistence. In the Great Plains region, Indians such as the Arapahos and Pawnees did not wander to the extent of their ancestors but pursued wild game within more or less fixed hunting zones. In the Southwest, the Hopi and Zuni tribes relied on agriculture, since edible plant and animal life was scarce in their desert environment. These natives even practiced irrigation. Perhaps they are best known for their flat-roofed, multitiered villages, which the Spanish called *pueblos*.

Eastern Indians on the Eve of Contact

In the East, where English explorers and settlers first made contact with Native Americans, dozens of small tribal groupings dotted the landscape. Southeastern Indians, including the Cherokees, Chickasaws, Creeks, Choctaws, and Seminoles, were more attuned to agriculture than to hunting because of lengthy growing seasons. Northeastern tribes, such as the Mahicans and Micmacs, placed more emphasis on hunting and gathering.

Eastern Woodland natives spoke several different languages but held many cultural traits in common. Perhaps linked to memories of the period of overkilling, they treated plant and animal life with respect. Essential to their religious values was the notion of an animate universe. They considered trees, plants, and animals to be spiritually alive (filled with *manitou*). As such, animals were not inferior to humans. They too organized themselves into nations, and through their "boss spirits" permitted some thinning of their numbers for humans to have food and survive. Boss spirits, however, would not tolerate overkilling. If tribes became gluttonous, animal nations could either leave the region or declare war, causing starvation and death.

The styles of Native American dwellings varied according to the particular group's customs, the climate in which they lived, and the materials readily available. Nomadic groups built temporary shelters of brush and bark, while Indians that engaged in farming constructed more permanent types of structures that might house one or several families.

Tribal *shamans,* or medicine men, communicated with the boss spirits and prescribed elaborate rules, or taboos, regarding the treatment of plants and animals. Indian parents, having mastered such customs, taught children like Tisquantum that nature contained the resources of life. Although intertribal trading was common, as was gift-giving in pottery, baskets, jewelry, furs, and wampum (conch and clam shells), religious values precluded tribal members from exploiting the landscape for the sake of acquiring great personal wealth.

Eastern Woodland parents introduced their children to many other concepts. Individual ownership of land was not known. Tribal boundaries consisted of geographic locales large enough to provide basic food supplies. Although individual dignity did matter, cooperation with tribal members rather than individual competitiveness was the essential ideal, even in sports. Eastern Woodland tribes enjoyed squaring off with one another in lacrosse matches, archery contests, and foot races. Betting and bragging occurred regularly, as did serious injuries in the heat of competition, but the matches had a decided group orientation. Individuals did not participate to gain personal glory but to bring accolades to their tribes.

The refinement of athletic skills also represented useful training for war. Intertribal warfare was sporadic and resulted from any number of factors, such as competition over valued hunting grounds. Skirmishes and the taking of a few lives by roving bands of warriors usually ended the conflict, but not necessarily the ill will, especially among different language groups. Festering tensions and language barriers worked against intertribal cooperation in repelling the Europeans.

Even though males served as warriors, they did not always control tribal decision making. Among the powerful Five Nations of Iroquois (Mohawks, Oneidas, Onondagas, Cayugas, and Senecas) in central New York, tribal organization was **matrilineal**. Women headed individual family units that in turn formed into clans. Clan leaders were also women, and they decided which males would sit on tribal councils charged with determining policies on diplomacy and war. Women held the power of removal as well, so males had no choice but to respect the authority of female clan heads. Among other Eastern Woodland Indians, women occasionally served as tribal *sachems* (chiefs), much to the shock of Europeans.

When European fishermen and explorers started making contact, an estimated 500,000 to 800,000 Indians inhabited the land between the North Atlantic coastline and the Appalachian Mountains. The Europeans, in a pattern that was essentially the same throughout the Americas, were initially curious as well as fearful in approaching the natives, but these feelings soon gave way to expressions of contempt. Judging all persons by their own cultural standards, Europeans came to regard the Indians as inferior. Native Americans looked and dressed differently. Their religious beliefs did not conform to European forms of Christianity. The men seemed lazy since women did the bulk of the farming, and they lacked a consuming drive to acquire personal wealth, leaving the mistaken impression of much "want in a land

The Atlantic Community, Late 1400s

Native Americans, Europeans, and Africans made up a triad of peoples around the Atlantic Ocean.

of plenty," as one historian has summarized European perceptions.

To make matters worse, the native populace, as was the case with Tisquantum's Patuxet tribe, quickly began to die in huge numbers, further confirming European perceptions that Indian peoples were inferior rather than merely different. These native "savages," or so Europeans stated, were blocking the path of a more advanced civilization desirous of expansion. Thus commenced what historians have come to call the "invasion" of America.

PREPARING EUROPE FOR WESTWARD EXPANSION

Nearly 500 years before Columbus's initial westward voyage, Europeans made their first known contacts with North America. Around A.D. 1000, the Vikings (Scandinavians) explored barren regions of the North Atlantic. Eric the Red led an expedition of Vikings to Greenland, and one of his sons, Leif Ericson, continued exploring south and westward, stopping at Baffin Island, Labrador, and Newfoundland (described as *Vinland*). There were some attempts at settlement, but none survived. The Viking voyages had no long-term impact because Europe was not yet ripe for westward expansion.

Changing Population Pressures

Most Europeans of the Middle Ages (approximately A.D. 500–1400) lived short, demanding lives. Many tilled the soil as peasants, owing allegiance to manor lords and eking out a meager subsistence. Their crops, grown on overworked soil, were not nutritious. Because they rarely ate fruits, they suffered from constipation and rickets among other diseases. These peasants worshipped as Roman Catholics, regularly attending church services that emphasized the importance of preparing for a better life after death. Meanwhile, the dominant concern was to survive long enough to help the next generation begin the cycle anew.

A variety of factors, including rapid population growth, gradually altered the established rhythms of life in the Middle Ages. Between A.D. 1000 and 1340, Europe's population doubled, reaching over 70 million people. Even with improved methods of

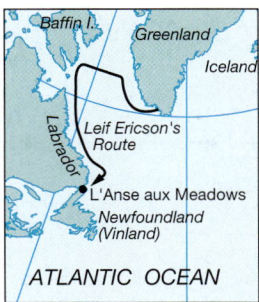

Vinland

Even though Leif Ericson made contact with North America about 500 years before Columbus, no permanent settlements resulted.

agricultural production, a new problem—overcrowding on the land—emerged. Overcrowding represents a condition in which too many individuals try to provide for themselves and their families on fixed parcels of farmland. To ease the pressure, manor lords forced some peasants off the land. These dispossessed persons struggled to avoid starvation. Some joined the growing class of beggars, or they became highway bandits. Others moved into the developing towns where they offered their labor for wages of any kind while seeking to acquire craft skills. Only a handful advanced beyond a marginal existence.

By 1340 Europe was bulging at the seams, but the knowledge and technology were not yet in place to facilitate the movement of people to distant regions. Then, suddenly, a frightening disaster relieved the population pressure. Italian merchant ships trading in Muslim ports in the eastern Mediterranean hauled rats as well as cargoes back to their home ports. These rats carried fleas infested with microbes that caused bubonic plague. The plague, or "Black Death," spread mercilessly through a populace already suffering less virulent maladies related to inadequate diet and unclean personal hygiene. When the plague struck the Italian city of Florence in 1348, for example, between half and two-thirds of the population of 85,000 died. More generally, between 1347 and 1353 about one-third of all Europeans died in a medical calamity not to be outdone until the plague and other killer diseases started wiping out Native Americans.

The unpeopling of Europe resulting from the Black Death temporarily checked any desire to find and inhabit new lands. In another two centuries rapid population growth, overcrowding, and consequent problems of destitution and starvation would again come to characterize life in Europe. By this time other factors were in place to facilitate the westward migration of peoples in search of new beginnings.

Crusades, Commerce, and the New Learning

Long before the Black Death, Europeans were gathering knowledge about previously unknown peoples and places. The Crusades, designed to oust the Muslim "infidels" from such Christian holy sites as Jerusalem, broadened their horizons. Sanctioned by the Roman Catholic church and begun in 1095, the Crusades lasted for two centuries. Although European warriors failed to break Muslim hegemony, they did discover that they could carry on trade with the Orient. They learned of spices that would preserve meats over long winters, fruits that would bring greater balance to diets, silk and velvet clothing, hand-crafted rugs, delicate glassware, and

This engraving depicts the horrible destruction of the "Black Death" in Florence, a city visited by the plague sixteen times in the thirteenth and fourteenth centuries. Between 1347 and 1353, the plague claimed the lives of nearly 20 million Europeans.

THE American Mosaic

Indian Scalping and European War Dogs

WHEN Native Americans and Europeans first came into contact, each seemed genuinely curious about the other. Curiosity, however, soon turned to mistrust, and mistrust to a state of unending warfare. Both sides employed "the tactics of remorseless terrorism" in their combat, as one student of early Indian-white relations has written, because both were fighting for control of the landscape—the natives to retain their ancient tribal homes and the Europeans to inhabit the same.

In their life-and-death struggle, Europeans and Indians drew upon long-accepted styles of waging combat. Neither showed much mercy toward the other. Europeans rationalized their acts of butchery by claiming they were dealing with "savages" who were at best "inhumanely cruel" and at worst "carnivorous beasts of the forest." Because of language barriers, the thoughts of Native Americans are not known, but they learned to fear and hate the invaders from across the ocean, and they too fought with a vengeance, although at times with more mercy than Europeans.

Long before the English first made contact, Eastern Woodland Indians regularly engaged in small-scale, intertribal wars. Their weapons included bows and arrows, knives, tomahawks, spears, and clubs. War parties did not attack in battle formations but used the forest as their cover as they ambushed enemies in surprise guerrilla-like raids. Employing hit-and-run tactics, intertribal combat rarely resulted in much bloodshed, since battles seldom lasted for more than a few minutes before attacking warriors melted back into the forest.

When possible, Indian war parties celebrated their victories by the taking of enemy scalps, which for them were war trophies filled with religious meaning. Native Americans believed the piece of scalp and hair sliced from an enemy's head contained the victim's living spirit, which now belonged to the holder of the scalp. To take a scalp, then, was to gain control over that person's spirit *(manitou)*. Even if victims survived scalping, which happened on occasion, they were spiritually dead, since they no longer possessed the essence of human life.

Because of their spiritual meaning and power, scalps were treated with great respect. Indians decorated them with jewelry and paint, and warriors kept them on display, even strapping them on their belts as symbols of individual prowess. In other instances warriors gave scalps to families who had lost relatives in battle. Since they contained life, scalps took the place of deceased tribal members.

When Europeans first saw scalps, they were not sure what to think. They certainly attached no spiritual significance to them. Frenchman Jacques Cartier, exploring along the St. Lawrence River in 1535, wrote about local Indians who showed him "the skins of five men's heads, stretched on hoops, like parchment." The local chief explained that the scalps were from Micmacs living to "the south, who waged war continually against his people." Just five years later in west Florida, natives killed two Spanish conquistadores exploring with Hernando de Soto. The Indians then "removed" the "head" of one victim, "or rather all around his skull—it is unknown with what skill they removed it with great ease—and carried it off as evidence of their deed."

Europeans quickly concluded that scalping was another barbarous practice of "savage" Native Americans. Also frightening was the way in which Indians conducted combat. They would not stand and fight in "civilized" fashion, holding to complex linear formations as Europeans did. Rather "they are always running and traversing from one place to another," complained de Soto, making it impossible for musket-wielding Europeans to shoot them down. Worse yet, an expert Indian bowman could easily "discharge three or four arrows" with great accuracy by the time musketeers went through the elaborate steps of preparing their cumbersome weapons for firing. This made combat with Native Americans particularly dangerous because, as de Soto concluded, an Indian bowman "seldom misses what he shoots at."

The Indian style of fighting caused a stream of negative commentary from various European New World adventurers. Natives did not fight fairly, they wrote, but used "cunning tricks" and "slippery designs" to defeat their adversaries. Rather than engaging in manly combat, they were "as greedy after their prey as a wolf," wanting above all else to mutilate their opponents by taking their scalps. The only effective way to deal with native tactics, reasoned these early adventurers, was to counter them with the most brutal

forms of corporal punishment then known—and commonly used—in Europe.

In times of combat the Europeans treated Indians as if they were criminals. As such, natives, in various combinations, would be hanged, drawn and quartered, disemboweled, and like the "savage" and "wild" Irish, beheaded. Captain Miles Standish, charged with protecting the Pilgrims, killed one troublesome Indian and then carried his head back to Plymouth where he had it publicly displayed. When the Dutch in New Netherland went to war with local natives in the 1640s, they regularly beheaded their opponents and had their "gory heads . . . laid in the streets of New Amsterdam, where the governor's mother kicked them like footballs."

Such wanton cruelty, when measured by modern standards, recently resulted in claims from some students of Native American history that Indians, before making contact with Europeans, did not scalp their enemies. Scalping, they claimed, was modeled on beheading but was a more efficient means of gaining war trophies for highly mobile Indian warriors not wanting to carry the extra weight of human heads.

Seeking to demonstrate the "barbarous" influence of "civilized" Europeans expanding westward, this line of reasoning has been thoroughly refuted. Among other forms of evidence, Indian cultural traditions and the astonishment of explorers who first saw scalps support the conclusion that Europeans learned about scalping from Indians and soon incorporated the practice into their arsenal of punishments.

In at least one area, however, European adventurers reached beyond accepted methods for exacting terror, pain, and death. The Spanish conquistadores used war dogs to maim and kill their victims. The English, who during the sixteenth century reveled in horror stories about Spanish New World barbarities (the so-called Black Legend), thought of war dogs as a new low point in human warfare. Yet within a few years of founding their first settlements, the English likewise were training and unleashing war dogs on Native Americans.

Apparently the favored breed was the English mastiff. These were huge, ugly dogs, weighing up to 150 pounds and naturally protective of their masters. In sixteenth-century England their owners trained them to "bait the bear, to bait the bull and other such like cruel and bloody beasts." The next logical step was to turn these dogs loose on the "heavy beast" in America. In retaliation for Opechancanough's 1622 massacre of Virginians, surviving settlers used dogs, presumably mastiffs, to track down and kill local Indians. War dogs participated in the slaughter of Pequot Indians in Connecticut during 1637 and would perform similar duty throughout the colonial period.

If prospects of facing the scalping knife filled European New World settlers with horror, war dogs, whether on guard duty or on the attack, represented an "extreme terror to the Indians," as a New England minister wrote in the early eighteenth century. This clergyman wanted yet more dogs "trained up to hunt Indians as they do the bear." He understood the nature of "total war" between Indians and whites in the bloody contest for the Americas, and he wanted to survive.

dozens of other commodities that would make European lives more comfortable.

Italian merchants, living in independent city-states such as Venice and Genoa, took the lead in developing the Mediterranean trade. Other European cities mushroomed in size at key trading points when Oriental goods started making their way from Italy into Switzerland, France, and Germany. One benefit of this striking increase in commercial activity was to create work for dislocated peasants. Also of major consequence was the rise of great merchants who devoted themselves to securing scarce commodities—and selling them for handsome profits.

The new wealth displayed by the great merchants promoted a pervasive spirit of material acquisition. The merchants, however, did more than merely reinvest profits in additional trading ventures. They also underwrote a resurgence in learning, known as the **Renaissance**. Beginning in Italy, the Renaissance soon captivated much of Continental Europe. New probings took place in all subjects. Learned individuals rediscovered the writings of such ancient scholars as Ptolemy, who had mapped the Earth, and Eratosthenes, who had estimated the circumference of the planet. By the mid-fifteenth century educated Europeans knew the world was not flat. Indeed, early in 1492, just a few months before Columbus sailed, a German geographer, Martin Behaim, constructed a round globe for all to see.

Enhanced geographical knowledge went hand in hand with developments in naval science. Before the fifteenth century, Europeans risked their lives when they did not sail within sight of land. The Muslims provided knowledge about the astrolabe and sextant and their uses as basic navigational instruments. Contact with the Arabs also introduced Europeans to more advanced ship and sail designs. Europeans soon abandoned their outmoded square-rigged galleys, which required oarsmen to maneuver these craft against the wind, in favor of lateen-rigged caravels. These vessels were sleeker in design, making them faster. Since their triangular sails could also swivel, the caravels were more mobile. Tacking, or sailing at angles into the wind, was now possible. Such nautical breakthroughs heightened prospects for worldwide exploration in the ongoing search for valuable trading commodities.

The adventures of Marco Polo (1254?–1324?) underscored the new learning and exemplified its relationship to commerce and exploration. Late in the thirteenth century, this young Venetian trader traveled throughout the Orient. He recorded his findings and told of unbelievable wealth in Asian kingdoms such as Cathay (China). Around 1450, Johannes Gutenberg, a German printer, perfected movable type, making it possible to reprint limitless copies of manuscripts, heretofore laboriously copied by hand. The first printed edition of Marco Polo's *Journals* ap-

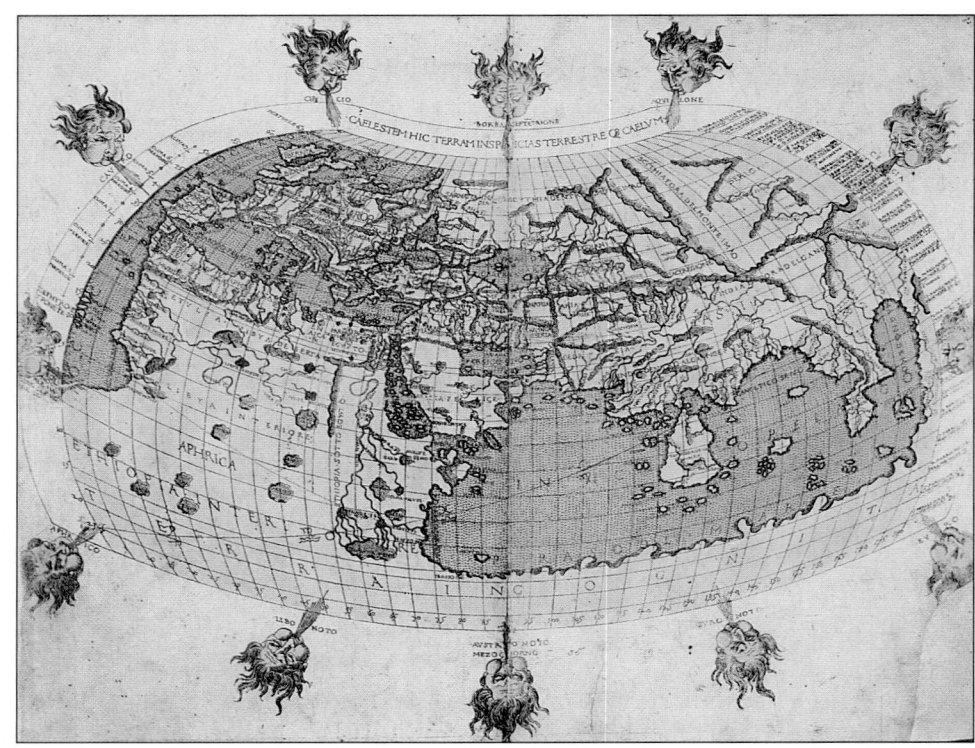

Ptolemy prepared his *Guide to Geography* in the second century A.D. He indicated that the world was round but underestimated the earth's circumference and imagined Asia as a larger continent than is actually the case. His work became part of Europe's new learning when widely republished after 1475.
Copyright © The British Museum.

peared in 1477. Merchants and explorers alike, among them Christopher Columbus, read Polo's *Journals*, which spurred them forward in their quest to gain complete access to Oriental riches.

Nation-States Support the First Explorations

Not all elements of European society embraced the new vitality. Powerful manor lords still controlled the countryside, and they made it difficult for merchants to move goods across their lands, unless traders paid heavy tolls. These nobles also sneered at monarchs wanting to collect taxes. Tapping into peasant manpower, manor lords quite often had stronger armies, leaving royal figures unable to enforce their will. Over time, merchants and monarchs started working together. Using mercantile capital, they formed armies that challenged the nobility.

The process of forming modern nation-states commenced during the fifteenth century. The marriage of Ferdinand of Aragon to Isabella of Castile in 1469 represented the beginnings of national unity in Spain. These joint monarchs hired mercenary soldiers to break the power of defiant nobles. In 1492 they also crushed the Muslims (Moors) inhabiting southern Spain, driving them as well as Jewish inhabitants out of the country. Working closely with the Roman Catholic church, Ferdinand and Isabella used inquisition torture chambers to break the will of those whose loyalty they doubted. By 1500 their subjects had become full-fledged Spaniards who expected to serve their nation with loyalty.

Portugal, France, and England also reckoned with the turbulent process of nation-making. John I led the way by consolidating Portugal in the 1380s. Louis XI, known as the "Spider King," was responsible for unifying France in the 1460s at the end of more than 100 years of intermittent but debilitating warfare with England. Two powerful English noble lines, the houses of York and Lancaster, fought endlessly and devastated themselves in the Wars of the Roses (1455–1485). Henry Tudor, who became Henry VII (reigned 1485–1509), arose from the chaos, worked to crush forever the power of the nobility, and initiated a lengthy internal unification process that set the stage for England's westward expansion.

Unification was critical to focusing national efforts on exploration, as demonstrated by Portugal. Secure in his throne, King John I was able to support his son, Prince Henry (1394–1460), called "the Navigator," in the latter's efforts to learn more about the world. Henry set up a school of navigation at Sagres on the rocky southwestern coast of Portugal. With official state support, he sent out ships on exploratory missions. When the crews returned, they worked to improve maps, sailing techniques, navigational procedures, and ship designs.

Initially, the emphasis was on learning, but then it shifted to a quest for valuable trade goods. Henry's mariners conquered such islands as the Azores and brought back raw wealth (gold, silver, and ivory) from the west coast of Africa. During the 1420s trading ties developed with Africans, including the first dealings in black slaves by early modern Europeans. The lure of wealth drove Portuguese ships farther south along the African coast. Bartholomeu Dias made it to the Cape of Good Hope in 1487. Ten years later, Vasco da Gama took a small flotilla around the lower tip of Africa and on to the riches of India.

Besides returning a 400 percent profit, da Gama's expedition led to the development of Portugal's Far Eastern empire. It also proved that the Muslim world, with its heavy trade tolls, could be circumvented in getting European hands on Oriental riches. None of this would have been possible without a unified Portuguese government able to tax the populace and thus sponsor Prince Henry's attempts to probe the boundaries of the unknown.

Ferdinand and Isabella were intensely aware of Portugal's triumphs when a young Genoese mariner, Christopher Columbus (1451–1506), asked them to underwrite his dream of sailing west to reach the Orient. Consumed by their struggle for internal unification, they refused him, but Columbus persisted. He had already contacted King John II of Portugal, who rebuffed him as "a big talker and boastful." Columbus also turned to France and England but gained no sponsorship. Ultimately, Queen Isabella reconsidered. She met Columbus's terms, which included 10 percent of all profits from his discoveries, and proclaimed him "Admiral of the Ocean Sea." Her decision, made possible by Spain's unification, had monumental consequences.

On August 3, 1492, Columbus and some 90 mariners set sail from Palos, Spain, in the *Niña, Pinta,* and *Santa María.* Using faulty calculations, the admiral estimated Asia to be no more than 4500 miles to the west (the actual distance is closer to 12,000 miles). Some 3000 miles out, his crew became fearful and almost rebelled. They wanted to return home, but he persuaded them to keep sailing west. Just two days later, on October 12, they landed on a small island in the Bahamas, which Columbus named San Salvador (holy savior). There they found hospitable natives, the Arawaks, whom Columbus described as "a loving people without covetous-

Columbus first landed on the Bahamian island that he named San Salvador. He described the local natives as peaceful and generous, an image that changed rapidly as conquistadores swept over the native populace in their rush to tap into the riches of the Americas.

ness." He called them Indians, a misnomer that stuck, because he believed he was near Asia (the Indies). Proceeding on, Columbus landed on Cuba, which he thought was Japan, and then on Hispaniola, where he traded for gold-laden native jewelry. In 1493 Columbus and his crew returned home to a hero's welcome and to funding for three more expeditions to America.

EXPLORERS, CONQUERORS, AND THE MAKING OF NEW SPAIN

A fearless explorer, Columbus proved to be an ineffective administrator and a poor geographer. He ended up in debtors' prison, and to his dying day in 1506 he never admitted to locating a world unknown to Europeans. Geographers named the western continents after another mariner, Amerigo Vespucci, a merchant from Florence who participated in a Portuguese expedition to South America in 1501. In a widely reprinted letter, Vespucci insisted that a new world had been found. His first name soon became associated with the two continents.

Columbus's significance lay elsewhere. His 1492 venture garnered enough extractable wealth to exhilarate the Spanish monarchs. They did not care whether Columbus had reached Asia, only that further exploratory voyages might produce unimaginable riches. Because they feared Portuguese interference, Ferdinand and Isabella moved quickly to validate their interests. They went to Pope Alexander VI, who issued a papal bull, *Inter Caetera*, that divided the unknown world between Portugal and Spain.

In 1494 the Spanish monarchs worked out a formal agreement with Portugal in the Treaty of Tordesillas, drawing a line some 1100 miles west of the Cape Verde Islands. All undiscovered lands to the west of the demarcation line belonged to Spain. Those to the east were Portugal's. Inadvertently, Ferdinand and Isabella had given away the easternmost portion of South America. In 1500 a Portuguese mariner, Pedro Alvares Cabral, laid claim to this territory, which came to be known as Brazil. Spain claimed title to everything else, which of course left nothing for emerging nation-states such as France and England.

The Spanish monarchs used their strong army, seasoned by the struggle for unification, as a weapon to conquer the Americas. These *conquistadores* did so with relish. Befitting their crusader's ideology, they agreed to subdue the natives and, with the support of church leaders, to convert them to Roman Catholicism. Bravery and courage, these warriors believed, would bring distinction to themselves and to Spain. Further, they could gain much personal wealth, even if shared with the Crown. Gold, glory, and the gospel formed a triad of factors motivating the Spanish conquistadores, and their efforts resulted in a far-flung American empire known as New Spain.

Conquistadores Overrun Native Americans

Before 1510 the Spanish confined their explorations and settlements to the Caribbean islands. The conquistadores parleyed with Indians, searched diligently for rare metals and spices, and listened to tales of fabulous cities of gold somewhere over the horizon. Most natives remained friendly, but they were hostile in some locales, such as the Lesser Antilles where the cannibalistic Caribs dined on more than one Spanish warrior.

Unwittingly, the conquistadores with their microbial weapons retaliated against all Indians—friend and foe alike. Natives on all the islands lacked the antibodies to fend off European diseases. Smallpox, typhoid, diphtheria, the measles, and various plagues and fevers took a rapid toll. In 1492, for example, more than 200,000 Indians inhabited Hispaniola. Just 20 years later, fewer than 30,000 were alive.

Voyages of Exploration

The European exploration of the Americas came in waves after Columbus's initial voyages in the late 1400s. In the 1500s Spain's American empire took shape, and in the early 1600s England, France, Holland, and Sweden located settlements north of New Spain along the Atlantic coast.

After 1510 the conquistadores moved onto the mainland. Vasco Núñez de Balboa reached Panama in 1513. He organized an exploratory expedition, cut across the isthmus, and became the first European to see the Pacific Ocean, which he dutifully claimed for Spain. The same year Juan Ponce de León, governor of Puerto Rico, led a party to Florida in search of gold and a rumored fountain of youth. Although disappointed on both counts, he claimed Florida for Spain.

Then in 1519 Hernán Cortés (1485–1547), a leader of great bravado, mounted his dramatic expedition against the Aztecs. Landing on the Mexican coast with 600 soldiers, his party began a difficult overland march toward Tenochtitlán. Along the

This Aztec drawing presumably represents Cortés's conquest of Tenochtitlán in 1519–1522.

way Cortés won to his side various tribes subservient to the Aztecs. These natives may have thought Cortés a god. They certainly admired his horses—unknown in America—as well as the armor and weapons of his soldiers. Still, so small an invading force, even if well armed, could never have prevailed over thousands of Aztec warriors if other factors had not intervened.

Aztec emperor Montezuma II, who feared that Cortés was the old Toltec war god Quetzalcoatl coming back to destroy the Aztecs, tried to keep the Spaniards out of Tenochtitlán. He offered mounds of gold and silver, but this gesture only intensified the conquistadores' greed. They boldly marched into the city and took Montezuma prisoner. The Aztecs finally drove off Cortés's army in 1520, but not before smallpox had broken out. Less than a year later, the Spaniards retook Tenochtitlán and claimed all Aztec wealth and political authority as their prize.

Carried away with success, Cortés's soldiers razed the city and boasted of their great prowess as warriors and the superiority of their weapons and knowledge of warfare. They even claimed that God had willed their victory. However, the microbes they brought with them were the true victors. As a participant wrote, when they reentered Tenochtitlán, "the streets, squares, houses, and courts were filled with bodies, so that it was almost impossible to pass. Even Cortés was sick from the stench in his nostrils."

European diseases resulted in at least 17 major epidemics in the Americas during the sixteenth century; there were 14 in Europe. One of these 17 epidemics broke the Aztecs' ability to keep resisting the Spanish. As additional epidemics struck, the native populace of 20 to 25 million in Mexico declined dramatically—by about 90 percent during the 50 years following the invasion of Cortés's small army.

Cortés's stunning victory spurred on many other conquistadores, such as aggressive Francisco Pizarro (1470–1541). With about 180 soldiers, he overwhelmed thousands of Incas in Peru, seizing the capital city of Cuzco in 1533 after hardly any fighting. Inca rulers, paralyzed by fear, provided little leadership in resisting the Spanish and their powerful microbial allies. Pizarro showed no mercy; he executed the great chief Atahualpa and proclaimed Spain's sovereignty. By the 1550s the Spanish had conquered much of the rest of South America.

To the north, various expeditions found nothing comparable to the wealth of the Aztecs and Incas. Four hundred men under Pánfilo de Narváez began a disastrous adventure in 1528. They landed in Florida and searched the Gulf Coast region before being shipwrecked in Texas. Only four men survived, one of whom, Cabeza de Vaca, wrote a tract telling of seven great cities laden with gold. Vaca's writings stimulated Hernando de Soto and 600 others, beginning in 1539, to investigate the lower Mississippi River valley. In 1540 another party under Francisco Vásquez de Coronado began exploring parts of New Mexico, Texas, Oklahoma, and Kansas. They were the first Europeans to see the Grand Canyon. During 1542–1543 mariners under Juan Rodríguez Cabrillo sailed along the California coast as far north as Oregon. None of these groups ever located the fabled cities, but they advanced geographic knowledge of North America while claiming everything they came in contact with for Spain.

Constructing the Spanish Empire

To keep out intruders and to maintain order in New Spain, the Spanish Crown set up two home-based administrative agencies in Madrid. The House of Trade formulated economic policies and provided for annual convoys of galleons, called plate fleets, to haul extractable forms of American wealth back to Spain. The Council for the Indies controlled all political matters in what became an autocratic, rigidly managed empire for the exclusive benefit of the parent state.

The Council for the Indies ruled through viceroys that headed four regional areas of administration. Viceroys, in turn, consulted with *audiencias* (appointed councils) on matters of local concern, but there were no popularly based representative assemblies. Normally, only pure-blooded Spaniards could influence local decision making—and only if they

Most of the Spanish colonists to the Americas were adventurers in search of fame and fortune or missionaries who hoped to convert the Native Americans to Christianity. Both groups used Indians as laborers to work the land, tend livestock, and process raw materials to help support the Spanish settlements.

had ties to councilors or viceroys. Those who questioned their political superiors soon learned there was little tolerance for divergent opinions.

During the sixteenth century the incentive to resettle in New Spain was lacking. Work was plentiful at home, and Spain's population was in decline, reflecting the government's constant warfare in Europe. Consequently, only about 200,000 Spaniards, a modest number, migrated to New Spain. Most migrants were young males looking for adventure and material riches. They did not find much of either, but a few became wealthy as manor holders, ranchers, miners, and government officials.

From the very outset, Spanish migrants complained about a shortage of laborers in America. One solution was the **encomienda system**, initially approved by the Crown to reward conquistadores for outstanding service. Favored warriors and settlers received land titles to Indian villages and the surrounding countryside. As *encomenderos,* or landlords, they agreed to educate the natives under their jurisdiction and to guarantee instruction in the Roman Catholic faith. In return, the landlords gained control of the labor of whole villages of people and received portions of annual crops and other forms of forced tribute in recognition of their efforts to "civilize" the native populace.

The *encomienda* system fostered serious problems. Landlords regularly abused the Indians, treating them like slave property. They maimed or put troublemakers to death and bought and sold many others as if they were commodities. The exploitation was so outrageous that one Dominican priest, Bartolomé de Las Casas (1474–1566), later a bishop in southern Mexico, repeatedly begged officials in Madrid to stop such barbarities.

In 1542 the Crown settled the issue by outlawing both the *encomienda* system and the enslavement of Indians. This ruling did not change matters that much. Governing officials continued to award pureblooded Spaniards vast landed estates *(haciendas)*, on which Indians lived in a state of peonage, cultivating the soil and sharing their crops with their landlords *(hacendados)*.

Since the native populace also kept dying from European diseases, a second solution to the labor problem was to import Africans. In 1501 the Spanish Crown authorized the first shipment of slaves to the Caribbean islands, a small beginning to what became a vast, forced migration of some 10 million human beings to the Americas.

Slavery as it developed in New Spain was harsh. *Hacienda* owners and mine operators wanted only young adult males who could literally be worked to death, then replaced by new shiploads of Africans. On the other hand, Spanish law and Roman Catholic doctrine restrained some brutality. The Church believed that all souls should be saved, and it recognized marriage as a sacrament, meaning that slaves could wed and aspire to family life. Spanish law even permitted slaves to purchase their freedom. Such allowances were well beyond those made in future English-speaking colonies, and many blacks, particularly those who became artisans and house servants in the cities, did gain their independence.

Also easing slavery's harsh realities was the matter of skin color gradation: The lighter the skin, the greater the range of privileges. Pure-blooded natives of Spain *(peninsulares)* were at the apex of society. Next came the creoles *(criollos),* or whites born in New Spain. Since so many of the first Spanish migrants were males, they often intermarried with Indians, their children forming the *mestizo* class; or they intermarried with Africans, their children making up the *mulatto* class. The mixture of skin colors in New Spain helped Africans escape some of the racial contempt experienced by blacks in English North America, where legal restrictions against racial intermarriage resulted in less skin color variation.

Success Breeds Envy and Contempt

Still, most slaves and Indians lived in privation at the bottom of New Spain's society. Many church officials, as suggested by the pleas of Las Casas, worked to ease their burdens. Las Casas even went so far as to denounce the enslavement of Africans; but the Crown ignored him, realizing that without slavery Spain would receive fewer shipments of gold, silver, and other valuable commodities.

As Spanish authority spread north into New Mexico, Arizona, California, and other areas, Franciscan, Dominican, and Jesuit friars opened missions and offered protection to natives who would accept Roman Catholic beliefs. Quite often local Indians simply incorporated Catholic doctrines into their own belief systems.

When in the late 1660s and early 1670s a prolonged drought followed by a devastating epidemic ravaged Pueblos living in the upper Rio Grande valley of New Mexico, these natives openly questioned their new Catholic faith—and conquering masters. Spanish friars and magistrates reacted harshly and imprisoned some of the leading dissidents. The Pueblos eventually rallied around a native spiritual leader named Popé. In 1680 they rose in rebellion and killed or drove some 2500 Spanish inhabitants out of New Mexico. By 1700 Spanish soldiers had reconquered the region, maiming and killing hundreds of Pueblos in the process. With their numbers already in rapid decline, the Pueblos never again seriously challenged what seemed like the ever-expanding reach of Spanish authority.

As it took shape, then, the Spanish empire was more brutal than tolerant and contained many sharp contrasts. The construction of European-like cathedrals and the founding of great universities could not mask the terrible price in native lives lost, the endemic poverty of surviving Indian and *mestizo* villagers on *haciendas*, or the brutal treatment of slaves in gold and silver mines. These contrasts reflected the acquisitive beginnings of New Spain, which operated first and foremost as a treasure chest for the monarchs back in Madrid.

The flow of wealth made Spain the most powerful—and envied—nation in Europe during the sixteenth century. Such success also became a source of contempt. When Las Casas, for example, published *A Very Brief Relation of the Destruction of the Indies* (1552), he described the Indians as "patient, meek, and peaceful...lambs" whom bloodthirsty conquistadores had "cruelly and inhumanely butchered." Las Casas's listing of atrocities became the basis of the "Black Legend," a tale that other Europeans started to employ as a rationale for challenging Spain's New World supremacy. They promised to treat Native Americans more humanely, but in reality their primary motivation was to garner a share of America's riches for themselves.

CHALLENGERS FOR NORTH AMERICA: FRANCE AND ENGLAND

When Henry VII of England realized how successful Columbus had been, he chose to ignore the Treaty of Tordesillas. He underwrote another Italian explorer, Giovanni Caboto (John Cabot), to seek Cathay on behalf of the Tudor monarchy. Cabot's was the first exploratory expedition to touch North America since the Viking voyages. He landed on Newfoundland and Cape Breton Island in 1497. A second expedition in 1498 ended in misfortune when Cabot was lost at sea. Still, his voyages served as the basis for English claims to North America.

Soon France joined the exploration race. In 1524 King Francis I authorized yet another Italian mariner, Giovanni da Verrazzano, to sail westward. Verrazzano tracked along the American coast from North Carolina to Maine. Unfortunately, during another voyage in 1528 he died somewhere in the Lesser Antilles, where either Spaniards hanged him as an intruder or Caribs killed him. More important for later French claims, Jacques Cartier mounted three expeditions to the St. Lawrence River area, beginning in 1534. He scouted as far inland as modern-day Quebec and Montreal. Cartier even started a colony in 1541–1542, but too much political turmoil in France diverted the Crown from supporting trading stations or permanent settlements.

Verrazzano and Cartier were among the first to show interest in finding an all-water route—the **Northwest Passage**—through North America to the Orient. Seeking a northerly route was partially a response to the epic voyage of Ferdinand Magellan (1519–1522) under the Spanish flag. Magellan's party circumnavigated the globe by sailing around the southern tip of South America and proved, once and for all, that the world was round and that a vast ocean lay between America and Asia. The Northwest Passage, had it existed, would have allowed the English and French, among other Europeans, to avoid contact with New Spain while gaining access to Oriental wealth, since no one, as yet, had found readily extractable riches in North America. Searching for the passage was also a challenge to the worldwide ambitions of Portugal and Spain, especially after 1529 when these two powers extended their demarcation line down through the Pacific Ocean.

The Protestant Reformation Stirs Deep Tensions

Throughout the sixteenth century, the monarchs of England and France did not directly challenge Spain's supremacy in the Americas. They had too many problems at home, such as those related to religious strife. The **Protestant Reformation** shattered the unity of the Roman Catholic church, convulsed Europe, and provoked bloody wars. At the same time, the Reformation helped stimulate many Europeans, experiencing repression at home because of their newfound beliefs, to consider moving and resettling elsewhere. This was particularly the case in England.

The Roman Catholic church was the most powerful institution in medieval Europe. When dissenters spoke out, they were invariably punished, unless they publicly recanted their heretical views. Then in 1517, Martin Luther (1483–1546), an obscure friar of the Augustinian order and a professor of Scripture at the University of Wittenberg in Germany, tacked "Ninety-Five Theses" on a local church door. Luther was upset with what he thought were a number of unscriptural practices, particularly the selling of **indulgences** in the form of cash payments to the church to make amends for sins. As a form of penance, individuals could purchase indulgences for themselves or for others, such as deceased loved ones, to assure quick journeys through purgatory to heaven.

Luther found no biblical basis for indulgences. He could not understand why the church, which he described as "wealthiest of the wealthy," wanted money from hard-pressed peasants to help complete such building projects as St. Peter's Basilica in Rome. He also despised agents who were selling indulgences with clever sayings like: "As soon as coin in the coffer rings, the soul from purgatory springs." Luther had agonized for years over the ways to earn God's grace. He concluded that faith was all that mattered, not ritual or good works. The papacy demanded that Luther recant his heretical notions, but he refused, knowing full well that his penalty would be excommunication from the church.

Among other ideas, Luther contended that people did not need priests to interpret scriptures. All persons should have the right to read the Bible for themselves in cultivating their own faith in God. Luther thus advocated a "priesthood of all believers" in comprehending the mysteries of Christianity. In effect, he was attacking the widespread illiteracy of his era. Luther envisioned an educated populace capable of improving its lot in life. By the 1550s the doctrines of Lutheranism had taken firm hold in parts of Germany and the Scandinavian countries, often in the wake of enormous social turmoil and bloodshed.

Once under way, the Reformation, as this religious reform movement came to be known, gained rapid momentum. It also took many forms. In England politics rather than theology dictated the split with Rome. Henry VIII (reigned 1509–1547) prided

Martin Luther's ideas spread quickly among Europeans. His call for reform helped spur the Protestant Reformation in opposition to the Roman Catholic church and caused political and social upheaval throughout Europe.
Philadelphia Museum of Art, Johnson Collection.

FIGURE 1.1
The Tudor Monarchy of England

In England, the Protestant Reformation took root in Henry VIII's obsession with producing a male heir to secure the Tudor line. Henry did not accept the Pope's ruling that he should remain married to Catherine of Aragon, and he severed his ties with Rome. The Tudors reached their height under Elizabeth I, Henry's daughter by his second wife, Anne Boleyn.

Henry VII (1485–1509) m. Elizabeth of York, daughter of Edward IV

Henry VIII (1509–1547) m. various wives

by Catherine of Aragon — Mary I (1553–1558)
by Anne Boleyn — Elizabeth I (1558–1603)
by Jane Seymour — Edward VI (1547–1553)

himself on his devotion to Roman Catholicism. In 1521 he published a *Defense of the Seven Sacraments*, which berated Luther for arguing in favor of only two sacraments—baptism and communion. The Pope responded by awarding Henry a new title, "Defender of the Faith." At the same time, Henry worried about producing a male heir. His queen, Catherine of Aragon, daughter of Ferdinand and Isabella, bore him six children; but only one, a daughter named Mary, survived early childhood. Henry still wanted a male heir to ensure perpetuation of the Tudor line. In 1527 he asked Pope Clement VII to annul his marriage. When the Pope refused, Henry severed all ties with Rome.

Henry's actions were also spurred by his infatuation with Anne Boleyn, who bore him Elizabeth before being beheaded as an alleged adulteress. Through a series of parliamentary acts, Henry closed monasteries and seized church property. In the 1534 Act of Supremacy he formally repudiated the Pope and declared himself God's regent over England. Henceforth, all subjects would belong to the Anglican (English) church. The Church of England, unlike the Lutheran church, was similar to Catholicism in doctrine and ritual.

After his death Henry's reformation became a source of internal political chaos. When his daughter Mary I (reigned 1553–1558) came to the throne, she tried to return England to the Roman Catholic faith. Her government persecuted Protestants relentlessly, condemning nearly 300 to fiery deaths at the stake. Her opponents dubbed her "Bloody Mary," and many church leaders fled the land. Some of these "Marian exiles" went to Geneva, Switzerland, to study with John Calvin, whose Biblical ideas formed the basis of the Reformed Protestant tradition.

John Calvin (1509–1564) was a French lawyer who had fled to Switzerland because of his controversial theological ideas. Brilliant and persuasive, he soon controlled Geneva and reordered life there according to his understanding of Scripture. Calvin believed God to be both all-powerful and wrathful. To avoid eternal damnation, persons had to gain God's grace through a conversion experience denoted by accepting Jesus Christ as their savior. All had to seek, insisted Calvin, even though God had already predestined who would be saved and who would be damned. Since no one could be sure which persons were God's chosen "saints," Calvin taught that correct moral behavior and outward prosperity—physical and mental as well as material—represented possible signs of divine favor.

Individuals disenchanted with Catholicism studied Calvin's famous *Institutes of the Christian Religion* (1536). Many, such as the Marian exiles, traveled to Geneva to learn more about the concepts that came to be known as **Calvinism**. Then they returned to their homelands eager to set up godly communities. Their numbers included founders of the German and Dutch Reformed churches, as well as Huguenots who eventually suffered from organized state persecution back in France. John Knox, another disciple of Calvin, established the Presbyterian church in Scotland.

The Marian exiles began reappearing in England after the death of Queen Mary. In time, they developed a large following and came to be known as "Puritans." They wanted to continue Henry's reformation, but now along theological lines. Fiercely dedicated to their beliefs, they had a startling impact on the course of English history, particularly after the time of Elizabeth I (reigned 1558–1603), when some of them moved to North America and others precipitated a civil war in England.

Defying the Supremacy of Spain

Spain's success in the Americas in combination with religious contention between Catholics and Protestants fostered unending turmoil among sixteenth-century nation-states. Some of the tension related to America, where French, Dutch, and English "sea dogs" attacked Spanish commerce or traded covertly within the empire. Some related to attempted Huguenot (French Protestant) settlements in South Carolina and Florida. Spain, cast as the primary defender of Roman Catholicism, fought back, using wealth extracted from America to pay for military forces capable of protecting its interests.

France remained overwhelmingly Roman Catholic but was at first tolerant of the Huguenots. The Crown, however, encouraged Huguenot emigration to America as a way to rid the realm of these zealous dissenters. Two attempts by Huguenots to settle in the Americas failed. Yet a third colonization undertaking occurred in 1564. These Huguenots lo-

The biblical views of John Calvin formed the basis of the reformed Protestant tradition. Calvin's followers included many Marian exiles—English Protestants who fled persecution during the reign of Mary I. Once back in England, they came to be called Puritans, some of whom would later settle New England.

cated in northern Florida and called their settlement site Fort Caroline.

Spanish officials responded decisively. In 1565 they sent out a small army under Pedro Menéndez de Avilés, who first set up a garrison at San Augustín (the beginnings of St. Augustine, the oldest European-style city in North America), then turned on the Huguenots. Menéndez's troops massacred the Fort Caroline settlers, killing 132 of them but sparing about 50 women and children. To make sure other outsiders, especially Protestants, understood the danger of trying to colonize in Spanish territory, Menéndez ordered his soldiers to hack up the bodies before dumping the remains into a river. The butchery of Menéndez helped curtail sixteenth-century French settlement ventures.

Raids on Spanish treasure ships served as another source of tension. As early as the 1520s French freebooters started attacking Spanish vessels. The most daring of the sea dogs were Englishmen such as John Hawkins and Francis Drake. During the 1560s and 1570s Hawkins traded illegally and raided for booty in New Spain. Drake's adventures were even more dramatic. With private financial backing, including funds from Queen Elizabeth, he began a voyage in 1577 that took him around the world. Drake attacked wherever Spanish ports of call existed before returning home in 1580. Elizabeth gratefully dubbed him a knight, not only for being the first Englishman to circumnavigate the globe but also for securing a 4600 percent profit for his investors.

Elizabeth's professions of innocence to the contrary, King Philip II of Spain suspected her of actively supporting the sea dogs, whom he considered piratical scum. Further, he was furious with the English for giving military aid to the Protestant Dutch, who since 1567 had been fighting to free themselves from Spanish rule. Philip so despised Elizabeth that he conspired with her Catholic cousin Mary Stuart, Queen of Scots, to overthrow the English Protestant government. Wary of such plots, Elizabeth had Mary beheaded in 1587, at which point Philip decided to conquer the troublesome English heretics.

Philip and his military advisers pulled together an armada of Spanish vessels. They planned to sail 130 ships, including many hulking galleons, through the English Channel, pick up thousands of Spanish troops fighting the Dutch, and then invade England. The expedition ended in disaster for the Spanish when a flotilla of English ships, most of them smaller but far more maneuverable than the slow-moving galleons, appeared in the channel under Drake's command and offered battle. Then the famous "Protestant Wind" blew the Spanish Armada to bits. The war with Spain did not officially end until 1604; however, the destruction of the Armada in 1588 established England's reputation as a naval power. It also demonstrated that little England, heretofore a minor kingdom, could prevail over Europe's mightiest nation, which caused some English subjects to press forward with plans to secure territories in North America.

England Prepares for Westward Expansion

Besides the diminished Spanish threat, other factors helped pave the way for England's westward expansion. None was more important than rapid population growth. During the sixteenth century, England's population doubled, reaching 4 million by the 1590s. Yet opportunities for employment and decent wages lagged behind the population explosion. The phenomenal growth of the woolen industry, for instance, forced peasants off the land as manor lords fenced in their fields to make pastures for sheep. Because of this **enclosure movement,** England in 1600 had three times as many sheep as people. Meanwhile, London and other cities exploded in size as persons displaced from the countryside poured in and subsisted as best they could under miserable conditions.

In addition, all Europeans faced the major problem of rapid inflation, a reflection of what has been called the **price revolution.** Between 1500 and 1600 the cost of goods and services spiraled upward by as much as 500 percent. The principal inflationary culprit was an overabundance of precious metal, mostly Spanish silver mined in America (7 million pounds in weight by about 1650) and then pumped into the European economy in exchange for various commodities. The amount of money in circulation expanded more quickly than did the supply of goods or services. As a result, prices jumped dramatically.

In England, even farmers who owned their own land struggled to make ends meet. What they had to pay for necessities rose faster than what they received in the marketplace for their agricultural produce. A prolonged decline in real income on top of heavy taxes under the Tudors left many independent farmers destitute. In time, the abundant land of America attracted great numbers of England's failing yeoman farmers and permanently poor (sometimes called "sturdy beggars").

Apparent overpopulation and so much poverty and suffering became powerful arguments for westward expansion. As the eminent Elizabethan expansionist Richard Hakluyt wrote in his influential *Discourse of Western Planting* (1584), "infinite numbers may be set to work" in America, "to the unburdening of the realm . . . at home." Hakluyt also viewed American settlements as the key to achieving national greatness, since colonies could serve as sources of valuable commodities. They would likewise stimulate England's shipbuilding industry. They would help "enlarge the glory of the gospel" by offering the Indians "sincere religion" in the form of the Protestant Anglican faith. Further, argued Hakluyt, no one, certainly not the native populace, could enjoy "humanity, courtesy, and freedom" in America unless England challenged Spain's tyrannical sway by planting true "liberty" in its overseas settlements.

As with other New World colonizers, the English viewed their motives as above reproach on all counts. Certainly Queen Elizabeth recognized the merits of Richard Hakluyt's arguments, especially as they related to increasing the power of her realm. Still, she was a tightfisted monarch who refused to plunge vast sums of royal funds into highly speculative American ventures. She preferred having her favored courtiers, such as those then subduing Ireland, expend their own capital and energies in the quest for riches across the Atlantic Ocean.

JOINING IN THE INVASION OF AMERICA

England's path to America lay through Ireland. Off and on over four centuries the English had conducted sporadic raids on the "wild" Irish, as they thought of their Gaelic-speaking neighbors. During Elizabeth's reign, these forays became routine. The goal was to gain political control of Ireland and to establish agricultural colonies, since ample food supplies had become a problem at home with the spread of the enclosure movement.

Sir Humphrey Gilbert's patent for founding the North American colonies established important guidelines for England's westward expansion.

Elizabeth named as governor one of her court favorites, Sir Humphrey Gilbert (1539?–1583), and instructed him to subdue the Irish. Gilbert did so with a vengeance, operating as if the only good Irish subject was one who had been beheaded. The Irish, a million strong, fought back relentlessly, causing the English "plantations" there to exist precariously as military outposts in an alien environment.

For Elizabethan courtiers, Ireland became a laboratory for learning how to crush one's adversaries. Assumptions of cultural superiority abetted the English onslaught. The conquerors condemned the Irish, who were Roman Catholics, as religious heathens. They faulted them for using the land improperly, since the Irish were not sedentary farmers but people of migratory habits who tilled the soil only when they needed food. England's expansionists held these same attitudes when they began their American settlements. This time, however, the Indians would be the wild, unkempt, "savage" peoples in need of subjugation or eradication.

The Roanoke Disaster

Sir Humphrey Gilbert was as intolerant and contemptuous of the Spanish as he was of the Irish. He resented their pretensions to everything in America. He dreamed of finding the Northwest Passage to facilitate a flow of Oriental riches back to England, and he was willing to risk his personal fortune in that quest. Gilbert had other visions as well, including the effective occupation of North America and the founding of American colonies. He appealed to Elizabeth for exclusive rights to carry out his plans, and she acceded in 1578.

Gilbert's patent represented an important statement with respect to future guidelines for England's westward expansion. On the monarch's authority, he could occupy "heathen and barbarous lands . . . not actually possessed of any Christian prince or people." He would share in profits from extractable wealth, as would the Crown. Even more significant, prospective settlers would be assured the same rights of Englishmen "as if they were born and personally resident" at home. Not guaranteeing fundamental liberties would have inhibited the development of American colonies.

Gilbert did not live to see his dreams fulfilled. He disappeared in a North Atlantic storm after searching for the Northwest Passage. In 1584 his half-brother, Sir Walter Raleigh (1552?–1618), requested permission to carry on Gilbert's work. Elizabeth agreed, and Raleigh took quick action. He sent out a reconnoitering party, which explored the North Carolina coast and surveyed Roanoke Island. Then in 1585 Raleigh sponsored an expedition of 600 men, many of them veterans of the Irish wars. After some raiding for booty in New Spain, Raleigh's adventurers sailed north and dropped off 107 men under Governor Ralph Lane at the chosen site.

Lane's party found the local Croatoan and Roanoak Indians to be friendly. Then diseases struck. "That people," an eyewitness exclaimed, "began to die very fast, and many in short space." In the spring

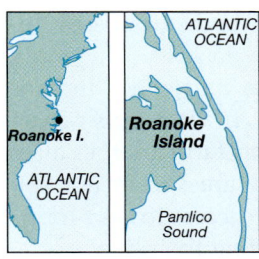

Roanoke Island

The fate of the lost colony of Roanoke Island may never be known. The settlement was too small and underfinanced to survive disease and continued strife with local natives.

of 1586 a local chief, Wingina, probably trying to protect his tribe from an illness "so strange that they neither knew what it was, nor how to cure it," moved inland. Ralph Lane went after the natives and ordered an attack, during which one of his men beheaded Wingina in the tradition of dealing with the "wild" Irish. Fortunately for Lane, Sir Francis Drake appeared and carried the English party away before the Indians counterattacked.

Raleigh persisted. He decided to send out families in 1587, with John White, a capable, gentle person, as their governor. White had been on the 1585 expedition. Besides preparing many famous drawings of native life in the Roanoke area, he had spoken out against butchering the Indians. White and the other 114 settlers arrived at Roanoke Island in late July. In mid-August his daughter Elinor gave birth to Virginia Dare, the first English subject born in America. A few days later, White sailed back to England to obtain additional supplies. The outbreak of warfare between Spain and England delayed his return, and he did not get back to Roanoke until 1590. Nothing was left, except the word CROATOAN carved on a tree.

What happened to the lost colony may never be known. No European saw the settlers again. Local Indians either killed or absorbed them into their tribes. As for Raleigh, he had ruined himself financially, proving that funding overseas ventures lay beyond the means of any one person. All that he had left was a patent that he gave up in the 1590s, a sense that colonizing in America was a hazardous undertaking at best, and a name, Virginia, which Raleigh had offered in thanks to his patron, Elizabeth, the Virgin Queen.

Merchant Capitalists Sponsor the Founding of Virginia

A few sixteenth-century English subjects did prosper in the wake of economic dislocation and spiraling inflation. Among these fortunate few were manufacturers of woolen goods and merchants who made Europe a major marketplace for English cloth. With their profits, these gentlemen of capital gained social respectability. Many purchased landed estates, and some even married into England's titled nobility. As members of the gentry class, they started pooling their capital and sponsoring risky overseas business ventures by investing in **joint-stock trading companies.**

In 1555 the Crown chartered the Muscovy Company, giving that business venture the exclusive right to develop England's trade with Russia. Having a monopoly made the enterprise more attractive to potential stockholders. Although they hoped to make handsome profits, they would lose no more than the money they had subscribed. Meanwhile, the company could draw on a large pool of working capital to underwrite its activities. Queen Elizabeth liked this model of business organization, which depended on private capital rather than royal funds to finance England's economic—and eventually political—expansion abroad. The Crown, of course, was to share in any profits.

The Muscovy Company was a success, and other joint-stock undertakings followed, such as the East India Company, chartered in 1600 to develop England's Far Eastern interests. Then in 1606 a charter for the Vir-

A Festive Dance is one of John White's drawings depicting life among the Native Americans in the village of Secoton, near the Roanoke settlement.

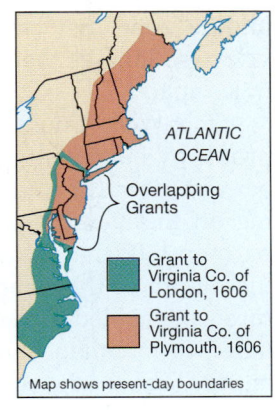

Conflicting Land Claims

ginia Company received royal approval. Ironically, even though this business enterprise failed its stockholders, company activities produced England's first enduring settlement in North America.

During the 1590s, English courtiers and merchant capitalists did not pick up on Raleigh's failed efforts. The ongoing war with Spain took precedence, and profits came easily from capturing Spanish vessels on the high seas. When peace returned, influential merchants stood ready to pool their capital, spread the financial risk, and pursue Raleigh's patent. They took their case to the new king, the Stuart monarch James I (reigned 1603–1625), who willingly granted them a generous trading company charter.

Initially, the Virginia Company had two sets of investors. The first, a group of London merchants, held Raleigh's patent. They had earned bountiful profits from other joint-stock ventures and were ready to take further risks. Foolishly, they dreamed of heaping piles of gold and silver. More realistically, they hoped to trade for valuable commodities with the native populace and to plant vineyards and silk-producing mulberry trees. The London merchants had first claim to all land between the Cape Fear River in southern North Carolina and present-day New York City.

In December 1606, they sent out 144 adventurers under Captain Christopher Newport aboard the *Susan Constant*, *Godspeed*, and *Discovery*. The crossing was difficult, and 39 men died. In May 1607 the survivors located on an island some 30 miles up the James River off Chesapeake Bay. They called their settlement, really meant as a trading post, Jamestown.

The second set of investors were from such West Country port towns as Plymouth. In response to bitter complaints over the years about London's dominance of joint-stock ventures, the Virginia Company granted the West Country merchants lands lying between the mouth of the Potomac River and northern Maine. Thus the charter allowed for an overlapping middle zone that both investor groups could develop, so long as their settlements were at least 100 miles apart.

The West Country merchants hoped to reap profits by harvesting great stands of American timber and from fur trading with the Indians and fishing off the New England coast. They dispatched a party in 1607 that located at Sagadahoc, Maine, near the mouth of the Kennebec River. These 44 adventurers squabbled incessantly among themselves and failed to maintain harmonious relations with local natives. Those who survived the first winter gave up and returned home in 1608. The Plymouth investors refused to expend more funds, and their patent fell dormant.

As with the Irish invasion, both groups of adventurers came forth in military fashion. They built forts to protect themselves from unfriendly Indians and Spanish raiding parties. In its early days, Jamestown functioned as an outpost in another alien environment. The early participants were not settlers. They wanted to get in, gain access to easy forms of wealth, and get out before losing their lives.

Struggling Jamestown Survives

That Jamestown survived is amazing. Newport's adventurers were miscast for the American wilderness. Many were second and third sons of English noblemen. Because of primogeniture and entail (laws that specified that only firstborn male heirs could inherit landed estates and family titles), these younger sons had to choose alternate careers. Many became lawyers, clergymen, or high-ranking military officers, but none toiled in the fields, as farming was hardly a gentleman's calling. When Jamestown ran short of food, these company adventurers still avoided agricultural work, preferring to search for gold, silver, or the Northwest Passage. Some starved to death as a result.

Besides gentleman-adventurers, other equally ill-prepared individuals, such as valets and footmen, joined the expedition. Their duties extended only to waiting on their aristocratic masters. Also present were goldsmiths and jewelers, plus a collection of ne'er-do-wells who knew no occupation but apparently functioned as soldiers under gentleman-officers in dealings with the natives.

The social and economic characteristics of these first adventurers suggest that the London investors may have modeled the expedition after the early Spanish conquests—with the idea of forcing local Indians to become agricultural workers as peons or slaves. As matters turned out, the natives supplied food, but even with their assistance, only 38 Englishmen were still alive by the early spring of 1608.

Another problem was the settlement site. Company directors had ordered the adventurers to locate on high ground far enough in-

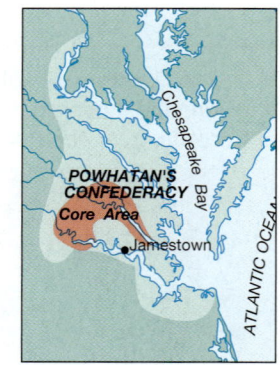

Powhatan's Confederacy

Powhatan's Confederacy, established for defense against aggressive neighbors, consisted of some 30 coastal tribes.

This imaginative drawing shows Native Americans sharing food with the Jamestown colonists. In fact, relations between the Indians and the English settlers were often quite thorny and several times erupted into open conflict.

land so as to go undetected by the Spanish. Jamestown Island met the second requirement, but it was a low, swampy place lying at a point on the James River where salt and fresh water mingled. The brackish water was "full of slime and filth," as one observer noted. The water could cause salt poisoning and was also a breeding ground for malaria, typhoid fever, and dysentery.

Several factors saved the Jamestown settlement. The local Indians under Powhatan, an Algonquian-speaking Pamunkey, initially offered sustenance. Powhatan had organized a confederacy of some 30 coastal tribes, numbering about 20,000 people, to defend themselves against aggressive interior neighbors. Powhatan tried to stay clear of the Jamestown adventurers, but when he was around them, he could not help but notice their large ships, gaudy body armor, and noisy firearms. He viewed the English as potential allies in warfare with interior tribes, a faulty assessment but one that kept him from wiping out the weakened adventurers.

At the same time, Company investors in London refused to quit. They kept sending out supplies and adventurers, as many as 800 more young men plus a few women in 1608 and 1609. Upon their arrival, however, many quickly died of malaria and other diseases. Others, debilitated from illnesses, were unable to work. They became a drain on Jamestown's precarious food supply.

In these early days the dynamic and ruthless local leadership of Captain John Smith (1580?–1631) kept the Jamestown outpost from totally collapsing. Smith had crossed the Atlantic with the original adventurers. Once in Jamestown, he emerged as a virtual dictator. Smith helped save many lives by imposing discipline and forcing everyone—gentleman or servant, sick or well—to adhere to one rule: "He who works not, eats not."

In October 1609 Smith returned to England after suffering severe burns from an accidental explosion of gunpowder. Lacking authoritarian leadership, the adventurers experienced a tragic "starving time" during the winter of 1609–1610. Hundreds died as food supplies, described as "moldy, rotten, full of cobwebs and maggots," gave out. Only about 60 persons survived by eating everything from rats to snakes, and there was even an alleged instance of cannibalism. One man completely lost his mind; he murdered his wife, then "powdered [salted] her up to eat her, for which he was burned" at the stake.

Smith's presence might not have averted the disaster. Too often, he, like the other early adventurers, had treated the Indians with contempt. Bad relations caused Powhatan to cut off food supplies. For some reason, however, the native leader did not seize the opportunity to wipe out Jamestown. Perhaps still hoping for an alliance, he simply allowed the feeble English to die on their own.

THE PEOPLE SPEAK

Powhatan Pleads for Peace and Harmony (1609)

The aging Chief Powhatan hoped to befriend the English adventurers who began appearing in the midst of his Confederacy in 1607. However, he quickly learned that they were just as likely to maim and kill his followers as to respond gratefully for the food that he was supplying them. Skeptics among the native populace started warning Powhatan that the English had but one goal—to kill them all and take their lands. In 1609, Powhatan, still hoping for peace, met with Captain John Smith and warned him of grave consequences should the English persist in their belligerent ways. The Jamestown adventurers did not listen. Powhatan cut off their food supplies, which resulted in the "starving time" of 1609–1610 and protracted warfare in the years ahead. Smith recorded the text of Powhatan's speech as follows:

> Captaine Smith, . . . I knowe the difference of peace and warre better than any in my Countrie. But now I am old, and ere long must die. My brethren, namely Opichapam, Opechankanough, and Kekataugh, my two sisters, and their two daughters, are distinctly each others successours. I wish their experience no lesse then mine, and your love to them, no less then mine to you: but this brute [rumor] from Nansamund, that you are come to destroy my Countrie, so much affrighteth all my people, as they dare not visit you. What will it availe you to take that perforce you may quietly have with love, or to destroy them that provide you food? What can you get by war, when we can hide our provision and flie to the woodes, whereby you must famish, by wronging us your friends? And whie are you thus jealous of our loves, seeing us unarmed, and both doe, and are willing still to feed you with that you cannot get but by our labours? Think you I am so simple not to knowe it is better to eate good meate, lie well, and sleepe quietly with my women and children, laugh, and be merrie with you, have copper, hatchets, or what I want being your friend; then bee forced to flie from all, to lie cold in the woods, feed upon acorns roots and such trash, and be so hunted by you that I can neither rest eat nor sleepe, but my tired men must watch, and if a twig but breake, everie one crie, there comes Captaine Smith: then must I flie I knowe not whether and thus with miserable feare end my miserable life, leaving my pleasures to such youths as you, which, through your rash unadvisednesse, may quickly as miserably ende, for want of that you never knowe how to find? Let this therefore assure you of our loves, and everie yeare our friendly trade shall furnish you with corn; and now also if you would come in friendly manner to us, and not thus with your gunnes and swords, as to invade your foes.

Source: Samuel G. Drake, *Biography and History of the Indians of North America* (Boston, 1841), 353.

Back in England, Virginia Company stockholders refused to concede defeat. By 1610 they realized that mineral wealth was an illusion, but still they sent out more people. One of them, John Rolfe, experimented with local tobacco plants, which produced a harsh-tasting crop. Rolfe, like the company, persisted. He procured some plants from Trinidad in the West Indies and grew a milder, more flavorful leaf. Tobacco soon became Virginia's gold and silver. The colony now had a valuable trading commodity, and settlements quickly spread along the banks of the James River. Englishmen had found an economic reason to stay in the Americas.

Dutch and French Adventurers

In the early 1600s the Spanish contented themselves with drawing wealth from their Caribbean basin empire. They did not challenge various European interlopers seeking to stake North American claims. Ultimately, Dutch settlements in New York were seized by the English, but France's efforts resulted in a Canadian empire capable of rivaling those of Spain and England.

Once fully liberated from Spanish domination at home, the Dutch grabbed at a portion of North America. In 1609 they sent out an English sea captain, Henry Hudson, to search for the Northwest Passage. He explored Delaware Bay, then the New York waterway that bears his name. Hudson made contact with the Iroquois Indians, probably the Mohawks, and talked of trade in furs. Broad-brimmed beaver hats were then the fashion rage in Europe, but fur supplies were dwindling. North America could become a new source of pelts, if the natives would cooperate. The Dutch established trading stations on Manhattan Island (later called New Amsterdam) and Albany (Fort Orange) in 1624. The Iroquois did their part in delivering furs, and the colony of New Netherland took hold under the auspices of the Dutch West India Company.

Chronology of Key Events

30,000–20,000 B.C.	First humans arrive in North America from Asia across what is now the Bering Strait	1497–1498	John Cabot's two voyages to Newfoundland and Cape Breton Island lay the basis for English claims to North America
8000–5000 B.C.	Central American Indians begin to practice agriculture	1501	Spain authorizes the first shipment of African slaves to the Caribbean islands
A.D. 300–900	Maya civilization flourishes in present-day Mexico and Guatemala	1517	Martin Luther's public protests against the sale of indulgences (pardons of punishment in Purgatory) mark the beginning of the Protestant Reformation
c. 900	Toltecs rise to power in the Valley of Mexico and later conquer the Mayas		
c. 1000	Vikings led by Leif Ericson reach Labrador and Newfoundland (*Vinland*)	1519	Hernán Cortés and 600 Spanish conquistadores begin the conquest of the Aztec empire
1095	European Christians launch the Crusades to capture the Holy Lands from Muslims	1527	Henry VIII of England begins to sever ties with the Roman Catholic church
c. 1100	Inca civilization emerges in what is now Peru	1531	Francisco Pizarro and 180 Spanish soldiers start the conquest of the Inca empire
1271	Marco Polo begins a 20-year journey to China	1534	Jacques Cartier explores the St. Lawrence River and claims the region for France
1347–1353	"Black Death" kills about one-third of Europe's population		
1420s	Prince Henry the Navigator of Portugal sends mariners to explore Africa's western coast	1542	Spain outlaws the *encomienda* system and the enslavement of Indians
c. 1450	Johannes Gutenberg, a German printer, develops movable type, the basis of modern printing	1585–1587	Sir Walter Raleigh sponsors England's first North American settlement at Roanoke Island in present-day North Carolina
1469	Ferdinand and Isabella marry and begin to unify Spain		
1492	Columbus makes the first of his voyages of discovery to the Americas	1607	English adventurers establish the first permanent English settlement at Jamestown in present-day Virginia
1494	Treaty of Tordesillas divides the known world between Portugal and Spain		

Profits from furs also helped motivate the French. In 1608 Samuel de Champlain set up an outpost at Quebec on the St. Lawrence River, and he found local Indians ready to trade. Quebec was the base from which New France spread. Yet only after 1663, when the Crown took control of managing the colony, did the French population in Canada grow significantly, reaching 10,000 people by the 1680s.

The French Canadians were energetic. Following Champlain's lead, they explored everywhere and claimed everything in sight. They established harmonious relations with dozens of different Indian nations, and they even joined in native wars as a way of solidifying trading ties. The French, with their small numbers, could not completely impose their cultural values. They did use the natives for their own purposes, especially in relation to the fur trade. At the same time, they also showed respect, which paid off handsomely when their many Indian allies willingly fought beside them in a series of imperial wars that beset America beginning in 1689.

Conclusion

Except in Canada, the Europeans who explored the Americas and began colonies after 1492 acted as foreign invaders. Although a few were at first curious, they generally viewed the natives as their adversaries, describing them as "worse than those beasts which are of the most wild and savage nature." Judgments of cultural superiority seemed to justify the destruction of Native Americans.

Still, there was a **Columbian exchange** of sorts. The Indians taught the Europeans about tobacco, corn, potatoes, varieties of beans, peanuts, tomatoes, and many other crops then unknown in Europe. In return, Europeans introduced the native populace to wheat, oats, barley, and rice, as well as to grapes for wine and various melons. The Europeans also brought with them domesticated animals, including horses, pigs, sheep, goats, and cattle. Horses proved to be important, particularly for Great Plains Indians, who used them in fighting against future generations of white settlers, just as tobacco production in the Chesapeake area had the unintended effect of attracting enough Europeans to end native control of that area.

Perhaps more than anything else, killer diseases served to unbalance the exchange. From the first moments of contact, great civilizations like the Aztecs and more humble groups like Tisquantum's Patuxets faced devastation. In some cases the Indians who survived, as in New Spain, had to accept the status of peons. Along the Atlantic coastline, survivors were drawn into the European trading network. In exchange for furs, the Indians wanted firearms to kill yet more animals whose pelts could be traded for still more guns and for alcohol to help them forget, even for a moment, what was happening to their way of life in the wake of European westward expansion.

The English would eventually send the most settlers. They left home for various reasons. Some, like the Pilgrims, crossed the Atlantic to avoid further religious persecution. Others, such as the Puritans, sought to build a holy community that would shine as a light upon Europe. Still others, including colonists in the Chesapeake Bay area, desired land for growing tobacco. The latter group wanted laborers to help them raise their crops. Unable to enslave the Indians, they ultimately borrowed from the Spanish model and enslaved Africans. In so doing, they forced blacks to enter their settlements in chains and to become a part of a peopling and unpeopling process that helped shape the contours of life in colonial America.

Suggestions for Further Reading

Alfred W. Crosby, *Ecological Imperialism: The Biological Expansion of Europe, 900–1900* (1986). Revealing examination of biological encounters that devastated Native Americans in the process of European westward expansion.

John Guy, *Tudor England* (1990). Admirable summary of the rise of a powerful monarchy, with implications for westward expansion, in the emerging nation-state of England.

Francis Jennings, *The Invasion of America: Indians, Colonialism, and the Cant of Conquest* (1976). Controversial introduction to discordant relations between Native Americans and Europeans with particular reference to white aggression in New England.

Steven Ozment, *The Age of Reform (1250–1550): An Intellectual and Religious History of Late Medieval and Reformation Europe* (1980). Balanced, readable investigation of growing religious tensions and the rise of Protestantism in Europe.

Ian K. Steele, *Warpaths: Invasions of North America* (1994). Broad-ranging assessment of European encounters with Native Americans and patterns of Indian resistance up to the 1760s.

Tzvetan Todorov, *The Conquest of America: The Question of the Other* (1992). Engrossing analysis of early Spanish conquests and the human dilemmas posed by cultural intolerance and conflict.

David J. Weber, *The Spanish Frontier in North America* (1992). Revisionist overview that treats the Spanish as much more than plunderers in their American explorations and settlements.

Overviews and Surveys

Daniel J. Boorstin, *The Americans: The Colonial Experience* (1958); Stephen Greenblatt, *Marvelous Possessions: The Wonder of the New World* (1992); James A. Henretta and Gregory H. Nobles, *Evolution and Revolution: American Society, 1600–1820* (1987); Alvin M. Josephy, Jr., *The Indian Heritage of America* (1991); D. W. Meinig, *The Shaping of America*, Vol. I: *Atlantic America, 1492–1800* (1986); Richard Middleton, *Colonial America: A History, 1585–1776*, 2d ed. (1996); Gary B. Nash, *Red, White, and Black: The Peoples of Early America*, 4th ed. (2000); Anthony Pagden, *European Encounters with the New World: From Renaissance to Romanticism* (1992); Jerome R. Reich, *Colonial America*, 2d ed. (1989);

Richard C. Simmons, *The American Colonies: From Settlement to Independence* (1981); David E. Stannard, *American Holocaust: Columbus and the Conquest of the New World* (1992); Wilcomb E. Washburn, *The Indian in America* (1975).

The First Discovery of America

James Axtell, *After Columbus: Essays in the Ethnohistory of Colonial North America* (1988), *The European and the Indian: Essays in the Ethnohistory of Colonial North America* (1981), and *The Invasion Within: The Contest of Cultures in Colonial North America* (1985); Henry W. Bowden, *American Indians and Christian Missions: Studies in Cultural Conflict* (1981); William Cronon, *Changes in the Land: Indians, Colonists, and the Ecology of New England* (1983); Alfred W. Crosby, *The Columbian Exchange: Biological and Cultural Consequences of 1492* (1972); William N. Denevan, ed., *The Native Population of the Americas in 1492* (1992); Henry F. Dobyns, *Their Number Become Thinned: Native American Population Dynamics in Eastern North America* (1983); Harold E. Driver, *The Indians of North America*, 2d ed. (1969); Brian M. Fagan, *The Great Journey: The Peopling of Ancient America* (1987); John S. Henderson, *The World of the Ancient Maya* (1981); Francis Jennings, *The Ambiguous Iroquois Empire: The Covenant Chain Confederation of Indian Tribes with English Colonies From Its Beginnings to the Lancaster Treaty of 1744* (1984), and *The Founders of America* (1993); Alvin M. Josephy, Jr., ed., *America in 1492* (1992); Yasuhide Kawashima, *Puritan Justice and the Indian: White Man's Law and Massachusetts, 1630–1763* (1986); Shepard Krech, III, ed., *Indians, Animals, and the Fur Trade: A Critique of Keepers of the Game* (1981); Peter C. Mancall, *Deadly Medicine: Indians and Alcohol in Early America* (1995); Calvin Martin, ed., *The American Indian and the Problem of History* (1987); James H. Merrell, *The Indians' New World: Catawbas and Their Neighbors From European Contact Through the Era of Removal* (1989); Paul C. Phillips and J. W. Smurr, *The Fur Trade*, 2 vols. (1960); Daniel K. Richter, *The Ordeal of the Longhouse: The Peoples of the Iroquois League in the Era of European Colonization* (1992); Neal Salisbury, *Manitou and Providence: Indians, Europeans, and the Making of New England, 1500–1643* (1982); Bernard Sheehan, *Savagism and Civility: Indians and Englishmen in Colonial Virginia* (1980); Timothy Silver, *A New Face on the Countryside: Indians, Colonists, and Slaves in South Atlantic Forests, 1500–1800* (1990); Margaret C. Szasz, *Indian Education in the American Colonies, 1607–1783* (1988); Alden T. Vaughan, *The New England Frontier: Puritans and Indians, 1620–1675*, rev. ed. (1995); J. Leitch Wright, Jr., *The Only Land They Knew: The Tragic Story of American Indians in the Old South* (1981).

Preparing Europe for Westward Expansion

Paul H. Chapman, *The Norse Discovery of America* (1981); Carlo M. Cipolla, *Guns, Sails, and Empires: Technological Innovation and the Early Phases of European Expansion, 1400–1700* (1985); Felipe Fernandez-Armesto, *Before Columbus: Exploration and Colonization From the Mediterranean to the Atlantic, 1229–1492* (1987); Valerie Flint, *The Imaginative Landscape of Christopher Columbus* (1992); E. L. Jones, *The European Miracle: Environments, Economies, and Geopolitics in the History of Europe and Asia*, 2d ed. (1987); William H. McNeill, *The Rise of the West: A History of the Human Community* (1991), and *Plagues and Peoples* (1976); Frederick J. Pohl, *The Viking Settlements of North America* (1972); Robert L. Reynolds, *Europe Emerges: Transition Toward an Industrial World-Wide Society, 600–1750* (1961).

Explorers, Conquerors, and the Making of New Spain

Charles R. Boxer, *The Portuguese Seaborne Empire, 1415–1825* (1969); David Carrasco, *Quetzalcoatl and the Irony of Empire: Myths and Prophecies in the Aztec Tradition* (1982); Inga Clendinnen, *Aztecs: An Interpretation* (1991); J. H. Elliott, *Imperial Spain, 1469–1716* (1963), and *The Old World and the New, 1492–1650* (1970); Charles Gibson, *The Aztecs Under Spanish Rule: A History of the Indians of the Valley of Mexico* (1964), and *Spain in America* (1966); J. R. Hale, *Renaissance Exploration* (1968); Clarence H. Haring, *The Spanish Empire in America* (1947); James Lockhart and Stuart B. Schwartz, *Early Latin America: A History of Colonial Spanish America and Brazil* (1983); Samuel E. Morison, *The European Discovery of America: The Southern Voyages, A.D. 1492–1616* (1979); J. H. Parry, *The Age of Reconnaissance* (1963), *The Spanish Seaborne Empire* (1966), and *The Discovery of South America* (1979); Daniel Peters, *The Incas* (1991); G. V. Scammell, *The World Encompassed: The First European Maritime Empires* (1981); Nathan Wachtel, *The Vision of the Vanquished: The Spanish Conquest of Peru Through Indian Eyes, 1530–1570* (1977); Silvio Zavala, *New Viewpoints on the Spanish Colonization of America* (1943).

Challengers for North America: France and England

Kenneth R. Andrews, *Trade, Plunder, and Settlement: The Genesis of the British Empire, 1480–1630* (1984); Carl Bridenbaugh, *Vexed and Troubled Englishmen, 1590–1642* (1967); Mildred Campbell, *The English Yeoman Under Elizabeth and the Early Stuarts* (1942); Patrick Collinson, *The Elizabethan Puritan Movement* (1967); G. R. Elton, *Reform and Reformation: England, 1509–1558* (1977); C. H. and Katherine George, *The Protestant Mind of the English Reformation* (1961); Peter Laslett, *The World We Have Lost, Further Explored*, 3d ed. (1984); Samuel E. Morison, *The European Discovery of America: The Northern Voyages, A.D. 500–1600* (1971); Wallace Notestein, *The English People on the Eve of Colonization, 1603–1630* (1954); Theodore K. Rabb, *Enterprise & Empire: Merchant and Gentry Investment in the Expansion of England, 1575–1630* (1967); Lacey Baldwin Smith, *This Realm of England, 1399–1688*, 3d ed. (1988); Lewis Spitz, *The Protestant Reformation, 1517–1559* (1985); Lawrence Stone, *The Crisis of the Aristocracy, 1558–1641* (1979); Michael Walzer, *The Revolution of the Saints: A Study in the Origins of Radical Politics* (1965); Keith Wrightson, *English Society, 1580–1680* (1982).

Joining in the Invasion of America

Charles R. Boxer, *The Dutch Seaborne Empire, 1600–1800* (1988); Carl Bridenbaugh, *Jamestown, 1544–1699* (1980); Nicholas P. Canny, *The Elizabethan Conquest of Ireland: A Pattern Established, 1565–76* (1976); Ralph Davis, *The Rise of the Atlantic Economies* (1973); W. J. Eccles, *The Canadian Frontier, 1534–1760,* rev. ed. (1983), and *France in America,* rev. ed. (1990); Paul E. Hoffman, *A New Andalucia and a Way to the Orient: The American Southeast During the Sixteenth Century* (1990); Alice P. Kenney, *Stubborn for Liberty: The Dutch in New York* (1975); Karen O. Kupperman, *Settling with the Indians: The Meeting of English and Indian Cultures in America, 1580–1640* (1980), and *Roanoke: The Abandoned Colony* (1984); James Lang, *Conquest and Commerce: Spain and England in the Americas* (1975); David B. Quinn, *The Elizabethans and the Irish* (1966), *North America from Earliest Discovery to First Settlements: The Norse Voyages to 1612* (1977), and *Set Fair for Roanoke: Voyages and Colonies, 1584–1606* (1985); Helen C. Rountree, *Pocahontas's People: The Powhatan Indians of Virginia Through Four Centuries* (1990); A. L. Rowse, *The Expansion of Elizabethan England* (1955), and *The Elizabethans and America* (1959); George L. Smith, *Religion and Trade in New Netherland: Dutch Origins and American Development* (1973); Allen W. Trelease, *Indian Affairs in Colonial New York: The Sixteenth Century* (1960).

Biographies

William J. Bouwsma, *John Calvin: A Sixteenth Century Portrait* (1988); Carolly Erickson, *The First Elizabeth* (1983); Erik H. Erikson, *Young Man Luther: A Study in Psychoanalysis and History* (1993); Felipe Fernandez-Armesto, *Columbus* (1991); Richard Marius, *Martin Luther* (1991); Samuel E. Morison, *Samuel de Champlain* (1972), and *Christopher Columbus, Mariner* (1955); Theodore K. Rabb, *Jacobean Gentleman: Sir Edwin Sandys, 1561–1629*; Kirkpatrick Sale, *The Conquest of Paradise: Christopher Columbus and the Columbian Legacy* (1992); Andrew Sinclair, *Sir Walter Raleigh and the Age of Discovery* (1984); Alden T. Vaughan, *American Genesis: Captain John Smith and the Founding of Virginia* (1991).

INTERNET RESOURCES

Index of Native American Resources on the Internet
http://hanksville.phast.umass.edu/misc/NAresources.html
A comprehensive source for Native American history and art.

Vikings in the New World
http://www.anthro.mankato.msus.edu/prehistory/vikings/vikhome.html
This site explores the history of some of the earliest European visitors to America.

Sir Francis Drake
http://www.mcn.org/2/oseeler/drake.htm
This comprehensive site covers much of Drake's life and voyages.

1492: An Ongoing Voyage
http://metalab.unc.edu/expo/1492.exhibit/Intro.html
An exhibit of the Library of Congress, Washington, D.C., with brief essays and images about early civilizations and contact in the Americas.

The Computerized Information Retrieval System on Columbus and the Age of Discovery
http://marauder.millersv.edu/~columbus/
The History Department and Academic Computing Services of Millersville University of Pennsylvania provide this text retrieval system containing over 1000 text articles from various magazines, journals, newspapers, speeches, official calendars, and other sources relating to various encounter themes.

Cahokia Mounds
http://medicine.wustl.edu/~mckinney/cahokia/cahokia.html
The Cahokia Mounds State Historical Site gives information about a fascinating pre-Columbian culture in North America.

Mexico Pre-Columbian History
http://www.mexonline.com/precolum.htm
This site provides information on the Aztecs, Maya, Mexica, Olmecs, Toltec, Zapotecs, and other pre-European cultures, as well as information on museums, archeology, language, and education.

The European Voyages of Exploration
http://www.acs.ucalgary.ca/HIST/tutor/eurvoya/
This University of Calgary site has images and texts for nearly every facet of European exploration.

The Discoverers' Web
http://www.win.tue.nl/cs/fm/engels/discovery/
Andre Engels maintains this most complete collection of information on the various efforts at exploration.

KEY TERMS

Matrilineal   (p. 9)

Renaissance   (p. 14)

Encomienda System   (p. 19)

Northwest Passage   (p. 20)

Protestant Reformation   (p. 21)

Indulgences   (p. 21)

Calvinism   (p. 22)

Enclosure Movement   (p. 23)

Price Revolution   (p. 23)

Joint-Stock Trading Companies   (p. 25)

Columbia Exchange   (p. 30)

REVIEW QUESTIONS

1. Describe the principal regions of the Americas, and discuss how factors such as climate and the environment affected the economic and social development of various Native American peoples before the time of Columbus. Why did Native Americans not offer more resistance to the first European explorers and settlers?

2. What factors were in place by the late fifteenth century that facilitated European exploration and, ultimately, expansion into the Americas? Why were Portugal and Spain the first to become involved in these exploratory ventures?

3. How did the European Renaissance and Protestant Reformation affect the process of European westward expansion? Was one more important than the other? If so, why?

4. Compare and contrast the Spanish colonial system and its organization and objectives to those of the English, French, and Dutch. What elements did they have in common? What were the most significant differences, if any?

5. Why did Native Americans fail in their attempts to live in harmony with or drive off the Europeans? What else could they have done to maintain rather than lose control of their ancient tribal lands? Was the Columbian exchange, then, a failure for the original inhabitants of the Americas?

Plan of a Slave-Ship.

Section of a Slave-Ship.

By the Honourable Sir William Johnson Bart. His Majesty's sole Agent and Super-Intendant of Indian Affairs for the Northern Depart

2

PLANTATIONS AND CITIES UPON A HILL, 1620–1700

FROM SETTLEMENTS TO SOCIETIES IN THE SOUTH
Searching for Laborers
To Be Like English Subjects at Home
Crushing Powhatan's Confederacy
A Model for Other Royal Colonies
Proprietary Maryland and the Carolinas

RELIGIOUS DISSENTERS COLONIZE NEW ENGLAND
The Rise of Puritan Dissenters at Home
Godly Mission to New England
Testing the Limits of Toleration
"Hivings Out" Provoke Bloody Indian Relations

FAMILIES, INDIVIDUALS, AND COMMUNITIES: SURVIVING IN EARLY AMERICA
Life and Death, North and South
Roles for Men, Women, and Children

COMMERCIAL VALUES AND THE RISE OF CHATTEL SLAVERY
Declension in New England
Stabilizing Life in the Chesapeake Region
The Beginnings of American Slavery
Shifting to Slavery in Maryland and Virginia
The World the Slaves Made

"Slaves excepted"

John Punch wanted his freedom. He was a black indentured servant who joined two white servants and tried to flee Virginia in 1640, only to be caught by local residents and brought before the governor's council, the colony's highest court. The judges ordered the flogging of each runaway—30 lashes well laid on. Then in a telling ruling, these officials revealed their thinking about the future status of blacks in England's North American colonies. The two whites had their terms of service extended by four years, but they ordered John Punch to "serve his said master . . . for the time of his natural life here or elsewhere."

Persons of African heritage were first transported to Virginia in 1619. In August of that year a Dutch vessel sailed north from the West Indies, where it had been trading or, more likely, stealing slaves from the Spanish. The Dutch ship entered Chesapeake Bay and sold some 20 "Negars," as John Rolfe described the human cargo, to settlers caught up in the early tobacco boom.

Virginia's first white settlers did not automatically assume that transplanted Africans were permanently unfree. They treated some blacks as indentured servants, a status that conveyed the prospect of personal freedom after four to seven years of laboring for someone else. English law did not recognize human slavery. The key phrase was *in favorem libertatis* (in favor of liberty), and the central tenet, wrote a contemporary legal authority, held that no person should ever "make or keep his brother in Christ, servile, bond, and underling forever unto him, as a beast rather than as a man."

Into the 1630s some black Virginians did gain their personal freedom. Others not only owned land but held servants of African origin as well, proof that permanent, inheritable slavery for blacks was a concept not yet fully developed in the Chesapeake Bay region.

By the 1640s, however, blacks faced a deteriorating legal status, ultimately leaving them outside the bounds of English liberty. In 1639 the new colony of Maryland guaranteed "all . . . Christians (slaves excepted)" the same "rights, liberties, . . . and free customs" as enjoyed by "any natural born subject of England." Worried about sporadic Indian raids, the Virginia assembly in 1640 ordered planters to arm themselves and "all those of their families which be capable of [bearing] arms . . . (excepting Negroes)." In 1643 the same assembly decreed that black women, like all adult males, would henceforth be "tithables"—those counted for local taxes because they worked in the fields. Black female servants planted, tended, and harvested tobacco crops while white female servants mainly performed household work—further evidence of discrimination based on skin color.

Local laws were catching up with the growing reality of lifetime slavery for blacks, as compared to

An African slave trader marches a group of yoked and chained captives—including women and children—from the interior of Africa to a trading post on the coast. There the captives awaited transport to the Americas.

temporary servitude for whites. In 1640 the Virginia council considered other runaway cases, besides that of John Punch. One of these involved a black named Emmanuel, who ran away with several whites. The judges handed out severe penalties, including whippings and extended terms of service for the whites. The leader of the group endured branding with an "R" on his face and had one of his legs shackled in irons for a year. Emmanuel received the same penalty, but the court made no mention of an extension of service. Apparently Emmanuel was already a slave for life.

Between 1640 and 1670 the distinction between short-term servitude for whites and permanent, inheritable slavery for blacks became firmly fixed. In appearance and by cultural and religious tradition, Africans were not like the English. As with the "wild" Irish and Indian "savages," noticeable differences translated into assumptions of inferiority, and blacks became "beastly heathens," not quite human.

Such thinking helped justify the mixing of words like "black" and "slave," so that by the 1690s slavery in the English colonies had emerged as a caste status for blacks only. Now fully excluded from the tradition of English liberty, local law defined Africans as chattels (movable property), and their masters held absolute control over their lives.

John Punch and Emmanuel were among those first African Americans in the Chesapeake Bay area who felt the stinging transition from servitude to slavery. They were also among the thousands of Europeans and Africans who helped settle England's North American colonies between 1620 and 1700. The societies and lifestyles of these migrants had many differences, as comparisons between the founding of the northern and southern colonies demonstrate. A common point for all migrants, regardless of status or condition, however, was their titanic struggle to survive in an alien land. Although thousands died, some 250,000 settlers inhabited England's mainland colonies by 1700, which resulted in the formation of another powerful European empire in the Americas.

FROM SETTLEMENTS TO SOCIETIES IN THE SOUTH

Smoking tobacco, wrote King James I, was "loathsome to the eye, hateful to the nose, harmful to the brain, [and] dangerous to the lungs." Despite the king's admonition, John Rolfe's experiments saved the Virginia Company—at least temporarily—by providing the struggling colony with an economic base. Early migrants grew tobacco with enthusiasm. The first exports occurred in 1617. By the mid-1630s Virginians were selling a million pounds a year, and by the mid-1660s annual tobacco crops for export reached 15 million pounds.

Company directors did not initially encourage the tobacco boom. Wanting a diversified economy, they sent out workers knowledgeable in the production of such commodities as silk, wine, glass, and iron, but all these efforts failed. Virginia's climate and soil were ideal for raising tobacco. Also, new land for cultivation was plentiful, since the "stinking weed" quickly depleted the soil of its minerals. Accepting reality, the London investors soon hailed tobacco as the savior of their venture. Other difficulties, however, cost the directors their charter, but not before company activities laid the basis for England's first enduring colony in North America.

Searching for Laborers

Life in early Virginia presented constant hardships. Migrants quickly succumbed to diseases such as malaria, typhoid fever, and dysentery. Survival, it seemed, depended upon "seasoning," or getting used to an inhospitable climate. Bad relations with Powhatan's Indians also was a source of mayhem and death, since the English and Native Americans fought in many isolated clashes. All told, the company convinced nearly 14,000 persons to attempt new lives in America. Only about 1150 were still alive and residing in the James River area in 1624, the year the company lost its charter.

Trying to overcome "a slaughter house" reputation, company leaders pursued various policies. Sir Thomas Smythe, a wealthy London merchant, used his boundless energy to keep the venture going. He tied company fortunes to England's potential for national greatness. His influence at court resulted in more generous charter rights in 1609 and 1612, the latter of which expanded company boundaries to include the island of Bermuda—soon a source of profitable cash crops. Also under Smythe's guidance, the company secured a steady supply of laborers. It also managed affairs in Virginia with an iron hand while attempting to improve Indian relations. Each activity was crucial to long-term development.

To encourage prospective laborers, company directors mounted publicity campaigns. These efforts helped neutralize Virginia's reputation as a death-

The rise of the tobacco industry in the colonies spurred tobacco consumption in England.

trap. More successful in securing workers was the development of the system of **indentured servitude,** modeled along the lines of contractual farm service. During early Stuart times, between one-fourth and one-third of England's families had servants. Many young men and women, having no access to land, made agreements to work for a year or more as farm laborers in return for food, lodging, and modest wages. They had few other prospects for employment and virtually no chance of gaining title to their own freehold farms.

In theory, Virginia held out the opportunity of potential economic independence for rapidly growing numbers of landless farm servants and the urban poor. As early as 1609, the mayor of London asked the company "to ease the city and suburbs of a swarm of unnecessary inmates." The challenge was to get these struggling poor to America. Persons without money needed only to sign bonded contracts, or indentures, in which they legally exchanged up to seven years of labor in return for passage costs. After completing their terms of service, their masters owed them "freedom dues," including clothing, farm tools, and in some cases land on which to begin anew as free persons.

The system of indentured servitude slowly took shape after 1609. At first, the company offered free passage along with shares of stock to those who signed up for seven years of labor. When terms were up, workers were to gain title to 100 acres of land as well as any stock dividends. The bait was eventual economic freedom, but even with so many unemployed persons in England, few applied. Getting by marginally or facing a hangman's noose remained more attractive than an early—and often brutal—death in America.

Some venturesome souls, mostly young, unattached males, signed on as company-managed laborers. To make sure these servants would take orders and work, Sir Thomas Smythe and his advisers gave dictatorial powers to their governors in Virginia. Lord De La Warr, a veteran of the Irish wars who arrived in 1610, organized the colony along military lines. He ruled by martial law, as did his surrogates, Sir Thomas Gates and Sir Thomas Dale, once he returned to England. Their *Lawes Divine, Moral, and Martiall* (1612) provided harsh penalties for even the smallest offenses.

Company servants were an undisciplined lot, less interested in work than in "bowling in the streets" of Jamestown, as an observer described their attitudes. When caught loafing, they paid with bloodied backs from public floggings, and when some laborers stole boats and tried to escape in 1612, Deputy Governor Gates showed no mercy. Their sentences included death by firing squad, hanging, or breaking upon the wheel, all as a warning to others with ideas of violating company contracts.

To Be Like English Subjects at Home

Stories of brutal treatment and high mortality rates undercut company efforts to secure a steady supply of laborers. Changes had to be made, and that process culminated when a reform-minded faction led by Sir Edwin Sandys prepared new instructions, since known as the "great charter" of 1618. The overriding goal was to frame incentives that would make risking settlement more attractive. Key provisions included an end to martial rule and a declaration assuring Virginians government "by those free laws which his Majesty's subjects live under in England." The charter promised a local representative assembly, which came to be known as the House of Burgesses. Its first deliberations took place in July 1619, a small cornerstone gathering pointing toward governments with a popular voice in England's North American colonies.

Besides guaranteeing political rights, the charter addressed economic incentives, including the notion of "private plantations" and **headrights.** Heretofore, the company controlled all acreage, but now potential settlers could purchase land without first serving as company laborers. Fifty acres per person would be given to those who migrated or those who paid for the passage of others to Virginia. Headrights would permit English families with funds to relocate and get title to enough property to grow tobacco and, perhaps, prosper. After all, Virginia had land in abundance but very few laborers, whereas England had a shortage of land and an oversupply of workers.

Even with these reforms, Virginia's unhealthful reputation kept families from migrating. English merchants and sea captains, however, developed a booming trade in indentured servants. They made substantial profits from delivering servants to labor-hungry planters and from headright patents, which they accumulated and sold to others with enough capital to purchase large tracts of land before migrating. In a few cases, buying up headrights resulted in the establishment of large plantations; still, three-fourths of all English settlers entering seventeenth-century Virginia were indentured servants.

The vast bulk of these migrants were single males under the age of 25 with no employment prospects in England. The unbalanced sex ratio concerned company officials. Wanting to give Virginia a "more settled" feeling, they contracted with 90 "uncorrupt" young women in 1619 to go to Jamestown and be sold as wives. The plan worked well, but because of other problems the company sent over only one more shipment of women. Stable family life was not a characteristic of the rough-and-tumble society of early Virginia.

Crushing Powhatan's Confederacy

Bickering, bloodshed, and death denoted relations with Powhatan's Indians as the English planted tobacco farms along the James River. John Rolfe's marriage to Powhatan's daughter, Pocahontas, in 1614, which implied a political alliance of sorts, eased tensions—but only briefly. Rolfe soon took Pocahontas to England, where she became an instant celebrity, and both of them encouraged settlement in Virginia. Unfortunately, while preparing to return home in 1616, Pocahontas contracted smallpox and died.

Two years later, Powhatan also died, leaving his more militant half-brother Opechancanough in charge of the Confederacy. Watching the growing English presence with misgivings, Opechancanough decided that slaughtering the intruders was the only means left to save his people. On Good Friday, March 22, 1622, his warriors struck everywhere. Before the massacre was over, the Indians killed 347 settlers, or about 30 percent of the English colonists, including John Rolfe. Opechancanough, however, had failed to exterminate the enemy, and in many ways the massacre of 1622 was the beginning of the end for Virginia's coastal natives. White settlers, now more convinced than ever that Indians were savages, took vengeance whenever they could.

Retreating inland, Opechancanough waited 22 years before striking again. The attack came in April 1644, and another 400 or more colonists died (about 5 percent of the white population). The 1644 massacre was a last desperate gasp by Virginia's coastal natives. The numbers of whites were now too overwhelming for total destruction. As for Opechancanough, the settlers took him prisoner. A white

This sketch of a Virginia native appeared in about 1645, shortly after Virginia's coastal Indians failed in their second attempt to drive out the white settlers.
Copyright © The British Museum

guard, seeking personal vengeance, shot the old, enfeebled native leader to death in 1646. That same year, Confederacy chiefs signed a treaty agreeing to submit to English rule. The survivors of Powhatan's once-mighty league eventually accepted life on a reservation, as many other remnant Indian peoples would be forced to do as Europeans pushed westward across the North American continent.

A Model for Other Royal Colonies

The massacre of 1622 was one of two fatal blows to the Virginia Company. James I had started to dream about huge sums of money flowing into the royal treasury from taxes on tobacco. Company leaders, trying to stabilize their debt-ridden interests after the massacre, negotiated an exclusive contract with the Crown to deliver tobacco to England with the king receiving tax revenues on every pound shipped. However, a rumor spread that company leaders intended to charge exorbitant fees for handling the tobacco. The Crown, as a second fatal blow, quickly voided the tobacco contract. Then the king's advisers used court proceedings to revoke the company charter, thereby dissolving the enterprise in 1624.

King James next declared Virginia a royal colony and sent out his own governor. He did not promise basic political rights to the settlers and canceled the privilege of a local assembly. In a virtual throwback to the days of martial law, the king authorized his officials to rule absolutely.

Neither James nor his son, King Charles I (reigned 1625–1649), were advocates of popular rights or representative forms of government. Rather, they adhered to **divine right** theories of kingship, which meant that monarchs were literally God's political stewards on earth.

Virginia's planters, however, would not be denied a voice in government, and the royal governors shrewdly called upon locally prominent men to serve as advisory councilors. The governors also began authorizing assemblies, conveniently referred to as conventions, to deal with local problems. Still, relations between royal governors and colonists could become turbulent. In 1634 one governor, Sir John Harvey, known as a "choleric and impatient" man, got into a fist fight with one of his councilors. He punched out his opponent's teeth and threatened to hang the other councilors. In response, the councilors had Harvey arrested and sent him back to England in chains.

In 1639 King Charles, facing popular dissent at home because of his high-handed rule, finally relieved some of the pressure by granting Virginians a representative assembly, thereby assuring some local participation in colony-related decision making. Unlike the Spanish and French, English subjects had refused to accede to political domination by a far-off parent nation. They would share in the decision making affecting their lives as colonists in America.

Proprietary Maryland and the Carolinas

Charles's concession suggests the expediency with which the Stuart kings viewed colonization. Assuring basic rights did attract more settlers, which in turn meant larger tobacco crops and more tax revenues for the Crown. Founding additional colonies, moreover, would enhance England's stature among the nations of Europe. These same settlements could be used as dumping grounds for troublesome groups in England, such as the Puritans. Vast stretches of territory could also be granted to court favorites. The Stuarts had the power to make wealthy men even wealthier by awarding them huge "proprietary" estates in America, which would foster loyalty among powerful gentlemen at court who might otherwise choose, at some point, to challenge the authority of the Crown.

Sir George Calvert, described as a "forward and knowing person," was one such favored courtier. Serving as James I's secretary of state, he took charge of dissolving the Virginia Company. A year later he converted to Roman Catholicism and had to leave the government. To reward his loyal service, however, the king named Calvert the first Lord Baltimore and granted him permission to colonize Newfoundland, an effort that failed. Then in 1632 Charles I awarded Calvert title to 10 million acres surrounding the northern end of Chesapeake Bay. The king named the territory "Maryland" after his own Catholic wife, Queen Henrietta Maria, and he named Calvert lord proprietor over these lands.

When Calvert died, his son Cecilius, the second Lord Baltimore, took charge and sent out the first settlement parties. The idea was for Maryland to function as a haven for persecuted Roman Catholics. Those Catholics who migrated received substantial personal estates in return for annual quitrents, or land taxes, paid to Lord Baltimore. Many more Protestants than Catholics secured land patents, also with quitrents. The colony soon bore a striking similarity to its Chesapeake neighbor Virginia, since Marylanders also devoted themselves to cultivating tobacco.

The Maryland charter granted the Baltimore proprietors absolute political authority, but in 1635 Cecilius Calvert, hoping to induce further settlements,

Chesapeake Settlements, 1650

FIGURE 2.1
The Stuart Monarchy of England

The Stuart monarchs adhered to divine right theories of kingship. They only reluctantly granted basic political rights to English settlers in America.

granted a representative assembly. As the colony grew, Catholics and Protestants dueled bitterly over control of local politics. In an attempt to protect the minority Catholics, Calvert proposed an Act of Religious Toleration in 1649, which guaranteed all adult males voting or officeholding rights, so long as they subscribed to the doctrine of the Trinity. Although not full toleration, this act, which the assembly approved, was a key step toward liberty of conscience. Still, bickering between Maryland's Catholic and Protestant settlers continued for several decades.

Religious warfare, meanwhile, convulsed England. During the 1640s civil war turned English subjects against one another. Puritan "Roundheads" rose up against the "Cavalier" supporters of Charles I, who had refused to let Parliament meet for several years. In 1649 the victorious Puritans showed willful contempt for divine right theories of kingship by beheading Charles. Oliver Cromwell, the leader of Puritan military forces, then took political control of England as Lord Protector. After Cromwell's death and a brief, disastrous period of rule by his son, Parliament invited Charles I's exiled son to reestablish the Stuart monarchy—in exchange for promises to assemble Parliament regularly and to support the Anglican church.

The restoration of Charles II (reigned 1660–1685) left the new king with many political debts. In 1663 he paid off eight powerful gentlemen by awarding them title to all lands lying south of Virginia and north of Spanish Florida. The region was already known as Carolus, the Latin equivalent of Charles. The new proprietors quickly set about the task of finding settlers for the Carolinas, which proved difficult because of a dramatic new boom in England's economy—and a consequent decrease in the numbers of unemployed subjects.

Trying to spark the settlement process, one of the proprietors, Sir Anthony Ashley Cooper, assisted by his brilliant secretary, political philosopher John Locke, produced the "Fundamental Constitutions for Carolina" (1669). This document spelled out unworkable plans for a complex social order in which "landgraves" and "caciques" held vast estates and functioned as an American nobility, but shared the responsibilities of local government with smaller landholders. More important, the proprietors offered attractive headright provisions of up to 150 acres per person, guarantees of a representative assembly and religious toleration, and a fateful promise that free persons "shall have absolute power and authority over . . . negro slaves."

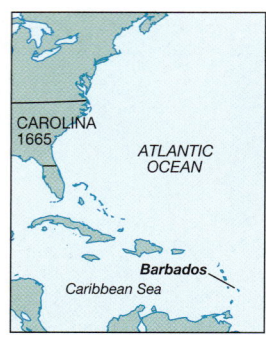

Barbadian Connection

Even with such generous terms, the Carolinas grew slowly. The Albemarle region of northeastern North Carolina developed as settlers spilled over from Virginia. William Byrd II, a prominent Virginia planter of the early eighteenth century, described the Albemarle inhabitants as having a "disposition to laziness for their whole lives." Most inhabitants subsisted marginally by exporting tobacco and various timber-derived products, including pitch, tar, and potash.

The proprietors focused on settling South Carolina. They contacted small-scale English farmers on the island of Barbados who were selling out to well-capitalized gentlemen building large sugar plantations. In 1670 a group of these Barbadians founded Charleston (then known as Charles Town), and a steady trade in deerskins and horsehides soon developed with interior natives. A few greedy migrants even dealt in humans by getting local Indians to capture tribal enemies, who were then sold off as slaves to the West Indies.

Picking up on the proprietors' promise, Barbadian migrants who owned slaves brought their chattels with them. Unlike in the Chesapeake area, slavery existed from the outset in South Carolina and took even firmer hold when rice production became the mainstay of economic activity after 1690. By the end of the seventeenth century, English colonists in the southern colonies had constructed their lives around the exportation of cash crops, particularly tobacco and rice, supported increasingly by black slave labor. Over time the institution of slavery gave white southerners a common identity—with serious long-term consequences.

RELIGIOUS DISSENTERS COLONIZE NEW ENGLAND

English men and women migrated to America for many reasons. Certainly the hope of economic betterment was a prime motivating factor, but in New England the initial emphasis reflected more directly on a communal desire to provide a hospitable environment for Calvinist religious values. Beginning in the 1620s New England emerged as a haven for religious dissenters of two types: **separatists,** such as the Pilgrims, and **nonseparatists,** such as the Puritans.

Separatists believed the Church of England to be so corrupt that it could not be salvaged. So as not to compromise their beliefs, their only course was to sever all ties with the Anglican church and establish their own religious communities of like-minded believers.

The dauntless band known as the Pilgrims were separatists from Scrooby Manor, a village in northeastern England. Facing official harassment, they fled to the Netherlands in 1608 but found it difficult to make a decent living there. Furthermore, they worried about their children, who not only were losing their sense of identity as English persons but also appeared "to degenerate and be corrupted" by frequent exposure to various worldly pleasures. As a result, Pilgrim leaders sought a land grant to settle in America, where they could set up their own religious community and worship as they pleased.

In September 1620 the first party of Pilgrims sailed west on the *Mayflower* under a land patent of the Virginia Company. Only one-third of the 102 migrants aboard were Pilgrims. The rest were employees of the London merchant Thomas Weston, who financed the venture in return for an exclusive seven-year monopoly over all trading commodities sent back to England. After surviving nine harrowing, storm-tossed weeks at sea, the *Mayflower* made first landfall on the northern tip of Cape Cod.

Knowing they were well to the north of Virginia territory and outnumbered by "strangers," the Pilgrims drafted a plan of government, called the Mayflower Compact, before proceeding to the mainland in December 1620 and selecting the site of Tisquantum's old Patuxet village for their permanent settlement. The Compact guaranteed settlers the right to elect governing officials to a representative assembly, but only Pilgrim "saints"—those who were church members—could vote. The Pilgrims would tolerate "strangers" in their midst and encourage them to seek God's grace—the basis of church membership—as long as they showed "due submission and obedience" to the authority of the congregation of church members. In this sense the Compact was not an advanced statement of popular government; its purpose was to assure the Pilgrims full political control of Plymouth Colony.

Plymouth Plantation struggled to survive. Under the effective, persistent leadership of Governor William Bradford, the settlers overcame all obstacles. Besides a deadly first winter, the Pilgrims had to reckon with no clear title to their land. In 1621 they obtained a proper patent, but several years passed before they fulfilled their financial obligations to Weston and a variety of other sponsors. They did so mostly by shipping fish and furs back to England.

English Barbadians settled Charleston, South Carolina. The local economy would develop around crops, such as rice, produced by slave labor.

At the outset the Pilgrims worked hard to maintain peace with local Indians. Under Miles Standish, the one professional soldier in their midst, they also trained for war, should serious discord with the natives develop. They certainly did not hesitate to discipline other whites in the region, such as the rowdy band of men at Thomas Morton's "Merry Mount" trading post not far from Plymouth. Not only was Morton selling alcohol and firearms, but his traders were regularly "dancing and frisking together" with native women around a maypole, in addition to "worse practices," according to Bradford. Morton's arming of the natives, as well as the lustful scenes at Merry Mount, incensed the Pilgrims. Above all else, they did not want to face the kind of massacre that had occurred in Virginia during 1622. With Standish in the lead, they closed down the Merry Mount post in 1628 and sent Morton packing off to England.

Slowly but surely the Pilgrim colony began to prosper, as recorded in Bradford's valuable account, *History Of Plymouth Plantation*, which covers the first 26 years of the colony's history. Through all of their adventures and travails, the Pilgrims never lost sight of their original purpose—freedom to worship God according to their own understanding of scripture. Their numbers increased to 7000 persons by 1691, the year they accepted annexation to the much more populous Puritan colony of Massachusetts Bay.

The Rise of Puritan Dissenters at Home

Far more numerous in England were nonseparatists, who wanted to "purify" rather than separate from the Church of England. The Puritans, as these dissenters were known, have often been characterized as prudish, ignorant bigots who hated the thought of having a good time. Modern historical research, however, has shattered this stereotype. The Puritans were reformers who, as recipients of John Calvin's legacy, took Biblical matters seriously. They believed that God's word should order the steps of every person's life. What troubled them most was their conviction that the Protestant Reformation in England had not gone far enough. They viewed the Church of England as "corrupt" in organization and guided by unscriptural doctrine; they longed for far-reaching institutional change that would rid the Anglican church of its imperfections. When church and state leaders harassed them, they responded in various ways, including the planting of a model utopian society—Massachusetts Bay Colony—in New England.

In the early 1600s the Puritans numbered in the hundreds of thousands. Their emphasis upon reading Scripture particularly appealed to literate members of the middle classes and lesser gentry—merchants, skilled craft workers, professionals, and freehold farmers. The Puritans prided themselves on hard work and the pursuit of one's "calling" as a way to glorify the Almighty. They also searched for signs of having earned God's saving grace through a personal conversion experience. The goal was to become one of God's "visible saints" on earth. To be a visible saint meant that a person was fit for church membership.

By comparison, the Church of England, as a state-supported institution, claimed all citizens, regardless of their spiritual nature, as church members. Besides this problem, the Anglican church, from the Puritan perspective, put too much emphasis on ritual. Its elaborate hierarchy of church officials did not include enough educated ministers who understood the Bible, let alone the need to teach parishioners to seek God's grace; rather, Anglican clergymen were the friends and relatives of the well connected. They were like "Mr. Atkins, curate of Romford, thrice presented for a drunkard," "Mr. Goldringe, parson of Laingdon Hills, . . . convicted of fornication," and "Mr. Cuckson, vicar of Linsell, . . . a pilferer, of scandalous life."

In his youth in Scotland, James Stuart, who became King James I, had regular dealings with John

A plaster statue of Governor William Bradford by Cyrus E. Dallin. There is no extant portrait of Bradford.

Knox and his Presbyterian (Scottish Puritan) followers. He developed a decided distaste for religious dissenters. "I will harry them out of the land," James boldly proclaimed after becoming king of England, "or else do worse." Like Queen Elizabeth before him, however, he endured the Puritans. He never felt secure enough in his own authority to test his will against their rapidly expanding influence.

During King James's reign, the Puritans moved aggressively to realize their goals. They built a political base from which to demand church reform by winning elections for seats in Parliament. James put up with their protests, but his son, Charles I, was more confrontational. He named William Laud, whom the Puritans considered a Roman Catholic in Anglican garb, as archbishop of the Church of England. Laud was particularly adept at persecuting his opponents. In response, the Puritans pushed a bill through Parliament denouncing "popish" practices in church and state. Finally, Charles used his royal prerogatives to disband Parliament and tried to rule by himself between 1629 and 1640, thus contributing to the advent of the bloody English Civil War.

In the late 1620s the Puritans were not ready for rebellion, but some in their numbers had decided upon an "errand into the wilderness." In 1629 they secured a joint-stock charter for the Massachusetts Bay Company. Investors knew they were underwriting the peopling of a utopian religious experiment in America. As for King Charles, the prospect of ridding the realm of thousands of Puritans was incentive enough to give royal approval to the Bay Company charter.

Godly Mission to New England

The Puritans organized their venture carefully. They placed their settlement effort under John Winthrop (1588–1649), a prominent lawyer and landholder. In 1630 some 700 Puritans crowded onto 11 ships and joined Winthrop in sailing to Massachusetts. They were the vanguard of what became the *Great Migration,* or the movement of an estimated 20,000 persons to New England by 1642. These men and women left not as indentured servants but as families fleeing the religious repression and worsening economic conditions of Charles I's England.

More than any other person, John Winthrop worked tirelessly to promote the Puritan mission. Before landing in Massachusetts Bay, he delivered a sermon entitled "A Model of Christian Charity," in which he asserted: "We must consider that we shall be as a **city upon a hill;** the eyes of all people are upon us." The Puritans' mission was to order human existence in the Bay Colony according to God's word. Their example, Winthrop and other company leaders hoped, would inspire England and the rest of Europe to change, thereby causing the full realization of the Protestant Reformation.

Curious events back in England facilitated attempts to build a model society in the wilderness.

John Winthrop led the Puritans to New England, where he served several terms as governor of the Massachusetts Bay Colony.

THE PEOPLE SPEAK

William Bradford's *History of Plymouth Plantation*

William Bradford (1590–1657) was a humble person who served several terms as the governor of Plymouth Plantation. In his spare moments he wrote vivid passages about what he and other Pilgrims experienced in crossing the Atlantic Ocean and building a new colony in the American wilderness. Scholars today regard Bradford's history, which was almost lost to posterity and was not published until the mid-nineteenth century, as a valuable source of information about the Pilgrims' quest to construct a godly society unfettered by Old World corruptions. Bradford's interpretive framework was providential in character. Like his fellow Pilgrims, he believed in an interventionist God who could either protect or destroy human beings. In the two passages that follow, Bradford describes how the Pilgrims survived both their harrowing voyage to America aboard the *Mayflower* and their terrible first winter in New England. For Bradford, God had saved them from destruction, which was proof that their quest to found a new society was a blessed undertaking.

[Aboard the *Mayflower*]

September 6 [1620]. These troubles being blown over, and now all being compact together in one ship, they put to sea again with a prosperous wind, which continued divers days together, which was some encouragement unto them; yet, according to the usual manner, many were afflicted with seasickness. And I may not omit here a special work of God's providence. There was a proud and very profane young man, one of the seamen, of a lusty, able body, which made him the more haughty; he would always be contemning the poor people in their sickness and cursing them daily with grievous execrations; and did not let to tell them that he hoped to help to cast half of them overboard before they came to their journey's end, and to make merry with what they had; and if he were by any gently reproved, he would curse and swear most bitterly. But it pleased God before they came half seas over, to smite this young man with a grievous disease, of which he died in a desperate manner, and so was himself the first that was thrown overboard. Thus his curses light on his own head, and it was an astonishment to all his fellows for they noted it to be the just hand of God upon him.

After they had enjoyed fair winds and weather for a season, they were encountered many times with cross winds and met with many fierce storms with which the ship was shroudly shaken, and her upper works made very leaky; and one of the main beams in the midships was bowed and cracked, which put them in some fear that the ship could not be able to perform the voyage. . . .

But in examining of all opinions, the master and others affirmed they knew the ship to be strong and firm under water; and for the buckling of the main beam, there was a great iron screw the passengers brought out of Holland, which would raise the beam into his place; the which being done, the carpenter and master affirmed that with a post put under it, set firm in the lower deck and otherways bound, he would make it sufficient. . . . So they committed themselves to the will of God and resolved to proceed.

[Disastrous First Winter]

But that which was most sad and lamentable was, that in two or three months' time half of their company died, especially in January and February, being the depth of winter, and wanting houses and other comforts; being infected with the scurvy and other diseases which this long voyage and their inaccommodate condition had brought upon them. So as there died some times two or three of a day in the foresaid time, that of 100 and odd persons, scarce fifty remained. And of these, in the time of most distress, there was but six or seven sound persons who to their great commendations, be it spoken, spared no pains night nor day, but with abundance of toil and hazard of their own health, fetched them wood, made them fires, dressed them meat, made their beds, washed their loathsome clothes, clothed and unclothed them. In a word, did all the homely and necessary offices for them which dainty and queasy stomachs cannot endure to hear named; and all this willingly and cheerfully, without any grudging in the least, showing herein their true love unto their friends and brethren; . . . And yet the Lord so upheld these persons as in this general calamity they were not at all infected either with sickness or lameness. . . .

But I may not here pass by another remarkable passage not to be forgotten. As this calamity fell among the passengers that were to be left here to plant, and were hasted ashore and made to drink water that the seamen might have the more beer, and one in his sickness desiring but a small can of beer, it was answered that if he were their own father he should have none. The disease began to fall amongst them also, so as almost half of their company died before they went away, and many of their officers and lustiest men, as the boatswain, gunner, three quartermasters, the cook and others. At which the Master was something strucken and sent to the sick ashore and told the Governor he should send for beer for them that had need of it, though he drunk water homeward bound. . . .

Source: William Bradford, *Of Plymouth Plantation, 1620–1647,* ed. with introduction by Samuel Eliot Morrison (New York, 1952), 58–59, 77–78.

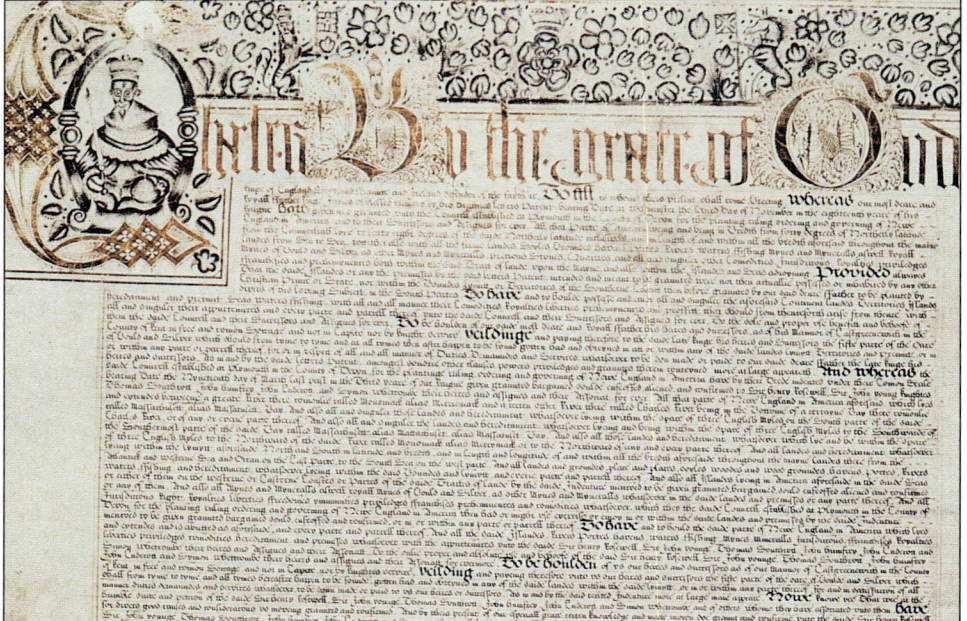

The Bay Colony charter served as the basis for government in Massachusetts until 1684, when the Crown had the charter nullified because settlers refused to stop acting so independently of England's authority.

For some reason, perhaps because of a well-placed bribe, the Bay Company charter did not specify a location for stockholder (General Court) meetings. Seizing the opportunity, Winthrop and others drafted the Cambridge Agreement in August 1629; they decided to carry the charter with them and hold all stockholder meetings in New England—3000 miles from meddlesome king's officials. Of the stockholders who migrated, all were fervent Puritans, which meant that decision making for the colony would be controlled in General Court sessions by a handful of men fully committed to the Puritan mission.

Once in Massachusetts, the stockholders soon faced challenges to their all-inclusive authority. Typical was a protest in 1632 by settlers who refused to pay taxes under the "bondage" of no voice in government. The solution was to create a category of citizenship known as "freeman." Freemen would be like stockholders; they could participate in government. As with the Pilgrims, however, only male church members gained full citizenship status as voters. The leaders assumed that these visible saints would not subvert the colony's mission.

The government of Massachusetts developed out of this arrangement. As the colony grew, the General Court became an elective assembly with freemen (full church members) from each town sending delegates to Boston to represent local concerns. The governorship, too, was elective on an annual basis, and John Winthrop dominated the office until his death in 1649. Ministers were not eligible for political offices, so the government was not technically a theocracy. Clergymen, however, met occasionally in synods and offered written advice to colony leaders regarding religious issues, which did affect political decision making.

Initially, Winthrop wanted all settlers to live in towns close to Boston, but with migrants pouring into the colony, that proved impossible. The General Court started to issue town charters, and settlements fanned out in semicircular fashion from Boston into the interior.

Designated proprietors guided the establishment of Puritan towns, emphasizing community control over individual lives. A 1635 law—later repealed—stated that inhabitants had to live within a half mile of the town church. Each family received a house lot near the village green, farmland away from the center of town, and access to pasture land and woodlots. Some towns perpetuated the European open-field system. Families gained title to strips of land in several fields and worked in common with other townspeople to bring in yearly crops. In other towns, families had all their farmland concentrated in one area.

These property arrangements reflected English patterns of land distribution as well as the desire to promote godly behavior, especially since some first-generation settlers were not Puritans. Village life was not wholly restrictive, however, so long as families viewed the Bay Colony, in the words of the Reverend John Cotton, as "the setting forth of God's house, which is His church."

Town leaders promoted harmonious living conditions. They set off lots for taverns, schools, and meeting houses. Taverns served as community centers in which people socialized and cheerfully drank alcohol, which they believed was essential to good health. School lots satisfied concerns about education. The Puritans advocated literacy so that everyone could read Scripture and "understand the principles of religion and . . . laws of the country." (The desire to have a learned clergy led to the founding of Harvard College in 1636.) Beginning in the 1640s, the General Court ordered each town to tax inhabitants to pay for formal schooling in reading and writing for all children. The meeting house was the gathering place for town meetings and church services. Church members had the duty to encourage non-Puritans in their midst to study the Bible, pray fervently, and seek God's grace so that they might also enjoy political and religious rights—as well as eternal salvation.

Testing the Limits of Toleration

The first generation of Puritans worked hard and prospered. Farming was the primary means of gaining a livelihood, although some coastal inhabitants took to shipbuilding, fishing, and mercantile activity. Prosperity did not stand in the way of serious internal controversies. These disagreements suggested how the Puritan system functioned on behalf of orthodoxy—and against diverse opinions—to assure adherence to the wilderness mission.

No Puritan was purer than Roger Williams (1603?–1683). When this well-educated clergyman arrived in Boston in 1631 and announced that "Bishop Laud pursued me out of the land," John Winthrop graciously welcomed him. Soon Williams received an offer to teach in the Boston church, but he refused because of rules about mandatory worship. To hold services with the unconverted in attendance was to be no purer than the Church of England. It "stinks in God's nostrils," Williams proclaimed.

So off Williams went, first to Salem and then to Plymouth Colony, where Governor William Bradford and the Pilgrims embraced him. Only the visible saints attended church services in Plymouth. The Pilgrims soon dismissed Williams for "strange opinions" having to do with questions of land ownership. He had become friendly with local Indians and had concluded that any Crown-based land patent was fraudulent—and that Puritans and Pilgrims alike were thieves because they had not purchased their land from the natives. Moving back to Salem, Williams next denounced Bay Colony leaders who meddled in church affairs. So long as churches were subject in any way to political influences, they would be as corrupt as the Church of England.

John Winthrop remained Williams's friend and kept advising him to keep his opinions to himself, but other Puritan leaders had endured enough. Orthodox adherence to the Puritan mission meant that this contentious young minister, no matter how logical in his criticisms, could not be tolerated. With Winthrop's reluctant approval, the General Court banished Williams in October 1635. To avoid being sent back to England, Williams fled to the Narragansett Indians, with whom he spent the winter and from whom he eventually purchased land for a new community—Providence, Rhode Island.

Partly because of Roger Williams's influence, the colony of Rhode Island took form as a center of religious toleration. Settlers there welcomed all faiths, including Judaism, and the government stayed out of matters of personal conscience. Personal conscience was truly sacred, Williams thought, which made him an advance agent for such concepts as religious freedom and separation of church and state.

Meanwhile, others such as Anne Hutchinson (1591–1643), also tested the limits of orthodoxy. Hutchinson was a woman of powerful mind and commanding presence who frightened leaders like John Winthrop. Hutchinson, the mother of 13 children, moved with her family to Boston in 1634, where she served as a midwife. She also spoke openly about her religious views, which had a strong mystical element. Once humans experienced saving grace, she believed, the "Holy Spirit illumines the heart," and God would offer direct revelation. This meant that his true saints no longer needed the church or the state to help order their daily existence.

Such ideas gained the label **Antinomian,** which Puritans defined as against the laws of human governance. To Winthrop, Hutchinson appeared as an ad-

Charged and convicted of spreading "dangerous opinions," Roger Williams was banished from Massachusetts Bay Colony in October 1635.

Tried for her controversial religious ideas before the General Court, Anne Hutchinson refused to recant. The court banished her from the Bay Colony.

vocate of social anarchy. She was threatening to ruin the Puritan mission, since human institutions of any kind would have no purpose, except to control the unregenerate. Winthrop viewed the Antinomian crisis as very serious, especially since the movement came to involve large numbers of people.

With Antinomian thinking spreading so rapidly, orthodox Puritans girded themselves for battle. In 1637 Bay Colony clergymen assembled in a synod and denounced Antinomianism as "blasphemous." They also insisted that Hutchinson's brother-in-law, the Reverend John Wheelwright, recant his Antinomian views. Wheelwright held his ground, and he was banished. He and his followers went off to found Exeter, New Hampshire.

Now the target was Hutchinson. Ordered to appear before the General Court, she masterfully defended herself for two days, only to be declared guilty of sedition for dishonoring her spiritual parents, Winthrop and the other magistrates. As "a woman not fit for our society," she too was banished. In the spring of 1638 she migrated to Rhode Island where she helped establish the community of Portsmouth.

"Hivings Out" Provoke Bloody Indian Relations

For those who accepted mainstream Puritan orthodoxy, Massachusetts was paradise compared to England. But for dissidents like the Antinomians, Bay Colony leaders seemed just as intolerant as Charles I or Archbishop Laud. As a result, they felt compelled to locate elsewhere, and that is how Rhode Island began. Eventually settlers there pulled themselves together into a confederation and, thanks to Roger Williams, gained a separate patent from Parliament in 1644. Then in 1663 King Charles II granted a more generous charter. Local political offices, even including the governorship, were to be elective, and the Crown also declared that no person should ever be "molested, ... [or] punished for any differences of opinion in matters of religion." This clause made Rhode Island a unique haven for religious freedom in Puritan New England.

Even before John Wheelwright's exodus to New Hampshire, a few hardy settlers had located in that region. Others established themselves along the coast of Maine. Massachusetts tried to maintain control of both areas, but in 1681 New Hampshire became a separate royal colony. The Bay Colony did sustain its authority over Maine by purchasing the land patents of rival claimants. This territory remained a thinly settled appendage of Massachusetts until it gained statehood in 1820.

Connecticut also started to emerge as a Puritan colony during the 1630s. The Reverend Thomas Hooker, who viewed John Winthrop as too dictatorial, led 100 settlers into the Connecticut River Valley in May 1636. By year's end, another 700 Puritans had followed Hooker's path, resulting in the founding of such towns as Hartford, Wethersfield, and Windsor. John Davenport guided a party of London Puritans to Boston in 1637 but after a few months decided that Winthrop was not dictatorial enough. He led his flock to the mouth of the Quinnipiac River, where they established New Haven.

In 1639 the three Connecticut river towns founded by Hooker adopted a plan of general government, known as the Fundamental Orders of Connecticut. Although based on the Bay Colony's political organization, this plan did permit all adult male property holders, not just church members, to vote, a step toward more inclusive franchise rights. Eventually, all the Connecticut settlements came together to form one political unit and gained a Crown charter (1662) as generous as Rhode Island's. Connecticut

Puritans, however, had little interest in encouraging religious diversity; as in Massachusetts, the Congregational church dominated spiritual life.

These "hivings out" from Massachusetts, as Winthrop called them, adversely affected relations with the native populace. A devastating smallpox epidemic in 1633 temporarily delayed Indian resistance. When Hooker's followers moved into the Connecticut River valley, they settled on land claimed by the Pequots, who decided to resist and struck at Wethersfield in April 1637, killing several people. A force of Puritans and Narragansett Indians, who hated the Pequots, retaliated a month later by surrounding and setting fire to the main Pequot village on the Mystic River. Some 400 men, women, and children died in the flames. "Horrible was the stink and scent thereof," wrote one Puritan, but destroying the Pequots "seemed a sweet sacrifice" to assure the peace and safety of those seeking to plant themselves on fertile Connecticut lands.

The Puritans were no worse than Virginians or Carolinians in their treatment of Native Americans. In some ways they tried to be better. The Bay Colony charter mandated that Indians be brought "to the knowledge... of the only true God and... the Christian faith." Most Puritans ignored this mandate, but the Reverend John Eliot devoted his ministry to converting the natives. Besides translating the Bible into an Algonquian tongue, he established four towns for "praying Indians," which by 1650 held a population of over 1000. Most of these natives did not actually seek conversion. They were remnant members of once vital tribes, and they were trying to survive while retaining as much of their cultural heritage as possible in the face of what had become an irreversible European tide of westward migration.

John Eliot was known as the Puritan Apostle to the Indians. Also shown below is the title page from the Bible as translated by Eliot into an Algonquian tongue.

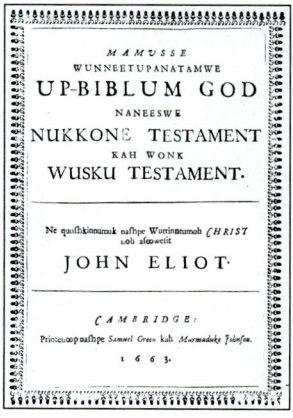

New England Colonies, 1650

FAMILIES, INDIVIDUALS, AND COMMUNITIES: SURVIVING IN EARLY AMERICA

Just as Opechancanough tried to wipe out the Virginians, Metacomet, better known to the Puritans as King Philip, attempted the same in New England. The son of Massasoit, a Wampanoag chieftain who, like Tisquantum, had aided the early Pilgrims, Metacomet felt threatened by the spread of white settlements. In 1671 the Pilgrims hauled him into court on the grounds of plotting against their colony and extracted a statement of submission to English authority. Thoroughly humiliated, Metacomet swore revenge.

The life-and-death struggle known as King Philip's War began during the summer of 1675 when various Indian tribes joined Metacomet's warriors in raiding towns along the Massachusetts-Connecticut frontier. Taking advantage of the settlers' habits, the natives often struck during Sunday church meetings. By early 1676 much of New England was in chaos. Metacomet's forces even attacked towns within 20 miles of Boston, but there were too many Puritans (around 50,000) and not enough Indians (fewer than 12,000) to annihilate the whites. When a "praying" Indian shot and killed Metacomet, King Philip's War rapidly lost its momentum.

Metacomet's warriors had leveled or done substantial damage to several towns, and around 2000 Puritan settlers died in the war. Roughly twice as many Indians lost their lives in what proved to be a futile effort to drive away the ever-expansive English. Still, King Philip's War was not the Indians' last gasp. In a few years remnant native groups started receiving support from the French in Canada and once again began attacking New England's frontier towns.

King Philip's War was very bloody. However, surviving in New England was less difficult than surviving in the Chesapeake region, as comparative experiences graphically reveal.

Life and Death, North and South

During the seventeenth century New England's population grew steadily by natural increase. Most of the 25,000 migrants crossed the ocean before the outbreak of England's civil war in the 1640s; yet by the end of the century some 93,000 colonists inhabited New England. In the Chesapeake, by comparison, as many as 100,000 persons had attempted settlement, but only about 85,000 were living in Virginia and Maryland in 1700. Had these two colonies not had a steady influx of new migrants, they might have ceased to exist altogether.

The Chesapeake colonists experienced shorter, less fertile lives than their New England counterparts. In 1640, for example, Chesapeake migrants had no more than a 50 percent chance of surviving their first year in America. Hot, steamy summers fostered repeated outbreaks of malaria and typhoid fever, which, along with dysentery and poisoning from brackish drinking water, killed thousands. New England's drinking water was safer, although Puritans generally preferred home-brewed beer, and the harsher winter climate helped kill off deadly germs. As a result, the Puritans enjoyed longer, healthier lives.

In New England 20 percent of all Puritan males who survived infancy lived into their seventies. Even with the hazards of childbirth, Puritan women lived almost as long. In Virginia and Maryland, men who survived into their early twenties had reached middle age; on the average, they would not live beyond

Population Comparison of New England and Chesapeake, Mid-1600s

Virulent disease and brackish water in the Chesapeake Bay region resulted in shorter life spans than in New England.

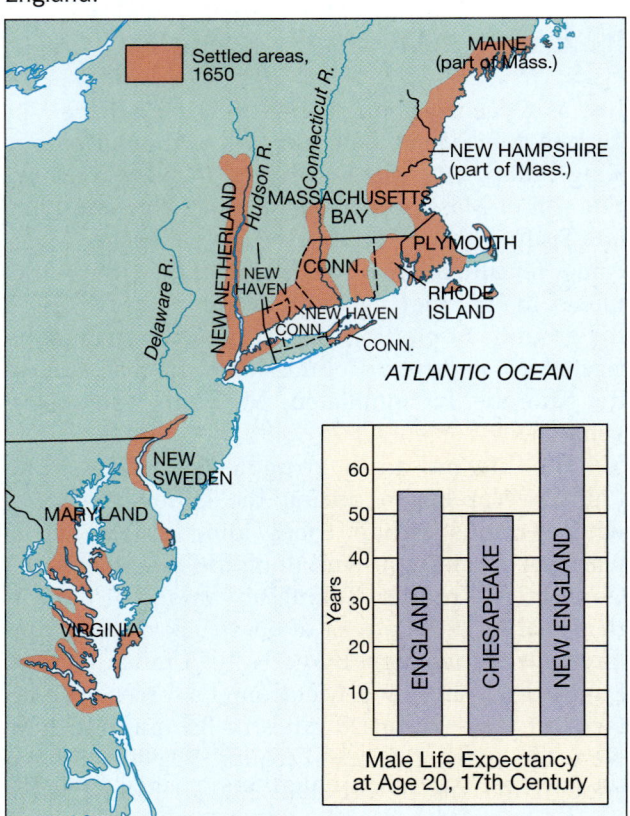

Living grandparents were a unique characteristic of New England families, as illustrated by this portrait of Abigail Gerrish and her grandmother.

their mid-forties. Women in their early twenties could not expect to survive too far beyond their late thirties. Given an average life expectancy of 50 to 55 years back in England, the Chesapeake region deserved its reputation as a human graveyard. In comparison early New England represented a utopian health environment.

Good health sustained life and meant longer marriages and more children. Men in New England were usually in their mid-twenties when they married, and their wives were only two to three years younger. Marriages lasted an average of 25 years before one or the other spouse died. Longevity also resulted in large families, averaging seven to eight children per household. In some locales, nine out of ten children survived infant diseases and grew to adulthood knowing not only their parents but their grandparents as well. Families with living grandparents were a unique characteristic of Puritan New England, reflecting life spans more typical of modern America than early modern Europe.

From a demographic perspective, then, New England families were far more stable and secure than those of the Chesapeake. Because Puritans crossed the Atlantic in family units, the ratio of women to men was more evenly balanced than in Virginia or Maryland, where most migrants were not married. Planters seeking laborers for their tobacco fields preferred young males, which skewed the gender ratio against women and retarded the development of family life. Before 1640 only one woman migrated to the Chesapeake for every six men; and as late as 1700, males still outnumbered females by a ratio of more than three to two.

The system of indentured servitude also affected population patterns. Servants could not marry until they had completed their terms. Typically, women were in their mid-twenties before they first wed, which in combination with short adult life expectancies curbed the numbers of children they could bear. Seventeenth-century Chesapeake families averaged only two to three children, and a quarter of them did not survive their first year of life. Marriages lasted an average of seven years before one or the other spouse died. Two-thirds of all surviving children lost one parent by the age of 18, and one-third lost both. Rarely did children know grandparents. Death was as much a daily reality as life for Chesapeake families, at least until the early eighteenth century when killer diseases stopped wreaking such havoc.

Roles for Men, Women, and Children

The early Puritans looked at their mission as a family undertaking, and they referred to families as "little commonwealths." Not only were families to "be fruitful and multiply," but they also served as agencies of education and religious instruction as well as centers of vocational training and social welfare. Families cared for the destitute and elderly; they took in orphans; and they housed servants and apprentices—all under one roof and subject to the authority of the father.

The Puritans carried **patriarchal** values across the Atlantic and planted them in America. New England law, reflecting its English base, subscribed to the doctrine of **coverture,** or subordinating the legal identity of women to their husbands, who were the undisputed heads of households. Unless there were prenuptial agreements, all property brought by women to marriages belonged to their mates. Husbands were responsible for assuring decency and good order in family life. They also represented their families in all community political, economic, and religious activities.

Wives also had major family responsibilities. "For though the husband be the head of the wife," the Reverend Samuel Willard explained, "yet she is the head of the family." The particular calling of mothers was to nurture their children in godly living, as well as to perform many other tasks—tending gardens, brewing beer, raising chickens, cooking, spinning, and sewing—when not helping in the planting and harvesting of crops.

Most Puritan marriages functioned in at least outward harmony. If serious problems arose, local churches and courts intervened to end the turmoil. Puritan law, again reflecting English precedent, made divorce quite difficult. The only legal grounds were bigamy, desertion, and adultery, and the process required the petitioning of assemblies for bills of separation. A handful of women, most likely battered or abandoned wives, effected their own divorces by setting up separate residences. On occasion the courts brought abusive husbands under control, such as a Maine man who brutally clubbed his wife for refusing to feed the family pig. Some instances occurred when wives defied patriarchalism, including one case involving a Massachusetts woman who faced community censure for beating her husband and even "egging her children to help her, bidding them knock him in the head."

Family friction arose from other sources as well, some of which stemmed from the absolute control that fathers exercised over property and inheritances. If sons wanted to marry and establish separate households, they had to conform to the will of their fathers, who controlled the land. Family patriarchs normally delayed the passing of property until sons had reached their mid-twenties and selected mates acceptable to their parents. Since parents also bestowed dowries on daughters as their contributions to new family units, romantic love had less to

THE American Mosaic

Childbirth in Early America

WHEN the *Mayflower* left Plymouth, England, September 16, 1620, on its historic voyage to the New World, 3 of its 102 passengers were pregnant. Elizabeth Hopkins and Susanna White were each in their seventh month of pregnancy. Mary Norris Allerton was in her second or third month.

Their pregnancies must have been excruciatingly difficult. After a few days of clear weather, the *Mayflower* ran into "fierce storms" that lasted for six of the voyage's nine and a half weeks. For days on end, passengers were confined to the low spaces between decks, while high winds blew away clothing and supplies and the ship tossed and rolled on the heavy seas.

While the ship was still at sea, Elizabeth Hopkins gave birth to a baby boy named Oceanus after his birthplace. Two weeks later, while the Mayflower was anchored off Cape Cod, Susanna White also had a baby boy. He was christened Peregrine, a name that means "pilgrim." Peregrine White would live into his eighties, but Oceanus Hopkins died during the Pilgrims' first winter in Plymouth. In the spring of 1621, Mary Norris Allerton died in childbirth; her baby was stillborn.

Childbirth in colonial America was a difficult and sometimes dangerous experience for women. During the seventeenth and eighteenth centuries, between 1 and 1.5 percent of all births ended in the mother's death—as a result of exhaustion, dehydration, infection, hemorrhage, or convulsions. Since the typical mother gave birth to between five and eight children, her lifetime chances of dying in childbirth ran as high as one in eight. This meant that if a woman had eight female friends, it was likely that one would die in childbirth.

Understandably, many colonial women regarded pregnancy with dread. In their letters, women often referred to childbirth as "the Dreaded apparition," "the greatest of earthly miserys," or "that evel hour I loock forward to with dread." Many, like New England poet Ann Bradstreet, approached childbirth with a fear of impending death. In a poem entitled "Before the Birth of One of Her Children," Bradstreet wrote,

How soon, my Dear, death may my steps attend,
How soon't may be thy lot to lose thy friend.

In addition to her anxieties about pregnancy, an expectant mother was filled with apprehensions about the survival of her newborn child. The death of a child in infancy was far more common than it is today. In the healthiest seventeenth-century communities, 1 infant in 10 died before the age of 5. In less healthy environments, 3 children in 10 died before their fifth birthday. Puritan minister Cotton Mather saw 8 of his 15 children die before reaching the age of 2. "We have our children taken from us," Mather cried out, "the Desire of our Eyes taken away with a stroke."

Given the high risk of birth complications and infant death, it is not surprising to learn that pregnancy was surrounded by superstitions. It was widely believed that if a mother-to-be looked upon a "horrible spectre" or was startled by a loud noise her child would be disfigured. If a hare jumped in front of her, her child was in danger of suffering a harelip. There was also fear that if the mother looked at the moon, her child might become a lunatic or sleepwalker. A mother's ungratified longings, it was thought, could cause a miscarriage or leave a mark imprinted on her child's body. At the same time, however, women were expected to continue to perform work until the onset of labor, since hard work supposedly made for an easier labor. Pregnant women regularly spun thread, wove fabric on looms, performed heavy lifting and carrying, milked cows, and slaughtered and salted down meat.

Today, most women give birth in hospitals under close medical supervision. If they wish, women can take anesthetics to relieve labor pangs. During the seventeenth and eighteenth centuries, the process of childbirth was almost wholly different. In colonial America, the typical woman gave birth to her children at home, while female kin and neighbors clustered at her bedside to offer support and encouragement. When the daughter of Samuel Sewall, a Puritan magistrate, gave birth to her first child on the last day of January 1701, at least eight other women were present at her bedside, including her mother, her mother-in-law, a midwife, a nurse, and at least four other neighbors.

Most women were assisted in childbirth not by a doctor but by a midwife. Most midwives were older women who relied on practical experience in delivering children. One midwife, Martha Ballard, who practiced in Augusta, Maine, delivered 996 babies with only 4 recorded fatalities. Skilled midwives were highly valued. Communities tried to attract experienced midwives by offering a

salary or a rent-free house. In addition to assisting in childbirth, midwives helped deliver the offspring of animals, attended the baptisms and burials of infants, and testified in court in cases of bastardy.

During labor, midwives administered no painkillers, except for alcohol. Pain in childbirth was considered God's punishment for Eve's sin of eating the forbidden fruit in the Garden of Eden. Women were merely advised to "arm themselves with patience" and prayer and to try, during labor, to restrain "those dreadful groans and cries which do so much discourage their friends and relations that are near them."

After delivery, new mothers were often treated to a banquet. At one such event, visitors feasted on "boil'd pork, beef, fowls, very good roast beef, turkey-pye, [and] tarts." Women from well-to-do families were then expected to spend three to four weeks in bed convalescing. Their attendants kept the fireplace burning and wrapped them in a heavy blanket in order to help them sweat out "poisons." Women from poorer families were generally back at work in one or two days.

During the second half of the eighteenth century, customs of childbirth began to change. One early sign of change was the growing insistence among women from well-to-do urban families that their children be delivered by male midwives and doctors. Many upper-class families assumed that in a difficult birth trained physicians would make childbirth safer and less painful. In order to justify their presence, physicians tended to take an active role in the birth process. They were much more likely than midwives to intervene in labor with forceps and drugs.

Another important change was the introduction in 1847 of two drugs—ether and chloroform—to relieve pain in childbirth. By the 1920s, the use of anesthesia in childbirth was almost universal. The practice of putting women to sleep during labor contributed to a shift from having children at home to having children in hospitals. In 1900, over 90 percent of all births occurred in the mother's home. But by 1940, over half took place in hospitals and by 1950, the figure had reached 90 percent.

The substitution of doctors for midwives and of hospital delivery for home delivery did little in itself to reduce mortality rates for mothers. It was not until around 1935, when antibiotics and transfusions were introduced, that a sharp reduction in the maternal mortality rate occurred. In 1900 maternal mortality was about 65 times higher than it is today, and not much lower than it had been in the mid-nineteenth century. By World War II, however, death in childbirth had been cut to its present low level.

In recent years, a reaction has occurred against the sterile impersonality of modern hospital delivery. Women today are much more likely than their mothers or grandmothers to want a "natural childbirth." Beginning in the 1960s, a growing number of women elected to bear their children without anesthesia, so that they could be fully conscious during childbirth. Many women also chose to have their husbands or a relative or a friend present during labor and delivery and to bear their children in special "birthing rooms" that provide a homelike environment. In these ways, many contemporary women have sought to recapture the broader support network that characterized childbearing in the colonial past, without sacrificing the tremendous advances that have been made in maternal and infant health.

do with mate selection than parental desires to unite particular family names and estates.

Puritans expected brides and grooms to learn to love one another as they went about their duty of conceiving and raising the next generation of children. In most cases spouses did develop lasting affection for one another, as captured by the gifted Puritan poet Anne Bradstreet in 1666 when she wrote to her "Dear and loving Husband":

> If ever two were one, then surely we.
> If ever man were lov'd by wife, then thee;
> If ever wife was happy in a man,
> Compare with me the women if you can.

Young adults who openly defied patriarchal authority were rare. Also unusual were instances of illegitimate children, despite the lengthy gap between puberty and marriage. As measured by illegitimate births, premarital sex could not have been that common in early New England. This is not a surprising finding among people living in closely controlled communities and seeking to honor the Almighty by reforming human society.

The experiences of seventeenth-century Chesapeake colonists were very different. The system of indentured servitude was open to abuse. Free planters ruled as patriarchs but with no sense of nurturing the next generation; rather, they presumed they were dealing with "simple people" who "professed idleness and will rather beg than work," as a contemporary claimed. The goal was to get as much labor as possible out of servants, since 40 percent died before completing their contracts. Disease was the major killer, but hard-driving planters also contributed to many early deaths.

Servants responded to cruel treatment in various ways. A few committed suicide. Others, like John Punch, ran away. Some killed farm animals, set buildings on fire, or broke tools. Local laws, as drafted by freeholding planters, specified harsh penalties. Besides floggings and brandings, resisting servants faced long extensions of service, as one unfortunate man learned after he killed three pigs belonging to his master. The court added six years to his term of service.

Indentured servitude also inhibited family life. Since servants could not marry, the likelihood of illicit sexual activity increased. Quite frequently, women became the unwilling sexual partners of lustful masters or male servants. Margerie Goold, for example, warded off attempted rape by her master in 1663, but another servant, Elizabeth Wild, was less successful. The planter, however, helped her induce an abortion. One-fifth of Maryland's indentured females faced charges of "bastardy," reflecting both a shortage of women and a labor system controlled by all-powerful masters. Finally in 1692, Virginia officials tried to improve the situation by adopting a statute that mandated harsh penalties for "dissolute masters" getting "their maids with child."

Widows and widowers in colonial America often remarried quickly, in the process creating households of persons of varying ages, many of whom might have no blood relation to one another.

Still, the fate of female and male servants was not always abuse or death. Some survived, gained title to land, and enjoyed, however briefly, personal freedom in America. A few women, usually widows, acquired influence. Margaret Brent, for example, controlled over 1000 acres in Maryland and served as the executor of Governor Leonard Calvert's estate in 1647. She even dared to demand the right to vote, a plea dismissed by male legislators.

Brent's case suggests that high death rates in combination with an unbalanced sex ratio may have, at least temporarily, enhanced the status of some Chesapeake women. English and colonial law recognized the category of *femes sole*, which permitted single, adult women and widows to own and manage property and households for themselves. Chesapeake women who outlived two or three husbands could acquire significant holdings through inheritances and then maintain control by requiring prenuptial contracts from future spouses. Once married, however, any property not so protected fell to new husbands because of *coverture*.

Since widowed mothers could presume they would outlive new husbands, most prenuptial contracts protected property for children by previous marriages. Indeed, few children grew to adulthood without burying one or both parents, and there were extreme cases like that of Agatha Vause, a Virginia child whose father, two stepfathers, mother, and guardian uncle all died before she was 11 years old.

The fragility of Chesapeake life resulted in complex family genealogies with some households containing children from three or four marriages. In some instances local Orphans' Courts had to take charge because all adult relatives had died. Because parents did not live that long, children quite often received their inheritances by their late teens, much earlier than in New England. This advantage meant only that economic independence, like death, came earlier in life.

COMMERCIAL VALUES AND THE RISE OF CHATTEL SLAVERY

By 1650 signs were abundant that the Puritan mission was in trouble. From the outset many non-Puritan settlers, including merchants in Boston, had shunned the religious values of the Bay Colony's founders. By the 1660s children and grandchildren of the migrating generation displayed less zeal about earning God's grace; they were becoming more like southern settlers in their eagerness to get ahead economically. By 1700 their search for worldly prosperity even brought some New Englanders into the international slave trade.

Declension in New England

Declension, or movement away from the ideals of the Bay Colony's founding fathers, resulted in tensions between settlers adhering to the original mission and those attracted to rising commercial values. Clergymen proposed a major compromise known as the **Half-Way Covenant** in 1662. The Covenant recognized that many children were not preparing for salvation, a necessary condition for full church membership, as their parents had done. The question was how to keep them—and their offspring—aspiring toward a spiritual life. The solution was half-way membership, which permitted the baptism of the children and grandchildren of professing saints. If still in the church, ministers and full members could continue to urge them to focus their lives on seeking God's eternal rewards.

Many communities disdained the Half-Way Covenant because of what it implied about changing values. As one minister wrote, too many individuals were acting "as if the Lord had no further work for his people to do but every bird to feather his own nest." With the passage of time, however, most accepted the covenant to help preserve some semblance of a godly society in New England.

Spreading commercial values took hold for many reasons, including the natural abundance of the New England environment and an inability to sustain fervency of purpose among American-born offspring who had not personally felt the religious repression of early Stuart England. Also, Puritans back in England, after overthrowing Charles I, generally ignored the model society in America, which left the impression that the mission had been futile, that no one back in Europe really cared.

The transition in values occurred gradually, as shown in various towns where families bought and sold common field strips so that all of their landholdings were in one place. The next step was to build homes on these sites and become "outlivers," certainly a more efficient way to practice agriculture, yet also a statement that making one's living was more important than daily participation in village life—with its emphasis on laboring together in God's love.

In Boston and other port towns, such as Salem, merchants gained increasing community stature because of their wealth. By the early eighteenth century some of them were earning profits by participating in the African slave trade. Retinues of household servants or, more properly, slaves taken from Africa, symbolized their newfound status.

Clergymen disapproved of these trends. Their sermons took on the tone of "jeremiads," modeled on the prophet Jeremiah who kept urging Israel to return to the path of godliness. In Calvinist fashion, they warned of divine retribution or "afflictions" from the Almighty, and they pointed to events like King Philip's War as proof that Jehovah was punishing New England. In 1679 the ministers met in another synod and listed several problems, everything from working on the Sabbath to swearing in public and sleeping during sermons. Human competitiveness and contention, they sadly concluded, were in ascendance. Worse yet, the populace, in its rush to garner worldly riches, showed little concern that Winthrop's "city upon a hill" was becoming the home of the acquisitive Yankee trader.

Stabilizing Life in the Chesapeake Region

By 1675 certain trends indicated that life in Maryland and Virginia could be something more than brief and unkind. The death rate was dropping; more children were surviving; the gender ratio was starting to balance out; and life expectancy was rising. By the early 1700s Chesapeake residents were living well into their fifties. This figure was comparable to longevity estimates for England but still 10 to 15 years shorter than that of New England. The patterns also indicate greater family stability, as shown by longer marriages and more children.

Not only did life become more stable, but also an elite group of families, controlling significant property and wealth, had begun to emerge. By 1700 the great tidewater families—the Byrds, Carters, Fitzhughs, Lees, and Randolphs, among others—were making their presence felt and had started to dominate social and political affairs in the Chesapeake area. These gentleman-planters aped the lifestyle of England's rural gentry class. They constructed lavish manor houses from which they ruled over their plantation estates, dispensing hospitality and wisdom as the most illustrious and powerful residents of their tobacco-producing region.

Such a person was William Byrd II (1674–1744), who inherited 26,000 fertile acres along the James River in 1705. He built the magnificent Westover plantation, raised a large family, served on the governor's council, and assumed, as he wrote to an English correspondent, that he was "one of the patriarchs" of Virginia society. By the time of his death, Byrd had holdings of 180,000 acres, and he owned at least 200 slaves.

Lavish estates like Westover plantation, built by William Byrd II on the James River, illustrate the wealth and social dominance of rising gentleman-planters in Virginia.

Byrd read widely, put together an impressive personal library, and wrote extensively on any subject that interested him. His "secret" diaries describe how he treated others, including his wife, Lucy Parke Byrd. When they argued, Byrd on occasion demonstrated his presumed masculine superiority with sexual bravado. In 1710 "a little quarrel" was "reconciled with a flourish... performed on the billiard table." Byrd's behavior was part of his assertive, self-confident manner. He was the master of everything on his magnificent plantation, making him a patriarch of the realm of Virginia.

For every great planter, there were dozens of small farmers who lacked the wealth to obtain land, slaves, and high status in society. Most eked out bare livings, yet they dreamed of the day when they, or their children, might live in the style of a William Byrd. Meanwhile, they deferred to their "betters" among the planter elite, who in turn "treated" them to large quantities of alcohol on election days and expressed gentlemanly concern about the welfare of their families. Such behavior was part of an ongoing bonding ritual among white inhabitants who, no matter how high or low in status, considered themselves superior to black slaves—whose numbers were now growing rapidly on the bottom rung of Maryland and Virginia society.

The Beginnings of American Slavery

The system of **perpetual servitude** that shaped the lives of persons of African heritage like John Punch and Emmanuel had ancient roots. However, slavery was dying out in much of Europe by the fifteenth century. Then the Portuguese mariners of Prince Henry started coasting along sub-Saharan Africa, making contact with various peoples and cultures, some of whom were willing to barter in human flesh as well as in gold and ivory. The first Portuguese expeditions represented the small beginnings of a trade that forcibly relocated an estimated 10 million Africans to the Americas during the next 350 years.

Africa, a continent of immense geographical diversity with vast deserts, grassy plains, and tropical rain forests, had a population of about 50 million people at the time of Columbus. Mighty kingdoms like Ghana had flourished in West Africa but had been overrun by Muslims from the north during the eleventh century, resulting in the empire of Mali and its magnificent trading and learning center, Timbuktu. Farther to the south in Guinea were smaller kingdoms such as Benin in which the populace farmed or worked at such crafts as pottery making, weaving, and metalworking. These cultures valued family life and were mostly matrilineal in the organization of kinship networks. They also had well-developed political systems and legal codes.

In addition, these kingdoms thrived on elaborate regional trading networks, which the Portuguese and other Europeans, offering guns and various iron products, tapped into easily. As time passed Europeans came to identify certain coastal areas with particular commodities. Upper Guinea contained the rice and grain coasts, and Lower Guinea the ivory, gold, and slave coasts.

Early modern European traders learned that some Africans held slaves—mainly individuals captured in tribal wars—who had the status of family members. The Portuguese found that coastal chiefs were willing to trade humans for European firearms, which they could use when attacking interior kingdoms. A new objective of this tribal warfare became the capturing of peoples who would then be transported back to the coast and sold into slavery in exchange for yet more European goods.

Once this vicious slave trading cycle began, it expanded rapidly. Decade after decade, thousands of Africans experienced the agony of being shackled in collars and ankle chains; marched in gangs, or *coffles*, to the coast; thrown into *barracoons*, or slave pens; and then packed aboard waiting European ships destined for ports of call in the Americas. One slave, Olaudah Equiano, who made the voyage during the eighteenth century, recalled the "loathsomeness of the stench" from overcrowded conditions, which made him "so sick and low" that he neither was "able to eat, nor had . . . the desire to taste anything."

Some Africans resisted by refusing to eat and starved to death. In response the Europeans made tools to break jaws and pry open mouths so that food could be jammed down unwilling throats. Other re-

Cramped and crowded conditions were common on the decks of slave vessels. As shown here, slaves invariably became emaciated from deficient food during their passage across the Atlantic.

sisters jumped overboard and drowned, but the Europeans soon placed large nets on the sides of their vessels. About 15 percent of those Africans forced onto slave ships did not survive. Those who did had to reckon with the frightening realization of having lost everything familiar in their lives—with no knowledge of what might happen next.

During the sixteenth century the Spanish and Portuguese started pouring Africans into their colonies. These slaves were not thought of as family members, but as disposable beings whose energy was to be used up in mining or agricultural operations. High mortality rates among the migrants did not seem to bother their European masters because more slave ships kept appearing on the horizon. As a result, areas such as Brazil and the West Indian sugar islands earned deserved reputations as centers of human exploitation and death.

Shifting to Slavery in Maryland and Virginia

The English North American colonies existed at the outer edge of the African slave trade until the very end of the seventeenth century. In 1650 the popula-

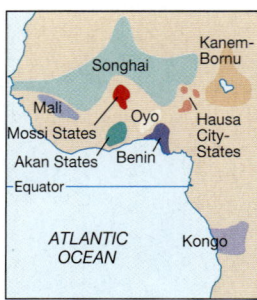

West African Kingdoms, Late 1400s

European and Portuguese traders in the late 1400s found the West African kingdoms rich with rice, gold, and slaves.

tion of Virginia approached 15,000 settlers, including only 500 persons of African descent. By comparison, the English sugar colony of Barbados already held 10,000 slaves, a majority of the population. English Barbadians had started to model their economy on that of other Caribbean sugar islands, whereas Virginians, with a steady supply of indentured servants, had not yet made the transition to slave labor.

Factors supporting a shift, however, were present by the 1640s, as evidenced in laws discriminating against Africans and court cases involving blacks like John Punch and Emmanuel. During the same decade, a few Chesapeake planters started to invest in Africans. Governor Leonard Calvert of Maryland, for example, asked "John Skinner mariner" to ship him "fourteen negro-men-slaves and three women-slaves." Planters like Calvert were ahead of their time because slaves cost significantly more to purchase than indentured servants. Yet for those who invested, they owned their laborers for their lifetimes and did not have to pay "freedom dues." Moreover, they soon discovered that Africans, having built up immunities to tropical diseases like malaria and typhoid fever, generally lived longer than white servants. Resistance to such diseases made Africans a better long-term investment, at least for well-capitalized planters.

Then in the 1660s two additional factors spurred on the shift toward slave labor. First, Virginia legislators in 1662 decreed that slavery was an inheritable status, "according to the condition of the mother." The law made yet unborn generations subject to slavery, a powerful incentive for risking an initial investment in human chattels. If slaves kept reproducing, planters would control a never-ending supply of laborers. Second, the numbers of new indentured servants began to shrink as economic conditions improved in England. With expanded opportunities for work, poorer citizens were less willing to risk life and limb for a chance at economic independence in America.

Also assisting the shift was the chartering of the Royal African Company in 1672 to develop England's role in the slave trade. Royal African vessels soon made regular visits to Chesapeake Bay. As the supply of slaves increased, asking prices started to drop—at the very time that the cost of buying indentured servants began to climb. In 1698 the company lost its monopoly, which spurred some New England traders to engage actively in the slave trade. Yankee merchants now had something in common with Chesapeake planters besides English roots and language. Both were profiting from the international traffic in human beings.

Population figures explain the rest. In 1670 Virginia contained about 40,000 settlers, which included an estimated 6000 white servants and 2000 black slaves. By 1700 the number of slaves had grown to 16,000, and by 1750 white Virginians owned 120,000 slaves—about 40 percent of the total population. The same general pattern characterized Maryland, where by 1750 there were 40,000 slaves—some 30 percent of the populace. In the Chesapeake area, indentured servitude was by then a moribund institution. White planters, great and small, now measured their wealth and status in terms of plantations and slaves owned and managed.

The World the Slaves Made

Historians once argued that slavery in English North America was harsher than the Spanish-American version. They pointed to the moderating influence of the Roman Catholic church, which mandated legal recognition of slave marriages as a sacramental right, and ancient legal precedents influencing Spanish law, which meant that slaves could earn wages for their labor in off hours and buy their freedom. Although Spanish laws may have been more humane, daily working and living conditions were not. Most slaves destined for Caribbean or South American settlements did not survive long enough to marry or enjoy other legal rights. By contrast, in North America, where early deaths were not as pervasive among migrants, slaves more easily reconstructed meaningful lives for themselves.

About 10 percent of those Africans coming to the colonies entered northern port towns like Boston and became domestic servants, craft workers, or in rare cases, farmhands out in the countryside. The rest labored in the South, mostly on small plantations where field work dominated their existence. These slaves had little chance for family life, at least in the early years, because planters purchased an average of three males for every female. In addition, southern law did not recognize slave marriages—in case masters wanted to sell off some of their chattels. Anglican church leaders accepted the situation. In New England, by comparison, the Congregational church insisted that slave marriages be recognized and respected by masters.

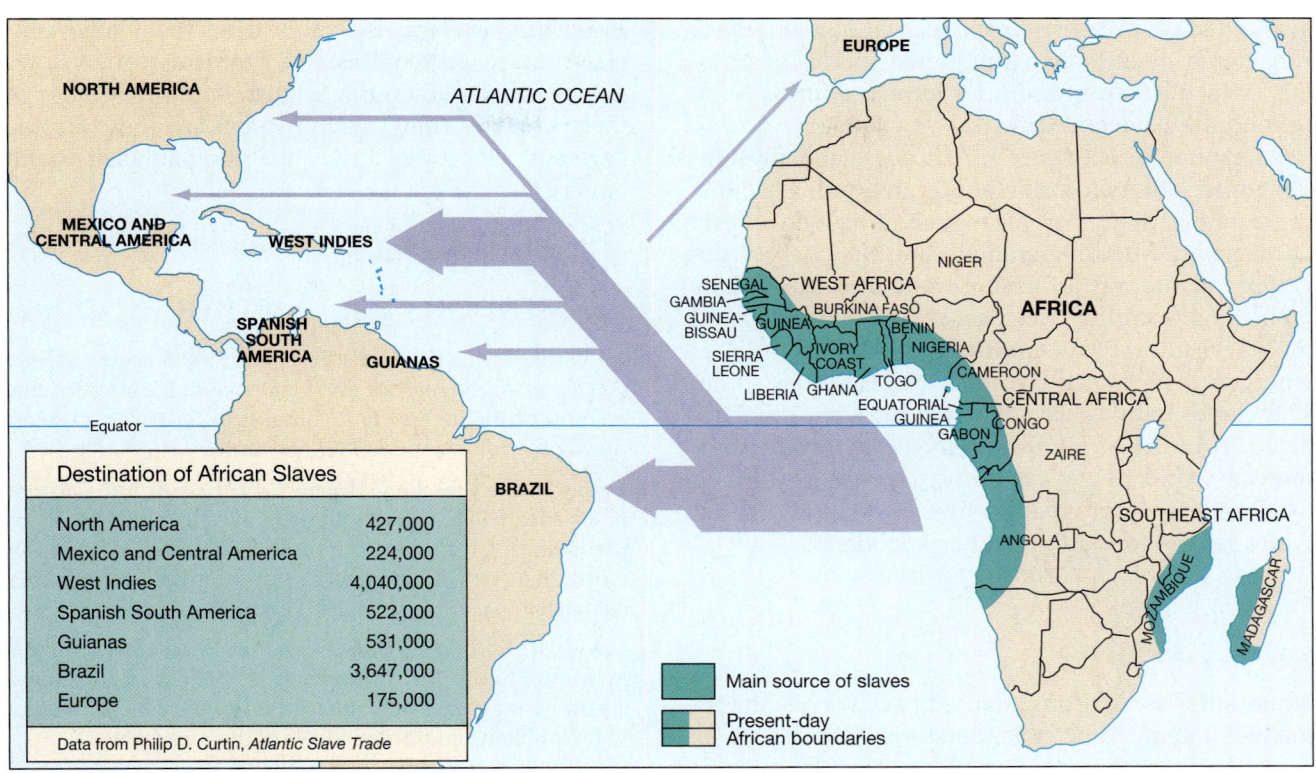

African Slave Trade

Central and South America represented the most common destination for slaves traded to the Americas between 1520 and 1810.

Destination of African Slaves	
North America	427,000
Mexico and Central America	224,000
West Indies	4,040,000
Spanish South America	522,000
Guianas	531,000
Brazil	3,647,000
Europe	175,000

Data from Philip D. Curtin, *Atlantic Slave Trade*

Facing a loss of personal freedom and pervasive racism, southern slaves made separate lives for themselves, particularly on large plantations where their substantial numbers allowed them to form their own communities in the slave quarters. Here they maintained African cultural traditions and developed distinctive forms of music. In South Carolina's sea island region, slaves continued to give their children African names, and they worked out a distinct dialect, known as *Gullah*, to communicate with one another in a unique combination of African and English sounds. In many places, female slaves managed slave quarter life, thus maintaining the matrilineal nature of African kinship ties.

Contrary to white owners' contentions, most slaves did not engage in promiscuous sexual relations. Whenever possible, they selected mates and had large families, even if slave quarter marriages had no standing in law. As a consequence, the ratio of men to women balanced itself out over time and in turn sped up natural population growth. Large families became a source of slave community pride. Natural increase also undercut the need to continue heavy importation of chattels. As a result, only 5 percent—an estimated 399,000 persons—of all imported Africans ended up in English North America.

Such comparisons are relative. Nowhere in the Americas did slavery function in an uplifting fashion. Although blacks on large southern plantations carried on traditional cultural practices, they still had to face masters or overseers who might whip them, sell off their children, or maim or kill them if they tried to run

The drawing *Old Plantation* shows that slaves, even though defined as property and without legal rights, succeeded in making meaningful lives for themselves in their own quarters.

away. Always present was the realization that whites considered them to be a subhuman species of property, which left scant room for human dignity in life beyond the slave quarters.

Despite the oppression, Africans made substantial contributions to colonial life. In South Carolina, for example, many early slave migrants were expert at raising and herding animals, and they helped develop and support a thriving trade in cattle. Others who came from the rice coast region of Africa used their agricultural skills in fostering South Carolina's emergence as a major center of rice production. These and many other contributions went unrecognized in the rush for profits in the maturing commercial world of the American colonies, except in the ironic sense of creating further demand among white settlers for additional black laborers.

Conclusion

Although most Africans adapted to slavery, some remained defiant. They stole food, broke farm tools, or in a few cases poisoned their masters. In rare instances they resorted to rebellion. In September 1739 twenty slaves in the Stono River area of South Carolina rose up, seized some weapons, killed a few whites, and started marching toward Spanish Florida. Within a few days frightened planters rallied together and crushed the Stono uprising by shooting or hanging the rebels.

The South Carolina legislature soon approved a more repressive slave code, which all but restricted the movement of blacks from their home plantations. No legislator gave thought to the other possibility, which was to abandon the institution of slavery. Even though long in development, slavery now supported southern plantation agriculture and the production of such cash crops as tobacco and rice.

Just as the southern colonies had made a fateful shift from servitude to slavery, New Englanders experienced another kind of transition. Slowly but surely, they had forsaken their utopian, religiously oriented mission into the wilderness. Service to mammon had started to replace loyalty to God and community. The religious side would remain, but the fervor of a nobler spiritual mission was in rapid decline by 1700. Material gain was now a quality shared by white English colonists in America—North and South.

Prosperity, which had come after so much travail and death, promoted a sense of unlimited opportunity in profiting from the abundance of the American environment. Other realities, however, were also taking shape. The colonists had learned that Crown officials now expected them to conform to new laws governing the emerging English empire. Because of these imperial rules, much turmoil lay ahead for the diversity of peoples now inhabiting English North America.

Suggestions for Further Reading

Ira Berlin, *Many Thousands Gone: The First Two Centuries of Slavery in North America* (1998). Detailed, highly readable account of the diverse and complex experiences of slaves during the colonial period and beyond.

David Hackett Fischer, *Albion's Seed: Four British Folkways in America* (1989). Broad-ranging investigation of the implantation of traditional cultural values and practices in North America by distinct groups of English-speaking colonists.

David D. Hall, *Worlds of Wonder, Days of Judgment: Popular Religious Belief in Early New England* (1990). Probing analysis of the mentality of ordinary Puritan settlers in relation to the publicly enunciated ideals of their leaders.

James Horn, *Adapting to a New World: English Society in the Seventeenth-Century Chesapeake* (1994). Comprehensive examination of migratory patterns and the construction of English society in the Chesapeake Bay region.

Jill Lepore, *The Name of War: King Philip's War and the Origins of American Identity* (1998). An evocative study of recollections and understanding of one of the bloodiest wars to take place on American soil.

Edmund S. Morgan, *American Slavery, American Freedom: The Ordeal of Colonial Virginia* (1975). Valuable discussion of the emergence of slavery in Virginia and the paradoxical evolution of freedom and slavery in British North America.

———, *The Puritan Dilemma: The Story of John Winthrop*, 2d ed. (1999). Classic introduction to Puritan religious beliefs and their implementation in the structure of life in Massachusetts Bay Colony.

Mary Beth Norton, *Founding Mothers and Fathers: Gendered Power and the Forming of American Society* (1996). A probing analysis of the evolution of gender relations in New England and the Chesapeake Bay region during the seventeenth century.

Peter H. Wood, *Black Majority: Negroes in Colonial South Carolina from 1670 Through the Stono Rebellion* (1974). Influential exploration of the lives and contributions of African-American slaves in the development of this Deep South colony.

Overviews and Surveys

Sydney E. Ahlstrom, *A Religious History of the American People* (1972); Bernard Bailyn, *Education in the Forming of American Society* (1960); Thomas Bender, *Community and*

Chronology of Key Events

1608	Pilgrims flee to Holland to avoid religious persecution in England
1617	Virginia begins to export tobacco
1619	The first persons of African descent arrive in Virginia; first representative assembly in English North America meets in Jamestown
1620	Pilgrims arrive at Cape Cod on the *Mayflower* and establish Plymouth Colony
1622	Opechancanough's Indians fail in an attempt to massacre all English settlers in Virginia
1624	English Crown takes control of Virginia; the Dutch begin to settle New York and name their colony New Netherland
1630	Puritans establish the Massachusetts Bay Colony
1632	Maryland becomes the first proprietary colony
1635	Leaders in Massachusetts Bay Colony banish Roger Williams
1636	Harvard College is founded; first permanent English settlements established in Connecticut and Rhode Island
1637–1638	Anne Hutchinson is convicted of heresy in Massachusetts and flees to Rhode Island
1640s	Legal status of African Americans in the Chesapeake Bay region deteriorates
1644	Second attempted Native American massacre of Virginia colonists fails
1646	Powhatan's Confederacy accepts English rule
1647	Massachusetts Bay Colony adopts the first public school law in the colonies
1649	Maryland's Act of Toleration affirms religious freedom for Christians in the colony; Charles I of England is beheaded
1660	Charles II is restored to the English throne
1664	English conquer New Netherland and rename the colony New York
1675–1676	King Philip's (Metacomet's) War inflicts heavy casualties on New Englanders
1681–1682	William Penn founds Pennsylvania as a "holy experiment" in which diverse groups of people can live together harmoniously
1688	Glorious Revolution drives James II from England
1732	Georgia is founded as a haven for debtors and a buffer colony against Spanish Florida
1739	Stono slave uprising occurs in South Carolina

Social Change in America (1978); Rowland Berthoff, *An Unsettled People: Social Order and Disorder in American History* (1971); Richard D. Brown, *Modernization: The Transformation of American Life, 1600–1865* (1976); David Brion Davis, *The Problem of Slavery in Western Culture* (1988), and *Slavery and Human Progress* (1984); John Hope Franklin and Alfred A. Moss, Jr., *From Slavery to Freedom: A History of African Americans,* 7th ed. (1994); Philip Greven, *The Protestant Temperament: Patterns of Child-Rearing, Religious Experience, and the Self in Early America* (1977); E. Brooks Holifield, *Era of Persuasion: American Thought and Culture, 1521–1680* (1989); Nathan I. Huggins, *Black Odyssey: The Afro-American Ordeal in Slavery* (1977); Steven Mintz and Susan Kellogg, *Domestic Revolutions: A Social History of American Family Life* (1988); Edwin J. Perkins, *The Economy of Colonial America,* 2d ed. (1988); John E. Pomfret and Floyd M. Shumway, *Founding the American Colonies, 1583–1660* (1970); Helena M. Wall, *Fierce Communion; Fam-*

ily and Community in Early America (1990); Robert V. Wells, *The Population of the British Colonies in America before 1776: A Survey of Census Data* (1975).

From Settlements to Societies in the South

Carl Bridenbaugh, *Myths and Realities: Societies of the Colonial South* (1952); Paul G. E. Clemens, *The Atlantic Economy and Colonial Maryland's Eastern Shore: From Tobacco to Grain* (1980); Converse D. Clowse, *Economic Beginnings of Colonial South Carolina, 1670–1730* (1971); Wesley Frank Craven, *The Southern Colonies in the Seventeenth Century, 1607–1689* (1949); David Galenson, *White Servitude in Colonial America: An Economic Analysis* (1981); David W. Jordan, *Foundations of Representative Government in Maryland, 1632–1715* (1987); Aubrey C. Land et al., eds., *Law, Society, and Politics in Early Maryland* (1977); Richard L. Morton, *Colonial Virginia*, 2 vols. (1960); James R. Perry, *The Formation of a Society on Virginia's Eastern Shore, 1615–1655* (1990); David B. Quinn, ed., *Early Maryland in a Wider World* (1982); M. Eugene Sirmans, *Colonial South Carolina, A Political History, 1663–1763* (1966); Abbot E. Smith, *Colonists in Bondage: White Servitude and Convict Labor in America, 1607–1776* (1971).

Religious Dissenters Colonize New England

David Grayson Allen, *In English Ways: The Movement of Societies and the Transferal of English Local Law and Custom to Massachusetts Bay in the Seventeenth Century* (1981); Bernard Bailyn, *The New England Merchants in the Seventeenth Century* (1955); Francis J. Bremer, *The Puritan Experiment* (1995); Charles E. Clark, *The Eastern Frontier: The Settlement of Northern New England, 1610–1763* (1970); Charles L. Cohen, *God's Caress: The Psychology of Puritan Religious Experience* (1986); Andrew Delbanco, *The Puritan Ordeal* (1989); Kai T. Erikson, *Wayward Puritans: A Study in the Sociology of Deviance* (1966); Stephen Foster, *The Long Argument: English Puritanism and the Shaping of New England Culture, 1570–1700* (1991), and *Their Solitary Way: The Puritan Social Ethic in the First Century of Settlement in New England* (1971); Richard P. Gildrie, *The Profane, the Civil, & the Godly: The Reformation of Manners in Orthodox New England, 1679–1749* (1994); Philip F. Gura, *A Glimpse of Sion's Glory: Puritan Radicalism in New England, 1620–1660* (1984); David D. Hall, *The Faithful Shepherd; A History of the New England Ministry in the Seventeenth Century* (1972); James Holstun, *A Rational Millennium: Puritan Utopias of Seventeenth-Century England and America* (1987); Stephen Innes, *Creating the Commonwealth: The Economic Culture of Puritan New England* (1995); Sydney V. James, *Colonial Rhode Island: A History* (1975); Lyle Koehler, *A Search for Power: The "Weaker Sex" in Seventeenth-Century New England* (1980); David Konig, *Law and Society in Puritan Massachusetts: Essex County, 1629–1692* (1979); George D. Langdon, Jr., *Pilgrim Colony: A History of New Plymouth 1620–1691* (1966); John Frederick Martin, *Profits in the Wilderness: Entre-preneurship and the Founding of New England Towns in the Seventeenth Century* (1991); Perry Miller, *Orthodoxy in Massachusetts, 1630–1650* (1961), *The New England Mind: The Seventeenth Century* (1953), and *The New England Mind: From Colony to Province* (1982); Edmund S. Morgan, *Visible Saints: The History of a Puritan Idea* (1963); Darrett B. Rutman, *American Puritanism: Faith and Practice* (1970); William K. B. Stoever, *A Faire and Easie Way to Heaven: Covenant Theology and Antinomianism in Early Massachusetts* (1988); Harry S. Stout, *The New England Soul: Preaching and Religious Culture in Colonial New England* (1986); Laurel Thatcher Ulrich, *Good Wives: Image and Reality in the Lives of Women in Northern New England, 1650–1750* (1982); David E. Van Deventer, *The Emergence of Provincial New Hampshire, 1623–1741* (1976); Robert E. Wall, Jr., *Massachusetts Bay: The Crucial Decade, 1640–1650* (1972).

Families, Individuals, and Communities: Surviving in Early America

Lois Green Carr et al., eds., *Colonial Chesapeake Society* (1988), and Carr et al., *Robert Cole's World: Agriculture and Society in Early Maryland* (1991); Wesley Frank Craven, *White, Red, and Black: The Seventeenth-Century Virginian* (1971); John Demos, *A Little Commonwealth: Family Life in Plymouth Colony* (1970); Philip J. Greven, Jr., *Four Generations: Population, Land, and Family in Colonial Andover, Massachusetts* (1970); Stephen Innes, *Labor in a New Land: Economy and Society in Seventeenth-Century Springfield* (1983); Douglas E. Leach, *Flintlock and Tomahawk: New England in King Philip's War* (1958); Judith Walzer Leavitt, *Brought to Bed: Childbearing in America, 1750–1950* (1986); Kenneth A. Lockridge, *A New England Town: The First Hundred Years, Dedham, Massachusetts, 1636–1736*, rev. ed. (1985); Paul R. Lucas, *Valley of Discord: Church and Society Along the Connecticut River, 1636–1725* (1976); Gloria L. Main, *Tobacco Colony: Life in Early Maryland, 1650–1720* (1982); Sally G. McMillen, *Motherhood in the Old South: Pregnancy, Childbirth, and Infant Rearing* (1990); Edmund S. Morgan, *The Puritan Family: Religion and Domestic Relations in Seventeenth-Century New England*, rev. ed. (1966); Darrett B. Rutman, *Winthrop's Boston: Portrait of a Puritan Town, 1630–1649* (1965), and with Anita H. Rutman, *A Place in Time: Middlesex County, Virginia, 1650–1750*, 2 vols. (1984); Catherine M. Scholten, *Childbearing in American Society* (1985); David E. Stannard, *The Puritan Way of Death* (1977); Thad W. Tate and David L. Ammerman, eds., *The Chesapeake in the Seventeenth Century: Essays on Anglo-American Society* (1979); Roger Thompson, *Sex in Middlesex: Popular Mores in a Massachusetts County, 1649–1699* (1986); Robert V. Wells, *Revolutions in Americans' Lives: A Demographic Perspective on the History of Americans, Their Families, and Their Society* (1982).

Commercial Values and the Rise of Chattel Slavery

T. H. Breen and Stephen Innes, *"Myne Owne Ground": Race and Freedom on Virginia's Eastern Shore, 1640–1676* (1980); Jay Coughtry, *The Notorious Triangle: Rhode Island and the*

African Slave Trade 1700–1807 (1981); Basil Davidson, *The African Genius: An Introduction to African Cultural and Social History* (1969); Richard S. Dunn, *Sugar and Slaves: The Rise of the Planter Class in the English West Indies, 1624–1713* (1972); Winthrop D. Jordan, *White over Black: American Attitudes Toward the Negro, 1550–1812* (1968); Herbert S. Klein, *Slavery in the Americas: A Comparative Study of Virginia and Cuba* (1967), and *The Middle Passage: Comparative Studies in the Atlantic Slave Trade* (1978); Allan Kulikoff, *Tobacco and Slaves: The Development of Southern Cultures in the Chesapeake, 1680–1800* (1986); Daniel C. Littlefield, *Rice and Slaves: Ethnicity and the Slave Trade in Colonial South Carolina* (1981); Edgar J. McManus, *Black Bondage in the North* (1973); Gerald W. Mullin, *Flight and Rebellion: Slave Resistance in Eighteenth-Century Virginia* (1972); Michael Mullin, *Africa in America: Slave Acculturation and Resistance in the American South and the British Caribbean, 1736–1831* (1992); Richard Olaniyan, ed., *African History and Culture* (1982); James Rawley, *The Transatlantic Slave Trade: A History* (1981); Daniel Blake Smith, *Inside the Great House: Planter Family Life in Eighteenth-Century Chesapeake Society* (1980); Hugh Thomas, *The Slave Trade: The Atlantic Slave Trade, 1440–1870* (1997); Donald R. Wright, *African Americans in the Colonial Era: From African Origins through the American Revolution* (1990).

Biographies

Kenneth A. Lockridge, *The Diary, and Life, of William Byrd II of Virginia, 1674–1744* (1987); Robert Middlekauff, *The Mathers: Three Generations of Puritan Intellectuals, 1596–1728* (1971); Edmund S. Morgan, *Roger Williams: The Church and the State* (1967); Bradford Smith, *Bradford of Plymouth* (1951).

Internet Resources

The Plymouth Colony Archive Project at the University of Virginia
http://www.people.virginia.edu/~jfd3a/
This site contains fairly extensive information about late seventeenth century Plymouth Colony.

DPLS Archive: Slave Movement During the 18th and 19th Centuries (Wisconsin)
http://dpls.dacc.wisc.edu/slavedata/index.html
This site explores the slave ships and the slave trade that carried thousands of Africans to the Americas.

Excerpts from Slave Narratives
http://vi.uh.edu/pages/mintz/primary.htm
The seventeenth- through nineteenth-century accounts of slavery housed in this site speak volumes about the many impacts of slavery.

Key Terms

Indentured Servitude (p. 38)
Headright (p. 39)
Divine Right (p. 40)
Separatists (p. 42)
Nonseparatists (p. 42)
"City upon a Hill" (p. 44)
Antinomian (p. 47)
Patriarchal (p. 51)
Coverture (p. 51)
Declension (p. 55)
Half-Way Covenant (p. 55)
Perpetual Servitude (p. 56)

Review Questions

1. What were the major difficulties that early English settlers in the area of Jamestown had to overcome? What developments allowed the Virginia colony to survive and endure?
2. Compare and contrast Indian-white relations in the Chesapeake and New England colonies. What were the differences and similarities? Did they matter in the end?
3. Describe the original mission of the Puritans who settled in New England. How did the Puritans attempt to implement their mission in the organization of their society? How successful were they in fulfilling their mission?
4. Compare and contrast the characteristics of living in New England and the Chesapeake colonies during the seventeenth century. Why did life seem so much harsher in the Chesapeake region than in New England?
5. What were the differences between indentured servitude and chattel slavery? What factors supported the shift from indentured servitude to slavery and the enslavement of Africans in the southern colonies?

3

PROVINCIAL AMERICA IN UPHEAVAL, 1660–1760

DESIGNING ENGLAND'S NORTH AMERICAN EMPIRE
  To Benefit the Parent Nation
  Seizing Dutch New Netherland
  Proprietary Difficulties in New York and New Jersey
  Planting William Penn's "Holy Experiment"

DEFYING THE IMPERIAL WILL: PROVINCIAL CONVULSIONS AND REBELLIONS
  Bacon's Bloody Rebellion in Virginia
  The Glorious Revolution Spills into America
  New England's Witchcraft Hysteria
  Settling Anglo-American Differences

MATURING COLONIAL SOCIETIES IN UNSETTLED TIMES
  An Exploding Population Base
  The "Europeanizing" of America
  Intellectual and Religious Awakening
  International Wars Beset America
  Showdown: The Great War for the Empire
  Allies as Enemies: Making War on the Cherokees

"Stripped and scourged and run the gauntlet"

Hannah Dustan (1657–1736) and Eliza Lucas (1722–1793) never knew one another. Dustan lived in the town of Haverhill on the Massachusetts frontier, and Lucas spent her adult years in the vicinity of Charleston, South Carolina. Even though of different generations, both were inhabitants of England's developing North American empire. Along with so many other colonists, perpetual imperial warfare profoundly affected their lives as England, France, and Spain repeatedly battled for supremacy in Europe and America between 1689 and 1763.

During the 1690s, as part of a war involving England and France, frontier New Englanders experienced devastating raids by Indian parties from French Canada. On the morning of March 15, 1697, a band of Abenakis struck Haverhill. Hannah Dustan's husband and seven of her children saved themselves by racing for the community's blockhouse. Hannah, who had just given birth a few days before, was not so fortunate. The Abenakis captured her, as well as her baby and midwife Mary Neff.

After some discussion, the natives "dashed out the brains of the infant against a tree," the well-known Puritan minister, the Reverend Cotton Mather, later wrote; but they decided to spare Hannah and Mary along with a few other captives. Their plan was to march these residents to the principal Abenaki village in Canada where they would "be stripped and scourged and [made to] run the gauntlet through the whole army of Indians." If they survived, they would be adopted into the tribe, literally to become white Indians.

The Abenakis split up their captives. Two male warriors, three women, and seven children escorted Hannah, Mary, and a young boy named Samuel Lenorson. Hannah, although still in a state of shock, maintained her composure as the party walked northward day after day. She prayed fervently for some means of escape.

Just before dawn one morning, she awoke to find all her captors sound asleep. Seizing the moment, she roused Mary and Samuel, handed them hatchets, and told them to crush as many skulls as possible. Suddenly the Indians were dying, and only two, a badly wounded woman and a child, escaped.

Hannah then took a scalping knife and finished the bloody work. When she and the other captives got back to Haverhill, they had ten scalps, for which the Massachusetts General Court awarded them a bounty of £50 in local currency. New Englanders hailed Hannah Dustan as a true heroine—a woman whose courage overcame the French and Indian enemies of England's empire in America.

Cotton Mather spread Dustan's story far and wide, hoping to rekindle the faith of New England's founders. If citizens would just "humble" themselves before God, he argued, the Almighty would stop afflicting society with the horrors of war and

This heroic statue of Hannah Dustan in Haverhill, Massachusetts, shows her with the hatchet she used to escape from her captors. Dustan brought the scalps back with her to Haverhill to prove her story and collect a bounty.

provide for the "quick extirpation" of all "bloody and crafty" enemies. Mather's jeremiad had little effect. The war soon ended, and New Englanders devoted themselves more than ever before to acquiring personal wealth.

After a long and full life, Hannah Dustan died in 1736. Two years later, George Lucas, a prosperous Antigua planter who was also an officer in the British army, moved to South Carolina, where he owned three rice plantations. He wanted to get his family away from the Caribbean region, since hostilities were brewing with Spain.

When war did come a year later, Lucas returned to Antigua to resume his military duties. Leaving an ailing wife, he placed his 17-year-old daughter Eliza in charge of his Carolina properties. The responsibility did not faze her; she wrote regularly to her "Dear Papa" for advice, and the plantations prospered. The war, however, disrupted rice trading routes into the West Indies, and planters needed other cash crops to be sold elsewhere. George Lucas was aware of the problem and sent Eliza seeds for indigo plants, the source of a valued deep-blue dye, to see whether indigo could be grown profitably in South Carolina.

With the help of knowledgeable slaves, Eliza conducted successful experiments. In 1744 a major dye broker in England tested her product "against some of the best French" indigo and rated it "in his opinion . . . as good." Just 22 years old, Eliza had pioneered a cash crop that brought additional wealth to Carolina's planters and became a major trading staple of the British empire.

Had Eliza chosen to marry before this time, she could have lost the legal independence to conduct her experiments; but she favored no suitor until she met and wed Charles Pinckney, a widower of great wealth and high social standing. In later life she took pride in the success of her children. Charles Cotesworth Pinckney (b. 1746) was a powerful voice in the Constitutional Convention of 1787, and Thomas Pinckney (b. 1750) represented President Washington during 1795 in negotiating an agreement called Pinckney's Treaty (see p. 202), which resolved western boundary questions with Spain.

A heralded woman of her generation, Eliza Lucas Pinckney died at the end of the revolutionary era, nearly 140 years after the birth of Hannah Dustan. Dustan's life paralleled the years in which England laid the foundations for a mighty empire in America. Between 1660 and 1700, the colonists offered resistance but had to adjust to new imperial laws governing their lives. Then a series of wars with France and Spain that affected both Dustan and Pinckney caused yet more turbulence. Even with so much upheaval, the colonies grew and prospered. After 1760 provincial Americans were in a position to question their subordinate relationship with England. The coming of the American Revolution cannot be appreciated without looking at the development of the English empire in America—and how that experience related to the lives of passing generations of colonists like Hannah Dustan and Eliza Lucas Pinckney.

Designing England's North American Empire

During the 1760s Benjamin Franklin tried to explain why relations between England and the colonies had turned sour. He blamed British trade policies designed to control American commerce. "Most of the statutes, or acts, . . . of parliaments . . . for regulating, directing, or restraining of trade," Franklin declared, "have been . . . political blunders . . . for private advantage, under pretense of public good." The trade system, he believed, had become both oppressive and corrupt.

Little more than a hundred years before, the colonists had traded as they pleased. After 1650, however, Oliver Cromwell and then the restored Stuart monarch Charles II (reigned 1660–1685) worked closely with Parliament to design trade policies that exerted greater control over the activities of the American colonists.

To Benefit the Parent Nation

Certain key ideas underlay the new, more restrictive policies. Most important was the concept of **mercantilism**, a term not invented until the late eighteenth century but one that describes what England's leaders set out to accomplish. Their goal was national greatness and, as one courtier told Charles II, the challenge was to develop "trade and commerce" so that it "draws [a] store of wealth" into England.

Mercantilist thinkers believed the world's supply of wealth was not infinite but fixed in quantity. Any nation that gained wealth automatically did so at the expense of another. In economic dealings, then, the most powerful nations always maintained a favorable balance of trade by exporting a greater value of goods than they imported. To square accounts, hard money in the form of gold and silver would flow into creditor nations. Governments controlling the most precious metals would be the most self-sufficient. They could use such wealth to stimulate internal economic development as well as to strengthen military forces, both of which were critical to economic survival and ascendancy over other nations.

Mercantilist theory also demonstrated how colonies could best serve their parent nations. Gold and silver extracted from Central and South America had underwritten Spain's rise to great power and glory in the sixteenth century. Although such easy wealth did not exist in eastern North America, the colonies could contribute to a favorable trade balance for England by producing such staple crops as tobacco, rice, and sugar, thus ending any need to import these goods from other countries.

The American provinces, in addition, could supply valuable raw materials—for example, timber products. England had plundered its own forests to have winter fuel and construct a strong naval fleet, making it necessary to import wood from the Baltic region. Now the colonies could help fill timber demands, again reducing foreign imports while supplying a commodity vital to national security. Great stands of American timber could also be fashioned into fine furniture and sold back to the colonists. Ideally, England's overseas colonies would serve as a source of raw materials and staple crops as well as a marketplace for manufactured goods.

Mercantilist thinking affirmed the principle that the colonies existed to benefit and strengthen the parent nation. As such, provincial economic and political activities required close management. To effect these goals, Parliament passed a series of Navigation Acts (1651, 1660, 1663, and 1673), which formed the cornerstone of England's commercial relations with the colonies and the rest of the world. The acts banned foreign merchants and vessels from participating in the colonial trade; proclaimed that certain **enumerated goods** could be shipped only to England or other colonies (the first list included dyewoods, indigo, sugar, and tobacco, and furs, molasses, rice, and wood products such as masts, pitch, and tar were added later); and specified that European goods destined for America had to pass through England.

Through the **Navigation System,** England became the central trading hub of its empire, which resulted in a great economic boom at home. Before 1660, for example, the Dutch operated the largest merchant fleet in Europe and dominated the colonial tobacco trade. With stimulus from the Navigation Acts, the shipbuilding industry began to boom in England as never before. By the late 1690s the English merchant fleet had outdistanced all competitors, including the Dutch, which seemed to bear out mercantilist ideas regarding one nation's strength coming at another's expense.

The ship's carpenter was typical of colonists who benefited from a thriving imperial economy. The colonies produced one-fourth or more of all English-registered vessels.

In the colonies the Navigation Acts had mixed effects. New Englanders, taking advantage of local timber supplies, bolstered their economy by heavy involvement in shipbuilding. By the early 1700s Americans were constructing one-fourth or more of all English merchant vessels. In the Chesapeake Bay region, however, the enumeration of tobacco resulted in economic problems. By the 1660s planters were producing too much tobacco for consumption in the British Isles alone. Because of the costs of merchandising the crop through England, the final market price was too high to support large sales in Europe. Consequently, the tobacco glut in England caused wholesale prices to decline, resulting in hard times in the Chesapeake region and much furor among planters.

Seizing Dutch New Netherland

Charles II learned from his father's mistakes. He never claimed divine authority in decision making; and so as not to appear too power hungry, he passed himself off at court as a sensuous, lazy, vulgar man whose major objectives were to attend horse races, tell bawdy jokes, and seduce women. His mistresses, like Nell Gwynn, became national celebrities and bore him at least 14 illegitimate children. When asked about his lustful ways, he replied, as if mocking the Puritans who had beheaded his father, "God will not damn a man for taking a little unregular pleasure by the way."

Charles often played the foppish fool, but he was an intelligent person with a vision for England's greatness. Besides urging Parliament to legislate the Navigation System, Charles pursued other plans for enhancing England's imperial power. None was more important than challenging Dutch supremacy over the Hudson and Delaware river valleys.

The precedent for attacking territory claimed by England's imperial rivals came in 1654 when Cromwell launched a fleet with 8000 troops to strike at the heart of New Spain. Cromwell's "Western Design" expedition failed to conquer the primary targets of Puerto Rico, Hispaniola, or the port city of Cartagena (located in modern-day Colombia). The fleet, however, seized the island of Jamaica, which in time became a center for illegal commerce with New Spain as well as a major slave trade marketing center.

Charles hated everything about Cromwell, which he proved by having the Lord Protector's corpse exhumed and hanged in public before a cheering crowd. Yet Charles borrowed freely from Cromwell's precedents. New Netherland, a colony having the geographic misfortune of lying between New England and the southern colonies, was an obvious target, especially since Dutch sea captains used New Amsterdam as a base for illegal trade with English settlers. To enforce the Navigation Acts, reasoned Charles and his advisers, the Dutch colony had to be conquered.

New Netherland was the handiwork of the Dutch West India Company, a joint-stock venture chartered in 1621. The company soon sent out a governor and employees to the Hudson River area to develop the fur trade with local Indians, particularly the Five Nations of Iroquois inhabiting upper New York west of Fort Orange (Albany).

Initially the company showed little interest in settlement, but its leaders had to reckon with food shortages. To encourage local agricultural production, the company announced in 1629 that vast landed estates, known as *patroonships*, would be made available to wealthy individuals who transported at least 50 families to New Netherland. The migrants would become tenant farmers for their masters, or *patroons*, who hoped to live like medieval lords on manorial estates. With the Dutch home economy booming, few subjects accepted these less-than-generous terms.

The New Netherland colony was also internally weak and unstable. The governors were a sorry lot, typified by Wouter van Twiller (served 1633–1638), who was pleasant, claimed a contemporary, only "as long as there is any wine." In 1643 his successor, William Kieft, started a war with natives around New Amsterdam (New York City) that devastated the colony's settlers. Facing bankruptcy in 1647, company directors called on Peter Stuyvesant to save the venture. Stuyvesant, however, became embroiled in many disputes with the settlers, whom he repeatedly infuriated with his highhanded policies.

Despite everything, New Netherland's population pushed toward 8000 by 1660, counting Puritans who had settled on Long Island. New Amsterdam was home to people from all over Europe, as well as many African slaves. The unpopularity of Stuyvesant, the absence of any voice in government, and the denial of freedom of worship separate from the Dutch Reformed church all combined to favor a possible English takeover.

In the early days of his monarchy, Charles II strengthened his political base at home by making generous land grants in America, such as rewarding eight loyal court favorites with the Carolinas patent (see p. 41). In 1664 the king gave his brother, James, the Duke of York, title to all Dutch lands in North America, on the obvious condition that they be conquered. James quickly hired Colonel Richard Nicolls to organize a small invasion fleet. When the flotilla appeared before New Amsterdam in August 1664, Stuyvesant could not rally the populace. With hardly an exchange of shots, New Netherland became the Duke of York's English province of New York.

Proprietary Difficulties in New York and New Jersey

Unlike his older brother, James was an inflexible person. Although hard-working, he was a humorless autocrat. He even treated his mistresses coldly, as if they were "given him by priests for penance," wrote one court wag. Nor was James sensitive to the political trends of his time. He hated Parliament for having executed his father and was intolerant of representative government.

Iroquois Nations

The Dutch West India Company developed the fur trade primarily with the Five Nations of Iroquois.

James's proprietary charter had no clause mandating a popular assembly for his colony, and he instructed Nicolls to make no concessions. As an adept administrator, Nicolls maneuvered around the issue by granting other rights. In his Articles of Capitulation, he confirmed the land titles of all inhabitants, including the Dutch. Next Nicolls announced the Duke's Laws, which provided for local government and guaranteed such basic liberties as trial by jury and religious toleration, so long as settlers belonged to and supported some church.

The Long Island Puritans kept pressing for a popularly elected assembly. They refused to pay local taxes, arguing that they were "enslaved under an arbitrary power." The absence of an assembly for New York's colonists remained a source of friction for several years. Finally, James conceded the point, and an assembly met for the first time in 1683. Once he became king in 1685, however, James disavowed further assembly meetings.

Making matters more confusing, in 1664 James turned over all his proprietary lands between the Hudson and Delaware rivers to John, Lord Berkeley, and Sir George Carteret, two court favorites who were also Carolina proprietors. Nicolls, however, did not learn of this grant until after he had offered some Puritans land patents in the eastern portion of what became the colony of New Jersey.

Until the end of the century, questions regarding proprietary ownership of New Jersey plagued the colony's development. Settlement proceeded slowly, with the population moving toward 15,000 by 1700. Most New Jersey colonists engaged in commercial farming and raised grain crops, which they marketed through New York City and Philadelphia, the two port towns that would dominate the region. Because of endless bickering over land titles and proprietary political authority, the Crown declared in 1702 that New Jersey would henceforth be a royal province.

Planting William Penn's "Holy Experiment"

During the English Civil War of the 1640s a number of radical religious sects—Ranters, Seekers, and Quakers among them—began to appear in England. Each represented a small band of fervent believers determined to recast human society in the mold of a particular religious vision. George Fox founded the Society of Friends. His followers came to be called "Quakers," because Fox, who went to jail many times, warned one judge to "tremble at the word of the Lord."

The Quakers adhered to many controversial ideas. They believed that all persons had a divine spark, or "inner light," which, when fully nurtured, allowed them to commune directly with God. Like Anne Hutchinson before them, they saw little need for human institutions. They had no ordained ministers and downplayed the importance of the Bible, since they could order their lives according to revelation received directly from God.

In addition, the Quakers held a unique social vision. All humans, they argued, were equal in the sight of God. Thus they wore unadorned black clothing and refused to remove their broad-brimmed hats when social superiors passed by them. Women had full access to leadership positions and could serve as preachers and missionaries. Members of the sect also refused to take legal oaths, which they considered a form of swearing, and they were pacifists, believing that warfare would never solve human problems. In time, Quakers became antislavery advocates, arguing that God did not hold some persons inferior because of skin color.

Early English Quakers were intensely fervent, and during the 1650s and 1660s they sent many witnesses of their faith to America. These individuals, about half of them women, fared poorly in the colonies. Puritan magistrates in Massachusetts told them of their "free liberty to keep away from us" and threw them out. Two Quaker males were so persistent in coming back to Boston that officials finally hanged them in 1659, and they gave a third witness, Mary Dyer, a gallows reprieve. Dyer, however, returned the next year, was hanged, and became a martyr to her vision of a more harmonious world.

William Penn (1644–1718) first became a Quaker in the early 1660s while a college student at Oxford. Hoping to cure his son's zealousness, Penn's father sent William on a tour of the Continent. Penn returned in a more worldly frame of mind, but he soon readopted Quaker beliefs. He was so outspoken that he even spent time in jail, but his father's high standing at court—he had supported the Stuart restoration—assured the family access to Charles II.

During the 1670s George Fox traveled to America, hoping to find a haven for his followers. He also encouraged William Penn to use his family connections to obtain a land grant. King Charles acceded to Penn's request for a proprietary charter in 1681, stating that the purpose was to "enlarge our British empire" and pay off a £16,000 debt long since due the estate of Penn's father. Years later, Penn claimed that Charles's real motivation was "to be rid of" the Quakers "at so cheap a rate" by conveying to him title to "a desert [wilderness] three thousand miles off."

Pennsylvania, which means Penn's woods, was hardly a desert. The tract was bountiful, and Penn tried to make the most of it, both as a sanctuary for oppressed religious groups and as a source of personal income from quitrents. He laid his plans carefully, making large grants to English Quakers, and he drew up a blueprint for a commercial center—Philadelphia, or the City of Brotherly Love. Penn sent agents to Europe in search of settlers, offering generous land packages with low annual quitrents. He also wrote his First Frame of Government (1682), which guaranteed a legislative assembly and full freedom of religion.

Like the Puritans before him, Penn had a utopian vision, in this case captured by the phrase **holy experiment.** Unlike the Puritans, Penn wanted to mold a society in which peoples of diverse back grounds and religious beliefs lived together harmoniously—a bold idea in an era not known for its toleration.

Determined to succeed, Penn sailed to America in 1682, landing first in the area known as the Three Lower Counties, later to become the colony of Delaware. He had purchased this strip of land from the Duke of York to assure an easy exit for commerce flowing out of Philadelphia to Atlantic trade routes. Until 1701, Delaware existed as an appendage of Pennsylvania, but then Penn granted the colonists there a separate assembly. Until the Revolution, however, the proprietary governors of Pennsylvania also headed Delaware's government.

Penn next journeyed upriver to lay out Philadelphia. Some settlers were already present, and during the next few years others migrated from England as well as from Wales, Scotland, Ireland, Holland, Germany, and Switzerland. Typical were Germans from the Rhineland who followed their religious leader, Francis Daniel Pastorius, and founded Germantown to the north of Philadelphia. From the very outset, Pennsylvania developed along pluralist lines, an early sign of what later characterized the cultural ideal of the United States as a whole.

Penn envisioned a "peaceable kingdom" and sought cordial relations with local Indians. Before traveling to America, he wrote to the Delawares, the dominant tribe in the region, explaining that the king of England "hath given me a great province." He asked that "we may always live together as neighbors and friends." True to his word, Penn met with the Delawares and told them that he would not take land from them unless sanctioned by tribal chieftains. What emerged was the "walking purchase" system in which the natives sold land based on the distance that a person could travel on foot in a day. Even though the system was open to abuse, Penn's goal was honest dealing, which had rarely been the case in other colonies.

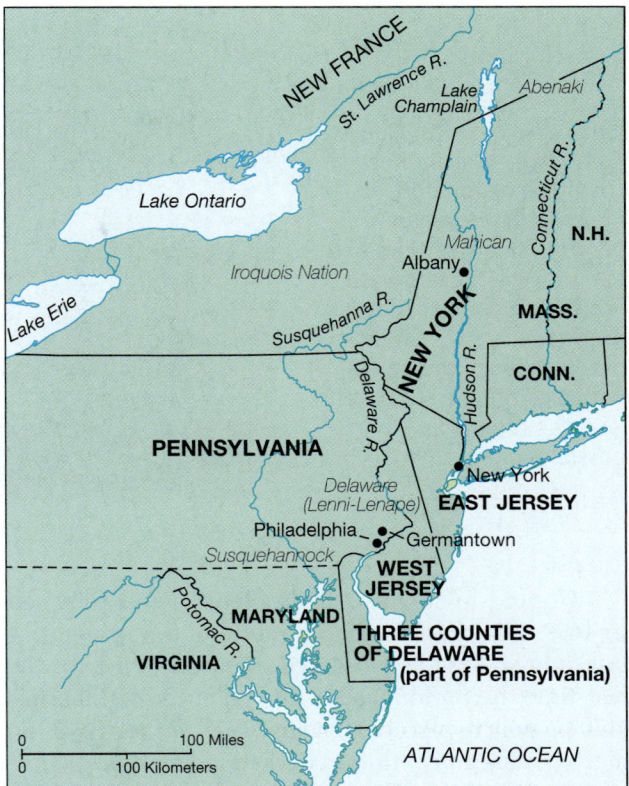

Middle Colonies, 1685

Completing these and other tasks, Penn returned to England in 1684 to encourage further settlement. That was no problem. Pennsylvania was very attractive, particularly for dissenter religious groups. By the early 1700s the population exceeded 20,000. Colonists poured through the booming port of Philadelphia and then fanned out into the fertile countryside. There they established family farms, raising livestock and growing abundant grain crops, which they marketed to the West Indies and Europe. The settlers prospered, and Pennsylvania gained a reputation as "one of the best poor man's countries in the world."

Still, not all was perfect in the peaceable kingdom. Religious sects segregated themselves, wanting little to do with one another. To Penn's dismay, life in Philadelphia was more raucous than pious. Drinking establishments and brothels sprang up in large numbers, and endless bickering characterized local politics. Quakers dominated the government but fought endlessly over the prerogatives of power. Penn thought these "brutish, . . . scurvy quarrels" were a "disgrace" to the colony, but his pleas for harmony went unheeded. Equally disturbing from his point of view, settlers refused to pay quitrents "to supply me with bread," yet he kept funding the colony's development.

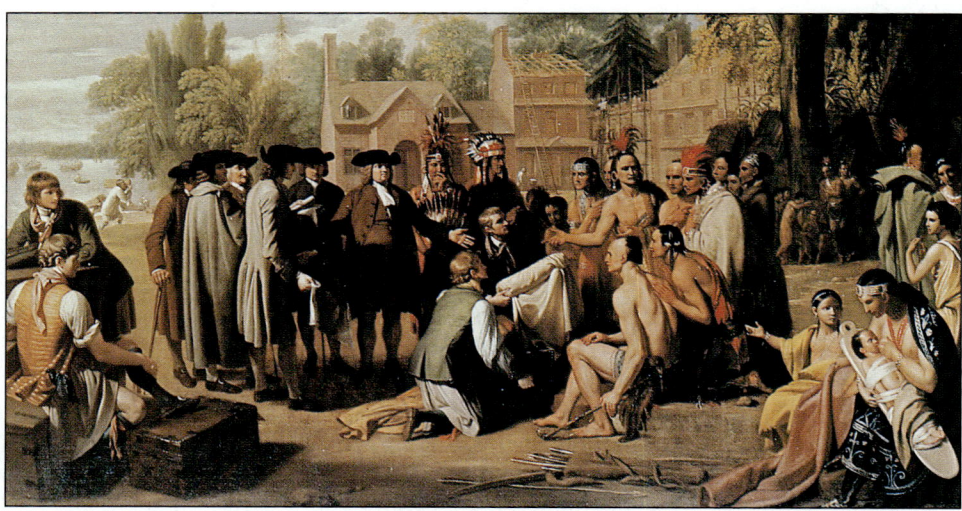

In his dealings with Native Americans, William Penn sought to negotiate land rights fairly. However, Pennsylvania's settlers and Penn's own officials were not so scrupulous. They used many underhanded means to push the native populace off ancient tribal lands as rapidly as possible.

Hoping to solve such problems, Penn returned in 1699. His presence had a moderating influence—but only so long as he stayed. Before leaving for the last time, he announced a new Charter of Liberties (1701), which placed all legislative authority in an elective assembly, to be checked only by a proprietary governor with the advice of a council of well-to-do local gentlemen. The charter served as the basis of Pennsylvania's unicameral government until the Revolution.

Peace, prosperity, pluralism, and religious toleration were the hallmarks of Penn's utopian vision. In his old age, however, he considered the "holy experiment" a failure. He concluded that peaceable kingdoms on earth lay beyond human reach. Having even spent time in prison for debts contracted on behalf of his colony, Penn died an embittered man in 1718. Still, by seeking a better life for all peoples, he helped infuse the American experience with a profound sense of social purpose.

In this idealized drawing of Quaker farmer David Twining's Pennsylvania homestead, the emphasis is on harmonious and peaceful relations.

DEFYING THE IMPERIAL WILL: PROVINCIAL CONVULSIONS AND REBELLIONS

Establishing the Middle Colonies was an integral part of England's imperial expansion within the framework of mercantilist thinking. Certainly the Dutch understood this, and they fought two wars with England (1664–1667 and 1672–1674), hoping to recoup their losses. In the second war they recaptured New York, only to renounce all claims in the peace settlement. After that time, the Dutch focused their activities on other parts of the world, even though some of their mariners continued to trade illegally with the English North American colonists.

Besides reckoning with the Dutch, Charles II and his advisers endeavored to shape the emerging empire in other ways. Crown representatives crossed the Atlantic to determine whether the colonists were cooperating with the Navigation System. Also traveling to America were the first customs officers, who were to collect duties on enumerated goods being traded between colonies—and then to foreign ports. Increasingly the Americans felt England's constraining hand, which in some locales resulted in violent confrontations.

Bacon's Bloody Rebellion in Virginia

With tobacco glutting the market in England, Virginia's economy went into a tailspin during the 1660s. The planters blamed the Navigation Acts, which stopped them from dealing directly with such foreign merchants as the Dutch. The planters' mood did not improve when, in 1667, Dutch war vessels captured nearly the whole English merchant fleet hauling the annual tobacco crop out of Chesapeake Bay, resulting in the virtual loss of a year's worth of labor, harvest, and income.

Besides economic woes, other problems existed. Some Virginians thought their long-time royal governor, Sir William Berkeley (1606–1677), had become a tyrant. Berkeley handed out patronage jobs to a few favored planters, known as the "Green Spring" faction (named after Berkeley's plantation). Such favors allowed the governor to dominate the assembly and levy heavy taxes at a time when settlers were suffering economically. As a consequence, some planters lost their property, and young males just completing terms of indentured service saw few prospects for ever gaining title to land and achieving economic independence. In 1670 Berkeley and the assembly approved a 50-acre property holding requirement for voting privileges. This action fed suspicions that the governor and his cronies were out to amass all power for themselves.

In 1674 young Nathaniel Bacon (1647–1676) jumped into the simmering pot. From a wealthy English family and educated at Cambridge, he had squandered his inheritance before reaching his mid-twenties. Bacon's despairing father sent him to Virginia with a stipend to start a plantation, hoping the experience would force his son to grow up. When Bacon arrived, Berkeley greeted him warmly, stating that "gentlemen of your quality come very rarely into this country."

Bacon was ambitious, and he sought acceptance among Berkeley's favored friends, who controlled the lucrative Indian trade. He asked the governor for a trading license, but Berkeley denied the request, feeling that the young man had not yet proven his worth. Incensed by his rejection, Bacon started opposing Berkeley at every turn. He organized other substantial planters—also not favored by Berkeley—into his own "Castle" faction (the name of his plantation), and he appealed to Virginia's growing numbers of property-less poor for support.

Stirrings among native peoples made matters worse. Far to the north in New York, the Five Nations of Iroquois had become more aggressive in their quest for furs. They started pushing other tribes southward toward Virginia, and some groups spilled onto frontier plantations, resulting in a few killings.

Bacon demanded reprisals, but Berkeley urged caution. A war, he stressed, would only add to Virginia's tax burdens. Bacon asked for a military commission, stating that he would organize an army of volunteers. The governor refused, at which point Bacon charged his adversary with being more interested in protecting profits from his Indian trading monopoly than in saving settlers' lives. Bacon pulled together a force of over 1000 men, described as "the scum of the country" by Berkeley's supporters, and indiscriminately started killing local natives.

In response, Berkeley declared Bacon "the greatest rebel that ever was in Virginia" and sent out militiamen to corral the volunteers, but Bacon's force eluded them. The governor also called a new assembly, which met at Jamestown in June 1676. Among reforms designed to pacify the "mutineers," the burgesses restored voting rights to all adult freemen, even if they did not own property. Events had gone too far, however, and a shooting war broke out. Before the fighting ceased, Bacon's force burned Jamestown to the ground, and Berkeley fled across Chesapeake Bay. What finally precipitated an end to the struggle was Bacon's death from dysentery in October 1676.

When Charles II learned of the uprising, he considered it an affront to royal authority and a threat to his tax revenues on tobacco. The colonists had to be disciplined, so he authorized a flotilla of 11 ships and 1000 troops to cross the Atlantic and restore order. By the time the troops arrived, Berkeley was back in control. Royal advisers with the king's army, however, removed the aging governor from office on the grounds that his policies had helped stir up trouble. Governors who placed self-interest above the need for stability and order in the empire would no longer be tolerated.

After 1676 the Crown started sending royal governors to Virginia with detailed instructions about managing the colony as an imperial enterprise—at times at the expense of local interests. In response, Virginia's leading gentleman-planters, previously divided into pro- and anti-Berkeley factions, settled their differences in the face of what they viewed as threats to local autonomy. They rallied the people to their side, got themselves elected regularly to the House of Burgesses, and worked together to protect the colony's interests.

This fundamental recasting of political lines was an important development. No longer would rising planter elite leaders fight to the death among themselves. They would stand united in defense of local rights and privileges, making sure Crown officials understood that harmony and stability depended on their showing basic respect for the welfare of the colonists.

The Glorious Revolution Spills into America

The king's reaction to Bacon's Rebellion fit a larger pattern of asserting more authority over America. New England, with its independent ways, was an obvious target. Back in the mid-1660s royal commissioners had visited Massachusetts and seen Dutch merchant vessels trading in Boston harbor in violation of the Navigation Acts. Puritan leaders were surly about the matter. "The laws of England . . . do not reach [to] America," they declared. Once back in England, the angry commissioners urged the Crown to take over the colony, but nothing happened—at least not for a few years.

Then in 1675 King Charles, seeking more effective control over the colonies, designated certain Privy Council members to serve as the Lords of Trade and Plantations. The lords, in turn, sent agents and customs officials to America. The most notorious was Edward Randolph, a grim, dedicated bureaucrat who never met a Puritan he liked. Soon he was bombarding the lords with negative reports. In response to Randolph's accusations the lords began legal proceedings and got the Bay Colony charter revoked in 1684.

Randolph was not solely responsible for voiding the charter. The Lords of Trade had developed plans for setting up two or three large administrative territories in North America. New England made a natural unit, based on geographic cohesion and forms of economic production. Charles thought the scheme too radical, but when James became king in 1685, the lords gained permission to set up the Dominion of New England, which stretched from Nova Scotia to the Delaware River.

James II liked the Dominion concept not only because it favored the Church of England but also because it centralized political power in the hands of a governor and a large advisory council made up of Crown appointees. Local representative assemblies would likewise cease to exist. James gladly wrote New York's local leaders and informed them that they would now exist under the authority of the Dominion. As for Connecticut and Rhode Island, the lords were working to void their charters in court.

From the outset the Dominion was a bad idea, perhaps made worse by naming as governor Sir Edmund Andros (1637–1714), a man of aristocratic bearing with impressive military credentials. Among his councilors was the despised Edward Randolph. Images of political tyranny wafted through Puritan minds when Andros debarked in Boston in late 1686 and demanded that a building be found for holding Anglican church services. It all smacked of garrison government in which the highest ranking military officer had complete authority, with no popular checks whatsoever.

Andros expected the Puritans to conform to the imperial will. He announced plans to rewrite all land deeds, none of which the General Court had awarded in the king's name and, then, to impose quitrents, which New Englanders had never paid. He announced import taxes to underwrite the expenses of his government, and he started prosecuting violators of the Navigation Acts.

Meanwhile, back in England, James II had created an uproar by pushing royal authority too far. In defiance of England's Protestant tradition, he flaunted his Roman Catholic beliefs and announced that his newborn son, now next in line for the throne, would be raised a Catholic. The thought of yet more turbulence over religious beliefs was too much for influential English leaders to bear. In December 1688 they drove James from the realm and offered the throne to his Protestant daughter, Mary, and her husband, the Dutch prince, William of Orange, as joint monarchs. As part of the Glorious Revolution, Parliament also placed strict limitations on royal prerogatives by adopting the Declaration of Rights (1689), which at long last assured Parliament an equal, if not dominant, voice in Britain's political affairs.

When news of the Glorious Revolution reached Boston, local Puritan leaders went into action. They believed wild rumors about James, who had fled to France, conspiring with Andros, French Canadians, and Indians to seize New England and turn it into a new bastion of Roman Catholicism. They seized the governor on April 18, 1689, threw him in jail, and then shipped him back to England. They did so, they insisted, to end Andros's arbitrary rule, and they asked William and Mary to restore their original corporate charter.

The coup in Massachusetts helped spark a rebellion in New York, where a volatile mix of ethnic and class tensions resulted in a violent upheaval. Francis Nicholson served in New York City as the Dominion's lieutenant governor. Wealthy Dutch and English landholders and merchants cooperated with his rule, which bred resentment among poorer Dutch and English settlers, such as the Puritans on Long Island. Jacob Leisler, a combative local merchant of German origin, also hated the favored families. They had snubbed him socially, despite his marriage to a wealthy Dutch widow. Even worse, from his point of view, they cared little about securing popular political rights.

When reports of the rumored "popish" plot and the Massachusetts coup reached New York, Leisler exhorted the anti-Nicholson settlers to rise up and defend themselves. He organized 500 of them into a military force, and on May 31 they captured Fort James which guarded New York harbor. Within a few days, Nicholson fled to England. Leisler set up an interim government and waited for advice from England, hoping that the new monarchs would make a permanent grant of a popularly based assembly. In addition, Leisler made no attempt to stop mobs from harassing and robbing wealthy families.

The third colony jolted by a revolt in 1689 was Maryland, where quarrels between Roman Catholics and Protestants remained a perpetual source of tension. The proprietary governor, William Joseph, tried to contain the popish conspiracy rumors, but John Coode, an anxious local planter, organized the Protestant Association to defend Marylanders from the impending slaughter. Rumormongers soon were whispering that the Catholic proprietor and his local governor were in on the plot. That was all Coode needed. He led 250 followers to St. Mary's, where in July 1689 they removed Joseph from office, called their own assembly, and then sent representatives to England to plead for royal government.

In a chain reaction, three political uprisings had occurred in the American colonies in just four months. Although each had its own individual character, the common issue, besides the rumored Catholic conspiracy, was the question of how extensive colonial rights would be in the face of tightening imperial administration. All the colonists could do now was wait to hear from the new monarchs—and hope for the best.

New England's Witchcraft Hysteria

William and Mary, at first, had little time to deal with the provincial rebellions. Warfare had broken out in Europe (the War of the League of Augsburg, 1689–1697). Spilling over into America, this contest caused havoc in the lives of frontier settlers like Hannah Dustan. French and Indian raiding parties made orphans of many children, including a few who ended up in Salem Village (now Danvers), Massachusetts, the center of the 1692 witchcraft episode.

Puritans, like most Europeans and colonists elsewhere, believed in witchcraft. They thought the devil could materialize in various shapes and forms, damaging lives at will. Satan's agents included witches and wizards, women and men possessed by his evil spirits. Eighty-one New Englanders had faced accusations of practicing witchcraft before 1692, 16 of whom were put to death. These numbers were insignificant in comparison to accused witches hunted down and executed in Europe.

Reasons abound for the outbreak of the witchcraft hysteria. By the early 1690s New Englanders had lost their charter, lived under the Dominion, rebelled against Edmund Andros, and engaged in war with the hated French. These unsettled conditions may have made the populace overly suspicious and anxious about evil influences in their midst.

In addition, specific tensions affected the Salem area. Salem Town, the port, was caught up in New England's commercial life while outlying settlers around Salem Village remained traditional in seeking God's grace before material wealth. Resentment by the villagers was growing, described even before 1690 as "uncharitable expressions and uncomely reflections tossed to and fro."

These tensions came out in the pattern of accusations when in early 1692 a few adolescent girls, among them some of the war orphans from Maine, started having their "fits." Anxious about their own

As the Salem witchcraft trials unfolded, the young "afflicted" girls became more bold in their accusations. They often fell into fits and shouted that the accused had cast evil satanic spells over them.

lives, the girls had asked Tituba, a local slave woman from the West Indies, to tell them their fortunes. She did so. Soon thereafter the girls started acting hysterically, observers claimed, as if possessed by Satan's demons. When asked to name possible witches, the girls did not stop with Tituba.

Before the hysteria ended, the "afflicted" girls made hundreds of accusations before a special court appointed to root the devil out of Massachusetts. With increasing frequency they pointed to more urbane, prospering citizens like those of Salem Town. The penalty for practicing witchcraft was death. Some 50 defendants, among them Tituba, saved themselves by admitting their guilt; but 20 men and women were executed (19 by hanging and 1 by the crushing weight of stones) after steadfastly refusing to admit that they had practiced witchcraft.

By the end of 1692 the craze was over, probably because too many citizens of rank and influence, including the wife of the new royal governor, Sir William Phips, had been accused of doing the devil's work. In time, most participants in the Salem witchcraft trials admitted to being deluded. While victims could not be brought back to life, the episode stood as a warning in the colonies about the dangers of mass hysteria at a time when Europeans were still actively ferreting out and prosecuting alleged witches. The playing out of events also helped sustain New England's transition to a commercial society by making traditional folk beliefs—and those who espoused them—appear foolish.

Settling Anglo-American Differences

In 1691 William and Mary began to address colonial issues. As constitutional monarchs, they were not afraid of popularly elected assemblies. In the case of Massachusetts they approved a royal charter that gave the Crown the authority to name royal governors and stated that all male property holders, not just church members, had the right to vote. On the other hand, the monarchs did not tamper with the established Congregational church, thereby reassuring old-line Puritans that conforming to the Church of England was not necessary so long as Bay Colony residents supported England's imperial aspirations.

New York also became a royal colony in 1691, complete with a local representative assembly. Henry Sloughter, the governor, delivered the news; but Jacob Leisler hesitated to step aside, fearing that Sloughter might be an agent of King James. Leisler's obstinacy led to his arrest and hasty trial for treason. His enemies gave all the testimony that the court needed to sentence him to a ghastly death by hanging, disemboweling, drawing and quartering and, if that were not enough, decapitation. It was little solace to Leisler's followers that Parliament, in later reviewing the evidence, declared him innocent of treason.

In Maryland's case the Calverts lost political control in 1692 in favor of royal government, although they still held title to the land and could collect quitrents. Shortly thereafter, a Protestant assembly banned Roman Catholics from political office. Not

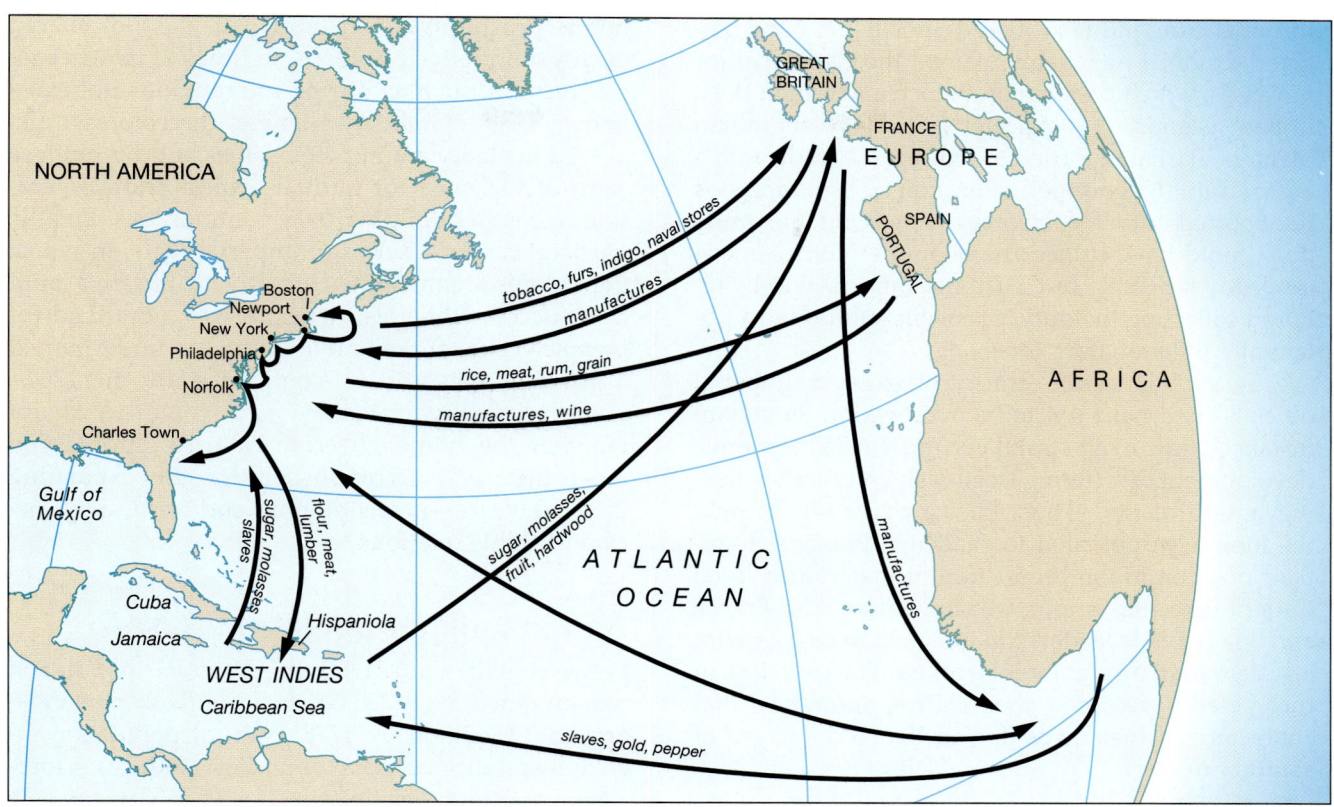

Colonial Trade Routes, 1750

until 1715 did the Calverts regain political control. By then the proprietary family had converted to Anglicanism and was no longer a threat to Protestant sensibilities.

The transformation revealed a movement toward the royal model of government in which the colonies established legislative assemblies to express and defend their local concerns. Crown-appointed governors, in turn, pledged themselves to enforce the Navigation Acts and other imperial laws. So long as the colonists cooperated, they would not face autocratic forms of government. Nor would the Crown permit the kind of loose freedom of earlier times, because in gaining basic rights, the colonists also accepted responsibility for conducting their daily affairs within the imperial framework. The Glorious Revolution and its reverberations in America had made this compromise possible.

Maintaining the delicate balance between imperial authority and local autonomy was the major challenge of the eighteenth century. Until the 1760s both sides succeeded in doing so. The Crown, for example, adopted the Navigation Act of 1696, which set up the Board of Trade and Plantations as an administrative agency to advise England's leaders on colonial issues. This act also mandated the establishment of vice-admiralty courts in America to punish with stiff penalties smugglers and others who violated the rules of trade.

The Board of Trade generally acted with discretion, even in recommending a few acts to restrain colonial manufacturers competing with home industries. Parliament in 1699 adopted legislation (the Woolen Act) that outlawed any exportation of woolen products from America or from one colony to another. The intent was to get the colonists to buy finished woolens from English manufacturers rather than develop their own industry. In 1732 the Hat Act barred the colonial production of beaver and felt hats. Then in 1750 Parliament passed the Iron Act, which forbade the colonists from building new facilities or expanding old ones for the manufacture of finished iron or steel products. On the other hand, the act encouraged them to keep preparing raw iron for final processing in England. As a whole, these acts had little adverse effect on the provincial economy. They simply reinforced fundamental mercantile notions regarding colonies as sources of raw materials and as markets for finished goods.

Occasionally, imperial leaders went too far, such as with the Molasses Act of 1733. In support of a thriving rum industry based mostly in New England, colonial merchants roamed the Caribbean for molasses, which cost less on French and Dutch West Indian islands. To placate British West Indian planters, Parliament tried to redirect the trade with a heavy duty (6 pence per gallon) on foreign molasses transported into the colonies. Enforcing the trade duty could have ruined the booming North American rum industry, but customs officers wisely ignored collecting the duty, a sensible solution to a potentially inflammatory issue.

As the eighteenth century progressed, imperial officials tried hard not to be overbearing. In certain instances they even stimulated provincial economic development by offering large cash bounties for raising indigo plants. (Thus, Eliza Lucas's efforts held the long-term potential to challenge France's dominant position in the production of that valued dye.) Caught up as the empire was in warfare with France and Spain, home leaders did not want to tamper with a system that, by and large, worked. The colonists, in turn, gladly accepted the relative autonomy that characterized their lives during the so-called era of **salutary neglect**.

MATURING COLONIAL SOCIETIES IN UNSETTLED TIMES

Stable relations with the parent nation and other factors nourished the maturing of the American provinces after 1700. Certainly a rapidly expanding population that nearly doubled every 20 years strengthened the colonies, as did widespread economic prosperity, even though it was not shared evenly among the populace. In times of internal social turmoil, such as during the religious upheaval known as the Great Awakening, the colonists disagreed heatedly among themselves but did not lose sight of the need for mutual respect and cooperation in further building their communities. Finally, participation in a series of imperial wars, in which the colonists contributed greatly to Britain's military success while also wresting yet more land for themselves from the native populace, underpinned a growing sense of self-confidence. By the 1760s, however, many colonists had come to doubt whether the home government truly appreciated what they had accomplished for the expanding British empire—portending an end to the long period of stable relations.

An Exploding Population Base

Between 1700 and 1760 the colonial population mushroomed from 250,000 to 1.6 million persons—and to 2.5 million by 1775. Natural population increase—predicated upon abundant land, early marriages, and high fertility rates—was only one source of the population explosion. Equally significant was the introduction of non-English peoples. Between 1700 and 1775 the British North American slave trade reached its peak, resulting in the involuntary entry of an estimated 250,000 Africans into the colonies. The black population grew from 28,000 in 1700 to over 500,000 in 1775, with most living as chattel slaves in the South. At least 40 to 50 percent of the African population increase in the colonies was attributable to the booming slave trade.

Among European groups, Scots-Irish and Germans predominated, although a smattering of French Huguenot, Swiss, Scottish, Irish, and Jewish migrants joined the westward stream. The Scots-Irish had endured many privations. Originally Presbyterian lowlanders from Scotland, they had migrated to Ulster (northern Ireland) in the seventeenth century at the invitation of the Crown. Once there, they harassed the Catholic Irish with a vengeance, only to face discrimination themselves when a new Parliamentary law, the Test Act of 1704, stripped non-Anglicans of political rights. During the next several years they also endured crop failures and huge rent increases from their English landlords.

In a series of waves between 1725 and 1775 over 100,000 Scots-Irish descended on North America, lured by reports of "a rich, fine soil before them, laying as loose...as the best bed in the garden." Philadelphia was their main port of entry. They then moved out into the backcountry where they squatted

TABLE 3.1
Colonial Population Growth, 1660–1780

Year	White	Black	Total
1660	70,200	2900	73,100*
1680	138,100	7000	145,100
1700	223,100	27,800	250,900
1720	397,300	68,900	466,200
1740	755,500	150,000	905,500
1760	1,267,800	325,800	1,593,600
1780	2,111,100	566,700	2,677,800

Note: All estimates rounded to the nearest hundred.
*Includes the population of New Netherland.
Source: The American Colonies: From Settlement to Independence by R. C. Simmons. Copyright © 1976 by R. C. Simmons. Reprinted by permission of Harold Matson, Inc.

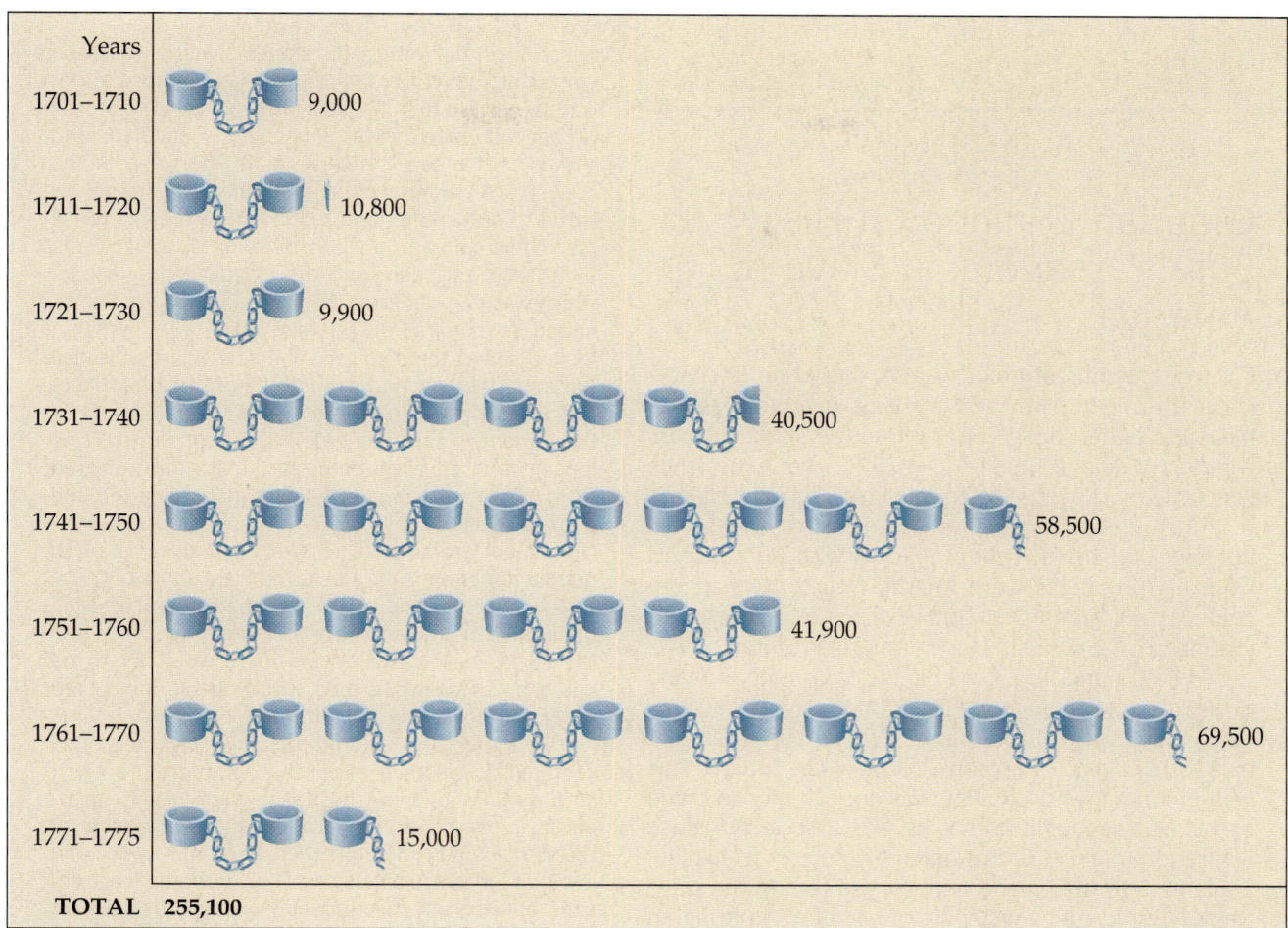

FIGURE 3.1
Slave Importation Estimates, 1701–1775

Source: R. C. Simmons, *The American Colonies: From Settlement to Independence.* Copyright © 1976 by R. C. Simmons. Reprinted by permission of Harold Matson Company.

on open land and earned reputations as bloodthirsty Indian fighters. In time, the Scots-Irish took the Great Wagon Road through the Shenandoah Valley and started filling in the southern backcountry.

Even before the first Scots-Irish wave, Germans from the area of the upper Rhine River began streaming into the Middle Colonies. Some, like Amish, Moravian, and Mennonite sectarians, fled religious persecution; others escaped from crushing economic circumstances caused by overpopulation, crop failures, and heavy local taxes. So many Germans came through Philadelphia that Benjamin Franklin questioned whether "Pennsylvania . . . [will] become a colony of aliens, who will shortly be so numerous as to Germanize us, instead of our Anglifying them." Franklin's worries could not stop the German migrants, whose numbers exceeded 100,000 by 1775.

Many destitute Germans crossed the Atlantic as **redemptioners.** This system was similar to indentured servitude, except that families migrated together and shippers promised heads of households a few days' time, upon arrival in America, to locate some person or group to pay for the family's passage in return for a set number of years of labor (usually three to six years per family member). If they failed, then ship captains held auctions at market with the expectation of making tidy profits. The redemptioner system was full of abuses, such as packing passengers on vessels like cattle and serving them worm-infested food. Hundreds died before seeing America. For those who survived, the dream of prospering someday as free colonists remained viable.

One reason for such optimism was that more settlers were enjoying longer life spans, as reflected in higher birth and lower death rates. Estimates indicate that post-1700 Americans were dying at an average of 20 to 25 per 1000 annually, but births numbered 45 to 50 per 1000 settlers.

THE PEOPLE SPEAK

Olaudah Equiano on His Ship Passage as a Slave to America

For free persons of great wealth, migrating to America in the eighteenth century was invariably an unpleasant undertaking. For unfree persons such as Olaudah Equiano (c. 1745–1797), the experience was truly mortifying. Stolen from his village in Nigeria by Africans involved in the slave trade, 11-year-old Equiano had to face the unknown with no sense of what his prospects were for the future. He had become one of about 250,000 Africans forced into migrating to the British North American colonies between 1700 and 1775. As events for young Equiano turned out, he was among the luckier slaves. A British naval officer purchased him in Virginia and later sold him to a Quaker merchant in the West Indies. This gentleman allowed Equiano the opportunity to trade on his own, enough so that he was able to purchase his freedom in 1766. For much of the rest of his life, Equiano lived in England and worked to halt the slave trade. His *Narrative* was part of his effort to bring an end to such human exploitation, as these passages about what he experienced on a slave ship attest.

> The first object which saluted my eyes when I arrived on the coast was the sea, and a slave ship, which was then riding at anchor, and waiting for its cargo. These filled me with astonishment, which was soon converted into terror, which I am yet at a loss to describe, nor the then feelings of my mind. When I was carried on board I was immediately handled, and tossed up, to see if I were sound, by some of the crew; and I was now persuaded that I had got into a world of bad spirits, and that they were going to kill me. Their complexions too differing so much from ours, their long hair, and the language they spoke, which was very different from any I had every heard, united to confirm me in this belief. . . . When I looked round the ship too, and saw a large furnace or copper boiling, and a multitude of black people of every description chained together, every one of our countenances expressing dejection and sorrow, I no longer doubted of my fate; and, quite overpowered with horror and anguish, I fell motionless on the deck and fainted.
>
> When I recovered a little, I found some black people about me, who I believed were some of those who brought me on board, and had been receiving their pay; they talked to me in order to cheer me, but all in vain. I asked them if we were not to be eaten by those white men with horrible looks, red faces, and long hair. They told me I was not. . . .
>
> I was not long suffered to indulge my grief; I was soon put down under the decks, and there I received such a salutation in my nostrils as I had never experienced in my life; so that, with the loathsomeness of the stench, and crying together, I became so sick and low that I was not able to eat, nor had I the least desire to taste any thing. I now wished for the last friend, death, to relieve me; but soon, to my grief, two of the white men offered me eatables; and, on my refusing to eat, one of them held me fast by the hands, and laid me across, I think, the windlass, and tied my feet while the other flogged me severely. I had never experienced any thing of this kind before. . . .

Longer lives reflected improved health and agricultural abundance. Colonists had plentiful supplies of food. Nutritious diets led to better overall health, making it easier for Americans to fight virulent diseases. Even the poorest people, claimed a New England doctor, had regular meals of "salt pork and beans, with bread of Indian corn meal," as well as ample quantities of home-brewed beer and distilled spirits. In the same period, food supplies in Europe were dangerously sparse. Thousands of western Europeans starved to death between 1740 and 1743 because of widespread crop failures.

The "Europeanizing" of America

Compared to Europe, America was a land of boundless prosperity. To be sure, however, the colonists accepted wide disparities in wealth, rank, and privilege as part of the natural order of life. They did so because of the pervasive influence of European values, such as the need for hierarchy and deference in social and political relations. The eighteenth century was still an era in which individuals believed in three distinct social orders—the monarchy, the aristocracy, and the "democracy" of common citizens. All persons had an identifiable place in society, fixed at birth; and to try to improve one's lot was to risk instability in the established rhythms of the universe.

These notions, dating back to Aristotle and other ancient thinkers, helped justify the highly stratified world of early modern Europe, featuring monarchical families such as the Tudors and Stuarts and bloodline aristocrats who passed hereditary titles from one generation to the next. Among those threatening Europe's established social order were ambitious commoners

> In a little time after, amongst the poor chained men, I found some of my own nation, which in a small degree gave ease to my mind. I inquired of them what was to be done with us? They gave me to understand we were to be carried to these white people's country to work for them. I then was a little revived, and thought, if it were no worse than working, my situation was not so desperate; but still I feared I should be put to than working, my situation was not so desperate; but still I feared I should be put to death, the white people looked and acted, as I thought, in so savage a manner; for I had never seen among any people such instances of brutal cruelty; and this not only shown toward us blacks, but also to some of the whites themselves....
>
> At last, when the ship we were in had got in all her cargo, they made ready with many fearful noises, and we were all put under deck.... The stench of the hold ... became absolutely pestilential. The closeness of the place, and the heat of the climate, added to the number in the ship, which was so crowded that each had scarcely room to turn himself, almost suffocated us. This produced copious perspirations, so that the air soon became unfit for respiration, from a variety of loathsome smells, and brought on a sickness amongst the slaves, of which many died, thus falling victims to the improvident avarice, as I may call it, of their purchasers. This wretched situation was again aggravated by the galling of the chains, now become insupportable; and the filth of the necessary tubs, into which the children often fell, and were almost suffocated. The shrieks of the women, and the groans of the dying, rendered the whole scene of horror almost inconceivable. Happily perhaps for myself I was soon reduced so low here that it was thought necessary to keep me almost always on deck; and from my extreme youth I was not put in fetters.
>
> In this situation I expected every hour to share the fate of my companions, some of whom were almost daily brought upon deck at the point of death, which I began to hope would soon put an end to my miseries. Often did I think many of the inhabitants of the deep much more happy than myself; I envied them the freedom they enjoyed, and as often wished I could change my condition for theirs....
>
> One day, when we had a smooth sea, and moderate wind, two of my wearied countrymen, who were chained together (I was near them at the time), preferring death to such a life of misery, somehow made through the nettings, and jumped into the sea; immediately another quite dejected fellow, who, on account of his illness, was suffered to be out of irons, also followed their example; and I believe many more would very soon have done the same, if they had not been prevented by the ship's crew, who were instantly alarmed. Those of us that were the most active were in a moment put down under the deck; and there was such a noise and confusion amongst the people of the ship as I never heard before, to stop her, and get the boat out to go after the slaves. However, two of the wretches were drowned, but they got the other, and afterwards flogged him unmercifully, for thus attempting to prefer death to slavery. In this manner we continued to undergo more hardships than I can now relate; hardships which are inseparable from this accursed trade. Many a time we were near suffocation, from the want of fresh air, which we were often without for whole days together. This, and the stench of the necessary tubs, carried off many....

Source: Olaudah Equiano, *The Interesting Narrative of the Life of Olaudah Equiano or Gustavus Vassa, the African* (New York, 1791).

who had acquired great wealth through commerce. They too craved public recognition and high status, and they tried to earn a place for themselves at the top of the social pyramid by aping the manners and customs of those born into privileged social stations.

The same could be said for wealthy elite families that had emerged in America by the early eighteenth century. In Virginia names like Byrd, Carter, and Lee were of the first rank; the Pinckneys and Rutledges dominated South Carolina; in New York the Livingstons and Schuylers were among the favored few with great estates along the Hudson River; and in Massachusetts those of major consequence included merchant families like the Hutchinsons and Olivers.

Elite families set themselves apart from the rest of colonial society by imitating English aristocratic lifestyles. Wealthy southern gentlemen used gangs of slaves to produce the staple crops that generated the income to construct lavish manor houses with elaborate formal gardens. Northern merchants built large residences of Georgian design and filled them with fashionable Hepplewhite or Chippendale furniture. Together, they thought of themselves as the "better sort," and they expected the "lower sort" (also described as the "common herd" or "rabble") to defer to their judgment in social and political decision making.

One characteristic, then, of the "Europeanizing" of colonial society was growing economic stratification, with extremes of wealth and poverty becoming more visible. In Chester County, Pennsylvania, where commercial farming was predominant, the wealthiest 10 percent of the people owned 24 percent of the taxable property in the 1690s, which jumped to 34 percent by 1760. Their gain came at the expense of the bottom 30 percent, who held 17 percent in the

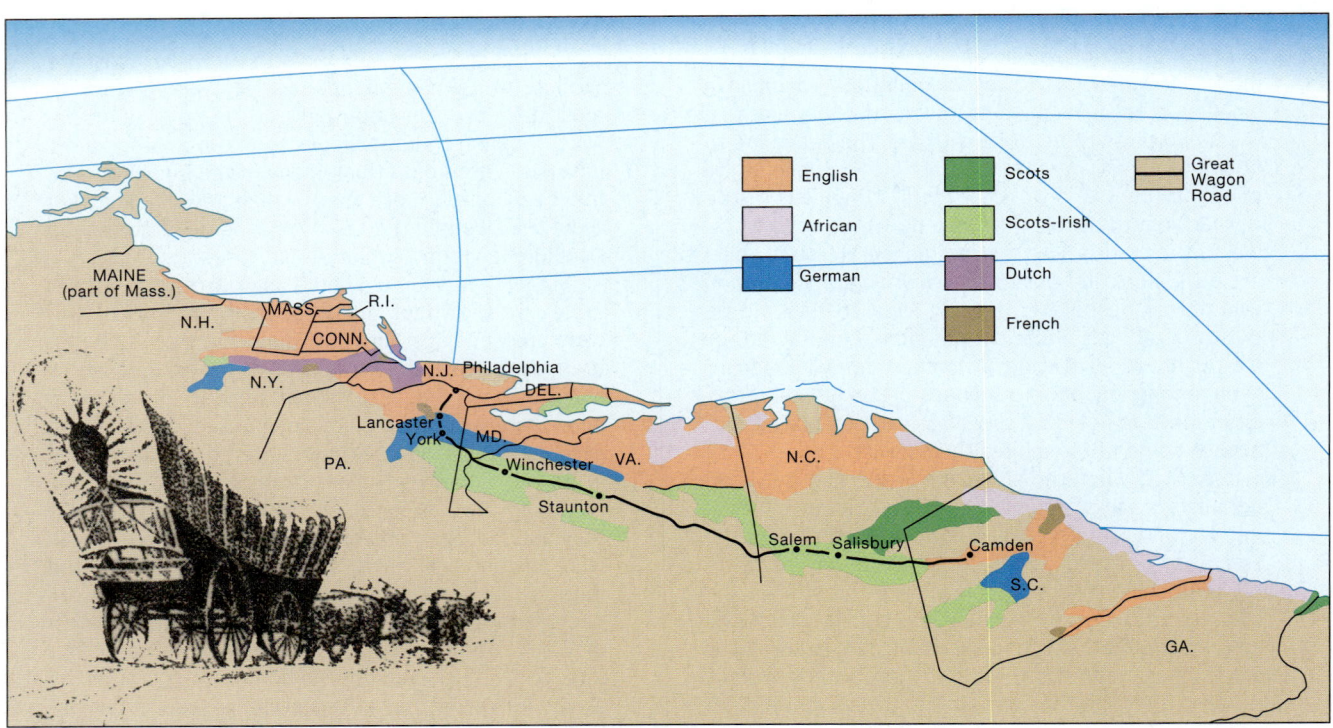

Distribution of Immigrant Groups and the Great Wagon Road, Mid-1700s

Many settlers carried their possessions in Conestoga wagons as they migrated south from Pennsylvania along the Great Wagon Road in search of new homesteads.

1690s but only 6 percent in 1760. The pattern was even more striking in urban areas like Boston and Philadelphia. By 1760 the top 10 percent controlled over 60 percent of the available wealth; the bottom 30 percent owned less than 2 percent.

Nevertheless, the colonies featured a large middle class, and it was still possible to get ahead in provincial America. Over 90 percent of the people lived in the countryside and engaged in some form of agricultural production. By European standards, property ownership was widespread, yet poverty was also common. Some of the worst instances were among urban dwellers, many of whom eked out the barest of livelihoods as unskilled day laborers or merchant seamen. These individuals at least enjoyed some personal freedom, which placed them above those persons trapped in slavery, who formed 20 percent of the populace but enjoyed none of its prosperity or political rights.

With colonial wealth concentrated in fewer and fewer hands, a second "Europeanizing" trend was toward the hardening of class lines. Elite families increasingly intermarried, and they spoke openly of an assumed right to serve as political stewards for the people. As one Virginia gentleman proclaimed in the 1760s, "men of *birth and fortune,* in every government that is free, should be invested with power, and enjoy higher honors than the people. If it were otherwise, their privileges would be less, and they would not enjoy an equal degree of liberty with the people."

Here was a classic statement of "deferential" thinking. Although widespread property holding allowed substantial numbers of free white males to vote, they most often chose among members of the elite to represent them in elective offices, particularly in colonial assemblies. Once elected, these stewards regularly contested with Crown-appointed governors and councilors in upper houses over the prerogatives of decision making. In colony after colony during the eighteenth century, elite leaders chipped away at royal authority, arguing that the assemblies were "little parliaments" with the same legislative rights in their respective territorial spheres as Parliament had over all British subjects.

More often than not, governors had only feeble backing from the home government and lost these disputes. Consequently, the assemblies gained many prerogatives, including the right to initiate all provincial money and taxation bills. Because governors depended on the assemblies for their salaries, they often approved local legislation not in the best interests of the Crown in exchange for bills appropri-

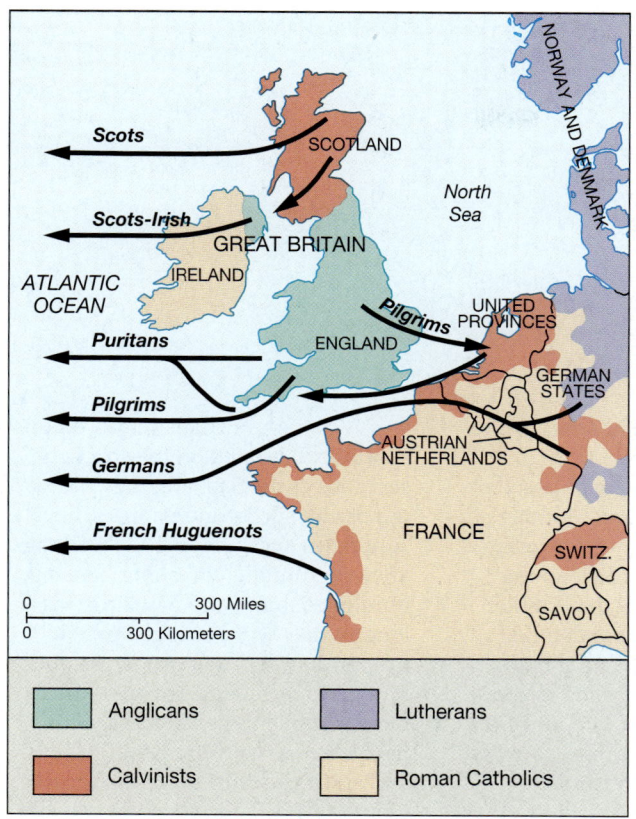

Western European Migration

Western Europeans, escaping religious persecution and dwindling food supplies, migrated in great numbers to North America.

Well-to-do colonists built stately homes and furnished them with fashionable furniture, in conscious imitation of the English aristocratic life-style.

ating their annual salaries. By the 1760s the colonial assemblies had thus emerged as powerful agencies of government.

As self-conscious, assertive elite leaders, colonial gentlemen also read widely and kept themselves informed about European political activities. They were particularly attracted to the writings of a band of "radical" Whig pamphleteers in England who repeatedly warned of ministerial officials who would use every corrupting device to grab all power and authority as potential tyrants at home. The radical Whigs spoke of the delicate fabric of liberty; and provincial leaders, viewing themselves as the protectors of American rights, were increasingly on guard, in case the Crown became too oppressive, as it had been during the 1680s in demanding conformity to the imperial will.

These colonial leaders took challenges to their local autonomy seriously. At least some in their number were ready to mobilize and lead the populace in resisting any new wave of perceived imperial tyranny, should a time ever come when the parent nation attempted to return to arbitrary government.

Intellectual and Religious Awakening

Besides politics, colonial leaders paid close attention to Europe's dawning Age of Reason, also called the **Enlightenment.** The new approach to learning was secular, based on scientific inquiry and the systematic collection of information. A major goal was to unlock the physical laws of nature, as the great English physicist Sir Isaac Newton (1642–1727), often considered the father of the Enlightenment, had done in explaining how the force of gravity held the universe together (*Principia Mathematica*, 1687).

Europe's intellectuals, heavily influenced by the English political thinker John Locke (1632–1704), tried to identify laws governing human behavior. In his *Essay Concerning Human Understanding* (1690), Locke described the human mind as a blank sheet (*tabula rasa*) at birth waiting to be influenced by the experiences of life. If people followed the insights of reason, social and political ills could be reduced or eliminated from society, and each person, as well as humanity as a whole, could advance toward greater harmony and perfection. As such, the key watchword of the Enlightenment was **rationalism,** meaning a firm trust in the ability of the human mind to solve earthly problems—with much less faith in the centrality of God as an active, judgmental force in the universe.

Like their counterparts in Europe, educated colonists pursued all forms of knowledge. Naturalists John Bartram of Pennsylvania and Dr. Alexander Garden of Charleston, South Carolina, were among those who systematically collected and classified American plants. The wealthy merchant James Logan of Philadelphia was a skilled mathematician who also conducted experiments in botany that revealed how pollen functioned as a fertilizing agent in corn.

THE American Mosaic

Colonial Pastimes

FOR much of the past 300 years, Puritans have been the subject of considerable bad press. Novelists and historians have pictured them as dour, sour individuals, dressed in black with faces cast in a permanently disapproving expression. H. L. Mencken, the twentieth-century opponent of what he saw as the Puritan legacy in America, defined Puritanism as "the haunting fear that some one, some where, may be happy." Thomas Babington Macaulay, the nineteenth-century English writer, perhaps best set the tone for Mencken. "The Puritan," Macaulay noted, "hated bear-baiting, not because it gave pain to the bear, but because it gave pleasure to the spectators."

Is there any truth to such broad-brushed stereotyping? What was the Puritans' attitude toward games, sports, and amusements? And how did their attitudes differ from southern Americans? The answers to such questions indicate the differences between Americans North and South.

Commenting on Puritan religious leaders Increase and Cotton Mather, one historian observed, "Though father and son walked the streets of Boston at noonday, they were only twilight figures, communing with ghosts, building with shadows." Certainly, as the quote suggests, the Puritan clergy were sober figures. They looked askance at frivolous behavior. Into this category they lumped sports, games, and amusements played for the pure joy of play. In 1647 the Massachusetts Bay Colony outlawed shuffleboard. A ban against bowling followed in 1650. Football and other sports were similarly treated.

Puritan leaders were opposed to any Sabbath amusements. Sunday was a day for worship—not work, and certainly not play. Remaining true to the teachings of the Prophet Isaiah, Cotton Mather condemned those who tried to justify Sabbath sports: "Never did anything sound more sorrowfully or odious since the day the World was first bless'd with such a day." Those who broke the Sabbath were punished. They were denied food, publicly whipped, or placed in stocks.

Nor did Puritans condone pit sports which matched animal against animal. Before the eighteenth century, pit sports (or blood sports) were popular and commonplace in Europe and the American South. People would travel long distances to watch dogs fight bulls, bears, badgers, or other dogs. Cockfighting was equally popular. Were these spectators cruel? Perhaps not. The "bloodied animals," noted a historian of humanitarianism, "were probably not victims of cruelty. Cruelty implies a desire to inflict pain and thus presupposes an empathic appreciation of the suffering of the object of cruelty. Empathy, however, seems not to have been a highly developed trait in premodern Europe."

Unlike Europeans and southerners, Puritans condemned such activity. They did empathize with the animals. "What Christen [sic] heart," wrote Puritan Philip Stubbes, "can take pleasure to see one poor beast to rent, teare, and kill another, and all for his foolish pleasure?"

Although Puritans outlawed pit sports and insisted on the strict observance of the Sabbath, they did not oppose all sports and games. They supported such activities as walking, archery, running, wrestling, fencing, hunting, fishing, and hawking—as long as they were engaged in at a proper time and in a proper manner. Moderate recreation devoid of gambling, drunkenness, idleness, and frivolousness could refresh the body and spirit and thus serve the greater glory of God. This last point was the most important for the Puritans. Recreations had to help men and women better serve God; they were never to be ends in themselves.

Different attitudes toward sports and games emerged in the southern colonies. Almost from the time of settlement, southerners exhibited an interest—oftentimes bordering on a passion—for various sports. They were particularly attracted to sports that involved opportunities for betting and demonstrations of physical prowess.

Cockfights attracted southerners from every class. The matches were advertised in newspapers and eagerly anticipated; at important events thousands of dollars in bets would change hands. For northern observers the entire affair attracted only scorn and disgust. Elkanah Watson, who traveled to the South in the mid-1800s, was upset to see "men of character and intelligence giving their countenance to an amusement so frivolous and scandalous, so abhorrent to every feeling of humanity, and so injurious in its moral influence."

Horse racing surpassed even cockfighting as a favorite southern pastime. Wealthy southerners liked to trace their ancestry to the English aristocracy, and they viewed horse racing and horse breeding as aristocratic occupations. In fact, by the eighteenth century the ownership of horses had taken on a cultural significance. As one student of the subject explained, "By the turn of the century possession of . . . these animals had become a social necessity. Without a horse, a planter felt despised, an object of ridicule. Owning even a slow footed saddle horse made the common planter more of a man in his own eyes as well as those of his neighbors."

Horse races matched owner against owner, planter against planter, in contests where large sums of money and sense of personal worth often rode on the outcome. In most races planters rode their own horses, making the outcome even more important. Intensely competitive men, planters sometimes cheated to win, and many races ended in legal courts rather than on the racetrack.

If planters willingly battled each other on the racetrack, they did not ride against their social inferiors. When James Bullocke, a tailor, challenged Mr. Mathew Slader to a race in 1674, the county court informed the tailor that it was "contrary to Law for a Labourer to make a race being a Sport for Gentlemen." For his efforts, the court fined Bullocke 200 pounds of tobacco and cask. Although laborers and slaves watched the contests, and even bet among each other, they did not mix socially with the gentry.

Unlike the Puritans who believed sports should serve God, southerners participated in sports as an outlet for their very secular materialistic, individualistic, and competitive urges. But neither North nor South had a modern concept of sports. Colonial Americans seldom kept records, respected equality of competition, established sports bureaucracies, standardized rules, or quantified results—all hallmarks of modern sports. Yet each section engaged in leisure activities that reflected their social and religious outlooks.

85

Benjamin Franklin epitomized Enlightenment thinking in the colonies. As a student of science he wanted to unlock the mysterious laws of nature, such as in his lightning experiments. Franklin was also a printer, inventor, philosopher, and statesman.

Courtesy of Mr. and Mrs. Wharton Sinkler Collection/Philadelphia Musem of Art.

Benjamin Franklin (1706–1790) became the best-known colonial student of science. In the early 1720s he organized the Junto, a club in Philadelphia devoted to exploring useful knowledge. In 1743 he helped found the American Philosophical Society, which focused on compiling scientific knowledge that would help "multiply the conveniences and pleasures of life." Flying his famous kite, Franklin himself performed experiments with lightning, seeking to reveal the mysteries of electrical energy. After publishing his *Experiments and Observations on Electricity* (1751), Franklin's fame spread throughout the Western world. The next year he invented the lightning rod (1752), which he first developed to protect his own home from the destructive energy contained in flashes of lightning.

Franklin was very much a man of secular learning. So were some clergymen, such as Boston's Cotton Mather, who dabbled in science without forsaking strongly held religious beliefs. During a deadly New England smallpox epidemic in 1720 and 1721, Mather was outspokenly in favor of inoculation, which involved purposely inducing slight infections. Many thought inoculations would only spread the disease, but Mather collected statistics that proved the procedure's preventive effects. Whereas 15 percent of uninoculated smallpox victims did not survive, just 3 percent died as a result of inoculation.

Mather conducted his experiment in the face of strong public opposition. Even local physicians railed against him, and one irate citizen threw a rock through the window of his home with the message: "Mather, you dog; damn you: I'll enoculate you with this, with a pox to you." Years would pass before most provincial Americans accepted inoculation as a sensible medical procedure for controlling deadly smallpox epidemics.

Unlike Mather, many ministers viewed the Enlightenment with great suspicion. Rationalism seemed to undermine orthodox religious values by reducing God to a prime mover who had set the universe in motion only to leave humans to chart their own destiny. (This system of thought was known as Deism.) Others perceived a decline in religious faith, as the populace rushed to achieve material rather than spiritual abundance. For some clergymen, the time was at hand for a renewed emphasis on vital religion.

During the 1720s and 1730s in Europe and America, some ministers started holding revivals. They did so in the face of dwindling church attendance in many locales. The first colonial outpouring of rejuvenated faith occurred during the mid-1720s in New Jersey and eastern Pennsylvania, where the determined Dutch Reformed minister, Theodorus Frelinghuysen, and his Presbyterian counterpart, Gilbert Tennent, attacked what the latter called the "presumptuous security" of his parishioners. Delivering impassioned sermons, these two ministers exhorted great numbers of people to seek after God's saving grace. Theirs was the first in a succession of revival "harvests" known collectively as the **Great Awakening.**

The next harvest came in New England. With each passing year fewer descendants of the Puritans showed interest in seeking God's grace and gaining full church membership. Attempting to reverse matters in the early eighteenth century, the longtime Congregational minister, Solomon Stoddard (c. 1643–1729) of Northampton, Massachusetts, threw open the doors of his church and encouraged everyone to join in communion services—the hallmark of full church membership. Stoddard's method worked, and he temporarily reversed the slide.

Then in 1734 Jonathan Edwards (1703–1758), who had succeeded Stoddard, his grandfather, in the

Jonathan Edwards (1703–1758) entered Yale before he was 13 years old, graduated in 1720, and was licensed to preach at the age of 19. In "Sinners in the Hands of an Angry God," he admonished his listeners to acknowledge their own sinfulness and thus take the necessary first step toward spiritual reawakening.

Although George Whitefield failed to convert Benjamin Franklin, the evangelist's eloquence moved Franklin to make a generous contribution to the preacher's collection.

Northampton pulpit, initiated a series of revival meetings aimed at young persons. Edwards was a learned student of the Enlightenment who argued that experiencing God's grace was essential to the full appreciation of the universe and its laws. Like his grandfather before him, he joyously preached about seeking redemption and salvation, soon noting that Northampton's inhabitants, both young and old, were now "full of love."

In 1741 Edwards delivered his best known sermon, "Sinners in the Hands of an Angry God." Preaching fervently, he reminded his listeners of the "manifold . . . abominations of your life," vividly picturing how each of them was "wallowing in sensual filthiness, as swine in mire." He also dangled his audience over "the abyss of *hell*" as a jarring reminder to place God at the center of human existence. Appealing to the senses more than to rational inquiry, Edwards felt, was the surest way to uplift individual lives, win souls for God, and improve society as a whole.

Such local revivals did not become broad and general until after the dynamic English preacher, George Whitefield (1714–1770), arrived in America. Whitefield was a disciple of John Wesley, the founder of the revival-oriented Methodist movement in England. Possessing a booming voice and charismatic presence, he preached with great simplicity, always stressing the essentials of God's "free gift" of grace for those seeking conversion. Even Benjamin Franklin, a confirmed skeptic, felt moved when Whitefield appeared in Philadelphia. He went to the meeting determined to give no money but relented in the end: Franklin confessed, "I emptied my pocket wholly into the collector's dish, gold and all."

Whitefield, known as the "grand itinerant," made seven preaching tours to the colonies, traveled thousands of miles, and delivered hundreds of sermons. Perhaps his most dramatic tour was to New England in the autumn of 1740. In Boston alone over 20,000 persons heard him preach in a three-day period. Concluding his tour in less than a month, Whitefield left behind churches full of congregants anxious to experience conversion and bask in the glow of their newfound fellowship with God.

The Awakening soon became a source of much contention, splitting America's religious community into **new** and **old light** camps. When in 1740 Gilbert

The Great Awakening, the religious revival that swept through the colonies in the mid-eighteenth century, swelled the ranks of many "New Light" denominations including the Baptists who founded the College of Rhode Island (later Brown University) in 1764.

Tennent preached his widely read sermon, "The Danger of an Unconverted Ministry," he expressed the feeling of many revivalists in advising their flocks of believers to shun clergymen who, although formally educated in theology, showed no visible signs of having gained God's saving grace. Thousands paid attention, and they started breaking away from congregations where ministers were suspect.

In response, Old Light clergymen, who at first rejoiced about having so many people return to the fold, began denouncing the Awakening as a fraudulent hoax being perpetrated by unlettered fools with no theological training. In New England ministers of the established Congregational church got their legislative assemblies to adopt anti-itinerancy laws, which barred traveling evangelists such as Whitefield and Tennent from preaching in their communities. The contention between Old Lights and New Lights became so heated in many New England towns that friends and neighbors, when not arguing, stopped speaking.

So much turmoil had significant long-term repercussions. Those feeling a new relationship with God were less willing to submit to established authority and more determined to speak out on behalf of basic liberties. Typical were colonists in New England who had started calling themselves Baptists. Under the resolute leadership of Isaac Backus, they demanded the right to separate completely from the established Congregational church, to which all citizens owed taxes, and the right to support their own ministers and churches. Theirs would be a long and hard-fought campaign to end state-supported religion.

The liberty to worship and support whatever church one pleased was a central outcome of the Awakening movement, as was a concern with the proper training of clergymen. Before the 1740s, the colonies had only three colleges: Harvard (1636), William and Mary (1693), and Yale (1701). In demanding toleration for diverse ideas, Presbyterian revivalists set up the College of New Jersey (1747, later Princeton), to train New Light clergymen; Baptists founded the College of Rhode Island (1764, later Brown); and the Dutch Reformed established Queen's College (1766, later Rutgers). In 1769 a New Light Congregational minister, Eleazar Wheelock, received a charter for Dartmouth College to carry the new-birth message to Native Americans. Only King's College (1757, later Columbia), founded by Anglicans, and the College of Philadelphia (1755, later the University of Pennsylvania) had no special interest in training New Light clergymen; but in recognizing growing religious pluralism, these two colleges regularly admitted students on a nonsectarian basis.

As the Great Awakening spread into the South, it had a variety of lasting effects. During the late 1740s and 1750s the Reverend Samuel Davies inspired the emergence of Presbyterian congregations in Virginia, thereby calling into question the authority of the established Anglican church. By the mid-1750s swelling numbers of Baptists were openly criticizing the mores of Virginia's planter elite. They started to demand, for example, the "entire banishment of *dancing, gaming,* and sabbath-day diversions."

Sometimes those in authority reacted viciously. A Virginia sheriff "violently jerked" a Baptist speaker off a platform and "beat his head against the ground" before administering "twenty lashes with his horse whip." The victim responded by returning to the stage and preaching even more vigorously "with a great deal of liberty." Persistence in the face of official hostility even led Awakening preachers to spread the gospel among the expanding slave population of the Chesapeake Bay region. This activity stimulated Protestant forms of worship among blacks, who did not forsake their African religious traditions but blended them with Christian faith in a savior who offered eternal life as well as hope for triumphing over oppression in their search for human freedom.

Throughout the British North American provinces, the Great Awakening caused its proponents to question established authority. It also provoked movement toward a clearer definition of fundamental human rights as well as a greater toleration of divergent ideas and the eventual acceptance of religious pluralism. These were hallmark legacies of the Awakening.

None of this came easily, and some of it—especially the emphasis on the search for personal liberty and freedom of conscience, along with the questioning of established authority—may have unwittingly helped prepare many colonists for the political rebellion against Great Britain that lay ahead. Historians have divided opinions on this subject, but most would agree that the Awakening demonstrated that American communities showed considerable strength and resiliency in weathering so much internal divisiveness—a sure sign that Britain's colonists had grown up and matured during the previous 100-year period.

International Wars Beset America

As the seventeenth century unfolded on the North American continent, Spain maintained its grip on Florida as well as on the Gulf coast. French Canadians, operating from bases in Montreal and Quebec, explored throughout the Great Lakes region and then down into the Mississippi Valley. In 1682 an expedition headed by René-Robert Cavelier, Sieur de La Salle, reached the mouth of the Mississippi River. La Salle, who dreamed of a mighty French empire west of the Appalachian Mountains, claimed the whole region for his monarch, Louis XIV.

La Salle's grand vision was ahead of its time. In 1699 the French located their first Louisiana country settlement at Biloxi, Mississippi. A second community soon sprang up on Mobile Bay (present-day Mobile, Alabama). Then in 1718 Jean Baptiste le Moyne, Sieur de Bienville, founded New Orleans, which be-

René-Robert Cavelier, Sieur de La Salle, claimed the whole of the Mississippi Valley for France. He inspired other French leaders with his dream of an empire encircling the British North American colonies.

came the French capital in the region. None of these posts contained a significant population, and they survived by developing close trading ties with various Indian nations.

The French monarchy, consumed by European affairs, did not actively encourage settlement in New France. As late as 1760, no more than 75,000 French subjects lived in all of Canada and the Mississippi Valley. Some farmed or fished, and others traded in furs. Because French numbers were so small, Native Americans did not fear losing ancient tribal lands to them. Solid relations with the Indians was an important advantage for the French, especially after European warfare spilled over into America. Having thousands of potential native allies willing to join in combat against the British colonists made the French a very dangerous foe in North America, as events proved during the imperial wars between 1689 and 1763.

Each of the four wars had a European as well as an American name. The first, the War of the League of Augsburg (1689–1697), known in the colonies as King William's War, was a limited conflict with no major battles in America. What made this war so frightening were bloody border raids—typical was the French and Indian attack on Hannah Dustan's Haverhill—that resulted in a total of about 650 deaths among the English colonists. The Treaty of Ryswick ended the contest without upsetting the balance of international power, since no major exchanges of territory occurred.

Five years later warfare erupted again when Louis XIV of France succeeded in placing his grandson, Philip of Anjou, on the Spanish throne. Other nations believed Louis intended to govern Spain himself, which they viewed as a serious threat to the European balance of power. What ensued was the War of the Spanish Succession (1702–1713), which the colonists called Queen Anne's War—named after the new English monarch Anne (reigned 1702–1714), another Protestant daughter of James II. This time, the British colonists found themselves dueling with Spain as well as France. The French and their native allies launched forays against frontier communities in New England. In 1702 South Carolinians assaulted the Spanish stronghold of St. Augustine, Florida, only to have to stave off a strong counterassault against Charleston four years later. In terms of casualties the war was not particularly bloody. The English colonists lost fewer than 500 persons over an 11-year period.

The peace settlement embodied in the Treaty of Utrecht was a virtual declaration of Britain's growing imperial might. The British realized major territorial gains, including Hudson Bay, Newfoundland, and Nova Scotia in Canada. In addition, they secured from Spain the strategically vital Rock of Gibraltar, guarding the entrance to the Mediterranean Sea, as well as the *Asiento*—a trading pact allowing the English to sell 4800 slaves annually in New Spain.

The scope of Britain's triumph, coming at the expense of its two major European rivals, deterred additional warfare for a quarter century, but further conflict seemed inevitable. In 1721 the Board of Trade urged the "enlarging and extending of the British settlements" in North America as "the most effectual means to prevent the growing power... of the French in those parts." Ten years later, board members called for the creation of a military colony in the buffer zone between South Carolina and Florida, and they talked of sending over convicted felons and other desperate persons to act as soldier-settlers.

General James Oglethorpe (1696–1785), a wealthy member of Parliament known for his "strong benevolence of soul," heard of these discussions and pursued the idea. A true philanthropist as well as imperialist, Oglethorpe hoped to roll back Spanish influence in America while improving the lot of England's downcast poor, especially imprisoned debtors. In 1732 King George II (reigned 1727–1760) issued a charter for Georgia, granting 21 trustees all the land between the Savannah and Altamaha rivers for 21 years to develop the region, after which the colony would revert to the Crown and function under royal authority.

Oglethorpe played on anti-Spanish sentiment, and large monetary donations poured in to under-

European Claims in North America, 1750

write the first settlements. Colonists, however, were hard to find, largely because of laws devised by Oglethorpe and the other trustees. To assure good order, they outlawed liquor. To promote personal industry and hard work as well as to spread out settlements in an effective defensive line, they limited individual grants to 500 acres, and they banned slavery. To guard against breaches in the settlement line, parcels of land could be passed only from father to son. Should no male heirs exist, grants would then revert to the trustees.

Those who did migrate to Georgia complained endlessly. Some wanted slaves; others, referring to Oglethorpe as "our perpetual dictator," called for a popular assembly; and they all demanded alcohol. The colony floundered as a social experiment to uplift the poor. The trustees admitted failure by turning Georgia back over to the Crown in 1752, a year ahead of schedule. By that time, they had already conceded on the issues of slavery and strong drink.

Thereafter, Georgia looked more and more like South Carolina, with large rice and indigo plantations sustaining the local economy. By 1770, the colony's populace was pushing toward 25,000, nearly half of whom were slaves.

The founding of Georgia angered the Spanish, as did England's cheating on the *Asiento* agreement, especially in relation to a clause that permitted only one English vessel a year to sell goods off the coast of Panama. The *one* turned into shiploads, involving reputed smugglers like Captain Robert Jenkins, whom the Spanish caught in 1731. As a warning to others, his captors cut off his ear. Seven years later Jenkins appeared before Parliament and held high the severed remains of his ear to affirm Spanish brutality. When asked to describe his feelings while facing mutilation, he boldly stated: "I commended my soul to God, and my cause to my country!"

Jenkins's testimony was part of an orchestrated campaign by powerful merchants in England to provoke anti-Spanish sentiment, with the hope of using cries for war to gain more trading rights in New Spain. In 1739 the War of Jenkins's Ear resulted. Then a dispute among rival European claimants over who belonged on the Austrian throne—male aspirants were upset by the rightful accession of Queen Maria Theresa—brought England and France to formal blows in the War of the Austrian Succession, which the colonists called King George's War (1744–1748).

In 1740, before the French became involved, James Oglethorpe mounted an unsuccessful expedition against Florida. In 1741 a combined British-colonial force attempted to capture the major Spanish port of Cartagena. The effort was a disaster, with three-fourths of the 3000 American troops dying from disease. Then in June 1745 a New England army achieved a brilliant victory against the French: After a lengthy siege some 4000 colonists under the command of William Pepperrell, a prominent merchant from Maine, captured the mighty fortress of Louisbourg, the so-called Gibraltar of the New World guarding the entrance to the St. Lawrence River. Here was a remarkable American victory, since the British offered only limited naval assistance.

The war cost the British colonists as many as 5000 lives, but the victory at Louisbourg represented the valued harvest of that sacrifice. In 1748 Britain approved the Treaty of Aix-la-Chapelle, a peace settlement that returned Louisbourg to the French in exchange for Madras, India, which the French had captured. The king's negotiators reasoned that Madras was of much greater value as a center for imperial trade—and expansion into other eastern markets—than a huge, non-income-producing fortress in the American wilderness. The colonists were furious about this decision, but they were powerless to do anything except complain among themselves about their subordinate—and unappreciated—status in the empire.

Showdown: The Great War for the Empire

The treaty of Aix-la-Chapelle really settled nothing. The three combatants were on a showdown course, and this time warfare would result from conflicting interests in America. In 1748 fur traders from Pennsylvania and Virginia began establishing contacts with natives in the Ohio River valley. The French, who had controlled the fur trade in that region, responded by warning all tribes to stop dealing with the land-hungry English who, as one French envoy stated, "are much less anxious to take away your peltries than to become masters of your lands."

TABLE 3.2
The Imperial Wars, 1689–1763

European Name	American Name	Dates	Peace Treaty
War of the League of Augsburg	King William's War	1689–1697	Ryswick
War of the Spanish Succession	Queen Anne's War	1702–1713	Utrecht
War of Jenkins's Ear		1739–1748	
War of the Austrian Succession	King George's War	1744–1748	Aix-la-Chapelle
Seven Years' War	French and Indian War*	1756–1763	Paris

*This term came into vogue when nineteenth-century historians first employed it. The colonists most often referred to this contest as "the war."

This observation was essentially correct. With the boom in colonial population, leading planters in Virginia were among those casting a covetous eye on the development of the Ohio valley. With the backing of London merchants one group formed the Ohio Company in 1747 and two years later secured a grant of 200,000 acres from the Crown. Should the company settle 200 families in the valley within seven years, its investors would receive a patent to an additional 300,000 acres.

Determined to secure the region against encroaching Anglo-American traders and land speculators, the French in the early 1750s started constructing a chain of forts in a line running southward from Lake Erie in western Pennsylvania. They decided to locate their principal fortress—and trading station—at the strategic point where the Monongahela and Allegheny rivers join to form the Ohio River (the site of modern-day Pittsburgh).

By 1753 the British ministry knew of these plans and ordered colonial governors to challenge the French advance and "repel force by force" if necessary. Virginia's Governor Robert Dinwiddie, an investor in the Ohio Company, acted quickly. He sent a young major of militia, 21-year-old **George Washington,** whose older half-brother Lawrence was also an Ohio Company investor, to northwestern Pennsylvania with a message to get out. Politely, the French declined.

In the spring of 1754 Washington led 200 Virginia soldiers toward the forks of the Ohio River and learned that the French were already there constructing Fort Duquesne. Foolishly, he skirmished with a French party, killing 10 and capturing 21. Washington then hastily retreated and constructed Fort Necessity, but a superior French and Indian force attacked on July 3. Facing extermination, Washington surrendered and signed articles of capitulation on July 4, 1754, which permitted him to lead his troops back to Virginia as prisoners of war. Out of these circumstances erupted a world war that cost France the whole of its North American empire.

At the very time (June 1754) that Washington was preparing to defend Fort Necessity, delegates from seven colonies had gathered in Albany, New York, to plan for their defense in case of war and to secure active support from the powerful Iroquois Confederacy. The Indian chiefs readily accepted 30 wagons loaded with gifts but did not promise to turn their warriors loose on the French. So as not to get caught on the losing side and face eviction from their ancient tribal lands in New York, the Iroquois assumed a posture of neutrality, waiting to see which side was winning the war. Some Senecas did fight for

This woodcut, displayed in the *Pennsylvania Gazette*, failed to overcome long-standing jealousies that thwarted attempts at intercolonial cooperation.

the French; but when the tide shifted in favor of the English after 1758, the Iroquois helped crush the French.

In other major business at the conference, delegates Benjamin Franklin and Thomas Hutchinson proposed an intercolonial plan of government, known as the Albany Plan of Union. The idea was to have a "grand council" made up of representatives from each colony who would meet with a "president general" appointed by the Crown to plan for defense, and even to tax the provinces on an equitable basis, in keeping the North American colonies secure from external enemies. The Plan of Union stirred little interest at the time, since the provincial assemblies were not anxious to share their prerogatives, especially that of taxation, with anyone. The plan's significance lay in its attempt to effect intercolonial cooperation against a common enemy—an important precedent for later years.

Leaders in England ignored the Albany Plan of Union, but the Fort Necessity debacle resulted in a fateful decision to send Major General Edward Braddock, an unimaginative 60-year-old officer who had never commanded troops in battle, to Virginia. Braddock arrived in February 1755 with two regiments of redcoats and orders to raise additional troops among the Americans. He eventually got his army of 3000 moving—Washington came along as a volunteer officer—toward Fort Duquesne. On July 9, about eight miles from the French fort, a much smaller French and Indian force nearly destroyed the British column, leaving two-thirds of Braddock's soldiers dead or wounded.

General Edward Braddock's failure to understand the nature of forest warfare and his underestimation of his opponents' abilities led to his disastrous defeat at Fort Duquesne. Braddock and his troops were ambushed by a force of French and Indian Warriors numbering less than half the size of the English group. The General was wounded in the attack and died three days later.

Washington, appalled by one of the worst defeats in British military history, spoke of being "most scandalously beaten by a trifling body of men." Braddock himself sustained mortal wounds; but before he died, he stated wryly: "We shall better know how to deal with them another time."

Braddock's defeat was an international embarrassment, yet King George II and his advisers hesitated to plunge into full-scale war. They knew the financial burden would be immense. Finally, a formal declaration of war came in May 1756. The Seven Years' War (1756–1763), later referred to in America as the French and Indian War, more accurately should be called "the great war for the empire." Certainly William Pitt (1708–1778), the king's new chief minister, viewed North America as the place "where England and Europe are to be fought for." Not a modest man, Pitt stated categorically that he alone could "save England and no one else can."

Pitt's strategic plan was straightforward. Letting King Frederick the Great of Prussia, Britain's ally, bear the brunt of warfare in Europe, Pitt placed the bulk of England's military resources in America with the intent of eradicating New France. He also advanced a group of talented young officers, such as General James Wolfe, over the heads of less capable men. His plans paid off in a series of carefully orchestrated military advances that saw Quebec fall in September 1759 to the forces of General Wolfe. Then in September 1760 with hardly an exchange of musket fire, Montreal surrendered to the army of General Jeffrey Amherst.

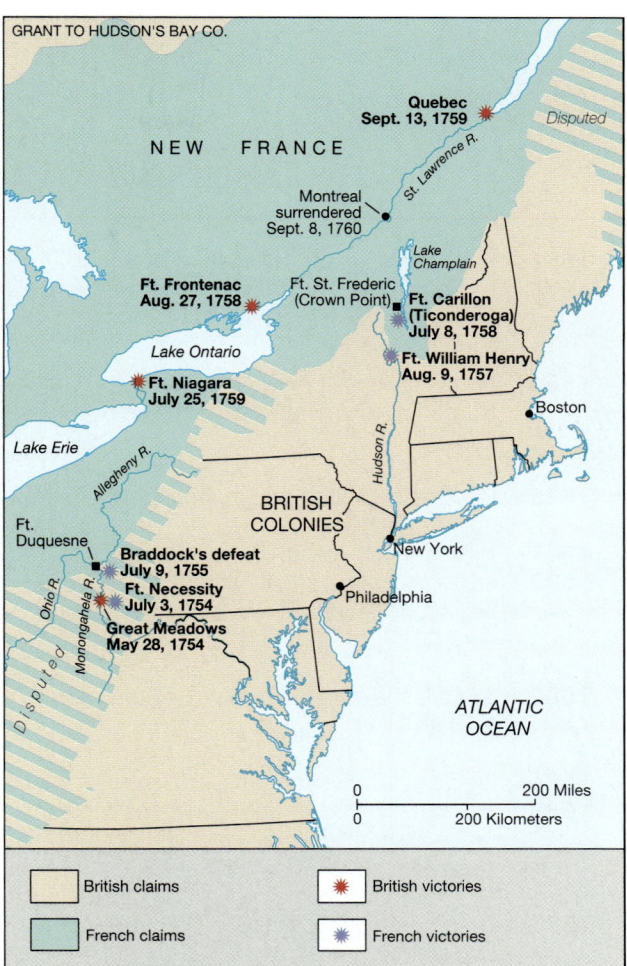

Significant Battles of the French and Indian War, 1756–1763

Allies as Enemies: Making War on the Cherokees

Unlike the Six Nations of Iroquois in New York, the four most powerful southern Indian nations—the Cherokees, Chickasaws, Choctaws, and Creeks—lacked unity of purpose when dealing with Europeans. The Choctaws, residing north and east of New Orleans, became heavily involved in trade with the French, who did not discourage them from engaging in warfare with the Chickasaws of northern Mississippi. The Creeks, who inhabited lands running north from Florida into central Alabama and western Georgia, successfully played off English, French, and Spanish trading interests in maintaining their territorial integrity. Sporadic warfare, however, denoted Creek relations with the Cherokees, whose territory encompassed the western portions of Virginia, North Carolina, and South Carolina as well as eastern Tennessee.

Chronology of Key Events

1651–1673	Parliament passes Navigation Acts to ensure that the colonies trade within the emerging English empire
1664	Dutch settlers in New Netherland surrender to the English, who rename the colony New York
1676	Bacon's Rebellion occurs in Virginia
1681–1682	William Penn founds Pennsylvania as a "holy experiment" in which diverse groups of people all live together homogeneously
1682	La Salle claims the Louisiana country for France
1684–1688	England revokes the Massachusetts Bay Colony charter and eliminates representative assemblies in all colonies east of New Jersey
1686	The Crown establishes the Dominion of New England
1688–1689	The English drive James II from the throne in the Glorious Revolution and replace him with William and Mary
1689	Massachusetts successfully rebels against the Dominion of New England; Leisler's Rebellion occurs in New York; Coode's uprising disrupts Maryland's government
1692	Witchcraft scare in Salem, Massachusetts, results in the execution of 20 women and men
1699	Parliament prohibits the export of woolen products from America
1733	Parliament passes the Molasses Act, which requires colonies to pay a high duty on molasses or rum imported from the foreign West Indies
1739–1740	George Whitefield begins preaching tours that turn local revivals into the Great Awakening
1749	Ohio Company obtains from the British government a 200,000-acre grant to western territory
1750	Parliament passes the Iron Act, which prohibits colonists from expanding the production of finished iron or steel products
1754	Albany Congress draws up a plan to unite the 13 colonies under a single government; George Washington defends Fort Necessity and helps to bring on the Seven Years' War
1759	British forces under General James Wolfe conquer Quebec; warfare erupts along the southern frontier between the Cherokee Nation and English settlers
1763	Treaty of Paris ends the Seven Years' War

At the time of the Seven Years' War, the Cherokees found themselves in a very vulnerable position. A devastating smallpox epidemic during the late 1730s had reduced their numbers by as much as 50 percent to about 10,000 persons. In seeking to restabilize themselves, the Cherokees drew closer to the English. They strengthened trading ties and generally ignored the ominous appearance of frontier settlers, among them many Scots-Irish, who were beginning to squat and farm in the easternmost portions of their tribal lands. After Braddock's defeat, the Cherokees even agreed to help fight the French, hoping in return to get lower prices for British trade goods along with increased supplies of gunpowder.

Then in 1758 a handful of Cherokee warriors coming home from service in the British ranks fell to fighting with western Virginia militiamen and settlers. Both sides lifted scalps, and two years of bloody combat ensued. The Cherokee War of 1759–1761 cost many lives and did not end until an expeditionary force of 2800 British regulars and frontier militiamen, accompanied by Indian support units, among them some Chickasaws, marched into the heart of Cherokee territory and destroyed at least 15 principal villages and hundreds of acres of crops. In the peace settlement that followed in December 1761, the Cherokees made land concessions along the eastern edge of their territory, based on the soon-to-be-broken promise that white settlers would not push beyond this boundary.

A determined people, the Cherokees eventually recovered from the devastation rained upon them in the midst of the Seven Years' War by their English allies. They would keep resisting, but in another seventy years they would have to accept, as would other Native Americans of the Southeast, resettlement in designated enclaves across the Mississippi River (see Chapter 10). Whether this long-term outcome would have been different had the southern nations found the means to rally together in some form of pan-Indian resistance movement will never be known.

Conclusion

The fall of the French empire in North America took place in the face of mounting antagonism between British military leaders and the colonists. Americans enlisted in provincial regiments and fought beside British redcoats, but most did not care for the experience. They found the king's regulars to be rough, crude, and morally delinquent. They viewed the king's officers as needlessly overbearing and aristocratic. They resented being treated as inferiors by the British.

Young George Washington explained how Virginia's recruits "behaved like men, and died like soldiers" during Braddock's defeat, as compared to the British regulars, who "behaved with more cowardice than it is possible to conceive." On the other hand, General James Wolfe later described provincial troops as "the dirtiest most contemptible cowardly dogs that you can conceive." The provincials, concluded another British officer, were a "naturally obstinate and ungovernable people, . . . utterly unacquainted with the nature of subordination in general."

The Americans were proud of their contributions to the triumphant British empire. They hoped the Crown would begin treating them with greater respect. Home government leaders, however, thought more like the British military officers in America. They believed that the colonists had done more to serve themselves than the British empire during the Seven Years' War. Because of so many problems related to the war, the Crown would soon prove to be less indulgent toward the "obstinate and ungovernable" American colonists.

Apparently the king's ministers had learned little from the previous 100 years of British-American history. Before 1690, when the laws by which the empire operated became too restrictive, colonial resistance ensued. After 1690, during the so-called era of salutary neglect, an accommodation of differences assured the Americans of basic rights and some local autonomy, so long as they supported the empire's economic and political objectives. Now more self-assertive than ever before, provincial Americans would once again resist imperial plans to make them more fully subordinate to the will of the parent nation. This time they would even challenge the bonds of empire.

Suggestions for Further Reading

Fred Anderson, *A People's Army: Massachusetts Soldiers and Society in the Seven Years' War* (1984). Prize-winning examination of colonists who went to war and came home disillusioned with the attitudes and values of their British comrades in arms.

Patricia U. Bonomi, *Under the Cope of Heaven: Religion, Society, and Politics in Colonial America* (1986). Balanced account of the Great Awakening in the framework of the firm commitment to religious beliefs among passing generations of English settlers.

John Demos, *The Unredeemed Captive: A Family Story from Early America* (1994). Fascinating study of a Puritan family captured by Indians during Queen Anne's War and one daughter's crossing of cultural boundaries by embracing the Mohawk way of life.

Carol F. Karlsen, *The Devil in the Shape of a Woman: Witchcraft in New England* (1987). Informative investigation that probes the meaning of witchcraft cases in assessing the constrained status of women in colonial society.

Douglas E. Leach, *Roots of Conflict: British Armed Forces and Colonial Americans, 1677–1763* (1986). Suggestive appraisal of the mounting mistrust between British regulars and American colonists that provoked imperial disunity pointing toward rebellion.

Philip D. Morgan, *Slave Counterpoint: Black Life and Culture in the Eighteenth-Century Chesapeake and Lowcountry* (1998). Thoroughly researched comparative study of the social, economic, and cultural interactions between black and white populations in Virginia and South Carolina.

Stephen S. Webb, *1676: The End of American Independence* (1984). Engaging analysis of Bacon's Rebellion, King Philip's War, and the long-term evolution of white-Indian and colonial-imperial relations.

Esmond Wright, *Franklin of Philadelphia* (1986). Highly readable biography about the amazingly talented Benjamin Franklin.

Overviews and Surveys

Wesley Frank Craven, *The Colonies in Transition, 1660–1713* (1968); Lawrence A. Cremin, *American Education, 1607–1783* (1970); John Morgan Dederer, *War in America to 1775: Before Yankee Doodle* (1990); John E. Ferling, *A Wilderness of Miseries: War and Warriors in Early America* (1980); Lawrence H. Gipson, *The British Empire Before the American Revolution*, 15 vols. (1936–1970); Jack P. Greene and J. R. Pole, eds., *Colonial British America* (1984), and Greene, *Peripheries and Center: Constitutional Development in the British Empire and the United States, 1607–1788* (1986); Richard Hofstadter, *America at 1750: A Social Portrait* (1971); Douglas E. Leach, *Arms for Empire: A Military History of the Colonies, 1607–1763* (1973); David S. Lovejoy, *Religious Enthusiasm in the New World* (1985); John J. McCusker and Russell R. Menard, *The Economy of British America, 1607–1789*, rev. ed. (1991); Alison G. Olson, *Anglo-American Politics, 1660–1775* (1973); Richard Slotkin, *Regeneration Through Violence: The Mythology of the American Frontier, 1600–1860* (1973); Gary M. Walton and James F. Shepherd, *The Economic Rise of Early America* (1979).

Designing England's North American Empire

Joyce O. Appleby, *Economic Thought and Ideology in Seventeenth-Century England* (1978); Thomas J. Condon, *New York Beginnings: The Commercial Origins of New Netherland* (1968); Wesley Frank Craven, *New Jersey and the English Colonization of North America* (1964); J. William Frost, *The Quaker Family in Colonial America* (1973); Joyce D. Goodfriend, *Before the Melting Pot: Society and Culture in New York City, 1664–1730* (1991); Joseph E. Illick, *Colonial Pennsylvania: A History* (1976); Michael Kammen, *Empire and Interest: The American Colonies and the Politics of Mercantilism* (1970); James T. Lemon, *The Best Poor Man's Country: A Geographical Study of Early Pennsylvania* (1972); Barry Levy, *Quakers and the American Family* (1988); Donna Merwick, *Possessing Albany, 1630–1710* (1990); Gary B. Nash, *Quakers and Politics: Pennsylvania, 1681–1726* (1968); Robert C. Ritchie, *The Duke's Province: Politics and Society in New York, 1660–1691* (1977); Sharon V. Salinger, *"To Serve Well and Faithfully": Labor and Indentured Servants in Pennsylvania, 1682–1800* (1987); Sally Schwartz, *"Mixed Multitude": The Struggle for Toleration in Colonial Pennsylvania* (1987); Jack M. Sosin, *English America and the Restoration Monarchy of Charles II* (1981); Stephen S. Webb, *The Governors-General: The English Army and the Definition of Empire, 1569–1681* (1979); Stephanie G. Wolf, *Urban Village: Germantown, Pennsylvania, 1683–1800* (1976); Arthur J. Worrall, *Quakers in the Colonial Northeast* (1980).

Defying the Imperial Will: Provincial Convulsions and Rebellions

Thomas J. Archdeacon, *New York City, 1664–1710: Conquest and Change* (1976); Paul Boyer and Stephen Nissenbaum, *Salem Possessed: The Social Origins of Witchcraft* (1974); Laurie Winn Carlson, *A Fever in Salem: The New England Witch Trials* (1999); Lois Green Carr and David W. Jordan, *Maryland's Revolution of Government, 1689–1692* (1974); John Putnam Demos, *Entertaining Satan: Witchcraft and the Culture of Early New England* (1982); Phillip S. Haffenden, *New England in the English Nation, 1689–1713* (1974); Chadwick Hansen, *Witchcraft at Salem* (1969); Peter Hoffer, *The Devil's Disciples: Makers of the Salem Witchcraft Trials* (1998); Richard R. Johnson, *Adjustment to Empire: The New England Colonies, 1675–1715* (1981); David S. Lovejoy, *The Glorious Revolution in America* (1972); Jerome R. Reich, *Leisler's Rebellion, 1664–1720* (1953); William L. Shea, *The Virginia Militia in the Seventeenth Century* (1983); Jack M. Sosin, *English America and the Revolution of 1688* (1982); Ian K. Steele, *The English Atlantic, 1675–1740: Communication and Community* (1986); Wilcomb E. Washburn, *The Governor and the Rebel: A History of Bacon's Rebellion* (1957).

Maturing Colonial Societies in Unsettled Times

Richard Aquila, *The Iroquois Restoration, 1701–1754* (1983); Bernard Bailyn, *The Origins of American Politics* (1968), *The Peopling of British North America* (1986), and *Voyagers to the West* (1986); Patricia U. Bonomi, *A Factious People: Politics and Society in Colonial New York* (1971), and *The Lord Cornbury Scandal: The Politics of Reputation in British America* (1998); J. M. Bumsted and John E. Van De Wetering, *What Must I Do to Be Saved? The Great Awakening* (1976); Richard L. Bushman, *From Puritan to Yankee: Character and the Social Order in Connecticut, 1690–1765* (1967), and *The Refinement of America: Persons, Houses, Cities* (1992); Kenneth Coleman, *Colonial Georgia: A History* (1976); Bruce C. Daniels, ed., *Power and Status: Officeholding in Colonial America* (1986); Robert J. Dinkin, *Voting in Provincial America, 1689–1776* (1977); A. Roger Ekirch, *Bound for America: The Transportation of British Convicts to the Colonies, 1718–1775* (1987); Edwin S. Gaustad, *The Great Awakening in New England* (1957); Jack P. Greene, *The Quest for Power: The Lower Houses of Assembly in the Southern Colonies, 1689–1776* (1963); Nathan O. Hatch and Harry S. Stout, eds., *Jonathan Edwards and the American Experience* (1988); Tom Hatley, *The Dividing Paths: Cherokees and South Carolinians Through the Revolution* (1993); Alan Heimert, *Religion and the American Mind: From the Great Awakening to the Revolution* (1966); James A. Henretta, *"Salutary Neglect": Colonial Administration Under the Duke of Newcastle* (1972); Christine Leigh Heyrman, *Commerce and Culture: The Maritime Communities of Massachusetts, 1690–1750* (1984); Rhys Isaac, *The Transformation of Virginia, 1740–1790* (1982); Francis Jennings, *Empire of Fortune: Crown, Colonies, and Tribes in the Seven Years' War* (1988); Stanley N. Katz, *Newcastle's New York, 1732–1753* (1968); Sung Bok Kim, *Landlord and Tenant in Colonial New York, 1664–1775* (1978); Frank Lambert, *Inventing the "Great Awakening"* (1999); Ned Landsman, *Scotland and Its First American Colony, 1683–1760* (1985); Henry F. May, *The Enlightenment in America* (1976); Richard Middleton, *The Bells of Victory: The Pitt-Newcastle Ministry and the Conduct of the Seven Years' War* (1985); Edmund S. Morgan, *Inventing the People: The Rise of Popular Sovereignty in England and America* (1988); Robert C. Newbold, *The Albany Congress* (1955); Howard H. Peckham, *The Colonial Wars, 1689–1762* (1964); William Pencak, *War, Politics, and Revolution in Massachusetts* (1981); William D. Piersen, *Black Yankees: Afro-American Subculture in Eighteenth-Century New England* (1988); J. R. Pole, *The Gift of Government: Political Responsibility from the Restoration to Independence* (1983); Thomas L. Purvis, *Proprietors, Patronage, and Money: New Jersey, 1703–1786* (1986); Alan Rogers, *Empire and Liberty: American Resistance to British Authority, 1755–1763* (1974); Harold E. Selesky, *War and Society in Colonial Connecticut* (1990); Timothy J. Shannon, *Indians and Colonists at the Crossroads of Empire: The Albany Congress of 1754* (2000); Mechal Sobel, *The World They Made Together: Black and White Values in Eighteenth-Century Virginia* (1987); Donna J. Spindel, *Crime and Society in North Carolina, 1663–1776* (1989); Carl E. Swanson, *Predators and Prizes: American Privateering and Imperial Warfare, 1739–1748* (1991);

James Titus, *The Old Dominion at War: Late Colonial Virginia* (1991); Alan Tully, *William Penn's Legacy: Pennsylvania, 1726–1755* (1977); Richard White, *The Middle Ground: Indians, Empires, and Republics in the Great Lakes Region, 1650–1815* (1991); Michael Zuckerman, *Peaceable Kingdoms: New England Towns in the Eighteenth Century* (1970).

Biographies

Elaine G. Breslaw, *Tituba, Reluctant Witch of Salem* (1996); Mary Maples Dunn, *William Penn: Politics and Conscience* (1967); Melvin B. Endy, Jr., *William Penn and Early Quakerism* (1973); Michael G. Hall, *Edward Randolph and the American Colonies* (1960), and *The Last American Puritan: Increase Mather, 1639–1723* (1988); Christopher M. Jedrey, *The World of John Cleaveland: Family and Community in New England* (1979); Paul E. Kopperman, *Braddock at the Monongahela* (1977); Franklin T. Lambert, *"Pedlar in Divinity": George Whitefield, 1737–1770* (1994); William G. McLoughlin, *Isaac Backus and the American Pietistic Tradition* (1967); Kenneth Silverman, *The Life and Times of Cotton Mather* (1984); Phinizy Spalding, *Oglethorpe in America* (1977); Patricia J. Tracy, *Jonathan Edwards, Pastor* (1980).

INTERNET RESOURCES

William Penn, Visionary Proprietor
http://xroads.virginia.edu/~CAP/PENN/pnhome.html
William Penn had an interesting life, and this site is a good introduction to the man and some of his achievements.

Witchcraft in Salem Village
http://etext.virginia.edu/salem/witchcraft/
Extensive archive of the 1692 trials and life in late seventeenth-century Massachusetts.

The Search for La Salle's Ship *La Belle*
http://www.thc.state.tx.us/Belle/index.html
This site covers the archaeological dig to recover the ship of one of America's famous early explorers.

Salem WitchcraftTrials (1692)
http://www.law.umkc.edu/faculty/projects/ftrials/salem/salem.htm
Images, chronology, court, and official documents from the University of Missouri—Kansas City Law School.

Colonial Documents
http://www.yale.edu/lawweb/avalon/18th.htm
The key documents of the Colonial Era are reproduced here, as are some of the important documents from earlier and later time periods in American History.

History Buff's Reference Library
http://www.historybuff.com/library/refseventeen.html
Brief journalistic essays on newspaper coverage of sixteenth- to eighteenth-century American history.

Benjamin Franklin Documentary History Web Site
http://www.english.udel.edu/lemay/franklin/
University of Delaware professor J. A. Leo LeMay tells the story of Franklin's varied life in seven parts on this intriguing site.

Jonathan Edwards
http://www.jonathanedwards.com/
Speeches by this famous minister of the Great Awakening are on this site.

The French and Indian War
http://digitalhistory.org
Digital History LTD provides extensive archives in this site, not intended for an exclusively academic audience.

The French and Indian War
http://web.syr.edu/~laroux/
This site is about French soldiers who came to New France between 1755 and 1760 to fight in the French and Indian War.

KEY TERMS

Mercantilism (p. 67)
Enumerated Goods (p. 68)
Navigation System (p. 68)
"Holy Experiment" (p. 71)
Salutary Neglect (p. 78)
Redemptioners (p. 79)
Enlightenment (p. 83)
Rationalism (p. 83)
Great Awakening (p. 86)
New Lights (p. 87)
Old Lights (p. 87)
George Washington (p. 92)

REVIEW QUESTIONS

1. Define *mercantilism* and trace its implementation in relation to England's North American colonies after 1650. Were the Navigation Acts a burden or a benefit to these colonies?

2. Compare and contrast the factors that led to the establishment of the Middle Colonies (New York, New Jersey, Pennsylvania, and Delaware) in relation to those that resulted in the founding of the New England and southern colonies. What were the most important differences and similarities?

3. What were the major reasons for the political and social upheavals in Virginia, Massachusetts, New York, and Maryland during the 1670s and 1680s? What impact did all of this turmoil have on the long-term development of the colonies?

4. What were the Enlightenment and the Great Awakening, and how did they affect colonial society, culture, and politics? How did these movements relate to the "Europeanizing" of the colonies?

5. Describe the ongoing military conflict among the British, French, and Spanish in the Americas from the 1690s through the 1750s. What competing interests were at stake, and why did the British ultimately emerge triumphant in 1763.

4

BREAKING THE BONDS OF EMPIRE, 1760–1775

PROVOKING AN IMPERIAL CRISIS
   A Legacy of War-Related Problems
   Getting Tough with the Americans
   Parliament Endorses Direct Taxes

"LIBERTY, PROPERTY, AND NO STAMPS"
   Emerging Patterns of Resistance
   Protest Takes a Violent Turn
   Resistance Spreads Across the Landscape
   Parliament Retreats

A SECOND CRISIS: THE TOWNSHEND DUTIES
   Formulating a New Taxation Scheme
   Mustering Further American Resistance
   A "Bloody Massacre" in Boston
   Parliament Backs Down Again

THE RUPTURING OF IMPERIAL RELATIONS
   The Necessity of Vigilance
   The Tea Crisis of 1773
   Parliament Adopts the Coercive Acts
   Hurling Back the Challenge: The First Continental Congress

"Truly the man of the Revolution"

Samuel Adams (shown here in an engraving by Paul Revere) believed that royalist leaders in Massachusetts wanted to destroy American liberties. He was an organizer of Boston's Sons of Liberty, a vigorous opponent of the Stamp Act, and eventually a leader in the movement for independence. Later he served as governor of Massachusetts.

Samuel Adams (1722–1803) was "truly the *man of the Revolution*," wrote Thomas Jefferson. In the port city of Boston, Massachusetts, Adams was the prime instigator of protest against the new wave of imperial policies adopted by King and Parliament after the Seven Years' War. He was an authentic popular leader, but he preferred to operate as anonymously as possible in guiding the resistance movement. Adams was by nature a secretive person who late in life destroyed many personal records relating to his revolutionary political activities. Perhaps he had something to hide.

"The great Mr. Adams," as one contemporary referred to him during the 1760s, had grown up with many advantages in life. His father, "Deacon" Samuel, was a prospering maltster (manufacturer of malt, a basic ingredient in beer and distilled spirits). The deacon wanted his son to become a Congregational minister, so he sent him off to Harvard College. In 1740 Samuel emerged with a bachelor's degree, a reputation for free spending and excessive drinking, for which he once paid a heavy fine, and little desire to become a clergyman. Always proud of his Puritan heritage, Adams remained a lifelong student of Scripture, but his primary career interest was politics.

The year 1740 turned out to be disastrous for Adams's father. As a community leader the deacon had become deeply involved in a plan to provide individuals with paper currency for local business transactions. The deacon and others established a "land bank" that would lend out money to persons who put up collateral in the form of real estate. The bank's paper money could then be used to purchase goods and services—and even pay debts as legal tender.

The directors of the Massachusetts Land Bank believed they were performing a public service. Wealthy merchants, however, thought otherwise. They viewed such paper currencies with great skepticism. Only money properly backed by **specie,** such as gold or silver, they argued, could hold its value in the marketplace. Under the leadership of a powerful local merchant, Thomas Hutchinson (1711–1780), they appealed to the royal governor, who declared the land bank illegal, a position sustained in 1741 by Parliament.

The crushing of the land bank cost Deacon Adams large sums of money that he had invested to help underwrite the venture. As a bank director, he became a defendant in lawsuits from others trying to regain funds. He never recovered financially. When the deacon died in 1748, he left his son a legacy of bitterness toward arbitrary royal authority and Crown favorites, such as Thomas Hutchinson, whose actions had ravaged his family's prosperity. In addition, the deacon left Samuel a bequest of lawsuits rather than a handsome patrimony.

Samuel Adams considered his father's ruin an instructive lesson in high-handed, oppressive government, a matter very much on his mind when he accepted an M.A. degree at Harvard's commencement in 1743. Although Samuel did not address those in attendance, his printed topic was "whether it be lawful to resist the supreme magistrate, if the commonwealth cannot be otherwise preserved?" Five years later he helped found a short-lived newspaper, the *Independent Advertiser,* in which he repeatedly warned his readers to be on guard against power-hungry royal officials, men under whose authority "our liberties must needs degenerate."

Having no desire to continue his father's business, Samuel barely kept his own family in food and clothing. What little income he earned came from a number of minor political offices. In 1746 he won election as a clerk of the Boston market; in 1753 he became town scavenger; and in 1756 he assumed duties as a collector of local taxes for the town government. He held the latter post until declining reelection in 1765. Samuel had no other choice, since he was £8000 behind in his tax collections and facing legal prosecution to produce the delinquent sum.

Samuel Adams had not taken the money for himself. He simply had not collected taxes from hard-pressed Bostonians who, like himself, were struggling to make ends meet. Adams regularly accepted any good explanation—the outbreak of illness in some families and the loss of jobs in others. Boston's economy was stagnant, and unskilled workers were especially hard pressed. As Adams was also aware, each time he did not enforce a collection he made a friend. By the early 1760s he had built up a loyal following of admirers who considered him a good and decent man committed to protecting their interests.

Even as he earned the gratitude of Boston's ordinary citizens, Adams did not lose sight of his adversaries. He particularly loathed Thomas Hutchinson, whose stature as a wealthy merchant with wide-ranging imperial connections had helped him gain a number of prominent offices. In 1758 Hutchinson secured a Crown appointment as the Bay Colony's lieutenant governor. He was already holding a local probate judgeship, was the ranking local militia officer, and was serving as an elected member of the governor's council (the upper house of the General Court). Then in 1760 Hutchinson received appointment to the post of chief judge of the superior court. His combined annual salary from these offices was around £400 sterling, ten times the amount of an average family's yearly income.

Samuel Adams worried about having so much power placed in the hands of one favored plural officeholder, especially Hutchinson, the very person he held most responsible for wrecking the land bank and his father's finances. In the days ahead when Hutchinson and other royal officials in Massachusetts tried to implement the new imperial policies, Adams was ready to protest and resist. His allies in the streets would be the ordinary people, and they set a particularly defiant example for the broader resistance movement throughout the 13 provinces. Whether Adams acted out of personal rancor toward Hutchinson or purely to defend American liberties was one of the secrets he carried to his grave, even as contemporaries remembered him both in Europe and America as "one of the prime movers of the late Revolution."

The outbreak of the American Revolution can be traced directly to the year 1763 when British leaders began to tighten the imperial reins. The colonists protested vigorously, and communications started to break down, so much so that a permanent rupture of political affections began to take place. No one in 1763 had any idea the developing crisis would shatter the bonds of empire. That, however, is exactly what took place when the American colonists, after a dozen years of bitter contention with their parent nation, finally proceeded to open rebellion in 1775.

PROVOKING AN IMPERIAL CRISIS

In 1763 British subjects everywhere toasted the Treaty of Paris which ended the Seven Years' War. The empire had gained territorial jurisdiction over French Canada and all territory east of the Mississippi River, except for a tiny strip of land around New Orleans that France deeded to Spain. The Spanish, in turn, who also took over French territory west of the Mississippi River, had to cede the Floridas to Britain to regain the Philippines and Cuba, the latter having fallen to a combined Anglo-American force in 1762. The British likewise made substantial gains in India. From the colonists' perspective, eradicating the French "menace" from North America was a cause for jubilation that should have signaled a new era of imperial harmony. Such was not to be the case.

A Legacy of War-Related Problems

For the chief ministers in Great Britain under the vigorous new monarch George III (reigned 1760–1820), who was 25 years old in 1763, the most pressing issue was Britain's national debt. During the Seven Years' War it had skyrocketed from £75 million to £137 million sterling. Annual interest payments on the debt amounted to £5 million alone. Advisers to the Crown worried about ways to get the debt under control, a most difficult problem considering the newly won territories that the home government now had to govern.

Closely linked to the debt issue was the question of American smuggling activity. Many colonial merchants, eager for profits of any kind, had traded illegally with the enemy during the war. Even though the Royal Navy had blockaded French and Spanish ports in the Caribbean, traders from New England

North America, 1763

With the signing of the Treaty of Paris, Great Britain received almost all of France's holdings in North America.

King George III, shown here in his coronation robes, was 22 when he acceded to the English throne in 1760.

and elsewhere used various pretexts to effect business deals. Some claimed to sail on missions of benevolence and exchanged prisoners of war to cover up illegal trading operations. These wily merchants and seamen carried more goods than prisoners, and the products they traded helped sustain the French and Spanish war efforts.

When chief war minister William Pitt, normally an advocate of American interests, learned in 1760 that 100 or more colonial vessels flying British flags were in the Spanish port of Montecristi, he sputtered with rage and ordered customs officers in North America to search inbound vessels with greater rigor. The minister was furious about such quasi-treasonous activity and was ready in 1763 to tighten controls on colonial commerce.

A host of issues relating to newly won territories to the north and west of the Anglo-American settlements also concerned the king's ministers. They especially worried about the financial burden of prolonged warfare on the frontier, should land-hungry white settlers keep pushing into Indian hunting grounds. The vacuum created by the end of French authority greatly concerned Native Americans. They had little reason to trust British traders and settlers. Trade goods, they soon found out, were suddenly more expensive in the absence of French competition. Furthermore, British officials hesitated to deal in firearms and gunpowder. Also aggravating relations were tribal suspicions that royal military officers had given them diseased blankets—taken from soldiers who had died of smallpox—during recent wartime parleys.

Native American prophets, among them Neolin, a Delaware Indian, started traveling among western tribes and arguing for resistance. Neolin urged a return to earlier tribal cultural practices and called for an alliance to drive the English from western forts. Pontiac, an Ottawa war chief who feared the loss of yet more land in the absence of French support, believed Neolin's words. He built a pan-Indian alliance that included Chippewas, Delawares, Hurons, Mingoes, Potawatomis, and Shawnees. Pontiac's initial targets were former French forts that the British now occupied and for which they refused to pay rents—as the French had regularly done in recognition of tribal ownership of the land.

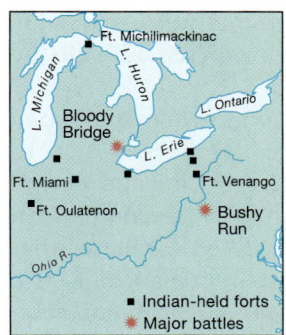

Pontiac's Rebellion

Pontiac, an Ottawa war chief, rebelled against white settlers who were moving onto tribal lands.

Beginning in May 1763, Pontiac's warriors struck with a vengeance at these posts, putting the major fortress at Detroit under heavy siege and attacking white settlements running in a southwesterly arc from New York through western Pennsylvania to Virginia. Only a severe drubbing at Bushy Run, Pennsylvania, in August 1763 turned the tide of bloody frontier warfare against the Indians. By autumn Pontiac's allies began drifting back to their villages, and they also lifted their siege of Detroit. When the final toll was taken, Pontiac's uprising had cost frontier white settlers some 2000 lives; a similar number of Native Americans died as well.

It fell to George Grenville (1712–1770), brother-in-law of William Pitt and a powerful leader in England, to solve these imperial problems. George III personally despised the humorless Grenville, but he needed the votes of Grenville's sizable following in Parliament, which was large enough to secure majorities for pressing legislative issues.

Grenville, who held strong anti-American feelings, became the king's chief minister in April 1763. In the common metaphor of the times, he viewed the provincials as spoiled children in need of a good spanking. As Grenville proclaimed before Parliament, "Great Britain protects America; America is bound to yield obedience." An ominous moment in British-American relations was at hand.

Getting Tough with the Americans

Grenville was not a rash man. A mercantilist in his thinking, he believed the colonists had forgotten their subordinate status in the empire. They needed to be reminded of their essential purpose, that of serving the parent nation. Having studied the issues carefully, Grenville struck hard on various fronts, leaving no doubt that a new era had dawned in Britain's administration of the American provinces.

Grenville made his first moves in early October 1763 through two administrative orders, each approved by the king's cabinet. The first, known as the Orders in Council of 1763, stationed British naval vessels in American waters with the intent of running down and seizing all colonial merchant ships suspected of illegal trading activity. Should juryless

This folk art painting depicts a well-to-do German farmer. The stock around his neck, his coat, and his walking stick all identify him with middle-class status.

Anderson, Elmer G. (American, active c. 1935). Pa. German Painted Wooden Box, c. 1937, watercolor and graphite on paper, .463 x .369 (18 1/4 x 14 1/2). Index of American Design, © 2000 Board of Trustees, National Gallery of Art, Washington.

vice-admiralty courts condemn these vessels on charges of smuggling, British naval captains and crews would share in profits from the public sales of both the erring colonial ships and their cargoes. The goal was to put an end to American smuggling while compelling the colonists to start paying more trade duties into royal coffers.

The second order, known as the Proclamation of 1763, dealt with the West. It addressed matters of government for the new British territories, including the temporary organization of such provinces as Quebec. It also mandated that a line be drawn from north to south along "the heads or sources of any of the rivers which fell into the Atlantic Ocean from the west and northwest." Deeply concerned by the news of Pontiac's uprising, the ministry's objective was to stop white incursions onto native lands. As such, territory west of the Proclamation line was forever to be "reserved to the Indians."

The Proclamation policy may have reflected some desire for humane treatment of Native Ameri-

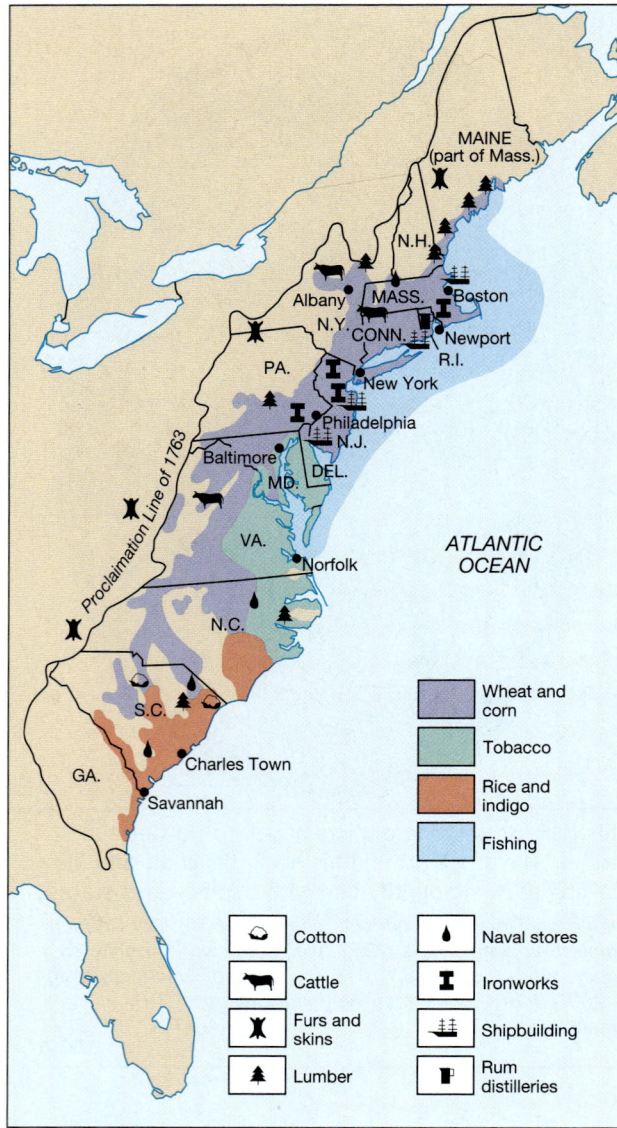

Colonial Products in the Mid-1700s

Proclamation policy determined that, at least initially, some of these redcoats would be ordered out onto the frontier.

The most critical matter was who would pay for these redcoats, an issue with the potential to provoke a serious imperial crisis if King and Parliament decided the colonists should assume that responsibility. Grenville had received estimates that the military force would cost at least £250,000 a year. Given the imposing home government debt, the chief minister soon went before Parliament with plans to tax His Majesty's subjects in America.

Grenville warmed to his task during 1764. He contacted the colonial agents who represented provincial interests in England and asked them for ideas about taxing the colonists. Not surprisingly, they had few thoughts. Nevertheless, fully intent on taxing the colonists, Grenville proceeded with Parliamentary legislation to do just that.

The Revenue Act of April 1764, usually called the Sugar Act, embodied a series of complex regulations relating to the loading and unloading of trading vessels. The purpose was to aid customs collectors in ferreting out smugglers. Even more important, the Sugar Act placed trade duties on a number of foreign goods—coffee, indigo, sugar, and wine—regularly purchased by the colonists. The bill also lowered the trade duty on foreign molasses from 6 to 3 pence per gallon (Parliament further reduced this duty to 1 penny in 1766.) The aim of revising downward the Molasses Act duty of 1733 (see p. 78) was to make the fee more collectible and to collect it—in contrast to the earlier period of lax enforcement.

Grenville projected initial annual revenue from the Sugar Act at £40,000. His stated objective was to help offset the costs of imperial administration, in this case only a portion of the sum needed to maintain British regulars in America. From the colonists' perspective, that was the problem with this legislation. The home government's purpose was something more than adopting slight trade duties that would adjust the flow of commerce in the imperial interest. In 1763, for instance, the colonists had paid only an estimated £1800 in imperial trade duties. (The Crown actually spent £8000 that year to operate the customs service in America.) A projected £40,000 in yearly revenue, by comparison, was a sure sign the home government intended to tax the Americans—and much more heavily than had ever been the case heretofore.

Taxation was what Grenville had most in mind; but he also had other concerns, as embodied in Parliament's passage in April of the Currency Act of 1764. This act represented an expansion of legislation directed against New England in 1751. Now the paper money of the colonial governments could no

cans; however, the cabinet's primary concern was to avoid costly Indian wars. Some cabinet leaders, furthermore, did not relish the prospect of American settlements spreading too far inland from the Atlantic coastline. If the colonists built communities across the mountains and out of the reach of the imperial trading network, they would of necessity begin manufacturing all sorts of products—and might, in time, compete with the British Isles for control of seaboard markets. From the imperial perspective, the parent nation's best interest lay in keeping the colonists on the eastern side of the Appalachian Mountains.

The Proclamation of 1763 also related to another policy decision of pivotal consequence. To keep control over both white settlers and Indians, the cabinet had already decided to garrison up to 10,000 British regulars in North America. Pontiac's uprising and the

longer be used as legal tender in payment of private debts. Nor could these governments issue any new paper bills, and the Crown expected them to retire what money they had in circulation within a reasonable time frame.

The logic behind this act was little different than that of wealthy merchants like Thomas Hutchinson when he denounced the Massachusetts Land Bank of 1740. Paper currencies could be highly inflationary, and wealthy creditors were invariably peevish about having to accept depreciated local money for debts. They only wanted to deal in hard coin. In 1764, unfortunately, the colonies were in the midst of a severe postwar depression. Reducing the provincial money supply only worsened conditions by forcing colonists to scramble in obtaining money to conduct business—let alone pay increased taxes. If nothing else, the timing of the Currency Act was terrible; it made the Crown appear incredibly insensitive about promoting the economic welfare of the colonies.

Parliament Endorses Direct Taxes

George Grenville was indifferent about the opinions of the colonists. His major goal was to raise a substantial tax revenue in the colonies. He finally got what he wanted with the Stamp Act of March 1765, the capstone of his imperial program. Through the Stamp Act, Parliament asserted for the first time ever its full authority to lay *direct* taxes, as opposed to *indirect* (or hidden taxes, such as trade duties) on the colonists.

The Stamp Act was not very subtle. To take effect on November 1, 1765, this legislation required Americans to pay for stamps attached to some 50 items, everything from newspapers, pamphlets, almanacs, and playing cards to port clearance papers for ships, land deeds, wills, and college diplomas. The price of the stamps varied according to the value of the particular items. Grenville estimated the tax would yield about £100,000 per year. All stamps would have to be paid for in hard currency, a virtual impossibility since specie (hard money) continually flowed to Britain to pay for imported goods. Also, violators could be prosecuted in juryless vice-admiralty courts, as well as in regular criminal courts.

George Grenville knew the colonists would not like the Stamp Act, but he justified the plan by declaring that "the [parent] nation has run itself into an immense debt to give them protection." The time had come for Americans to pay for the benefits of being part of the mightiest empire in the western world. Grenville was not asking the colonists to help reduce the home debt, only to assist in meeting the actual costs of imperial administration. For that reason, Parliament earmarked Stamp Act revenues for maintaining the redcoats in America.

Grenville used three lines of reasoning in arguing for the Stamp Act. First, citizens in England had been paying stamp taxes for years. Second, the colonial public debt amounted to only £2.6 million, as compared to £137 million in England. On a per capita basis, each person living in Britain owed approximately 20 times as much as each American (£18 as compared to 18 shillings). With such a light per capita public debt load, the colonists could afford a heavier tax burden. Third, to counter arguments about taxation without representation, Grenville employed the concept of **virtual representation.** He maintained that all English subjects, regardless of where they resided in the empire, enjoyed representation in Parliament. His assertion was that members of Parliament (M.P.s), when they made legislative decisions, did not just represent particular constituents at home but every imperial subject, including all colonial Americans.

Testaments to virtual representation found favor in Parliament, where little pro-American sentiment existed, but proved unconvincing to the colonists. Grenville's thinking, moreover, did not encompass the whole picture. From an economic point of view, if from no other, the colonies were invaluable to the British empire. The provinces so stimulated the home economy, particularly with regard to buying manufactured goods, that a serious trade deficit had developed for the colonists. They had gotten into the habit of importing much more from the British Isles than they exported in return. The trade deficit amounted to £1.6 million for the year 1760. By the early 1770s provincial Americans owed more than £4 million to English and Scottish creditors. This was a major reason that hard money was so difficult to come by in America. It was being drained off constantly to pay these debts.

By only looking at specific governmental costs, Grenville had missed an essential point. Provincial subjects were not just taking from the empire; they also provided a ready, indeed, captive market for British-manufactured commodities. In this sense the Americans were paying a significant price, as measured by the trade deficit, in support of the parent nation.

A few members of Parliament appreciated the inherent value of the provinces and did not think of the colonists as overindulged children. Colonel Isaac Barré, who had served under General James Wolfe at Quebec, was one such person. "They grew by your neglect of them," he stated sharply during the Stamp Act debates in Parliament. Now, the tightening imperial grip would cause "the blood of those *sons of liberty* to recoil within them. . . . And remember I this day told you so, that same spirit of freedom which actuated that people at first, will accompany them still." Barré's words were prophetic. The Stamp Act would truly arouse the Americans.

"LIBERTY, PROPERTY, AND NO STAMPS"

Certainly the colonists were not plotting independence in 1763. They were proud to be subjects of the far-flung British empire, stretching as it did from India in the East across the globe to some 30 American colonies in the West, including such Caribbean islands as Barbados and Jamaica. With the elimination of the French threat in North America, mainland colonists were also experiencing a buoyant new sensation of freedom. Paradoxically, the toughened imperial program came at the very time when the colonists, now needing much less government protection from across the ocean, hoped for a continuation if not expansion of the local autonomy to which they had become accustomed. Psychologically, they were ready for anything but new imperial constraints on their lives.

Emerging Patterns of Resistance

As the Grenville program took shape, the colonists evidenced various emotions. Dismay gave way to disappointment and anger. Initial reactions involved petitioning King and Parliament for a redress of grievances. By the summer of 1765 colonial protest took an extralegal turn as Americans resorted to such tactics of resistance as crowd intimidation and violence, economic boycott, and outright defiance of imperial law. The colonists did not think of themselves as Britain's children. Through their tactics of resistance they were asking to be treated more like adults. Few British officials, however, comprehended this message.

The first statements of protest were quite mild, expressed in a flurry of petitions and pamphlets that laid out an American position with respect to essential political rights. In reaction to the Sugar Act of 1764, Stephen Hopkins of Rhode Island expressed the sentiments of many in his widely read pamphlet, *The Rights of Colonies Examined*. He stated that "British subjects are governed only agreeable to laws to which [they] themselves have [in] some way consented." Hopkins then warned his fellow colonists: "Those who are governed at the will ... of others, and whose property may be taken from them by taxes, or otherwise, without their own consent, and against their will, are in the miserable condition of slaves." Hopkins's words may be summarized in the phrase "no taxation without representation"—the core argument against Parliamentary taxation.

In many ways protest by pamphlet and petition was so mild in tone during 1764 that George Grenville did not hesitate to argue for more comprehensive taxation plans. The intensity of American ill feeling in reaction to the Stamp Act thus shocked the home government.

First news of the Stamp Act arrived in the provinces during April 1765, which left ample time to organize resistance before its November 1 effective date. Colonial protest soon became very turbulent, with Samuel Adams's Boston taking the lead in the use of more confrontational forms of resistance.

In Massachusetts, as in many other provinces, a small number of royal officials enjoyed the parent nation's political patronage. This group held the most prominent offices in colonial government, and they were known as the "royalist" or "court" political faction. Besides Lieutenant Governor and Chief Justice Thomas Hutchinson, other leading members of the royalist faction were Governor Francis Bernard, Secretary and Councilor Andrew Oliver, and Associate Justice and Councilor Peter Oliver (Andrew's younger brother). Hutchinson and the Oliver brothers were natives of New England and had all graduated from Harvard College. They were interrelated by marriage, and they were among the wealthiest citizens in America.

Even though these gentlemen were at the apex of provincial society, their opponents in the "popular" or "country" faction did not defer to them. Besides Samuel Adams, another local leader, the brilliant

---

The Stamp Act, which required Americans to purchase stamps for everything from playing cards to marriage licenses, provoked intense colonial protest. Some newspaper printers expressed their outrage by using a skull and crossbones to mark the spot where the stamp was to be embossed, as shown here in the October 31, 1765, issue of the *Pennsylvania Journal* and *Weekly Advertiser*.

Thomas Hutchinson was key leader of the royalist political faction in Massachusetts.

lawyer James Otis, Jr., viewed the likes of Hutchinson and the Oliver brothers with contempt. In 1760 when Bernard became governor and appointed Hutchinson to the chief judgeship, he ignored the claims of assembly speaker James Otis, Sr., who had been promised this post by an earlier governor. Enraged by Bernard's slight to his father, Otis stated that he would "kindle such a fire in the province as shall singe the governor, though I myself perish in the flames."

Otis was soon speaking out on behalf of American rights and against royal appointees charged with enforcing imperial laws in Massachusetts. Before the end of 1760, for instance, customs collectors in the Bay Colony had started to use blanket search warrants, known as **writs of assistance,** to catch suspected smugglers, particularly those rumored to be trading with the enemy. The writs did not require any form of prior evidence to justify searches; as such, many respected attorneys in England questioned their legality, since they violated the fundamentals of due process in cases of search and seizure.

In 1761 on behalf of merchants in Boston, some number of whom were certainly smugglers, Otis argued against the writs in a well-publicized case before the Massachusetts superior court. Chief Justice Hutchinson ruled in favor of the writs, politely explaining how they were also then in use in England.

In turn, Otis declared that the power of King and Parliament had specified boundaries, implying that only tyrants would uphold the use of writs.

Otis and the merchants may have lost, but they had put Hutchinson in an embarrassing position. They portrayed him as a person blinded to the protection of fundamental legal rights because of his insatiable lust for offices and power. Unfortunately for Otis, he would in a few years lose his mental stability. As a consequence, after the mid-1760s Samuel Adams assumed overall leadership of the popular rights faction in Massachusetts politics.

Adams won his first term to the Assembly in 1765 as a representative from Boston. The emerging Stamp Act crisis gave him an opportunity to launch a simultaneous attack on both unacceptable imperial policies and his old political adversaries. The combined assault commenced in August 1765, shortly after citizens learned that none other than Andrew Oliver was the Bay Colony's proposed Stamp Act distributor.

Protest Takes a Violent Turn

Samuel Adams did not participate directly in crowd actions, nor did the informal popular rights governing body, known as the **Loyal Nine.** (Adams and Otis were not members of this group but were the principal guides in directing the politics of defiance.) The Loyal Nine communicated specific protest plans to men like Ebenezer Mackintosh, a shoemaker living in the South End of town, and Henry Swift, a cobbler from the North End. Before 1765 these two craft workers were leaders of "leather apron" gangs (workers' associations) from their respective districts. The North End and South End gangs, as the "better sort" of citizens called them, were in reality fraternal organizations providing fellowship for artisans, apprentices, and day laborers.

Each year these leather apron workers looked forward to November 5, known as Pope's Day—referring to an alleged plot in 1605 by Guy Fawkes, a Roman Catholic, to blow up Parliament. November 5 was a traditional anti-Catholic holiday during which leaders like Swift and Mackintosh, holding high crude effigies of the devil and the pope, led throngs of North and South End workers in a march through the streets. These working people vented their anti-Catholic emotions and their fears of satanic influences as they marched; they also readied themselves for the annual fistfight that invariably took place after the two groups converged on the center of Boston. The fighting was so vicious in 1764 that at least one person died.

During the summer of 1765 Samuel Adams and the Loyal Nine convinced the North and South End associators to stop fighting among themselves and to unite in defense of essential political liberties. This juncture proved a critical step in ending any attempted implementation of the Stamp Act in Massachusetts.

On the morning of August 14, 1765, the local populace awoke to find an effigy of Peter Oliver (and a boot, representing Lord Bute, Grenville's predecessor) hanging in an elm tree—later called the Liberty Tree—in the South End of Boston. An appalled Governor Bernard demanded removal of the figures; but no one touched them, knowing they were under the protection of the associators—in time called the Sons of Liberty. That evening Ebenezer Mackintosh, who soon gained the title "Captain General of Liberty Tree," solemnly removed the effigies and exhorted the thousands of Bostonians present to join in a march through the streets. Holding the effigies high on a staff, Mackintosh and Swift led what was an orderly procession. As they marched, the people shouted: "Liberty, Property, and No Stamps."

The crowd worked its way to the dockyards, where the Sons of Liberty ripped apart a warehouse recently constructed by Andrew Oliver. Rumor had it that Oliver intended to store his quota of stamps there. Next, the crowd moved toward Oliver's stately home, which the family had fled. Some of the Sons of Liberty tore up the fence, ransacked the first floor, and imbibed from the well-stocked wine cellar. Others gathered on a hill behind the Oliver residence. Materials from Oliver's warehouse as well as his wooden fence provided kindling for a huge bonfire that ultimately consumed the effigies even as the working men and women of Boston cheered enthusiastically. This crucial crowd action was over by midnight.

Early the next morning, as Hutchinson later wrote, the thoroughly intimidated Oliver "despairing of protection, and finding his family in terror and distress, ... came to the sudden resolution to resign his office before another night." Mackintosh's crowd, rather than Crown officials, now were in control of Boston. After this action of August 14, moreover, no one thought at all about assuming Oliver's stamp distributorship. Intimidating threats and selective property destruction had preserved the interests of the community over those of the Crown.

Had Boston's Sons of Liberty and their leaders been solely concerned with rendering the Stamp Act unenforceable, they would have ceased their rioting after Oliver's resignation; however, they had other accounts to settle. A misleading rumor began circulating through the streets, claiming that Thomas Hutchinson was very much in favor of the Stamp Act, indeed had even helped write the tax plan. As a result, the Sons of Liberty appeared again on the evening of August 26. After a few other intimidating stops, the crowd descended upon Hutchinson's opulent home, one of the most magnificent in the province. They ripped it apart. As the lieutenant governor later described the scene, "they continued their possession until daylight" and "demolished every part of it, except for walls, as lay in their power."

Who started the rumor remains a moot point, but Hutchinson's political enemies were well known. Further, some Bostonians may have vented their frustrations with the depressed local economy by ransacking the property of a well-placed person with key imperial connections who was prospering during difficult times. Whatever the explanation, royal author-

Crowds protesting imperial policies—in this case burning tax officials in effigy—were normally made up of ordinary citizens, particularly the working poor.

ity in the Bay Colony had suffered another setback. The looming threat of crowd violence gave Samuel Adams and his popular rights faction a powerful presence that Hutchinson and other royalist officials never overcame.

Resistance Spreads Across the Landscape

By rendering the office of stamp distributor powerless, Boston had established a prototype for resistance. Colonists elsewhere were quick to act. Before the end of the month Augustus Johnston, Rhode Island's stamp distributor-designate, had been cowed into submission. In September Maryland's distributor, Zachariah Hood, not only resigned but fled the province after a crowd destroyed his home. Jared Ingersoll was the victim in Connecticut. The local Sons of Liberty met him on the road to Hartford, surrounded him, and demanded his resignation. They then rode with him to Hartford where the staid Ingersoll renounced the office in public, threw his periwig in the air, and cheered for liberty—to the delight of a menacing crowd. By November 1 virtually no one was foolish or bold enough to distribute stamps in America. Only Georgians experienced a short-lived implementation of the despised tax.

While the colonists employed intimidation and violence, they also petitioned King and Parliament. Assembly after assembly prepared remonstrances stating that taxation without representation was a fundamental violation of the rights of English subjects. Patrick Henry, a young and aggressive backcountry Virginia lawyer, had a profound influence on these official petitions. Henry first appeared in the Virginia House of Burgesses (lower house of the Assembly) in mid-May 1765. The session, meeting in Williamsburg, was coming to a close. Only a handful of burgesses were still present when Henry proposed seven resolutions. They endorsed the first four, which reiterated the no taxation without representation theme, but rejected the fifth as too categorical a denial of Parliament's authority. Henry did not bother to present his remaining two resolutions.

Some newspapers in other provinces reprinted all seven resolutions. The fifth stated that the Virginia Assembly held "the only exclusive right and power to lay taxes and impositions upon the inhabitants of this colony." The sixth asserted that Virginians were "not bound to yield obedience to any law" not approved by their own assembly. The seventh indicated that anyone thinking otherwise would "be deemed an enemy by His Majesty's colony."

Patrick Henry first served in the Virginia House of Burgesses in May 1765 and presented a series of resolutions condemning the Stamp Act.

These three resolutions read as if the Virginia burgesses had denied King and Parliament all legislative power over the American provinces. They seemed to advocate some form of dual sovereignty in which the American assemblies held final authority over legislative matters in America—comparable in scope to Parliament's authority over the British Isles. This was a radical concept, indeed too radical for the Virginia burgesses. Still, the reprinting of all seven of the Virginia Resolutions, as they came to be known, encouraged other assemblies to prepare strongly worded petitions during the summer and fall of 1765.

An important example of intercolonial unity, also bearing on the petitioning process, was the **Stamp Act Congress,** held in New York City during October 1765. At the urging of James Otis, Jr., the Massachusetts General Court called for an intercolonial congress to draft a joint statement of grievances. Nine colonies responded, and 27 delegates appeared in New York.

The delegates to the Stamp Act Congress were mostly cautious gentlemen from the upper ranks of society. Their "declarations" on behalf of American rights had a far more conciliatory tone than the Virginia Resolutions. They attested to "all due subordination to that august body, the Parliament of Great Britain." Since "from their local circumstances" Americans could not easily be represented in Parliament, the only way to protect "all the inherent rights and liberties" of the colonists was for Parliament to relinquish its right of taxation, more or less on a permanent basis, to the provincial assemblies. With these words the congress disbanded, having shown that leaders from different colonies could meet together and agree on common principles. The congress also suggested that unified resistance was possible, should events necessitate further intercolonial actions.

Another, more telling blow to the Stamp Act was a widespread economic boycott. Merchants in New York City were the first to act. On October 31 they pledged not to order "goods or merchandise of any nature, kind, or quality whatsoever, usually imported from Great Britain, . . . unless the Stamp Act be repealed." Within a month merchants in the other principal port cities, including Boston and Philadelphia, drafted similar agreements.

On November 1, 1765, commerce in the colonies came to a halt. Trading vessels remained in ports because no stamped clearance papers could be obtained. Courts ceased functioning, since so many legal documents required stamps. Newspapers stopped publication, at least temporarily. For all of their bravado the Americans really did not want to defy the law. As November gave way to December, however, popular leaders began to apply various forms of pressure on more timid citizens. By the beginning of 1766 colonial business and legal activity started returning to normal, and newspaper editors commenced printing again—all in open defiance of the Stamp Act.

George Grenville had grossly miscalculated. Not willing to be treated as errant children, the colonists, in defending their liberties, sent petitions to Parliament, intimidated and harassed royal officials, destroyed property, cut off the importation of British goods, and, finally, openly defied the law. Americans hoped for a return to the old days of salutary neglect, but they could not be sure whether the king's ministers would back down in the face of such determined resistance.

Parliament Retreats

Instability in the British cabinet, as much as American protest, helped bring about repeal of the Stamp Act. George III had never liked Grenville. In July 1765 the king asked him to step aside in favor of the Marquis of Rockingham, who was more sympathetic toward the Americans. Rockingham's political coalition was brittle, and his term as chief minister lasted just long enough to bring about repeal of the Stamp Act.

Looking for political allies, Rockingham took advantage of pressure from English traders and manufacturers who were extremely worried about the American boycott. He also linked arms with William Pitt, England's most influential politician. Pitt was eloquent in the repeal debates before Parliament. He exhorted his fellow M.P.s to recognize the colonists as "subjects of this kingdom equally entitled . . . to all

In this political cartoon, mournful political leaders in England carry the dead Stamp Act to its grave after its repeal in 1766.

the natural rights of mankind and peculiar privileges of Englishmen." The M.P.s listened and in March 1766 repealed the Stamp Act.

Home government leaders had by no means accepted colonial arguments. They insisted on a face-saving statement designed to make sure everyone understood that King and Parliament were the supreme legislative voices of the empire. In conjunction with rescinding the Stamp Act, the M.P.s approved the Declaratory Act, which denied the claims of American assemblies to "the sole and exclusive right of imposing duties and taxes... in the colonies." The Declaratory Act forcefully asserted that Parliament had "full power and authority to make laws and statutes..., *in all cases whatsoever*." Repealing the Stamp Act had been only for the sake of imperial harmony; Parliament still had the right to tax all British subjects anytime it chose. The M.P.s had stated their position—and in terms at odds with the stance taken by the Americans.

A SECOND CRISIS: THE TOWNSHEND DUTIES

What everyone needed in 1766 was an extended cooling-off period, but that was not to happen. The Rockingham ministry, which might well have left the colonists alone, collapsed in the summer of 1766. George III called for a new cabinet. He wanted William Pitt to become his chief minister. In poor health, Pitt agreed to organize a ministry in return for peerage status as the Earl of Chatham. He retired to the House of Lords, letting others provide for legislation in the House of Commons. One man in particular, Chancellor of the Exchequer Charles Townshend (1725–1767), sometimes called "Champagne Charlie" because of his penchant for that bubbly drink, charged into the leadership void. To the amazement of many, Townshend proclaimed that he knew how to tax the colonists. The result was the ill-advised Townshend Duties of 1767.

Formulating a New Taxation Scheme

Benjamin Franklin, who was in England serving as an agent for various colonies, inadvertently helped formulate Townshend's plan. In a lengthy interview before Parliament during the repeal debates, Franklin, who was out of touch with American sentiment, stated emphatically that the colonists only objected to *direct* or "internal" taxes, such as those embodied in the Stamp Act. They did not object, he claimed, to *indirect* or "external" taxes, which may be defined as duties placed on trade goods for the purpose of obtaining imperial revenue. Pointing out that Franklin was the most respected of all American colonists, Townshend seized on this distinction as the basis for his taxation plan.

Townshend believed the Americans had to be taxed, if for no other reason than to establish once and for all the indivisible sovereignty of King and Parliament. In June 1767 Parliament agreed by authorizing the Townshend Duties, which were nothing more than import duties on a short list of trade items: British-manufactured glass, paper and lead products, painters' colors, and a three-pence-a-pound duty on tea. Townshend declared that his plan would net the Crown £35,000 to £40,000 per year. In time, once the colonists got used to paying the duties, the list of taxable products could be lengthened. Meanwhile, the revenue would help defray the costs of royal governments in America.

At first, it appeared that Townshend knew what he was doing. His scheme was subtle and generated very little colonial opposition. Except for tea, the duties were on luxury items, rarely used by the majority of colonists. The tea tax could be evaded by opening illicit trading connections with Dutch tea merchants—and Americans were still quite adept at the art of smuggling.

Mustering Further American Resistance

Late in the year John Dickinson, a landholder and lawyer residing in the area of Philadelphia, began publishing a series of newspaper essays, soon thereafter printed as a pamphlet entitled *Letters from a Farmer in Pennsylvania*. Dickinson assailed Townshend's logic. The colonists, he pointed out, had not distinguished between internal and external taxes. Certainly they had long accepted duties designed "to regulate trade" and facilitate the flow of imperial commerce. However, they now faced trade duties "for the single purpose" of raising revenue. Taxes disguised as trade duties, warned a suspicious Dickinson, were "a most dangerous innovation," having the potential to turn the colonists into "abject slaves." Yet Dickinson, a man of considerable wealth who feared the destructive potential of violent crowds, urged moderation in resistance; he called for the colonial assemblies merely to petition Parliament, hoping the M.P.s would listen to reason.

In February 1768 the Massachusetts General Court, at the prompting of Samuel Adams, sent a Circular Letter to the other assemblies with arguments

THE American Mosaic

Those Hated Customs Informers

BENEDICT Arnold, who later became famous for turning against the American cause of liberty, was a prospering merchant in New Haven, Connecticut, before the Revolution. One of Arnold's trading vessels returned from the West Indies during January 1766 and managed to unload its cargo of rum and molasses without paying the required trade duties. Like hundreds of other colonial merchants, Arnold thought nothing of evading imperial customs collectors in American port towns. The economy was depressed, and many merchants were struggling to avoid bankruptcy. In addition, many argued that not paying duties at a time when the colonists were demanding repeal of the Stamp Act was a justifiable form of protest against the willfulness of the home government.

In attempting to stop colonial smuggling, British customs officers were in regular contact with informers, or local inhabitants who listened for rumors in the streets and secretly provided evidence about merchants evading the law. Informers expected cash payments for their services, and if vice-admiralty courts ruled against an offending merchant, informers sometimes shared in profits gained from the sale of confiscated cargoes. To be an informer could be lucrative, but it also assured the wrath of local citizens, should colonists caught smuggling find out who had broken the unwritten law of noncooperation with customs collectors.

Peter Boles was a seaman in the employ of Benedict Arnold who had helped to unload the smuggled cargo. Late in January he approached Arnold and asked for extra wages, implying that the money would help keep him quiet. Arnold responded tersely that he did not hand out bribes. Boles went straight to the New Haven customs office. The chief collector was not there, so the informer announced his intention to return later with important information.

When Arnold learned of Boles's action, he sought out the mariner, "gave him a little chastisement," and told him to get out of New Haven. Boles agreed to leave, but two days later he was still in town. Arnold, now backed by a number of seamen, confronted Boles at a local tavern and forced him to sign a prepared confession. "Being instigated by the devil," Boles acknowledged that "I justly deserve a halter for my malicious and cruel intentions." He also promised "never to enter the same [town] again."

Four hours later, at 11 P.M., Boles was still tippling at the tavern. This time Arnold returned with yet more followers. The party grabbed Boles and dragged the informer to the town's whipping post, where he "received forty lashes with a small cord, and was conducted out of town." Peter Boles was not heard from again.

Boles's punishment outraged more law-abiding community leaders. Arnold and a few members of his crowd were arrested for disturbing the peace, which ultimately cost each of them a small fine. In response, Arnold organized a demonstration and parade. Dozens of citizens participated in this evening spectacle, which saw effigies of the local magistrates who had issued the arrest warrants carried through the streets on pretended gallows and then consumed in a huge bonfire. As Arnold wrote later, these magistrates had acted as if they wanted to "vindicate, protect, and caress an informer," rather than stand up for American rights when colonial trade "is nearly ruined by the . . . detestable Stamp and other oppressive acts." Vigilante justice for "infamous informers" like Boles, Arnold maintained, was an effective way to loosen the stranglehold of imperial restrictions on provincial commerce and, at the same time, defend basic rights.

The whipping and banishment of Boles were relatively mild punishments. Angry crowds often covered informers with tar and feathers before strapping them onto wooden rails and "riding" them out of town. In some cases, such as that of Ebenezer Richardson of Boston, informers nearly lost their lives. A combative person and occasional employee of the customs office, Richardson provided damaging information about a prominent local merchant in 1766, for which this informer was " frequently abused by the people." Then in early 1770 Richardson gained the community's wrath by defying citizens enforcing Boston's nonimportation agreement protesting the Townshend Duties. Events got out of hand, and he became known as the greatest "monster of the times."

Since August 1768, when Bostonians accepted Samuel Adams's call for nonimportation, an informal group known as "the Body" directed the harassment of violators. Merchants who kept importing British goods endured much abuse as "importers." Roving bands of citizens struck at night, breaking windows and defacing importers' property; the damage included coating walls with a combination of mud and feces known

> O MURD'RER! RICHARDSON! with their latest breath
> Millions will curse you when you sleep in death!
> Infernal horrors sure will shake your soul
> When o'er your head the awful thunders roll.
> Earth cannot hide you, always will the cry
> Of Murder! Murder! haunt you 'till you die!
> To yonder grave! with trembling joints repair,
> Remember, SEIDER'S corps lies mould'ring there;

as "Hillsborough treat." During the day, crowds moved from location to location, posting large wooden hands pointing toward the shops of offending merchants. As customers came and went, they received verbal abuse while dodging flying handfuls of Hillsborough treat.

On February 22, 1770, a crowd visited such a shop in Boston's North End, unfortunately across the street from Richardson's residence. The ever-belligerent informer suddenly appeared and, in the face of verbal taunts and flying debris, tried to remove the hand. Soon he retreated to his house with the crowd, including many boys, following close behind. "Come out, you damn son of a bitch," they shouted, and they started to break the windows. Inside, Richardson and another man loaded their muskets. When the crowd tried to enter the house, the informer first warned his assailants and then fired. He severely wounded an 11-year-old boy, Christopher Seider, who died several hours later. Only the intervention of well-known patriot gentlemen saved Richardson from being lynched.

Samuel Adams and other popular leaders in Boston took full advantage of this ugly incident. They planned an elaborate funeral during which some 2500 mourners solemnly marched in front and back of Seider's coffin from Liberty Tree to the burial ground. Hundreds more lined the streets as the procession passed by. Popular rights advocate John Adams considered young Seider a martyr to the cause of liberty. Lieutenant Governor Thomas Hutchinson was less charitable. Had his political adversaries had the power to restore Seider's life, he declared, they "would not have done it, but would have chosen the grand funeral."

Christopher Seider's death and emotional funeral were signs of the tension filling the streets of Boston over such imperial legislation as the Townshend Duties. That British redcoats were present to help enforce imperial law and keep the populace under control only made matters worse. In the week following Seider's funeral, there was a dramatic increase in incidents of troop baiting, including the fight at John Gray's ropemaking establishment, all of which culminated in the Boston Massacre.

As for Ebenezer Richardson, he soon stood trial on the charge of willfully murdering Seider. His argument was self-defense. His wife and two daughters were in the house and had been struck by eggs, stones, and flying Hillsborough treat. The Superior Court judges realized that manslaughter was the proper charge, not "damn him—hang him—murder not manslaughter," the phrase enraged Bostonians shouted as the jurors left the courtroom to deliberate on a verdict.

The jury pronounced Richardson guilty of murder; however, the court, headed by Thomas Hutchinson, initiated a series of legal actions that in 1772 secured Richardson's freedom by king's pardon. Now an outcast, Boston's most notorious informer tried to find work, only to be reviled and sent on his way. Finally, he secured employment with the customs office in Philadelphia, but more than once he disappeared to avoid a coat of tar and feathers because everywhere colonists knew Richardson as the "execrable villain, . . . as yet unhanged" customs informer who had shot down young Christopher Seider.

TABLE 4.1 Estimated Population of Colonial Port Towns Compared to London, England (1775)	
London	700,000
Philadelphia	28,000
New York City	23,000
Boston	16,000
Charleston	12,000
Newport	11,000
Baltimore	10,000

London, the capital of the British empire, had an enormous population by the standards of the largest cities in the colonies. The king's ministers were aware of this striking discrepancy, and they regarded American port towns like Boston as minor trading outposts in which a few well-trained redcoats could easily restore order among protesting colonists. Lord Hillsborough certainly believed so, but events proved him wrong.

commissioners found it virtually impossible to walk the streets or carry out their official duties without harassment.

More serious trouble erupted in June 1768 when a crowd attacked local customs collectors who had seized John Hancock's sloop *Liberty* on charges of smuggling in a cargo of Madeira wine. (Hancock was notorious for illegal trading.) For their personal safety, the new commissioners fled to Fort Castle William in Boston harbor. Even before the *Liberty* riots, they had sent reports to Hillsborough about the unruly behavior of Bostonians, and they had asked for military protection.

In the wake of the August 1765 Stamp Act riots, royalist political faction leaders had likewise talked in private about calling for military support. Governor Bernard demurred, thinking that the presence of redcoats might provoke even greater turmoil in the streets. Hillsborough, however, was not going to tolerate such abusive behavior from the Bostonians, even in the absence of a formal gubernatorial request for troops. Just before the *Liberty* riots took place, the American secretary issued orders for four regiments of redcoats to proceed to Boston. The troops were "to give every legal assistance to the civil magistrate in the preservation of the public peace; and to the officers of the revenue in the execution of the laws of trade and revenue."

When the first redcoats arrived in the fall of 1768 without serious incident, members of the royalist political faction went about their duties with newfound courage. Many inhabitants hoped that crowd rule, civil anarchy, and open harassment were tactics of the past.

Samuel Adams and the popular rights faction, however, kept demanding more resistance. On August 1, 1768, they convinced an enthusiastic town meeting to accept a nonimportation boycott of British goods. New Yorkers signed a similar agreement a few days later. Philadelphians refused at first to go along with their two northern neighbors, bowing to the pressure of influential merchants. Somewhat reluctantly, they finally joined the trade boycott in February 1769. Pressure from South Carolina's popular leader, Christopher Gadsden, backed by threats of crowd action, convinced Charleston merchants to come around in August 1769. A year had passed, but now all the major port cities had endorsed yet another trade boycott in defense of political liberties.

The colonists did more than boycott. In some communities talk was rife about producing manufactured goods, such as woolen cloth, in direct defiance of imperial restrictions. With the boycott in full force wealthier citizens could no longer get the most fashionable fabrics from London, and popular lead-

predicated on Dickinson's widely reprinted pamphlet and his call for petitions. If the British ministry had ignored the Massachusetts document, nothing of consequence might have happened. However, Wills Hill, Lord Hillsborough (1718–1793), who had recently taken the new cabinet post of Secretary for American Affairs, overreacted and provoked needless conflict.

Hillsborough considered the Circular Letter insubordinate. He quickly fired off orders to Governor Bernard to confront the General Court and demand an apology. If the delegates refused (they did overwhelmingly), Bernard was to dissolve the assembly and call for new elections. In addition, Hillsborough sent his own circular letter to the other colonial governors, insisting that they not allow their assemblies "to receive or give any countenance to this seditious paper" from Massachusetts. If they did, such assemblies were also to be dissolved. The result of Hillsborough's actions actually strengthened the colonists' resolve when new elections swelled the ranks of delegates firmly committed to resisting any form of Parliamentary taxation.

Just as the Massachusetts Circular Letter infuriated Hillsborough, so did the rough treatment experienced by royal customs officials, particularly in Boston where the Crown had recently located a new five-man Board of Customs Commissioners. When members of the board, which was to coordinate all customs collections in America, arrived at the end of 1767, jeering crowds greeted them at the docks. The

British redcoats landed at Boston's Long Wharf in 1768 with orders to put an end to ongoing political unrest in that port city.

ers encouraged them to join poorer colonists in wearing homespun cloth—a sign of personal sacrifice for the cause. Some leaders urged all "genteel ladies" to master the skills of spinning and weaving. The *Boston Gazette* asked "Daughters of Liberty" everywhere to:

> First then throw aside your high top knots of pride
> Wear none but your own country linen
> Of economy boast. Let your pride be the most
> To show clothes of your make and spinning.

Upper-class women, by and large, remained skeptical. They did not like the itchy feeling of homespun, and they considered spinning and weaving to be beneath their station in society. For poorer women, particularly those in the port cities, the trade boycott generated opportunities for piecemeal work in the production of homespun cloth. Such labor meant extra income, but there was virtually no long-term effect in improving the lot of the poor in America. Homespun was abundant, and the market price remained quite low. While wealthier women itched, complained, and worried about losing their status, poorer women were virtually donating their labor to the defense of American rights. For them the term "sacrifice" held a special meaning.

A "Bloody Massacre" in Boston

The citizens of Boston deeply resented the redcoats in their midst. When the king's troops had first debarked in October 1768, a concerned local minister proclaimed: "Good God! What can be worse to a people who have tasted the sweets of liberty! Things have come to an unhappy crisis, . . . and the moment there is any bloodshed all affection will cease."

Besides symbolizing political tyranny, the redcoats also competed for scarce jobs because, when not on duty, their officers allowed them to work for extra wages on a piecemeal basis. As a result, the troops made hard economic times even harder for day laborers, semiskilled workers, and other poorer Bostonians already suffering from the prolonged economic depression besetting their community.

Throughout 1769 troop baiting by Boston's working men and women had resulted in fistfights and bloodied faces. Bad feelings continued to mount as winter snows covered the ground. Then on March 2, 1770, an ugly confrontation took place. A young off-duty soldier, Patrick Walker, entered John Gray's ropemaking establishment and asked for work. Seizing the opportunity to be insulting, one of Gray's workers snorted: "Well, then go and clean my shit-house." Taken aback, the soldier snapped in response: "Empty it yourself." Upset and angry, Walker fled amid taunts and threats from other laborers.

Walker told his story to comrades like Mathew Kilroy and William Warren of the 29th regiment. He convinced several of them to join him in teaching these workers a lesson. The soldiers soon appeared at Gray's, and a general brawl ensued before Gray's workers drove off the redcoats. This nasty fight would have been lost to history had it not been an important precursor to the so-called Boston Massacre three days later.

Effective propaganda, such as Paul Revere's engravings of the Boston Massacre, helped increase outrage over the event. Here, the British soldiers appear to be firing without provocation into an innocent-looking crowd.

Revere, Paul, Boston Massacre, 1770. U.S., 1735–1818. Engraving after Henry Pelham, hand-colored by Christian Remik (1726–after 1783) 10 1/4 x 8 5/8 in. Gift of Watson Grant Cutter. Courtesy, Museum of Fine Arts, Boston.

Monday, March 5, was bitterly cold, but heated emotions among workers and soldiers could have melted the deep piles of snow in the streets. A number of isolated fights had occurred over the weekend, but an eerie calm pervaded on Monday because Boston's working people had decided to challenge the redcoats' continued presence in their community. Toward evening small parties of day laborers, apprentices, and merchant seamen began milling about in the streets, eventually moving toward King Street, the site of the Customs House. Here a lone redcoat was on guard duty, and the growing crowd pressed in on him.

Then a small detachment from the 29th regiment, including privates Kilroy and Warren, appeared. After rescuing their isolated comrade, the redcoats retreated to the steps of the customs house with the Boston crowd harassing them with mud, snowballs, and rocks every step of the way. Captain Thomas Preston tried to steady his squad, but one of his soldiers, fearing for his life, panicked. He leveled his musket and shot into the crowd. Ignoring Preston's orders to stop, other soldiers also fired their weapons. Before the shooting was over, a number of civilians lay wounded and dying.

All told, five colonists lost their lives, including Samuel Gray, a relative of John Gray and a participant in the March 2 brawl; seventeen-year-old Samuel Maverick, brother-in-law of shoemaker Ebenezer Mackintosh; and Crispus Attucks, an unemployed mulatto merchant seaman. Bostonians would soon hail these men as martyred heroes in the struggle to defend American liberties.

Captain Preston and his troops faced trials for murder. The court found all but two of the redcoats innocent on the grounds of having been forced into a life-threatening situation by an enraged crowd of citizens. Private Kilroy and another soldier were declared guilty of manslaughter. By pleading benefit of clergy they had their thumbs seared with a hot branding iron before being sent back to their regiment.

Long before these verdicts, royal officials removed the hated redcoats from Boston. In this sense the working citizens of Boston had won—at the cost of five lives. They had freed their community of British regulars and unwanted economic competition. Just as important, the Boston Massacre caused colonists everywhere to ask just how far King and Parliament would go to sustain the imperial will. With lives now lost, Americans would be increasingly wary of British government actions that might result in some detestable form of political tyranny. In sum, the legacy of the Boston Massacre was even greater mistrust of the parent nation's intentions.

Parliament Backs Down Again

The colonists' trade boycott seriously hurt merchants and manufacturers in the British Isles. By the beginning of 1770 the Townshend program had netted only about £20,000 in revenue, a paltry sum when compared to the loss in American trade, estimated to be as high as £7 million. Once again, the colonists had found the means to get Parliament to reevaluate its position.

It may have been fortunate for Charles Townshend that he died unexpectedly in September 1767. He did not have to listen to the abuse that his infamous duties took before Parliament in early 1770. By that time the Pitt ministry had collapsed. In January 1770 George III asked amiable Lord Frederick North (1732–1792) to form a new cabinet and give some direction to drifting governmental affairs.

North, listening to the wrath of powerful merchants and manufacturers in the British Isles, moved quickly to settle differences with America. He went before Parliament on March 5, 1770 (ironically the same day as the Boston Massacre) and called for repeal of the Townshend Duties, except for the tax on tea, which was to stand as a face-saving, symbolic reminder of Parliament's right to tax and legislate for the Americans in all cases whatsoever. As with the Stamp Act confrontation, the colonial trade boycott of 1768–1770 most certainly had a telling effect. King and Parliament had backed down again—but for the last time.

THE RUPTURING OF IMPERIAL RELATIONS

Lord North was a sensible leader who wanted to avoid taxation schemes and other forms of legislation that could provoke more trouble. He understood that imperial relations had been strained almost to a breaking point by too many controversial policies thrown at the colonists in too short a time after so many years of salutary neglect. North carefully avoided challenging the Americans between 1770 and 1773. In turn, the colonial resistance movement clearly waned. For a while, then, there were no new issues to stir further conflict—only old problems needing resolution.

When Parliament stepped back from the Townshend Duties, most colonists wanted to end the boycott and return to normal trade relations, despite the irritating tax on tea. That duty, they knew, could be avoided by the continued smuggling of Dutch tea. Slowly, economic relations with Great Britain improved, and His Majesty's subjects in England and America enjoyed a brief period of mutually beneficial economic prosperity.

The Necessity of Vigilance

Political relations were not so resilient. Many colonists had become very suspicious of the intentions of home government officials. Provincial leaders tried to explain what had happened since 1763 by drawing on the thoughts of England's "radical" **whig** opposition writers of the early eighteenth century. Men such as John Trenchard and Thomas Gordon, who had penned an extended series of essays known as *Cato's Letters* (1720–1723), had repeatedly warned about corruption in government caused by high ministerial officials lusting after power. If such officials were not stopped, citizens like the colonists would find themselves stripped of all liberties and living in a state of tyranny (often described as **political slavery**).

What took firm hold during the 1760s was an American worldview, or ideology, that saw liberties under attack by such grasping, power-hungry leaders as George Grenville and Charles Townshend in England and their royalist puppets in America, personified by such officials as Thomas Hutchinson and Andrew Oliver. Evidence of a conspiracy seemed overwhelming to those attempting to explain what had happened. Obvious signs included the hovering presence of British redcoats in such places as Boston and ships of the Royal Navy patrolling American waters, all during peacetime. The colonists had been cut off from frontier lands, and—perhaps worst of all from their perspective—they had experienced three willful attempts to tax them, literally to deprive them of property without any voice in the matter.

As never before, great numbers of colonists doubted the goodwill of the home government. Even if Lord North was behaving himself and keeping Parliament in check, many were sure that ministerial inaction was nothing more than a trick designed to lull Americans into a false sense of security while conspiring royal officials devised new and even more insidious plans to strip them of basic political rights.

Popular leaders exhorted the citizenry to be vigilant at all times. They employed various devices to ensure that the defense of liberties was not forgotten. In Boston Samuel Adams and his political lieutenants declared March 5 to be an annual commemorative holiday to honor the five fallen martyrs of the Massacre. Each year there was a large public meeting and grand oration to stir memories and to remind the populace of the possible dangers of a new ministerial assault.

Local confrontations also kept emotions stirred up. One such incident occurred in June 1772 and involved a Royal Naval vessel, the *Gaspée*, that regu-

Tension increased between British leaders and the American colonists when in June 1772 Rhode Islanders burned the *Gaspée*, a Royal Naval vessel charged with patrolling the area for smugglers.

THE PEOPLE SPEAK

Dr. Joseph Warren's Boston Massacre Oration (1772)

Just 31 years old in 1772, Joseph Warren was a seasoned veteran of the political struggles in Massachusetts between the popular rights faction of Samuel Adams and the royalist clique of Thomas Hutchinson. Warren graduated from Harvard College in 1759. He then turned to the study of medicine while also nurturing his political skills as an advocate of American rights. He became a favorite of Samuel Adams, who saw in Warren a keenly intelligent person who also possessed extraordinary speaking talent. On the second anniversary of the massacre, March 5, 1772, Warren stood before a huge assemblage in Boston and presented an oration about that terrible confrontation—and its larger meaning. He appealed to history in warning his audience about the dangers of standing armies, and he passionately described how much destruction the king's troops were so capable of producing. His words had a certain prophetic quality, at least for Warren himself. Just a little over three years later he died at the hands of British regulars in the midst of combat during the Battle of Bunker Hill.

> The ruinous consequences of standing armies to free communities may be seen in the histories of Syracuse, Rome, and many other once flourishing states; some of which have now scarce a name! Their baneful influence is most suddenly felt when they are placed in populous cities; for, by a corruption of morals, the public happiness is immediately affected! . . . And this will be more especially the case when the troops are informed that the intention of their being stationed in any city is to overawe the inhabitants. That this was the avowed design of stationing an armed force in this town is sufficiently known; and we, my fellow citizens, have seen, we have felt the tragical effects! *The fatal fifth of March, 1770, can never be forgotten.* The horrors of *that dreadful night* are but too deeply impressed on our hearts. Language is too feeble to paint the emotion of our souls, when our streets were stained with the blood of our brethren—when our ears were wounded by the groans of the dying, and our eyes were tormented with the sight of the mangled bodies of the dead.
>
> When our alarmed imagination presented to our view our houses wrapped in flames, our children subjected to the barbarous caprice of the raging soldiery, our beauteous virgins exposed to all the insolence of unbridled passion, our virtuous wives, endeared to us by every tender tie, falling sacrifice to worse than brutal violence, and perhaps like the famed Lucretia, distracted with anguish and despair, ending their wretched lives by their own fair hands. When we beheld the authors of our distress parading in our streets, or drawn up in a regular *battalia*, as though in a hostile city, our hearts beat to arms; we snatched our weapons, almost resolved by one decisive stroke to avenge the death of our slaughtered brethren, and to secure from future danger all that we held most dear: but propitious heaven forbade the bloody carnage and saved the threatened victims of our too keen resentment, not by their discipline, not by their regular array, no, it was royal George's livery that proved their shield—it was that which turned the pointed engines of destruction from their breasts. The thoughts of vengeance were soon buried in our inbred affection to Great Britain, and calm reason dictated a method of removing the troops more mild than an immediate resource to the sword. With united efforts you urged the immediate departure of the troops from the town—you urged it, with a resolution which ensured success—you obtained your wishes, and the removal of the troops was effected without one drop of their blood being shed by the inhabitants. . . .

Source: Merrill Jensen, ed., *English Historical Documents*, Vol. 9: *American Colonial Documents to 1776* (New York, 1969), 756–757.

larly patrolled for smugglers in the waters off Rhode Island. The ship's crew and its captain, William Dudingston, were very efficient. Finally, Rhode Islanders had endured enough. One day they sent out a sloop that purposely flaunted itself before the *Gaspée*. Suspecting illicit trading activity, Dudingston gave chase but ran aground as the smaller vessel swept close to shore. That evening, a crowd, disguised as Indians, descended upon the stranded ship and burned it. One of the crowd delivered the supreme insult by firing a load of buckshot into Dudingston's buttocks.

Crown officials were furious about the *Gaspée's* destruction. They set up a royal commission of inquiry but never obtained any conclusive evidence regarding the perpetrators of this crowd action. Curiously, popular leaders, ignoring the reasons that the *Gaspée* was in American waters in the first place, set up a hue and cry about the royal commission. They feared that the intention was to send suspects to England for trial. Consequently, several provincial assemblies established **committees of correspondence** to communicate with one another, should home government leaders appear to jeopardize liberties of any kind—in this case holding trials of persons outside districts where they had allegedly committed crimes. These correspondence committees were soon writing back and forth regarding problems over tea.

The Tea Crisis of 1773

The final assault on American rights, as the colonists perceived reality, grew out of a rather inconspicuous piece of legislation known as the Tea Act of 1773. When Lord North proposed this bill, he had no idea that it would precipitate a disastrous sequence of events; indeed, he was hardly thinking about the American provinces. His primary concern was the East India Company, a joint-stock trading enterprise that dated back to the early seventeenth century whose officials ruled over British interests in India.

Once enormously prosperous, the company had descended into desperate economic straits by the early 1770s. One reason was that the recent colonial boycott had cost the company its place in the American tea market. With tea warehouses bulging, company directors sought marketing concessions from Parliament. They asked to have the authority to ship tea directly from India to America rather than through England, which would lower the final market price. In May 1773 King and Parliament acceded to this request and, in turn, forced the company to give up some of its political authority in India.

To reduce costs further, the company proceeded to name its own tea agents in the major American ports. The agents were to function as local distributors for 6 percent commissions. The net effect of these changes was to make company tea much more competitive with, if not cheaper than, smuggled Dutch blends—a fact that pleased Lord North very much.

North was even more pleased to have found a way, he thought, to get the Americans to accept the tea tax—and, symbolically at least, recognize Parliament's sovereignty. How could they refuse cheaper tea, even with the Townshend duty added to the price? The chief minister should have listened to the M.P. who warned him during the debates on the Tea Act that "if we don't take off the duty they won't take the tea."

In September 1773 the company dipped into its warehouses and readied its first American consignment of 600,000 pounds of tea worth £60,000. Vigilant Americans were waiting. Conditioned by years of warding off undesirable imperial legislation, they were looking for signs of further conspiratorial acts. A small economic saving meant nothing in the face of what they believed to be another, more insidious plot to reduce them to a state of political slavery. East India Company tea had to be resisted.

Once again, the port city of Boston became the focal point of significant protest. In early November a crowd took to the streets and tried to intimidate the tea agents (among them Thomas and Elisha Hutchinson, sons of Thomas who was now the royal governor) into resigning. The merchant agents, who had not received official commissions as yet, refused to submit; the crowd did not press the matter, waiting for a more timely moment to force resignations.

On November 28 the first tea ship, the *Dartmouth*, docked in Boston. The local customs collectors fled to Fort Castle William, and the local committee of correspondence, headed by Samuel Adams and his associates, put guards on the *Dartmouth* and two other tea ships entering the port within the next few days. Repeatedly the popular rights faction insisted that the three tea ships be sent back to England. But Governor Hutchinson refused. This native-son royal governor could be fair-minded but also stubborn, and this time Hutchinson decided that a showdown was necessary. He called on Royal Naval vessels in the vicinity to block off the port's entrance.

According to imperial law, unclaimed cargo had to be unloaded after 20 days in port and then sold at public auction. Since the tea ships could not escape the harbor, Hutchinson fully expected to have the vessels unloaded after the 20-day waiting period. Once the tea had been sold at auction, the Townshend duty would be paid from the revenues obtained, and the governor would have upheld the law of King and Parliament. Hutchinson's determination to stand firm on behalf of imperial authority—and against his troublesome, long-time local enemies—proved to be a bad idea.

The waiting period for the *Dartmouth* was over on December 16. That day a mass meeting of local citizens took place at Old South Church. The Samuel Adams faction made one last attempt to communicate the gravity of the situation to Hutchinson. They sent a messenger to him with a very clear message—remove the tea ships or else. Hutchinson refused again. Late in the day, Adams appeared before the huge gathering and reportedly shouted: "This meeting can do no more to save the country." The moment for crowd action had come. Several dozen artisans, apprentices, and day laborers, led by Ebenezer Mackintosh, went to the docks disguised as Indians. They clambered onto the tea ships and dumped 342 chests of tea valued at £10,000 into the harbor. It took them nearly three hours to complete the work of the Boston Tea Party.

Tea confrontations occurred later in other ports, but none were as destructive as that in Boston. Philadelphians used the threat of tar and feathers to convince local officials to send back the first tea ships to arrive there. The governor of South Carolina outmaneuvered the local populace and managed to get the tea landed, but the company product lay rotting in a warehouse and was never sold. New Yorkers had to wait until the spring of 1774 for tea ships to appear in their port. They jeered loudly at the docks, and an intelligent sea captain raised anchor and fled for the high seas. Once again, then, the Bostonians stood out for their bold defiance of imperial law.

Parliament Adopts the Coercive Acts

The Boston Tea Party shocked Lord North and other British leaders. North decided that the "rebellious" Bostonians had to be taught a lesson, and Parliament adopted a series of legislative bills, collectively known as the *Coercive Acts*. Although King and Parliament aimed these laws at Massachusetts, the Coercive Acts held implications for colonists elsewhere who believed that the tyrannical parent nation was using the Tea Party as a pretext for the final destruction of American liberties.

King George III signed the first act, known as the Boston Port Bill, into law at the end of March 1774. This act closed the port of Boston, making trade illegal until such time as local citizens paid for the tea. In May Parliament passed the Massachusetts Government Act and the Administration of Justice Act. The first suspended the colony's royal charter (which dated to 1691), vastly expanded the powers of the royal governor, abolished the elective council (upper house of the General Court), and replaced that body with appointed councilors of the Crown's choosing. Town meetings could be held only with the governor's permission, except for annual spring election gatherings.

Governor Hutchinson never exercised this vastly expanded range of authority. Distraught by the Tea Party, he asked for a leave of absence and traveled to England. The Crown replaced him with General Thomas Gage, Britain's North American military commander, who held the governorship until the final disruption of royal government in the Bay Colony.

The Administration of Justice Act provided greater protection for customs collectors and other imperial officials in Massachusetts. If they injured or killed anyone while carrying out their official duties, the governor would have the right to move trials to some other colony or to England. The assumption was that local juries were too biased to render fair judgments.

Finally, in early June 1774 Parliament sanctioned the fourth coercive bill, which was an amendment to the Quartering Act of 1765. The earlier law had outlined procedures relating to housing for the king's regulars and had specifically excluded the use of private dwellings of any kind. The 1774 amendment gave General Gage the power to billet his troops anywhere, including unoccupied private homes, so long as the army paid fair rental rates. Parliament passed this law because Gage was bringing several hundred troops to Boston with him.

The colonists also viewed the Quebec Act, approved in June 1774, as another piece of coercive legislation. Actually, this bill mainly concerned itself with the territorial administration of Canada by providing for a royal governor and a large appointed advisory council, but no popularly elected assembly. Roman Catholicism was to remain the established religion for the French-speaking populace. In addition, the Ohio River was to become the new southwestern boundary of Quebec.

Ever-vigilant colonial leaders viewed the Quebec Act as confirming all the worst tendencies of imperial rule over the past decade. Parliament had denied local representative government; it had ratified the establishment of a branch of the Christian faith that was repugnant to militantly Protestant Americans, especially New Englanders; and it had wiped out the claims of various colonial governments to millions of acres of western land, in this case all of the Ohio country. The latter decision particularly infuriated well-placed provincial land speculators, among them Benjamin Franklin and George Washington, who had fixed on this region for future development and population expansion. The Quebec Act, concluded thousands of Americans, smacked of abject political slavery.

Even without the Quebec Act, Lord North had made a tactical error by encouraging Parliament to pass so much legislation. The port bill punishing Boston was one thing; some Americans believed the Bostonians had gone too far and deserved some chas-

Quebec Act of 1774

By making the Ohio River the new southwest boundary of Quebec, the Quebec Act cut into land the colonists wanted for expansion.

tisement. The sum total of the Coercive Acts, however, caused widespread concern because they seemed to violate the sanctity of local political institutions, to distort normal judicial procedures, and to favor military over civil authority. For most colonists the acts resulted in feelings of solidarity with (rather than separateness from) the Bostonians, a critical factor in generating a unified resistance movement.

Hurling Back the Challenge: The First Continental Congress

News of the full array of Coercive Acts provoked an outburst of intercolonial activity, the most important expression of which was the calling of the **First Continental Congress.** This body began its deliberations in Philadelphia on September 5, 1774. Gentlemen of all political persuasions were in attendance (Georgia was the only colony not represented). Among the more radical delegates were Samuel Adams and his younger cousin John, as well as Patrick Henry. George Washington was present, mostly silent in debates but firmly committed to defending fundamental rights. Conservative delegates included Joseph Galloway of Pennsylvania and John Jay of New York. The core question was how confrontational the Congress should be. The more cautious delegates wanted to find some nonhostile means to settle differences with Britain, but the radicals believed that only a well-organized resistance effort would induce home government leaders to back down yet a third time.

As the largest American city and a central geographic point, Philadelphia was a logical location for delegates of the First Continental Congress to gather in 1774.

Political maneuvering for control of the Congress began even before the sessions got under way. Conservative delegates favored meeting in the Pennsylvania State House, a building symbolizing ties with British rule. The radicals argued in favor of Carpenter's Hall, a gathering place for Philadelphia's laborers. The delegates chose the latter building, thus seeming to identify with the people and their desire to preserve political liberties. Then the radicals insisted on naming Charles Thomson, a popular leader in Philadelphia, secretary for the Congress. Thomson gained the post and was able to design the minutes so that more confrontational actions stood out in the official record.

These signs foreshadowed what was to come. Accounts of the work of the First Continental Congress make clear that Samuel Adams, Patrick Henry, and others of their radical persuasion dominated the proceedings. Although they went along with the preparation of an elaborate petition to Parliament, known as the "The Declaration of Colonial Rights and Grievances," these experienced molders of the colonial protest movement demanded much more. They drew upon the old weapons of resistance that had caused King and Parliament to retreat before, and they added a new cudgel. Just in case they could not convince home government leaders to repeal the Coercive Acts, they argued that Americans should begin to prepare for war.

To ensure that Congress moved in the right direction, Samuel Adams and his political allies back in Massachusetts had done some careful planning. Their efforts came to light on September 9, 1774, when a convention of citizens in Suffolk County (Boston and environs) adopted a series of resolutions written by Dr. Joseph Warren. Once approved, Paul Revere, talented silversmith and active member of Adams's popular rights faction, rode hard for Philadelphia. Revere arrived in mid-September and laid the Suffolk Resolves before Congress. Not only did these statements strongly profess American rights, but they also called for a complete economic boycott and the rigorous training of local militia companies, just in case military action became necessary to defend lives, liberty, and property against the redcoats of Thomas Gage.

Congress approved the Suffolk Resolves—and with them the initial step in organization for a possible military showdown. The delegates also committed themselves to a plan of economic boycott, which became known as the Continental Association. The association represented a comprehensive plan mandating the nonimportation and nonconsumption of British goods, to be phased in over the next few months, as well as the nonexportation of

Chronology of Key Events

1760 George III becomes King of England

1763 Treaty of Paris ends the Seven Years' War (February); Pontiac begins an unsuccessful Indian rebellion on the western frontier (May); Orders in Council station Royal Naval vessels in American waters to run down smugglers (October); Proclamation of 1763 forbids white settlement west of the Appalachian Mountains (October)

1764 Sugar Act levies new trade duties on coffee, indigo, sugar, and wine (April); Currency Act prohibits colonial governments from issuing paper money and requires all debts to be paid in hard money (April)

1765 Stamp Act—which requires stamps to be affixed to all legal documents, almanacs, newspapers, pamphlets, and playing cards, among other items—provokes popular protests (March–December); Quartering Act directs colonists to provide barracks, candles, bedding, and beverages to soldiers stationed in their area (May); representatives from nine colonies at the Stamp Act Congress in New York City deny that Parliament has the right to tax the colonists (October)

1766 Parliament repeals the Stamp Act, but asserts its authority to tax the colonies in the Declaratory Act (March)

1767 Townshend Duties Act imposes taxes on imported glass, lead, paint, paper, and tea to defray the cost of colonial administration (June)

1768 British troops ordered to Boston (June); colonists begin to mount a trade boycott of British goods to protest the Townshend Duties (August)

1770 Boston Massacre leaves five colonists dead and others wounded (March)

1772 Rhode Island colonists attack and burn British naval vessel *Gaspée* (June)

1773 Tea Act allows the East India Company to sell tea directly to American retailers (May); Boston Tea Party occurs when a band of "Indians" boards three British vessels and dumps 342 chests of tea into Boston Harbor (December)

1774 Coercive Acts close the port of Boston (March), modify the Massachusetts charter (May), provide for trials outside colonies when royal officials are accused of serious crimes (May), and call for billeting of troops in unoccupied private homes (June); Quebec Act expands the boundaries of Quebec to the Mississippi and Ohio rivers (June); First Continental Congress, meeting in Philadelphia, protests oppressive Parliamentary legislation, votes to boycott trade with Britain, and defeats the Galloway Plan of Union (September–October)

---

colonial products should Parliament not retreat within a year.

The association also called on every American community to establish a local committee of observation and inspection charged with having all citizens subscribe to the boycott. In reality, the association was a loyalty test. Citizens who refused to sign were about to become outcasts from the cause of liberty. The term of derision applied to them was *tory;* however, they thought of themselves as *loyalists*—maintaining their allegiance to the Crown.

The only conciliatory countercharge of any consequence during the first Congress came from Joseph Galloway, a wealthy Philadelphia lawyer who had long served as Pennsylvania's speaker of the house. Galloway desperately wanted to maintain imperial ties because he feared what the "common sort" of citizens might do if that attachment should be irrevocably severed. He could imagine nothing but rioting, dissipation, and the confiscation of the property of economically successful colonists. For Galloway, the continuation of any kind of political and social order in America depended on the stabilizing influence of British rule.

Galloway drew from the Albany Plan of Union of 1754 (see p. 92) in proposing a central government based in America that would be superior to the provincial assemblies. This government would consist of a "grand council" elected by colonial assemblymen and a "president general" appointed by the Crown. Grand council legislation would have to gain Parliament's approval; at the same time imperial acts from King and Parliament would have to secure the assent of the grand council and president before becoming law.

Galloway's Plan of Union, as his blueprint came to be known, represented a structural alternative that would allow Americans a greater voice in imperial decisions affecting the colonies—and also foreshadowed the future commonwealth organization of the British empire. The more radical delegates, however, belittled it as an idea that would divert everyone from the task of the moment, which was to get King and Parliament to rescind the Coercive Acts. In a close vote the delegates remanded Galloway's plan to a committee, where it lay dormant for lack of majority support.

Later, at the urging of the radicals, Secretary Thomson expunged all references to Galloway's plan from the official minutes of Congress. He did so on the grounds of displaying full unity of purpose in resisting the home government. As for Galloway, he faced growing harassment as a loyalist in the months ahead and eventually fled to the British army for protection.

When the First Continental Congress ended its deliberations in late October 1774, its program was one of continued defiance. The delegates understood the course they had chosen. One of their last acts was to call for the Second Continental Congress, to convene in Philadelphia on May 10, 1775, "unless the redress of grievances, which we have desired, be obtained before that time."

As the fall of 1774 gave way to another cold winter, Americans awaited the verdict of King and Parliament. Would the Coercive Acts be repealed, or would the course of events lead to war? Local committees of observation and inspection were busily at work encouraging—and in some cases coercing—the populace to boycott British goods. Local militia companies were vigorously training. Even as they prepared for war, the colonists hoped that George III, Lord North, and Parliament would choose a less strident course. They would soon learn that imperial leaders had dismissed the work of the First Continental Congress, having decided the parent nation could not retreat a third time.

Conclusion

In September 1774 Lord North remarked: "The die is now cast, the colonies must either submit or triumph." Once-harmonious relations between Britain and America had become increasingly discordant between 1763 and the end of 1774. The colonists refused to accept undesirable imperial acts, and they successfully resisted such taxation plans as the Stamp Act and the Townshend Duties. In the process they came to believe that ministerial leaders in England were engaging in a deep-seated plot to deprive them of their fundamental liberties. When something as inconsequential as the Townshend duty on tea precipitated yet another crisis in 1773, neither side was willing to disengage. By early 1775 both had decided to show their resolve.

A small incident that well illustrates the deteriorating situation occurred in Boston during March 1774. At the state funeral of Andrew Oliver, the Bay Colony's most recent lieutenant governor and former stamp distributor-designate, a large gathering of ordinary citizens came out to watch the solemn procession. As Oliver's coffin was slowly lowered into the ground, these Bostonians, many of them veterans of the American resistance movement, suddenly burst into loud cheers.

This open expression of disaffection for the memory of so locally prominent a royalist leader epitomized the acute strain in British-American relations. Symbolically, the cheers almost seemed like a testament on behalf of the burial of imperial authority in America. Such striking changes in attitudes, over just a few years, pointed toward the fateful clash of arms known as the War for American Independence.

Suggestions for Further Reading

Bernard Bailyn, *The Ideological Origins of the American Revolution* (1967). Broadly influential, Pulitzer Prize-winning examination of the role of "radical" whig ideas in provoking the Revolution.

Ian R. Christie and Benjamin W. Labaree, *Empire or Independence, 1760–1776* (1976). Engaging appraisal of the reasons for revolution from the perspectives of British policymakers and ordinary American colonists.

Edmund S. and Helen M. Morgan, *The Stamp Act Crisis*, 3d ed. (1995). Classic account of the political, social, and constitutional aspects of the first major political confrontation pointing toward revolution.

Gary B. Nash, *The Urban Crucible: Social Change, Political Consciousness, and the Origins of the Revolution* (1979). Challenging analysis of the lives of ordinary persons in Boston, New York City, and Philadelphia, and the factors that propelled them toward revolution.

Gordon S. Wood, *The Radicalism of the American Revolution* (1992). Winner of a Pulitzer Prize focusing on pre-Revolutionary social and political values and the transformations wrought by the Revolution.

Alfred F. Young, *The Shoemaker and the Tea Party: Memory and the American Revolution* (1999). Fascinating account of an ordinary Bostonian who participated in key events pointing toward rebellion against the British.

Overviews and Surveys

Bernard Bailyn, *The Origins of American Politics* (1968); Colin Bonwick, *The American Revolution* (1991); Richard Maxwell Brown, *Strain of Violence: Historical Studies of American Violence and Vigilantism* (1975); Robert M. Calhoon, *Revolutionary America: An Interpretive Overview* (1976); Edward Countryman, *The American Revolution* (1985); Marc Egnal, *A Mighty Empire: The Origins of the Revolution* (1988); Lawrence Henry Gipson, *The Coming of the Revolution, 1763–1775* (1954); Merrill Jensen, *The Founding of a Nation, 1763–1776* (1968); Stephen G. Kurtz and James H. Hutson, eds., *Essays on the American Revolution* (1973); James Kirby Martin, *In the Course of Human Events: An Interpretive Exploration of the Revolution* (1979); Robert Middlekauff, *The Glorious Cause, 1763–1789* (1982); Edmund S. Morgan, *The Birth of the Republic, 1763–89*, 3d ed. (1993); Robert E. Shalhope, *The Roots of Democracy: American Thought and Culture, 1760–1800* (1990); Neil R. Stout, *The Perfect Crisis: The Beginning of the Revolutionary War* (1976); Harry M. Ward, *The American Revolution: Nationhood Achieved, 1763–1788* (1995); Esmond Wright, *Fabric of Freedom, 1763–1800*, rev. ed. (1978).

Provoking an Imperial Crisis

Robert A. Becker, *Revolution, Reform, and the Politics of American Taxation, 1763–1783* (1980); Colin Bonwick, *English Radicals and the American Revolution* (1977); John Brewer, *Party Ideology and Popular Politics at the Accession of George III* (1976); John L. Bullion, *A Great and Necessary Measure: George Grenville and the Genesis of the Stamp Act, 1763–1765* (1982); Ian R. Christie, *Crisis of Empire, 1754–1783* (1966); John Derry, *English Politics and the American Revolution* (1976); Joseph A. Ernst, *Money and Politics in America, 1755–1775* (1973); Daniel M. Friedenberg, *Life, Liberty, and the Pursuit of Land: The Plunder of Early America* (1992); Eric Hinderaker, *Elusive Empires: Constructing Colonialism in the Ohio Valley, 1673–1800* (1997); Michael Kammen, *A Rope of Sand: Colonial Agents, British Politics, and the Revolution* (1968); Lewis B. Namier, *England in the Age of the American Revolution*, rev. ed. (1961), and *The Structure of Politics at the Accession of George III*, rev. ed. (1957); Howard H. Peckham, *Pontiac and the Indian Uprising* (1947); Francis Philbrick, *The Rise of the West, 1754–1830* (1965); John Shy, *Toward Lexington: The Role of the British Army in the Coming of the Revolution* (1965); Jack M. Sosin, *Whitehall and the Wilderness: The Middle West in British Colonial Policy, 1760–1775* (1961), and *The Revolutionary Frontier, 1763–1783* (1967); Neil R. Stout, *The Royal Navy in America, 1760–1775* (1973); Robert W. Tucker and David C. Hendrickson, *The Fall of the First British Empire* (1982); Carl Ubbelohde, *The Vice-Admiralty Courts and the American Revolution* (1960); Franklin B. Wickwire, *British Subministers and Colonial America, 1763–1783* (1966).

"Liberty, Property, and No Stamps" and A Second Crisis: The Townshend Duties

Paul Gilje, *Road to Mobocracy: Popular Disorder in New York City, 1763–1834* (1987); Dirk Hoerder, *Crowd Action in Revolutionary Massachusetts, 1765–1780* (1977); Pauline R. Maier, *From Resistance to Revolution: Colonial Radicals and the Development of Opposition to Britain, 1765–1776* (1972), and *The Old Revolutionaries: Political Lives in the Age of Samuel Adams*, rev. ed. (1990); Charles S. Olton, *Artisans for Independence: Philadelphia Mechanics and the Revolution* (1975); Peter Shaw, *The Character of John Adams* (1976), and *American Patriots and the Rituals of Revolution* (1981); Peter D. G. Thomas, *British Politics and the Stamp Act Crisis* (1975), and *The Townshend Duties Crisis: The Second Phase of the Revolution, 1767–1773* (1987); John W. Tyler, *Smugglers and Patriots: Boston Merchants and the Advent of the Revolution* (1986); John J. Waters, Jr., *The Otis Family in Provincial and Revolutionary Massachusetts* (1968); Hiller B. Zobel, *The Boston Massacre* (1970).

The Rupturing of Imperial Relations

David Ammerman, *In the Common Cause: American Response to the Coercive Acts of 1774* (1974); Richard R. Beeman, *The Evolution of the Southern Backcountry: A Case Study of Lunenburg County, Virginia, 1746–1832* (1984); Ruth H. Bloch, *Visionary Republic: Millennial Themes in American Thought, 1756–1800* (1985); T. H. Breen, *Tobacco Culture: The Mentality of the Great Tidewater Planters* (1985); Richard D. Brown, *Revolutionary Politics in Massachusetts: The Boston Committee of Correspondence, 1772–1774* (1970); Edwin G. Burrows and Michael Wallace, "The Ideology and Psychology of National Liberation," *Perspectives in American History*, 6 (1972), pp. 167–306; Richard L. Bushman, *King and People in Provincial Massachusetts* (1985); H. Trevor Colbourn, *The Lamp of Experience: Whig History and the Intellectual Origins of the Revolution* (1965); Jere R. Daniell, *Experiment in Republicanism: New Hampshire Politics and the Revolution, 1741–1794* (1970); Bernard Donoughue, *British Politics and the American Revolution: The Path to War, 1733–1775* (1964); A. Roger Ekirch, "Poor Carolina": *Politics and Society in North Carolina, 1729–1776* (1981); Jay Fliegelman, *Prodigals and Pilgrims: The American Revolution Against Patriarchal Authority, 1750–1800* (1982); Larry R. Gerlach, *Prologue to Independence: New Jersey in the Coming of the Revolution* (1976); Ronald Hoffman, *A Spirit of Dissension: Economics, Politics, and the Revolution in Maryland* (1973); Woody Holton, *Forced Founders: Indians, Debtors, Slaves, and the Making of the Revolution in Virginia* (1999); Benjamin W. Labaree, *The Boston Tea Party* (1964); David S. Lovejoy, *Rhode Island Politics and the Revolution, 1760–1776* (1958); Stephen E. Lucas, *Portents of Rebellion: Rhetoric and Revolution in Philadelphia, 1765–1776* (1976); Bernard Mason, *The Road to Independence: The Revolutionary Movement in New York, 1773–1777* (1966); John A. Neuenschwander, *The Middle Colonies and the Coming of the American Revolution* (1973); Gregory H. Nobles, *Divisions Throughout the Whole: Politics and Society in Hampshire County, Massachusetts, 1740–1775*

(1983); J. G. A. Pocock, *The Machiavellian Moment: Florentine Political Thought and the Atlantic Republican Tradition* (1975); Bruce Ragsdale, *A Planter's Republic: The Search for Economic Independence in Virginia* (1996); Caroline Robbins, *The Eighteenth-Century Commonwealthman* (1959); Clinton Rossiter, *Seedtime of the Republic: The Origin of the American Tradition of Political Liberty* (1953); Richard A. Ryerson, *The Revolution Is Now Begun: The Radical Committees of Philadelphia, 1765–1776* (1978); David Curtis Skaggs, *Roots of Maryland Democracy, 1753–1776* (1973); Alan Taylor, *Liberty Men and Great Proprietors: The Maine Frontier, 1760–1820* (1990); Peter D. G. Thomas, *Tea Party to Independence: The Third Phase of the Revolution, 1773–1776* (1991).

Biographies

Bernard Bailyn, *The Ordeal of Thomas Hutchinson* (1974); Richard R. Beeman, *Patrick Henry* (1974); John Brooke, *King George III* (1972); John H. Cary, *Joseph Warren* (1961); Noble E. Cunningham, Jr., *In Pursuit of Reason: Thomas Jefferson* (1987); John Ferling, *The First of Men: George Washington* (1988), and *John Adams* (1992); William M. Fowler, Jr., *The Baron of Beacon Hill: John Hancock* (1979), and *Samuel Adams: Radical Puritan* (1997); Don R. Gerlach, *Philip Schuyler and the Revolution in New York, 1733–1777* (1964); E. Stanly Godbold, Jr., and Robert W. Woody, *Christopher Gadsden* (1982); David Freeman Hawke, *Franklin* (1976); Christopher Hibbert, *George III* (1999); James L. McKelvey, *George III and Lord Bute* (1973); John C. Miller, *Sam Adams: Pioneer in Propaganda* (1936); Lewis B. Namier and John Brooke, *Charles Townshend* (1964); Sheila Skemp, *William Franklin: Son of a Patriot, Servant of a King* (1990); Peter D. G. Thomas, *Lord North* (1976); Andrew S. Walmsley, *Thomas Hutchinson and the Origins of the American Revolution* (1999).

Internet Resources

The Leslie Brock Center for the Study of Colonial Currency
http://www.virginia.edu/~econ/brock.html
This site includes useful primary and secondary documents on early American currency.

Canada History
http://www.civilization.ca/index1e.html
Canada and the United States shared a colonial past but developed differently in the long run. This site is a part of the virtual museum of the Canadian Museum of Civilization Corporation.

Key Terms

Specie   (p. 100)
Vice-Admiralty Courts   (p. 103)
Virtual Representation   (p. 105)
Writs of Assistance   (p. 107)
Loyal Nine   (p. 107)
Stamp Act Congress   (p. 109)
Whigs   (p. 117)
Political Slavery   (p. 117)
Committees of Correspondence   (p. 119)
First Continental Congress   (p. 121)

Review Questions

1. How did Great Britain's overwhelming success in the Seven Years' War (the French and Indian War in America) help produce an imperial crisis with the English colonies in North America after 1763?

2. Why did the Stamp Act cause such immense fury among the colonists? What various nonviolent and violent tactics were employed by the colonists in resisting British policy actions? Which proved to be most effective, and why?

3. What motivated George Grenville, Charles Townshend, and Lord Frederick North to attempt to tax the Americans? Prepare a brief defense of British colonial policies between 1763 and 1774.

4. The Boston Massacre and the Boston Tea Party were pivotal events in the colonial resistance movement. Examine both events by considering their short-term and long-term causes as well as their wide-reaching consequences.

5. Why did the combination of the Coercive Acts and the Quebec Act prove to be a legislative tactical blunder for Lord North's administration? How did the colonists respond to these measures, and why did their response seem to imply rebellion?

5

THE TIMES THAT TRIED MANY SOULS, 1775–1783

RECONCILIATION OR INDEPENDENCE
The Shooting War Starts
Moderates Versus Radicals in Congress
The Expanding Martial Conflict
Lord Dunmore's Proclamation of Emancipation
Resolving the Independence Question

WITHOUT VISIBLE ALLIES: THE WAR IN THE NORTH
Britain's Massive Military Buildup
The Campaign for New York
Saving the Cause at Trenton
The Real Continentals

RESCUING THE PATRIOTS: TOWARD GLOBAL CONFLICT
France Offers Covert Assistance
The British Seize Philadelphia
Capturing Burgoyne's Army at Saratoga

THE WORLD TURNED UPSIDE DOWN
Revamping British Strategy
The Tide of War Turns at Last
Franco-American Triumph at Yorktown
A Most Generous Peace Settlement

"Starve, dissolve, or disperse"

Joseph Plumb Martin was a dedicated patriot soldier, one of 11,000 men and women who formed the backbone of General George Washington's Continental army. When that force entered its Valley Forge winter campsite in December 1777, the soldiers' trail could "be tracked by their blood upon the rough frozen ground," Martin recorded despondently. The Continentals were "now in a truly forlorn condition,—no clothing, no provisions, and as disheartened as need be." They had fought hard against British regulars and Hessians that summer and autumn but had not prevented the army of General Sir William Howe from taking Philadelphia, the rebel capital. Washington had chosen Valley Forge as a winter encampment because, as a hilly area, it represented an easily defensible position some 20 miles northwest of Philadelphia, should Howe's soldiers venture forth from their far more comfortable quarters.

Washington was very worried about the conditions facing his troops. If something was not done, and soon, he stated, "this army must inevitably . . . starve, dissolve, or disperse." Private Martin thought the same. The weather was bitterly cold, but the Continentals, using what energy they had left, constructed "little shanties" described as "scarcely gayer than dungeon cells."

Making matters even more grim was the lack of food and clothing. Martin claimed that, upon first entering Valley Forge, he went a full day and two nights without anything to eat, "save half a small pumpkin, which I cooked by placing it upon a rock, the skin side uppermost, and making fire upon it." His comrades fared no better. Within two days of moving into Valley Forge, a common grumble could be heard everywhere: "No Meat! No Meat!" By the first of January the words had become more ominous: "No bread, no soldier!"

Thus began a tragic winter of desperation for Washington's Continentals. Some 2500 soldiers, or nearly one fourth of the troops, perished before the army broke camp in June 1778. They died from exposure to the elements, malnutrition, and such virulent diseases as typhus and smallpox. Not uncommonly, soldiers languished for days in their rudely constructed huts because they were too weak to drill or to participate in food-hunting expeditions. Sometimes for lack of straw and blankets, they simply froze to death in their beds. To add to the woes of the camp, more than 500 of the army's horses starved to death that winter. Their carcasses could not be buried in the frozen ground, which only magnified the deplorable sanitation conditions and the consequent spread of disease.

Under such forsaken circumstances, hundreds of soldiers deserted. If Washington had not let his troops leave camp to requisition food in the countryside or if there had not been an unusually early shad run in the Schuylkill River, which flowed behind the encampment, the army might well have perished.

Commentators have usually attributed the extreme suffering at Valley Forge to the severe weather and a complete breakdown of the army's supply system. Actually, weather conditions were no worse than in other years. Certainly a major reason for the deprivation at Valley Forge was widespread civilian indifference toward an army made up of the poor, the expendable, and the unfree in American society.

Joseph Plumb Martin clearly thought this was the case. He was a young man from Connecticut, without material resources, who had first enlisted during 1776 at the very peak of patriot enthusiasm for the war—sometimes called the **rage militaire.** He soon learned that soldiering had few glorious moments. Camp life was both dull and dangerous, given the many killer diseases that ravaged armies of the era, and battle was a frightening experience. Before 1776 was over, Martin had faced the hurtling musket balls and bloodied bayonets of British soldiers in the Continental army's futile attempt to defend New York City and vicinity. He did not renew his enlistment and returned to Connecticut.

For a poor, landless person, economic prospects at home were not much better than serving for promises of regular pay in the Continental army. So in 1777 Martin stepped forth again and agreed to enlist as a substitute for some local gentlemen being threatened by an attempted draft. For a specified sum of money (Martin "forgot the sum"), he became their substitute. As Martin later wrote, "they were now freed from further trouble, at least for the present, and I had become the scapegoat for them."

The experiences of Martin typified those of many others who performed long-term Continental service on behalf of the cause of liberty. After an initial rush to arms in defiance of British authority in 1775, the harsh realities of military life and pitched battles

George Washington led a bedraggled, half-starved army of 11,000 men and women into Valley Forge in December 1777.

dampened patriot enthusiasm to the point that by December 1776 the Continental army all but ceased to exist. Washington's major task became that of securing enough troop strength and material support to shape an army capable of standing up time after time to British forces.

The commander in chief found his long-term soldiers among the poor and deprived persons of revolutionary America. In addition, major European nations such as France, Spain, and Holland also came to the rescue with additional troops, supplies, and vital financial support. Working together, even in the face of so much popular indifference, these allies-in-arms outlasted the mighty land and sea forces of Great Britain, making possible a generous peace settlement in 1783 that guaranteed independence for the group of former British colonies that now called themselves the 13 United States.

RECONCILIATION OR INDEPENDENCE

Crown officials in England gave scant attention to the acts of the First Continental Congress. They believed the time had come to teach the American provincials a military lesson. George III explained why: The colonists, he asserted, "have boldly thrown off the mask and avowed nothing less than a total independence of the British legislature will satisfy them." The king's impression was inaccurate, but it lay behind the decision to turn the most powerful military machine in the western world, based on its record in recent wars, against the troublemakers in America and to crush resistance to British authority once and for all.

The Shooting War Starts

During the winter of 1774–1775 the king's ministers prepared for what they expected to be a brief but decisive demonstration of military force. General Gage received "secret" orders to employ the redcoats under his command "to arrest and imprison the principal actors and abettors" of rebellion; however, if the likes of Samuel Adams, John Hancock, and Joseph Warren could not be captured, then Gage was to challenge in any way he deemed appropriate "this rude [American] *rabble* without plan, without concert, and without conduct... unprepared to encounter with a regular force." Above all else, Gage was to strike hard with a crushing blow.

In a series of related showdown decisions, King and Parliament authorized funds for a larger force of regular troops in America and named three high-

ROAD TO WAR, 1763–1776

WAR FOR AMERICAN INDEPENDENCE

1763	Orders in Council	Places British naval vessels in American waters during peacetime to run down smugglers, thereby threatening highly profitable illegal trading activities.
	Proclamation of 1763	Denies colonists access to western lands with the purpose of avoiding frontier warfare with Native Americans; infuriates land-hungry settlers searching for tillable farmland.
1764	Sugar Act	Designed to collect trade duty on foreign molasses and toughen other trading regulations.
	Currency Act	Requires colonial governments to stop issuing paper currencies heretofore used to conduct local business transactions and pay private debts.
1765	Stamp Act	Unprecedented legislation to tax colonists directly; heavily resisted through crowd actions and the boycotting of British trade goods.
	Quartering Act	Shifts onto the colonists the financial burden of paying for the housing of imperial troops stationed in America.
1767	Townshend Duties	Another plan to tax the colonists, this time indirectly through a series of trade duties; provokes further resistance.
1770	Boston Massacre	Local crowd action against hated redcoats results in the death of five persons who are transformed into martyrs in the defense of American liberties.
1772	*Gaspée* Affair	Rhode Islanders destroy British naval vessel charged with seizing smugglers, thereby incensing the Crown.
	Committee organization	Colonial assemblies organize committees of correspondence to communicate about imperial policies; Massachusetts establishes local committees to be vigilant in relation to possible acts of tyranny.
1773	Tea Act	Colonists defy this plan to market cheaper tea with the Townshend duty attached; Boston Tea Party sets the tone of resistance.
1774	Coercive Acts	Crown closes port of Boston and makes various modifications in the Massachusetts government, actions that many colonists consider tyrannical.
	First Continental Congress	Offers something less than an olive branch in calling for a complete economic boycott of British trade goods and advising colonists to prepare for possible war.
1775	Lexington and Concord	Warfare breaks out when British regulars attempt to seize powder and arms at Concord.
	Lord Dunmore's Proclamation	Offers freedom to slaves and indentured servants in Virginia who who will fight for the Crown.
	Invasion of Canada	Patriot attempt to conquer Quebec Province as the fourteenth colony in rebellion does not succeed.

1776	Common Sense	Thomas Paine demands independence and denounces colonists too faint-hearted to break free of perceived British tyranny.
	Massive British buildup	Crown musters huge martial force, including Hessians, to put down the American rebellion.
	Declaration of Independence	Second Continental Congress proclaims American desire to become a separate nation.

ranking generals—William Howe, Henry Clinton, and "Gentleman Johnny" Burgoyne—to sail to Boston and join Gage. George III also declared Massachusetts to be in a state of rebellion, which permitted redcoats to shoot down suspected rebels on sight should that be necessary to quell opposition. Eventually this decree would be applied to all 13 provinces.

General Gage received the ministry's secret orders in mid-April 1775. Being on the scene, he was not quite as convinced as his superiors about American martial weakness. Gage had repeatedly urged caution in his reports to home officials, but now he had no choice; he had to act. Because the rebel leaders had already gotten word of the orders and fled to the countryside, Gage decided upon a reconnaissance in force mission. He would send a column of regulars to Concord, a town some 20 miles northwest of Boston that served as a storage point for patriot gunpowder and related military supplies. Once there, the troops were to seize or destroy as much weaponry and ammunition as possible. Gage hoped this maneuver could be effected without bloodshed; he feared the onset of full-scale warfare if patriot lives were lost.

After dark on April 18 some 700 British troops under Lieutenant Colonel Francis Smith moved out across Boston's back bay. Popular leaders monitored this deployment, and soon Paul Revere and William Dawes were riding through the countryside alerting the populace to what was happening. In Lexington, 5 miles east of Concord and on the road that the king's troops had taken, 70 militiamen, trained to respond at a moment's notice, gathered at the local tavern with their captain, John Parker. Samuel Adams and John Hancock were also present. Obviously outnumbered, the Minutemen debated possible actions. They decided to respond to the redcoats' provocative incursion into the countryside by acting as an army of observation.

Parker and his men lined up across the village green as the British column bore down on them at dawn (Adams and Hancock, as known enemies, fled into the woods). The Minutemen were not there to exchange shots, but to warn the regulars against trespassing on the property of free-born British subjects. As the redcoats came closer, Parker tried to shout out words to this effect. He could not be heard. A mysterious shot rang out just as the Minutemen, having made their protest, turned to leave the green. The shot caused troops at the front of the British column to level their arms and fire. Before order was restored, several of Parker's men lay wounded, mostly shot in their backs. Eight of them died in what was the opening volley of the War for American Independence.

The redcoats regrouped and continued their march to Concord. Once there, a detachment moved out to cross the Old North Bridge in search of weapons and gunpowder. Rallying militiamen repulsed them. Falling back to the center of town, the redcoats left behind three dead comrades. Now blood had been spilled on both sides.

Lieutenant Colonel Smith began to worry that his column might be cut to pieces by harassing citizen-soldiers, so he ordered a retreat. The rest of the day turned into a rout as an aroused citizenry fired away at the British from behind trees and stone fences. Only a relief column of some 1100 troops, which Gage had the foresight to send out, saved Smith's column. Final casualty figures showed 273 redcoats dead or wounded, as compared to 95 colonists. Lexington and Concord were clear blows to the notion of the invincibility of British arms and suggested that American citizens, when defending their own property, could and would hold their own against better-trained British soldiers.

As word of the bloodshed spread, New Englanders rallied to the patriot banner. Within days thousands of colonists poured into hastily assembled military camps surrounding Boston. Thomas Gage and his soldiers were now trapped, and they could only hope that promised reinforcements would soon reach them. The *rage militaire* was on. Everyone, it seemed, wanted to be a temporary soldier—and fire a few shots at a redcoat or two before returning home again.

This painting, based on an eyewitness sketch, shows British troops under Lieutenant Colonel Francis Smith marching into Concord to destroy patriot stores of gunpowder and military supplies.

Most colonists believed the ministry would soon regain its senses and quickly restore all American rights rather than engage in warfare. They did not realize that imperial leaders were irrevocably committed to eradicating all American resistance, or that the conflict would become a long and grueling war in which the fortitude to endure would determine the eventual winner.

Moderates Versus Radicals in Congress

The shadow of Lexington and Concord loomed heavily as the **Second Continental Congress** convened in Philadelphia in May 1775. Despite the recent bloodshed, very few delegates had become advocates of independence. New Englanders like Samuel and John Adams were leaning that way, but the vast majority held out hope for a resolution of differences. By the summer of 1775 two factions had emerged in Congress: the one led by New Englanders, favoring a formal declaration of independence, and the opposing reconciliationist or moderate faction, whose strength lay in the Middle Colonies and whose most influential leader was John Dickinson of Pennsylvania. The two factions debated every issue with regard to possible effects on the subject of independence. The moderates remained the dominant faction into the spring of 1776, but then the weight of the spreading rebellion swung the pendulum decisively toward those favoring independence.

Early congressional wrangling centered on the organization of the Continental army. In mid-June 1775 the delegates, at the urging of the New Englanders, voted to adopt the patriot forces around Boston as a Continental military establishment. They asked the other colonies to supply additional troops and unanimously named wealthy Virginia planter George Washington, who had been appearing in Congress in his military uniform, to serve as commander in chief. Washington had qualifications for the job, including his combat experiences during the Seven Years' War. Also, he was a southerner. His presence at the head of the army was a way to involve the other colonies, at least symbolically, in what was still a localized conflict being fought by New Englanders.

Although the delegates agreed about the need for central military planning and coordination, the moderates worried about how British officials would view the formation of an independent American army. At the urging of John Dickinson, they wanted Congress to prepare a formal statement explaining this bold action. In early July the delegates approved the "Declaration of the Causes and Necessity for Taking up Arms," which they sent to England. The purpose of a Continental force, the "Declaration" stressed, was not "to dis-

George Washington, who regularly appeared in Congress in military uniform, was a natural choice to serve as the Continental army's commander in chief.
Metropolitan Museum of Art, Bequest of Grace Wilkes, 1922.

solve that union which has so long and so happily subsisted between us." Rather, Congress had formed the army to assure the defense of American lives, liberty, and property until "hostilities shall cease on the part of the aggressors, and all danger of their being renewed shall be removed, and not before." Given home government attitudes about American intentions, this document received scant ministerial attention.

The moderates were persons caught in a bind. Even though deeply concerned about American rights, they feared independence. Like many other colonists of substantial wealth, they envisioned internal chaos in the colonies without the stabilizing influence of British rule. They also doubted whether a weak, independent American nation could long survive among aggressive European powers.

The moderates thus tried to keep open the channels of communication with the British government. Characteristic of such attempts was John Dickinson's "Olive Branch" petition, approved by Congress in July 1775. This document stated that "our breasts retain too tender a regard for the kingdom from which we derive our origin" to want independence. It implored George III to intercede with Parliament and find some means to preserve English liberties in America. Like so many other petitions, the Olive Branch had little impact in Britain. By the autumn of 1775 the home government was already mobilizing for full-scale war. This was one form of a response to the Olive Branch. The other was a public declaration that all the colonies were now in open rebellion.

The Expanding Martial Conflict

Congressional moderates accomplished little, except to delay a declaration of independence. The war kept spreading, making a formal renunciation of British allegiance seem almost anticlimactic. On May 10, 1775, citizen-soldiers under Vermont's Ethan Allen and Connecticut's Benedict Arnold seized the once-mighty fortress of Ticonderoga at the southern end of Lake Champlain. This action netted the Americans more than 100 serviceable artillery pieces that would eventually be deployed to help drive British forces from Boston.

Taking Ticonderoga raised the question of luring Canada into the rebellion. Many hoped that Quebec Province would become the fourteenth colony, so much so that Congress approved a two-pronged invasion in the late summer of 1775. One column under General Richard Montgomery, a former British officer who had resettled in America, traveled down Lake Champlain and seized Montreal. The second column under Colonel Benedict Arnold proceeded on a harrowing march through the woods of Maine and finally emerged before the walls of Quebec City. Early on the morning of December 31, 1775, combined forces under these two commanders boldly tried to take the city but were repulsed. Montgomery lost his life, Arnold was seriously wounded, and great numbers of patriot troops were killed or captured. The rebel attempt to seize Canada had failed. This effort, however, made it increasingly difficult to argue that the colonists were only interested in defending their homes and families until political differences with Britain could be resolved.

Back in Boston, meanwhile, generals Howe, Clinton, and Burgoyne arrived in May 1775 and urged General Gage to resume the offensive against the New Englanders. That opportunity came on June 17 just after patriot forces moved onto Charlestown peninsula north of Boston's back bay. The rebels planned to dig in on Bunker Hill but constructed the most extended portions of their line on Breed's Hill closer to Boston. After lengthy debate the British generals decided upon a frontal assault by some 2500 troops under William Howe's command to show the rebels the awesome power of concentrated British arms.

That afternoon, as citizens in Boston watched the misnamed Battle of Bunker Hill from rooftops, Howe's detachment made three separate charges, finally dislodging the patriots, who were running out of ammunition. This engagement was the bloodiest of the whole war. The British suffered 1054 casualties—40 percent of the redcoats engaged. American casualties amounted to 411, or 30 percent. Among those slain was Samuel Adams's close political associate, Dr. Joseph Warren, mourned by patriots everywhere.

The realization that patriot soldiers had been driven from the field undermined the euphoria that followed the rout of the redcoats at Lexington and Concord. Still, the British gained little advantage because they had failed to pursue the fleeing rebels. They remained trapped in Boston, surrounded by thousands of armed and angry colonists. Henry Clinton summarized matters best when he called Bunker Hill "a dear bought victory," adding dryly that "another such would have ruined us."

Lord Dunmore's Proclamation of Emancipation

New England and Canada did not long remain the only theaters of war. Before the end of 1775 fighting erupted in the South. In Virginia the protagonist was John Murray, Lord Dunmore, who was the last royal governor of the Old Dominion. In May 1774 Dunmore had dissolved the Assembly because the burgesses called for a day of fasting and prayer in support of the Bostonians. Incensed at Dunmore's arbitrary action, Virginia's gentleman-planters started meeting in provincial conventions, acting as if royal authority no longer existed.

Dunmore resented such impudence. In June 1775 he fled Williamsburg and announced that British subjects still loyal to the Crown should join him in bringing the planter elite to its senses. Very few citizens came forward. By autumn Dunmore, who used a naval vessel in Chesapeake Bay as his headquarters, had concluded that planter resistance could only be broken by turning Virginia's slaves against their masters. On November 7, 1775, he issued an emancipation proclamation. It read in part: "And I do hereby further declare all indentured servants, Negroes, or others . . . free, that are able and willing to bear arms."

LEXINGTON AND CONCORD

The Shot Heard 'Round the World

AFTER the bloody skirmish at Lexington, Lieutenant Colonel Francis Smith's redcoats marched toward their intended target, the village of Concord, which served as a central storage point for patriot powder and arms. Smith's troops were to "seize and destroy" these military goods.

Just east of Concord, Smith's column found the road blocked by 250 Minutemen under Major John Buttrick. Choosing not to fight, Buttrick ordered his citizen-soldiers to retreat. They did so in disciplined fashion, marching into Concord just ahead of the redcoats and then to higher ground a mile north of the village across Old North Bridge.

Colonel Smith soon had his troops out hunting for supplies. He sent six companies up to North Bridge to seize any powder and weapons stored at farms in that area. Once there, Captain Lawrence Parsons led three companies across the bridge, right past the patriot militia. Captain Walter Laurie secured the bridge with the remaining companies.

At this juncture, just a little before 10 A.M., Buttrick's Minutemen saw a cloud of smoke rising from the village. The British were burning Concord's liberty tree, along with some gun carriages. An alarmed patriot officer shouted, "Would you let them burn down our town?" Angered by this prospect, Buttrick's troops advanced and engaged Laurie's redcoats; both contingents fired at each other across the bridge. The British, sustaining several casualties, fell back to Concord in reacting to these shots "heard 'round the world."

By late morning, Smith realized that the local patriots, fearing an incursion, had earlier that week moved most of the military supplies to other locales. The redcoat mission was a failure. Worse yet, hundreds of militiamen, enraged by news of events at Lexington, were gathering behind trees and stone fences, just waiting for Smith's retreat.

Had General Gage not sent out a relief force under Hugh, Lord Percy, Smith's redcoats might have been exterminated. The two British columns linked up just east of Lexington. By sundown, they had reached Charlestown peninsula, just north of Boston, having barely survived the opening encounter of the War for American Independence.

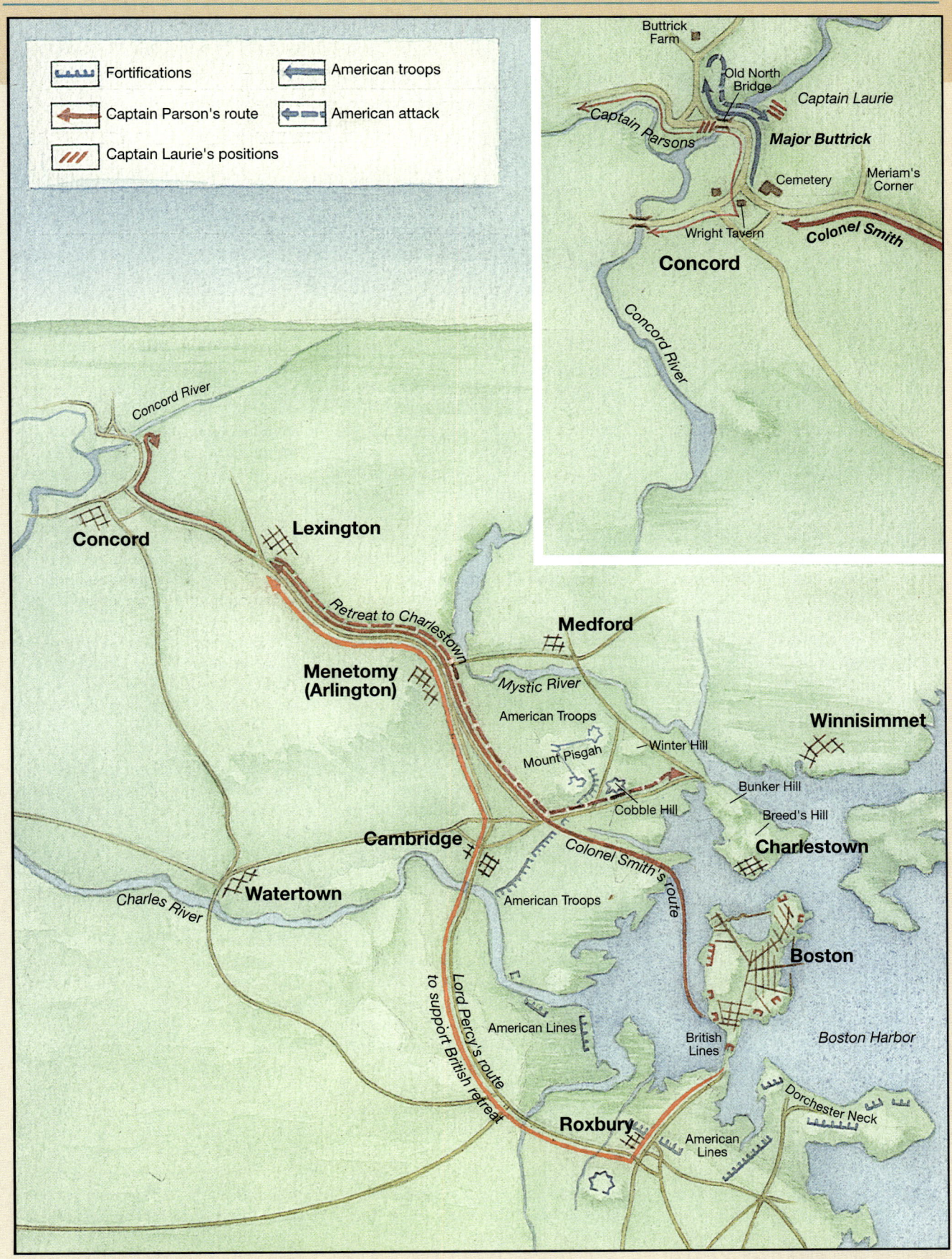

THE American Mosaic

The Battle of Bunker Hill

EARLY on Friday evening, June 16, 1775, rebel military leaders held an urgent meeting in Cambridge, Massachusetts. Intelligence had just reached them that redcoats under Lieutenant General Thomas Gage would soon attempt to break out of Boston. The British plan was to cross the body of water south of Boston, take Dorchester Heights, then sweep north through Cambridge, the patriot army command base, and send the rebels, now numbering well over 10,000 volunteers, reeling back into the countryside. The target date for this operation was Sunday, June 18.

The assembled rebel officers decided to divert the British from their plans by moving patriot lines yet closer to Boston. They gave orders to Colonel William Prescott to fortify Bunker Hill on Charlestown peninsula, just to the north of Boston. The rebels would now control terrain from which they could cannonade British vessels in the harbor and even the city, if necessary. Should the British attempt to dislodge the rebels, they would have to storm up a hill rising 130 feet above sea level into withering patriot fire.

Before midnight on June 16, Prescott, leading more than 1000 troops, reached Bunker Hill. At this point he called together the other officers, including Colonel Richard Gridley, an experienced military engineer, to discuss the placement of earthworks. As they studied the terrain around them, they could see another hill some 600 yards closer to Boston, which rose sharply to 75 feet above sea level. Gridley recommended a line of trenches and a redoubt on that site. Bunker Hill, the group concluded, should serve as a secondary line of defense.

Moving forward as quietly as possible, the Americans dug in rapidly on Breed's Hill, knowing that daylight would expose their activity. At dawn on Saturday, June 17, sailors on board a British war vessel in the harbor spied the new rebel position and opened up with artillery fire. The cannonade awoke everyone in the vicinity, including Gage, who soon met in a council of war with three other generals—William Howe, Henry Clinton, and John Burgoyne—all of whom had recently arrived in Boston.

Gage, despite his superior rank as commander of British military forces in North America, deferred to the three major generals in his presence. Since Gage had repeatedly urged caution in handling the rebels, many home leaders had started asking whether he was too timid for the task at hand. The appearance of Howe, Clinton, and Burgoyne, he knew, was hardly a vote of confidence.

During the imperial wars, British military officers had repeatedly characterized the colonists as fainthearted fighters. Reflecting this attitude, the three generals could not fathom how Gage had gotten his troops trapped in Boston by untrained, disorganized, and ill-disciplined rebels. The generals, not surprisingly, demanded an immediate offensive against Prescott's troops. They hoped for a victory so crushing that rebel resistance would disintegrate completely.

Then they debated tactics. Henry Clinton wanted to seize control of the narrow neck of land behind Bunker Hill connecting Charlestown peninsula to the mainland. That maneuver would trap Prescott's force, which then could be defeated and captured in detail. Howe and Burgoyne favored a direct frontal assault. The rebels would wither and run, they argued, in the face of concentrated, disciplined British arms. Gage reluctantly agreed to a frontal assault. He hoped the other generals were correct, that the Americans would flee rather than fight, but deep inside he expected heavy casualties.

British regulars were very well trained soldiers. They would rather stand up to furious enemy fire than to the wrath of their officers and the brutal military penalties for insubordination of any kind. Insolence toward an officer or attempted desertion resulted in punishments of up to 1000 lashes well laid on, which few persons could survive.

New soldiers received rigorous training in the basics of combat. When deployed in front of the enemy, they moved easily from column formations into three battle lines. After troops in the first line fired their smoothbore muskets, affectionately known as the "Brown Bess," they reloaded as their comrades in the next two lines stepped in front of them and fired their muskets in turn.

Smoothbore muskets were inaccurate weapons with an effective range of less than 80 yards. Experienced soldiers going through the steps of ramming powder and ball down the barrel could rarely get off more than two shots a minute. Thus most battle casualties came from bayonet wounds when competing armies, once having fired three or four

rounds at very close range, charged forward and engaged in hand-to-hand combat. The bayonet, fastened to the end of the musket, was the major killing weapon of eighteenth-century European-style warfare, and the proficient soldier more often stabbed than shot his opponent to death.

Knowing all of this, General Howe, whom Gage placed in charge of the assault, envisioned an overwhelming victory over a motley band of rebels. By 3 P.M., more than 2000 redcoats had been ferried across the bay and were ready to advance. Howe sent forward troops on his left under General Robert Pigot directly at Breed's Hill to divert the Americans. In turn, he led his column along the shore to break through a patriot line behind a rail fence. He expected to sweep these defenders aside in a classic flanking maneuver, then swing sharply to the left and cut Prescott's soldiers off from retreat as they dueled with Pigot's redcoats on their front. Bayonets would finish the expected rout.

Galling rebel fire frustrated the first British assault. The patriots held off shooting until the last possible moment, then unleashed a furious series of blasts. The redcoats staggered and fell back. Wrote one British officer with Howe, we "were served up in companies against the grass fence, without being able to penetrate. . . . Most of our grenadiers and light infantry, in presenting themselves, lost three-fourths, and many nine-tenths, of their men." Far to the left Pigot's soldiers also ran back from the blistering volleys of musket fire being laid down by Prescott's defenders.

Retreating on all fronts, the British regrouped and then tried to execute Howe's plan a second time. "It was surprising," wrote an observer, to watch the redcoats "step over . . . dead bodies, as though they had been logs of wood." Once again, exclaimed one British officer, "an incessant stream of fire" forced them back. From his vantage point in Boston, General Burgoyne described what was happening as "a complication of horror . . . more dreadfully terrible" than anything he had ever seen. He wondered whether "defeat" would bring on "a final loss to the British empire in America."

At this critical juncture, Howe, reinforced by 400 fresh troops, decided to throw everything against the redoubt, where, unknown to him, Prescott's troops were running out of ammunition. Now the British, with regimental pride at stake, shouted "push on, push on." Within minutes they overran the Americans, most of whom lacked bayonets to defend themselves. Prescott's coolness under heavy fire resulted in an orderly retreat, but most of the rebel casualties occurred among defenders who did not evacuate in time. Included among them was Samuel Adams's valued political associate, Dr. Joseph Warren, already wounded but who died from bayonet wounds inflicted by an enraged redcoat who apparently recognized him and cried out that agitators like Warren were responsible for such horrible carnage.

The misnamed Battle of Bunker Hill was over within little more than an hour. Most of the patriots did escape, having no way of knowing that they had participated in the bloodiest fight of the Revolutionary War. The figure of 1465 combined casualties shocked everyone in what General Clinton called "a dear bought victory." The British had really gained nothing of consequence, since the American patriots still controlled the countryside surrounding Boston and Charlestown peninsula.

Dunmore hoped that Virginia's slaves would break their chains and join with him in teaching their former masters that talk of liberty was a two-edged sword. The plan backfired. Irate planters suppressed copies of the proclamation and spread the rumor of a royal hoax designed to lure blacks into Dunmore's camp so that he could sell them to the owners of West Indian sugar plantations, where inhuman working conditions and very high mortality rates prevailed. Still, as many as 2000 slaves took their chances and escaped to the royal standard.

Those blacks who first fled became a part of **Dunmore's Ethiopian regiment,** which made the mistake of engaging Virginia militiamen in a battle at Great Bridge in December 1775. Having had no time for even the fundamentals of military training, the regiment took a drubbing. This battle ended any semblance of royal authority in Virginia. Dunmore and his following soon retreated to a flotilla of vessels in Chesapeake Bay. During the next few months the numbers of royalist adherents kept growing, but then smallpox struck, killing hundreds of people. In the summer of 1776 Dunmore sailed away, leaving behind planters who more closely guarded their human property while demanding independence from those in Britain whom they denounced as tyrants.

Resolving the Independence Question

Lord Dunmore's experiences highlighted the collapse of British political authority. Beginning in the summer of 1775, colony after colony witnessed an end to royal government. To fill the void, the patriots elected ad hoc provincial congresses. These bodies functioned as substitute legislatures and dealt with pressing local issues. They also took particular interest in suppressing suspected loyalists.

During that same summer Massachusetts asked the Continental Congress for permission to establish a more enduring government based on a written constitution. After ousting its royal governor, New Hampshire followed suit. These requests forced Congress to act. The delegates did so in early November, stating that Massachusetts, New Hampshire, and any others might adopt "such a form of government, as . . . will best produce the happiness of the people," yet only if written constitutions specified that these governments would exist until "the present dispute between Great Britain and the colonies" came to an end. The moderates realized that new state governments, as much if not more than a separate army, had the appearance of de facto independence. They did everything they could to prevent a total rejection of British political authority in America.

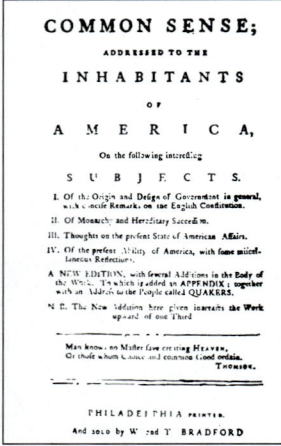

Thomas Paine's *Common Sense*, first published in January 1776, urged the colonists to embrace independence and a bold new world of political freedom.

John Dickinson led the campaign in Congress to suppress discussion of a declaration of independence. In early November 1775 he got the Pennsylvania Assembly to instruct its congressional delegates to "dissent from, and utterly reject, any propositions . . . that may cause or lead to a separation from our mother country." New York, Delaware, Maryland, and South Carolina soon adopted similar instructions. Thus there was to be no resolution of the independence question before 1776.

Events outside of Congress were about to overwhelm the moderates. In January 1776 Thomas Paine, a recent migrant from England who had once been a corsetmaker's apprentice, published a pamphlet entitled **Common Sense.** It became an instant best-seller, running through 25 editions and 120,000 copies over the next three months.

Common Sense electrified the populace with its dynamic, forceful language. Paine communicated a sense of urgency about moving toward independence. He attacked congressional moderates for not being bold enough to break with the past, and he likewise denounced the British monarchy, writing: "The folly of hereditary right in Kings, is that nature disapproves it . . . by giving mankind *an ass for a lion.*" He encouraged Americans to adopt republican forms of government, since "every spot of the old world is overrun with oppression." The fate of all humans everywhere, he concluded, hung in the balance. *Common Sense* put severe pressure on the moderates, but they held on doggedly, hoping against hope that Great Britain would turn from its belligerent course and begin serious negotiations with Congress.

At the end of February 1776 another significant incident took place in the form of a short, bloody battle between loyalists and patriot militia at Moore's Creek Bridge in North Carolina. This engagement resulted in more than a rout of local **tories.** Now facing a shooting war, North Carolina's provincial congress reversed instructions to its congressional delegates and allowed them to discuss independence and vote on a plan of national government. Soon thereafter the Virginians, furious about Lord Dunmore's activities, issued similar instructions. Then leaders in Rhode Island, impatient with everyone else, boldly declared their own independence in early May.

On June 7, 1776, Richard Henry Lee, speaking on behalf of the Virginia provincial convention, presented formal resolutions to Congress. Lee urged "that these United Colonies are, and of right ought to be, free and independent states, . . . and that all political connection between them and the State of Great Britain is, and ought to be, totally dissolved." The resolutions also called for the creation of a national government and the formation of alliances with foreign nations in support of the war effort.

Within a few days Congress established two committees, one headed by John Dickinson to produce a plan of central government and another to prepare a statement on independence. Thomas Jefferson (1743–1826), a tall, young Virginian, agreed to write a draft text on independence, which the committee laid before Congress on Friday, June 28. John Adams was expecting "the greatest debate of all" on Monday, July 1. In the session that day Dickinson spoke forcefully against a formal severance of ties with Great Britain. Americans, he argued, could not endure against superior British arms, especially "when we are in so wretched a state of preparation" for war. Nor did he think that significant foreign aid from France and other nations would be readily forthcoming. Moving forward with independence, he concluded, would be like reading "a little more in the Doomsday Book of America."

The delegates listened politely, but Dickinson was no longer in step with the mood of Congress. At the end of the day they voted on Lee's resolutions, and nine state delegations gave their assent. Political maneuvering produced what could be described as a unanimous vote the next day when 12 states voted affirmatively. New York's delegates had not yet received instructions from leaders back home, so they abstained, even though they were now personally in favor of independence. By so overwhelming a ratification of Lee's resolutions, Congress technically declared independence on Tuesday, July 2.

Congress next turned to the consideration of Jefferson's draft, which one delegate in a classic understatement called "a pretty good one." The delegates made only a few changes. They deleted a controversial statement blaming the slave trade on the king as well as a phrase repudiating friendship with the British people. By Thursday evening, July 4, 1776, everything was in place, and Congress unanimously adopted Jefferson's document, a masterful explanation of the reasons why the colonists were seeking independence.

The Declaration of Independence proclaimed to the world that Americans had been terribly mis-

Delegates to the Second Continental Congress formally debated whether to declare independence on July 1, 1776. After making minor modifications in Jefferson's draft, they unanimously approved the Declaration of Independence on July 4.

treated by their parent nation. Much of the text represents a summary list of grievances, ranging from misuse of a standing army of redcoats in the colonies and the abuse of the rightful powers of popularly elected colonial assemblies to the ultimate crime, starting an unjustified war against loyal subjects. The Declaration blamed George III for the pattern of tyranny. He had failed to control his ministers, thereby abandoning his role as a true servant of the people.

Besides grievances, the Declaration also offered a long-range vision. Jefferson believed the Revolution would succeed only if Americans acted with a clear and noble purpose. Since "all men are created equal" and have "certain unalienable rights," which Jefferson defined as "life, liberty, and the pursuit of happiness," Americans needed to dedicate themselves to the establishment of a whole new set of political relationships guaranteeing all citizens fundamental liberties. The great task facing the revolutionary generation would be to institute republican forms of government, based on the rule of law and human reason. Governments had "to effect" the "safety and happiness" of all persons in the name of human decency, and all persons would be obligated to work for the greater good of the whole community.

Through Jefferson's words, the patriots of 1776 committed themselves to uplifting humanity in what they viewed as a world overrun by greed, petty ambition, and political tyranny. They would not realize their lofty purpose, however, unless they found the means to defeat the huge British military force arriving in America at the very time that Congress was debating and approving the Declaration of Independence.

WITHOUT VISIBLE ALLIES: THE WAR IN THE NORTH

British officials had made a great blunder in 1775. Disdaining the colonists as "a set of upstart vagabonds, the dregs and scorn of the human species," they had woefully underestimated their opponent. Lexington and Concord drove home this reality. Although the king's civil and military leaders continued to presume their superiority, they became far more serious about waging war. They had come to realize that snuffing out the rebellion was a complex military assignment, given the sheer geographic size of the colonies and the absence of a strategically vital center, such as a national capital, that, if captured, would end the contest. They also understood that the use of an invading army was not the easiest way to regain the political allegiance of a people no longer placing such great value on being British subjects.

Britain's Massive Military Buildup

Directing the imperial war effort were King George, Lord North, and Lord George Germain (1716–1785), who became the American secretary in 1775. Germain, who during the Seven Years' War had been court-martialed on charges of cowardice in battle and thrown out of the British army, was a surprisingly effective administrator. He proved adept at dealing with the bureaucratic and inefficient imperial military machine. His skills became evident in planning for the campaign of 1776—the largest land and sea offensive executed by any western nation until the Allied invasion of North Africa in 1942.

Step by step, Germain pulled the elements together. Of utmost importance was overall campaign strategy. It involved concentrating as many troops as possible on the port of New York City, where great numbers of loyalists lived, then subduing the surrounding countryside as a food and supply base. Loyalists would be used to reinstitute royal government, and the king's forces would engage and crush the rebel army. The American will to resist had to be shattered, and Germain hoped the king's forces could do so in only one campaign season. The longer the rebels lasted, he thought, the greater would be their prospects for success.

Next was the matter of assembling the military forces. It was not the practice in Britain, or elsewhere in Europe, to draw upon all able-bodied, adult males. By and large the middle classes were exempt from service because they were considered productive members of society. The rank and file would come from two sources. First would be the poorer, less productive subjects in the British Isles either recruited or dragooned into service. Since life in European armies was often brutal, it was not always possible to convince or coerce even the most destitute of subjects to sign enlistment papers.

A second source would be the principalities of Germany. Before the end of the war, six German states procured 30,000 soldiers. Some 17,000 came from Hesse-Cassel, where the local head of state coerced many unwilling subjects into service. In return, he received cash payments from the British Crown for each soldier supplied. **Hessians** and downtrodden Britons, including many Irish subjects, thus became the backbone of His Majesty's army.

Certainly as significant a matter as troop recruitment was military leadership. Home government leaders viewed General Gage as too timid and too respectful of Americans. The king recalled Gage in October 1775, naming William Howe (1729–1814) to replace him as commander in chief. William's brother Richard, Admiral Lord Howe (1726–1799), took charge of the naval flotilla that transported thousands of troops to America in 1776.

Lord Germain expected the Howe brothers to use their combined land and naval forces to smash and bayonet the rebels into submission. However, they did not turn out to be fearsome commanders. Politically, they identified with Whig leaders in England who believed the colonists had some legitimate grievances. They intended to move in careful steps, using the presence of so many well-trained regulars to persuade Americans to sign loyalty oaths and renounce the rebellion. In failing to achieve the strategic objective of wiping out patriot resistance in only one campaign season, the less than daring Howe brothers actually helped save the patriot cause from early extinction.

The Campaign for New York

Not yet aware of the scale of British mobilization, New Englanders cheered loudly in mid-March 1776 when William Howe took redcoats and loyalists in tow and fled by sea to Halifax, Nova Scotia. British control of Boston had become untenable because Washington placed the cannons captured at Ticonderoga on Dorchester Heights overlooking the city. Howe's choice was to retreat or be bombarded into submission. Washington, however, did not relax. For months he had predicted the British would strike at New York City. He was absolutely right.

The king's army soon converged on Staten Island, across the bay from Manhattan. William Howe, sailing south from Halifax, arrived with 10,000 soldiers at the end of June. During July, even as Americans learned about the Declaration of Independence, more and more British troops appeared, another 20,000 by mid-August. They came in some 400 transports escorted by 70 naval vessels and 13,000 sailors under Admiral Lord Howe's supervision. All told, the Howe brothers had some 43,000 well-supplied, well-trained, and well-armed combatants. By comparison, George Washington had 28,000 troops on his muster rolls, but only 19,000 were present and fit for duty in August. Even worse, the bulk of the rebel army lacked good weapons or supplies and was deficient in training and discipline.

The decision to defend New York, which the Continental Congress insisted upon and to which Washington acceded, was one of the great rebel blunders of the war. Completely outnumbered, the American commander unwisely divided his soldiers between Manhattan and Brooklyn Heights, separated by the East River. The Howe brothers responded on August 22 by landing troops at Gravesend, Long Island, thereby putting them in an excellent position to trap Washington's force in Brooklyn. For some inexplicable reason, however, Lord Howe chose not to move his naval vessels into the East River, which would have sealed off Washington's escape route. The rebels took a severe beating from the redcoats and Hessians, but they escaped back across the East River. Washington had been lucky, and he clearly learned from his error. Never again did he place his troops in so potentially disastrous a position.

Although Washington's officers wanted to burn New York City to keep the British from using this port city as a base for military operations, Congress vetoed the proposal. When a fire broke out on September 20, 1776, the British and the Americans accused one another of starting the conflagration.

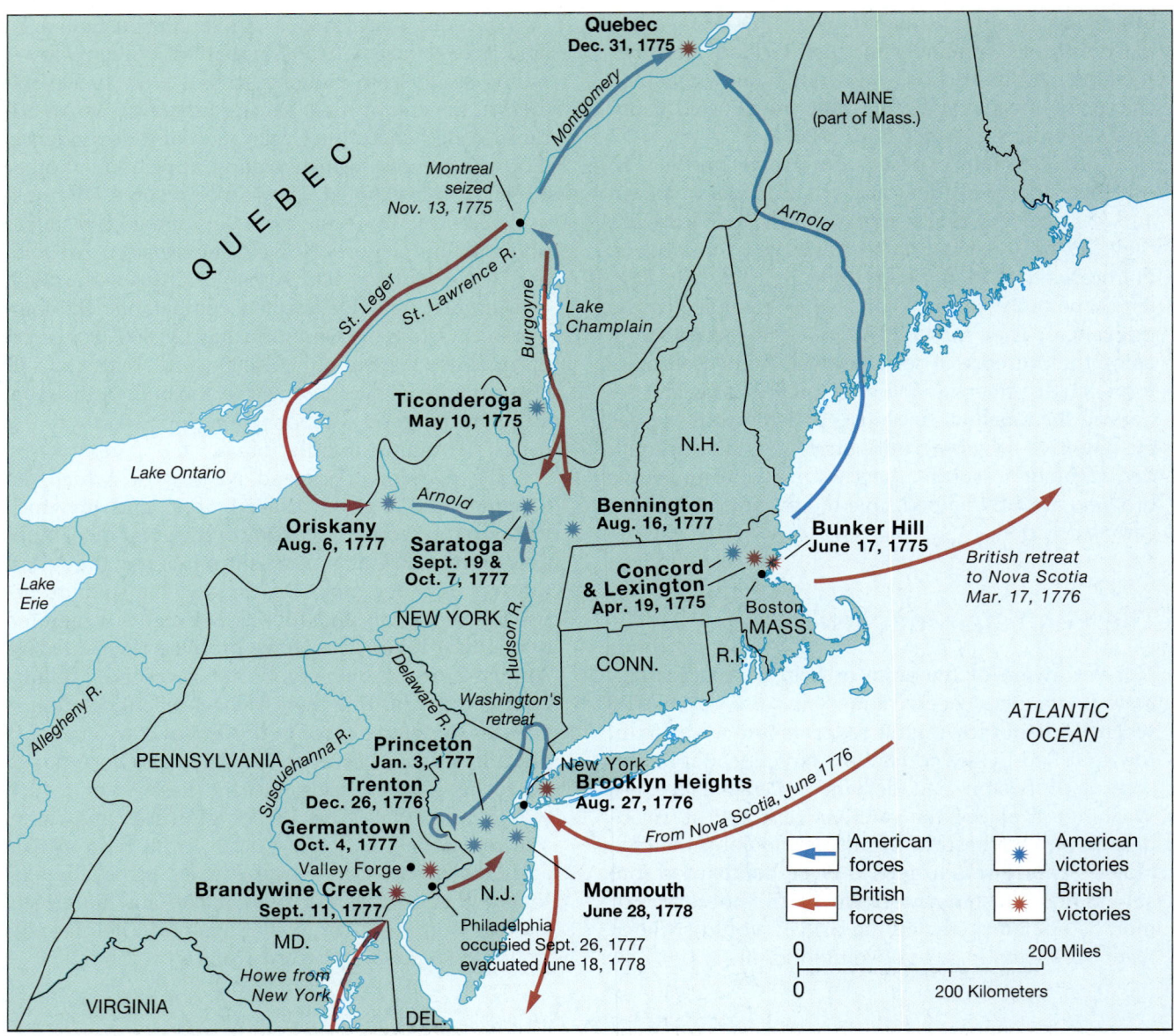

Northern Theater of War, 1775–1778

The Howe brothers moved along indecisively through the rest of the campaign season. Every time they had the advantage, they failed to destroy the rebel army. They drove Washington's forces northward out of Manhattan, then wheeled about and captured some 2000 rebels defending Fort Washington (November 16, 1776), located high on a bluff overlooking the Hudson River. Two days later a British column under Charles, Lord Cornwallis (1738–1805), nearly bagged another sizable patriot contingent at Fort Lee in New Jersey, across from Fort Washington. One of Washington's most talented field commanders, Nathanael Greene of Rhode Island, managed to extricate his force just in time.

Washington had already moved into New Jersey. He ordered a retreat, hoping to get his soldiers across the Delaware River and into Pennsylvania before the aggressive Cornwallis caught up with the dispirited rebel band. By early December 1776 what remained of Washington's army had reached Pennsylvania.

Saving the Cause at Trenton

As the half-starving, battle-wearied patriot troops fled, hundreds of them also deserted. They had learned that British muskets and bayonets could maim and kill. Others, ravaged by disease or wounded in battle, were left behind along the way with the hope of their receiving decent treatment from the enemy. The American army was on the verge of extinction. Washington wrote in mid-December, "I think the game is pretty near up.... No man, I believe, ever had a greater choice of difficulties and less means to extricate himself from them." Knowing he had virtually destroyed his prey, William Howe ordered his troops into winter camps and returned to New York City. He was sure mopping up operations could be easily completed in the spring of 1777.

At this juncture George Washington earned his credentials as an innovative commander. He assessed his desperate position and decided upon a bold counterstroke. The success of this maneuver might save his army; defeat would surely ruin it. With muster rolls showing only 6000 troops, Washington divided his soldiers into three groups and tried to recross the icy Delaware River on Christmas evening. Their targets were British outposts in New Jersey. Of the three contingents, only Washington's near-frozen band of 2400 troops accomplished this daring maneuver.

At dawn they reached Trenton, where Colonel Johann Rall's unsuspecting Hessians were still groggy with liquor from their Christmas celebration. The engagement was over in a moment. Four hundred enemy troops escaped, but the Continentals captured almost 1000 Hessians. Within another few days the elated Americans again outdueled British units at Princeton. Stunned by this flurry of rebel activity, Howe redeployed his New Jersey outposts in a semicircle much closer to New York.

Washington had done much more than regain lost ground. He had saved the Continental army from virtual extinction. Never again during the war would the British come so close to total victory—and all because of Howe's failure to demolish Washington's shattered forces when the opportunity was there.

Also of importance was Howe's decision to pull in his outposts. As the British army had marched across New Jersey, it lured thousands of neutrals and loyalists under its banner. These individuals signed loyalty oaths, thus identifying themselves publicly as enemies of the Revolution. As the British army drew back toward New York, the fury of local patriots descended on these tory neighbors whose true allegiance had been revealed.

Time and again throughout the war, British military commanders committed the error of not sustaining support for the king's friends in America. They rarely took advantage of the reservoir of loyal subjects, an estimated 20 percent of the populace, who stood ready to fight the rebels and to do anything else within reason to assure a continuation of British rule. Before the war was over an es-

Diversity of dress among American soldiers was common, but more common was the fact that few soldiers ever had the prescribed clothing.

timated 50,000 loyalists formed into nearly 70 regiments to help the British army regain control in America. British commanders, however, largely used this valuable source of troop strength ineffectively. They did not really trust loyalists or respect their fighting prowess. Their attitude was that loyalists were just colonists, a part of the "rude" American rabble. Such presumed superiority represented a major blindspot, when an essential military task involved regaining the allegiance of enough citizens to effect a complete revival of imperial political authority in America.

On the rebel side, the Trenton and Princeton victories did not result in a revived outpouring of popular support for Washington's army. When the Continentals were in flight across New Jersey, Thomas Paine stepped forth with his first *Crisis* paper. He begged the populace to rally at this moment of deep desperation. "These are the times that try men's souls," Paine stated forcefully. "The summer soldier and the sunshine patriot will, in this crisis, shrink from the service of his country; but he that stands it now, deserves the love and thanks of man and woman." Many read Paine's words, but the massive British campaign effort of 1776 had snuffed out the *rage militaire*.

The Real Continentals

One of the greatest problems facing Washington and the Continental Congress after 1776 was sustaining the rebel army's troop strength. In May 1777 the commander in chief had only 10,000 soldiers, of whom 7363 were present and fit for duty. This number increased substantially during the summer and fall, although only an estimated 11,000 Continentals entered Valley Forge. For the remainder of the war Washington's core of regulars rarely was more sizable. At times, as few as 5000 soldiers stood with him.

Certainly after his experiences in 1776, Washington understood that he must maintain "a respectable army" in the field, hoping ultimately to break Britain's will to continue the fight. He needed troops who would commit themselves to long-term service (three years or the duration), would submit to rigorous training and discipline, and would accept privation in the field. These were hardly glamorous prospects, especially when service often entailed death or dismemberment. Still, Washington, Congress, and the states could promise cash bounties for enlisting, as well as regular pay, decent clothing, adequate food, and even land at war's end. For people who had nothing to lose, long-term service in the Continental army was at least worth considering.

After 1776 the rank and file of the Continental army came to be made up of economically hard pressed and unfree citizens. Private Joseph Plumb Martin was probably better off than most who enlisted—or were forced into service. The bulk were young (ranging in age from their early teens to mid-twenties), landless, unskilled, poverty-stricken males whose families were likewise quite poor. Also well represented were indentured servants and slaves who stood as substitutes for their masters in return for guarantees of personal freedom at the war's end.

In 1777 Massachusetts became the first state to authorize the enlistment of African Americans—both slaves and freemen. Rhode Island soon followed suit by raising two black regiments. Southern states were far more reluctant to allow slaves to substitute for their masters. Maryland and Virginia ultimately did so, which caused one patriot general to query why so many "sons of freedom" seemed so anxious "to trust their all to be defended by slaves." Add to these groups captured British soldiers and deserters, particularly Hessians and Irishmen, as well as tories and criminals who were often given a choice between military service or the gallows, and a composite portrait of the real Continental army begins to emerge.

Eighteenth-century armies also accepted women in the ranks. Like their male counterparts, they were invariably living on the margins of society. These women "on the ration" (more literally half rations) must be differentiated from so-called camp followers—those who marched along with their husbands or lovers or were prostitutes. Women in service performed various functions, ranging from caring for the sick and wounded, cooking, and mending clothes to scavenging battlefields for clothing and equipment and burying the dead. On occasion they became directly involved in combat. Such a person was hard-drinking Margaret "Dirty Kate" Corbin. Her husband, a cannoneer, was shot dead when British forces attacked and captured Fort Washington in November 1776. Kate Corbin stepped forth, took his place, and helped fire the artillery piece until she also sustained a serious

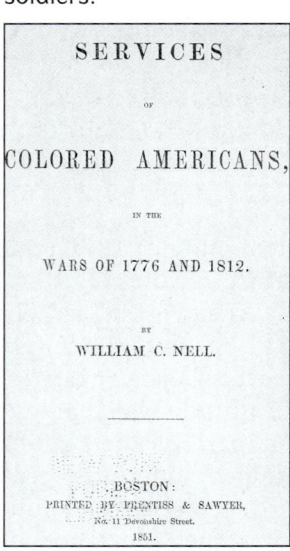

The title page of a first edition on the history of African-American soldiers.

Deborah Sampson served in the army under the name of Timothy Thayer.

THE PEOPLE SPEAK

Thomas Paine's *American Crisis I* (December 1776)

In 1774 Benjamin Franklin, then residing in England, urged Thomas Paine to resettle in America and make his living as a writer. Paine was 37 years old at the time and had failed at virtually everything. He had nothing to lose, so he sailed for Philadelphia, where he gained the opportunity to become one of the great pamphleteers of the Revolution. His *Common Sense* (January 1776) was a runaway bestseller and clearly helped push American patriots toward independence. "We have it in our power to begin the world over again," Paine wrote excitedly in *Common Sense,* but that possibility depended on beating the British militarily. By the end of 1776 the Continental army was struggling to survive, having been shoved by British forces all the way across New Jersey into Pennsylvania. Paine, traveling with the army, penned his first *Crisis* paper to assist in reviving patriot fervor for the cause of liberty. His words, though powerful, had little effect in getting more Americans to commit to long-term military service against the British, a chronic patriot problem after 1776.

> These are the times that try men's souls. The summer soldier and the sun-shine patriot will, in this crisis, shrink from the service of his country: but he that stands it *now*, deserves the thanks of man and woman. Tyranny, like hell, is not easily conquered: yet we have this consolation with us, that the harder the conflict, the more glorious the triumph. What we obtain too cheap, we esteem too lightly: 'tis dearness only that gives every thing its value. Heaven knows how to set a proper price upon its goods; and it would be strange, indeed, if so celestial an article as freedom should not be highly rated. Britain, with an army to enforce her tyranny, has declared that she has a right, not only to tax, but 'to bind us in all cases whatsoever:' and if being bound in that manner is not slavery, there is not such a thing as slavery upon earth. Even the expression is impious: for so unlimited a power can belong only to God. . . .
>
> I turn, with the warm ardour of a friend, to those who have nobly stood, and are yet determined to stand the matter out. I call not upon a few, but upon all; not on this state, or that state, but on every state. Up and help us. Lay your shoulders to the wheel. Better have too much force than too little, when so great an object is at stake. Let it be told to the future world, that in the depth of winter, when nothing but hope and virtue could survive, that the city and the country, alarmed at one common danger, came forth to meet and to repulse it. Say not that thousands are gone: turn out your tens of thousands: throw not the burden of the day upon providence, but show your faith by your good works, that God may bless you. It matters not where you live, or what rank of life you hold; the evil or the blessing will reach you all. The far and the near, the home counties and the back, the rich and the poor, shall suffer or rejoice alike. The heart that feels not now, is dead. The blood of his children shall curse his cowardice, who shrinks back at a time when a little might have saved the whole and made them happy. I love the man that can smile in trouble—that can gather strength from distress, and grow brave by reflection. It is the business of little minds to shrink; but he, whose heart is firm, and whose conscience approves his conduct, will pursue his principles unto death. My own line of reasoning is to myself, as strait and clear as a ray of light. Not all the treasures of the world, so far as I believe, could have induced me to support an offensive war; for I think it murder: but if a thief break into my house—burn and destroy my property, and kill, or threaten to kill me and those that are in it, and to 'bind me in all cases whatsoever,' to his absolute will, am I to suffer it? . . . Let them call me rebel, and welcome; I feel no concern from it; but I should suffer the misery of devils, were I to make a whore of my soul, by swearing allegiance to one whose character is that of a sottish, stupid, stubborn, worthless, brutish man. . . .
>
> This is our situation—and who will, may know it. By perseverance and fortitude, we have the prospect of a glorious issue; by cowardice and submission, the sad choice of a variety of evils—a ravaged country—a depopulated city—habitations without safety—and slavery without hope—our homes turned into barracks and bawdy-houses for Hessians—and a future race to provide for, whose fathers we shall doubt of! Look on this picture, and weep over it! and if there yet remains one thoughtless wretch, who believes it not, let him suffer it unlamented.
>
> *December, 1776*

Source: Thomas Paine, *American Crisis I* (December 1776).

wound, from which she eventually recovered. The British army allowed 1 woman in the ranks for every 10 men; the Continental ratio was closer to 1 in 15.

Whether male or female, a unifying characteristic of Washington's post-1776 Continentals was poverty and, in many cases, lack of personal freedom—much like their counterparts in the British army. As a group, they repeatedly risked their lives in return for promises: food, clothing, pay, and even land on which to make a decent living after the war. Their dreams of future opportunity depended upon the success of the rebellion, and that is one reason why they willingly endured, even though the far more prosperous civilian populace ignored their privation at such encampments as Valley Forge.

RESCUING THE PATRIOTS: TOWARD GLOBAL CONFLICT

The struggles of the American rebels did not go unobserved in European diplomatic circles. France and Spain, in particular, hoped to see the rebellion succeed. Their concerns, however, were not wholly altruistic. Territorial losses sustained during the Seven Years' War had swung the European balance of power decisively toward Great Britain. From the perspective of the Duc de Choiseul, France's foreign minister, the growing rift between Britain and America after 1763 represented an opportunity to deflate the puffed-up British lion. Losing the colonies would weaken the British empire immeasurably. France, concluded Choiseul, could only benefit from the Americans gaining their independence.

Neither Choiseul nor his protégé, the Comte de Vergennes, who became France's foreign minister in 1774, were beacons of the Age of Enlightenment. They supported monarchism, not republicanism, and they had little interest in fostering political liberties. As hardened and cynical diplomatic veterans, they hoped to take advantage of the American rebellion. If they could shape events properly, they would enhance France's stature at the expense of an old and despised enemy. As Vergennes stated privately, "Providence had marked out this moment for the humiliation of England."

France Offers Covert Assistance

Before 1775, the French sent spies to America not only to report on events but, when possible, to help stir up ill-will toward Britain. Shortly after Congress established its Committee of Secret Correspondence in late November 1775 to open negotiations with other nations regarding war-related support, a young French aristocrat, Achard de Bonvouloir, appeared in Philadelphia. Although acting like a private citizen, Bonvouloir was actually an agent of Vergennes. His government, he told committee members, stood ready to support the rebel cause with arms and other war goods. Vergennes's role would be to provide secret assistance to the patriots while maintaining a public stance of disinterested neutrality. The French foreign minister did not want France to get caught between the colonies and England, should the Americans falter on the battlefield or suddenly reconcile differences. If the rebels demonstrated their long-term resolve and proved worthy in combat, then France would enter the war and help crush the British.

Vergennes was a master manipulator in the court of Louis XVI (reigned 1774–1793). In 1775 one of his diplomatic agents, the courtier Pierre-Augustin Caron de Beaumarchais (1732–1799), perhaps best known for writing librettos for the *Marriage of Figaro* and the *Barber of Seville,* made contacts with prominent Americans in London. Beaumarchais reported back to Vergennes, and the two of them pushed hard for the formation of a private trading company, **Roderigue Hortalez & Cie.,** the sole purpose of which was to funnel war *matériel* to the patriots. Vergennes had already convinced the Spanish government to join France in making possible the American purchases by loaning money to the rebel Congress.

Meanwhile, congressional delegates had selected one of their colleagues, Connecticut merchant Silas Deane, to travel to Europe in search of loans and war goods. In July 1776 Deane made his first contact with Beaumarchais, who informed him that the structure was already in place to provide covert aid to the rebels. A delighted Deane soon was working with Beaumarchais and others in obtaining supplies.

Although some of the merchandise was shoddy, much of it was invaluable to the patriot cause. Shipments made in 1777, for example, mostly went to the Continental army's Northern Department in upstate New York where weapons, gunpowder, tents, clothing, and shoes were in desperately short supply. French goods sustained the patriot army that defeated John Burgoyne's British army at Saratoga. Secret French aid, with a smaller portion from Spain, strengthened the rebel cause immeasurably, thereby helping the patriots to endure until the French governement came out publicly against Great Britain.

In September 1776 Congress designated two additional commissioners to join Deane in France. They were Benjamin Franklin and Arthur Lee,

Richard Henry's irascible younger brother who had lived for many years in England and had met Beaumarchais in 1775. Franklin, well-known before his arrival in Paris (he had been admitted to the French Academy of Sciences during 1772 in recognition of his electrical experiments), dominated the American delegation, whose assignment was to seek full diplomatic recognition and a formal alliance. The aging Philadelphian became a popular celebrity. With his simple dress, witty personality, worldly charm, and shrewd mind, he embodied the ideals of republicanism. Painted likenesses of him appeared everywhere, even one place that Franklin did not find very flattering—inside chamber pots.

Much more than the Philadelphian's personal charm and skillfulness as a diplomat produced an alliance. Vergennes kept pronouncing France's neutrality to avoid serious problems with the British. Invariably at public gatherings, Vergennes all but snubbed the three commissioners. In private, however, he kept priming the government of Louis XVI to build up its land and naval forces in preparation for entering the war, should circumstances warrant such a decisive move. Britain's military failures in 1777 triggered formal French intervention on behalf of the patriots.

The British Seize Philadelphia

Sir William Howe had ideas of his own regarding how to conduct the war in America. He may have been a good tactician in battle, but he had little appreciation of strategy. The home government's plan—called the **Hudson Highlands strategy**—for 1777 was to send an army under John Burgoyne south from Canada through the Lake Champlain corridor. In turn, Howe was to move troops up the Hudson River, eventually linking with Burgoyne at Albany. The overall objective was to cut off New England from the rest of the colonies before sweeping eastward in reconquering the very region that had been the seedbed of rebellion.

Sir William favored going after and destroying the main Continental army. During May and June 1777 he tried to lure Washington into a climactic battle, but the American commander refused the bait and held to a very defensible position in New Jersey's Watchung Mountains.

At this juncture Howe made a decision that may have cost Britain the war. All but abandoning the primary campaign goal of joining up with Burgoyne, he resolved to seize Philadelphia, the rebel capital, hoping at the same time to catch and crush Washington's Continentals as they moved into eastern Pennsylvania to protect the rebel capital. Howe loaded 15,000 soldiers onto vessels in New York harbor and sailed out to sea in the middle of the campaign season.

Howe's flotilla came up through Chesapeake Bay in August, landing at Head of Elk in Maryland. On September 11 the British mauled Washington's Continentals at Brandywine Creek, southwest of Philadelphia. The engagement, however, did not destroy the rebel army. Within another two weeks Sir William proudly led his troops into Philadelphia; yet, except for the establishment of comfortable winter quarters, the British commander had accomplished nothing of consequence. The Continental Congress had already moved westward to York, Pennsylvania. Howe's presence cheered local loyalists. All British proponents felt relief when Washington's attack on British troops at Germantown on October 4 failed. Then the realization began to sink in that chasing after the main rebel army and seizing the enemy's capital had represented a hollow quest that cost the British dearly.

Capturing Burgoyne's Army at Saratoga

The 1777 British descent from Canada had been planned carefully, at least on paper. One of its many aspects involved the use of Native-American allies as auxiliary troops. When the war broke out, both sides had asked the tribes of the North, particularly the powerful Six Nations of Iroquois, to remain neutral in what the Continental Congress called a "family quarrel." Soon, trying to gain every possible advantage, neither side could resist tapping into Indian manpower. Guy Johnson, Britain's Superintendent of Indian Affairs in the northern colonies, invited various tribes to fight under the king's banner. Similarly, American commissioners requested direct assistance. The British held the advantage in gifts and supplies, especially arms and gunpowder. In addition, they had the better argument, since colonial settlers were the obvious culprits in seizing tribal lands, whereas British officials had tried to stop these encroachments by insisting that territory west of the Appalachians was a permanent Indian reserve.

The army of General John Burgoyne (1722–1792), strengthened by hundreds of Indians now on the warpath, moved southward out of Canada in mid-June. The main column of nearly 8000 pushed into Lake Champlain and drove the rebels from Fort Ticonderoga in early July. A second column of 1700 under Colonel Barry St. Leger proceeded up the St. Lawrence River and onto Lake Ontario, before sweeping south toward Fort Schuyler (formerly Fort Stanwix) at the western end of the Mohawk Valley. St. Leger's troops

The American victories at Saratoga thwarted the British plan to defeat the colonies by dividing them. Benedict Arnold led the Americans to victory but credit for the success went to General Horatio Gates. Frustrated by the lack of recognition he felt he deserved for his military service and leadership, Arnold eventually switched his allegiance to the British.

were to act as a diversionary force. Soon they had 750 desperate rebel defenders of Fort Schuyler under siege. Seemingly nothing could stop these two columns, which were to converge again in Albany.

After seizing Ticonderoga, Burgoyne became more tentative about his southward movement. Like William Howe in 1776, he did not take his opponent seriously enough. Under the leadership of General Philip Schuyler, the Continental army's Northern Department had started to rally. The rebels blocked Burgoyne's path by cutting down trees, ripping up bridges, and moving boulders into fording points on streams. Soon the British advance had been slowed to less than a mile a day. Then Congress confused matters by replacing Schuyler—New Englanders considered him too aristocratic in his behavior—with General Horatio Gates.

Burgoyne, meanwhile, was having problems controlling his Native-American allies. In late July a few of them murdered and scalped a young woman, Jane McCrea, who was betrothed to one of his loyalist officers. Burgoyne refused to punish the culprits, fearing he might drive off all his native allies. Despite his forbearance, the Indians found traveling with the slow moving British army tedious at best; most retreated back to Canada before the end of August. Moreover, not disciplining Jane McCrea's murderers conveyed a message of barbarism that helped convince at least some frontier New England militiamen, worried about shielding their own families from possible Indian depredations, to take up arms and come forward in support of the Continentals.

Just as bad for the British, St. Leger's diversionary force ran into trouble. Militiamen in the Mohawk Valley under General Nicholas Herkimer, in alliance with Oneidas and Tuscaroras of the Six Nations, tried to break through to Fort Schuyler. On August 6, 1777, they clashed with St. Leger's loyalists and Indians, among them Mohawks, Cayugas, and Senecas (also of the Six Nations) at the Battle of Oriskany. Herkimer and nearly half of his column were killed or wounded that day, one of the bloodiest of the war.

Oriskany represented the beginning of the end for the once mighty Iroquois nation, whose tribes were now hopelessly divided and consuming each other in combat. When war chieftain Joseph Brant (Thayendanegea) of the Mohawks led numerous bloody frontier raids for the British, a Continental army expedition under General John Sullivan marched into central New York in 1779 and destroyed every Iroquois village it came upon. After the Revolutionary War ended, the more aggressive Iroquois migrated north to Canada or west into the Ohio country, where they fought to keep out white settlers; others, less militant, moved onto reservations in western New York.

St. Leger's victory was temporary. Continentals under Benedict Arnold rushed west from the Albany area and drove off St. Leger without a second major fight. Arnold sent a dim-witted local loyalist into St. Leger's camp with fabricated news of thousands of rebel soldiers moving rapidly toward Fort Schuyler. The Indians, already upset by the loss of so many warriors at Oriskany, quickly broke camp and fled,

Joseph Brant (Thayendanegea), a Mohawk war chieftain, believed the Iroquois could not remain neutral and that their only chance was to side with the British.

leaving the British colonel no alternative but to retreat back into Canada.

Burgoyne had now lost his diversionary force. He suffered another major setback on August 16 when New Hampshire militiamen under General John Stark overwhelmed some 900 Hessians who were out raiding for supplies near Bennington in the Vermont territory. Burgoyne's army was all but entrapped some 30 miles north of Albany along the Hudson River. In two desperate battles (September 19 and October 7) the British force tried to find a way around the well-entrenched rebels, but the brilliant field generalship of Benedict Arnold inspired the Americans to victory. Burgoyne finally surrendered what remained of his army—some 5000 soldiers and auxiliaries—to General Gates on October 17, 1777.

According to one British soldier on the Saratoga surrender field, "we marched out, ... with drums beating and the honors of war, but the drums seemed to have lost their former inspiring sounds, ... as if almost ashamed to be heard on such an occasion." Losing Burgoyne's army was an unnecessary disaster for Britain, caused primarily by William Howe's unwillingness to work in concert with Burgoyne and follow through on the Hudson Highlands strategy. The victory was a momentous triumph for the Americans and a key factor in convincing Vergennes that France could now commit itself publicly to the rebel cause.

On February 6, 1778, the French government signed two treaties with the American commissioners. The first, the Treaty of Amity and Commerce, recognized American independence and encouraged the development of close trading ties. For Vergennes the prospect of conducting—and perhaps even dominating—international trade with the Americans was another way to weaken the British. Still, trading concessions were really not enough to entice the French into an alliance. What Vergennes and Louis XVI really wanted was the opportunity to strike devastating military blows at the British. They knew the Treaty of Amity and Commerce would likely provoke Britain into an act of war with France, so they insisted upon a second agreement, the more entangling Treaty of Alliance, by which the young United States and France would stand as "good and faithful" allies in the event of such hostilities.

On March 20 Louis XVI formally greeted the American commissioners at court and announced that the new nation had gained France's diplomatic recognition. In June 1778 a naval battle in the English Channel involving British and French warships resulted in formal warfare between these two powers. The drum beat for British rule over the 13 states had now taken on the cadence of a death march.

THE WORLD TURNED UPSIDE DOWN

When George Washington learned about the French alliance, he declared a holiday for "rejoicing throughout the whole army." On that spring day in early May 1778, the Continentals at Valley Forge thoroughly enjoyed themselves. They had much to celebrate. They had survived the winter, and they had also benefited from the rigorous field training of colorful Baron Friedrich von Steuben, a pretended Prussian nobleman who had volunteered to teach the soldiery how to fight in more disciplined fashion. Equally important was the announcement of open, direct aid from France, which would include not only land troops but critical naval support. Having gained the formal backing of a powerful European nation certainly enhanced prospects for actually beating the British. Washington, so elated by this turn in events, even winked at the issuance of "more than the common quantity of liquor" to his soldiers, which he knew would result in "some little drunkenness among them."

Revamping British Strategy

The American alliance with France changed the fundamental character of the War for Independence. British officials realized that they were no longer just contending with upstart rebels in America. They were getting themselves ensnared in a world war. France, with its well-trained army and highly mobile navy, had the ability to strike British territories anytime and anywhere it chose. While renouncing any desire to retake Canada, the French did have designs on the valuable British sugar islands in the Caribbean. They built up troop strength in the French West Indies and soon had a four-to-one advantage in that region.

The British military problem became even more complex in 1779 when Spain joined the war but only after signing a secret agreement with France—the Convention of Aranjuez—stipulating that Louis XVI's military forces were not to stop fighting until the Spanish regained the Rock of Gibraltar (lost to the British at the end of the War of the Spanish Succession in 1713). Then in late 1780 the British declared war on the Netherlands, partly so they could capture the Dutch Caribbean island of St. Eustatius, which served as a key point of exchange for American patriots in obtaining war supplies from Dutch merchants.

The dawning reality of world war threatened the British empire with major territorial losses across the globe. One result was a redesigned imperial war plan—the **Southern strategy**—for reconquering the rebellious American provinces. The assumption was that his Majesty's troops could no longer be massed against the American rebels; instead, they would have to be dispersed to threatened points, such as islands in the West Indies.

The first step came in May 1778 when General Sir Henry Clinton (1738?–1795), who had taken over as North American commander from a discredited William Howe, received orders to evacuate Philadelphia. In June Clinton's troops retreated to New York City, narrowly averting a disastrous defeat by Washington's pursuing Continentals at Monmouth Court House (June 28) in central New Jersey. Clinton was to hang on as best he could at the main British base, but he would have to accept a reduction in forces for campaigns elsewhere. The process of dispersal began during the autumn of 1778. Sir Henry avoided major battles with Washington's army in the North while he implemented the Southern strategy.

Crown officials mistakenly assumed that, in the South, loyalists existed in far greater numbers than in the North. In a slight modification of the Hudson Highlands strategy, the idea was to employ the king's friends, primarily as substitutes for depleted British forces, in partisan (guerrilla) warfare. Bands of armed loyalists would operate in conjunction with a main redcoat army to break patriot resistance, beginning in Georgia and then moving in carefully planned steps northward. As soon as any rebel-dominated region had been fully resecured for the Crown, royal government would be reintroduced. Ultimately through attrition, the whole South would be brought back into the British fold, opening the way for eventual subjugation of the North.

The Southern strategy required patience as well as careful nurturing of loyalist sentiment. Both seemed very possible when a detachment of 3500 redcoats sailed south from New York City in November 1778 and quickly reconquered Georgia.

Until the French alliance the South was a secondary theater of war, marked mostly by sporadic partisan fighting between loyalists and rebel militia. Indian-white relations were bloodier. As in the North with Iroquois, both sides maneuvered to gain favor with the Cherokees, Chickasaws, Creeks, and Choctaws. These four nations had a total of about 10,000 warriors, compared to an estimated 2000 among the northern Iroquois.

John Stuart, Britain's Superintendent of Indian Affairs in the southern colonies, had a network of agents working among the native populace. Late in 1775 he focused on winning over the Cherokees and Creeks, who had the most warriors, urging them to fight in concert with loyalists. Stuart was particularly successful with the Cherokees, who had recovered somewhat from their losses during the Seven Years' War. Led by the Overhill chieftain Dragging Canoe (Chincohacina), Cherokee war parties in the summer of 1776 attacked frontier settlements from Virginia to South Carolina, massacring settlers who had unwisely moved onto traditional tribal hunting grounds.

Dragging Canoe's raids had two major effects. First, in September 1776 hundreds of Virginia and North Carolina frontiersmen came together as militia and wreaked mayhem on the most easterly Cherokee towns. During October the Virginians proceeded farther west to the Overhill Cherokee villages. Dragging Canoe and his warriors retreated, promising to foreswear further assistance to the British. This

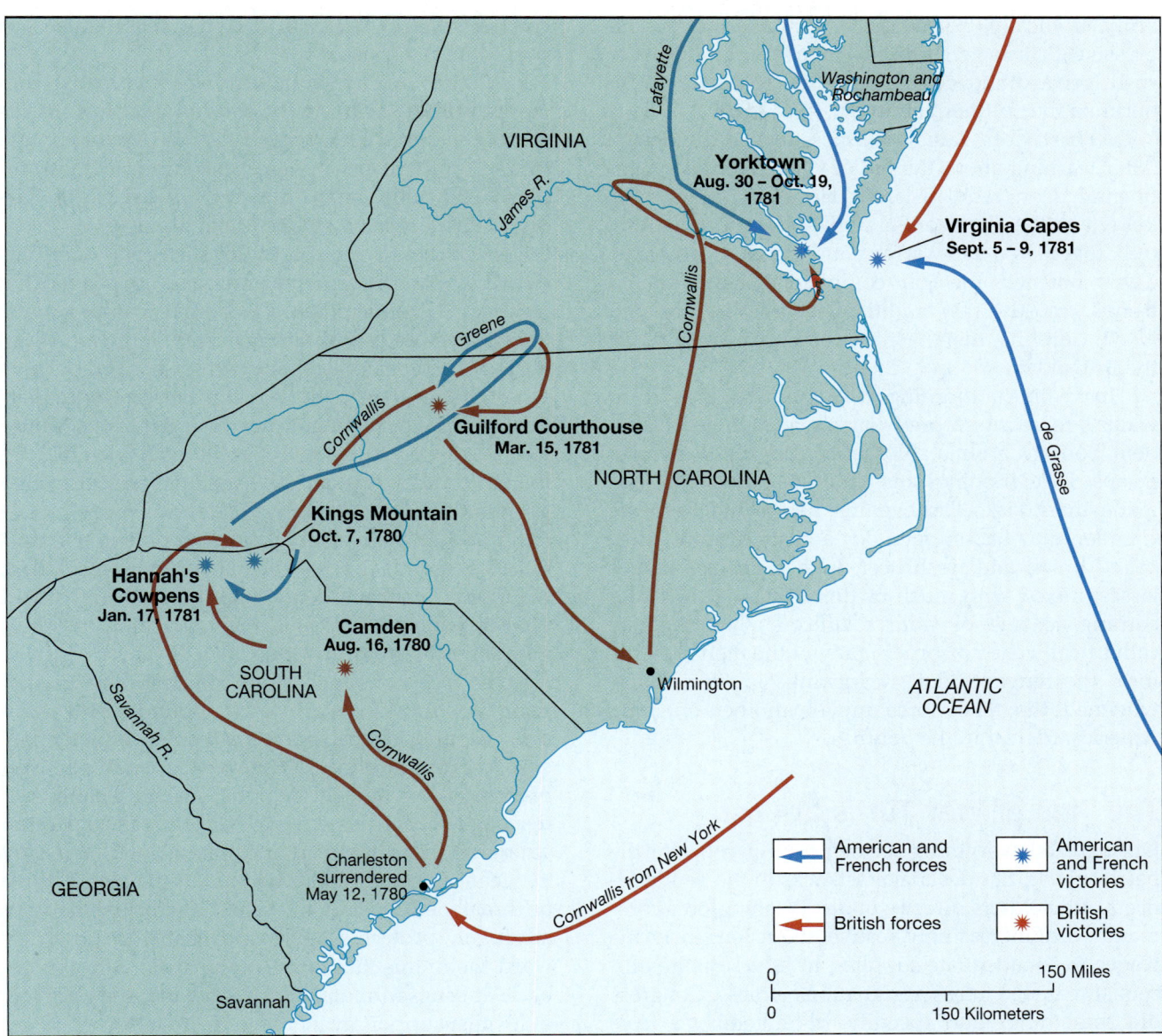

Southern Theater of War, 1780–1781

agreement took the Cherokees out of the war. Second, the other major nations, seeing what had happened, snubbed John Stuart's agents and backed off from the "family quarrel." By 1777 the southern Indians had been neutralized. Although a band of Creeks did support the British after their invasion of Georgia, Native Americans did not figure prominently in Britain's post-1778 strategy.

Sir Henry Clinton, who was probably less decisive than William Howe, was slow to expand on the redcoats' success in Georgia. Finally, in late 1779 he sailed with 7600 troops toward his target—Charleston, South Carolina. There General Benjamin Lincoln, with just 3000 Continental regulars and a smattering of militia, found himself completely outnumbered and trapped when part of Clinton's force moved inland and cut off escape routes. Facing prospects of extermination, Lincoln surrendered without much of a fight on May 12, 1780. This was the only occasion during the war that the British captured an American army.

Clinton's victory at Charleston was the second success in the Southern strategy. The British commander sailed back to New York in high spirits, leaving behind Lord Cornwallis to secure all of South Carolina. Clinton had ordered Cornwallis to advance with careful steps, making sure that loyalist partisans always had firm control of territory behind his army. Ironically, Cornwallis was one of the few aggressive British generals in America. His desire to rush forward and get on with the fight helped undermine the Southern strategy.

At first, Cornwallis's boldness reaped dividends. After learning about the fall of Charleston, the Continental Congress ordered Horatio Gates, now known as the "hero of Saratoga," to proceed south, pull together a new army, and check Cornwallis. Gates botched the job completely. He gathered troops, mostly raw militiamen, in Virginia and North Carolina, then hastily rushed his soldiers into the British lair.

Early on the morning of August 16, 1780, Cornwallis's force intercepted Gates's column near Camden, South Carolina. Not only did the American troops lack training, but tainted provisions had made them sick. The evening before the Battle of Camden they had supped on "a hasty meal of quick baked bread and fresh beef, with a dessert of molasses, mixed with mush or dumplings," which, according to one of Gates's officers, "operated so cathartically as to disorder many of the men" just before the engagement. Cornwallis's army overwhelmed the rebel force in yet another crushing American defeat in the South.

The Tide of War Turns at Last

During 1780 everything seemed to go wrong for the patriot cause. Besides major setbacks in the South, officers and soldiers directly under Washington's command were increasingly restive about long overdue wages and inadequate supplies. In July 1780 the officers threatened mass resignations unless Congress did something—and speedily. In September a frustrated Benedict Arnold switched his allegiance to the British. By the end of 1780 Continental army troop strength fell below 6000. Then, as the new year dawned, Washington faced successive mutinies among his hardened veterans in the Pennsylvania and New Jersey lines. The Continental army seemed to be disintegrating, so much so that the commander in chief put aside plans for a possible strike against New York City. Even though French troops under the Comte de Rochambeau were now in the vicinity, his own Continental numbers were too few to pursue such an elaborate venture.

Quite simply, the British seemed to be winning the endurance contest of wills: One despondent Continental officer wrote, "It really gives me great pain to think of our public affairs; where is the public spirit of the year 1775? Where are those flaming *patriots* who were ready to sacrifice their lives, their fortunes, their all, for the public?" At no time during the war, except for those dark days just before Washington's counterstrike at Trenton, had the rebel cause appeared more forlorn.

What could not yet be seen was that British successes in the South moved the redcoats toward far greater failure. Encouraged by its victories, the British southern army overreached itself. After Camden, Cornwallis started pushing toward North Carolina. His left wing under Major Patrick Ferguson, whose soldiers were mostly loyalists, was soon under the eye of growing numbers of "over-the-mountain" frontiersmen. Their goal was to protect their homesteads and families from Ferguson's loyalists, who repeatedly shot down or hanged patriots who fell into their path. Feeling their presence, Ferguson began retreating. When he spied Kings Mountain, Ferguson calculated that he and his 1100 followers could withstand any assault from atop that promontory. On October 7, 1780, the over-the-mountain force attacked from all sides. Ferguson fell mortally wounded; the rest of his column was killed, wounded, or captured; and the frontiersmen hanged nine of Ferguson's loyalists as a warning to others who might fight for the king.

The Battle of Kings Mountain destroyed the left wing of Cornwallis's army. Compounding the damage, the main British force had not completely secured South Carolina. Whenever Cornwallis moved his troops to a new locale, rebel guerrilla bands under such leaders as "Swamp Fox" Francis Marion emerged from their hiding places and wreaked vengeance on tories who had aided the British force or threatened rebels. Once again, the British had not effectively protected citizens favorably disposed toward them; this failing in combination with the debacle at Kings Mountain cut deeply into the reservoir of loyalist support available to Cornwallis.

Despite these reverses, Cornwallis seemed unconcerned. Like his fellow officers, he held Americans in contempt, believing it was only a matter of time until

Rebel guerrilla leaders like Francis Marion kept the patriot cause alive in South Carolina. In this scene, Marion is leading his troops across the Pee Dee River.

superior British arms would destroy the rebels. However, Cornwallis did not bargain on facing the likes of General Nathanael Greene (1742–1786), who replaced Gates as the Southern Department commander. Greene arrived in North Carolina during December 1780. Not surprisingly, very few troops were available for duty and, as Greene stated despondently, the "appearance" of those in camp "was wretched beyond description."

Greene was a military genius. Violating the military maxim of massing troop strength as much as possible, he decided to divide his soldiers into three small groups, one of which would work with partisan rebel bands. The idea was to let Cornwallis chase after the other two columns of just over 1000 each, until the redcoats were worn out. At that point Greene would stand and fight.

The aggressive Cornwallis took the bait. He went after Greene and sent a detached force after the other rebel column headed by shrewd, capable General Daniel Morgan of Virginia. Morgan's troops lured the onrushing British into a trap at Hannah's Cowpens in western South Carolina on January 17, 1781. Only 140 of the some 1100 British soldiers escaped being killed, captured, or wounded.

Meanwhile, Cornwallis relentlessly pursued Greene, who kept retreating northward before swinging back into central North Carolina. Then, on March 15, 1781, the rebels squared off for battle at Guilford Courthouse. The combatants fought throughout the afternoon, when the Americans abandoned the field. Greene's force had inflicted 506 casualties, as compared to taking 264 of their own. Cornwallis had gained a technical victory, but his troops were exhausted from Greene's game of "fox and hare," and the rebels were still very much in the field.

Franco-American Triumph at Yorktown

Cornwallis retreated to the seacoast to rest his army, then decided to take over British raiding operations in Virginia, which had begun in January 1781 under turncoat Benedict Arnold. In storming northward, Cornwallis totally abandoned the Southern strategy. Nathanael Greene was now free to reassert full patriot authority in the states south of Virginia.

Back in New York, General Clinton fumed. He wanted to discipline his subordinate but was too timid to do so. Instead, he sent Cornwallis orders in July to establish a defensive base in Virginia and to refrain from conducting any offensive operations until such time as Clinton issued further orders. A most reluctant Cornwallis selected Yorktown, with easy access to Chesapeake Bay.

At this juncture everything fell into place for the Americans. Washington learned from General Rochambeau that a French naval fleet would be making its way north from the West Indies. If that fleet could seal off the entrance to Chesapeake Bay and combined Franco-American land forces could surround Cornwallis's army, a major victory would be in the making.

The rebel commander seized the opportunity. Washington and Rochambeau began marching soldiers south from New York, leaving only enough troops behind to keep Clinton tied down. In early September the French fleet, after dueling with British warships, took control of Chesapeake Bay. As the month came to a close, some 7800 French troops and 9000 Continentals and militiamen surrounded the British army of 8500 at Yorktown. Cornwallis wrote Clinton: "If you cannot relieve me very soon you must expect to hear the worst."

Using traditional siege tactics, Washington and Rochambeau slowly squeezed Cornwallis into submission. On October 17 a lone British drummer marched toward the Franco-American lines with a white flag showing. Two days later, on a bright, sunny autumn afternoon, the army of Charles, Lord Cornwallis, marched out from its lines in solemn procession and laid down its arms. As these troops did so, their musicians played an appropriate song, "The World Turned Upside Down." The surrender at Yorktown was an emotional scene. A second British army had been captured in America, and the

With combined Franco-American forces, General Washington put Yorktown under siege in October 1781 and entrapped General Cornwallis's army.

lingering question was whether Great Britain still had the resolve to continue the war.

A Most Generous Peace Settlement

An accumulation of wounds, with the great Franco-American victory at Yorktown being the most damaging, brought the British to the peace table. As early as 1778 Britain had felt the effects of world war. Daring seaman John Paul Jones (1747–1792), known as the "father of the American navy," had conducted damaging raids along the English and Scottish coasts during that year. In 1779, while sailing in the North Sea, Jones lost his own warship, the *Bon Homme Richard*, but captured the British war frigate *Serapis* in a dramatic naval engagement, all within sight of England.

By 1781 French and Spanish warships were attacking British vessels at will in the English Channel, and French warships threatened British possessions in the West Indies. France and Spain were about to launch a major expedition against Gibraltar. In the spring of 1781 a Spanish force under Bernardo de Gálvez captured a sizable British garrison at Pensacola, Florida, and the British soon experienced defeats as far away as India. The allies had demonstrated they could carry the war anywhere, even to the shores of England, suggesting the possibility of much greater damage to the far-flung British empire than just the loss of 13 rebellious colonies in North America.

Keenly aware of these many setbacks, Lord North received the news about Yorktown "as he would have taken a [musket] ball in the breast." In March 1782 North's ministry collapsed, and a new cabinet opened negotiations with designated American peace commissioners—Benjamin Franklin, John Adams, and John Jay—in France. On November 30, 1782, the representatives agreed to preliminary peace terms, pending final ratification by both governments. The other belligerents also started coming to terms, largely because the naval war had turned

Chronology OF KEY EVENTS

1775	The shot "heard 'round the world"—the first military clashes between British troops and colonists take place at Lexington and Concord (April); Second Continental Congress begins meeting in Philadelphia (May); fighting breaks out in New York, Massachusetts, and Canada (May–December); Continental army forms under the command of George Washington (June)
1776	Thomas Paine publishes *Common Sense* (January); Continental Congress adopts the Declaration of Independence (July); Virginia, North Carolina, and South Carolina frontiersmen neutralize southern Indians (July–November); British rout rebel soldiers in vicinity of New York City (August–November); American forces defeat British units at Trenton (December)
1777	Massachusetts begins enlisting free African Americans for Continental service (April); British forces seize Philadelphia after defeating Washington's troops at Brandywine Creek in Pennsylvania (September); American forces capture General Burgoyne's army at Saratoga (October)
1778	American patriots form an alliance with France (February–March); John Paul Jones raids along the British coastline (April–May); British troops invade the Deep South and conquer Savannah, Georgia (December)
1779	Spain joins the war against Britain
1780	British forces defeat American armies at Charleston (May) and Camden (August), South Carolina, but lose at Kings Mountain (October); Benedict Arnold, caught in his efforts to exchange West Point for a commission in the British army, flees to the British (September); British declare war on the Dutch (December)
1781	American forces defeat British soldiers at Hannah's Cowpens (January) in western South Carolina and fight to a draw at Guilford Courthouse (March) in central North Carolina; British surrender to combined Franco-American forces at Yorktown, Virginia (October)
1783	Treaty of Paris ends the War for American Independence

against France and Spain and British troops had saved Gibraltar. All parties signed the final peace accords at Paris on September 3, 1783.

The major European powers now recognized the 13 rebellious colonies as a separate nation. Further, the peace accords established the Mississippi River as the western boundary line of the new nation and 31° north latitude as the southern boundary. Based on Gálvez's success, Britain returned the lands south of this line, constituting Florida, to Spain.

Although the American commissioners failed to obtain Canada, they had gained title to the vast reserve of Indian territory lying between the Appalachian Mountains and the Mississippi River. The treaty was silent about the rights of Indians, whose interests the British ignored, despite repeated promises during the war to protect the lands of Native Americans who joined the king's cause. All told, effective bargaining by the American peace commissioners gave the former colonists a huge geographic base on which to build their new republic.

The peace settlement also contained other important provisions. Britain recognized American fishing rights off the coast of eastern Canada, thus sustaining a major New England industry. The British promised not to carry away slaves when evacuating their troops (which they did anyway). At the same time, they demanded that prewar American debts be paid in full to British creditors (few actually would be paid) and insisted upon the complete restoration of the rights and property of loyalists. The American commissioners agreed to have Congress make such a recommendation to the states (which they generally ignored). The peace treaty, then, both established American independence and laid the groundwork for future conflict.

Conclusion

The rebellious Americans came out remarkably well in 1783. They emerged victorious not only in war but at the peace table as well. The young republic had endured over its parent nation, Great Britain, and with invaluable assistance from foreign allies, particularly France, had earned its freedom from European monarchism and imperialism. On the other hand, no one knew for sure whether the young United States could sustain its independence or have much of a future as a separate nation, given the many internal problems facing the 13 sovereign states.

Among those who did not cheer heartily at the prospect of peace were the officers and soldiers of the Continental army. They had made great personal sacrifices and had every reason to be proud of their accomplishments; however, they deeply resented the lack of civilian support that had plagued their efforts throughout the long conflict. Even in leaving the service, wrote Private Joseph Plumb Martin, the Continentals were "turned adrift like old worn-out horses" without just financial compensation for their services. Still, they had the personal satisfaction of knowing that their pain and suffering had sustained the grand vision of 1776, which would only prevail if revolutionary Americans resolved among themselves their many differences—especially those relating to the process of implanting republican ideals in the social and political fabric of the new nation.

SUGGESTIONS FOR FURTHER READING

Colin G. Calloway, *The American Revolution in Indian Country: Crisis and Diversity in Native American Villages* (1995). Thoughtful presentation of the ways in which eight Indian communities dealt with the American Revolution, viewed from the native as opposed to the British-American perspective.

Stephen Conway, *The War of American Independence, 1775–1783* (1995). Suggestive study that depicts the contest with Britain as the first modern war, a description usually reserved for the French Revolutionary and Napoleonic wars of a later period.

Jonathan R. Dull, *A Diplomatic History of the American Revolution* (1985). Succinct, incisive treatment of the competing national interests and rivalries that affected the outcome of the Revolutionary War.

David Hackett Fischer, *Paul Revere's Ride* (1994). Engaging narrative of Revere's life and the battles of Lexington and Concord in the context of New England's folkways.

Pauline Maier, *American Scripture: Making the Declaration of Independence* (1997). Fresh evaluation of the factors that helped shape Thomas Jefferson's landmark document.

James Kirby Martin and Mark Edward Lender, *A Respectable Army: The Military Origins of the Republic, 1763–1789* (1982). Overview analysis of Revolutionary ideals in contact with the realities of who served in the Continental army, their reasons for fighting, and their contributions to the nation-making process.

Charles Royster, *A Revolutionary People at War: The Continental Army and American Character, 1775–1783* (1979). Widely read study of the ways in which the Revolutionary populace perceived their involvement in the martial contest with Britain.

John Shy, *A People Numerous and Armed: Reflections on the Military Struggle for American Independence*, rev. ed. (1990). Classic essays illuminating the nature of eighteenth-century military values and practices and how the Revolutionary War helped foster a sense of national identity.

Overviews and Surveys

John R. Alden, *The American Revolution, 1775–1783* (1954); Jeremy Black, *War for America: The Fight for Independence,*

1775–1783 (1991); Lawrence D. Cress, *Citizens in Arms: The Army and the Militia in American Society to the War of 1812* (1982); R. Ernest Dupuy, et al., *The American Revolution: A Global War* (1977); John Ferling, ed., *The World Turned Upside Down: The American Victory in the War of Independence* (1988); Sylvia R. Frey, *The British Soldier in America* (1981); Don Higginbotham, *The War of American Independence, 1763–1789* (1971), ed., *Reconsiderations on the Revolutionary War* (1978), and *War and Society in Revolutionary America* (1988); Ronald Hoffman and Peter J. Albert, eds., *Arms and Independence: The Military Character of the American Revolution* (1984); Piers Mackesy, *The War for America, 1775–1783* (1964); Holly A. Mayer, *Belonging to the Army: Camp Followers and Community during the Revolution* (1996); Charles P. Neimeyer, *America Goes to War: The Continental Army* (1996); Dave R. Palmer, *The Way of the Fox: American Strategy in the War for America, 1775–1783* (1975); Eric Robson, *The American Revolution in Its Political and Military Aspects, 1763–1783* (1955); Reginald C. Stuart, *War and American Thought: From the Revolution to the Monroe Doctrine* (1982); Robert K. Wright, Jr., *The Continental Army* (1984).

Reconciliation or Independence

Joseph L. Davis, *Sectionalism in American Politics, 1774–1787* (1977); H. James Henderson, *Party Politics in the Continental Congress* (1974); Merrill Jensen, *The Articles of Confederation: An Interpretation of the Social-Constitutional History of the American Revolution, 1774–1781* (1940); Jackson Turner Main, *The Sovereign States, 1775–1783* (1973); Jerrilyn Greene Marston, *King and Congress: The Transfer of Political Legitimacy, 1774–1776* (1987); Jack N. Rakove, *The Beginnings of National Politics: An Interpretive History of the Continental Congress* (1979).

Without Visible Allies: The War in the North

Rodney Atwood, *The Hessians* (1980); George A. Billias, ed., *George Washington's Generals* (1964), and ed., *George Washington's Opponents* (1969); Richard Buel, Jr., *Dear Liberty: Connecticut's Mobilization for the Revolutionary War* (1980); John C. Dann, ed., *The Revolution Remembered: Eyewitness Accounts of the War for Independence* (1980); Barbara Graymont, *The Iroquois in the American Revolution* (1972); Robert A. Gross, *The Minutemen and Their World* (1976); Robert McConnell Hatch, *Thrust for Canada: The American Attempt on Quebec in 1775–1776* (1979); Richard M. Ketchum, *The Winter Soldiers* (1973); James Kirby Martin, ed., *Ordinary Courage: The Revolutionary War Adventures of Joseph Plumb Martin*, 2d ed. (1999); Max M. Mintz, *Seeds of Empire: The American Revolutionary Conquest of the Iroquois* (1999); John S. Pancake, *1777: The Year of the Hangman* (1977); Gary Alexander Puckrein, *The Black Regiment in the American Revolution* (1978); Jonathan Gregory Rossie, *The Politics of Command in the American Revolution* (1975); Steven Rosswurm, *Arms, Country, and Class: The Philadelphia Militia and "Lower Sort" During the Revolution, 1775–1783* (1987); Paul H. Smith, *Loyalists and Redcoats: A Study in British Revolutionary Policy* (1964).

Rescuing the Patriots: Toward Global Conflict

Samuel F. Bemis, *The Diplomacy of the American Revolution*, rev. ed. (1957); Light Townsend Cummins, *Spanish Observers and the American Revolution, 1775–1783* (1992); Ronald Hoffman and Peter J. Albert, eds., *Diplomacy and Revolution: The Franco-American Alliance of 1778* (1981); Reginald Horsman, *The Diplomacy of the New Republic, 1776–1815* (1985); James H. Hutson, *John Adams and the Diplomacy of the American Revolution* (1980); Lawrence S. Kaplan, ed., *The American Revolution and "A Candid World"* (1977); Richard B. Morris, *The Peacemakers: The Great Powers and American Independence* (1965); Charles R. Ritcheson, *British Politics and the American Revolution* (1954); H. M. Scott, *British Foreign Policy in the Age of the American Revolution* (1991); William C. Stinchcombe, *The American Revolution and the French Alliance* (1969); Gerald Stourzh, *Benjamin Franklin and American Foreign Policy*, 2d ed. (1969); Richard W. Van Alstyne, *Empire and Independence: The International History of the American Revolution* (1965); Paul A. Varg, *Foreign Policies of the Founding Fathers* (1963).

The World Turned Upside Down

Lawrence E. Babits, *A Devil of a Whipping: The Battle of Cowpens* (1998); R. Arthur Bowler, *Logistics and the Failure of the British Army in America, 1775–1783* (1975); John Buchanan, *The Road to Guilford Courthouse* (1997); E. Wayne Carp, *To Starve the Army at Pleasure: Continental Army Administration and American Political Culture, 1775–1783* (1984); Jeffrey J. Crow and Larry E. Tise, eds., *The Southern Experience in the American Revolution* (1978); John Morgan Dederer, *Making Bricks Without Straw: Nathanael Greene's Southern Campaign and Mao Tse-Tung's Mobile War* (1983); Jonathan R. Dull, *The French Navy and American Independence, 1774–1787* (1975); William M. Fowler, Jr., *Rebels Under Sail: The American Navy During the Revolution* (1976); W. Robert Higgins, ed., *The Revolutionary War in the South* (1979); Ronald Hoffman, Thad W. Tate, and Peter J. Albert, eds., *An Uncivil War: The Southern Backcountry During the American Revolution* (1985); Lee Kennett, *The French Forces in America, 1780–1783* (1977); Henry Lumpkin, *From Savannah to Yorktown* (1981); George S. McCowen, Jr., *The British Occupation of Charleston, 1780–82* (1972); James H. O'Donnell, III, *Southern Indians in the American Revolution* (1973); John S. Pancake, *This Destructive War: The British Campaign in the Carolinas, 1780–1782* (1985); John E. Selby, *The Revolution in Virginia, 1775–1783* (1988); David Syrett, *The Royal Navy in American Waters* (1989), and *Shipping and the American War, 1775–83: A Study of British Transport Organization* (1970); John A. Tilley, *The British Navy and the American Revolution* (1987); Russell F. Weigley, *The Partisan War: The South Carolina Campaign of 1780–1782* (1970).

Biographies

Edward J. Cashin, *The King's Ranger: Thomas Brown and the Revolution on the Southern Frontier* (1989); Marcus Cunliffe, *George Washington: Man and Monument*, rev. ed. (1982); Don R. Gerlach, *Proud Patriot: Philip Schuyler and the War of Independence, 1775–1783* (1987); Louis R. Gottschalk, *Lafayette*

Joins the American Army (1937); Ira D. Gruber, *The Howe Brothers and the American Revolution* (1972); Richard J. Hargrove, Jr., *General John Burgoyne* (1983); Don Higginbotham, *Daniel Morgan* (1961), and *George Washington and the American Military Tradition* (1985); James Kirby Martin, *Benedict Arnold, Revolutionary Hero* (1997); David B. Mattern, *Benjamin Lincoln and the American Revolution* (1995); Max M. Mintz, *The Generals of Saratoga: John Burgoyne and Horatio Gates* (1990); Samuel E. Morison, *John Paul Jones* (1959); Orville T. Murphy, *Charles Gravier, Comte de Vergennes* (1982); Paul David Nelson, *General Horatio Gates* (1976), and *Anthony Wayne: Soldier of the Early Republic* (1985); Louis W. Potts, *Arthur Lee: A Virtuous Revolutionary* (1981); Hugh F. Rankin, *Francis Marion: The Swamp Fox* (1973); Thomas J. Schaeper, *France and America in the Revolutionary Era: Jacques-Donatien Leray de Chaumont, 1725–1803* (1995); Hal T. Shelton, *General Richard Montgomery: From Redcoat to Rebel* (1994); Willard M. Wallace, *Traitorous Hero: Benedict Arnold* (1954); Franklin B. and Mary Wickwire, *Cornwallis: The American Adventure* (1970); William B. Willcox, *Portrait of a General: Sir Henry Clinton in the War of Independence* (1964).

INTERNET RESOURCES

Exploring the West from Monticello: An Exhibition of Maps and Navigational Instruments
http://www.lib.virginia.edu/exhibits/lewis_clark/home.html
Maps and charts reveal knowledge and conceptions about the known and the unknown. This site includes a number of eighteenth century maps.

Georgia's Rare Map Collection
http://scarlett.libs.uga.edu/darchive/hargrett/maps/colamer.html
http://scarlett.libs.uga.edu/darchive/hargrett/maps/revamer.html
These two sites contain maps for Colonial and Revolutionary America.

LVA Colonial Records Project—Index of Digital Facsimiles of Documents on Early Virginia
http://eagle.vsla.edu/colonial/
This site contains numerous early documents, but it is unguided and a little difficult to use.

Thomas Paine National Historical Association
http://www.dpipc.com/cdadesign/paine/home.html
This official site contains a large archive of Paine's works and information about the Association.

Maryland Loyalists and the American Revolution
http://www.erols.com/candidus/index.htm
This look at Maryland's loyalists promotes the author's book, but it has good information about an underappreciated phenomenon, including loyalist songs and poems.

Revolution Era Documents
http://www.geocities.com:80/Athens/Forum/9061/USA/revolution/rev.html
The Historical Text Archive has numerous useful documents for the period of the Revolution.

The American Revolution
http://revolution.h-net.msu.edu/
This site accompanies the PBS series Revolution with essays and resource links.

KEY TERMS

Rage Militaire (p. 128)
Second Continental Congress (p. 132)
Dunmore's Ethiopian Regiment (p. 138)
Common Sense (p. 138)
Tory (p. 139)
Hessians (p. 140)
Roderigue Hortalez & Cie. (p. 146)
Hudson Highlands Strategy (p. 147)
Southern Strategy (p. 150)

REVIEW QUESTIONS

1. What is meant by the concept *rage militaire*? What factors account for the widespread desire of the American colonists to challenge Great Britain militarily by the spring and summer of 1775?

2. Why were so many leaders in the Second Continental Congress so hesitant about moving toward formal independence? Discuss the text of the Declaration of Independence. How does the Declaration both summarize colonial grievances and provide a bold vision for the future of an independent American republic?

3. Examine the composition of British and American military forces. How did the Continental army change as the war progressed beyond 1775 and 1776? Who were the real Continentals, and what did they accomplish as the backbone of Washington's "respectable" army?

4. Assess the role of European powers such as the French, Spanish, and Dutch and the role of Native Americans in the colonists' fight for independence. Of these groups, did any seem to benefit from their support of the rebel cause? If so, how? If not, why not?

5. Why did the Americans emerge victorious in the Revolutionary War? Explain how all three of the following contributed to that final triumph—American strengths, British weaknesses, and the global diplomatic and strategic situation. How did these factors help secure a favorable peace settlement in 1783?

6

SECURING THE REPUBLIC AND ITS IDEALS, 1776–1789

ESTABLISHING NEW REPUBLICAN GOVERNMENTS
People Victorious: The New State Governments
The Articles of Confederation

CRISES OF THE CONFEDERATION
Struggle to Ratify the Articles
Turmoil over Financing the War
Threatened Military Coup: The Newburgh Conspiracy
Drifting Toward Disunion
Daniel Shays's Rebellion

HUMAN RIGHTS AND SOCIAL CHANGE
In Pursuit of Religious Freedom
The Propertyless Poor and the West
Women Appeal for Fundamental Liberties
The Dilemma of Race and Racism

SECOND NEW BEGINNING, NEW NATIONAL GOVERNMENT
The Framers of the Constitution
A Document Constructed by Compromises
The Ratification Struggle

"Others may never feel tyrannic sway"

Nancy Shippen was a product of Philadelphia's best lineage. Because she was born in 1763, the political turmoil leading to rebellion did not affect her early life. As a privileged daughter in an upper-class family, her duty was to blossom into a charming woman, admired for her beauty and social graces rather than her intellect. Nancy's education consisted of the refinement of skills that would please and entertain—dancing, cultivating her voice, playing musical instruments, painting on delicate china, and producing pieces of decorative needlework.

Had Nancy shown any interest in politics, an exclusively masculine preserve, she would have shocked everyone, including her father, William Shippen. Shippen was a noted local physician who espoused independence in 1776. That was his prerogative as paterfamilias; where he led, according to the customs of the time, his family followed. Indeed, he was a proud father in 1777 when, at his urging, Nancy displayed her patriotic virtue by sewing shirt ruffles for General Washington.

Three hundred miles away in Boston, another woman by the name of Phillis Wheatley was also reckoning with the American Revolution. Her life had been very different from Nancy's. Born on Africa's West Coast around 1753, she had been snatched from her parents by slave catchers. At the Boston slave market, Mrs. Susannah Wheatley, looking for a young female slave to train in domestic service, noticed her. In Phillis the Wheatley family got much more; their new slave yearned to express her thoughts and feelings through poetry.

Conventional wisdom dictated that slaves should not be educated. Exposure to reading and writing might make them resentful, perhaps even rebellious. Sensing Phillis's talents, the Wheatley family defied convention. She mastered English and Latin, even prepared translations of ancient writings. By 1770 some of her poems had been published, followed in 1773 by a collection entitled *Poems on Various Subjects, Religious and Moral*. In one verse addressed to Lord Dartmouth, Britain's secretary for American affairs, she queried:

> I young in life, by seeming cruel fate
> Was snatch'd from Afric's fancy'd seat:
> Such was my case. And can I then but pray
> Others may never feel tyrannic sway?

Experiencing the tyranny of slavery influenced Phillis's feelings about the presence of redcoats in Boston. Late in 1775 she sent a flattering poem to George Washington. He responded gratefully and called her words "striking proof of your great poetical talents."

Little as Phillis Wheatley and Nancy Shippen had in common, they lived during an era in which men thought of all women, regardless of their rank in society, as second-class human beings. Phillis carried the additional burden of being black in an openly racist society. Like other women in revolutionary America, they could only hope that the ideals of human liberty might someday apply to them.

Nancy Shippen had two male tyrants in her life. The first was her father William, who in 1781 forced her into marriage with Henry Beekman Livingston, a son of one of New York's most powerful and wealthy families. The man she truly loved had only "honorable expectations" of a respectable income. So her father insisted that Nancy wed Livingston. The rejected suitor wanted to know "for what reason in this *free* country a lady ... must be married in a hurry and given up to a man whom she dislikes." None of the Shippens responded. In truth, the answer was that Nancy legally belonged to her father until she became the property of the second tyrant in her life—her husband Henry.

The marriage was a disaster, most likely because Henry was a philanderer. Nancy eventually took her baby daughter and moved back to her family. She wanted full custody of the child, who by law was the property of her husband. Henry made it clear that he would never give up his legal rights to his daughter, should Nancy embarrass him in public by seeking a bill of divorcement. Even if she had defied him, divorce bills were very hard to get because they involved proving adultery or desertion.

To keep actual custody of her daughter, Nancy accepted her entrapment. Several years later Henry relented and arranged for a divorce, but by that time Nancy's spirit was broken. This former belle of Philadelphia society lived on unhappily in hermit-like fashion until her death in 1841. Having been so favored at birth, her adult years were a personal tragedy, primarily because of her legal dependence on the will of men.

Although from different social and racial backgrounds, Nancy Shippen and Phillis Wheatley shared one characteristic: As women, they were second-class citizens in Revolutionary America.

Phillis Wheatley, by comparison, enjoyed some personal freedom before her untimely death in 1784. Mr. and Mrs. Wheatley died during the war period, and their will provided for Phillis's emancipation. She married John Peters, a free black man, and bore him three children. But John Peters was poor, and Phillis had scant time for poetry. Free blacks rarely got decent jobs, and Phillis struggled each day to help her family avoid destitution. She lived long enough to see slavery being challenged in the northern states; nevertheless, she died knowing that African Americans, even when free, invariably faced racial discrimination, which caused families like hers to exist on the margins of revolutionary society.

The experiences of Phillis Wheatley and Nancy Shippen raise basic questions about the character of the Revolution. Did the cause of liberty really change the lives of Americans? If it was truly a movement to end tyranny, secure human rights, and ensure equality of opportunity, then why did individuals like Wheatley and Shippen benefit so little? A major reason was that white, adult males of property and community standing put much greater emphasis on establishing an independent nation between 1776 and 1789 than on securing human rights. Still, the ideology of liberty could not be denied. Primarily, the revolutionary era saw the creation of a new nation and the articulation of fundamental ideals regarding human freedom and dignity—ideals that have continued to shape the course of American historical development.

ESTABLISHING NEW REPUBLICAN GOVERNMENTS

Winning the war and working out a favorable peace settlement represented two of three crucial elements that made for a successful rebellion. The third centered on the formation of stable governments, certainly a challenging assignment because that process involved the careful definition of how governments should function to support life, liberty, and property (or happiness, as Jefferson framed the triad). A monarchical system, indeed any other capable of producing political tyranny, everyone agreed, was unacceptable. A second point of consensus was that governments should be republican in character. Sovereignty, or ultimate political authority, previously residing with King and Parliament, should be vested in the people. After all, political institutions presumably existed to serve them. As such, citizens should be governed by laws, not by power-hungry officials, and laws should be the product of the collective deliberations of representatives elected by the citizenry.

Defining the core ideals of **republicanism**—popular sovereignty, rule by law, and legislation by elected representatives—was not a source of disagreement. Revolutionary leaders, however, argued passionately about the organization and powers of new governments, both state and national, as well as the extent to which basic political rights should be put into practice. At the heart of the debate was the concept of **public virtue:** whether citizens were capable of subordinating their self-interest to the greater good of the whole community. Although some leaders answered in the affirmative, others did not. Their trust or distrust of the people directly affected how far they were willing to go in implementing republican ideals.

Leaders who believed that citizens could govern themselves and not abuse public privileges for private advantage were in the vanguard of political thinking in the western world. As such, they may be called radicals. They were willing to establish "the most democratic forms" of government, as Samuel Adams so aptly capsulized their thinking.

More cautious, elitist revolutionary leaders feared what the masses might do without the restraining hand of central political authority. As one of them wrote: "No one loves liberty more than I do, but of all tyranny I most dread that of the multitude." These leaders remained attached to traditional notions of hierarchy and deference in social and political relationships. They still thought that the "better sort" of citizens—men of education, wealth, and proven ability, whom they now defined as "natural aristocrats"—should be the stewards who guided the people. For such leaders the success of the Revolution depended on transferring power from the despoilers of liberty in Britain to "enlightened" gentlemen like themselves in America. As a precaution against a citizenry abusing liberties, they wanted a strong central government to replace King and Parliament, a government controlled by cautious revolutionaries in the interests of national political stability.

People Victorious: The New State Governments

In the wake of collapsing British authority during 1775 and 1776, **radical** and **cautious revolutionaries** squared off in constitutional conventions. Their heated debates produced ten new state constitutions

Table 6.1
Personal Wealth and Occupations of Approximately 900 Representatives Elected to Prewar and Postwar Assemblies (Expressed in Percentages)

	New Hampshire, New York, and New Jersey		Maryland, Virginia, and South Carolina	
	Prewar	Postwar	Prewar	Postwar
Property holdings				
Over £5000	36%	12%	52%	28%
£2000–£5000	47	26	36	42
Under £2000	17	62	12	30
Occupations				
Merchants and lawyers	43%	18%	23%	17%
Farmers*	23	55	12	26

Source: Derived from Jackson T. Main, "Government by the People: The American Revolution and the Democratization of the Legislatures," *William and Mary Quarterly*, 3d ser., 23 (1966), p. 45.

*Plantation owners with slaves are not included with farmers.

by the end of 1777, plus a plan of national government written by the Continental Congress. Connecticut and Rhode Island kept their liberal colonial charters, which had provided for the popular election of executive officials, and simply deleted all references to British sovereignty; Massachusetts ratified a new state constitution in 1780.

The first constitutional settlement of the Revolution shows that leaders who had firm faith in the people prevailed over those who did not, based on three essential characteristics. First, there was general agreement that governments derive their authority from the consent of the governed. This principle of popular sovereignty has prevailed to this day. Second, although state constitution-makers varied in their commitment, free, white, adult male citizens (about 20 percent of the total population) gained expanded voting and office holding rights. The movement clearly was toward greater popular participation in governmental decision making. Third, the central government would not have the power to inhibit the state governments and the people in the management of the republic's political affairs.

Pennsylvanians produced the most democratic of the first state constitutions. Decision-making authority resided in an annually elected unicameral, or one-chamber, assembly. All white male citizens, with or without property, could now vote for legislators. By comparison, Maryland's constitution-framers were much less trusting. They maintained a three-tiered structure of government, reminiscent of that of King and two houses of Parliament. Potential voters had to meet modest propertyholding requirements (at least a £30 valuation in local currency). At a minimum, those elected to the lower house had to own a 50-acre freehold farm while those chosen for the upper house needed to demonstrate a net worth of £1000 in local currency. For the governor the requirement was £5000. In Pennsylvania ordinary citizens could control their own political destiny, but in Maryland wealthier citizens were to act as stewards for the people, hence continuing the tradition of deferential politics. The other state constitutions varied between these two extremes.

Only New Jersey defined the electorate without regard to gender. Its 1776 constitution gave the vote to "all free inhabitants" meeting minimal property qualifications. This permitted some women to vote. Since all property in marriage belonged to husbands, New Jersey had technically extended franchise rights only to widows and spinsters (very few divorced women were to be found anywhere in America). Nonetheless, great numbers of married women went to the polls regularly. Not until 1807 did New Jersey disenfranchise females, on the alleged grounds that they were more easily manipulated by self-serving political candidates. For a brief time, then, at least one state regarded women—not just free, white, adult males—as a legitimate voice in government. Even though the experiment worked, this concept proved too radical for the customary male-dominated political culture of revolutionary America.

Because of the first state constitutions, male citizens with more ordinary family backgrounds, less personal wealth, and a greater diversity of occupations began to hold higher political offices after the Revolution started. As an excited citizen noted in late 1776, elected delegates to the new Virginia assembly were more "plain and of consequence, less disguised, but I believe to be full[y] as honest, less intriguing, more sincere." Not "so politely educated, nor so highly born," these delegates were "the people's men (and the people in general are right)." Radical leaders throughout the states heartily endorsed these sentiments.

TABLE 6.2

Family and Personal Wealth of Approximately 450 Executive Officials* in Late Colonial and Early Revolutionary Governments (Expressed in Percentages)

	Family Wealth†		Personal Wealth	
	1774	1777	1774	1777
Over £5000	40%	26%	65%	37%
£2000–£5000	34	33	29	52
Under £2000	26	41	6	11

Source: Derived from James Kirby Martin, *Men in Rebellion: Higher Governmental Leaders and the Coming of the American Revolution* (New Brunswick, NJ: Rutgers University Press, 1973).

*Officeholders included are governors, lieutenant governors, secretaries, treasurers, members of upper houses of assemblies (councilors before the Revolution), attorneys general, chief judges, and associate judges of the highest provincial and state courts.

†Refers to the wealth of parents. A higher percentage of late colonial leaders (74 percent) than early revolutionary leaders (59 percent) came from upper-class and upper-middle-class families.

New Jersey extended the right to vote to all free inhabitants until 1807 when a new state law specifically limited the franchise to free white male citizens.

The Articles of Confederation

In June 1776 the Continental Congress called for a plan of national government. John Dickinson, the well-known reluctant revolutionary who refused to vote for independence, took the lead. Concerned about losing the stabilizing influence of British authority, Dickinson proposed a muscular central government in the draft constitution his committee presented to Congress. The Confederacy was to be called "THE UNITED STATES OF AMERICA" and was to exist "for their common defense, the security of their liberties, and their mutual and general welfare." Not surprisingly, the states would have little authority. Each would retain only "as much of its present laws, rights and customs, as it may think fit ... in all matters that shall not interfere with the Articles of this Confederation."

The exigencies of war kept interrupting congressional debate on Dickinson's draft. Furthermore, the radical revolutionaries who dominated Congress in late 1776 and 1777 did not like this plan. They feared power too far removed from the people. After all, they had rebelled against a distant government that they had perceived as tyrannical. When Congress finally completed revisions in November 1777, the delegates had turned Dickinson's draft inside out. The Articles now stated: "Each state retains its sovereignty, freedom and independence, and every power, jurisdiction and right, which is not ... expressly delegated to the United States, in Congress assembled."

As a testament to the sovereignty of the 13 states, each had to ratify the Articles before this plan could go into full operation. At most the central government could coordinate activities among the states. It could manage the war, but it lacked taxation authority to support that effort. If Congress needed money (it obviously did), it could "requisition" the states. The states, however, would decide for themselves whether they would send funds to Congress.

Fundamentally penniless and powerless, the Confederation government represented the optimistic view that a virtuous citizenry did not require the constraining hand of central authority. This bold vision—fully in line with the rejection of King and Parliament as a remote, autocratic central government—pleased radicals like Samuel Adams, Thomas Paine, and Thomas Jefferson. Jefferson wrote glowingly of the "ease" with which the people "had deposited the monarchical and taken ... republican government," as effortlessly as "throwing off an old and putting on a new suit of clothes." Cautious revolutionaries still harbored grave doubts, and events over the next few years convinced them that the first constitutional settlement had all but doomed the experiment in republicanism to failure.

CRISES OF THE CONFEDERATION

Internal difficulties soon beset the young American republic. Cautious revolutionaries viewed the years between 1776 and 1787 as a "critical period" because of problems encountered with the sovereign states and the people. These difficulties included ratifying the Articles of Confederation, establishing a national domain west of the Appalachian Mountains, finding some means to pay for the war, achieving stable diplomatic relations with foreign powers, and guarding against domestic upheavals.

Over time, those who advocated a strong central government formed an informal political alliance, and they have since come to be known as the **nationalists**. With each passing year the nationalists became more and more frustrated by the Confederation. In 1787 they finally overwhelmed their opposition by pressing for and getting a new plan of national government.

Struggle to Ratify the Articles

Given the wartime need for national unity in the face of a common enemy, Congress asked each state to approve the Articles of Confederation quickly. Overcoming much indifference, 12 states had finally ratified by January 1779—but Maryland still held out.

The propertied gentlemen who controlled Maryland's revolutionary government objected to one specific provision in the Articles. Although Dickinson's draft had designated all lands west of the Appalachians as a *national domain*, belonging to all the people for future settlement, the final version left these lands in the hands of states having sea-to-sea clauses in their colonial charters—a logical extension of the principle of state sovereignty. Maryland, having a fixed western boundary, had no such western claim. Nor did Rhode Island, New Jersey, Pennsylvania, or Delaware.

Maryland's leaders refused to be cut off from western development. In public they talked in terms of high principle. Citizens from "landless" states should have as much right to resettle in the West as inhabitants of "landed" states. Equal access was not the only issue, however. Many Maryland leaders had invested in pre-Revolution land companies trying to gain title to large parcels of western territory. They had done so by appealing to the Crown and by making purchases from individual Native Americans, who without tribal approval often "sold" rights in return for alcohol and other "gifts." Wanting to avoid costly frontier warfare, the Crown had promulgated the Proclamation of 1763 (see p. 103) and thereafter refused to recognize any such titles. After independence there was new hope for these land speculators, but only if the Continental Congress rather than some of the states controlled the West.

The Maryland Assembly adamantly refused ratification unless the landed states agreed to turn over their charter titles to Congress. Virginia, which had the largest claim, including the vast region north of the Ohio River that came to be known as the "Old Northwest," faced the most pressure. Forsaking local land speculators for the national interest, the Virginia Assembly broke the deadlock in January 1781 by agreeing to cede its claims to Congress.

Had self-interest not been involved, ratification would have followed quickly; however, covetous Maryland leaders still held out. They pronounced Virginia's grant unacceptable because of a condition not permitting Congress to award lands on the basis of Indian deeds. Fortunately for the republic, the war intervened. In early 1781, with the British raiding in the Chesapeake Bay region, Marylanders became quite anxious about their defense. Congressional leaders urged ratification in exchange for promises of Continental military support. All but cornered, the Maryland Assembly reluctantly gave in and approved the Articles of Confederation.

March 1, 1781, the day formal ratification ceremonies finally took place, elicited only muted celebrations. Some cheered "the union," at long last "indissolubly cemented," as an optimist wrote. Certainly, too, the prospect of a national domain for a rapidly expanding population pleased many citizens. The nationalists, on the other hand, believed that Maryland's behavior showed how self-interest could be masked as public virtue. With so many problems needing solutions, they wondered how long the republic could endure when any sovereign state had the capacity to thwart the will of the other 12.

Turmoil over Financing the War

From the outset financial problems plagued the new central government. Under the Articles, Congress had no power of taxation; it repeatedly asked the states to pay a fair proportion of war costs. The states, also hard pressed for funds, rarely sent in more than 50 percent of their requisitions. Meanwhile, soldiers like Joseph Plumb Martin endured shortages of food, clothing, camp equipment, and pay. As a result, with each passing month the army grew increasingly angry about its role as a creditor to the republic.

The lack of tax revenues forced Congress to resort to various expedient measures to meet war costs. Between 1775 and 1780 it issued some $220 million in paper money, or Continental dollars. Lacking any financial backing, these "Continentals" became so worthless by 1779 that irate army officers complained how "four months' pay of a private [soldier] will not procure his wretched wife and children a single bushel of wheat." In addition, Congress, largely to get military supplies, issued interest-bearing certificates of indebtedness. Because Congress lacked the means to pay interest, these certificates, which also circulated as money, rapidly lost value. In 1780 Congress attempted to refinance Continental dollars at a 40 to 1 ratio, but the plan failed. Had it not been for grants and loans from allies like France and the Netherlands, the war effort might well have floundered.

Deeply disturbed by these conditions, many nationalists in the Continental Congress acted forcefully to institute financial reform. Their leader was the wealthy Philadelphia merchant, Robert Morris (1734–1806), sometimes called the "financier of the Revolution," who became Congress's Superintendent of Finance in 1781. His assistant superintendent, Gouverneur Morris (no relation), a wealthy New Yorker

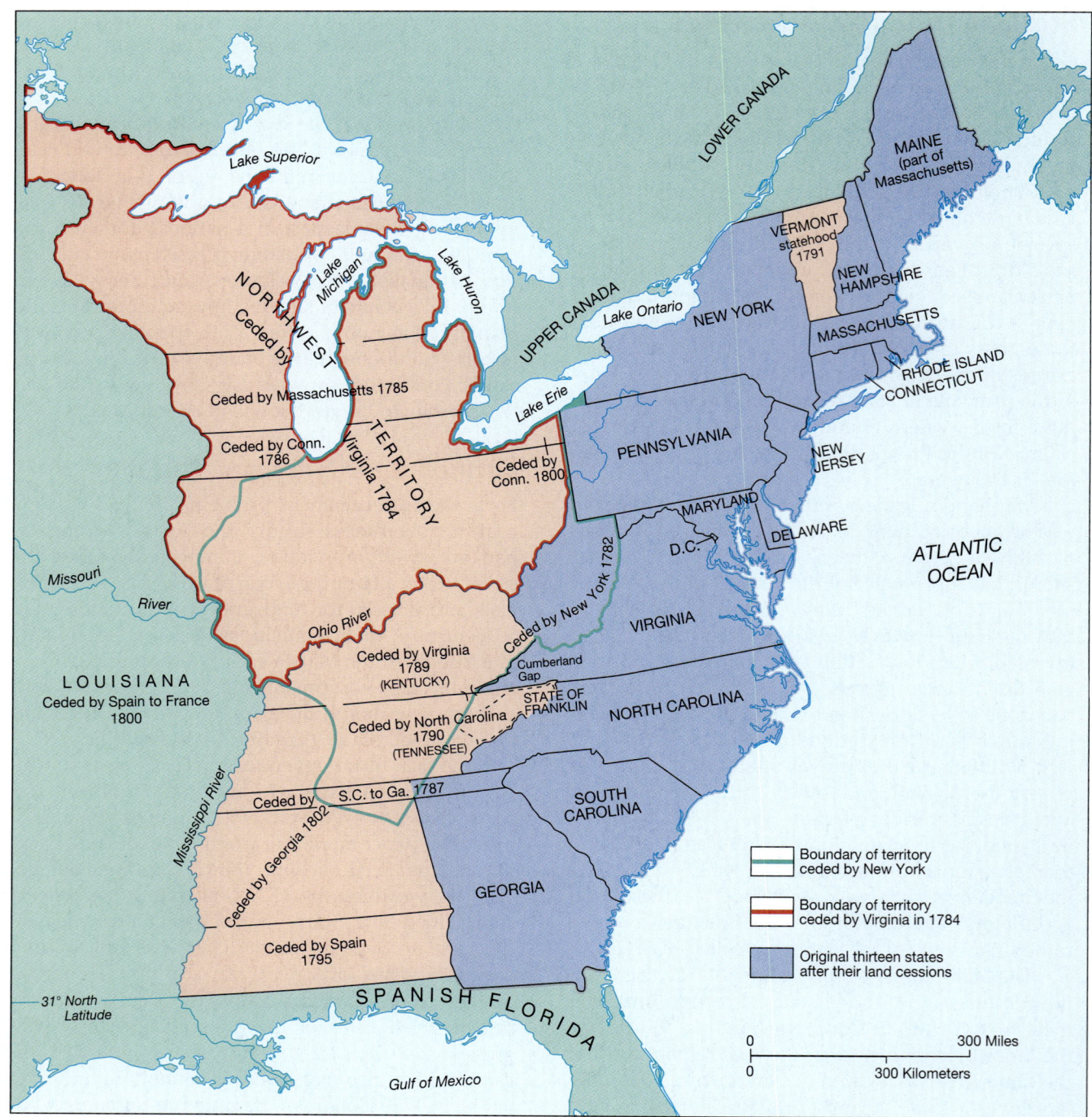

Western Land Claims Ceded by the States

The battle over conflicting state claims to western lands was a major issue facing the Continental Congress.

then practicing law in Philadelphia, was also critical to shaping the events that lay ahead, as were Alexander Hamilton of New York and James Madison of Virginia. Hamilton summarized their feelings this way: "The Confederation . . . gives the power of the purse too entirely to the state legislatures. . . . That power, which holds the purse strings absolutely, must rule."

At the urging of the nationalists, congressional delegates approved the Impost Plan of 1781. It called for import duties of 5 percent on all foreign trade goods entering the United States, the revenues to belong to Congress. These funds could be used to pay the army, to back a stable national currency, and, ultimately, to meet foreign loan obligations. Because

Gouverneur Morris (left) and Robert Morris (right) were key figures in the nationalist drive for financial reform.

the Plan would allow Congress some taxation authority, the delegates recommended it in the form of an amendment to the Articles. Amendments required the approval of all 13 states.

Reluctant as they were to share taxation powers with the central government, many state leaders agreed with Robert Morris, who had warned: "The political existence of America depends on the accomplishment of this [Impost] plan." Twelve states had ratified by the autumn of 1782. Only Rhode Island hesitated. With so little land to tax, the easiest way to fund its own war debt was to collect state import duties. If a choice had to be made, state interests came first. The Assembly voted against ratification. Once again local interests had prevailed; a single state had blocked the will of the other 12.

In this crucial matter the nationalists had allies. Most prominent were disgruntled officers in the Continental army. Rarely had the soldiers been paid, and in 1780 the officers had exacted from Congress a promise of half-pay postwar pensions as their price for staying in the service. Without a fixed source of revenue, Congress lacked the ability to meet these obligations.

After a group of high-ranking officers learned about Rhode Island's decision, they sent a menacing petition to Congress in December 1782. It stated; "We have borne all that men can bear—our property is expended—our private resources are at an end." With no likelihood of pensions being funded, they insisted upon five years of full pay when mustering out of the service. Even with British troops still on American soil, the angry officers warned Congress: "Any further experiments on their patience may have fatal effects."

Threatened Military Coup: The Newburgh Conspiracy

For years Continental officers and soldiers alike had complained about the ungenerous treatment they received from revolutionary leaders and civilians. Convinced that the general populace had lived well at home while the army endured privation, sickness, and death in the field, they spoke out passionately about the absence of citizen virtue. As one officer bluntly wrote, "I hate my countrymen."

After the British force at Yorktown surrendered, Washington moved 11,000 troops north to the vicinity of Newburgh, New York. From this campsite on the Hudson River, the Continental army waited for peace terms and kept its eye on British forces in New York City. As peace negotiations dragged on during 1782, officers and soldiers worried about being demobilized without back pay and promised pensions. When Rhode Island refused to ratify the Impost Plan, their worst fears seemed to be realized.

Curiously, when the congressional nationalists received the officers' hotly worded petition, they were more pleased than alarmed. They soon devised a scheme to use these threats to extort taxation authority from the states. If need be, they would encourage the army to go back into the field and threaten the civilian populace with a military uprising. The danger, of course, was that the army might get out of control, seize the reins of government, and push the Revolution toward some form of military dictatorship.

When the states refused to be bullied, the nationalists turned to George Washington in February 1783. As his former military aide, Alexander Hamilton (1757?–1804), wrote to him, the critical issue was "the establishment of general funds.... In this the influence of the army, properly directed, may cooperate." Washington refused to help; perhaps better than anyone in revolutionary America, he understood that military power had to remain subordinate to civilian authority, or the republic would never be free.

At this juncture, Robert Morris and other congressional nationalists began "conspiring" with General Horatio Gates, second in command at Newburgh, who had often dreamed of replacing Washington at the head of the Continental army. Gates made his move in early March. He authorized two Newburgh Addresses, both prepared by members of his staff. The addresses warned the officers to "suspect the man [Washington] who would advise to more moderation and forbearance." If peace comes, let nothing separate you "from your arms but death," or at least not until the army had realized financial justice. The first address instructed the officers to attend a meeting to vent grievances—and take action. Dismayed, Washington called this proposal "disorderly"; he nevertheless approved a meeting for March 15. He would not attend, he stated, but would let Gates chair the gathering.

Despite his promise, Washington appeared at this showdown meeting. He pleaded with the officers to temper their rage and not go back into the field. That would destroy everything the army had accomplished during eight long years of war. The officers appeared unmoved. Then preparing to read a letter, Washington reached into his pocket, pulled out spectacles, and put them on. The officers, never having seen their commander wear eyeglasses before, started to murmur. Sensing a mood shift, Washington calmly stated, "Gentlemen, you must pardon me. I have grown gray in your service and now find myself growing blind." These heartfelt words caught the angry officers off guard. They recalled that they, as exemplars of truly virtuous citizenship, likewise had offered their lives for a cause larger than any of them. Many openly wept, even as the threat of a possible mutiny, or worse, a military coup directed against the states and the people, suddenly came to an end.

Washington promised to do everything in his power to secure "complete and ample justice" for the army. He did send a circular letter to the states imploring them to give more power to Congress. He warned them that "the Union could not be of a long duration" with a central government lacking in the capacity "to regulate and govern the general concerns of the Confederated republic." The states ignored Washington's plea for a strengthened national government.

Even though British troops were still in New York City, Washington also started "furloughing" soldiers, so that further troublesome incidents would not occur. After leaving the army one angry group of Pennsylvania Continentals marched on Philadelphia in June 1783. They surrounded Independence Hall (the Pennsylvania State House), where Congress held its sessions. In threatening fashion these veterans refused to leave until they received back pay. The frightened delegates asked the Pennsylvania government to have local militia troops protect them, but state officials turned down their request. Amid the taunts and jeers of the angry soldiers, the delegates finally abandoned Independence Hall. They never came back.

Thoroughly humiliated by armed soldiers and a state government that would not defend them, the delegates first moved to Princeton, New Jersey, then to Annapolis, Maryland, and finally to New York City. One newspaper, in mocking the central government, spoke of "the itinerant genius of Congress," a body that would "float along from one end of the continent to the other" as would a hot-air balloon.

Many citizens did not seem to care much one way or the other, since Congress was so lacking in authority. Nationalist leaders, on the other hand, kept trying to redress the balance of power between the impotent central government and the sovereign states. They drafted the Impost Plan of 1783, but this proposal, too, failed to secure unanimous state ratification. The plan was still languishing in late 1786, but by that time the nationalists were pursuing other avenues of change.

Drifting Toward Disunion

Despite the Paris peace settlement and the final removal of British troops, most citizens were engaged in another battle beginning in late 1783—this one against a hard-hitting economic depression. It had many sources. Planters in the South had lost about 60,000 slaves, many of whom the British had carried off. In addition, crop yields for 1784 and 1785 were small, largely because of bad weather. Farmers in New England reeled from the effects of new British trade regulations—in essence turning the Navigation system against the independent Americans. The Orders in Council of 1783 prohibited the sale of many American agricultural products in the British West Indies, formerly a key market for New England goods, and required many commodities to be conveyed to and from the islands in British vessels. The orders represented a serious blow to New England's agricultural, shipping, and shipbuilding trades.

Making matters even worse, merchants in all the states rushed to reestablish old trading connections with their British counterparts. These overly optimistic traders quickly became oversupplied with British goods on easy credit terms. They soon discovered that they could not sell these commodities to citizens feeling the effects of the postwar depression. Many American merchants thus faced total economic ruin by 1785.

The central government could do little. Congress did send John Adams to Britain in 1785 as the first minister from the United States. Adams, however, made no headway in getting British officials to back off from the Orders in Council. He dejectedly reported to Congress: British leaders "rely upon our disunion" to avoid negotiations.

To add to these economic woes, significant postwar trading ties did not develop with France. In fact, American exports to France far exceeded the value of imports (by roughly $2 million a year during the 1780s). The same held true with the Dutch. Even though some venturesome merchants sent a trading vessel—the *Empress of China*—to the Far East in 1784, all the new activity was insignificant in comparison to the renewed American dependency on British manufactured goods. The former colonists stayed glued to the old imperial trading network; decades would pass before they would gain full economic independence.

Some merchants, primarily from the Middle Atlantic states, were anxious to break free of Britain's economic hold. An opportunity presented itself in 1784 after Congress named John Jay (1745–1829), one of the Paris peace commissioners, to be its secretary for foreign affairs. Jay soon started negotiations with Don Diego de Gardoqui, Spain's first minister to the United States. Gardoqui talked about his government's concern that Americans, now streaming into the trans-Appalachian west, would in time covet Spanish territory beyond the Mississippi River. To stem the tide, Gardoqui informed Congress that Spain would not allow the Mississippi to serve as an outlet for western agricultural goods. To ease possible bad feelings, Gardoqui offered an advantageous commercial treaty.

Jay and a number of powerful merchants from the Middle Atlantic states saw merit in the Spanish proposal. They viewed western development—settlements were sprouting in Kentucky and Tennessee—as a potential threat to eastern economic dominance. Meanwhile, Gardoqui had Spanish agents circulating through the west. They encouraged settlers to become Spanish subjects in return for trade access to the Mississippi River—a means to protect Spanish holdings beyond the Mississippi. Basically these agents did little more than stir up resentment, both toward Spain and eastern leaders like Jay, who appeared to be selling out western interests for a commercial treaty of undetermined value.

When Jay reported on his discussions to Congress in August 1786, tempers flared. The southern states voted as a bloc against any such treaty, which represented a mortal blow to the Jay-Gardoqui negotiations. Southerners and westerners remained suspicious that Jay and his eastern merchant allies would not hesitate to abandon them altogether for petty commercial

Named in 1784 as secretary for foreign affairs, John Jay was unsuccessful in his efforts to negotiate trade accords with Spain. *Copyright © Collection of the New-York Historical Society.*

gains. Some leaders in Congress, as one delegate explained, began to speak "lightly of a separation and dissolution of the Confederation." Such talk helped galvanize the nationalists for dramatic action, as did a rebellion that now convulsed Massachusetts.

Daniel Shays's Rebellion

Postwar economic conditions were so bad in several states that citizens began demanding tax relief from their governments. In western Massachusetts desperate farmers complained about huge property tax increases by the state government to pay off the state's war debt. Taxes on land rose by more than 60 percent in the period from 1783 to 1786, exactly when a depressed postwar economy meant that farmers were getting little income from the sale of excess agricultural goods.

Local courts, in the absence of tax payments, started to seize the property of persons like Daniel Shays (1747?–1825), a revolutionary war veteran. Some lost their freehold farms, and in certain cases the courts remanded delinquent taxpayers to debtors' prison. Viewing their plight in terms of tyranny, the farmers of western Massachusetts believed they had the right to break the chains of political oppression, just as they had done in resisting British rule a few years before. This time, however, the perceived enemy was their own state government.

The **Shaysites,** as they came to be known, tried to resist in orderly fashion. They first met in impromptu conventions and sent petitions to the state assembly. Getting no relief, they turned to more confrontational means of resistance. In late August 1786 an estimated 1000 farmers poured into Northampton and shut down the county court. This crowd action represented the first of many such closures. By popular mandate citizens would no longer permit judges to seize property or condemn people to debtors' prison as the penalty for not paying taxes.

State leaders in Boston started to panic, fearing the "rebels" would soon descend upon them. Desperately, they conducted an emotional public appeal for funds. Frightened Bostonians opened their purses. They subscribed £5000 to pay for an eastern Massachusetts army headed by former Continental general Benjamin Lincoln. Lincoln's assignment was to march his army into western parts of the state and subdue the Shaysites.

The insurrection soon fizzled. Lacking weapons and suffering in bitterly cold weather, Daniel Shays and his followers lacked the essentials to sustain themselves. To get weapons, they attacked the federal arsenal at Springfield on January 25, 1787. A few well-placed cannon shots, which resulted in 24

Shays's Rebellion in Massachusetts convinced many citizens that the American republic needed a strong central government, if for no other reason than to control domestic insurrections.

Shaysite casualties (including 4 killed), drove them off. In early February the eastern Massachusetts army, after pursuing the western rebels through a driving snowstorm, fell upon Shays's followers at Petersham. Lincoln's force quickly routed the largely weaponless farmers. The Petersham engagement, along with tax relief from the assembly and amnesty for the leaders of the rebellion, ended the uprising.

Shays's Rebellion, however, held broader significance. The confrontation further coalesced the nationalists. Wrote George Washington: "Good God! . . . There are combustibles in every state, which a spark might set fire to." Only a national government of "energy" could save the republic from sinking "into the lowest state of humiliation and contempt." The nationalists thus intensified their campaign for a new constitutional settlement, one designed to bring the self-serving sovereign states and the people under control.

HUMAN RIGHTS AND SOCIAL CHANGE

The years between 1776 and 1787 represented much more than a time of mounting political confrontation between nationalists and localists. This period also witnessed the establishment of many fundamental human rights. When Thomas Jefferson penned his famous words, "all men are created equal," he informed George III that kings were not superior to the people by some assumed right of birth. Jefferson went on to say that all human beings had "certain unalienable rights," or rights literally beyond governmental control. Republican governments had the responsibility to guarantee and respect these rights, including "life, liberty, and the pursuit of happiness" for all citizens.

Americans had likewise rebelled against Britain to preserve property rights. Tyrannical governments, for example, threatened property through taxation without representation. In trying to protect property rights while expanding human rights, revolutionary leaders learned that the two could clash. They found it much easier to guarantee human rights when property rights, such as those relating to the ownership of slaves, were not also at stake. Thus the revolutionary era produced some striking contradictions in efforts to enshrine greater freedom for all persons living in the new American nation.

In Pursuit of Religious Freedom

Since the days of the Great Awakening, dissenter religious groups had expressed opposition to established churches in the colonies. The Baptists were particularly outspoken. They wanted official toleration and an end to taxes used exclusively for state-supported churches. A major breakthrough came in 1776, thanks to George Washington's close friend George Mason, who wrote the Virginia Declaration of Rights, a document appended to the new state constitution. It guaranteed all citizens equal entitlement "to the free exercise of religion, according to the dictates of conscience." This statement provided for official toleration of dissenter sects but did not halt taxes going exclusively to the established Anglican church.

Three years later, Thomas Jefferson, with the support of Baptists from the backcountry, took up the cause. Jefferson presented legislation calling for the complete separation of church and state. On and off for seven years, the Virginia assembly debated this bill. In 1786 the will of those who argued for complete freedom of conscience, including the right to believe nothing and support no church, prevailed. In later years Jefferson would be labeled an atheist for his part in guaranteeing religious freedom. For him the Virginia Statute of Religious Freedom was just as significant as the Declaration of Independence, and he had these sentiments engraved on his tombstone.

Disestablishment quickly followed in other states, particularly in the South where the Anglican church (soon to become the Protestant Episcopal Church of America) had been dominant. In New England, only Rhode Islanders, following in the tradition of Roger Williams, had enjoyed full latitude in worship. With the Revolution the cause of religious freedom started to move forward in other New England states. Lawmakers began letting citizens decide which local church to support with their tax monies. This development represented a partial victory for individuals who preferred worshipping as Baptists or Presbyterians, but Congregationalism was still the established state church, continuing a pattern of official favoritism dating back to Puritan times. Complete separation of church and state, including the right not to support any church or to deny all religious creeds, did not occur in New England until the early nineteenth century.

Freedom of religion was one among a number of fundamental rights to make headway during the revolutionary era. Several of the states adopted bills of rights similar to Virginia's, guaranteeing freedom of speech, assembly, and the press, as well as trials by jury. Other states started revising their legal codes, making penalties for crimes less harsh. There was a sense that criminals could become useful citizens, which eventually resulted in prisons oriented more toward rehabilitation. Fewer crimes would now carry the death penalty.

In Virginia, Thomas Jefferson revised the state legal code. His work put an end to such feudal practices as primogeniture and entail (passing and committing property only to eldest sons through the generations). Running through all these acts was the republican assumption that citizens should have the opportunity to lead productive lives, uninhibited by laws violating personal conscience or denying the opportunity to acquire property.

The Propertyless Poor and the West

Gaining property remained only a dream for many revolutionary Americans. At least 20 percent of the population lived at the poverty level or below, eking out precarious existences as unskilled laborers. Indeed, wealth was more unevenly distributed in 1800 than in 1750. The striking increase in almshouses and other relief organizations was evidence in itself that poverty was spreading, especially in the large port cities.

One missed opportunity to help the poor related to the property of an estimated 500,000 loyalists, of whom one-fifth fled permanently to such places as England, Canada, the Bahamas, and various West Indian islands. State governments seized their land and other forms of property, worth millions, which could have been redistributed to poorer citizens. Instead, the states quickly sold off confiscated property to the highest bidders as a source of wartime revenues. This practice favored persons of wealth with investment capital and preempted any substantial redistribution of property.

Another opportunity lay with the enormous trans-Appalachian frontier. Washington's Continental soldiers, who ranked among the poorest members of revolutionary society, had been promised access to western lands for long-term service. When they mustered out in 1783, they received land warrant certificates. To survive, most veterans soon exchanged these paper certificates for the bare necessities of life. Consequently, very few were ever able to begin anew in the Ohio country, once military tracts had been set aside and surveyed.

Wilderness Road

One of the most famous frontiersmen of his day, Daniel Boone blazed the Wilderness Road to Kentucky in 1775.

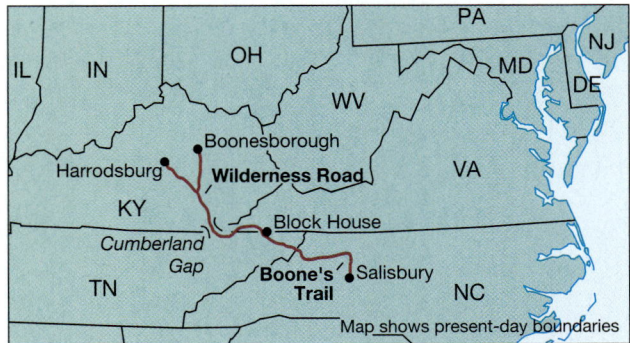

Still, western lands remained a source of hope for economically downtrodden soldiers and civilians alike. In 1775 explorer Daniel Boone laid out the "Wilderness Road" to Kentucky. Others, like rugged Simon Kenton, scouted down the Ohio River from Pittsburgh. Where these frontiersmen went, thousands of land-hungry easterners soon followed. By 1790 Kentucky contained a population of 74,000, and Tennessee held 36,000. These settlers paid dearly for their invasion of Native-American lands. The Shawnees, Cherokees, and Chickasaws fought back in innumerable bloody clashes. The white death toll reached 1500. Besides losing ancient tribal lands, Native Americans also suffered considerable casualties.

White settlements in Kentucky and Tennessee generated pressure to open territory north of the Ohio River. After ceding the Old Northwest to the United States in 1783, however, the British did not abandon their military posts there. To maintain the lucrative fur trade, they bolstered the Miamis, Shawnees, Delawares, and remnant groups of the Iroquois nation with a steady supply of firearms. Americans foolish enough to venture north of the Ohio River rarely survived, and the region remained closed to large numbers of westward-moving settlers well into the 1790s.

Despite these circumstances, Congress was eager to open the Ohio country. With this goal in mind, the delegates approved three land ordinances. The 1784 Ordinance provided for territorial government and guaranteed settlers they would not remain in permanent colonial status. When enough people (later specified at 60,000) had moved in, a constitution could be written, state boundaries set, and admission to the union as a full partner would follow. The 1785 Ordinance called for orderly surveying of the region. Townships of 6 miles square were to be laid out in gridlike fashion—each township to contain 36 sections of 640 acres each with proceeds from the sale of the sixteenth section to be used to finance public education. The Northwest Ordinance of 1787 refined governmental arrangements, gave a bill of rights to prospective settlers, and proclaimed slavery forever banned north of the Ohio River—a prohibition that Thomas Jefferson had sought but failed to get included in the 1784 Ordinance. In providing for orderly development and eventual statehood, the land ordinances may well have been the most significant legislation of the Confederation-period Congress.

The ordinances, however, were not fully enlightened. Congress, in its continuing search for revenue, viewed the Old Northwest as a source of long-term income. The smallest parcel individual settlers could buy was 640 acres, priced at $1.00 per acre, and there were to be no purchases on credit. Families of modest means, let alone poorer ones, could not meet such terms. As a result, Congress dealt mainly with well-to-do land speculators—and even extended them deeds to millions of acres on credit no less! These decisions cut off the poorest citizens from the West, unless they were willing to squat on uninhabited land until driven off, which thousands did to survive economically.

First Territorial Survey

Thomas Hutchins, a native of New Jersey, directed the first survey of territorial lands.

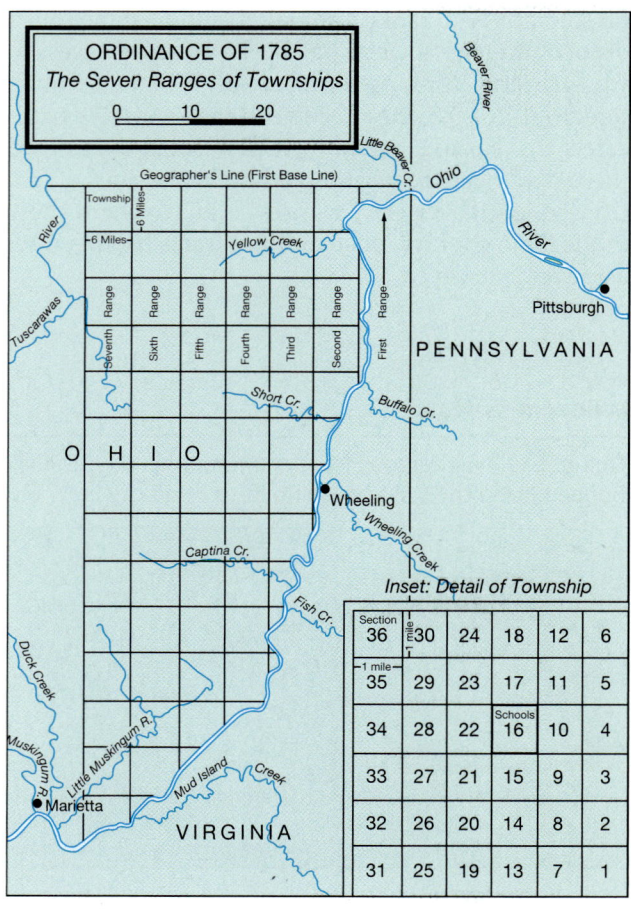

Women Appeal for Fundamental Liberties

Like the poor, women experienced little success in improving their lot during the revolutionary era. Among their advocates was Abigail Adams. In the spring of 1776 she wrote to her husband John, then in Philadelphia arguing for independence, and admonished him to "remember the ladies, and be more generous and favorable to them than your ancestors."

As if joking with his wife, John Adams replied by asking whether American women were now working in league with the British ministry. Should political independence come, he wrote, "we know better than to repeal our masculine system," claim-

THE PEOPLE SPEAK

Abigail Adams Exhorts Her Husband to "Remember the Ladies" (1776)

In the spring of 1776 John Adams, who had become a staunch advocate of independence, was attending the Second Continental Congress in Philadelphia. His wife Abigail (1744–1818) was back in Massachusetts tending to the family homestead and their children. Abigail was a brilliant, insatiably curious person. She corresponded regularly with her husband, repeatedly asking him for news about the momentous events of the day. Moreover, she offered her own opinions, such as in late March 1776 when she wrote to John about the inferior status of women in American society. Should independence come about, Abigail wanted to see a real revolution as well that would include a vast expansion of social, political, and legal rights for women. In his reply, John was somewhat dismissive of Abigail's words. Her statement, however, did not go away but served as an important rallying cry for women as they struggled to obtain a full measure of equal rights for themselves over the next two centuries of United States history.

ABIGAIL TO JOHN ADAMS
Braintree March 31 1776

... I long to hear that you have declared an independancy—and by the way in the new Code of Laws which I suppose it will be necessary for you to make I desire you would Remember the Ladies, and be more generous and favourable to them than your ancestors. Do not put such unlimited power into the hands of the Husbands. Remember all Men would be tyrants if they could. If perticuliar care and attention is not paid to the Laidies we are determined to foment a Rebelion, and will not hold ourselves bound by any Laws in which we have no voice, or Representation.

That your Sex are Naturally Tyrannical is a Truth so thoroughly established as to admit of no dispute, but such of you as wish to be happy willingly give up the harsh title of Master for the more tender and endearing one of Friend. Why then, not put it out of the power of the vicious and the Lawless to use us with cruelty and indignity with impunity. Men of Sense in all Ages abhor those customs which treat us only as the vassals of your Sex. Regard us then as Beings placed by providence under your protection and in imitation of the Supreem Being make use of that power only for our happiness.

JOHN TO ABIGAIL ADAMS
Ap. 14. 1776

... As to your extraordinary Code of Laws, I cannot but laugh. We have been told that our Struggle has loosened the bands of Government every where. That Children and Apprentices were disobedient—that schools and Colledges were grown turbulent—that Indains slighted their Guardians and Negroes grew insolent to their Masters. But your Letter was the first Intimation that another Tribe more numerous and powerfull than all the rest were grown discontented.—This is rather too coarse a Compliment but you are so saucy, I wont blot it out.

Depend upon it, We know better than to repeal our Masculine systems. Altho they are in full Force, you know they are little more than Theory. We dare not exert our Power in its full Latitude. We are obliged to go fair, and softly, and in Practice you know We are the subjects. We have only the Name of Masters, and rather than give up this, which would compleatly subject Us to the Despotism of the Peticoat, I hope General Washington, and all our brave Heroes would fight. I am sure every good Politician would plot, as long as he would against Despotism, Empire, Monarchy, Aristocracy, Oligarchy, or Ochlocracy.—A fine Story indeed. I begin to think the Ministry as deep as they are wicked. After stirring up Tories, Landjobbers, Trimmers, Bigots, Canadians, Indians, Negroes, Hanoverians, Hessians, Russians, Irish Roman Catholicks, Scotch Renegadoes, at last they have stimulated the to demand new Priviledges and threaten to rebell.

Source: L. H. Butterfield, et al., eds. *The Adams Papers*, Series II: *Adams Family Correspondence*, Vol 1: December 1761–May 1776 (New York, 1965), 369–371, 381–383.

ing that men "have only the name of masters." John Adams knew very well that by law and social practice, women were legally dependent on men, as the case of Nancy Shippen so vividly illustrates.

Women gained no significant political rights during the revolutionary period, except briefly in New Jersey. Yet they contributed enthusiastically to the cause. Some, like "The Association" headed by Esther DeBerdt Reed of Philadelphia, called themselves "daughters of liberty" and met regularly to make clothing for the Continental army. Others, such as Mary Ludwig Hays McCauly of Carlisle, Pennsyl-

In her letters to her husband John, Abigail Adams spoke out in support of women's rights, but her message received little sympathetic attention.

The concept of **republican motherhood** had potentially liberating qualities. The calling of republican mothers was to manage the domestic sphere of family life, just as husbands were to take responsibility for the family's economic welfare. This duty reduced traditional male dominance in all family matters. Elevating the role of women in family life may also have affected the nature of courtship by putting more emphasis upon affection than on parental control in the making of marriages. However, the immediate effect of this emerging tendency should not be exaggerated, as Nancy Shippen's experiences indicate.

If women were to be responsible for instilling republican values in future generations, they needed more and better schooling. During the 1780s and 1790s some states started taxing the populace for the support of elementary education. Massachusetts broke new ground in 1789 by requiring its citizens to pay for female as well as male elementary education. In addition, these two decades saw the opening of many new private schools, such as the Young Ladies Academy of Philadelphia (founded in 1787). The academies offered more advanced education to daughters of well-to-do families in subjects traditionally reserved for males, such as mathematics, science, and history. This was a major breakthrough be-

vania, were not so well off economically. Living on a sparse income as a domestic servant, she accompanied her husband to war. A tough-talking, plucky woman, Mary helped fire a rebel artillery piece at the Battle of Monmouth Court House in June 1778 and was almost hit by a flying British cannon ball, which passed between her legs. To this she replied: "It was lucky it did not pass a little higher, for in that case it might have carried away something else." Later generations, worried lest America's youth be corrupted by Mary's earthy manner, redefined her role as a water bearer to troops and turned her into the far more feminine "Molly Pitcher," a change in persona that would have made Mary laugh. After the Revolution she lived in near poverty as a charwoman, although she did obtain a small war pension a few years before her death in 1832.

What held the greatest promise for women, at least for those of middling and affluent economic status, was the ideology of republicanism, which directly influenced family life by offering a broadened definition regarding the role of mothers. Patriot leaders repeatedly asserted that the republic would collapse without virtuous citizens. Hence a special task for mothers was to implant strong moral character and civic virtue in their children, especially their sons, so they would uphold the obligations of disinterested citizenship for the good of the nation.

Judith Sargent Murray, here portrayed by American artist John Singleton Copley, was an early proponent of equal educational opportunities for women.

cause popular lore held that too much exposure to "masculine" subjects would addle the minds of young women. The female academies quickly demonstrated otherwise.

Still, the emphasis in expanding opportunities for middle- and upper-class women was upon service to the family and the republic, not on individual development and self-fulfillment. That is what bothered Judith Sargent Murray of Massachusetts, who wrote extensively about the need for comparable educational experiences for men and women. Murray insisted that women could exist independently of men and lead satisfying lives, but she was very much ahead of her times.

Most men in revolutionary America resisted further change for women. As a Marylander insisted in 1790, pursuit of the principle that "all mankind are born equal" was being "taken in too extensive a sense" in relation to females, and would undermine "those charms which it is the peculiar lot of the fair sex to excel in." Thus while republican motherhood offered potentially higher status, most men still thought of women as a form of property whose existence should be devoted to masculine welfare and happiness.

The Dilemma of Race and Racism

Revolutionary ideology placed a premium on such terms as liberty and equality. Almost everyone recognized that it was inconsistent to employ such terms, yet hold 500,000 African Americans (one-fifth of the population in 1776) in perpetual bondage. Phillis Wheatley addressed this incongruity in her poem to Lord Dartmouth. Lord Dunmore also pointed it out dramatically in November 1775 when he offered emancipation to Virginia's slaves (see p. 134) in return for bearing arms against their rebellious masters.

For generations colonial Americans had taken slavery for granted, as if the institution were part of the natural order of life. All of the talk about liberty and political slavery during the 1760s and 1770s began to undermine this unquestioning attitude, so much so that even slaveholding patriots like Patrick Henry asked whether holding persons in bondage was not "repugnant to humanity . . . and destructive to liberty?" Some revolutionary leaders decisively answered "yes."

These leaders did something else; they went into action. In 1774 Philadelphians, among them Benjamin Franklin, organized an abolition society. Pressure from this group and from antislavery Quakers resulted in Pennsylvania's becoming the first state (1780) to declare human bondage illegal. Soon other Northern states followed, modeling their emancipa-

Slave Concentration, 1790

Many Americans considered slavery irreconcilable with the revolution's themes of liberty and equality.

tion laws on Pennsylvania's, which specified that children born to slave mothers had to be set free by the age of 28. By 1800 slavery was a dying institution in the North.

Slaves themselves were also very active in challenging human bondage. Quok Walker of Massachusetts ran away from his master in April 1781 and sought refuge with a friendly neighbor. His master located Walker a few days later and accosted him with a whip. Although beaten severely, Walker stood his ground. He sued for his freedom, pointing out that the new state constitution had proclaimed that "all men are born free and equal." The State Superior Court upheld Walker in 1783, signaling the beginning of the end of slavery in Massachusetts.

Many revolutionary leaders hoped the campaign to abolish slavery would extend into the South. During the 1780s there were some positive signs. After 1783 only South Carolina and Georgia were

The American Mosaic

Birth Control in the Early Republic

ONE of the most hotly debated questions in late eighteenth-century America and Europe was whether human beings were capable of improvement. Famous philosophers of the Enlightenment argued that people were naturally good and that all of society's problems could be solved by the application of reason. English philosopher William Godwin described the future in particularly glowing terms. He wrote that in the future "there would no longer be a handful of rich and a multitude of poor.... There will be no war, no crime, no administration of justice, as it is called, and no government. Beside this there will be no disease, anguish, melancholy, or resentment."

On the other side of the debate on human perfectibility was a young Anglican clergyman, Thomas Robert Malthus. Parson Malthus argued that human perfection was unattainable because human population growth would inevitably exceed the growth of the world's food supply. He asserted—on the basis of figures collected by Benjamin Franklin—that population tends to increase geometrically (1, 2, 4, 8) while subsistence only grows arithmetically (1, 2, 3, 4). Ultimately population would be held in check by famine, war, and disease.

Malthus's gloomy vision of the future failed to come true because large numbers of people began to limit the number of children through the use of birth control. Nowhere was the limitation of births more striking than in the United States. In 1800 the American birthrate was higher than the birthrate in any European nation. The typical American woman bore an average of 7 children. She had her first child around the age of 23 and proceeded to bear children at two-year intervals until her early forties. Had the American birthrate remained at this level, the nation's population would have reached 2 billion by 1990.

Late in the eighteenth century, however, Americans began to have fewer children. Between 1800 and 1900 the birthrate fell 40 percent and even more sharply among the middle and upper classes. Where the typical American mother bore 7 children in 1800, the average number of children had fallen to 3.5 in 1900. And instead of giving birth to her last child at the age of 40 or later, by 1900 the typical American woman bore her last child at the age of 33. The decline of the birthrate is such an important historical breakthrough that it has its own name: *the demographic transition*.

The sharp decline in birthrates is a phenomenon easier to describe than to explain. The drop in fertility was not the result of sudden improvements in contraceptive devices. The basic birth control techniques used before the Civil War—coitus interruptus (withdrawal), douching, and condoms—were known in ancient times. Ancient Egyptian papyri and the Old Testament describe cervical caps and spermicides, while ancient Greek physicians were aware of the contraceptive effects of douching. Contraception was not unknown in the past, it was simply used haphazardly and ineffectively. Nor was the imposition of limits on birthrates a result of urbanization. Although fertility fell earliest and most rapidly in the urban Northeast, the decline in fertility occurred in all parts of the country, in rural as well as urban areas and in the South and West as well as the Northeast.

What accounted for the declining birthrate? In part, the reduction in fertility reflected the growing realization among parents that in an increasingly commercial and industrial society children were no longer economic assets who could be productively employed in household industries or bound out as apprentices or servants. Instead, children required significant investment in the form of education to prepare them for respectable careers and marriages. The emergence of a self-conscious middle class concerned about social mobility and maintaining an acceptable standard of living also encouraged new limits on family size.

The shrinking size of families also reflected a growing desire among women to assert control over their lives. Much of the impetus behind birth control came from women who were weary of an unending cycle of pregnancy, birth, nursing, and new pregnancy. A letter written by a sister of Harriet Beecher Stowe suggests the desperation felt by many women who were single-handedly responsible for bearing and rearing a family's children. "Harriet," her sister observed, "has one baby put out for the winter, the other at home, and number three will be here the middle of January. Poor thing, she bears up wonderfully well.... She says she shall not have any more children, she knows for certain for one while."

How did Americans limit births? Periodic abstinence—or what is now known as the rhythm method—was the most widely advocated method of birth control. Unfortunately, knowl-

> **" A Beautiful Invention."**—The very thing that every Gentleman needs. Samples sent free for 15 cts. Address   **H. ALEXANDERS,**
> 3550   Houghton, Mich.

edge about women's ovulation cycle, menstruation, and conception was largely inaccurate and most advice writers suggested that the "safe period" was the ten days halfway between menstrual periods—which is in fact the time when a woman is most likely to conceive.

Other principal methods of contraception included coitus interruptus—withdrawal prior to ejaculation—and douches of the vagina after intercourse. Less common was the insertion of a sponge soaked in a spermicidal fluid into the vagina. None of these methods, however, were especially effective in preventing conception since each of these techniques can still allow small amounts of semen to reach the fallopian tubes. Other popular forms of contraception were heavily influenced by superstition. These included ingestion of teas concocted out of fruitless plants; having a woman engage in violent movements immediately after intercourse; and having intercourse on an inclined plane in order to prevent the sperm from reaching the egg or to prevent the egg from leaving the ovary.

Charles Goodyear's discovery in 1839 of the vulcanization of rubber permitted the mass production of an inexpensive and effective birth control device, the condom. But during the nineteenth century condoms were mainly used for protection against venereal disease, not for birth control.

Given the ineffectiveness of other methods of contraception, it is not surprising to learn that abortion was a major method of population control. By 1860, according to one estimate, 20 percent of pregnancies were terminated by abortion, compared to 30 percent today. Some of the popular practices for inducing abortion included taking hot baths, jumping off tables, performing heavy exercises, having someone jump on a pregnant woman's belly, drinking nauseating concoctions, and poking sharp instruments into the uterus.

Why were abortions so widespread during the nineteenth century? In part, it reflected the general ignorance of the reproductive process. It was not until 1827 that the existence of the human egg was established. Before that time it was believed by many scientists that the human sperm constituted a miniature person that grew into a baby in the mother's womb. Thus there was no modern notion of a moment of conception when egg and sperm unite.

Furthermore, for most of the nineteenth century, it was difficult to determine whether a woman was pregnant or simply suffering menstrual irregularity. A woman only knew she was pregnant for sure when she could feel the child stir within her. This occurs around the fourth or fifth month of pregnancy and in most jurisdictions abortions prior to this time were not considered crimes. It was not until the late nineteenth century that most jurisdictions in the United States declared abortions to be criminal offenses.

The decline in the birthrate carried far-reaching consequences for family life. First of all, motherhood and the strain of pregnancy ended earlier for women. They had an increasing number of years when young children were no longer their primary responsibility. It also meant that parents were free to invest more time, energy, and financial resources in each individual child.

still involved in the international slave trade. Maryland, Delaware, and Virginia passed laws making it easier for planters to manumit (free) individual slaves. George Washington was one among a few wealthy planters who took advantage of Virginia's **manumission** law. He referred to slavery as a "misfortune" that sullied revolutionary ideals, and in his will he made provision for the liberation of his slaves.

Washington was unusual. Far more typical was Thomas Jefferson. In his *Notes on the State of Virginia* (1785), he called slavery "a perpetual exercise" in "the most unremitting despotism." Fearing the worst should human bondage continue, he wrote: "I tremble for my country when I reflect that God is just." Such thinking led him to propose in Congress during 1784 that slavery never be allowed to spread north of the Ohio River. Jefferson, however, could not bring himself to free his own slaves. His chattels formed the economic base of his way of life. Their labor gave him the time that he needed for politics and, ironically, the time to work so persuasively on behalf of human liberty.

Support for his lifestyle was not the only reason Jefferson held back. He was representative of his times in believing blacks to be inherently inferior to whites. In his *Notes*, he made a number of comparisons of ability that were disparaging toward blacks, such as in the category of reasoning power. Trying to prove his point, Jefferson scoffed at the poems of Phillis Wheatley, which he described as "below the dignity of criticism." Jefferson thought, too, that the emancipation of African Americans would result in racial war and "the extermination of the one or the other race." Thus a man who labored so diligently for human rights in his own lifetime remained in bondage to the racist concepts of his era.

Negative racial attitudes were the norm in revolutionary America, as the growing number of freed African Americans learned again and again. Because of the general abolition and individual manumission movements, the free black population approached 60,000 by 1790 and 108,000 by 1800 (11 percent of the total African-American population). Like the some 5000 black Continental army veterans, Phillis Wheatley, and George Washington's former slaves, these individuals repeatedly had to struggle to survive in a hostile society.

Not only did they survive, but they led noteworthy lives. Benjamin Banneker (1731–1806) was such a person. He grew up in a free black family in Maryland, attended an interracial Quaker school, and became a talented mathematician, astronomer, and surveyor. During the 1790s he published a series of almanacs and also served on the commission that de-

Absalom Jones (top) established St. Thomas's African Episcopal Church of Philadelphia, while Richard Allen founded the African Methodist Episcopal Church in the United States (bottom).

signed the new federal city of Washington, D.C. Throughout his life Banneker successfully disproved, as he wrote to Jefferson in 1791, the "train of absurd and false ideas and opinions" regarding the innate intelligence of African Americans.

Unlike Banneker, who spent his whole life in Maryland, many free blacks moved to the large northern port cities, where slavery was a fading threat. They built their own neighborhoods, and skilled workers opened shops to serve one another. Other urban free blacks, including both males and females, performed domestic service at low wages for well-to-do white families, but they did so as free persons with the opportunity to fashion independent lives for themselves.

Free African Americans also established their own schools and churches. With the assistance of the New York Society for the Promotion of Manumission, blacks helped found the African Free School in New York City during 1787. At first the school faced opposition from whites, who worried about educating blacks. This school survived, however, and would train hundreds of students in the fundamentals of reading and mathematics. In Delaware, Richard Allen, who purchased his own freedom in 1777, became a powerful preacher within the Methodist ranks. After enduring incidents of intimidation from unfriendly whites, Allen moved to Philadelphia in 1786 where he became the founder of the African Methodist Episcopal Church. African Baptist and African Presbyterian denominations also developed in the northern port cities, and these churches provided opportunities for formal education, since African-American children were rarely welcome in white schools.

Whether in the North or the South, the reality most often was overt discrimination. As a group, free African Americans responded by providing for one another and believing in a better day when revolutionary ideals regarding human freedom and liberty would have full meaning in their lives. In this sense they still had much in common with their brethren in slavery.

SECOND NEW BEGINNING, NEW NATIONAL GOVERNMENT

In 1787 many revolutionary leaders were more concerned about internal political stability than securing human rights. With all the talk of breaking up the Confederation, with Shays's Rebellion not yet completely quelled, and with the states arguing endlessly about almost everything, political leaders believed that matters of government should take primacy, or the republican experiment might be forever lost. Certainly the nationalists felt this way, and they were pushing hard for a revision of the first constitutional settlement.

In September 1786 representatives from five states met briefly in Annapolis, Maryland, to discuss pressing interstate commercial problems. Those present included such strong nationalists as Alexander Hamilton, John Dickinson, and James Madison. Since so few states were represented, the delegates abandoned their agenda in favor of an urgent plea asking all the states to send delegates to a special constitutional convention for remedying "such defects as exist" in the Articles of Confederation.

This time the states responded, largely because of the specter of civil turmoil associated with Shays's Rebellion. Twelve states—Rhode Island refused to participate—named 74 delegates, 55 of whom would attend the Constitutional Convention in Philadelphia. As the Continental Congress instructed the delegates in February 1787, their purpose was to revise the Articles of Confederation, making them "adequate to the exigencies . . . of the union." Some nationalists, however, had other ideas. They wanted a whole new plan of national government. Their ideas would dominate the proceedings from beginning to end, and their determination produced the Constitution of 1787.

The Framers of the Constitution

The men who gathered in Philadelphia were successful lawyers, planters, and merchants of education, wealth, and wide-ranging accomplishments, not ordinary citizens. They represented particular states, but most of them thought in national terms, based on experiences like serving in the Continental Congress and the Continental army. They feared for the future

James Madison, a strong nationalist, has been called the "father of the Constitution" for his plan of national government. He became the nation's fourth president.

of the republic, unless the weak central government was strengthened as a means of containing the selfishness of particular states. They seized this opportunity for change and made the most of it.

Among those present during the lengthy proceedings, which stretched from May 25 to September 17, was the revered George Washington, who served as the convention's president. Other notable leaders included James Madison, Alexander Hamilton, Gouverneur and Robert Morris, and John Dickinson. Benjamin Franklin, at 81, was the oldest delegate. He offered his finely tuned diplomatic tact in working out compromises that kept the proceedings moving forward.

Although the delegates disagreed vehemently over particular issues, they never let their differences deflect them from their main purpose—to find the constitutional means for an enduring republic. The Constitution was not perfect, as Benjamin Franklin stated on the last day of the convention, but it did bring stability and energy to national government—and it has endured.

A Document Constructed by Compromises

Had the nationalists been doctrinaire, their deliberations would have collapsed. They held fast to their objective—providing for a strong central government—but were flexible about ways to achieve their goal. Thus they were able to compromise on critical issues. The first great points of difference dealt with the structure of government and whether states should be represented equally or according to population distribution. The eventual compromise required the abandonment of the Articles of Confederation.

Slight of build and reserved, James Madison of Virginia (1751–1836) has been called the "father of the Constitution." A diligent student of history and politics, he drafted a proposed plan of national government, then made arrangements to have it presented by Edmund Randolph, Virginia's governor and a more adept public speaker, at the outset of the convention. This strategy worked, and the delegates gave the "Virginia Plan" their undivided attention. The plan outlined a three-tiered structure with an executive branch and two houses of Congress. Madison also envisioned a separate judicial branch.

Delegates from the less populous, smaller states objected. Under the Virginia Plan representatives to the two chambers of Congress would be apportioned to the states according to population, whereas under the Articles, each state, regardless of population, had an equal voice in national government. For such delegates as lawyer William Paterson of New Jersey, the latter practice ensured that the interests of the smaller states would not be sacrificed to those of the more populous, larger states. Paterson countered with his "New Jersey Plan" on June 15. It retained equal voting in a unicameral national legislature, and it also vested far greater authority, including the powers of taxation and regulation of interstate and foreign commerce, in the central government. Paterson's plan was far more consistent with the convention's original charge—an argument in its favor.

On June 19 the delegates voted to adopt a three-tiered structure of government, but they did not resolve the question of how the states should be represented in the two new legislative branches. The convention had reached an impasse, and some delegates now threatened to leave. At the end of June Benjamin Franklin made one of his well-timed speeches. He urged everyone present to put aside "our little partial local interests" so that future generations would not "despair of establishing governments by human wisdom and leave it to chance, war, and conquest."

The advice of Franklin and others calling for unity of purpose helped ease tensions. By July 12 the delegates had hammered out a settlement. Central to the "Great Compromise," which saved the convention from dissolving, was an agreement providing for proportional representation in the lower house (favoring the more populous states) and equality of representation in the upper house (favoring the less populous states). In the upper house each state would have two senators. Although the senators could vote independently of each other, they could also operate in tandem to protect state interests.

Having passed this crucial hurdle, the convention turned to other issues, not the least of which was slavery. Delegates from the Deep South wanted guarantees that would prevent any national tampering with their chattel property. Some Northerners, however, including those who had supported abolition in their states, preferred constitutional restrictions on slavery.

For a while, compromise did not seem possible. In the heat of debate South Carolinian Pierce Butler blurted out that the North and the South were "as different as . . . Russia and Turkey." Later on, Pennsylvania delegate Gouverneur Morris, a firm antislavery advocate, suggested that it was impossible "to blend incompatible things." Finally, both sides made concessions for the sake of union. What they produced was the first major national compromise on the continuation of slavery (to be followed by others, including the Compromises of 1820 and 1850).

In the North-South compromise of 1787, the delegates left matters purposely vague. By mutual agreement, the Constitution neither endorsed nor condemned slavery, nor can that word be found in the text. It did guarantee Southerners that slaves would count as "three-fifths" of white persons for purposes of determining representation in the lower house. While this meant more congressional seats for the South, direct taxes would also be based on population, including "three-fifths of all other persons." Thus the South would also pay more in taxes. The delegates also agreed to prohibit any national legislation against the importation of slaves from abroad until 1808.

Although these clauses gave implicit recognition to slavery, it should be noted that the Northwest Land Ordinance of 1787, adopted by the Continental Congress in New York at the same time, forever barred slavery north of the Ohio River. The timing has led some historians to conclude that inhibiting the spread of slavery was also part of the compromise, representing a major concession to northern interests.

The North-South compromise kept the convention and the republic together by temporarily mollifying most delegates on an extremely divisive issue. Still, slavery was so remarkably inconsistent with the ideals of human liberty that the problem could not be sidestepped for long.

A third set of issues provoking compromise had to do with the office of president. Nobody seemed sure what range of authority the national executive should have, how long the term of office should be, or how the president should be elected. By early September the delegates, fatigued by endless debates and extremely hot weather during three months of meetings, settled these questions quickly. The office of the president was potentially powerful. Besides serving as commander in chief of military forces, the incumbent could fashion treaties with foreign powers, subject to ratification by a two-thirds vote of the Senate. The president could veto congressional legislation, which both houses of Congress could only override with two-thirds majorities. Congress, in turn, had an important check on the president. It could impeach the executive if presidential powers were abused. Four years seemed like a reasonable term of office, and reelection would be permitted.

To help insulate the president from manipulation by public opinion, the delegates made the office indirectly elective. They did so by creating the electoral college. Each state would have the same number of electors as representatives and senators. In states that permitted popular voting for the presidency, citizens would cast ballots for electors who favored particular candidates. In turn the electors would meet and vote for the person they favored. The candidate with a majority of electoral college votes would become president. The person with the second highest total would become vice president. Should the electors fail to reach a majority decision (this happened in the elections of 1800 and 1824), the election would be turned over to the House of Representatives, where each state would have one vote in choosing a president.

The subject of the presidency might have been more contentious had no person of George Washington's universally acclaimed stature been on the scene. Washington was the one authentic popular hero and symbol of national unity to emerge from the Revolution, and the delegates were already thinking of him as the first president. Since he was so fully trusted as a firm apostle of republican principles who had disdained the mantle of a military dictator, defining the mode of election and powers of the national executive were not insurmountable tasks.

The Ratification Struggle

Thirty-nine delegates affixed their signatures to the proposed Constitution on September 17, 1787. Benjamin Franklin hoped that more of the delegates would sign, and he echoed the thoughts of those who did so by indicating that "there are several parts of this Constitution which I do not at present approve. . . . It therefore astonishes me, Sir," he stated, "to find this system approaching so near to perfection as it does." Pointing toward a seal with a carving of the sun on the president's chair, Franklin concluded: "At length I have the happiness to know that it is a rising and not a setting sun."

The delegates who signed the Constitution of 1787 knew there would be significant opposition because their plan cut so heavily into state authority. So they made the shrewd move of agreeing that only nine states needed to ratify the Constitution—through special state conventions rather than through state legislatures—to allow the new central government to commence operations. The nationalists were not going to let one or two states destroy months of work—and what they viewed as the best last hope for a languishing republic.

In another astute move, the nationalists started referring to themselves as **Federalists,** and they disarmed their opponents by calling them **Antifederalists**. Actually, the Antifederalists were the real federalists; they wanted to continue the confederation of sovereign states, and they sought to keep power as close as possible to the people, mostly in the hands of state governments. This manipulation of terminology may have gotten some local Federalist candidates elected to state ratifying conventions, thus helping to secure victory for the Constitution.

George Washington (on the podium) presided at the Constitutional Convention in Philadelphia during the summer of 1787. Washington was a popular hero and a natural choice to serve as the first president of the United States.

The nationalists were also very effective in explaining the Convention's work. The essence of their argumentation appeared in **The Federalist Papers,** a series of 85 remarkably cogent newspaper essays written by James Madison, Alexander Hamilton, and John Jay on behalf of ratification in New York. Under the pseudonym "Publius," they discussed various aspects of the Constitution and tried to demonstrate how the document would ensure political stability and provide enlightened legislation.

The new government, they asserted, had been designed to protect the rights of all citizens. No one self-serving faction ("a landed interest, a manufacturing interest, a mercantile interest, a monied interest"), whether representing a minority or majority of citizens, could take power completely and deprive others of their liberties and property. The Constitution would check and balance these interest groups because basic powers (executive, legislative, judicial) would be divided among the various branches of government. Furthermore, the system was truly federal, they argued, because much decision-making authority remained with the states as a further protection against power-hungry, self-serving factional interest groups.

Beyond these advantages, the Constitution embodied the principle of representative republicanism, as Madison explained in *Federalist No. 10.* Large election districts for the House of Representatives would make it more difficult for particular interest groups to manipulate elections and send "unworthy candidates" to Congress. Citizens of true merit, hence, could rise up, emerge triumphant, and then meet in Congress to enact laws beneficial for all citizens of the republic.

The nationalists admitted they were overturning the first constitutional settlement of 1776. The emphasis would now be on a national government whose acts would be "the supreme law of the land." Federal leaders would be drawn from citizens of learning and wealth, many like those nationalists who had never fully trusted the people. From their perspective the people had failed the test of public virtue. They had shown more concern for their individual welfare than in making material or personal sacrifices to support the Continental war effort. They had formed into troublesome factions like the Maryland land speculators and the Massachusetts rebel followers of Daniel Shays, all to the detriment of the republic's political stability.

The nationalists, now expecting to function as the new nation's political stewards, did not repudiate the principle of popular sovereignty. Rather, they enshrined it in such concepts as representative republicanism. The people were to have a political voice, in the abstract at least, and they were to remain the constituent authority of American government. Their stewards, supposedly detached from selfish concerns, could now more easily check narrow interests inhibiting stable national development.

The Antifederalists understood, and they viewed this new settlement with grave alarm. One writer, "Centinel," stated that the Constitution would support "in practice a *permanent* ARISTOCRACY" of self-serving, wealthy citizens. Another, calling himself "Philadelphiensis," saw in the Constitution "a conspiracy against the liberties of his country, concerted by a few *tyrants*, whose views are to lord it over the rest of their fellow citizens."

These arguments, reminiscent of those that had stirred up revolutionary fervor in the 1760s and 1770s, lay at the heart of the Antifederalist critique of the proposed Constitution. Leading Antifederalists, among them Samuel Adams, Patrick Henry, and Richard Henry Lee, still had negative images of the distant British government, too far removed from the people to be checked in any effective way. Having rebelled against what they perceived as the tyranny of the British imperial government, they were not anxious to approve a plan for a new central government with enough power to threaten the states and the people with yet more political tyranny. They preferred life under the Articles of Confederation.

The Antifederalists failed to counter nationalist momentum. Close calls occurred in some ratifying conventions, such as in Massachusetts, New York, and Virginia. The well-organized nationalists were always ready to counter Antifederalist complaints. When some complained about the absence of a national bill of rights guaranteeing each citizen fundamental liberties, they promised that the first Congress would prepare one. When some demanded a second convention that would not overturn but modify the Articles of Confederation, they argued that the new government should first be given a chance. If it did not work, the nationalists stated, they would support another convention.

Once the New Hampshire convention voted to ratify on June 21, 1788, the necessary nine states had given their approval. The two large states of Virginia and New York were still not in the fold, however, so everyone hesitated. Virginia was the most populous state, and New York was fourth behind Pennsylvania and Massachusetts. In addition, both Virginia and New York were so strategically located that it would have been virtually impossible to operate the new national government without their involvement.

Promises of a bill of rights helped bring the Virginia convention around in a close vote (89 yeas to 79 nays) on June 25. A month later after much skillful Federalist maneuvering, including promises of a second constitutional convention should the 1787 plan fail to work, the dominant Antifederalists in New York's ratifying convention conceded enough votes for ratification to occur by the slim margin of 30 yeas to 27 nays. New York thus became the "eleventh pillar" of the union. Since the constitution did succeed, as demonstrated by George Washington's presidential administration, arguments for a second convention faded away.

TABLE 6.3
Ratification of the Constitution of 1787

State	Date	Vote Yes	Vote No
Delaware	December 7, 1787	30	0
Pennsylvania	December 12, 1787	46	23
New Jersey	December 18, 1787	38	0
Georgia	January 2, 1788	26	0
Connecticut	January 9, 1788	128	40
Massachusetts	February 6, 1788	187	168
Maryland	April 26, 1788	63	11
South Carolina	May 23, 1788	149	73
New Hampshire	June 21, 1788	57	47
Virginia	June 25, 1788	89	79
New York	July 26, 1788	30	27
North Carolina*	November 21, 1789	194	77
Rhode Island†	May 29, 1790	34	32

*On July 21, 1788, the first ratifying convention in North Carolina voted 184 to 84 not to consider approval of the Constitution. The vote recorded is that of the second convention.

†Rhode Island not only refused to participate in the Philadelphia Constitutional Convention but also decided not to call a state ratifying convention. Only after the United States Senate threatened to sever commercial ties with Rhode Island did the state government agree to a convention that reluctantly approved the Constitution.

Chronology OF KEY EVENTS

1775 Daniel Boone blazes the "Wilderness Road" to Kentucky; Lord Dunmore calls for the emancipation of Virginia's slaves (November)

1775–1777 Ten states adopt new state constitutions

1776–1777 Congress drafts the Articles of Confederation

1780 Pennsylvania becomes the first state to provide for the emancipation of slaves

1781 Articles of Confederation are finally ratified by all the states

1782 Rhode Island refuses to ratify the Impost Plan to provide Congress a tax revenue, thereby precipitating the threat of a military coup—the Newburgh Conspiracy

1783 Washington defuses the threat of a military coup

1784 Land Ordinance of 1784 guarantees western settlers territorial government

1785 Land Ordinance of 1785 provides for the survey and sale of western lands

1786 Virginia adopts Jefferson's Statute of Religious Freedom separating church and state (January); Jay-Gardoquí negotiations fail to produce a trading alliance with Spain (August); Shays's Rebellion gains momentum (August–December); Annapolis Convention calls for a national constitutional convention (September)

1787 Constitutional Convention convenes in Philadelphia (May); Congress passes the Northwest Ordinance, forever barring slavery north of the Ohio River (July)

1788 Hamilton, Madison, and Jay publish 85 essays on behalf of the Constitution, known as *The Federalist Papers*; Constitution is ratified by the necessary number of states

CONCLUSION

In 1776 those radical revolutionaries who believed in a virtuous citizenry had sought to expand popular participation in government. By and large they succeeded. This first constitutional settlement proved to be unsatisfactory, however, largely because the weak central government under the Articles of Confederation lacked the authority to support even the minimal needs of the new nation. Blaming the states and the people, the nationalist leaders produced a second constitutional settlement in 1787 by drafting a plan for a more powerful central government. It was to be above the people and the states, strong enough to establish and preserve national unity and stability.

The new national government began functioning in April 1789. No sooner had these "diffusive and established" gentlemen started to govern, however, than they fell to fighting among themselves over a host of controversial issues. To gain allies, they turned back to the people. Against the wishes of many nationalists, some leaders started to organize political parties and urged the citizenry to support their candidates as a means of stopping the opposition. By the mid-1790s the people were emerging as much more than a token voice in national politics. Concepts of deference and stewardship were now in full retreat; common citizens were at last becoming the true foundation of what would one day be a system of political democracy.

The years between 1776 and 1789 thus secured the republic and republican ideals. On the other hand, notions regarding each American's right to enjoy life, liberty, happiness, and property in an equalitarian society fell far short of full implementation. Women remained second-class citizens, and the shackles of slavery and racist thinking still manacled African Americans. Even with the opening of the trans-Appalachian West, which came at the expense of thousands of Native Americans, poorer citizens found it difficult to gain access to farmland on which they could provide for themselves and secure their personal prosperity. Although future generations would argue and fight, even to the point of a bloody civil war, over how best to realize the full potential of republican ideals, there was no denying their rudimentary presence. In this sense the years before 1789 had witnessed a revolution in human expectations.

Suggestions for Further Reading

Gregory Evans Dowd, *A Spirited Resistance: The North American Indian Struggle for Unity, 1745–1815* (1992). Incisive account of militant Native-American resistance in reaction to white expansion into the trans-Appalachian West.

Sylvia R. Frey, *Water from the Rock: Black Resistance in a Revolutionary Age* (1991). Revisionist investigation of southern slaves and how they sought to make better lives for themselves out of the turmoil of the Revolutionary era.

Robert A. Gross, ed., *In Debt to Shays: The Bicentennial of an Agrarian Rebellion* (1993). Illuminating essays focusing on Shays's Rebellion and the many problems besetting ordinary citizens in late eighteenth-century America.

Merrill Jensen, *The New Nation, 1781–1789* (1950). Classic examination of "critical period" politics and the nationalist mind-set of the Founding Fathers.

Jean B. Lee, *The Price of Nationhood: The American Revolution in Charles County* (1994). Suggestive appraisal of the impact of the Revolution on the inhabitants of this Maryland county.

Mary Beth Norton, *Liberty's Daughters: The Revolutionary Experience of American Women, 1750–1800* (1980). Valuable study of ways in which the Revolution affected the roles women defined for themselves.

Jack N. Rakove, *Original Meanings: Politics and Ideas in the Making of the Constitution* (1996). Prize-winning analysis of the ideas, concerns, and intentions that both shaped and gave meaning to the Constitution of 1787.

Gordon S. Wood, *The Creation of the American Republic, 1776–1787* (1969). Influential analysis of changing conceptions of political thought and culture culminating in the Constitution of 1787 and a new national government.

Overviews and Surveys

Richard R. Beeman, et al., eds., *Beyond Confederation: Origins of the Constitution and American National Identity* (1987); Robert M. Calhoon, *Dominion and Liberty: Ideology in the Anglo-American World* (1994); Edward Countryman, *The American Revolution* (1985); Staughton Lynd, *Class Conflict, Slavery, and the United States Constitution* (1967); Forrest McDonald, *E Pluribus Unum: The Formation of the American Republic, 1776–1790* (1965); Edmund S. Morgan, *Inventing the People: The Rise of Popular Sovereignty in England and America* (1988); Richard B. Morris, *The Forging of the Union, 1781–1789* (1987); Alfred F. Young, ed., *The American Revolution: Explorations in the History of American Radicalism* (1976).

Establishing New Republican Governments

Willi Paul Adams, *The First American Constitutions* (1980); Edward Countryman, *A People in Revolution: Political Society in New York, 1760–1790* (1981); Robert J. Dinkin, *Voting in Revolutionary America* (1982); Jackson Turner Main, *The Upper House in Revolutionary America, 1763–1788* (1967), and *Political Parties Before the Constitution* (1973); James Kirby Martin, *Men in Rebellion: Higher Governmental Leaders and the Coming of the Revolution* (1973); Jerome J. Nadelhaft, *The Disorders of War: The Revolution in South Carolina* (1981); Stephen E. Patterson, *Political Parties in Revolutionary Massachusetts* (1973); J. R. Pole, *Political Representation in England and the Origins of the American Republic* (1966); Garry Wills, *Cincinnatus: George Washington and the Enlightenment* (1984).

Crises of the Confederation

John L. Brooke, *The Heart of the Commonwealth: Worcester County, Massachusetts, 1713–1861* (1989); Thomas Doerflinger, *A Vigorous Spirit of Enterprise: Merchants and Economic Development in Revolutionary Philadelphia* (1986); E. James Ferguson, *The Power of the Purse: American Public Finance, 1776–1790* (1961); Dall W. Forsythe, *Taxation and Political Change in the Young Nation, 1781–1833* (1977); Van Beck Hall, *Politics Without Parties: Massachusetts, 1780–1791* (1972); Ronald Hoffman and Peter J. Albert, eds., *Sovereign States in an Age of Uncertainty* (1981); Richard H. Kohn, *Eagle and Sword: The Federalists and Military Establishment in America, 1783–1802* (1975); Peter S. Onuf, *The Origins of the Federal Republic: Jurisdictional Controversies in the United States, 1775–1787* (1983), and *Statehood and Union: The Northwest Ordinance* (1987); Irwin H. Polishook, *Rhode Island and the Union, 1774–1795* (1969); Norman K. Risjord, *Chesapeake Politics, 1781–1800* (1978); Charles R. Ritcheson, *Aftermath of Revolution: British Policy, 1783–1795* (1969); Malcolm Rohrbough, *The Trans-Appalachian Frontier, 1775–1850* (1978); David Szatmary, *Shays' Rebellion* (1980); Robert J. Taylor, *Western Massachusetts in the Revolution* (1954); Alfred F. Young, *The Democratic-Republicans of New York, 1763–1797* (1967).

Human Rights and Social Change

John K. Alexander, *Render Them Submissive: Responses to Poverty in Philadelphia, 1760–1800* (1980); Lee L. Bean, et al., *Fertility Change on the American Frontier* (1990); Ira Berlin and Ronald Hoffman, eds., *Slavery and Freedom in the Age of the American Revolution* (1983); Wallace Brown, *The Good Americans* (1969); Joy Day Buel and Richard Buel, Jr., *The Way of Duty: A Woman and Her Family in Revolutionary America* (1984); Robert McCluer Calhoon, *The Loyalists in Revolutionary America, 1760–1781* (1973); David Brion Davis, *The Problem of Slavery in the Age of Revolution, 1770–1823* (1975); Carl N. Degler, *At Odds: Women and the Family in America from the Revolution to the Present* (1980); Linda Grant De-

Pauw and Conover Hunt, *"Remember the Ladies": Women in America, 1750–1815* (1976); Philip S. Foner, *Labor and the American Revolution* (1977); Linda Gordon, *Woman's Body, Woman's Right: Birth Control in America* (1976); Adele Hast, *Loyalism in Revolutionary Virginia* (1982); Norman Edwin Himes, *Medical History of Contraception* (1970); J. Franklin Jameson, *The American Revolution Considered as a Social Movement* (1926); Sidney and Emma N. Kaplan, *The Black Presence in the Era of the American Revolution*, rev. ed. (1989); Linda Kerber, *Women of the Republic: Intellect and Ideology in Revolutionary America* (1980); Allan Kulikoff, *The Agrarian Origins of American Capitalism* (1992); Duncan J. MacLeod, *Slavery, Race, and the American Revolution* (1974); Jackson Turner Main, *The Social Structure of Revolutionary America* (1965); John C. Miller, *The Wolf by the Ears: Thomas Jefferson and Slavery* (1977); James C. Mohr, *Abortion in America* (1978); Gary B. Nash, *Forging Freedom: Philadelphia's Black Community, 1720–1840* (1988), and *Race and Revolution* (1990); William H. Nelson, *The American Tory* (1961); Mary Beth Norton, *The British-Americans: The Loyalist Exiles in England, 1774–1789* (1972); Theda Perdue, *Slavery and the Evolution of Cherokee Society, 1540–1866* (1979); Merrill D. Peterson, *Thomas Jefferson and the New Nation* (1970); Janice Potter, *The Liberty We Seek: Loyalist Ideology in New York and Massachusetts* (1983); Benjamin Quarles, *The Negro in the American Revolution* (1961); Donald L. Robinson, *Slavery in the Structure of American Politics, 1765–1820* (1971); Marylynn Salmon, *Women and the Law of Property in Early America* (1986); Billy G. Smith, *The "Lower Sort": Philadelphia's Laboring People, 1750–1800* (1990); Merril D. Smith: *Breaking the Bonds: Marital Discord in Pennsylvania, 1730–1830* (1991); Gregory A. Stiverson, *Poverty in a Land of Plenty: Tenancy in Eighteenth-Century Maryland* (1977); James W. St. G. Walker, *The Black Loyalists: The Search for a Promised Land in Nova Scotia and Sierra Leone, 1783–1870* (1976); John Todd White, "The Truth About Molly Pitcher," in James Kirby Martin and Karen R. Stubaus, eds., *The American Revolution: Whose Revolution?* rev. ed. (1981), pp. 99–105; Shane White, *Somewhat More Independent: The End of Slavery in New York City, 1770–1810* (1991); Arthur Zilversmit, *The First Emancipation: The Abolition of Slavery in the North* (1967).

Second New Beginning, New National Government

John K. Alexander, *The Selling of the Constitutional Convention: A History of News Coverage* (1990); Charles A. Beard, *An Economic Interpretation of the Constitution of the United States* (1913); Stephen R. Boyd, *The Politics of Opposition: Antifederalists and the Acceptance of the Constitution* (1979); Christopher Collier and James L. Collier, *Decision in Philadelphia* (1986); Linda Grant DePauw, *The Eleventh Pillar: New York State and the Federal Constitution* (1966); Michael Kammen, *A Machine That Would Go by Itself: The Constitution in American Culture* (1986); Jackson Turner Main, *The Antifederalists: Critics of the Constitution, 1781–1788* (1961); Frederick W. Marks, III, *Independence on Trial: Foreign Affairs and the Constitution*, 2d ed. (1986); Forrest McDonald, *We the People: The Economic Origins of the Constitution* (1958), and *Novus Ordo Seclorum: The Intellectual Origins of the Constitution* (1985); Clinton Rossiter, *1787: The Grand Convention* (1966); Robert A. Rutland, *The Ordeal of the Constitution: The Antifederalists and the Ratification Struggle of 1787–88* (1966); Garry Wills, *Explaining America: The Federalist* (1981).

Biographies

Lance Banning, *The Sacred Fire of Liberty: James Madison and the Founding of the Federal Republic* (1996); George A. Billias, *Elbridge Gerry* (1976); Fawn Brodie, *Thomas Jefferson: An Intimate History* (1974); Roger J. Champagne, *Alexander McDougall* (1975); Christopher Collier, *Roger Sherman's Connecticut: Yankee Politics and the Revolution* (1971); Jacob E. Cooke, *Alexander Hamilton* (1982); John Mack Faragher, *Daniel Boone* (1992); Eric Foner, *Tom Paine and Revolutionary America* (1976); John P. Kaminski, *George Clinton: Yeoman Politician of the New Republic* (1993); Elizabeth P. McCaughey, *From Loyalist to Founding Father: William Samuel Johnson* (1980); Merrill D. Peterson, *Thomas Jefferson and the New Nation* (1970); Jack N. Rakove, *James Madison and the Creation of the American Republic* (1990); C. Edward Skeen, *John Armstrong, Jr., 1758–1843* (1981); Sheila Skemp, *Judith Sargent Murray* (1998); Laurel Thatcher Ulrich, *A. Midwife's Tale: The Life of Martha Ballard, 1785–1812* (1990); Clarence L. Ver Steeg, *Robert Morris: Revolutionary Financier* (1954); Lynne Withey, *Dearest Friend: A Life of Abigail Adams* (1981); Rosemarie Zagarri, *A Woman's Dilemma: Mercy Otis Warren and the American Revolution* (1995).

INTERNET RESOURCES

Northwest Territory Alliance
http://www.nwta.com/main.html
This Revolutionary Era reenactment organization site contains several links and is an interesting look at historical reenactment.

Archiving Early America
http://earlyamerica.com/
Old newspapers are excellent windows into the issues of the past. This site includes the Keigwin and Matthews collection of historic newspapers.

Biographies of the Founding Fathers
http://www.colonialhall.com/
This site provides information about the men who signed the Declaration of Independence and includes a trivia section.

Religion and the Founding of the American Republic
http://lcweb.loc.gov/exhibits/religion/religion.html
This Library of Congress site is an online exhibit about religion and the creation of the United States.

Several Federalist Papers with Special Reference to the Government's Power to Tax
http://www.taxhistory.org/federalists/
The Federalist Papers, a series of 85 essays designed to encourage ratification of the United States Constitution, pro-

vide important insight about the history of U.S. federal taxation.

The Federalist Papers
http://www.law.emory.edu/FEDERAL/federalist/
A collection of the most important *Federalist Papers,* a series of documents designed to convince people to support the new Constitution.

The Constitution and the Amendments
http://www.law.emory.edu/FEDERAL/usconst.html
A searchable site to the Constitution, especially useful for its information about the Bill of Rights and other constitutional amendments.

Documents from the Continental Congress and the Constitutional Convention, 1774–1789
http://memory.loc.gov/ammem/bdsds/bdsdhome.html
The Continental Congress Broadside Collection (253 titles) and the Constitutional Convention Broadside Collection (21 titles) contain 274 documents relating to the work of Congress and the drafting and ratification of the Constitution. Items include extracts of the journals of Congress, resolutions, proclamations, committee reports, treaties, and early printed versions of the United States Constitution and the Declaration of Independence. Most broadsides are one page in length; others range from 2 to 28 pages.

KEY TERMS

Republicanism   (p. 162)
Public Virtue   (p. 162)
Radical Revolutionaries   (p. 162)
Cautious Revolutionaries   (p. 162)
Nationalists   (p. 164)
Shaysites   (p. 169)
Republican Motherhood   (p. 174)
Manumission   (p. 178)
Federalists   (p. 181)
Antifederalists   (p. 181)
The Federalist Papers   (p. 182)

REVIEW QUESTIONS

1. Examine the major points of disagreement between radical and reluctant revolutionaries. What characterized their viewpoints regarding the concept of public virtue, and how did these differences affect constitution making during the Revolutionary era?

2. What were some of the numerous internal problems that plagued the early American republic? In what ways were these problems aggravated by having a weak national government under the Articles of Confederation and sovereign power granted to the states?

3. Compare and contrast the Newburgh Consipiracy of 1783 with Shays's Rebellion of 1786–1787. In what ways did these two events relate to the drive for a stronger national government, and what was their significance?

4. What were some of the contradictions between the Revolution's rhetoric of liberty and actual conditions faced by such groups as African Americans, women, and the propertyless poor? What effect, if any, did the rhetoric of liberty have on these groups during the Revolution and beyond?

5. Explain why the Constitution of 1787 might be described as a bundle of compromises? How did this plan of government address the major problems that had beset the struggling Confederation of states between 1776 and 1787? Why did the Constitution raise prospects for long-term political stability?

7

THE FORMATIVE DECADE, 1790–1800

THE ROOTS OF AMERICAN ECONOMIC GROWTH

IMPLEMENTING THE CONSTITUTION
Establishing the Machinery of Government
Defining the Presidency
Alexander Hamilton's Financial Program

THE BIRTH OF POLITICAL PARTIES
World Events and Political Polarization
1793 and 1794: Years of Crisis
Washington Retires

A NEW PRESIDENT AND NEW CHALLENGES
The Presidency of John Adams
A New National Capital
The Quasi War with France
The Alien and Sedition Acts

THE REVOLUTION OF 1800

An "outrageous and wretched scandalmonger"

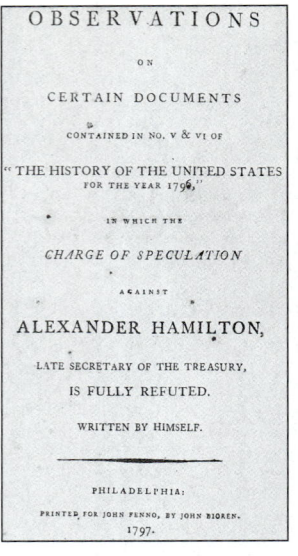

Alexander Hamilton responded to journalist James Thomson Callender's charges that he had engaged in illegal financial speculations by publishing a detailed denial.

A critic called James Thomson Callender "the most outrageous and wretched scandalmonger of a scurrilous age." Callender, a pioneering muckraking journalist, during the 1790s published vicious attacks on George Washington, John Adams, Alexander Hamilton, and other leading political figures. Today, Callender is best known as the journalist who first published the story that Thomas Jefferson had a decades-long affair with one of his slaves.

Born in Scotland in 1758, Callender became a clerk and writer and an early proponent of Scottish independence from Britain. Indicted for sedition in 1793, he fled to Philadelphia, where he made a living as a congressional reporter and a political propagandist.

Profoundly suspicious of Treasury Secretary Alexander Hamilton's financial program and his pro-British views on foreign affairs, Callender used his pen to discredit Hamilton. In 1797 he published evidence—probably provided by supporters of Thomas Jefferson—that Hamilton had an adulterous extramarital affair with a woman named Maria Reynolds. Callender also accused Hamilton of involvement in illegal financial speculations with Reynolds's husband, an unsavory character who had been convicted of fraud and dealing in stolen goods. Hamilton acknowledged the affair, but denied the corruption charges, claiming that he was a victim of blackmail. Nevertheless, Hamilton's public reputation was hurt, and he never held public office again.

In 1798 Hamilton's political party, the Federalist party, pushed the Sedition Act through Congress, making it a crime to attack the government or the president with false, scandalous, or malicious statements. In 1800 Callender was one of several journalists indicted, tried, and convicted under the law. He was fined $200 and sentenced to nine months in prison, where he found himself "surrounded by thieves of every description."

By the time Callender was released, Thomas Jefferson had been elected president. Callender expected the new administration to refund his fine and appoint him to a government job. When repayment of the fine was delayed and Jefferson refused to appoint him as a postmaster, Callender struck back. In 1802, a year before his death, Callender publicly accused Jefferson of having a lifelong liaison with his slave Sally Hemings.

Sally Hemings was the half-sister of Jefferson's deceased wife Martha. Her mother had been impregnated by her master, John Wayles, the father of Martha Jefferson. Sally Hemings herself bore five mulatto children out of wedlock. Callender insisted that Jefferson fathered the children. Jefferson's defenders denied the assertion. In 1998 DNA testing indicated that Thomas Jefferson fathered at least one of Sally Hemings's children.

Despised by his critics as a "traitorous and truculent scoundrel," Callender defended himself on strikingly modern grounds: that the public had a right to know the moral character of people it elected to public office. Although he has often been dismissed as a "pen for hire," willing to defame anyone, Callender's work underscores one of the most radical consequences of the American Revolution. The revolution gave new meaning to the idea of popular sovereignty and ensured that ordinary Americans would be the ultimate arbiters of American politics. Passionately rejecting the notion that common people should express deference toward the educated and well-to-do, Callender aimed his political commentary at artisans and at immigrants who flocked to seaport towns during the 1790s. Scandal, sensation, and suspicion of the powerful were the appeals he used to attract readers.

Politically and economically, the 1790s was the nation's formative decade. During this time the United States implemented the new Constitution, adopted a bill of rights, created its first political parties, and built a new national capital city in Washington, D.C. The 1790s were also years of rapid economic and demographic growth, the time when the new United States established a strong and vigorous national government and a prosperous, growing economy.

THE ROOTS OF AMERICAN ECONOMIC GROWTH

Early in August 1790, David Howe, an assistant federal marshal, began the difficult task of counting all the people who lived in Hancock County, Maine. One of 650 federal census takers, charged with making "a just and perfect enumeration and description of all persons" in the United States, he began by writing down his own name followed by his wife's and child's. He next listed the names of all the other people who lived in his hometown of Penobscot, then proceeded to crisscross the Maine coast, recording the names of 9549 residents. In March 1791 he submitted his findings: 2436 free white males, 16 and older; 4544 free white females; 2631 white children; and 38 "other free persons" (including Peter Williams, "a black," and his wife and child).

The United States was the first nation in history to institute a periodic national census. Since 1790, the country has tried to count each woman, man, and child every ten years. The first census asked just six simple questions, yet when supplemented by other statistical information, it provides a treasure chest of information about the social and economic life of the American people.

Taking the nation's first census was an extraordinarily difficult challenge. The nation's sheer physical size—stretching across 867,980 square miles from Georgia to Maine—made it impossible to make an accurate count. Many people refused to speak to census takers; some because they feared that this was

The Constitution provided for a census every ten years. The first census, conducted in 1790, estimated the population of the United States at 3.9 million people. The jug, made in England after the 1790 census, shows the figures gathered in that census.

the first step toward enactment of new taxes, others because they believed that the Bible prohibited census taking. To make matters worse, census takers were abysmally paid; they received just $1 for every 150 rural residents and $1 for every 300 city dwellers counted. Indeed, the pay was so low that one judge found it difficult to find "any person whatever" to take the census.

What was the United States like in 1790? According to the first census, the United States contained just 3,929,214 people, about half living in the northern states, half in the South. At first glance, the population seems quite small (it was only about a quarter the size of England's and a sixth the size of France's), but it was growing extraordinarily rapidly. Just 1.17 million in 1750, the population would pass five million by 1800.

The 1790 census revealed a nation still overwhelmingly rural in character. In a population of nearly four million, only two cities had more than 25,000 people. Yet the urban population, while small, was growing extremely rapidly, especially in the West where frontier towns like Louisville started to sprout.

In 1790, most Americans still lived on the Atlantic coast. Nevertheless, the West was the most rapidly growing part of the nation. During the 1790s, the population of Kentucky and Tenessee increased nearly 300 percent, and by 1800, Kentucky had more people than five of the original 13 states.

The first census also revealed an extraordinarily youthful population, with half the people under the age of 16. Extraordinarily diverse, a fifth of the entire population was African American. Three-fifths of the white population was English in ancestry and another fifth was Scottish or Irish. The remainder was of German, Dutch, French, Swedish, or other background.

Records indicate that the American economy was still quite undeveloped. There were fewer than 100 newspapers in the entire country, three banks (with a total capital of less than $5 million), and three insurance companies; yet, the United States was perched on the edge of an extraordinary decade of growth.

Over the next ten years, American society made tremendous economic advances. During the 1790s, states chartered almost ten times more corporations, banks, and transportation companies than during the 1780s. Exports climbed from $29 million to $107 million; cotton production rose from 3000 bales to 73,000. Altogether, eleven mechanized mills were built in the country during the 1790s, laying the foundations of future economic growth.

In 1800, as in 1790, the United States remained a nation of farms, plantations, and small towns, of yeomen farmers, slaves, and artisans. Nevertheless, the nation was undergoing far-reaching social and economic transformations. Improvements in education were particularly striking. Between 1783 and 1800, Americans founded 17 new colleges and a large number of female academies.

Why did the United States experience such rapid growth during the 1790s? In part, the answer lies in European wars, pitting France against Britain, that increased demand for U.S. products and stimulated American shipping and trade. But the answer also lies in critical political developments, especially enactment of a financial program that secured the nation's credit.

IMPLEMENTING THE CONSTITUTION

The United States was the first modern nation to achieve independence through a successful revolution against colonial rule. Although many colonies in the nineteenth and twentieth centuries followed the example of the United States in winning independence through revolution, few were as successful in subsequent economic and political development. Even the United States, however, struggled to establish itself in its first decade under the Constitution.

The new nation faced severe economic and foreign policy problems. A huge debt remained from the Revolution, and paper money issued during and after the war was virtually worthless. Along with these pressing economic problems were foreign threats to the new nation's independence. In violation of the peace treaty of 1783 ending the Revolutionary War, Britain continued to occupy forts in the Old Northwest, and Spain refused to recognize the new nation's southern and western boundaries. In 1790, economic problems, domestic political conflict, and foreign policy issues challenged the new nation in its efforts to establish a stable republic.

Establishing the Machinery of Government

The first task facing American leaders was to establish the machinery of government. The new United States government consisted of 75 post offices, a large debt, a small number of unpaid clerks, and an army of just 46 officers and 672 soldiers. There was no federal court system, no navy, and no system for collecting taxes.

It fell to Congress to take the initial steps toward putting the new national government into operation: To raise revenue, it passed a tariff on imported goods and an excise tax on liquor; to encourage American shipping, it imposed duties on foreign vessels; and to

---

In its first session, Congress organized a federal judicial system as part of the new national government. This depiction of an early courthouse was drawn in 1804 by Lewis Miller.

provide a structure for the executive branch of the government, it created departments of State, Treasury, and War. By the Judiciary Act of 1789, Congress organized a federal court system, which consisted of a Supreme Court with six justices, a district court in each state, and three appeals courts.

To strengthen popular support for the new government, Congress also approved a **Bill of Rights** in the form of ten amendments to the Constitution. These first amendments guaranteed the rights of free press, free speech, and free exercise of religion; the right to peaceful assembly; and the right to petition government. The Bill of Rights also ensured that the national government could not infringe on the right to trial by jury. In an effort to reassure Antifederalists that the powers of the new government were limited, the tenth amendment "reserved to the States respectively, or to the people" all powers not specified in the Constitution.

Defining the Presidency

The Constitution provided only a broad outline of the office and powers of the president. It would be up to George Washington, as the first president, to define the office, and to establish many precedents regarding the president's relationship with the other branches of government. It was unclear, for example, whether the president was personally to run the executive branch or, instead, act like a constitutional monarch and delegate responsibility to the vice president and executive officers, called the **cabinet**. Washington favored a strong and active role for the president. Modeling the executive branch along the lines of a general's staff, Washington consulted his cabinet officers and listened to them carefully, but he made the final decisions, just as he had done as commander in chief.

The relationship between the executive and legislative branches was also uncertain. Should a president, like Britain's prime minister, personally appear before Congress to defend administration policies? Should the Senate have sole power to dismiss executive officers? The answers to such questions were not clear. Washington insisted that the president could dismiss presidential appointees without the Senate's permission. A bitterly divided Senate approved this principle by a single vote.

With regard to foreign policy, Washington tried to follow the literal words of the Constitution, which stated that the president should negotiate treaties with the advice and consent of the Senate. He appeared before the Senate to discuss a pending Indian treaty. The senators, however, refused to provide immediate answers and referred the matter to a committee.

This figurative drawing depicts President George Washington meeting with his first cabinet—Secretary of War Henry Knox, Secretary of State Thomas Jefferson, and Secretary of the Treasury Alexander Hamilton—at Washington's Mount Vernon home.

"This defeats every purpose of my coming here," Washington declared. In the future he negotiated treaties first and then sent them to the Senate for ratification.

The most difficult task that the president faced was deciding whom to nominate for public office. For secretary of war, Washington nominated Henry Knox, an old military comrade, who had held a similar position under the Articles of Confederation. As postmaster general, he named Samuel Osgood of Massachusetts, who carried out his tasks in a single room with the help of two clerks. For attorney general, he tapped fellow Virginian Edmund Randolph, and for chief justice of the Supreme Court, he selected New Yorker John Jay. Washington nominated another Virginian, Thomas Jefferson, for secretary of state. He named his former aide-de-camp, the 34-year-old Alexander Hamilton, to head the Treasury Department.

Alexander Hamilton's Financial Program

The most pressing problems facing the new government were economic. As a result of the revolution, the federal government had acquired a huge debt: $54 million including interest. The states owed another $25 million. Paper money issued under the

Continental Congresses and Articles of Confederation was worthless. Foreign credit was unavailable.

Ten days after **Alexander Hamilton** became Treasury Secretary, Congress asked him to report on ways to solve the nation's financial problems. Hamilton, a man of strong political convictions, immediately realized that he had an opportunity to create a financial program that would embody his political principles.

Hamilton believed that the nation's stability depended on an alliance between the government and citizens of wealth and influence. No society could succeed, he maintained, "which did not unite the interest and credit of rich individuals with those of the state." Unlike Thomas Jefferson, Hamilton doubted the capacity of common people to govern themselves. "The people are turbulent and changing," he maintained, "they seldom judge or determine right."

To keep the masses in check, Hamilton favored a strong national government. Born in the British West Indies, Hamilton never developed the intense loyalty to a state that was common among many Americans of the time. He wanted to create a unified nation and a powerful federal government, intending to use government fiscal policies to strengthen federal power at the expense of the states and "make it in the immediate interest of the moneyed men to cooperate with government in its support."

The paramount problem facing Hamilton was the national debt. Hamilton argued that it was vital for the nation to repay the debts in order to establish the credit of the federal government. He proposed that the government assume the entire indebtedness—principal and interest—of the federal government and the states. His plan was to retire the old depreciated obligations by borrowing new money at a lower interest rate.

This proposal ignited a firestorm of controversy, because states like Maryland, Pennsylvania, North Carolina, and Virginia had already paid off their war debts. They saw no reason why they should be taxed by the federal government to pay off the debts of states like Massachusetts and South Carolina. Others opposed the scheme because it would provide enormous profits to speculators who had bought bonds from revolutionary war veterans for as little as 10 or 15 cents on the dollar. Many of these financial speculators were associates of Hamilton or members of Congress who knew that Hamilton's report would recommend full payment of the debt.

For six months, a bitter debate raged in Congress. The nation's future seemed in jeopardy until a compromise orchestrated by James Madison and Thomas Jefferson secured passage of Hamilton's plan. In exchange for Southern votes in Congress, Hamilton promised his support for locating the future national capital on the banks of the Potomac River, the border between two southern states, Virginia and Maryland.

Hamilton's debt program was a remarkable success. Funding and assumption of the debt created pools of capital for business investment and firmly established the credit of the United States abroad. By demonstrating Americans' willingness to repay their debts, he made America a good credit risk attractive to foreign investors. European investment capital poured into the new nation in large amounts.

Hamilton's next objective was to create a Bank of the United States, modeled after the Bank of England, to issue currency, collect taxes, hold government funds, and make loans to the government and borrowers. This proposal, like his debt scheme, unleashed a storm of protest.

One criticism directed against the bank was that it threatened to undermine the nation's republican values. Banks—and the paper money they issued—would simply encourage speculation, paper shuffling, and corruption. Some opposed the bank on constitutional grounds. Adopting a position known as **strict construction,** Thomas Jefferson and James Madison charged that a national bank was unconstitutional since the Constitution did not specifically give Congress the power to create a bank. Other grounds for criticism were that the bank would subject America to foreign influences (because foreigners would have to purchase a high percentage of the bank's stock) and give a propertied elite disproportionate influence over the nation's fiscal policies (since private investors would control the bank's board of directors). Worse yet, the bank would increase the public debt, which, in turn, would add to the nation's tax burden. Under Hamilton's plan, the bank would raise capital by selling stock to private investors. Investors could pay for up to three-quarters of the bank stock they purchased with government bonds of indebtedness. The burden of financing the bank, therefore, would ultimately rest on the public treasury.

Hamilton responded to the charge that a bank was unconstitutional by formulating the doctrine of **implied powers.** He argued that Congress did have the power to create a bank since the Constitution granted the federal government authority to do anything "necessary and proper" to carry out its constitutional functions (in this case its fiscal duties). This represented the first attempt to defend a **loose interpretation** of the Constitution. Hamilton also defended his bank plan on another ground. He asserted that his plan would transform the public debt into a public good by using it to expand credit, finance business expansion, and provide a much needed pool of capital.

In 1791 Congress passed a bill creating a national bank for a term of 20 years, leaving the question of the bank's constitutionality up to President Washington. After listening to Madison, Jefferson, and Hamilton, the president reluctantly decided to sign the measure out of a conviction that a bank was necessary for the nation's financial well-being.

The first **Bank of the United States,** like Hamilton's debt plan, was a great success. It helped regulate the currency of private banks. It provided a reserve of capital on which the government and private investors drew. It helped attract foreign investment to the credit-short new nation. In 1811, however, the jealousy of private commercial banks convinced Congress to allow the bank, which had been chartered for a maximum of 20 years, to expire.

The final plank in Hamilton's economic program was a proposal to aid the nation's infant industries. In his *Report on Manufactures* (1791), Hamilton argued that the nation's long-term interests "will be advanced, rather than injured, by the due encouragement of manufactures." Through high tariffs designed to protect American industry from foreign competition, government bounties and subsidies, and internal improvements of transportation, he hoped to break Britain's manufacturing hold on America.

Opposition to Hamilton's proposal came from many quarters. Many Americans feared that the proposal would excessively cut federal revenues by discouraging imports. Shippers worried that the plan would reduce foreign trade. Farmers feared the proposal would lead foreign countries to impose retaliatory tariffs on agricultural products. Many southerners regarded the plan as a brazen attempt to promote northern industry and commerce at the South's expense, since it provided no assistance to agriculture.

The most eloquent opposition to Hamilton's proposals came from Thomas Jefferson, who believed that the growth of manufacturing threatened the values of an agrarian way of life. Hamilton's vision of America's future directly challenged Jefferson's ideal of a nation of freehold farmers, tilling the fields, communing with nature, and maintaining personal freedom by virtue of landownership. Manufacturing, Jefferson believed, should be left to European cities, which he considered to be cesspools of human corruption. Like slaves, factory workers would be manipulated by their masters, who not only would deny them satisfying lives but also would make it impossible for them to think and act as independent citizens.

Alexander Hamilton offered a remarkably modern economic vision based on investment, industry, and expanded commerce. Most strikingly, it was an economic vision that had no place for slavery. Before the 1790s, the American economy—North and South—was intimately tied to a transatlantic system of slavery. States south of Pennsylvania depended on slave labor to produce tobacco, rice, indigo, and cotton. The northern states conducted their most profitable trade with the slave colonies of the West Indies. A member of New York's first antislavery society, Hamilton wanted to reorient the American economy away from slavery and trade with the slave colonies of the Caribbean.

Congress rejected most of Hamilton's proposals to aid industry. Nevertheless, the debate over Hamilton's plan carried with it fateful consequences. Fundamental disagreements had arisen between Hamiltonians and Jeffersonians over the federal government's role, constitutional interpretation, and distinct visions of how the republic should develop. To resolve these fundamental differences, Americans would create modern political parties—parties the writers of the Constitution never wanted nor anticipated.

THE BIRTH OF POLITICAL PARTIES

When George Washington assembled his first cabinet, there were no national political parties in the United States. In selecting cabinet members, he paid no attention to partisan labels and simply chose the

The National Bank of the United States, which opened in Philadelphia in 1791, was a key part of Alexander Hamilton's economic plan for a strong central government.

individuals he believed were best qualified to run the new nation. Similarly, the new Congress had no party divisions. In all the states, except Pennsylvania, politics was waged not between parties but rather between impermanent factions built around leading families, political managers, ethnic groups, or interest groups such as debtors and creditors.

By the time Washington retired from the presidency in 1797, the nature of the American political system had changed radically. The first president devoted part of his "Farewell Address" to denouncing "the baneful effects of the Spirit of Party," which had come to dominate American politics. Local and state factions had given way to two competing national parties, known as the **Federalists** and the **Republicans.** They nominated political candidates, managed electoral campaigns, and represented distinctive outlooks or ideologies. By 1796 the United States had produced its first modern party system.

The framers of the Constitution had not prepared their plan of government with political parties in mind. They associated parties with the political factions and interest groups that dominated the British government and hoped that in the United States the "better sort of citizens," rising above popular self-interest, would debate key issues and reach a harmonious consensus regarding how best to legislate for the nation's future. Thomas Jefferson reflected widespread sentiments when he declared in 1789, "If I could not go to heaven but with a party, I would not go there at all."

Yet despite a belief that parties were evil and posed a threat to enlightened government, political factions gradually coalesced into political parties during Washington's first administration. To build support for his financial program, Alexander Hamilton relied heavily on government patronage. Of 2000 federal officeholders appointed between 1789 and 1801, two-thirds were Federalist party activists, who used positions as postmasters, tax collectors, judges, and customs house officials to favor the interests of the Federalists. By 1794 Hamilton's faction had evolved into the first national political party in history capable of nominating candidates, coordinating votes in Congress, staging public meetings, organizing petition campaigns, and disseminating propaganda.

Hamilton's opponents struck back. James Madison and his ally Thomas Jefferson saw in Hamilton's program an effort to establish the kind of corrupt patronage society that existed in Britain; that is, one with a huge public debt, a standing army, high taxes, and government-subsidized monopolies. Hamilton's aim, declared Jefferson, was to assimilate "the American government to the form and spirit of the British monarchy."

World Events and Political Polarization

World events intensified partisan divisions. On July 14, 1789, the Bastille, a hated royal fortress, was stormed by 20,000 French men and women, an event that marked the beginning of the French Revolution. For three years France experimented with a constitutional monarchy. Then, in 1792, the revolution took a violent turn. In August Austrian and Prussian troops invaded France to put an end to the revolution. French revolutionaries responded by officially deposing King Louis XVI and placing him on trial. He was found guilty and, in January 1793, beheaded. France declared itself a republic and launched a reign of terror against counterrevolutionary elements in the population. Three hundred thousand suspects were arrested; 17,000 were executed. A general war erupted in Europe pitting revolutionary France against a coalition of European monarchies, led by Britain. With two brief interruptions, this war would last 23 years.

Many Americans reacted enthusiastically to the overthrow of the French king and the creation of a French republic. The French people appeared to have joined America in a historic struggle against royal absolutism and aristocratic privilege. More cautious observers expressed horror at the cataclysm sweeping France. The French Revolution, they feared, was not merely a rebellion against royal authority, but a mass assault against property and Christianity. Conservatives urged President Washington to support England in its war against France.

Washington believed that involvement in the European war would weaken the new nation before it had firmly established its own independence. He proposed to keep the country "free from political connections with every other country, to see them independent of all, and under the influence of none." The president, however, faced a problem. During the War for American Independence, The United States had signed an alliance with France (see pp. 149). Washington took the position that while the United States should continue to make payments on its war debts to France, it should refrain from directly supporting the new French republic. In April 1793 he issued a proclamation of neutrality, stating that the "conduct" of the United States would be "friendly and impartial toward the belligerent powers."

1793 and 1794: Years of Crisis

During 1793 and 1794 a series of explosive new controversies further divided the followers of Hamilton and Jefferson: Washington's administration confronted a French effort to entangle America in its war with England, an armed rebellion in western Pennsylvania, several Indian uprisings, and the threat of war with Britain. These controversies intensified party spirit and promoted an increase in voting along party lines in Congress.

Citizen Genêt Affair
In April 1793 "Citizen" Edmond Charles Genêt, minister of the French Republic, arrived in the United States. His mission was to persuade American citizens to join in France's "war of all peoples against all kings." Genêt proceeded to pass out military commissions as part of a plan to attack Spanish New Orleans, and letters authorizing Americans to attack British commercial vessels. Washington regarded these activities as clear violations of U.S. neutrality and demanded that France recall its hotheaded minister. Fearful that he would be executed if he returned to France, Genêt requested and was granted political asylum, bringing his ill-fated mission to an end. However, the Genêt affair did have an important effect—it intensified party feeling. From Vermont to South Carolina, citizens organized Democratic-Republican clubs to celebrate the triumphs of the French Revolution. Hamilton suspected that these societies really existed to stir up grass-roots opposition to the Washington administration. Jefferson hotly denied these accusations, but the practical consequence was to further divide followers of Hamilton and Jefferson.

Whiskey Rebellion
The outbreak of popular protests in western Pennsylvania against Hamilton's financial program further intensified political polarization. To help fund the nation's war debt, Congress in 1791 passed Hamilton's proposal for a whiskey excise tax. Frontier farmers objected to the tax on whiskey as unfair. On the frontier, because of high transportation costs, the only practical way to sell surplus corn was to distill it into whiskey. Thus, frontier farmers regarded a tax on whiskey in the same way as American colonists had regarded Britain's stamp tax.

By 1794 western Pennsylvanians had had enough. Like the Shaysites of 1786, they rose up in defense of their property and the fundamental right to earn a decent living. Some 7000 frontiersmen marched on Pittsburgh to stop collection of the tax. Determined to set a precedent for the federal government's authority, Washington gathered an army of 15,000 militiamen to disperse the rebels. In the face of this overwhelming force, the uprising collapsed. Two men were convicted of treason but later pardoned by the president. The new government had proved that it would enforce laws enacted by Congress.

Thomas Jefferson viewed the Whiskey Rebellion from quite a different perspective. He saw the fiendish hand of Hamilton in putting down what he called a rebellion that "could never be found." Hamilton had "pronounced and proclaimed and

President Washington is reviewing the troops at Fort Cumberland, Maryland. These troops formed part of the force of 15,000 militiamen Washington assembled to disperse the Whiskey Rebellion in western Pennsylvania, a protest against the whiskey excise tax.
Gift of Edgar William and Bernice Chrysler Garbisch, 1963, Metropolitan Museum of Art.

The American Mosaic

Yellow Fever in Philadelphia: Pills and Politics

DEATH stalked the streets of Philadelphia in 1793 in the form of a yellow fever epidemic. The first case appeared in August, and by the time the epidemic disappeared in November, yellow fever had killed 10 percent of the city's population, while another 45 percent had fled in terror. At the height of the epidemic, Philadelphia was a city under siege, with city services interrupted; communications impaired; the port closed; the economy in shambles; and people locked in their homes, afraid to venture beyond their doorsteps. To make matters worse, the city's leaders—unable to reach agreement on what caused the disease or what should be done to combat it—attacked each other in endless debates. The result was that Philadelphia, America's premiere city, all but shut down.

Philadelphia's plight is not hard to explain, for yellow fever is a pulverizing, terrifying disease. Caused by a virus, the disease is spread by the female mosquito. Yellow fever's early symptoms are nearly identical to those of malaria; the victim feels flush and then develops chills, followed by a sizzling fever, accompanied by a severe headache or backache. The fever lasts for two or three days, and then the patient usually enjoys a remission.

Mild cases of yellow fever stop here. For the less fortunate, however, remission soon gives way to jaundice (hence "yellow" fever), and the victim starts to hallucinate. Massive internal hemorrhaging follows, and the sufferer starts vomiting huge quantities of black blood. Next, the victim goes into a coma. A lucky few emerge from the coma to escape death, but the vast majority die from internal bleeding.

If any American city seemed well equipped to handle a medical crisis, it was Philadelphia. It was the nation's leading center of medicine, home to the prestigious College of Physicians, America's first medical school (1765), and to America's most famous physician, Dr. Benjamin Rush, a founder of the Pennsylvania Society for Promoting the Abolition of Slavery and a signer of the Declaration of Independence. The City of Brotherly Love could also point with pride to Franklin's Pennsylvania Hospital (1752), the first hospital in America and a model facility for the poor.

Yet for all of its luster, Philadelphia's medical community was no match for yellow fever. The basic problem was that doctors in 1793 could not agree on what caused the disease, how it spread, or how to treat it. Many physicians, including Dr. Rush, cited local factors. They blamed the disease on the decaying vegetation and rotting filth that littered Philadelphia's streets and docks, producing an atmospheric "miasma" that was carried by the wind, infecting anyone who breathed its noxious fumes. Rejecting local causes, other physicians argued that yellow fever was a contagious disease. It had been imported to Philadelphia, they insisted, by the 2000 French refugees who had fled the revolution (and a yellow fever epidemic!) in Haiti to seek political asylum in the United States.

Physicians in 1793 had no way of settling the dispute. Those who blamed the epidemic on dirty streets sounded just as believable as those who pointed an accusing finger at sickly foreigners. What made the controversy truly remarkable, however, was the extent to which it became embroiled in politics, for what began as a purely medical debate quickly degenerated into a raging political battle.

With very few exceptions, the doctors who insisted that yellow fever was contagious were Federalists, while the anticontagionists were almost all Jeffersonian Republicans. Taught by the French Revolution to be wary of free-thinking political ideas, Federalist doctors regarded yellow fever as just another unwanted French import. Ablaze with pro-French sympathies, anticontagionist Republicans saw the French refugees as honored friends who brought virtue rather than death. The source of the epidemic, they insisted, lay with unvirtuous filth at their doorsteps.

Partisan leaders tried desperately to bend this medical debate to their political advantage. To Federalists, the doctrine of importation demanded that the United States protect itself from the French menace. Therefore, trade with French West Indian islands should be suspended; French refugees who had gained entry to the United States should be quarantined and future refugees excluded. Republicans, by contrast, denounced these demands as a federal plot to ruin profitable trade with the West Indies and to infect Americans with a new disease—hatred of all things French. Nor was their concern unfounded, for public hysteria was definitely building. At one point, amid persistent rumors that the French had poisoned the public drinking wells in preparation for a full-scale invasion, Philadelphians threatened violence against the innocent refugees.

At the height of the turmoil, politics even influenced how physicians treated the victims of yellow fever. At the beginning of the epidemic, doctors were pretty evenly divided, without regard to politics, into two schools. One prescribed stimulants—quinine bark, wine, and cold baths; while the other recommended bleeding—drawing off huge quantities of the patient's blood. (Dr. Rush had long been an advocate of the bleeding treatment. He recommended removing about four-fifths of the patient's blood supply, more than enough to kill all but the unkillable!)

Alexander Hamilton was personally responsible for converting this medical squabbling into a political issue. After managing to survive an attack of yellow fever, he published a ringing testimonial to the life-saving properties of the bark and wine cure. The treatment had been prescribed, he declared, by Dr. Edward Stevens of Philadelphia, a longtime friend of Hamilton. Dr. Stevens was the only physician in the City of Brotherly Love who was a publicly confessed Federalist.

A few days after his testimonial appeared, Hamilton published a second article in which he ridiculed Dr. Rush's "new treatment." Hamilton's attack was immediately echoed by Federalist editors across the country, and in the wake of their articles, the public came to regard "bark" as the Federalist cure and "bleeding" as the Republican cure.

The controversy over yellow fever raged until the epidemic ended in the fall. Philadelphia's struggle against yellow fever was one of the many times that Americans would infuse their discussions of health problems with nonmedical concerns. In future epidemics, notions of class, race, individual virtue, and even gender would color public discussions of health, just as surely as politics enlivened the medical debate over yellow fever in Philadelphia in 1793 when the republic was young.

armed against" the people for the sheer pleasure of suppressing liberties. And further, Jefferson claimed, Hamilton had done so because westerners no longer supported Washington's administration. He had used the army to stifle legitimate opposition to unfair government policies.

Clearing the Ohio Country of Native Americans

The end of the American Revolution unleashed a mad rush of white settlers into frontier Georgia, Kentucky, Tennessee, Ohio, and western New York. To allow whites to occupy lands in central Georgia, the United States bribed a Creek leader, Alexander McGilvray, to sign a peace treaty in 1790. In New York, following the Revolution, large-scale land acquisitions by whites forced Native Americans to migrate (the Mohawk moved to Canada) or to settle (like the Seneca) on small, impoverished, and unproductive reservations. In Kentucky and Tennessee, clashes between Cherokees, Chickasaws, Shawnees, and frontier settlers between 1784 and 1790 left some 1500 whites dead or captured, but ultimately warfare forced many Native Americans to migrate north of the Ohio River.

To clear the Ohio country, President Washington dispatched three armies. Twice, a confederacy of eight tribes led by Little Turtle, chief of the Miamis, defeated American forces. But, in 1794, a third army defeated the Indian alliance. A 3000-man force under Anthony Wayne overwhelmed 1000 Native Americans at the Battle of Fallen Timbers in northwestern Ohio. Under the Treaty of Greenville (1795), Native Americans ceded much of the present state of Ohio in return for cash and a promise that the federal government would treat the Indian nations fairly in land dealings.

Native Americans responded to the loss of land and declining population in a variety of ways. One response was cultural renewal, the path taken by the Seneca, who lived in upstate New York. Displaced from their traditional lands and suffering the psychological and cultural disintegration brought on by epidemic disease, the Seneca revitalized their culture under the leadership of a prophet named Handsome Lake. Handsome Lake preached a new religion that blended Quaker and traditional Iroquois beliefs, which helped the Seneca adapt to a changing social environment while maintaining many traditional practices and religious tenets. Most strikingly, the prophet endorsed the demand of Quaker missionaries that the traditional Iroquois sexual division of labor emphasizing male hunting and female horticulture be replaced. Instead, men took up farming, even though this had been traditionally viewed as women's work.

Another response to cultural disruption was the formation of loosely knit Indian confederacies. In the Great Lakes region, the Shawnees, Delawares, and other Indian peoples banded together in an effort to resist white expansion, while across the Mississippi, the Chippewas, Fox, Kickapoos, Ottawas, Potawatomis, Sauks, and Sioux formed another confederation. But the ability of these confederacies to obstruct expansion depended on military support from Britain.

The Continuing Threat from Britain

The year 1794 brought a crisis in America's relations with Britain. For a decade, Britain had refused to evacuate forts in the Old Northwest as promised in the treaty ending the Revolution. Control of those forts impeded white settlement of the Great Lakes region and allowed the British to monopolize the fur trade. Frontiersmen believed that British officials at those posts sold firearms to Native Americans and incited uprisings against white settlers. War appeared imminent when British warships stopped 300 American ships carrying food supplies to France and to France's overseas possessions, seized their cargoes, and forced seamen suspected of deserting from British ships into the British navy.

Washington acted decisively to end the crisis. After Anthony Wayne's soldiers overwhelmed Indians at the Battle of Fallen Timbers, the president sent Chief Justice John Jay to London to seek a negotiated settlement with the British. The United States's strongest bargaining chip was a threat to join an alliance of European trading nations to resist British trade restrictions. Alexander Hamilton undercut Jay by secretly informing the British minister that the United States would not join the alliance.

Jay secured the best agreement he could under the circumstances. Britain agreed to evacuate its forts on American soil and promised to cease harassing American ships (provided the ships did not carry contraband to Britain's enemies). Britain agreed to pay damages for the ships it had seized, to permit trade with Indians, and to carry on restricted trade with the British West Indies; however, Jay failed to win concessions on a host of other American grievances, such as British incitement of the Indians and Britain's routine searching of American ships for escaping deserters.

As a result of the debate over Jay's Treaty, the first party system fully emerged. Publication of the terms of the treaty unleashed a storm of protest from the emerging Jeffersonian Republicans. Republican newspapers and pamphlets denounced the treaty as craven submission to British imperial power and to wealthy commercial, shipping, and trading interests.

British Posts and Indian Battles

Because Americans still felt threatened by the continuing British refusal to evacuate forts and by Native American uprisings in the Northwest, John Jay, the first chief justice of the United States, was sent to negotiate a treaty with Great Britain.

Angry Republicans denounced John Jay's treaty as submission to British power and hanged his effigy in Charleston, South Carolina.

In New York, a mob pelted Alexander Hamilton with stones. In Boston, graffiti appeared on a wall: "Damn John Jay! Damn everyone who won't damn John Jay!! Damn everyone that won't put lights in his windows and sit up all night damning John Jay!!!"

Washington never anticipated the wave of outrage that greeted his decision to sign the treaty. Republicans accused him of forming an Anglo-American alliance, and they made his last years in office miserable by attacking him for conducting himself like a "tyrant." James Thomson Callender denounced Washington in particularly negative terms: "If ever a nation was debauched by a man, the American Nation has been debauched by Washington.... If ever a nation has been deceived by a man, the American Nation has been deceived by Washington." It was even suggested that he should be impeached because he had overdrawn his $25,000 salary. Privately, Washington complained that he was being compared to the Roman emperor "Nero" and to a "common pickpocket."

They sought to kill the treaty in the House of Representatives by refusing to appropriate the funds necessary to carry out the treaty's terms unless the president submitted all documents relating to the treaty negotiations. Washington refused to comply with the House's request for information, thereby establishing the principle of executive privilege. This precedent gives the chief executive authority to withhold information from Congress on grounds of national security. In the end, fear that rejection of the Jay Treaty would result in disunion or war convinced the House to approve the needed appropriations.

Washington's popularity returned within a few months when he was able to announce that a treaty had been negotiated with Spain opening up the Mississippi River to American trade. Spain, fearing joint British and American action against its American colonies, recognized the Mississippi River as the new nation's western boundary and the 31st parallel (the northern border of Florida) as America's southern boundary. In addition, Pinckney's Treaty (1795)—also known as the Treaty of San Lorenzo—granted Americans the right to navigate the Mississippi River as well as the right to export goods, duty free, through New Orleans, which was still a Spanish city.

Washington Retires

President Washington was now in a position to retire gracefully. He had avoided war, crushed the Native Americans, pushed the British out of western forts, established trade with selected parts of Asia, and opened the Northwest Territory to settlement. In his **Farewell Address,** published in a Philadelphia newspaper in September 1796, Washington warned his countrymen against the growth of partisan divisions. In foreign affairs, he warned against long-term alliances. Declaring the "primary interests" of America and Europe to be fundamentally different, he argued that "it is our true policy to steer clear of permanent alliance with any portion of the foreign world."

A New President and New Challenges

Washington's decision to retire set the stage for one of the most critical presidential elections in American history. The election of 1796 was the first in which voters could choose between competing political parties; it was also the first election in which candidates were nominated for the vice presidency. It was a critical test of whether the nation could transfer power through a contested election.

The Federalists chose John Adams, the first vice president, as their presidential candidate, and the Republicans selected Thomas Jefferson. In an effort to attract southern support, the Federalists named Thomas Pinckney of South Carolina as Adams's running mate. The Republicans, hoping to win votes in New York and New England, chose Aaron Burr of New York as their vice presidential nominee.

Both parties appealed directly to the people, rallying supporters through the use of posters, handbills, and mass rallies. Republicans portrayed their candidate as "a firm Republican" while they depicted his opponent as "the champion of rank, titles, and hereditary distinctions." Federalists countered by condemning Jefferson as the leader of a "French faction" intent on undermining religion and morality.

In the popular voting, Federalists drew support from New England; commercial, shipping, manufacturing, and banking interests; Congregational and Episcopalian clergy; professionals; and farmers who produced for markets. Republicans attracted votes from the South and from smaller planters; backcountry Baptists, Methodists, and Roman Catholics; small merchants, tradesmen, and craftsmen; and subsistence farmers.

John Adams won the election, despite backstage maneuvering by Alexander Hamilton against him. Hamilton developed a complicated scheme to elect Thomas Pinckney, the Federalist candidate for vice president. Under the electoral system originally set up by the Constitution, each presidential elector was allowed to vote twice, with the candidate who received the most votes becoming president, while the candidate who came in second was elected vice president. According to Hamilton's plan, southern electors would drop Adams's name from their ballots, while still voting for Pinckney. Thus Pinckney would receive more votes than Adams and be elected president. When New Englanders learned of this plan, they dropped Pinckney from their ballots, ensuring that Adams won the election. When the final votes were tallied, Adams received 71 votes, only 3 more than Jefferson. As a result, Jefferson became vice president.

The Presidency of John Adams

The new president was a 61-year-old Harvard-educated lawyer who had been an early leader in the struggle for independence. Short, bald, overweight, and vain (he was known, behind his back, as "His Rotundity"), **John Adams** had found the vice presidency extremely frustrating. He complained to his wife Abigail: "My country has contrived for me the most insignificant office that ever the invention of man contrived or his imagination conceived."

His presidency also proved frustrating. He had failed to win a decisive electoral mandate and was saddled with the opposition leader as his vice president. He faced intense challenges within his own party and continuing problems from France throughout his four years in office. He avoided outright war with France, but he destroyed his political career in the process.

A New National Capital

John Adams was the first president to live in what would later be called the White House. In 1800 the national capital moved to Washington, D.C., from

John Adams was elected the second president of the United States by only three electoral votes. During his presidency, he strengthened the military and averted war with France.

Philadelphia (in 1790 it had moved to Philadelphia from New York).

In planning the city of Washington, the architect Benjamin Latrobe hoped that "the days of Greece may be revived in the woods of America." Like many other late-eighteenth-century Americans, he hoped to build a country that would emulate the spirit of the ancient Greek and Roman republics.

The White House and the Capitol were designed along classical lines. Greek Revival architecture became the dominant style, influencing the design not only of government buildings but also houses. Many new towns received classical names, such as Syracuse and Troy. Government institutions, like the Senate, also acquired classical names.

When John Adams moved into the unfinished executive mansion, only 6 of the structure's 30 rooms were plastered; the main staircases were not installed for another four years. The mansion's grounds were cluttered with workers' shanties, privies, and stagnant pools of water. The president's wife, Abigail, hung laundry to dry in the East Room.

The nation's Capitol was also uncompleted. Construction of the building's central portion had not even begun. All that stood were the House and Senate wings connected by a covered boardwalk.

The city of Washington consisted of a brewery, a half-finished hotel, an abandoned canal, an empty warehouse and wharf, and 372 "habitable" dwellings, "most of them small miserable huts." Cows and hogs ran freely in the capital's streets, and snakes frequented the city's many bogs and marshes. A bridge, supported by an arch of 13 stones—symbolizing the first 13 states—had collapsed. The entire population consisted of 500 families and some 300 members of government. A visitor saw "no fences, gardens, nor the least appearance of business."

The Quasi War with France

A decade after the Constitution was written, the United States faced its most serious international crisis: an undeclared naval war with France. In Jay's Treaty, France perceived an American tilt toward Britain, especially in the provision permitting the British to seize French goods from American ships in exchange for financial compensation. France retaliated by launching an aggressive campaign against American shipping, particularly in the West Indies, capturing hundreds of vessels flying the United States flag.

Adams attempted to negotiate with France, but the French government refused to receive the American envoy and suspended commercial relations. Adams then called Congress into special session. Determined not to permit the United States to be "humiliated under a colonial spirit of fear and a sense of inferiority," he recommended that Congress arm American merchant ships, purchase new naval vessels, fortify harbors, and expand the artillery and cavalry. To pay for it all, Adams recommended a series of new taxes. By a single vote, a bitterly divided House of Representatives authorized the president to arm American merchant ships, but it postponed consideration of the other defense measures.

Adams then sent three commissioners to France to try to negotiate a settlement. Charles Maurice de Talleyrand, the French foreign minister, continually postponed official negotiations. In the meantime, three emissaries of the French minister (known later simply as X, Y, and Z) said that the only way the Americans could see the minister was to pay a bribe of $250,000 and provide a $10 million loan. The indignant American commissioners refused. When word of the "XYZ affair" became known in the United States, it aroused a popular demand for war. The popular slogan was "millions for defense, but

Abigail Adams supervises the work of a maidservant hanging laundry in the East Room of the White House.

not one cent for tribute." The Federalist-controlled Congress authorized a standing army of 20,000 troops, established a 30,000-man reserve army, and created the nation's first navy department. It also unilaterally abrogated America's 1778 treaty with France.

Adams named George Washington commanding general of the United States Army, and, at Washington's insistence, designated Alexander Hamilton second in command. During the winter of 1798, 14 American warships backed by some 200 armed merchant ships captured some 80 French vessels and forced French warships out of American waters and back to bases in the West Indies. But the president refused to ask Congress for an official declaration of war. Thus, this conflict is known as the quasi war.

Despite intense pressure to declare war against France or to seize territory belonging to France's ally, Spain, President Adams managed to avert a full-scale war and achieve a peaceful settlement. Early in 1799, with the backing of moderate Federalists and Republicans, Adams proposed reestablishing diplomatic relations with France. When more extreme Federalists refused to go along with the plan, Adams threatened to resign and leave the presidency in the hands of Vice President Jefferson.

In 1800, after seven months of wearisome negotiations, negotiators worked out an agreement known as the Convention of 1800. The agreement freed the United States from its alliance with France; in exchange, America forgave $20 million in damages caused by the illegal seizure of American merchant ships during the 1790s.

Adams kept the peace, but at the cost of a second term as president. The more extreme Federalists reacted furiously to the negotiated settlement. Hamilton vowed to destroy Adams: "If we must have an enemy at the head of Government, let it be one whom we can oppose, and for whom we are not responsible."

The Alien and Sedition Acts

During the quasi war, the Federalist-controlled Congress attempted to suppress political opposition and stamp out sympathy for revolutionary France by enacting four laws in 1798 known as the **Alien and Sedition acts.** The Naturalization Act lengthened the period necessary before immigrants could receive citizenship from 5 to 14 years. The Alien Act gave the president the power to imprison or deport any foreigner believed to be dangerous to the United States. The Alien Enemies Act allowed the president to deport enemy aliens in time of war. Finally, the Sedition Act made it a crime to attack the government with "false, scandalous, or malicious" statements or writings. Adams, bitterly unhappy with the "spirit of falsehood and malignity" that threatened to undermine loyalty to the government, signed the measures.

The Alien acts were so broadly written that hundreds of foreign refugees—French intellectuals, Irish nationalists, and English radicals—fled to Europe fearing detention. But it was the Sedition Act that produced the greatest fear within the Republican opposition. Federalist prosecutors and judges used the Sedition Act to attack leading Republican newspapers, securing indictments against 25 people, mainly Republican editors and printers. Ten people were eventually convicted, one a Republican Representative from Vermont.

One of the most notorious uses of the law to suppress dissent took place in July 1798. Luther Bald-

In the early days of the Republic, political dissent sometimes escalated into physical violence. This fight between Republican Matthew Lyon and Federalist Roger Griswold took place on the floor of Congress on February 15, 1798. Lyon was later arrested for violating the Sedition Act by publishing in his newspaper a letter attacking the government.

win, the pilot of a garbage scow, was arrested in a Newark, New Jersey, tavern on charges of criminal sedition. While cannons roared through Newark's streets to celebrate a presidential visit to the city, Baldwin was overheard saying "that he did not care if they fired through [the president's] arse." For his drunken remark, Baldwin was arrested, locked up for two months, and fined.

Republicans accused the Federalists of conspiring to subvert fundamental liberties. In Virginia, the state legislature adopted a resolution written by James Madison that advanced the idea that states have the right to determine the constitutionality of federal law, and pronounced the Alien and Sedition acts unconstitutional. Kentucky's state legislature went even further, adopting a resolution written by Thomas Jefferson that declared the Alien and Sedition acts "void and of no force." The Kentucky resolution raised an issue that would grow increasingly important in American politics in the years before the Civil War: Did states have the power to declare acts of Congress null and void? In 1799, however, no other states were willing to go as far as Kentucky and Virginia.

With the Union in danger, violence erupted. In the spring of 1799 German settlers in eastern Pennsylvania rose up in defiance of federal tax collectors. President Adams called out federal troops to suppress the so-called Fries Rebellion. The leader of the rebellion, an auctioneer named John Fries, was captured, convicted of treason, and sentenced to be hanged. Adams followed Washington's example in

THE PEOPLE SPEAK

Gabriel's Revolt

In 1800 a group of slaves in Virginia plotted to seize the city of Richmond. Led by a man known as Gabriel, the insurrection was inspired in part by the slave revolt that began in the French colony of St. Domingue (Haiti) in 1791. It was also motivated by the ideals of liberty and natural rights that had led the American colonists to revolt against Britain. About 30 of the accused conspirators were executed, and many others were sold as slaves to Spanish and Portuguese colonies. Here, a visitor to Virginia describes why one of the slaves had decided to participate in Gabriel's revolt.

> In the afternoon I passed by a field in which several poor slaves had lately been executed, on the charge of having an intention to rise against their masters. A lawyer who was present at their trials at Richmond, informed me that on one of them being asked, what he had to say to the court on his defence, he replied, in a manly tone of voice: "I have nothing more to offer than what General Washington would have had to offer, had he been taken by the British and put to trial by them. I have adventured my life in endeavouring to obtain the liberty of my countrymen, and am a willing sacrifice in their cause: and I beg, as a favour, that I may be immediately led to execution. I know that you have pre-determined to shed my blood, why then all this mockery of a trial?"

Source: Robert Sutcliff, *Travels in Some Parts of North America in the Years 1804, 1805, & 1806* (Philadelphia: B. & T. Kite, 1812).

the Whiskey Rebellion and pardoned Fries, but Republicans feared that the Federalists were prepared to use the nation's army to suppress dissent.

THE REVOLUTION OF 1800

In 1800 the young republic faced another critical test: Could national leadership pass peacefully from one political party to another? Once again, the nation had a choice between John Adams and **Thomas Jefferson.** But this election was more than a contest between two men; it was also a real party contest for control of the national government. Deep substantive and ideological issues divided the two parties and partisan feelings ran deep. Federalists feared that Jefferson would reverse all the accomplishments of the preceding 12 years. A Republican president, they thought, would overthrow the Constitution by returning power to the states, dismantling the army and navy, and overturning Hamilton's financial system.

The Republicans charged that the Federalists, by creating a large standing army, imposing heavy taxes, and using federal troops and the federal courts to suppress dissent, had shown contempt for the liberties of the American people. They worried that the Federalists' ultimate goal was to centralize power in the national government and involve the United States in the European war on the side of Britain.

The contest was one of the most vigorous in American history; emotions ran high. Federalist opponents called Jefferson an "atheist in religion, and a fanatic in politics." They claimed he was a drunkard, an enemy of religion, and the father of numerous mulatto children. Timothy Dwight, the president of Yale, predicted that a Jefferson administration would see "our wives and daughters the victims of legal prostitution; soberly dishonored; speciously polluted."

Jefferson's supporters responded by charging that President Adams was a warmonger, a spendthrift, and a monarchist who longed to reunite Britain with its former colonies. Republicans even claimed that the president had sent General Thomas Pinckney to England to procure four mistresses, two for himself and two for Adams. Adam's response: "I do declare if this be true, General Pinckney has kept them all for himself and cheated me out of my two."

The election was extremely close. The Federalists won all of New England's electoral votes, while the Republicans dominated the South and West. The final outcome hinged on the results in New York. Rural New York supported the Federalists, and Republican fortunes therefore depended on the voting in New York City. There, Jefferson's running mate, **Aaron Burr**, had created the most successful political organization the country had yet seen. Burr organized rallies, established ward committees, and promoted loyal supporters for public office. Burr's efforts paid off; Republicans won a majority in New York's legislature, thus giving the state's 12 electoral votes to Jefferson and Burr. Declared one Republican: The election "has been conducted . . . in so miraculous a manner that I cannot account for it but from the intervention of a Supreme Power and our friend Burr the agent."

Table 7.1
Election of 1800

Candidate	Party	Electoral Vote
T. Jefferson	Republican	73
J. Adams	Federalist	65

Thomas Jefferson described his election as president in 1800 as a "revolution." His goal was to reverse the centralizing policies of the Federalists.

Jefferson appeared to have won by a margin of eight electoral votes. But a complication soon arose. Because each Republican elector had cast one ballot for Jefferson and one for Burr, the two men received exactly the same number of electoral votes.

Under the Constitution, the election was now thrown into the Federalist-controlled House of Representatives. Instead of emphatically declaring that he would not accept the presidency, Burr failed to say anything. So the Federalists faced a choice. They could help elect the hated Jefferson—whom they had called "a brandy-soaked defamer of churches," "a contemptible hypocrite"—or they could throw their support to the opportunistic Burr—considered by Federalists to be "a profligate," "a voluptuary." Hamilton disliked Jefferson, but he believed he was a far more honorable man than Burr, whose "public principles have no other spring or aim than his own aggrandizement." Most other Federalists supported the New Yorker.

As the stalemate persisted, Virginia and Pennsylvania mobilized their state militias. Recognizing "the certainty that a legislative usurpation would be resisted by arms," as Jefferson noted, the Federalists finally backed down. On February 17, 1801, after six days of balloting and 36 ballots, the House of Representatives finally elected Thomas Jefferson the third president of the United States. And as a result of the election, Congress adopted the Twelfth Amendment to the Constitution, by which electors in the Electoral College cast one ballot for president and a separate and distinct ballot for vice president.

CONCLUSION

Sometime between 2:00 A.M. and 3:00 A.M., on December 13, 1799, George Washington woke his wife,

Chronology of Key Events

1789 First session of Congress meets; Electoral College names George Washington the first president; Washington selects the first cabinet; Federal Judiciary Act establishes federal court system; French Revolution begins

1790 Congress adopts Hamilton's proposal to fund the national debt at full value and to assume all state debts from the Revolutionary War

1791 Bank of the United States is established; Congress adopts an excise tax on distilled liquors; the Bill of Rights becomes part of the Constitution

1793 King Louis XVI of France is beheaded and war breaks out in Europe; Washington issues the Proclamation of Neutrality; Citizen Genêt affair

1794 Jay's Treaty with Britain; Whiskey Rebellion in western Pennsylvania; General Anthony Wayne defeats an Indian alliance at the Battle of Fallen Timbers in Ohio

1795 Treaty of Greenville opens Ohio to white settlement; Pinckney's Treaty is negotiated with Spain

1796 Washington issues Farewell Address warning against political factionalism and foreign entanglements

1797 John Adams is inaugurated as second president

1798 Adams reports XYZ Affair to Congress; undeclared naval war with France begins; Alien and Sedition acts give the president the power to imprison or deport dangerous foreigners and make it a crime to attack the government with "malicious" statements or writings; Virginia and Kentucky resolutions, drawn up by Jefferson and Madison, declare the Alien and Sedition acts unconstitutional

1800 Washington, D.C., replaces Philadelphia as the nation's capital; Convention of 1800 supplants treaties of 1778 with France

1801 House of Representatives elects Thomas Jefferson as third president

---

complaining of severe pains. Martha Washington called for an overseer, who inserted a lancet in the former president's arm and drew blood. Over the course of that day and the next, doctors arrived and attempted to ease General Washington's pain by applying blisters, administering purges, and additional bloodletting—eventually removing perhaps four pints of Washington's blood. Medical historians generally agree that Washington needed a tracheotomy (a surgical operation into the air passages), but this was too new a technique to be risked on the former president, who died on December 14.

During the early weeks of 1800 every city in the United States commemorated the death of the former leader. In Philadelphia, an empty coffin, a riderless horse, and a funeral cortege moved through the city streets. In Boston, business was suspended, cannons roared, bells pealed, and 6000 people—a fifth of the city's population—stood in the streets to express their last respects for the fallen general. In Washington, Richard Henry Lee delivered the most famous eulogy: "First in war, first in peace, and first in the hearts of his countrymen."

In 1789 it was an open question whether the Constitution was a workable plan of government. It was still unclear whether the new nation could establish a strong and vigorous national government or win the respect of foreign nations. For a decade, the new nation battled threats to its existence. It faced bitter party conflict, threats of secession, and foreign interference with American shipping and commerce.

By any standard, the new nation's achievements were impressive. During the first decade under the Constitution, the country adopted a bill of rights, protecting the rights of the individual against the power of the central government; enacted a financial program that secured the government's credit and stimulated the economy; and created the first political parties that directly involved the enfranchised segment of the population in national politics. In the face of intense partisan conflict, the United States became the first nation to transfer peacefully political power from one party to another as a result of an election. A nation, strong and viable, had emerged from its baptism by fire.

SUGGESTIONS FOR FURTHER READING

Stanley Elkins and Eric McKitrick, *The Age of Federalism: The Early American Republic, 1788–1800* (1993). Examines the major political and diplomatic controversies of the period from the beginning of the U.S. government under the Constitution to Thomas Jefferson's election as president.

James Roger Sharp, *American Politics in the Early Republic: The New Nation in Crisis* (1993). Vividly recaptures the atmosphere of passion, suspicion, and fear that marked the country's first 12 years under the new Constitution.

Overviews and Surveys

Jacob E. Cooke, "The Federalist Age: A Reappraisal," in George A. Billias and Gerald N. Grob, eds., *American History: Retrospect and Prospect* (1971); John R. Howe, *From the Revolution Through the Age of Jackson* (1973); Seymour M. Lipset, *The First New Nation: The United States in Perspective* (1963); John C. Miller, *The Federalist Era, 1789–1801* (1960); Robert E. Shalhope, *The Roots of Democracy: American Thought and Culture, 1760–1800* (1990).

Implementing the Constitution

Margo J. Anderson, *The American Census: A Social History* (1988); Richard R. Beeman, *The Old Dominion and the New Nation, 1788–1801* (1972); Thomas E. Cronin, ed., *Inventing the American Presidency* (1989); Noble Cunningham, Jr., *The United States in 1800: Henry Adams Revisited* (1988); Richard H. Kohn, *Eagle and Sword: The Federalists and the Creation of the Military Establishment in America, 1783–1802* (1975); Forrest McDonald, *The Presidency of George Washington* (1974); Carl Prince, *The Federalists and the Origins of the U.S. Civil Service* (1977); John Rhodehamel, *The Great Experiment: George Washington and the American Republic* (1998); Robert A. Rutland, *The Birth of the Bill of Rights, 1776–1791* (1955); Barry Schwartz, *George Washington: The Making of an American Symbol* (1987); Bernard Schwartz, *The Great Rights of Mankind: A History of the American Bill of Rights* (1977); Gerald Stourzh, *Alexander Hamilton and the Idea of Republican Government* (1970); Leonard D. White, *The Federalists: A Study in Administrative History* (1948).

The Birth of Political Parties

Harry Ammon, *The Genêt Mission* (1973); Joyce Appleby, *Capitalism and a New Social Order: The Republican Vision of the 1790s* (1984); James M. Banner, *To the Hartford Convention: The Federalists and the Origins of Party Politics in Massachusetts, 1789–1815* (1970); Lance Banning, *The Jeffersonian Persuasion* (1978); Richard Beeman, *The Old Dominion and the New Nation, 1788–1801* (1972); Samuel Flagg Bemis, *Jay's Treaty* (1923), and *Pinckney's Treaty* (1926); Doron Ben-Atar and Barbara B. Oberg, *Federalists Reconsidered* (1998); Steven R. Boyd, ed., *The Whiskey Rebellion* (1985); Richard Buel, Jr., *Securing the Revolution: Ideology in American Politics, 1789–1815* (1972); William N. Chambers, *Political Parties in a New Nation* (1963); Joseph Charles, *The Origins of the American Party System* (1956); Jerald A. Combs, *The Jay Treaty* (1970); Noble E. Cunningham, Jr., *The Jeffersonian Republicans: The Formation of Party Organization, 1789–1801* (1957); David Brion Davis, *Revolutions: Reflections on American Equality and Foreign Liberations* (1990); Alexander De Conde, *Entangling Alliance: Politics and Diplomacy Under George Washington* (1958); Felix Gilbert, *To the Farewell Address* (1961); Paul Goodman, *The Democratic-Republicans of Massachusetts* (1964); Sanford W. Higginbotham, *The Keystone in the Democratic Arch: Pennsylvania Politics, 1800–1816* (1952); John F. Hoadley, *Origins of American Political Parties, 1789–1803* (1986); Ronald Hoffman and Peter J. Albert, eds., *Launching the "Extended Republic": The Federalist Era* (1996); Richard Hofstadter, *The Idea of a Party System: The Rise of Legitimate Opposition in the United States, 1780–1840* (1969); Lawrence S. Kaplan, *Jefferson and France: An Essay on Politics and Political Ideas* (1967); Eugene P. Link, *Democratic-Republican Societies, 1790–1800* (1942); Gilbert L. Lycan, *Alexander Hamilton and American Foreign Policy: A Design for Greatness* (1970); Conor Cruise O'Brien, *The Long Affair: Thomas Jefferson and the French Revolution* (1996); Carl E. Prince, *New Jersey's Jeffersonian Republicans* (1967); Norman Risjord, *Chesapeake Politics, 1781–1800* (1978); Arthur M. Schlesinger, Jr., ed., *History of United States Political Parties, Volume I: 1798–1860: From Factions to Parties* (1973); Bernard Schwartz, *The Great Rights of Mankind: A History of the American Bill of Rights* (1977); Louis M. Sears, *George Washington and the French Revolution* (1960); Thomas P. Slaughter, *The Whiskey Rebellion* (1986); James Morton Smith, *Freedom's Fetters: The Alien and Sedition Laws and American Civil Liberties* (1956); Paul A. Varg, *Foreign Policies of the Founding Fathers* (1963); Patricia Watlington, *The Partisan Spirit* (1972); Alfred F. Young, *The Democratic Republicans of New York* (1967); John Zvesper, *Political Philosophy and Rhetoric: A Study of the Origins of American Party Politics* (1977).

A New President and New Challenges

Ralph Adams Brown, *The Presidency of John Adams* (1975); Manning J. Dauer, *The Adams Federalists* (1953); Alexander De Conde, *The Quasi-War: Politics and Diplomacy of the Undeclared War with France, 1797–1801* (1966); John R. Howe, *The Changing Political Thought of John Adams* (1966); Lawrence S. Kaplan, *Colonies into Nation: American Diplo-*

macy, 1763–1801 (1972); Stephen G. Kurtz, *The Presidency of John Adams: The Collapse of Federalism, 1795–1800* (1957); Leonard W. Levy, *Legacy of Suppression: Freedom of Speech and Press in Early American History* (1960); John C. Miller, *Crisis in Freedom: The Alien and Sedition Acts* (1951); John R. Nelson, *Liberty and Property: Political Economy and Policymaking in the New Nation* (1987); Bradford Perkins, *The First Rapprochement: England and the United States, 1795–1805* (1955); Peter Shaw, *The Character of John Adams* (1976); William Stinchcombe, *The XYZ Affair* (1980).

The Revolution of 1800

David Hackett Fischer, *The Revolution of American Conservatism: The Federalist Party in the Era of Jeffersonian Democracy* (1965); Robert M. Johnstone, Jr., *Jefferson and the Presidency: Leadership in the Young Republic* (1978); Linda K. Kerber, *Federalists in Dissent* (1970); A. M. Schlesinger, Jr., and Fred L. Israel, eds., *History of American Presidential Elections, 1789–1968* (1971); Daniel Sisson, *The American Revolution of 1800* (1974).

Biographies

Charles Akers, *Abigail Adams: An American Woman* (1980); Irving Brant, *James Madison*, 6 vols. (1941–1961); Fawn M. Brodie, *Thomas Jefferson: An Intimate History* (1974); Richard Brookhiser, *Alexander Hamilton* (1999), and *Founding Father: Rediscovering George Washington* (1996); Jacob Ernest Cooke, *Alexander Hamilton* (1982); Marcus Cunliffe, *George Washington: Man and Monument* (1958); Noble E. Cunningham, Jr., *In Pursuit of Reason: The Life of Thomas Jefferson* (1987); James Thomas Flexner, *George Washington*, 4 vols. (1965–1972); Douglas Southall Freeman, *George Washington: A Biography*, 7 vols. (1948–1957); Ralph Ketcham, *James Madison* (1971); Phyllis Lee Levin, *Abigail Adams* (1987); Milton Lomask, *Aaron Burr*, 2 vols. (1979–1982); Paul K. Longmore, *Invention of George Washington* (1988); Dumas Malone, *Jefferson and His Time*, 6 vols. (1948–1981); John C. Miller, *Alexander Hamilton* (1959); Broadus Mitchell, *Alexander Hamilton*, 2 vols. (1957–1962); Merrill Peterson, *The Jefferson Image in the American Mind* (1960), and *Thomas Jefferson and the New Nation* (1970); William M. S. Rasmussen and Robert S. Tilton, *George Washington* (1999); Lynne Withey, *Dearest Friend: A Life of Abigail Adams* (1981).

Internet Resources

The Electoral College
http://www.nara.gov/fedreg/ec-hmpge.html
This National Archives and Records Administration site explains how the electoral college works.

George Washington Papers
http://www.virginia.edu/~gwpapers/
Information on the publishing project, with selected documents, essays, and an index of the published volumes.

George Washington at Home
http://www.mountvernon.org/
Pictures and documents of Mount Vernon, the home of the first president, George Washington.

George Washington Papers at the Library of Congress, 1741–1799
http://memory.loc.gov/ammem/gwhtml/gwhome.html
This site, "the complete George Washington Papers from the Manuscript Division at the Library of Congress consists of approximately 65,000 documents. This is the largest collection of original Washington documents in the world."

White House Historical Association
http://www.whitehousehistory.org/whha/default.asp
This site contains a timeline of the history of the White House and several interesting photos and links.

John Adams
http://www.whitehouse.gov/WH/glimpse/presidents/html/ja2.html
This site contains biographical information about the second president, his inaugural address, and links to his more quotable phrases.

Key Terms

Bill of Rights   (p. 193)
Cabinet   (p. 193)
Alexander Hamilton   (p. 194)
Strict Construction   (p. 194)
Implied Powers   (p. 194)
Loose Interpretation   (p. 194)
Bank of the United States   (p. 195)
Federalists   (p. 196)
Republicans   (p. 196)
Farewell Address   (p. 202)
John Adams   (p. 202)
Alien and Sedition Acts   (p. 204)
Thomas Jefferson   (p. 205)
Aaron Burr   (p. 206)

Review Questions

1. What were the most serious problems facing the new nation when George Washington became president?
2. What strengths and skills did George Washington bring to the presidency?
3. What measures did Alexander Hamilton propose to create a strong central government and a prospering economy? Why did his opponents oppose these measures?
4. Which set of ideas and programs—Alexander Hamilton's or Thomas Jefferson's—best addressed the new country's needs?
5. Why did George Washington warn against permanent alliances and party divisions in his Farewell Address?
6. Why did Congress enact the Alien and Sedition Acts? Why did the Jeffersonians oppose these measures?

8

THE JEFFERSONIANS IN POWER, 1800–1815

JEFFERSON TAKES COMMAND
   Who Was Thomas Jefferson?
   Jefferson's Goal: To Restore Republican Government
   Reforming the Federal Government
   War on the Judiciary
   International Conflict
   Disunionist Conspiracies

THE AMERICAN EAGLE CHALLENGES THE FRENCH TIGER AND THE BRITISH SHARK
   "Dambargo"
   A Second War of Independence
   Early Defeats
   The Tide Turns
   The War's Significance

"A dangerous man"

On the morning of June 18, 1804, a visitor handed a package to former treasury secretary Alexander Hamilton. Inside was a newspaper clipping and a terse three-sentence letter. The clipping said that Hamilton had called Vice President Aaron Burr "a dangerous man, and one who ought not to be trusted with the reins of government." It went on to say that Hamilton had "expressed" a "still more despicable opinion" of Burr—apparently a bitter personal attack on Burr's public and private morality, not merely a political criticism. The letter, signed by Burr, demanded a "prompt and unqualified" denial or an immediate apology.

Hamilton and Burr had sparred verbally for decades. Hamilton regarded Burr as an unscrupulous man and considered him partly responsible for a duel in 1801 that had left his son Philip dead. Burr, in turn, blamed Hamilton for his defeat in the race for governor of New York earlier in the year. When, after three weeks, Hamilton had failed to respond to his letter satisfactorily, Burr insisted that they settle the dispute according to the code of honor.

Shortly after 7 A.M., on July 11, 1804, Burr and Hamilton met on the wooded heights of Weehawken, New Jersey, a customary dueling ground directly across the Hudson River from New York. Hamilton's son died there in a duel in 1801.

Hamilton's second handed Burr one of two pistols equipped with hair-spring triggers. After he and Burr took their positions ten paces apart, Hamilton raised his pistol on the command to "Present!" and fired. His shot struck a tree a few feet to Burr's side. Then Burr fired. His shot struck Hamilton in the right side and passed through his liver. Hamilton died the following day.

The popular view was that Hamilton had intentionally fired to one side, while Burr had slain the Federalist leader in an act of cold-blooded murder. In fact, historians do not know whether Burr was guilty of willful murder. Burr had no way of knowing whether Hamilton had purposely missed. Hamilton, after all, had accepted the challenge, raised his pistol, and fired. According to the code of honor, if Burr missed on his first try, Hamilton would have a second chance to shoot.

The states of New York and New Jersey wanted to try Burr for murder; New Jersey actually indicted him. The vice president fled through New Jersey by foot and wagon to Philadelphia, then took refuge in Georgia and South Carolina, until the indictments were quashed and he could finish his term in office.

The Jeffersonian era—the period stretching from 1800 to 1815—was rife with conflict, partisan passion, and larger-than-life personalities. On the domestic front, a new political party, the Republicans, came to office for the first time and a former vice president was charged with treason against his coun-

On July 11, 1804, Vice President Aaron Burr critically wounded Alexander Hamilton in a duel.

try. The era was also marked by foreign policy challenges. Pirates, operating from bases on the coast of North Africa, harassed American shipping and enslaved American sailors. Britain and France interfered with American shipping. Finally, the United States once again waged war with Britain, the world's strongest power. These developments raised profound questions: Could the country peacefully transfer political power from one party to another? Could the country preserve political stability? And most important of all, could the nation preserve its neutral rights and national honor in the face of grave threats from Britain and France?

JEFFERSON TAKES COMMAND

Thomas Jefferson's goal as president was to restore the principles of the American Revolution. In his view, a decade of Federalist party rule had threatened republican government. Not only had the Federalists levied oppressive taxes, stretched the provisions of the Constitution, and established a bastion of wealth and special privilege in the creation of a national bank, they also had subverted civil liberties and expanded the powers of the central government at the expense of the states. A new revolution was necessary, "as real a revolution in the principles of our government as that of 1776 was in its form." What was needed was a return to basic republican principles.

Beginning with his very first day in office, Jefferson sought to demonstrate his administration's commitment to republican principles. At noon, March 4, 1801, Jefferson, clad in clothes of plain cloth, walked from a nearby boardinghouse to the new United States Capitol in Washington. Without ceremony, he entered the Senate chamber and took the presidential oath of office. In his inaugural address Jefferson sought to allay fear that he planned a Republican reign of terror. "We are all Republicans," he said, "we are all Federalists." Echoing George Washington's Farewell Address, he asked his listeners to set aside partisan and sectional differences and remember that "every difference of opinion is not a difference of principle." He also laid out the principles that would guide his presidency: a frugal, limited government; reduction of the public debt; respect for states' rights; encouragement of agriculture; and a limited role for government in peoples' lives. He committed his administration to repealing oppressive taxes,

Republicans celebrated Thomas Jefferson's victory in the election of 1800 with a flag inscribed: "T. Jefferson President . . . John Adams no more."

slashing government expenses, cutting military expenditures, and paying off the public debt.

Who Was Thomas Jefferson?

In 1962 President John F. Kennedy hosted a White House dinner for America's Nobel Laureates. He told the assemblage that this was "probably the greatest concentration of talent and genius in this house except perhaps for those times when Thomas Jefferson ate alone."

Thomas Jefferson, the nation's third president, was a man of many talents. Though best known for his political accomplishments, he was also an architect, inventor, philosopher, planter, scientist, and talented violinist. Jefferson was an extremely complex man, and his life was filled with apparent inconsistencies. An idealist who repeatedly denounced slavery, the "Apostle of Liberty" owned 200 slaves when he wrote the Declaration of Independence and freed only five slaves at the time of his death. A vigorous opponent of all forms of human tyranny and staunch defender of human equality, he adopted a patronizing attitude toward women, declaring that their proper role was to "soothe and clam the minds of their husbands." Yet Jefferson remains this country's most eloquent exponent of democratic principles. A product of the Enlightenment, Jefferson was a stalwart defender of political freedom, equality, and re-

THE PEOPLE SPEAK

Religion in the Early Republic

During the late eighteenth and early nineteenth centuries, America's churches were deprived of state tax support. Nevertheless, church membership soared, largely due to the success of religious revivals in converting thousands of Americans. Peter Cartwright (1785–1872), a Methodist minister in frontier Kentucky, Tennessee, and Illinois, describes the revival at Cane Ridge, Kentucky, which touched off a wave of revivals that continued until the Civil War. In 1846, Cartwright ran for Congress in Illinois but was defeated by a young Springfield attorney named Abraham Lincoln.

> Somewhere between 1800 and 1801, in the upper part of Kentucky, at a memorable place called "Cane Ridge," there was appointed a sacramental meeting by some of the Presbyterian ministers, at which meeting, seemingly unexpected by ministers or people, the mighty power of God was displayed in a very extraordinary manner; many were moved to tears, and bitter and loud crying for mercy. The meeting was protracted for weeks. Ministers of almost all denominations flocked in from far and near. The meeting was kept up by night and day. Thousands heard of the mighty work, and came on foot, on horseback, in carriages and wagons. It was supposed that there were in attendance at times during the meeting from twelve to twenty-five thousand people. Hundreds fell prostrate under the mighty power of God, as men slain in battle. Stands were erected in the woods from which preachers of different Churches proclaimed repentance toward God and faith in our Lord Jesus Christ, and it was supposed, by eye and ear witnesses, that between one and two thousand souls were happily and powerfully converted to God during the meeting. It was not unusual for one, two, three, and four to seven preachers to be addressing the listening thousands at the same time from the different stands erected for the purpose. The heavenly fire spread in almost every direction. It was said, by truthful witnesses, that at times more than one thousand persons broke into loud shouting all at once, and that the shouts could be heard for miles around.
>
> From this camp-meeting, for so it ought to be called, the news spread through all the Churches, and through all the land, and it excited great wonder and surprise; but it kindled a religious flame that spread all over Kentucky and through many other states. And I may here be permitted to say, that this was the first camp-meeting ever held in the United States, and here our camp-meetings took their rise.

Source: W. P. Strickland, ed., *Autobiography of Peter Cartwright, The Backwoods Preacher* (New York: Carlton & Porter, 1856), 30–33.

---

ligious and intellectual freedom. He was convinced that the yeoman farmer, who worked the land, provided the backbone of democracy. He popularized the idea that a democratic republic required an enlightened and educated citizenry and that government has a duty to assist in the education of a meritocracy based on talent and ability.

Jefferson's Goal: To Restore Republican Government

As president, Jefferson strove to return the nation to republican values. Through his personal conduct and public policies he sought to return the country to the principles of democratic simplicity, economy, and limited government. He took a number of steps to rid the White House of aristocratic customs that had prevailed during the administrations of Washington and Adams. He introduced the custom of having guests shake hands instead of bowing stiffly; he also placed dinner guests at a round table, so that no individual would sit in a more important place than any other. In an effort to discourage a "cult of personality," he refused to sanction public celebrations of his birthday declaring, "The only birthday I ever commemorate is that of our Independence, the Fourth of July." Jefferson also repudiated certain "monarchical practices" that had marked the Washington and Adams presidencies. Jefferson refused to ride in an elegant coach or host elegant dinner parties and balls and wore clothes made of homespun cloth. To dramatize his disdain for pomp and pageantry, he received the British minister in his dressing gown and slippers.

Jefferson believed that presidents should not try to impose their will on Congress, and consequently he refused on policy grounds to initiate legislation openly or to veto congressional bills. Convinced that presidents Washington and Adams had acted like British monarchs by personally appearing before Congress and requesting legislation, Jefferson simply sent Congress written messages. Not until the presi-

One of Thomas Jefferson's inventions was this polygraph machine, which made copies of Jefferson's letters as he wrote them.

dency of Woodrow Wilson would another president publicly address Congress and call for legislation.

Jefferson matched his commitment to republican simplicity with an emphasis on economy in government. His ideal was "a wise and frugal Government, which shall . . . leave [Americans] free to regulate their own pursuits of industry and improvement." He slashed army and navy expenditures, cut the budget, eliminated taxes on whiskey, houses, and slaves, and fired all federal tax collectors. He reduced the army to 3000 soldiers and 172 officers, the navy to 6 frigates, and foreign legations to 3—in Britain, France, and Spain. His budget cuts allowed him to cut the federal debt by a third, despite the elimination of all internal taxes.

Jefferson did not conceive of government in entirely negative terms. Convinced that ownership of land and honest labor in the earth were the firmest bases of political stability, Jefferson persuaded Congress to cut the price of public lands and extend credit to purchasers in order to encourage landownership and rapid western settlement. A firm believer in the idea that America should be the "asylum" for "oppressed humanity," he moved Congress to reduce the residence requirement for citizenship from 14 to 5 years. In the interest of protecting civil liberties, he allowed the Sedition Act to expire in 1801, freed all people imprisoned under the act, and refunded their fines. And finally, to ensure that the public knew the names and number of all government officials, Jefferson ordered publication of a register of all federal employees.

In one area Jefferson felt his hands were tied. He considered the Bank of the United States "the most deadly" institution to republican government. But Hamilton's bank had been legally chartered for 20 years and Jefferson's secretary of the treasury, Albert Gallatin, said that the bank was needed to provide credit for the nation's growing economy. So Jefferson allowed the bank to continue to operate, but he weakened its influence by distributing the federal government's deposits among 21 state banks. "What is practicable," Jefferson commented, "must often control pure theory."

Contemporaries were astonished by the sight of a president who had renounced all the practical tools of government: an army, a navy, and taxes. Jefferson's actions promised, said a British observer, "a sort of Millennium in government." Jefferson's goal was, indeed, to create a new kind of government, a republican government wholly unlike the centralized, corrupt, patronage-ridden one against which Americans had rebelled in 1776.

Reforming the Federal Government

Jefferson thought that one of the major obstacles to restoring republican government was the 3000 Federalist officeholders. Of the first 600 political appointees named to federal office by presidents Washington and Adams, all but 6 were Federalists. Even after learning of his defeat, Adams appointed Federalists to every vacant government position. His most dramatic postelection appointment was naming **John Marshall,** a Federalist, chief justice of the Supreme Court.

Jefferson was committed to the idea that government office should be filled on the basis of merit, not political connections. Only government officeholders guilty of malfeasance or incompetence should be fired. Nothing more should be asked of government officials, he felt, than that they be honest, able, and loyal to the Constitution. Jefferson wholly rejected the idea that a victorious political party had a right to fill public offices with loyal party supporters.

Although many Republicans felt that Federalists should be replaced by loyal Republicans, Jefferson declared that he would remove only "midnight" appointees who had been named to office by President Adams after he learned of his electoral defeat.

War on the Judiciary

When Thomas Jefferson took office, not a single Republican was serving as a federal judge. In Jefferson's view, the Federalists had prostituted the federal judiciary into a branch of their political party and intended to use the courts to frustrate Republican plans. "From that battery," said Jefferson, "all the works of republicanism are to be beaten down and erased."

The first major political battle of Jefferson's presidency involved his effort to weaken Federalist control of the federal judiciary. The specific issue that provoked Republican anger was the **Judiciary Act of 1801,** which was passed by Congress five days before Adams's term expired. The law created 16 new federal judgeships, positions which Adams promptly filled with Federalists. Even more damaging from a Republican perspective, the act strengthened the power of the central government by extending the jurisdiction of the federal courts over bankruptcy and land disputes, which were previously the exclusive domain of state courts. Finally, the act reduced the number of Supreme Court justices effective with the next vacancy, delaying Jefferson's opportunity to name a new Supreme Court justice.

Jefferson's supporters in Congress repealed the Judiciary Act, but the war over control of the federal courts continued. One of Adams's "midnight appointments" to a judgeship was William Marbury, a loyal Federalist. Although approved by the Senate, Marbury never received his letter of appointment from Adams. When Jefferson became president, Marbury demanded that the new secretary of state, James Madison, issue the commission. Madison refused and Marbury sued, claiming that under section 13 of the Judiciary Act of 1789, the Supreme Court had the power to issue a court order that would compel Madison to give him his judgeship.

The case threatened to provoke a direct confrontation between the judiciary on the one hand and the executive and legislative branches of the federal government on the other. If the Supreme Court ordered Madison to give Marbury his judgeship, the secretary of state was likely to ignore the Court, and Jeffersonians in Congress might try to limit the high court's power. This is precisely what had happened in 1793 when the Supreme Court had ruled that a state might be sued in federal court by nonresidents. Congress had retaliated by initiating the Eleventh Amendment, which restricted such suits.

In his opinion in **Marbury v. Madison,** John Marshall, the new chief justice of the Supreme Court, ingeniously expanded the court's power without directly provoking the Jeffersonians. Marshall conceded that Marbury had a right to his appointment but ruled the Court had no authority to order the secretary of state to act, since the section of the Judiciary Act that gave the Court the power to issue an order was unconstitutional. "A law repugnant to the constitution is void," Marshall declared. "It is emphatically the province and duty of the judicial department to say what the law is." For the first time, the Supreme Court had declared an act of Congress unconstitutional.

Marbury v. *Madison* was a landmark in American constitutional history. The decision firmly established the power of the federal courts to review the constitutionality of federal laws and to invalidate acts of Congress when they are determined to conflict with the Constitution. This power, known as **judicial review,** provides the basis for the important place that the Supreme Court occupies in American life today.

John Marshall, the fourth chief justice of the United States, expanded the Court's power in *Marbury* v. *Madison* by establishing the right of judicial review. He thus gave the federal courts the power to determine the constitutionality of federal laws and congressional acts.

Marshall's decision in *Marbury* v. *Madison* intensified Republican party distrust of the courts. Impeachment, Jefferson and his followers believed, was the only way to be rid of judges they considered unfit or overly partisan and make the courts responsive to the public will. "We shall see who is master of the ship," declared one Jeffersonian. "Whether men appointed for life or the immediate representatives of the people . . . are to give laws to the community." Federalists responded by accusing the administration of endangering the independence of the federal judiciary.

Three weeks before the Court handed down its decision in *Marbury* v. *Madison,* congressional Republicans launched impeachment proceedings against Federal District Judge John Pickering of New Hampshire. An alcoholic, who may have been insane, Pickering was convicted and removed from office.

On the day of Pickering's conviction, the House voted to impeach Supreme Court Justice Samuel Chase, a staunch Federalist and a signer of the Declaration of Independence. From the bench, he had openly denounced equal rights and universal suffrage and accused the Jeffersonians of atheism and being power hungry. Undoubtedly, Chase was guilty of unrestrained partisanship and injudicious statements. An irate President Jefferson called for Chase's impeachment.

Chase was put on trial for holding opinions "hurtful to the welfare of the country." But the real issue was whether Chase had committed an impeachable offense, since the Constitution specified that a judge could be removed from office only for "treason, bribery, or other high crimes" and not for partisanship or judicial misconduct. In a historic decision that helped to guarantee the independence of the judiciary, the Senate voted to acquit Chase. Although a majority of the Senate found Chase guilty, seven Republicans broke ranks and denied Jefferson the two-thirds majority needed for a conviction. "Impeachment is a farce which will not be tried again," Jefferson commented.

Chase's acquittal had momentous consequences for the future. If the Jeffersonians had succeeded in removing Chase, they would probably have removed other Federalist judges from the federal bench. However, since Chase's acquittal, no further attempts have ever been made to remove federal judges solely on the grounds of partisanship or to reshape the federal courts through impeachment. Despite the Republicans' active hostility toward an independent judiciary, the Supreme Court had emerged as a vigorous third branch of government.

International Conflict

In his inaugural address, Thomas Jefferson declared that his fondest wish was for peace. "Peace is my passion," he repeatedly insisted. As president, however, Jefferson was unable to realize his wish. Like Washington and Adams before him, Jefferson faced the difficult task of preserving American independence and neutrality in a world torn by war and revolution.

The Barbary Pirates

Jefferson's first major foreign policy crisis came from the "Barbary pirates" who preyed on American shipping off the coast of North Africa. In 1785, Algerian pirates boarded an American merchant schooner sailing off the coast of Portugal, took its 21-member crew to Algeria, and enslaved them for twelve years. During the next eight years, 100 more American hostages were seized from American ships. In 1795 Congress approved a $1 million ransom for their release, and by 1800, one-fifth of all federal revenues went to the North African states as tribute.

Early in Jefferson's first term, he refused to pay additional tribute. Determined to end the humiliating demands, he sent warships to the Mediterranean to enforce a blockade of Tripoli. The result was a pro-

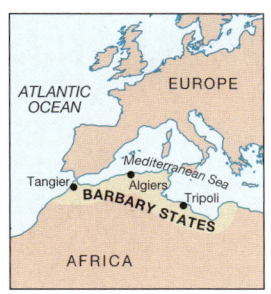

Barbary States

Thomas Jefferson's first foreign policy crisis occurred when he refused to pay tribute to the Barbary States for the release of hostages captured by Algerian pirates. Instead, he sent eight ships to enforce a blockade of Tripoli.

Burning of the *Philadelphia*

To avenge the capture of 307 crew members of the U.S. frigate *Philadelphia*, Lt. Stephen Decatur, Jr., and a small band of sailors boarded the ship and set it afire in 1804.

The American Flag was raised over New Orleans in 1803 after the Louisiana Purchase.

tracted conflict with Tripoli, which lasted until 1805. Tripoli eventually agreed to make peace, though the United States continued to pay other Barbary states until 1816.

The Louisiana Purchase

At the same time that conflict raged with the Barbary pirates, a more serious crisis loomed on the Mississippi River. In 1795 Spain granted western farmers the right to ship their produce down the Mississippi River to New Orleans, where their cargoes of corn, whiskey, and pork were loaded aboard ships bound for the east coast and foreign ports. In 1800 Spain secretly ceded the Louisiana territory to France and closed the port of New Orleans to American farmers. Westerners, left without a port from which to export their goods, exploded with anger. Many demanded war.

The prospect of French control of the Mississippi alarmed Jefferson. Spain had held only a weak and tenuous grip on the Mississippi, but France was a much stronger power. Jefferson feared the establishment of a French colonial empire in North America blocking American expansion. The United States appeared to have only two options: diplomacy or war.

The president sent James Monroe to join Robert Livingston, the American minister to France, with instructions to purchase New Orleans and as much of the Gulf Coast as they could for $2 million. Circumstances played into American hands when France failed to suppress a slave rebellion in Haiti. One hundred thousand slaves, inspired by the French Revolution, had revolted, destroying 1200 coffee and 200 sugar plantations. In 1800 France sent troops to crush the insurrection and reconquer Haiti, but they met a determined resistance led by a former slave named **Toussaint Louverture.** Then, they were wiped out by mosquitoes carrying yellow fever. "Damn sugar, damn coffee, damn colonies," Napoleon exclaimed. Without Haiti, which he regarded as the centerpiece of an American empire, Napoleon had little interest in keeping Louisiana.

Two days after Monroe's arrival, the French finance minister unexpectedly announced that France was willing to sell not just New Orleans but all of Louisiana Province, a territory extending from Canada to the Gulf of Mexico and westward as far as the Rocky Mountains. The American negotiators agreed on a price of $15 million, or about 4 cents an acre.

Since the Constitution did not give the president specific authorization to purchase land, Jefferson considered asking for a constitutional amendment empowering the government to acquire territory. In Congress, Federalists bitterly denounced the purchase, fearing that the creation of new western states

On his expedition with Meriwether Lewis to explore the Louisiana Territory, William Clark kept a detailed journal of field notes and drawings. This drawing shows how the Chinook Indians flattened their infants' heads by binding them between two boards.

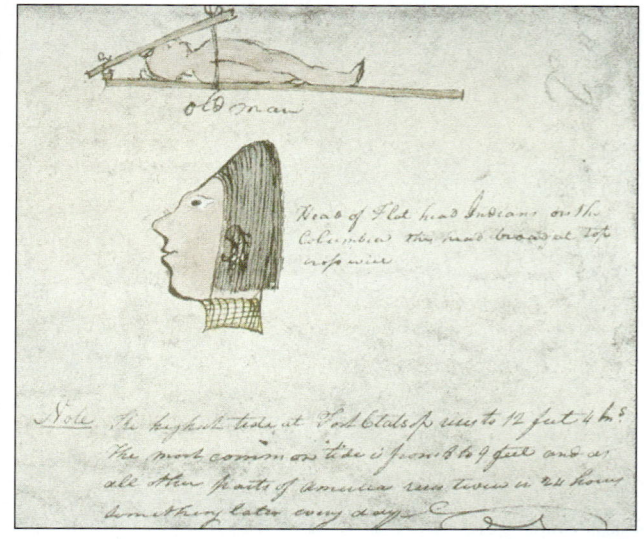

The Louisiana Purchase and Route of Lewis and Clark

No one realized how much territory Jefferson had acquired through the Louisiana Purchase until Lewis and Clark explored the far West.

would weaken the influence of their party. In the end Jefferson, fearing that Napoleon might change his mind, simply sent the agreement to the Senate, which ratified it. "The less said about any constitutional difficulty, the better," he stated. In a single stroke, Jefferson had doubled the size of the country.

To gather information about the geography, natural resources, wildlife, and peoples of Louisiana, President Jefferson dispatched an expedition led by his private secretary Meriwether Lewis and William Clark, a Virginia-born military officer. For 2 years Lewis and Clark led some 30 soldiers and 10 civilians up the Missouri River as far as present-day central North Dakota and then west to the Pacific.

Disunionist Conspiracies

Anger over the acquisition of Louisiana led some Federalists to consider secession as a last resort to restore their party's former dominance. One group of Federalist congressmen plotted to establish a "Northern Confederacy," which would consist of New Jersey, New York, the New England states, and Canada.

Alexander Hamilton repudiated this scheme, and the conspirators turned to Vice President Aaron Burr. In return for Federalist support in his campaign for the governorship of New York, Burr was to swing New York into the Northern Confederacy. Burr was badly beaten, in part because of Hamilton's opposition. Incensed and irate, Burr challenged Hamilton to the duel described at the beginning of this chapter.

The duel ruined Burr's career as a politician and made him a fugitive from the law. The Republican party stripped away his control over political patronage in New York. In debt, disgraced, on the edge of bankruptcy, the desperate Burr became involved in a conspiracy for which he would be put on trial for treason.

During the spring of 1805 Burr traveled to the West, where he and an old friend, James Wilkinson, commander of United States forces in the Southwest and military governor of Louisiana, hatched an adventurous scheme. It is still uncertain what the conspirators' goal was, since Burr, in his efforts to attract support, told different stories to different people. Spain's minister believed that Burr planned to set up an independent nation in the Mississippi Valley. Others reported that he planned to seize Spanish territory in what is now Texas, California, and New Mexico. The British minister was told that for $500,000 and British naval support, Burr would separate the states and territories west of the Appalachians from the rest of the Union and create an empire with himself as its head.

In the fall of 1806 Burr and some 60 schemers traveled down the Ohio River toward New Orleans to assess possibilities and perhaps to incite disgruntled French settlers to revolt. Wilkinson, recognizing that the scheme was doomed to failure, decided to betray Burr. He wrote a letter to Jefferson describing a "deep, dark, wicked, and widespread conspiracy, . . . to seize on New Orleans, revolutionize the territory, and carry an expedition against Mexico."

Burr fled, but was finally apprehended in the Mississippi Territory. He was then taken to the circuit court in Richmond, Virginia, where, in 1807, he was tried for treason. Jefferson, convinced that Burr was a dangerous man, wanted a conviction regardless of the evidence. Chief Justice John Marshall, who presided over the trial, was equally eager to discredit Jefferson. Ultimately, Burr was acquitted. The reason for the acquittal was the Constitution's very strict definition of treason as "levying war against the United States" or "giving . . . aid and comfort" to the nation's enemies. In addition, each overt act of treason had to be attested to by two witnesses. The prosecution was unable to meet this strict standard; as a result of Burr's acquittal, few cases of treason have ever been tried in the United States.

Was Burr guilty of conspiring to destabilize the United States and separate the West by force? Probably not. The prosecution's case rested largely on the unreliable testimony of co-conspirator James Wilkinson, who was a spy in the pay of Spain while also a U.S. army commander and governor of Louisiana. What, then, was the purpose of Burr's mysterious scheming? It appears likely that the former vice president was planning a filibuster expedition—an unauthorized military attack—on Mexico, which was then controlled by Spain. The dream of creating a western republic in Mexico, Florida, or Louisiana appealed to many early nineteenth-century Americans—especially to those who feared that a European power might seize Spain's New World colonies unless America launched a preemptive strike. Alexander Hamilton himself, back in 1798, had proposed a plan to conquer Louisiana and the Floridas.

To the end of his life, Burr denied that he had plotted treason against the United States. Asked by one of his closest friends whether he had sought to separate the West from the rest of the nation, Burr responded with an emphatic "No!" "I would as soon have thought of taking possession of the moon and informing my friends that I intended to divide it among them."

THE AMERICAN EAGLE CHALLENGES THE FRENCH TIGER AND THE BRITISH SHARK

In 1804, Jefferson was easily reelected, carrying every state except Connecticut and Delaware. He received 162 electoral votes to only 14 for his Federalist opponent, Charles C. Pinckney. Although his second term began, he later wrote, "without a cloud on the horizon," storm clouds soon gathered as a result of renewed war in Europe. Jefferson faced the difficult challenge of keeping the United States out of the European war, while defending the nation's rights as a neutral country.

In May 1803, only two weeks after Napoleon sold Louisiana to the United States, France declared war on Britain. As part of his overall strategy to bring Britain to its knees, Napoleon instituted the "Continental System," a policy of economic warfare that closed European ports to British goods and ordered the seizure of any neutral vessel that carried British goods or stopped in a British port. Britain retaliated in 1807 by issuing Orders in Council, which required all neutral ships to land at a British port to obtain a trading license and pay a tariff. Britain threatened to seize any ship that failed to obey the Orders in Council. United States shipping was

---

In the election of 1804, Thomas Jefferson dropped Aaron Burr from the Republican ticket and replaced him with another New Yorker, George Clinton.

Copyright © Collection of the New-York Historical Society.

REPUBLICANS

Turn out, turn out and save your Country from ruin !

From an *Emperor*—from a *King*—from the iron grasp of a *British Tory Faction*—an unprincipled banditti of British speculators. The hireling tools and emissaries of his majesty king George the 3d have thronged our city and diffused the poison of principles among us.

DOWN WITH THE TORIES, DOWN WITH THE BRITISH FACTION,

Before they have it in their power to enslave you, and reduce your families to distress by heavy taxation. Republicans want no Tribute-liars—they want no ship Ocean-liars—they want no Rufus King's for Lords —they want no Varick to lord it over them—they want no Jones for senator, who fought with the British against the Americans in time of the war.—But they want in their places such men as

Jefferson & Clinton,

who fought their Country's Battles in the year '76

caught in the crossfire. By 1807 France had seized 500 ships and Britain nearly 1000.

The most outrageous violation of America's neutral rights was the British practice of **impressment.** The British navy desperately needed sailors. Unable to procure sufficient volunteers, the British navy resorted to seizing—impressing—men on streets, in taverns, and on British merchant ships. When these efforts failed to muster sufficient men, the British began to stop foreign ships and remove seamen alleged to be British subjects. By 1811 nearly 10,000 American sailors had been forced into the British navy, although an undetermined number were actually deserters from British ships who made more money sailing on U.S. ships.

Outrage over impressment reached a fever pitch in 1807 when the British man-of-war *Leopard* fired three broadsides at the American naval frigate *Chesapeake* as the American crew had refused to allow British officers to search the American ship for Royal Navy deserters. The blasts killed 3 American sailors and wounded 18 more. British authorities then boarded the American ship and removed 4 sailors, only 1 of whom was really a British subject.

"Dambargo"

In a desperate attempt to stave off war, for which it was ill-prepared, and to win respect for America's neutral rights, the United States imposed an **embargo** on foreign trade. Convinced that American trade was vital to European industry, Jefferson persuaded Congress in late 1807 to adopt a policy of "peaceable coercion": a ban on all foreign shipping and exports.

Jefferson regarded the embargo as an idealistic experiment—a moral alternative to war. Jefferson was not a doctrinaire pacifist, but he had long advocated economic coercion as an instrument of diplomacy. Now he had a chance to put his ideas into practice.

The embargo was an unpopular and costly failure. It hurt the American economy far more than it did the British or French and resulted in widespread smuggling. Without the European export market, harbors filled with idle ships, and nearly 30,000 sailors found themselves jobless. The embargo resuscitated the Federalist party, which regained power in several New England states and made substantial gains in the Congressional elections of 1808. "Would to God," said one American, "that the embargo had done as little evil to ourselves as it has done to foreign nations!"

Jefferson believed that Americans would cooperate with the embargo out of a sense of patriotism. Instead, evasions of the embargo were widespread, and smuggling flourished, particularly through Canada, and early in 1809, just three days before Jefferson left office, Congress repealed the embargo. In effect for 15 months, the embargo exacted no political concessions from either France or Britain. But it had produced economic hardship, evasion of the law, and political dissension at home. Upset by the failure of his policies, the 65-year-old Jefferson looked forward to his retirement: "Never did a prisoner, released from his chains, feel such relief as I shall on shaking off the shackles of power."

The problem of American neutrality now fell to Jefferson's hand-picked successor, **James Madison.** "The Father of the Constitution" was small in stature and frail in health. A quiet and scholarly man, who secretly suffered from epilepsy, Madison brought a keen intellect and a wealth of experience to the presidency. At the Constitutional Convention, he had played a leading role in formulating the principles of federalism and separation of powers that underlie the American system of government. As a member of Congress, he had sponsored the Bill of Rights and founded the Republican party. As Jefferson's secretary of state, he had kept the United States out of the Napoleonic wars and was committed to using economic coercion to force Britain and France to respect America's neutral rights.

In 1809 Congress replaced the failed embargo with the **Non-Intercourse Act,** which reopened trade with all nations except Britain and France.

Violations of American neutrality continued, and a year later Congress replaced the Non-Intercourse Act with a new measure, **Macon's Bill No. 2.** This policy reopened trade with France and Britain. It stated, however, that if either Britain or France agreed to respect America's neutral rights, the United States would immediately stop trade with the other nation. Napoleon seized on this new policy in an effort to entangle the United States in his war with Britain. In the summer of 1810, he announced repeal of all French restrictions on American trade. Even though France continued to seize American ships and cargoes, President Madison snapped at the bait. In early 1811 he cut off trade with Britain and recalled the American minister.

For 19 months the British went without American trade, but gradually economic coercion worked. Food shortages, mounting unemployment, and increasing inventories of unsold manufactured goods led the British to end its trade restrictions (though not the British navy's policy of impressment). Unfortunately, Prime Minister Perceval was assassinated before he actually revoked the restrictions. When the restrictions were finally suspended on June 16, it was too late. President Madison had asked Congress for a declaration of war on June 1. A divided House and Senate concurred. The House voted to declare war on Britain by a vote of 79 to 49; the Senate by a vote of 19 to 13.

A Second War of Independence

Why did the United States declare war on Britain in 1812? Resentment at British interference with American rights on the high seas was certainly the most loudly voiced grievance. British trade restrictions, impressment of thousands of American seamen, and British blockades humiliated the country and undercut America's national honor and neutral rights.

But if British harassment of American shipping was the primary motivation for war, why then did the prowar majority in Congress come largely from the South, the West, and the frontier, and not from northeastern shipowners and sailors? The vote to declare war on Britain divided along sharp regional lines. Representatives from western, southern, and frontier states voted 65 to 15 for war, while representatives from New England, New York, and New Jersey, states with strong shipping interests, voted 34 to 14 against war.

Northeastern Federalists and a handful of Republicans from coastal regions of the South regarded war with Britain as a grave mistake. The United

At the Battle of Tippecanoe, U.S. troops led by General William Henry Harrison routed the small force of Native Americans under the Shawnee Prophet, Tenskwatawa.

States, they insisted, could not hope to challenge successfully British supremacy on the seas, and the government could not finance a war without bankrupting the country. Southerners and westerners, in contrast, were eager to avenge British insults against American honor and British actions that mocked American sovereignty on land and sea. Many southerners and westerners blamed British trade policies for depressing agricultural prices and producing an economic depression. War with Britain also offered another incentive: the possibility of clearing western

THE ROAD TO WAR

1807	**Leopard-Chesapeake Affair**	British man-of-war H.M.S. *Leopard* fires upon the American warship U.S.S. *Chesapeake*, killing three; then the British forcibly remove four alleged deserters, bringing the United Sates and Great Britain to the brink of war.
	Embargo Act	Prohibits all American trade with foreign nations.
1809	**The Non-Intercourse Act**	Reopens overseas commerce except to Britain and France; trade with these countries is to be reinstituted if they halt interference with American shipping.
1810	**Macon's Bill No. 2**	Restores trade with Britain and France but stipulates that if either country lifts its restrictions on neutral trade, the United States would terminate trade with the other.
	Trade Disputes	France informs the United States that it will repeal its trade restrictions if the United States halts trade with Britain; United States forbids trade with Britain.
	Congressional Elections	Voters sweep the "War Hawks" into Congress.
1811	**The Battle of Tippecanoe**	Battle in Indiana Territory shatters the influence of the Shawnee Prophet, Tenskwatawa.
1812	**Declaration of War**	Congress declares war against Britain on grounds of British impressment of American seamen, interference with trade, and blockading of American ports.

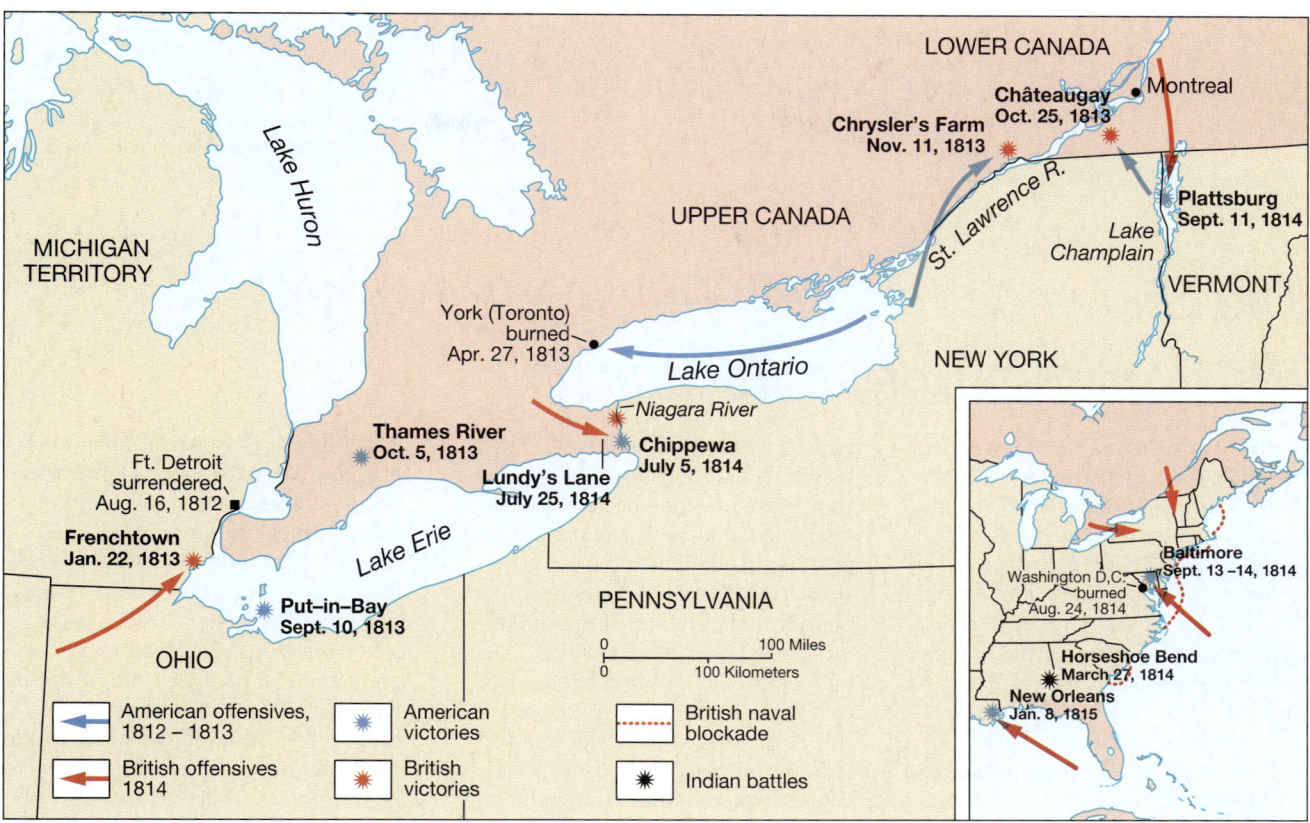

The War of 1812

lands of Indians by removing the Indians' strongest ally—the British. And finally, many westerners and southerners had their eye on expansion, viewing war as an opportunity to add Canada and Spanish-held Florida to the United States.

Weary of Jefferson and Madison's patient and pacifist policy of economic coercion, voters swept 63 of the 142 representatives out of Congress in 1810 and replaced them with young Republicans that Federalists dubbed "War Hawks." These second-generation Republicans avidly supported national expansion and national honor. They elected Henry Clay, a representative from frontier Kentucky, Speaker of the House on his very first day in Congress. Clay then assigned other young Republicans, such as John C. Calhoun, a freshman representative from South Carolina, to key House committees.

Staunchly nationalist and rabidly anti-British, eager for territorial expansion and economic growth, the young Republicans regarded the Napoleonic Wars in Europe as an unparalleled opportunity to defend national honor, assert American interests, and conquer Canada and Florida.

Further contributing to their prowar fervor was the belief that the British incited Native Americans on the frontier to attack. Anti-British feeling soared in November 1811, when General William Henry Harrison precipitated a fight with a Native-American alliance led by the Shawnee Prophet, Tenskwatawa, at Tippecanoe Creek in Indiana. More than 60 American soldiers were killed and 100 were wounded. Since British guns were found on the battlefield, young Republicans concluded that the British were responsible for the incident.

Early Defeats

Although Congress voted strongly in favor of war, the country entered the conflict deeply divided. Not only would many New Englanders refuse to subscribe to war loans, some merchants would actually ship provisions that Britain needed to support its army, which was fighting Napoleon in Europe. Moreover, the United States was woefully unprepared for war. The army consisted of fewer than 7000 soldiers and the navy was grotesquely overmatched.

The American strategy called for a three-pronged invasion of Canada and heavy harassment of British shipping. The attack on Canada, however, was a disastrous failure. At Detroit, 2000 American troops surrendered to a much smaller British and Native-American

THE American Mosaic

The Shawnee Prophet Tenskwatawa and His Warrior Brother Tecumseh

DURING the last years of the eighteenth century, defeat, disease, and death were the bitter lot of Native Americans living in the Northwest Territory. In 1794 an American expeditionary force led by Major General "Mad" Anthony Wayne crushed an opposing Indian army at the Battle of Fallen Timbers near present-day Toledo, Ohio. This decisive victory eventually forced Native Americans to give up 25,000 square miles of land north of the Ohio River.

Forty-five thousand land-hungry white settlers poured into the Ohio Country during the next six years. They spread a variety of killer diseases, including smallpox, influenza, and measles, in their wake. Whole villages succumbed, and hundreds of natives died. High Indian mortality rates did not bother the intruding whites, who also considered the arbitrary "murdering of the Indians in the highest degree meritorious," according to William Henry Harrison, the territorial governor. Aggressive frontier settlers likewise infringed on Indian hunting grounds and rapidly killed off wild game that provided the natives with basic sustenance. Deprived of their ancestral homelands, faced with severe food shortages, and enduring a drastic loss of population, Native Americans in the Old Northwest saw the fabric of their society coming apart. Tribal unity eroded, villages broke apart, and violent disputes became widespread. To escape from their problems, some natives turned to alcohol for the mind-numbing relief it provided them.

One of the Native Americans who suffered from the breakdown of Indian society was a Shawnee youth named Laulewasika. A few months before he was born in 1774, white frontiersmen—they had crossed into the Ohio Country in violation of a recent treaty—killed his father, a respected Shawnee warrior chief. Shortly thereafter, his despondent mother, a Creek, fled westward, leaving behind her children to be raised by relatives.

As a young man Laulewasika lacked direction. He became a dissolute, drunken idler, known only for the handkerchief he wore to cover up the facial disfigurement he suffered when he lost an eye during an accident. Then in 1805 in the midst of a frightening epidemic, Laulewasika underwent a powerful transformation. Overcome by images of his own wickedness, he fell into a deep trance during which he met the Indian Master of Life. On the basis of this mystical experience, Laulewasika embarked on a crusade "to reclaim the Indians from bad habits." Adopting the name Tenskwatawa, meaning "the open door," he first called upon Indians everywhere to stop drinking the white traders' alcohol. He soon broadened his appeals. Like other Native-American revitalization prophets before and after him, Tenskwatawa vigorously demanded an end to intertribal fighting, a return to ancestral ways, and a complete rejection of all aspects of white civilization. His central message was native unity as the key to blocking further white encroachments on ancient tribal lands.

Tenskwatawa's reputation reached a high point in 1806 after Governor William Henry Harrison demanded the performance of a miracle. "If he is a prophet," an almost mocking Harrison said to some Indians, "ask him to cause the sun to stand still, the moon to alter its course, . . . or the dead to rise from their graves. If he does these things, you may then believe he has been sent from God." Tenskwatawa obliged. Most likely learning from the British about an upcoming solar eclipse, he pronounced that he would make the sun disappear on the morning of June 16. When the shadow of the moon darkened the rays of the sun that day, the prophet's fame and message of unity spread far and wide among Native Americans.

The doctrines of Tenskwatawa were not solely his own. His older brother, the famed Shawnee war chief Tecumseh (1768–1813), had come to recognize the futility of fighting piecemeal against the whites. He also emerged as a firm advocate of a broad-based Indian alliance. In conjunction with the Shawnee Prophet, he struggled to convince Native Americans as far north as Wisconsin, as far west as Arkansas, and as far south as Florida to join together in blocking white expansion.

Besides working to build an alliance, Tecumseh's immediate goal was to save Indiana territory, or "the country of Indians," for the native populace. In 1808 he and Tenskwatawa relocated their tribal village in northwestern Indiana along the shoreline of the Tippecanoe River where it flowed into the Wabash River. The presence of the so-called Prophet's Town greatly worried Governor Harrison, since it served as a mecca for Indian unification. In reaction Harrison directly challenged

The Field Museum, Neg# A93851, Chicago.

the growing influence of the Shawnee brothers. He conducted negotiations with friendly local chiefs and plied them with alcohol until they turned over title to 3 million acres in Indiana for the paltry sum of $7000 and an annuity of $1750. This precipitous act put Harrison on a collision course with Tecumseh and Tenskwatawa.

Harrison eventually held a meeting with the outraged Shawnee brothers. The governor told them they could surely place their faith in treaties with the United States, but not before Tecumseh, a spellbinding orator, had queried: "How can we have confidence in the white people? When Jesus Christ came upon the earth, you killed Him and nailed Him to a cross. You thought He was dead, but you were mistaken." Harrison did not miss the point. Tecumseh and Tenskwatawa intended to revitalize Native Americans so that they too would regain life as a united nation of peoples and put an end to legalized land grabbing as provided for in such treaties as the one recently negotiated by Harrison.

Tecumseh needed time to build his alliance, and he soon set off on another of his journeys to convince his native brethren to put aside their petty tribal squabbles and prepare to rise up as one to resist the whites. He warned Tenskwatawa to avoid any conflict with Harrison, but the prophet did not listen. In November 1811, while Tecumseh was away in the south attempting to rally support, Harrison approached the Prophet's Town with an army of nearly 1000 men. Tenskwatawa rose to the bait and allowed some 450 warriors to attack the Americans. What followed was a rout. As the battle raged, the prophet called upon the Master of Life to protect his native fighters. His prayer failed. Harrison's troops drove off the warriors and then sacked and burned the village. In so doing, they destroyed the prophet's credibility and prestige. They also inadvertently gave Harrison the kind of impressive military victory that helped him successfully secure the presidency of the United States in 1840. "Tippecanoe and Tyler Too" was Harrison's catchy electioneering slogan.

Tecumseh returned home from his trip a few months later. He was in an optimistic frame of mind, believing the grand native alliance could yet become reality. Then he saw the devastated village. Shocked and enraged that his brother had challenged Harrison's force, he angrily denounced Tenskwatawa and sent him packing westward into obscurity. In frustration Tecumseh likewise abandoned his dream of a pan-Indian alliance, since he now doubted whether his native brethren had the patience to plan and work together. Then, in his own words, he "swore . . . eternal hatred—the hatred of an avenger" against white settlers everywhere. He would rally what warriors he could and fight with all his strength in the name of his way of life until death relieved him of the anguish he felt for the collapsing world of his native brethren.

When the War of 1812 broke out, Tecumseh allied himself with the British in his final effort to halt American expansion. In October 1813, after U.S. forces compelled the British to retreat from the area around Detroit, the Shawnee warrior and an army consisting of Indian and British troops tried to halt the American advance at the Thames River in the eastern part of Canada's Ontario Province. The day before the climactic encounter, Tecumseh told his native followers: "Brother warriors, we are about to enter an engagement from which I shall not return. My body will remain on the field of battle." Tecumseh's premonition was correct. The next afternoon he died from multiple wounds in combat. With his demise the vision of pan-Indian resistance to white encroachment on native lands in the Middle West also perished.

force. An attack across the Niagara River, near Buffalo, resulted in 900 American prisoners of war when the New York State militia refused to provide support. Along Lake Champlain, a third army retreated into American territory after failing to cut undefended British supply lines. By the end of 1812, British forces controlled key forts in the Old Northwest, including Detroit and Fort Dearborn, the future site of Chicago. The only consolation for the Americans was a string of naval victories in single ship encounters.

In 1813 America suffered new failures. In January, an American army advancing toward Detroit was defeated and captured in the swamps west of Lake Erie. Then, in April, Americans staged a raid across Lake Ontario to York (now Toronto). American soldiers set fire to the two houses of the provincial parliament, an act that brought retaliation in the burning of Washington, D.C., by the British. A plan to capture Montreal in the fall of 1813 also ended without an attack.

Only a series of unexpected victories at the end of the year raised American spirits. On September 10, 1813, America won a major naval victory at the Battle of Lake Erie near Put-in-Bay at the western end of Lake Erie. There, Master-Commandant Oliver Hazard Perry successfully engaged six British ships. Though Perry's flagship, the *Lawrence*, was disabled in the fighting, he went on to capture the British fleet. He reported his victory with the stirring words, "We have met the enemy and they are ours."

The Battle of Lake Erie was America's first major victory of the war. It forced the British to abandon Detroit and retreat toward Niagara. On October 5, 1813, Major General William Henry Harrison overtook the retreating British army and their Native-American allies at the Thames River. He won a decisive victory in which the Indian leader Tecumseh was killed, thereby ending the fighting strength of the northwestern Indians.

The Tide Turns

In early 1814, prospects for an American victory dimmed. In the spring, Britain defeated Napoleon in Europe, freeing 18,000 veteran British troops to participate in an invasion of the United States. The British planned to invade the United States at three points: upstate New York across the Niagara River and Lake Champlain, the Chesapeake Bay, and New Orleans. The London *Times* accurately reflected the confident English mood: "Oh, may no false liberality, no mistaken lenity, no weak and cowardly policy interpose to save the United States from the blow! Strike! Chastise the savages, for such they are.... Our demands may be couched in a single word—Submission!"

At Niagara, however, a small American army stopped the British advance, and on Lake Champlain, American naval forces commanded by Thomas Macdonough placed British supply lines in jeopardy, forcing 11,000 British troops to retreat into Canada. Outnumbered more than three to one, American forces had halted Britain's invasion from the north.

In a second attempt to invade the United States, Britain landed 4000 soldiers on the Chesapeake Bay coast and marched on Washington, D.C. where untrained soldiers lacking uniforms and standard equipment were protecting the capital.

On August 24, 1814, British troops avenged an American attack on York, Ontario, by marching into Washington, D.C. and setting fire to the Capitol and the White House.

The result was utter chaos. While President Madison was inspecting the troops and offering encouragement, he narrowly escaped capture by British forces. On August 24, 1814, the British humiliated the nation by capturing and burning Washington, D.C. President Madison and his wife Dolley were forced to flee the capital—carrying with them many of the nation's treasures, including the Declaration of Independence and Gilbert Stuart's portrait of George Washington. For 72 hours, the president was forced to hide in the Virginia and Maryland countryside. The British arrived so soon after the president fled that the officers dined on a White House meal that had been prepared for the Madisons and 40 invited guests.

Britain's next objective was Baltimore. To reach the city, British warships had to pass the guns of Fort McHenry, which was manned by 1000 American soldiers. Waving atop the fort was the largest garrison flag ever designed—30 feet by 42 feet. On September 13, 1814, British warships began a 25-hour bombardment of Fort McHenry. British vessels anchored two miles off shore—close enough so that their guns could hit the fort, but too far for American shells to reach them.

All through the night British cannons bombarded Fort McHenry. At dawn on September 14, Francis Scott Key, a young lawyer detained on a British ship, saw the flag still waving over the fort's ramparts. The Americans had repulsed the British attack, with only 4 soldiers killed and 24 wounded. Key was so moved by the American victory that he wrote a poem entitled "The Star-Spangled Banner" on the back of an old envelope. The song was destined to become the young nation's national anthem.

The country still faced grave threats in the South. In 1813 the Creek Indians, encouraged by the British, attacked American settlements in what are now Alabama and Mississippi. Frontiersmen from Georgia, Mississippi, and Tennessee, led by Major General **Andrew Jackson,** retaliated and succeeded in defeating the Creeks in March 1814, at the battle of Horseshoe Bend in Alabama. When the Creek War ended, Jackson proceeded to cut British supply lines in the South. He knew that Spain, supposedly neutral, allowed Britain to use the Florida port of Pensacola as a base of operations for a planned invasion of New Orleans. In a week, Jackson marched from Mobile, Alabama, to Pensacola and seized the city, forcing the British to delay their invasion.

But, on January 8, 1815, the British fleet and a battle-tested 10,000-man army finally attacked New Orleans in an attempt to seize control of the mouth of the Mississippi River. To defend the city, Jackson assembled a ragtag army, including French pirates, Choctaw Indians, western militia, and freed slaves. Although British forces outnumbered Americans by more than two to one, American artillery and sharpshooters stopped the invasion. American losses totaled only 8 dead and 13 wounded, while British casualties were 2036, including their commanding officer. Almost 400 British soldiers were killed. Ironically, American and British negotiators in Ghent, Belgium, had signed the peace treaty ending the War of 1812 two weeks earlier. Britain, convinced that the American war was so difficult and costly that nothing would be gained from further fighting, agreed to return to the conditions that existed before the war. Left unmentioned in the peace treaty were the issues over which the Americans had fought the war—impressment, naval blockades, and the British Orders in Council.

The War's Significance

Although often treated as unimportant, a minor footnote to the bloody European war between France and Britain, the **War of 1812** was crucial for the United States. First, it effectively destroyed the Indians' ability to resist American expansion east of the Mississippi. Native Americans were crushed in the

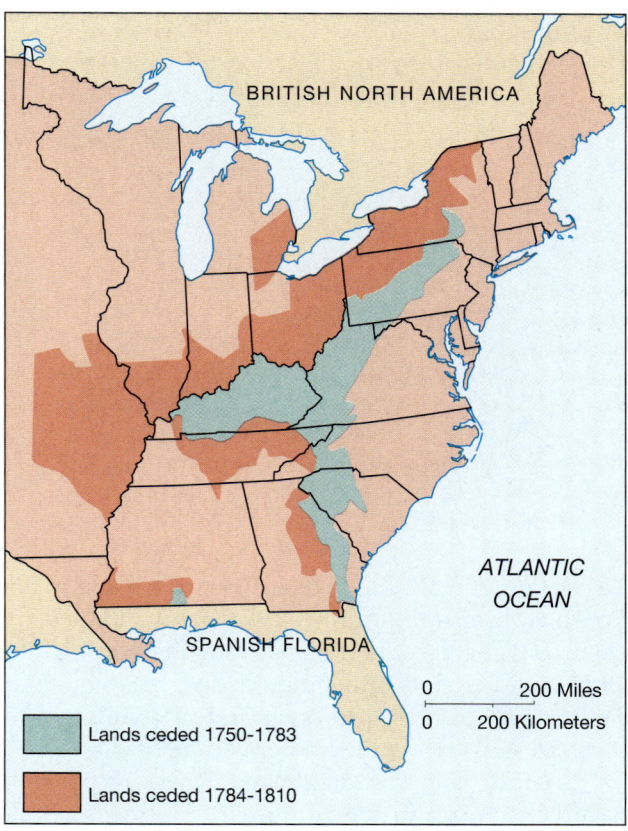

Indian Land Cessions

Before the War of 1812, Native Americans had already ceded much of their land to the federal government.

Chronology of Key Events

1801 John Marshall becomes chief justice; House of Representatives elects Thomas Jefferson as the third president; Jefferson sends eight ships to enforce a blockade of Tripoli

1802 Republican Congress repeals Judiciary Act of 1801

1803 *Marbury* v. *Madison* upholds the principle of judicial review; Jefferson purchases Louisiana Territory from Napoleon for $15 million or 4 cents an acre; war resumes in Europe

1804 Lewis and Clark expedition sets out from St. Louis to explore Louisiana Territory; Vice President Aaron Burr kills Alexander Hamilton in a duel; impeachment of federal district Judge John Pickering and Supreme Court Justice Samuel Chase

1807 Aaron Burr is charged with treason; U.S. naval frigate *Chesapeake* is attacked by British man-of-war *Leopard*; Embargo Act

1809 Embargo Act is repealed; James Madison is sworn in as fourth president; Non-Intercourse Act prohibits trade with Britain and France

1810 Macon's Bill No. 2 reopens trade with Britain and France, but says that if either country removes its trade restrictions, the United States will halt trade with the other nation; young Republicans who protest British interference with American shipping and favor expansion win congressional elections

1811 Madison, believing that France had repealed its restrictions on American shipping, stops trade with Britain; Battle of Tippecanoe in Indiana; Congress allows the charter of Bank of the United States to lapse

1812 Congress declares war against Britain; Americans surrender Detroit to British

1813 Captain Oliver Perry defeats British naval forces at the Battle of Lake Erie; General William Henry Harrison defeats British and northwestern Indians at Battle of the Thames

1814 General Andrew Jackson defeats Creek Indians at Battle of Horseshoe Bend; British burn Washington, D.C.; Commander Thomas Macdonough defeats British fleet on Lake Champlain; British invasion is turned back at Plattsburgh, New York; Hartford Convention meets; United States and Britain sign Treaty of Ghent, which ends the War of 1812

1815 Jackson defeats British at Battle of New Orleans

North by General William Henry Harrison and in the South by General Andrew Jackson. Abandoned by their British allies, the Indians made the best treaties they could. Reluctantly, they ceded most of their lands north of the Ohio River and in southern and western Alabama to the U.S. government.

Second, the war strengthened America's position relative to Spain in the South and Southwest. It allowed the United States to rewrite its boundaries with Spain and solidify control over the lower Mississippi River and the Gulf of Mexico. Although the United States failed to conquer Canada or defeat the British empire, it had fought the world's strongest power to a stalemate. Spain recognized the significance of this fact, and in 1819 Spanish leaders abandoned Florida and agreed to an American boundary running clear to the Pacific Ocean.

Third, the Federalist party never recovered from its opposition to the war. Many Federalists believed that the War of 1812 was really fought to help Napoleon in his struggle against Britain, and they opposed the war by refusing to pay taxes, boycotting war loans, and refusing to furnish troops. In December 1814, delegates from New England gathered in Hartford, Connecticut, where they recommended a series of constitutional amendments to restrict the power of Congress to wage war, regulate commerce, and admit new states. The delegates also supported a one-term president (in order to break the grip of Virginians on the presidency) and abolition of the three-fifths compromise (which increased the political clout of the South), and talked of seceding if they did not get their way.

The proposals of the **Hartford Convention** became public knowledge at the same time as the terms of the Treaty of Ghent and the American victory in the Battle of New Orleans. Euphoria over the war's end led many people to brand the Federalists as traitors. The party never recovered from this stigma and disappeared from national politics.

CONCLUSION

Early in the evening of February 11, 1815, the British sloop *Favourite*, flying a flag of truce, entered New York Harbor bearing copies of the peace treaty ending the War of 1812. By 8:30 P.M., the news had spread throughout the city. Bells pealed and cannons boomed. Cheering crowds congregated in the streets, carrying candles. Despite bungling, incompetence, and threats of disunion, the new nation had fought Britain to a draw and affirmed its independence. *Niles' Register* summed up the prevailing mood: "Who would not be an American? Long live the Republic! All hail! Last asylum of oppressed humanity."

Between 1800 and 1815, the Jeffersonian Republicans had increased the nation's size, opened new lands to western settlement, and won international respect for American independence. In a climate of war and revolution, the new nation acquired Louisiana and the Southeast, defeated powerful Indian confederations in the Northwest and South, and evicted British troops from American soil. What emerged from this period was a strong, confident, and united nation.

SUGGESTIONS FOR FURTHER READING

Donald R. Hickey, *The War of 1812* (1989). Ably examines the War of 1812.

Drew McCoy, *The Elusive Republic: Political Economy in Jeffersonian America* (1980) and *The Last of the Fathers: James Madison and the Republican Legacy* (1989). Offer extensive information on Jeffersonian republicanism.

Merrill Peterson, *Thomas Jefferson and the New Nation* (1970). An especially valuable biography of Thomas Jefferson.

Overviews and Surveys

Donald R. Hickey, *The War of 1812* (1989); John R. Howe, *From the Revolution Through the Age of Jackson* (1973); Jean V. Matthews, *Toward A New Society: American Thought and Culture, 1800–1830* (1991); John Mayfield, *The New Nation, 1800–1845*, rev. ed. (1982); James Roger Sharp, *American Politics in the Early Republic* (1993); Marshall Smelser, *The Democratic Republic, 1801–1815* (1968).

Jefferson Takes Command

Henry Adams, *History of the United States During the Administrations of Thomas Jefferson [and] of James Madison*, 9 vols., (1889–1891); James H. Broussard, *The Southern Federalists, 1800–1816* (1978); Robert Lowry Clinton, *Marbury v. Madison and Judicial Review* (1989); Edward S. Corwin, *The "Higher Law" Background of American Constitutional Law* (1929); Noble E. Cunningham, Jr., *The Jeffersonian Republicans in Power: Party Operations, 1801–1809* (1963), and *The Process of Government Under Jefferson* (1978); Alexander De Conde, *The Affair of Louisiana* (1976); D. O. Dewey, *Marshall Versus Jefferson: The Political Background of Marbury v. Madison* (1970); Richard E. Ellis, *The Jeffersonian Crisis: Courts and Politics in the Young Republic* (1971); David Hackett Fischer, *The Revolution of American Conservatism: The Federalist Party in the Era of Jeffersonian Democracy* (1965); Charles G. Haines, *The American Doctrine of Judicial Supremacy*, 2d ed. (1932); George Lee Haskins and Herbert A. Johnson, *History of the Supreme Court of the United States*, vol. 2, *Foundations of Power: John Marshall, 1801–1815* (1981); C. William Hill, *The Political Theory of John Taylor* (1977); Ray W. Irwin, *Diplomatic Relations of the United States with the Barbary Powers* (1931); Robert M. Johnstone, Jr., *Jefferson and the Presidency: Leadership in the Young Republic* (1978); Linda K. Kerber, *Federalists in Dissent* (1970); Ralph Ketcham, *Presidents Above Party: The First American Presidency, 1789–1829* (1984); Shaw Livermore, *The Twilight of Federalism* (1962); Drew McCoy, *The Elusive Republic: Political Economy in Jeffersonian America* (1980); Forrest McDonald, *The Presidency of Thomas Jefferson* (1976); David M. Mayer, *The Constitutional Thought of Thomas Jefferson* (1994); R. Kent Newmyer, *The Supreme Court Under Marshall and Taney* (1968); Howard B. Rock, *Artisans of the New Republic: The Tradesmen of New York City in the Age of Jefferson* (1979); Robert E. Shalhope, *John Taylor of Caroline: Pastoral Republican* (1980); Daniel Sisson, *The American Revolution of 1800* (1974); Marshall Smelser, *The Democratic Republic, 1801–1815* (1968); Charles G. Steffen, *The Mechanics of Baltimore: Workers and Politics in the Age of Revolution* (1984); Shannon C. Stimson, *The American Revolution in the Law: Anglo-American Jurisprudence Before John Marshall* (1990); Robert W. Tucker and David C. Hendrickson, *Empire of Liberty: The Statecraft of Thomas Jefferson* (1990); Leonard D. White, *The Jeffersonians: A Study in Administrative History, 1801–1829* (1951); James S. Young, *The Washington Community, 1800–1828* (1966).

The American Eagle Challenges the French Tiger and the British Shark

James Banner, *To the Hartford Convention* (1970); Samuel Flagg Bemis, *John Quincy Adams and the Foundations of American Foreign Policy* (1949); Roger H. Brown, *The Republic in Peril: 1812* (1964); Gregory Dowd, *A Spirited Resistance: The North American Indian Struggle for Unity* (1991); H. S. Halbert and T. H. Ball, *The Creek War of 1813 and 1814* (1969); David S. Heidler and Jeanne T. Heidler, eds., *Encyclopedia of the War of 1812* (1997); Reginald Horsman, *The Causes of the War of 1812* (1962); Drew R. McCoy, *The Last of the Fathers: James Madison and the Republican Legacy* (1989); Bradford Perkins, *Castlereagh and Adams: England and the United States, 1812–1823* (1964), and *Prologue to War: England and the United States, 1805–1812* (1961); Robert A. Rutland, *Madison's Alternatives: The Jeffersonian Republicans and the Coming of War* (1975), and *The Presidency of James Madison* (1990); R. A. Rutland, ed., *James Madison and the American Nation* (1994); Burton Spivak, *Jefferson's English Crisis: Commerce, Embargo, and the Republican Revolution* (1979); J. C. A. Stagg, *Mr. Madison's War: Politics, Diplomacy, and Warfare in the Early American Republic, 1783–1830* (1983).

Biographies

Leonard Baker, *John Marshall: A Life in Law* (1974); Alexander Balinky, *Albert Gallatin: Fiscal Theories and Policies* (1958); Lance Banning, *The Sacred Fire of Liberty: James Madison and the Founding of the American Republic* (1995); Irving Brant, *James Madison*, 6 vols. (1941–1961); Fawn M. Brodie, *Thomas Jefferson: An Intimate History* (1974); Andrew Burstein, *The Inner Jefferson* (1995); Noble E. Cunningham, Jr., *In Pursuit of Reason: The Life of Thomas Jefferson* (1987); R. David Edmunds, *Shawnee Prophet* (1983), and *Tecumseh and the Quest for Indian Leadership* (1984); Joseph J. Ellis, *American Sphinx: The Character of Thomas Jefferson* (1997); Ralph Ketcham, *James Madison* (1971); Milton Lomask, *Aaron Burr*, 2 vols. (1979–1982); Dumas Malone, *Jefferson and His Time*, 6 vols. (1948–1981); Drew R. McCoy, *The Last of the Fathers: James Madison and the Republican Legacy* (1989); John C. Miller, *Alexander Hamilton* (1959); Broadus Mitchell, *Alexander Hamilton*, 2 vols. (1957–1963); Merrill Peterson, *The Jefferson Image in the American Mind* (1960); M. Peterson, *Thomas Jefferson and the New Nation* (1970); Arnold A. Rogow, *A Fatal Friendship: Alexander Hamilton and Aaron Burr* (1998); Robert Allen Rutland, *James Madison* (1987); Ernest Spaulding, *His Excellency George Clinton* (1938); Raymond Walters, Jr., *Albert Gallatin: Jeffersonian Financier and Diplomat* (1957).

Internet Resources

Thomas Jefferson
http://www.pbs.org/jefferson/
A companion site to the Public Broadcasting Service series on Jefferson, especially important because it contains a fine collection of other people's view of Jefferson.

Some Writings of Thomas Jefferson
http://www.geocities.com/Athens/Forum/9061/USA/early/jeff.html
This site features many of Jefferson's noted writings as well as some that are less well known.

Thomas Jefferson on Politics and Government
http://etext.virginia.edu/jefferson/quotations/
Selected quotations from Jefferson that reveal a strong libertarian bent make up this topical Web site.

Thomas Jefferson Online Resources at the University of Virginia
http://etext.virginia.edu/jefferson/
Mr. Jefferson's University—the University of Virginia—houses this site with numerous online resources about Jefferson and his times.

The Jefferson Bibliography Database
http://etext.virginia.edu/jefferson/bibliog/
This invaluable site compiles and annotates a bibliography of works on Jefferson from 1826 to 1990.

Lewis and Clark PBS Web Site from PBS
http://www.pbs.org/lewisandclark/
This is a companion site to Ken Burns' documentary containing a timeline of the expedition, a collection of related links, a bibliography, and over 800 minutes of unedited, full-length RealPlayer interviews with seven experts featured in the film.

The War of 1812
http://members.tripod.com/~war1812/index.html
In-depth and varied information about the War of 1812.

Key Terms

John Marshall   (p. 215)
Judiciary Act of 1801   (p. 216)
Marbury v. *Madison*   (p. 216)
Judicial Review   (p. 216)
Toussaint Louverture   (p. 218)
Impressment   (p. 221)
Embargo of 1807   (p. 221)
James Madison   (p. 221)
Non-Intercourse Act   (p. 221)
Macon's Bill No. 2   (p. 221)
Andrew Jackson   (p. 226)
War of 1812   (p. 227)
Hartford Convention   (p. 227)

Review Questions

1. In what ways did Thomas Jefferson seek to conciliate the Federalists after he became president? In what ways did he implement his own principles?
2. What steps did President Jefferson take to reduce Federalist influence over the judiciary?

3. Why is *Marbury* v. *Madison* a landmark in American legal history?
4. How did Britain and France threaten American shipping? What steps did President Jefferson and President Madison take to pressure the French and British to recognize American neutrality?
5. Who favored war with Britain in 1812 and why? Who opposed the war and why?
6. Why did the United States fare poorly during the early stages of the War of 1812? Why was the United States ultimately able to fight Britain to a draw?
7. What was the significance of the War of 1812?

9

NATIONALISM, ECONOMIC GROWTH, AND THE ROOTS OF SECTIONAL CONFLICT, 1815–1824

THE GROWTH OF AMERICAN NATIONALISM
  Neo-Hamiltonianism
  Strengthening American Finances
  Protecting American Industry
  Conquering Space
  Judicial Nationalism
  Defending American Interests in Foreign Affairs

THE GROWTH OF THE AMERICAN ECONOMY
  Accelerating Transportation
  Speeding Communications
  Transforming American Law
  Resistance to Technological Innovation
  Early Industrialization
  The Growth of Cities

THE GROWTH OF POLITICAL FACTIONALISM AND SECTIONALISM
  The Panic of 1819
  The Missouri Crisis

"No smoking, drinking, or swearing"

As the year 1810 began, Francis Cabot Lowell, a 36-year-old Boston importer, was bitterly discouraged. His health was failing and, as a result of war between Britain and France and the U.S. policy of discouraging trade by embargo and other legislation, his importing business was in ruins. Uncertain about which way to turn, he decided to travel abroad. While overseas, he discovered his life's calling. In Britain, he marveled at textile factories at Manchester. Although it was illegal to export textile machinery or plans, Lowell carefully studied the power looms and secretly made sketches of the designs.

Upon his return to Boston in 1813, Lowell constructed textile machinery superior to any he had seen in England. The next year, in Waltham, Massachusetts, he and two associates spent a half million dollars to build the world's first factory able to convert raw cotton into cloth by power machinery under one roof.

To staff his new textile mill, Lowell chose a labor force different from that found in any previous factory. Determined to avoid the misery of England's textile mills, Lowell recruited his labor force not from the families of the poor or from young children but from among the virtuous daughters of New England farmers, who agreed to work in Lowell's mill for two or three years as a way of earning a dowry or an independent income. Because spinning and weaving had long been performed by women in the home, and because young women were willing to work for half or a third the wages of young men, they seemed to offer a perfect solution to the factory's labor needs.

To break down the prejudice against factory work as degrading and immoral, the company announced that it would employ only women of good moral character. It threatened to fire any employee guilty of smoking, drinking, lying, swearing, or any other immoral conduct. To keep a close watch over employees' moral character, the company required employees to attend church and provided boardinghouses where mill girls lived under the careful supervision of housekeepers of impeccable character. Within a few years, the new factory was overwhelmed with job applicants and was "more puzzled to get rid of hands than to employ them."

The opening of the Boston Manufacturing Company's textile mill in 1814 marked a symbolic beginning to a new era in the nation's history. For Americans, the end of the War of 1812 unleashed a surge of nationalism, dramatic industrial growth, and rapid expansion to the West. In the years ahead, the United States would undergo an economic transformation, symbolized by improvements in transportation and agriculture, rapid urban growth, and many technological innovations.

In the aftermath of the war, patriotic fervor swept aside bitter political and sectional divisions. Intense nationalism was apparent in the adoption of programs to promote national economic growth, a series of Supreme Court decisions establishing the supremacy of the federal government and expanding the powers of Congress, and the proud assertion of American interest and power in foreign policy.

Paradoxically, it was during these years of nationalism and growth, known to contemporaries as the **Era of Good Feelings,** that sectional and political conflicts were exacerbated. Westward expansion, the rapid growth of industry in the North, and the strengthening of the federal government created problems that dominated American political life for the next 40 years.

The new textile mills offered a source of income to daughters of New England farmers.

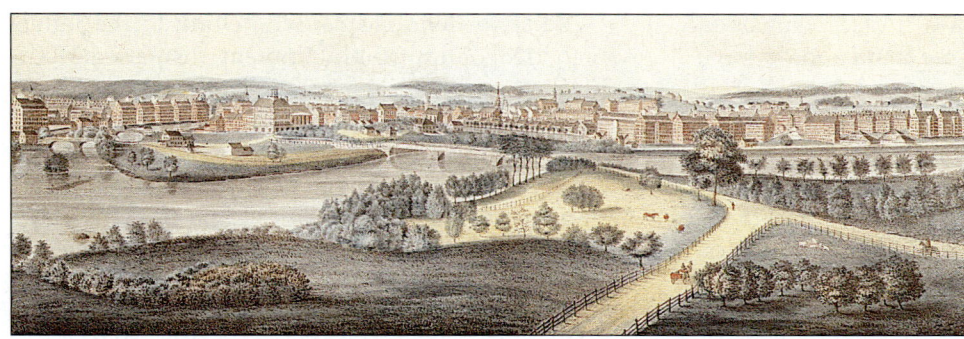

Lowell, Massachusetts, along the Merrimack River, was one of the first American mill towns.

THE GROWTH OF AMERICAN NATIONALISM

Early in the summer of 1817, as a conciliatory gesture toward the Federalists who had opposed the War of 1812, **James Monroe,** the nation's fifth president, embarked on a goodwill tour through the North. Everywhere Monroe went, citizens greeted him warmly, holding parades and banquets in his honor. In Federalist Boston, a crowd of 40,000 welcomed the Republican president. John Quincy Adams expressed amazement at the acclaim with which the president

THE PEOPLE SPEAK

Growing Up Female in the Early Republic

During the early nineteenth century, a new life stage emerged. Called "girlhood," it was a period of relative independence when a growing number of young women attended school or worked outside of a home. In her autobiography, the poet Lucy Larcom describes her girlhood and the growing expectation that young women had to prepare themselves for an independent life. After her father's death when she was 11, Lucy had to leave school and go to work in a Lowell, Massachusetts, textile mill. At first, she found mill work exciting, but she soon felt frustrated by the routine and the lack of education.

> It was not in my mother's nature closely to calculate costs, and in this way there came to be a continually increasing leak in the family purse. The older members of the family did everything they could, but it was not enough. I heard it said one day, in a distressed tone, "The children will have to leave school and go into the mill" . . .
>
> I thought it would be a pleasure to feel that I was not a trouble or a burden or expense to anybody. So I went to my first day's work in the mill with a light heart. The novelty of it made it seem easy, and it really was not hard, just to change the bobbins on the spinning-frames every three quarters of an hour or so, with half a dozen other little girls who were doing the same thing. . . .
>
> And for a little while it was only a new amusement; I liked it better than going to school and "making believe" I was learning when I was not. . . .
>
> I never cared much for the machinery. The buzzing and hissing and whizzing of pulleys and rollers and spindles and flyers around me often grew tiresome. . . .
>
> There were compensation for being shut in to daily toil so early. The mill itself had its lessons for us. But it was not, and could not be, the right sort of life for a child, and we were happy in the knowledge that, at the longest, our employment was only to be temporary. . . .
>
> But alas! I could not go [to high school]. The little money I could earn—one dollar a week, beside the price of my board—was needed in the family. . . .
>
> In the older times it was seldom said to little girls, as it always has been said to boys, that they ought to have some definite plan, while they were children, what to be and do when they were grown up. There was usually but one path open before them, to become good wives and housekeepers. . . . But girls, as well as boys, must often have been conscious of their own peculiar capabilities,—must have desired to make use of their individual powers. When I was growing up, they had already begun to be encouraged to do so.

Lucy Larcom, *A New England Girlhood* (Boston: Houghton Mifflin and Co., 1889), pp. 42–45, 120–121, 152–157.

was greeted: "Party spirit has indeed subsided throughout the Union to a degree that I should have thought scarcely possible."

A Federalist newspaper, reflecting on the end of party warfare and the renewal of national unity, called the times the "Era of Good Feelings." The phrase accurately describes the period of James Monroe's presidency, which, at least in its early years, was marked by a relative absence of political strife and opposition. With the collapse of the Federalist party, the Jeffersonian Republicans dominated national politics. Reflecting a new spirit of political unity, the Republicans adopted many of the nationalistic policies of their former opponents, establishing a second national bank, a protective tariff, and improvements in transportation.

To the American people, James Monroe was the popular symbol of the Era of Good Feelings. A dignified and formal man, Monroe was the last president to don the fashions of the eighteenth century. He wore his hair in a powdered wig tied in a queue and dressed himself in a cocked hat, a black broadcloth tailcoat, knee breeches, long white stockings, and buckled shoes. His political values, too, were those of an earlier day. Like George Washington, Monroe worked to eliminate party and sectional rivalries by his attitudes and behavior. He hoped for a country without political parties, governed by leaders chosen on their merits. So great was his popularity that he won a second presidential term by an electoral college vote of 231 to 1. A new era of national unity appeared to have dawned.

Neo-Hamiltonianism

Traditionally, the Republican party stood for limited government, states' rights, and a strict interpretation of the Constitution. By 1815, however, the party had adopted former Federalist positions on a national bank, protective tariffs, a standing army, and national roads.

In a series of policy recommendations to Congress at the end of the War of 1812, President Madison revealed the extent to which Republicans had adopted Federalist policies. He called for a program of national economic development directed by the central government, which included creation of a second Bank of the United States to provide for a stable currency, a protective tariff to encourage industry, a program of internal improvements to facilitate transportation, and a permanent 20,000-man army. In subsequent messages, he recommended an extensive system of roads and canals, new military academies, and establishment of a national university in Washington.

Old-style Republicans, who clung to the Jeffersonian ideal of limited government, dismissed Madison's proposals, but his nationalistic program found enthusiastic support among the new generation of political leaders. Convinced that inadequate roads, the lack of a national bank, and dependence on foreign imports had nearly resulted in a British victory in the war, these young leaders were eager to use the federal government to promote national economic development.

Henry Clay, John C. Calhoun, and Daniel Webster were the principal leaders of the second generation of American political life—the period stretching from the War of 1812 to almost the eve of the Civil War. Each was destined to become the preeminent spokesman of his region—Clay of the West, Calhoun of the South, Webster of the North. Each possessed extraordinary oratorical talent. Each served in the cabinet as secretary of state or secretary of war. They died within a few months of each other in the early 1850s.

The leader of this group was **Henry Clay,** a Republican from Kentucky. Clay was one of the so-called War Hawks who had urged President Madison to wage war against Britain. After the war, Clay became one of the strongest proponents of an active federal role in national economic development. He used his position as Speaker of the House to advance an economic program that he later called the "American System." According to this plan, the federal government would erect a high protective tariff to keep out foreign goods, stimulate the growth of industry, and create a large urban market for western and southern farmers. Revenue from the tariff, in turn, would be used to finance internal improvements of roads and canals to stimulate the growth of the South and West.

Another leader of postwar nationalism was **John C. Calhoun,** a Republican from South Carolina. Calhoun, like Clay, entered Congress in 1811 and later served with distinction as secretary of war under Monroe and as vice president under both John Quincy Adams and Andrew Jackson. Later, Calhoun became the nation's leading exponent of states' rights, but at this point he seemed to John Quincy Adams, "above all sectional and factious prejudices more than any other statesman of this Union..."

The other dominant political figure of the era was **Daniel Webster.** Nicknamed "the Godlike Daniel" for his magnificent speaking style, Webster argued 168 cases before the Supreme Court. When he entered Congress as a Massachusetts Federalist, he opposed the War of 1812, the creation of a second national bank, and a protectionist tariff. But, later in his career, after industrial interests supplanted shipping and importing interests in the Northeast, Webster became a staunch defender of the national bank and a

Eager to use the federal government to promote economic development, young politicians Senator Henry Clay of Kentucky (left), Congressman John C. Calhoun of South Carolina, (center), and Senator Daniel Webster of Massachusetts (right) supported a protective tariff to stimulate industry, a national bank to promote economic growth, and federally funded aid for transportation. Calhoun, elected to the Senate from South Carolina in 1832, became the nation's leading defender of states' rights, even defending his state's asserted right to "nullify" federal law within its territory.

high tariff and perhaps was the nation's strongest exponent of nationalism and strongest critic of states' rights. His argument that the United States was not only a union of states but a union of people—would later be developed by Abraham Lincoln.

Strengthening American Finances

The severe financial problems created by the War of 1812 led to a wave of support for the creation of a second national bank. The demise of the first Bank of the United States just before the War of 1812 had left the nation ill-equipped to deal with the war's financial demands. To finance the war effort, the government borrowed from private banks at high interest rates. As demand for credit rose, the private banks issued bank notes greatly exceeding the amount of gold or silver that they held. One Rhode Island bank issued $580,000 in notes backed up by only $86.48 in gold and silver. The result was high inflation. Prices jumped 40 percent in just two years.

To make matters worse, the United States government was unable to redeem millions of dollars deposited in private banks. In 1814, after the British burned the nation's capital, many banks outside of New England stopped redeeming their notes in gold or silver. Soldiers, army contractors, and government securities holders went unpaid, and the Treasury temporarily went bankrupt. After the war was over, many banks still refused to resume payments in gold or silver.

In 1816, Congress voted by a narrow margin to charter a second Bank of the United States for 20 years and give it the privilege of holding government funds without paying interest for their use. Supporters of a second national bank argued that it would provide a safe place to deposit government funds and a convenient mechanism for transferring money between states. Supporters also claimed that a national bank would promote monetary stability by regulating private banks. A national bank would strengthen the banking system by refusing to accept the notes issued by overspeculative private banks and ensuring that bank notes were readily exchangeable for gold or silver. Opposition to a national bank came largely from private banking interests and traditional Jeffersonians, who considered a national bank to be unconstitutional and a threat to republican government.

Protecting American Industry

The War of 1812 provided tremendous stimulus to American manufacturing. It encouraged American manufacturers to produce goods previously imported from overseas. By 1816, 100,000 factory work-

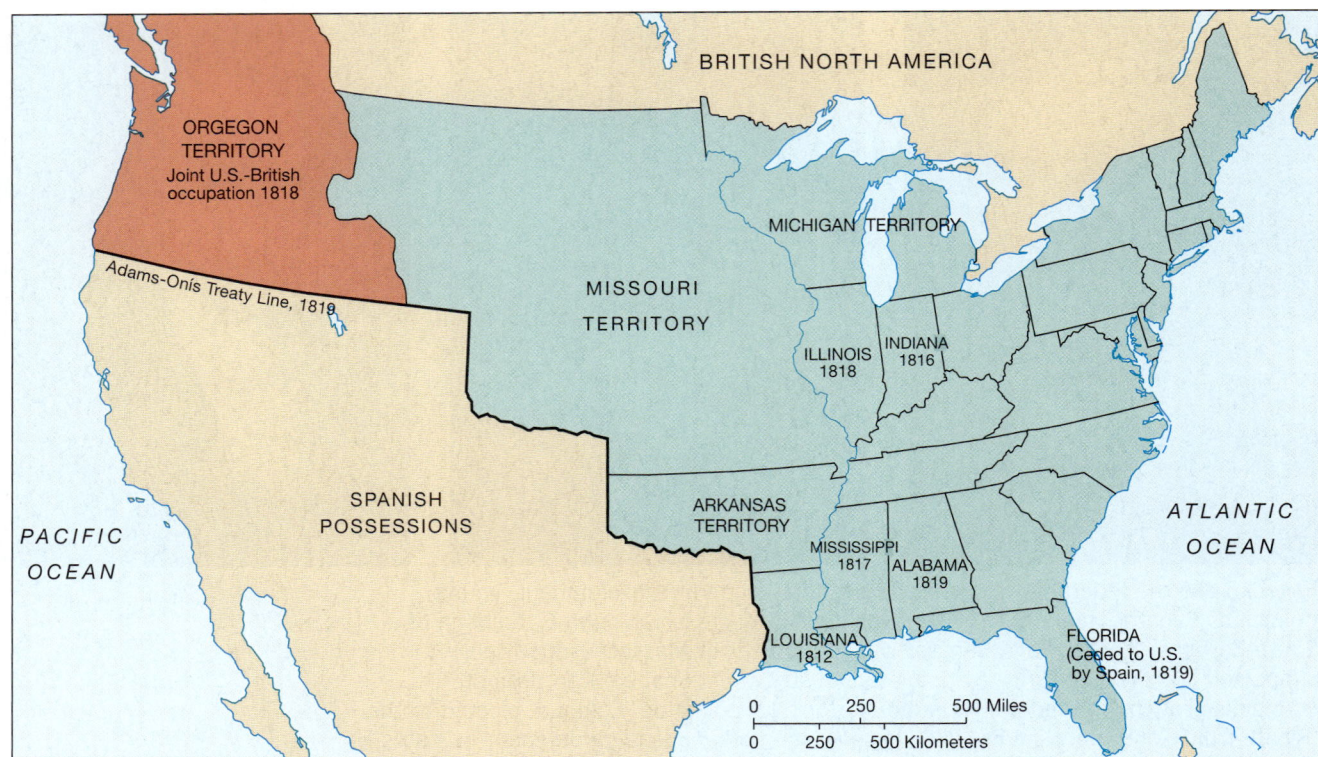

The United States in 1819

ers, two-thirds of them women and children, produced more than $40 million worth of manufactured goods a year. Capital investment in textile manufacturing, sugar refining, and other industries totaled $100 million.

Following the war, however, cheap British imports flooded the nation, threatening to undermine local industries. Congress responded to the flood of imports by continuing a tariff set during the War of 1812 to protect America's infant industries from low-cost competition. With import duties ranging from 15 to 30 percent on cotton, textiles, leather, paper, pig iron, wool, and other goods, the tariff promised to protect America's growing industries from foreign competition. Shipping and farming interests opposed the tariff on the grounds that it would make foreign goods more expensive to buy and would provoke foreign retaliation.

Conquering Space

Prior to 1812, westward expansion had proceeded slowly. Most Americans were nestled along the Atlantic coastline. More than two-thirds of the new nation's population still lived within 50 miles of the Atlantic seaboard, and the center of population rested within 18 miles of Baltimore. Only two roads cut across the Allegheny Mountains, and no more than half a million pioneers had moved as far west as Kentucky, Tennessee, Ohio, or the western portion of Pennsylvania. Cincinnati was a town of 15,000 people; Buffalo and Rochester, New York, did not yet exist. Kickapoos, Miamis, Wyandots, and other Native-American peoples populated the areas that would become the states of Illinois, Indiana, Michigan, and Wisconsin, while Cherokees, Chickasaws, Choctaws, and Creeks considered the future states of Alabama, Mississippi, and western Georgia their territory.

Between 1803, when Ohio was admitted to the Union, and the beginning of the War of 1812, not a single new state was carved out of the west. Thomas Jefferson estimated in 1803 that it would be a thousand years before settlers occupied the region between the Alleghenies and the Mississippi.

The end of the War of 1812 unleashed a rush of pioneers to Indiana, Illinois, Ohio, northern Georgia, western North Carolina, Alabama, Mississippi, Louisiana, and Tennessee. Congress quickly admitted five states to the Union: Louisiana in 1812, Indiana in 1816, Mississippi in 1817, Illinois in 1818, and Alabama in 1819. Pioneers demanded cheaper land and clamored for better transportation to move goods to eastern markets.

Farmers demanded that Congress revise legislation to make it easier to obtain land. Originally, Congress viewed federal lands as a source of revenue, and public land policies reflected that view. Under a policy adopted in 1785 and reaffirmed in 1796, the federal government only sold land in blocks of at least 640 acres. Although the minimum allotment was reduced to 320 acres in 1800, federal land policy continued to retard sales and concentrate ownership in the hands of a few large land companies and wealthy speculators.

In 1820 Congress sought to make it easier for farmers to purchase homesteads in the west by selling land in small lots suitable for operation by a family. Congress reduced the minimum allotment offered for sale from 320 to 80 acres. The minimum price per acre fell from $2 to $1.25. The second Bank of the United States encouraged land purchases by liberally extending credit. The result was a boom in land sales. For a decade, the government sold approximately a million acres of land annually.

Westward expansion also created a demand to expand and improve the nation's roads and canals. In 1808 Albert Gallatin, Thomas Jefferson's Treasury secretary, proposed a $20 million program of canal and road construction. As a result of state and sectional jealousies and charges that federal aid to transportation was unconstitutional, the federal government funded only a single turnpike, the National Road, at this time stretching from Cumberland, Maryland, to Wheeling, Virginia (later West Virginia), but much later extending westward from Baltimore through Ohio and Indiana to Illinois.

In 1816 John C. Calhoun introduced a new proposal for federal aid for road and canal construction. Failure to link the nation together with an adequate system of transportation would, Calhoun warned, lead "to the greatest of calamities—disunion." "Let us," he exclaimed, "bind the republic together with a perfect system of roads and canals. Let us conquer space." Narrowly, Calhoun's proposal passed. But on the day before he left office, Madison vetoed the bill on constitutional grounds.

Despite this setback, Congress did adopt major parts of the nationalist neo-Hamiltonian economic program. It had established a second Bank of the United States to provide a stable means of issuing money and a safe depository for federal funds. It had enacted a tariff to raise duties on foreign imports and guard American industries from low-cost competition. It had also instituted a new public land policy to encourage western settlement. In short, Congress had translated the spirit of national pride and unity that the nation felt after the War of 1812 into a legislative program that placed the national interest above narrow sectional interests.

Judicial Nationalism

The decisions of the Supreme Court also reflected the nationalism of the postwar period. With John Marshall as chief justice, the Supreme Court greatly expanded its powers, prestige, and independence. When Marshall took office, in the last days of John Adams's administration in 1801, the Court met in the basement of the Capitol and was rarely in session for more than six weeks a year. Since its creation in 1789, the Court had only decided 100 cases.

In a series of critical decisions, the Supreme Court greatly expanded its authority. As previously noted (p. 216), *Marbury* v. *Madison* (1803) established the Supreme Court as the final arbiter of the Constitution and its power to declare acts of Congress unconstitutional. *Fletcher* v. *Peck* (1810) declared the Court's power to void state laws. *Martin* v. *Hunter's Lessee* (1816) gave the Court the power to review decisions by state courts.

After the War of 1812, Marshall wrote a series of decisions that further strengthened the powers of the national government. ***McCulloch v. Maryland*** (1819) established the constitutionality of the second Bank of the United States and denied to states the right to exert independent checks on federal authority. The case involved a direct attack on the second Bank of the United States by the state of Maryland, which had placed a tax on the bank notes of all banks not chartered by the state.

In his decision, Marshall dealt with two fundamental questions. The first was whether the federal government had the power to incorporate a bank. The answer to this question, the Court ruled, was yes because the Constitution granted Congress implied

The Conestoga wagon carried people and goods in the rush of westward expansion. Settlers moved west and north along the Ohio and Mississippi rivers before moving to open farmlands further inland.

John Marshall established many basic principles of constitutional law in the 34 years he served as chief justice of the United States. Marshall and the six other members of the Supreme Court appear on the podium in this 1822 painting of the House of Representatives by Samuel F. B. Morse.

powers to do whatever was "necessary and proper" to carry out its constitutional powers—in this case, the power to manage a currency. In a classic statement of "broad" or "loose" construction of the Constitution, Marshall said, "Let the end be legitimate, let it be within the scope of the Constitution, and all means which are plainly adapted to that end, which are not prohibited, but consistent with the letter and spirit of the Constitution, are constitutional."

The second question raised was whether a state had the power to tax a branch of the Bank of the United States. In answer to this question, the Court said no. The Constitution, the Court asserted, created a new government with sovereign power over the states. "The power to tax involves the power to destroy," the Court declared, and the states do not have the right to exert an independent check on the authority of the federal government.

During the postwar period, the Supreme Court also encouraged economic competition and development. In *Dartmouth v. Woodward* (1819) the Court promoted business growth by establishing the principle of sanctity of contracts. The case involved the efforts of the New Hampshire legislature to alter the charter of Dartmouth College, which had been granted by George III in 1769. The Court held that a charter was a valid contract protected by the Constitution and that states do not have the power to alter contracts unilaterally.

In *Gibbons v. Ogden* (1824), the Court broadened federal power over interstate commerce. The Court overturned a New York law that had awarded a monopoly over steamboat traffic on the Hudson River, ruling that the Constitution had specifically given Congress the power to regulate commerce.

Under John Marshall, the Supreme Court became the final arbiter of the constitutionality of federal and state laws. The Court's role in shifting sovereign power from the states to the federal government was an important development. It would become increasingly difficult in the future to argue that the union was a creation of the states, that states could exert an independent check on federal government authority, or that Congress's powers were limited to those specifically conferred by the Constitution.

Defending American Interests in Foreign Affairs

The War of 1812 stirred a new nationalistic spirit in foreign affairs. In 1815, this spirit resulted in a decision to end the raids by the Barbary pirates on American commercial shipping in the Mediterranean. For 17 years the United States had paid tribute to the ruler of Algiers. In March 1815, Captain Stephen Decatur and a fleet of ten ships sailed into the Mediterranean, where they captured two Algerian gunboats, towed the ships into Algiers harbor, and threatened to bombard the city. As a result, all the North African states agreed to treaties releasing American prisoners without ransom, ending all demands for American tribute, and providing compensation for American vessels that had been seized.

After successfully defending American interests in North Africa, Monroe acted to settle old grievances with the British. Britain and the United States had left a host of issues unresolved in the peace treaty ending the War of 1812, including disputes over boundaries, trading and fishing rights, and rival claims to the Oregon region. The two governments moved quickly to settle these issues. The Rush-Bagot Agreement (1817) removed most military ships from the Great Lakes. In 1818, Britain granted American fishermen the right to fish in eastern Canadian waters, agreed to the 49th parallel as the boundary between the United States and Canada from Minnesota to the Rocky Mountains, and consented to joint occupation of the Oregon region.

The critical foreign policy issue facing the United States after the War of 1812 was the fate of Spain's crumbling New World empire. A source of particular concern was Florida, which was still under Spanish control. Pirates, fugitive slaves, and Native Americans used Florida as a sanctuary and as a jumping off point for raids on settlements in Georgia. In December 1817, to end these incursions, Monroe authorized General Andrew Jackson to lead a punitive expedition against the Seminole Indians in Florida. Jackson not only attacked the Seminoles and destroyed their villages but overthrew the Spanish governor. He also court-martialed and executed two British citizens whom he accused of inciting the Seminoles to commit atrocities against Americans.

Jackson's actions provoked a furor in Washington. Spain protested Jackson's acts and demanded that he be punished. Secretary of War John C. Calhoun and other members of Monroe's cabinet urged the president to reprimand Jackson for acting without specific authorization. In Congress, Henry Clay called for Jackson's censure. Secretary of State Adams, however, saw in Jackson's actions an opportunity to wrest Florida from Spain.

Instead of apologizing for Jackson's conduct, Adams declared that the Florida raid was a legitimate act of self-defense. Adams informed the Spanish government that it would either have to police Florida effectively or cede it to the United States. Convinced that American annexation was inevitable, Spain ceded Florida to the United States in the Adams-Onis Treaty of 1819. In return, the United States agreed to honor $5 million in damage claims by Americans against Spain, and renounced, at least temporarily, its claims to Texas.

At the same time, European intervention in the Pacific Northwest and Latin America threatened to become a new source of anxiety for American leaders. In 1821, Russia claimed control of the entire Pacific coast from Alaska to Oregon and closed the area to foreign shipping. This development coincided with rumors that Spain, with the help of its European allies, was planning to reconquer its former colonies in Latin America. European intervention threatened British as well as American interests. Not only did Britain have a flourishing trade with Latin America, which would decline if Spain regained its New World colonies, but it also occupied the Oregon region jointly with the United States. In 1823, British Foreign Minister George Canning proposed that the United States and Britain jointly announce their opposition to further European intervention in the Americas.

Monroe initially regarded the British proposal favorably. But his secretary of state, John Quincy Adams, opposed a joint Anglo-American declaration. Secure in the knowledge that the British would use their fleet to support the American position, Adams convinced President Monroe to make an independent declaration of American policy. In his annual message to Congress in 1823, Monroe outlined the principles that have become known as the **Monroe Doctrine.** He announced that the Western Hemisphere was henceforth closed to any further European colonization, declaring that the United States would regard any attempt by European nations "to extend their system to any portion of this hemisphere as dangerous to our peace and safety." European countries with possessions in the hemisphere—Britain, France, the Netherlands, and Spain—were warned not to attempt expansion. Monroe also said that the United States would not interfere in internal European affairs.

For the American people, the Monroe Doctrine was the proud symbol of American hegemony in the Western Hemisphere. Unilaterally, the United States had defined its rights and interests in the New World. It is true that during the first half of the nineteenth century the United States lacked the military power to enforce the Monroe Doctrine and depended on the British navy to deter European intervention in the Americas, but the nation had clearly warned the European powers that any threat to American security would provoke American retaliation.

THE GROWTH OF THE AMERICAN ECONOMY

At the beginning of the nineteenth century, the United States was an overwhelmingly rural and agricultural nation. Most Americans lived on farms or in villages with fewer than 2500 inhabitants. The nation's population was small and scattered over a vast geographical area—just 5.3 million, compared to Britain's 15 million and France's 27 million.

Transportation and communications had changed little over the previous half-century. A coach ride between Boston and New York took three days. South of the Mason-Dixon line, except for a single stagecoach that traveled between Charleston and Savannah, no public transportation of any kind could be found.

American houses, clothing, and agricultural methods were surprisingly primitive. Fifty miles inland, half the houses were log cabins, lacking even glass windows. Farmers planted their crops in much the same way as had their parents and grandparents. Few farmers practiced crop rotation or used fertilizers or drained fields. They made plows out of wood, allowed their swine to run loose, and left their cattle outside except on the coldest nights.

Manufacturing was also still quite backward. In rural areas, farm families grew their own food, produced their own soap and candles, wove their own blankets, and constructed their own furniture. The leading manufacturing industries, iron making, textiles, and clothes making, employed only about 15,000 people in mills or factories.

After the War of 1812, however, the American economy grew at an astonishing rate. The 25 years that followed Andrew Jackson's victory at New Orleans represented a critical period for the nation's economic growth, during which the United States overcame a series of serious obstacles that had stood in the way of sustained economic expansion. Improved transportation, rapid urbanization, increased farm productivity, and technological innovation transformed a rural, agricultural nation into one of the world's industrial leaders.

Accelerating Transportation

At the outset of the nineteenth century, the lack of reliable, low-cost transportation was a major barrier to American industrial development. The stagecoach, slow and cumbersome, was the main form of transportation. Twelve passengers, crowded along with their bags and parcels, traveled at just 4 miles an hour. In Connecticut and Massachusetts, Sunday travel was still forbidden by law.

Wretched roads plagued travelers. Larger towns had roads paved with cobblestones, but most roads were simply dirt paths left muddy and rutted by rain. The presence of tree stumps in the middle of many roads posed a serious obstacle to carriages. Charles Dickens aptly described American roads as a "series of alternate swamps and gravel pits."

In 1791 builders first inaugurated a new era in transportation with the construction of a 66-mile-long turnpike between Philadelphia and Lancaster, Pennsylvania. This stimulated a craze for toll road construction. By 1811, 135 private companies in New York had invested $7.5 million in 1500 miles of road. By 1838, Pennsylvania had invested $37 million to build 2200 miles of turnpikes.

Despite the construction of turnpikes, the cost of transporting freight over land remained high. Because water transportation was cheaper, farmers often shipped their produce down the Mississippi, Potomac, or Hudson rivers by flatboat or raft. Unfortunately, water transportation was slow and few vessels were capable of going very far upstream. The trip downstream from Pittsburgh to New Orleans took a month; the trip upstream against the current took four months. Steam power offered the obvious solution, and inventors built at least 16 steamships before Robert Fulton successfully demonstrated the commercial practicality of steam navigation. In 1807 he sailed a 160-ton side-wheeler, the *Clermont*, 150 miles from New York City to Albany in only 32 hours. "Fulton's folly," as critics mockingly called it, opened a new era of faster and cheaper water transportation.

The building of canals further revolutionized water transportation. In 1825, the state of New York opened the Erie Canal, which connected the Great Lakes to the Atlantic Ocean. The canal was a stupendous engineering achievement. Three thousand workers, using hand labor, toiled for 8 years to build the canal. They built 84 locks, each 15 feet wide and 90 feet long, to raise or lower barges 10 feet at a time.

The main form of public transportation in the early nineteenth century was the stagecoach. Unprotected from the weather, 12 passengers traveled with baggage between their knees at only 4 miles per hour.
Rogers Fund, 2942 Metropolitan Museum of Art.

In 1807, Robert Fulton demonstrated the feasibility of steam travel by launching his 160-ton side-wheeler, the *Clermont*, on the Hudson river.

Built almost entirely with state and local funding, "Clinton's Ditch"—named after the Erie Canal's chief backer, Governor DeWitt Clinton—sparked an economic revolution. Before the canal was built, it cost $100 and took 20 days to transport a ton of freight from Buffalo to New York City. After the canal was opened, the cost fell to $5 a ton and transit time was reduced to 6 days. By 1827, as a result of the canal, wheat from central New York state could be bought for less in Savannah, Georgia, than wheat grown in Georgia's interior.

The success of the Erie Canal led other states to embark on expensive programs of canal building. Pennsylvanians spent $10 million to build a canal between Philadelphia and Pittsburgh. The states of Illinois, Indiana, and Ohio launched projects to connect the Ohio and Mississippi rivers to the Great Lakes. By 1840, 3326 miles of canals had been dug at a cost of $125 million.

Cities like Baltimore and Boston that were unable to reach the West with canals experimented with the railroad, a novel form of transportation. Early railroads suffered from nagging engineering problems and vociferous opposition. Brakes were wholly inadequate, consisting of wooden blocks operated by a foot pedal. Boilers exploded so frequently that passengers had to be protected by bales of cotton. Engine sparks set fire to fields and burned unprotected passengers. One English traveler counted 13 holes burned in her dress after a short ride.

Vested interests, including turnpike and bridge companies, stagecoaches, ferries, and canals, sought laws to prohibit trains from carrying freight. A group of Boston doctors warned that bumps produced by trains traveling at 15 or 20 miles an hour would lead to many cases of "concussion of the brain." An Ohio school board declared that "such things as railroads ... are impossibilities and rank infidelity."

Nonetheless, it quickly became clear after 1830 that railroads were destined to become the nation's chief means of moving freight. During the 1830s, construction companies laid down 3328 miles of track, roughly equal to all the miles of canals in the country. With an average speed of 10 miles an hour, railroads were faster than stagecoaches, canalboats, and steamboats, and, unlike water-going vessels, could travel in any season.

The greatest engineering feat of the Erie Canal took place at the town of Lockport, where seven locks, each capable of raising or lowering a barge ten feet, were constructed.

Lockport on the Erie Canal, 1832. Munson-Williams-Proctors Institute Museum of Art, Utica, New York.

The transportation revolution sharply reduced the cost of shipping goods to market and stimulated agriculture and industry. New roads, canals, and railroads speeded the pace of commerce and strengthened ties between the East and West.

Speeding Communications

Poor communications had also impeded development. During the 1790s, it took 3 weeks for a letter to travel from New York to Cincinnati or Detroit and 4 weeks to arrive in New Orleans. In 1799 it took 1 week for news of George Washington's death to reach New York City from Virginia.

By the early 1830s, a decade before Samuel F. B. Morse invented the telegraph, the transmission of information had improved considerably as a result of improved roads and faster sailing ships. In 1831 it took just 15.5 hours for the text of Andrew Jackson's State of the Union address to travel from Washington to New York. By 1841 a letter traveled between New York and New Orleans in 9 days and between New York and Cincinnati in 5 days—three times faster than in 1815.

The volume of information transmitted also increased considerably. In 1790 the United States had just 92 newspapers, with a total annual circulation of less than 4 million. By 1820 the number of papers published had jumped to 512, with an annual circulation of 50 million. When Alexis de Tocqueville, a French observer, visited the United States in 1831, he was shocked at the amount of information available even in frontier regions: "I do not think that in the most enlightened rural districts of France there is an intellectual movement either so rapid or on such a scale as in this wilderness."

Transforming American Law

The growth of an industrial economy in the United States required a shift in American law. At the beginning of the nineteenth century, American law was rooted in concepts that reflected the values of a slowly changing, agricultural society. The law presumed that goods and services had a just price, independent of supply and demand. Courts forbade many forms of competition and innovation in the name of a stable society. Courts and judges legally protected monopolies and prevented lenders from charging high rates of interest. The law allowed property owners to sue for damages if a mill built upstream flooded their land or impeded their water supply. After 1815, however, the American legal system favored economic growth, profit, and entrepreneurial enterprise.

By the 1820s, courts, particularly in the Northeast, had begun to abandon many traditional legal doctrines that stood in the way of a competitive market economy. Courts dropped older doctrines that assumed that goods and services had an objective price, independent of supply and demand. Courts rejected many usury laws, which limited interest rates, and increasingly held that only the market could determine interest rates or prices or the equity of a contract.

To promote rapid economic growth, courts and state legislatures gave new powers and privileges to private firms. Companies building roads, bridges, canals, and other public works were given the power to appropriate land; private firms were allowed to avoid legal penalties for fires, floods, or noise they caused on the grounds that the companies served a public purpose. Courts also reduced the liability of companies for injuries to their own employees, ruling that an injured party had to prove negligence or carelessness on the part of an employer in order to collect damages. The legal barriers to economic expansion had been struck down.

Resistance to Technological Innovation

At the beginning of the nineteenth century, the United States lagged far behind Europe in the practical application of science and technology. There was probably just one steam engine in regular operation in the United States in 1800, one hundred years after simple engines had first been used in Europe. Inventors like Oliver Evans, who opened the first automated flour mill in 1785, and Samuel Fitch, who created the first American steamboat in 1786, failed because they were unable to finance their projects or persuade the public to use their inventions.

The inadequate state of higher education also slowed technological innovation. At the beginning of the nineteenth century, Harvard, the nation's most famous college, graduated just 39 men a year, no more than it had graduated in 1720. Harvard's entire undergraduate faculty consisted of the college president, a professor of theology, a professor of mathematics, a professor of Hebrew, and four tutors. All the nation's libraries put together contained barely 50,000 volumes.

By the 1820s, however, the United States had largely overcome resistance to technological innovation. When Friedrich List, a German traveler, visited the United States in the 1820s, he was astonished by the amount of public interest in technology. "Everything new is quickly introduced here," List wrote.

"There is no clinging to old ways; the moment an American hears the word 'invention' he pricks up his ears."

How had Americans overcome resistance to technological innovation? The answer lies in the efforts of literally hundreds of inventors, tinkerers, and amateur scientists, who transformed European ideas into practical technologies. Their inventions inspired in Americans a boundless faith in technology.

Early American technology was pioneered largely by self-taught amateurs, whose zeal and self-assurance led them to create inventions that trained European scientists did not attempt. As early as the 1720s, it was known that electricity could be conducted along a wire to convey messages, but it was not until 1844 that an American artist and inventor named Samuel F. B. Morse demonstrated the practicality of the telegraph and devised a workable code for sending messages. A Frenchman built the first working steamship in 1783, but it was 24 years later that Robert Fulton, an American, produced the first commercially successful steamship. Eighteenth-century Europeans knew that ether would induce unconsciousness, but it was not until 1842 that a Georgia surgeon named Crawford Long used ether as an anesthetic.

Early Industrialization

In the 1820s and 1830s, America became the world's leader in adopting mechanization, standardization, and mass production. Manufacturers started to adopt labor-saving machinery that allowed workers to produce more goods at lower costs. So impressed were foreigners with these methods of manufacture that they called them the **American system of production.**

The single most important figure in the development of the American system of production was **Eli Whitney,** the inventor of the cotton gin. In 1798, Whitney persuaded the U.S. government to award him a contract for 10,000 muskets to be delivered within two years. Until then, rifles had been manufactured by skilled artisans, who made individual parts by hand and then carefully fitted the pieces together. When Whitney made his offer, the federal arsenal at Springfield, Massachusetts, was capable of producing only 245 muskets in two years. Whitney's idea was to develop precision machinery that would allow a worker with little manual skill to manufacture identical gun parts that would be interchangeable from one gun to another. The first year he produced 500 muskets.

Other industries soon adopted the American system of production. As early as 1800 manufacturers of wooden clocks began to use interchangeable parts. Makers of sewing machines used mass production techniques as early as 1846, and the next year, manufacturers mechanized the production of farm machinery.

Innovation was not confined to manufacturing. During the years following the War of 1812, American agriculture underwent a transformation nearly as profound and far-reaching as the revolution taking place in industry. No longer cut off from markets by the high cost of transportation, farmers began to grow larger crop surpluses and to specialize in cash crops. A growing demand for cotton for England's textile mills led to the introduction of long-staple cotton from the West Indies into the islands and lowlands of Georgia and South Carolina. Eli Whitney's invention of the cotton gin in 1793—which permitted an individual to clean 50 pounds of short-staple cotton in a single day, 50 times more than could be

With Eli Whitney's cotton gin, the amount of cotton fiber that a slave could separate from seed each day increased from 1 pound to 50 pounds.

This painting, dated 1832–1834, by Russell Smith depicts a saltworks, one of the leading industrial enterprises of the early nineteenth century.

cleaned by hand—made it practical to produce the crop in the South. Other cash crops raised by southern farmers included rice, sugar, flax for linen, and hemp for rope fibers. In the Northeast, the growth of mill towns and urban centers created a growing demand for hogs, cattle, sheep, corn, wheat, wool, butter, milk, cheese, fruit, vegetables, and hay to feed horses.

As production for the market increased, farmers began to demand improved farm technology. In 1793 Charles Newbold, a New Jersey farmer, spent his entire fortune of $30,000 developing an efficient cast-iron plow. Farmers refused to use it, fearing that iron would poison the soil and cause weeds to grow. Twenty years later, a Scipio, New York, farmer named Jethro Wood patented an improved iron plow made out of interchangeable parts. Unlike wooden plows, which required two people and four oxen to plow an acre in a day, Wood's cast-iron plow allowed one person and one yoke of oxen to plow the same area. Demand was so great that manufacturers infringed on Wood's patents and produced thousands of copies of this new plow yearly.

A shortage of farm labor encouraged many farmers to adopt labor-saving machinery. Prior to the introduction in 1803 of the cradle scythe—a rake used to cut and gather up grain and deposit it in even piles—a farmer could not harvest more than half an acre a day. The horse rake—a device introduced in 1820 to mow hay—allowed a single farmer to perform the work of eight to ten people. The invention in 1836 of a mechanical thresher, used to separate the wheat from the chaff, helped to halve the hours of labor required to produce an acre of wheat.

By 1830 the roots of America's future industrial growth had been firmly planted. Back in 1807, the nation had just 15 or 20 cotton mills, containing approximately 8000 spindles. By 1831 the number of spindles in use totaled nearly a million and a quarter. Factory production made household manufacture of shoes, clothing, textiles, and farm implements obsolete. The United States was well on its way to becoming one of the world's leading manufacturing nations.

The Growth of Cities

At the beginning of the nineteenth century, the United States was a nation of farms and rural villages. Only four cities had more than 10,000 inhabitants. Boston, which in 1800 contained just 25,000 inhabitants, looked much as it had prior to the Revolution. Its streets, still paved with cobblestones, were unlighted at night. New York City was so small that Wall Street (which is located near Manhattan Island's tip) was considered to be uptown and Broadway was a country drive. New York City's entire police force, which only patrolled at night, consisted of 2 captains, 2 deputies, and 72 assistants.

During the 1820s and 1830s, the nation's cities grew at an extraordinary rate. The urban population increased 60 percent a decade, five times as fast as that of the country as a whole. In 1810, New York City's population was less than 100,000. Two decades later it was more than 200,000. Western cities grew particularly fast.

The chief cause of the increase was the migration of sons and daughters away from farms and villages. The growth of commerce drew thousands of farm children to the cities to work as bookkeepers, clerks, and salespeople. The expansion of factories demanded thousands of laborers, mechanics, teamsters, and operatives. The need of those in rural areas to use services available only in urban centers also promoted the growth of cities, particularly in the West. Farmers needed their grain milled and their livestock butchered. In response, a grain processing and meat-packing industry sprouted up in "Porkopolis," Cincinnati. Manufacturers in Lexington produced hemp sacks and ropes for Kentucky farmers, and Louisville businesses cured and marketed tobacco.

Pittsburgh's growth illustrates these processes at work. Frontier farmers needed products made of iron, such as nails, horseshoes, and farm implements. Pittsburgh lay near western Pennsylvania's coal fields. Because it was cheaper to bring the iron ore to the coal supply for smelting than to transport the

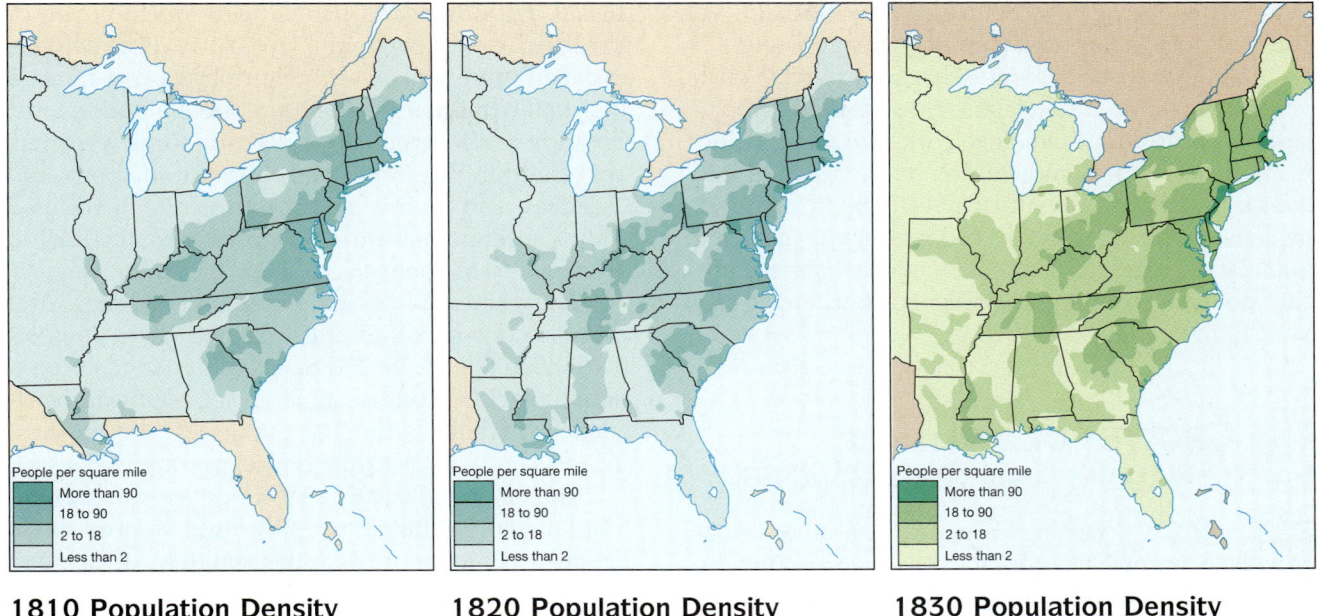

1810 Population Density

1820 Population Density

1830 Population Density

coal to the side of the iron mine, Pittsburgh became a major iron producer. Iron foundries and blacksmith shops proliferated. So did glass factories, which required large amounts of fuel to provide heat for glassblowing. As a result, Pittsburgh's population tripled between 1810 and 1830.

As urban areas grew many problems were exacerbated, including the absence of clean drinking water, the lack of cheap public transportation, and most importantly, poor sanitation. Sanitation problems led to heavy urban mortality rates and frequent epidemics of typhoid, dysentery, typhus, cholera, and yellow fever.

Most city dwellers used outdoor privies, which emptied into vaults and cesspools that sometimes leaked into the soil and contaminated the water supply. Kitchen wastes were thrown into ditches; refuse was thrown into trash piles by the side of the streets. Every horse in a city deposited as much as 20 pounds of manure and urine on the streets each day. To help

Broadway, New York, c. 1834. By the 1830s numerous street trades were operating on Broadway, which had evolved into an urban thoroughfare traversed by a variety of vehicles, including the urban stagecoach.

remove the garbage and refuse, many cities allowed packs of dogs, goats, and pigs to scavenge freely.

Although elite urbanites began to enjoy such amenities as indoor toilets, the cities' poorest inhabitants lived in slums. On New York's lower east side, many men, women, and children were crowded into damp, unlighted, ill-ventilated cellars with 6 to 20 persons living in a single room. Despite growing public awareness of the problems of slums and urban poverty, conditions remained unchanged for several generations.

THE GROWTH OF POLITICAL FACTIONALISM AND SECTIONALISM

The Era of Good Feelings began with a burst of nationalistic fervor. The economic program adopted by Congress, including a national bank and a protective tariff, reflected the growing feeling of national unity. The Supreme Court promoted the spirit of nationalism by establishing the principle of federal supremacy. Industrialization and improvements in transportation also added to the sense of national unity by contributing to the nation's economic strength and independence and by linking the West and the East together.

But this same period also witnessed the emergence of growing factional divisions in politics, including a deepening sectional split between the North and South. A severe economic depression between 1819 and 1822 provoked bitter division over questions of banking and tariffs. Geographic expansion exposed latent tensions over the morality of slavery and the balance of economic power. Political issues that arose during the Era of Good Feelings dominated American politics for the next 40 years.

The Panic of 1819

In 1819 a financial panic swept across the country. The growth in trade that followed the War of 1812 came to an abrupt halt. Unemployment mounted, banks failed, mortgages were foreclosed, and agricultural prices fell by half. Investment in western lands collapsed.

In Richmond, property values fell by half. In Philadelphia, 1808 individuals were committed to debtors' prison. In Boston, the figure was 3500.

For the first time in American history, the problem of urban poverty commanded public attention. In New York in 1819, the Society for the Prevention of Pauperism counted 8000 paupers out of a population of 120,000. The next year, the figure climbed to 13,000. Fifty thousand people were unemployed or irregularly employed in New York, Philadelphia, and Baltimore, and one foreign observer estimated that half a million people were jobless nationwide. To address the problem of destitution, newspapers appealed for old clothes and shoes for the poor, and churches and municipal governments distributed soup. Baltimore set up 12 soup kitchens in 1820 to give food to the poor.

The panic had several causes, including a dramatic decline in cotton prices, a contraction of credit by the Bank of the United States designed to curb inflation, an 1817 congressional order requiring hard-currency payments for land purchases, and the closing of many factories due to foreign competition.

The panic unleashed a storm of popular protest. Many debtors agitated for "stay laws" to provide relief from debts as well as the abolition of debtors' prisons. Manufacturing interests called for increased protection from foreign imports, but a growing number of southerners believed that high protective tariffs, which raised the cost of imported goods and reduced the flow of international trade, were the root of their troubles. Many people clamored for a reduction in the cost of government and pressed for sharp reductions in federal and state budgets. Others, particularly in the South and West, blamed the panic on the nation's banks and particularly the tight-money policies of the Bank of the United States.

By 1823 the panic was over. But it left a lasting imprint on American politics. The panic led to demands for the democratization of state constitutions, an end to restrictions on voting and officeholding, and heightened hostility toward banks and other "privileged" corporations and monopolies. The panic also exacerbated tensions within the Republican party and aggravated sectional tensions as Northerners pressed for higher tariffs while Southerners abandoned their support of nationalistic economic programs.

The Missouri Crisis

In the midst of the panic, a crisis over slavery erupted with stunning suddenness. It was, Thomas Jefferson wrote, like "a firebell in the night." Missouri's application for statehood ignited the crisis, and the issue raised involved the status of slavery west of the Mississippi River.

East of the Mississippi, the Mason-Dixon line and the Ohio River formed a boundary between the North and South. States south of this line were slave states; states north of this line had either abolished slavery or adopted gradual emancipation policies.

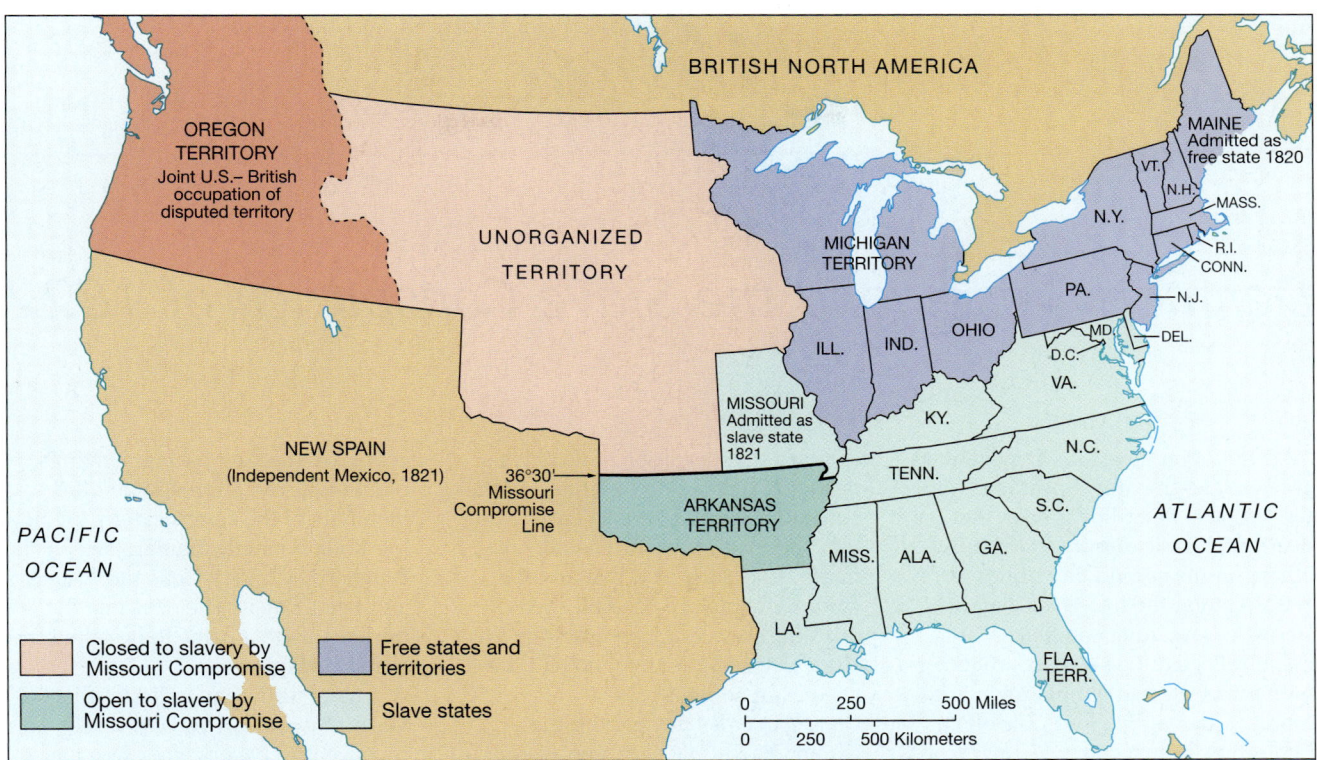

Missouri Compromise

The agreement reached in the Missouri Compromise temporarily settled the argument over slavery in the territories.

West of the Mississippi, however, no clear line demarcated the boundary between free and slave territory.

Representative James Tallmadge, a New York Republican, provoked the crisis in February 1819 by introducing an amendment to restrict slavery in Missouri as a condition of statehood. The amendment prohibited the further introduction of slaves into Missouri and provided for emancipation of all children of slaves at the age of 25. Voting along ominously sectional lines, the House approved the Tallmadge Amendment, but the amendment was defeated in the Senate.

Southern and Northern politicians alike responded with fury. Southerners condemned the Tallmadge proposal as part of a northeastern plot to dominate the government. They declared the United States to be a union of equals, claiming that Congress had no power to place special restrictions upon a state.

Talk of disunion and civil war was rife. Senator Freeman Walker of Georgia envisioned "civil war . . . a brother's sword crimsoned with a brother's blood." Northern politicians responded with equal vehemence. Said Representative Tallmadge, "If blood is necessary to extinguish any fire which I have assisted to kindle, I can assure you gentlemen, while I regret the necessity, I shall not forbear to contribute my mite." Northern leaders argued that national policy, enshrined in the Northwest Ordinance, committed the government to halt the expansion of the institution of slavery. They warned that the extension of slavery into the West would inevitably increase the pressures to reopen the African slave trade.

Mass meetings convened in a number of cities in the Northeast. The vehemence of anti-Missouri feeling is apparent in an editorial that appeared in the New York *Advertiser:* "THIS QUESTION INVOLVES NOT ONLY THE FUTURE CHARACTER OF OUR NATION, BUT THE FUTURE WEIGHT AND INFLUENCE OF THE FREE STATES. IF NOW LOST— IT IS LOST FOREVER." Never before had passions over the issue of slavery been so heated or sectional antagonisms so overt.

Compromise ultimately resolved the crisis. In 1820, the Senate narrowly voted to admit Missouri as a slave state. To preserve the sectional balance, it also voted to admit Maine, which had previously been a part of Massachusetts, as a free state, and to prohibit the formation of any further slave states from the territory of the Louisiana Purchase north of 36°30' north latitude. Henry Clay then skillfully steered the compromise through the House, where a handful of anti-

THE American Mosaic

Denmark Vesey and the Slave Conspiracy of 1822

"DO not open your lips! Die silent, as you shall see me do." Speaking from the gallows, Peter Poyas soon met his death with stoic dignity—as did five others on the second day of July in 1822. Among the five was Denmark Vesey, whose quiet composure at death reflected the steely courage with which he had led blacks in and around Charleston, South Carolina, in plotting insurrection. As their trials revealed, for over a year Vesey and his lieutenants had planned, recruited, and hoarded the provisions for the fight. Only betrayal by a few slaves had prevented what could well have become the bloodiest slave revolt in America's history.

Many whites were surprised at the revelation of Vesey's leadership. In their eyes he seemed to have few grievances. Born in the late 1760s in either Africa or the Caribbean, he served as a slave to Captain Joseph Vesey, a Bermuda slave trader who settled in Charleston in 1783 as a slave broker and ship merchandiser. In 1800 Denmark Vesey won $1500 in the East Bay Lottery. He then purchased his freedom for $600 and opened a carpentry shop; by 1817 he had amassed savings of several thousand dollars. He was literate and well traveled. He had once been offered the opportunity to return to Africa as a free man and rejected it. "What did he have to be upset about?" many whites must have asked. Well, for one thing, his wife and several of his children were still in bondage. He also deeply resented white interference in the lives of free blacks as well as slaves.

Vesey was a proud man and frequently rebuked friends who acquiesced to such traditional displays of deference as bowing to whites on the street. One remembered Vesey telling him "all men were born equal, and that he was surprised that anyone would degrade himself by such conduct; that he would never cringe to whites, nor ought any who had the feelings of a man."

As in cities throughout the nation, blacks in Charleston were meeting oppression by forging their own institutions and creating self-affirming communities. A key part of this process was religious independence. At the close of the War of 1812 black Methodists in Charleston outnumbered white ones ten to one. After an unsuccessful attempt by blacks to control their destinies within the white church, Morris Brown went to Philadelphia and was ordained by the African Methodist Episcopal church. In 1818, following a dispute over a burial ground, more than three-fourths of the 6000 black Methodists of Charleston withdrew from the white-led churches. Morris Brown was appointed bishop, and the African Church of Charleston was established.

White authorities regarded such independent churches as possible seedbeds of radicalism. Thus they harassed church meetings and jailed church leaders. Beginning in 1820 legislation was passed to reduce the free black population of South Carolina. Finally, in 1821, the city of Charleston closed the Hampstead Church, which had been the leader of the independent church movement—and which included Denmark Vesey among its members. That closing became the spark that ignited Vesey to action. He began holding meetings, often in his own home, with other members of the congregation, including Rolla Bennett, "Gullah Jack" Pritchard, Monday Gell, and Ned and Peter Poyas. They became the nucleus of what came to be called the Vesey Conspiracy.

Later testimony indicates that Vesey was well aware of several recent events that convinced him that the tide of history was changing. Foremost was the successful slave rebellion in Haiti that began in 1791. Vesey "was in the habit of reading to me all the passages in the newspapers that related to St. Domingo, and apparently every pamphlet he could lay his hands on that had any connection with slavery," one rebel testified. Vesey was also knowledgeable about the debates over Missouri statehood; the same rebel reported, "He one day brought me a speech which he told me had been delivered in congress by a Mr. [Rufus] King on the subject of slavery; he told me this Mr. King was the black man's friend, that he, Mr. King, had declared . . . that slavery was a great disgrace to the country."

Vesey used religion as a potent force to spur blacks to join him in armed rebellion. At almost every meeting he "read to us from the Bible, how the children of Israel were delivered out of Egypt from bondage." He also frequently used the passage: "Behold the day of the Lord cometh, and thy spoil shall be divided in the midst of thee. For I shall gather all nations against Jerusalem to battle; and the city shall be taken." In addition, "Gullah Jack," born in Africa, was known as a powerful conjurer, and many were

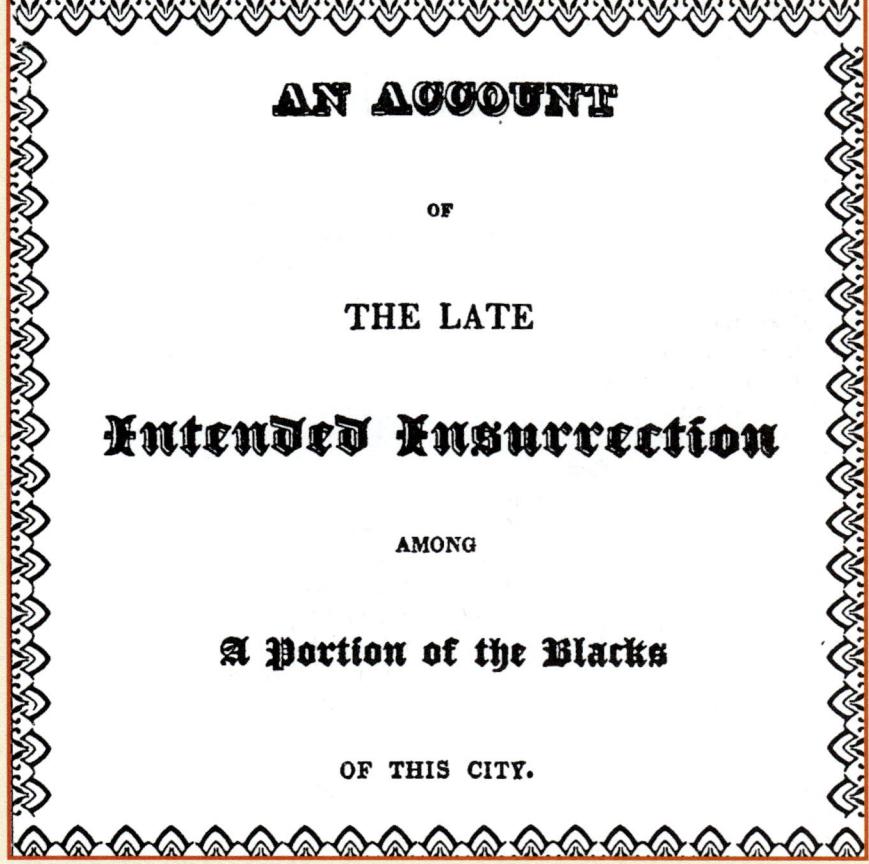

convinced his power could protect them from harm.

There was a distinctly Pan-African cast to the conspiracy. A number of the leaders had lived in either Africa or the Caribbean. One of them, Monday Gell, had apparently corresponded with the president of Haiti. Charleston blacks were told that "Santo Domingo and Africa will assist us to get our liberty, if we will only make the motion first." The motion they planned was bold indeed. They were to attack the city at seven different points, capture weapons at the arsenal, set fire to the city, and kill all whites they encountered.

The plan was bold but not rashly undertaken. They prepared for a deadline in the second week of July 1822. Large numbers were needed and available. Blacks outnumbered whites ten to one in the area surrounding Charleston, and recruiting extended to plantations as far away as 80 miles. The big problem was a shortage of arms until the arsenal was taken. So blacksmiths began making bayonets and spikes. Anything that could be used as a weapon was hoarded, along with gunpowder. Draymen, caters, and butchers were recruited to supply horses. Hundreds of blacks from all classes and occupations were contacted, but the nucleus remained skilled artisans, free and slave, from Charleston.

The dangers of advance planning and a widespread network were leaks and betrayal. For months luck held, but in late May 1822 a slave reported an attempt to recruit him to the insurrection. As authorities began to investigate, the betrayals escalated, and the authorities deployed military force to quash the rebellion before it had a chance to get started. Ten slaves were arrested on June 17 and 18, and the court began hearings. On June 22 Vesey was captured and stood trial the next day, while "Gullah Jack," the only major leader still free, tried to continue the revolt. Three days after the July 2 executions "Gullah Jack" was arrested. By August 9 more than 30 blacks had been hanged and many more deported.

White retaliation was swift and sure. So was white hysteria. The executions were public, and blacks were forbidden to dress in black or wear black crepe to mourn the dead. Examples were also made of the informers, who were freed and granted lifetime annuities. Finally, whites responded to Vesey's conspiracy with further antiblack legislation.

On the surface little good came from Denmark Vesey's bold plan. Its chances of success were meager at best. During Vesey's sentencing, the presiding magistrate told him, "It is difficult to imagine what *infatuation* could have prompted you to attempt an enterprise so wild and visionary. You were a free man; were comparatively wealthy; and enjoyed every comfort, compatible with your situation. You had therefore, much to risk and little to gain. From your age and experience you *ought* to have known, that success was impracticable." Nevertheless, Vesey took his indomitable stand. While recruiting for the Union army, the great black abolitionist Frederick Douglass called upon blacks "to remember Denmark Vesey."

Chronology OF KEY EVENTS

1785	Oliver Evans opens the first automated flour mill	1819	Panic of 1819; Spain cedes Florida to the United States and recognizes the western limits of the Louisiana Purchase in the Adams-Onis Treaty; *Dartmouth* v. *Woodward* upholds the sanctity of contracts; *McCulloch* v. *Maryland* upholds the constitutionality of the second Bank of the United States
1786	Samuel Fitch demonstrates his first steamboat		
1793	Samuel Slater opens the first American textile mill at Pawtucket, Rhode Island; Eli Whitney invents the cotton gin		
1807	Robert Fulton's *Clermont* demonstrates practicality of steam-powered navigation	1820	Missouri Compromise prohibits slavery in the northern half of the Louisiana Purchase; Missouri enters the union as a slave state and Maine as a free state
1814	First factory to turn raw cotton into cotton cloth opens in Waltham, Massachusetts		
1815	Congress declares war on Algiers	1822	Denmark Vesey's slave insurrection in South Carolina is exposed
1816	Second Bank of the United States is chartered; Protective Tariff is passed; James Monroe is elected fifth president	1823	President James Monroe opposes any further European colonization or interference in the Americas, establishing the principle now known as the Monroe Doctrine
1817–1818	General Andrew Jackson invades Florida; Rush-Bagot convention between Britain and United States establishes American fishing rights and U.S.-Canadian boundary	1824	*Gibbons* v. *Ogden* broadens federal power over interstate commerce
		1825	Erie Canal opens

slavery representatives, fearful of the threat to the Union, threw their support behind the proposals.

Southerners won a victory in 1820, but they paid a high price. While many states would eventually be organized from the Louisiana Purchase area north of the compromise line, only two (Arkansas and part of Oklahoma) would be formed from the southern portion. If the South was to defend its political power against an antislavery majority, it had but two options in the future. It would either have to forge new political alliances with the North and West, or it would have to acquire new territory in the Southwest. The latter would inevitably reignite northern opposition to the further expansion of slavery.

The Era of Good Feelings ended on a note of foreboding. Although compromise had been achieved, it was clear that sectional conflict had not been resolved, only postponed. Sectional antagonism, Jefferson wrote, "is hushed, indeed, for the moment. But this is a reprieve only, not a final sentence. A geographical line, coinciding with a marked principle, moral and political, once conceived and held up to the angry passions of men, will never be obliterated; and every new irritation will mark it deeper and deeper." John Quincy Adams agreed. The Missouri crisis, he wrote, is only the "title page to a great tragic volume."

CONCLUSION

The Era of Good Feelings came to a formal close on March 4, 1825, the day that John Quincy Adams was inaugurated as the nation's sixth president. Adams, who had served eight years as his predecessor's secretary of state, believed that James Monroe's terms in office would be regarded by future generations of Americans as a "golden age." In his inaugural address, he spoke with pride of the nation's achievements since the War of 1812. A strong spirit of nationalism pervaded the nation and the country stood united under a single political party, the Republicans. The nation had settled its most serious disputes with England and Spain, extended its boundaries to the Pacific, asserted its diplomatic independence, encouraged the wars for national independence in Latin America, had developed a strong manufacturing system, and had begun to create a system of transportation adequate to a great nation.

The Era of Good Feelings marked a period of dramatic growth and intense nationalism, but it also witnessed the emergence of new political divisions as well as growing sectional animosities. The period following the War of 1812 brought rapid growth to cities, manufacturing, and the factory system in the North, while the South's economy remained centered on slavery and cotton. These two great sections were developing along diverging lines. Whether the spirit of nationalism or the spirit of sectionalism would triumph was the great question that would dominate American politics over the next four decades.

SUGGESTIONS FOR FURTHER READING

Jeremy Atack and Peter Passell, *A New Economic View of American History*, 2nd ed. (1994) and Charles Sellers, *The Market Revolution, 1815–1846* (1991). Analyze thoroughly American economic development after 1815.

William Barney, *The Passage of the Republic* (1987). Offers a highly informative overview of the period.

Ernest R. May, *The Making of the Monroe Doctrine* (1975). Examines American foreign policy during this period.

Overviews and Surveys

William Barney, *The Passage of the Republic: An Interdisciplinary History of Nineteenth-Century America* (1987); W. Elliot Brownlee, *Dynamics of Ascent: A History of the American Economy*, 2d ed. (1988); Stuart Bruchey, *The Roots of American Economic Growth, 1607–1861* (1965); George Dangerfield, *The Awakening of American Nationalism* (1965), and *The Era of Good Feelings* (1952); Robert Heilbroner, *The Economic Transformation of America*, 2d ed. (1984); John R. Howe, *From the Revolution Through the Age of Jackson* (1973); John Mayfield, *The New Nation, 1800–1845*, rev. ed. (1982); Douglas C. North, *The Economic Growth of the United States, 1790–1860* (1961); Sidney Ratner, James H. Soltow, and Richard Sylla, *The Evolution of the American Economy* (1979).

The Growth of American Nationalism

Samuel Flagg Bemis, ed., *The American Secretaries of State and Their Diplomacy*, vol. 4 (1928); Edward M. Burns, *The American Idea of Mission: Concepts of National Purpose and Destiny* (1957); Robert K. Faulkner, *The Jurisprudence of John Marshall* (1968); Lloyd C. Gardner et al., *Creation of the American Empire: U.S. Diplomatic History* (1973); C. C. Griffin, *The United States and the Disruption of the Spanish Empire* (1937); George Lee Haskins and Herbert A. Johnson, *History of the Supreme Court of the United States*, vol. 2, *Foundations of Power: John Marshall, 1801–1815* (1981); Ernest R. May, *The Making of the Monroe Doctrine* (1975); Frederick W. Merk, *Manifest Destiny and Mission in American History: A Reinterpretation* (1963), and *The Monroe Doctrine and American Expansionism, 1843–1849* (1966); Paul C. Nagel, *One Nation Indivisible: The Union in American Thought, 1776–1861* (1964); Dexter Perkins, *The Monroe Doctrine* (1927); Gregg Russell, *John Quincy Adams and the Public Virtues of Diplomacy* (1995).

The Growth of the American Economy

Richard A. Bartlett, *The New Country: A Social History of the American Frontier, 1776–1890* (1974); Alfred D. Chandler, Jr., ed., *The Railroads: The Nation's First Big Business* (1965), and *The Visible Hand* (1977); Howard Chudacoff, *The Evolution of American Urban Society* (1975); Victor S. Clark, *History of Manufactures in the United States, 1607–1860*, 2 vols. (1916–1928); Thomas C. Cochran, *Frontiers of Change: Early Industrialism in America* (1981); Robert F. Dalzell, Jr., *Enterprising Elite: The Boston Associates and the World They Made* (1987); Clarence H. Danhof, *Change in Agriculture: The Northern United States, 1820–1870* (1969); Paul David, *Technical Choice, Innovation and Economic Growth* (1975); Lance Davis et al., *American Economic Growth: An Economist's History of the United States* (1972); Everett Dick, *The Lure of the Land: A Social History of the Public Lands* (1970); Joseph A. Durrenberger, *Turnpikes: A Study of the Toll Road Movement* (1968); John Faragher, *Sugar Creek* (1986); Albert Fishlow, *American Railroads and the Transformation of the Antebellum Economy* (1965); Paul W. Gates, *The Farmer's Age: Agriculture, 1815–1860* (1960); Sigfried Giedion, *Mechanization Takes Command* (1948); Carter Goodrich, ed., *Canals and American Economic Development* (1961), and *Government Promotion of American Canals and Railroads, 1800–1890* (1960); Ralph D. Gray, *The National Waterway: A History of the Chesapeake and Delaware Canal*, 2d ed. (1989); Erik F. Haites, James Mak, and Gary M. Walton, *Western River Transportation: The Era of Early Internal Development, 1810–1860* (1975); David Hamer, *New Towns in the New World: Images and Perceptions of the Nineteenth-Century Urban Frontier* (1990); Oscar and Mary Handlin, *Commonwealth: A Study of the Role of Government in the American Economy*, rev. ed. (1969); Louis Hartz, *Economic Policy and Democratic Thought* (1948); Morton Horwitz, *The Transformation of American Law, 1780–1860* (1977); David A. Hounshell, *From the American System to Mass Production* (1984); Louis C. Hunter, *Steamboats on the Western Rivers* (1949); James Willard Hurst, *Law and the Conditions of Freedom in the Nineteenth-Century United States* (1956), and *The Legitimacy of the Business Corporation in the Law of the United States, 1780–1970* (1970); David J. Jeremy, *Transatlantic Industrial Revolution: The Diffusion of Textile Technologies Between Britain and America, 1790–1830s (1981); Arthur M. Johnson and Barry Supple, Boston Capitalists and Western Railroads: A Study in the Nineteenth Century Railroad Investment Process (1967); John F. Kasson, Civilizing the Machine: Technology and Republican Values in America, 1776–1900 (1976); Darwin P. Kelsey, ed., Farming in the New Nation (1972); Susan Previant Lee and Peter Passell, A New Economic View of American History (1979); Leonard W. Levy, The Law of the Commonwealth and Chief Justice Shaw (1957); Timothy R. Mahoney, River Towns in the Great West: The Structure of Provincial Urbanization in the American Midwest, 1820–1870 (1990); Blake McKelvey, American Urbanization: A Comparative History (1973); Nathan Miller, The Enterprise of a Free People: Aspects of Economic Development in New York State During the Canal Period, 1792–1838 (1962); Zane Miller, The Urbanization of America (1973); Eric H. Monkkonen, America Becomes Urban: The Development of U.S. Cities and Towns (1988); William Nelson, The Americanization of the Common Law: The Impact of Legal Change on Massachusetts Society, 1760–1830 (1975); James D. Norris, R. G. Dun and Co., 1841–1900 (1978); Douglas C. North, Growth and Welfare in the American Past, 2d ed. (1974); F. S. Philbrick, The Rise of the West, 1754–1830 (1965); Glenn Porter and Harold C. Livesay, Merchants and Manufacturers: Studies in the Changing Structure of Nineteenth-Century Marketing (1971); J. Potter, "The Growth of Population in America, 1700–1860" in D. V. Glass and D. E. C. Eversley, eds., Population in History (1965); Allan R. Pred, Urban Growth and the Circulation of Information (1973); Malcolm J. Rohrbough, The Land Office Business (1960), and The Trans-Appalachian Frontier (1978); Nathan Rosenberg, Technology and American Economic Growth (1972); Harry Scheiber, Ohio Canal Era: A Case Study of Government and the Economy, 1820–1861 (1969); Leo F. Schnore, ed., The New Urban History: Quantitative Explorations by American Historians (1975); Ronald E. Shaw, Canals for a Nation: The Canal Era in the United States (1990), and Erie Water West: A History of the Erie Canal, 1792–1854 (1966); Carl Siracusa, A Mechanical People: Perceptions of the Industrial Order in Massachusetts, 1815–1880 (1979); Merritt Roe Smith, Harpers Ferry Armory and the New Technology (1977); John R. Stilgoe, Borderland: Origins of the American Suburb (1988); John F. Stover, Iron Road to the West: American Railroads in the 1850s (1978), and The Life and Decline of the American Railroad (1970); Alan Taylor, William Cooper's Town (1995); George Rogers Taylor, The Transportation Revolution (1951); Jon C. Teaford, The Municipal Revolution in America: Origins of Modern Urban Government, 1650–1825 (1975); Peter Temin, Causal Factors in American Economic Growth in the Nineteenth Century (1975), and Iron and Steel in Nineteenth Century America (1964); Stephan Thernstrom and Richard Sennett, eds., Nineteenth-Century Cities: Essays in the New Urban History (1969); Robert L. Thompson, Wiring a Continent: The History of the Telegraph Industry in the United States, 1832–1866 (1947); Dale Van Every, The Final Challenge: The American Frontier, 1804–1845 (1964); Richard C. Wade, The Urban Frontier (1959); Caroline F. Ware, The Early New England Cotton Manufacture (1931); Sam Bass Warner, Jr., The Private City: Philadelphia in Three Periods of Its Growth (1968), and The Urban Wilderness (1972); James W. Whitaker, ed., Farming in the Midwest, 1840–1900 (1974).

The Growth of Political Factionalism and Sectionalism

David Brion Davis, The Problem of Slavery in the Age of Revolution, 1770–1823 (1975); Don E. Fehrenbacher, The South and Three Sectional Crises (1980); Staughton Lynd, Class Conflict, Slavery and the United States Constitution (1967); Duncan J. MacLeod, Slavery, Race, and the American Revolution (1974); Glover Moore, The Missouri Controversy (1953); D. L. Robinson, Slavery in the Structure of American Politics, 1765–1820 (1971); Murray N. Rothbard, The Panic of 1819: Reactions and Policies (1962).

Biographies

Harry Ammon, James Monroe: The Quest for National Identity (1971); Leonard Baker, John Marshall: A Life in Law (1974); Samuel Flagg Bemis, John Quincy Adams and the Foundations of American Foreign Policy (1949), and John Quincy Adams and the Union (1956); Evan Cornog, The Birth of Empire: Dewitt Clinton and the American Experience, 1769–1828 (1998); Richard Current, Daniel Webster and the Rise of National Conservatism (1955); Gerald T. Dunne, Justice Joseph Story and the Rise of the Supreme Court (1970); Clement Eaton, Henry Clay and the Art of American Politics (1957); Mary W. M. Hargreaves, The Presidency of John Quincy Adams (1985); John Horton, James Kent: A Study in Conservatism (1939); George A. Lipsky, John Quincy Adams: His Theory and Ideas (1950); J. H. Powell, Richard Rush: Republican Diplomat (1942); F. N. Stites, John Marshall: Defender of the Constitution (1981); Barbara M. Tucker, Samuel Slater and the Origins of the American Textile Industry, 1790–1860 (1984); Glyndon G. Van Deusen, The Life of Henry Clay (1937); Charles M. Wiltse, John C. Calhoun: Nationalist, 1782–1828 (1944).

INTERNET RESOURCES

Prairietown, Indiana
http://www.indianapolis.in.us/cp/stories.html
This fictional model of a town and its inhabitants on the early frontier says much about America's movement westward and the everyday lives of Americans.

The Seminole Indians of Florida
http://www.seminoletribes.com/
Before he was president, Andrew Jackson began a war against the Seminole Indians.

Whole Cloth: Discovering Science and Technology Through American Textile History
http://www.si.edu/lemelson/centerpieces/whole_cloth/
The Jerome and Dorothy Lemelson Center for the Study of Invention and Innovation/Society for the History of Tech-

nology put together this site, which includes excellent activities and sources concerning early American manufacturing and industry.

The National Road
http://www.connerprairie.org/ntlroad.html
The National Road was a hot political topic in the early republic and was part of the beginning of the development of America's infrastructure.

Nineteenth Century Scientific American Online
http://www.history.rochester.edu/Scientific_American/
Magazines and journals are windows through which we can view society. This site provides online editions of one of the more interesting nineteenth-century journals.

KEY TERMS

Era of Good Feelings   (p. 234)

James Monroe   (p. 235)

Henry Clay   (p. 236)

John C. Calhoun   (p. 236)

Daniel Webster   (p. 236)

McCullough v. Maryland   (p. 239)

Dartmouth v. Woodward   (p. 240)

Monroe Doctrine   (p. 241)

American System of Production   (p. 245)

Eli Whitney   (p. 245)

REVIEW QUESTIONS

1. Why is the period following the War of 1812 called the "Era of Good Feelings"? What political, social, and economic developments contributed to a growing sense of nationalism after the conflict?

2. In what ways did the Supreme Court strengthen the authority of the national government?

3. What problems had to be overcome for the United States to develop a vigorous economy? How did the United States overcome the problems of scarce labor and poor transportation and communication?

4. Identify the main provisions of the Monroe Doctrine.

5. Explain how the Panic of 1819 and the Missouri Crisis ended the "Era of Good Feelings" and helped produce new sectional and party divisions.

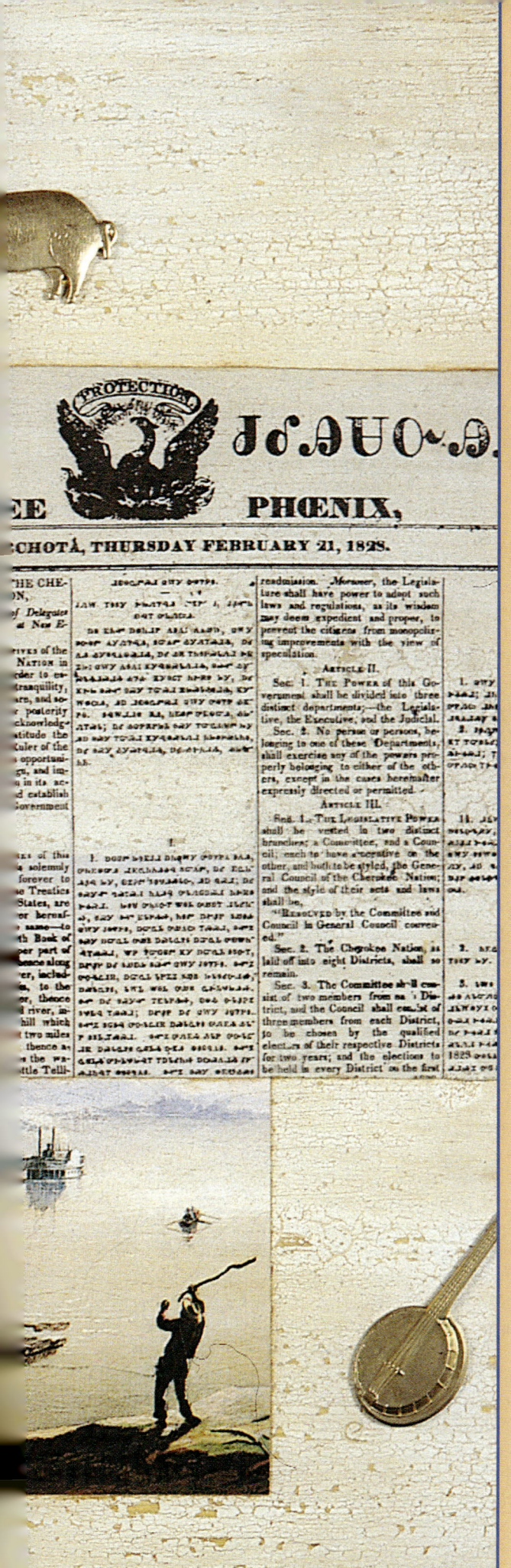

10

POWER AND POLITICS IN JACKSON'S AMERICA

POLITICAL DEMOCRATIZATION
  The Expansion of Voting Rights
  Popular Attacks on Privilege

THE REBIRTH OF PARTIES
  Birth of the Second Party System
  The Presidency of John Quincy Adams
  The "American System" and the "Tariff of Abominations"
  The Election of 1828

ANDREW JACKSON: THE POLITICS OF EGALITARIANISM
  Expanding the Powers of the Presidency
  Clearing the Land of Indians
  Sectional Disputes over Public Lands and Nullification
  The Bank War
  The Jacksonian Court
  Jackson's Legacy

RISE OF A POLITICAL OPPOSITION
  A Party Formed by Coalition
  Who Were the Whigs?

The "people's" candidate

It was, without a doubt, one of the most exciting, colorful, and dirty presidential campaigns in American history. In 1840, William Henry Harrison, a military hero best known for fighting an alliance of Indians at the Battle of Tippecanoe in 1811, challenged the Democratic incumbent, Martin Van Buren, for the presidency.

Harrison's campaign began on Monday, May 4, 1840, when a huge procession made up of an estimated 75,000 people marched through the streets of Baltimore to celebrate Harrison's nomination by the Whig party convention. Although Harrison was college educated and brought up on a plantation with a workforce of some 200 slaves, his Democratic opponents had already dubbed him the "log cabin" candidate, who was happiest on his backwoods farm sipping hard cider. In response, Harrison's supporters enthusiastically seized on this image and promoted it in a number of colorful ways. They distributed barrels of hard cider, passed out campaign hats and placards, and mounted eight log cabins on floats.

Harrison's campaign brought many innovations to the art of electioneering. For the first time, a presidential candidate spoke out on his own behalf. Previous candidates had let others speak for them.

Harrison's backers also coined the first campaign slogans: "Tippecanoe and Tyler Too," "Van, Van is a used up man," and "Matty's policy, 12½ cents a day and french soup, Our policy, 2 Dollars a day and Roast Beef." They staged log-cabin raisings, including the erection of a 50-by–100-foot cabin on Broadway in New York City. They sponsored barbecues, including one in Wheeling, Virginia (now West Virginia), where a crowd devoured 360 hams, 26 sheep, 20 calves, 1500 pounds of beef, 8000 pounds of bread, 1000 pounds of cheese, and 4500 pies. Harrison's campaign managers even distributed whiskey bottles in the shape of log cabins, filled by the E. C. Booz Distillery of Philadelphia, thereby adding the word "booze" to the American vocabulary.

While defending their man as the "people's" candidate, Harrison's backers heaped an unprecedented avalanche of personal abuse on his Democratic opponent. The Whigs accused President Van Buren of eating off of golden plates and lace tablecloths, drinking French wines, perfuming his whiskers, and wearing a corset. Whigs in Congress denied Van Buren an appropriation of $3665 to repair the White House lest he turn the executive mansion into a "palace as splendid as that of the Caesars." The object of this rough and colorful kind of campaigning was to show that the Democratic candidate harbored aristocratic leanings, while Harrison truly represented the people.

The Harrison campaign provided a number of effective lessons for future politicians, most notably an emphasis on symbols and imagery over ideas and substance. Fearful of alienating voters and dividing the Whig party, the political convention that nominated Harrison agreed to adopt no party platform. Harrison himself said not a single word during the campaign about his principles or proposals. He closely followed the suggestion of one of his advisers that he "rely entirely on the past" (that is, his reputation as a general and victor over the Indians) and offer no indication "about what he thinks now, or what he will do hereafter."

The new campaign techniques produced an overwhelming victory. In 1840, voter turnout was

In 1840 the Whig party tried to mobilize voter support for William Henry Harrison by distributing gaily colored handkerchiefs and whiskey bottles shaped like log cabins.

Copyright © Collection of the New-York Historical Society. Harrison Kerchief.

the highest it had ever been in a presidential election: nearly 80 percent of eligible voters cast ballots. The log cabin candidate for president won 53 percent of the popular vote and a landslide victory in the electoral college.

POLITICAL DEMOCRATIZATION

When James Monroe began his second term as president in 1821, he rejoiced at the idea that the country was no longer divided by political parties, which he considered "the curse of the country," breeding disunity, demagoguery, and corruption. Yet even before Monroe's second term had ended, new political divisions had already begun to evolve, creating an increasingly democratic system of politics.

In 1821, American politics was still largely dominated by deference. Competing political parties were nonexistent and voters generally deferred to the leadership of local elites or leading families. Political campaigns tended to be relatively staid affairs. Direct appeals by candidates for support were considered in poor taste. Election procedures were, by later standards, quite undemocratic. Most states imposed property and taxpaying requirements on the white adult males who alone had the vote, and they conducted voting by voice. Presidential electors were generally chosen by state legislatures. Given the fact that citizens had only the most indirect say in the election of the president, it is not surprising that voting participation was generally extremely low, amounting to less than 30 percent of adult white males.

Between 1820 and 1840, a revolution took place in American politics. In most states, property qualifications for voting and officeholding were repealed; and voting by voice was largely eliminated. Direct methods of selecting presidential electors, county officials, state judges, and governors replaced indirect methods. Because of these and other political innovations, voter participation skyrocketed. By 1840 voting participation had reached unprecedented levels. Nearly 80 percent of adult white males went to the polls.

A new two-party system, made possible by an expanded electorate, replaced the politics of deference to and leadership by elites. By the mid-1830s, two national political parties with marked philosophical differences, strong organizations, and wide popular appeal competed in virtually every state. Professional party managers used partisan newspapers, speeches, parades, rallies, and barbecues to mobilize popular support. Our modern political system had been born.

The Expansion of Voting Rights

The most significant political innovation of the early nineteenth century was the abolition of property qualifications for voting and officeholding. Hard times resulting from the panic of 1819 led many people to demand an end to property restrictions on voting and officeholding. In New York, for example, fewer than two adult males in five could legally vote for senator or governor. Under the new constitution adopted in 1821, all adult white males were allowed to vote, so long as they paid taxes or had served in the militia. Five years later, an amendment to the state's constitution eliminated the taxpaying and militia qualifications, thereby establishing universal white manhood suffrage. By 1840, universal white manhood suffrage had largely become a reality. Only three states—Louisiana, Rhode Island, and Virginia—still restricted the suffrage to white male property owners and taxpayers.

In order to encourage popular participation in politics, most states also instituted statewide nominating conventions, opened polling places in more convenient locations, extended the hours that polls were open, and eliminated the earlier practice of voting by voice. This last reform did not truly institute the secret ballot, which was only adopted beginning in the 1880s, since voters during the mid-nineteenth century usually voted with straight-ticket paper ballots prepared by the political parties themselves. Each party had a different colored ballot, which voters deposited in a publicly viewed ballot box, so that those present knew who had voted for which party. By 1824 only 6 of the nation's 24 states still chose presidential electors in the state legislature, and eight years later the only state still to do so was South Carolina, which continued this practice until the Civil War.

In addition to removing property and tax qualifications for voting and officeholding, states also reduced residency requirements for voting. Immigrant males were permitted to vote in most states if they had declared their intention to become citizens. During the nineteenth century, 22 states and territories permitted immigrants who were not yet naturalized citizens to vote. States also allowed voters to choose presidential electors, governors, and county officials.

While universal white manhood suffrage was becoming a reality, restrictions on voting by African Americans and women remained in force. Only one state, New Jersey, had given unmarried women property holders the right to vote following the Rev-

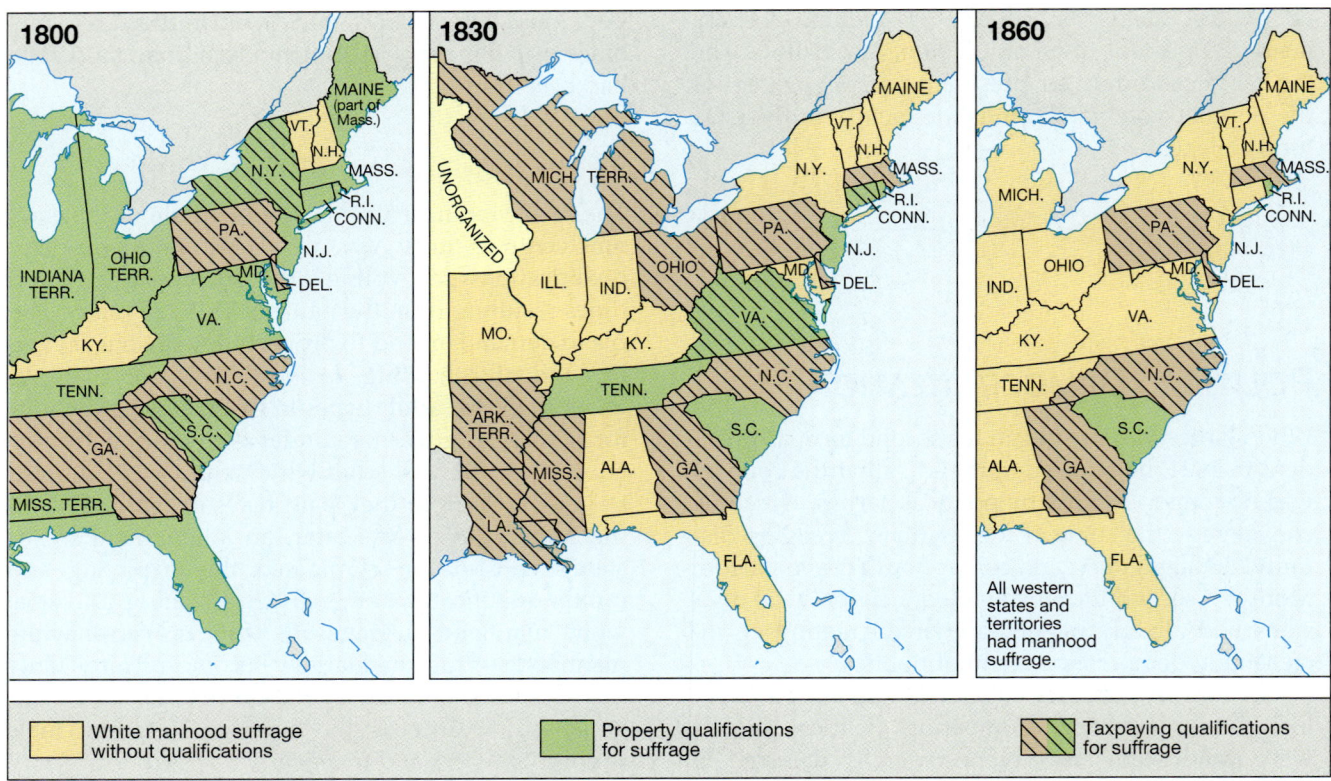

Extension of Male Suffrage

Some states and territories reserved the suffrage to white male property holders and taxpayers, while others permitted an alternative such as a period of residence.

olution, but the state rescinded this right at the time it extended suffrage to all adult white men. Most states also explicitly denied the right to vote to free African Americans. By 1858 free blacks were eligible to vote in just four northern states: New Hampshire, Maine, Massachusetts, and Vermont.

Popular Attacks on Privilege

The democratic impulse that swept the country in the 1820s was also apparent in widespread attacks on special privilege and aristocratic pretension. Established churches, the bench, and the legal and medical professions all saw their elitist status diminished.

The judiciary became more responsive to public opinion through election, rather than appointment, of judges. To open up the legal profession, many states dropped formal training requirements to practice law. Some states also abolished training and licensing requirements for physicians, allowing unorthodox "herb and root" doctors, including many women, to compete freely with established physicians.

The surge of democratic sentiment had an important political consequence: the breakdown of deferential politics and its terminology. The eighteenth-century language of politics—which included such terms as "faction," "junto," and "caucus"—was rooted in an elite-dominated political order. During the first quarter of the nineteenth century, a new democratic political vocabulary emerged that drew its words from everyday language. Instead of "standing" for public office, candidates "ran" for office. Politicians "log-rolled" (made deals) or "straddled the fence" or promoted "pork barrel" legislation (programs that would benefit their constituents).

During the first quarter of the nineteenth century, local elites lost much of their influence. They were replaced by professional politicians. In the 1820s, political innovators such as Martin Van Buren, the son of a tavernkeeper, and Thurlow Weed, a newspaper editor in Albany, New York, devised new campaign tools such as torchlight parades, subsidized partisan newspapers, and nominating conventions. These political bosses and manipulators soon discovered that the most successful technique for arousing popular interest in politics was to attack a privileged group or institution that had used political influence to attain power or profit.

The "Anti-Masonic party" was the first political movement to win widespread popular following using this technique. In the mid-1820s, a growing num-

By attacking special privilege and demanding equality of opportunity for all citizens, the Anti-Masonic party won broad support in New York and other Northern states.

ber of people in New York and surrounding states had come to believe that members of the fraternal order of Freemasons, who seemed to monopolize many of the region's most prestigious political offices and business positions, had used their connections to enrich themselves. They noted, for instance, that Masons held 22 of the nation's 24 governorships.

Then, in 1826, in the small town of Batavia, New York, William Morgan, a former Mason, disappeared. Morgan had written an exposé of the organization in violation of the order's vow of silence, and rumor soon spread that he had been tied up with heavy cables and dumped into the Niagara River. When no indictments were brought against the alleged perpetrators of Morgan's kidnapping and presumed murder, many upstate New Yorkers accused local constables, justices of the peace, and judges, who were members of the Masons, of obstruction of justice.

By 1830 the Anti-Mason movement had succeeded in capturing half the vote in New York State and had gained substantial support throughout New England. In the mid-1830s, the Anti-Masons were absorbed into a new national political party, the Whigs.

THE REBIRTH OF PARTIES

The first years of the new republic had given rise to two competing political parties, the Federalists and the Republicans. The first two parties, unlike the present-day political parties, tended to have a strong sectional character, with the Federalists dominant in New England and the Republicans elsewhere.

After the War of 1812, the nation reverted to a period of one-party government in national politics. The decline of the Federalist party created the illusion of national political unity, but appearances were deceptive. Without the discipline imposed by competition with a strong opposition party, the Republican party began to fragment into cliques and factions.

During James Monroe's presidency, the Republican party disintegrated as a stable national organization. Following his overwhelming victory in 1816, Monroe sought to promote the ideal expressed by George Washington in his Farewell Address: a nation free of partisan divisions. Like Washington, he appointed rival factional leaders, such as John Quincy Adams and John C. Calhoun, to his cabinet. He refused to use federal patronage to strengthen the Republican party. He also took the position that Congress, not the president, was the best representative of the public will and therefore should define public policy.

The absence of a strong leader, however, led to the fragmentation of the Republican party during Monroe's administration. Factional and sectional rivalries grew increasingly bitter and party machinery fell into disuse.

Birth of the Second Party System

Over time, local and personal factions began to coalesce into a new political party system. Three critical factors contributed to the creation of the second party system. The first was the financial panic of 1819 and the subsequent depression.

The panic resulted in significant political differences over such issues as debt relief, banking and monetary policy, and tariffs. Farmers, particularly in the South and West, demanded enactment of stay laws to postpone repayment of debts. Many artisans and farmers blamed banks for causing the panic by printing an excess of worthless paper money. They demanded that bank notes be replaced by hard money, gold and silver coinage. These groups often

THE American Mosaic

The Cholera Epidemic of 1832: Sinners and Saints

IN the spring of 1832, Americans braced themselves for an attack by cholera—what one historian has called "the classic epidemic disease of the nineteenth century." They knew it was coming. Throughout the preceding year, newspapers had reported with alarm the disease's escape from its Asian homeland and its westward march across Europe. The press had turned shrill when cholera crossed the Atlantic Ocean—the last great barrier that shielded the Americas from this horrible plague—and struck Canada in June 1832. Despite the certainty that the disease would soon reach the United States, however, neither the federal, state, nor local governments did much to prevent or even prepare for an epidemic.

Nothing in their inventory of illnesses, not even the ravages of smallpox or malaria, had prepared Americans for the terror that seized them when cholera finally appeared. Their fear is easily understood: Cholera killed approximately half of those who contracted it, and it struck with unbelievable rapidity. A New Yorker who survived the 1832 epidemic testified that he was walking down the street when he suddenly fell forward on his face "as if knocked down with an axe."

Cholera's symptoms, which mimic those of severe arsenic poisoning, are indeed spectacular. The onset of the disease is marked by acute diarrhea, uncontrollable vomiting, and violent abdominal cramps. Within hours, this sudden and massive loss of fluids causes dehydration, and the victim's extremities feel cold, the face turns blue, and the feet and hands appear dark and swollen. Unless proper medical treatment is provided, death can follow within a few hours after the first symptoms appear, or, at most, within a few days. Even more than its devastating symptoms, it was the disease's ability to kill so swiftly that terrorized the public. "To see individuals well in the morning & buried before night, retiring apparently well & dead in the morning is something which is appalling to the boldest heart," exclaimed another survivor of America's first cholera epidemic.

The cause of cholera was not discovered until 1883 when Robert Koch, the famous scientist, led a commission to Egypt that isolated *Vibrio comma*, the guilty bacterium. These deadly germs settle in the intestines of their victims, following a journey along any one of several pathways that lead to the human digestive tract. Although dirty hands or raw fruits and vegetables often transmit the disease, most cholera epidemics are spread by polluted drinking water from sewage-contaminated water systems.

Unfortunately, America's cities in 1832 harbored more than enough filth to nurture an epidemic. New York was especially dirty. Residents were required by law to pile their garbage in the gutter in front of their homes for removal by the city, but it seldom got collected. (With their characteristic sense of humor, New Yorkers dubbed these piles of stinking, decomposing garbage "corporation pie.") The only effective "sanitary engineers" in New York were the thousands of swine that roamed the streets gorging themselves on the refuse.

Thanks to this filth, cholera unleashed a great plague of death when it reached New York. Thousands died in the epidemic, producing so many bodies that the undertakers could not keep up with the volume and had to stack corpses in warehouses and public buildings to await burial. In short, cholera hit New York with the same force with which yellow fever had knocked Philadelphia to its knees in 1793 (see pp. 198–199).

In the midst of their suffering, New Yorkers could not help but wonder why some people contracted the disease while others escaped it. To answer this question, America's physicians espoused a doctrine of predisposing causes. People who kept God's laws, they explained, had nothing to fear, but the intemperate and the filthy stood at great risk. In fact, physicians elaborated their warnings about "predisposing" or "exciting" causes into a jeremiad against sin. Impiety, imprudence, idleness, drunkenness, gluttony, and sexual excess all left their devotees weakened and "artificially stimulated" their bodies to be vulnerable to cholera.

Because the disease was "decidedly vulgar," physicians predicted that it would confine itself largely to the lower classes—specifically, to blacks and to the Irish, who were thought by upper-class individuals to be the most intemperate and debauched members of society. Here, then, was a classic example of how the medical profession appropriated

social attitudes regarding class and race to blame the victims of disease for their suffering.

The doctors appeared to be right, but for the wrong reasons. Cholera was indeed a "poor man's plague"; sin, however, was not the explanation. The upper classes suffered less because they fled the cities for country homes and lodges where pure water and low population density prevented infection. The poor, by contrast, could not afford to leave: they had to remain and take their chances.

Most of New York's lower classes lived in tiny, unvented apartments where entire families (and perhaps a boarder or two) occupied a single room; the most wretched subsisted in unfurnished cellars whose walls glistened with sewage and slime every time it rained. Instead of pure water imported in hogsheads from fresh water springs in the countryside (the only water the wealthy would touch), the poor drew their drinking water from the river or from contaminated shallow wells. Though New Yorkers had long joked that their water was an excellent purgative, they might as well have called it "liquid death" when cholera swept the land.

Once cholera struck, physicians found that none of the traditional remedies of heroic medicine worked. In addition to bloodletting, they treated their patients with laudanum (the main ingredient of which was opium), tobacco smoke, enemas, and huge doses of calomel, a chalky mercury compound employed as a cathartic. In desperation, one of New York's leading physicians (a practical thinker) even recommended plugging the patient's rectum with beeswax to halt the diarrhea.

Many Americans turned to quacks or treated themselves with home remedies. It made no difference. Those who survived the epidemic did so in spite of the medical care they received, not because of it.

Cholera receded from the land almost as quickly as it had come. By the fall of 1832 the epidemic had spent its fury, and by the winter it was gone. When it struck again in 1866, Americans had learned how to battle the disease. They no longer talked about cholera in moral terms as God's vengeance on the poor and the wicked. Instead, they approached it as a social problem amenable to human intervention. They imposed quarantines, opened emergency hospitals, increased the powers of health authorities, removed the trash and garbage from city streets, and cleaned up municipal water supplies. The contrast between 1832 and 1866 could not have been more complete.

Within the span of two generations, the public changed the way it viewed disease. American physicians became more scientific in handling and treating the sick—eloquent testimony to the medical advances in a modernizing society.

disagreed with probusiness interests, which called for the extension of credit, higher tariffs to protect infant industries, and government-financed transportation improvements to reduce the cost of trade.

A second source of political division was southern alarm over the slavery debates in Congress in 1819 and 1820. Many southern leaders feared that the Missouri crisis (see pp. 248–249, 252) might spark a realignment in national politics along sectional lines. Such a development, John Quincy Adams wrote, was "terrible to the South—threatening in its progress the emancipation of all their slaves, threatening in its immediate effect that Southern domination which has swayed the Union for the last twenty years." Anxiety over the slavery debates in 1819 and 1820 induced many southerners to seek political alliances with the North. As early as 1821, Old Republicans in the South—who opposed high tariffs, a national bank, and federally funded internal improvements—had begun to form a loose alliance with Senator Martin Van Buren of New York and the Republican party faction he commanded.

The third major source of political division was the selection of presidential candidates. The "Virginia dynasty" of presidents, a chain that had begun with George Washington and included Thomas Jefferson, James Madison, and James Monroe, was at its end by 1824. Traditionally, a caucus of the Republican party's members of Congress selected the Republican party's candidate. At the 1824 caucus, the members met in closed session and chose William Crawford, Monroe's secretary of the Treasury, as the party's candidate. Not all Republicans, however, supported this method of nominating candidates and therefore refused to participate.

When Crawford suffered a stroke and was left partially disabled, four other candidates emerged: Secretary of State John Quincy Adams, the son of the nation's second president and the only candidate from the North; John C. Calhoun, Monroe's secretary of war, who had little support outside of his native South Carolina; Henry Clay, the Speaker of the House; and General Andrew Jackson, the hero of the Battle of New Orleans and victor over the Creek and Seminole Indians. About the latter, Thomas Jefferson commented dryly, one might as well try "to make a soldier of a goose as a President of Andrew Jackson."

In the election of 1824, Jackson received the greatest number of votes both at the polls and in the electoral college, followed (in electoral votes) by Adams, Crawford, and then Clay. But he failed to receive the constitutionally required majority of the electoral votes. As provided by the Twelfth Amendment of the Constitution, the election was therefore thrown into the House of Representatives, which was required to choose from among the top three vote-getters in the electoral college. There, Henry Clay persuaded his supporters to vote for Adams, commenting acidly that he did not believe "that killing two thousand five hundred Englishmen at New Orleans" was a proper qualification for the presidency. Adams was elected on the first ballot.

The Philadelphia *Observer* charged that Adams had made a secret deal to obtain Clay's support. Three days later, Adams's nomination of Clay as secretary of state seemed to confirm the charges of a "corrupt bargain." Jackson was outraged, since he could legitimately argue that he was the popular favorite. The general exclaimed, "The Judas of the West has closed the contract and will receive the thirty pieces of silver."

The Presidency of John Quincy Adams

John Quincy Adams was one of the most brilliant and well-qualified men ever to occupy the White House. A deeply religious, intensely scholarly man, he read Biblical passages at least three times a day—once in English, once in German, and once in French. He was fluent in seven foreign languages, including Greek and Latin. During his remarkable career as a diplomat and secretary of state, he negotiated the treaty that ended the War of 1812, acquired the Floridas, and conceived the Monroe Doctrine.

But Adams lacked the political skills and personality necessary to create support for his program. Like his father, Adams lacked personal warmth. His adversaries mockingly described him as a "chip off the old iceberg."

Adams's problems as president did not arise exclusively from his temperament. His misfortune was to serve as president at a time of growing partisan

Table 10.1
Election of 1824

Candidate	Party	Popular Vote	Electoral Vote
J. Q. Adams	No party designations	113,122	84
Jackson		151,271	99
Clay		47,531	37
Crawford		40,856	41

divisions. The Republican party had split into two distinct camps. Adams and his supporters, known as National Republicans, favored a vigorous role for the central government in promoting national economic growth, while the Jacksonian Democrats demanded a limited government and strict adherence to laissez-faire principles.

John Quincy Adams won the election of 1824 in the House of Representatives even though Andrew Jackson received the most popular votes.

As the only president to lose both the popular vote and the electoral vote, Adams faced hostility from the start. Jackson and his supporters accused the new president of "corruptions and intrigues" to gain Henry Clay's support. Acutely aware of the fact that "two-thirds of the whole people [were] averse" to his election as president, Adams promised in his inaugural address to make up for this with "intentions upright and pure; a heart devoted to the welfare of our country." A staunch nationalist, Adams proposed an extraordinary program of federal support for scientific and economic development that included a national university, astronomical observatories ("lighthouses of the skies"), federal funding of roads and canals, and exploration of the country's territory—all to be financed by a high tariff.

Adams's advocacy of a strong federal government and a high tariff enraged defenders of slavery and states' rights advocates who clung to traditional Jeffersonian principles of limited government and strict construction of the Constitution. They feared that any expansion of federal authority might set a precedent for interference with slavery. Thomas Jefferson himself condemned Adams's proposals, declaring in a stinging statement that they would undermine the states and create a national elite—"an aristocracy . . . riding and ruling over the plundered ploughman and beggarded yeomanry."

Adams met with further frustration because he was unwilling to adapt to the practical demands of politics. Adams made no effort to use his patronage powers to build support for his proposals and refused to fire federal officeholders who openly opposed his policies. During his entire term in office he removed just 12 incumbents, and these only for gross incompetence. He justified his actions by saying that he did not want to make "government a perpetual and unremitting scramble for office."

Adams's Indian policies also cost him supporters. Although he, like his predecessor Monroe, wanted to remove Native Americans in the south to an area west of the Mississippi River, he believed that the state and federal governments had a duty to abide by Indian treaties and to purchase, not merely annex, Indian lands. Adams's decision to repudiate and renegotiate a fraudulent treaty that stripped the Georgia Creek Indians of their land outraged land-hungry southerners and westerners.

Even in the realm of foreign policy, his strong suit prior to the presidency, Adams encountered difficulties. His attempts to acquire Texas from Mexico through peaceful means failed, as did his efforts to persuade Britain to permit more American trade with the British West Indies.

The "American System" and the "Tariff of Abominations"

President Adams was committed to using the federal government to promote national economic development. His program included a high protective tariff to promote industry, the sale of public lands at low prices to encourage western settlement, federally financed transportation improvements, expanded markets for western grain and southern cotton, and a strong national bank to regulate the economy.

Adams's secretary of state, Henry Clay, called this economic program the **American system** because it was supposed to promote growth in all parts of the country. But the program infuriated southerners who believed that it favored Northeastern industrial interests at their region's expense. Southerners particularly disliked a protective tariff, since it raised the cost of manufactured goods, which they did not produce.

Andrew Jackson's supporters in Congress sought to exploit the tariff question in order to embarrass Adams and help Jackson win the presidency in 1828. They framed a bill, which became known as the **Tariff of Abominations,** to win support for Jackson in Kentucky, Missouri, New York, Ohio, and Pennsylvania while weakening the Adams administration in New England. The bill raised duties on iron, hemp, and flax (which would benefit westerners), while lowering the tariff on woolen goods (to the detriment of New England textile manufacturers). John Randolph of Virginia accurately described

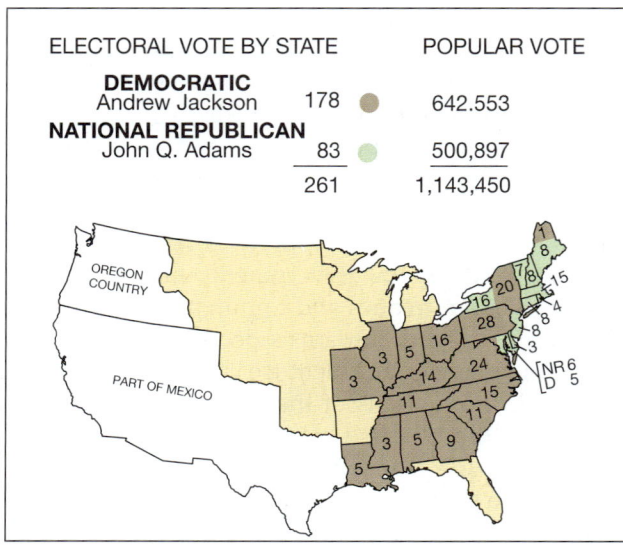

Election of 1828

the object of the bill as an effort to encourage "manufactures of no sort or kind, except the manufacture of a President of the United States."

The Tariff of Abominations created a political uproar in the South, where it was denounced as unconstitutional and discriminatory. The tariff, southerners insisted, was essentially a tax on their region to assist northern manufacturers. South Carolina expressed the loudest outcry against the tariff. At a public meeting in Charleston, protesters declared that a tariff was designed to benefit "one class of citizens [manufacturers] at the expense of every other class." Some South Carolinians called for revolutionary defiance of the national government.

Vice President John C. Calhoun, a skilled logician well versed in political theory, offered a theoretical framework for Southern discontent. Retreating from his early nationalistic position, the South Carolinian anonymously published the "South Carolina Exposition," an essay that advanced the principle of **nullification.** A single state, Calhoun maintained, might overrule or "nullify" a federal law within its own territory, until three-quarters of the states had upheld the law as constitutional. In 1828 the state of South Carolina decided not to implement this doctrine but rather to wait and see what attitude the next president would adopt toward the tariff.

The Election of 1828

"J. Q. Adams who can write" squared off against "Andy Jackson who can fight" in the election of 1828, one of the most bitter campaigns in American history. Jackson's followers repeated the charge that Adams was an "aristocrat" who had obtained office as a result of a "corrupt bargain." The Jackson forces also alleged that the president had used public funds to buy personal luxuries and had installed gaming tables in the White House. They even charged that Mrs. Adams had been born out of wedlock.

Adams's supporters countered by digging up an old story that Jackson had begun living with his wife before she was legally divorced from her first husband (which was technically true, although neither Jackson nor his wife Rachel knew her first husband was still living). They called the general a slave trader, a gambler, and a backwoods buffoon who could not spell more than one word out of four correctly. One Philadelphia editor published a handbill picturing the coffins of 12 men allegedly murdered by Jackson in numerous duels.

The Jackson campaign in 1828 was the first to appeal directly for voter support through a professional political organization. Skilled political organizers, like Martin Van Buren of New York, Amos Kendall of Kentucky, and Thomas Ritchie of Virginia, created an extensive network of campaign committees and subcommittees to organize mass rallies, parades, and barbecues, and to erect hickory poles, Jackson's symbol.

For the first time in American history, a presidential election was the focus of public attention, and voter participation increased dramatically. Twice as many voters cast ballots in the election of 1828 as in 1824, four times as many as in 1820. As in most previous elections, the vote divided along sectional lines. Jackson swept every state in the South and West and Adams won the electoral votes of every state in the North except Pennsylvania and part of New York.

Contemporaries interpreted Jackson's resounding victory as a triumph for political democracy. Jackson's supporters called the vote a victory for the "farmers and mechanics of the country" over the "rich and well born." Even Jackson's opponents agreed that the election marked a watershed in the nation's political history, signaling the beginning of a new democratic age. One Adams supporter said bluntly, "a great revolution has taken place."

ANDREW JACKSON: THE POLITICS OF EGALITARIANISM

Supporters of Adams regarded Jackson's victory with deep pessimism. A justice of the Supreme Court declared, "The reign of King 'Mob' seems triumphant." But enthusiasts greeted Jackson's victory as a great triumph for the people. At the inaugural, a cable stretched in front of the east portico of the Capitol to keep back the throngs snapped under the pres-

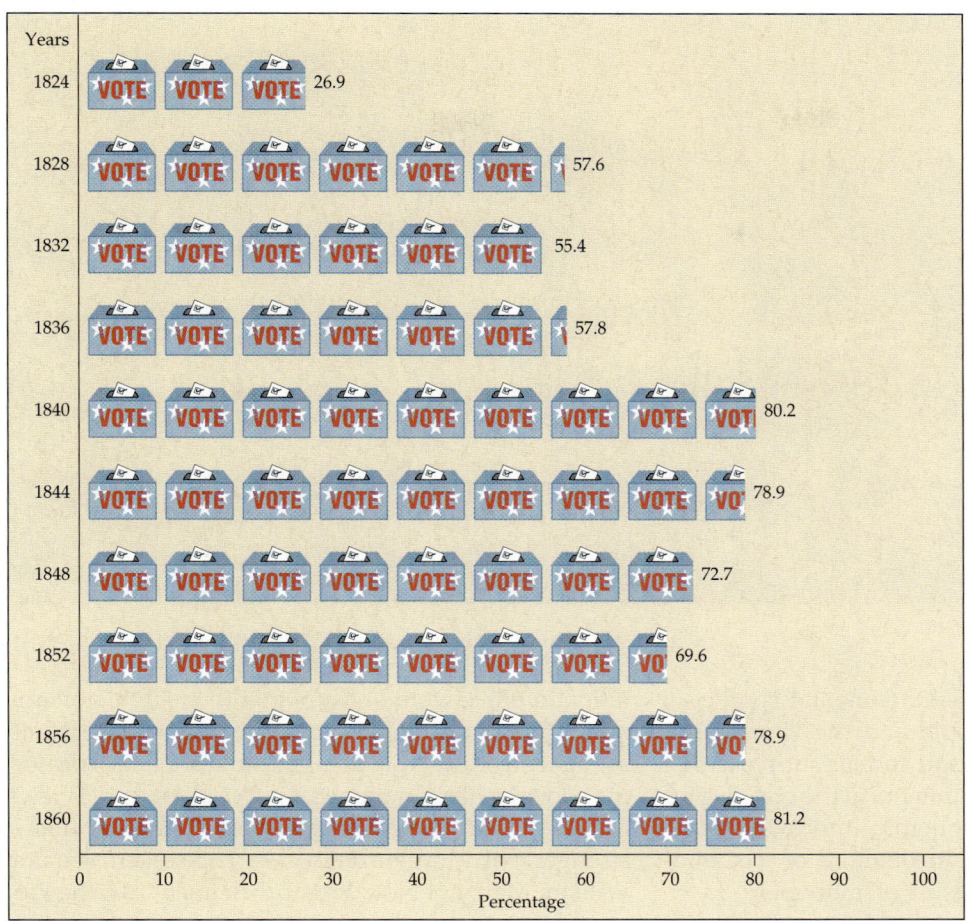

Voter Population and Turnout, 1824–1860

sure of the surging crowd. As many as 20,000 well-wishers attended a White House reception to honor the new president, muddying rugs, breaking furniture, and damaging china and glassware. "It was a proud day for the people," commented one Kentucky newspaperman. "General Jackson is their own President."

In certain respects, Jackson was truly a self-made man. Born in 1767 in a frontier region along the North and South Carolina border, he was the first president to be born in a log cabin. His father, a poor farmer from northern Ireland, died two weeks before his birth, while his mother and two brothers died during the American Revolution. At the age of 13, Jackson volunteered to fight in the American Revolution. He was taken prisoner and a British officer severely slashed Jackson's hand and head when the boy refused to shine the officer's shoes.

Jackson soon rose from poverty to a career in law and politics, becoming Tennessee's first congressman, a senator, and judge on the state supreme court. Although he would later gain a reputation as the champion of the common people, in Tennessee he was allied by marriage, business, and political ties to the state's elite. As a land speculator, cotton planter, and attorney, he accumulated a large personal fortune and acquired more than 100 slaves. His candidacy for the presidency was initially promoted by speculators, creditors, and elite leaders in Tennessee who hoped to exploit Jackson's popularity in order to combat antibanking sentiment and fend off challenges to their dominance of state politics.

Expanding the Powers of the Presidency

In office, Jackson greatly enhanced the power and prestige of the presidency. While each member of Congress represented a specific regional constituency, only the president, Jackson declared, represented all the people of the United States.

Jackson convinced many Americans that their votes mattered. He espoused a political ideology of "democratic republicanism" that stressed the common peoples' virtue, intelligence, and capacity for self-government. He also expressed a deep disdain for the "better classes," which claimed a "more enlightened wisdom" than common men and women.

Twenty thousand people attended a reception for President Jackson at the White House, trampling rugs, breaking furniture, and damaging china.

Endorsing the view that a fundamental conflict existed between working people and the "nonproducing" classes of society, Jackson and his supporters promised to remove any impediments to the ordinary citizen's opportunities for economic improvement. According to the Jacksonians, inequalities of wealth and power were the direct result of monopoly, favoritism, and special privileges, which made "the rich richer and the powerful more potent." Only free competition in an open marketplace would ensure that wealth would be distributed in accordance with each person's "industry, economy, enterprise, and prudence." The goal of the Jacksonians was to remove all obstacles that prevented farmers, artisans, and small shopkeepers from earning a greater share of the nation's wealth.

Nowhere was the Jacksonian ideal of openness made more concrete than in Jackson's theory of rotation in office, known as the **spoils system.** In his first annual message to Congress, Jackson defended the principle that public offices should be rotated among party supporters in order to help the nation achieve its republican ideals. Performance in public office, Jackson maintained, required no special intelligence or training, and rotation in office would ensure that the federal government did not develop a class of corrupt civil servants set apart from the people. His supporters advocated the spoils system on practical political grounds, viewing it as a way to reward party loyalists and build a stronger party organization. As Jacksonian Senator William Marcy of New York proclaimed, "To the victor belongs the spoils."

Known as a champion of the common people, President Jackson greatly expanded the powers of the presidency.

The spoils system opened government positions to many of Jackson's supporters, but the practice was neither as new nor as democratic as it appeared. During his first 18 months in office, Jackson replaced fewer than 1000 of the nation's 10,000 civil servants on political grounds, and fewer than 20 percent of federal officeholders were removed during his administration. Moreover, many of the men Jackson appointed to office had backgrounds of wealth and social eminence. Further, Jackson did not originate the spoils system. By the time he took office, a number of states, including New York and Pennsylvania, practiced political patronage.

Clearing the Land of Indians

The first major political controversy of Jackson's presidency involved Indian policy. At the time Jackson took office, 125,000 Native Americans still lived east of the Mississippi River. Cherokee, Choctaw, Chickasaw, and Creek Indians—60,000 strong—held millions of acres in what would become the southern cotton kingdom stretching across Georgia, Alabama, and Mississippi. The key political issues were whether these Native-American groups would be permitted to block white expansion and whether the U.S. government and its citizens would abide by previously made treaties.

Since Jefferson's presidency, two conflicting policies, assimilation and removal, had governed the treatment of Native Americans. Assimilation encouraged Indians to adopt the customs and economic practices of white Americans. The government provided financial assistance to missionaries in order to Christianize and educate Native Americans and convince them to adopt single-family farms. Proponents defended assimilation as the only way Native Americans would be able to survive in a white-dominated society.

By the 1820s, the Cherokee had demonstrated the ability of Native Americans to adapt to changing conditions while maintaining their tribal heritage. Sequoyah, a leader of these people, had developed a written alphabet. Soon the Cherokee opened schools, established churches, built roads, operated printing presses, and even adopted a constitution.

The other policy—**removal**—was first suggested by Thomas Jefferson as the only way to ensure the survival of Native American cultures. The goal of this policy was to encourage the voluntary migration of Indians westward to tracts of land where they could live free from white harassment. As early as 1817, James Monroe declared that the nation's security depended on rapid settlement along the Southern coast and that it was in the best interests of Native Americans to move westward. In 1825 he set before Congress a plan to resettle all eastern Indians on tracts in the West where whites would not be allowed to live.

After initially supporting both policies, Jackson favored removal as the solution to the controversy. This shift in federal Indian policy came partly as a result of a controversy between the Cherokee nation and the state of Georgia. The Cherokee people had adopted a constitution asserting sovereignty over their land. The state responded by abolishing tribal rule and claiming that the Cherokee fell under its jurisdiction. The discovery of gold on Cherokee land triggered a land rush, and the Cherokee nation sued to keep white settlers from encroaching on their territory. In two important cases, *Cherokee Nation* v. *Georgia* in 1831 and *Worcester* v. *Georgia* in 1832, the Supreme Court ruled that states could not pass laws conflicting with federal Indian treaties and that the federal government had an obligation to exclude white intruders from Indian lands. Angered, Jackson is said to have exclaimed: "John Marshall has made his decision; now let him enforce it."

The primary thrust of Jackson's removal policy was to encourage Native Americans to sell their homelands in exchange for new lands in Oklahoma and Arkansas. Such a policy, the president maintained, would open new farmland to whites while offering Indians a haven where they would be free to develop at their own pace. "There," he wrote, "your white brothers will not trouble you, they will have

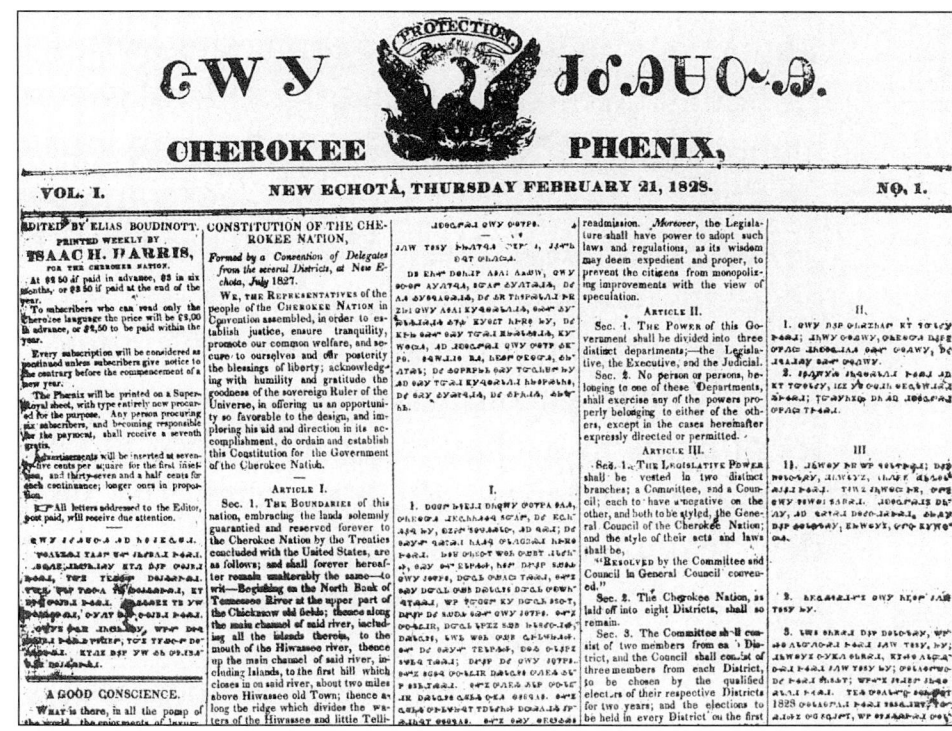

In 1809 a Cherokee named Sequoyah began to devise an alphabet consisting of letters based on English, Greek, and Hebrew. The Cherokee nation's weekly newspaper, the *Cherokee Phoenix*, was printed with this alphabet.

no claims to the land, and you can live upon it, you and all your children, as long as the grass grows or the water runs, in peace and plenty."

Pushmataha, a Choctaw chieftain, called on his people to reject Jackson's offer. Far from being a "country of tall trees, many water courses, rich lands and high grass abounding in games of all kinds," the promised preserve in the West was simply a barren desert. Jackson responded by warning that if the Choctaw refused to move west, he would destroy their nation.

During the winter of 1831, the Choctaw became the first tribe to walk the "Trail of Tears" westward. Promised government assistance failed to arrive, and malnutrition, exposure, and a cholera epidemic killed many members of the nation. Then, in 1836, the Creek suffered the hardships of removal. About 3500 of the tribe's 15,000 members died along the westward trek. Those who resisted removal were bound in chains and marched in double file.

Emboldened by the Supreme Court decisions declaring that Georgia law had no force on Indian territory, the Cherokees resisted removal. Fifteen thousand Cherokee joined in a protest against Jackson's policy: "Little did [we] anticipate that when taught to think and feel as the American citizen ... [we] were to be despoiled by [our] guardian, to become strangers and wanderers in the land of [our] fathers, forced to return to the savage life, and to seek a new home in the wilds of the far west, and that without [our] consent." The federal government bribed a faction of the tribe to leave the land in exchange for transportation costs and $5 million, but most Cherokees held out until 1838, when the army evicted them from their land. All told, 4000 of the 15,000 Cherokee died along the trail to Indian territory in what is now Oklahoma.

A number of other tribes also organized resistance against removal. In the Old Northwest, the Sauk and Fox Indians fought the Black Hawk War (1832) to re-

Trail of Tears (Indian Removal)

Andrew Jackson's Indian removal policy was known to many Native Americans as the Trail of Tears. Native Americans were herded westward off their lands in order to open the territory for expansion. The trek brought death to perhaps one-fourth of those who set out.

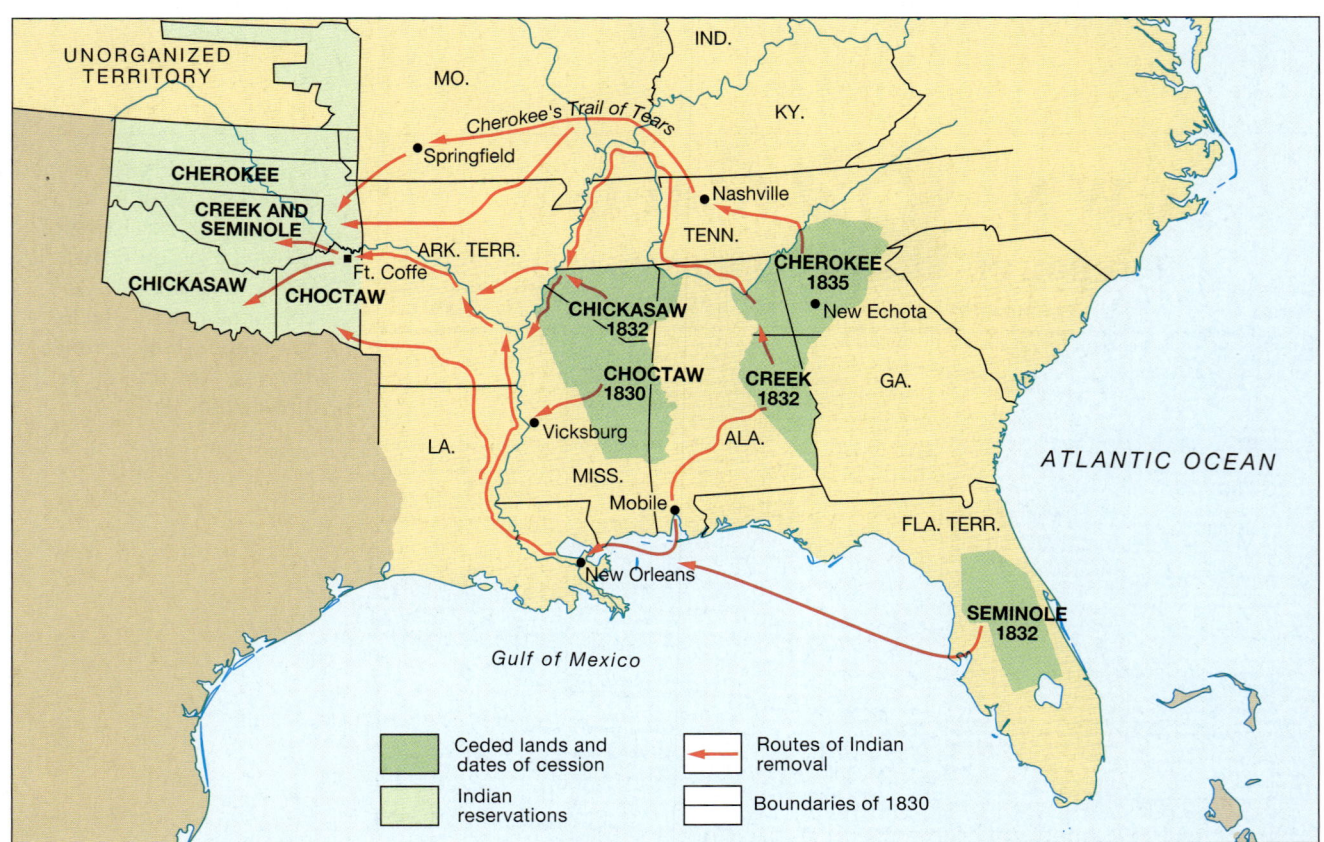

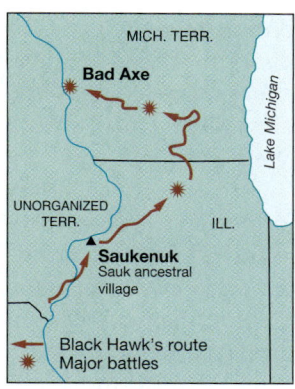

Black Hawk War

The Sauk and Fox resisted removal and fought the Black Hawk War to recover ceded lands in Illinois and Wisconsin. The U.S. army and the Illinois state militia ruthlessly suppressed the Native Americans.

cover ceded tribal lands in Illinois and Wisconsin. The Indians claimed that when they had signed the treaty transferring title to their land, they had not understood the implications of the action. "I touched the goose quill to the treaty," said Chief Black Hawk, "not knowing, however, that by that act I consented to give away my village." The United States army and the Illinois state militia ended the resistance by wantonly killing nearly 500 Sauk and Fox men, women, and children who were trying to retreat across the Mississippi River. In Florida, the military spent seven years putting down Seminole resistance at a cost of $20 million and 1500 casualties, and even then succeeding only after the treacherous act of kidnapping the Seminole leader Osceola during peace talks.

By twentieth-century standards, Jackson's Indian policy was both callous and inhumane. Despite the semblance of legality—94 treaties were signed with Indians during Jackson's presidency—Native-American migrations to the West almost always occurred under the threat of government coercion. Even before Jackson's death in 1845, it was obvious that tribal lands in the West were no more secure than Indian lands had been in the East. In 1851 Congress passed the Indian Appropriations Act, which sought to concentrate the western Native-American population on reservations.

Why were such morally indefensible policies adopted? Because many white Americans regarded Indian control of land and other natural resources as a serious obstacle to their desire for expansion and as a potential threat to the nation's security. Even had the federal government wanted to, it probably lacked the resources and military means necessary to protect the eastern Indians from encroaching white farmers, squatters, traders, and speculators. By the 1830s, a growing number of missionaries and humanitarians agreed with Jackson that Indians needed to be resettled westward for their own protection. Removal failed in large part because of the nation's commitment to limited government and its lack of

THE PEOPLE SPEAK

The Cherokee Nation Protests Against Jackson's Removal Policy (1836)

The Cherokee nation did not respond passively to President Andrew Jackson's efforts to evict them from their land. They challenged the removal policy in court. In 1836, 15,000 members of the nation submitted a protest to Congress, denouncing the evils of the removal policy and declaring that the agreements that supposedly justified their removal from their homelands had been obtained by fraud.

> It will be seen, from the numerous subsisting treaties . . . that . . . in consideration of valuable concessions made by the Cherokee nation, the United States solemnly guaranteed to said nation all their lands . . . and pledged the faith of the government, that "all white people who have intruded, or may hereafter intrude on the lands reserved for the Cherokees, shall be removed by the United States. . . ." The Cherokees were happy and prosperous under a scrupulous observance of treaty stipulations by the government of the United States, and from the fostering hand extended over them, they made rapid advance in civilization, morals, and the arts and sciences. Little did they anticipate, that when taught to think and feel as the American citizen, and to have with him a common interest, they were to be *despoiled by their guardian*, to become strangers and wanderers in the land of their fathers, forced to return to the savage life, and to seek a new home in the wilds of the far west, and that without their consent. An instrument purporting to be a treaty with the Cherokee people, has recently been made public by the President of the United States, that will have such an operation if carried into effect. This instrument, the delegation aver before the civilized world, and in the presence of Almighty God, is fraudulent, false upon its face, made by unauthorized individuals, without the sanction, and against the wishes, of the great body of the Cherokee people. Upwards of fifteen thousand of those people have protested against it, solemnly declaring they will never acquiesce. . . .

Source: "Memorial and Protest of the Cherokee Nation," June 22, 1836, Exec. Doc. No. 286, 24th Cong., 1st sess., pp. 1–2.

experience with social welfare programs. Contracts for food, clothing, and transportation were awarded to the lowest bidders, many of whom failed to fulfill their contractual responsibilities. Indians were resettled on semiarid lands, unsuited for intensive farming. The tragic outcome was readily foreseeable.

The problem of preserving native cultures in the face of an expanding nation was not confined to the United States. Jackson's removal policy can only be properly understood when seen as part of a broader process: the political and economic conquest of frontier regions by expanding nation states. During the early decades of the nineteenth century, Western nations were penetrating into many frontier areas, including the steppes of Russia, the pampas of Argentina, the veldt of South Africa, the outback of Australia, and the American West. In each of these regions, national expansion was justified on the grounds of strategic interest (to preempt settlement by other powers) or in the name of opening valuable land to white settlement and development. And in each case, expansion was accompanied by the removal or wholesale killing of native peoples.

Sectional Disputes over Public Lands and Nullification

Bitter sectional disputes arose during Jackson's presidency over public lands and the tariff. After the Revolutionary War, the federal government owned one-quarter billion acres of public land; the Louisiana Purchase added another half-billion acres to the public domain. These public lands constituted the federal government's single greatest resource.

In 1820, to promote the establishment of farms, Congress encouraged the rapid sale of public land by reducing the minimum land purchase from 160 to just 80 acres at a price of $1.25 per acre. Still, a variety of groups favored even easier terms for land sales. Squatters, for example, who violated federal laws that forbade settlement prior to the completion of public surveys, pressured Congress to adopt preemption acts that would permit them to buy the land they occupied at the minimum price of $1.25 when it came up for sale. Urban workingmen—agitating under the slogan "Vote Yourself a Farm"—demanded free homesteads for any American who would settle the public domain. Transportation companies, which built roads, canals, and later railroads, called for grants of public land to help fund their projects.

In Congress, two proposals—"distribution" and "graduation"—competed for support. Under the distribution proposal, which was identified with Henry Clay, Congress would distribute the proceeds from the sale of public lands to the states, which would use it to finance transportation improvements. Senator Thomas Hart Benton of Missouri offered an alternative proposal, graduation. He proposed that Congress gradually reduce the price of unsold government land and finally freely give away unpurchased land.

At the end of 1829, a Connecticut senator proposed a cessation of public land sales. This transformed the debate over public lands into a sectional battle over the nature of the union. Senator Benton denounced the proposal as a brazen attempt by manufacturers to keep laborers from settling the West, fearing that westward migration would reduce the size of the urban workforce and therefore raise their wage costs.

Benton's speech prompted Robert Y. Hayne, a supporter of John C. Calhoun, to propose an alliance of southern and western interests based on a low tariff and cheap land. Affirming the principle of nullification, he called on the two sections to unite against attempts by the Northeast to stengthen the powers of the federal government.

Daniel Webster of Massachusetts answered Hayne in one of the most famous speeches in American history. The United States, Webster proclaimed, was not simply a compact of the states. It was a creation of the people, who had invested the Constitution and the national government with ultimate sovereignty. If a state disagreed with an action of the federal government, it had a right to sue in federal court or seek to amend the Constitution, but it had no right to nullify a federal law. That would inevitably lead to anarchy and civil war. It was delusion and folly to think that Americans could have "Liberty first and Union afterwards," Webster declared. "Liberty and Union, now and forever, one and inseparable."

Jackson revealed his position on the questions of states' rights and nullification at a Jefferson Day dinner on April 13, 1830. Fixing his eyes on Vice President John C. Calhoun, Jackson expressed his sentiments with the toast: "Our Union: It must be preserved." Calhoun responded to Jackson's challenge and offered the next toast: "The Union, next to our liberty, most dear. May we always remember that it can only be preserved by distributing equally the benefits and burdens of the Union."

Relations between Jackson and Calhoun had grown increasingly strained. Jackson had learned that when Calhoun was secretary of war under Monroe he had called for Jackson's court-martial for his conduct during the military occupation of Florida in 1818. Jackson was also angry because Mrs. Calhoun had snubbed the wife of Secretary of War John H. Eaton, because Mrs. Eaton was the twice-married

In his famous oration, Senator Daniel Webster answered Senator Robert Hayne's call for states' rights, proclaiming, "Liberty and Union, now and forever, one and inseparable."

daughter of a tavernkeeper. Because Jackson's own late wife Rachel had been snubbed by society (partly because she smoked a pipe, partly because she had unknowingly married Jackson before a divorce from her first husband was final), the president had empathy for young Peggy Eaton. In 1831, Jackson reorganized his cabinet and forced Calhoun's supporters out. The next year, Calhoun became the first vice president to resign his office, when he became a senator from South Carolina.

In 1832, in an effort to conciliate the South, Jackson proposed a lower tariff. Revenue from the existing tariff (together with the sale of public lands) was so high that the federal debt was quickly being paid off; in fact on January 1, 1835, the United States Treasury had a balance of $440,000, not a penny of which was owed to anyone—the only time in U.S. history when the government was completely free of debt. The new tariff adopted in 1832 was somewhat lower than the Tariff of 1828 but still maintained the principle of protection. In protest, South Carolina's fiery "states' righters" declared both the Tariff of 1832 and the Tariff of 1828 null and void. To defend nullification, the state legislature voted to raise an army.

Jackson responded by declaring nullification illegal and then asked Congress to empower him to use force to execute federal law. Congress promptly enacted a Force Act. Privately, Jackson threatened to "hang every leader . . . of that infatuated people, sir, by martial law, irrespective of his name, or political or social position." He also dispatched a fleet of eight ships and a shipment of 5000 muskets to Fort Pinckney, a federal installation in Charleston harbor.

In Congress, Henry Clay, the "great compromiser" who had engineered the Missouri Compromise of 1820, worked feverishly to reduce South Carolina's sense of grievance. "He who loves the Union must desire to see this agitating question brought to a termination," he said. In less than a month, he persuaded Congress to enact a compromise tariff with lower levels of protection. South Carolinians backed down, rescinding the ordinance nullifying the federal tariff. As a final gesture of defiance, however, the state adopted an ordinance nullifying the Force Act.

In 1830 and 1831 South Carolina stood alone. No other southern state yet shared South Carolina's fear of federal power or its militant desire to assert the doctrine of states' rights. South Carolina's anxiety had many causes. By 1831 declining cotton prices and growing concern about the future of slavery had turned the state from a staunch supporter of economic nationalism into the nation's most aggressive advocate of states' rights. Increasingly, economic grievances fused with concerns over slavery. In 1832, the Palmetto State was one of just two states the majority of whose population was made up of slaves. By that year events throughout the hemisphere made South Carolinians desperately uneasy about the future of slavery. In 1831 and 1832 militant abolitionism had erupted in the North, slave insurrections had occurred in Southampton County, Virginia, and Jamaica, and Britain was moving to emancipate all slaves in the British Caribbean.

By using the federal tariff as the focus of their grievances, South Carolinians found an ideal way of debating the question of state sovereignty without debating the morality of slavery. Following the Missouri Compromise debates, a slave insurrection led by Denmark Vesey had been uncovered in Charleston in 1822. By 1832 South Carolinians did not want to stage debates in Congress that might bring the explosive slavery issue to the fore and possibly incite another slave revolt.

The Bank War

The major political issue of Jackson's presidency was his war against the second Bank of the United States. The banking system at the time Jackson assumed the presidency was completely different than it is today. At that time, the federal government coined only a limited supply of hard money and printed no paper money at all. The principal source of circulating currency—paper bank notes—was private commercial banks (of which there were 329 in 1829), chartered by the various states. These private, state-chartered banks supplied the credit necessary to finance land purchases, business operations, and economic growth. The notes they issued were promises to pay in gold or silver, but they were backed by a limited amount of precious metal and they fluctuated greatly in value.

In 1816, the federal government had chartered the **second Bank of the United States** partly in an effort to control the notes issued by state banks. By demanding payment in gold or silver, the national bank could discipline overspeculative private banks. But the very idea of a national bank was unpopular for various reasons. Many people blamed it for causing the Panic of 1819. Others resented its political influence. For example, Senator Daniel Webster was both the bank's chief lobbyist and a director of the bank's Boston branch. Wage earners and small-business owners blamed it for economic fluctuations and loan restrictions. Private banks resented its privileged position in the banking industry.

In 1832, Henry Clay, Daniel Webster, and other Jackson opponents in Congress, seeking an issue for that year's presidential election, passed a bill rechartering the second Bank of the United States. The bank's charter was not due to expire until 1836, but Clay and Webster wanted to force Jackson to take a clear probank or antibank position. Jackson had frequently attacked the bank as an agency through which speculators, monopolists, and other seekers after economic privilege cheated honest farmers and mechanics. Now, his adversaries wanted to force him either to sign the bill for recharter, alienating voters hostile to the bank, or veto it, antagonizing conservative voters who favored a sound banking system.

Jackson vetoed the bill in a forceful message that condemned the bank as a privileged "monopoly" created to make "rich men . . . richer by act of Congress." The bank, he declared, was "unauthorized by the Constitution, subversive of the rights of the States, and dangerous to the liberties of the people." In the presidential campaign of 1832, Henry Clay tried to make an issue of Jackson's bank veto, but Jackson swept to an easy second-term victory, defeating Clay by 219 electoral votes to 49.

Jackson interpreted his reelection as a mandate to undermine the bank still further. In September 1833, he ordered his Treasury secretary to divert federal revenues from the Bank of the United States to selected state banks, which came to be known as "pet" banks. The secretary of the Treasury and his assistant resigned rather than carry out the president's order. It was only after Jackson appointed a second new secretary that his order was implemented. Jackson's decision to divert federal deposits from the national bank prompted his adversaries in the Senate to formally censure the president's actions as arbitrary and unconstitutional. The bank's president, Nicholas Biddle, responded to Jackson's actions by reducing loans and calling in debts. "This worthy President," said Biddle, "thinks that because he has scalped Indians and imprisoned Judges he is to have his way with the Bank. He is mistaken." Jackson retorted: "The Bank . . . is trying to kill me, but I will kill it."

Jackson's decision to divert funds drew strong support from many conservative businesspeople who believed that the bank's destruction would increase the availability of credit and open up new business opportunities. Jackson, however, hated all banks, and believed that the only sound currencies were gold and silver. Having crippled the Bank of the United States, he promptly launched a crusade to replace all bank notes with hard money. Denouncing "the power which the moneyed interest derives from a paper currency," the president prohibited banks that received federal deposits from issuing bills valued at less than $5. Then, in the Specie Circular of 1836, Jackson prohibited payment for public lands in anything but gold or silver. That same year, in another antibanking measure, Congress voted to deprive pet banks of federal deposits. Instead, nearly $35 million in surplus funds was distributed to the states to help finance internal improvements.

To Jackson's supporters, the presidential veto of the bank bill was a principled assault on a bastion of wealth and special privilege. His efforts to curtail the circulation of bank notes was an effort to rid the country of a tool used by commercial interests to exploit farmers and working men and women. To his critics, the veto was an act of economic ignorance that destroyed a valuable institution that promoted monetary stability, eased the long-distance transfer of funds, provided a reserve of capital on which

As this anti-Jackson cartoon illustrates, defenders of the second Bank of the United States regarded Jackson's banking policies as a threat to the nation's economic health.

other banks drew, and helped regulate the bank notes issued by private banks. Jackson's effort to limit the circulation of bank notes was a misguided act of a "backward-looking" president, who failed to understand the role of a banking system in a modern economy.

The effect of Jackson's banking policies remains a subject of debate. Initially, land sales, canal construction, cotton production, and manufacturing boomed following Jackson's decision to divert federal funds from the bank. At the same time, however, state debts rose sharply and inflation increased dramatically. Prices climbed 28 percent in just three years. Then in 1837, just after the election of Jackson's successor Democrat Martin Van Buren, a deep financial depression struck the nation. Cotton prices fell by half. In New York City, 50,000 people were thrown out of work and 200,000 lacked adequate means of support. Hungry mobs broke into the city's flour warehouse. From across the country came "ru-

This anti-Democratic cartoon lays the blame for the Panic of 1837 on Jackson and his fiscal policies. His Specie Circular of 1836 has led to a run on the bank as panicked citizens try to exchange their paper bills for gold and silver. Debtors, unable to pay the soaring prices for food and other necessities, are being herded into the sheriff's office. A woman and her child are forced to beg for alms, while workers, idled by unemployment, hold the tools of their trade or slump in discouragement. Other targets of the cartoonist's criticism are the immigrants and drunkards pictured on the left side of the cartoon.

mor after rumor of riot, insurrection, and tumult." Not until the mid-1840s would the country fully pull out of the depression.

Who was to blame for the **Panic of 1837**? One school of thought holds Jackson responsible, arguing that his banking policies removed a vital check on the activities of state-chartered banks. Freed from the regulation of the second Bank of the United States, private banks rapidly expanded the volume of bank notes in circulation, contributing to the rapid increase in inflation. Jackson's Specie Circular of 1836, which sought to curb inflation by requiring that public land payments be made in hard currency, forced many Americans to exchange paper bills for gold and silver. Many private banks lacked sufficient reserves of hard currency and were forced to close their doors, triggering a financial crisis.

Another school of thought blames the panic on factors outside of Jackson's control. A surplus of cotton on the world market caused the price of cotton to drop sharply, throwing many southern and western cotton farmers into bankruptcy. Meanwhile, in 1836, Britain suddenly raised interest rates, which drastically reduced investment in the American economy and forced a number of states to default on loans from foreign investors.

If Jackson's policies did not necessarily cause the panic, they certainly made recovery more difficult. Jackson's hand-picked successor, Martin Van Buren, responded to the economic depression in an extremely doctrinaire way. A firm believer in the Jeffersonian principle of limited government, Van Buren refused to provide government aid to business.

Fearful that the federal government might lose funds it had deposited in private banks, Van Buren convinced Congress in 1840 to adopt an independent treasury system. Under this proposal, federal funds were locked up in insulated subtreasuries, which were totally divorced from the banking system. As a result the banking system was deprived of funds that might have aided recovery.

The Jacksonian Court

Presidents' judicial appointments represent one of their most enduring legacies. In his two terms as president, Andrew Jackson appointed five of the seven justices on the Supreme Court. To replace Chief Justice John Marshall, who died in 1835, Jackson selected his Treasury secretary, Roger B. Taney, who would lead the court for nearly three decades. Under Taney, the first chief justice to wear trousers instead of knee breeches, the Court broke with tradition and sought to extend Jacksonian principles of promoting individual opportunity by removing traditional restraints on competition in the marketplace. The Taney Court upheld the doctrine of limited liability for corporations and provided legal sanction to state subsidies for canals, turnpikes, and railroads. Taken together, the decisions of the Taney Court played a vital role in the emergence of the American system of free enterprise.

One case in particular, that of *Charles River Bridge* v. *Warren Bridge*, raised an issue fundamental to the nation's future economic growth: whether state-granted monopolies would be allowed to block competition from new enterprises. In 1828, the state of Massachusetts chartered a company to build a bridge connecting Boston and neighboring Charlestown. The owners of an existing bridge sued, claiming that their 1785 charter included an implied right to a monopoly.

In its decision, the Court ensured that monopolistic privileges granted in the past would not be allowed to interfere with public welfare. The Court held that contracts conferred only explicitly stated rights. Any ambiguity in wording should be construed in the public interest. The decision epitomized the ideals of Jacksonian democracy: a commitment to removing artificial barriers to opportunity and an emphasis upon free competition in an open marketplace.

Jackson's Legacy

Andrew Jackson was one of the nation's most resourceful and effective presidents. In the face of hostile majorities in Congress, he carried out his most important policies, affecting banking, internal improvements, Native Americans, and tariffs. As president, Jackson used the veto power more often than had all earlier presidents together during the preceding 40 years, and used it in such a way that he succeeded in representing himself as the champion of the people against special interests in Congress. In addition, his skillful use of patronage and party organization and his successful manipulation of public symbols helped create the nation's first modern political party with truly national appeal.

And yet, despite his popular appeal, Jackson's legacy is a matter of great dispute among historians. His Indian policies continue to arouse passionate criticism, while his economic policies, contrary to his reputation as the president of the common man, did little to help small farmers, artisans, and working people. In fact, his policies actually weakened the ability of the federal government to regulate the nation's economy. Indeed, many historians now believe that slaveholders—not small farmers or working people—benefited most. His Indian policy helped to open new lands for slaveowners, and his view of limited government forestalled federal interference with slavery.

RISE OF A POLITICAL OPPOSITION

Although it took a number of years for Jackson's opponents to coalesce into an effective national political organization, by the mid-1830s the Whig party, as the opposition came to be known, was able to battle the Democratic party on almost equal terms throughout the country.

A Party Formed by Coalition

The party was formed in 1834 as a coalition of National Republicans, Anti-Masons, and disgruntled Democrats, who were united by their hatred of "King Andrew" Jackson and his "usurpations" of congressional and judicial authority, came together in 1834 to form the **Whig party.** The party took its name from the seventeenth-century British Whig group that had defended English liberties against the usurpations of pro-Catholic Stuart Kings.

In 1836 the Whigs mounted their first presidential campaign, running three regional candidates against Martin Van Buren: Daniel Webster, the senator from Massachusetts who had substantial appeal in New England; Hugh Lawson White, who had appeal in the South; and William Henry Harrison, who fought an Indian alliance at the Battle of Tippecanoe and appealed to the West and to Anti-Masons in Pennsylvania and Vermont. The party strategy was to throw the election into the House of Representatives, where the Whigs would unite behind a single candidate. Van Buren easily defeated all his Whig opponents, winning 170 electoral votes to just 73 for his closest rival.

Following his strong showing in the election of 1836, William Henry Harrison received the united support of the Whig party in 1840. Benefiting from the Panic of 1837 and from a host of colorful campaign innovations as described at the beginning of this chapter, Harrison easily defeated Van Buren by a vote of 234 to 60 in the electoral college.

Unfortunately, the 68-year-old Harrison caught cold while delivering a two-hour inaugural address in the freezing rain. Barely a month later he died of pneumonia, the first president to die in office. His successor, John Tyler of Virginia, was an ardent defender of slavery, a staunch advocate of states' rights, and a former Democrat, whom the Whigs had nominated in order to attract Democratic support to the Whig ticket.

A firm believer in the principle that the federal government should exercise no powers other than those expressly enumerated in the Constitution, Tyler rejected the entire Whig legislative program, which called for reestablishment of a national bank, an increased tariff, and federally funded internal improvements.

John Tyler's opponents mocked him as "His Accidency" because he was the first vice president to take office as president upon the death of his predecessor.

The Whig party was furious. An angry mob gathered at the White House, threw rocks through the windows, and burned the president in effigy. To protest Tyler's rejection of the Whig political agenda, all members of the cabinet but one resigned. Tyler became a president without a party. "His Accidency" vetoed nine bills during his four years in office, more than any previous one-term president, frustrating Whig plans to recharter the national bank and raise the tariff while simultaneously distributing proceeds of land sales to the states. In 1843 Whigs in the House of Representatives made Tyler the subject of the first serious impeachment attempt, but the resolutions failed by a vote of 127 to 83.

Curiously, it was during John Tyler's tumultuous presidency that the nation's new two-party system achieved full maturity. Prior to Tyler's ascension to office, the Whig party had been a loose conglomeration of diverse political factions unable to agree on a party platform. Tyler's presidency increased unity among Whigs who found common cause in their opposition to his policies. Never before had party identity been so high or partisan sentiment so strong.

Who Were the Whigs?

The Jacksonians made a great effort to persuade voters to identify their own cause with Thomas Jefferson and their Whig opponents with Alexander Hamilton. A radical Jacksonian Democrat made the point bluntly. "The aristocracy of our country ... continually contrive to change their party name," wrote Frederick Robinson. "It was first Tory, then Federalist, then no party, then amalgamation, then National Republican, now Whig." In spite of Democratic charges to the contrary, however, the Whigs were not

Chronology of Key Events

1820 Land Act reduces price of public land to $1.25 per acre

1821 New York State Constitutional Convention eliminates property qualification for voting

1824 House of Representatives elects John Quincy Adams as sixth president

1825 President Monroe calls for voluntary removal of Native Americans in the east to lands west of the Mississippi River

1826 Disappearance of William Morgan touches off Anti-Masonic movement in New York State

1828 John C. Calhoun's "South Carolina Exposition" spells out the doctrine of nullification; Congress passes Tariff of Abominations; Andrew Jackson is elected seventh president

1830 Indian Removal Act provides funds to purchase Indian homelands in exchange for land in present-day Oklahoma and Arkansas; Webster-Hayne debate on land policy and nature of the union; Anti-Masons hold the first national party convention

1832 Jackson vetoes the bill to recharter the second Bank of the United States; John C. Calhoun becomes the first vice president to resign; South Carolina nullifies the federal tariff; United States defeats the Sauk and Fox Indians in the Black Hawk War

1833 Congress adopts "Compromise Tariff," lowering tariff rates, but also passes "Force Bill," authorizing Jackson to enforce federal law in South Carolina

1835 Roger B. Taney succeeds John Marshall as chief justice

1836 Jackson issues the Specie Circular; Martin Van Buren is elected eighth president

1837 Panic of 1837; *Charles River Bridge* v. *Warren Bridge* decides against monopoly privilege, rejecting the notion of implied rights in contracts and ruling that ambiguities in charters should be resolved in the favor of public welfare

1840 Congress passes Van Buren's Independent Treasury Act; William Henry Harrison, a Whig, is elected ninth president

1841 Harrison's death makes John Tyler the tenth president; Dorr Rebellion against suffrage restrictions in Rhode Island is put down

---

simply a continuation of the Federalist party. Like the Democrats, the Whigs drew support from all parts of the nation. Indeed, the Whigs often formed the majority of the South's representatives in Congress. Like the Democrats, the Whigs were a coalition of sectional interests, class and economic interests, and ethnic and religious interests.

Democratic voters tended to be small farmers, residents of less-prosperous towns, and the Scots-Irish and Catholic Irish. Whigs tended to be educators and professionals; manufacturers; business-oriented farmers; British and German Protestant immigrants; upwardly aspiring manual laborers; free blacks; and active members of Presbyterian, Unitarian, and Congregational churches. The Whig coalition included supporters of Henry Clay's American System, states' righters, religious groups alienated by Jackson's Indian removal policies, and bankers and businesspeople frightened by the Democrats' antimonopoly and antibank rhetoric.

Whereas the Democrats stressed class conflict, Whigs emphasized the harmony of interests between labor and capital, the need for humanitarian reform, and leadership by men of talent. The Whigs also idealized the "self-made man," who starts "from an humble origin, and from small beginnings rise[s] gradually in the world, as a result of merit and industry." Finally, the Whigs viewed technology and factory enterprise as forces for increasing national wealth and improving living conditions.

In 1848 and 1852 the Whigs tried to repeat their successful 1840 presidential campaign by nominating military heroes for the presidency. The party won the 1848 election with General Zachary Taylor, an Indian fighter and hero of the Mexican War, who had boasted that he had never cast a vote in a presidential election. Like Harrison, Taylor confined his campaign speeches to uncontroversial platitudes. "Old Rough and Ready," as he was known, died after just 1 year and 127 days in office. Then, in 1852, the Whigs nominated another Indian fighter and Mexican War hero, General Winfield Scott, who carried just four states for his dying party. "Old Fuss and Feathers," as he was called, was the last Whig nominee to play an important role in a presidential election.

Conclusion

A political revolution occurred in the United States between 1820 and 1840. Those two decades saw the abolition of property qualification for voting and officeholding, the elimination of voting by voice, an increase in voter participation, and the emergence of a new party system. Unlike America's first political parties, the Federalists and Republicans, the Jacksonian Democrats and the Whigs were parties with grassroots organization and support in all parts of the nation.

Andrew Jackson, the dominant political figure of the period, spelled out the new democratic approach to politics. In the name of eliminating special privilege and promoting equality of opportunity, he helped institute the national political nominating convention, defended the spoils system, destroyed the second Bank of the United States, and opened millions of acres of Indian lands to white settlement. A strong and determined leader, Jackson greatly expanded the power of the presidency. When South Carolina asserted the right of a state to nullify the federal tariff, Jackson made it clear that he would not tolerate defiance of federal authority. No matter how one evaluates his eight years in the White House, there can be no doubt that he left an indelible stamp on the nation's highest office; indeed, on a whole epoch in American history.

Suggestions for Further Reading

Donald B. Cole, *The Presidency of Andrew Jackson* (1993), and Richard Latner, *The Presidency of Andrew Jackson* (1979). Provide general overviews of Jackson's presidency.

Daniel Feller, *The Jacksonian Promise* (1995). An up-to-date reinterpretation of the Jacksonian era.

Michael Holt, *Rise and Fall of the American Whig Party* (1999). A thorough reappraisal of Jackson's political opposition.

Daniel Walker Howe, *The Political Culture of the American Whigs* (1979). Examines the political ideologies of the Whig party.

Edward Pessen, *Jacksonian America*, rev. ed. (1978), and Harry L. Watson, *Liberty and Power* (1990). Offer insightful surveys of the Jacksonian era.

Robert Remini, *Andrew Jackson and the Course of American Freedom* (1981), and *Andrew Jackson and the Course of American Democracy* (1984). Major biographies of Andrew Jackson.

Peter Temin, *The Jacksonian Economy* (1969). Reexamines Jackson's economic and banking policies.

Anthony F. C. Wallace, *The Long, Bitter Trail: Andrew Jackson and the Indians* (1993). Analyzes Jackson's Indian policies.

Overviews and Surveys

John Ashworth, *Slavery, Capitalism, and Politics in the Antebellum Republic* (1995); James MacGregor Burns, *The Crosswinds of Freedom: The Vineyard of Liberty* (1982); Ronald P. Formisano, "Toward a Reorientation of Jacksonian Politics: A Review of the Literature, 1959–1975," *Journal of American History*, 63 (1976); Edward Pessen, *Jacksonian America: Society, Personality, and Politics*, rev. ed. (1978); Robert V. Remini, *The Revolutionary Age of Andrew Jackson* (1976); Arthur M. Schlesinger, Jr., *The Age of Jackson* (1945); Harry L. Watson, *Liberty and Power: The Politics of Jacksonian America* (1990).

Political Democratization

Henry Christman, *Tin Horns and Calico: A Decisive Episode in the Emergence of Democracy* (1945); Ronald Formisano, *Transformation of Political Culture: Massachusetts Parties, 1790s–1840s* (1983); Paul Goodman, *Toward a Christian Republic: Antimasonry and the Great Transition in New England* (1988); Merrill Peterson, ed., *Democracy, Liberty and Property: The State Constitutional Conventions of the 1820s* (1966); Lorman Ratner, *Anti-Masonry: The Crusade and the Party* (1969); W. P. Vaughn, *The Antimasonic Party in the United States, 1826–1843* (1983); Chilton Williamson, *American Suffrage: From Property to Democracy, 1760–1860* (1960).

The Rebirth of Parties

Lee Benson, *The Concept of Jacksonian Democracy: New York as a Test Case* (1961); Steven C. Bullock, *Revolutionary Brotherhood: Freemasonry and the Transformation of the American Social Order* (1996); James S. Chase, *Emergence of the Presidential Nominating Convention, 1789–1832* (1973); Donald B. Cole, *Jacksonian Democracy in New Hampshire, 1800–1851* (1970); Ronald Formisano, *The Birth of Mass Political Parties: Michigan, 1827–1861* (1971); Marvin E. Gettleman, *The Dorr Rebellion: A Study in American Radicalism, 1833–1849* (1973); M. J. Heale, *The Presidential Quest: Candidates and Images in American Political Culture, 1787–1852* (1982); Richard

Hofstadter, *The Idea of a Party System: The Rise of Legitimate Opposition in the United States, 1780–1840* (1969); Robert Kelley, *The Cultural Pattern in American Politics: The First Century* (1979); Peter D. Levine, *The Behavior of State Legislative Parties in the Jacksonian Era, New Jersey, 1829–1844* (1977); Shaw Livermore, *The Twilight of Federalism: The Disintegration of the Federalist Party, 1815–1830* (1962); Richard P. McCormick, *The Second American Party System* (1966), and *The Presidential Game: The Origins of American Presidential Politics* (1982); Edward Pessen, *Riches, Class, and Power Before the Civil War* (1973); Robert V. Remini, *The Election of Andrew Jackson* (1963), and *Martin Van Buren and the Making of the Democratic Party* (1959); Arthur M. Schlesinger, Jr., ed., *History of U.S. Political Parties, 1789–1860: From Factions to Parties* (1973); Arthur M. Schlesinger, Jr. and Fred L. Israel, eds., *History of American Presidential Elections, 1789–1968* (1971); Joel Silbey, *The American Political Nation, 1838–1893* (1991), and *The Partisan Imperative: The Dynamics of American Politics Before the Civil War* (1985); J. Mills Thornton III, *Politics and Power in a Slave Society: Alabama, 1800–1860* (1977); Harry L. Watson, *Jacksonian Politics and Community Conflict: The Emergence of the Second Party System in Cumberland County, North Carolina* (1981).

Andrew Jackson: The Politics of Egalitarianism

William L. Anderson, ed., *Cherokee Removal: Before and After* (1991); John Ashworth, *"Agrarians" and "Aristocrats": Party Political Ideology in the United States, 1837–1846* (1983); Jean H. Baker, *Affairs of Party: The Political Culture of Northern Democrats in the Mid-Nineteenth Century* (1983); Amy Bridges, *A City in the Republic: Antebellum New York and the Origins of Machine Politics* (1984); Matthew A. Crenson, *The Federal Machine: Beginnings of Bureaucracy in Jacksonian America* (1975); James C. Curtis, *Andrew Jackson and the Search for Vindication* (1976); Angie Debo, *And Still the Waters Run: The Betrayal of the Five Civilized Tribes* (1940); A. H. DeRosier, Jr., *The Removal of the Choctaw Indians* (1970); B. W. Dippie, *The Vanishing American: White Attitudes and U.S. Indian Policy* (1982); Cecil Eby, *"That Disgraceful Affair": The Black Hawk War* (1973); Richard Ellis, *The Union at Risk: Jacksonian Democracy, States' Rights, and the Nullification Crisis* (1987); Daniel Feller, *Public Lands in Jacksonian Politics* (1984); William W. Freehling, *Prelude to Civil War: The Nullification Controversy in South Carolina, 1816–1836* (1966); Michael D. Green, *The Politics of Indian Removal: Creek Government and Society in Crisis* (1982); Charles G. Haines and Foster H. Sherwood, *The Role of the Supreme Court in American Government and Politics, 1835–1864* (1957); Bray Hammond, *Banks and Politics in America: From the Revolution to the Civil War* (1957); Stanley I. Kutler, *Privilege and Creative Destruction: The Charles River Bridge Case* (1971); Richard Latner, *The Presidency of Andrew Jackson: White House Politics, 1829–1837* (1979); John M. McFaul, *The Politics of Jacksonian Finance* (1972); R. C. McGrane, *The Panic of 1837* (1924); William G. McLoughlin, *Cherokee Renascence in the New Republic* (1986); James H. Merrell, *The Indians' New World: Catawbas and Their Neighbors from European Contact Through the Era of Removal* (1989); Marvin Meyers, *The Jacksonian Persuasion* (1957); Roger L. Nichols, *Black Hawk and the Warrior's Path* (1992); M. D. Peterson, *Olive Branch and Sword: The Compromise of 1833* (1982); F. P. Prucha, *American Indian Policy in the Formative Years* (1962); Fritz Redlich, *The Molding of American Banking: Men and Ideas* (1951); Robert Remini, *The Legacy of Andrew Jackson* (1988); Hugh Rockoff, *The Free Banking Era* (1975); Ronald N. Satz, *American Indian Policy in the Jacksonian Era* (1975); Bernard Schwartz, *From Confederation to Nation: The American Constitution, 1835–1877* (1973); W. G. Shade, *Banks or No Banks: The Money Issue in Western Politics, 1832–1865* (1972); J. R. Sharp, *The Jacksonians versus the Banks* (1970); W. B. Smith and A. H. Cole, *Fluctuations in American Business, 1790–1860* (1935); Paul Studenski and Herman E. Krooss, *Financial History of the United States*, 2d ed. (1963); Peter Temin, *The Jacksonian Economy* (1969); Richard H. Timberlake, Jr., *The Origins of Central Banking in the United States* (1978); J. Van Fenstermaker, *The Development of American Commercial Banking, 1782–1837* (1965); Herman J. Viola, *Thomas L. McKenney: Architect of America's Early Indian Policy* (1974); Anthony F. C. Wallace, *The Long, Bitter Trail: Andrew Jackson and the Indians* (1993); John William Ward, *Andrew Jackson: Symbol for an Age* (1955); Philip Weeks, *Farewell, My Nation: The American Indian & the United States, 1820–1890* (1990); Leonard D. White, *The Jacksonians: A Study in Administrative History, 1829–1861* (1954); Jean Alexander Wilburn, *Biddle's Bank: The Crucial Years* (1967).

Rise of a Political Opposition

Thomas Brown, *Politics and Statesmanship: Essays on the American Whig Party* (1985); Daniel Walker Howe, *The Political Culture of the American Whigs* (1979); Lawrence Frederick Kohl, *The Politics of Individualism: Parties and the American Character in the Jacksonian Era* (1989); Thomas H. O'Connor, *Lords of the Loom: The Cotton Whigs and the Coming of the Civil War* (1968).

Biographies

Irving H. Bartlett, *Daniel Webster* (1978); Maurice G. Baxter, *One and Inseparable: Daniel Webster and the Union* (1984), and *Henry Clay and the American System* (1995); Norman D. Brown, *Daniel Webster and the Politics of Availability* (1969); Alfred A. Cave, *An American Conservative in the Age of Jackson: The Political and Social Thought of Calvin Colton* (1969); William N. Chambers, *Old Bullion Benton: Senator from the New West* (1956); Oliver Perry Chitwood, *John Tyler: Champion of the Old South* (1939); Freeman Cleaves, *Old Tippecanoe: William Henry Harrison and His Time* (1939); Donald B. Cole, *Martin Van Buren and the American Political System* (1984); Richard N. Current, *Daniel Webster and the Rise of National Conservatism* (1955), and *John C. Calhoun* (1963); James C. Curtis, *The Fox at Bay: Martin Van Buren and the Presidency, 1837–1841* (1970); Robert F. Dalzell, Jr., *Daniel Webster and the Trial of American Nationalism, 1843–1852* (1973); Martin Duberman, *Charles Francis Adams, 1807–1886* (1961); Robert G. Gunderson, *The Log Cabin Campaign*

(1957); Richard Hofstadter, *The American Political Tradition* (1948); Robert J. Morgan, *A Whig Embattled: The Presidency Under John Tyler* (1954); Jerome Mushkat and Joseph G. Raybeck, *Martin Van Buren* (1997); Paul C. Nagel, *John Quincy Adams* (1997); Sydney Nathans, *Daniel Webster and Jacksonian Democracy* (1973); John Niven, *John C. Calhoun and the Price of Union* (1988), and *Martin Van Buren: The Romantic Age of American Politics* (1983); Lynn Hudson Parsons, *John Quincy Adams* (1998); Robert V. Remini, *Andrew Jackson and the Course of American Empire, 1767–1821* (1977), *Andrew Jackson and the Course of American Freedom, 1822–1832* (1981), *Andrew Jackson and the Course of American Democracy, 1833–1845* (1984), and *Martin Van Buren and the Making of the Democratic Party* (1959); G. G. Van Deusen, *The Life of Henry Clay* (1937).

Internet Resources

Jacksonian Era Medicine and Life
http://www.indianapolis.in.us/cp/jmed.html
Survival was far from certain in the Jacksonian Era. This site discusses some of the reasons and some of the possible cures of the times.

The University of Pennsylvania in 1830
http://www.upenn.edu/AR/1830/
This "virtual tour" shows what a fairly typical campus looked like and what student life was like at one of the larger universities in the Antebelllum Era.

1830s Clothing
http://www.connerprairie.org/clothing.html
See how clothing worn in the early republic was quite different from what you are wearing now.

Key Terms

American System [of Henry Clay]   (p. 265)
Tariff of Abominations   (p. 265)
Nullification   (p. 266)
Spoils System   (p. 268)
Removal [Indian Removal Policy]   (p. 269)
Second Bank of the United States   (p. 274)
Panic of 1837   (p. 276)
Whig Party   (p. 277)

Review Questions

1. What changes took place in voting, nominating procedures, party organization, and campaign strategies between 1820 and 1840?
2. What new political parties emerged in the 1820s and 1830s? How did these parties differ?
3. What groups were denied political participation under Jacksonian democracy?
4. Why did settlers want to move Native Americans west of the Mississippi River? How did Native Americans try to resist removal? Why is the removal of the Native Americans from their homelands in the Southeast known as the Trail of Tears?
5. Why did South Carolina try to nullify the federal tariff? What was President Jackson's reaction? How was the controversy resolved?
6. Why was President Jackson opposed to the Second Bank of the United States? What actions did he take to weaken the bank?
7. How did President Jackson strengthen the presidency?

11

AMERICA'S FIRST AGE OF REFORM

SOURCES OF THE REFORM IMPULSE
Social Problems on the Rise
A New Moral Sensibility
The Second Great Awakening
Religious Diversity

MORAL REFORM

SOCIAL REFORM
The Problem of Crime in a Free Society
The Struggle for Public Schools
Asylums for Society's Outcasts

RADICAL REFORM
Early Antislavery Efforts
The Rise of Abolitionist Sentiment in the North
Abolitionist Arguments and Public Reaction
Division Within the Antislavery Movement
The Birth of Feminism
Catalyst for Women's Rights
Utopian Communities

ARTISTIC AND CULTURAL FERMENT
American Transcendentalism
A Literary Renaissance
Ethnic Voices
American Art

AMERICAN POPULAR CULTURE
The Popular Novel
Forms of Popular Entertainment

"And a'n't I a woman?"

She was born into slavery around 1797 in New York State's Hudson River Valley, 80 miles from New York City. As a slave, she was known simply as "Isabella." But a decade and a half after escaping from bondage, she adopted a new name. As **Sojourner Truth,** she became a legend in the struggle to abolish slavery and extend equal rights to women.

The youngest of some 10 or 12 children, she grew up in a single room in a dark and damp cellar, sleeping on straw on top of loose boards. For 16 years, from 1810 to 1826, she served as a household slave in upstate New York, and was sold five times. One owner beat her so savagely that her arms and shoulders bore scars for the rest of her life. She bore a fellow slave five children, only to see at least three of her offspring sold away. In 1826, just a year before slavery was finally abolished in the state, she fled after her owner broke a promise to free her and her husband. She took refuge with a farm family that later bought her freedom.

Isabella then moved to New York City, carrying only a bag of clothing and 25 cents. There she supported herself as a domestic servant. It was a period of intense religious excitement, and, although she lacked formal schooling, Isabella began to preach at camp meetings and on street corners.

In 1843, Isabella took on the name Sojourner Truth, convinced that God had called on her to wander the country and boldly speak out the truth. Her fame as a preacher, singer, and orator for abolition and women's rights spread quickly and three incidents became the stuff of legend. During the late 1840s, when the black abolitionist Frederick Douglass expressed doubt about the possibility of ending slavery peacefully, she replied forcefully: "Frederick, is God dead?" Several years later, in a speech before a woman's rights convention in Akron, Ohio, in 1851, she demanded that Americans recognize that impoverished African American women were women too, reportedly saying: "I could work as much and eat as much as a man—when I could get it—and bear de lash as well! And a'n't I a woman?" And in 1858, when a hostile audience insisted that the six-foot tall orator spoke too powerfully to be a woman, she reportedly bared her breasts before them.

During the Civil War, she took an active role promoting the Union cause, collecting food and supplies for black troops and struggling to make emancipation a war aim. When the war was over, she traveled across the North, collecting signatures on petitions calling on Congress to set aside western land for former slaves. At her death in 1883, she could rightly be remembered as one of the nation's most eloquent opponents of discrimination in all forms.

The decades before the Civil War saw the birth of the American reform tradition. Reformers launched unprecedented campaigns to educate the deaf and the blind, rehabilitate criminals, extend equal rights to women, and abolish slavery. Our modern systems of free public schools, prisons, and hospitals for the infirm and the mentally ill are all legacies of this first generation of American reform.

SOURCES OF THE REFORM IMPULSE

What factors gave rise to the reform impulse and why was it unleashed with such vigor in pre–Civil War America? Reformers had many different reasons for wanting to change American society. Some hoped to remedy the distresses created by social disorder, violence, and widening class divisions. Others found motivation in a religious vision of a godly society on earth.

Social Problems on the Rise

During the early nineteenth century, poverty, lawlessness, violence, and vice appeared to be increasing at an alarming rate. In New York, the nation's largest city, crime rose far faster than in the overall popula-

A legend in the abolitionist and women's rights movements, Sojourner Truth was born into slavery around 1797 and escaped from bondage in 1826.

tion. Between 1814 and 1834, the city's population doubled, but reports of crime quadrupled. Gangs, bearing such names as Plug Uglies and Bowery B'hoys, prowled the streets, stealing from warehouses and private residences. Public drunkenness was a common sight. By 1835, there were nearly 3000 drinking places in New York—one for every 50 persons over the age of 15. Prostitution also generated concern. By 1850, a reported 6000 "fallen women" strolled the city streets. Mob violence evoked particular fear. In a single decade, 1834–1844, 200 incidents of mob violence occurred in New York. Adding to the sense of alarm were scenes of heart-wrenching poverty, such as children standing barefoot outside hotels, selling matches.

Social problems were not confined to large cities like New York. During the decades before the Civil War, newspapers reported hundreds of incidences of duels, lynchings, and mob violence. In the slave states and southwestern territories men frequently resolved quarrels by dueling. In one 1818 duel between two cousins, the combatants faced off with shotguns at four paces! Lynchings too were widely reported. In 1835, the citizens of Vicksburg, Mississippi, attempted to rid the city of gambling and prostitution by raiding gaming houses and brothels and lynching five gamblers. In urban areas, mob violence increased in frequency and destructiveness. Between 1810 and 1819 there were 7 major riots; in the 1830s there were 115.

A nation in which the vice president had to carry a gun while presiding over the Senate—lest senators attack each other with knives or pistols—seemed to confirm criticism by Europeans that democracy inevitably led to anarchy. Incidents of crime and violence led many Americans to ask how a free society could maintain stability and moral order. Americans sought to answer this question through religion, education, and social reform.

A New Moral Sensibility

More than anxiety over lawlessness, violence, and vice sparked the reform impulse during the first decades of the nineteenth century. America's revolutionary heritage, the philosophy of the Enlightenment, and religious zeal all contributed to a sensitivity to human suffering and a boundless faith in humankind's capacity to improve social institutions.

Many pre–Civil War reformers saw their efforts as an attempt to realize the ideals enshrined in the Declaration of Independence. Invoking the principles of liberty and equality set forth in the Declaration, abolitionists such as William Lloyd Garrison attacked slavery and feminists such as Elizabeth Cady Stanton called for equal rights for women.

The philosophy of the **Enlightenment,** with its belief in the people's innate goodness and with its rejection of the inevitability of poverty and ignorance, was another important source of the reform impulse. Those who espoused the Enlightenment philosophy argued that the creation of a more favorable moral and physical environment could alleviate social problems.

Religion further strengthened the reform impulse. Almost all the leading reformers were devoutly religious men and women who wanted to deepen the nation's commitment to Christian principles. Two trends in religious thought—religious liberalism and evangelical revivalism—strengthened reformers' zeal. **Religious liberalism** was an emerging form of humanitarianism that rejected the harsh Calvinist doctrines of original sin and predestination. Its preachers stressed the basic goodness of human nature and each individual's capacity to follow the example of Christ.

William Ellery Channing (1780–1842) was America's leading exponent of religious liberalism, and his beliefs, proclaimed in a sermon he delivered in Baltimore in 1819, became the basis for American Unitarianism. The new religious denomination stressed individual freedom of belief, a united world under a single God, and the mortal nature of Jesus Christ, whom individuals should strive to emulate. Channing's beliefs stimulated many reformers to work toward improving the conditions of the physically handicapped, the criminal, the impoverished, and the enslaved.

The Second Great Awakening

Enthusiastic religious revivals swept the nation in the early nineteenth century, providing further religious motivation for the reform impulse. On August 6, 1801, some 25,000 men, women, and children gathered in the small frontier community of Cane Ridge, Kentucky, in search of religious salvation. Twenty-five thousand was a fantastically large number of people at a time when the population of the whole state of Kentucky was a quarter million, and the state's largest city, Lexington, had only 1795 residents. The Cane Ridge camp meeting went on for a week. Baptists, Methodists, and ministers of other denominations joined together to preach to the vast throng. Within three years, similar revivals occurred throughout Kentucky, Tennessee, and Ohio. This great wave of religious fervor became known as the **Second Great Awakening.**

The American Mosaic

Gouging Fights and Backcountry Honor

NOBODY ever called them pretty. Eastern and European travelers to the American southern back-country employed many descriptive and emotive adjectives— disgusting, brutal, savage, uncivilized, disgraceful, barbaric, unsightly—but never once pretty. And, indeed, backcountry fights, whether called "gouging" matches, "rough-and-tumble" contests, or "no holds barred" battles, were not attractive affairs. Men fought all out, using fists, hands, feet, elbows, knees, teeth, and whatever other part of their anatomy promised to do bodily damage to their opponents. Capturing the temper of these battles, Anglican minister Charles Woodmason counseled, "I would advise you when You do fight Not to act like Tygers and Bears as these Virginians do—Biting one anothers Lips and Noses off, and *gouging* one another—that is, thrusting out one anothers Eyes, and kicking one another on the Cods, to the Great damage of many a Poor Woman."

The goal of a gouging match was the disfigurement of one's opponent. This could be accomplished in any number of ways, but the most popular was eye gouging. Fighters manicured their fingernails hard and sharp so that they could use them as a fulcrum to pry out their adversary's eye. On seeing a renowned fighter badly mauled, a passerby remarked, "'You have come off badly this time; I doubt?' 'Have I,' says he triumphantly, showing from his pocket at the same time an eye; which he had extracted during the combat, and preserved as a trophy."

Reading descriptions of these sanguinary contests provokes a series of questions. Who would engage in such activities? And why? Were the contests considered sports or manifestations of blood feuds? And what of the spectators and the law—did they enjoy and allow and condone such barbarities? Finally, what do the contests tell us about the society in which they flourished?

Gouging centered in the region of rivers and largely untamed backcountry south of the Ohio River. It was a land of dangers and violence and early deaths. Organized groups of Native Americans threatened settlers. Wild animals roamed the heavily wooded forests. Outlaws practiced their professions almost unchecked by the law. High infant mortality rates, short life expectancies, dangerous occupations, and random violence stood as grim reminders that life in this region of nature was, as philosopher Thomas Hobbes once noted, "solitary, poor, nasty, brutish, and short."

The men who disfigured each other in gouging matches had been hardened by their environment and their occupations. Many worked on the rivers as roustabouts, rivermen, or gamblers. Others were hunters, herders, or subsistence farmers. No plantations dotted their world; no landed aristocrats dominated them. As a leading historian of the subject commented, "the upland folk lived in an intensely local, kin-based society. Rural hamlets, impassable roads, and provincial isolations—not growing towns, internal improvements, or international commerce—characterized the backcountry."

The work these men performed was physically demanding and dangerous. Working on a Mississippi barge or trapping game in the backcountry exposed men to all the forces of nature and did not foster a gentle view of life. Death and pain were everywhere to be seen. Mark Twain remembered such men from his boyhood experiences in a raw river town: "Rude, uneducated, brave, suffering terrific hardships with sailor-like stoicism; heavy drinkers, coarse frolickers . . . , heavy fighters, reckless fellows, every one, elephantinely jolly, foul witted, profane, prodigal of their money, bankrupt at the end of the trip, fond of barbaric finery, prodigious braggarts." They were not Jacksonian men on the make or respectable churchgoers. Rather they were men who worked hard, played hard, and drank hard.

Since they spent most of their lives in the company of other men, much of their sense of self-worth came from how their companions viewed them. They did not use money or piety as yardsticks for measuring the worth of a man. Bravery, strength, conviviality, and a jealous sense of personal honor determined the cut of a man. The ability to drink, boast, and fight with equal ability marked a backcountry Renaissance man.

Question a man's honor and you questioned in the most profound sense his manhood. If aristocratic Southerners dueled over such slights, backcountry laborers gouged over them. Northerners found this touchy sense of honor perplexing. Philip Vickers Fithian, a New Jerseyite who traveled to the South in the 1770s, commented about the reason for one fight, "I suppose either that they are lovers, and one has in Jest or reality some way supplanted the other; or has in

a merry hour called him a *Lubber* or a *Thick-Skull*, or a *Buckskin*, or a *Scotsman*, or perhaps one has mislaid the other's hat, or knocked a peach out of his Hand, or offered him a dram without wiping the mouth of the Bottle." Any excuse, thought Fithian, could lead to mortal combat. But he misread the situation. In truth, any insult, no matter how slight, could be judged serious enough to provoke violence.

Once men exchanged angry words and angrier challenges, their combat provided entertainment for their companions. At the fights, drinking and boasting continued, and the line between participant and spectator was hazy. One fight often led to another and general melees were not uncommon. Were such contests sports? Probably not, but it was not a question that anyone would have posed. Just as there was little distinction between participant and spectator, there was little difference between sport and battery.

Gouging matches were certainly not civilized affairs, and as civilized behavior and culture penetrated the backcountry, men ceased to settle their differences in such brutal contests. This is not to say that they stopped fighting. Rather they "defended their honor" in more "civilized" ways. Bowie knives, swords, and pistols replaced honed thumbnails and filed teeth as the weapons of choice. And these "affairs of honor" were held before a few solemn witnesses rather than a host of cheering friends.

But if gouging became a relic of another age, it remained a particularly telling relic. It provides an important clue to the values of the southern backcountry. How men fought—just as how they worked or played—indicates much about their lives. The men who gouged led strenuous, often violent lives. They were not the sort of men to turn pale at the sight of blood or even at the sight of an eyeless eye socket. They admired toughness, fearlessness, and even meanness—not piety, gentleness, and sensitivity.

During an earlier time, it was considered an unmanly sign of fear for a person to carry a weapon. But more refined sensibilities reversed this notion. By the mid-nineteenth century weapon carrying had become an indication of manliness.

Americans turned to revival meetings in times of social and economic upheaval. These meetings, which stressed new-birth conversions, could last for days.

The revivals inspired a widespread sense that the nation was standing close to the millennium, a thousand years of peace and benevolence when sin, war, and tyranny would vanish from the earth. Evangelical leaders urged their followers to reject selfishness and materialism and repent their sins. To the revivalists, sin was no metaphysical abstraction. Luxury, high living, indifference to religion, preoccupation with worldly and commercial matters—all were denounced as sinful. If men and women did not seek God through Christ, the nation would face divine retribution. **Evangelical revivals** helped instill in Americans a belief that they had been chosen by God to lead the world toward "a millennium of republicanism."

Charles Grandison Finney (1792–1875), the "father of modern revivalism," led revivals throughout the Northeast. Finney became the North's leading revivalist. Despite his lack of formal theological training, he was remarkably successful in converting souls to Christ. Finney's message was that anyone could experience a redemptive change of heart and a resurgence of religious feeling. He prayed for sinners by name; he held meetings that lasted night after night for a week or more; he set up an "anxious bench" at the front of the meeting, where the almost-saved could receive special prayers. He also encouraged women to participate actively in revivals. If only enough people converted to Christ, Finney told his listeners, the millennium—Christ's reign on earth—would arrive within three years.

Revival meetings attracted both frontier settlers and city folk, slaves and masters, farmers and shopkeepers. The revivals had their greatest appeal among isolated farming families on the western and southern frontier and among upwardly mobile merchants, shopkeepers, artisans, skilled laborers in the expanding commercial and industrial towns of the North. They also drew support from social conservatives who feared that America would disintegrate into a state of anarchy without the influence of evangelical religion. Above all, revivals attracted large numbers of young women, who took an active role organizing meetings, establishing church societies, and editing religious publications.

Religious Diversity

The early nineteenth century was a period of extraordinary religious ferment. Church membership climbed steeply, until three-quarters of all Americans were affiliated with a church. The religious landscape grew increasingly diverse. A number of older denominations—notably the Baptists, Catholics, and Methodists—expanded rapidly while a host of new denominations and movements arose, including the African Methodist Episcopal church, the Disciples of Christ, the Mormons, and the Unitarian and Universalist churches.

During the late eighteenth century, church membership was low and falling. Deism—a movement that emphasized reason rather than revelation and denied that a divine creator interfered with the workings of the universe—and skepticism seemed to be spreading. A French immigrant claimed that "religious indifference is imperceptibly disseminated from one end of the continent to the other." Yet by 1830, foreign observers considered the United States the most religious country in the western world.

Religious revivals played a critical role in this outpouring of religion. In part, revivalism represented a response to the growing separation of church and state that followed the American Revolution. When states deprived established churches of state support (as did Virginia in 1785, Connecticut in 1818, and Massachusetts in 1833), Protestant ministers held revivals to ensure that America would remain a God-fearing nation. The popularity of revivals also reflected the hunger of many Americans for an emotional religion that downplayed creeds and rituals and instead emphasized conversion.

No religious group grew more rapidly during the pre–Civil War era or faced more bitter hostility than the Roman Catholic Church. From just 25,000 members and 6 priests in 1776, the Catholic church in America grew to 3 million members in 1860. With English, French, German, Irish, and Mexican members, it was not only the nation's largest denomination, it was also America's first multicultural church. Concerned that many immigrants were only nominally Catholic, the Church established urban missions and launched religious revivals to strengthen Catholics' religious identity. Somewhat similar to the Protestant evangelical revivals, the Catholic revivals featured rousing sermons and encouraged piety, fervor, and devotion. By establishing its own schools and system of hospitals, orphanages, and benevolent societies, the Church sought to help Catholics preserve their faith in the face of Protestant proselytizing.

Prejudice and discrimination led African Americans to create their own churches. The first were established in Philadelphia, after the city's black Methodists were ordered to sit in a segregated gallery. Between 1804 and 1815, African Americans formed their own Baptist, Methodist, and Presbyterian churches in eastern cities. In 1816, the African Methodist Episcopal church, the first autonomous black denomination, was founded.

Another religious group that grew sharply before the Civil War was American Jewry. At the beginning of the nineteenth century, there were only about 2000 Jews in the United States, 6 Jewish congregations, no Jewish newspapers, and not a single rabbi. By 1860, when the number of American Jews had climbed to 150,000, Jewish newspapers reached readers in 1250 communities, and Jews had served in the legislatures of Georgia, Indiana, New York, North Carolina, and South Carolina. Jews faced less discrimination and hostility than Catholics, in part because the Jewish community was scattered and in part because most Jews shed the distinctive dress, long sideburns, and other customs that set European Jews apart. Yet, although they adapted to American life in many ways, Jews vigorously resisted threats to their identity, strongly opposing state laws that limited public office to Christians, bans against commerce on the Christian Sabbath, and the recitation of Christian prayers in schools.

MORAL REFORM

The earliest reformers wanted to persuade Americans to adopt more godly personal habits. They set up associations to battle profanity and Sabbath breaking, to place a Bible in every American home, and to curb the widespread heavy use of hard liquor. By discouraging drinking and gambling and encouraging observance of the Sabbath, reformers hoped to "restore the government of God."

One of the most dramatic attempts at moral reform involved Magdalene societies, which sought in the 1830s and 1840s to rehabilitate prostitutes and discourage male solicitation. The New York Moral Reform Society had 15,000 members in 1837 and had branches in New England and upstate New York. Members walked into brothels and prayed for the prostitutes, publicized in the newspapers the names of men who patronized prostitutes, visited prostitutes in jails, and lobbied for state laws that would make male solicitation of prostitutes a crime.

The most extensive moral reform campaign, however, was that against drinking, which was an integral part of American life. Many people believed

The temperance movement of the 1830s and 1840s used religious revivalist tactics to frighten drinkers into taking the "pledge" to abstain from drinking.

that downing a glass of whiskey before breakfast was conducive to good health. Instead of taking coffee breaks, people took a dram of liquor at 11 and again at 4 o'clock as well as drinks after meals "to aid digestion" and a nightcap before going to sleep. Campaigning politicians offered voters generous amounts of liquor during campaigns and as rewards for "right voting" on election day. On the frontier, one evangelist noted, "a house could not be raised, a field of wheat cut down, nor could there be a log rolling, a husking, a quilting, a wedding, or a funeral without the aid of alcohol."

Easily affordable to even the poorest Americans—a gallon of whiskey cost 25 cents in the 1820s—consumption had risen markedly since the beginning of the century. The supply of alcohol increased as farmers distilled growing amounts of corn into cheap whiskey, which could be transported more easily than bulk corn. By 1820 the typical adult American consumed more than 7 gallons of absolute alcohol a year (compared to 2.6 gallons today).

Reformers sought to alter the cultural norms that encouraged alcohol consumption by identifying liquor as the cause of a wide range of social, family, and personal problems. Many middle-class women blamed alcohol for the abuse of wives and children and the squandering of family resources. Many businesspeople identified drinking with crime, poverty, and inefficient and unproductive employees.

The stage was set for the appearance of an organized movement against liquor. In 1826 the nation's first formal national **temperance** organization—the American Society for the Promotion of Temperance—was born. Led by socially prominent clergy and laypeople, the new organization called for total abstinence from distilled liquor. Within 3 years, 222 state and local antiliquor groups were laboring to spread this message.

By 1835 an estimated 2 million Americans had taken the "pledge" to abstain from hard liquor. Temperance reform drew support from many southerners and westerners who were otherwise indifferent or hostile to reform. Their efforts helped reduce annual per capita consumption of alcohol from 7 gallons in 1830 to 3 gallons a decade later, forcing 4000 distilleries to close.

The sudden arrival of hundreds of thousands of immigrants from "heavy drinking" cultures heightened the concerns of temperance reformers. Between 1830 and 1860, nearly 2 million Irish arrived in the United States along with an additional 893,000 Germans. In Ireland, land was in such short supply that many young men were unable to support a family by farming. The only solution was to delay marriage and socialize with other young men in "bachelor groups," a ritual that often involved heavy drinking. These immigrants probably drank no more than most native-born Americans before the 1830s, but increasingly heavy drinking was regarded as a problem demanding government action.

Two new approaches to the temperance movement arose during the 1840s. The first was the Washingtonian movement in which reformed alcoholics sought to reform other drinkers. As many as 600,000 drinkers took the Washingtonian pledge of total abstinence. The second approach was a campaign to restrict the manufacture and sale of alcohol, culminating in adoption of the nation's first statewide prohibition law in Maine in 1851, which led to prohibition laws often being referred to as "Maine laws." Convinced that moral suasion was ineffective, a minister argued strongly in behalf of prohibition laws: "You might almost as well persuade the chained maniac to leave off howling, as to persuade him to leave off drinking."

SOCIAL REFORM

The nation's first reformers tried to improve the nation's moral and spiritual values by distributing Bibles and religious tracts, promoting observance of the Sabbath, and curbing drinking. Beginning in the 1820s a new phase of reform—social reform—spread across the country, directed at crime, illiteracy, poverty, and disease. Reformers sought to solve these social problems by creating new institutions to deal with them—including prisons, public schools, and asylums for the deaf, the blind, and the mentally ill.

The Problem of Crime in a Free Society

Before the American Revolution, punishment for crimes generally involved some form of corporal punishment, ranging from the death penalty for serious crimes to public whipping, confinement in stocks, and branding for lesser offenses. Jails were used as temporary confinement for criminal defendants awaiting trial or punishment. Conditions in these early jails were abominable. Cramped cells held large groups of offenders of both sexes and all ages; debtors were confined with hardened criminals. Prisoners customarily had to pay the expenses of food and lodging.

During the pre–Civil War decades reformers began to view crime as a social problem—a product of environment and parental neglect—rather than the

As early as the 1820s, urban slums like New York City's Five Points began to appear. These areas of poverty, crime, filth, and violence attracted beggars, pimps, prostitutes, and hoodlums.

result of original sin or innate human depravity. Reformers believed it was the duty of a humane society to remove the underlying causes of crime, to sympathize and show patience toward criminals and to try to reform them, instead of whipping or confining them in stocks.

Revulsion over the spectacle of public punishment led to the rapid construction of penal institutions in which the "disease" of crime could be quarantined and inmates could be gradually rehabilitated in a carefully controlled environment. Two rival prison systems competed for public support. After constructing Auburn Prison, New York State authorities adopted a system in which inmates worked in large workshops during the day and slept in separate cells at night. Convicts had to march in lockstep and refrain from speaking or even looking at each other. In Pennsylvania's Eastern State Penitentiary, constructed in 1829, authorities placed even greater stress on the physical isolation of prisoners. Every prison cell had its own exercise yard, work space, and toilet facilities. Under the Pennsylvania plan, prisoners lived and worked in complete isolation from each other. Called "penitentiaries" or "reformatories," these new prisons reflected the belief that hard physical labor and solitary confinement might encourage introspection and instill habits of discipline that would rehabilitate criminals.

The legal principle that a criminal act should be legally punished only if the offender was fully capable of distinguishing between right and wrong opened the way to one of the most controversial aspects of American jurisprudence—the **insanity defense.** The question arose dramatically in 1835 when a deranged Englishman named Richard Lawrence walked up to President Andrew Jackson and fired 2 pistols at him from a distance of 6 feet. Incredibly, both guns misfired, and Jackson was unhurt. Lawrence believed that Jackson's attack on the second Bank of the United States had prevented him from obtaining money that would have enabled him to claim the English throne. The court, ruling that Lawrence was clearly suffering from a mental delusion, found him insane and not subject to criminal prosecution; instead, he was confined to an asylum for treatment of his mental condition.

Another major effort in social reform was the drive to outlaw **capital punishment.** Before the 1830s, most states reduced the number of crimes punishable by death and began to perform executions out of public view, lest the public be stimulated to acts of violence by the spectacle of hangings. In 1847 Michigan became the first modern jurisdiction to outlaw the death penalty; Rhode Island and Wisconsin soon followed.

Imprisonment for debt also came under attack. As late as 1816, an average of 600 residents of New York City were in prison at any one time for failure to pay debts. More than half owed less than $50. New York's debtor prisons provided no food, furniture, or fuel for their inmates, who would have starved without the assistance of relatives or the charity of humane societies. In a Vermont case, state courts imprisoned a man for a debt of just 54 cents,

The design of Eastern State Penitentiary in Pennsylvania reflected the principle that the way to correct criminal behavior was to keep the convicts in strict isolation. Confined in solitude, convicts were to reflect upon their crimes and be penitent—hence, the term *penitentiary*.

and in Boston a woman was taken from her three children as a result of a $3 debt.

Increasingly, reformers regarded imprisonment for debt as irrational, since imprisoned debtors were unable to work and pay off their debts. Piecemeal reform led to the abolition of debtor prisons, as states eliminated the practice of jailing people for trifling debts, and then forbade the jailing of women and veterans.

The Struggle for Public Schools

Of all the ideas advanced by antebellum reformers, none was more original than the principle that all American children should be educated to their full capacity at public expense. Reformers viewed education as the key to individual opportunity and the creation of an enlightened and responsible citizenry. Reformers also believed that public schooling could be an effective weapon in the fight against juvenile crime and an essential ingredient in the education and assimilation of immigrants.

From the early days of settlement, Americans attached special importance to education. During the seventeenth century, the New England Puritans required every town to establish a public school supported by fees from all but the very poorest families (a requirement later repealed). In the late eighteenth century, Thomas Jefferson popularized the idea that a democratic republic required an enlightened and educated citizenry. Early nineteenth-century educational reformers extended these ideas and struggled to make universal public education a reality. As a result of their efforts, the northern states were among the first jurisdictions in the world to establish tax-supported, tuition-free public schools.

At the beginning of the nineteenth century, the United States had the world's highest literacy rate—approximately 75 percent. Apprenticeship was a major form of education, supplemented by church schools, charity schools for the poor, and private academies for the affluent. Many youngsters learned to read in informal dame schools, in which a woman would take girls and boys into her own home. Formal schooling was largely limited to those who could afford to pay. Many schools admitted pupils regardless of age, mixing young children with young adults in their twenties. A single classroom could contain as many as 80 pupils.

The campaign for public schools began in earnest in the 1820s, when religiously motivated reformers advocated public education as an answer to poverty, crime, and deepening social divisions.

At first, many reformers championed Sunday schools as a way "to reclaim the vicious, to instruct the ignorant, to secure the observance of the Sabbath... and to raise the standard of morals among the lower classes of society." But soon, reformers began to call for public schools.

Horace Mann (1796–1859) of Massachusetts, the nation's leading educational reformer, led the fight for government support for public schools. As a state legislator, in 1837 Mann took the lead in establishing a state board of education and his efforts resulted in a doubling of state expenditures on education. He also won state support for teacher training, an improved curriculum in schools, the grading of pupils by age and ability, and a lengthened school year. He was also partially successful in curtailing the use of corporal punishment. In 1852, three years after Mann left office to take a seat in the U.S. Congress, Massachusetts adopted the first compulsory school attendance law in American history.

Horace Mann led the struggle for public schools in Massachusetts and established the first state board of education. His reforms included a lengthened school year and grading pupils by age and ability.

Educational opportunities, however, were not available to all. Most northern cities specifically excluded African Americans from the public schools. Finally, in 1855, Massachusetts became the first state to admit students to public schools without regard to "race, color, or religious opinions."

In 1832, **Prudence Crandall**, a Quaker school-teacher in Canterbury, Connecticut, sparked a major controversy by admitting Sarah Harris, the daughter of a free black farmer, into her

Prudence Crandall, a Quaker schoolteacher, was jailed for teaching free African-American children.

school. After white parents withdrew their children from the school, the young schoolteacher tried to turn her school into an institution for the education of free blacks. Hostile neighbors broke the school's windows, contaminated its well with manure, and denied its students seats on stagecoaches and in pews in church. In 1833, after the state adopted a law making it a crime to teach black students who were not residents of Connecticut, state authorities arrested Crandall. She was tried twice, convicted, and jailed. After her release, a local mob attacked Crandall's school building with crowbars and attempted to burn the structure. It never opened again.

Women and religious minorities also experienced discrimination. For women, education beyond the level of handicrafts and basic reading and writing was largely confined to separate female academies and seminaries for the affluent. Emma Hart Willard opened one of the first academies offering an advanced education to women in Philadelphia in 1814. Many public school teachers showed an anti-Catholic bias by using texts that portrayed the Catholic church as a threat to republican values and reading passages from a Protestant version of the Bible. Beginning in New York City in 1840, Catholics decided to establish their own system of schools in which children would receive a religious education as well as training in the arts and sciences.

In higher education a few institutions opened their doors to African Americans and women. In 1833 Oberlin College, where Charles G. Finney taught, became the nation's first co-educational college. Four years later, Mary Lyon established the first women's college, Mount Holyoke, to train teachers and missionaries. A number of western state universities also admitted women. In addition, three colleges for African Americans were founded before the Civil War, and a few other colleges, including Oberlin, Harvard, Bowdoin, and Dartmouth, admitted small numbers of black students.

The reform impulse brought other changes in higher education. At the beginning of the nineteenth century, most colleges offered their students, who usually enrolled between the ages of 12 and 15, only a narrow training in the classics designed to prepare them for the ministry. During the 1820s and 1830s, in an effort to adjust to the "spirits and wants of the age," colleges broadened their curricula to include the study of history, literature, geography, modern languages, and the sciences. The entrance age was also raised and the requirements demanded of students were broadened.

The number of colleges also increased. Most of the new colleges, particularly in the South and West, were church-affiliated, but several states established state universities. Before the Civil War, 16 states provided some financial support to higher education, and by the 1850s, New York City offered tuition-free education from elementary school to college.

Asylums for Society's Outcasts

A number of reformers devoted their attention to the problems of the mentally ill, the deaf, and the blind. In 1841, **Dorothea Dix** (1802–1887), a 39-year-old former schoolteacher, volunteered to give religious instruction to women incarcerated in the East Cambridge, Massachusetts, House of Correction. Inside the House of Correction, she was horrified to find mentally ill inmates dressed in rags and confined to a single dreary, unheated room. Shocked by what she saw, she embarked on a lifelong crusade to reform the treatment of the mentally ill.

After a two-year secret investigation of every jail and almshouse in Massachusetts, Dix issued a report to the state legislature. The mentally ill, she found, were mixed indiscriminately with paupers and hardened criminals. Many were confined "in cages, closets, cellars, stalls, pens! Chained, naked, beaten with rods and lashed into obedience." Dix then carried her campaign for state-supported asylums nationwide, persuading more than a dozen state legislatures to improve institutional care for the insane.

Through the efforts of reformers such as Thomas Gallaudet and Samuel Gridley Howe, institutions to care for the deaf and blind began to appear. In 1817, **Thomas Hopkins Gallaudet** (1787–1851) established the nation's first school in Hartford, Connecticut, to teach deaf-mutes to read and write, read lips, and communicate through hand signals. **Samuel Gridley Howe** (1801–1876), the husband of Julia Ward Howe, composer of the "Battle Hymn of the Republic," accomplished for the blind what Gallaudet achieved for the deaf. He founded the country's first school for the blind in Boston and produced printed materials with raised type.

RADICAL REFORM

The initial thrust of reform—moral reform—was to rescue the nation from infidelity and intemperance. A second line of reform, social or humanitarian reform, attempted to alleviate such sources of human misery as crime, cruelty, disease, and ignorance. Additionally, a third line of reform, radical reform, sought national regeneration by eliminating slavery and racial and sexual discrimination.

Early Antislavery Efforts

As late as the 1750s, no church had discouraged its members from owning or trading in slaves. Slaves could be found in each of the 13 American colonies, and before the American Revolution, only the colony of Georgia had temporarily sought to prohibit slavery (because its founders did not want a workforce that would compete with the convicts they planned to transport from England).

By the beginning of the nineteenth century, however, protests against slavery had become widespread. By 1804 nine states north of Maryland and Delaware had either emancipated their slaves or adopted gradual emancipation plans. Both the United States and Britain in 1808 outlawed the African slave trade.

The emancipation of slaves in the northern states and the prohibition against the African slave trade generated optimism that slavery was dying. Congress in 1787 had barred slavery from the Old Northwest, the region north of the Ohio River to the Mississippi River. The number of slaves freed by their masters had risen dramatically in the upper South during the 1780s and 1790s, and more antislavery societies had been formed in the South than in the North. At the present rate of progress, predicted one religious leader in 1791, within 50 years it will "be as shameful for a man to hold a Negro slave, as to be guilty of common robbery or theft."

By the early 1830s, however, the development of the Cotton Kingdom proved that slavery was not on the road to extinction. Despite the end of the African slave trade, the slave population had continued to grow, climbing from 1.5 million in 1820 to over 2 million a decade later.

A widespread belief that blacks and whites could not coexist and that racial separation was necessary encouraged futile efforts at deportation and overseas **colonization.** In 1817 a group of prominent ministers and politicians formed the American Colonization Society to resettle free blacks in West Africa, encourage planters voluntarily to emancipate their slaves, and create a group of black missionaries who would spread Christianity in Africa. During the 1820s, Congress helped fund the cost of transporting free blacks to Africa.

A few blacks supported African colonization in the belief that it provided the only alternative to continued degradation and discrimination. **Paul Cuffe** (1759–1817), a Quaker sea captain who was the son of a former slave and an Indian woman, led the first experiment in colonization. In 1815 he transported 38 free blacks to the British colony of Sierra Leone, on the western coast of Africa, and devoted thousands of his own dollars to the cause of colonization. In 1822 the American Colonization Society established the colony of Liberia, in west Africa, for resettlement of free American blacks.

It soon became apparent that colonization was a wholly impractical solution to the nation's slavery problem. Each year the nation's slave population rose by roughly 50,000, but in 1830 the American Colonization Society succeeded in persuading only 259 free blacks to migrate to Liberia, bringing the total number of blacks colonized in Africa to a mere 1400.

The Rise of Abolitionist Sentiment in the North

Initially, free blacks led the movement condemning colonization and northern discrimination against African Americans. As early as 1817, more than 3000 members of Philadelphia's black community staged a protest against colonization, at which they denounced the policy as "little more merciful than death." In 1829 **David Walker** (1785–1830), the free black owner of a second-hand clothing store in Boston, issued the militant *Appeal to the Colored Citizens of the World.* The appeal threatened insurrection and violence if calls for the abolition of slavery and improved conditions for free blacks were ignored. The next year, some 40 black delegates from 8 states held the first of a series of annual conventions denouncing slavery and calling for an end to discriminatory laws in the northern states.

The idea of abolition received impetus from **William Lloyd Garrison** (1805–1879). In 1829 the 25-year-old white Bostonian added his voice to the outcry against colonization, denouncing it as a cruel hoax designed to promote the racial purity of the northern population while doing nothing to end slavery in the South. Instead, he called for "immediate emancipation." By immediate emancipation, he meant the immediate and unconditional release of slaves from bondage without compensation to slaveowners.

In 1831, Garrison founded *The Liberator,* a militant abolitionist newspaper that was the country's first publication to demand an immediate end to slavery. On the front page of the first issue, he defiantly declared: "I will not equivocate—I will not excuse—I will not retreat a single inch—AND I WILL

BE HEARD." Incensed by Garrison's proclamation, the state of Georgia offered a $5000 reward to anyone who brought him to the state for trial.

Within 4 years, 200 antislavery societies had appeared in the North. In a massive propaganda campaign to proclaim the sinfulness of slavery, they distributed a million pieces of abolitionist literature and sent 20,000 tracts directly to the South.

Abolitionist Arguments and Public Reaction

Abolitionists attacked slavery on several grounds. Slavery was illegal because it violated the principles of natural rights to life and liberty embodied in the Declaration of Independence. Justice, said Garrison, required that the nation "secure to the colored population . . . all the rights and privileges that belong to them as men and as Americans." Slavery was sinful because slaveholders, in the words of abolitionist Theodore Weld, had usurped "the prerogative of God." Masters reduced a "God-like being" to a manipulable "THING." Slavery also encouraged sexual immorality and undermined the institutions of marriage and the family. Not only did slave masters sexually abuse and exploit slave women, abolitionists charged, but in some older southern states, such as Virginia and Maryland, they bred slaves for sale to the more recently settled parts of the Deep South.

Slavery was economically retrogressive, abolitionists argued, because slaves, motivated only by fear, did not exert themselves willingly. By depriving their labor force of any incentive for performing careful and diligent work, by barring slaves from acquiring and developing productive skills, planters hindered improvements in crop and soil management. Abolitionists also charged that slavery impeded the development of towns, canals, railroads, and schools.

Antislavery agitation provoked a harsh public reaction in both the North and the South. The U.S. postmaster general refused to deliver antislavery tracts to the South. In each session of Congress between 1836 and 1844 the House of Representatives adopted gag rules allowing that body automatically to table resolutions or petitions concerning the abolition of slavery.

Mobs led by "gentlemen of property and standing" attacked the homes and businesses of abolitionist merchants, destroyed abolitionist printing presses, disrupted antislavery meetings, and terrorized black neighborhoods. Crowds pelted abolitionist reformers with eggs and even stones. During antiabolitionist rioting in Philadelphia in October 1834, a white mob destroyed 45 homes in the city's black community. A year later, a Boston mob dragged Garrison through the streets and almost lynched him before authorities removed him to a city jail for his own safety.

In 1837, the abolitionist movement acquired its first martyr when an antiabolitionist mob in Alton, Illinois, murdered Reverend Elijah Lovejoy, editor of a militant abolitionist newspaper. Three times mobs destroyed Lovejoy's printing presses and attacked his house. When a fourth press arrived, Lovejoy armed himself and guarded the new press at the warehouse. The antiabolitionist mob set fire to the warehouse, shot Lovejoy as he fled the building, and dragged his mutilated body through the town.

William Lloyd Garrison, a leader of radical abolitionism, sought immediate freedom for slaves without compensation to their owners.

Photo is the gift of I.N. Phelps Stokes, Edward S. Hawes, Alice Mary Hawes, Marion Augusta Hawes, 1937. Metropolitan Museum of Art.

Division Within the Antislavery Movement

Questions over strategy and tactics divided the antislavery movement. At the 1840 annual meeting of the American Anti-Slavery Society in New York, abolitionists split over such questions as women's right to participate in the administration of the organization and the advisability of nominating abolitionists as independent political candidates. Garrison won control of the organization, and his opponents promptly walked out. From this point on, no single organization could speak for abolitionism.

One group of abolitionists looked to politics as the answer to ending slavery and founded political parties for that purpose. The **Liberty party,** founded in 1839 under the leadership of Arthur and Lewis Tappan, wealthy New York City businessmen, and James G. Birney, a former slaveholder, called on Congress to abolish slavery in the District of Columbia, end the interstate slave trade, and cease admitting new slave states to the Union. The party also sought the repeal of local and state "black laws" in the North, which discriminated against free blacks, much as segregation laws would in the post-Reconstruction South. The Liberty party nominated Birney for president in 1840 and again in 1844. Although it gathered fewer than 7100 votes in its first campaign, it polled some 62,000 votes 4 years later and captured enough votes in Michigan and New York to deny Henry Clay the presidency.

In 1848 antislavery Democrats and Whigs merged with the Liberty party to form the Free Soil party. Unlike the Liberty party, which was dedicated to the abolition of slavery and equal rights for African Americans, the **Free Soil party** narrowed its demands to the abolition of slavery in the District of Columbia and the exclusion of slavery from the federal territories. The Free Soilers also wanted a homestead law to provide free land for western settlers, high tariffs to protect American industry, and federally sponsored internal improvements. Campaigning under the slogan "free soil, free speech, free labor, and free men," the new party polled 300,000 votes (or 10 percent) in the presidential election of 1848 and helped elect Whig candidate Zachary Taylor.

Other abolitionists, led by Garrison, took a more radical direction, advocating civil disobedience and linking abolitionism to other reforms such as women's rights, world government, and international peace. Garrison and his supporters established the New England Non-Resistance Society in 1838. Members refused to vote, to hold public office, or to bring suits in court. In 1854 Garrison attracted notoriety by publicly burning a copy of the Constitution, which he called "a covenant with death and an agreement with Hell" because it acknowledged the legality of slavery.

African Americans played a vital role in the abolitionist movement, staging protests against segregated churches, schools, and public transportation. In New York and Pennsylvania, free blacks launched petition drives for equal voting rights. Northern blacks also had a pivotal role in the "underground railroad," which provided escape routes for southern slaves through the northern states and into Canada. African-American churches offered sanctuary to runaways, and black "vigilance" groups in cities such as New York and Detroit battled slave catchers who sought to recapture fugitive slaves.

Fugitive slaves, such as William Wells Brown, Henry Bibb, and Harriet Tubman, advanced abolitionism by publicizing the horrors of slavery. Their firsthand tales of whippings and separation from spouses and children combated the notion that slaves were contented under slavery and undermined belief in racial inferiority. Tubman risked her life by making 19 trips into slave territory to free as many as 300 slaves. Slaveholders posted a reward of $40,000 for the capture of the "Black Moses."

Frederick Douglass was the most famous fugitive slave and black abolitionist. The son of a Maryland slave woman and an unknown white father, Douglass was separated from his mother and sent to work on a plantation when he was 6 years old. At the age of 20, in 1838, he escaped to the North using the papers of a free black sailor. In the North, Douglass became the first runaway slave to speak out against slavery. When many Northerners refused to believe that this eloquent orator could possibly have been a slave, he responded by writing an autobiography that identified his previous owners by name. Although he initially allied himself with William Lloyd Garrison, Douglass later started his own newspaper, *The North Star,* and supported political action against slavery.

By the 1850s, many blacks had become pessimistic about defeating slavery. Some African Americans looked again to colonization as a solution. In the 15 months following passage of the federal Fugitive Slave Law in 1850, some 13,000 free blacks fled the North for Canada. In 1854, Martin Delany (1812–1885), a Pittsburgh doctor who had studied medicine at Harvard, organized the National Emigration Convention to investigate possible sites for black colonization in Haiti, Central America, and West Africa.

Other blacks argued in favor of violence. Black abolitionists in Ohio adopted resolutions encouraging slaves to escape and called on their fellow citi-

Fugitive slave, abolitionist, and later spy for the Union during the Civil War Harriet Tubman is pictured here at the extreme left with some of the slaves she helped escape. She led at least 19 raids into slave territory to escort more than 300 slaves to freedom in the northern states and Canada. Frederick Douglass (right) gained public notice by giving a powerful speech against slavery. He opposed not only slavery but all forms of racial discrimination.

zens to violate any law that "conflicts with reason, liberty and justice, North or South." A meeting of fugitive slaves in Cazenovia, New York, declared that "the State motto of Virginia, 'Death to Tyrants,' is as well the black man's as the white man's motto." By the late 1850s, a growing number of free blacks had concluded that it was just as legitimate to use violence to secure the freedom of the slaves as it had been to establish the independence of the American colonies.

Over the long run, the fragmentation of the antislavery movement worked to the advantage of the cause. Henceforth, Northerners could support whichever form of antislavery best reflected their views. Moderates could vote for political candidates with abolitionist sentiments without being accused of radical Garrisonian views or of advocating violence for redress of grievances.

The Birth of Feminism

The women's rights movement was a major legacy of radical reform. At the outset of the century, women could not vote or hold office in any state, they had no access to higher education, and they were excluded from professional occupations. American law accepted the principle that a wife had no legal identity apart from her husband. She could not be sued, nor could she bring a legal suit; she could not make a contract, nor could she own property. She was not permitted to control her own wages or gain custody of her children in case of separation or divorce. Under many circumstances she was even deemed incapable of committing crimes.

Broad social and economic changes, such as the development of a market economy and a decline in the birthrate, opened employment opportunities for women. Instead of bearing children at two-year intervals after marriage, as was the general case throughout the colonial era, during the early nineteenth century women bore fewer children and ceased childbearing at younger ages. During these decades the first women's college was established, and some men's colleges first opened their doors to women students. More women were postponing marriage or not marrying at all; unmarried women gained new employment opportunities as "mill girls" and elementary school teachers; and a growing number of women achieved prominence as novelists, editors, teachers, and leaders of church and philanthropic societies.

Although there were many improvements in the status of women during the first half of the century, women still lacked political and economic status when compared with men. As the franchise was extended to larger and larger numbers of white males, including large groups of recent immigrants, the gap in political power between women and men widened. Even though women made up a core of supporters for many reform movements, men excluded them from positions of decision making and relegated them to separate female auxiliaries. Additionally, women lost economic status as production shifted away from the household to the factory and workshop. During the late eighteenth century, the need for a cash income led women and older children to engage in a variety of household industries, such as weaving and spinning. Increasingly, in the nineteenth century, these tasks were performed in factories and mills, where the workforce was largely male.

The fact that changes in the economy tended to confine women to a sphere separate from men had important implications for reform. Since women were believed to be uncontaminated by the competitive struggle for wealth and power, many argued that they had a duty—and the capacity—to exert an uplifting moral influence on American society.

Catharine Beecher (1800–1878) and Sarah J. Hale (1788–1879) helped lead the effort to expand women's roles through moral influence. Beecher, the eldest sister of Harriet Beecher Stowe, was one of the nation's most prominent educators before the Civil War. A woman of many talents and strong leadership, she wrote a highly regarded book on domestic science and spearheaded the campaign to convince school boards that women were suited to serve as schoolteachers. Hale edited the nation's most popular women's magazines, the *Ladies Magazine* and *Godey's Ladies Book*. She led the successful campaign to make Thanksgiving a national holiday (during Lincoln's administration), and she also composed the famous nursery rhyme "Mary Had a Little Lamb."

Both Beecher and Hale worked tirelessly for women's education (Hale helped found Vassar College). They gave voice to the grievances of women—the abysmally low wages paid to women in the needle trades (12.5 cents a day), the physical hardships endured by female operatives in the nation's shops and mills (where women worked 14 hours a day), and the minimizing of women's intellectual aspirations. Even though neither woman supported full equal rights for women, they were important transitional figures in the emergence of feminism. Each significantly broadened society's definition of "women's sphere" and assigned women vital social responsibilities: to shape their children's character, morally to uplift their husbands, and to promote causes of "practical benevolence."

Other women broke down old barriers and forged new opportunities in a more dramatic fashion. Frances Wright (1795–1852), a Scottish-born reformer and lecturer, received the nickname "The Great Red Harlot of Infidelity" because of her radical ideas about birth control, liberalized divorce laws, and legal rights for married women. In 1849 Elizabeth Blackwell (1821–1910) became the first American woman to receive a degree in medicine. A number of women became active as revivalists. Perhaps the most notable was Phoebe Palmer (1807–1874), a Methodist preacher who ignited religious fervor among thousands of Americans and Canadians.

Catalyst for Women's Rights

A public debate over the proper role of women in the antislavery movement, especially their right to lecture to audiences composed of both sexes, led to the first organized movement for women's rights. By the mid-1830s more than a hundred female antislavery societies had been created, and women abolitionists were circulating petitions, editing abolitionist tracts, and organizing antislavery conventions. A key question was whether women abolitionists would be permitted to lecture to "mixed" audiences of men and women. In 1837 a national women's antislavery convention resolved that women should overcome this taboo: "The time has come for women to move in that sphere which providence has assigned her, and no longer remain satisfied with the circumscribed limits which corrupt custom and a perverted application of Scripture have encircled her."

Angelina Grimké (1805–1879) and her sister **Sarah** (1792–1873)—two sisters from a wealthy Charleston, South Carolina, slaveholding family—were the first women to break the restrictions and widen women's sphere through their writings and lectures before mixed audiences. In 1837 Angelina gained national notoriety by lecturing against slavery to audiences that included men as well as women. Shocked by this breach of the separate sexual spheres ordained by God, ministers in Massachusetts called on their fellow clergy to forbid women the right to speak from church pulpits. Sarah Grimké in 1840 responded with a pamphlet entitled *Letters on the Condition of Women and the Equality of the Sexes*, one of the first modern statements of feminist principles. She denounced the injustice of lower pay and denial of equal educational opportunities for women. Her pamphlet expressed outrage that women were "regarded by men, as pretty toys or as mere instruments of pleasure" and were taught to believe that marriage is "the *sine qua non* [indispensable element] of human happiness and human existence." Men and women, she concluded, should not be treated differently, since both were endowed with innate natural rights.

In 1840, after the American Anti-Slavery Society split over the issue of women's rights, the organization named three female delegates to a World Anti-Slavery Convention to be held in London later that year. There, these women were denied the right to participate in the convention on the grounds that their participation would offend British public opinion. The convention relegated them to seats in a balcony.

Eight years later, Lucretia Mott (1793–1880), who earlier had been denied the right to serve as a delegate to the World Anti-Slavery Convention, and **Elizabeth Cady Stanton** (1815–1902) organized the first women's rights convention in history. Held in July 1848 at Seneca Falls, New York, the convention drew up a Declaration of Sentiments, modeled on the Declaration of Independence, which opened with the phrase "All men and women are created equal." It named 15 specific inequities suffered by women, and after detailing "a history of repeated injuries and usurpations on the part of men toward woman," the document concluded that "he has endeavored, in every way that he could, to destroy her confidence in her own powers, to lessen her self-respect, and to make her willing to lead a dependent and abject life."

Among the resolutions adopted by the convention, only one was not ratified unanimously—that women be granted the right to vote. Of the 66 women and 34 men who signed the Declaration of Sentiments at the convention (including black abolitionist Frederick Douglass), only two lived to see the ratification of the women's suffrage amendment to the constitution 72 years later.

By midcentury women's rights conventions had been held in every northern state. Despite ridicule from the public press—the *Worcester* (Massachusetts) *Telegraph* denounced women's rights advocates as "Amazons"—female reformers contributed to important, if limited, advances against discrimination. They succeeded in gaining adoption of Married Women's Property Laws in a number of states, granting married women full control over their own income and property. A New York law passed in 1860 gave women joint custody over children and the right to sue and be sued, and in several states women's rights reformers secured adoption of permissive divorce laws. A Connecticut law, for example, granted divorce for any "misconduct" that "permanently destroys the happiness of the petitioner and defeats the purposes of the marriage relationship."

Utopian Communities

Between the 1820s and 1840s, individuals who believed in the perfectibility of the social and political order founded hundreds of "utopian communities." These experimental communal societies were called utopian communities because they provided blueprints for an ideal society.

The characteristics of these communities varied widely. One of the earliest perfectionist societies was popularly known as the Shakers. Founded in 1776 by "Mother" Ann Lee, an English immigrant, the Shakers believed that the millennium was at hand and that the time had come for people to renounce sin. Shaker communities regarded their male and female members as equals; thus, both sexes served as elders and deacons. Aspiring to live like the early Christians, the Shakers adopted communal ownership of property and a way of life emphasizing simplicity. Dress was kept simple and uniform. Shaker architecture and furniture are devoid of ornament—no curtains on windows, carpets on floors, or pictures on walls—but they are pure and elegant in form.

A Quaker minister, feminist, and the mother of six children, Lucretia Mott was an ardent opponent of slavery and often faced angry and violent mobs.

THE PEOPLE SPEAK

Women's Rights: Seneca Falls Declaration and Resolutions (1848)

At the first convention in history dedicated to equal rights for women, held in Seneca Falls, New York, in 1848, the delegates adopted a "Declaration of Sentiments." Drafted by Elizabeth Cady Stanton and modeled on the Declaration of Independence, it listed a series of injuries that women had suffered at the hands of men and declared that women and men shared the same inalienable rights.

> We hold these truth to be self-evident: that all men and women are created equal. . . .
>
> The history of mankind is a history of repeated injuries and usurpations on the part of man toward woman, having in direct object the establishment of an absolute tyranny over her. To prove this, let facts be submitted to a candid world.
>
> He has never permitted her to exercise her inalienable right to the elective franchise.
>
> He has compelled her to submit to laws, in the formation of which she had no voice.
>
> He has withheld from her rights which are given to the most ignorant and degraded men—both natives and foreigners.
>
> Having deprived her of this first right of a citizen, the elective franchise, thereby leaving her without representation in the halls of legislation, he has opposed her on all sides.
>
> He has made her, if married, in the eye of the law, civilly dead.
>
> He has taken from her all rights in property, even to the wages she earns.
>
> He has made her, morally, an irresponsible being, as she can commit many crimes with impunity, provided they be done in the presence of her husband. In the covenant of marriage, she is compelled to promise obedience to her husband, he becoming, to all intents and purposes, her master—the law giving him power to deprive her of her liberty, and to administer chastisement.
>
> He has so framed the laws of divorce, as to what shall be the proper causes, and in case of separation, to whom the guardianship of children shall be given, as to be wholly regardless of the happiness of women—the law, in all cases, going into a false supposition of the supremacy of man, and giving all power into his hands.
>
> After depriving her of all rights as a married woman, if single, and the owner of property, he has taxed her to support a government which recognizes her only when her property can be made profitable to it.
>
> He has monopolized nearly all the profitable employments, and from those she is permitted to follow, she receives but a scanty remuneration. He closes against her all avenues to wealth and distinction which he considers most honorable to himself. As a teacher of theology, medicine, or law, she is not known. . . .
>
> He has endeavored, in every way that he could, to destroy her confidence in her own powers, to lessen her self-respect, and to make her willing to lead a dependent and abject life.

Source: Seneca Falls Declaration and Resolutions, 1848, in Susan B. Anthony, Elizabeth Cady Stanton, and Matilda Joslyn Gage, eds., *History of Woman Suffrage* (Rochester, 1889), 1: 75–80.

The two most striking characteristics of the Shaker communities were their dances and abstinence from sexual relations. The Shakers believed that religious fervor should be expressed through the head, heart, and mind, and their ritual religious practices included shaking, shouting, and dancing. Viewing sexual intercourse as the basic cause of human sin, the Shakers also adopted strict rules concerning celibacy. They attempted to replenish their membership by admitting volunteers and taking in orphans. Today, the Shakers have all but died out. Fewer than 20 members survived in the 1990s.

Another utopian effort was Robert Owen's experimental community at New Harmony, Indiana, which reflected the influence of Enlightenment ideas. Owen, a paternalistic Scottish industrialist, was deeply troubled by the social consequences of the industrial revolution. Inspired by the idea that people are shaped by their environment, Owen purchased a site in Indiana where he sought to establish common ownership of property and abolish religion. At New Harmony the marriage ceremony was reduced to a single sentence and children were raised outside of their natural parents' home. The community lasted just three years, from 1825 to 1828.

Some 40 utopian communities based their organization on the ideas of the French theorist Charles Fourier, who hoped to eliminate poverty through the establishment of scientifically organized cooperative communities called "phalanxes." Each phalanx was to be set up as a "joint-stock company," in which profits were divided according to the amount of

Officially named "The United Society of Believers in Christ's Second Appearing," the Shakers received their popular name from the movements they made during their religious dances.

money members had invested, their skill, and their labor. Fourier coined the term *feminism*, and in the phalanxes, women received equal job opportunities and equal pay, equal participation in decision making, and the right to speak in public assemblies. Although one Fourier community lasted for 18 years, most were unsuccessful.

The currents of radical antislavery thought inspired Frances Wright, a fervent Scottish abolitionist, to found Nashoba Colony in 1826, near Memphis, Tennessee, as an experiment in interracial living. She established a racially integrated cooperative community in which slaves were to receive an education and earn enough money to purchase their own freedom. Publicity about Fanny Wright's desire to abolish the nuclear family, religion, private property, and slavery created a furor, and the community dissolved after only four years.

Perhaps the most successful—and notorious—experimental colony was John Humphrey Noyes's Oneida Community. A lawyer who was converted in one of Charles Finney's revivals, Noyes believed that the millennium would occur only when people strove to become perfect through an "immediate and total cessation from sin."

In Putney, Vermont, in 1835 and in Oneida, New York, in 1848, Noyes established perfectionist communities that practiced communal ownership of property and "complex marriage." Complex marriage involved the marriage of each member of the community to every member of the opposite sex. Exclusive emotional or sexual attachments were forbidden, and sexual relations were arranged through an intermediary in order to protect a woman's individuality and give her a choice in the matter. Men were required to practice *coitus interruptus* (withdrawal) as a method of birth control, unless the group had approved of the couple's conceiving offspring. After the Civil War, the community conducted experiments in eugenics, the selective control of mating to improve the hereditary qualities of children. Other notable features of the community were mutual criticism sessions and communal child rearing. Noyes left the community in 1879 and fled to Canada to escape prosecution for adultery. As late as the early 1990s descendants of the original community could be found working at the Oneida silverworks, which became a corporation after Noyes's departure.

ARTISTIC AND CULTURAL FERMENT

In the late eighteenth century, many Americans wondered whether their country's infant democracy could produce great works of art. The revolutionary generation drew its models of art and architecture from the world of classical antiquity, especially the Roman republic. The new United States had few professional writers or artists. It lacked a large class of patrons to subsidize the arts. It published few magazines and housed only a single art museum. Above all, America seemed to lack the traditions out of which artists and writers could create great works.

Europeans treated American culture with contempt. They charged that America was too commercial and materialistic, too preoccupied with money and technology to produce great art and literature. "In the four quarters of the globe," asked one English critic, "who reads an American book? or goes to an American play? or looks at an American picture or statue?"

On August 31, 1837, a 34-year-old former Unitarian minister named Ralph Waldo Emerson (1803–1882) answered these critics. As he stood at the pulpit of the First Parish Church of Cambridge, Massachusetts—the very spot where Anne Hutchinson had been examined for heresy two centuries earlier—he delivered a talk, entitled "The American Scholar," that would be called America's "intellectual Declaration of Independence." In his address, Emerson urged Americans to cast off their "long apprenticeship to the learning of other lands" and abandon subservience to English models and create distinctly American forms of art rooted in the facts of American life.

Even before Emerson's call for a distinctly American culture, a number of authors had already begun to create literature emphasizing native scenes and characters. Washington Irving (1783–1859), who was probably the first American to support himself as a man of letters, demonstrated the possibility of creating art out of native elements in his classic tales

"Rip Van Winkle" (1818) and "The Legend of Sleepy Hollow" (1820).

The poet Henry Wadsworth Longfellow was even more successful in transforming American legends into the stuff of art and reaching a broad popular audience. His narrative poems dramatizing scenes from America's past made such figures as Paul Revere, Miles Standish, John Alden, Priscilla Mullins, and Hiawatha household names. His simple evocative lines have been cherished by generations of American children:

> Under the spreading chestnut tree
> The village smithy stands;
>
> I shot an arrow into the air,
> It fell to earth, I knew not where;
>
> There was a little girl
> Who had a little curl
> Right in the middle of her forehead.

Ironically, this popular poet was a "Boston Brahmin" (a member of one of Boston's leading families), an expert in linguistics, a professor of modern languages at Harvard, and a translator of the latest European poetry.

James Fenimore Cooper (1789–1851) was another successful mythmaker. His works gave us such staples of western fiction as the lone frontiersman, the faithful Indian companion, and the kidnap, chase, and rescue. He also made such words and phrases as "paleface," "on the warpath," and "war paint" part of the American vocabulary.

Born in Burlington, New Jersey, the son of a land speculator, Cooper grew up in the frontier community of Cooperstown in central New York. At 13, he enrolled at Yale but was expelled for blowing open a classmate's door with a charge of gunpowder and roping a donkey onto a professor's chair. He then went to sea as a common sailor. In 1819, following his return to Cooperstown, Cooper was reading a popular novel of the day aloud to his wife. He tossed the book aside and claimed that he could write a better one. His wife dared him to try, and during the remaining 32 years of his life he wrote 34 books.

In his second and third novels, *The Spy* (1821) and *The Pioneers* (1823), Cooper created one of the most enduring archetypes in American culture. His hero, the frontiersman Natty Bumppo (also known as Hawkeye, Leatherstocking, and Pathfinder) was an American knight errant at home in the wilderness. He became the prototype not only for future trappers and scouts, but also for countless cowboys, detectives, and superheroes found in popular American fiction and film. Part of Natty Bumppo's appeal was

Natty Bumppo, the legendary American frontiersman created by James Fenimore Cooper, from the frontispiece of Cooper's *Last of the Mohicans*. Bumppo, the hero of Cooper's Leatherstocking tales, has been called the most famous character in American fiction.

that he gave expression to many of the misgivings early nineteenth-century Americans had about the cost of progress (his last words were "Let me sleep where I have lived—beyond the din of settlements"). An acute social critic, Cooper railed against the destruction of the natural environment, the violence directed at Native Americans, and the rapaciousness and materialism of an expansive American society.

American Transcendentalism

On the afternoon of September 19, 1836, a number of Boston's leading young intellectuals met at the Boston home of the Reverend George Ripley. Ralph Waldo Emerson, who would shortly deliver his "American Scholar" address, was there, as was Bronson Alcott, a pioneering educational reformer and the father of novelist Louisa May Alcott. Orestes Brownson, a staunch advocate of the rights of workers, also attended. Their goal was "to see how far it would be possible for earnest minds to meet." Soon, other important thinkers joined the meetings, including novelist Nathaniel Hawthorne, feminist editor

Margaret Fuller, educator Elizabeth Peabody, and pencilmaker and poet Henry David Thoreau. So abstract and incomprehensible were their discussions to those outside their circle that unkind wits dubbed the group the "Transcendentalist Club." The nickname stuck, and these important thinkers, authors, and reformers came to be called transcendentalists.

The **transcendentalists** were a group of young New Englanders, mostly of Unitarian background, who found liberal religion too formal and rationalistic to meet their spiritual and emotional needs. Logic and reason, they believed, were incapable of explaining the fundamental mysteries of human existence. Where, then, could people find answers to life's fundamental problems? The deepest insights, the transcendentalists believed, were to be found within the human individual, through intuition.

The transcendentalists shared a common outlook: a belief that each person contains infinite and godlike potentialities; an emphasis on emotion and the senses over reason and intellect; and a glorification of nature as a creative, dynamic force in which people could discover their true selves and commune with the supernatural. Like the romantic artists and poets of Europe, they emphasized the individual, the subjective, the imaginative, the personal, the emotional, and the visionary.

The central figure in transcendentalism was **Ralph Waldo Emerson.** Trained, like his father, to be a liberal Unitarian minister, Emerson found his parents' faith unsatisfying. Unitarian theology and ritual, he wrote, was "corpse cold"; it was the "thin porridge or cold tea" of genteel Bostonians. Emerson's life was marked by personal tragedy and illness—his father died when he was a boy; his first wife died after less than two years of marriage; his firstborn son died at the age of five; a brother went insane. Consequently, Emerson could never believe that logic and reason offered answers to life's mysteries.

Appalled by the complacency, provinciality, and materialism of Boston's elite, the 29-year-old Emerson resigned as minister of the prestigious Second Church of Boston in 1832. Convinced that no external answers existed to the fundamental problems of life, he decided to look inward and "spin my thread from my own bowels." In his essays and public lectures, Emerson distilled the essence of the new philosophy: All people contain seeds of divinity, but society, traditionalism, and lifeless religious institutions thwart the fulfillment of these potentialities. In his essay "Nature" (1836), Emerson asserted that God's presence is inherent in both humanity and nature and can best be sensed through intuition rather than through reason. In his essay "Self-Reliance" (1841), he called on his readers to strive for true individuality in the face of intense social pressures for conformity: "Society everywhere is in conspiracy against the manhood of every one of its members.... The virtue in most request is conformity.... Whoso would be a man must be a nonconformist."

Essayist Ralph Waldo Emerson was one of the foremost intellectual figures of his era. His philosophy, called transcendentalism, espoused the belief that people can transcend ordinary understanding and find truth through intuition.

Although Emerson himself was not an active reformer (he once wrote that whenever he saw a reformer, he felt like asking, "What right, Sir, do you have to your one virtue?"), his philosophy inspired many reformers far more radical than he. His stress on the individual, his defense of nonconformity, and his vocal critique of the alienation and social fragmentation that had accompanied the growth of cities and industry led others to try to apply the principles of transcendentalism to their personal lives and to society at large.

Henry David Thoreau (1817–1862) was one of the transcendentalists who strove to realize Emersonian ideals in his personal life. A pencilmaker, surveyor, and poet, Thoreau, like Emerson, was educated at Harvard. He felt nothing but contempt for social conventions and wore a green coat to chapel because Harvard's rules required black. After college, he taught school and worked at his father's pencil factory, but these jobs brought him no fulfillment.

In March 1845, the 28-year-old Thoreau, convinced that his life was being frittered away by details, walked into the woods near Concord, Massachusetts, to live alone. He put up a cabin near Walden Pond as an experiment—to see if it was possible for a person to live truly free and uncommitted: "I went into the woods because I wished to live deliberately, to front only the essential facts of life, and see if I could not learn what it had to teach, and not, when I came to die, discover that I had not lived." The aim of his experiment was to break free from the distractions and artificialities of life, to shed himself of needless obligations and possessions, and to establish an original relationship with nature. His motto was "simplify, simplify."

Henry David Thoreau said he went to live in solitude in the woods because he wished to "front only the essential facts of life."

The title page from the first edition of Thoreau's *Walden*, published in 1854.

During his 26 months at Walden Pond, he constructed his own cabin, raised his own food ("seven miles of beans"), observed nature, explored his inner self, and kept a 6000-page journal. He served as "self-appointed inspector of snow-storms and rain-storms," "surveyor of forest-paths," and protector of "wild-stock." He also spent a night in jail, for refusing to pay taxes as a protest against the Mexican-American War. This incident led him to write the classic defense of nonviolent direct action, "Civil Disobedience."

Another figure who sought to realize transcendentalist ideals in her personal life was Margaret Fuller (1810–1850), editor of the transcendentalist journal *The Dial*. Often mocked as an egotist, she once said: "I know all the people worth knowing in America, and I find no intellect comparable to my own." She did indeed possess one of nineteenth-century America's towering minds. She was the first woman to use the Harvard College library and later became one of the nation's first woman journalists, writing for Horace Greeley's New York *Tribune*. A determined social reformer, she became a leading advocate of women's rights, publishing *Woman in the Nineteenth Century* in 1845. The book, in which she called for the complete equality of women, became a central work of the emerging women's rights movement. A partisan in Rome's revolution of 1849, she shocked Bostonians by taking an Italian revolutionary nobleman, 11 years her junior, as her lover, and bearing his child out of wedlock (they secretly married later). She died in a shipwreck off Long Island, at the age of 40, along with her husband and son. Edgar Allan Poe spoke for many Americans when he said of her: "Humanity is divided into men, women, and Margaret Fuller."

Another key figure in the transcendentalist circle was Bronson Alcott (1799–1888), a pioneer in the areas of child development and education. Often ridiculed—reviewers mockingly described one of his books as "clear as mud"—Alcott was far ahead of his time in his conception of education, which he viewed as a process of awakening and drawing out children's intellectual and moral capacities through dialogue, individualized instruction, nature study, and encouragement of creative expression through art and writing. Critics scoffed at his techniques, particularly his rejection of corporal punishment and his substitution of "vicarious atonement," a method of child discipline in which Alcott had naughty children spank him. When his own daughters misbehaved, Alcott went without dinner. Convinced that adults had a great deal to learn about children's physical, intellectual, and moral development, Alcott recorded 2500 pages of observations on the first years of his daughters' lives (including Louisa May, who later wrote *Little Women* and *Little Men*). He also published his dialogues with pupils on such controversial topics as the meaning of the Christian gospel and the processes of conception and birth.

Two dramatic attempts to apply the ideas of transcendentalism to everyday life were Brook Farm, a community located near Boston, and Fruitlands, a utopian community near Harvard, Massachusetts. In 1841, George Ripley, like Emerson a former Unitarian clergyman, established Brook Farm in an attempt to substitute transcendentalist ideals of "brotherly cooperation," harmony, and spiritual fulfillment for the "selfish competition," class division, and alienation that increasingly characterized the larger society. "Our ulterior aim is nothing less than Heaven on Earth," declared one community member. Brook Farm's residents, who never numbered more than 200, supported themselves by farming, teaching, and manufacturing clothing. The most famous member of the community was Nathaniel Hawthorne, who based his 1852 novel *The Blithedale Romance* on his experiences there. The community lasted in its original form just three years.

In 1843, Bronson Alcott and others attempted to form a "New Eden" at Fruitlands—a community where they could achieve human perfection through high thinking, manual labor, and dress and diet reform. Practices at Fruitlands included communal ownership of property, frequent cold water baths, and a diet based entirely on native grains, fruits, herbs, and roots. Residents wore canvas shoes and linen tunics, so as not to have to kill animals for leather or use slave-grown cotton. Division of labor by gender, however, remained traditional. Responsibility for housekeeping and food preparation fell on Alcott's wife Abba. Asked by a visitor if there were any beasts of burden at Fruitlands, Abba Alcott replied: "There is one woman."

A Literary Renaissance

Emerson's 1837 plea for Americans to cease imitating Europeans, speak with their own voices, and create art drawn from their own experiences coincided with an extraordinary burst of literary creativity. Nathaniel Hawthorne, Herman Melville, Edgar Allan Poe, Harriet Beecher Stowe, and Walt Whitman, like Emerson and Thoreau, produced literary works of the highest magnitude, yet in their own time many of their greatest works were greeted with derision, abuse, or indifference. It is a tragic fact that with the sole exception of Harriet Beecher Stowe, none of pre–Civil War America's greatest writers was able to earn more than a modest income from his or her books (on Harriet Beecher Stowe, see pp. 390–391).

During his lifetime, Edgar Allan Poe (1809–1849) received far more notoriety from his legendary dissipation than from his poetry or short stories. The Boston-born son of two poor actors, Poe was raised by a Richmond, Virginia, merchant after his father abandoned the family and his mother died. For two years he went to the University of Virginia and briefly attended West Point, but drinking, gambling debts, and bitter fights with his guardian cut short his formal education. At the age of 24, he married a 13-year-old second cousin, who died a decade later of tuberculosis, brought on by cold and starvation. Found drunk and unconscious in Baltimore in 1849, Poe died at the age of 40.

Sorely underappreciated by contemporaries, Poe invented the detective novel; edited the *Southern Literary Messenger*, one of the country's leading literary journals; wrote incisive essays on literary criticism; and produced some of the most masterful poems and frightening tales of horror ever written. His literary techniques inspired a

Edgar Allan Poe, shown here in a self-portrait, is known for his haunting stories and poems, his literary theories, and his invention of the modern detective story.

number of important French writers, including Charles Baudelaire, Stéphane Mallarmé, and Paul Valéry. Poe said that his writing style consisted of "the ludicrous heightened into the grotesque; the fearful coloured into the horrible; the witty exaggerated into the burlesque; the singular wrought into the strange and mystical."

Nathaniel Hawthorne (1804–1864), the author of *The Scarlet Letter* (1850), one of America's towering works of fiction, did not consider himself a novelist. He wrote "romances," he insisted—imaginative representations of moral problems, rather than novelistic depictions of social realities. A descendant of one of the Salem witch-trial judges, the Salem-born Hawthorne grew up in a somber and solitary atmosphere. His father, a sea captain, perished on a voyage when his son was just 4 years old, and Hawthorne's mother spent the remainder of her life in mourning. After attending Bowdoin College, where Henry Wadsworth Longfellow and future president Franklin Pierce were among his classmates, he began to write. It would not be until 1837, however, when he published *Twice-Told Tales*, that the 33-year-old Hawthorne first gained public recognition. He lived briefly at Brook Farm and participated in the transcendentalist circle, but did not share their idealistic faith in humanity's innate goodness.

Hawthorne was a secretive, painfully shy man. But no pre–Civil War author wrote more perceptively about guilt—sexual, moral, and psychological. "In the depths of every human heart," he wrote in an early tale, "there is a tomb and a dungeon, though the lights, the music, the revelry above may cause us to forget their existence, and the buried ones, or prisoners whom they hide." In his fiction, Hawthorne, more than any other early nineteenth-century American writer, challenged the larger society's faith in science, technology, progress, and humanity's essential goodness. Many of his greatest works project nineteenth-century concerns—about women's roles, sexuality, and religion—onto seventeenth-century Puritan settings. Some of his stories examine the hubris of scientists and social reformers who dare tamper with the natural environment and human nature.

Herman Melville (1819–1891), author of *Moby Dick* (1851), possibly America's greatest romance, had little formal education and claimed that his intellectual development did not begin until he was 25. By then, he had already seen his father go bankrupt and die insane, worked as a cabin boy on a merchant ship, served as a common seaman on a whaling ship, deserted in the Marquessa Islands, escaped on an Australian whaler, and been imprisoned in Tahiti. He drew on these experiences in his first two books, *Typee* (1846) and *Omoo* (1847), which were popular successes, but his third book *Mardi* (1849), a complex blend of political and religious allegory, metaphysics, and cosmic romance, failed miserably, foreshadowing the reception of his later works.

Part of a New York literary circle called Young America, Melville dreamed of creating a novel as vast and energetic as the nation itself. In *Moby Dick*, he produced such a masterwork. Based on the tale of "Mocha-Dick," a gigantic white whale that sank a whaling ship, *Moby Dick* combined whaling lore and sea adventure into an epic drama of human arrogance, producing an allegory that explores what happens to a people who defy divine limits. Tragically, neither *Moby Dick* nor Melville's later works found an audience, and Melville spent his last years as a deputy customs collector in New York. He died in utter obscurity, and his literary genius was rediscovered only in the 1920s.

In 1842, Ralph Waldo Emerson lectured in New York and called for a truly original American poet who could fashion verse out of "the factory, the railroad, and the wharf." Sitting in Emerson's audience was a 22-year-old New York printer and journalist named Walt Whitman (1819–1892). A carpenter's son with only five years of schooling, Whitman soon became Emerson's ideal of the native American poet, with the publication of *Leaves of Grass* in 1855. "A mixture of Yankee transcendentalism and New York rowdyism," *Leaves of Grass* was, wrote Emerson, "the most extraordinary piece of wit & wisdom that America has yet contributed." Most reviewers, however, reacted scornfully to the book, deeming it "trashy, profane & obscene" for its sexual frankness. A sprawling portrait of America, encompassing every aspect of American life, from the steam-driven Brooklyn ferry to the use of ether in surgery, the volume opens not with the author's name but simply with his daguerreotype (a forerunner of the photograph). Unconventional in style—Whitman invented "free verse" rather than use conven-

In the poem "Song of Myself" from the collection *Leaves of Grass*, Walt Whitman declared "The United States themselves are essentially the greatest poem." This "carpenter portrait" of the author accompanied the first edition of *Leaves of Grass*, published in 1855.

tionally rhymed or regularly metered verse—the volume stands out as a landmark in the history of American literature for its celebration of the diversity, the energy, and the expansiveness of pre–Civil War America.

Ethnic Voices

During the years preceding the Civil War, America's ethnic and racial minorities began to publish novels, poems, histories, and autobiographies that explored what it meant to be an outsider in a predominantly white, Anglo-Saxon, Protestant society. The result was a unique body of ethnic writing chronicling the distinctive experience and changing self-image of ethnic Americans.

One of the earliest forms of African American literature was the slave narrative, graphic first-person accounts of life in bondage, written by former slaves, including William Wells Brown, Frederick Douglass, and Josiah Henson (he was Harriet Beecher Stowe's model for Uncle Tom). These volumes not only awoke readers to the hardships and cruelties of life under slavery, they also described the ingenious strategies that fugitive slaves used to escape from bondage. William and Ellen Craft, for example, disguised themselves as master and slave; Henry "Box" Brown had himself crated in a box and shipped north.

The 1850s saw the publication of the first four novels by African Americans. William Wells Brown's *Clotel* (1853), written by an abolitionist and escaped slave, offers a fictional reworking of the story that Thomas Jefferson fathered several children by a slave mistress. In *The Garies and Their Friends* (1857), Frank Webb, a Philadelphia free black, describes the destructive effects of prejudice, discrimination, and racial violence on two families, one lower class and the other, wealthier, with a white husband and a mulatto wife. In *Blake* (1859), one of the most militant novels produced during the nineteenth century, Martin R. Delany, a physician and a reform activist, tells the story of a black Cuban who repudiates organized religion and seeks to liberate blacks in Cuba and the United States. Harriet Jacobs, a poverty-stricken free black from Massachusetts, blends autobiography and fiction in *Incidents in the Life of a Slave Girl* (1859), which tells the story of an orphan who is indentured to an abusive white family, but who nevertheless achieves self-respect and self-reliance. Each of these novels draws on unique African American elements—including folklore and oral traditions—and gives expression to a distinctive "double consciousness," an awareness of being both African and American.

Native Americans, too, produced firsthand accounts of their lives. Among the most notable is the *Life of Ma-Ka-Tai-Me-she-kia-Kiak or Black Hawk* (1833), a classic spiritual and secular biography, in which the Sauk warrior explains why he resisted white efforts to seize Indian land in northwestern Illinois during the Black Hawk War (1832). William Apes, a Pequod, published one of the earliest histories from an Indian vantage point in 1836. John Rollin Ridge, a Cherokee journalist, published the first novel by an Indian in 1850, *The Life and Adventures of Joaquin Murieta*, which recounts the heroic adventures of a Robin Hood–like bandit in California who protects Mexican Americans from white exploitation. Much more than a simple adventure story, this novel is also a thinly veiled protest of the treatment of Native Americans by someone who had personally experienced the removal of the Cherokees from their tribal homelands in Georgia.

Mexican Americans responded to the arrival into the Southwest of white Americans through a variety of literary forms, including *corridos* (ballads), *chistes* (jokes), and autobiographies. The earliest autobiographical narrative was published by Padre Antonio José Martínez in 1838. Martínez resisted Father Jean-Baptiste Lamy's efforts to Americanize Catholic religious practices in New Mexico, a subject later treated in Willa Cather's 1927 novel *Death Comes to the Archbishop*. Other notable early autobiographies, written by José Antonio Mechaca and Juan Séguin, chronicle the decline of the landed Tejano elite following the Texas Revolution.

The famine years of the late 1840s—a period of massive Irish Catholic immigration and intense anti-Catholic prejudice—inspired a number of Irish American immigrants to reflect on their experience through fiction. Such authors as John Boyce, Hugh Quigley, and Mary Anne Sadlier used fiction to chronicle the sufferings of famine-stricken Ireland, the wrenching transatlantic passage, the disorientation of rural immigrants resettling in American cities, and the need for religious faith to help immigrants adjust to a challenging new environment. Sadlier, an orphan who migrated from Ireland in 1844, was the most prolific and influential nineteenth-century Irish American novelist. Her 18 novels on Irish history and immigrant life offer a wealth of information about the famine generation and its religious beliefs and practices.

American Art

If Americans could produce literary masterpieces, were they also capable of creating visual art that would rival that of Europe? At the end of the eigh-

Thomas Cole, *Schroon Mountain, The Adirondacks*, 1838. This painting captures the sense of awe at the grandeur and scenic beauty of the American landscape associated with artists of the Hudson River school.

teenth century, this seemed doubtful. Artistic implements, such as paints, brushes, and canvases, were difficult to obtain, and professional artists were few in number. Although a number of talented portrait painters—including John Singleton Copley, Charles Willson Peale, and Gilbert Stuart—appeared during the last half of the eighteenth century, most painters were simply skilled craftspeople, who devoted most of their time to painting houses, furniture, or signs.

Perhaps the biggest obstacle to the development of the visual arts was the fact that the revolutionary generation associated art with luxury, corruption, sensual appetite, and aristocracy. Commented one person: "When a people get a taste for the fine arts, they are ruined."

During the early nineteenth century, however, artists succeeded in overcoming public hostility toward the visual arts. One way artists gained a degree of respectability was through historical painting. The American public hungered for visual representations of the great events of the American Revolution, and works such as John Trumbull's Revolutionary War battle scenes and his painting of the Declaration of Independence (1818) fed the public's appetite. Romantic landscape paintings also attracted a large popular audience. Portrayals of the American landscape by artists of the Hudson River school, such as Thomas Cole, Albert Bierstadt, and Frederick Church, evoked a sense of the immensity, power, and grandeur of nature, which had not yet been completely tamed by an expansive American civilization.

A more favorable public attitude toward art was also evident in public campaigns to erect patriotic monuments, to landscape homes, and to beautify cities by restoring town greens and commons, constructing the first urban parks, and building the first modern "park" cemeteries. At the beginning of the nineteenth century, public monuments and statues were rarities; town commons were muddy, ill-kept areas, often containing buildings and packs of animals; houses lacked lawns; and cemeteries were unlandscaped collections of graves located near town centers.

Beginning in 1825, when an obelisk was erected at Bunker Hill to commemorate that Revolutionary War battle, Americans began to construct patriotic monuments. Around the same time, homeowners began to beautify their homes with lawns and landscaping, while cities established the nation's first urban parks. Construction of Mount Auburn cemetery in the 1830s in a pastoral setting outside Boston marked the beginning of the modern park cemetery, where the living could commune with the spirit of the dead (though the site was initially popular because it was a "green space" that could be used as a picnic ground). These beautification campaigns represented a response to the urban and industrial growth of cities that already threatened to destroy the physical beauty of city environments.

AMERICAN POPULAR CULTURE

Existing alongside the literary and artistic achievements of Emerson, Thoreau, and Melville was a vibrant popular culture. Consisting of penny newspapers, dime novels, minstrel shows, and other forms of popular amusement, this commercialized mass culture began to emerge at the beginning of the nineteenth century. By the eve of the Civil War, mass-circulation newspapers, inexpensive popular novels, and popular theater had become staples of American life.

One important aspect of popular culture was the penny press. Before the American Revolution, newspapers were few in number, expensive, short, small in circulation, infrequently printed, and aimed at a narrow audience. As late as 1765, there were only 23 weekly newspapers in all of the American colonies and no daily papers at all. At six cents a copy, these papers were out of reach of a popular audience; the contents of their four-page issues—announcements of ship arrivals, piracies, court actions, and maritime news—were of interest only to merchants. It was not until 1783, that the first daily newspaper, the *Pennsylvania Evening Post*, began to be published.

After the Revolution, political newspapers expressing the viewpoint of a particular political faction began to flourish. In the 1830s, when the development of the steam printing press dramatically cut printing costs and speeded production, the first mass-circulation newspapers began to appear. The first penny newspapers, Horatio David Sheppard's New York *Morning Post* and Benjamin H. Day's New York *Sun*, began publication in 1833.

The *Sun*, the first American paper to use newsboys to hawk papers on the street, soon discovered other ways of increasing its circulation. In the summer of 1835, the *Sun* announced that British astronomer Sir John Herschel had made "astronomical discoveries of the most wonderful description." With a new and powerful telescope, he had discovered "planets in other solar systems" and, most remarkably, the winged inhabitants of the moon. As a result of the "Great Moon Hoax," the *Sun's* circulation soared from 10,000 to 19,000. The *Sun's* success inspired other publishers to use hoaxes and stories of murders, railroad accidents, cannibalism, and freaks of nature—horror, gore, and perversity—to build circulation. English novelist Charles Dickens thought that appropriate names for newspapers would be the New York *Sewer* and the New York *Stabber*.

During the 1830s and 1840s, the modern mass-circulation newspaper emerged. Journalistic pioneers, such as James Gordon Bennett of the New York *Herald*, introduced features that we still associate with the daily newspaper, including crime stories, gossip columns, editorials, stock tables, and sports pages.

Along with the modern newspaper came magazines. From just 5 American magazines in 1794, the number rose to nearly 100 in 1825 and 600 in 1850. By 1850, there were magazines for almost every imaginable audience, with the proliferation of children's magazines, scientific journals, literary reviews, women's magazines, religious periodicals, and comics.

The Popular Novel

In 1860 an Oswego, New York, printer named Erastus Beadle, issued his first dime novel, *Malaeska, The Indian Wife*. Critics attacked this book and others about heroes such as Daniel Boone as "devil-traps for the young," but within three years, Beadle had sold more than 2.5 million copies.

Well before Erastus Beadle introduced the dime novel (which usually sold for a nickel), opportunistic publishers had already produced murder trial transcripts, criminals' biographies, pirate tales, and westerns targeted at working-class and frontier readers. The respectable middle-class tended to read sentimental domestic tales, such as Susan Warner's *The Wide, Wide World*, one of the most popular mid-nineteenth-century novels; sentimental love poetry, by authors such as Lydia Sigourney, "the sweet singer of Hartford"; or morally high-minded adventure tales, such as Richard Henry Dana, Jr.'s *Two Years Before the Mast* (1840) or historian Francis Parkman's *The Oregon Trail* (1847). Less educated Americans, however, favored adventure novels and urban crime novels.

Popular southern writers such as William Gilmore Simms and Robert Montgomery Bird produced tales of pirates and sea monsters for working-class and younger readers, and popular northern writers such as George Lippard, author of *New York: Its Upper Ten and Lower Million*, and Ned Buntline, author of *The Mysteries and Miseries of New York*, created tales of urban poverty and criminality. Although not great works of literature, the urban crime novels, in particular, offered valuable social commentary, providing graphic details of aspects of pre–Civil War American life, such as teenage prostitution, urban poverty, class division, and social inequity, that were absent from the works of more respectable writers such as Washington Irving.

Much of the most popular American fiction produced before the Civil War was written by women. Although Nathaniel Hawthorne dismissed female novelists as "mere scribbling women," their works offered psychologically and sociologically insightful descriptions of drunken husbands brutalizing their wives, amoral men seducing and abandoning trusting young women, and callous employers exploiting ill-paid seamstresses and maids. The earliest woman-authored novel—Susanna Rowson's *Charlotte Temple* (1791), a story of a trusting heroine lured from her English home by a British officer and abandoned into poverty and premature death in New York—dealt with seduction and betrayal. At a time when the rate of illegitimate births was sharply rising (approaching 10 percent in New England), such stories offered a stark warning to young women.

By the 1820s, the form of women's literature most in demand was the "domestic novel," which typically described the "trials and triumphs" of a young woman who encounters hardships in a hostile society and discovers the resources within herself to surmount these difficulties. Authors such as Maria Cummins, Catharine Sedgwick, and Susan Warner gave expression to an early feminist vision. Their books upheld "feminine" values—of duty, tenderness, and self-sacrifice—as an alternative to the acquisitive, pecuniary values of the dominant society and called on women to attain a sense of self-respect and self-worth.

Forms of Popular Entertainment

A freewheeling, irreverent spirit pervaded American popular culture before the Civil War—a spirit typified by P. T. Barnum, nineteenth-century America's most famous purveyor of popular entertainment. A Connecticut Yankee born in Bridgeport in 1810, Barnum is reputed to have said that "there is a sucker born every minute." A staunch advocate of temperance, antislavery, and women's rights, Barnum made a fortune through pioneering campaigns of advertising and self-promotion. A critic said that an appropriate motto for Barnum would be: "Lie and swindle as much as you please . . . but be sure you read your Bible and drink no brandy!"

Throughout his life, the "prince of humbugs" never stopped believing that the public enjoyed having its wits tested. He got his start exhibiting a slave woman named Joice Heth, whom he claimed was 161 years old and had served as George Washington's nursemaid (an autopsy later revealed that she was 80 at her death). Barnum achieved fame and fortune from his 25-cent American Museum in New York, which contained the "Feejee mermaid," which had the head of a monkey and the body of a fish; a working model of Niagara Falls; the 25-inch-tall General Tom Thumb; and Jumbo, an immense white elephant. After the Civil War, Barnum closed his museum and opened "the greatest show on earth," a spectacular three-ring circus. With his hoaxes, humbugs, and shameless self-promotion, Barnum epitomized the buoyant, irreverence of antebellum popular culture—which taught Americans to pay gladly for entertainment.

A rowdy, boisterous spirit was particularly evident in popular humor. The word "grotesque" sums up a defining characteristic of American humor before the Civil War. Employing crude language, wild exaggeration, pungent images, and incongruity, the writings of such early American humorists as James Kirke Paulding and George Washington Harris paved the way for the later success of Artemus Ward, Bret Harte, and Mark Twain.

No form of humor was more popular than the tall tale, an incredibly exaggerated account of improbable events. The most famous comic hero was Davy Crockett, loosely based on the life of the frontier hero and Whig politician who died at the Alamo. More than 50 wildly popular Crockett almanacs and humor pamphlets described him as a high-spirited resourceful braggart, "half-man, half-alligator." He is depicted as an ardent opponent of corruption in business and politics, who spends his leisure time riding on streaks of lightning, and lighting his pipe with the sun.

American popular culture found one of its most well-received forms of expression on the stage. A typical night at the theater included not only a play, but various musical interludes and a comic opera, as well as demonstrations of magic tricks, tightrope walking, fireworks, acrobatics, or pantomime. Melodramas were an especially popular form of theatrical entertainment, often describing a villain's efforts to strip a young maiden of her virtue and fortune. Emphasizing action over characterization, melodramas were filled with thrilling fights, daring escapes, and breathtaking rescues, and featured elaborate scenery, including working waterfalls and volcanoes.

Critics condemned the theater as a "Synagogue of Satan" that attracted "the most depraved and yet the most enticing companions the community affords." Antebellum theaters were rowdy places where liquor dealers and prostitutes plied their wares, and audiences interacted directly with actors and musicians. Theatergoers were not passive spectators. They ate during performances and expressed their praise with boisterous clapping. When they were displeased, they yelled and hissed and pelted actors with rotten eggs, stones, and even chairs. Some performances actually ignited riots—usually when an English actor was accused of insulting the United States. The most famous, the Astor Place Riot of 1849, resulted in dozens of injuries.

Oratory was a particularly popular form of entertainment. Americans attended sermons, political speeches, poetry readings, and public lectures with an enthusiasm unmatched in American history. The lyceum movement, founded by Josiah Holbrook, a Connecticut farmer, in 1826, sponsored traveling lec-

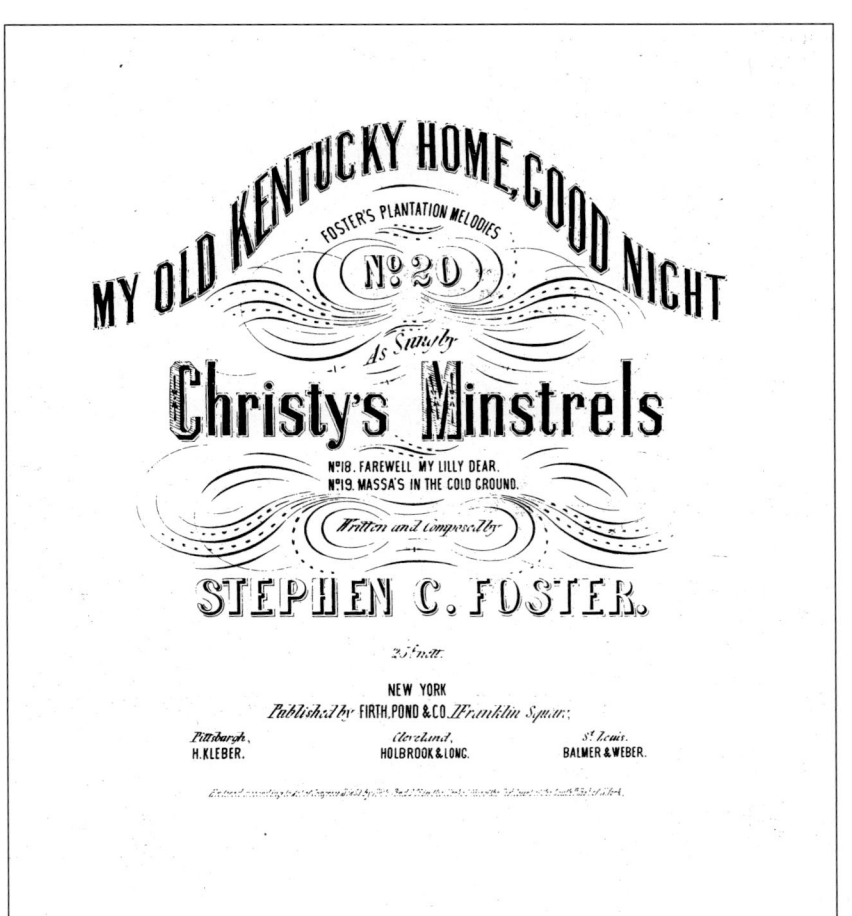

Although Stephen Foster actually knew little about the South, his songs, such as "Old Folks at Home" and "My Old Kentucky Home," gave expression to a sentimental picture of the antebellum South. Foster also wrote songs for blackface minstrel shows, like Christy's Minstrels, a popular form of entertainment in the 1830s and 1840s.

tures on the arts, literature, philosophy, religion, and science, including such prominent figures as Ralph Waldo Emerson and the Whig politician Daniel Webster.

Perhaps the most distinctive feature of pre–Civil War popular culture was the minstrel show. The first uniquely American entertainment form, the minstrel show provided comedy, music, dance, and novelty acts to audiences hungry for entertainment. Offering humor that ranged from comedy skits to slapstick and one-liners—often mocking pompous politicians and pretentious professionals—the minstrel shows also introduced many of America's most enduring popular songs, including "Turkey in the Straw" and "Dixie."

Minstrel shows popularized the songs of Stephen Foster (1826–1864), the most acclaimed American composer of the mid-nineteenth century. Foster wrote more than 200 songs during his lifetime, mainly sentimental ballads and love songs (such as "Old Folks at Home," "My Old Kentucky Home," and "Beautiful Dreamer") and uptempo, rhythmic comic songs (such as "Camptown Races" and "Oh! Susanna"). At a time when the country was undergoing rapid urbanization and industrialization, Foster's music responded to a deep nostalgia for a sim-

Chronology of Key Events

1776	Mother Ann Lee founds the first Shaker community in America near Albany, New York
1801	Cane Ridge, Kentucky, revival meeting
1807	Congress outlaws the African slave trade
1816	American Colonization Society is founded
1819	Washington Irving publishes "Rip Van Winkle"
1825	Charles Finney leads his first religious revivals in New York State; Robert Owen founds New Harmony community in Indiana
1826	American Society for the Promotion of Temperance is founded
1829	David Walker issues his *Appeal to the Colored Citizens of the World*
1831	William Lloyd Garrison begins publishing the militant abolitionist newspaper, *The Liberator*
1833	First penny newspapers—New York *Sun* and New York *Morning Post*—are published; first coeducational college in the United States—Oberlin—is founded
1834	Antiabolitionist rioting takes place in Philadelphia
1837	Emerson presents his address on the "American Scholar"; Angelina Grimké lectures to mixed audiences of men and women; Massachusetts creates first state board of education and appoints Horace Mann secretary; abolitionist Elijah P. Lovejoy is killed by a proslavery mob in Alton, Illinois
1838	Frederick Douglass escapes from slavery
1840	Washington temperance movement begins; Liberty party is founded; and James G. Birney runs for president as Liberty party candidate; Sarah Grimké publishes *Letters on the Condition of Women and the Equality of the Sexes,* one of the earliest public defenses of sexual equality
1841	Dorothea Dix begins crusade on behalf of the mentally ill; Brook Farm is founded
1843	"Isabella" takes name Sojourner Truth and begins to speak out on behalf of women's rights and against slavery
1845	Henry David Thoreau begins living at Walden Pond
1848	First women's rights convention is held in Seneca Falls, New York; Free Soil party receives 10 percent of presidential vote
1849	Astor Place riot in New York city
1850	Nathaniel Hawthorne publishes *The Scarlet Letter*
1851	Herman Melville publishes *Moby Dick*
1852	Massachusetts adopts the first compulsory education law; Harriet Beecher Stowe's *Uncle Tom's Cabin* sells a million copies in its first year and a half
1854	Henry David Thoreau publishes *Walden*
1855	Walt Whitman publishes *Leaves of Grass*

pler era. Although Foster died in utter poverty—at the age of 37 in the paupers' wing of New York's Bellevue Hospital, with just 37 cents in his pocket—he, more than any other composer stimulated popular enthusiasm for American music.

The minstrel shows are difficult to interpret, in part because they relied on blackfaced humor that we find particularly abhorrent. Reflecting the racism of the broader society, minstrel shows presented a denigrating portrayal of African Americans. Racial stereotypes were the minstrel shows' stock in trade. Actors wore grotesque makeup, spoke in ludicrous dialects, and presented plantation life in a highly romanticized manner. Yet if the minstrel shows expressed the virulent racism of many white Americans, the blackfaced minstrel had another side. His humor frequently mocked whites and challenged traditional values. Moreover, the shows often incorporated elements of African-American folklore and showed black men and women outwitting white masters.

Pseudoscience also captured the popular fancy during the decades before the Civil War. During the early nineteenth century, science was advancing so rapidly that it was difficult to distinguish authentic scientific discoveries from hoaxes. Before the Civil War, Americans were fascinated by a variety of pseudosciences. Phrenology linked human character to the shape of and bumps on a person's skull. Animal magnetism was the belief in a universal electrical fluid influencing physics and even human psychology. Audiences flocked to see demonstrations of mesmerism (the control of a hypnotized person by a medium) and spiritualism (the direct communication with spirits of the deceased through trance visions or seances).

Phrenology had particular appeal to pre–Civil War Americans. Discovered by a physician from Vienna named Franz Gall and imported into the United States in 1832, phrenology exerted an extraordinary impact on popular culture. One American phrenology journal claimed a circulation of 50,000, and many employers required prospective employees to have their heads read. One of the earliest examples of a "science" of human behavior, phrenology held that distinct portions of the brain were devoted to distinct impulses—such as combativeness, amativeness (sexual love), and adhesiveness (comradely affection)—and that peoples' mental attributes could be read through their facial features. Phrenology claimed to offer young men and women a way to evaluate potential spouses and employers a tool for judging potential employees.

Conclusion

The pre–Civil War reform era came to a symbolic end in 1865 when William Lloyd Garrison, the abolitionist, closed down his militant abolitionist newspaper *The Liberator* and called on the American Anti-Slavery Society to disband. Its mission, he announced, had been accomplished.

The first half of the nineteenth century witnessed the rise of the first secular movements in history to educate the deaf and the blind, care for the mentally ill, extend equal rights to women, and abolish slavery. Inspired by the revolutionary ideals of the Declaration of Independence and the Bill of Rights, the Enlightenment faith in reason, and liberal and evangelical religious principles, educational reformers created a system of free public education; prison reformers constructed specialized institutions to reform criminals; temperance reformers sought to end the drinking of liquor; and utopian socialists established ideal communities to serve as models for a better world.

America's first age of reform was also an era of extraordinary intellectual and artistic ferment. The decades preceding the Civil War witnessed the growth of a mass audience for art, literature, and drama; the rise of a vibrant commercial mass culture; and the popularization of some of the most distinctive products of American culture, including the penny press, the minstrel show, and the western adventure novel. Authors such as James Fenimore Cooper and Henry Wadsworth Longfellow created a distinctly American literature employing native scenes and characters. The Transcendentalists developed a philosophy that rejected external authority and tradition and instead emphasized each person's infinite potentialities and glorified nature as a creative force. And especially during the 1850s, a host of writers—including Nathaniel Hawthorne, Harriet Jacobs, and Herman Melville—produced works of literature that rank among the greatest ever produced in this country.

The Civil War brought this period of ferment and experimentation to a close. The war's grim brutality undercut the spirit of hope and boundless possibilities that had pervaded pre–Civil War America. Nevertheless, the reformers, writers, and artists of the early nineteenth century would stand as an example and an inspiration to future generations of Americans.

Suggestions for Further Reading

Robert Abzug, *Cosmos Crumbling: American Reform and the Religious Imagination* (1994) shows how religious ideals and motives influenced the major reforms of the pre–Civil War era, including abolition, temperance, and woman's rights.

Steven Mintz, *Moralists and Modernizers: America's Pre-Civil War Reformers* (1995) offers an overview and interpretation of America's first age of reform, combining portraits of leading reformers with discussions of religion and specific reform movements.

Ronald G. Walters, *American Reformers, 1815–1860* (1997) examines the beliefs, rhetoric, and tactics of leading reformers.

Overviews and Surveys

Richard Carwardine, *Evangelicals and Politics in Antebellum America* (1993); Whitney R. Cross, *The Burned Over District: The Social and Intellectual History of Enthusiastic Religion in Western New York, 1800–1850* (1950); David Brion Davis, ed., *Antebellum Reform* (1967); Lori D. Ginzberg, *Women and the Work of Benevolence: Morality, Politics, and Class in the Nineteenth-Century United States* (1990); Clifford S. Griffin, *The Ferment of Reform, 1830–1860* (1967); George M. Marsden, *Religion and American Culture* (1990); Alice Felt Tyler, *Freedom's Ferment: Phases of American Social History to 1860* (1962).

Sources of the Reform Impulse

Jon Butler, *Awash in a Sea of Faith: Christianizing the American People* (1990); Patricia Cline Cohen, *The Murder of Helen Jewett: The Life and Death of a Prostitute in Nineteenth-Century New York* (1998); Paul A. Gilje, *Rioting in America* (1996); David Grimsted, *American Mobbing* (1998); Nathan O. Hatch, *Democratization of American Christianity* (1989); Curtis D. Johnson, *Islands of Holiness: Rural Religion in Upstate New York, 1790–1860* (1989); Paul Johnson, *A Shopkeeper's Millennium: Society and Revivals in Rochester, New York, 1815–1837* (1978); P. E. Johnson and Sean Wilentz, *The Kingdom of Matthias* (1994); John F. Kasson, *Rudeness and Civility: Manners in Nineteenth-Century Urban America* (1990); Jama Lazerow, *Religion and the Working Class in Antebellum America* (1995); Perry Miller, *The Life of the Mind in America from the Revolution to the Civil War* (1965), Timothy L. Smith, *Revivalism and Social Reform in Mid-19th Century America: From the Colonial Era to the Twentieth Century* (1957); William R. Sutton, *Journeymen for Jesus: Evangelical Artisans* (1998); John Wigger, *Taking Heaven by Storm: Methodism and the Rise of Popular Christianity* (1998); Forrest G. Wood, *The Arrogance of Faith: Christianity and Race in America* (1990).

Moral Reform

John R. Bodo, *The Protestant Clergy and Public Issues, 1812–1848* (1954); Anne M. Boylan, *Sunday School: The Formation of an American Institution, 1790–1880* (1988); Charles C. Cole, Jr., *The Social Ideas of the Northern Evangelists* (1954); Jed Dannenbaum, *Drink and Disorder: Temperance Reform in Cincinnati From the Washington Revival to the WCTU* (1984); Charles I. Foster, *An Errand of Mercy: The Evangelical United Front, 1790–1837* (1960); Clifford S. Griffin, *Their Brothers' Keepers: Moral Stewardship in the United States, 1800–1865* (1983); Joseph R. Gusfield, *Symbolic Crusade: Status Politics and the American Temperance Movement*, 2nd ed. (1986); Robert L. Hampel, *Temperance and Prohibition in Massachusetts* (1982); Mark Lender and James Kirby Martin, *Drinking in America: A History*, rev. ed. (1987); John R. McKivigan, *The War Against Proslavery Religion: Abolitionism and the Northern Churches, 1830–1865* (1984); W. J. Rorabaugh, *The Alcoholic Republic: An American Tradition* (1979); Ian R. Tyrell, *Sobering Up: From Temperance to Prohibition in Antebellum America, 1800–1860* (1979).

Social Reform

David Allmendinger, *Paupers and Scholars: The Transformation of Student Life in Nineteenth-Century New England* (1975); Robert H. Bremner, *From the Depths: The Discovery of Poverty in the United States* (1992); Lawrence Cremin, *American Education: The National Experience, 1783–1876* (1980); Norman Dain, *Concepts of Insanity in the United States, 1789–1865* (1964); Allen F. Davis and Mark H. Haller, eds., *The Peoples of Philadelphia: A History of Ethnic Groups and Lower-Class Life, 1790–1940* (1973); David Brion Davis, *Homicide in American Fiction, 1798–1860: A Study in Social Values* (1957); Albert Deutsch, *The Mentally Ill in America: A History of Their Care and Treatment*, 2d ed. (1949); Ellen Dwyer, *Homes for the Mad: Life Inside Two Nineteenth-Century Asylums* (1987); Ruth Elson, *Guardians of Tradition: American Schoolbooks of the Nineteenth Century* (1964); Michael Feldberg, *The Turbulent Era: Riot and Disorder in Jacksonian America* (1980); Gerald Grob, *The State and the Mentally Ill: A History of Worcester State Hospital in Massachusetts, 1830–1920* (1966); Joseph M. Hawes, *Children in Urban Society: Juvenile Delinquency in Nineteenth-Century America* (1971); Joel T. Headley, *Great Riots of New York, 1712–1873* (1971); W. Eugene Hollon, *Frontier Violence: Another Look* (1974); Mary Ann Jimenez, *Changing Faces of Madness: Early American Attitudes and Treatment of the Insane* (1987); Carl F. Kaestle, *Pillars of the Republic: Common Schools and American Society, 1780–1860* (1983); Carl F. Kaestle and Maris A. Vinovskis, *Education and Social Change in Nineteenth-Century Massachusetts* (1980); Michael B. Katz, *The Irony of Early School Reform: Educational Innovation in Mid-Nineteenth-Century Massachusetts* (1968); Roger Lane, *Policing the City, Boston, 1822–1855* (1967), and *Violent Death in the City: Suicide, Accident and Murder in Nineteenth Century Philadelphia* (1979); Vincent P. Lannie, *Public Money and Parochial Education: Bishop Hughes, Governor Seward, and the New York School Controversy* (1968); W. David Lewis, *From Newgate to Dannemora; The Rise of the Penitentiary in New York, 1796–1848* (1965); Louis P. Masur, *Rites of Execution: Capital Punishment and the Transformation of American Culture, 1776–1865* (1989); Michael Meranze, *Laboratories of Virtue: Punishment, Revolution, and Authority in Philadelphia* (1996); Donald H. Meyer, *The Instructed Conscience: The Shaping of the American National Ethic* (1972); Raymond A. Mohl, *Poverty in New York, 1783–1825* (1971); Leonard L. Richards, "Gentlemen of Property and Standing": Anti-Abolition Mobs in Jacksonian America* (1970); James F. Richardson, *The New York Police: Colonial Times to 1901* (1970); David Rothman, *The Discovery of the Asylum: Social Order and Disorder in the New Republic*, rev. ed. (1991); Lee Soltow and Edward Stevens, *The Rise of Literacy and the Common School in the United States: A Socioeconomic Analysis to 1870* (1981); David Tyack and Elisabeth Hansot, *Learning Together: A History of Coeducation in American Public Schools* (1992); David B. Tyack, *The One Best System: A History of American Urban Education* (1974); Paul O. Weinbaum, *Mobs and Demagogues: The New York Response to Collective Violence in the Early Nineteenth Century* (1979); Thomas A. Woody, *A History of Women's Education in the United States*, 2 vols. (1929).

Radical Reform

Howard Bell, *A Survey of the Negro Convention Movement, 1830–1861* (1953); Barbara J. Berg, *The Remembered Gate:*

Origins of American Feminism, The Woman and the City, 1800–1860 (1978); Arthur E. Bestor, Jr., *Backwoods Utopias: The Sectarian and Owenite Phases of Communitarian Socialism in America, 1663–1829,* 2nd ed. (1970); R. J. M. Blackett, *Building an Antislavery Wall: Black Americans in the Atlantic Abolitionist Movement, 1830–1860* (1983); Frederick J. Blue, *Free Soilers: Third Party Politics, 1848–54* (1973); Jeanne Boydston, *Home and Work: Housework, Wages and the Ideology of Labor in the Early Republic* (1990); Maren Lockwood Carden, *Oneida: Utopian Community to Modern Corporation* (1971); Christopher Clark, *The Communitarian Moment: The Radical Challenge of the Northampton Association* (1995); Nancy F. Cott, *The Bonds of Womanhood: "Woman's Sphere" in New England, 1780–1835* (1977); David Brion Davis, *The Problem of Slavery in the Age of Revolution, 1770–1823* (1975), and *Slavery and Human Progress* (1984); Carl N. Degler, *At Odds: Women and the Family in America from the Revolution to the Present* (1980); Merton L. Dillion, *Slavery Attacked: Southern Slaves and Their Allies* (1990); Chris Dixon, *Perfecting the Family: Antislavery Marriages in Nineteenth-Century America* (1997); Ann Douglas, *The Feminization of American Culture* (1977); Donald Egbert and Stow Persons, eds., *Socialism in American Life,* 2 vols. (1952); Barbara Leslie Epstein, *The Politics of Domesticity: Women, Evangelism, and Temperance in Nineteenth-Century America* (1981); Sara Evans, *Born for Liberty: A History of Women in America* (1989); Michael Fellman, *The Unbounded Frame: Freedom and Community in Nineteenth-Century American Utopianism* (1973); Robert S. Fogarty, *All Things New: American Communes and Utopian Movements, 1860–1914* (1990); Lawrence Foster, *Religion and Sexuality: Three American Communal Experiments of the Nineteenth Century* (1981); George Fredrickson, *The Black Image in the White Mind: The Debate on Afro-American Character and Destiny, 1817–1914* (1971); Larry Gara, *Liberty Line: The Legend of the Underground Railroad* (1961); Paul Goodman, *Of One Blood: Abolition and the Origins of Racial Equality* (1998); Carl J. Guarneri, *The Utopian Alternative: Fourierism in Nineteenth-Century America* (1991); J. F. C. Harrison, *Quest for the New Moral World: Robert Owen and the Owenites in Britain and America* (1969); Stanley Harrold, *The Abolitionists and the South, 1831–1861* (1995); Blanche Hersh, *The Slavery of Sex: Feminist-Abolitionists in America* (1978); Nancy A. Hewitt, *Women's Activism and Social Change: Rochester, New York, 1822–1872* (1984); Mark Holloway, *Heavens on Earth: Utopian Communities in America,* 2d ed. (1966); Victor B. Howard, *Conscience and Slavery: The Evangelical Domestic Missions, 1837–1861* (1990); Nancy Isenberg, *Sex and Citizenship in Antebellum America* (1998); David M. Jacobs, *Courage and Conscience: Black and White Abolitionists in Boston* (1993); Julie Roy Jeffrey, *The Great Silent Army of Abolition: Ordinary Women in the Antislavery Movement* (1998); Howard Jones, *Mutiny on the Amistad* (1987); Rosabeth Moss Kanter, *Commitment and Community: Communes and Utopias in Sociological Perspective* (1972); Louis J. Kern, *An Ordered Love: Sex Roles and Sexuality in Victorian Utopias: The Shakers, the Mormons, and the Oneida Community* (1981); Carol A. Kolmerten, *Women in Utopia: The Ideology of Gender in American Owenite Communities* (1990); Aileen Kraditor, *Means and Ends in American Abolitionism: Garrison and His Critics on Strategy and Tactics* (1969); Alma Lutz, *Crusade for Freedom: Women of the Antislavery Movement* (1968); Carleton Mabee, *Black Freedom* (1970); John R. McKivigan, *The War Against Proslavery Religion: Abolitionism and the Northern Churches, 1830–1865* (1984); John R. McKivigan and Stanley Harrold, eds., *Antislavery Violence* (1999); John R. McKivigan and Mitchell Snay, eds., *Religion and the Antebellum Debate Over Slavery* (1998); Keith Melder, *Beginnings of Sisterhood: The American Women's Rights Movement, 1800–1850* (1977); Lucretia Mott, *Slavery and "The Woman Question"; Lucretia Mott's Diary of Her Visit to Great Britain to Attend the World's Anti-Slavery Convention of 1840* (1952); Raymond L. Muncy, *Sex and Marriage in Utopian Communities; Nineteenth-Century America* (1973); Charles Nordhoff, *The Communistic Societies of the United States, from Personal Visit and Observation* (1875); John Humphrey Noyes, *History of American Socialisms* (1870); Jane H. Pease, *They Who Would Be Free: Blacks' Search for Freedom, 1830–1861* (1974); Jane H. and William H. Pease, *Black Utopia: Negro Communal Experiment in America* (1963); Lewis Perry and Michael Fellman, eds., *Antislavery Reconsidered* (1979); Carla L. Peterson, *Doers of the Word: African-American Women Speakers and Writers in the North* (1995); Donald E. Pitzer, *America's Communal Utopias* (1997); Benjamin Quarles, *Black Abolitionists* (1969); Nicholas V. Riasanovsky, *The Teaching of Charles Fourier* (1969); C. Duncan Rice, *The Rise and Fall of Black Slavery* (1975); Mary P. Ryan, *Cradle of the Middle Class: The Family in Oneida County, New York, 1790–1865* (1981), and *Womanhood in America from Colonial Times to the Present,* 3d ed. (1983); Karen Sánchez-Eppler, *Touching Liberty: Abolition, Feminism, and the Politics of the Body* (1993); Richard H. Sewell, *Ballots for Freedom: Antislavery Politics in the United States, 1837–1860* (1976); Gerald Sorin, *Abolitionism: A New Perspective* (1972); John C. Spurlock, *Free Love: Marriage and Middle Class Radicalism in America, 1825–1860* (1988); Phillip J. Staudenraus, *The African Colonization Movement* (1961); Stephen J. Stein, *The Shaker Experience in America: A History of the United Society of Believers* (1992); James Brewer Stewart, *Holy Warriors: The Abolitionists and American Slavery* (1996); Vernon L. Volpe, *Forlorn Hope of Freedom: The Liberty Party in the Old Northwest, 1838–1848* (1990); Carol Wilson, *Freedom at Risk: The Kidnapping of Free Blacks in America, 1780–1865* (1994); William E. Wilson, *The Angel and the Serpent: The Story of New Harmony* (1964); Nancy Woloch, *Women and the American Experience* (1984); Donald R. Wright, *African Americans in the Early Republic* (1993); Jean Fagan Yellin, *Women & Sisters; Antislavery Feminists in American Culture* (1989); Jean Fagan Yellin and John C. Van Horne, eds., *Abolitionist Sisterhood: Women's Political Culture in Antebellum America* (1994); Arthur Zilversmit, *The First Emancipation: The Abolition of Slavery in the North* (1967).

Artistic and Cultural Ferment

Harold Bloom, ed., *Henry David Thoreau* (1987), and *Henry David Thoreau's Walden* (1987); Paul F. Boller, Jr., *American Transcendentalism 1830–1860: An Intellectual Inquiry* (1974); Lawrence Buell, *New England Literary Culture from Revolu-*

tion Through Renaissance (1986); Mary Kupiec Cayton, Emerson's Emergence (1990); Ann Fabian, Card Sharps, Dream Books, & Bucket Shops: Gambling in Nineteenth-Century America (1990); Jon W. Finson, The Voices That Are Gone: Themes in Nineteenth-Century American Popular Song (1994) Len Gougeon, Virtue's Hero: Emerson, Antislavery, and Reform (1990); Neil Harris, The Artist in American Society: The Formative Years, 1790–1860 (1982), and Humbug: The Art of P. T. Barnum (1973); Richard Lebeaux, Young Man Thoreau (1977); Lawrence Levine, Highbrow/ Lowbrow: The Emergence of Cultural Hierarchy in America (1988) F. O. Matthiessen, American Renaissance (1941); Michael Meyer, Several More Lives to Live: Thoreau's Political Reputation in America (1977), Perry Miller, The Life of the Mind in America: From the Revolution to the Civil War (1965); Joel Myerson, ed., Critical Essays on Henry David Thoreau's Walden (1988); Anne C. Rose, Transcendentalism as a Social Movement, 1830–1850 (1981) and Voices of the Marketplace: American Thought and Culture, 1830–1860 (1995).

American Popular Culture

Ann Fabian, Card Sharps, Dream Books, & Bucket Shops: Gambling in Nineteenth-Century America (1990); Jon W. Finson, The Voices That Are Gone: Themes in Nineteenth-Century American Popular Song (1994); Neil Harris, Humbug: The Art of P. T. Barnum (1973); Lawrence Levine, Highbrow/Lowbrow: The Emergence of Cultural Hierarchy in America (1988); Russel B. Nye, Society and Culture in America, 1830–1860 (1974); Ronald J. Zboray, A Fictive People: Antebellum Economic Development and the American Reading Public (1993).

Biographies

Robert Abzug, Passionate Liberator: Theodore Dwight Weld and the Dilemma of Reform (1980); Lois Banner, Elizabeth Cady Stanton: A Radical for Woman's Rights (1980); Thomas J. Brown, Dorothea Dix (1998); Frank L. Byrne, Prophet of Prohibition: Neal Dow and His Crusade (1961); Charles Capper, Margaret Fuller: An American Romantic Life (1992); Charles Crowe, George Ripley: Transcendentalist and Utopian Socialist (1967); Hugh Davis, Joshua Leavitt: Evangelical Abolitionist (1990); Merton Dillon, Elijah P. Lovejoy, Abolitionist Editor (1961); Isabelle Webb Entrikin, Sarah Josepha Hale and Godey's Lady's Book (1946); Edward Farrison, William Wells Brown: Author and Reformer (1969); Betty Fladeland, James Gillespie Birney: Slaveholder to Abolitionist (1955); Frank O. Gatell, John Gorham Palfrey and the New England Conscience (1963); David L. Gollaher, A Voice for the Mad: The Life of Dorothea Dix (1995); Lawrence B. Goodheart, Abolitionist, Actuary, Atheist: Elizur Wright and the Reform Impulse (1990); Cyril Griffith, African Dream: Martin R. Delany and the Emergence of Pan-African Thought (1975); Keith J. Hardman, Charles Grandison Finney (1987); Ralph Volney Harlow, Gerrit Smith, Philanthropist and Reformer (1939); Joan D. Hedrick, Harriet Beecher Stowe, A Life (1993); Carolyn L. Karcher, The First Woman in the Republic: A Cultural Biography of Lydia Maria Child (1994); Gerda Lerner, The Grimké Sisters from South Carolina: Pioneers for Women's Rights and Abolition (1967); Katherine Du Pre Lumpkin, The Emancipation of Angelina Grimké (1974); Carleton Mabee, Sojourner Truth (1993); Helen E. Marshall, Dorothea Dix: Forgotten Samaritan (1937); Waldo E. Martin, Jr., The Mind of Frederick Douglass (1984); William McFeely, Frederick Douglass (1991); Milton Meltzer, Tongue of Flame: The Life of Lydia Maria Child (1965); Walter M. Merrill, Against Wind and Tide: A Biography of William Lloyd Garrison (1963); Jonathan Messerli, Horace Mann: A Biography (1972); Nell Painter, Sojourner Truth (1996); Jane H. Pease, Bound with Them in Chains (1972); Benjamin Quarles, Frederick Douglass (1948); David S. Reynolds, Walt Whitman's America (1995); A. H. Saxon, P. T. Barnum: The Legend and the Man (1989); Richard H. Sewell, John P. Hale and the Politics of Abolition (1965); Kathryn Kish Sklar, Catharine Beecher: A Study in American Domesticity (1973); James Brewer Stewart, Joshua R. Giddings and the Tactics of Radical Politics (1970), and Wendell Phillips, Liberty's Hero (1986); Benjamin P. Thomas, Theodore Weld, Crusader for Freedom (1950); John L. Thomas, The Liberator, William Lloyd Garrison (1963); Robert David Thomas, The Man Who Would Be Perfect: John Humphrey Noyes and the Utopian Impulse (1977); Nancy Tomes, A Generous Confidence: The Art of Asylum Keeping, Thomas Story Kirkbride and the Origins of American Psychiatry (1984); Albert J. Von Frank, The Trials of Anthony Burns (1998); Bertram Wyatt-Brown, Lewis Tappan and the Evangelical War Against Slavery (1969).

INTERNET RESOURCES

America's First Look into the Camera: Daguerreotype Portraits and Views, 1839–1862
http://memory.loc.gov/ammem/daghtml/daghome.html
The Library of Congress's daguerreotype collection consists of more than 650 photographs dating from 1839 to 1864. Portraits, architectural views, and some street scenes make up most of the collection.

Votes for Women: Selections from the National American Woman Suffrage Association Collection, 1848–1921
http://memory.loc.gov/ammem/naw/nawshome.html
This Library of Congress site contains 167 books, pamphlets, and other artifacts documenting the suffrage campaign.

By Popular Demand: "Votes for Women" Suffrage Pictures, 1850–1920
http://memory.loc.gov/ammem/vfwhtml/vfwhome.html
Portraits, suffrage parades, picketing suffragists, an anti-suffrage display, and cartoons commenting on the movement make up this Library of Congress site.

Women in America, 1820–1842
http://xroads.virginia.edu/~HYPER/DETOC/FEM/home.htm
This University of Virginia site takes a look at women in antebellum America.

Godey's Ladies Book Online
http://www.history.rochester.edu/godeys/
Here is online text of this interesting nineteenth century journal.

Important Black Abolitionists
http://www.loc.gov/exhibits/african/influ.html
An exhibit site, with pictures and text, that discusses some key African American abolitionists and their efforts to end slavery, from the Library of Congress.

The Alexis de Tocqueville Tour Exploring Democracy in America
http://www.tocqueville.org/
Text, images, and teaching suggestions are a part of this companion site to C-SPAN's recent programming on de Tocqueville.

KEY TERMS

Sojourner Truth   (p. 284)
Enlightenment   (p. 285)
Religious Liberalism   (p. 285)
William Ellery Channing   (p. 285)
Second Great Awakening   (p. 285)
Evangelical Revivalism (revivals)   (p. 288)
Charles Grandison Finney   (p. 288)
Temperance   (p. 290)
Insanity Defense   (p. 291)
Capital Punishment   (p. 291)
Imprisonment for Debt   (p. 291)
Horace Mann   (p. 292)
Prudence Crandall   (p. 292)
Dorothea Dix   (p. 293)
Thomas Hopkins Gallaudet   (p. 293)
Samuel Gridley Howe   (p. 293)
Colonization   (p. 294)
Paul Cuffe   (p. 294)
David Walker   (p. 294)
William Lloyd Garrison   (p. 294)
Liberty Party   (p. 296)
Free Soil Party   (p. 296)
Frederick Douglass   (p. 296)
Angelina and Sarah Grimké   (p. 298)
Elizabeth Cady Stanton   (p. 299)
Transcendentalists   (p. 303)
Ralph Waldo Emerson   (p. 303)
Henry David Thoreau   (p. 303)

REVIEW QUESTIONS

1. Describe the social and religious roots of the reform movements of the early nineteenth century.
2. In what ways did moral reformers try to change the behavior of early nineteenth-century Americans? How successful were they?
3. Describe the efforts of pre–Civil War reformers in each of the following areas: (a) educational reform; (b) the treatment of criminals; and (c) the treatment of the mentally ill.
4. Why did the abolition movement arouse resentment among many Northerners as well as many Southerners?
5. Why did a movement for women's rights emerge in the mid-nineteenth century? Identify the movement's achievements.
6. In what ways did American literature and art give expression to a distinctive national identity in the years before the Civil War?

12

THE DIVIDED NORTH, THE DIVIDED SOUTH

A DIVIDED CULTURE

THE EMERGENCE OF A NEW INDUSTRIAL ORDER IN THE NORTH
The Transformation of the Rural Countryside
The Disruption of the Artisan System of Labor
The Introduction of the Factory System
Labor Protests
The Movement for a Ten-Hour Day
The Laboring Poor
Immigration Begins
The Divided North

SOUTHERN DISTINCTIVENESS
The Plantation Legend
The Old South: Images and Realities
Impact of Slavery on the Southern Economy
Growth of a Distinctive Southern Identity
The Decline of Antislavery Sentiment in the South
"Reforming" Slavery from Within
Southern Nationalism
Southern Radicalism

SLAVERY
The Legal Status of Slaves
Slave Labor
Material Conditions of Slave Life
Slave Family Life
Slave Cultural Expression
Slave Resistance
Free African Americans

"Some other means of cultivating their estates"

In the early 1790s, slavery appeared to be a dying institution. Slave imports into the New World were declining and slave prices were falling because the crops grown by slaves—tobacco, rice, and indigo—did not generate enough income to pay for their upkeep. In Maryland and Virginia, planters were replacing tobacco, a labor-intensive crop that needed a slave labor force, with wheat and corn, which did not. At the same time, leading Southerners, including Thomas Jefferson, denounced slavery as a source of debt, economic stagnation, and moral dissipation. A French traveler reported that people throughout the South "are constantly talking of abolishing slavery, of contriving some other means of cultivating their estates."

Then **Eli Whitney** of Massachusetts gave slavery a new lease on life. Even as a teenager, Whitney was considered a mechanical genius. At the age of 12, he produced a violin that "made tolerable good musick." At 15 he took over his father's workshop in Westborough, Massachusetts, and began manufacturing nails. By the time he was 18, he had begun to produce hat pins for women's bonnets and men's walking sticks. But young Whitney hoped to become something more than a clever mechanic, and at the age of 23 he abandoned his father's workshop and entered college.

In 1792, just after graduating from Yale, Whitney traveled south in search of employment as a tutor. His journey was filled with disasters. During the boat trip, he became seasick. Before he could recover, his boat ran aground on rocks near New York City. Then he contracted smallpox. The only good thing to happen during his journey was that he was befriended by a charming Southern widow named Catharine Greene, whose late husband, General Nathanael Greene, had been a leading general during the American Revolution. When he arrived in the South, Whitney discovered that his promised salary as a tutor had been cut in half. So he quit the job and accepted Greene's invitation to visit her plantation near Savannah, Georgia.

During his visit, Whitney became intrigued with the problem encountered by southern planters in producing short-staple cotton. The booming textile industry had created a high demand for the crop, but it could not be marketed until the seeds had been extracted from the cotton boll, a laborious and time-consuming process.

From a slave known only by the name Sam, Whitney learned that a comb could be used to remove seeds from cotton. In just ten days, Whitney devised a way of mechanizing the comb. Within a month, Whitney's cotton engine (gin for short) could separate fiber from seeds faster than 50 people working by hand.

Whitney's invention revitalized slavery in the South by stimulating demand for slaves to raise short-staple cotton. Between 1792, when Whitney arrived on the Greene plantation, and 1794, the price of slaves doubled. By 1825 field hands, who brought $500 apiece in 1794, were worth $1500. As the price of slaves rose, so too did the number of slaves. During the first decade of the nineteenth century, the number of slaves in the United States increased by 33 percent; during the following decade (after the African slave trade became illegal), the slave population grew another 29 percent.

As the institution of slavery expanded in the South, it declined in the North. In 1777, Vermont's constitution outlawed slavery, making it the first area in the New World to prohibit slavery. Judicial decisions freed slaves in Massachusetts and New Hampshire, and other northern states adopted gradual emancipation acts. By the beginning of the nineteenth century, the new republic was fatefully divided into a slave section and a free section.

While seeking employment in the South, Yankee schoolteacher Eli Whitney developed a simple machine for separating cotton from its seeds. The "cotton gin" met the increasing demand for cotton and breathed new life into the institution of slavery.

A Divided Culture

By 1860 most Americans believed that the Mason-Dixon line divided the nation into two distinctive cultures: a commercial North and an agrarian South. This belief—that the cultures of the North and South were fundamentally different—was not a new idea on the eve of the Civil War. During the bitter political battles of the 1790s, New England Federalists pictured the South as a backward, economically stagnant society in which manual labor was degraded and wealth was dissipated in personal luxury. Many Southern Republicans countered by denouncing the corrupt, grasping, materialistic society of the North.

Many factors contributed to this sense of sectional difference. Diction, work habits, diet, and labor systems distinguished the two sections. One section depended on slave-based agriculture; the other emphasized commercial agriculture based on family farms and a developing industrial sector resting on wage labor.

The North was over 50 percent more populous than the South. Urban centers grew as European immigrants arrived in greater and greater numbers. Commerce, financial institutions, manufacturing, and transportation were developing rapidly. In contrast, the South had primitive transportation facilities, and it had smaller and fewer cities. Most important of all, a third of the South's population lived in slavery.

Despite these differences, the pre–Civil War North and South shared many important characteristics. Both regions were predominantly rural, both had booming economies, and both were engaged in speculation and trade. They shared western expansion, the enactment of democratic political reforms, and the same national political parties. Nevertheless, most Americans thought of their nation as divided into two halves, a commercial civilization and an agrarian civilization, each operating according to entirely different sets of values.

THE EMERGENCE OF A NEW INDUSTRIAL ORDER IN THE NORTH

To all outward appearances, life in the North in 1790 was not much different than in 1740. The vast majority of the people—more than 90 percent—still lived and worked on farms or in small rural villages. Less than 1 Northerner in 13 worked in trade or manufacturing.

Conditions of life remained primitive. The typical house—a single-story one- or two-room log or wood frame structure—was small, sparsely furnished, and afforded little personal privacy. Sleeping, eating, and work spaces were not sharply differentiated, and mirrors, curtains, upholstered chairs, carpets, desks, and bookcases were luxuries enjoyed only by wealthy families.

Even prosperous farming or merchant families lived simply. Many families ate meals out of a common pot or bowl, just as their ancestors had in the seventeenth century. Standards of cleanliness remained exceedingly low. Bedbugs were constant sleeping companions, and people seldom bathed or even washed their clothes or dishes.

Daily life was physically demanding. Most families made their own cloth, clothing, and soap. Because they lacked matches, they lit fires by striking a flint again and again with a steel striker until a spark ignited some tinder. Because there was no indoor plumbing, chamber pots had to be used and emptied. Homes were usually heated by a single open fireplace and illuminated by candles. Housewives hand-carried water from a pump, well, or stream and threw the dirty water or slops out the window. Family members hauled grain to a local grist mill or else milled it by hand. They cut, split, and gathered wood and fed it into a fireplace.

But by 1860, profound and far-reaching changes had taken place. Commercial agriculture had replaced subsistence agriculture. Household production had been supplanted by centralized manufacturing outside the home. And nonagricultural employment had begun to overtake agricultural employment: Nearly half of the North's population made a living outside the agricultural sector.

These economic transformations were all results of the industrial revolution, which affected every aspect of life. It raised living standards, transformed the work process, and relocated hundreds of thousands of people across oceans and from rural farms and villages into fast-growing industrial cities.

The most obvious consequence of this revolution was an impressive increase in wealth, per capita income, and commercial, middle-class job opportunities. Between 1800 and 1860, output increased 12-fold, and purchasing power doubled. New middle-class jobs proliferated. Increasing numbers of men found work as agents, bankers, brokers, clerks, merchants, professionals, and traders.

Living standards rose sharply, at least for the rapidly expanding middle class. Instead of making cloth and clothing at home, families began to buy them. Instead of hand milling grains, an increasing number of families began to buy processed grains. Kerosene lamps replaced candles as a source of light; coal replaced wood as fuel; friction matches replaced crude flints. Even poorer families began to cook their food on cast-iron cookstoves and to heat their rooms with individual-room heaters. The advent of railroads and the first canned foods brought year-round variety to the northern diet.

The industrial revolution led to rising standards of living that enabled white, middle-class families, like the one shown here, to enjoy new household comforts. Portraits and other artwork adorn the walls, bric-a-brac and knickknacks line the mantel. The fire in the fireplace provides heat, but the woman sews by the light of the kerosene lamp on the table. The middle-class wife and mother was expected to maintain a comfortable home that would provide her husband with rest and refuge from the pressures of work and business. Child rearing came to be guided by affection and patient instruction, rather than punishment and intimidation.

Physical comfort increased markedly. Padded seats, spring mattresses, and pillows became more common. By 1860 many urban middle-class families had central heating, indoor plumbing, and wall-to-wall carpeting.

Houses became larger and more affordable. The invention in the 1830s of the balloon frame—a lightweight house frame made up of boards nailed together—as well as prefabricated doors, window frames, shutters, and sashes resulted in larger and more reasonably priced houses. The cost of building a house fell by 40 percent, and two-story houses, with four or five rooms, became increasingly common.

A revolution in values and sensibility accompanied these changes in the standard of living. Standards of cleanliness and personal hygiene rose sharply. People bathed more frequently, washed their clothes more often, and dusted, swept, and scrubbed their houses more regularly. Standards of propriety also rose. The respectable classes began to blow their noses into handkerchiefs, instead of wiping them with their sleeves, and to dispose of their spittle in spittoons.

Northerners regarded all of these changes as signs of progress. A host of northern political leaders, mainly Whigs and later Republicans, celebrated the North as a region of bustling cities, factories, railroads, and prosperous farms and independent craftsmen—a stark contrast to an impoverished, backward, slave-owning South, suffering from soil exhaustion and economic and social decline.

Although the industrial revolution brought many material benefits, critics decried its negative consequences. Labor leaders deplored the bitter suffering of factory and sweatshop workers, the breakdown of craft skills, the vulnerability of urban workers to layoffs and economic crises, and the maldistribution of wealth and property. Conservatives lamented the disintegration of an older household-centered economy in which husbands, wives, and children had labored together. Southern writers, such as George Fitzhugh, argued that the North's growing class of free laborers were slaves of the marketplace, suffering even more insecurity than the South's chattel slaves, who were provided for in sickness and old age.

During the early nineteenth century, the industrial revolution transformed northern society, altering the way people worked and lived and contributing to growing sectional differences between the North and South. How and why did the industrial revolution occur when it did? What were its consequences? How did it fuel sectional antagonisms?

The Transformation of the Rural Countryside

In 1790 most farm families in the rural North produced most of what they needed to live. Instead of using money to purchase necessities, families entered into complex exchange relationships with relatives and neighbors and bartered to acquire the goods they

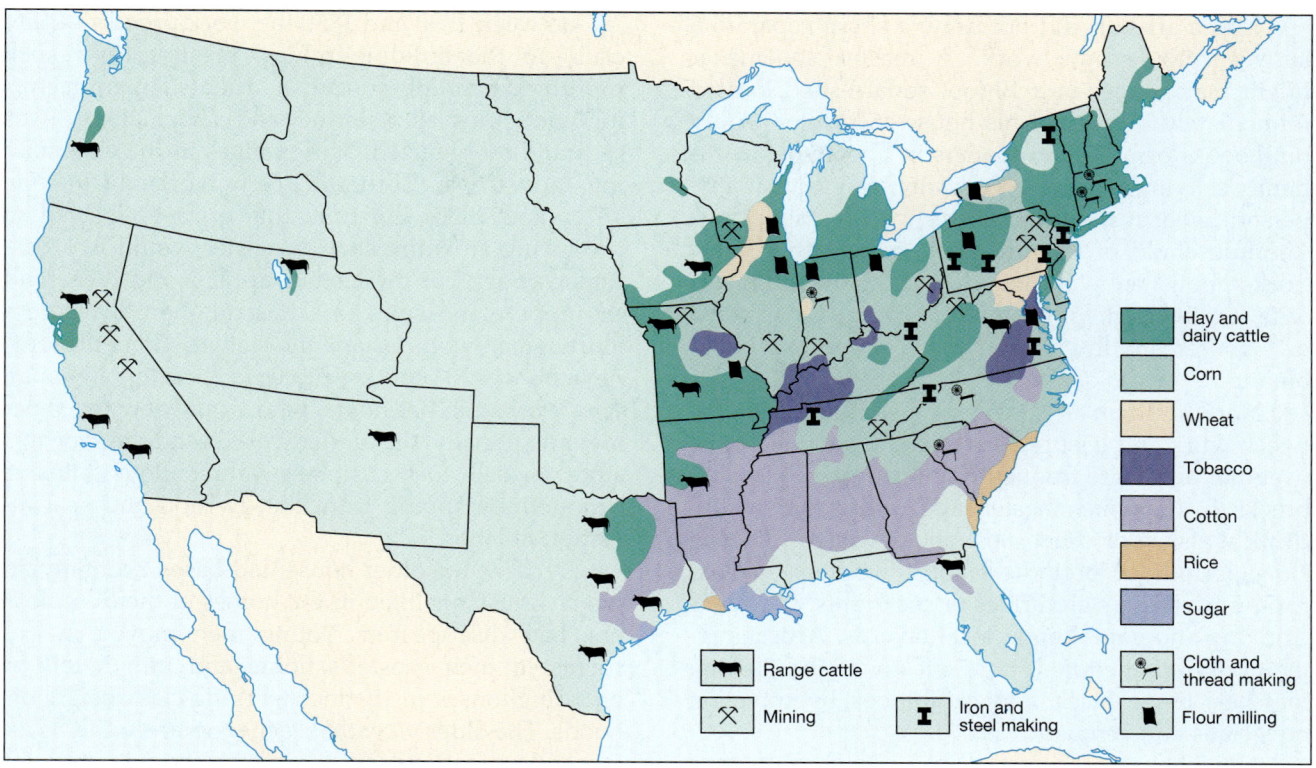

Agriculture and Industry, 1850

needed. To supplement their meager incomes, farm families often did piecework for shopkeepers and craftsmen. In the late eighteenth century these "household industries" provided work for thousands of men, women, and children in rural areas. Shopkeepers or master craftsmen supplied farm families with raw materials and paid them piece rates to produce such items as linens and farm utensils.

Between 1790 and the 1820s, a new pattern emerged. Subsistence farming gave way to commercial agriculture as farmers increasingly began to grow cash crops for sale and used the proceeds to buy goods produced by others. In New Hampshire farmers raised sheep for wool; in western Massachusetts they began to fatten cattle and pigs for sale to Boston; in eastern Pennsylvania they specialized in dairy products.

After 1820, the household industries that had employed thousands of women and children began to decline. They were replaced by manufacturing in city shops and factories. New England farm families began to buy their shoes, furniture, cloth, and sometimes even their clothes ready-made. Small rural factories closed their doors, and village artisans who produced for local markets found themselves unable to compete against cheaper city-made goods. As local opportunities declined, many long-settled farm areas suffered sharp population losses. Convinced that "agriculture is not the road to wealth, nor honor, nor to happiness," thousands of young people left the fields for cities.

The Disruption of the Artisan System of Labor

In the late eighteenth century, the North's few industries were small. Skilled craftspeople, known as *artisans* or *mechanics*, performed most manufacturing in small towns and larger cities. These craftspeople manufactured goods in traditional ways—by hand in their own homes or in small shops located nearby—and marketed the goods they produced. Matthew Carey, a Philadelphia newspaperman, personified the early nineteenth-century artisan-craftsman. He not only wrote articles and editorials that appeared in his newspaper, he also set the paper's type, operated the printing press, and hawked the newspaper.

The artisan class was divided into three subgroups. At the highest level were self-employed master craftspeople. They were assisted by skilled journeymen, who owned their own tools but lacked the capital to set up their own shops, and by apprentices, teenage boys who typically worked for three years in exchange for training in a craft.

Urban artisans did not draw a sharp separation between home and work. A master shoemaker might make shoes in a 10-foot square shed located immediately in back of his house. A printer would bind books or print newspapers in a room below his family's living quarters. Typically, a master craftsperson lived in the same house with his assistants. The household of Everard Peck, a Rochester, New York, publisher, was not unusual. It included his wife, his children, his brother, his business partner, a day laborer, and four journeyman printers and bookbinders.

Nor did urban artisans draw a sharp division between work and leisure. Work patterns tended to be irregular and were frequently interrupted by leisure breaks during which masters and journeymen would drink whiskey or other alcoholic beverages. During slow periods or periodic layoffs, workers enjoyed fishing trips and sleigh rides or cockfights, as well as drinking and gambling at local taverns. Artisans often took unscheduled time off to attend boxing matches, horse races, and exhibitions by traveling musicians and acrobats.

The first half of the nineteenth century witnessed the decline of the artisan system of labor. Skilled tasks, previously performed by artisans, were divided and subcontracted to less expensive unskilled laborers. Small shops were replaced by large "machineless" factories, which made the relationship between employer and employee increasingly impersonal. Many master craftspeople abandoned their supervisory role to foremen and contractors and substituted unskilled teenage boys for journeymen. Words like *employer*, *employee*, *boss*, and *foreman*—descriptive of the new relationships—began to be widely used.

Between 1790 and 1850 the work process—especially in the building trades, printing, and such rapidly expanding consumer oriented manufacturing industries as tailoring and shoemaking—was radically reorganized. The changes in the shoemaking industry in Rochester, New York, during the 1820s and 1830s illustrate this process. Instead of producing an entire shoe, a master would fit a customer, rough-cut the leather uppers, and then send the uppers and soles to a boardinghouse, where a journeyman would shape the leather. Then, the journeyman would send the pieces to a binder, a woman who worked in her home, who would sew the shoes together. Finally, the binder would send the shoe to a store for sale to a customer. Tremendous gains in productivity sprang from the division and specialization of labor.

By 1850, the older household-based economy, in which assistants lived in the homes of their employers, had disappeared. Young men moved out of rooms in their master's home and into hotels or boardinghouses in distinct working-class neighborhoods. The older view that each worker should be attached to a particular master, who would supervise his behavior and assume responsibility for his welfare, declined. This paternalistic view was replaced by a new conception of labor as a commodity, like cotton, that could be acquired or disposed of according to the laws of supply and demand.

The Introduction of the Factory System

In 1789 the Pennsylvania legislature placed an advertisement in British newspapers offering a cash bounty to any English textile worker who would migrate to the state. Samuel Slater, who was just finishing an apprenticeship in a Derbyshire textile mill, read the ad. He went to London, booked passage to America, and landed in Philadelphia. There he learned that Moses Brown, a Quaker merchant, had just completed a mill in Pawtucket, Rhode Island, and needed a manager. Slater applied for the job and received it, along with a promise that if he made the factory a success he would receive all the business's profits, less the cost and interest on the machinery.

On December 21, 1790, the mill opened. Seven boys and two girls, all between the ages of 7 and 12, operated the little factory's 72 spindles. Slater soon discovered that these children, "constantly employed under the immediate inspection of a [supervisor]," could produce three times as much as whole families working in their homes. To keep the children awake and alert, Slater whipped them with a

In the factory system of production, machines lowered the costs of producing goods, but workers faced increasing demands to tend more machines and put out greater numbers of items.

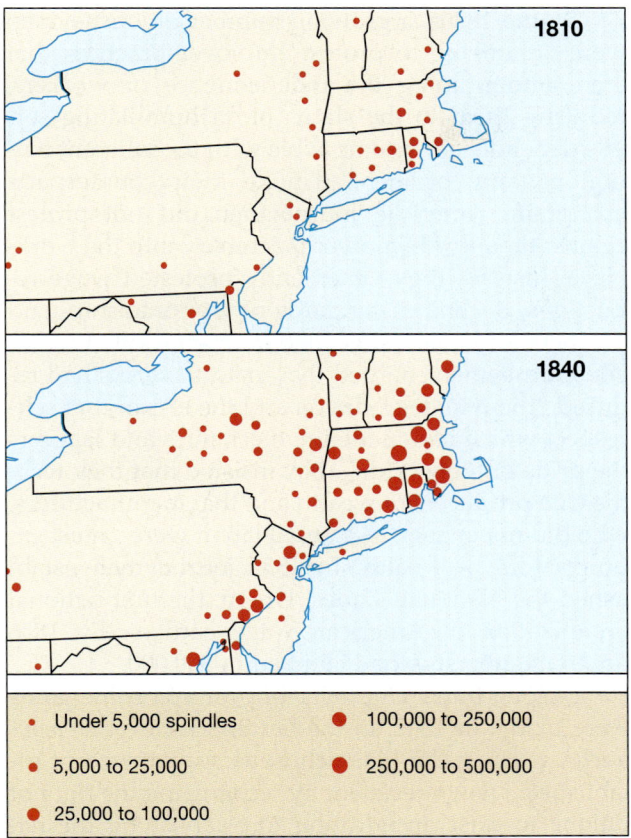

Cotton Textile Industry

During the first half of the nineteenth century, unmarried women made up a majority of the workforce in cotton textile mills and a substantial minority of workers in factories manufacturing ready-made clothing, hats, and shoes. Women were also employed in significant numbers in the manufacture of buttons, furniture, gloves, gunpowder, shovels, and tobacco.

Unlike farm work or domestic service, employment in a mill offered female companionship and an independent income. Wages were twice what a woman could make as a seamstress, tailor, or schoolteacher. Furthermore, most mill girls viewed the work as only temporary before marriage. Most worked in the mills fewer than four years, and frequently interrupted their stints in the mill for several months at a time with trips back home.

By the 1830s, increasing competition among textile manufacturers caused deteriorating working conditions that drove native-born women out of the mills. Employers cut wages, lengthened the workday, and required mill workers to tend four looms instead of just two. Hannah Borden, a Fall River, Massachusetts, textile worker, was required to have her loom running at 5 A.M. She was given an hour for breakfast and half an hour for lunch. Her workday ended at 7:30 P.M., 14½ hours after it had begun. For a 6-day workweek, she received between $2.50 and $3.50.

The mill girls militantly protested the wage cuts. In 1834 and again in 1836, the mill girls went out on strike. An open letter spelled out the workers' complaints: "sixteen females [crowded] into the same hot, ill-ventilated attic"; a workday "two or three hours longer . . . than is done in Europe"; and work-

leather strap or sprinkled them with water. On Sundays the children attended a special school Slater founded for their education.

The opening of Slater's mill marked the beginning of a widespread movement to consolidate manufacturing operations under a single roof. During the last years of the eighteenth century, merchants and master craftspeople who were discontented with the inefficiencies of their workforce created the nation's first modern factories. Within these centralized workshops, employers closely supervised employees, synchronized work to the clock, and punished infractions of rules with heavy fines or dismissal. In 1820, only 350,000 Americans worked in factories or mills. Four decades later, on the eve of the Civil War, the number had soared to 2 million.

For an inexpensive and reliable labor force, many factory owners turned to child labor. During the early phases of industrialization, textile mills and agricultural tool, metal goods, nail, and rubber factories had a ravenous appetite for cheap teenage laborers. In many mechanized industries, from a quarter to over half of the workforce was made up of young men or women under the age of 20.

Young women made up the bulk of the workforce in the early textile mills.

During the 1830s, rapid inflation and mounting competition for jobs encouraged the growth of unions. By 1836, an estimated 300,000 American workers were union members.

ers compelled to "stand so long at the machinery . . . that varicose veins, dropsical swelling of the feet and limbs, and prolapsus uter[us], diseases that end only with life, are not rare but common occurrences."

During the 1840s, fewer and fewer native-born women were willing to work in the mills. "Slavers," which were long, black wagons that criss-crossed the Vermont and New Hampshire countryside in search of mill hands, arrived empty in Rhode Island and Massachusetts mill towns. Increasingly, employers replaced the native-born mill girls with a new class of permanent factory operatives: immigrant women from Ireland.

Labor Protests

In 1806 journeyman shoemakers in New York City organized one of the nation's first labor strikes. The workers' chief demands were not higher wages and shorter hours. Instead, they protested the changing conditions of work. They staged a "turn-out" or "stand-out," as a strike was then called, to protest the use of cheap unskilled and apprentice labor and the subdivision and subcontracting of work. The strike ended when a court ruled that a labor union was guilty of criminal conspiracy if workers struck to obtain wages higher than those set by custom. The court found the journeyman shoemakers guilty and fined them $1 plus court costs.

By the 1820s, a growing number of journeymen were organizing to protest employer practices that were undermining the independence of workers, reducing them to the status of "a humiliating servile dependency, incompatible with the inherent natural equality of men." Unlike their counterparts in Britain, American journeymen did not protest against the introduction of machinery into the workplace. Instead, they vehemently protested wage reductions, declining standards of workmanship, and the increased use of unskilled and semiskilled workers. Journeymen charged that manufacturers had reduced "them to degradation and the loss of that self-respect which had made the mechanics and laborers the pride of the world." They insisted that they were the true producers of wealth and that manufacturers, who did not engage in manual labor, were unjust expropriators of wealth. In 1834 journeymen established the National Trades' Union, the first national organization of American wage earners. By 1836 union membership had climbed to 300,000.

Despite bitter employer opposition, some gains were made. In 1842, in the landmark case *Commonwealth* v. *Hunt*, the Massachusetts supreme court established a new precedent by recognizing the right of unions to exist. In addition to establishing the nation's first labor unions, journeymen also formed political organizations, known as Working Men's parties, as well as mutual benefit societies, libraries, educational institutions, and producers' and consumers' cooperatives. Working men and women published at least 68 labor papers, and they agitated for free public education, reduction of the workday, and abolition of capital punishment, state militias, and imprisonment for debt. Following the Panic of 1837, land reform was one of labor's chief demands. One hundred sixty acres of free public land for those who would actually settle the land was the demand, and "Vote Yourself a Farm" became the popular slogan.

The Movement for a Ten-Hour Day

Labor's greatest success was a campaign to establish a ten-hour workday in most major northeastern cities. In 1835 carpenters, masons, and stonecutters in Boston staged a seven-month strike in favor of a ten-hour day. The strikers demanded that employers reduce excessively long hours worked in the summer and spread them throughout the year. Quickly, the movement for a ten-hour workday spread to Philadelphia, where carpenters, bricklayers, plasterers, masons, leather dressers, and blacksmiths went on strike. Textile workers in Paterson, New Jersey, were the first factory operatives to strike for a reduction in work hours. Soon, women textile operatives in Lowell added their voices to the call for a ten-hour day, contending that such a law would "lengthen the lives of those employed, by giving them a greater opportunity to breathe the pure air of heaven" as well as provide "more time for mental and moral cultivation."

In 1840 the federal government introduced a ten-hour workday on public works projects. In 1847 New Hampshire became the first state to adopt a ten-hour day law. It was followed by Pennsylvania in 1848. Both states' laws, however, included a clause that allowed workers to voluntarily agree to work more than a ten-hour day. Despite the limitations of these state laws, agitation for a ten-hour day did result in a reduction in the average number of hours worked, to approximately 11½ by 1850.

The Laboring Poor

In January 1850, police arrested John McFeaing in Newburyport, Massachusetts, for stealing wood from the wharves. McFeaing pleaded necessity and a public investigation was conducted. Investigators found McFeaing's wife and four children living "in the extremity of misery. The children were all scantily supplied with clothing and not one had a shoe to his feet. There was not a stick of firewood or scarcely a morsel of food in the house, and everything betokened the most abject want and misery." McFeaing's predicament was not uncommon at that time.

The quickening pace of trade and finance during the early nineteenth century not only increased the demand for middle-class clerks and shopkeepers, it also dramatically increased demand for unskilled workers, who earned extremely low incomes and led difficult lives.

In 1851 Horace Greeley, editor of the New York *Tribune*, estimated the minimum weekly budget needed to support a family of five. Essential expenditures for rent, food, fuel, and clothing amounted to $10.37 a week. In that year, a shoemaker or a printer earned just $4 to $6 a week, a male textile operative $6.50 a week, and an unskilled laborer just $1 a week. The only manual laborers able to earn Greeley's minimum were blacksmiths and machinists.

Frequent unemployment compounded the problems of the unskilled. In Massachusetts upward of 40 percent of all workers were out of a job for part of a year, usually for four months or more. Fluctuations in demand, inclement weather, interruptions in transportation, technological displacement, fire, injury, and illness all could leave workers jobless.

Typically, a male laborer earned just two-thirds of his family's income. The other third was earned by wives and children. Many married women performed work in the home, such as embroidery and making artificial flowers, tailoring garments, or doing laundry. The wages of children were critical for a family's standard of living. Children under the age of 15 contributed 20 percent of the income of many working-class families. These children worked not because their parents were heartless, but because children's earnings were absolutely essential to the family's survival.

To provide protection against temporary unemployment, many working-class families scrimped and saved to buy a house or maintain a garden. In Newburyport, Massachusetts, many workers bought farm property on the edge of town. On New York City's East Side, many families kept goats and pigs. Ownership of a house was a particularly valuable source of security, since a family could always obtain extra income by taking in boarders and lodgers.

Immigration Begins

During the summer of 1845, a "blight of unusual character" devastated Ireland's potato crop, the basic staple in the Irish diet. A few days after potatoes were dug from the ground, they began to turn into a slimy, decaying, blackish "mass of rottenness." Expert panels, convened to investigate the blight's cause, suggested that it was a result of "static electricity" or the smoke that billowed from railroad locomotives or "mortiferous vapours" rising from un-

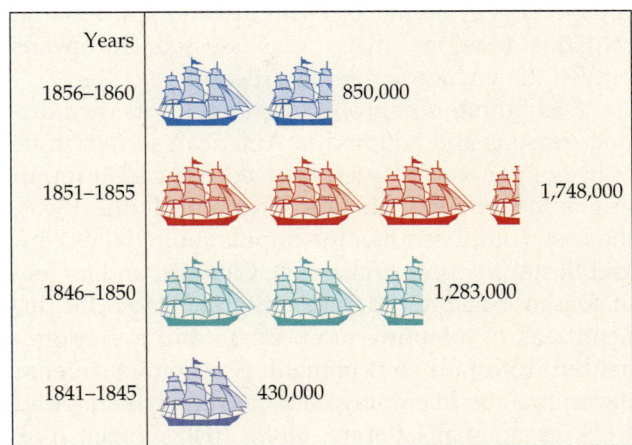

FIGURE 12.1
Total Immigration, 1841–1860

derground volcanoes. In fact, the cause was a fungus that had traveled from America to Ireland.

"Famine fever"—dysentery, typhus, and infestations of lice—soon spread through the Irish countryside. Observers reported seeing children crying with pain and looking "like skeletons, their features sharpened with hunger and their limbs wasted, so that there was little left but bones, their hands and arms." Masses of bodies were buried without coffins, a few inches below the soil.

Over the next ten years, 750,000 Irish died and another 2 million left their homeland for Great Britain, Canada, and the United States. Freighters, which carried American and Canadian timber to Europe, offered fares as low as $17 to $20 between Liverpool and Boston—fares subsidized by English landlords eager to be rid of the starving peasants. As many as 10 percent of the emigrants perished while still at sea. In 1847, 40,000 (or 20 percent) of those who set out from Ireland died along the way. "If crosses and tombs could be erected on water," wrote the U.S. commissioner for emigration, "the whole route of the emigrant vessels from Europe to America would long since have assumed the appearance of a crowded cemetery."

At the beginning of the nineteenth century, only about 5000 immigrants arrived in the United States each year. During the 1830s, however, immigration climbed sharply as 600,000 immigrants poured into the country. This figure jumped to 1.7 million in the 1840s, when harvests all across Europe failed, and reached 2.6 million in the 1850s. Most of these immigrants came from Germany, Ireland, and Scandinavia, pushed from their homelands by famine, eviction from farmlands by landlords, political unrest, and the destruction of traditional handicrafts by factory enterprises. Attracted to the United States by the prospects of economic opportunity and political and religious freedom, many dispossessed Europeans braved the voyage across the Atlantic.

Each immigrant group migrated for its own distinct reasons and adapted to American society in its own unique ways. Poverty forced most Irish immigrants to settle in their port of origin. By the 1850s, the Irish comprised half the population of New York and Boston. Young, unmarried, Catholic, and largely of peasant background, the immigrants faced the difficult task of adapting to an urban and a predominantly Protestant environment. Confronting intense discrimination in employment, most Irish men found work as manual laborers, while Irish women took jobs mainly in domestic service. Discrimination had an important consequence: It encouraged Irish immigrants to become actively involved in politics. With a

Immigrants from Europe, hoping for economic opportunity and a better life in the United States, crowd the deck of a ship bound for America. Crop failures across Europe hit Ireland particularly hard as blight destroyed the potato crop—the single crop on which poor Irish farmers depended on for their livelihood—several times between 1845 and 1855. More than 1 million Irish died of starvation or disease during this time of the "Great Hunger." Almost 2 million emigrated, about 80 percent of them to the United States. Without any industrial skills or experience, many of the new immigrants could find work only in unskilled labor or domestic service.

strong sense of ethnic identity, high rates of literacy, and impressive organizational talents, Irish politicians played an important role in the development of modern American urban politics.

Unlike Irish immigrants, who settled primarily in northeastern cities and engaged in politics, German immigrants tended to move to farms or frontier towns in the Midwest and were less active politically. While some Germans fled to the United States to escape political persecution following the revolutions of 1830 and 1848, most migrated for quite a different reason: to sustain traditional ways of life. The industrial revolution severely disrupted traditional patterns of life for German farmers, shopkeepers, and practitioners of traditional crafts (like baking, brewing, and carpentering). In the Midwest's farmland and frontier cities, including Cincinnati and St. Louis, they sought to reestablish old German lifeways, setting up German fraternal lodges, coffee circles, and educational and musical societies. German immigrants carried important aspects of German culture with them, which quickly became integral parts of American culture, including the Christmas tree and the practice of Christmas gift giving, the kindergarten, and the gymnasium. Given Germany's

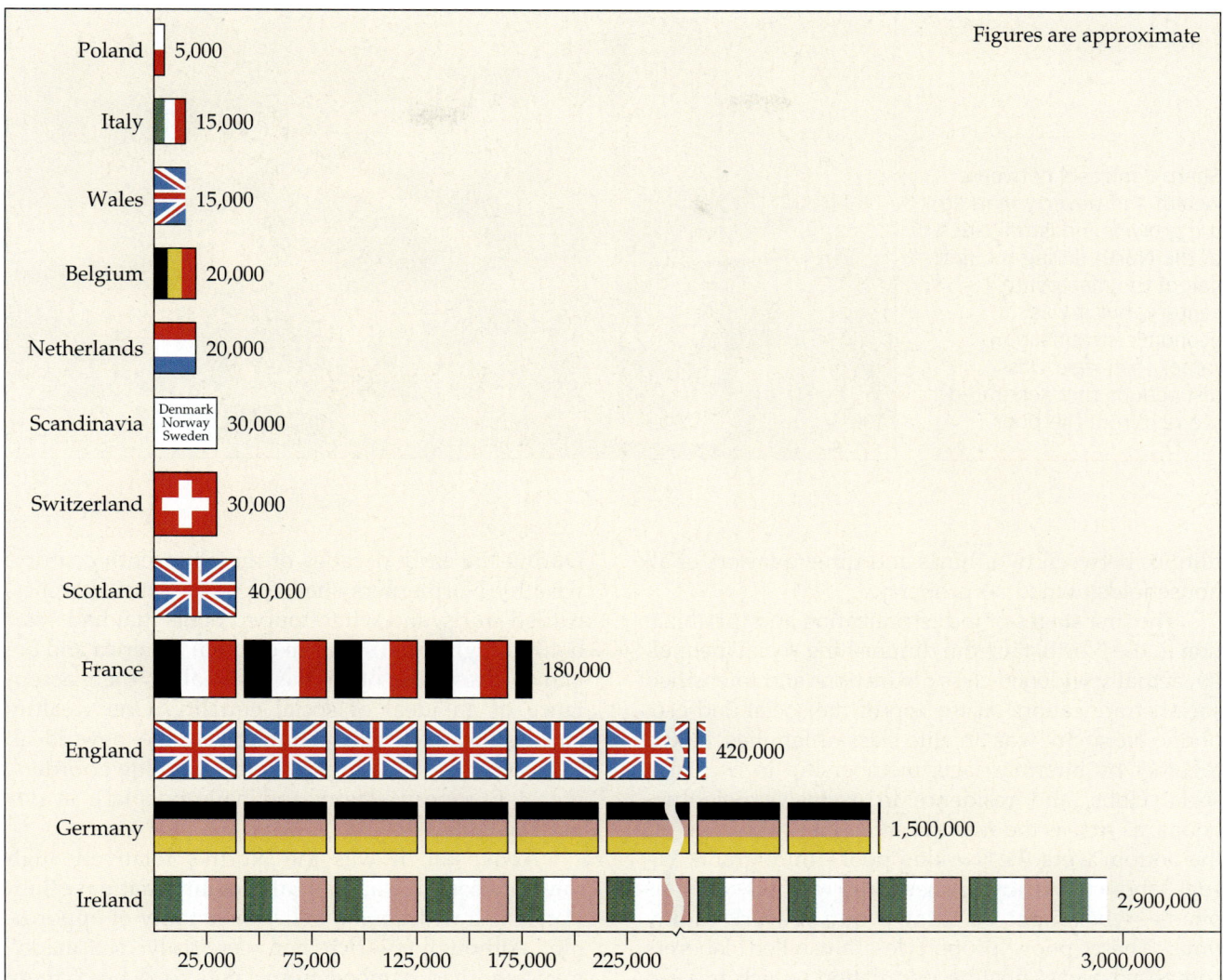

FIGURE 12.2
Immigration by Country of Origin, 1840–1860

strong educational and craft traditions, it is not surprising that German immigrants would be particularly prominent in the fields of engineering, optics, drug manufacture, and metal and tool making, as well as in the labor movement.

The Divided North

During the decades preceding the Civil War, it was an article of faith among Northerners that their society offered unprecedented economic equality and opportunity, free of rigid class divisions and glaring extremes of wealth and poverty. It was a land where even a "humble mechanic" had "every means of winning independence which are extended only to rich monopolists in England." How accurate is this picture of the pre–Civil War North as a land of opportunity, where material success was available to all?

In fact, the percentage of wealth held by those at the top of the economic hierarchy appears to have increased substantially before the Civil War. While the proportion of wealth controlled by the richest 10 percent rose from 50 percent in the 1770s to 70 percent in 1860, the real wages of unskilled northern workers stagnated or, at best, rose modestly. By 1860 half of all free whites held fewer than 1 percent of the North's real and personal property, while the richest 1 percent owned 27 percent of the region's wealth—a level of inequality comparable to that found in early nineteenth-century Europe and greater than that found in the United States today. In towns as different as Stonington, Connecticut, and Chicago,

Sharp contrasts between wealth and poverty marked the growing industrial cities of the North during the first half of the nineteenth century, but it was economic stratification rather than rigid class distinctions that separated the rich from the poor.

Illinois, between two-thirds and three-quarters of all households owned no property.

The first stages of industrialization and urbanization in the North, far from diminishing social inequality, actually widened class distinctions and intensified social stratification. At the top of the social and economic hierarchy was an elite class of families, linked together by intermarriage, membership in exclusive social clubs, and residence in exclusive neighborhoods, as rich as the wealthiest families of Europe. At the bottom were the working poor—immigrants, casual laborers, African Americans, widows, and orphans—who might be thrown out of work at any time. These poor, propertyless unskilled laborers composed a vast floating population, which trekked from city to city in search of work. They congregated in urban slums like Boston's Ann Street and New York's Five Points, where starving children begged for pennies and haggard prostitutes plied their trade.

Between these two extremes were family farmers and a rapidly expanding urban middle class of northern shopkeepers, merchants, bankers, agents, and brokers. This was a highly mixed group that ranged from prosperous entrepreneurs and professionals to hard-pressed journeymen, who found their skills increasingly obsolete.

Does this mean that the pre–Civil War North was not the fluid, "egalitarian" society that Jacksonians claimed? The answer is a qualified "no." In the first place, the North's richest individuals, unlike Europe's aristocracy, were a working class, engaged in commerce, insurance, finance, shipbuilding, manufacturing, landholding, real estate, and the professions. More important, wealthy Northerners publicly rejected the older Hamiltonian notion that the rich and well-born were superior to the masses of people.

During the early decades of the nineteenth century, wealthy Northerners shed the wigs, knee breeches, ruffled shirts, and white-topped boots that had symbolized high social status in colonial America and began to dress like other men, signaling their acceptance of an ideal of social equality. One wealthy Northerner succinctly summarized the new ideal: "These phrases, the higher orders, and lower orders, are of European origin, and have no place in our Yankee dialect."

Above all, it was the North's relatively high rates of economic and social mobility that gave substance to a widespread belief in equality of opportunity. Although few rich men were truly "self-made" men who had climbed from "rags to riches," there were many dramatic examples of upward mobility and countless instances of more modest climbs up the ladder of success. Industrialization rapidly increased the number of nonmanual jobs in commerce, industry, and the professions. There were new opportunities for lawyers, bookkeepers, business managers, brokers, and clerks. Giving additional reinforcement to the belief in opportunity was a remarkable rate of physical mobility. Each decade, fully half the residents of northern communities moved to a new town.

Even at the bottom of the economic hierarchy, prospects for advancement increased markedly after 1850. During the 1830s and 1840s, less than one unskilled worker in ten managed in the course of a decade to advance to a white-collar job. After 1850, the percentage doubled. The sons of unskilled laborers were even more likely to advance to skilled or white-collar employment. Even the poorest unskilled laborers often were able to acquire a house and a savings account as they grew older, and their children did better yet. It was the reality of physical and economic mobility that convinced the overwhelming majority of Northerners that they lived in a uniquely open society, in which differences in wealth or status were the result of hard work and ambition.

SOUTHERN DISTINCTIVENESS

In 1785 Thomas Jefferson jotted down a brief list of differences between North and South.

In the North they are:

cool
sober
laborious
independent
jealous of their own liberties and just to those of others
interested
chicaning
superstitious and hypocritical in their religion.

In the South they are:

fiery
voluptuary
indolent
unsteady
zealous for their own liberties, but trampling on those of others
generous
candid
without attachment or pretensions to any religion but that of the heart.

Pre–Civil War Americans regarded Southerners as a distinct people, who possessed their own values and ways of life. It was widely though mistakenly believed that the North and South had originally been settled by two distinct groups of immigrants, each with its own ethos. Northerners were said to be the descendants of seventeenth-century English Puritans, while Southerners were the descendants of England's country gentry. In the eyes of many pre–Civil War Americans this contributed to the evolution of two distinct kinds of Americans: the aggressive, individualistic, money-grubbing Yankee and the southern cavalier. According to the popular stereotype, the cavalier, unlike the Yankee, was violently sensitive to insult, indifferent to money, and preoccupied with honor.

The Plantation Legend

During the three decades before the Civil War, popular writers created a stereotype, now known as the **plantation legend,** that described the South as a land of aristocratic planters, beautiful southern belles, poor white trash, faithful household slaves, and superstitious fieldhands.

This image of the South as "a land of cotton" where "old times" are "not forgotten" received its most popular expression in 1859 in a song called "Dixie," written by a Northerner named Dan D. Emmett to enliven shows given by a troupe of black-faced minstrels on the New York stage. In the eyes of many Northerners, uneasy with their increasingly urban, individualistic, commercial society, the culture of the South seemed to have many things absent from the North—a leisurely pace of life, a clear social hierarchy, and an indifference to money.

The Old South: Images and Realities

Despite the strength of the plantation stereotype, the South was, in reality, a diverse and complex region. Though Americans today often associate the old South with cotton plantations, large parts of the South were unsuitable for plantation life. In the mountainous regions of eastern Tennessee and western Virginia, few plantations and few slaves were to be found. Nor did southern farms and plantations

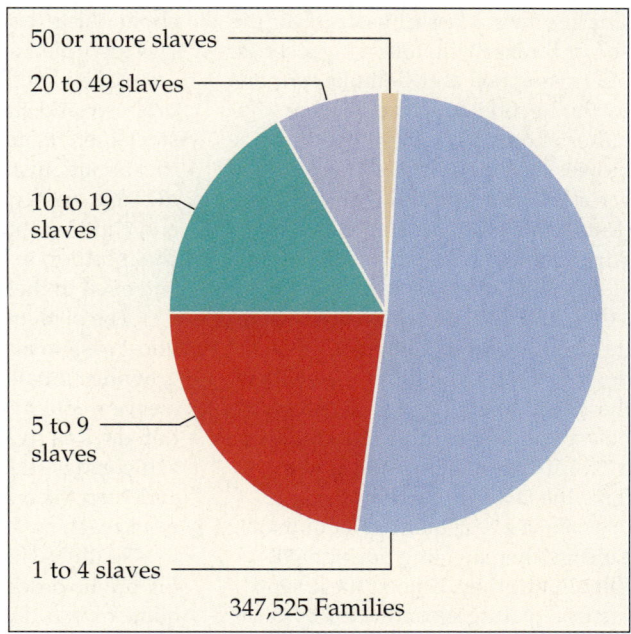

FIGURE 12.3
Slaveowning Population, 1850

The American Mosaic

Policing the Pre–Civil War City

DURING the mid-1830s, a wave of rioting without parallel in earlier American history swept the nation. In April 1834, in New York, three days of rioting pitting pro-Democrat against pro-Whig gangs erupted during municipal elections. In July, another New York mob stormed the house of a prominent abolitionist, carried the furniture into the street, and set it on fire. Over the next two days, a mob gutted New York's Episcopal African Church and attacked the homes of many of the city's African Americans. The state militia had to be called out to quell the disturbances.

Rioting was not confined to New York City. On August 11, 1834, a mob composed of lower-class men and boys sacked and burned a convent in Charlestown, Massachusetts, near the site of Bunker Hill, following a series of impassioned anti-Catholic sermons by the Reverend Lyman Beecher, the father of novelist Harriet Beecher Stowe. Two months later, a proslavery riot swept through Philadelphia, destroying 45 homes in the city's African American community.

Altogether there were at least 115 incidents of mob violence during the 1830s, compared to just 7 incidents in the 1810s and 21 incidents in the 1820s. *Niles' Register*, a respected newspaper of the time, reported that a "spirit of riot or a disposition to 'take the law into their own hands' prevails in every quarter." Abraham Lincoln, then a young Springfield, Illinois, attorney, echoed these sentiments. "Outrages committed by mobs," he lamented, had become "the everyday news of the times."

Mob violence during the 1830s had a variety of sources. A rate of urban growth faster than that in any previous decade was one major contributor to social turbulence during the 1830s. Urban populations grew by 60 percent and the sharp upsurge in foreign immigration heightened religious and ethnic tensions. The number of immigrants entering the country jumped from 5000 a year at the beginning of the century to over 50,000 annually during the 1830s.

Another source of violence came with abolitionism, which emerged at the beginning of the decade and produced a violent reaction. The belief that abolitionists favored miscegenation—interracial marriages of African Americans and whites—enflamed anti-African American sentiment. The mobs that attacked African American homes and churches, burned white abolitionists' homes and businesses, and disrupted antislavery meetings were often led by "gentlemen of property and standing." These old-stock merchants and bankers feared that abolitionist appeals to the middle class and especially to women and children threatened their patriarchal position in local communities and even in their own families.

The birth of a new two-party political system also contributed to a growing climate of violence. Mob violence frequently broke out on election days as rival Democratic and Whig gangs tried to steal ballot boxes and keep the opposition's voters from reaching local polling places.

Traditional methods of preserving public order proved totally inadequate by the 1830s. Earlier in time, the nation's cities were "policed" by a handful of unpaid, untrained, ununiformed, and unarmed sheriffs, aldermen, marshals, constables, and nightwatchmen. In New England towns, tithingmen armed with long black sticks tipped with brass patrolled streets searching for drunkards, disorderly children, and wayward servants.

These law officers were not a particularly effective deterrent to crime. Nightwatchmen generally held other jobs during the day and sometimes slept at their posts at night. Sheriffs, aldermen, marshals, and constables made a living not by investigating crimes or patrolling city streets but by collecting debts, foreclosing on mortgages, and serving court orders. Victims of crime had to offer a reward if they wanted these unpaid law officers to investigate a case.

This early system of maintaining public order worked in previous decades when the rates of serious crime were extremely low and citizens had informal mechanisms that helped maintain order. Most cities were small and compact and lacked any distinct working-class ghettoes. Shopkeepers usually lived at or near their place of business and apprentices, journeymen, and laborers tended to live in or near the house of their master. Under these circumstances, the poor and the working class were subject to close supervision by their social superiors. By the mid-1830s, however, this older pattern of social organization had clearly broken down. Class-segregated neighborhoods grew increasingly common. Youth gangs, organized along ethnic and neighborhood lines, proliferated. Older mechanisms of social control weakened.

After 1830, drunken brawls, robberies, beatings, and murders all in-

creased in number. Fear of crime led city leaders to look for new ways of preserving public order. Many municipal leaders regarded the new professional police force established in London in 1829 by the British Parliament as a model. London's police, nicknamed "bobbies" after Prime Minister Robert Peel, were trained, full-time professionals. They wore distinctive uniforms to make them visible to the public, patrolled regular beats, and lived in the neighborhoods they patrolled.

Initially, resistance to the establishment of professional police forces in American cities was intense. Taxpayers feared the cost of a police force. Local political machines feared the loss of the night watch as a source of political patronage. During the late 1830s and 1840s, rising crime rates overcame opposition to the establishment of a professional police force. Boston appointed the nation's first police officers in 1838.

In New York City, the turning point came in 1841 following the unsolved murder of Mary Rogers, who worked in a tobacco shop. On July 25, 1841, she disappeared. Three days later, the body of the "beautiful cigar girl" was found in a river. The coroner said she had died not from drowning but from being abused and murdered by a gang of ruffians. The case aroused intense passion in New York City, prompting vocal demands for an end to waterfront gangs. But the city's constables said that they would only investigate the murder if they were promised a substantial reward. The public was outraged. In 1844, the New York state legislature authorized the establishment of a professional police force to investigate crimes and patrol streets in New York City.

The life of a mid-nineteenth-century police officer was exceptionally hard. In many cities, members of gangs, like New York's Bowery B'hoys, Baltimore's Rip Raps, and Philadelphia's Schuylkill Rangers, actually outnumbered police officers. Young toughs regularly harrassed police officers. Many officers resisted wearing uniforms on the grounds that any distinctive dress made them readily identifiable targets for street gangs. In New York City, four officers were killed in the line of duty in a single year.

After 1850, in large part as a result of more efficient policing, the number of street disorders in American cities began to drop. Despite the introduction of the Colt revolver and other easily concealed and relatively inexpensive handguns during the middle years of the century, homicide rates, too, began to decline. By the eve of the Civil War, the nation's cities had become far less violent and far more orderly places than they had been two decades before.

devote their efforts exclusively to growing cotton or other cash crops, such as rice and tobacco. Unlike the slave societies of the Caribbean, which produced crops exclusively for export, the South devoted much of its energy to raising food and livestock.

The pre–Civil War South encompassed a wide variety of regions that differed geographically, economically, and politically. Such regions included the Piedmont, Tidewater, coastal plain, piney woods, Delta, Appalachian mountains, upcountry, and a fertile "black belt"—regions that clashed repeatedly over such political questions as debt relief, taxes, apportionment of representation, and internal improvements.

The white South's social structure was much more complex than the popular stereotype of proud aristocrats disdainful of honest work and ignorant, vicious, exploited poor whites. The old South's intricate social structure included many small slaveowners and relatively few large ones.

Actually, large slaveholders were extremely rare. In 1860 only 11,000 Southerners—three-quarters of one percent of the white population—owned more than 50 slaves; a mere 2358 owned as many as 100 slaves. However, although large slaveholders were few in number, they owned most of the South's slaves. Over half of all slaves lived on plantations with 20 or more slaves and a quarter lived on plantations with more than 50 slaves.

Slave ownership was relatively widespread. In the first half of the nineteenth century, one-third of all southern white families owned slaves, and a majority of white southern families either owned slaves, had owned them, or expected to own them. These slaveowners were a diverse lot. A few were African American, mulatto, or Native American; one-tenth were women; and more than one in ten worked as artisans, businesspeople, or merchants rather than as farmers or planters. Few led lives of leisure or refinement. The average slaveowner lived in a log cabin rather than a mansion and was a farmer rather than a planter. The average holding varied between four and six slaves, and most slaveholders possessed no more than five.

White women in the South, despite the image of the hoop-skirted southern belle, suffered under heavier burdens than their northern counterparts. They married earlier, bore more children, and were more likely to die young. They lived in greater isolation, had less access to the company of other women, and lacked the satisfactions of voluntary associations and reform movements. Their education was briefer and much less likely to result in opportunities for independent careers.

The plantation legend was misleading in still other respects. Slavery was neither dying nor unprofitable. In 1860 the South was richer than any country in Europe except England, and it had achieved a level of wealth unmatched by Italy or Spain until the eve of World War II.

The southern economy generated enormous wealth and was critical to the economic growth of the entire United States. Well over half of the richest 1 percent of Americans in 1860 lived in the South. Even more important, southern agriculture helped finance early nineteenth-century American economic growth. Before the Civil War, the South grew 60 percent of the world's cotton, provided over half of all U.S. export earnings, and furnished 70 percent of the cotton consumed by the British textile industry. Cotton exports paid for a substantial share of the capital and technology that laid the basis for America's industrial revolution. In addition, precisely because the South specialized in agricultural production, the North developed a variety of businesses that provided services for the southern states, including textile and meat processing industries and financial and commercial facilities.

Impact of Slavery on the Southern Economy

Although slavery was highly profitable, it had a negative impact on the southern economy. It impeded the development of industry and cities and contributed to high debts, soil exhaustion, and a lack of technological innovation. The philosopher and poet Ralph Waldo Emerson said that "slavery is no

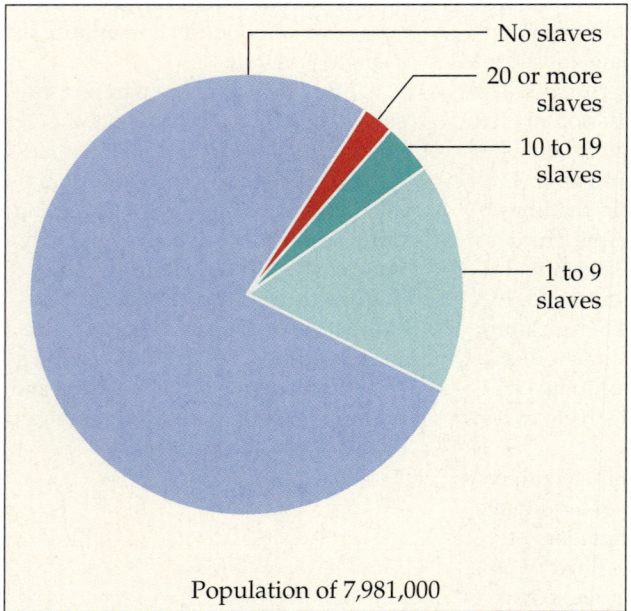

FIGURE 12.4
Southern White Population, 1860

scholar, no improver; it does not love the whistle of the railroad; it does not love the newspaper, the mail-bag, a college, a book or a preacher who has the absurd whim of saying what he thinks; it does not increase the white population; it does not improve the soil; everything goes to decay." There appears to be a large element of truth in Emerson's observation.

The South, like other slave societies, did not develop urban centers for commerce, finance, and industry on a scale equal to those found in the North. Virginia's largest city, Richmond, had a population of just 15,274 in 1850. That same year, Wilmington, North Carolina's largest city, had only 7264 inhabitants, while Natchez and Vicksburg, the two largest cities in Mississippi, had fewer than 3000 white inhabitants.

Southern cities were small because they failed to develop diversified economies. Unlike the cities of the North, southern cities rarely became processing or finishing centers and southern ports rarely engaged in international trade. Their primary functions were to market and transport cotton or other agricultural crops, supply local planters and farmers with such necessities as agricultural implements, and produce the small number of manufactured goods, such as cotton gins, needed by farmers.

An overemphasis on slave-based agriculture led Southerners to neglect industry and transportation improvements. As a result, manufacturing and transportation lagged far behind in comparison to the North. In 1860 the North had approximately 1.3 million industrial workers, whereas the South had 110,000, and northern factories manufactured nine-tenths of the industrial goods produced in the United States.

The South's transportation network was primitive by northern standards. Traveling the 1460 overland miles from Baltimore to New Orleans in 1850 meant riding five different railroads, two stagecoaches, and two steamboats. Most southern railroads served primarily to transport cotton to southern ports, where the crop could be shipped on northern vessels to northern or British factories for processing.

Because of high rates of personal debt, Southern states kept taxation and government spending at much lower levels than did the states in the North. As a result, Southerners lagged far behind Northerners in their support for public education. Illiteracy was widespread. In 1850, 20 percent of all southern white adults could not read or write, while the illiteracy rate in New England was less than half of 1 percent.

Because large slaveholders owned most of the region's slaves, wealth was more stratified than in the North. In the Deep South, the middle class held a relatively small proportion of the region's property, while wealthy planters owned a very significant portion of the productive lands and slave labor. In 1850, 17 percent of the farming population held two-thirds

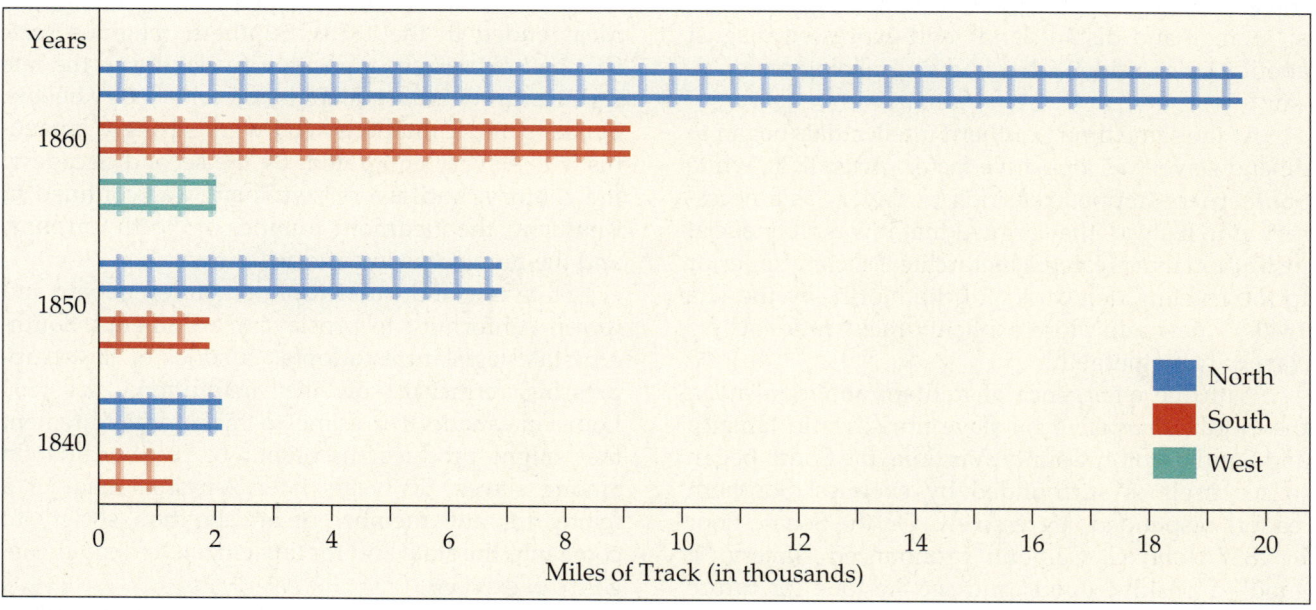

FIGURE 12.5
Railroad Growth, 1840–1860

An overemphasis on slave-based agriculture led Southerners to neglect transportation improvements.

of all acres in the rich cotton-growing regions of the South.

There are indications that during the last decade before the Civil War slave ownership was increasingly concentrated in fewer and fewer hands. As soil erosion and exhaustion diminished the availability of cotton land, scarcity and heavy demand forced the price of land and slaves to rise beyond the reach of most, and in newer cotton-growing regions, yeomen farmers were pushed off the land as planters expanded their holdings. In Louisiana, for example, nearly half of all rural white families owned no land. During the 1850s, the percentage of the total white population owning slaves declined significantly. By 1860, the proportion of whites holding slaves had fallen from about one-third to one-fourth. As slave and land ownership grew more concentrated, a growing number of whites were forced by economic pressure to leave the land and move to urban centers.

Growth of a Distinctive Southern Identity

Beginning in the 1830s, the South developed a new and aggressive sense of "nationalism" that was rooted in its sense of distinctiveness and its perception that it was ringed by enemies. The South began to conceive of itself more and more as the true custodian of America's revolutionary heritage. Southern travelers who ventured into the North regarded it as a "strange and distant land" and expressed disgust about its vice-ridden cities and its grasping materialism.

At the same time, southern intellectuals began to defend slavery as a positive factor. After 1830, white Southerners stopped referring to slavery as a necessary evil. Instead, they argued that it was a beneficial institution that created a hierarchical society superior to the leveling democracy of the North. By the late 1840s, a new and more explicitly racist rationale for slavery had emerged.

With the emergence of militant abolitionism in the North, sharpened by slave uprisings in Jamaica and Southampton County, Virginia, the South began to see itself as surrounded by enemies. Southern leaders responded aggressively. On the Senate floor in 1837, John C. Calhoun pronounced slavery "a good—a positive good" and set the tone for future southern proslavery arguments. Before the 1830s, southern statements on slavery had been defensive; afterward, they were defiant.

In the 1840s, a growing number of southern ministers, journalists, and politicians began to denounce the North's form of capitalism as "wage slavery." The condition of free labor, they argued, was actually "worse than slavery," because slaveholders, unlike greedy northern employers, provide for their employees "when most needed, when sickness or old age has overtaken [them]." Northern workers, they declared, were simply "slaves without masters."

During the 1840s, more and more Southerners defended slavery on explicitly racial grounds. In doing so, they drew on new pseudoscientific theories of racial inferiority. Some of these theories came from Europe, which was seeking justification of imperial expansion over nonwhite peoples in Africa and Asia. Other racist ideas were drawn from northern scientists, who employed an elaborate theory of "polygenesis," which claimed that Africans and whites were separate species.

The Decline of Antislavery Sentiment in the South

During the eighteenth century, the South was unique among slave societies in its openness to antislavery ideas. In Delaware, Maryland, and North Carolina, Quakers freed more than 1500 slaves and sent them out of state. Scattered Presbyterian, Baptist, and Methodist ministers and advisory committees condemned slavery as a sin "contrary to the word of God." As late as 1827, the number of antislavery organizations in the South actually outnumbered those in the free states by at least four to one.

The South's historical openness to antislavery ideas ended in the 1830s. Southern religious sects that had expressed opposition to slavery in the late eighteenth century modified their antislavery beliefs. Quakers and Unitarians who were strongly antagonistic to slavery emigrated. By the second decade of the century, antislavery sentiment was confined to Kentucky, the Piedmont counties of North Carolina, and the mountains in eastern Tennessee.

State law and public opinion stifled debate and forced conformity to proslavery arguments. Southern state legislatures adopted a series of laws suppressing criticism of the institution. In 1830 Louisiana made it a crime to make any statement that might produce discontent or insubordination among slaves. Six years later, Virginia made it a felony for any member of an abolition society to come into the state and for any citizen to deny the legality of slavery.

The silent pressure of public opinion also limited public discussion of the slavery question. College presidents or professors suspected of sympathizing with abolitionists lost their jobs. Mobs attacked editors who dared to print articles critical of slavery. One Richmond, Virginia, editor fought eight duels in two years to defend his views on slavery. In Parkville, Missouri, and Lexington, Kentucky, crowds dismantled printing presses of antislavery newspapers. An "iron curtain" was erected against the invasion of antislavery propaganda.

Only once, in the wake of Nat Turner's famous slave insurrection in 1831, did a southern state openly debate the possibility of ending slavery. These debates in the Virginia legislature in January and February 1832 ended with the defeat of proposals to abolish slavery.

James G. Birney was one of many Southerners to discover that it was hopeless to work for slave emancipation in the South. Birney was born into a wealthy Kentucky slaveholding family, and, like many members of the South's slaveowning elite, was educated at Princeton. After graduation, he moved to Huntsville, Alabama, where he practiced law and operated a cotton plantation. In Huntsville, he developed qualms about slavery and began to work as an agent for the American Colonization Society. Soon, his doubts about slavery had grown into an active hatred for the institution. He returned to Kentucky, emancipated his slaves, and in 1835 organized the Kentucky Anti-Slavery Society.

In Kentucky, Birney quickly discovered that public opinion vehemently opposed antislavery ideas. A committee of leading citizens in Danville informed him that they would not permit him to establish an antislavery newspaper in the city. When Birney announced that he would go through with his plans anyway, the committee bought out the paper's printer, and the town's postmaster announced that he would refuse to deliver the newspaper. In a final effort to publish his paper, Birney moved across the Ohio River into Cincinnati, but a mob destroyed his press while the city's mayor looked on.

The defense of slavery after 1830 also led to hostility toward all social reforms. One southern newspaper editor declared that the South "has uniformly rejected the isms which infest Europe and the Eastern and Western states of this country." Many Southerners spoke proudly of rejecting the reforms that flourished in the North. The South, said one South Carolina scientist, was "the breakwater which is to stay that furious tide of social and political heresies now setting toward us from the shores of the old world." Only the temperance movement made headway in the South.

"Reforming" Slavery from Within

Many white Southerners felt genuine moral doubts about slavery. For the most part, however, these doubts were directed into efforts to reform the institution by converting slaves to Christianity, revising slave codes to make them less harsh, and making slavery conform to the ideal depicted in the Old Testament.

During the early eighteenth century, ministers from such denominations as the Quakers, Moravians, and Anglicans launched the first concerted campaigns to convert slaves in the American colonies to Christianity. Missionaries established schools and taught several thousand slaves to read and recite Scripture. They stressed that Christian slaves would make more loyal and productive workers, less likely to stage insurrections. The Great Awakening of the 1730s and 1740s stimulated renewed efforts to promote Christianization, but was not until the early nineteenth century that most slaveowners expressed concern for converting their slaves to Christianity.

There were also early nineteenth-century efforts to ameliorate the harshness of the early slave codes. The eighteenth-century codes permitted owners to punish slaves by castration and cutting off limbs. Slaveholders had no specific obligations for housing, feeding, or clothing slaves, and many observers reported seeing slaves half-clothed or naked. Few eighteenth-century masters showed any concern for slave marriages, families, or religion.

During the early nineteenth century, the southern states enacted new codes regulating the punishment of slaves and setting minimum standards for maintenance. State legislatures defined killing a

In a particularly cruel twist, an African slave is forced to whip a fellow slave as the white slave owner watches. Punishments and tortures that slaves might be forced to endure included, in addition to whipping, chaining, confinement, and branding.

slave with malice as murder and made dismemberment and some other cruel punishments illegal. Three states forbade the sale of young slave children from their parents, and four states permitted slaves to be taught to read and write.

Many of the new laws went unenforced, but they suggest that a new code of values and behavior was emerging. Paternalism was the defining characteristic of this new code. According to this new ideal, slaveholding was "a duty and a burden" carrying strict moral obligations. A humane master of a plantation was supposed to show concern for the spiritual and physical well-being of his slaves.

These minimal efforts to reform slavery were, however, accompanied by tighter restrictions on other aspects of slave life. Private manumissions were made illegal. Southern states instituted the death penalty for any slaves involved in plotting a rebellion. Most states prohibited slaves from owning firearms, horses, or drums, which might be used during an insurrection; these states also placed tight restrictions on slave funerals and barred African-American preachers from conducting religious services unless a white person was present. In order to restrict contact between free African Americans and slaves, a number of southern states required manumitted slaves to leave the state. Other restrictive laws quarantined vessels containing black sailors and imprisoned those who stepped on shore.

Southern Nationalism

Seeking to free their region from cultural, economic, and religious dependence on the North, southern "nationalists" sought to promote southern economic self-sufficiency, to create southern-oriented educational and religious institutions, and to develop a distinctive southern literature. Beginning in 1837, southern leaders held the first of a series of commercial conventions in an attempt to diversify the southern economy and to rescue the South from northern "pecuniary and commercial supremacy."

Efforts to develop the southern economy were surprisingly successful. Southern railroad mileage quadrupled between 1850 and 1860—although southern track mileage still trailed that of the free states by 14,000. By 1860 Richmond manufactured more tobacco than any other America city and exported more goods to South American than any other American port, including New York.

Other southern nationalists strove to create southern-oriented educational institutions to protect the young from, in Jefferson's words, "imbibing opinions and principles in discord" with those of the South. Schoolbooks, declared one southern magazine, "have slurs and innuendoes at slavery; the geographies are more particular in stating the resources of the Northern States; the histories almost ignore the South; the arithmetics contain in their examples reflections upon the Southern states."

The struggle for independent southern colleges achieved considerable success. By 1860 Virginia had 23 colleges and Georgia had 32, while New York had 17 colleges and Massachusetts just 8. In 1856 the University of Virginia had 558 students, compared to only 361 at Harvard.

Regional independence was also called for in religion. Due in large part to fear of antislavery agitation, southern Baptists, Methodists, and Presbyterians sought to sever their denomination affiliations with northern churches. In the early 2000s, only the Baptists remain divided.

Southerners also called for a distinctive and peculiarly southern literature. More than 30 periodicals were founded with the word "Southern" in their title, all intended to "breathe a Southern spirit, and sustain a strictly Southern character." Authors such as Nathaniel Beverly Tucker and William Gilmore Simms called on the South to write on southern themes and to overcome the taunts of "Englishmen and Northernmen" that they were intellectually inferior.

Southern Radicalism

By the early 1850s, a growing number of aggressive Southerners had moved beyond earlier calls for separate southern factories, colleges, and churches. Militant nationalists called for the reopening of the slave trade and aggressive annexations of new slave territory in Latin America and the Caribbean.

In a bid to acquire new lands for slavery a filibustering expedition was launched from New Orleans in 1851 to secure Cuba for the South. After this failed, extreme southern nationalists supported the efforts of William Walker, "the gray-eyed man of destiny," to extend slave labor into Latin America. In 1853, with considerable southern support, Walker raised a private army and unsuccessfully invaded Mexico. Two years later, he launched the first of three invasions of Nicaragua. On his final foray in 1860, he was taken prisoner by a British officer, handed over to Honduran authorities, and, at the age of 36, executed by a firing squad. In the late 1850s, another group of ardent southern expansionists, the Knights of the Golden Circle, developed plans to create an independent slave empire stretching from Maryland and Texas to northern South America and the West Indies. The only practical effect of these schemes was to arouse northern opinion against an aggressive southern slaveocracy.

SLAVERY

The primary distinguishing characteristic of the South was its dependence on slave labor. During the decades before the Civil War, 4 million African Americans, one-third of the South's population, labored as slaves.

Two unrelated incidents suggest the complexity of the institution of slavery. The first took place in 1811. Lilburne and Isham Lewis, two nephews of Thomas Jefferson, ordered Lilburne's slaves to lash a slave named George to the kitchen floor of their southwest Kentucky farm. The 17-year-old slave had run away, returned, and then broken a treasured pitcher. Enraged and probably drunk, Lilburne seized an ax and nearly decapitated the young slave. Then the brothers had their terrorized slaves dismember the victim and throw the pieces on the fire.

The second picture of slavery is from 1825. In that year, Joseph Davis, a Mississippi planter, met Robert Owen, the Scottish industrialist and utopian reformer. Inspired by Owen's vision of society operating according to the principles of voluntary cooperation, Davis attempted to reorganize his plantation at Davis Bend, 30 miles south of Vicksburg. Davis provided slave families with two-room cabins and supplied food freely. His most famous innovation was a form of self-government for the slave community. No slave of the more than 300 on his plantation could be punished without being tried and convicted by a jury of his peers. Later, Joseph's younger brother, Jefferson Davis, the future president of the Confederacy, put a similar system into practice on his plantation.

In general, slaves were overworked, poorly clad, and inadequately housed and received the minimum of medical care. Debt, the death of a master, or merely the prospect of economic gain frequently tore slave husbands from wives and slave parents from children. And yet, as brutal and destructive as the institution of slavery was, slaves were not defenseless or emasculated victims. They were able to sustain ties to their African past and to maintain a cultural life. Through religion, folklore, music, and family life as well as more direct forms of resistance, slaves were able to sustain a vital culture supportive of human dignity.

The Legal Status of Slaves

Every southern state enacted a **slave code** that defined the slaveowners' power and the slaves' status as property. The codes stated that a slave, like a domestic animal, could be bought, sold, and leased. A master also had the right to compel a slave to work. The codes prohibited slaves from owning property, testifying against whites in court, or from making contracts. Slave marriages were not recognized by law. Under the slave codes, slavery was lifelong and hereditary, and any child born to a slave woman was the property of her master.

The slave codes gave slaves limited legal rights. To refute abolitionist contentions that slavery was unjust and inhumane, southern legislators adopted statutes regulating slaves' hours of labor and establishing certain minimal standards for slave upkeep. Most states also defined the wanton killing of a slave as murder, prohibited cruel and unusual punishments, and extended to slaves accused of capital offenses the right to trial by jury and legal counsel. Whipping, however, was not regarded by southern legislatures as a cruel punishment, and slaves were

Hardworking slaves on a plantation pick and carry cotton while white overseers look on.

prohibited from bringing suit to seek legal redress for violations of their rights.

The main goal of the slave codes, however, was to regulate slaves' lives. Slaves were forbidden to strike whites or use insulting language toward white people, hold a meeting without a white person present, visit whites or freed slaves, or leave plantations without permission. The laws prohibited whites and free blacks from teaching slaves to read and write, gambling with slaves, or supplying them with liquor, guns, or poisonous drugs. Most of the time, authorities loosely enforced these legal restrictions, but whenever fears of slave uprisings spread, enforcement tightened.

Slave Labor

Simon Gray was a slave. He was also the captain of a Mississippi River flatboat and the builder and operator of a number of sawmills. Emanuel Quivers, too, was a slave. He worked at the Tredegar Iron Works of Richmond, Virginia. Andrew Dirt was also a slave. He was an overseer.

Slaves performed all kinds of work. During the 1850s, half a million slaves lived in southern towns and cities, where they were hired out by their owners to work in ironworks, textile mills, tobacco factories, laundries, shipyards, and mechanics' homes. Other slaves labored as lumberjacks, as deckhands and fire tenders on river boats, and in sawmills, gristmills, and quarries. Many other slaves were engaged in construction of roads and railroads. Most slaves, to be sure, were field hands, raising cotton, hemp, rice, tobacco, and sugar cane. But even on plantations not all slaves were menial laborers. Some worked as skilled artisans such as blacksmiths, shoemakers, or carpenters; others held domestic posts, such as coachmen or house servants; and still others held managerial posts. At least two-thirds of the slaves worked under the supervision of black foremen of gangs, called drivers. Not infrequently they managed the whole plantation in the absence of their masters.

For most slaves, slavery meant backbreaking field work on small farms or larger plantations. On the typical plantation, slaves worked "from day clean to first dark." Solomon Northrup, a free black who was kidnapped and enslaved for 12 years on a Louisiana cotton plantation, wrote a graphic description of the work regimen imposed on slaves: "The hands are required to be in the cotton field as soon as it is light in the morning, and, with the exception of ten or fifteen minutes, which is given them at noon to swallow their allowance of cold bacon, they are not permitted to be a moment idle until it is too dark to see, and when the moon is full, they often times labor till the middle of the night." Even then, the slaves' work was not over; it was still necessary to feed swine and mules, cut wood, and pack the cotton. At planting time or harvest time, work was even more exacting as planters required slaves to stay in the fields 15 or 16 hours a day.

To maximize productivity, slaveowners assigned each hand a specific set of tasks throughout the year. During the winter, field slaves ginned and pressed cotton, cut wood, repaired buildings and fences, and cleared fields. In the spring and summer, field hands

The dirt-floored, poorly ventilated, roughly built log one-room huts in which slaves lived were breeding grounds for disease. When slave owners realized they were losing the productive labor of their frequently ill slaves, they provided them with sturdier, better constructed cabins—still made of logs, but with wooden floors and glazed windows.

plowed and hoed fields, killed weeds, and planted and cultivated crops. In the fall, slaves picked, ginned, and packed cotton, shucked corn, and gathered peas. Elderly slaves cared for children, made clothes, and prepared food.

Labor on large plantations was as rigidly organized as in a factory. Under the gang system, which was widely used on cotton plantations, field hands were divided into plow gangs and hoe gangs, each commanded by a driver. Under the task system, mainly used on rice plantations, each hand was given a specific daily work assignment.

Because slaves had little direct incentive to work hard, slaveowners combined a variety of harsh penalties with positive incentives. Some masters denied disobedient slaves passes to leave the plantation or forced them to work on Sundays or holidays. Other planters confined disobedient hands to private or public jails, and one Maryland planter required a slave to eat the worms he had failed to pick off tobacco plants. Chains and shackles were widely used to control runaways. Whipping was a key part of the system of discipline and motivation. On one Louisiana plantation, at least one slave was lashed every four and one-half days. In his diary, Bennet H. Barrow, a Louisiana planter, recorded flogging "every hand in the field," breaking his sword on the head of one slave, shooting another slave in the thigh, and cutting another with a club "in 3 places very bad."

But physical pain alone was not enough to elicit hard work. To stimulate productivity, some masters gave slaves small garden plots and permitted them to sell their produce. Others distributed gifts of food or money at the end of the year. Still other planters awarded prizes, holidays, and year-end bonuses to particularly productive slaves. One Alabama master permitted his slaves to share in the profits of the cotton, peanut, and pea crops.

Material Conditions of Slave Life

Deprivation and physical hardship were the hallmarks of life under slavery. It now seems clear that the material conditions of slave life may have been even worse than those of the poorest, most downtrodden free laborers in the North and Europe. Although the material conditions for slaves improved greatly in the nineteenth century, slaves remained much more likely than southern or northern whites to die prematurely, suffer malnutrition or dietary deficiencies, or lose a child in infancy.

Plantation records reveal that over half of all slave babies died during their first year of life—a rate twice that of white babies. Although slave children's death rate declined after the first year of life, it remained twice the white rate. The average slave's small size indicates a deficient diet. At birth, over half of all slave children weighed less than 5 pounds—or what is today considered underweight. Throughout their childhoods, slaves were smaller than white children of the same age. The average slave children did not reach 3 feet in height until their fourth birthdays. At that age they were 5 inches shorter than a typical child today and about the same height as a child in present-day Bangladesh. At 17, slave men were shorter than 96 percent of present-day American men, and slave women were smaller than 80 percent of American women.

The slaves' diet was monotonous and unvaried, consisting largely of cornmeal, salt pork, and bacon. Only rarely did slaves drink milk or eat fresh meat or vegetables. This diet provided enough bulk calories to ensure that slaves had sufficient strength and energy to work as productive field hands, but it did not provide adequate nutrition. As a result, slaves were small for their ages, suffered from vitamin and protein deficiencies, and were victims of such ailments as beriberi, kwashiorkor, and pellagra. Poor nutrition and high rates of infant and child mortality contributed to a short average life expectancy—just 21 or 22 years compared to 40 to 43 years for whites.

The physical conditions in which slaves lived were appalling. Lacking privies, slaves had to urinate and defecate in the cover of nearby bushes. Lacking any sanitary disposal of garbage, they were surrounded by decaying food. Chickens, dogs, and pigs lived next to the slave quarters, and in consequence, animal feces contaminated the area. Such squalor contributed to high rates of dysentery, typhus, diarrhea, hepatitis, typhoid fever, and intestinal worms.

Slave quarters were cramped and crowded. The typical cabin—a single, windowless room, with a chimney constructed of clay and twigs and a floor made up of dirt or planks resting on the ground—ranged in size from 10 feet by 10 feet to 21 feet by 21 feet. These small cabins often contained five, six, or more occupants. On some plantations, slaves lived in single-family cabins; on others, two or more shared the same room. On the largest plantations, unmarried men and women were sometimes lodged together in barracklike structures. Josiah Henson, the Kentucky slave who served as the model for Harriet Beecher Stowe's Uncle Tom, described his plantation's cabins this way:

> We lodged in log huts.... Wooden floors were an unknown luxury. In a single room were huddled, like cattle, ten or a dozen persons, men, women, and chil-

dren. . . . There were neither bedsteads nor furniture. . . . Our beds were collections of straw and old rags. . . . The wind whistled and the rain and snow blew in through the cracks, and the damp earth soaked in the moisture till the floor was muddy as a pig sty.

Slave Family Life

In 1858, after being sold away from his family, a Georgia slave named Abream Scriven wrote the following words to his wife: "Give my love to my dear father and mother and tell them good bye for me. . . . My dear wife for you and all my children my pen cannot express the grief I feel to be parted from you. I remain your true husband until death."

Slavery severely strained family life. Slave sales frequently broke up slave families. During the Civil War, nearly 20 percent of former slaves reported that an earlier marriage had been terminated by "force." The sale of children from parents was even more common. Over the course of a lifetime, the average slave had a fifty-fifty chance of being sold at least once and was likely to witness the sale of several members of his or her immediate family.

Even in instances in which marriages were not broken by sale, slave husbands and wives often resided on separate farms and plantations and were owned by different individuals. On large plantations, one slave father in three had a different owner than his wife and could visit his family only at his master's discretion. On smaller holdings divided ownership occurred even more frequently. The typical farm and plantation were so small that it was difficult for many slaves to find a spouse at all. As a former slave put it, men "had a hell of a time getting a wife during slavery."

Other obstacles stood in the way of an independent family life. Living accommodations undermined privacy. Many slaves had to share their single-room cabins with relatives and other slaves who were not related to them. On larger plantations, food was cooked in a common kitchen and young children were cared for in a communal nursery while their parents worked in the fields. Even on model plantations, children between the ages of 7 and 10 were taken from their parents and sent to live in separate cabins.

Slavery imposed rigid limits on the authority of slave parents. Nearly every slave child went through an experience similar to one recalled by a young South Carolina slave named Jacob Stroyer. Stroyer was being trained as a jockey. His trainer beat him regularly, for no apparent reason. Stroyer appealed to his father for help, but his father simply said to work harder, "for I cannot do anything for you." When Stroyer's mother argued with the trainer, she was whipped for her efforts. From this episode, he learned a critical lesson: The ability of slave parents to protect their own children was sharply limited.

Of all the evils associated with slavery, abolitionists most bitterly denounced the sexual abuse suffered by slave women. Abolitionists claimed that slaveholders adopted deliberate policies to breed slaves for sale in the lower South—"like oxen for the shambles"—and kept "black harems" and sexually exploited slave women. Some masters did indeed take slave mistresses and concubines. One slave, Henry Bibb, said that a slave trader forced Bibb's wife to become a prostitute.

Planters also sought to increase slave birthrates through a variety of economic incentives. Many slaveholders gave bounties in the form of cash or household goods to mothers who bore healthy children and increased rations and lightened the workload of pregnant and nursing women.

And yet, despite the constant threat of sale and family breakup, African Americans managed to forge strong family ties and personal relationships; despite the fact that southern law provided no legal sanction for slave marriages, most slaves established *de facto* arrangements that were often stable over long periods of time; despite frequent family disrup-

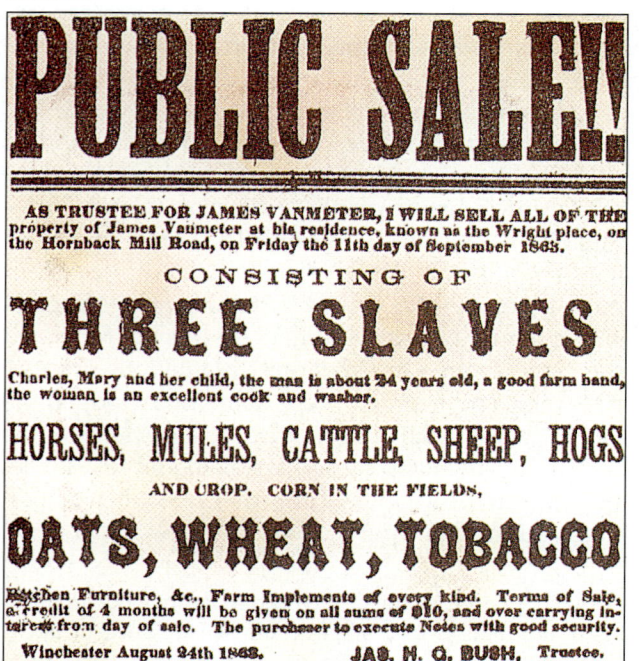

Slavery's worst evil was that it reduced people to the status of property. Under slavery, slaves could be bought, sold, leased, and traded away from their families.

tion, a majority of slaves grew up in families headed by a father and a mother. Nuclear family ties stretched outward to an involved network of extended kin. Through the strength and flexibility of their kin ties, African Americans fought the psychologically debilitating effects of slavery.

Contrary to what early nineteenth-century abolitionists charged, the sexual life of slaves was not casual or promiscuous nor did slave women become mothers at a particularly early age. Some slave women, like some white women, engaged in intercourse and bore children before settling into a permanent union. Most slave women settled into long-lasting monogamous relationships in their early twenties, which lasted, unless broken by sale, until she or her husband died.

Slave Cultural Expression

Notwithstanding the harshness and misery of life under slavery, slaves developed a distinctive life and culture. Through their families, their religion, and their cultural traditions, slaves were able to nurture an autonomous culture and community, beyond the direct control of their masters.

During the late eighteenth and early nineteenth centuries, slaves embraced Christianity, but they molded and transformed it to meet their own needs. Slave religious beliefs were a mixture of African traditions and Christianity. From their African heritage, slaves brought a hopeful and optimistic view of life, which contrasted sharply with evangelical Protestantism's emphasis on human sinfulness. In Protestant Christianity the slaves found an emphasis on love and the spiritual equality of all people that strengthened their ties to others. Many slaves fused the concepts of Moses, who led his people to freedom, and Jesus, who suffered on behalf of all humankind, into a promise of deliverance in this world.

A major form of African American religious expression was the **spiritual.** Slave spirituals, such as "Go Down Moses" with its refrain "let my people go," indicated that slaves identified with the history of the Hebrew people, who had been oppressed and enslaved, but who achieved eventual deliverance.

In addition to the spiritual, storytelling was another important form of slave cultural expression. Slave folktales were much more than amusing stories; slaves used them to comment on the people around them and to convey lessons for everyday living. Among the most popular slave folktales were animal trickster stories, like the Brer Rabbit tales, derived from similar African stories, which told of powerless creatures who achieve their will through wit and guile rather than power and authority. These tales taught slave children how they had to function in a white-dominated world and held out the promise that the powerless would eventually triumph over the strong.

Slave Resistance

It was a basic tenet of the proslavery argument that slaves were docile, contented, faithful, and loyal.

Slave religious expression, like that depicted in this 1860 painting *Plantation Burial*, by John Antrobus, often combined the beliefs and practices of white Christian slave owners with rituals imported from Africa.

"Our slave population is not only a happy one," said a Virginia legislator, "but it is a contented, peaceful, and harmless one."

In fact, there is no evidence that the majority of slaves were contented. One scholar has identified more than 200 instances of attempted insurrection or rumors of slave resistance between the seventeenth century and the Civil War. And many slaves who did not directly rebel made their masters' lives miserable through a variety of indirect protests against slavery, including sabotage, stealing, malingering, murder, arson, and infanticide.

Four times during the first 31 years of the nineteenth century, slaves attempted major insurrections. In 1800, a 24-year-old Virginia slave named **Gabriel**, who was a blacksmith, led a march of perhaps 50 armed slaves on Richmond. The plot failed when a storm washed out the road to Richmond, giving the Virginia militia time to arrest the rebels. White authorities executed Gabriel and 25 other conspirators.

In 1811 in southern Louisiana, between 180 and 500 slaves, led by Charles Deslondes, a free mulatto from Haiti, marched on New Orleans, armed with axes and other weapons. Slaveowners retaliated by killing 82 blacks and placing the heads of 16 leaders on pikes.

In 1822 **Denmark Vesey,** a former West Indian slave who had been born in Africa, bought his freedom, and moved to Charleston, South Carolina. There he devised a conspiracy to take over the city on a summer Sunday when many whites would be vacationing outside the city. Using his connections as a leader in the African Church of Charleston, Vesey drew support from skilled African-American artisans, carpenters, harnessmakers, mechanics, and blacksmiths as well as from field slaves. Before the revolt could take place, however, a domestic slave of a prominent Charlestonian informed his master. The authorities proceeded to arrest 131 African Americans and hang 37.

The best known slave revolt took place nine years later in Southampton County in southern Virginia. On August 22, 1831, **Nat Turner,** a trusted Baptist preacher, led a small group of fellow slaves into the home of his master Joseph Travis and killed the entire Travis household. By August 23, Turner's force had increased to between 60 and 80 slaves and had killed more than 50 whites. The local militia counterattacked and killed about 100 African Americans. Twenty more slaves, including Turner, were later executed. Turner's revolt sparked a panic that spread as far south as Alabama and Louisiana. One Virginian worried that "a Nat Turner might be in any family."

Slave uprisings were much less frequent and less extensive in the American South than in the West Indies or Brazil. Outright revolts did not occur more often because the chances of success were minimal and the consequences of defeat catastrophic. As one Missouri slave put it, "I've seen Marse Newton and Marse John Ramsey shoot too often to believe they can't kill" a slave.

The conditions that favored revolts elsewhere were absent in the South. In Jamaica, slaves outnumbered whites ten to one, whereas in the South whites were a majority in every state except Mississippi and South Carolina. In addition, slaveholding units in the South were much smaller than in other slave societies in the Western Hemisphere. Half of all U.S. slaves worked on units of 20 or less; in contrast, many sugar plantations in Jamaica had more than 500 slaves.

The unity of the white population in defense of slavery made the prospects for a successful rebellion bleak. In Virginia in 1830, 100,000 of the state's 700,000 whites were members of the state militia. Finally, southern slaves had few havens to which to escape. The major exception was the swamp country in Florida, where former slave **maroons** joined with Seminole Indians in resisting the U.S. army.

Recognizing that open resistance would be futile or even counterproductive, most plantation slaves expressed their opposition to slavery in a variety of subtle ways. Most day-to-day resistance took the form of breaking tools, feigning illness, doing shoddy work, stealing, and running away. These acts of resistance most commonly occurred when a master or overseer overstepped customary bounds. Through these acts, slaves tried to establish a right to proper treatment.

Free African Americans

In 1860, 488,000 African Americans were not slaves. After the American Revolution, slaveowners freed thousands of slaves, and countless others emancipated themselves by running away. In Louisiana, a large free Creole population had emerged under Spanish and French rule, and in South Carolina a Creole population had arrived from Barbados. The number of free blacks in the Deep South increased rapidly with the arrival of thousands of light-colored refugees from the slave revolt in Haiti.

Free African Americans varied greatly in status. Most lived in poverty, but in a few cities, such as New Orleans, Baltimore, and Charleston, they worked as skilled carpenters, shoemakers, tailors, and millwrights. In the lower South, a few achieved high occupational status and actually bought slaves of their own. One of the wealthiest former slaves was William Ellison, the son of a slave mother and a

THE PEOPLE SPEAK

Slave Resistance

One of the first fugitive slaves to speak out publicly against slavery, Frederick Douglass electrified audiences with his firsthand accounts of slavery. Women's rights advocate Elizabeth Cady Stanton recalled her first glimpse of Douglass: "He stood there like an African prince, majestic in his wrath, as with wit, satire, and indignation he graphically described the bitterness of slavery and the humiliation of subjection." When many Northerners refused to believe that this eloquent orator could possibly have been a slave, he responded by writing an autobiography that identified his previous owners by name. Here, Douglass describes his battle with a brutal "slave-breaker."

> If at any one time of my life . . . I was made to drink the bitterest dregs of slavery, that time was during the first six months of my stay with Mr. [Edward] Covey. We worked in all weather. It was never too hot or too cold. . . . The longest days were too short for him, and the shortest nights too long for him. I was somewhat unmanageable when I first went there, but a few months of this discipline tamed me. Mr. Covey succeeded in breaking me. I was broken in body, soul, and spirit. My natural elasticity was crushed, my intellect languished, the disposition to read departed, the cheerful spark that lingered about my eye died; the dark night of slavery closed in upon me; and behold a man transformed into a brute! . . .
>
> You have seen how a man was made a slave; you shall see how a slave was made a man. On one of the hottest days of the month of August, 1833 . . . my strength utterly failed me; I was seized with a violent aching of the head, attended with extreme dizziness; I trembled in every limb. . . .
>
> Mr. Covey . . . asked me what was the matter. I told him as well as I could, for I scarce had strength to speak. He then gave me a savage kick in the side, and told me to get up. I tried to do so, but fell back in the attempt. He gave me another kick. . . . At this moment I resolved to go to my master, enter a complaint, and ask his protection. In order to do this, I must that afternoon walk seven miles; and this undertaking. . . . I . . . started on my way, through bogs and briers . . . tearing my feet sometimes at every step. . . . I arrived at master's store. I then presented an appearance enough to affect any but a heart of iron. My hair was all clotted with dust and blood, my shirt was stiff with briers and thorns. . . . Master Thomas ridiculed the idea that there was any danger of Mr. Covey's killing me, and said . . . that I must go back to him, come what might. . . .
>
> All went well till Monday morning. . . . Long before daylight, I was called to go and rub, curry, and feed the horses. I obeyed, and was glad to obey. But whilst thus engaged . . . Mr. Covey entered the stable with a long rope; and just as I was halfway out of the loft, he caught hold of my legs, and was about tying me. As soon as I found what he was up to, I gave a sudden spring. . . . But at this moment—from whence came the spirit I don't know—I resolved to fight; and suiting my action to the resolution, I seized Covey hard by the throat; and as I did so, I rose. He held on to me, and I to him. My resistance was so entirely unexpected, that Covey seemed taken all aback. He trembled like a leaf. This gave me assurance. . . .
>
> The battle with Mr. Covey was the turning-point in my career as a slave. It rekindled the few expiring embers of freedom, and revived within me a sense of my own manhood. It recalled departed self-confidence, and inspired me again with a determination to be free.

Source: Frederick Douglass, *Narrative of the Life of Frederick Douglass, An American Slave* (Boston, 1845).

---

white planter. As a slave apprenticed to a skilled artisan, Ellison had learned how to make cotton gins, and at the age of 26 bought his freedom with his overtime earnings. At his death in 1861, he had acquired the home of a former South Carolina governor, a shop, lands, and 63 slaves worth more than $100,000.

Free people of color occupied an uneasy middle ground between the dominant whites and the masses of slaves. Legally, courts denied them the right to serve on juries or to testify against whites. Some, like William Ellison, distanced themselves from those black people who remained in slavery and even bought and sold slaves. Others identified with slaves and poor free slaves and took the lead in establishing separate African American churches.

In addition to the more than 250,000 free African Americans who lived in the South, another 200,000 of them lived in the North. Although they made up no more than 3.8 percent of the population of any northern state, free African Americans faced intense legal, economic, and social discrimination, which kept them desperately poor. They were prohibited from marrying whites and were forced into the lowest paying jobs. Whites denied them equal access to education, relegated them to segregated jails, ceme-

Although many free African Americans lived in poverty, some worked as skilled carpenters, tailors, millwrights, or sawyers.

teries, asylums, and schools, forbade them from testifying against whites in court, and, in all but four states—New Hampshire, Maine, Massachusetts, and Vermont—denied them the right to vote.

In the North as well as the South, most free African Americans faced economic hardship and substandard living conditions. Northern African Americans typically lived in tenements, sheds, and stables. An 1847 visitor described the typical black dwelling in Philadelphia as "a desolate pen," 6 feet square, without windows, beds, or furniture, possessing a leaky roof and a floor so low in the ground "that more or less water comes in on them from the yard in rainy weather." According to the *New York Express,* the principal residence of a free black in that city was a house with eight or ten rooms, "and in these are crowded not infrequently two or three hundred souls."

During the 1830s or even earlier, African Americans in both the North and South began to suffer from heightened discrimination and competition from white immigrants in both the skilled trades and such traditional occupations as domestic service. In the late 1850s, the plight of free African Americans worsened. In states such as South Carolina and Maryland, they faced a new crisis. White mechanics and artisans, bitter over the competition they faced from free people of color, demanded that the states legislate the reenslavement of African Americans. During the winter of 1859, politicians in the South Carolina legislature introduced 20 bills restricting the freedom of African Americans. None passed. The next summer, Charleston officials went house to house, demanding that free people of color provide documentary proof of their freedom and threatening to reenslave those who lacked evidence. A panic followed, and hundreds of free blacks emigrated to the North. Some 780 emigrated from South Carolina before secession; 2000 more left during the first month and a half of 1861.

CONCLUSION

In 1857 **Hinton Rowan Helper,** the son of a western North Carolina farmer, published one of the most politically influential books ever written by an American. Entitled *The Impending Crisis of the South,* the book argued that slavery was incompatible with economic progress. Using statistics drawn from the 1850 census, Helper maintained that by every possible measure, the North was growing far faster than the South and that slavery was the cause of the South's economic backwardness.

Helper's thesis was that southern slavery was inefficient and wasteful, inferior in all respects to the North's free labor system. Helper argued that slavery was incompatible with economic progress; it impoverished the South, degraded labor, inhibited urbanization, thwarted industrialization, and stifled innovation. A rabid racist, Helper accompanied a call for the abolition of slavery with a demand for black colonization overseas. He concluded his book with a call for the South's nonslaveholders to overthrow the region's planter elite.

Helper's book created a nationwide furor. A leading antislavery newspaper distributed 500 copies a day, viewing the book as the most effective propaganda against slavery ever written. Many Southerners burned it, fearful that it would divide the white population and undermine the institution of slavery.

By 1857, when Helper's book appeared, the North and South had become in the eyes of many Americans two distinct civilizations, with their own

Chronology of Key Events

1790	Samuel Slater opens the nation's first textile mill in Pawtucket, Rhode Island
1793	Eli Whitney obtains a patent for the cotton gin
1800	Gabriel slave insurrection is uncovered in Richmond, Virginia
1806	Journeyman shoemakers in New York stage one of the nation's first labor strikes
1811	Charles Deslondes's slave insurrection in southern Louisiana is suppressed
1822	Denmark Vesey's slave rebellion is uncovered in South Carolina
1831	Nat Turner's slave insurrection in Southhampton County, Virginia
1832	Virginia legislature defeats proposal to abolish slavery
1834	National Trades' Union is organized; Massachusetts mill girls stage their first strike
1837	Panic of 1837 begins
1838	Boston establishes the nation's first modern police force
1840	Ten-hour day is established for federal employees
1842	Massachusetts supreme court, in *Commonwealth* v. *Hunt,* recognizes unions' right to exist
1844	Methodist church divides over slavery issue
1845	Potato blight strikes Ireland; Baptists split over the slavery issue
1848	Revolutions in Europe; Free Soil party is organized to oppose expansion of slavery into new territories
1857	Hinton Helper publishes *The Impending Crisis of the South*

distinctive sets of values and ideals: one increasingly urban and industrial, the other committed to slave labor. Although the two sections shared many of the same ideals, ambitions, and prejudices, they had developed along diverging lines. In increasing numbers, Northerners identified their society with progress and believed that slavery was an intolerable obstacle to innovation, self-improvement, and commercial and economic growth. A growing number of Southerners, in turn, regarded their rural and agricultural society as the true embodiment of republican values. The great question before the nation was whether it could continue to exist half slave, half free.

SUGGESTIONS FOR FURTHER READING

William J. Cooper, Jr., *The South and the Politics of Slavery* (1978) and Cooper and Thomas E. Terrill, *The American South* (1990) are valuable studies of the pre–Civil War South.

Peter Kolchin, *American Slavery, 1619–1877* (1993) offers an insightful overview of slavery.

Sean Wilentz, *Chants Democratic: New York City and the Rise of the American Working Class, 1788–1850.* (1984) provides extensive information on the antebellum northern working class.

Overviews and Surveys

Daniel Boorstin, *The Americans: The National Experience* (1965); Russel B. Nye, *Society and Culture in America, 1830–1860* (1974); Edward Pessen, *Jacksonian America: Society, Personality, and Politics,* rev. ed. (1978).

The Emergence of a New Industrial Order in the North

Hal S. Barron, *Those Who Stayed Behind: Rural Society in Nineteenth-Century New England* (1984); Mary H. Blewett,

Men, Women, and Work: Class, Gender, and Protest in the New England Shoe Industry (1988); Stuart Blumin, The Emergence of the Middle Class: Social Experience in the American City (1989), and The Urban Threshhold (1976); John L. Brooke, The Heart of the Commonwealth: Society and Political Culture in Worcester County, Massachusetts (1989); Christopher Clark, The Roots of Rural Capitalism: Western Massachusetts, 1780–1860 (1990); Dennis Clark, The Irish in Philadelphia (1973); Kathleen N. Conzen, Immigrant Milwaukee, 1836–1860 (1976); Allen F. Davis and Mark H. Haller, eds., The Peoples of Philadelphia (1973); Alan Dawley, Class and Community: The Industrial Revolution in Lynn (1976); Hasia R. Diner, Erin's Daughters in America (1983); Robert Doherty, Society and Power: Five New England Towns, 1800–1860 (1977); Thomas Dublin, Women at Work: The Transformation of Work and Community in Lowell, Massachusetts, 1826–1860 (1979); Faye E. Dudden, Serving Women: Household Service in Nineteenth-Century America (1983); Robert Ernst, Immigrant Life in New York City, 1825–1863 (1949); John Faragher, Sugar Creek (1986); Michael Feldberg, The Turbulent Era: Riot and Disorder in Jacksonian America (1980); Michael Frisch, Town into City: Springfield, Massachusetts and the Meaning of Community, 1840–1880 (1972), and Philadelphia, 1800–1880 (1989); Richard Stott and J. Ritchie Garrison, Landscape and Material Life in Franklin, Massachusetts, 1770–1860 (1991); David A. Gerber, The Making of an American Pluralism; Buffalo, New York, 1825–60 (1989); Howard M. Gitelman, Workingmen of Waltham (1974); Arthur Gribben, ed., The Great Famine & the Irish Diaspora in America (1999); Steven Hahn and Jonathan Prude, eds., The Countryside in the Age of Capitalist Transformation (1985); Oscar Handlin, Boston's Immigrants, rev. ed. (1959); Marcus L. Hansen, The Atlantic Migration, 1607–1860 (1940); William F. Hartford, Working People of Holyoke (1990); Joel T. Headley, Great Riots of New York, 1712–1873 (1970); Willard A. Heaps, Riots, U.S.A., 1765–1970 (1970); Susan Hirsch, Roots of the American Working Class: The Industrialization of Crafts in Newark, 1800–1860 (1978); Joan M. Jensen, Loosening the Bonds: Mid-Atlantic Farm Women, 1750–1850 (1986); Maldwyn A. Jones, American Immigration (1960); Alice Kessler-Harris. Out to Work: A History of Wage-Earning Women in the United States (1982); Alexander Keyssar, Out of Work: The First Century of Unemployment in Massachusetts (1986); Peter R. Knights, The Plain People of Boston, 1830–1860 (1971); Roger Lane, Policing the City; Boston, 1822–1855 (1967), and Violent Death in the City: Suicide, Accident and Murder in Nineteenth Century Philadelphia (1979); Jack Larkin, The Transformation of Everyday Life (1989); Bruce Laurie, Artisans into Workers (1989), and Working People of Philadelphia (1980); Kerby A. Miller, Emigrants and Exiles: Ireland and the Irish Exodus to North America (1985); Brian C. Mitchell, The Paddy Camps: The Irish of Lowell (1988); Eric H. Monkkonen, Police in Urban America (1981); Edward Pessen, Most Uncommon Jacksonians: Radical Leaders of the Early Labor Movement (1967), and Riches, Class and Power Before the Civil War (1973); Jonathan Prude, The Coming of Industrial Order: Town and Factory Life in Rural Massachusetts, 1810–1860 (1983); Leonard D. Richards, "Gentlemen of Property and Standing": Anti-Abolitionist Mobs in Jacksonian America (1970); James F. Richardson, The New York Police: Colonial Times to 1901 (1970), and Urban Police in the United States (1974); Howard Rock, Paul Gilje, and Robert Asher, eds., American Artisans (1995); W. J. Rorabaugh, The Craft Apprentice (1986); Steven J. Ross, Workers on the Edge: Work, Leisure, and Politics in Industrializing Cincinnati (1985); Billy G. Smith, The "Lower" Sort: Philadelphia's Laboring People, 1750–1800 (1990); Lee Soltow, Men and Wealth in the United States, 1850–1870 (1975); Christine Stansell, City of Women: The Female Laboring Poor in New York, 1789–1860 (1986); Allen Steinberg, The Transformation of Criminal Justice: Philadelphia, 1800–1880 (1989); Richard Stott, Workers in the Metropolis: Class, Ethnicity, and Youth in Antebellum New York City (1990); Philip Taylor, The Distant Magnet: European Emigration to the U.S.A. (1971); Stephan Thernstrom, Poverty and Progress, Social Mobility in a Nineteenth Century City (1964), and The Other Bostonians (1973); Anthony F. C. Wallace, Rockdale: The Growth of an American Village in the Early Industrial Revolution (1978); Norman Ware, The Industrial Worker, 1840–1860 (1924); Paul O. Weinbaum, Mobs and Demagogues: The New York Response to Collective Violence (1979); Sean Wilentz, Chants Democratic: New York City and the Rise of the American Working Class, 1788–1850 (1984).

Southern Distinctiveness

Edward L. Ayers, Vengeance and Justice: Crime and Punishment in the 19th Century American South (1984); Fred Bateman and Thomas Weiss, A Deplorable Scarcity: The Failure of Industrialization in the Slave Economy (1981); Carol Bleser, ed., In Joy and In Sorrow: Women, Family, and Marriage in the Victorian South (1991); John B. Boles and Evelyn Thomas Nolen, Interpreting Southern History (1987); Blaine A. Brownell and David R. Goldfield, eds., The City in Southern History (1977); Dickson D. Bruce, Jr., Violence and Culture in the Antebellum South (1979); Orville Vernon Burton and Robert C. McMath, Jr., eds., Class, Conflict and Consensus: Antebellum Southern Community Studies (1982); Randolph B. Campbell, A Southern Community in Crisis: Harrison County, Texas, 1850–1880 (1983); Randolph B. Campbell and Richard G. Lowe, Wealth and Power in Antebellum Texas (1977); Jane Turner Censer, North Carolina Planters and Their Children, 1800–1860 (1984); Catherine Clinton, The Plantation Mistress: Woman's World in the Old South (1982); William J. Cooper, Jr., South and the Politics of Slavery (1978); William J. Cooper, Jr., and Thomas E. Terrill, The American South: A History (1990); Carl N. Degler, The Other South: Southern Dissenters in the Nineteenth Century (1974); Clement Eaton, The Freedom-of-Thought Struggle in the Old South, rev. ed. (1964); Drew Gilpin Faust, A Sacred Circle: The Dilemma of the Intellectual in the Old South (1977), The Ideology of Slavery, 1830–1860 (1981), and James Henry Hammond and the Old South (1982); James D. Foust, The Yeoman Farmer and Westward Expansion of U.S. Cotton Production (1975); Elizabeth Fox-Genovese, Within the Plantation Household (1988); George Fredrickson, The Black Image in the White Mind (1971); Alison Goodyear Freehling, Drift Toward Dissolution: The Virginia Slavery Debate of 1831–1832

(1982); Jean E. Friedman, *The Enclosed Garden: Women and Community in the Evangelical South, 1830–1900* (1985); Eugene D. Genovese, *The Political Economy of Slavery* (1965), *The Slaveholders' Dilemma: Freedom and Progress in Southern Conservative Thought* (1992), and *The World the Slaveholders Made* (1969); Kees Gispen, ed., *What Made the South Different?* (1990); David R. Goldfield, *Cotton Fields and Skyscrapers: Southern City and Region, 1607–1980* (1982); George D. Green, *Finance and Economic Development in the Old South* (1972); Kenneth S. Greenberg, *Masters and Statesmen* (1985); J. William Harris, *Plain Folk and Gentry in a Slave Society* (1985); Michael S. Hindus, *Prison and Plantation: Crime, Justice, and Authority in Massachusetts and South Carolina, 1767–1878* (1980); Cynthia A. Kierner, *Beyond the Household: Women's Place in the Early South, 1700–1835* (1998); Rachel N. Klein, *Unification of a Slave State: The Rise of the Planter Class in the South Carolina Backcountry* (1990); Suzanne Lebsock, *The Free Women of Petersburg, 1784–1860* (1984); Raimondo Luraghi, *The Rise and Fall of the Plantation South* (1978); Edward Magdol and Jon L. Wakelyn, eds., *The Southern Common People* (1980); Donald G. Mathews, *Religion in the Old South* (1977); Robert E. May, *The Southern Dream of a Caribbean Empire, 1854–1861* (1973); John McCardell, *The Idea of a Southern Nation* (1979); John Hebron Moore, *The Emergence of the Cotton Kingdom in the Old Southwest* (1988); James Oakes, *The Ruling Race* (1982), and *Slavery and Freedom: An Interpretation of the Old South* (1990); Anne Firor Scott, *The Southern Lady: From Pedestal to Politics, 1830–1930* (1970); Steven M. Stowe, *Intimacy and Power in the Old South* (1987); Michael Tadman, *Speculators and Slaves: Masters, Traders, and Slaves in the Old South* (1989); Ronald T. Takaki, *A Pro-Slavery Crusade: The Agitation to Reopen the African Slave Trade* (1971); William R. Taylor, *Cavalier and Yankee: The Old South and the American National Character* (1961); Larry E. Tise, *Proslavery: A History of the Defense of Slavery* (1987); Jack K. Williams, *Dueling in the Old South* (1980); Harold D. Woodman, *King Cotton & His Retainers: Financing & Marketing the Cotton Crop of the South, 1800–1825* (1968); Ralph A. Wooster, *The People in Power: Courthouse and Statehouse in the Lower South, 1850–1860* (1969), and *Politicians, Planters, and Plain Folk: Courthouse and Statehouse in the Upper South, 1850–1860* (1975); Gavin Wright, *The Political Economy of the Cotton South* (1978); Bertram Wyatt-Brown, *Southern Honor: Ethics and Behavior in the Old South* (1982).

Slavery

Ira Berlin, *Slaves Without Masters: The Free Negro in the Antebellum South* (1974); Eugene H. Berwanger, *The Frontier Against Slavery: Western Anti-Negro Prejudice and the Slavery Extension Controversy* (1967); John W. Blassingame, *The Slave Community: Plantation Life in the Antebellum South*, rev. ed. (1979), and *Slave Testimony: Two Centuries of Letters, Speeches, Interviews, and Autobiographies* (1977); Tommy L. Bogger, *Free Blacks in Norfolk, Virginia* (1997); John B. Boles, *Black Southerners, 1619–1869* (1983); John H. Bracey, Jr., August Meier, and Elliott Rudwick, eds., *American Slavery: The Question of Resistance* (1971); James O. Breeden, ed., *Advice Among Masters: The Ideal in Slave Management in the Old South* (1980); Michael Craton, ed., *Roots and Branches: Current Directions in Slave Studies* (1979); Daniel J. Crowley, ed., *African Folklore in the New World* (1977); Leonard P. Curry, *The Free Black in Urban America, 1800–1850* (1981); Paul A. David et al., eds., *Reckoning with Slavery* (1976); Charles B. Dew, "The Slavery Experience," in John B. Boles and Evelyn Thomas Nolen, eds., *Interpreting Southern History* (1987); Seymour Drescher and Stanley Engerman, eds., *A Historical Guide to World Slavery* (1998); Douglas R. Egerton, *Gabriel's Rebellion* (1993); Dena J. Epstein, *Sinful Tunes and Spirituals: Black Folk Music to the Civil War* (1977); Paul D. Escott, *Slavery Remembered* (1979); Patience Essah, *A House Divided: Slavery and Emancipation in Delaware* (1996); Paul Finkelman and Joseph C. Miller, eds., *Macmillan Encyclopedia of World Slavery* (1998); Robert William Fogel, *Without Consent or Contract: The Rise and Fall of American Slavery* (1989); John Hope Franklin and Loren Schweninger, *Runaway Slaves* (1999); David Barry Gaspar and Darlene Clark Hine, eds., *More Than Chattel: Black Women and Slavery in the Americas* (1996); Eugene D. Genovese, *From Rebellion to Revolution: Afro-American Slave Revolts in the Making of the Modern World* (1979), and *Roll, Jordan, Roll: The World the Slaves Made* (1974); Claudia D. Goldin, *Urban Slavery in the American South, 1820–1860* (1976); Michael A. Gomez, *Exchanging Our Country Marks: The Transformation of African Identities* (1998); Virginia Meacham Gould, ed., *Chained to the Rock of Adversity: To Be Free, Black, and Female in the Old South* (1998); Herbert G. Gutman, *The Black Family in Slavery and Freedom, 1750–1925* (1976), and *Slavery and the Numbers Game* (1975); Janet Sharp Hermann, *The Pursuit of a Dream* (1981); Peter P. Hinks, *To Awaken My Afflicted Brethren: David Walker and the Problem of American Slave Resistance* (1996); Graham Russell Hodges, *Slavery and Freedom in the Rural North* (1997); Joseph E. Holloway, *Africanisms in American Culture* (1990); James Oliver Horton, *Free People of Color* (1993); James O. Horton and Lois E. Horton, *In Hope of Liberty: Culture, Community and Protest Among Northern Free Blacks* (1997); Larry Hudson, *To Have and To Hold: Slave Work and Family Life* (1997); Michael P. Johnson and James L. Roark, *Black Masters: A Free Family of Color in the Old South* (1984), and eds., *No Chariot Let Down: Charleston's Free People of Color on the Eve of the Civil War* (1984); James Hugo Johnston, *Race Relations in Virginia & Miscegenation in the South, 1776–1860* (1970); Jacqueline Jones, *Labor of Love, Labor of Sorrow* (1985); Charles Joyner, *Down by the Riverside: A South Carolina Slave Community* (1984); Wilma King, *Stolen Childhood: Slave Youth in Nineteenth-Century America* (1995); Kenneth F. Kiple and Virginia Himmelsteib King, *Another Dimension to the Black Diaspora: Diet, Disease, and Racism* (1981); Peter Kolchin, *American Slavery* (1993); Lawrence Levine, *Black Culture and Black Consciousness* (1977); Ronald L. Lewis, *Coal, Iron, and Slaves* (1979); Leon Litwack, *North of Slavery: The Negro in the Free States* (1961); Donald G. Mathews, *Religion in the Old South* (1977); Stephanie McCurry, *Masters of Small Worlds: Yeoman Households, Gender Relations, and the Political Culture of the Antebellum South Carolina Low Country* (1995); Joanne Pope Melish, *Disowning Slavery: Gradual*

Emancipation and "Race" in New England, 1780–1860 (1998); Randall M. Miller and John David Smith, *Dictionary of Afro-American Slavery* (1997); Gary B. Mills, *The Forgotten People: Cane River's Creoles of Color* (1977); Thomas D. Morris, *Southern Slavery and the Law* (1996); Patricia Morton, ed., *Discovering the Women in Slavery* (1996); Michael Mullin, ed., *American Negro Slavery* (1976); Gary B. Nash, *Forging Freedom: The Formation of Philadelphia's Black Community* (1988); Gary B. Nash and Jean R. Soderlund, *Freedom by Degrees: Emancipation and Its Aftermath in Pennsylvania* (1991); Stephen B. Oates, *The Fires of Jubilee: Nat Turner's Fierce Rebellion* (1975); Leslie Howard Owens, *This Species of Property: Slave Life and Culture in the Old South* (1976); Stephan Palmié, ed., *Slave Cultures and the Culture of Slavery* (1995); Peter J. Parish, *Slavery: History and Historians* (1989); Jane H. and William H. Pease, *They Who Would Be Free: Blacks' Search for Freedom, 1830–1861* (1990); Richard Price, ed., *Maroon Societies: Rebel Slave Communities in the Americas*, 2d ed. (1979); Albert J. Raboteau, *Slave Religion: The "Invisible Institution" in the Antebellum South* (1978); George P. Rawick, *From Sundown to Sunup: The Making of the Black Community* (1972); Junius P. Rodriguez, *Historical Encyclopedia of World Slavery* (1997); Willie Lee Rose, ed., *A Documentary History of Slavery in North America* (1976), and *Slavery and Freedom* (1982); Todd L. Savitt, *Medicine and Slavery* (1978); William K. Scarborough, *The Overseer: Plantation Management in the Old South* (1966); Mark M. Smith, *Debating Slavery* (1998); Kenneth M. Stampp, *The Peculiar Institution: Slavery in the Antebellum South* (1956); Robert S. Starobin, ed., *Denmark Vesey: The Slave Conspiracy of 1822* (1970), and *Industrial Slavery in the Old South* (1970); Dorothy Sterling, ed., *We Are Your Sisters: Black Women in the Nineteenth Century* (1984); Brenda E. Stevenson, *Life in Black and White: Family and Community in the Slave South* (1996); Sterling Stuckey, *Slave Culture* (1987); Midori Takagi, "Rearing Wolves to Our Own Destruction": *Slavery in Richmond, Virginia* (1999); Mark Tushnet, *The American Law of Slavery, 1810–1860* (1981); William L. Van Deburg, *The Slave Drivers* (1979); Michael Vlach, *The Afro-American Tradition in Decorative Arts* (1978); Richard C. Wade, *Slavery in the Cities: The South 1820–1860* (1964); Alan Watson, *Slave Law in the Americas* (1989); Thomas L. Webber, *Deep Like the Rivers: Education in the Slave Quarter Community, 1831–1865* (1978); Marli F. Weiner, *Mistresses and Slaves* (1998); Steven Weisenberger, *Modern Medea: A Family Story of Slavery and Child-Murder in the Old South* (1998); Deborah Gray White, *Ar'n't I a Woman: Female Slaves in the Plantation South* (1985); T. Stephen Whitman, *The Price of Freedom: Slavery and Manumission in Baltimore* (1997); Joel Williamson, *New People: Miscegenation and Mulattoes in the United States* (1980); Donald R. Wright, *African Americans in the Early Republic* (1993).

Internet Resources

"Been Here So Long": Selections from the WPA American Slave Narratives
http://newdeal.feri.org/asn/index.htm
Slave narratives are some of the more interesting primary sources about slavery.

Exploring Amistad
http://amistad.mysticseaport.org/main/welcome.html
Mystic Seaport runs this site, which includes extensive collections of historical resources relating to the revolt and subsequent trial of enslaved Africans.

Africans in America: America's Journey Through Slavery
http://www.pbs.org/wgbh/aia/home.html
This PBS site contains images and documents recounting slavery in America.

Amistad Trials (1839–1840)
http://www.law.umkc.edu/faculty/projects/ftrials/amistad/AMISTD.HTM
Images, chronology, court and official documents comprise this site by Dr. Doug Linder at University of Missouri—Kansas City Law School.

Slave Narratives
http://metalab.unc.edu/docsouth/neh/neh.html
This site presents the telling narratives of several slaves, housed at the Documents of the American South collection and the University of North Carolina.

The Settlement of African Americans in Liberia
http://www.loc.gov/exhibits/african/perstor.html
This site contains images and text relating to the colonization movement to return African Americans to Africa.

Underground Railroad
http://www.cr.nps.gov/delta/under.htm
Best and most extensive National Park Service site about the Underground Railroad, with special reference to the lower Mississippi Valley.

Key Terms

Eli Whitney (p. 320)

Plantation Legend (p. 331)

Slave Codes (p. 339)

Spirituals (p. 343)

Gabriel (p. 344)

Denmark Vesey (p. 344)

Nat Turner (p. 344)

Maroons (p. 344)

Hinton Rowan Helper (p. 346)

Review Questions

1. In what ways were Northerners and Southerners similar? In what ways were they different?

2. How was industrialization both a force for unity and a force for division in the pre–Civil War United States?

3. How did the northern economy change during the early nineteenth century?

4. Why did an increasing number of immigrants come to the United States during the 1840s and 1850s? Why did some Americans resent the immigrants?
5. How did the invention of the cotton gin affect southern society?
6. Why did some Southerners try to promote industry and a distinctive southern culture during the 1840s and 1850s?
7. Explain how the size of a plantation and the crop grown affected the conditions under which slaves worked and lived.
8. How were enslaved African Americans able to sustain a sense of dignity and independence under slavery? In what ways did they resist slavery?

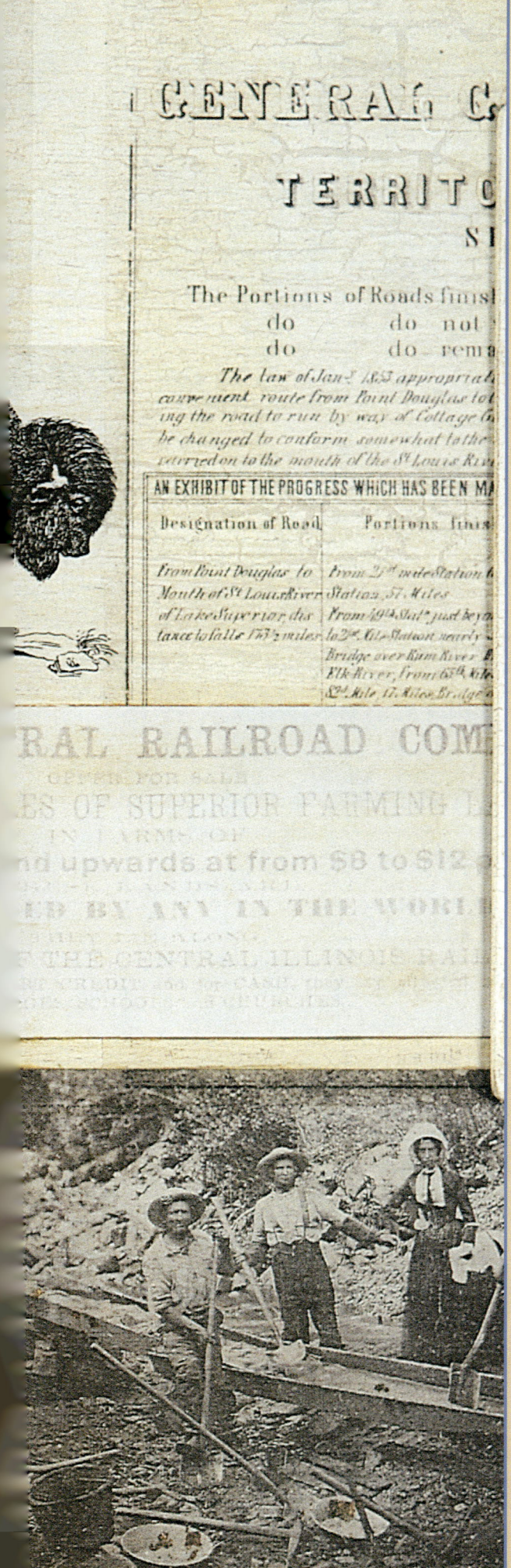

13

Cultures Collide in the Far West

The Hispanic and Native American West
- Spanish America
- The Mission System
- Impact of Mexican Independence
- Native Americans
- Impact of Contact

The Surge Westward
- Opening the West
- Pathfinders
- Mountain Men
- Trailblazing
- Settling the Far West
- Life on the Trail

Manifest Destiny
- Gone to Texas
- The Texas Question
- Webster-Ashburton Treaty
- Oregon
- The Mormon Frontier

War with Mexico
- Why War?
- The War
- War Fever and Antiwar Protests
- Peace
- The Fate of Mexican Americans
- The War's Significance
- Political Crisis of the 1840s
- The Gold Rush

"Vampires, in the guise of men"

In 1920 an enormously popular figure burst onto the Hollywood screen. Zorro, a California version of Robin Hood, was Hollywood's first swashbuckling hero. Played by some of Hollywood's biggest stars—including Douglas Fairbanks, Sr., and Tyrone Power—Zorro was a gifted horseman and master of disguise. He wore a mask, wielded a cape and a sword with panache, and announced his presence by slashing the letter Z on a wall. Like the legendary English outlaw, he robbed from the rich and gave to the poor—but he had a crucial difference: he was Hispanic. In more than a dozen feature films and a long-running Walt Disney television series, Don Diego Vegas, the son of a prominent wealthy California *alcalde* (administrator and judge), deeply resents the exploitation of California's peasants. He adopts the secret identity of Zorro, robs tax collectors, and returns the money to the poor.

Zorro was the fictional creation of a popular novelist named Johnston Culley. But the figure he portrayed—the social bandit protecting the interests of ordinary Mexicans (and later Mexican Americans) in the Southwest—was based on reality. Especially after Americans moved into the Southwest, many Mexicans struggled to preserve their culture, economy, and traditional rights. Some Mexicans in Texas and California—such as the legendary Joaquín Murieta—turned to banditry as a way to resist exploitation and avenge injustice. Though called *bandidos*, these figures did not rob banks or stage coaches; instead, they sought to protect the rights and interests of poorer Mexicans and Mexican Americans.

One of the most famous social bandits was Juan Nepomuceno Cortina of Texas. Born in 1824 to a wealthy, established family, Cortina fought for Mexico in its war with the United States, between 1846 and 1848. After the war, he saw many Mexicans reduced to second-class citizenship, mistreated by local police officers and Texas Rangers, and cheated out of their cattle and land. "Flocks of vampires, in the guise of men," he wrote, robbed Mexicans "of

Joaquín Murieta turned to banditry to avenge the mistreatment of Mexicans in California.

their property, incarcerated, chased, murdered, and hunted [them] like wild beasts." In July 1859, he saw a marshal in Brownsville beating a Mexican farmhand. Cortina ordered the marshal to stop, and when he refused, shot him in the shoulder. Then, in September, Cortina and other Mexicans raided Brownsville, proclaimed a Republic of the Rio Grande, and raised the Mexican flag. A force consisting of Texas Rangers and the United States Army eventually forced Cortina and his supporters to retreat into Mexico. Cortina would later serve as governor of the Mexican state of Tamaulipas.

Until recently, American popular culture presented the story of America's westward expansion largely from the perspective of white Americans. Countless western novels and films depicted the westward movement primarily through the eyes of explorers, missionaries, soldiers, trappers, traders, and pioneers. Theodore Roosevelt captured their perspective in a book entitled *The Winning of the*

West, an epic tale of white civilization conquering the western wilderness. But there are other sides to the story. To properly understand America's surge to the Pacific, one must understand it from multiple perspectives, including the viewpoint of the people who already inhabited the region: Mexicans and Native Americans.

THE HISPANIC AND NATIVE AMERICAN WEST

When Americans ventured westward, they did not enter uninhabited land. Large parts of the Far West were inhabited by Native Americans and Mexicans, who had lived on those lands for hundreds of years and established their own distinctive ways of life.

Spanish America

Until 1821, Spain ruled the area that now includes the states of Arizona, California, Colorado, Nevada, New Mexico, Texas, and Utah. Spanish explorers, priests, and soldiers first entered the area in the early sixteenth century, half a century before the first English colonists arrived at Jamestown. Between 1528 and 1800 Spain established imperial claims and isolated outposts in an area extending from Mexico to Montana and from California to the Mississippi River. Spain established permanent settlements in the region partly as a way to keep out other European powers. In the late sixteenth century, Spain planted a colony in New Mexico and a century later built the first settlements in what is now Arizona and Texas. In the late eighteenth century, fears of British and Russian occupation of the Pacific Coast led Spain also to establish outposts in California.

Unlike England or France, Spain did not actively encourage settlement or economic development in its northern empire. Instead, Spain concentrated much of its energies in Mexico. Spain restricted manufacturing and trade and discouraged migration to regions north of Mexico. In 1821, the year Mexico gained its independence, Spanish settlement was concentrated in just four areas: in southern Arizona, along California's coast, in New Mexico, and in Texas. Santa Fe, Spain's largest settlement, had only 6000 Spanish inhabitants, and San Antonio a mere 1500.

Despite these small numbers, Spain would leave a lasting cultural imprint on the entire region. Such institutions as the rodeo and the cowboy (the *vaquero*) had their roots in Spanish culture. Place names, too, bear witness to the Spanish heritage: Los Angeles, San Diego, and San Francisco were founded by Spanish explorers and priests. To this day, Spanish architecture—adobe walls, tile roofs, wooden beams, and intricate mosaics—continues to characterize the Southwest. By introducing horses and livestock, Spanish colonists and missionaries transformed the southwestern economy and that area's physical appearance. As livestock devoured the region's tall, native grasses, a new and distinctively southwestern environment arose, one of cactus, sagebrush, and mesquite.

The first American cowboys borrowed the clothing and customs of Mexican cowhands known as *vaqueros*.

Between 1769 and 1823, Spain built 21 missions between San Diego and San Francisco. Here Native Americans perform a dance at the San Francisco mission in 1816.

California Missions

Mission life reached its peak of development in California.

The Mission System

The Spanish clergy, particularly Jesuits and Franciscans, played a critical role in settling the Southwest using the mission system. Their missions were designed to spread Christianity among, and establish control over, native populations. In some areas, they forced Indians to live in mission communities, where the priests taught them weaving, blacksmithing, candle-making, and leather-working, and forced them to work in orchards, workshops, and fields for long hours. The missions were most successful in New Mexico (despite an Indian revolt in 1680) and California and far less successful in Arizona and Texas.

Mission life reached its peak in California, an area Spain did not begin to colonize until 1769. Spain built 21 missions between 1769 and 1823, extending from San Diego northward to Sonoma. By 1830, 30,000 of California's 300,000 Native Americans worked on missions, where they harvested grain and herded 400,000 cattle, horses, goats, hogs, and sheep.

Impact of Mexican Independence

By the early nineteenth century, resistance to Spanish colonial rule was growing. In 1810, Miguel Hidalgo y Costilla, a Mexican priest, led a revolt against Spain, which, although short-lived, represented the beginning of Mexico's struggle for independence. Mexican independence was finally achieved in 1821.

The War of Independence marked the beginning of a period of far-reaching change in the Southwest. Among the most important consequences of the collapse of Spanish rule was the opening of the region to American economic penetration. Mexican authorities in New Mexico and Arizona allowed American

After it won its independence from Spain, Mexico secularized the missions and divided the land into ranchos. This painting shows a master of a rancho in the Mexican Southwest.

traders to bring American goods into the area and trappers to hunt for beaver. Texas and California were also opened to American commerce and settlement. By 1848, Americans made up about half of California's non-Indian population.

Mexican independence also led to the demise of the mission system. After the revolution the missions were "secularized"—broken up and their property sold or given away to private citizens. In 1833–1834, the Mexican government confiscated California mission properties and exiled the Franciscan friars. As a result, mission properties fell into private hands. By 1846, mission land and cattle had passed into the hands of 800 private landowners called *rancheros*, who controlled 8 million acres of land in units called *ranchos*, which ranged in size from 4500 to 50,000 acres. These ranchos were run like feudal estates. They were worked by Native Americans, who were treated like slaves. Indeed, the death rate of Native Americans who worked on ranchos was twice that among southern slaves.

Comanche Chasing Buffalo with Bows and Lances, by George Catlin. Catlin lived in many different nations of the Plains and produced an important record of Native American life, both in his book *Letters and Notes on the Manners, Customs and Condition of the North American Indians*, published in 1841, and in hundreds of sketches, engravings, and paintings.

Native Americans

In 1840, before large numbers of pioneers and farmers crossed the Mississippi, at least 300,000 people lived in the Southwest, on the Great Plains, in California, and on the northwest Pacific Coast. This population was divided into more than 200 nations whose lifestyles ranged from sedentary farming to nomadic hunting and gathering. Their social organization was equally diverse, each nation having its own language, religious beliefs, kinship patterns, and system of government.

The best-known of the western Indians are the 23 Indian tribes—including the Cheyenne and Sioux—who lived on the Great Plains and hunted buffalo, antelope, deer, and elk for subsistence. For many present-day Americans, the Plains Indians, riding on horseback, wearing warbonnets, and living in tepees, are regarded as the typical American Indians. In fact, however, the Plains Indians first acquired the horse from the Spanish in the sixteenth century. Not until the middle of the eighteenth century did these tribes have a large supply of horses and not until the early to mid-nineteenth century did most Plains Indians have firearms.

South and west of the Plains, in the huge, arid region that is now Arizona and New Mexico, sophisticated farmers, like the Hopi, Zuni, and other Pueblo groups, coexisted alongside migratory hunters, like the Apaches and Navajos. In the Great Basin, the harsh barren region between the Sierra Nevada and the Rocky Mountains, nations like the Paiutes and the Gosiutes lived on berries, nuts, roots, insects, and reptiles.

More than 100,000 Native Americans lived in California when the area was acquired by the United States in 1848. Most lived in small villages in the winter but moved during the rest of the year gathering wild plants and seeds, hunting small game, and fishing in the ocean and rivers.

The large number of tribes living along the northwest Pacific Coast developed an elaborate social hierarchy based on wealth and descent. These people found an abundant food supply in the sea, coastal rivers, and forests. They took salmon, seal, whale, and otter from the coastal waters and hunted deer, moose, and elk in the forests.

Impact of Contact

Contact with white traders, trappers, and settlers caused a dramatic decline in Native American populations. In California, disease and deliberate campaigns of extermination on the part of settlers killed 70,000 Native Americans between 1849 and 1859. In the Great Basin, trappers shot Gosiutes and Paiutes for sport. In Texas, the Karankawas and many other nations in the area largely disappeared. Further west, Comanche, Kiowa, and Apache warriors bitterly resisted white encroachment on their land.

Nations in the Pacific Northwest and northern Plains struggled desperately to slow the pioneers' surge westward. The Nez Perce and Flathead nations expelled American missionaries from their lands, and the Snake, Cheyenne, Shasta, and Rogue River nations tried futilely to cut emigrant roots. The federal government employed the army to protect pioneers and forced western Native Americans to cede 147 million acres of land to the United States between 1853 and 1857.

THE SURGE WESTWARD

Early in April 1846, 87 pioneers led by George Donner, a well-to-do 62-year-old farmer, set out from Illinois for California. As this group of pioneers headed westward, they never imagined the hardship that awaited them. Like many emigrants, they were ill-prepared for the dangerous trek. The pioneers' 27 wagons were loaded not only with necessities, but with fancy foods, liquor, and such luxuries as built-in beds and stoves.

In Wyoming, the party decided to take a shortcut, having read in a guidebook that pioneers could save 400 miles by cutting south of the Great Salt Lake. At first the trail was "all that could be desired," but soon huge boulders and dangerous mountain passes slowed the expedition to a crawl. During one stretch, the party traveled only 36 miles in 21 days. In late October, the Donner party reached the eastern Sierra Nevada and prepared to cross the Truckee Pass, the last remaining barrier before they arrived in California's Sacramento Valley. They climbed the high Sierra ridges in an attempt to cross the pass, but early snows blocked their path.

Trapped, the party built crude tents covered with clothing, blankets, and animal hides, which were soon buried under 14 feet of snow. The pioneers intended to slaughter their livestock for food, but many of the animals perished in 40-foot snowdrifts. To survive, the Donner party was forced to eat mice, their rugs, and even their shoes. In the end, surviving members of the party escaped starvation only by eating the flesh of those who died.

Finally, in mid-December, 17 men and women made a last-ditch effort to cross the pass to find help. They took only a six-day supply of rations, consisting of finger-sized pieces of dried beef—two pieces per person per day. During a severe storm two of the group died. The surviving members of the party "stripped the flesh from their bones, roasted and ate it, averting their eyes from each other, and weeping." More than a month passed before seven frostbitten survivors reached an American settlement. By then, the rest had died and two Native American guides had been shot and eaten.

Relief teams immediately sought to rescue the pioneers still trapped near Truckee Pass. The situation that the rescuers found was unspeakably gruesome. Surviving members of the Donner party were delirious from hunger and overexposure. One survivor was found in a small cabin next to the cannibalized body of a young boy. Of the original 87 members of the party, only 47 survived.

Donner Party
Western emigrants like the Donner party were ill-prepared for the dangers of travel to the Far West.

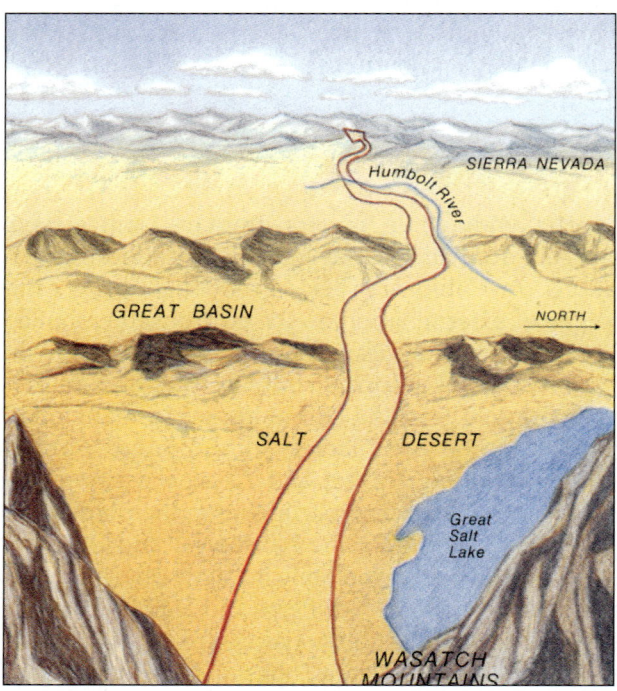

Margaret Reed was one of only 47 survivors of the original party of 87 pioneers to reach California.

It took white Americans a century and a half to expand as far west as the Appalachian Mountains, a few hundred miles from the Atlantic coast. It took another 50 years to push the frontier to the Mississippi river. By 1830, fewer than 100,000 pioneers had crossed the Mississippi.

During the 1840s, however, tens of thousands of Americans ventured beyond the Mississippi River. Inspired by the new vision of the West as a paradise of plenty, filled with fertile valleys and rich land, thousands of families chalked GTT ("Gone to Texas") on their gates or painted "California or Bust" on their wagons and joined the trek westward. By 1850 pioneers had pushed the edge of American settlement all the way to Texas, the Rocky Mountains, and the Pacific Ocean.

Opening the West

Before the nineteenth century, mystery shrouded the Far West. Mapmakers knew very little about the shape, size, or topography of the land west of the Mississippi River. French, British, and Spanish trappers, traders, and missionaries had traveled the Upper and Lower Missouri River, and the British and Spanish had explored the Pacific Coast, but most of western North America was unknown to white Americans or Europeans.

The popular conception of the West was largely a mixture of legend and guesswork. Even educated people like Thomas Jefferson believed that the West was populated by primeval beasts, that a "Northwest Passage" connected the Missouri River and the Pacific Ocean, and that only a single ridge of mountains, known as the "Stony Mountains," needed to be crossed before one could see the Pacific Ocean.

Pathfinders

In 1803, President Thomas Jefferson appointed his personal secretary, Meriwether Lewis, and William Clark, a former U.S. military officer, to explore the Missouri and Columbia rivers as far as the Pacific Ocean. As a politician interested in the rapid settlement and commercial development of the West, Jefferson wanted Lewis and Clark to establish American claims to the region west of the Rocky Mountains, gather information about furs and minerals in the region, and identify sites for trading posts and settlements. The president also instructed the expedition to collect information covering the diversity of life in the West, ranging from climate, geology, and plant growth to fossils of extinct animals and Indian religions, laws, and customs.

Guided by the Native American woman Sacajewa, Meriweather Lewis and army captain William Clark led a party of 34 soldiers and 10 civilians up the Missouri River, across the northern Rocky Mountains, and along the tributaries of the Columbia river to the Pacific Ocean. Sergeant Patrick Glass, a member of the expedition, kept a journal recording the events and adventures of the two-year journey. This drawing shows Clark and his men building a line of huts.

In 1806, the year that Lewis and Clark returned from their 8000-mile expedition, a young army lieutenant named Zebulon Pike left St. Louis to explore the southern border of the Louisiana Territory, just as Lewis and Clark had explored the territory's northern portion. Traveling along the Arkansas River, Pike saw the towering peak that bears his name. He and his party then traveled into Spanish territory along the Rio Grande and Red River. Pike's description of the wealth of Spanish towns in the Southwest attracted American traders to the region.

Pike's report of his expedition, published in 1810, helped to create one of the most influential myths about the Great Plains: that this region was nothing more than a "Great American Desert," a treeless and waterless land of dust storms and starvation. "Here," wrote Pike, is "barren soil, parched and dried up for eight months of the year... [without] a speck of vegetation." This image of the West as a region of wild beasts and deserts received added support from another government-sponsored expedition, one led by Major Stephen H. Long in 1820 in search of the source of the Red River. Long's report described the West as "wholly unfit for cultivation, and ... uninhabitable by a people depending upon agriculture for their subsistence." This report helped implant the image of the "Great American Desert" even more deeply in the American mind, retarding western settlement for a generation.

The view of the West as a dry, barren wasteland was not fully offset until the 1840s when another government-sponsored explorer, John C. Frémont, mapped much of the territory between the Mississippi Valley and the Pacific Ocean. His glowing descriptions of the West as a paradise of plenty captivated the imagination of many midwestern families who, by the 1840s, were eager for new lands to settle.

Mountain Men

Traders and trappers were more important than government explorers in opening the West to white settlement. Mountain men trapped beaver and bartered with Native Americans for pelts. They blazed the great western trails through the Rockies and Sierra Nevada and stirred the popular imagination with stories of redwood forests, geysers, and fertile valleys in California and Oregon. These men also undermined the ability of western Native Americans to resist white incursions by making them dependent on manufactured goods and pitting tribes against one another. They killed off animals that provided a major part of the Great Plains hunting economy, distributed alcohol, and spread disease.

When Lewis and Clark completed their expedition, they brought back reports of rivers and streams teeming with beaver and otter in the northern Rockies. Starting in 1807, keelboats ferried fur trappers up the Missouri River. By the mid-1830s these "mountain men" had marked out the overland trails that would lead pioneers to Oregon and California.

The Rocky Mountain Fur Company played a central role in opening the western fur trade. Instead of buying skins from the Native Americans, the company ran ads in St. Louis newspapers asking for white trappers willing to go to the wilderness. In 1822, it sent a hundred trappers along the upper Missouri River. Three years later the company introduced the "rendezvous" system, under which trappers met once a year at an agreed-on meeting place to barter pelts for supplies. "The rendezvous," wrote one participant, "is one continued scene of drunkenness, gambling, and brawling and fighting, as long as the money and the credit of the trappers last."

At the same time that mountain men searched for beaver in the Rockies and along the Columbia River, other groups trapped furs in the Southwest, at that time part of Mexico. In 1827, Jedediah Smith and a party of 15 trappers, after nearly dying of thirst, discovered a westward route to California. Jim Beckwourth, a mountain man who was the son of a Virginia slave, later discovered a pass through the Sierra Nevada that became part of the overland trail to California.

In 1827 Jedediah Smith led a party of trappers through Utah, across the Colorado River, then across the Mojave Desert and the San Bernardino Mountains to the Pacific.

The western fur trade lasted only until 1840, when the last annual rendezvous was held. Beaver hats for gentlemen went out of style in favor of silk hats; thus the era of the mountain man, dressed in a fringed buckskin suit, came to an end. Fur-bearing animals had been trapped out, and profits from trading, which amounted to as much as 2000 percent during the early years, fell steeply. Instead of hunting furs, some trappers became scouts for the United States Army or pilots for the wagon trains that were beginning to carry pioneers to California and Oregon.

Trailblazing

The Santa Fe and Oregon trails were the two principal routes to the Far West. William Becknell, an American trader, opened the Santa Fe Trail in 1821. His 800-mile journey from Missouri to Santa Fe took two months. When he could find no water, Becknell drank blood from a mule's ear and the contents of a buffalo's stomach. Ultimately, the trail tied the New Mexican Southwest economically to the United States and hastened American penetration of the region.

The Santa Fe Trail served primarily commercial functions. From the early 1820s until the 1840s, an average of 80 wagons and 150 traders used the trail each year. Mexican settlers in Santa Fe purchased cloth, hardware, glass, and books. On their return east, American traders carried Mexican blankets, beaver pelts, wool, mules, and silver. By the 1830s, traders had extended the trail into California with branches reaching Los Angeles and San Diego. By the 1850s and 1860s more than 5000 wagons a year took the trail across long stretches of desert, dangerous water crossings, and treacherous mountain passes. The Santa Fe Trail made the New Mexican Southwest economically dependent on the United States and brought Americans into the areas that became Arizona, California, and New Mexico.

In 1811 and 1812 fur trappers marked out the Oregon Trail, the longest and most famous pioneer route in American history. This trail crossed about 2000 miles from Independence, Missouri, to the Columbia River country of Oregon. During the 1840s, 12,000 pioneers traveled the trail's entire length to Oregon.

Travel on the Oregon Trail was a tremendous test of human endurance. The journey by wagon train took six months. Settlers encountered prairie fires, sudden blizzards, and impassable mountains. Cholera and other diseases were common; food, water, and wood were scarce. Only the stalwart dared brave the physical hardship of the westward trek.

Settling the Far West

During the 1840s thousands of pioneers headed westward toward California and Oregon. In 1841, the first party of 69 pioneers left Missouri for California, led by an Ohio schoolteacher named John Bidwell. The members of the party knew little about western travel: "We only knew that California lay to the west." The hardships the party endured were nearly unbearable. They were forced to abandon their wagons and eat their pack animals, "half roasted, dripping with blood." But American pioneering of the Far West had begun. Over the next 25 years, 350,000 more made the trek along the overland trails.

The rugged pioneer life was not a new experience for most of the early western settlers. Most pioneers migrated to the Far West from states that border the Mississippi River—Arkansas, Illinois, Louisiana, and Missouri—which had only recently acquired statehood. Either these settlers or their parents had already moved several times before reaching the Mississippi Valley.

Life on the Trail

Each spring, pioneers gathered at Council Bluffs, Iowa, and Independence and St. Joseph, Missouri, to

Western Trails

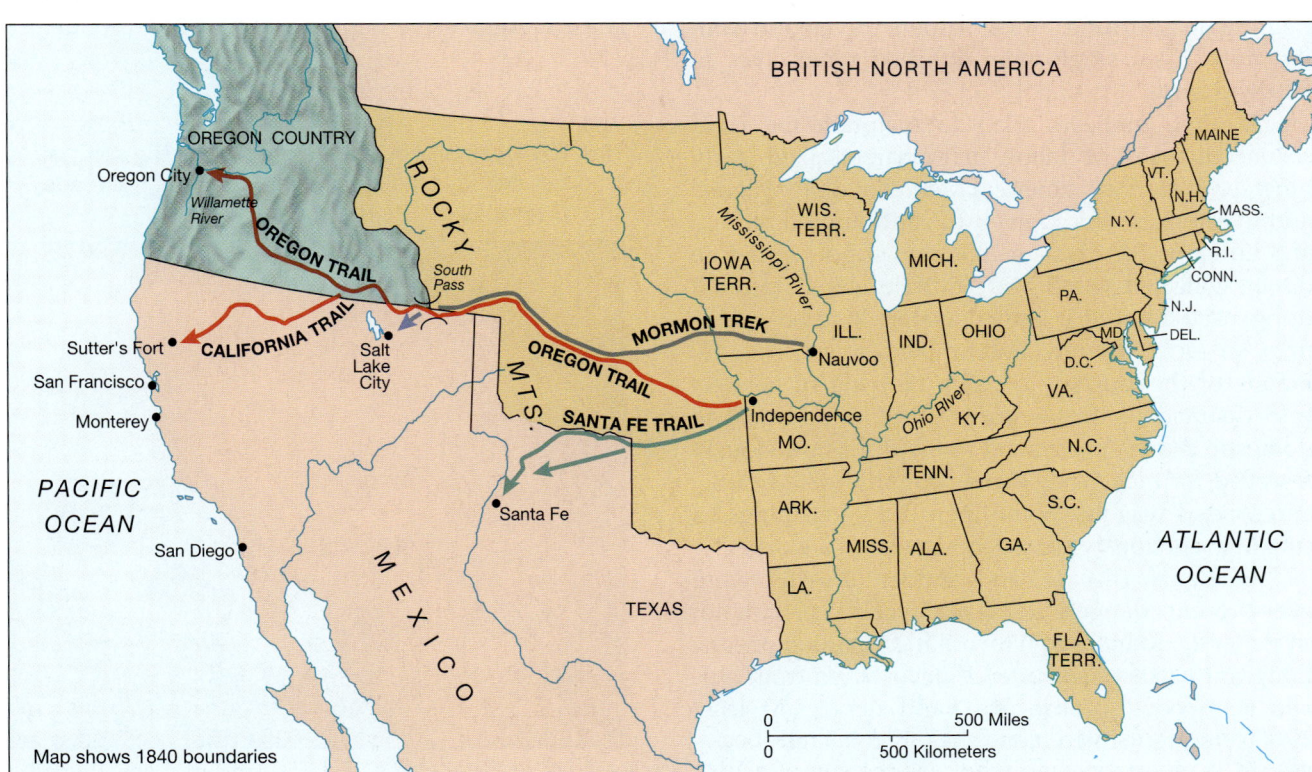

Life along the westward trails was a tremendous test of human endurance. Pioneers encountered arid desert, difficult mountain passes, dangerous rivers, and quicksand.

begin a 2000-mile journey westward. For many families, the great spur for emigration was economic. The financial depression of the late 1830s, accompanied by floods and epidemics in the Mississippi Valley, forced many to pull up stakes and head west. Said one woman: "We had nothing to lose, and we might gain a fortune." Most settlers traveled in family units. Even single men attached themselves to family groups.

At first, pioneers tried to maintain the rigid sexual division of labor that characterized early nineteenth-century America. Men drove the wagons and livestock, stood guard duty, and hunted buffalo and antelope for extra meat. Women got up before dawn, collected wood and "buffalo chips" (animal dung used for fuel), hauled water, kindled campfires, kneaded dough, and milked cows. The demands of the journey forced a blurring of gender-role distinctions for women who, in addition to domestic chores, performed many duties previously reserved for men. They drove wagons, yoked cattle, and loaded wagons. Some men did such things as cooking, previously regarded as women's work.

Accidents, disease, and sudden disaster were ever-present dangers. Diseases such as typhoid, dysentery, and mountain fever killed many pioneers. Emigrant parties also suffered devastation from buffalo stampedes, prairie fires, and floods. At least 20,000 emigrants died along the Oregon Trail.

Still, despite the hardships of the experience, few emigrants ever regretted their decision to move west. As one pioneer put it: "Those who crossed the plains . . . never forgot the ungratified thirst, the intense heat and bitter cold, the craving hunger and utter physical exhaustion of the trail. . . . But there was another side. True they had suffered, but the satisfaction of deeds accomplished and difficulties overcome more than compensated and made the overland passage a thing never to be forgotten."

MANIFEST DESTINY

In 1845 an editor named John L. O'Sullivan referred in a magazine to America's "manifest destiny to overspread the continent allotted by Providence for the free development of our yearly multiplying millions." One of the most influential slogans ever coined, the term *manifest destiny* expressed the romantic emotion that led Americans to risk their lives to settle the Far West.

The idea that America had a special destiny to stretch across the continent motivated many people to migrate west. Manifest destiny inspired a 29-year-old named Stephen F. Austin to talk of grandly colonizing the Mexican province of Texas with "North American population, enterprise and intelligence." It led expansionists—united behind the slogan "54°40' or fight!"—to demand that the United States should own the entire Pacific Northwest all the way to Alaska. Aggressive nationalists invoked the idea to

This 1879 painting by John Gast depicts the spirit of manifest destiny leading pioneers, farmers, railroads, and telegraphs across the continent.

justify the displacement of Native Americans from their land, war with Mexico, and American expansion into Cuba and Central America. More positively, the idea of manifest destiny also inspired missionaries, farmers, and pioneers, who dreamed only of transforming plains and fertile valleys into farms and small towns.

Gone to Texas

In 1822, when the first caravan of American traders traversed the Santa Fe Trail and the first hundred fur trappers searched the Rocky Mountains for beaver, a small number of Americans followed trails to another frontier—Texas.

American settlement in Texas began with the encouragement of first the Spanish and then the Mexican governments. In the summer of 1820, Moses Austin, a bankrupt 59-year-old Missourian, asked Spanish authorities for a large Texas land tract that he would promote and sell to American pioneers. The following year the Spanish government gave him permission to settle 300 families in Texas. Spain welcomed the Americans for two reasons—to provide a buffer against illegal U.S. settlers, who were creating problems in east Texas even before the grant was made to Austin, and to help develop the land, since only 3500 native Mexicans had settled in Texas (which was then part of the Mexican state of Coahuila y Tejas).

Moses Austin soon died, but his son Stephen carried out his dream to colonize Texas. By 1824, he had attracted 272 colonists to Texas and persuaded the new government of Mexico that encouragement of American immigration was the best way to develop the area. To promote colonization, Mexico in 1825 gave land agents 67,000 acres of land for every 200 families that they brought to Texas. Mexico imposed two conditions on land ownership: settlers had to become Mexican citizens and convert to Roman Catholicism. By 1830 there were 16,000 Americans in Texas.

As the Anglo population swelled, Mexican authorities grew increasingly suspicious of the growing American presence in Texas, and in 1827 the government sent General Manuel de Mier y Terán to investigate the situation. In his report Terán warned that unless the Mexican government took timely measures, American settlers in Texas were certain to rebel. Differences in language and culture, Terán believed, had produced bitter enmity between the colonists and native Mexicans. The colonists, he noted, refused to learn the Spanish language, maintained their own separate schools, and conducted

One of the most colorful leaders of the struggle for Texas independence, Sam Houston lived for a time with the Cherokee, was a popular hero of the Creek War, and later served as a congressman and governor of Texas.

San Jacinto Museum of History, Houston.

most of their trade with the United States. They complained bitterly that they had to travel more than 500 miles to reach a Mexican court and resented the efforts of Mexican authorities to deprive them of the right to vote.

To reassert its authority over Texas, the Mexican government reaffirmed its constitutional prohibition against slavery throughout Mexico, established a chain of military posts occupied by convict soldiers, levied customs duties, restricted trade with the United States, and decreed an end to further American immigration. These actions might have provoked Texans to revolution. But in 1832 **General Antonio López de Santa Anna** became Mexico's president. Colonists hoped that he would make Texas a self-governing state within the Mexican republic, separate from the much more populous Coahuila, thereby eliminating any reason for rebellion. Once in power, however, Santa Anna proved to be far less liberal than many Americans had be-

Antonio López de Santa Anna (1797–1876) dominated Mexican politics for 30 years following the country's independence from Spain, serving as president five times.

lieved. In 1834 he overthrew Mexico's constitutional government, abolished state governments, and made himself dictator. When Stephen Austin went to Mexico City to try to settle the Texans' grievances, Santa Anna imprisoned him in a Mexican jail for a year.

On November 3, 1835, American colonists adopted a constitution and organized a temporary government but voted overwhelmingly against declaring independence. A majority of settlers hoped to attract the support of Mexican liberals in a joint effort to depose Santa Anna and restore power to the state governments, hopefully including a separate state of Texas.

While holding out the possibility of compromise, the Texans prepared for war. The provisional government elected Sam Houston, a former Tennessee governor and close friend of Andrew Jackson, to lead whatever military forces he could muster. In the middle of 1835 scattered local outbursts erupted against Mexican rule. Then, in 1836, a band of 300 to 500 Texans captured Mexico's military headquarters in San Antonio. The Texas Revolution was under way.

Soon the ominous news reached Texas that Santa Anna himself was marching north with 7000 soldiers to crush the revolt. In actuality, Santa Anna's army was not particularly impressive; it was filled with raw recruits and included many Maya American troops who spoke and understood little Spanish. When Houston learned that Santa Anna's initial goal was to recapture San Antonio, he ordered the city abandoned. But Texas rebels decided to defend the town and made their stand at an abandoned Spanish mission, the Alamo. The Texans were led by William Travis and Jim Bowie and included the frontier hero David Crockett.

For 12 days Mexican forces laid siege to the Alamo. At 5 A.M., March 6, 1836, Mexican troops scaled the mission's walls. By 8 A.M., the fighting was over. One hundred eighty-three defenders lay dead, including several Mexicans who had fought for Texas independence.

Two weeks after the defeat at the Alamo, James Fannin and his men surrendered to Mexican forces near Goliad with the understanding that they would be treated as prisoners of war. Instead, Santa Anna ordered more than 350 Texans shot.

These defeats, however, had an unexpected side effect. They gave Sam Houston time to raise and train an army. Volunteers from the American South flocked to his banner. On April 21 his army of less than 800 men surprised and utterly defeated Santa Anna's army as it camped out on the San Jacinto River, east of present-day Houston. The next day Houston's army captured Santa Anna himself and forced him to sign a treaty granting Texas its independence, a treaty that was never ratified by the Mexican government because it was acquired under duress.

For most Mexican settlers in Texas, defeat meant that they would be relegated to second-class social, political, and economic positions. The new Texas constitution denied citizenship and property rights to those who failed to support the revolution. All persons of Hispanic ancestry were considered in the "denial" category unless they could prove otherwise. Consequently, many Mexican landowners fled the region.

Texas grew rapidly following independence. In 1836, 5000 immigrants arrived in Texas, boosting its population to 30,000. By 1847 its population had reached 140,000. The region also grew economically. Although cotton farming dominated the Texas economy, cattle were becoming an increasingly important industry. Many Mexican landowners abandoned cattle after the Texas Revolution, and by the 1840s, large numbers of wild cattle roamed the range. By 1850, the first American cowboys were driving 60,000 cattle a year to New Orleans and California.

The Texas Question

Texas had barely won its independence when it decided to become a part of the United States. A referendum held soon after the Battle of San Jacinto showed Texans favoring annexation by a vote of 3277 to 93.

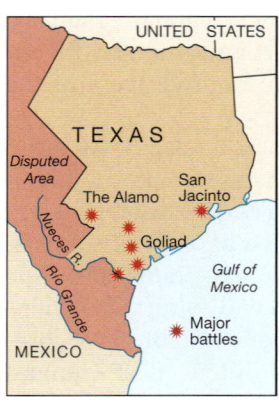

Texas Revolution

The revolution left Texas a lone republic, unrecognized by Mexico and unwanted by the United States.

The annexation question became one of the most controversial issues in American politics in the late 1830s and early 1840s. The issue was not Texas but slavery. The admission of Texas to the Union would upset the sectional balance of power in the U.S. Senate, just as the admission of Missouri had threatened 15 years earlier. President Andrew Jackson, acutely conscious of the opposition to admitting Texas as a slave state, agreed only to recognize Texan independence. In 1838, John Quincy Adams, then a member of the House of Representatives, staged a 22-day filibuster that successfully blocked annexation. It appeared that Congress had settled the Texas question. For the time being, Texas would remain an independent republic.

At this point, proslavery Southerners began to popularize a conspiracy theory that would eventually bring Texas into the Union as a slave state. In 1841 John Tyler, an ardent defender of slavery, succeeded to the presidency on the death of William Henry Harrison. Tyler and his secretary of state, John C. Calhoun, argued that Britain was scheming to annex Texas and transform it into a haven for runaway slaves. According to this theory, British slave emancipation in the West Indies had been a total economic disaster, and the British now hoped to undermine slavery in the American South by turning Texas into a British satellite state. In fact, British abolitionists, but not the British government, were working to convince Texas to outlaw slavery in exchange for British foreign aid. Sam Houston did his part to excite American fears by conducting highly visible negotiations with the British government. If the United States would not annex Texas, Houston warned, Texas would seek the support of "some other friend." In the spring of 1844 Calhoun hammered out an annexation treaty with Texas diplomats, but the agreement failed to gain the required two-thirds majority for Senate ratification.

The Texas question became the major political issue in the presidential campaign of 1844. **James K. Polk,** the Democratic candidate, was a strong supporter of annexation, and his victory encouraged Tyler to attempt to annex Texas again in the waning months of his administration. This time Tyler submitted the measure in the form of a resolution, which required only a simple majority of both houses. Congress narrowly approved the resolution in 1845, making Texas the twenty-eighth state.

Webster-Ashburton Treaty

Today, the 4000-mile United States–Canadian border is one of the world's most peaceful international boundaries. During the decades before the Civil War, by contrast, the border between the United States and British America was the scene of constant tensions. In 1837 many Americans viewed an insurrection in eastern Canada as an opportunity to annex the country. Americans who lived near the Canadian border aided the rebels, and in one incident several hundred western New Yorkers crossed into Canada and staged an abortive attack on a band of British soldiers. After British forces suppressed the uprising, New Yorkers provided safe haven for the insurrection's leaders. When the rebels began to launch raids into Canada from western New York State, Canadian officials crossed the U.S. border, killed a Canadian rebel, and burned an American ship, the *Caroline*, which had supplied the rebels. When Americans demanded an apology and reparations, Canadian officials refused. Almost immediately, another dispute erupted over the Maine boundary as American and Canadian lumberjacks and farmers battled for possession of northern Maine and western New Brunswick.

The Webster-Ashburton Treaty of 1842 settled these controversies. The treaty awarded the United States most of the disputed territory in Maine and New Brunswick and guaranteed free navigation on many rivers and lakes along the Canadian border. The Webster-Ashburton Treaty left one major border controversy unresolved: the Canadian-American boundary in the Pacific Northwest.

Oregon

Disputes between the United States and Britain over the "Oregon" country emerged early in the nineteenth century. In 1810 John Jacob Astor, an American who had made a fortune in the Great Lakes fur trade, decided to open a trading post, named Astoria, at the mouth of the Columbia River. He hoped the post would secure a monopoly over the western fur trade for shipping the furs to eager customers in China. The venture failed, however, and for nearly two decades the fur trade was dominated by the British Hudson's Bay Company.

As British fur traders expanded their activities in the Pacific Northwest, American politicians grew alarmed that Britain would gain sovereignty over the region. American diplomats moved quickly to solidify American claims to Oregon. Spain, Russia, Britain, and the United States all claimed rights to the Pacific Northwest. In 1818 Britain and the United States agreed that nationals of both countries could trade in the region; this agreement was renewed in 1827. In 1819 American negotiators persuaded Spain to cede its claims to Oregon to the United States, and

THE American Mosaic

Tejanos at the Alamo

GENERAL Antonio López de Santa Anna, backed by some 2400 Mexican troops, put the Alamo under siege on February 23, 1836. On that day Santa Anna ordered the hoisting of a red flag, meaning "no quarter," or no mercy toward potential prisoners of war. This only hardened the resolve of the Alamo's small contingent of defenders, including the legendary Jim Bowie, Davy Crockett, and William Barret Travis. Also inside the Alamo were men like Juan Seguin and Gregorio Esparza. They represented a handful of Tejano defenders. As native residents of Texas (named the province of Tejas in 1691 by the conquering Spanish), they despised Santa Anna for having so recently overthrown the Mexican Constitution of 1824 in favor of dictatorship.

San Antonio was a center of the Tejano population of Texas. Juan Seguin's father, Don Erasmo, was a wealthy local rancher who in earlier years had encouraged the opening of the Mexican province of Coahuila y Tejas to nonnatives from the United States. Most of the Americans settled far to the east of San Antonio, but those who traveled to the Tejano settlements knew Don Erasmo as a generous host who entertained lavishly at his *hacienda*, "Casa Blanca." His son Juan was also locally prominent and had helped immeasurably in driving Mexican troops under General Martin Perfecto de Cós, Santa Anna's brother-in-law, out of San Antonio late in 1835. His reward was a commission as a captain of Texas cavalry.

Much less is known about Gregorio Esparza. He lived with his wife and four children in San Antonio when Juan Seguin recruited him for his cavalry company. When Santa Anna's advance troops appeared on February 23, Esparza quickly gathered up his family and rushed for protection behind the thick walls of the old Spanish mission known locally as the Alamo.

The Alamo defenders were in an all but impossible position, especially with Santa Anna tightening his siege lines every day. Inside the Alamo, the defenders looked to Jim Bowie for leadership, but he was seriously ill with pneumonia. So they accepted orders from William Barret Travis. With 1000 troops, Travis had argued, the Alamo would never fall. His numbers, however, were hardly more than 150. As a result, Travis regularly sent out couriers with urgent messages for relief. His words were direct. He would never "surrender or retreat." He would "die like a soldier who never forgets what is due to his own honor and that of his country." For those at the Alamo, the alternatives were now "Victory or death."

Late in February Travis, who would gain only 32 troops as reinforcements, prepared yet another appeal, this time addressed to Sam Houston, commander-in-chief of the Texas army. Time was running out, Travis wrote. "If they overpower us," he explained, "we hope posterity and our country will do our memory justice. Give me help, oh my country!" Travis handed the message to Juan Seguin, who borrowed Jim Bowie's horse and rode off with his aide, Antonio Cruz, under the cover of a driving rainstorm. They eventually found Houston, far to the east, but there was nothing anyone could do now to save those defenders still with Travis.

Early on the morning of March 6, 1836, the Alamo fell to 1800 attacking Mexican soldiers. The fighting was so brutal that 600 of Santa Anna's troops lay dead or wounded before the last of the 183 defenders faced mutilation from countless musket balls, bayonet thrusts, or summary executions after the battle. Gregorio Esparza was torn to shreds as the Mexicans reached the church inside the courtyard. Only women, children, Colonel Travis's slave Joe, and one Tejano, who claimed that he was a prisoner, survived. Later that day Mrs. Esparza got permission to bury her husband with Christian rites. Santa Anna issued orders to have the bodies of all other defenders heaped into piles and set on fire.

During the next several weeks Santa Anna's troops pushed steadily eastward with the goal of destroying another Texas army being hastily assembled by Sam Houston. The Seguins, father and son, played key parts in providing resistance. Don Erasmo worked furiously to collect needed food supplies, and Juan led troops in harassing and delaying the Mexican column, all of which aided in the staging of Houston's stunning victory over Santa Anna at the Battle of San Jacinto on April 21, 1836—the day the Republic of Texas secured its independence.

As the Texas Revolution gained momentum in late 1835 and early 1836, Tejanos had to choose which side to support. Some hoped that uniting with the Americans would force Santa Anna to renounce his dictatorship in favor of the liberal 1824 constitution. Few Tejanos actually favored independence because they knew that Americans held them in

contempt. This caused men like Gregorio Esparza's brother to join Santa Anna's army and fight against the Alamo defenders. He suspected that heavy-handed rule under the Mexican dictator could not be worse and might well be better than living under culturally and racially intolerant Americans.

From the very outset, Americans entering Texas spoke of Tejanos and Mexicans as debased human beings, comparable in many ways to Native American "savages" blocking the westward movement of white European civilization. In 1831 colonizer Stephen F. Austin wrote: "My object, the sole and only desire of my ambitions since I first saw Texas, was to . . . settle it with an intelligent, honorable, and enterprising people." Four years later Austin still wanted to see Texas "Americanized, that is, settled by a population that will harmonize with their neighbors on the East, in language, political principles, common origin, sympathy, and even interest." The success of the Texas Revolution, from Austin's point of view, would ensure that Americans pouring into the region would not be ruled by what they considered an inferior native populace.

Increasingly, before and after 1836, American migrants employed terms of racial and cultural derision to describe the native Tejanos. They were the most "lazy, indolent, poor, starved set of people as ever the sun shined upon"; they were "slaves of popish superstitions and despotism"; and they would "spend days in gambling to gain a few bits" rather than "make a living by honest industry." With their mixture of blood from Spanish, Native American, and African parents, the native populace represented a "mongrel" race, a "swarthy looking people much resembling . . . mulattoes."

Worse yet, according to the Americans, they behaved at times like depraved, violent, less-than-human creatures as personified by Santa Anna at the Alamo and by Mexican troops later at Goliad, where nearly 400 captured rebels were systematically shot to death. Wrote one American veteran of the Texas Revolution late in life: "I thought that I could kill Mexicans as easily as I could deer and turkeys." He apparently did so while shouting: "Remember the Alamo! Remember Goliad!"

This veteran, like so many others looking back at the days of the Texas Revolution, only recalled selected portions of the Alamo story. They talked of the bravery of Bowie, Crockett, and Travis but ignored the courage of Tejanos like Don Erasmo and Juan Seguin and Gregorio Esparza. Nor did they remember that Juan Seguin received an honorable military discharge before serving as mayor of San Antonio until 1842, when Anglo rumormongers accused him of supporting an attempted military invasion from Mexico. To save himself, Seguin had to flee across the border. Eventually he returned to his native Texas and quietly lived out his days far removed from the public limelight. No doubt Seguin wondered whether he had made the right decision in not joining the side of Santa Anna, especially as he experienced the racial and cultural malice directed at Mexican Americans as the United States surged forward toward the Pacific. Although his thoughts are not known, it is fortunate that his story and those of other Tejano resisters have not been forgotten. Surely they too deserve remembrance as heroes of the Alamo and the Texas Revolution.

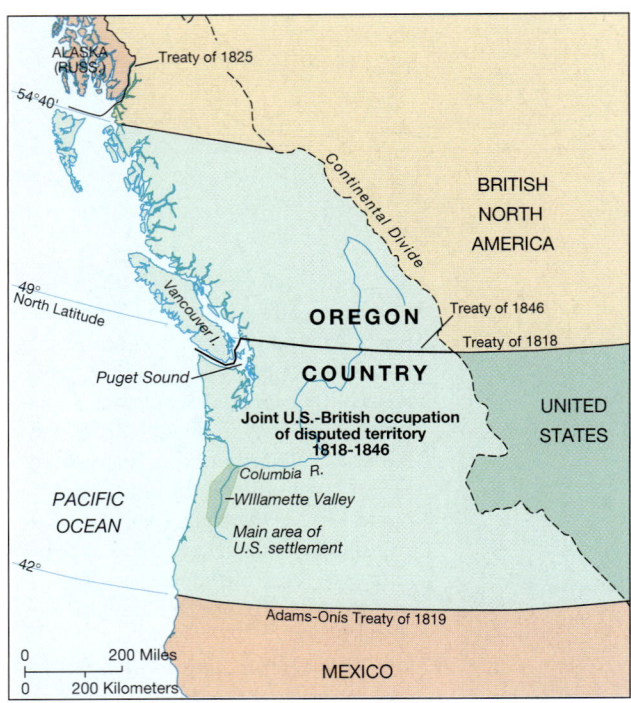

Oregon Country, Pacific Northwest Boundary Dispute

The United States and Great Britain nearly came to blows over the disputed boundary in Oregon.

two years later Secretary of State John Quincy Adams warned Russia that the United States would oppose any Russian attempts to occupy the territory.

But U.S. politicians, merchants, and fur traders were unsuccessful in promoting American settlement of Oregon. In the end, it was neither commerce nor politics, but religion that led to American settlement of the region.

The first missionaries arrived in Oregon in 1834. The most famous were Marcus Whitman, a young doctor, and his wife Narcissa Prentiss Whitman, who were sent west in 1836 by the Methodists. The couple founded a mission near present-day Walla Walla, Washington, and persisted in their efforts to convert Native Americans to Christianity until 1847, when a severe epidemic of measles broke out in the area. Many Native Americans blamed the epidemic on white missionaries, and the Whitmans and 12 others were murdered.

Before his death, Marcus Whitman made an epic 3000-mile journey to Boston, during which he publicized the attractions of the Pacific Northwest and the need to offset British influence in the region. On his return trip to Oregon in 1843, Whitman guided nearly 900 immigrants along the Oregon trail. By the mid-1840s, 6000 Americans had moved to Oregon.

The rapid influx of land-hungry Americans into Oregon in the mid-1840s forced Britain and the United States to decide the status of Oregon. In the presidential election of 1844, the Democratic party demanded the "re-occupation" of Oregon and the annexation of the entire Pacific Northwest coast up to the edge of Russian-held Alaska, which was fixed at 54°40'. This demand helped James K. Polk win the presidency in 1844.

In truth, Polk had little desire to go to war with Britain. As an ardent proslavery Southerner, he did not want to add new free states to the Union. Furthermore, he believed that the northernmost portions of the Oregon country were unsuitable for agriculture. Therefore, in 1846—despite the expansionist slogan "54°40' or fight!"—he readily accepted a British compromise to extend the existing United States–Canadian boundary along the 49th parallel from the Rocky Mountains to the Pacific Ocean.

The Mormon Frontier

Pioneers migrated to the West for a variety of reasons. Some moved west in the hope of economic and social betterment, others out of a restless curiosity and an urge for adventure. The Mormons migrated for an entirely different reason—to escape religious persecution.

The Mormon church had its beginnings in upstate New York, which was a hotbed of religious fervor. Methodist, Baptist, Presbyterian, and Universalist preachers all eagerly sought converts. Fourteen-year-old **Joseph Smith, Jr.**, the son of a farmer, listened closely to these preachers but was uncertain which way to turn.

In the spring of 1820, Smith went into the woods near Palmyra, New York, to seek divine guidance. According to his account, a brilliant light revealed "two personages," who announced that they were God the Father and Christ the Savior. They told him that all existing churches were false and that the true church of God was about to be reestablished on earth.

In 1823, Smith had another revelation that told him of the existence of buried golden plates that contained a lost section from the Bible describing a tribe of Israelites that had lived in America. Smith wrote that he unearthed the golden plates and four years later translated them into English. The messages on the plates were later published as the *Book of Mormon*.

By the 1830s Smith attracted several thousand followers from rural areas of the North and the frontier Midwest. The converts were usually small farmers, mechanics, and traders who had been displaced by the growing commercial economy and who were

Saints [Mormons] *Driven from Jackson County, Missouri*, by C. C. A. Christensen. Mormon settlements in Missouri were repeatedly attacked and destroyed by mobs between 1832 and 1839, when the Mormons moved to Illinois.

repelled by the rising tide of liberal religion and individualism in early nineteenth-century America.

Because Smith said that he conversed with angels and received direct revelations from God, local authorities threatened to indict him for blasphemy. He and his followers responded by moving to Ohio, where they built their first temple and experimented with an economy planned and controlled by the church. From Ohio, the Mormons moved to Missouri. There, proslavery mobs attacked the Mormons, accusing them of inciting slave insurrections. Fifteen thousand Mormons fled Missouri after the governor proclaimed them enemies who "had to be exterminated, or driven from the state."

In 1839, the Mormons resettled along the east bank of the Mississippi River in Nauvoo, Illinois, which soon grew into the second largest city in the state. Both Illinois Whigs and Democrats eagerly sought support among the Mormons, who usually voted as a bloc. In exchange for their votes, the state legislature awarded Nauvoo a special charter that made the town an autonomous city-state, complete with its own 2000-man militia.

But trouble arose again. A dissident group within the church published a newspaper denouncing the practice of polygamy and attacking Joseph Smith for trying to become "king or lawgiver to the church." On Smith's orders, city officials destroyed the dissidents' printing press. Under the protection of the Illinois governor, Smith and his brother were then confined to a jail cell in Carthage, Illinois. Late in the afternoon of June 27, 1844, a mob broke into Smith's cell, shot him and his brother, and threw their bodies out of a second-story window.

Why did the Mormons seem so menacing? Anti-Mormonism was rooted in a struggle for economic and political power. Individualistic frontier settlers felt threatened by Mormon communalism. By voting as their elders told them to and controlling land as a bloc, Mormons seemed to have an unfair advantage in the struggle for wealth and power.

Mormonism was also denounced as a threat to fundamental social values. Protestant ministers railed against it as a threat to Christianity because Mormons rejected the legitimacy of the established churches and insisted that the *Book of Mormon* was sacred Scripture, equal in importance to the Bible. The Mormons were also accused of corrupt moral values. Before the church changed its rules in 1890, some Mormons practiced polygyny, which they saw as an effort to reestablish the patriarchal Old Testament family. Polygamy also served an important social function by absorbing single or widowed women into Mormon communities. Contrary to popular belief, it was not widely practiced. Altogether, only 10 to 20 percent of Mormon families were polygamous and nearly two-thirds involved a man and two wives.

After Joseph Smith's murder, the Mormons decided to migrate across a thousand miles of unsettled prairie and desert in search of a new refuge outside the boundaries of the United States. In 1846 a new leader, **Brigham Young,** led the Mormons to the Great Salt Lake. As governor of the Mormon state of Deseret and later as governor of Utah, Young oversaw the building of Salt Lake City and 186 other Mormon communities, developed church-owned businesses, and established cooperative irrigation projects.

Early nineteenth-century American society attached enormous importance to individualism, secularism, monogamous marriage, and private property, and the Mormons were believed to threaten each of these values. But in a larger sense the Mormons' aspirations were truly American. They sought nothing less than the establishment of the Kingdom of God on earth—a dream that was, of course, not new in this country. In seeking to build God's kingdom the Mormons were carrying on a quest that had been begun by their Puritan ancestors two centuries before.

War with Mexico

When Brigham Young led the Mormons west, he was seeking a homeland outside the boundaries of the United States. But even before he arrived at the Great Salt Lake during the summer of 1847, Utah, as well as California, Nevada, and parts of Arizona, Colorado, New Mexico, and Wyoming, became part of the United States as a result of a war with Mexico.

Why War?

Fifteen years before the United States plunged into civil war, it fought a war against Mexico that added a half million square miles of territory to the United States. Not only was it the first American war fought almost entirely outside the United States, it was also the first American war to be reported by daily newspapers as it was occurring. It was also a controversial war that bitterly divided American public opinion. Finally, it was the war that gave young military officers such as Ulysses S. Grant, Robert E. Lee, Thomas ("Stonewall") Jackson, William Tecumseh Sherman, and George McClellan their first experience in a major conflict.

The underlying cause of the Mexican War was the inexorable movement of American pioneers into the Far West. As Americans marched westward, they moved into land claimed by Mexico, and inevitably Mexican and American interests clashed.

The immediate reason for the conflict was the annexation of Texas in 1845. Despite its defeat at San Jacinto in 1836, Mexico refused to recognize Texan independence and warned the United States that annexation would be tantamount to a declaration of war. In early 1845, when Congress voted to annex Texas, Mexico cut diplomatic relations, but took no further action.

Polk told his commanders to prepare for the possibility of war. He ordered American naval vessels in the Gulf of Mexico to position themselves outside Mexican ports. Secretly, he warned the Pacific fleet to prepare to seize ports along the California coast in the event of war. Anticipating a possible Mexican invasion of Texas, he dispatched American forces in Louisiana to Corpus Christi.

The Road to War

Events Leading To The Mexican-American War

1821	Spain allows Moses Austin to settle 300 American families in Texas; Mexico gains its independence from Spain
1827	Mexico establishes a chain of military posts in Texas and decrees an end to further American immigration
1834	General Santa Anna declares Mexico a dictatorship
1836	American settlers are defeated in the siege of the Alamo; Americans win the battle of San Jacinto; Texas gains independence
1845	Congress annexes Texas; Mexico cuts diplomatic ties with the United States
1846	Mexican cavalry crosses the Rio Grande; United States declares war

Peaceful settlement of the two countries' differences still seemed possible. In the fall of 1845, the president sent an envoy, John Slidell, to Mexico with a proposal to settle the disputes peacefully. The most significant controversies concerned Texas's boundary and the Mexican government's failure to compensate American citizens for losses during Mexico's years of political turmoil. Slidell was authorized to cancel the damage claims and pay $5 million in reparations if the Mexicans agreed to recognize the Rio Grande as the southwestern boundary of Texas (earlier the Spanish government had defined the Texas boundary as the Nueces River, 130 miles to the north of the Rio Grande). No Americans lived between the Nueces and the Rio Grande, although many Mexicans lived in the region.

Polk not only wanted to settle the boundary and claims disputes, he also wanted to acquire Mexico's two northwestern provinces, California and New Mexico. He directed Slidell to offer up to $5 million for the province of New Mexico—which included Nevada and Utah and parts of four other states—and up to $25 million for California.

Polk was anxious to acquire California because in mid-October 1845 he had been led to believe that Britain was on the verge of making California a protectorate. It was widely believed that Mexico had agreed to cede California to Britain as payment for outstanding debts. Immediate preventive action seemed necessary. Polk therefore instructed his consul in Monterey to encourage Californians to agitate for annexation by the United States. He also dispatched a young Marine Corps lieutenant, Archibald H. Gillespie, to California, apparently to foment revolt against Mexican authority.

The Mexican government, already incensed over the annexation of Texas, refused to negotiate. The Mexican president, José Herrera, refused to receive Slidell and ordered his leading commander, General Mariano Paredes y Arrillaga, to assemble an army and reconquer Texas. Paredes proceeded to topple Herrera's government and declared himself president, but he also refused to receive Slidell.

The failure of Slidell's mission led Polk to order Brigadier General Zachary Taylor to march 3000 troops from Corpus Christi, Texas, to "defend the Rio Grande." Late in March 1846 Taylor and his men set up camp along the Rio Grande, directly across from the Mexican city of Matamoros, on a stretch of land claimed by both Mexico and the United States.

On April 25, a Mexican cavalry force crossed the Rio Grande and clashed with a small American squadron, forcing the Americans to surrender after the loss of several lives. Polk used this episode as an excuse to declare war.

The Mexican War was the nation's first war to be reported in newspapers as it was happening.

Hours before he received word of the skirmish on May 9, Polk and his cabinet had already decided to press for war with Mexico. On May 11, Polk asked Congress to acknowledge that a state of war already existed. "Mexico," the president announced, "has passed the boundary of the United States, has invaded our territory, and shed American blood upon the American soil." Congress responded with a declaration of war.

The Mexican War was extremely controversial. Its supporters blamed Mexico for the hostilities because it had severed relations with the United States, threatened war, refused to receive an American emissary, and refused to pay the damage claims of American citizens. Opposition leaders denounced the war as an immoral land grab by an expansionist power against a weak neighbor that had been independent barely two decades. The war's critics claimed that Polk deliberately provoked Mexico into war by ordering American troops into disputed territory. A Delaware senator declared that ordering Taylor to the Rio Grande was "as much an act of aggression on our part as is a man's pointing a pistol at another's breast."

Critics argued that the war was an expansionist power play dictated by an aggressive southern slaveocracy intent on acquiring more land for cotton cultivation and more slave states to better balance the northern free states in the U.S. Senate. "Bigger pens to cram with slaves" was the way poet James Russell Lowell put it. Others blamed the war on expansion-minded Westerners who were hungry for land, and on eastern trading interests, which dreamed of establishing "an American Boston or New York" in San Francisco to increase trade with Asia. Mexicans denounced the war as a brazen attempt by the United States to seize Mexican territory.

The War

American strategy was based on a three-pronged attack. Colonel Stephen Kearny had the task of securing New Mexico, naval forces under Commodore John D. Sloat blockaded the California coast, and General Zachary Taylor invaded Mexico.

Kearny easily accomplished his mission. In less than two months he marched his 1700-man army more than a thousand miles. On August 16, 1846, he occupied Santa Fe and declared New Mexico's inhabitants American citizens. In California, American settlers in the Sacramento Valley, fearful that Mexican authorities were about to expel them, revolted even before reliable reports of the outbreak of war reached the area. The so-called Bear Flag Revolt soon came to an end, and by January 1847 U.S. naval forces under Commodore Robert F. Stockton and an expeditionary force under Captain John C. Frémont had brought the region under American control.

Meanwhile, the main U.S. army under Taylor's command had taken Matamoros, and by late September captured Monterrey, Mexico's largest northern city.

Although the American invasion of Mexico's northernmost provinces was completely successful, the Mexican government did not surrender. In June 1846 Colonel A. W. Doniphan led 856 Missouri cavalry volunteers 3000 miles across mountains and desert into the northern Mexican province of Chihuahua. He occupied El Paso and then captured the capital city of Chihuahua. Further south, 6000 volunteers under the command of Zachary Taylor held their ground against a Mexican force of 15,000 at the battle of Buena Vista on February 22 and 23, 1847.

Despite an impressive string of American victories, Mexico still refused to negotiate. Switching strategy, Polk ordered General Winfield Scott to invade central Mexico from the sea, march inland, and capture Mexico City. On March 9, 1847, the Mexicans allowed an American force of 10,000 men to land unopposed at Veracruz on the Gulf of Mexico. Scott's army then began to march on the Mexican capital. On April 18, at a mountain pass near Jalapa, a 9000-man American force met 13,000 Mexican troops and in bitter hand-to-hand fighting forced the Mexicans to flee. As Scott's army pushed on toward Mexico City, it stormed a Mexican fortress at Contreras and then routed a large Mexican force at Churubusco on August 19 and 20.

For two weeks, from August 22 to September 7, Scott observed an armistice to allow the Mexicans to consider peace proposals. When the negotiations failed, Scott's 6000 remaining men attacked El Molino del Rey and stormed Chapultepec, a fortified castle guarding Mexico City's gates.

The fortified castle at Chapultepec was the last major obstacle General Winfield Scott had to overcome in his conquest of Mexico City in 1847. Scott won the gun battle at Chapultepec on September 12 and over the next two days he and his men breached the walls surrounding Mexico City.

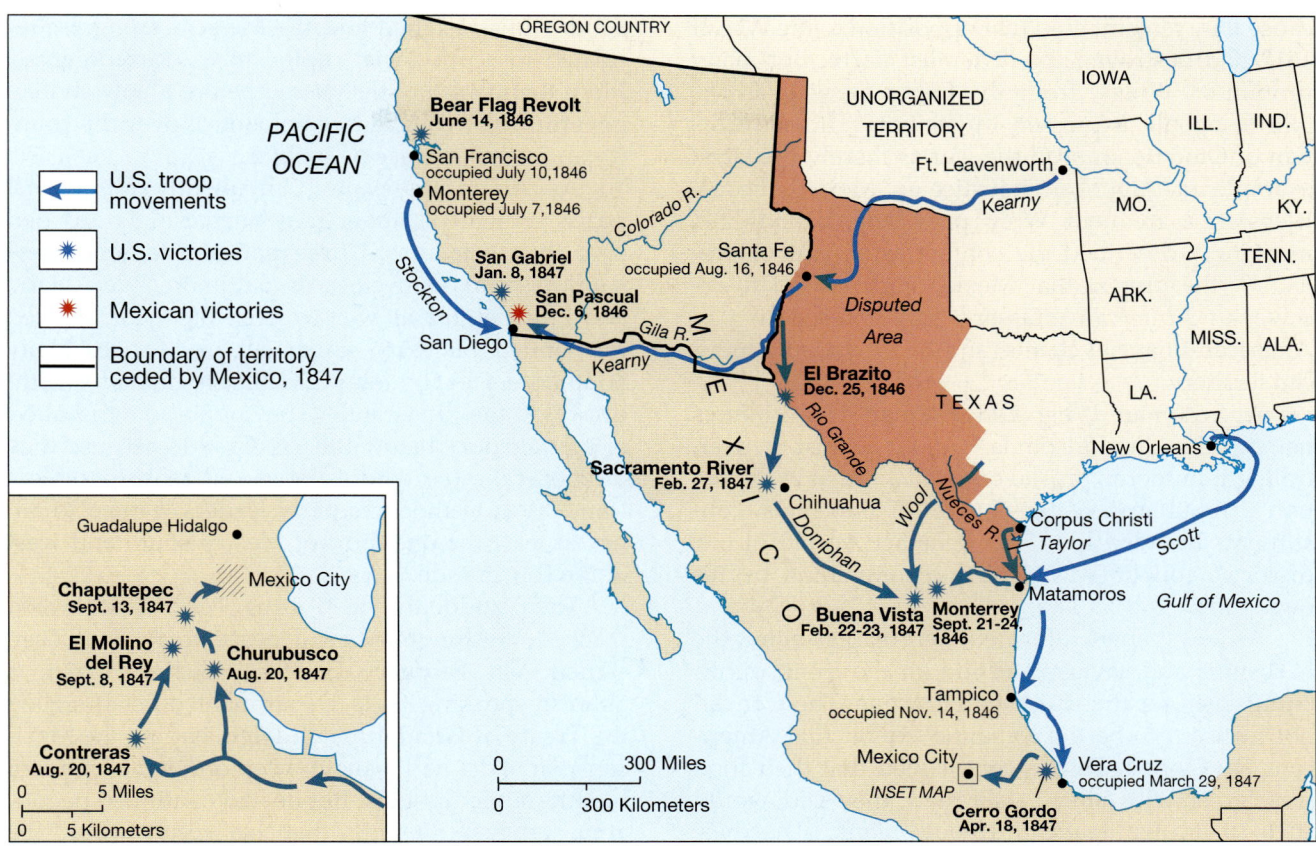

Mexican-American War

The Mexican-American War would increase the nation's size by one-third.

Despite the capture of their capital, the Mexicans refused to surrender. Hostile crowds staged demonstrations in the streets, and snipers fired shots and hurled stones and broken bottles from the tops of flat-roofed Mexican houses. To quell the protests, General Scott ordered the streets "swept with grape and canister" and artillery "turned upon the houses whence the fire proceeded." Outside the capital, belligerent civilians attacked army supply wagons and, guerrilla fighters harassed American troops.

War Fever and Antiwar Protests

During the first few weeks following the declaration of war, a frenzy of prowar hysteria swept the country. Two hundred thousand men responded to a call for 50,000 volunteers. Novelist Herman Melville observed, "a military ardor pervades all ranks.... Nothing is talked about but the halls of the Montezumas." In New York, placards bore the slogan "Mexico or Death." Many newspapers, especially in the North declared that the war would benefit the Mexican people by bringing them the blessings of democracy and liberty. The *Boston Times* said that an American victory "must necessarily be a great blessing" because it would introduce "the reign of law where license has existed for a generation."

In Philadelphia, 20,000 turned out for a prowar rally, and in Cincinnati, 12,000 celebrated Zachary Taylor's victories with cannon salutes, parades, and speeches. In Tennessee, 30,000 men volunteered for 3000 positions as soldiers, prompting one applicant to complain that it was "difficult even to purchase a place in the ranks." The war was particularly popular in the West. Of the 69,540 men who were accepted for service, more than 40,000 were from the western states.

From the war's very beginning, however, a small but highly visible group of intellectuals, clergy, pacifists, abolitionists, and some Whig and Democratic politicians denounced the war as brutal aggression against a "poor, feeble, distracted country." Abolitionist William Lloyd Garrison's militant newspaper, the *Liberator*, expressed open support for the Mexican people: "Every lover of Freedom and humanity throughout the world must wish them the most triumphant success."

Most Whigs supported the war—in part because two of the leading American generals, Zachary Taylor and Winfield Scott, were Whigs, and in part because they remembered that opposition to the War of 1812 had destroyed the Federalist party. But many prominent Whigs, from the South as well as the North, openly expressed opposition. Thomas Corwin of Ohio denounced the war as merely the latest example of American injustice to Mexico. Daniel Webster, a frequent Whig presidential candidate, mockingly described the conflict as a "war of pretexts"—the pretext that Mexico had refused to receive an American emissary, had refused to pay American financial claims, and had invaded American territory.

A freshman Whig congressman from Illinois named Abraham Lincoln lashed out against the war, calling it immoral, proslavery, and a threat to the nation's republican values. One of Lincoln's constituents branded him "the Benedict Arnold of our district," and he was denied renomination by his own party.

As newspapers informed their readers about the hardships and savagery of life on the front, public enthusiasm for the war began to wane. The war did not turn out to be the romantic exploit that Americans envisioned. Troops complained that their food was "green with slime"; their meat, they said, would stick "if thrown against a smooth plank." Diarrhea, amoebic dysentery, measles, and yellow fever ravaged American soldiers. Seven times as many Americans died of disease and exposure as died of battlefield injuries. Of the 90,000 Americans who served in the war, only 1721 died in action. Another 11,155 died from diseases and exposure to the elements.

Public support for the war was further eroded by reports of brutality against Mexican civilians. After one of their members was murdered, the Arkansas volunteer cavalry surrounded a group of Mexican peasants and began an "indiscriminate and bloody massacre of the poor creatures." A young lieutenant named George G. Meade reported that volunteers in Matamoros robbed the citizens, stole their cattle, and killed innocent civilians "for no other object than their own amusement." If only a tenth of the horror stories were true, General Winfield Scott wrote, it was enough "to make Heaven weep, & every American of Christian morals blush for his country."

During wartime the party in power has often lost support. The Mexican War was no exception. In the congressional election of 1846, which took place half a year after the outbreak of war, the Democrats lost control of the House of Representatives to the Whigs.

Peace

Difficult negotiations followed the war. After American troops entered Mexico City, Mexican president Santa Anna resigned and the Mexican Congress retreated to a provincial capital to try to reorganize. More than two months passed before a new civilian government was able to gain control over the country and name a peace negotiator.

As Americans waited impatiently for a final peace settlement, they grew increasingly divided over their war aims. Ultraexpansionists, who drew support from such cities as Baltimore, New York, and Philadelphia as well as from the West, wanted the United States to annex all of Mexico. Many Southerners, led by John C. Calhoun, called for withdrawal to the Rio Grande. They opposed annexation of any territory below the Rio Grande because they did not want to extend American citizenship to Mexicans. Most Democratic party leaders wanted to annex at least the one-third of Mexico south and west of the Rio Grande.

Then suddenly on February 22, 1848, word reached Washington that a peace treaty had been signed. On February 2, 1848, Nicholas Trist, a Spanish-speaking State Department official, signed the **Treaty of Guadalupe Hidalgo,** ending the Mexican War. Trist had actually been ordered home two months earlier by Polk, but he had continued negotiating anyway, fearing that his recall would be "deadly to the cause of peace."

According to the treaty, Mexico ceded to the United States only those areas that Polk had originally sought to purchase. Mexico ceded California, Nevada, New Mexico, Utah, and parts of Arizona, Colorado, Kansas, and Wyoming to the United States for $15 million and the assumption of $3.25 million in debts owed to Americans by Mexico. The treaty also settled the Texas border dispute in favor of the United States, placing the Texas-Mexico boundary at the Rio Grande.

Ultraexpansionists called on Polk to throw out the treaty, but a war-weary public wanted peace. Polk quickly submitted the treaty to the Senate which ratified it overwhelmingly. The war was over.

The Fate of Mexican Americans

The 80,000 Mexicans who lived in the Southwest did not respond to the Mexican War with a single voice. Some welcomed the Americans; many others, recognizing the futility of resistance, responded to the American conquest with ambivalence. A number openly resisted the American military advance. For example, in 1847, disaffected Mexicans and Pueblos in Taos, New Mexico, staged an unsuccessful revolt, in which they killed the American-imposed governor. One observer described the dominant view: "The native sons have hope that the Americans will tire of a long and stubborn war and that in some time they will be left to live in their land in peace and tranquility."

Although American officials promised to protect Mexican property and religious rights and the Treaty of Guadalupe Hidalgo explicitly guaranteed Mexicans "all the rights of citizens," they quickly found themselves reduced to second-class citizenship.

In Texas—where memories of the Alamo fueled anti-Mexican sentiment—Mexicans found themselves increasingly outnumbered and outvoted. By 1850, Anglos outnumbered Mexican Americans in Texas 20 to 1. While delegates to Texas's constitutional convention rejected a motion to restrict voting to "white persons," violent intimidation kept Mexican Americans from the polls. In south Texas, large landowners and political bosses used their economic power to manipulate the votes of Mexican American cowboys and laborers.

In California, too, Mexican Americans were outnumbered and vulnerable to discrimination. During the early years of the Gold Rush, Mexican Americans were robbed, beaten, and lynched with impunity. The 1850 Foreign Miners' Tax imposed a $20 a month tax on Mexican American miners, even though the Treaty of Guadalupe Hidalgo had granted them citizenship. In 1855 the state legislature outlawed bullfights, refused to provide for translation of laws into Spanish (as required by the state constitution), and adopted an antivagrancy act aimed at Mexican American laborers.

Only in New Mexico—where Mexican Americans made up a majority of the population—did Mexican Americans play an important political role. With sizable representation in territorial and local government, Spanish-speaking New Mexicans were able to prevent discriminatory legislation. The New Mexico Constitution, for example, prohibited school segregation, reaffirmed the rights conferred in the Treaty of Guadalupe Hidalgo, and made Spanish and English equal languages of government. At that time, New Mexico included much of Arizona and Colorado. Anglo New Mexicans convinced Congress

THE PEOPLE SPEAK

Mexican Americans Defend Their Land and Rights (1859)

A Robin Hood-like figure defended Mexican Americans in Texas against discrimination and violent intimidation. Juan Nepomuceno Cortina (1824–1892) was born south of the Rio Grande River to an established family and fought for Mexico in its war with the United States. In 1859, he saw a marshal in Brownsville in southern Texas beating a Mexican farmhand. Cortina ordered the marshal to stop and, when he refused, shot him in the shoulder. Then, Cortina proclaimed a Republic of the Rio Grande and raised the Mexican flag. The Texas Rangers and the U.S. Army eventually forced him to retreat into Mexico. But he continued to conduct raids across the Mexican-Texas border until Mexico, under intense U.S. pressure, imprisoned him in 1876.

> The Mexicans who inhabit this wide region, some because they were born therein, others because since the treaty [of] Guadalupe Hidalgo, they have been attracted to its soil . . . and the advantages of wise government. . . .
>
> Mexicans! When the State of Texas began to receive the new organization [government after it entered the Union] . . . flocks of vampires, in the guise of men, came and scattered themselves in the settlements, without any capital, except the corrupt heart and the most perverse intentions. . . . Many of you have been robbed of your property, incarcerated, chased, murdered, and hunted like wild beasts, because your labor was fruitful, and because your industry excited the vile avarice which led them. A voice infernal said, from the bottom of their soul, "kill them; the greater will be our gain!" . . .
>
> Mexicans! Is there no remedy for you? Inviolable laws, yet useless, serve, it is true, certain judges and hypocritical authorities, cemented in evil and injustice, to do whatever suits them. . . . The wicked way in which many of you have been oftentimes involved in persecution . . . is well known; these crimes being hid from society under the shadow of a horrid night, those implacable people with the haughty spirit which suggests impunity for a life of criminality. . . .
>
> Mexicans! . . . To me is entrusted the work of breaking the chains of your slavery, and that the Lord will enable me, with powerful arm, to fight against our enemies, in compliance with the requirements of that Sovereign Majesty, who, from this day forward, will hold us under His protection. On my part, I am ready to offer myself as a sacrifice for your happiness. . . .

Source: Juan Nepomuceno Cortina, "Proclamation to the Mexican Americans of South Texas," 36 Congress, 1 Session, House Executive Document No. 52: "Difficulties on Southwestern Frontier," pages 79–82.

to create a separate Colorado Territory in 1861 and a separate Arizona Territory in 1862 partly to gain political control of those areas.

Across the Southwest, Mexican Americans lost land, despite provisions in the Treaty of Guadalupe Hidalgo that guaranteed Spanish and Mexican land grants and Mexican American property rights. In California, many Mexicans were forced to sell land to pay onerous taxes that fell heaviest on the Spanish-speakers. In Texas, speculators purchased many Mexican land grants, and squatters simply seized abandoned land. In Arizona and New Mexico, where it took years of expensive litigation to confirm land titles, many Mexicans sold land to pay legal bills. In New Mexico, litigation over land claims was still dragging on in the 1970s.

Loss of land had important implications for the future. Increasingly, Mexican American men were forced to support themselves as migratory unskilled laborers in mines, on farms, and on railroads, and women found employment as domestic servants and farm laborers. Displaced from their land, Mexican Americans were forced to live in segregated neighborhoods and communities, known as *barrios* and *colonias*.

The discovery of gold in California drew thousands who hoped to find their fortunes there. Most came from eastern North America, but substantial numbers also came from Europe, Australia, South America, and China. Some sought their fortunes in the minefields; others looked for opportunity supplying the miners with necessities.

The War's Significance

The story of America's conflict with Mexico tends to be overshadowed by the story of the Civil War, which began only a decade and a half later. In fact, the conflict had far-reaching consequences. It increased the nation's size by a third, but it also created deep political divisions that threatened the nation's future.

The most significant result of the Mexican War was to reignite the question of slavery in the western territories—the very issue that had divided the country in 1819. Even before the war began, philosopher Ralph Waldo Emerson predicted that the United States would "conquer Mexico, but it will be as the man who swallows the arsenic which will bring him down in turn. Mexico will poison us." The war convinced a growing number of Northerners that southern slaveowners had precipitated the conflict in order to open new lands to slavery and acquire new slave states. And most significant of all, the war weakened the party system and made it increasingly difficult for congressional leaders to prevent the issue of slavery from dominating congressional activity.

Political Crisis of the 1840s

Before the Mexican War, the major political issues that divided Americans were questions of tariffs, banking, internal improvements, and land. Political positions on these issues largely divided along party lines. After the outbreak of war with Mexico a new issue began to dominate American politics—the extension of slavery in the western territories. Public opinion began to polarize and party cohesion began to break down as party factional and sectional divisions grew more important than traditional party coalitions.

The question of slavery burst into the public spotlight one summer evening in 1846. Congressman David Wilmot, a Pennsylvania Democrat, introduced an amendment, known as the **Wilmot Proviso,** to a war appropriations bill. The proviso forbade slavery in any territory acquired from Mexico. Throughout the North, thousands of working men and women and farmers feared that free workers would be unable to compete successfully against slave labor. "If slavery is not excluded by law," said one northern congressman, "the presence of the slave will exclude the laboring white man."

Southerners denounced the Wilmot Proviso as "treason to the Constitution." Polk tried to quiet the debate between "southern agitators and northern fa-

Territorial Growth to 1853

natics" by assuring moderate Northerners that slavery could never take root in the arid Southwest, but his efforts were to no avail. With the strong support of Westerners, the amendment passed the House twice, but was defeated in the Senate. Although the Wilmot Proviso did not become law, the issue it raised—the extension of slavery into the western territories—contributed to the growth of political factionalism.

Growing sectional tensions were also evident in the founding of the Free Soil party in 1848. This sectional party opposed the westward expansion of slavery and favored free land for western homesteaders. Under the slogan "free soil, free speech, free labor, and free men," the party nominated Martin Van Buren as its presidential nominee in 1848 and polled 291,000 votes. This was enough to split the Democratic vote and throw the election to Whig candidate Zachary Taylor.

Up until the last month of 1848, the debate over slavery in the Mexican cession seemed academic. Most Americans thought of the newly acquired territory as a wasteland filled with "broken mountains and dreary desert." Then, in a farewell address, Polk electrified Congress with news that gold had been discovered in California—and suddenly the question of slavery was of inescapable importance.

The Gold Rush

On January 24, 1848, less than 10 days after the signing of the peace treaty ending the Mexican War, James W. Marshall, a 36-year-old carpenter and handyman, noticed several bright bits of yellow mineral. Marshall was building a sawmill in California's Sacramento Valley for John A. Sutter, a Swiss-born rancher. To test if the bits were fool's gold, which shatters when struck by a hammer, or real gold, which is malleable, Marshall "tried it between two rocks, and found that it could be beaten into a different shape but not broken. He told the men working with him: "Boys, by God, I believe I have found a gold mine."

On March 15, 1849, a San Francisco newspaper, the *Californian*, printed the first account of Marshall's discovery. Within two weeks the paper had lost its staff and was forced to shut down its printing press. In its last edition, it told its readers: "The whole country, from San Francisco to Los Angeles . . . resounds with the sordid cry of Gold! Gold! Gold!

Chronology of Key Events

1803	Louisiana Purchase
1804	Lewis and Clark Expedition sets out from St. Louis to explore the northern region of Louisiana Purchase territory
1810	Mexican War for Independence against Spanish rule begins; John Jacob Astor attempts to plant a trading post in Oregon
1811–1812	Fur trappers mark out the Oregon Trail
1818	United States and Britain agree to joint occupation of Oregon
1819	Spain cedes its claims to Oregon to the United States
1821	Mexico gains independence from Spain; first American traders traverse the Santa Fe Trail; Stephen Austin founds American colony in Texas
1822	The Rocky Mountain Fur Company begins to send trappers into the frontier
1830	Joseph Smith, Jr., founds Church of Christ, later renamed Church of Jesus Christ of Latter-Day Saints
1833–1834	Mexican government confiscates California missions
1834	Santa Anna overthrows Mexico's constitutional government and makes himself dictator; first American missionaries arrive in Oregon
1835	Scattered local outbursts erupt in Texas against Mexican rule
1836	Texas Revolution
1838	John Quincy Adams's filibuster defeats move to annex Texas
1841	First party of pioneers leaves Missouri for California; Congress recognizes squatters' rights in the Preemption Bill
1844	Joseph Smith, Jr., assassinated at Carthage, Illinois
1845	Texas is admitted as twenty-eighth state; Mexican government breaks off diplomatic relations with the United States
1846	The United States declares war on Mexico; Britain and the United States divide Oregon along 49th parallel; Donner party becomes trapped in Sierra Nevada; Brigham Young leads the Mormons to the Great Salt Lake Valley; Wilmot Proviso, barring slavery from any territory acquired from Mexico, is proposed.
1848	Gold is discovered at Sutter's Mill in California; Treaty of Guadalupe Hidalgo ends the Mexican War
1849	Gold rush brings 80,000 gold prospectors to California

while the field is left half-planted, the house half-built, and everything neglected but the manufacture of picks and shovels."

In 1849, 80,000 men arrived in California—half by land and half by ship, around the tip of South America or across the isthmus of Panama. Only half were Americans; the rest came from Europe, Latin America, and China. Soldiers deserted; sailors jumped ship; husbands abandoned wives; apprentices ran away from their masters; farmers and businesspeople deserted their livelihoods. Within a year, California's population had swollen from 14,000 to 100,000.

The gold rush transformed California from a quiet society into one that was wild, unruly, ethnically diverse, and violent. In San Francisco alone there were more than 500 bars and 1000 gambling dens. There were a thousand murders in San Francisco during the early 1850s, but only one conviction. "Forty-niners" slaughtered Native Americans for sport, drove Mexicans from the mines on penalty of death, and sought to restrict the immigration of foreigners, especially the Chinese. Since the military government was incapable of keeping order, leading merchants formed vigilance committees, which attempted to rule by lynch law and the establishment of "popular" courts.

California's gold rush era lasted less than a decade. By the mid-1850s, the lone miner who prospected for gold with a pick, a shovel, and a washpan was already an anachronism. Mining companies using heavy machinery replaced the individual prospector. Systems of dams exposed whole river bottoms. Drilling machines drove shafts 700 feet into the earth. Hydraulic mining machines blasted streams of water against mountainsides. The mythical era of California gold mining had already come to a close.

Conclusion

By 1860 the gold rush was over. Prospectors had found more than $350 million worth of gold. Certainly, some fortunes were made, but few struck it rich. Even James W. Marshall, who discovered the first gold bits, and John A. Sutter, on whose ranch the gold was first found, died penniless.

By 1850 the American flag flew over an area that stretched from sea to sea. In the span of just five years the United States had increased its size by a third and acquired an area that now includes the states of Arizona, California, Colorado, Idaho, Nevada, New Mexico, Oregon, Texas, Utah, Washington, and Wyoming.

The exploration and settlement of the Far West is one of the great epics of nineteenth-century history. But America's dramatic territorial expansion also created severe problems. In addition to providing the United States with its richest mines, greatest forests, and most fertile farmland, the Far West intensified the sectional conflict between the North and South and raised the fateful and ultimately divisive question of whether slavery should be permitted in the western territories. Could democratic political institutions resolve the question of slavery in the western territories? That question would dominate American politics in the 1850s.

Suggestions for Further Reading

Patricia Nelson Limerick, *The Legacy of Conquest: The Unbroken Past of the American West* (1987). Reinterprets the history of the West as a region where diverse peoples struggled for control of land, resources, and cultural dominance. Richard White, *"It's Your Misfortune and None of My Own": A New History of the American West* (1991). Offers a comprehensive history of the American West incorporating the most recent historical scholarship.

Overviews and Surveys

Ray A. Billington, *The Far Western Frontier, 1830–1860* (1956), and *Westward Expansion*, 5th ed. (1982); William Cronon, George Miles, and Jay Gitlin, eds., *Under an Open Sky: Rethinking America's Western Past* (1992); Bernard DeVoto, *The Year of Decision: 1846* (1943), and *Across the Wide Missouri* (1947); Richard Drinnon, *Facing West: The Metaphysics of Indian-Hating and Empire-Building* (1980); Thomas R. Hietala, *Manifest Design: Anxious Aggrandizement in Late Jacksonian America* (1985); Reginald Horsman, *Race and Manifest Destiny: The Origins of American Racial Anglo-Saxonism* (1981); Anne Farrar Hyde, *An American Vision: Far Western Landscape and National Culture* (1990); Howard R. Lamar, ed., *New Encyclopedia of the American West* (1998); Frederick Merk, *History of the Westward Movement* (1978); Clyde A. Milner, II, Carol A. O'Connor, and Martha A. Sandweiss, *Oxford History of the American West* (1994); Martin Ridge and Ray A. Billington, eds., *America's Frontier Story* (1969); Albert K. Weinberg, *Manifest Destiny* (1935); Richard White and Patricia Nelson Limerick, *The Frontier in American Culture* (1994); Donald Worcester, *Under Western Skies: Nature and History in the American West* (1992).

The Hispanic and Native-American West

Rodofo Acuña, *Occupied America: A History of Chicanos*, 3d ed. (1988); Arnando Alonzo, *Tejano Legacy* (1998); Robert F. Berkhofer, Jr., *The White Man's Indian: Images of the American Indian from Columbus to the Present* (1978); Albert Camarillo, *Chicanos in California* (1984); John R. Chávez, *The Lost Land* (1984); Arnoldo De León, *The Tejano Community, 1836–1900* (1982), and *They Called Them Greasers: Anglo Attitudes Toward Mexicans in Texas, 1821–1900* (1983); Sarah Deutsch, *No Separate Refuge: Culture, Class, and Gender on an Anglo-Hispanic Frontier in the American Southwest* (1987); Edward P. Dozier, *The Pueblo Indians of North America* (1970); Harold E. Driver, *Indians of North America*, 2d ed. (1969); Fred Eggan, *The American Indian* (1966); Jack Forbes, *Native Americans of California and Nevada*, rev. ed. (1982); Thomas D. Hall, *Social Change in the Southwest, 1350–1880* (1989); Robert F. Heizer and Alan Almquist, *The Other Californians* (1971), and with M. A. Whipple, eds., *California Indians*, 2d ed. (1971); Alice Kehoe, *North American Indians: A Comprehensive Account* (1981); Robert H. Lowie, *Indians of the Plains* (1963); Cecil Robinson, *Mexico and the Hispanic Southwest in American Literature* (1977); Robert Rosenbaum, *Mexicano Resistance in the Southwest* (1981); Robert F. Spencer and Jesse D. Spencer, *The Native Americans: Ethnology and Backgrounds of the North American Indians*, 2d ed.

(1977); W. R. Swagerty, ed., *Scholars and the Indian Experience: Critical Reviews of Recent Writings in the Social Sciences* (1984); Wilcomb Washburn, *The Indian in America* (1975); David J. Weber, *The Mexican Frontier, 1821–1846: The American Southwest Under Mexico* (1982).

The Surge Westward

Stephen Ambrose, *Undaunted Courage: Meriwether Lewis, Thomas Jefferson, and the Opening of the American West* (1996); Gloria G. Cline, *Exploring the Great Basin* (1963); William Cronon, *Nature's Metropolis: Chicago and the Great West* (1991); R. L. Duffus, *The Santa Fe Trail* (1930); John Mack Faragher, *Women and Men on the Overland Trail* (1979); William H. Goetzmann, *Army Exploration in the American West, 1803–1863* (1959), and *Exploration and Empire: Explorer and Scientist in the Winning of the West* (1966); Julie Roy Jeffrey, *Frontier Women: The Transmississippi West, 1840–1880* (1979); Michael P. Malone, ed., *Historians and the American West* (1983); Dale L. Morgan, *Jedediah Smith and the Opening of the West* (1953); Sandra L. Myres, *Westering Women and the Frontier Experience, 1800–1915* (1982); Francis Parkman, *The Oregon Trail* (1849); Gerald Rawling, *The Pathfinders* (1964); Glenda Riley, *The Female Frontier* (1988); Lillian Schlissel, *Women's Diaries of the Westward Journey* (1982), and with Byrd Gibbens and Elizabeth Hampsten, *Far from Home: Families of the Western Journey* (1989); Joanna Stratton, *Pioneer Women* (1981); Richard Slotkin, *The Fatal Environment: The Myth of the Frontier in the Age of Industrialization* (1985); John Unruh, *The Plains Across: The Overland Emigrants and the Trans-Mississippi West* (1979); David J. Wishart, *The Fur Trade of the American West* (1979).

Manifest Destiny

Leonard J. Arrington, *Great Basin Kingdom* (1958), and with Davis Bitton, *The Mormon Experience* (1979); Gunther Barth, *Instant Cities: Urbanization and the Rise of San Francisco and Denver* (1975); William C. Binkley, *The Texas Revolution* (1952); John L. Brooke, *The Refiner's Fire: The Making of Mormon Cosmology* (1994); Robert Calvert and Arnoldo De León, *The History of Texas* (1990); Randolph Campbell, *Sam Houston and the American Southwest* (1993); Malcolm Clark, Jr., *Eden Seekers: The Settlement of Oregon, 1818–1862* (1981); Robert B. Flanders, *Nauvoo: Kingdom on the Mississippi* (1965); Norman F. Furniss, *The Mormon Conflict, 1850–1859* (1960); Robert Gottlieb and Peter Wiley, *America's Saints: The Rise of Mormon Power* (1984); Norman A. Graebner, *Empire on the Pacific* (1955); Klaus Hansen, *Quest for Empire: The Political Kingdom of God and the Council of Fifty in Mormon History* (1967); Sam W. Haynes and Christopher M. Morris, eds., *Manifest Destiny and Empire* (1997); Robert F. Heizer and Alan J. Almquist, *The Other Californians: Prejudice and Discrimination Under Spain, Mexico, and the United States* (1971); Marvin S. Hill and James B. Allen, eds., *Mormonism and American Culture* (1972); Frederick Merk, *Fruits of Propaganda in the Tyler Administration* (1971), *The Oregon Question: Essays in Anglo-American Diplomacy and Politics* (1967); and *Slavery and the Annexation of Texas* (1972); William Mulder and A. Russell Mortensen, eds., *Among the Mormons: Historic Accounts by Contemporary Observers* (1958); David M. Pletcher, *The Diplomacy of Annexation: Texas, Oregon, and the Mexican War* (1973); Earl Pomeroy, *The Pacific Slope: A History* (1965); Jan Shipps, *Mormonism: The Story of a New Religious Tradition* (1985); Wallace Stegner, *The Gathering of Zion: The Story of the Mormon Trail* (1964); Anders Stephanson, *Manifest Destiny* (1995); Philip Taylor, *Expectations Westward: The Mormons and the Emigration of Their British Converts in the Nineteenth Century* (1966); Grant Underwood, *The Millenarian World of Early Mormonism* (1993).

War with Mexico

K. Jack Bauer, *The Mexican War, 1846–1848* (1974); Walton Bean, *California: An Interpretive History*, 3d ed. (1978); Warren A. Beck and David A. Williams, *California: A History of the Golden State* (1972); Paul H. Bergeron, *The Presidency of James K. Polk* (1987); Gene M. Brack, *Mexico Views Manifest Destiny, 1821–1846: An Essay on the Origins of the Mexican War* (1975); Kinley J. Brauer, *Cotton Versus Conscience: Massachusetts Whig Politics and Southwestern Expansion, 1843–1848* (1967); William R. Brock, *Parties and Political Conscience, 1840–1850* (1979); Seymour V. Connor and Odie B. Faulk, *North America Divided: The Mexican War, 1846–1848* (1971); Eric Foner, "The Wilmot Proviso Revisited," *Journal of American History*, 56 (1969); Paul W. Gates, ed., *California Ranchos and Farms, 1846–1862* (1967); Richard Griswold Del Castillo, *Treaty of Guadalupe Hidalgo* (1990); Neal Harlow, *California Conquered: War and Peace on the Pacific, 1846–1850* (1982); J. S. Holliday, *The World Rushed In* (1981); Robert Johannsen, *To the Halls of the Montezumas: The Mexican War in the American Imagination* (1985); Rudolph M. Lapp, *Blacks in Gold Rush California* (1977); James M. McCaffrey, *Army of Manifest Destiny: The American Soldier in the Mexican War* (1992); Frederick Merk, "Dissent in the Mexican War," Samuel E. Morison et al., eds., in *Dissent in Three American Wars* (1970); Robert Ryal Miller, *Shamrock and Sword: Saint Patrick's Battalion in the U.S.-Mexican War* (1989); C. W. Morrison, *Democratic Politics and Sectionalism: The Wilmot Proviso Controversy* (1967); Rodman W. Paul, *California Gold: The Beginning of Mining in the Far West* (1947), and *Mining Frontiers of the Far West, 1848–1880* (1963); R. H. Peterson, *Manifest Destiny in the Mines: A Cultural Interpretation of Anti-Mexican Nativism in California, 1848–1853* (1975); Andrew F. Rolle, *California: A History*, 4th ed. (1987); Alexander Saxton, *The Indispensable Enemy: Labor and the Anti-Chinese Movement in California* (1971); John H. Schroeder, *Mr. Polk's War: American Opposition and Dissent* (1973); Kevin Starr, *Americans and the California Dream, 1850–1915* (1973); John E. Weems, *To Conquer a Peace: The War Between the United States and Mexico* (1974); Richard Bruce Winders, *Mr. Polk's Army* (1997).

Biographies

Leonard J. Arrington, *Brigham Young: American Moses* (1985); Richard L. Bushman, *Joseph Smith and the Beginnings of Mormonism* (1984); K. Jack Bauer, *Zachary Taylor* (1985); John S. D. Eisenhower, *Agent of Destiny: The Life and Times of General Winfield Scott* (1997); Sam Haynes, *James K. Polk and the Expansionist Impulse* (1996); Charles G. Sellers, *James K. Polk: Continentalist* (1966).

INTERNET RESOURCES

Pioneering the Upper Midwest: Books from Michigan, Minnesota, and Wisconsin, ca. 1820–1910
http://memory.loc.gov/ammem/umhtml/umhome.html
This Library of Congress site looks at first-person accounts, biographies, promotional literature, local histories, ethnographic and antiquarian texts, colonial archival documents, and other works from the seventeenth to the early twentieth century. It covers many topics and issues that affected Americans in the settlement and development of the upper Midwest.

The Mexican-American War Memorial Homepage
http://sunsite.unam.mx/revistas/1847
Images and text explain the causes, courses, and outcomes of the Mexican-American War.

On the Trail in Kansas
http://www.ukans.edu/carrie/kancoll/galtrl.htm
This Kansas Collection site holds several good primary sources with images concerning the Oregon Trail and America's early movement westward.

The Era of the Mountain Men
http://www.xmission.com/~drudy/amm.html
Private letters can speak volumes about the concerns and environment of the writers and recipients. Letters from early settlers west of the Mississippi River are offered on this site.

The Donner Party
http://members.aol.com/danmrosen/donner/index.htm
This site includes logs from the infamous party that resorted to extreme measures to survive. It also has images of the region.

National Museum of the American Indian, 1846–1996
http://www.si.edu/organiza/museums/amerind/start.htm
The Smithsonian Institution maintains this site providing information about this museum.

KEY TERMS

General Antonio López de Santa Anna   (p. 363)

James K. Polk   (p. 365)

Joseph Smith, Jr.   (p. 368)

Brigham Young   (p. 370)

Treaty of Guadalupe Hidalgo   (p. 374)

Wilmot Proviso   (p. 376)

REVIEW QUESTIONS

1. Describe the role of each of the following in the settlement of the Far West: (a) trappers and traders; (b) government explorers; and (c) missionaries.
2. Why did Anglo American settlers in Texas rebel against the Mexican government?
3. What is the meaning of the phrase "manifest destiny"? Explain why Americans expanded west of the Mississippi River during the 1840s.
4. Why did the United States and Mexico go to war in 1846? Why did the war arouse bitter controversy?

14

THE HOUSE DIVIDED

THE CRISIS OF 1850
The South's Dilemma
The Compromise of 1850: The Illusion of Sectional Peace
The Fugitive Slave Law

DISINTEGRATION OF THE PARTY SYSTEM
The Know Nothings
Young America
The Kansas-Nebraska Act
Revival of the Slavery Issue

THE GATHERING STORM
"Bleeding Kansas" and "Bleeding Sumner"
The Election of 1856
The Supreme Court Speaks
The Lecompton Constitution: "A Swindle and a Fraud"

CRISIS OF THE UNION
The Lincoln-Douglas Debates
Harpers Ferry

The "slave power" conspiracy

Early in 1864, a New York economist named John Smith Dye published a book entitled *The Adder's Den or Secrets of the Great Conspiracy to Overthrow Liberty in America.* In his volume, Dye set out to prove that for more than 30 years a ruthless southern "slave power" had engaged in a deliberate, systematic plan to subvert civil liberties, pervert the Constitution, and extend slavery into the western territories.

In Dye's eyes, the entire history of the United States was the record of the South's repeated plots to expand slavery. An arrogant and aggressive "slave power," he maintained, had entrenched slavery in the Constitution, caused financial panics to sabotage the North's economy, dispossessed Indians from their native lands, and fomented revolution in Texas and war with Mexico in order to expand the South's slave empire. Most important of all, he insisted, the southern slaveocracy had secretly assassinated two presidents by poison and unsuccessfully attempted to murder three others.

According to Dye, this campaign of political assassination began in 1835 when John C. Calhoun, outraged by Andrew Jackson's opposition to states' rights and nullification, encouraged a deranged man named Richard Lawrence to kill Jackson. This plot failed when Lawrence's pistols misfired. Six years later, in 1841, Dye argued, a successful attempt was made on William Henry Harrison's life. After he refused to cooperate in a southern scheme to annex Texas, Harrison died of symptoms resembling arsenic poisoning. This left John Tyler, a strong defender of slavery, in the White House.

The next president to die at the hands of the slave power, according to Dye, was Zachary Taylor. A Louisiana slave owner who had commanded American troops in the Mexican War, Taylor had shocked Southerners by opposing the extension of slavery into California. Just 16 months after taking office, Taylor died suddenly of acute gastroenteritis, caused, claimed Dye, by arsenic poisoning. (A 1991 post-mortem examination of Taylor's remains disproved

In 1864, New York economist John Smith Dye argued that the slave power had secretly poisoned two presidents—William Henry Harrison and Zachary Taylor—and had conspired to murder three others.

this theory.) He was succeeded by Vice President Millard Fillmore, who was more sympathetic to the southern cause. Just three years later, Dye maintained, an attempt was made on Millard Fillmore's successor, Franklin Pierce, a New Hampshire Democrat whom the slave power considered unreliable. On the way to his inauguration, Pierce's railroad car derailed and rolled down an embankment. The president and his wife escaped injury, but their 12-year-old son was killed. From that point on, Pierce toed the southern line.

According to Dye, the next attempt came on February 23, 1857. President-elect James Buchanan, a Pennsylvania Democrat, was dining at Washington's National Hotel. Buchanan had won the Democratic presidential nomination in the face of fierce southern opposition, and, in Dye's view, the slaveocracy wanted to remind Buchanan who was in charge. Southern agents sprinkled arsenic on the lump sugar used by Northerners to sweeten their tea. Because Southerners drank coffee and used granulated sugar, no Southerners were injured. According to Dye, 60 Northerners, including the President, were poisoned and 38 died. Frightened by this brush with death, Buchanan became a reliable tool of the slave power.

In fact, no credible evidence supports any of John Smith Dye's sensational allegations. Historians have uncovered no connection between John C. Calhoun and the assassination attempt on Andrew Jackson; nor have they found any proof that Harrison's and Taylor's deaths resulted from poisoning or that southern agents derailed Pierce's train; nor have they located any evidence at all that 60 Northerners were poisoned at the dinner for President-elect Buchanan. Yet even if his charges were without foundation, Dye was not alone in interpreting events in conspiratorial terms. His book *The Adder's Den* was only one of the most extreme examples of conspiratorial charges that had been made by abolitionists since the late 1830s.

By the 1850s, a growing number of Northerners had come to believe that an aggressive southern slave power had seized control of the federal government and threatened to subvert republican ideals of liberty, equality, and self-rule. At the same time, an increasing number of Southerners had begun to believe that antislavery radicals dominated northern politics and would "rejoice" in the ultimate consequences of abolition—race war and racial amalgamation that would surely follow emancipation. Sectional animosities were becoming increasingly ideological and inflamed, moving the torn nation closer to secession and civil war.

During the 1850s, the American political system was incapable of containing the sectional disputes between the North and South that had smoldered for more than half a century. One major political party—the Whigs—collapsed. Another—the Democrats—split into northern and southern factions. With the breakdown of the party system, the issues raised by slavery exploded. The bonds that had bound the country for more than seven decades began to unravel.

THE CRISIS OF 1850

In 1849 an expedition of Texas slaveowners and their slaves arrived in the California gold fields. As curious prospectors looked on, the Texans staked out claims and put their slaves to work panning for gold. White miners considered it unfair that they should have to compete with slave labor. They held a mass meeting and resolved "that no slave or Negro should own claims or even work in the mines." They ordered the Texans out of the gold fields within 24 hours.

Three days later, the white miners elected a delegate to a convention that had been called to frame a state constitution for California and to apply for admission to the Union. At the convention, the miners' delegate proposed that "neither slavery nor involuntary servitude" should ever "be tolerated" in California. The convention adopted his proposal unanimously.

In California white miners refused "to swing a pick side by side with the Negro." Their delegate to the California constitutional convention of 1849 proposed that "neither salvery nor industry servitude . . . shall ever be tolerated in this state."

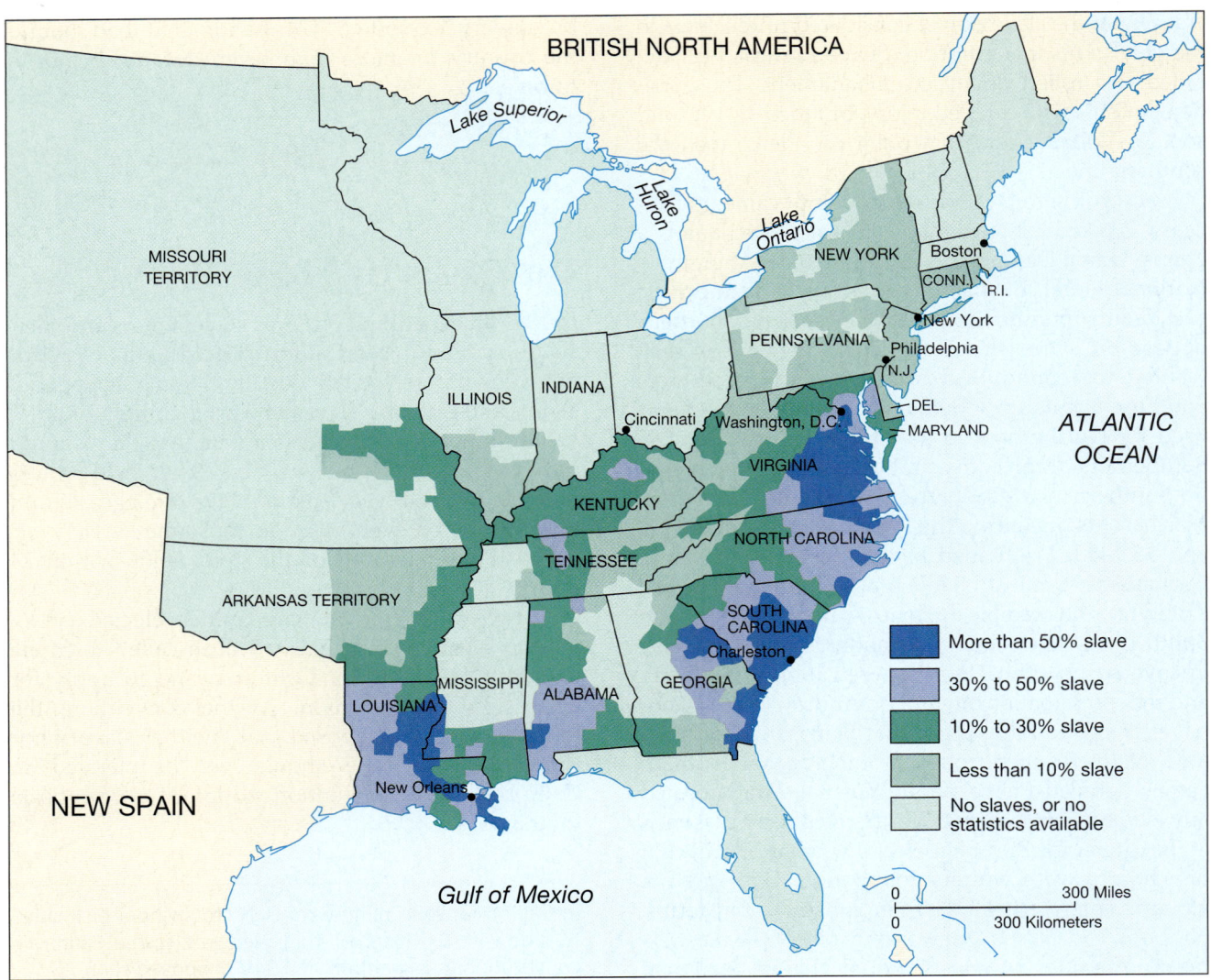

Slave Concentration, 1820

California's application for admission to the Union as a free state in September 1849 raised the question that would dominate American politics during the 1850s: would slavery be allowed to expand into the West or would the West remain free soil? It was the issue of slave expansion—and not the morality of slavery—that would make antislavery a respectable political position in the North, polarize public opinion, and initiate the chain of events that would lead the United States to civil war.

California's application for statehood made slavery's expansion an unavoidable political issue. Southerners feared that California's admission as a free state would upset the sectional balance of power. The free states already held a commanding majority in the House of Representatives because they had a much greater population than did the slave states. Therefore, the political power of proslavery Southerners depended on maintaining a balance of power in the Senate. Since the Missouri Compromise, Congress had paired the admission of a free state and a slave state. In 1836 and 1837, Congress had admitted Arkansas as a slave state and Michigan as a free state. In 1845 Florida and Texas had joined the Union as slave states, but Congress restored the sectional balance by admitting Iowa as a free state in 1846 and Wisconsin in 1848. If California was admitted as a free state, there would be 16 free states and only 15 slave states. The sectional balance of power in the Senate would be disrupted, and the South feared that it would lose its ability to influence political events.

The instability of the Democratic and Whig parties, and the growing political power of northern opponents of slave expansion, further dimmed chances of a peaceful compromise. When the

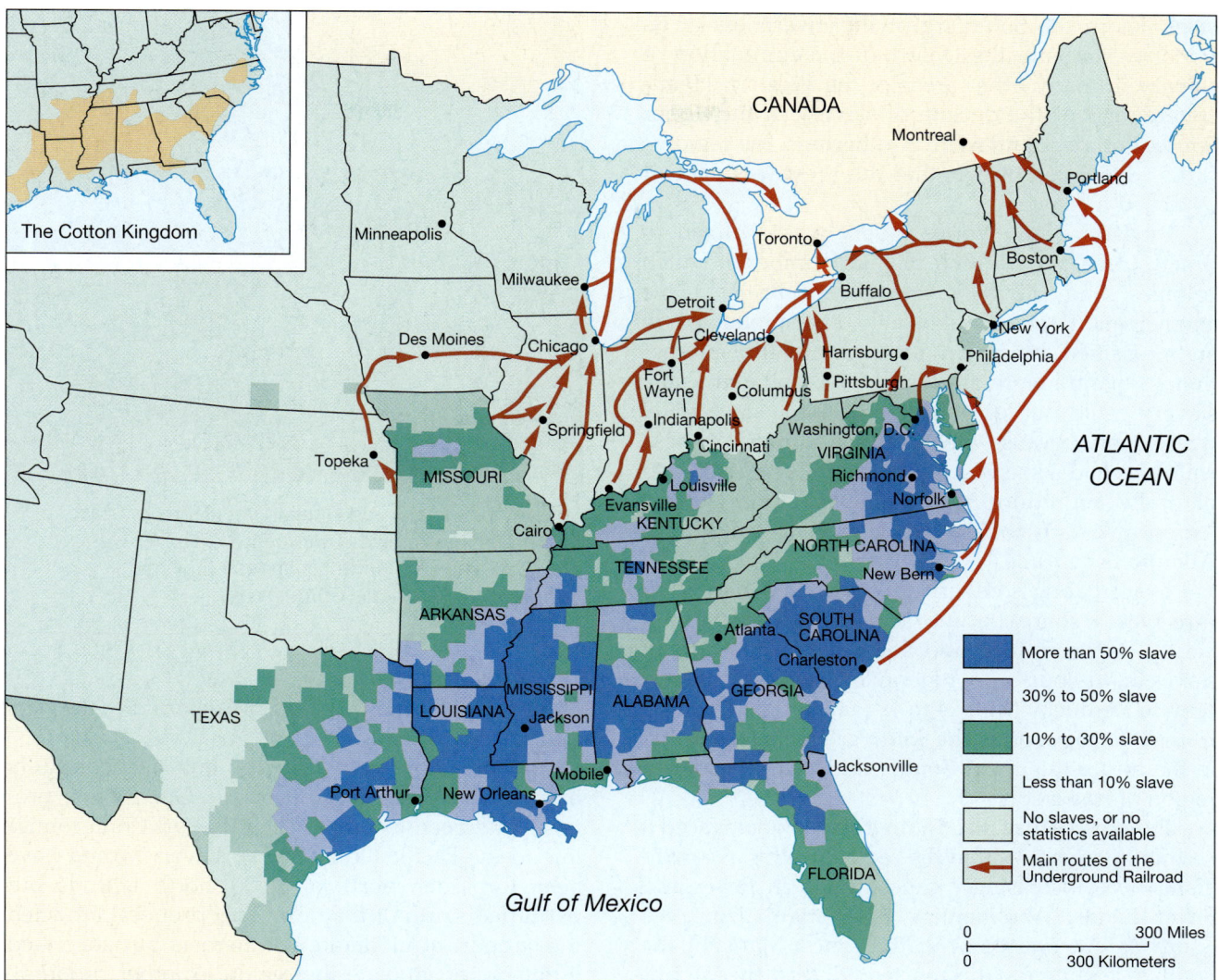

Slave Concentration, 1860/The Cotton Kingdom

As shown here, northern African Americans were providing escape routes for slaves along the underground railroad. Slaveowning Southerners feared that the end of slavery would reduce their economic and political status in the Union.

Thirty-first Congress convened in December 1849, neither the Democrats nor the Whigs had a stable majority. Southern Whigs were deserting their party in droves, and northern and southern Democrats were badly split. The parties were so divided that it took 3 weeks and 63 ballots simply to elect the Speaker of the House.

In the North, opponents of the westward expansion of slavery made striking gains, particularly within the Democratic party. Coalitions of Democrats and Free Soilers in Connecticut, Illinois, Indiana, Massachusetts, New York, Ohio, Vermont, and Wisconsin elected congressmen determined to prevent southern expansion. Every northern state legislature, except Iowa's, asserted that Congress had the power and duty to exclude slavery from the territories.

Southern hotspurs talked openly of secession. Robert Toombs of Georgia declared that if the North deprived the South of the right to take slaves into California and New Mexico, "I am for disunion." Such bold talk inched the South closer to secession.

The South's Dilemma

Why were the South's political leaders so worried about whether slavery would be permitted in the West when geography and climate made it unlikely that slavery would ever prosper in the area? The answer lies in the South's growing awareness of its minority status in the Union, of the elimination of slavery in many other areas of the Western Hemisphere, and of the decline of slavery in the upper South. For more and more Southerners, the region's future depended on whether the West was opened or closed to slavery.

By 1850, New World slavery was confined to Brazil, Cuba, Puerto Rico, a small number of Dutch colonies, and the American South. British slave emancipation in the Caribbean had been followed by an intensified campaign to eradicate the international slave trade. In areas such as Brazil and Cuba, slavery could not long survive once the slave trade was cut off, because the slave populations of these countries had a skewed sex ratio and were unable to naturally reproduce their numbers. Only in the American South could slavery survive without the Atlantic slave trade.

Exacerbating southern fears about slavery's future was a sharp decline in slavery in the upper South. Between 1830 and 1860, the proportion of slaves in Missouri's population fell from 18 to 10 percent; in Kentucky from 24 to 19 percent; in Maryland from 23 to 13 percent. The South's leaders feared that in the future the upper South would soon become a region of free labor.

By mid-century, the South's slaveowners faced a further dilemma. Within the region itself, slave ownership was increasingly concentrated in fewer and fewer hands. Abolitionists were stigmatizing the South as out of step with the times. Many of the South's leading politicians feared that these criticisms of slavery would weaken lower-class white support for slavery.

The desire to ensure the support for slavery among poorer whites led some Southereners to agitate for reopening the African slave trade, believing that nonslaveholding Southerners would only support the institution if they had a chance to own slaves themselves. But most Southern leaders believed the best way to perpetuate slavery was through westward expansion, and they wanted concrete assurance that Congress would not infringe on the right to take slaves into the western territories. Without such a guarantee, declared an Alabama politician, "This union cannot stand."

The Compromise of 1850: The Illusion of Sectional Peace

Ever since David Wilmot had proposed in 1846 that slavery be prohibited from any territory acquired from Mexico, opponents of slavery had argued that Congress possessed the power to regulate slavery in

Seventy-three-year-old Henry Clay pleads his case for sectional compromise. The Senate chamber was so crowded when he made his speech that the temperature reached 100 degrees.

all of the territories. Ardent proslavery Southerners vigorously disagreed.

Politicians had repeatedly but unsuccessfully tried to work out a compromise. One simple proposal had been to extend the Missouri Compromise line to the Pacific Ocean. Thus, slavery would have been forbidden north of 36°30' north latitude but permitted south of that line. This proposal attracted the support of moderate Southerners but generated little support outside the region. Another proposal, supported by two key Democratic senators, Lewis Cass of Michigan and Stephen Douglas of Illinois, was known as squatter sovereignty or **popular sovereignty.** It declared that the people actually living in a territory should decide whether or not to allow slavery.

Henry Clay, the aging statesman known as the "Great Compromiser," for his efforts on behalf of the Missouri Compromise and the Compromise Tariff of 1832 (which resolved the nullification crisis), once again appealed to Northerners and Southerners to place national patriotism ahead of sectional loyalties. He believed that compromise could be effective only if it addressed all the issues dividing the two regions. He proposed that California be admitted as a free state; that territorial governments be established in New Mexico and Utah without any restrictions on slavery; that Texas relinquish its claims to land in New Mexico in exchange for federal assumption of Texas's unpaid debts; that Congress enact a stringent and enforceable fugitive slave law; and that the slave trade—but not slavery—be abolished in the District of Columbia.

Clay's proposal ignited an eight-month debate in Congress and led John C. Calhoun to threaten Southern secession. On March 4, 1850, Calhoun, the "Sentinel of the South," offered his response to Clay's compromise proposal. Calhoun was dying of tuberculosis and was too ill to speak publicly, so his speech was read by a colleague. He warned the North that the only way to save the Union was to "cease the agitation of the slave question," concede "to the South an equal right" to the western territories, return runaway slaves, and accept a constitutional amendment that would protect the South against northern violations of its rights. In the absence of such concessions, Calhoun argued, the South's only option was to secede.

Three days later, Daniel Webster, the North's most spellbinding orator, abandoned his previous opposition to the expansion of slavery into the western territories and threw his support behind Clay's compromise. "Mr. President," he began, "I wish to speak today not as a Massachusetts man, nor as Northern man, but as an American. . . . I speak today for the preservation of the Union. Hear me for my cause." The 68-year-old Massachusetts Whig called on both sides to resolve their differences in the name of patriotism. The North, he insisted, could afford to be generous because climate and geography ensured that slavery would never be profitable in the western territories. He concluded by warning his listeners that "there can be no such thing as a peaceable secession."

Webster's speech provoked a storm of outrage from northern opponents of compromise. Senator William H. Seward of New York called Webster a "traitor to the cause of freedom." But Webster's speech did have one important effect. It reassured moderate Southerners that powerful interests in the North were committed to compromise.

Still, opposition to compromise was fierce. Whig President Zachary Taylor argued that California, New Mexico, Oregon, Utah, and Minnesota should all be admitted to statehood before the question of slavery was addressed—a proposal that would have given the North a 10-vote majority in the Senate. William H. Seward, speaking for abolitionists and other opponents of slave expansion, denounced the compromise as conceding too much to the South and proclaimed that there was a "higher law" than the Constitution, a law that demanded an end to slavery. At the same time, many Southern extremists bridled at the idea of admitting California as a free state. In July, northern and southern senators opposed to the very idea of compromise joined ranks to defeat a bill that would have admitted California to the Union and organized New Mexico and Utah without reference to slavery.

Compromise appeared to be dead. A bitterly disappointed and exhausted Henry Clay dejectedly left the Capitol, his efforts apparently for naught. Then with unexpected suddenness the outlook changed. On the evening of July 9, 1850, President Taylor died of gastroenteritis, five days after taking part in a Fourth of July celebration dedicated to the building of the Washington Monument. Taylor's successor was Millard Fillmore, a 50-year-old New Yorker who was an ardent supporter of compromise.

In Congress, leadership in the fight for a compromise passed to Stephen Douglas, a Democratic senator from Illinois. An arrogant and dynamic leader, 5 feet 4 inches in height, with stubby legs, a massive head, bushy eyebrows, and a booming voice, Douglas was known as the "Little Giant." Douglas abandoned Clay's strategy of gathering all issues dividing the sections into a single "omnibus" bill. Instead, he introduced Clay's proposals one at a time. In this way, he was able to gather support from varying coalitions of Whigs, Democrats, Northerners, and Southerners on each issue. At the same time, banking and business interests as well as speculators in Texas bonds lobbied and even bribed members of Congress to support compromise. Despite these manipulations, the compromise proposals never succeeded in gathering solid congressional support. In the end, only 4 senators and 28 representatives voted for every one of the measures. Nevertheless, they all passed.

As finally approved, the compromise admitted California as a free state, allowed the territorial legislatures of New Mexico and Utah to settle the question of slavery in those areas, set up a stringent federal law for the return of runaway slaves, abolished the slave trade in the District of Columbia, and gave Texas $10 million to abandon its claims to territory in New Mexico east of the Rio Grande.

The compromise created the illusion that the territorial issue had been resolved once and for all. "There is rejoicing over the land," wrote one Northerner, "the bone of contention is removed; disunion, fanaticism, violence, insurrection are defeated." Sectional hostility had been defused; calm had returned. But, as one southern editor correctly noted, it was "the calm of preparation, and not of peace."

The Fugitive Slave Law

The most divisive element in the Compromise of 1850 was the **Fugitive Slave Law,** which permitted any African American to be sent South solely on the affidavit of anyone claiming to be his or her owner. As a result, free African Americans were in danger of being placed in slavery. The law also stripped runaway slaves of such basic legal rights as the right to a jury trial and the right to testify in one's own defense. The law further stipulated that accused runaways stand trial in front of special commissioners, not a judge or a jury, and that the commissioners be paid $10 if a fugitive was returned to slavery but only $5 if the fugitive was freed—a provision that many Northerners regarded as a bribe to ensure that any African American accused of being a runaway would be found guilty. Finally, the law required all U.S. citizens and U.S. marshals to assist in the capture of escapees. Anyone who refused to aid in the capture of a fugitive, interfered with the arrest of a slave, or tried to free a slave already in custody was subject to a heavy fine and imprisonment.

The Fugitive Slave Law kindled widespread outrage in the North and converted thousands of Northerners to the free soil doctrine that slavery should be barred from the western territories. "We went to bed one night old-fashioned, conservative, compromise, Union Whigs," wrote a Massachusetts factory owner, "and waked up stark mad Abolitionists."

Efforts to enforce the new law provoked wholesale opposition. Riots directed against the law broke out in many cities. In Christiana, Pennsylvania, in 1851, a gun battle broke out between abolitionists and slave catchers, and in Wisconsin, an abolitionist editor named Sherman M. Booth freed Joshua Glover, a fugitive slave, from a local jail. In Boston,

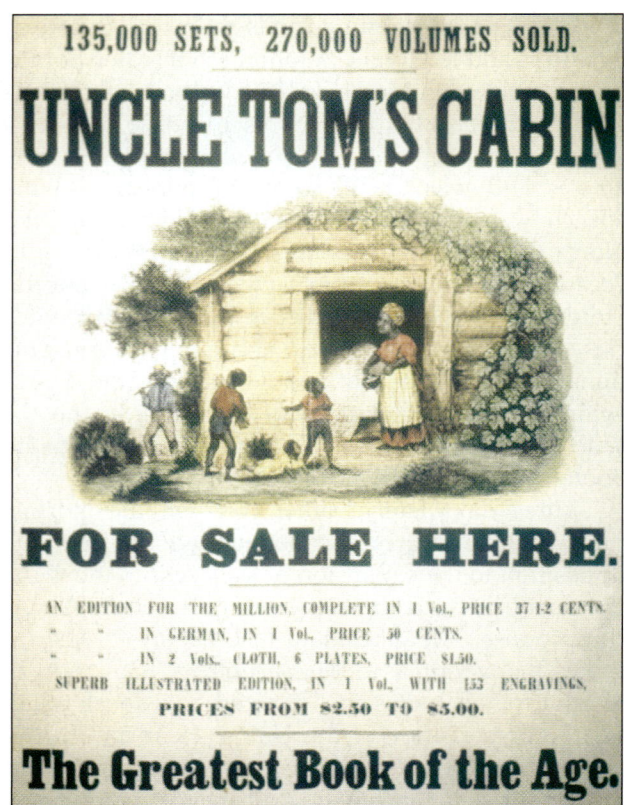

Apologists for slavery denounced *Uncle Tom's Cabin* as inaccurate. Harriet Beecher Stowe responded by writing *The Key to Uncle Tom's Cabin*, which provided documentary proof of the abuses she described in her novel.

Copyright © Collection of The New-York Historical Society.

No part of the Compromise of 1850 drew more outrage from Northerners than the Fugitive Slave Law. An Ohio congressman defiantly stated: "Let the President drench our land of freedom in blood; but he will never make us obey that law."

federal marshals and 22 companies of state troops were needed to prevent a crowd from storming a courthouse to free a fugitive named Anthony Burns.

Eight northern states attempted to invalidate the law by enacting "personal liberty" laws that forbade state officials from assisting in the return of runaways and extended the right of jury trial to fugitives. Southerners regarded these attempts to obstruct the return of runaways as a violation of the Constitution and federal law.

The free black communities of the North responded defiantly to the 1850 law. Northern blacks provided about 1500 fugitive slaves with sanctuary along the Underground Railroad to freedom. Others established vigilance committees to protect blacks from hired kidnappers who were searching the North for runaways. And 15,000 free blacks, convinced that they could never achieve equality in America, emigrated to Canada, the Caribbean, and Africa after adoption of the federal law.

One northern moderate who was repelled by the Fugitive Slave Law was a 41-year-old Maine

Harriet Beecher Stowe.
Gift of I.N. Phelps Stokes, Edward S. Hawes, Alice Mary Hawes, Marion Augusta Hawes/Metropolitan Museum of Art.

mother of six named Harriet Beecher Stowe. In 1852 she published *Uncle Tom's Cabin,* the single most widely read attack on slavery ever written. Stowe had learned about slavery while living in Cincinnati, Ohio, across from slaveholding Kentucky. Her book awakened millions of Northerners to the moral evil of slavery. Southerners denounced Stowe as a "wretch in petticoats," but in the North the book sold a million copies in sixteen months. No novel has ever exerted a stronger influence on American public opinion. Legend has it that when President Lincoln met Mrs. Stowe during the Civil War, he said, "So this is the little woman who made this big war."

DISINTEGRATION OF THE PARTY SYSTEM

As late as 1850, the two-party system was, to all outward appearances, still healthy. Every state, except for South Carolina, had two effective political parties. Both the Democratic party and the Whigs were able to attract support in every section and in every state in the country. Voter participation was extremely high, and in presidential elections neither party was able to gain more than 53 percent of the popular vote. Then, in the space of just five years, the two-party system began to disintegrate in response to two issues: massive foreign immigration and the reemergence of the issue of the expansion of slavery.

The Know Nothings

The most momentous shift in party sentiment in American history took place in the early 1850s following the rise of a party vigorously opposed to immigrants and Catholics. This party, which was known as the American party or **Know Nothing Party,** crippled the Whig party, weakened the Democratic party, and made the political system incapable of resolving the growing crisis over slavery.

Hostility toward immigrants and Catholics had deep roots in American culture. The Protestant religious revivals of the 1820s and 1830s stimulated a "No Popery" movement. Prominent northern clerics, mostly Whig in politics, accused the Catholic Church of conspiring to overthrow democracy and subject the United States to Catholic despotism. Popular fiction offered graphic descriptions of priests seducing women during confession and nuns cutting unborn infants from their mothers' wombs and throwing them to dogs. A popular children's game was called "break the Pope's neck." Anti-Catholic sentiment culminated in mob rioting and in the burning of churches and convents. In 1834, for example, a Philadelphia mob rampaged through Irish neighborhoods, burning churches and houses.

A massive wave of immigration from Ireland and Germany after 1845 led to a renewed outburst of antiforeign and anti-Catholic sentiment. Between 1846 and 1855, more than three million foreigners arrived in America. In cities such as Chicago, Milwaukee, New York, and St. Louis, immigrants actually outnumbered native-born citizens. Nativists—ardent opponents of immigration—capitalized on deep-seated Protestant antagonism toward Catholics, working-class fear of economic competition from cheaper immigrant labor, and resentment among native-born Americans of the growing political power of foreigners. Nativists charged that Catholics were responsible for a sharp increase in poverty, crime, and drunkenness and were subservient to a foreign leader, the Pope.

To native-born Protestant workers, the new immigrants posed a tangible economic threat. Economic slumps in 1851 and 1854 resulted in severe unemployment and wage cuts. Native workers blamed Irish and German immigrants for their plight. The immigrants also posed a political threat. Concentrated in the large cities of the eastern seaboard, Irish immigrants voted as blocs and quickly built up strong political organizations.

One example of anti-Catholic hostility was the formation of a secret fraternal society made up of native-born Protestant working men. This secret society, "The Order of the Star Spangled Banner," soon formed the nucleus of a new political party known as

THE American Mosaic

Physicians and Planters, Prescription for Slave Medical Care

"SO perverse and stubbornly foolish are these people," one slaveholder wrote of his bondsmen, "they are either running into the hospital without cause or braving such a disease as cholera, by concealing the symptoms." Maintenance of slaves' health presented masters with diverse dilemmas. In the continual battle of wills between slaves and their owners over the amount and type of work to be performed, pretending to be sick became a form of "striking" for some slaves. Due to the state of medicine at the time, however, other slaves feared the cure more than the disease. Determining who really was sick was a tricky but crucial matter. Complicating the task were issues of profits, humanitarianism, and racism. Sick slaves could produce few profits; dead slaves none. At the same time, to provide healthy living conditions and constant medical care cost money, which cut into profits. Most masters liked to see themselves as paternalists who took good care of their "slave children." Planters and physicians consequently spent much time trying to determine appropriate responses to slave illnesses.

Feigning illness was an art that some slaves learned through trial and error. Some complaints worked better than others, as the Virginia slave James L. Smith discovered. He detested shooing crows from the cornfield but knew that if he acted sick "they will give me something that will physic me to death." That something was frequently ipecac, which induced vomiting. In response to an earlier stomach complaint Smith's mistress had "made me drunk with whiskey"—a state he had not enjoyed. So he finally decided to claim to have injured his leg and stayed in his room, eating less, to give his claim credibility. Two weeks later, after the crows had deserted the cornfield for the cherry orchard, Smith "began to grow better very fast."

For the same reason that Smith avoided certain imaginary complaints, a number of slaves concealed symptoms of real diseases. Most masters called in the doctor only after the failure of home remedies—many of which had unpleasant and occasionally fatal side effects. Treatment by a physician was not always better. Nineteenth-century medical science was still primitive and had cures for only a handful of conditions. Otherwise doctors resorted to the use of excessive drugs and diuretics, leeching and bloodletting, purging and sweating, all of which caused discomfort and often weakened the body's ability to fight the disease. Many slaves therefore preferred to treat themselves with herbal cures that had been quietly passed down through the generations. Some home remedies in the slaves' quarters were superior to those of whites and were occasionally reported in medical journals. Others, however, were based on superstition, and conjurers sometimes caused treatable diseases to progress to irreversible states. For some slaves the decision to conceal an illness was an act of independence. Even though an unannounced illness meant they had to continue to work while sick, some slaves preferred that to surrendering their bodies to the care of white owners and physicians.

Once planters had overcome the hurdle of determining which slaves were ill, they then had to decide on a course of action. Here humanitarian and profit concerns frequently intersected. Slaveowners were concerned about slaves' health for essentially three reasons: protecting their financial investment, preventing the spread of illness to themselves and their families, and concern for the slaves as human beings. The decision of when to call in a doctor was difficult even for those with the best intentions. To his overseer, Thomas Jefferson specified certain illnesses for which physicians should be summoned as they could provide "certain relief," but insisted that "in most other cases they oftener do harm than good."

For many reasons home care was the first resort of most planters in all cases except those in which the value of professional care was obvious. Treatments for some illnesses were fairly standardized, well known, and easily performed by laymen. Many planters questioned the need to pay a doctor to treat such maladies. Through various suppliers, they obtained such commonly used drugs as calomel, castor oil, ipecac, laudanum, opium, camphor, and quinine. They consulted various household medical guides about proper dosages. Frequently the home cures worked as well as or better than professional services. Often, however, planters misdiagnosed. Even if the improper treatment made the condition no worse, it prolonged the course of the illness until too late for effective treatment.

Some slaveholders consciously waited until everything else had failed before they called in a doctor. Planter Robert Garter of Virginia sent a dying patient to a physician with a note: "I do not wish to continue prac-

tice any longer on Peter—and now I deliver him to you." Such actions infuriated doctors, who were then blamed for their low cure rates. On some plantations where the doctor was not summoned until death was at hand, slaves superstitiously began to link the doctor's arrival with life's departure, giving them another reason to conceal their symptoms.

There were limits to paternalism. The growing knowledge of the impact of environment on health did not induce many planters to improve the living quarters or diets of their bondsmen. That cut into profits too drastically for the perceived benefits. Hence inadequate diets, clothing, and shelter dramatically decreased slaves' health. Economic and humane considerations were offset by a racism that placed less value on slave life. Landon Carter administered rattlesnake powder to his slaves during an attack of "bilious fever." It seemed to help but produced unpleasant side effects. "I wish my own fears did not prevent my giving it to my Children," Carter wrote in his diary—displaying a willingness to "experiment" on slaves that was not uncommon for physicians or planters. Slaves had no authority to refuse any kind of treatment.

African Americans were sometimes treated differently from whites because of perceived physiological differences. A number of the perceptions were accurate assessments distilled from experience. Physicians could not help but note variations in the susceptibility to specific diseases or in the response to treatment between the two groups. Modern researchers have found physiological bases for some of their observations, such as the effect of the sickle-cell trait—more common in African Americans than in the rest of the population—on some malarial viruses. At the time, however, those differences were often used and exaggerated as justification for both slavery and inadequate health care. Some asserted that African American bodies were uniquely suited for hard labor as well as slavery—a proposal not supported by mortality statistics.

Samuel W. Cartwright of Louisiana was a leading medical apologist for slavery. He argued that African Americans were intellectually inferior because dark pigmentation was more than skin deep. "Even the negro's brain and nerves," he wrote, "are tinctured with a shade of pervading darkness." To support his claims of African American bodies and minds being built for slavery, Cartwright explained all "unslavelike" behavior as diseases peculiar to African Americans. Careless habits were a symptom of what he called *Dysaetesia Aethipica*. Slaves who ran away were affected with *Drapetomania*. He could not accept that either could be rational forms of resistance to slavery. The health care of slaves illustrates the interplay of medicine and public values. Physicians became apologists for slavery and built lucrative careers on treating "Negro illnesses." Although slaves often sought to control their medical destinies through secret self-treatment, ultimate authority over their bodies rested in the property rights of their owners. Those owners most frequently acted on the basis of self-interest, which sometimes, but not always, coincided with benevolence. Few valued African American life as highly as white. Medical care, like most other life-and-death matters, was controlled by the white establishment.

After Philadelphia's Catholic bishop convinced the city's board of education in 1844 to use both the Catholic and Protestant versions of the Bible in schools, a vicious anti-Catholic riot erupted.

the Know Nothing or the American party. The party received its name because when members were asked about the workings of the party, they were supposed to reply, "I know nothing."

The sudden growth of the **Know Nothing party** is one of the most extraordinary stories in American political history. In the North, the Know Nothings drew support from many native-born Protestants hostile toward Catholics and immigrants. In the South and in the border states, the party attracted voters disturbed by the mounting sectional disputes over slavery. Throughout the country, the Know Nothings capitalized on a popular longing for new political leaders.

By 1855 the Know Nothings had captured control of the legislatures in New England, except in Vermont and Maine, and were the dominant opposition party to the Democrats in New York, Pennsylvania, Maryland, Virginia, Tennessee, Georgia, Alabama, Mississippi, and Louisiana. In the presidential election of 1856, the party supported Millard Fillmore and won more than 21 percent of the popular vote and 8 electoral votes. In Congress, the party had 5 senators and 43 representatives. Between 1853 and 1855, the Know Nothings replaced the Whigs as the nation's second largest party.

Respectable public opinion spoke out vehemently against the dangers posed by the party. In 1855 an Illinois Whig politician named Abraham Lincoln denounced the Know Nothings in eloquent terms:

> I am not a Know-Nothing. How could I be? How can any one who abhors the oppression of Negroes be in favor of degrading classes of white people? Our progress in degeneracy appears to me pretty rapid, as a nation we began by declaring "all men are created equal." We now practically read it, "all men are created equal, except Negroes." When the Know-Nothings get control, it will read "all men are created equal, except Negroes, and foreigners, and Catholics." When it comes to this I should prefer emigrating to some country where they make no pretense of loving liberty—to Russia, for example, where despotism can be taken pure and without the base alloy of hypocrisy.

By 1856, however, the Know Nothing party was already in decline. Many Know Nothing officeholders were relatively unknown men with little political experience. In the states where they gained control, the Know Nothings proved unable to enact their legislative program, which included a 21-year residency period before immigrants could become citizens and vote, a limitation on political officeholding to native-born Americans, and restrictions on the sale of liquor.

After 1855 the Know Nothing party was supplanted in the North by a new and explosive sectional party, the Republicans. By 1856 northern workers felt more threatened by the southern slave power than by the Pope and Catholic immigrants. At the same time, fewer and fewer Southerners were willing to support a party that ignored the question of the expansion of slavery. As a result, the Know Nothing party rapidly dissolved.

Nevertheless, the Know Nothings left an indelible mark on American politics. The Know Nothing movement eroded loyalty to the national political parties, helped destroy the Whig party, and undermined the capacity of the political system to contain the divisive issue of slavery.

Young America

For nearly four years following the Compromise of 1850, agitation over the question of the expansion of slavery abated. Most Americans were weary of the continuing controversy and turned their attention away from politics to focus instead on railroads, cotton, and trade. The early 1850s were dominated by dreams of greater American influence abroad—in areas such as Asia, the Caribbean, and Central America. Majestic clipper ships raced from New York to China in as few as 104 days. Steamship and railroad promoters launched ambitious schemes to build transit routes across Central America to link California and the Atlantic Coast.

In 1853 Commodore Matthew Perry sailed into Tokyo Bay with two steam frigates and two sailing ships, ending Japan's era of isolation from the western world. The whole world appeared to be opening up to American influence.

Franklin Pierce, a New Hampshire Democrat elected as the nation's fourteenth president in 1852, tried to unite the country with an aggressive program of foreign expansion called "Young America." He sought to annex Hawaii, expand American influence in Honduras and Nicaragua, and acquire new territory from Mexico and Spain. He announced that his administration would not be deterred "by any timid forebodings of evil" raised by the slavery question. But each effort to expand the country's boundaries only provoked new sectional disputes because any acquisition would have posed the question of its status with regard to slavery.

Pierce was the first "doughface" president. He was, in the popular phrase, "a Northern man with Southern principles." Many Northerners suspected that Pierce's real goal was the acquisition of new territory for slavery. This suspicion was first raised in 1853, when the president instructed James Gadsden, his minister to Mexico, to purchase as much Mexican territory as possible, to provide a route for a southern railroad from New Orleans to California.

Cuba was the next object of Pierce's ambitions. Southern slaveholders coveted Cuba's 300,000 slaves. Other Americans wanted to free Cuba's white population from Spanish rule. In 1854 Pierce instructed his ambassador to Spain to offer $130 million for Cuba, but Spain refused the offer. That same year, at a meeting in Ostend, Belgium, three of Pierce's diplomatic ministers (including a future Democratic president, James Buchanan) sent a dispatch, later titled the Ostend Manifesto, to the secretary of state. It urged the military seizure of Cuba if Spain continued to refuse to sell the island. The Ostend Manifesto outraged Northerners, who regarded it as a brazen attempt to expand U.S. slavery in defiance of Spain's sovereign rights.

Commodore Matthew Perry's display of armor and technology led Japan to accept the Treaty of Kanagawa, opening Japanese ports to American trade. These drawings were done by artists dispatched by Japanese officials to keep a visual record of Perry's activities.

The Kansas-Nebraska Act

In 1854, less than four years after the Compromise of 1850, a piece of legislation was introduced in Congress that revived the issue of the expansion of slavery, shattered all illusions of sectional peace, and reordered the political landscape by destroying the Whig party, dividing the Democratic party, and creating the Republican party. Ironically, the author of this legislation was Senator Stephen A. Douglas, the very man who had pushed the earlier compromise through Congress—and a man who had sworn after the passage of the Compromise of 1850 that he would never make a speech on the slavery question again.

As chairman of the Senate Committee on Territories, Douglas proposed that the area west of Iowa and Missouri—which had been set aside as a permanent Indian reservation—be organized as the Nebraska territory and opened to white settlement. Douglas had sought to achieve this objective since 1844, but southern congressmen had objected because Nebraska was located in the northern half of the Louisiana Purchase where the Missouri Compromise prohibited slavery. To forestall southern opposition, Douglas's original bill ignored both the Missouri Compromise and the status of slavery in the Nebraska territory. It simply provided that Nebraska, when admitted as a state, could enter the Union "with or without slavery," as its "constitution may prescribe."

Southern senators, however, demanded that Douglas add a clause specifically repealing the Missouri Compromise and stating that the question of slavery would be determined on the basis of popular sovereignty. Douglas relented to southern pressure. In its final form, Douglas's bill created two territories, Kansas and Nebraska, and declared that the Missouri Compromise was "inoperative and void." With solid support from southern Whigs and southern Democrats and the votes of half of the northern Democratic congressmen, the measure passed. On May 30, 1854, President Pierce signed the measure into law.

Why did Douglas risk reviving the slavery question? His critics accused him of yielding to the southern pressure because of his presidential ambitions and a desire to enhance the value of his holdings in Chicago real estate and western lands. They charged that the Illinois senator's chief interest in opening up Kansas and Nebraska was to secure a right-of-way for a transcontinental railroad that would make Chicago the transportation center of mid-America.

Douglas's supporters, on the other hand, pictured him as a statesman laboring for western development and a sincere believer in popular sovereignty as a solution to the problem of slavery in the western territories. Douglas had long insisted that the democratic solution to the slavery issue was to allow the people who actually settled a territory to decide whether slavery would be permitted or forbidden. Popular sovereignty, he believed, would allow the nation to "avoid the slavery agitation for all time to come." Moreover, he believed that because of climate and geography slavery could never be extended into Kansas and Nebraska anyway.

To understand why Douglas introduced the **Kansas-Nebraska Act,** it is important to realize that by 1854 political and economic pressure to organize Kansas and Nebraska had become overwhelming. Midwestern farmers agitated for new land. A southern rail route had been completed through the Gadsden Purchase in December 1853, and promoters of a northern route for a transcontinental railroad viewed territorial organization as essential. Missouri slaveholders, already bordered on two sides by free states, believed that slavery in their state was doomed if they were surrounded by a free territory. All wanted to see the region opened to settlement.

Revival of the Slavery Issue

Neither Douglas nor his southern supporters anticipated the extent and fury of northern opposition to the Kansas-Nebraska Act. Opponents denounced it as "a gross violation of a sacred pledge." They burned so many figures of Douglas from trees, the Illinois senator joked, "I could travel from Boston to Chicago by the light of my own effigy."

Douglas predicted that the "storm will soon spend its fury," but it did not subside. Northern Free Soilers regarded the Missouri Compromise line as a "sacred compact" that had forever excluded slavery from the northern half of the Louisiana Purchase. Now, they feared that under the guise of popular sovereignty, the southern slave power threatened to spread slavery across the entire western frontier.

No single piece of legislation ever passed by Congress had more far-reaching political consequences. The Kansas-Nebraska Act brought about nothing less than a dramatic realignment of the two-party system. Conservative Whigs abandoned their party and joined the Democrats, while northern Democrats with free soil sentiments repudiated their own elected representatives. In the elections of 1854, 44 of the 51 northern Democratic representatives who voted for the act were defeated.

The chief beneficiary of these defections was a new political organization, the Republican party. A combination of diverse elements, it stood for the belief that slavery must be barred from the western ter-

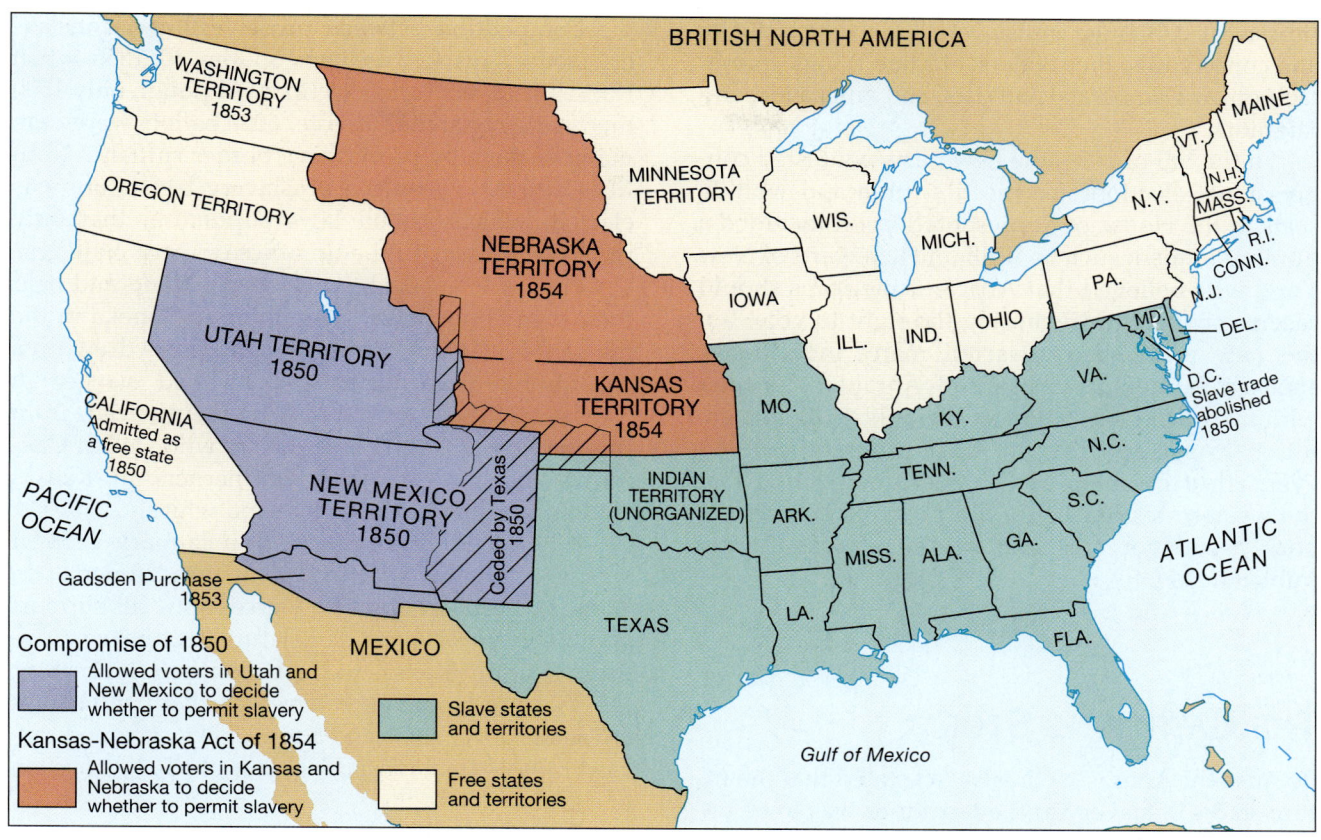

Compromise of 1850/Kansas-Nebraska Act

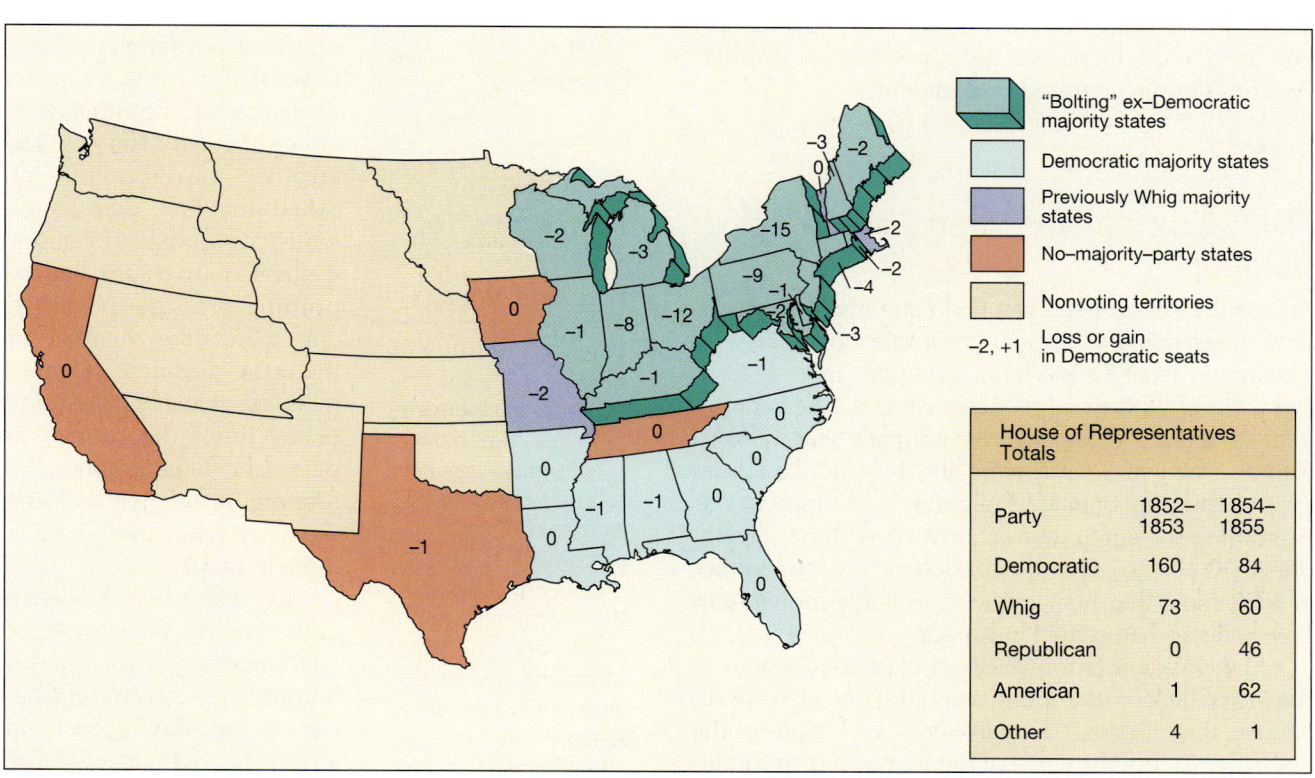

Gains and Losses in the Congressional Election of 1854

The sectional rift grew even sharper after the Kansas-Nebraska Act.

ritories. It contained antislavery radicals, moderate and conservative Free Soilers, old-line Whigs, former Jacksonian Democrats, nativists, and antislavery immigrants.

In the fall of 1854, the new party contested congressional elections for the first time and won 46 seats in the House of Representatives. It included a number of men, such as William H. Seward of New York, who believed that African Americans should receive civil rights, including the right to vote. But the new party also attracted many individuals, such as Salmon P. Chase and Abraham Lincoln, who favored colonization as the only workable solution to slavery. Despite their differences, however, all of these groups shared a conviction that the western territories should be saved for free labor. "Free labor, free soil, free men," was the Republican slogan.

THE GATHERING STORM

Because the Kansas-Nebraska Act stated that the future status of slavery in the territories was to be decided by popular vote, both antislavery northerners and proslavery southerners competed to win the region for their section. Because Nebraska was too far north to attract slave owners, Kansas became the arena of sectional conflict. For six years, proslavery and antislavery factions fought in Kansas as popular sovereignty degenerated into violence.

"Bleeding Kansas" and "Bleeding Sumner"

Across the drought-stricken Ohio and Mississippi valleys, thousands of land-hungry farmers hoped to stake a claim to part of Kansas's 126,000 square miles of territory. Along with these pioneers came a small contingent of settlers whose express purpose was to keep Kansas free soil. Even before the 1854 act had been passed, the New England Emigrant Aid Company was promoting the emigration of antislavery New Englanders to Kansas to "vote to make it free." By the summer of 1855, more than 9000 pioneers—mainly midwestern Free Soilers—had settled in Kansas.

Slaveholders from Missouri expressed alarm at the activities of the Emigrant Aid Society. In response, they formed "Social Bands" and "Sons of the South" to "repel the wave of fanaticism which threatens to break upon our border." One Missouri lawyer told a cheering crowd that he would hang any "free soil" emigrant who came into Kansas.

Competition between proslavery and antislavery factions reached a climax on May 30, 1855, when Kansas held territorial elections. Although only 1500 men were registered to vote, 6000 ballots were cast, many of them by proslavery "border ruffians" from Missouri. As a result, a proslavery legislature was elected, which passed laws stipulating that only proslavery men could hold office or serve on juries.

Free Soilers called the election a fraud and held their own "Free State" convention in Topeka in the fall of 1855. At this convention, delegates drew up a constitution that not only prohibited slavery in Kansas but also barred free African Americans from the territory. Like the Free Soilers who settled California and Oregon, most northerners in Kansas wanted the territory to be free and white.

When Congress convened in January 1856, it was confronted by two rival governments in Kansas. President Franklin Pierce threw his support behind the proslavery legislature and asked Congress to admit Kansas to the Union as a slave state.

Violence broke out between northern and southern settlers over rival land claims, town sites, and railroad routes—and, most dangerous of all, the question of slavery.

In one episode, when a proslavery grand jury indicted several members of the Free Soil Topeka government for high treason, 800 proslavery men, many from Missouri, marched into Lawrence, Kansas, to arrest the leaders of the antislavery government. The posse burned the local hotel, called the Free Soil Hotel, looted a number of houses, destroyed two antislavery printing presses, and killed one man. One member of the posse declared: "Gentlemen, this is the happiest day of my life. I determined to make the fanatics bow before me in the dust and kiss the territorial laws. I have done it, by God."

On May 19, 1856—two days before the "sack of Lawrence"—Senator Charles Sumner of Massachusetts began a two-day speech in which he denounced "The Crime Against Kansas." In his speech, Sumner charged that there was a southern

Bleeding Kansas

When the territory of Kansas was established under the principle of popular sovereignty, violence erupted between proslavery and antislavery forces. A preview of the Civil War occurred when a proslavery mob from Missouri ransacked antislavery Lawrence, Kansas. The term "Bleeding Kansas" became a battle cry for antislavery advocates.

Between May and September 1856, terrorism and guerrilla warfare swept across Kansas, leaving 200 dead and $2 million in property damage. In one incident, Kansas Free Soilers fired on a proslavery settlement at the Battle of Hickory Point.

conspiracy to make Kansas a slave state. He proceeded to argue that a number of southern senators, including Senator Andrew Butler of South Carolina, stood behind this conspiracy. Launching into a bitter personal diatribe, Sumner accused Senator Butler of taking "the harlot, Slavery," for his "mistress" and proceeded to make fun of a medical disorder from which Senator Butler suffered. At the rear of the Senate chamber, Stephen Douglas muttered: "That damn fool will get himself killed by some other damned fool."

Two days later, Senator Butler's nephew, Congressman Preston Brooks of South Carolina, entered a nearly empty Senate chamber. Brooks was convinced that he had a duty to "avenge the insult to my State." Sighting Sumner at his desk, Brooks charged at him and began striking the Massachusetts senator over the head with a cane. He swung so hard that the cane broke into pieces. Brooks caned Sumner, rather than challenging him to a duel, because he regarded the Senator as his social inferior. Thus, he wanted to use the same method slaveholders used to chastise slaves. Although it took Sumner three years to recover from his injuries and return to his Senate seat, he promptly became a martyr to the cause of freedom in the the North, where a million copies of his "Crime Against Kansas" speech were distributed. In the South, Brooks was hailed as a hero. Merchants in Charleston bought the congressman a new cane, inscribed "Hit him again." A vote to expel Brooks from Congress failed because every Southern representative but one voted against the measure. Instead, Brooks was censured. He promptly resigned his seat and was immediately reelected.

The caning of Sumner had repercussions in strife-torn Kansas. John Brown, a devoted Bible-quoting Calvinist who believed he had a personal responsibility to overthrow slavery, announced that the time had come "to fight fire with fire" and "strike terror in the hearts of proslavery men." The next day, in reprisal for the "sack of Lawrence" and the assault on Sumner, Brown and six companions dragged five proslavery men and boys from their beds at Pottawatomie Creek, split open their skulls with a sword, cut off their hands, and laid out their entrails.

A war of revenge erupted in Kansas. Columns of proslavery Southerners ransacked free farms, while they searched for Brown and the other "Pottawatomie killers." Armed bands looted enemy stores and farms. At Osawatomie, proslavery forces attacked John Brown's headquarters, leaving a dozen men dead. John Brown's men killed four Missourians, and proslavery forces retaliated by blockading the free towns of Topeka and Lawrence. Before it was over, guerilla warfare in eastern Kansas left 200 dead.

Clutching a pen in one hand and a copy of his "Crime Against Kansas" speech in the other, Senator Charles Sumner attempts to defend himself against an attack by South Carolina Congressman Preston Brooks.

The Election of 1856

The presidential election of 1856 took place in the midst of Kansas's civil war. President Pierce hoped for renomination to a second term in office, but northern indignation over the Kansas-Nebraska Act led the Democrats to seek out a less controversial candidate. On the seventeenth ballot, northern and western Democrats succeeded in winning the nomination for James Buchanan, a 65-year-old Pennsylvania bachelor, who had been minister to Great Britain during the struggle over the Kansas-Nebraska bill. The dying Whig party and the southern wing of the Know Nothing party nominated former President Millard Fillmore.

The Republican party held its first national convention in Philadelphia and adopted a platform denying the authority of Congress and of territorial legislatures "to give legal existence to slavery" in the territories. The convention nominated the dashing young explorer and soldier John C. Frémont for president as young Republicans chanted, "Free Speech, Free Soil and Frémont." Frémont was a romantic figure who had led more than a dozen major explorations of the Rocky Mountains and Far West. After accepting the Republican nomination, he declared that Kansas should be admitted to the Union as a free state. This was his only public utterance during the entire 1856 campaign. A few weeks later, the northern wing of the Know Nothing party threw its support behind Frémont.

The election was one of the most bitter in American history and the first in which voting divided along rigid sectional lines. The Democratic strategy was to picture the Republican party as a hotbed of radicalism. Democrats called the Republicans the party of disunion and described Frémont as a "black abolitionist" who would destroy the union. Republicans responded by accusing the Democrats of being accomplices in a conspiracy to extend slavery.

Although Buchanan garnered only 45 percent of the popular vote because of the presence of Fillmore, he narrowly carried five northern states, giving him a comfortable margin in the electoral college. Buchanan won 174 electoral college votes to 114 for Frémont and 8 for Fillmore.

The election results showed how polarized the nation had become. The South, except for Maryland, voted solidly Democratic. Frémont did not receive a single vote south of the Mason-Dixon line. At the same time, the northernmost states were solidly Republican.

In their first presidential campaign, the Republicans had made an extraordinarily impressive showing. Eleven free states voted for Frémont. If only two more states had voted in his favor, the Republicans would have won the election.

The Supreme Court Speaks

In his inaugural address, Buchanan declared that "the great object of my administration will be to arrest... the agitation of the slavery question in the North." He then predicted that a forthcoming Supreme Court decision would once and for all settle the controversy over slavery in the western territories. Two days after Buchanan's inauguration, the high court handed down its decision.

On March 6, 1857, the Supreme Court finally decided a question that Congress had evaded for decades: whether Congress had the power to pro-

In the sweeping Dred Scott (left) decision, Chief Justice Roger Taney (right) sought to resolve the constitutional questions raised by slavery. The decision, which remained a major source of controversy until the eruption of the Civil War, intensified divisions between proslavery and antislavery factions.

hibit slavery in the territories. Repeatedly, Congress had declared that this was a constitutional question that the Supreme Court should settle. Now, for the first time, the Supreme Court offered its answer.

The case originated in 1846, when a Missouri slave, **Dred Scott,** sued to gain his freedom. Scott argued that while he had been the slave of an army surgeon, he had lived for four years in Illinois, a free state, and Wisconsin, a free territory, and that his residence on free soil had erased his slave status. By a 7–2 margin, the Court ruled that Dred Scott had no right to sue in federal court, that the Missouri Compromise was unconstitutional, and that Congress had no right to exclude slavery from the territories.

All nine justices rendered separate opinions, but Chief Justice Taney delivered the opinion that expressed the position of the Court's majority. His opinion represented a judicial defense of the most extreme proslavery position.

The chief justice made two sweeping rulings. The first was that Dred Scott had no right to sue in federal court because neither slaves nor free blacks were citizens of the United States. At the time the Constitution was adopted, the chief justice wrote, blacks had been "regarded as beings of an inferior order" with "no rights which the white man was bound to respect."

Second, Taney declared that Congress had no right to exclude slavery from the federal territories since any law excluding slave property from the territories was a violation of the Fifth Amendment prohibition against the seizure of property without due process of law. For the first time since *Marbury* v. *Madison* in 1803, the Court declared an act of Congress unconstitutional. The Missouri Compromise was unconstitutional, the Court declared, because it prohibited slavery north of 36°30'. Newspaper headlines summarized the Court's rulings: "SLAVERY ALONE NATIONAL—THE MISSOURI COMPROMISE UNCONSTITUTIONAL—NEGROES CANNOT BE CITIZENS—THE TRIUMPH OF SLAVERY COMPLETE."

In a single decision, the Court sought to resolve all the major constitutional questions raised by slavery. It declared that the Declaration of Independence and the Bill of Rights were not intended to apply to African Americans. It stated that the Republican party platform—barring slavery from the western territories—was unconstitutional. And it ruled that Stephen Douglas's doctrine of "popular sovereignty"—which stated that territorial governments had the power to prohibit slavery—was also unconstitutional.

Republicans reacted with scorn. The decision, said the *New York Tribune*, carried as much moral weight as "the judgment of a majority of those congregated in any Washington barroom." Radical abolitionists called for secession. Many Republicans—including an Illinois politician named Abraham Lincoln—regarded the decision as part of a slave power conspiracy to legalize slavery throughout the United States.

The Dred Scott decision was a major political miscalculation. In its ruling, the Supreme Court sought to solve the slavery controversy once and for all. Instead the Court intensified sectional strife, undercut possible compromise solutions to the divisive issue of the expansion of slavery, and weakened the moral authority of the judiciary.

The Lecompton Constitution: "A Swindle and a Fraud"

Late in 1857, President Buchanan faced a major test of his ability to suppress the slavery controversy. In September, proslavery forces in Kansas met in Lecompton, the territorial capital, to draft a constitution that would bring Kansas into the Union as a slave state. Recognizing that a proslavery constitution would be defeated in a free and fair election, proslavery delegates withheld the new state charter from the territory's voters. Instead, they offered voters a referendum on whether they preferred "the constitution with slavery" or "the constitution without slavery." In either case, however, the new constitution guaranteed slave ownership as a sacred right. Free Soilers boycotted the election and, as a result, "the constitution with slavery" was approved by a 6000-vote margin.

President Buchanan—afraid that the South would secede if Kansas were not admitted to the Union as a slave state—accepted the proslavery Lecompton constitution as a satisfactory application of the principle of popular sovereignty. He then demanded that Congress admit Kansas as the sixteenth slave state.

Stephen Douglas was aghast. "A small minority" of proslavery men in Kansas, he said, had "attempted to cheat and defraud the majority by trickery and juggling." Appalled by this travesty of the principle of popular sovereignty, Douglas broke with the Buchanan administration.

After a rancorous debate, the Senate passed a bill that admitted Kansas as a slave state under the Lecompton constitution. But the House of Representatives rejected this measure and instead substituted a compromise, known as the English bill, which allowed Kansans to vote on the proslavery constitution. As a thinly veiled bribe to encourage Kansans to ratify the document, the English bill offered Kansas a huge grant of public land if it approved the Lecompton constitution. In 1858, while federal troops guarded the polls, Kansas voters overwhelmingly rejected the proslavery constitution.

The bloody battle for Kansas had come to an end. Free Soilers took control of the territorial legislature and repealed the Kansas territorial slave code. Stripped of any legal safeguards for their slave property, most Kansas slaveowners quickly left the territory. When the federal census was taken in 1860, just two slaves remained in Kansas.

But the nation would never be the same. To antislavery Northerners, the Lecompton controversy showed that the slave power was willing to subvert democratic processes in an attempt to force slavery on a free people. In Kansas, they charged, proslavery forces had used violence, fraud, and intimidation to expand the territory open to slavery. To the more extreme opponents of slavery in the North, the lesson was clear. The only way to preserve freedom and democratic procedures was to destroy slavery and the slave power through force of arms.

CRISIS OF THE UNION

In 1858, Senator William H. Seward of New York examined the sources of the conflicts between the North and the South. Some people, said Seward, thought the sectional conflict was "accidental, unnecessary, the work of interested or fanatical agitators, and therefore ephemeral." But Seward believed that these people were wrong. The roots of the conflict went far deeper. "It is an irrepressible conflict," Seward said, "between opposing and enduring forces."

By 1858, a growing number of Northerners were convinced that two fundamentally antagonistic societies had evolved in the nation, one dedicated to freedom, the other opposed. They had come to believe that their society was locked in a life-and-death struggle with a southern society dominated by an aggressive slave power, which had seized control of the federal government and imperiled the liberties of free people. Declared the *New York Tribune:* "We are not one people. We are two peoples. We are a people for Freedom and a people for Slavery. Between the two, conflict is inevitable."

At the same time, an increasing number of Southerners expressed alarm at the growth of anti-slavery and anti-South sentiment in the North. They were convinced that Republicans would not only insist on halting slavery's expansion but would also seek to undermine the institution where it already existed. As the decade closed, the dominant question of American political life was whether the nation's leaders could find a peaceful way to resolve the differences separating the North and South.

The Lincoln-Douglas Debates

The critical issues dividing the nation—slavery versus free labor, popular sovereignty, and the legal and political status of African Americans—were brought into sharp focus in a series of dramatic forensic duels during the 1858 election campaign for U.S. senator from Illinois. The campaign pitted a little-known lawyer from Springfield named Abraham Lincoln against Senator Stephen A. Douglas, the front-runner for the Democratic presidential nomination in 1860. (Senators, at the time, were elected by state legislators, and Douglas and Lincoln were actually campaigning for candidates from their party for the state legislature.)

The contest received intense national publicity. One reason for the public attention was that the political future of Stephen Douglas was at stake. Douglas had openly broken with the Buchanan administration over the proslavery Lecompton constitution and had joined with Republicans to defeat the admission of Kansas to the Union as a slave state. Now, many wondered, would Douglas assume the leadership of the free soil movement?

The public knew little about the man the Republicans selected to run against Douglas. Lincoln had been born on February 12, 1809, in a log cabin and grew up on the wild Kentucky and Indiana frontier. At the age of 21, he moved to Illinois, where he worked as a clerk in a country store, became a local postmaster and a lawyer, and served four terms in the lower house of the Illinois General Assembly. A Whig in politics, Lincoln was elected in 1846 to the U.S. House of Representatives, but his stand against the Mexican War had made him too unpopular to win reelection. After the passage of the Kansas-Nebraska Act in 1854, Lincoln reentered politics, and in 1858 the Republican party nominated him to run against Douglas for the Senate.

Lincoln accepted the nomination with the famous words: "'A house divided against itself cannot stand.' I believe this Government cannot endure permanently half-slave and half-free." He did not believe the Union would fall, but he did predict that it would cease to be divided. Lincoln proceeded to argue that Stephen Douglas's Kansas-Nebraska Act and the Supreme Court's Dred Scott decision were part of a conspiracy to make slavery lawful "in all the States, old as well as new—North as well as South."

For 4 months Lincoln and Douglas crisscrossed Illinois, traveling nearly 10,000 miles and participating in seven face-to-face debates before crowds of up to 15,000.

During the course of the debates, Lincoln and Douglas presented two sharply contrasting views of the problem of slavery. Douglas argued that slavery was a dying institution that had reached its natural limits and could not thrive where climate and soil were inhospitable. He asserted that the problem of slavery could best be resolved if it were treated as essentially a local problem. Lincoln, on the other hand, regarded slavery as a dynamic, expansionistic institution, hungry for new territory. He argued that if Northerners allowed slavery to spread unchecked, slaveowners would make slavery a national institution and would reduce all laborers, white as well as black, to a state of virtual slavery.

The sharpest difference between the two candidates involved the issue of African Americans' legal rights. Douglas was unable to conceive of African Americans as anything but inferior to whites, and he was unalterably opposed to their citizenship. "I want citizenship for whites only," he declared. Lincoln said that he, too, was opposed to granting free blacks full legal rights. But he insisted that African Americans were equal to Douglas and "every living man" in their right to life, liberty, and the fruits of their own labor.

The debates reached a climax on a damp, chilly August 27. At Freeport, Illinois, Lincoln asked Douglas to reconcile the Supreme Court's Dred Scott decision, which denied Congress the power to exclude slavery from a territory, with popular sovereignty. Could the residents of a territory "in any lawful way" exclude slavery prior to statehood? Douglas replied that the residents of a territory could exclude

The question of the legal status of slavery in the territories was the major issue Illinois senatorial candidates Stephen A. Douglas and Abraham Lincoln discussed in their series of seven debates in 1858. Lincoln lost the Senate race to Douglas, nicknamed the "Little Giant" in reference to his short stature but outstanding oratorical skills. The debates, however, helped bring Lincoln to national prominence, and two years later he defeated Douglas for the presidency.

slavery by refusing to pass laws protecting slaveholders' property rights. "Slavery cannot exist a day or an hour anywhere," he declared, "unless it is supported by local police regulations."

Any way he answered, Douglas was certain to alienate northern Free Soilers or proslavery Southerners. The Dred Scott decision had given slave owners the right to take their slavery into any western territories. Now Douglas said that territorial settlers could exclude slavery, despite what the Court had ruled. Douglas won reelection, but his cautious statements antagonized Southerners and northern Free Soilers alike.

In the final balloting, the Republicans outpolled the Democrats. But the Democrats had gerrymandered the voting districts so skillfully that they kept control of the state legislature.

Although Lincoln failed to win a Senate seat, his battle with Stephen Douglas had catapulted him into the national spotlight and made him a serious presidential possibility in 1860. As Lincoln himself noted, his defeat was "a slip and not a fall."

Harpers Ferry

On August 19, 1859, John Brown, the Kansas abolitionist, and Frederick Douglass, the celebrated African American abolitionist and former slave, met in an abandoned stone quarry near Chambersburg, Pennsylvania. For three days, the two men discussed whether violence could be legitimately used to free the nation's slaves. The Kansas guerrilla leader asked Douglass if he would join a band of raiders who would seize a federal arsenal and spark a mass uprising of slaves. "When I strike," Brown said, "the bees will begin to swarm, and I shall need you to help hive them."

As Robert E. Lee's marines broke through the brick walls of John Brown's stronghold at Harpers Ferry, Brown "felt the pulse of his dying son with one hand and held his rifle with the other," and commanded his men with the utmost composure.

THE PEOPLE SPEAK

John Brown Defends His Raid on Harpers Ferry (1859)

At the very end of his trial in a Virginia court for treason, conspiracy, and murder, John Brown delivered a five-minute speech in which he defended his raid on Harpers Ferry.

> I have, may it please the Court, a few words to say.
>
> In the first place, I deny everything but what I have all along admitted: of a design on my part to free slaves. I intended certainly to have made a clean thing of that matter, as I did last winter, when I went into Missouri and there took slaves without the snapping of a gun on either side, moving them through the country, and finally leaving them in Canada. I designed to have done the same thing again on a larger scale. That was all I intended. I never did intend murder, or treason, or the destruction of property, or to exercise or incite slaves to rebellion, or to make insurrection.
>
> I have another objection, and that is that it is unjust that I should suffer such a penalty. . . . Had I so interfered in behalf of the rich, the powerful, the intelligent, the so-called great . . . it would have been all right. Every man in this Court would have deemed it an act worthy of reward rather than punishment.
>
> This Court acknowledges . . . the validity of the law of God. I see a book kissed, which I suppose to be the Bible, or at least the New Testament, which teaches me that all things whatsoever I would that men should do to me, I should do even so to them. It teaches me, further, to remember them that are in bonds as bound with them. I endeavored to act up to that instruction. I say I am yet too young to understand that God is any respecter of persons. I believe that to have interfered as I have done . . . in behalf of His despised poor, I did no wrong, but right. Now, if it is deemed necessary that I should forfeit my life for the furtherance of the ends of justice, and mingle my blood further with the blood of my children and with the blood of millions in this slave country whose rights are disregarded by wicked, cruel, and unjust enactments, I say let it be done.

Source: John Brown, "Last Statement to the Court," in *The Life and Execution of Captain John Brown, Known as "Old Brown of Ossawatomie"* (New York, 1859).

"No," Douglass replied. Brown's plan, he knew, was suicidal. Brown had earlier proposed a somewhat more realistic plan. According to that scheme, Brown would have launched guerrilla activity in the Virginia mountains, providing a haven for slaves and an escape route into the North. That scheme had a chance of working, but Brown's new plan was hopeless.

Up until the Kansas-Nebraska Act, abolitionists were averse to the use of violence. Opponents of slavery hoped to use moral suasion and other peaceful means to eliminate slavery. But by the mid-1850s, the abolitionists' aversion to violence had begun to fade. In 1858 William Lloyd Garrison complained that his followers were "growing more and more warlike." On the night of October 16, 1859, violence came, and John Brown was its instrument.

Brown's plan was to capture the federal arsenal at Harpers Ferry, Virginia (now West Virginia), and arm slaves from the surrounding countryside. His long-range goal was to drive southward into Tennessee and Alabama, raiding federal arsenals and inciting slave insurrections. Failing that, he hoped to ignite a sectional crisis that would destroy slavery.

At eight o'clock Sunday evening, October 16, John Brown led a raiding party of approximately 21 men toward Harpers Ferry, where they captured the lone night watchman and cut the town's telegraph lines. Encountering no resistance, Brown's raiders seized the federal arsenal, an armory, and a rifle works along with several million dollars worth of arms and munitions. Brown then sent out several detachments to round up hostages and liberate slaves.

But Brown's plans soon went awry. As news of the raid spread, many townspeople and local militia companies cut off Brown's escape routes and trapped his men in the armory. Twice, Brown sent men carrying flags of truce to negotiate. On both occasions, drunken mobs, yelling "Kill them, kill them," gunned the men down.

Two days later U.S. Marines, commanded by Colonel Robert E. Lee and Lieutenant J. E. B. Stuart, arrived in Harpers Ferry. Brown and his men took refuge in a fire engine house and battered holes through the building's brick wall to shoot through. A hostage later described the climactic scene: "With one son dead by his side and another shot through, he felt the pulse of his dying son with one hand and held his rifle with the other and commanded his men . . . encouraging them to fire and sell their lives as dearly as they could."

Later that morning, Colonel Lee's marines stormed the engine house and rammed down its doors. Brown and his men continued firing until the leader of the storming party cornered Brown and knocked him unconscious with a sword. Five of Brown's party escaped, ten were killed, and seven, including Brown himself, were taken prisoner.

A week later, John Brown was put on trial in a Virginia court, even though his attack had occurred on federal property. During the six-day proceedings, Brown refused to plead insanity as a defense. He was found guilty of treason, conspiracy, and murder, and was sentenced to die on the gallows.

The trial's high point came at the very end when Brown was allowed to make a five-minute speech. His words helped convince thousands of Northerners that this grizzled man of 59, with his "piercing eyes" and "resolute countenance," was a martyr to the cause of freedom. Brown denied that he had come to Virginia to commit violence. His only goal, he said, was to liberate the slaves. "If it is deemed necessary," he told the Virginia court, "that I should forfeit my life for the furtherance of the ends of justice and mingle my blood . . . with the blood of millions in this slave country whose rights are disregarded by wicked, cruel, and unjust enactments, I say let it be done."

Brown's execution was set for December 2. Before he went to the gallows, Brown wrote one last message: "I . . . am now quite certain that the crimes of this guilty land will never be purged away but with blood." At 11 A.M., he was led to the execution site, a halter was placed around his neck, and a sheriff led him over a trapdoor. The sheriff cut the rope and the trapdoor opened. As the old man's body convulsed on the gallows, a Virginia officer cried out: "So perish all enemies of Virginia!"

Across the North, church bells tolled, flags flew at half-mast, and buildings were draped in black bunting. Ralph Waldo Emerson compared Brown to Jesus Christ and declared that his death had made "the gallows as glorious as the cross." William Lloyd Garrison, previously the strongest exponent of nonviolent opposition to slavery, announced that Brown's death had convinced him of "the need for violence" to destroy slavery. He told a Boston meeting that "every slave holder has forfeited his right to live" if he opposed immediate emancipation.

Prominent northern Democrats and Republicans, including Stephen Douglas and Abraham Lincoln, spoke out forcefully against Brown's raid and his tactics. Lincoln expressed the views of the Republican leadership when he denounced Brown's raid as an act of "violence, bloodshed, and treason" that deserved to be punished by death. But southern whites refused to believe that politicians like Lincoln and Douglas represented the true opinion of most Northerners. These men condemned Brown's "invasion," observed a Virginia senator, "only because it failed."

Chronology of Key Events

1846	Wilmot Proviso, banning slavery from any territory acquired from Mexico, is proposed
1850	Compromise of 1850
1852	Harriet Beecher Stowe publishes *Uncle Tom's Cabin*
1853	Gadsden Purchase from Mexico
1854	Ostend Manifesto calls on the United States to acquire Cuba from Spain; Commodore Matthew Perry negotiates a treaty opening Japan to American trade; Kansas-Nebraska Act reignites sectional controversy over slavery; "Bleeding Kansas" begins; conventions of Free Soilers form the Republican party
1856	"Sack of Lawrence"—proslavery Missourians loot and burn several buildings in Lawrence, Kansas; "Bleeding Sumner"—Congressman Preston Brooks of South Carolina beats Senator Charles Sumner of Massachusetts with a cane; John Brown's raid on Pottawatomie Creek, Kansas
1857	Dred Scott decision
1858	Kansas voters reject the Lecompton constitution; Lincoln-Douglas debates
1859	John Brown's raid at Harpers Ferry

Conclusion

For 40 years the debate over the extension of slavery had divided North and South. National leaders had tried on several occasions to reach a permanent, workable solution to the problem, without success. With the collapse of the Whigs and the rise of the Republicans, the American political process could no longer contain the fierce antagonisms and mutual distrust that separated the two regions.

In 1859, John Brown's raid convinced many white Southerners that a majority of Northerners wished to free the slaves and incite a race war. Southern extremists, known as "fire-eaters," told large crowds that John Brown's attack on Harpers Ferry was "the first act in the grand tragedy of emancipation, and the subjugation of the South in bloody treason." After Harpers Ferry, Southerners increasingly believed that secession and creation of a slaveholding confederacy were now the South's only options. A Virginia newspaper noted that there were "thousands of men in our midst who, a month ago, scoffed at the idea of a dissolution of the Union as a madman's dream, but who now hold the opinion that its days are numbered." The final bonds that had held the Union together had come unraveled.

Suggestions for Further Reading

Tyler Anbinder, *Nativism and Slavery: The Northern Know Nothings and the Politics of the 1850s* (1992) and William E. Gienapp, *Origins of the Republican Party* (1987). Analyze shifts in voting patterns in the 1850s.

William J. Cooper, Jr., *Liberty and Slavery* (1983). Examines white southern attitudes on the eve of the Civil War. Eric Foner, *Free Soil, Free Labor, Free Men* (1970). Explores northern attitudes.

Don E. Fehrenbacher, *The Dred Scott Case* (1978). Thoroughly examines this landmark Supreme Court decision.

William W. Freehling, *The Road to Disunion* (1990); Bruce Levine, *Half Slave and Half Free: The Roots of the Civil War* (1992); David M. Potter, *The Impending Crisis* (1976); and Kenneth M. Stampp, *America in 1857* (1990). Explore the causes of the Civil War.

Overviews and Surveys

Philip D. Curtin, *The Rise and Fall of the Plantation Complex* (1990); David Brion Davis, *The Slave Power Conspiracy and the Paranoid Style* (1970); Eric Foner and Olivia Mahoney, *A House Divided: America in the Age of Lincoln* (1990); William W. Freehling, *The Road to Disunion: Secessionists at Bay, 1776–1854* (1990); Michael Holt, *The Political Crisis of the 1850s* (1978); James M. McPherson, *Ordeal by Fire* (1982); William L. Neumann, *America Encounters Japan: From Perry to MacArthur* (1963); Allan Nevins, *The Ordeal of the Union* (1947), and *The Emergence of Lincoln,* 2 vols. (1950); Roy F. Nichols and Eugene H. Berwanger, *The Stakes of Power, 1845–1877,* rev. ed. (1982); John Niven, *The Coming of the Civil War, 1837–1861* (1990); David Potter, *The Impending Crisis, 1848–1861* (1976); James A. Rawley, *Secession: Disruption of the American Republic, 1844–1861* (1990); Joel H. Silbey, *The American Political Nation, 1838–1893* (1991), and *The Partisan Imperative: The Dynamics of American Politics Before the Civil War* (1985); Kenneth Stampp, *The Imperiled Union* (1980).

The Crisis of 1850

William L. Barney, *The Road to Secession: A New Perspective on the Old South* (1972); John Barrywell, *Love of Order: South Carolina's First Secession Crisis* (1982); Stanley W. Campbell, *The Slave Catchers: Enforcement of the Fugitive Slave Law, 1850–1860* (1970); William J. Cooper, *Liberty and Slavery* (1983), and *The South and the Politics of Slavery, 1828–1856* (1978); Barbara J. Fields, *Slavery and Freedom on the Middle Ground* (1985); Holman Hamilton, *Prologue to Conflict: The Crisis and Compromise of 1850* (1964); Joseph G. Rayback, *Free Soil: The Election of 1848* (1970).

Disintegration of the Party System

Thomas Alexander, *Sectional Stress and Party Strength* (1967); Carleton Beales, *Brass Knuckles Crusade: The Great Know-Nothing Conspiracy* (1960); Ray Allen Billington, *The Protestant Crusade, 1800–1860* (1938); Eric Foner, *Free Soil, Free Labor, Free Men: The Ideology of the Republican Party* (1970); Paul W. Gates, *Fifty Million Acres: Conflicts over Kansas Land Policy, 1854–1890* (1954); William E. Gienapp, *Origins of the Republican Party* (1987); Charles G. Hamilton, *Lincoln and the Know-Nothing Movement* (1954); Michael F. Holt, *Forging a Majority: The Formation of the Republican Party in Pittsburgh, 1848–1860* (1969); James C. Malin, *The Nebraska Question, 1852–1854* (1953); Stuart C. Miller, *The Unwelcome Immigrant* (1969); John R. Mulkern, *The Know-Nothing Party in Massachusetts* (1990); Alice Nichols, *Bleeding Kansas* (1954); Roy F. Nichols, "The Kansas-Nebraska Act: A Century of Historiography," *Mississippi Valley Historical Review,* 43 (1956); W. Darrell Overdyke, *The Know-Nothing Party in the South* (1950); James A. Rawley, *Race and Politics: "Bleeding Kansas" and the Coming of the Civil War* (1969); Joel H. Silbey, *The Shrine of Party: Congressional Voting Behavior, 1841–1852* (1967), and *The Transformation of American Politics, 1840–1860* (1967); Thomas P. Slaughter, *Bloody Dawn: The Christiana Riot and Racial Tensions in the Antebellum North* (1991); Mark W. Summers, *The Plundering Generation: Corruption and the Crisis of the Union* (1987).

The Gathering Storm

Dale Baum, *The Civil War Party System: The Case of Massachusetts, 1848–1876* (1984); Robert M. Cover, *Justice Accused* (1975); Don E. Fehrenbacher, *The Dred Scott Case: Its Signifi-*

cance in American Law and Politics (1978); Paul Finkelman, *An Imperfect Union: Slavery, Federalism and Comity* (1981); Eric Foner, *Free Soil, Free Labor, Free Men: The Ideology of the Republican Party before the Civil War* (1970); A. Leon Higginbotham, Jr., *In the Matter of Color: Race and the American Legal Process* (1978); Michael F. Holt, *Forging a Majority: The Formation of the Republican Party in Pittsburgh, 1848–1860* (1969); Stanley I. Kutler, *The Dred Scott Decision* (1967); Stephen E. Maizlish, *The Triumph of Sectionalism: The Transformation of Ohio Politics* (1983); William Lee Miller, *Arguing About Slavery* (1996); Thomas D. Morris, *Free Men All: The Personal Liberty Laws of the North* (1974); Michael A. Morrison, *Slavery and the American West* (1997); Arthur M. Schlesinger, Jr., and Fred L. Israel, eds., *History of U.S. Political Parties* (1973); Hans L. Treffouse, *The Radical Republicans* (1969); Edward L. Widmer, *Young America: The Flowering of Democracy in New York City* (1998).

Crisis of the Union

Jules Abels, *Man on Fire: John Brown and the Cause of Liberty* (1971); Elizabeth Ammons, ed., *Critical Essays on Harriet Beecher Stowe* (1979); Hannah Page Wheeler Andrews, *Time and Variations: Uncle Tom's Cabin as Book, Play, and Film* (1979); R. O. Boyer, *The Legend of John Brown* (1973); Don E. Fehrenbacher, *Prelude to Greatness: Lincoln in the 1850s* (1962); Paul Finkelman, ed., *His Soul Goes Marching On: Responses to John Brown* (1995); Charles H. Foster, *The Rungless Ladder: Harriet Beecher Stowe and New England Puritanism* (1970); Thomas F. Gossett, *Uncle Tom's Cabin and American Culture* (1985); Theodore R. Hovet, *The Master Narrative: Harriet Beecher Stowe's Subversive Story of Master and Slave* (1988); Henry V. Jaffa, *Crisis of the House Divided: An Interpretation of the Issues in the Lincoln-Douglas Debates* (1959); Ellen Moers, *Harriet Beecher Stowe and American Literature* (1978). Truman Nelson, *The Old Man: John Brown at Harper's Ferry* (1973); Benjamin Quarles, *Allies for Freedom: Blacks and John Brown* (1974), and *Blacks on John Brown* (1972); Edward J. Renehan, Jr., *The Secret Six* (1995); Jeffrey Rossbach, *Ambivalent Conspirators: John Brown, the Secret Six, and a Theory of Slave Violence* (1982); Louis Ruchames, ed., *John Brown: The Making of a Revolutionary* (1969); Kenneth M. Stampp, *America in 1857* (1990); David Zarefsky, *Lincoln, Douglas, and Slavery* (1990).

Biographies

John R. Adams, *Harriet Beecher Stowe* (1989); Richard Current, *The Lincoln Nobody Knows* (1963); David Herbert Donald, *Lincoln* (1995); Robert W. Johannsen, *Stephen A. Douglas* (1973); William S. McFeely, *Frederick Douglass* (1991); Samuel Eliot Morison, *"Old Bruin": Commodore Matthew C. Perry, 1794–1858* (1967); William L. Neumann, *America Encounters Japan: From Perry to MacArthur* (1963); John Niven, *John C. Calhoun and the Price of Union* (1988); Stephen B. Oates, *To Purge This Land with Blood: A Biography of John Brown*, 2d ed. (1984), and *With Malice Toward None: The Life of Abraham Lincoln* (1977); William E. Parrish, *David Rice Atchison of Missouri* (1961); Robert V. Remini, *Henry Clay: Statesman for the Union* (1991); Damon Wells, *Stephen Douglas: The Last Years, 1857–1861* (1971).

INTERNET RESOURCES

Daniel Webster: Dartmouth's Favorite Son
http://grafton.dartmouth.edu:8005/~dw/
Dartmouth College provides texts and images concerning famous alumnus Daniel Webster.

Secession Era Editorials Project
http://history.furman.edu/~benson/docs/
Furman University is digitizing editorials about the secession crisis and already includes scores of them on this site.

John Brown Trial Links
http://www.law.umkc.edu/faculty/projects/ftrials/Brown.html
For information about the trial of John Brown, this site provides a list of excellent links.

Abraham Lincoln and Slavery
http://odur.let.rug.nl/~usa/H/1990/ch5_p6.htm
This site discusses Lincoln's views and action concerning slavery, especially the Lincoln-Douglas debates.

Bleeding Kansas
http://www.ukans.edu/carrie/kancoll/galbks.htm
Contemporary and later accounts of America's rehearsal for the Civil War make up this University of Kansas site.

KEY TERMS

Popular Sovereignty (p. 388)
Fugitive Slave Law (p. 389)
Know Nothing Party (p. 391)
Kansas-Nebraska Act (p. 396)
Dred Scott (p. 400)

REVIEW QUESTIONS

1. Why did California's application for statehood cause heated debate in Congress?
2. In what ways did Southerners benefit from the Compromise of 1850? In what ways did Northerners benefit?
3. Why did the Fugitive Slave Law anger many Northerners?
4. What issue led to the formation of the Republican party?
5. How was the issue of slavery to be decided in Kansas and Nebraska? Why did the status of slavery in Kansas become a divisive issue during the 1850s?
6. What did the Supreme Court rule in the Dred Scott decision? What was the ruling's significance?
7. What were the major differences in the attitudes of Abraham Lincoln and Stephen Douglas toward slavery?
8. Why did John Brown's raid convince many Southerners that their states should secede from the Union?

15

A Nation Shattered by Civil War, 1860–1865

From Secession to Full-Scale War
Electing a New President
Secession Rends the Union
Lincoln Takes Command
An Accounting of Resources

"Forward to Richmond!" and "On to Washington!"
Planning the Union Offensive
Yankee Reverses and Rebel Victories in the East
Federal Breakthrough in the West

To and From Emancipation: The War on the Home Front
An Abundance of Confederate Shortages
Directing the Northern War Effort
Issuing the Emancipation Proclamation
Emancipation Tests Northern Resolve

Breaking Confederate Resistance, 1863–1865
The Tide Turns: Gettysburg and Vicksburg
Crushing Blows from Grant and Sherman
Total War Forces Surrender

"We will make our stand"

Looking eastward from Sharpsburg into the mountains of western Maryland, General Robert E. Lee uttered the fateful words: "We will make our stand." Behind him was the Potomac River and to his front was Antietam Creek. Having invaded Union territory in early September 1862, Lee dispersed his Army of Northern Virginia, some 50,000 strong, across the countryside to capture strategic points such as Harpers Ferry and to rally the citizens of this border slaveholding state behind the Confederate cause. Now he issued orders for his troops to reassemble with all haste at Sharpsburg. A major battle was in the making. General George B. McClellan's Army of the Potomac, numbering nearly 100,000 soldiers, was rapidly descending upon Lee's position.

Early on the morning of September 17, the great battle began. As the day progressed, Union forces attacked in five uncoordinated waves, which allowed Lee to maneuver his heavily outnumbered troops from point to point, warding off federal assaults. As usual, Lee calculated his opponent's temperament correctly. McClellan was too timid to throw everything into the battle at once. As darkness fell, the Confederates still held their lines. Lee knew, however, that if McClellan attacked again the next morning, the southern army might well be annihilated.

Among those rebel troops who had marched into Maryland was 25-year-old Thomas Jefferson Rushin. He had grown up secure in his social station as the second son of Joel Rushin, a prospering west Georgia cotton planter who owned 21 slaves. Thomas was anxious to show those far-off "Black Republican" Yankees that Southern gentlemen would never shrink from battle in defense of their way of life. He enlisted in Company K of the Twelfth Georgia Volunteers in June 1861. At 5:30 A.M. on September 17, 1862, Sergeant Rushin waited restlessly north of Sharpsburg—where the first Union assault occurred.

As dawn beckoned, Rushin and his comrades first heard skirmish fire, then the booming of cannons. Out in an open field they soon engaged Yankee troops appearing at the edge of a nearby woods. The Twelfth Georgia Volunteers stood their ground until they pulled back at 6:45 A.M. By the time that order came, 62 of the Georgians lay dead or wounded, among them the lifeless remains of Thomas Jefferson Rushin.

To the south of Sharpsburg, the battle would soon heat up. At 9:00 A.M. General Ambrose E. Burnside's Union soldiers prepared to cross a stone bridge over Antietam Creek. On the other side was sharply rising ground, on top of which troops in gray waited, ready to shoot at any person bold enough to venture onto what became known as Burnside Bridge.

The Eleventh Connecticut Volunteers were among those poised for the advance. Included in their number was 18-year-old Private Alvin Flint, Jr., who had enlisted a few months before in Company D. He was from Hartford, where his father, Alvin, Sr., worked in a papermaking factory. Flint's departure from home was sorrowful because his mother had just died of consumption. A few weeks later he received word that his younger sister had succumbed to the same disease.

Flint's own sense of foreboding must have been overwhelming as he charged toward the bridge. In an instant, he became part of the human carnage, as minié balls poured down from across the bridge. Bleeding profusely from a mortal wound, he died before stretcher-bearers from the Ambulance Corps could reach him.

Flint had not known that his father and younger brother had recently joined another Connecticut regiment, affording Alvin, Sr., the chance to visit the

The human toll of the Civil War was overwhelming for contemporaries and remains so for later generations. Thomas Jefferson Rushin (left) and Alvin Flint, Jr. (right), were young casualties of the Battle of Antietam.

battlefield a month later in search of his son's remains. Deeply distressed, his father wrote the *Hartford Courant* and decried the loss of "my boy" who "was brutally murdered" because of this "hellish, wicked rebellion." "Oh how dreadful was that place to me," he wrote in agony, where his son "had been buried like a beast of the field!"

Fifty-three-year-old Alvin Flint, Sr., gave up, returned to his regiment, and marched toward Fredericksburg, Virginia, where another major battle took place in December 1862. A month later the two remaining Flints died of typhoid fever, a disease then raging through the Army of the Potomac.

As the human toll mounted higher and higher, Civil War battlefields became hallowed ground. Southerners named these sites after towns while Northerners named them for nearby landmarks like rivers and streams. In the South the Battle of Sharpsburg symbolized a valiant stand against overwhelming odds. In the North the Battle of Antietam represented a turning point in the war because Union troops, at last, controlled the field of combat after Lee, astonished that McClellan did not continue the fight, ordered a retreat back into Virginia on the evening of September 18.

Different names for the same battle could not change the results. With 23,000 dead and wounded soldiers, Antietam turned out to be the bloodiest one-day action of the Civil War. Before the slaughter ended in 1865, total casualties reached 1.2 million people, including 620,000 dead—more than the total number of United States troops who lost their lives in World Wars I and II combined. Back in April 1861, when the Confederates fired on Fort Sumter, no one foresaw such carnage. No one imagined bodies as "thick as human leaves" decaying in fields around Sharpsburg, or how "horrible" looking would be "the faces of the dead."

The coming of the Civil War could be compared to a time bomb ready to explode. The fundamental issue was slavery, or more specifically whether the "peculiar institution" would be allowed to spread across the American landscape. Southerners feared that northern leaders would use federal authority to declare slavery null and void throughout the land. The South made its stand on the principle of states' rights and voted to secede. The North, in response, went to war to save the Union, but always lurking in the background was the issue of permitting the continued existence of slavery. The carnage of the war settled the matter. A few days after Antietam, President Abraham Lincoln announced the Emancipation Proclamation, which transformed the Civil War into a struggle to end slavery—and the way of life it supported—as a means of destroying Confederate resistance and preserving the federal Union.

FROM SECESSION TO FULL-SCALE WAR

On April 23, 1860, the Democratic party gathered in Charleston, South Carolina, to select a presidential candidate. No nominating convention faced a more difficult task. The delegates argued bitterly among themselves, and many southern delegates walked out of the convention. The breaking up of the Democratic party cleared the way for Lincoln's election, which in turn provoked the secession of seven southern states by February 1861. As the Union fell apart, all Americans watched closely to see how "Honest Abe," the "Railsplitter" from Illinois, would handle the secession crisis.

Electing a New President

Even before the Democratic convention met, evidence was abundant that the party was crumbling. Early in 1860 Jefferson Davis of Mississippi introduced a series of resolutions in the U.S. Senate calling for federal protection of slavery in all western territories. More extreme **fire-eaters,** such as William L. Yancey of Alabama, not only embraced Davis's proposal but announced that he and others would leave the convention if the party did not defend their inalienable right to hold slaves and nominate a Southerner for president. After the convention rejected an extreme proslavery platform, delegates from eight southern states walked out.

Those who remained tried to nominate a candidate, but after dozens of ballots no one received a two-thirds majority. So the delegates gave up and agreed to reconvene in Baltimore in another six weeks. That convention also failed to produce a consensus. Finally, in two separate meetings, northern delegates named Stephen A. Douglas as their candidate, and southern delegates chose John C. Breckinridge of Kentucky.

To confuse matters further, a short-lived party, the Constitutional Unionists, emerged. This coalition of former Whigs, Know Nothings, and Unionist Democrats adopted a platform advocating "no political principle other than the Constitution of the country, the union of the states, and the enforcement of the laws." The Constitutional Unionists nominated John

This 1860 cartoon shows Abraham Lincoln, "the fittest of all candidates," outdistancing his opponents.

Bell of Tennessee, who enjoyed some support in the border states and drew votes away from both Douglas and Breckinridge, thereby making it easier for the sectional Republican party to carry the election.

When the Republicans gathered in Chicago during mid-May, they were very optimistic, especially with the Democrats hopelessly divided. Delegates constructed a platform with many promises, including high tariffs in an appeal to gain the support of northern manufacturers and a homestead law in a bid to win the backing of citizens wanting free farmland. On the slave expansion issue there was no hint of compromise. "The normal condition of all the territory of the United States is that of freedom," the platform read, and no federal, state, or local legislative body could ever "give legal existence to slavery in any territory." The platform, however, did not call for an end to slavery in states where that institution already existed.

To ensure victory, Republican party regulars sought a candidate, as one of them stated, "of popular origin, ... who had no record to defend and no radicalism of an offensive character." This left out Senator William H. Seward, the front-runner, who was widely known as a strong antislavery advocate. Seward fell short of a majority on the first ballot. Then the skilled floor managers of Abraham Lincoln, the local favorite from Illinois—the Republican party had failed to carry this state in 1856—started what became a landslide for their candidate.

The 1860 presidential campaign took place in a lightning-charged atmosphere of threats and fears bordering on hysteria. Rumors of slave revolts, town burnings, and the murder of women and children swept the South. Newspapers reported the imminence of John Brown–style invasions and of slaves

Election of 1860

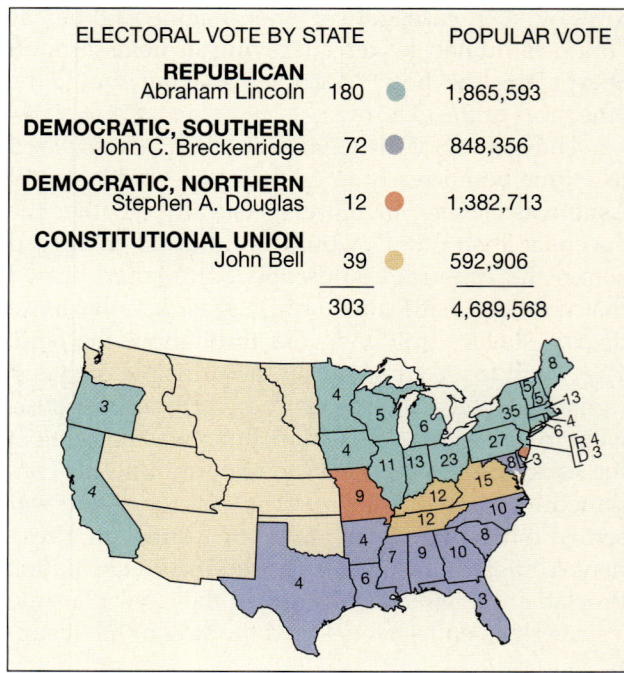

stockpiling strychnine to poison water supplies. In one Alabama town, a mob hanged a stranger, thinking him to be an abolitionist. Across the South militia companies armed themselves and started to drill just in case that "black-hearted abolitionist fanatic" Lincoln won the election.

According to custom, Lincoln stayed home during the campaign and let others speak for him. His supporters inflamed sectional tensions by bragging that slavery would never survive their candidate's presidency. Stephen Douglas, desperately trying "to save the Union," announced, "I will go South." He embarked on the first nationwide speaking tour of a presidential nominee. Once under way, southern Democrats asked Douglas to withdraw from the election in favor of Breckinridge, whom they thought had a better chance to beat Lincoln. Douglas refused, asserting that only he could defeat the Republican candidate.

On election day, November 6, 1860, Lincoln won only 39.9 percent of the popular vote, but he received 180 electoral college votes, 57 more than the combined total of his opponents. The vote was purely sectional; Lincoln's name did not appear on the ballots of 10 southern states. Even when totaling all the popular votes against him, Lincoln still would have won in the electoral college by 17 votes because he carried the most populous states—all in the North. His election dramatically demonstrated to Southerners their minority status.

Secession Rends the Union

Lincoln said to a friend during the campaign that Southerners "have too much good sense, and good temper, to attempt the ruin of the government." He told others he would support a constitutional amendment protecting slavery where it already existed, but Southerners believed otherwise. The choice for the South, as the Mississippi secession convention framed the alternatives, was either to "submit to degradation, and to the loss of [slave] property worth four billions," or to leave the Union. No matter what, "the South will never submit" was the common refrain. Secession, then, meant liberation from the oppression of Black Republicans.

South Carolina led the way when its legislature, in the wake of Lincoln's victory, unanimously called for a secession convention. On December 20, 1860, the delegates voted 169 to 0 to leave the Union. The rationale had long since been developed by John C. Calhoun. State authority was superior to that of the

Secession

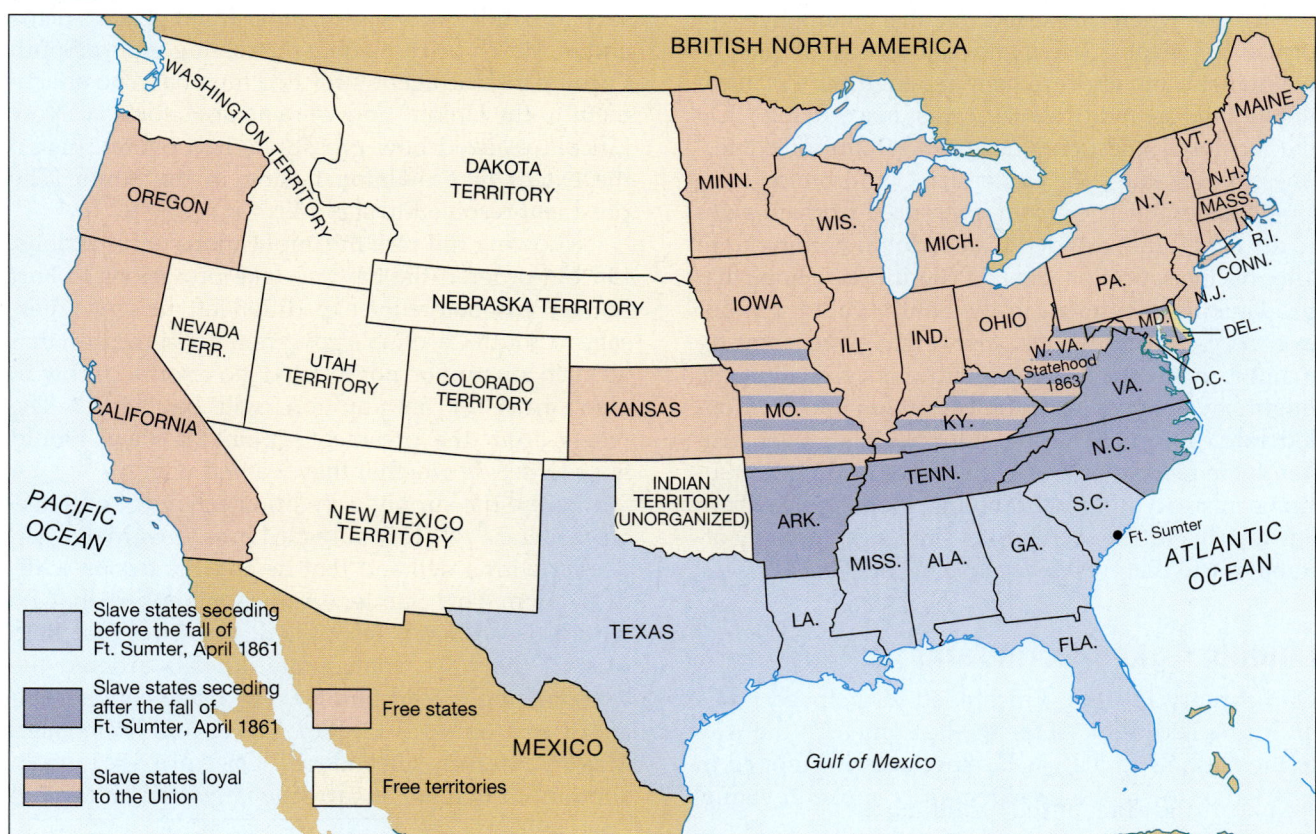

nation, and as sovereign entities, states could as freely leave as they had freely joined the Union. South Carolina, as the delegates proclaimed, had "resumed her position among the nations of the world."

By early February 1861 the states of Georgia, Florida, Alabama, Mississippi, Louisiana, and Texas had also voted for secession. Representatives from the seven states first met in Montgomery, Alabama, on February 8 and proclaimed a new nation, the Confederate States of America. They elected Jefferson Davis provisional president and wrote a plan of government, which they modeled on the federal Constitution except for their emphasis on states' rights. The southern government would consist of an executive branch headed by a president, a two-house Congress, and a Supreme Court. The Confederate constitution limited the president to a single six-year term, required a two-thirds vote of Congress to admit new states or enact appropriations bills, and forbade protective tariffs and government funding of internal improvements.

For some Northerners, such as newspaper editor Horace Greeley of the *New York Tribune*, the intelligent course was to let the "wayward sisters" of the South "depart in peace." A more conciliatory approach, as suggested in December 1860 by Senator John J. Crittenden of Kentucky, was to enshrine the old Missouri Compromise line of 36°30' in a constitutional amendment that would also promise no future restrictions on slavery where it existed. Neither alternative appealed to Lincoln. Secession was unconstitutional, he maintained, and appeasement, especially any plan endorsing the spread of slavery, was unacceptable. "On the territorial question," he stated, "I am inflexible." These words killed the Crittenden Compromise.

President-elect Lincoln, pressured from all sides to do something, decided instead to do nothing until after his inauguration. He had continued to hope that pro-Unionist sentiment in the South would win out over secessionist feelings. Also, eight slave states remained in the Union and controversial statements might have pushed some or all of them into the Confederate camp. Lincoln would make his moves prudently, indeed so carefully that some leading Republicans misread him as a bumbling, inept fool. William Seward, his future secretary of state, even politely offered to run the presidency on Lincoln's behalf.

Lincoln Takes Command

On February 11, 1861, Lincoln left his beloved home of Springfield, Illinois, for the last time. All the way to the nation's capital, as his special train stopped in town after town, the president-elect spoke in vague, conciliatory terms. Between stops, he worked on his inaugural address, which embodied his plan.

On March 4, Lincoln raised his hand and swore to uphold the Constitution as the nation's sixteenth president. Then he read his inaugural address, with its powerful but simple message. The Union was "perpetual," and secession was illegal. To resist federal authority was both "insurrectionary" and "revolutionary." As president, he would support the Union by maintaining possession of federal properties in the South. Then Lincoln appealed to the southern people: "We are not enemies, but friends." And he warned: "In your hands, my dissatisfied countrymen, and not in mine, is the momentous issue of civil war.... You can have no conflict without yourselves being the aggressors."

Even as he spoke, Lincoln knew the seceding states had taken possession of all federal military installations within their borders—with the principal exceptions of Fort Sumter, guarding the entrance to Charleston harbor, and Fort Pickens along the Florida coast at Pensacola. The next day Lincoln received an ominous report. Major Robert Anderson, in command of Fort Sumter, was running out of provisions and would have to abandon his position within six weeks unless resupplied.

Lincoln had a month to back off or decide on a showdown. He consulted his cabinet, only to get sharply conflicting advice. Finally, he sent an emissary to South Carolina to gather intelligence. At the end of March he received a distressing report. South Carolinians, the agent informed him, had "no attachment to the Union" and were anxious for war. Now Lincoln realized how grossly he had overestimated the extent of pro-Union feeling in the South. The president resolved to stand firm.

Knowing full well the implications of his actions, Lincoln ordered the navy to take provisions to Fort Sumter. Just before the expedition left, he sent a message to South Carolina's governor, notifying him that "if such attempt be not resisted, no effort to throw in men, arms, or ammunition, will be made." The rebels, from the president's point of view, would have to decide whether they wanted war.

Before the supply expedition arrived, Confederate General P. G. T. Beauregard presented Major Anderson with a demand that he and his troops withdraw from Fort Sumter. Anderson replied that he would do so if not resupplied. Knowing that help was on the way, Confederate officials ordered the cannonading of Fort Sumter. The firing commenced at 4:30 A.M. on April 12, 1861. Thirty-four hours later, Major Anderson surrendered. On April 15, Lincoln announced that an "insurrection" existed and called for 75,000 volunteers to put down the South's rebellion. The Civil War had begun.

An Accounting of Resources

The firing on Fort Sumter caused both jubilation and consternation. Most citizens thought a battle or two would quickly end the conflict, so they rushed to enlist, not wanting to miss the action. The emotional outburst was particularly strong in the South where up to 200,000 enthusiasts tried to join the fledgling Confederate military machine. Several thousand had to be sent home, since it was impossible to muster them into the service in so short a time with even the

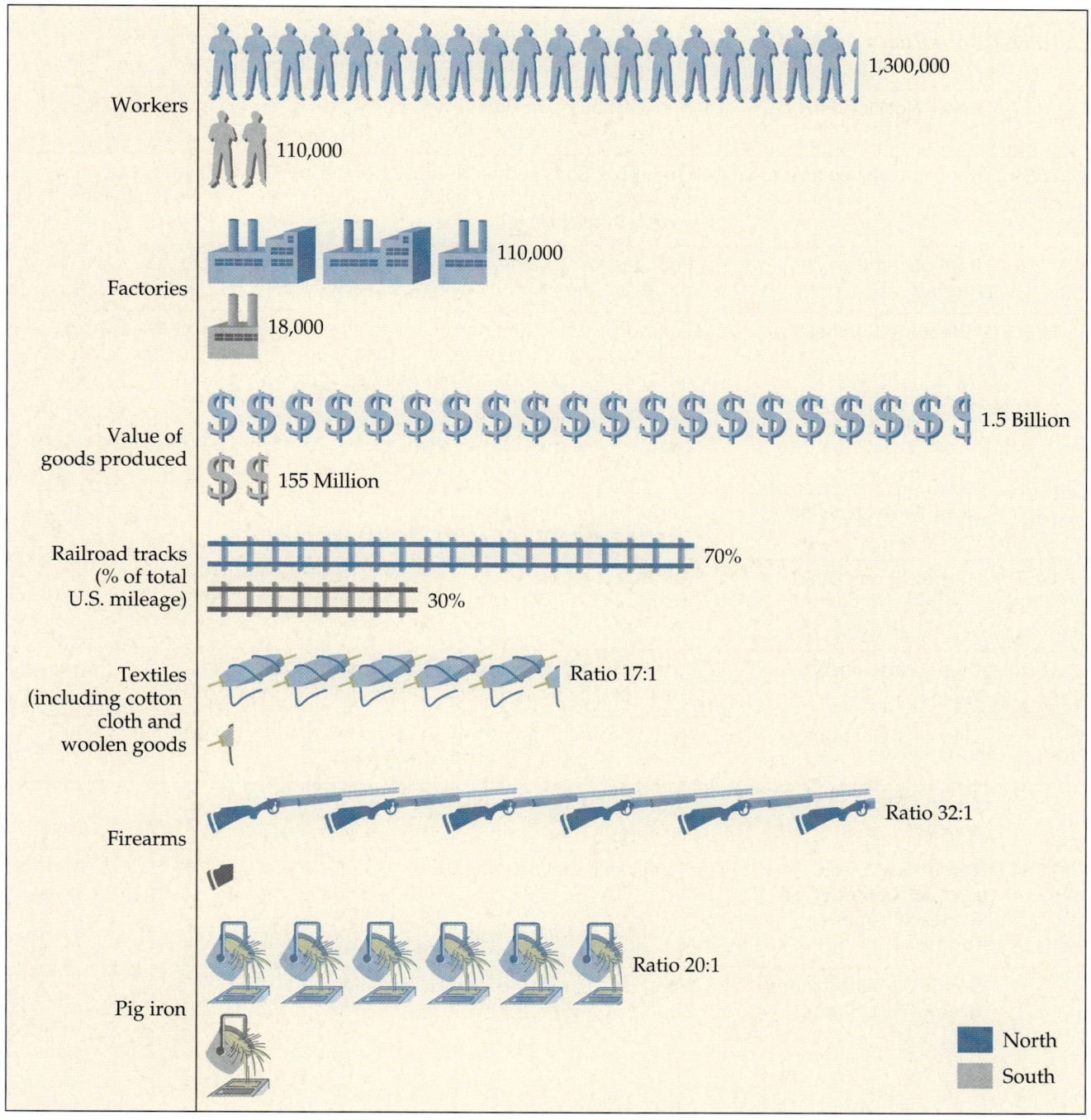

FIGURE 15.1
Resources, North and South

THE ROAD TO WAR

CIVIL WAR

1850	Compromise of 1850	Series of acts which appear to settle sectional strife over slavery; most controversial feature was a strict law for the return of fugitive slaves.
1852	*Uncle Tom's Cabin*	Harriet Beecher Stowe's novel, which sells a million copies in 18 months, arouses antislavery sentiment in the North.
	Know Nothing Party	Anti-Catholic, anti-immigrant party grows largely at the expense of the Whig party, weakening the party system.
1854	Kansas-Nebraska Act	Organizes Kansas and Nebraska territories and provides that slavery in those territories will be decided on the basis of popular sovereignty; reopens issue of slavery in the territories.
	Republican Party formed	Founded by opponents of the Kansas-Nebraska Act, the party is committed to halting slavery's westward expansion.
1856	"Bleeding Sumner"	Senator Charles Sumner of Massachusetts denounces "The Crime Against Kansas"; three days later, Representative Preston Brooks of South Carolina beats him unconscious with a cane.
	"Bleeding Kansas"	Proslavery Kansans attack Lawrence, center of free soil settlers; a band led by John Brown avenges the "Sack of Lawrence" by killing five people at Pottawatomie Creek.
1857	Dred Scott decision	Declares the Missouri Compromise unconstitutional and holds that Negroes are not citizens of the United States.
1859	Harpers Ferry Raid	An armed group led by John Brown seizes the federal arsenal at Harpers Ferry, Virginia; Brown is subsequently executed for treason.
1860	Democratic party splits	Northern Democrats nominate Stephen Douglas for president; Southern Democrats nominate John Breckinridge.
	Lincoln's election	Republican candidate Abraham Lincoln, committed to halting the westward spread of slavery, wins election.
	South Carolina secedes	The Union begins to disintegrate.
1861	Ten other states secede; Confederate States of America forms	Compromise efforts fail.
	South Carolina troops fire on Fort Sumter	President Lincoln responds by declaring a state of insurrection and calls for 75,000 volunteers to put down the rebellion.

bare essentials of war—uniforms, weapons, camp equipment, and food rations.

Professional military men like Lieutenant Colonel Robert E. Lee, who had experienced combat in the Mexican War, were less enthusiastic. "I see only that a fearful calamity is upon us," he wrote. Lee was anxious "for the preservation of the Union," but he felt compelled to defend the "honor" of Virginia, should state leaders vote for secession. If that happened, he would resign his military commission and "go back in sorrow to my people and share the misery of my native state."

On April 17, Virginians seceded in direct response to Lincoln's declaration of an insurrection. By late May, North Carolina, Tennessee, and Arkansas had also voted to leave the Union, meaning that 11 states containing a population of nearly 9 million people, including 3.5 million slaves, ultimately proclaimed their independence. On the other hand, four slaveholding states bordering the North—Delaware, Maryland, Kentucky, and Missouri—equivocated about secession. Lincoln understood that sustaining the loyalty of the border states was critical. Besides making it more difficult for the Confederates to carry the war into the North, their presence gave the Union, with 23 million people, a decisive population edge, a major asset should a prolonged military struggle ensue.

Set in this frame, Robert E. Lee's gloom reflected more than a personal dilemma about conflicting loyalties; it also related to a realistic appraisal of what were overwhelming northern advantages going into the war. The value of northern property was twice that of the South; the banking capital advantage was 10 to 1, and it was 8 to 1 in investment capital. The North could easily underwrite the production of war goods, whereas the South would have to struggle, given its scarce capital resources and an industrial capacity far below that of the North. In 1861 there were just 18,000 Confederate manufacturing establishments employing 110,000 workers. By comparison, the North had 110,000 establishments utilizing the labor of 1.3 million workers.

By other crucial resource measures, such as railroad mileage, representing the capacity to move armies and supplies easily, the Union was far ahead of the Confederacy. The North had 22,000 miles of track, as compared to 9000 for the South. In 1860 U.S. manufacturers produced 470 locomotives, only 17 of which were built in the South. That same year the North produced 20 times as much pig iron, 17 times the clothing, and 32 times as many firearms. Indeed, Northern factories manufactured nearly 97 percent of all firearms, a major reason that the Confederacy could not absorb all those enthusiasts who wanted to enlist in the spring of 1861. The South went to war with a serious weapons shortage.

Despite the South's valiant efforts to produce war goods, the advantage of material resources in the North took its toll. This photograph shows the equipment used by General Grant during his Southern campaigns.

What is remarkable is that the South, despite this imbalance, performed so well in the early going and that the North fared so poorly. Among the South's assets, at least in 1861, was sheer geographic size. As long as the Confederacy maintained a defensive military posture, the North would have to demonstrate an ability to win more than an occasional battle. It would have to conquer a massive region. This factor alone emboldened Southern leaders. In analogies alluding to the American Revolution, they discussed how the British, with superior resources, had failed to reconquer the colonies. If Southerners maintained their resolve, something more likely to happen when soldiers were defending homes and families, nothing, it appeared, could extinguish their desire for national independence.

In addition, the South held an initial advantage in generalship. When secession occurred, regular army officers, some of them trained at West Point, had to decide which side to serve. Most, like Robert E. Lee, stood with their states. There were about 300 available West Pointers, and some 120 joined the Confederate army. Of those senior in age, the South gained more initial talent with Lee (54), Joseph E. Johnston (54), and Albert Sidney Johnston (58), when compared to the North's draw of Henry W. Halleck (46), Joseph Hooker (47), and George G. Meade (46).

As mature senior commanders, men like the two Johnstons and Lee quickly gravitated to the top of the new Confederate command structure. The Union structure, however, was already in place, with the aging hero of the Mexican War, "Old Fuss and Feathers" Winfield Scott (74) serving as general in chief in April 1861. Younger West Pointers, such as Ulysses S. Grant (39), William Tecumseh Sherman (41), and George B. McClellan (34), were not even in the service. Grant had developed a drinking problem after the Mexican War and was running a general store in Illinois; Sherman had fared poorly as a banker in San Francisco and was heading a military academy in Louisiana; and McClellan was in the railroad business. So even with their West Point credentials, Grant and Sherman had to work through the pack of lackluster military professionals in line ahead of them.

Then there was the matter of civilian leadership. At the outset the South appeared to have the advantage. Jefferson Davis, the Confederacy's new president, possessed superb qualifications. Besides being a wealthy slaveholder, he had a West Point education, had fought in the Mexican War, had served in Congress, and had been Franklin Pierce's secretary of war (1853–1857). Further, he looked like a president. "He bears the marks of greatness," wrote an admirer in 1862, because "above all, the gentleman is apparent, the thorough, high-bred, polished gentleman."

Jefferson Davis was named provisional president of the Confederate States of America in 1861. He faced the difficulty of establishing a new government while at the same time fighting an ongoing war.

Appearances, however, were deceptive. Davis was a hard-working but often ineffective administrator. He would not delegate authority and became tangled up in details; he surrounded himself with weak assistants; he held strong opinions on all subjects; and he was invariably rude with those who disagreed with him. Perhaps worst of all, he was not an inspirational leader, something the South desperately needed after war weariness set in. A close associate aptly described Davis in 1865: "Few men could be more chillingly, freezingly cold."

Abraham Lincoln, by comparison, lacked the outward demeanor of a cultured gentleman. Republican campaign literature of 1860 stated: "We know Old Abe does not look very handsome, but if all the ugly men in the U.S. vote for him, he will surely be elected." Worse yet, Lincoln's credentials were unimpressive. He had little formal schooling; he spent an impoverished childhood in Kentucky and Indiana before moving to Illinois and succeeding as a country lawyer; he had served only one term in Congress; and he had virtually no military experience, except for a brief stint as a militia captain during the Black Hawk War (1832). As Lincoln liked to joke, he "fought, bled, and came away" barely alive—not because of contact with "fighting Indians" but because of "many bloody struggles with the mosquitoes."

Many Northerners shook their heads as Lincoln entered the White House. With his tall, thin frame and long legs, he seemed to stumble as he walked, half hunched over in baggy clothes. When he listened, he appeared to be daydreaming; yet he did listen, and when he spoke in return, stated one newspaper reporter, "the dull, listless features dropped like a mask." Citizens soon found that Lincoln viewed himself as a man of the people, eager to do anything necessary to save the Union. They saw him bear up under unbelievable levels of criticism. Even those who disagreed with him came to admire his ability to reflect and think through the implications of proposed actions—and then to move forward decisively. As "Old Abe" or "Father Abraham," he emerged as an inspirational leader in the North's drive for victory.

"FORWARD TO RICHMOND!" AND "ON TO WASHINGTON!"

War hysteria was pervasive after Fort Sumter, and Southerners exuded confidence. As a Virginian wrote, "all of us are ... ripe and ready.... I go for taking Boston and Cincinnati. I go for wiping them out." Another, having sent forth five sons, offered his daughter who "desires me to say ... that if you will furnish her with suitable arms she will undertake deeds of daring that will astonish many of the sterner sex." Northerners were equally delirious with war fever. In New York a woman reported on "the terrible excitement" of a city full of "excited crowds" reveling in "the incessant movement and music of marching regiments."

The populace clearly wanted a fight. Throughout the North the war cry was "Forward to Richmond!" referring to the Virginia city 100 miles south of Washington that had been selected as the permanent

The departure of the Seventh Regiment from New York conveys the sense of enthusiasm everyone had early in the war.

capital of the Confederacy. Throughout the South anyone shouting "On to Washington!" could expect to hear cheering voices in return. The land between the two capitals soon became a major combat zone. President Lincoln, bowing in mid-July to pressure for a demonstration of Union superiority in arms, ordered General Irvin McDowell and 30,000 half-trained **Billy Yanks** to engage General P. G. T. Beauregard and his **Johnny Rebs,** who were gathering at sleepy Manassas Junction, lying near a creek called Bull Run, 25 miles southwest of the federal capital.

The Battle of Bull Run (First Manassas) occurred on Sunday, July 21. Citizens of Washington packed picnic lunches and went out to observe the engagement. Because the battlefield soon became shrouded in smoke, they saw little except Union soldiers finally breaking off and fleeing past them in absolute panic for their lives. Bull Run had its glorious moments, such as when Virginians under Thomas J. Jackson held onto a key hill despite a crushing federal assault. This stand earned Jackson his nickname, "Stonewall," and he became the South's first authentic war hero. The North had no heroes. As Union troops straggled back into Washington, they "looked pretty well whipped." Bull Run, with 2700 Union and 2000 Confederate casualties, proved to Lincoln that the warring sections were in for a long-term struggle.

Planning the Union Offensive

Bull Run showed the deficiencies of both sides. Union troops had not been trained well enough to stand the heat of battle. The Confederates were so disorganized after sweeping their adversaries from the field that they could not take advantage of the rout and strike a mortal blow at Washington. Lincoln now realized, too, that he had to develop a comprehensive strategy—a detailed war plan—to break the South's will of resistance. Also, he needed to find young, energetic generals who could organize Union forces and guide them to victory. Devising a war strategy proved to be much easier than locating military leaders with the capacity to execute those plans.

Well before Bull Run, Lincoln had turned to Winfield Scott for an overall strategic design, and the general in chief came up with the **Anaconda Plan**—which, like the snake, was capable of squeezing the resolve out of the Confederacy. The three essential coils included a full naval blockade of the South's coastline to cut off shipments of war goods and other supplies from Europe; a campaign to gain control of the Mississippi River, thereby splitting the Confederacy into two parts; and a placement of armies at key points to ensure that Southerners could not wiggle free of the squeeze. Once accomplished, Scott predicted, pro-Unionists would rise up, discredit secessionist hotheads, and lead the South back into the Union, all in a year's time.

Lincoln liked certain features. He ordered the blockade, a seemingly impossible assignment, given

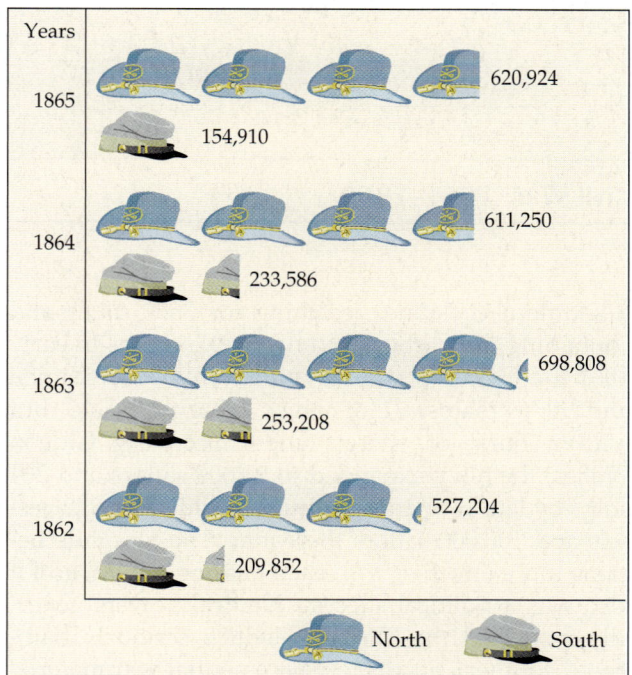

FIGURE 15.2

Comparative Troop Strength, North and South

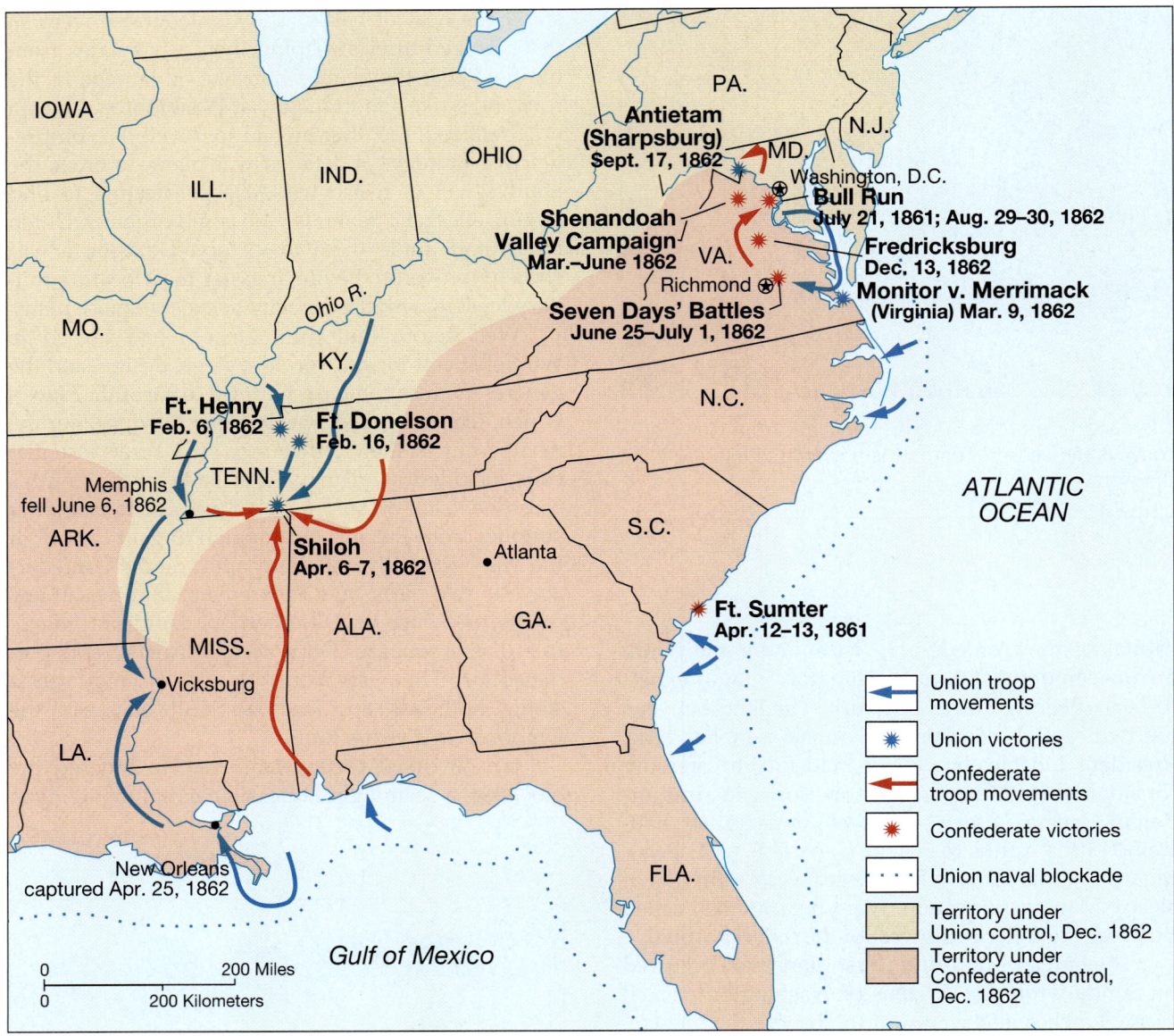

Civil War, 1861–1862

a southern coastline stretching for 3550 miles and containing 189 harbors and navigable rivers. In early 1861 the United States Navy had only 7600 seamen and 90 warships, 21 of which were unusable. But with a burst of energy under Secretary Gideon Welles, the navy expanded to 20,000 sailors and 264 ships by late 1861 and continued building to 650 vessels and 100,000 sailors thereafter. The blockade became more effective with each passing month, and it also was a political success. Neutral powers generally respected the blockade, which seriously hampered southern efforts to gain essential war matériel from abroad.

Lincoln also agreed with Scott that splitting the Confederacy was critical. He ordered Generals Henry W. Halleck, headquartered in St. Louis, and Don Carlos Buell, based in Louisville, to build great armies for the western theater. The president likewise worked with the Navy Department to devise the means to gain control of the Mississippi River. The latter effort resulted in the risky campaign of Captain David G. Farragut, whose fleet of 24 wooden ships and 19 mortar vessels captured New Orleans on April 25, 1862. Farragut's triumph was a major first step in cutting the South apart and crippling dreams of independence.

The third aspect of the Anaconda Plan, Lincoln thought, was naive. Fort Sumter had convinced him that the slaveholding elite had too powerful a grip on the southern populace to expect any significant rallying of pro-Unionists. Nor should armies sit on the sidelines or train endlessly and wait for a decisive battle. After all, Bull Run had accomplished little except to embarrass Lincoln. By July 1861 the president was talking about truly muscular federal armies, mightier than anything the South, with its limited resources, could ever muster. After Bull Run he got Congress to authorize the enlistment of 500,000 additional volunteer troops, far beyond the number recommended by Scott.

For a man with no formal training in military strategy, Lincoln was way ahead of the generals immediately surrounding him. As he explained to one of them, "we have the greater numbers," and if "superior forces" could strike "at different points at the same time," breakthroughs would occur, and the South could then be disemboweled from the inside. Lincoln's thinking pointed toward unrestrained total war, implying the complete destruction of the South, if need be, to save the Union.

The former militia captain needed ranking officers who viewed overall strategy as he did. Lincoln hoped he had found such a person in George B. McClellan, whom he brought to Washington to replace McDowell. McClellan happened to be in the public eye because he had just directed a small force in saving the territory of western Virginia from Confederate raiders. (West Virginia joined the Union as a separate state in 1863.) McClellan turned out to be one of Lincoln's mistakes.

Yankee Reverses and Rebel Victories in the East

George McClellan was a man of great bravado who had finished second in his West Point class and authored a book on the art of war. He could organize and train troops like no one else, as evidenced by his command of the Army of the Potomac. He was also an inspiring leader, adored by his troops. With his usual brashness McClellan told Lincoln: "I can do it all." Unfortunately, the cocksure commander was incapable of using effectively what he had wrought.

Lincoln gave McClellan everything necessary to do the job. Not only did the president place him at the head of the Army of the Potomac, which at peak strength numbered 150,000 troops, but he made him general in chief after Winfield Scott retired in the fall of 1861. The problem was McClellan's unwillingness to move his showcase force into combat. When Lincoln called for action, McClellan demanded more soldiers. The rebels, he claimed from spy reports, had 220,000 troops at Manassas Junction—the actual number was closer to 36,000. To counter this mythical force, McClellan wanted at least 273,000 men before entering the field.

To give McClellan his due, his approach to the war was different from Lincoln's. He intended to maneuver his army but avoid large battles. He wanted to save soldiers' lives, not expend them. He thought he could threaten Southerners into submission by getting them to realize the futility of standing up to so superior a force—and so brilliant a general in command.

For Lincoln, now convinced that only crushing victories orchestrated along several fronts could break the Confederate will, McClellan had contracted a bad case of "the slows." In January 1862 the angry president laughed and told a friend, "I am thinking of taking the field myself." By March he no longer covered his feelings. So that McClellan would concentrate on actual fighting, Lincoln removed him as general in chief and ordered him to use the Army of the Potomac.

What followed was the Peninsula campaign. McClellan transported his army down through Chesapeake Bay, landing between the York and James rivers, about 75 miles to the southeast of Richmond. In May his army moved forward at a snail's pace, which allowed the Confederates time to mass 70,000 troops. By the end of the month McClellan's advance units were approaching the outskirts of Richmond. Rebel forces under Joseph E. Johnston struck the main Union army near the Chickahominy River on May 31 and June 1. The Battle of Seven Pines cost a total of 10,000 casualties, among them a seriously wounded General Johnston.

Johnston's misfortune opened the way for Robert E. Lee, then advising President Davis on military matters, to assume command of the Army of Northern Virginia. Evaluating his opponent, Lee called in "Stonewall" Jackson's corps from the Shenandoah Valley and aggressively went after the Union army. McClellan all but panicked. Insisting that his army now faced 200,000 rebels (the number was 90,000), he re-

At first, Robert E. Lee was an adviser to Jefferson Davis. Then, on June 1, 1862, Davis appointed him to command the Confederate Army of Northern Virginia. After the war, Lee encouraged reconciliation between the North and the South.

treated after two inconclusive fights north of the Chickahominy. What ensued was the Battle of the Seven Days (June 25–July 1) in which combined casualties reached 30,000, two-thirds sustained by the Confederates. Still, Lee's offensive punches prevailed—and saved Richmond. McClellan soon boarded his troops on waiting transport ships and returned to Washington.

The aggressive Lee, meanwhile, sensed other opportunities. In defending Richmond the rebels had abandoned their advanced post at Manassas Junction. A Union force numbering 45,000 under General John Pope moved into position there. Having just come in from the western theater, Pope was as blind to danger as McClellan was cautious. He thought the enemy a trifle and kept exhorting his officers to "study the probable lines of retreat of our opponents." What Pope did not factor in was the audacity of Lee, who, once sure of McClellan's decision to retreat, wheeled about and rushed northward straight toward Pope.

Lee broke all the rules by dividing his force and sending Jackson's corps in a wide, looping arc around Pope. On August 29, Jackson began a battle known as Second Bull Run (Second Manassas). When Pope turned to face Jackson, Lee hit him from the other side. The battle raged for another day and ended with Union troops again fleeing for Washington. Combined casualties were 19,000 (10,000 for the North).

Even with another monstrous body count, the Army of the Potomac had gained nothing in over a year's campaigning. A tired, frustrated Lincoln said: "We might as well stop fighting." The president knew he had to get the war off dead center, and he was already devising plans to do so, which included an emancipation proclamation. Lee gave Lincoln the opportunity to announce that document when he led his victorious army into Maryland in early September, moving toward Antietam and yet another rendezvous with McClellan.

Federal Breakthrough in the West

The two Union western commanders, Henry W. Halleck and Don Carlos Buell, also suffered from "the slows." Neither responded to Lincoln's pleas for action. Halleck, however, was not afraid to let his subordinates take chances. Brigadier General Ulysses S. Grant had a good idea about how to break through 50,000 Confederate troops—under the overall command of General Albert Sidney Johnston—spread thinly along a 150-mile line running westward from Bowling Green, Kentucky, to the Mississippi River. The weak points were the two rebel forts, Henry and Donelson, guarding the Tennessee and Cumberland rivers in far northern Tennessee.

ANTIETAM

"We Will Make Our Stand"

As George B. McClellan moved his Army of the Potomac into Maryland during September 1862, in pursuit of Robert E. Lee's Army of Northern Virginia, a Union soldier stumbled upon cigars lying in a field wrapped in a piece of paper. The paper was a copy of Lee's orders regarding his invasion of Maryland. The Confederate general had divided his force to strike at such vulnerable federal posts as Harpers Ferry.

McClellan now had the opportunity to destroy separate components of Lee's army. The methodical Union general did speed up his advance but not at a fast enough pace to take advantage of circumstances.

Learning of McClellan's discovery, Lee issued urgent orders for his units to reassemble at Sharpsburg. Most critical were "Stonewall" Jackson's soldiers, who had easily captured Harpers Ferry and a Union garrison of 12,000 on September 15. Had McClellan attacked Lee on the 16th before Jackson's troops covered the 15 miles from Harpers Ferry to Sharpsburg, he might have crushed his opponent. As usual, McClellan acted slowly, preferring to refine his battle plan for the 17th.

There was nothing wrong with the plan. The idea was to throw the weight of Union troops against Lee's left flank, north of Sharpsburg. Meanwhile, General Ambrose E. Burnside was to create a diversion by crossing the stone bridge over Antietam Creek southeast of town, thereby pinning down rebels that could be shifted to support Lee's left flank.

The Union army, however, never got its punches coordinated. Three assaults on Lee's left, from dawn until late morning, proved futile. Then the battle shifted toward the center, where soldiers fought along a sunken farm road, since known as Bloody Lane. In the early afternoon, Burnside finally got his troops across the bridge. They threatened to crush Lee's right flank before a column of Confederates rushing north from Harpers Ferry cut off their thrust.

Antietam was the bloodiest day of the war. Once again, President Lincoln was furious with McClellan's unaggressive generalship, and he eventually removed him from command. More important, the appearance of a Union victory, based on Lee's retreat back into Virginia, gave Lincoln what he needed, the opportunity to announce his Emancipation Proclamation.

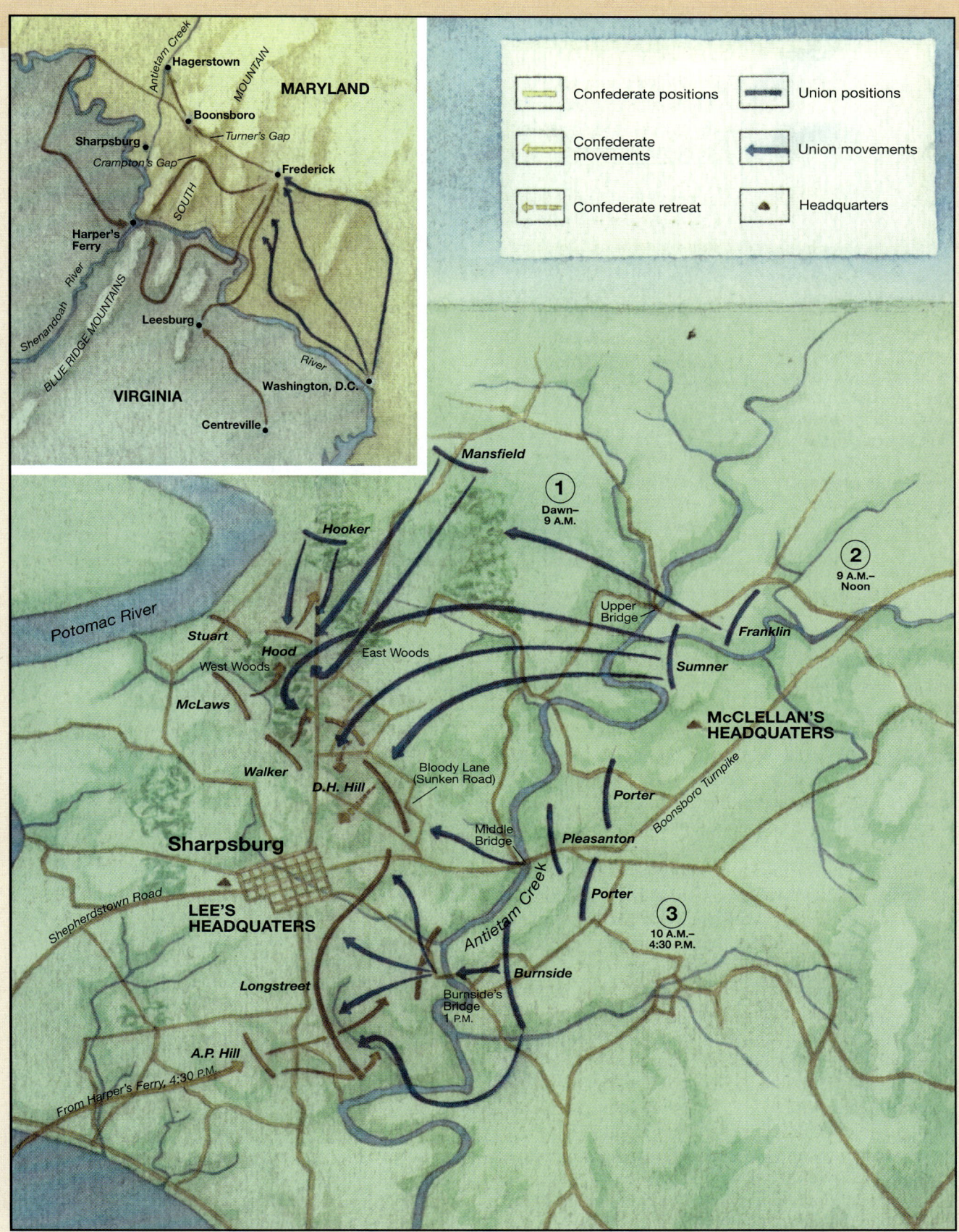

Ulysses S. Grant was criticized for his command tactics early in the war, but Lincoln remained supportive of him throughout. Grant later became the eighteenth president of the United States.

Grant sensed that a combined land and river offensive might reduce these forts, thereby cutting through the rebel defensive line and opening states such as Tennessee to full-scale invasion. Working with Flag Officer Andrew H. Foote, who commanded the Union gunboats, the Federals captured both forts in February 1862. Grant even earned the nickname "Unconditional Surrender" when he told the Fort Donelson commander to choose between capitulation or annihilation, which netted the Union side 15,000 rebel prisoners.

After puncturing the Confederate line, Grant's army of 40,000 poured into Tennessee, following after Johnston, who retreated all the way to Corinth in northern Mississippi. Cautioned by Halleck "to strike no blow until we are strong enough to admit no doubt of the result," Grant settled his army in at Pittsburgh Landing, 25 miles north of Corinth along the Tennessee River—with advanced lines around a humble log church bearing the name Shiloh. There he waited for reinforcements marching south under Buell. Flushed with confidence, Grant did not bother to order a careful posting of picket guards.

When Johnston received additional troops under Beauregard, he decided to attack. At dawn on April 6, 40,000 rebels overran Grant's outer lines, and for two days the battle raged before the Federals drove off the Confederates. The Battle of Shiloh (Pittsburgh Landing) resulted in 20,000 combined casualties. General Johnston died the first day from a severe leg wound, which cost the South a valued commander. Grant, so recently hailed as a war hero, now faced severe criticism for not having secured his lines. Some even claimed that he was dead drunk when the rebels first struck, undercutting—at least for the moment—thoughts of elevating him to higher command.

With other Union victories along the Mississippi corridor, and with Farragut's capture of New Orleans, the Union western offensive was making headway. The only portion of the Mississippi River yet to be conquered was a 110-mile stretch running north from Port Hudson, Louisiana, to Vicksburg, Mississippi. Since the rebels had powerful artillery batteries trained on the river, Union gunboats could not pass through this strategic zone and complete the dissection of the Confederacy. General Grant would redeem his reputation in 1863 by conquering Vicksburg after a prolonged siege.

TO AND FROM EMANCIPATION: THE WAR ON THE HOME FRONT

Rarely a man of humor, Jefferson Davis laughed when he read a letter from a young woman demanding that her soldiering boyfriend be sent home to wed her. Even though "I is willin" to marry him, she wrote, the problem was "Jeem's capt'in," who "ain't willin" to let him leave the front. She begged Davis to intervene, promising that "I'll make him go straight back when he's done got married and fight just as hard as ever." Thinking it good for morale, Davis ordered the leave. True to his bride's word, "Jeem," once married, did return to his unit in one of thousands of incidents involving ordinary citizens who were trying to maintain the normal rhythms of life in the midst of a terrible war.

Keeping up morale—and the will to endure at all costs—was a major challenge for both sides, once citizens at home accepted the reality of a long and bloody conflict. How civilian leaders in the North and the South handled these problems had a direct bearing on the outcome of the conflict. Northern leaders, drawing on greater resources, proved more adept at finding solutions designed to keep up morale while breaking the southern will to continue the war.

An Abundance of Confederate Shortages

With their society lacking an industrial base, southern leaders realized the great need to secure material aid from Europe, just as the American colonists had received vital foreign support to sustain their rebellion against Britain. Overconfident secession enthusiasts expected Europe's dependence on cotton to assure them unofficial assistance, if not diplomatic recognition as an independent nation. "Cotton," predicted the *Charleston Mercury*, "would bring England to her knees." It did not. A glut then existed in the European marketplace, and British textile manufacturers after 1861 turned to Egypt, India, and Brazil as sources for new supplies of cotton.

Some British leaders saw advantages to a prolonged war in which the Union and Confederacy ripped each other apart. Wrote Lincoln's minister to Russia, "I saw at a glance where the feeling of England was. They hoped for our ruin! They are jealous of our power. They care neither for the South nor the North." In addition, Britain had long since abandoned slavery, and leaders had moral qualms about publicly recognizing a slave power. Having so little to gain except the possible destruction of the rising—and still much-hated—American nation, the English government chose to remain on the sidelines. Queen Victoria announced her country's neutrality in May 1861.

Despite concerted southern diplomatic efforts, other European nations followed Britain's lead and officially ignored the Confederacy. Some of these countries depended heavily on northern grain crops to help feed their populace. Grain rather than "king cotton" was most vital to their national well-being.

The Confederacy, however, received small amounts of clandestine aid from Europe. In 1862 English shipyards constructed two commerce raiders, the *Florida* and the *Alabama*, before protests from the Lincoln administration ended such activity. By 1865 blockade runners had transported an estimated 600,000 European-produced weapons into southern ports. The Richmond government also obtained about $710 million in foreign loans, secured by promises to deliver cotton; but the tightening Union naval blockade made the exportation of cotton difficult, discouraging further European loans because of the mounting risk of never being paid back.

From the very outset, Union naval superiority was a critical factor in isolating the South. There was a moment of hope in March 1862, when a scuttled U.S. naval vessel, the *Merrimack*, now covered with iron plates, given a huge ram, and renamed the CSS *Virginia*, steamed out into Norfolk Bay and battered a fleet of wooden Union blockade vessels. Losing engine power, the *Virginia* retreated, then returned the next day to discover a new adversary, the USS *Monitor*, also clad in iron and ready to fight. The *Virginia* held its own in the ensuing battle but finally backed away, as if admitting that whatever the South tried, the North could counter it effectively. The Confederacy simply lacked the funds to build a naval fleet of any consequence, a disadvantage that allowed the Union navy to dominate the sea lanes.

The effects of cutting the South off from external support were profound. By the spring of 1862 citizens at home were experiencing many shortages—and getting mad about it. Such common items as salt, sugar, and coffee had all but disappeared, and shoes and clothing were at a premium. In 1863 bread riots broke out in several southern cities, including Richmond, where citizens demanded basic food amid shouts of, "we are starving." Shortages abetted rapid inflation, as did the overprinting of Confederate dollars. The central government put a total of $1.5 billion into circulation to help pay for the war.

Although neither the *Monitor* (foreground) nor the *Merrimack* (*CSS Virginia*) won a decisive victory when they met, they helped introduce a new era in naval warfare by demonstrating the superior capacity of ironclads over wooden vessels.

Between 1861 and 1865 prices spiraled upward on the average of 7000 percent.

Once it was obvious that cotton would not bring significant foreign support, Jefferson Davis tried to turn adversity to advantage by urging citizens to raise less cotton and grow more food. Farm women, thrown into new roles as heads of households with husbands and older sons off at war, did so, but then Richmond-based tax collectors appeared and started seizing portions of these crops—wheat, corn, and peas—to feed the armies. For struggling wives, this was too much. Many wrote their husbands and begged them to come home. Some did, thus aggravating an increasing desertion problem.

Most Southerners, in trying to comprehend so many difficulties, blamed their central government. When the Confederate Congress, for example, enacted a conscription act in April 1862—the first draft law in U.S. history—because of rapidly declining enlistments, a North Carolina soldier wrote: "I would like to know what has been done to the main principle for which we are now fighting—*States' Rights!*—Where is it? ... When we hear men comparing the despotism of the *Confederacy* with that of the Lincoln government—*something must be wrong*." The fault lay with power-hungry leaders like Davis, many argued, not with a political philosophy inherently at odds with the need for effective, centralized military planning to defeat the North's war machine.

In the months that followed, accusations of political high-handedness in Richmond could be heard everywhere. The draft law, for example, allowed individuals to purchase substitutes, and with rapid inflation, avoiding service became solely a wealthy man's prerogative. When the central government in October 1862 exempted from the draft all those managing 20 or more slaves, ordinary citizens were furious with their planter leaders. Some started referring to the contest as "a rich man's war and a poor man's fight."

These were very serious problems. In defending the institution of slavery, wealthy planters had touted states' rights to rally their more humble neighbors on behalf of independence. With all the shortages and sacrifices, however, disaffection with these same planters was on the rise because they were violating the tenets of states' rights and adopting laws favoring their class. In combination with a dawning realization that the North had overpowering resources and numbers, some Southerners were concluding, even before the end of 1862: "The enemy is superior to us in everything but courage." Courage, especially when leaders in Richmond appeared to be so self-serving, could not be sustained in perpetuity.

Directing the Northern War Effort

Although Abraham Lincoln focused most of his energies on military matters, he did not neglect other vital areas, including diplomatic relations with foreign powers and domestic legislation. His diplomatic objective was to keep European nations from supporting the Confederacy, and his domestic goal was to maintain high levels of popular support for the war effort. Lincoln was successful on both counts, but he took many risks, the most dramatic being his announcement of an emancipation proclamation.

Unlike Jefferson Davis, Lincoln delegated authority whenever he could. In foreign affairs he relied heavily on Secretary of State William Seward, whom European leaders came to regard as hotheaded but effective. Early in the war, for example, Lord John Russell, Britain's foreign secretary, met briefly—and unofficially—with fire-eating William L. Yancey, who was in London to seek diplomatic recognition for the Confederacy. When informed of the meeting, Seward drafted a strong letter, which Lincoln toned down, all but threatening the British with war. Russell never saw the text, but he learned about it and decided not to meet again with commissioners of the Confederacy. "For God's sakes," Russell stated, "let us if possible, keep out of it." Certainly Britain had nothing to gain by provoking the Union too much, especially over so remote a possibility as according the Confederacy diplomatic recognition.

There were some intense diplomatic moments, such as in November 1861, when the U.S. warship *San Jacinto* intercepted a British packet vessel, the *Trent*, and seized two Confederate envoys, James M. Mason and John Slidell, who were on their way to the courts of Europe. England vehemently protested such an overt violation of maritime law—stopping and searching neutral vessels on the high seas. The often-bellicose Seward took these complaints seriously, and he and Lincoln, with the skillful help of the U.S. Ambassador to England, Charles Francis Adams, the son and grandson of two former presidents, smoothed matters over by apologizing for the *Trent* affair and releasing the envoys from jail.

Then, a few months later, Seward received reports that English shipyards were completing two ironclad ram vessels, similar to the CSS *Virginia*. This time the United States threatened serious repercussions. In response, British officials confiscated the ironclads, thus averting another crisis. All in all, Seward and Lincoln helped convince the major European powers that they could "commit no graver error than to mix...in our affairs." With Europe maintaining a posture of neutrality, the North could fully concentrate on defeating the South.

Also helping the Yankee cause was wartime prosperity, which Lincoln and a Republican-dominated Congress tried to sustain. In 1862 Congress passed the Homestead Act, which granted 160 acres free to individuals who agreed to farm that land for at least five years; the Morrill Land Grant Act, which offered immense parcels of public land to states that established agricultural colleges; and the Pacific Railway Act, which laid the basis for constructing a transcontinental railroad after the war. Under the leadership of Lincoln's treasury secretary, Salmon P. Chase, Congress approved National Banking acts in 1863 and 1864, which clamped down on irresponsible financial practices and provided for a uniform national currency. Also, the Republican Congress, to protect the North's manufacturing interests from foreign competition, approved tariff acts that raised import duties nearly 50 percent.

Under the watchful eye of Secretary Chase, the government likewise resorted to various expedients to finance the war effort. In 1861 Congress approved a modest income tax with rates that fell only on the wealthy. The government also taxed the states, borrowed heavily (around $2.2 billion), and issued **greenbacks,** a fiat currency that, like Confederate dollars, had no backing in gold or silver but held its value better because of slowly growing confidence in the Union war effort. At no time did the Lincoln administration need to confiscate farm goods, a morale booster in and of itself.

Historians have debated whether the economic boom in the North generated by the Civil War sped up the process of industrialization in the United States. By some measures, such as the annual rate of economic growth during the 1860s, the war injured the economy. No decade in American history before the Great Depression years of the 1930s saw less economic growth, but most of this seeming downturn had to do with the destruction of the southern economy. By war's end in 1865, two-fifths of all southern

TABLE 15.1
Previous Occupations of Sampled White Union and Confederate Soldiers*

Civil War soldiers came rather evenly from all occupational categories, an indication that fighting the war did not fall disproportionately on any one economic group. Confederate claims to the contrary, Union armies were not made up heavily of the foreign-born. Although 31 percent of all white northern males of military age were foreign-born, only 26 percent of white Union soldiers were nonnatives. By comparison, some 10 percent of all southern troops were foreign-born, even though only 7.5 percent of Confederate males of military age were nonnatives. The South, then, drew more heavily on its supply of foreign-born residents than did the North, just as the Confederacy called upon a far greater proportion of its eligible population (90 percent as compared to 40 percent for the Union) to fight the war. Running out of troops by late 1864, the only source left for the South was the slave population.

Occupational Categories	Union Troops	Total Male Population North (1860 census)	Confederate Troops	Total Male Population South (1860 census)
Farmers and farm laborers (includes southern planters)	47.5	42.9	61.5	57.5
Skilled laborers	25.1	24.9	14.1	15.7
Unskilled laborers	15.9	16.7	8.5	12.7
White collar and commercial	5.1	10.0	7.0	8.3
Professional	3.2	3.5	5.2	5.0
Miscellaneous and unknown	3.2	2.0	3.7	0.8

Source: Ordeal by Fire: The Civil War and Reconstruction by James M. McPherson. Copyright © 1982 by Alfred A. Knopf, Inc. Reprinted by permission.

*All numbers are in percentages.

---

livestock had been killed; more than half of the Confederacy's farm machinery had been destroyed; and countless plantations and family farms had been ruined. In the North, by comparison, per capita commodity output rose by 56 percent during the decade of the 1860s, and the amount of working capital to underwrite business activity expanded by 50 percent. Entrepreneurs, John D. Rockefeller and Andrew Carnegie among them, made huge profits from war contracts. Their new-found capital base and ideas about the advantages of large-scale business organization certainly foreshadowed the rapid postwar transition to a full-scale industrial economy.

The intense level of governmental activity resulted in charges that Lincoln's real purpose was to become a dictator. These accusations started soon after Fort Sumter, when the new president, acting by himself since Congress was not then in session, declared an insurrection and began a military buildup. Shortly thereafter, secession-minded Marylanders attacked Yankee troops moving through Baltimore to the federal capital. To quell such turbulence, Lincoln suspended the writ of habeas corpus in Maryland and ordered the arrest and jailing of leading advocates of secession, including Baltimore's mayor and several state legislators.

The question of whether the president had the power to curtail constitutionally guaranteed rights, even when facing wartime emergencies, quickly produced a response from Supreme Court Chief Justice Roger B. Taney, a Marylander himself. In a federal circuit court case, *Ex Parte Merryman* (1861), Taney proclaimed Lincoln's action illegal by arguing that only Congress had the authority to suspend writs of habeas corpus in times of rebellion. Lincoln ignored Taney's ruling, and John Merryman, one of those arrested, languished in a military prison with no set trial date on vague charges of having incited Marylanders to secede from the Union.

During the war Lincoln authorized the arrest of some 14,000 dissidents and had them jailed without any prospect for trials. He was careful, however, not to suppress his political opponents, particularly leading members of the Democratic party. The president worked to have open and fair elections, operating on a distinction between legitimate dissent in support of the nation and willful attempts to subvert the Union. Most agree that Lincoln, given the tense wartime climate, showed sensitivity toward basic rights. At the same time he clearly tested the limits of presidential powers.

Some of his political opponents, mostly Peace Democrats who favored negotiating an end to the war and letting the South leave the Union, regularly described Lincoln as a doer of all evil. These **Copperheads,** as their detractors called them, had some support in the Midwest. They rallied around individuals such as Congressman Clement L. Vallandigham of Ohio. In 1863 Union military officials arrested him on nonspecific charges, but Lincoln ordered him set free and banished to the South. Vallandigham then moved to Canada where he conducted a vigorous election campaign to become governor of Ohio, which he decisively lost. Lincoln wisely ignored the matter, hoping that Vallandigham and other Peace Democrats, who most of all liked to bewail the **Emancipation Proclamation,** could not muster enough popular support to undermine the Union cause.

Issuing the Emancipation Proclamation

Abraham Lincoln believed fervently in the ideals of the Declaration of Independence, which gave Americans "the right to rise" out of poverty, as he described his own experience, and "get through the world respectably." He also admired the Declaration's emphasis on human liberty, which made chattel slavery inconsistent with the ideals of the Revolution. Slavery, he wrote as early as 1837, was "founded both on injustice and bad policy."

After becoming president, Lincoln promised not to interfere with slavery in established southern states. When warfare began, he seemed to move with indecisive steps toward emancipation. His only war aim, he claimed well into the spring of 1862, was to save the Union. When in August 1861 General John C. Frémont, then heading federal military operations in Missouri, declared an end to slavery in that state, the president not only rescinded the proclamation but severely rebuked Frémont by removing him from command in Missouri.

For a person who despised slavery, Lincoln held back in resolving the emancipation question for many reasons. First, he did not want to drive slaveholding border states such as Missouri into the Confederacy. Second, he worried about pervasive racism; white Northerners had willingly taken up arms to save the Union, but he wondered whether they would keep fighting to liberate the slave population. Third, if he moved too fast, he reasoned, he

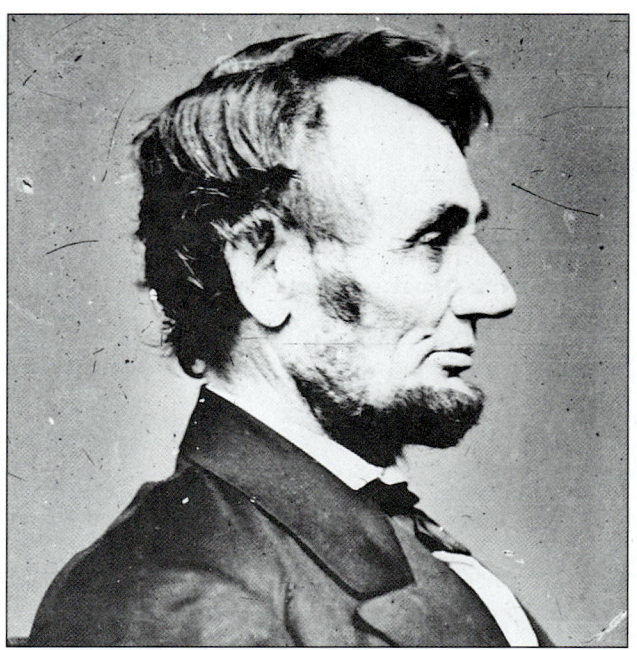

With the Emancipation Proclamation, Abraham Lincoln provided a new rationale for the war beyond the original goal of preserving the Union.

might lose everything, including the Union itself, should northern peace advocates seize upon popular fears of emancipation and create an overwhelming demand to stop the fighting in favor of southern independence. Fourth, he had personal doubts as to whether black Americans and white Americans could ever live together in freedom.

For all these reasons Lincoln moved cautiously, allowing people and events to decide the issue. He did not seek close identity with radical Republicans in Congress, led by Charles Sumner and Benjamin Wade in the Senate and Thaddeus Stevens in the House, men who built a strong coalition in favor of ending slavery. When these same radicals scoffed at his proposals for compensated emancipation at $500 a head, or for colonization in Central America or Liberia, he stated, "I can only go just as fast as I can see how to go." Lincoln did support a series of radical-sponsored bills adopted by Congress in the spring and early summer of 1862. One act abolished slaveholding in the nation's capital and western territories; and a second bill, the Confiscation Act, freed all slaves belonging to rebel masters fighting against the Union.

By the summer of 1862, Lincoln had finally made up his mind. The war's death toll, he now reasoned, had become too great; all the maiming and killing had to have some larger purpose, transcending the primary objective of preserving the Union. For Lincoln, the military contest had become a test to see whether the republic, at long last, had the capacity to live up to the ideals of the American Revolution. This could be determined only by announcing the Emancipation Proclamation.

Lincoln knew he was gambling with northern morale at a time when Union victories were all but nonexistent, when enlistments were in decline, and when war weariness had set in. He was aware that racists, such as the person who wrote and called him a "god-damned black nigger," would spread their poison far and wide. So the president waited for the right moment, such as after an important battlefield triumph, to quiet his critics, who would surely say that emancipation was a desperate measure designed to cover up presidential mismanagement of the war.

As a shrewd politician, Lincoln began to prepare Northerners for what was coming. He explained to readers of Horace Greeley's *New York Tribune* in late August: "If I could save the Union without freeing *any* slave, I would do it; and if I could save it by freeing *all* the slaves, I would do it; and if I could save it by freeing some and leaving others alone, I would also do that." Sidestepping any pronouncement of high ideals in public, the president would treat his assault on slavery as a war measure designed to ensure total military victory.

On September 22, 1862, five days after the Battle of Antietam, Lincoln announced his preliminary Emancipation Proclamation, which called on Southerners to lay down their arms and return to the Union by year's end or to accept the abolition of slavery. Getting no formal response, on January 1, 1863, he declared all slaves in the Confederacy "forever free." The final document called emancipation "an act of justice, warranted by the Constitution upon military necessity." Out of necessity, too, slavery could continue to exist in the four Union border states—to ensure a united front against the rebels.

In private, Lincoln referred to the horrible carnage at Antietam as "an indication of Divine will" that had forever "decided the question" of emancipation "in favor of the slaves." He did not see how slavery, even in the loyal border states, could long outlast the war, and he happily envisioned a republic now moving forward toward the realization of its ideals.

Lincoln did something else in the wake of Antietam. He fired George McClellan for not using his superior troop strength to destroy Lee's army when the opportunity had so clearly presented itself. In trying to save soldiers' lives, Lincoln reasoned, McClellan's timidity would actually cost thousands more in the days ahead. So the president kept searching for a commander with the capacity to bring down the Confederacy in a war now dedicated to abolishing slavery as a means to preserve the Union.

Emancipation Tests Northern Resolve

Reaction to the preliminary proclamation varied widely. With Democrats in Congress calling for Lincoln's impeachment, some cabinet members urged the president to reconsider. They also feared repercussions in the upcoming November elections. The Republicans did lose seats, but they still controlled Congress, despite the efforts of many Democrats to smear "Black Republican" candidates. Certainly, too, frustration with so many battlefield reverses, as much as news of the proclamation, hurt the Republicans at the polls.

Others, however, criticized Lincoln for not going far enough. Abolitionists chided him for offering only half a loaf, and female activists like Susan B. Anthony and Elizabeth Cady Stanton formed the Woman's Loyal National League, dedicated to the eradication of slavery in all the states. Foreign opinion generally applauded Lincoln, although a few commentators made caustic remarks about a curious new "principle" that no American would henceforth be allowed to own slaves "unless he is loyal to the United States."

In the Confederacy, the planter elite played on traditional racist attitudes and used the proclamation to rally citizens wavering in their resolve. Here was proof, shouted planter leaders, that every indignity the South had suffered was part of a never-ending abolitionist plot to stir up slave rebellions and "convert the quiet, ignorant black son of toil into a savage incendiary and brutal murderer."

Back in the North, African Americans were jubilant. Wrote Frederick Douglass, "We shout for joy that we live to record this righteous decree." Standing outside the White House on New Year's Day, 1863, a group of African Americans sang praises to the president, shouting that "they would hug him to death" if he would "come out of that palace" and greet them. For African Americans the Civil War meant liberation at last.

Up until this point, black Americans had found the war frustrating. Federal officials had blocked their attempts to enlist. Not wanting to stir up racial violence, Lincoln had danced around the issue. Most early African American enlistments were in the navy. Finally, in 1862, Secretary of War Edwin M. Stanton, with the president's backing, called for the enlistment of African Americans—North and South—in land forces. In a model program, Colonel Thomas Wentworth Higginson, one of the financial sponsors of radical abolitionist John Brown, worked with former slaves in the Sea Island region of South Carolina, an area under Union control, to mold them into a well-trained regiment (the 1st South Carolina Volunteers). They fought effectively in the coastal region running south to Florida.

THE PEOPLE SPEAK

Frederick Douglass Calls upon African Americans to Take up Arms Against the Confederacy (1863)

Escaping to the North in 1838, former slave Frederick Douglass gained widespread fame as a leading black abolitionist. For years he spoke out passionately against the institution of chattel slavery, and he rejoiced at the news of Lincoln's Emancipation Proclamation. Douglass then took an activist's role in encouraging African Americans to join Union military forces. He became an unofficial recruiter for Robert Gould Shaw's Massachusetts 54th Infantry, the first black regiment organized in the North, in which two of his own sons served. In his recruiting appeal that follows, Douglass offered many reasons why African Americans should enlist and fight in a war now being waged, he hoped, as much to end slavery as to save the Union:

> When the first rebel cannon shattered the walls of [Fort] Sumter and drove away its starving garrison, I predicted that the war then and there inaugurated would not be fought out entirely by white men. Every month's experience during these dreary years has confirmed that opinion. A war undertaken and brazenly carried on for the perpetual enslavement of colored men, calls logically and loudly for colored men to help suppress it. Only a moderate share of sagacity was needed to see that the arm of the slave was the best defense against the arm of the slaveholder. Hence with every reverse to the national arms, with every exulting shout of victory raised by the slaveholding rebels, I have implored the imperiled nation to unchain against her foes, her powerful black hand. Slowly and reluctantly that appeal is beginning to be heeded. Stop not now to complain that it was not heeded sooner. It may or may not have been best that it should not. This is not the time to discuss that question. Leave it to the future. When the war is over, the country is saved, peace is established, and the black man's rights are secured, as they will be, history with an impartial hand will dispose of that and sundry other questions. Action! Action! not criticism, is the plain duty of this hour. Words are now useful only as they stimulate to blows. The office of speech now is only to point out when, where, and how to strike to the best advantage. There is no time to delay. The tide is at its flood that leads on to fortune. From East to West, from North to South, the sky is written all over, "Now or never."
>
> Liberty won by white men would lose half its luster. "Who would be free themselves must strike the blow." "Better even die free, than to live slaves." This is the sentiment of every brave colored man amongst us. There are weak and cowardly men in all nations. We have them amongst us. They tell you this is the "white man's war"; that you will be "no better off after than before the war"; that the getting of you into the army is to "sacrifice you on the first opportunity." Believe them not; cowards themselves, they do not wish to have their cowardice shamed by your brave example. Leave them to their timidity, or to whatever motive may hold them back. I have not thought lightly of the words I am now addressing you. The counsel I give comes of close observation of the great struggle now in progress, and of the deep conviction that this is your hour and mine. In good earnest then, and after the best deliberation, I now for the first time during this war feel at liberty to call and counsel you to arms. By every consideration which binds you to your enslaved fellow-countrymen, and the peace and welfare of your country; by every aspiration which you cherish for the freedom and equality of yourselves and your children; by all the ties of blood and identity which make us one with the brave black men now fighting our battles in Louisiana and in South Carolina, I urge you to fly to arms, and smite with death the power that would bury the government and your liberty in the same hopeless grave. . . .

Source: *Douglass's Monthly,* March 1863, Rochester, New York.

The success of Higginson's troops broke down some racial stereotypes by demonstrating that African Americans could master the art of war. No regiment proved that more dramatically than the 54th Massachusetts Infantry. Like all other black regiments, the 54th trained separately from white units and received its commands from white officers. This regiment prepared itself for combat during the spring of 1863 under 25-year-old Robert Gould Shaw, the scion of a wealthy Boston antislavery family. Then the unit shipped out to the front lines in coastal South Carolina.

On July 18, 1863, the 54th Massachusetts Infantry led an early evening assault against an army more than twice its numbers that was defending Fort Wagner, a major bastion protecting Charleston harbor for the Confederacy. Eventually repulsed after fierce fighting, the 54th experienced more than a 40 percent casualty rate that evening. Shaw, who had complete confidence in his troops, was shot dead in the charge. After the battle the rebel defenders tried to mock Shaw, even in death as a Confederate stated, by burying him in a common grave "with his niggers!" Their attempted insult failed. Shaw became a mar-

Despite an excellent record in combat, black soldiers often found themselves the victims of discrimination. Black regiments were kept separate from white units and were commanded by white officers.

tyred war hero in the North, and his surviving troops, wrote one of them, swore "Revenge for our galant Curnel." The 54th still expected "to Plant the Stars and Stripes on the City of Charleston" or die in the effort, this soldier declared with conviction.

Before the war ended, 179,000 African Americans had served in the Union army (10 percent of total land forces), and another 29,000 in the navy (25 percent of total naval forces). About 135,000 were former slaves, delighted to be free at last of their masters. Some 44,000 died fighting to save the Union and to defend the prize of freedom for black Americans. Twenty-four received the Congressional Medal of Honor for extraordinary bravery in battle. Among them was Sergeant William H. Carney of the 54th Massachusetts, whose citation praised him for grabbing the regimental flag after its bearer was shot down and leading the troops forward into the outer works of Fort Wagner. Carney, a runaway slave from Virginia, then planted the flag and engaged in hand-to-hand combat. Severely wounded, he reluctantly retreated with flag in hand, not suspecting that he would become the first African American Medal of Honor recipient in the Civil War—and in American history.

Because of the Emancipation Proclamation, African Americans could "march through...fine thoroughfares," explained one black observer, as "Negro soldiers!—with banners flying." Still, as they marched, they received lower pay until protests ended such discrimination in 1864; and they quite often drew menial work assignments, such as digging latrines and burying the dead after battle. Emancipation, African Americans soon realized, was just the beginning of a monumental struggle that lay ahead—beyond the Civil War—to overcome the prejudice and hatred that had locked them in slavery for over two centuries.

BREAKING CONFEDERATE RESISTANCE, 1863–1865

During the spring of 1863, Union war sentiment sagged to a low point. Generals kept demanding

Although outnumbered nearly two to one, the Confederates soundly defeated the northern army under the command of General Joseph Hooker at the Battle of Chancellorsville in May, 1863. The four days of fighting cost each side thousands of casualties. A major loss for the Southerners was General Thomas A. "Stonewall" Jackson, who was accidentally wounded by his own troops and died of pneumonia a few days later.

THE American Mosaic

Pickett's Charge at Gettysburg

FOR two days the death toll mounted, but nothing conclusive had yet happened in the Battle of Gettysburg. Late on the evening of July 2, 1863, General Robert E. Lee made the momentous decision. The next afternoon, on the third day of fighting, 13,000 troops under the command of Major General George E. Pickett would attack the center of the Union line, which stretched for 3 miles south of Gettysburg along Cemetery Ridge, a mile to the east of Lee's 5-mile line along Seminary Ridge. His soldiers, Lee believed with pride, could do anything. The question was whether, in the face of concentrated enemy fire, they could drive off their adversaries and achieve a victory so crushing that it would result in independence for the South.

Late on the morning of July 3, Pickett's officers and men started to assemble under the cover of woods along Seminary Ridge. The fear of death lurked among them, but they spoke of courage and the need "to force manhood to the front." In numerous engagements they had seen their comrades die in ghastly ways from metal hurled by Yankee weapons. They suppressed thoughts of death as best they could and prayed for God's help in girding themselves up for battle.

Like their commanders, these "Johnny Rebs" were battle-hardened veterans who knew what to expect as they marched across the open fields toward Cemetery Ridge. At first, solid shot from enemy artillery, fired mostly from cannons called Napoleons, would fly at them from up to a mile away. As they moved closer, within 400 yards or so, enemy cannons would unleash canisters, or large tin cans filled with lethal cast-iron pellets. Once in flight, the cans fell away, and the pellets ripped human beings to shreds. Within 200 yards, if not before, "Billy Yanks" would start firing their rifled muskets, the basic infantry weapon of the Civil War. With grooves inside the barrel, the rifled musket shot the minié ball, really an elongated bullet, up to 400 yards or more with accuracy. For Civil War soldiers, all of these weapons made the offensive charge a deadly proposition.

To reduce enemy firepower, Lee ordered a heavy cannonade to weaken the Union center. He hoped to knock out enemy artillery units and cause mayhem among the massed infantry on Cemetery Ridge. The bombardment began at 1:00 P.M. and lasted for over one and a half hours. Federal cannons quickly responded in what proved to be the greatest artillery barrage of the Civil War. One officer compared the noise to "that from the falls of Niagara." Another stated "that the earth shook as if in fright." When Southern officers spotted Union cannoneers pulling their artillery pieces back to greater cover, they concluded that much damage had been done. They were wrong. Sensing that so great a cannonade would be followed by an infantry attack, Brigadier General Henry J. Hunt, artillery chief for the Army of the Potomac, had ordered his units to regroup and reload with canister shot.

As the battlefield fell silent, another drama played itself out. Lieutenant General James Longstreet, Lee's valuable deputy, was adamantly opposed to the assault, believing it would only produce a senseless slaughter. Still, as Pickett's corps commander, his responsibility was to order the charge. A little after 2:30 P.M., Pickett rode up to Longstreet and said: "General, shall we advance?" Longstreet looked away and made no reply. The handsomely dressed Pickett, described by one officer as a "desperate-looking character" with long, flowing locks of hair, saluted and stated grandly: "I am going to lead my division forward, sir."

Soon Pickett was riding among the assembled regiments and shouting: "Up men and to your posts! Don't forget today that you are from old Virginia." The afternoon was excruciatingly hot, and the soldiers had been lying down to protect themselves from the Union cannonade. Now with officers urging them into line, the men were soon ready to leave the woods and press forward with red battle flags unfurled before them. Even before the advance, a few soldiers fell to the ground, suffering from "seeming sunstroke," but more likely from fear. As for the rest, wrote a rebel lieutenant, they formed a "beautiful line of battle."

From the Union vantage point on Cemetery Ridge, officers and soldiers whispered back and forth that "the enemy is advancing." The waiting Yankees "grew pale" as they crouched behind stone fences and hastily constructed earthworks. Pickett's front stretched for half a mile, and the rebels moved forward in three battle lines, "man touching man, rank pressing rank, and line supporting line." At first, Union artillery fire was sporadic, cutting only occasional holes in Pickett's proud lines. When soldiers fell, torn to bits

by cannon balls, those beside them closed ranks, as if nothing had happened.

While the Confederates advanced, Union infantry troops held their fire, reported Major General Winfield S. Hancock, whose corps took the brunt of Pickett's Charge. Then when Pickett's front line closed to about 300 yards, Union officers gave the command to fire. Hunt's artillery belched forth with canister shot, and a hailstorm of minié balls flew through the air. Rebel officers suddenly realized how little damage Lee's cannon barrage had done. They had been deceived by Hunt's decision to pull back his cannons. There was no serious weakness in the Union line.

Still the Confederates came on, now at double-quick step, determined to break through or to die honorably in the attempt. Rebel soldiers leveled their muskets, yet few got off shots before being struck down. Only 5000 men reached the stone wall, where they temporarily breached the Union line. Those who made it were shot, stabbed by bayonets, captured, or driven back in hand-to-hand combat. In little more than 20 minutes Pickett's Charge was all over. Wrote General Hancock afterward, the Confederates "were repulsed . . . and sought safety in flight or by throwing themselves on the ground to escape our fire. Their battle flags were ours and the victory was won."

Retreating as best they could, fewer than half of the rebels got back to Seminary Ridge. Pickett, a survivor among the officers, rode up to Lee in tears and shouted that his division had been massacred. Lee replied softly: "Never mind, general; all this has been *my* fault. It is *I* who have lost this fight, and you must help me out of it in the best way you can." Then Lee rode among the broken soldiers, soothing them by saying over and over again: "All this will come right in the end. . . . All good men must rally."

Gettysburg was the high mark of human carnage during the Civil War. Combined Union and Confederate losses of 50,000 or more after three days of battle were greater than total British and American casualties in eight years of fighting during the War for American Independence. The huge increase in human carnage reflected many changes in the conduct of war over the previous 80 years. Armies had grown dramatically in size, and significant technological improvements in weaponry, as represented in the expanded range and accuracy of the rifled musket over its smoothbore predecessor, turned Civil War battlefields into deadly killing zones.

Soldiers of Robert E. Lee's generation had been trained in the advantages of offensive tactical maneuvers. The massed charge of infantry troops during the Mexican War of 1846–1848, in which Lee and many other high-ranking Civil War officers fought, had worked in storming positions without great loss of life. This was before the United States had fully adopted the rifled musket, which occurred during the 1850s.

After Gettysburg, Lee never attempted another massed charge of soldiers. His army fought primarily on the defensive until its surrender in April 1865. And as Union troops buried slain rebels after Lee's retreat on July 4, they spoke of how the Confederates had "advanced magnificently, unshaken by shot and shell" into the jaws of death. Certainly, too, more than one Yankee reflected on the irony of the words painted on a sign hanging from a tree on Cemetery Hill: "All persons found using firearms in these grounds will be prosecuted with the utmost rigor of the law."

more troops; yet with the exception of African American enlistees, few stepped forth as new volunteers. Congress faced this reality in March and passed a Conscription Act, which provided for the drafting of males between the ages of 20 and 45. Draftees could buy exemptions for $300.00—an average wage for half a year—or hire substitutes. All told, federal conscription produced 166,000 soldiers, roughly three-fourths of whom were substitutes.

Conscription infuriated many Northerners, particularly day laborers who lacked the income to buy their way out of the service. Riots took place in several cities. The worst were in New York where Irish workers, sensing a plot to force them into the Union army so that newly freed slaves would get their jobs, vented their rage in mid-July 1863. The rampaging started when workers assaulted a building in which a draft lottery was taking place. For a week the streets were not safe, particularly for African Americans, who in a few cases were beaten to death or hanged by roaming mobs. Only the intervention of federal troops ended the New York draft riots, but not before at least 100 people had died.

Moderate Republicans wondered whether the northern war effort could outlast such serious turmoil on the home front, but Lincoln would not back down on emancipation. As a Senate leader said of him, "he is stubborn as a mule when he gets his back up." The president kept approaching the war effort with the same grim determination, even as he continued his search for a commanding general with the talent and tenacity to achieve total military victory.

The Tide Turns: Gettysburg and Vicksburg

Before relieving McClellan of command, Lincoln had named a new general in chief, Henry W. Halleck. "Old Brains," as the soldiers called him because of his West Point education and voluminous writings on military strategy, moved to Washington from the western theater in the summer of 1862. Life in the field was one thing; life in the nation's capital was another. The pressures of office caused Halleck to have a nervous breakdown.

Lincoln did not replace Halleck but functioned as his own general in chief until the spring of 1864. His greatest frustration was with commanders of the Army of the Potomac, which the masterful Robert E. Lee kept subjecting to embarrassing defeats. After dismissing McClellan, Lincoln named General Ambrose E. Burnside, famous for his huge sideburns, to head the eastern army. Burnside did not have "the slows." He rushed his troops south and, on December 13, 1862, foolishly engaged Lee in a frontal assault at Fredericksburg, Virginia. His force outnumbered Lee's by a ratio of three to two; but Burnside's casualties that day were nearly 11,000, as compared to under 5000 for the Army of Northern Virginia.

Shattered by the defeat, Burnside offered strong hints to Lincoln about finding a replacement. Lincoln accommodated him and elevated "Fighting Joe" Hooker, whose ambitions to command the Army of the Potomac were well-known. Hooker did raise sagging troop morale, even if his headquarters, according to one critic, represented "a combination of barroom and brothel." With self-assurance, Hooker promised Lincoln that he could capture Richmond. The president only wanted to know when, reminding Hooker that the hen was the wisest of all animals "because she never cackles until the egg is laid."

Moving south in late April 1863, Hooker got 75,000 troops across the Rappahannock River and quickly squared off with Lee's Confederates in what became a bloody brawl known as the Battle of Chancellorsville (May 1–4). The intense action resulted in a combined casualty count of 21,000 before Hooker pulled back across the river on the evening of May 5. "Stonewall" Jackson, shot accidentally by his own pickets, died a few days later, costing the South an authentic military genius. As for Hooker, the embarrassment of Chancellorsville soon brought to an end his command of the Army of the Potomac.

At this juncture, with the war taking such a toll on the Virginia countryside, Lee asked Jefferson Davis for permission to lead his troops northward into Pennsylvania. There they could disrupt rail traffic, live off the land, intimidate civilians, and, most important, try to win a battle so overwhelming that Lincoln would be forced to accept peace terms favorable to the Confederacy. During June, Lee executed his plan, and the Army of the Potomac tagged along far to the east, keeping an eye fixed on the Confederate offensive challenge. Late in the month, Lincoln asked George G. Meade, a lackluster but competent general, to assume command. On July 1, 1863, the two armies squared off against one another just west of a small Pennsylvania town called Gettysburg.

The Battle of Gettysburg, lasting three days, was the bloodiest engagement of the war, with combined casualties of over 50,000. On the third day, hoping that he could split and rout his adversary, Lee massed soldiers under General George E. Pickett for an assault on the center of the Union line. Pickett's Charge, sometimes called "the high tide of the Confederacy," saw some 13,000 rebels hurtling across a mile of open, gradually rising fields. For the Union soldiers it was a turkey shoot, costing Lee at least 7000 casualties. Late the next day, Lee retreated, his army battered but not yet broken. Rather than boldly pursuing, the Union

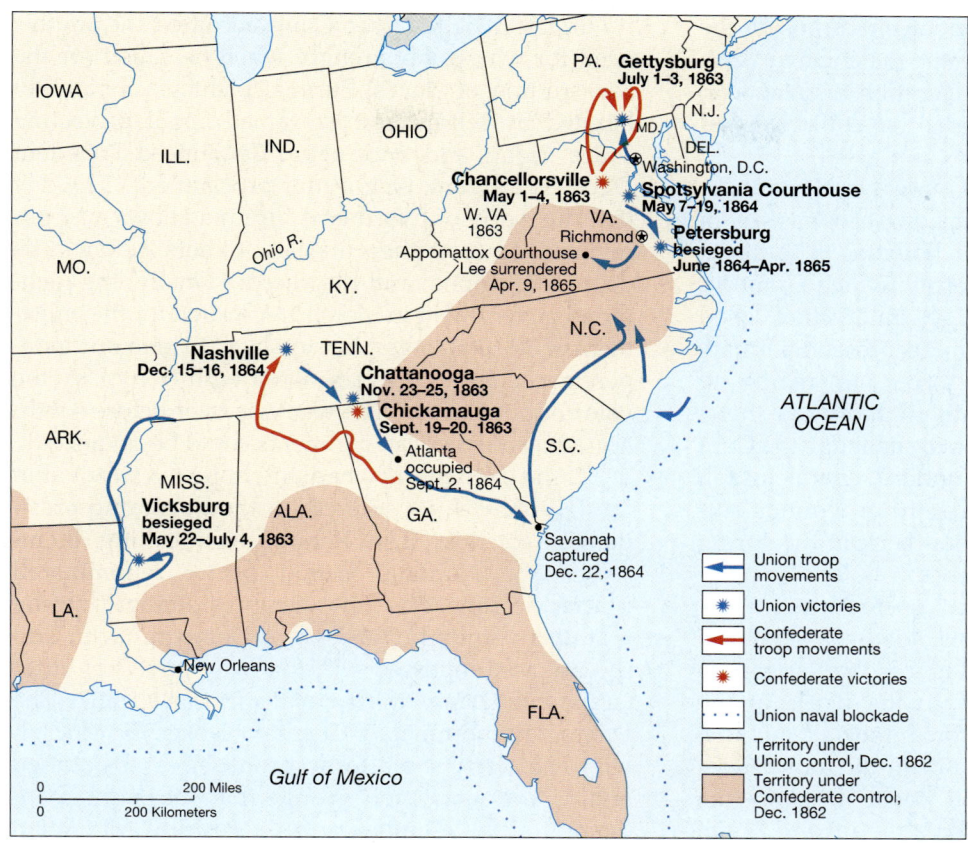

Civil War, 1863–1865

force followed along at a safe distance, causing Lincoln to accuse Meade of acting like "an old woman trying to shoo her geese across the creek."

Still, Gettysburg was a decisive battle. Never again would Lee have the troop strength to carry the war into enemy territory. Further, the timing of the engagement was important, because the federal siege of Vicksburg on the Mississippi River was just ending successfully.

Early in 1863 General Grant had secured permission to attempt the reduction of that city. Through a series of intricate maneuvers, he moved 75,000 troops south through eastern Arkansas into Louisiana, then swept east across the Mississippi River and slowly turned west in a wide arc, securing his lines against rebel marauders along the way. By late May, Grant had Vicksburg under siege, and his artillery bombarded that city and its defenders for six weeks. Reduced to living in caves and eating rats, troops under General John C. Pemberton and local citizens held out valiantly until they could take no more. On July 4, 1863, the day after Pickett's Charge, Grant accepted Vicksburg's surrender. A few days later rebel defenders capitulated at Port Hudson, Louisiana. Union forces had finally severed the Confederacy.

With these triumphs the war had turned against the South. The combat was far from over, Lincoln fully appreciated, as he rode a train to Gettysburg to dedicate a national memorial cemetery before a large crowd in November 1863. At Gettysburg he urged all citizens to "resolve that these dead shall not have died in vain; . . . and that government of the people, by the people, for the people, shall not perish from the earth."

Crushing Blows from Grant and Sherman

Vicksburg revived Grant's tarnished reputation, and after Union forces suffered an embarrassing defeat at the Battle of Chickamauga in northwestern Georgia on September 19–20, 1863, Lincoln named him overall commander of western forces. Once in the vicinity, Grant quickly restored federal fortunes in the campaign to capture Chattanooga, Tennessee (November 1863). Now the opportunity was at hand to plunge an army into Georgia to cut away at the heart of the Confederacy.

Early in 1864, Lincoln decided to name Grant general in chief, despite critics who described the western commander as a dirty, uncouth little man who drank too much whiskey—to which Lincoln reputedly said that if he could get the brand name he would send abundant supplies to his other generals. Grant arrived in Washington during March and soon unveiled his war plan. Promising to limit "the carnage . . . to a single year," Grant wanted Union armies to advance on "a common center" inside the Confederacy. They were to pursue the enemy relentlessly. Further, in a virtual declaration of **total war,** he wanted to destroy all property that could be used to support the rebel armies.

To ensure no faint-hearted maneuvers, Grant decided to travel with General Meade, who was still in command of the Army of the Potomac. The target was not Richmond but Lee's army, which Grant intended to grind into dust. The general in chief called on his old ally, General William Tecumseh Sherman, then commanding western forces, to march to Atlanta and destroy key southern railheads there. As Sherman proceeded, he was to challenge the Confederate Army of Tennessee under General Joseph E. Johnston, who had recovered from wounds suffered while defending Richmond back in the spring of 1862.

Grant and Sherman began operations in May 1864, and the spectacle made for blood-soaked newspaper headlines. Grant moved across the Rappahannock River and engaged Lee in the Battle of the Wilderness (May 5–6). Union forces took a drubbing, but something was different. They did not retreat but rolled southeastward in what became the month-long campaign for Virginia. Again and again, Johnny Rebs and Billy Yanks clashed at such places as Spotsylvania Courthouse (May 7–19) and Cold Harbor (June 1–3), within a few miles of Richmond. Finally, the two exhausted armies settled along siege lines at Petersburg, 20 miles southeast of the Confederate capital, with Grant waiting for Lee's army to disintegrate.

There had been nothing quite like the Virginia campaign before. Grant started with 120,000 soldiers, and half of them were casualties by early June. To preserve his army, Lee lived up to one of his nicknames, "King of Spades," by repeatedly ordering his troops to dig up earth, indeed anything, to provide cover from the relentless fury of federal minié balls flying at them. By the time Lee reached the Petersburg trenches in mid-June, his army had been reduced by more than a third, to 40,000.

In the North, Peace Democrats called Grant a "butcher," but the general in chief, with Lincoln's backing, held tight to the war plan. Winning was now only a matter of time since the president, as the manager of the Union's superior resources, could supply more troops and keep waging a war of attrition. The South, however, had little manpower left to draw on. Of an estimated 1.2 million white males between the ages of 16 and 50, some 90 percent had already seen Confederate military service; the comparable figure for the North was 40 percent.

In late 1864 Jefferson Davis admitted the South's need for new troop strength when he called for the conscription of slaves. Furious planters, apparently blinded by self-interest, screamed about protecting states' rights and once again denounced President Davis as a tyrant. One leader proclaimed: "The day that the Army of [Northern] Virginia allows a Negro regiment to enter their lines as soldiers they will be degraded, ruined, and disgraced." Finally, the Richmond government in March 1865 called for the enlistment of 300,000 slaves, but too late "to gain our independence," as a Georgian noted with irony, "by the valor of our slaves." The war was over before southern African American regiments could be organized.

If the Confederacy had any hope for survival in the fall of 1864, it centered on the upcoming presidential election. The Republicans, calling themselves the National Union party, renominated Lincoln in June. His new vice presidential running mate was Andrew Johnson, a Democrat who had served as Tennessee's Union war governor after Grant's invasion of that state in early 1862. The Democrats nominated General George B. McClellan. The party's platform promised a negotiated end to the war, even should that mean independence for the Confederacy—a position McClellan himself thought too extreme to support. A despairing Lincoln, looking at the horrible casualty figures in Virginia, feared repudiation at the polls by a populace too sickened by the carnage to let him finish the fight.

Lincoln's pessimism proved groundless. He had not counted on General Sherman's army, moving slowly toward Atlanta in the face of stout rebel resistance. In early September, Sherman wired the president: "Atlanta is ours, and fairly won." News of the capture of this major Confederate railroad and manufacturing center thrilled Northerners. The Confederacy was obviously in serious trouble. Voters gave Lincoln a resounding victory. On November 8, 1864, he received 55 percent of the popular vote and 212 electoral college votes, as compared to just 21 for McClellan. Lincoln's reelection especially pleased Union soldiers in the field, such as one of Sherman's corporals, who wrote excitedly that his comrades now marched forward "with our Hartes contented nowing that we have a president that will not declare peace on no other terms then an Uncondishnell Surrender."

Total War Forces Surrender

In the eighteenth century, warfare rarely affected the whole populace. Armies were small, and combat could be conducted in war zones away from population centers. By comparison, the Civil War touched nearly every American life. Families gave fathers and sons to the armed services; and women assumed the management of farms or moved to the cities and took jobs to keep factories humming in the production of war goods. Hundreds of women, more rigidly segregated from combat than had been the case at the time of the American Revolution, became nurses who fought to save thousands of lives.

Serving the fallen was grim work. Too often hospitals were centers of filth, horrible agony, and death. Such women as Dorothea Dix, superintendent of Union army nurses, and Clara Barton, who later founded the American Red Cross (1881), endured incredible personal privation to comfort those in pain. Still, they could hardly relieve the suffering. Medicine was too primitive to cope with such killer diseases as typhoid fever and malaria that swept through army camps and cut down Alvin Flint, Sr., and thousands of other soldiers.

Since physicians lacked a sense of the importance of sterilization, germs spread rapidly as surgeons cut off arms and legs to save wounded soldiers from gangrene poisoning. Troops on both sides would have agreed with the Alabama private who wrote in 1862: "I beleave the doctors kills more than they cure." Of those who survived the crude surgery of the times, only a small portion recovered in the type of clean, well-managed hospital run by Sally L. Tompkins in Richmond. Indeed, Confederate leaders did not officially permit the use of female nurses until the autumn of 1862. Once they did, they found that death rates were lower than in hospitals employing only male nurses.

To force an end to all the suffering and killing, General Sherman, after taking Atlanta, proposed to march his troops first eastward to Savannah, Georgia, then north toward Grant's army in Virginia. He intended to "demonstrate the vulnerability of the South," he wrote, "and make its inhabitants feel that war and individual ruin are synonymous terms." Before year's end Sherman's soldiers cut a 60-mile-wide swath through Georgia. Then, in Jan-

TABLE 15.2
Incidence of Disease Among Union Soldiers

Sickness was a chronic problem in both the Union and Confederate armies. White federal troops were ill on the average of 2.50 times a year, and black soldiers were ill on the average of 3.33 times a year. Black soldiers also died at a more rapid rate from their illnesses. There is no satisfactory explanation for these higher rates.

	Whites	Blacks
Average annual number of sick cases per 1000 troops	2435	3299
Average annual number of deaths from sickness per 1000 troops	53.4	143.4

Source: From *The Life of Billy Yank: The Common Soldier of the Union* by Bell Irvin Wiley. Copyright 1952 © by Bell I. Wiley. Reprinted by permission of Louisiana State University Press.

Sally L. Tompkins opened a private hospital in Richmond to care for wounded Confederate soldiers after the first Battle of Bull Run.

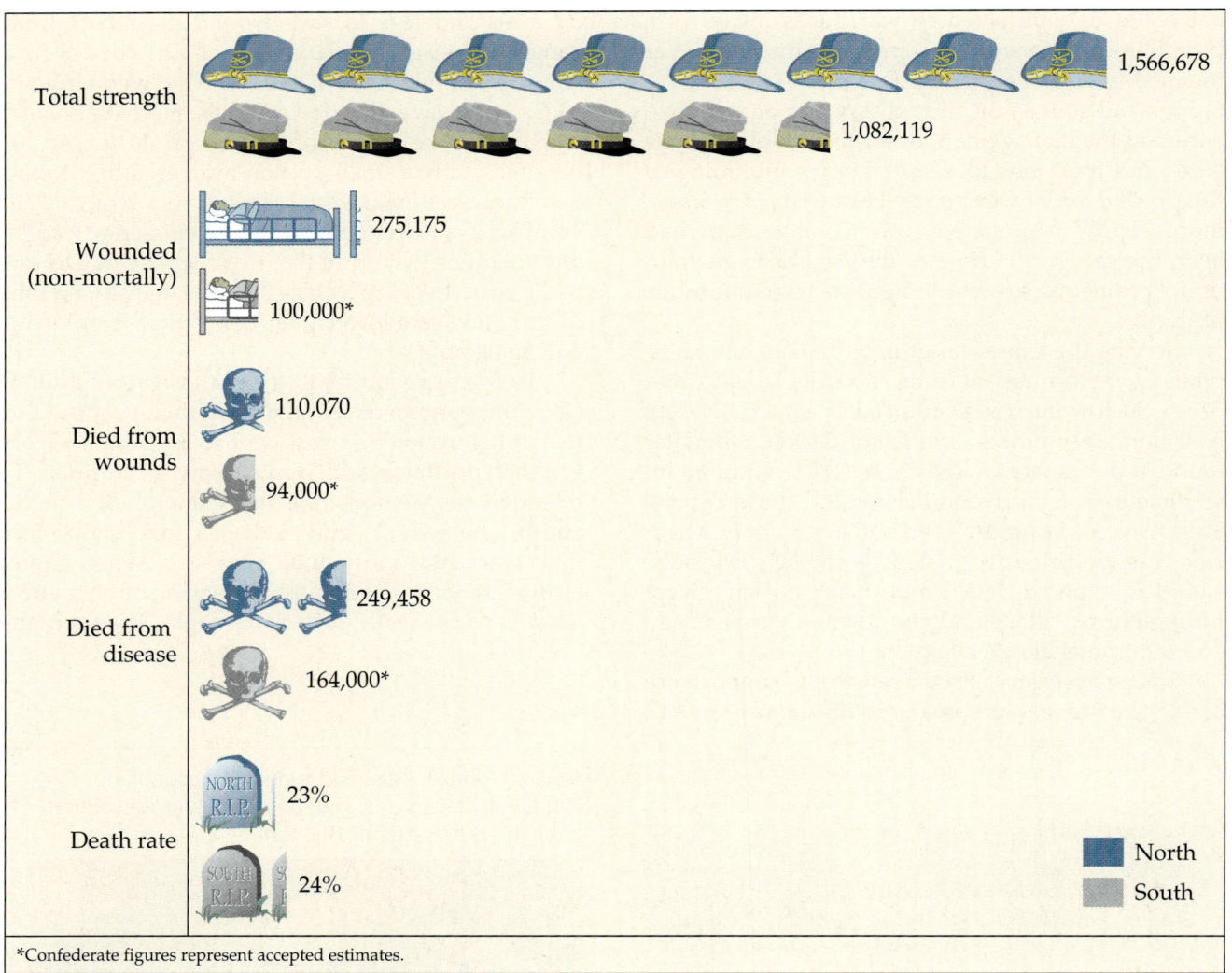

FIGURE 15.3
The Human Cost of War

Many soldiers died as a result of inadequate care of wounds and diseases.

uary 1865, they entered South Carolina, which they thought of as "the birth place of Dark Treason" against the Union. "South Carolina cried out the first for war," penned an Iowa soldier, "and she shall have it to her hearts content." In systematic fashion Sherman's army broke the southern will to keep fighting by burning and leveling everything in sight.

As word of Sherman's devastating march reached Lee's troops in the Petersburg trenches, they deserted in droves, wanting to return home to help protect their loved ones. By late March, Lee's Army of Northern Virginia had fewer than 35,000 troops, compared to Grant's total of 115,000. The situation was all but hopeless, so the Confederate commander ordered a retreat to the west, and Richmond fell on April 3. Grant's soldiers moved quickly to encircle the disintegrating rebel army. They soon had their prey entrapped.

On April 9, 1865, Lee met with Grant and surrendered at Appomattox. The two generals reminisced for a few moments about their previous service in the Mexican War. They said goodbye, but not before Grant graciously allowed the Confederates to keep their horses—they had to give up their arms—so that they could more easily plow their fields and plant crops after returning home. Lee's surrender served as a signal to other Confederate forces to lay down their arms and accept military defeat. The Civil War, at long last, had ended.

Chronology of Key Events

1860 Democratic party links along sectional lines; Republican nominee Abraham Lincoln is elected the sixteenth president (November); Senator John J. Crittenden offers a series of compromise proposals to end the sectional crisis (December); South Carolina votes to secede from the Union (December)

1861 Six Deep South States—Georgia, Florida, Alabama, Mississippi, Louisiana, and Texas—secede (January–February); Confederate States of America is formed by the seceding states (February); Fort Sumter falls to Confederate artillery (April); Lincoln declares an "insurrection," calls for volunteer troops, and announces a naval blockade (April); western section of Virginia breaks away to form West Virginia and later joins the Union in 1863 (June); South wins at Bull Run, or First Manassas (July)

1862 Union forces penetrate the South's western defenses, seizing Forts Henry and Donelson in Tennessee and capturing Memphis, Tennessee; Corinth, Mississippi; and New Orleans, Louisiana (February–June). Confederacy adopts a draft law (April); Homestead Act offers 160 acres of western acreage to citizens who will occupy and improve the land for five years (May); in the Battle of the Seven Days, the Second Battle of Bull Run (Second Manassas), and the Battle of Fredericksburg, Confederates prevent Union forces from breaking through to Richmond (June–December); Morrill Act gives states land grants to endow agricultural colleges (July); at Antietam (Sharpsburg), McClellan's army halts a Confederate offensive into Maryland and forces Lee to retreat to Virginia (September); Lincoln issues preliminary Emancipation Proclamation—all slaves in states still in rebellion on January 1, 1863, would be freed (September)

1863 National Bank Act creates nation's first centralized banking system (February); the Union passes a draft law (March); Congress affirms Lincoln's suspension of habeas corpus to persons who resist the draft, discourage enlistments, or aid the rebel cause (March); Lee leads army into Pennsylvania (June); Confederates are defeated at Gettysburg and forced to withdraw to Virginia (July); capture of Vicksburg and Port Hudson place Mississippi River under Union control (July); New York City faces violence in draft riots (July); African American soldiers in 54th Massachusetts regiment lead assault on Fort Wagner in Charleston harbor (July); Union army secures strategic railroad center at Chattanooga, Tennessee (November)

1864 General Ulysses S. Grant pursues Lee's army through Virginia to Confederate entrenchments at Petersburg (May–June); William T. Sherman's army marches from Chattanooga and takes Atlanta, then marches through Georgia (May–December); Union General Philip H. Sheridan's army takes control of the Shenandoah Valley (September–October); Four Southern state governors recommend using slaves as Confederate soldiers (October)

1865 Lee retreats from his Richmond-Petersburg defenses and surrenders at Appomattox (April); John Wilkes Booth assassinates Lincoln at Ford's Theater in Washington, D.C., and Andrew Johnson becomes the seventeenth president (April)

Conclusion

At noon on Good Friday, April 14, 1865, a crowd gathered to watch Major General Robert Anderson raise over Fort Sumter the very same U. S. flag that he had surrendered four years earlier. A genuinely moved Anderson said: "I thank God that I have lived to see this day." Then he hoisted up the "weather-beaten, frayed, and shell-torn old flag" as Union naval vessels out in Charleston harbor fired their cannons in salute. Citizens at the fort wept and cheered, realizing that the national tragedy was finally over, a tragedy that had forever sealed the fate of secession. The states, while far from reunited, would continue together as a nation.

Just a few hours later another shot rang out, this time in the nation's capital. John Wilkes Booth, a Confederate sympathizer and racist fanatic who hated Abraham Lincoln for emancipating African Americans, gained access to the presidential box at Ford's Theater and assassinated the president at point blank range. At 7:22 A.M. the next morning, four years to the day after he had declared an insurrection and called up federal troops, Lincoln died quietly at the age of 56.

In his last days Lincoln felt the elation of knowing that a war begun to preserve the Union had achieved its objective. Further, in recognition of the horrible price in lives maimed and destroyed, he took pride in the elimination of slavery from the American landscape, which he called the "act" that would put "my name . . . into history." Lincoln had also started to speak openly of citizenship for African Americans as part of his reconstruction plans. Even as the American people mourned his passing, they too turned to the difficult task of how best to bring the South—defeated, destroyed, but still with a dogged streak of defiance—back into the United States.

SUGGESTIONS FOR FURTHER READING

Catherine Clinton and Nina Silber, eds., *Divided Houses: Gender and the Civil War* (1992). Challenging essays focusing on gender-related issues, including prescribed identities for men and women during the Civil War era.

David Herbert Donald, *Lincoln* (1995). Highly readable, perceptive one-volume biography of the nation's sixteenth president.

Joseph T. Glatthaar, *Forged in Battle: The Civil War Alliance of Black Soldiers and White Officers* (1990). Valuable analysis of racial attitudes as reflected in the wartime service experiences of African Americans.

Howard Jones, *Union in Peril: The Crisis over British Intervention in the Civil War* (1992). Important revisionist analysis of the reasons the Confederacy failed to gain powerful foreign allies, a serious impediment to securing independence.

James M. McPherson, *Battle Cry of Freedom: The Civil War Era* (1988). Winner of a Pulitzer Prize, the best detailed introduction to the war period in its broad-ranging complexities.

Emory M. Thomas, *General Robert E. Lee: A Biography* (1995). Balanced one-volume study of the talented—and charismatic—Confederate general and folk hero.

Maris A. Vinovskis, ed., *Toward a Social History of the American Civil War: Exploratory Essays* (1990). Suggestive essays focusing on the ways in which the Civil War affected civilian and community life in the North.

Overviews and Surveys

Bruce Catton, *The Centennial History of the Civil War*, 3 vols. (1961–1965); Henry S. Commager, ed., *The Blue and the Gray*, 2 vols., rev. ed. (1973); William C. Davis, "A Government of Our Own": The Making of the Confederacy (1994); David Donald, *Liberty and Union* (1978), and ed., *Why the North Won the Civil War* (1960); Shelby Foote, *The Civil War*, 3 vols. (1958–1974); Joseph T. Glatthaar, *Partners in Command: The Relationships Between Leaders in the Civil War* (1994); Alvin M. Josephy, Jr., *The Civil War in the American West* (1991); Richard M. McMurry, *Two Great Rebel Armies: An Essay in Confederate Military History* (1989); James M. McPherson, *Drawn with the Sword: Reflections on the Civil War* (1996), *For Cause and Comrades: Why Men Fought in the Civil War* (1997), and *Ordeal by Fire: The Civil War and Reconstruction*, 2d ed. (1992); Allan Nevins, *The War for the Union*, 4 vols. (1959–1971); Phillip Shaw Paludan, *"A People's Contest": The Union and Civil War, 1861–1865* (1988); Charles P. Roland, *The American Iliad: The Story of the Civil War* (1991); Emory M. Thomas, *The Confederate Nation, 1861–1865* (1979).

From Secession to Full-Scale War

Michael C. C. Adams, *Our Masters the Rebels* (1978); Bern Anderson, *By Sea and By River* (1962); William L. Barney, *The Road to Secession* (1972), and *The Secessionist Impulse: Alabama and Mississippi in 1860* (1974); Steven A. Channing, *Crisis of Fear: Secession in South Carolina* (1970); Richard N. Current, *Lincoln and the First Shot* (1963); Michael F. Holt, *The Rise and Fall of the American Whig Party: Jacksonian Politics and the Onset of the Civil War* (1999); Randall C. Jimerson, *The Private Civil War: Popular Thought During the Sectional Conflict* (1988); Michael P. Johnson, *Toward a Patriarchal Republic: The Secession of Georgia* (1977); Charles R. Lee, *The Confederate Constitutions* (1963); David M. Potter, *Lincoln and His Party in the Secession Crisis*, 2d ed. (1962); Donald E. Reynolds, *Editors Make War: Southern Newspapers in the Secession Crisis* (1970); Kenneth M. Stampp, *And the War Came: The North and the Secession Crisis, 1860–1861* (1950); Emory M. Thomas, *The Confederacy as a Revolutionary Experience* (1971); Bell I. Wiley, *The Road to Appomattox* (1956); Ralph A. Wooster, *The Secession Conventions of the South* (1962).

"Forward to Richmond!" and "On to Washington!"

Michael Barton, *Goodmen: The Character of Civil War Soldiers* (1981); Thomas L. Connelly and Archer Jones,

The Politics of Command: Factions and Ideas in Confederate Strategy (1973); Paul D. Escott, After Secession: Jefferson Davis (1978); Joseph A. Frank and George A. Reaves, "Seeing the Elephant": Raw Recruits at the Battle of Shiloh (1989); William A. Frassanito, America's Bloodiest Day: Antietam (1978); Gary W. Gallagher, ed., The Antietam Campaign (1999), and The Confederate War (1997); Paddy Griffith, Battle Tactics of the Civil War (1989); Earl J. Hess, Liberty, Virtue, and Progress: Northerners and Their War for the Union (1988); Archer Jones, Civil War Command and Strategy (1992); Gerald F. Linderman, Embattled Courage: Combat in the American Civil War (1987); Reid Mitchell, Civil War Soldiers: Their Expectations and Experiences (1988), and The Vacant Chair: The Northern Soldier Leaves Home (1993); James I. Robertson, Soldiers Blue and Gray (1988), and The Stonewall Brigade (1963); Frank E. Vandiver, Rebel Brass: The Confederate Command System (1956); Bell I. Wiley, The Life of Johnny Reb (1943), and The Life of Billy Yank (1952); T. Harry Williams, Lincoln and His Generals (1952), and McClellan, Sherman, and Grant (1962).

To and From Emancipation: The War on the Home Front

Thomas B. Alexander and Richard E. Beringer, The Anatomy of the Confederate Congress (1972); Stephen V. Ash, When the Yankees Came: Conflict and Chaos in the Occupied South (1995); Dale Baum, The Civil War Party System (1984); Herman Belz, A New Birth of Freedom: The Republican Party and Freedmen's Rights (1976); Stuart L. Bernath, Squall Across the Atlantic: Civil War Prize Cases (1970); Allan G. Bogue, The Congressman's Civil War (1989); Victoria E. Bynum, The Politics of Social and Sexual Control in the South, 1840–1865 (1992); Dudley T. Cornish, The Sable Arm: Negro Troops in the Union Army, 2d ed. (1987); LaWanda Cox, Lincoln and Black Freedom (1981); Beth G. Crabtree and James M. Patton, eds., "Journal of a Secesh Lady" (1979); David P. Crook, The North, the South, and the Powers, 1861–1865 (1974), and Diplomacy During the American Civil War (1975); Wayne K. Durrill, War of Another Kind: A Southern Community in the Great Rebellion (1990); Drew Gilpin Faust, The Creation of Confederate Nationalism (1988), and Mothers of Invention: Women of the Slaveholding South in the Civil War (1996); Norman B. Ferris, The Trent Affair (1977); Eric Foner, Politics and Ideology in the Age of the Civil War (1980); John Hope Franklin, The Emancipation Proclamation (1963); George M. Fredrickson, The Inner Civil War (1965); J. Matthew Gallman, Mastering Wartime: A Social History of Philadelphia During the Civil War (1990); Louis Gerteis, From Contraband to Freedman: Federal Policy Toward Southern Blacks, 1861–1865 (1973); Brian A. Jenkins, Britain & the War for the Union, 2 vols. (1974–1980); Jacqueline Jones, Labor of Love, Labor of Sorrow (1985); Ervin L. Jordan, Jr., Black Confederates and Afro-Yankees in Civil War Virginia (1995); Frank L. Klement, The Copperheads in the Middle West (1960); Elizabeth A. Leonard, Yankee Women: Gender Battles in the Civil War (1994); Leon F. Litwack, Been in the Storm So Long (1979); Mary E. Massey, Bonnet Brigades: Women and the Civil War (1966); James M. McPherson, The Struggle for Equality (1964), and Abraham Lincoln and the Second American Revolution (1990); Clarence L. Mohr, On the Threshold of Freedom: Masters and Slaves in Civil War Georgia (1986); Robert M. Myers, ed., The Children of Pride: Georgia and the Civil War (1972); Mark E. Neely, Jr., The Fate of Liberty: Abraham Lincoln and Civil Liberties (1991); Benjamin Quarles, The Negro in the Civil War (1953); George C. Rable, Civil Wars: Women and the Crisis of Southern Nationalism (1989), and The Confederate Republic: A Revolution Against Politics (1994); Willie Lee Rose, Rehearsal for Reconstruction: The Port Royal Experiment (1964); Joel H. Silbey, A Respectable Minority: The Democratic Party in the Civil War Era (1977); Hans L. Trefousse, The Radical Republicans (1969); V. Jacque Voegeli, Free But Not Equal: The Midwest and the Negro (1967); Gordon H. Warren, Fountain of Discontent: The Trent Affair (1981); Forrest G. Wood, Black Scare: Racist Response to Emancipation and Reconstruction (1968); C. Vann Woodward, ed., Mary Chesnut's Civil War (1981), and with Elisabeth Muhlenfeld, eds., The Private Mary Chesnut (1984).

Breaking Confederate Resistance, 1863–1865

Richard E. Beringer, Herman Hattaway, Archer Jones, and William N. Still, Jr., Why the South Lost the Civil War (1986); Iver Bernstein, The New York City Draft Riots (1990); David W. Blight, Frederick Douglass' Civil War (1989); Robert F. Durden, The Gray and the Black (1972); William A. Frassanito, Gettysburg (1975), and Grant and Lee (1983); Joseph T. Glatthaar, The March to the Sea and Beyond (1985); U. S. Grant, Personal Memoirs, 2 vols. (1885–1886); Edward Hagerman, The American Civil War and the Origins of Modern Warfare (1988); Herman Hattaway and Archer Jones, How the North Won (1983); Lawrence L. Hewitt, Port Hudson: Confederate Bastion on the Mississippi (1987); Jay Luvaas, The Military Legacy of the Civil War (1959); Grady McWhiney and Perry D. Jamieson, Attack and Die: Civil War Military Tactics and the Southern Heritage (1982); Mark E. Neely, Confederate Political Prisoners and the Myth of Southern Constitutionalism (1999); James L. Roark, Masters Without Slaves (1977); Charles Royster, The Destructive War: Sherman, Jackson, and the Americans (1991); Steven E. Woodworth, Davis and Lee at War (1995), and Jefferson Davis and His Generals: The Failure of Confederate Command in the West (1990).

Biographies

Thomas L. Connelly, The Marble Man: Robert E. Lee (1977); David Donald, Lincoln Reconsidered (1956); Martin Duberman, Charles Francis Adams (1961); Michael Fellman, Citizen Sherman (1995); Douglas S. Freeman, R. E. Lee: A Biography, 4 vols. (1934–1935); John F. Marszalek, Sherman: A Soldier's Passion for Order (1993); William S. McFeely, Frederick Douglass (1991), and Grant: A Biography (1981); Alan T. Nolan, Lee Considered: General Robert E. Lee and Civil

War History (1991); Stephen B. Oates, *With Malice Toward None: Abraham Lincoln* (1977), *Abraham Lincoln: The Man Behind the Myths* (1984), and *A Woman of Valor: Clara Barton and the Civil War* (1994); Stephen W. Sears, *George B. McClellan: The Young Napoleon* (1988); Brooks D. Simpson, *Let Us Have Peace: Ulysses S. Grant* (1991); Benjamin P. Thomas, *Abraham Lincoln* (1953); Emory M. Thomas, *Bold Dragoon: J. E. B. Stuart* (1986); Hans L. Trefousse, *Andrew Johnson: A Biography* (1989); Frank E. Vandiver, *Mighty Stonewall* (1957); Jeffrey D. Wert, *General James Longstreet* (1994).

Internet Resources

The American Civil War Homepage
http://funnelweb.utcc.utk.edu/~hoemann/cwarhp.html
This site has a good collection of hypertext links to the most useful identified electronic files about the American Civil War.

The Valley of the Shadow: Living the Civil War in Pennsylvania and Virginia
http://jefferson.village.virginia.edu/vshadow/vshadow.html
This project tells the histories of two communities on either side of the Mason-Dixon line during the Civil War. It includes a narrative and an electronic archive of sources.

Civil War @ Charleston
http://www.awod.com/gallery/probono/cwchas/cwlayout.html
This site covers the history of the Civil War in and around Charleston, South Carolina.

Abraham Lincoln Association
http://www.alincolnassoc.com/
This site allows you to search digital versions of Lincoln's papers.

The Papers of Jefferson Davis
http://www.ruf.rice.edu/~pjdavis/jdp.htm
This site tells about the collection of Jefferson Davis Papers and includes a chronology of his life, a family genealogy, some key Davis documents on-line, and a collection of related links.

Crisis at Fort Sumter
http://www.tulane.edu/~latner/CrisisMain.html
This well-crafted use of hypermedia with assignments or problems explains and explores the events in and around the start of the Civil War.

U.S. Civil War Center
http://www.cwc.lsu.edu/
This is a site whose mission is to "locate, index, and/or make available all appropriate private and public data regarding the Civil War and to promote the study of the Civil War from the perspectives of all professions, occupations, and academic disciplines."

American Civil War (1861–1865) Archive
http://users.iamdigex.nef/bdboyle/cw.html
This excellent site marshals diverse information about the Civil War.

Civil War Women
http://scriptorium.lib.duke.edu/collections/civil-war-women.html
This site includes original documents, links, and biographical information about several women and their lives during the Civil War.

History of African Americans in the Civil War—United States Colored Troops
http://www.itd.nps.gov/cwss/africanh.html
This National Park Service site explores the history of the USCT (United States Colored Troops).

Assassination of President Abraham Lincoln
http://memory.loc.gov/ammem/alhtml/alrintr.html
Part of the American Memory series with an introduction, time line, and gallery.

Selected Civil War Photographs
http://lcweb2.loc.gov/ammem/cwphome.html
Library of Congress site with more than 1000 photographs, many from Matthew Brady.

A Time Line of the Civil War
http://www.historyplace.com/civilwar/index.html
A complete time line of the Civil War, well illustrated with photographs.

National Civil War Association
http://www.ncwa.org/info.html
One of the many Civil War reenactment organizations in the United States.

Key Terms

Fire-eaters   (p. 411)
Billy Yank   (p. 419)
Johnny Reb   (p. 419)
Anaconda Plan   (p. 419)
Greenbacks   (p. 426)
Copperheads   (p. 428)
Emancipation Proclamation   (p. 428)
Total War   (p. 436)

Review Questions

1. Examine the numerous problems that contributed to the dissolution of the Democratic Party and the consequences this breakup had for the coming of the Civil War. Why did Abraham Lincoln's election prompt secession?

2. Evaluate the reasons for the Civil War by considering the following: On what principles did the South secede from the Union? On what principles did the North go to war? How did these principles change during the course of the war?

3. Compare and contrast the strengths and weaknesses of the North and the South as the Civil War started. Be sure to include a survey of available resources as well as an assessment of the political leadership of the two regions.

4. Compare and contrast the military leaders, strategies, and tactics of the North and the South. How effective were the various generals in the battlefield?

5. Discuss the role of slavery as an issue during the Civil War. What were the experiences of African Americans? Why did Lincoln issue the Emancipation Proclamation? How did Northerners and Southerners react to the proclamation?

6. Assess the ways in which the Civil War became a "total war." What did the war accomplish, and why

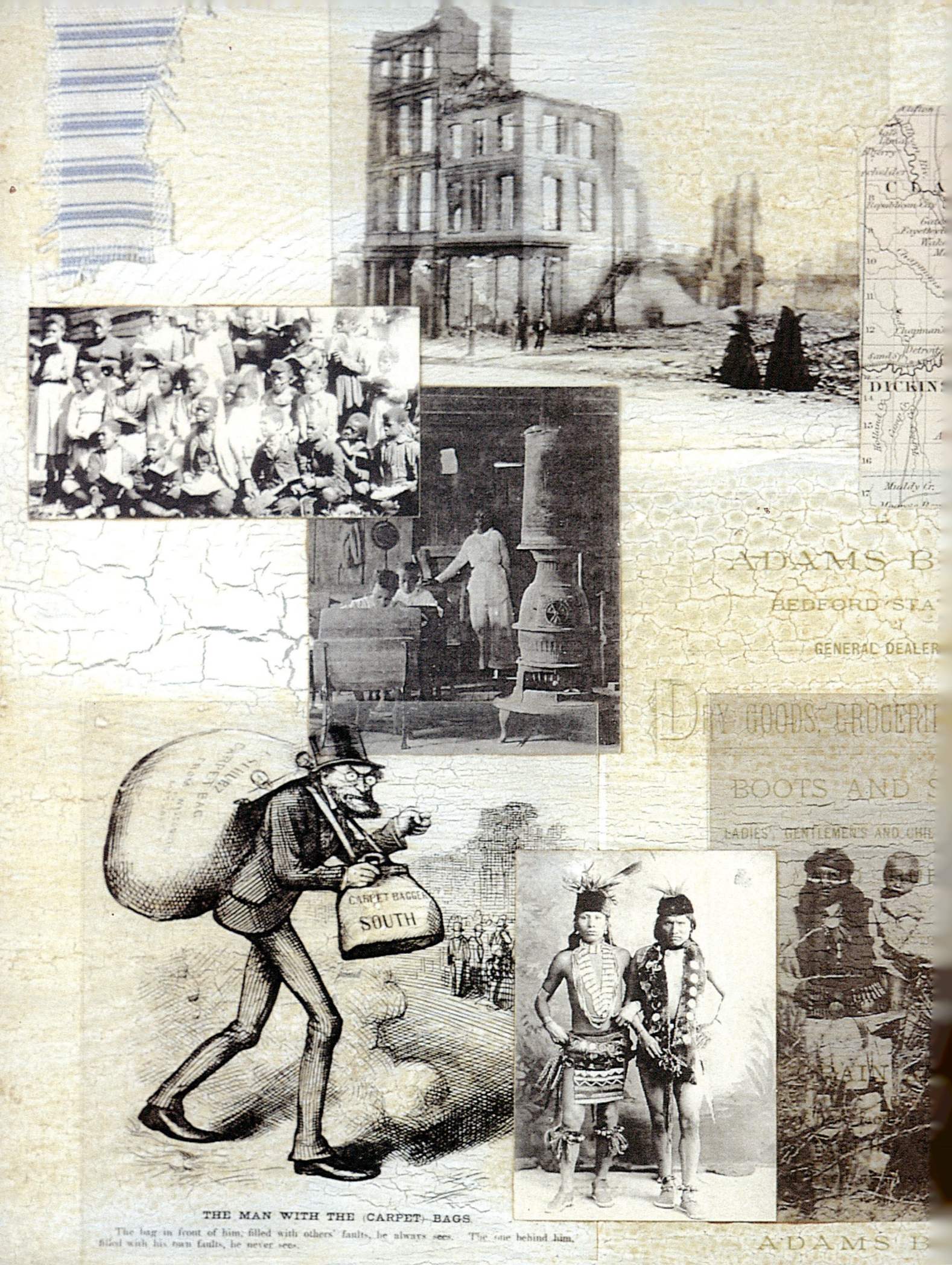

16

THE NATION RECONSTRUCTED: NORTH, SOUTH, AND THE WEST, 1865–1877

POSTWAR CONDITIONS AND ISSUES
  The War's Impact on Individuals
  Unresolved Issues

PRESIDENTIAL RECONSTRUCTION
  Lincoln's Plan
  Johnson's Plan
  Black Codes in the South

CONGRESSIONAL RECONSTRUCTION
  "Radical" Reconstruction
  Black Suffrage

RECONSTRUCTION IN THE SOUTH
  Carpetbaggers, Scalawags, and Black Republicans
  Character of Republican Rule
  Black and White Economic and Social Adaptation
  Violent White Resistance

RECONSTRUCTION IN THE NORTH AND WEST
  Northern Shifts in Attitudes
  Western Expansion, Racism, and Native Americans
  Final Retreat from Reconstruction

"I'd like tuh see any man put me outer dis house"

As Thomas Pinckney approached El Dorado, his plantation on the Santee River in South Carolina, he felt a quiver of apprehension. Pinckney, a captain in the defeated Confederate army, had stayed the night with neighbors before going to reclaim his land. "Your negroes sacked your house," they reported, "stripped it of furniture, bric-a-brac, heirlooms, and divided these among themselves. They got it in their heads that the property of whites belongs to them." Pinckney remembered the days when his return home had been greeted with slaves' chants of "Howdy do, Master! Howdy do, Boss!" Now he was welcomed with an eerie silence. He did not even see any of his former slaves until he went into the house. There, a single servant seemed genuinely glad to see him, but she pleaded ignorance as to the whereabouts of any others. He lingered about the house until after the dinner hour. Still no one appeared, so he informed the servant that he would return in the morning and expected to see all his former slaves.

On his ride back the next day, Pinckney nostalgically recalled his days as a small boy when the slaves had seemed happy to see him as he accompanied his mother on her Saturday afternoon rounds. He could not believe he had any reason to fear his "own people" whom he "could only remember as respectful, happy and affectionate." He probably mistook their previous displays of submissiveness as expressions of a genuine affection that would not be altered by freedom. Yet he was armed this time, and after summoning his former slaves, he quickly noticed that they too were armed. Their sullen faces reflected their defiant spirits.

Pinckney told them, "Men, I know you are free. I do not wish to interfere with your freedom. But I want my old hands to work my lands for me. I will pay wages." They remained silent as he gave further reassurances. Finally one responded, "O yes, we gwi wuk! We gwi wuk fuh ourse'ves. We ain' gwi wuk fuh no white man." Pinckney was confused and asked how they expected to support themselves and where they would go. They quickly informed him that they intended to stay and work "right here on de lan' whar we wuz bo'n an' whar belongs tuh us." One former slave, dressed in a Union army uniform, stood beside his cabin, brought his rifle down with a crash, and declared, "I'd like tuh see any man put me outer dis house."

Pinckney had no intention of allowing the former slaves to work the land for themselves. He joined with his neighbors in an appeal to the Union commander at Charleston, who sent a company of troops and addressed the blacks himself. They still refused to work under his terms, so Pinckney decided to "starve" them into submission. He denied them access to food and supplies. Soon his head plowman begged food for his hungry family, claiming he wanted to work, "But de other niggers dee won' let me wuk." Pinckney held firm, and the man returned several days later saying, "Cap'n, I come tuh ax you tuh lemme wuk fuh you, suh." Pinckney pointed him to the plow and let him draw his rations. Slowly, his other former slaves drifted back to work. "They had suffered," he later recalled, "and their ex-master had suffered with them."

All over the South this scenario was acted out with variations, as former masters and former slaves sought to define their new relationships. Whites tried to keep the blacks a dependent labor source; African Americans struggled to win as much independence as possible. Frequently Union officials were called upon to arbitrate; the North had a stake in the final outcome. At the same time the other sections of the nation faced similar problems of determining the status of heterogeneous populations whose interests were sometimes in conflict with the majority. The war had reaped a costly harvest of death and hostility, but at the same time it accelerated the modernization of the economy and society. Western expansion forced Americans to deal with the often hostile presence of the Plains Indians; the resumption of large-scale immigration raised issues of how to adapt to an increasingly pluralistic society made up of many different ethnic and religious groups. More and more the resolution of conflicting interests became necessary: farmer versus industrialist, whites versus blacks, Republicans versus Democrats, Indians versus settlers, North versus South, management versus labor, immigrant versus native born, men versus women, one branch of government versus another. Complicating these issues were unresolved questions about federal authority, widespread racial prejudice in both North and South, and

Although former slaves hoped that emancipation would release them from supervised gang labor in cotton fields, many were forced to sign yearly labor contracts and work under conditions similar to what they had endured under slavery.

strongly held beliefs in the sanctity of property rights.

Reconstruction offered an opportunity to balance conflicting interests with justice and fairness. In the end, however, the government was unwilling to establish ongoing programs and permanent mechanisms to protect the rights of minorities. As on Pinckney's plantation, economic power usually became the determining factor in establishing relationships. Northerners were distracted by issues related to industrialization and Westerners by conflicts with the Plains Indians. Authorities sacrificed the interests of both African Americans and the Indians of the West to the goals of national unity and economic growth. Yet in the ashes of failure were left two cornerstones on which the future could be built—the Fourteenth and Fifteenth amendments to the Constitution.

POSTWAR CONDITIONS AND ISSUES

General William T. Sherman proclaimed, "War is all hell." Undoubtedly it was for most soldiers and civilians caught up in the actual throes of battle and for the families of the 360,000 Union and 258,000 Confederate soldiers who would never return home. The costs of war, however, were not borne equally. Many segments of the North's economy were stimulated by wartime demands, and with the once powerful southern planters no longer there, Congress enacted programs to aid industrial growth. Virtually exempt from the devastation of the battlefield, the North built railroads and industries and increased agricultural production at the same time that torn-up Southern rails were twisted around trees, Southern factories were put to the torch, and Southern farmland lay choked with weeds.

In 1865 Southerners were still reeling from the bitter legacy of total war. General Philip Sheridan announced that after his troops had finished in the Shenandoah Valley even a crow would have to carry rations to fly over the area. One year after the war, Carl Schurz noted that along the path of Sherman's march the countryside still "looked for many miles like a broad black streak of ruin and desolation." Much of what was not destroyed was confiscated, and emancipation divested Southerners of another $2 billion to $4 billion in assets. The decline of southern wealth has been estimated at more than 40 percent during the four years of war.

The War's Impact on Individuals

Returning soldiers and their wives had to reconstruct relationships disrupted by separation—and the assumption of control by the women on farms and plantations. War widows envied them that adjustment. While the homeless wandered, one plantation mistress moaned, "I have not one human being in the wide world to whom I can say 'do this for me.'" Another noted, "I have never even so much as washed out a pocket handkerchief with my own hands, and now I have to do all my work." Southerners worried about how to meet their obligations; Confederate currency and bonds were worthless except as collectors' items—and even as collectors' items, they were too plentiful to have much value. One planter remarked dryly that his new son "promises to suit the times, having remarkably large hands as if he might one day be able to hold plough handles." Many white Southerners, rich and poor, suffered a self-induced paranoia. They imagined the end of slavery would bring a nightmare of black revenge, rape, and pillage unless whites retained social control.

For four million former slaves, emancipation had come piecemeal, following the course of the Northern armies. It was not finalized until the ratification of the Thirteenth Amendment in December 1865. Most slaves waited patiently for the day of freedom, continuing to work the plantations but speaking up

The American Mosaic

Day of Jubilo: Slaves Confront Emancipation

ROOTED in Africa, the oral tradition became one of the tools slaves used to maintain a sense of self-worth. Each generation heard the same stories, and story-telling did not die with slavery. The day that slaves first learned of their emancipation remained vivid in their own minds and later in those of their descendants. The great-grandchildren of a strong-willed woman named Caddy relished the family account of her first taste of freedom:

> Caddy threw down that hoe, she marched herself up to the big house, then she looked around and found the mistress. She went over to the mistress, she flipped up her dress and told the white woman to do some thing. She said it mean and ugly. This is what she said: *Kiss my ass!*

Caddy's reaction was not typical. There was no typical response. Reminiscences of what was called the "Day of Jubilo" formed a tapestry as varied as the range of personality. Some, however, seem to have occurred more frequently than others. Many former slaves echoed one man's description of his and his mother's action when their master announced their emancipation: "Jes like tarpins or turtles after 'mancipation. Jes stick our heads out to see how the land lays."

Caution was a shrewd and realistic response. One of the survival lessons in slavery had been not to trust whites too much. This had been reinforced during the war when Union troops moved through regions proclaiming emancipation only to depart, leaving blacks at the mercy of local whites. One elderly slave described the aftermath to a Union correspondent. "Why, the day after you left, they jist had us all out in a row and told us they was going to shoot us, and they did hang two of us; and Mr. Pierce, the overseer, knocked one with a fence rail and he died the next day. Oh, Master! we seen stars in de day time."

Environment played a role in slaves' reactions to the Day of Jubilo. Urban slaves frequently enjoyed more freedom than plantation slaves. Even before emancipation such black social institutions as schools and churches emerged in many cities. When those cities were liberated, organized celebrations occurred quickly. In Charleston 4000 black men and women paraded before some 10,000 spectators. Two black women sat in one mule-drawn cart while a mock auctioneer shouted, "How much am I offered?" In the next cart a black-draped coffin was inscribed with the words "Slavery is Dead." Four days after the fall of Richmond blacks there held a mass rally of some 1500 people in the First African Church.

Knowledge of their freedom came in many forms to the slaves. Rural slaves were less likely to enjoy the benefits of freedom as early as urban slaves. Many heard of the Emancipation Proclamation through the slave grapevine or from Union soldiers long before its words became reality for them. Masters sometimes took advantage of the isolation of their plantations to keep their slaves in ignorance or to make freedom seem vague and frightening. Their ploys usually failed, but learned patterns of deference made some former slaves unwilling to challenge their former masters. Months after emancipation one North Carolina slave continued to work without compensation, explaining to a northern correspondent, "No, sir; my mistress never said anything to me that I was to have wages, nor yet that I was free; nor I never said anything to her. Ye see I left it to her honor to talk to me about it, because I was afraid she'd say I was insultin' to her and presumin', so I wouldn't speak first. She ha'n't spoke yet." There were, however, limits to his patience; he intended to ask her for wages at Christmas.

Numerous blacks described the exuberance they felt. One elderly Virginia man went to the barn, jumped from one stack of straw to another, and "screamed and screamed!" A Texan remembered, "We all felt like horses" and "everybody went wild." Other blacks recalled how slave songs and spirituals were updated, and "purty soon ev'ybody fo' miles around was singin' freedom songs."

Quite a few slaves learned of freedom when a Union officer or Freedmen's Bureau agent read them the Emancipation Proclamation—often over the objections of the master. "Dat one time," Sarah Ford declared, "Massa Charley can't open he mouth, 'cause de captain tell him to shut up, dat he'd do the talkin'." Some masters, however, still sought to have the last word. A Louisiana planter's wife announced immediately after the Union officer departed, "Ten years from today I'll have you all back 'gain."

Fear did not leave all slaves as soon as their bondage was lifted. Jenny Proctor of Alabama recalled that her fellow slaves were stunned by the news. "We didn' hardly know what he means. We jes' sort of huddle 'round together like scared rabbits, but after we knowed what he mean, didn' many of us go, 'cause we didn' know where to of went." James Lucas, a former slave of Jefferson Davis, explained, "folks dat ain' never been free don' rightly know de *feel* of bein' free. Dey don' know de meanin' of it."

Former slaves quickly learned that one could not eat or wear freedom. "Dis livin' on liberty," one declared, "is lak young folks livin' on love after they gits married. It just don't work." They searched for the real meaning of liberty in numerous ways. Some followed the advice of a black Florida preacher, "You ain't none 'o you, gwinter feel rale free till you shakes de dus ob de Ole Plantashun offen you feet," and moved. Others declared their independence by legalizing their marriages and taking new names or publicly using surnames they had secretly adopted while in slavery. "We had a real sho' nuff weddin' wid a preacher," one recalled. "Dat cost a dollar." When encouraged to take his old master's surname, a black man declared, "Him's nothing to me now. I don't belong to he no longer, an' I don't see no use in being called for him." Education was the key for others. "If I nebber does do nothing more while I live," a Mississippi freedman vowed, "I shall give my children a chance to go to school, for I considers education next best ting to liberty."

Most came to a good understanding of the benefits and limits of their new status. One explained, "Why, sar, all I made before was Miss Pinckney's, but all I make now is my own." Another noted, "You could change places and work for different men." One newly freed slave wrote his brother, "I's mighty well pleased tu git my eatin' by de 'sweat o' my face, an all I ax o' ole masser's tu jes' keep he hands off o' de Lawd Almighty's property, fur *dat's me*." A new sense of dignity was cherished by many. An elderly South Carolina freedman rejoiced, "Don't hab me feelins hurt now. Used to hab me feelins hurt all de times. But don't hab em hurt now, no more." Charlie Barbour exulted over one thing: "I won't wake up some mornin' fer fin' dat my mammy or some ob de rest of my family am done sold." Most agreed with Margrett Millin's answer when she was asked decades later whether she had liked slavery or freedom better. "Well, it's dis way. In slavery I owns nothin'. In freedom I's own de home and raise de family. All dat cause me worryment and in slavery I has no worryment, but I takes de freedom."

more boldly. Sometimes the Yankees came, proclaimed them free, and then left them to the mercy of their masters. Most, therefore, reacted cautiously to test the limits of their new freedom.

Many African Americans had to leave their plantations, at least for a short time, to feel liberated. A few were confused as to the meaning of freedom and thought they would never have to work again. Soon, most learned they had gained everything—and nothing. As Frederick Douglass, the famous black abolitionist, noted, the freedman "was free from the individual master but a slave of society. He had neither money, property, nor friends."

The wartime plight of homeless and hungry blacks as well as whites impelled Congress to take unprecedented action, establishing on March 3, 1865, the Bureau of Refugees, Freedmen, and Abandoned Lands (**Freedmen's Bureau**), within the War Department. The bureau was to provide "such issues of provisions, clothing, and fuel" as were needed to relieve "destitute and suffering refugees and their wives and children." Never before had the national government assumed responsibility for relief. Feeding and clothing the population had not been deemed its proper function. Considered drastic action, warranted only by civil war, the bureau was supposed to operate for just a year, but was extended for five years.

Under Commissioner Oliver O. Howard, the bureau had its own courts to deal with land and labor disputes. Agents in every state provided rations and medical supplies and helped to negotiate labor contracts between former slaves and landowners. The quality of the service rendered to the former slaves depended on the ability and motivation of the individual agents. One of the most lasting benefits of the Bureau was the schools it established. During and after the war, African Americans of all ages flocked to schools to taste the previously forbidden fruit of education. The former slaves shrewdly recognized the keys to the planters' power—land, literacy, and the vote. The white South had legally denied all three to African Americans in slavery, and now many former slaves were determined to have them all.

Some former bondsmen had a firmer grasp of reality than their "liberators." Southern whites had long claimed to "know our Negroes" better than outsiders could. Ironically, this was proven false, but the reverse *was* true. Ex-slaves knew their ex-masters very well. One freedman pleaded, "Gib us our own land and we can take care ourselves; but widout land, de ole massas can hire us or starve us, as dey please." The events on Pinckney's plantation proved the wisdom of that statement.

Later generations have laughed at the widespread rumor among former slaves that they were to receive "forty acres and a mule" from the government, but the rumor did have some basis. During the war, General Sherman was plagued with swarms of former slaves following his army, and in January 1865 he issued Special Field Order 15 setting aside a strip of abandoned coastal lands from Charleston, South Carolina, to Jacksonville, Florida, for the exclusive use of former slaves. African Americans were to be given "possessory titles" to 40-acre lots. Three months later, the bill establishing the Freedmen's Bureau gave the agency control of thousands of acres of abandoned and confiscated lands to be rented to "loyal refugees and freedmen" in 40-acre plots for three-year periods with an option to buy at a later date. By June 1865, 40,000 African Americans were cultivating land. In the Sea Islands and elsewhere, they proved they could be successful independent farmers. Yet land reform was not a popular cause among whites. Although a few congressmen continued to advocate land confiscation and redistribution, the dream of "forty acres and a mule" was a casualty of the battle for control of Reconstruction when Andrew Johnson's pardons returned most confiscated lands. Indeed, the issue of economic security for the former slaves was obscured by other questions that seemed more important to whites.

Unresolved Issues

At war's end some issues had been settled, but at a terrible cost. As historian David Potter noted, "slav-

Freed persons realized that education was a key to real freedom and flocked to schools opened by the Freedmen's Bureau, the American Missionary Association, and other groups.

ery was dead, secession was dead, and six hundred thousand men were dead." A host of new problems had arisen from the nature of civil war and the results of that war as well as the usual postwar dislocations. Many questions remained that shaped Reconstruction.

The first of these concerned the status of the former slaves. They were indeed free, but were they citizens? The Dred Scott decision (1857) had denied citizenship to all African Americans. Even if it were decided that they were citizens, what rights were conferred by that citizenship? Would they be segregated as free blacks in the antebellum North had often been? Also, citizenship did not automatically confer suffrage; women were proof of that. Were the freedmen to be given the ballot? These weighty matters were complicated by racial prejudice as well as constitutional and partisan questions.

The Constitution had been severely tested by civil war, and many felt it had been twisted by the desire to save the Union. Once the emergency was over, how were constitutional balance and limits to be restored? Except during the terms of a few strong presidents, Congress had been the most powerful branch of government during the nation's first 70 years. Lincoln had assumed unprecedented powers, and Congress was determined to regain its ascendancy. The ensuing battle directly influenced Reconstruction policies and their implementation.

Secession was dead, but what about states' rights? Almost everyone agreed that a division of power between the national and state governments was crucial to the maintenance of freedom. The fear of centralized tyranny remained strong. There was reluctance to enlarge federal power into areas traditionally controlled by the states, even though action in some of those areas was essential to craft the kind of peace many desired. Hesitation to reduce states' rights produced timid and compromised solutions to such issues as suffrage.

Another constitutional question concerned the status of the former Confederate states and how they were to be readmitted to the Union. There was no constitutional provision for failed secession, and many people debated whether the South had actually left the Union or not. The query reflected self-interest rather than an intellectual inquiry. Ironically, Southerners and their Democratic sympathizers now argued that the states had never legally separated from the rest of the nation, thus denying validity to the Confederacy in order to quickly regain their place in the Union. Extremists on the other side—**Radical Republicans**—insisted that the South had reverted to the status of conquered territory, forfeiting all rights as states. Under territorial governments, Representative Thaddeus Stevens declared, Southerners could "learn the principles of freedom and eat the fruit of foul rebellion." Others, including Lincoln, believed that the Confederate states had remained in the Union but had forfeited their rights. This constitutional hair-splitting grew out of the power struggle between the executive and legislative branches to determine which had the power to readmit the states and on what terms.

Influencing all these issues were partisan politics. Although not provided for in the Constitution, political parties had played a major role in the evolving American government. The road to war had disrupted the existing party structure—killing the Whig party, dividing the Democratic party, and creating the Republican party. The first truly sectional party, the Republican party had very few adherents in the South. Its continued existence was dubious in the face of the probable reunion of the Northern and Southern wings of the Democratic party. Paradoxically, the political power of the South, and in turn the Democratic party, was increased by the abolition of slavery. As slaves, only three-fifths of African Americans had been counted for representation; with the end of slavery, all African Americans would be counted. Thus the Republican party's perceived need to make itself a national party also colored the course of Reconstruction.

PRESIDENTIAL RECONSTRUCTION

Early in the conflict, questions regarding the reconstruction of the nation were secondary to winning the war—without victory there would be no nation to reconstruct. Nonetheless, Lincoln had to take some action as Union forces pushed into the South. Authority had to be imposed in the reclaimed territory, so the president named military governors for Tennessee, Arkansas, and Louisiana in 1862 after federal armies occupied most of those states. He also began formulating plans for civilian government for those states and future Confederate areas as they came under the control of Union forces. The result was a Proclamation of Amnesty and Reconstruction issued in December 1863 on the constitutional basis of the president's power to pardon.

Lincoln's Plan

Called the 10 percent plan, Lincoln's provisions were incredibly lenient. Rebels could receive presidential pardon by merely swearing their future allegiance to the Union and their acceptance of the end of slavery. In other words, former Confederates were not required to say they were sorry—only to promise they would be good in the future. A few people were excluded from pardons, such as Confederate military and civilian officers. After only 10 percent of the number who had voted in 1860 had taken the oath, a state could form a civilian government. When such states produced a constitution outlawing slavery, Lincoln promised to recognize them as reconstructed. He did not demand any provisions for protecting black rights or allowing black suffrage.

Tennessee, Arkansas, and Louisiana met Lincoln's requirements and soon learned they had only cleared the first barrier in what became a long obstacle course. Radical Republicans, such as Representative Thaddeus Stevens of Pennsylvania and Senator Charles Sumner of Massachusetts, were outraged by the president's generosity. They thought the provisions did not adequately punish Confederate treason, restructure Southern society, protect the rights of African Americans, or aid the Republican party. The Radicals were in a minority, but many moderate Republicans were also dismayed by Lincoln's leniency, and shared the Radical view that Reconstruction was a congressional, not a presidential, function. As a result Congress recognized neither the three states' elected congressmen nor their electoral votes in the 1864 election.

After denying the president's right to reconstruct the nation, Congress drew up a plan for reconstruction: the Wade-Davis Bill. Its terms were much more stringent, yet not unreasonable. A majority, rather than 10 percent, of each states' voters had to declare their allegiance in order to form a government. Only those taking "ironclad" oaths of their past Union loyalty were allowed to participate in the making of new state constitutions. Barely a handful of high-ranking Confederates, however, were to be permanently barred from political participation. The only additional requirement imposed by Congress was the repudiation of the Confederate debt; Northerners did not want Confederate bondholders to benefit from their "investment in treason" at a cost to loyal taxpayers. Congress would determine when a state had met these requirements.

Constitutional collision was postponed by Lincoln's pocket veto of the bill and his assassination on April 14, 1865. While most of the nation mourned, some Radicals rejoiced at the results of John Wilkes Booth's action. Lincoln had been a formidable opponent and had articulated his position on the South in his second inaugural address. Calling for "malice toward none" and "charity for all," he proposed to "bind the nation's wounds" and achieve "a just and lasting peace." His successor, Andrew Johnson, on

North Carolina–born Andrew Johnson, a former governor of Tennessee and a U.S. senator from that state, was the only senator from a seceding state to remain loyal to the Union. In 1862 Lincoln appointed him military governor of Tennessee, and in 1864 Johnson was selected as Lincoln's running mate.

the other hand, had announced, "Treason is a crime, and crime must be punished." Johnson was a Tennessee Democrat and Unionist; he had been the only Southerner to remain in the Senate after his state seceded. Placed on the 1864 Republican "Union" ticket as a gesture of unity, Johnson's political affiliation was less than clear, but some considered him a weaker opponent than Lincoln. Radical Senator Benjamin Wade proclaimed, "By the gods there will be no trouble now in running this government."

Radicals found comfort in, but miscalculated, Johnson's hatred of the planters. He hated them for their aristocratic domination of the South, not for their slaveholding. Born of humble origins in Raleigh, North Carolina, and illiterate until adulthood, Johnson entered politics in Tennessee as a successful tailor. A champion of the people, he called the planters a "cheap purse-proud set . . . not half as good as the man who earns his bread by the sweat of his brow." Favoring free public education and a homestead act, Johnson was elected mayor, congressman, governor, and senator, before being appointed military governor of Tennessee and then becoming vice president. Although he shared the Radicals' hatred and distrust of the planters, he was a firm believer in black inferiority and did not support the Radical aim of black legal equality. He also advocated strict adherence to the Constitution and strongly supported states' rights.

Johnson's Plan

In the end Johnson did not reverse Lincoln's lenient policy. Congress was not in session when Johnson became president so he had about eight months to pursue policies without congressional interference. He issued his own proclamation of amnesty in May 1865 that excluded everyone with taxable property worth more than $20,000. Closing one door, he opened another by providing for personal presidential pardons for excluded individuals. By year's end he had issued about 13,000 pardons. The most important aspect of the pardons was Johnson's claim that they restored all rights, including property rights. Thus many former slaves with crops in the ground suddenly found their masters back in charge—a disillusioning first taste of freedom that foreclosed further attempts at widespread land redistribution.

Johnson's amnesty proclamation did not immediately end the Radicals' honeymoon period with him, but his other proclamation issued on the same day caused deep concern. In it, he announced plans for the reconstruction of North Carolina—a plan that would set the pattern for all southern states. A native Unionist was named provisional governor with the power to call a constitutional convention elected by loyal voters. Omitting Lincoln's 10 percent provision, Johnson did eventually require ratification of the Thirteenth Amendment, repudiation of Confederate debts, and state constitutional provisions abolishing slavery and renouncing secession. He also recommended limited black suffrage, primarily to stave off congressional attempts to give the vote to all black males.

The presidential plan fell short of the Radicals' hopes, but many moderates might have accepted it if the South had complied with the letter and the spirit of Johnson's proposals. Instead, Southerners seemed determined to ignore their defeat, even to make light of it. The state governments, for the most part, met the minimum requirements (Mississippi and South Carolina refused to repudiate the debt and Mississippi declined to ratify the Thirteenth Amendment). Their apparent acceptance, however, grew out of a belief that very little had actually changed, and Southerners proceeded to show almost total disregard for northern sensibilities. Presenting themselves, like prodigal sons, for admission to Congress were four Confederate generals, six Confederate cabinet officials, and as the crowning indignity, Confederate Vice President Alexander H. Stephens. Most Northerners were not exceedingly vindictive. Still the North did expect some sign of change and hoped for some indication of repentance by the former rebels.

Black Codes in the South

At the very least, Northerners expected adherence to the abolition of slavery, and the South was blatantly forging new forms of bondage. African Americans were to be technically free, but Southern whites expected them to work and live as they had before emancipation. To accomplish this, the new state governments enacted a series of laws known as the **Black Codes.** This legislation granted certain rights denied to slaves. Freedmen had the right to marry, own property, sue and be sued, and testify in court. Complex legalisms, however, often took away what was apparently given. Black Codes in all states prohibited racial intermarriage. Some forbade freedmen to own certain types of property, such as alcoholic beverages and firearms. Most so tightly restricted

Black Codes and vagrancy laws sharply curtailed the freedom of former slaves. In this sketch the provost guard in New Orleans is rounding up vagrant blacks in 1864.

black legal rights that they were practically nonexistent. Black Codes imposed curfews on African Americans, segregated them, and outlawed their right to congregate in large groups.

The Black Codes did more than merely provide means of racial control; they also sought to fashion a labor system as close to slavery as possible. Some required that African Americans obtain special licenses for any job except agricultural labor or domestic service. Most mandated the signing of yearly labor contracts, which sometimes required African Americans to call the landowner "master" and allowed withholding wages for minor infractions. To accomplish the same objective, Mississippi prohibited black ownership or even rental of land. Mandatory apprenticeship programs took children away from their parents, and vagrancy laws allowed authorities to arrest blacks "wandering or strolling about in idleness" and use them on chain gangs or rent them out to planters for as long as a year.

When laws failed, some southern whites resorted to violence. In Memphis, whites resented the presence of black troops at nearby Fort Pickering. A local paper asserted "the negro can do the country more good in the cotton field than in the camp" and chastised "the dirty, fanatical, nigger-loving Radicals of this city." In May 1866 a street brawl erupted between white policemen and recently discharged black soldiers. That night, after the soldiers had returned to the fort, white mobs attacked the black section of the city, with the encouragement of the police and local officials, one of whom urged the mob to "go ahead and kill the last damned one of the nigger race." The reign of terror lasted over 40 hours and left 46 blacks and 2 whites dead. This and other outbreaks of violence disgusted northern voters.

Most Northerners would not have insisted on black equality or suffrage, but the South had regressed too far. Some Black Codes were even identical to the old slave codes, with the word negro substituted for slave. At the same time, reports of white violence against blacks filtered back to Washington. It is no wonder that upon finally reconvening in December 1865, Congress refused to seat the representatives and senators from the former Confederate states and instead proceeded to investigate conditions in the South.

CONGRESSIONAL RECONSTRUCTION

To discover what was really happening in the South, Congress established the Joint Committee on Reconstruction, which conducted inquiries and interviews that provided graphic and chilling examples of white repression and brutality toward African Americans. Prior to the committee's final report, even moderates were convinced that action was necessary. In early 1866 Congress passed a bill to extend the life of the Freedmen's Bureau. The bill also granted the agency new powers to establish special courts for disputes concerning former slaves and to promote black education. Johnson vetoed it, claiming that the bureau was constitutional only in wartime conditions. Now, he claimed, the country had returned "to a state of peace and industry."

Southern whites frequently vented their frustration on blacks. Following a Radical Republican meeting in New Orleans on July 30, 1866, rioting erupted; 37 blacks and 3 white sympathizers were killed in the fighting.

At first Johnson prevailed; his veto was not overridden. Then he made a mistake. In an impromptu speech on Washington's birthday, Johnson launched into a bitter attack on the Joint Committee on Reconstruction. Even moderates were offended. In mid-March 1866 Congress passed the Civil Rights Act. It declared that "all persons born in the United States and not subject to any foreign power, excluding Indians not taxed," were citizens and entitled to "full and equal benefit of all laws." Congress was responding to the Black Codes, but Johnson deemed the bill both unconstitutional and unwise. He vetoed it. This time, however, Congress overrode the veto. It then passed a slightly revised Freedmen's Bureau bill in July and enacted it over Johnson's veto. Even though the South had ignored much of Johnson's advice, such as granting limited suffrage to blacks, he stubbornly held to his conviction that reconstruction was complete and labeled his congressional opponents as "traitors."

His language did not create a climate of cooperation. Congress was concerned about the constitutional questions he raised and his challenge to congressional authority. To protect its handiwork and establish an alternate program of reconstruction, it drafted the Fourteenth Amendment. Undoubtedly the most significant legacy of Reconstruction, the first article of the amendment defined citizenship and its basic rights. Every person born in the United States and subject to its jurisdiction is declared a citizen. It also forbids any state from abridging "the privileges and immunities" of citizenship, from depriving any person of "due process of law," and from denying citizens the "equal protection of the laws." Although 100 years passed before its provisions were enforced as intended, the amendment has been interpreted to mean that states as well as the federal government are bound by the Bill of Rights—an important constitutional change that paved the way for the civil rights decisions and laws of the twentieth century.

The remaining four sections of the amendment spelled out Congress's minimum demands for postwar change and was the South's last chance for a lenient peace. A creation of the congressional moderates, the amendment did not require black suffrage but reduced the "basis of representation" proportionately for those states not allowing it. Former Confederate leaders were also barred from holding office unless pardoned by Congress—not the president. Finally, neither Confederate war debts nor compensation to former slaveholders were ever to be paid. The amendment, which passed Congress in June 1866, was then sent to the states for ratification.

"Radical" Reconstruction

Everyone assumed that the 1866 congressional elections would be a referendum on the Fourteenth

TABLE 16.1
Reconstruction Amendments, 1865–1870

Amendment	Main Provisions	Congressional Passage (2/3 majority in each house required)	Ratification Process (3/4 of all states including ex-Confederate states required)
13	Slavery prohibited in United States	January 1865	December 1865 (27 states, including 8 southern states)
14	1. National citizenship 2. State representation in Congress reduced proportionally to number of voters disfranchised 3. Former Confederates denied right to hold office	June 1866	Rejected by 12 southern and border states, February 1867 Radicals make readmission of southern states hinge on ratification Ratified July 1868
15	Denial of franchise because of race, color, or past servitude explicitly prohibited	February 1869	Ratification required for readmission of Virginia, Texas, Mississippi, Georgia Ratified March 1870

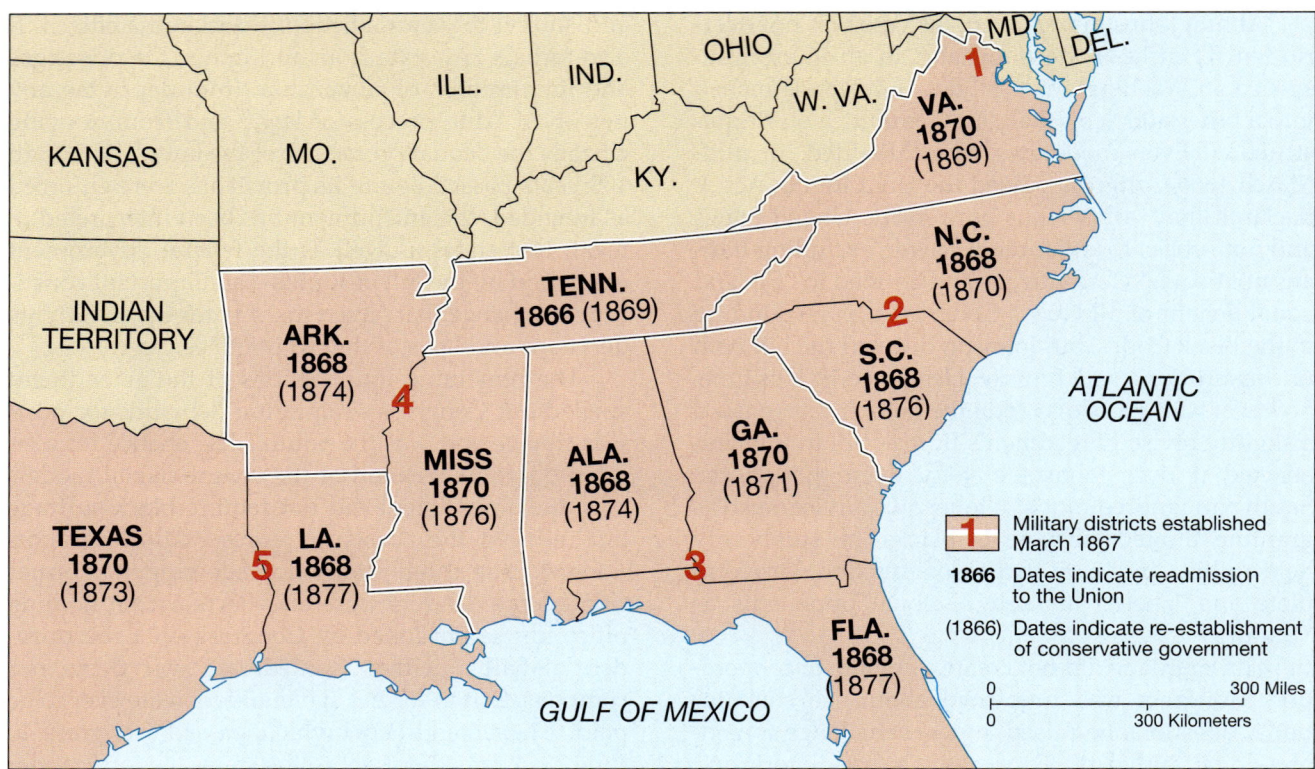

Reconstruction and Redemption

Amendment and that their position would prevail. At President Johnson's urging, all former Confederate states but Tennessee refused to ratify it. In the end the Republicans won overwhelming victories, which they interpreted as a mandate for congressional reconstruction. The election results along with the South's intransigence finally gave the Radicals an upper hand. In 1867 Congress passed the **Military Reconstruction Act** that raised the price of readmission. The act declared all existing "Johnson governments," except Tennessee's, void and divided the South into five military districts headed by military governors granted broad powers to govern. Delegates to new constitutional conventions were to be elected by all qualified voters—a group that by congressional stipulation included black males and excluded former Confederate leaders. Following the ratification of a new state constitution providing for black suffrage, elections were to be held and the state would be required to ratify the Fourteenth Amendment. When that amendment became part of the Constitution and Congress approved the new state constitutions, the states would be granted representation in Congress once again.

Obviously, Johnson was not pleased with the congressional plan; he vetoed it, only to see his veto overridden. Nevertheless, as commander in chief he reluctantly appointed military governors, and by the end of 1867 elections had been held in every state except Texas. Because many white Southerners boycotted the elections, the South came under the control of Republicans supported by Union forces. In a way, however, Southerners had brought more radical measures upon themselves by their inflexibility. As the *Nation* declared in 1867,

> Six years ago, the North would have rejoiced to accept any mild restrictions upon the spread of slavery as a final settlement. Four years ago, it would have accepted peace on the basis of gradual emancipation. Two years ago, it would have been content with emancipation and equal civil rights for the colored people without the extension of suffrage. One year ago, a slight extension of the suffrage would have satisfied it.

Congress realized the plan it had enacted was unprecedented and subject to challenge by the other two branches of government. To check Johnson's power to disrupt, Congress took two other actions on the same day it passed the Military Reconstruction Act. The Command of the Army Act limited presidential military power. The Tenure of Office Act re-

This 1868 cartoon portrays President Johnson as a child who cannot safely handle the Constitution.

quired Senate consent for the removal of any official whose appointment had required the Senate's confirmation. It was meant in part to protect Secretary of War Edwin M. Stanton, who supported the Radicals.

The Supreme Court had also shown its willingness to challenge Reconstruction actions in two important cases of 1866. In *Ex parte Milligan* the justices struck down the conviction of a civilian by a military tribunal in an area where civil courts were operating. Another decision ruled as void a state law barring former Confederates from certain professions on the basis that the act was *ex post facto*. Nevertheless, other decisions reflected a hesitation to tackle some of the thornier issues of Reconstruction. Important cases were pending, and Congress acted in March 1868 to limit the court's power to review cases. Because the congressional action was clearly constitutional, the Supreme Court acquiesced and in *Texas* v. *White* (1869) even acknowledged congressional power to reframe state governments.

President Johnson was not so accommodating. He sought to sabotage military reconstruction by continuing to pardon former Confederates, removing military commanders who were Radical sympathizers, and naming former Confederates to federal positions. Congress was angry but could not find adequate grounds for impeachment. Johnson did not attempt to mend fences. After an unsuccessful attempt to replace Secretary of War Stanton with Ulysses S. Grant, on February 21 he named Lorenzo Thomas to the cabinet position. Stanton also refused to surrender and barricaded himself in his office. On February 24, the House voted impeachment.

The Senate was given 11 articles of impeachment for its trial of the president. Eight related to the violation of the Tenure of Office Act and another to a violation of the Command of the Army Act. Only the last 2 reflected the real reasons for congressional action. Those articles accused Johnson of "inflammatory and scandalous harangues" against Congress

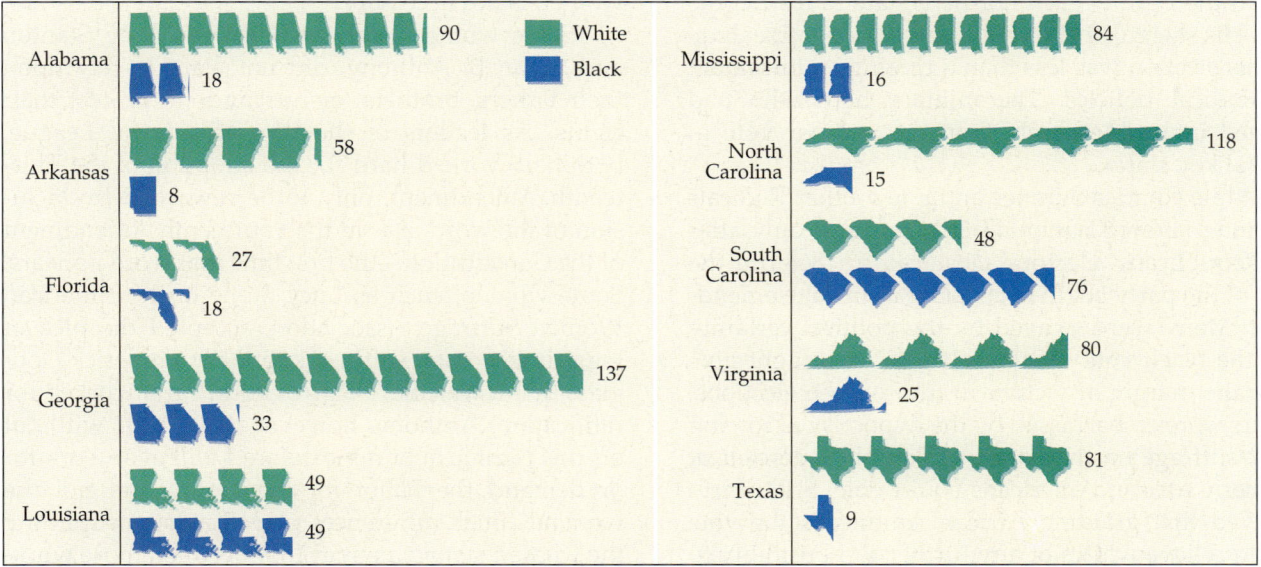

FIGURE 16.1

Composition of State Constitutional Conventions under Congressional Reconstruction and of "unlawfully devising and contriving" to obstruct congressional will. The heated and bitter trial lasted from March 5 to May 26. Johnson did not attend, but his lawyers made a good legal case that he had not technically violated the Tenure of Office Act since Stanton had been appointed by Lincoln. They tried to keep the trial focused on indictable offenses. Radical prosecutors continued to argue that Johnson had committed "high crimes and misdemeanors," but they also asserted that a president could be removed for political reasons, even without being found legally guilty of crimes—a position James Madison had supported during the drafting of the Constitution.

The vote for conviction fell one short of the required two-thirds majority, when seven Republicans broke ranks and voted against conviction. This set the precedent that a president must be guilty of serious misdeeds to be removed from office. The outcome was a political blow to the Radicals, costing them some support. The action, however, did make Johnson more cooperative for the last months of his presidency.

Black Suffrage

In the 1868 presidential election, the Republicans won with Ulysses S. Grant, whose Civil War victories made his name a household word. He ran on a platform that endorsed congressional reconstruction, urged repayment of the national debt, and defended black suffrage in the South as necessary but supported the right of each northern state to restrict the vote. His slogan, "Let us have peace," was appealing, but his election was less than a ringing endorsement for Radical policies. The military hero who had seemed invincible barely won the popular vote in several key states.

While Charles Sumner and a few other Radicals had long favored national black suffrage, only after the Republicans' electoral close call in 1868 did the bulk of the party begin to consider a suffrage amendment. Many were swayed by the political certainty that the black vote would be theirs and might give them the margin of victory in future close elections. Others were embarrassed by the hypocrisy of forcing black suffrage on the South while only 7 percent of northern African Americans could vote. Still others believed that granting African Americans the vote would relieve whites of any further responsibility to protect black rights.

Suffrage supporters faced many objections to such an amendment. One was based on the lack of popular support. At that time only seven northern states granted blacks the right to vote, and since 1865, referendum proposals for black suffrage in eight states had been voted down. In fact, only in Iowa and Minnesota (both containing minuscule black populations) had voters supported the extension of the vote. The amendment was so unpopular that, ironically, it could never have won adoption without its ratification by the southern states, where black suffrage already existed.

A more serious challenge was the question of whether Congress could legislate suffrage at all. Before Reconstruction the national government had never taken any action regarding the right to vote; suffrage had been considered not a right but a privilege which only the states could confer. The Radical answer was that the Constitution expressly declared that "the United States shall guarantee to every State in this Union a republican form of government." Charles Sumner further asserted that "anything for human rights is constitutional" and that black rights could only be protected by black votes.

Senator George Vickers sarcastically asked, "does not the doctrine of human rights asserted by the senator apply as well to females as to males?" Although he was "no advocate for woman suffrage," he noted that "if the Congress of the United States had been composed exclusively of women we should have had no civil war. We might have had a war of words, but that would have been all." When one senator did propose female suffrage, a colleague informed him that "to extend the right of suffrage to negroes in this country I think is necessary for their protection; but to extend the right of suffrage to women is not necessary."

Some women, such as Elizabeth Cady Stanton and Susan B. Anthony, did not want to rely upon their fathers, brothers, or husbands to protect their rights. As leaders of the Women's Loyal League, both had worked hard for the adoption of the Thirteenth Amendment, only to be rewarded by inclusion of the word *male* in the Fourteenth Amendment of the Constitution—the first time that word appears. Some women, such as Lucy Stone of the American Woman Suffrage Association, accepted the plea of long-time woman suffrage supporter Frederick Douglass that it was the "Negro's hour," and worked for ratification. Anthony, however, vowed "[I will] cut off this right arm of mine before I will ever work for or demand the ballot for the Negro and not the woman." Such differences played a role in splitting the women's movement in 1869 between those working for a national suffrage amendment and those who concentrated their efforts on the state level. Anthony and Stanton founded the National Woman Suffrage Association to battle for a constitutional amendment and other feminist reforms. Others be-

Susan B. Anthony (left) moved from temperance work to join with Elizabeth Cady Stanton in 1869 to form the National Woman Suffrage Association.

came disillusioned with that approach and established the American Woman Suffrage Association, which focused on obtaining suffrage on a state-by-state basis.

Actually, women did not lose much by not being included in the Fifteenth Amendment. To meet the various objections, compromise was necessary. The resulting amendment did not grant the vote to anyone. It merely stated that the vote could not be denied "on account of race, color, or previous condition of servitude." Suffrage was still essentially to be controlled by the states, and other bases of exclusion were not deemed unconstitutional. These loopholes would eventually allow white Southerners to make a mockery of the amendment.

Although congressional reconstruction was labeled "Radical," compromise had instead produced another essentially moderate plan. What Congress did *not* do is as important as what it did. It did not even guarantee the right to vote. There was only one execution for war crimes and only Jefferson Davis was imprisoned for more than a few months. For all but a handful, former Confederates were not permanently barred from voting or holding office. By 1872 only about 200 were still denied the right to hold office. Most local Southern governments were undisturbed. Land as well as rights were restored to former rebels, eliminating the possibility of extensive land redistribution. Most areas that had traditionally been the states' domain remained so, free from federal meddling. For example, no requirements were placed on the states to provide any education to former slaves. The only attempt by the national government to meet the basic needs of its citizens was the temporary Freedmen's Bureau—justified only as an emergency measure. The limited nature of Reconstruction doomed it as an opportunity to provide means for the protection of minority rights.

Such congressional moderation reflected the spirit of the age. Enduring beliefs in the need for strict construction of the Constitution and in states' rights presented formidable barriers to truly radical changes. Property rights were considered sacrosanct—even for "traitors." Cherished ideals of self-reliance and the conviction that a person determined his or her own destiny led many to support Horace Greeley's so-called root, hog, or die approach to the black problem. By ending the threat of slavery, he argued, "we may soon break up our Freedmen's Bureaus and all manner of coddling devices and let the negroes take care of themselves." Few agreed with Charles Sterns who argued that even a hog could not root without a snout—that there could be no equality of opportunity where one group had long been allowed an unfair advantage. Many instead sided with an editorialist for the *New York Herald* who wrote of the bill to extend the life of the Freedmen's Bureau: "The bill ought to be called an act to support the negroes in idleness by the honest labor of white people, or an act to establish a gigantic and corrupt political machine for the benefit of the radical faction and a swarm of officeholders." Clearly the idea of affirmative action or even equal opportunity had less support then than it did 100 years later.

Tainting every action was the widespread conviction that African Americans were not equal to whites. Many Northerners were more concerned with keeping blacks in the South than with abstract black rights. In 1866, for example, New York Senator Roscoe Conkling catered to the northern fear of black immigration while calling for support of the Fourteenth Amendment:

> Four years ago mobs were raised, passions were aroused, votes were given, upon the idea that emancipated negroes were to burst in hordes upon the North. We then said, give them liberty and rights in the South, and they will stay there and never come into a cold climate. We say so still, and we want them let alone, and that is one thing that this part of the amendment is for.

Even Radical Representative George Julian admitted to his Indiana constituents, "the real trouble is that we hate the negro. It is not his ignorance that offends us, but his color."

The plan for Reconstruction evolved fitfully, buffeted first one way and then another by the forces of the many issues unresolved at war's end. If permanent changes were very limited, nonetheless precedents had been set for later action, and for a brief time congressional reconstruction brought about the most democratic governments the South had ever seen—or would see for another hundred years.

RECONSTRUCTION IN THE SOUTH

Any dictated peace would probably have been unpalatable to Southern whites. They were especially leery of any action that seemed to threaten white supremacy—whether or not that was the intended result. Even before the war, suspicion greeted every Northern move. Southerners continued to see a radical abolitionist behind every bush.

Most Southerners criticized and condemned the Freedmen's Bureau from its first day to its last. Many believed its agents were partial to African Americans. As one Mississippi planter declared, "The negro is a sacred animal. The Yankees are about negroes like the Egyptians were about cats." Actually there was a great diversity in the background and goals of bureau agents. Some were idealistic young New Englanders who, like the Yankee schoolmarms, came south to aid in the transition to freedom. Others were army officers whose first priority was to maintain order—often by siding with the landowners. All were overworked, underpaid, and under pressure.

The results of bureau actions were mixed in regard to conditions for African Americans. The agents helped to negotiate labor contracts that African Americans were forced to sign to obtain rations. Frequently the wages were well below the rate at which slaves had been hired out by their owners before the war. While it should be remembered that money was scarce at the time, these contracts helped to keep African Americans on the farm—someone else's farm. On the other hand, between 1865 and 1869 the bureau issued over 21 million rations, of which about 5 million went to whites. Thus it showed that the government could establish and administer a massive relief program, as it would again do during the depression of the 1930s. The bureau also operated more than 40 hospitals, opened hundreds of schools, and accomplished the Herculean task of resettling some 30,000 people displaced by the war.

Carpetbaggers, Scalawags, and Black Republicans

Until Congressional Reconstruction, Southern governments were largely unchanged. Afterwards however, Republican officeholders joined bureau agents in directing the course of Reconstruction. Despised by many whites, these men, depending on their origins, were derisively labeled "carpetbaggers," "scalawags," and "nigrahs." Opponents considered all three groups despicable creatures whose "black and tan" governments were tyrannizing native whites, while engaged in an orgy of corruption. Myths created about Southern Republicans lingered long after the restoration of Democratic party rule.

Northerners who came to the South during or after the war and became engaged in politics were called **carpetbaggers**. They supposedly arrived with a few meager belongings in their carpetbags, which would expand to hold ill-gotten gains from looting an already devastated South. Probably what most infuriated whites was the carpetbaggers' willingness to cooperate with African Americans. Calling them "a kind of political dry-nurse for the negro population," native whites accused the carpetbaggers of cynically exploiting former slaves for their own gain. Many agreed with the charge that the carpetbaggers were standing "right in the public eye, stealing and plundering, many of them with both arms around ne-

Northerners who engaged in politics in the South before or after the war were called carpetbaggers. This cartoon shows Grant and Union soldiers propping up carpetbag rule with bayonets, while the "Solid South" staggers under the weight.

groes, and their hands in their rear pockets, seeing if they cannot pick a paltry dollar out of them."

White Southerners who voted for Republicans were labeled **scalawags.** The term, said to be derived from Scalloway, "a district in the Shetland Islands where small, runty cattle and horses were bred," had been used previously as a "synonym for scamp, loafer, or rascal." Thus southern white Republicans were depicted as people "paying no taxes, riding poor horses, wearing dirty shirts, and having no use for soap." Such men were said to have "sold themselves for office" and become a "subservient tool and accomplice" of the carpetbaggers.

Most detested by white Southerners were the black Republicans. Having long characterized African Americans as inferior creatures dependent on white management for survival, Southerners loathed the prospect of blacks in authority. They feared that the former slaves would exact payment for their years of bondage. Democrats also knew that racism was their best rallying cry to regain power. Thus Reconstruction governments were denounced for "Ethiopian minstrelsy, Ham radicalism in all its glory." Whites claimed ignorant freedmen, incapable of managing their own affairs, were allowed to run the affairs of state with disastrous results.

Such legends persisted for a long time, despite contrary facts. Southern whites had determined even before Reconstruction began that it would be "the most galling tyranny and most stupendous system of organized robbery that is to be met with in history." The truth was, as W. E. B. Du Bois later wrote, "There is one thing that the white South feared more than negro dishonesty, ignorance, and incompetency, and that was negro honesty, knowledge, and efficiency." To a surprising degree they got what they most feared.

Black voters were generally as fit to vote as the millions of illiterate whites enfranchised by Jacksonian democracy. Black officials as a group were as qualified as their white counterparts. In South Carolina two-thirds of them were literate, and in all states most of the acknowledged leaders were well educated and articulate. They usually had been members of the Northern or Southern free black elite or part of the slave aristocracy of skilled artisans and household slaves. Hiram Revels, a U.S. senator from Mississippi, was the son of free blacks who had sent him to college in the North. James Walker Hood, the presiding officer of the North Carolina constitutional convention of 1867, was a black carpetbagger from Pennsylvania who came to the state as an African Methodist Episcopal Zion missionary. Some, such as Francis Cardoza of South Carolina, were the privileged mulatto sons of white planters. Cardoza had been educated in Scottish and English universities.

In a historic first, seven African Americans were elected to the Forty-first and Forty-second Congresses. Between 1869 and 1901, two African Americans became senators and 20 served in the House.

During Reconstruction 14 such men served in the U.S. House of Representatives and 2 in the Senate. By 1901, 6 others were elected to the House, before Southern black political power was effectively demolished.

Even if black Republicans had been incompetent, they could hardly be held responsible for the perceived abuses of so-called black reconstruction. Only in South Carolina did African Americans have a majority of the delegates to the constitutional convention provided for by the Reconstruction Acts. Neither did they dominate the new governments; only for a two-year period in South Carolina did blacks control both houses of the legislature. None were elected governor, although P. B. S. Pinchback, the lieutenant governor of Louisiana, did serve as acting governor for a short time. When the vote was restored to ex-Confederates, African Americans comprised only one-third of the voters of the South, and only in two states did they have a majority.

Actually, carpetbaggers dominated most Republican governments to an extent not warranted by their numbers. They accounted for less than 1 percent of the party's voters but held a third of the offices. Their power was especially obvious in the higher offices. Over half of the South's Republican governors and almost half of the Republican congressmen and senators were former Northerners. Although some carpetbaggers did resemble their stereotypes, most did not. Many had come south before black enfranchisement and could not have predicted political futures based on black votes. Most were Union veterans whose wartime exposure to the region convinced

African Americans eagerly participated in politics when allowed. As depicted in this sketch of the 1867 election in the nation's capital, they served as polling place judges and lined up as early as 2 A.M. to vote.

them that they could make a good living there without having to shovel snow. Some brought with them much needed capital for investment in their new home. A few came with a sense of mission to educate blacks and reform southern society.

Obviously, if African Americans constituted only a third of the population and carpetbaggers less than 1 percent, those two groups had to depend on the votes of a sizable number of native white Southerners to obtain office in some regions of the South. Those men came from diverse backgrounds. Some scalawags were members of the old elite of bankers, merchants, industrialists, and even some planters who, as former Whigs, favored the "Whiggish" economic policies of the Republican party and hoped to control and use the black vote for their own purposes. On discovering their inability to dominate the Republican governments, most of these soon drifted into alliance with the Democrats. The majority of southern white Republican voters were yeomen farmers and poor whites from areas where slavery had been unimportant. They had long resented planter domination and had opposed secession.

To win their vote the Republicans appealed to class interests. In Georgia they proclaimed, "Poor White men of Georgia: Be a Man! Let the Slave-holding aristocracy no longer rule you. Vote for a constitution which educates your children free of charge; relieves the poor debtor from his rich creditor; allows a liberal homestead for your families; and more than all, places you on a level with those who used to boast that for every slave they were entitled to three-fifths of a vote in congressional representation." Many accepted such arguments and joined African Americans to put Republicans into office. The coalition, however, was always shaky, given the racism of poor whites. The scalawags actually represented a swing vote that finally swung toward the Democratic party of white supremacy later in the 1870s.

Character of Republican Rule

While the coalition lasted, the Republican governments became the most democratic that the South had ever had. More people could vote for more offices, all remaining property requirements for voting and office holding were dropped, representation was made fairer through reapportionment, and more offices became elective rather than appointive. Salaries for public officials made it possible to serve without being wealthy. Most important, universal male suffrage was enacted with the support of black legislators. Ironically, by refusing to deny southern whites what had been denied to them—the vote—African Americans sowed the seeds of their own destruction.

The Republican state constitutions, which brought the South firmly into the mainstream of national reform, often remained in effect years after the end of Reconstruction. Legislatures abolished automatic imprisonment for debt and reduced the use of the death penalty. More institutions for the care of the indigent, orphans, mentally ill, deaf, and blind were established. Tax structures were overhauled, reducing head taxes and increasing property taxes to relieve somewhat poorer taxpayers. At the same time, southern railroads, harbors, and bridges were rebuilt.

Reforms also affected the status of women, increasing their rights in the possession of property and divorce. Although giving women legal control of their property was mainly intended to protect the families of their debt-ridden husbands, African Americans in particular pushed for more radical changes. When William Whipper's motion to give South Carolina women the vote did not receive a second, he declared:

> However frivolous you may think it, I know the time will come when every man and woman in this country will have the right to vote. I acknowledge the superiority of woman. There are large numbers of the sex who have an intelligence more than equal to our own. Is it right or just to deprive these intelligent beings of the privileges which we enjoy? The time will come

when you will have to meet this question. It will continue to be agitated until it must ultimately triumph.

The area in which black legislators had the most success was laying the foundations for public education. Antebellum provisions for public schools below the Mason-Dixon line were meager to nonexistent. In every state African Americans were among the main proponents of state-supported schools, but most accepted segregated facilities as necessary compromises. Some black parents did not even desire integration; they believed their children could not flourish in environments tainted by white supremacy. By 1877 some 600,000 blacks were in schools, but only the University of South Carolina and the public schools of New Orleans were integrated.

As desirable as many of the new social services were, they required money and money was scarce. Railroads and bridges also needed to be rebuilt. The necessary tax increases were bound to be unpopular, as were soaring state debts. Both were blamed on corruption, with some justification. Louisiana governor Henry C. Warmouth netted some $100,000 in a year in which his salary was only $8000. A drunken South Carolina governor signed an issue of state bonds for a woman in a burlesque show. One black man was paid $9000 to repair a bridge with an original cost of only $500. Contracts for rebuilding and expanding railroads, subsidies to industries, and bureaucracies for administering social services offered generous opportunities for graft and bribery. When these occurred, southern whites loudly proclaimed that they knew it would happen if shifty former slaves were given the keys to the till.

Actually, although African Americans received a large share of the blame, they received little of the profit. A smaller percentage of blacks than whites were involved in the scandals. Also the corruption that the Democrats denounced at every turn was rather meager compared with the shenanigans of such contemporary northern Democratic regimes as the Boss Tweed Ring of New York. There seemed to be an orgy of national corruption that infected both parties. Indeed, in the South a Democratic state treasurer who came to office after Reconstruction deserves the dubious distinction of being the largest embezzler of the era.

The "tyranny" that so distressed southern whites did not include wholesale disfranchisement or confiscation of their lands. In fact, the demands of most African Americans were quite reasonable and moderate. Their goals were expressed by the declarations of the many postwar black conventions, such as a Virginia one in 1865 that declared, "All we ask is an *equal chance* with the white *traitors* varnished and japanned with the oath of amnesty."

Black and White Economic and Social Adaptation

Just as the former slaves on Thomas Pinckney's plantation had learned, blacks everywhere soon realized that the economic power of whites had diminished little. If anything, land became more concentrated in the hands of a few. In one Alabama county, the richest 10 percent of landowners increased their share of landed wealth from 55 to 63 percent between 1860 and 1870. Some African Americans, usually through hard work and incredible sacrifice, were able to obtain land. The percentage of blacks owning property increased from less than 1 to 20 percent. Indeed, African Americans seemed to fare better than poor whites. One observer noted, "The negro, bad as his condition is, seems to me, on the whole, to accommodate himself more easily than the white to the change of situation." The truth of his assertion is reflected in the fact that the percentage of whites owning land dropped from 80 to 67 percent. Increasingly, poor blacks and whites became agricultural laborers on someone else's land.

The black landless farmers, like the slaves before them, were not mere pawns. If they could not control their destinies, at least they could shape them. As one northern observer wrote, "They have a mine of strategy to which the planter sooner or later yields." Through strikes and work slowdowns, African Americans resisted contract and wage labor because working in gangs under white supervision smacked too much of slavery. When they could not own land, they preferred to rent it, but the few who had the cash to do so found few southern whites would risk the wrath of their neighbors by breaking the taboo against renting to blacks.

Sharecropping emerged both as a result of blacks' desire for autonomy and whites' lack of cash. Landowners gave blacks as well as poor whites a plot of land to work in return for a share of the crops. Freedom from white supervision was so desirable to former slaves that they sometimes hitched mule teams to their old slave cabins and carried them off to their assigned acres. To put distance between themselves and slavery, many black men would not allow their wives and children to work in the fields.

Sharecropping at first seemed to be a good bargain for African Americans because they frequently negotiated their way to a half-share of the crops. Their portion of the profits from southern agriculture, including all provisions, rose from 22 percent under slavery to 56 percent by the end of Reconstruction. Moreover, they were making more for working less. Fewer family members worked and black men labored shorter hours; as a group African Americans worked one-third fewer hours than under slavery. Per capita black income increased quickly after the war to about one-half that of whites, but then it stagnated.

Sharecropping later proved to be disastrous for most blacks and poor whites. They needed more than land to farm; they also required seeds, fertilizers, and provisions to live on until they harvested their crops. To obtain these they often borrowed against their share of the crops. Falling crop prices, high credit rates, and sometimes cheating by creditors left many to harvest a growing burden of debt with each crop. In many states, when the Democrats regained power, laws favoring creditors were passed. These led to debt peonage for many sharecroppers.

If most former slaves did not win economic freedom, they benefited from freedom in other ways. It was no longer illegal to learn to read and write, and African Americans pursued education with much zeal. Many even paid as much as 10 percent of their limited incomes for tuition. They began to learn the fundamentals, and a growing number also sought higher education. Between 1860 and 1880 over 1000 African Americans earned college degrees. Some went north to college, but most went to 1 of the 13 southern colleges established by the American Missionary Association or by black and white churches with the assistance of the Freedmen's Bureau. Such schools as Howard and Fisk were a permanent legacy of Reconstruction.

African Americans were also able to enjoy and expand their rich cultural heritage. Religion was a central focus for most, just as it had been in slavery. Withdrawing from white congregations with segregated pews and self-serving sermons on the duty of servants to their masters, blacks everywhere established separate black churches. The membership in such antebellum denominations as the African Methodist Episcopal soared. In essence, black Christians declared their religious independence, and their churches became centers of political and social activities as well as religious ones. As one carpetbagger noted, "The colored preachers are *the great power* in controlling and uniting the colored vote." The churches also functioned as vehicles for self-help and sources of entertainment.

Most African Americans desired racial intermingling no more than whites. Many could not feel free until they had removed themselves and their children as far as possible from white arrogance. They created separate congregations and acquiesced to segregated schooling. Nevertheless, they did not want to be publicly humiliated by such measures as separate railroad cars. They frequently used their limited political power to protect civil rights through clauses in state constitutions and legislation, as well as by appeals for the enforcement of national laws. Consequently, black Southerners did enjoy the use of public facilities to a greater degree than they would during the 75 years following Reconstruction.

The very changes that gave African Americans hope during Reconstruction distressed poor whites. Black political equality rankled them, but much more serious was their own declining economic status. As their landownership declined, more whites became dependent on sharecropping and low-wage jobs, primarily in the textile industry. Even these meager opportunities were eagerly greeted; as one North Carolina preacher proclaimed, "Next to God, what this town needs is a cotton mill." Economic competition between poor whites and blacks was keen, but their common plight also favored cooperation based on class interest. The economic pressures applied by the white elite frequently hurt both groups as well as middle-class yeomen farmer, and for brief periods during Reconstruction they warily united in politics. Invariably, however, these attempts were shattered by upper-class appeals to white supremacy and racial unity.

Ironically, although poor whites were perceived by nearly everyone as the group most hostile to blacks, the two shared many aspects of a rich Southern cultural heritage. Both groups developed colorful dialects. For each, aesthetic expression was based on utility—reflecting their need to use wisely what little they had. Their quilts were not merely functional but often quite beautiful. In religion and recreation, their experiences were similar. At camp meetings and revivals, poor whites practiced a highly emotional religion, just as many black Southerners did. Both groups spun yarns and sang songs that reflected the perils of their existence and provided folk heroes. They also shared many superstitions as well as useful folk remedies. Race, however, was a potent wedge between them that upper-class whites frequently exploited for their own political and economic goals.

Planters no longer dominated the white elite; sharecropping turned them and others into absentee landlords. The sons of the old privileged families joined the growing ranks of lawyers, railroad entrepreneurs, bankers, industrialists, and merchants. In some ways, the upper and middle classes began to merge, but in many places the old elite and their sons still enjoyed a degree of deference and political leadership. Their hostility toward African Americans was not as intense, largely because they possessed means of control. When their control slipped, however, they also became ranting racists.

So strongly were all southern whites imbued with a belief in white superiority that most could not imagine total black equality. A Freedmen's Bureau agent reported in 1866 that "a very respectable old citizen . . . swore that, if he could not thrash a negro who insulted him, he would leave the country." White attitudes toward blacks were as irrational as they were generalized. Most whites exempted the blacks they knew from such generalizations. As an Alabama planter declared in 1865, "If all were like some of mine I wouldn't say anything. They're as intelligent and well behaved as anybody. But I can't stand free niggers anyhow!"

Violent White Resistance

Large numbers of whites engaged in massive resistance to Reconstruction. Unlike the resistance of southern blacks 100 years later, however, this brand of resistance was not passive but very aggressive. In 1866, some bored young men in Pulaski, Tennessee, organized a social club with all the trappings of fraternal orders—secret rituals, costumes, and practical jokes. They soon learned that their antics intimidated African Americans; thenceforth the **Ku Klux Klan** grew into a terrorist organization, copied all over the South under various names. A historian of the Klan asserts that it "whipped, shot, hanged, robbed, raped, and otherwise outraged Negroes and Republicans across the South in the name of preserving white civilization." A major goal of the Klan was to intimidate Republican voters and restore Democrats to office. In South Carolina, when blacks working for a scalawag began to vote, Klansmen visited the plantation and "whipped every nigger man they could lay their hands on." The group's increasing lawlessness alarmed many people and led to congressional action. The Klan was broken up by three Enforcement Acts (1870–1871) that gave the president the right to suspend habeas corpus against "armed combinations" interfering with any citizen's right to vote. In 1871 Grant did so in nine South Carolina counties. Disbanding the Klan, however, did little to decrease southern violence or the activities of similar terrorist groups.

Some black Southerners were probably never allowed to vote freely. At the peak of Reconstruction, fewer than 30,000 federal troops were stationed in the entire South—hardly enough to protect the rights of 4.5 million African Americans. As troops were being withdrawn, Democrats sought to regain control of their states. They made appeals to white supremacy and charged the Republicans with corrup-

This attempted lynching was photographed by a federal agent who stopped it. This 1871 engraving is based on that photograph.

tion. Without secret ballots landowners could threaten sharecroppers with eviction for "improper" voting. In addition to economic intimidation, violence against African Americans escalated in most states as the Democrats increased their political power. When victory seemed close, Democrats justified any means to the desired end that they called "redemption." A South Carolina Democratic campaign plan in 1876 urged, "Never threaten a man individually. If he deserves to be threatened, the necessities of the times require that he should die. A dead Radical is very harmless." One Democratic candidate for governor in Louisiana proclaimed, "We shall carry the next election if we have to ride saddle-deep in blood to do it." In six heavily black counties in Mississippi such tactics proved highly successful—reducing Republican votes from more than 14,000 in 1873 to only 723 in 1876. Beginning with Virginia and Tennessee in 1869, by 1876 all but three states—Louisiana, Florida, and South Carolina—had Democratic "Redeemer" governments. The final collapse of Reconstruction became official the following year with the withdrawal of federal troops from the three unredeemed states.

RECONSTRUCTION IN THE NORTH AND WEST

In the end, the South could be said to have lost the war but won the peace. After 1877 Southern whites found little resistance to their efforts to forge new in-

THE PEOPLE SPEAK

Testimony Against the Klan

The terrorism committed by the Ku Klux Klan is documented in the published proceedings of the Joint Committee on Reconstruction. Here Daniel E. Smith of Mississippi tells of his narrow escape from a lynching in his testimony before the committee.

Question. Have you ever been attacked by disguised men?

Answer. Yes, sir.

Question. You may state the particulars to the committee.

Answer. After I came here in 1866, and was near Brooksville, a gentleman up there named Elm tried to hire my wife, and told me he would give me a school on the place, if I would let my wife go and wait on him. When I mentioned it to her she was not willing to go there. I would not try to force her there, and he fell out with me about it. After he fell out with me about it, he met me, and asked me what sort of way I had done, and cursed me. I told him I thought I done my duty; that my wife was not willing to go. He told me he generally made negroes like me do as he wanted them to do; he didn't ask no negro what they did; he generally made them do it; and a good many words passed between us. I told him I thought I had done my duty. He threatened to kill me a time or two up there if I did not do it. When I was coming from Brooksville one night, I saw two men up here in the road before me, with white sheets around them. They lit off of horses and told me to stop. They knowed I was going to Brooksville; they always knew it; for I was teaching a colored school near Brooksville, and always went to Brooksville Saturday evening, and sometimes it was after night before I returned home. In returning back I saw two people with sheets around them, and when they ordered me to stop I did so, and they got down and asked if that was Daniel Smith. I told them it was not, it was Alleck Billips. He was a man that resembles me very much, and was about my height, and, it being dark, they could not tell whether it was me or not, and I don't think they had taken very particular notice of my features and face. They drew a rope out, and said if it had been Daniel H. Smith they aimed to hang him with that rope that night. Then they went on and asked me if I had been a good negro to my master Charley; that was Charley Sherrod. I told them I had been very good and obedient to him, and got away from them that night by telling them that falsehood. The year after that, or a shorter time than a year, I moved away from there down here to where I am now. . . .

Question. What is the feeling among the whites, so far as you have conversed with them or heard an expression of opinion in relation to colored suffrage or negroes voting?

Answer. Well, sir, they do not believe in it. . . . Out in the part of the county where I live I have known a great many of them to tell the colored people, so as to disappoint them, that there was no election—that it had all been given over. A great many ignorant people would think the employer knew, and that he told them the truth. They would deprive them in that way of their votes. And, again, they would tell them to take their wagons, and go to such a place, and haul so and so away from there. They would manage in all such ways to keep the black people away. Since I have been in the State they came to me and asked me when the election was, and I would tell them. I do not believe, sir, that the generality, the majority of the white people that were around in the neighborhood, generally appreciated me very much on account of my being a negro. I have heard them speak so very bitterly, though I have always behaved myself to them and been very obedient, and never put myself in the way to create any disturbance in any way. . . .

Question. Do the white people here favor the colored people buying lands and having homes?

Answer. No, sir. . . . [T]hey say that if you suffer the colored people here to own land they cannot get any laborers then, for where a colored man owns a piece of land, as many as can do so will go to their own land, and that will defeat them from getting labor.

Question. So that the white owners of the soil you think are generally opposed to your people becoming owners of land?

Answer. Yes, sir; or stocks [livestock] in any way; they don't believe in that. I have known a great many people that have lost their stock. Sometimes the employers would go out and shoot the stock down, if they found them in the wrong place. They did not tell them who killed them.

Testimony of Daniel H. Smith, Macon, Mississippi, November 7, 1871, in U.S. Congress. *Testimony Taken by the Joint Select Committee to Inquire into the Condition of Affairs in the Late Insurrectionary States.* Government Printing Office, Washington, D.C., Vol. II, pp. 570–573, 574, 1872.

stitutions to replace both the economic benefits and racial control of slavery. By 1910 they had devised a system of legalized repression that gave whites many of the benefits of slavery without all the responsibilities. Surely this was not what the North had envisioned after Appomattox. How did it happen? Much of the answer is found in events occurring in the North and West.

Northern Shifts in Attitudes

The basic cause for the decline of Reconstruction can be seen in an 1874 conversation between two northern Republicans during which one declared that the people were "tired out with this wornout cry of 'Southern Outrages!!!' Hard times and heavy taxes make them wish the . . . 'everlasting nigger' were in [hell] or Africa. . . . It is amazing the change that has taken place in the last two years in the public sentiment." A shifting political climate, economic hard times, increasing preoccupation with other issues, and continued racism combined to make most Northerners wash their hands of the responsibility for the protection of black rights.

Although his slogan "Let us have peace" was appealing, Ulysses S. Grant proved to be a poor choice for the presidency. Not only was he politically inexperienced, but he also lacked a taste for politics. Haunted by a fear of failure and socially insecure, Grant was too easily influenced by men of wealth and prestige. He made some dismal appointments and remained loyal to individuals who did not merit his trust. The result was a series of scandals. Grant was not personally involved, but his close association with the perpetrators blemished both his and his party's image. The first major scandal surfaced in 1872; it involved Credit Mobilier, a dummy construction company used to milk money from railroad investors in order to line the pockets of a few insiders, including Vice President Schuyler Colfax and a number of other prominent Republicans. Later, bribes and kickback schemes surfaced that involved Indian trading posts, post office contracts, and commissions for tax collection. Such revelations as well as the corruption in some southern Republican governments did little to enhance the public image of the party, and Democrats were quick to make corruption a major issue in both the North and the South.

Although by the 1872 presidential election, there had only been a hint of scandal, some Republicans were disenchanted. In that election the Republican party was split; a number, calling themselves Liberal Republicans, formed a separate party. They supported their own candidate, *New York Tribune* editor Horace Greeley, rather than Grant. Among Greeley's campaign pledges was a more moderate southern policy. Even with the Democrats also nominating Greeley, Grant easily won reelection, but the fear of disgruntled Republicans merging with Democrats remained. By 1874 Republicans were becoming aware that the black vote would not save them. That year Democrats captured the House and gained in the Senate, following further revelations of Republican corruption.

At least as detrimental to Republican political fortunes was a depression that followed the Panic of 1873, which was caused by overinvestment in railroads and risky financial deals. Lasting six years, it was the most serious economic downturn the nation had yet experienced. Whatever their cause, depressions usually result in "voting the rascals out." Democratic fortunes were bound to rise as the people's fell. Yet economic distress had an even wider impact on Reconstruction. People's attention became focused on their pocketbooks rather than on abstract ideals of equality and justice.

Actually, the Panic of 1873 merely brought into clearer focus the vast changes occurring in the North during Reconstruction. The South had never had the undivided attention of the rest of the nation. Such events as the completion of the first transcontinental railroad in 1869 often overshadowed reports of "Southern outrages." The United States was experiencing the growing pains of economic modernization and western expansion. The Republican platform of 1860 had called for legislation favoring both of these as well as stopping the expansion of slavery. Comprised of diverse interest groups, the party went through a battle for its soul during Reconstruction. For a while the small abolitionist faction had gained some ascendancy due to postwar developments. By the late 1870s, however, the Republican party had forsaken its reformist past to become a protector of privilege rather than a guarantor of basic rights. In effect, Republicans and Democrats joined hands in conservative support of railroad and industrial interests.

Western Expansion, Racism, and Native Americans

The major reason for the decline of Reconstruction was the pervasive belief in white supremacy. There could be little determination to secure equal rights for those who were considered unequal in all other respects. Reconstruction became a failed opportunity to resolve justly the status of one minority, and the climate of racism almost ensured failure for others as well. Western expansion not only diverted attention from Reconstruction but also raised the question of what was to be done about the Plains Indians. They, too, were considered inferior to whites. William H. Seward, who later became secretary of state, spoke for most white Americans when in 1860 he described blacks as "a foreign and feeble element like the Indians, incapable of assimilation." Indeed, while Reconstruction at first offered hope to African Americans, for Native Americans hope was fading.

In the end, African Americans were oppressed; Native Americans were exterminated or separated into shrinking reservations. From the white viewpoint the reason was obvious. As a so-called scientific treatise of the 1850s explained, "The *Barbarous* races of America . . . although nearly as low in intellect as the Negro races, are essentially untameable. Not merely have all attempts to civilize them failed, but also every endeavor to enslave them." Because most Africans, like Europeans, depended on agriculture rather than hunting, they adapted more easily to agricultural slavery. Black labor was valuable, if controlled; Native Americans were merely barriers to expansion.

Cultural Differences When settlers first began moving onto the Great Plains, they encountered about 250,000 Plains Indians and 13 million buffalo. Some groups, including the Zuni, Hopi, Navaho, and Pawnee, were fairly settled and depended on gardening and farming. Others, such as the Sioux, Apache, and Cheyenne, however, were nomadic hunters who followed the buffalo herds over vast tracts of land. These herds played a crucial role in most Plains Indians' culture—providing almost all the basic necessities. Indians ate the buffalo meat, made clothing and teepees out of the hides, used the fats for cosmetics, fashioned the bones into tools, made thread from the sinews, and even burned dried buffalo droppings as fuel. To settlers, however, the buffalo were barriers to western expansion. The herds interfered with construction, knocked over telegraph poles and fences, and could derail trains during stampedes.

Other cultural differences caused misunderstandings between settlers and Native Americans. Among Anglo-Americans, capitalism fostered competition and frontier living promoted individualism. On the other hand, Plains Indians lived in tribes based on kinship ties. As members of an extended family that included distant cousins, Indians were taught to place the welfare of the group over the interests of the individual. The emphasis within a tribe was on cooperation rather than competition. Some tribes might be richer than other tribes, but there was seldom a large gap between the rich and the poor within a tribe.

Power as well as wealth was usually shared. Tribes were loosely structured rather than tightly organized. Chiefs seldom had much individual power. The Cheyenne, for example, had a council of 44 to advise the chief. Instead of having a lot of political power, chiefs were generally religious and ceremonial leaders. Anglo-Americans did not always understand their limited power. Whites incorrectly believed that an individual Indian could make decisions and sign agreements that would be considered legal by their fellow Indians.

Another major cultural difference between the newly arriving settlers and the Plains Indians was their attitudes toward the land. Most Native Americans had no concept of private property. Chief Joseph of the Nez Percé eloquently expressed the view: "The earth was created by the assistance of the sun, and it should be left as it was. . . . The country was made without lines of demarcation, and it is no man's business to divide it."

Native Americans refused to draw property lines and borders because of how they viewed the place of people in the world. Whites tended to see land, plants, and animals as resources to be exploited. Native Americans, on the other hand, stressed the unity of all life—and its holiness.

Most of the Plains Indians believed that land could be utilized but never owned. The idea of owning land was as absurd as owning the air people breathed. To some, the sacredness of the land made farming against their religion. Chief Somohalla of the Wanapaun explained why his people refused to farm. "You ask me to plow the ground! Shall I take a knife and tear my mother's bosom? . . . You ask me to cut grass and make hay and sell it, and be rich like white men! But how dare I cut off my mother's hair?"

Chief Joseph of the Nez Percé expressed the views of Native Americans who had no concept of owning the earth. He proclaimed, "The earth and myself are of one mind."

Indians had great reverence for all land. In addition, some particular pieces of land were considered especially sacred or holy. Certain bodies of water were seen as sources of healing and sites for worship. Some areas were burial grounds, where the spirits of ancestors were believed to reside. White settlers had little understanding of or respect for such Indian sentiments. The results could be tragic where interests collided.

From the white viewpoint, the most significant characteristic of many of the Plains Indian tribes, such as the Cheyenne, Sioux, and Arapaho, was their ability as mounted warriors. Using horses introduced by the Spanish, they had resisted white encroachment for two centuries. Most had no desire for assimilation; they merely wanted to be left alone. "If the Indians had tried to make the whites live like them," one Sioux declared, "the whites would have resisted, and it was the same way with the Indians."

Although some tribes could coexist peacefully with settlers, the nomadic tribes had a way of life that was incompatible with miners, railroad developers, cattle ranchers, and farmers. To Anglo-Americans the Indians were barriers to expansion. They agreed with Theodore Roosevelt that the West was not meant to be "kept as nothing but a game reserve for squalid savages." Thus U.S. Indian policy focused on getting more territory for white settlement. Prior to Reconstruction this was done by signing treaties that divided land between Native Americans and settlers and restricted the movement of each on the lands of the other. Frequently Indian consent was fraudulently obtained, and white respect for Indian land depended on how desirable it was for settlement. As the removal of the Southern Cherokees to Oklahoma had shown in the 1830s, compatibility of cultures did not protect Native Americans from the greed of whites.

During the Civil War, Sioux, Cheyenne, and Arapaho braves rejected the land cessions made by their chiefs. Violence against settlers erupted as frontier troop strength was reduced to fight the Confederacy. The war also provided an excuse to nullify previous treaties and pledges with the Native Americans resettled in Oklahoma under Andrew Jackson's Indian removal policy. Some did support the Confederacy, but all suffered the consequences of Confederate defeat. Settlers moved into the most desirable land, pushing the Indians farther south and west. Some Native Americans began to resist.

Confrontation and Annihilation By the close of the Civil War, Indian hostility had escalated, especially after an 1864 massacre. The territorial governor of Colorado persuaded most of the warring Cheyennes and Arapahos to come to Fort Lyon on Sand Creek, promising them protection. Colonel J. M. Chivington's militia, however, attacked an Indian

Indian Battles and Reservations

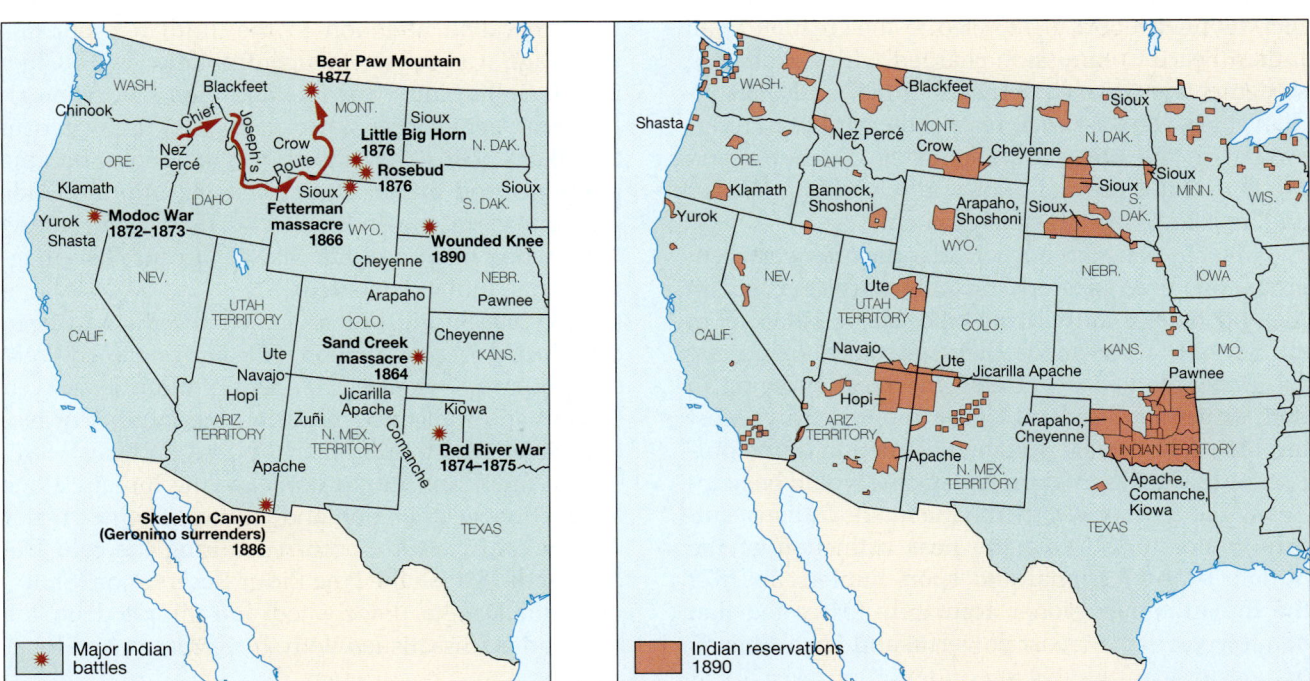

A Native-American watercolor rendering of the Battle of Little Bighorn depicts its aftermath. As Sitting Bull and others stand watching, Sioux and Cheyenne warriors ride horseback over the corpses of Custer (left center) and his troops.

camp flying a white flag and the American flag and killed hundreds of Native American men, women, and children. The following year Congress established a committee to investigate the causes of conflict. Its final report in 1867 led to the creation of an Indian Peace Commission charged with negotiating settlements. At two conferences in 1867 and 1868, Indian chiefs were asked to restrict their tribes to reservations in the undesirable lands of Oklahoma and the Black Hills of the Dakotas in return for supplies and assistance from the government.

Most Indians did not consider the offer very generous. Some acquiesced and others resisted, but in the end federal authorities subdued or killed them all. Several factors made their resistance unsuccessful. Railroads had penetrated the West, bringing in both settlers and federal troops more rapidly. Most important, however, was the destruction of the buffalo herds. Just as modern Americans would be helpless without oil or electricity, the Plains Indians' culture could not survive the near extinction of the buffalo by professional and sport hunters. In 1872 the Indian commissioner accurately forecasted that in a few years the "most powerful and hostile bands of today" would be "reduced to the condition of supplicants for charity."

In 1876, the final year of Reconstruction, Lieutenant Colonel George A. Custer's defeat at Little Bighorn called attention to the "Indian problem." The stage was set for this confrontation with Chief Sitting Bull's Sioux warriors and their Cheyenne allies two years earlier when gold was discovered in the Black Hills. The territory suddenly became tempting, and miners began pouring into the lands guaranteed to the Indians only five years before. "The white man is in the Black Hills just like maggots," one Indian lamented.

Despite Sitting Bull's victory, the die had been cast during Reconstruction. All that remained were "mopping up" exercises. Federal authorities solved the Indian problem by reducing the number of Native Americans to a level that posed no threat. Still, white Americans would not leave the Indians alone to practice their religion and culture. The last major bloody confrontation occurred during the cold December of 1890 on the Pine Ridge Reservation (Sioux) in South Dakota. Poorly fed and supplied on the reservation, dissatisfied with their present, and long-

This photograph, showing the mass burial of the victims after the massacre at Wounded Knee, illustrates the callous disregard of the value of Native American lives.

ing for the glories of their past, members of the Teton Sioux took up the "Ghost Dance," a harmless ritual that promised the faithful the mystical disappearance of the whites and the return of their lands. An inept government agent overreacted, calling in troops to suppress the Ghost Dance and arrest the Sioux leader Sitting Bull, whom the government considered the focal point of Indian resistance. When Indian police killed Sitting Bull, some Sioux took up arms and left the reservation. Near Wounded Knee Creek, U.S. soldiers, armed with rapid-fire Hotchkiss guns, attempted to disarm the Indians. When one Indian resisted, soldiers opened fire, killing more than 300 men, women, and children. The Battle of Wounded Knee, which resembled more a slaughter than a battle, ended the violent era of Indian and white relations.

Ethnocide and Assimilation

By the time of Wounded Knee, the U.S. government had adopted a policy that emphasized ethnocide rather than genocide. An assault on tribalism, ethnocide—the calculated destruction of a culture—was an attempt by white Americans to force Native Americans to assimilate into their culture. Although not as bloody as the Indian wars, ethnocide was even more destructive to Native-American societies.

At the heart of this new policy was the destruction of the reservation system. Reservations encouraged tribal unity, and, as such, distinctiveness from white American society. Congress believed that the solution was to treat Indians less like members of individual tribes and more like autonomous individuals. As a first step, in 1871 Congress had ruled that no Indian tribe "shall be acknowledged or recognized as an independent nation, tribe or power, with whom the United States may contract by treaty." Then in an attempt to destroy Indian culture, in 1887 Congress passed the **Dawes Severalty Act,** which authorized the president to divide tribal lands and redistribute the lands among tribal members, giving 160 acres to each head of a family and lesser amounts to bachelors, women, and children. Although the plots would be held in trust for 25 years to prevent Indians from immediately selling the land, the object of the legislation was to make Indians individual landowners. In addition, all Native Americans receiving land grants were also made citizens of the United States.

Dawes was motivated by what he believed were the best interests of the Native Americans. Like other reformers, he believed that the most effective solution to the Indian problem was to assimilate Indians into mainstream white American culture. To this end, other reformers opened Indian schools to teach Indian children to be mechanics and farmers and to train them for citizenship. Richard Pratt, an army officer who founded the Carlisle Indian Industrial School in Pennsylvania in 1879, maintained that the fastest and surest way to assimilate Indians was to remove Indian children from reservations and send them to boarding schools in the East. By 1905 there were 25 boarding schools patterned after Carlisle. The schools emphasized ruthless assimilation. The "Rules for Indian Schools" called for compulsory observation of the Christian Sabbath, all formal and casual conversation in English, and instruction in "the sports and games enjoyed by white youth, such as baseball, hopscotch, croquet, marbles, bean bags, dominoes, checkers." Even more boarding schools were established on reservations to serve the same ends. What surprised reformers the most, however, was the failure of these schools to break tribal loyalties or destroy Indian culture.

While the reformers opened schools, Congress continued its efforts to break up the reservations. The Curtis Act of 1898 ended tribal sovereignty in Indian Territory, voiding tribal control of mineral rights, abolishing tribal laws and courts, and imposing the laws and courts of the United States on the Indians. The Dead Indian Act (1902) permitted Indians to sell allotted lands they had inherited, thereby circumventing the 25-year trust period imposed by the Dawes Act. Four years later, Congress continued its assault on the trust period with the Burke Act, which eliminated the trust period altogether and allowed the secretary of interior to decide when Indians were competent to manage their own affairs. Finally, in 1924 Congress enacted the Snyder Act, which granted all Indians born in the United States full citizenship. As far as Congress was concerned, the United States had now assimilated its true natives.

Reformers believed that these acts would end the tribal system and lead to assimilation. The legislation, however, served only the land interests of white Americans. By 1932 the allotment program had taken 90 million acres of land away from tribal control. Far from being assimilated, Indians saw their own culture attacked and partially destroyed, while at the same time they were never fully accepted into the dominant American culture.

Final Retreat from Reconstruction

The exact nature of the Native Americans' status, like that of African Americans, was determined after Reconstruction was over. The treatment of both, as well as of immigrants, would be justified by the increasingly virulent racism of whites, which was given "scientific" support by the scholars of the late nineteenth century. The patriotism engendered by the 1876 centennial of the Declaration of Independence also fostered a desire for unity among white Americans at the expense of nonwhites.

By 1876, fewer Americans championed black rights than had at the close of the war. Neither could Northerners who believed that the only good Indian was a dead Indian condemn southern whites for their treatment of African Americans. Some of the old abolitionist Radicals had grown tired of what had become a protracted and complex problem. They therefore justified their withdrawal from the fight by the failures of some southern Reconstruction governments. Those least likely to do so, such as Thaddeus Stevens and Charles Sumner, were dead. Until his death in 1874, Sumner had struggled to get Congress to pass a civil rights act that would spell out more specifically the guarantees of the Fourteenth Amendment. He proposed that segregation of all public facilities, including schools, be declared illegal and the right of African Americans to serve on juries specified. After his death, in part as a tribute to him but mostly as one provision of a larger political bargain, Congress enacted the Civil Rights Act of 1875. The act did not include Sumner's clause on schools and did not provide any means of enforcement. For African Americans it was a paper victory that marked an end of national action on their behalf. Never effectively enforced, the act was rendered totally impotent by Supreme Court decisions of the late nineteenth century.

By 1876 all the elements were present for a national retreat on Reconstruction: the distraction of economic distress, a deep desire for unity among whites, the respectability of racism, a frustrated weariness with black problems by former allies, a growing conservatism on economic and social issues, a changing political climate featuring a resurgence of the Democratic party, and finally a general public disgust with the failure of Reconstruction. The presidential election of that year sealed the fate of Reconstruction and brought about an official end to it.

Corruption was a major issue in the 1876 election and the Democrats chose Samuel J. Tilden, a New Yorker whose claim to fame was breaking up the notorious Boss Tweed Ring. The Republicans nominated Rutherford B. Hayes, a man who had offended few—largely by doing little. Although Hayes had been elected governor of Ohio three times, to one observer he was "a third rate nonentity, whose only recommendation is that he is obnoxious to no one." As would become typical of most elections during the decades following Reconstruction, the campaign did not focus on any burning issues. The Democrats ran against Republican corruption. The Republicans ran against Democratic violence in the South. "Our strong ground," Hayes wrote, "is the dread of a solid South, *rebel rule*, etc., etc. . . . It leads people away from 'hard times'; which is our deadliest foe."

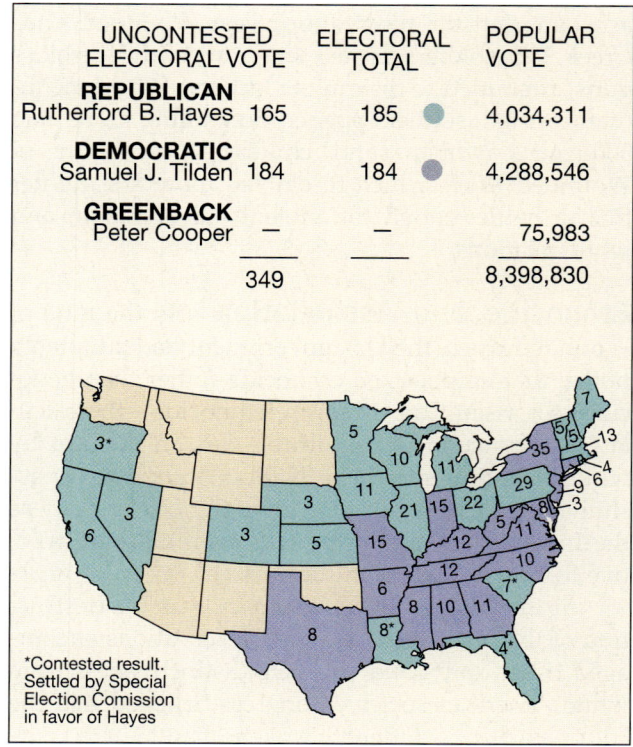

Election of 1876

The election itself was so riddled with corruption and violence that no one can ever know what would have happened in a fair election. One thing is certain. The Democrats gained strength. Tilden won the popular vote and led Hayes in undisputed electoral votes 184 to 165. However, 185 votes were needed for election, and 20 votes were disputed—19 of them from Louisiana, Florida, and South Carolina. They were the only Southern states still under Republican rule with the backing of federal troops. In each, rival election boards sent in different returns.

With no constitutional provision for such an occurrence, the Republican Senate and Democratic House established a special commission to decide which returns were valid. The 15-member Electoral Commission had 5 members each from the House, the Senate, and the Supreme Court. At first it was evenly divided with 7 Republicans and 7 Democrats; politically independent Supreme Court Justice David Davis was the swing vote. Illinois Democrats then made a mistake and selected Davis as their senator. Thus, a Republican justice was appointed to replace him on the Electoral Commission, which proceeded to vote along party lines, 8 to 7, to give all the disputed votes to Hayes. Democrats were outraged, and a constitutional crisis seemed in the making if a united Democratic front in the House voted to reject the commission's findings.

A series of agreements between Hayes's advisors and Southern Democratic congressmen averted the crisis. In what came to be called the **"Compromise of 1877,"** Hayes agreed to support federal aid for Southern internal improvements, especially a transcontinental railroad. He also promised to appoint a southern Democrat to his cabinet and to allow southern Democrats a say in the allocation of federal offices in their region. Most important, however, was his pledge to remove the remaining federal troops from the South. In return southern Democrats promised to protect black rights and to support the findings of the Electoral Commission. On March 2, the House voted to accept the report and declare Hayes the presidential winner by an electoral vote of 185 to 184. After taking office, Hayes removed the troops, and the remaining Republican governments in the South soon collapsed.

Scholars once considered the Compromise of 1877 an important factor in the end of Reconstruction. Actually, its role was more symbolic than real; it merely buried the corpse. The battle for the Republican party's soul had been lost by its abolitionist faction well before the election of 1876. The Democratic party had never sought to extend or protect blacks' rights. The Supreme Court began to interpret the Fourteenth and Fifteenth amendments very nar-

This 1871 cartoon shows President Hayes as a railroad conductor ushering two Louisiana carpetbaggers out of the state.

rowly, stripping them of their strength. Thus African Americans were left with a small number of allies, and one by one many of their rights were lost during the next four decades.

CONCLUSION

As the Civil War ended, many unresolved issues remained. The most crucial involved the status of the former slaves and of the former Confederate states. The destinies of both were inextricably intertwined. Anything affecting the status of either influenced the fate of the other. Quick readmission of the states with little change would doom black rights. Enforced equality of African Americans under the law would create turbulence and drastic change in the South. This difficult problem was further complicated by constitutional, economic, and political considerations, ensuring that the course of Reconstruction would be chaotic and contradictory.

Presidential Reconstruction under both Lincoln and Johnson favored rapid reunification and white unity more than changes in the racial structure of the South. The South, however, refused to accept a meaningful end of slavery, as was blatantly demonstrated by the Black Codes. Congressional desire to reestablish legislative supremacy and the Republican need to build a national party combined with this southern intransigence to unite Radical and moder-

Chronology of Key Events

1863 Lincoln proclaims 10 percent plan for Reconstruction, which requires states to abolish slavery and have 10 percent of the citizens who had voted in the 1860 election subscribe to an oath to support the Constitution and the Union

1864 Lincoln vetoes Wade-Davis Bill on grounds that it imposes too severe conditions on the readmission of the seceded states; Sand Creek Massacre of Indians in Colorado

1865 Congress establishes Freedmen's Bureau to aid former slaves and refugees; Confederate army surrenders at Appomattox; John Wilkes Booth assassinates Lincoln at Ford's Theater in Washington, D.C.; Andrew Johnson becomes seventeenth president; Thirteenth Amendment is ratified, abolishing slavery

1866 Civil Rights Act provides that all persons born in the United States are citizens and possess equal legal and property rights; Fourteenth Amendment is proposed

1867 Reconstruction Act, passed over Johnson's veto, divides the South into five military districts, each governed by an army general. It requires each state to adopt a constitution disqualifying former Confederate officials from holding office to grant black citizens the right to vote, and to ratify the Fourteenth Amendment

1868 House of Representatives impeaches President Johnson; he escapes conviction in the Senate by one vote; Fourteenth Amendment is ratified; it guarantees citizenship to black Americans; Indian peace conference leads to establishment of reservations in Oklahoma and the Black Hills of the Dakotas; Ulysses S. Grant is elected eighteenth president

1870 Fifteenth Amendment is ratified; outlaws the exclusion from voting on the basis of race

1870–1871 Ku Klux Klan Acts are passed, which outlaw use of force to prevent people from voting and authorize use of federal troops to enforce the laws; Tweed Ring in New York City is exposed

1872 Credit Mobilier scandal is exposed

1876 Custer is defeated at Little Bighorn; disputed presidential election between Tilden and Hayes

1877 Electoral Commission awards disputed ballots to Republican Rutherford B. Hayes, who becomes nineteenth president

ate Republicans on the need to protect black rights and to restructure the South. What emerged from congressional reconstruction were Republican governments that expanded democracy and enacted needed reforms but were deeply resented by many southern whites. At the core of that resentment was not disgust over incompetence or corruption but hostility to black political power in any form.

Given the pervasiveness of racial prejudice, what is remarkable is not that the Freedmen's Bureau, the constitutional amendments, and the civil rights legislation did not produce permanent change but that these actions were taken at all. Cherished ideas of property rights, limited government, and self-reliance, as well as an almost universal belief in black inferiority, almost guaranteed that the experiment would fail. The first national attempt to resolve fairly and justly the question of minority rights in a pluralistic society was abandoned in less than a decade. After Native American populations had been decimated, the government sought to eradicate all elements of their culture that differed from that of the dominant society. Indians, blacks, and women saw the truth of the Alabama planter's words of 1865: "Poor elk—poor buffaloe—poor Indian—poor Nigger—this is indeed a white man country." However, less than a century later seeds planted by the amendments would finally germinate, flower, and be harvested.

Suggestions for Further Reading

Richard Nelson Current, *Those Terrible Carpetbaggers* (1988). Refutes the longstanding myth that northerners in the South after the Civil War were ill-educated people whose only goal was private gain.

Eric Foner, *Nothing But Freedom: Emancipation and Its Legacy* (1983). Compares and contrasts the post-emancipation experience of African Americans with that of former slaves in the Caribbean.

Eric Foner, *Reconstruction: America's Unfinished Revolution, 1863–1877* (1988). Comprehensive history of the period, which emphasized African-Americans' central role in defining the period's political and social agenda.

Leon Litwack, *Been in the Storm So Long: The Aftermath of Slavery* (1979). Examines the varied responses of African Americans in the South to emancipation.

Mark W. Summers, *The Era of Good Stealings* (1993). Investigates political corruption during the Reconstruction period.

Joel Williamson, *The Crucible of Race* (1984). Explores the evolution of Southern race relations after Reconstruction.

Overviews and Surveys

Eric Anderson and Alfred A. Moss, Jr., *The Facts of Reconstruction: Essays in Honor of John Hope Franklin* (1992); Mary Francis Berry and John W. Blassingame, *Long Memory: The Black Experience in America* (1982); W. E. B. DuBois, *Black Reconstruction in America 1860–1880* (1935); Eric Foner and Olivia Mahoney, *America's Reconstruction: People and Politics After the Civil War* (1995); Jay R. Mandle, *Not Slave, Not Free: The African-American Experience Since the Civil War* (1992); James McPherson, *Ordeal by Fire* (1982); James G. Randall and David Donald, *The Civil War and Reconstruction*, 2d ed. (1969); Kenneth M. Stampp, *The Era of Reconstruction, 1865–1877* (1965).

Postwar Conditions and Issues

Herman Belz, *Emancipation and Equal Rights: Politics and Constitutionalism in the Civil War Era* (1976); John H. and LaWanda Cox, *Politics, Principles, and Prejudice* (1963); John Hope Franklin, *Reconstruction After the Civil War*, 2d Ed. (1994); William C. Harris, *With Charity for All: Lincoln and the Reconstruction of the Union* (1997); Peter Kolchin, *First Freedom: The Responses of Alabama's Blacks to Emancipation and Reconstruction* (1972); J. Morgan Kousser and James McPherson, eds., *Region, Race, and Reconstruction* (1982); Rembert W. Patrick, *Reconstruction of the Nation* (1967); James Roark, *Masters Without Slaves* (1977); Willie Lee Rose, *Rehearsal for Reconstruction* (1964); James Sefton, *The United States Army and Reconstruction, 1865–1877* (1967); Ted Tunnell, *Crucible of Reconstruction* (1984).

Presidential Reconstruction

Richard H. Abbott, *The Republican Party and the South, 1855–1877: The First Southern Strategy* (1986); Michael Les Benedict, *A Compromise of Principle* (1974); William R. Brock, *An American Crisis* (1963); LaWanda Cox, *Lincoln and Black Freedom* (1981); David Donald, *The Politics of Reconstruction* (1965); William B. Hesseltine, *Lincoln's Plan of Reconstruction* (1960); Peyton McCrary, *Abraham Lincoln and Reconstruction* (1978); Eric McKitrick, *Andrew Johnson and Reconstruction* (1960); James M. McPherson, *The Struggle for Equality: Abolitionists and the Negro in the Civil War and Reconstruction* (1964); Patrick W. Riddleberger, *1866: The Critical Year Revisited* (1979); Hans L. Trefousse, *The Radical Republicans* (1969).

Congressional Reconstruction

Michael Les Benedict, *The Impeachment of Andrew Johnson* (1973); Ellen DuBois, *Feminism and Suffrage* (1978); William Gillette, *The Right to Vote* (1969); Harold M. Hyman, *A More Perfect Union* (1973); Joseph James, *The Framing of the Fourteenth Amendment* (1956); Stanley I. Kutler, *The Judicial Power and Reconstruction Politics* (1968); Hans L. Trefousse, *The Impeachment of a President* (1975); Xi Wang, *The Trial of Democracy: Black Suffrage and Northern Republicans, 1860–1910* (1997).

Reconstruction in the South

Dan T. Carter, *When the War Was Over: The Failure of Self-Reconstruction in the South, 1865–1867* (1985); Stephen J. DeCanio, *Agriculture in the Postbellum South* (1974); Laura F. Edwards, *Gendered Strife & Confusion: The Political Culture of Reconstruction* (1997); Paul D. Escott, *Many Excellent People* (1985); Barbara Jeanne Fields, *Slavery and Freedom on the Middle Ground: Maryland During the Nineteenth Century* (1985); Eric Foner, *Nothing But Freedom* (1983); Herbert G. Gutman, *The Black Family in Slavery and Freedom* (1976); Steven Hahn, *The Roots of Southern Populism* (1983); William C. Harris, *The Day of the Carpetbagger* (1979); Thomas Holt, *Black over White* (1977); Gerald Jaynes, *Branches Without Roots: Genesis of the Black Working Class in the American South, 1862–1882* (1986); Jay R. Mandle, *The Roots of Black Poverty* (1978); William E. Montgomery, *Under Their Own Vine and Fig Tree: The African-American Church in the South, 1865–1900* (1993); Robert C. Morris, *Reading, 'Riting and Reconstruction* (1981); Otto H. Olsen, ed., *Reconstruction and Redemption in the South* (1980); Michael Perman, *The Road to Redemption: Southern Politics, 1869–1879* (1984); Lawrence N. Powell, *New Masters: Northern Planters During the Civil War and Reconstruction* (1980); Howard Rabinowitz, *Race Relations in the Urban South* (1978); George C. Rable, *But There Was No Peace: The Role of Violence in the Politics of Reconstruction* (1984); Peter J. Rachleff, *Black Labor in the South: Richmond, Virginia, 1865–1890* (1984); Roger L. Ransom and Richard Sutch,

One Kind of Freedom: The Economic Consequences of Emancipation (1977); Edward Royce, *The Origins of Southern Sharecropping* (1993); Joe Gray Taylor, *Louisiana Reconstructed* (1974); Allen Trelease, *White Terror* (1971); Ted Tunnell, *Crucible of Reconstruction* (1984); Jonathan M. Wiener, *Social Origins of the New South: Alabama, 1860–1885* (1978); Sarah Woolfolk Wiggins, *The Scalawag in Alabama Politics* (1977); Joel Williamson, *After Slavery: The Negro in South Carolina During Reconstruction* (1965), and *A Rage for Order: Black-White Relations in the American South Since Emancipation* (1986).

Reconstruction in the North and West

Ralph K. Andrist, *The Long Death: The Last Days of the Plains Indians* (1964); Robert F. Berkhofer, *The White Man's Indian* (1978); Eugene H. Berwanger, *The West and Reconstruction* (1981); George Pierre Castile and Robert L. Bee, eds., *State and Reservation: New Perspectives on Federal Indian Policy* (1992); William Y. Chalfant, *Cheyennes at Dark Water Creek: The Last Fight of the Red River War* (1997); Charles Fairman, *Reconstruction and Reunion*, 2 vols. (1971–1987); David A. Gerber, *Black Ohio and the Color Line, 1860–1915* (1976); William Gillette, *Retreat from Reconstruction* (1979), and *The Right to Vote* (1969); Norris Handley, Jr., ed., *The American Indian* (1974); Nell Irvin Painter, *The Exodusters* (1977); Keith Ian Polakoff, *The Politics of Inertia* (1973); Francis Paul Prucha, *American Indian Policy in Crisis* (1975); David Roberts, *Once They Moved Like the Wind: Cochise, Geronimo, and the Apache Wars* (1993); Nina Silber, *The Romance of Reunion: Northerners and the South, 1865–1900* (1993); Mark W. Summers, *Railroads, Reconstruction and the Gospel of Prosperity* (1984); Orlan J. Svingen, *The Northern Cheyenne Indian Reservation, 1877–1900* (1993); Ronald T. Takaki, *Iron Cages* (1979); Wilcomb E. Washburn, *The Indian in America* (1975), and *Red Man's Land/White Man's Law* (1971); Elliott West, *The Contested Plains: Indians, Goldseekers, & the Rush to Colorado* (1998); C. Vann Woodward, *Reunion and Reaction* (1951).

Biographies

Fawn M. Brodie, *Thaddeus Stevens* (1959); David Donald, *Charles Sumner and the Rights of Man* (1970); Robert W. Larson, *Red Cloud: Warrior-Statesman of the Lakota Sioux* (1997); Erik S. Lunde, *Horace Greeley* (1980); William S. McFeely, *Yankee Stepfather: General O. O. Howard and the Freedmen* (1968), *Grant: A Biography* (1981), and *Frederick Douglass* (1990); Sally M. Miller, ed., *John Muir: Life and Work* (1993); John G. Neihardt, *Black Elk Speaks* (1932); Michael F. Steltenkamp, *Black Elk: Holy Man of the Oglala* (1993); Hans L. Trefousse, *Andrew Johnson* (1989); Robert M. Utley, *The Lance and the Shield: The Life and Times of Sitting Bull* (1993); Joseph D. Wert, *Custer: The Controversial Life of George Armstrong Custer* (1996).

INTERNET RESOURCES

Diary and Letters of Rutherford B. Hayes
http://www.ohiohistory.org/places/hayes/search/index.cfm
The Rutherford B. Hayes Presidential Center in Fremont, Ohio maintains this searchable database of Hayes's writings.

Images of African Americans from the 19th Century
http://digital.nypl.org/schomburg/images_aa19/
The New York Public Library—Schomburg Center for Research in Black Culture site contains numerous visuals.

Freedmen and Southern Society Project (University of Maryland, College Park)
http://www.inform.umd.edu/ARHU/Depts/History/Freedman/home.html
This site contains a chronology and sample documents from several print collections or primary sources about emancipation and freedom in the 1860s.

Andrew Johnson
http://www.whitehouse.gov/WH/glimpse/presidents/html/aj17.html
White House history of Johnson.

Ulysses S. Grant
http://www.whitehouse.gov/WH/glimpse/presidents/html/ug18.html
White House history of Grant.

Indian Affairs: Laws and Treaties, Complied and Edited by Charles J. Kappler (1904)
http://www.library.okstate.edu/kappler
This digitized text at Oklahoma State University includes pre-removal treaties with the Five Civilized Tribes and other tribes.

Native American Documents Project
http://www.csusm.edu/projects/nadp/nadp.htm
California State University at San Marcos has several digital documents relating to Native Americans on this site.

Geronimo
http://odur.let.rug.nl/~usa/B/geronimo/geronixx.htm
This site contains biographical and autobiographical information about this famous Native American who resisted European American domination.

KEY TERMS

Freedmen's Bureau   (p. 450)

Radical Republicans   (p. 451)

Black Codes   (p. 453)

Military Reconstruction Act   (p. 456)

Carpetbaggers   (p. 460)

Scalawags   (p. 461)

Sharecropping   (p. 463)

Ku Klux Klan   (p. 465)
Dawes Severalty Act   (p. 471)
"Compromise of 1877"   (p. 473)

REVIEW QUESTIONS

1. How were the war and Reconstruction's impacts on black and white southerners interrelated, and how did the impacts affect the actions of each?
2. To what extent were white southerners responsible for what they considered to be the harsh conditions of Congressional Reconstruction?
3. Just how radical was "Radical Reconstruction"?
4. What factors led to the decline of Reconstruction?
5. How were white Americans' treatments of African Americans and Native Americans similar, and how did they differ?

17

EMERGENCE AS AN ECONOMIC POWER

AMERICA: LAND OF PLENTY
  Mineral and Geographic Possibilities
  Technological Change
  An Expanding Railroad Network

CREATING A FAVORABLE CLIMATE: THE ROLE OF IDEOLOGY, POLITICS, AND FINANCE
  Social Darwinism and the Gospel of Wealth
  Laissez-Faire in Theory and Practice
  Corporations and Capital Formation

THE RISE OF BIG BUSINESS
  Controlling Competition
  New Managerial Styles and an Expanding Middle Class
  Mass Marketing, Assembly Lines, and Mass Production
  The Power of Bigness

VARIETIES OF ECONOMIC CHANGE IN THE WEST AND SOUTH
  Western Expansion and Exploitation
  The Changing Nature of Farming
  The New South

WORKING IN INDUSTRIAL AMERICA
  The Conditions of Work
  Worker Discontent
  Early Labor Violence
  Unorganized and Organized Labor

"I want to congratulate you on being the richest man in the world"

On a cold winter night in December 1900, 75 of the richest, most influential American businessmen gathered at the New York University Club for a dinner to honor Charles Schwab, president of Carnegie Steel Company. Seated to the honoree's right was J. P. Morgan, the powerful investment banker and consolidator of industry. He had been placed there so that he would not miss a word of Schwab's speech. When Schwab finally spoke, what he delivered was a veiled threat instead of a speech. With pretended innocence he rhapsodized over a bright future of stability and low prices for the steel industry. This future was to be ushered in by the formation of a scientifically integrated firm—one that combined all phases of the industry from the production of raw steel to the manufacture of finished products.

Morgan did not miss the point. Previously, Carnegie Steel had limited its operations to making raw steel. For several years before this dinner Morgan and others had been busily creating trusts among the producers of such finished steel products as tubes and wire. Trusts, which were often-successful attempts to unite smaller competing firms in order to control markets and raise prices, often used this combined power to put remaining competitors out of business. The steel products trusts, however, had a problem. Andrew Carnegie's company was the largest supplier of raw steel and he hated trusts.

When American Tin Plate Company threatened to cancel its orders with Carnegie Steel unless he refused to sell to its competitors, Carnegie decided to beat them at their own game. He joined several informal arrangements to fix prices, known as "pools," only to sabotage them from within. Morgan and his cohorts soon realized that depending on Carnegie for raw steel would doom their consolidation schemes. Consequently, in July 1900 National Tube, American Steel and Wire, and American Hoop canceled all contracts with Carnegie. They were going to produce their own steel or buy it from others—and put Carnegie out of business.

Rather than surrender, Carnegie continued his policy of spending money to make money. He telegraphed instructions to his company's officers: "Crisis has arrived, only one policy open; start at once hoop, wire, nail mills. . . . Extend coal and coke roads, announce these; also tubes. . . . Have no fear as to result, victory certain. Spend freely for finishing mills, railroads, boat lines." Carnegie knew he could produce superior products at cheaper prices. After Schwab assured him that they could manufacture tubes at a price $10 a ton cheaper than National Tube, he decided to pay no dividends on common stock and announced plans to build a $12-million tube plant.

The antiquated and scattered plants of his competitors would have been no match for Carnegie's new ones. Panicked promoters scurried to J. P. Morgan in the weeks before the testimonial dinner. Few doubted Federal Steel president Elbert Gary's assertion that Carnegie could "have driven entirely out of business every steel company in the United States." Carnegie, however, wanted to retire. Schwab's speech was aimed at producing a bargain, not a war. After the dinner Morgan fired dozens of questions at Schwab. Later they held an all-night session at Morgan's house. In the early hours of the next day Morgan finally said, "Well, if Andy wants to sell, I'll buy. Go find his price."

Schwab approached Carnegie on the golf course, where he might be more inclined to cooperate. Carnegie listened, then asked Schwab to return the next day for an answer. At that time Carnegie handed him a slip of paper with his asking price of $480 million written in pencil. When Schwab gave Morgan the offer, he glanced at it and replied, "I accept the price." A few days later Morgan stopped by Carnegie's office, shook hands on the deal and stated, "Mr. Carnegie, I want to congratulate you on being the richest man in the world."

Two of the best had locked in combat, and both emerged victors. Carnegie had his millions to endow libraries, and anything else that struck his fancy. Morgan was able to found United States Steel Corporation which became a colossus even among the existing giants of American industry. It was capitalized at $1.4 billion, a figure three times larger than the annual budget of the United States government. These outcomes for Carnegie and Morgan reflected momentous changes occurring after the Civil War. The

Lavish displays of wealth were common in the business world, as exemplified by this 1901 dinner meeting of officials of the Carnegie Steel Company to celebrate the formation of United States Steel.

United States moved out of the ranks of second-rate industrial powers and became the leader. By 1900 its manufacturing output exceeded the combined totals of Great Britain, France, and Germany. The speed with which this happened seems more suited to fairy tales than reality. As Andrew Carnegie exclaimed in 1886, "The old nations of the earth creep on at a snail's pace; the Republic thunders past with the rush of an express."

Many yardsticks supported his assertion. Between 1870 and 1914 U.S. railroad mileage increased from 53,000 to 250,000—more than the combined railroad mileage of the rest of the world. Almost every sector of the economy grew in multiples of two or more from the 1860s to 1900. Land under agricultural production doubled; the gross national product was six times larger; the amount of manufactured goods per person tripled.

This phenomenal growth had resulted from the foundations laid by antebellum industrial development, the abundance of the land and its people, technological breakthroughs, and a favorable business climate—ideologically, financially, legally, and politically. The rapidity of change first produced chaotic conditions, which eventually led to new managerial styles and finally to economic consolidation and the rise of such supercorporations as United States Steel.

Forces of economic change swept through all sections and all segments of the economy. The profound alterations of the social order that resulted touched virtually every aspect of life. Much of what is now commonplace—electric lights, petroleum products, the telephone, the skyscraper, the hand-held camera, the typewriter—was largely unknown prior to the Civil War. The natures of work and marketing were drastically transformed, affecting all social relationships. The new order produced a few big winners, such as Carnegie and Morgan, but there were more losers.

AMERICA: LAND OF PLENTY

In 1847 Walt Whitman boasted, "Yankeedoodledom is going ahead with the resistless energy of a sixty-five-hundred-horse-power steam engine.... Let the Old World wag on under its cumbersome load of form and conservatism; we are of a newer, fresher race and land. And all we have to say is, to point to fifty years hence and say, 'Let those laugh who win.'" By 1897 Americans were laughing. Their victory was facilitated by the abundance of the nation's new land, new people, and new ideas. Western expansion, increasing immigration, and numerous inventions ushered in a new era.

Mineral and Geographic Possibilities

It wasn't until the nineteenth century that Americans began to realize the vast wealth that their territorial expansion had brought. Most spectacular was the discovery of gold in California in the 1840s. That discovery sparked frenzied prospecting all through the West. Each new discovery led to "rushes," creating mining towns almost overnight. Between 1850 and the 1880s thousands of men and women of almost every ethnic background helped create makeshift social institutions whenever and wherever strikes were made.

Wherever it moved, the mining frontier tended to follow the same pattern. Adventurous optimists would search for the elusive glint of precious metals. After living weeks or months at subsistence level, many would go home poorer. Although a few did strike it rich, inexpensive and inefficient mining methods quickly exhausted the more easily obtainable supplies of precious metals. Extracting ore from beneath the ground and in veins of quartz was expensive. It required large amounts of capital best raised by mining syndicates. Frequently financed by Eastern and European investors, these syndicates bought prospectors' claims for a fraction of their value.

As mining became an organized business, its focus moved to less exotic but more useful minerals such as copper, lead, talc, zinc, and quartz. These fed the growing demands of Eastern industries. By the 1880s mining no longer represented easy riches for pioneering individuals; it had become an integrated part of the nation's modern industrial economy.

Emerging basic industries such as steel and petroleum, and those producing electric power, depended on large supplies of various minerals. New processing techniques to produce steel led to increased demand for iron. Copper became a key resource in such new fields as oil refining, electrical generation and conduction, and telephone communications. A shift from water wheels to coal-burning steam engines sparked a spectacular rise in coal mining.

Even more dramatic was the rise in the importance of petroleum. Many people were aware of large oil reserves in Pennsylvania because it seeped into streams and springs. Early demand was mainly for making patent medicines of dubious value. Encouraged by reports of its potential use as a lighting source and lubricating oil, Pennsylvania businessman George Bissell funded the first drilling efforts. In 1859 his employee, Edwin L. Drake, tapped the first oil well, in Titusville, Pennsylvania. Commonly labeled "Drake's folly," the well marked the beginning of another new industry. Oil was indeed needed to lubricate the increasing number of machine parts, and in the 1870s about 20 million barrels were being produced annually. John D. Rockefeller and others built refineries to refine the oil into kerosene, which was used as a popular form of illumination, displacing candles before it itself was replaced by electricity.

The growing demand led to the search for "liquid gold" in the Southwest. In 1901 a well at Spindletop, Texas, shot a 160-foot stream of oil into the air. New sources of oil led to the development of the gasoline engine in the twentieth century, exemplifying how abundant natural resources and technology often interacted—each shaping the evolution of the other.

Technological Change

Seldom has technology so dramatically transformed so much of people's lives in a single generation. Bewildering as the changes sometimes were in the late nineteenth century, the public generally welcomed new inventions with wide-eyed wonder and nationalistic pride. Many public events were like mass rituals to the new god of technology. Parades and thanksgiving services as well as the ringing of the Liberty Bell greeted the completion of the first transcontinental railway at Promontory Point, Utah, in May 1869. Awed sightseers crammed expositions celebrating "progress." At the 1876 Philadelphia Centennial Exposition, visitors saw for the first time the Corliss engine, bicycles, the typewriter, the elevator, the telephone, and even the "floor covering of the future"—linoleum. By the time of the World's Columbian Exposition at Chicago in 1893, the Corliss engine was obsolete, and many of the miracles of 1876 were commonplace "necessities." The impact of new inventions was enormous. Whereas only 276 inventions were recorded during the Patent Office's first decade, 22,000 patents were issued in the year 1893.

Technological change during the era affected the lives of individuals far more than any political or philosophical development. Offices became mechanized with the invention of the typewriter in 1867 and the development of a practical adding machine in 1888. As clerical work became more necessary and required less skill, it became classed as women's work with lower pay scales. Electric streetcars profoundly changed the character of urban development by accelerating the move to the suburbs.

Innovations in communication unified a collection of island communities into a nation. The com-

The Columbian Exposition of 1893 in Chicago celebrated the enormous technological progress of the late nineteenth century. In the Palace of Electricity many visitors saw their first electric lamp.

pletion of a telegraphic cable across the Atlantic in 1866 increased the nation's links with the rest of the world. New inventions in printing made popular newspapers with wide circulations a reality—along with mass advertising. Photographic advances culminated in George Eastman's Kodak handheld camera in 1888. However, few, if any, inventions rivaled the impact of Alexander Graham Bell's 1876 "toy." Telephones rapidly became necessities—more than 1.5 million were installed by 1900.

The new inventions increasingly relied on cheap and efficient sources of electricity. The names of Thomas Edison and George Westinghouse stand above the rest in this area. Edison began his career peddling candy and newspapers on trains, but he soon became a telegrapher and invented various improvements to it. The success of his ideas convinced him to go into the "invention business." Establishing a research lab at Menlo Park, New Jersey, in 1876, he promised to produce "a minor invention every ten days and a big thing every six months or so." In 1877 he invented the phonograph and in 1879 the incandescent light bulb, as well as hundreds of other devices over the years, such as a better telephone, the dictaphone, the mimeograph, the dynamo, motion pictures, and an electric distribution for lighting transmission. With backing from banker J. P. Morgan, he created the first electric company in 1882 in New York City, and formed the Edison General Electric Company in 1888 to produce light bulbs.

In his Menlo Park, New Jersey, laboratory, Thomas Edison, who eventually obtained over 1000 patents, aimed at practicality in his inventions. He is shown listening to his phonograph in 1888.

Edison's only serious mistake was his choice of direct electrical current, which limited the range of transmission to a radius of about two miles. George Westinghouse developed an alternating current system in 1886 that soon supplanted direct current, forcing even Edison's companies to make the switch. Westinghouse also acquired and improved an electric motor that had been invented by Croatian immigrant Nikola Tesla in 1888.

An Expanding Railroad Network

Americans developed a love/hate relationship with the railroads. The same locomotive that inspired Walt Whitman's rhapsody to its "fierce throated beauty" was described by Frank Norris in 1901 as "the leviathan, with tentacles of steel clutching into the soil, the soulless Force, the iron-hearted Power, the Master, the Colossus, the Octopus." Despite differing visions, no one doubted the importance of the railroads. They played a crucial role in forging a new society, transforming a continent of isolated communities into a unified nation with an interdependent economy. Rails brought raw materials to population centers, making possible large factories that mass-produced goods. Those goods were then shipped to national markets over the same rails.

Early railroads were strictly local affairs, however. Although there were already 35,000 miles of rails by 1865, few lines linked up in any rational way. Having 11 different rail gauges meant that both goods and passengers had to be unloaded from one set of cars and reloaded onto another set—sometimes at a depot on the opposite side of town. Between New York and Chicago, for example, cargo had to be unloaded and reloaded as many as six times.

Unlike many European rail systems, American railroads grew with little advance planning or government regulation, sprouting like weeds in populous areas where immediate profits could be made. While too many railroads served some sections in the East, prior to 1869 there were no transcontinental lines linking the East and West coasts due to the high cost of construction. Large amounts of capital were required in the East but a return on the investment came quickly. In the West railroads often preceded settlement and, therefore, demand for their lines. Transcontinental routes were needed, however, and land grants became the solution. Contemporary and later analysts have questioned the size of those grants, but they undoubtedly had the desired effect. By the turn of the century there were five transcontinental routes.

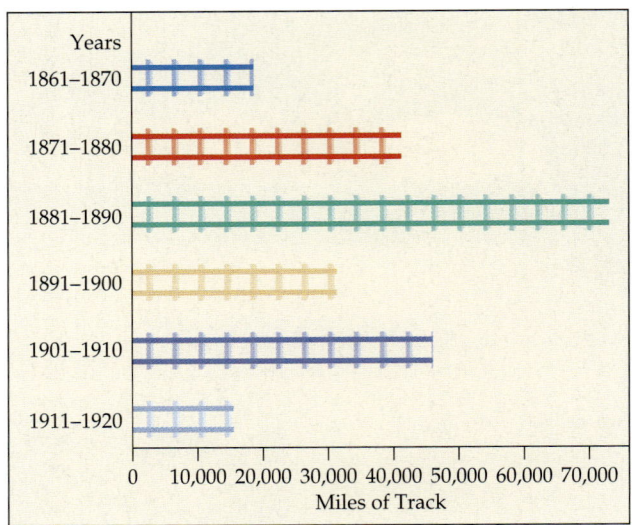

FIGURE 17.1
Railroad Construction, 1861–1920

By 1865 there were 35,000 miles of railroad, but few lines connected in any logical way to provide direct routes from one location to another.
Source: U.S. Bureau of the Census, 1975.

At the same time, after some fierce competitive battles, a few eastern railroad companies gained control of many of the local lines. When the dust settled, there were four main trunklines in the Northeast and five in the Southeast. The average track length of a railroad grew from a mere 100 miles in 1865 to over 1000 miles two decades later. Gauges were also standardized, and a more efficient rail system emerged.

CREATING A FAVORABLE CLIMATE: THE ROLE OF IDEOLOGY, POLITICS, AND FINANCE

An abundant harvest requires good soil, favorable climatic conditions, and adequate fertilization. Materials and machinery were the "seeds" of industrialization, but the bountiful economic harvest of the late nineteenth century depended first on the "good soil" of popular support fostered by intellectual and cultural justifications. Favorable government policies created a desirable "climate," while legal and financial developments provided the needed "fertilizer." The combination produced not only more but also larger industries.

Social Darwinism and the Gospel of Wealth

Expanding economic opportunities fostered cutthroat competition from which fewer and fewer winners emerged. The road to wealth taken by the new captains of industry was strewn with ruined competitors and broken labor movements. Ruthlessness not only seemed to become increasingly necessary, it was also transformed into a virtue by the twin ideologies of **Social Darwinism** and the "gospel of wealth."

For men like Andrew Carnegie the writings of Social Darwinists Herbert Spencer and William Graham Sumner helped relieve unwelcome guilt. "I remember that light came as in a flood and all was clear," Carnegie noted, after reading Spencer's writings. Spencer and his followers applied the biological concepts of Charles Darwin to the workings of society. Natural selection allowed the fittest individuals to survive and flourish in the marketplace. Survival of the fittest supposedly enriched not only the winners but also society as a whole. Human evolution would produce what Spencer called "the ultimate and inevitable development of the ideal man" through a culling process.

According to the Social Darwinists, poverty and slums were as inevitable as the concentration of wealth. Spencer pleaded that "there should not be a forcible burdening of the superior for the support of the inferior." His disciple Sumner declared, "If we do not like the survival of the fittest, we have only one possible alternative, and that is the survival of the unfittest." Both argued that governmental or charitable intervention to improve the conditions of the poor interfered with the functioning of natural law and prolonged the life of "defective gene pools" to the detriment of society as a whole.

The so-called fittest naturally greeted "scientific" endorsement of their elite positions with eagerness. John D. Rockefeller told his Baptist Sunday school class, "The growth of large business is merely the survival of the fittest. This is not an evil tendency in Business. It is merely the working out of a law of nature and a law of God." Some who found the ruthlessness of Social Darwinism unpalatable sought their justification in religious rationales. Since colonial times, the Protestant work ethic had denounced idleness and viewed success as evidence of being among the "elect"—God's chosen people. Building upon this base, apologists constructed the **gospel of wealth**.

Some simply and boldly announced God's sanction of their wealth: Rockefeller asserted, "God gave me my riches." Carnegie produced a written, logically argued rationale: "Not evil, but good, has come to the race," he wrote, "from the accumulation of wealth by those who have the ability and energy that produces it." The masses would waste any extra income "on the indulgence of appetite." "Wealth, passing through the hands of the few," Carnegie wrote, "can be a much more potent force for the elevation of our race than if it had been distributed in small sums to the people themselves." In other words, the "fittest" could best decide what other people needed. In Carnegie's case, he took that responsibility seriously, distributing over

---

THE PEOPLE SPEAK

The Gospel of Wealth

The religious support for wealth is illustrated by Russell Conwell, a lawyer and Baptist minister. This is one version of the "Acres of Diamonds" speech that Conwell gave approximately 6,000 times between 1861 and 1925.

> Money is power, and you ought to be reasonably ambitious to have it. You ought because you can do more good with it than you could without it. Money printed your Bible, money builds your churches, money sends your missionaries, and money pays your preachers, and you would not have many of them, either, if you did not pay them. I am always willing that my church should raise my salary, because the church that pays the largest salary always raises it the easiest. You never knew an exception to it in your life. The man who gets the largest salary can do the most good with the power that is furnished to him. Of course he can if his spirit be right to use it for what it is given to him.
>
> I say, then, you ought to have money. If you can honestly attain unto riches in Philadelphia, it is your Christian and godly duty to do so. It is an awful mistake of these pious people to think you must be awfully poor in order to be pious.
>
> Some men say, "Don't you sympathize with the poor people?" Of course I do, or else I would not have been lecturing these years. I won't give in but what I sympathize with the poor, but the number of poor who are to be sympathized with is very small. To sympathize with a man whom God has punished for his sins, thus to help him when God would still continue a just punishment, is to do wrong, no doubt about it, and we do that more than we help those who are deserving. While we should sympathize with God's poor—that is, those who cannot help themselves—let us remember there is not a poor person in the United States who was not made poor by his own shortcomings, or by the shortcomings of some one else. It is all wrong to be poor anyhow. Let us give in to that argument and pass that to one side.

Source: Russell H. Conwell, *Acres of Diamonds*, 1915, pp. 17–22, Harper & Brothers, New York, NY.

The caption of "What has he done? He laughs and talks in school. He loves to be idle. Does he not look bad?" in *McGuffey's First Eclectic Reader* illustrates the role of education in stressing discipline and hard work.

$300 million to such philanthropic causes as the founding of libraries and the Carnegie Foundation.

Among the most effective apologists for the wealthy were religious leaders of the era. In 1901 Bishop William Lawrence, for example, proclaimed, "Godliness is in league with riches." Not only did the elite deserve their riches, but the poor were responsible for their low status. The eminent preacher Henry Ward Beecher argued that "no man suffers from poverty unless it be more than his fault—unless it be his sin."

Thus, according to both scientific and religious thought, the maldistribution of wealth was not only inevitable but also desirable. Probably more important, though, was the support for this idea provided by popular culture. *McGuffey Readers* stressed the virtue of hard work and its inevitable rewards. Novelist Horatio Alger penned many stories in which the heroes rose from poverty to comfortable middle-class status through a combination of diligence and good luck. Popular literature reinforced the idea that success always came to those who deserved it, in America, the land of opportunity.

Laissez-Faire in Theory and Practice

The prevailing economic theory also lent respectability to greed and to the idea that government should not intervene in the economy. In 1776 Adam Smith presented arguments in *The Wealth of Nations* that would long be used to explain the workings of a free economy and to prescribe government's role in that economy. Smith asserted that the market was directed and controlled by an "invisible hand" composed of a multitude of individual choices. If government did not meddle, competition would naturally lead to the production of desired goods and services at reasonable prices—the natural laws of supply and demand. In short, if everyone were free to act according to self-interest, the resulting economy would be best suited to meet society's needs.

Acceptance of the "invisible hand" of supply-and-demand economic theory naturally led to a policy called **"laissez-faire."** Government was to leave the economy alone and not disrupt the operation of these natural forces. Business leaders naturally endorsed the theory's rejection of governmental regulation, yet they saw no contradiction in asking for government aid and subsidies to foster industrialization. And to a large extent the industrialists got what they wanted—a laissez-faire policy that left them alone, except to help. Ironically, this distortion of theory helped produce an economy where business consolidation wreaked havoc upon the very competition needed for natural regulation of the economy.

Business freedom of action boggles the modern mind. No laws protected the consumer from adulterated foods, spurious claims for ineffective or even dangerous patent medicines, the sale of stock in nonexistent companies, or unsafe and overpriced transportation services. No national regulating agency of any kind existed prior to the establishment of the Interstate Commerce Commission in 1887. The proclamation "Let the buyer beware" asked people to make decisions and choices without enough information to protect their interests.

While denying support and protection to consumers or workers, government at all levels aided businesspeople. Alexander Hamilton's vision of an industrializing nation fostered by favorable governmental action, which had never entirely died, was rejuvenated by the Republican party. In 1860 the

Popular culture at the turn of the century reinforced the American Dream. In the Horatio Alger stories, the hero always escapes poverty through hard work and good fortune and joins the middle class.

party pledged to enact higher tariffs, to subsidize the completion of a transcontinental railroad, and to establish a stable national banking system. The Republican victory undoubtedly helped create a favorable environment for rapid industrialization. There was no sharp break with the past, however, nor did business gain a great victory over agriculture. The pattern of governmental aid to business was, as one historian has noted, "like certain kinds of embroidery . . . boldly visible but not of simple design." No form of aid was without antebellum precedents and most had wide public support. Both the motives behind many actions and their results were mixed. At the same time, agriculture was far from unrepresented and powerless, as can be seen by the passage of the Homestead and Morrill Land Grant acts, which provided free land to settlers and financed agricultural education.

Another government aid to business was the tariff. Tariffs had a long history. At first, such American industries as steel needed to be protected from European competition to survive. Yet even after Carnegie greatly reduced the cost of steel production, the tariff remained. Without foreign competition, businesspeople were able to make higher profits by charging higher prices, which consumers came to resent. Tariffs were nevertheless widely viewed as serving the national interest by fostering economic independence.

Additional forms of subsidy were also meant to serve the public good. Dwarfing all others were the land grants to railroads. During the 1860s Congress granted 20 square miles of public land in alternating sections to the Union Pacific and Central Pacific railroads for each mile of track laid by the two railroads, to spur completion of a transcontinental route. Only the scale of these grants was new—railroads had already received nearly 20 million acres of federal land prior to the war. By the time the grants ended, railroad developers had received a total of 130 million acres of federal land and some 51 million acres of state land. Congress gave all those acres to a handful of people—creating some of America's wealthiest families. In return the government paid only half fare to move troops and supplies, the value of the remaining land increased, and the uniting of the East and West aided the entire economy.

Business also benefited from favorable labor and financial legislation and low-interest loans. Individuals exploited these policies for personal gain, and the results were not uniformly positive. Although never unlimited or unrestricted, aid to business enjoyed wide public support at first. Indeed, nationalism and patriotism accompanied the process of industrialization. Many Americans took pride in the nation's growing economic power. When John D. Rockefeller explained his business activities by saying, "I wanted to participate in the work of making our country great," his words fell on sympathetic ears. Only after the problems of industrialization became more apparent did the public begin to cry "foul."

Corporations and Capital Formation

Although corporations were certainly not new, changes dating from the Jacksonian period paved the way for their postwar domination of the economy. Businesspeople had once been required to apply to a state legislature for a charter; by the 1830s they could incorporate on their own, provided they met certain standards. Following the Civil War, courts also began to affirm the principle of limited

This drawing illustrates the dangers of unregulated patent medicines, and the unpopularity of trusts.

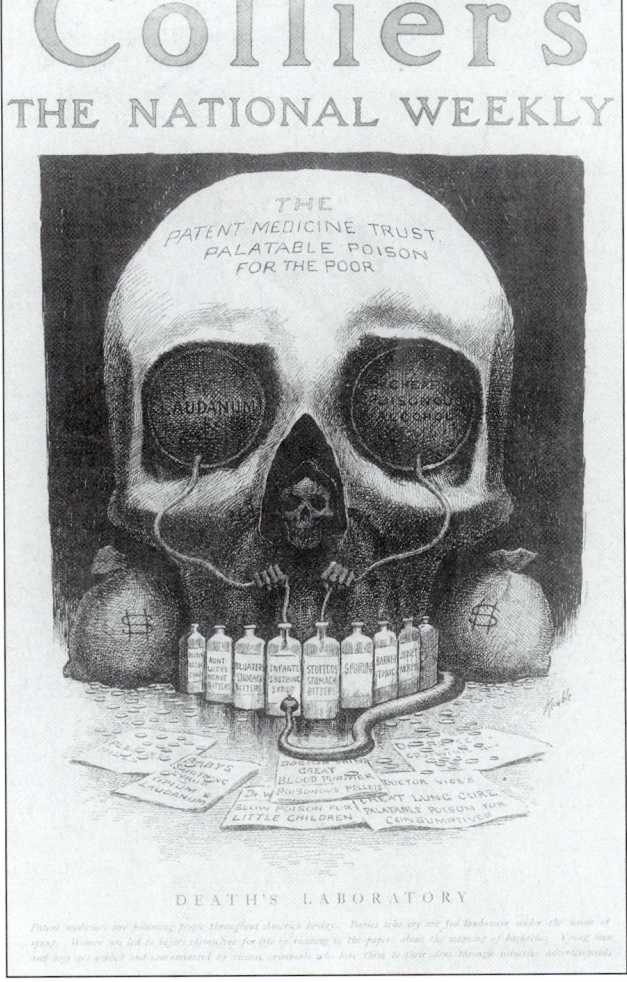

liability. Previously, bankruptcy could bring not only the loss of one's investment but also seizure of personal property by creditors. A corporation's liability eventually became limited to its assets—making investment a safer and more desirable venture. One knew just how much could be lost.

In *Santa Clara County* v. *The Southern Pacific Railroad* (1886) the Supreme Court perverted the Fourteenth Amendment by ruling that a corporation was a legal "person" and therefore entitled to all the protections granted by the amendment, such as equal protection of the law. Corporations were also eventually granted the "right" to "reasonable" profits—to be determined by the courts, not the state.

Corporations not only received "equal protection," they became privileged "persons." Real human beings whose rights were protected by the Constitution were also held responsible for illegal activities. There were no handcuffs or jail cells large enough for "corporate persons." Punishing individuals for corporate crimes was difficult because corporate directors were considered to be merely employees of the company. A popular saying noted that a corporation had "neither a soul to be damned nor a body to be kicked." Such advantages helped spur the growth of corporations—by 1904 almost 70 percent of all manufacturing employees worked for corporations.

Perhaps the greatest advantage of corporations was their ability to raise large amounts of capital. The expansion of industry in the late nineteenth century required big infusions of money. Farmers needed new machinery to increase productivity; manufacturers needed new plants to utilize the latest technology; cities needed new construction to service the needs of the urban population.

From where was all this money to come? Some, of course, was generated by the rising gross national product—the total value of goods and services produced in one year—which grew from $225 per person in 1870 to nearly $500 in 1900. New technology increased productivity and put "extra" money into the hands of middle- and upper-class people–money not required to meet physical needs. Many chose to use the extra money, or capital, to make more money by investing it.

Increasing amounts of this capital were invested in manufacturing partly because investment bankers such as J. P. Morgan marketed corporate stocks and bonds. Foreign investment was also important; by 1900 Europeans had $3.4 billion invested in the United States, which represented approximately one-third of the almost $10 billion invested in manufacturing. This was indeed rich fertilizer for growth.

The net result of the favorable conditions of the late nineteenth century was the industrial supremacy

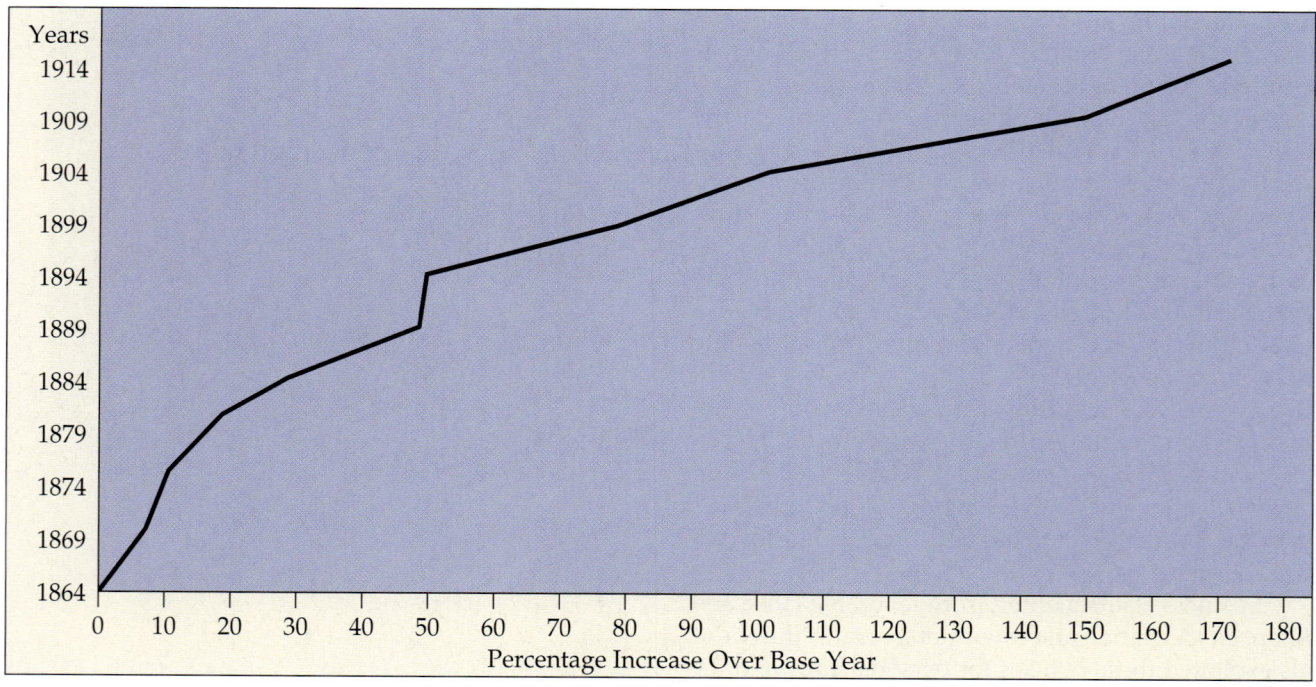

FIGURE 17.2
Index of U.S. Manufacturing Production, 1864–1914

of the United States. Vast mineral wealth, technological breakthroughs, growth of railroads, popular support, beneficial government policies, liberal corporation laws, and the availability of capital fostered this transformation and Americans reveled in it. At first these favorable conditions worked like overfertilized land—too many plants were produced for the available space and resources. This overgrowth created chaos until such entrepreneurs as Andrew Carnegie found ways to prune away their rivals.

THE RISE OF BIG BUSINESS

"You might as well endeavor to stay the formation of clouds, the falling of rains, the flowing of streams, as to attempt . . . to prevent the organization of industry." These words of John D. Rockefeller's attorney described what he considered to be the inevitable domination of entire industries by large corporations. The impact of the consolidation of industry was enormous. As companies grew larger, new management styles and more white-collar workers were needed. Mass production increased—profoundly changing the nature of work for industrial laborers. Giant corporations thus amassed great power over production, people, and politics.

Controlling Competition

Most business leaders did not really advocate free enterprise fueled by competition. To them competition meant chaos, and they sought to eliminate it. J. P. Morgan, one historian wrote, "did not really believe in the free enterprise system, and like most ardent socialists, he hated the waste, duplication, and clutter of unrestrained competition."

After a period of intense competition in the railroad industry, a few rail barons consolidated lines often by using unscrupulous methods, seemingly to carve up the nation at will, as illustrated by this cartoon.

As America's first big business, the railroad industry was also the first to confront the problems of competition. In some regions too many companies were after the same traffic. Some railroads desperately wooed shippers by giving lower rates for bulk shipments and long hauls. They also gave "rebates"—secret kickbacks below their published prices—to some preferred customers. They then sought to make up for that lost revenue by overcharging smaller shippers.

Such tactics did not solve the railroads' problems, however, especially when rate wars broke out. In the 1870s some railroad managers tried cooperation as a cure for competition. They formed "pools," regional federations to divide traffic equitably and to raise rates to increase profits. Pools were not legally enforceable, however, and greed frequently doomed many.

For the railroads, consolidation—often through ruthless tactics—rather than cooperation became the key to controlling competition. The former shipping magnate Cornelius Vanderbilt gained control of the New York Central Railroad in 1867 by buying two key lines that connected with it. He then refused to accept any rail cars going to or from the Central. In response to criticism Vanderbilt replied, "Can't I do what I want with my own?" Elsewhere other buyouts and mergers eventually reduced the number of competitors—especially after the economic depressions of the 1870s and 1890s.

Like the railroads, the oil industry suffered from the proliferation of small companies and dramatically fluctuating prices. John D. Rockefeller, founder of the Standard Oil Company, lamented that "the butcher, the baker, and the candlestick maker began to refine oil." Rockefeller first tried a combination of pooling and rebates to deal with this problem. In 1872 he organized the South Improvement Company—a combine of oil refiners and railroad directors aimed at dividing the oil carriage trade between the railroads. In return for a guaranteed share of the shipments, Rockefeller convinced the railroads to give rebates. Eventually Rockefeller was able to obtain rebates not only on the oil he shipped but also on the shipments of his competitors. Thus Rockefeller could undersell his competitors, whom he often bought out during times of economic depression.

Although such techniques allowed Rockefeller to ultimately control 90 percent of the oil business, legal problems arose from Standard Oil's far-flung holdings. His solution was the *trust*. In 1882 he convinced the major stockholders in a number of refineries to surrender their stock to a board of nine trustees. In return the stockholders received trust certificates that entitled them to a share of the joint profits of all the refineries. Because pools had no legal standing, they could be manipulated by some members to the detriment of other members. In a trust, however, competitive actions were of no benefit. Everyone shared all losses and gains. Soon trusts began popping up throughout the economy.

Andrew Carnegie rose from an immigrant bobbin-boy in a textile mill to control the U.S. steel industry.

Andrew Carnegie disliked pools and trusts, but he found other ways to gain a competitive edge. One of these was **vertical integration**—buying the sources of his raw materials (iron ore and coke) and later many of the transportation facilities needed to distribute his product. He thus was able to bring down his costs and control his supply and shipping costs, resulting in lower final product prices.

The key to Carnegie's success was his ability to cut costs without lowering quality. He used such traditional measures as wage cuts and increased hours for workers, but he also constantly explored new methods of increasing productivity. When told that a plant had broken all records the previous week, he replied "Congratulations! Why not do it every week?" He did not focus only on short-term profits but was willing to invest in expensive new technology to lower long-term costs of production. He reportedly opened one board meeting with the question, "Well, what shall we throw away this year?"

Carnegie often boasted that he knew almost nothing about making steel—he hired experts to do that. He did know how to run a company and make money. By effectively using all the economies of scale available to large firms, Carnegie was able to undersell and destroy most of the steel companies that had sprung up in response to the increased demand from railroads and industry. He also was a master at exploiting downturns in business cycles. Most of his acquisitions were made during economic depressions, when prices were lower. Although competitors and labor movements suffered from Carnegie's actions, the result was better steel at cheaper prices. And cheap steel aided the expansion of the railroads and the rise of other industries.

Of course, Carnegie was well-paid for providing these benefits—receiving around $350 million

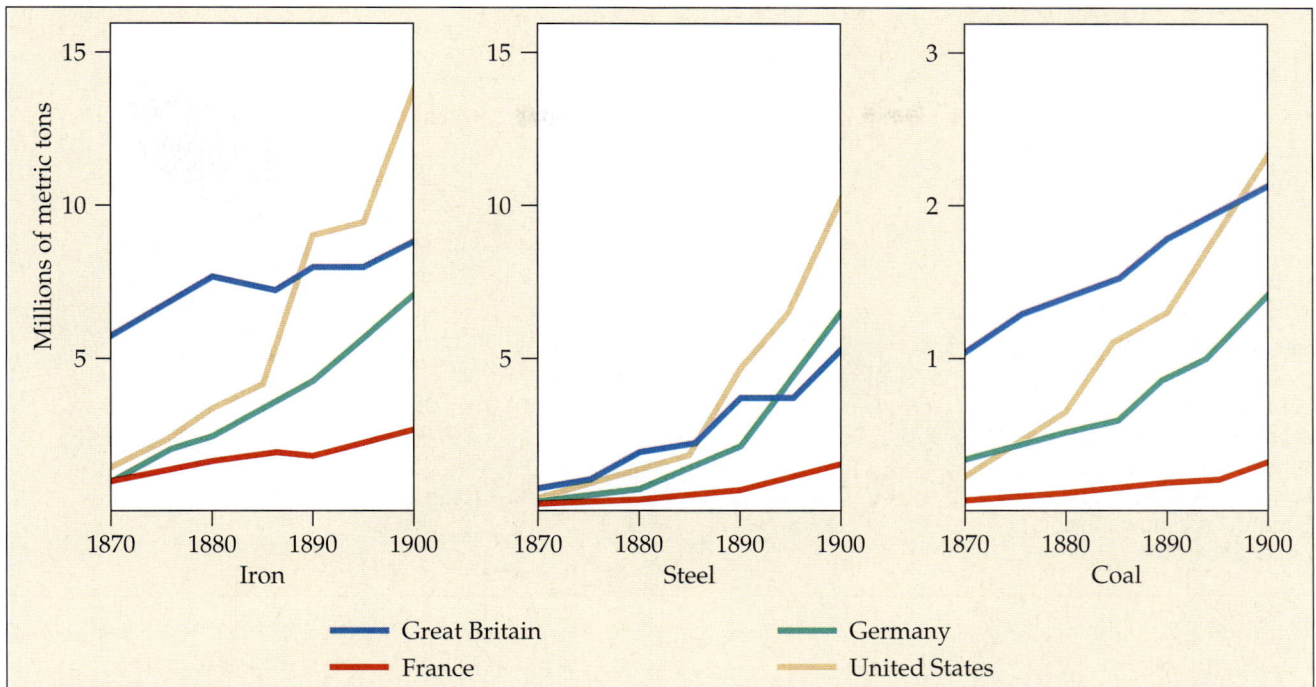

FIGURE 17.3
Iron, Steel, and Coal Production, 1870–1900

Source: Carl N. Degler, The Age of Economic Revolution. Copyright © 1977 by Scott, Foresman and Co.

dollars when he sold Carnegie Steel to J. P. Morgan. That sale illustrates another factor in consolidation: bankers. Morgan and other bankers often stepped in during economic panics to reorganize bankrupt companies. They chewed up failing companies and railroads and spat them out as single supercorporations. The result was a more orderly economy and increased production, but at the price of centralizing vast economic power into the hands of a few unelected individuals. One wit quipped when U.S. Steel was formed: "God created the world in 4004 B.C. and J. P. Morgan reorganized it in 1901."

New Managerial Styles and an Expanding Middle Class

Consolidation into giant corporations created the need for new management techniques, and again the railroads pioneered. As railroad companies grew larger, their activities covered hundreds of miles and employed thousands of workers. Safety and market conditions required that the entire system operate as a single unit under a tight schedule, which caused managerial problems. In the beginning, as one railroad expert wrote, "management had been personal and autocratic; the superintendent, a man gifted with energy and clearness of perception, molded the property to his own will. But as the properties grew, he found himself unable to give his personal attention to everything. Undaunted, he sought to do everything and do it well. He ended by doing nothing."

Railroad management thus required a division of responsibilities and a level of coordination previously unknown in business. Erie Railroad employee Daniel McCallum created the first organizational table for an American company in the 1850s. It had a chain of command moving from local train agents to the president and board of directors, and responsibilities were divided on a functional basis, with top management separate from daily operations. Since railroads also needed better accounting procedures to keep track of the monies collected and paid out, management and accounting of funds became the function of the controller's office.

Other large businesses began to adopt the accounting methods, hierarchical administrative structures, and divisions of responsibilities pioneered by the railroads. "Middle management" was thus created to coordinate the operations of far-flung local plants and bring reports to top executives. Big businesses were now run by bureaucracies

Because the emergence of gigantic trusts concentrated economic power into relatively few hands, many people saw the trusts as the real "bosses of the Senate," as shown in this political cartoon.

staffed by white-collar workers, who had no role in founding the companies they served but who began to work their way up the bureaucratic ladder.

A profound consequence of the new economic order was the expansion of the middle class. Corporations needed accountants, middle managers, clerical workers, and sales representatives. Urban growth created demands for professionals, shopkeepers, and government employees. Between the Civil War and the 1890s the average earnings of the middle class rose nearly 30 percent. By 1900 more than a third of urban families owned their homes. The middle class clearly derived benefits from and had a stake in the new economic order.

Mass Marketing, Assembly Lines, and Mass Production

Both the urban population boom and the transportation revolution created markets unparalleled in vastness and accessibility. But such markets would not have inevitably led to mass production and mass marketing without the public's acceptance of standardized goods. Several factors made Americans more receptive than Europeans to such goods. Class distinctions, although not absent, were more blurred and became increasingly so with the availability of ready-made clothing. Also, physical mobility broke down many of the local loyalties so prevalent in Europe. These factors created opportunities that modern mass advertising was quick to exploit. Nowhere were changes greater than in the food industry.

Food processors originally only produced limited quantities for nearby markets. When transportation advances widened distribution areas, producers used wholesale merchants and agents to sell their goods to the public. Then the communication revolution transformed the marketing of consumer goods. Manufacturers could now peddle their wares directly to the consumer. Rather than selling nonperishable foods by the barrel to wholesalers, they now packaged them in smaller containers of standard size and weight. By 1900, they were spending $90 million annually to convince Americans of the advantages of specific brand names—modern advertising had embarked on its unending quest to shape public tastes.

Meanwhile the same drastic transformation was taking place in the meat-packing business. The railroads again played a key role by opening up the grazing ranges of the Great Plains. Because of its rail network, Chicago quickly became the major funnel through which cattle were distributed from West to East. Cattle were shipped from its Union Stock Yards to slaughterhouses on the outskirts of eastern cities. The meat was then distributed through local butchers to city residents.

A major problem was stock deterioration during long train journeys. Until the advent of the refrigerated car, the only alternative was pickling or curing meat—processes that had made Chicago the pork-packing center but were not as well suited to beef.

Gustavus Swift, a Boston cattle buyer who had moved to Chicago, hired an engineer to design a refrigerated train car for safely shipping fresh meat long distances, with the first successful shipment in

1877. Swift also recognized the possibilities of centralized slaughtering, one of which was using all waste products (horns into buttons, hooves into glue, for example) and thus increasing profits. Eventually he formed glue, fertilizer, soap, and glycerin factories. People said that he used every part of the pig except the squeal.

Swift also pioneered assembly-line mass production. He subdivided the slaughtering and packing process into numerous distinct jobs as carcasses moved along on overhead conveyor belts. There was little wasted motion, and, as one of Swift's superintendents noted, "If you need to turn out a little more, you speed up the conveyor a little and the men speed up to keep pace."

The Power of Bigness

The creation of the gigantic U.S. Steel Corporation was not an isolated occurrence. By 1904 a single firm in each of 50 different industries accounted for 60 percent or more of the total output in that industry. The transition from local, independently owned shops and factories to giant national corporations with impersonal boards of directors dramatically altered the work and leisure time of the American people. For individuals the transition was often painful, and the economy experienced a frightening cycle of boom and bust. Periodic depressions rocked the nation, causing widespread unemployment and business failures.

Big business also created a class of millionaires who flaunted ostentatious homes and lavish life-styles. For example, during the 1897 depression Mr. and Mrs. Bradley Martin gave a costume ball to which they invited most of the richest people in New York. The Waldorf-Astoria Hotel was redecorated to resemble the palace at Versailles in France. The hostess was dressed as Mary, Queen of Scots and wore an enormous ruby necklace that had once adorned Queen Marie Antoinette. One guest came in a $10,000 suit of armor inlaid with gold. Those few hours of entertainment cost the Martins $369,000.

This portrait of the family of William Astor illustrates the lavish life-style of the rich. Their parties were especially ostentatious—at one, guests smoked cigarettes rolled in one hundred dollar bills after drinking coffee.

A drawing of the Bradley Martin ball by an artist for *Harper's Weekly*.

In 1890 about 11 million of the 12.5 million families in the United States averaged less than $380 a year in income, so it is obvious that all did not share equally in the economic expansion of the era. Wealth had always been concentrated and industrialization only continued the trend. In 1890 the bulk of wealth was concentrated in less than 10 percent of the population, while 0.03 percent of the population controlled 20 percent of the wealth. Many people resented or envied the life-styles such wealth provided, and they feared the power it produced.

Government and organized labor remained relatively small while big business grew. Business leaders wielded enormous power over many phases of American life. Some of their actions benefited the nation but were taken in a high-handed manner. For example, to simplify schedules, in 1883 railroad owners established four time zones—without consulting any branch of government. And some of the freewheeling railroad barons only aggravated the fears such arbitrary power raised. Vanderbilt once remarked, "What do I care about the law? Hain't I got the power?" Another time a member of the Pennsylvania legislature reportedly said, "Mr. Speaker, I move we adjourn unless the Pennsylvania Railroad has some more business to conduct."

VARIETIES OF ECONOMIC CHANGE IN THE WEST AND SOUTH

Although most industrialization occurred in the Northeast, all regions of the country experienced profound changes as a national, interdependent economy emerged. Some of the forces feeding the growth of industry also fueled agricultural expansion. Rural population kept growing, although not as rapidly as urban population. Even as the number of farms and farmers more than doubled, farmers became a minority of the population. Most of the new farmers were in the West, where new settlers competed with existing populations to exploit the region's economic potential. Demand by urban dwellers for food sparked a farming revolution made possible by mechanization and scientific agriculture. For a variety of reasons, the South failed to keep pace with the rest of the nation. Despite numerous efforts to forge a "New South," the region's economy failed to keep pace with the rest of the nation.

Western Expansion and Exploitation

Confrontations between miners—the first actors in the drama of western expansion—and Native Americans foreshadowed the eventual expulsion of the American Indians from land that had been "given" to them "forever." But "forever" lasted only until the white men realized the region's true value. From then on, competition for resources among a diverse number of populations marked the history and culture of the West, creating a distinctly American mosaic. Anglo-Americans came to dominate Western economic development, but their lives and how they worked were shaped by earlier Native American and Hispanic societies as well as by African-American and Asian immigrants.

In addition to mineral wealth, the region had two other plentiful resources: grass and cattle. Western ranching was born. At first, ranching did not require much capital. Both the cows and grass were free. By 1860, there were some five million head of wild Texas longhorn, descendants of cattle imported by Spanish colonists. They replaced the buffalo that were being hunted to virtual extinction. Although cattle were so plentiful that they were considered almost worthless in the West, steers sold for $30 to $50 a head in Chicago. All that was needed was a way to get them there. Joseph G. McCoy realized the potential for profit and established the first "cowtown" at Abilene, Kansas, where he built stock pens and loading chutes. Cowboys would "drive" cattle there for shipment by rail to Chicago. Other cowtowns arose as some six million head of cattle were driven to such sites between 1866 and 1888.

Since longhorns were not easily captured or herded on foot, settlers used methods of the Mexican vaquero, the predecessor of the American cowboy. Herding cattle while mounted on horses was hard, dirty work. One participant wrote, "It was tiresome grimy business for the attendant punchers, who travelled over in a cloud of dust, and heard little but the constant chorus from the crackling of hoofs and ankle joints, from the bellows, lows, and bleats of the trudging animals." Romantic stories both glorified and whitened the cowboys, at least one-third of whom were Mexicans and African Americans. The heyday of the working cowboy was brief, however, for ranching, like mining, soon turned into a more organized business.

Profits from a successful drive were very good—about 40 percent. Such figures naturally attracted eastern investors, and soon the use of long cattle drives declined as other ways of producing profit were found. The lean, rangy longhorns, better suited to enduring the long drive than to producing choice, juicy steaks, became even less desirable after traveling long distances. As the rail network expanded into Texas, ranchers switched to breeding the longhorns with superior imported stock to improve the quality of the beef.

Cattle breeders, who needed large tracts of grassland for grazing, usually just appropriated land from the public domain. During this open-range era, high profits attracted even more investors. Eventually the ranchers joined other segments of the economy that were outproducing demand. Beef prices dropped from $30 to $10 a head in 1885 and 1886. Poorer producers fell victim to the low prices, challenges to their land claims from sheepherders and farmers, and bad weather. A winter of terrible blizzards following the scorching summer of 1886 led to the deaths of 90 percent of western cattle.

Battles for supremacy between economic competitors in the West provoked sometimes bloody confrontations. By the 1890s these skirmishes had largely ended, leading some to claim that the "Wild West" was tamed. Those ranchers who remained established legal title to their grazing lands, surrounded them with barbed wire, and practiced scientific breeding and feeding of their stock. The forces of economic consolidation had now reached ranching—making it another business requiring large amounts of capital.

The post–Civil War development of the West initiated a pattern of federal intervention in the management of land and resources to an extent unknown

Joseph A. Glidden's invention of barbed wire provoked range wars between cattlemen and farmers.

in other regions. Laissez-faire economics were never practiced in the West. As elsewhere, government intervention at first helped some more than others. Large tracts of public lands were given away or sold cheaply. Laws enacted to promote socially desirable goals, all had large loopholes that were exploited by cattlemen and land speculators.

The Homestead Act, meant to promote settlement, gave 160 free acres to those who would cultivate it for five years. The Desert Land Act granted 640 acres at $1.25 an acre to anyone who would irrigate the land. The Timber Culture Act, based on the theory that trees increased rainfall, awarded 160 acres to anyone who would plant trees on a quarter of the land. Cattlemen and speculators fraudulently claimed to have met the terms of the grants or hired dummy entrymen to stake claims for them—a bucket of water was sometimes the only basis for claims of irrigation. Lumber barons in California, Nevada, Oregon, and Washington similarly utilized other land-granting laws, such as the Timber and Stone Act of 1878, which allowed people to buy 160-acre plots "unfit for cultivation" and "valuable chiefly for timber" at an incredibly low $2.50 an acre. Thus, much of the newly discovered wealth of the West ended up in the hands of a few winners in the great land lottery.

Before they were transformed into capital-intensive businesses, mining, cattle, and lumber operations offered some quick, easy riches. Farming, however, required more patience to make any profit. By the time farmers arrived in the new West, much of the best land had already been appropriated, although most of the 274 million acres distributed under the terms of the Homestead Act were eventually purchased from speculators and cattlemen by bona fide settlers. Other farmers bought land from the railroads, which was promoting settlement to increase traffic in isolated areas. Railroad companies often provided easy credit terms and extolled western opportunities in flyers and speeches.

Many farming pioneers soon learned that railroad propaganda sometimes overstated the promise of the West. When they arrived, they discovered not only a shortage of wood and water but an overabundance of severe weather, insects, and social isolation. The houses they built of "bricks" cut from

THE American Mosaic

The Wild West

AT 6 P.M. on April 5, 1892, a mysterious train, its shades tightly drawn, pulled out of Cheyenne, Wyoming, the state capital, bound for Casper, 200 miles to the northwest. Aboard the train were 46 vigilantes heavily armed with an impressive array of weapons including army rifles, dynamite, and strychnine. The train had been chartered by Wyoming's cattle kings. The vigilantes' mission: kill Johnson County settlers suspected of cattle rustling.

For more than two decades, the cattlemen had accused homesteaders of land grabbing and cattle theft. Juries refused to convict the small stockmen, so the cattle barons responded by taking the law into their own hands. In one incident, on the night of July 20, 1889, ten cattlemen captured two homesteaders and hanged them from a stunted pine tree. Altogether six or seven suspected rustlers were shot or hanged. Despite lynchings and shootings, the rustling continued. In the summer of 1891, the cattle barons decided to launch an armed invasion of Johnson County and kill the most notorious rustlers. The Wyoming Stock Growers' Association, asked to provide names of suspected rustlers, compiled a list of 70 purported cattle thieves. The invasion was scheduled for the following spring.

On Saturday, April 9, 1892, the vigilantes killed two suspected rustlers at K C Ranch near the southern edge of Johnson County. Word quickly spread to Buffalo, Wyoming, the county seat, 46 miles to the north. There, 200 small stockmen formed a posse to avenge the murders. They caught up with the vigilantes at the T A Ranch, 14 miles south of Buffalo, and surrounded them.

Before they could be captured, however, the cavalry rode to the rescue early on Wednesday, April 13. Wyoming's acting governor and the state's senators had sent frantic telegrams to President Benjamin Harrison declaring that a state of insurrection existed in Johnson County and asking that the U.S. cavalry be sent in to quell the disturbances. The invaders, who included several federal marshals and state officials, were escorted out of Johnson County. Although they charged with first-degree murder, the charges were later dropped. The Johnson County war was over.

Today it is commonly assumed that the roots of violence in American society lie in our frontier heritage of violence and lawlessness. According to popular mythology—disseminated by dime novels, pulp newspapers, and television and movie westerns— the frontier was a lawless land populated by violent men: outlaws, stagecoach robbers, gunslingers, vigilantes, claim jumpers, cattle rustlers, horse thieves, Indian fighters, border ruffians, and mule skinners.

But how violent was the Wild West? Certain forms of violence and lawlessness were indeed common: warfare between Native Americans and whites, attacks on Chinese and Mexican minorities, vigilantism, rowdyism, drunkenness, opium addiction, gambling, vigilante executions, stagecoach robberies, and gunfights. Racially motivated acts of brutality represented the ugliest side of frontier violence. In 1871, in one of the most gruesome incidents, ranchers in California's Sacramento Valley tracked 30 Digger Indians into a cave and shot them, saving the children for last because they "could not bear to kill them with [a] 56-calibre Spencer rifle. 'It tore them up so bad.'" Instead, the children were shot with a 38-calibre Smith and Wesson revolver.

Chinese immigrants faced particular hostility. In Los Angeles, on October 24, 1871, a white mob stormed the city's Chinatown district and murdered between 20 and 25 Chinese men and women. In Rock Springs, Wyoming Territory, on September 2, 1885, a heavily armed white mob attacked the town's Chinatown, set fire to the coal miners' shacks, and shot at fleeing workers, killing 50, 10 percent of the town's Chinese population. A few days later, in Seattle, Washington Territory, a mob killed Chinese hop pickers asleep in their tents. In November, a Tacoma mob routed Chinese immigrants out of their dwellings, loaded them into wagons, and dumped them outside of town.

African Americans and Hispanics also encountered frontier violence. At least 373 black freedmen were lynched or murdered in 40 Texas counties between June 1865 and June 1868. In California, some 15,000 Mexican, Chilean, and Peruvian gold hunters were driven out of the gold fields by threats of lynching, branding, whipping, and ear cropping. Said one white miner: "Give 'em a fair jury trial and rope 'em with all the majesty of the law."

The lack of courts of law and police forces in the West gave rise to frontier committees of vigilance—extralegal committees organized to suppress and summarily punish murderers, counterfeiters, corrupt government officials, and horse and

cattle thieves. In a single year in California, 1855, 47 people were executed by mobs, 9 by legal tribunals, and 10 by sheriffs or police officers. Between 1865 and 1890, 27 vigilante movements that arose in Texas pursued outlaws like John Wesley Hardin. A final wave of vigilantism originated in rural southern Indiana in 1887. Known as the White Cap movement, local rural committees flogged drunks, prostitutes, and men who failed to support their families.

The most notorious perpetrators of frontier violence were the outlaws and gunmen, like Belle Starr, Billy the Kid, Black Bart, Frank and Jesse James, John Wesley Hardin, the Younger brothers, Butch Cassidy and the Sundance Kid, and the Dalton Gang, who held up stagecoaches and trains, robbed banks, and stole horses and cattle. Hardin and the Jameses—who ironically were the sons of ministers—as well as the Younger brothers learned outlaw strategy as Confederate guerrillas during the Civil War. Hardin, who was probably the most prolific murderer, killed over 20 men between 1868, when he was 15, and 1878, when he was finally captured. Frank and Jesse James, America's most renowned bank and train robbers, staged at least 26 daring robberies between 1866 and 1881 in Missouri, taking in half a million dollars. Black Bart (born Charles E. Boles) robbed 27 stagecoaches in 28 attempts in California between 1875 and 1882, using an empty shotgun as his only weapon. Most popular accounts of Western banditry, however, appear to be grossly exaggerated and romanticized. Bat Masterson, who, according to legend, killed 30 men in gunfights, actually killed only 3. Billy the Kid, who supposedly killed 1 man for each of his 21 years of life, also apparently killed only 3.

Kansas's cattle towns, legend holds, witnessed a killing every night. But in fact in Abilene, Caldwell, Dodge City, Ellsworth, and Wichita, a grand total of 45 homicides took place during a 15-year span, 1.5 homicides per cattle trading season, never exceeding five in one year. In Deadwood, South Dakota, where Wild Bill Hickok was shot in the back while playing poker in 1876, only four homicides—and no lynchings—took place in the town's most violent year. And in Tombstone, Arizona, the "town too tough to die" and the site of the shootout at the OK Corral (where Marshall Virgil Earp, his brothers Wyatt and Morgan, and gambler Doc Holliday, hurled the Clanton brothers "into eternity in the duration of a moment") only five men were killed during the city's deadliest year.

Despite the omnipresence of rifles, knives, and revolvers and the prevalence of saloons, gambling houses, and bordellos, rape, robbery, and burglary were relatively rare. "We could go to sleep in our cabins," wrote one miner, "with our bag of gold dust under our pillows minus locks, bolts or bars, and feel a sense of absolute security."

Because of the scarcity of trees on the Plains, both black and white settlers built homes with "bricks" of sod. With walls two to three feet thick, the houses were cozy but gloomy, providing solid protection from the elements.

thick prairie sod were functional but bleak. At first, many farmers managed only to eke out a bare subsistence. Eventually, however, Western farmers were caught up in the dramatic forces of change that had already transformed other sectors of the economy.

The Changing Nature of Farming

By the time Congress passed the Homestead Act in 1862, most of the arable land east of the Mississippi was already taken. The established farmers of the Old Northeast adapted fairly well to the changing economy and were generally prosperous. Most did not try to compete with the new wheat and corn areas of the West. Instead they turned their efforts to supplying the rapidly growing urban areas with fresh vegetables, dairy products, poultry, and pigs. They also profited from rising land values by selling extra acres to residential and industrial developers at high prices. Although they may not have liked all the changes, most received a reasonable share of the fruits of economic expansion. The same could not be said for many farmers in the West and South.

The challenges of farming were much greater in the West. New agricultural techniques and adaptations to the environment were required. The scarcity of trees not only dictated the building of sodhouses but also made the cost of fencing prohibitive. Until the development of barbed wire in 1874, crops were not easily protected from the millions of roaming cattle.

A more serious problem was the lack of water. Farmers came to believe they had found solutions by using new varieties of seed, pumping water from far below the ground surface with windmills, and using cultivation techniques known as dry farming. In reality their success had resulted mainly from abnormally wet summers in the 1870s, as they learned when climate conditions returned to normal. During the good times, however, optimism flourished. As one Kansas official noted: "Most of us crossed the Mississippi with no money but with a vast wealth of hope and courage. Haste to get rich has made us borrowers, and the borrowing has made booms, and the booms have made men wild, and Kansas became a vast asylum covering 50,000 square miles." Then came the droughts. By 1900 two-thirds of the homesteaders had failed, and farmers returned east with signs saying, "In God We Trusted; in Kansas We Busted." Westerners learned earlier than many Americans that the environment can't always be conquered.

In the South, the Civil War had crippled agriculture. Wartime devastation destroyed half the region's farm equipment and killed one-third of its draft animals. The death of slavery also ended the plantation system. The number of farms doubled from 1860 to 1880, but the number of landowners remained the same. The size of the average farm dropped by more than half, as sharecropping and tenancy rose. At the very time the rest of the economy was consolidating, Southern agriculture was marching off in the opposite, less efficient direction. A shortage of cash forced Southern farmers to borrow against future crops. Crop liens and high credit costs kept a lot of black and white farmers trapped in a cycle of debt and poverty.

Although many Plains and Southern farmers were losers in the changing economy, both winners and losers were playing essentially the same game—

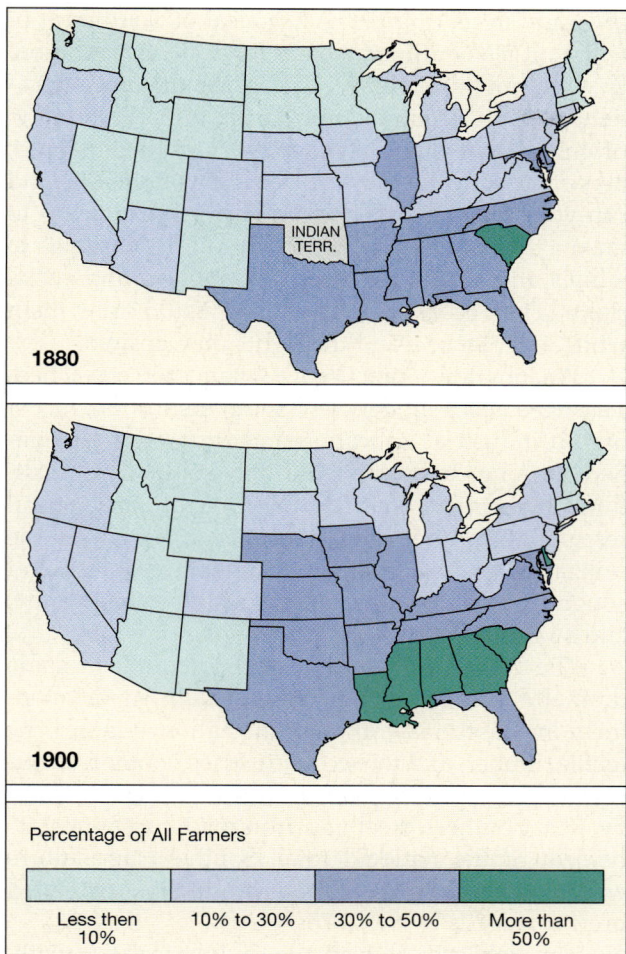

Rise of Tenancy

dramatically as they had in factories. After the mechanization of wheat farming, the hours required to farm one acre dropped from 61 to 3, and the per acre cost of production fell from $3.65 to $0.66. Machines entered every phase of agriculture, and farmers began to learn "scientific agriculture" at land-grant colleges that Congress had established under the Morrill Land Grant Act of 1862. Researchers, at agricultural experiment stations (funded by the Hatch Act of 1887) explored ways to increase production and found new uses for overabundant crops. Farmers were not opposed to all government aid to the economy.

Mechanization brought economies of scale to agriculture, but they were not as easily exploitable. Although some bonanza farmers in the Dakotas cultivated 100,000 acres and more, the average farm remained at 150 acres. The farms of the West were usually much larger than average because dry-farming techniques produced low yields per acre. To succeed, then, Western farmers needed more acres and more machines to work those acres; both cost money. Thus, like businesspeople, farmers needed access to capital. Unable to sell shares in their enterprise, most obtained personal loans using their land, machinery, and crops as collateral. As production increased, however, prices fell; to counteract lower profits farmers further expanded production in a self-defeating downward spiral. Mortgage indebtedness grew two and a half times faster than agricultural wealth.

One solution to overproduction was to expand markets, which required cheap and reliable transportation facilities. Railroads, therefore, had as much impact in agriculture as in industry. Instead of selling surplus food to the local cobbler, American farmers fed distant urban masses at home and abroad; 20 percent of agricultural production was exported. Thus farmers' profits now hinged on many factors beyond their control—such as the size of harvests in Argentina. Marketing became a key to success. One farm editor declared: "The work of farming is only half done when the crop is out of the ground."

Most farmers at first celebrated their status as businesspeople. Agricultural expansion initially was as dramatic as that of industry, but then farmers began to lose ground. In 1860 farmers owned 50 percent of the nation's wealth and received 30 percent of the national income. By 1910 those figures had dropped to 20 and 18 percent, respectively, and farmers were becoming a minority of the population. When they realized that they could not adapt as well as industri-

the commercialization of farming. As in manufacturing, the elements were specialization, new technology, mechanization, expanded markets, heavier capital investment, and reliance on interstate transportation. At first many changes were wholeheartedly embraced by farmers.

Most farmers agreed with a farm journal's assertion: "Agriculture, like all other business, is better for its subdivision, each one growing that which is best suited for his soil, climate, and market." Specialization became apparent in the decline of subsistence farming and the growing importance of cash crops, although general farming continued. Outside of the South, small gardens and stock raising usually supplemented cash crops. In Dixie, however, cotton reigned supreme, and landowners and merchants often forced tenant farmers to plant all available acres with cotton.

Technology revolutionized agriculture as inventions increased productivity on the farms as

alists to the new economic order, farmers began to assert the superiority of rural culture. However, their functions were far removed from that of the independent, self-sufficient yeoman farmer.

The New South

Like the farmers, many Southerners wholeheartedly endorsed the new economic order at first. Some even saw the South's salvation in the destruction of slavery, proclaiming the emergence of a **"New South."** Henry W. Grady, editor of the *Atlanta Constitution*, wrote and traveled extensively to proclaim the region's unlimited opportunities. Grady envisioned three major changes from the Old South: diversified farming, industrialization, and racial accommodation and cooperation. To win support for these changes, New South spokesmen linked the new order to the virtues of romanticized versions of the Old South and the "lost cause" of the Confederacy. Confederate heroes were named to boards of directors and appeals to Southern nationalism were made. The defeated South was encouraged to take up a new battle—for industrial supremacy. As one historian wrote, the "romance of the past was used to underwrite the materialism of the present."

At the Cotton States Exposition of 1895 in Atlanta, an African-American spokesman for the New South emerged. Booker T. Washington, principal of Tuskegee Normal and Industrial Institute in Macon County, Alabama, was asked by the exposition's white organizers to give an address. His speech, known as the "Atlanta Compromise," rivaled those of Grady in its optimistic appraisal of Southern potential. It also outlined a basis for racial cooperation. If whites would allow African Americans educational and economic opportunity, Washington promised that blacks "will buy your surplus land, make blossom the waste places in your fields, and run your factories." He urged African Americans to make themselves economically indispensable to whites and forego agitation for political and social rights. Their economic importance would bring them white acceptance—and the rights they desired.

Washington practiced what he preached. Tuskegee was a model New South institution, focusing on industrial education and promoting diversified farming. It boasted the only all-black agricultural experiment station. Director of agricultural research, George Washington Carver, advocated the utilization of undeveloped Southern resources and sought to expand markets for such crops as peanuts and sweet potatoes.

The New South optimism was based on some dramatic changes in the region. Railroad development increased faster than in the nation at large. The textile, timber, and tobacco industries boomed. Birmingham grew into a major producer of raw steel, and by 1890 Southern steel and iron made up almost 20 percent of the national total. Southern agriculture was also recovering—cotton production exceeded prewar records by the 1870s.

The tobacco and textile industries especially seemed to bring the dream of industrialization to life. Both were based on major Southern crops. In the 1880s, James B. Duke introduced the cigarette industry to the region, following a path similar to that of

Booker T. Washington's close ties to business and political leaders are illustrated by this photo of Washington with (from left to right) Robert C. Ogden, President William Taft, and Andrew Carnegie.

other captains of industry. Duke was a North Carolina tobacco grower when he encountered in 1881 a machine that rolled cigarettes. He bought the patent and proceeded to change American tastes to suit his purposes. Previously, most tobacco users either chewed the weed or smoked pipes or cigars. Duke enclosed "trading cards," featuring pictures and stories of popular heroes, in packs of cigarettes to lure youngsters into smoking. At the same time he was buying out competitors. In 1890 he created a trust through which he controlled 150 companies in an almost perfect monopoly until 1911, when federal antitrust actions disbanded the trust.

Though entirely homegrown, Duke's enterprise had no distinctly Southern characteristics. The same was not true of the textile industry. Its development was flavored with a kind of regional revivalism and paternalism. A good example was the founding of Salisbury Cotton Mills. In 1887 the town of Salisbury, North Carolina, had done little to recover from the war. It was poor, dirty, and full of saloons. Then a lean, intense Tennessee preacher named Mr. Pearson came to town and set up a big tent, and preached that Salisbury needed to go to work. Idleness had bred corruption; building a cotton mill was the most Christian act his hearers could perform. The result was Salisbury Cotton Mills.

The evangelical appeal of the cotton mill crusade tended to create a myth that the mills were mainly built and run to aid the lower classes. The creation of "mill towns" helped to promote the image of mill owners as "fathers" to their employees. The company built houses, stores, schools, and even churches for the workers. In reality, many mill owners proved not to be such good fathers. By local custom African Americans were excluded from the textile mills. Mill workers tended to be poor whites; often an entire family worked an average of 12 hours a day. Wages were as low as 50 cents a day and were usually not paid in cash, but in "trade checks." The trade checks were accepted as rent for company houses or to buy goods in company stores. Some merchants and landlords would not accept the checks at face value. So some mill workers never saw any cash. They merely turned their trade checks back over to the mill owners in return for supplies and housing. The result was high profits that caused the textile boom in the South—the number of mills grew from 161 in 1880 to 400 in 1900.

Despite all these signs of progress, major obstacles prevented the South's economy from keeping pace with that of the rest of the nation. Southern agriculture remained trapped in the inefficient sharecropping system and in single-crop agriculture. By 1880 the South was not growing enough food to feed its people. Poor nutrition thus added bad health and disease to the region's problems.

The persistent ideology of white supremacy not only doomed Booker T. Washington's vision of African-American advancement but also helped keep the South mired in poverty. Race relations actually worsened in the 1890s as white Southerners struggled to keep black Southerners "in their place" (see Chapter 19). In 1896 the Supreme Court ruled in *Plessy v. Ferguson* that separate accommodations for African Americans did not violate the Fourteenth Amendment if the facilities were substantially equal in quality. The effect was to legalize segregation—a disaster for both black and white Southerners. Accommodations were never really equal, and African Americans suffered from inferior schools and services. At the same time, keeping most of the black third of the Southern population in ignorance and poverty depressed wage scales and the tax base needed to support public education and other services.

Another key to the South's relative poverty was its shortage of capital. Reliance on slavery and cotton had enriched the Old South but helped impoverish the New South. While the North was using its capital to build canals, railroads, cities, and factories, the South used its profits to buy more slaves. Emancipatio meant the loss of about $4 billion, and the Civil War brought devastation. Before the war the South had seen little reason to use its capital to build factories and cities. After the war, it no longer had the capital to do those things.

Southerners sought to attract outside investment by means of industrial expositions and hundreds of publications and speeches, as well as by tax exemptions and land grants. In the late nineteenth century, Northern dollars did flow south, replacing Sherman's armies. However, the use of Northern capital in most industries also meant that the profits went to Northerners as well. A good example of how this worked is what happened to the timber industry. In the postwar era, over 60 percent of the nation's forests were located in the South. A growing demand for lumber to build cities thus made timber the region's leading industry and number one employer. Yet in the end, the South was probably left poorer rather than richer by the exploitation of its timber.

Corrupt state governments allowed Northerners and foreigners to obtain vast tracts of timberland at prices far below their actual value. Temporary logging camps were set up and manned mainly by low-paid African-American workers, who were, in the words of one visitor, "single, homeless, and possessionless." Once an area was stripped of its trees, the camp moved on to a new one. The overcutting of

Southern forests destroyed many of them and created erosion and flooding problems. Most of the timber was turned into raw lumber at sawmills and sold to Northern factories to be made into finished products. Only in North Carolina did a significant furniture industry develop. The South therefore remained in a colonial economic position by selling unfinished raw materials, such as lumber, at low prices to the North to be converted into manufactured goods, goods that it had to buy at prices higher than it had received for the raw materials.

For all the above reasons the South's progress did not alter its position at the bottom of the economic ladder. Although its share of national manufacturing doubled between 1880 and 1920, it rose only to 10 percent of the total—roughly the same percentage it had at the start of the Civil War. Per capita income increased 21 percent, but fell from 60 percent of that of the North in 1860 to 40 percent in 1900. As in the West, the South's reliance on Northern capital kept the majority of profits going elsewhere. By the late 1880s farmers in both regions, however, would unite to oppose the changes brought by industrial capitalism.

WORKING IN INDUSTRIAL AMERICA

In the post—Civil War era, perhaps no group experienced more changes than the working class. Factories sprang up near or in cities, whose populations were being swelled by rural immigrants from both abroad and the farmlands of America. City life and factory work profoundly changed the lives of these new arrivals. For many the transition was extremely painful; they were being asked to transform radically their visions of themselves and their places in the world.

The Conditions of Work

Was it worth it? Was the price paid of industrialization worth the benefits native-born and immigrant labor received? This is not a simple question to answer. In fact, each laborer might have answered it differently, since wages played an important role in a laborer's attitude. In general, wages rose and prices fell during the late nineteenth and early twentieth centuries. Exactly how much is a question of heated historical debate. One economic historian estimated that when adjusted for changes in the price level, real annual earnings increased from approximately $300 in 1860 to more than $425 in 1890. Other historians believe those estimates are overly optimistic, contending that wages tended to stagnate, especially in the large textile industries. All, however, admit that the pace of wages and earnings lagged well behind the spectacular growth in the American economy.

Even with modest improvements in wages, laborers continually battled poverty. More often than not, the prosperity of a family depended on how many members of that family worked. Carroll D. Wright, chief of the Massachusetts Bureau of the Statistics of Labor, expressed the matter plainly in 1882: "A family of workers can always live well, but the man with a family of small children to support, unless his wife works also, has a small chance of living properly." The material quality of life often depended more on circumstances than on occupation or wages.

Take, for example, two hard-working union coal miners who earned $1.50 a day and were studied in 1883 by the Illinois Bureau of Labor Statistics. The first worked only 30 weeks in 1883, and his total income was $250. He lived with his wife and five children in a $6-per-month, two-room, crowded but neat tenement apartment. During the year, he spent only $80 on food, mainly bread, salted meat, and coffee. His income was barely enough to allow his family to maintain a minimal standard of living. His existence was precarious: strikes, layoffs, sickness, or injury could easily throw him and his family into abject poverty.

The second miner worked full time in 1883 and earned $420. He had a wife and four children, three of whom were also miners, and who brought home an additional $1000. They all lived comfortably in their own six-room house perched on an acre of land. They ate well, spending $900 a year on food—steak, butter, potatoes, bacon, and coffee comprised a typical breakfast. They bought books and enjoyed a full leisure life.

In many working-class families, fathers and sons, mothers and daughters, and often aunts, uncles, and grandparents—all contributed to the family economy. Carroll D. Wright in the United States Census of 1880 warned, "the factory system necessitates the employment of women and children to an injurious extent, and consequently its tendency is to destroy family life and ties and domestic habits, and ultimately the home." In truth, however, the opposite was probably true. Economically, families worked as a single entity; the desires of any individual often had to be sacrificed for the good of the family. Far from destroying the family, working for the family economy often strengthened it.

During the first decade of the twentieth century, social workers conducted numerous studies to determine how much money was needed to sustain a typical working-class existence for a year. Estimates for

A family economy was an important part of survival in America in this time period. This family earned extra money by arranging artificial flowers at home.

New York City ranged between $800 and $876 for a family of four, $505 for a single man, and $466 for a working woman. Many of New York's laborers fell painfully below the recommended minimum, and single women lived particularly difficult lives. In New York women earned about half as much as men—the majority made less than $300 per year. One woman worker described her meager existence: "I didn't live, I simply existed. I couldn't live that [which] you could call living.... It took me months and months to save up money to buy a dress or a pair of shoes.... I had the hardest struggle I ever had in my life."

Conditions for African Americans, Asians, and Mexicans in America were even worse. They were given the most exhausting and dangerous work, paid the least, and were fired first during hard economic times. For a black sharecropper farming a patch of worked-over soil in Mississippi, or a Chinese miner carrying nitroglycerin down a hole in a Colorado mountain, or a Mexican working on a Texas ranch, $300 per year would have seemed a kingly sum.

There were clear divisions among workers. At the top were the highly skilled laborers. Mostly English-speaking, generally Protestant, and almost exclusively white, they were paid well, had good job security, and considered themselves elite craftsmen. Below them were the semiskilled and unskilled workers, most of whom were immigrants from southern and eastern Europe, spoke halting if any English, and were Catholics or Jews. They lacked job security and had to struggle for a decent existence. At the bottom were the nonwhite and women workers, usually semi- and unskilled, for whom even a decent existence was normally out of reach.

Hours of work varied widely. Long hours were not new—farm workers and artisans often labored from sunup to sundown. The tempo and quality of their labor was different, however. During summer months and harvest season, the work was intense, but it slowed down during the shorter days of winter. There was always time for fishing, horse racing, visiting, and tavern-going. Preindustrial workshops similarly mixed work with fellowship. If the workdays were long, they were also sociable. As they worked, laborers talked, joked, laughed, and even drank.

Nor was time measured out in teaspoons. Punctuality was not the golden virtue it became during industrialization. In the early nineteenth century, household clocks were rare and many of them possessed only a single hand. Cheap, mass-produced pocket watches did not become readily available until the Civil War. Certainly the idea of punching a time clock was alien to the preindustrial worker, who might think in terms of hours but not minutes.

Preindustrial labor, then, was done in a more relaxed atmosphere. This is not meant to romanticize it. Farm work and shop labor could be hard and dangerous, but there were not sharp lines between labor and leisure. Gambling, storytelling, singing, debating, and drinking formed a crucial part of the workday. Thrift, regularity, sobriety, orderliness, punctuality—hallmarks of an industrial society—were virtues not rigorously observed.

The new concept of time changed not only how people worked but also how they regarded the worker. The most prominent feature of nineteenth- and early twentieth-century New England mill towns was the giant factory bell towers. Before clocks and watches, the bell towers served a utilitarian function. They told the laborers when to get out of bed, be at work, eat lunch, and go home. The importance of time was literally drilled home in a brochure prepared by the International Harvester Corporation to teach Polish laborers the English language. "Lesson One" read:

> I hear the whistle. I must hurry.
> I hear the five minute whistle.
> It is time to go into the shop.
> I take my check from the gate board and hang it on the department board.
> I change my clothes and get ready to work.
> The starting whistle blows.
> I eat my lunch.
> It is forbidden to eat until then.

Factory owners demanded standards of work, behavior, and punctuality that left the industrial worker little leisure time or energy. Workers campaigned unsuccessfully for an eight-hour workday during the late nineteenth century.

that stated their goal. "Eight Hours for Work, Eight Hours for Rest, Eight Hours for What We Will." A popular song of the day captured the ideal.

> We mean to make things over;
> We're tired of toil for naught;
> We may have enough to live on,
> But never an hour for thought.
> We want to feel the sunshine,
> We want to smell the flowers;
> We are sure that God has willed it,
> And we mean to have eight hours.

The reality, however, fell far short of this ideal. It is difficult to generalize about hours since they varied considerably from occupation to occupation. In 1890, for example, bakers averaged over 65 hours a week, steelworkers over 66, and canners nearly 77. Even as late as 1920, skilled workers still averaged 50.4 hours a week and the unskilled 53.7 hours. Before the 1930s, workers regarded an 8-hour day or even a 10-hour day as an unattainable dream.

The new ideals of industrial America created even more work for women. The increased emphasis on cleanliness led to a demand for tidier homes. As a result, women now devoted more time to cleaning, dusting, and scrubbing. New washable cotton fabrics increased the amount of laundering. And more varied diets meant women spent more time plucking feathers from chickens, soaking and blanching hams, roasting coffee beans, grinding whole spices and sugar, and cooking meals. By 1900 the typical housewife worked six hours a day on just two tasks: meal preparation and cleaning—in addition to the time she already spent on other household tasks.

Worker Discontent

Although workers complained regularly about wages and hours, they were equally disturbed by several other aspects of industrialization. The late-nineteenth-century industries differed from the preindustrial workshop in four important areas: size, discipline, mechanization, and displacement of skill. The huge new factories, employing hundreds or even thousands of laborers, needed an organized, disciplined workforce. Workers were carefully regulated to ensure maximum productivity. Work itself became formalized and structured, and several levels of bureaucrats separating the owner from workers emerged. There was an incredible boom in productivity, and the informal preindustrial workshop,

> The whistle blows at five minutes of starting time.
> I get ready to go to work.
> I work until the whistle blows to quit.
> I leave my place nice and clean.
> I put all my clothes in the locker.
> I must go home.

The lesson also perfectly describes the ideal industrial worker: punctual, hardworking, clean, and sober.

Given this new standard of work and time demanded by factory owners, laborers were reluctant to work the preindustrial dawn-to-dusk workday. In 1889 hundreds of trade unionists paraded through the streets of Worcester, Massachusetts, behind a banner

with its handful of employees, was an inevitable casualty.

Mechanization also caused an erosion of certain skilled trades. Newly invented machines performed tasks previously done by skilled artisans. For example, once a single tailor took a piece of cloth, cut it, fashioned it, and sewed it into a pair of pants; by 1859 a Cincinnati clothing factory had divided the process into 17 different semiskilled jobs. This replacement of highly skilled by semiskilled workers was characteristic of the factory system. By the end of the century, it appeared to many observers that *all* work was being mechanized and moving toward a factory mode. Even farmers followed the mechanization march. By the early 1880s, one Dakota Territory wheat farm—or "food factory" as a critic called it—stretched over 30,000 acres, used 20 reapers and 30 steam-powered threshers, and employed 1000 field hands. Workers did not know their bosses, but this impersonality was offset by a remarkable increase in output.

In the long run, industrialization brought much to many. From a worker's perspective, however, industrialization was often an inhumane process. Factory labor tended to be monotonous, and machines made work more dangerous. Industrial accidents were alarmingly common—careless or tired workers sacrificed fingers, hands, arms, and sometimes even lives. Frequent production speedups increased the chances of injury. In one year at Armour's meat-packing plant in Chicago, 22,381 workers were injured or became ill. Conditions were much the same at Swift's meat-packing plant.

To make matters even worse, owners concerned with production quotas and cost efficiency, often assumed an uncaring attitude toward their laborers. Many were indeed insensitive. One factory manager even proclaimed, "I regard my people as I regard my machinery. So long as they can do my work for what I choose to pay them, I keep them, getting out of them all I can. What they do or how they fare outside my walls I don't know, nor do I consider it my business to know. They must look out for themselves as I do myself."

Where once it was workers who determined their production and work pace, factory managers with stopwatches now made laborers account for their time by seconds. Workers particularly resented scientific time-motion experts who strove to get the maximum production out of every laborer. Frederick W. Taylor, the father of "scientific management," believed that his ideas benefited labor as well as management. Instead, his aim "to induce men to act as nearly like machines as possible" promoted monotony and displaced workers—especially skilled ones.

Workers did not passively accept industrialization and the changes it caused. They resisted change at almost every step and they had formidable weapons at their disposal. On one level, resistance entailed a simple, individual decision not to change completely. Despite demanding a steady, dependable workforce, factory managers were plagued by chronic absenteeism. Immigrant workers refused to labor on religious holidays, and in some towns factories had to shut down on the day the circus arrived. Across America, heavy drinking on Sunday led to "blue Monday," a euphemism for absenteeism.

Another form of individual protest was quitting. Most industrial workers changed jobs at least every three years, and in many industries the annual turnover rate was over 100 percent. Some quit because they were bored, "forced to work too hard," or because they were struck by spring wanderlust and simply wanted to move on. Others quit because of severe discipline, unsafe working conditions, or low wages. This compulsive quitting was a clear indication that perhaps 20 percent of the workforce never came to terms with industrialization.

Workers were similarly quick to take collective action. The late nineteenth century witnessed the most sustained and violent industrial conflict in the nation's history. Strikes were as common as political corruption during the period—Bureau of Labor Statistics estimated that 9668 strikes and lockouts occurred between 1881 and 1890. Although most of these conflicts were relatively peaceful, some were so

Workers at Swift's meat-packing plant wield huge cleavers as they impassively go about their tasks. A slip of the cleaver could mean the loss of a limb or even a life.

violent that citizens across the nation feared that America was moving toward another revolution.

Early Labor Violence

An early, violent conflict occurred in the anthracite coal region of eastern Pennsylvania. During the depression of the mid-1870s, mine owners agreed to cut wages and increase workloads in the mines. This sort of oppression was nothing new to the Irish, and they responded much as they had in the Old Country, Ireland. While the Workingmen's Benevolent Association (WBA) battled owners at the negotiating table, the Ancient Order of Hibernians, a secret fraternal society of Irish immigrants, and its inner circle, the Molly Maguires, waged a violent guerrilla war in the coalfields in 1877. They disrupted the operation of several mines and attacked a handful of mining officials.

The mine owners infiltrated the group with a secret agent, James McParlan, who agreed to inform on his fellow Irishmen for the Pinkerton agency. While McParlan was gathering information, the WBA went on strike. Disorder and violence followed. Through the local press, management convinced much of the community that there was a direct link between the WBA, the Mollies, and the bloodshed. The tactic worked and the strike was broken. A short time later, McParlan's testimony was used to destroy both the Mollies and the WBA. Altogether, 20 Mollies were convicted and executed after sensational trials. It was a scenario that industrialists would use again and again. Their greatest weapon against strikers was the community's fear of violence.

The same depression that convulsed the Pennsylvania coalfields shook the rest of the country. To keep from going under, many businessmen cut rates and attempted to recoup their losses by reducing labor costs. This was true especially in the highly competitive railroad business. Workers, most often unskilled, suffered repeated wage cuts. Workingmen, one railroad worker declared in 1877, "know what it is to bring up a family on ninety cents a day, to live on beans and cornmeal week in and week out, to run in debt at the stores until you cannot get trusted any longer, to see the wife breaking down under privation and distress, and the children growing up sharp and fierce like wolves day after day because they don't get enough to eat." That knowledge drove many workers to desperate lengths.

During the dog days of mid-July 1877, the Baltimore and Ohio Railroad (B&O) announced its third consecutive 10 percent wage cut. Angry, frustrated, hot, and hungry railroad workers along the line, led by the new Trainmen's Union, went on strike. When trouble followed, B&O workers seized an important junction at Martinsburg, West Virginia. The state militia and local sheriffs sympathized with the workers but could not end the strike. President Rutherford B. Hayes sent in federal troops to protect an army of strikebreakers.

From Martinsburg the strike spread. Railroad workers walked off their jobs, and trains sat unused. The strike paralyzed transportation in the Midwest and much of the industrial Northeast. Violence and destruction seemed to be everywhere. In Baltimore the state militia shot into a mob and killed ten persons; in Pittsburgh rioters burned 2000 freight cars, looted stores, and torched railroad buildings; in Buffalo, Chicago, and Indianapolis workers and police engaged in bloody battles.

When local police and state militiamen failed to control the situation, President Hayes ordered more federal troops in to do the job. Eventually, superior force restored peace and the trains started rolling again, but not before more than a hundred strikers were killed. Like most spontaneous strikes, the Great Strike of 1877 failed. But the anger it revealed frightened America. Although some authorities labeled the disturbances as the work of communist agitators, more thoughtful observers knew workers had legitimate grievances. For owners and workers alike, the strike was a lesson. Owners learned that workers were not merely passive partners in the industrial process. Labor learned that when pressed, the federal government was not neutral—it would side with capital.

At the same time, economic consolidation increased the power of industrialists such as Carnegie,

The Great Railroad Strike, 1877

During the spontaneous uprising that followed the railroad strike of 1877 two-thirds of the nation's track was paralyzed for two weeks and millions of dollars worth of railroad property was destroyed.

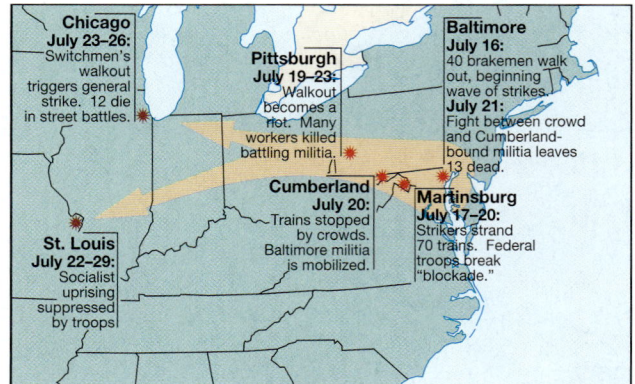

The famous Haymarket Square riot of 1886 began as a peaceful protest meeting. The arrest and conviction of eight local radicals without any real evidence against them sent a message to workers: police and public opinion side with the industrialists.

Rockefeller, and Swift. The power of industrialists can be seen in the famous **Haymarket Square riot** of 1886. In 1885, skilled molders at McCormick Harvester Machine Company in Chicago won a 15 percent pay increase after a strike. Reacting angrily to the union's activities, McCormick introduced pneumatic molders that could be run by unskilled workers. The skilled workers went on strike again in 1886, but with different results. The combination of McCormick's forces and local police ensured the safety of an army of strikebreakers and the plant's output continued until the strike was broken.

Tempers, however, remained high, and violence resulted. In May, after the strike ended, police and workers clashed once again, and a number of laborers were killed and wounded. Disturbed by the violence used by police in defense of industrialists' positions, August Spies, a Chicago anarchist and labor agitator who edited the radical newspaper *Arbeiter Zeitung*, called for a protest meeting in Haymarket Square, a location that could hold 20,000 persons. On the evening of May 4, a small and generally unenthusiastic crowd of about 3000 labor supporters gathered in the rain. The speeches were dull and the listeners were peaceful. But as the meeting was breaking up, local police unexpectedly charged the crowd. Then somebody—to this day no one knows who—threw a bomb into the melee, killing both police and protesters. Surrounded by a fog of confusion and anger, the police opened fire, shooting protesters and even, accidentally, each other.

Industrialists, city officials, ministers, and the local press convinced a bewildered public that the bombing was a prelude to anarchistic revolution. Police arrested eight local radicals, including Spies, and charged them with conspiracy. Despite no real evidence against them, the eight were tried and convicted, and seven were sentenced to be hanged. One man committed suicide in his cell and three were eventually pardoned, but Spies and three others were executed. For radicals, labor agitators, and unionists, the message was clear: Police and public opinion were on the side of the industrialists.

The excessive violence of the Molly Maguires, the Great Strike of 1877, and the Haymarket Square riot were not necessarily typical of disputes between labor and management. Although labor violence continued in the 1890s, with such dramatic episodes as the Homestead strike and the Pullman strike (see Chapter 19), late-nineteenth-century labor disputes often were settled peacefully. In most cases, however, management was the winner. Only in small towns, where prolabor and anti-industrial sentiment knew no class lines, did labor battle management on anything approaching even terms.

Unorganized and Organized Labor

Historians have used the term *robber barons* to characterize late-nineteenth-century industrialists. Whether "robber" is accurate or not is debatable, but "baron" is a fitting description. They controlled their industries as medieval barons ruled their fiefs. Their word was usually final, and such a modern concept as democracy did not find a sympathetic environment inside factory walls. A Pennsylvania coal miner described the situation accurately: "They find monopolies as strong as government itself. They find capital as rigid as absolute monarchy. They find their so-called independence a myth, and that their subjection to power is as complete as when their forefathers were part and parcel of the baronial estate."

In the last third of the nineteenth century, labor was unable to form an organization powerful enough to deal with capital on equal terms. Before 1900, most unions were weak, with goals that were often out of touch with the changing American economy. In addition, the labor force itself was divided along ethnic, racial, gender, and craft lines. During this period, however, labor attempted to overcome its own divisions and fumble its way toward a clearer vision of what were its own best interests.

Before the 1870s most American unions were locally rooted, craft-based organizations. They were geared to the small workshop of Jacksonian America, not to the large modern factory. The first union to attempt to organize all workers was the short-lived

National Labor Union (NLU), founded in Baltimore in 1866. Besides shorter work hours and higher wages, the NLU supported the rights of women and African Americans, monetary reform, and worker-owned industries. As one of their leaders said, the "only way by which the toiling masses can protect themselves against the unjust claims and soul-crushing tyranny of capital" was for "themselves to become capitalists." Rich in ideas and solutions, the NLU was poor in organization and finances, and it died during the depression of the mid-1870s.

The NLU's mission was carried on by the Noble and Holy Order of the **Knights of Labor.** Begun in 1869 as a secret fraternal order as well as a union, the Knights remained small and unimportant until 1878 when it went public. Led by Terence V. Powderly, a machinist and former mayor of Scranton, Pennsylvania, in 1881 the Knights opened its membership not only to "any person working for wages but to anyone who had at any time worked for wages." The Knights excluded only bankers, lawyers, liquor dealers, speculators, and stockbrokers, whom they viewed as money manipulators and exploiters.

Complete worker solidarity was the Knights' goal. "An injury to one is an injury to all," they proclaimed. They welcomed and spoke for all laborers—women and men, black and white, immigrant and native, unskilled and skilled. Like the NLU, the Knights rejected industrial capitalism and favored cooperatively owned industries. "The aim of the Knights of Labor," Powderly emphasized, "is to make each man his own employer." Although critics at the time labeled the Knights "wild-eyed, utopian visionaries," they are best understood in the context of exploited workers searching for a less exploitive alternative to industrial capitalism. If their statements were extreme, their suffering was real.

An able leader, Powderly called for reforms of the currency system, the abolition of child labor, regulation of trusts' and monopolies, an end to alien contract labor networks, and government ownership of public utilities. By nature a diplomatic, good-natured man, he favored peaceful arbitration of labor disputes and opposed strikes. He also opposed the formation of narrow trade unions, instead advocating that skilled workers should assist the unskilled. Harmony and fellowship ultimately dominated his vision of America's future. Consensus, not conflict, was his goal.

The Knights' rhetoric found receptive listeners among American workers, and membership rolls grew during the early 1880s. Then came 1884, the beginning of what labor historians have called "the great upheaval." Strikes erupted in the coalfields of Pennsylvania and Ohio and the railroad yards of Missouri and Illinois. The labor conflicts continued into 1885 and 1886. Labor won some, but by no means all, of the strikes. Although its role was small, the Knights were associated with several important labor victories. By mid-1886 perhaps 750,000 workers had joined the Knights.

From that high point, however, the Knights declined rapidly. From the start, they could not weld together the diverse rank and file. Administrative and organizational problems surfaced, and Powderly's relatively conservative leadership was opposed by more radical members, who fully accepted strikes and conflict. The Haymarket Square bombing in 1886 branded all unions as un-American and violent in the public mind. By 1893, when Powderly was driven from office, the Knights' membership had declined alarmingly. Weakened and divided, it failed to survive the depression of the mid-1890s.

Unlike the NLU and the Knights, the **American Federation of Labor** (AFL) did not aspire to remake society. Its leaders accepted industrial capitalism and rejected partisan politics and the dreams of radical visionaries. Instead they concentrated on practical, reachable goals—higher wages, shorter workdays, and improved working conditions. Most importantly, they only recruited skilled laborers, recognizing that easily replaceable unskilled workers were in a poor position to negotiate with employers.

Formed in 1886 by the coming together of skilled-trade unions, the AFL was led ably by Samuel Gompers, a Jewish immigrant from England who had been the president of a New York cigar makers' union. Like many cigar makers, Gompers was well, if informally, educated. Cigar-rolling was a quiet job, and the rollers often employed one of their number as a reader. As a boy Gompers not only learned a skill, but he absorbed the leading political, economic, and literary ideas of his day. "In fact," Gompers later wrote, "these [readings and] discussions in the shops were more like public debating societies . . . 'labor forums.'"

As the head of the AFL for almost 40 years, Gompers used his considerable "moral power" and organizational ability to fight for *achievable* goals. American laborers were divided over religious, racial, ethnic, gender, and political issues, but they all desired higher wages, more leisure time, and greater liberty. Working out of his eight-by-ten-foot office, and using tomato boxes for filing cases, Gompers battled for those unifying issues. He focused on the world around him, not on the best of all possible worlds. Once effectively organized, he maintained, labor could deal with capital on equal terms.

Gompers's approach toward working with capital and organizing labor proved successful in the long

Chronology of Key Events

1856 Bessemer steelmaking process is invented

1859 Edwin Drake drills the first commercial oil well in Titusville, Pennsylvania

1861 Morrill Tariff is passed; first of a series of high protective tariffs

1862 Homestead Act gives 160 acres of free public land to those who will cultivate it for five years; Morrill Land Grant Act establishes many technical and agricultural colleges

1866 National Labor Union is founded in Baltimore; Cyrus W. Field lays the first successful transatlantic telegraph cable

1869 First transcontinental railroad is completed on May 10

1870 John D. Rockefeller founds Standard Oil Company

1873 Timber Culture Act awards 160 acres of public land to anyone who will plant trees on a quarter of the land

1876 Alexander Graham Bell invents the telephone

1877 Thomas Edison invents the phonograph; Desert Land Act grants 640 acres at $1.25 per acre to anyone who will irrigate the land; Great Strike paralyzes railroad transportation from Midwest and most of Northeast; 20 Molly Maguires are convicted and executed for terrorism in Pennsylvania coalfields

1879 Edison invents the incandescent lightbulb

1883 Railroad companies divide country into time zones

1885 George Westinghouse introduces alternating current for transmitting electricity

1886 *Santa Clara County* v. *Southern Pacific Railroad* decision rules that a corporation is a legal entity entitled to constitutional protection; Haymarket Square riot erupts in Chicago; American Federation of Labor is founded in Columbus, Ohio, by Samuel Gompers

1888 George Eastman produces the first hand-held camera

1892 Homestead, Pennsylvania, steelworkers strike

1894 Pullman strike by railroad workers leads to nationwide boycott railroad

1895 Booker T. Washington's "Atlanta Compromise" speech advocates that African Americans focus on achieving economic success as a basis for social and political equality

1896 *Plessy* v. *Ferguson* decision rules that the principle of "separate but equal" does not deprive African Americans of civil rights guaranteed under the Fourteenth Amendment

1901 Andrew Carnegie sells his steel company for almost $500 million to a group that is forming U.S. Steel

---

run. Before 1900, however, the AFL was not more successful than the Knights or the NLU. In fact, workers benefited little from unions before the turn of the century. Fewer than 5 percent of American workers joined trade unions, and the major areas of industrial growth were the least unionized. Nevertheless, the experimentation during the late nineteenth century taught workers valuable lessons: to combat the power of capital, labor needed equal power. During the twentieth century labor would move closer to that power.

Conclusion

In one generation the United States became the economic colossus of the world. After a heated period of intense competition, mergers forged supercorporations that controlled the majority of their industries. This economic expansion and consolidation provided many benefits. In some cases people were able to buy superior goods at cheaper prices. (As Edwin Atkinson noted in 1886, "Did Vanderbilt keep any of you down by saving you two dollars and seventy-five cents on a barrel of flour, while he was making fourteen cents?") And social mobility did increase. Although some skilled artisans slipped downward on the social ladder, upward mobility rates usually doubled the downward rates. Of course not all shared equally. Few duplicated Andrew Carnegie's transition from rags to riches.

Average annual incomes rose steadily for almost all classes of workers, although wage increases rarely equaled the rising cost of living. Nevertheless, most families' standard of living improved because more members of the family worked for wages. Items that had been considered luxuries soon became viewed as necessities.

Individuals, however, paid huge social costs for these advances. Some paid a disproportionate share. Patterns of working and living changed dramatically. Many workers' new status imperiled their independence. Personal relationships were being replaced by impersonal, contractual arrangements. Workers confronted the changes, and some sought to organize themselves to offset the overwhelming advantages enjoyed by management. In short, all of the late nineteenth century is the story of profound transformation as well as an adaptation and adjustment to a new social and economic order.

SUGGESTIONS FOR FURTHER READING

Walter Licht, *Industrializing America: the Nineteenth Century* (1995). Presents an up-to-date interpretation of the growth of industry and its consequences for American workers.

David Montgomery, *The Fall of the House of Labor: The Workplace, The State, and American Labor Activism, 1865–1925* (1987). Examines labor's responses to the growth of industry.

Carroll W. Pursell, *The Machine in America: A Social History of Technology* (1995). Provides a thorough examination of the growth of mechanization in U.S. industry.

Ronald Takaki, *A Different Mirror: The Making of Multicultural America* (1993). Retells American history from the perspective of ethnic and minority groups.

Alan Trachtenberg, *The Incorporation of America: Culture and Society in the Gilded Age* (1982). Explores intellectual and artistic responses to late nineteenth-century industrialization.

Ricahrd White, *"It's Your Misfortune and None of My Own": A History of the American West* (1991). Stresses the federal government's role in Western development.

Overviews and Surveys

Sean Dennis Cashman, *America in the Gilded Age: From the Death of Lincoln to the Rise of Theodore Roosevelt*, 3rd ed. (1993); Carl N. Degler, ed., *The Age of the Economic Revolution, 1876–1900* (1977); John A. Garraty, *The New Commonwealth, 1877–1890* (1968); Ray Ginger, *The Age of Excess: The United States From 1877 to 1914*, 2d ed. (1975); Morton Keller, *Affairs of State: Public Life in Late Nineteenth Century America* (1977); Jacqueline Jones, *The Dispossessed: America's Underclasses from the Civil War to the Present* (1992); Edward C. Kirkland, *Industry Comes of Age: Business, Labor, and Public Policy, 1860–1877* (1961); William Leach, *Land of Desire: Merchants, Power, and the Rise of a New American Culture* (1993); Nell Irvin Painter, *Standing at Armageddon: The United States, 1877–1919* (1987); Robert Wiebe, *The Search for Order, 1877–1920* (1967).

America: Land of Plenty

Ruth Schwartz Cowan, *A Social History of American Technology* (1997); George H. Daniels, *Science in American Society: A Social History* (1971); Sigfried Giedion, *Mechanization Takes Command: A Contribution to Anonymous History* (1948); Samuel P. Hays, *The Response to Industrialism, 1885–1914*, 2d ed. (1995); Robert Higgs, *The Transformation of the American Economy* (1971); Leo Marx, *The Machine in the Garden: Technology and the Pastoral Ideal in America* (1964); Elting E. Morison, *From Know-How to Nowhere: The Development of American Technology* (1974), and *Men, Machines, and Modern Times* (1966); D. F. Noble, *America by Design: Science, Technology, and the Rise of Corporate Capitalism* (1977); Nathan Rosenberg, *Technology and American Economic Growth* (1972).

A Favorable Climate: The Role of Ideology, Politics, and Finance

Robert Bannister, *Social Darwinism: Science and Myth in Anglo-American Social Thought* (1979); W. Elliot Brownlee, *Dynamics of Ascent: A History of the American Economy*, 2d ed. (1988); Thomas C. Cochran, *Business in American Life: A History* (1972); Sidney Fine, *Laissez-faire and the General Welfare State: A Study of Conflict in American Thought* (1956); Milton Friedman and Anna J. Schwartz, *Monetary History of the United States, 1867–1960* (1963); Louis Galambos, *The Public Image of Big Business in America, 1880–1940: A Quantitative Study in Social Change* (1975); Elliot J. Gorn, ed., *The McGuffey Readers: Selections from the 1879 Edition* (1998); Richard Hofstadter, *Social Darwinism in American Thought*, rev. ed. (1992); T. Jackson Lears, *No Place of Grace: Antimodernism and the Transformation of American Culture, 1880–1920* (1981); Robert

McCloskey, *American Conservatism in the Age of Enterprise, 1865–1910: A Study of William Graham Sumner, Stephen J. Field, and Andrew Carnegie* (1951); Daniel T. Rodgers, *The Work Ethic in Industrial America, 1850–1920* (1978); Martin Sklar, *The Corporate Reconstruction of American Capitalism, 1890–1916: The Market, the Law, and Politics* (1988); John L. Thomas, *Alternative America: Henry George, Edward Bellamy, Henry Demarest Lloyd, and the Adversary Tradition* (1983); Christopher L. Tomlins, *The State and the Unions: Labor Relations, Law, and the Organized Labor Movement in America, 1880–1960* (1985); James Weinstein, *The Corporate Ideal in the Liberal State, 1900–1918* (1968).

The Rise of Big Business

Alfred D. Chandler, *The Visible Hand: The Managerial Revolution in American Business* (1977); Thomas Cochran, *Railroad Leaders, 1845–1890* (1953); Francis L. Eames, *The New York Stock Exchange* (1894); Jonathan Hughes, *The Vital Few: American Economic Progress and Its Protagonists* (1966); Matthew Josephson, *The Robber Barons: The Great American Capitalists, 1861–1901* (1962); Robert Kanigel, *The One Best Way: Frederick Winslow Taylor and the Enigma of Efficiency* (1997); Maury Klein, *The Flowering of the Third America: The Making of an Organizational Society, 1850–1920* (1993); Daniel Nelson, *Managers and Workers: Origins of the New Factory System in the United States, 1880–1920* (1975); Glenn Porter, *The Rise of Big Business, 1865–1920*, 2d ed. (1992); William G. Roy, *Socializing Capital: The Rise of the Large Industrial Corporation in America* (1997); Philip Scranton, *Endless Novelty: Specialty Production and American Industrialization, 1865–1925* (1997); George R. Taylor and Irene D. Neu, *The American Railroad Network, 1861–1890* (1956); Peter Temin, *Iron and Steel in Nineteenth-Century America* (1964); Daniel Yergin, *The Prize: The Epic Quest for Oil, Money and Power* (1991); Olivier Zunz, *Making America Corporate, 1870–1920* (1990).

Varieties of Economic Change in the West and South

Blake Allmendinger, *The Cowboy: Representations of Labor in an American Work Culture* (1992); Gunther Barth, *Instant Cities: Urbanization and the Rise of San Francisco and Denver* (1975); Ray A. Billington, *Westward Expansion*, 5th ed. (1982); Allan G. Bogue, *From Prairie to Corn Belt: The Life of the Social Activist Kate Richards O'Hare* (1963); Orville Vernon Burton and Robert C. McMath, Jr., eds., *Toward a New South?: Studies in Post–Civil War Southern Communities* (1982); Anne M. Butler, *Uncommon Common Women: Ordinary Lives of the West* (1996); David L. Carlton, *Mill and Town in South Carolina, 1880–1920* (1982); Thomas D. Clark, *Frontier America: The Story of the Westward Movement*, 2d ed. (1969), with Albert D. Kirwan, *The South Since Appomattox: A Century of Regional Change* (1967); William C. Culberson, *Vigilantism: Political History of Private Power in America* (1990); Edward E. Dale, *The Range Cattle Industry, 1865 to 1925*, rev. ed. (1969); Pete Daniel, *Breaking the Land: The Transformation of Cotton, Tobacco, and Rice Cultures Since 1880* (1985); David Dary, *Cowboy Culture: A Saga of Five Centuries* (1981); Everett Dick, *The Sod-House Frontier, 1854–1890: A Social History of the Northern Plains From the Creation of Kansas & Nebraska to the Admission of the Dakotas* (1937); Philip Durham and E. L. Jones, *The Negro Cowboys* (1965); Robert R. Dykstra, *The Cattle Towns* (1968); Paul Gaston, *The New South Creed* (1970); P. W. Gates, *History of Public Land Law Development* (1968); Dewey Grantham, Jr., *The Democratic South* (1963); Melvin Greenhut and W. Tate Whitman, eds., *Essays in Southern Economic Development* (1964); William S. Greever, *Bonanza West: The Story of the Western Mining Rushes, 1848–1900* (1963); Steven Hahn, *The Roots of Southern Populism: Yeoman Farmers and the Transformation of the Georgia Upcountry, 1850–1890* (1983); Katherine Harris, *Long Vistas: Women and Families on Colorado Homesteads* (1993); Robert Higgs, *Competition and Coercion: Blacks in the American Economy, 1865–1914* (1977); Robert V. Hine, *The American West*, 2d ed. (1984); W. Eugene Hollon, *Frontier Violence: Another Look* (1974); Julie Roy Jeffrey, *Frontier Women: The Trans-Mississippi West, 1840–1880* (1979); Terry G. Jordan, *Trails to Texas: Southern Roots of Western Cattle Ranching* (1981); J. Morgan Kousser, *The Shaping of Southern Politics: Suffrage Restriction and the Establishment of the One-Party South, 1880–1910* (1974); Howard R. Lamar, *The Far Southwest, 1846–1912: A Territorial History* (1966); Patricia Nelson Limerick, *The Legacy of Conquest: The Unbroken Past of the American West* (1987); Roger D. McGrath, *Gunfighters, Highwaymen, and Vigilantes: Violence on the Frontier* (1984); Melton A. McLaurin, *Paternalism and Protest: Southern Cotton Mill Workers and Organized Labor* (1971); Gregory H. Nobles, *American Frontiers: Cultural Encounters and Continental Conquest* (1997); Earl Pomeroy, *The Pacific Slope: A History of California, Washington, Idaho, Utah, and Nevada* (1965); Roger Ransom and Richard Sutch, *One Kind of Freedom: The Economic Consequences of Emancipation* (1977); Glenda Riley, *Building and Breaking Families in the American West*, (1996); R. M. Robbins, *Our Landed Heritage: The Public Domain, 1776–1936* (1942); Duane A. Smith, *Rocky Mountain Mining Camps: The Urban Frontier* (1967); Henry Nash Smith, *Virgin Land: The West as Symbol and Myth* (1978); Frederick Jackson Turner, *The Frontier in American History* (1920); Carroll Van West, *Capitalism on the Frontier: Billings and the Yellowstone Valley in the Nineteenth Century* (1993); C. Vann Woodward, *Origins of the New South, 1877–1913* (1951), and *The Strange Career of Jim Crow*, 3d ed. (1974); Gavin Wright, *Old South, New South: Revolutions in the Southern Economy Since the Civil War* (1986); Sally Zanjani, *A Mine of Her Own: Women Prospectors in the American West, 1850–1950* (1997); Liping Zhu, *A Chinaman's Chance: The Chinese on the Rocky Mountain Mining Frontier* (1997).

Working in Industrial America

Paul Avrich, *The Haymarket Tragedy* (1984); James R. Barrett, *Work and Community in the Jungle: Chicago's Packing-*

house Workers, 1894–1922 (1987); Susan Porter Benson, Counter Cultures: Saleswomen, Managers, and Customers in American Department Stores, 1890–1940 (1986); Lindy Biggs, The Rational Factory: Architecture, Technology, and Work in America's Age of Mass Production (1996); John Bodnar, Immigration and Industrialization: Ethnicity in an American Mill Town (1977); Jeanne Boydston, Home and Work: Housework, Wages, and the Ideology of Labor in the Early Republic (1990); David Brody, Steelworkers in America (1960); Wayne G. Broehl, Jr., The Molly Maguires (1964); Robert V. Bruce, 1877: Year of Violence (1959); John R. Commons, et al., History of Labor in the United States, 4 vols. (1918–1935); Ruth Schwartz Cowan, More Work for Mother: The Ironies of Household Technology From the Open Hearth to the Microwave (1983); Melvyn Dubofsky, Industrialism and the American Worker, 2d ed. (1985), and We Shall Be All: A History of the Industrial Workers of the World, 2d ed. (1988); Leon Fink, Workingmen's Democracy: The Knights of Labor and American Politics (1983); Wendy Gamber, The Female Economy: The Millinery and Dressmaking Trades, 1860–1930 (1997); Victor Greene, The Slavic Community on Strike: Immigrant Labor in Pennsylvania Anthracite (1968); Gerald Grob, Workers and Utopia (1961); Herbert Gutman, Work, Culture, and Society in Industrializing America (1976); Jacqueline Hall, et al., Like a Family: The Making of a Southern Cotton Mill World (1987); Tamara Hareven and Randolph Langenbach, Amoskeag: Life and Work in an American Factory City (1979), and Hareven, Family and Industrial Time: The Relationship Between the Family and Work in a New England Industrial Community (1982); Alice Kessler-Harris, Out to Work: A History of Wage-Earning Women in the United States (1982); William H. Harris, The Harder We Run: Black Workers Since the Civil War (1982); Victoria C. Hattam, Labor Visions and State Power: The Origins of Business Unionism in the United States (1993); David Katzman, Seven Days a Week: Women and Domestic Service in Industrializing America (1978); Stuart B. Kaufman, Samuel Gompers and the Origins of the AFL (1973); Susan Kennedy, If All We Did Was to Weep at Home: A History of White Working-Class Women in America (1979); Kevin Kenny, Making Sense of the Molly Maguires (1998); S. J. Kleinberg, The Shadow of the Mills: Working-Class Families in Pittsburgh, 1870–1907 (1989); Clayton D. Laurie and Ronald H. Cole, The Role of Federal Military Forces in Domestic Disorders, 1877–1945 (1997); Susan Levine, Labor's True Woman: Carpet Weavers, Industrialization, and Labor Reform in the Gilded Age (1984); Glenna Matthews, "Just a Housewife": The Rise and Fall of Domesticity in America (1987); David Montgomery, Beyond Equality: Labor and the Radical Republicans (1967), and Workers' Control in America: Studies in the History of Work Technology and Labor Struggles (1979); Stephen H. Norwood, Labor's Flaming Youth: Telephone Operators and Worker Militancy, 1878–1923 (1990); Annegret S. Ogden, The Great American Housewife: From Helpmate to Wage Earner, 1776–1986 (1986); Daniel T. Rodgers, The Work Ethic in Industrial America, 1850–1920 (1978); Gerald Rosenblum, Immigrant Workers: Their Impact on American Labor Radicalism (1973); Roy A. Rosenzweig, Eight Hours for What We Will: Workers and Leisure in an Industrial City, 1870–1920 (1983); David Shannon, The Socialist Party of America: A History (1955); Peter Shergold, Working-Class Life: The American Standard in Comparative Perspective, 1899–1913 (1982); Susan Strasser, Never Done: A History of American Housework (1982); Sharon Hartman Strom, Beyond the Typewriter: Gender, Class, and the Origins of Modern American Office Work, 1900–1930 (1992); Leslie W. Tentler, Wage-Earning Women: Industrial Work and Family Life in the United States, 1900–1930 (1979); Daniel J. Walkowitz, Worker City, Company Town: Iron and Cotton-Worker Protest in Troy and Cohoes, New York, 1855–84 (1978); Norman Ware, The Labor Movement in the United States, 1860–1895 (1929).

Biographies

Andy Adams, Log of a Cowboy: A Narrative of the Old Trail Days (1927); Frederick Lewis Allen, The Great Pierpont Morgan (1949); Robert V. Bruce, Bell: Alexander Graham Bell and the Conquest of Solitude (1973); Julius Grodinsky, Jay Gould, His Business Career, 1867–1892 (1957); Louis R. Harlan, Booker T. Washington: The Making of a Black Leader, 1856–1901 (1972), and Booker T. Washington: The Wizard of Tuskegee, 1901–1915 (1983); David F. Hawke, John D.: The Founding Father of the Rockefellers (1950); Maury Klein, The Life and Legend of Jay Gould (1986); Harold C. Livesay, Andrew Carnegie and the Rise of Big Business (1975), and Samuel Gompers and Organized Labor in America (1978); Linda O. McMurry, George Washington Carver: Scientist and Symbol (1981); Allan Nevins, Study in Power: John D. Rockefeller, Industrialist and Philanthropist, 2 vols. (1953); Raymond B. Nixon, Henry W. Grady: Spokesman of the New South (1943); Joseph G. Rosa, Wild Bill Hickok: The Man and the Myth (1996); Nick Salvatore, Eugene V. Debs, Citizen and Socialist (1982); Andrew Sinclair, Corsair: The Life of J. Pierpont Morgan (1981); Karen Holliday Taner, Doc Holliday: A Family Portrait (1998); Robert M. Utley, Billy the Kid: A Short and Violent Life (1989); Joseph F. Wall, Andrew Carnegie (1970), and Alfred I. du Pont: The Man and His Family (1990); George Wheeler, Pierpont Morgan and Friends (1973).

INTERNET RESOURCES

The Northern Great Plains, 1880–1920: Photographs from the Fred Hultstrand and F. A. Pazandak Photograph Collections
http://memory.loc.gov/ammem/award97/ndfahtml/ngphome.html
This American Memory site from the Library of Congress contains "two collections from the Institute for Regional Studies at North Dakota State University" with "900 photographs of rural and small town life at the turn of the century." Included are "images of sod homes and the people who built them; images of farms and the machinery that made them prosper; and images of one-room schools and the children that were educated in them."

"California as I Saw It": First-Person Narratives of California's Early Years, 1849–1900
http://memory.loc.gov/ammem/cbhtml/cbhome.html
This site is a part of the American Memory Series and contains "full text and illustrations of 190 works documenting

the formative era of California's history through eyewitness accounts." It covers the Gold Rush, the interaction of various groups, and the settling of the region.

Home on the Range/Cowboy Heritage
http://history.cc.ukans.edu/heritage/old_west/cowboy.html
This site tells this history of the cattle trails and towns like Dodge City with useful text, links, documents, and maps.

Heroes and Villains in Kansas
http://www.ukans.edu/carrie/kancoll/galhero.htm
The Kansas Collection Gallery of both famous and little known people who made up the history of the state.

Alexander Graham Bell Family Papers at the Library of Congress
http://memory.loc.gov/ammem/bellhtml/bellhome.html
This site contains papers from 1862 to 1939 but includes a chronology, images, selected documents, and interpretive essays about Bell.

The Richest Man in the World: Andrew Carnegie
http://www.pbs.org/wgbh/pages/amex/carnegie
This American Experience/PBS site provides images and text about Carnegie's life and activities.

Anarchist Archive at Pitzer University
http://www.pitzer.edu/~dward/Anarchist_Archives/archivehome.html
This archive includes classic anarchist texts, especially information and graphics for the Haymarket Riot.

John D. Rockefeller and the Standard Oil Company
http://www.micheloud.com/FXM/SO/
This study with accompanying images by François Micheloud tells of the rise of Rockefeller and his mammoth company.

National Refinery Company
http://www.enarco.com/
This positive history of the company reflects the industrial changes of late-nineteenth-century America.

KEY TERMS

Social Darwinism (p. 485)
Gospel of Wealth (p. 485)
Laissez-Faire (p. 486)
Trust (p. 490)
Vertical Integration (p. 490)
"New South" (p. 500)
Plessy v. *Ferguson* (p. 501)
Haymarket Square Riot (p. 507)
Knights of Labor (p. 508)
American Federation of Labor (p. 508)

REVIEW QUESTIONS

1. What factors aided the rapid expansion of American industry in the late nineteenth century?
2. How did scholarship and popular culture support the concentration of wealth?
3. What led to the consolidation of business, and how did the rise of big business change marketing and manufacturing techniques?
4. What impact did national economic trends have in the South and West?
5. How did the nature of work change, and what were workers' responses to those changes?

18

THE RISE OF AN URBAN SOCIETY AND CITY PEOPLE

THE NEW IMMIGRANTS
   "Birds of Passage"
   In Search of a New Home

NATIVISM: THE ANTI-IMMIGRANT REACTION
   Sources of Conflict
   Closing the Golden Door

NEW CITIES AND NEW PROBLEMS
   City Technology
   The Segregated City
   The Problems of Growth
   From Private City to Public City

CITY CULTURE
   Night Life and Day Life
   From the Genteel Tradition to Realism and Naturalism
   Describing the Urban Jungle
   Painting Urban Reality
   The Sounds of the City

ENTERTAINING THE MULTITUDES
   Of Fields and Cities
   "I Can Lick Any Sonofabitch in the House"
   The Excluded Americans
   From Central Park to Coney Island
   The Magic of the Flickering Image
   The Agony of Painless Escape

"Murder with a hatchet"

Andrew Borden had, as the old Scotch saying goes, short arms and long pockets. He was cheap not because he had to be frugal but because he hated to spend money. He had dedicated his entire life to making and saving money, and tales of his unethical and parsimonious business behavior were legendary in his home town of Fall River, Massachusetts. Local gossips maintained that as an undertaker he cut off the feet of corpses so that he could fit them into undersized coffins that he had purchased at a very good price. Andrew, however, was not interested in rumors or the opinions of other people; he was more concerned with his own rising fortunes. By 1892 he had amassed over half a million dollars, he controlled the Fall River Union Savings Bank, and he served as the director of the Globe Yard Mill Company, the First National Bank, the Troy Cotton and Manufacturing Company, and the Merchants Manufacturing Company.

Andrew was rich, but he did not live like a wealthy man. Instead of living alongside the other prosperous Fall River citizens in the elite neighborhood known as the Hill, Andrew resided in an area near the business district called the Flats. He liked to save time as well as money, and from the Flats he could conveniently walk to work. For his daughters Lizzie and Emma, whose eyes and dreams focused on the Hill, life in the Flats was an intolerable embarrassment. Their house was a grim, boxlike structure lacking both comfort and privacy. Since Andrew believed that running water on each floor was a wasteful luxury, the only washing facilities were a cold-water faucet in the kitchen and a laundry room water tap in the cellar. Also in the cellar was the only toilet in the house. To make matters worse, the house was not connected to the Fall River gas main. Andrew preferred to use kerosene to light his house. Although it did not provide as good light or burn as cleanly as gas, it was less expensive. To save even more money, he and his family frequently sat in the dark.

Preconceived notions of Victorian womanhood saved Lizzie Borden from being convicted of murdering her father and stepmother.

The Borden home was far from happy. Lizzie and Emma, ages 32 and 42 in 1892, strongly disliked their stepmother Abby and resented Andrew's penny-pinching ways. Lizzie especially felt alienated from the world around her. Although Fall River was the largest cotton-manufacturing town in America, it offered few opportunities for the unmarried daughter of a prosperous man. Society expected a woman of Lizzie's social position to marry, and while she waited for a proper suitor, her only respectable social outlets were church and community service. So Lizzie taught a Sunday School class and was active in the Woman's Christian Temperance Union, the Ladies' Fruit and Flower Mission, and other organizations. She kept herself busy, but she was not happy.

In August 1892, strange things started to happen in the Borden home—after Lizzie and Emma learned that Andrew had secretly changed his will. Abby became violently ill. In time so did the Borden maid Bridget Sullivan and Andrew himself. Abby told a neighborhood doctor that she had been poisoned, but Andrew refused to listen to her wild ideas. Shortly thereafter, Lizzie went shopping for prussic acid, a deadly poison, that she said she needed to clean her sealskin cape. When a Fall River druggist refused her request, she left the store in an agitated state. Later in the day, she told a friend that she feared an unknown enemy of her father's was after him. "I'm afraid somebody will do something," she said.

On August 4, 1892, Bridget awoke early and ill, but she still managed to prepare a large breakfast of johnnycakes, fresh-baked bread, ginger and oatmeal cookies with raisins, and some three-day-old mutton and hot mutton soup. After eating a hearty meal, Andrew left for work. Bridget also left to do some work outside. This left Abby and Lizzie in the house alone. Then somebody did something very grisly. As Abby was bent over making the bed in the guest room, someone moved into the room unobserved and killed her with an ax.

Andrew came home for lunch earlier than usual. He asked Lizzie where Abby was, and she said she did not know. Unconcerned, Andrew, who was not feeling well, lay down on the parlor sofa for a nap.

He never awoke. Like Abby, he was slaughtered by someone with an ax. Lizzie "discovered" his body, still lying on the sofa. She called Bridget, who had taken the back stairs to her attic room: "Come down quick; father's dead; somebody came in and killed him."

Experts have examined and reexamined the crime, and most have reached the same conclusion: Lizzie killed her father and stepmother. In fact, Lizzie was tried for the gruesome murders. Despite a preponderance of evidence, however, an all-male jury found her not guilty, a verdict arrived at without debate or disagreement. A woman of Lizzie's social position, they affirmed, simply could not have committed such a terrible crime.

Even before the trial began, newspaper and magazine writers had judged Lizzie innocent for the same reason. As historian Kathryn Allamong Jacob, an expert on the case, noted, "Americans were certain that well-brought-up daughters could not commit murder with a hatchet on sunny summery mornings." Criminal women, they believed, originated in the lower classes and even looked evil. A criminologist writing in the *North American Review* commented, "[The female criminal] has coarse black hair and a good deal of it. . . . She has often a long face, a receding forehead, overjutting brows, prominent cheek bones, an exaggerated frontal angle as seen in monkeys and savage races, and nearly always square jaws." They did not look like round-faced Lizzie and did not belong to the Ladies' Fruit and Flower Mission.

Jurors and editorialists alike judged Lizzie according to their preconceived notions of Victorian womanhood. They believed that such a woman was gentle, docile, and physically frail, short on analytical ability but long on nurturing instincts. "Women," wrote an editorialist for *Scribner's*, "are merely large babies. They are shortsighted, frivolous and occupy an intermediate stage between children and men." Too uncoordinated and weak to accurately swing an ax and too gentle and unintelligent to coldly plan a double murder, a woman of Lizzie's background simply had to be innocent because of her basic innocence.

Even as Lizzie was being tried and found innocent, Victorian notions were being challenged elsewhere. In the larger cities of America, a new culture based on freedoms, not restraints, was taking form. Anything was possible, or at least so some people claimed. Immigrants could become millionaires and women could vote and hold office. Rigid Victorian concepts crumbled under the weight of new ideas, but the price of the new freedoms was high. In both the cities and the culture that flourished within them, a new order had to be constructed out of the chaos of freedom.

THE NEW IMMIGRANTS

On October 28, 1886, President Grover Cleveland traveled to New York Harbor to watch the unveiling of the Statue of Liberty. A gift from France, Frederic Auguste Bartholdi's grand statue was meant to symbolize solidarity between the two republics, but for Americans and incoming immigrants, it was a simple symbol of welcome, the statue's torch lighting the path to a better future.

In popular theory, the promise of America exerted a powerful pull on Europe and Asia. The United States stood for political freedom, social mobility, and economic opportunity. Since the first settlers landed in Jamestown, millions of immigrants had responded to the American magnet. At no time was immigration as great as in the late nineteenth and early twentieth centuries. Between 1860 and 1890, more than 10 million immigrants arrived on America's shores; between 1890 and 1920 over 15 million more arrived.

Seen in a worldwide context, however, the United States' pull was less powerful than Europe's push. Almost every European country—from Ireland in the northwest to Greece in the southeast—experienced a dramatic population increase during the nineteenth century. Advances in medicine and public health standards reduced infant mortality rates and increased life expectancies, but available land and food supplies did not increase to meet the new population demands. Twenty or so years later, when the "baby boomers" reached maturity, emigration increased sharply. (The United States was not the only country to lure immigrants from Europe—millions more emigrated to Australia, New Zealand, South Africa, Canada, Brazil, Argentina, and other underpopulated areas of the globe.)

Historians have divided immigration to the United States into two categories: old and new. The source of the "old" immigration was for the most part northern and western Europe—England, Ireland, France, Germany, and Scandinavia. Immigrants were mostly Protestants (except for the Irish Catholics) and always white; a majority were literate and had lived under constitutional forms of government. Assimilation for them was relatively easy. But this pattern fundamentally changed beginning in the 1880s. The next wave of immigration came from eastern and southern Europe—Greeks, Poles, Rus-

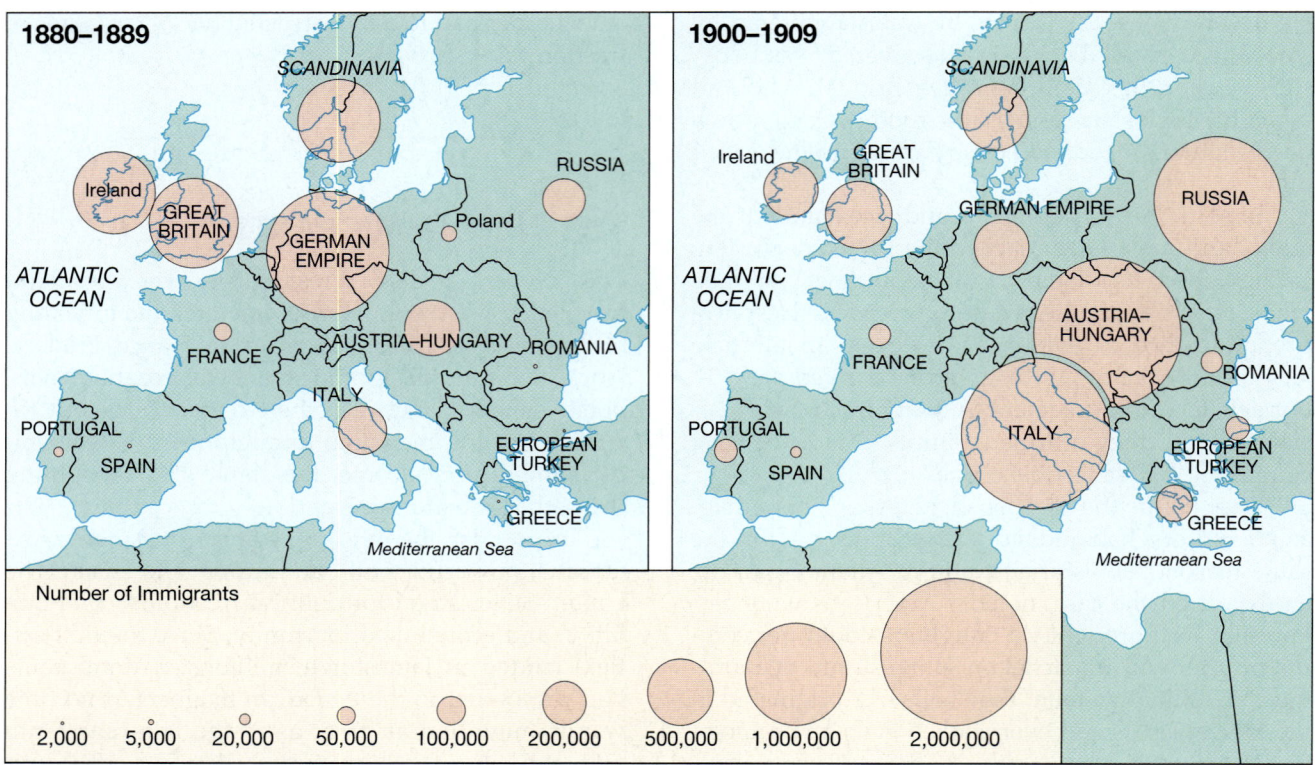

Immigration, 1880–1889 and 1900–1909

The source of old immigration was primarily northern and western Europe—England, Ireland, Germany, and Scandinavia. By the 1890s a wave of new immigrants began to arrive from eastern and southern Europe.

sians, Italians, Slavs, Turks. These people found assimilation more difficult; politically, religiously, and culturally, they differed greatly from both the earlier immigrants and native-born Americans.

More than geography differentiated the new immigrants. Their reasons for leaving Europe, their visions of America, and their settlement patterns in the United States varied dramatically. Conditions in southern and eastern Europe were right for the push to America at this time.

With the abolition of serfdom, peasants were free to emigrate; and with the rise in population, young men faced job, land, and food shortages. Too, railroads and steamships made travel faster and less expensive. During the 1880s, British and German steamships carried immigrants across the Atlantic for as little as $8, and by the turn of the century the trip took only five and a half days.

"Birds of Passage"

Essentially there were two types of immigrants—permanent immigrants and migrant workers. The people in the second group, often called **birds of passage,** never intended to make the United States their home. Unable to earn a livelihood in their home countries, they came to America, worked and saved, and then returned home. Most were young men in their teens and twenties. They left behind their parents, young wives, and children, indications that their absence would not be too long. Before 1900, an estimated 78 percent of Italian immigrants and 95 percent of Greek immigrants were men. Many traveled to America in the early spring, worked until late fall, and returned to the warmer climates of their southern European homes for the winter. Some fully intended to return home, but for one reason or another—love, hardship, early death—did not. Overall, 20 to 30 percent of all immigrants did return home.

Italian immigration patterns are a good example of the activity of the birds of passage. Beginning in the 1870s, Italian birthrates rose and mortality rates fell. Population pressure became severe, especially in *Il Mezzogiorno*, the southern and poorest provinces of Italy. The central government, dominated by northerners and concerned only with northern interests,

Many immigrants who looked on their stay in the United States as temporary sought jobs that might have paid a little better but were dangerous and physically demanding.

seemed unconcerned about the impoverished southern provinces. Heavily taxed and hurt by high protective tariffs on northern industrial goods, Italians in southern Italy sank deeper into poverty.

Then even nature joined the opposition. Natural disasters rocked southern Italy during the first decade of the twentieth century. Earthquakes caused untold devastation in the provinces of Basilicata and Calabria. Vesuvius erupted and buried a town near Naples. Then Etna erupted. The cruelest blow came in 1908 when an earthquake and tidal wave swept through the Strait of Messina between Sicily and the Italian mainland and killed hundreds of thousands of people.

The jobs that Italian men sought reflected their attitude toward America. They did not look for careers; occupations that provided opportunity for upward economic mobility were alien to them. Unlike most earlier immigrants, they did not want to farm in America or even own land, both of which implied a permanence that did not figure in their plans. Instead, Italians headed for the cities, where labor was needed and wages were relatively good. Particularly attracted to heavy construction jobs, they supplied the muscle that dug tunnels and canals, laid railroad tracks, and constructed bridges and roads. Expecting their stay in America to be short, they lived as inexpensively as possible under conditions that native-born families considered intolerable.

While they received good wages, they seldom forgot their homes in Italy. One nostalgic Italian admitted, "Doctor, we brought to America only our brains and our arms. Our hearts stayed there in the little house in the beautiful fields of our Italy." For women, adjustment to America was even more difficult. They often wore black clothing, an old-country practice that symbolized self-sacrifice, misery, and determination.

The same feelings of loneliness and alienation were also felt by many Chinese immigrants in the United States. Beginning in the mid-1860s, they emigrated to America to work building the Central Pacific railroad, and when that project was completed they sought jobs in western mining towns and cities. Normally only men emigrated, and they lived frugally and sent much of their wages to their families back in China. Their dream was almost always to return home, not to forge a new life in America.

Italians and Chinese were not the only birds of passage. The same forces that had initiated their flight—population pressure, unemployment, hunger, and the breakdown of agrarian societies—sent Greeks, Slavs, Japanese, Mexicans, French Canadians, and inhabitants of scores of other nations to the United States. Seeking neither permanent homes nor citizenship, they desired only an opportunity to work for a living, hoping to save enough money to return to a better life in the country of their birth. Always the land *they* coveted was some distant home, not in the United States.

In Search of a New Home

In contrast to the birds of passage were the **permanent immigrants,** for whom America offered political and religious freedom as well as economic opportunity. The promise of America was especially appealing to members of ethnic and religious minorities who were persecuted, abused, and despised in their homelands. Germans from Slavic countries, Greeks from Romania, Serbs from Hungary, Turks from Bulgaria, Poles from Russia—for these men and women home held few warm associations.

Czarist Russia, for example, was notoriously and historically inhospitable to many minorities. In 1907, 250,000 "Russians" emigrated from Russia. But who were these Russians? More than 115,000 were Jews, and another 73,000 were Poles. Others were Finns, Germans, and Lithuanians. Only a small percentage were of Russian ethnic stock.

The Jews were the prototypical new immigrants; they fled nearly unbearable hardships. Millions of Jews had maintained a relatively stable communal life in Poland until the eighteenth century when Russia, Prussia, and Austria conquered and divided the country. Most of the Polish Jews lived under Russian rule, and the quality of their lives took an immediate and drastic downward turn. Russian authorities

Hester Street on New York City's Lower East Side, in a photograph from 1907, was home to thousands of Jewish immigrants from Russia and eastern Europe. The immigrants crowded into the tenements lining the street, which bustled with peddlers and pedestrians.

drove Jews out of commerce and forced them into an area known as the Pale of Settlement, home to over 90 percent of Russian Jews. There they toiled as farmers on the poor soil of the steppes or earned a living as artisans or craftsmen in impoverished villages. There, too, Russian officials burned their books, disrupted their religious practices, and occasionally even broke up their families.

Starting in 1881, when the liberal Russian Czar Alexander II was assassinated, conditions for Jews in Russia went rapidly from bad to worse to intolerable. Laws restricted Jewish businesses, prevented Jewish land ownership, and limited Jewish education. Pogroms, legally sanctioned mob attacks against Jews, killed and injured thousands. Sometimes at the whim of authorities, Russian Cossacks burned Jewish houses and destroyed Jewish possessions.

For Jews, then, emigration offered a chance for a far better life than that in the Pale of Settlement. Dr. George M. Price, one of the several million Jews who left Russia for America during the late nineteenth century, expressed the feelings of these immigrants for their homeland. In his diary he wrote: "Sympathy for Russia? How ironical it sounds! Am I not despised? Am I not urged to leave? Do I not hear the word zhid (Jew) constantly? Can I even think that some consider me a human capable of thinking and feeling like others? Do I not rise daily with the fear lest the hungry mob attack me? . . . It is impossible . . . that a Jew should regret leaving Russia." Compared to Russia, the United States seemed like heaven to Price.

Because these Jewish immigrants came to the United States to stay, their form of immigration differed substantially from that of the generally young, male birds of passage. Jews, like other permanent immigrants, tended to come to America in family units, men and women, young and old. They brought their life savings and most valuable possessions with them, never expecting to see again what they left behind. The move to America thus was financially and physically taxing, and once in America, whole families had more expenses than the young male birds of passage.

Since America was now their home, Jewish men looked for jobs that offered future opportunities rather than simply work for wages. They were not drawn to unskilled labor in the steel mills and mines or even in construction. Many Jews had skills, for the uncertain life of the Russian Pale had taught them not to depend on land or commerce. In the Pale a Jew's greatest possession was the ability to do something that could not be taken away, a skilled craft. First in the Pale and then in America, Jews were tailors and seamstresses, cigar makers and toy makers, tanners and butchers, carpenters, joiners, roofers, and masons, coppersmiths and blacksmiths. They had the knowledge and ability to perform the thousands of skilled tasks needed in an urban environment.

NATIVISM: THE ANTI-IMMIGRANT REACTION

Native-born citizens and new immigrants confronted each other in America's cities. Tensions often ran high, as seen in the 1891 Hennessy case. A feud between gangs on the New Orleans docks had turned violent, and Joe and Pete Provenzano were arrested and tried for attempting to massacre the rival gang. The trial took a sensational turn when David Hennessy, the New Orleans superintendent of police, asserted that he had evidence that a secret Sicilian organization known as the Mafia was involved in the affair. Shortly after Hennessy made his bold charges, he was gunned down by five armed men. Before he died, Hennessy was heard to say, "The dagos shot me."

The crime raised a hue and cry against Sicilians. Local police, urged on by Mayor Joseph Shakespeare to "arrest every Italian you come across, if necessary," arrested scores. Eleven Sicilians were brought to trial, but a jury failed to convict them. A local mob promptly took matters into its own hands and shot or clubbed to death nine suspects and hanged the other two. As far as most natives of New Orleans were concerned, justice had been done.

Many other Americans seemed to agree. Editorial writers praised the mob action and damned the vile "un-American" Italians. Across the country anti-Italian rhetoric became ugly, and wild rumors ricocheted like bullets. Some said that the Italian fleet was headed toward America's east coast; others claimed that uniformed Italians were going through military drills in the streets of New York City. One thing was clear, noted an editorial writer in the *Review of Reviews:* Congress had to pass immigration legislation to keep out "the refuse of the murder-breeds of Southern Europe."

Although the Hennessy case soon faded from the front pages of American newspapers, the emotions it generated and revealed were very real. Native-born Americans harbored deep suspicion of and resentment toward immigrants, especially those from Asia and southern and eastern Europe. American industrialists saw in the immigrants a bottomless pool of dependable, inexpensive labor, but other Americans saw something far different and much less promising. Workers saw competition. Protestants saw Catholics and Jews. Educators saw illiterate hordes. Politicians saw peasants, unfamiliar with the workings of republicanism, democracy, and constitutionalism, and—even worse—perhaps contaminated by a belief in socialism, communism, or anarchism. Social Darwinists saw a mass of dark-skinned, thick-browed, bent-backed people who were far "below" northern and western Europeans on the evolutionary ladder. In short, native-born Americans, heirs of a different culture, religion, and complexion, saw something alien and inferior, perhaps even dangerous, in these new immigrants.

They reacted accordingly. They posted signs: "No Jews or Dogs Allowed." They called the Chinese "coolies," and the Mexicans "bean heads." Overall, they created an atmosphere of hostility that too often spilled over into open violence. In 1891 in a New Jersey mill town, 500 tending boys in a glassworks rioted when the management hired 14 young Russian Jews. During an 1895 labor conflict in the southern Colorado coal fields, American miners killed 6 Italians. When Slavic coal miners went on strike in 1897 in eastern Pennsylvania, local citizens massacred 21 Polish and Hungarian workers. On the West Coast, Chinese workers were subject to regular and vicious attacks. Especially during economic hard times, native-born Americans lashed out against the new immigrants.

Sources of Conflict

Nativism, as this anti-immigrant backlash was called, took many forms. Racial nativism, the subject of thousands of books and articles, is the best remembered. Using such criteria as complexion, size of cranium, length of forehead, and slope of shoulders, university professors such as Wisconsin's Edward Alsworth Ross and popular writers such as Madison Grant judged the immigrants from southern and eastern Europe as inferior to most native-born Americans. University professors and scientists gave credibility to such theories of innate racial and ethnic inferiority, and popular writers readily accepted the stereotypes. Jacob Riis, a Danish immigrant who became an urban reformer in America and wrote the popular book *How the Other Half Lives* (1890), characterized Italians as "born gamblers" who lived destitute and disorderly lives, Chinese as secretive and addicted to every vice, and Jews as "enslaved" by their pursuit of gold as well as living amidst filth.

Religious differences reinforced ethnic variations. Overwhelmingly Catholic and Jewish, the new immigrants challenged the Protestant orthodoxy in America. Anti-Catholicism, noted a leading student of nativism, "blossomed spectacularly" during the late nineteenth century. Many Americans regarded the pope as the anti-Christ and Catholics as his evil minions. And it was widely believed that the authoritarian bent of the Catholic mind made it incompatible with democratic institutions.

Native-born Americans viewed Jews with even greater suspicion, attributing the characteristics of Shakespeare's Shylock to Jews as a whole. "Money is their God," wrote Jacob Riis. Other writers commented that Jews were tactless, tasteless, and pushy. Eventually many social clubs, country clubs, hotels, and universities excluded Jews, arguing that money alone could not purchase respectability.

The Leo Frank case painfully demonstrated the ubiquitous anti-Semitism in American society. Frank, a Cornell University graduate and a son of a wealthy New York merchant, managed an Atlanta pencil factory. In 1914 one of the factory hands, Mary Phagan, was found murdered on the premises. Frank was tried and convicted on flimsy evidence, but the case soon became an international cause célèbre. After reviewing the case, the governor of Georgia commuted Frank's death sentence to life imprisonment. The decision outraged native Georgia whites. They boycotted Jewish merchants and clamored for Frank's blood. Finally, a group of citizens from Mary Phagan's home town took Leo Frank from a state prison, transported him 175 miles across the state, and coldly hanged him. As news of the hanging spread, people gathered to gaze at the sight and shout "Now we've got you! We've got you now!" In the 1980s, new evidence in the Phagan case proved Frank innocent, and

Georgia's Board of Pardons granted him a posthumous pardon. But dispassionate justice was scarce in the weeks after Frank's death.

Orators used the Frank case as an object lesson. Tom Watson, the fiery Georgia politician, warned listeners, "From all over the world, the Children of Israel are flocking to this country, and plans are on foot to move them from Europe *en masse* . . . to empty upon our shores the very scum and dregs of the *Parasite Race*." Watson believed that Congress should stop the flow of immigrants before America was flooded by the waves of eastern and southern Europeans.

Many congressmen agreed. They too harbored strong suspicions that every boat that docked at Ellis Island contained a swarm of socialists, communists, and anarchists prepared to foment revolution. As unfounded as their fears were, they could always point to isolated cases of radicalism among immigrants. They drew attention, for example, to Leon Czolgosz, born only months after his eastern European parents arrived in America. After embracing anarchism, Czolgosz shot and killed President William McKinley on September 6, 1901.

Most Americans resented the new immigrants, however, for purely economic reasons. American workers, particularly the unskilled, believed that immigrants depressed wages by their willingness to "work cheap." An iron worker complained: "Immigrants work for almost nothing and seem to be able to live on wind—something which I cannot do." Even skilled workers maintained that the birds-of-passage immigrants were unwilling to support any union efforts to improve working conditions in America. Samuel Gompers, himself an immigrant and head of the American Federation of Labor, believed that the immigrants from eastern and southern Europe and from Asia were ignorant, unskilled, and unassimilable. Calling for strong restrictive legislation, he said, "Some way must be found to safeguard America."

In the 1890s, a terrible depression disrupted the normal economic and social course of America, and the new immigrants became a convenient scapegoat for the nation's myriad ills. People elevated racial prejudice and rumors to universal truths. Native-born Americans blamed crime on Italians and prostitution on the Chinese; they claimed that the social ills of America's expanding cities—corruption, poor sanitation, violence, crime, disease, pollution—were the fault of the new immigrants. And they looked to the federal government for relief and protection.

Closing the Golden Door

The first immigrants attacked were those who were the most different from native-born Americans—the Chinese. The more than 160,000 Chinese who entered the United States between 1868 and 1882 laid down railroad tracks and mined for gold, silver, and coal. Unlike native-born Americans and most members of other immigrant groups, they did not consider cooking, washing, and ironing as "women's work," and in these areas they were particularly successful. Perhaps too successful.

"Americans are not all bad," noted Lee Chew, a Chinese immigrant, "nor are they wicked wizards. Still . . . their treatment of us is outrageous."

During the depression of the mid-1870s the Chinese came under increasingly bitter and violent attack. Labor and political leaders, especially in California, demanded an end to Chinese immigration. But the provisions of the Burlingame Treaty (1868) with China encouraged the Chinese to immigrate to America and establish citizenship.

Eventually Congress responded to the pressure for restriction. In 1880, China gave the United States Congress the right "to regulate, limit or suspend," though not to prohibit, the immigration of Chinese workers to the United States. The golden door quickly slammed shut. The Chinese Exclusion Act of

This political cartoon depicts the 1882 Chinese Exclusion Act, which barred Chinese laborers from entering the United States for ten years.

1882 suspended Chinese immigration for ten years and drastically restricted the rights of the Chinese already in the United States. In 1892 Congress extended the act for another ten years, and then in 1902 extended it indefinitely.

The legislation established a precedent for the future exclusion of other immigrants. By the 1890s most Americans agreed that the country should restrict "undesirable" immigrants. But how, for example, could Congress close America's door to southern and eastern Europeans while still leaving it open for northern and western Europeans? Politicians came up with the idea of a literacy test. As early as the late 1880s economist Edward W. Bemis proposed that the United States exclude all male adults who could not read and write their own language. He maintained that such a law would effectively stop the flow of eastern and southern Europeans into America. The idea soon had the backing of the influential Republican Senator Henry Cabot Lodge of Massachusetts and the equally important Immigration Restriction League.

In 1896 Lodge pushed through Congress a literacy test bill that would have excluded any adult immigrant unable to read 40 words in his own language. Lodge's timing was poor. The bill reached the desk of Democratic President Grover Cleveland two days before his second term expired. Cleveland promptly vetoed the measure, suggesting that the bill tested prior opportunities and that America stood for open opportunities.

Cleveland's veto neither ended the demand for restrictive legislation nor killed the idea of a literacy test. Subsequent presidents William Howard Taft and Woodrow Wilson also vetoed similar pieces of legislation. In 1917, on the eve of America's entry into World War I, Wilson vetoed a literacy test bill on the grounds that it was "not a test of character, of quality, or of personal fitness." Congress nevertheless passed the act over Wilson's veto.

World War I made even chillier the already cold climate for immigrants from southern and eastern Europe. Those born in the polyglot Austro-Hungarian Empire were now considered the enemy, and others were watched with deep suspicion. This was especially true after the 1917 Bolshevik Revolution in Russia. Once again American authorities regarded Jews from Russia as potential revolutionaries. Responding to this fear, in 1918 and 1920 Congress passed legislation to exclude or deport anarchists and other "dangerous radicals."

The generation-long battle over restriction was to end with a clear victory for nativism. In the early 1920s Congress discovered its own solution: the quota system. The Emergency Quota Act (1921) limited immigration according to a nation-based quota system—no more than 3 percent of any given nationality in America in 1910 could annually immigrate to the United States. In 1924 the **National Origins Act** lowered the quota to 2 percent of each nationality residing in America in 1890. By using 1890 as the base year, the act was clearly aimed at restricting eastern and southern Europeans, for there were far fewer of the new immigrants in America in 1890 than in 1910. Although in 1927 the base year was changed to 1920, the National Origins Act had achieved its desired result. America's doors were no longer fully open to eastern and southern Europeans, and it was completely closed to Asians. An important era in American history had ended.

Despite the prejudice against them, immigrants contributed greatly to the growth of industrial America. They and their fellow workers—native-born white and black Americans—built the railroads that crisscrossed the country; mined the gold and silver that made other men rich; and labored in the oilfields, steel mills, coal pits, packing plants, and factories that made such names as Rockefeller, Carnegie, Swift, and Westinghouse famous. Without these men and their companions, there would have been no industrialization. In the process they made the United States an ethnically rich nation, as well as help to transform the country into an increasingly urban nation.

New Cities and New Problems

The physical layout of the mid-nineteenth-century city was strikingly different from its twentieth-century counterpart. In an age before reliable mass transportation, when only the rich could afford carriages, the majority of city dwellers walked to and from work. Even America's largest cities—New York, Philadelphia, and Boston—were thus compact and crowded, their sizes limited to about a two-mile radius from center city, or the distance a person could walk in half an hour.

Inside the cities, houses, businesses, and factories were strewn about willy-nilly. Tightly packed near the waterfront were shops, banks, warehouses, and business offices, and not far away were the residences of the people who owned those enterprises or worked in them. There was little residential segregation. The rich may have occupied the finest houses in the center city, but the poor lived in the alleys and dirty streets close by. People dealt with people in a congested, highly personalized world. Rich and poor, native-born and immigrant, black and white—

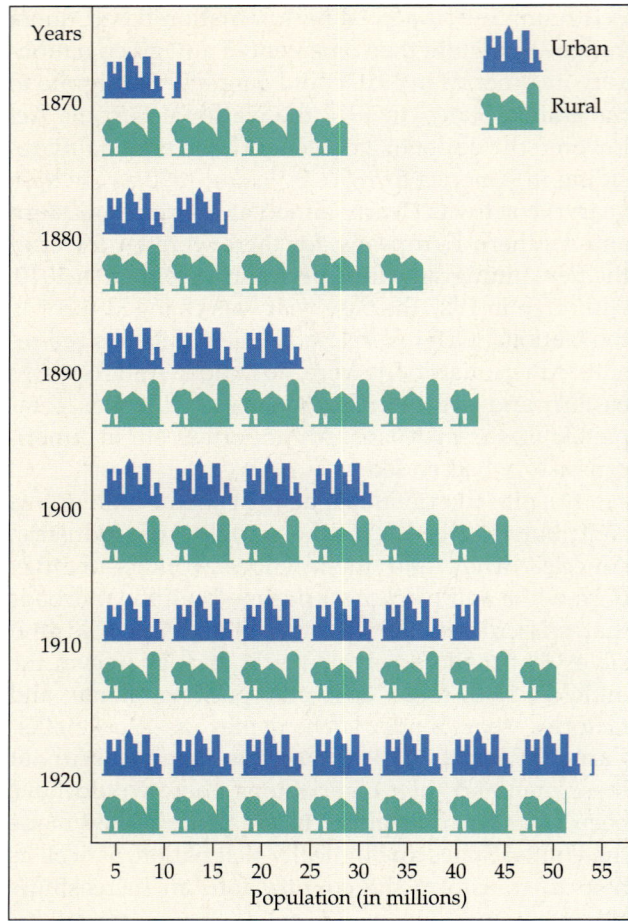

FIGURE 18.1

Urban and Rural Population, 1870–1920

Immigrants and native-born migrants from rural areas contributed to the urban population explosion in this 50-year span.

they all walked along the same streets and worked in the same area.

During the last third of the century, however, booming industrialization and immigration shattered this arrangement. Like twin children, factories and cities each helped the other to reach its physical potential. In 1860, before America's industrial surge, 20 percent of the population lived in cities. By 1900 almost 40 percent of the population lived in cities or towns, and that figure climbed to over 50 percent in 1920. The numbers of large cities (those with a population of over 100,000) increased at an even faster rate. In 1860, America had only 9 large cities; in 1900 there were 38; in 1920, 68.

Immigrant and native sources fueled the urban explosion. Most of the late-nineteenth-century immigrants came from rural communities, but they settled in America's industrial heartland. In 1920, 87 percent of Irish immigrants, 89 percent of Russians, 84 percent of Italians and Poles, 80 percent of Hungarians, and 75 percent of Austrians, British, and Canadians lived in cities. For every industrial worker who moved to the countryside, 20 farmers moved to urban America. As in Europe and Asia, rural opportunities in the United States were dwindling at the same time that the population was growing. Thus, for each farm son who became a farm owner, 10 farm sons moved to the cities.

Black migration from the rural South to the urban North further expanded the labor pool in the industrial cities. Slowly at first, blacks left the land of their bondages determined to forge a better life for themselves and their families in the northern cities. Between 1897 and 1920 almost one million African Americans left the South, and 85 percent of those settled in the urban North.

City Technology

Even the largest of the "walking" cities was unprepared to meet the demands the newcomers placed on it. Cities were already crowded, and construction technology was not yet sufficiently advanced to accommodate new arrivals. In time, however, engineers and scientists discovered ways to expand cities. Horizontal and vertical growth changed the

During the early decades of the twentieth century, hundreds of thousands of African Americans left the rural South for the cities of the industrial North.

skyline and living conditions of urban America during the half-century after 1870.

Better transportation facilities solved the most basic limitation of the walking city, although at first only the wealthy and those with some money benefited. As early as the 1830s, the horse-drawn omnibus could carry 12 to 20 passengers along a fixed route for between 6 and 12 cents. Faster than walking, it was also expensive, certainly beyond the means of an unskilled laborer who earned less than one dollar a day. Similarly the commuter railroads, which also dated back to the 1830s and 1840s and cost between 12 and 25 cents to ride, served only the wealthier classes. Constructed and owned by entrepreneurs, omnibuses and commuter railways existed only for the comfort of people who could pay.

The horse railway expanded the city for the middle-class urbanites, white-collar workers, and skilled workers. For 5 cents, these horse-drawn omnibuses carried passengers over steel rails at a speed of 6 to 8 miles per hour. In southern and border towns, mules, which tended to live longer, pulled the omnibuses. By the 1880s, over 300 American cities and towns had constructed horsecar lines, which significantly expanded the size of cities. Now a person could live 5 miles from his or her place of work and still be there in less than an hour. The age of walking was almost over.

The horsecar was not always as safe or as comfortable as its developers planned. Travelers complained about pickpockets, tobacco juice, and overcrowding. Entrepreneurial conductors sometimes packed 80 persons into a car designed for 25 and used underfed, overworked horses that struggled day after day until they dropped from exhaustion and were left to die. Drivers worked long hours for little pay and sat exposed to the weather in the front or rear of the cars. In the winter, cold winds whipped their faces and froze their fingers around the reins. One hardened streetcar conductor remarked, "I feel that I could almost digest cobblestones."

For hillier cities like San Francisco and Pittsburgh, the cable car, introduced during the 1870s, proved a blessing for humans and horses alike. Utilizing steam power, cable cars were faster and cleaner than horse-drawn transportation. Even relatively flat cities such as Kansas City and Chicago installed cable cars. Because it was pulled by a moving underground cable, engineers believed it would be the public transportation of the future—but its problems were considerable. Expensive to install and quick to break down, the cable car soon gave way to the **electric trolley,** which was cheaper to run and more dependable.

In 1888, former naval engineer Frank Sprague converted the horsecar network of Richmond, Virginia, to electricity. Employing electrical current in overhead wires, these trolleys could operate in stop-and-go traffic and travel at average speeds of 10 to 12 miles per hour. American cities quickly climbed aboard the electric bandwagon. By 1902, 97 percent of urban transit mileage had been electrified, and trolleys connected not only city with suburb but also city with city. By 1920 a person could travel from Boston to New York entirely by trolleys known as interurbans.

This watercolor of New York City's Bowery at night by W. Louis Sonntag, Jr. shows how steam, steel, and electricity played a major part in transforming cities.

Called "one of the most rapidly accepted innovations in the history of technology," trolleys were not without their problems: overhead wires gave cities a weblike appearance; in winter the electric wires snapped from the cold and created dangerous situations; and they sometimes frightened horses, thus aggravating traffic problems. By the 1890s, the mixture of horsecars, cable cars, and trolleys jostling each other and pedestrians on city streets created immense traffic jams. English science fiction writer H. G. Wells found Chicago streets in 1906 "simply chaotic—one hoarse cry for discipline."

Engineers searching for other solutions to clogged streets designed electric-powered elevated railway lines and underground subways. Each helped ease mass transportation. The Chicago "el" (elevated railway) and the New York City subway satisfied the urban traffic engineers and even occasionally stirred the souls of artists. W. Louis Sonntag, Jr.'s beautiful watercolor captured New York City's Bowery in 1896, in which, illuminated by electric lights, an electric el and trolley pass in the night.

Mass transportation allowed cities to spread miles beyond their cores, but steel and glass permitted cities to reach for the sky. At midcentury, church spires still dominated the urban skyline. Few buildings were higher than five stories. But that would change, as a real-estate columnist wrote in the *Chicago Tribune* in 1888: "Chicago has thus far had but three directions, north, south, and west, but there are indications now that a fourth is to be added and that it is to cut a larger figure in the coming decade than all the others. The new direction is zenithward. Since water hems in the business center on three sides and a nexus of railroads on the south, Chicago must grow upward."

Architects could not design buildings much higher than ten stories, using traditional brick-and-masonry construction. In 1885 New York architect William LeBaron Jenney solved this problem by using light masonry over an iron and steel skeleton. Although only ten stories high his Home Insurance Building in Chicago was the first true skyscraper in history. Materials like steel, light masonry, and eventually glass revolutionized building construction, and the use of electric elevators made tall buildings functional.

Skyscrapers changed the profile of American cities as surely as industrialism altered the American landscape. Returning to America from Europe in 1906, novelist Henry James observed "the multitudinous skyscrapers standing up to the view . . . like extravagant pins in a cushion already overplanted, and stuck in as in the dark, anywhere and anyhow."

What disturbed James's sensibilities excited most Americans. The skyscraper symbolized American possibilities. Businesspeople and industrialists even used skyscrapers to glorify their own accomplishments. In 1913, President Woodrow Wilson pressed the button that lit up the Woolworth Building. At 792 feet, it was the largest building in America, a monument to five-and-ten-cents king Frank Woolworth. This hauntingly beautiful structure, which freely adapted aspects of Gothic and Moorish construction, truly was "the Cathedral of Commerce."

The Segregated City

With the outward and upward growth of cities came an end to the more personal walking city. Mass transportation freed the upper and middle classes from having to live in the city core. Voicing their decision with their feet, they scampered for the "streetcar suburbs," where, popular theory held, the water was purer, the trees fuller, and the air fresher. They commuted to work and no longer mixed daily with their economic inferiors.

The working class moved into the areas and even houses deserted by wealthier families. In New York City the large stately brownstone homes that had served the upper classes were divided into small apartments that satisfied the new demand for inexpensive housing. Of course, the houses had not been designed to be used as multiunit apartments, and there were numerous problems. Heatless, sunless, and poorly ventilated rooms became increasingly common.

Ethnic groups and races, like economic classes, tended to stake out particular neighborhoods in the new larger cities, and real-estate brokers and landlords restricted blacks and immigrants to specific areas. Black ghettos emerged in the major northern cities for the first time. And in Chicago, New York, Boston, and Philadelphia, English became a foreign language in ethnic neighborhoods, which reproduced in their finer details Old World conditions. Familiar faces, foods, churches, and speech patterns comforted lonely immigrants.

Since members of the ethnic working class were too poor for even moderately priced mass transit, they tended to settle close to their places of work. In New York City, Jews and Italians lived within walking distance of the Lower East Side garment factories. In Chicago, the Poles and Lithuanians who worked in the meat-packing industry awoke in the morning and went to sleep at night hearing the sounds of dying animals and smelling the stench of the stockyards.

Just as new residential trends separated rich and poor, prices for real estate in the central business district shot up at an incredible rate, sometimes as much as 1000 percent a decade in the late nineteenth century. Only businesses and industries could afford the new prices, so the central cities were turned over to high-income businesses, banks, warehouses, railroad terminals, and the recently developed department stores. It became an area where money was made, not where people lived.

The Problems of Growth

By the 1890s, British observers despaired over what had become of the once small American cities. The uncontrolled growth, they suggested, had created ugliness on an almost unprecedented scale. English traveler Charles Philips Trevelyan graphically described the horrors of industrial Pittsburgh:

> A cloud of smoke hangs over it by day. The glow of scores of furnaces light the river banks by night. It stands at the junction of two great rivers, the Monongahela which flows down in a turbid yellowish stream, and the Allegheny which is blackish.... All nations are jumbled up here, the poor living in tenement dens or wooden shanties thrown up or dumped down with little reference to roads or situation, whenever a new house is wanted. It is the most chaotic city, and as yet there is no public spirit or public consciousness to make conditions healthy or decent.

Numerous American observers echoed Trevelyan's observations. American cities were unprepared for the incredible growth they experienced during the late nineteenth century. Housing, clean water, competent police, and adequate public services were all in short supply. Health standards were low everywhere and scientists had barely begun to study the problems and diseases created by crowded urban conditions. To make matters worse, the people who moved to the cities usually came from rural areas and were not familiar with city life.

Crime plagued rich and poor. Pickpockets, robbers, con artists, and violent gangs roamed the streets and alleyways of American cities. Urban police forces had been established in the 1830s and 1840s. In the 1850s, police forces wore uniforms and badges and carried clubs and revolvers but still could not control or seriously curtail urban crime. In fact, during this earlier period, police were often expected to clean streets, inspect boilers, or run poorhouses as well as prevent crime and maintain public order. In addition, police often took bribes from saloon keepers and streetwalkers to overlook illegal activities and even intimidated voters on election day.

They owed their loyalty to the political boss who appointed them, not to some abstract public. Not until the end of the century would attempts to bring professionalism and civil service reform to police departments be successful.

Housing presented an even more pressing problem. Immigrants disembarking at the ports of entry and farmers arriving by train needed places to live, which created both opportunities and problems. The building industry was one of the great urban boom industries, and its leaders largely determined the shape and profile of the modern city. Equipped with a lofty disregard for public opinion, like other businesspeople they worked in an essentially unregulated economic world and were bent on maximizing their profits.

When it came to urban housing, money talked. In large cities from New York to San Francisco the rich built stately homes with high ceilings, European furnishings, and spacious rooms. Even the apartments of the upper classes were designed and constructed by gifted architects and artisans. The beautiful Dakota Apartments, Central Park West at Seventy-second Street, still stands as one of the architectural triumphs of the period.

Tenement apartments on the Lower East Side of New York were overcrowded, filthy, and dangerous.

On the other hand, undermaintained tenements—built to minimal codes but designed to cram the largest number of people into the smallest amount of space—greeted urban newcomers without money. Like skyscrapers, the tenements made use of vertical space by piling family upon family into small, poorly lit, badly ventilated apartments. By 1900 portions of the Jewish Tenth Ward in New York City's Lower East Side had reached population density levels of 500,000 people per one square mile and as many as one person per square foot of land in the most crowded areas. To be in the land of tenements, noted writer William Dean Howells, "is to inhale the stenches of the neglected streets, and to catch the yet fouler and dreadfuller poverty-smell which breathes from the open doorways.... It is to see the work-worn look of mothers, the squalor of the babies, the haggish ugliness of the old women, and the slovenly frowziness of the young girls."

Dumbbell tenements—with a dumbbell-shaped indentation in the middle to allow better ventilation—were the most notorious examples of exploitative urban housing. Although they conformed to the Tenement Reform Law of 1879, which required all rooms to have access to light and air, they made maximum use of standard 25- by 100-foot urban lots. Although the problems inherent in the dumbbell tenement were obvious from the first, the design was not outlawed in New York until 1901. Their use, in fact, spread east to Boston and west to Cincinnati and Cleveland.

Street conditions, unlike housing, were more democratic in that they plagued rich and poor alike. People dumped trash and horses unloaded their own pollution onto dirty city thoroughfares. Spring rains turned the streets into fetid quagmires, and winter freezes left them with hard deep ruts. Well into the 1870s, pigs roamed the streets of most cities, rooting for food in the garbage and further polluting the environment. When trolleys began to replace horses as the primary form of urban transportation, editorialists predicted that air pollution would soon come to an end. As late as 1900, however, there were still 150,000 horses in New York City, each producing between 20 and 30 pounds of manure a day.

Waste not dumped onto the streets often found its way into the rivers that flowed through the major cities or into the harbors that bordered them. By the turn of the century, 13 million gallons of sewage were emptied each day into the Delaware River, the major source for Philadelphia's drinking water. Even more polluted was Pittsburgh's Golden Triangle, where the Allegheny and Monongahela rivers meet to form the Ohio River. It could have just as aptly been dubbed the black triangle for all the industrial waste poured into it.

The establishment of dump sites did little to solve the terrible garbage problem. The Reverend Hugh Miller Thompson described the conditions in a New Orleans dump to a meeting of the American Public Health Association in 1879: "Thither were brought the dead dogs and cats, the kitchen garbage and the like, and duly dumped. This festering rotten mess was picked over by rag-pickers and wallowed over by pigs, pigs and humans contesting for a living in it, and as the heaps increased, the odors increased also, and the mass lay corrupting under a tropical sun, dispersing the pestilential fumes where the winds carried them."

The overcrowded housing, polluted streets and rivers, and uncollected garbage contributed to the notoriously unhealthy urban environment. Unfortunately, advances in medicine and public health to cope with the consequences of such problems lagged behind technological and industrial progress. Diseases ranging from yellow fever and smallpox to diphtheria and typhoid claimed thousands of victims. In 1878 a yellow fever epidemic moved along the Mississippi River—5150 people died in Memphis, another 3977 in New Orleans. Known as the American Plague, the disease struck without warning and often led to a rapid, painful death. Walter Reed's discovery in 1900 that the disease was carried by the *Aedes aegypti* mosquito led to a cure for this dreaded scourge.

The smallpox virus proved more persistent. Although not as deadly as yellow fever, it struck more people and left millions of pockmarked faces. Like diphtheria and scarlet fever, smallpox flourished in the overcrowded and garbage-strewn cities. During the late nineteenth century, health wardens were unsuccessful in limiting the diseases, mostly because they were party hacks who owed their jobs to political loyalty rather than knowledge of public health.

Death, suffering, and massive inconvenience eventually prodded city officials to move toward a more systematic approach to their problems. Trained experts slowly replaced political appointees. Remarkable progress came in the 1880s with the development of the germ theory, which linked contagious disease to environmental conditions.

Health officials and urban engineers vigorously attacked the sewage and water problems. Discussing the importance of a good sewer system, one Baltimore engineer noted in 1907 that Paris is "the center of all that is best in art, literature, science, and architecture, and is both clean and beautiful. In the evolution of this ideal attainment, its sewers took at least a leading part." Without good sewers and clean drinking water, urban civilization was almost a contradiction of terms. Cities replaced cesspools and backyard

THE PEOPLE SPEAK

How the Other Half Lives

The Danish immigrant Jacob Riis began his journalistic career as a police reporter for the *New York Tribune,* where he learned to capture the colorful details of urban life and evoke emotional responses from his readers. Increasingly a social activist, Riis expanded a series of lectures, a collection of photographs, and a long article in *Scribner's Magazine* into his 1890 book *How the Other Half Lives.* This passage on New York City tenement life during the summer vividly illustrates the unfortunate combination of poverty, heat, and teeming, squalid conditions.

> With the first hot nights in June police dispatches, that record the killing of men and women by rolling off roofs and windowsills while asleep, announce that the time of greatest suffering among the poor is at hand. It is in hot weather, when life indoors is well-nigh unbearable with cooking, sleeping, and working, all crowded into the small rooms together, that the tenement expands, reckless of all restraint. Then a strange and picturesque life moves upon the flat roofs. In the day and early evening mothers air their babies there, the boys fly their kites from the housetop, undismayed by police regulations, and the young men and girls court and pass the growler. In the stifling July nights, when the big barracks are like fiery furnaces, their very walls giving out absorbed heat, men and women lie in restless, sweltering rows, panting for air and sleep. Then every truck in the street, every crowded fire escape, becomes a bedroom, infinitely preferable to any the house affords. A cooling shower on such a night is hailed as a heaven-sent blessing in a hundred thousand homes.
>
> Life in the tenements in July and August spells death to an army of little ones whom the doctor's skill is powerless to save. When the white badge of mourning flutters from every second door, sleepless mothers walk the streets in the gray of the early dawn, trying to stir a cooling breeze to fan the brow of the sick baby. There is no sadder sight than this patient devotion striving against fearfully hopeless odds. Fifty "summer doctors," especially trained for this work, are then sent into the tenements by the Board of Health, with free advice and medicine for the poor. Devoted women follow in their track with care and nursing for the sick. Fresh-air excursions run daily out of New York on land and water; but despite all efforts the gravediggers in Calvary work overtime, and little coffins are stacked mountains high on the deck of the Charity Commissioners' boat when it makes its semi-weekly trips to the city cemetery.

Source: Jacob A. Riis, *How the Other Half Lives: Studies among the Tenements of New York, 1890,* pp. 109–110 (reprinted 1970) Belknap Press. Reprinted by permission of Harvard University Press.

---

privies with modern sewer systems, and most large cities turned to filtration and chlorination to assure a supply of pure water.

From Private City to Public City

In the areas of housing, pure water, and clean streets, the battle lines in most cities were drawn between individual profits and public need. Individual entrepreneurs had shaped the modern American city. They laid the horsecar and trolley lines; constructed the skyscrapers, apartments, and tenements; and provided water for the growing urban population. They worked, planned, and invested, fully expecting to earn huge profits. Because their pocketbooks came before their civic responsibilities, they provided good housing and services for only those city dwellers who could pay for it.

Historians have called this type of city the "private city." Using the profit motive to determine urban growth created numerous problems. It led to waste and inefficiency, for example competing trolley lines, where promoters could turn a profit; and such inconveniences as poorly cleaned streets, from which little money was to be made. But most important, it was contrary to planned urban growth. Urban entrepreneurs, generally unconcerned about the city as a whole, regarded parks as uneconomic use of real estate and battled against the idea of zoning. In the end, they contributed to the ugliness and problems of Pittsburgh, New York, Chicago, and other American cities.

By the turn of the century, however, urban engineers and other experts began calling for planned urban growth and more concern for city services. Advocates of the "public city," their aim was efficient, clean, healthy cities where rich and poor could enjoy a decent standard of life. Most urban planning advocates were college-educated professionals who brought knowledge, administrative expertise, and a taste for bureaucracy to government service. After

1900 they would increasingly dominate the quest for better services and more public responsibility, but in many cities their voices were heard too late. The scars of the private city remained on the urban landscape.

CITY CULTURE

It was almost like magic. At 3:00 P.M. on September 4, 1882, Thomas Edison's chief electrician threw the switch at the inventor's Pearl Street station in New York City. Four hundred electric lights went on. For the first time Wall Street buildings were illuminated by the brightest and clearest of all artificial lighting. "It was not until 7 o'clock, when it began to be dark that the electric light made itself known and showed how bright and steady it was," commented a *New York Times* reporter. In the *Times* offices, where 52 Edison lights illuminated the night, "it seemed almost like writing by daylight." Just as trolleys spelled the end for the horse car, electric lights eventually replaced gaslights, candles, and kerosene and oil lamps.

Night Life and Day Life

Electricity soon bathed America's leading cities in white light, making night day. In the rural regions life revolved around the sun. Farmers awoke with the sun, labored during the daylight hours, and went to sleep soon after the sun disappeared over the horizon. Although one's labor changed depending on the season, the order of one's day was changeless. In cities and industries, however, night became more than just a time to rest. Labor and leisure soon claimed their share of the night.

Nighttime labor proved a plague for the working class, but nighttime leisure animated the lives of the wealthy. For Broadway's "fast set," the real fun began after the theaters closed. They moved down the Great White Way, stopping at an exclusive restaurant for a late-night dinner, dining on shrimp Mornay, beef marguery, canape of crab meat, bisque de crème, and other such exotic dishes. Lorenzo Delmonico, the Swiss immigrant who founded New York's most famous restaurant, popularized ices and green vegetables and made meals that rivaled the best in Paris. Eating became a refined pleasure, not just a physical necessity.

Not only did city dwellers consume different types of food, the middle and upper classes consumed more of everything. This shift in consumption patterns signaled a break with the past. The traditional Victorian ethos emphasized production and values—thrift, self-control, delayed gratification, and hard work—that encouraged production. But with industrial success came a general fear of overproduction. Increasingly, advertisers and economic advisors in various ways attempted to transform Americans from "savers" to "spenders." They told people to abandon the traditional laissez-faire economic thinking (which viewed scarcity as an inevitable and fundamental fact of life) and to give in to their desire for luxury.

This new attitude was fostered in large American cities by department stores and hotels. John Wanamaker in Philadelphia, Marshall Field in Chicago, and Rowland H. Macy in New York opened department stores that catered to and pampered the middle and upper classes by offering an unequaled range of products and quality service. The architecture and interior decoration of the department stores, with their grand entrances, marble staircases, chandeliers, stained glass, plush carpets, and wood paneling, inspired extravagance. Spending came easily when the shopper was made to feel like royalty. Grand hotels like the Waldorf Astoria in New York and the Palmer House in Chicago provided the same luxury. The austerity doctrines of the early nineteenth century were easily forgotten amidst such splendor.

It is difficult to imagine the impression electric lights, fruit salads, department stores, and grand hotels made on the people who lived in or visited American cities. They underscored a style of life clearly different from what existed in rural America. City life presented a strange new world that produced in American writers, painters, and musicians feelings of excitement and revulsion. This ambivalence formed the basis of a new urban culture, which combined the energies and experiences of all city people—black and white, male and female, immigrant and native-born.

From the Genteel Tradition to Realism and Naturalism

Frank Norris was born in Chicago, grew up in San Francisco, and lived for a time in Paris. Restlessly moving about the world looking for action, he traveled to Cuba to report on the Spanish-American War, and to South Africa to chronicle the Boer War. In his journalism and novels, he told the truth, feeding his readers bloody slices of the real world. He battled "false views of life, false characters, false sentiments, false morality, false history, false philosophy, false emotions, false heroism." Shortly before he died at 32 of appendicitis in 1902, he boasted, "I never truckled. I never took off the hat to fashion and held it out for pennies. I told them the truth. They liked it or they didn't like it. What had that to do with me? I told them the truth."

The truth. How literature had changed from the previous generation! At the end of the Civil War, American literary tradition had little to do with harsh truth. Controlled by a literary aristocracy in Boston, literature conformed to the "genteel tradition." Great writers endeavored to reinforce morality, not portray reality. Real life was too sordid, corrupt, and mean; far too coarse, violent, and vulgar. James Russell Lowell spoke for other genteel writers when he commented that no man should describe any activity that would make his wife or daughter blush. Sex, violence, and passion were taboo.

Out of rural America came the first challenge to this genteel tradition. Local colorists like Bret Harte, who set his stories in the rough mining camps of the West, emphasized regional differences and used regional dialects to capture the flavor of rural America. Local colorists emphasized, however, humor and innocence, rather than pressing social issues.

Mark Twain, whose real name was Samuel Langhorne Clemens, was the only one to transcend the genre. Like a local colorist, he used regional dialects, humor, and sentimentality, but he also explored the darker impulses of human nature. His classic, *The Adventures of Huckleberry Finn* (1884), exposed the greed, violence, corruption, alcoholism, and racism in American society. As Huck and runaway slave Jim travel down the Mississippi River toward freedom, they encounter a society based on a perversion of Christian ethics. Nowhere is Twain more insightful than when he deals with American racism. In one scene, Huck invents a story about a riverboat explosion. A woman asks if anyone was injured. "No'm," Huck responds. "Killed a nigger." Relieved, she replies, "Well, it's lucky; because sometimes people do get hurt."

The impact of industrialism and city life on the American character did not much interest Twain. It did, however, fascinate most of the other great writers of his generation. Equipped with camera eyes and critical minds, they wanted to show American life in all its harsh and sordid reality. The realism movement soon replaced the genteel sentimentality of the previous generation. Defined by its leader William Dean Howells as "the truthful treatment of material," realism depicted average individuals dealing with concrete ethical choices in realistic circumstances. Even style became secondary. "Who cares for a fine style," Norris wrote in 1899. "Tell your yarn and let your style go to the devil. We don't want literature, we want life."

As realism matured in the largely unregulated and highly competitive cities, it turned into the more

Samuel Langhorne Clemens, better known as Mark Twain, wrote humorous and insightful novels about problems in nineteenth-century America.

pessimistic **naturalism,** which was influenced by the writings of Charles Darwin, Karl Marx, and Sigmund Freud. The individual was seen as a helpless victim in a world in which biological, social, and psychological forces determined his or her fate. Naturalists were particularly interested in the effect of the uncaring forces of industrialization and urbanization on people's lives.

Describing the Urban Jungle

The premier naturalistic writer was Theodore Dreiser. Unlike most earlier American novelists, he was not Protestant, Anglo-Saxon, or respectable middle-class. His German-Catholic immigrant father's life was the flip side of the American success story. After a promising beginning, the family slid deeper

Novelist Theodore Dreiser, writing in the naturalist style, described urban social problems, often portraying characters as helpless victims of their environment.

and deeper into poverty. Dreiser knew what it was like to subsist on potatoes and fried mush, and all his life he dreaded winter, which reminded him of his most painful days of poverty. Sympathetic to those who suffered similarly, he wrote, "Any form of distress—a wretched, down-at-heels neighborhood, a poor farm, an asylum, a jail, or an individual or group of individuals anywhere that seemed to be lacking in the means of subsistence or to be devoid of the normal comforts of life—was sufficient to set up in me thoughts and emotions, which had a close kinship to actual and severe physical pain."

Dreiser left his home in Indiana at 16 and went to Chicago, where he became first a journalist and then a novelist. Unlike better-educated writers, Dreiser had no genteel tradition to shed or rebel against. With his plodding style and atrocious English, Dreiser lacked every writing tool except genius. His first novel, *Sister Carrie* (1900), unflinchingly describes the effect of modern urban society on the lives of one woman and one man. Carrie travels to Chicago from the countryside in search of happiness, which she equates with material possessions, but she discovers only poverty, exploitation, and hardship. The likable, friendly Carrie sinks ever deeper into physical and moral despair.

Like Dreiser, Stephen Crane was also interested in the effects of poverty and urban life on individual character. In his first novel, *Maggie: A Girl of the Streets* (1893), a girl raised in a New York City slum loses, in rapid order, her innocence, her virginity, and her life. It was not a story of a character being rewarded or punished—Maggie was an honest, cheerful person—but rather being a victim of her environment. Poverty determined Maggie's, and later Carrie's, fate.

Naturalistic writers challenged the traditional idea that individuals had the power to control their own destinies. The cherished frontier ideal of rugged individualism seemed poor protection against the forces of urban poverty and industrial exploitation. Carrie was no match for the sweatshop owner, and Maggie's innocence was merely a target in her environment. Neither book was a blueprint for reform, but they did suggest a pressing need for change.

Painting Urban Reality

Unlike Europe, America did not have proud literary, artistic, or musical traditions—no Parthenon, no Rembrandt, no Beethoven. America's asset was land, thousands of square miles of wild land. "American scenery," wrote the artist Thomas Cole, "has features, and glorious ones, unknown to Europe. The most distinctive, and perhaps the most impressive, characteristic of American scenery is its wildness."

American artists shared with American writers and social critics a general aesthetic and philosophical dislike of the city. As Americans moved west, artists continued to focus on the landscape. Albert Bierstadt exaggerated the drama of the Rocky Mountains, but his pictures thrilled eastern and western Americans alike. Even the great, late-nineteenth-century realists—Winslow Homer, Thomas Eakins, and John LaFarge—harbored a suspicion, if not an outright fear, of the city. To be sure, Eakins's work demonstrated a profound respect for the machine, but his admiration did not extend to the city.

By the end of the century, however, the varied urban landscape began to intrigue artists. Steel bridges; colorful immigrant costumes; smoke-filled, congested streets; clashing boxers; washed clothes hanging between tenements; pigeons soaring over flat apartment roofs—each demonstrated the everyday beauty of the city. The energy, conflict, and power of the city seemed to explode with artistic possibilities. When a critic noted that the fighters' faces in George Bellows's *Stag at Starkey's* were hidden, Bellows replied, "Who cares what a prize fighter looks like. It's his muscles that count."

Appropriately enough, the center of this new movement was New York City. The leader of the school—often called Ashcan because of its urban orientation—was Robert Henri, an artistic and political radical. Skyscrapers thrilled him, and he saw beauty in the most squalid slum. He was joined by other artists who shared his love of city life and political radicalism. Generally impressionistic in style, the paintings used unmixed primary colors and quick brush strokes to produce a general impression of a scene. But they were more concerned with content than technique. As George Luks sneered at a critic, "Technique, did you say? My slats! Say, listen, you—it's in you or it isn't. Who taught Shakespeare technique? Guts! Guts! Life! Life! That's my technique."

Like Theodore Dreiser, who admired the Ashcan school, Henri and his followers used their talent to show problems in the growing cities. Bellows's *Cliff*

John Sloan's *Sunday, Women Drying Their Hair*, 1912, is an urban portrait typical of the Ashcan school. The school got its name because the artists preferred to paint the unglamorous, everday aspects of city life.

Dwellers portrayed teeming life but also overcrowded tenement conditions; *Steaming Streets* underscored the problems of urban traffic. And George Luks's *Hester Street* illuminated the excitement but also the packed conditions of the Jewish section of Lower New York.

Maturing along with the Ashcan painters was a second school of artists who also drew inspiration from the urban landscape. Labeled modernists, they championed the pure freedom of nonrepresentational abstract painting. Their intellectual leader was Alfred Stieglitz, whose studio at 291 Fifth Avenue in New York was used to exhibit the modernist paintings. The modernists were also drawn to the conflict and power of the city. Painter John Marin observed, "I see great forces at work, great movements, the large buildings and the small buildings, the warring of the great and the small. . . . I can hear the sound of their strife, and there is great music being played."

In 1913 the Ashcanners and the modernists participated in the most important art exhibition in American history. Held at the Sixty-ninth Regiment Armory in New York City, the show also included works by Cézanne, Van Gogh, Picasso, Marcel Duchamp, Georges Braque, and Juan Gris, the leaders of the European post-impressionists. The Armory Show drew some sharp criticism; Duchamp's cubist *Nude Descending a Staircase*, for example, was called "an explosion in a shingle factory." Other critics and collectors maintained that the exhibition marked a new age for American art. "The members of this association have shown you that American artists—young American artists, that is—do not dread . . . the ideas or the culture of Europe," noted leading collector John Quinn. "This exhibition will be epoch-making." Its most important result was to fuse European and American art movements. It further signaled the ascendancy of the modernists, who would dominate the next generation of American art.

The Sounds of the City

Before the nineteenth century, music critics regarded American music as decidedly inferior to European music; America had produced no great classical composers in the European tradition. Modern American music, uninfluenced by those traditions, was from the very first the language of the oppressed. American blacks adapted the rhythms and melodies of Africa to meet American conditions. Out of the marriage came the work songs of Mississippi slaves, the street cries of Charleston fish and fruit vendors, and spirituals, deeply emotional religious songs. Unlike European music, which was based on a 12-note scale, African music centered on rhythmic complexity with notes that did not conform to the standard scale. Repetition, call and response, and strong beat became the hallmarks of African-American music.

The two music traditions, African and European, existed independently in the United States until the 1890s. But when Jim Crow laws legally and forcefully separated the races in New Orleans, it had unexpected results for American music. Before the 1890s wealthy half-white, half-black Creoles who followed European musical traditions lived in the affluent downtown section of New Orleans. Segregation, however, forced them uptown, where the poorer blacks who followed African musical traditions lived. Although the two groups did not mix socially, they did forge a new musical style–**jazz.**

This musical form, based on improvisation within a structured band format, used both the African and European traditions. Such early New Orleans jazz bands as Buddy Bolden's Classic Jazz Band and Joe "King" Oliver's Creole Jazz Band pioneered the style. Bolden had grown up in the uptown region, where Baptist churches stood next to voodoo parlors and music provided the background for prayer, work, and play. His powerful, moody musical grace mesmerized audiences. But his music came from the soul of a troubled man. Plagued by syphilis and alcoholism, in 1907 he went berserk during a street parade and spent the rest of his life in a mental hospital.

In Storyville, the New Orleans red-light district, the jazz musicians, freed from manual labor during the day, honed their musical skills and explored the possibilities of their instruments. Charlie "Sweet Lovin'" Galloway, Ferdinand "Jelly Roll" Morton, Robert "Baby" Dodds, Bunk Johnson, Sidney Bechet, Alphonse Picou, and especially Louis Armstrong, entertained Storyville customers.

Storyville became a mecca for jazz musicians and a hotbed of raucous city culture. Alphonse Picou recalled the days before Storyville was officially closed with fond nostalgia: "Those were happy days, man, happy days. Buy a keg of beer for one dollar and a bag of food for another. . . . Talking 'bout wild and wooly! There were two thousand registered girls and must have been ten thousand unregistered. And all crazy about clarinet blowers."

Ragtime and the blues also flourished in Storyville. Tony Jackson, Scott Joplin, and Jelly Roll Morton played ragtime, a syncopated piano style that needed only one performer and was popular as café and bordello entertainment. Joplin, a Texas-born African American who had formal musical training, wrote several scores of popular rags, and his "Maple Leaf Rag" (1899) probably sold a million copies in sheet music form. Morton also advanced ragtime, developing the piano swing beat. Blues musicians—mostly African Americans from the Mississippi Delta region raised outside of European music traditions—performed in cheap saloons and expressed the pain of life in a hostile world.

During World War I, government officials closed Storyville, charging it was a health hazard. As the houses of prostitution closed their doors, the talented black musicians headed north—to St. Louis, Chicago, Memphis, Kansas City, and New York. They continued to play jazz and it continued to evolve. White musicians, trained in the European tradition, also contributed to this new American musical form. Bix Beiderbecke from Davenport, Iowa, for example, who formed a Chicago-based jazz band, used more instruments, replaced the African banjo with the guitar, and moved away from improvisation.

The larger jazz bands that dominated music during the next generation were an outgrowth of the New Orleans sound, the result of the mixture of European and African musical traditions. It could only have happened in the fertile atmosphere of the cities, where old and new, black and white, immigrant and native-born combined to create new literary, artistic, and musical forms.

ENTERTAINING THE MULTITUDES

City sports, like city music, were loud and raucous. They moved to the beat of the trolley cars, steel wheels on steel tracks, not horses' hooves on dusty farm roads. Before the urbanization of the late nineteenth century, American sports and games tended to be informal and participant-oriented. Rules varied from region to region, and few people even considered the standardization of rules desirable. By 1900 this cozy informality had all but disappeared. Entertainment became a major industry, and specialized performers competed for the right to entertain the multitudes.

The emergence of commercialized entertainment was the result of changes in both American technology and values. Transportation improvements allowed professional entertainers and sports teams to move across America more easily and cheaply, and technological advances in the popular press, telegraph, and telephone allowed the results of games and entertainment news to quickly spread throughout the country. Also the Victorian notion that entertainment was somehow suspect began to decline. Drawing on Puritan criticisms of play and recreation and a Republican ideology that was hostile to luxury, hedonism, and extravagance, the Victorians had tended to associate theaters, dance halls, circuses, and organized sports with such vices as gambling, swearing, drinking, and immoral sexual behavior. Popular entertainments were judged guilty by association.

In the second half of the nineteenth century, however, these prejudices were challenged. Members of the Victorian counterculture revered play, gratification, and revelry more than the virtues of hard work, punctuality, delayed gratification, and

Jazz combined European and African musical styles into a new musical form. Here King Oliver's Creole Jazz Band poses for a rare picture.

self-control. At first, members of the counterculture tended to be immigrants and bachelors. Irish, German, and eastern and southern European immigrants brought with them a culture at odds with Victorian notions of work and play. In addition, immigrants tended to marry later than native-born Americans; even at midcentury 40 percent of men between the ages of 25 and 35 were unmarried. These men thus formed a "bachelor subculture" that revolved around saloons, gambling halls, race tracks, boxing rings, billiard rooms, and cockpits. As the Victorian economic and social order began to crumble toward the end of the century, upper-class and then middle-class Americans became interested in the activities of the bachelor subculture. The result: a new attitude toward sports and leisure.

Of Fields and Cities

"Baseball," wrote Mark Twain, "is the very symbol, the outward and visible expression of the drive and push and struggle of the raging, tearing, booming nineteenth century." Baseball captured the bustle and hustle of city life. More than any other sport of the period, baseball was an urban game. All of the early professional teams were located in cities and most of the paid players were products of the cities.

The mythology of the sport, however, still lingers—that Abner Doubleday "invented" baseball in 1839, when he laid out the first baseball diamond in the pastoral village of Cooperstown, New York. In fact, however, if anyone can be said to have invented a sport that actually evolved, it was Alexander J. Cartwright, Jr., a New York City stationery-bookstore owner who in 1845 set down the first written rules for the game.

The symbols of the game also recalled America's rural past. Unlike most modern sports, no clock governed the pace of a baseball game. In crowded, dirty cities, baseball was played on open, grassy fields with such bucolic names as Sportsman Park, Ebbets Field, and the Polo Grounds. (Yankee Stadium, opened in 1923, was the first baseball enclosure to veer from the rural tradition.) The field even had fences and bullpens, and the game was played during the planting and harvesting seasons of spring, summer, and fall.

If the symbols and mythology of baseball were rural, the game itself was very urban. Team managers, like their industrialist counterparts, preached the values of hard work, punctuality, thrift, sobriety, and self-control to their players. Baseball, they emphasized, was like modern life, ruthlessly competitive and demanding sacrifice for the "good of the team." As Mr. Clayton, a character in an 1891 baseball novel, explained, "We can't work and we can't play, we can't learn and we can't make money without getting some of other people's help." Like modern corporate society, then, modern sports reinforced the idea of teamwork.

During the last third of the nineteenth century, as men like Rockefeller and Carnegie struggled to bring order to their industrial empires, modern baseball took form. Rules were standardized, for one thing. In the early years of baseball, a base runner could be thrown out by hitting him with the ball as he ran between the bases. Organizers outlawed such violent relics of the past. Then owners attempted to make the sport suitable for the urban middle class. They banned the spitball, arranged games to fit the urban professionals' schedules, fined players for using profanity, and encouraged women to attend the games.

Most important, the owners formed competitive professional leagues centered in the industrial cities of America. In 1869 Harry Wright took his all-professional Cincinnati Red Stockings on a barnstorming tour. Traveling on the recently completed transcontinental railroad, they played teams from New York City to San Francisco and compiled a record of 57 wins, no losses, and 1 tie. In one year the team traveled 11,877 miles by rail, stage, and boat, and entertained more than 200,000 spectators.

The Cincinnati club taught the rest of America, as one journalist commented, that "steady, temperate habits and constant training are all conditions precedent to all first class professional organizations." It also demonstrated to entrepreneurs that there was money to be made in professional sports. In 1876 William A. Hulbert and several associates formed the National League, which was organized around owners and clubs, not players. In business terms, the league was a loosely organized cartel designed to eliminate competition among franchises for players. League officials eventually devised the "reserve clause," which effectively bound a player to the team that held the rights to him and further undermined his ability to negotiate for higher salary. Although the National League was known as a "rich man's" league because it charged a 50-cent admission price, it was certainly not a rich player's league.

In 1890 the players revolted and formed the Players' League. Headed by lawyer and star player John Montgomery Ward, the Players' League was an experiment in workers' control of an industry. In words similar to those used by workers in industry, the players' "manifesto" of 1889 claimed, "There was a time when the [National] League stood for integrity and fair dealing. Today it stands for dollars and cents. . . . Players have been bought, sold, and exchanged, as though they were sheep, instead of

American citizens..." Although lofty in ideals, the Players' League was badly managed and lasted only one year.

With its failure, the National League increased its control over professional baseball. It either crushed rival leagues or absorbed them. In 1903, for example, after a short business war the National League entered into a partnership with the American League. The only losers were the players, whose salaries decreased with the absence of competition. Nevertheless, the sport's popularity soared. By 1909, when President William Howard Taft established the practice of the president opening each season by throwing out the first ball, baseball had become the national pastime.

"I Can Lick Any Sonofabitch in the House"

Only boxing rivaled baseball in popularity during the late nineteenth century. Like baseball, boxing began as a largely unstructured sport, but by 1900 entrepreneurs had reorganized the activity into a profitable business. Although it remained illegal in most parts of America, it produced some of the first national sports heroes.

Bare-knuckle boxing, the forerunner of modern boxing, was a brutal, bloody sport. Two men fought bare-fisted until one could not continue. A round lasted until one of the men knocked or threw down his opponent. At that point both men rested for 30 seconds and then started to fight again. Fights could and often did last over 100 rounds and as long as 7 or 8 hours. After such a fight it took months for the fighters to recover.

Boxers, unlike baseball players, were often from poor immigrant families. Irish-Americans dominated the sport during the late nineteenth century, and they used boxing as a means of social mobility. Such men as John Morrissey, James C. Heenan, and John L. Sullivan became national legends during the period. Morrissey, for instance, was born in Ireland, lived in poverty in Troy, New York, gained fame as a prizefighter, and eventually became a leading New York gambler and politician. By the time he died, he had served two terms in Congress and made a fortune.

The Great John L. (John L. Sullivan), however, eclipsed Morrissey in popularity. He became the best-known American athlete of the nineteenth century. "Excepting General Grant," one newspaperman wrote, "no American has received such ovations as Sullivan." Born in Boston of Irish immigrant parents, Sullivan was a loud, boastful man who loved to fight. He often walked into a saloon and claimed he could outfight and outdrink "any sonofabitch in the house." After he won the bare-knuckle world heavyweight title in 1882, tales of his punching power and his unrestrained attacks on Victorian morality spread across the country.

During the 1880s, Sullivan watched his sport move toward greater respectability. Boxing, like baseball, underwent a series of reforms. The traditional challenge system of arranging fights was replaced by modern promotional techniques pioneered by New Orleans athletic clubs. Fighters deserted bare-fisted combat and started wearing gloves. Most important of all, professional boxers adopted the **Marquis of Queensberry Rules,** which standardized a round at three minutes, allowed a one-minute rest period between rounds, and outlawed all wrestling throws and holds. The new rules also replaced the fight to the finish with a fight to a decision over a specified number of rounds. Although the new rules did not reduce the violence, they did provide for more orderly bouts.

With the advent of the Queensberry Rules, the factory system effectively invaded boxing. Just as workers lost control of the pace of work, fighters no longer could determine the pace of the action. Under the old rules prizefighters could tacitly agree to slow down the action in order to catch their breath or simply exchange boasts and oaths. Now a bell and a referee told them when to fight and when to rest.

John L. Sullivan won the last bare-knuckle championship contest. In 1889 he defeated Jake Kilrain in a fight held near Richburg, Mississippi. It was an illegal fight, but it attracted spectators from all social classes. Bat Masterson, the gunfighter and gambler, served as timekeeper, and he was joined at ringside by wealthy sons of southern aristocrats, gamblers, and sporting men of every variety. The fight lasted for 75 rounds, and both boxers drank whiskey between rounds. After winning the epic fight, Sullivan gained even greater fame.

In 1892 Sullivan lost the title to James J. Corbett in a legal gloved contest fought in New Orleans. Nicknamed "Gentleman Jim," Corbett's scientific boxing style and smooth manners outside the ring demonstrated that boxing had gained some respectability. In fact, by the 1890s boxing was no longer a working-class sport. Like baseball, it had become an organized, structured, and profitable business. All that was left of the older sport was the legend of the Great John L.—the boisterous, crude, lovable, man-child. As he told future novelist Theodore Dreiser shortly after the Corbett fight: "I'm ex-champion of the world, defeated by that little dude from California, but I'm still John L. Sullivan—ain't that right. Haw! Haw! They can't take that away from me, can they? Haw! Haw! Have some more champagne, boy."

The Excluded Americans

Although promoters talked about the democratic nature of sports, this was far from the case. To be sure, a number of Irish and German men—often immigrants or sons of immigrants—prospered in professional sports, but far more Americans were excluded from the world of sports.

In large cities the lines between social classes tended to blur, much to the discomfort of the wealthy who struggled to separate themselves from the hoi polloi. The rich moved to the suburbs and employed other methods of residential segregation to isolate themselves. Another tactic to protect their exclusive status was to allow their children only to marry within their narrow group of acquaintances. They also used sports and athletic clubs to set themselves apart. "Gentlemen and ladies," as they styled themselves, they only wanted to compete against opponents of similar dress, speech, education, and wealth.

One way to exclude the masses was to engage in sports that only the very rich could play. Yachting and polo, for example, demanded nearly unlimited free time, expensive equipment, and a retinue of hired helpers.

In 1884 the New York Yacht Club was founded, quickly gaining as members a "succession of gentlemen ranking high in the social and financial circles" in the city. By the 1890s every major eastern seaboard city had its exclusive yacht club, and each summer the richest yacht owners sailed their splendid vessels to Newport, Rhode Island, the most exclusive of the summer colonies.

Athletic clubs devoted to track and field, golf, and tennis were similarly exclusive. The members of Shinnecock Hills, one of the oldest golf clubs in America, prided themselves not only on the beauty of their course but on their social standing. Such exclusive clubs also had elaborate social calendars filled with dress balls and formal dinners. When sporting events were scheduled, participation and even the privilege of watching were normally on an invitation-only basis.

Wealthy patrons also advocated the code of amateurism to separate the greedy professionals—who often came from the poorer classes—from more prosperous athletes who participated in a sport simply for the love of the game. The constitution of the British Amateur Rowing Association, for example, included in their definition of amateur one who had never "been employed in or about boats, or in manual labour, for money or wages"; and who was not "by trade or employment for wages a mechanic, artisan or labourer, or engaged in any menial duty." The revival of the Olympic Games in 1896 strengthened the amateur code. (When it was discovered, for example, that Jim Thorpe, an Oklahoma Indian who had attended the Carlisle Indian School and who won the decathlon and the pentathlon in the 1912 Stockholm Games, had played baseball for a minor league professional team during the summer of 1909, the International Olympic Committee stripped him of his medals.)

Although amateurism was a subtle attack on the working class, sports leaders moved more forcefully against African Americans. During the 1870s and 1880s, blacks and whites competed against each other on a fairly regular basis. A number of blacks even rose to become world champions. Marshall W. "Major" Taylor was hailed as the "Fastest Bicycle Rider in the World"; Isaac Murphy rode to three Kentucky Derby victories; and George Dixon and other blacks won boxing titles. During the 1890s, however, most sports became segregated.

Jim Crow laws came to boxing during this period. John L. Sullivan steadfastly refused to fight African-American boxers. In 1892 he issued his famous challenge to fight all contenders: "In this challenge I include all fighters—first come, first served—who are white. I will not fight a Negro. I never have and I never shall." True to his word, the Boston Strong Boy never did. The same year, lightweight champion George Dixon administered a terrible beating to white challenger Jack Skelly in New Orleans. After the fight, the editor of the *New Orleans Times-Democrat* wrote that it was "a mistake to match a negro and a white man, a mistake to bring the two races together on any terms of equality, even in the prize ring." After 1892 the number of "mixed bouts" declined rapidly.

Organized baseball also excluded African Americans during the 1890s. Several owners integrated their professional baseball teams during the 1880s, but the trend toward segregation that led to the landmark court case, *Plessy* v. *Ferguson* (1896), overtook baseball. In 1889 baseball's *Sporting News* announced that "race prejudice exists in professional baseball ranks to a marked degree, and the unfortunate son of Africa who makes his living as a member of a team of white professionals has a rocky road to travel." The observation was accurate. By 1892 major league baseball was all white, to remain so until Jackie Robinson broke the "color barrier" in 1946.

Cultural expectations and stereotypes also limited the development of women athletes. Scientists spoke confidently about women's "arrested evolu-

THE American Mosaic

College Football Wars

ALTHOUGH the year was 1905, the story is hauntingly familiar: colleges, football, corruption. Henry Beach Needham in an article in *McClure's* charged that college football had become a professional endeavor, that players were paid performers who cared little for their studies. One example was James J. Hogan, Yale's team captain and star player who knew how to make the most out of an "amateur" sport. At the age of 27, he agreed to play football for Yale. In return, Yale paid his tuition, gave him a $100-a-year scholarship, housed him in rooms at its most luxurious dormitory, and fed him at the University Club. In addition, Hogan and two other players received all the profits from the sale of game programs; Hogan was also appointed the American Tobacco Company's agent in New Haven and received a commission on every package of cigarettes sold in the area. Finally, after each season—but during the school term—Hogan was given a ten-day vacation trip to Cuba.

Hogan was by no means unique. In an age of unregulated football competition, it was each school for itself, each player for himself. Money talked and school spirit was for the students in the stands. Players were more mercenaries than students; their loyalty was constantly on the auction block. Andrew Smith demonstrated this principle in 1902. On October 4, Smith played an exceptional game for Pennsylvania State University against a powerhouse Penn team. The next Monday he had transferred schools and was practicing with Penn, a college that had also "drafted" players from Middlebury, Colorado College, Lafayette, and Peddie. Lafayette College had little cause for complaint. Fielding H. Yost, who coached the University of Michigan for three decades, was an undergraduate at West Virginia at that time. During one season, an undefeated Lafayette "hired" Yost to play against the also unbeaten Penn. After the game, Yost "transferred" back to West Virginia.

Critics charged that football was undermining the very ethics that college professors were laboring to instill into students. As early as 1893, E. L. Godkin, editor of the influential *The Nation*, noted that the leading colleges were losing their educational orientation and becoming "huge training grounds for young gladiators, around whom as many spectators roar as roared in the Flavian amphitheatre." More than a decade later, Charles W. Eliot, president of Harvard, complained bitterly that each fall undergraduates at his university seemed totally obsessed by football, talking about or thinking about little else. Godkin and Eliot found an unlikely kindred spirit in John S. Mosby, who had led the Confederate Mosby's Raiders during the Civil War. Although he had been suspended from the University of Virginia in 1853 for shooting a fellow student, Mosby continued to think of the school as his alma mater. In 1909 the old Raider wrote, after a tragic accident there, "I do not think football should be tolerated where the youth of the country are supposed to be taught literature, science and humanity. The game seems to overshadow everything else at the University."

By the turn of the century, the number of athletes killed or injured in football games had reached an alarming level. In 1909 Virginia halfback Archer Christian died shortly after being injured in a game against Georgetown. Mosby asked, "I believe that cock-fighting is unlawful in Virginia: Why should better care be taken of a game chicken than a school boy?"

Other critics pondered the same question—during the 1909 season 30 boys were killed and 216 seriously injured in football games. The most publicized death of that season was Army's captain Eugene Byrne. He was fatally injured in a game against Harvard. The event was so shocking that the game was immediately halted, and the Army-Navy game of that year was canceled. Byrne was buried with full military honors, while thousands mourned his senseless death and questioned the place of college football in American society.

The nature of football emphasized brutality and violence. Today the team with the ball has four plays to make a 10-yard first down, but during the late-nineteenth and early-twentieth centuries the offensive team had three plays to make a 5-yard first down, and passing was severely restricted, both by the rules and by tradition. As a result, coaches emphasized "mass plays" that directed the maximum amount of force against one isolated player or point on the field. The flying wedge was the most notorious mass play. It entailed players grouping themselves in a V formation and starting to run before the ball was put into play. At the last moment the ball was snapped and passed to a player within the wall of the wedge. The wedge of runners then crashed into their stationary opponents. Given that equipment

was crude—players often played without helmets and no helmet had a facemask—this use of a massed brute force injured hundreds of players each year.

If such plays were not bad enough, referees rarely enforced rules against slugging, kicking, and piling on. Victory was the supreme object; and any method seemed justified in the pursuit of that goal. One Princeton player confessed to a reporter that he and his teammates were coached to eliminate dangerous opponents during the early minutes of a game. A writer for the *Nation* believed this ruthless drive for victory illustrated a fundamental American characteristic: "The spirit of the American youth, as of the American man, is to win, 'to get there,' by fair means or foul; and the lack of moral scruple which pervades the struggles of the business world meets with temptations equally irresistible in the miniature contests of the football field."

By the end of the particularly brutal 1905 season many educators, journalists, and politicians had decided that college football served no educational good and did considerable harm. Professor Shailer Mathews of Chicago's Divinity School labeled football "a social obsession—a boy-killing, education-prostituting, gladiatorial sport." President Theodore Roosevelt stepped in and tried to clean up the game, and officials altered the rules of the sport, but a number of universities chose to drop football from their athletic programs. Columbia, Union, Northwestern, Stanford, and the University of California led the abolitionist movement.

Critics continued to level charges of brutality, commercialism, and corruption against football between 1905 and 1910. The 1905 rules had not lessened the violence, and deaths continued to shock concerned Americans. In 1910 the rules of football were once again altered. In the most important change, the forward pass as

we know it today was legalized. Although football conservatives continued for several years to ignore the new offensive weapon, the pass came into its own in 1913. That year a highly regarded Army team filled an open date in its schedule with a small Indiana school called Notre Dame. During the game Notre Dame quarterback Charley Dorais threw perfectly timed passes to his favorite end Knute Rockne. The result was a 35–13 upset by the Irish of Notre Dame. By the end of the season other teams had adopted the new tactic and passes filled the autumn air. The age of the mass play was over.

Passing made football even more exciting, and after 1913 criticism of the sport generated little support. Continuing scandals over brutality, commercialism, and corruption led more to attacks on individual schools than against football as a college sport. Indeed, by 1917 football reigned unrivaled as college's supreme sport and public spectacle.

tion." Compared to men, women were considered weak and uncoordinated, athletically retarded because of their narrow sloping shoulders, broad hips, underdeveloped muscles, and short arms and legs. Women might ride a bicycle or gently swing a croquet mallet, but men ridiculed women who were interested in serious competitive athletics. The cult of domesticity, which idealized women as nurturers and maintained that women's proper sphere was the home, also militated against female participation in competitive sports.

Even during the 1890s, when the tall, commanding Gibson Girl was the physical ideal and women were becoming more interested in sports and exercise, women's athletics developed along different lines than men's. Male and female physical educators decided that women's sports should be noncompetitive, promote women's physical and mental qualities, and make them more attractive to men. They also believed that sports and exercise would sublimate female sexual drives. As renowned physical educator Dudley A. Sargent noted: "No one seems to realize that there is a time in the life of a girl when it is better for her and for the community to be something of a boy rather than too much of a girl."

But tomboyish behavior had to stop short of abrasive competition. Lucille Eaton Hill, director of physical training at Wellesley College, urged women to "avoid the evils which are so apparent . . . in the conduct of athletics for men." She and other female physical educators encouraged widespread participation rather than narrow specialization. Spectator and professional sports were left to the men. It was not until 1924 that women were allowed to compete in Olympic track and field events, and even then on a limited basis.

From Central Park to Coney Island

Like sports, parks changed to satisfy new urban demands. Uneasy about the urban environment, mid-nineteenth-century park designers saw in parks an antidote for the tensions and anxieties caused by city living. Frederick Law Olmsted, the most famous park architect, believed cities destroyed community ties and fostered ruthless competition. He designed Central Park to serve as a rural retreat in the midst of New York City. Surrounded by trees, streams, and ponds, city dwellers would be moved toward greater sociability. "No one who has closely observed the conduct of the people who visit [Central] Park," Olmsted declared, "can doubt that it exercises a distinctly harmonizing and refining influence upon the most unfortunate and most lawless classes of the city—an influence favorable to courtesy, self-control,

and temperance." But Olmsted was occasionally upset by the behavior of a "certain class" of visitors who believed "that all trees, shrubs, fruit and flowers are common property" and who refused to behave according to Olmsted's ideal.

Other leaders of Victorian culture shared Olmsted's vision. They believed that culture and leisure activities should smooth the rough edges of the urban masses. They built parks, libraries, and museums. Both the Metropolitan Museum of Art in New York and the Museum of Fine Arts in Boston opened in 1870. Visitors to these repositories of culture were expected to behave in an orderly, respectful manner. Museum officials frowned upon laughing, talking, coughing, shouting, and loud demonstrations of enthusiasm.

Many urbanites, however, wanted more excitement than the quiet world of Central Park and the new museums. This was clearly seen at the World's Columbian Exposition of 1893 in Chicago. The most popular area of the World's Fair was the Midway, the center of commercial amusements. Visitors eagerly rode the Ferris wheel, frequented the "40 Ladies from 40 Nations" exhibition, and watched "Little Egypt" perform her exotic dances. Parks and entertainment that amused, not soothed, attracted the most people.

Entrepreneurs were quick to recognize and satisfy the public's desire for entertainment. During the 1890s a series of popular amusement parks opened in Coney Island, New York. Unlike Central Park, which was constructed as a rural retreat, the Coney Island parks glorified the sense of adventure and excitement of the cities, and offered exotic, dreamland landscapes; wonderful, novel machines; and a free and loose social environment. Men could remove their coats and ties, and both sexes could enjoy a rare personal freedom. As one immigrant claimed, for the young, "privacy could be had only in public."

Coney Island also exemplified new values. If Central Park reinforced self-control, sobriety, and delayed gratification, Coney Island stressed the emerging consumer-oriented values of extravagance, gaiety, abandon, revelry, and instant gratification. It attracted working-class Americans who longed for at least a taste of the "good life." A person might never own a mansion in Newport, but for a few dimes he could experience the exotic pleasures of Luna Park or Dreamland Park.

Even the rides in the amusement parks were designed to create illusions and break down reality. Mirrors distorted people's images, and rides threw them off balance. At Luna Park, the Witching Waves simulated the bobbing of a ship in high seas, and the Tickler featured spinning circular cars that threw riders together. "Such rides," wrote a student of Coney

Coney Island provided a temporary escape from the pressures of urban life. Its sense of informality and sheer excitement attracted people of every class.

Island, "served in effect as powerful hallucinogens, altering visitors' perceptions and transforming their consciousness, dispelling everyday concerns in the intense sensations of the present moment. They allowed customers the exhilaration of whirlwind activity without physical exertion, of thrilling drama without imaginative effort."

The Magic of the Flickering Image

Coney Island showed workers that machines could liberate as well as enslave. The motion picture industry, in turn, offered a less expensive, more convenient escape. During the early twentieth century the motion picture developed into a major popular culture form, one that reflected the hopes and ambitions, fears and anxieties of an urban people.

In 1887 when Thomas Edison moved his research laboratory from Menlo Park to Orange, New Jersey, he gave William K. L. Dickson, one of his leading inventors, the task of developing a motion picture apparatus. Edison envisioned a machine "that should do for the eye what the phonograph did for the ear." Working closely with Edison, Dickson developed the Edison kinetophonograph, a machine capable of showing film in synchronization with a phonograph record. The idea of talking pictures, however, was not as popular as the moving pictures themselves. Further refinements by Edison and other inventors made silent moving pictures a commercial reality.

The first movies, as the new form was soon called, presented brief vaudeville turns or glimpses of everyday life. Such titles as *Fred Ott's Sneeze, Chinese Laundry, The Gaiety Girls Dancing, Dentist Scene,* and *Highland Dance* tell the full content of each 3- or 4-minute film. Filmmakers soon began to experiment with such techniques as editing and intercutting separate "shots" to form a dramatic narrative. In 1903 Edwin S. Porter's *The Great Train Robbery,* the first western and the first film to exploit the violence of armed robbery, fully demonstrated the commercial possibilities of the movie. The 12-minute film mesmerized audiences.

During the early twentieth century, movies developed a strong following in ethnic, working-class neighborhoods. Local entrepreneurs converted stores and saloons into nickelodeons and introduced immigrants to a silent world of promise, inexpensive and short escapes from the grimmer realities of urban life. Describing the experience of visiting a nickelodeon, Abraham Cahan, editor of the *Jewish Daily Forward,* wrote in 1906: "People must be entertained and five cents is little to pay. A movie lasts half an hour. If it isn't too busy you can see it several times. They open in the afternoon and customers, mostly men and women, eat fruit and have a good time." In addition, since the movies were silent, knowledge of English was not required for enjoyment.

Ministers, politicians, and other guardians of traditional Victorian morality were quick to criticize the new form of entertainment. Their fears were summarized by Nebraska's superintendent of schools Joseph R. Fulk. Movies, he said, "engendered idleness and cultivated careless spending" at the "expense of earnest and persistent work." Worse yet, they stirred "primitive passions," encouraged "daydreaming," and fostered "too much familiarity be-

Early nickelodeons were cramped and uncomfortable, but they provided endless leisure enjoyments for both immigrants and native-born Americans.

tween boys and girls." Soon local boards of censorship formed to protect innocent boys and girls, and some not so innocent men and women, from being corrupted by movies.

In the cities, censorship movements ultimately failed. Attempts by white, native-born American entrepreneurs to control the new industry similarly failed. Ironically, while films were beginning to attract middle-class audiences, control of the industry began to shift to immigrant entrepreneurs, most of whom were Jews from eastern Europe who proved better able than native-born businessmen to develop the possibilities of the medium. The immigrants emerged from a culture that valued laughter, cooperation, and entertainment, which allowed them to make movies that appealed to Americans.

They were committed to giving the people what they wanted, not to the traditional Victorian code of morality. As Samuel Goldwyn, one of the best immigrant filmmakers, observed, "If the audience don't like a picture, they have a good reason. The public is never wrong. I don't go for all this thing that when I have a failure, it is because the audience doesn't have the taste or education, or isn't sensitive enough. The public pays the money. It wants to be entertained. That's all I know." Film moguls started producing feature-length films and moved the industry from the East Coast to sunny Hollywood, where they could shoot outdoors and, incidentally, escape union difficulties. While such "stars" as Charlie Chaplin, Douglas Fairbanks, and Mary Pickford captured the hearts of America, producers such as Adolph Zukor, William Fox, Louis B. Mayer, Carl Laemmle, and Harry Warner forged a multimillion-dollar industry.

The Agony of Painless Escape

At the same time as popular culture was exploring the theme of mechanized instant gratification, however, Americans were seeking escape in other, more ominous forms. Like the whirring machines at Coney Island and the flickering images on the silent silver screen, the mindless escape of narcotics attracted millions of Americans. During the late nineteenth and early twentieth centuries, as the nation underwent the trauma of industrialization and urbanization, Americans took drugs in unprecedented amounts. Apologists blamed this development on the Civil War, claiming that soldiers became addicted to morphine after using it as a painkiller. Yet France, Germany, Great Britain, Russia, and Italy also fought wars in the second half of the nineteenth century, and their drug addiction rates were far below those of the United States.

Part of the problem was that before 1915 there were few restrictions on the importation and use of opium, its derivatives, and cocaine. Physicians routinely prescribed opiates for a wide range of ailments, and patent medicine manufacturers used morphine, laudanum, cocaine, or heroin in their concoctions. William Hammond, former surgeon general of the army, swore by cocaine and drank a glass of a cocaine drink with each meal. The Hay Fever Association officially recommended cocaine as an effective remedy. Coca-Cola used cocaine as one of its secret ingredients, and the Parke-Davis Company produced coca-leaf cigarettes, cheroots, and a Coca Cordial. Vin Mariani, a wine product containing cocaine and endorsed by Pope Leo XIII, was advertised as "a perfectly safe and reliable diffusable stimulant and tonic; a powerful aid to digestion and assimilation; admirably adapted for children, invalids, and convalescents."

By the late 1890s cocaine's harmful effects had become obvious. Journalists and government officials linked it to urban crime and racial unrest in the South. Eventually, angry citizens and the federal and state governments launched the first great American crusade against cocaine. It culminated with the Har-

Chronology of Key Events

1869 First professional baseball team, the Cincinnati Red Stockings, begins a barnstorming tour of America

1870 The Metropolitan Museum of Art in New York and the Museum of Fine Arts in Boston open

1871 Great Chicago fire claims 300 lives, destroys 17,500 buildings, and leaves 100,000 people homeless

1873 Cable car is introduced in San Francisco

1878 Yellow fever epidemic causes 5150 deaths in Memphis and 3977 in New Orleans

1879 New York City adopts Tenement Reform Law, requiring all rooms to have access to light and air

1882 Chinese Exclusion Act suspends Chinese immigration for ten years; extended in 1892 and 1902; electric lighting comes into widespread use for the first time in New York City

1884 Mark Twain's *The Adventures of Huckleberry Finn* is published

1885 William LeBaron Jenney erects the Home Insurance Building in Chicago, the first true skyscraper

1886 Statue of Liberty is unveiled

1887 W. K. L. Dickson and Thomas Edison develop motion pictures

1888 Richmond, Virginia, introduces the electric-power trolley

1892 James J. Corbett wins heavyweight boxing title from John L. Sullivan; Stephen Crane publishes his first novel, *Maggie: A Girl of the Streets*

1896 President Cleveland vetoes literacy requirement for adult immigrants

1899 Scott Joplin composes "Maple Leaf Rag"

1900 Theodore Dreiser publishes his first novel, *Sister Carrie*

1903 Edwin S. Porter's *The Great Train Robbery* is the first American film to tell a story

1912 Jim Thorpe, an Oklahoma Indian, wins the decathlon and pentathlon at the 1912 Olympic Games in Stockholm

1913 Artists from the Ashcan and modernist schools participate in the Armory Show in New York City

1914 Harrison Anti-Narcotic Act controls the distribution of opiates and cocaine

1921 Emergency Quota Act provides that no more than 3 percent of a nationality already in America in 1910 could immigrate annually to the United States

1924 National Origins Act lowers the immigration quota to 2 percent of each nationality already residing in the United States in 1890

---

rison Anti-Narcotic Act in 1914, which controlled the distribution of opiates and cocaine; but drug addiction remained a problem in cities well into the 1920s.

Robert Louis Stevenson's *Dr. Jekyll and Mr. Hyde*, which he wrote while under the influence of cocaine, described the dangers of challenging society's standards and altering one's personality, but in America's cities a new culture had taken shape. Advocates of this culture opposed Victorian restraints, glorified the freedoms of urban life, and at the same time worried about the implications of a liberated life-style.

Social, as well as economic, freedom came with a price. By the 1890s many Americans believed that some new form of regulation was needed to check the social and economic freedom unleashed in urban America.

Conclusion

On January 17, 1906, Marshall Field, the dry-goods merchant and founder of the large Chicago department store that bears his name, died. "The first as well as the richest citizen" in Chicago, noted the *New York Sun,* Field left his children over $140 million. Americans questioned how one man could accumulate such a fortune. "No man could earn a million dollars honestly," said politician William Jennings Bryan. Another critic suggested that Field's fortune was made at the expense of his more than 10,000 employees, 95 percent of whom earned $12 dollars a week or less: "The female sewing-machine operators, who make the clothes which are sold in the Field establishment, get $6.75 per week. . . . The makers of socks and stockings are paid: finishers, $4.75 per week of fifty-nine working hours . . . knitters, $4.75 per week of fifty-nine and one-half working hours."

Most Americans, however, focused more on what Field offered shoppers than what he paid his employees. Marshall Field, A. T. Stewart, Rowland H. Macy, John Wanamaker—their very names conjured visions of miles and miles of consumer goods. These men brought order to shopping and emphasized standardization of products. In their department stores in New York, Chicago, and Philadelphia, customers could purchase ready-made clothes, jewelry, toys, sheet music, cutlery, and a wide range of other products. Serving urban markets and satisfying urban desires, they also provided a safe haven for urban shoppers. Inside one of the great department stores, consumers were isolated from the garbage in the streets, the filth in the air, and the sounds of traffic and commerce that dominated the outside world. They chose not to think about the workers who made the goods they purchased.

The orderly world of the department store and the chaotic one of the streets were both products of the urban entrepreneurs who fashioned the modern cities. In pursuit of profits they were capable of producing dazzling monuments to commerce and terrible tributes to greed. The same spirit that built the Woolworth Building and the Dakota Apartments also constructed dumbbell tenements, but by 1900, their days of absolute dominance were numbered. Although they would remain a vital part of American capitalism, in the future they would be rivaled by governmental planners—people who wanted to extend the smooth, efficient order of the department store to the outside streets.

The emergence of the great cities changed American life, and more than just economically. Eventually they came to dominate the American imagination. In the cities, the clash of ideas and beliefs, of peoples and traditions created an exciting, new heterogeneous culture. The result was evident at places such as Coney Island and at the Armory Show; it was visible in many of the movies, and it was audible at a New Orleans jazz café. As the nineteenth century drew to a close, a new culture was clearly emerging. It would add a new element to the new century.

SUGGESTIONS FOR FURTHER READING

Lois W. Banner, *American Beauty* (1983). Charts changing standards of beauty in America.

John Bodnar, *The Transplanted: A History of Immigrants in Urban America* (1985). Rejects an older interpretation that viewed immigrants as peasants whose cultures were uprooted in the course of migration.

Roger Daniels, *Coming to America: A History of Immigration and Ethnicity in American Life* (1990). Offers a thorough history of immigrants to the United States.

Leonard Dinnerstein, *The Leo Frank Case* (1968). Case history of anti-Semitism and violence in America.

Caroline Golab, *Immigrant Destinations* (1977). Study of immigrant work in industrial America.

John F. Kasson, *Amusing the Millions: Coney Island at the Turn of the Century* (1978). Uses Coney Island to illustrate changes in American values from agrarian, to industrial, to consumption.

Lawrence W. Levine, *Highbrow/Lowbrow: The Emergence of Cultural Hierarchy in America* (1988). Demonstrates that popular culture can be fascinating without being trivialized.

Kerby A. Miller, *Emigrants and Exiles: Ireland and the Irish Exodus to North America* (1985). First-rate study of why many Irish left Ireland and how they were received in America.

Robert H. Wiebe, *The Search for Order, 1870–1920* (1967). Classic synthesis of major historical trends in turn-of-the-century America.

Overviews and Surveys

Thomas J. Archdeacon, *Becoming American: An Ethnic History* (1983); Leonard Dinnerstein, *Natives and Strangers: Blacks, Indians, and Immigrants in America* (1990); John Garraty, *The New Commonwealth* (1968); Charles N. Glaab and A. Theodore Brown, *A History of Urban America,* 3d ed. (1983); David R. Goldfield and Blaine A. Brownwell, *Urban America: From Downtown to No Town* (1979); Oscar Handlin, *The Uprooted,* 2d ed. (1973); Samuel Hays, *The Response to Industrialism, 1885–1914* (1957); Jacqueline Jones, *The Dispossessed: America's Underclasses from the Civil War to the Present* (1992); Maldwyn Allen Jones, *American Immigration,* 2d ed. (1992); Alan M. Kraut, *The Huddled Masses* (1982); Raymond A. Mohl, *The New City: Urban America in the Industrial Age, 1860–1920* (1985);

Lewis Mumford, *The City in History: Its Origins, Its Transformations, and Its Prospects* (1961); Gerald Sorin, *A Time for Building: The Third Migration, 1880–1920* (1992); Jon C. Teaford, *Twentieth-Century American City*, 2d ed. (1993); Rudolph J. Vecoli and Suzanne M. Sinke, eds., *A Century of European Migrations, 1830–1930* (1991); Sam Bass Warner, Jr., *The Urban Wilderness* (1972).

The New Immigrants

Rodolfo Acuña, *Occupied America: A History of Chicanos* (1988); Josef J. Barton, *Peasants and Strangers: Italians, Rumanians, and Slovaks in an American City, 1890–1950* (1975); Maurice Biolette, *The Franco Americans* (1976); John W. Briggs, *The Italian Passage: Immigrants to Three American Cities, 1890–1930* (1978); Jack Chen, *The Chinese of America* (1980); Hasia R. Diner, *Erin's Daughters in America: Irish Immigrant Women in the Nineteenth Century* (1983); John Duff, *The Irish in the United States* (1971); David M. Emmons, *The Butte Irish* (1989); Elizabeth Ewen, *Immigrant Women in the Land of Dollars: Life and Culture in the Lower East Side* (1985); Richard Gambino, *Blood of My Blood: The Dilemma of the Italian-Americans* (1974); Mario García, *Desert Immigrants: The Mexicans of El Paso, 1880–1920* (1981); Susan A. Glenn, *Daughters of the Shtetl: Life and Labor in the Immigrant Generation* (1990); Marilyn Halter, *Between Race and Ethnicity: Cape Verdean American Immigrants, 1860–1965* (1993); Yuji Ichioka, *The Issei: The World of the First Generation Japanese Americans, 1885–1924* (1988); Thomas Kessner, *The Golden Door: Italian and Jewish Immigrant Mobility in New York City, 1880–1915* (1977); Harry Kitano, *Japanese Americans*, 2d ed. (1976); Helena Znaniecka Lopata, *Polish Americans: Status Competition in an Ethnic Community* (1976); Joseph Lopreato, *Italian Americans* (1970); Ande Manners, *Poor Cousins* (1972); Charles C. Moskos, Jr., *Greek Americans: Struggle and Success*, 2d ed. (1989); Cecyle S. Neidle, *America's Immigrant Women* (1975); Humbert S. Nelli, *Italians in Chicago, 1880–1930: A Study in Ethnic Mobility* (1970), and *The Business of Crime: A Documentary Study of Organized Crime in the American Economy* (1976); Walter Nugent, *The Great Transatlantic Migrations, 1870–1914* (1993); William Petersen, *Japanese Americans* (1971); Andrew F. Rolle, *The Immigrant Upraised* (1968), and *The Italian Americans* (1980); Theodore Saloutos, *The Greeks in the United States* (1964); Henry Tsai Shih-shan, *China and the Overseas Chinese in the United States, 1868–1911* (1983); Stephan Thernstrom, *Poverty and Progress: Social Mobility in a Nineteenth-Century American City* (1964), and *The Other Bostonians* (1973); Susan Cotts Watkins, ed., *After Ellis Island: Newcomers and Natives in the 1910 Census* (1994); Sydney Weinberg, *The World of Our Mothers: Lives of Jewish Immigrant Women* (1988); Mark Wyman, *Round-Trip to America: The Immigrants Return to Europe, 1880–1930* (1993); Virginia Yans-McLaughlin, *Family and Community: Italian Immigrants in Buffalo, 1880–1930* (1977); Olivier Zunz, *The Changing Face of Inequality: Urbanization, Industrial Development, and Immigrants in Detroit* (1982).

Nativism: The Anti-Immigrant Reaction

David H. Bennett, *The Party of Fear: From Nativist Movements to the New Right in American History* (1988); Robert Carlson, *The Americanization Syndrome: The Quest for Conformity* (1987); Mark Haller, *Eugenics* (1963); Leo Hershkowitz, *Tweed's New York: Another Look* (1977); John Higham, *Strangers in the Land*, 2d ed. (1988); Gerd Korman, *Industrialization, Immigrants, and Americanizers* (1967); Richard M. Linkh, *American Catholicism and European Immigrants, 1900–1924* (1975); Seymour Mandelbaum, *Boss Tweed's New York* (1965); Paul McBride, *Culture Clash* (1975); Stuart C. Miller, *The Unwelcome Immigrant: The American Image of the Chinese, 1785–1882* (1969); Thomas J. Pavlak, *Ethnic Identification and Political Behavior* (1976); Diane Ravitch, *The Great School Wars: A History of New York City Public Schools* (1974); Alexander Saxton, *The Indispensable Enemy: Labor and the Anti-Chinese Movement in California* (1971).

New Cities and New Problems

Elaine S. Abelson, *When Ladies Go A-Thieving: Middle-Class Shoplifters in the Victorian Department Store* (1989); John M. Allswang, *Bosses, Machines and Urban Voters*, rev. ed., (1986); Andrew Alpern, *Apartments for the Affluent: A Historical Survey of Buildings in New York* (1975); Nelson M. Blake, *Water for the Cities* (1956); Charles W. Cheape, *Moving the Masses: Urban Public Transit in New York, Boston, and Philadelphia, 1800–1912* (1980); Howard P. Chudacoff, *Mobile Americans: Residential and Social Mobility in Omaha, 1880–1920* (1972); Michael H. Ebner, *Creating Chicago's North Shore: A Suburban History* (1988); Dean R. Esslinger, *Immigrants and the City: Ethnicity and Mobility in a Nineteenth-Century Midwestern Community* (1975); Phillip J. Ethington, *The Public City: The Political Construction of Urban Life in San Francisco, 1850–1900* (1994); David M. Fine, *The City, The Immigrant and American Fiction, 1880–1920* (1977); Robert M. Fogelson, *Big-City Police* (1977); Kenneth Fox, *Better City Government: Innovation in American Urban Politics, 1850–1937* (1977); Clifton Hood, *722 Miles: The Building of the Subways and How They Transformed New York* (1993); Thomas J. Jablonsky, *Pride in the Jungle: Community and Everyday Life in Back of the Yards Chicago* (1993); Maury Klein and Harvey A. Kantor, *Prisoners of Progress: American Industrial Cities, 1850–1920* (1976); Roger Lane, *Policing the City: Boston, 1822–1885* (1967), and *Violent Death in the City* (1979); Peter McCaffery, *When Bosses Ruled Philadelphia: The Emergence of the Republican Machine, 1867–1933* (1993); Blake McKelvey, *American Urbanization: A Comparative History* (1973); Clay McShane, *Technology and Reform* (1974); Harold M. Mayer and Richard C. Wade, *Chicago* (1969); Martin V. Melosi, *Garbage in the Cities: Refuse, Reform, and the Environment* (1982), and (ed.) *Pollution and Reform in the American Cities, 1870–1930* (1980); Gilbert Osofsky, *Harlem: The Making of a Ghetto* (1966); Harold L. Platt, *The Electric City: Energy and the Growth of the Chicago Area, 1880–1930* (1991); Bradley R. Rice, *Progressive Cities* (1977); Christine M. Rosen, *The Limits of Power: Great Fires and the Process of City Growth in America* (1986); Karen Sawislak, *Smoldering*

City: Chicagoans and the Great Fire, 1871–1874 (1995); Martin J. Schiesl, *The Politics of Efficiency: Municipal Administration and Reform in America, 1800–1920* (1977); Carl Smith, *Urban Disorder and the Shape of Belief: The Great Chicago Fire, the Haymarket Bomb, and the Model Town of Pullman* (1994); Allan H. Spear, *Black Chicago: The Making of a Negro Ghetto, 1890–1920* (1967); John Stilgoe, *Borderland: Origins of the American Suburb, 1820–1939* (1988); Jon C. Teaford, *The Unheralded Triumph: City Government in America, 1870–1900* (1984); David Ward, *Poverty, Ethnicity, and the American City, 1840–1925: Changing Conceptions of the Slum and the Ghetto* (1989); William S. Worley, *J. C. Nichols and the Shaping of Kansas City* (1990).

City Culture

Gunther Barth, *City People: The Rise of Modern City Culture in Nineteenth-Century America* (1980); Susan P. Benson, *Counter Cultures: Saleswomen, Managers, and Customers in American Department Stores, 1890–1940* (1986); Edward Berlin, *Ragtime: A Musical and Cultural History* (1980); Burton J. Bledstein, *The Culture of Professionalism: The Middle Class and the Development of Higher Education in America* (1976); Stuart Blumin, *The Emergence of the Middle Class: Social Experience in the American City, 1760–1900* (1989); Paul Boyer, *Urban Masses and Moral Order in America, 1820–1920* (1978); Sarah Burns, *Inventing the Modern Artist: Art and Culture in Gilded Age America* (1996); Susan Curtis, *Dancing to a Black Man's Tune: A Life of Scott Joplin* (1994); Blanche H. Gelfant, *The American City Novel*, 2d ed. (1970); James Gilbert, *Perfect Cities: Chicago's Utopias of 1893* (1991); Martin Green, *New York, 1913: The Armory Show and the Paterson Strike Pageant* (1988); Neil Leonard, *Jazz and the White Americans* (1962); Walter Benn Michaels, *The Gold Standard and the Logic of Naturalism: American Literature at the Turn of the Century* (1987); William L. O'Neill, *Divorce in the Progressive Era* (1967); David J. Pivar, *Purity Crusade: Sexual Morality and Social Control, 1868–1900* (1973); W. J. Rorabaugh, *The Alcoholic Republic: An American Tradition* (1979); Sheila M. Rothman, *Woman's Proper Place: A History of Changing Ideals and Practices, 1870 to the Present* (1978); Lewis O. Saum, *The Popular Mood of America, 1860–1890* (1990); William J. Schafer and Johannes Riedel, *The Art of Ragtime* (1973); David Shi, *Facing Facts: Realism in American Thought and Culture, 1850–1920* (1994); Thomas J. Schlereth, *Victorian America: Transformations in Everyday Life, 1876–1915* (1991); Vincent Scully, *American Architecture and Urbanism* (1969).

Entertaining the Multitudes

Melvin L. Adelman, *A Sporting Time: New York City and the Rise of Athletic Culture* (1986); Robert C. Allen, *Horrible Prettiness: Burlesque and American Culture* (1991); Reid Badger, *The Great American Fair: The World's Columbian Exposition and American Culture* (1979); David F. Burg, *Chicago's White City of 1893* (1976); Dominick Cavallo, *Muscles and Morals: Organized Playgrounds and Urban Reform, 1880–1920* (1981); John E. DiMeglio, *Vaudeville U.S.A.* (1973); Perry Duis, *The Saloon: Public Drinking in Chicago and Boston, 1880–1920* (1983); Lewis A. Erenberg, *Steppin' Out: New York Nightlife and the Transformation of American Culture, 1890–1930* (1981); Charles E. Funnell, *By the Beautiful Sea: The Rise and High Times of That Great American Resort, Atlantic City* (1975); Warren Goldstein, *Playing for Keeps: A History of Early Baseball* (1989); Elliott Gorn, *The Manly Art: Bare-Knuckle Prize Fighting in America* (1986); Stephen Hardy, *How Boston Played: Sport, Recreation, and Community, 1865–1915* (1982); T. J. Jackson Lears, *No Place of Grace: Antimodernism and the Transformation of American Culture, 1880–1920* (1981); Larry May, *Screening Out the Past: The Birth of Mass Culture and the Motion Picture Industry* (1980); Donald J. Mrozek, *Sport and American Mentality, 1880–1910* (1983); James D. Norris, *Advertising and the Transformation of American Society, 1865–1920* (1990); Kathy Peiss, *Cheap Amusements: Working Women and Leisure in Turn-of-the-Century New York* (1986); Steven A. Riess, *Touching Base: Professional Baseball and American Culture in the Progressive Era* (1980); Roy Rosenzweig, *Eight Hours for What We Will: Workers and Leisure in an Industrial City, 1870–1920* (1983); Robert Sklar, *Movie-Made America*, rev. ed. (1994).

Biographies

Marianne Doezema, *George Bellows and Urban America* (1992); Neil Harris, *Humbug: The Art of P. T. Barnum* (1973); Michael T. Isenberg, *John L. Sullivan and His America* (1988); Peter Levine, *A. G. Spalding and the Rise of Baseball* (1985); Randy Roberts, *Papa Jack: Jack Johnson and the Era of White Hopes* (1983), and *Jack Dempsey: The Manassa Mauler* (1979); Laura Wood Roper, *FLO: A Biography of Frederick Law Olmsted* (1973); Elizabeth Stevenson, *Park Maker: A Life of Frederick Law Olmsted* (1977).

INTERNET RESOURCES

A Short History of American Labor
http://www.unionweb.org/history.htm
This brief essay is adapted from AFL-CIO *American Federationist*, March 1981.

American Labor History
http://www.geocities.com/CollegePark/Quad/6460/AmLabHist/index.html
This site takes a general look at the history of labor in America.

Samuel Gompers Papers at the University of Maryland
http://www.inform.umd.edu/HIST/Gompers/web1.html
This site includes information about the papers project but also has a photo gallery, selected documents, and a brief history of the first president of the American Federation of Labor.

Columbian Exposition of 1893
http://xroads.virginia.edu/~MA96/WCE/title.html
This site has a virtual tour of the fair along with contemporary reactions and modern analysis.

Key Terms

Birds of Passage   (p. 518)

Permanent Immigrants   (p. 519)

Nativism   (p. 521)

National Origins Act   (p. 523)

Electric Trolley   (p. 525)

Dumbbell Tenements   (p. 528)

Naturalism   (p. 531)

Jazz   (p. 534)

Marquis of Queensberry Rules   (p. 536)

Coney Island   (p. 540)

Review Questions

1. How did the "new immigrants" of the late nineteenth and early twentieth century differ from previous immigrants to America?
2. What was nativism? What forms did it take? Why did so many native-born Americans embrace it?
3. What problems plagued the growing American city? Why?
4. How did literature, art, and music reflect both the social tensions and possibilities of the new American cities?
5. Were new entertainment choices in sports, parks, and movies a tightening of the new industrial order, a release from it, or both?

19

END-OF-THE-CENTURY CRISIS

EQUILIBRIUM AND INERTIA: THE NATIONAL POLITICAL SCENE
    Divided Power: The Parties and the Federal Government
    Subtle Differences: The Bases of Party Loyalty
    The Business of Politics: Party Organization
    The Struggle for Inclusion: Women and Politics

STYLE OVER SUBSTANCE: GOVERNMENT IN THE GILDED AGE, 1877–1892
    Hayes and the "Money Question"
    Garfield, Arthur, and the Patronage Issue
    Cleveland, the Railroads, and Tariffs
    Harrison and Big Business
    Legislative Activity on Minority Rights and Social Issues

REVOLT OF THE WEST AND SOUTH
    Grievances: Real and Imagined
    The Farmers Organize
    The Agrarian Agenda
    Emergence of the Populist Party

DEPRESSION AND TURBULENCE IN THE 1890S
    The Roots and Results of the Depression
    Expressions of Worker Discontent
    Deteriorating Race Relations
    The Tide Turns: The Election of 1896

"You shall not crucify mankind upon a cross of gold"

On July 9, 1896, William Jennings Bryan rose to speak to the delegates at the Democratic National Convention in Chicago. "I thought I had never seen a handsomer man," a reporter wrote, "young, tall, powerfully built, clear-eyed, with a mane of black hair which he occasionally thrust back with his hand." Thirty-six-year-old Bryan was the son of a circuit court judge who was a Baptist deacon; his mother was a devout Methodist. Bryan, elected to Congress from Nebraska in 1890, was thus steeped in both religion and politics from an early age.

As the cry for "free silver" swept the rural areas of the West and South, Bryan took up the cause. "I don't know anything about free silver," he admitted. "The people of Nebraska are for free silver and I am for free silver. I will look up the arguments later." In the 1890s the slogan referred to expanding the amount of money in circulation by coining more silver dollars. Farmers believed that such inflation of the currency would raise crop prices and alleviate their heavy debt burdens. Many rural residents felt the national government had not been responsive to their needs—that both political parties had been captured by industrialists, railroad owners, and bankers. In 1896 silver was a symbol for popular grievances—it represented rural values, the common people, and a growing discontent with northeastern political domination.

By the time of the Democratic convention the Republicans had nominated William McKinley and adopted a platform calling for the gold standard (or currency backed entirely by gold supplies in the federal treasury). The Democrats were divided between the "silverites" and the "Gold Democrats," monetary conservatives who supported President Grover Cleveland. Control of the party by northeasterners was being challenged by southern and western delegates when Bryan finally rose to speak.

Called "the Great Commoner," Bryan voiced the frustrations of farmers with the failure of traditional politicians to meet their needs. "We have petitioned," he cried, "and our petitions have been scorned; we have entreated, and our entreaties have been disregarded; we have begged, and they have mocked when our calamity came. We beg no longer; we entreat no more; we petition no more. We defy them!"

He enthralled the crowd from the beginning, but his closing words created pandemonium. "We will answer the demand for a gold standard," he roared, "by saying to them: 'You shall not press down upon the brow of labor this crown of thorns, you shall not crucify mankind upon a cross of gold.'" Closing with his arms outstretched as if he were nailed to a cross, he won the Democratic nomination and cinched the victory of the party's silverites.

Cleveland supporters were unwilling to accept Bryan's "foul pit of repudiation, socialism, [and] anarchy," and one declared "I am a Democrat still—very still." Because many party regulars deserted him and nearly half the Democratic newspapers opposed him, Bryan was able to raise only the meager sum of about $500,000. Low on funds he took his campaign directly to the people, appealing to sectional and class animosities: "Probably the only passage in the Bible read by some financiers is that about the wise men of the East. They seem to think that wise men have been coming from that direction ever since."

Bryan relied on his oratorical genius and electrifying charisma rather than money. Between August and November he traveled more than 18,000 miles, visiting 27 states and giving 600 speeches. His youth sustained him as he made his own travel arrangements, bought his own tickets, carried his own bags, rode in public cars, and walked from train stations to hotels late at night. He was often called upon to give unscheduled speeches—when one Indiana crowd awakened him, he spoke in his nightshirt.

With a Republican campaign fund of more than $3.5 million, McKinley had no need to follow Bryan's course. "I might just as well put up a trapeze in my front lawn and compete with some professional athlete as to go out speaking against Bryan," he said. Between June and November, McKinley left his home in Canton, Ohio, for only three days. Railroads provided cheap excursion rates to Canton, so every day except Sunday, crowds of up to 50,000, thronged to McKinley's lawn, from where he conducted his "front porch" campaign. The gatherings were hardly spontaneous, however. His staff organized the groups by occupation or interest, screened each delegation's remarks, and planned each event in detail, right down to brass bands and banners.

In the 1896 election, Republicans sought to convince voters that William Jennings Bryan, shown here at an outdoor rally, was a radical who threatened American values and institutions, while William McKinley, would guarantee stability, order, and integrity.

In contrast to Bryan's speeches, McKinley's were calm and dispassionate, stressing national unity rather than division. "We are all dependent on each other, no matter what our occupation may be," he declared. "All of us want good times, good wages, good markets; and then we want good money always." From his front porch he addressed some 750,000 people from 30 states. The Republicans also spent more for printing than Bryan raised for his entire campaign. By the campaign's end Republicans had sent 200 million pamphlets in several languages to 15 million voters, and some 250 paid speakers toured 27 states.

On election day Bryan and his wife rose at 6:30 A.M. and voted at a local fire station in Omaha, Nebraska. He then gave seven speeches in his hometown before collapsing, exhausted, in bed that evening. McKinley walked to his polling place and stood in line to vote. He then returned home to wait for the returns—his lawn and porch in worse shape than he was. All over the nation politicians and just plain people waited to find out which man and party would preside over the dawning of the twentieth century.

The 1896 election occurred near the end of a decade of turbulence that saw violence toward the labor movement, rising racial tensions, militancy among farmers, and discontent among the unemployed—all of which had intensified after a major depression began in 1893. The social fabric seemed to be unraveling, which is why this election was considered so important. For the first time since the 1870s voters were given a clear choice between two very different candidates and platforms.

Following Reconstruction, national politics were colorful but not very significant. No important policy differences separated the two major parties at the national level; the campaigns revolved around personalities, gimmicks, emotional slogans, and local issues. As elections were trivialized, they became a major source of entertainment, and voters turned out in record numbers. For its triumph of style over substance in politics as well as culture the era is known as the "Gilded Age," a term taken from the title of a novel by Mark Twain and Charles Dudley Warner. By 1890 both the Democratic and Republican parties had lost touch with the sentiments of large blocks of voters—especially those in the West and South. The losers in the great national race toward economic modernization began to question its assumptions. They raised their voices in the 1890s but, unable to unite around a workable agenda they failed to win many battles at that time. The issues they raised, however, appeared regularly on political agendas in the twentieth century.

EQUILIBRIUM AND INERTIA: THE NATIONAL POLITICAL SCENE

American politics have often seemed odd to Europeans. Never was this more true than in the closing decades of the nineteenth century. Commenting on American politics in his 1898 book, *The American Commonwealth,* Lord James Bryce wrote that "neither party has any principles, any distinctive tenets. Both have traditions. Both claim to have tendencies. Both have certainly war cries, organizations, interests enlisted in their support. But those interests are in the main interests of getting or keeping the patronage of government.... All has been lost, except office or the hope of it."

Patronage, or the granting of political favors and offices, became more important than issues to the two major parties for many reasons. In close elections the parties had to be careful not to alienate potential supporters. Most people also believed in limited government. Political parties were therefore organized more to win offices than to govern. The result was a failure by government to deal effectively with the enormous changes wrought by industrialization and urbanization.

Divided Power: The Parties and the Federal Government

Both the Democratic and Republican parties emerged from Reconstruction with sizable and stable constituencies. For the 20 years between 1876 and 1896 they shared a rare equality of political power. Elections were so close that until 1896 no president won office with a majority of the popular vote; the average popular vote margin was 1.5 percent. Two (Hayes and Harrison) even entered the presidency without a plurality. Republicans occupied the White House for 12 years, Democrats for 8. During only three two-year periods did the same party control the presidency and both houses of Congress—Democrats once and Republicans twice. Most of the time Congress itself was split, with Democrats generally taking the House and the Republicans the Senate. Very few seats shifted parties in any given election.

The party division of Congress inevitably weakened the presidents of the era. None was elected to consecutive terms. Calling them "the lost Americans," one observer noted that "their gravely vacant and bewhiskered faces mixed, melted, swam together" in the public mind. Lord Bryce claimed none of them "would have been remembered had he not been President." To be fair, all were competent men, most with considerable public service, and some with distinguished war records. One reason they were so forgettable was the era's concept of the presidency. Many agreed with Cleveland's assertion that the office "was essentially executive in nature." "I did not come here to legislate," he said. Presidents were only supposed to implement efficiently and honestly laws passed by Congress—occasionally vetoing ill-advised legislation. Even though these presidents did turn back many of the encroachments on presidential authority that began in Andrew Johnson's term, none considered it his duty to propose legislation.

Some found the office frustrating. After James Garfield moved from leadership roles in the House of Representatives to the presidency, he lamented, "I have heretofore been treating of the fundamental principles of government, and here I am considering all day whether A or B should be appointed to this or that office." Even representatives and senators were frequently frustrated, however, because congressional action was often stalemated. In the House, outdated and complex rules hampered action. Party discipline was practically impotent in both houses, and since neither controlled both houses for more than a two-year term, there was little possibility of formulating and enacting any coherent legislative program.

The lack of legislative action did not seem a serious problem at the start of the Gilded Age. Most people rejected the idea of an activist government—widely accepted doctrines of laissez-faire and Social Darwinism limited what people expected of government. The Social Darwinist William Graham Sumner once proclaimed that government had "at bottom ... two chief things ... with which to deal. They are the property of men and the honor of women. These it has to defend against crime." Both parties basically accepted a narrow vision of federal responsibility. When vetoing a small appropriation for drought relief in Texas, Democrat Cleveland asserted that "though the people support the Government, the Government should not support the people."

Such antigovernment sentiment tended to increase the power of the judicial branch. Many saw the courts as a bastion against governmental interference in the economy, and the courts certainly fulfilled that role. On the basis of the Fourteenth Amendment, judges were especially active in striking down state laws regulating business. The courts narrowly interpreted the Constitution on federal authority—ruling that the power to tax did not extend to personal incomes and that the power to regulate interstate commerce applied only to trade, not manufacturing. Congress indirectly gave judges more power by enacting vague laws that relied upon the courts for both definition and enforcement.

Subtle Differences: The Bases of Party Loyalty

One consequence of the equality of power shared by the Democrats and Republicans was the reluctance of either party to chance losing voters by taking clear positions on most contemporary issues. This reluctance may also have been based on the memories of the divisive 1860 election and its devastating impact on party and national unity. In addition, there was widespread agreement on many issues. Few members of either party questioned the pace or cost of industrialization; neither saw any need for federal action to regulate the economy. When a Democratic president replaced a Republican one in 1893, one of Andrew Carnegie's managers wrote the industrialist, "I cannot see that our interests are going to be affected one way or another by the change in administration." Business leaders had so little to fear from either party that they contributed generously to both.

Until 1896 the parties did share numerous similarities. Both were led by wealthy men but still tried to appeal to wage earners and farmers as well as merchants and manufacturers. Most members of both parties believed in protective tariffs and "sound currency." Both rejected economic radicalism and activist programs to aid workers. Presidents of both parties sent federal troops to break up strikes.

Ironically, for all their similarities the parties evoked fierce loyalty from a heterogeneous mix of people. One reason party platforms were so innocuous as to be interchangeable is that both parties were composed of factions and coalitions of "strange bedfellows." Because of its past abolitionist connections the Republican party retained the support of many activist reformers, idealists, and African Americans. Yet most Republicans came from established, "old stock" families. The more wealth a man had, the more likely he was to vote Republican. The party therefore was a curious combination of "insiders" and "outsiders."

The Democrats were even more mixed. The party's constituents sometimes seemed united mainly by opposition to the Republicans on various grounds. One Republican leader complained, "The Republican party does things, the Democratic party criticizes; the Republican party achieves, the Democratic party finds fault." Several generations later humorist Will Rogers quipped, "I don't belong to an organized party; I'm a Democrat." His words were certainly true of the Democratic party of the Gilded Age. The party contained such disparate elements as Southern whites, immigrants, Catholics, and Jews.

For historical and cultural reasons, party loyalty was frequently determined by the three factors of region, religion, and ethnic origin. The regional factor was most evident in the support white Southerners gave to the Democratic party. To vote for the party of abolition and Reconstruction was considered treason and a threat to white supremacy. Republicans could count on heavy support from New England for the opposite reasons. To New Englanders, the Democrats were members of the party of traitorous rebellion against the Union. With little hope of winning southern white votes, Union loyalty was one issue the Republicans did not need to tiptoe around. They frequently "waved the bloody shirt," reminding Northerners that the Democrats had caused the Civil War. In 1876 one Republican declared, "Every man that tried to destroy this nation was a Democrat.... Soldiers, every scar you have on your heroic bodies was given to you by a Democrat."

For various reasons immigrants had long gravitated toward the Democratic party. Many were members of the poorest classes, which traditionally voted Democratic. In the 1850s anti-immigration Know Nothing party members joined the Republican ranks, reinforcing immigrants' ties to the Democrat party. Most of the "new immigrants" of the Gilded Age settled in cities controlled by Democratic political machines that won immigrants' loyalty by meeting their needs. As immigration swelled, increasing Democratic strength, Republicans became more and more restrictionist. In fact, immigration policy was one of the very few substantive issues on which the parties took clearly different stands.

Religious affiliations also helped determine party loyalty—partly because of the positions on immigration. Many of the late-nineteenth-century immigrants were Catholics and Jews who were suspicious of the Protestant-dominated Republican party. There were also fundamental differences in the religious orientation of most Republicans and Democrats. Republicans tended to belong to *pietistic* sects that based salvation on good works and moral behavior. Democrats, on the other hand, leaned toward *ritualistic* religions that emphasized faith and observance of church rituals above adherence to strict codes of moral conduct.

Pietistic Republicans frequently sought to legislate morality, supporting prohibition of alcohol and enforcement of Sunday blue laws, which barred various activities on the Sabbath—including baseball. Many Democrats did not believe that personal morality could or should be a matter of state concern. A Chicago Democrat explained, "A Republican is a man who wants you t' go t' church every Sunday. A Democrat says if a man wants t' have a glass of beer on Sunday he can have it."

The roots and constituencies of the parties thus created differences in their outlooks. The Republicans became the "party of morality," the Democrats the "party of personal liberty." Democrats not only rejected government interference in their personal life; in the nineteenth century, they were also more suspicious of government action of any sort. Some quoted Democrat Albert Gallatin's dictum: "We are never doing as well as when we are doing nothing."

Because of their mixed constituencies, however, the differences and divisions *within* parties were as great, and sometimes greater, than those between the parties. Democrats could count on the South for all its electoral votes, but southern Democrats frequently broke party ranks when voting on legislation. They sometimes voted with western Republicans on acts favorable to farmers. They were, however, fundamentally conservative men of Whiggish tendencies who usually voted with northern Republicans on financial and economic issues, as well as on immigration restriction. In a bizarre political arrangement, southern Democrats also voted with northern Republicans at times in order to receive a share of the patronage.

The Republicans were even more deeply divided into factions. One group, led by Roscoe Conkling, was labeled the "Stalwarts." Followers of James G. Blaine of Maine were called "Half-breeds." The only significant item of dispute between the two was who would receive the numerous jobs the president could make appointments to. Because the distribution of patronage was a prime function of both parties of the era, the division was bitter. When Conkling was asked if he intended to campaign for Blaine for president in 1884, he snapped that he did not engage in criminal activities.

One faction of the Republican party, however, did have some ideological basis. It was composed of reformers whose primary concern was honest and effective government. They had bolted the party in 1872 because of the corruption of the Grant regime, and they bolted again in 1884, supporting Democratic candidate Grover Cleveland for president. Party regulars ridiculed them, calling them "goo-goos" for their idealistic good government crusade. They were finally labeled **"Mugwumps"**—a joke that asserted they had their "mugs" on one side of the fence and their "wumps" on the other.

The divisions in the Republican party reflected the fact that the politicians of the day were less concerned with issues and ideology than with winning office and distributing patronage. Lord Bryce observed that American politicians could be differentiated from European ones by the fact "that their whole time is frequently given to political work, that many of them draw an income from politics . . . that . . . they are proficient in the acts of popular oratory, of electioneering, and of party management."

The Business of Politics: Party Organization

Gilded Age politicians were very serious about their careers. They worked hard at both "party management" and "electioneering." The result was the largest voter turnout in the nation's history. In the elections from 1860 to 1900 an average of 78 percent of eligible voters cast ballots. Outside of the South (where African Americans were increasingly prevented from voting and where the Democratic nomination determined the general election), the turnout sometimes reached 90 percent.

There was one main difference in Republican and Democratic party organization. Republicans generally depended on strong state organizations, while Democrats tended to rely on urban political machines to win and control votes. Since city governmental structures did not keep pace with the huge population increases, political machines based on ward captains provided many of the services for which government would later be held responsible. This machine also helped immigrants and rural migrants adjust to city life. One ward boss noted: "There's got to be in every ward somebody that any bloke can come to—no matter what he's done—and get help. Help, you understand, none of your law and justice, but help." Politicians took their pay in votes from the people, bribes from legal and illegal businesses, and graft from contractors. The system worked so well that the Democrats usually carried the big cities.

For both parties, recruiting and maintaining party voters was a game for professionals. Republicans in Pennsylvania compiled a list of 800,000 voters with notations as to their reliability as party loyalists. Politics was a rough and sometimes corrupt game. Conkling warned, "Parties are not built by deportment, or by ladies' magazines, or gush." In 1888 when newly elected Benjamin Harrison pro-

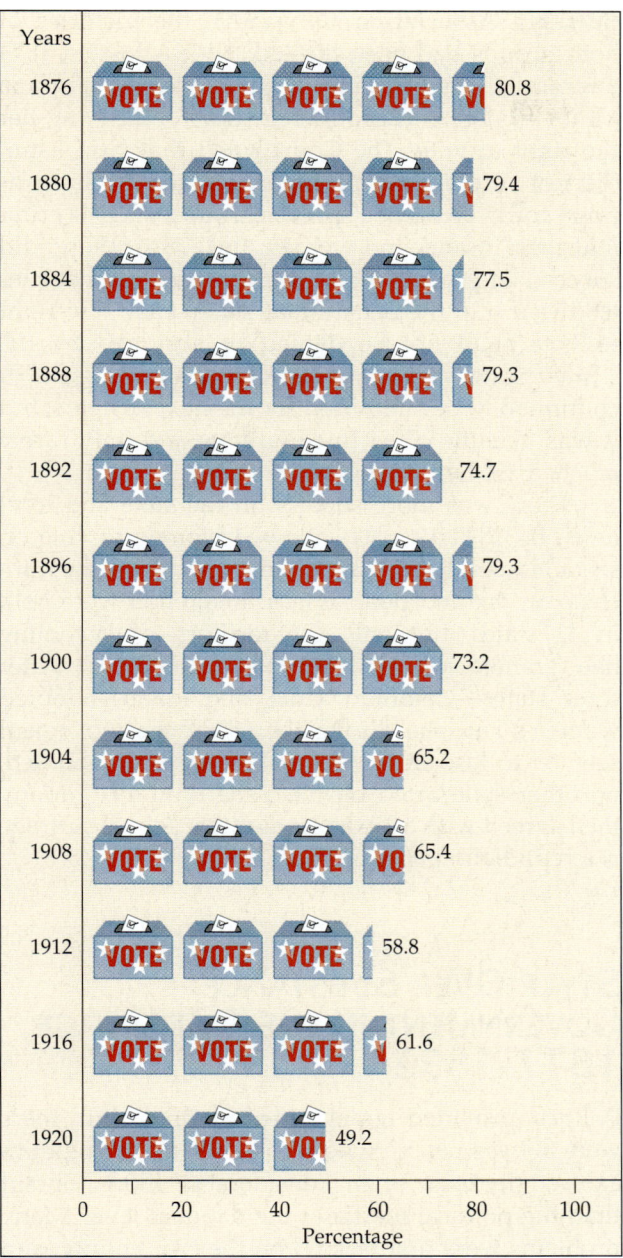

FIGURE 19.1

Voter Participation in Presidential Elections, 1876–1920

fair count in Mississippi since 1875, that we have been preserving the ascendancy of white people by revolutionary methods. In other words, we have been stuffing ballot boxes, committing perjury, and here and there in the state carrying the elections by fraud and violence."

Gilded Age politics was not dull. One could almost claim that the business of politics was entertainment. One observer remarked, "What the theatre is to the French, or the bull fight... to the Spanish... [election campaigns] and the ballot box are to *our* people." The drama of emotional tent meetings rivaled circuses, and the pageantry of parades provided excitement. Almost everyone got caught up in the elections, frequently displaying such paraphernalia as buttons, handkerchiefs, hats, banners, and posters emblazoned with their party's symbol or slogan. In 1888 one tobacco company enclosed in its packages pictures similar to baseball cards of the 25 presidential hopefuls. Politics was undoubtedly a prime form of mass entertainment.

Many politicians surely must have enjoyed their status as "media stars" and folk heroes. For some whose ethnic or class backgrounds closed conventional doors of opportunity, politics provided a vehicle of upward social mobility, similar to professional entertainment and athletics or trade union leadership. Yet politics as a vocation offered other rewards. Elected and appointed officials not only received salaries but many also openly accepted gifts from

Gimmicks in Gilded Age political campaigns, such as this Bryan donkey, stirred public interest, resulting in the highest voter turnouts in the nation's history.

claimed, "Providence has given us the victory," Republican party boss Matt Quay snorted, "Providence hadn't a damn thing to do with it." Quay then added that Harrison "would never know how close a number of men were impelled to approach the gates of the penitentiary to make him president." Electoral corruption was not limited to one party. In the same year a Mississippi Democrat admitted: "It is no secret that there has not been a full vote and a

lobbyists and free passes from railroads. They sometimes used their governmental status to promote their private interests. James G. Blaine of Maine expressed no qualms about accepting stock concessions from an Arkansas railroad that he had aided in getting a federal land grant. One quip claimed that the United States had the best Congress money could buy.

The Struggle for Inclusion: Women and Politics

Politics could be a rough and dirty business—one many considered inappropriate for women. Increasingly women disagreed. After an 1869 split in the suffrage movement, the National Woman Suffrage Association (NWSA), led by Elizabeth Cady Stanton and Susan B. Anthony, fought for the vote on the national level through the courts and a proposed constitutional amendment. At the same time the American Woman Suffrage Association (AWSA), headed by Lucy Stone and Julia Ward Howe, sought victories at the state level.

Up to the point in 1890 when the groups merged to form the **National American Woman Suffrage Association (NAWSA),** the victories of both groups had been limited. NWSA lost an 1874 Supreme Court decision in a suit filed by Virginia Minor against a St. Louis registrar for denying her the right to vote. The Court ruled that citizenship did not automatically confer the vote and that suffrage could be denied specific groups, such as criminals, the insane, and women. In 1878 Anthony did succeed in getting a constitutional amendment introduced into the Senate that stated that "the right to vote shall not be denied or abridged by the United States or by any state on account of sex." It continued to be submitted for the next 18 years, but it was usually killed in committee and only rarely reached the Senate floor.

There was more success on the state and local level. By 1890 19 states allowed women to vote on school issues, and 3 states extended women the franchise on tax and bond issues. Referenda were held in 11 states, but only the territory of Wyoming had granted women full political equality. After three states—Colorado, Utah, and Idaho—adopted women's suffrage during the 1890s, the movement seemed to lose steam. As male resistance mounted, no other state acted on the issue until 1910. Many men agreed with a Texas senator that "equal suffrage is a repudiation of manhood."

In 1869 Wyoming became the first territory to allow women to vote in all territorial elections. It later refused to enter the Union without women's suffrage.

STYLE OVER SUBSTANCE: GOVERNMENT IN THE GILDED AGE, 1877–1892

Politics provided great entertainment, but there were always people who wanted more. Local political activity was often considerably more vibrant than the political inertia at the national level. Many problems were first tackled on the city, county, and state levels before becoming a part of the national agenda. Such issues as the currency and tariffs could only be solved at the national level, but others, such as demands for clean government, were undertaken at all levels. On the whole, the states responded more vigorously than the national government to the problems created by economic changes—only to have the Supreme Court sometimes tie their hands. Out of frustration, people began to look to Washington for solutions, but the presidents and Congress responded timidly. National elections still focused mainly on trivial issues. When backed to the wall, Congress would enact laws to quiet popular cries for action, but such laws were often limited in scope and unenforceable.

Hayes and the "Money Question"

After the disputed election of 1876 almost created a constitutional crisis, the presidency was snatched from Democrat Samuel J. Tilden and given to Rutherford B. Hayes. A series of bargains was needed for the acceptance of the 8 to 7 vote of the electoral commission that named Hayes president. His administration was thus from the start tainted with snide references to him as "His Fraudulence" and "Old 8 to 7." He was actually honest and competent, and did much to establish the Republican party as the "party of morality" after the corruption of the Grant regime. His wife also helped to link Republicans with morality by her refusal to serve strong drinks—earning her the label of "Lemonade Lucy." One guest at a White House party remarked in disgust that "the water flowed like champagne."

Hayes is now probably best remembered for removing the remaining federal troops from the South—marking the end of Reconstruction. At the time, however, economics rather than race relations occupied the public's mind. Hayes came into office more than three years into an economic depression that began with the panic of 1873. That depression raised the "money question," which continued to crop up for more than two decades.

At the root of this issue—as complex as it was heated—was a long period of deflation following the Civil War. Price levels dropped because the production of goods was growing faster than the supply of money. Farmers are not necessarily hurt by a general deflation if all prices fall equally and the farmers debt levels are low. Wheat, corn, and cotton prices, however, declined more than other prices in the late nineteenth century, and farmers had also borrowed heavily to expand production. They were thus caught in a debt squeeze—their mortgage payments remained high while the prices they received fell. For example, a farmer who borrowed $1000 with a 25-year mortgage to buy a farm in 1868 had to produce over twice as much cotton to make the mortgage payment in 1888. The farmer received virtually nothing for doubled efforts, but the creditor received not only interest for the use of the money but also an additional bonanza—dollars now worth twice as much as those lent.

Debtors in all occupations began blaming their problems on deflation and saw inflation of the currency as the cure—for them it was a moral issue, a

In this Greenback party cartoon from the 1870s, a gold-nosed government octopus puts a stranglehold on U.S. farmers, laborers, and small businesses. The Greenbackers wanted to distribute more money to more of the American people and opposed specie (gold) payments on bonds.

question of justice. One way to inflate currency was to increase the number of legal tender paper "greenbacks" first issued during the war. Supporters of that solution organized the **Greenback party** in 1874. Instead, two years before Hayes entered the White House, Congress enacted the Resumption Act of 1875 to eliminate paper money not backed by gold or silver.

After the Resumption Act, some inflationists turned their attention to silver. The nation had been on a bimetallic standard since the 1790s. The dollar was based on both gold and silver, and for years dollars were coined at a 16 to 1 mint ratio—16 times as much silver as gold. By the 1870s this ratio did not reflect the market prices of the metals. Silver prices got so high that producers sold it on the open market rather than take it to the mint to be coined. Unable to buy silver at that ratio, Congress passed the Coinage Act of 1873, which halted the minting of silver dollars.

Soon after, the discovery of large deposits of silver drove prices down again. Then it was in the interest of both silver miners and inflationists to return to the coining of silver at 16 to 1. The two groups formed a large lobby that wrested minor concessions from Congress. The Bland-Allison Act of 1878 required the government to buy between $2 and $4 million worth of silver each month. Like much of the legislation of the Gilded Age, the Bland-Allison Act proved to be a cosmetic answer to popular demands. It neither raised silver prices nor inflated the currency significantly. Inflationists remained unhappy, and the Greenback party nominated former Union general James B. Weaver of Iowa for president in the 1880 election.

Garfield, Arthur, and the Patronage Issue

As in earlier elections neither of the two major parties focused on substantial issues in the 1880 election, but instead relied on slogans and gimmicks to win votes. The battle for the Republican nomination was between the Half-Breed and Stalwart factions. After Hayes refused to run for a second term in 1880, stalwarts hoped to run Grant again, but the Republican convention became deadlocked. On the thirty-sixth ballot the party picked James A. Garfield, a veteran but relatively unknown Ohio congressman. To conciliate the Stalwarts, Chester A. Arthur, a Conkling henchman, became the vice-presidential nominee.

The Democrats nominated an even more obscure figure, General Winfield Scott Hancock, whose only claim to fame was being a hero of the Battle of Gettysburg. He was described as "a good man weighing 250 pounds." Garfield was also bland, but he had the advantage of a log cabin birth and a brief career on a canal towpath—giving rise to a popular Republican campaign slogan: "From the towpath to the White House." The 1880 election was one of the closest of the century in popular vote. Garfield received a mere 39,000 vote plurality out of almost 10 million ballots cast. Greenback nominee Weaver came in a distant third, gaining only 3.4 percent of the popular vote.

Returning prosperity and a tragic event focused attention on the issue of patronage, overshadowing the currency question. Four months after Garfield's inauguration he was shot twice by a deranged office-seeker, Charles Guiteau, who exclaimed, "I am a Stalwart. Arthur is now President of the United States." A native of Vermont, Arthur attended Union College, became an abolitionist lawyer, and then held a series of appointed offices. Considered by many to be a party hack, Arthur surprised them by becoming a champion of governmental reform.

The Mugwumps and others had become increasingly concerned with corruption in government. In the 1873 novel that gave the era its label of the Gilded Age, Mark Twain and Charles Dudley Warner wrote, "The present era of indelible rottenness is not Democratic, it is not Republican, it is national. Politics are not going to cure more ulcers like these, nor the decaying body they fester upon." Because of the pervasiveness of the corruption, some saw no way out. "All being corrupt together," E. L. Godkin, editor of *The Nation*, wrote, "what is the use of investigating each other?"

Some reformers believed that one answer to the problem of corruption was the reformation of the **"spoils system"** of patronage. Since the early 1800s government jobs had been considered the "spoils" of political victory, to be awarded to loyal party workers regardless of their qualifications. Between 1865 and 1891 problems grew as federal positions tripled from 53,000 to 166,000. Indeed, presidents of the era spent much of their time making some 100,000 appointments—most of which were in the postal service. That number of jobs provided incentives to precinct and ward bosses to get out the vote, but such inventions as the typewriter began to make it necessary for government workers to have skills other than getting people to vote.

After Garfield's assassination, Congress finally took action. With the support and encouragement of President Arthur, Congress enacted the **Pendleton Act** in 1883, which outlawed political contributions by appointed officeholders. It also established competitive examinations for federal positions to be

Charles Guiteau shoots President Garfield as Secretary of State Blaine looks on in horror. After suffering for two and a half months, the President died on September 19, 1881. Guiteau, whose behavior during his trial suggested insanity, was convicted on January 25, 1882, and hanged on June 30.

given by the Civil Service Commission. The rather timid act only applied to about 10 percent of government employees, and some self-serving motives contributed to its passage. Since it was to apply only to future appointees and protected incumbents, the Democrats called it "a bill to perpetuate in office the Republicans who now control the patronage of the Government." In the same manner, every president elected after its enactment increased the number of positions protected from political removal—usually to prevent his appointees from being removed. The political system thus was becoming modernized, but some questioned whether it was being improved.

Cleveland, the Railroads, and Tariffs

By the time of the 1884 election, Arthur's actions had won more favor from the public than from his party. The Republicans bypassed him and nominated James G. Blaine, who was far from bland. He was so handsome and charismatic that a colleague's wife once remarked, "Had he been a woman, people would have rushed off to send expensive flowers." Indeed, Blaine had almost all the qualities of a successful presidential candidate: a phenomenal memory for names and faces, eloquent oratory, and a quick wit. He was, however, tainted politically. While in Congress he had become very rich without any visible means of outside income. Letters circulated that implied Blaine was up for sale to the railroads. He was more than the Mugwumps could stomach; they could not support him.

Realizing the potential advantage of a Mugwump defection, the Democrats selected Grover Cleveland, a reform governor of New York. Neither physically attractive nor charismatic, he did have one appealing quality. He was honest. As one supporter explained, "We love him for the enemies he has made." Cleveland and Blaine did not disagree on the major issues, so their campaign revolved around personalities and became one of the most scurrilous in the nation's history.

Blaine's tainted past was obvious fodder for the Democrats' campaign. At torchlit rallies Democrats chanted: "Blaine! Blaine! James G. Blaine! Continental liar from the state of Maine!" Unable to find a shred of evidence to challenge Cleveland's honesty, Republicans publicized a more personal scandal. Cleveland, a bachelor, had supported an illegitimate child since 1874, even though his paternity was questionable. Thus Republicans countered Democratic chants with "Ma! Ma! Where's my pa? Going to the White House? Ha! Ha! Ha!" In the end Cleveland's victory may have been due to an indiscretion by a Blaine supporter, who had labeled the Democrats as the party of "rum, Romanism, and rebellion." Even though Blaine's mother was Catholic, Democrats were able to rally Catholic voters to win key states.

The major legislation of Cleveland's first presidency resulted from public pressure and court actions. The power and discriminatory rates of the railroads frightened and angered many Americans, and actions to regulate the railroads had started at the state level. Beginning with the establishment in

In this cartoon, Grover Cleveland's alleged illegitimate child is used to impugn "Grover the Good's" well-known political integrity.

Public anger over railroad power, as expressed in this political cartoon, finally pushed Congress to pass the Interstate Commerce Act in 1887.

1869 of a regulatory commission in Massachusetts, by 1880 there were railroad commissions in 14 states. Farmers and their allies, especially in the Midwest, got stronger legislation enacted that set maximum rates and charges within their states.

The railroad men naturally attacked these laws through the courts. At first they lost. In the 1877 *Munn* v. *Illinois* decision, the Supreme Court ruled that when "private property is affected with a public interest it . . . must submit to be controlled by the public for the common good." Nevertheless, states had difficulty regulating railroads chartered by other states and doing business across state lines. Then in the 1886 *Wabash, St. Louis & Pacific Railway Company* v. *Illinois* case the Supreme Court took away the rights of states to even try by ruling that only Congress had the right to regulate interstate commerce.

Pressure began to build for federal action, and Congress finally responded to the demands by passing the Interstate Commerce Act, which Grover Cleveland signed into law in February 1887. It prohibited pools, rebates, and rate discriminations; provided that all charges by the railroads should be "reasonable and just"; and established the **Interstate Commerce Commission (ICC).** Although significant as the first federal regulatory agency, the commission's power was woefully limited. It could investigate charges against the railroads and issue "cease and desist" orders, but these could only be enforced by the courts.

Conservative courts soon nullified 90 percent of the commission's orders; between 1887 and 1905 the Supreme Court decided against the ICC in 15 of 16 cases. By 1892 railroad attorney Richard S. Olney wrote, "The Commission, as its functions have now been limited by the Courts, is, or can be made of great use to the railroads. It satisfies the popular clamor for a government supervision of railroads, at the same time that such supervision is almost entirely nominal." One railroad executive admitted, "There is not a road in the country that can be accused of living up to the rules of the Interstate Commerce Commission."

The Interstate Commerce Act temporarily satisfied "popular clamor" without alienating railroad owners, so it did not become a partisan issue for either party. However, during Cleveland's term, a major issue on which Democrats and Republicans actually differed emerged: the tariff. Although both parties supported these taxes on imports to raise revenue and to protect American products from being undersold by foreign competitors, the difference lay in how high these tariffs should be. Regardless of party, congressmen voted their constituents' interests, which made few of them consistent on the issue. "I am a protectionist for every interest which I am sent here by my constituents to protect," one Democratic senator explained.

Like most Democrats, Cleveland had long been less enthusiastic about high tariffs than Republicans. While in office he found that existing tariff rates were producing treasury surpluses that were tempting congressmen to propose programs and appropriations that he considered dangerous expansions of federal activities. A moralistic man, Cleveland was deeply opposed to governmental involvement in the economy and social issues. He thus became an advocate of tariff reduction. In 1887, at his urging, the Democratic House enacted moderate reductions, but the Republican Senate blocked the bill. Cleveland then proceeded to make the tariff a focus of his reelection bid in 1888.

Harrison and Big Business

In 1888 the Democrats renominated Cleveland and wrote tariff reduction into their platform. The Republicans chose Benjamin Harrison and cheerfully picked up the gauntlet—denouncing Cleveland's "free trade" as unpatriotic. They also promised generous pensions to veterans. Voters at last were given some choice on a real issue. The result was a viciously corrupt and close election. Harrison's campaign chairman, Matt Quay, proceeded to "put the manufacturers of Pennsylvania under the fire and fry all the fat out of them." He asked them to make large contributions to the Republican party as insurance against lowered tariff rates. When Cleveland lost, many blamed his defeat on his taking too clear a stand on an issue. Republicans erroneously interpreted his narrow defeat as a mandate for protectionism. Congress then enacted the McKinley Tariff, which raised average duties to the highest level yet, but the Republicans misread public sentiment. The McKinley Tariff was very unpopular.

Both high tariffs and trusts were becoming distasteful to many Americans. Popular demand for legislative action against trusts had been growing during the 1880s. Again action started on the state level; 15 southern and western states had passed antitrust legislation by the mid-1880s. Of course, companies simply incorporated in more sympathetic states. The laws were ineffective and likely to be overturned by federal courts, but they did reflect popular distaste for the monopolies. Congress responded to these rumblings by enacting the **Sherman Antitrust Act** in 1890. On the surface it seemed to doom the trusts, prohibiting any "contract, combination in the form of trust or otherwise, or conspiracy in restraint of trade or commerce." As with the Interstate Commerce Act, appearances were deceiving. One senator explained that Congress had wanted to pass "some bill headed 'A bill to Punish Trusts' with which to go to the country" to aid their reelection.

Until 1901 the act was virtually unenforced—the Justice Department had instituted only 14 suits and failed to get convictions in most of them. The Supreme Court also emasculated the law in *United States* v. *E. C. Knight Co.* (1895), ruling that it applied to commerce but not manufacturing. Thus, the subject of that suit, a sugar trust controlling 98 percent of the industry, was not held in violation. Indeed, the only effective use made of the act in its first decade was as a tool to break up labor strikes by court injunctions.

In 1890 popular pressure also led to further action on the currency question. Following the Bland-Allison Act of 1878, the money supply continued to grow too slowly for the expanding economy. By 1890 pressure to coin more silver was growing. Congress responded with the Sherman Silver Purchase Act, which required the government to buy 4.5 million ounces of silver each month at the unrealistic ratio of 16 to 1. Paper money to pay for the purchases was redeemable in gold or silver, keeping the inflationary impact minimal. The act was a compromise that satisfied no one; the silver issue grew more heated in the 1890s.

Legislative Activity on Minority Rights and Social Issues

To African Americans the Republicans remained the party of black rights, but after the election of 1876 the party did less and less to earn that label. By 1890, however, increasing southern assaults on African-American voting rights finally moved some Republicans to action. Senator Henry Cabot Lodge and others drafted the Lodge Bill, a federal elections bill that sought to protect voter registration and guarantee fair congressional elections by establishing mechanisms to investigate charges of voting fraud and to deal with disputed elections.

Southern white response was rapid and bitter. The *Florida Times-Union* charged: "The gleam of federal bayonets will again be seen in the South." Northern Democrats lent their support to southern outrage. Cleveland exclaimed, "It is a dark blow at the freedom of the ballot." Although in 1890 Republicans controlled both houses of Congress, they finally bartered away the Lodge Election Bill to gain support for the McKinley Tariff. Protection of manufacturers was more important to them than the protection of African Americans.

In that same year Republicans also let the Blair Education Bill die. This bill would have provided federal aid to schools, mostly African American, that did not get a fair share of local and state funds. The Blair Bill marked the last glimpse of the party's dying abolitionist roots as well as the loss of party idealism. The Fifty-first Congress wanted to alleviate treasury surpluses to protect tariffs, but in the end the only group to receive substantial aid was Union Army veterans, who were voted pensions by the so-called Billion-Dollar Congress in 1890.

Other measures of the era affected minorities—but usually in a negative way. Southern white Democrats enacted discriminatory legislation against African Americans at the local and state level. A movement for immigration restriction, usually initiated by Republicans, led to the Chinese Exclusion Act of 1882 and other legislation that banned certain categories of immigrants and gave the federal government control of overseas immigration. The 1887 Dawes Act attacked the roots of American Indian culture by trying to make Native Americans homesteading farmers, which resulted, unintentionally, in making them dependent wards of the state.

Although most social issues received short shrift at the federal level, some received passionate attention at the local and state level. The two main ones—education and prohibition—were essentially Republican issues. An Iowa Republican slogan called for "a school house on every hill, and no saloon in the valley." Many people were alarmed by the increased use of alcohol—annual consumption of beer rose from 1.6 to 6.9 gallons per capita from 1850 to 1880. Republicans moved beyond the educational focus of the temperance movement to attempt to make drinking alcohol a crime. They also sought to increase compulsory school attendance, but these efforts were often linked to moves to undermine parochial schools and schools that taught immigrants in their native tongues. In most areas these Republican actions backfired, losing more voters than they gained. For example, Republicans had once predicted "Iowa will go Democratic when Hell goes Methodist," but in 1890 the state fell to their opponents.

By 1890 very little effective national legislation had been adopted to deal with the problems of a pluralistic society experiencing rapid social and economic change. Resulting partly from a political equilibrium that bred inertia, concepts of the limited nature of governmental responsibility also did not provide impetus for action. Public demands for change were nevertheless growing. No group challenged the status quo more than the farmers.

Revolt of the West and South

Cries for change naturally came from the losers in the new economic order, and among the greatest losers were American farmers. Their failure to thrive in the expanding economy convinced many that the cards had been stacked against them. After seeking various other solutions to their problems, farmers turned to politics—taking up Populist leader Mary E. Lease's cry "to raise less corn and more hell." Their

By the late 1880s many farmers were already suffering from severe economic dislocation. In this 1889 cartoon a poor, hungry farmer gazes at a banquet being enjoyed by tariff-gorged industrialists; in the back Congressman McKinley is pouring whiskey.

success was limited, but they did lead the first American mass movement to reject Social Darwinism and laissez-faire. They also promoted the "radical" idea that "it is the duty of government to protect the weak, because the strong are able to protect themselves." Some even questioned basic tenets of industrial capitalism.

Grievances: Real and Imagined

In 1887 North Carolina editor Leonidas L. Polk summed up the views of many farmers: "There is something radically wrong in our industrial system. There is a screw loose.... The railroads have never been so prosperous, and yet agriculture languishes. The banks have never done a better ... business, and yet agriculture languishes. Manufacturing enterprises never made more money, ... and yet agriculture languishes. Towns and cities flourish and 'boom,' ... and yet agriculture languishes."

The basic cause of the farmers' problems was the decline of agricultural prices—primarily because of overproduction. Farmers had a hard time believing, however, that they were producing too much. Kansas governor Lorenzo Dow Lewelling wondered how "there were hungry people ... because there was too much bread" and "so many ... poorly clad ... because there was too much cloth."

Overproduction was an abstract, invisible enemy, so many farmers sought more tangible, personal villains such as the railroads, bankers, and monopolists. As "Sockless" Jerry Simpson claimed, "It is a struggle between the robbers and the robbed." Farmers believed they were being robbed by high freight and credit costs, an unfair burden of taxation, middlemen who exploited their marketing problems, and an inadequate currency.

Although there was no conspiracy by the "monopolists" to fleece the farmers, there was a germ of truth in farmers' grievances. Freight rates were higher for western farmers because of the long distances to markets and the scattered and seasonal nature of grain shipments. Although these farmers generally paid the same interest rates as easterners, they were more dependent on mortgages to finance their operations than were the corporations, who could market stocks and bonds to raise needed capital. Southern farmers also had to pay dearly, through higher credit prices for goods obtained by crop liens. Large debts increased farmers' marketing problems. All the crops in a region were usually harvested at the same time, and farmers had to sell them immedi-

FIGURE 19.2

Price Indexes for Consumer and Farm Products, 1865–1913

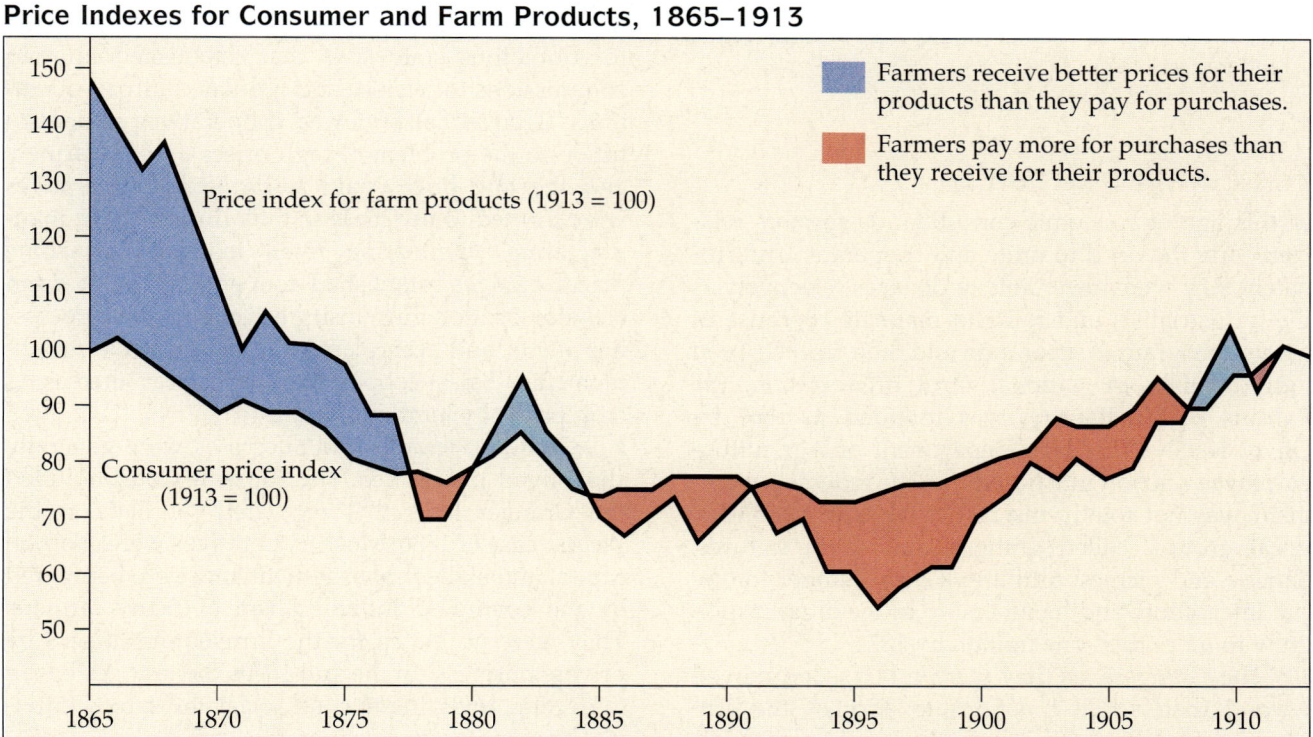

ately to pay off loans. Middlemen took advantage of the glutted markets—buying the crops at low prices and selling them when prices rose. Sometimes their profit margin was greater than that of the farmer who had gotten up before dawn every day and worked long hours to produce the goods. The unfairness of this galled farmers, living as they did isolated from the excitement and modern conveniences of the city. (The isolation was especially hard on the women, who were, as one writer noted, "not much better than slaves. It is a weary, monotonous round of cooking and washing and mending and as a result the insane asylum is 1/3d filled with wives of farmers.")

Governmental policy seemed to hurt more than help. Property taxes hit farmers hard because they had a lot of land but little income. The tariffs affected most farmers both by raising the prices they paid for goods and by making it harder for them to sell their crops on the international market. The deflationary policy of the federal government especially hurt because of the farmers' great indebtedness. Every economic downturn brought a wave of farm foreclosures and frustration. Thousands of dreams died slowly, as one Kansas farmer's letter reveals.

> At the age of 52 years, after a long life of toil, economy and self-denial, I find myself and family virtually paupers. With hundreds of cattle, hundreds of hogs, scores of good horses, and a farm that rewarded the toil of our hands with 16,000 bushels of golden corn, we are poorer by many dollars than we were years ago. What once seemed a neat little fortune and a house of refuge for our declining years ... has been rendered valueless.

This lithograph illustrates the breadth of Grange activities with panels depicting musicals, sewing bees, courtships, dances, and care for the aged.

The Farmers Organize

In this age of economic consolidation farmers realized early the need to unite and cooperate. Unfortunately they were never able to do so as effectively as the industrialists and railroad magnates because of greater geographic separation and their frontier-bred individualism. A national farm organization, the **Patrons of Husbandry,** was founded in 1867 by Oliver Kelley. This U.S. Department of Agriculture employee's action illustrated that the federal government was not totally insensitive to farm problems. Local groups, called granges, sponsored lectures, dances, and picnics, fulfilling a deep hunger for social interaction, and membership in the organization grew to more than one million by 1874.

The Grangers, as they were called, soon moved beyond their social functions to address the economic grievances of the farmers. Focusing their actions on railroad regulation, they were responsible for numerous state laws that established railroad commissions to oversee and regulate railroad operations. Grangers also viewed cooperatives as one solution to the problem of high prices paid *by* farmers and the low prices paid *to* farmers. Cooperatives were formed to purchase in bulk directly from manufacturers, eliminating retail markups. In some places granges established cooperative banks, grain elevators, cotton gins, insurance companies, processing plants, and even plants to manufacture farm implements. Sales cooperatives aimed at increasing crop prices by joint marketing.

Granger victories and successes were generally short-lived and limited. The Supreme Court nullified the Granger laws that regulated railroads in the *Wabash* case of 1886. Most cooperatives were short on capital and skilled management and were hampered by the continued individualism of many farmers. They were no match for the unrelenting attacks by private business. In the late 1870s the granges began to decline, reverting to rural social clubs, but continued to operate some cooperative stores.

Economic grievances remained, and farmers' organizational efforts shifted to the Alliance movement. Milton George, the editor of the Chicago-based *Western Rural,* organized a northwestern Alliance in 1880. Never very effective, by the late 1880s it was mainly a paper organization. The Alliance movement in the South was more radical and more successful. Started in 1877 as a frontier farmers' club in Lampasas County, Texas, it grew into the Grand State Alliance in 1879. Beginning in 1886, under the new leadership of Dr. Charles W. Macune, the southern Alliance spread rapidly by organizing new locals and absorbing existing farm groups in the South and other regions. At the same time a separate Colored Alliance was established. By 1890 the southern Alliance was a national organization with about 1.5 million members—with an additional 1 million members in its African-American affiliate.

Like the Grangers, Alliancemen sought to establish cooperatives, mostly without long-term success. They also conducted wider social and educational programs and boasted about 1000 affiliated newspapers. Self-help, however, proved inadequate, so in 1890 they turned to political action. In the 1890 elections southern Alliancemen tried to capture their state Democratic parties rather than supplant them. Because Northwest and Great Plains farmers were not burdened with such intense party loyalty or the complication of the racial issue, they established independent third parties. Regardless of the form of the organization, Alliancemen sought political solutions to their problems.

The Agrarian Agenda

The demands of the farmers mixed rhetoric, radicalism, and realism. Their words expressed an anger that was flaring white-hot after years of smouldering resentment. No one voiced that anger better than Kansas homesteader Mary E. Lease.

> Wall Street owns the country. It is no longer a government of the people, by the people and for the people, but a government of Wall Street, by Wall Street and for Wall Street. The great common people of this country are slaves, and monopoly is the master. The West and South are bound and prostrate before the manufacturing East.... Our laws are the output of a system which clothes rascals in robes and honesty in rags. The parties lie to us and the political speakers mislead us.

Farmers' words rang with a rejection of aspects of capitalism that in retrospect seems radical. Their rhetoric divided the nation into "haves" and "have-nots." "There are but two sides," one manifesto proclaimed. "On the one side are the allied hosts of monopolies, the money power, great trusts and railroad corporations.... On the other are the farmers, laborers, merchants and all the people who produce wealth.... Between those two there is no middle ground." To farmers, government either stood by idly or actively aided the monopolists as the "fruits of the toil of millions are stolen to build up colossal fortunes for a few."

Kansas homesteader and radical activist Mary E. Lease urged farmers to "raise less corn and more hell."

Their rhetoric earned scorn from critics, who labeled the leaders "hayseed socialists." To be fair, there were some unsavory aspects to the movement: A few agrarians espoused simplistic and often anti-Semitic conspiracy theories, and some flamboyant demagogues—such as "Pitchfork Ben" Tillman of South Carolina—exploited rural anger for personal political ambitions. With a mixture of contempt and fear, critics called the rural reformers "crackpot radicals."

By Gilded Age standards the farmers' demands *were* radical—even though most were adopted in the twentieth century. Their most socialistic ideas called for government ownership and operation of the railroads and the telegraph and telephone, although they did not desire state ownership of all productive property. As landowners, farmers rejected socialism, but some did believe that these transportation and communication facilities were "natural monopolies" that could only be run efficiently under centralized management and were, besides, too important to the public welfare to be in the hands of private monopolies for profit.

The remainder of the agrarian political agenda reflected a realistic and moderate response to the farmers' problems. To ease their credit crisis they advocated an inflated, more flexible currency and the subtreasury plan. Considered by the Alliancemen to be the keystone of their program, subtreasuries (federal warehouses) were to be constructed as places where farmers could store their crops and receive treasury notes amounting to 80 percent of the crops' market value. Relieved from the pressure to sell immediately, farmers could wait for prices to rise to sell their crops and then pay back their subtreasury advances plus small interest and storage fees. Farmers saw the plan as a solution to the twin evils of the crop lien and depressed prices at harvest time. To finance government programs farmers called for a graduated income tax based upon the ability to pay.

Farmers believed that many of their ailments could be relieved by a more responsive, activist government. They therefore proposed political changes to "restore the government of the Republic to the hands of 'the plain people,' with which class it originated." Among the proposed changes were initiative and referendum, direct primaries, the direct election of United States senators, and the use of a secret ballot.

Initiative and **referendum** would allow people to propose legislation through petitions and enact laws by popular vote—thereby bypassing the state legislatures that seemed unwilling to act on their grievances. Direct primaries would let "the people" vote on political party candidates rather than having party leaders pick the candidates. In the same manner, people would directly elect senators instead of allowing state legislatures to select them. All of these proposals were intended to give citizens more control over their government. To make those changes effective a secret ballot was needed to protect voters from economic intimidation by employers and creditors or physical intimidation by threats of violence.

Although the farmers did not address the fundamental problem of overproduction, adoption of the agrarian demands could have relieved somewhat the agricultural distress fueling their anger. Thus it was that farmers became increasingly involved in political organization.

Emergence of the Populist Party

In 1890 Alliancemen entered politics in the West and the South with remarkable success. Under independent party banners, western Alliancemen elected a governor in Kansas, gained control of four state legislatures, and elected U.S. senators from Kansas and Nebraska. Working through the existing Democratic state parties, southern Alliancemen elected four governors, 44 congressmen, and several senators.

Western Alliancemen interpreted this success as a mandate to establish a national third party. At a May 1891 meeting in Cincinnati they failed to convince the southern Alliancemen to join them. By 1892, however, the Southerners were disillusioned

The Populist party was a coalition of western and southern farm organizations, urban laborers, Grangers, and Greenbackers. This hostile cartoonist ridiculed as lunacy the Populist platforms.

with Alliance-backed Democrats who failed to support the subtreasury system. Overcoming their apprehension of third parties, the Alliances joined hands in St. Louis to create the **People's,** or **Populist, party**. In July 1892 the Populist party's national convention in Omaha drafted a platform and gave its presidential nomination to James B. Weaver, the former Union general who had been the Greenback party nominee in 1880. To symbolize the unity of the party they nominated former Confederate officer James G. Field for vice president. The Populist platform included all the agrarian agenda: the subtreasury plan; an income tax; free coinage of silver to inflate the currency; government ownership of railroads, telephone, and telegraph; and the political reforms intended to restore government to "the hands of the people."

Most Populists were small-scale farmers in the South and West whose farms were minimally mechanized. Most relied on a single cash crop, had unsatisfactory access to credit, and lived in social isolation some distance from towns and railroads. In other words, their existence was marginal in all respects.

The majority owned some land, but sizable numbers of sharecroppers and tenant farmers joined the party. Prosperous, large-scale, diversified farmers found little appeal in the party's platforms or activities.

Because the Populists realized the need to broaden the base of their constituency, the Omaha platform also included planks to appeal to urban workers. They advocated an eight-hour day, immigration restriction, and the abolition of the Pinkerton system that supplied strikebreakers to management. One plank promised "fair and liberal" pensions to veterans. In the South some Populists, such as Tom Watson of Georgia, sought to woo African-American voters. "You are kept apart," he told audiences of black and white farmers, "that you may be separately fleeced of your earnings. You are made to hate each other because upon that hatred is rested the keystone of the arch of financial despotism which enslaves you both."

The Populists conducted colorful campaigns, which one Nebraska Democrat called a blend of "the French Revolution and a western religious revival." Their anger fostered a revolutionary spirit that appealed to large numbers of farmers. In 1892 Weaver became the first third-party candidate to win over one million votes. He carried Kansas, Colorado, Idaho, and Nevada for a total of 22 electoral votes. Populist strength in such mining states as Colorado reflected the appeal to silver miners of the party's demand for inflation by means of the free and unlimited coinage of silver at 16 to 1. On the other hand, the Populists failed to carry a single southern state, largely because of voting fraud, Democratic cries of white supremacy, and economic intimidation of many African-American voters. Nevertheless, it was a remarkable showing for a new party, revealing the extent of popular discontent. The next year brought the panic of 1893, which produced even more discontent and gave the Populists great hopes for the election of 1896.

DEPRESSION AND TURBULENCE IN THE 1890S

Social harmony became somewhat strained in the late 1880s with such violent episodes as the Haymarket Square riot of 1886. Economic "losers," mainly workers and farmers, were already becoming restless. The depression following the panic of 1893 intensified their suffering. Naturally, turbulence increased, setting the stage for an attempt to unite the losers in a quest for political power in the election of 1896.

The Roots and Results of the Depression

While the Populists made their bid for office in the election of 1892, the two major parties were involved in a rerun of the 1888 election. Once again Cleveland and Harrison faced each other over the issue of the tariff. The presence of the unpopular McKinley Tariff created a different outcome, and Cleveland entered the White House—just in time for the panic of 1893.

The depression started in Europe and spread to the United States as overseas buyers reduced their purchases of American goods as well as their American investments. Their unloading of some $300 million of investments caused American gold to leave the country to pay for these securities. Thus supplies of currency dropped, which led to rapidly falling prices. There had also been serious overexpansion of the economy, especially in railroad construction. Confidence faltered, the stock market crashed, and banks failed.

During the depression that followed, unemployment reached 20 percent of the work force, farm prices dropped to new lows; and farm foreclosures reached new highs. Sharp wage cuts and massive layoffs took place in virtually every industry. Historian Henry Adams lamented, "Men died like flies under the strain, and Boston grew suddenly old, haggard, and thin." Still opposed to direct federal aid, President Cleveland responded to the suffering by repealing the Sherman Silver Purchase Act and selling lucrative federal bonds to a banking syndicate headed by J. P. Morgan in an effort to protect the nation's gold reserves.

The Democrats did act on their campaign issue, passing the Wilson-Gorman Tariff that reduced rates by 10 percent. Reformers were disappointed with the moderate cuts but were appeased by a provision placing a 2 percent tax on incomes. That provision, however, was declared unconstitutional in *Pollock* v. *The Farmer's Loan and Trust Co.* in 1895. In the face of massive suffering, many people wanted the government to do more.

Expressions of Worker Discontent

Violence had begun to escalate in labor-management relations in the late 1880s and continued into the 1890s. In 1892 Andrew Carnegie and the Amalgamated Association of Iron and Steel Workers clashed at Carnegie's Homestead plant outside of Pittsburgh. In an effort to crush the union, Carnegie had slashed wages and—expecting a confrontation—had fortified his steel mills, hired strikebreakers, and employed

Striking workers from Carnegie's Homestead steel plant outside Pittsburgh used guns and dynamite to try to keep Pinkerton guards from approaching the plant on barges from a nearby river.

the Pinkerton Agency to protect them. This done, Carnegie departed for Scotland on a fishing trip and left his manager, Henry Clay Frick, to do battle with the union.

On July 5, strikers and Pinkerton agents fought their first battle. Smoke from cannons, rifles, dynamite, and burning oil filled the hot summer air. Ten men were killed and another 70 were wounded, as the strikers won the first engagement. When Frick appealed to the governor of Pennsylvania for help, the governor dispatched 8000 militiamen to Homestead "to protect law and order"—a phrase normally synonymous with defense of industrialists' property.

The fighting continued until late July when an anarchist from Chicago named Alexander Berkman took matters into his own hands. He went to Frick's office, shot the manager twice, and stabbed him seven times before being subdued. Frick lived and police arrested Berkman. Although Berkman had no connection with the steel union, the local and national press linked unionism with radicalism. Shortly afterward, strikebreakers went to work—the union was defeated and destroyed by the powerful forces of capital, government, and press.

During the depression, employers frequently cut wages to preserve profits. In 1894, for example, the workers in the Pullman plant at Chicago had their wages reduced several times while their rent for company-owned housing remained the same. When management refused to negotiate with the union, members of the American Railway Union (ARU) refused to handle any cars made in the Pullman plant. The boycott totally disrupted railroad traffic in the Midwest. Railroad executives appealed to Illinois governor John Altgeld for help, but the liberal politician refused to interfere. The executives then turned to U.S. Attorney General Richard Olney, a former railroad corporation lawyer. Olney and President Cleveland responded quickly, using the excuse of protecting the mails to come to the aid of the railroad managers. Over Altgeld's protest, the government sent 2000 troops to the Chicago area, and a federal court issued a blanket injunction that virtually ordered union leaders to discontinue the strike. When ARU president Eugene V. Debs defied the injunction, he was imprisoned. Only after federal troops arrived did violence occur. Within two days, bitter fighting had broken out, railcars were burned, and over $340,000 worth of damage had been done to railroad property. Force—absolute, final, and federal—crushed the Pullman strike. Such unified repressive force drove some workers to the political left.

Prior to 1894, the badly divided Socialist Labor party, led by the abrasive Daniel DeLeon, had a minuscule membership. After the Pullman strike Eugene V. Debs emerged from prison a socialist and made socialism more respectable. Born in Indiana in 1855, the balding Debs had the common touch and

Eugene V. Debs was the Socialist Party of America's presidential nominee four times. Here Debs addresses a crowd of railroad workers during one of his campaigns.

delivered with a Hoosier twang a version of socialism based upon distinctly American values. The movement thus acquired a fiery and effective orator. "Many of you think you are competing," Debs would declare. "Against whom? Against Rockefeller? About as I would if I had a wheelbarrow and competed with the Santa Fe [railroad]." Around the nucleus of his personality the larger and stronger Socialist Party of America began to form and directly challenge unrestrained capitalism.

The mass suffering during the depression also provoked some to ask the federal government to provide work for the unemployed. Jacob S. Coxey, a short, quiet Ohio businessman, was one who advocated putting men to work on the roads. They were to be paid by the printing of $500 million in legal tender paper money, which would also help to inflate the currency. He organized the Army of the Commonwealth of Christ to march to Washington and demand action. When about 500 of the marchers straggled into the capital on May 1, 1894, their leader was arrested for walking on the grass. Federal authorities beat and arrested his "troops." Although **"Coxey's Army"** fell far short of his dream of a demonstration of 400,000 jobless workers, their actions did get the attention of the public. Forty-three newspaper reporters accompanied them, reporting almost every detail of the march. One journalist quipped, "Never in the annals of insurrection has so small a company of soldiers been accompanied by such a phalanx of recording angels."

Businessman Jacob S. Coxey is shown leading his army of unemployed workers into Washington, D.C., where he was arrested and his army dispersed by club-wielding police.

Deteriorating Race Relations

The turbulent 1890s was also one of the worst decades of racial violence in the nation's history. It stemmed from class as well as race conflict. The Populist leader Tom Watson was right when he told black and white farmers that the Democrats were using race as a wedge to keep them apart.

Although the Populists failed to unite blacks and whites on the basis of class interests, the attempt led to considerable bloodshed. Whites shed white blood, but more frequently they spilled black blood. Lynching became a tool for controlling both black votes and actions. Under the pretext of "maintaining law and order," vigilante mobs hanged, mutilated, and burned African Americans in increasing numbers. During the 1890s an average of two to three black Southerners were lynched each week.

It is probably not coincidental that attempts to limit African-American voting began in earnest precisely at the time that farmer unrest arose. Mississippi led the way in finding ways to skirt the Fifteenth Amendment. Without mentioning "race,

The growing number of lynchings in the 1890s launched Ida B. Wells's crusade against mob rule.

color, or previous condition of servitude," the 1890 Mississippi constitution established poll taxes, literacy tests, and residency requirements, all aimed at reducing black voting. A key element of the literacy tests was the requirement that voters be able to explain what they read to the satisfaction of the voter registrars—African Americans found registrars extremely hard to satisfy. The Supreme Court displayed its disregard for black rights by upholding the so-called Mississippi Plan in *Williams* v. *Mississippi*, and other states soon adopted similar measures. Later, to woo lower-class white voters, grandfather clauses were added—providing exemptions from these requirements based on voting eligibility prior to the Reconstruction Acts. These clauses applied to all adult white males and to no African Americans.

Once whites stripped away black political power other black rights toppled. With no need to cater to African-American voters, whites soon began to pass discriminatory legislation. Most wanted to use segregation as a means of racial control, but the Fourteenth Amendment raised constitutional questions. The Supreme Court removed that barrier. After several rulings that limited constitutional protection of black rights, in the 1896 *Plessy* v. *Ferguson* decision the Court finally ruled that public accommodations for blacks could be "separate but equal." With segregation now legalized, for the next two decades southern states frantically passed legislation—known as "Jim Crow" laws—to make legal the separation of the races. When the frenzy stopped, some states had even passed laws prohibiting interracial checker playing and requiring textbooks used in black schools to be stored in separate rooms from those used in white schools.

Segregation and the exclusion of African Americans from public facilities had long existed in a haphazard way based on custom. As this informal and inconsistent arrangement was converted into a legalized system of repression, violence erupted, and no one stepped in to protect African Americans. The popularity of Booker T. Washington's 1895 "Atlanta Compromise," with its plea for racial cooperation, is easily understandable under the conditions it was delivered. Both whites and blacks were eager to find a way out of the bloodshed. More militant black voices, however, such as that of Memphis newspaper editor Ida B. Wells, insisted on federal action to prevent lynching.

Fissures seemed to be opening up along a number of the seams in American society. The turbulence was enough to provoke the Democratic party to respond to popular demands for economic relief and political reform in 1896, creating a dilemma for the Populists.

The Tide Turns: The Election of 1896

After the Republicans nominated William McKinley and the Democrats chose William Jennings Bryan, the Populists were left with an impossible choice. When Bryan and the Democrats endorsed silver, the Populists had their thunder stolen. They had hoped to ride silver to power because of the growing popularity of the issue. William H. Harvey's pro-silver book *Coin's Financial School* had become a best-seller in 1894. Instead of picking up silverite bolters from the major parties as they had expected to do, the Populists were now faced with a real problem. To nominate someone else would split the silver votes and ensure a victory for McKinley. Yet to nominate Bryan meant a loss of their identity and momentum.

Many Populists argued fervently against "fusion" with the Democrats, who focused almost exclusively on silver at the expense of the rest of the Populist demands. Watson and others viewed the obsession with silver as "a trap, a pitfall, a snare, a menace, a fraud, a crime against common sense and common honesty." In the end Populists bit the bullet and nominated Bryan for president but chose Tom Watson for vice president rather than the Democratic choice, Arthur Sewall.

"God's in his Heaven, all's right with the world!" Republican campaign manager Mark Hanna wired McKinley when he learned of the Republican victory. McKinley carried the popular vote 7.1 million to 6.5 million and the electoral votes 271 to 176. The defeat of Bryan and the silver forces brought an end to political equilibrium. Millions of Democrats left their party, and the Republican party became the majority party. Republicans then won the presidency in seven of the nine contests between 1896 and 1928, and controlled both houses of Congress 17 of the next 20 sessions. One basic reason for the Republican victory of 1896 was the bad luck of the Democrats to be in power when the depression came. Republicans gleefully noted in 1894, "We were told in the old times that the rich were getting richer and the poor were getting poorer. To cure that imaginary ailment our political opponents have brought on a time when everybody is getting poorer."

The Populists, of course, suffered the most from the election results: Their party disappeared. The attempt to unite farmers and labor, blacks and whites,

---

THE PEOPLE SPEAK

Lynch Law in America

After three personal friends of Ida B. Wells were lynched in Memphis, Tennessee, she crusaded against the evil of mob rule through articles, pamphlets, speeches, and two lecture tours of Great Britain. Here she describes the grisly nature of lynching in an article based upon one of her speeches.

> Not only are two hundred men and women put to death annually, on the average, in this country by mobs, but these lives are taken with the greatest publicity. In many instances the leading citizens aid and abet by their presence when they do not participate, and the leading journals inflame the public mind to the lynching point with scare-head articles and offers of rewards. Whenever a burning is advertised to take place, the railroads run excursions, photographs are taken, and the same jubilee is indulged in that characterized the public hangings of one hundred years ago. There is, however, this difference: in those old days the multitude that stood by was permitted only to guy or jeer. The nineteenth century lynching mob cuts off ears, toes, and fingers, strips off flesh, and distributes portions of the body as souvenirs among the crowd. If the leaders of the mob are so minded, coal-oil is poured over the body and the victim is then roasted to death. This has been done in Texarkana and Paris, Tex., in Bardswell, Ky., and in Newman, Ga. In Paris the officers of the law delivered the prisoner to the mob. The mayor gave the school children a holiday and the railroads ran excursion trains so that the people might see a human being burned to death. In Texarkana, the year before, men and boys amused themselves by cutting off strips of flesh and thrusting knives into their helpless victim. At Newman, Ga., of the present year, the mob tried every conceivable torture to compel the victim to cry out and confess, before they set fire to the faggots that burned him. But their trouble was all in vain—he never uttered a cry, and they could not make him confess.

Originally published in *Arena*, January 1900, pp. 15–24.

THE American Mosaic

"Rise Brothers!": The Black Response to Jim Crow

AFRICAN Americans had long struggled against white prejudice and repression. During Reconstruction constant vigilance was needed to protect and expand newly won rights. Some efforts were in vain, but a few successes had helped curb the growth of segregation. For example, African Americans in Savannah, Georgia, succeeded in desegregating their city's streetcar system in 1872 by boarding the so-called white cars, threatening legal action, and boycotting the Jim Crow cars. Beginning in the 1890s, however, a rising tide of virulent white racism eventually confounded black attempts to resist being made into second-class citizens. With a new determination white Southerners stripped African Americans of their voting rights, passed segregation laws, and lynched those who refused to cooperate.

Once whites had won the battle and the smoke had cleared from the battlefields, the mythology of African-American submission and acceptance began to prevail. Booker T. Washington became a symbol of black cooperation and accommodation. Selected passages of his 1895 Atlanta address, the "Atlanta Compromise," were heralded as the "will of blacks." Other voices were ignored. Few quoted the words of John Hope, a professor at a black college in Nashville, the next year. Hope exhorted African Americans:

> Rise, Brothers! Come let us possess this land. Never say "Let well enough alone." Cease to console yourself with adages that numb the moral sense. Be discontented. Be dissatisfied.... Be restless as the tempestuous billows on the boundless sea. Let your dissatisfaction break mountain-high against the walls of prejudice and swamp it to the very foundation. Then we shall not have to plead for justice nor on bended knee crave mercy; for we shall be men. Then and not until then will liberty in its highest sense be the boast of our Republic!

Many African Americans responded to the new wave of discrimination by employing every available tactic to protest the loss of their rights. Before disfranchisement was completed, black officeholders made impassioned speeches and lobbied their white colleagues to oppose to discriminatory legislation. Activists organized local "Negro Rights," "Emancipation," and "Colored Uplift" groups that wrote strongly worded resolutions and organized petition drives. Individuals and groups launched legal challenges in the courts. Some tested the new laws by breaking them. Protest meetings were held. Boycotts of newly segregated facilities occurred in New Orleans, Savannah, Jacksonville, Richmond, and other southern cities. The black press often fearlessly attacked white actions; a Bay Minette, Alabama, paper counseled, "The best remedy for lynching is a good Winchester rifle." Finally, a few engaged in the ultimate protest—armed resistance.

Two very different examples illustrate the nature and results of African-American protest at the turn of the century. The first, a Savannah streetcar boycott in 1906, had many similarities to the Montgomery bus boycott of 1955—the main exception being the outcome. The second, the story of Robert Charles, demonstrates that this early civil rights movement had its share of martyrs.

At the beginning of the twentieth century both whites and blacks of Savannah were proud that their city had been immune to the lynching virus. In 1906 it was also one of the few southern cities without a single Jim Crow law on its books. Race relations were better than average, though not ideal. Of the city's 72,000 residents 54 percent were African American, but the white minority exercised a firm, if benevolent, control. There were only three black public officials, and they held positions allotted to blacks by law. Nevertheless, the black community had spawned a leadership class that commanded some respect from the white establishment and enjoyed a measure of political clout. They had thus been able to turn back all previous attempts to enact segregation.

The year 1906, however, brought increased racial tension throughout the South, with several outbreaks of violence, including those in Brownsville, Texas, and in Georgia where the bitter gubernatorial campaign of Hoke Smith aroused white prejudice. Savannah whites began to urge city leaders to get into the "new order of things" and exclude African Americans from both politics and social contact with whites. On September 12, 1906, the city adopted a law that required separate seating in streetcars and empowered the police to arrest anyone sitting in the wrong place.

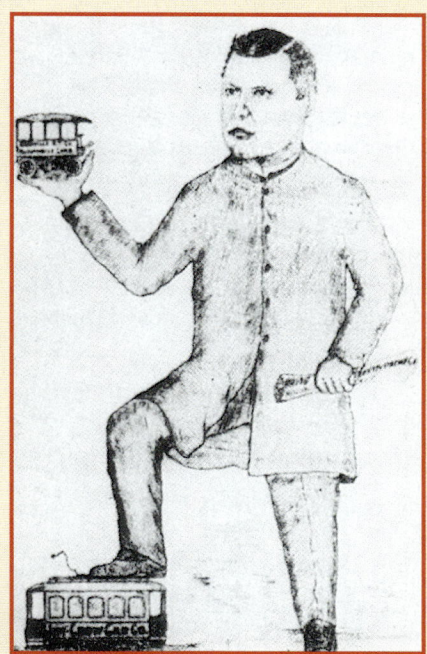

The African-American elite—leading ministers, physicians, and businessmen—had already formed a committee to lobby against the ordinance. Once the law was passed, they immediately organized a boycott. In the churches, ministers urged compliance with the boycott and the black *Savannah Tribune* declared: "Let us walk! walk! and save some nickels. . . . Do not trample on your pride by being 'jim crowed.' Walk!" Black hackmen reduced their fares for boycotters from 25 cents to 10 cents. One group attempted to form the United Transportation Company to compete with white lines. Those rich enough to own wagons drove themselves and friends to town.

Many who could get no other transportation heeded the words of their leaders and walked. It was reported that the mayor's secretary had given his maid carfare to bring two large suitcases from his home to city hall. When she arrived late and soaked with perspiration, he discovered that she had followed her minister's advice and refused to ride the streetcar. The local white paper noted that trolley after trolley went by with the back seats vacant. The boycott was almost total.

City authorities responded much as Montgomery authorities did in 1955. They cracked down on unlicensed hacks and harassed licensed ones. African Americans remained firm for some time—even after it became apparent that the boycott was not going to change white minds. As late as May 1908, two years after the start of the boycott, the streetcar line admitted that no more than 80 percent of blacks had returned to the cars. Without action by the federal government, even economic loss could not persuade whites to abandon segregation.

Savannah blacks suffered inconvenience to protest the infringement of their rights, but Robert Charles paid a much higher price. A quiet, intense young man in his twenties who worked at odd jobs, he supported black emigration to Africa as a response to white prejudice in the South. He read a lot and collected weapons but broke no laws. One night in July of 1900 he sat on a front porch in New Orleans talking quietly with a friend. Near midnight three police officers arrived with drawn pistols and flailing billy clubs to arrest him.

Charles responded to the attempted arrest by drawing his own gun and shooting one of the officers. Wounded himself, he then fled—not to safety but to rearm with a rifle. Charles then moved from one hiding place to another, leaving a trail of five dead police officers and a dozen wounded ones. A mob of over a thousand whites joined police in the manhunt, frequently firing indiscriminately into the African-American community. Finally surrounded, Charles was burned out of his hiding place and immediately riddled with bullets. As was customary, the mob then badly mutilated the body. They killed the man but not the spirit. African-American newspaper woman Ida Wells-Barnett investigated the incident and ended her report with the words: "The white people of this county may charge that he was a desperado, but to the people of his own race Robert Charles will always be regarded as the 'hero of New Orleans.'" Later, his willingness to fight police brutality with retaliatory violence would be renewed by the Black Panthers in the 1960s.

Even heroic actions failed to protect African-Americans' rights from the onslaught of discrimination at the dawn of the new century. Nevertheless these men and women added to the heritage of protest that would reap rewards a half-century later—when the media were more sympathic and the federal government finally decided that it was in the national interest to protect the rights of all citizens.

Chronology of Key Events

1867 The Grangers, first national farmers' organization, is founded

1873 "Crime of '73": Coinage Act declares that gold alone would be minted to back paper money

1877 Southern Farmers' Alliance is founded in Texas; *Munn* v. *Illinois* upholds the constitutionality of state regulation of railroads

1878 Bland-Allison Act requires the U.S. Treasury to buy $2 to $4 million of silver a month in order to inflate the currency

1881 President James A. Garfield mortally wounded at a Washington, D.C., train station, Chester Arthur becomes twenty-first president

1883 Pendleton Act classifies approximately 15,000 federal jobs as civil service positions to be awarded only after a competitive examination

1886 *Wabash, St. Louis, & Pacific Railway Company* v. *Illinois* reverses *Munn* v. *Illinois* and states that only Congress can regulate commerce between states

1887 Congress establishes the Interstate Commerce Commission, the first federal regulatory commission, to regulate railroads

1890 National Woman Suffrage Association and American Woman Suffrage Association merge to form the National American Woman Suffrage Association; Congress passes Sherman Antitrust Act, forbidding restraints on trade; Sherman Silver Purchase Act increases amount of silver that had to be purchased annually and allows the Treasury to issue paper money based on silver; Mississippi becomes first southern state to adopt poll taxes, literacy tests, and residency requirements to restrict African-American voting

1892 Populist party is formed and receives over a million votes in presidential race; violent Homestead, Pennsylvania, steel strike erupts

1893 Severe economic depression begins

1894 Pullman workers strike; Coxey's Army marches on Washington, D.C., to protest unemployment and to urge a public works program to relieve unemployment

1895 *United States* v. *E. C. Knight Co.* weakens Sherman Antitrust Act by stating that law does not apply to companies that operate exclusively in one state; *Pollock* v. *Farmer's Loan and Trust Co.* declares a federal income tax unconstitutional

1896 *Plessy* v. *Ferguson* decision rules that the principle of "separate but equal" does not deprive blacks of civil rights guaranteed under the Fourteenth Amendment; Republican William McKinley defeats Democrat William Jennings Bryan to become the twenty-fifth president

1900 Gold Standard Act places the nation on the gold standard

---

failed. Like the Socialists and other radicals, the Populists were never able to recruit organized labor in order to forge a broadly based working-class movement. American Federation of Labor president Samuel Gompers and other labor leaders argued that farmers were capitalists, not wage earners, and that their goals were not compatible with labor's interests. For example, the inflation that farmers wanted would raise food prices to the detriment of workers already living close to the margin. In the South race proved to be more important than class, and many disillusioned white Populists such as Tom Watson became anti-black activists following their defeat. They joined gladly with the Democrats to curtail African-American suffrage. The Democrats had stirred up the issue of racism to defeat the Populists and then were unable to put the genie back into the bottle. In many states they were replaced by less elitist, bigoted demagogues.

Americans had come to a turning point in 1896 and chose the conservative path. The Republican administration quickly raised duties with the Dingley Tariff of 1897. Three years later the Gold Standard Act officially put the nation on the gold standard by requiring all money to be redeemable in gold. Ironically, new discoveries of gold and more efficient extracting methods brought the inflation that farmers had sought from silver. Prosperity began to return, and the Republicans could point with pride to their slogan, "The Full Dinner Pail." That prosperity sapped the strength of the agrarian movement as rising farm prices eased farmers' economic distress. And such inventions and services as the telephone and rural free delivery of mail decreased farmers' isolation—especially after mail-order catalogs began to arrive from Montgomery Ward's and Sears, Roebuck.

Conclusion

After Reconstruction, national politics entertained the masses and voter turnout reached all-time highs. At the same time, the emerging problems of industrialization challenged the traditional roles of state and federal governments. The failure of either major party to dominate the federal government created some degree of political inertia. Competing for voters, the parties differed little in their laissez-faire support of business or their primary concern with the spoils of office. Most people supported the government's nonintervention in the economy and society until problems escalated for farmers, workers, and minorities. State and local governments made efforts to solve emerging problems, but many ills seemed to require federal action. Political inertia in Washington bred crisis after crisis as problems remained unresolved.

Finally, in the West and South a challenge to unrestrained capitalism arose from the losers in the race toward industrialism and economic expansion. Led by disgruntled farmers, the Populist party sought to unite large segments of the American population on the basis of class interest. In 1896 the Democratic party responded by nominating William Jennings Bryan. As a result, the presidential election of that year provided a real choice for American voters. The victory of conservative William McKinley brought about the death of Populism, but many of the problems the farmers addressed in the 1890s continued into the twentieth century. Time vindicated the farmers' demands. A large number of their rejected solutions were adopted in the first two decades of the new century, and most of their remaining agenda was enacted in modified form during the New Deal of the 1930s.

Suggestions for Further Reading

Ed Ayers, *The Promise of the New South: Life After Reconstruction* (1992). Provides a thorough examination of diverse aspects of Southern culture following Reconstruction.

Sean Dennis Cashman, *America in the Gilded Age: From the Death of Lincoln to the Rise of Theodore Roosevelt* 3d ed. (1993) A thorough account of politics and society during the late nineteenth century.

Lawrence Goodwyn, *Democratic Promise: The Populist Moment in America* (1976). An interpretation that focuses on the Populists' attempt to expand democracy.

William F. Holmes, ed., *American Populism* (1994). Comprehensive collection of significant interpretations of the Populist movement.

Michael Kazin, *The Populist Persuasion: An American History* (1995). Analyzes the various functions that Populism has served in American politics.

Robert C. McMath, *American Populism: A Social History 1877–1898* (1993). Presents an up-to-date account of the Populism and its supporters.

Overviews and Surveys

Vincent P. DeSantis, *The Shaping of Modern America, 1877–1916* (1973); Harold U. Faulkner, *Politics, Reform, and Expansion, 1890–1900* (1959); John A. Garraty, *The New Commonwealth, 1877–1890* (1968); Ray Ginger, *The Age of Excess: The United States From 1877 to 1914* (1965); John D. Hicks, *The Populist Revolt: A History of the Farmers' Alliance and the People's Party* (1931); Richard Hofstadter, *The Age of Reform* (1955); Alan Trachtenberg, *The Incorporation of America: Culture and Society in the Gilded Age* (1982).

Equilibrium and Inertia: The National Political Scene

John Allswang, *Bosses, Machines, and Urban Voters* (1977); William R. Brock, *Investigation and Responsibility* (1984); John M. Dobson, *Politics in the Gilded Age: A New Perspective on Reform* (1972); Rebecca Edwards, *Angels in the Machinery: Gender in American Party Politics from the Civil War to the Progressive Era* (1997); J. Rogers Hollingsworth, *The Whirligig of Politics: The Democracy of Cleveland and Bryan* (1963); Richard Jensen, *The Winning of the Midwest: Social and Political Conflicts, 1888–1896* (1971); Morton Keller, *Affairs of State: Public Life in Nineteenth Century America* (1977); Paul Kleppner, *The Cross of Culture: A Social Analysis of Midwestern Politics, 1850–1900* (1970), and *The Third Electoral System, 1853–1892* (1979); Michael E. McGerr, *The Decline of Popular Politics: The American North, 1865–1928* (1986); Robert D. Marcus, *GOP: Political Structure in the Gilded Age, 1880–1896* (1971); Horace S. Merrill, *Bourbon Democracy in the Middle West, 1865–1896* (1953); H. Wayne Morgan, *From Hayes to McKinley* (1969); David J. Rothman,

Style Over Substance: Government in the Gilded Age, 1877–1892

Ballard C. Campbell, *Representative Democracy* (1980); Justus D. Doenecke, *The Presidencies of James A. Garfield & Chester A. Arthur* (1981); Eleanor Flexner, *Century of Struggle: The Women's Rights Movement in the United States*, rev. ed. (1975); Margaret Forster, *Significant Sisters: The Grassroots of Active Feminism, 1839–1939* (1984); Lewis L. Gould, *The Presidency of William McKinley* (1980); Stanley P. Hirshson, *Farewell to the Bloody Shirt: Northern Republicans and the Southern Negro* (1962); Ari A. Hoogenboom, *Outlawing the Spoils: The Civil Service Reform Movement* (1961); Aileen Kraditor, *The Ideas of the Woman's Suffrage Movement, 1890–1920* (1965); Gerald W. McFarland, *Mugwumps, Morals, and Politics 1884–1920* (1975); Arnold M. Paul, *Conservative Crisis and the Rule of Law: Attitudes of Bar and Bench, 1887–1895* (1969); Gretchen Ritter, *Goldbugs and Greenbacks: The Antimonopoly Tradition and the Politics of Finance in America* (1997); Theda Skocpol, *Protecting Soldiers and Mothers: The Political Origins of Social Policy in the United States* (1992); John G. Sproat, *The Best Men: Liberal Reformers in the Gilded Age* (1968); Mark Wahlgren Summers, *The Era of Good Stealings* (1993); Tom E. Terrill, *The Tariff, Politics, and American Foreign Policy, 1874–1901* (1973); Allen Weinstein, *Prelude to Populism: Origins of the Silver Issue, 1867–1878* (1970).

The Farmers Revolt

Peter H. Argersinger, *Populism and Politics: William Alfred Peffer and the People's Party* (1974); Allan G. Bogue, *Money at Interest: The Farm Mortgage on the Middle Border* (1955); Paul W. Glad, *McKinley, Bryan, and the People* (1964); Sheldon Hackney, *Populism to Progressivism in Alabama* (1969); Steven Hahn, *The Roots of Southern Populism: Yeomen Farmers and the Transformation of the Georgia Upcountry, 1850–1890* (1983); Robert McMath, Jr., *Populist Vanguard: A History of the Southern Farmers' Alliance* (1975); Walter T. K. Nugent, *The Tolerant Populists: Kansas Populism and Nativism* (1963); Jeffrey Ostler, *Prairie Populism: The Fate of Agrarian Radicalism in Kansas, Nebraska, and Iowa, 1880–1892* (1993); Bruce Palmer, *Man over Money: The Southern Populist Critique of American Capitalism* (1980); Norman Pollack, ed., *The Populist Mind* (1967); Barton C. Shaw, *The Wool-Boys: Georgia's Populist Party* (1984).

Depression and Turbulence in the 1890s

W. Fitzhugh Brundage, *Under Sentence of Death: Lynching in the South* (1997); John P. Diggins, *The American Left in the Twentieth Century* (1973); Robert F. Durden, *The Climax of Populism: The Election of 1896* (1965); Glenda Elizabeth Gilmore, *Gender and Jim Crow: Women and the Politics of White Supremacy in North Carolina, 1896–1920* (1996); Charles Hoffmann, *The Depression of the Nineties: An Economic History* (1970); Stanley L. Jones, *The Presidential Election of 1896* (1964); J. Morgan Kousser, *The Shaping of Southern Politics: Suffrage Restriction and Establishment of the One-Party South, 1880–1910* (1974); Paul Krause, *The Battle for Homestead, 1880–1892* (1992); Charles Lofgren, *The Plessy Case: A Legal-Historical Interpretation* (1987); Donald L. McMurry, *Coxey's Army: A Study of the Industrial Army Movement of 1894* (1929); Samuel T. McSeveney, *The Politics of Depression* (1972); Howard N. Rabinowitz, *Race Relations in the Urban South, 1865–1890* (1978); William G. Ross, *A Muted Fury: Populists, Progressives, and Labor Unions, 1890–1937* (1994); David Traxel, *1898: The Birth of the American Country* (1998); C. Vann Woodward, *The Strange Career of Jim Crow*, rev. ed. (1974).

Biographies

Paolo Coletta, *William Jennings Bryan: Political Evangelist* (1964); Richard Digby-Junger, *The Journalist as Reformer: Henry Demarest Lloyd and Wealth Against Commonwealth* (1996); Ray Ginger, *Bending Cross: A Biography of Eugene Victor Debs* (1949); Paul W. Glad, *The Trumpet Soundeth: William Jennings Bryan and His Democracy* (1960); Louis Koenig, *Bryan: A Biography of William Jennings Bryan* (1971); Linda O. McMurry, *To Keep the Waters Troubled: The Life of Ida B. Wells* (1998); Allan Nevins, *Grover Cleveland: A Study in Courage* (1932); Allan Peskin, *Garfield: A Biography* (1978); Thomas Reeves, *Gentleman Boss: The Life of Chester Alan Arthur* (1975); Martin Ridge, *Ignatius Donnelly: The Portrait of a Politician* (1962); Nick Salvatore, *Eugene V. Debs: Citizen and Socialist* (1982); Charles Morrow Wilson, *The Commoner: William Jennings Bryan* (1970); C. Vann Woodward, *Tom Watson: Agrarian Rebel* (1938).

INTERNET RESOURCES

African American Perspectives: Pamphlets from the Daniel A. P. Murray Collection, 1818–1907
http://memory.loc.gov/ammem/aap/aaphome.html
This collection includes writings of famous African Americans including Frederick Douglass, Booker T. Washington, Ida B. Wells-Barnett, Benjamin W. Arnett, Alexander Crummel, and Emanuel Love.

The Era of William McKinley
http://www.history.ohio-state.edu/projects/mckinley/default.htm
This site contains numerous images from various stages of William McKinley's career along with a brief biographical essay. This Ohio State University site also has a section with an excellent collection of cartoons from the era.

Politics and Power: The United States Senate, 1869–1901 (1966); Leonard D. White, *The Republican Era, 1869–1901* (1958); R. Hal Williams, *Years of Decision: American Politics in the 1890s* (1978).

Gilded Age (1890) to World War I
http://www.emayzine.com/lectures/Gilded~1.htm
This site is a good overview essay of the era.

This Gilded Page
http://www.wm.edu/~srnels/gilded.html
This site has links to scores of Gilded Age and Progressive Era documents.

A Righteous Cause: A Documentary on the Life of William Jennings Bryan
http://www.c7p.com/screen/bryan/index.html
Produced and Directed by William S. Murray, III, this site contains Bryan images and speeches.

1896 The Grand Realignment
http://jefferson.village.virginia.edu/seminar/unit8/home.htm
This University of Virginia site contains biographical information, images, cartoons, and related links about the pivotal 1896 election.

KEY TERMS

Mugwumps   (p. 554)
National American Woman Suffrage Association (NAWSA)   (p. 556)
Greenback Party   (p. 558)
Spoils System   (p. 558)
Pendleton Act   (p. 558)
Interstate Commerce Commission (ICC)   (p. 560)
Sherman Antitrust Act   (p. 561)
Patrons of Husbandry   (p. 564)
Initiative   (p. 566)
Referendum   (p. 566)
People's (Populist) Party   (p. 566)
Coxey's Army   (p. 569)

REVIEW QUESTIONS

1. What roles did the two major political parties play in the late nineteenth century?
2. How did events shape political concerns during the Gilded Age?
3. Why and how did the farmers and workers revolt?
4. How did conditions for African Americans deteriorate at the end of the century?

20

IMPERIAL AMERICA, 1870–1900

CONGRESSIONAL CONTROL AND THE REDUCTION OF AMERICAN POWER
Trimming the State Department
Reducing the Military
Seward's Dream

THE SPIRIT OF AMERICAN GREATNESS
American Exceptionalism
Sense of Duty
Search for Markets
The New Navy
Large Policy

THE EMERGENCE OF AGGRESSION IN AMERICAN FOREIGN POLICY
Confronting the Germans in Samoa
Teaching Chile a Lesson
Plucking the Hawaiian Pear
Facing Down the British

THE WAR FOR EMPIRE
The Spirit of the 1890s
The Cuban Revolution
The Yellow Press
The Spanish-American War
Freeing Cuba
The Imperial Debate
The War to Crush Filipino Independence
Keeping the Doors Open

579

"A colossus of ignorance"

Dreams of expansion came easily to Americans during the nineteenth century. For most of the century they expanded westward, moving into Texas and Kansas, pushing across the Great Plains, and occupying California and the Pacific Northwest. But they did not restrict their dreams to the millions of acres between Mexico and Canada. They cast covetous eyes toward Central America and the islands of the Caribbean and the Pacific. Plans to annex Nicaragua, Cuba, Santo Domingo, the Virgin Islands, Hawaii, and Samoa fired politicians' imaginations. Before the Civil War, the debate over slavery blocked these larger expansionist efforts. Once the Union was preserved, however, expansionists returned to their plans with revived energy and enthusiasm.

President Ulysses S. Grant had a pet expansionist project of his own—the Dominican Republic, the eastern two-thirds of the Caribbean island of Santo Domingo. The island was rich in mineral resources, possessed an important natural harbor, and its inhabitants were eager to buy American products. Most importantly for Grant, who was ever mindful of America's race problem, the Dominicans were black. The island could serve as a frontier for black Americans, a retreat from Ku Klux Klan harassment.

With so much to gain, Grant put his full political weight behind annexation. His conduct was less than presidential. First, he sent his personal secretary and close friend Orville Babcock to Santo Domingo on a "fact-finding" mission. Unimpressed by the islanders, Babcock reported: "The people are indolent and ignorant. The best class of people are the American Negroes who have come here from time to time." But Babcock was convinced that the Dominican Republic was a commercial and strategic prize worthy of annexation. What was more, Buenaventura Baez, the unscrupulous president of the republic, was eager to sell his country. With the money he would make from the transaction, Baez hoped to establish residence in Paris or Madrid, because, as Babcock noted, the Dominican Republic was "a dull country."

Unrest around him added fuel to Baez's willingness to sell. Both neighboring Haiti and a strong force of Dominican rebels threatened his government. So difficult was Baez's position that Babcock had to order a United States Navy ship to protect the Baez government during the annexation negotiations, which were completed in the late fall of 1869. The promise of American dollars had convinced Baez that his country should belong to the United States.

Grant was pleased. The treaty of annexation, however, would have to be ratified by the Senate, a body more difficult to satisfy than Baez's government. Grant decided to forgo presidential protocol and personally visit Charles Sumner, the chairman of the Senate Foreign Relations Committee. On the evening of January 2, 1870, Grant called at Sumner's Washington home on Lafayette Park. Sumner recalled later that Grant was drunk at the time. Drunk or sober, Grant was certainly in earnest. He energetically discussed the need to annex the Dominican Republic. Sumner listened, then replied: "Mr. President, I am an Administration man, and whatever you do will always find in me the most careful and candid consideration." Grant departed, believing he had won Sumner's full support. In fact, he had only won the powerful Massachusetts senator's "candid consideration."

After consideration and considerable investigation, Sumner decided that the entire annexation scheme was distasteful. He was disturbed by Babcock's and Baez's unethical financial dealings and was enraged that the United States Navy had been used to keep the Dominican president in power. Sumner was not a man to mince words. Labeled "probably the most intolerant man that American history has ever known," he accused Grant of being "a colossus of ignorance." By a vote of 5 to 2, the Foreign Relations Committee voiced its disapproval of the treaty of annexation.

Grant was furious. His son later recalled, "I never saw Father so grimly angry." Known for his bulldog tenacity during the Civil War, Grant was not about to quit. He hinted that if the United States did not take the Dominican Republic, one of the European powers would; he even reported the results of a rigged plebiscite in which the Dominicans supposedly supported annexation by the suspiciously lopsided vote of 15,169 to 11. Grant's efforts failed. On June 30, 1870, the Senate rejected the treaty. Defining America's duty toward the island, Sumner said, "Our duty is as plain as the Ten Commandments.

Elected president in 1868, U. S. Grant showed little aptitude for the office.

Kindness, beneficence, assistance, aid, help, protection, all that is implied in good neighborhood, these we must give freely, bountifully, but their independence is as sacred to them as is ours to us."

The failed attempt to annex the Dominican Republic is important for the themes it underscored. It demonstrated both the desire for expansion by the president and his advisers and the power of Congress in foreign affairs. For the remainder of the century the scenario would be repeated again and again, often with differing results. Gradually presidents wrested more control over foreign affairs from Congress. And Congress, for its part, accepted a more expansionist foreign policy. As presidents and Congress found common ground, America expanded outward into the Caribbean and the Pacific, although the expansion took different forms. Sometimes the United States annexed countries outright; other times it was content to exercise less forceful control over nominally independent countries. The results were the same. The United States ultimately acquired an overseas empire and expanded its influence over the Western Hemisphere.

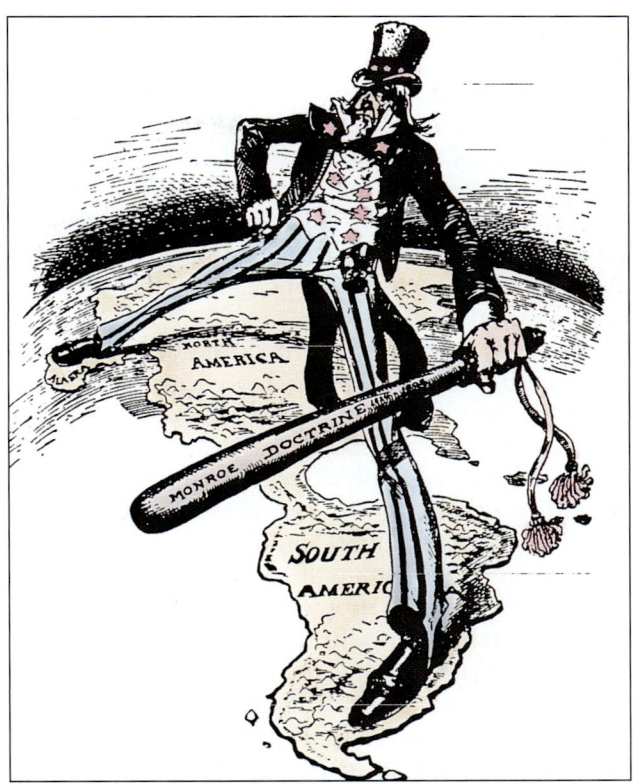

During the turn of the century, the United States increasingly tried to influence the affairs of the Americas. Here, Uncle Sam assumes a forceful attitude.

Congressional Control and the Reduction of American Power

In 1869, when Grant took office, congressmen and other Americans held the State Department and the diplomatic service in low esteem. No majestic building housed the State Department—it was headquartered in a former orphan asylum. Nor was the post of secretary of state as great a prize as it had been. Once regarded as a stepping-stone to the presidency, politicians increasingly viewed the post as a reward for outstanding party men or the refuge for defeated presidential aspirants. Even the diplomats themselves did not escape criticism. One newspaper editor said the diplomatic service was too often used as "gilt edged pigeon holes for filing away Americans, more or less illustrious, who are no longer particularly wanted at home."

Trimming the State Department

The irreverent treatment of the State Department reflected a congressional and national mood. Concerns over the currency, civil service reform, Reconstruction, taxation, the tariff, Indian fighting, and railroad building dwarfed interest in foreign affairs. During the 1870s and 1880s, when a powerful Congress largely dictated foreign policy, the spirit of Washington's Farewell Address and the Monroe Doctrine guided the country. Washington had counseled America to steer clear of foreign entanglements and Monroe had made isolationism from Europe a national obsession. Separated from a powerful Europe by the cold North Atlantic, Congress saw no reason to spend time or money on the State Department or foreign affairs.

Using its control over the budget as a sword, Congress trimmed the State Department to the bone. In 1869, Congress allowed the State Department a paltry 31 clerks; by 1881 presidential efforts had succeeded in raising that number to a still inadequate 50. Politicians who considered the foreign service "a nursery of snobs" viewed diplomats as an expensive, nearly useless luxury. A few reformers even advocated the abolition of the foreign service. They argued that two oceans protected America and that international lawyers could be hired to handle serious international crises.

Reducing the Military

The sword that trimmed the State Department was also used to pare the United States army and navy.

When the Civil War ended and peace returned, Congress quickly reduced the country's military might, making the United States a weaker country. In 1865 the United States had the largest and perhaps the most powerful navy in the world, with 971 vessels. To be sure, it was a ragtag navy, composed of just about any vessel that would float, ranging from the powerful *Monitor*-class ironclads to modest yachts. Within nine months of Appomattox, the fleet had been reduced to 29.

As Congress watched unconcerned, the navy declined intellectually as well. To begin with, there were far too many officers. Although after the post–Civil War reductions the United States navy was less than one-tenth as large as Great Britain's, it contained over half as many officers. With promotions based strictly upon length of service, any officer who lived long enough could become an admiral. This system of promotion almost guaranteed poor leadership. The world's best navies converted to steel and steam, but U.S. naval leaders remained tied to wood and sails. The U.S. navy quickly became a joke. In 1881 authorities claimed, with some justification, that a single modern ship of the Chilean navy could destroy the entire United States fleet.

The power and effectiveness of the army were similarly reduced. On May 23, 1865, with the Civil War just ended, Union bluecoats marched down Pennsylvania Avenue in a victory parade. There were over 100,000 soldiers. It took an hour for General Meade's cavalry to pass the reviewing stand. "Marching twelve abreast, the general's infantry consumed another five hours." The next day thousands of General Sherman's men repeated the performance, marching briskly "like the lords of the world!"

The sight would not be repeated for over 50 years. Demobilization occurred quickly and haphazardly. In May 1865 the army contained 1,034,064 volunteers; by November 1866 only 11,043 remained in uniform. Eventually Congress slashed the number of even the regular troops. By the end of Reconstruction, Congress had reduced the army to a distant echo of its former self. In 1876 maximum strength stood at 27,442 troops.

Certainly, in 1876 the United States did not need an active foreign service and a powerful army and navy to secure its borders. No countries threatened America. Geography defended the United States, and the European balance of power discouraged European designs on any part of the Western Hemisphere. At the same time, the relative weakness of America's foreign service, army, and navy discouraged the United States from attempting to extend its influence beyond its own borders. All in all, most congressmen were entirely happy with the situation.

Seward's Dream

Not everyone in government agreed with congressional leadership in foreign affairs. Regularly during the 1860s and 1870s, presidents or their secretaries of state called for a more forceful, expansionist foreign policy. **William Henry Seward** of New York, who served as secretary of state for Lincoln and Johnson, was such a man. A cold and vain man with a weak chin and a prominent nose, Seward dreamed of an American empire that would dominate the Pacific and Caribbean basins. During his term as secretary of state, he advocated a vigorous expansionism. He negotiated with Denmark to purchase the Danish West Indies (Virgin Islands), with Russia to buy Alaska, and with Santo Domingo for the Dominican harbor of Samana Bay. In addition, his plan for an American empire encompassed Haiti, Cuba, Iceland, Greenland, Honduras's Tigre Island, and Hawaii.

Congress, not sharing Seward's vision, balked. During Seward's term, America did acquire the Midway Islands in the middle of the Pacific Ocean, but few Americans even noticed the addition. The purchase of Alaska in 1867 drew more comments, most of them negative. Congressmen grumbled over the treaty. Some senators claimed that $7.2 million was too much money for a frozen wasteland that only Eskimos and seals could love. Others cracked jokes about "Johnson's Polar Bear Garden" and "Frigidia." But in the end the Senate, influenced by a few well-placed bribes, reluctantly ratified the treaty.

Articulate and aggressive anti-imperialists blocked the remainder of Seward's dreams. During the late 1860s and the 1870s congressional power was at high tide. Seward and President Andrew Johnson were no match for Sumner and Thaddeus Stevens and their colleagues in Congress. Congressmen consistently found other issues more pressing than foreign affairs. Some pushed for money to enact a fair Reconstruction policy. Others freely gave money to railroad construction companies and Union veterans, such gifts contributing significantly to their reelection. But they drew America's purse strings tight when confronted with most expansionist schemes.

THE SPIRIT OF AMERICAN GREATNESS

Although Congress was reluctant to endorse expansionist schemes, during the last third of the nineteenth century many other citizens had become convinced that the United States had to adopt a more aggressive and forceful foreign policy. Their reasons varied. Some believed expansion would be good for

American business. Others felt America had a duty to spread its way of life to less fortunate countries. Still others maintained that economic and strategic security required that the country acquire overseas bases. Behind all the arguments, however, rested a common assumption: The United States was a great and important country, and it should start acting the part.

American Exceptionalism

For many Americans it started with God's plan. The idea of **American exceptionalism**—that the nation houses God's chosen people—has deep roots in the country's history. Puritan concepts of "a city upon a hill" mixed easily with talk of the greatness of republicanism and democracy and the manifest destiny of America. The teachings of Social Darwinists added "scientific proof" to the concept of American exceptionalism. With such Darwinian phrases as "natural selection" and "survival of the fittest," American intellectuals praised the course of American history. Charles Darwin himself noted that "the wonderful progress of the United States, as well as the character of the people, are the results of natural selection; the more energetic, restless, and courageous men from all parts of Europe have emigrated during the last ten or twelve generations to that great country."

Such ideas found a warm reception in America. There was, however, a dark side to American exceptionalism, and too many Americans were quick to endorse it: If white Anglo-Saxon Americans were biologically superior, then other races and other nations had to be inferior. During the late nineteenth century, such Social Darwinists as Herbert Spencer in England and John Fiske in the United States helped make racism intellectually acceptable. Catering to Anglo-Saxon audiences, Social Darwinists advanced pseudoscientific theories to "prove" the superiority of Anglo-Saxons.

From the idea of superiority to the acceptance of domination was a short step. If Americans were God's and Darwin's chosen people, why shouldn't they dominate and uplift less fortunate countries and peoples? This was the question that advocates of a more aggressive American foreign policy asked their audiences. Senator Albert J. Beveridge of Indiana spoke for many Americans when he told Congress,

> God has not been preparing the English-speaking and Teutonic peoples for a thousand years for nothing but vain and idle self-admiration. No! He has not made us the master organizers of the world to establish a system where chaos reigns.... He has given us the spirit of progress to overwhelm the forces of reaction

THE PEOPLE SPEAK

March of the Flag

Few American leaders articulated the nation's expansionist impulse as clearly or unapologetically as Indiana Senator Albert J. Beveridge. His "March of the Flag" speech, first delivered in Indianapolis' Tomlinson Hall in September 1898, argued that Americans possessed a unique responsibility for their less "civilized" neighbors.

> In this campaign, the question is larger than a party question. It is an American question. It is a world question. Shall the American people continue their march toward the commercial supremacy of the world? Shall free institutions broaden their blessed reign as the children of liberty wax in strength, until the empire of our principles is established over the hearts of all mankind? . . .
>
> The Opposition tells us that we ought not to govern a people without their consent. I answer, The rule of liberty that all just government derives its authority from the consent of the governed, applies only to those who are capable of self-government. We govern the Indians without their consent, we govern our territories without their consent, we govern our children without their consent. How do they know that our government would be without their consent? Would not the people of the Philippines prefer the just, humane, civilizing government of this Republic to the savage, bloody rule of pillage and extortion from which we have rescued them?
>
> And, regardless of this formula of words made only for enlightened, self-governing people, do we owe no duty to the world? Shall we turn these peoples back to the reeking hands from which we have taken them? Shall we abandon them, with Germany, England, and Japan hungering for them? Shall we save them from those nations, to give them a self-rule of tragedy? . . .
>
> Will you say by your vote that American ability to govern has decayed; that a century's experience in self-rule has failed of a result? Will you affirm by your vote that you are an infidel to American power and practical sense? Or will you say that ours is the blood of government; ours the heart of dominion; ours the brain and genius of administration? Will you remember that we do but what our fathers did—we but pitch the tents of liberty farther westward, farther southward—we only continue the march of the flag?

Source: Albert J. Beveridge, "The March of the Flag" (printed in the *Indianapolis Journal*, September 17, 1898. *The Meaning of the Times*, 1908). Bobbs-Merrill, Indianapolis.

throughout the earth. He has made us adept in government that we may administer government among savage and senile peoples.

Sense of Duty

Religious leaders also noted the duty that American exceptionalism implied. Talk of the "white man's burden" and the duty of "advanced" peoples was rife during the period. Protestant missionaries carried their faith and beliefs to the far corners of the world, but the benefits of their message extended well beyond preaching salvation and saving souls. They also extolled the virtues of American civilization, which included everything from democracy and rule by law to sanitation, material progress, sewing machines, and cotton underwear. Defining good and bad, progress and savagery by American standards, they attempted to alter native customs and beliefs to conform to a single American model.

Popular writer and religious leader Reverend Josiah Strong voiced what other missionaries and true believers acted upon. In 1885 Strong published *Our Country: Its Possible Future and Present Crisis*, a book that quickly sold 170,000 copies and was translated into dozens of languages. "The Anglo-Saxon," Strong wrote, "is the representative of two great ideas . . . civil liberty [and] a pure *spiritual* Christianity." These two ideas, he added, are destined to elevate all mankind, and "the Anglo-Saxon . . . is divinely commissioned to be . . . his brother's keeper." He firmly believed that it was America's destiny and duty to expand and spread its influence. Quoting the Bible while speaking to Anglo-Saxon Americans, he intoned, "Prepare ye the way of the Lord!"

Search for Markets

Strong's message was not lost on the business leaders of America. They fully agreed that missionaries should preach the benefits of American material progress as well as the glories of the Protestant faith. Looking south toward Latin America and west toward Asia, American businesspeople and farmers saw vast virgin markets for their industrial and agricultural surpluses as well as endless sources of raw materials. Sensing that American markets, filled with low-paid workers, offered few new opportunities, they entertained fabulous visions of hungry Latin Americans and shoeless Chinese.

By the late nineteenth century, the United States was the leading industrial and agricultural country in the world, but domestic consumption did not keep pace with the galloping production. In addition,

Many foreign missionaries sought to unite the people of the world by extolling the virtues of American civilization. White missionaries are shown meeting with blacks in Africa.

throughout the period the government pursued tight-money policies, and laborers' real income only modestly grew. The result was a boom-and-bust economy: spectacular growth and severe depressions. In fact, in the 25 years after 1873, the country suffered through three depressions: 1873 to 1878, 1882 to 1885, and 1893 to 1897.

During depression years, foreign trade seemed a necessity. Depressions meant farm foreclosures and industrial unemployment, problems that led to social unrest. The Grange and Populist movements, the two largest agrarian revolts, originated in cotton and wheat areas during depression years. And such labor confrontations as the violent railroad strikes of 1877, Chicago's Haymarket riot of 1886, and the Pullman strike of 1894 occurred during lean economic times. For many Americans the issue was simple: The United States had to acquire foreign markets or face economic hardship and revolution at home. As one industrial spokesman put it: The time has come for the United States to pursue "an intelligent and spirited foreign policy," one in which the government would "see to it" that the country had adequate foreign markets. If force proved necessary, then so be it.

The State Department was in full agreement. William Henry Seward and Hamilton Fish, Johnson's and Grant's secretaries of state, believed firmly that America needed new markets. Seward called the potentially bottomless markets of Asia "the prize," and he wanted the United States to acquire islands in the Pacific as stepping-stones toward that prize. He similarly believed that the United States should extend its economic control to include Canada and Latin America. Hamilton Fish agreed with the hoarse-voiced, cigar-chewing Seward. Although, like Seward, he had to contend with a cautious, isolationist Congress, Fish made several important strides toward the Asia markets. During his term as secretary of state, the United States signed treaties and established more formal relations with Hawaii and Samoa, two Pacific island groups that would later become part of the American empire.

During the late 1870s and 1880s, economic hard times quickened the search for new markets. Rutherford B. Hayes's secretary of state William Evarts valued a good story; he once told a British minister that George Washington had been able to throw a dollar across the Rappahannock River because a dollar went farther in those days. Evarts also valued dollars, and he felt Americans needed far more of them. As secretary of state, he worked toward an American commercial empire. He hoped that unexploited Asian and Latin American markets would guarantee continual economic growth and social tranquility for all Americans.

James G. Blaine and Frederick T. Frelinghuysen, who served as secretaries of state for James Garfield and Chester Arthur, concentrated their efforts on Latin American markets. Blaine later recounted that during his short stay in the State Department in 1881 he followed two principles: "first, to bring about peace . . . ; second, to cultivate such friendly commercial relations with all American countries as would lead to a large increase in the export trade of the United States." When Blaine was forced out of office after Garfield's assassination, Frelinghuysen continued his policies. He successfully negotiated bilateral reciprocity treaties with many Latin American countries, which lowered tariffs and thus stimulated trade between the United States and Latin America.

By the mid-1880s, expansion efforts combined with economic and social problems at home convinced Congress to reevaluate its isolationist policies. The West was settled, the Native Americans defeated, the Union reconstructed, and the railroads built. It was now time to look at our oceans not as defensive barriers but as paths toward new markets and increased prosperity. There was one final problem: America's navy and merchant marine seemed woefully unfit for the challenge.

The New Navy

British writer and wit Oscar Wilde was close to the truth when he had one of his fictional characters reply to an American woman who complained that her country had no ruins and no curiosities: "No ruins! No curiosities! You have your Navy and your manners!" By 1880 the United States Navy was a sad joke.

If America hoped to compete for world markets, it had to upgrade its navy. During the 1880s and early 1890s advocates of a "New Navy" moved Congress to action. The transformation from a "heterogeneous collection of naval trash" to a great navy occurred in two stages. The face-lift began in 1883, during the administration of Chester A. Arthur. Prodded by the president, Congress passed an act providing for three small cruisers and a dispatch boat, the beginning of the famous White Squadron. More vessels soon followed. Under the direction of President Grover Cleveland and his able secretary of the navy, William Whitney, the White Squadron grew in size, and naval bureaucracy and fleet personnel improved.

By 1890 great gains had been made, but there were still serious problems. The White Squadron was not a world-class navy. Its ships were lightly armored, fast cruisers, ideal for hit-and-run missions but inadequate for any major naval engagement. While Britain and Germany were building large, heavily armored battleships capable of bombarding and damaging coastal cities, the United States continued to think of naval warfare in terms of commerce raiding.

Benjamin F. Tracy, Benjamin Harrison's secretary of war, was determined to change American naval thinking. Tracy had a very modern view of what defense entailed. To adequately defend America's interests, Tracy called for ships that could "raise blockades" and attack an enemy's coast, "for a war, though defensive in principle, may be conducted most effectively by being offensive in its operations." In fact, Tracy maintained that proper defense might even include shooting first: "The nation that is ready to strike the first blow will gain an advantage which its antagonist can never offset." Such a first-strike definition of defense meant one thing: The United States needed to build modern, armored battleships. Tracy wanted two battleship fleets, one for the Atlantic and another for the Pacific.

Tracy's program was endorsed in Congress by such "Big Navy" advocates as Senator Eugene Hale of Maine and Representative Henry Cabot Lodge of Massachusetts. They found Congress in the mood to act. As one senator said, "You can not negotiate without a gun." In 1890, Congress appropriated money for the construction of three first-class battleships and a heavy cruiser. It was the beginning of a new, very much offensive navy for the United States. Reviewing his accomplishments in 1891, Tracy boasted: "The sea will be the future seat of empire. And we shall rule it as certainly as the sun doth rise."

Talk of empire, navy, trade, and national greatness came together in 1890 in the publication of a monumentally important book, *The Influence of Sea Power upon History,* by Captain Alfred Thayer Mahan. Mahan, who was attached to the Naval War College, was more comfortable around books than on ships. Although he had served throughout the world, he had the look, temperament, and inclinations of a college don. His masterpiece set forward the simple thesis that naval power was the key to national greatness. Taking Greece, Rome, and England as examples, he attempted to demonstrate that countries rise to world power through expanding their foreign commerce and protecting that commerce with a strong navy. Without a powerful navy, Mahan emphasized, a nation can never enjoy full prosperity and security. Without a strong navy, in short, no nation could ever hope to be a world power.

Large Policy

Mahan's writings and Tracy's proposal were applauded by American politicians and businesspeople who felt it was time for the United States to assume the rights and responsibilities of world-power status. These were important citizens—men of wealth, education, and influence. Some like Whitelaw Reid, editor of the *New York Tribune,* helped shape public opinion through their editorials. Others like Henry Cabot Lodge, Theodore Roosevelt, Albert J. Beveridge, and John Hay were powerful politicians and administrators. They were vocal nationalists who believed that the United States was destined to be the greatest of world powers. Increasingly after 1890, these and other men of like mind dominated and shaped America's foreign policy.

These expansionists often shared common experiences and beliefs. Most were prosperous Republicans from old-line American families, and most had traveled abroad widely. Anglo-Saxon by heritage, they tended to be ardent Anglophiles, full of praise for Great Britain's imperial efforts. They believed that the United States should join "Mother England" in administering to the "uncivilized" corners of the globe. As Beveridge noted, without the work of Anglo-Saxons "the world would relapse into barbarism and night.... We are trustees of the world's progress, guardians of its righteous place."

Lodge and other expansionists called for a bold foreign policy, what they called the **"large policy."** They advocated the construction of a canal through Central America to allow American ships to move between the Atlantic and Pacific oceans more rapidly. To protect the canal, the United States would have to exert control over Cuba and the other strategically located Caribbean islands. Next America would have to acquire coaling stations and naval bases across the Pacific. Secure bases in Hawaii, Guam, Wake Island, and the Philippines would allow the United States to exploit the seemingly limitless Asian market. Finally, a powerful navy would have to protect the entire American empire.

In the end, then, all of their plans were rooted in the theme of a strong navy. Like his friend Mahan, Lodge was a student of history. "It is the sea power which is essential to the greatness of every splendid people," he said. It had enabled Rome to crush the Carthaginians, England to defeat Napoleon, and the North to win the Civil War. Without the power of a strong navy, Lodge believed that America could never experience real peace and security: "All the peace the world has ever had has been obtained by fighting, and all the peace that any nation... can ever have, is by readiness to fight if attacked." For Lodge as for Tracy, thoughts of peace and war often ran together and appeared in the same sentences.

THE EMERGENCE OF AGGRESSION IN AMERICAN FOREIGN POLICY

"To be prepared for war is the most effectual means to promote peace," said Theodore Roosevelt. The more such politicians talked about peace, the closer war seemed. It is not coincidental that the United States launched a more belligerent foreign policy at the same time it was building and launching more powerful ships. The two developments originated from the same source: a ready acceptance of force as the final arbiter of international disputes. Before the turn of the century, the acceptance of force would lead to the Spanish-American War of 1898; between 1885 and 1897, during the presidencies of Benjamin Harrison and Grover Cleveland, the same attitudes almost caused several other wars. The Spanish-American War was not an aberrant event. Rather it was the result of a more aggressive American foreign policy, one aimed at acquiring both world respect and an empire.

Confronting the Germans in Samoa

Changing American attitudes toward foreign policy first became apparent in relation to Samoa, a group of 14 South Pacific volcanic islands with splendid natural harbors. In 1872 an American negotiated a treaty with a tribal chief to grant the United States rights to a naval station at Pago Pago. Although an antiexpansionist Senate took no action on the treaty, expansionists kept trying. In 1878 the Senate did rat-

America's attempt to gain the Samoan islands as coaling stations along the route to Australia led to a diplomatic crisis with Germany.

ify a similar treaty, which formally committed the United States to Samoa. Unfortunately for the United States, German Chancellor Otto von Bismarck had also decided that Samoa should belong to Germany. As a result of the intricacies of European politics, England sided with the "iron chancellor." President Cleveland and his secretary of state, Thomas F. Bayard, firmly disagreed with the Europeans. Germany and the United States were set on a collision course.

When a conference between the three countries held in Washington in 1887 failed to solve the problem, war seemed closer still. Neither Germany nor the United States had much money invested in the islands, but both felt their national pride was at stake. "We must show sharp teeth," remarked Bismarck. Cleveland, for his part, dispatched three warships to Samoa. Nature, however, had the most powerful weapon. On the morning of March 16, 1889, a typhoon swept across Samoa, destroying both American and German warships anchored in Apia harbor.

The violent winds seemed to calm the ruffled emotions of the United States and Germany. "Men and nations," wrote the *New York World*, "must bow before the decrees of nature." The same year as the typhoon, Germany, the United States, and England met for another conference, this one in Berlin. Without consulting the Samoans, they decided to partition the islands. Everyone seemed satisfied—except the Samoans, who were deprived of their independence and saddled with an unpopular king. The plan lasted until 1899, when Germany and the United States ended the facade of Samoan independence and officially made colonies of the islands. The United States was granted Tutuila, with the harbor of Pago Pago, and several smaller islands. Many expansionists believed that America's aggressive stand against Germany had paid handsome dividends.

Teaching Chile a Lesson

American expansionists had something to gain from their confrontation with Germany over Samoa. Pago Pago was, after all, "the most perfectly landlocked harbor that exists in the Pacific Ocean." It was an ideal coaling station for ships running between San Francisco and Australia. American troubles with Chile, however, are more difficult to understand. Trade and strategic policy played only small roles. More than anything else, touchy pride and jingoism pushed the United States toward war with Chile.

Had people not died, the background to the confrontation would have been amusing. In 1891 a revolutionary faction, which the United States had opposed, gained control of the Chilean government and initiated a foreign policy that was unfriendly toward America. Shortly thereafter, on October 16, 1891, an American cruiser, the *Baltimore*, anchored off the coast of Chile. About 100 members of its crew were sent ashore on leave at Valparaiso. Some sailors retired to the local True Blue Saloon. An officer who arrived on the scene later said that the men had gone ashore "for the purpose of getting drunk" and that by evening they were "probably drunk, properly drunk." As the men left the saloon, a riot broke out. An angry, anti-American mob attacked the sailors, killing 2 and injuring 16. To make matters worse, the Chilean police, who had done nothing to halt the fighting, carried the surviving Americans off to jail.

It was an unfortunate affair, and the United States loudly protested, demanding a formal apology and "prompt and full reparation." The Chilean government refused. President Harrison, a former Union general who prided himself on his patriotism and was easily swayed by jingoism, threatened to break off diplomatic relations—a serious step toward war—unless the United States received an immediate apology. When Secretary of State James G. Blaine tried to counsel moderation, Harrison angrily replied, "Mr. Secretary, that insult was to the uniform of United States sailors."

Public opinion sided with Harrison. The *New York Sun* commented that "we must teach men who will henceforth be called snarling whelps of the Pacific that we cannot be snapped at with impunity." Angry young Theodore Roosevelt insisted, "For two nickels he would declare war himself . . . and wage it sole." Finally the Chilean government backed down, apologizing for the attack on the sailors and paying a $75,000 indemnity.

The threat of force had again carried the day. Advocates of the New Navy and aggressively nationalistic Americans cheered Harrison's actions. Few Americans heeded Edwin L. Godkin, editor of *The Nation*, who wrote, "Navy officers dream of war and talk and lecture about it incessantly. The Senate debates are filled with predictions of impending war and with talk of preparing for it at once. . . . Most truculent and bloodthirsty of all, jingo editors keep up a din day after day about the way we could cripple one country's fleet and destroy another's commerce, and fill heads of boys and silly men with the idea that war is the normal state of a civilized country."

Plucking the Hawaiian Pear

Throughout the late nineteenth century, Hawaii figured prominently in American foreign policy planning. Earlier in the century, the islands had been a favorite place for American missionaries. Many went to Hawaii to spread Christianity and ended up settling and raising their families in the tropical paradise. More important still was the islands' location. Not only were they ideally situated along the trade routes to Asia, but they offered a perfect site for protecting the Pacific sea lanes to the American west coast and to the potential locations of an isthmus canal. In Hawaii, missionary, economic, and strategic concerns met in complete harmony.

By the mid-1880s, Congress was willing to accept expansionists' dreams for Hawaii. A treaty between Hawaii and the United States, ratified in 1887, set aside Pearl Harbor for the exclusive use of the American navy. By that time the islands were already economically tied to the United States. An 1875 treaty had allowed Hawaiians to sell their sugar in the United States duty-free, giving them a two-cents-per-pound advantage over other foreign producers. The legislation encouraged American speculators to invest in Hawaiian sugar and to import Chinese and Japanese laborers to the islands to work on the large plantations. The investments returned incredibly high dividends, and for a time business boomed.

Problems arose suddenly in 1890. The McKinley Tariff Act removed all tariffs on foreign sugar and protected domestic sugar producers by awarding American sugar a bounty of two cents per pound. Hawaiian sugar prices plummeted. The American

Queen Liliuokalani assumed the Hawaiian throne in 1891. Strongly nationalistic, she sought to purge white influence from Hawaii. She was overthrown by white islanders with the aid of American sailors and marines.

minister in Honolulu estimated that the McKinley Tariff cost Hawaiian producers $12 million. And in 1891 the government of the islands changed. **Queen Liliuokalani** ascended the throne. A poet and a composer interested in humanitarian work, she nevertheless initiated a strongly anti-American policy. She wanted to purge American influences in Hawaii and disfranchise all white men except those married to native women.

The white population in Hawaii reacted quickly. On January 17, 1893, three days after the queen dismissed the legislature and proclaimed a new constitution, white islanders overthrew her government. Supported by American officials, sailors, and marines, the revolution was fast, almost bloodless, and successful. Foreign minister John L. Stevens then proclaimed Hawaii an American protectorate and wired his superiors in Washington that "the Hawaiian pear is now fully ripe, and this is the golden hour for the United States to pluck it."

The Harrison administration, due to leave office on March 4, negotiated a treaty of annexation with "indecent haste" and sent it to the Senate for ratification. Public sentiment cheered Harrison's actions. But before the Senate could ratify the treaty, Cleveland took office. An anti-imperialist, Cleveland had grave misgivings about the revolution, America's reaction, and the treaty. Five days after his inauguration, he recalled the treaty from the Senate and sent a special agent, James H. Blount of Georgia, to Hawaii to investigate the entire affair. After a careful investigation, Blount reported to Cleveland that the majority of native Hawaiians opposed annexation and that on moral and legal grounds the treaty was unjustified. Cleveland accepted Blount's report and killed the treaty.

The controversy, however, was not over. A white American minority continued to govern Hawaii. To correct the situation, Cleveland sent another representative, Albert S. Willis, to Hawaii to convince the new government to step down and allow Queen Liliuokalani to return to the throne. Willis failed in his mission. "Queen Lil" refused to promise full amnesty for the revolutionaries if she were returned to power. "My decision would be," she said, "as the law directs, that such persons should be beheaded." In addition, newly elected President Sanford B. Dole, head of a large Hawaiian pineapple corporation, refused to leave office. In the end, Cleveland washed his hands of the entire matter, and the revolutionaries proclaimed an independent Hawaiian republic on July 4, 1894. Four years and three days later, during the Spanish-American War, the United States finally annexed Hawaii.

Facing Down the British

Potentially the most serious conflict America faced during the 1890s originated in a dispute over a strip of land in a South American jungle. Venezuela and British Guiana shared a common border, but both claimed land the other side said was theirs. For almost 50 years this dispute remained peacefully unsettled, until the discovery of gold in the region in the 1880s increased the importance of the issue. It was a rich deposit—the largest nugget ever discovered, 509 ounces, was found there—and both Britain and Venezuela wanted it. In response to Venezuelan requests for help, the United States several times offered to arbitrate the matter, and each time Britain refused the offer.

By June 1895 Cleveland and his new secretary of state, Richard Olney, two short-tempered men, had decided that Britain's actions violated the spirit, if not the letter, of the Monroe Doctrine. (Ever since a cancer operation had left him with an artificial jaw of vulcanized rubber, Cleveland had been irritable.) Olney, who had persuaded Cleveland to use federal troops to put down the Pullman strike in Chicago the year before, was a man of strong ideas who did not shrink from the use of force. In a strongly worded message to Great Britain, Olney demanded that Britain submit the dispute to arbitration, hinting that the United States might intervene militarily if its wishes were not honored.

Lord Salisbury, Britain's prime minister, foreign secretary, and consummate aristocrat, did not reply to Olney's note for four months; he then answered, in effect, that the dispute did not involve either the United States or the Monroe Doctrine and would America kindly mind its own business. Olney was furious. Americans throughout the country felt insulted. When Cleveland read the message he became "mad clean through." In a special message to Congress, he asked for funds to establish a commission to determine the actual Venezuelan boundary. He also insisted that he would use force if necessary to maintain that boundary against any aggressors. Both houses of Congress unanimously approved Cleveland's request. The excitement of war was in the air.

The violence of America's reaction surprised Salisbury and British officials. England, increasingly involved in a conflict in South Africa, certainly did not want war. Salisbury reversed his position and allowed a commission to arbitrate the dispute. In the end, the arbitral tribunal gave Britain most of the land it claimed.

America, however, felt it was the real winner. Cleveland had faced the British lion and won. The Monroe Doctrine and American prestige soared to new heights. More important for the future, Cleveland's actions, coupled with his handling of the Hawaiian revolution, significantly increased the power of the president over foreign affairs. Future presidents would not soon relinquish that control.

THE WAR FOR EMPIRE

During the Venezuela crisis many Americans seemed to invite and look forward to the prospect of war. Theodore Roosevelt, who was determined to atone for the failure of his father to fight in the Civil War and to be the first in war even if he were the last in peace, wrote: "Let the fight come if it must; I don't care whether our sea coast cities are bombarded or not; we would take Canada." For Roosevelt, war would be an ennobling experience. It would test and validate American greatness. "All the great masterful races," Roosevelt wrote, "have been fighting races; and the minute that a race loses the hard fighting virtues, then... it has lost its proud right to stand as the equal of the best."

The Spirit of the 1890s

Throughout the 1890s other Americans echoed Roosevelt's war cries. Viewed as a whole, it was a decade of strident nationalism and aggressive posturing. It was also a troubled and violent decade. Racked by the depression of 1893, frustrated by the problems created by monopolies and overproduction, and plagued by internal strife, Americans turned on each other, often with violent results. Strikes in Pullman, Illinois, and Homestead, Pennsylvania, saw laborers battle federal and state authorities. Populist protest dramatized the widening gulf between city and country, rich and poor. Anarchists and socialists talked about the need for violent solutions to complex problems.

American heroes of all stripes reflected this aggressive mood. In saloons across the country, heavyweight boxing champion John L. Sullivan defiantly boasted, "I can lick any sonofabitch in the house." In the parlors of the wealthy, Roosevelt stressed, "Cowardice in a race, as in an individual, is the unpardonable sin." Between Sullivan and Roosevelt, and the Americans that admired both men, was a bond forged by the love of violence and power.

This attitude led to the glorification of war and jingoistic nationalism. During the mid-1890s a remarkable interest in Napoleon gripped the nation—between 1894 and 1896 28 books were written about the Corsican general. In public schools throughout the country, administrators instituted daily flag salutes and made the recitation of the new pledge of allegiance mandatory. Even the popular music of the day had a particularly martial quality. Such marches as John Philip Sousa's "Stars and Stripes Forever" (1897) captured the aggressive, patriotic, and boisterous mood of the country.

As the disputes with Germany, Chile, and Great Britain demonstrated, neither the American people nor its leaders feared war. The horrors of the Civil War were dying with the generation that had known them. A younger generation of men, filled with romantic conceptions of battle and heroism, now openly sought a war of their own. Some Washington politicians even began to view war as a way to unite the country, to quell the protests of angry farmers and laborers.

The Cuban Revolution

Oftentimes the mood of a nation governs the reaction to and interpretation of events. Such was the case with America's attitude toward the Cuban Revolution. In 1895, while Sousa was writing energetic marches and Americans were cheering new boxing heroes, an independence revolt broke out in Cuba. It was not the first time the Cubans took up arms in pursuit of independence. During the Ten Years' War (1868–1878) Cuban patriots had unsuccessfully fought for independence from their Spanish rulers. The war was bloody and violent, and Cubans actively sought American support; but the United States, guided by a policy of isolationism, steered clear.

By 1895, however, cautious isolationism was out of step with the country's aggressive tempo. From the start of this revolution, Americans expressed far more than casual interest in the rebellion. American business had invested over $50 million in Cuba and the annual trade between the two countries totaled almost $100 million. Once the revolution started, insurgents burned crops in the fields, and the trade between Cuba and the United States slowed to a trickle. Overall, however, economics played a relatively unimportant role in forming America's attitude toward the revolution.

Humanitarianism was a far more important factor. In Cuba's valiant fight, Americans saw a reenactment of their own war for independence. The resourceful Cubans made sure that Americans stayed well supplied with stories of Spanish atrocities and Cuban heroism. The Cuban junta—central revolutionary committee—established bases in New York City and Tampa, Florida, and daily provided American newspapers with stories aimed at sympathetic American hearts.

Not all the stories were false. The Cuban—and Spanish—suffering was real enough. Unable to defeat the Spanish army in the field, Cuban revolutionaries resorted to guerilla tactics. They burned sugarcane fields and blew up mills. They destroyed railroad tracks and bridges. They vowed to win their independence or destroy Cuba in the process. Supported by the populace, the guerillas succeeded in turning Cuba into an economic and military nightmare for Spanish officials.

In 1896 Spain sent Governor-General Valeriano Weyler y Nicolau to Cuba to crush the rebellion. A man of ruthless clarity, he understood the nature of guerila warfare. Guerrillas could not be defeated by conventional engagements. Their generals did not imitate the tactics of Napoleon; they were not concerned with flanking maneuvers and cavalry charges. Their weapons were patience and endurance and popular support. Weyler knew this, and he decided to fight the guerrillas on their own terms.

His first plan was to rob the guerrillas of their base of support, the rural villages and the sympathetic peasants. He divided the island into military districts and relocated Cubans into guarded camps. He forced over a half million Cubans from their homes and crowded them into shabbily constructed and unsanitary camps. The food was bad, the water worse. Disease spread with frightful speed and horrifying results. Perhaps 200,000 Cubans died in the camps as Weyler earned the sobriquet "the Butcher." After inspecting the camps, Senator Renfield Proctor of Vermont reported on the plight of the Cuban people to Congress: "Torn from their homes, with foul earth, foul air, foul water, and foul food or none, what wonder that one-half have died and that one-quarter of the living are so diseased that they cannot be saved?... Little children are still walking about with arms and chest terribly emaciated, eyes swollen, and abdomens bloated to three times the natural size."

The Yellow Press

In the United States reports of the suffering Cuban masses filled the front pages of newspapers. In New York City, William Randolph Hearst's *New York Journal* and Joseph Pulitzer's *New York World* used the junta's lurid stories as ammunition in a newspaper war. Newspaper reporters freely engaged in **"yellow journalism,"** exaggerating already sad and inhumane conditions. Most stories had a sensational twist. One particularly incendiary drawing by Frederic Remington, the famous western artist sent to Cuba by Hearst, pictured three leering Spanish officials searching a nude Cuban woman. Hearst ran the picture five columns wide on the second page of the *Journal*, and the edition sold close to one million copies, the largest newspaper run in history until then. Neither the picture nor the story, however, mentioned that Spanish women—not men—conducted the search, although men had conducted other such searches. Such coverage biased American opinion against Spain. It also sold newspapers. When Hearst bought the *Journal* in 1895 it had a daily circulation of 77,000 copies; by the summer of 1898 sales had increased to over 1.5 million daily.

"Yellow journalism" and the more sober coverage of the standard press persuaded many Americans to call for U.S. intervention in the Cuban Revolution. Grover Cleveland, however, was not easily moved by newspaper reports. His administration wanted to protect American interests in Cuba but was dead set against any sort of military intervention in the conflict. Without recognizing the revolutionaries, he worked to convince Spain to grant "home rule." But when he left office in early 1897, the revolution in Cuba was raging as violently as ever. Cleveland passed the Cuban problem to his successor William McKinley. Like Cleveland, McKinley deplored war. He had fought bravely in the Civil War, and he knew the horrors of war firsthand. Before he would even consider military intervention, McKinley was determined to exhaust every peaceful alternative.

McKinley displayed strength and patience. As many influential Americans called for U.S. intervention, McKinley worked diplomatically to end the fighting. Rather than inflame public opinion, he attempted to remove the issue from public debate. In his inaugural address, for example, he did not even mention Cuba. For a time it appeared that his efforts would succeed. In October 1897 a new government in Spain moved toward granting more autonomy to Cuba. It removed Weyler and promised to end his hated reconcentration program. Spain, said McKinley, was following "honorable paths." Patience and cool heads, he hoped, would carry the day.

Spain moved with glacial slowness. Some of its reforms were half-hearted, others were merely designed to calm American emotions. In Cuba the bloodshed continued. As Spanish officials and Cuban revolutionaries ignored or denounced Spain's "honorable paths," pressure on McKinley to take stronger action mounted. In May 1897 he dispatched his trusted political friend William J. Calhoun of Ohio to Cuba to provide him with an independent report on the conditions on the island. Calhoun's report confirmed the grim picture presented in American newspapers. "The country outside of the military posts was practically depopulated," Calhoun noted. "I did not see a house, a man, woman or child; a horse, mule or cow, not even a dog; I did not see a

This *New York Journal* sketch by Frederic Remington of Spanish officials searching a Cuban woman on an American steamer shocked the nation. Such "yellow journalism," or exaggeration of the facts, played an important role in persuading Americans to call for intervention in the Cuban Revolution.

sign of life, except an occasional vulture or buzzard sailing through the air. The country was wrapped in the stillness of death and the silence of desolation." By January of 1898 the president looked as defeated as his diplomatic efforts. He had to take drugs to sleep, his skin was pasty, and his dark eyes seemed to be sinking farther back into his head. Two events in February would end any hope of a diplomatic solution and lead to the Spanish-American War.

William Randolph Hearst had often told his reporters: "Don't wait for things to turn up. Turn them up!" He did just that in early February 1898. With the help of the Cuban junta, Hearst acquired a private letter from Enrique Dupuy de Lôme, the Spanish minister in the United States, to a Spanish friend of his in Cuba. The letter contained de Lôme's unguarded and undiplomatic opinion of McKinley. Reprinted on the front page of the *Journal* on February 9, 1898, Hearst labeled the letter: "Worst insult to the United States in Its History." De Lôme called McKinley "weak and a bidder for the admiration of the crowd." He accused the American president of being a hypocrite and a "would-be politician." Even worse, de Lôme suggested that Spain's new peace policy was mere sham and propaganda.

The letter infuriated the American public. As one leader rejoiced to the delight of the Cuban junta, "The de Lôme letter is a great thing for us."

Less than a week later a second event rocked America. On the still evening of February 15, an explosion ripped apart the *Maine*, a U.S. battleship anchored in Havana harbor. The ship quickly sank, killing over 250 officers and men. An 1898 investigation ruled that an external explosion had sunk the *Maine*. A 1976 study, however, blamed the sinking on an internal explosion. In truth, no one knows the who, how, and why answers. Americans at the time,

The sinking of the *Maine* was one of the major events leading to the Spanish-American War. It is still uncertain who or what caused the explosion that sank the ship.

however, were not in an impartial or philosophical mood. They blamed Spain. One diplomatic historian commented, " **'Remember the *Maine!*'** became a national watch word.... In a Broadway bar a man raised his glass and said solemnly, 'Gentlemen, remember the *Maine!*' Through the streets of American cities went the cry, 'Remember the *Maine!* To Hell with Spain!' "

War was in the air, and it is doubtful if McKinley or any other president could have long preserved peace. Congress was ready for war. On March 6, McKinley told a leading congressman, "I must have money to get ready for war." Congress responded on March 8 by passing the "Fifty Million Bill" (the amount of McKinley's request) without a single dissenting vote. Although McKinley continued to work for a diplomatic solution to the crisis, his efforts lacked his earlier energy and optimism. By early April, diplomacy had reached its end.

On April 11, an exhausted McKinley sent a virtual war message to Congress. He asked for authority to use force to end the Cuban war. His message mixed talk of commerce with lofty humanitarianism. America must take up the "cause of humanity," he wrote, and stop the "very serious injury to the commerce, trade, and business of our people, and the wanton destruction of property."

On April 19 Congress officially acted. It proclaimed Cuba's independence, called for Spain's evacuation, and authorized McKinley to use the army and navy to achieve those ends. In the Teller Amendment, Congress added that the United States had no intention of annexing Cuba for itself. For some Americans it was a great and noble decision. Senator Albert Beveridge, one of the great speakers of his day, intoned: "At last, God's hour has struck. The American people go forth in a warfare holier than liberty—holy as humanity." For the men and boys who would have to fight the battles, the war would soon seem considerably less noble.

The Spanish-American War

There is no simple explanation for the Spanish-American War. Economics and imperial ambitions certainly played a part, but no more so than did humanitarianism and selfless concern for the suffering of others. McKinley tried to find a peaceful solution, but he failed. The unpredictability of events and the mood of the nation were more powerful than the president.

In theory America had prepared for war with Spain. In 1897 the Navy Department had drawn up contingency plans for a war against Spain for the liberation of Cuba. It had envisioned a war centered mainly in the Caribbean, but the navy had plans to attack the Philippine Islands, which belonged to Spain, and even the coast of Spain, if necessary. In the Caribbean, the plan was to blockade Cuba and assist an army invasion of the island. On paper, neatly written and soundly reasoned, America was well prepared for a war that seemed more of a military exercise than a deadly struggle.

In reality, the military was not physically ready for war. The process of mobilizing troops was chaotic and the training given volunteers was inadequate. In addition, the army faced severe supply shortages, with volunteers suffering the most. They were herded into camps, often without such basic equipment as tents and mess kits. Long before they ever faced enemy guns or even saw Cuba, they battled wet uniforms, bad food, and deadly sanitary conditions. Far more volunteers died in stateside camps than were killed by Spanish bullets.

For African-American troops, regular and volunteers, racism aggravated already difficult conditions. They too were plagued by spoiled beef, thick wool uniforms, and unsanitary conditions. Also, since most of the large camps were located in the South—in places such as Tampa, New Orleans, Mobile, and Chickamauga Park, Tennessee—they had to battle Jim Crow laws and other forms of racial hostility. They saw signs that proclaimed "Dogs and niggers not allowed" and were pelted by rocks. Once in the camps, they were given the lowest military assignments. George W. Prioleau, a black chaplain, could not help but wonder: "Is America any better than Spain?"

While the agony of mobilization was taking place, the navy moved into action. During the tense weeks before the United States went to war against Spain, Theodore Roosevelt, then acting secretary of the navy, joyfully followed McKinley's orders and wired his friend Commodore George Dewey, leader of America's Asiatic Squadron: "KEEP FULL OF COAL, IN THE EVENT OF DECLARATION OF WAR [WITH] SPAIN, YOUR DUTY WILL BE TO SEE THAT THE SPANISH SQUADRON DOES NOT LEAVE THE ASIATIC COAST, AND THEN OFFENSIVE OPERATIONS IN PHILIPPINE ISLANDS." Dewey had been anxiously waiting just that order.

At the break of light on the morning of May 1, 1898, he struck. In a few hours of fighting, he destroyed Spain's Asiatic fleet in Manila Bay. It was a stunning victory. Only one American died, from heat prostration manning a ship's overworked boiler. "You have made a name for the nation, and the Navy, and yourself," Roosevelt wrote Dewey. Americans rejoiced in the quick victory. Newspapers were filled with stories of American heroics. One not-very-accomplished poet captured the public mood:

> Oh, dewey was the morning
> Upon the first of May,
> And Dewey was the Admiral,
> Down in Manila Bay.
> And dewey were the Spaniard's eyes,
> Them orbs of black and blue;
> And dew we feel discouraged?
> I do not think we dew.

Not every victory came so easily. Closer to home, in the Caribbean theater, the war was much more prosaic. The main Spanish forces in Cuba controlled the strategically important Santiago Bay. To defeat the Spanish would require the combined efforts of the army and the navy. With this in mind, McKinley ordered Major General William R. Shafter, commander of the 5th Corps, from Tampa to Santiago. The trip to Cuba set the tone for the entire expedition. Delays, confused orders, and other problems slowed the process. Some 17,000 American troops were forced to spend 19 days on crowded transports, sweating in their woolen uniforms, eating unappetizing travel rations, and thinking about what lay ahead. Finally, toward the end of June, and with the help of Cuban rebels, American troops landed at the ports of Daiquiri and Siboney.

From there they moved toward Santiago. The distance was not great—Santiago Bay was only about 15 miles from the coastal town of Siboney. But the road to Santiago was little more than a rutted, dirt trail. When it rained, wagons became mired in the mud, streams swelled and made fording treacherous, and the troops suffered in the jungle humidity. Slowly the army moved forward, more concerned with broken wagons and tropical diseases than Spanish soldiers.

On July 1, American soldiers learned firsthand the horrors of battle. Between the American position and Santiago were Spanish troops in the tiny hamlet of El Caney and along the San Juan Heights, a ridge to the east of Santiago. From the first, American plans broke down in the face of stiff Spanish opposition. There were no romantic charges, no idealized warfare. The American troops that struggled up Kettle and San Juan hills moved very slowly and suffered alarming casualties. Although outnumbered more than ten to one, Spanish soldiers made U.S. troops pay for every foot they advanced. After America finally secured the enemy positions, correspondent Richard H. Davis wrote, "Another such victory as that of July 1 and our troops must retreat."

General Shafter was frankly worried and even considered retreat. Grossly overweight and gout-ridden, Shafter had neither the disposition nor the ability to lead an energetic campaign. Fortunately for him, Spain's forces in Cuba were even less ready to fight. In Santiago, Spanish soldiers faced shortages of food, water, and ammunition. On July 3, the Spanish squadron tried to break an American blockade and force its way out of Santiago Bay. The act was a suicidal move. American guns destroyed the Spanish fleet and killed some 500 Spanish sailors. Only one American died in the decisive engagement. When his men broke out in a yell of joy, Captain Philip of the *Texas* said, "Don't cheer, men, the poor devils are dying."

Little fighting remained. On July 17 the leading Spanish general in Cuba surrendered to Shafter. Timid in war, Shafter was petty in victory. He refused to permit any naval officers to sign the capitulation document, nor would he allow any Cubans to participate in the surrender negotiations and cere-

Spanish-American War, Cuban Theater

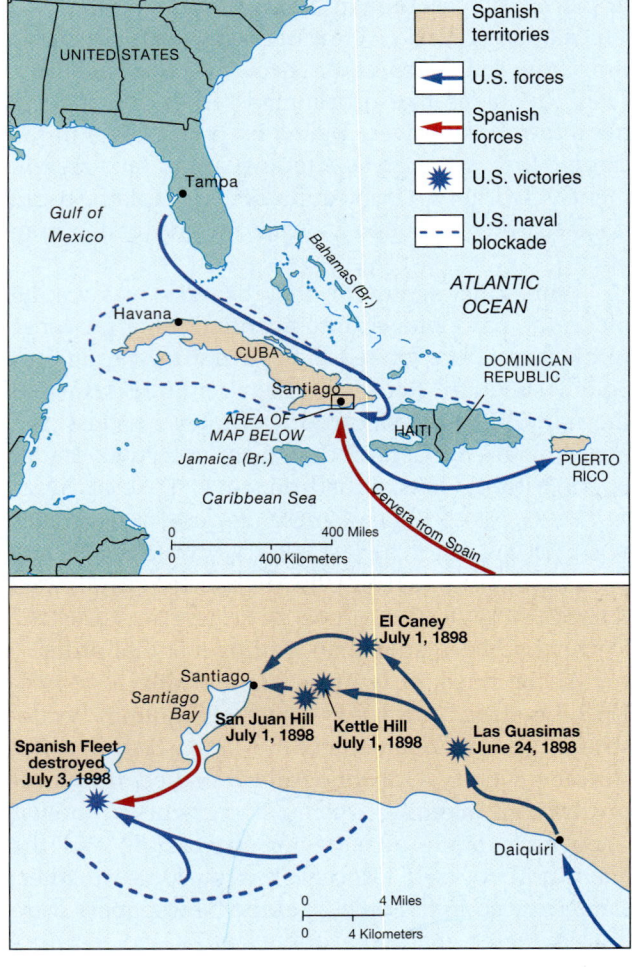

monies. It was a sad moment. The Cubans who had fought so long and bravely for their independence were denied the glory of their success.

Before the full Spanish surrender, the United States extended its influence in the Caribbean. In late July, General Nelson A. Miles invaded Puerto Rico, Spain's other Caribbean colony. Without any serious resistance, U.S. forces took the island. Finally, on August 12, Spain surrendered, granting Cuban independence and ceding Puerto Rico and Guam to the United States. Both countries agreed to settle the fate of the Philippines at a postwar peace conference to be held in Paris.

For America, it had been a short, successful war. Spanish bullets killed only 379 Americans, the smallest number in any of America's declared wars. Disease and other problems cost over 5000 more lives. If the army's mobilization had been chaotic, its troops had performed heroically under fire. And the navy, which took most of the credit for winning the war, demonstrated the wisdom of its planners. Finally, the war served to bring the North and South closer together as the two sections fought alongside each other rather than against each other. All in all, many Americans agreed with U.S. Ambassador to England John Hay that it had been a "splendid little war."

There was nothing little about the consequences of the war. With the Spanish-American War the United States became an imperial power. The war also increased America's appetite for overseas territories. The McKinley administration used the war to annex Hawaii and part of Samoa. In addition, at the Paris Peace Conference the United States wrested the Philippines, Puerto Rico, and Guam from Spain. Although the United States paid Spain $20 million for the Philippines, there was no question that Spain was forced to negotiate under duress. These new imperial possessions gave the United States strategic bases in the Caribbean and along the trade routes to Asia.

Freeing Cuba

Many Americans favored the annexation of Cuba. In the land grab that ended the war, the idealism of the Teller Amendment and the war's beginning was all but forgotten. When the war ended, U.S. troops stayed in Cuba, and the country was ruled by an American-run military government. Particularly under General Leonard Wood, the military government helped Cuba recover from its terrible conflict with Spain. Wood restored the Cuban economy and promoted reforms in the legal system, education, sanitation, and health care. Neither Wood nor McKinley, however, was willing to grant Cuba its immediate independence. In his annual message of December 1898, McKinley noted that American troops would stay in Cuba until "complete tranquility" and a "stable government" existed on the island.

The United States finally recognized Cuban independence in 1903. But it was a limited independence. According to the **Platt Amendment** to the Army Appropriation Bill of 1901, Cuba could exercise self-government, but it could sign no treaties that might limit its independence. The amendment also gave the United States the right to maintain two naval bases on Cuba. Should, in the judgment of the United States, Cuban independence ever be threatened, the Platt Amendment authorized the United States to intervene in Cuba's internal and external affairs. The amendment was also written into the 1901 Cuban constitution. In short, for Cuba, independence had the look and feel of an American protectorate.

The Imperial Debate

Compared to the Philippines, Cuba was a minor problem. McKinley's decision to annex the Philippines pleased some Americans and angered many more. Businessmen who dreamed of the rich Asian markets applauded McKinley's decision. Naval strategists similarly believed it was a wise move. They argued that if the United States failed to take the Philippines, then Germany, Japan or England probably would. Finally, Protestant missionaries favored annexation to facilitate their efforts to Christianize the Filipinos. That the Filipinos already favored Roman Catholicism did not seem to dampen the fervor of the Protestant missionaries.

Opposed to the annexation of the Philippines was a heterogeneous group of Americans who called themselves anti-imperialists. The group included such notable Americans as agrarian leader William Jennings Bryan, steel magnate Andrew Carnegie, labor organizer Samuel Gompers, writers Mark Twain and William Dean Howells, reformers Lincoln Steffens and Jane Addams, university presidents Charles W. Eliot of Harvard and David Starr Jordan of Stanford, and politicians George Frisbie Hoar of Massachusetts and "Pitchfork Ben" Tillman of South Carolina.

Their reasons for being anti-imperialist were as varied as their occupations and backgrounds. Some were high-minded idealists who believed that the Filipinos had the right to govern themselves. Others had more selfish reasons. Samuel Gompers, for example, feared that annexation would lead to an in-

THE American Mosaic

Theodore Roosevelt and the Rough Riders

ABOARD the *Yucatan*, anchored off the coast of Cuba, Theodore Roosevelt (TR) received the news on the evening of June 21, 1898. He and his men, a volunteer cavalry regiment dubbed the Rough Riders, had received their orders to disembark from the safety of the ship and join the fighting ashore. It was a welcomed invitation, celebrated with cheers, war dances, songs, boasts, and toasts. "To the Officers—may they get killed, wounded or promoted," urged one toast that captured the mood aboard the ship.

Roosevelt and many men of his generation looked forward to war, greedily anticipating the chance to prove their mettle in battle. They had been raised on stories of the Civil War, stories that over the years had taken on the golden gloss of time. Tales of Shiloh, Chancellorsville, Antietam, and Gettysburg; of Robert E. Lee, Ulysses S. Grant, and Stonewall Jackson; of battles won and causes lost had fired their imaginations. The Spanish-American War was their chance to experience firsthand what they had long only heard about from their fathers' and uncles' lips.

Few men wanted the war more than Roosevelt. Son of a wealthy New York family, he was competitive by nature and enjoyed all physical sports. He also loved history, writing books about American wars and heroic deeds. And for Roosevelt there was perhaps even a deeper motivation. During the Civil War his father, the man he admired above everyone else, had hired a substitute soldier to serve for him. Thousands of other wealthy men had done the same, but for Theodore such a course was unmanly. During a war, he believed, able-bodied men should be in a uniform, not dressed in mufti. He would not repeat his father's mistake. When the Spanish-American War was declared, TR quickly resigned his post as assistant secretary of the navy and joined the fray. In his own mind, he could do nothing else. In *The Rough Riders*, his memoirs of the war, he quoted a poem by Bret Harte, whose last verse was:

"But when won the coming battle,
What of profit springs therefrom?
What if conquest, subjugation,
Even greater ills become?"
But the drum
Answered, "Come!"

And come Roosevelt did.

The men who followed him were kindred spirits. They were rough riders, the men who with Roosevelt formed the First United States Volunteer Cavalry regiment. Some were Ivy Leaguers from Harvard, Yale, and Princeton who belonged to the most exclusive clubs in Boston and New York City. Many had been college athletes, stars in football, tennis, and track and field, men for whom war was a grand playing field. Others were Westerners—cowboys, hunters, frontier sheriffs, Indian fighters, Texas Rangers, prospectors—"a splendid set of men," wrote Roosevelt, "tall and sinewy, with resolute, weather-beaten faces, and eyes that looked a man straight in the face without flinching." Such men were accustomed to riding horses, shooting rifles, and living off the land.

Bucky O'Neill was something of a Rough Rider ideal. Indian fighter and sheriff of Prescott, Arizona, Bucky could shoot with the hunters, exchange stories with the prospectors, and philosophize with the college graduates. Roosevelt once overheard Bucky and Dr. Robb Church, the former Princeton football player who served as the surgeon for the Rough Riders, "discussing Aryan word roots together, and then sliding off into a review of the novels of Balzac, and a discussion as to how far Balzac could be said to be the founder of the modern realistic school of fiction." Once when Bucky and Roosevelt were leaning on the ship's railing searching the Caribbean sky for the Southern Cross, the old Indian fighter asked, "Who would not risk his life for a star?" TR agreed that great risk was part of greatness.

Brimming with enthusiasm, perhaps a bit innocent in their naiveté, the Rough Riders viewed Cuba as a land of stars, a place to win great honors or die in the pursuit. Like many of his men, TR believed "that the nearing future held . . . many chances of death, of honor and renown." And he was ready. Dressed in a Brooks Brothers uniform made especially for him and with several extra pairs of spectacles sewn in the lining of his Rough Rider hat, Roosevelt prepared to meet his destiny.

In a land of beauty, death often came swiftly. As the Rough Riders and other soldiers moved inland toward Santiago, snipers fired on them. The high-speed Mauser bullets seemed to come out of nowhere, making a *z-z-z-z-z-eu* as they moved through the air or a loud *chug* as they hit flesh. Since the Spanish snipers used smokeless gunpowder, no puffs of smoke betrayed their positions.

On their first day in Cuba, the Rough Riders experienced the

"blood, sweat, and tears" of warfare. Dr. Church looked "like a kid who had gotten his hands and arms into a bucket of thick red paint." Some men died, and others, dying, lay where they had been shot. The reality of war strikes different men differently. It horrifies some, terrifies others, and enrages still others. Sheer exhilaration was the best way to describe Roosevelt's response to the death and danger. Even sniper fire could not keep TR from jumping up and down with excitement.

On July 1, 1898, the Rough Riders faced their sternest task. Moving from the coast toward Santiago along the Camino Real, the main arm of the U.S. forces encountered an entrenched enemy. Spread out along the San Juan Heights, Spanish forces commanded a splendid position. As American troops emerged from a stretch of jungle, they found themselves in a dangerous position. Once again the sky seemed to be raining Mauser bullets and shrapnel. Clearly, the Heights had to be taken. Each hour of delay meant more American casualties.

The Rough Riders were deployed to the right to prepare to assault Kettle Hill. Once in position, they faced an agonizing wait for orders to charge. Most soldiers hunched behind cover. Bucky O'Neill, however, casually strolled up and down in front of his troops, chain-smoked cigarettes, and shouted encouragement. A sergeant implored him to take cover. "Sergeant," Bucky remarked, "the Spanish bullet isn't made that will kill me." Hardly had he finished the statement when a Mauser bullet ripped into his mouth and burst out of the back of his head. Even before he fell, Roosevelt wrote, Bucky's "wild and gallant soul had gone out into the darkness."

Finally the orders came. On foot the Rough Riders moved up Kettle Hill toward the Spanish guns. It was a slow, painful, heroic charge. Bullets, sounding "like the ripping of a silk dress," cut down a number of Roosevelt's men. But unable to stop the push of the American forces, the Spanish gave way, leaving their fortified positions and running for safety.

From the heights of Kettle Hill, Roosevelt watched another U.S. attack on nearby San Juan Hill. Once again feeling the wolf rising in his heart, he led his men toward the new objective. Again the fighting was difficult. Again the Spanish gave way. By the end of the day, American forces had taken the San Juan Heights. Before them was Santiago and victory. "The great day of my life," as TR called it, was over.

"Another such victory like that of July 1," wrote Richard Harding Davis, "and our troops must retreat." Indeed, casualties ran high, and the Rough Riders suffered the heaviest losses. But the fighting helped to break the Spanish resistance. It was the last really difficult day of fighting in the war. Perhaps more importantly, the day made Roosevelt a national hero. Aided by his ability at self-promotion, TR used the event as a political stepping-stone. "I would rather have led the charge," he later wrote, "than served three terms in the U.S. Senate."

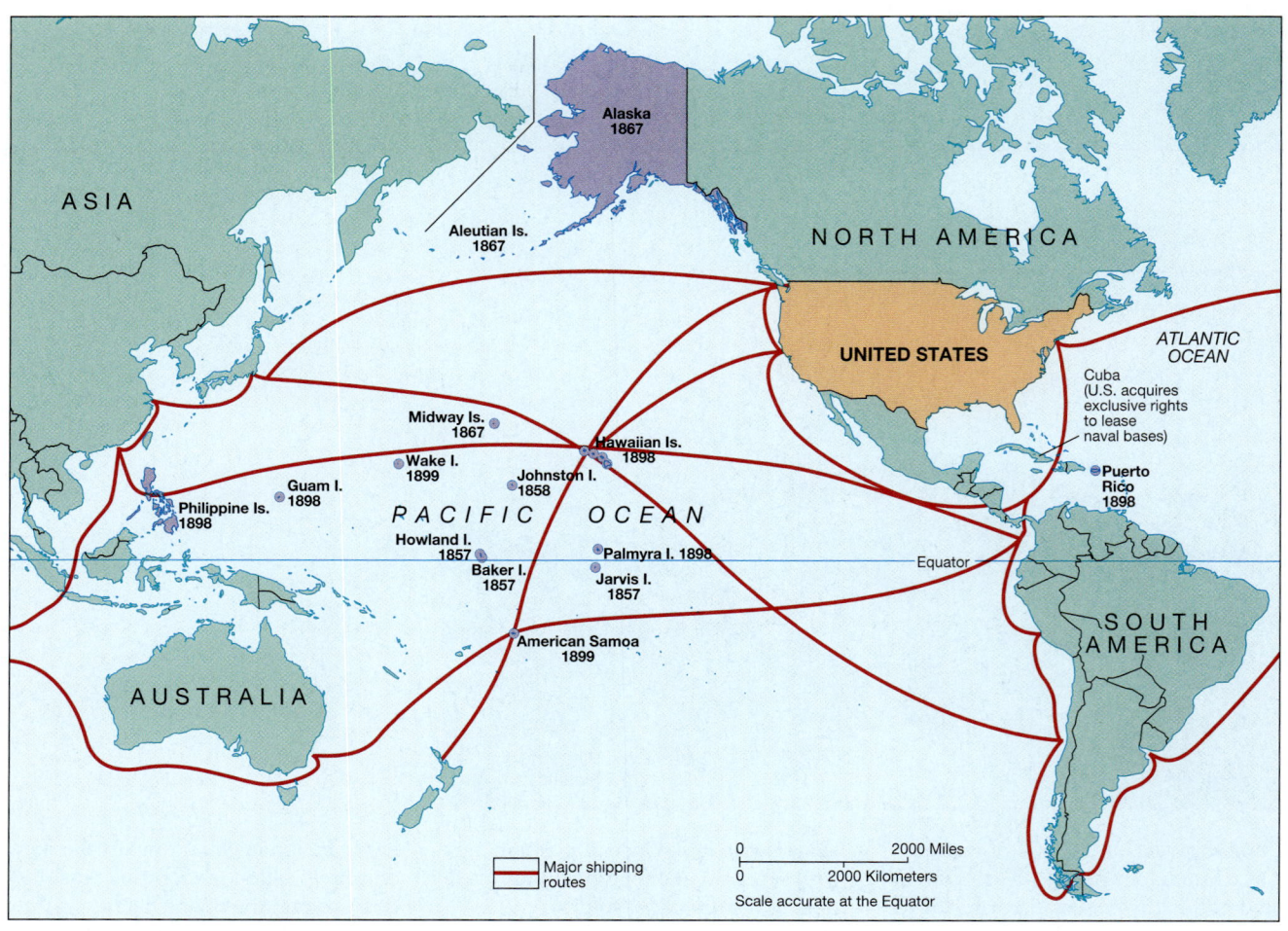

American Empire

With the Treaty of Paris, the United States gained an expanded colonial empire that included Puerto Rico, Alaska, Hawaii, parts of the Samoan islands, Guam, the Philippines, and a chain of Pacific islands.

flux of Filipino workers into the United States and hurt the American labor movement. Still others opposed annexation for base racial grounds. The annexation of "dependencies inhabited by ignorant and inferior races," noted *The Nation* editor E. L. Godkin, could only lead to renewed racial problems.

During early 1899 the imperial debate raged on. Journalists editorialized, speakers pontificated, and humorists detailed the absurdities of both sides. Mark Twain asked, "Shall we . . . go on conferring our Christianity upon the peoples that sit in darkness, or shall we give those poor things a rest?" Twain's thoughtful questions about all the uproar changed very few opinions. Even Andrew Carnegie's offer to write a personal check for $20 million to buy the independence of the Philippines failed to end the debate. Ultimately, imperialists and anti-imperialists had different visions for America, and no bridge could span the gulf between.

The issue was settled on February 6, 1899, when the Senate voted on the Treaty of Paris. Strained tempers were evident in the tense atmosphere. Imperialist Senator Henry Cabot Lodge called the treaty fight the "closest, most bitter, and most exciting I have ever known, or ever expect to see in the Senate." For a time it appeared that the imperialists would not be able to muster the two-thirds majority needed to ratify the treaty. Anti-imperialist and titular leader of the Democratic party William Jennings Bryan ironically saved the imperialist cause. Not wanting to prolong the war by rejecting the treaty, he urged Democratic anti-imperialists to vote for ratification. By the close vote of 57 to 27 the Senate ratified the treaty. Undoubtedly Bryan hoped to use the issue of Philippine independence to capture the presidency in 1900, but it was not to be. With ratification of the treaty, the issue lost its sense of urgency and Americans grew tired of the debate.

The War to Crush Filipino Independence

Filipino independence, however, was not an abstract debate in the Philippines. Imperialist arguments about duty, destiny, defense, and dollars were lost on independence-minded Filipinos, led by Emilio Aguinaldo, who had fought bravely against the Spanish both before and after Dewey arrived in Manila. They had battled for their own independence, not to replace Spain with the United States as their colonial master. When it was clear that the United States did not have Filipino interests at heart, Aguinaldo and his followers resumed their fight for independence. Like the Cubans, the Filipinos held dear the cause of freedom. Like the Spanish, the United States was not willing to grant that freedom.

Between 1899 and 1902 American troops and Filipino revolutionaries fought an ugly and destructive colonial war. Mark Twain's *The War Prayer* captured the mood of the fighting: "O Lord our God, help us to tear their soldiers to bloody shreds with our shells . . . , blast their hopes, blight their lives, protract their bitter pilgrimage." American soldiers faced a difficult task. Some did not know what they were fighting for, whose interests they were defending, or what rights they were protecting. Others regarded the Filipinos as subhuman. They referred to them as "niggers" and "gugus," and they regarded the notion of Philippine independence as a joke.

African-American troops fighting to destroy Filipino freedom faced an even greater and more painful dilemma. Many black soldiers readily identified with Filipino aspirations. Some white officers even suspected, as journalist Stephen Bonsel noted in 1902, that "the negro soldiers were in closer sympathy with the aims of the native populations than they were with those of their white leaders and the policy of the United States." Although the majority of black troops professionally followed the orders of their white officers, an unusually large number deserted. Bonsel suggested that, unlike white deserters, blacks left the army "for the purpose of joining the insurgents," with whose struggle they identified.

For black and white soldiers alike, however, the actual fighting was bloody and frustrating. After suffering serious losses in conventional fighting, Aguinaldo turned to guerrilla warfare. His forces fought only when victory was certain, usually ambushing small patrols. They burned bridges, destroyed railroads, sniped, and sabotaged. They filled pits with sharpened stakes and tortured prisoners. Some American captives had their ears cut off, and many Filipinos who supported the United States were hacked to death with bolos or buried alive. Aguinaldo's hope was that eventually the game would not be worth the prize, and that the American president would call his troops home.

McKinley was not about to do any such thing, and American troops proved just as vicious as the Filipino insurgents. Atrocities committed by American soldiers became alarmingly common. Americans used the "water cure" to obtain information. This entailed forcing a

After the United States acquired the Philippine islands through conquest and purchase, Emilio Aguinaldo led the struggle for Philippine independence. Filipino resistance to the U.S. presence in the Philippine islands continued through mid-1902, even after U.S. troops captured Aguinaldo in 1901.

prisoner to drink gallons of water and then emptying his stomach quickly with a kick or a punch. In one especially violent campaign General Jacob H. Smith ordered his subordinates to take no prisoners: "I wish you to kill and burn ... the more you kill and burn the better it will please me. I want all persons killed who are capable of bearing arms in actual hostilities against the United States." In the last category he included any male 10 years or older.

In another campaign, American leaders used the same tactics that had made the Spanish General Weyler infamous in Cuba. They tried to destroy the guerrilla base by herding more than 300,000 civilians into concentration zones. Death, disease, starvation, and suffering increased in the concentration centers. "Suburbs of hell" one American commander called them. Industrialist and anti-imperialist Andrew Carnegie seethed to a U.S. peace commissioner in the Philippines, "You seem to have about finished your work of civilizing the Filipinos. About 8000 of them have been completely civilized and sent to Heaven."

Although the fighting continued, Aguinaldo faced serious difficulties. Most of his leaders came from the upper classes, and they had little interest in bettering the lives of poorer Filipinos, a fact that hurt recruitment. Looking for a political solution, Aguinaldo hoped that Bryan would defeat McKinley for the presidency in 1900 and thereby install an anti-imperialist in the White House. The November election dashed Aguinaldo's hopes. Five months later American troops captured the Filipino leader. This, coupled with American reform efforts designed to improve transportation, education, and public health in the Philippines, doomed the Philippine independence movement. By July 4, 1902, the American victory was complete. However, approximately 4200 Americans and over 20,000 Filipino soldiers had died. Perhaps another 200,000 Filipino civilians died of famine, disease, and war-related incidents. The United States paid Spain $20 million for the Philippines, which it had won control of after the ceasefire. But it cost another $400 million to crush the Philippine independence movement.

Keeping the Doors Open

The struggle against the Filipinos led to congressional investigations and shocked many Americans. Political and business leaders, however, continued to believe that the Philippines were worth the fight because the islands were of strategic importance both as a military base and a stepping-stone toward the Asian markets. Yet policy-makers understood the popular mood; they knew that the American public would be hostile to any U.S. military venture into Asia *just* to support trade.

To prevent other countries from carving up China, in 1899 Secretary of State John Hay issued an **"open door" note.** Hay believed that imperial competition in China was dangerous and economically inefficient. It stimulated costly anticolonial resistance and rebellion and gave no incentive to European countries to improve their economic efficiency. Hay's Open Door note was an attempt to prevent further European partitioning of the Manchu empire and to protect the principle of open trade in China. Under the terms of the Open Door Policy, all countries active in China would respect each other's trading rights by imposing no discriminating duties and closing no ports within their spheres of influence. Although most European countries expressed little interest in Hay's Open Door Policy—which, after all, benefited the United States the most—in 1900 Hay announced that the European powers had accepted his proposal.

American soldiers stand guard over captured Filipino guerrillas in 1899. Expansionism raised questions of whether the native peoples of acquired lands had the same rights as American citizens.

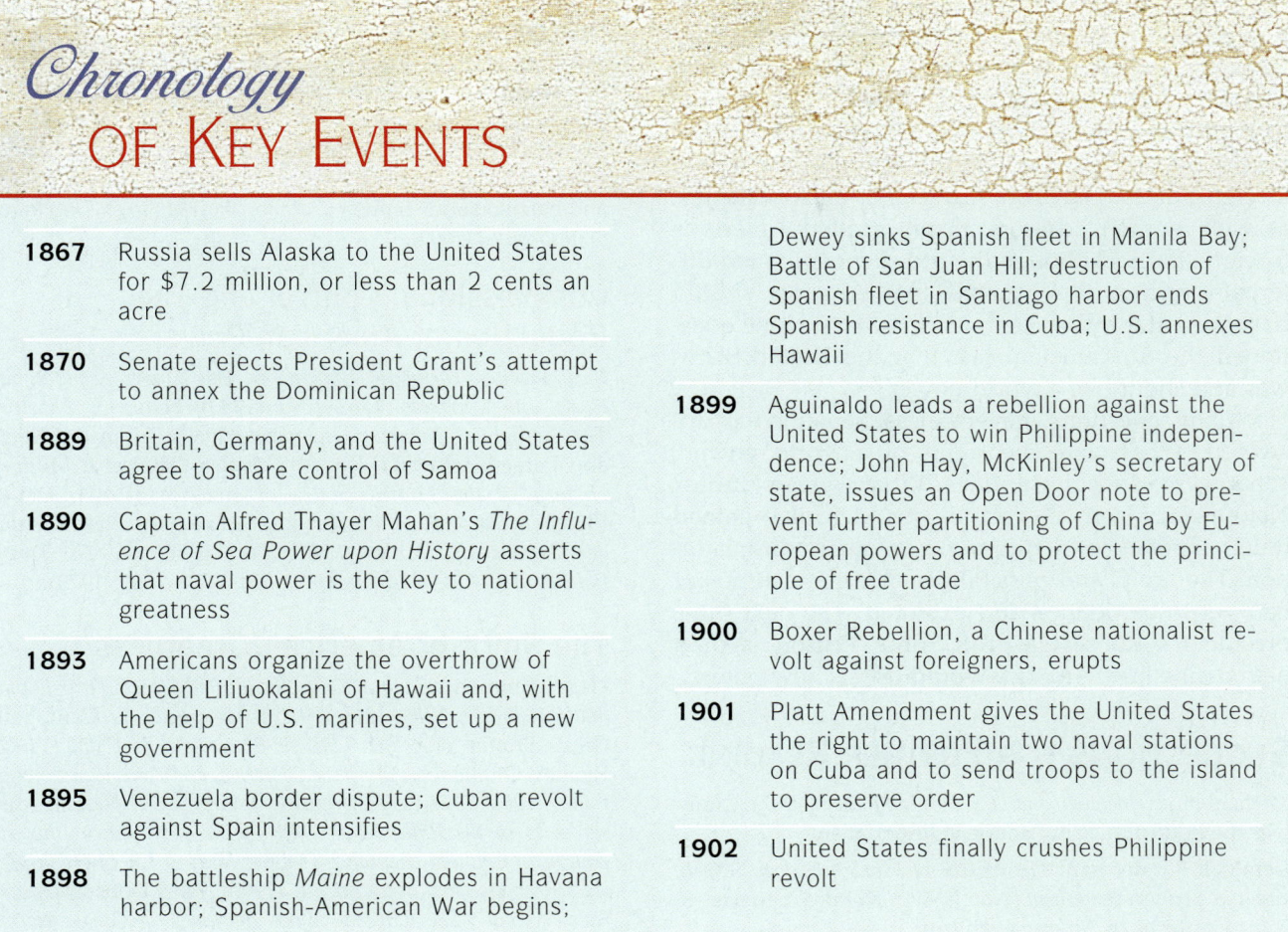

Chronology of Key Events

1867	Russia sells Alaska to the United States for $7.2 million, or less than 2 cents an acre
1870	Senate rejects President Grant's attempt to annex the Dominican Republic
1889	Britain, Germany, and the United States agree to share control of Samoa
1890	Captain Alfred Thayer Mahan's *The Influence of Sea Power upon History* asserts that naval power is the key to national greatness
1893	Americans organize the overthrow of Queen Liliuokalani of Hawaii and, with the help of U.S. marines, set up a new government
1895	Venezuela border dispute; Cuban revolt against Spain intensifies
1898	The battleship *Maine* explodes in Havana harbor; Spanish-American War begins; Dewey sinks Spanish fleet in Manila Bay; Battle of San Juan Hill; destruction of Spanish fleet in Santiago harbor ends Spanish resistance in Cuba; U.S. annexes Hawaii
1899	Aguinaldo leads a rebellion against the United States to win Philippine independence; John Hay, McKinley's secretary of state, issues an Open Door note to prevent further partitioning of China by European powers and to protect the principle of free trade
1900	Boxer Rebellion, a Chinese nationalist revolt against foreigners, erupts
1901	Platt Amendment gives the United States the right to maintain two naval stations on Cuba and to send troops to the island to preserve order
1902	United States finally crushes Philippine revolt

The Chinese themselves had other plans. In the late spring of 1900 a group of Chinese nationalists, known as Boxers, besieged the Legation Quarter in Peking, calling for the expulsion or death of all westerners in China. The Boxers, whose Chinese name better translates as "Righteous and Harmonious Fists," were a quasi-religious organization that believed deeply in magic and maintained that all its members were impervious to western bullets. As a joint European and American rescue force proved, bullets could and would kill Boxers. By late summer, 1900, westernizers had crushed the Boxer Rebellion.

Additional troops in China threatened Hay's Open Door Policy, On July 3, 1900, during the tensest moment of the Boxer Rebellion, he issued a second Open Door note, calling on all western powers to preserve "Chinese territorial and administrative entity" and uphold "the principle of equal and impartial trade with all parts of the Chinese Empire." Once again, few European countries paid attention to Hay's Open Door Policy. Mutual distrust and the fear of provoking a general European war—more than any American plan—prevented the major European powers from dismembering China. Out of Hay's Open Door Policy notes came the idea, held mostly in America, that the United States was China's protector. It was another example of the increasingly active role the United States had taken in world affairs.

Conclusion

Thirty-two years separated the inauguration of Ulysses S. Grant and the assassination of William McKinley, but during that generation, America and the presidency changed radically. Part of the change can be attributed to growth—industry boomed, the population swelled, agricultural production increased. The growth was also psychological. During those years many Americans achieved a new sense of confidence, and their vision broadened. After 250 years of looking westward across America's seemingly limitless acres of land, they began to look toward the oceans and consider the possibilities of a new form of expansion. Talk of world power, world outlook, and world responsibilities colored their rhetoric.

This outward thrust was accompanied and enhanced by the growth of presidential power. Grant worked hard for the annexation of the Dominican Republic, but Congress blocked his efforts. By the turn of the century, however, Congress clearly expected the president to lead the nation in the area of foreign affairs. Harrison, Cleveland, and McKinley, as well as their advisers, firmly guided America's foreign affairs. Although the presidents pursued different policies, they agreed that America should have a greater influence in world affairs. None questioned the fundamental fact that the United States was and should be a world power.

Many questions, nevertheless, remained unanswered. What were the rights of a world power? What were its responsibilities? What were its duties? Neither Harrison, Cleveland, nor McKinley gained much experience in running a colonial administration. The limits and possibilities of American power had yet to be defined and explored. The next three presidents—Roosevelt, Taft, and Wilson—would help define how America would use its new power.

SUGGESTIONS FOR FURTHER READING

Michael Hunt, *Ideology and U.S. Foreign Policy* (1987). Examines the issue of race in American imperialism.

Gerald F. Linderman, *The Mirror of War: American Society and the Spanish-American War* (1974). Relates patterns of war to patterns in American culture.

Stuart C. Miller, *"Benevolent Assimilation": The American Conquest of the Philippines, 1899–1903* (1982). Classic study of war in the Philippines.

H. Wayne Morgan, *America's Road to Empire* (1967). Short but interesting history of the origins of the American war with Spain.

David F. Trask, *The War with Spain in 1898* (1981). Most detailed study of the Spanish-American War.

William A. Williams, *The Tragedy of American Diplomacy*, 2d ed. (1972). Pioneering but controversial study of economic motives in American imperialism.

Overviews and Surveys

William H. Becker and Samuel F. Wells, Jr., eds, *Economics and World Power: An Assessment of American Diplomacy Since 1789* (1984); Gail Bederman, *Manliness and Civilization: A Cultural History of Gender and Race in the United States, 1880–1917* (1995); Robert L. Beisner, *From the Old Diplomacy to the New, 1865–1900* (1975), and *Twelve Against Empire: The Anti-Imperialists, 1898–1900* (1968); Charles S. Campbell, Jr., *Transformation of American Foreign Relations, 1865–1900* (1976); Warren I. Cohen, ed., *New Frontiers in American-East Asian Relations* (1983); B. Franklin Cooling, *Gray Steel and Blue Water Navy: The Formative Years of America's Military Industrial Complex* (1979); Arthur Power Dudden, *The American Pacific: From the Old China Trade to the Present* (1992); David F. Healy, *U.S. Expansionism: Imperialist Urge in the 1890s* (1970), and *Drive to Hegemony: The United States in the Caribbean* (1988); Michael Hunt, *The Making of a Special Relationship: The United States and China to 1914* (1983); Walter LaFeber, *The New Empire: An Interpretation of American Expansion* (1963), and *The American Search for Opportunity, 1865–1913* (1993); Tenant S. McWilliams, *The New South Faces the World* (1988); Thomas G. Paterson, et al., *American Foreign Policy*, 2 vols., 3d ed. (1988), and Paterson and Stephen C. Rabe, *Imperial Surge: The United States Abroad* (1992).

Congressional Control and The Reduction of American Power

Paul Holbo, *Tarnished Expansion: The Alaska Scandal, the Press, and Congress, 1867–1871* (1983); Henry E. Mattox, *The Twilight of Amateur Diplomacy* (1989); Allan R. Millett and Peter Maslowski, *For the Common Defense: A Military History of the United States of America* (1984); David Pletcher, *The Awkward Years: American Foreign Relations under Garfield and Arthur* (1963); Tom E. Terrill, *The Tariff, Politics, and American Foreign Policy, 1874–1901* (1973).

The Spirit of American Greatness

Henry Blumenthal, *France and the United States: Their Diplomatic Relation, 1789–1914* (1970); Alexander E. Campbell, *Great Britain and the United States, 1895–1903* (1960); Richard Challener, *Admirals, Generals, and American Foreign Policy, 1889–1914* (1973); Kenton J. Clymer, *Protestant Missionaries in the Philippines, 1898–1916: An Inquiry Into the American Colonial Mentality* (1986); Warren I. Cohen, *America's Response to China*, 3d ed. (1990); John Dobson, *America's Ascent: The United States Becomes a Great Power, 1880–1914* (1978); James A. Field, Jr., *America and the Mediterranean World, 1776–1882* (1969); Thomas J. McCormick, *China Market: America's Quest for Informal Empire, 1893–1901* (1967); Bradford Perkins, *The Great Rapprochement: England and the United States, 1895–1914* (1968); James Reed, *The Missionary Mind and American East Asia Policy* (1985); Emily Rosenberg, *Spreading the American Dream: American Economic and Cultural Expansion, 1890–1945* (1982); Marilyn B. Young, *Rhetoric of Empire: American China Policy, 1895–1901* (1968).

The Emergence of Aggression in American Foreign Policy

David Anderson, *Imperialism and Idealism: American Diplomats in China, 1861–1898* (1985); Phillip Darby, *Three Faces of Imperialism: British and American Approaches to Asia and Africa, 1870–1970* (1987); R. P. Gilson, *Samoa 1830 to 1900* (1970); Kenneth J. Hagan, *American Gunboat Diplomacy and the Old Navy, 1877–1889* (1973); Walter R. Herrick, *The American Naval Revolution* (1966); Akira Iriye, *Across the Pacific* (1967); Paul M. Kennedy, *The Samoa Tangle: A Study in Anglo-German-American Relations, 1878–1900* (1974); Paul A.C. Koistinen, *Mobilizing for Modern War: The Political Economy of American Warfare, 1865–1917* (1997); John L. Offner, *An Unwanted War: The Diplomacy of the United States and Spain over Cuba, 1895–1898* (1992); Thomas J. Osborne, *Empire Can Wait: American Opposition to Hawaiian Annexation, 1893–1898* (1981); William A. Russ, Jr., *The Hawaiian Revolu-*

tion, 1893–94 (1959); Thomas D. Schoonover, *The United States in Central America, 1860–1911: Episodes of Social Imperialism and Imperial Rivalry in the World System* (1991); Merze Tate, *The United States and the Hawaiian Kingdom* (1965).

The War for Empire

Jules R. Benjamin, *The United States and the Origins of the Cuban Revolution* (1990); H. W. Brands, *Bound to Empire: The United States and the Philippines* (1992); Frank Freidel, *The Splendid Little War* (1958); John M. Gates, *Schoolbooks and Krags: The United States Army in the Philippines, 1898–1902* (1973); Willard B. Gatewood, Jr., "Smoked Yankees" and the Struggle for Empire (1971), and *Black Americans and the White Man's Burden, 1898–1903* (1975); Lewis L. Gould, *The Presidency of William McKinley* (1980); David Healy, *U.S. Expansionism: The Imperialist Urge in the 1890s* (1970); Lester D. Langley, *The Banana Men: American Mercenaries and Entrepreneurs in Central America, 1880–1930* (1995); Ernest R. May, *Imperial Democracy: The Emergence of America as a Great Power* (1961), and *American Imperialism*, rev. ed. (1991); Glenn May, *Battle for Batangas* (1991); H. Wayne Morgan, *From Hayes to McKinley* (1969), and ed. *The Gilded Age*, rev. ed. (1970); Louis Pérez, Jr., *Cuba under the Platt Amendment, 1902–1934* (1986), and *Cuba Between Empires, 1878–1902* (1983); Julius W. Pratt, *Expansionists of 1898* (1936); Goran Rystad, *Ambiguous Imperialism* (1975); Daniel B. Schirmer, *Republic or Empire* (1972); E. Berkeley Tompkins, *Anti-Imperialism in the United States* (1970); Richard E. Welch, Jr., *Response to Imperialism: The United States and the Philippine-American War, 1899–1902* (1979); Leon Wolff, *Little Brown Brother: How the United States Purchased and Pacified the Philippines* (1961).

Biographies

Howard Beale, *Theodore Roosevelt and the Rise of America to World Power* (1956); Kenton J. Clymer, *John Hay: The Gentleman as Diplomat* (1975); David Donald, *Charles Sumner and the Rights of Man* (1970); John A. Garraty, *Henry Cabot Lodge* (1953); Lewis J. Gould, *The Presidency of Theodore Roosevelt* (1991); H. Wayne Morgan, *William McKinley and His America* (1963); Allan Nevins, *Grover Cleveland* (1932), and *Hamilton Fish*, rev. ed. (1957); Ernest N. Paolino, *The Foundations of the American Empire: William Henry Seward and U.S. Foreign Policy* (1973); Ronald Spector, *Admiral of the New Empire: The Life and Career of George Dewey* (1974); John M. Taylor, *William Henry Seward* (1991); Richard W. Turk, *The Ambiguous Relationship: Theodore Roosevelt and Alfred Thayer Mahan* (1987); Richard E. Welch, Jr., *The Presidencies of Grover Cleveland* (1988); William C. Widenor, *Henry Cabot Lodge and the Search for an American Foreign Policy* (1980).

Internet Resources

William McKinley and the Spanish-American War
http://www.history.ohio-state.edu/projects/mckinley/SpanAmWar.htm
Part of Ohio State University's site about William McKinley, this part highlights the Spanish-American War with an essay and photos.

Sentenaryo/Centennial: The Philippine Revolution and Philippine-American War
http://www.boondocksnet.com/centennial/index.html
Jim Zwick organizes primary documents, images, and essays focusing upon the Philippines and American involvement.

Anti-Imperialism in the United States, 1898–1935
http://www.boondocksnet.com/ail98-35.html
Jim Zwick edits this extensive site, collating a large number of primary documents about anti-imperialism in America.

Photos of the Philippine-American War
http://www.msstate.edu/Archives/History/USA/filipino/filipino.html
The Philippine-American War is one of the least discussed military engagements in American history. Many tactics employed then were later used in the Vietnam war.

Imperialism Web Page
http://www.smplanet.com/imperialism/toc.html
Focusing on the period around the turn of the century, this site puts much information about American imperialism in one place.

Key Terms

William Henry Seward (p. 582)
American Exceptionalism (p. 583)
The Influence of Sea Power upon History (p. 586)
Large Policy (p. 586)
Queen Liliuokalani (p. 588)
Lord Salisbury (p. 589)
Yellow Journalism (p. 591)
"Remember the *Maine*!" (p. 593)
Platt Amendment (p. 595)
Open Door Note (p. 600)

Review Questions

1. How did Congress discourage overseas expansion following the Civil War?
2. What factors drove Americans to pursue an expansionist foreign policy?
3. Why did the American government take an aggressive imperial stance in areas like Samoa, Chile, Hawaii, and Venezuela?
4. Why did the United States government decide to fight the Spanish-American War?
5. How did the Spanish-American War affect Americans? Cubans? Filipinos?

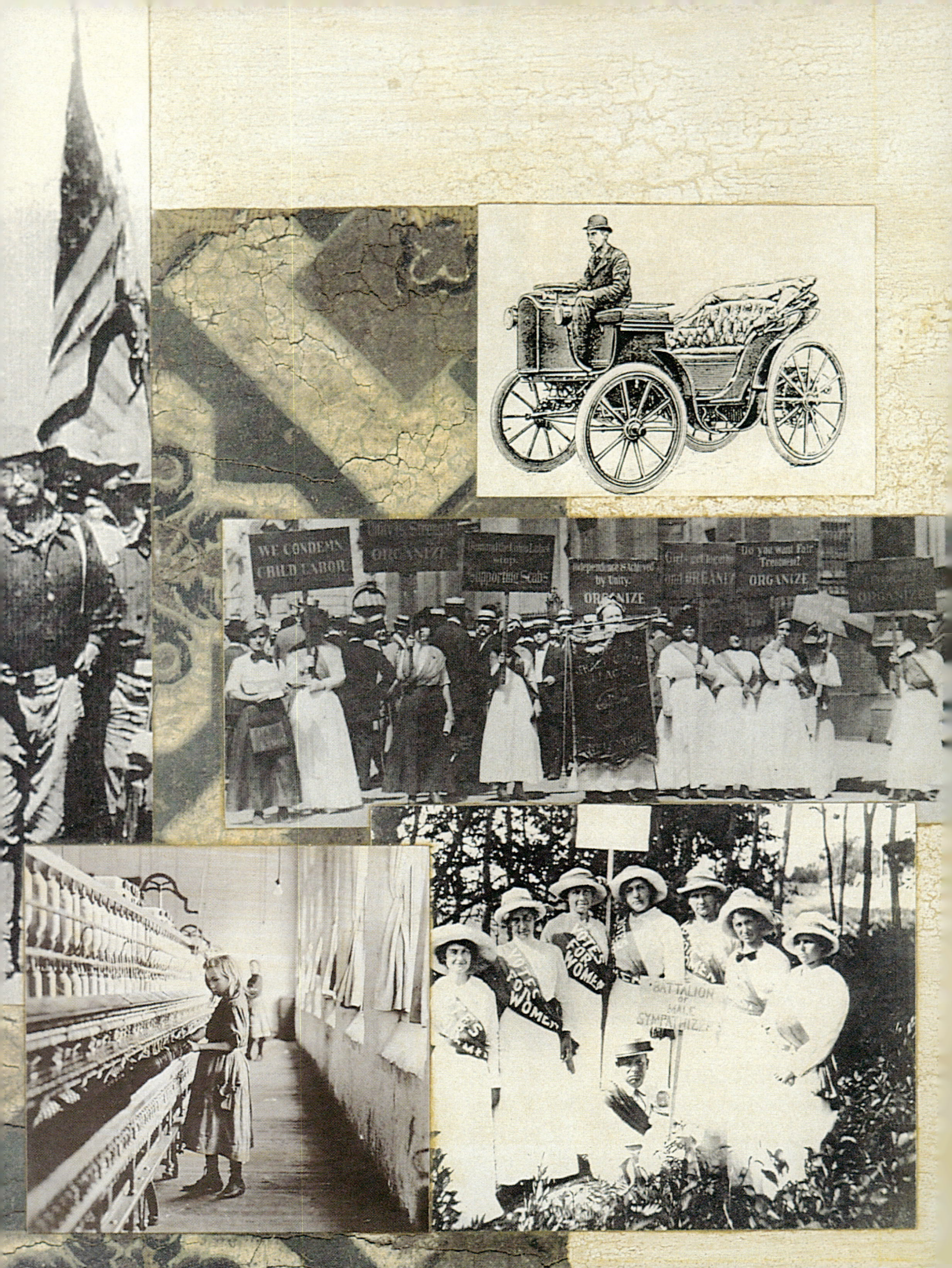

21

THE PROGRESSIVE STRUGGLE, 1900–1917

THE PROGRESSIVE IMPULSE
  America in 1901
  Voices for Change
  The Muckrakers

PROGRESSIVES IN ACTION
  The Drive to Organize
  Urban Beginnings
  Reform Reaches the State Level

PROGRESSIVISM MOVES TO THE NATIONAL LEVEL
  Roosevelt and New Attitudes Toward Government Power
  Taft and Quiet Progressivism
  Wilson and Moral Progressivism

PROGRESSIVISM IN THE INTERNATIONAL ARENA
  Big Stick Diplomacy
  Dollar Diplomacy
  Missionary Diplomacy

PROGRESSIVE ACCOMPLISHMENTS, PROGRESSIVE FAILURES
  The Impact of Legislation
  Winners and Losers

"We object to being called here to meet a criminal"

Times had changed by 1902 when George F. Baer declared "anthracite mining is business and not a religious, sentimental or academic proposition." Those tough-minded words might have won public approval at an earlier time, but many believed that Baer, spokesperson for mine owners in Pennsylvania, was merely being pigheaded. His words were in response to a request by John Mitchell of the United Mine Workers (UMW) for arbitration of a labor dispute. There was an unusual amount of support for the coal miners' position. Exposés had increased popular awareness of miserable working conditions, and the union's demands seemed reasonable: a 9-hour day, recognition of the union, a 10 to 20 percent increase in wages, and a fair weighing of the coal mined. Mitchell repeatedly stated the miners' willingness to accept arbitration, both before and after 50,000 miners walked out of the pits in May 1902.

Skillfully led, the coal miners stood firm month after month. By September, coal reserves were running short and prices were rising. With winter approaching, empty coal bins began multiplying, even in schools and hospitals. Baer remained stubborn. "The rights and interests of the laboring man," he declared, "will be protected and cared for—not by the labor agitators, but by the Christian men to whom God in his infinite wisdom has given the control of property interests in this country." This proclamation of the Gospel of Wealth fell on deaf ears. Newspaper after newspaper expressed disgust with the mine owners, and some tentatively suggested government ownership of the mines.

On October 3, President Theodore Roosevelt, temporarily in a wheelchair as a result of an accident, presided over a conference at the White House. Attending were Mitchell, Baer, Attorney General Philander C. Knox, and other labor leaders and mine operators. Baer was not in a mood to be cooperative. "We object to being called here to meet a criminal," he told a reporter, "even by the President of the United States." Refusing to speak directly to Mitchell, Baer urged Roosevelt to prosecute UMW leaders under the Sherman Antitrust Act and to use federal troops to break the strike, just as Cleveland had done in the 1894 Pullman strike. While Mitchell "behaved like a gentleman" according to Roosevelt, Baer was obstinate, concluding one diatribe against unions by calling "free government...a contemptible failure if it can only protect the lives and property and secure comfort of the people by compromise with violators of law and instigators of violence and crime."

Irritated with Baer, Roosevelt declared, "If it wasn't for the high office I hold I would have taken him by the seat of the breeches and the nape of the neck and chucked him out of that window." When the owners returned to Pennsylvania, they took actions that indicated they might use force to break the strike. Roosevelt's response was to begin preparations to send 10,000 federal troops to take over and operate the mines. This action jolted opponents of state socialism, who induced banker J. P. Morgan to get involved. Serving as a broker, Morgan was able to patch together a compromise under which the miners returned to work and Roosevelt appointed a commission to arbitrate the dispute.

The commission and its findings illustrate a number of aspects of the turn-of-the-century reforms labeled "progressivism." Originally, the commission was to consist of an army engineer, a mining engineer, a businessperson "familiar with the coal industry," a federal judge, and an "eminent sociologist"—reflecting a progressive tendency to call upon "experts" to conduct public affairs. Its composition was also decidedly probusiness, and even the addition of two other members and the appointment of a labor leader as the "eminent sociologist" did not redress this imbalance. As a result, its findings were essentially conservative: a 10 percent wage increase and reduction of working hours to 8 a day for a handful of miners and to 9 for most. The union did not receive recognition, and the traditional manner of weighing coal was continued. The commission also suggested a 10 percent increase in the price of coal. Business influence on other progressive responses to social problems generally produced similar moderate solutions that frequently brought industrialists as many benefits as losses.

Nevertheless, Roosevelt's actions did add some new rules to the game. For the first time, a president did not give knee-jerk support to business. Government became not merely a champion of the status quo but also an arbiter of change. Demands from the middle class and from workers motivated this retreat from laissez-faire. By 1902 many middle-class citizens had rejected management's heavy-handed tactics, which had often ended in chaos and conflict.

President Theodore Roosevelt, surrounded here by coal miners after their 1902 strike, set a precedent by threatening the use of force against management rather than labor. John Mitchell (right), leader of the United Mine Workers of America, rose from working in the mines to become one of the most respected labor leaders in America.

They sought a more orderly, stable, and just society through government intervention. Workers also began to flex their political muscles, electing sympathetic mayors in a number of cities. Like the coal miners, Americans of all classes were learning the limits of individualism and the benefits of joining together in organizations to accomplish their goals. National leaders such as Roosevelt began to recognize the need for change in order to preserve stable government and the capitalistic system. Roosevelt justified his actions in 1902 as a way to save "big propertied men ... from the dreadful punishment which their folly would have brought upon them." He stood, he declared, "between them and socialistic action." For a variety of motives, a plethora of legislation was enacted—sometimes with unintended results.

THE PROGRESSIVE IMPULSE

Americans exalted progress as a basic characteristic of their nation's distinctiveness. Technology was reshaping the human environment in dramatic ways. The pace of change was dizzying. Then in the late 1890s, people seemed to stop, catch their breath, and look around at their brave, new world. Much filled them with pride, but some of what they saw seemed outmoded or disruptive. Problems, however, appeared eminently solvable. Modern minds were explaining and harnessing natural forces. Could they not also understand and control human behavior? Could they not eliminate conflict and bring harmony to competing interests through some simple adjustments in the system? Americans increasingly answered "Yes" and called themselves "progressives." Many agreed with Thomas Edison's observation, "We've stumbled along for awhile, trying to run a new civilization in old ways, but we've got to start to make this world over."

America in 1901

The twentieth century opened with a rerun of the 1896 election between William Jennings Bryan and William McKinley. Although the outcome was the same, much was different. "I have never known a Presidential campaign so quiet," Senator Henry Cabot Lodge noted. By 1900 the crises of the 1890s had largely passed. Prosperity had returned and was shared by many. The nation also reveled in its newfound international power following the Spanish-American War. The social fabric seemed to be on the mend, but memories of the depression still haunted Americans, and society's blemishes appeared more and more intolerable to many.

As the nation reached adulthood, a number of ugly moles and warts had indeed come to the surface. Unequal distribution of wealth and income persisted. One percent of American families possessed nearly seven-eighths of its wealth. Four-fifths of Americans lived on a subsistence level, while a handful lived in incredible opulence. In 1900, Andrew Carnegie's income was $23 million; the average working man earned $500. The wealth of a few was increased by the exploitation of women and children. To feed their families women worked for wages as low as $6 a week. The sacrifice of the country's young to the god of economic growth was alarming. One reporter undertook to do a child's job in the mines for one day and wrote, "I tried to pick out the pieces of slate from the hurrying stream of coal, often missing them; my hands were bruised and cut within a few minutes; I was covered from head to foot with coal dust, and for many hours afterwards I was expectorating some of the small particles of anthracite I had swallowed."

Working conditions were equally horrifying in other industries, and for many Americans housing conditions were as bad or worse. One investigator described a Chicago neighborhood, remarking on the "filthy and rotten tenements, the dingy courts and tumble-down sheds, the foul stables and dilapidated outhouses, the broken sewer pipes, the piles of garbage fairly alive with diseased odors." At the same time the Vanderbilts summered in a "cottage" of 70 rooms, and wealthy men partied in shirts with diamond buttons.

The middle class did not experience either extreme. Its members did have their economic grievances, however. Prosperity increased the cost of living by 35 percent in less than a decade, while many middle-class incomes remained fairly stable. Such people were not poor, but they believed they were not getting a fair share of the prosperity. Many came to blame the monopolies and watched with alarm as trusts, proving to be immune from the Sherman Act, proliferated rapidly. Nearly three-fourths of all trusts in 1904 had been created since 1898. Decreasing competition seemed to threaten America's status as the land of opportunity.

People came to believe that they had to find political solutions to the nation's problems. To achieve that goal they had to wrest government from the hands of a few and return it to the "people." The great democratic experiment seemed to have run awry. Wealthy industrialists bought state and federal legislators; urban political machines paid for votes with money from bribes; Southern elections had become both bloody and corrupt.

Most problems were not new in 1901; neither were the proposed solutions. What came to be called progressivism was rooted in the Gilded Age. Whereas reform had been a sideshow earlier, it now became a national preoccupation. Progressivism was more broadly based and enjoyed greater appeal than any previous reform movement. The regional differences of the North, South, and West shaped reformers' concerns but not their intensity. The entire na-

Breaker boys employed by the mines worked in dirty, dismal, and dangerous surroundings that robbed them of their childhood. Conditions were much the same in textile mills.

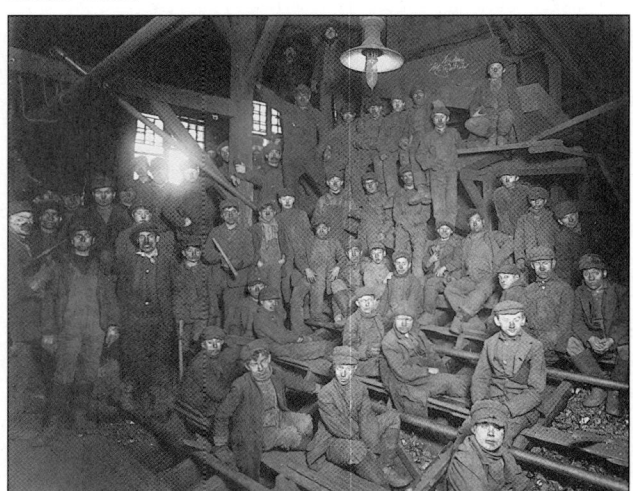

tion had experienced war or depression, never reform. One reason it did so now was the diversity and pervasiveness of the voices calling for change.

Voices for Change

By 1900, Americans had done nothing less than reinterpret their understanding of their world. Under the old, classical interpretation, the universe was governed by absolute and unchangeable law. There was divine logic to all and truth was universal—the same at all times and in all places. Humanity's chore was to discover these truths, not to devise new ones. Under this vision, public policy should be aligned with natural laws; to attempt to change the course of those laws through man-made law was to court disaster. Such logic justified the concentration of wealth as well as the lack of governmental regulation of business and assistance to the poor and weak.

Social Darwinism, laissez-faire economics, and the Gospel of Wealth never enjoyed total acceptance. Throughout the Gilded Age, challenges and alternative visions chipped away at their bases of support. The earlier challengers, however, either offered rather radical or simplistic alternatives. In 1879 Henry George wrote *Progress and Poverty*. As the title implies, he early recognized the unequal distribution of the fruits of economic growth. His solution was a "single tax" on the "unearned increment" of land values. He wanted to tax those who benefited from land speculation and rising property values without producing anything. In essence he attacked the premise of capitalism that said that one could use money to make more money without providing other goods or services. In *Looking Backward* (1888) Edward Bellamy provided a glimpse of a utopian society based upon a state-controlled economy propelled by cooperation rather than competition. Such writings profoundly influenced the Populists, the Socialists, and many who called themselves progressive.

Although critics dismissed the likes of George as crackpots, some respectable voices arose from the worlds of arts and literature, academia, the law, organized religion, and journalism. Realist writers described the world as it was, not as it should be. Instead of romantic heroes battling for abstract ideals, their characters were ordinary people dealing with concrete problems. The naturalists portrayed the powerlessness of the individual against the uncaring forces of urbanization and industrialization. Artists of the Ashcan school painted urban scenes teeming with problems as well as life. Art and literature thus became mirrors of social concerns (see Chapter 18).

A revolution was also taking place in the academic world. Two important changes were the democratization of higher education and the revolt against formalism. From 1870 to 1910 the number of colleges and universities nearly doubled, and their enrollment grew from 52,000 in 1870 to 600,000 in 1920. Higher education became less elitist, white, religious, and male, as women came to account for 47.3 percent of students in 1920 and African-American enrollment grew to over 20,000. Increasingly, their professors came from the middle class as well. Such students and teachers had little interest in supporting the status quo.

Also undermining the status quo was the revolt against formalism. Previous academics had sought to explain the world by formulating abstract, universal theories. The new scholars, especially in the emerging social sciences, turned this approach on its head. They began instead by collecting concrete data. In field after field that data did not support the so-called natural laws propounded by their predecessors. Knowledge, philosopher and educator John Dewey proclaimed, was "no longer an immobile solid; it has been liquefied."

Theories had prescribed limits to human action; facts became weapons for change. Classical economists asserted earlier that self-interested economic decisions by individuals in a freely competitive economy would naturally regulate markets through the laws of supply and demand. The new economists, calling themselves "institutional economists," conducted field research to learn how the economy actually worked. Their findings challenged the laissez-faire doctrines of the classicists on two levels: (1) that free competition existed and (2) that human decisions were based on purely economic motivations.

These women in a physics class illustrate the growing presence of women in college during the Progressive Era.

To continue policies based on competition was absurd, they argued, in an economy dominated by monopolies. In *Theory of the Leisure Class* (1899) and *The Instinct of Workmanship* (1914), economist Thorstein Veblen demonstrated the power of noneconomic motives. For example, vanity prompted the newly rich to indulge in "conspicuous consumption" well beyond their economic needs. For many economists "natural laws" were, in the words of Richard T. Ely, "used as a tool in the hands of the greedy."

A group of sociologists, calling themselves **"Reform Darwinists,"** rejected Spencer's Social Darwinism as another tool of exploitation. They accepted evolutionary principles and the influence of environment but denied that people were merely pawns manipulated by natural forces. Human intelligence was an active force that could control and change the environment, especially when people worked together. A leading Reform Darwinist, Lester Frank Ward, proclaimed, "The individual has reigned long enough. The day has come for society to take its affairs into its own hands and shape its own destinies." Ward called for "rational planning" and "social engineering" in his *Dynamic Sociology* (1883).

Legal scholars joined the assault on formalism in both books and court decisions. During the Gilded Age, courts had read laissez-faire principles into their interpretation of the Constitution. Decisions striking down regulatory and reform legislation invoked such abstract principles as the sanctity of property rights and contracts. In theory all such rights were equal before the law; reality was a different matter. For example, in *Lochner* v. *New York* (1905) the Supreme Court struck down a New York law limiting bakers' working hours. The law, the Court ruled, violated the bakers' rights to bargain freely and to make contracts. Most workers, however, had no real power to bargain, and maintaining that myth merely increased management's already overwhelming advantage.

A new breed of jurists challenged laissez-faire justice. Dean Roscoe Pound of the Harvard Law School advocated "sociological jurisprudence," calling for "the adjustment of principles and doctrines to the human conditions they are to govern rather than assumed first principles." Supreme Court Justice Oliver Wendell Holmes, Jr., rejected the idea that laws had ever been the logical result of pure, universal principles. He argued that laws should be based on "the felt necessities of the time." Lawyer Louis D. Brandeis successfully argued these ideas in 1908. That year the Supreme Court upheld a law in *Muller* v. *Oregon* that set a ten-hour workday for women working in Oregon laundries, primarily because social research documented the damage done to women's health by long hours of work.

As Americans began to reject absolute truths and universal principles, the question remained of how to determine right from wrong and good from bad. Philosopher William James with his doctrine of **pragmatism** provided an answer. "The ultimate test for us of what a truth means," he wrote, "is the conduct it dictates or inspires." Inherited ideas and principles needed scientific scrutiny before being accepted as guides to social development. As a distinctly American philosophy, pragmatism found many adherents. One of them, John Dewey, applied its principles to education. Requiring rote memorization of a static body of facts, he believed, did not meet the needs of individuals in a dynamic, changing environment. Instead, education should be based on experience to prepare students to assume personally fulfilling roles in society. In schools modeled after Dewey's Laboratory School at the University of Chicago, students engaged in activities that taught problem solving by doing rather than reading.

The literary and intellectual currents of the era helped to set the stage for reform by combining optimism, idealism, and a tough-minded practicality. Yet the educated elite were probably reflecting rather than shaping public opinion. Priests and preachers influenced far more people than professors. The impact of organized religion on progressivism was profound. It was no coincidence that Teddy Roosevelt's supporters marched around the hall singing "Onward Christian Soldiers" at the 1912 convention.

The confrontation between the church and the city produced the **Social Gospel** movement. Urban clergymen saw ravaged bodies that needed to be healed before souls could be saved. As a young Baptist minister in the dismal New York neighborhood "Hell's Kitchen," Walter Rauschenbusch described the poor coming to his church for aid. "They wore down our threshold, and they wore away our hearts...one could hear human virtue cracking and crunching all around." Following the lead of William Graham Taylor at the Chicago Theological Seminary, theology schools added courses in Christian sociology to teach "the application of our common Christianity to... social conditions." Social Gospelers used the tools of scientific inquiry to root out and solve human

In 1889 Jane Addams founded Hull House, a social settlement in Chicago. A "Social Gospeler," Addams turned to Christian ideals to solve social problems.

problems in order to usher in the "Kingdom of God on Earth." Many settlement house workers, such as Jane Addams, sought to put their faith into action for "the joy of finding the Christ that lieth in man, but which no man can unfold save in fellowship." The Social Gospelers advocated a kind of sacred humanism.

Progressivism was dominated by, but not limited to, Protestantism. The 1891 encyclical, *Rerum Novarum,* by Pope Leo XIII, inspired such Catholic priests as Father John A. Ryan to declare "a small number of very rich men have been able to lay upon the masses of people a yoke little better than slavery itself" and "no practical solution of this question will ever be found without the assistance of the church." Such Catholics as Alfred E. Smith and Robert F. Wagner became prominent progressive politicians. Others such as Jewish lawyer Louis Brandeis illustrated that the reform sentiment was not exclusively Christian.

The Muckrakers

A final spark that ignited public interest in reform was popular journalism. The expansion of education and cities provided a mass audience for low-priced magazines. Such journals as *Collier's* and *McClure's* sold for only 10 cents and could only succeed if large numbers of people bought them. Their editors quickly rediscovered people's fascination with evil. Investigative reporters peered beneath all sorts of rocks and brought to light corruption in almost every facet of society. Their vivid, indignant accounts sold magazines but appalled some of the elite. Teddy

Ida Tarbell became one of the most influential muckrakers after the 1904 publication of her *History of the Standard Oil Company*.

Roosevelt compared the writers to the character in John Bunyan's *The Pilgrim's Progress,* who was too engrossed in raking muck to look up and accept a celestial crown. Thus these chroniclers came to be called **muckrakers**.

Most of their exposés came out serially in magazines; others were published as books, but all titillated the public. John Spargo wrote on child labor, "Statistics cannot express the withering of child lips in the poisoned air of factories; the tired strained look of child eyes that never dance to the glad music of souls tuned to Nature's symphonies." David Graham Phillips argued, "The United States Senate is a larger factor than your labor and intelligence, you average American, in determining your income. And the Senate is a traitor to you!" State legislatures were little better, as was shown by journalist William Allen White's investigation in Missouri. "The legislature met biennially, and enacted such laws as the corporations paid for and such as were necessary to fool the people." In *Following the Color Line* journalist and author Ray Stannard Baker exhorted, "Whether we like it or not the whole nation . . . is tied by unbreakable bonds to its Negroes, its Chinamen, its slum-dwellers, its thieves, its murderers, its prostitutes. We cannot elevate ourselves by driving them back either with hatred, violence or neglect; but only by bringing them forward: by service." Ida Tarbell called Standard Oil "one of the most gigantic and dangerous conspiracies ever attempted." In similar, stirring words Lincoln Steffens denounced urban politics in *The Shame of the Cities,* and the socialist Upton Sinclair described the horrifying conditions in the meat-packing industry in *The Jungle.*

One might believe these men and women were cynical mudslingers, but that was not how they saw themselves: "We muckraked," said Baker, "not because we hated our world, but because we loved it. We were not hopeless, we were not cynical, we were not bitter." The public sometimes missed the intended message. Sinclair's goal in *The Jungle* was a socialist critique of the exploitation of labor in the meat-packing industry, but as he ruefully noted, "I aimed at the nation's heart and hit it in the stomach." After a few years, muckraking tended to degenerate into sloppy research and wild, unsubstantiated charges. Yet the publishers of the more than 2000 muckraking books and articles who aimed at the nation's pocketbooks hit a number of Americans in the heart.

PROGRESSIVES IN ACTION

Voices of change echoed a genuine transformation of popular sentiment. Americans of all classes began

The American Mosaic

The White Plague

DURING the Progressive Era, the rise of scientific ways of thinking cleared the way for reformers and health officers to launch a campaign against the disease most identified with industrialization—tuberculosis (TB). During the nineteenth century, TB was aptly called "the Captain of All the Men of Death." It killed more people and caused more sickness than any other disease in the western world. Its very name conjures up images of fetid sweatshops and sulfurous mills where long working hours and physical exhaustion broke the health of men, women, and children; of urban slums and overcrowded tenements rotten with disease; and, finally, of emaciated, ghostlike wretches, feverish with infection, gasping for breath, coughing up mouthfuls of blood, and staring hollow-eyed into space waiting for death.

In a sense, TB mirrors the complexity of the industrial revolution, for just as the transformation of the economy was multifaceted, TB is not one but many diseases. TB is merely the generic name for a host of infections caused by tubercle bacilli, isolated in 1882 by Robert Koch, the famous German scientist. The most common (and most feared) is pulmonary tuberculosis, a chronic, debilitating disease of the lungs; it can kill its victims in a few months but usually requires several years to complete the task. Other common forms of the disease include meningeal TB, which produces an inflammation of the membranes surrounding the brain; TB of the spine, which causes a hunchback deformity of the spine; lupus, TB of the skin; and miliary TB, a generalized infection that occurs when the tubercle bacilli are distributed by the bloodstream throughout the body, producing small nodules on most organs.

Because the term *tuberculosis* did not appear in print until around 1840, most Americans knew the disease as consumption, which seemed the perfect metaphor since victims of the disease gradually wasted away from debilitating fever, weight loss, night sweats, chronic cough, and copious sputum decorated toward the end with the bright red blood spots that denoted advanced pulmonary tuberculosis.

In less polite society, consumptives were called *lungers,* a term of derision. Throughout the nineteenth century, many people associated TB with poverty and attached a social stigma to the disease. Others believed that TB was caused by some hereditary defect; for them, the perplexing problem was why the disease hit some families harder than others. In Ralph Waldo Emerson's family, for example, he and three of his brothers suffered from the disease, while his fellow transcendentalist, Henry David Thoreau, lost his father, a sister, and a grandfather to TB before dying from the disease himself.

Paradoxically, despite its dreadful symptoms and terrifying ability to wipe out entire families, TB was romanticized on both sides of the Atlantic. For many writers, it became a metaphor for comparing decay in nature to disease in man. Thus, Henry Thoreau, upon seeing the first splashes of red in the green maple leaves of autumn, could write in 1852 in his *Journal Intime:* "Decay and disease are often beautiful, like . . . the hectic glow of consumption."

In fact, the Age of Romanticism's much heralded "doom and gloom" may have derived at least in part from the sadness and melancholy caused by the deaths of loved ones from TB—especially the death of young adults, for whom the disease had a special affinity. John Keats, the quintessential romantic poet, succumbed to TB at 26; Emily Brontë, author of the powerful *Wuthering Heights,* was cut down tragically at 30. The novels of the day, Charles Dickens's *David Copperfield,* for one, are positively littered with the corpses of people killed in the bloom of youth by the "White Plague."

The disease also broke its share of hearts in the theater and at the opera. Alexander Dumas lamented the death from TB of a beautiful heroine in *La Dame aux Camelias,* which in its English translation became the play, *Camille, or the Fate of a Coquette,* later adapted by Verdi for the opera as *La Traviata.* An identical fate befell the heroine in the play, *La Bohème,* which inspired Puccini's opera of the same name.

Under the spell of this heart-wrenching romanticism, writers, poets, and artists created a new and profoundly twisted ideal of feminine beauty: the dying angel, smitten by consumption, whose physical appeal was somehow enhanced by her mal-

 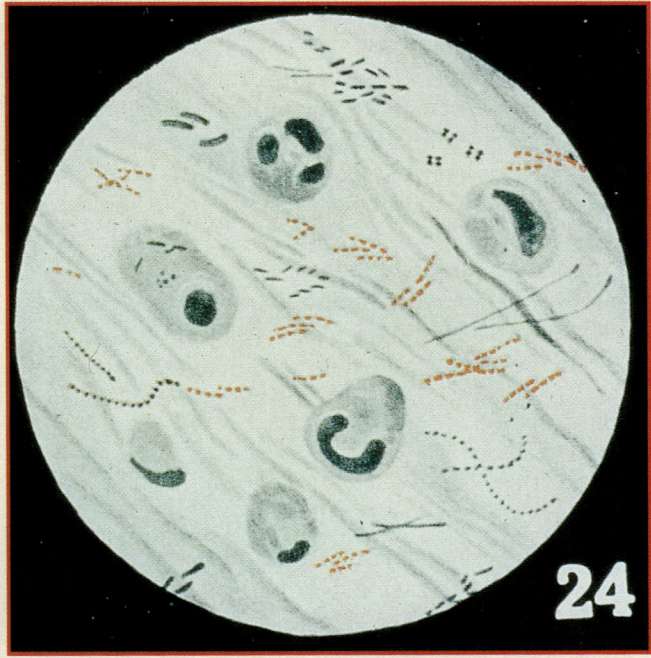

ady. One gravely ill woman confided to her diary, "I cough continually! But for a wonder, far from making me look ugly, this gives me an air of languor that is very becoming." As depicted by writers, the dying female consumptive was, to her fingertips, an exquisitely fragile creature, the very embodiment of both the romantic and the Victorian ideal of frail feminine beauty. Her languid pallor was rendered even more pale by the generous application of whitening powders; and her slender body, with its swanlike neck and elongated limbs, was adorned in thin, sheer white clothing of cotton or linen, giving her an ethereal quality, as a spirit not quite of this earth.

Numerous artists struggled to capture this image on canvas, including Gabriel Rossetti of the Pre-Raphaelite school, who idealized tall, slender women "with cadaverous bodies and sensual mouths." Reducing this image to a word portrait, Henry James described Janet Burden, one of the leading Pre-Raphaelite models, as "strange, pale, livid, gaunt, silent, and yet in a manner graceful and picturesque." To another observer the same woman looked "as if she had walked out of an Egyptian tomb at Luxor."

As the nineteenth century drew to a close, however, the romantic view of life gradually lost its hold on the public's imagination. Instead of celebrating TB, writers, joined by health reformers, saw TB through the lens of realism. They linked the disease to poverty, unsafe working conditions, overcrowded housing, poor diet, and the failure of government to safeguard the public's health. Rather than glorifying consumptives, this change in attitude depicted them as the victims of a cruel, punishing illness. TB was no longer something to spark the artistic imagination; it was now a microbial insult to mankind and an indictment against the society that tolerated it.

calling themselves "progressives" and sought to reform whichever social evil captured their attention. Most believed problems could be legislated away; their typical response to injustice or sin was "There ought to be a law." At the same time they rejected the individualism of Social Darwinism and believed that progress would come through cooperation rather than competition. Thus they organized themselves by droves into groups that shared their own particular vision of human progress.

The diversity of new organizations reflected the breadth of reform activity. Indeed, so varied were the aims of people calling themselves progressive that to call progressivism a single movement is a mistake. The only unity lay in the idea that people could improve society. Most progressives, however, were middle-class moderates who abhorred radical solutions. Motivated by a fear and hatred of class conflict, such progressives sought to save the capitalists from their own excesses and thereby salvage the system. Their goal was an orderly and harmonious society.

The Drive to Organize

Organizing was a major activity at the turn of the century. Such professional groups as the American Medical Association (AMA) and the American Historical Association emerged in their modern form. These groups reflected the rise of a new professionalism that helped to create a body of "experts" who aided progressives wanting to impose order and efficiency on social institutions. The organizations themselves also acted to bring change. The AMA was reorganized in 1901, and by 1910 its membership had increased from 8400 to more than 70,000. Its major goal was to improve professional standards. Governments assisted by enacting laws that required licenses to practice medicine. In 1910 a Carnegie Foundation study recommended minimum standards for medical education. Widespread acceptance of its report closed dozens of marginal medical schools, several of which trained minority doctors. Professionalization thus reduced the number of practitioners. Although this did help weed out incompetents, it also increased the incomes of the remaining practitioners and often reduced minority participation. Order, stability, and improved standards came at the cost of decreased opportunity for some.

Given the religious bent of progressive thought, a number of church-related organizations also arose. One of the most important was the Federal Council of Churches of Christ in America. Founded in 1908, it was an interdenominational group that advocated safer working conditions, the abolition of child labor, shorter workweeks, higher wages, workmen's compensation, old-age pensions, and "the most equitable division of the products of industry that can ultimately be devised."

To a large extent, middle-class women led in the organization of reform. Technology and domestic help lessened the burdens of running a home for these women, but a stigma remained on paid employment. Women's clubs provided an outlet for the energies and abilities of many competent and educated women. Local organizations flourished and in 1890 joined to form the General Federation of Women's Clubs. In the next two decades, reform groups founded and led mainly by women sprang up.

The majority of activist, middle-class women became involved in movements closely linked to their assigned social roles as guardians of morality and nurturers of the family. Many worked through such religious groups as the Young Women's Christian Association. Numerous others joined in a resurgence of prohibitionism. The **Woman's Christian Temperance Union (WCTU)**, led by Frances Willard, revived a flagging prohibition movement and by 1898 had 10,000 local branches. It was assisted by the Anti-Saloon League (organized in 1893) and such church organizations as the Temperance Society of the Methodist Episcopal church.

Some of the prohibitionists were Protestant fundamentalists who considered the consumption of alcohol a sin; others were concerned with its social impact. Urban reformers constantly saw the consequences of alcohol abuse in domestic violence, accidents, and pauperism. Alcohol was the root of so many social problems that to ignore it was like "bailing water out of a tub with the tap turned on; letting the ... liquor traffic run full blast while we limply stood around and picked up the wreckage." The physically devastating effects of alcoholism were reported by the AMA. Many in the Anti-Saloon League were also dismayed by the part played by drinking establishments in machine politics.

The idea of legislating morality for the good of society spilled over into the sexual sphere. A major area of concern was prostitution, and its opponents had a variety of motivations. Some stressed its role in the spread of venereal disease; others deplored the exploitation of women and the double standard that allowed only men sexual freedom. For some it was morally wrong; to others it was just one more social evil—a product of environment rather than original sin. Many linked it with immigration as they did alcohol abuse. The crusade against this age-old problem had deep roots, but at the turn of the century it followed a typically progressive path. Muckraking journalists enraged the public with lurid accounts of "white slavery" rings that kidnapped young women and forced them into prostitution. The next step was to pressure local governments to establish commissions to study the issue. Most reports stressed the economic roots. One prostitute asked an investigator, "Do you suppose I am going back to earn five or six dollars a week in a factory, when I can earn that amount any night and often much more?"

Some people believed prostitution was merely a symptom of a larger disease, and they became "purity crusaders." Dr. Will K. Kellogg wrote "The exorbitant demands of the sexual appetites encountered among civilized people are not the result of a normal instinct, but are due to the incitements of an abnormally stimulating diet, including alcohol, the seduction of prurient literature and so-called art, and the temptations of impure associations." After a national Purity Congress in 1895, the purity crusaders lobbied not only for the prohibition of alcohol and prostitution but also for such things as censorship and the regulation of narcotics.

Progressive social reform had two aims: control and justice. Women were deeply involved in social justice as well as control movements like prohibition. Middle-class women had long dominated humanitarian work, but during the 1890s their work took on a new aggressiveness. Women came to believe that aid to the poor was an inadequate response to society's ills; they wanted to attack the causes of poverty. They sought to improve wages and working conditions, especially for women, and to protect children from exploitation. To this end, they started several organizations. The National Consumers League, led by former Illinois factory inspector Florence Kelly, lobbied for protective legislation for women and children as well as better working and living conditions for all. Kelly became a leading advocate of child labor laws and was joined in this cause by Alabama clergyman Edgar Gardner Murphy, who proposed the formation of the National Child Labor Committee in 1904. Like most progressives, child labor reformers gathered data and photographs to document horrors for legislators at the local, state, and finally federal level.

African-American women were among the most active of the reformers. The growing black middle class produced increasing numbers of educated women. Unlike their white counterparts, most engaged in paid employment. More than financial need alleviated the stigma of employment for African-American women. They were expected to play a larger role in society. Journalist Lucy Wilmot Smith explained that although the white woman "has had to contest with her brother every inch of the ground for recognition; the Negro man, having had his sister by his side on plantations and in rice swamps, keeps her there, now that he moves in other spheres." In addition to working, black women engaged in reform. Ida B. Wells (later Wells-Barnett) launched an antilynching campaign that resulted in the expulsion of both her and her newspaper, the *Free Speech*, from Memphis, Tennessee, in 1893. In 1895 she joined with other clubwomen to form what became the National Association of Colored Women.

Some reformers were not content to be merely advocates for the poor and the weak; they wanted to become directly involved with such people to educate and organize them to help themselves. Here again middle-class women played a key role. Foremost among such activities was the **settlement house movement.** Following the lead of Jane Addams of Hull House in Chicago, many young college-educated women moved into slum neighborhoods to live and work with those they sought to help. "From the first," Addams wrote, "it seemed understood that we were ready to perform the humblest neighborhood services. We were asked to wash the newborn babies, and to prepare the dead for burial, to nurse the sick, and to 'mind the children.'"

More than unselfishness motivated such women. One worker confessed that settlement houses gratified her "thirst to know how the other half lives." Some educated women wanted more freedom than marriage and part-time volunteer work seemed to offer. One appeal of settlement work was that men did not control it. A result was a growing social feminism that cut across class lines. An example was the founding of the National Women's Trade Union League in 1905.

Alarmed by the unhealthy child-care practices of many immigrants, visiting nurses went to immigrant homes to teach such things as the proper bathing of babies.

Susan B. Anthony, a founder of the National Woman Suffrage Association in 1869 and vice president and president of the National American Woman Suffrage Association from 1890 to 1900, fought for women's right to vote on the national level through an amendment to the U.S. Constitution. The Nineteenth Amendment (sometimes called the Anthony Amendment) guaranteeing woman suffrage was adopted in 1920, fourteen years after Anthony's death.

progressive reforms, however, did eventually convince many people that women not only deserved the right to vote but also that their political participation would be socially beneficial. Jane Addams asserted, "If women have in any sense been responsible for the gentler side of life which softens and blurs some of its harsher conditions may they not have a duty to perform in our American cities?" Arguments based on women's "special role," however, cut both ways. In articles with such titles as "Famed Biologist's Warning on the Peril in Votes to Women," writers charged that voting was so "unnatural" for women that pregnant women would miscarry and nursing mothers' milk would cease to flow. As during the fight for ratification of the Equal Rights Amendment in the 1970s, not all opponents were male. Mrs. A. J. George of the National Association Opposed to Woman Suffrage declared, "The Woman-suffrage movement is an imitation-of-man movement, and as such, merits the condemnation of every normal man and woman."

In the face of such opposition, suffragists began to escalate their demands for the vote. Many became convinced that only national action would be effective. Thus the National American Woman Suffrage Association, led by Carrie Chapman Catt after 1915, began a broad-based campaign for an amendment to the U.S. Constitution. More militant women followed the young Quaker, Alice Paul, who founded the National Woman's party in 1914. She preferred the tactics of British suffragists who had picketed, gone on hunger strikes, and actively confronted both politicians and police.

Another group in the social justice movement

Through it, wealthy supporters organized women workers, joined their strikes, and trained leaders.

At first such activity seemed to draw attention away from the suffrage movement. Women's roles in

Women employed a variety of tactics in their fight for the vote. Here Dr. Anna Howard Shaw and Carrie Chapman Catt lead 20,000 marchers down Fifth Avenue in New York City.

sought to improve relations between blacks and whites. White Southerners had continued to devise forms of racial control to replace slavery. Their solution became a three-legged stool: legal segregation, disfranchisement, and violence. From the beginning, African Americans resisted white efforts to suppress them. In city after city, they utilized every tool and tactic that would prove successful in the 1960s. They marched, they lobbied legislative bodies, they petitioned, they challenged discriminatory legislation in courts, and they boycotted segregated streetcars. Under the leadership of Booker T. Washington, they also tried conciliation. Nothing stemmed the rising tide of racism.

As conditions worsened Washington seemed to grow even more accommodating, at least in public. His influence with white politicians and philanthropists as well as his control of much of the black press gave him incredible power, which he used ruthlessly on occasion. Behind the scenes, he supported protest activities, using code names and secret funds. Educated African Americans, however, became increasingly disenchanted with his public performance. They also resented his suppression of dissent by fellow blacks. The so-called anti-Bookerite radicals found their spokesperson in W. E. B. Du Bois. Unlike Washington, who had been born into slavery and educated at an industrial school, Du Bois was born to free parents in Massachusetts and became the first African American to receive a doctorate from Harvard.

Gifted with staggering intellectual brilliance, Du Bois expressed the frustrations and dreams of his fellow blacks in *The Souls of Black Folks* (1903). Of being black in America, he wrote, "one ever feels his twoness—an American, a Negro, two souls, two thoughts, two unreconciled strivings, two warring ideals in one dark body." In that book he also penned a polite but devastating critique of Washington's leadership. He objected to Washington's failure to recognize the importance of the vote, his emphasis on industrial education at the expense of higher education, his reluctance to criticize as well as praise white actions, and his willingness to give up previously won rights.

Relations between the two men deteriorated steadily after 1903, even though immediate methods rather than ultimate goals separated them. Both wanted the full acceptance of African Americans as first-class citizens. To Washington, the best route was self-help and educating the masses. To these ends, he made Tuskegee Institute into an impressive institution staffed entirely by blacks. Du Bois, on the other hand, was more integrationist and believed the key to black advancement was in cultivating what he called the "Talented Tenth." To him, more

THE PEOPLE SPEAK

An Account of the Proceedings of the Trial of Susan B. Anthony

From the inception of the women's rights movement, suffragists had argued for the right of women to vote, using all available tactics. This transcription of the 1872 trial of Susan B. Anthony for illegally attempting to register to vote demonstrates one of those methods—court challenges to the constitutionality of prohibiting woman suffrage. At the conclusion of the trial, Anthony was found guilty and required to pay a fine of $100 plus court costs.

> The only alleged ground of illegality of the defendant's vote is that she is a woman. If the same act has been done by her brother under the same circumstances, the act would have been not only innocent, but honorable and laudable; but having been done by a woman it is said to be a crime. The crime therefore consists not in the act done, but in the simple fact that the person doing it was a woman and not a man, I believe this is the first instance in which a woman has been arraigned in a criminal court, merely on account of her sex.
>
> Women have the same interest that men have in the establishment and maintenance of good government; they are to the same extent as men bound to obey the laws; they suffer to the same extent by bad laws, and profit to the same extent by good laws; and upon principles of equal justice, as it would seem, should be allowed equally with men, to express their preference in the choice of law-makers and rulers. But however that may be, no greater *absurdity*, to use no harsher term, could be presented, than that of rewarding men and punishing women, for the same act, *without giving to women any voice in the question which should be rewarded, and which punished.*
>
> I am aware, however, that we are here to be governed by the Constitution and laws as they are, and that if the defendant has been guilty of violating the law, she must submit to the penalty, however unjust or absurd the law may be. But courts are not required to so interpret laws or constitutions as to produce absurdity or injustice, so long as they are open to a more reasonable interpretation. . . .

Source: Votes for Women: Selections from the National American Woman Suffrage Association Collection 1848–1926.

W. E. B. Du Bois, shown here in the editorial offices of *The Crisis* at the New York headquarters of the NAACP, was at first the only African American to hold a significant office in the organization.

of the limited education funds should go to train the ablest 10 percent of African Americans for eadership through liberal arts and professional schooling. Although most African Americans saw value in both approaches, the dispute became bitter and divisive.

In 1905 Du Bois joined William Monroe Trotter in forming the Niagara Movement, an organization devoted to two main objectives: opposition to Washington's leadership and demands for "full manhood rights." Only about 50 educated African-Americans—mainly Northerners—joined, and the movement struggled to exist in the face of unrelenting sabotage by Washington. It played an important role, however, in convincing northern white progressives that an alternative to Washington was desirable. When a white mob in Springfield, Illinois, went on a rampage against African Americans, concerned whites joined with Du Bois and Ida B. Wells-Barnett to found the **National Association for the Advancement of Colored People (NAACP)** in 1909. At first the group was led and dominated by whites; Du Bois was the only African American to hold a responsible position, as editor of its journal *The Crisis*. The organization became more black over time, but the focus of its activities remained essentially the same: education and propaganda, court challenges to discrimination, and lobbying for such legislation as a federal antilynching law.

The drive to organize pervaded all of society, creating such diverse groups as the Boy Scouts of America (1910), the Rotary Club (1915), the National Collegiate Athletic Association (1906), the National Birth Control League (1915), and even the Aero Club of America (1905) to popularize "ballooning as a sport, especially among the more wealthy class." Americans came to believe in cooperative efforts to reach goals. In unprecedented numbers they also began to look to government for answers—starting at the city level and moving up to Washington.

Urban Beginnings

Progressivism was a response to emerging problems and first confronted the most visible ones, many of which were found in the cities. Incredibly rapid increases in urban populations outpaced the ability of "small-town" governments to meet the challenges. Political machines provided needed services but came under attack in the 1890s as inefficient and corrupt. Middle- and upper-class reformers demanded that governments operate "on a strict business basis" and be run "not by partisans, [n]either Republican nor Democratic, but by men who are skilled in business management and social service."

Urban reformers' victories included the secret ballot and voter registration in some cities. Then in 1900, a model for efficient, nonpartisan city government emerged from the chaos created when a devastating hurricane killed more than 6000 people in Galveston, Texas. Local government broke down and the state legislature appointed a five-man commission to run the city. The idea had spread to over 400 cities by World War I. A refinement was added in 1913, when in the wake of a disastrous flood, the government of Dayton, Ohio, hired a city manager to run the city on a day-to-day basis.

The cost of efficiency was decreased democracy. Indeed, some urban reformers were openly antidemocratic. One wrote in 1901, "Ignorance should be excluded from control. City business should be carried on by trained experts selected on some other principle than popular suffrage." The ward system, under which aldermen were elected by district, was seen as a problem because, as a Chicago businessman noted in 1911, "Men of successful experience and ability large enough to do justice to public affairs will seldom live and bring up families in the poorer wards." The reformers naively sought to take politics out of government, but by "politics" they often meant the voice of people not like themselves. Nevertheless, these goals contradicted broader support for democracy, and by 1914 most city commissioners were required to run for election—although often, in at-large elections rather than by district.

Middle-class progressives sometimes found their will thwarted by lower-class voters. Breaking up urban machines often destroyed the informal welfare networks that met the needs of the poor. When that happened, the poor rejected the new efficiency. In 1901, the Tammany Hall machine recaptured New

York with the campaign slogan "To hell with reform." Poor immigrants did not accept that their ignorance and "foreign ways" were at the root of urban problems. "It is not so much the under crust," one declared, "as the upper crust that endangers the interests of the people."

In a number of cities, voters elected mayors who sympathized with working-class desires. Tom L. Johnson, elected mayor of Cleveland in 1901, rejected efforts to impose middle-class morality on the poor. "I am not trying to enforce Christianity," he proclaimed, "only make it possible." To this end he expanded social services and brought about the public ownership of the waterworks, gas and electric utilities, and public transportation, thereby reducing their costs to the poor. After his election in 1899, Mayor Samuel "Golden Rule" Jones sought to establish the "Cooperative Commonwealth, the Kingdom of Heaven on Earth," in Toledo, Ohio. Until his death in 1904, he worked to provide free kindergartens, free playgrounds, free golf courses, and free concerts. He also reformed the police department, substituting light canes for the heavy clubs carried by patrolmen and prohibiting the jailing of people without charges. He made some powerful enemies and once declared, "Everyone is against me but the people." Most urban liberals depended on working-class voters.

The move toward public ownership of utilities was most avidly supported by the Socialists, who showed growing strength on the local level. In 1910 a Socialist was elected mayor of Milwaukee, and in the next year 70 other socialists were elected in towns and cities across the nation. By 1912 about 1000 held offices in 33 states and 160 cities. Their rising power, however, helped trigger a backlash by middle-class voters, who favored regulatory commissions rather than public ownership of utilities.

Urban progressivism was obviously not a coherent, unified movement. Different groups at different times succeeded in different cities. Social services were cut to lower business taxes in some cities and expanded in others. In most cities the evils of overcrowded, unhealthy tenements were attacked with varying degrees of success with such measures as building codes. By the turn of the century, however, more and more people began to look to the states to solve problems.

Reform Reaches the State Level

Regardless of their objectives, many urban reformers eventually dabbled in state politics. The city had little power and the federal government seemed too remote. Thus the states became major battlegrounds for reform. The form and leadership of state progressivism were as diverse and complex as urban progressivism. In the South, most progressives worked through the Democratic party; in the Midwest and on the Pacific Coast, progressives captured the Republican party. In the industrial Northeast, progressives emerged in both major parties, but the Democrats were the more successful. In some cases progressive governors, such as Al Smith of New York, were the products of urban machines that embraced reform to hold onto their electorates. Others, such as Robert La Follette of Wisconsin, were Republican regulars who bypassed party leaders to ride reform to power. In the South, reform governors were elected by startlingly diverse constituencies. In Mississippi, small-town lawyer and editor James K. Vardaman was elected by poor white farmers, the "redneck" vote. In Georgia, the urban middle class was the main support of Hoke Smith, publisher of the *Atlanta Journal*.

State progressives pursued four major goals: (1) providing "direct democracy," (2) protecting the public by regulating the economy, (3) increasing state services, and (4) establishing social control. One progressive creed was dramatically stated by writer and journalist William Allen White: "The voice of the people is indeed the will of God." By World War I many states had adopted political procedures designed to give the people a more direct say in running the government. An initiative allowed voters to propose legislative changes, usually by petition; a referendum gave the public a mechanism for voting directly on controversial legislation; recall provided a way to remove elected officials. Many states also established direct primaries. Other states adopted measures to cleanse electoral procedures, including the secret ballot, voter registration, and corrupt practices legislation. The drive for direct democracy culminated in the Seventeenth Amendment to the Constitution (1913), which substituted the popular election of senators for their election by state legislatures.

The victories of women suffragists at the state level also expanded democracy—especially in the West. In that region the relatively barren environment and the frontier conditions endured by early settlers caused husbands and wives to work together as partners to survive. The Anglo conflict with existing Hispanic and Native American cultures may have also fostered a unity that created more equality. At any rate, Washington state gave women the vote in 1910. California did so the next year, and four other western states had followed suit by 1916. That year Jeannette Rankin was elected to Congress from Montana. These victories encouraged efforts to obtain a constitutional amendment allowing women to vote.

Progressive actions by states to protect the public and regulate the economy took many forms. In the West the emphasis was on regulating railroads and utilities, reflecting the region's Populist heritage. The region was also especially vulnerable to rate discrimination because of its remoteness and the long distances to markets. Legislatures created commissions to regulate the rates charged by both railroads and utilities. At the same time, taxes on corporations were increased. For example, after La Follette's election as governor of Wisconsin in 1900, state revenues from taxes on railroads grew from $1.9 million to $3.4 million.

In the industrialized states, workmen's compensation became a major goal. Horror stories about industrial accidents had long abounded, and muckrakers further inflamed the public. Then in 1911 a major tragedy chilled the hearts of Americans. A fire broke out at the Triangle Shirtwaist Company in New York just 30 minutes before closing time. The doors were locked to prevent workers from leaving early, and many fire escape ladders were either broken or missing. By the time the flames were doused, 147 workers, mainly women and girls, had lost their lives—47 had jumped to their deaths, littering the street with bodies. The Triangle fire was the worst example of escalating industrial accidents. The only recourse for most maimed workers or their widowed spouses was to sue the company, which for many was not a realistic option. Some workers did get large settlements, however, which represented an unpredictable cost to businesses. Gradually, the idea of mandatory insurance grew in popularity, with the support of many factory owners. Between 1910 and 1916, 32 states enacted **workmen's compensation laws.**

The work of the National Child Labor Committee and other organizations moved states to legislate protection for women and children. Progressives gathered evidence of the harm done to both by long working hours and unsafe, unhealthy conditions. State action was necessary, they argued, for two reasons: Women and children could not protect themselves and the nation's future depended on the health of both. By 1916, 32 states had laws regulating the hours worked by women and children, 11 had specified minimum wages for women, and every state regulated child labor in some manner. Other protective legislation included building and sanitary codes, which benefited all workers.

A number of states also expanded social services. Because of lobbying by settlement house workers, by 1914 some 20 states had provided mother's pensions to widows or abandoned wives with dependent children. The sums paid were meager, however, ranging from $2 to $15 a month for the first child and lesser amounts for the rest. Funding for education also increased. A major area of reform was the expansion of compulsory education to the high school level. Support often came from businesses, which saw public education as a means of preparing individuals for life in an industrial society. As a result, very few public schools were modeled on John Dewey's progressive educational doctrines. Instead of promoting personal development, education, in the industrialists' minds, should inculcate discipline and punctuality. Hence school bells trained one for factory whistles and letter grades taught the value of individual initiative. Governments also made school organization more businesslike, with increased power given to school superintendents and principals, who were expected to be trained in management techniques.

The flip side of state social justice legislation was increased efforts at social control. Prohibitionists won many victories in the states, especially in the South. That region provided fertile soil for prohibitionists because of the strength of Protestant fundamentalism and the so-called race problem. One southern prohibitionist argued that African Americans were "a child race in the South, and if drunkenness causes three-fourths of the crime ascribed to it, whiskey must be taken out of the Negro's hands," and that it was the duty "of the stronger race to forego its own personal liberty for the protection of the weaker race." Between 1907 and 1909 Georgia, Mississippi, North Carolina, Tennessee, and Alabama adopted state prohibition; 14 other states had joined them by 1916.

The move toward social control infected all regions. Between 1907 and 1917, 16 states passed laws authorizing sterilization of various categories of allegedly unfit individuals. Social control measures were usually directed at minorities, so the South naturally offered the most extreme examples, but California progressives excluded Asians almost as ruthlessly. Southern whites trumpeted segregation as a reform, and they had the approval of many northern progressives. Even race relations muckraker Ray Stannard Baker wrote, "As for the Jim Crow laws in the South, many of them, at least, are at present necessary to avoid clashes between the ignorant of both races." Segregation was often enacted under progressive governors—a paradox only if the general progressive tendency toward social control is ignored.

In most ways, southern progressivism was for whites only. Increased school funding was common, but the bulk went to educating white children. The discrepancies between the amounts spent accelerated, making even more of a lie of the *Plessy* v. *Ferguson* (1896) formula of "separate but equal" facilities. In 1919 southern states spent an average of $12.16 per white student and $3.29 per black student. Racism remained a potent force. As governor of Mississippi from 1903 to 1907, James K. Vardaman pursued progressive reforms in such

This temperance lithograph portrays with religious fervor the path ahead for those who board the "Inebriate's Express."

areas as convict-lease (a system by which states rented out their prisoners to private interests to provide a cheap labor source), school funding, and railroad regulation. At the same time he defended lynching, saying "We would be justified in slaughtering every Ethiopian on earth to preserve unsullied the honor of one Caucasian home."

The legacy of progressivism in the states was mixed, as were the motives of reformers. Regardless of their goals, most came to look to the federal government for help. One reformer expressed their frustration. "When I was in the city council . . . fighting for a shorter work day, [my opponents] told me to go to the legislature; now [my fellow legislators] tell me to go to Congress for a national law. When I get there and demand it, they will tell me to go to hell."

PROGRESSIVISM MOVES TO THE NATIONAL LEVEL

When McKinley was reelected in 1900, few expected a national reform leader, and but for a quirk of fate they would have been right. As the 1900 Republican convention rolled around, party leaders realized they had a problem. Theodore Roosevelt had become a national hero in the wake of the Spanish-American War, but he had angered party regulars by supporting regulatory legislation as governor of New York. When they decided to "bury" Roosevelt in the vice presidency, presidential adviser and politician Mark Hanna warned, "Don't you realize that there's only one life between that madman and the White House?" On September 6, 1901, anarchist Leon Czolgosz shot McKinley. Eight days later that one life was gone, and Roosevelt was president. It was not immediately apparent, however, that he would usher in reform. Many remembered that during the Pullman strike Roosevelt had suggested shooting the strikers. Most therefore did not expect the action he took in the 1902 coal strike. That year, however, became the first in a decade and a half of snowballing reform that would result in a massive amount of legislation and four constitutional amendments by 1920.

Roosevelt and New Attitudes Toward Government Power

Roosevelt became the most forceful president since Abraham Lincoln, but few men have looked or sounded less presidential. He was short, nearsighted, beaver-toothed, and talked in a high-pitched voice. A frail, asthmatic child, he seemed intent on proving his manliness. His life became a robust adventure of sports, hunting, and camping. Once he took a foreign diplomat skinny-dipping in the Potomac. His exuberance, vitality, and wit captivated most Americans. They called him "Teddy" and named a stuffed bear after him. To understand him, an observer declared, one had to remember "the president is really only six years old." He was not a simple man, however. His hobbies included writing history books, and he displayed a keen intellect that he had honed at Harvard.

Born into an aristocratic Dutch family in New York, Roosevelt rejected a leisurely life for the rough and tumble world of politics, which his friends declared was an occupation for saloonkeepers and such. He replied that he "intended to be one of the governing class." His privileged background made him an unlikely candidate for a reformer, yet he ended up making reform both fun and respectable. He saw himself as a conservative but declared, "The only true conservative is the man who resolutely sets his face toward the future." The conservatives of his time, however, rejected his call for change and continued to insist on laissez-faire policies and limited government.

Roosevelt, on the other hand, shared two progressive sentiments. One was that government should be efficiently run by able, competent people. The other was that industrialization had created the need for expanded governmental action. "A simple and poor society," he observed, "can exist as a democracy on the basis of sheer individualism. But a rich and complex society cannot so exist." As a result of these two sentiments, Roosevelt reorganized and revitalized the executive branch, modernized the army command structure and the consular service, and pursued the federal regulation of the economy that characterized twentieth-century America.

Although he was later remembered more for his "trust-busting" and "Square Deal," Roosevelt considered conservation his greatest domestic accomplishment. It was the topic of his first presidential address. "We are prone to think of the resources of this country as inexhaustible, this is not so," he later warned Congress. Roosevelt used presidential power to add almost 150 million acres to national forests and to preserve valuable coal and water sites for national development. With his ally, Chief Forester Gifford Pinchot, he sponsored a National Conservation Congress in 1908. Roosevelt's actions won both praise and condemnation.

The conservation movement, then as well as later, divided into two camps. Naturalist John Muir and the Sierra Club (formed in 1892) wanted to preserve the scenic beauty and biological diversity of the West. Most businesspeople and Westerners wanted government action only to promote orderly economic exploitation of resources. In 1902 they supported the Newlands Reclamation Act, which began many years of federally sponsored irrigation and reclamation projects (for details of this and other federal legislation see Table 21.1). Furious, however, about the withdrawal from sale of so many acres of federal land, they led a move to limit presidential authority to do so. Western and business influences usually prevailed in such disputes. For the West a scarcity of water was the main ecological problem, and its solution was a regional priority. In 1913 the city of San Francisco won a dispute over a dam that had flooded one of the most beautiful areas of Yosemite National Park in order to solve the city's water shortage.

Some businesspeople already disliked Roosevelt for his conservation policies, but he aggravated others with two actions in 1902. The first was his handling of the coal strike, which served notice that the government could no longer be counted on to come automatically to the aid of management in labor disputes. The second was a suit against Northern Securities Company under the Sherman Antitrust Act. Roosevelt's trust-busting was an answer to progressive prayers. Antimonopoly was a strong component of progressivism. Most agreed with Louis Brandeis that "if the Lord had intended things to be big, he would have made men bigger—in brains and character." Antitrust action had not been undertaken on a large scale in the cities and states only because federal action seemed necessary.

Northern Securities, a highly unpopular combination of northwestern railroad systems engineered by such heavyweights as James J. Hill and J. P. Morgan, was a wise choice for action. Its unpopularity reflected the West's concern for railroad regulation. The suit infuriated Hill, who complained, "It seems hard that we should be compelled to fight for our lives against the political adventurers who have never done anything but pose and draw a salary." In 1904 the Supreme Court ordered the company's dissolution. That same year, in a case against the major meat packers, the Court also reversed the *E. C. Knight* ruling that exempted manufacturing from federal antitrust law.

The rulings pleased Roosevelt, who rejected the Court's earlier narrow, strict interpretations of the Constitution. Instead, he believed that the Constitution "must be interpreted not as a straight-jacket . . . but as an instrument designed for the life and healthy growth of the Nation." In his desire to expand federal power, he was once credited with asking "What's the Constitution between friends?" Yet Roosevelt was not a complete convert to trust-busting.

"This is an age of combination," he wrote, "and any effort to prevent all combination will be not only useless, but in the end vicious." At the same time he believed "of all the forms of tyranny the least attractive and the most vulgar is the tyranny of mere wealth." Thus he attacked trusts that abused their power and left alone trusts that acted responsibly.

Theodore Roosevelt is shown here campaigning in New Castle, Wyoming, as the Republican candidate in 1903.

He preferred to negotiate differences, and to do so he established in 1904 a Bureau of Corporations within the Department of Commerce and Labor, created the year before.

Campaigning on the promise to provide a "Square Deal" to all Americans, Roosevelt easily defeated Democratic candidate Alton B. Parker in the 1904 presidential election. Now elected in his own right, he launched into expanding the regulatory power of the federal government. His top priority, over the objections of conservative Republican senators, was to control effectively the railroads by expanding the power of the Interstate Commerce Commission (ICC). Although the Elkins Act, passed in 1903, had already eliminated rebates, Roosevelt wanted to go further and give the ICC the power to set rates. Through shrewd political maneuvering he got this with the Hepburn Act of 1906, although he had to give up his demand for limited court review of rate decisions.

The publication of Upton Sinclair's *The Jungle* in that same year caused a consumer uproar for regulation of the food and drug industries. A chemist in the Agriculture Department, Harvey W. Wiley had long been analyzing food products for chemical adulteration by testing additives on volunteers known as the "Poison Squad." His data were supplemented by an investigation of the meat-packing industry ordered by Roosevelt, which proved the truth of Sinclair's charges of filth and contamination. As a result, Congress passed the Pure Food and Drug Act and the Meat Inspection Act on the same day in 1906. By 1908 Roosevelt had left his indelible mark on the nation and decided not to run for re-election. He cast his support to William Howard Taft, who easily defeated William Jennings Bryan, the Democratic nominee and loser for the third time. Roosevelt then retired and went to hunt lions in Africa, a move that led J. P. Morgan to toast "Health to the Lions."

Taft and Quiet Progressivism

William Howard Taft brought to the presidency a distinguished record of public service. An Ohio lawyer, he had served as a federal judge, the first civil governor of the Philippines, and secretary of war. He did not, however, look presidential; he weighed more than 350 pounds, which led to rumors that a special bathtub was to be installed in the White House. Unlike his predecessor, he was far from charismatic and indeed quite shy. Legalistic and precise, he was neither a fiery writer nor speaker. In short, he was incapable of rallying public support for any cause, and reformers were especially skeptical about him. As a judge he had been called the "injunction standard bearer" by labor leaders. When soldiers shot into the crowd at the Haymarket riot, he confided, "they have only killed six as yet. This is hardly enough to make an impression."

Table 21.1
Progressive Era Legislation and Amendments

Year	Act	Provisions
1902	Newlands Reclamation	Set aside proceeds from the sale of federal land for irrigation and reclamation projects
1903	Elkins	Outlawed rebates to favored shippers; federal courts could issue injunctions to stop rate discrimination
1906	Pure Food and Drug	Made it a crime to sell adulterated foods or medicine; required correct labeling of the contents of certain substances
1906	Meat Inspection	Required governmental approval of sanitary conditions in meat-packing plants; prohibited use of dangerous chemicals or preservatives; government paid inspection costs
1906	Hepburn	Gave ICC the power to set railroad rates, subject to court review
1909	Payne-Aldrich Tariff	Raised most tariff rates, while reducing or eliminating the rates for very few products
1910	Mann-Elkins	Extended jurisdiction of the ICC to telephone and telegraph companies; gave ICC further power to suspend rate increases; rulings were still subject to court review
1910	Mann	Outlawed the transportation of women across state lines for "immoral purposes"
1913	Sixteenth Amendment	Gave Congress the right to impose an income tax
1913	Seventeenth Amendment	Provided for the direct election of senators by the people rather than by state legislatures
1913	Underwood-Simmons Tariff	Substantially reduced tariff rates; levied an income tax rising from 1 percent on incomes over $4000 to 4 percent on incomes over $10,000
1913	Federal Reserve	Reformed the banking and currency system; created 12 regional banks that were privately owned but responsible to the Federal Reserve Board, which was appointed by the president; the Board had the ability to regulate the amount of currency (federal reserve notes) through its transactions with the regional banks
1914	Federal Trade Commission	Created FTC, composed of 5 members, to oversee business transactions; could publicize infractions and issue cease and desist orders, which were subject to court review
1914	Clayton Antitrust	Outlawed unfair business practices that reduced competition; held company officials liable for actions; specifically exempted farm and labor groups from its provisions, limited the use of court injunctions against strikers
1914	Harrison Anti-Narcotic	Listed "controlled substances" that could only be sold with a doctor's prescription required manufacturers to keep records of the manufacture and sale of such substances
1916	Federal Farm Loan	Provided farmers with cheap credit through 12 farm loan boards
1916	Keating-Owen	Outlawed the sale of goods made by children from interstate commerce
1916	Adamson	Provided for an eight-hour workday for workers on interstate railroads
1916	Workman's Compensation	Established a workmen's compensation system for federal employees

Taft was indeed more conservative than Roosevelt, especially in his view of governmental power. "The lesson must be learned," he argued, "that there is only a limited zone within which legislation and governments can accomplish good." Further, he declared, "We can, by passing laws which cannot be enforced, destroy that respect for laws . . . which has been the strength of people of English descent everywhere." On the other hand, his respect for the law extended to the Sherman act. "We are going to enforce that law or die in the attempt," he promised, and his administration prosecuted far more cases than Roosevelt's had.

In his own quiet way Taft was as sympathetic to reform as Roosevelt. He supported the eight-hour workday and favored legislation to improve mine safety. He also urged passage of the Mann-Elkins Act of 1910 to increase the power of the ICC. The Six-

Without federal regulation, meat packers exploited workers and allowed rats and other contaminants to be processed with meat in making sausages.

teenth and Seventeenth amendments were initiated under his presidency. Purity crusaders also won a victory in 1910 with the passage of the Mann Act against prostitution.

Nevertheless, Taft was not forceful enough to effectively overcome the growing divisions within the Republican party. The conservatives, led by powerful Senator Nelson W. Aldrich of Rhode Island, were determined to draw the line against further reform. At the same time, progressive Republicans such as Robert La Follette of Wisconsin and George Norris of Nebraska were growing rebellious. Conflict came on several fronts. One was the tariff. In his campaign Taft had promised a lower tariff, but in the end he accepted the much compromised Payne-Aldrich Tariff. While placing many nonessential items on the duty-free list, it actually raised some key duties. It disappointed reformers immensely. Listing such duty-free items as silkworm eggs, canary birdseed, hog bristle, leeches, and skeletons, the political humorist Finley Peter Dunne had his fictional bartender, Mr. Dooley, proclaim, "The new tariff puts these familyer commodyties within the reach iv all." Taft had suffered a defeat but foolishly did not admit it. He called the tariff the "best" ever passed. In reality he backed down on his pledges because he believed the president should not interfere unduly with the legislative branch. And he simply had an accommodating personality. One Republican griped, "The trouble with Taft is that if he were Pope he would think it necessary to appoint a few Protestant Cardinals."

Caught in the middle of several conflicts, Taft eventually alienated the progressive wing of his party as well as Teddy Roosevelt. He first supported and then abandoned party insurgents who challenged the power of conservative Speaker of the House "Uncle Joe" Cannon of Illinois. Later, when Gifford Pinchot protested a sale of public lands by

Groomed for the presidency by his predecessor and easily elected to the office in 1908, William Howard Taft found his presidential duties onerous. Here, he participates in an activity he found far more enjoyable.

Robert La Follette in Cumberland, Wisconsin, in 1897. La Follette, known for progressive reforms as governor of and U.S. senator from Wisconsin, was on the progressive side of the split in the Republican party between progressives rebelling against Taft and conservatives opposing further reforms.

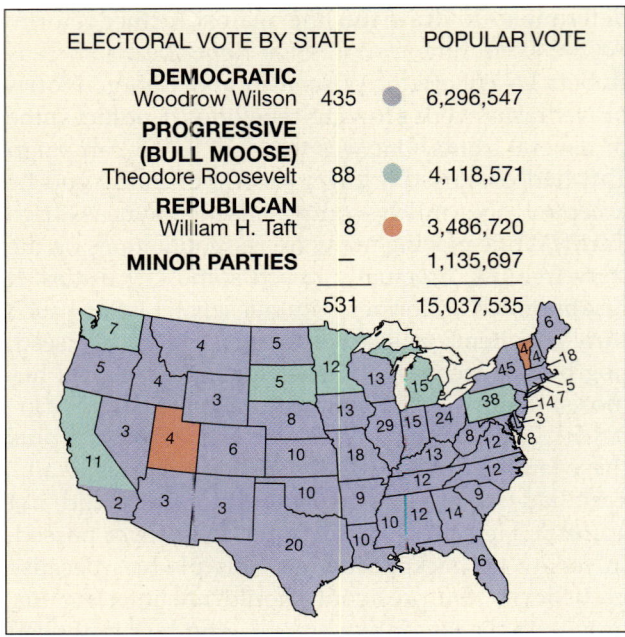

Election of 1912
Woodrow Wilson did not receive a majority of the popular vote, but the split in the Republican party gave him the majority of the votes in the electoral college.

Secretary of the Interior Richard A. Ballinger, Taft fired Pinchot from his position as chief of the Forest Service, which infuriated both conservationists and Roosevelt. The latter was also irritated by Taft's antitrust prosecutions. He believed that a case had been pursued against U.S. Steel to embarrass him: The investigation exposed a deal Roosevelt had made with J. P. Morgan in 1907 in return for the banker's aid in stemming a financial panic.

By 1912 progressive Republicans were ready to bolt the party if Taft were renominated, and Roosevelt declared his intention to run. The fight for the nomination became bitter. Taft called Roosevelt's supporters "political emotionalists or neurotics." Roosevelt labeled Taft's people as "men of cold heart and narrow mind, who believe we can find safety in dull timidity and dull inaction." As president, Taft was able to control the convention. The defeated Roosevelt walked out with his supporters and formed a third party, known as the **Progressive or Bull Moose party**.

Many leading reformers attended the Progressive convention, which often resembled a religious revival, with hymn singing and marches. Its platform endorsed such wide-ranging reforms as abolition of child labor; federal old-age, accident, and unemployment insurance programs; an eight-hour workday; and women's suffrage. At Roosevelt's request, however, a plank supporting equality for African Americans was deleted. Calling the major parties "husks with no real soul," he accepted the third party's nomination.

With the Republicans divided, Democratic chances of recapturing the White House increased. A former Republican senator lamented that his party's only unanswered question was "Which corpse gets the most flowers?" The scent of victory led to a hard fight for the Democratic nomination, which New Jersey's progressive governor, Woodrow Wilson, won on the forty-sixth ballot. The Socialist party nominated Eugene V. Debs, making it a four-way race.

As soon became apparent, the real battle was between Wilson and Roosevelt. It was marked by an unusually high level of debate over the proper role of government in a modern, industrialized society. Wilson declared, "What this country needs above everything else is a body of laws which will look after the men who are on the make rather than the men who are already made." Labeling his program "New Freedom," his aim was the restoration of competition and his tool was to be trustbusting.

Roosevelt, on the other hand, believed that big business was not necessarily bad, but he proclaimed, "Somehow or other we shall have to work out methods of controlling the big corporations without paralyzing the energies of the business community." His answer was "New Nationalism"—the expansion of federal regulatory activities to control rather than dismantle the trusts. Big government would offset the power of big business. Their rhetoric differed sharply, but in their presidencies both Roosevelt and Wilson practiced a little of both "New Nationalism" and "New Freedom."

The split in the Republican party enabled the Democrats to capture not only the White House but also the Senate. Democrats also consolidated their control of the House, so Wilson entered the presidency with his party solidly in power. Nevertheless, Wilson did not receive a majority of the popular vote. He got 6.3 million votes, Roosevelt 4.1 million, Taft 3.5 million, and Debs nearly 1 million. In the electoral college, however, Wilson won an impressive 435 votes to Roosevelt's 88 and a mere 8 for Taft.

Wilson and Moral Progressivism

As the third progressive-era president, Woodrow Wilson differed from his predecessors in both appearance and leadership style. He looked very much like the moralistic professor he was. The son and grandson of Presbyterian ministers, Wilson was raised in the South and practiced law in Atlanta before receiving his doctorate from Johns Hopkins University in Baltimore. His book *Congressional Government* was published in 1895, and he became

A distinguished professor, Woodrow Wilson brought both competence and a grim moral determination to the presidency.

president of Princeton University in 1902 before being elected governor of New Jersey. His religion was an important factor in his personality. "My life would not be worth living," he declared, "if it were not for the driving power of religion."

Wilson was not the kind of man whom people named stuffed animals after or gave nicknames. His self-righteousness was not endearing. One politician noted that when Wilson "said something to me . . . I didn't know whether God or him was talking." Although much less charismatic, Wilson did resemble Roosevelt in being a better speaker than Taft and in his view of the role of the president. Roosevelt had called the presidency a "bully pulpit," and Wilson agreed that the president should be the "political leader of the nation" because "his is the only national voice in politics." Unlike Taft, he argued that the president must be "as much concerned with the guidance of legislation as with the just and orderly execution of the laws."

Wilson's activism coincided with growing demands for further reform. Investigations and amendments launched earlier came to fruition during his presidency. The result was an outpouring of legislation. In 1913, his first year in office, the Sixteenth Amendment was ratified, allowing the imposition of a federal income tax. It appeared as a provision of the Underwood Tariff, which was passed in a special session of Congress that year. Wilson called the session to redeem a campaign pledge to lower duties as part of the New Freedom goal of restoring competition. During the tariff hearings, lobbyists were so plentiful that Wilson complained, "a brick wouldn't be thrown without hitting one of them." This time, however, they did not all prevail. Congress significantly lowered duties for the first time since the Civil War. To recoup lost revenues, a graduated tax of from 1 to 6 percent was placed on personal incomes of $3000 and over.

Congress passed banking reform the same year. Following the panic of 1907, congressional investigations were launched into its causes. Everyone, including bankers, had come to believe the nation's banking system needed to be stabilized by governmental action. The question was *how* to do it. Wall Street wanted a centralized system owned and controlled by bankers. Others wanted a more decentralized system owned or controlled by the government. The Federal Reserve Act of 1913 was a compromise. It established the **Federal Reserve System** of 12 regional banks owned by bankers but under the control of a presidentially appointed Federal Reserve Board.

Prohibitionists won their first national victory with the Webb-Kenyon Act of 1913, which increased the power of states to enforce their own prohibition laws. The next year those concerned with the large amounts of narcotics in patent medicines rejoiced over the passage of the Harrison Anti-Narcotic Act. It required a doctor's prescription for the sale of any drug on a list of controlled substances. In 1914 Congress took action to deal with monopolies and to regulate business. In September it established the Federal Trade Commission to replace the Bureau of Corporations. The five-person body was charged with investigating alleged violations of antitrust law and could issue cease and desist orders against corporations found guilty of unfair trade practices. The next month the Clayton Antitrust Act sought to close some of the loopholes of the Sherman act and limit court actions against labor unions.

At that point Wilson believed he had accomplished his agenda. He was not a supporter of further labor legislation or farm-credit plans. A firm opponent of paternalism, he said, "The old adage that God takes care of those who take care of themselves is not gone out of date. No federal legislation can change that thing. The minute you are taken care of by the government you are wards, not independent men." As the election of 1916 approached, however, progressives reminded Wilson of the importance of the farm and labor vote. Legislation to win those votes soon followed. Farmers were given the Federal Farm Loan Act and federal supplemental funding for agricultural specialists in each county; labor leaders got the Keating-Owen Child Labor Act; railroad workers got the Adamson Act to limit their work hours; and federal employees got the Workman's Compensation Act. Progressives were also pleased by Wilson's appointment of Louis Brandeis to the Supreme Court. All of these actions helped ensure Wilson's victory over the Republican nominee Charles Evans Hughes in 1916.

PROGRESSIVISM IN THE INTERNATIONAL ARENA

Many progressives did not believe that progress was limited by national boundaries. In their eyes, human beings had the capacity to create a more just and orderly society both at home and abroad. The progressive spirit was optimistic, and progressive victories on the home front expanded Americans' confidence in their ability to solve problems—even on the international level. This confidence was further bolstered by the nation's economic growth and victory in the Spanish-American War.

Everyone agreed that by 1900, America's status in the world had changed. How to respond to those changes was the question. Just as people differed over what alterations, if any, were required in domestic policies, various visions of a new American foreign policy also emerged. For some, progressivism simply redefined and reinvigorated the old ideas of manifest destiny. The United States would solve its problems at home and then remake the world in its own image. Such a new world order would also open up new markets for America's industrial and agricultural surpluses. Other progressives believed that democratic principles required that all people, even foreigners, be free to determine their own destinies. Order and justice were two progressive goals that sometimes conflicted, and that conflict was also apparent in the international arena.

Big Stick Diplomacy

Theodore Roosevelt's foreign policy reflected the same vigor he displayed in everything else he did. His "macho" foreign policy emerged from his belief that a man's mission was to "work, fight, and breed." He believed progress and order could benefit the world as well as the nation. He also asserted that Congress was "not well fitted for the shaping of foreign policy" and expanded presidential power in the conduct of diplomacy. It was his destiny to deal with the legacies of increased power and influence from the Spanish-American War. Order having been restored in Cuba and the Philippines by 1903, Roosevelt launched the United States into the role of policeman. His doctrine was to "speak softly and carry a big stick," but he really only lived up to the second half of the slogan.

Possession of the Philippines caused concern over turbulent Asian politics. Most alarming was the emergence of Japan as a power after its unexpected victories in the Russo-Japanese War (1904–1905). Often playing the role of arbiter at home, Roosevelt now shifted his arena and mediated an end to the war at a Portsmouth, New Hampshire, conference in August 1905—an action that won him a Nobel Peace Prize. Japan remained a formidable rival, however, and agreements were later reached to respect each other's Asian interests. In the Pacific, Roosevelt displayed his "big stick" by sending a fleet of 16 battleships, called the "Great White Fleet," on a 1907 to 1909 around-the-world tour with conspicuous stops in the Pacific, including Japan. His intent was to intimidate the Japanese, but he failed to halt their growing power.

Within the Western Hemisphere, Roosevelt was even less reluctant to threaten or use force. In 1906 he responded to Cuban demonstrations against the Platt Amendment and insurrection by sending in marines, who stayed until 1909. "I am doing my best," he declared, "to persuade the Cubans that if only they will be good, they will be happy. I am seeking the very minimum of interference necessary to make them good." The marines could be very persuasive.

Progress and strategic considerations also demanded that a canal in Central America link the Atlantic and Pacific oceans. Roosevelt was determined to make it happen. There were two possible routes: one through Nicaragua and one across the Panamanian isthmus, which belonged to Colombia. A French company had made a start in Panama, but it ran out of funds and was reorganized as the New Panama Canal Company. The new company's major asset was its concession from Colombia that extended to 1904.

Three commissions appointed to determine the route recommended Nicaragua, primarily because the New Panama Canal Company demanded $190 million for its rights, property, and previous work. The company's stockholders, however, were mainly Americans and frantic to convince Congress to choose the Panamanian route. They dropped their demand to $40 million, contributed profusely to campaign funds, and hired a full-time lobbyist—Philippe Bunau-Varilla, the French

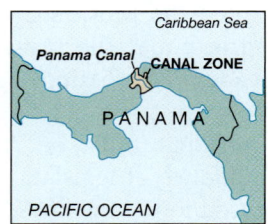

Panama Canal
The Panama Canal provided a strategic shipping and military link between the Atlantic and the Pacific oceans.

chief engineer of the original company. In June 1902, Congress authorized efforts to secure the rights to a Panamanian canal. The Hay-Herrán Treaty provided the United States with rights to a 6-mile-wide zone in return for a $10 million payment to Colombia and an annual rental fee of $250,000. As in America, ratification required the consent of the Colombian senate, which in August 1903 rejected the treaty unanimously. Its motive was probably to delay the treaty until 1904, when the New Panama Canal Company's concession expired and Colombia might receive some of the $40 million originally earmarked for the company.

Roosevelt was furious. "The blackmailers of Bogota," he roared, should not be allowed "permanently to bar one of the future highways of civilization." He drafted a message to Congress proposing to take the canal zone by force but never delivered it. A different solution was found, Bunau-Varilla engineered a Panamanian revolution by providing people with a national constitution, flag, and anthem as well as assurances that the United States would not let their revolt fail. He was right. Most Colombian troops were prevented from even getting to the so-called revolution by the USS *Nashville*. Three days after its start, Roosevelt recognized the independence of the Republic of Panama. U.S. Secretary of State John Hay and the French citizen Bunau-Varilla, who had demanded to be made ambassador to the United States, then quickly drafted the Hay–Bunau-Varilla Treaty with essentially the same terms as the Hay-Herrán Treaty—only now the payment went to the rebels, not Colombia.

American actions enraged people all over the world. At first Roosevelt denied any part in the revolution, but he eventually admitted, "I took the Canal Zone and let Congress debate; and while the debate goes on the Canal does also." In 1914, the canal, a monument to both progress and Yankee imperialism, was completed. It was a big investment, one that required protection from foreign military vessels.

At the same time, Latin American countries sometimes fell behind in debt payments to such European powers as Britain and Germany. As a result those two nations blockaded Venezuela in 1902 to 1903. A year later, Roosevelt announced that the United States would assume the responsibility of seeing that the nations of the Caribbean behaved themselves and paid their debts. European intervention, therefore, would not be necessary. Known as the Roosevelt Corollary to the Monroe Doctrine, this policy justified U.S. intervention in such places as the Dominican Republic, Nicaragua, and Haiti. Roosevelt's **"big stick" diplomacy** established America as the "police of the Western Hemisphere"—a role that would last long into the twentieth century.

Dollar Diplomacy

Before becoming president, William Howard Taft had served as governor-general in the Philippines and as Roosevelt's troubleshooter in Cuba. These experiences had convinced Taft of two principles. The first was the need for order and stability; the second was the limited capacity of armed force for solving problems. He also realized that the United States had a new source of power—its economic clout. From 1898 to 1909, American overseas investments had risen from about $800 million to more than $2.5 billion.

Called "dollar diplomacy," Taft's approach was to use dollars instead of bullets to ensure stability and order. He wanted American capital to replace European capital in Latin America in order to increase U.S. influence there. When British bondholders wanted to collect their debts from Honduras in 1909, Taft asked American financiers to assume the debt. In 1910 he convinced New York bankers to take over the assets of the National Bank of Haiti. When needed, however, Taft also wielded a big stick. He refused to recognize a revolution in Nicaragua until the leaders agreed to accept American credits to pay off British debts and sent marines to punctuate his point.

Missionary Diplomacy

As in domestic policies, Woodrow Wilson's foreign policy differed more in style than substance from his predecessors. Wilson's moralism did not stop at national boundaries. Indeed his sermonistic foreign policy has sometimes been called "missionary diplomacy." His gospel was American-style democracy. "When properly directed," he declared, "there is no people not fitted for self-government." That direction was to come from the United States. He spoke of "releasing the intelligence of America for the service of mankind" and proclaimed "every nation needs to be drawn into the tutelage of America."

The rhetoric was different from his predecessors, but the results were the same. Renouncing both big stick and dollar diplomacy, Wilson nevertheless used similar measures to maintain stability and order in the Caribbean. He sent marines to the Dominican Republic and Haiti and kept them in Nicaragua. His interventionism ran into more trouble in Mexico, where the overthrow of long-time dictator Porfirio Díaz in 1911 began a cycle of revolution.

General Porfirio Díaz ruled Mexico with an iron hand from the early 1870s to 1910. As dictator, he brought order to his nation and opened Mexico to foreign investors. Under his protective hand a flood of foreign businesspeople rushed in to tap Mexico's rich mineral wealth, build railroads, and exploit the

American Interventions in the Caribbean
Early in the twentieth century, the United States took it upon itself to police the Western Hemisphere and often took action when it judged Latin American countries were not running their affairs properly.

agricultural sector of its economy. On the eve of World War I, Americans valued their holdings in Mexico at $1 billion. Yet only a handful of wealthy Mexicans benefited from their nation's economic development. The political stability Díaz brought to Mexico came at the expense of individual liberties. He crushed political opposition and turned a deaf ear to pleas for land reform.

In 1910, his opponents revolted and to the world's amazement Díaz proved to be a paper tiger. Unable to extinguish a series of small revolts that sprang up across Mexico, he fled the country. Mexico's new leader was Francisco I. Madero, an idealist who championed the middle class's aspirations for democracy and the peasant class's demands for land reform. Madero had hardly settled into the presidency before new revolts broke out, plunging Mexico into chaos. On February 22, 1913, less than two weeks before William Howard Taft's term as president ended, Madero and his vice president were assassinated by federal troops under the command of General Victoriano Huerta, who immediately proclaimed himself Mexico's new ruler. Despite the urgent recommendations of his ambassador to Mexico, President Taft did not extend diplomatic recognition to Huerta's government, leaving the issue to be resolved by Wilson.

President Wilson refused to recognize Huerta's government, calling it a "government of butchers." Wilson regarded Mexico's new strong man as a murderer and a usurper, a ruler who symbolized all that was wrong with Latin American governments. Wilson believed that diplomatic recognition implied moral approval and could never sanction a government that had seized power by substituting bullets for ballots. He wrote one diplomat, "The United States intends not merely to force Huerta from power but to exert every influence it can to secure Mexico a better government under which all contracts and business concessions will be safer than they have ever been." Americans considered protection of contracts and concessions very important—American businesses controlled 75 percent of Mexico's mines, 60 percent of its oil, and 70 percent of its rubber.

Huerta's claims to power were shaky. Following Madero's assassination, several political factions in Mexico revolted against Huerta. Emiliano Zapata led an army against federal troops in Morelos, a mountainous state in southern Mexico. In the north, Venustiano Carranza, the governor of Coahuila, declared himself the first chief of the Constitutionalist forces and won the allegiance of several powerful regional leaders, including Pancho Villa, Alvaro Obregón, and Pablo González.

Because Huerta was not able to defeat his opponents in battle, his claim to controlling Mexico was suspect; and his apparent weakness only strengthened President Wilson's decision to withhold diplomatic recognition. American policy was designed to aid Huerta's opponents, particularly Carranza, who appealed strongly to Wilson as a tool for restoring democracy to Mexico. As Wilson confided to a British diplomat, "I am going to teach the South American republics to elect good men."

However noble his ambition, Wilson allowed his animus against Huerta to trigger an American invasion of Mexico. In April 1914, Mexican officials arrested several American sailors in Tampico, a seaport on Mexico's east coast; detained a mail courier; and delayed an official Department of State dispatch. Wilson used these minor incidents to precipitate a showdown with Huerta's government—less than two weeks later American troops invaded the port city of Veracruz. At least 200 Mexicans died in the fighting that followed and another 300 were wounded, most of them noncombatant civilians. American troops remained in Veracruz for six months.

None of Mexico's warring factions approved the invasion and subsequent occupation of Veracruz. In fact, no issue has produced more bitterness in Mexico against the United States—not even the Mexican-American War. To Mexicans their defeat in the 1840s inflicted a serious wound to their national pride, but they saw the war as a lesson in power politics. Manifest destiny was a harsh policy, but Mexicans could understand the motives from which it sprang. Americans wanted American land, and they took it. What made the invasion of Veracruz so galling was that President Wilson clothed American aggression, in the words of one historian, "with the sanctimonious raiment of idealism." Because he insisted his acts were moral, Wilson "aroused both the hatred and the scorn of the Mexicans—hatred over the invasion but a deep scorn for what they saw as his hypocrisy."

In one sense, Wilson got what he wanted in Mexico. Huerta's government collapsed in 1915, and Carranza became the new president. In the larger sense, however, the United States was the big loser. Mexicans deeply resented Wilson's arrogant assumption that he had the right to intervene in their internal affairs. Even after Huerta was overthrown, civil war continued between Carranza's government forces and rebels led by Pancho Villa. In an attempt to draw America into the fracas, Villa launched a raid into New Mexico in March 1916. The tactic worked. Wilson sent an expedition led by General John Pershing to capture Villa. American troops failed to find him, but soon were 300 miles deep into Mexican territory by January 1917 and on the brink of war with Carranza's government. By then, however, America was being drawn into World War I, and Wilson decided to withdraw the troops. Although Wilson eventually got the kind of government he wanted for Mexico, Mexicans continued to believe that their government was their business and deeply resented the American intervention.

American involvement in World War I diverted attention from more than Mexico. Domestic reform took a back seat to "making the world safe for democracy." Yet war always brings changes on the home front. The nation shifted gears, but progressivism did not entirely die. Indeed prohibitionists, woman suffragists, and immigration restrictionists won their greatest victories in the wake of war.

PROGRESSIVE ACCOMPLISHMENTS, PROGRESSIVE FAILURES

The twentieth century began with great optimism about the power of human beings to shape their destinies. Progress, people believed, could be legislated. Efficient, noncorrupt government could provide order and stability, promote social justice, and improve personal morals. Groups organized to promote their goals, and more and more of them began to win their objectives. In the 1920s, however, some began to realize that legislation had not always had its desired effect, that not everyone had benefited equally, and that change had been far from radical.

The Impact of Legislation

Measured by direct results most progressive reforms proved disappointing. In some cases unintended consequences actually worked against the intended goals of laws. This often occurs when ideals confront reality. Solving one problem frequently creates another. Nevertheless, progressives established important precedents that opened doors to later, more effective reform.

Attempts to promote direct democracy were among the least effective. Direct election of senators did not seem to alter the kinds of people elected. Initiative, referendum, and recall were rarely used, and then not by people in general. The expense and organization needed for petition drives were beyond the reach of any but well-financed pressure groups. An unintended result of democratization was to increase the power of urban machines. Bosses may have had to work a little harder, but most were still able to dominate primaries as well as elections. The move toward popular voting increased the political power of populous cities and the machines that controlled them. The greatest failing of the movement was a dramatic drop in voter participation. Nevertheless, in some states, such as Wisconsin, government did become more responsive to public needs, and urban machines often adopted reform measures to maintain power.

Other kinds of urban reforms had varying results. In some, government did indeed become more efficiently and economically run. The competency and honesty of officials generally increased. An occasional consequence, however, was decreased social services in less affluent neighborhoods. This was more likely to happen where the commissioner-manager system was adopted—usually in midsize cities without a tradition of machine politics. In other cities municipally owned utilities lowered rates, providing some real relief for the poor.

Attempts to regulate the railroads on either the state or national level rarely produced dramatic benefits for the general public. The chief advocates and beneficiaries of railroad regulation were frequently large shipping interests that did not share lower costs with consumers. With the Hepburn Act, Roosevelt did accomplish his primary goal of giving the ICC the power to set rates. The provision allowing court review of its decisions, however, made the act more significant as a precedent for expanded governmental power than as an immediate solution to problems. The courts ruled in favor of the railroads in most rate disputes.

Antimonopoly actions also did not always produce the intended results. For example, the breakups of Standard Oil and the American Tobacco Company did not increase competition or lower prices. Perhaps the only legislation to fulfill the promise of New Freedom was the Underwood Tariff, and it was reversed by the tariff legislation of the 1920s. The Clayton Antitrust Act was widely, and correctly, considered too vague for effective enforcement. The general counsel of the American Anti-Boycott Association analyzed the provision to exempt labor organizations from antitrust legislation; he declared that the law "makes few changes in existing law as relating to labor unions, injunctions and contempts of court, and those are of slight practical importance." Later court decisions proved his assessment accurate.

The Federal Trade Commission (FTC) did not become an aggressive watchdog either. One of Wilson's cabinet members reported that the president viewed it as "a counsellor and friend to the business world," rather than as a "policeman to wield a club over the head of the business community." His appointments were fairly probusiness, and appointments made in the 1920s were even more so. In the end, the FTC proved beneficial to big business by protecting firms from unexpected suits and by outlawing some "unfair trade practices," many of which had promoted competition at the expense of stability. On the other hand, the FTC was also an important precedent for the regulation of business.

Proclaimed victories for labor frequently turned out to be more symbolic than real. In the arbitration of the 1902 coal strike, for example, what the United Mine Workers did not receive is very significant: The union did not win recognition. As the 1920s would show, organized labor did not emerge from the progressive era any stronger. Yet symbolism can be important. The precedent that the government would not automatically support the demands of management was later built upon during the New Deal of the 1930s.

Some labor legislation did bring benefits but also produced unintended results. Child labor laws in combination with compulsory education legislation decreased the number of children from ages 10 to 15 who were working for wages, from 1 in 5 in 1900 to 1 in 20 by 1930. During those same years, the number of students enrolled in secondary education increased by 800 percent. Both were desirable results, but in the short run at least, it was a mixed blessing for the poor. The incomes of a family's children were often crucial to its welfare, and no alternatives were provided. As one historian noted, "Child labor laws treated the symptoms and made the disease—poverty—worse." Much the same can be said about limits imposed on women's working hours. Laws establishing minimum wages for women helped somewhat to offset earning losses resulting from child labor legislation. In any event, laws such as the Child Labor Act were declared unconstitutional in the 1920s.

Workmen's compensation laws were an improvement over existing procedures but were not an unqualified victory of labor over management. Indeed, businesspeople eventually welcomed the relief from the growing number of suits instituted by hungry lawyers on a contingency-fee basis. By agreeing to take a percentage of any damage awards and to charge no fee for lost cases, attorneys made it possible for poor workers to take legal action. The award schedule in most compensation plans provided payments far below what some lawyers had been winning in court. Workers, however, were guaranteed at least some compensation. For the industrialists, a predictable premium replaced the uncertainty of court actions, decreasing risks and increasing stability in the cost of doing business.

The establishment of the Federal Reserve System also enhanced order and stability. Everyone benefited from the maintenance of cash reserves for emergencies, a more flexible currency, and national check-clearing facilities. The banking system became more resistant to panics but, as 1929 would prove, not immune to them. Wall Street was not a big loser here. Three of the five seats on the Federal Reserve Board went to large bankers, and the New York Federal Reserve bank quickly came to dominate the system. The new system, in other words, was a significant improvement, but far from a radical change.

From the consumer's point of view, the Pure Food and Drug Act and the Meat Inspection Act were great victories. After the advent of mass production and mass marketing, only federal action could provide adequate protection from adulteration of the nation's foodstuffs. Unintended beneficiaries, however, were the large drug and meat-packing companies, which could more easily afford the increased expenses of meeting required production standards. The effect was thus anticompetitive. Lobbying by the big meat packers also affected the final form of the legislation. Their victories included government payment of inspection costs and the deletion of the requirement to date canned meat. Like much progressive legislation, the final act did provide protection for consumers, but in a way agreeable to big business. Swift, one of the largest meat packers, even endorsed its passage in an advertisement declaring, "It is a wise law."

Other progressive legislation left mixed legacies. Roosevelt's conservation measures prevented wanton squandering of resources but also aided the larger lumber companies. Morality legislation made undesirable activities illegal but at the same time more profitable for organized crime. It also fostered widespread disrespect for the law. With a maximum rate of 6 percent, the income tax did little to redistribute the huge fortunes of such men as J. P. Morgan but did establish an important tool for later use. A significant precedent was set by the Adamson Act, through which the federal government first dabbled in wage and hour legislation. Many other progressive reforms were illusory or short-lived. In the 1920s, lax enforcement and hostile court decisions reversed many of them. Nevertheless, laissez-faire had suffered an irreversible blow. That was a major accomplishment and perhaps as much as many progressives wanted.

Winners and Losers

Before the era ended, people from almost every class and occupation had sought to take advantage of the climate of change to promote their interests. Obviously not all were equally successful. Few were unqualified winners or losers, but some gained far more than others, and some lost more than they gained. Clearly, large corporations were among the biggest winners. One historian labeled the movement "the triumph of conservatism." Given the basic moderation of all three presidents and most congressmen, as well as the resources and influence of big business, this may have been inevitable. It was not, however, the original intention of all legislation. To label most progressives as conservative is a gross mistake. They rejected the strict laissez-faire principles of nineteenth-century conservatives and embraced a vision of a more activist government.

Other winners included members of the growing body of middle-class technocrats. At all levels of government the search for orderly, efficient management created new job opportunities for engineers, health professionals, trained managers, and other experts. Reforms that diminished the influence of political parties also increased the power of special-interest groups working for particular social and economic goals. Consumers of all classes shared benefits from government regulation.

Theodore Roosevelt gave the appearance of supporting African Americans when he invited Booker T. Washington to the White House, but like many white leaders, he did not promote equality between blacks and whites.

Chronology of Key Events

1879 Henry George's *Progress and Poverty* proposes a tax on land as a means of controlling illegitimate profits

1888 Edward Bellamy's *Looking Backward* depicts a utopian society guided by cooperation rather than competition

1889 Jane Addams founds Hull House

1901 President William McKinley is assassinated; Theodore Roosevelt becomes the twenty-sixth president

1902 Oregon, South Dakota, and Utah become first states to adopt initiative and recall; Roosevelt threatens to use troops to run coal mines when owners refuse to negotiate; Roosevelt charges Northern Securities with violating the Sherman Antitrust Act, and in 1904, the U.S. Supreme Court orders the company's breakup

1903 In *The Souls of Black Folks,* W.E.B. DuBois attacks Booker T. Washington for abandoning the goal of equal rights; Wisconsin becomes the first state to adopt primary elections; Elkins Act bars railroad rebates

1904 Lincoln Steffens's *Shame of the Cities* exposes corruption in city government; United States obtains right to build the Panama Canal; announcement of Roosevelt Corollary to the Monroe Doctrine, asserting the right of the United States to exercise international police power in the Caribbean

1905 Roosevelt helps negotiate an end to a war between Russia and Japan, and wins a Nobel Peace Prize for his efforts

1906 Upton Sinclair's *The Jungle* exposes unsanitary conditions in the meat-packing industry; Meat Inspection Act enforces health and sanitary standards in meat-packing industry; Pure Food and Drug Act prohibits the use of harmful additives and misleading advertisements of drugs; Hepburn Act gives the Interstate Commerce Commission the right to set maximum freight rates

1907 Roosevelt dispatches 16 battleships (the Great White Fleet) on an around-the-world cruise

1908 Staunton, Virginia, hires the first city manager

1909 National Association for the Advancement of Colored People (NAACP) is founded to protect the rights of black Americans

1910 Mann-Elkins Act allows Interstate Commerce Commission to regulate railroad rates even without complaints from shippers

1912–1917 12 states adopt minimum wage laws for women; 30 states adopt workmen's compensation insurance (industrial accident insurance)

1912 Roosevelt and his supporters launch the Progressive ("Bull Moose") party; Democrat Woodrow Wilson is elected the twenty-eighth president

1913 Sixteenth Amendment gives Congress the power to levy an income tax; Underwood-Simmons Tariff substantially lowers duties on imports and imposes a graduated income tax; Seventeenth Amendment requires direct election of senators; Federal Reserve System is created to supervise banking system and regulate money supply

1914 Federal Trade Commission is established to preserve economic competition by preventing unfair business practices; Clayton Antitrust Act prohibits interlocking corporate directorates and predatory pricing policies; U.S. Navy captures Mexican port of Veracruz

1915 U.S. marines are dispatched to Haiti

1916 U.S. troops enter Mexico to search for Pancho Villa; U.S. marines are sent to Dominican Republic

1919 Eighteenth Amendment prohibits manufacture and sale of liquor

1920 Nineteenth Amendment grants women the right to vote

In general most of the winners were white, urban, Protestant, and middle class. This was true even though working-class ethnic groups won victories in some cities and states. They and small businesspeople were among those who both lost and gained. African Americans came closest to being unqualified losers. For them, the only lasting advances came from establishing organizations. The NAACP survived to become an important force later in the century, and self-help organizations provided aid to many. Other victories were mainly token; the defeats were concrete.

In the South, and often in the North as well, African Americans were clearly losers on the local level. At the same time black relations with the federal government also deteriorated. Of the three presidents, Roosevelt was the most sympathetic. In 1901, he invited Booker T. Washington to dine at the White House, consulted with him on some southern appointments, and named a few African Americans to federal positions. His actions hardly reflected an acceptance of black equality, however. He believed, "as a race and in the mass they are altogether inferior to whites." One of his speeches to Congress seemed to condone lynching. Most disturbing to African Americans was his handling of an incident in Brownsville, Texas, in 1906. There, white townspeople and black soldiers met in a shoot-out. No one could determine exactly what had happened, but that did not deter Roosevelt from ordering dishonorable discharges for 167 black soldiers without court-martial.

When Taft became president, he approved of southern disfranchisement and appointed white-supremacist Republicans to federal jobs. These actions by the two Republicans convinced some African Americans, including W. E. B. Du Bois, to support Wilson in 1912. That was a mistake. The influence of Wilson's southern upbringing and advisers became apparent when he allowed his cabinet to segregate federal employees and to demote black officeholders, especially those "who boss white girls." Jim Crow moved to Washington, and Wilson's defense of these actions indicated the blindness and paternalism of many white progressives on race:

> It is true that the segregation of the colored employees in the several departments was begun upon the initiative and at the suggestion of the heads of departments, but as much in the interest of the negroes as for any other reason, with the approval of some of the most influential negroes I know, and with the idea that the friction, or rather the discontent and uneasiness, which had prevailed in many departments would thereby be removed. It is as far as possible from being a movement against the negroes. I believe it to be in their interest.

It seems that white progressives often seemed to feel they knew the best interests of those not like them, at home and abroad.

CONCLUSION

At the start of the new century, Americans confronted the urban squalor, poverty, powerful monopolies, corrupt and inefficient government, disorder, and despair that had accompanied rapid industrialization and urbanization. They were determined to do something to achieve more social justice and stability. Numerous solutions were proposed and victories won. In the end, however, Americans rejected radicalism and ignored major problems.

Once again the nation resolutely refused to come to terms with its ethnic and cultural diversity. Rather than protect minorities, most actions infringed on their personal liberties and sought to control rather than accommodate their differences. Women won some victories, but the majority of Americans did not accept the radical feminists' vision of true equality. Socialists' dreams of a peaceful, democratic redistribution of the country's wealth fell on deaf ears. In the end, there was no significant change in the distribution of either wealth or power. The United States had weeded and tidied up its social garden, not replanted it. Although that garden produced bitter fruit for some people, many Americans benefited. Also, the vigor and diversity of progressive actions brought to light many problems and provided later generations with a body of experience in dealing with them.

SUGGESTIONS FOR FURTHER READING

John Whiteclay Chambers, *The Tyranny of Change: America in the Progressive Era, 1890–1920,* 2nd ed. (1992). Offers a thorough and up-to-date history of Progressivism.

John Milton Cooper, *The Warrior and the Priest: Woodrow Wilson and Theodore Roosevelt* (1983). Examines the lives, philosophies, and actions of the key Progressive presidents.

Morton Keller, *Regulating a New Society: Public Policy and Social Change in America, 1900–1933* (1994). Assesses government responses to the social problems of the early twentieth century.

James T. Kloppenberg, *Uncertain Victory: Social Democracy and Progressivism in European and American Thought, 1870–1920* (1986). Places the major thinkers of the Progressive era in comparative perspective.

Martin J. Sklar, *The Corporate Reconstruction of American Capitalism, 1890–1916: The Market, the Law and Politics* (1988). Analyzes relationships between business and government during the Progressive era.

Overviews and Surveys

Paul Boyer, *Urban Masses and Moral Order in America, 1820–1920* (1978); Robert M. Crunden, *Ministers of Reform: The Progressives' Achievement in American Civilization* (1982); Arthur Ekrich, *Progressivism in America* (1974); Lewis L. Gould, *Reform and Regulation: American Politics from Roosevelt to Wilson* (1986); Richard Hofstadter, *Age of Reform* (1955); Gabriel Kolko, *The Triumph of Conservatism* (1963); Arthur S. Link and Richard L. McCormick, *Progressivism* (1983); Robert Wiebe, *The Search for Order* (1967).

The Progressive Impulse

Richard Abrams, *The Burdens of Progress* (1978); Jerold S. Auerbach, *Unequal Justice: Lawyers and Social Change in Modern America* (1976); Steven J. Diner, *A Very Different Age: Americans of the Progressive Era* (1998); Harold U. Faulkner, *The Quest for Social Justice, 1898–1914* (1931); Andrew Feffer, *The Chicago Pragmatists and American Progressivism* (1993); Louis Filler, *The Muckrakers*, rev. ed. (1976); Samuel Haber, *Efficiency and Uplift: Scientific Management in the Progressive Era* (1964); Thomas Haskell, *The Emergence of Professional Social Science* (1977); William R. Hutchison, *The Modernist Impulse in American Protestantism* (1976); Samuel Konefsky, *The Legacy of Holmes and Brandeis* (1956); David W. Marcell, *Progress and Pragmatism: James, Dewey, Beard, and the American Idea of Progress* (1974); David W. Noble, *The Progressive Mind*, rev. ed. (1981); Frank Tariello, *The Reconstruction of American Political Ideology* (1982); John L. Thomas, *Alternative America: Henry George, Edward Bellamy, Henry Demarest Lloyd, and the Adversary Tradition* (1983); Laurence Veysey, *The Emergence of the American University* (1970); James Weinstein, *The Corporate Ideal in the Liberal State, 1900–1918* (1968); Morton White, *Social Thought in America: The Revolt Against Formalism* (1975); Harold S. Wilson, *McClure's Magazine and the Muckrakers* (1970).

Progressives in Action

Mark Aldrich, *Safety First: Technology, Labor, and Business in the Building of American Work Safety, 1870–1939* (1997); Mansel G. Blackford, *The Lost Dream: Business and City Planning on the Pacific Coast, 1890–1920* (1993); John D. Buenker, *Urban Liberalism and Progressive Reform* (1973); Norman H. Clark, *Deliver Us From Evil: An Interpretation of Prohibition* (1976); Allen F. Davis, *Spearheads for Reform: The Social Settlements and the Progressive Movement, 1890–1914* (1967); Rene J. Dubos, *The White Plague: Tuberculosis, Man, and Society* (1952); Nancy S. Dye, *As Equals and Sisters: Feminism, the Labor Movement, and the Women's Trade Union League of New York* (1980); Dewey Grantham, *Southern Progressivism: The Reconciliation of Progress and Tradition* (1983); Sheldon Hackney, *Populism to Progressivism in Alabama* (1969); Melvin G. Holli, *Reform in Detroit: Hazen S. Pingree and Urban Politics* (1969); Charles F. Kellogg, *NAACP: A History of the National Association for the Advancement of Colored People* (1967); Maury Klein, *The Flowering of the Third America: The Making of an Organizational Society, 1850–1920* (1993); Regina G. Kunzel, *Fallen Women, Problem Girls: Unmarried Women and the Professionalization of Social Work, 1890–1945* (1993); Elisabeth Lasch-Quinn, *Black Neighbors: Race and the Limits of Reform in the American Settlement House Movement, 1890–1945* (1993); Ellen Condliffe Lagemann, *A Generation of Women: Education in the Lives of Progressive Reformers* (1979); William A. Link, *The Paradox of Southern Progressivism, 1880–1930* (1992); Roy Lubove, *The Progressives and the Slums, 1890–1917* (1962); Richard L. McCormick, *From Realignment to Reform: Political Change in New York State, 1893–1910* (1981); August Meier, *Negro Thought in America, 1880–1915* (1963); George E. Mowry, *California Progressives* (1951); Bradley R. Rice, *Progressive Cities: The Commission Government Movement* (1977); Ruth Rosen, *The Lost Sisterhood: Prostitution in America, 1900–1918* (1982); Bruce M. Stave, *Urban Bosses, Machines, and Progressive Reformers*, 2d ed. (1984); Eleanor J. Stebner, *The Women of Hull House: A Study in Spirituality, Vocation, and Friendship* (1997); Edward A. Stettner, *Shaping Modern Liberalism: Herbert Croly and Progressive Thought* (1993); Rosalyn Terborg-Penn, *African American Women in the Struggle for the Vote, 1850–1920* (1997); David P. Thelen, *The New Citizenship: Origins of Progressivism in Wisconsin* (1972); James H. Timberlake, *Prohibition and the Progressive Movement* (1963); Walter I. Trattner, *Crusade for the Children* (1970); Irwin Yellowitz, *Labor and the Progressive Movement in New York State* (1965).

Progressivism Moves to the National Level

John D. Buenker, *The Income Tax and the Progressive Era* (1985); Paolo E. Coletta, *The Presidency of William Howard Taft* (1973); James Holt, *Congressional Insurgents and the Party System* (1969); James Penick, Jr., *Progressive Politics and Conservation: The Ballinger-Pinchot Affair* (1968); James Oliver Robertson, *No Third Choice: Progressives in Republican Politics, 1916–1921* (1983); Richard West Sellars, *Preserving Nature in the National Parks: A History* (1997); Robert Stanley, *Dimensions of Law in the Service of Order: Origins of the Federal Income Tax, 1861–1913* (1993).

Progressivism in the International Arena

P. Edward Haley, *Revolution and Intervention: The Diplomacy of Taft and Wilson with Mexico, 1910–1917* (1970); Walter LaFeber, *The Panama Canal*, rev. ed. (1989); Lester Langley, *The United States and the Caribbean* (1980); Dana G. Munro, *Intervention and Dollar Diplomacy in the Caribbean, 1900–1921* (1964); Thomas F. O'Brien, *The Revolutionary Mission: American Enterprise in Latin America, 1900–1945* (1996); Whitney Perkins, *Constraints of Empire: The United States and Caribbean Interventions* (1981); Robert E. Quirk, *An Affair of Honor: Woodrow Wilson and the Occupation of Veracruz* (1962); John Womack, *Zapata and the Mexican Revolution* (1968).

Progressive Accomplishments, Progressive Failures

Paul D. Casdorph, *Republicans, Negroes, and Progressives in the South, 1912–1916* (1981); John Dittmer, *Black Georgia in the Progressive Era, 1900–1920* (1977); Jack Temple Kirby, *Darkness at the Dawning: Race and Reform in the Progressive South* (1972); Robert Wiebe, *Businessmen and Reform* (1962).

Biographies

Howard K. Beale, *Theodore Roosevelt and the Rise of America to World Power* (1956); John M. Blum, *The Republican Roosevelt*, 2d ed. (1977), and *Woodrow Wilson and the Politics of Morality* (1956); Allen F. Davis, *American Heroine: Jane Addams* (1973); William Harbaugh, *The Life and Times of Theodore Roosevelt*, rev. ed. (1963); Louis R. Harlan, *Booker T. Washington: The Making of a Black Leader, 1856–1901* (1972), and *The Wizard of Tuskegee, 1901–1915* (1983); Arthur S. Link, *Wilson*, 5 vols. (1947–1965), and *Woodrow Wilson and the Progressive Era* (1954); Daniel Nelson, *Frederick W. Taylor and the Rise of Scientific Management* (1980); David Riesman, *Thorstein Veblen* (1953); Elliott M. Rudwick, *W. E. B. DuBois* (1960); David P. Thelen, *Robert La Follette and the Insurgent Spirit* (1976).

INTERNET RESOURCES

Edward Bellamy
http://www.vineyard.net/vineyard/history/pdgech3.htm
This is a fine essay about Edward Bellamy and some of the movements and ideas he inspired.

The American Experience: America 1900
http://www.pbs.org/wgbh/pages/amex/1900/
This site is the companion site to the PBS documentary. It includes audio clips of respected historians on the economics, politics, and culture of 1900, a primary source database, a timeline of the year, downloadable software to compile your family tree, and other materials.

The Evolution of the Conservation Movement, 1850–1920
http://memory.loc.gov/ammem/amrvhtml/conshome.html
This American Memory site brings together scores of primary sources and photographs about "the historical formation and cultural foundations of the movement to conserve and protect America's natural heritage."

The Triangle Shirtwaist Factory Fire, March 25, 1911
http://www.ilr.cornell.edu/trianglefire/
The Kheel Center for Labor-Management Documentation and Archives at Cornell University put together this excellent site composed of oral histories, cartoons, images, and essays.

Labor-Management Conflict in American History
http://www.history.ohio-state.edu/projects/laborconflict/
This site at Ohio State University includes primary accounts of some of the major events in the hsitory of labor-management conflict in the late nineteenth and early twentieth centuries.

An American Factory: The Westinghouse Works, 1904
http://lcweb2.loc.gov/ammem/papr/west/westhome.html
Part of the American Memory Project at the Library of Congress, this site provides a glimpse inside and turn-of-the-century factory.

African-American Women Writers of the 19th Century
http://digital.nypl.org/schomburg/writers_aa19/
The New York Public Library's Schomburg Center for Research in Black Culture maintains this site that contains a large number of digital texts by African American women of the nineteenth century.

Touring Turn-of-the-Century America: Photographs from the Detroit Publishing Company, 1880–1920
http://memory.loc.gov/ammem/detroit/dethome.html
This Library of Congress collection has thousands of photographs from turn-of-the-century America.

The Theodore Roosevelt Association
http://www.theodoreroosevelt.org/
This official site contains biographical and research information about this famous American.

Woodrow Wilson
http://www.ipl.org/ref/POTUS/wwilson.html
This page contains basic factual data about his election and presidency, speeches, and on-line biographies.

KEY TERMS

Reform Darwinists   (p. 610)
Pragmatism   (p. 610)
Social Gospel   (p. 610)
Muckrakers   (p. 611)
Woman's Christian Temperance Union (WCTU)   (p. 614)
Settlement House Movement   (p. 615)
National Association for the Advancement of Colored People (NAACP)   (p. 618)
Workmen's Compensation Laws   (p. 620)
Progressive (Bull Moose) Party   (p. 626)
Federal Reserve System   (p. 627)
"Big Stick" Diplomacy   (p. 629)

REVIEW QUESTIONS

1. What factors led to an increased spirit of reform at the turn of the century?
2. Who were the "progressives," and how did they respond to the problems they perceived?
3. What was the impact of presidential leadership on the course of progressivism?
4. How did the "progressive spirit" influence foreign affairs?
5. Who were the winners and losers of progressivism? Why?

22

THE UNITED STATES AND WORLD WAR I

THE ROAD TO WAR
    The Guns of August
    American Neutrality
    Allied Violations of Neutrality
    Submarine Warfare
    Preparedness Campaign
    The Election of 1916
    The End of Neutrality

AMERICAN INDUSTRY GOES TO WAR
    Voluntarism
    "Hooverizing"
    Peace with Labor
    Financing the War

THE AMERICAN PUBLIC GOES TO WAR
    Selling the War
    Political Repression
    Wartime Reform
    African Americans and the Great
      Migration

THE WAR FRONT
    The War at Sea
    Raising an Army
    The Defeat of Germany

SOCIAL UNREST AFTER THE WAR
    Mounting Racial Tension
    Labor Unrest and the Red Scare

THE TREATY OF VERSAILLES
    The Fourteen Points
    Discord Among the Victors
    The Struggle for Ratification
    The Election of 1920

"The intellectual hero of World War I"

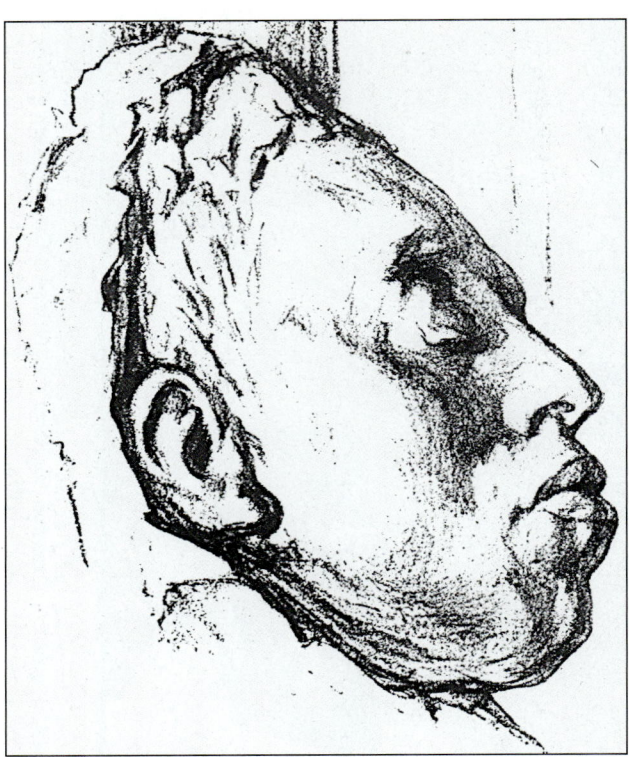

This drawing of American critic, essayist, and pacifist Randolph Stillman Bourne was done by Arthur G. Dove from the death mask by James Earle Fraser.

Disillusioned writers of the 1920s honored Randolph Silliman Bourne as "the intellectual hero of World War I," yet his appearance was anything but heroic. Theodore Dreiser called Bourne "as frightening a dwarf as I had ever seen." An unusually messy forceps delivery crushed one side of Bourne's skull at birth, leaving him with a misshapen ear, a partially paralyzed face, and a mouth permanently askew in a horrible grimace. Then, when he was four, an attack of spinal tuberculosis twisted his frame and left him a hunchback dwarf.

Bourne's brain, however, was razor sharp. He started reading at the age of two, and by the time he entered school, he had finished entire books, including the Bible. A brilliant student, Bourne attended Columbia University where he studied under Franz Boaz, the father of cultural anthropology; John Dewey, the famed educator and apostle of pragmatism; and Charles A. Beard, the historian who stressed the economic motives of the founding fathers.

Bourne left college on the eve of World War I determined to become a writer. Drawn by the intense intellectual ferment of the day, he settled in New York's Greenwich Village, where self-styled literary radicals had declared war on the smugness and optimism of American culture. Bourne's interests ranged wide and far but he made his reputation as a critic of America's entrance into World War I.

Bourne loathed President Woodrow Wilson, but he directed his choicest barbs at fellow intellectuals who supported Wilson's policies. In effect, he accused them of not doing their job as thinkers—of not subjecting the president's high-sounding rhetoric to the fierce scrutiny required to sharpen public debate. Instead of questioning Wilson's policies, they had betrayed their duty by "opening the sluices and flooding the public with the sewage of the war spirit."

Bourne refused to endow the war with lofty purposes. In his judgment, World War I was not a struggle to make the world safe for democracy; it was nothing more than "frenzied mutual suicide." To those who argued that this war would be different, that this war could somehow be converted into an instrument of progress and democracy, Bourne replied that World War I would unleash "all the evils that are organically bound up with it." America's allies would reject Wilson's call for a "peace without victory," Bourne cautioned, because "war determines its own end—victory." Eschewing a just peace, they would try to win the war and "then grab what they can."

On the home front, warned Bourne, there would be "clumsily levied taxes and the robberies of imperfectly controlled private enterprises," the suppression of civil liberties, and the growth of big government. "War is the health of the State," he declared in one of his most famous lines. "It automatically sets in motion throughout society those irresistible forces for uniformity, for passionate cooperation with the Government in coercing into obedience the minority groups and individuals which lack the larger herd sense."

Like many of his contemporaries, Bourne feared the state. During wartime the state's power grew exponentially, making it "the inexorable arbiter and determinant of men's businesses and attitudes and opinions." The individual would lose every conflict with the state. "It will be coercion from above that will do the trick rather than patriotism from below," he warned.

Most alarming of all, the war would kill reform by diverting public attention from the unfinished work of progressivism. It would "leave the country spiritually impoverished because of the draining away of sentiment into the channels of war."

A few days after the Armistice was signed in 1918, Bourne died, a victim of the influenza epidemic that killed 500,000 Americans that winter—five times the number that died in World War I. Although he had no visible impact on Wilson's administration, Bourne raised important questions about the relationship between the individual and the state during wartime, and many of his fears proved prophetic. In the end, the United States had little choice but to enter the conflict on the side of the Allies, but the war itself was a terrible human tragedy. World War I did not make "the world safe for democracy" or serve as the "war to end all wars" as President Wilson promised. Rather, World War I sowed the seeds of World War II.

THE ROAD TO WAR

World War I killed more people—more than 9 million soldiers, sailors, and flyers and another 5 million civilians—involved more countries—28—and cost more money—$186 billion in direct costs and another $151 billion in indirect costs—than any previous war in history. It was the first war in which parties used airplanes, tanks, long-range artillery, submarines and poison gas. It left at least 7 million men permanently disabled.

World War I probably had more far-reaching consequences than any other preceding war. Politically, it resulted in the downfall of four monarchies—in Russia in 1917, in Austria-Hungary and Germany in 1918, and in Turkey in 1922. It contributed to the Bolshevik rise to power in Russia in 1917 and the triumph of fascism in Italy in 1922.

Economically, the war severely disrupted European economies and allowed the United States to become the world's leading creditor and industrial power. The war also had vast social consequences, including the mass murder of Armenians in Turkey and an influenza epidemic that killed over 25 million people worldwide.

The event that triggered World War I was the assassination of Archduke Franz Ferdinand, the heir to

Archduke Francis Ferdinand and his wife Sophie, leave the Senate House in Sarajevo on June 28, 1914. Five minutes after this photograph was taken, the nineteen-year-old Serbian nationalist Gavrilo Princip assassinated them both, triggering World War I. Within weeks of the assassination, Germany, Turkey, Italy, and Austria-Hungary were at war with Britain, France, and Russia.

the Austro-Hungarian throne. On June 28, 1914, Gavrilo Princip, a Serbian nationalist, assassinated the archduke while Ferdinand and his wife were riding through Sarajevo, the provincial capital of Bosnia in the Balkans. The assassination provoked outrage in Austria-Hungary, which wanted to punish Serbia for the assassination and intimidate other minority groups whose independence struggles threatened the empire's stability.

A complicated system of military alliances transformed the Balkan crisis into a full-scale European war. After consulting with its ally Germany, Austria-Hungary sent Serbia an ultimatum. Serbia accepted most of Austria-Hungary's demands and agreed to mediate the rest, but Austria-Hungary was unwilling to compromise and on July 28, declared war on Serbia. Meanwhile, Russia, vowing to defend Serbia if it was attacked, began to mobilize, while France, in turn, promised to support Russia. Germany demanded that Russia halt its military buildup; Russia refused. Germany responded by declaring war on Russia on August 1, and on France two days later.

World War I caught most people by surprise. Lulled by a century of peace, many observers had come to regard armed conflict as an anachronism, a dead relic rendered unthinkable by human progress. Convinced that the major powers had advanced too far morally and materially to fight, these optimists believed that nation-states would settle disputes through diplomacy. By the end of the century, peace societies abounded on both sides of the Atlantic, nur-

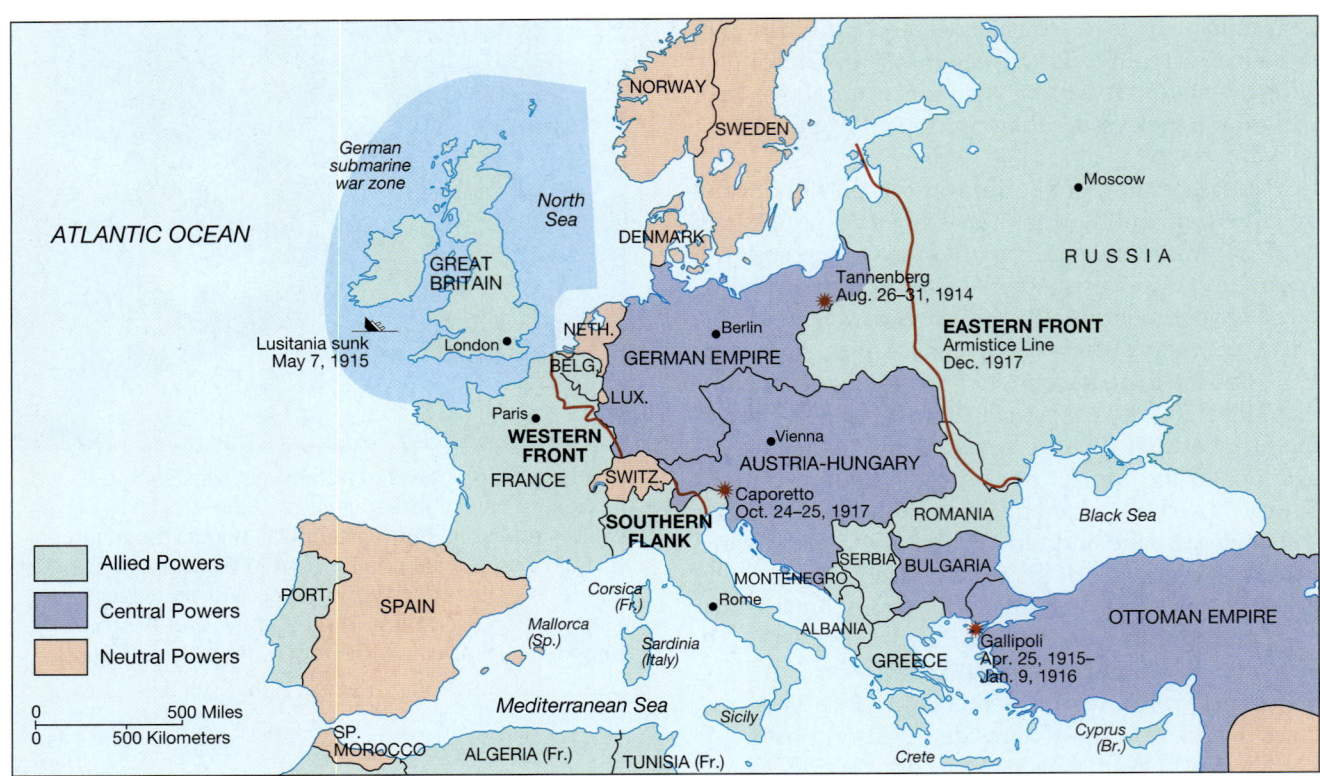

European Alliances and Battlefronts

turing visions of a world without war, and the Hague Conferences of 1899 and 1907 seemed to bear out these hopes by codifying international law in order to establish procedures for the peaceful resolution of conflict. World War I shattered these dreams, demonstrating that death and destruction had not yet been banished from human affairs.

The Guns of August

Faced by Russia to the east and France to the west, Germany believed that its only hope for victory was to strike first. The German military plan, originally devised by General Alfred von Schlieffen in 1905, called for a small force to defend Germany's eastern border, while a much larger German army raced across Belgium into France.

Germany's plan involved a violation of international law. Belgium was a neutral country, and Britain was committed to its defense. Thus a German invasion was certain to bring Britain into the war. Germany asked for permission to move its troops through Belgium, but King Albert, the country's monarch, refused, saying "Belgium is a nation, not a road." Germany decided to press ahead anyway; its forces invaded Belgium on August 3.

The German military strategy worked better on paper than it did in practice. While fierce resistance by 200,000 Belgian soldiers did not stop the German advance, it did give Britain and France time to mobilize their forces. Meanwhile, Russia mobilized faster than expected, forcing Germany to divert 100,000 troops to the eastern front. German hopes for a quick victory were dashed at the first battle of the Marne in September 1914, when a retreating French army launched a powerful counterattack, assisted by 6000 troops transported to the front by 1200 Parisian taxicabs.

After the **Allies** halted Germany's massive offensive through France and Belgium at the Marne River, the Great War bogged down into trench warfare and a ghastly stalemate ensued. Congealed lines of men, stretching from the English Channel to the Swiss border, formed an unmovable battle front across northern France. Four million troops burrowed into trenches that were 6 to 8 feet deep and wide enough for two men to pass, and which stretched for 450 miles. The soldiers of both sides, ravaged by tuberculosis and plagued with lice and rats, stared at each other across barren expanses called "no man's land," fighting pitched battles over narrow strips of blood-soaked earth.

Life in the trenches, as seen in this photograph of British soldiers in 1916, was often cramped, uncomfortable, and miserable. Many men tried to make the best of it by surrounding themselves with personal effects.

To end the stalemate, Germany introduced several military innovations in 1915, but none proved decisive. Germany dispatched submarines to prevent merchant ships from reaching Britain; it added poison chlorine gas to its military arsenal at the second battle of Ypres in northern France; and it dropped incendiary bombs over London from a zeppelin. Other innovations that distinguished World War I from previous conflicts were airplanes, tanks, and hand grenades. But it was the machine gun that did most of the killing. The grim cycle repeated itself countless times: officers cried "Attack!"; men rose in waves; and the opposing forces opened fire with machine guns, spewing out death at the rate of eight bullets per second. When the war ended, Germany had lost 1,800,000 men; Russia, 1,700,000; France, 1,385,000; Austria-Hungary, 1,200,000; and Great Britain, 947,000.

In a fateful attempt to break the deadlock, German forces adopted a new objective in 1916; to kill so many French soldiers that France would be forced to sue for peace. The German plan was to attack the French city of Verdun, a psychologically important town in northeastern France, and bleed the French dry. The battle, the war's longest, lasted from February 21, 1916 through July, and engaged 2 million soldiers. When it ended, Verdun had become a symbol of wartime futility. France had suffered 315,000 casualties, Germany 280,000. The town was destroyed, but the front had not moved.

With fighting on the western front deadlocked, action spread to other arenas. A British soldier and writer named T. E. Lawrence (better known as "Lawrence of Arabia"), organized revolts against the Ottoman territories in Syria, Palestine, Iraq, and the Arabian peninsula. With Germany preoccupied in Europe, Japanese and British commonwealth forces seized German islands in the Pacific, while British forces conquered German colonies in Africa.

The military stalemate produced political turmoil across Europe. On Easter Monday, 1916, some 1500 Irish Catholics seized buildings in Dublin and declared Ireland an independent republic. Fighting raged for a week before British forces suppressed the rebellion. British reprisals created great sympathy for the rebels. In 1919, renewed fighting broke out between British forces and supporters of Irish independence.

In Czarist Russia, wartime casualties, popular discontent, and shortages of food, fuel, and housing touched off revolution and civil war. In March 1917 strikes and food riots erupted in the Russian capital of Petrograd. Soldiers called in to quell the strikes joined the uprising; and on March 15, Czar Nicholas II abdicated. The czarist regime was replaced by a succession of weak provisional governments which tried to keep Russia in World War I. On November 7 communist Bolsheviks led by V. I. Lenin overthrew the provisional government, promising "Peace to the army, land to the peasants, ownership of the factories to the workers."

In 1917, after two and a half years of fighting, 5 million troops were dead and the western front remained deadlocked. This was the situation that awaited the United States in 1917.

American Neutrality

Like the combatants, Americans did not see the war coming. Most felt relieved when President Woodrow Wilson issued an official declaration of neutrality on August 4, 1914. Many citizens did not believe their nation's interest and security hinged on the war's outcome. Mindful of the wisdom embodied in Washington's Farewell Address, steeped in a long tradition of isolation from Europe's wars, and shielded from the hostilities by the Atlantic Ocean, they hoped to escape the insanity.

Two weeks after the official declaration of **neutrality** Wilson asked his countrymen to remain impartial "in thought as well as in action." Yet the president himself could not meet this standard. Privately, his sympathies lay with the Allies, especially Great Britain, whose culture and government he had long admired. Moreover, with the notable exception of William Jennings Bryan, his first secretary of state, Wilson's closest advisers all favored Great Britain.

The American Mosaic

The First Day of the Somme

DURING the American Civil War Richard J. Gatling hoped to become wealthy by selling the Union army his hand-cranked precursor to the machine gun, the Gatling gun. It could unleash up to 200 rounds a minute, as compared to the 2 to 3 rounds a minute from a rifled musket being loaded and fired by a well-trained soldier. Gatling considered his weapon "providential," the ultimate device, he wrote to Abraham Lincoln, for "crushing the rebellion." After the war Gatling even spoke of social benefits. His gun would ease the pain and suffering of war. Only one soldier would be needed "to do as much battle duty as a hundred" because of its "rapidity of fire." His weapon would "supersede the necessity of large armies, and consequently exposure to battle and disease would be greatly diminished."

Hiram Maxim, another inventor, offered a major improvement to Gatling's weapon in 1884 when he demonstrated a mechanism that would permit the gun to fire automatically, simply by depressing the trigger—the modern rapid-firing machine gun was born. Because of such technological breakthroughs, water-cooled machine guns capable of shooting 600 rounds a minute were commonplace in the arsenal of weapons used by the armies engaged in World War I. The Maxim guns, as they were generically known, could spray an area with bullets and easily destroy companies of soldiers trained well enough to fire their breechloading rifles only 15 times a minute. The machine gun proved to be an effective killing weapon.

More sophisticated weapons did not, as Richard Gatling had assured his customers, result in any reduction in the size of wartime armies. During Europe's Age of Industrialization the major powers built up ever-larger military forces, as if only huge masses of troops could defeat the enhanced firepower of new weapons such as the machine gun.

When the armies of Europe first collided in August 1914 after Germany's penetration through Belgium, a stark reality became clear. Firepower, both in the form of small arms and large artillery, was so overwhelming that neither side could defeat the other without virtual annihilation. What emerged were opposing lines of trenches along what was called the western front, running without interruption south from the North Sea all the way through France to the border of Switzerland. For the next three years combat became a horrible contest in which one side or the other periodically tried to break through these trench lines.

The Battle of the Somme was in many ways typical of trench warfare. Up until June 1916 this sector in northeastern France was inactive. German divisions had been present since September 1914 and had constructed three defensive lines of trenches running back from "no man's land," an area some 500 to 1000 yards wide on the other side of which were trenches manned by the Allies—the British to the north and the French to the south of the Somme River. Because of a fearsome struggle occurring far to the south at Verdun, the Allied high command, after preliminary planning, decided in May 1916 to mount a massive offensive in the Somme sector.

If German lines could be permanently ruptured, then it would be possible to roll up enemy divisions on their flanks. German soldiers would face surrender or retreat, thus breaking the military deadlock in favor of the Allies. To breech the German trenches in coordinated fashion along a stretch of 50 miles involved detailed planning, considering the thousands of troops and massive firepower that the Allies faced. Further, surprise attacks were impossible. German artillery and machine-gun operators could obliterate waves of soldiers trying to cross no man's land, even before they reached the barbed wire placed in front of the German trenches. The alternative was to prepare the way with an extended artillery bombardment.

The Battle of the Somme was launched with a seven-day cannonade. During the last week of June some 50,000 British artillerists fired 2,960,000 rounds at the German trenches. By evening of the second day, wrote an observer, "some sectors of the German front line were already unrecognizable and had become crater fields." The next day the British started releasing clouds of chlorine gas, hoping that it would seep down into dugouts 20 or more feet belowground where German soldiers were at that moment living, surviving, and listening carefully for the climactic fury of the bombardment, a sure sign that the infantry assault was to begin.

At 6:30 A.M., on July 1, 1916, one hour before infantry troops were to

644

advance, the cannonade reached "an intensity as yet unparalleled . . . along the whole front." German soldiers noticed the difference and knew that the moment of reckoning was near. The whole course of the battle would depend on their ability to get back aboveground, set up their machine guns, and begin firing before enemy infantry overran them. It was a moment for which they had repeatedly trained.

As zero hour approached, thousands of British and French soldiers made final preparations in their trenches. Their assignment was to secure control of the second German line by the end of the day. Soon they would climb up scaling ladders and jump over the top, then listen for the sounds of whistles from their platoon leaders to guide them across no man's land. Most found themselves "sweating at zero hour," supposedly from "nervous excitement." Many had attended church services the previous day. Explained one British soldier, "I placed my body in God's keeping, and I am going into battle with His name on my lips." Everyone received a warm breakfast and a healthy ration of rum to settle their jittery nerves.

Promptly at 7:30 A.M., the race began. "Over the top" went hundreds of thousands of British and French troops. Up out of their dugouts came German soldiers. In most areas the Germans were ready with time to spare. Their machine gun and artillery fire cut a third of the British battalions to shreds before they reached what remained of the first German trenches.

British soldiers who survived witnessed unbelievable sights. One watched as "two men suddenly rose into the air vertically, 15 feet perhaps," as a German shell hit the ground ahead of him. "They rose and fell with the easy, graceful poise of acrobats," he noted, as they died. Another saw men "falling forward," stating that it was "some time before I realized they were hit." In one company only three soldiers made it to the German barbed wire. Their leader, a lieutenant, looked around in amazement and said: "God, God, where's the rest of the boys?"

Hardly over the top, a British sergeant heard the "patter, patter" of German machine guns. "By the time I'd gone another ten yards," he explained, "there seemed to be only a few men left around me; by the time I had gone twenty yards, I seemed to be on my own. Then I was hit myself." This sergeant was among the fortunate. In some sectors, British soldiers who evaded machine-gun fire and reached the other side "were burned to death by [German] flame throwers."

From the British perspective, the fighting went poorly that day. By evening they had not captured the German second line, but they had suffered 60,000 casualties, including 21,000 dead. By comparison, the Germans, who got most of their machine guns up and operating, experienced only 6000 casualties.

The battle, however, had just begun. It would rage in fits and starts until November 18, 1916, when the Allies decided that a breakthrough in the Somme sector was not attainable. By that time the British had suffered 420,000 casualties, the French an estimated 200,000. No one knows exactly how many soldiers the Germans lost, but a fair guess would be in the 500,000 to 600,000 range. Yet virtually no ground had been lost or gained by either side.

It is not surprising, then, that the Allies rejoiced when the Americans finally entered the war. They needed more than loans and war goods to achieve total victory. Field Marshal Joseph Joffre, the former French commander-in-chief, said it all when he arrived in the United States after Congress declared war in April 1917. Declared Joffe with his usual bluntness: "We want men, men, men."

Robert Lansing, who succeeded Bryan as secretary of state; Walter Hines Page, ambassador to the Court of St. James; and Colonel Edward House, Wilson's alter ego, pushed the president to side with England and her Allies. Yet Wilson saw the war's causes as complicated and obscure; simple prudence dictated that the United States avoid taking sides.

Internal divisions underscored the wisdom of neutrality. Wilson knew his countrymen felt deeply divided over the war. Ties of language and culture prompted many Americans to side with the Allies, and, as the war progressed, the British adeptly exploited these bonds with anti-German propaganda. After the German invasion of neutral Belgium, for example, British propagandists depicted the Germans as sadistic brutes who committed atrocities against civilians. Yet the **Central Powers** had their sympathizers, too. Approximately one-third of the nation, 32 million people, were either foreign-born or the children of immigrants, and the roots of more than 10 million of these were the nations of the Central Powers. Furthermore, millions of Irish Americans sided with the Central Powers because they hated the English.

Domestic politics reinforced Wilson's determination to remain neutral. In 1914 the United States stood at the end of two decades of bitter social and political debate. Labor unrest, corporate growth, trust-busting, and the arrival of 12 million new immigrants since the turn of the century had opened deep fissures in American society. As Wilson struggled to correct these problems through legislation, he feared his domestic program would be endangered if neutrality failed. "Every reform we have won will be lost if we go into this war," declared Wilson in 1914.

Allied Violations of Neutrality

Because German armies held the edge in the land war, Great Britain had no choice but to press its naval superiority. Like Thomas Jefferson and James Madison a century earlier, President Wilson confronted a Great Britain bent upon ruling the waves, and no less than his predecessors in the White House, Wilson fought to protect neutral rights. During the early part of the war, British efforts to control the seas repeatedly posed threats to Anglo-American relations.

Immediately after war erupted, the British navy attempted to blockade Europe. In February 1915 British ships mined the North Sea and started seizing American vessels bound for neutral countries, often without offering compensation. The British captured not only war materiel but also noncontraband items, including food and cotton, bound for neutral nations such as Holland for reshipment to Germany. In 1916 Britain blacklisted some 87 American companies accused of trading with Germany and censored the mail coming from Europe to the United States.

These actions, coupled with England's ruthless suppression of the Irish Rebellion in 1916, infuriated Wilson. In retaliation, the State Department bombarded England with a flurry of firm protests. These objections were consistently undermined, however, by Walter Hines Page, the pro-British American ambassador at the Court of St. James. On one occasion, for example, Page delivered a long dispatch to Sir Edward Grey, the British foreign secretary, and declared: "I have now read the dispatch but I do not agree with it; let us consider how it should be answered." Although the British interpreted Wilson's ardent defense of neutral rights as petty, legalistic quibbling, they realized they could not push Wilson too far, since they needed American trade to survive.

Wilson could have ended the controversy over neutral rights by clamping an embargo on trade with the belligerents, but he refused to take this action because wartime trade was stimulating the American economy. The United States had been in a recession when Wilson entered office in 1913, and the war had quadrupled its exports to the Allied nations.

The huge volume of trade quickly exhausted the Allies' cash reserves, forcing them to ask the United States for credit. Secretary of State William Jennings Bryan, a near pacifist and the only member of Wilson's cabinet who supported strict neutrality, opposed their requests. After hesitating several months, Wilson agreed in October 1915 to permit loans to belligerents, a decision that favored Great Britain and France far more than Germany. By 1917 American loans to the Allies had soared to $2.25 billion; loans to Germany stood at a paltry $27 million. The United States became a creditor nation for the first time, giving Americans a strong economic interest in an Allied victory.

Submarine Warfare

Given Britain's overwhelming naval superiority, Germany decided to rely on a new weapon, the submarine, and on February 4, 1915, Germany proclaimed a "war zone" around the British Isles. Henceforth, they declared, all enemy merchant ships that entered the zone would be torpedoed without warning, and neutral ships would not be guaranteed safe passage. Germany was bluffing. It had only four submarines in the area, but Germany intended to use the threat of submarine warfare to terrorize and in-

Crew on the deck of a German World War I submarine at sea. The German U-boat (*Unterseeboot*) violated the International law that required a warship to warn a passenger or merchant vessel before it attacked. The U-boat struck silently and without warning.

timidate its enemies until it could build enough ships to enforce its threats.

A new development in naval technology, the submarine posed serious challenges to international law. The law required ships that attacked other vessels on the high seas to warn their intended victims, allow time for passengers to reach lifeboats, and then rescue survivors after the sinking. Moreover, merchant vessels suspected of transporting contraband had to be "visited and searched" before being attacked. A silent assassin whose effectiveness depended on the element of surprise, the submarine had to strike from below the surface in violation of international law.

Wilson's approach to foreign affairs was both legalistic and moralistic. He expected nation-states to behave like gentlemen; and, above all, that meant living up to the letter of international law and respecting the rights of every nation. To Wilson, German submarines were committing criminal acts. In contrast to British violations of American neutrality, which merely resulted in property losses, submarine warfare threatened to kill innocent civilians. In unusually blunt language, he warned Berlin that it would be held "strictly accountable" for American lives lost to submarine attacks. While international law did not guarantee the safety of neutrals who traveled on belligerent ships, Wilson acted as though it did.

On March 28, 1915, a German submarine torpedoed the *Falaba,* a British liner, killing 104 passengers, including one American. "PIRACY," "SHOCKING BLOODTHIRSTINESS," "BARBARISM RUN MAD," screamed the American press in banner headlines. Wilson was furious, but Secretary of State Bryan reminded the president of numerous British violations of American neutrality in her attempt to blockade Germany.

On May 1, the German Embassy took out ads in New York newspapers warning Americans not to travel on Allied ships. Undeterred, 197 Americans sailed for the British Isles on board the **Lusitania,** the queen of the British-owned Cunard fleet. On May 7, 1915, a German submarine torpedoed the *Lusitania* off the coast of Ireland. The ship sank in 18 minutes, killing 1198 persons, 128 of them Americans. The public was shocked and outraged. It did not seem to matter that the *Lusitania* (like the *Falaba*) was transporting munitions in her hull and had secret orders to ram submarines on sight.

In a sharply worded dispatch, Wilson ordered Germany to apologize for the sinking, compensate the victims, and pledge to stop attacking merchant ships. When Berlin equivocated, Wilson sent a second *Lusitania* note repeating his demands. This time the Germans met him halfway, expressing regret over the *Lusitania* and agreeing to pay an indemnity. However, the Imperial Government refused to stop sinking merchant ships without warning, explaining that Germany's survival depended on full use of the submarine.

Convinced that Wilson's policies would lead to war, Bryan resigned from the cabinet to protest what he saw as a dangerous tilt toward Great Britain in American policy. For his part, Wilson knew that the issue of submarine warfare had not been resolved. "I can't keep the country out of war," he admitted privately. "Any little German lieutenant can put us into war at any time by some calculated outrage."

Events soon showed how right he was. On March 24, 1916, a German submarine attacked the *Sussex,* an unarmed French passenger ship, killing more than 80 and severely wounding 7 Americans. Wilson threatened to sever diplomatic relations unless Germany promised to stop sinking all merchant and passenger ships without warning. Anxious to keep the United States neutral, Berlin agreed. The so-called *Sussex* pledge reduced tensions between the United States and Germany for the remainder of 1916, but the fragile peace depended solely on German restraint.

Preparedness Campaign

As the submarine threatened to draw the United States into the fighting, the American people and their leaders debated whether or not to make ready for war. Initially, Wilson's policy toward preparedness was cautious. In December 1914 he told Congress, "We never have had, and while we retain our present principles and ideals we never shall have, a large standing army."

Many Americans saw the issue differently. Wilson increasingly found himself assailed by prominent and highly vocal critics who insisted that the best way to preserve peace was to prepare for war. The pugnacious Theodore Roosevelt called the president "the popular pacifist hero," while another critic growled that the Germans were "standing by their torpedoes, the British by their guns, and Wilson by strict accountability." As Tin Pan Alley produced songs with titles such as "I Did Not Raise My Boy to Be a Coward," the National Security League, headed by General Leonard Wood, organized volunteer military training programs across the country.

Yet Wilson also felt pressured by groups opposed to war. Socialists such as Eugene V. Debs dismissed the war as a struggle for assets among capitalist nations. Radicals such as anarchist Emma Goldman and "Big Bill" Haywood, head of the Industrial Workers of the World, shared this view and advocated violent resistance to preparedness. Liberal reformers such as Randolph Bourne feared that war would destroy the spirit of progressivism. Most troubling of all, Wilson had to worry about opposition from within his own party. Speaking for the peace Democrats, former Secretary of State William Jennings Bryan warned that a preparedness campaign would transform the United States into "a vast armory with skull and crossbones above the door."

In the end, Wilson shifted ground and threw his support behind a moderate preparedness program. Throughout January and February 1916, he stumped the country demanding a military force powerful enough to protect the nation's honor. In June 1916, Congress increased the army from 90,000 to 175,000 men, and a few months later appropriated more than $500 million for new ships. Though of small importance militarily, both acts drew fire from those who predicted that armaments would lead to war.

At the height of the preparedness controversy, Wilson had to beat back a serious challenge to his control of American foreign policy. During the early months of 1916, Congress considered separate resolutions sponsored by Senator Thomas Gore of Oklahoma and Representative Jeff McLemore of Texas. Fearing that Wilson's defense of neutral rights would draw the United States into the conflict, the Gore and McLemore resolutions sought to prevent future incidents by prohibiting Americans from traveling on ships owned by belligerent nations and by prohibiting American vessels or neutral vessels from transporting American citizens and contraband "at one and the same time." Both resolutions enjoyed strong support in Congress, and for a while their passage appeared inevitable, but Wilson threw his power and prestige into a furious attack on both measures, insisting that if the United States accepted any abridgment of neutral rights "many other humiliations would follow." In the end, Congress accepted his argument and the Gore and McLemore resolutions went down in defeat.

The Election of 1916

Despite his own support for military preparedness, Wilson decided to make peace the key issue in his bid for reelection in 1916. The Republicans chose Charles Evans Hughes, a former governor of New York and a Supreme Court justice who had earned a solid reputation as a liberal. His nomination demonstrated the GOP's determination to regain progressive support and avoid the split that had put Wilson in the White House four years earlier. Wilson labeled the Republicans "the party of war" and charged that Hughes's election would plunge the United States into Europe's madness. "He kept us out of war" became the Democrats' rallying cry.

The race was extremely close. On election eve the *New York Times* and the *New York World* both awarded victory to Hughes, who went to bed believing he had won. He ran well in traditional Republican strongholds such as the Midwest (he won Illinois, Indiana, and Michigan) and the large eastern states. However, Wilson won in the electoral college by a vote of 277 to 254, with a popular vote margin of 9.1 million to Hughes's 8.5 million.

A careful analysis of Wilson's victory reveals that the Democrats won because they managed to fuse progressivism with the cause of peace. Wilson carried the Solid South, Ohio, Maryland, and New Hampshire, but he owed his victory to voters west of the Mississippi River, where he took every state except Oregon, Iowa, South Dakota, and Minnesota. This was the section of the country where peace sentiment ran highest and the opposition to preparedness was strongest.

The End of Neutrality

Interpreting his reelection as a vote for peace, Wilson attempted to mediate an end to the war. In 1917, Wilson urged both sides to embrace his call for "peace

THE ROAD TO WAR

WORLD WAR I

1914	Archduke Franz Ferdinand assassinated	After the murder of the Crown Prince of Austria, Austria-Hungary declares war on Serbia; other war declarations follow; real war erupts when Germany invades Belgium.
	American neutrality	President Woodrow Wilson urges Americans to be "impartial in thought as well as action."
1915	Submarine warfare	President Wilson warns Germany that he will hold it responsible for the loss of American lives and property resulting from submarine warfare.
	Lusitania sunk	A British passenger liner is sunk without warning by a German submarine; 128 Americans are among the 1198 fatalities.
1917	U.S.-German relations chill	President Wilson breaks diplomatic relations with Germany, citing the resumption of unrestricted submarine warfare.
	The Zimmermann telegram	Sent from the German foreign minister to the German ambassador in Mexico, it proposes that Mexico enter the war in return for Arizona, New Mexico, and Texas.
	Merchant ships armed	President Wilson authorizes the arming of American merchant ships.
	Declaration of war	President Wilson asks Congress to declare war, stating that "the world must be made safe for democracy."

without victory," but neither welcomed his overtures. Randolph Bourne was right. Above all else, the belligerents wanted victory.

Any hope for a negotiated settlement ended when Germany announced that after February 1, 1917, all vessels caught in the war zone, neutral or belligerent, armed or unarmed, would be sunk without warning. Driven to desperation by the British blockade and unable to break the impasse on land, Germany had decided to risk everything on a furious U-boat campaign designed to starve Britain into submission. The German high command expected the United States to declare war in retaliation, but they believed their submarines could deliver a knockout blow before America could mobilize.

Members of his cabinet pressed Wilson to declare war, but he broke diplomatic relations instead. Though critics accused the president of shaking first his fist and then his finger, Wilson refused to budge, largely because he viewed war as a defeat for reason. For weeks he seemed indecisive and confused, unable to accept the fact that "strict accountability" demanded war once the Germans started sinking American ships.

The **Zimmermann telegram** snapped Wilson out of his daze. In January, British cryptographers had intercepted a secret message from Arthur Zimmermann, the German foreign minister, to the German ambassador to Mexico, proposing an alliance between Germany and Mexico in the event Germany went to war with the United States. Germany promised to help Mexico recover the territory it had lost in the 1840s, roughly the present-day states of Texas, New Mexico, California, and Arizona. The British revealed the scheme to Wilson in late February, hoping to draw the United States into the war.

The Zimmermann telegram convinced Wilson and millions of Americans that Germany would stop at nothing to satisfy her ambitions—goals that posed a serious danger to America's rights and security. Late in February, Wilson asked Congress for permission to arm American merchant ships. The House approved, but 11 pacifists in the Senate filibustered against the bill. Dismissing his Senate opponents as

THE PEOPLE SPEAK

Woodrow Wilson, Address to Congress (1917)

When World War I erupted in Europe during his first term as President, Woodrow Wilson vowed to remain neutral. Despite his promises of peace in the election of 1916, President Wilson finally bowed to mounting pressures, particularly German submarine attacks on Americans, to enter World War I. The following is an excerpt from his impassioned address to Congress asking them to declare war on Germany in April, 1917.

> I have called the Congress into extraordinary session because there are serious, very serious choices of policy to be made, and made immediately, which it was neither right nor constitutionally permissible that I should assume the responsibility of making.
>
> On the third of February last I officially laid before you the extraordinary announcement of the Imperial German Government that on and after the first day of February it was its purpose to put aside all restraints of law or of humanity and use its submarines to sink every vessel that sought to approach either the ports of Great Britain and Ireland or the western coasts of Europe or any of the ports controlled by the enemies of Germany within the Mediterranean. . .
>
> I was for a little while unable to believe that such things would in fact be done by any government that had hitherto subscribed to the humane practices of civilized nations. International law had its origin in the attempt to set up some law which would be respected and observed upon the seas, where no nation had right of dominion and where lay the free highways of the world. . . . The minimum of right the German Government has swept aside under the plea of retaliation and necessity and because it had no weapons which it could use at sea except these which it is impossible to employ as it is employing them without throwing to the winds all scruples of humanity or of respect for all understandings that were supposed to underlie the intercourse of the world. I am not now thinking of the loss of property involved, immense and serious as that is, but only of the wanton and wholesale destruction of the lives of non-combatants, men, women, and children, engaged in pursuits which have always, even in the darkest periods of modern history, been deemed innocent and legitimate. Property can be paid for; the lives of peaceful and innocent people cannot be. The present German submarine warfare against commerce is a warfare against mankind.
>
> It is a war against all nations. American ships have been sunk, American lives taken, in ways which it has stirred us very deeply to learn of, but the ships and people of other neutral and friendly nations have been sunk and overwhelmed in the waters in the same way. There has been no discrimination. The challenge is to all mankind. Each nation must decide for itself how it will meet it. The choice we make for ourselves must be made with a moderation of counsel and a temperateness of judgement befitting our character and our motives as a nation. We must put excited feeling away. Our motive will not be revenge or the victorious assertion of the physical might of the nation, but only the vindication of right, of human right, of which we are only a single champion. . . .

"a little band of willful men, representing no opinion but their own," Wilson issued an executive order on March 12, arming merchant ships and instructing them to shoot submarines on sight.

At this critical juncture, with the United States and Germany virtually at war, the Russian Revolution erupted. Suddenly, the czar's government was swept away, and in its place stood the provisional government of a Russian Republic, complete with a representative parliament. Given his penchant for framing issues in moral terms, Wilson could now view the Allies in a new light: With the only autocratic regime among the Allies transformed overnight into a fledgling democracy, the war truly seemed to pit the forces of democracy against the forces of despotism.

Pale and solemn, Wilson delivered his war message to Congress on April 2. The United States "had no quarrel with the German people," he insisted, but their "military masters" had to be defeated in order to make the world "safe for democracy." The next day the Senate approved the war resolution, 82 to 6; the House followed on April 6, 373 to 50. The president signed the declaration on April 7, 1917, and America was at war.

For more than two years Wilson had worked frantically to keep the United States at peace: why did he now lead the nation to war? True, cultural ties with Great Britain predisposed the United States to favor the Allies, and enormous volumes of trade and loans strengthened those ties. Yet cultural bonds and money did not decide the issue. Wilson, reluctantly,

> With a profound sense of the solemn and even tragical character of the step I am taking and of the grave responsibilities which it involves, but in unhesitating obedience to what I deem my constitutional duty, I advise that the Congress declare the recent course of the Imperial German Government to be in fact nothing less than war against the government and people of the United States; that it formally accept the status of belligerent which has thus been thrust upon it; and that it take immediate steps not only to put the country in a more thorough state of defense but also to exert all its power and employ all its resources to bring the Government of the German Empire to terms and end the war. . . .
>
> We have no quarrel with the German people. We have no feeling towards them but of sympathy and friendship. It was not upon their impulse that their government acted in entering this war. It was not with their previous knowledge or approval. It was a war determined upon as wars used to be determined upon in the old, unhappy days when peoples were nowhere consulted by their rulers and wars were provoked and waged in the interest of dynasties or of little groups of ambitious men who were accustomed to use their fellow men as pawns and tools. . . .
>
> We are accepting this challenge of hostile purpose because we know that in such a Government, following such methods, we can never have a friend; and that in the presence of its organized power, always lying in wait to accomplish we kow not what purpose, there can be no assured security for the democratic Governments of the world. We are now about to accept gauge force of the nation to check and nullify its pretensions and its power. We are glad, now that we see the facts with no veil of false pretense about them, to fight thus for the ultimate peace of the world and for the liberation of its peoples, the German peoples included: for the rights of nations great and small and the privilege of men everywhere to choose their way of life and of obedience. The world must be made safe for democracy. Its peace must be planted upon the tested foundations of political liberty. We have no selfish ends to serve. We desire no conquest, no dominion. We seek no indemnities for ourselves, no material compensations for the sacrifices we shall freely make. We are but one of the champions of the rights of mankind. We shall be satisfied when those rights have been made as secure as the faith and the freedom of nations can make them. . . .
>
> It is a distressing and oppressive duty, Gentlemen of the Congress, which I have performed in thus addressing you. There are, it may be, many months of fiery trial and sacrifice ahead of us. It is a fearful thing to lead this great peaceful people into war, into the most terrible and disastrous of all wars, civilization itself seeming to be in the balance. But the right is more precious than peace, and we shall fight for the things which we have always carried nearest our hearts,—for democracy, for the right of those who submit to authority to have a voice in their own Governments, for the rights and liberties of small nations, for a universal dominion of right by such a concert of free peoples as shall bring peace and safety to all nations and make the world itself at last free. To such a task we can dedicate our lives and our fortunes, everything that we have, with the pride of those who know that the day has come when America is privileged to spend her blood and her might for the principles that gave her birth and happiness and the peace which she has treasured. God helping her, she can do no other.
>
> Source: *New York Times,* April 3, 1917.

drew the sword, because he concluded that German submarines violated international law and made a mockery of America's long-standing commitment to freedom of the seas. His strong defense of neutral rights left him no choice but to declare war once Germany resumed its attacks on American ships.

One additional factor carried great weight for Wilson—his desire to help shape the peace. By entering the war, the United States would be guaranteed a place at the peace table. "I hate this war," an anguished Wilson confided to one of his aides, "and the only thing I care about on earth is the peace I am going to make at the end of it."

Most Americans supported Wilson's call to arms. John Dewey, the famed educator, spoke for progressives when he described war as an ugly reality that had to be converted into an instrument for benefiting mankind. Randolph Bourne disagreed. "If the war is too strong for you to prevent," he asked pointedly, "how is it going to be weak enough for you to control and mold to your liberal purposes?"

AMERICAN INDUSTRY GOES TO WAR

The United States entered the Great War unprepared. Americans had no idea of what the war would ask of them as a society. Decisions had to be made about mobilization, but the public had not yet formed a consensus on the proper role of government in society, especially during wartime. As a result, Wilson hesitated to place the economy on a wartime footing by decree. Instead, he tried to create a system of economic incentives that would encourage Americans to support the war in a spirit of voluntary cooperation.

Voluntarism

It took nearly a year to organize an effective war administration. Wilson established a war cabinet with six key boards, conferring broad power on the central government. The War Industries Board (WIB), organized early in 1918 under the leadership of Bernard M. Baruch, a Wall Street financier, assumed the task of managing the economy by fixing prices, setting priorities, and reducing waste. To increase production, the WIB appealed to the profit motive, permitting earnings to triple during the war.

The Fuel Administration, the War Trade Board, the Shipping Board, and the U.S. Railroad Administration adopted similar policies. Under the slogan "Mine More Coal," the Fuel Administration increased production by two-fifths and conserved supplies through voluntary "lightless nights" and "gasless Sundays." By spending $500 million on new equipment and repairs, offering large profits to railroads and high wages to workers, the Railroad Administration established an efficient rail system under national control.

"Hooverizing"

Agricultural production came under the jurisdiction of the Food Administration headed by Herbert Hoover, a mining engineer and self-made millionaire who had served with distinction as director of relief operations in Belgium. Appealing to the spirit of patriotism, he preached "the gospel of the clean plate." Americans **"Hooverized"** with wheatless Mondays and Wednesdays, meatless Tuesdays, and porkless Thursdays and Saturdays.

No foe of profits, Hoover set farm prices at high levels to encourage production, stabilized the grain market by guaranteeing farmers a minimum price, and purchased raw sugar and then sold it to refineries at a fixed rate. The policies worked. Overall, real farm incomes rose 30 percent during the war, food production increased by one-quarter, domestic food consumption fell, and America's food shipments to the Allies tripled.

Peace with Labor

The government also made concessions to labor. Wilson addressed the American Federation of Labor (AFL) convention in November 1917, the first time a president had so honored the trade union movement. Important policy shifts followed. Gradually, Wilson recognized labor's right to organize and engage in collective bargaining, and he sanctioned other key demands, including the eight-hour workday. To settle

Wilson's administration opposed militant labor unions like the Industrial Workers of the World (IWW), shown here striking against Oliver Steel in Pennsylvania. Such strikes did little to help the war effort at home.

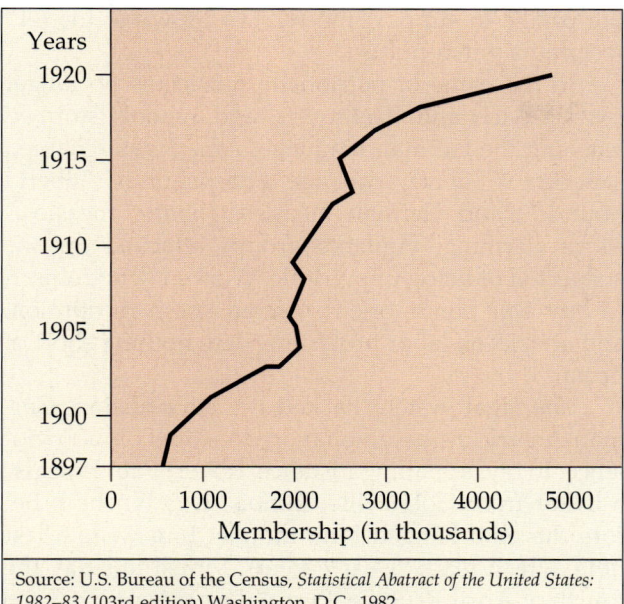

FIGURE 22.1
Labor Union Membership, 1897–1920

workweek), and AFL membership jumped from 2.7 million in 1916 to 4 million in 1919.

Financing the War

By 1920 the war had cost the nation $33.5 billion—33 times the federal government's revenues in 1916. Conservatives favored a regressive tax policy: consumption taxes, borrowing, and, if necessary, a slight increase in income taxes. Reformers and radicals demanded a progressive tax policy: inheritance and excess profits taxes coupled with higher income taxes. Wilson walked the middle ground, but the heaviest burdens fell on the wealthy, through taxes on large incomes, corporate profits, and estates.

World War I brought an important change in the sources of federal tax revenues. Before the war nearly three-quarters of federal revenues had come from excise and customs taxes. After the war, America's tax structure shifted from taxing consumption to taxing wealth, proof that progressives had won an important victory in the struggle to make upper-income groups pay a large share of the cost of government. On the tax issue Randolph Bourne was wrong.

THE AMERICAN PUBLIC GOES TO WAR

Although Wilson preferred to rely on voluntary efforts rather than mandated government interference, federal powers were greatly expanded during World War I. Wilson's decision to substitute voluntarism for statutory controls on industry placed the burden of supporting the war on the profit motive and the public's sense of patriotism. This policy avoided a clash between Wilson and industry that would have resulted from strict government control over the economy, but it did so at a huge cost to civil liberties.

Selling the War

Throughout the war the government directed its coercion at people rather than industries, largely through the **Committee on Public Information (CPI).** Ably led by George W. Creel, the CPI created America's first propaganda agency. Creel immediately drafted a voluntary censorship agreement with newspapers to keep sensitive military information out of print. The CPI hired hundreds of musicians, writers, and artists to stage a patriotic campaign, sponsored 75,000 speakers who delivered four-minute war pep talks in

labor disputes, Wilson created the National War Labor Board (WLB). Though it lacked legal authority, the WLB had the president's backing and a commitment from industry and labor to accept its decisions.

While Wilson embraced the AFL, his administration opposed the militant Industrial Workers of the World (IWW, also called "Wobblies"). From the textile mills of New England to the logging camps of the Pacific Northwest and steel companies in between, the Wobblies demanded higher wages and better working conditions, and they went out on strike to win them. Because the Wobblies frequently employed the rhetoric of class warfare to dramatize their demands, their strikes frightened many Americans who feared social revolution. Businessmen played upon these fears to demand suppression of the so-called radical unions.

The AFL shrewdly separated its union from these more militant workers, pledging not to strike for the duration of the war. The AFL supported the war and joined the administration's attack on socialist critics. In return, the AFL won a voice in homefront policy. Union men occupied seats in wartime agencies, where they pushed for the eight-hour workday and staved off pressure from employers bent on preserving the open shop. Real income of manufacturing workers and coal miners rose by one-fifth between 1914 and 1918, hours were reduced (by 1919 half the labor force had achieved a 48-hour

Hollywood and Tin pan Alley did their parts to encourage patriotism by putting out a multitude of war films and a large number of music pieces like the one shown here.

vaudeville and movie theaters across the country, and got movie stars to sell war bonds.

Indeed, the CPI found a powerful ally in Hollywood. Quick to perceive the link between patriotism and profits, studio moguls cranked out scores of crude propaganda films with titles such as *The Prussian Cur*, *The Claws of the Hun*, and *To Hell with the Kaiser*, which reduced World War I to a conflict between good and evil, Allied heroes and Central Powers villains. Songwriters did their best to foster patriotism by pumping out a series of catchy tunes with titles like "Keep the Home Fires Burning" and "Over There."

Popular culture reflected the CPI's influence. Suddenly, dissent meant treason, Germans devolved into Huns, and all German Americans spied for the fatherland. At its best the CPI may have sold war bonds, discouraged war stoppages, and convinced the public to support the war; at its worst the CPI fostered a witch-hunt.

In the name of patriotism, musicians no longer played Bach and Beethoven, and schools stopped teaching the German language. Americans renamed sauerkraut "liberty cabbage"; dachshunds, "liberty hounds"; and German measles, "liberty measles." More alarming, vigilante groups attacked anyone suspected of being unpatriotic. Workers who refused to buy war bonds often suffered harsh retribution, and attacks on labor protesters were nothing short of brutal.

The legal system backed the suppression. German Americans became favored victims of mob violence. In one appalling instance, Robert Paul Praeger, a baker from Colinsville, Illinois, was lynched. Before the mob hanged him, they let him write a last note, which read: "Dear Parents, I must this day the fourth of April 1918 die. Please dear parents pray for me." A jury acquitted the lynch mob in less than half an hour, while a band played patriotic songs in the courthouse.

Political Repression

The government fueled the hysteria. In June 1917 Congress passed the Espionage Act, which gave postal officials the authority to ban newspapers and magazines from the mails and threatened individuals convicted of obstructing the draft with $10,000 fines and 20 years in jail. Congress passed the Sedition Act of 1918, which made it a federal offense to use "disloyal, profane, scurrilous, or abusive language" about the Constitution, the government, the American uniform, or the flag. The government prosecuted over 2100 people under these acts. Randolph Bourne's prediction that civil rights would fall victim to the power of the state rang true.

Political dissenters bore the brunt of the repression. Eugene V. Debs, who urged socialists to resist militarism, went to prison for nearly three years. Another Socialist, Kate Richards O'Hare served a year in prison for stating that the women of the United States were "nothing more nor less than brood sows, to raise children to get into the army and be made into fertilizer."

Labor radicals offered another ready target for attack. In July 1917 in Cochise County, Arizona, armed men, under the direction of a local sheriff, rounded up 1186 strikers at the Phelps Dodge copper mine. They placed these workers, many of Mexican descent, on railroad cattle cars without food or water, and left them in the New Mexico desert, 180 miles away. The *Los Angeles Times* editorialized: "The citizens of Cochise County have written a lesson that the whole of America would do well to copy."

The IWW never recovered from government attacks during World War I. In September 1917 the Justice Department staged massive raids on IWW officers, arresting 169 of its veteran leaders. The administration's purpose was, as one attorney put it, "very largely to put the IWW out of business."

The Supreme Court later approved the attacks on civil liberties. Oliver Wendell Holmes, the court's leading champion of civil liberties, upheld the Espionage Act in Schenck v. United States (1919), ruling that the conviction of Charles T. Schenck for distributing leaflets urging draftees to oppose the war did not violate Schenck's free speech rights. Holmes delivered the famous "clear and present danger" doctrine, which held that there are circumstances (like "a man falsely shouting fire in a theater") that pose such a threat to public order that First Amendment protections do not apply. In U.S. v. Debs (1919), the court, with Holmes's support, again approved the Espionage Act, upholding the conviction of Eugene Debs, the Socialist Party leader, who opposed the war. In a third case, Abrams v. United States (1919), Holmes reversed himself, returning to his support for "free trade in ideas," but he was outvoted seven to two. The American Civil Liberties Union (ACLU) was founded during World War I to defend the First Amendment.

World War I did not *cause* repression, it merely intensified old fears. Many Americans clung to the image of the United States as a strong, isolated country, inhabited by old stock, white, middle-class Protestants. Their vision no longer reflected reality, but the war offered them a chance to lash out at those who had changed America. Immigrants, radical labor organizers, socialists, anarchists, Communists, and critics of any kind became victims of intolerance.

Wartime Reform

The war hysteria bred a curious alliance between superpatriots and old-style reformers. Prohibitionists had little difficulty turning World War I to their advantage. They had been winning victories at the state level since the middle of the nineteenth century, but they did not enjoy any success at the federal level until 1917 when Congress prohibited the use of grain for the production of alcoholic beverages, insisting that foodstuffs must be used to feed America's soldiers and Allies. Prohibitionists joined the anti-German craze, warning that German Americans controlled the nation's breweries. Congress passed the Eighteenth Amendment in 1917 and the final state

Members of the National Woman's Party, led by Alice Paul (on the balcony), celebrate their right to vote at their headquarters in Washington, D.C., in 1920.

ratified the amendment two months after the Armistice. The Volstead Act, which banned the manufacture, transportation, and sale of alcoholic beverages, took effect in 1920.

Like prohibition, women's suffrage benefited from the emergency atmosphere of World War I. Although radical suffragists, led by Alice Paul of the National Women's Party, refused to back the war as long as women could not vote, most women's organizations supported the war effort. Wilson appointed suffragists Carrie Chapman Catt and Anna Howard Shaw as directors of the Women's Committee of the Council of National Defense. Thousands of women joined the Red Cross and the American Women's Hospital Service and served overseas as nurses, physicians, clerks, and ambulance drivers. Thousands more enlisted after the army established the Army Corps of Nurses in 1918.

Suffragists demanded the vote in return for their support of the war. Wilson had long opposed women's suffrage, but political reality ultimately forced his hand. Most western states had granted women the vote before he entered the White House. When Illinois fell in line in 1914, followed by Rhode Island and New York in 1917, pressure started building for national action. Alice Paul pressed the issue by organizing around-the-clock picketing in front of the White House. Determined to prevent women's suffrage from becoming a political issue in the congressional elections of 1918, Wilson told the Senate that the vote for women "is vital to the winning of the war." In 1919, shortly after the Armistice, Congress passed the Nineteenth Amendment, granting women the right to vote. Ratification followed in the summer of 1920.

Apart from voting rights, World War I brought few permanent changes for women. Women had hoped the war would open new jobs for them. Instead, employment opportunities proved meager and brief. Of the one million women who found work in war-related industries, the majority had held jobs before the war. Labor unions opposed hiring women and tolerated their presence solely as a wartime necessity. As the Central Federated Union of New York put it: "the same patriotism which induced women to enter industry during the war should induce them to vacate their positions after the war." Fewer than half of the women who took jobs in heavy industry during the war still held them in 1919, and the number of women who remained in the work-force in 1920 dropped below the 1910 figures.

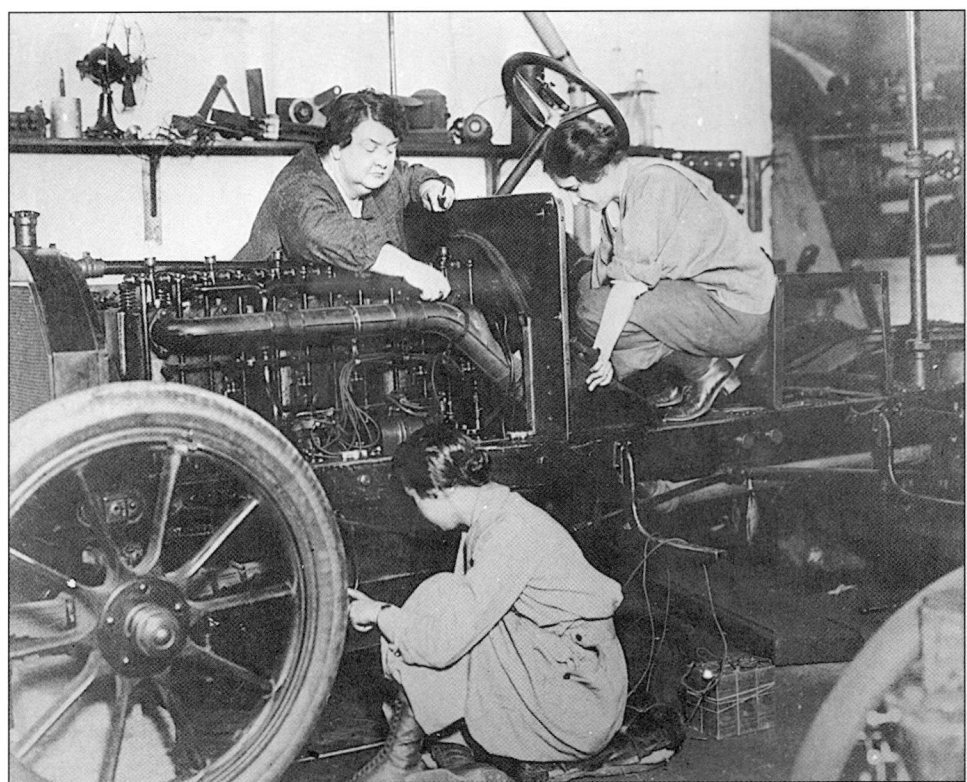

During the war, many women took jobs previously held by men. Here a group of women assemble an automobile in a factory.

African Americans and the Great Migration

Like women, African Americans wanted to use the war to improve their status. While the government had given African Americans little reason to shed their blood, most African-American newspapers backed the war. W. E. B. Du Bois urged African Americans to "close ranks" with whites, declaring, "If this is our country, then this is our war." Du Bois hoped that by demonstrating patriotism and bravery, African Americans could win public respect and earn better treatment after the war.

At first military leaders denied African Americans even the right to fight for their country. When the National Association for the Advancement of Colored People (NAACP) and other African-American organizations protested, however, the army agreed to compromise. Following the Civil War example, the army created black regiments commanded almost exclusively by white officers. Black regiments committed to battle fought bravely, but most African-American soldiers in Europe never got the chance to prove their valor. Instead, they were assigned to move supplies. While two-thirds of the American Expeditionary Force saw combat, only one-fifth of African-American troops did so. Even so, 14.4 percent of African-American soldiers lost their lives, compared with 6.3 percent of white soldiers.

The 369th infantry Regiment returned from the war in February 1919. They were awarded the *Croix de Guerre* (war cross) for bravery in the Meuse-Argonne campaign.

African-American soldiers faced segregation and humiliation. When the war ended, they were denied the right to march in the victory parade down Paris's Champs-Elysées boulevard, even though Africans from European colonies were permitted to do so.

Back home the record was equally mixed. In the decades following the Civil War a steady trickle of African Americans had left the South to search for jobs in northern cities. During World War I the trickle became a flood. Plagued by the boll weevil, low cotton prices, and unrelenting white repression, sharecroppers longed for change. By November 1918 the **"Great Migration"** had brought half a million southern African Americans to the "Land of Hope."

Many found jobs in northern factories and packing houses. The labor force in Chicago's packing houses had been 97 percent white in 1901, but by 1918 they employed 10,000 African Americans—over 20 percent of the workforce. The labor force in the northern steel industry had been virtually all white in 1900, but by 1920 African Americans held 10 percent of those jobs. Still, regardless of the industry, discrimination forced many to the bottom of the ladder, where they took over the menial, backbreaking jobs that had been vacated by Slavic and Italian workers, the prior most recent wave of immigrants.

The Great Migration angered many southerners. The price of cotton tripled during the war, southern planters, fearing the loss of their labor force, resorted to intimidation and mob violence to stop the exodus. Like their ancestors who had taken the underground railroad to freedom, many African Americans who moved to the North during World War I had to travel under cover of darkness.

Northern whites opposed the Great Migration, too. Manufacturers welcomed the cheap labor (especially as strikebreakers), but most Northerners felt threatened by the newcomers. Middle-class whites feared changes in the racial composition of their society, while immigrants resented the competition for jobs and housing. Increasingly, Northerners turned to segregation, discrimination, and violence; and African Americans, hoping for a better life in the North, fought back. Race riots erupted in 26 cities in 1917, with the most serious violence occurring in East St. Louis, where at least 39 African Americans died in the fighting.

Clearly, World War I meant different things to different groups: for the administration, a test of the limits of voluntarism; for businessmen and technocrats, a chance to pull the levers of government; for nativists and superpatriots, an excuse to lash out at "undesirable" elements; for radicals and dissenters, repression and hardship; for manufacturers and farmers, high profits; for reformers, victories on women's suffrage and prohibition; for trade unions, the right to organize for better pay; and for African Americans, a chance to escape from southern poverty.

THE WAR FRONT

The United States entered World War I without a large army or the ships to transport one to Europe. Six weeks before Congress declared war, the army had not even drafted plans to organize a large military force. At first confident the Allies were winning, Wilson hoped to limit America's contribution to supplies, financial credit, and moral support. In truth, the Allies were ready to collapse. The French army was in the throes of mutiny. Soldiers were tired of suicidal assaults ordered by inept generals, and the submarine offensive had reduced Britain to a six-week supply of food.

The War at Sea

With the Allies ready to collapse due to huge casualties, low morale, and dwindling food supplies, Wilson ordered the United States Navy to act immediately. American ships relieved the British of patrolling the Western Hemisphere while another portion of the fleet steamed to the north Atlantic to combat the submarine menace. Six destroyers reached Ireland on May 4; 35 ships had arrived by July; and 343 ships were patrolling the seas surrounding England by the war's end.

To cut down losses of merchant ships, which in April alone totaled 881,027 tons, the Americans proposed a convoy system—using warships to escort merchant ships to Great Britain. By December the convoy system had cut losses in half.

Raising an Army

Wilson's choice to lead the American Expeditionary Force (AEF) was Major General John J. "Black Jack" Pershing. Despite urgent requests from Allied commanders, Pershing refused to send raw recruits to the front, and he rejected demands that American units be integrated into British and French regiments. Instead, Pershing insisted on keeping American troops as independent units under his command. To bolster Allied morale while the army trained, the War Department hurriedly dispatched the First Division to France, where it marched through Paris on July 4, 1917, to the cheers of thousands.

A bitter debate erupted over how to raise the troops. Despite heavy pressure from Theodore Roosevelt and others who favored a volunteer army, Wilson insisted on conscription, and Congress passed the Selective Service Act on May 18, 1917. More than 23 million men registered during World War I, and 2,810,296 draftees served in the armed forces.

To assign soldiers to the right military tasks, the army launched an ambitious program of psychological testing. "If the Army machine is to work smoothly and efficiently," declared Robert M. Yerkes, the man who presided over the effort, "it is as important to fit the job to the man as to fit the ammunition to the gun." Yerkes saw the war as an opportunity to establish the academic legitimacy of psychology by providing a vital service to the nation.

Though the tests supposedly measured native intelligence, in reality they favored men with the most schooling, and thus reinforced the class structure of American society. Native-born whites, who possessed academic skills, achieved the highest scores, while recent immigrants consistently scored lowest.

Apart from selecting officers, the army made little use of the test data. Ordinary soldiers were not assigned tasks on the basis of test scores. After the war, however, Yerkes boldly proclaimed that mental testing had "helped to win the war." All it really accomplished was to sell the public on the idea of mental testing and lay the groundwork for a thriving peacetime industry. After the war, numerous businesses adopted mental tests to screen personnel, and many colleges began requiring them for admission. Few legacies of the war had a more lasting or widespread impact on American society.

The Defeat of Germany

As the American army trained, the situation in Europe deteriorated. Mutiny within the French army was spreading (ten divisions were now in revolt); the eastern front dissolved in March when the Bolsheviks, who had seized power in Russia in November, accepted Germany's peace terms; and German and Austrian forces all but routed the Italian armies. In fact, by late 1917 the war had come down to a race between American mobilization and Germany's war machine.

On March 21, 1918, the Germans launched a massive offensive on the western front in the Valley of the Somme in France. For a time, it looked as though the Germans would succeed. Badly bloodied, the Allied forces lost ground. But with German troops barely 50 miles from Paris, Marshal Ferdinand

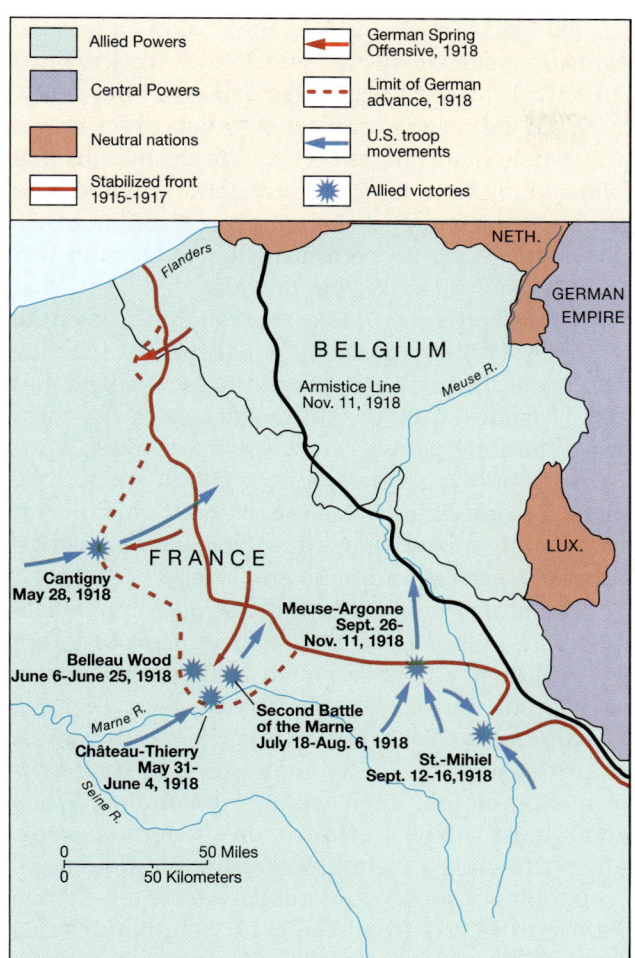

United States Participation on the Western Front

mer of 1918 broke the opposition, and within a few months the Central Powers faced certain defeat. The Austro-Hungarian Empire asked for peace; Turkey and Bulgaria stopped fighting; and Germany requested an armistice. In a direct slap at the kaiser, Wilson announced that he would negotiate only with a democratic regime in Germany. When the military leaders and the kaiser wavered, a brief revolution forced the kaiser to abdicate, and a civilian regime assumed control of the government.

Germany's new government immediately accepted the armistice and agreed to negotiate a treaty. At 11:00 A.M., November 11, 1918, the guns stopped. Throughout the Western world, crowds filled the streets to celebrate peace.

SOCIAL UNREST AFTER THE WAR

Peace did not restore stability to the United States. Jubilation over the Armistice quickly dissolved into fear, unleashing the forces of conformity, vigilantism, and repression. Attacks centered on African Americans, organized labor, and political dissidents—the very groups old-stock citizens blamed for the changes in American society that they found most threatening. The Wilson administration led the attacks or did nothing to stop them, as government officials found new enemies at home to replace those abroad. Echoing Bourne's earlier warnings, Frederick Howe, the commissioner of immigration

Foch, the leader of the French army, assumed command of the Allied forces. Foch's troops, aided by 85,000 American soldiers, launched a furious counteroffensive, hitting the Germans hard in a series of bloody assaults. By the end of October the German army had been pushed back to the Belgian border.

During the final months of fighting, American troops hit Europe like a tidal wave. In June 279,000 American soldiers crossed the Atlantic; in July over 300,000; in August, 286,000. All told, 1.5 million American troops arrived in Europe during the last six months of the war.

Fresh and battle-ready, Pershing's forces made the crucial difference in the war. Germany had enjoyed numerical superiority when American troops first arrived, but by the end of the war the Allies could field 600,000 more men than the Germans. Buoyed by the fresh manpower, the Allies pressed their advantage. Their furious offensive in the sum-

On November 11, 1918, American troops celebrated the news of the Armistice on the western front, while the Western world rejoiced at home.

under President Wilson, later confided: "I became distrustful of the state. It seemed to want to hurt people; it showed no concern for innocence; it aggrandized itself and protected its powers by unscrupulous means."

Mounting Racial Tension

Race relations deteriorated badly after the war, as tensions rose in the North because of competition for jobs and housing. In the South, whites felt threatened by the return of 400,000 African-American veterans, many of whom had been trained in the use of firearms, even if they had not seen actual combat. Moreover, many of the veterans had served in France, where they were treated as equals, and southern whites feared they would demand the same treatment at home. Determined to keep African Americans down, southern whites instituted a reign of terror. In 1919, 10 African-American veterans were lynched (several still in uniform); 14 were burned at the stake. All told, 70 lynchings occurred in the first year of peace.

As the heat of summer brought tensions to a boil, race riots broke out in 25 cities. The worst violence erupted on a Chicago beach where 17-year-old Eugene Williams strayed into waters claimed by whites. A rock-throwing mob kept him from reaching shore, and Williams drowned. Fighting broke out when police refused to arrest his killers. Thirteen days of street violence followed, leaving 38 dead, 578 injured, and 1000 families homeless. Racial injustice remained a defining feature of American life throughout the Progressive Era, despite American efforts abroad to make the world "safe for democracy."

Labor Unrest and the Red Scare

Labor was another trouble spot. Most workers had demonstrated their patriotism by not striking during the war, but the Armistice ended their truce with management. High inflation, job competition from returning veterans, and government policies all contributed to labor's discontent. Of the three, inflation hit workers the hardest. Food prices more than doubled between 1915 and 1920; clothing costs more than tripled. Wilson had made peace with trade unions only as a wartime necessity. After the fighting stopped, he removed wartime controls on industry, and business leaders closed ranks to roll back wartime concessions to workers.

The first strike came four days after the Armistice, when textile workers in New York walked out for a 15-percent wage hike and a 44-hour workweek. To the surprise of most observers, the workers won. Many more strikes occurred in the months that followed. Strikers ranged from clothing workers to actors. By the end of 1919 more than 4 million workers (a staggering 20 percent of the workforce) had staged over 3600 strikes nationwide.

The strikes, however, left the labor movement in shambles. Well-established unions affiliated with the AFL came through the turmoil in good shape, but unions made up of unskilled workers in the mass production industries, such as the United Mine Workers or the steelworkers, went down for the count. The message was clear: without government backing, organized labor could not win against the united strength of antiunion employers.

The strikes frightened middle- and upper-class Americans, who feared the country might be swept by revolution. The government made matters worse by blaming the strikes on Communists. In 1919, Russian Bolsheviks called for socialists and workers in Europe and the United States to seize their governments and join the worldwide revolution. When Communist revolts erupted in eastern Europe, Americans braced themselves for trouble at home.

A bomb scare brought public fears to a head. On the eve of May 1 (May Day), 1919, authorities discovered 20 bombs in the mail of prominent capitalists, including John D. Rockefeller and J. P. Morgan, Jr., as well as government officials like Supreme Court justice Oliver Wendell Holmes. A month later, bombs exploded in eight American cities. Anarchists were probably responsible, but the public blamed the Communists.

Fear sparked by the labor unrest, communism, and the bombings plunged the United States into the "Red Scare." Every threat to national security, real or imagined, fed the public's anxiety. In Washington, D.C., in May 1919, a man who refused to stand during the Star Spangled Banner at a victory pageant was shot by an enraged sailor while the crowd cheered; in Hammond, Indiana, in February 1919, a jury took two minutes to acquit a man who had killed an immigrant for yelling "To Hell with the United States."

Vigilantism flourished as juries across the country acquitted individuals accused of violent acts against Communists. In the Washington lumber town of Centralia, American Legionnaires stormed the IWW office on Armistice Day. Four attackers died in the fight, and townspeople lynched an IWW member in reprisal. Federal officials then moved to break the IWW's back by prosecuting 165 Wobblie leaders, who received prison sentences of up to 25 years.

Congress joined the attack on radicalism. In May 1919 the House refused to seat Victor Berger, a Milwaukee Socialist, after he was convicted of sedition. The House again denied him his seat following a special election in December 1919. Not until his reelection in 1922, after the government had dropped its charges, did Congress seat him.

Attorney General A. Mitchell Palmer led the attack on radicalism. Determined to become president in 1920, Palmer hoped to ride a wave of public hysteria against radicalism into the White House. To root out sedition, he created a General Intelligence Division (the precursor of the Federal Bureau of Investigation) in the Justice Department under the direction of J. Edgar Hoover. Hoover collected the names of thousands of known or suspected Communists and made plans for a coordinated government attack on their headquarters.

In November 1919 Palmer struck with lightning speed at radicals in 12 cities. The raids netted 250 arrests, a small taste of what was to follow. A second series of raids in 33 cities came in January. This time Palmer's men arrested more than 4000 alleged Communists, many of whom were jailed without bond, beaten, and denied food and water for days. Local authorities freed most of them in a few weeks, except for 600 aliens, who were deported.

Palmer insisted he was ridding the country of the "moral perverts and hysterical neurasthenic women who abound in communism." To cooler heads, however, his tactics gave off the unmistakable odor of a police state. Suddenly on the defensive, Palmer tried to rally public support by predicting a second wave of terrorist attacks on May Day, 1920. Federal troops went on alert, and police braced themselves in cities across the country, but May Day came and went without incident. Suddenly Palmer looked more like dead wood than presidential timber. His bid for the White House fizzled, and the Red Scare faded into memory.

THE TREATY OF VERSAILLES

Long before the war's military outcome became clear, the Allies started planning for peace, signing secret treaties and plotting harsh peace terms for Germany. Their schemes made a mockery of Wilson's call for "peace without victory." Wilson felt a punitive treaty would sow the seeds of future wars. He repeatedly elaborated his ideas on the interdependence of democracy, free trade, and liberty, and on January 8, 1918, he unveiled the **Fourteen Points,** his personal peace formula.

The Fourteen Points

Among other things, Wilson called for "open covenants openly arrived at," freedom of the seas, free trade, arms reduction, and self-determination. Other points demanded partial or full independence for minorities and a recognition of the rise of nationalist sentiments. The fourteenth point, which Wilson considered the heart of his plan, called for a **League of Nations,** an international organization to promote world peace by guaranteeing the territorial integrity of all nations.

Economically, the Fourteen Points projected Wilson's vision of liberal capitalism onto a world stage. His call for freedom of the seas and free trade was designed to protect free-market capitalism from monopolistic restrictions and open huge markets to booming American industries. Self-determination would offer independence to Europe's minorities and thereby delight millions of recent immigrants back in the United States, most of whom were drifting into the Democratic party. The League of Nations would enable the world to police aggression and spare the United States that responsibility.

When the tide of war turned in favor of the Allies in 1918, peace forces within Germany agreed to surrender on the basis of the Fourteen Points. They overthrew the kaiser's regime, paving the way for Wilson to make good on his promise of peace without victory.

Wilson's personal prestige peaked with the Armistice. Europeans saw him as the moral leader of the Western democracies, and his authority rested not only on words but on might. Economically, the United States was now the most powerful nation on earth. It had been spared the devastation of war; its economy was booming; and its armed forces, in sharp contrast to Europe's exhausted armies, had barely geared up for battle.

Yet Wilson proved to be his own worst enemy in marshaling support for his peace plans. His first mistake was in asking voters to support Democratic candidates at the polls in 1918 if they wished him to continue as their "unembarrassed spokesman." His request offended the Republicans who had faithfully supported the administration throughout the war. When voters gave Republicans a narrow majority (primarily reflecting local issues), Wilson looked as if he had lost a national referendum on his leadership.

The American Peace Commission's composition further alienated Congress. Wilson elected to take

Table 22.1
Woodrow Wilson's Fourteen Points, 1918: Success and Failure in Implementation

#	Point	Status
1.	Open covenants of peace openly arrived at	Not fulfilled
2.	Absolute freedom of navigation upon the seas in peace and war	Not fulfilled
3.	Removal of all economic barriers to the equality of trade among nations	Not fulfilled
4.	Reduction of armaments to the level needed only for domestic safety	Not fulfilled
5.	Impartial adjustment of colonial claims	Not fulfilled
6.	Evacuation of all Russian territory; Russia to be welcomed into the society of free nations	Not fulfilled
7.	Evacuation and restoration of Belgium	**Fulfilled**
8.	Evacuation and restoration of all French lands; return of Alsace-Lorraine to France	**Fulfilled**
9.	Readjustment of Italy's frontiers along lines of Italian nationality	Compromised
10.	Self-determination for the former subjects of the Austro-Hungarian Empire	Compromised
11.	Evacuation of Rumania, Serbia, and Montenegro; free access to the sea for Serbia	Compromised
12.	Self-determination for the former subjects of the Ottoman Empire; secure sovereignty for Turkish portion	Compromised
13.	Establishment of an independent Poland, with free and secure access to the sea	**Fulfilled**
14.	Establishment of a League of Nations affording mutual guarantees of independence and territorial integrity	Not fulfilled

Source: Data from G. M. Gathorne-Hardy, *The Fourteen Points and the Treaty of Versailles,* Oxford Pamphlets on World Affairs, no. 6, 1939); and Thomas G. Paterson et al., *American Foreign Policy, A History Since 1900,* 2nd ed., Vol. 2, pp. 282–293.

---

personal responsibility for negotiating the peace, a role no previous president had assumed. In addition, he named only one Republican to the five-man commission; the other three men were loyal Democrats. The failure to include a prominent Republican senator, such as Henry Cabot Lodge of Massachusetts, the newly elected chairman of the powerful Senate committee on Foreign Relations, was a serious tactical error. The treaty had to be approved by two-thirds of the Senate, and Republicans picked up five new Senate seats in the congressional elections of 1918, giving them a two-vote majority.

Discord Among the Victors

The delegates, who arrived in Europe early in January 1919, confronted three basic issues: territory, reparations, and future security. On each of these issues, Wilson and the Allies disagreed. Early in the war the Allies had decided to divide Germany's territorial possessions among themselves, but the Fourteen Points called for self-determination. Devastated by the war, the Allies (especially France) wanted to saddle Germany with huge reparations to pay for the war. The Fourteen Points rejected punishment, arguing it would only lead to future wars. On the issue of security, France wanted Germany dismembered while the other Allies favored treaties and alliances.

Only five nations played an important role in the proceedings (the Allies refused to allow Russia's Communist government to participate). Prime Minister David Lloyd George of Great Britain proved to be Wilson's staunchest ally, yet he also defended Britain's colonial ambitions and insisted on reparations. Premier Georges Clemenceau of France was determined to break up the German empire and bleed the German people dry in order to rebuild France. He wryly remarked, "God gave us the Ten Commandments and we broke them. Wilson gave us his Fourteen Points—we shall see."

Premier Vittorio Orlando of Italy was bent on pressing Italy's territorial ambitions in the Tyrol and on the Adriatic. When Wilson refused to sanction Italy's sovereignty over the largely Yugoslav population near Fiume, Orlando stormed out of the peace conference in disgust. The final important negotiator was Count Nobuaki Makino, the spokesman for Japan, who demanded control over German interests in the Far East. He also insisted upon a statement of racial equality in the League of Nations charter—a demand the Allies rejected.

At the January peace conference in Paris, Wilson met with British Prime Minister David Lloyd George, Italian Premier Vittorio Orlando, and French Premier Georges Clemenceau. Not pictured is Count Nobuaki Makino of Japan, the fifth nation to play an important role in the proceedings.

The Russians were conspicuous by their absence at Versailles. Allied leaders, furious at the Bolsheviks for negotiating a separate peace with Germany at Brest-Litovsk in March 1918, refused to assign V. I. Lenin's "Red" government a place at the peace conference. Indeed, the Allies had earlier decided to intervene militarily in the Russian Revolution, and even as their spokesmen met in Versailles, Allied armies were fighting in Russia on the side of the "White," or anti-Communist, forces.

Personally, Wilson despised the Bolsheviks, and, in keeping with his response to Huerta's regime in Mexico, he refused to extend diplomatic recognition to Lenin's government. Moreover, much as he had with Mexico, Wilson did not stop to ponder how Russians would react to finding American soldiers on their soil. To help rescue Czech troops trapped by the Germans in northern Russia, Wilson sent 5000 American soldiers to the Soviet Union in 1918, where they joined British troops. The following year Wilson sent 9000 American troops to Siberia to help evacuate Czech troops through Vladivostok. Wilson hoped American troops in Russia would save the Czechs and discourage any Japanese designs on Siberia. In addition, he wanted this show of force to bolster the anti-Communist forces in Russia by weakening the Bolsheviks' claims to power. Consequently, the United States dragged its feet and did not withdraw its last troops from Russia until 1920.

American Military Forces in Russia, 1918

The Bolsheviks deeply resented these heavy-handed efforts to undermine their regime. Yet the invasion of Russian soil by American troops was not the only reason for the intense hatred that developed between Lenin and Wilson. As the architect of the Bolshevik Revolution, Lenin emerged as Wilson's chief rival for world leadership. Where Wilson offered liberal democracy and limited social change, Lenin championed communism, social revolution, and swift changes. Wilson was determined to see his vision of the future, not Lenin's, carry the day at Versailles.

To achieve any treaty at all, Wilson had to compromise. Though he fought gallantly, he could not overcome the combined strength of his opponents. In the end he tried to scale down their demands and pinned his hopes on the League of Nations. Under the territorial compromise, the Allies gained control of Germany's colonies as "mandates" under the League of Nation's supervision. Japan acquired Germany's Pacific islands under mandate and assumed Germany's economic interest in China's Shantung peninsula. In eastern Europe, the delegates created the nation states of Poland, Yugoslavia, Czechoslovakia, Estonia, Latvia, Lithuania, and Finland. Europe's political map for the first time roughly resembled its linguistic and cultural map.

Security proved more difficult to negotiate. Over the misgivings of most delegates, Wilson insisted on making the League of Nations an integral part of the final treaty. Dubious that any international organization could protect its borders, France demanded a buffer zone. To satisfy Clemenceau, the delegates gave France control over Alsace-Lorraine for 10 years and placed the coal-rich Saar Basin under the League of Nations for 15 years. After Wilson and Lloyd George both signed security treaties guaranteeing these arrangements, France grudgingly agreed to join the League of Nations.

Despite promises of a just peace, the treaty imposed a harsh settlement on Germany, saddling the country with a $34-billion reparations bill, far more than Germany could pay. In addition, Germany lost territories that contained German people: Alsace-Lorraine to France, the Saar Basin to a League protectorate, a corridor containing the port of Danzig to Poland, and Upper Silesia to Czechoslovakia. Moreover, under the terms of the war guilt clause in the reparations bill, Germany accepted the blame for World War I, agreed to dismantle its war machine, and pledged not to rearm in the future. Germany felt betrayed. Clearly, this was not a peace based upon the Fourteen Points. Rather, it brought to life Bourne's prediction of victors who "grab what they can."

Wilson derived no joy from the **Treaty of Versailles.** He accepted the treaty's territorial and punitive provisions in order to ensure the adoption of the League of Nations, which he hoped would secure world peace and eventually redress the treaty's inequities. The League consisted of a general assembly that included all member states and an executive council composed of the United States, Great Britain, France, Italy, Japan, and four other states to be elected by the assembly. But the heart of the League was clearly Article 10, which pledged all members "to respect and uphold the territorial integrity and independence of all members of the League." It embodied Wilson's dream of an international organization that would keep the peace by giving all nations (large and small) equality and protection.

Europe After World War I

The Struggle for Ratification

Wilson knew the treaty faced stiff opposition back home. In February 1919, 39 Senate Republicans had signed a petition warning they would not approve the League in its present form. To court domestic support, Wilson persuaded the delegates in Europe to acknowledge the Monroe Doctrine, omit domestic issues from the League's purview, and permit member states to withdraw after two years' notice. Though he worked to include provisions the Senate wanted, Wilson refused to separate the League from the treaty.

Senate opposition broke into three groups. The first, 14 "irreconcilables," were staunch isolationists who opposed the League of Nations in any form. Though their attack was broad-based, they concentrated their fire on Article 10, which called for the mutual protection of the territorial integrity of all member states. Critics charged that the article gave the League the authority to commit American troops to foreign military actions.

Henry Cabot Lodge of Massachusetts spoke for the second group of critics, the "strong reservationists." Parodying Wilson's "Fourteen Points," Lodge offered 14 amendments, called the "Lodge" reservations. The most important decreed that the United States "assumes no obligation" to protect the independence or territory boundaries of any other nation, or to send American troops for such purposes unless Congress should so order. Lodge and his followers were basically in favor of the treaty and could have been won over if Wilson had agreed to their modifications.

The third group of opponents, the "limited reservationists," could have been assuaged by relatively minor alterations. They approached international affairs as cautious nationalists, favoring an independent foreign policy as the best tool for protecting American interests. With their backing and the support of Senate Democrats, the treaty would have passed easily.

As Wilson sailed back to the United States, polls suggested that most Americans favored the League in some form. All he had to do was compromise and the treaty would pass. Instead, Wilson descended on Washington in July itching for a fight. Dismissing his opponents as "blind and little provincial people," he declared that the "Senate must take its medicine." His use of a medical metaphor was telling, for Wilson's health had seriously deteriorated under the strain of the war.

Fearing Senate debate had eroded popular support for the treaty, Wilson decided to take his case directly to the people. Against his doctor's advice, he launched a nationwide tour in September 1919, covering 8000 miles in 33 days and delivering 32 major addresses. Totally exhausted, Wilson collapsed on September 25 in Pueblo, Colorado. Four days after returning to Washington, he suffered a severe stroke that paralyzed the left side of his body. Unable to work, he did not meet with his cabinet for more than six months. Since the law made no provision for removing an incapacitated president, Wilson's second wife, Edith Bolling Wilson, assisted by a few close aides, ran the government, operating under a cloak of silence about the president's condition.

As the Senate vote on the treaty drew near, Wilson remained intransigent, telling his wife: "Better a thousand times to go down fighting than to dip your colors to dishonorable compromise." He ordered all Democrats to vote against the treaty if it contained any changes. On November 19, the Senate defeated the revised version of the treaty, 55 to 39; a few minutes later the Senate defeated the treaty without changes, 39 to 53.

The Senate's failure to reach a compromise must be blamed on Wilson. When the treaty's supporters tried again in March, many of the Democrats disobeyed the president and voted for a revised version. But 23 Democrats followed Wilson's orders, and the treaty fell 7 votes short of adoption. It would be wrong, however, to interpret the treaty's defeat as an endorsement of isolationism. In essence, the Senate rejected both isolationism and Wilsonian internationalism in favor of preserving a nationalistic foreign policy that would allow the United States to act independently.

The Election of 1920

Unable to accept defeat, Wilson decided to make the election of 1920 a "solemn referendum" on the League: the election of a Democrat would signify approval of the treaty; a Republican victory would mean the treaty's death. At best the president's proposal offered a dubious test of the public's support for the treaty. National elections rarely turn on a single issue.

When the Democratic convention met in San Francisco, the delegates ignored Wilson's pathetic anglings for a third term and nominated Governor James M. Cox of Ohio. To round out the ticket, they selected the assistant secretary of the navy, Franklin D. Roosevelt, for vice president, largely to capitalize on the magic Roosevelt name. The Republicans nominated Senator Warren G. Harding of Ohio. A stal-

The refusal of the Senate to ratify the Treaty of Versailles and join the League of Nations is satirized in this political cartoon.

wart party regular on domestic issues, Harding had voted for the Treaty of Versailles with the Lodge reservations.

While Cox barnstormed the country, campaigning unequivocally for the League of Nations and the Treaty of Versailles, Harding waffled on the issue. Tired of foreign crusades, the people wanted to repudiate Wilson's ardent internationalism, and they did just that, giving Harding 61 percent of the popular vote. (Eugene V. Debs, the Socialist candidate, won 919,799 votes, even though he was then serving a prison term for opposing American involvement in the war.) In the electoral college, Harding trounced Cox 404 to 127.

Wilson's fragile coalition of 1916 had collapsed. Many Democrats, disillusioned by the costs of the war, either stayed at home or switched parties. Angered by the Treaty of Versailles, ethnic Americans (Germans, Italians, and the Irish in particular) abandoned the Democrats in droves. Western states and the Midwest went Republican as well, for despite their wartime prosperity, many farmers believed that Wilson's agricultural policies had favored cotton

Chronology of Key Events

1914	World War I begins in Europe
1915	U.S. marines are dispatched to Haiti; German submarine sinks the British passenger ship *Lusitania*, killing 1198 passengers, including 128 Americans
1916	Germany promises to suspend unannounced submarine attacks in *Sussex* pledge
1917	Germany resumes submarine attacks; Zimmermann telegram, secret note to German ambassador in Mexico, proposing Mexico and Japan join Central Powers if the United States enters the war in Europe; United States enters the war; Espionage Act passed, imposing fines and jail sentences for aiding the enemy or obstructing recruitment; Russian Revolution begins; War Industries Board is created to coordinate industrial production
1918	Wilson's Fourteen Points outline a plan for peace; National War Labor Board is created to arbitrate disputes between labor and management; Sedition Act passes, punishing any expression of disloyalty to the American government or flag; Germany surrenders
1919	Treaty of Versailles ends World War I
1920	In raids authorized by Attorney General Palmer many suspected Communists are arrested; Senate rejects Treaty of Versailles; Nineteenth Amendment grants women the right to vote; Republican Warren Harding is elected twenty-ninth president

growers in the South over grain producers of the Midwest. The Solid South remained a bastion of Democratic strength, but it did not have nearly enough votes to elect a president.

Harding interpreted his victory as a mandate to reject the League. America never joined the League of Nations, opening the way for those who later blamed the United States for the rise of fascism in Italy and Nazism in Germany. Critics, including a number of later historians, went so far as to claim that America's failure to join the League caused World War II. Instead of peace without victory, the war's main legacy turned out to be bitterness and suspicion.

Conclusion

World War I made Randolph Bourne a prophet. The changes in American life between 1914 and 1919 bore out his fear that war obliterates idealism and brings out the dark side of the human spirit. World War I accelerated social and economic changes, expanded the power of the federal government, and unleashed extraordinary fears that led to attacks on labor unions, African Americans, immigrants, Socialists, and Communists. Similar confusion gripped America's foreign policy. The United States emerged from the Great War as the premier economic power on earth, with global interests requiring protection. Tired and disillusioned, Americans attempted to flee their responsibilities rather than make global political commitments commensurate with their new economic interests.

The result was an upsurge in isolationist sentiment in the United States during the 1920s and 1930s that made it very difficult for America's leaders to respond strongly to the rise of despotic governments in Europe and the Far East. The Great War did not make the world "safe for democracy." It left humankind a legacy of bitterness, hatred, and suspicion, creating rich soil for the seeds of future conflicts.

In 1920, however, most Americans felt too tired and too disillusioned to give much thought to the future. Harding's promise of a return to "normalcy" struck a responsive chord. Millions of Americans thought he meant resurrecting rural villages and a small farm economy, restoring Anglo-Protestant culture, and forgetting about the rest of the world. The 1920s proved they were in for a surprise.

Suggestions for Further Reading

Lloyd Ambrosus, *Woodrow Wilson and the American Diplomatic Tradition* (1988). Presents a comprehensive account of American diplomacy during and after the war.

Robert H. Ferrell, *Woodrow Wilson and World War I, 1917–1921,* (1985). Thoroughly analyzes the president's responses to the conflict.

Martin Gilbert, *The First World War* (1994). Discusses the conflict's causes and fighting.

David M. Kennedy, *Over Here: The First World War and American Society* (1980). Examines the war's impact on the homefront.

Michael J. Lyons, *World War I* (1994). Offers a comprehensive account of the conflict.

Herbert F. Margulies, *The Mild Reservations and the League of Nations Controversy in the Senate* (1989). Explores the reasons the Senate rejected American membership in the League of Nations.

Arthur Walworth, *Wilson and His Peacemakers: American Diplomacy at the Paris Peace Conference* (1986). Examines the contentious debates surrounding the Treaty of Versailles.

Overviews and Surveys

Randolph S. Bourne, *War and the Intellectuals: Collected Essays, 1915–1919* (1964); Edward M. Coffman, *The War to End All Wars: the American Military Experience in World War I* (1998); Foster R. Dulles, *America's Rise to World Power, 1898–1954* (1955); Modris Eksteins, *Rites of Spring: The Great War and the Birth of the Modern Age* (1989); Robert H. Ferrell, *Woodrow Wilson and World War I, 1917–1921* (1985); Lloyd C. Gardner, *Safe for Democracy: The Anglo-American Response to Revolution, 1913–1923* (1984); Otis L. Graham, Jr., *The Great Campaigns: Reform and War in America, 1900–1928* (1971); Ellis W. Hawley, *The Great War and the Search for a Modern Order: A History of the American People and Their Institutions, 1917–1933* (1979); William E. Leuchtenburg, *The Perils of Prosperity, 1914–32* (1958); Emily S. Rosenberg, *Spreading the American Dream: American Economic and Cultural Expansion 1890–1945* (1982); Bernadotte Schmitt and Harold C. Vedeler, *The World in the Crucible: 1914–1919* (1984); Daniel M. Smith, *The Great Departure: The United States and World War I, 1914–1920* (1965).

The Road to War

John M. Cooper, Jr., *The Vanity of Power: American Isolationism and the First World War, 1914–1917* (1969) and *The Warrior and the Priest: Woodrow Wilson and Theodore Roosevelt* (1983); Patrick Devlin, *Too Proud to Fight: Woodrow Wilson's Neutrality* (1974); Ross Gregory, *The Origins of American Intervention in the First World War* (1971); George F. Kennan, *The Decision to Intervene* (1958) and *Russia Leaves the War* (1956); N. Gordon Levin, Jr., *Woodrow Wilson and World Politics: America's Response to War and Revolution* (1968); Arthur S. Link, *Woodrow Wilson: Revolution, War and Peace* (1979); Ernest R. May, *The World War and American Isolation, 1914–1917* (1959); Barbara Tuchman, *The Guns of August* (1962).

American Industry Goes to War

William J. Breen, *Uncle Sam at Home, 1917–1919* (1984); Valerie Jean Conner, *The National War Labor Board: Stability, Social Justice, and the Voluntary State in World War I* (1983); Robert D. Cuff, *The War Industries Board: Business-Government Relations During World War I* (1973); Leslie Midkiff Debauche, *Reel Patriotism: The Movies and World War I* (1997); Charles Gilbert, *American Financing of World War I* (1970); Maurine Weiner Greenwald, *Women, War, and Work: The Impact of World War I on Women Workers in the United States* (1980); Stephen Skowronek, *Building a New American State: The Expansion of National Administrative Capacities, 1877–1920* (1982); Stephen L. Vaughn, *Holding Fast the Inner Lines: Democracy, Nationalism, and the Committee on Public Information* (1980); Neil A. Wynn, *From Progressivism to Prosperity: World War I and American Society* (1986).

The American Public Goes to War

Rodolfo Acuña, *Occupied America*, 3d ed. (1988); Arthur E. Barbeau and Florette Henri, *The Unknown Soldiers: Black American Troops in World War I* (1974); Allan M. Brandt, *No Magic Bullet: A Social History of Venereal Disease in the United States Since 1880* (1985); Nancy K. Bristow, *Making Men Moral: Social Engineering During the Great War* (1996); John Whiteclay Chambers II, *To Raise an Army: The Draft Comes to Modern America* (1987); Wayne Cornelius, *Building the Cactus Curtain: Mexican Migration and U.S. Responses from Wilson to Carter* (1980); Lettie Gavin, *American Women in World War I: They Also Served* (1997); Maurine W. Greenwald, *Women, War, and Work: The Impact of World War I on Women Workers* (1980); James R. Grossman, *Land of Hope: Chicago, Black Southerners, and the Great Migration* (1989); David M. Kennedy, *Over Here: The First World War and American Society* (1980); K. Austin Kerr, *Organized for Prohibition: A New History of the Anti-Saloon League* (1985); Daniel J. Kevles, *In the Name of Eugenics: Genetics and the Uses of Human Heredity* (1985); Frederick C. Luebke, *Bonds of Loyalty: German-Americans and World War I* (1974); Carole Marks, *Farewell—We're Good and Gone: The Great Black Migration* (1989); John F. McClymer, *War and Welfare: Social Engineering in America, 1890–1925* (1980); Paul L. Murphy, *World War I and the Origin of Civil Liberties in the United States* (1979); Gerald W. Patton, *War and Race: The Black Officer in the American Military* (1981); H. C. Peterson and Gilbert C. Fite, *Opponents of War 1917–1918* (1957); William Preston, Jr., *Aliens and Dissenters: Federal Suppression of Radicals, 1903–1933* (1963); John A. Thompson, *Reformers and War: American Progressive Publicists and the First World War* (1987); Stephen L. Vaughn, *Holding Fast the Inner Lines: Democracy, Nationalism, and the Committee on Public Information* (1980).

The War Front

Arthur E. Barbeau and Florette Henri, *The Unknown Soldiers: Black American Troops in World War I* (1974); Edward M. Coffman, *The War to End Wars: The American Military Experience in World War I* (1968); Harvey DeWeerd, *President Wilson Fights His War: World War I and the American Intervention* (1968); Russell F. Weigley, *The American Way of War: A History of United States Military Strategy and Policy* (1973).

Social Unrest After the War

Wesley M. Bagby, *The Road to Normalcy: The Presidential Campaign and Election of 1920* (1962); David Brody, *Labor in Crisis: The Steel Strike of 1919* (1965); Richard C. Cortner, *A Mob Intent on Death: The NAACP and the Arkansas Riot Cases* (1988); Paul Fussell, *The Great War and Modern Memory* (1975); Christine A. Lunardini, *From Equal Suffrage to Equal Rights: Alice Paul and the National Woman's Party, 1910–1928* (1986); Robert K. Murray, *The Red Scare: A Study in National Hysteria, 1919–1920* (1955); Burl Noggle, *Into the Twenties: The United States from Armistice to Normalcy* (1974); Francis Russell, *A City in Terror: 1919, the Boston Police Strike* (1975); Arthur M. Schlesinger, Jr., *The Crisis of the Old Order, 1919–1933* (1957); William Tuttle, Jr., *Race Riot: Chicago and the Red Summer of 1919* (1970).

The Treaty of Versailles

Thomas A. Bailey, *Woodrow Wilson and the Great Betrayal* (1945), and *Woodrow Wilson and the Lost Peace* (1944); Warren F. Kuehl, *Seeking World Order: The United States and International Organization to 1920* (1969); N. Gordon Levin, Jr., *Woodrow Wilson and World Politics: America's Response to War and Revolution* (1968); Herbert F. Margulies, *The Mild Reservationists and the League of Nations Controversy in the Senate* (1989); Arno J. Mayer, *Politics and Diplomacy in Peacemaking: Containment and Counterrevolution at Versailles, 1918–1919* (1967) and *Wilson vs. Lenin: Political Origins of the New Diplomacy, 1917–1918* (1959); Ralph A. Stone, *The Irreconcilables: The Fight Against the League of Nations* (1970); William C. Widenor, *Henry Cabot Lodge and the Search for an American Foreign Policy* (1980).

Biographies

Robert W. Cherny, *A Righteous Cause: The Life of William Jennings Bryan* (1985); Kendrick A. Clements, *William Jennings Bryan, Missionary Isolationist* (1982); Stanley Coben, *A. Mitchell Palmer: Politician* (1963); Yvonne Klein, ed., *Beyond the Homefront: Women's Autobiographical Writing of the Two World Wars* (1997); Lawrence W. Levine, *Defender of the Faith: William Jennings Bryan, The Last Decade, 1915–1925* (1965); Arthur S. Link, *Wilson*, 5 vols. (1947–1965); James R. Vitelli, *Randolph Bourne* (1981); Edwin A. Weinstein, *Woodrow Wilson: A Medical and Psychological Biography* (1981).

Internet Resources

Bill Haywood Trial (1907)
http://www.law.umkc.edu/faculty/projects/ftrials/haywood/haywood.htm
This site contains images, chronology, and court and official documents maintained by Dr. Doug Linder at University of Missouri—Kansas City Law School.

World War I Document Archive
http://www.lib.byu.edu/~rdh/wwi/
This archive contains sources about World War One in general, not just America's involvement.

The Great Influenza Epidemic
http://www.pbs.org/wgbh/pages/amex/influenza/
This PBS site reveals the impact of the flu epidemic of 1918.

Documents from the Women's Liberation Movement
http://scriptorium.lib.duke.edu/wlm/
Primary documents online from the Special Collections Library at Duke University provide firsthand information about the women's liberation movement.

The Women's Suffrage Movement
http://www.rochester.edu/SBA/hisindx.html
This site includes a chronology, important texts relating to women's suffrage, and biographical information on Susan B. Anthony and Elizabeth Cady Stanton.

World War One: Trenches on the Web
http://www.worldwar1.com/index.html
This site provides a mass of data concerning the prosecution of the world's first global war.

The Great Migration in Chicago
http://lcweb.loc.gov/exhibits/african/afam011.html
This site looks at the black experience in the Great Migration through the lens of one prominent destination.

National Geographic and the Titanic
http://www.nationalgeographic.com/society/ngo/explorer/titanic/movie.html
This site offers historical perspective and balanced coverage of this tragic event.

Key Terms

Allies (p. 642)
Neutrality (p. 643)
Central Powers (p. 646)
Lusitania (p. 647)
Zimmermann telegram (p. 649)
Hooverizing (p. 652)
Committee on Public Information (CPI) (p. 653)
Great Migration (p. 657)
Fourteen Points (p. 661)
League of Nations (p. 661)
Treaty of Versailles (p. 664)

REVIEW QUESTIONS

1. Could the United States have avoided entering the war?
2. Did World War I propaganda serve as a mobilizing or a suppressing force for Americans?
3. How did President Wilson ensure the participation of American industry in World War I?
4. How did World War I differ from previous wars?
5. Why did the end of World War I bring tension to the homefront?
6. Was Congress justified in rejecting the League of Nations?

23

MODERN TIMES, 1920–1929

THE EMERGENCE OF MODERN AMERICA
Urban Growth
The Rise of a Consumer Economy

THE FORMATION OF MODERN AMERICAN CULTURE
Mass Entertainment
Spectator Sports
Low-Brow and Middle-Brow Culture
The Avant-Garde
The Sex Debate

THE CLASH OF CULTURES
The New Woman
Prohibition
The Scopes Trial
Xenophobia and Restricting Immigration
The Ku Klux Klan
African-American Protests
The Harlem Renaissance

THE REPUBLICAN RESTORATION
Handsome Harding
Silent Cal
The Twilight of Progressivism
The Election of 1928

THE GREAT CRASH
Speculative Manias
The Market Crashes
Why It Happened

"Biological duty"

In 1898 the Physicians Club of Chicago held a symposium on "sexual hygiene" to give its members some practical tips on marriage counseling. To those married women who wanted information on birth control, Chicago physicians were to offer this advice: "Get a divorce and vacate the position for some other woman, who is able and willing to fulfill all a wife's duties as well as to enjoy her privileges."

Most Americans shared this view. To the male custodians of morality, birth control challenged patriarchy. It would lead to sexual promiscuity and an epidemic of venereal diseases, they charged, and weaken the family by raising the divorce rate. Many women condemned birth control just as soundly. Taught from childhood to embrace the cult of domesticity, they accepted childbearing as their "biological duty" and rejected birth control as immoral and radical.

Yet by 1950 most Americans regarded birth control as a public virtue rather than a private vice. The person most responsible for this amazing transformation was Margaret Sanger, a tireless crusader who possessed an iron will and the soul of a firebrand. Sanger's mother, Margaret Higgins, bore 11 children, all weighing ten pounds or more; Michael Higgins, her father, worked as a stonecutter. Her mother died of pulmonary tuberculosis at 43; her father lived to 84. For the rest of her life, Sanger blamed her mother's suffering on the absence of effective family planning.

An unhappy marriage also pushed Sanger toward reform work. While still in nursing school, she married William Sanger, an architect and would-be artist. After bearing three children in rapid succession, Sanger overcame her own struggle with tuberculosis, finished school, and began a nursing career. Feeling trapped by married life and determined to achieve her own identity, Margaret plunged into New York's labor movement.

Convinced that large families placed a terrible economic burden on poor people, Sanger came to regard family planning as the most important issue of her day because it could make abortion, as well as unwanted babies, unnecessary. When male labor leaders refused to add contraception to their reform

Margaret Sanger, a nurse who had watched many women suffer from unwanted births and die from illegal abortions, was one of the founders of the modern American birth control movement. After spending a year studying medical literature and learning about contraceptives, Sanger began publishing the journal *The Woman Rebel*.

agenda, Sanger left the labor movement, resolving to make birth control her life's work.

From 1914 to 1937 Sanger campaigned to make birth control morally acceptable. She built a network of clinics where women could get accurate information about contraception and obtain inexpensive, reliable birth control devices. After World War II she helped organize the international planned parenthood movement and played a key role in the development of "the pill." Through her birth control work, Margaret Sanger probably had a greater influence on the world than any other American woman of her day.

Sanger played a key role in the transition to modern times. By promoting birth control, she helped alter American sexual behavior, redefine women's role in society, and redistributed power within the family. But the birth control movement represented just one symptom of a society in flux, one in which urban growth, ethnic diversity, and economic development set the stage for controversy.

The 1920s was a decade of exciting social changes and deep cultural conflicts. The most obvious signs of change were the growth of cities, with their huge ethnic populations; the rise of a consumer-oriented economy, evident in the spread of cars, electricity, and a host of new appliances; and the spread of mass entertainment, such as spectator sports, radio, and the movies. But a deeper transformation was also under way, a "revolution in morals and manners." Sexual mores and gender roles underwent dramatic shifts.

For many Americans, these changes represented a liberation from the restrictions of the country's Victorian past. But for others, especially those who lived in the more rural and provincial parts of the country, morals seemed to be decaying and the United States seemed to be changing in undesirable ways. The result was a thinly veiled "cultural civil war," in which a pluralistic society clashed bitterly over such issues as foreign immigration, evolution, and race.

Wets battled drys, Darwinists ridiculed fundamentalists, nativists denounced the "new immigrants," and rural folks denounced the dubious morals of city dwellers. None of these disputes was new. Each was a continuing, if sharpening, controversy that had been building for decades. At bottom, these conflicts were the unavoidable growing pains of a nation struggling to come to grips with cultural pluralism and changing values.

THE EMERGENCE OF MODERN AMERICA

Americans in the 1920s were the first to wear ready-made, exact-sized clothing, the first to play electric phonographs or use electric vacuum cleaners or listen to commercial radio broadcasts or drink fresh orange juice year round. In countless ways, large and small, American life was transformed during the 1920s, at least in the nation's growing towns and cities, where the majority of Americans now lived. Cigarettes, cosmetics, and synthetic fabrics such as rayon became staples of American life. Public opinion polling, sex education, newspaper gossip columns, illuminated billboards, commercial airplane flights—all were novelties during the 1920s. In that decade, the United States became a modern consumer society.

Urban Growth

For more than four decades, the Empire State Building was the largest building in the world, rising 102 stories above New York City's Fifth Avenue. The 1454-foot-high building cost nearly $41 million to erect, but when it was finished in 1930, it stood half-empty—a symbol of a decade's broken dreams.

All across America, urban skylines were transformed. Urban growth drove up land values and reshaped the skyline of America's cities, especially in central business districts, where office space more than doubled during the 1920s. Skyrocketing land prices forced architects to build "up" instead of "out," launching the first great era of skyscrapers. By 1929, the United States had 377 buildings with more than 20 stories.

According to the census of 1920 more Americans dwelled in cities than in the country. For the first time in its history, the United States became a predominantly urban society. Most urbanites lived

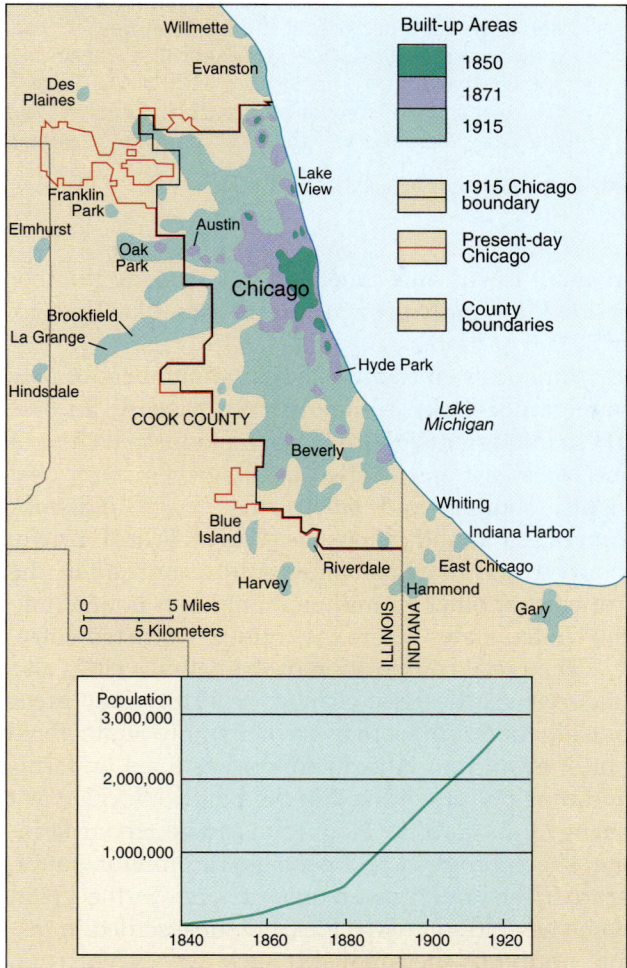

Growth of Chicago

THE PEOPLE SPEAK

Margaret Sanger, "Happiness in Marriage" (1926)

Margaret Sanger, one of the founders of the birth control movement, saw family planning as the key to women's liberation. Middle-class women in particular took up the cause, seeing in Sanger's ideas an escape from the restrictions of traditional womanhood. In the excerpt below, Sanger describes the ideal marriage and family situation.

> We must recognize that the whole position of womanhood has changed today. Not so many years ago it was assumed to be a just and natural state of affairs that marriage was considered as nothing but a preliminary to motherhood. A girl passed from the guardianship of her father or nearest male relative to that of her husband. She had no will, no wishes of her own. Hers not to question, but merely to fulfil duties imposed upon her by the man into whose care she was given.
>
> Marriage was synonymous with maternity. But the pain, the suffering, the wrecked lives of women and children that such a system caused, show us that it did not work successfully. Like all other professions, motherhood must serve its period of apprenticeship.
>
> Today women are on the whole much more individual. They possess as strong likes and dislikes as men. They live more and more on the plane of social equality with men. They are better companions. We should be glad that there is more enjoyable companionship and real friendship between men and women.
>
> This very fact it is true, complicates the marriage relation, and at the same time ennobles. Marriage no longer means the slavish subservience of the woman to the will of the man. It means, instead, the union of two strong and highly individualized natures. Their first problem is to find out just what the terms of this partnership are to be. Understanding full and complete cannot come all at once, in one revealing flash. It takes time to arrive at a full and sympathetic understanding of each other, and mutually to arrange lives to increase this understanding. Out of the mutual adjustments, harmony must grow and discords gradually disappear.
>
> These results cannot be obtained if the problem of parenthood is thrust upon the young husband and wife before they are spiritually and economically prepared to meet it. For naturally the coming of the first baby means that all other problems must be thrust aside. That baby is a great fact, a reality that must be met. Preparations must be made for its coming. The layette must be prepared. The doctor must be consulted. The health of the wife may need

in small towns and cities, but a surprising number resided in rapidly growing large cities, like Chicago, of 50,000 or more.

America's cities attracted large numbers of new immigrants from southern and eastern Europe. These immigrants poured into the industrial cities of the Northeast and Midwest, filling them with new sights, sounds, and smells that many old-stock Americans found offensive. World War I briefly stopped the flow of immigrants, but after the armistice another 3.2 million immigrants poured into the United States before the country restricted entry.

The racial composition of the nation's cities also underwent a decisive change. In 1910, urban areas outside the South were overwhelmingly white; three out of every four African Americans lived on farms and nine out of ten lived in the South. World War I changed that profile. Hoping to escape tenant farming, sharecropping, and peonage, 1.5 million southern African Americans moved to cities in the 1920s. Some went to southern cities, but most settled in major northern metropolises such as New York, Philadelphia, Cleveland, and Chicago. During the 1910s and 1920s, Chicago's African-American population grew 148 percent, Cleveland's by 307 percent, Detroit's by 611 percent.

During this massive movement of people, competition for available housing became a major source of friction. In city after city, whites closed ranks against African Americans, blocking access to white neighborhoods. Cities passed municipal residential segregation ordinances; white realtors refused to show houses in white areas to African Americans; and white property owners formed "neighborhood improvement associations," largely in order to keep African Americans out. After the Supreme Court declared municipal resident segregation ordinances unconstitutional in 1917, whites resorted to the restrictive covenant, a formal deed restriction that bound white property owners in a given neighborhood to sell only to whites. Those who broke such agreements could be sued by "damaged" neighbors. Not until 1948 did the Supreme Court strike down restrictive covenants. Zoning laws offered an even

consideration. The young mother will probably prefer to go to the hospital. All of these preparations are small compared to the regime after the coming of the infant.

Now there is a proper moment for every human activity, a proper season for every step in self-development. The period for cementing the bond of love is no exception to this great truth. For only by the full and glorious living through these years of early marriage are the foundations of an enduring and happy married life rendered possible. By this period the woman attains a spiritual freedom. Her womanhood has a chance to bloom. She wins a mastery over her destiny; she acquires self-reliance, poise, strength, a youthful maturity. She abolishes fear. Incidentally, few of us realize, since the world keeps no repugnance by young mothers who are the victims of undesired maternity. Nor has science yet determined the posibilities of a generation conceived and born of conscious desire.

In the wife who has lived through a happy marriage, for whom the bonds of passionate love have been fully cemented, maternal desire is intensified and matured. Motherhood becomes for such a woman not a penalty or a punishment, but the road by which she travels onward toward completely rounded self-development. Motherhood thus helps her toward the unfolding and realization of her higher nature.

Her children are not mere accidents, the outcome of chance. When motherhood is a mere accident, as so often it is in the early years of careless or reckless marriages, a constant fear of pregnancy may poison the days and nights of the young mother. Her marriage is thus converted into a tragedy. Motherhood becomes for her a horror instead of a joyfully fulfilled function.

Instead of being a self-determined and self-directing love, everything is henceforward determined by the sweet tyranny of the child. I have known of several young mothers, despite a great love for the child, to rebel against this intolerable situation. Vaguely feeling that this new maternity has rendered them unattractive to their husbands, slaves to a deadly routine of bottles, baths and washing, they have revolted. I know of innumerable marriages which have been wrecked by premature parenthood.

Love has ever been blighted by the coming of children before the real foundations of marriage have been established. Quite aside from the injustice done to the child who has been brought accidentally into the world, this lamentable fact sinks into insignificance when compared to the injustice inflicted by chance upon the young couple, and the irreparable blow to their love occasioned by premature or involuntary parenthood.

For these reasons, in order that harmonious and happy marriage may be established as the foundation for happy homes and the advent of healthy and desired children, premature parenthood must be avoided. Birth Control is the instrument by which this universal problem may be solved.

Source: Margaret Sanger, *Happiness in Marriage*, 1926. Reprinted by permission.

---

more subtle way of segregating cities. Originally designed to keep businesses and industry out of residential neighborhoods, zoning restrictions had become the tool of choice for segregating people on the basis of wealth by the 1930s.

Racial animosity, restrictive covenants, and zoning restrictions confined African Americans to certain neighborhoods. The decade following World War I saw the development of scores of American cities within cities. The largest was Harlem, in upper Manhattan; 200,000 African Americans lived in a neighborhood that had been virtually all white fifteen years before. These "black metropolises" resembled the ethnic ghettoes of the late nineteenth and early twentieth centuries, with one major difference—racial prejudice made it all but impossible for their residents to escape.

While a growing number of African Americans migrated to central cities, many white members of the country's new middle class of white-collar employees moved to fast-growing suburbs, which new forms of transportation had made possible. After the Civil War, trolleys and streetcars permitted workers to move beyond the walking radius of the factories. During the 1920s, the automobile opened up vast new regions for housing, giving people numerous options about where to live. Once the exclusive domain of the well-to-do, the suburbs were now widely accessible.

Yet optimists who hoped to escape the city's congestion by moving to the suburbs were too optimistic. The sharp rise in road construction following the Federal Highway Act of 1916 produced complicated lateral traffic flows within cities, and traffic congestion got worse. City planners counterattacked with traffic circles, synchronized stoplights, and divided dual highways, but nothing could free motorists from rush hour and holiday traffic jams.

The Rise of a Consumer Economy

Two automotive titans—Henry Ford and Alfred Sloan—symbolized the profound transformations that took place in American industry during the

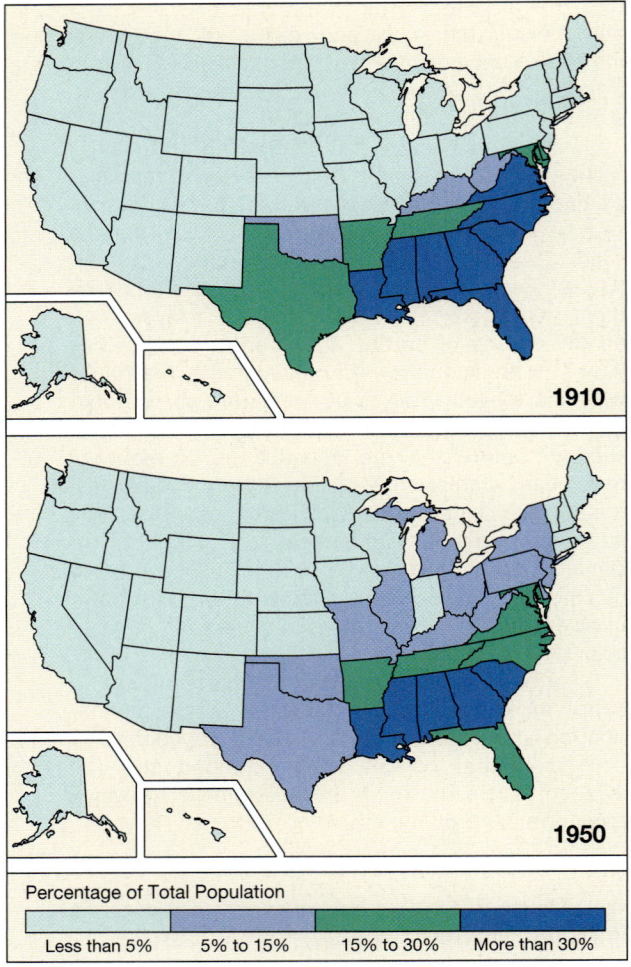

African-American Population, 1910 and 1950

Alfred Sloan, the president of General Motors from 1923 to 1941, built his company into the world's largest automaker not by refining the production process but by adopting new approaches to advertising and marketing. Sloan summed up his philosophy with these blunt words: "The primary object of the corporation was to make money, not just make cars." Unlike Ford, a farmer's son who wanted to produce an inexpensive, functional vehicle with few frills, Sloan was convinced that Americans were willing to pay extra for luxury and prestige. He advertised his cars as symbols of wealth and status, and in 1927 introduced the yearly model change, to convince motorists to trade in old models for newer ones with flashier styling. He also developed a series of divisions that were differentiated by status, price, and level of luxury, with Chevrolets less expensive than Buicks or Cadillacs. To make his cars affordable, he set up the nation's first national consumer credit agency in 1919. If Henry Ford demonstrated the efficacy of mass production, Sloan revealed the importance of merchandising in a modern consumer society.

Cars were the symbol of the new consumer society that emerged in the 1920s. In 1919, there were just 6.7 million cars on American roads. By 1929, there were more than 27 million—nearly one car for every household in the United States. With car manufacturers and banks encouraging the public to buy the car of their dreams on credit, the American love affair with the car truly began. A quarter of all American families purchased a car in 1929. About 60 percent bought it on credit, often paying interest rates of 30 percent or more.

Cars revolutionized the American way of life. Enthusiasts claimed the automobile promoted family togetherness through evening rides, picnics, and weekend excursions. Critics decried squabbles between parents and teenagers over use of the automobile, and an apparent decline in church attendance resulting from Sunday outings. Worst of all, charged critics, automobiles gave young people freedom and privacy, serving as "portable bedrooms" that couples could take anywhere.

The automobile also transformed the American landscape, quickly obliterating all traces of the horse and buggy past. During the 1920s, the country doubled its system of roads and highways. The nation spent over $2 billion annually building and maintaining roads; by 1929 there were 852,000 miles of roads in the United States, compared to just 369,000 in 1920. The car also brought with it pollution, congestion, and nearly 30,000 traffic deaths a year.

The automobile industry provided an enormous stimulus for the national economy. By 1929, the industry produced 12.7 percent of all manufacturing

1910s and 1920s. In 1913, the 50-year-old Ford revolutionized American manufacturing by introducing the automated assembly line. By using conveyor belts to bring automobile parts to workers, he reduced the assembly time for a Ford car from 12½ hours in 1912 to just 1½ hours in 1914. Declining production costs allowed Ford to cut prices—six times between 1921 and 1925, reducing a new Ford's cost to just $290. This was less than three months wages for an average American worker, and it made cars affordable for the average family. To lower employee turnover and raise productivity, Ford also introduced a minimum daily wage of $5 in 1914—twice what most workers earned—and shortened the workday from nine hours to eight. Twelve years later, Ford reduced his workweek from six days to five. Ford demonstrated the logic of mass production: expanded production allows manufacturers to reduce costs and therefore increase the number of products sold, and higher wages allow workers to buy more products.

output, and employed 1 out of every 12 workers. Automobiles in turn stimulated the growth of steel, glass, and rubber industries, along with gasoline stations, motor lodges, campgrounds, and the hot-dog stands that dotted the nation's roadways.

Other emblems of the consumer economy were the telephone and electricity. As more and more of America's homes received electricity, new appliances followed—refrigerators, washing machines, vacuum cleaners, and toasters quickly took hold. Advertisers claimed that "labor-saving" appliances would ease the sheer physical drudgery of housework, but they did not shorten the average housewife's workweek. Women now had to do more because standards of cleanliness kept rising. Sheets had to be changed weekly; the house had to be vacuumed daily. In short, social pressure expanded household chores to keep pace with the new technology. Far from liberating women, appliances imposed new standards and pressures.

Ready-to-wear clothing was another important innovation in America's expanding consumer economy. During World War I, the federal government defined standard clothing sizes to help the nation's garment industry meet the demand for military uniforms. Standard sizes meant that it was now possible to mass-produce ready-to-wear clothing. Since there was no copyright on clothing designs until the 1950s, garment manufacturers could pirate European fashions and reproduce them using less expensive fabrics.

Even the public's eating habits underwent far-reaching shifts, as Americans began to consume fewer starches (like bread and potatoes) and more fruit and sugar. But the most striking development was the shift toward processed foods. Important innovations in food processing occurred during World War I, as manufacturers learned how to efficiently can and freeze foods. Processed foods saved homemakers enormous amounts of time in peeling, grinding, and cutting.

Accompanying the rise of new consumer-oriented businesses were profound shifts in the ways that business operated. To stimulate sales and increase profits, businesses expanded advertising, offered installment credit, and created the nation's first regional and national chains.

The nation's first million-dollar advertising campaign was for Uneeda Biscuits and its patented waterproof box, demonstrating the power of advertising. During the 1920s, advertising agencies hired psychologists to design the first campaigns. They touted products by building up name-brand identification, creating memorable slogans, manipulating endorsements by doctors or celebrities, and appealing to consumers' hunger for prestige and status. By 1929, American companies were spending $3 billion annually to advertise their products, five times more than in 1914.

The use of installment credit soared during the 1920s. Banks offered the country's first home mortgages, while manufacturers of everything from cars to irons allowed consumers to pay "on time." About 60 percent of all furniture and 75 percent of all radios were purchased on the installment plan. In contrast to a Victorian society that had placed a high premium on thrift and saving, the new consumer society emphasized spending and borrowing.

A fundamental shift took place in the American economy during the 1920s. The nation's families spent a declining proportion of their income on necessities—food, clothing, and utilities—and an increasing share on appliances, recreation, and a host of new consumer products. As a result, older industries, such as textiles, railroads, and steel, declined, while newer industries, such as appliances, automobiles, aviation, chemicals, entertainment, and processed foods, surged ahead rapidly.

During the 1920s, the chain-store movement revolutionized retailing. Chains like Woolworths, five-and-dime stores, multiplied across the country. Besides drugstore and cigar-store chains, there were also interlocking networks of banks and utility companies. These banks and utilities played a critical role in promoting the financial speculation of the late 1920s that would become one of the causes of the Great Depression.

The Formation of Modern American Culture

Many of the defining features of modern American culture emerged during the 1920s. The best-seller, the book club, the record chart, the radio, the talking picture, and spectator sports all became popular forms of mass entertainment. But the primary reason the 1920s stand out as one of the most important periods in American cultural history is because the decade produced a generation of artists, musicians, and writers who were among the most innovative and creative in the country's history.

Mass Entertainment

Of all the new appliances to enter the nation's homes during the 1920s, none had a more revolutionary impact than radio. Sales soared from $60 million in 1922 to $426 million in 1929. The first commercial radio station began broadcasting in 1919, and during the

1920s, the nation's airwaves were filled with musical variety shows and comedies.

Radio drew the nation together by bringing news, entertainment, and advertisements to more than ten million households. Radio blunted regional differences and imposed similar tastes and lifestyles. No other media had the power to create heroes and villains so quickly; when Charles Lindbergh became the first person to fly nonstop across the Atlantic from New York to Paris in 1928, the radio brought his incredible feat into American homes, transforming him into a celebrity overnight.

Radio also brought the nation decidedly unheroic images. The nation's most popular radio show, "Amos 'n Andy," which first aired in 1926 on Chicago's WMAQ, spread vicious racial stereotypes into homes whose white occupants knew little about African Americans. Other minorities fared no better. The Italian gangster and the tightfisted Jew became stock characters in radio programming.

The phonograph was not far behind the radio in importance. The 1920s saw the record player enter American life in full force. Piano sales sagged as phonograph production rose from just 190,000 in 1923 to 5 million in 1929.

The popularity of jazz, blues, and "hillbilly" music fueled the phonograph boom. Novelist F. Scott Fitzgerald called the 1920s the "Jazz Age"—and the decade was truly jazz's golden age. Duke Ellington wrote the first extended jazz compositions; Louis Armstrong popularized "scat" (singing of nonsense syllables); Fletcher Henderson pioneered big band jazz; and trumpeter Jimmy McPartland and clarinetist Benny Goodman popularized the Chicago school of improvisation.

The blues craze erupted in 1920, when a black singer named Mamie Smith released a recording called "Crazy Blues." The record became a sensation, selling 75,000 copies in a month and a million copies in seven months. Recordings by Ma Rainey, the "Mother of the Blues," and Bessie Smith, the "Empress of the Blues," brought the blues, with its poignant and defiant reaction to life's sorrows, to a vast audience.

"Hillbilly" music broke into mass culture in 1923, when a Georgia singer named "Fiddlin' John" Carson sold 500,000 copies of his recordings. "Country" music's appeal was not limited to the rural South or West; city people, too, listened to country songs, reflecting a deep nostalgia for a simpler past.

The single most significant new instrument of mass entertainment was the movies. Movie attendance soared, from 50 million patrons a week in 1920 to 90 million weekly in 1929. Americans spent 83 cents of every entertainment dollar going to the movies—and three-fourths of the population went to a movie theater every week.

During the late teens and 1920s, the film industry took on its modern form. In cinema's earliest days, the film industry was based in the nation's theatrical center—New York. By the 1920s, the industry had relocated to Hollywood, drawn by cheap land and labor, the ready accessibility of varied scenery, and a climate ideal for year-round filming. Each year, Hollywood released nearly 700 movies, dominating worldwide film production. By 1926, Hollywood had captured 95 percent of the British and 70 percent of the French markets.

A small group of companies consolidated their control over the film industry and created the "studio system" that would dominate film production for the next thirty years. Paramount, 20th-Century Fox, MGM, and other studios owned their own production facilities, ran their own worldwide distribution networks, and controlled theater chains committed to showing their companies' products. In addition, they kept certain actors, directors, and screenwriters under contract.

The popularity of the movies soared as films increasingly featured glamour, sophistication, and sex appeal. New kinds of movie stars appeared: the mysterious sex goddess, personified by Greta Garbo; the passionate hot-blooded lover, epitomized by Rudolph Valentino; and the flapper, with her bobbed hair and skimpy skirts. New film genres also debuted, including swashbuckling adventures, sophisticated comedies, and tales of flaming youth and the new sexual freedom. Americans flocked to see Hollywood spectacles such as Cecil B. DeMille's *Ten Commandments* (1923) with its "cast of thousands" and dazzling special effects.

Like radio, movies created a new popular culture, with common speech, dress, behavior, and heroes. And like radio, Hollywood did its share to reinforce racial stereotypes by denigrating minority groups. The radio, the electric phonograph, and the silver screen all molded and mirrored mass culture.

Spectator Sports

Spectator sports attracted vast audiences in the 1920s. The country yearned for heroes in an increasingly impersonal, bureaucratic society, and sports, as well as the film industry, provided them. Prize fighters like Jack Dempsey became national idols. Team sports flourished, but Americans focused on individual superstars, people whose talents or personalities made them appear larger than life. Knute Rockne and his

Spectator sports became popular in the 1920s. Heroes of the day included men like "Red" Grange (left) of the University of Illinois and "Babe" Ruth (right) of the New York Yankees.

"Four Horsemen" at Notre Dame spurred interest in college football, and professional football began during the 1920s. In 1925, Harold "Red" Grange, the "Galloping Ghost" halfback for the University of Illinois, attracted 68,000 fans to a professional football game at Brooklyn's Polo Grounds.

Baseball drew even bigger crowds than football. The decade began with the sport mired in scandal. In 1920, three members of the Chicago White Sox told a grand jury that they and five other players had thrown the 1919 World Series. As a result of the "Black Sox" scandal, eight players were banished from the sport. But baseball soon regained its popularity, thanks to George Herman ("Babe") Ruth, the sport's undisputed superstar. Up until the 1920s Ty Cobb's defensive brand of baseball, with its emphasis on base hits and stolen bases, had dominated the sport. Ruth transformed baseball into the game of the home-run hitter. In 1921, the New York Yankee slugger hit 59 home runs—more than any other team combined. In 1927, the "Sultan of Swat" hit 60.

Low-Brow and Middle-Brow Culture

"It was a characteristic of the Jazz Age," novelist F. Scott Fitzgerald wrote, "that it had no interest in politics at all." What, then, were Americans interested in? Entertainment was Fitzgerald's answer. Parlor games like Mah Jong and crossword puzzles became enormously popular during the 1920s. Americans hit golf balls, played tennis, and bowled. Dance crazes like the fox trot, the Charleston, and the jitterbug swept the country.

New kinds of pulp fiction found a wide audience. Edgar Rice Burroughs' *Tarzan of the Apes* became a runaway best-seller. For readers who felt concerned about urbanization and industrialization, the adventures of the lone white man in "dark Africa" revived the spirit of frontier individualism. Zane Grey's novels, such as *Riders of the Purple Sage,* enjoyed even greater popularity, with their tried but true formula of romance, action, and a moralistic struggle between good and evil, all in a western setting.

Other readers wanted to be titillated, as evidenced by the boom in "confession magazines." Urban values, liberated women, and Hollywood films had all relaxed Victorian standards. Confession magazines rushed to fill the vacuum, purveying stories of romantic success and failure, divorce, fantasy, and adultery. Writers survived the censors' cut by placing moral tags at the end of their stories, in which readers were advised to avoid similar mistakes in their own lives.

Readers too embarrassed to pick up a copy of *True Romance* could read more urbane magazines such as *The New Yorker* or *Vanity Fair,* which offered entertainment, amusement, and gossip to those with more sophisticated tastes. They could also join the Book-of-the-Month Club or the Literary Guild, both of which were founded during the decade.

The Avant-Garde

Few decades have produced as many great works of art, music, or literature as the 1920s. At the decade's beginning, American culture stood in Europe's shadow. By the decade's end, Americans were leaders in the struggle to liberate the arts from older canons of taste, form, and style. It was during the twenties that Eugene O'Neill, the country's most talented dramatist, wrote his greatest plays, and that William Faulkner, Ernest Hemingway, F. Scott Fitzgerald, and Thomas Wolfe published their first novels.

American poets of the 1920s—such as Hart Crane, e.e. cummings, Countee Cullen, Langston Hughes, Edna St. Vincent Millay, and Wallace Stevens—experimented with new styles of punctuation, rhyming, and form. Likewise, artists like Charles Demuth, Georgia O'Keeffe, and Joseph Stella challenged the dominant realist tradition in American art and pioneered nonrepresentational and expressionist art forms.

The 1920s marked America's entry into the world of serious music. It witnessed the founding of fifty symphony orchestras and three of the country's most prominent music conservatories—Julliard, Eastman, and Curtis. The decade also produced America's first great classical composers—including Aaron Copland and Charles Ives—and witnessed George Gershwin create a new musical form by integrating jazz into symphonic and orchestral music.

Members of the "Lost Generation" of writers felt disillusioned with an American culture obsessed with money and devoid of spiritual vitality. Two of the Lost Generation's most prominent members were Ernest Hemingway (left) and F. Scott Fitzgerald (right).

World War I had left many American intellectuals and artists disillusioned and alienated. Neither Wilsonian idealism nor Progressive reformism appealed to America's postwar writers and thinkers, who believed that the crusade to end war and to make the world safe for democracy had been a senseless mistake.

During the 1920s, many of the nation's leading writers exposed the shallowness and narrow-mindedness of American life. The United State was a nation awash in materialism and devoid of spiritual vitality, a "wasteland," wrote the poet T. S. Eliot, inhabited by "hollow men." No author offered a more scathing attack on middle-class boorishness and smugness than Sinclair Lewis, who in 1930 became the first American to win the Nobel Prize for Literature. In *Main Street* (1920) and *Babbitt* (1922) he satirized the narrow-minded complacency and dullness of small-town America, while in *Elmer Gantry* (1922) he exposed religious hypocrisy and bigotry.

As editor of *Mercury* magazine, H. L. Mencken wrote hundreds of essays mocking practically every aspect of American life. Calling the South a "gargantuan paradise of the fourth rate," and the middle class the "booboisie," Mencken directed his choicest barbs at reformers, whom he blamed for the bloodshed of World War I and the gangsters of the 1920s. "If I am convinced of anything," he snarled, "it is that Doing Good is in bad taste."

The writer Gertrude Stein defined an important group of American intellectuals when she told Ernest Hemingway in 1921, "You are all a lost generation." Stein was referring to the expatriate novelists and artists who had participated in the Great War only to emerge from the conflict convinced that it was an exercise in futility. In their novels, F. Scott Fitzgerald and Hemingway foreshadowed a philosophy now known as "existentialism"—which maintains that life has no transcendent purpose and that each individual must salvage personal meaning from the void. Hemingway's fiction lionized toughness and "manly virtues" as a counterpoint to the softness of American life. In *The Sun Also Rises* (1926) and *A Farewell to Arms* (1929) he emphasized meaningless death and the importance of facing stoically the absurdities of the universe. In the conclusion of *The Great Gatsby* (1925), Fitzgerald gave pointed expression to an existentialist outlook: "so we beat on, boats against the current, borne back ceaselessly into the past."

The Sex Debate

"If all girls at the Yale prom were laid end to end, I wouldn't be surprised," sighed Dorothy Parker, the official wit of New York's smart set. Parker's quip captured the public's perception that America's morals had taken a nosedive. Practically every newspaper featured articles on prostitution, venereal disease, sex education, birth control, and the rising divorce rate.

City life nurtured new sexual attitudes. With its crowded anonymity, urban culture eroded sexual inhibitions by relaxing community restraints on individual behavior. Cities also promoted secular, consumer values, and city people seemed to tolerate, if not welcome, many forms of diversity.

While cities provided the ideal environment for liberalized sexual values, Sigmund Freud provided the ideal psychology. A Vienna physician, Freud revolutionized academic and popular thinking about human behavior by arguing that unconscious sexual anxieties cause much of human behavior. Freud also explained that sexual desires and fears develop in infancy and stay with people throughout their lives. During the 1920s, Freud's theories about the sexual unconscious were widely debated by physicians, academics, advice columnists, women's magazine writers, and preachers.

The image of the **"flapper"**—the liberated woman who bobbed her hair, painted her lips, raised her hemline, and danced the Charleston—personified the public's anxiety about the decline of traditional morality. In the 1950s Alfred C. Kinsey, a sex researcher at Indiana University, found that women born after 1900 were twice as likely to have had premarital sex as their mothers, with the most pronounced changes occurring in the generation reaching maturity in the early 1920s.

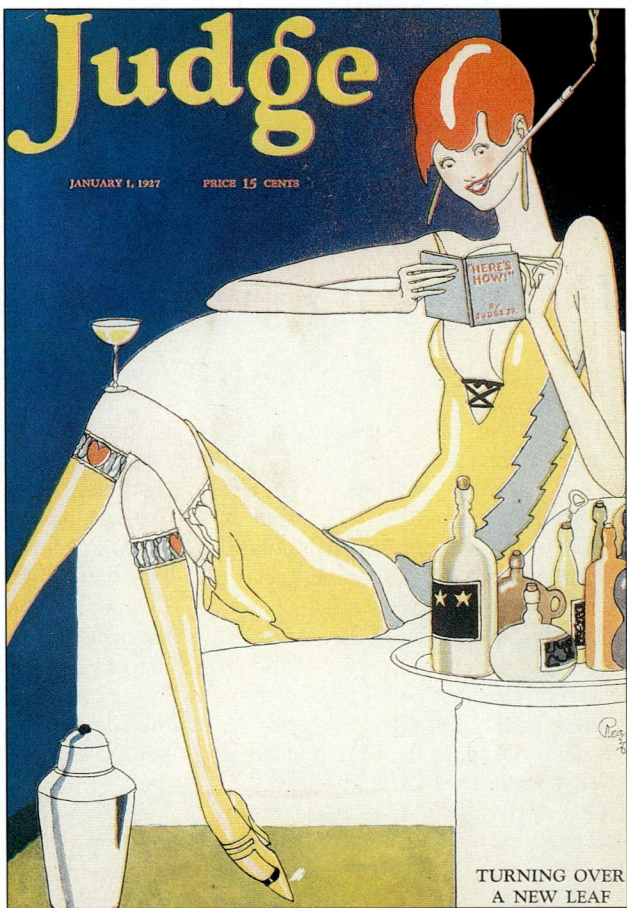

The image of the "flapper," who bobbed her hair, bared her knees, and smoked and drank in public, alarmed a public still clinging to Victorian codes of morality.

Sexual permissiveness had eroded Victorian values, but the "new woman" posed less of a challenge to traditional morality than her critics feared. Far from being promiscuous, her sexual experience before marriage was generally limited to one or two partners, one of whom she married. In practice, this narrowed the gap between men and women and moved society toward a single standard of morality. Instead of turning to prostitutes, men made love with their sweethearts, who in many instances became their wives.

THE CLASH OF CULTURES

The 1920s was a decade of intense cultural conflict. No longer a nation of farms and villages, the United States had become a nation of factories and cities. The Protestant culture of rural America was being undermined by the secular values of an urban soci-

THE American Mosaic

The Sexual Revolution of the Early 1900s

DURING the 1800s, public sexual attitudes in the United States were rooted in a moral code known as "civilized sexual morality." This sexual code condemned public discussion of sexual matters, held that sexual relations outside marriage were the blackest of sins, and declared that the only legitimate purpose of sexual relations was reproduction. Foreign travelers were invariably struck by Americans' sexual prudery. In the United States, they reported, a chicken breast was called a bosom and a piano leg was called a limb and was covered with lace trousers.

This strict sexual code drew support from a large medical literature that declared that any violation of the tenets of civilized morality would be detrimental to a person's health. Respected physicians insisted that loss of semen through masturbation or excessive sexual intercourse would produce "urinary difficulties, disorders of the genital organs, spinal diseases, weakness of the brain, loss of memory, epilepsy, insanity, apoplexy, abortions, premature births, and extreme feebleness, morbid predispositions, and an early death of offspring." Medical authorities also warned that women were too frail physically and too sensitive spiritually to engage in frequent intercourse and that "the majority of women (happily for them) are not very much troubled with sexual feelings of any kind." Above all, physicians warned that individuals who had sexual relations outside of marriage ran a high risk of contracting incurable venereal diseases.

The Victorian sexual code was a public ideal, not an accurate description of reality. Prostitution flourished in turn-of-the-century America. Every large city had at least one red-light district. In New York, there was the Tenderloin; in Chicago, the Levee; in New Orleans, Storyville; in San Francisco, the Barbary Coast. Early-twentieth-century vice commissions estimated that there were "not less" than a quarter of a million prostitutes in the country. In Chicago, an estimated quarter of the city's males visited prostitutes annually, and paid them $15 million a year. Pornography was also widespread.

Nor were nineteenth-century women necessarily the prudish, asexual, sexually ignorant figures popularized in Victorian mythology. An early sexual survey of the attitudes of 45 well-educated women, mainly born before 1870, reported that most enjoyed intercourse and experienced orgasm.

Nevertheless, the values of civilized sexual morality dominated polite society and received strong public backing from the broad-based crusade to suppress vice. A "purity crusade" had arisen in the 1860s and 1870s in response to proposals to legalize and regulate prostitution. In almost every major city in the country, former abolitionists like William Lloyd Garrison, feminists like Susan B. Anthony, temperance advocates, and ministers joined forces to defeat legalized prostitution. Prostitution, they argued, was a menace "to the chastity of our women and the sanctity of the home." It exploited poor women to satisfy male lust and endangered respectable women, who were often infected with syphilis and gonorrhea by their husbands.

In later years, the purity forces broadened their aims. In addition to fighting prostitution, they also sought to protect the family by outlawing abortion, restricting the sale of alcohol, stamping out pornography, censoring nudity in the arts, enforcing the Sabbath through enactment of "blue laws," suppressing the use of narcotics, and stopping the flow of birth control information through the mails.

The self-appointed leader of the purity forces was a staunch crusader named Anthony Comstock. Born on a farm in New Canaan, Connecticut, Comstock, as a youth, had been so upset by an impulse to masturbate that he feared he might be driven to commit suicide. While serving with a Connecticut regiment in the Civil War he had been appalled by the pornographic French postcards circulated among soldiers. After the war he moved to New York, where he became active in the Young Men's Christian Association, and was shocked by the prevalence of prostitutes and of vendors selling obscene books.

In 1873, Comstock persuaded Congress to pass a federal law banning from the mails "every obscene, lewd, lascivious or filthy book, pamphlet, paper, letter, writing, print or other publication of an indecent character." Comstock was then appointed special agent of the Post Office and made responsible for arresting those who used the mail in violation of the law. "Morals, not art or literature," was Comstock's motto. He took credit for hounding 16 persons to their deaths.

By 1910, Comstock and the purity forces had achieved many of their legislative goals. They had successfully pushed for state laws to restrict

divorce; raised the age of consent for sexual intercourse (from 7, in some states, to 18); imposed tests for venereal disease prior to marriage; and criminalized abortion. The purity crusaders also won passage of a federal statute that defined the mailing of birth control information a felony.

The years just before World War I witnessed a series of sharp challenges to the nineteenth-century code of sexual purity. Radical new ideas about marriage were publicized and debated. Swedish feminist Ellen Key preached a scheme of "unwed motherhood"; Edith Ellis, wife of British sex researcher Havelock Ellis, advocated trial marriage and "semi-detached marriage" in which each spouse occupied a separate domicile; still others advocated "serial marriage" and easier divorce. Greenwich Village bohemians and political radicals advocated, and to some extent practiced, free love. Psychologists, including Havelock Ellis, G. Stanley Hall, and Sigmund Freud, attacked the notion that women lacked sexual impulses.

Sexual conduct was also changing rapidly. The first scientific sex surveys indicated that women who came to maturity after the turn of the century were much more likely than their mothers to engage in sex before marriage and outside it. Women who were born around 1900 were two to three times as likely to have premarital intercourse compared to women born before 1900. They were also more likely to experience orgasm. Among men, premarital sexual experience did not increase, but it occurred less often with prostitutes and more frequently with other women.

Public alarm over the changes occurring in American sexual experience culminated in the first decade of the 1900s in an explosion of concern over "white slavery"—prostitution—and the "black plague"—venereal disease. Many lurid books appeared—with such titles as *The Traffic in Souls, The House of Bondage,* and *The Shame of a Great Nation*—that explained how innocent young girls were seduced by panderers and, through the use of a chloroformed cloth, a hypodermic needle, or a drugged drink, forced into prostitution. Congress attacked the problem of "white slavery" in 1910 by adopting the Mann Act, which made it a crime to transport women across state lines for immoral purposes. During World War I, Congress provided states with federal funds to set up facilities to detain and rehabilitate women apprehended as prostitutes. Fifteen thousand women were detained during the war. Sex was becoming a subject of open public debate and direct government involvement.

During the 1920s, the drift toward sexual liberalization continued. Journalists wrote in bewilderment about a new social phenomenon, the flapper, the independent, assertive, pleasure-hungry, young woman, "making love lightly, boldly, and promiscuously." Systematic sex surveys showed that the incidence of premarital intercourse was continuing to rise and that an increasing number of young women had slept with men other than their future husbands. Half of the women born in the first decade of the twentieth century and two-thirds of those born in the second decade had engaged in intercourse before marriage. Meanwhile, contraceptive practices were also changing dramatically. Instead of relying heavily on douching or coitus interruptus as a form of birth control, younger women were using the more effective and less disruptive diaphragm.

This growing sexual permissiveness evoked a sharp reaction. Purity forces renewed their crusade to discourage indecent styles of dancing, immodest dress, and impure books and films. Religious journals denounced popular dance styles as "impure, polluting, corrupting, debasing, destroying spirituality, [and] increasing carnality." A bill was introduced in the Utah state legislature to fine and imprison women who wore, on the streets, skirts "higher than three inches above the ankle." In the Ohio legislature it was proposed that cleavage be limited to two inches and that the sale of any "garment which unduly displays or accentuates the lines of the female figure" be prohibited. Four states and many cities established censorship boards to review films, and many other cities broke up red-light districts and required licenses for dance halls. But despite these efforts, a sexual revolution had begun that has continued to this day.

ety. Country against city, native against immigrant, Protestant against Catholic and Jew, fundamentalist against liberal, conservative against progressive, wet against dry—bitter confrontations erupted as the United States underwent a colossal identity crisis as it struggled to come to terms with secular values and cultural pluralism. The chief battlegrounds in this "cultural civil war" were gender, immigration, prohibition, and the teaching of evolution in public schools.

The New Woman

In 1920, after 72 years of struggle, American women received the right to vote with the passing of the **Nineteenth Amendment.** Reformers talked about female voters uniting to clean up politics, improve society, and end discrimination.

At first, male politicians moved aggressively to court the women's vote, passing legislation guaranteeing women's right to serve on juries and hold public office. Congress also passed legislation to set up a national system of women's and infant's health care clinics as well as a constitutional amendment prohibiting child labor, a measure supported by many women's groups.

But the early momentum quickly dissipated, as the women's movement divided from within and faced growing hostility from without. The major issue that split feminists during the 1920s was a proposed **Equal Rights Amendment** to the Constitution outlawing discrimination based on sex. The issue pitted the interests of professional women against those of working class women, many of whom feared that the amendment would prohibit "protective legislation" that stipulated the minimum wages and maximum work hours of female workers.

The women's movement also faced mounting external opposition. During the Red Scare following World War I, the War Department issued the "Spider Web" chart that linked feminist groups to foreign radicalism. Many feminist goals went down to defeat in the mid-1920s. The Supreme Court struck down a minimum wage law for women workers, while Congress failed to fund the system of health care clinics.

Women also did not win new opportunities in the workplace. Although the American workforce included eight million women in 1920, more than half were African American or foreign-born. Domestic service remained the largest occupation, followed by secretarial work, typing, and clerking—all low-paying jobs. The American Federation of Labor (AFL) remained openly hostile to women because it did not want females competing for men's jobs. Female professionals, too, made little progress. They consistently received less pay than their male counterparts. Moreover, they were concentrated in traditionally "female" occupations such as teaching and nursing.

Prohibition

Prohibition exposed deep fissures in American society. The issue turned on the class, ethnic, and religious makeup of individual communities.

At first prohibition's apparent success muted its critics. Distilleries and breweries shut down, saloons locked their doors, arrests for drunkenness declined, and alcohol-related deaths all but disappeared. Compliance, however, had less to do with piety and public support than the law of supply and demand: since illegal liquor remained in short supply, its price rose beyond the average worker's means.

Private enterprise filled the void. Smugglers supplied wealthy imbibers, but the less affluent had to rely on small-time operators who produced for local

FIGURE 23.1
Women in the Workforce, 1900–1940

Although the number of women in the workplace rose from 1900 to 1940, they were mostly concentrated in only a few fields.

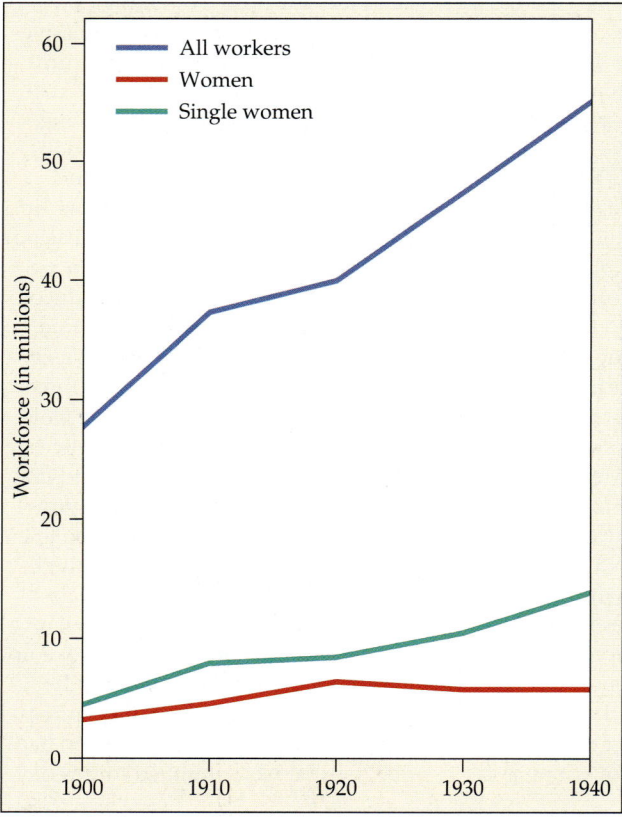

consumption. Much of this liquor ran the gamut from swill to poison. Hundreds, perhaps thousands, died from drinking these illegal concoctions.

Neither federal nor state authorities had enough funds to enforce prohibition. New York's mayor estimated that it would require a police force of 250,000 to enforce prohibition—and another 250,000 to police the police. In fact, only about 2200 agents across the country enforced the law. Lax enforcement, coupled with huge profits, enticed organized crime to enter bootlegging. Long a fixture of urban life, with gambling and prostitution as its base, organized crime had operated on a small, local scale. Liquor, however, demanded production plants, distribution networks, and sales forces. Bootlegging turned into a gold mine for organized crime. By the late 1920s liquor sales generated revenue in excess of $2 billion annually. Chicago's Al Capone had a gross income of $60 million in 1927.

From the outset, cynics had insisted that prohibition could not be enforced. They were right. Particularly in large cities, people openly defied the law. In New York City, 7000 arrests for liquor law violations resulted in 17 convictions. On more than one occasion journalists saw President Warren G. Harding's bootlegger deliver cases of liquor to the White House in broad daylight.

In 1923 New York became the first state to repeal its enforcement law, and by 1930 six more states had followed suit. Others remained firmly committed to prohibition. After a presidential commission reported prohibition could not be enforced, Congress finally repealed it in 1933, making liquor control a state and local matter.

The campaign to outlaw cigarette smoking was closely allied to the prohibition movement. Opposition to tobacco was not new. During the nineteenth century the antitobacco campaign remained an appendage of the temperance movement. After the introduction of machine-made cigarettes in the 1880s, however, opponents concentrated their fire specifically on the "little white slavers."

As early as the Civil War, a few cities had banned smoking in restaurants, theaters, public buildings, trolleys, and railway cars. After antismokers organized the National Anti-Cigarette League in 1903, scores of prominent leaders joined the crusade. By 1923, 14 states had outlawed the sale of cigarettes, prompting calls for a constitutional amendment for national prohibition. By the end of the decade, however, every state had repealed its law against cigarette sales. A national consensus had not formed against tobacco, and the tobacco industry opposed every effort to restrict the sale of cigarettes, spending millions of dollars on advertisements.

The Scopes Trial

During the late nineteenth century, Charles Darwin's theory of evolution produced a momentous split within the ranks of American Protestantism. Earlier in the century, virtually all American Protestant denominations were united in the belief that the findings of science confirmed the teachings of religion. But Darwin's theory shattered that consensus. Religious liberals argued that religion had to accommodate to the teachings of modern science. Religious fundamentalists sought to preserve the basic tenets of Protestant faith against liberal criticisms.

The split between religious liberals and fundamentalists widened in the early twentieth century. A religious revival in Topeka, Kansas, in 1901, marked the beginning of Pentecostalism, a movement that emphasizes the spiritual gifts conferred by the Holy Spirit, including the ability to "speak in tongues" (an unknown, but divinely inspired language) and the power of prayer to heal the sick. By arguing that the Biblical age of miracles had not ended, Pentecostals directly challenged the ideas of religious modernists. *The Fundamentals,* 12 volumes by anonymous authors published between 1910 and 1915, argued that there were certain Christian doctrines that must be accepted without question, including the infallibility of the

When biology teacher John Scopes taught evolutionary theory to his class, the state of Tennessee brought him to trial. The well-publicized trial emphasized the split between religious fundamentalists and those who advocated scientific and academic freedom.

Bible, the authenticity of the miracles described in the Scriptures, and the virgin birth of Jesus Christ. Although the fundamentalist and Pentecostal movements began in the North, they attained their greatest support in the South.

During the 1920s, conflict erupted between fundamentalists and liberals over the teaching of evolution in public schools, a clash that culminated in the celebrated **Scopes "Monkey Trial."** In 1925 the Tennessee legislature passed a bill that prohibited the teaching of evolution in public schools. Immediately afterwards, a 24-year-old science teacher, John Scopes, from Dayton, Tennessee, provoked a test case by declaring publicly that he taught biology from an evolutionary standpoint.

Scopes was brought to trial in the summer of 1925. William Jennings Bryan, rural America's defender of the faith, agreed to join the team of prosecutors, and Clarence Darrow, the celebrated trial lawyer and self-proclaimed agnostic, volunteered his services to defend Scopes.

The trial opened on July 10, 1925. As "Holy Rollers" from the surrounding regions held revivals and religious zealots exhorted people to read their Bibles, huge crowds poured into Dayton to watch Bryan and Darrow do combat. Near the end of testimony the defense surprised everyone by asking Bryan to take the stand as an expert witness on the Bible. His simple, direct answers to Darrow's sarcastic questions revealed an unshakable faith in the literal truth of the Bible. Bryan insisted "it is better to trust in the Rock of Ages than to know the ages of rocks."

The outcome was never in doubt. Scopes admitted he had broken the law. He was convicted and fined $100. (Tennessee's supreme court later rescinded the fine on a technicality.) What gave the trial its drama was the clash between Bryan and Darrow and the opposite images of America they represented. Bryan, who died five days after the trial ended, left the courtroom believing he had carried the day. His opponents, however, thought he had been humiliated and they proclaimed the Scopes trial a victory for academic freedom. In the end, the Scopes trial merely illustrated how little tolerance secular and fundamentalist groups had for each other.

Xenophobia and Restricting Immigration

Cultural fears unleashed a new wave of nativism in the 1920s. Organized labor, bent upon protecting high wages, resented competition from cheap labor; staunch nativists and superpatriots warned that foreign influences would corrupt the American charac-

Many people felt that Italian-born, self-admitted anarchists Sacco and Vanzetti, shown here in handcuffs in a painting by Ben Shahn, were persecuted for their immigrant status and radical views rather than for any real crime. Their trial became an important symbol in the fight for civil liberties and brought about violent protest in America and abroad.

Ben Shahn, *Bartolomeo Vanzetti and Nicola Sacco* from the Sacco-Vanzetti series of twenty-three paintings (1931–32). Tempera on paper over composition board, $10\frac{1}{2}$ x $14\frac{1}{2}$" (26.7 x 36.8 cm). Gift of Abby Aldrich Rockefeller, Jr. Photograph © The Museum of Modern Art, New York.

ter; and assorted businessmen denounced immigrants as dangerous radicals.

To protect the United States these groups demanded drastic changes in the nation's immigration policy. Congress passed the **National Origins Act of 1924,** establishing an annual immigration quota of 2 percent of each national group counted in the 1890 census, and barring Asians entirely. Since southern and eastern Europeans did not begin arriving in large numbers until the turn of the century, the law gave western and northern Europeans a big edge over the "new immigrants."

Hostility to immigrants also surfaced in the Sacco and Vanzetti case. On April 15, 1920, two unidentified gunmen robbed a payroll messenger from a shoe factory in South Braintree, Massachusetts, killing a paymaster and a guard. Two Italian immigrants, Nicola Sacco and Bartolomeo Vanzetti, both avowed anarchists, were arrested and charged with the crime. Although the state failed to prove its case, prosecutors succeeded in parading before the jury the radical political views of both men. On July 14, 1921, Sacco and Vanzetti were convicted and sentenced to death.

The trial and conviction brought a storm of protest from Italian-Americans, liberals, and civil rights advocates. Despite lengthy appeals, the conviction was upheld, and Sacco and Vanzetti, asserting their innocence to the end, went to the electric chair on August 23, 1927.

The Ku Klux Klan

Fear of political radicals and ethnic minorities found its most strident voice during the 1920s in the rebirth of the **Ku Klux Klan.** The secret organization, led by Colonel William Joseph Simmons, stood for "100 percent pure Americanism" and limited its membership to white, native-born Protestants. Membership remained modest until Simmons hired two advertising specialists, Edward Young Clarke and Elizabeth Tyler, to market the Klan nationwide.

Clarke and Tyler hired an army of organizers to canvass the country selling memberships in the Klan. Working on commission and molding their pitch to match their clientele, the salesmen enjoyed astounding success. By 1921 the Klan had become a national organization with over 90,000 paying members; by 1925 it claimed a membership of five million. The Klan was strongest in the South, but it had a large following in the Southeast, the Far West, and the Midwest. Its natural habitat was not the countryside, but middling towns and small cities as well as larger cities like Chicago and Detroit. Most members were not "poor white trash," but members of the lower middle class from old-stock, respectable families.

In the mid-1920s the Klan was a political force to reckon with. It influenced the election of several governors and members of state legislatures. The Klan also sought to intimidate individuals, using night ridings, cross burnings, tar and featherings, public beatings, and lynching as forms of coercion. The Klan did not limit its wrath to ethnic and religious "offenders," but also lashed out against wife-beaters, drunkards, bootleggers, gamblers—anyone who violated time-honored standards of morality.

In the end poor leadership and the absence of a political program destroyed the Klan. Once they attained office, Klan-supported officials offered no constructive legislation. Even more damaging, several Klan leaders became involved in sex scandals, and several more were indicted for corruption. By 1930 the white sheets and cross burnings had vanished from public view, only to return again a few decades later when the civil rights movement challenged white supremacy.

African-American Protests

Many African Americans believed that the sacrifices of African-American soldiers during World War I would be repaid when the war was over. It was not to be. The federal government denied African-American soldiers the right to participate in the victory march down Paris's Champs-Elysées boulevard. In the 25 race riots that took place in 1919, 10 of the 70 African-American victims were veterans of World War I.

African Americans did not respond passively to these outrages. Already, in the 1910s, they had stepped up their protests against discrimination. Closely identified with Booker T. Washington's conciliatory approach to race relations, the National Urban League, organized in 1911 by social workers, white philanthropists, and conservative African-American leaders, concentrated on finding jobs for urban African Americans. Despite the nation's postwar prosperity, African Americans made scant progress on the job front during the 1920s.

Leaving economic issues to the Urban League, the **National Association for the Advancement of Colored People (NAACP),** formed in 1909, concentrated on civil rights and legal action. The NAACP won important Supreme Court decisions against the grandfather clause (1915) and restrictive covenants (1917). The NAACP also fought school segregation in northern cities during the 1920s, and lobbied hard, though unsuccessfully, for a federal antilynching bill. Though progress on these fronts was not made until after World War II, the NAACP became the nation's leading civil rights organization.

African-American radicals dismissed the Urban League and the NAACP as too conservative. A. Philip Randolph, the editor of the Socialist monthly the *Messenger* called for a "New Negro" who would meet violence with violence to end discrimination and achieve racial equality. Randolph urged African-American workers to seek admission to trade unions.

No black leader was more successful in touching the aspirations and needs of the mass of African

The Ku Klux Klan exploited postwar confusion and fear of things "un-American." Although the Klan had originally flourished in small, rural towns across the South, during the 1920s it spread to working-class and middle-class neighborhoods of large cities, where people felt threatened by the influx of African-American and immigrant workers.

Marcus Garvey, a charismatic Jamaican, encouraged black pride. His Universal Negro Improvement Association (UNIA) included one million members worldwide.

Americans than Marcus Garvey. A flamboyant and charismatic figure from Jamaica, Garvey rejected integration and preached racial pride and self-help. He declared that Jesus Christ and Mary were black and he exhorted his followers to glorify their African heritage and revel in the beauty of their skin.

In 1917 Garvey moved to New York, where he organized the American branch of the Universal Negro Improvement Association (UNIA), the first mass movement in African-American history. Convinced that African Americans would never achieve full equality in the United States, Garvey called on blacks to regard Africa as their homeland. By the mid-1920s, Garvey's organization had 700 branches in 38 states and the West Indies and published a newspaper with as many as 200,000 subscribers. The UNIA operated grocery stores, laundries, restaurants, printing plants, clothing factories, and a steamship line.

In the mid-1920s, Garvey was charged with mail fraud, jailed, and finally deported. Still, the "Black Moses" left behind a rich legacy. At a time when magazines and newspapers overflowed with advertisements for hair straighteners and skin lightening cosmetics, Garvey's message of racial pride struck a responsive chord in many African Americans.

The Harlem Renaissance

The movement for African-American pride found its cultural expression in the **Harlem Renaissance**—the first self-conscious literary and artistic movement in African-American history.

For over three decades, African Americans had shown increasing interest in African-American history and folk culture. As early as the 1890s, W.E.B. Du Bois, Harvard's first African-American Ph.D., began to trace African-American culture in the United States to its African roots; Fisk University's Jubilee Singers introduced Negro spirituals to the general public; and the American Negro Academy, organized in 1897, promoted African-American literature, arts, music, and history. A growing spirit of racial pride was evident, as a group of talented writers, including Charles Chestnut, Paul Lawrence Dunbar, and James Weldon Johnson, explored life in African-American communities; as the first Negro dolls appeared; and as all-Negro towns were founded in Whitesboro, New Jersey, and Allensworth, California.

Artist Archibald Motley, Jr., one of the black painters of the 1920s Harlem Renaissance, celebrated the energy and excitement of the era there in *Black Belt* (1934). Motley, who was born in New Orleans and raised in Chicago, trained at the Art Institute of Chicago. He said he believed art to be governed by "personality, intensity and sympathy" and it is these qualities that enliven his works, such as this dynamic urban scene.

Archibald Motley Jr., *Black Belt*, 1934. Oil on canvas, $31^{7}/_{8}$" x $39^{1}/_{4}$", Hampton University Museum, Hampton, VA.

Signs of growing racial consciousness proliferated during the 1910s. Fifty new African-American newspapers and magazines appeared in that decade, bringing the total to 500. The Associated Negro Press, the first national African-American press agency, was founded in 1919. In 1915, Carter Woodson, a Harvard Ph.D., founded the first permanent Negro historical association—the Association for the Study of Negro Life and History—and began publication of the *Journal of Negro History*.

During the 1920s, Harlem, in upper Manhattan, became the capital of black America, attracting African-American intellectuals and artists from across the country and the Caribbean as well. Soon, the Harlem Renaissance was in full bloom. The poet Countee Cullen eloquently expressed black artists' long-suppressed desire to have their voices heard: "Yet do I marvel at a curious thing: To make a poet black, and bid him sing!"

Many of the greatest works of the Harlem Renaissance sought to recover links with African and folk traditions. In "The Negro Speaks of Rivers," the poet Langston Hughes reaffirmed his ties to an African past: "I looked upon the Nile and raised the pyramids above it." In "Cane" (1923), Jean Toomer—the grandson of P. B. S. Pinchback, who served briefly as governor of Louisiana during Reconstruction—blended realism and mysticism, poetry and prose, to describe the world of the black peasantry in Georgia and in the ghetto of Washington, D.C.

A fierce racial consciousness and a powerful sense of racial pride animated the literature of the Harlem Renaissance. The West Indian–born poet Claude McKay expressed the new spirit of defiance and protest with militant words: "If we must die—oh let us nobly die . . . dying, but fighting back!"

THE REPUBLICAN RESTORATION

The Republican party dominated American politics in the 1920s. When Republican leaders promised to restore prosperity, most Americans embraced the conservative rhetoric, hoping to find in politics the stability they found lacking in their culture. Talk about trust-busting and regulating big business gave way in New Era politics to calls for a partnership between government and industry, one that would promote the interests of American corporations at home and abroad.

Handsome Harding

By and large the presidents of the New Era were mediocre figures. Senator Warren G. Harding of Ohio, who led off the decade, suited the times perfectly.

Harding's administration was fraught with scandals involving bribes and kickbacks within his cabinet and inner circle, as illustrated in this political cartoon.

Handsome enough to be a movie star, he not only looked great, but promised voters what they wanted: a return to "normalcy." He appeared to be a moderate, responsible leader who would avoid extremes and guide the country into a decade of prosperity.

Harding, a fun-loving man who liked to play poker, drink whiskey, and shoot the breeze with old pals, left government to his cabinet members and to the Supreme Court. Political conservatives all, they equated the people's interests with those of big business, championing American business interests abroad, denouncing government regulation, and slashing taxes on the rich.

Business leaders had contributed $8 million to the GOP's campaign chest in 1920; in return they expected the federal government to roll back the gains organized labor had made during World War I. They were not disappointed. Under the leadership of Chief Justice William Howard Taft, the Court took a narrow view of federal power, assigning the responsibility for protecting individual citizens to the states. During the 1920s the Court outlawed picketing, overturned national child labor laws, and abolished minimum wage laws for women.

The decade's most capable figure was Herbert Hoover, secretary of commerce under both Harding and his successor, Calvin Coolidge. A successful engineer, Hoover abhorred destructive competition and waste in the economy, which he proposed to eliminate through "associationism." Hoover called for voluntary trade associations to foster cooperation in industry and agriculture through commissions, trade practice controls, and ethical standards. By 1929 more than 2000 trade associations were busily at work implementing Hoover's vision of a stable and prosperous economy. No other Harding appointment matched Hoover's talent and vision.

In fact, several of Harding's appointees proved to be disasters. Harding found it difficult to say "no" to old friends and cronies, members of the so-called Ohio Gang, when they asked for government jobs. In the end this motley assortment of political hacks and hangers-on plunged his administration into disgrace, as major scandals involving bribes and kickbacks erupted in the Justice Department and in the Veterans Bureau. Shortly after these disclosures, Harding died of a cerebral embolism, on August 2, 1923. Immediately after his death, more misdeeds came to light. In the infamous Teapot Dome oil scandal, Secretary of the Interior Albert B. Fall was convicted of accepting $360,000 in bribes in exchange for leasing drilling rights on federal naval oil reserves, the first cabinet member in American history convicted for crimes in office. Attorney General Harry Daugherty, accused of accepting payoffs for selling German chemical patents controlled by the Alien Property Office, was forced to resign in disgrace.

Silent Cal

The election of 1924 symbolized, in a variety of ways, the tensions and concerns of the 1920s. Despite the Harding scandals, President Calvin Coolidge remained extremely popular, largely because of the nation's prosperity. Deeply divided over such issues as immigration, prohibition, and the Ku Klux Klan, the Democrats balloted 103 times before nominating a compromise candidate, John W. Davis, a Wall Street attorney.

A coalition of labor leaders, social workers, and former progressives bolted both major parties and formed the Progressive party, which nominated Wisconsin Senator Robert La Follette for president. Their platform called for government ownership of natural resources, abolition of child labor, elimination of monopolies, and increased taxes on the rich. In the end, no issue could match the GOP's prosperity crusade. Coolidge won the election by a comfortable margin.

Coolidge was a stern-faced, tight-lipped New Englander. Born in Plymouth Notch, Vermont, where five generations of Coolidges had worked the same family farm, he epitomized the rural values threatened by immigration, urbanization, and industrialization. As governor of Massachusetts, Coolidge had crushed a police strike in Boston in 1919 by calling out the National Guard, prompting the Republicans to give him the number two slot on their ticket in 1920.

Coolidge had no desire to be a strong president in the tradition of a Teddy Roosevelt or a Woodrow Wilson. A firm believer in the wisdom of inactivity, Coolidge slept ten hours a night, napped every afternoon, and seldom worked more than four hours a day. A staunch conservative, Coolidge was positively consumed by his reverence for the corporate elite. Government, he believed, should do everything in its power to promote business interests. While Coolidge set the tone for his administration, he left it to his cabinet members, the courts, and Congress to devise strategies for consummating the marriage between business and government.

The Twilight of Progressivism

The government's tilt toward business signaled a retreat from progressivism. With the Democrats in disarray and Teddy Roosevelt's wing of the GOP all but dead, conservative Republicans were riding high. Still, the reform impulse did not disappear entirely during the 1920s. A small band of beleaguered reformers, led by Robert La Follette of Wisconsin and George Norris of Nebraska, kept progressivism alive in Congress, where they worked for farm relief, child labor laws, and regulation of wages and working hours for women.

In keeping with their historic pattern, progressives had better luck at the state and local level than at the federal level, where they ran into stiff opposition from Congress or from Coolidge himself. Social workers and women's groups spearheaded campaigns that sponsored a broad range of welfare legislation. By 1930, 43 states had passed laws providing assistance to women with dependent children, and 34 states had adopted workers' compensation laws. Under the leadership of Governor Alfred Smith, New York granted women a 40-hour workweek and instituted the nation's first public housing program.

Welfare opponents counterattacked, arguing labor reforms would increase production costs and leave states that passed welfare legislation at a competitive disadvantage with states without such laws. Asked to choose between social welfare programs and jobs, Congress, along with most states, opted for jobs.

The Election of 1928

After Coolidge announced his retirement from politics in 1928, the Republicans nominated Herbert Hoover, while the Democrats turned to Alfred E. Smith. Since both parties adopted nearly identical platforms, the election turned on personalities and images. Few elections have pitted opponents who better defined the two faces of America—one rural, the other urban.

A native of Iowa, Hoover depicted himself as a simple farmboy who, through hard work and pluck, had grown up to become wealthy and famous. Orphaned as a boy and cared for by a variety of relatives, Hoover worked his way through Stanford University, earning a degree in mining engineering. Brilliant and hard-working, he was a millionaire 12 years after landing his first engineering job. As a self-made man, Hoover presented a portrait of a safe, reassuring world.

Herbert Hoover, the consummate self-made man, was in office only a few months when the stock market crashed.

Yet Hoover was also a spokesman for the future. He thought the federal government had a responsibility to coordinate the competing interests of a modern economy. He accepted the reality of industrialization, technology, governmental activism, and global markets, and in contrast to Harding and Coolidge, Hoover believed the president should lead the nation. According to Hoover, technology and expertise would make economic prosperity a permanent feature of American life.

The son of immigrants, Smith was an Irish Catholic from Hell's Kitchen in New York City. He had started public life with nothing and had climbed the political ladder as a faithful son of the New York Democratic machine. Smith also represented the future, not so much in terms of science, technology, and organization, but in terms of cultural pluralism and urbanization. America's future lay with her cities, and the cities contained large groups of ethnic Americans struggling for acceptance and their share of the good life.

Aided by prosperity, Hoover coasted to an easy victory. Smith was hurt by his failure to bridge the North-South, urban-rural split in the Democratic party; by anti-Catholic sentiment; and by his opposition to prohibition. Yet even in defeat, Smith's campaign revealed the most significant political change of the 1920s—the growing power of urban and ethnic voters and the shrinking influence of the rural element within the Democratic party.

Herbert Hoover's election marked the climax of New Era politics. As president he advocated total cooperation between government and business. Optimistic businesspeople, bankers, and stockbrokers applauded Hoover's promises, predicting a future of prosperity and progress. Ironically, the stock market crashed before their cheers had stopped echoing.

THE GREAT CRASH

Few people ever see their name enter the English language, but Charles Ponzi did. A "Ponzi scheme" has become synonymous with wild speculation. In September 1919, Ponzi was a 42-year-old former vegetable dealer with just $150 to his name. He promised to return $15 to anyone who lent him $10 for 90 days. His plan, he explained, was to buy foreign currencies at low prices and sell them at higher prices. After newspapers reported his scheme, dollars began to pour in—$1 million a week.

It was too good to be true. Ponzi took in $15 million in eight months—and less than $200,000 was ever returned to investors.

Speculative Manias

Ponzi symbolized the "get-rich-quick" mentality that infected the public during the 1920s. A vivid example was the Florida land boom. During the 1920s, sun-worshipping northerners discovered Florida's warm winter climate and its sun-drenched beaches. Could there be a safer investment? Real estate promoters—including the former presidential candidate William Jennings Bryan—offered seafront lots to investors for 10 percent down. Investors snapped up the properties—much of which turned out to be swamp and scrub land. Prices skyrocketed. A lot 40 miles from Miami sold for $20,000. A beach lot sold for $75,000. Ponzi himself sold lots "near Jacksonville"—actually 65 miles west of the city; he divided each acre into 23 lots.

In the fall of 1926 the bubble burst. Two hurricanes ripped through Florida, killing more than 400 people. Property valued at $1 billion in 1925 dropped to $143 million in 1928.

A wave of similar stock swindles and business frauds took place during the 1920s. But the most striking manifestation of the decade's speculative frenzy was the stock market boom of 1928 and 1929. After rising steadily during the 1920s, stock prices began to soar in March 1928. Between March 3, 1928, and September 3, 1928, AT&T rose from $179\frac{1}{2}$ to $335\frac{5}{8}$, General Motors from $139\frac{3}{4}$ to $181\frac{7}{8}$, and Westinghouse from $91\frac{5}{8}$ to 313. By the beginning of the fall of 1929, stock prices were four times higher than five years before.

Brokerage houses lured investors into the market by selling stock on margin, requiring investors to only put down 10 or 20 percent of the stock's price in cash and borrowing the rest. By 1929, 1.5 million Americans had invested in securities.

Boosters like John Jacob Raskob, the chairman of the Democratic Party, encouraged ordinary people to invest in stocks. In an article in the *Ladies' Home Journal* entitled "Everybody Ought to be Rich," he explained that a person who invested $15 a month in the stock market for 20 years would have a nest egg of $80,000. Leading economists encouraged investors to believe that the stock market would continue to rise. At the end of October 1929, the seemingly endless surge in stock prices came to a crashing halt.

The Market Crashes

On Thursday, October 24, 1929, an unprecedented wave of sell orders shook the New York Stock Exchange. Stock prices tumbled, falling $2, $5, and even $10 between trades. As prices fell, brokers required investors who had bought stock on margin to put up money to cover their loans. To raise money, many investors dumped stocks for whatever price the stocks could fetch. During the first three hours of trading, stock values plunged by $11 billion.

At noon, a group of prominent bankers met at the offices of J. P. Morgan and Company. To stop the hemorrhaging of stock prices, the bankers' pool agreed to buy stocks well above the market. At 1:30 P.M. they put their plan into action. Within an hour, U.S. Steel was up $15 a share, AT&T up $22, General Electric up $21, Mongtomery Ward up $23.

Even though the market recovered its morning losses, public confidence was badly shaken. Rumors spread that 11 stock speculators had killed themselves and that government troops were surrounding the exchange to protect traders from an angry mob. President Hoover sought to reassure the public by declaring that the "fundamental business of the country . . . is on a sound and prosperous basis."

Prices held steady on Friday, then slipped on Saturday. Monday, however, brought fresh disaster. Eastman Kodak plunged $41 a share, AT&T went down $24, New York Central Railroad, $22. The worst was yet to come—**Black Tuesday,** October 29, the day the stock market experienced the greatest crash in its history.

As soon as the stock exchange's gong sounded, a mad rush to sell began. Trading volume soared to an unprecedented 16,410,030 shares, and the average price of a share fell 12 percent. Stocks were sold for whatever price they would bring. White Sewing Machine had reached a high of $48 a share. One purchaser—reportedly a messenger boy—bought a block of the stock for $1 a share.

The bull market of the late 1920s was over. By 1932, the index of stock prices had fallen from a 1929 high of 210 to 30. Altogether, between September 1929 and June 1932, the nation's stock exchanges lost $179 billion in value.

The great stock market crash of October 1929 brought the economic prosperity of the 1920s to a symbolic end. For the next ten years, the United States was mired in a deep economic depression. By 1933, unemployment had soared to 25 percent of the workforce, up from just 3.2 percent in 1929. Industrial production declined by 50 percent. In 1929, before the crash, investment in the U.S. economy totaled $16 billion. By 1933, the figure had fallen to $340 million, a decrease of 98 percent.

This newspaper headline from Friday, October 25, 1929, tried to reassure the public that the economy was fundamentally sound, only four days before Black Tuesday. The economy's downward spiral continued through 1932, when prices were 80 percent below their 1929 highs.

Why It Happened

Economists have been hard pressed to explain why "prosperity's decade" ended in financial disaster. In 1929, the American economy appeared to be extraordinarily healthy. Employment was high and inflation was virtually nonexistent. Industrial production had risen 30 percent between 1919 and 1929 and per capita income had climbed from $520 to $681. The United States accounted for nearly half the world's industrial output. Still, the seeds of the Depression were already present in the "boom" years of the 1920s.

For many groups of Americans, the prosperity of the 1920s was a cruel illusion. Even during the most prosperous years of the Roaring Twenties, most families lived below what contemporaries defined as the poverty line. In 1929, economists considered $2500 the income necessary to support a family. In that year, more than 60 percent of the nation's families earned less than $2000 a year, the income necessary for basic necessities; and over 40 percent of all families earned less than $1500 annually. Although labor productivity soared during the 1920s because of electrification and more efficient management, wages stagnated or fell in mining, transportation, and manufacturing.

Prosperity bypassed specific groups of Americans entirely. A 1928 report on the condition of Native Americans found that half earned less than $500 and that 71 percent lived on less than $200 a year. Mexican Americans, too, had failed to share in the prosperity. During each year of the 1920s, 25,000 Mexicans migrated to the United States. Most lived in conditions of extreme poverty. A survey found that a substantial minority of Mexican Americans had virtually no meat or fresh vegetables in their diet; 40 percent said that they could not afford to give their children milk.

The farm sector had been mired in depression since 1921. Farm prices had been depressed ever since the end of World War I, when European agriculture revived and grain from Argentina and Australia entered the world market. Strapped with long-term debts, high taxes, and a sharp drop in crop prices, farmers lost ground throughout the 1920s. In 1910, a farmer's income was 40 percent of a city worker's. By 1930, it had sagged to just 30 percent.

The decline in farm income reverberated throughout the economy. Millions of farmers defaulted on their debts, placing tremendous pressure on the banking system. Between 1920 and 1929, more than 5000 of the country's 30,000 banks failed.

Because of the banking crisis, thousands of small businesspeople failed because they could not secure loans. Thousands more went bankrupt because they had lost their working capital in the stock market crash. A heavy burden of consumer debt also weakened the economy. Consumers built up an unmanageable amount of consumer installment and mortgage debt, taking out loans to buy cars, appliances, and homes in the suburbs. To repay these loans, consumers cut back sharply on discretionary spending.

Drops in consumer spending then led inevitably to reductions in production and subsequent worker layoffs. Unemployed workers then spent less, and the cycle repeated itself.

A poor distribution of income compounded the country's economic problems. During the 1920s, there was a pronounced shift in wealth and income toward the very rich. Between 1919 and 1929, the share of income received by the wealthiest 1 percent of Americans rose from 12 percent to 19 percent, while the share received by the richest 5 percent jumped from 24 percent to 34 percent. Over the same period, the poorest 93 percent of the nonfarm population actually saw its disposable income fall. Because the rich tend to spend a high proportion of their income on luxuries—such as large cars, entertainment, and tourism—and save a disproportionately large share of their income, there was insufficient demand to keep employment and investment at a high level.

Even before the onset of the Depression, business investment had begun to decline. Residential construction boomed between 1924 and 1927, but in 1929 housing starts fell to less than half the 1924 level. A major reason for the depressed housing market was the 1924 immigration law that had restricted foreign immigration. Soaring inventories also led businesses to reduce investment and production. During the mid-1920s, manufacturers expanded their productive capacity and built up excessive inventories. At the decade's end, they cut production back sharply, directing their surplus funds into stock market speculation.

The Federal Reserve, the nation's central bank, played a critical, if inadvertent, role in weakening the economy. In an effort to curb stock market speculation, the Federal Reserve slowed the growth of the money supply, then allowed that supply to fall dramatically after the stock market crash, producing a wrenching "liquidity crisis." Consumers found themselves unable to repay loans, while businesses did not have the capital to finance business operations. Instead of actively stimulating the economy by cutting interest rates and expanding the money supply—the way monetary authorities fight recessions today—the Federal Reserve allowed the country's money supply to decline by 27 percent between 1929 and 1933.

Finally, Republican tariff policies damaged the economy by depressing foreign trade. Anxious to protect American industries from foreign competitors, Congress passed the Fordney-McCumber Tariff of 1922 and the Hawley-Smoot Tariff of 1930, raising tariff rates to unprecedented levels. American tariffs stifled international trade, making it difficult for European nations to pay off their debts. As foreign economies foundered, those countries imposed trade barriers of their own, choking off

Chronology of Key Events

1914	Marcus Garvey organizes the Universal Negro Improvement Association (UNIA), in Jamaica, to promote black migration to Africa, with first U.S. UNIA branch in Harlem in 1917
1915	Ku Klux Klan is revived and claims 4 million members by 1924
1917–1925	Some 600,000 black Americans migrate to northern industrial cities
1919	Labor unrest includes a nationwide steel strike, a coal miners' strike, a general strike in Seattle, and a police strike in Boston; race riots erupt in over 20 cities; Eighteenth Amendment bans the manufacture and sale of alcoholic beverages
1920	Palmer raids arrest suspected Communists; Massachusetts trial of two Italian anarchists, Nicola Sacco and Bartolomeo Vanzetti, begins on charges of murder, and they are executed in 1927; Sinclair Lewis's *Main Street* exposes the complacency of small-town life
1921	Warren Harding's inauguration as the twenty-ninth president begins 12 years of Republican control of the presidency; Revenue Act slashes taxes on higher incomes; European immigration is restricted to a quota of 3 percent of the population of a nationality living in the United States in 1910
1922	Fordney-McCumber Tariff raises duties on imports
1923	President Harding dies; Calvin Coolidge becomes the thirtieth president
1924	Congress reduces immigration quota to 2 percent of the population of a nationality living in the United States in 1890; Senate committee begins an investigation of Teapot Dome oil-leasing scandal
1925	Scopes trial, the celebrated "Monkey Trial," attacks the teaching of evolution in public schools; F. Scott Fitzgerald's *The Great Gatsby* criticizes the American success ethic
1926	New revenue act further reduces tax rates on high incomes
1929	Herbert Hoover is inaugurated as the thirty-first president; annual quota of immigrants is reduced to about 152,000; stock market crashes
1930	Hawley-Smoot Tariff raises import duties to unprecedented levels

U.S. exports. By 1933, international trade had plunged 30 percent.

All these factors left the economy ripe for disaster. Yet the depression did not strike instantly; it infected the country gradually, like a slow-growing cancer. Measured in human terms, the Great Depression was the worst economic catastrophe in American history. It hit urban and rural areas, blue- and white-collar families alike. In the nation's cities, unemployed men took to the streets to sell apples or shine shoes. Thousands of others hopped freight trains and wandered from town to town, looking for jobs or handouts.

Unlike most of Western Europe, the United States had no federal system of unemployment insurance. The relief burden fell on state and municipal governments working in cooperation with private charities, such as the Red Cross and the Community Chest. Created to handle temporary emergencies, these groups lacked the resources to alleviate the massive suffering created by the Great Depression. Poor southerners, whose states had virtually no relief funds, were particularly hard hit.

Urban centers in the North fared little better. Most city charters did not permit public funds to be spent on work relief. Adding insult to injury, several states disqualified relief clients from voting, while other cities forced them to surrender their automobile license plates. "Prosperity's decade" had ended in economic disaster.

Conclusion

In 1931, a journalist named Frederick Lewis Allen published a volume of popular history that did more to shape the popular image of the 1920s than any book ever written by a professional historian. Entitled *Only Yesterday*, it depicted the 1920s as a cynical, hedonistic interlude between the Great War and the Great Depression, a decade of dissipation, of jazz bands, raccoon coats, bathtub gin, flappers, flagpole sitters, bootleggers, and marathon dancers. Allen argued that World War I shattered Americans' faith in reform and moral crusades. The younger generation proceeded to rebel against traditional taboos while their elders engaged in an orgy of speculation.

In fact, however, the twenties present a much more complicated picture than that summed up by such catchphrases as "The Jazz Age" or "The Age of Flaming Youth." Janus, the two-faced god of antiquity, offers a more accurate symbol for America in the 1920s. The nation's image was divided, with one profile looking optimistically to the future and the other staring longingly at the past. Caught between the disillusionment of World War I and the economic malaise of the Great Depression, the 1920s witnessed a gigantic struggle between an old and a new America. Immigration, race, alcohol, evolution, gender politics, sexual morality—all became major cultural battlefields during the twenties. But what World War I started, the Great Depression interrupted. The intense cultural upheavals of the 1920s gave way to the equally intense economic debates of the 1930s and cultural politics took a back seat to the politics of survival.

SUGGESTIONS FOR FURTHER READING

Stanley Coben, *Rebellion Against Victorianism: The Impetus for Cultural Change in 1920s America* (1991). Analyzes social and intellectual changes during the 1920s.

Ann Douglas, *Terrible Honesty: Mongrel Manhattan in the 1920s* (1995). Examines the intellectual and artistic ferment in New York City.

John A. Garraty, *The Great Depression* (1986). Discusses the causes of the depression.

Ellis W. Hawley, *The Great War and the Search for Modern Order: A History of the American People and Their Institutions, 1917–1933*, 2d ed. (1992). Presents an interpretive overview of the period.

Roderick Nash, *The Nervous Generation: American Thought, 1917–1930* (1970). Analyzes intellectual and artistic innovation from World War I to the Great Depression.

Geoffrey Perrett, *America in the Twenties* (1982). Offers an overview of social and cultural developments of the decade.

Overviews and Surveys

Frederick Lewis Allen, *Only Yesterday: An Informal History Of the Nineteen-Twenties* (1931); Paul A. Carter, *Another Part of the Twenties* (1977), and *The Twenties in America*, 2d ed. (1975); David J. Goldberg, *Discontented America: The United States in the 1920s* (1999); Ellis Hawley, *The Great War and the Search for Modern Order: A History of the American People and Their Institutions, 1917–1933*, 2nd ed. (1992); John D. Hicks, *Republican Ascendancy, 1921–1933* (1960); William E. Leuchtenburg, *The Perils of Prosperity, 1914–32* (1958); Geoffrey Perrett, *America in the Twenties* (1982).

The Emergence of Modern America

Erik Barnouw, *A Tower of Babel: A History of Broadcasting in the United States to 1933* (1966); Robert Crunden, *From Self to Society, 1919–1941* (1972); James J. Flink, *The Car Culture* (1975); Lewis F. Fried, *Makers of the City* (1990); Kenneth T. Jackson, *Crabgrass Frontier: The Suburbanization of the United States* (1985); Peter J. Ling, *America and the Automobile: Technology, Reform, and Social Change* (1990); Fred J. MacDonald, *Don't Touch That Dial! Radio Programming in American Life, 1920–1960* (1979); Roland Marchand, *Advertising the American Dream: Making Way for Modernity, 1920–1946* (1985); John B. Rae, *The Road and the Car in American Life* (1971).

The Formation of Modern American Culture

Loren Baritz, ed., *The Culture of the Twenties* (1970); Edward Behr, *Prohibition: Thirteen Years that Changed America* (1996); Lynn Dumenil, *The Modern Temper: American Culture and Society in the 1920s* (1995); Paula Fass, *The Damned and the Beautiful: American Youth in the 1920s* (1977); Frederick Hoffman, *The Twenties: American Writing in the Postwar Decade*, rev. ed. (1962); David Gerard Hogan, *Selling 'Em by the Sack: White Castle and the Creation of American Food* (1997); Ed Larson, *Summer for the Gods: The Scopes Trial and America's Continuing Debate Over Science and Religion* (1997); Roderick Nash, *The Nervous Generation: American Thought, 1917–1930* (1970); Kathy J. Ogren, *The Jazz Revolution: Twenties America and the Meaning of Jazz* (1989); Daniel Pope, *The Making of Modern Advertising* (1983); Robert Sklar, *Movie-Made America: A Cultural History of American Movies* (1975).

The Clash of Values

Houston A. Baker, Jr., *Modernism and the Harlem Renaissance* (1987); Dorothy M. Brown, *Setting a Course: American Women in the 1920s* (1987); Susan D. Becker, *The Origins of the Equal Rights Amendment* (1981); Kathleen M. Blee, *Women of the Klan: Racism & Gender in the 1920s* (1991); Albert Camarillo, *Chicanos in a Changing Society* (1979); William H. Chafe, *The American Woman: Her Changing Social, Economic, and Political Role* (1972); David Chalmers, *Hooded Americans: The First Century of the Ku Klux Klan, 1865–1965* (1965); Mark Thomas Connelly, *The Response to Prostitution in the Progressive Era* (1980); Nancy Cott, *The Grounding of Modern Feminism* (1987); Robert A. Divine, *American Immigration Policy, 1924–1952* (1957); John D'Emilio and Estelle B. Freedman, *Intimate Matters: A History of Sexuality in America* (1988); Peter G. Filene,

Him/Her/Self Sex Roles in Modern America (1986); David H. Fischer, *Growing Old In America* (1978); Ellen Fitzpatrick, *Endless Crusade: Women Social Scientists and Progressive Reform* (1990); Norman Furniss, *The Fundamentalist Controversy, 1918–1931* (1954); Ray Ginger, *Six Days or Forever? Tennessee v. John Thomas Scopes* (1958); Penina Migdal Glazer and Miriam Slater, *Unequal Colleagues: The Entrance of Women into the Professions, 1890–1940* (1987); Robert A. Goldberg, *Hooded Empire* (1981); Linda Gordon, *Woman's Body, Woman's Right: A Social History of Birth Control in America* (1976); Vivian Gornick, *The Romance of American Communism* (1977); John Higham, *Strangers in the Land: Patterns of American Nativism, 1860–1925* (1955); John B. Holway, *Black Diamonds: Life in the Negro Leagues From the Men Who Lived It* (1989); Nathan Huggins, *Harlem Renaissance* (1971); Kenneth T. Jackson, *The Ku Klux Klan in the City* (1967); Ira Katznelson, *Black Men, White Cities: Race Politics and Migration in the United States, 1900–30, and Britain, 1948–68* (1973); Don S. Kirshner, *City and Country: Rural Responses to Urbanization in the 1920s* (1970); Kenneth Kusmer, *A Ghetto Takes Shape: Black Cleveland, 1870–1930* (1976); J. Stanley Lemons, *The Woman Citizen: Social Feminism in the 1920s* (1973); David Levering Lewis, *When Harlem Was in Vogue* (1981); Leonard Moore, *Citizen Klansmen* (1991); Gilbert Osofsky, *Harlem: The Making of a Ghetto: Negro New York, 1890–1930*, 2d ed. (1971); James Reed, *From Private Vice to Public Virtue: The Birth Control Movement and American Society* (1978); Ricardo Romo, *East Los Angeles: History of a Barrio* (1983); Ruth Rosen, *The Lost Sisterhood: Prostitution in America, 1900–1918* (1982); Ernest Sandeen, *The Roots of Fundamentalism* (1970); Andrew Sinclair, *Prohibition* (1962); Leslie W. Tentler, *Wage-Earning Women: Industrial Work and Family Life in the United States, 1900–1930* (1979); Theodore Vincent, *Black Power and the Garvey Movement* (1971); Winifred D. Wandersee, *Women's Work and Family Values, 1920–1940* (1981); Nancy Weiss, *The National Urban League, 1910–1940* (1974); William Young and David E. Kaiser, *Postmortem: New Evidence in the Case of Sacco and Vanzetti* (1985).

The Republican Restoration

Gary Alchon, *The Invisible Hand of Planning: Capitalism, Social Science, and the State in the 1920s* (1985); LeRoy Ashby, *The Spearless Leader: Senator Borah and the Progressive Movement in the 1920s* (1972); Gary Dean Best, *The Politics of American Individualism: Herbert Hoover in Transition, 1918–1921* (1976); David Burner, *The Politics of Provincialism: The Democratic Party in Transition, 1918–1932* (1968); Clarke Chambers, *Seedtime of Reform, 1918–1932* (1963); Douglas B. Craig, *After Wilson: The Struggle for the Democratic Party* (1992); Paula Eldot, *Governor Alfred E. Smith: The Politician as Reformer* (1983); John D. Hicks and Theodore Saloutos, *Twentieth-Century Populism: Agricultural Discontent in the Midwest, 1900–1939* (1951); Allan Lichtman, *Prejudice and the Old Politics: The Presidential Election of 1928* (1979); Robert K. Murray, *The Harding Era: Warren G. Harding and His Administration* (1969), and *The Politics of Normalcy* (1973); Burl Noggle, *Teapot Dome: Oil and Politics in the 1920s* (1962); Thomas B. Silver, *Coolidge and the Historians* (1982); Robert H. Zieger, *Republicans and Labor, 1919–1929* (1969).

The Great Crash

William J. Barber, *From New Era to New Deal: Herbert Hoover, the Economists, and American Economic Policy, 1921–1933* (1985); Irving Bernstein, *The Lean Years: A History of the American Worker, 1920–1933* (1960); David Brody, *Workers in Industrial America: Essays on the Twentieth-Century Struggle* (1980); Alfred Chandler, *Strategy and Structure: Chapters in the History of the Industrial Enterprise* (1962); Martin L. Fausold, *The Presidency of Herbert Hoover* (1985); John Kenneth Galbraith, *The Great Crash, 1929* (1955); Ellis W. Hawley, *The Great War and the Search for a Modern Order: A History of the American People and Their Institutions, 1917–1933*, 2d ed. (1992); Sanford M. Jacoby, *Employing Bureaucracy: Managers, Unions, and the Transformation of Work in American Industry* (1985); David C. Jones, *Empire of Dust: Settling and Abandoning the Prairie Dry Belt* (1987); C.P. Kindleberger, *The World in Depression, 1929–1939* (1973); Jim Potter, *The American Economy Between the World Wars*, rev. ed. (1985); James Prothro, *The Dollar Decade: Business Ideas in the 1920s* (1954); Albert U. Romasco, *The Poverty of Abundance: Hoover, the Nation, and the Depression* (1965); Jordan A. Schwarz, *Interregnum of Despair: Hoover, Congress, and the Depression* (1970); Robert Sobel, *The Great Bull Market: Wall Street in the 1920s* (1968); George Soule, *Prosperity Decade: From War to Depression, 1917–1929* (1947); Peter Temin, *Did Monetary Forces Cause the Great Depression?* (1976).

Biographies

David Burner, *Herbert Hoover: A Public Life* (1979); Ellen Chesler, *Woman of Valor: Margaret Sanger and the Birth Control Movement in America* (1992); William Harbaugh, *Lawyer's Lawyer: The Life of John W. Davis* (1973); Matthew Josephson and Hannah Josephson, *Al Smith: Hero of the Cities* (1969); David Kennedy, *Birth Control in America: The Career of Margaret Sanger* (1970); Lawrence Levine, *Defender of the Faith: William Jennings Bryan, 1915–1925* (1965); Richard Lowitt, *George W. Norris* (1971); Manning Marable, *W.E.B. Du Bois: Black Radical Democrat* (1986); Donald R. McCoy, *Calvin Coolidge: The Quiet President* (1967); George Nash, *The Life of Herbert Hoover—The Engineer* (1983); Randy Roberts, *Jack Dempsey: The Manassa Mauler* (1979); Francis Russell, *The Shadow of Blooming Grove: Warren G. Harding in His Times* (1968); Andrew Sinclair, *The Available Man: The Life Behind the Masks of Warren Gamaliel Harding* (1965); Richard N. Smith, *An Uncommon Man: The Triumph of Herbert Hoover* (1984); David P. Thelen, *Robert M. La Follette and the Insurgent Spirit* (1976); William Allen White, *A Puritan in Babylon: The Story of Calvin Coolidge* (1938).

INTERNET RESOURCES

Margaret Sanger Papers Project
http://www.nyu.edu/projects/sanger
This site at New York University contains information about Margaret Sanger and digital versions of several of her works.

Automotive History at the Michigan Electronic Library
http://mel.lib.mi.us/business/autocenter/auto-history.html
This page has several links to sites about automotive history in America.

National Arts and Crafts Archives at the Arts and Crafts Society
http://arts-crafts.com/_b35c69ed/archive/archive.html
This site serves as a guide to materials on the Arts & Crafts Movement that lasted roughly from 1890 to 1929.

Harlem 1900–1940: An African-American Community
http://www.si.umich.edu/CHICO/Harlem
The New York Public Library's Schomburg Center for Research in Black Culture hosts this site that includes a database, a timeline, and an exhibit.

William P. Gottlieb Photographs of the Golden Age of Jazz
http://memory.loc.gov/ammem/wghtml/wghome.html
The Music Division of the Library of Congress has numerous images, audio, and scanned articles from the 1940s.

Negro Leagues Baseball Online Archive
http://www.negroleaguebaseball.com/
Essays about desegregation, baseball, and Jim Crow as well as images of teams and players comprise much of this site.

Popular Culture in the 1920s
http://www.louisville.edu/~kprayb01/1920s,Society-Index.html
This site looks at how the 1920s set the stage for many aspects of modern popular culture.

The Scopes Trial
http://xroads.virginia.edu/~UG97/inherit/1925home.html
This site gives a general description of the trial and the issues surrounding it.

Temperance and Prohibition
http://www.cohums.ohio-state.edu/history/projects/prohibition/
This site looks at the temperance movement over time and contains many informative links.

The Flapper
http://www.pandorasbox.com/flapper.html
This site contains many links to information about the popular culture of the 1920s with special reference to the flapper.

The Calvin Coolidge Experience
http://www.geocities.com/CapitolHill/4921/
This site is an unusual look at one of America's less colorful presidents.

KEY TERMS

Flapper   (p. 681)
Nineteenth Amendment   (p. 684)
Equal Rights Amendment   (p. 684)
Prohibition   (p. 684)
Scopes "Monkey Trial"   (p. 686)
National Origins Act of 1924   (p. 686)
Ku Klux Klan   (p. 687)
National Association for the Advancement of Colored People (NAACP)   (p. 687)
Harlem Renaissance   (p. 688)
Black Tuesday   (p. 692)

REVIEW QUESTIONS

1. What factors contributed to the emergence of modern American culture in the 1920s?
2. How did the appearance of new forms of art and entertainment change American society in the 1920s?
3. What were the major points of conflict within the emerging modern American culture?
4. Why did conservative politics dominate such a seemingly liberal culture as 1920s America?
5. Would government intervention have prevented the stock market crash in 1929?

24

THE AGE OF ROOSEVELT

THE GREAT DEPRESSION IN GLOBAL PERSPECTIVE

THE HUMAN TOLL
The Dispossessed
Private and Public Charity

PRESIDENT HERBERT HOOVER RESPONDS
Conservative Responses
Government Loans

FRANKLIN ROOSEVELT AND THE FIRST NEW DEAL
The Election of 1932
The First 100 Days
The New Dealers
The Farmers' Plight
The National Recovery Administration
Jobs Programs
Roosevelt's Critics

THE SECOND NEW DEAL
The Wagner Act
Social Security
The Election of 1936

THE NEW DEAL, WOMEN, AND MINORITY GROUPS
Women
African Americans
Mexican Americans
Native Americans

THE NEW DEAL IN DECLINE
Court Packing
The Depression of 1937

POPULAR CULTURE DURING THE GREAT DEPRESSION
Artistic and Literary Endeavors
Hollywood During the Great Depression

"Shakespeare in overalls"

Woody Guthrie often inscribed the phrase "This machine surrounds hate and destroys it" on his guitars.

To fans of authentic folk music, Woodrow Wilson "Woody" Guthrie was a "Shakespeare in overalls," the finest American frontier balladeer of the twentieth century. His nasal, high-pitched singing voice was definitely an acquired taste, but Guthrie's lyrics were at once simple and penetrating. He sang of vagabonds who wandered in search of work, of union men who saw their comrades on the picket lines knocked to the ground by company goons, and of farmers who watched with horror as their land dried up and turned into a dust bowl. In short he put to music the hardships and struggles of working-class Americans trapped in the Great Depression.

Guthrie drew his material from his life. Born in 1912, Woody grew up in Oklahoma and the Texas Panhandle in a family star-crossed by disasters. When he was still a boy his older sister died from setting herself on fire; his father, once a prosperous land speculator, sank into alcoholism; and his mother slipped slowly into madness and had to be committed to the state mental hospital.

In the face of these tragedies the Guthrie household simply dissolved, leaving Woody pretty much on his own. He passed the time by learning to play the guitar and harmonica. Eventually, he dropped out of school and became a drifter, driven by an internal restlessness that kept him on the road for the rest of his life.

Guthrie spent the Great Depression riding the rails, playing his music, and visiting "his" people, in the boxcars, hobo jungles, and migrant camps from Oklahoma to California. He saw families sleeping on the ground and children with distended bellies who cried from hunger while guards hired to protect the orchards prevented them from eating fruit that lay rotting on the ground. Over time a quiet anger began to eat at him and he blamed the nation's "polli-Tish-uns" for not doing more to relieve the people's suffering.

By 1940 Guthrie had recorded several albums of Dust Bowl ballads and union protest songs. His homegrown radicalism made him an instant hit with socialist and communist intellectuals and entertainment figures who saw his music as a powerful weapon in the class struggle. They saw Guthrie as an authentic folk hero, the very embodiment of the proletarian artist. In truth, Guthrie held more radical political views than most Americans, but he aptly fulfilled his role as the "voice of the people" by putting to music the most important themes to emerge in American life during the 1930s—the common man's defiant pride, his will to survive in the face of adversity, and the extraordinary love Americans felt for their country.

In "God Blessed America" (which later generations of Americans would recognize by its first line, "This land is your land, this land is my land"), Guthrie sang of "endless skyways," "golden valleys," "diamond deserts," and "wheat fields waving," evoking the country's grandeur with a poet's sense of beauty. What gave the song its power, however, was the idea that America belonged to the people; every verse closed with the refrain, "God blessed America for me."

Even in the depths of the Great Depression, Guthrie found much of enduring value in America. In ballad after ballad, he celebrated the fortitude and dignity of the American people. They provided the glue that held things together while President Franklin D. Roosevelt experimented with policies and programs designed to promote relief, recovery, and reform.

THE GREAT DEPRESSION IN GLOBAL PERSPECTIVE

Unlike previous economic downturns, which generally were confined to a handful of nations or specific regions, the Great Depression was a global phenomenon. Africa, Asia, Australia, Europe, and North and South America all suffered from the economic collapse. International trade fell 30 percent, as most nations tried to protect their industries by raising tariffs on imported goods. These "beggar-thy-neighbor" trade policies were a major reason why the depression persisted as long as it did.

Also, in contrast to the relatively brief economic "panics" of the past, the Great Depression dragged on with no end in sight. As it deepened, the depression had far-reaching political consequences. One response to it was military dictatorship—a response found in Argentina and many countries in Central America. Western industrialized countries cut back sharply on the purchase of raw materials and other commodities. The collapse in raw material and agricultural commodity prices led to social unrest, resulting in the rise of military dictatorships that promised to maintain order.

A second response to the depression was fascism and militarism—a response found in Germany, Italy, and Japan. In Germany, Adolf Hitler and his Nazi party promised to restore the country's economy and rebuild its military. After becoming chancellor in 1932, Hitler outlawed labor unions, restructured German industry into a series of cartels, and, after 1935, instituted a massive program of military rearmament that ended high unemployment. In Italy, fascism arose under the leadership of Italian dictator Benito Mussolini even before the depression's onset. In Japan, militarists seized control of the government during the 1930s. In an effort to relieve the depression, Japanese military officers conquered Manchuria, a region rich in raw materials, in 1931, and coastal China in 1937.

A third response to the depression was totalitarian communism. In the Soviet Union, the Great Depression helped solidify Joseph Stalin's grip on power. In 1928, Stalin instituted a planned economy. His first Five-Year Plan called for rapid industrialization and "collectivization" of small peasant farms under government control. To crush opposition to his program, which required peasant farmers to give their products to the government at low prices, Stalin exiled millions of peasants to labor camps in Siberia, instituting a program of terror called the Great Purge. Historians estimate that as many as 20 million Soviets died during the 1930s as a result of famine and deliberate killings.

A fourth and final response to the depression was welfare capitalism, which could be found in countries such as Canada, Great Britain, and France. Under welfare capitalism, the government assumed ultimate responsibility for promoting a reasonably fair distribution of wealth and power and providing security against the risks of bankruptcy, unemployment, and destitution.

The economic decline brought on by this depression was steeper and more protracted in the United States than in other industrialized countries. The unemployment rate rose higher and remained higher longer than in any other western society. While European countries significantly reduced unemployment by 1936, as late as 1939, when World War II began in Europe, the American jobless rate still exceeded 17 percent, not dropping below 14 percent until 1941.

The Great Depression transformed the American political and economic landscape. It produced a major political realignment, creating a coalition of big-city ethnics, African Americans, and Southern Democrats committed, to various degrees, to interventionist government. It strengthened the federal presence in American life, spawning such innovations as national old-age pensions, unemployment compensation, aid to dependent children, public housing, federally subsidized school lunches, insured bank deposits, the minimum wage, and stock market regulation. It fundamentally altered labor relations, producing a revived labor movement and a national labor policy protective of collective bargaining. It transformed the farm economy by introducing federal price supports and rural electrification. Above all, the Great Depression produced a fundamental shift in public attitudes. It led Americans to view the federal government as their agency of action and reform and the ultimate protector of public well-being.

THE HUMAN TOLL

Even after more than half a century, images of the Great Depression remain firmly etched in the American psyche—breadlines, soup kitchens, tin-can shanties and tarpaper shacks known as **"Hoovervilles,"** penniless men and women selling apples on street corners, and gray battalions of "Arkies" and "Okies" packed into Model A Fords heading out to California.

The economic collapse was staggering in its dimensions. Unemployment jumped from less than 3 million in 1929 to 4 million in 1930, 8 million in 1931, and 12½ million in 1932. By 1932, a quarter of the nation's families did not have a single employed wage earner. Only one company in ten failed to cut pay, and in 1932, three-quarters of all workers were on part-time schedules, averaging just 60 percent of the normal workweek.

Appalling in dimension, the collapse was terrifying in its scope and impact. By 1933 average family income had tumbled 40 percent, from $2300 in 1929

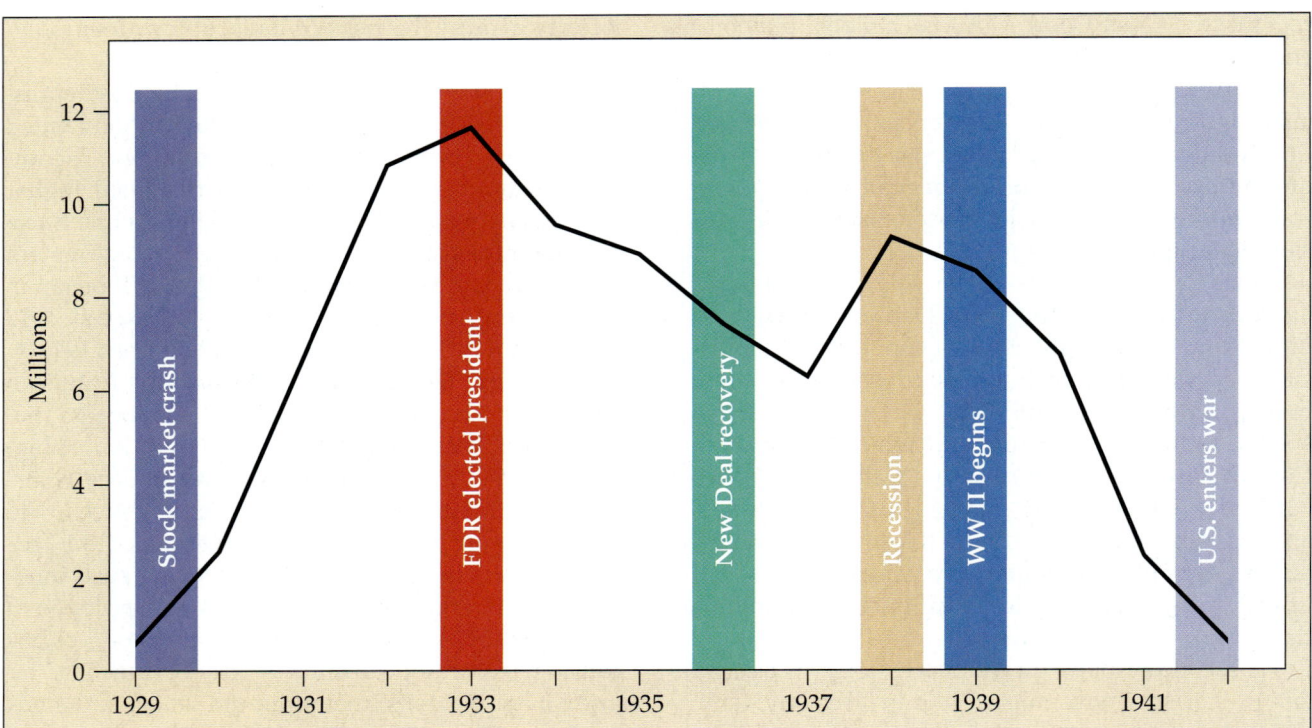

FIGURE 24.1
Unemployment, 1929–1942

down to just $1500 four years later. In the Pennsylvania coalfields, three or four families crowded together in one-room shacks and lived on wild weeds. In Arkansas, families were found inhabiting caves, and in Oakland, California, whole families lived in sewer pipes.

Vagrancy shot up as many families were evicted from their homes for nonpayment of rent. The Southern Pacific Railroad boasted that it threw 683,000 vagrants off its trains in 1931. Free public flophouses and missions in Los Angeles provided beds for 200,000 of the uprooted.

Many families sought to cope by planting gardens, canning food, buying day-old bread, and using cardboard and cotton for shoe soles. Despite a steep drop in food prices, many families did without milk or meat. To save money, families neglected medical and dental care.

President Herbert Hoover declared, "Nobody is actually starving. The hoboes are better fed than they have ever been." But in New York City in 1931 there were 20 known cases of starvation; in 1934, there were 110 deaths from hunger.

The Great Depression had a powerful impact on families. It forced couples to delay marriage and drove the birthrate below the replacement level for the first time in American history. The divorce rate fell—for the simple reason that many couples could not afford to maintain separate households or pay legal fees. But rates of desertion soared—by 1940, 1.5 million married women were living apart from their husbands. More than 200,000 vagrant children wandered the country because of the breakup of their families.

The depression inflicted a heavy psychological toll on jobless men. With no wages to reinforce their authority, many men lost power as primary decision makers. Large numbers of men lost their self-respect, became immobilized, and stopped looking for work, while others turned to alcohol or became self-destructive or abusive to their families.

In contrast to the men, many women saw their status rise during the depression. To supplement the family income, married women entered the work force in large numbers. Although most women worked in menial occupations, the fact that they were employed and bringing home paychecks elevated their position within the family and gave them a say in family decisions.

Despite the hardships it inflicted, the Great Depression drew some families closer together. Families had to devise strategies for getting through hard times because their survival depended on it. They pooled their incomes, moved in with relatives in order to cut expenses, and did without. Many families drew comfort from their religion, sustained by the hope things would turn out well in the end, while others placed their faith in themselves, in their own dogged determination to survive that so impressed observers like Woody Guthrie. But many Americans no longer believed the problems could be solved by people acting alone or through voluntary associations. Increasingly, they looked to the federal government for help.

The Dispossessed

Economic hardship and loss visited all sections of the country. Doctors and lawyers saw their incomes fall 40 percent. But no groups suffered more from the depression than African Americans and Mexican Americans.

A year after the stock market crashed, 70 percent of Charleston's black population and 75 percent of Memphis's was unemployed. In Macon County, Alabama, home of Booker T. Washington's famous Tuskegee Institute, most black families lived in homes without wooden floors, windows, or sewage disposal and subsisted on salt pork (pork fat cured in salt), hominy grits, corn bread, and molasses. Income averaged less than a dollar a day.

Conditions were also distressed in the North. In Chicago and other large northern cities, most African Americans lived in "kitchenettes." Six-room apartments, previously rented for $50 a month, were di-

Table 24.1
Depression Shopping List: 1932–1934

Automobiles		Household Items		Toys	
Pontiac Coupe	$ 585.00	Silverplate flatware,		Doll carriage	$ 4.98
Chrysler Sedan	995.00	26 pieces	$4.98	Sled	1.45
Dodge	595.00	Double-bed sheets	.67	Tricycle	3.98
Studebaker	840.00	Bath towel	.24	Bicycle	10.95
Packard	2150.00	Wool blanket	1.00	Fielder's glove and	
Chevrolet ton pick-up		Wool rug (98'×128')	5.85	ball	1.25
truck	650.00				
Clothing		**Appliances**		**Food**	
Women's		Electric iron	$ 2.00	Sirloin steak/lb.	$.29
Mink coat	$585.00	Electric coffee		Rib roast/lb.	.22
Leopard coat	92.00	percolator	1.39	Bacon/lb.	.22
Cloth coat	6.98	Electric mixer	9.95	Ham/lb.	.31
Wool dress	1.95	Vacuum cleaner	18.75	Chicken/lb.	.22
Wool suit	3.98	Electric washing		Pork chops/lb.	.20
Wool sweater	1.69	machine	47.95	Salmon (16 oz can)	.19
Silk stockings	.69	Gas stove	23.95	Milk (quart)	.10
Leather shoes	1.79	Electric sewing		Butter/lb.	.28
		machine	24.95	Eggs (dozen)	.29
Men's				Bread (20 oz loaf)	.05
Overcoat	$11.00	**Furniture**		Coffee/lb.	.26
Wool suit	10.50			Sugar/lb.	.05
Trousers	2.00	Dining room set,		Rice/lb.	.06
Shirt	.47	8-piece	$46.50	Potatoes/lb.	.02
Pullover sweater	1.95	Lounge chair	19.95	Tomatoes (16 oz.	
Silk necktie	.55	Double bed and		can)	.09
Stetson hat	5.00	mattress	14.95	Oranges/dozen	.27
Shoes	3.85	Mahogany coffee		Cornflakes (8 oz.	
		table	10.75	box)	.08
Air Travel		Chippendale sofa	135.00		
New York to Chicago,		Louis XV walnut dining			
round trip	$86.31	table	124.00		
Chicago to Los Angeles,		Wing chair	39.00		
round trip	207.00	Grand Piano	395.00		

vided into six kitchenettes renting for $8 dollars a week, assuring landlords of a windfall of an extra $142 a month.

The depression hit Mexican-American families especially hard. Mexican Americans faced serious opposition from organized labor, which resented competition from Mexican workers as unemployment rose. Bowing to union pressure, federal, state, and local authorities "repatriated" more than 400,000 people of Mexican descent to prevent them from applying for relief. Since this group included many United States citizens, the deportations constituted a gross violation of civil liberties.

Private and Public Charity

The economic crisis of the 1930s overwhelmed private charities and local governments. In south Texas, the Salvation Army provided a penny per person each day. In Philadelphia, even though private and public charities distributed $1 million a month in poor relief, this provided families with only $1.50 a week for groceries. In 1932, total public and private relief expenditures amounted to $317 million—$26 for each of the nation's 12½ million jobless.

PRESIDENT HERBERT HOOVER RESPONDS

When the Great Depression struck, most political and economic leaders had regarded recessions as inevitable, a natural part of the business cycle. The prevailing economic theory held that government intervention was both unnecessary and unwise. Previous financial panics had failed to elicit much response from government; and many economists in 1929 continued to extol the virtues of inaction, arguing that the economy would recover by itself. President Herbert Hoover disagreed. Though Hoover saw the Great Crash as a temporary slump in a fundamentally healthy economy, he believed the president should try to facilitate economic recovery.

Conservative Responses

First, Hoover resorted to old-fashioned "jawboning." Shortly after the stock market crashed, he summoned business and labor leaders to the White House. Industrial leaders promised to maintain prices and wages, and labor spokesmen pledged not to strike or demand higher wages. While Hoover remained hopeful voluntary measures would suffice, businesses struggled to survive, forcing employers to lay off workers.

Next, the president tried cheerleading. The contrast between Hoover's speeches and conditions in the country was jarring. According to Hoover, the economy in 1930 was fundamentally sound, and recovery was just around the corner. His rosy pronouncements prompted critics to accuse Hoover of being insensitive to the unemployed and the dispossessed. Cynics called the shantytown slums on the edges of cities "Hoovervilles." Newspapers became "Hoover blankets" and empty pockets turned inside out, "Hoover flags."

Neither cruel nor insensitive, Hoover was tormented by the suffering of the poor. Yet he could not bring himself to sanction large-scale federal public works programs because he honestly believed that recovery depended on the private sector, because he wanted to maintain a balanced budget, and because he feared federal relief programs would undermine individual character by making recipients dependent on the state.

Government Loans

When jawboning and cheerleading failed to revive the economy, Hoover reluctantly adopted other measures. In 1932 Congress created the Reconstruction Finance Corporation (RFC) and authorized it to loan $2 billion to banks, savings and loan associations,

Bank failures wiped out the life savings of many prudent Americans.

railroads, and life insurance companies. Blaming the depression on tight credit, Hoover believed federal loans would enable businesses to increase production and hire workers. The same principle applied to the Federal Home Loan Bank System (FHLBS), created by Congress in July 1932 to lend up to $500 million to savings and loan associations to revive the construction industry.

Yet by early 1933 Hoover's agencies had failed to make a dent in the Great Depression. The real problem was not tight credit but the soft demand for goods, a problem that flowed both from the chronic low wages paid to the bulk of American workers and the massive layoffs following the Great Crash. It was a vicious cycle. Unemployed workers could not buy goods, so businesses cut back production and laid off additional workers. Businesspeople did not ask banks for working capital loans, which the RFC and FHLBS were created to provide, because they had no interest in increasing production.

Franklin Roosevelt and the First New Deal

In June 1932, Franklin D. Roosevelt received the Democratic presidential nomination. At first glance he did not look like a man who could relate to other peoples' suffering, for Roosevelt had spent his entire life in the lap of luxury. A fifth cousin of Teddy Roosevelt, he was born in 1882 to one of New York's oldest and wealthiest families. He attended Groton, an exclusive private school, then went to Harvard University and Columbia Law School. After three years in the New York state senate, Roosevelt was tapped by President Wilson to serve as assistant secretary of the navy in 1913. His status as the rising star of the Democratic party was confirmed when James Cox chose Roosevelt as his running mate in the presidential election of 1920.

The Election of 1932

Handsome and outgoing, Roosevelt seemed to have a bright political future. Then disaster struck. In 1921 he contracted polio, which left him paralyzed from the waist down and confined to a wheelchair for the rest of his life. Instead of retiring, however, Roosevelt labored diligently to return to public life. "If you had spent two years in bed trying to wiggle your toe," he later declared, "after that anything would seem easy."

Buoyed by an exuberant optimism and devoted political allies, Roosevelt won the governorship of New York in 1928, one of the few Democrats to survive the Republican landslide. Surrounding himself with able advisers, Roosevelt labored to convert

Roosevelt was charming and charismatic, and many people felt he was genuinely interested in their concerns. Here Roosevelt meets with a miner during his 1932 campaign.

Members of the Bonus Army poured into Washington, D.C., from every part of the country during the spring and summer of 1932.

New York into a laboratory for reform, involving conservation, old-age pensions, public works projects, and unemployment insurance.

In his acceptance speech before the 1932 Democratic convention in Chicago, Roosevelt promised "a **New Deal** for the American people." Although his speech contained few concrete proposals, Roosevelt radiated confidence, giving many desperate voters hope. He even managed during the campaign to turn his lack of a blueprint into an asset, promising to experiment.

The Republicans stuck with Hoover, but what little chance he had for reelection was dashed by his callous treatment of the **"Bonus Army."** A bedraggled collection of unemployed veterans and their families, the Bonus Army marched on Washington in the spring of 1932 to ask Congress for immediate payment of their war service bonuses, which did not come due until 1945. More than 15,000 strong, they erected a shantytown, camped out in vacant lots, and occupied empty government buildings. Though the House voted to give them what they wanted, the Senate killed the bill after Hoover lobbied against it.

Most of the veterans then left Washington, D.C., but a few thousand stayed behind because they had no place to go. At Hoover's request, Congress appropriated $100,000 to help the remaining veterans return home. When police tried to evict some of the marchers in late July, a riot broke out in which two policemen and two marchers died. Hoover then ordered General Douglas MacArthur to use federal troops to remove them from government buildings. Exceeding his orders, MacArthur used tanks and tear gas to drive the veterans from the city. Newsmen captured the melee in vivid photographs, which papers carried the next day.

Although Hoover was appalled by what happened, he publicly accepted the responsibility and endorsed MacArthur's charge that the bonus marchers included dangerous radicals who wanted to overthrow the government. Most Americans were outraged by the government's harsh treatment of the Bonus Army, and Hoover encountered resentment everywhere he campaigned.

Upon learning of the Bonus Army incident, Franklin D. Roosevelt remarked: "Well, this will elect me." Roosevelt was correct—he buried Hoover in November, winning 22,809,638 votes to Hoover's 15,758,901, and 472 to 59 electoral votes. The Democrats also won commanding majorities in both houses of Congress.

Roosevelt appealed to a wide range of voters, wooing southerners back into the Democrat fold and attracting new groups of voters, including young people, women, and ethnic Americans. Urban Catholics, Jews, and members of the Eastern Orthodox Church voted overwhelmingly for Roosevelt. The 1932 election was the first of many in which these groups would support strongly the Democratic party.

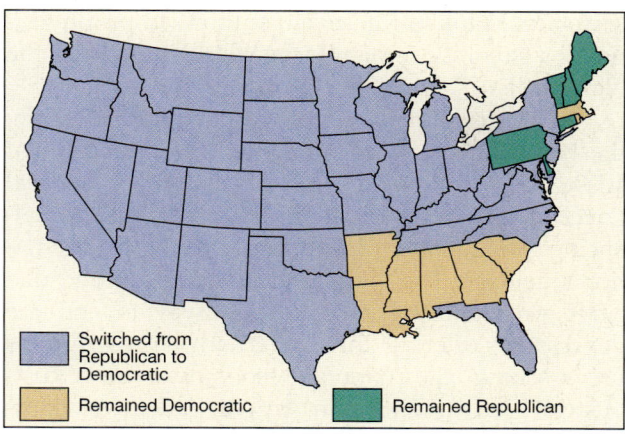

Electoral Shift, 1928 and 1932

The First 100 Days

The nation's plight on March 4, 1933, the day Franklin Roosevelt assumed the presidency, was desperate. A quarter of the nation's workforce was jobless. About 9000 banks, holding the savings of 27 million families, had failed since 1929—1456 in 1932 alone. Farm foreclosures were averaging 20,000 a month. The public was frantic for action. Hamilton Fish, a conservative Republican Congressman from New York, promised the president that Congress would "give you any power that you need."

In his inaugural address, Roosevelt expressed confidence that his administration could end the depression. "The only thing we have to fear," he declared, "is fear itself." The president promised decisive action. He called Congress into special session and demanded "broad executive power to wage a war against the emergency, as great as the power that would be given me if we were in fact invaded by a foreign foe." In his **first 100 days** in office, the president pushed 15 major bills through Congress, which would reshape every aspect of the economy, from banking and industry to agriculture and social welfare.

He attacked the bank crisis first, declaring a national bank holiday, which closed all banks. In just four days, his aides drafted the Emergency Banking Relief Act, which permitted solvent banks to reopen under government supervision, and allowed the RFC to buy the stock of troubled banks and keep them open until they could be reorganized. The law also gave the president broad powers over the Federal Reserve System. The law radically reshaped the nation's banking system; it passed Congress in eight hours.

To generate support for his program, Roosevelt appealed directly to the people. On March 12, eight days after he took office, he conducted the first of many radio **"fireside chats."** Using the radio the way later presidents would exploit television, he explained what he had done in plain, simple terms and told the public to have "confidence and courage." When the banks reopened the following day, people demonstrated their faith by making more deposits

TABLE 24.2
Legislation Enacted During the First Hundred Days March 9–June 16, 1933

March 9	Emergency Banking Relief Act
March 20	Economy Act
March 22	Beer-Wine Revenue Act
March 31	Unemployment Relief Act
March 31	Civilian Conservation Corps Act
May 12	Agricultural Adjustment Act
May 12	Federal Emergency Relief Act
May 18	Tennessee Valley Authority Act
May 27	Securities Act of 1933
June 5	Gold Repeal Joint Resolution
June 13	Home Owners' Refinancing Act
June 16	Farm Credit Act
June 16	Banking Act of 1933
June 16	Emergency Railroad Transportation Act
June 16	National Industrial Recovery Act

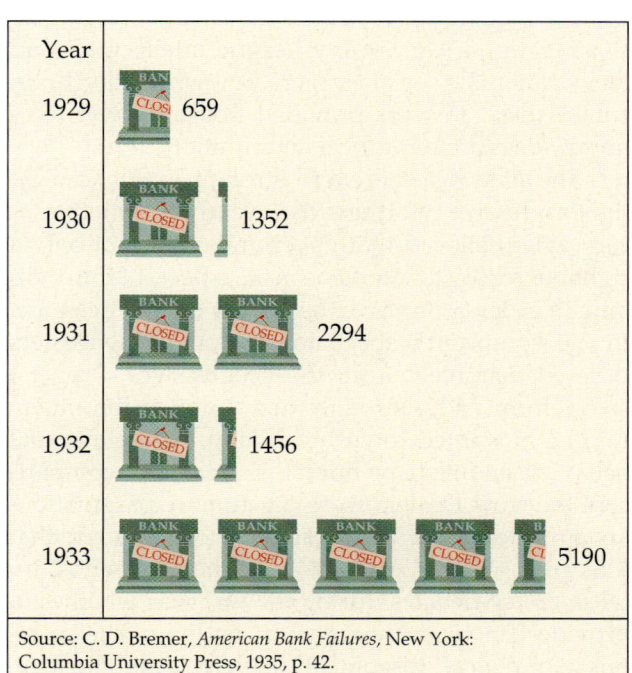

Source: C. D. Bremer, *American Bank Failures*, New York: Columbia University Press, 1935, p. 42.

FIGURE 24.2
Bank Failures, 1929–1933

than withdrawals. One of Roosevelt's key advisers did not exaggerate when he later boasted, "Capitalism was saved in eight days."

The president quickly pushed ahead on other fronts. The Federal Emergency Relief Act pumped $500 million into state-run welfare programs. The Homeowners Loan Act provided the first federal mortgage financing and loan guarantees. The Glass-Steagall Act provided a federal guarantee on all bank deposits under $5000 (with creation of the Federal Deposit Insurance Corporation), separated commercial and investment banking, and strengthened the Federal Reserve's ability to stabilize the economy.

In addition, Roosevelt took the nation off the gold standard, devalued the dollar, and ordered the Federal Reserve System to ease credit. Other important laws passed during the 100 days included the Agricultural Adjustment Act, the nation's first system of agricultural price and production supports; the National Industrial Recovery Act, the first major attempt to plan and regulate the economy; and the Tennessee Valley Authority Act, the first direct government involvement in energy production.

The New Dealers

Franklin Roosevelt brought a new breed of government officials to Washington. Previously, most government administrators were wealthy patricians, businessmen, or political loyalists. Roosevelt, however, looked to new sources of talent, bringing to Washington a team of Ivy League intellectuals and New York State social workers. Known as the **"brain trust,"** these advisers provided Roosevelt with economic ideas and oratorical ammunition.

The New Dealers were strongly influenced by the Progressive reformers of the early twentieth century, who believed that government had not only a right but a duty to intervene in all aspects of the economy in order to improve the quality of American life. In one significant respect, however, the New Dealers differed decisively from the Progressives. Progressive reform had a strongly moral dimension; many reformers wanted to curb drinking, regulate sexual behavior, and reshape human character. In comparison, the New Dealers were much more pragmatic—an attitude vividly illustrated by an incident that took place during World War I. One of the most intense policy debates during the war was whether to provide American troops with condoms. The secretary of the navy, Josephus Daniels, rejected the idea, fearing that it would corrupt the troops' morals. While Daniels was on vacation, however, his undersecretary, Franklin Roosevelt, authorized prophylactics for sailors. Moral reform would not drive the New Deal.

Apart from their commitment to pragmatism, the New Dealers were unified in their rejection of laissez-faire orthodoxy—the idea that the federal government's responsibilities were confined to balancing the federal budget and providing for the nation's defense. The New Dealers did, however, disagree profoundly about the best way to end the depression, offering three alternative prescriptions for rescuing the nation's economy. The "trustbusters," led by Thurman Arnold, called for vigorous enforcement of antitrust laws to break up concentrated business power. The "associationalists" wanted to encourage cooperation between business, labor, and government by establishing associations and codes supported by the three parties. The economic planners, led by Rexford Tugwell, Adolph Berle, and Gardiner Means, wanted to create a system of centralized national planning.

The Farmers' Plight

Roosevelt moved aggressively to address the crisis facing the nation's farmers. No group was harder hit by the depression than farmers and farm workers. Farm income fell a staggering two-thirds during the depression's first three years. In one day, a quarter of Mississippi's farm acreage was auctioned off to pay debts.

The farmers' problem, ironically, was that they grew too much. Worldwide crop production soared—a result of more efficient farm machinery, stronger fertilizers, and improved plant varieties—but demand fell, as people ate less bread, Europeans imposed protective tariffs, and consumers replaced cotton with rayon. The glut caused prices to fall. To meet farm debts in 1932, farmers had to grow 2.5 times as much corn as in 1929, 2.7 times as much wheat, and 2.4 times as much cotton.

As farm incomes fell, farm tenancy soared; two-fifths of all farmers worked on land that they did not own. The Gudgers, a white southern Alabama sharecropping family of six, illustrated the plight of tenants, who were slipping deeper and deeper into debt. Each year, their landlord provided them with 20 acres of land, seed, an unpainted one-room house, a shed, a mule, fertilizer, and $10 a month. In return, they owed him half their corn and cotton crop and 8 percent interest on their debts. In 1934 they were $80 in debt; by 1935, their debts had risen another $12.

Nature itself seemed to have turned against farmers. In the South, the boll weevil devoured the cotton crop, while on the Great Plains, the top soil literally blew away, piling up in ditches like "snow drifts in winter." The Dust Bowl produced unparalleled human tragedy, but it had not occurred by accident. Although the Plains had always been a harsh, arid, inhospitable environment, a covering of tough grass-roots called sod allowed the land to retain moisture and support vegetation. During the 1890s, however, overgrazing by cattle severely damaged the sod. Then, during World War I, farmers driven by the demand for wheat, used gasoline-powered tractors to plow large sections of the prairie for the first time. The fragile skin protecting the prairie was stripped away. When, beginning in 1930, drought struck and temperatures soared, the wind began to blow the soil away.

Tenant farmers found themselves evicted from their land. By 1939, a million Dust Bowl refugees and other tenant farmers left the Plains to work as itinerant produce pickers in California. Whole counties were depopulated as a result.

The New Deal attacked farm problems through a variety of programs. Rural electrification programs meant that for the first time, Americans in Appalachia, the Texas hill country, and other areas would have the opportunity to share in the benefits of electric light and running water. As late as 1935 more than 6 million of America's 6.8 million farms had no electricity. Unlike their sisters in the city, farmwomen had no washing machines, refrigerators, or vacuum cleaners. Private companies insisted that it would be prohibitive to provide electrical service to rural areas.

Roosevelt disagreed. He wanted to break the private monopoly of electric power in rural areas, envisioning a future in which electric power would serve broader goals, including flood control, soil conservation, reforestation, diversification of industry, and a general improvement in the quality of life for rural Americans. Settling on the 40,000-square-mile valley of the Tennessee River as a test site, Roosevelt decided to put the government into the electric business.

Two months after he took office Congress passed a bill creating the Tennessee Valley Authority (TVA). The bill authorized the TVA to build 21 dams to generate electricity for tens of thousands of farm families. In 1935 Roosevelt signed an executive order creating the Rural Electrification Administration (REA) to bring electricity generated by government dams to America's hinterland.

Nor was electricity the only benefit the New Deal bestowed on farmers. The Soil Conservation Service helped farmers battle erosion; the Farm Credit Administration provided some relief from farm foreclosures, and the Commodity Credit Corporation permitted farmers to use stored products as collateral for loans. Roosevelt's most ambitious farm program, however, was the Agricultural Adjustment Act (AAA).

The AAA, led by Secretary of Agriculture Henry Wallace, sought a partnership between the government and major producers. Together the new allies would raise prices by reducing the supply of farm goods. Under the AAA, the large producers, acting through farm cooperatives, would agree upon a "domestic allotment" plan that would assign acreage quotas to each producer. Participation would be voluntary. Farmers who cut production to comply with the quotas would be paid for land left fallow.

Unfortunately for its backers, the AAA got off to a horrible start. Because the 1933 crops had already been planted by the time Congress established the AAA, the administration ordered farmers to plow their crops under, paying them over $100 million to destroy 10 million acres of cotton. The government also purchased and slaughtered six million pigs, salvaging only one million pounds for the needy. The public neither understood nor forgave the agency for destroying food while jobless people went hungry.

Overall, the AAA's record was mixed. It raised farm income, but did little for sharecroppers and tenant farmers, the groups hardest hit by the agricultural crisis. Farm incomes doubled between 1933 and 1936, but those with large farms reaped most of the benefits. Many large landowners used government payments to purchase tractors and combines allowing them to mechanize farm operations, increasing crop yields and reducing the need for sharecroppers and tenants. An unintentional consequence of the New Deal farm policies was to force at least 3 million small farmers off the land. For all its inadequacies, however, the AAA established the precedent for a system of farm price supports, subsidies, and surplus purchases that continues more than half a century later.

The National Recovery Administration

To help industry and labor, Roosevelt asked for—and Congress passed—the National Industrial Recovery Act (NIRA), which authorized establishment of the **National Recovery Administration** (NRA). The NRA sought to revive industry through rational planning. Representatives of business, labor, and government would establish codes of fair practices that would set prices, production levels, minimum wages, and maximum hours within each industry. The NRA also supported workers' right to join labor unions. By ending ruinous competition, overproduction, labor conflicts, and by deflating prices, the NRA sought to stabilize the economy.

Led by General Hugh Johnson, the new agency got off to a promising start. By midsummer 1933, over 500 industries had signed codes covering 22 million workers. By the end of the summer the nation's ten largest industries had been won over, as well as hundreds of smaller businesses. All across the country businesses displayed the Blue Eagle, the insignia of the NRA, in their windows.

The NRA's success was short-lived, however. Instead of creating a smooth-running corporate state, Johnson presided over a chorus of endless squabbling. The NRA boards, dominated by representatives of big business, drafted codes that favored their interests over those of small competitors. Moreover, even though they controlled the new agency from the outset, many leaders of big business resented the NRA for interfering in the private sector. Many quipped that the NRA stood for "national run-around."

For labor the NRA was a mixed blessing. On the positive side, the codes abolished child labor and established the precedent of federal regulation of minimum wages and maximum hours. Under the National Industrial Recovery Act, union membership was expanded by the drawing of large numbers of unskilled workers into unions. On the negative side, however, the NRA codes set wages in most industries well below what labor demanded, and large occupational groups, such as farm workers, fell outside the codes' coverage.

Jobs Programs

Harry Hopkins, one of Roosevelt's most trusted advisers, asked why the federal government could not simply hire the unemployed and put them to work. Reluctantly, Roosevelt agreed, and the first major program to attack unemployment through public works was the Public Works Administration (PWA). It was supposed to serve as a "pump-primer," providing people with money to spend on industrial products. In six years the PWA spent $6 billion, building such projects as Brownsville, Texas's port, the Grand Coulee Dam, and Chicago's sewer system. Unfortunately, the man who headed the program, Harold Ickes, was so concerned about potential graft and scandal that the PWA did not spend enough money to significantly reduce unemployment.

Appointed administrator of the Federal Emergency Relief Administration in 1933, Harry Hopkins oversaw the distribution of $500 million in federal funds as outright grants (rather than loans) to state relief agencies.

One of the New Deal's most famous jobs programs was the Civilian Conservation Corps (CCC). By mid-1933, 300,000 jobless young men between the ages of 18 and 25 went to work in the nation's parks and forests. For $30 a month, CCC workers planted saplings, built fire towers, restocked depleted streams with fish, and restored historic battlefields. Workers lived in wilderness camps, earning money that they passed along to their families. Despite its immense popularity, the CCC failed to make a serious dent in depression unemployment. It excluded women, imposed rigid quotas on African Americans, and offered employment to only a small number of the young people who needed work.

Far more ambitious was the Civil Works Administration (CWA), established in November 1933. Under the energetic leadership of Harry Hopkins, the CWA put 2.6 million men to work in its first month. Within two months it employed 4 million men building 250,000 miles of road, 40,000 schools, 150,000 privies, and 3700 playgrounds. In March 1934, however, Roosevelt scrapped the CWA because he (like Hoover) did not want to run a budget deficit or create a permanent dependent class.

Roosevelt badly underestimated the severity of the crisis. As government funding slowed down and economic indicators leveled off, the depression deepened in 1934, triggering a series of violent strikes. The climax came on Labor Day, 1934, when 500,000 garment workers launched the single largest strike in the nation's history. All across the nation, critics attacked Roosevelt for not doing enough to combat the depression, charges that did not go unheeded in the White House.

Following the congressional elections of 1934, in which the Democrats won 13 new House seats and 9 new Senate seats, Roosevelt abandoned his hopes for a balanced budget, deciding that bolder action was required. He had lost faith in government planning and the proposed alliance with business. This left only one other road to recovery—government spending. Encouraged by the CCC's success, he decided to create more federal jobs for the unemployed.

In January 1935 Congress passed the Emergency Relief Appropriation Act, which created the Works Progress Administration (WPA), Roosevelt's program to employ 3.5 million workers at a "security wage"—twice the level of welfare payments but well below union scales. To head the new agency,

For $30 a month, workers in the Civilian Conservation Corps (CCC) planted trees and dug drainage ditches. Such federal work relief programs helped many retain their self-respect.

The WPA program employed artists like Jackson Pollock, Willem de Kooning, and Ben Shahn to decorate public buildings with murals that celebrated American culture.

Roosevelt again turned to Harry Hopkins. Since the WPA's purpose was to employ men quickly, Hopkins opted for labor-intensive tasks, creating jobs that were often makeshift and inefficient. Jeering critics said the WPA stood for "We Piddle Along," but the agency built many worthwhile projects. In its first five years alone the WPA constructed or improved 2500 hospitals, 5900 schools, 1000 airport fields (including New York's La Guardia Airport), and nearly 13,000 playgrounds. By 1941 it had pumped $11 billion into the economy.

The WPA's most unusual feature was its spending on cultural programs. While folksingers like Woody Guthrie honored the nation in ballads, other artists were hired to catalog it, photograph it, paint it, record it, and write about it. In photojournalism; for example, the Farm Security Administration (FSA) employed scores of photographers to create a pictorial record of America and its people. Under the auspices of the WPA, the Federal Writers Project sponsored an impressive set of state guides and dispatched an army of folklorists into the backcountry in search of tall tales. Oral historians collected slave narratives, and musicologists compiled an amazing collection of folk music.

Valuable in their own right, the WPA's cultural programs had the added benefit of providing work for thousands of writers, artists, actors, and other creative people. In addition, these programs established the precedent of federal support to the arts and the humanities, laying the groundwork for future federal programs to promote the life of the mind in the United States.

The WPA marked the zenith of Roosevelt's influence over Congress. Following its passage, Congress dallied for several months over the remainder of his program. By 1935, opposition came from both the right and the left, as the New Deal's failure to end the depression led to growing frustration.

Roosevelt's Critics

Many conservatives regarded Roosevelt's programs as infringements on the rights of the individual, while a growing number of critics argued that they did not go far enough. Three figures stepped forward to challenge Roosevelt: Huey Long, a Louisiana senator; Father Charles Coughlin, a Catholic priest from Detroit; and Francis Townsend, a retired California physician.

Of the three, Huey Long attracted the widest following. Ambitious, endowed with supernatural energy, and totally devoid of scruples, Long was a fiery, spell-binding orator in the tradition of southern populism. As governor and then U.S. senator, he ruled Louisiana with an iron hand, keeping a private army equipped with submachine guns and a "deduct box," where he kept funds deducted from state employees' salaries. Yet the people of Louisiana loved him because he attacked the big oil companies, increased state spending on public works, and improved public schools. Although he backed Roosevelt in 1932,

Long quickly abandoned the president and opposed the New Deal as too conservative.

Huey Long was immensely popular, especially among the poor. Part of his appeal lay in his style; he dressed in vanilla ice cream white suits and called himself "the Kingfish," after a character in the popular radio show "Amos 'n Andy." By playing up his country origins and ridiculing the rich, Long became a popular legend.

Early in 1934 Long announced his "Share Our Wealth" program. Vowing to make "Every Man a King," he promised to soak the rich by imposing a stiff tax on inheritances over $5 million and by levying a 100 percent tax on annual incomes over $1 million. The confiscated funds, in turn, would be distributed to the people, guaranteeing every American family an annual income of no less than $2000—in Long's words more than enough to buy "a radio, a car, and a home." Roosevelt had to take him seriously, for a Democratic poll revealed that Long could attract three to four million voters to an independent presidential ticket.

Like Long, Father Charles Coughlin was an early supporter who turned sour on the New Deal. Speaking on the radio to an estimated 30 million Americans from his Catholic parish in a Detroit suburb, Coughlin blamed the depression on greedy bankers and challenged Roosevelt to solve the crisis by nationalizing banks and inflating the currency. When Roosevelt refused to heed his advice, Coughlin broke with him and formed the National Union for Social Justice.

Roosevelt's least likely critic was Dr. Francis Townsend, a California public health officer who found himself unemployed at the age of 67, with only $100 in savings. Seeing many people in similar or worse straits, Townsend embraced old-age relief as the key to ending the depression. In January 1934 Townsend announced his plan, demanding a $200 monthly pension for every citizen over the age of 60. In return, recipients had to retire and spend their entire pension every month within the United States. Younger Americans would inherit the jobs vacated by senior citizens, and the economy would be stimulated by the increased purchasing power of the elderly. Although critics lambasted the Townsend plan as ludicrous, several million Americans found his plan refreshingly simple.

THE SECOND NEW DEAL

Alarmed by his critics, Roosevelt slowly abandoned his dream of building a coalition that would unite all Americans behind the New Deal. Previously, he had seen himself as an honest broker attempting to reconcile the conflicting demands of widely diverse interest groups. Now Roosevelt stopped trying to please everyone and started inching to the left. In June 1935, Roosevelt refused to dismiss Congress for summer vacation, vowing to make its members swelter in the Washington heat until they passed his new legislative agenda. The result was the "Second Hundred Days."

The Wagner Act

In 1930, only 3.4 million workers belonged to labor unions—down from 5 million in 1920. Union members were confined to a few industries, such as construction, railroads, and local truck delivery. Workers in the nation's major industries, like autos and steel, remained unorganized.

As the depression dragged on, bitter labor-management warfare erupted, with auto and steel workers and longshoremen becoming involved in violent strikes. In all, 1.5 million workers went on strike in 1934. In August, textile workers staged the largest strike the country had ever seen. In Massachusetts, 110,000 workers struck, 60,000 in Georgia—a total of 500,000 workers in 20 states. While some of the strikes aimed at higher wages, fully a third demanded union recognition.

Labor unrest forced the federal government to step into labor relations and forge a compromise between management and labor. Under the **Wagner Act** (the National Labor Relations Act) of 1935, the federal government guaranteed the right of employ-

TABLE 24.3
Later New Deal Legislation

1934	Farm Mortgage Refinancing Act
	Gold Reserve Act
	Civil Works Emergency Relief Act
	Home Owners' Loan Act
	Farm Mortgage Foreclosure Act
	Bank Deposit Insurance Act
	Silver Purchase Act
	Securities Exchange Act
	Labor Dispute Joint Resolution
	Railway Pension Act
	Communication Act
1935	Emergency Relief Appropriation Act
	National Labor Relations Act
	Social Security Act
	Public Utility Holding Company Act
	Work Relief Act
1937	National Housing Act
	Bankhead-Jones Farm Tenancy Act
1938	Fair Labor Standards Act

ees to form unions and to bargain collectively. The act also set up the National Labor Relations Board (NLRB), which had the power to prohibit unfair labor practices by employers.

During the mid-1930s, a bitter dispute broke out within labor's ranks. It involved an issue that had been simmering for half a century: Should labor focus its efforts on unionizing skilled workers; or should labor go after all workers in industry, regardless of skill level? The country's major labor federation, the American Federation of Labor (AFL), consisted of craft unions organized by occupation. In late 1935, a group of union leaders formed the Committee of Industrial Organization (CIO) to organize unskilled workers in America's mass-production industries. The CIO formed unions in the auto, glass, radio, rubber, and steel industries; by the end of 1937, it had more members than the AFL—3.7 million against 3.4 million.

A 44-day sit-down strike in Flint, Michigan, in 1937 forced General Motors to recognize the United Auto Workers. A few weeks later, U.S. Steel accepted unionization without a strike, but the "Little Steel" companies—Bethlehem, Inland, National, Republic, and Youngstown Sheet & Tube—vowed to resist the steelworkers union. In May 1937, police in South Chicago opened fire on marchers at the Republic mill, killing ten. Soon after, the strike was broken, but in 1941, the National Labor Relations Board ordered "Little Steel" to recognize the United Steelworkers of America and reinstate all workers fired for union activity.

Social Security

A goal of reformers since the Progressive Era, the 1935 **Social Security Act** aimed to alleviate the plight of America's visible poor—dependent children, the elderly, and the handicapped. A major political victory for Roosevelt, the Social Security Act was a triumph of social legislation. It offered workers 65 or older monthly stipends based on previous earnings, and it gave the indigent elderly small relief payments, financed by the federal government and the states. In addition, it provided assistance to blind and handicapped Americans, and to dependent children who did not have a wage-earning parent. The act also established the nation's first federally sponsored system of unemployment insurance. Mandatory payroll deductions levied equally on employees and employers financed both the retirement system and the unemployment insurance.

While conservatives argued that the Social Security Act placed the United States on the road to socialism, the legislation profoundly disappointed reformers, who demanded "cradle to grave" protection as the birthright of every American. The new system authorized pitifully small payments; its retirement system left huge groups of workers uncovered, including migrant workers, civil servants, domestic servants, merchant seamen, and day laborers; its budget came from a regressive tax scheme that placed a disproportionate tax burden on the poor; and it did not provide health insurance.

Despite these criticisms, the Social Security Act introduced a new era in American history. It committed the government to a social welfare role by providing for elderly, disabled, dependent, and unemployed Americans. By doing so, the act greatly expanded the public's sense of entitlement and the support people expected government to give to all citizens.

The remaining "must legislation" of the Second Hundred Days included utilities regulation (Public Utility Holding Company Act), banking reform, and a new tax proposal. Yet none of these measures represented a drastic change in American politics or society. On the whole, the **Second New Deal** merely sought to make capitalism more humane. The majority of Americans did not want dramatic changes, and Roosevelt never contemplated, much less achieved, a social revolution. He made no attacks on private property; the well-to-do retained their privileges; wealth was not redistributed; and the poor remained poor.

To hear many wealthy conservatives tell it, however, Roosevelt was a wild-eyed radical who threatened the very foundation of capitalism. William Randolph Hearst ordered his newspapers to substitute the words "Raw Deal" for "New Deal." Firmly committed to a balanced budget, conservatives viewed heavy government spending as sacrilege, and they were appalled by the growth of bureaucracy in Washington, D.C. Conservatives feared government's growth would increase federal power at the expense of states' rights and individual liberties, and they believed Roosevelt would raise rich people's taxes to finance his relief programs. Viewing Roosevelt as a traitor to his class, many wealthy Americans saw the election of 1936 as their chance to save the country.

The Election of 1936

To carry its banner in 1936, the Republicans picked Alfred M. Landon of Kansas, the only Republican governor who survived the 1934 elections. Landon was far more liberal than many of his backers. He had opposed the Ku Klux Klan, backed business regulation, and supported many New Deal programs. A

THE PEOPLE SPEAK

Francis Perkins, "The Social Security Act" (1935)

The Social Security Act of 1935 is one of the most significant of the New Deal programs. By providing aid to the elderly, the unemployed, and the handicapped, Social Security marked the beginning of the "welfare state," the embodiment of the idea that society should provide security for its members. Secretary of Labor Frances Perkins, one of Roosevelt's most controversial cabinet appointees, made the following radio address to announce the new program to the public.

People who work for a living in the United States of America can join with all other good citizens on this forty-eighth anniversary of Labor Day in satisfaction that the Congress has passed the Social Security Act. This act establishes unemployment insurance as a substitute for haphazard methods of assistance in periods when men and women willing and able to work are without jobs. It provides for old-age pensions which mark great progress over the measures upon which we have hitherto depended in caring for those who have been unable to provide for the years when they no longer can work. It also provides security for dependent and crippled children, mothers, the indigent disabled and the blind.

Old people who are in need, unemployables, children, mothers and the sightless, will find systematic regular provisions for needs. The Act limits the Federal aid to not more than $15 per month for the individual, provided the State in which he resides appropriates a like amount. There is nothing to prevent a State from contributing more than $15 per month in special cases, and there is no requirement to allow as much as $15 from either State or Federal funds when a particular case has some personal provision and needs less than the total allowed.

Following essentially the same procedure, the Act as passed provides for Federal assistance to the States in caring for the blind, a contribution by the States of up to $15 a month to be matched in turn by a like contribution by the Federal Government. The Act also contains provision for assistance to the States in providing payments to dependent children under sixteen years of age. There also is provision in the Act for cooperation with medical and health organizations charged with rehabilitation of physically handicapped children. The necessity for adequate service in the fields of public and maternal health and child welfare calls for the extension of these services to meet individual community needs.

Consider for a moment those portions of the Act which, while they will not be effective this present year, yet will exert a profound and far-reaching effect upon millions of citizens. I refer to the provision for a system of old-age benefits supported by the contributions of employer and employees, and to the section which sets up the initial machinery for unemployment insurance.

Old-age benefits in the form of monthly payments are to be paid to individuals who have worked and contributed to the insurance fund in direct proportion to the total wages earned by such individuals in the course of their employment subsequent to 1936. The minimum monthly payment is to be $10, the maximum $35. These payments will begin in the year 1942 and will be to those who have worked and contributed. . . .

Federal legislation was framed in the thought that the attack upon the problems of insecurity should be a cooperative venture participated in by both the Federal and State Governments, preserving the benefits of local administration and national leadership. It was thought unwise to have the Federal Government decide all questions of policy and dictate completely what the States should do. Only very necessary minimum standards are included in the Federal measure leaving wide latitude to the States. . . .

The social security measure looks primarily to the future and is only a part of the administration's plan to promote sound and stable economic life. We cannot think of it as disassociated from the Government's program to save the homes, the farms, the businesses and banks of the Nation, and especially must we consider it a companion measure to the Works Relief Act which does undertake to provide immediate increase in employment and corresponding stimulation to private industry by purchase of supplies.

Our social security program will be a vital force working against the recurrence of severe depressions in the future. We can, as the principle of sustained purchasing power in hard times makes itself felt in every shop, store and mill, grow old without being haunted by the spectre of a poverty-ridden old age or of being a burden on our children. . . .

The passage of this act, with so few dissenting votes and with so much intelligent public support is deeply significant of the progress which the American people have made in thought in the social field and awareness of methods of using cooperation through government to overcome social hazards against which the individual alone is inadequate. . . .

Source: Copyright © 1935 Vital Speeches of the Day.

"Mother, Wilfred wrote a bad word!"
MCKAY IN ESQUIRE

Some Americans felt capitalism was threatened under Roosevelt's New Deal. This 1938 *Esquire* cartoon captures the mood of disapproval prevalent among certain parts of the population at the time.

poor public speaker, Landon offered few alternatives to Roosevelt's programs.

To win in 1936, the Republicans needed help from a third party to splinter the Democrats, but this assistance never arrived. Huey Long's organization fell apart following his assassination in 1935; Francis Townsend's campaign, already weakened by passage of the Social Security Act in 1935, collapsed in the spring of 1936 under charges of corruption; and by 1936 Father Coughlin had been reduced to an abusive name-caller who had been publicly rebuked by the Catholic church.

Roosevelt enjoyed the race, lashing out at "economic royalists" who opposed the New Deal. Positive economic indicators helped the Democrats. In 1936 industrial output more than doubled its 1933 figures, and the national income rose half again as much. In the election Roosevelt carried every state but Maine and Vermont. Democrats won an equally lopsided victory in the congressional races, resulting in 331 Democrats to 89 Republicans in the House and 76 Democrats to 16 Republicans in the Senate.

The 1936 Democratic victory rested on a broad base of support. Roosevelt's backers included poor people, organized labor, urban ethnics, the Democratic South, African Americans, and many intellectuals. A formidable alliance of diverse groups, Roosevelt's New Deal coalition would shape the contours of American politics for decades to come.

THE NEW DEAL, WOMEN, AND MINORITY GROUPS

Eleanor Roosevelt deserves much of the credit for the progress made by minorities. The first president's wife to stake out an independent public position, she provided the social conscience of the New Deal. The First Lady worked tirelessly to persuade her husband and the heads of government agencies to hire well-qualified women and African Americans. More courageous than her husband and less restricted politically, she did not hesitate to take a public stand on civil rights. When the Daughters of the American Revolution refused in 1939 to grant the black contralto Marian Anderson permission to sing in Washington's Constitution Hall, Mrs. Roosevelt arranged for a concert on the steps of the Lincoln Memorial on Easter Sunday.

Women

Women achieved measured progress under the New Deal. Prior to the depression, women had dominated both social work and the voluntary associations that provided charity for the poor and unemployed. Since the same skills were needed to combat the depression, women joined the throngs of professionals who rushed to Washington to work in New Deal programs.

Once there, women formed a tightly knit network of professionals who supported each other's careers. Frances Perkins, the secretary of labor and the first woman cabinet member in American history, brought many women into government. Molly Dewson, the director of the Women's Division of the Democratic Committee, helped place women throughout the administration. By 1939 women held one-third of all positions in the independent agencies and almost one-fifth of the jobs in the executive departments.

African Americans

Until the New Deal, African Americans had shown their traditional loyalty to the party of Lincoln by voting overwhelmingly Republican. By the end of Roosevelt's first administration, however, one of the most dramatic voter shifts in American history had occurred. In 1936, 75 percent of black voters supported the Democrats. Blacks turned to Roosevelt in part because his spending programs gave them a measure of relief from the depression and in part because the Republicans—the Grand Old Party (GOP)—had done little to repay their earlier support.

Still, Roosevelt's record on civil rights was modest at best. Instead of using New Deal programs to promote civil rights, the administration consistently bowed to the forces of discrimination. In order to pass major New Deal legislation, Roosevelt needed the support of southern Democrats. Time and time again, he backed away from equal rights to avoid antagonizing southern whites, although his wife did take a public stand in support of civil rights.

Most New Deal programs discriminated against blacks. The NRA, for example, not only offered whites the first crack at jobs but authorized separate and lower pay scales for African Americans. The Federal Housing Authority (FHA) refused to guarantee mortgages for blacks who tried to buy homes in white neighborhoods, and the CCC maintained segregated camps. Furthermore, the Social Security Act excluded those job categories traditionally filled by blacks.

Mary McLeod Bethune, a member of the advisory committee for the National Youth Administration, meets here with Eleanor Roosevelt.

The story in agriculture was particularly grim. Since 40 percent of all black workers made their living as sharecroppers and tenant farmers, the AAA acreage reduction hit blacks hard. White landlords could make more money by leaving land untilled than by putting land into production. As a result, the AAA's policies forced more than 100,000 African Americans off the land in 1933 and 1934. Even more galling to black leaders, the president failed to support an antilynching bill and a bill to abolish the poll tax. Roosevelt feared that conservative southern Democrats, who had seniority in Congress and controlled many committee chairmanships, would block his bills if he tried to fight them on the race question.

Yet the New Deal did record a few gains in civil rights. Roosevelt named Mary McLeod Bethune, a black educator, to the advisory committee of the National Youth Administration (NYA), and thanks to her efforts, African Americans received a fair share of NYA funds. The WPA was colorblind, and blacks in northern cities benefited from its work relief programs. Harold Ickes, a strong supporter of civil rights who had several African Americans on his staff, poured federal funds into black schools and hospitals in the South. Most blacks appointed to New Deal posts, however, served in token positions as advisers on black affairs.

Mexican Americans

Like African Americans, most Mexican Americans reaped few benefits from the New Deal. Affected in much the same way as sharecroppers and tenant farmers, many Mexican-American migrant workers lost their jobs due to AAA acreage reductions or competition in the fields from unemployed whites.

Still, the New Deal offered Mexican Americans a little help. The Farm Security Administration established camps for migrant farm workers in California, and the CCC and WPA hired unemployed Mexican Americans on relief jobs. Many, however, did not qualify for relief assistance because, as migrant workers, they did not meet residency requirements. Furthermore, agricultural workers were not eligible for benefits under workers' compensation, Social Security, and the National Labor Relations Act.

Native Americans

The so-called Indian New Deal was the only bright spot in the administration's treatment of minorities. In the late nineteenth century, American Indian policy had begun to place a growing emphasis on erasing a distinctive Native American identity. To weaken the authority of Native American leaders, Congress in 1871 ended the practice of treating Indian groups as sovereign nations. To undermine traditional Native American justice systems, Congress, in 1882, created a Court of Indian Offenses, to try Native Americans who violated government laws and rules. Native American schools took Native American children away from their families and sought to strip them of their heritage. Schoolchildren were required to trim their hair and speak English and were prohibited from practicing Native American religions.

The culmination of these policies was the 1887 Dawes Act, which allocated reservation lands to individual Native Americans. The purpose of the act was to encourage Native Americans to become farmers, but the plots were too small to support a family or to raise livestock. Government policies further reduced Native American–owned lands from 155 million acres to just 48 million acres in 1934.

When Roosevelt became president in 1933, he appointed John Collier, a leading reformer, as Commissioner of Indian affairs. At Collier's request, Congress created the Indian Emergency Conservation Program (IECP), a CCC-type project for the reservations that employed more than 85,000 Native Americans. Collier also made certain that the PWA, WPA, CCC, and NYA hired Native Americans.

Collier had long been an opponent of the 50-year-old government allotment program that had broken up and distributed Native American lands. In 1934 he persuaded Congress to pass the Indian Reorganization Act, which terminated the allotment program of the Dawes Severalty Act of 1887; provided funds for Native American groups to purchase new land; offered government recognition of Native American constitutions; and repealed prohibitions on Native American languages and customs. That same year, federal grants were provided to local school districts, hospitals, and social welfare agencies to assist Native Americans.

THE NEW DEAL IN DECLINE

In his second inaugural address in early 1937, Franklin Roosevelt promised to press for new social legislation. Yet instead of pursuing new reforms, he allowed his second term to bog down in political squabbles. And he wasted his energies on an ill-conceived battle with the Supreme Court and an abortive effort to purge the Democratic party.

Court Packing

On "Black Monday," May 27, 1935, the Supreme Court struck down a basic part of Roosevelt's program of recovery and reform. A kosher chicken dealer sued the government, charging that the NRA was unconstitutional. In its famous "dead chicken" decision, *Schechter Poultry Corporation* v. *United States*, the court agreed, declaring that Congress had delegated excessive authority to the president and had improperly involved the federal government in regulating interstate commerce.

In June 1936, the court ruled another of the measures enacted during the 100 days—the Agricultural Adjustment Act—unconstitutional. Then, six months later, the high court declared invalid a New York state minimum-wage law. Roosevelt was aghast. The court, he charged, had established a "'no-man's land' where no Government—State or Federal—can

Fearful that the Supreme Court would invalidate the Social Security Act and other measures, Roosevelt proposed in 1937 that he be allowed to appoint an additional justice for every court member over the age of 70, up to a total of six.

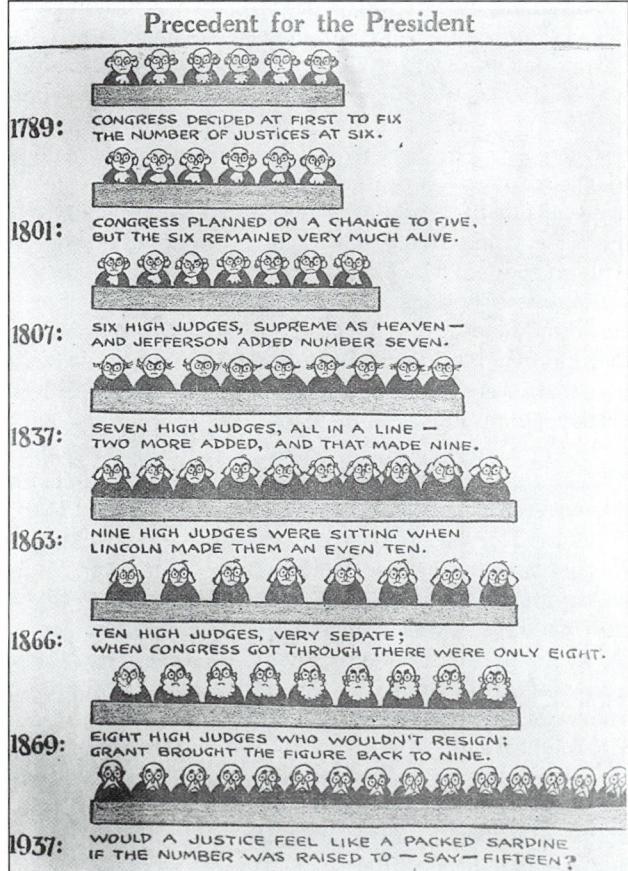

The American Mosaic

The Tuskegee Syphilis Study

THE South in the 1930s was the section of the United States that most resembled the underdeveloped nations of the world. Its people (white and black) remained mostly rural; they were less well-educated than other Americans; and they made decidedly less money.

As a group, African Americans in the South were among the poorest of the poor—virtual paupers, chronically unemployed, without benefit of sanitation, adequate diet, or the rudiments of hygiene. They suffered from a host of diseases, including tuberculosis, syphilis, hookworm, pellagra, rickets, and rotting teeth; and their death rate far exceeded that of whites.

Despite their evident need, few blacks received proper medical care. In fact, many African Americans lived outside the world of modern medicine, going from cradle to grave without ever seeing a doctor. There was a severe shortage of black physicians, and many white physicians refused to treat black patients. In addition, there were only a handful of black hospitals in the South, and most white hospitals either denied blacks admission or assigned them to often overcrowded segregated wings.

But poverty as much as racism was to blame for the medical neglect of African Americans. Medical care in the United States was offered on a fee-for-services basis, and the simple truth was that many African Americans were too poor to be able to afford medical care.

To combat this and other problems, the federal government in 1912 united all its health-related activities under the Public Health Service (PHS). Over the next few decades, the PHS distinguished itself by launching attacks on hookworm, pellagra, and a host of other illnesses. In no field was it more active than in its efforts to fight venereal diseases.

Health reformers knew that not only was syphilis a killer, but it was also capable of inflicting blindness, deafness, and insanity on its victims. Furthermore, they saw the disease as a serious threat to the family because they associated it with prostitution and loose morals in general, thus adding a moral dimension to their medical concerns.

Taking advantage of the emergency atmosphere of World War I, progressive reformers pushed through Congress in 1918 a bill to create a special Division of Venereal Diseases within the PHS. The PHS officers who launched this new offensive against syphilis began with high motives, and their initial successes were impressive. By 1919, they had established over 200 health clinics, which treated over 64,000 patients who could not otherwise have afforded health care.

In the late 1920s, the PHS joined forces with the Rosenwald Fund (a private philanthropic foundation based in Chicago) to develop a syphilis control program for African Americans in the South. Most doctors assumed that blacks suffered a much higher infection rate than whites because blacks abandoned themselves to sexual promiscuity. And once infected, the argument went, African Americans remained infected because they were too poor and too ignorant to seek medical care.

To test these theories, the PHS selected communities in six different southern states, examined the local African-American populations to ascertain the incidence of syphilis, and offered free treatment to those who were infected. This pilot program had hardly gotten underway, however, when the stock market collapse forced the Rosenwald Fund to terminate its support. The PHS was left without sufficient funds to follow up its syphilis control work among African Americans in the South.

Macon County, Alabama, was the site of one of those original pilot programs. Its county seat, Tuskegee, was the home of the famed Tuskegee Institute. It was in and around Tuskegee that the PHS had discovered an infection rate of 35 percent among those tested, the highest incidence in the six communities studied. In fact, despite the presence of the Tuskegee Institute, which boasted a well-equipped hospital that might have provided low-cost health care to African Americans in the region, Macon County was home to the worst poverty and the most sickly residents the PHS discovered anywhere in the South. It was precisely this ready-made laboratory of human suffering that prompted the PHS to return to Macon County in 1932. Since they could not afford to treat syphilis, the PHS decided to document the damage inflicted on its victims by launching a scientific study of the effects of untreated syphilis on African-American males. Many white Southerners (including physicians) believed that although practically all blacks had syphilis, it did not harm them as severely as it did whites. PHS officials knew that syphilis was a serious threat to the health of African Americans, and they intended to use the results of the study

to pressure southern state legislatures into appropriating funds for syphilis control work among rural blacks.

Armed with these good motives, the PHS launched the Tuskegee Study in 1932. It involved approximately 400 African-American males who tested positive for the disease and 200 nonsyphilitic black males to serve as controls. In order to secure cooperation, the PHS told the local residents that they had returned to Macon County to treat the ill men. The PHS did not inform them that they had syphilis. Instead, the men were told that they had "bad blood," a catch-all phrase rural blacks used to describe a host of ailments.

The PHS had not intended to treat the men, but state health officials demanded, as the price of their cooperation, that the men be given at least enough medication to render them noninfectious. Consequently, all of the men received a little treatment. No one worried much about the glaring contradiction of offering treatment in a study of supposedly untreated syphilis (the reasoning being that the men had not received enough treatment to cure them). Thus, the experiment was scientifically flawed from the outset.

Although the original plan called for only a one-year experiment, the Tuskegee Study continued until 1972—partly because many of the health officials became fascinated by the scientific potential of a long-range study of syphilis. No doubt others rationalized the study by telling themselves that the men were too poor to afford proper treatment, or that too much time had passed for treatment to be of any benefit. Some health officials may even have seen the men as clinical material rather than human beings.

At any rate, the Tuskegee Study killed approximately 100 African-American men, who died as a direct result of syphilis; scores went blind or insane, and still others endured lives of chronic ill health from syphilis-related complications. Throughout their suffering, the PHS made no effort to treat the men, and on several occasions even took steps to prevent them from getting treatment on their own. As a result, the men did not receive penicillin when that "wonder drug" became widely available after World War II.

During those same four decades civil protests raised America's concern for the rights of African Americans, and the ethical standards of the medical profession changed dramatically. These changes had no impact on the Tuskegee Study, however. PHS officials published no fewer than 13 scientific papers on the experiment (several appearing in the nation's leading medical journals), and the PHS routinely presented sessions on it at medical conventions. The Tuskegee Study only ended in 1972 because a "whistle-blower" in the PHS named Peter Buxtun leaked the story to the press. Health officials at first tried to defend their actions, but public outrage quickly silenced them, and they agreed to end the experiment. As part of an out-of-court settlement, the survivors were finally treated for syphilis, and the men, and the families of the deceased, received small cash payments.

The 40-year deathwatch had finally ended, but its legacy can still be felt today. In the wake of its hearings, Congress enacted new legislation to protect the subjects of human experiments. The Tuskegee Study left behind a host of unanswered questions about the social and racial attitudes of the medical establishment in the United States. It served as a cruel reminder of how class distinctions and racism could negate ethical and scientific standards.

function." Roosevelt feared that every New Deal reform—such as the prohibition on child labor or regulation of wages and hours—was at risk. In 1936, his supporters in Congress responded by introducing over a hundred bills to curb the judiciary's power.

After his landslide reelection in 1936, the president proposed a controversial "**court-packing scheme.**" In an effort to make his opponents on the Supreme Court resign so he could replace them with justices more sympathetic to his policies, Roosevelt announced a plan to add one new member to the Supreme Court for every judge who had reached the age of 70 without retiring (six justices were over 70). To offer a carrot with the stick, Roosevelt also outlined a generous new pension program for retiring federal judges.

The court-packing scheme was a political disaster. Conservatives and liberals alike denounced Roosevelt for attacking the separation of powers, and critics accused him of trying to become a dictator. Fortunately, the Court itself ended the crisis by shifting ground. In two separate cases the Court upheld the Wagner Act and approved a Washington state minimum-wage law, furnishing proof that it had softened its opposition to the New Deal.

Yet Roosevelt remained too obsessed with the battle to realize he had won the war. He lobbied for the court-packing bill for several months, squandering his strength on a struggle that had long since become a political embarrassment. In the end, the only part of the president's plan to gain congressional approval was the pension program. Once it passed, Justice Willis Van Devanter, the most obstinate New Deal opponent on the Court, resigned. By 1941 Roosevelt had named five justices to the Supreme Court. Few legacies of the president's leadership proved more important, for the new "Roosevelt Court" significantly expanded the government's role in the economy and in civil liberties.

The Depression of 1937

The sweeping Democratic electoral victory in 1936 was followed by a deep economic relapse known as the "Roosevelt Recession." In just a few months, industrial production fell by 40 percent; unemployment rose by 4 million; stock prices plunged 48 percent.

Several factors contributed to the "little depression," of which the most important was a blunder in fiscal policy. Secretary of the Treasury Henry Morgenthau urged Roosevelt to cut federal spending in an effort to balance the federal budget and restore business confidence. Reassured by good economic news in 1936, Roosevelt slashed government spending the following year. The budget cuts knocked the economy into a tailspin. Roosevelt's virulent attacks on "economic royalists" also undermined business confidence.

By the end of 1938 the reform spirit was gone. A conservative alliance of southern Democrats and northern Republicans in Congress blocked all efforts to expand the New Deal. In the congressional elections of 1938, Roosevelt campaigned against five conservative senators who opposed the New Deal; but all won reelection. The failed purge intensified the conservative-liberal split within the Democratic party by showing conservatives they could defy the president with impunity. Roosevelt may not have been able to pass any new measures, but his opponents could not dismantle his programs. The New Deal ended in stalemate, but several reforms had been ensconced as permanent features of American politics.

POPULAR CULTURE DURING THE GREAT DEPRESSION

The popular culture of the 1930s was fraught with contradictions. It was, simultaneously, a decade of traditionalism and of modernist experimentation, of sentimentality and "hard-boiled" toughness, of longings for a simpler past and fantastic dreams of the future.

Beset by deep anxieties and insecurities, many Americans in the 1930s hungered for heroes. Popular culture offered many: superheroes like Superman and Batman, who appeared in the new comic books of the 1930s; tough, hard-boiled detectives in the fiction of Dashiell Hammett and Raymond Chandler; and radio heroes like "The Lone Ranger" or "The Shadow."

Artistic and Literary Endeavors

Seeing modern society as excessively individualistic and fragmented, many prominent intellectuals of the time looked to the past. Eleven leading white southern intellectuals, known as the Southern Agrarians, issued a manifesto titled *I'll Take My Stand*, urging a return to an agrarian way of life. Another group of distinguished intellectuals known as the New Humanists, led by Irving Babbitt and Paul Elmer More, extolled classical civilization as a bulwark against modern values. One of the decade's leading social critics was Lewis Mumford. In volumes like *Technics and Civilization* (1934), he examined how the values of a pre-machine culture could be blended into modern capitalist civilization.

And yet, for all the emphasis on tradition, the 1930s was also a decade in which modernism in the arts and architecture became increasingly pronounced. Martha Graham developed American modern dance. William Faulkner experimented with "stream-of-consciousness" in *As I Lay Dying* (1930) and other novels, while John Dos Passos's avant-garde trilogy, *U.S.A.*, combined newspaper headlines, capsule biographies, popular song lyrics, and fiction to document the disintegration of depression-era society. Nothing better illustrated the concern with the future than the 1939 New York World's Fair, the self-proclaimed "Fair of the Future," which promised to show fairgoers "the world of tomorrow."

The depression was, in certain respects, a powerful unifying experience. A new phrase, "the American way of life," entered the language—as did public opinion polls and statistical surveys that gave the public a better sense of what the "average American" thought, voted, and ate. The new photojournalism that appeared in new magazines like *Life* helped create a common frame of reference. Yet regional, ethnic, and class differences occupied an important place in the literature of the 1930s. The great novels of the decade successfully combined social criticism and rich detail about the facets of American life in specific social settings. In his novels of fictional Yoknapatawpha County, William Faulkner explored the traditions and history of the South. James T. Farrell's *Studs Lonigan* trilogy (1932–1935) analyzed the impact of urban industrial decay on Catholic youth, while Henry Roth's *Call It Sleep* (1934) traced the assimilation of Jewish youth into American life. John Steinbeck's *Grapes of Wrath* (1939) examined the struggle of a poor Oklahoma farming family migrating to California. Richard Wright's classic *Native Son* (1940) discussed the ways that poverty and prejudice in Chicago drove a young African American to crime.

Hollywood During the Great Depression

During the Great Depression, Hollywood played a valuable psychological role, providing reassurance to a demoralized nation. Even at the depth of the depression, 60 to 80 million Americans attended movies each week.

During the depression's earliest years, movies reflected a despairing public's mood, as Tommy-gun toting gangsters, haggard prostitutes, and sleazy backroom politicians and lawyers appeared on the screen. Screen comedies released in these years expressed an almost anarchistic disdain for traditional institutions and values. The Marx Brothers spoofed everything from patriotism to universities; W. C. Fields ridiculed families; and Mae West used sexual innuendo to poke fun at the middle-class code of sexual propriety.

A renewed sense of optimism generated by the New Deal combined with industry self-censorship to produce new kinds of films during the second half of the depression. G-men, detectives, western heroes, and other defenders of law and order replaced gangsters. Audiences enjoyed Frank Capra comedies and dramas in which little men stood up against corruption and restored America to itself. A new comic genre—the screwball comedy—presented a world in which rich heiresses wed impoverished young men, keeping alive a vision of America as a classless society.

In the face of economic disaster, the fantasy world of the movies sustained a traditional American faith in individual initiative, in government, and a common American identity transcending social class.

CONCLUSION

At the end of 1938, Harry Hopkins observed that the American people had become "bored with the poor, unemployed, and insecure." The New Deal was over. From a purely economic perspective, the New Deal barely made a dent in the Great Depression. Roosevelt's programs suffered from poor planning and moved with considerable caution. Roosevelt simply could not bring himself to support huge federal budgets. As a result, government expenditures stayed below $10 billion a year, not nearly enough to fuel economic recovery. World War II, not the New Deal, snapped America out of the depression, for then and only then did unemployment disappear.

Whatever its shortcomings, the New Deal did blunt the worst effects of the Great Depression. By means of economic reforms and public works projects Roosevelt managed to preserve the public's faith in capitalism and in democratic government at a time when both seemed on the verge of collapse. Roosevelt accomplished this, in large measure, by reaching out to groups that Washington had largely neglected in the past. The Social Security program, while it ignored many, made the government responsible for old-age pensions and welfare payments to citizens who could not support themselves. The NIRA and the Wagner Act encouraged the growth of unions; minimum wage laws benefited many workers; and the Fair Labor Standards Act finally abolished child labor in industry (though it remained in agriculture). While the New Deal stopped far short of providing equal treatment under the law

Chronology of Key Events

1928 Herbert Hoover is elected thirty-first president

1929 Stock market crashes

1930 Hawley-Smoot Tariff raises import duties to unprecedented levels

1932 Congress creates Reconstruction Finance Corporation to lend money to banks, railroads, and insurance companies; Bonus Army, a group of veterans demanding immediate payment of World War I bonuses, is dispersed by federal troops in Washington, D.C.; to revive the construction industry, Congress creates the Federal Home Loan Bank System to lend money to savings and loan associations; Franklin Roosevelt is elected thirty-second president

1933 Emergency Banking Relief Act addresses banking crisis; Roosevelt conducts the first of many "fireside chats" over national radio; Civilian Conservation Corps puts young people to work conserving natural resources; Federal Emergency Relief Act provides relief payments to the unemployed through local and state welfare agencies; Civil Works Administration offers employment to over 4 million people; Agricultural Adjustment Act sets up a system of farm price supports and production limits; National Industrial Recovery Act authorizes industrial codes regulating production, prices, and working conditions and provides funds for public works projects; Tennessee Valley Authority constructs dams and hydroelectric plants in the Tennessee River valley; Twenty-first Amendment repeals prohibition; Glass-Steagall Act creates the Federal Deposit Insurance Corporation to insure savings accounts against bank failure; Farm Credit Administration provides low-interest loans for farmers.

1934 Dr. Francis Townsend proposes a $200 monthly pension for every citizen over 60; former supporter, "radio priest" Father Charles Coughlin, breaks with Roosevelt and forms the National Union for Social Justice; Senator Huey Long of Louisiana announces his "Share Our Wealth" program to provide every American family with a guaranteed annual income; Indian Reorganization Act provides funds for tribes to purchase land, offers recognition of tribal constitutions, and repeals prohibitions on Native American customs

1935 *Schechter Poultry Corporation* v. *United States* declares National Industrial Recovery Act unconstitutional; Emergency Relief Appropriation Act creates Works Progress Administration and National Youth Administration; National Labor Relations Act guarantees workers' right to organize and bargain collectively; Public Utility Holding Company Act is passed to prevent monopolies in gas and electricity distribution; Social Security Act creates a federal system of old-age pensions and state-run unemployment compensation programs

1937 Roosevelt proposes his "court-packing" scheme

1938 Fair Labor Standards Act bans child labor and establishes minimum wages and maximum hours

---

for minorities, it offered them a measure of relief from the depression.

The New Deal encouraged Americans to look to the White House for strong executive leadership. Roosevelt responded to situations with decisive action, and the public increasingly expected the other branches of government to support presidential initiatives. Roosevelt's administrative style—creating special agencies to handle specific problems and placing people in charge who answered directly to him—further enhanced presidential power. On a purely partisan level, the New Deal enabled Roosevelt to forge a Democratic coalition of diverse groups—labor, African Americans, urban ethnics, intellectuals, and southern whites—that helped shape American politics for the next several decades.

Above all, the New Deal made the federal government responsible for safeguarding the nation's economic health. Prior to the 1930s, if people were asked how the government affected them, they probably thought in terms of state or even local government. The New Deal, however, made the federal government such a daily presence in peoples' lives that they now expected Washington to involve itself in everything from farm subsidies to the sale of stocks and securities.

SUGGESTIONS FOR FURTHER READING

Alan Brinkey, *The End of Reform: New Deal Liberalism in Recession and War* (1995). Analyzes the reasons for the New Deal's decline.

Kenneth S. Davis, *FDR: The New York Years* (1985), *FDR: The New Deal Years* (1986), *FDR: Into the Storm* (1993). Recent biographies of the president.

Melvyn Dubovsky and Stephen Burnwood, eds., *Women and Minorities During the Great Depression* (1990). Examines issues confronting women and minority groups during the depression.

Mario T. Garcia, *Mexican-American Leadership, Ideology, and Identity* (1989). Analyzes the Depression's impact on Mexican-Americans and the community's responses.

William E. Leuchtenburg, *The Supreme Court Reborn: The Constitutional Revolution in the Age of Roosevelt* (1995). Explores the impact of the Depression on constitutional law.

Robert S. McElvaine, *The Great Depression: America, 1929–1941* (1984). Offers a thorough treatment of America during the Depression.

Michael E. Parrish, *Anxious Decades: America in Prosperity and Depression* (1992). Provides insights into America during the 1930s.

Lois Scharf, *To Work and to Wed: Female Employment and Feminism in the Great Depression* (1980). Examines the impact of the Depression on women.

Harvard Sitkoff, ed., *Fifty Years Later: The New Deal Evaluated.* (1985) Offers recent assessments of various aspects of the New Deal.

T. H. Watkins, *The Great Depression: America in the 1930s* (1993). Offers an up-to-date account of the Depression decade.

Overviews and Surveys

Michael Bernstein: *The Great Depression: Delayed Recovery and Economic Change in America, 1929–1939* (1988); Roger Biles, *A New Deal for the American People* (1991), and *The New Deal and the South* (1995); James M. Burns, *Roosevelt: The Lion and the Fox* (1956); Sean Dennis Cashman, *America in the Twenties and Thirties* (1989); Paul K. Conkin, *The New Deal*, 2d ed. (1975), and *The Southern Agrarians* (1988); Peter Fearon, *War, Prosperity, and Depression: The U.S. Economy, 1917–1945* (1988); Otis L. Graham, Jr., *The New Deal: The Critical Issues* (1971); Robert L. Heilbroner and Aaron Singer, *The Economic Transformation of America* (1977); David M. Kennedy, *Freedom from Fear: The American People in Depression and War, 1929–1945* (1999); Jack Temple Kirby, *Rural Worlds Lost: The American South, 1920–1960* (1987); William E. Leuchtenburg, *Franklin D. Roosevelt and the New Deal* (1963), *The Perils of Prosperity, 1914–32* (1958), and *The FDR Years: On Roosevelt and His Legacy* (1997); Albert U. Romasco, *The Politics of Recovery: Roosevelt's New Deal* (1983); Page Smith, *Redeeming the Time: A People's History of the 1920s and the New Deal* (1987); Studs Terkel, *Hard Times: An Oral History of the Great Depression* (1970).

The Human Toll

Robert S. McElvaine, ed., *Down and Out in the Great Depression: Letters from the "Forgotten Man"* (1983); James H. Jones, *Bad Blood: The Tuskegee Syphilis Experiment, A Tragedy of Race and Medicine*, 2d ed. (1992); Robin D. G. Kelly, *Hammer and Hoe: Alabama Communists During the Great Depression* (1990); Steven Mintz and Susan Kellogg, *Domestic Revolutions: A Social History of American Family Life* (1983); Bernard Sternsher, *Hitting Home: The Great Depression in Town and Country* (1989); Nan Elizabeth Woodruff, *As Rare as Rain: Federal Relief in the Great Southern Drought of 1930–31* (1985).

Herbert Hoover Responds

William J. Barber, *From New Era to New Deal: Herbert Hoover, the Economists, and American Economic Policy* (1985); Roger Daniels, *The Bonus March: An Episode of the Great Depression* (1971); Mark Dodge, *Herbert Hoover and the Historians* (1989); Glen H. Elder, Jr., *Children of the Great Depression: Social Change in Life Experience* (1974); Martin L. Fausold, *The Presidency of Herbert Hoover* (1985); Donald J. Lisio, *Hoover, Blacks, and Lily-Whites* (1985), and *The President and Protest: Hoover, Conspiracy, and the Bonus Riot* (1974); Albert U. Romasco, *The Poverty of Abundance, Hoover, the Nation, the Depression* (1965); Jordan A. Schwarz, *Interregnum of Despair: Hoover, Congress, and the Depression* (1970); Gene Smith, *The Shattered Dream: Herbert Hoover and the Great Depression* (1984); Winifred D. Wandersee, *Women's Work and Family Values, 1920–1940* (1981); Joan Hoff-Wilson, *Herbert Hoover: Forgotten Progressive* (1975).

Franklin Roosevelt and the First New Deal

Sue Bridwell Beckham, *Depression Post Office Murals and Southern Culture* (1989); Bernard Bellush, *The Failure of the NRA* (1975); Donald R. Brand, *Corporatism and the Rule of Law: A Study of the National Recovery Administration* (1988); David E. Conrad, *The Forgotten Farmers: The Story of the Sharecroppers in the New Deal* (1965); Frank Freidel, *Franklin D. Roosevelt: Launching the New Deal* (1973); James N. Gregory, *American Exodus: The Dust Bowl Migration and Okie*

Culture in California (1989); Robert F. Himmelberg, *The Origins of the National Recovery Administration* (1976); R. Douglas Hurt, *The Dust Bowl: An Agricultural and Social History* (1981); Jerre Mangione, *The Dream and the Deal: The Federal Writers' Project, 1935–1943* (1972); Robert S. McElvaine, *The Great Depression: America, 1929–1941* (1984); Joseph P. Lash, *Dealers and Dreamers: A New Look at the New Deal* (1988); David Milton, *The Politics of U.S. Labor: From the Great Depression to the New Deal* (1982); Michael Parrish, *Securities Regulation and the New Deal* (1970); Gail Radford, *Modern Housing for America: Policy Struggles in the New Deal Era* (1996); Elliot Rosen, *Hoover, Roosevelt, and the Brain Trust* (1984); John Salmond, *The Civilian Conservation Corps, 1933–1942: A New Deal Case Study* (1967); James E. Sargent, *Roosevelt and the Hundred Days* (1981); Ronald W. Schatz, *The Electrical Workers: A History of Labor at General Electric and Westinghouse, 1923–1960* (1983); Bonnie Schwartz, *The Civil Works Administration* (1984); Paul S. Taylor, *On the Ground in the Thirties* (1983); Ronald C. Tobey, *Technology as Freedom: The New Deal and the Electrical Modernization of the American Home* (1996); Graham White and John Maze, *Harold Ickes and the New Deal* (1985); Donald Worster, *Dust Bowl: The Southern Plains in the 1930s* (1979).

The Second New Deal

Irving Bernstein, *A Caring Society: The New Deal, the Worker, and the Great Depression* (1985); Alan Brinkley, *Voices of Protest: Huey Long, Father Coughlin, and the Great Depression* (1982); Robert F. Burk, *The Corporate State and the Broker State: The Du Ponts and American National Politics, 1925–1940* (1990); Keith Dix, *What's a Coal Miner to Do? The Mechanization of Coal Mining* (1988); Sidney Fine, *Sit-Down: The General Motors Strike of 1936–1937* (1969); Steven Fraser, *Labor Will Rule: Sidney Hillman and the Rise of American Labor* (1991); Philip J. Funigiello, *Toward a National Power Policy: The New Deal and the Electric Utility Industry, 1933–1941* (1973); Ellis Hawley, *The New Deal and the Problem of Monopoly: A Study in Economic Ambivalence* (1966); Dorothy Healey and Maurice Isserman, *Dorothy Healey Remembers: A Life in the Communist Party* (1990); James A. Hodges, *New Deal Labor Policy and the Southern Cotton Textile Industry, 1934–1941* (1986); Harvey Klehr, *The Heyday of American Communism: The Depression Decade* (1984); Roy Lubove, *The Struggle for Social Security, 1900–1935*, 2d ed. (1986); Thomas McCraw, *TVA and the Power Fight, 1933–1939* (1971); Greg Mitchell, *The Campaign of the Century: Upton Sinclair's Race for Governor of California* (1992); Bruce Nelson, *Workers on the Waterfront: Seamen, Longshoremen, and Unionism in the 1930s* (1988); Nell Irvin Painter, *The Narrative of Hosea Hudson: His Life as a Negro Communist in the South* (1979); James T. Patterson, *Congressional Conservatism and the New Deal* (1967); Richard Polenberg, *Reorganizing Roosevelt's Government, 1936–1939* (1966); Vicki L. Ruiz, *Cannery Women, Cannery Lives: Mexican Women, Unionization, and the California Food Processing Industry* (1987).

The New Deal, Women, and Minority Groups

Dan T. Carter, *Scottsboro: A Tragedy of the American South*, rev. ed. (1979); William H. Chafe, *The American Woman: Her Changing Social, Economic, and Political Role, 1920–1970* (1972); Cletus E. Daniel, *Bitter Harvest: A History of California Farmworkers, 1870–1941* (1981); Sara M. Evans, *Born for Liberty: A History of Women in America* (1989); Suzanne Forrest, *The Preservation of the Village: New Mexico's Hispanics and the New Deal* (1989); Mario T. Garcia, *Mexican Americans: Leadership, Ideology, and Identity* (1989); Nancy L. Grant, *TVA and Black Americans: Planning for the Status Quo* (1990); William H. Harris, *Keeping the Faith: A. Philip Randolph, Milton P. Webster, and the Brotherhood of Sleeping Car Porters, 1925–1937* (1977); Abraham Hoffman, *Unwanted Mexican Americans in the Great Depression, Repatriation Pressures, 1929–1939* (1974); James H. Jones, rev. ed., *Bad Blood: The Tuskegee Syphilis Experiment, A Tragedy of Race and Medicine* (1992); Lawrence C. Kelly, *The Assault on Assimilation: John Collier and the Origins of Indian Policy Reform* (1983); Harry A. Kersey, Jr., *The Florida Seminoles and the New Deal, 1933–1942* (1989); Alice Kessler-Harris, *Out to Work: A History of Wage-Earning Women in the United States* (1982); Suzanne Mettler, *Gender and Federalism in New Deal Public Policy* (1988); Kenneth Philip, *John Collier's Crusade for Indian Reform, 1920–1954* (1977); Mark Reisler, *By the Sweat of Their Brow: Mexican Immigrant Labor in the United States, 1900–1940* (1976); Lois Scharf, *To Work and to Wed: Female Employment, Feminism, in the Great Depression* (1980); Susan Ware, *Beyond Suffrage: Women in the New Deal* (1981); Nancy J. Weiss, *Farewell to the Party of Lincoln: Black Politics in the Age of FDR* (1983); Raymond Wolters, *Negroes and the Great Depression: The Problem of Economic Recovery* (1970); Robert L. Zangrando, *The NAACP Crusade Against Lynching, 1909–1950* (1980).

The New Deal in Decline

Alan Brinkley, *The End of Reform: New Deal Liberalism in Recession and War* (1995); Steve Fraser and Gary Gerstle, eds., *The Rise and Fall of the New Deal Order, 1930–1980* (1989); William E. Leuchtenburg, *The Supreme Court Reborn: The Constitutional Revolution in the Age of Roosevelt* (1995); Harvard Sitkoff, ed., *Fifty Years Later: The New Deal Evaluated* (1985).

Popular Culture During the Great Depression

Daniel Aaron, *Writers on the Left: Episodes in American Literary Communism* (1961); Andrew Bergman, *We're in the Money: Depression America and Its Films* (1971); Lizbeth Cohen, *Making a New Deal: Industrial Workers in Chicago* (1990); Richard H. Pells, *Radical Visions and American Dreams: Culture and Social Thought in the Depression Years* (1973); Gerald

Weales, *Canned Goods as Caviar: American Film Comedy of the 1930s* (1985).

Biographies

John Barnard, *Walter Reuther and the Rise of the Auto Workers* (1983); David Burner, *Herbert Hoover* (1979); Melvyn Dubovsky and Warren Van Tine, *John L. Lewis* (1977); Steven Fraser, *Labor Will Rule: Sidney Hillman and the Rise of American Labor* (1991); Thomas Kessner, *Fiorella H. La Guardia and the Making of Modern New York* (1989); Joe Klein, *Woody Guthrie* (1980); Joseph Lash, *Eleanor and Franklin* (1971); Jim McJimsey, *Harry Hopkins* (1987); Arthur Schlesinger, Jr., *The Age of Roosevelt*, 3 vols. (1957–1960); Richard N. Smith, *An Uncommon Man: The Triumph of Herbert Hoover* (1984); Geoffrey C. Ward, *A First-Class Temperament: The Emergence of Franklin Roosevelt* (1989); T. Harry Williams, *Huey Long* (1969).

INTERNET RESOURCES

Voices from the Dust Bowl: The Charles L. Todd and Robert Sonkin Migrant Worker Collection, 1940–1941
http://memory.loc.gov/ammem/afctshtml/tshome.html
Farm Security Administration (FSA) studies of migrant work camps in central California in 1940 and 1941 are the bulk of this site. The collection includes audio recordings, photographs, manuscript materials, and publications.

New Deal Network
http://newdeal.feri.org/
This database includes photographs, political cartoons, and texts—including speeches, letters, and other historic documents—from the New Deal period.

Franklin Delano Roosevelt
http://www.ipl.org/ref/POTUS/fdroosevelt.html
This site provides information about FDR, the only president to serve more than two terms.

Picture Archive: Photographs of the Great Depression, 1935–1942
http://www.corbis.com/fdr/fsa/map.html
These photographs reveal the real impact of the Great Depression on American life.

Newspaper Events Not Big in History
http://www.ybi.com/brink/author/1933/index.html
This site lists dozens of events that were front-page news in 1933 but failed to make the history books.

A New Deal for the Arts
http://www.nara.gov/exhall/newdeal/newdeal.html
Artworks, documents, and photographs recount the federal government's efforts to fund artists in the 1930s in the National Archives site.

Price of Civilization: Tax in War and Depression 1933–1946
http://www.taxhistory.org/civsite/
This site is part of the Tax History Project, at Tax Analysts. It includes thousands of searchable pages of documents and analysis and is part of a larger site that contains a cartoon gallery and WWII era posters.

KEY TERMS

Hoovervilles   (p. 701)

New Deal   (p. 706)

Bonus Army   (p. 706)

First 100 Days   (p. 707)

Fireside Chats   (p. 707)

Brain Trust   (p. 708)

National Recovery Administration   (p. 709)

Wagner Act   (p. 712)

Social Security Act   (p. 713)

Second New Deal   (p. 713)

Court Packing   (p. 720)

REVIEW QUESTIONS

1. How did the global economic situation compare with the Depression in the United States?
2. What were the most notable effects of the Depression on the general population?
3. Did President Hoover realize the magnitude of the economic crisis?
4. How did the New Deal change Americans' perception of the role of federal government?
5. What was the most significant feature of the Second New Deal? Why? Did the New Deal change the status of women and minorities in the United States?
6. What caused the decline of the New Deal?
7. How did popular culture during the Depression reflect the American landscape?

25

THE END OF ISOLATION: AMERICA FACES THE WORLD, 1920–1945

DIPLOMACY BETWEEN THE WARS
American Diplomacy During the 1920s
United States Policy Toward Latin America
The Isolationist Mirage

THE COMING OF WORLD WAR II
Conflict in the Pacific
Italy
Germany
The American Response to Hitler
War Begins
"The Arsenal of Democracy"
A Collision Course in the Pacific
Pearl Harbor

AMERICA MOBILIZES FOR WAR
Mobilizing the Economy
Taming Inflation
Election of 1944
Molding Public Opinion

SOCIAL CHANGES DURING THE WAR
Women
African Americans
Mexican Americans
Fear of Enemy Aliens
Internment of Japanese Americans

THE WAR IN EUROPE
The Grand Alliance
Early Axis Victories
Stemming the German Tide
Liberating Europe
The Yalta Conference

THE WAR IN THE PACIFIC
Island Hopping
The Dawn of the Atomic Age
The Manhattan Project
Hiroshima and Nagasaki

The "final solution to the Jewish problem"

At 3 P.M., January 27, 1945, Russian troops of the 100th and 107th divisions entered Auschwitz, a village in southern Poland 30 miles west of Krakow. There, inside Auschwitz's concentration camps, they found 7600 inmates along with World War II's most terrible secret: the Holocaust. Two days later, the U.S. 7th Army liberated Dachau, another infamous Nazi death camp, located just outside Munich. The liberators could scarcely believe what they saw: starving prisoners, bones protruding from their skin, serial numbers tattooed on their arms; stacks of half-burned corpses, and piles of human hair.

Auschwitz was not the first Nazi concentration camp—that dubious distinction belonged to Dachau, which was set up in 1933—but it was the most infamous; 1.6 million people died there. Of the victims, 1.3 million were Jews and 300,000 were Gypsies, Polish Catholics, and Russian prisoners of war. Altogether, people from 28 nations lost their lives at Auschwitz, including the disabled, homosexuals, political prisoners, and others deemed unfit to live in Adolf Hitler's Third Reich.

Auschwitz had two main areas. "Auschwitz I" contained a gas chamber, a crematorium, housing for prisoners used in slave labor, and Dr. Josef Mengele's "medical research" station. "Auschwitz II–Birkenau" contained only gas chambers and crematoria. It was here that cattle cars dumped their exhausted passengers, who then entered through a gate inscribed with the false promise "Work Will Make You Free." SS guards directed each new arrival to the left or the right. The healthy and strong went to the right. The weak, the elderly, and the very young went up a ramp to the left—to the gas chambers, disguised as showers. Inmates were told that the showers would be used to disinfect them, but there was no plumbing and the showerheads were fake. Guards injected a poison gas, Zyklon B, through openings in the ceilings and walls; when the deadly gas had done its work, the bodies were cremated. The ashes were used as road filler and fertilizer, or simply dumped into surrounding ponds and fields.

Auschwitz was a product of Adolf Hitler's belief that Germans constituted a master race that had a right to kill those they deemed inferior. "Nature is cruel, therefore we too may be cruel," Hitler stated in 1934. "If I can send the flower of the German nation into the hell of war . . . then surely I have a right to remove millions of an inferior race that breeds like vermin!"

In 1941 and 1942, the Nazi *Führer* (leader) initiated the "Final Solution to the Jewish Problem." The Nazis did their best to disguise their murderous scheme behind euphemisms and camouflage, but the truth sometimes slipped out. Heinrich Himmler, the official in charge of carrying out the final solution, explained to his top officers: "In public we will never speak of it. I am referring to the annihilation of the Jewish people. In our history, this is an unwritten and never-to-be written page of glory."

In the spring of 1944, four prisoners escaped from Auschwitz, carrying tangible proof of the Nazi's systematic program of mass murder. American and British leaders learned in mid-July what was happening at Auschwitz, but they rejected pleas to bomb the gas chambers or the roads and rail lines leading to the camps.

This was not the first time that western help had failed to come. During the 1930s, the U.S. State Department blocked efforts by Jewish refugees to migrate to the United States. Between 1933 and 1945, the United States allowed in only 132,000 Jewish refugees, just 10 percent of the quota allowed by law. This opposition to Jewish immigration reflected widespread anti-Semitism. As late as 1939, opinion polls indicated that 53 percent of Americans agreed with the statement "Jews are different and should be restricted." In the end, less than 500,000 Jews (out of 6.5 million) survived in Nazi-occupied Europe.

The Holocaust was an appalling and unique tragedy in human history. Never before had a sovereign state, with the cooperation of bureaucrats, industrialists, and civilians, sought to systematically exterminate an entire people. Yet many wonder whether Auschwitz's terrible lesson has been learned. Despite the establishment of the state of Israel, improved Christian-Jewish relations, and heightened sensitivity to racism, many Americans remain ignorant of the past. More than half a century after the liberation of Auschwitz, "ethnic cleansing" and the persecution of religious, racial, and ethnic groups continues in Bosnia, China, Guatemala, India, Sri Lanka, Turkey, and elsewhere.

No war in history killed more people or destroyed more property than World War II. Alto-

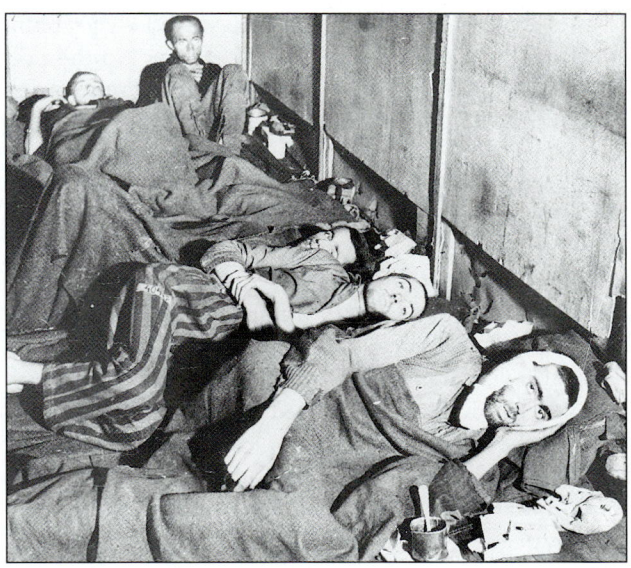

The scenes that greeted the troops who liberated Auschwitz in January 1945 almost defied belief. Perhaps as many as 12,000 people were slaughtered each day at Auschwitz.

gether, 70 million people served in the armed forces during the war; of these, some 7.5 million Soviet troops died in World War II, along with 3.5 million Germans, 1.25 million Japanese, and 400,000 Americans. Civilian deaths were even higher. At least 19 million Soviet civilians, 10 million Chinese, and 6 million European Jews lost their lives during the war.

More than any previous war in history, World War II was a total war. Some 70 nations took part in the war, and fighting took place on the continents of Europe, Asia, and Africa, as well as on the high seas. Entire societies participated, either as soldiers, war workers, or victims of occupation and mass murder. In the United States, the war had vast repercussions: it ended unemployment, brought millions of married women into the workforce, initiated sweeping changes in the lives of the nation's minority groups, and dramatically expanded government's presence in American life. Finally, World War II marked the beginning of the nuclear age.

DIPLOMACY BETWEEN THE WARS

World War I had left the public suspicious of foreign crusades. In 1936, eight Princeton undergraduates formed the Veterans of Future Wars. The organization demanded a bonus of $1000 for every man between the ages of 18 and 36—payable immediately, so that they could enjoy it before being forced to fight the "next war." A women's auxiliary, the Future Gold Star Mothers, demanded government pensions for women, so that they could afford to visit their sons' graves in Europe.

Americans wanted to retreat from foreign affairs. "The people have had all the war, all the taxation, and all the military service they want," declared President Calvin Coolidge in 1925. During the 1920s and much of the 1930s, the United States concentrated on improving its status in the Western Hemisphere and on avoiding European entanglements.

American Diplomacy During the 1920s

During the 1920s, Republican leaders debated joining and ultimately refused to join the League of Nations or the World Court. Such commitments, they feared, might involve the United States too deeply in global politics. Yet Washington remained keenly interested in preserving international stability and tried to promote world peace through diplomatic means.

In 1921 representatives of nine Asian and European nations met in Washington to discuss ways to ease tensions in the Pacific. Secretary of State Charles Evans Hughes stunned the meeting by making specific proposals for disarmament. He called for a ten-year moratorium on the construction of battleships and an agreement that for every five naval vessels owned by the United States or Britain, Japan could have three, and France and Italy one and three-fourths. To win support for what the Japanese delegates called a ratio of "Rolls-Royce, Rolls-Royce, Ford," the United States and Great Britain agreed not to improve their fortifications in the Far East, especially in the Philippines. To appease Japanese resentment at its inferior position, the United States, Britain, and France also agreed in the Four-Party Treaty of 1922 to consult with Japan before going to war in Asia. Neither treaty, however, contained any provision for enforcement.

In 1928 the French foreign minister, Aristide Briand, and Secretary of State Frank B. Kellogg attempted to outlaw war. The Kellogg-Briand Pact, which was eventually signed by 62 nations, renounced war as an instrument for resolving international disputes. If attacked, however, the signatories could defend themselves by force. While it raised hopes for peace and earned Kellogg the Nobel Peace Prize, the Kellogg-Briand Pact had no chance of preventing future bloodshed, since it, too, lacked an enforcement mechanism.

United States Policy Toward Latin America

Twenty times between 1898 and 1932, the United States intervened militarily in the Caribbean and Central America, suppressing popular uprisings in Nicaragua, seizing customs houses in Cuba, occupying Haiti (for 17 years), and supplying military and financial aid to friendly parties in the Mexican Revolution. Despite repeated American interventions, however, the region remained unstable.

During the 1920s Republican administrations inched away from gunboat diplomacy and tried to develop better relations with Latin America. Although progress was uneven and Washington's policies occasionally reverted to heavy-handed interventions, the thrust of Republican diplomacy during the 1920s clearly anticipated the shift toward improved relations with Latin America. In 1924, for example, the United States pulled the marines out of the Dominican Republic, and the following year American troops left Nicaragua, only to be sent back a few months later when a revolution broke out. But the real test of the United States' desire for improved relations came in Mexico.

Following Alvaro Obregón's election as president of Mexico in 1920, the Mexican government threatened to expropriate American-owned oil properties. The oil companies demanded government intervention, and in 1927 President Calvin Coolidge appointed Dwight Morrow, a partner in the firm of J. P. Morgan and Company, as ambassador. Mexicans expected the worst; one newspaper declared, "after Morrow come the marines." They were wrong. One of Morrow's first actions was to change the sign on the embassy to read "United States Embassy," rather than "American Embassy." It was a small gesture, but its significance was not lost on the Mexicans, who had long resented the United States' arrogance in appropriating a continental adjective. Morrow's diplomacy paid handsome dividends, and in 1927 Mexico once again recognized American-owned oil properties.

President Herbert Hoover continued the diplomacy of reconciliation. He announced plans to withdraw marines from Nicaragua and Haiti, and he resisted pressure from Congress to establish a customs receivership in El Salvador when the government there defaulted on its bonds. In 1930 Hoover approved a document written by Undersecretary of State J. Reuben Clark. The Clark Memorandum repudiated the Roosevelt Corollary to the Monroe Doctrine, which for 25 years had justified U.S. intervention in Latin America.

In his first inaugural address, President Franklin D. Roosevelt dedicated the United States "to the policy of the good neighbor." Secretary of State Cordell Hull stunned Latin America in December 1933 at the Seventh Pan-American Conference by declaring, "no state has the right to intervene in the international or external affairs of another." The marines left Nicaragua in 1933 and Haiti in 1934. The United States also nullified the Platt Amendment, thereby surrendering the right to intervene in the affairs of Cuba; and it gave Panama its political independence. Furthermore, when Mexico finally expropriated foreign oil properties in 1938, Roosevelt rejected calls to send in troops and let the action stand. The **Good Neighbor Policy** did not solve all the problems with Latin America, but it promoted better relations just when the United States needed hemispheric solidarity to meet the threat of global war.

The Isolationist Mirage

During the Great Depression, isolationist sentiment surged. In 1935, 150,000 college students participated in a nationwide Student Strike for Peace and half a million signed pledges saying that they would refuse to serve in the event of war.

Antiwar sentiment was not confined to undergraduates. Disillusionment over World War I fed opposition to foreign entanglements. "We didn't win a thing we set out for in the last war," said Senator Gerald Nye of North Dakota. "We merely succeeded, with tremendous loss of life, to make secure the loans of private bankers to the Allies." The overwhelming majority of Americans agreed; an opinion poll in 1935 found that 70 percent of Americans believed that intervention in World War I had been a mistake.

Isolationist ideas spread through American popular culture during the mid-1930s. The Book-of-the-Month Club featured a volume entitled *Merchants of Death*. Its author contended that the United States had been drawn into the European war by international arms manufacturers, who had deliberately fomented conflict in order to market their products. From 1934 to 1936, a congressional committee, chaired by Senator Nye, investigated charges that false Allied propaganda and unscrupulous Wall Street bankers had dragged Americans into the European war. In April 1935—the eighteenth anniversary of America's entry into World War I—50,000 veterans held a peace march in Washington, D.C.

By 1938, however, pacifist sentiment was fading. A rapidly modernizing Japan was seeking to acquire raw materials and territory on the Asian mainland; a revived Germany was rebuilding its military power and grabbing land bloodlessly on its eastern borders; and Italy was trying to restore Roman glory through military might.

THE COMING OF WORLD WAR II

The modern world had never known a leader like Adolf Hitler. A charismatic and spellbinding orator, Hitler possessed a unique ability to articulate a nation's darkest fears and hatreds and then turn them to his own twisted purposes. Winston Churchill offered a profound truth when he described Hitler as the "monstrous product of former wrongs and shame."

Hitler exploited the psychological injuries inflicted on Germans by World War I. Rare indeed was the German who did not feel stunned by his country's sudden, unexpected defeat or who did not seethe with anger over the harsh peace imposed by the victors. Hitler's great genius (and history's great tragedy) was his ability to tap into his countrymen's anger and resentment. Exploiting the ugly strain of anti-Semitism in German culture, he claimed that the country's economic woes were the result of a conspiracy of German Jews. Hitler also attacked the Treaty of Versailles, telling his countrymen that they would regain their national honor only if they abrogated the treaty. Purged of so-called Jewish traitors, cleared of the blame for causing the war, freed from onerous reparation payments, and rescued from emasculating disarmament, Germany would rise anew and reclaim her position as a world leader.

The 1920s had prepared many Germans to embrace a leader who promised to restore national pride. The Treaty of Versailles had saddled Germany with a reparations bill of $34 billion in 1921. Unable to make the interest payments, let alone the principal, Germany staggered beneath the burden until its economy dissolved into severe unemployment and hyperinflation. Forty million marks were worth one cent.

Confronted by Germany's imminent economic collapse, the United States offered a measure of relief. In 1924 Charles Dawes, a prominent American banker, worked out a proposal (the Dawes Plan) that reduced the reparations bill and provided Germany with an American loan. With prodding from the United States, Great Britain and France cut reparations to $2 billion, but even that proved too much when the Great Depression struck. Germany entered the 1930s with its economy in shambles, providing fertile soil for Adolf Hitler.

Hitler's drive for political power began in 1919, when he joined the small National Socialist Workers' Party (later known as the Nazis), which demanded that all Jews be deprived of German citizenship and that all German-speakers be united in a single country. A brilliant propagandist and organizer, Hitler gave the Nazi movement a potent symbol, the swastika; raised party membership to 15,000 by 1923; and formed a private army, the storm troopers, to attack his political opponents. In the fall of 1923, Hitler engineered a revolt, the Beer-Hall Putsch, to overthrow Germany's five-year-old Weimar Republic. It was a dismal failure; the National Socialist Party was ordered dissolved and Hitler was imprisoned for nine months.

While in prison, he wrote a book titled *Mein Kampf* (My Struggle) which laid out his beliefs and vision for Germany. He called on Germans to repudiate the Versailles Treaty, rearm, conquer countries with large German populations like Austria and Czechoslovakia, and seize *lebensraum* (living space) for Germans in Russia.

Following his release from prison, Hitler persuaded the German government to lift its ban on the National Socialist Party. In 1928, the Nazis polled just 810,000 votes in German elections, but by 1930, after the depression began, they polled 6½ million votes. Two years later Hitler ran for president. He lost, but received 13½ million votes, 37 percent of all votes cast. The Nazis had suddenly become the single largest party in the German parliament, and in January 1933, Germany's president appointed Hitler to the post of chancellor. A year and a half later Hitler was dictator of Germany.

Within months of becoming chancellor, Hitler's National Socialist government banned labor unions, imposed newspaper censorship, and outlawed all other political parties. The regime established a secret police force, the Gestapo, to suppress all opposition, and required all children ten years and older to join Nazi youth groups. By 1935, Hitler had transformed Germany into a fascist state, with the government exercising total control over all political, economic, and cultural activities.

Anti-Semitism was an integral part of Hitler's political program. The 1935 Nuremberg Laws forbade intermarriage between Jews and Germans, restricted Jewish property rights, and barred Jews from the civil service, the universities, and all professional and managerial occupations. On the night of November 9, 1939—a night now known as *Kristallnacht* (the night of the broken glass)—the Nazis imprisoned more than 20,000 Jews in concentration camps and destroyed more than 200 synagogues and 7500 Jewish businesses.

A reviving Germany was not the only threat to world peace. While Hitler busied himself with rearming Germany, occupying the Rhineland, annexing Austria, and seizing Czechoslovakia, Japan attacked China, and Italy attacked Ethiopia.

Conflict in the Pacific

Another major threat to international stability following World War I came in the Far East. Chronically short of raw materials, Japan was desperate to establish political and cultural hegemony in Asia. In September 1931 Japan invaded Manchuria, reducing the Chinese province to a puppet state. President Hoover, a peaceful man, rejected American military intervention. He also refused to impose economic sanctions against Japan, fearing that such reprisals might hurt American exports or, worse yet, lead to war. Instead, Hoover applied the Stimson Doctrine, which revived the Wilsonian policy of refusing to recognize governments established by force.

Expecting bolder measures, Japan ignored America's slap on the wrist and concluded that the United States would not use military might to oppose Japan's designs on the Far East. In 1934, Japan terminated the Five-Power Naval Treaty of 1922, which had limited its naval power in the Pacific, and in 1937 invaded China. In response, the League of Nations sponsored a conference that same year in Brussels. As the delegates debated whether or not to impose economic sanctions against Japan, the United States announced it would not support sanctions. The conference adjourned after passing a report that mildly criticized Japanese aggression.

Any doubts regarding United States willingness to appease Japan vanished a few weeks later. In December 1937 Japanese aircraft bombed the *Panay*, a U.S. gunboat stationed on the Yangtze River near Nanking, killing three Americans. While the attack angered the public, few called for war as they had following the sinking of the *Maine* or the *Lusitania*. Secretary of State Cordell Hull sent sharply worded protests to Tokyo, but the United States quickly accepted Japan's "profound apology," which included indemnities for the injured and the relatives of the dead, promises against future attacks, and punishment of the pilots responsible for the bloodshed. In short, by the end of 1937, as one historian has noted, "America's Far Eastern Policy had retreated to inaction."

Italy

Mussolini's Italy posed another threat to world peace. Benito Mussolini, Italy's fascist dictator from 1922 to 1943, promised to restore his country's martial glory. Surrounded by storm troopers dressed in black shirts, Mussolini delivered impassioned speeches from balconies, while crowds chanted "Duce! Duce!"

His opponents mocked him as the "Sawdust Caesar," but for a time his admirers included Winston Churchill and humorist Will Rogers. Cole Porter, the popular songwriter, referred to the Italian leader in one of his smash hits: "You're the top," he wrote, "you're Mussolini."

Mussolini invented a political philosophy known as fascism, extolling it as an alternative to socialist radicalism and parliamentary inaction. By fascism, he meant one-party government, strict government control of business and labor, and severe restrictions on personal liberty. Fascism, he promised, would end political corruption and labor strife while maintaining capitalism and private property. It would make trains run on time. Like Hitler's Germany, fascist Italy adopted anti-Semitic laws banning marriages between Christian and Jewish Italians, restricting Jews' right to own property, and removing Jews from positions in government, education, and banking.

One of Mussolini's goals was to create an Italian empire in North Africa. In 1912 and 1913, Italy conquered Libya. In 1935, Mussolini provoked war with Ethiopia, conquering the country in eight months. Two years later, Mussolini sent 70,000 Italian troops to Spain to help Francisco Franco defeat the republican government in the Spanish Civil War.

Germany

The third threat to world peace came from a revived Germany. Hitler had vowed to reclaim Germany's position as a world leader. True to his vow to reclaim Germany's position as a world leader, Hitler pulled Germany out of the League of Nations and secretly began to rearm. In 1935 he publicly announced that he was building an air force and a 550,000-man-strong army. He also declared that Germany would have a peacetime draft, a clear violation of the Treaty of Versailles.

In 1936, Hitler concentrated on forging alliances with nations that shared Germany's taste for expansion and aggression. First he signed the Anti-Comintern Pact (forerunner of a full-scale military al-

Axis Takeovers in Europe, 1936–1939

liance) with Japan. Next, he formed the Rome-Berlin Axis with Italy. Finally, he reoccupied the Rhineland, the German-speaking region between the Rhine River and France. Once again, France and Great Britain did nothing to oppose Hitler's bold advance, for they believed (or wanted to believe) that the Rhineland would satisfy his expansionist ambitions.

But the Rhineland only whetted Hitler's appetite. Intent on reuniting all German-speaking peoples of Europe under the "Third Reich," Hitler annexed Austria in 1938 and imprisoned the country's chancellor. Once again, the British and the French acquiesced, hoping Austria would be Hitler's last stop. Later that year he demanded the Sudetenland, the German-speaking region of western Czechoslovakia.

This time France and Great Britain felt compelled to act. In September 1938 Edouard Daladier, the premier of France, and Neville Chamberlain, Britain's prime minister, met with Hitler in Munich, Germany, to ask whether he had further designs on Europe. Fearing that they could not count on each other to use force, British and French leaders eagerly accepted Hitler's promises not to seek additional territory in Europe. In less than a year, Munich would become synonymous with shameful appeasement and Chamberlain would be vilified for believing Hitler's lies.

By 1938, then, Hitler had kept his promise to avenge the humiliations Germans had suffered at Versailles. Germany's frontiers were larger than they had been in 1914, the country was rearmed, and German national pride had been restored. In addition, Germany had acquired powerful allies in Japan and Italy. All this had transpired virtually unopposed by the victors of World War I. The member states of League of Nations had offered only feeble protests and failed to act. Everyone hoped the Germans, Italians, and Japanese would be satisfied with their acquisitions and stop their expansions. In retrospect, such hopes were clearly wrong, but at the time they did not appear unfounded. Western leaders assumed they were dealing with reasonable and responsible men; they had no way of knowing appeasement would only fuel the Axis dictators' appetites for expansion.

In late summer, Hitler took one further step. On August 24, 1939, Germany and the Soviet Union signed a nonaggression treaty. In exchange for the pact, Hitler agreed to grant the Soviet Union a sphere of influence over eastern Poland, Estonia, Latvia, Finland, and Bessarabia (northeastern Romania), while Stalin approved Germany's designs on western Poland and Lithuania. With his eastern front protected from attack, Hitler was now prepared for war.

Benito Mussolini and Adolf Hitler share their diplomatic triumph over France and England in Munich in 1938, after the signing of the Munich Pact.

The American Response to Hitler

The United States responded to Europe's turmoil with caution. Preoccupied with the Great Depression, President Roosevelt had little time or energy to deal with foreign affairs. Yet America's timidity also reflected the strength of its isolationist sentiment. Congress, not the president, played the dominant role in foreign affairs for much of the 1930s, and Congress was determined to keep the United States out of another European conflict.

Roosevelt's first diplomatic initiative involved the Soviet Union. Hoping to expand foreign trade and to use the Soviet Union to balance Japan in the Far East, he formally recognized the Soviet Union in 1933, provoking the wrath of isolationists and anti-Communists alike.

Privately, Roosevelt opposed the growth of isolationist sentiment in the United States during the early and mid-1930s. In his view, the United States, like it or not, had to play an important role in world affairs because it had become a major world power. But Roosevelt's freedom to act was severely limited by isolationists in Congress. Between 1935 and 1937, Congress passed three separate neutrality laws, which clamped an embargo on arms sales to belligerents, forbade American ships from entering war zones and prohibited them from being armed, and barred Americans from traveling on belligerent ships, respectively. Clearly, Congress was determined not to repeat what it regarded as the mistakes that had plunged the United States into World War I.

The neutrality laws troubled Roosevelt. Convinced that these laws posed a serious threat to presidential power, Roosevelt delivered a speech in October 1937 in which he spoke of the need to "quarantine the aggressors." But he immediately retreated into silence when it became clear the public did not support vigorous action. This was where matters stood when Hitler decided to take advantage of the world's indecisiveness.

War Begins

At daybreak on September 1, 1939, mechanized German forces poured across the Polish border, while German bombers and fighters attacked Polish railroads from the air. On September 17, Russia attacked Poland from the east. Poland was overrun within three weeks.

The key to Germany's success was a new military strategy known as *blitzkrieg* ("lightning war"). Blitzkrieg stressed speed, force, and surprise; by closely coordinating air power and mechanized ground forces, Germany ripped through its adversary's defenses.

Hitler's armies devastated Poland with their tremendous force and firepower. Here soldiers drive through a town battered by repeated bombings.

Britain and France declared war on Germany on September 3, 1939, two days after the German invasion began, but they did little while Poland fell. France moved its troops to its famous Maginot Line, a supposedly invincible line of defensive fortifications built to protect France's eastern border. No fighting took place in late 1939 and early 1940, leading some to call this a "phony war."

Then in April 1940, German freighters sailed secretly into Norway's major ports and the port of Copenhagen, Denmark's capital, their holds filled with German troops. The Danes, taken completely by surprise, surrendered in two hours; the Norwegians held out until June, when they, too, capitulated. British troops had tried to assist Norway, but were forced to retreat due to a lack of air support.

Following the Norway debacle, British Prime Minister Neville Chamberlain was forced to resign. He was replaced by Winston Churchill, who, since 1932, had been warning about the danger Hitler posed. Upon becoming prime minister, Churchill told the British people that he had nothing to offer them but "blood, toil, tears, and sweat" in their fight to resist foreign aggression.

In May 1940, Hitler began his assault on western Europe. He outflanked France's Maginot Line by attacking Belgium, Luxembourg, and the Netherlands before driving his forces into France. Luxembourg surrendered in one day; Holland in five. A British expeditionary force rushed across the English Channel to try to stop the German offensive. But a German tank thrust forced the British to retreat to the French seaport of Dunkirk. With the British force nearly surrounded, Hitler had a chance to crush his opponents. But Britain's Royal Air Force held off German bombers long enough to allow a flotilla of yachts, ferries, and fishing boats to evacuate 338,000 Allied troops across the English Channel.

British forces had been driven from the continent. Worse yet, they had been forced to leave their weapons and tanks behind. Britain turned to the United States for help. President Roosevelt responded to the Dunkirk disaster by ordering U.S. military arsenals to send all available war materiel to Britain to replace the lost equipment.

During World War I, France held out against the Germans for four years. This time, French resistance lasted two weeks. Germany began its assault on France June 5; its troops entered Paris June 14; and on June 22, a new French government, made up of pro-German sympathizers, was set up at Vichy. In just six weeks, Germany had conquered most of continental Europe.

Convinced that Britain would negotiate with him (in order to keep control of its empire), Hitler decided against an immediate invasion of Britain. But Churchill refused to bargain. Defiantly, he told his people that he would resist any German assault: "We shall fight on the beaches . . . we shall fight in the streets . . . we shall never surrender."

Hitler was furious. First, he unleashed German submarines against British shipping. Then in July he sent his air force, the Luftwaffe, to destroy Britain from the air. At the time the assault began the Royal Air Force (RAF) had just 704 serviceable planes, while Germany had 2682 bombers and fighters ready for action. Throughout July and August the Luftwaffe attacked airfields and radar stationed on Britain's southern and eastern coast. Then, in September, Hitler shifted strategy and began to bomb civilian targets in London. These air raids, known collectively as the blitz, continued through the fall and winter. In May 1941, the blitz ended. The RAF, while outnumbered, had won the Battle of Britain. Churchill expressed his nation's gratitude with famous words: "Never in the field of human conflict was so much owed by so many to so few."

Having failed in his bid to destroy Britain with air power, Hitler again shifted strategy and invaded the Soviet Union. The attack, which began June 22, 1941, violated the German-Soviet nonaggression pact. Hitler's goal was to seize Soviet food, oil, and slave labor for Germany. At first, the Nazi war machine seemed invincible. By fall, Hitler's armies had overrun the grain fields of Ukraine and were approaching Moscow and Leningrad. But instead of pressing ahead toward Moscow, as his generals advised, Hitler decided to seize Leningrad and occupy the Ukraine. By the time he was ready to advance on Moscow, temperatures had plunged to 40 degrees below zero. In the frigid cold, German troops suffered frostbite and their equipment broke down.

The week between December 6 and 11, 1941, proved to be one of the most pivotal in the entire war. On December 6, Soviet forces repulsed the German attack on Moscow; it was Hitler's first military defeat. The next day, Japanese forces attacked the American naval base at Pearl Harbor, Hawaii, bringing the United States into the war. On December 11, Hitler declared war on the United States.

"The Arsenal of Democracy"

Like Wilson before him, Roosevelt responded to Europe's war by declaring America's neutrality. Unlike the idealistic Wilson, however, he did not ask his countrymen to be "neutral in thought as well as in action." After France fell, Roosevelt feared a German victory would threaten America's future security, and he resolved to save England at all costs—including war.

Before he could rescue Britain, however, Roosevelt first had to regain control of American foreign policy. Soon after Germany invaded Poland, he pushed a fourth neutrality act through Congress. It modified the earlier legislation by permitting belligerents to purchase war materials, provided they paid cash and carried the goods away in their own ships. This act was pro-British because England controlled the Atlantic. Acting on his own authority, Roosevelt then rushed thousands of planes and guns to Britain. In September 1940 he persuaded Congress to pass the first peacetime draft in American history and signed an executive agreement with Great Britain transferring 50 destroyers to England in exchange for 99-year leases on eight British bases in the Western Hemisphere. Most Americans supported the destroyers-for-bases deal.

Fearing Roosevelt was duplicating Wilson's mistakes, isolationists opposed the tilt toward Britain. Strongest in the Midwest, they represented the entire spectrum of political thought, including Republicans such as Senators Arthur Vandenberg of Michigan and Robert Taft of Ohio; Democrats such as Joseph Kennedy, ambassador to Great Britain; and progressives such as Wisconsin's Senator Robert La Follette. Their most powerful argument was that Europe's war did not threaten "fortress America." Germany had no designs on the Western Hemisphere, they insisted. The United States should therefore sit this war out.

The war dominated the election of 1940. Running for an unprecedented third term, Roosevelt handily defeated Republican challenger Wendell Willkie, 27 million votes to 22 million votes, and 449 electoral votes to 82.

During the campaign, Willkie charged Roosevelt with maneuvering the United States into the European war. On the eve of the election, Roosevelt responded, offering these reassuring words to American parents: "I have said this before, but I shall say it again and again: your boys are not going to be sent into any foreign wars." In actuality, however, events were drawing the country closer to war.

After the election, Churchill informed Roosevelt that England had run out of money and could no longer purchase war supplies. Consequently, the president replaced "cash and carry" with a **"lend-lease" bill,** which Congress passed after a bitter debate and Roosevelt signed in March 1941.

To cement the Anglo-American bond, Roosevelt met with Churchill in August 1941 on board the USS *Augusta* off the coast of Newfoundland. There they negotiated the Atlantic Charter, which pledged mutual support for democracy, freedom of the seas, arms reductions, and a just peace. In everything but name the United States and Great Britain were now allies.

While the public strongly supported aid for Great Britain, many Americans balked at helping the Russians, who had been invaded by Germany in June 1941. Roosevelt, however, immediately offered lend-lease aid to the Soviet Union, and in November 1941 the United States allocated $1 billion in aid to the Soviets. While critics denounced Roosevelt, Churchill, who knew wars often made strange bedfellows, supported the decision wholeheartedly. By 1945 America's allies had received $50 billion, four times the amount loaned to the allies in World War I.

Kneeling in prayer near the Capitol in Washington, D.C., members of the "Mother's Crusade" against the lend-lease bill plead for Congress not to pass the measure.

In April 1941 the United States went beyond financial assistance by constructing bases in Greenland and escorting convoys as far as Iceland to protect them from German submarines. The American navy started tracking German submarines and signaling their locations to British destroyers. After a German submarine attacked an American destroyer in September, Roosevelt ordered the navy to "shoot on sight" any German ships in the waters around Iceland. Yet the president stopped short of asking Congress for a formal declaration of war; for a few more months the United States maintained the fiction of neutrality.

A Collision Course in the Pacific

Thanks to the public's preoccupation with Europe, Roosevelt had a relatively free hand in the Far East, where Japan was seeking to acquire large parts of China and the western Pacific. Yet Japan's dream of expansion clashed with the two main pillars of America's Far Eastern policy—preserving the "Open Door" for trade, and protecting China's territorial integrity.

After Japan invaded China in 1937, relations between Washington and Tokyo deteriorated rapidly. The United States pressured Japan to withdraw, but Tokyo refused. In July 1939 Secretary of State Cordell Hull, aware that American exports fueled Japan's war machine, threatened to impose economic sanctions. Roosevelt, however, held back, fearing Japan would attack the Dutch East Indies to secure the oil it needed.

Events quickly forced Roosevelt's hand. In 1940 Japan occupied northern Indochina, an obvious step

In little more than an hour, the surprise attack at Pearl Harbor killed more than 2400 American sailors and damaged or sunk eight battleships, including the USS *Arizona*, pictured here.

toward the Dutch East Indies. Late in September, Roosevelt placed an embargo on scrap iron and steel, hoping economic sanctions would strengthen moderates in Japan who wished to avoid conflict with the United States.

When these actions failed to deter Japanese aggression, Roosevelt froze Japanese assets in the United States and cut off steel, oil, and aviation fuel exports to Japan. Hurt by these sanctions, Japan negotiated with the United States throughout 1941. Instead of compromising, however, the United States asked Japan to withdraw immediately from Indochina and China, concessions that would have ended Japan's dream of economic and military hegemony in Asia.

In a last-ditch effort to avoid war, Japan promised not to march further south, not to attack the Soviet Union, and not to declare war against the United States if Germany and America went to war. In return, Japan asked the United States to abandon China. Roosevelt refused. In October 1941 the Japanese government fell and General Hideki Tojo, the leader of the militants, seized power. War was imminent.

Most military experts expected Japan to attack the Dutch East Indies to secure oil and rubber. Before striking there, however, Japan moved to neutralize American naval power in the western Pacific.

Pearl Harbor

At 7:02 A.M., December 7, 1941, an Army mobile radar unit set up on Oahu Island in Hawaii picked up the tell-tale blips of approaching aircraft. The two privates operating the radar contacted the Army's General Information Center, but the duty officer there told them to remain calm; the planes were probably American B-17s flying in from California. In fact, they were Japanese aircraft that had been launched from six aircraft carriers 200 miles north of Hawaii.

At 7:55 A.M., the first Japanese bombs fell on **Pearl Harbor,** the main base of the U.S. Pacific Fleet. Moored in the harbor were more than 70 warships, including 8 of the fleet's 9 battleships. There were also 2 heavy cruisers, 29 destroyers, and 5 submarines. Four hundred airplanes were stationed nearby.

Japanese torpedo bombers, flying just 50 feet above the water, launched torpedoes at the docked American warships. Japanese dive bombers strafed the ships' decks with machine gun fire, while Japanese fighters dropped high-explosive bombs on the aircraft sitting on the ground. Within half an hour, the U.S. Pacific Fleet was virtually destroyed. The U.S. battleship *Arizona* was a burning hulk. Three other large ships—the *Oklahoma*, the *West Virginia*, and the *California*—were sinking.

A second attack took place at 9 A.M., but by then the damage had already been done. Seven of the eight battleships were sunk or severely hit. Out of 400 aircraft, 188 had been destroyed and 159 were seriously damaged. Altogether, 2403 Americans died during the Japanese attack on Pearl Harbor; another 1178 were wounded. Japan lost just 55 men.

Militarily it was not a total disaster. Japan had failed to destroy Pearl Harbor's ship-repair facilities, the base's power plant, and its fuel tanks. Even more important, three U.S. aircraft carriers, which had been on routine maneuvers, escaped destruction. But it was a devastating blow nonetheless. That same day, Japanese forces also launched other attacks throughout the Pacific, striking Guam, Hong Kong, Malaya, Midway Island, the Philippine Islands, and Wake Island.

The next day, President Roosevelt appeared before a joint session of Congress to ask for a declaration of war. He began his address with these famous words: "Yesterday, December 7, 1941—a date that will live in infamy—the United States of America was suddenly and deliberately attacked by naval and air forces of the Empire of Japan." Congress declared war on Japan, with only one dissenting vote.

AMERICA MOBILIZES FOR WAR

After Pearl Harbor, practically everyone agreed on what had to be done: jump-start the economy, raise an army, and win the war. Yet the economic challenges facing the United States were truly mind-boggling. New plants had to be built and existing ones expanded; raw materials had to be procured and distributed where needed; labor had to be kept on the job; production had to be raised; and all this had to be accomplished without producing soaring inflation.

Mobilizing the Economy

Following the declaration of war, Roosevelt easily made the switch from reformer to war leader, telling reporters that "Dr. New Deal" had to be replaced by "Dr. Win-the-War." Like Wilson before him, Roosevelt wished to avoid government controls. He, too, would fail. World War II created a huge (and apparently permanent) federal bureaucracy. In January 1942 Roosevelt created the **War Production Board (WPB)** to "exercise general responsibility" over the economy.

Business leaders responded coolly to the call for economic conversion. With profits already high because of the war in Europe, many industrialists did not wish to jeopardize their position in the domestic market by converting factories to military production. Others worried about getting stuck with inflated capacity after the war ended.

To gain their support, the government suspended competitive bidding, offered cost-plus contracts, guaranteed low-cost loans for retooling, and paid huge subsidies for plant construction and equipment. Lured by huge profits, the American auto industry began to produce war vehicles and construct new factories, like the huge Willow Run plant near Detroit, to build airplanes. In 1940, 6000 planes rolled off Detroit's assembly lines; by 1942 production had soared to 47,000, and by the end of the war it had exceeded 100,000, more than doubling Roosevelt's goal.

Consumer industries prospered, too. Robert W. Woodruff of Coca-Cola made his 5-cent drink the most widely distributed consumer product in the world by convincing the army that soldiers needed Coke to refresh their fighting spirit. Backed by government subsidies, Woodruff built an international network of plants, and then purchased them at a fraction of their cost after the war, ensuring Coca-Cola's postwar supremacy in the soft drink industry.

Most military contracts went to big businesses because large-scale production simplified buying. At Roosevelt's insistence the Justice Department stopped prosecuting antitrust violators, a policy that accelerated business consolidations. Overall, industrial profits doubled, but small industries, lacking the capital to convert to war production, got crowded away from the federal trough.

When he saw the production figures of American industry during World War II, Winston Churchill smiled broadly and exclaimed, "Nothing succeeds like excess!" Great Britain's bulldog of a prime minister was right: Allied armies won the decisive battles of World War II, but the Allied victory rested squarely on America's economic might. Within a year of the Japanese attack on Pearl Harbor, the output of the nation's war industries outstripped that of all the Axis countries combined; by 1944, it was twice as great. By the war's end, industrial production had soared an astonishing 96 percent.

Government-sponsored research became a major new industry during World War II. To counter Germany's scientific and technological superiority, Roosevelt created the Office of Scientific Research and Development (OSRD) in 1942. Federal funds supported the development of radar, flame throwers, antiaircraft guns, rockets, and even new medicines. Thanks in large part to penicillin and new blood plasma techniques, the death rate of wounded soldiers who reached medical installations was half that of World War I. Antimalarial drugs and insecticides dramatically reduced the incidence of mosquito-carried diseases among troops in the Mediterranean and in the Pacific.

No less than industry, American agriculture performed impressively during World War II. To encourage production, Roosevelt allowed farmers to make large profits by setting crop prices at high levels. Good weather, mechanization, and a dramatic increase in the use of fertilizers did the rest.

The distribution of profits in agriculture followed the same pattern as in industry: most went to large-scale operators who could afford expensive machinery and fertilizers. Many small farmers, saddled with huge debts from the depression, abandoned their farms for jobs in defense plants or the armed services.

Overall, the war brought unprecedented prosperity to Americans. Per capita income rose from $373 in 1940 to $1074 in 1945, and total personal income went from $81 billion to $182 billion during the same years. The total income of families increased dramatically as large numbers of women joined the workforce, creating millions of two-income families. In fact, World War II brought Americans more money than they could spend, for the production of consumer goods could not keep pace with the new buying power.

Taming Inflation

The shortages led to inflation. Prices rose 18 percent between 1941 and the end of 1942. Apples sold for ten cents apiece; the price of a watermelon soared to $2.50; and oranges reached an astonishing $1.00 a dozen.

Many goods were unavailable regardless of price. To conserve steel, glass, and rubber for war industries, the government halted production of cars in December 1941. A month later, production of vacuum cleaners, refrigerators, radios, sewing machines, and phonographs ceased. Altogether, production of nearly 300 items deemed nonessential to the war effort—including coat hangers, beer cans, and toothpaste tubes—was banned or curtailed.

Congress responded to surging prices by establishing the Office of Price Administration (OPA) in January 1942, with the power to freeze prices and wages, control rents, and institute rationing of scarce items. The OPA quickly rationed foodstuffs. Every month, each man, woman, and child in the country received two ration books—one for canned goods and one for meat, fish, and dairy products. Meat was limited to 28 ounces per person a week; sugar to 8 to 12 ounces; and coffee, a pound every 5 weeks. Rationing was soon extended to tires, gasoline, and shoes. Drivers were allowed a mere 3 gallons a week, while pedestrians were limited to two pairs of shoes a year.

In addition to rationing, Washington attacked inflation by reducing the public's purchasing power. The administration encouraged the sale of war bonds, which not only helped finance the war but also absorbed more than 7 percent of the real personal income of Americans. Taxation was also used to combat inflation. To cool off consumer purchasing power, Congress passed the Revenue Act of 1942, which raised corporate taxes, increased the excess profits tax, and levied a 5 percent withholding tax on anyone who earned more than $642 a year. Tax reforms forced citizens to pay more than 40 percent of the war's total cost as the war progressed, laying the foundation for postwar tax policies. Wage controls offered another tool for controlling inflation. The War Labor Board (WLB), established in 1942, had the power to set wages, hours, and working conditions.

These programs, working together, brought inflation under control. After 1942 the annual inflation rate did not exceed 1.5 percent. Still, the administration's methods pleased no one. Everyone groused about taxes; manufacturers and farmers denounced price controls as an attack on their profits; and labor officials condemned wage freezes as an assault on their incomes.

Yet American workers clearly reaped a bonanza from World War II. Because the war created 17 million new jobs at the exact moment when 15 million men and women entered the armed services, unemployment virtually disappeared. After Pearl Harbor, labor soared to an absolute premium, drawing into the workforce previously unemployed and underemployed groups such as women, teenagers, African Americans, senior citizens, and the handicapped. Under the benevolent hand of government protection, unions rebounded from their sharp decline of the 1920s and early 1930s.

Despite these gains, labor unrest increased throughout the war. After Pearl Harbor union officials pledged not to strike until the war ended, but inflation and wage restrictions quickly eroded their goodwill. The number of work stoppages rose from 2960 in 1942 to 4956 in 1944, though most ended quickly and did not harm the war effort.

In contrast to the president, Congress took a hostile stand toward labor. Over Roosevelt's veto, Congress passed the Smith-Connally Act, which banned strikes in war industries, authorized the president to seize plants useful to the war effort, and limited political activity by unions. The Smith-Connally Act reflected a resurgence of conservatism, both in Congress and in the country at large. Though the Democrats continued to maintain a thin majority in both houses of Congress throughout the war, a coalition of Republicans and conservative Democrats after 1942 could defeat any measure.

Beginning in 1943 Roosevelt's opponents led a successful attack against the New Deal, refusing to fund the Civilian Conservation Corps, the Works Progress Administration, the National Youth Administration, and the National Resources and Planning Board. According to conservatives, these agen-

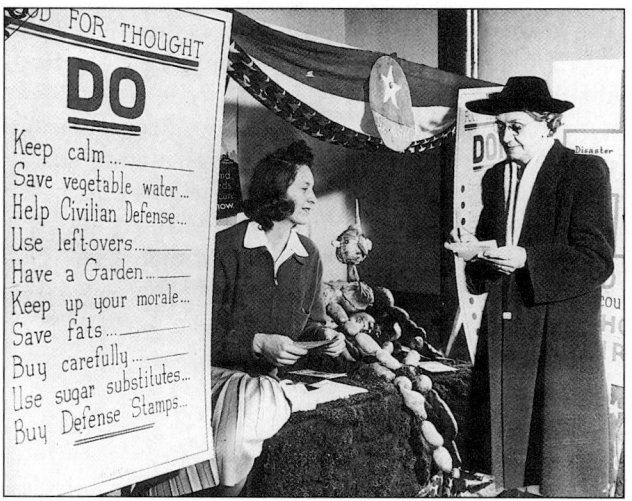

At a consumer conservation booth in West Dundee Township, Illinois, women offered "food for thought" in an attempt to help the war effort.

cies had dangerously expanded federal power and deserved to die.

Election of 1944

With reform in retreat, the Republicans expected to win the election of 1944. Thomas E. Dewey, the dapper young governor of New York, won his party's nomination on the first ballot. While Dewey accepted the New Deal as part of American life, he opposed its expansion. No distance separated the two major candidates on foreign affairs.

Roosevelt easily captured his party's nomination for a fourth term. Because his health was deteriorating badly his choice of a vice president was more important than ever. Roosevelt allowed the Democratic convention to select a nominee, and it picked Harry S Truman of Missouri, best known as leader of a Senate committee investigating corruption in defense spending.

The 1944 campaign revitalized Roosevelt. He unveiled plans for a "GI Bill of Rights," promising liberal unemployment benefits, educational support, medical care, and housing loans for veterans, which Congress approved overwhelmingly in 1944. Unwilling to switch leaders while at war, the public stuck with Roosevelt to see the crisis through.

Molding Public Opinion

Having witnessed the mistakes of World War I, Roosevelt did not want government propaganda to arouse or fuel false hopes. Shortly before Pearl Harbor, he created the Office of Facts and Figures under Archibald MacLeish, the Librarian of Congress. A poet, MacLeish became embroiled in bureaucratic struggles with government agencies, the armed services, and the Office of Strategic Services. By 1944 the government had all but abandoned its efforts to shape public opinion about the war.

Private enterprise filled the void. Movies, comic strips, newspapers, books, and advertisements reduced the war to a struggle between good and evil as the Allies engaged in mortal combat with Japan and Germany. The Japanese bore the brunt of the propaganda, especially during the first two years of fighting. Caricatured with thick glasses and huge buck teeth, public portraits of the Japanese grew more ugly and vicious as deeply ingrained racism fed the stereotypes, reviving old fears of the "yellow peril."

Germans, by contrast, elicited more complex attitudes in Americans, largely because passions were not inflamed by racism. At first, Americans blamed Hitler for the war. As eyewitness accounts of German atrocities began to filter back from the front, however, the public's views shifted. Americans

Bill Maudlin's cartoon characters, Willie and Joe, were popular not only at home but also among soldiers abroad.

gradually came to blame not just the Nazis, but all Germans, for the war.

Motion pictures emerged as the most important instrument of propaganda during World War II. After Pearl Harbor, Hollywood immediately enlisted in the war cause. The studios quickly copyrighted movie titles like "Yellow Peril" and "V for Victory." Hollywood's greatest contribution to the war effort was in the area of morale. Combat films produced during the war emphasized patriotism, group effort, and the value of sacrifice for a larger cause. They portrayed World War II as a peoples' war, typically featuring a group of men from diverse ethnic backgrounds who were thrown together, tested on the battlefield, and molded into a dedicated fighting unit. Wartime films also featured women serving as combat nurses, riveters, welders, and long-suffering mothers who kept the home fires burning.

SOCIAL CHANGES DURING THE WAR

World War II produced important changes in American life, some trivial, others profound. One striking change involved fashion. To conserve wool and cotton, dresses became shorter, and vests and cuffs disappeared, as did double-breasted suits, pleats, and ruffles.

More significant was a tremendous increase in mobility. The war set families in motion, pulling them off farms and out of small towns, and packing them into large urban areas.

War industries sparked the urban growth. Detroit's population exploded as the automotive industry switched to war vehicles. Washington, D.C., became another boomtown, as tens of thousands of new workers staffed the swelling ranks of the bureaucracy. The most dramatic growth occurred in California, however. Of the 15 million civilians who moved across state lines during the war, over 2 million went to California to work in defense industries.

Women

The war had a dramatic impact on women. Easily the most visible change involved the sudden appearance of large numbers of women in uniform. The military organized women into auxiliary units with special uniforms, their own officers, and, amazingly, equal pay. By 1945 more than 250,000 women had joined the **Women's Army Corps (WAC),** the Army Nurses Corps, the Women Accepted for Voluntary Emergency Service (WAVES), the Navy Nurses Corps, the Marines, and the Coast Guard.

Women also substituted for men on the home front. The war challenged the conventional image of female behavior, as "Rosie the Riveter" became the popular symbol of women who abandoned traditional female occupations to work in defense industries.

Women paid a price for their economic independence, though. Outside employment did not free wives from domestic duties. The same women who put in full days in offices and factories went home to cook, clean, shop, and care for children. They had not one job, but two, and the only way they could fill both was to sacrifice relaxation, recreation, and sleep. Outside employment also raised the problem of child care. A few industries, such as Kaiser Steel, offered day-care facilities, but most women had to make their own informal arrangements.

Social critics had a field day attacking women. Social workers blamed working mothers for the rise in juvenile delinquency during the war, while other critics condemned women for their immodesty, self-indulgence, drinking, dress standards, and sexual promiscuity.

Amid this confusion, many women elected to cling to the familiar by embracing the traditional roles of housewives and mothers. Between 1941 and 1945, the marriage rate reached new heights: 105 marriages per every 1000 women between the ages of 17 and 29, well above 89.1, the rate during the "normal" years of 1925 to 1929. The birthrate increased, too, rebounding

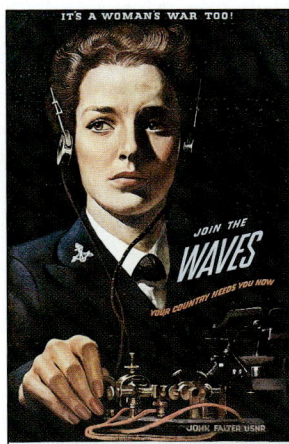

During the war, a growing number of women not only joined the armed forces but also helped out in the labor force at home by filling jobs normally held by men.

sharply from the all-time low of 18 to 19 per 1000 people during the depression. In 1943 the birthrate jumped to 22.7, and by 1946 it had reached 25, where it remained, with modest fluctuations, for the rest of the decade. Overall, the "baby boom" did not signal a return to large families; rather, the birthrate rose because women married at younger ages and had their families earlier in life.

Hasty marriages between young partners often proved brittle. Wartime separations forced newlyweds to develop new roles and become self-reliant, and many couples later found it difficult to reestablish their relationships. Rather than remain in unhappy marriages, they often opted for divorce. In 1946 the American courts granted a record 600,000 divorces. By 1950 the divorce rate stood at one quarter of the marriages, well above the prewar levels.

Yet Americans had not given up on marriage. The divorce rate had been climbing steadily (except during the depression years when many people could not afford to get married or divorced) since 1900. Furthermore, most Americans who divorced during the 1940s promptly remarried. They had rejected their mates, not marriage.

African Americans

During World War II, African Americans waged battles on two fronts. They helped the country win the war overseas and pressed for equal rights at home. African Americans called this dual struggle for victory against fascism and discrimination the "Double V" campaign. They played many critical roles in the war effort. About a million African Americans served in the armed forces during World War II, about half serving overseas. The armed forces were segregated, and many African-American soldiers complained that they were treated like prisoners of war. Nevertheless, all-black units like the famous "Tuskegee Airmen" (the 99th Pursuit Squadron), which flew combat missions in Europe; the 92nd Division, which suffered 3161 casualties in campaigns in Italy; and the 761st Tank Battalion, which fought at the Battle of the Bulge, played pivotal battlefield roles.

World War II helped reshape the nation's race relations. In 1941, the overwhelming majority of the nation's African-American population—10 out of 13 million—lived in the South, primarily in rural areas. During the war, more than one million African Americans migrated to the North and West—twice the number during World War I—and more than two million found work in defense industries. Yet African Americans continued to be the last hired and the first fired, and other forms of discrimination remained blatant, especially in housing and employment.

African-American leaders fought discrimination vigorously. In the spring of 1941 (months before America entered the war), the president of the Brotherhood of Sleeping Car Porters, A. Philip Randolph, with strong backing from the National Association for the Advancement of Colored People (NAACP), called for 150,000 people to march on Washington to protest discrimination in defense industries. Embarrassed and concerned, Roosevelt issued an executive order prohibiting discrimination in defense industries and creating the Fair Employment Practices Commission (FEPC). But the FEPC's tiny staff lacked the power and resources to enforce its decisions. During the war the FEPC did not even process most complaints, and contractors ignored 35 of the 45 compliance orders the commission issued.

African Americans fared no better in the public sector. Most African Americans in the federal bureaucracy worked as janitors, and the armed services treated its African-American soldiers as second-class citizens. The marines excluded blacks; the navy used them as servants; and the army created separate black regiments commanded mostly by white officers. The Red Cross even segregated blood plasma.

Not surprisingly, racial tensions deepened during the war. The number of African-American GIs rose from 100,000 in 1941 to 700,000 in 1944. Many joined the armed services hoping to find social mobility. Instead, they encountered segregation and discrimination. They resented white officials who denounced Nazi racism but remained silent about discrimination at home. Northern African Americans stationed in the South found race relations shocking.

Conditions in the civilian sector were no better. As urban areas swelled with defense workers, housing and transportation shortages exacerbated racial tensions. In 1943 a riot broke out in Detroit in a federally sponsored housing project. Polish Americans wanted African Americans barred from the new apartments named, ironically, in honor of Sojourner Truth, the ex-slave abolitionist and poet. White soldiers from a nearby base joined the fighting, and other federal troops had to be brought in to disperse the mobs. The violence left 35 African Americans and 9 whites dead.

Similar conflicts erupted across the nation, exposing in each instance the same jarring contradiction: white Americans espoused equality abroad but practiced discrimination at home. A 1942 survey showed that many African Americans sympathized with the Japanese struggle to expel white colonialists from the Far East. Significantly, the same survey revealed that a majority of white industrialists in the South preferred a German victory to racial equality in America.

Many African Americans responded to the rising tensions by joining civil rights organizations—during World War II, the NAACP, for example, intensified its legal campaigns against discrimination. Its membership grew from 50,000 to 500,000 as large numbers of African Americans and middle-class whites demanded racial equality.

Some African Americans, however, considered the NAACP too slow and too conciliatory. Rejecting legal action, the Congress of Racial Equality (CORE), founded in 1942, organized a series of "sit-ins." Civil disobedience produced a few victories in the North, but the South's response was brutal. While civil rights activists made few gains during World War II, they did forge new demands and tactics that would shape the civil rights movement after the war.

Federal officials did little to advance civil rights. Personally, Roosevelt sympathized with African Americans, but he feared losing the Solid South's support if he moved too rapidly on the race issue. Thus, while he admitted African-American leaders to the White House to hear their grievances, Roosevelt seldom took action. Eleanor Roosevelt remained the conscience of the administration, voicing her sympathy for civil rights at every juncture, but the president refused to take the political risks needed to end discrimination and promote racial equality.

Mexican Americans

World War II affected Mexican Americans no less than African Americans and women. Almost 400,000 Mexican Americans served in the armed forces during the war. As soldiers, they expanded their contacts with American society, for the first time visiting new parts of the country in which large groups of people held few prejudices against them. For Mexican Americans in the civilian sector, jobs in industry provided an escape hatch from the desperate poverty of migratory farm labor. In New Mexico, for example, about one-fifth of the rural Mexican American population left for war-related jobs.

The need for farm workers rose dramatically after Pearl Harbor. To meet the demand, the United States established the *bracero* (work hands) program in 1942; by 1945 several hundred thousand Mexican workers had immigrated to the Southwest. Commercial farmers welcomed them, but labor unions resented the competition, leading to animosity and discrimination against Mexicans and Mexican Americans alike.

In Los Angeles, ethnic tensions erupted into violence. White society both feared and resented newly formed Mexican-American youth gangs, whose members celebrated their ethnicity by wearing flamboyant "zoot suits" and by tattooing their left hands. In June 1943 hundreds of white sailors on liberty from nearby naval bases invaded downtown Los Angeles. Eager to put down the Mexican-American youths, they attacked the "zooters" and riots broke out for several nights. The local press blamed Mexican-American gangs, and the riots did not end until military police ordered sailors back to their ships.

Despite outbursts of violence and discrimination, World War II benefited the poor of all races. Thanks to full employment and progressive taxation, people at the bottom had income redistributed in their favor. Before the war there were 12 families with an income under $2000 for every family with an income over $5000; after the war the ratio was almost even. Still, the gains made by poor people came from the state of the economy (the need for soldiers and workers), not from federal policies or the efforts of organized labor.

Fear of Enemy Aliens

On December 8, 1941, Roosevelt issued an executive order regarding enemy aliens. It suspended naturalization proceedings for Italian, German, and Japanese immigrants, required them to register, restricted their mobility, and prohibited them from owning items that might be used for espionage and sabotage, such as cameras and shortwave radios. In practice, however, the government did not accord enemy aliens the same treatment: Italian and German aliens received lenient treatment, while Japanese aliens suffered gross injustices.

Approximately 600,000 Italian aliens lived in the United States in 1940. In general, the government treated them well throughout the war, administering the enemy alien laws with compassion. On Columbus Day, 1942 (just before the congressional elections), Roosevelt lifted the enemy alien designation for Italians and established simplified naturalization procedures. German aliens received similar treatment; though less numerous (264,000) and not as politically important to the Democrats, Roosevelt's administration treated them fairly throughout the war.

Jewish refugees complicated the German question. Reflecting a nasty strain of anti-Semitism, Congress in 1939 refused to raise immigration quotas to admit 20,000 Jewish children fleeing Nazi oppression. Instead of relaxing immigration quotas, American officials worked in vain to persuade Latin American countries and Great Britain to admit Jewish refugees. Other officials, such as Assistant Secretary of State Breckinridge Long, the chief administrator for immigration policy, insisted that winning the war offered the best means for rescuing European Jews. Bitterly anti-Semitic in his private views, Long

Location of Nazi Concentration and Death Camps

argued that any relaxation of the quota system would permit Nazi spies to slip into the country along with legitimate refugees.

While the futile debates dragged on, Hitler's death camps killed helpless victims at the rate of 2000 an hour. As late as 1944, American officials who knew the ghastly truth even publicly downplayed reports of genocide in the press.

Finally, in January 1944, Secretary of the Treasury Henry Morgenthau, forced the issue. The only Jew in the Cabinet, Morgenthau presented to Roosevelt the "Report to the Secretary on the Acquiescence of this Government in the Murder of the Jews." Shamed into action, Roosevelt created the War Refugee Board, which, in turn, set up refugee camps in Italy, North Africa, and the United States. But America's response offered too little, too late. During the 18 months of the War Refugee Board's existence, Hitler killed far more Jews than the War Refugee Board saved.

Internment of Japanese Americans

Like Jews, Japanese Americans got a bitter taste of discrimination during World War II. Barred from migrating to the United States by the Immigration Act of 1924, they comprised only a tiny portion of the population in 1941—no more than 260,000 people; 150,000 lived in Hawaii, with the remaining 110,000 concentrated on the West Coast, where they worked mostly as small farmers or businesspeople serving the Japanese community. After Pearl Harbor, rumors spread about Japanese troops preparing to land in California, where they allegedly planned to link up with Japanese Americans and Japanese aliens poised to strike as a fifth column for the invasion.

On February 19, 1942, Roosevelt authorized the Department of War to designate military areas and to exclude any or all persons from them. Armed with this power, military authorities im-

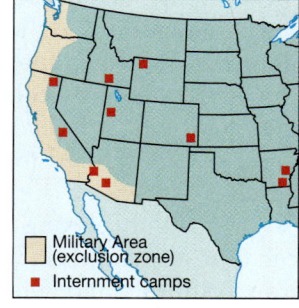

Location of Internment Camps for Japanese Americans

mediately moved against Japanese aliens. In Hawaii, where residents of Japanese ancestry formed a large portion of the population and where the local economy depended on their labor, the military did not force Japanese Americans to relocate. On the West Coast, however, military authorities ordered the Japanese to leave, making no distinction between aliens and citizens. Forced to sell their property for pennies on the dollar, most Japanese Americans suffered severe financial losses. Relocation proved next to impossible, as no other states would take them.

When voluntary measures failed, Roosevelt created the War Relocation Authority. It resettled 100,000 Japanese Americans in ten camps scattered across six western states and Arkansas called relocation camps. Resembling minimum security prisons, these concentration camps locked American citizens who had committed no crimes behind barbed wire. They were crowded into ramshackle wooden barracks where they lived one family to a room furnished with nothing but cots and bare light bulbs, forced to endure bad food, inadequate medical care, and poorly equipped schools.

Nearly 18,000 Japanese-American men won release from the camps to fight for the United States Army. Most served with the 100th Infantry Battalion and the 442nd Regimental Combat Team. In Italy, the 442nd sustained nearly 10,000 casualties, with

Japanese Americans of all ages, tagged like pieces of luggage, await their relocation to one of ten detention camps in seven states. This family was from Hayward, California.

3600 Purple Hearts, 810 Bronze Stars, 342 Silver Stars, 123 divisional citations, 47 Distinguished Service Crosses, 17 Legions of Merit, 7 Presidential Unit Citations, and 1 Congressional Medal of Honor. In short, they fought heroically for the United States, emerging as the most decorated military unit in World War II. In one of the most painful scenes in American history, Japanese-American parents, still locked inside concentration camps, received posthumous Purple Hearts for their sons.

Japanese Americans protested their treatment, claiming numerous civil rights violations. Citing national security considerations, the Supreme Court backed the government, 6 to 3, in *Korematsu* v. *United States* (1944). But in a dissenting opinion, Frank Murphy admitted federal policy had fallen "into the ugly abyss of racism." On December 18, 1944, in the *Endo* case, the Supreme Court ruled that a civilian agency, the War Relocation Authority, had no right to incarcerate law-abiding citizens. Two weeks later the federal government began closing down the camps, ending one of the most shameful chapters in American history.

THE WAR IN EUROPE

The Grand Alliance

Following Pearl Harbor, the **Axis Powers** of Germany, Japan, and Italy faced the **Grand Alliance,** composed of the United States, Great Britain, Free France, and the Soviet Union. Yet from the beginning the Grand Alliance was an uneasy coalition, born of necessity and racked with tension. Apart from the need to defeat the enemy, the Allies found it difficult to agree on anything.

Winston Churchill, Great Britain's prime minister, approached international affairs in spheres-of-influence, balance-of-power terms. He wanted to block Soviet expansion and was determined that Britain play a major role in postwar Europe. Furthermore, he wanted Britain to emerge form the war with its colonial empire intact.

France's goals reflected the vision of one man—General Charles de Gaulle, who after the fall of France in 1940 had established in London a French government-in-exile. Above all, de Gaulle wanted to restore France to greatness. By nature aloof and suspicious, he fought to retain his country's empire, and as the war progressed American officials came to regard de Gaulle as a political extremist. In policy disputes, he often sided with Britain to oppose American and Soviet demands.

Joseph Stalin spoke for the Soviet Union. The son of a cobbler, Stalin rose to power by crushing all political rivals during the turbulent years following the Bolshevik revolution. Iron-willed, deeply paranoid, and bold as a thief, "Uncle Joe" enjoyed a well-deserved reputation as a formidable negotiator. Throughout World War II, he pressed for a postwar settlement that would guarantee the Soviet Union's future security and open new lands for Communism. To protect the Soviet Union from future attacks, Stalin insisted upon Germany's total destruction. As additional insurance, he demanded parts of Poland and Finland and all of the Baltic states. Eastern Europe would then form a buffer against future aggression from the West, provide colonies for rebuilding the Soviet economy, and add new territory to the Communist world map.

Roosevelt had his own ideas about how the world should look after the war. In broad terms, he opposed colonialism and the spread of Communism; and he supported open markets, democratic elections to counter spheres of influence, and a new League of Nations to promote world peace. Among these objectives, anticolonialism and support for free markets were his top priorities, and both goals reflected Roosevelt's remarkable ability to join political principle with economic advantage.

No less than his counterparts, Roosevelt's personality shaped his policies. Because he disliked the rough and tumble of hard bargaining, he tried to avoid clashes with other leaders by postponing difficult decisions and by relying too heavily on his personal charm. In addition, Roosevelt's pragmatic approach to problem solving made him seek compromises whenever possible, which meant that he often sacrificed principles in order to preserve Allied cooperation.

From the outset, then, dissent riddled the Grand Alliance. In pursuit of its own national interests, each ally had a separate agenda, its own set of demands, and its own vision of the how the world map should look when the war ended. Given these conflicts, the Allies could look forward not to harmony but to clashes over military strategy throughout the war, bitter debates over peace terms at the war's end, and decades of international strife in the postwar era.

Early Axis Victories

For six months after Pearl Harbor, Japan looked unbeatable. Japanese forces captured Guam, Wake Island, the Philippines, Hong Kong, and Malaya and slashed deep into Burma. General Douglas MacArthur was driven from the Philippines in March 1942. In a matter of months Japanese troops had conquered a vast expanse of territory extending from the Gilbert Islands through the Solomons and from New Guinea to Burma, leaving India and Australia vulnerable to attack.

Nor did the Allied cause look any brighter in Europe. During the first ten months of 1942, German submarines sank over 500 American merchant ships. On the Russian front, German troops pressed toward Stalingrad, and in North Africa, where German Field Marshal Erwin Rommel, the famous "Desert Fox," was sweeping toward the Suez Canal, the situation seemed equally bleak. In short, 1942 opened badly for the Allies. Axis victories in the Pacific, Europe, and Africa served notice the war would be long and costly.

Stemming the German Tide

Roosevelt decided to assign Germany top priority for two reasons: First, he doubted Hitler could be dislodged from Europe if Britain fell; and, second, Roosevelt wanted to placate Stalin, whose troops were bearing the brunt of the German war machine. As the Germans drove deep into Soviet territory in 1942, Stalin demanded a second front in France to force Germany to divide her armies, thereby relieving some of the pressure on the Soviet Union.

By the autumn of 1942 the tide was beginning to turn on the eastern front. In September the Red Army won a key victory at Stalingrad. Then the Soviets launched a furious counterattack, beginning the long drive to push the Germans back across the Ukraine. Despite Soviet victories and Stalin's repeated pleas for a second front, the Allies, at Churchill's insistence, decided to attack the Germans in North Africa instead of France. Stalin saw this as a betrayal and his suspicions deepened.

Allied victories in Africa seemed to confirm Churchill's wisdom. British Field Marshal Sir Bernard Montgomery drove the Germans back to Tunis in October, and in November 1942 General Dwight D. Eisenhower led a force of 400,000 Allied soldiers in a full-scale invasion of North Africa. Complete victory in North Africa came on May 12, 1943, when the remnants of the Axis armies surrendered. Germany and Italy had both suffered a major defeat and Allied shipping could now cross the Mediterranean in safety.

Cheered by North African victories, Churchill and Roosevelt met in Casablanca, French Morocco, in January 1943. Stalin did not attend, explaining he could not leave the Soviet Union at this critical juncture of the war. Haunted by ghastly memories of World War I and fearing a premature invasion of France might bog down into trench-style warfare, Churchill pushed hard for an attack on Sicily and then Italy. The United States initially opposed the plan, arguing it would delay the invasion of France, but Churchill prevailed. With the promised invasion of France again put on hold, Churchill and Roosevelt moved to reassure Stalin. Vowing publicly to make peace with the Axis powers only on the basis of unconditional surrender, the two leaders also renewed their pledge to open a second front.

Sicily fell in August 1943 after a campaign of slightly more than a month. Victory in Italy, however, did not come cheaply. The terrain was mountainous, and the Germans offered savage resistance. Stalin deeply resented the commitment of Allied troops there, which further postponed the long-promised second front in France. Moreover, since Soviet troops had not fought in the Italian campaign, Roosevelt and Churchill did not allow Stalin to participate in organizing an occupation government there. The next time Stalin wanted a voice in a region he made certain to have his armies on site.

Liberating Europe

In November 1943 Roosevelt, Churchill, and Stalin held their first face-to-face conference, meeting in Teheran, the capital of Iran. Buoyed by military success, Stalin sounded conciliatory as they discussed a second front. The leaders set May 1944 as the target date for Operation OVERLORD, the code name for the invasion of France. To increase the odds for success, Stalin promised to coordinate Russia's spring offensive with the invasion.

Once the leaders turned to postwar issues, however, the conference dissolved into bitter controversy. Stalin demanded Soviet control over Eastern Europe and insisted Germany be divided into several weak states. Opposing both demands, Churchill proposed democratic governments for Eastern Europe, especially in Poland, for which England had gone to war, and argued that the balance of power in postwar Europe required a united Germany. Roosevelt, on the other hand, knew Stalin had the inside track in Eastern Europe. Convinced he could handle "Uncle Joe," Roosevelt decided to leave territorial questions to a postwar international organization dominated by the victors. Apart from reaching agreement on the second front, the Teheran Conference merely aired the leaders' conflicting demands.

In preparation for the invasion, the Allies instituted saturation bombing German territory. They dropped 2,697,473 tons of bombs, killing 305,000 civilians and damaging over 5.5 million homes. The air raids were supposed to wipe out the German war machine and break the people's will to resist, but missions such as the firebombing of Dresden, which killed 100,000 people, convinced many Germans that Hitler's ravings about the evil Allies were true, and that stiffened their will to fight.

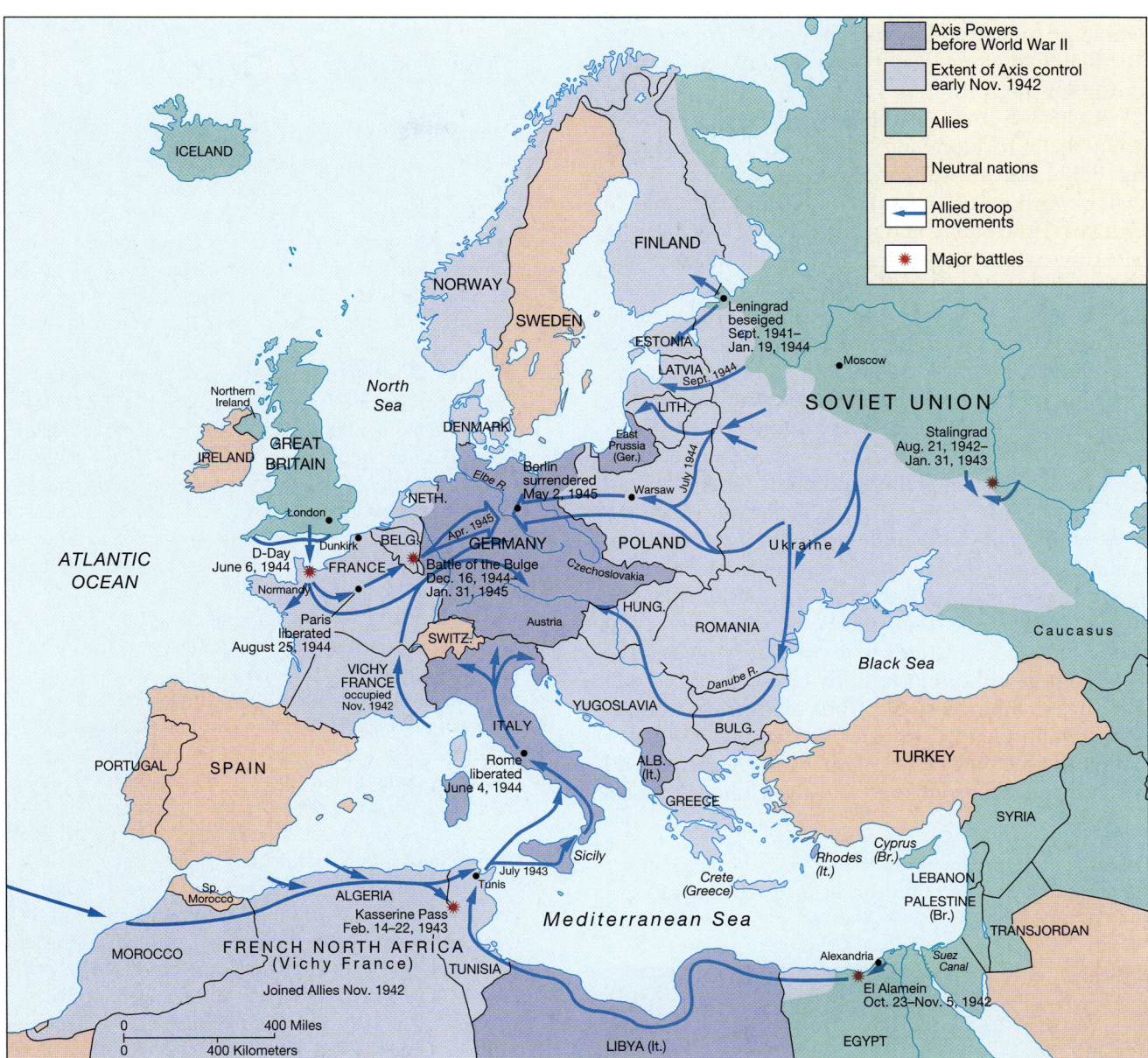

World War II, European Theater

As the bombers pounded Germany the Allies prepared for the invasion of France, massing more than 3 million soldiers in England under the command of General Dwight D. Eisenhower. **D-Day** came on June 6, 1944. After two weeks of desperate fighting on the beaches of Normandy, the Allies began to push inland. A month later Allied troops were sweeping across Europe in a race for Berlin. They liberated Paris in August, and by mid-September Allied forces had crossed the German border. True to his word, Stalin synchronized his spring offensive with the invasion. Soviet troops engaged the Germans in furious combat all across Eastern Europe, tying up men and materials that otherwise could have been hurled against the Allies.

On December 16, 1944, German troops launched a massive counteroffensive. In the Battle of the Bulge, German armored divisions slashed 60 miles to the Franco-Belgian border before being defeated by General George Patton's Third Army. By January 1945 Soviet troops had captured Warsaw, and by February they were within 45 miles of Berlin.

The Yalta Conference

With victory in Europe at hand, Roosevelt, Churchill, and Stalin met in February 1945 at **Yalta**, on the Black Sea, to settle the shape of the postwar world. They concurred on the partition of Germany, but there the agreement stopped. Stalin wanted $20 billion in reparation payments from Germany, half of which would go to Russia. Churchill opposed him, rejecting any plan that would leave Germany financially prostrate after the war.

Eastern Europe was the most divisive issue at Yalta. Stalin had long insisted on Soviet control over the Baltic states (Estonia, Lithuania, and Latvia), as well as portions of Finland, Poland, and Romania. In October 1944 Stalin and Churchill met secretly in Moscow, where they agreed to divide Eastern Europe into British and Soviet spheres for the duration of the war. Consistent with these earlier demands, Stalin laid claim to eastern Poland at the **Yalta Conference,** reminding Churchill and Roosevelt that since he had not opposed their political decisions in Italy, he would not tolerate any interference in Eastern Europe. Under pressure from Roosevelt and Churchill, however, Stalin grudgingly agreed to hold free elections in Poland itself, promising that any new government formed there would include democratic elements. Yet as one of Roosevelt's chief military advisers warned the president, Stalin tacked so many amendments onto the Polish agreement that the Soviets "could stretch it all the way from Yalta to Washington without technically breaking it."

The remaining issues at Yalta proved less troublesome. Stalin pledged to enter the war against Japan within three months after Germany surrendered, and he renewed his promise to join the United Nations.

Stalin, Roosevelt, and Churchill at their meeting at Yalta in February 1945 to discuss the state of the postwar world.

LANDINGS ON D-DAY

The Longest Day

For the Allies in World War II, the D-Day landing on June 6, 1944, was the long-planned, long-anticipated blow against Nazi Germany. Originally scheduled for 1942, it had been pushed back first to 1943 and finally to 1944. Although both the Soviet Union and impatient Americans had clamored for an earlier invasion, Prime Minister Winston Churchill of Great Britain, who remembered the difficulties of Dunkirk, counseled caution.

The cross-channel invasion was a risky proposition and an immense undertaking. During early 1944, the Allies moved thousands of aircraft, tanks, trucks, jeeps, and men into southeastern England, moving soldiers to joke that if the invasion was long postponed, England would tilt and sink into the Channel. Then there were the imponderables no amount of careful planning could predict: weather, visibility, the state of the Channel.

As much as possible General Dwight D. Eisenhower, who was the overall commander of the invasion, tried to deceive the Germans into believing that the invasion would take place at the Pas de Calais, around Boulogne, Calais, and Dunkirk. It appears that Hitler did believe that the Allies would strike there. Instead, Ike centered his attack further to the west, along the French coast between Cherbourg and Le Havre. Altogether, the Allies assaulted five beaches and dropped paratroopers and airborne infantry into three sites.

Further east, British paratroopers were given the task of securing the left flank by gaining control of the Orne River. American paratroopers were given the job of securing the right flank along the Merderet River. In between these two points, the Allies landed on five beaches: Sword (British), Juno (Canadian), Gold (British), Omaha (American), and Utah (American). All totaled, 2,876,000 soldiers, sailors, and airmen; 11,000 aircraft; and over 2000 vessels played a part in the invasion.

At several beaches, especially Utah, the Allies met little opposition. At others, notably Omaha, the story was much different and losses were heavy. More than 2000 Americans were killed or wounded securing Omaha beach on June 6. But by the end of that "longest day" the Allies had accomplished their goal. They were back in France and ready to move east toward Germany.

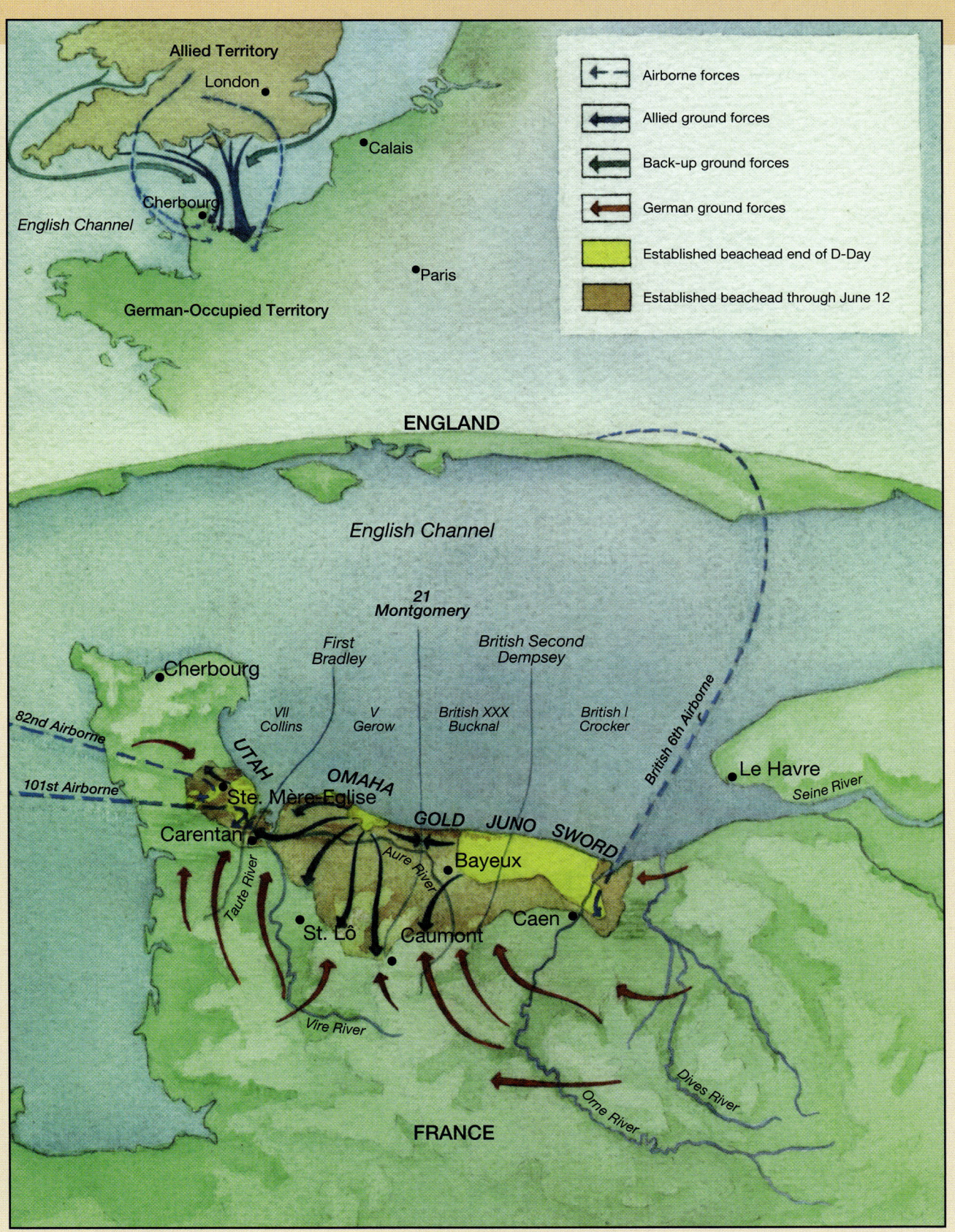

Roosevelt considered both concessions to be important victories because he wanted Soviet help in defeating Japan and because he remained hopeful the United Nations could negotiate peaceful solutions to the disputes between the United States and the Soviet Union after the war.

Critics have denounced Roosevelt for his role at Yalta, insisting Stalin would have surrendered Eastern Europe had Roosevelt held firm. This argument seriously discounts Stalin's obsession with protecting his homeland from future attacks. The Soviet Union had paid a staggeringly high price for victory in World War II. When the war finally ended, the country had suffered approximately 18 million military and civilian deaths. Stalin's determination to maintain Soviet control of Eastern Europe was also bolstered by the fact that the Red Army occupied Eastern Europe in the spring of 1945. Stalin was not about to lose at the conference table what he had won on the battlefield.

Allied victories came rapidly after the Battle of the Bulge. On March 4, American troops reached the Rhine River, and in April they joined forces with the Soviet army 60 miles south of Berlin. After Roosevelt's death on April 12, however, Stalin immediately tested the new president, Harry S Truman. Stalin ordered the execution of democratic leaders in Eastern Europe and replaced them with Communist governments. Truman deplored Stalin's disregard for the Yalta agreements, but like Roosevelt he refused to fight the Soviets to save Eastern Europe. Instead, he followed General Eisenhower's advice about finishing off Germany. On April 22 Soviet troops reached Berlin and occupied the city after house-to-house fighting, and on April 30 Hitler committed suicide. Germany surrendered one week later. On May 8, 1945, the Allies celebrated V-E (Victory in Europe) Day.

THE WAR IN THE PACIFIC

On December 7, 1941, Japan had launched an offensive incredible in its scale. A thousand Japanese warships attacked an area comprising one-third of the earth's surface, including Guam, Hong Kong, Malaya, Midway Island, the Philippine Islands, and

World War II, Pacific Theater

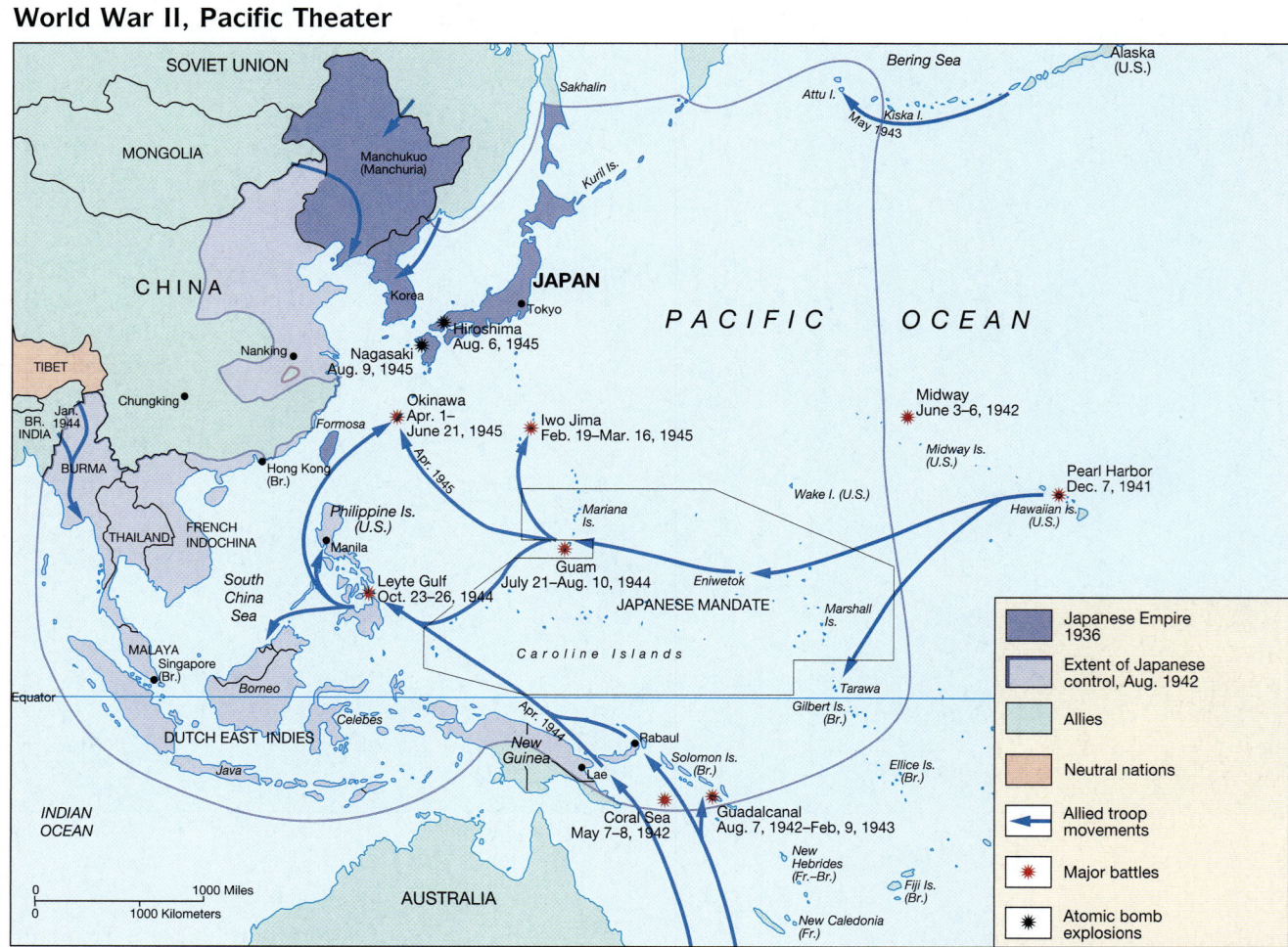

Wake Island. The offensive was a stunning success. Hong Kong was overrun in 18 days; Wake Island in two weeks; Singapore held out for two months. By May, the Japanese had also captured the islands of Borneo, Bali, Sumatra, and Timor. In addition, Japan had taken Rangoon, Burma's main port, and seized control of the rich tin, oil, and rubber resources of southeast Asia.

But by mid-summer of 1942, American forces had halted the Japanese advance. In May, a Japanese troop convoy was intercepted and destroyed by the U.S. Navy at Coral Sea, preventing a Japanese attack on Australia. In early June, at Midway Island in the Central Pacific, the Japanese launched an aircraft carrier offensive to cut American communications and isolate Hawaii to the east. In a three-day naval battle the Japanese lost three destroyers, a heavy cruiser, and four carriers. The Battle of Midway broke the back of Japan's navy.

Island Hopping

On August 7, 1942, the 1st Marine Division attacked Guadalcanal in the Solomon Islands; after six months of hard fighting they drove the Japanese troops into the sea, securing the Allied supply line to Australia. The victory also protected the Allies' eastern flank, enabling General Douglas MacArthur, commander of southwest Pacific forces, to seize the northern coast of nearby New Guinea in September 1943. Instead of assaulting Japanese strong points on the island, MacArthur leapfrogged up the coast. By capturing isolated positions, MacArthur cut Japanese supply lines and forced Japanese troops to abandon their fortifications. By July 1944 MacArthur's forces controlled all of New Guinea.

Meanwhile, Admiral Chester Nimitz's naval and marine forces in the Central Pacific were "island hopping" toward Japan, capturing important positions, building airstrips, and then moving on to the next island. After securing the Gilbert Islands and the Marshall Islands, Nimitz attacked Saipan, Tinian, and Guam, from which the Americans could strike the main Japanese islands with B-29 bombers. Determined to protect their homeland against air raids, Japanese commanders resolved to fight to the last man. In the battle for Saipan, 30,000 of the island's 32,000 Japanese defenders died, and 6000 of the island's 12,000 Japanese civilians committed suicide rather than surrender. Tinian and Guam fell to the Americans in early August, and B-29s began regular bombing raids over Japan in November 1944.

On October 21, 1944, General MacArthur invaded the Philippines. That same month the navy won a stunning victory at the Battle of Leyte Gulf,

On October 21, 1944, General Douglas MacArthur, commander of the Southeast Pacific forces, splashed ashore in the Philippines with the 96th division.

where the Japanese lost virtually their entire remaining battle fleet. American submarines now controlled Pacific shipping lanes, sealing the Japanese Islands off from military and food supplies. In January, Allied forces invaded Luzon, the main island of the Philippines, and Allied troops claimed victory five months later.

While MacArthur was reclaiming the Philippines, the American island-hopping strategy was entering its final phase. By early March the island of Iwo Jima fell to U.S. marines. Its capture enabled fighter planes to link up with B-29s heading out of Saipan, providing escorts for their raids on Japan. On April 1, 1945, American troops attacked Okinawa, 350 miles southwest of Japan. Japanese resistance was fierce. Kamikaze attacks (suicide flights by Japanese pilots) rose dramatically. Okinawa fell in June, after 70,000 Japanese soldiers had died defending it. In the meantime, B-29s firebombed Japan, killing more than 330,000 civilians and cutting deeply into war production.

Confronted with certain defeat, many moderate leaders in Japan wanted to avoid an invasion, but strong factions within the military vowed to keep fighting. In an effort to save Japan, the Emperor switched his support to the peace party in February 1945. He then sent out peace feelers to Stalin, who in turn conveyed them to Truman at the Potsdam Conference in July 1945.

The Dawn of The Atomic Age

Few presidents have been asked to conduct diplomacy with less preparation than Harry S Truman.

THE American Mosaic

Hiroshima and Nagasaki

ON July 16, 1945, the Atomic Age became reality. The place was Alamogordo Air Force Base in the southern desert region of New Mexico. The occasion was the first successful detonation of an atomic bomb. Observers witnessed "a blinding flash that lighted the entire northwestern sky." Next came "a huge billow of smoke," followed by "an enormous ball of what appeared to be fire and closely resembled a rising sun." Dr. J. Robert Oppenheimer, the chief scientist in charge of the team that designed the weapon, was so astonished by the scale of the blast that he recalled the Hindu quotation: "I am become death, shatterer of worlds."

Back in 1939 two brilliant scientists, Albert Einstein and Enrico Fermi, both of whom had fled fascism and anti-Semitism in Europe, warned President Roosevelt that German nuclear physicists under Adolf Hitler's control might well be trying to develop such a bomb. Roosevelt realized the implications, and he set in motion what became the "Manhattan Project," a top-secret effort involving civilian scientists and army engineers to apply the theory of nuclear fission to a bomb. Hitler's scientists never succeeded, but in July 1945, with the war over in Europe, the United States now had a weapon with the potential to threaten civilization itself. The question was whether the bomb would be used against Japan, the last of the Axis powers still at war.

The Japanese were a formidable foe. Since 1942 U.S. troops had been rolling back their empire, all the way to the shore of Japan and the Chinese mainland by the summer of 1945. The casualty toll was horrendous. Japanese soldiers fought with a sense of personal honor that struck Americans as fanatical. They would not surrender when beaten but would fight to their death. To do otherwise would be to disgrace themselves, their families, and their emperor, whom they considered a god.

At first, in defending Pacific islands such as Guadalcanal (August 1942–February 1943), Japanese soldiers mounted suicidal *banzai* charges. They ran forward in waves at U.S. troops, inflicting massive damage before being shot down. Later, on islands such as Iwo Jima (February–March 1945), they used elaborate networks of underground bunkers to wreak havoc, so effectively that U.S. casualties started to reach the 50 percent range. By 1945 the Japanese were unleashing kamikaze raids in which pilots sacrificed themselves for the glory of the empire by dive-bombing their planes into U.S. naval vessels. In the bloody battle of Okinawa (April–June 1945), kamikaze pilots flew some 2800 planes into American ships, inflicting 10,000 casualties and sinking 28 vessels and damaging 325 others.

American soldiers, as well as the U.S. public at large, neither understood nor respected Japanese martial values. Explained a Marine Corps general, to shoot "a Jap . . . was like killing a rattlesnake." A Guadalcanal veteran stated that the Japanese soldier "possessed considerable cleverness; he could not be classified as an intellectual. He was more of an animal. He could live on a handful of rice." Almost universally, Americans used terms of racial derision to describe an enemy that had not only mounted the "sneak attack" on Pearl Harbor but now refused to surrender when beaten.

Such attitudes affected the development of a comprehensive U.S. war plan, known as Operation DOWNFALL, that was constructed on the assumption that only a full-scale invasion of Japan would bring total victory in the Pacific. The first phase of the plan, called Operation OLYMPIC, involved an assault on Kyushu, the southernmost island of Japan, to begin in November 1945. The Joint Chiefs of Staff presented OLYMPIC to President Truman in June and stated that American casualties could reach 268,000 (out of 767,000 participants). The Japanese still had 2.3 million soldiers ready to fight and another 4 million citizens trained in the use of arms. If they battled to the death, as they had so far, American casualties, the Joint Chiefs predicted, would exceed 1 million by the time U.S. troops conquered the main island of Honshu in 1946 or 1947.

Because of the bloody price everyone expected to pay, high-ranking American officials were anxious to involve Russia—attacking through Manchuria and Korea—in the final crushing of Japan. At Yalta in February 1945 President Roosevelt secured pledges of Soviet assistance. Then at Potsdam in July, President Truman seemed much less interested. Having just learned of the test results in New Mexico, Truman told Joseph Stalin of "a new weapon of unusual destructive force." Stalin, however, would not be cast aside. He still wanted the territory (the lower half of Sakhalin Island, the Kurile Islands, and certain considerations in Manchuria) promised at Yalta. The Soviet leader thus "hoped" the United States "would make good use" of the weapon "against the Japanese," but the Russians would not be denied their part in the invasion or the promised territory.

Meanwhile, a committee of American scientists and military officers were working at selecting possible targets. Some advocated a demonstration at a preannounced neutral site as a way of cajoling the Japanese into sur-

render, but others feared what might happen should the bomb prove to be a dud—all leverage would then be lost. Finally, with great reluctance, these advisers agreed that there was "no acceptable alternative to direct military use" of the bomb.

In public, Truman never admitted to any qualms about the decision to employ the new weapon, but in private, he wondered how "we as the leader of the world for common welfare" could drop "this terrible bomb." Still, he accepted the responsibility for many reasons. He hoped to save thousands of American lives by avoiding a full invasion of Japan against soldiers who fought like "savages, ruthless, merciless, and fanatic." Likely, too, Truman and his advisers feared the expansionism of the Communist regime of Joseph Stalin. Using the bomb might prove a great point of leverage in dealing with the Soviets in the days ahead.

While Truman and others considered the alternatives, a select unit of the Army Air Force, flying B-29s, made a series of practice bomb runs over Japan. Since these planes did not attack, as they had so often before in firebombing cities like Tokyo, no one paid much attention. Then on August 6, 1945, at a few minutes past 8:00 A.M., three B-29s at 31,600 feet of altitude appeared over Hiroshima. Colonel Paul Tibbets, piloting the lead bomber, *Enola Gay*, turned the controls over to Major Thomas Ferebee, the bombardier officer, who completed the run. It took 45 seconds, as *Enola Gay* banked away quickly, for the atomic bomb to reach the ground. As the fireball erupted toward the sky, nearly 100,000 people, including thousands of soldiers at the headquarters of Japan's Second General Army just 2000 yards from ground zero, died instantly. Three days later, in the absence of a firm willingness of the Japanese to surrender, a second bomb flattened Nagasaki and killed about 35,000 people. Thousands more perished later from serious burns, radiation poisoning, and other devastating effects of the two bombings.

The dropping of the atomic bombs gave peace advocates in Japan the muscle they needed to overcome the militarists. When on August 10 Emperor Hirohito agreed to seek peace terms, the war faction reluctantly acceded, but only after General Anami Korechika, the war minister, upheld his honor on August 14 by committing suicide. He could not bear hearing Hirohito's proclamation of surrender.

When American troops training for Operation OLYMPIC heard about the surrender, they rejoiced. "We would not be obliged to run up the beaches near Tokyo assault-firing while being mortared and shelled," wrote one soldier. "We are going to live. We are going to grow up to adulthood after all." They did not realize how different the world would be with nuclear weapons in the hands of the two superpowers to emerge from World War II. For a moment, however, General Douglas MacArthur understood. After the Japanese surrender ceremony on September 2, 1945, he stated: "We have had our last chance. If we do not devise some greater and more equitable system, Armageddon will be at our door."

THE PEOPLE SPEAK

That Day at Hiroshima

Alexander Leighton, research leader of a Morale Division team from the U.S. Strategic Bombing Survey, arrived in Hiroshima in December of 1945, four months after the explosion of the atomic bomb. Most allied leaders regarded the atomic weapons as mere bombs, but from Leighton's account, the bombs that devastated Hiroshima and Nagasaki possessed more destructive power than could be imagined.

> . . . About seven o'clock on the morning of August 6 there was an air-raid warning and three planes were reported in the vicinity. No one was much disturbed. For a long time B-29s flying over in small numbers had been a common site. At some future date, Hiroshima might suffer an incendiary raid from masses of planes such as had devastated other Japanese cities. With this possibility in mind there had been evacuations, and firebreaks were being prepared. But on this particular morning there could be no disaster from just three planes.
>
> By 7:30 the "all clear" had sounded and people were thinking again of the day's plans, looking forward to their affairs and engagements of the morning and afternoon. The castle keep stood in the sun. Children bathed in the river. Farmers labored in the fields and fishermen on the water. City stores and factories got under way with their business.
>
> In the heart of the city near the buildings of the Prefectural Government and at the intersection of the busiest streets, everybody had stopped and stood in a crowd gasping up at three parachutes floating down through the blue air.
>
> The bomb exploded several hundred feet above their heads.
>
> The people for miles around Hiroshima, in fields, in the mountains, and on the bay, saw a light that was brilliant even in the sun, and felt heat. A countrywoman was going out to her farm when suddenly, "I saw a light reflected on the mountain and then a streak just like lightning came. . . ."
>
> In the heart of the city death prevailed and few were left to tell us about it. That part of the picture has to be reconstructed, as in archaeology, from the remains.
>
> The crowd that stood gazing upward at the parachutes went down withered and black, like a burned-out patch of weeds. Flames shot out of the castle keep. Trolleys bulging with passengers stopped, and all died at once, leaving burned figures standing supporting each other and fingers fused to the straps. The military at their barracks and offices were wiped out. So too were factories full of workers, including students from schools, volunteers from neighboring towns working on the firebreaks, children scavenging for wood, the Mayor's staff, and the units for air-raid precaution, fire, welfare, and relief. The larger war industries, since they were on the fringe of the city, were for the most part not seriously damaged. Most of the personnel in the Prefectural Government offices were killed, though the Governor himself happened to be in Tokyo. In hospitals and clinics, patients, doctors, and nurses all died together, as did the priests and pastors of the temples and churches. Of 1780 nurses, 1654 were

He had risen to power as a loyal machine politician in Kansas City. Both as vice president and former senator from Missouri he knew next to nothing about foreign affairs, especially since Roosevelt kept him in the dark, neither seeking his counsel nor confiding in him. When Roosevelt's death elevated him to the White House, Truman told reporters: "I felt like the moon, the stars, and all planets had fallen on me." Yet Truman brought certain assets to the challenge. A man who possessed the courage of his convictions, he fully intended to be a strong president and to make decisions resolutely.

Truman's first test came at Potsdam, a suburb of Berlin, where the Allied leaders convened in July 1945 for their last wartime meeting. Though new to the job, Truman had been in office long enough to believe Roosevelt had been too soft on Stalin, whom he viewed as a liar and a bully. Yet like his predecessor Truman did not wish to risk a showdown over Eastern Europe, largely because his military advisers insisted the United States still needed the Soviet Union's help against Japan. The Potsdam Declaration of July 26 demanded immediate "unconditional surrender," warning that any other action would lead to "prompt and utter destruction."

During the Potsdam negotiations, Truman learned that American scientists had successfully tested the first atomic bomb. Hoping to impress Stalin, Truman told him in a conversation one evening the United States now possessed a new weapon of awesome power. Stalin blithely replied he trusted the United States would make good use of it against Japan.

The Manhattan Project

In 1939, Albert Einstein wrote a letter to President Roosevelt, warning him that the Nazis might be able to build a weapon with incredible destructive potential: an atomic bomb. The idea seemed impossible,

killed, and 90 percent of the doctors in Hiroshima were casualties. . . .

People who were in buildings that sheltered them from the instantaneous effects that accompanied the flash were moments later decapitated or cut to ribbons by flying glass. Others were crushed as walls and floors gave way even in buildings that maintained their outer shells erect. In the thousands of houses that fell, people were pinned below the wreckage, not killed in many cases, but held there till the fire that swept the city caught up with them and put an end to their screams. . . .

A doctor who was at a military hospital outside Hiroshima said that about an hour after the bomb went off, "many, many people came rushing to my clinic. They were rushing in all directions of the compass from the city. Many were stretcher cases. Some had their hair burned off, were injured in the back, had broken legs, arms, and thighs. The majority of the cases were those injured from glass; many had glass imbedded in the body. Next to the glass injuries, the most frequent were those who had their faces and hands burned, and also the chest and back. Most of the people arrived barefooted; many had their clothes burned off. Women were wearing men's clothing and men were wearing women's. They had put on anything they could pick up along the way. . . ."

Hiroshima, of course, never had been prepared for a disaster of the magnitude which overtook it, but in addition the organized sources of aid that did exist were decimated along with everything else. As a result, rescue had to come from surrounding areas, and soon trucks and trains were picking up the wounded, while hospitals, schools, temples, assembly halls, and tents were preparing to receive them. However, the suburbs and surrounding areas were overwhelmed by the rush of immediate survivors out of the bombed region and so, for about a day, help did not penetrate far into the city. This, together with the fact that survivors who were physically uninjured were stunned and bewildered, resulted in great numbers of the wounded dying from lack of aid.

The vice-mayor of a neighboring town that began receiving the wounded about 11:30 in the morning said, "Everybody looked alike. The eyes appeared to be a mass of melted flesh. The lips were split up and also looked like a mass of molten flesh. Only the nose appeared the same as before. The death scene was awful. The patient would turn blue and when we touched the body the skin would stick to our hands. . . ."

The wife of a soldier who had been with the Hiroshima troops said, "My husband was a soldier and so he was to die, but when it actually happened, I wondered why we did not all go with him. They called me and I went to see. I was to find him in the heap, but I decided against looking at the bodies. I want to remember him as he was—big and healthy, not some horribly charred body. If I saw that it would remain forever in my eyes. . . ."

The destroyed heart of Hiroshima consisted of 4.7 square miles, and the best estimates indicate that the mortality rate was 15,000 to the square mile. For many days funeral processions moved along the roads and through the towns and villages all around Hiroshima. The winds were pervaded by the smell of death and cremating. At night the skies were lit with the flames of funeral pyres. . . .

Source: Alexander Leighton, "That Day in Hiroshima" in the *Atlantic Monthly,* October 1946. Reprinted by permission of Alexander Leighton.

---

and at first scientists worked on the project largely on their own. Then on December 2, 1942, Enrico Fermi, an Italian refugee, demonstrated that it was possible to produce a nuclear chain reaction. In an old squash court beneath the University of Chicago's football field, he built the world's first nuclear reactor. Fermi's reactor produced the first self-sustained, controlled nuclear chain reaction.

To ensure that the United States developed a bomb before Nazi Germany, the federal government started the **Manhattan Project,** a secret $2-billion program with 120,000 employees. At Los Alamos, New Mexico; Oak Ridge, Tennessee; and Hanford, Washington, the world's top physicists—including many Jewish refugees from Germany—worked in secrecy to develop the new weapon.

At dawn on July 16, 1945, in the New Mexico desert near Alamogordo, the Manhattan Project's scientists watched the first atomic bomb explode. There was a blinding flash of pink, blue, red, and yellow light. The heat generated by the bomb at that instant was ten thousand times hotter than the sun. The explosion broke windows 125 miles away.

President Harry S Truman had never heard of the Manhattan Project until he was sworn in. It was during the Potsdam negotiations that he learned that American scientists had tested the first atomic bomb. Many scientists who worked on the Manhattan Project, as well as several key political figures, pleaded with Truman not to use the bomb because they foresaw its implications for a postwar arms race with the Soviet Union. Others, arguing from a moral position, wanted the United States to warn the Japanese about the bomb's terrifying power, giving them a chance to surrender. Truman rejected these arguments and approved the use of the new weapon.

Hiroshima and Nagasaki

On the morning of August 6, 1945, the *Enola Gay,* a B-29 Superfortress, took off from a tiny Pacific atoll bound for Hiroshima, Japan's eighth-largest city. At 8:15 A.M., the plane released an atomic bomb nicknamed "Little Boy." The explosion when it hit began as a pinpoint of light that grew into a fireball half a mile across. A cloud of smoke rose upward, gradually assuming the shape of a giant mushroom 50,000 feet high.

On the ground, 4.7 square miles of central Hiroshima was obliterated. Buildings melted, steel bridges burned, the city's river caught fire. Peoples' shadows were photographed onto walls and sidewalks. Black rain containing radioactive dust fell on the city, leaving red splotches on the bodies it touched. Between 80,000 and 140,000 people were killed or fatally wounded.

Three days later, on August 9, another B-29, the *Bock's Car*, dropped a second bomb, this time on the city of Nagasaki. About 35,000 people were killed. The following day Japan sued for peace. On September 2, 1945, Japanese officials surrendered unconditionally to General Douglas MacArthur aboard the battleship U.S.S. *Missouri* in Tokyo Bay. World War II was over.

President Truman's decision to order the atomic bombings has been the subject of intense historical debate. Truman's defenders argue that the bombs ended the war quickly, avoiding the necessity of a costly invasion and the probable loss of tens of thousands of Americans lives and hundreds of thousands of Japanese lives. According to some intelligence estimates, an invasion might have cost 268,000 American casualties, with Japanese costs several times that figure.

Truman's defenders also argue that Hiroshima and Nagasaki were legitimate targets with both military bases and war industry, and their civilian populations had been showered with leaflets warning them to evacuate. Finally, they argue that two bombs were ultimately necessary to end the war. They note that even after the atomic bomb had fallen on Hiroshima, the Japanese war minister implored the nation's Supreme Council "for one last great battle on Japanese soil—as demanded by the national honor. . . . Would it not be wondrous for this whole nation to be destroyed like a beautiful flower."

Truman's critics argue that the war might have ended even without the atomic bombings. They maintain that the Japanese economy would have been strangled by a continued naval blockade and forced to surrender by conventional firebombing. The revisionists also contend that the president had options apart from using the bombs. They believe that it might have been possible to induce a Japanese surrender by a demonstration of the atomic bomb's power or by providing a more specific warning of the damage it could produce or by guaranteeing the Emperor's position in postwar Japan.

The revisionists also believe that estimates of potential American casualties were grossly inflated after the war to justify the bombing. And finally, they argue that the bomb might have been dropped mainly to justify its cost or to scare the Soviet Union. The Soviet Union entered the Japanese war August 8, and some revisionists charge that the bombings were designed to end the war before the Red army could occupy northern China.

The bomb dropped on Hiroshima on August 6, 1945, marked the first use of a nuclear weapon in warfare. The bomb, carrying a destructive force equal to 20,000 tons of TNT, obliterated nearly 60 percent of the city.

THE ROAD TO WAR

WORLD WAR II

1939	Germany invades Poland	World War II begins.
	Neutrality Act of 1939	Allows the sale of arms to belligerents.
1940	Arms sales to Britain	The U.S. agrees to sell Britain surplus and outmoded arms.
	Destroyers for bases	The U.S. gives 50 American destroyers to Britain in exchange for British bases in the Western Hemisphere.
	Embargo imposed	President Roosevelt imposes an embargo on the export of scrap steel and iron to Japan.
	Draft instituted	The military draft goes into effect.
	"Arsenal of Democracy"	President Roosevelt announces that the U.S. will be the "arsenal of democracy."
1941	Lend-Lease	President Roosevelt signs the Lend-Lease Act empowering the president to lend war materiel to countries whose freedom is vital to U.S. interests.
	Assets frozen	President Roosevelt freezes assets of Germany, Italy, and Japan in the United States and closes German and Italian consulates.
	Pearl Harbor attacked	Japanese forces attack the naval base at Pearl Harbor, Hawaii, killing 2403 Americans, sinking or disabling 19 ships, and destroying some 150 planes.
	Declaration of war	Declaring December 7 "a date that shall live in infamy," President Roosevelt asks Congress to declare war against Japan. Germany declares war on the United States on December 11, 1941.

CONCLUSION

Fifty years after the United States brought World War II to an end by dropping two atomic bombs on Japan, a major public controversy erupted over plans to exhibit the fuselage of the *Enola Gay* at the Smithsonian Institution's Air and Space Museum. As originally conceived, the exhibit, titled "The Last Act: The Atomic Bomb and the End of World War II," was designed to provoke debate about the decision to drop atomic bombs. Museum visitors would be encouraged to reflect on the morality of the bombing and to ask whether the bombs were necessary to end the war.

The proposal generated a firestorm of controversy. The part of the script that produced the most opposition stated: "For most Americans, this ... was a war of vengeance. For most Japanese it was a war to defend their unique culture against Western imperialism." Another controversial section addressed the question: "Would the bomb have been dropped on the Germans?" The answer began "Some have argued that the United States would never have dropped the bomb on the Germans, because Americans were more reluctant to bomb 'white people' than Asians."

Veterans groups considered the proposed exhibit too sympathetic to the Japanese, that it portrayed them as victims of racist Americans hell-bent on revenge for Pearl Harbor. They called the exhibit an insult to the U.S. soldiers who fought and died during the war and complained that it paid excessive attention to Japanese casualties and suffering and insufficient attention to Japanese aggression and atrocities. The U.S. Senate unanimously passed a resolution calling a revised version of the exhibit "unbalanced

Chronology of Key Events

1921 Washington Naval Conference places limits on construction of large warships

1922 Mussolini seizes power in Italy

1924 Dawes Plan to help Germany pay war reparations

1928 Kellogg-Briand Pact renounces war "as an instrument of national policy"; Clark Memorandum states that the United States does not have a right to intervene militarily in the affairs of Latin American nations

1931 Japan invades Manchuria

1932 Stimson Doctrine declares that the United States would not recognize Japanese territorial gains in China

1933 Adolf Hitler is appointed chancellor of Germany; Roosevelt announces Good Neighbor Policy, withdraws marines from Haiti, and nullifies Platt Amendment

1935 Neutrality Act allows president to bar arms sales to nations at war (is extended in 1936 to bar loans to belligerents and in 1937 to bar shipments of nonmilitary goods)

1936 German troops reoccupy the Rhineland; Spanish Civil War begins

1937 Japan invades China

1938 Germany annexes Austria; Munich Pact hands over a third of Czechoslovakia to Nazi Germany

1939 Soviet Union and Germany sign a nonaggression pact; World War II begins following Germany's invasion of Poland

1940 United States transfers 50 destroyers to Britain in exchange for bases in Newfoundland and the Caribbean; United States institutes first peacetime military draft; Roosevelt is elected to third term

1941 Lend-Lease Act allows United States to lend war materials to Britain; Roosevelt issues order prohibiting discrimination in defense industries; Germany invades USSR; United States sets embargo on scrap metal, oil, and fuel to Japan; Japan attacks Pearl Harbor, killing over 2400 U.S. soldiers and sailors; United States enters World War II

1942 Congress creates the Office of Price Administration to control prices and ration scarce goods; President Roosevelt authorizes internment of 112,000 West Coast Japanese Americans; Philippine Islands surrender to Japan; U.S. Navy wins a major victory at Midway Island in the central Pacific; British and U.S. forces land in French North Africa

1943 British and U.S. forces defeat Axis forces in North Africa; U.S. marines secure control of Guadalcanal in the Solomon Islands; Soviets halt German drive into Soviet Union; Allies invade Italy; Mussolini is overthrown and new Italian government surrenders to Allies

1943–1944 U.S. marines and navy seize islands of Tarawa, Kwajelin, Wake, and Guam in central Pacific and New Guinea in South Pacific

1944 U.S. Supreme Court upholds legality of the forced relocation of Japanese Americans; D-Day—Allies launch amphibious invasion of northern France; U.S. forces begin an invasion of Philippine Islands and aerial attacks on Japan; Bretton Woods conference draws up plans for International Monetary Fund and International Bank to finance postwar economic recovery; Dumbarton Oaks conference makes plans for creation of United Nations; German troops launch counteroffensive in the Ardennes Forest along Belgium-Luxembourg border

1945 At Yalta, Roosevelt, Churchill, and Stalin discuss Soviet entry into the war against Japan, the postwar division of Europe, and plans for the United Nations; Roosevelt dies; Harry S Truman becomes thirty-third president; Germany surrenders; Potsdam conference plans postwar settlement in Europe and final attack on Japan; United States drops atomic bombs on Hiroshima and Nagasaki; Japan surrenders

and offensive" and reminding the museum of "its obligation to portray history in the proper context of its time."

In the end, the Smithsonian decided to scale back the exhibit, displaying the *Enola Gay's* fuselage along with a small plaque. In announcing the decision, a Smithsonian official explained, "In this important anniversary year, veterans and their families were expecting, and rightly so, that the nation would honor and commemorate their valor and sacrifice. They were not looking for analysis and, frankly, we did not give enough thought to the intense feelings such an analysis would evoke."

World War II cost America one million casualties and over 300,000 deaths. In both domestic and foreign affairs, its consequences were far-reaching. It had an immediate and spectacular impact on the economy by ending the Great Depression. Fueled by government contracts, the economy expanded dramatically, soaring to full employment and astounding the world with its productivity. Labor unions also grew during the war as the government adopted pro-union policies, continuing the New Deal's sympathetic treatment of organized labor.

Presidential power expanded enormously during World War II, anticipating the rise of what postwar critics termed the "imperial presidency." The Democrats reaped a political windfall from the war. Roosevelt rode the wartime emergency to unprecedented third and fourth terms, preserving the New Deal coalition so effectively that many people wondered if the Republicans would ever elect another president. Despite such victories, however, the reform spirit had waned, a victim, it seemed, of the country's unmistakable swing to the right in politics.

The war's social effects varied from group to group. For most people, it had a disruptive influence—separated families, overcrowded housing, and a shortage of consumer goods. The war also accelerated the movement from the countryside to the cities, and it challenged gender and racial roles, opening new opportunities for women and minority groups. Yet sexual and racial barriers remained, highlighting reforms left unfinished at home, even as American troops fought totalitarian forces abroad.

In foreign policy, the many disagreements between the Allies on military strategy and peace terms foreshadowed the major conflicts that dominated the postwar era. Gone forever was the notion of fortress America, isolated and removed from world affairs. In its place stood a strong internationalist state, determined to exercise power on a global scale. Second only to the victory the Allies won for freedom, the war's most important legacy was the end of isolation and the rise of America's commitment to international security.

SUGGESTIONS FOR FURTHER READING

Michael C.C. Adams, *The Best War Ever* (1994). Offers a succinct interpretation of the impact of World War II on American troops and the homefront.

P.M.H. Bell, *The Origins of the Second World War in Europe*, 2d ed. (1989). Examines the conflict's causes.

John Ellis, *Brute Force: Allied Strategy and Tactics in the Second World War* (1990). Discusses military strategy.

Akira Iriye, *The Origins of the Second World War in Asia and the Pacific* (1987). Analyzes the roots of war with Japan.

Geoffrey Perrett, *There's a War to Be Won* (1991). Investigates the combat experience.

William O'Neill, *A Democracy at War: America's Fight at Home and Abroad in World War II* (1993). Presents an excellent overview of American involvement in the conflict.

Allan M. Winkler, *Home Front U.S.A.* (1986). Explores the impact of the conflict on American society.

Overviews and Surveys

Selig Adler, *The Uncertain Giant: American Foreign Policy Between the Wars* (1969); Albert R. Buchanan, *The United States and World War II*, 2 vols. (1964); Sean Dennis Cashman, *America, Roosevelt, and World War II* (1989); Martha Hoyle, *A World in Flames: A History of World War II* (1970); Warren F. Kimball, *Forged in War: Roosevelt, Churchill, and the Second World War* (1996); Robert Leckie, *The Wars of America*, rev. ed., 2 vols. (1981); Gerald D. Nash, *The Crucial Era: The Great Depression and World War II*, 2d ed. (1992); Maria Emilia Paz, *Strategy, Security, and Spies: Mexico and the U.S. as Allies in World War II* (1997); Geoffrey Perrett, *Days of Sadness, Years of Triumph, 1939–1945* (1973); Pamela Rotner Sakamoto, *Japanese Diplomats and Jewish Refugees: A World War II Dilemma* (1998); Studs Terkel, ed., *"The Good War": An Oral History of World War Two* (1984); Russell F. Weigley, *The American Way of War: A History of United States Military Strategy and Policy* (1973); Gordon Wright, *The Ordeal of Total War, 1939–1945* (1968).

Diplomacy Between the Wars

Charles Chatfield, *For Peace and Justice: Pacifism in America, 1914–1941* (1971); Charles DeBenedetti, *Origins of the Modern American Peace Movement, 1915–1929* (1978); Warren Cohen, *Empire without Tears: American Foreign Relations, 1921–1933* (1987); Frank Costigliola, *Awkward Dominion: American Political, Economic, and Cultural Relations with Europe* (1984); Michael Dunne, *The United States and the World Court, 1920–1935* (1988); Robert H. Ferrell, *Peace in Their Time: Men Who Led Us In and Out of War, 1914–1945* (1953); Irwin F. Gellman, *Good Neighbor Diplomacy* (1979); Richard M. Ketchum, *The Borrowed Years, 1938–1941* (1989); Manfred Jonas, *Isolationism in America, 1935–1941* (1966); Joan Hoff-Wilson, *American Business and Foreign Policy, 1920–1933* (1971); John E. Wiltz, *In Search of Peace: The Senate Munitions Inquiry* (1963); Bryce Wood, *Making of the Good Neighbor Policy* (1961).

The Coming of World War II

Thomas A. Bailey and Paul B. Ryan, *Hitler vs. Roosevelt: The Undeclared Naval War* (1979); Robert J. Butow, *Tojo and the Coming of the War* (1961); Warren I. Cohen, *America's Response to China*, 3d ed. (1990); Wayne S. Cole, *America First: The Battle Against Intervention, 1940–1941* (1953), and *Roosevelt and the Isolationists* (1983); James V. Compton, *The Swastika and the Eagle: Hitler, the United States, and the Origins of World War II* (1967); Robert Dallek, *Franklin D. Roosevelt and American Foreign Policy, 1932–1945* (1979); Robert A. Divine, *Illusion of Neutrality* (1962), and *Second Chance: The Triumph of Internationalism During World War II* (1967); Herbert Feis, *The Road to Pearl Harbor* (1950); Robert Edwin Herzstein, *Roosevelt & Hitler: Prelude to War* (1989); Akira Iriye, *After Imperialism: The Search for a New Order in the Far East, 1921–1931* (1965); Warren F. Kimball, *The Most Unsordid Act: Lend-Lease, 1939–1941* (1982); Joseph P. Lash, *Roosevelt and Churchill, 1939–1941* (1976); Marvin V. Melosi, *The Shadow of Pearl Harbor: Political Controversy over the Surprise Attack* (1977); Gordon W. Prange, *At Dawn We Slept: The Untold Story of Pearl Harbor* (1981); David Reynolds, *The Creation of the Anglo-American Alliance: 1937–41* (1982); Bruce Russet, *No Clear and Present Danger: A Skeptical View of the United States Entry into World War II* (1972); Michael Schaller, *The U.S. Crusade in China 1938–1945* (1979); John E. Wiltz, *From Isolation to War: 1931–1941* (1968); Roberta Wohlstetter, *Pearl Harbor: Warning and Decision* (1962).

America Mobilizes for War

John Morton Blum, *V Was for Victory: Politics and American Culture During World War II* (1976); David Brinkley, *Washington Goes to War* (1988); Frank W. Fox, *Madison Avenue Goes to War* (1975); William K. Klingaman, *1941: Our Lives in a World on the Edge* (1988); Paul A. C. Koistinen, *The Hammer and the Sword: Labor, the Military, and Industrial Mobilization, 1920–1945* (1979); Clayton Koppes and Gregory Black, *Hollywood Goes to War: How Politics, Profits, and Propaganda Shaped World War II Movies* (1987); Nelson Lichtenstein, *Labor's War at Home: The CIO in World War II* (1982); Richard Lingeman, *Don't You Know There's a War On? The American Home Front, 1941–1945* (1970); Richard Polenberg, *The War and Society: The United States, 1941–1945* (1972); David R. Segal, *Recruiting for Uncle Sam: Citizenship and Military Manpower Policy* (1989); Harold G. Vatter, *The U.S. Economy in World War II* (1985); Gerald T. White, *Billions for Defense: Government Financing by the Defense Plant Corporation During World War II* (1980).

Social Changes During the War

Alison R. Bernstein, *American Indians and World War II* (1991); Karen Anderson, *Wartime Women: Sex Roles, Family Relations, and the Status of Women During World War II* (1981); Allan Berube, *Coming Out Under Fire: The History of Gay Men and Women in World War Two* (1990); A. Russell Buchanan, *Black Americans in World War II* (1977); D'Ann Campbell, *Women at War with America: Private Lives in a Patriotic Era* (1984); Dominic J. Capeci, Jr., *Race Relations in Wartime Detroit* (1984); John Costello, *Virtue Under Fire: How World War II Changed Our Social and Sexual Attitudes* (1985); Richard M. Dalfiume, *Desegregation of the U.S. Armed Forces: Fighting on Two Fronts, 1939–1953* (1969); Roger Daniels, *Concentration Camps USA: Japanese Americans and World War* (1971), and *Prisoners Without Trial: Japanese Americans in World War II* (1993); Richard Drinnon, *Keeper of Concentration Camps: Dillon S. Myer and American Racism* (1987); Charity Adams Earley, *One Woman's Army: A Black Officer Remembers the WAC* (1989); Audrie Girdner and Alme Loftig, *The Great Betrayal: The Evacuation of the Japanese-Americans During World War II* (1969); Sherna Berger Gluck, *Rosie the Riveter Revisited: Women, the War, and Social Change* (1987); Anne Bosanko Green, *One Woman's War: Letters Home from the Women's Army Corps, 1944–1946* (1989); Chester W. Gregory, *Women in Defense Work During World War II: An Analysis of the Labor Problem and Women's Rights* (1974); Susan M. Hartmann, *The Home Front and Beyond: American Women in the 1940s* (1982); Peter H. Irons, *Justice at War: The Story of the Japanese American Internment Cases* (1983); Glen Jeansonne, *Women of the Far Right: The Mother's Movement and World War II* (1996); George Lipsitz, *Rainbow at Midnight: Labor and Culture in the 1940s* (1989); Deborah E. Lipstadt, *Beyond Belief: The American Press and the Coming of the Holocaust* (1993); Mauricio Mazón, *The Zoot-Suit Riots: The Psychology of Symbolic Annihilation* (1984); August Meier and Elliot Rudwick, *CORE, 1942–1968* (1973); Gunnar Myrdal, *An American Dilemma* (1944); Robert Shogan and Thomas Craig, *The Detroit Race Riot: A Study in Violence* (1964); William M. Tuttle, Jr., *"Daddy's Gone to War": The Second World War in the Lives of America's Children* (1993); Neil Wynn, *The Afro-American and the Second World War* (1976).

The War in Europe

James MacGregor Burns, *Roosevelt: Soldier of Freedom* (1970); Diane Shaver Clemens, *Yalta* (1970); Michael D. Doubler, *Closing with the Enemy: How GIs Fought the War in Europe* (1994); Kent Roberts Greenfield, *American Strategy in World War II: A Reconsideration* (1963); Eric Larabee, *Commander in Chief: Franklin Delano Roosevelt, His Lieutenants, and Their War* (1987); Ronald Schaffer, *Wings of Judgment: American Bombing in World War II* (1985); Michael Sherry, *The Rise of American Air Power* (1987); Bradley F. Smith, *The Shadow Warriors: O.S.S. and the Origins of the C.I.A.* (1983); Gaddis Smith, *American Diplomacy During the Second World War, 1941–1945* (1965); John Snell, *Illusion and Necessity: The Diplomacy of Global War, 1939–1945* (1963); Mark A. Stoler, *The Politics of the Second Front: American Military Planning and Diplomacy in Coalition Warfare, 1941–1943* (1977).

The War in the Pacific

John Costello, *The Pacific War* (1981); John W. Dower, *War Without Mercy: Race and Power in the Pacific War* (1986); Roger Hilsman, *American Guerrilla: My War Behind Japanese Lines* (1990); Akira Iriye, *Power and Culture: The Japanese-American War* (1981); Gordon W. Prange, *Miracle at Midway* (1982); Ronald H. Spector, *Eagle Against the Sun: The American War with Japan* (1985).

The Dawn of the Atomic Age

Gar Alperovitz, *Atomic Diplomacy: Hiroshima and Potsdam*, rev. ed. (1985); Robert Butow, *Japan's Decision to Surrender* (1954); Herbert Feis, *The Atomic Bomb and the End of World War II* (1966); Gregg Herkin, *The Winning Weapon: The Atomic Bomb in the Cold War: 1945–1950* (1980); Robert Jungk, *Brighter than a Thousand Suns: A Personal History of the Atomic Scientists* (1958); Dan Kurzman, *Day of the Bomb: Countdown to Hiroshima* (1986); Martin J. Sherwin, *A World Destroyed: The Atomic Bomb and the Grand Alliance* (1975); Dennis Wainstock, *The Decision to Drop the Atomic Bomb* (1996).

Biographies

Saul Alinsky, *John L. Lewis* (1949); Mark S. Foster, *Henry J. Kaiser: Builder in the Modern American West* (1989); Warren F. Kimball, *The Juggler: Franklin Roosevelt as Wartime Statesman* (1991); Michael Schaller, *Douglas MacArthur: The Far Eastern General* (1989); Barbara Tuchman, *Stilwell and the American Experience in China, 1911–45* (1971).

INTERNET RESOURCES

A People at War
http://www.nara.gov/exhall/people/people.html
This National Archives Exhibit takes a close look at the contributions millions of Americans made to the war effort.

Powers of Persuasion—Poster Art of World War II
http://www.nara.gov/education/teaching/posters/poster.html
These powerful posters at the National Archives were part of the battle for the hearts and minds of the American people.

America from the Great Depression to World War II: Photographs from the FSA and OWI, ca. 1935–1945
http://memory.loc.gov/ammem/fsowhome.html
These images in the Farm Security Administration–Office of War Information Collection show Americans from all over the nation experiencing everything from despair to triumph in the 1930s and 1940s.

A-Bomb WWW Museum
http://www.csi.ad.jp/ABOMB/
This site offers information about the impact of the first atomic bomb as well as the background and context of weapons of total destruction.

The United States Holocaust Memorial Museum
http://www.ushmm.org/index.html
This is the official Web site of the Holocaust Museum in Washington, D.C.

World War II Era Links
http://wrightmuseum.org/links.html
The Wright Museum maintains this page with its many links to information about the World War II era.

World War II Pictures
http://www.corbis.com/FDR/ww2.html
This Corbis site houses many pictures about the second world war and American involvement in the conflict.

Tuskegee Airmen
http://www.wpafb.af.mil/museum/history/prewwii/ta.htm
The Air Force Museum at Wright-Patterson Air Force Base maintains this site about the African American pilots of World War II.

Abraham Lincoln Brigade Archives
http://www.alba-valb.org
This Brandeis University site has posters and photographs from the Spanish civil war and the unit of American volunteers who fought in it.

World War II Resources: Primary Source Materials on the Web
http://www.sunsite.unc.edu/pha/index.html
This site has a large number of searchable primary texts from all aspects of World War II.

The Enola Gay Controversy
http://www.glue.umd.edu/~enola/
This comprehensive site at the University of Maryland explores all facets of the dropping of the first atomic bomb in 1945 from the development of the bomb to controversy around the recent Smithsonian exhibit.

Manzanar Project
http://www.mvhs.srvusd.k12.ca.us/~mleck/man/Default.html
A site that explores Japanese internment in World War II.

KEY TERMS

Good Neighbor Policy   (p. 730)
Lend-Lease Act   (p. 736)
Pearl Harbor   (p. 737)
War Production Board (WPB)   (p. 738)
Women's Army Corps (WAC)   (p. 741)
Axis Powers   (p. 745)
Grand Alliance   (p. 745)
Joseph Stalin   (p. 745)
D-Day   (p. 747)
Yalta Conference   (p. 747)
Manhattan Project   (p. 755)

REVIEW QUESTIONS

1. What characterized U.S. diplomacy between the world wars?
2. Why did the Neutrality Acts fail to keep the United States out of World War II?
3. How did mobilization for World War II differ from that for World War I?
4. How did World War II change the roles and status of women and minorities in the United States?
5. How crucial was U.S. involvement in the European war?
6. Could the use of the atomic bombs have been avoided? How?

26

WAGING PEACE AND WAR

CONTAINING THE RUSSIAN BEAR
Origins of the Cold War
A World Divided
Tough Talk
The Marshall Plan: "Saving Western Europe"

THE CONTAINMENT POLICY
Berlin Test
Troubling Times
The Korean War

THE COLD WAR AT HOME
Adjusting to Peace
Confronting the Demands of Labor
Failure of the Fair Deal
Searching for the Enemy Within
The Rise and Fall of Joseph McCarthy

THE PARANOID STYLE
HUAC Goes to Hollywood
"What's Wrong with Our Kids Today?"

"I am not and never have been..."

It was Sunday, August 27, 1948. Whittaker Chambers appeared calm as he answered questions on "Meet the Press," a weekly radio news show. Chambers's appearance, like most of his life, was a deception. He knew he was on enemy ground and that questions were the ammunition of the war. "I sought not to let myself be crowded," he later recalled, "not to lose my temper during the baiting." Chambers was very still, waiting for the inevitable question. He didn't have to wait long. Edward T. Folliard, a reporter for the *Washington Post*, asked, "Are you willing to say now that Alger Hiss is or ever was a Communist?" Chambers paused a second before answering, for the answer could open him up to a slander or libel suit. Then came his terse, important reply: "Alger Hiss was a Communist and may be now."

The road to "Meet the Press" had begun for Chambers a generation before 1948. It was one paved with unhappiness. His father, Jay, had left his wife Laha for a time, returning after three years. He demonstrated no love or affection for his wife or children. Whittaker remembers that his father—who never allowed his children to call him "Papa"—dined alone and seldom spoke, except perhaps to say "don't." Home experiences left Chambers rebellious and feeling unwanted. After being forced to withdraw from Columbia for writing a mildly sacrilegious play, he flirted with radical political philosophies, moved through a succession of love affairs, and kicked about Europe. In 1926 his brother Richard committed suicide. It was the most painful event in Chambers's life, and for several months he was inconsolable. Almost as a form of therapy, he committed himself fully to another family—the Communist party. During his time of troubles, it gave his life a direction and a purpose.

During the late 1920s and early 1930s, as the United States sank deeper and deeper into the Great Depression, other Americans joined Chambers in the Communist party. Feeling betrayed by the capitalist order, they looked toward the Soviet Union for economic and political inspiration. The Soviet Union, under Joseph Stalin, appeared less affected by the depression than the capitalist West. Still more Americans joined the Communist party because only the Soviets seemed to be standing up against the Fascist threat posed by Hitler, Mussolini, and Franco. For Chambers and his comrades, then, the Red Star represented the future and the hope of the world.

Chambers met Alger Hiss in 1934, when they both belonged to the same Communist "cell" in Washington, D.C. In appearance and personality they were almost perfect opposites. Chambers was sloppy; his clothes always seemed rumpled, and his face had a sleepy, slightly disinterested cast. Hiss was cut from different cloth. Handsome and aristocratic-looking, Hiss's career was marked by ambition and achievement. He was an honors student at Johns Hopkins University and Harvard Law School; he was a favorite of future Supreme Court justice Felix Frankfurter; he clerked for the legendary Oliver Wendell Holmes. Popular with influential superiors and his co-workers, Hiss obviously seemed singled out as one of the best and brightest, as one who would succeed. And he did. He acted as a counsel for the Agricultural Adjustment Administration, worked for the Senate committee investigating the munitions industry, went to the Yalta Conference with President Roosevelt, helped to organize the United Nations, and served as president of the Carnegie Endowment for International Peace.

Through these years of his impressive career, Hiss worked with Whittaker Chambers for the Communist party. It was while Hiss served as a legal assistant for the Senate committee investigation of the munitions industry that he became close friends with Chambers. He allowed Chambers to use his Washington, D.C., apartment for two months, gave him an automobile, and even permitted him to stay in his

Bureaucrat Alger Hiss (left), accused of being a Communist spy by Whittaker Chambers (right), was convicted of perjury (in his second trial for perjury; the first ended in a hung jury). This episode helped heighten American fear of communism at home.

home on several occasions. Although Hiss would later deny that he knew Chambers—and then admit that he knew him slightly under a different name—the evidence is clear on one point: the very different men had formed a close friendship. It was during that period of friendship in the mid-1930s, Chambers later testified, that Hiss began to give him secret government documents.

Like many of his American comrades, Chambers later, in the late 1930s, abandoned the ideology of communism and lost faith in the Soviet Union. There were sound reasons for this break. For the true believers of the early 1930s, the Soviet Union was the light that failed. By 1938 news of Stalin's purges, which would eventually lead to the deaths of millions of Soviets, had reached the West. Such gross disregard for humanity shook many American Communists. In addition, in 1939 Stalin signed a nonaggression pact with Hitler's Germany. Once seen as the bulwark against Nazi expansion, the Soviet Union now joined Germany in dividing Poland. Although during World War II the United States and the Soviet Union were forced together as allies, Communist ideology ceased to attract many American followers.

Chambers not only quit the Communist party, he turned against it with vengeful wrath. As an editor for *Time* magazine, he openly criticized Communist tactics and warned about the evils of the Soviet Union. The passage of time only increased his rage. Finally in 1948 he went before the House Un-American Activities Committee (HUAC) and told his life story, carefully naming all his former Communist party friends and associates. Of all the people he named, the one who attracted the most attention was the brilliant young New Dealer Alger Hiss.

Hiss of course denied Chambers's allegations. He too appeared before HUAC. Well-dressed and relaxed despite a too-tight collar, he testified, "I am not and never have been a member of the Communist party.... I have never followed the Communist party line, directly or indirectly. To the best of my knowledge, none of my friends is a Communist." As he smilingly answered questions, he confidently stood on his record of public service. Unlike his nervous, rumpled accuser, Hiss was the picture of placid truthfulness. His testimony satisfied most of the committee members, even the Republicans.

Not all were satisfied, however. After listening to both Chambers and Hiss, Republican Richard Nixon, a junior congressman from California, still was not sure Hiss was as innocent as he seemed. As one psychohistorian bluntly put it, Hiss "was everything Nixon was not." Nixon's background of struggle contrasted sharply with Hiss's career, and Nixon believed Hiss treated him "like dirt." At Nixon's insistence, Hiss and Chambers were brought together face to face before HUAC. It was at that meeting that Chambers demonstrated his encyclopedic knowledge about Hiss—his family—and his life. He discussed the furniture in the other man's house and his hobbies. Chambers showed beyond any doubt that at one time he had been close to Hiss. For once Hiss's confident equanimity vanished. He challenged Chambers to make his accusations in public, where he would not be protected against a libel suit.

Chambers accepted the challenge, and on "Meet the Press" he repeated his charges. Hiss hesitated for a month and then sued Chambers for defamation. During the involved trials that followed, Chambers proved his case. He even produced a series of classified, microfilmed documents he had stored in a hollowed-out pumpkin on his Maryland farm. Experts testified that the classified documents had been written in Hiss's hand or typed on his Woodstock typewriter. Hiss was indicted for perjury by a federal grand jury. Although the first trial ended in a hung jury, the second trial was far less satisfactory for Hiss. In January 1950 he was found guilty of perjury and sentenced to five years in prison.

The Hiss-Chambers affair was one of the major episodes of the late 1940s. Those years were a time of momentous changes. America took an active and aggressive stand in world affairs and accepted the responsibilities and problems of world leadership. Across the globe it clashed with the Soviet Union over a series of symbolic and real issues in what was labeled the Cold War. These ideological and economic battles affected American domestic and foreign policy. During the late 1940s and early 1950s Americans attacked the Communist threat inside as well as outside the United States. In an atmosphere charged with fear, anxiety, paranoia, and hatred, the United States waged peace and war with equal emotional intensity.

CONTAINING THE RUSSIAN BEAR

During World War II, when the United States and the Soviet Union were allies, **Joseph Stalin** was known as Uncle Joe. The media and Hollywood portrayed him as a stern but fair leader and pictured communism as strikingly like capitalism. Warner Brothers' 1943 film *Mission to Moscow* was particularly kind to Stalin, who appeared on screen as a gentle, pipe-smoking, sad-eyed friend of America.

The onset of the Cold War was due in part to the growing divergence between the United States and the Soviet Union after World War II. At Potsdam, Britain's Prime Minister Clement Attlee, President Truman, and Stalin tried unsuccessfully to decide the future of Poland and Germany.

In reality Joseph Stalin was a determined, ruthless leader who, over the years, had systematically eliminated his actual and suspected political rivals. Between 1933 and 1938 he violently eliminated over 850,000 members of the Communist party, and perhaps one million more died in labor camps. He was apparently suspicious of almost everyone, inside and outside of the Soviet Union. If his attitude was extreme, it was not totally irrational. Twice in his lifetime Russia had been invaded from the West. Twice Germans had pushed into his country, killing millions upon millions of Russians. Russia suffered almost 4 million military and civilian deaths in World War I, and more than 20 million in World War II. For Stalin, the West stood unalterably opposed to communism. He would take what he could from the West, but he would never trust westerners.

Stalin, however, was not the only suspicious world leader. The newest Western leader, President Harry Truman, was wary of Stalin but did not exactly regard him as the enemy, at least not in 1945—after all, the Soviet Union and America had been allies during World War II. When Truman took office on April 12, 1945, he assumed he could deal with Stalin. Advisers told him that Stalin was a tough, no-nonsense leader. These were characteristics that the tough, no-nonsense Truman could appreciate. His first meeting with Stalin at Potsdam confirmed his initial assessment of the Soviet leader. "I like Stalin," Truman wrote his wife Bess. "He is straightforward. Knows what he wants and will compromise when he can't get it."

Potsdam was the light before the long dark tunnel. Truman was overly optimistic about his ability to work with Stalin. Totally different backgrounds and philosophies separated the two leaders from the start, and the directions in which they led their countries drove them further apart. The United States and the Soviet Union emerged from World War II as the two most powerful countries in the world, even though the Soviet Union had suffered tremendous industrial, agricultural, and human losses during the war. Both countries were inexperienced as world leaders, but both knew exactly what they wanted, and what they wanted guaranteed future conflicts. The result was the Cold War.

Origins of the Cold War

For Western leaders and their diplomats, World War II had a successful but not neat ending. Too many questions were left unanswered, too many issues unresolved. At Yalta and then at Potsdam the leaders of the Soviet Union, Great Britain, and the United States discussed the future of Poland and Germany, but no firm conclusions were reached. Afraid of further straining the already uneasy wartime alliance, they decided to leave such thorny issues to the future. When the future arrived in August 1945 after America dropped two atomic bombs on Japan, the fates of Eastern Europe and Germany were as yet undetermined, as was the relationship between the United States and the Soviet Union.

When Germany had invaded Poland in early September 1939, England and France had come to the aid of Poland. The Soviet Union had not. Instead, the Soviets had invaded Poland from the east and gobbled up a large section of the country. In 1941, however, Germany invaded the Soviet Union and forced Stalin to join the Grand Alliance against Hitler. For the remainder of World War II, the Soviets had battled heroically against Germany on the eastern front. The West contributed weapons and supplies in this theater of the war, but it was the Red Army working alone that drove the Germans out of Eastern Europe. When the war ended, the Soviets controlled all of Eastern Europe from Stettin on the Baltic Sea to Trieste on the Adriatic Sea.

Had the Soviet Union liberated Eastern Europe or simply replaced Germany as the master of the region? That was the crucial question of 1945. The debate centered on the fate of Poland: Truman insisted that the Soviets allow free and democratic elections in Poland. Certainly, Truman conceded, the Soviets had the right to expect any Polish government to be friendly toward the Soviet Union, but he expected Stalin to give Poland its complete freedom. Poland's fate was no abstract diplomatic issue to millions of Americans of Eastern European origins who pressed Truman to take a tough stand. Truman complied. In a profanity-laced tirade, he told Soviet Foreign Minister V. M. Molotov that America would not tolerate Poland being made into a Soviet puppet state. Stalin, however, would not give away Poland or any other territory the Red Army occupied simply because of Truman's colorful phrases. Twice during the twentieth century Germany had invaded Russia through Poland. Stalin was determined it would never happen again. As he had bluntly stated at Yalta, "For the Russian people, the question of Poland is not only a question of honor but also a question of security . . . of life and death for the Soviet Union."

Confronted by an inflexible opponent, Truman played his trump card. He threatened to cut off economic aid to the Soviet Union. Devastated by World War II, the Soviet Union needed the aid, but Stalin believed Poland was more important. Rather than abandon Poland, Stalin accepted the loss of American money. In the end, Truman was powerless. Americans would certainly not accept a war with the Soviet Union to reliberate Poland, and in 1945 the Soviet Union was not about to leave Poland voluntarily. Although there was no war, there was one important casualty: relations between America and the Soviet Union were strained to the breaking point.

A World Divided

The controversy over Poland indicated the direction of postwar Soviet-American relations. The two countries were divided by substantial issues, the most important of which was the degree of control they should and did have over other nations. At the end of the war both nations occupied large areas of land. America's control was based on the strength of its economy as much as its military position. Even as the country demobilized, American leaders were confident that they could use foreign aid to exert influence on the future development of the world. They were also confident that what was good for America would be good for the world. The Soviet Union's control in all of Eastern Europe—Hungary, Romania, Bulgaria, and Czechoslovakia, as well as Poland—depended on the physical presence of the Red Army. Stalin freely granted America and England their spheres of influence, but he wanted the West to recognize his own.

Truman refused. A believer in free trade, national self-determination, and the virtues of democracy, he opposed Stalin's use of military force as a diplomatic weapon. The irony of the United States's position was clearly seen by political commentator Walter Lippmann: "While the British and the Americans held firmly . . . the whole position in Africa and the Mediterranean . . . and the whole of Western Germany . . . they undertook by negotiation and diplomatic pressure to reduce Russia's position in Eastern Europe."

Approaching the issues from different perspectives, the Soviet Union and America arrived at different conclusions. After World War II ended, they agreed on very little. The fate of Germany illustrates the basic conflict between the two powers. The Soviets wanted to punish Germany by stripping the country of its industry and imposing harsh reparation payments. Only a prostrate Germany, unarmed and unthreatening, would satisfy Stalin. As Truman lost confidence in the Soviet Union, he came to believe in the need for a strong Germany to act as a block against Soviet expansion. The result of these conflicting approaches was, literally, a divided Germany. Occupied by the Red Army, East Germany became a Soviet satellite. West Germany fell under the American, British, and French spheres of influence and soon became part of the postwar democratic alliance. Not until the early 1990s would Germany again be united.

Control over atomic weapons also divided the two powers. America developed and used the first atomic bomb—demonstrating to the world that it possessed not only the scientific knowledge to construct the bomb but also the will to use the weapon. Publicly Truman seemed favorable to international control of the world's fissionable materials. But privately he used the threat of the bomb in his negotiations with the Soviet Union. America, Secretary of War Henry L. Stimson commented, wore the "weapon rather ostentatiously on our hip."

Stalin reacted with suspicion and bitterness to this contradictory policy, distrusting any atomic control plan that originated in the United States. Rather

Europe After World War II

than make Stalin more manageable, America's atomic diplomacy stiffened his resolve and made him cling even more firmly to Eastern Europe as a buffer. At a high-level meeting in the Kremlin he announced his own plan: "A single demand of you, comrades: provide us with atomic weapons in the shortest possible time. You know that Hiroshima has shaken the whole world. The equilibrium has been destroyed. Provide the bomb. It will remove a great danger from us." The result: an atomic arms race, not international cooperation.

By early 1946 U.S.-Soviet relations were badly strained. In February of that year, Stalin warned all Soviet citizens that there would never be a lasting peace with the capitalistic West; economic sacrifices and perhaps more warfare lay ahead. Supreme Court Justice William Douglas labeled the speech "the declaration of World War III." The next month Winston Churchill traveled to Fulton, Missouri, to give a lecture of his own. With Truman by his side, he announced that "from Stettin in the Baltic to Trieste in the Adriatic, an iron curtain has descended across the continent"; only a combined Anglo-American effort could lift the curtain. Fortunately, Churchill emphasized, "God has willed" the atomic bomb to America. Dramatic words, ominous warnings, threats and counterthreats—the Cold War clearly had been declared.

Tough Talk

Although real issues divided America and the Soviet Union, the emotionally charged rhetoric and the emergence of Cold War myths hardened the battle lines. Truman's public pronouncements lacked the tact and language of a diplomat. He also remembered how the British and the French had given in to Hitler at the Munich Conference of 1938. Equating Stalin's goals with Hitler's, however, was a grave mistake. Stalin was concerned more with security than expansion; he wanted to protect his country from a future attack, not initiate World War III. As George Kennan, America's leading expert on the Soviet Union, later observed, "The image of a Stalinist Russia poised and yearning to attack the West, and deterred only by our possession of atomic weapons, was largely a creation of the Western imagination."

The Munich example and the get-tough talk turned American public opinion against the Soviet Union. Leading American diplomat Dean Acheson warned, "I think it is a mistake to believe that you can, at any time, sit down with the Russians and solve problems." Comments of this sort were aired over and over in public as the media began to build a new, more menacing image of Stalin. The pipe in hand and sad, soft eyes of Uncle Joe quickly faded in late 1945 and early 1946. News stories emphasized confrontation, conflict, and controversy. Talk turned no longer toward how to avoid an explosive conflict but rather how to win it. In the mind of the public, the Soviet Union soon became the once and future enemy of America.

The situation was exacerbated by Britain's decline. England, like much of the rest of Europe, suffered terribly during World War II. The war shattered its economy, and burned-out buildings and miles of fresh graves silently testified to the country's physical and human losses. By early 1947 Britain could no longer stand as the leader of the Western democracies. At an emergency meeting with Secretary of State George C. Marshall, the British ambassador in Washington announced that his country could no longer economically support Greece and Turkey in their fight against Communist rebels. If these two countries, which were vitally important because of their position between the Soviet Union and the Mediterranean and the Middle East, were to be kept as Western allies, the United States had to aid their cause.

Truman was prepared to assume the burden, but there were doubts whether the country was. Republicans had regained control of Congress in the November 1946 elections, and they were not anxious to shoulder expensive new foreign programs. In addition, rapid demobilization after World War II had drastically reduced the size and effectiveness of the American military forces. Still, something had to be done. Truman's advisers and congressional leaders recommended that he speak directly to the American people. But as Republican Senator Arthur Vandenberg

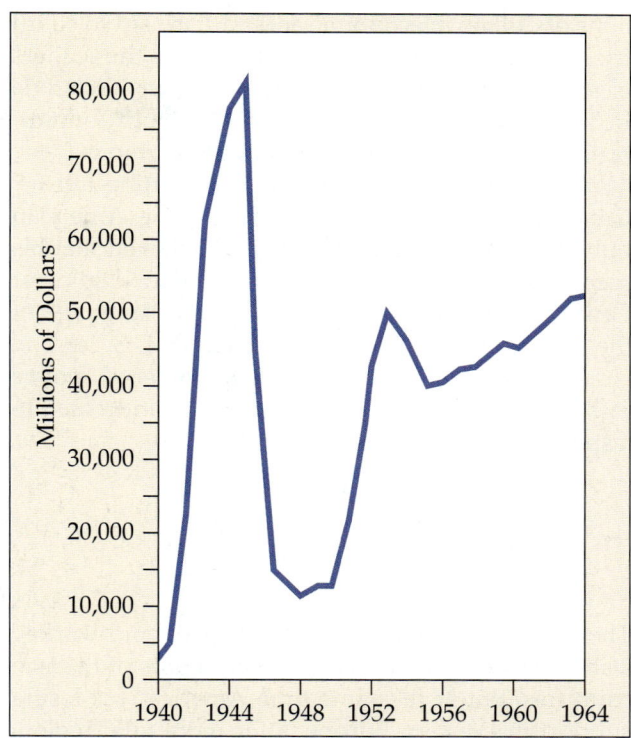

FIGURE 26.1
National Defense Budgets, 1940–1964

warned, to win public support the president would have to "scare the hell out of the American people."

On March 12, 1947, Truman appeared before a joint session of Congress and described the Greek and Turkish situations as battles between the forces of light and the legions of darkness. "At the present moment in world history nearly every nation must choose between alternative ways of life," he said. "One way of life is based upon the will of the majority, and is distinguished by free institutions, representative government, free elections, guarantees of individual liberty, freedom of speech and religion, and freedom from political oppression. The second way of life is based upon the will of a minority forcibly imposed upon the majority. It relies upon terror and oppression." Congress sounded its approval as Truman came to his climactic sentence: "I believe that it must be the policy of the United States to support free peoples who are resisting attempted subjugation by armed minorities or outside pressures." Labeled the **Truman Doctrine,** the statement set the course U.S. foreign policy would follow during the next generation.

Specifically, Truman called for economic and financial aid to "save" Greece and Turkey. Congress responded by appropriating $400 million. By later standards it was a paltry sum, but it was a significant beginning. In the future, America would send billions of dollars in economic and military aid to countries fighting communism, even though the leaders of some of those nations were themselves dictators. In Truman's morality play, however, "anti-Communists" and "free peoples" became synonymous.

Although Truman succeeded in getting aid for Greece and Turkey and in arousing the American public, a few foreign policy experts believed that his scare tactics did more harm than good. Diplomat George Kennan deplored the sweeping language of the Truman Doctrine, which placed U.S. aid to Greece "in the framework of a universal policy rather than in that of a specific decision addressed to a specific set of circumstances."

The Marshall Plan: "Saving Western Europe"

The millions of dollars sent to Greece and Turkey stabilized the pro-American governments of the two countries. But at the same time America was losing support in Western Europe, a far more vital region. The region lacked the money to rebuild its war-torn economies and scarred cities. To make matters worse, the winters of 1946 and 1947 were brutally cold. News reports from early 1947 told the sad story. Snow buried thousands of sheep in northern England; between December 1 and February 8, 40 residents of Berlin and 68 of Hamburg died from the cold; Holland was short of food; Italy was inundated by floods; and across the continent the weather report was always the same: "cold or very cold." The winter hardships were a boon to the Communist party, which made marked gains. American leaders assumed that economic distress would continue to breed political extremism. *New York Times* correspondent Anne O'Hare McCormick told Americans: "The extent to which democratic government survives on [the] continent depends on how far this country is willing to help it survive." Truman concurred, and so did his advisers. They were upset by the emerging view in Europe of selfish, exploitative Americans. Describing the typical occupation soldier in Germany, an army chaplain wrote, "There he stands in his bulging clothes, fat, overfed, lonely, a bit wistful, seeing little, understanding less—the Conqueror, with a chocolate bar in one pocket and a package of cigarettes in the other. . . . The chocolate bar and the cigarettes are about all that he, the Conqueror, has to give the conquered."

At the Harvard University commencement on June 5, 1947, Secretary of State George C. Marshall announced a plan to give Europe more. After describing the severe problems facing Europe, Marshall suggested that America could not afford to send a Band-Aid to cover the deep European wounds. "A cure rather than a mere palliative" was in order—Europe needed massive economic blood transfusions. He told his audience that the cost might seem high. Without America's help, however, "economic, social, and political deterioration of a very grave character" would result. And from a more selfish point of view, America needed a strong, democratic Europe to provide rich markets for American goods and to act as a check against Soviet westward expansion.

In early 1948 Congress appropriated $17 billion to be spent over the next four years for the European Recovery Program (ERP), more popularly called the **Marshall Plan.** The program put food in the mouths of hungry children, coal in empty furnaces, and money in near-empty banks. More importantly, it rebuilt the economic infrastructure of Western Europe and restored economic prosperity to the region. In the process it created stable markets for American goods. Americans were proud of the Marshall Plan, and Europeans were moved by it. Winston Churchill judged it "the most unsordid act in history." All told, the Marshall Plan greatly restored America's prestige abroad.

The Marshall Plan also fostered the economic integration of Western Europe by curbing nationalistic economic policies. "A healthy Europe," John Foster Dulles remarked, could not be "divided into small compartments." Although the process toward a single economic unit in Western Europe was slow and occasionally painful, it did move forward. The European Payments Union was created in 1950, the European Coal and Steel Authority in 1951, and the European Economic Community (Common Market) in 1958. In the final analysis, the Marshall Plan served both America's Cold War strategy and plans for an economic internationalism.

THE CONTAINMENT POLICY

Money, even billions of dollars, could not substitute for a concrete foreign policy to guide U.S. actions, an explicit policy that mixed the international idealism of the Truman Doctrine and the economic realism of the Marshall Plan with the will to meet the real or perceived Soviet threat. The policy was not long in coming. In July 1947, the journal *Foreign Affairs* contained an article entitled "The Sources of Soviet Conduct" by "Mr. X." The article provided a blueprint for the policy of containment, which would influence American foreign policy for at least the next generation.

"Mr. X" was George Kennan, the government's foremost authority on the Soviet Union. Kennan had spent his adult life in the U.S. foreign service and was stationed in Moscow during World War II. Although he believed Russians were a "great and appealing people," he distrusted the Soviet government. In the article, Kennan argued that Soviet communism was driven by two engines: the need for a repressive dictatorship at home and the belief that there could never be any sense of community or true accord with the capitalist West. In fact, the Kremlin used the supposed threat from capitalism to justify its continued dictatorship. But, he continued, Stalin and the leaders in the Kremlin were more interested in security than expansion. Russia would only expand when allowed to by American weakness. It could be *contained* to its present borders by a politically, economically, and militarily active United States. What was needed was "the adroit and vigilant application of counter-force at a series of constantly shifting geographical and political points, corresponding to the shifts and maneuvers of Soviet policy." Kennan even suggested that if the United States was firm in its resolve to contain Soviet expansion, "the possibility remains . . . that Soviet power . . . bears within it the seeds of its own decay." In short, Kennan held out the hope of complete victory in the Cold War.

Although Kennan later remarked that he was talking about the political containment of a political threat, in 1947 his article was read as primarily a military blueprint. As such, it satisfied hard-liners but was challenged by many other politicians and respected political commentators. Walter Lippmann challenged Kennan's policy in a series of newspaper articles later published as *The Cold War: A Study in U.S. Foreign Policy* (1947). Containment, Lippmann commented, allowed the Soviet Union largely to decide when and where its battles against America would take place, and it promised to tie the United States to small, unstable "client" countries that would be political, economic, and military drains on America. Seeing that the plan was primarily focused on Western European problems, Lippmann suggested that if followed it might well lead America into a land war in Asia, where the idea of victory would be a cruel delusion. America, Lippmann maintained, was not in the military, economic, or strategic position to implement containment. Lippmann found it "hard to understand how Mr. X could have recommended such a strategic monstrosity."

Containment involved confronting the spread of communism across the globe and, as Americans soon learned, its price was high. It meant supporting allies around the world with billions of dollars in military and economic aid, and it meant thousands of Americans dying in foreign lands. Since containment was a defensive policy, it involved a prolonged Cold War. Unlike World War I and World War II, the Cold War emphasized the doctrine of limited wars fought for limited goals. And in this arrangement, Kennan noted, "Man would have to recognize . . . that the device of military coercion would have . . . only relative—never an absolute—value in the pursuit of political objectives." It was a policy bound to breed frustration and anxiety—certain to influence domestic as well as foreign policy.

Berlin Test

During the late 1940s containment seemed to fit American needs. American-Soviet tensions centered particularly on the future of Germany. The United States maintained that the economic revival of Western Europe depended on a reindustrialized and prosperous Germany. The Soviets believed that a reindustrialized Germany was a dangerous Germany. An early conflict over the two different viewpoints occurred in Berlin, a divided city located in the heart

During 1948 and 1949, an American and British airlift brought close to 7000 tons of food and fuel each day to Soviet-blockaded West Berlin.

of East Germany, deep within the Soviet zone. Future Soviet Premier Nikita Khrushchev called democratic West Berlin a "bone in the throat" of Russia. In June 1948, Stalin decided to remove the bone by stopping all road and rail traffic between West Germany and Berlin. It was a crisis tailor-made for the containment policy. Stalin had picked the time and place. Now Truman had to decide upon a response.

He chose the sky. Stalin could close highways and railways, but he could not effectively close the skyways. For almost one year America and Britain kept West Berlin alive and democratic by a massive airlift. Food, coal, clothing, and all other essentials were flown daily into Berlin. It was a heroic feat, a triumph of technology. Western pilots logged 277,264 flights into West Berlin; they hauled in 2,343,315 tons of food, fuel, medicine, and clothing. Finally on May 12, 1949, Stalin lifted his blockade of West Berlin. For Stalin, the success of the airlift had become an embarrassment for the Soviet Union. In the West, containment had passed an important test.

Troubling Times

Truman scored a series of triumphs during 1947 and 1948. The Truman Doctrine, the Marshall Plan, and the Berlin Airlift strengthened his popularity at home and U.S. prestige abroad. In the election of 1948 Truman won a remarkable upset victory over Thomas E. Dewey. Then in 1949 eleven Western democracies joined the United States in signing the North Atlantic Treaty Organization (NATO) agreement, a mutual defense pact. NATO signified America's position as the leader of the Western Alliance, and it conformed to the containment policy. But difficult times for Truman, containment, and America lay ahead. In late August 1949, American scientists detected traces of radioactive material in the Soviet atmosphere. The cause was as clear as a mushroom-shaped cloud. The Soviets had the bomb—a full decade before American intelligence expected it.

Between 1945 and 1949 the threat of the bomb had given teeth to American policy. It was America's check on the Red Army, and U.S. policy-makers seldom allowed Soviet leaders to forget it. In 1945 Secretary of State James F. Byrnes told his Soviet counterpart V. M. Molotov, "If you don't cut out all this stalling and let us get down to work, I am going to pull an atomic bomb out of my hip pocket and let you have it." Now Molotov had one in his hip pocket. Truman responded by asking his scientists to accelerate the development of a hydrogen bomb; and Congress responded by voting appropriations for Truman's latest defense requests. Of such events and decisions are the humble origins of arms races.

On the heels of the Soviet bomb came more unwelcome news—the establishment of the Communist government in China after a bitter civil war. The war between Mao Tse-tung (Mao Zedong) and Chou En-lai's (Zhou Enlai's) Communists and Chiang Kai-shek's (Jiang Jieshi's) Nationalists had been raging since the 1930s. The United States had strongly

The celebration of the first anniversary of Mao Tse-tung's rule in 1950 brought many Chinese to the streets of Peking.

backed Chiang during the civil war, providing him with more than $3 billion in aid between 1945 and 1949. But the aid was unable to prop up a government that was structurally unsound, inefficient, and corrupt. In the first week of May 1949, Chiang fled across the Formosa Strait to Taiwan, and on September 21, Mao proclaimed Red China's sovereignty. With Chiang in Taiwan and Mao on the mainland, China became two countries.

The Truman administration tried to put the best face possible on the turn of events. Secretary of State Dean Acheson issued a thousand-page white paper explaining how Mao had won the civil war. It detailed the rampant corruption in the Nationalist government and Chiang's many mistakes. Assessing the role of the United States, Acheson concluded, "Nothing that this country did or could have done within the reasonable limits of its capabilities could have changed that result . . . it was the product of internal Chinese forces, forces which this country tried to influence but could not."

For the American public, however, that explanation was not good enough. The China most Americans knew, as one historian put it, was associated with novelist "Pearl Buck's peasants, rejoicing in the good earth . . . dependable, democratic, warm, and above all pro-American." Journalists supported this image during World War II. Americans were told that there were two types of Asians—the good Chinese and the evil Japanese. In 1941 *Time* magazine even ran an article entitled "How to Tell Your Friends From the Japs." It confidently reported, "the Chinese expression is likely to be more placid, kindly, open; the Japanese more positive, dogmatic, arrogant."

Republicans and supporters of Chiang in America blamed Truman for "losing" China. Led by Henry Luce, the influential publisher of *Time* and *Life* and the Chinese-born son of American missionaries, an informal group known as the **China Lobby** blasted the Truman administration. They claimed "egg-sucking phony liberals" had "sold China into atheistic slavery." The China Lobby believed that America had far more influence than it actually had, that a country that contained 6 percent of the earth's population could control the other 94 percent. They were wrong, but millions of Americans took their loud cries seriously.

"China lost itself," Acheson countered. "We picked a bad horse," Truman admitted. But given the political pressure at home, Truman was not about to change mounts in the middle of the race. Reversing America's traditional policy of recognizing de facto governments, Truman refused to recognize the Communist People's Republic of China. Instead he insisted that Chiang's Nationalist government on Taiwan was the legitimate government of China. It was an unrealistic policy, but one that future presidents found politically difficult to reverse. The United States and the People's Republic of China did not establish formal relations until 1979.

The Korean War

The rhetoric of the Truman administration tended to simplify complex issues, intensify the Cold War rivalry, and tie foreign policy to domestic politics. Failure abroad could have calamitous consequences for politicians at home. "If you can't stand the heat, get out of the kitchen," Truman often said. By 1950 the kitchen had become hotter. After "China fell," Truman was more determined than ever to contain communism.

The mood of the Truman administration is clearly evident in **National Security Council Paper Number 68 (NSC-68),** one of the most important documents of the Cold War. Completed in April 1950, it expressed the views of foreign-policy planners Paul Nitze and Dean Acheson that communism was a monolithic world movement directed from the Kremlin; it advocated "an immediate and large-scale build-up in our military and general strength of our allies with the intention of righting the power balance and in the hope that through means other than all-out war we could induce a change in the nature of the Soviet system." NSC-68 extended the Truman

American occupation troops stationed in Japan joined South Korean allies in a retreat that ended up in the southeast area of Korea, where they managed to hold off the North Korean forces.

THE PEOPLE SPEAK

NSC-68

In 1950, at the height of the Cold War—in the wake of "Lost" China and the Alger Hiss trial—President Harry Truman ordered the National Security Council to conduct "a reexamination of our objectives in peace and war and of the effect of these objectives on our strategic plans." The resulting document, NSC-68, is regarded by many as the blueprint of the Truman administration's Cold War policy. Filled with specific policies and statistics advocating a rapid military buildup, NSC-68 opens with a general description of the perceived chasm between American and Soviet values.

> The free society values the individual as an end in himself, requiring of him only that measure of self-discipline and self-restraint which make the rights of each individual compatible with the rights of every other individual. . . .
>
> From this idea of freedom with responsibility derives the marvelous diversity, the deep tolerance, the lawfulness of the free society. This is the explanation of the strength of free men. It constitutes the integrity and the vitality of a free and democratic system. . . .
>
> The idea of freedom is the most contagious idea in history, more contagious than the idea of submission to authority. For the breadth of freedom cannot be tolerated in a society which has come under the domination of an individual or group of individuals with a will to absolute power. Where the despot holds absolute power—the absolute power of the absolutely powerful will—all other wills must be subjugated in an act of willing submission, a degradation willed by the individual upon himself under the compulsion of a perverted faith. . . .
>
> The same compulsion which demands total power over all men within the Soviet state without a single exception, demands total power over all Communist Parties and all states under Soviet domination. Thus Stalin has said that the theory and tactics of Leninism as expounded by the Bolshevik party are mandatory for the proletarian parties of all countries. . . . The antipathy of slavery to freedom explains the iron curtain, the isolation, the autarchy of the society whose end is absolute power. . . .
>
> Thus unwillingly our free society finds itself mortally challenged by the Soviet system. No other value system is so wholly irreconcilable with ours, so implacable in its purpose to destroy ours, so capable of turning to its own uses the most dangerous and divisive trends in our own society, no other so skillfully and powerfully evokes the elements of irrationality in human nature everywhere, and no other has the support of a great and growing center of military power.

Source: Ernest R. May, *American Cold War Strategy: Interpreting NSC 68*. Copyright ©1993 Bedford Books of St. Martin's Press.

Doctrine and called for America to protect the world against the spread of communism. The cost would be great—NSC-68 estimated it at 20 percent of the gross national product, or over a 300-percent increase in military appropriations—but planners warned that without the commitment America faced the prospect of a world moving toward communism.

Truman realized that NSC-68 "meant a great military effort in time of peace. It meant doubling or tripling the budget, increasing taxes heavily, and imposing various kinds of economic controls." And he doubted whether Congress would accept such a peacetime buildup. He never got a chance to find out, for in June 1950 America went to war in Korea.

Korea, like Germany, was a divided country. When the Japanese surrendered its forces in Korea after World War II, Soviet troops accepted the surrender north of the 38th parallel, American troops south of that line. With the deepening of the Cold War, the temporary division line became permanent. North of the 38th parallel, Communist Kim Il Sung governed North Korea. Supported by the Soviet Union, Kim forged a modern, disciplined army during the late 1940s. In South Korea, 75-year-old President Syngman Rhee, who received strong aid and support from the United States, opposed any reconciliation with Communist North Korea. But, as Secretary of State Acheson noted in an unfortunate speech before the National Press Club on January 12, 1950, South Korea lay outside America's primary "defense perimeter." Should an attack occur, Acheson emphasized, the "initial resistance" must come from "the people attacked."

On June 25, 1950, the attack occurred. In an orderly, coordinated offensive, North Korea sent 90,000 men across the 38th parallel into South Korea, where they faced a weak, disorderly South Korean army. It was a mismatch of epic proportions, and

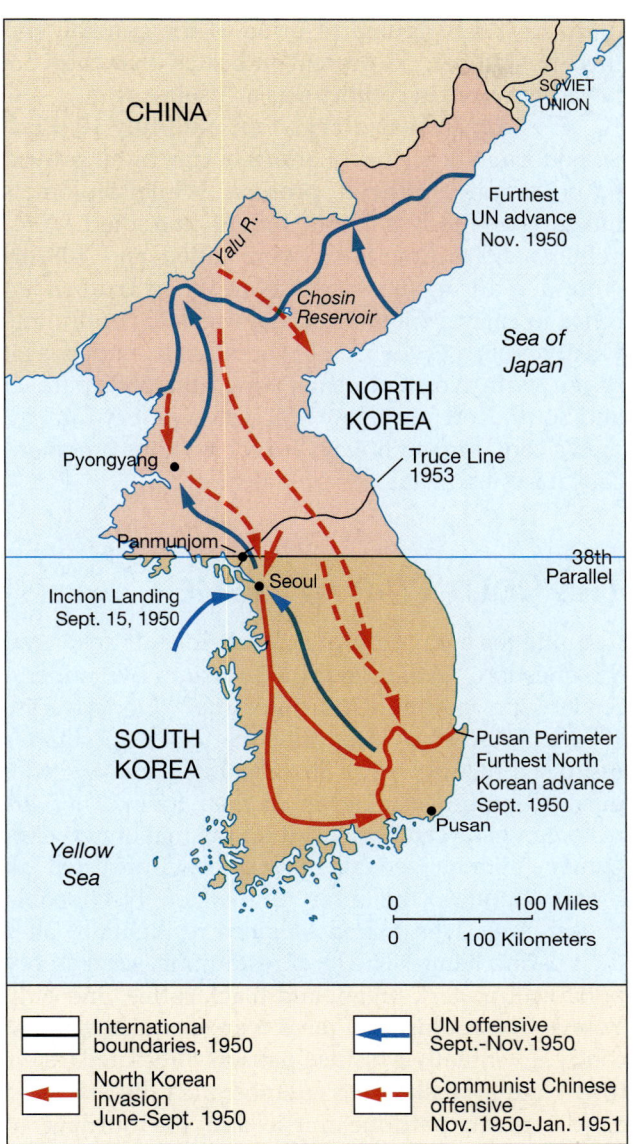

Korean War

South Korean troops quickly mounted an all-out retreat. As the monsoon rains drenched the rice paddies and mountains, Korea moved swiftly toward unification under Kim's Communist government.

Why did North Korea attack? At the time, the Truman administration believed that the Soviets directed the assault. It regarded Kim as little more than a puppet whose strings were manipulated in Moscow. There is little evidence, however, to support this contention. More likely, internal Korean politics dictated the course of events. Kim's position in North Korea was threatened by organized opposition from a rival political party. The invasion of South Korea, therefore, may have been launched to undercut that movement. Certainly Kim informed Stalin of the impending invasion, but the idea and the timing were probably his own.

Truman had just finished a Saturday dinner in Independence, Missouri, when Acheson telephoned him with news of the invasion. His reaction was as rapid and as certain as North Korea's attack. Since both Koreas were technically wards of the United Nations, the Truman administration took the matter to the Security Council. With the Soviet Union absent (it was boycotting the United Nations over the refusal of the organization to seat the People's Republic of China), the Security Council by a 9 to 0 vote condemned the North Korean assault and demanded an immediate cease-fire. Encouraged by the United Nations's prompt action and without consulting Congress, Truman pledged American support to South Korea and strengthened the military position of the United States in Asia.

Truman termed the conflict a "UN police action" and, in fact, a number of UN members sent troops, but for all practical purposes it was a war that initially matched the United States and South Korea against North Korea. Air force advisers told Truman that they could stop the North Korean advance by bombing the Communist supply line. They convinced Truman that ground forces would not be needed. Truman's advisers seemed convinced that the Asians would turn and run at the first show of Western force. Although the bombs destroyed miles of roads and bridges, they did not slow the North Korean advance.

On June 30, Truman took the fateful step of ordering American occupation troops stationed in Japan to proceed to Korea. They soon joined their South Korean allies in a headlong retreat. For six weeks the allies fell steadily back until they stabilized a perimeter in southeast Korea around the port city of Pusan. With their offensive halted, North Korean troops mounted a siege. To the surprise of the world, the Pusan perimeter held firm.

For American soldiers it had been a painful and disappointing two months. They were fighting in an unfamiliar country for an unsatisfactory objective. Truman's announced goal was simply to restore the 38th parallel as the border between the two Koreas. Victory then was defined as a stalemate. Corporal Stephen Zeg of Chicago expressed the feeling of other soldiers when he commented, "I'll fight for my country, but I'll be damned if I see why I'm fighting to save this hellhole."

But fighting they were, and **General Douglas MacArthur** was determined to reverse the military situation of the war. A bold, even arrogant man, firmly fixed in his opinions and certain of his ability to command in battle, MacArthur decided to split his forces and launch a surprise attack against the North Korean's rear. On the morning of September 15, 1950, American marines began an amphibious attack on Inchon, a port city, wrote one historian, "about as large as Jersey City, as ugly as Liverpool, and as dreary as Belfast." MacArthur's military advisers warned him against the move, noting that Inchon possessed every natural and geographic handicap. MacArthur, however, was confident of victory. It was a bold, risky maneuver—a bold, risky, successful maneuver.

Faced with an enemy to their front and their rear, North Korean troops retreated across the border. By the beginning of October those North Korean soldiers who were not captured or killed were above the 38th parallel. Truman had achieved his stated objective. But the warrior in MacArthur wanted more—he wanted victory on the battlefield. And he said so, loudly and publicly. In private the Truman administration was moving toward MacArthur's position. Containment was giving way to a policy of liberation. After receiving MacArthur's reassurances at a private meeting on Wake Island, Truman decided to allow U.S. forces to move across the 38th parallel and "liberate" North Korea. Like MacArthur's Inchon landing, it was a bold plan, one predicated on the widely held American belief that China would not intervene in the conflict.

This time boldness failed. North Korea was a difficult country to invade. The American army had no reliable maps and mountainous terrain rendered traditional military tactics impossible. In addition, as MacArthur's forces moved recklessly north toward Manchuria, Chinese officials sent informal warnings to the United States that unless the advance stopped, their country would enter the fray. MacArthur ignored Chinese warnings and his own intelligence reports and kept moving.

Communist China struck in late November. Over 300,000 troops poured across the border and attacked unprepared American forces radically altering the nature of the war. Victory was now out of the question. Only MacArthur continued to talk about an absolute victory. If a nation was going to fight a war, he sermonized, it should fight to win. In Washington, however, the Truman administration was shifting back to the pre-Inchon policy of containment. When MacArthur publicly criticized the administration's newest approach, an angry Truman recalled him and replaced him with General Matthew B. Ridgway. In America Truman's sacking of "Mac" raised a firestorm of protest. An April 1951 Gallup poll reported that 66 percent of Americans disapproved of Truman's firing of the general, and then in October, 56 percent indicated that they believed the Korean conflict was a "useless war."

The Korean War dragged on until July 10, 1951, when formal peace negotiations began, but it proved to be a long, difficult process. While diplomats talked, American soldiers fought and died. Altogether, 34,000 Americans were killed and 103,000 wounded during the Korean War. When Truman left office in early 1953 the carnage was still continuing. Finally on July 26, 1953, the war officially ended, as it began, with North Koreans above the 38th parallel and South Koreans below it. It was a victory for Truman's containment policy, but for millions of Americans it somehow tasted like defeat.

THE COLD WAR AT HOME

Commie for a day. It was a theme idea. It answered the question, "What would it be like to live under a Soviet-type, communist dictatorship?" On May Day 1950, at Mosinee, Wisconsin, American Legionnaires disguised themselves as Soviet soldiers and staged a mock Communist takeover of their town. They arrested and summarily locked up the mayor and clergymen, nationalized all businesses, confiscated all firearms, and rid the library of rows of objectionable books. They even forced Mosinee residents to alter their eating habits. The local restaurants served only potato soup, dark bread, and black coffee, and only Young Communist Leaguers were permitted to eat candy. Eventually Mosinee patriots "liberated" their town, and at dusk a mass democratic rally was held amidst much patriotic music and the burning of Communist literature.

For most of Mosinee's citizens it was an edifying experiment. "We really learned about what 100 percent communism would be like," one resident observed. They concluded that life under communism was hardly worth living. Many found intolerable the lack of such basic freedoms as privacy, speech, press, religion, and decent food. One participant confessed, "I know some people who even drove to [neighboring] Wausau to get something to eat. In Russia I guess you wouldn't be able to get anything else anywhere."

Although there is an element of humor to Mosinee's Red May Day, behind the events was a national mood that was far from funny. As Truman waged the Cold War abroad, Cold War issues gradually came to dominate the American domestic scene. During the ensuing Red Scare, the fear of communism disrupted American life, and the freedoms that

Americans took for granted came under attack. At home as well as abroad, Americans battled real and imagined Communist enemies.

Adjusting to Peace

Truman and his advisers approached the end of World War II with their eyes on the past. They were uneasy about the future: Memories of the Great Depression and the painful social and economic adjustment after World War I clouded their thinking. They knew that massive wartime spending, not the New Deal, had ended the Great Depression, and they worried that peace might bring more economic suffering. Peace with prosperity was their goal.

The solution to the problems of converting back to a peacetime economy, Truman believed, lay in the continuation, at least for a time, of wartime government economic controls. During the war, the Office of Price Administration (OPA) had controlled prices and held inflation in check. After Japan surrendered, Truman asked Congress to continue price controls and outlined a program for economic reconversion. To ensure future prosperity, Truman advocated such economic measures as a 65-cents-an-hour minimum wage, nationalization of the housing industry, and stronger fair employment practices legislation.

Congress responded half-heartedly, passing the Employment Act of 1946. Although it was less than Truman had requested, it did provide the institutional framework for more government control over the economy. The act created the Council of Economic Advisors to help "promote free competitive enterprise, to avoid economic fluctuations ... and to maintain employment, production, and purchasing power." During the decades after 1946, the council exerted a powerful influence over economic policy.

On the other hand, Republicans and southern Democrats balked against a return to more "New Dealism." Congress destroyed the OPA by relaxing its controls, a policy that created immediate inflation. Congress's refusal to pass Truman's economic package did not tumble America into another depression. In truth, the American economy was basically sound. Wartime employment and wartime saving had created a people whose money was burning holes in their pockets. They wanted peacetime goods—automobiles, houses, Scotch whiskey, nylon stockings, and red meat. Given the demand and the short supply, inflation was inevitable. In addition, the short supply of consumer goods increased black-market activities. Americans offered bribes for preferential treatment from car salesmen, butchers, and landlords, but as industries converted to peacetime production, consumer supplies rose to meet the new demands.

Confronting the Demands of Labor

The death of the OPA led to demands for higher wages as well as to higher prices. During the war labor unions had taken "no strike" pledges, and it was through their efforts that America became the "arsenal of democracy." Workers labored long and hard, agreeing to speedups and higher production quotas. Virtually no production time was lost to strikes.

The end of the war signaled the start of the strike season as workers demanded rewards for their wartime efforts and their loss of overtime pay. During 1946 over 4.5 million laborers struck, and 107,476,000 workdays were lost to strikes. If labor's cause was just, its timing was disastrous. After clashing repeatedly with an obstreperous Congress, Truman was in no mood to coddle labor. When two national railway brotherhoods threatened to disrupt the transportation system, Truman proposed to draft the workers. On national radio he announced, "The crisis at Pearl Harbor was the result of action by a foreign enemy. The crisis tonight is caused by a group of men within our country who place their private interests above the welfare of the nation." Confronted by hostile public opinion and an unsympathetic president, the brotherhoods went back to work.

Labor was angry. United Mine Workers leader John L. Lewis told reporters, "You can't mine coal with bayonets." As winter approached, Lewis took his men out on strike. The prospect of a cold winter created anxiety, and Truman reacted angrily, threatening to take over the mines. He then appealed directly to the miners, asking them to go back to work for the good and warmth of the nation. It worked. Lewis called off the strike. Truman's prestige and confidence soared.

Truman's gains were labor's losses. The congressional elections of 1946, which brought to power the conservative Republican-controlled Eightieth Congress, added to labor's problems. Led by Robert Taft, Congress pushed through the Labor-Management Relations Act of 1947 (better known as the **Taft-Hartley Act**), which was passed over Truman's veto. It outlawed the closed shop (a business or industry in which all the employees were required to join a union), gave presidents power to delay strikes by declaring a "cooling-off" period, and curtailed the political and economic power of organized labor. The act reflected the country's increasingly conservative mood.

Failure of the Fair Deal

Political experts expected America to vote Republican in the 1948 presidential elections. Truman's policies had angered liberals, labor, Southerners, and most of Congress. Moreover, Democrats had occupied the White House since 1933. Republicans reasoned that it was time for a change. They nominated Thomas E. Dewey of New York, the GOP candidate in 1944. The Democrats stayed with Truman, even though large numbers of Southerners and liberals deserted the party to follow third-party movements. Southerners, angered by Truman's support of civil rights, formed the States' Rights Democratic party—better known as the Dixiecrats—and nominated Governor J. Strom Thurmond of South Carolina for president. Liberals joined with Communists to form the Progressive party, which nominated FDR's former vice president Henry A. Wallace for president.

An underdog from the start, Truman rolled up his sleeves and took his cause to the people by train, the 17-car "Presidential Special." As it moved across the country, Truman blasted the "do-nothing" Eightieth Congress at each stop. "If you send another Republican Congressman to Washington, you're a bigger bunch of suckers than I think you are," he lectured. "Give 'em hell, Harry!" was the popular refrain. By contrast, Dewey sat tight, seemingly more concerned with his fastidious appearance than his bland speeches. His cold personality failed to move American voters. "I don't know which is the chillier experience—to have Tom ignore you or shake your hand," noted a Truman supporter. "You have to get to know Dewey to dislike him," added another.

By election day Truman had closed the gap. The old Roosevelt coalition—midwestern farmers, urban ethnic groups, organized labor, African Americans, and Southerners—remained sufficiently strong to send Truman back to the White House. Neither the Dixiecrats nor the progressives hurt Truman in any substantial way, since most Democrats chose to remain in the center of the party with Truman rather than drift toward the radical fringes. Truman's victory was a testimony to the legacy of FDR as well as Truman's scrappiness, and to the often overlooked fact that Democrats outnumbered Republicans in the nation.

"Keep America Human With Truman," read one of his campaign posters. In 1949 he announced a plan to do just that. Known as the **Fair Deal,** the legislative package included an expansion of Social Security, federal aid to education, a higher minimum wage, federal funding for public housing projects, a national plan for medical insurance, civil rights legislation for minorities, and other measures to foster social and economic justice. As Truman explained, "I expect to give every segment of our population a fair deal." At the core of the Fair Deal was his belief that government-controlled economic expansion blunts extremism from the right and left and ensures prosperity.

Congress took Truman's package, stripped off the wrapping, threw away some of the contents, and sent it back to the president for his signature. Congress did extend Social Security, raise the minimum wage to 75 cents an hour, and further developed several New Deal programs. But the more original proposals of the Fair Deal—civil rights legislation, a national health insurance program, an imaginative farm program, and federal aid to education—were rejected by a Congress that opposed anything defined as "creeping socialism."

Truman, as well as Congress, contributed to the ultimate failure of the Fair Deal to achieve its objectives. Republicans and Southerners did join forces in opposition to civil rights and government spending programs, but Truman demonstrated an almost total inability to work with Congress on domestic issues. In addition, by 1949 foreign policy dominated the president's attention and claimed an increasing share of the federal budget.

Searching for the Enemy Within

While Congress removed the heart from Truman's Fair Deal, Cold War winds were chilling the coun-

Most pollsters predicted that Republican candidate Thomas E. Dewey would win the 1948 presidential election, but in a stunning political upset the voters re-elected President Truman.

Widespread protesting, both for and against Julius and Ethel Rosenberg, was common after their conviction for treason in 1951 and subsequent execution in 1953.

try's political landscape. The tough diplomatic rhetoric of Truman, Acheson, and other policy-makers encouraged Americans to view the rivalry between the Soviet Union and the United States in simplistic terms. America became the "defender of free people," the Soviet Union the "atheistic enslaver of millions." Every time a world event did not go America's way, it was seen as a Soviet victory. In this world of black-and-white thinking, the suspicion that "enemies within" America were secretly aiding the Soviet cause took shape. Soon, talk of American "atomic spies" giving information to the Soviets and State Department officials sabotaging U.S. foreign policy became common.

Were spies working against American interests to further the Soviet cause? Unquestionably, yes. In 1945 Igor Gouzenko, a Soviet embassy official in Ottawa, defected to the West, carrying with him documents that detailed a Communist spy ring working in Canada and the United States. The evidence led to the arrests of two British physicists, Dr. Alan Munn May and Dr. Klaus Fuchs, who had worked on the Manhattan Project. Fuchs implicated a group of American radicals—Harry Gold, David Greenglass, Morton Sobell, and **Julius and Ethel Rosenberg**. Clearly these individuals had passed atomic secrets to the Soviets during the war. Whether or not this information helped the Soviet Union to develop an atomic bomb is largely conjecture.

The damage done by British spies Kim Philby, Guy Burgess, and Donald Maclean is more certain. The three men held high British diplomatic and intelligence posts and were privy to sensitive American CIA and British Secret Intelligence Service (SIS) information. In 1951 Burgess and Maclean defected to the Soviet Union, where they were joined by Philby in 1963. There is considerable circumstantial evidence that the information they passed to the

Soviet Union severely compromised American Cold War intelligence and may have been influential in the Chinese intervention in the Korean War.

There were certainly spies, but the issue soon outgrew the question of mere espionage and became an instrument of partisan politics. Republicans accused Democrats of being "soft" on communism—in fact, of harboring spies in the State Department and other government agencies. Richard M. Nixon, who was elected to Congress in 1946, announced that Democrats were responsible for "the unimpeded growth of the communist conspiracy in the United States." As proof Republicans pointed to the "fall" of China, the atomic bomb in the Soviet Union, and Alger Hiss in the State Department.

Truman reacted to such criticism as early as 1947 by issuing Executive Order 9835, which established the Federal Employee Loyalty Program, authorizing the FBI to investigate all government employees. Although the search disclosed no espionage or treason, thousands of employees were forced to resign or were fired because their personal lives or past associations did not meet government inspection. Homosexuality, alcoholism, unpaid debts, contribution to left-wing causes, support of civil rights—all became grounds for dismissal.

Truman also used the anti-Communism issue to drum up support for his foreign policy. At the end of World War II public opinion polls revealed that few Americans regarded communism as a serious problem. Republican charges and Truman's loyalty program, however, encouraged citizens to profess 100 percent Americanism. In 1947 the president sent a special "Freedom Train" across the country to exhibit important national documents, including the Truman Doctrine. By 1950 communism had become a more visible issue at home as well as abroad.

Ethel and Julius Rosenberg paid the supreme price for being Communists. At least one may have been a spy, but the death penalty was not mandatory for their crime. But their "diabolical conspiracy to destroy a God-fearing nation," according to Judge Irving R. Kaufman, had given the Soviets the bomb "years before our best scientists predicted." He ordered the couple's execution for treason. On June 19, 1953, the Rosenbergs, parents of two young sons, died in the electric chair.

The Rise and Fall of Joseph McCarthy

More than any other person, Wisconsin Senator Joseph McCarthy capitalized on the anti-Communism issue. Although he did not start the crusade or even join it until 1950, the entire movement bears the name "McCarthyism." His career, which was the cause of so much suffering for so many, illuminated the price the country had to pay for temporarily placing anti-Communism above the Constitution.

Elected to the Senate in 1946, McCarthy spent four years in relative obscurity, all the while demonstrating his incompetence and angering his colleagues. Then on February 9, 1950, he gave a Lincoln's Birthday address in Wheeling, West Virginia. Warning his audience about the threat of communism to America, he boldly announced, "While I cannot take the time to name all of the men in the State Department who have been named as members of the Communist Party and members of a spy ring, I have in my hand a list of 205 . . . a list of names that were known to the Secretary of State and who nevertheless are still working and shaping the policy of the State Department." McCarthy had no real list; he had no names. Simply put, he was lying. But within days he became a national sensation.

McCarthy dealt in simple solutions for complex problems. He told Americans that the United States could control the outcome of world affairs if it would get the Communists out of the State Department. It was those "State Department perverts," those "striped-pants diplomats" who "gave away" Poland, "lost" China, and allowed the Soviet Union to develop the bomb. It was the "bright young men who are born with silver spoons in their mouths" who were "selling the Nation out." His arguments found receptive ears among Catholics who had relatives in Eastern Europe, political outsiders who resented the power of the "Ivy League Eastern Establishment," supporters of Chiang, and pragmatic Republicans who wanted to return to the White House in 1952. McCarthy's support only grew with the outbreak of the Korean War in the early summer of 1950.

McCarthy's origins were humble; he worked his way through high school and a Catholic college and intentionally cultivated the image of a bull in a china shop. With his beetle brow, he looked the part of a movie villain. He was in all ways the opposite of Secretary of State Dean Acheson, whose Ivy League degrees, waxed mustache, and aristocratic accent were a flapping red flag to McCarthy. Throughout the early 1950s McCarthy bitterly attacked "Red Dean" and the State Department. But in the end, McCarthy ferreted out no Communists, espionage agents, or traitors.

McCarthy's basic tactic was never defend. Caught in a lie, he told another; when one case dis-

Senator Joseph McCarthy's downfall came about as a result of his unsubstantiated charges of Communist infiltration throughout the army.

solved, he created another. He attacked Truman and Eisenhower, Acheson and Marshall, the State Department and the U.S. Army. No authority or institution frightened him. In 1954 his campaign against the army became so bitter that the Senate arranged special hearings. Televised between April 22 and June 17, the Army-McCarthy hearings attracted a high audience rating. It was the first time that most Americans saw McCarthy in action—the bullying of witnesses, the cruel innuendo, the tasteless humor. At one point he attempted to ruin a young lawyer's career in order to discredit the lawyer's associate, Joseph Welch, the army's chief counsel. Welch unsuccessfully tried to stop McCarthy. Appalled, the chief counsel interrupted, "Until this moment, Senator, I think I never really gauged your cruelty or your recklessness.... Have you no sense of decency, sir, at long last?"

He didn't, and a large television audience saw that he didn't. McCarthy's consequent downfall was as rapid as his rise. When the polls showed that his popularity had swung sharply downward, his colleagues mounted an offensive. On December 2, 1954, the Senate voted to "condemn" McCarthy for his unsenatorial behavior. Newspapers stopped printing his outlandish charges. He sank back into relative obscurity and died on May 2, 1957.

The end of the Korean War and McCarthy's downfall signaled the end of the Red Scare. The Cold War remained, but most Americans soon realized that there was no significant domestic Communist threat. They learned that an occasional spy was part of the price that free societies pay for their personal freedom, and that "McCarthyism" can be the result of a curtailment of that freedom.

THE PARANOID STYLE

The Cold War mentality left its imprint on politics and culture during the late 1940s and early 1950s. A certain "paranoid style" permeated the early Cold War years. Defining the term, historian Richard Hofstadter wrote:

> It is, above all, a way of seeing the world and of expressing oneself.... The distinguishing thing about the paranoid style is... that its exponents see... a "vast" or "gigantic" conspiracy as *the motive force* in historical events.... The paranoid spokesman sees the fate of this conspiracy in apocalyptic terms—he traffics in the birth and death of whole worlds, whole political orders, whole systems of human values.... Since what is at stake is always a conflict between absolute good and absolute evil, the quality needed is not a willingness to compromise but the will to fight things out to the finish.

The nature of the fight against communism contributed to the paranoid style. Politicians warned Americans that communism silently and secretly destroyed a country from within. Although allegedly directed from Moscow, its aim was subversion through the slow destruction of a country's moral fiber. No one knew which institution it would next attack, or when. It might be the State Department or the YMCA; it might be the presidency, the army, the movie industry, or the Cub Scouts. Politicians counseled vigilance. They told Americans to watch for the unexpected, to suspect everyone and everything. As a result, between 1945 and 1955 a broad spectrum of institutions, organizations, and individuals came under suspicion. Whether it was the Mafia or the fluoridation of drinking water, Americans sought the answers to complex problems in the workings of conspiracies.

THE American Mosaic

The Kefauver Crime Committee

IN May 1950, at the very moment that Senator Joseph McCarthy was beginning his crusade against the domestic political threat posed by communism, the U.S. Senate created a special committee to investigate another "enemy within": organized crime. The nation appeared to be in the midst of an unprecedented wave of lawlessness. A memorandum to the president reported that a serious crime was committed in the United States every 18.7 seconds. Aggravated assault was up 68.7 percent over prewar averages; rape was up 49.9 percent. Burglary, murder, robbery, prostitution, gambling, and racketeering all were on the increase. Criminologists attributed the postwar crime wave to such factors as the wartime disruption of families, shortages of goods during and after the war, and a continuing public demand for illicit gambling. But journalists, citizen crime commissions, and the Federal Bureau of Narcotics identified another villain: organized crime.

Estes Kefauver, an ambitious 47-year-old first-term Tennessee Democratic senator, originally proposed a congressional investigation of organized crime in January 1949. The Truman administration, already rocked by charges of fiscal mismanagement, financial irregularities, and favors to businessmen, feared that any inquiry might link urban Democratic political machines to criminal activities. For a time, the administration succeeded in blocking a potentially embarrassing investigation. But on April 6, 1950, the bodies of two gangsters were found in a Kansas City, Missouri, Democratic political club under a photograph of President Truman. The Democratic-controlled Senate quickly authorized the investigation of organized crime.

For the next 15 months, the committee held hearings in 14 major cities and took testimony from more than 800 witnesses. The committee immediately attracted national attention by linking individuals close to Florida's Democratic governor, Fuller Warren, to a bookmaking syndicate controlled by Al Capone's mob in Chicago. Subsequent hearings in Kansas City and Chicago revealed widespread examples of political corruption and influence peddling.

Television made the Kefauver committee's hearings among the most influential in American history. While the Kefauver committee did not hold the first televised congressional hearings (it was actually the fifth congressional committee to allow TV cameras into a hearing room), it was the first to attract a massive number of viewers. As many as 20 to 30 million Americans watched spellbound as crime bosses, bookies, pimps, and hitmen appeared on their television screens. They listened intently as the committee's chairman informed them that "there is a secret international government-within-a-government" in the United States, controlling gambling, vice, and narcotics traffic and infiltrating legitimate businesses, protected by corrupt police officers, prosecutors, judges, and politicians.

The high point of the investigation occurred in New York City, where the committee held televised hearings beginning on March 12, 1951, and lasting eight days. Over 50 witnesses testified before the committee, but public interest centered on the alleged boss of the New York underworld Frank Costello, alias Francisco Castaglia, alias Frank Severio. Costello was purportedly head of the organized crime family previously run by Vito Genovese and Charles Luciano.

In his initial appearance before the committee, Costello's lawyer objected to having his client's face televised. Technicians proceeded to focus the cameras on Costello's hands. The result was television at its most powerful. As committee counsel Rudolph Halley fired questions, Costello was seen nervously ripping sheets of paper to shreds, drumming his fingers on the table top, and clenching his fist.

During the New York hearings, daytime television audiences grew from a minuscule 1.5 percent of homes to a phenomenal 26.2 percent. In the New York metropolitan area an average of 86.2 percent of all individuals watching television watched the hearings, twice the number that had watched the World Series the previous October. The New York City electric company had to add a generator to supply power for all the television sets in use. Commented *Life* magazine: "The week of March 12, 1951, will occupy a special place in history.... [People] had suddenly gone indoors into living rooms, taverns and clubrooms, auditoriums and backoffices. There, in eerie half-light, looking at millions of small frosty screens, people sat as if charmed.... Never before had the attention of the nation been riveted so completely on a single matter."

The Kefauver committee failed to produce effective crime-fighting legislation, but it did heighten public awareness of the problem of political

corruption and organized crime, and generated pressure to enforce existing law. In the aftermath of the committee's investigation, more than 70 local crime commissions were established. The Special Rackets Squad of the FBI launched 46,000 investigations, and by 1957, federal prosecutors had won 874 convictions and recovered $336 million. The committee's hearings were largely responsible for the defeat of proposals to legalize gambling in Arizona, California, Massachusetts, and Montana.

The investigation was important in one other respect. The Kefauver committee played a vital role in popularizing the myth that organized crime in the United States was an alien import, brought to the United States by Italian, and especially by Sicilian, immigrants in the form of the Mafia, a highly centralized, secret organization, that used violence and deceit to prey on the weaknesses and vices of the public. In its report, the committee asserted that much of the responsibility for gambling, loan sharking, prostitution, and narcotics trafficking lay in two major syndicates.

In fact, the committee's conclusion—that organized crime was rooted in a highly centralized ethnic conspiracy—was an error. Most organized crime in the United States is organized on a municipal and regional, rather than a national, basis. And despite the image portrayed in such epics as Mario Puzo's *The Godfather*, diverse ethnic groups have participated in such sophisticated crimes as large-scale gambling, loan sharking, narcotics trafficking, and labor racketeering.

Today, the power of the nation's traditional Mafia families appears to be dwindling. Since the mid-1980s, more than 100 top Cosa Nostra leaders have been sentenced to long prison terms. In Detroit, Kansas City, Milwaukee, New England, New Jersey, Philadelphia, and St. Louis, where Mafia gangs once influenced the construction, trucking, trash collection, and garment manufacturing industries, Mafia strength has sharply declined. The decline of the mob, however, does not mean the end of organized crime; rival crime groups have stepped in and taken over such activities as illegal gambling and drug trafficking.

HUAC Goes to Hollywood

The House of Representatives had established the **House Un-American Activities Committee** (**HUAC**) in the late 1930s to combat subversive right-wing and left-wing movements. Its history was less than distinguished. From the first it tended to see subversive Communists everywhere at work in American society. HUAC even announced that the Boy Scouts were infiltrated by Communists. During the late 1940s and the early 1950s HUAC picked up the tempo of its investigations, which it conducted in well-publicized sessions. Twice during this period HUAC "traveled" to Hollywood to investigate Communist infiltration in the film industry.

HUAC first went to Hollywood in 1947. Although it didn't find the party line preached in the movies, it did call a group of radical screenwriters and producers into its sessions to testify. Asked if they were Communists, a group of leftist filmmakers known as the "Hollywood Ten" refused to answer questions about their political beliefs. As Ring Lardner, Jr., one of the ten, said, "I could answer . . . but if I did, I would hate myself in the morning." They believed that the First Amendment protected them. In the politically charged late 1940s, however, their rights were not protected. Those who refused to divulge their political affiliations were tried for contempt of Congress, sent to prison, and blacklisted.

HUAC went back to Hollywood in 1951. This time it called hundreds of witnesses from both the political right and the political left. Conservatives told HUAC that Hollywood was littered with "Commies." Walt Disney even recounted attempts to have Mickey Mouse follow the party line. Of the radicals, some talked and others didn't. To cooperate with HUAC entailed "naming names"—that is, informing on one's friends and political acquaintances. Again, those who refused to name names found themselves unemployed and unemployable.

The HUAC hearings and blacklistings convinced Hollywood producers to make strongly anti-Communist films. Between 1947 and 1954 they released more than 50 such films. Most were second-rate movies, starring third-rate actors. The films assured Americans that Communists were thoroughly bad people—they didn't have children, they exhaled cigarette smoke too slowly, they murdered their "friends," and they went berserk when arrested. As one film historian has commented, the Communists in these anti-Communist films even looked alike; most were "apt to be exceptionally haggard or disgracefully pudgy," and there was certainly "some-

Movies like *Rebel Without a Cause*, starring James Dean, depicted the futility and hopelessness of American youth in the 1950s.
Film Stills Archive/The Museum of Modern Art, New York.

thing terribly wrong with a woman if her slip straps showed through her blouse."

The films may have been bad civics lessons, but they did have an impact. They seemed to confirm HUAC's position that Communists were everywhere, that subversives lurked in every shadow. They reaffirmed the paranoid style and helped to justify McCarthy's harangues and Truman's Cold War rhetoric.

"What's Wrong with Our Kids Today?"

At the same time as it was turning out films about serious but bumbling Communists, Hollywood was producing movies that contributed to the fear that something was terribly wrong with the youth of America. Films such as *The Wild One* (1954), *Blackboard Jungle* (1955), and *Rebel Without a Cause* (1955) portrayed adolescents as budding criminals, emerging homosexuals, potential fascists, and pathological misfits—everything but perfectly normal kids.

FBI reports and congressional investigations reinforced the theme of the moral decline of America's adolescents. J. Edgar Hoover, head of the FBI, linked the rise in juvenile delinquency to the decline in the influence of family, home, church, and local community institutions. Youths had moved away from benign authority toward the temptations of popular culture, which, Hoover said, "flout indecency and applaud lawlessness."

Frederic Wertham, a psychiatrist who studied the problem extensively, agreed, emphasizing particularly the pernicious influence of comic books. He believed that crime and horror comic books fostered racism, fascism, and sexism in their readers. In his book *Seduction of the Innocent* (1954), Wertham even linked homosexuality to the reading of comics. Describing how the comic *Batman* could lead to homosexuality, Wertham quoted one of his male patients: "I remember the first time I came across the page mentioning the 'secret bat cave.' The thought of Batman and Robin living together and possibly having sex relations came to my mind, . . . I felt I'd like to be loved by someone like Batman or Superman." Far from being an unheard voice, Wertham's attack generated congressional investigations of and local attacks against the comic book industry. In response, the industry passed several self-regulatory codes designed to restrict the violent and sexual content of comic books.

For a number of critics, sports were an antidote to the ills of wayward youths. "Organized sport is one of our best weapons against juvenile delinquency," remarked J. Edgar Hoover. Youths who competed for championship trophies felt no inclination to compete for "wrist watches, bracelets and automobiles that belong to other people." Nor would they turn to Communism. As Senator Herman Welker of Idaho bluntly put it, "I never saw a ballplayer who was a Communist."

Given these widespread beliefs, the sports scandals of the early 1950s shocked the nation and raised fresh questions about the morality of American adolescents. In February 1951 New York authorities disclosed that players for the City College of New York (CCNY) basketball team had accepted money to fix games. By the time the investigations ended, Long Island University, New York University, Manhattan College, St. John's, Toledo, Bradley, and Kentucky were implicated in the scandal, which involved forging transcripts, paying players, and fixing games. In August 1951 the scandal moved to football. This one involved academic cheating, not point shaving, and was confined to one school—the United States Military Academy at West Point. Altogether, Academy officials dismissed 90 cadets, half of them football players, for violations of the school's honor code.

The West Point scandal, especially, struck at the nation's heart, for half a world away in Korea American soldiers were battling to contain communism. What of their moral fiber? They too had read comics, watched films written by left-wing screen writers, and been exposed to "subversive" influences. Did they have the "right stuff"? These questions swirled around the Korean prisoner-of-war (POW) controversy. Early reports suggested that American POWs in Korea were different from, and inferior to, those of World War II. Journalists portrayed them as undisciplined, morally weak, susceptible to "brainwashing," uncommitted to traditional American ideals, and prone to collaborate with their guards.

What was wrong? Who was corrupting the youth of America? The Republican *Chicago Tribune* blamed the New Deal. The Communist *Daily Worker* said it was the fault of Wall Street, bankers, and greedy politicians (the paranoid style, after all, had no party affiliation). Other Americans, without being too specific, simply felt that there was some ominous force working within America against America.

Adherents to the paranoid style dealt more in vague perceptions than concrete facts. They reacted more to what *seemed* to be true than to what actually was true. In fact, sociologists and historians have demonstrated that Korean POWs behaved in much the same way as POWs from earlier wars. Juvenile delinquency was not on an upswing during the late 1940s and 1950s. And alien subversive forces were not undermining American morality. In retrospect, we know this. But the rhetoric of the Cold War and McCarthyism created a political atmosphere that proved fertile for the paranoid style.

CONCLUSION

By 1953 and 1954 there were indications of a thaw in the Cold War. First came the death of Joseph Stalin, which was officially announced on March 5, 1953. Shortly thereafter Georgi Malenkov told the Supreme Soviet, the highest legislative body of the Soviet Union: "At the present time there is no disputed or unresolved question that cannot be settled peacefully by mutual agreement. . . . This applies to our relations with all states, including the United States of America." That summer the Korean War ended in a stalemate that allowed both the United States and the Communist forces to save face. In America, 1954 saw the fall of McCarthy. Certainly these events did not

Chronology of Key Events

1938 House Un-American Activities Committee (HUAC) is created to investigate Fascist or Communist subversion

1945 United Nations is founded

1947 Truman Doctrine declares that the United States will provide military and economic aid to allies faced by external aggression or internal subversion; Truman establishes a federal program to investigate the loyalty of government employees; Marshall Plan provides $17 billion over four years to Western Europe to aid in its economic recovery; Taft-Hartley Act, passed over President Truman's veto, bans the closed shop, restricts union political contributions, and allows courts to delay strikes threatening health or safety; HUAC investigates Communist infiltration of the film industry

1948 State of Israel proclaimed; United States, Britain, and France merge their zones of occupation in Germany to form an independent nation, West Germany; Soviet Union blockades Berlin; ex-Communist Whittaker Chambers charges that former State Department official Alger Hiss gave him secret government documents

1949 NATO is founded; Berlin blockade ends; Mao Zedong's Communist forces win China's civil war; Soviet Union successfully tests an atomic bomb

1950 NSC–68 argues that the United States must commit itself to whatever military steps are necessary to stop the spread of Communism; Senator Joseph McCarthy claims he has the names of 205 State Department employees who were members of the Communist party; North Korean troops cross the 38th parallel, beginning the Korean War; UN forces invade North Korea; Chinese troops enter North Korea and force UN troops to retreat across the 38th parallel

1951 Negotiations to work out a cease-fire in Korea begin; HUAC conducts a second investigation of Communist subversion in Hollywood; Ethel and Julius Rosenberg are sentenced to death for espionage

1953 Dwight D. Eisenhower is inaugurated as the thirty-fourth president; cease-fire signed in Korean War

1954 Army-McCarthy hearings; U.S. Senate censures McCarthy for "conduct unbecoming a member"

---

end the paranoid style in either America or the Soviet Union, but they did ease the tension.

In addition, by 1954 both the United States and the Soviet Union had become more comfortable in their positions as world powers. Leaders in both countries had begun to realize that neither side could readily win the Cold War. Between 1945 and 1954 each side had carved out spheres of influence. The Soviet Union and its sometime-ally China dominated most of Eastern Europe and the Asian mainland. America and its allies controlled Western Europe, North and South America, most of the Pacific, and to a lesser extent Africa, the Middle East, and Southeast Asia. Throughout much of the Third World, however, emerging nationalistic movements would challenge both U.S. and Soviet influences.

In the United States, the containment policy was seldom even debated. The Truman Doctrine and muscular internationalism governed foreign policy decisions, but economic and political questions lingered. How much would containment cost? Where would the money come from? Which Americans would pay the most? Would it mean the end of liberal reform? Over the next decade American leaders would wrestle with these and other questions.

Suggestions for Further Reading

Gar Alperovitz, *Atomic Diplomacy,* rev. ed. (1985). Controversial study that ignited a serious second look at the reasons for America's use of atomic weapons.

Larry Ceplair and Steven Englund, *The Inquisition in Hollywood* (1980). Studies the impact of Washington on Hollywood and Hollywood's impact on America.

Stanley I. Kutler, *The American Inquisition: Justice and Injustice in the Cold War* (1982). A series of poignant studies of the human consequences of the domestic side of the Cold War.

Walter LeFeber, *America, Russia, and the Cold War,* 7th ed. (1993). The frequently updated story of the great rivalry of the second half of the twentieth century.

David McCullough, *Truman* (1992). Sprawling biography of Harry Truman and the world that made him.

David M. Oshinsky, *A Conspiracy So Immense: The World of Joe McCarthy* (1983). A fascinating biography of a man who gave his name to an age.

Allen Weinstein, *Perjury: The Hiss-Chambers Case* (1978). A detailed examination of Alger Hiss's guilt.

Daniel Yergin, *Shattered Peace* (1977). Well-written, balanced exploration of the origins of the Cold War.

Overviews and Surveys

Stephen E. Ambrose, *Rise to Globalism: American Foreign Policy Since 1938,* 5th ed. (1988); H. W. Brands, *Inside the Cold War* (1991); William H. Chafe, *The American Woman* (1972); Warren I. Cohen, *America in the Age of Soviet Power, 1945–1991* (1993); Richard Crockatt, *The Fifty Years War: The United States and the Soviet Union in World Politics, 1941–1991* (1995); John Diggins, *The Proud Decades: America in War and Peace, 1941–1960* (1988); John Lewis Gaddis, *The United States and the Cold War* (1992) and *We Now Know: Rethinking Cold War History* (1997); Alonzo Hamby, *The Imperial Years* (1976); Godfrey Hodgson, *America in Our Time* (1976); R. W. Leopold, *The Growth of American Foreign Policy* (1962); William Leuchtenburg, *A Troubled Feast,* rev. ed. (1983); William Manchester, *The Glory and the Dream* (1974); Thomas J. McCormick, *America's Half-Century* (1989); Thomas G. Paterson and Robert J. McMahon, *The Origins of the Cold War,* 3d ed. (1991); Emily and Norman Rosenberg, *In Our Times,* 5th ed. (1995); Frederick F. Siegel, *A Troubled Journey* (1984); Lawrence Wittner, *Cold War America,* rev. ed. (1978); Randall B. Woods and Howard Jones, *Dawning of the Cold War* (1991); Howard Zinn, *Postwar America, 1945–1971* (1973).

Containing the Russian Bear and the Containment Policy

Gar Alperovitz, *The Decision to Use the Atomic Bomb, and the Architecture of an American Myth* (1995); Terry H. Anderson, *The United States, Great Britain and the Cold War, 1944–1947* (1981); James Aronson, *The Press and the Cold War* (1970); Stanley D. Bachrack, *The Committee of One Million: "China Lobby" Politics, 1953–1971* (1976); Richard J. Barnet, *The Giants: Russia and America* (1977); Ronald J. Caridi, *The Korean War and American Politics* (1969); Gordon H. Chang, *Friends and Enemies: The United States, China, and the Soviet Union, 1948–1972* (1990); Bernard C. Cohen, *The Public's Impact on Foreign Policy* (1972); Frank Costigliola, *France and the United States: The Cold Alliance Since World War II* (1992); Bruce Cumings, *The Origins of the Korean War,* 2 vols. (1981–1990); Lynn Etheridge Davis, *The Cold War Begins: Soviet-American Conflict over Eastern Europe* (1974); A. W. DePorte, *Europe Between the Superpowers: The Enduring Balance,* 2d ed. (1986); Richard B. Finn, *Winners in Peace: MacArthur, Yoshida, and Postwar Japan* (1992); D. F. Fleming, *The Cold War and Its Origins,* 2 vols. (1961); Rosemary Foot, *A Substitute for Victory* (1990); John L. Gaddis, *The United States and the Origins of the Cold War, 1941–1947* (1972), and *Strategies of Containment: A Crucial Appraisal of Postwar American National Security Policy* (1982); Lloyd C. Gardner, *Architects of Illusion: Men and Ideas in American Foreign Policy, 1941–1949* (1970); Marshall I. Goldman, *Détente and Dollars: Doing Business with the Soviets* (1975); Michael Hogan, *The Marshall Plan* (1987); Akira Iriye, *The Cold War in Asia* (1974); Howard Jones, *A New Kind of War: America's Global Strategy and the Truman Doctrine in Greece* (1989); Burton Kaufman, *Trade and Aid* (1982); Joyce and Gabriel Kolko, *The Limits of Power: The World and U.S. Foreign Policy, 1945–1954* (1972); Bennett Kovrig, *The Myth of Liberation: East-Central Europe in U.S. Diplomacy and Politics Since 1941* (1973); Bruce Kuklick, *American Policy and the Division of Germany* (1972); Steven Hugh Lee, *Outposts of Empire: Korea, Vietnam, and the Origins of the Cold War in Asia, 1949–1954* (1995); Melvyn P. Leffler, *A Preponderance of Power: National Security, the Truman Administration, and the Cold War* (1991), and *The Specter of Communism: The United States and the Origins of the Cold War* (1994); Ralph B. Levering, *The Public and American Foreign Policy, 1918–1978* (1978), and *The Cold War, 1945–1987,* 2d ed. (1988); Louis Liebovich, *The Press and the Origins of the Cold War, 1944–1947* (1988); Robert James Maddox, *Weapons for Victory: The Hiroshima Decision Fifty Years Later* (1995); Vojtech Mastny, *Russia's Road to the Cold War, 1941–1945* (1979); Ernest R. May, *The Truman Administration and China, 1945–1949* (1975); Ernest R. May, ed., *American Cold War Strategy: Interpreting NSC-68* (1993); David Mayers, *George Kennan and the Dilemmas of U.S. Foreign Policy* (1993); Wilson D. Miscamble, *George F. Kennan and the Making of American Foreign Policy* (1992); Thomas Paterson, *On Every Front: The Making and Unmaking of the Cold War,* rev. ed. (1992); David Rees, *Korea: The Limited War* (1964); Martin Sherwin, *A World Destroyed: The Atomic Bomb and the Grand Alliance* (1975); John W. Spanier, *The Truman-MacArthur Controversy and the Korean War* (1959); William Stueck, *The Korean War: An International History* (1995); Hugh Thomas, *Armed Truce: The Beginnings of the Cold War* (1986); Adam B. Ulam, *Expansion and Coexistence: The History of Soviet Foreign Policy, 1917–73, 2d ed. (1974); William Welch, *American Images of Soviet Foreign Policy* (1970); Allen S. Whiting, *China Crosses the Yalu: The Decision to Enter the Korean War* (1960); Lawrence Wittner, *American Intervention in Greece, 1943–1949* (1982).

The Cold War at Home

Edwin R. Bayley, *Joe McCarthy and the Press* (1981); H. W. Brands, *The Devil We Knew: Americans and the Cold War* (1993); Jeff Broadwater, *Eisenhower and the Anti-Communist Crusade* (1992); David Caute, *The Great Fear: The Anti-Communist Purge under Truman and Eisenhower* (1978); Richard Freeland, *The Truman Doctrine and the Origins of McCarthyism* (1972); Richard M. Fried, *Men Against McCarthy* (1976), and *Nightmare in Red* (1990); Walter Goodman, *The Committee* (1968); Robert Griffith, *The Politics of Fear*, 2d ed. (1987); Alonzo Hamby, *Beyond the New Deal: Harry S Truman and American Liberalism* (1973); Susan M. Hartmann, *Truman and the 80th Congress* (1971); Fred Inglis, *The Cruel Peace: Everyday Life and the Cold War* (1991); Richard S. Kirkendall, *Harry S. Truman, Korea, and the Imperial Presidency* (1975); Harvey Klehr, John Early Haynes, and Fridrikh Igorevich Firsov, *The Secret World of American Communism* (1995); R. Alton Lee, *Truman and Taft-Hartley* (1966); Samuel Lubell, *Future of American Politics*, 2d ed. (1956); Maeva Marcus, *Truman and the Steel Seizure Case* (1977); Allen J. Matusow, *Farm Policies and Politics in the Truman Years* (1967); Gary May, *Un-American Activities: The Trials of William Remington* (1994); John H. Neville, *The Press, the Rosenbergs, and the Cold War* (1995); Michael Rogin, *The Intellectuals and McCarthy* (1967); Athan Theoharis, *Seeds of Repression: Harry S. Truman and the Origins of McCarthyism* (1971).

The Paranoid Style

Paul Boyer, *By the Bomb's Early Light: American Thought and Culture at the Dawn of the Atomic Age* (1994); Stephen Fox, *Blood and Power: Organized Crime in Twentieth-Century America* (1990); Eric Goldman, *The Crucial Decade and After* (1961); Richard Hofstadter, *The Paranoid Style in American Politics and Other Essays* (1965); William Howard Moore, *The Kefauver Committee and the Politics of Crime* (1974); Victor Navasky, *Naming Names* (1980); Nora Sayre, *Running Time: Films of the Cold War* (1982); Stephen J. Whitfield, *The Culture of the Cold War* (1991).

Biographies

Dean Acheson, *Present at the Creation: My Years in the State Department* (1969); Charles E. Bohlen, *Witness to History, 1929–1969* (1973); Douglas Brinkley, *Dean Acheson: The Cold War Years, 1953–1971* (1992); David Callahan, *Dangerous Capabilities: Paul Nitze and the Cold War* (1990); Clark Clifford with Richard Holbrooke, *Counsel to the President, A Memoir* (1991); Robert J. Donovan, *Conflict and Crisis* (1977), and *Tumultuous Years* (1982); Robert H. Ferrell, *George C. Marshall* (1966), and *Harry S Truman and the Modern American Presidency* (1983); Charles L. Fontenay, *Estes Kefauver* (1980); Gregory A. Fossedal, *Our Finest Hour: Will Clayton, the Marshall Plan, and the Triumph of Democracy* (1993); Joseph Bruce Gorman, *Kefauver* (1971); Alonzo L. Hamby, *Man of the People: A Life of Harry S. Truman* (1995); Walter L. Hixson, *George F. Kennan* (1989); Ronald McGlothlen, *Controlling the Waves: Dean Acheson and U.S. Foreign Policy in Asia* (1993); David S. McLellan, *Dean Acheson* (1976); Robert P. Newman, *Owen Lattimore and the "Loss" of China* (1992); James T. Patterson, *Mr. Republican: A Biography of Robert A. Taft* (1972); Thomas C. Reeves, *The Life and Times of Joe McCarthy* (1982); Edward L. and Frederick H. Schapsmeier, *Prophet in Politics: Henry A. Wallace and the War Years, 1940–1965* (1971); Gaddis Smith, *Dean Acheson* (1972); Ronald Steel, *Walter Lippmann and the American Century* (1980); Anders Stephanson, *Kennan and the Art of Foreign Policy* (1989); Mark A. Stoler, *George C. Marshall* (1989); Harry S Truman, *Memoirs*, 2 vols. (1955–1956).

INTERNET RESOURCES

Harry S Truman
http://www.ipl.org/ref/POTUS/hstruman.html
This page contains basic factual data about his election and presidency, speeches, and on-line biographies.

Harry S Truman Library
http://www.trumanlibrary.org
This presidential library has numerous photos and several important primary documents.

Senator Joe McCarthy
http://www.webcorp.com/mccarthy/
This webcorp site includes audio clips of McCarthy's speeches.

Korean War Project
http://www.onramp.net/~hbarker
This site has information about the war and is a guide to resources on the Korean War.

Cold War
http://cnn.com/SPECIALS/cold.war/
This is the companion site to the CNN Perspectives series on the Cold War. It contains a lot of information including interactive timelines and a quiz.

Key Terms

Joseph Stalin   (p. 765)

Truman Doctrine   (p. 769)

Marshall Plan   (p. 770)

The China Lobby   (p. 773)

National Security Council Paper Number 68 (NSC-68) (p. 773)

General Douglas MacArthur   (p. 775)

Taft-Hartley Act   (p. 777)

The Fair Deal   (p. 778)

Julius and Ethel Rosenberg   (p. 779)

House Un-American Activities Committee (HUAC)   (p. 784)

Review Questions

1. During the war effort, Americans viewed the Soviet Union as an ally. How did this view so rapidly deteriorate by 1947?
2. What was the policy of containment? How did it shape America's response to the invasion of South Korea?
3. How did Joseph McCarthy become such a powerful and influential senator in the early 1950s?
4. What role did popular culture—movies, comic books, sports, etc.—play in creating a domestic mood of paranoia?

27

IKE'S AMERICA

QUIET CHANGES
 "I Like Ike"
 "Dynamic Conservatism"
 A Country on Wheels
 Ike, Dulles, and the World
 A New Face in Moscow
 1956: The Dangerous Year
 The Troubled Second Term
 Sputnik and Sputtering Rockets
 Third-World Challenges
 Not with a Bang, But a Whimper

WE SHALL OVERCOME
 Taking Jim Crow to Court
 A Failure of Leadership
 The Word from Montgomery

THE SOUNDS OF CHANGE
 Father Knows Best
 The Other Side of the Coin
 The Meaning of Elvis
 A Different Beat

"What else could we do?"

Mose Wright and his three boys, seated in the "colored" section of the courtroom, attended the trial of Roy Bryant and J. W. Milam, accused of killing Emmett Till in Mississippi.

Mose Wright stood and surveyed the courtroom. Most of the faces he saw were white. The two accused men were white. The 12 jurors were white. The armed guards were white. Slowly, Wright, a 64-year-old African-American sharecropper, extended his right arm. "Thar he," Wright answered, pointing at J. W. Milam. He then pointed at Roy Bryant, the second defendant. In essence, Wright was accusing the two whites of murdering Emmett Till, his 14-year-old nephew—accusing them in a segregated courtroom in Sumner, Mississippi. Wright later recalled that he could "feel the blood boil in hundreds of white people as they sat glaring in the courtroom. It was the first time in my life I had the courage to accuse a white man of a crime, let alone something as terrible as killing a boy. I wasn't exactly brave and I wasn't scared. I just wanted to see justice done."

It was 1955, but the march of racial justice in the South had been painfully slow. In 1954 the Supreme Court of the United States, in the landmark *Brown* v. *Board of Education of Topeka* decision, had ruled that segregated schooling was "inherently unequal." News of the *Brown* decision drew angry comments and reactions from all corners of the Jim Crow South. Mississippi Senator James Eastland told his constituents that the decision destroyed the Constitution of the United States and counseled, "You are not obliged to obey the decisions of any court which are plainly fraudulent." Throughout Dixie, Klansmen burned crosses while other white leaders hastily organized Citizens' Councils. Self-proclaimed protectors of white America vowed "to make it difficult, if not impossible, for any Negro who advocates desegregation to find and hold a job, get credit, or renew a mortgage."

Into the racially charged atmosphere of August 1955 came Emmett Till. Taking a summer vacation from his home on the South Side of Chicago, he rode a train to visit relatives living near Money, Mississippi. Emmett had known segregation in Chicago, but nothing like what he discovered in Money, where shortly before his arrival an African-American girl had been "flogged" for "crowding white people" in a store.

Emmett's mother told him what to expect and how to act: "If you have to get on your knees and bow when a white person goes past, do it willingly." But Emmett had a mind and a mouth of his own. In Chicago, he told his cousins, he was friends with plenty of white people. He even had a picture of a white girl, *his* white girl, he said. "Hey," challenged a listener, "there's a [white] girl in that store there. I bet you won't go in there and talk to her."

Emmett accepted the challenge. He entered Bryant's Grocery and Meat Market, browsed about, and bought some bubble gum. As he left, he said, "Bye, Baby" to Carolyn Bryant and gave a "wolf call" whistle. Outside an old black man told Emmett to scat before the woman got a pistol and blew "his brains out." The advice sounded sage enough, so Emmett beat a hasty retreat.

A few days later Roy Bryant returned to Money after hauling shrimp from Louisiana to Texas. What his wife told him is unknown, but it was enough to make him angry. After midnight that Saturday night, he and his half brother, J. W. "Big" Milam, drove to Mose Wright's unpainted cabin. They demanded the "boy who done the talkin'." Mose tried to explain that Emmett was from "up nawth," that he "ain't got good sense" and was unfamiliar with southern ways. The logic of the argument was lost on the two white men, one of whom told Mose that if he caused trouble he would never see his next birthday.

Various stories have been told about what happened during the next few hours. One thing is for certain: Emmett Till did not live much past daybreak. According to Milam and Bryant's account, they had only meant to scare the northern youth. But Emmett did not beg for mercy. Therefore they *had* to kill him. "What else could we do?" Milam asked. "He was hopeless. I'm no bully; I never hurt a nigger in my life. I like niggers in their place. I know how to work 'em. But I just decided it was time a few people got put on notice."

Three days later Emmett's badly beaten body was found in the Tallahatchie River. A gouged-out eye, crushed forehead, and bullet in his skull gave evidence to the beating he took. Around his neck, attached by barbed wire, was a 75-pound cotton gin fan. At the request of his mother, the local sheriff sent the decomposing body to Chicago for burial.

Mamie Bradley, Emmett's mother, grieved openly and loudly. Contrary to the wishes of Mississippi authorities, she held an open-casket funeral. Thousands of African-American Chicagoans attended the viewing, and the African-American press closely followed the episode. *Jet* magazine even published a picture of the mutilated corpse. In the African-American community the Till murder case became a cause célèbre. In a land that valued justice, would any be found in Mississippi?

In Money, white Southerners rallied to Bryant and Milam's side. Supporters raised a $10,000 defense fund, and southern editorials labeled the entire affair a "Communist plot" to destroy southern society. By the time the trial started, American interest seemed focused on Mississippi. Few people, however, expected that Bryant and Milam would be judged guilty because few expected any African Americans would testify against white men in Mississippi.

Mose Wright proved the folly of common wisdom. He dramatically testified against the white men. So did several other relatives of Emmett Till. But in his closing statement, John C. Whitten, one of the five white defense attorneys, told the all-white, all-male jury: "Your fathers will turn over in their graves if [Milam and Bryant are found guilty] and I'm sure that every last Anglo-Saxon one of you has the courage to free these men in the face of that [outside] pressure."

The jury returned a "not guilty" verdict in one hour and seven minutes. "If we hadn't stopped to drink a pop, it wouldn't have taken that long," one juror commented. On that day in 1955 there was no justice in Sumner, Mississippi. Michigan Congressman Charles Diggs, who sat with other African Americans in the rear section of the segregated courtroom, recalled, "I certainly was angered by the decision, [but] I was not surprised by it. And I was strengthened in my belief that something had to be done about the dispensation of justice in that state." Roy Wilkins of the NAACP remarked that "there is in the entire state no restraining influence of decency, not in the state capital, among the daily newspapers, the clergy, not among any segment of the so-called lettered citizens."

But if there was no justice that day, there were clear signs of change. An African-American man had demanded justice in white-controlled Mississippi. Soon—very soon—other voices would join Mose Wright's. Their peaceful but insistent cries would be heard over the surface quiet of Dwight Eisenhower's America. They would force America to come to terms with its own ideology. After a heroic struggle against fascism and during a cold conflict against communism, Americans no longer could ignore racial injustice and inequality at home.

It was time for change. During the late 1940s and the 1950s the process began. Slow, painful, poignant, occasionally uplifting—the march toward justice moved forward. It was part of other significant social and economic changes taking place in America. Against the backdrop of Eisenhower's calm assurances, a new country was taking shape.

QUIET CHANGES

Most white Americans during the late 1940s and the early 1950s were unconcerned about the struggles of their African-American compatriots. Perhaps some admired Jackie Robinson's efforts on the baseball field, but few made the connection between integration in sports and civil rights throughout society. Other concerns seemed more urgent. In November 1952 the Korean War was dragging into its third year, and the chances for a satisfactory peace were fading. Joseph McCarthy was still warning Americans about the Communist infiltration of the U.S. government. Political corruption had stained the Truman administration. At the polls Americans were ready to vote for change.

"I Like Ike"

Republicans certainly felt it was time for change. The Democrats had occupied the White House for the previous 20 years. In 1952 they ran Governor Adlai Stevenson of Illinois for the presidency. A political moderate and a vocal anti-Communist, the witty, sophisticated Stevenson was burdened by Truman's unpopularity. His Republican opponent was Dwight David Eisenhower, a moderate, anti-Communist war hero. The Republican campaign strategy was summarized in a formula—K_1C_2. Eisenhower promised that if elected he would first end the war in Korea then battle communism and corruption at home. The nation responded. Eisenhower was swept into office. He even carried several southern states and cut into the urban-ethnic coalition of the Democrats.

"I Like Ike" campaign buttons and posters captured the public sentiment. There was much to like. Few people had advanced so far while making so few enemies. Ike's was the classic Horatio Alger success story. Although born in Texas, he was raised in Abilene, Kansas, the northern terminus of the Chisholm Trail. An accomplished athlete and a good student, Ike earned an appointment to West Point, where he graduated in 1915 among "the class on which the stars fell." (Fifty-nine of the 164 graduates of the class would rise to the rank of brigadier general or higher.)

As an army officer, Eisenhower demonstrated rare organizational abilities and a capacity for complex detail work. If by 1939 he had only risen to the rank of lieutenant colonel, he had nonetheless impressed his superiors. With the outbreak of World War II, he was promoted with startling rapidity. In fact, in 1942 General George Marshall passed over 366 more senior officers to promote Eisenhower to major general and appoint him commander of the European Theater of Operations. It was Ike who planned and oversaw America's invasions of North Africa, Sicily, and Italy and who led the combined British-American D-Day invasion of France. By the end of the war, Ike was a four-star general and an international hero.

Ike's ability to win the loyalty of others and work with people of diverse and difficult temperaments would serve him well as a politician. But during the early postwar years, he expressed no interest in holding political office. "I cannot conceive of any set of circumstances that could drag out of me permission to consider me for any political post from dog catcher to Grand High Supreme King of the Universe," he told a reporter in 1946. And indeed there is no evidence that Ike had ever voted or had any party affiliation before running for the presidency on the Republican ticket in 1952.

Eisenhower did have strong beliefs concerning America's domestic and foreign policies. His fiscal conservatism led him to the Republican party, and his internationalism convinced him to run for the presidency. He did not want to see an isolationist Republican elected in 1952, and the early front-runner was isolationist Robert Alphonso Taft, the powerful Ohio senator. Once Ike had defeated Taft for the nomination, his victory over Stevenson was almost anticlimactic.

Almost overnight the image of Eisenhower was transformed from one of a master military organizer to one of mumbling, bumbling, smiling incomprehensibility. Reporters commented on his friendly smile, engaging blue eyes, and his mangled syntax. As a young officer Eisenhower had written striking speeches for Douglas MacArthur, and as a World War II general he had impressed reporters with the precision of his thought. Commenting on Ike's speaking style, FDR's press secretary said, "He knows his facts, he speaks freely and frankly, and he has a sense of humor, he has poise, and he has command."

Had Eisenhower somehow sunk into senility on taking office? Certainly not. He sensed that the country needed a rest from 20 years of active presidents. Rather than needing an earthshaker, the country needed a "dirt smoother." The result was the "hidden-hand leadership" of Ike. In public he seemed everyone's favorite grandfather and golfing buddy, friendly, outgoing, quick to please, but only slightly interested in being president. Although he had read widely in both military history and the classics, he insisted publicly that he only read westerns, and those not too closely. But throughout his eight years in office, Eisenhower focused closely on his two major priorities: U.S.-Soviet relations and a balanced budget. These issues, not civil rights or other important social concerns, occupied most of his attention.

"Dynamic Conservativism"

Eisenhower saw himself as a forward-looking Republican. He called himself a conservative, "but an extremely liberal conservative," one who was concerned with fiscal prudence but not at the expense of human beings. Ike termed his approach **"modern Republicanism"** and "dynamic conservativism," by which he meant, "conservative when it comes to money matters and liberal when it comes to human beings." In practice this approach led the Eisenhower administration to cut spending while not rolling back New Deal social legislation.

George Humphrey, a conservative Ohio industrialist, served as Eisenhower's treasury secretary. More conservative than Eisenhower, Humphrey believed that the federal government should shift more fiscal responsibilities to the state and private sectors. He did succeed in getting Congress to abolish the Reconstruction Finance Corporation (see Chapter 24) and turn over off-shore oil rights to the seaboard states. The *New York Times* called this latter piece of legislation, the Submerged Land Act, "one of the greatest and surely the most unjustified give-away programs in all the history of the United States." On the whole, however, Eisenhower's domestic programs were hardly reactionary.

During Ike's two terms the country made steady and at times spectacular economic progress. In 1955 the minimum wage was raised from 75 cents to $1 per hour, and during the 1950s the average family income rose 15 percent and real wages went up 20 percent. And work was plentiful. During the decade, unemployment averaged only 4.5 percent per year, a figure close to the magical 4 percent economists considered "full employment." Stable prices, full employment, and steady growth were the economic hallmarks of the 1950s. "American labor has never had it so good," AFL-CIO chief George Meany told his associates in 1955. Although the population increased by 28 million people, the country was on the whole better housed and fed than ever before. The output of goods and services rose 15 percent. Especially for white Americans, "modern Republicanism" seemed a viable alternative to New Dealism.

A Country on Wheels

If Eisenhower labored to curtail the role of the federal government in some areas, he expanded it in other places. As an expert on military logistics, Ike frequently expressed concern about the sad state of the American highway system. During World War II he had been impressed by Hitler's system of *Autobahnen,* which allowed the German dictator to deploy troops to different parts of Germany with incredible speed. From his first days in office, Eisenhower worked for legislation to improve America's highway network.

The highway lobby agreed. Following the philosophy that what was good for General Motors was good for the country, the highway lobby—a loose collection of pressure groups that included representatives from the automobile, trucking, bus, oil, rubber, asphalt, and construction industries—pushed for a new federally subsidized interstate highway system. Not only would such a project provide millions of new jobs, it would contribute to a safer America by making it easier to evacuate major cities in the event of a nuclear attack.

As a result of presidential and lobby pressure, in 1956 Congress passed the **National System of Interstate and Defense Highways Act,** the most significant piece of domestic legislation enacted under Eisenhower. As planned, the system would cover 41,000 (later expanded to 42,500) miles, cost $26 billion, and take 13 years to construct. Although it took longer to complete and cost far more than Congress projected, it did provide the United States with the world's most extensive superhighway system. Secretary of Commerce Sinclair Weeks estimated that the act would create 150,000 new construction jobs and rank as "the greatest public works program in history."

More than any other piece of legislation, it also changed America. The commitment to internal combustion engines altered the culture and landscape of America. It accelerated the decline of the inner city and the flight to the suburbs. The downtown portions of cities, once thriving with commerce and excitement, rapidly turned into ghost towns. As downtown businesses, hotels, and theaters closed, suburban shopping malls with multiscreen cinemas and roadside motels began to dot the American highway landscape. Drive-in theaters, gasoline service stations, mobile homes, and multicar garages signified the birth of a new extended society, one without center or focus. Indeed, highway construction was simply one expression of Americans' obsession with the automobile during the 1950s and 1960s. After being deprived of new cars during the war—when the maximum speed limit was 35 miles per hour—Americans adopted the new automobile philosophy of bigger is better and the biggest and fastest is the best. In 1952 over 52 million cars crowded American roads, and that number doubled during the next 20 years.

New home architecture exemplified America's mobile-minded culture. The garage, once separated from and located behind the house, achieved a new position. By the 1960s the average home devoted more space to the family automobiles than to individual family members. With access to the house itself—usually through the kitchen—the garage had become an integrated part of the house and the car an important member of the family.

America's commitment to highways and cars created numerous problems. Mass transportation suffered most conspicuously. Streetcars and commuter railroads languished, as did the country's major interstate railroads. Since highway construction

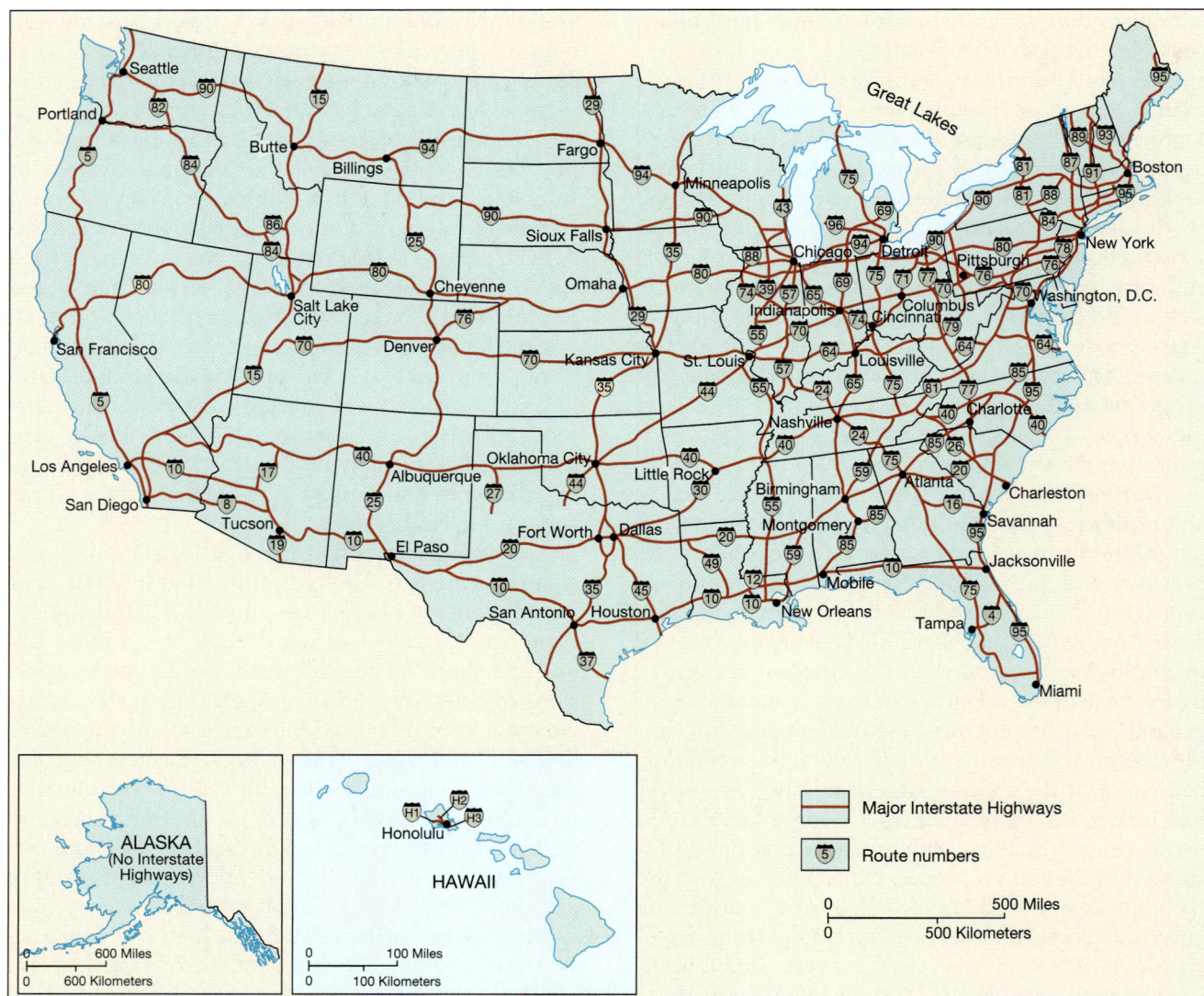

United States Interstate Highway System

The 1956 plan to create an interstate highway system drastically changed America's landscape and culture.

was financed by a nondivertible gasoline tax, government often ignored mass transit. In the years since the end of World War II, 75 percent of government expenditures for transportation have gone for highways as opposed to 1 percent for urban mass transit. As a result, those not able to use automobiles—the old, the very young, the poor, the handicapped—became victims of America's automobile obsession.

Ike, Dulles, and the World

For Eisenhower, "modern Republicanism" was more than simply a domestic economic credo. It also implied an internationalist foreign policy. As with domestic policy, Ike preferred to operate behind the scenes in foreign policy. But he did make all major foreign policy decisions.

The point man for Ike's foreign policy was Secretary of State John Foster Dulles. International diplomacy was in his blood. Dulles's maternal grandfather had served as Benjamin Harrison's secretary of state, and one of his uncles, Robert Lansing, had occupied the same post under Woodrow Wilson. In 1919, as a young man, Dulles had been part of the American delegation to the Versailles Peace Conference. After World War II, he helped organize the United Nations and then served as a delegate. In addition, throughout his life Dulles was a careful student of foreign affairs and international politics.

Eisenhower noted, there was "only one man I know who has seen *more* of the world and talked with more people and *knows* more than [Dulles] does—and that's me."

Dulles's experience and knowledge were somewhat offset by his rigidity and excessive moralism. If Americans felt comfortable calling President Eisenhower "Ike," not even close friends called Dulles "Jack." Plain and as unpolished as granite, Dulles took himself, his Presbyterian religion, and the world seriously. "His face," commented an associate, "was permanently lined with an expression of unhappiness mingled with faint distaste—the kind of face that, on those rare occasions when it was drawn into a smile, looked as though it ached in every muscle to get back into its normal shape." Dulles tended to see opposition to communism in religious terms. A friend recalled a conversation in which China's Chiang Kai-shek and South Korea's Syngman Rhee were criticized. Offended, Dulles announced: "No matter what you say about them, those two gentlemen are modern-day equivalents of the founders of the church. They are Christian gentlemen who have suffered for their faith."

Although Eisenhower and Dulles had strikingly different public styles, they shared a common vision of the world. Both were internationalists and cold warriors who believed that the Soviet Union was the enemy and that the United States was and should be the protector of the free world. Peace was their objective—but never a peace won by appeasement. To keep honorable peace, both were willing to consider the use of nuclear weapons and go to the brink of war. As Dulles said in 1956, "You have to take some chances for peace, just as you must take chances in war."

Occasionally Dulles's impassioned anti-Communist rhetoric obscured the actual policies pursued by the Eisenhower administration. In public Dulles rejected the containment doctrine as a "negative, futile and immoral policy" and advocated the "liberation" of Eastern Europe. It was time to "roll back" the Iron Curtain, he said, and if nuclear weapons were needed to achieve America's objectives—well, then, so be it. In public Dulles constantly flexed his—and America's—muscles.

In reality, Eisenhower's objectives were far more limited and his approach toward foreign policy much more cautious. Eisenhower supported containment, but not as practiced by Truman. In Eisenhower's eyes, Truman's approach was unorganized and far too expensive. Ike believed that the United States could not support every country that claimed to be fighting communism. As historian Charles C. Alexander noted, "The chief lesson Eisenhower and his associates drew from Korea was that limited wars, fought with conventional weaponry on the periphery of the Communist world, only drained the nation's resources and weakened its allies' resolve." If America continued Truman's shotgun policies, the

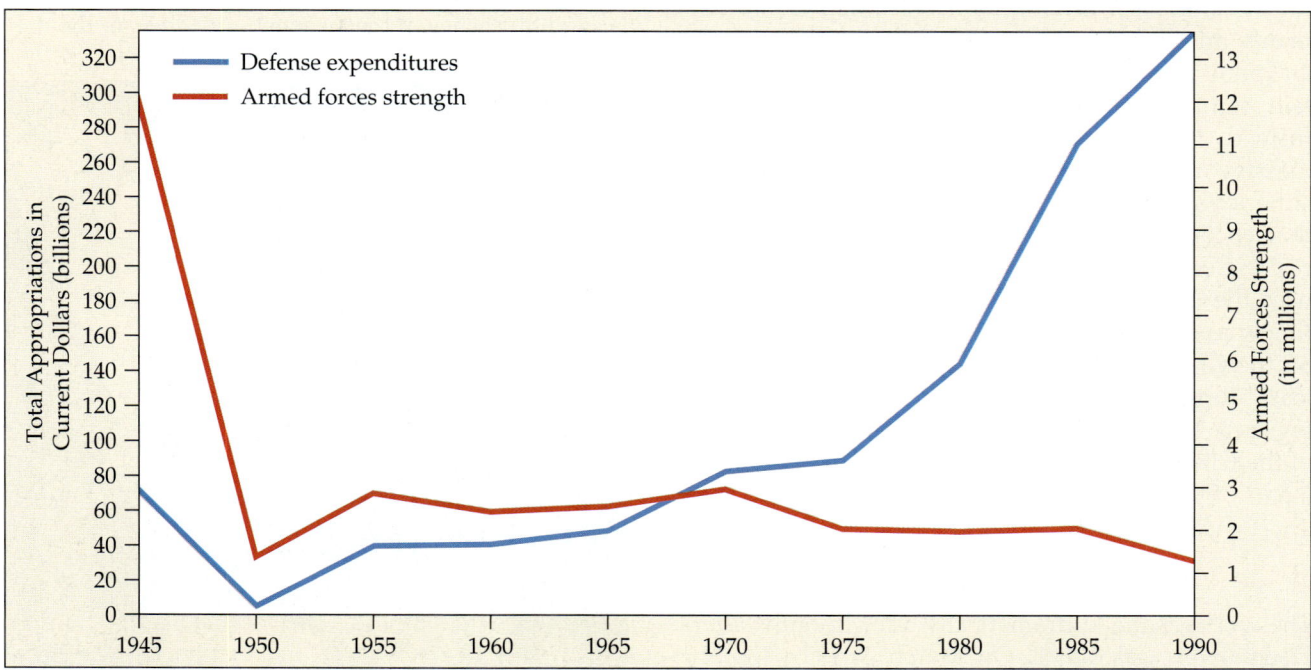

FIGURE 27.1
Defense Expenditures, Armed Forces Strength, 1945–1990

costs would soon become higher than Americans would be willing to pay. A change, Ike maintained, was needed.

Eisenhower termed his adjustments of the containment doctrine the **"New Look."** Ike's program began with the idea of saving money. To do this he decided to emphasize nuclear weapons over conventional weapons, assuming that the next major war would be a nuclear conflict. This "more bang for the buck" program drew angry criticism. Congressional hawks claimed that Eisenhower was "putting too many eggs in the nuclear basket," and liberals suggested that the program would inevitably lead to nuclear destruction.

Whatever the criticisms, the New Look did save money. While air and missile forces were expanded, the army's budget was trimmed of all its fat and much of its bone. In fact, if Eisenhower had had his way, the army would have been completely reorganized. The results of Eisenhower's approach were dramatic. In 1953 defense cost $50.4 billion. By 1956 Eisenhower had reduced the defense budget to $35.8 billion. In addition, during the same period troop levels were reduced by almost one-third. Future presidents did not so much reverse Eisenhower's approach as enlarge it. They continued the nuclear buildup started by Eisenhower, and at the same time insisted on increased spending on conventional weapons. The result was an ever-escalating defense budget.

The New Look took an unconventional approach to conventional warfare. Ike had learned from Truman's mistakes in Korea. America could not send weapons and men to all corners of the world to contain communism. It was a costly, deadly policy. Instead, the New Look emphasized the threat of massive retaliation to keep order and reinforced America's position with a series of foreign alliances that encouraged indigenous troops and peoples to resist Communist expansion. Finally, Eisenhower used the CIA as a covert foreign policy arm. Through timely assassinations and political coups engineered by the CIA, Eisenhower was able to prevent—or at least forestall—the emergence of anti-American regimes. While historians argue about the morality of the CIA's covert operations, they were very much a part of the New Look.

A New Face in Moscow

The world changed dramatically a few months after Eisenhower took office. On March 5, 1953, Joseph Stalin, the Soviet dictator whom Ike knew personally, died. Always fearful of rivals, Stalin did not groom a successor. The result was a power struggle within the Kremlin, from which **Nikita Khrushchev** emerged as the winner.

Khrushchev looked like a cross between a Russian peasant and Ike himself. Short, rotund, and bald, he had a warm smile and alert eyes. Unlike Stalin, Khrushchev enjoyed meeting people, making speeches, and traveling abroad. If occasionally he lost his temper and uttered belligerent remarks—he once even took off his shoe and pounded it on a table at the United Nations—Khrushchev did try to lessen the tensions between the Soviet Union and the United States.

Ike shared Khrushchev's dream for peaceful coexistence between the two world leaders. In fact, Eisenhower used Stalin's death as an opportunity to extend an olive branch. The Soviet Union peacefully responded. During 1955 the nations resolved several thorny issues: the Soviets repatriated German prisoners of war who had been held in the Soviet Union since World War II, established relations with Greece and Israel, and gave up claims to Turkish territory. The Soviet Union's most significant action was to withdraw from its occupation zone of Austria. Until the massive changes in Eastern Europe in 1990 and 1991, it was the only time that the Soviet Union withdrew from territory that it had seized during the war.

A worker from the Kiev region greets Soviet Premier Nikita Khrushchev at the Twentieth Congress of the Communist party in the Soviet Union.

The cold winter of the Cold War seemed to be over. Khrushchev condemned Stalin's excesses, and Eisenhower talked guardedly about a new era of cooperation. In July 1955, the two leaders met in Geneva, Switzerland, for a summit conference. During the meeting, Eisenhower suggested that the United States and the Soviet Union allow aerial surveillance and photography of each other's nations to lessen the chance of a possible surprise attack. Khrushchev rejected this "open skies" proposal, calling it "a very transparent espionage device." Actually, although the meeting achieved few tangible results, the two leaders seemed to be working toward the same peaceful ends. Against Dulles's advice, Eisenhower even smiled when posing for pictures with the Soviets. "A new spirit of conciliation and cooperation" had been achieved, Ike announced. Unfortunately, "the Spirit of Geneva" would not survive the confrontations ahead.

1956: The Dangerous Year

Neither Eisenhower nor Khrushchev was completely candid. While working for "peaceful coexistence," both still had to satisfy critics at home. In Washington, Dulles continued to call for the "liberation" of Eastern Europe and to hint that the United States would rally behind any Soviet-dominated country that struck a blow for freedom. In reality, Eisenhower was not about to risk war with the Soviet Union to come to the defense of Poland, Hungary, or Czechoslovakia.

At the same time, Khrushchev made speeches that condemned Stalin's domestic crimes and foreign policy mistakes, endorsed "peaceful coexistence" with the West, and indicated a willingness to allow greater freedom behind the "Iron Curtain."

Poland took Khrushchev at his word and moved in a more liberal, anti-Stalinist direction. Wladyslaw Gomulka, who represented the nationalistic wing of the Polish Communist party, gained power in Poland and moved his country away from complete Soviet domination. Claiming that "there is more than one road to socialism," Gomulka announced that Poles would defend with their lives their new freedoms. Since Poland did not attempt to withdraw from the Soviet bloc, Khrushchev allowed Poland to move along its more liberal course.

What Poland had won, Hungary wanted—and perhaps a bit more. On October 23, 1956, students and workers took to the streets in Budapest loudly demanding changes. They knocked over a gigantic statue of Stalin and desecrated it with freedom slogans and graffiti. As in Poland, they forced a political change. Independent Communist Imre Nagy replaced a Stalinist leader. The Soviets peacefully recognized the new government. Pressing his luck, Nagy then announced that he planned to pull Hungary out of the Warsaw Pact—the Soviet-dominated defense community created in response to the signing of the NATO Pact—and allow opposition political parties.

Khrushchev sent Soviet tanks and soldiers into Budapest to crush what he now termed a "counterrevolution" and the work of "fascist reactionary elements." Students with bricks and hastily made Molotov cocktails were no match for the Red Army. The Soviets kidnapped Nagy (and later executed him), killed hundreds of demonstrators, and brutally restored their control over Hungary. All the while the Eisenhower administration just watched, demonstrating that the notion of "liberation" was mere rhetoric, not policy. Ike even refused a CIA request to parachute weapons and supplies to the Hungarian freedom fighters. Hungary, said Ike, was "as inaccessible to us as Tibet."

Actually, at the time of the Soviet move into Budapest, Eisenhower was more concerned with the troubled Western alliance. The source of the problem was Egypt, whose nationalistic leader, President Gamal Abdel Nasser, was struggling to remain neutral in the Cold War. The United States had attempted to win Nasser's favor by promising to finance the construction of the Aswan High Dam on the Nile. But when Nasser recognized the People's Republic of China and pursued amicable relations with the Soviet Union, the Eisenhower administration withdrew the proposed loan. Neither Dulles nor Eisenhower was happy with Nasser's fence-sitting diplomacy.

Nasser struck back. On July 26, he nationalized the Suez Canal, the waterway linking the oil-rich Gulf of Suez and the Mediterranean. Half of Western Europe's oil came through the Suez Canal, which Ike believed was essential to the security of Western Europe. "And it will be run by Egyptians," Nasser added in an emotional message to the world. If Eisenhower was upset, British and French leaders were outraged, loudly claiming that the seizure threatened their Middle Eastern oil supplies. Eisenhower counseled caution, but Britain, France, and Israel resorted to "drastic actions." On October 29, Israel invaded Egypt and Britain and France used the hostilities as a pretext to seize the Suez Canal.

Eisenhower was furious. He told Dulles to inform the Israelis that "goddamn it, we're going to apply sanctions, we're going to the United Nations, we're going to do everything that there is so we can stop this thing."

Ike stood on the high ground, uncomfortably aligned with the Soviet Union. Without law there can be no peace, he claimed, adding, "and there can be no law—if we were to invoke one code of international conduct for those who oppose us—and another for our friends." Cut off from American support and faced with angry Soviet threats, Britain, France, and Israel halted their operations on November 6, the same day Eisenhower overwhelmingly defeated Adlai Stevenson and was reelected for a second term.

Taken together, the Hungarian and the Suez crises strained America's relations with both the Soviet Union and Western Europe. "The spirit of Geneva" was being replaced by a more hostile mood. Nowhere was this better seen than in the 1956 Olympic Games, held in Melbourne, Australia, only two weeks after the November incidents. Egypt, Lebanon, and Iraq refused to take part in any Games that included Britain, France, and Israel. And in the water polo competition, a match between the Soviet Union and Hungary quickly deteriorated into a form of aquatic warfare. The contest had to be halted before its official end, as the pool ran red with blood.

The Troubled Second Term

In foreign affairs, Eisenhower's second term was less successful than his first. Although he restrained military spending and shrewdly utilized information gathered by U-2 spy missions, his actions received more criticism at home and abroad. Age and health may have contributed to this turn of events. During his first four years in office, Ike suffered a heart attack and a bout with ileitis, which entailed a serious operation. During his second term, he was more apt to take vacations and play golf and bridge with his close friends. John Foster Dulles's health was also declining. During the Suez crisis doctors discovered that he had cancer. Acute physical pain punctuated his last years as secretary of state and he died in 1959.

Sputnik and Sputtering Rockets

More than ill health plagued Ike's foreign policy. Soviet technological advances created a mood of edginess in American foreign policy and military circles. In 1957 the Soviet Union successfully placed a tiny transmitter encased in a 184-pound steel ball into an orbit around earth. They called the artificial satellite *Sputnik*—Russian for "fellow traveler of Earth"—but the humor of the name was lost on most Americans,

U.S. efforts to compete with the Soviet Union's space advances suffered a major setback when the *Vanguard* exploded two seconds after takeoff on December 6, 1957.

who were too concerned about Soviet rocket advances to laugh.

Less than one month later, the Soviet Union launched its second *Sputnik*, this one built on a larger and grander scale. It weighed 1120 pounds, contained instruments for scientific research, and carried a small dog named Laika who was wired with devices to gauge the effects of extragravitational flight on animal functions. If the first *Sputnik* demonstrated that the Soviets had gained the high ground, the second indicated that they intended to go higher and to place men in space.

Before the end of 1957, the United States tried to respond with a satellite launch of its own. Code-named *Vanguard,* the satellite was placed on the top of a three-stage navy rocket that was ignited on December 6. Describing the "blast off," a historian wrote, "It wobbled a few feet off the pad and exploded. The grapefruit-sized American rival to *Sputnik* fell to the ground and beeped its last amid geysers of smoke." It was the first of a series of highly publicized American rocket launches that ended with the sputtering sound of failure.

Sputnik forced Americans to question themselves and their own values. Had the country become soft and overly consumer oriented? While Soviet students were studying calculus, physics, and chemistry, had American students spent too much time in shop, home economics, and driver education classes? More importantly, did *Sputnik* give the Soviet Union a military superiority over the United States? If a Soviet rocket could put a thousand-pound ball in orbit could the same rocket armed with a nuclear warhead hit a target in the United States? Such questions disturbed ordinary Americans and U.S. policymakers alike.

In truth, Americans overrated the importance of *Sputnik.* It was not all that it seemed. As German-born Wernher von Braun, one of America's leading rocket scientists, would later demonstrate, launching a satellite was no great accomplishment. It simply took rockets with great thrust. Delivering a warhead to a specific target was quite another matter. That entailed sophisticated guidance systems, which the Soviet Union had certainly not developed.

Sputnik then did not demonstrate Soviet technological superiority. It did, however, indicate the willingness of Soviet leaders to place military advancement ahead of the physical well-being of their citizens. As a French journalist noted, the price of *Sputnik* was "millions of pots and shoes lacking." The Soviet Union lagged behind the West in diet, health care, education, housing, clothing, and transportation.

American policy-makers reacted to the illusion of Soviet success. Congress appropriated more money for "defense-related" research and funneled more dollars into higher education in the United States. In fact, *Sputnik* was a tremendous boon for education. In an attempt to improve science and mathematics skills, Congress passed the National Defense Education Act (1958) to help finance the undergraduate and graduate educations of promising students. The Eisenhower administration jumped into the "space race," determined to be the swiftest. A leading historian of space measured the success of Eisenhower's effort by noting, "more new starts and technical leaps occurred in the years before 1960 than in any comparable span. Every space booster and every strategic missile in the American arsenal, prior to . . . the 1970s, date from these years."

Third-World Challenges

If *Sputnik* was largely an illusionary challenge, nationalist movements in the Third World created more serious problems. Eisenhower's response to such movements varied from case to case. On the one hand, he opposed Britain and France's efforts to use naked physical aggression to whip Egypt into line. On the other hand, Ike employed covert CIA operations to achieve his foreign policy goals. In 1953 the CIA planned and executed a coup d'état which replaced a popularly elected government in Iran with a pro-American regime headed by Shah Mohammad Reza Pahlavi. One year later the CIA masterminded the overthrow of a leftist government in Guatemala and replaced it with an unpopular but strongly pro-American government. In 1958, Ike ordered marines from America's Sixth Fleet into Lebanon after Lebanese Moslems threatened a revolt against the Beirut government dominated by the Christian minority. But the short-term benefits of these CIA activities came with long-term costs. Increasingly, the United States became identified with unpopular, undemocratic, and intolerant right-wing regimes. Such actions tarnished America's image in the Third World.

The problems of Eisenhower's approach toward the Third World were clearly seen in his handling of the Cuban Revolution. In 1959, revolutionary Fidel Castro overthrew Fulgencio Batista, a right-wing dictator who had encouraged American investments in Cuba at the expense of the Cuban people. Before the revolution, in fact, American companies owned 90 percent of Cuban mining operations, 80 percent of its utilities, and 40 percent of its sugar operations. Castro quickly set about to change the situation. He confiscated land and properties in Cuba owned by Americans, executed former Batista officials, built hospitals and schools, ended racial segregation, improved workers' wages, and moved leftward. Before long, Castro had begun to jail writers and critics, hold public executions, postpone elections, and condemn the United States as the "vulture . . . feeding on humanity."

Instead of waiting for Cuba's anti-American feelings to subside, Eisenhower decided to move against Castro. He gave the CIA permission to plan an attack on Cuba by a group of anti-Castro exiles, a plan that would culminate with the disastrous Bay of Pigs invasion (see Chapter 29). As one of his last acts as president, in 1961 Eisenhower severed diplomatic relations with Cuba. Such actions only increased Castro's anti-American resolve and further drove him into the arms of the Soviet Union.

Ultimately, the Truman and Eisenhower brands of containment were unsuccessful in dealing with nationalistic independence movements. Such movements dominated the post–World War II world. Between 1944 and 1974, for example, 78 countries won their independence. These included more than one billion people, or close to one-third of the world's population. By using a political yardstick to evaluate these movements, American presidents since Truman have made critical mistakes that have lowered the image of the United States in the Third World and given ammunition to Third World politicians who have pandered to anti-American emotions.

Not with a Bang, But a Whimper

Going into his last year in office, Eisenhower hoped to improve on the foreign policy record of his second term. Since his last meeting with Khrushchev in Geneva, the Cold War had intensified. In particular, the Soviets were once again threatening to cut off Western access to West Berlin, an action Eisenhower feared might lead to a nuclear war. To solve the problem—or at least to neutralize it—Eisenhower invited Khrushchev to visit the United States. The Soviet leader toured Iowa farms, visited Hollywood, and was generally warmly received by the American people. Turning to politics, he spent two days in private talks with Eisenhower at Camp David, where the two agreed to a formal summit meeting set for May 1960 in Paris.

The two world leaders never again had serious talks. Just before the meeting the Soviets shot down an American U-2 spy plane over their territory. So sophisticated was the plane's surveillance equipment, it could read a newspaper headline from 10 miles above the earth's surface or take pictures of the earth's surface 125 miles wide and 3000 miles long. During the previous few years, U-2 missions had kept Eisenhower abreast of Soviet military developments and convinced him that *Sputnik* posed no military threat to the United States. Nevertheless, the existence of such planes was a military secret, and U-2 pilots had strict orders to self-destruct their planes rather than be forced down in enemy territory. (For crash landings in neutral countries, the pilots carried a silk banner with the same statement in 14 languages: "I bear no malice toward your people. If you help me you will be rewarded.")

Assuming that the pilot had followed orders, Eisenhower responded to the Soviet charges of spying by publicly announcing that the Soviets had shot down a weather plane that had blown off course. Un-

Soviet Premier Nikita Khrushchev visited the United States in September 1959, meeting with President Eisenhower and then touring the country. In Washington Khrushchev presented Eisenhower with a model of the sphere which a Soviet rocket had landed on the moon.

fortunately for Ike, the pilot, Francis Gary Powers, had not followed orders, and the Soviets had him and the wreckage of his plane. Trying to save the summit, Khrushchev offered Eisenhower a way to save face. The Soviet leader indicated that he was sure that Eisenhower had not known about the flights. Eisenhower, however, accepted full personal responsibility and refused to apologize for actions he deemed were in defense of America. Rather than appear soft himself, Khrushchev refused to engage in the Paris summit.

Eisenhower's presidency ended on this note of failure—a chance to improve Soviet-American relations had been lost. But this end to his presidency should not obscure his positive accomplishments. He had ended one war, kept America out of several others, limited military spending, and presided over seven and a half years of relative peace. Like George

Washington, when Eisenhower left office he issued warnings to America about possible future problems. In particular, he noted, the "military-industrial complex"—an alliance between government and business—could threaten the democratic process in the country. As Eisenhower remarked early in his presidency, "Every gun that is made, every warship launched, every rocket fired signifies, in the final sense, a theft from those who hunger and are not fed, those who are cold and are not clothed."

WE SHALL OVERCOME

When Dwight Eisenhower took office in early 1953 almost everywhere in the United States racism—often institutionalized, sometimes less formal—was the order of the day. Below the Mason-Dixon line it reached its most virulent form in the Jim Crow laws that governed the everyday existence of southern blacks. Whites framed the Jim Crow laws to separate the races and to demonstrate to all the superiority of whites and the inferiority of African Americans. Jim Crow dictated that whites and blacks eat in separate restaurants, drink from separate water fountains, sleep in separate hotels, and learn in separate schools.

Jim Crow subjected African Americans to daily degradation and soul-destroying humiliation. Blacks had to give way on sidewalks to whites, tip their hats, and speak respectfully. African Americans addressed whites of all ages as Mr., Mrs., or Miss; whites addressed African Americans of all ages by their first names. Although the underpinning of the Jim Crow laws was the "separate but equal" doctrine enunciated in *Plessy* v. *Ferguson* (1896), both blacks and whites realized that subjugation, not equality, was the object of the laws. Jim Crow even leaped over national boundaries. When a waitress at a Howard Johnson's in Dover, Delaware, refused to serve a glass of orange juice to the finance minister of Ghana, America's image abroad suffered.

North of Dixie the situation was not much better. To be sure, rigid Jim Crow laws did not exist, but, informally, blacks were excluded from the better schools, neighborhoods, and jobs. Whites argued that the development of ghettos was a natural process, not some sort of racist agreement between white realtors. Such, however, was not the case. William Levitt, the most famous post–World War II suburban housing developer, attempted to keep African Americans out of his developments. A passage in the New York Levittown covenant read: "No dwelling shall be used . . . by members of other than the Caucasian race, but the employment and mainte-

Jim Crow laws were not limited to restaurants or hotels in cities. This roadside sign shows that segregation was common in areas outside southern metropolitan locations.

nance of other than Caucasian domestic servants shall be permitted." Even after the courts struck down such restrictions, Levitt instructed his realtors not to sell to blacks. Indeed, *Shelley* v. *Kraemer* (1948), the court case that stated that state courts could not uphold housing restrictions, only declared such restrictions legally unenforceable; it did not outlaw such practices per se. To break a racially motivated housing restriction, a black had to take the initiative and force a court test.

THE American Mosaic

Integration in Sports

ON April 18, 1946, the sports world focused on a baseball field in Jersey City, an industrial wasteland on the banks of the Passaic River. It was the opening day for the Jersey City Giants of the International League. Their opponents were the Montreal Royals, the Brooklyn Dodgers' leading farm team. Playing second base for the Royals was Jackie Roosevelt Robinson, a pigeon-toed, highly competitive, marvelously talented African-American athlete. The stadium was filled with curious and excited spectators, and in the press box sportswriters from New York, Philadelphia, Baltimore, and cities further west fidgeted with their typewriters. It was not just another season-opening game. Professional baseball, America's national game, was about to be integrated.

Since the late nineteenth century professional baseball and most other professional team sports had prohibited interracial competition. White athletes played for the highest salaries, in the best stadiums, before the most spectators. During the same years black teams barnstormed the country playing where they could and accepting what was offered. For them, the pay was low, the stadiums rickety, and the playing conditions varied between bad and dangerous. The *Plessy* v. *Ferguson* ideal of "separate but equal" was a cruel joke.

During the period of forced segregation, whites stereotyped African-American athletes. Since colonial times whites had maintained that blacks were instinctive rather than thoughtful, physical rather than intellectual, complacent rather than ambitious. As athletes, whites believed blacks were physically gifted but lazy, undisciplined, and wholly lacking in competitive drive. Disregarding the success of black athletes in individual sports whites clung to the racist theory that nature had fashioned blacks to laugh and sing and dance and play, but not to sacrifice, train, work, compete, and win.

The most successful African-American athletes and teams catered to these stereotypes. The Harlem Globetrotters, for example, played the role of Sambo in sweats. Started in 1927 by white Chicago entrepreneur Abe Saperstein, the all-black Harlem Globetrotters basketball team presented African-American athletes as wide-eyed, toothy, camera-mugging clowns. White audiences loved their antics—Marques Haynes dribbling circles around his hopeless white opponents while the rest of the Trotters stretched out on the floor feigning sleep; Meadowlark Lemon hiding the basketball under his jersey and sneaking down the court to make a basket; Goose Tatum slam-dunking while reading a comic book; all of them cavorting around with deflated, lopsided, or balloon balls, throwing confetti-filled water buckets on an indulgent crowd, and deviously getting away with every conceivable infraction of the rules.

Saperstein insisted that "his boys" conform off as well as on the court. As a Trotter veteran told new teammate Connie Hawkins, "Abe don't care what you do with colored, but don't let him catch you with no white broads . . . And don't let him see you with a Cadillac. He don't stand for that either." Nor did Saperstein allow his players to contradict whites. He wanted only "happy darkies," not "uppity niggers," on his team.

The Indianapolis Clowns were the Harlem Globetrotters of baseball. They played in grass skirts and body paint and engaged in comedy as much as baseball. Pregame routines included acrobatics and dancing, exaggerated black English, minstrel slapstick, and grinning, always lots of grinning. How could any reasonable person expect major league performances out of people playing baseball in grass skirts and war paint?

Jackie Robinson came to bat in the first inning. His very presence had ended segregation in "organized baseball." Now he wanted to strike a blow against the racist stereotyping. Nervous, he later recalled that his palms seemed "too moist to grip the bat." He didn't even swing at the first five pitches. On the sixth pitch he hit a bouncing ball to the shortstop who easily threw him out. It was a start of sorts.

In the third inning Robinson took his second turn at bat. With runners on first and second, he lashed out at the first pitch and hit it over the left-field fence 330 feet away. In the press box Wendell Smith and Joe Bostic, two African-American reporters for the *Amsterdam News*, "laughed and smiled. . . . Our hearts beat just a little faster and the thrill ran through us like champagne bubbles." According to another account, among the white sportswriters "there were some very long faces."

Robinson wasn't through for the day. In the fifth inning he had a bunt single, stole second, advanced to third on a ground ball, and, faking an

attempt to steal home, forced a balk and scored. It was a virtuoso performance. During the remainder of the game he had two more hits, another stolen base, and forced a second balk. In the field he was tough, intense, and smart, a reverse image of the stereotypical black athlete. It was a fine day for Robinson and his supporters. "Baseball took up the cudgel of democracy," Bostic wrote, "and an unassuming, but superlative Negro boy ascended the heights of excellence to prove the rightness of the experiment. And prove it in the only correct crucible for such an experiment—the crucible of white hot competition."

The success of Jackie Robinson in baseball led to the integration of the other major professional sports. In 1946 the Cleveland Rams moved their football franchise to Los Angeles, and to boost ticket sales they signed African Americans Kenny Washington and Woody Strode, both of whom had played football with Robinson at UCLA. Professional football thus became the next to be integrated. In 1950 the Boston Celtics of the National Basketball Association signed Chuck Cooper of Duquesne to a professional contract, and the New York Knicks signed Nat "Sweetwater" Clifton away from the Harlem Globetrotters, over Abe Saperstein's bitter protests. The same year, the United States Lawn Tennis Association allowed African Americans to compete at Forest Hills. In a relatively short time integration came to American professional sports.

The process was not without individual pain. Robinson especially became the object of hate mail, death threats, and racial slurs. Opposition runners spiked him and pitchers threw at him. Off the field he faced a life of segregated restaurants, clubs, theaters, and neighborhoods. Patient, witty, and quick to forgive, he endured extraordinary humiliation. He became an American hero, but he paid dearly. Throughout the 1946 and 1947 seasons Robinson was plagued by headaches, bouts of depression, nausea, and nightmares. Talking about the pressures on her husband, Rachel Robinson recalled, "There were the stresses of just knowing that you were pulling a big weight of a whole lot of people on your back . . . I think Jackie felt . . . that there would be serious consequences if he didn't succeed and that one of them would be that nobody would try again for a long time." Of course, other African-American players also confronted trials on and off the field, but as Robinson's teammate Roy Campanella said, "nothing compared to what Jackie was going through."

Integration in sports preceded integration in society at large. But in both sports and the civil rights movement, racial gains were paid for by individuals willing to risk serious hardships. Change seldom came easily and the struggle never ended quickly. In baseball, for example, as late as 1988 many white bureaucrats still resisted the idea of African-American managers, resorting to the same racial stereotyping that had plagued America for over 350 years.

When Ike left office in 1961, segregation remained largely unchanged. In that year, John Howard Griffin's book *Black Like Me* gave white America a stark look at the daily life of millions of African Americans. After shaving his head and darkening his skin chemically, Griffin traveled about the South to experience what it was like to live as a black in Jim Crow America. He described the humiliating search for hotels, restaurants, and restrooms in a land where for blacks unequal facilities were a constant and no facilities always a real possibility. He also described how blacks came to each other's aid and support. A national best-seller that sold over five million copies, Griffin's tale shocked and shamed many whites who never realized—or even considered—the plight of black Americans.

During Eisenhower's years in office, however, African Americans did make some significant strides in their quest for civil rights. In particular, during the decade after 1954 African Americans won a series of legal victories that in theory if not always in practice buried Jim Crow. They were years of joy and years of sadness, when the best as well as the worst aspects of the American character were clearly visible.

Taking Jim Crow to Court

World War II underscored the yawning gap between the promise and reality of life in America. Fighting against Nazi racist theories helped to draw attention to real racial problems at home. At the start of the war, defense industry managers refused to hire African Americans, and the races were segregated in the armed services. The war and a threat by African-American leader A. Philip Randolph to organize a protest march on Washington led to some changes. Executive Order 8802 prohibited discrimination in the war industries. But the outbreak of the Detroit race riot during the hot summer of 1943 demonstrated that African Americans were dissatisfied with racial conditions at home. "Our war is not against Hitler and Europe," claimed one African-American columnist, "but against the Hitlers in America."

After the war conditions improved at a snail's pace. With an eye on African-American Democratic northern voters, Truman established the President's Committee on Civil Rights, which issued a report that most white politicians ignored. While Truman called for "fair employment throughout the federal establishment" and ordered the racial desegregation of the armed services, southern politicians proclaimed the need to return to the embrace of Jim Crow. "No Negro will vote in Georgia for the next four years," Eugene Talmadge promised after he was elected governor of Georgia. And in Congress, Southerners like Senator Theodore G. Bilbo railed

Some children attended segregated schools, but others, such as these African-American children in West Memphis, Arkansas, were crammed into the sanctuary of a church for their classes.

against Truman's moderate racial reforms. Opposing Truman's plan for universal military training, Bilbo exhorted, "If you draft Negro boys into the army, give them three good meals a day and let them shoot craps and drink liquor around the barracks for a year, they won't be worth a tinker's dam thereafter."

By the late 1940s African Americans had realized that they would have to lead the fight against racial injustice. In the early years of the battle, the NAACP spearheaded the struggle. But the organization faced a number of problems, both within and outside the African-American community. For example, many believed the NAACP was racist and elitist. The organization was staffed by educated middle-class African Americans who seemed out of touch with the majority of their race. Worse yet, many African Americans charged that the NAACP was staffed by light-skinned blacks because it accepted the theory that mulattos were more aggressive, enterprising, and ambitious than their pure-blooded counterparts.

Outside of the African-American community, the NAACP encountered a hostile white society. In Congress, southern Democrats—there were few southern Republicans—opposed any assault on segregation—the prevailing form of institutionalized racism.

Given this racial climate, the NAACP moved cautiously. Instead of attacking segregation head-on and demanding full equality, the organization chose to chip away at the legal edges of Jim Crow. The separate but equal doctrine was particularly vulnerable. In *Missouri ex rel Gaines* (1938), *Sweatt* v. *Painter* (1950), and *McLaurin* v. *Board of Regents* (1950), the NAACP lawyers demonstrated the impossibility, even the absurdity, of applying the separate but equal yardstick to graduate education and law schools. In all three cases, the Supreme Court agreed. If, the court implied, separate but equal educational systems were to be continued, then states had to pay more than lip service to equality.

In grade school and high school education, just as in graduate education, the South translated separate but equal to read "separate and highly unequal." In South Carolina's Clarendon County, for example, 75 percent of the students were African American, but the white minority received 60 percent of the educational funds. On the average, the county spent $179 per year on each white student and $43 per year on each African-American student. Educational resources were separate, but highly unequal.

Intellectual and financial considerations were not the only factors that precluded equality. Psychologists argued that segregation instilled feelings of inferiority among African-American children. Psychologist Kenneth Clark conducted a simple test with African-American children attending segregated schools. He showed the children two dolls, one black and the other white. In one case, of the 16 children tested, 10 said they liked the white doll better, 11 added that the black doll looked "bad," and 9 remarked that the white doll looked "nice." Recalling the tests, Clark noted, "The most disturbing question—and the one that really made me, even as a scientist, upset—was the final question: 'Now show me the doll that's most like you.' Many of the children became emotionally upset when they had to identify with the doll they had rejected. These children saw themselves as inferior, and they accepted the inferiority as part of reality." When asked that question, one child even smiled and pointed to the black doll: "That's a nigger. I'm a nigger."

It was inhumane to continue such psychological damage, the NAACP concluded. In 1952 the NAACP consolidated a series of cases under the name of the first case—*Brown* **v.** *Board of Education of Topeka*—which challenged the very existence of the separate but equal doctrine. The Supreme Court listened to the arguments and began its extended deliberation. Then in September 1953 Chief Justice Fred M. Vinson, who seemed to be leaning against ending segregation, died of a heart attack.

President Eisenhower named Earl Warren to take Vinson's place. It was a political, not an ideological, appointment. Formerly governor of California, Warren had helped Ike win the Republican nomination in 1952. Appointment as Chief Justice of the United States was a fine reward. On the surface, minorities had little reason to suspect that Warren would be on their side. During World War II he had been active in the relocation of 100,000 Japanese Americans into internment camps; but in the years after that action, Warren realized that his action had been a mistake. The *Brown* case offered him a second chance.

After working to achieve unanimity in the court, Warren read the Court's decision on May 17, 1954. "Does segregation of children in public schools solely on the basis of race, even though the physical facilities and other tangible factors may be equal, deprive children of the minority group of equal educational opportunities?" Warren asked. "We believe it does," he answered. "To separate them from others of similar age and qualifications solely because of their race generates a feeling of inferiority as to their status in the community that may affect their hearts and minds in a way very unlikely ever to be undone." In public education, he concluded, the "separate but equal" doctrine has no place. "Separate educational facilities are inherently unequal."

The *Chicago Defender* labeled the *Brown* decision "a second emancipation proclamation," and the *Washington Post* called it "a new birth of freedom." But such Court decisions have to be enforced. As Charles Houston, a leading NAACP lawyer, remarked, "Nobody needs to explain to a Negro the difference between the law in the books and the law in action."

A Failure of Leadership

A year after the *Brown* decision, the Supreme Court ruled that schools should desegregate "with all deliberate speed." It was a vague, cautious, legally meaningless phrase. Perhaps it was the price Warren had to pay for the previous year's unanimous verdict. In any case, the second decision placed the burden of desegregation into the hands of local, state, and national leaders. If the process was to be accomplished with the minimum amount of conflict, those leaders would have to be firm in their resolve to see justice done. Such, however, would not be the case.

On the national level, Eisenhower moved uncomfortably and cautiously on the issue of civil rights and desegregation. He did not see racism as a great moral issue, and believed that the *Brown* decision had been a mistake, for which he blamed Earl Warren. He later asserted that the appointment of Warren had been the "biggest damn fool mistake" he had ever made. When questioned about the decision in 1954, he claimed, "I don't believe you can change the hearts of men with laws or decisions."

The brand of Ike's leadership and his ambitions for the Republican party further weakened his response. His behind-the-scenes approach—the "hidden-hand" style—led him to avoid speaking out clearly and forcefully on the subject. Moral outrage was not his style. In addition, he was popular in the South and harbored hopes of bringing that section of the country into the Republican party. Finally, his commitment to integration was lukewarm at best, and he placed controlling military spending above desegregating the South. Therefore, instead of deploring the killing of Emmett Till and other atrocities by southern whites, Eisenhower kept quiet.

In the South, Eisenhower's silence was often as deadly as bullets. If Eisenhower had acted decisively in support of the *Brown* v. *Board of Education* decision—if he had placed the full weight of his office behind desegregation—there is some evidence that the South would have complied peacefully with the verdict. By not acting forcefully, however, Eisenhower strengthened the position of Southerners who equated desegregation with death. "Ending segregation," Governor James F. Byrnes of South Carolina said, "would mark the beginning of the end of civilization in the South as we have known it."

The **Little Rock crisis** demonstrated the failure of national and state leadership. In 1957 in Little Rock, Arkansas, school officials were ordered to desegregate. As they prepared to do so, Governor Orval Faubus, locked in a reelection fight, intervened. Announcing that any integration attempt would disrupt public order, he sent in the National Guard to prevent black children from entering Central High. While Eisenhower quietly tried to maneuver behind the scenes, a crisis was brewing. On the morning of September 23, 1957, when black children attempted to attend school, they were inhospitably greeted by an angry mob chanting, "two, four, six, eight, we ain't going to integrate."

Television turned the ugly episode into a national drama. Millions of Americans for the first time witnessed violent racism, as angry whites moved around the defenseless children like hungry sharks. Television gave a face to racism, a concept that for many white Americans was still an abstraction. It showed the reality of hate and racism in the South. For the first but not last time, television aided the cause of civil rights by conveying the human suffering caused by racism.

To restore order, Eisenhower federalized the Arkansas National Guard and sent one thousand paratroopers from the 101st Airborne Division to Little Rock. It was the first time since Reconstruction that a president had ordered troops to the South. Although their presence desegregated Central High School in 1957, the following year Faubus closed Little Rock's public schools, declaring "I stand now and always in opposition to integration by force or at bayonet point." Taken together, Faubus's short-sighted political moves and Eisenhower's refusal to take action until public order had been disrupted created a crisis that more thoughtful leadership might have avoided.

The Word from Montgomery

This failure on the part of white leaders convinced African Americans that court orders would not magically produce equal rights. The fight would be difficult, the march long. Many realized this even before the Little Rock crisis. On a cold afternoon in 1955 in Montgomery, Alabama, **Rosa Parks,** a well-respected African-American seamstress who was ac-

Paratroopers escorted African-American students to and from school in Little Rock, Arkansas, after violence erupted when the schools were instructed to desegregate.

Rosa Parks's arrest (left) for refusing to move to the back of a bus led to citywide bus boycotts throughout 1956. (Right) Martin Luther King, Jr., shown here seated in second row left, was one of the first to ride the buses when the bus systems were integrated.

tive in the NAACP, took a significant stride toward equality. She boarded a bus and sat in the first row of the "colored" section. The white section of the bus quickly filled, and according to Jim Crow rules, African Americans were expected to give up their seats rather than force whites—male or female—to stand. The time came for Mrs. Parks to give up her seat. She stayed seated. When told by the bus driver to get up or he would call the police, she said, "You may do that." Later she recalled that the act of defiance was "just something I had to do." The bus stopped, the driver summoned the police, and Rosa Parks was arrested.

African-American Montgomery rallied to Mrs. Parks's side. Like her, they were tired of riding in the back of the bus, tired of giving up their seats to whites, tired of having their lives restricted by segregation laws. Local leaders decided to organize a boycott of Montgomery's white-owned and white-operated bus system. They hoped that economic pressure would force changes that court decisions could not. For the next 381 days, more than 90 percent of Montgomery's African-American citizens participated in a heroic and successful demonstration against racial segregation. Among African Americans, the common attitude toward the protest was voiced by an elderly woman when a black leader offered her a ride. "No," she replied, "my feets is tired, but my soul is rested."

To lead the boycott, Montgomery African Americans turned to the new minister of the Dexter Avenue Baptist Church, a young man named Martin Luther King, Jr. Reared in Atlanta, the son of a respected and financially secure minister, King had been educated at Morehouse College, Crozier Seminary, and Boston University, from which he earned a doctorate in theology. King was an intellectual, excited by ideas and deeply influenced by the philosophical writings of Henry David Thoreau and Mahatma Gandhi as well as by the teachings of Jesus, all of whom believed in the power of nonviolent, direct action.

King's words as well as his ideas stirred people's souls. At the start of the Montgomery boycott he told his followers:

> There comes a time when people get tired. We are here this evening to say to those who have mistreated us so long that we are tired—tired of being segregated and humiliated, tired of being kicked about by the brutal feet of oppression . . . We've come here tonight to be saved from the patience that makes us patient with anything less than freedom and justice . . . If you protest courageously and yet with dignity and Christian love, in the history books that are written in future generations, historians will have to pause and say "there lived a great people—a black people—who injected a new meaning and dignity into the veins of civilization."

In King, civil rights had found a genuine spokesman, one who preached a doctrine of change guided by the Christian ideal of love and not by racial hatred. "In our protest," he observed, "there will be no cross burnings. No white person will be taken from his home by a hooded Negro mob and brutally murdered. There will be no threats and no intimidation."

The success of the Montgomery boycott inspired nonviolent protests elsewhere in the South. Increasingly, young African Americans took the lead. Violence and biased law enforcement did not stop the protesters. Indeed, within a few months of the successful conclusion of the Montgomery boycott, demonstrations erupted in 54 cities in 9 states. The protesters were arrested, jailed, beaten, and even knocked off their feet by high-pressure fire hoses, but still they pressed on.

The protests were widely reported in the country's newspapers and televised nightly on the news shows. Americans everywhere were confronted with the stark reality of segregation. Ignorance of the situation became an impossibility; and as the violence continued, national pressure mounted on white politicians to take decisive action. By the early 1960s the word from Montgomery had reinforced the *Brown* decision. It was time for freedom to become a reality. (See Chapter 30 for further discussion of civil rights.)

THE SOUNDS OF CHANGE

Beginning in the 1970s, American advertisers started to market a new commodity—the fifties. They marketed it as a Golden Decade, a carefree time before the assassination of John F. Kennedy, the Vietnam War, and Watergate. According to the popular myth, kids in the 1950s thought "dope" referred to a dull-witted person, parents married for life, and major family problems revolved around whether or not sis had a date for the prom. This image of the decade has taken different forms. *Happy Days* presented it on television; *American Grafitti* detailed it on the silver screen. It was an age of innocence, tranquility, and static charm. In truth, however, that carefully packaged Golden Decade never existed. Instead, the decade was alive with dynamic, creative tensions.

Father Knows Best

The stock television situation comedy (sitcom) of the 1950s centered on a white family with a happily married husband and wife and two—or sometimes three—well-adjusted children. Most often, the family lived in a white, two-story suburban home, from which the father ventured daily to his white-collar job. Mothers stayed home to tend the children. *Father Knows Best* was the classic example of this genre. It ran from 1954 to 1962 and signaled an optimistic outlook through its title song, "Just Around the Corner There's a Rainbow in the Sky."

The picture these sitcoms presented of America was not entirely inaccurate. Starting after World War II, Americans moved steadily toward the suburbs, which during the 1950s grew six times faster than cities. Several factors contributed to this migration. The high price of urban real estate had driven industries out of the cities, and as always in American history, the population followed the jobs. By 1970 suburban areas had more manufacturing jobs than the central cities. In addition, developers were building abundant, inexpensive homes, which newly married couples, aided by VA and FHA loans, purchased. Of the 13 million homes constructed during the 1950s, 11 million were built in the suburbs.

Nor was the television image of a lily-white suburbia misleading. A far greater percentage of whites than African Americans moved to the suburbs. In 1950 African Americans were 12.5 percent of America's urban population and 4.9 percent of the country's suburban population. By 1970 the urban figure had climbed to 20.5 percent with the suburban num-

Television programs of the 1950s often centered around a happy, well-adjusted suburban family with two or three children.

Table 27.1
Population of Metropolitan Areas, by Region, Size, and Race, 1950–1970

Year		Inner City	Suburbs	African-American Population as Percent of Inner City	African-American Population as Percent of Suburbs
1950	White	43,001,634	33,248,836		
	Black	6,194,948	1,736,521	12.5	4.9
	Other	216,210	102,531		
1970	White	49,430,443	71,148,286		
	Black	13,140,331	3,630,279	20.5	4.8
	Other	1,226,169	843,303		

Source: Data taken from *Historical Statistics of the United States*, Bicentennial Edition, vol. 1, p. 40.

ber declining modestly to 4.8 percent. Housing and job restrictions worked to keep African Americans in the central cities while allowing whites to fill the suburban areas.

Even the image of the suburban housewife preoccupied with her husband and her family was socially sanctioned. American women in the 1950s had babies as never before. The population of the United States increased by under 10 million in the 1930s, 19 million in the 1940s, and a staggering 30 million in the 1950s. During the 1950s the nation's growth rate approached that of India. The best-sellers list indicated America's concern with children: between 1946 and 1976 the pocket edition of Dr. Benjamin Spock's *Baby and Child Care* sold over 23 million copies, ranking it behind only the Bible and the combined works of Mickey Spillane and Dr. Seuss.

During that age of remarkable fertility, popular writers glorified the role of the mother. The bestseller *Modern Woman: The Lost Sex* went as far as to say that an independent woman was "a contradiction in terms." The ideal woman, writers observed, was content being a wife and a mother or, in a word, a homemaker. "Women must boldly announce," wrote novelist Sloan Wilson, "that no job is more exacting, more necessary, or more rewarding than that of housewife and mother." In the 1950s women married younger and had children sooner than they had in the previous two decades.

The Other Side of the Coin

Father Knows Best and other shows portrayed an ideal world where serious problems seldom intrude and where life lacks complexity. In fact, the move to suburbia and the changes in family life forced Americans to reevaluate many of their beliefs. Cultural critics, for example, claimed that life in suburbia fostered mindless conformity. Lewis Mumford described suburbs as "a multitude of uniform, unidentifiable houses, lined up inflexibly, at uniform distances, on uniform roads, in a treeless communal wasteland, inhabited by people of the same class, the same income, the same age group."

Some writers feared the United States had become a country of unthinking consumers driven by advertisers to desire only the latest gadget. Americans bought automobiles, houses, and electrical appliances as never before. Thirty percent more Americans owned homes in 1970 than in 1940. Between 1945 and 1960 the number of cars in the country increased by 133 percent and the use of electricity tripled. This consumerism fueled the tremendous economic growth between 1945 and 1970. Clearly, buying was good for the American economy, but

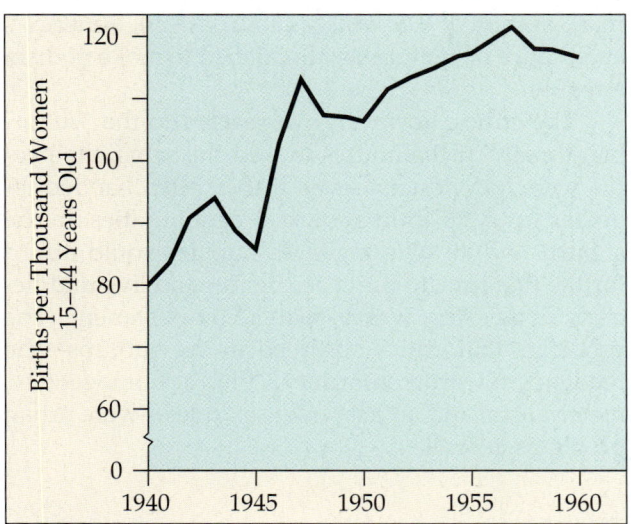

Figure 27.2
American Birthrate, 1940–1960

The People Speak

Images and Illusions

In 1946, a few thousand Americans owned television sets. By 1950, TVs were in 5 million households, a number that increased at a rate of around 5 million a year for the rest of the decade. To some social critics, it was the culmination of what historian Daniel Boorstin called the "graphic revolution"—an ability to quickly transmit images through print, radio, film, and now television. In his 1961 book *The Image,* Boorstin illustrated how a culture suffused in quick images and illusions had transformed American life, with some very dire consequences.

> We expect the papers to be full of news. If there is no news visible to the naked eye, or to the average citizen, we still expect it to be there for the enterprising newsman. The successful reporter is one who can find a story, even if there is no earthquake or assassination or civil war. If he cannot find a story, then he must make one—by the questions he asks of public figures, by the surprising human interest he unfolds from some commonplace event, or by "the news behind the news." If all this fails, then he must give us a "think piece"—an embroidering of well-known facts, or a speculation about startling things to come.
>
> This change in our attitude toward "news" is not merely a basic fact about the history of American newspapers. It is a symptom of a revolutionary change in our attitude toward what happens in the world, how much of it is new, and surprising, and important. Toward how life can be enlivened, toward our power and the power of those who inform and educate and guide us, to provide synthetic happenings to make up for the lack of spontaneous events. Demanding more than the world can give us, we require that something be fabricated to make up for the world's deficiency. This is only one example of our demand for illusions.
>
> Many historical forces help explain how we have come to our present immoderate hopes. But there can be no doubt about what we now expect, nor that it is immoderate. Every American knows the anticipation with which he picks up his morning newspaper at breakfast or opens his evening paper before dinner, or listens to the newscasts every hour on the hour as he drives across country, or watches his favorite commentator on television interpret the events of the day. Many enterprising Americans are now at work to help us satisfy these expectations. Many might be put out of work if we should suddenly moderate our expectations. But it is we who keep them in business and demand that they fill our consciousness with novelties, that they play God for us.

Source: Reprinted with the permission of Schribner, a Division of Simon & Schuster from *The Image* by Daniel J. Boorstin. Copyright © 1961 Daniel J. Boorstin; copyright renewed 1989.

---

was it beneficial to the individuals who spent more and more of their time in their cars and watching their televisions? Cultural observers despaired.

Some women also expressed frustration about their roles as wives and mothers. One poll of the 1934 graduates of the best women's colleges reported that one out of every three women felt unfulfilled. Although many women worked, cultural stereotyping prevented most of them from rising to the higher-paying, more prestigious positions. In addition, Betty Friedan, a leader in the women's rights movement, noted that women who did place a career above marriage or family were regarded as abnormal.

The problems of suburban life were explored in numerous films, novels, articles, and advice books. The film *Invasion of the Body Snatchers* (1956) is an outstanding example of the perceived fear that suburbia had created a nation of conformists. In the movie, the inhabitants of the town of Santa Mira are turned into emotionless shells by giant pods from outer space. The pod-people utterly lack individuality; as one explains, podism means being "reborn into an untroubled world, where everyone's the same." In that world, "there is no need for love or emotion." For such cultural critics as David Riesman, author of *The Lonely Crowd* (1955), America's acceptance of conformity threatened to make podism a reality.

The critics, however, overreacted to the "suburban threat." If the houses looked the same, the people were individuals—even if they often banded together to try to form suburban communities. In the suburbs, white working-class families could afford for the first time to purchase homes and live middle-class lives. This was a real accomplishment. The problems that critics observed in the suburbs—the tendency toward conformity, cultural homogeneity, materialism, and anxiety over sex roles—were urban problems as well.

The Meaning of Elvis

The harshest critics of "suburban values" were American youths. Their criticism took different forms. Some of it was thoughtful and formalized, the result of the best efforts of young intellectuals. At other times it took a more visceral form, a protest that came from the gut rather than the mind. Of the second type, none was more widely embraced by youths—or roundly attacked by adults—than **rock and roll.**

Rock and roll was the bastard mulatto child of a heterogeneous American culture. It combined black rhythm and blues with white country music. It was made possible by the post–World War II demographic changes. The movement of southerners to the cities of the upper South and North threw together different musical traditions and forged an entirely new sound. Its lyrics and heavy beat challenged the accepted standards of "good taste" in music. Confronting conventional morality, rock and roll was openly vulgar. The very term—"rock 'n' roll"—had long been used in blues songs to describe lovemaking, and early black rock-and-roll singers glorified physical relationships. Little Richard sang:

> I'm gonna RIP IT UP!
> I'm gonna rock it up!
> I'm gonna shake it up. I'm gonna ball it up!
> I'm gonna RIP IT UP and ball tonight.*

From its emergence in the early 1950s, rock and roll generated anger and criticism. In the South, white church groups attacked it as part of an NAACP plot to corrupt the morals of southern youths and foster integration. In Hartford, Connecticut, Dr. Francis J. Braceland described rock and roll as "a communicable disease, with music appealing to adolescent insecurity and driving teenagers to do outlandish things . . . It's cannibalistic and tribalistic." Particularly between 1954 and 1958, there were numerous crusades to ban rock and roll from the airways.

Most of the criticism of rock and roll focused on Elvis Presley, who more than any other artist most fully fused country music with rhythm and blues. In his first record, he gave the rhythm-and-blues song "That's All Right Mama" a country feel and the country classic "Blue Moon over Kentucky" a rhythm-and-blues swing. It was a unique exhibition of genius. In addition, Presley exuded sexuality. When he appeared on the Ed Sullivan Show, network executives instructed cameramen to avoid shots of Elvis's suggestive physical movements. Finally, Presley upset segregationists by performing

Elvis Presley, one of the great pioneers of rock-and-roll music, was the target of much controversy throughout his life.

"race music." Head of Sun Records Sam Phillips had once claimed, "If I could find a white man who had the Negro sound and the Negro feel, I could make a million dollars." Presley was that white man.

In the end, however, the protests implicit in Elvis Presley and rock and roll were largely co-opted by middle-class American culture. Record producers, most of whom were white, smoothed the jagged edges of rock and roll. Sexually explicit recordings were rewritten and rerecorded—a process known as "covering"—by white performers and then sold to white youths. African-American singer Joe Turner, for example, recorded "Shake, Rattle and Roll" for an African-American audience. Its lyrics ran:

> Get out of that bed,
> And wash your face and hands.
> Get into the kitchen,
> Make some noise with the pots and pans.
> Well you wear low dresses,
> The sun comes shinin' through.
> I can't believe my eyes,
> That all of this belongs to you.*

The white group Bill Haley and the Comets "covered" the song for a white audience. The new version stated:

---

* *Rip it Up* Robert A. Blackwell/John S. Marascalco. Copyright © 1956 Renewed 1984 Venice Music Inc. All Rights Controlled and Administered by SBK Blackwood Music Inc. Under License from ATV Music (Venice). All Rights Reserved. International Copyright Secured. Used by Permission.

* *Shake, Rattle and Roll*, words and music by Charles Calhoun. Copyright © 1954 (Renewed) Unichappel Music. (BMI). All Rights Reserved. Warner Bros. Publications, Miami, FL 33014

Get out in that kitchen,
And rattle those pots and pans.
Roll my breakfast
'Cause I'm a hungry man.
You wear those dresses,
Your hair done up so nice.
You look so warm,
But your heart is cold as ice.

In the second version all references to beds and bodies have been eliminated; by 1959 rock and roll had become an accepted part of mainstream American culture.

A Different Beat

Rock-and-roll artists never rejected the idea of success in America. If they challenged conventional sexual mores and tried to create a unique sound, they accepted the rewards of success in a capitalistic society. Elvis Presley translated success into a steady stream of Cadillacs and conventional, unchallenging films. Not all youth protests, however, were so easily absorbed into middle-class culture. The Beat movement, for example, questioned the values at the heart of that culture.

The Beat Generation extolled the very thing that conventional Americans abhorred, and they rejected what the others prized. Beats scorned materialism, traditional family life, religion, traditional sexuality, and politics. They renounced the American Dream. Instead, they valued spontaneity and intuition, searching for truth through Eastern mysticism and drugs. Although whites formed the rank and file of the Beat Generation, they glorified the supposedly "natural" life of African Americans, a life representing (at least for whites) pure instinctual drives. They adopted African-American music and the jive words of the black lexicon. Terms such as *cat, solid, chick, Big Apple,* and *square,* were all absorbed into the Beat vocabulary.

Allen Ginsberg was the leading poet of the Beat Generation. A graduate of Columbia University, where he was influenced by the lifestyle of New York City lowlifes and artists, Ginsberg moved to San Francisco in the mid-1950s. There, surrounded by kindred souls, Ginsberg came to accept his homosexuality and preached a life based on experimentation. He also developed an authentic poetic voice. In 1955 he wrote "Howl," the prototypical Beat poem, while he was under the influence of drugs. "Howl" is a literary kaleidoscope, a breathless succession of stark images and passionate beliefs. In a unique but soon to be widely imitated style, Ginsberg declared,

> I saw the best minds of my generation destroyed by madness, starving hysterically naked,
> dragging themselves through the negro streets at dawn looking for an angry fix . . .

Ginsberg and Jack Kerouac, the leading Beat novelist, outraged adults but discovered followers on college campuses and in cities across America. They tapped an underground dissatisfaction with the prevailing blandness of conventional culture. In this, their appeal was similar to that of rock and roll. Both were scattering seeds that would bear fruit during the next decade.

Allen Ginsberg was educated at the University of California, Berkeley, and at Columbia University. His poetry expressed the Beat Generation's dissatisfaction with conventional middle-class values.

Conclusion

Ike's America was both more and less than what it seemed. In foreign and domestic affairs, Eisenhower appeared to allow his subordinates to run the country, when in reality he made the important decisions.

Chronology of Key Events

1944 — GI Bill of Rights grants veterans financial aid for education and government loans for building houses and starting businesses

1947 — 25-year-old Jackie Robinson becomes the first black player in major league baseball

1948 — President Truman bans segregation in armed forces

1953 — Dwight D. Eisenhower becomes thirty-fourth president; Stalin dies; Nikita Khrushchev emerges as leader of the Soviet Union; CIA helps bring Shah Mohammad Reza Pahlavi to power in Iran

1954 — CIA masterminds overthrow of leftist government of Guatemala; *Brown* v. *Board of Education of Topeka* decision holds that "separate educational facilities are inherently unequal"

1955 — Emmett Till murdered; black residents of Montgomery, Alabama, organize a bus boycott to protest segregation; Eisenhower and Khrushchev hold summit in Geneva, Switzerland

1956 — Soviet troops crush Hungarian uprising; Suez crisis; United States begins interstate highway system

1957 — Eisenhower sends troops to Little Rock, Arkansas, to enable black students to enroll in formerly all-white public schools; Soviet Union launches the first satellite, *Sputnik*

1958 — U.S. marines intervene in Lebanon; Congress passes the National Defense Education Act to provide federal aid to schools and colleges

1959 — Fidel Castro leads Cuban Revolution against the regime of Fulgencio Batista

1960 — U–2 spy plane is shot down over the Soviet Union

Whether it was national highways or the Middle East, Eisenhower's vision of order helped shape American policy. He was more influential than most Americans during the 1950s realized.

If Eisenhower was more active than he appeared, then the country was more dynamic than it seemed on the surface. Although critics railed against the conformity of suburban America, everywhere there were signs of change. During the 1950s African Americans quickened the pace of their struggle for equality, and youths experimented with alternatives to traditional behavior. And increasingly these two rebellions merged to form a distinct subculture. During the 1960s, the war in Vietnam would give a political edge to that subculture.

Suggestions for Further Reading

Taylor Branch, *Parting the Waters: America in the King Years, 1954–1963* (1988). Fascinating epic study of the first decade of the civil rights movement.

Robert A. Caro, *The Power Broker: Robert Moses and the Fall of New York* (1974). A long, detailed, intriguing look at power politics in New York City.

John D'Emilio and Estelle Freedman, *Intimate Matters: A History of Sexuality in America* (1988). An open look at an important topic normally ignored by historians.

David Garrow, *Bearing the Cross: Martin Luther King, Jr., and the Southern Christian Leadership Conference* (1986). A prize-winning biography of the most important civil rights leader.

Kenneth Jackson, *The Crabgrass Frontier: The Suburbanization of the United States* (1985). The reasons for, and the impact of, the suburb.

Richard Kluger, *Simple Justice: The History of* Brown v. Board of Education *and Black America's Struggle for Equality* (1976). A detailed and humane examination of one of the most important Supreme Court cases of the twentieth century.

Melton A. McLaurin, *Separate Pasts: Growing Up White in the Segregated South* (1987). A close look at everyday relations between the races.

Greil Marcus, *The Mystery Train,* 3d ed. (1990). This group of essays gives one of the best looks at the meaning of Elvis Presley.

Overviews and Surveys

Stephen E. Ambrose, *Rise to Globalism: American Foreign Policy Since 1938*, 5th ed. (1988); H. W. Brands, Jr., *Cold Warriors: Eisenhower's Generation and American Foreign Policy* (1988); William H. Chafe, *The Unfinished Journey*, 3d ed. (1995), and *The American Woman* (1972); Warren I. Cohen, *America in the Age of Soviet Power, 1945–1991* (1993); Alonzo Hamby, *The Imperial Years* (1976); Godfrey Hodgson, *America in Our Time* (1976); Walter LaFeber, *America, Russia, and the Cold War*, 7th ed. (1993); Emily and Norman Rosenberg, *In Our Times*, 5th ed. (1995); Frederick F. Siegel, *A Troubled Journey* (1984); Pauline Winand, *Eisenhower, Kennedy, and the United States of Europe* (1993); Lawrence Wittner, *Cold War America*, rev. ed. (1978).

Quiet Changes

Charles Alexander, *Holding the Line: The Eisenhower Era, 1952–1961* (1975); Chester L. Cooper, *The Lion's Last Roar: Suez, 1956* (1978); Robert A. Divine, *The Sputnik Challenge: Eisenhower's Response to the Soviet Satellite* (1993), and *Eisenhower and the Cold War* (1981); Tom Engelhardt, *The End of Victory Culture: Cold War America and the Disillusioning of a Generation* (1995); Fred I. Greenstein, *The Hidden-Hand Presidency: Eisenhower as Leader* (1982); Peter L. Hahn, *The United States, Great Britain, and Egypt, 1945–1956* (1991); Richard Immerman, *The CIA in Guatemala* (1982); Madeleine Kalb, *The Congo Cables: The Cold War in Africa—from Eisenhower to Kennedy* (1982); William R. Louis and Roger Owens, eds., *Suez 1956: The Crisis and the Consequences* (1989); Clay McShane, *Down the Asphalt Path: The Automobile and the American City* (1994); Richard Melanson and David Mayers, eds., *Reevaluating Eisenhower: American Foreign Policy in the 1950s* (1987); Stephen G. Rabe, *Eisenhower and Latin America: The Foreign Policy of Anti-Communism* (1988); John B. Rae, *The Road and the Car in American Life* (1971); Mark H. Rose, *Interstate: Express Highway Politics, 1939–1989*, rev. ed. (1990); Stephen Schlesinger and Steven Kinzer, *Bitter Fruit: The Untold Story of the American Coup in Guatemala* (1982); John W. Sloan, *Eisenhower and the Management of Prosperity* (1991); James Sundquist, *Politics and Policy: The Eisenhower, Kennedy, and Johnson Years* (1968); Richard Welch, Jr., *Response to Revolution: The United States and the Cuban Revolution, 1959–1961* (1985).

We Shall Overcome

Numan V. Bartley, *The Rise of Massive Resistance: Race and Politics in the South During the 1950s* (1969); Jack Bass, *Unlikely Heroes: The Dramatic Story of the Southern Judges of the Fifth Circuit* (1981); Sally Belfrage, *Freedom Summer* (1965); William Berman, *The Politics of Civil Rights in the Truman Administration* (1970); Albert Blaustein and Clarence Clyde Ferguson, Jr., *Desegregation and the Law*, 2d ed. (1962); Robert F. Burk, *The Eisenhower Administration and Black Civil Rights* (1984); William H. Chafe, *Civilities and Civil Rights: Greensboro, North Carolina, and the Black Struggle for Equality* (1980); Robert Conot, *Rivers of Blood, Years of Darkness* (1967); Richard Dalfiume, *Desegregation of the U.S. Armed Forces: Fighting on Two Fronts, 1939–1953* (1969); John Dittmer, *Local People: The Struggle for Civil Rights in Mississippi* (1994); David Garrow, *Protest at Selma* (1978); Steven Lawson, *Black Ballots: Voting Rights in the South, 1944–1969* (1976), and *Running for Freedom: Civil Rights and Black Politics in America Since 1941* (1991); Manning Marable, *Race, Reform, and Rebellion: The Second Reconstruction in Black America, 1945–1990* (1991); Donald R. McCoy and Richard T. Ruetten, *Quest and Response: Minority Rights and the Truman Administration* (1973); August Meier and Elliott Rudwick, *CORE: A Study in the Civil Rights Movement, 1942–1968* (1973); Benjamin Muse, *The American Negro Revolution* (1968); Gunnar Myrdal, *An American Dilemma*, 2 vols. (1944); William L. O'Neill, *American High: The Years of Confidence, 1945–1960* (1986); James Peck, *Freedom Ride* (1962); Howell Raines, *My Soul Is Rested: Movement Days in the Deep South Remembered* (1977); Harvard Sitkoff, *The Struggle for Black Equality* (1981); Morton Sosna, *In Search of the Silent South: Southern Liberals and the Race Issue* (1977); Thomas J. Sugrue, *The Origins of the Urban Crisis: Race and Inequality in Postwar Detroit* (1996).

The Sounds of Change

Kent Anderson, *Television Fraud* (1978); Erik Barnouw, *Tube of Plenty*, 2d ed. (1990); Carl Belz, *The Story of Rock*, 2d ed. (1972); Paul A. Carter, *Another Part of the Fifties* (1983); William H. Chafe, *Women and Equality* (1977); Bruce Cook, *The Beat Generation* (1971); Marcus Cunliffe, *The Literature of the United States*, 4th ed. (1986); Scott Donaldson, *The Suburban Myth* (1969); James Flink, *The Car Culture* (1975); Betty Friedan, *The Feminine Mystique* (1963); John Kenneth Galbraith, *The Affluent Society*, 4th ed. (1984); Herbert Gans, *The Levittowners* (1967); Charlie Gillett, *The Sound of the City: The Rise of Rock and Roll*, rev. ed. (1984); Michael Harrington, *The Other America: Poverty in the United States* (1962); Molly Haskell, *From Reverence to Rape: The Treatment of Women in the Movies*, 2d ed. (1987); Margot A. Henrikson, *Dr. Strangelove's America: Society and Culture in the Atomic Age* (1997); Will Herberg, *Protestant, Catholic, Jew* (1955); Jerry Hopkins, *The Rock Story* (1970); Pauline N. Kael, *I Lost It at the Movies* (1965); Marcus Klein, comp., *The American Novel since World War II* (1969); W. T. Lhamon, Jr., *Deliberate Speed: The Origins of a Cultural Style in the American 1950s* (1990); David Marc, *Demographic Vistas: Television in American Culture* (1984); Karal Ann Marling, *As Seen on TV: The Visual Culture of Everyday Life in the 1950s* (1995); Douglas Miller and Marion Nowak, *The Fifties: The Way We Really Were* (1977); James T. Patterson, *America's Struggle Against Poverty, 1900–1980* (1981); Ned Polsky, *Hustlers, Beats, and Others* (1967); David M. Potter, *People of Plenty: Economic Abundance and the American Character* (1954); David Riesman, *The Lonely Crowd* (1950); Stephen M. Rose, *The Betrayal of the Poor: The Transformation of Community Action* (1972); Lynn Spigel, *Make Room for TV: Television and the Family Ideal in Postwar America* (1992); I. F. Stone, *The Haunted Fifties* (1963); Michael Wood, *America in the Movies* (1975).

Biographies

Stephen E. Ambrose, *Eisenhower,* 2 vols. (1983–1984); Jervis Anderson, *A. Philip Randolph* (1973); Robert J. Donovan, *Eisenhower* (1956); Peter Goldman, *The Death and Life of Malcolm X,* 2d ed. (1979); Alex Haley, *Autobiography of Malcolm X* (1965); Townsend Hoopes, *The Devil and John Foster Dulles* (1973); David L. Lewis, *King,* 2d ed. (1978); Peter Lyon, *Eisenhower: Portrait of the Hero* (1974); Anne Moody, *Coming of Age in Mississippi* (1968); Stephen B. Oates, *Let the Trumpet Sound: The Life of Martin Luther King, Jr.* (1982).

INTERNET RESOURCES

Levittown: Documents of an Ideal American Suburb
http://www.uic.edu/~pbhales/Levittown/
The postwar boom in housing made suburban living the cultural norm in America and shaped a generation. The story of the classic suburb, Levittown, is told on this site in pictures and text.

Fifties Web
http://www.fiftiesweb.com/
This entertaining site tells about and samples music and television from the 1950s. It also includes a related links page.

1950s America
http://dept.english.upenn.edu/~afilreis/50s/home.html
This site by Professor Al Filreis of the University of Pennsylvania contains a large array of 1950s literature and images in an alphabetical index.

Eisenhower National Historic Site
http://www.nps.gov/htdocs4/eise/home.htm
This National Park Service site has photographs of Eisenhower, quotes, and lists of his best and worst actions as President.

Dwight D. Eisenhower Library
http://www.eisenhower.utexas.edu/
This site has mainly photos, but it includes an interesting collection of campaign images for all the presidents.

The History of NATO
http://www.cnn.com/SPECIALS/1999/nato/
This site from CNN Interactive has an excellent timeline and images telling the history of the North Atlantic Treaty Organization.

KEY TERMS

Modern Republicanism   (p. 794)
National System of Interstate and Defense Highways Act (p. 795)
The New Look   (p. 798)
Nikita Khrushchev   (p. 798)
Sputnik   (p. 800)
Brown v. *Board of Education of Topeka*   (p. 807)
Little Rock Crisis   (p. 808)
Rosa Parks   (p. 808)
Rock and Roll   (p. 813)
The Beat Generation   (p. 814)

REVIEW QUESTIONS

1. How did the election of Dwight Eisenhower reflect the national mood of the 1950s, both in domestic and international affairs?
2. What strides did Eisenhower and Khrushchev make toward thawing the Cold War? What barriers remained?
3. What gains did African-Americans make in the 1950s toward ending segregation? What tactics did they adopt?
4. In what ways are television's stereotypes of American life in the 1950s accurate? In what ways do they obscure more nonconformist aspects of American culture?

28

POWER SHIFTS: THE EMERGENCE OF THE SOUTH AND WEST

THE EMERGENCE OF THE SOUTHERN RIM
    From the Long Hot Summer to the Sunbelt
    A Shift in Race Relations
    The Business of the South Is Business

THE MYTH AND REALITY OF THE WEST
    Packaging the West
    Washington and the West
    From Extraction to Diversification
    The Problems and Benefits of Growth

POLITICS WESTERN STYLE
    An Aberration or an Omen?
    Shifting Party Loyalties
    The Politics of Liberation

"The genuine article"

There was something about actor John Wayne that simply intrigued other people. He was like his country—oversized, powerful, and dramatic; part Daniel Boone, part Mike Fink, and all American. He was the Ringo Kid framed against a Monument Valley butte, holding a gun in one hand and a saddle in the other; he was Sergeant John M. Stryker telling his men to "Saddle up" before assaulting Iwo Jima; he was Thomas Dunson parting a sea of longhorns to get to Montgomery Clift; he was Captain Nathan Brittles reading the inscription on his "brand-new silver watch"; he was all those men on horseback or performing a service for their country or taking matters into their own hands—Captain Kirby York and Captain Rockwell Torrey, Pittsburgh Markham and Cole Thornton, Sean Thornton and Hondo Lane, Ethan Edwards and Tom Doniphon, George Washington McLintock and Rooster Cogburn—memorable characters from memorable films. Over the years he lost the smooth, fresh handsomeness of his youth. His hair fell out, his waist thickened, his face became lined and weathered. But the changes seemed to have made him even more appealing. His face seemed to take on a chiseled, Mount Rushmore quality, as if it had existed forever. Perhaps it was that quality, his granite sense of permanence, that attracted such awe. As much as any man of his century, he had become a symbol of America. As cultural critic Eric Bentley wrote, John Wayne was "the most important American of our time.... In the age when the image is the most important thing, Wayne is the principal image."

Yet during the late 1960s and 1970s no American seemed more out of step with the social and cultural changes in America than John Wayne. His critics charged that he was a political Neanderthal, a monument to such outmoded concepts as rugged individualism and sentimental patriotism. Since the 1920s he had starred in over 150 films in which he played varieties of the same character: the independent man of action who rode tall in the saddle, confronted evil on deserted streets at high noon, and protected innocent men and women. About his character—and indeed himself—there was a certain surliness, a roughness about the edges that manifested itself in his

Born Marion Michael Morrison in Winterset, Iowa, in 1907, John "Duke" Wayne came to symbolize the man of the West—honest, brave, upright, and true—in his movie roles. As cattleman Thomas Dunston in *Red River* (1948), he led his Texas longhorns on the 1000-mile long drive along the Chisholm Trail from San Antonio, Texas, to the railroad center at Abilene, Kansas.

coarse, blunt language and bull-in-a-china-closet behavior, yet no one who watched his films doubted what he stood for or where he would be when the trouble began.

But during the years of Lyndon Johnson's Great Society and protests against the war in Vietnam, John Wayne's simplistic attitudes and patriotism seemed naive. He preached individuality in an age of bureaucracy and *laissez-faire* in an era of social engineering. Liberal critics asserted that he was a dangerous superpatriot and attacked his 1968 film *The Green Berets*, which defended America's role in Vietnam. *New York Times* reviewer Renata Adler wrote that the film was "unspeakable,... stupid,... rotten and false"; another critic called it "immoral, in the deepest sense." The attacks confused Wayne. "I am an ... honest-to-goodness, flag-waving patriot," he told reporters. "It's kind of a sad thing when a normal love of country makes you a superpatriot."

Wayne responded to his critics with his own scathing denunciation of liberalism. He could not abide freeloaders and reserved his sharpest barbs for what he felt were the weakest links in liberalism's chain of being—crime, welfare, and affirmative action. Perhaps his views on evil and justice had been shaped by his own Western movies, but he believed that some people were just badly flawed and incapable of even minimally acceptable social behavior except when the threat of swift punishment hung permanently over their heads. "I don't go along with . . . this new thing of genuflecting to the downtrodden," he told a reporter in 1969. "We ought to go back to praising the kids who get good grades, instead of making excuses for the ones who shoot the neighborhood groceryman." And he insisted that society had not only the right but the absolute duty to punish criminal behavior.

Just as he deplored coddling criminals, he opposed most welfare programs, which he claimed robbed clients of self-respect and personal responsibility. A firm believer in individual charity, he scoffed at the idea of government charity, especially when it was financed by his and his friends' money. "I don't want any handouts from a benevolent government," he explained in 1970. "I do not want the government to take away my human dignity and ensure me of anything more than normal security." To his way of thinking, entitlement programs were addictions, monkeys on the back of America, and a terrible disservice to recipients. "You never do anybody a favor giving them something for nothing," he said. "You take away their survival instincts, their ambition, and their self-respect."

If liberals condemned Wayne's views, conservatives in the 1980s and 1990s embraced them. For millions of Americans John Wayne—tall, rugged, forthright, and independent—became the embodiment of the American ethos. President Jimmy Carter, against whom Wayne campaigned in 1976, said John Wayne was "bigger than life. In an age of few heroes, he was the genuine article. But he was more than a hero; he was the symbol of many of the qualities that make America great . . . ." And Irish actress Maureen O'Hara remarked, "To the people of the world, John Wayne is not just an actor. . . . John Wayne is the United States of America. He is what they believe it to be. He is what they hope it to be. And he is what they hope it will always be." Finally, in 1995, sixteen years after his death, a Harris Poll listed Wayne as America's Leading Movie Star.

Certainly no American of the twentieth century is more identified with America than John Wayne. In his 1990 novel *The Golden Orange*, popular writer Joseph Wambaugh attested to the power of Wayne as a symbol and an idol. Wambaugh writes of a soft-

John Wayne won an Academy Award for his performance in *True Grit* (1969), but the Oscar may have honored as much all the heroic characters he played in his more than 150 films. Embodying the image of the rugged hero, Wayne played leading roles in all but 11 of the movies in which he appeared.

ball tournament held in Southern California where all the teams are encouraged to select "imaginative" names—the cruder the better. "And yet, the *only* caveat insofar as picking out a name is that no entrant can, in any way, denigrate the United States of America, or John Wayne. *That* is how profanity gets defined in *these* parts."

To America and to the world John Wayne was the embodiment of another ethos as well: the American West. Not only did he play western roles and live in Southern California, in so many ways he spoke for the West. In his films, easterners were often portrayed as corrupt and effete, men who controlled power to the detriment of "the people"; westerners were portrayed as freedom-loving, independent sorts who wanted only to escape the domination of eastern bankers and land agents. This resentment of the political and economic power of the East helped to shape twentieth-century western—as well as southern and southwestern—history. It helped explain Richard Nixon's sense that he was an outsider and the conservative political revolts led by Barry Goldwater and Ronald Reagan. Indeed, by the 1980s and 1990s the beliefs John Wayne espoused underlay a great power shift in the United States.

The Emergence of the Southern Rim

The central political, social, economic, and cultural fact of the second half of the twentieth century has been the gradual shift in power from the older industrial states and cities of the northeast and upper midwest to the southern and western rim of the United States. This rim—circling half the country from the Chesapeake region to Raleigh and Charlotte; south to Atlanta, Jacksonville, Miami, and Tampa; west to Birmingham, New Orleans, Houston, Dallas, San Antonio, Albuquerque, Phoenix, San Diego, and Los Angeles; then north up the coast of California to San Francisco Bay, to Oregon, and on to Seattle—has experienced the country's greatest growth and economic success. It has been and continues to be the destination for millions of immigrants from Asia, Mexico, and Central America, the spawning ground of new political ideas, and the most fertile area for cultural expression. Since 1964, all of the country's elected presidents—Lyndon Johnson, Richard Nixon, Jimmy Carter, Ronald Reagan, George Bush, and Bill Clinton—have either been born or claim residence in the South and West.

It is a region that defies hasty attempts at labeling. Is it the home of Ronald Reagan's conservatism or Jimmy Carter's liberalism? Merle Haggard's redneck revolt or San Francisco's Summer of Love? John Wayne's go-for-your-gun philosophy or Robert Redford's passion for the wilderness? It is all of these and more. But above anything else, this southern and western rim has defined itself by two measures: first, by its antithesis to the East; and second, by its concern for individual liberty. Like a John Wayne movie, the two go together. Running through much of southern and western political and cultural rhetoric is the idea that the East—especially the economic power of Wall Street and the political power of Washington—threatens individualism.

From The Long Hot Summer to the Sunbelt

When World War II ended, the South was the poorest, most economically backward section of the United States. Per capita income was barely one-half that of the national average, and income distribution was badly skewed. Pockets of the South in South Carolina, Georgia, Mississippi, and Louisiana seemed never to have recovered from the Civil War, and other regions in Appalachia had *never* had a prosperous time. Altogether, the South was the "Nation's No. 1" economic problem.

Changes since 1945 have been remarkable, though not uniform. Poverty still plagues much of the inner South, especially the rural sections of Alabama, Arkansas, Kentucky, Mississippi, and Tennessee. The South as a whole continues to lag behind the nation in funding for public education, high school graduation rates, health standards, working conditions, and hourly wages. But along the rim of the South—from the Chesapeake Bay down to Florida and over to Texas—and in the cities and suburbs of the Carolinas, Georgia, and Louisiana, prosperity has replaced poverty.

No one factor accounts for the changes. Technology, politics, and social and cultural shifts have aided the rise of the "New South." Perhaps it all began with the end of the long hot summer. If the Northeast and Midwest had cold winters, the South had uncomfortably hot, long summers, normally accompanied by high humidity, mosquitoes, and disease. In the areas closest to the Gulf of Mexico, summer conditions often began in April and lasted well into October. It was not a climate that encouraged immigration or industrial relocation.

Wealthy southerners tried to escape the oppressive heat and humidity by building houses with high ceilings, long breezeways, large windows, bedroom transoms, and broad awnings. With the invention in 1882 of the electric fan—or "whirligig" as it was called in the South—the urban middle class also found some relief from the heat if not the humidity. But the urban poor and rural dwellers lacking electric power found little comfort. During the first half of the twentieth century, however, engineers developed and refined the technology of "air-conditioning," an electrical system that simultaneously cooled, circulated, dehumidified, and cleansed air. First used in southern textile and tobacco industries, by the 1920s and 1930s air-conditioning had spread into the better hotels, first-run movie theaters, Pullman railroad cars, and some public buildings. By the end of the 1930s theater owners knew that they could vastly increase ticket sales by installing air-conditioning and putting up frost-covered signs advertising "20 DEGREES COOLER INSIDE."

But it was not until after World War II that most southerners felt the impact of air-conditioning. Air-conditioning spread to department stores, banks, government buildings, hospitals, schools, and, finally, homes and automobiles. Home air-conditioning soared after the introduction in 1951 of an inexpensive, efficient window unit. By 1960, 18 percent of all southern homes had either window units or central air-conditioning. That number topped 50 percent in 1970 and almost 75 percent by 1980. Still, there were limitations. In 1980, for example, 79.9 percent of

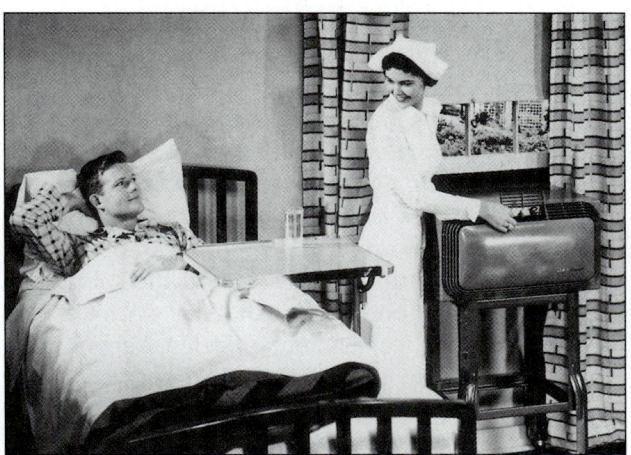

A nurse adjusts the air-conditioning for the comfort of the patient in a hospital room.

urban houses had air-conditioning, compared to 59.2 percent of rural houses.

"The South of the 1970s could claim air-conditioned shopping malls, domed stadiums, dugouts, green-houses, grain elevators, chicken coops, aircraft hangers, crane cabs, off-shore oil rigs, cattle barns, steel mills, and drive-in movies and restaurants," wrote one historian. In Texas, the South's most air-conditioned state, even the Alamo has central air, and the annual cost for air-conditioning in Houston exceeded the gross national product of some Third World countries. The victory over heat also had great significance. It has helped to promote "the Americanization of Dixie" by removing one obstacle to the movement of people to the region. During the first half of the twentieth century more Americans moved out of the South than moved into the region. The exodus began to slow in the 1950s, and during the 1960s the trend reversed: more people moved into the South than left. The *New York Times* called the 1970 census "The Air-Conditioned Census." "The humble air-conditioner," a *Times* editorialist wrote, "has been a powerful influence in circulating people as well as air in this country."

The innovation also encouraged industries to relocate to the South, the history of which had been dominated by agriculture. At the time of Pearl Harbor, more than 40 percent of all southerners were farmers. Forty years later only 3 to 4 percent of southerners were farmers. The spread of industry southward has provided new sources of income and jobs. With the decline of heavy industry in the 1960s and 1970s, many manufacturers have relocated to the South where they could buy less expensive land, pay fewer taxes and lower wages, and avoid union difficulties.

If air-conditioning eased this industrial transition, it also opened the South to tourism. The reality of the long, hot summer gave way to the ideal of the Sunbelt—a vision of year-round golf, Christmas barbecues, and life without snow tires. Vacationers flocked to southern resorts, from Hilton Head, South Carolina, in the southeast to Scottsdale, Arizona, in the southwest. Older Americans moved to the South and West when they retired. Without air-conditioning such demographic shifts would have been difficult to imagine. "Can you conceive a Walt Disney World . . . in the 95-degree summers of central Florida without air-conditioned hotels, attractions and shops?" a newspapers editorialist asked. "Can you see a Honeywell or Sperry or anyone else opening a big plant where their workers would have to spend much of their time mopping brows and cursing mosquitoes?"

A Shift in Race Relations

More than air-conditioning, however, accounted for the change in the South. Race relations, long the defining characteristic of the region, also underwent profound changes. Institutional racism, as characterized by a series of Jim Crow laws (see Chapter 19), died a slow death in Dixie. Throughout the 1940s white southerners ignored the stirring of racial progress taking place in the North, and even after the 1954 *Brown* v. *Board of Education of Topeka* decision, which delivered the most decisive blow to the concept of separate but equal, many white southerners refused to accept racial change. During the 1950s and early 1960s such southern politicians as Governor Lester Maddox of Georgia, Governor Ross Barnett of Mississippi, and Governor George Wallace of Alabama fought rear-guard actions against any change in the racial status quo. (See Chapters 27 and 30 for more detail on the quest for civil rights.)

But change did come. Civil rights acts in 1957, 1960, and 1964 struck down the legal basis of Jim Crow, and the Voting Rights Act of 1965 gave African Americans in the South (and elsewhere) the instrument to win even more changes. Such organizations as the Southern Christian Leadership Conference, the Congress for Racial Equality, and the Student Nonviolent Coordinating Committee struggled to ensure the reality of change. The end result was a new South—certainly not one where all racial problems had been solved or the distinction between black and white had been eliminated, but one that was at least confronting the question of race.

Perhaps **Jimmy Carter** from Plains, Georgia, best demonstrated the changes in the South. Carter grew up in a segregated South, in a county that resisted civil rights laws and all attempts to eradicate racial distinctions. Martin Luther King, Jr., had spent time in one of the county's jails, and in the 1960s white officials attempted to enforce illegal segregation statutes. But when Carter won the state's governorship in 1970, he announced that the South had entered a new age: "I say to you quite frankly that the time for racial discrimination is over.... No poor, rural, weak, or black person should ever have to bear the burden of being deprived of the opportunity of an education, a job, or simple justice." As a symbol of his fresh approach, he ordered a portrait of Martin Luther King, Jr., hung in the state capitol.

Advances against racism opened a new age of prosperity in the South. Attitudes expressed by Jimmy Carter and other politicians like him announced that the desire for progress in the South had finally overcome the desire for white supremacy. Since the 1870s proponents of the New South had called for southerners to stop living in the past, to renounce overt racism, and to accept industrialism. Only then, they argued, would the South enjoy the same material progress as the North. Though it took almost a century for the new ethos to emerge—aided by Supreme Court decisions and Congressional legislation—by the 1970s it had gained a firm foothold, especially in southern cities. It was no coincidence that urban business leaders became some of the most influential advocates of desegregation.

The Business of the South Is Business

Although talk of a New South—an economically diversified South—had begun almost as soon as the Civil War ended, it took almost one hundred years to make the transition from a fine idea to a reality. Before World War II, most of the talk about southern industrialism and prosperity was mere boosterism, and the profits from what little industry had developed usually flowed north. Thanks largely to the federal government, the southern economy did grow during the 1940s. During the war, Uncle Sam invested almost $9 billion in the South, mostly in defense-related activities. Although the government spent even more in other regions, the war provided the greatest infusion of cash and jobs in the South's history. At Oak Ridge, Tennessee, for example, where uranium was processed for atomic bombs, over 100,000 new jobs were created.

Throughout the region the story was much the same. Government shipyards in Newport News, Norfolk, Charleston, Tampa, Mobile, Pascagoula, New Orleans, and Houston provided hundreds of thousands of jobs. Aircraft, oil refinery, chemical, aluminum, and tin milling plants created many more. The South's industrial capacity increased by 40 percent, and per capita income tripled.

After the war the government closed some but not all of the bases and production facilities. As late as 1980, 24 of the Army's major American posts were located in the South, and almost half the soldiers in uniform were stationed below the Mason-Dixon line. In 1980 alone, the Department of Defense spent more than $50 billion in the South, or 39.5 percent of its budget. Together, the bases and plants gave the South a start from which to grow.

In the late 1960s and 1970s the South enjoyed spectacular growth. For investors, businesspeople, and industrialists, the region had certain natural advantages. Labor was cheaper and labor unions were weaker in the South than in the North. In addition, the South offered industry cheaper land, lower taxes, and fewer regulations. As industry in the Midwest declined—the result of high taxes, labor strife, technological obsolescence, and government interference—the South became an attractive place for industrial resettlement. The Midwest became known as the Rustbelt, the South as the Sunbelt. Rust and Sun, decay and growth—Americans quickly responded to the images. By the 1960s the South had reversed its century-old problem of outmigration—more people were moving into the region than out.

The 1970s were boom years in the southern Sunbelt. Young, well-educated northerners moved into the region looking for economic opportunity, and middle-class retirees relocated to the Carolinas and Florida to take advantage of the sun and lower cost of living. At the same time, northern and foreign capital poured into the South for industrial expansion. In the years immediately following World War II, Ford and General Motors built plants in Georgia; in the last third of the twentieth century Nissan and Saturn set up shop in Tennessee, Toyota in Kentucky, BMW in South Carolina, and Mercedes-Benz in Alabama. Critics of the southern automobile plants charged that state officials paid too high a price, that the subsidies and incentives offered the companies—including tax-free municipal bonds to subsidize construction and millions of dollars to train workers—negated the creation of new jobs. But the new plants *did* mean jobs; they *did* mean economic growth. While the wages and benefits in the new factories were below national averages, they were usually well above local averages.

Urbanization accompanied industrialization, and the South's traditional dependency on agricul-

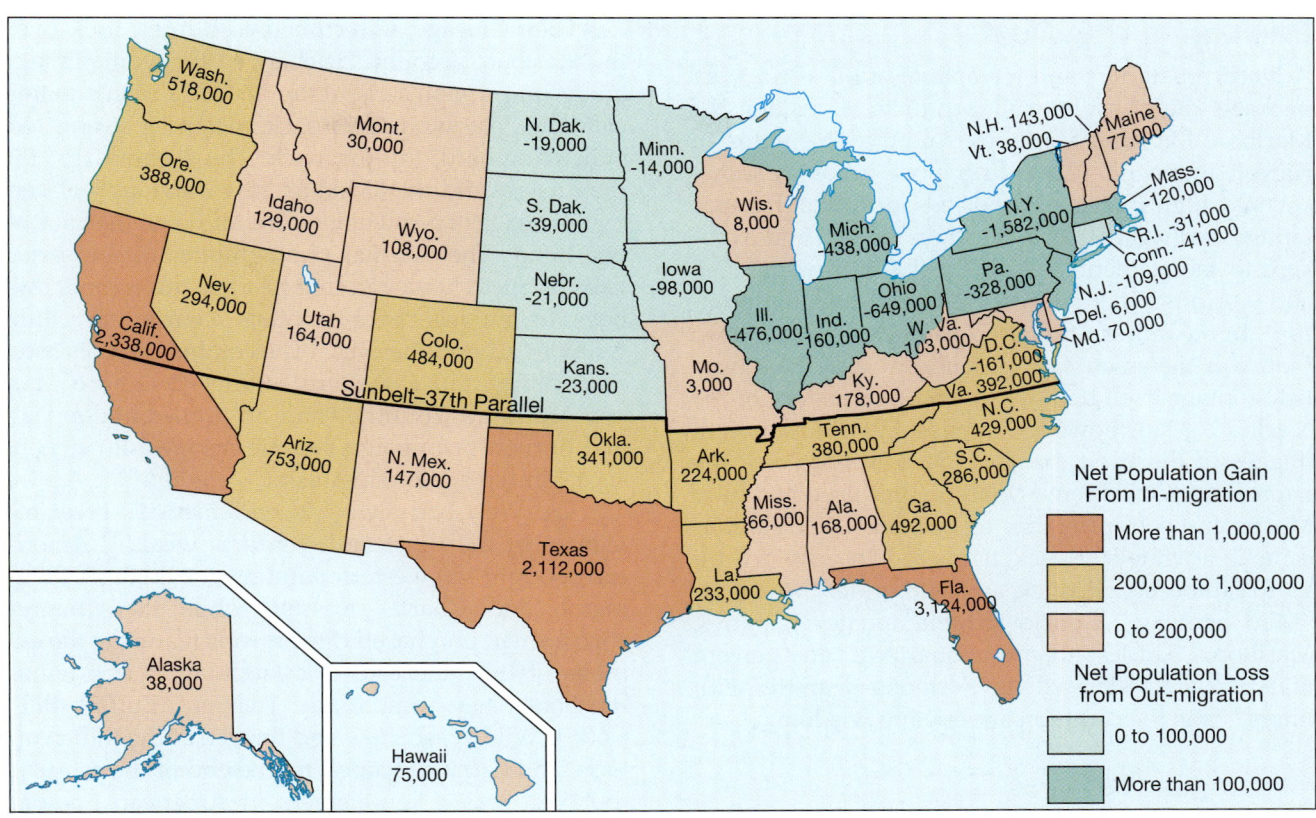

Migration to the Sunbelt, 1970–1981

ture declined. As the percentage of southerners engaged in farming fell from 40 to 3 or 4 percent during the period from 1941 to 1981, the number of farms shrank from 2.9 million to 949,000. The transition from rural to urban, from farm to industry, brought with it a human toll of pain and suffering. Thousands of country music and blues songs lament the agony of transition. Songs like "Detroit City" and "Cotton Mill Colic" emphasize the coldness of factory towns and the numbing boredom of industrial work.

Progress, desegregation, and increasing industrialism have not cost the South its distinctiveness. Throughout the second half of the twentieth century, regional and sectional pride remained stronger below the Mason-Dixon line than above it. For example, in one sociological study about 90 percent of people living in North Carolina responded that they believed they lived in the "best state." In Massachusetts only about 40 percent of the residents so answered. Similarly, regional identifications—such as "southern" or "northern," "Dixie" or "Yankee"—in businesses remained much stronger in the South than the North. The popular magazine *Southern Living*, aimed at the southern middle class, illustrated the continued appeal of regional identity in its stories about southern football and tailgate parties, Bourbon advertisements, and recipes for wild game.

While many lament the passing of the traditional South, many more celebrate the new levels of prosperity. The South has become more like the rest of the country, a land where rich suburbs and pockets of poverty coexist, and strip mall and fast-food restaurants compete with older, family-run operations.

THE MYTH AND REALITY OF THE WEST

The West is an image and a bundle of myths firmly ingrained in the American imagination. It is a tactile image. It can be touched as well as seen, smelled as well as read. It has been portrayed in thousands of Westerns on movie and television screens, and in even more novels and short stories. And unlike tales about Puritan settlers or cotton planters, its appeal has not diminished with the end of the twentieth century.

Packaging the West

Advertisers understand the appeal of the West; they package the West to sell products. Consider the Marlboro Man and Marlboro Country. This figure of rugged independence, riding alone across a snow-covered high plateau or a dried-out range, his face tanned and weathered by work in the sun and exposure to the elements, became a fixture in American and world popular culture in the mid-twentieth century. In the minds of many consumers, the Marlboro Man was the essence of masculinity, and the advertising image itself became an icon. The history of the Marlboro Man, however, suggests just how potent images of the West are. In 1954, Marlboro was the name brand of a filtered cigarette produced by Philip Morris and sold primarily to women. The cigarettes came in a white soft pack, had a red "beauty tip" filter to camouflage lipstick, and sold under the slogan, "Mild as May." Considered effeminate cigarettes, Marlboros had less than one-quarter of one percent market share. "Men will never smoke cigarettes with filters," was the common advertising wisdom.

One of the most widespread of the Western images in advertising was the Marlboro Man, who invited smokers to "Come to Marlboro Country."

Then Chicago advertiser Leo Burnett took over the Marlboro account. He changed the woman's cigarette into a man's cigarette, in fact a man's man's cigarette. The white soft pack became a strong red and white hard, flip-top pack. The "beauty tip" bit the dust, as did the "Mild as May" slogan, replaced by the image of a cowboy with a tattoo on the back of one hand. The original photographer of the series later recalled, however, that he used pilots, not cowboys, for models "because pilots seem to have little wrinkles around the eyes." The combination of rustic masculinity and a western setting—Marlboro Man and Marlboro Country—had an immediate appeal, and Burnett's campaign became the most financially successful in advertising history.

The West had always been America's great romance. In the nineteenth century, wealthy Americans bought the western paintings of Frederic Remington and Charles Russell, while their poorer countrymen purchased dime novels featuring the exploits of Billy the Kid, Doc Holliday, or the James Brothers. They went to see William "Buffalo Bill" Cody's Wild West Show and thrilled at the Indian attacks and narrow escapes. By the end of the century, the West was a key element in American popular culture, and it seemed in the blood of the people.

The popular nineteenth-century, western formulas carried over into the twentieth century. In the pulp fiction, short stories, and novels of Zane Grey, Max Brand, Ernest Haycox, Alan Le May, and Louis L'Amour, Americans received a steady supply of guns, guts, and grit. Grey's preachy western tales proved endlessly popular in the first half of the century, and no writer has had more films made of his works. L'Amour has been one of the biggest selling writers in the second half of the century. By the 1980s, his western novels had sold over 200 million copies.

If the West translated well to the printed page, it found its true medium on the silver screen. The marriage between Hollywood and the West has been a long one. Although it was filmed in New Jersey, *The Great Train Robbery* (1903) portrayed a train hold-up, the formation of a posse, a horseback chase, and dance hall scene; it was the earliest fiction western film. Thousands more followed. In the 1920s Broncho Billy Anderson, Tom Mix, and Hoot Gibson portrayed the western hero in scores of silent films. In the 1930s, during Hollywood's first decade of sound production, the "B" westerns of such actors as John Wayne, Buck Jones, and Gene Autry were popular attractions in small theaters in the South, Midwest, and West. After the success of *Stagecoach* in 1939, "A" westerns began to dominate the biggest theaters in the nation's largest cities. The great western boom carried through World War II into the early decades of television in the 1950s and 1960s.

The millions of Americans who watched westerns every year received civic instruction along with their entertainment. The message of many of the westerns was that Washington and Wall Street, the seats of national political and economic power, could not be trusted. John Wayne's westerns, for example, told the story of a West besieged by evil—ruthless merchants, monopolistic land and water agents, greedy bankers, and corrupt government officials. Innocent people are shot at, beaten up, and left for dead; they are cheated, robbed, and chased off their land. Order is restored only by a tough, independent man with a gun. Although some films deal with the threat of Native Americans, the vast majority center on the dangers inherent in Washington bureaucrats and big-city bankers.

Washington and the West

For many real-life westerners, John Wayne's message and the circumstances of his films were not that far from the truth. By the late nineteenth century the battles between U.S. settlers in the West and their Hispanic and Native American opponents had ended and the West had been conquered. But the new western leaders soon grew to resent the economic and political power of the East. Throughout the late nineteenth century and the twentieth century there were revolts against the entrenched power of the East. Populists fought against discriminatory railroad freight rates, a banking industry centralized east of the Mississippi, corporate greed, and high protective tariffs. Talk of the "financial dictatorship" of Wall Street and the "Eastern corporate aristocracy" came easily to hard-pressed farmers and ranchers living in the West.

Yet at the same time that Westerners were complaining about federal power, they received more than their share of federal dollars. The prosperity of the post–World War II West was largely financed and constructed by Washington, D.C. Although the federal government had always pumped money into the West, the investment steeply increased in the 1930s. Disappointed by fellow westerner President Herbert Hoover's agricultural and cattle programs, conservation policies, and opposition to federally funded public power, westerners, like most other Americans, turned against him in 1932 and supported Franklin D. Roosevelt. FDR did not disappoint them. His New Deal provided relief in the form of jobs, agricultural price supports, farm loans, and rural electrification.

But more importantly, Roosevelt enthusiastically supported western dam, power, and irrigation projects. In particular, he promoted the Central Valley Project on the Sacramento River to divert water from northern California to provide water, irrigation, and electric power for the rest of the state; the completion of the Hoover (Boulder) Dam on the Colorado River to provide water and electric power for southern California, the Imperial Valley, and the southwest; the Grand Coulee Dam on the Columbia River to provide electric power, irrigation, flood control, and navigational improvements in the northwest; and Colorado-Big Thompson Project to provide electric power in eastern Colorado.

The various dam projects helped to turn the West, in the words of historian Donald Worster, into "a modern **hydraulic society,** which is to say, a social order based on the intensive manipulation of water and its products in an arid setting." By 1978 the Census of Agriculture reported that the West had one-tenth of the world's irrigated land—43,668,834 acres—and nine of the top ten agriculturally productive counties in the United States. California, with eight of those counties, was the most agriculturally productive state in the country.

World War II accelerated the growth of the West at the same time that it created new bonds between Washington and the region. "Never in western his-

Water regulation projects often helped foster the tourist industry in the West. This view of the Shasta Dam and Reservoir, part of the Central Valley Project on the Sacramento River in California, is from a high point above the tourists' vista point overlooking the dam.

tory," wrote historian Richard White, "did changes come so quickly or have such far-reaching consequences as between 1941 and 1945. It was as if someone had tilted the country: people, money, and soldiers all spilled west. That tilt came from the federal bureaucracies, which devoted a disproportionate share of their enlarged resources to western development." During the war the federal government spent $70 billion in the western states and poured $40 billion more into factories, military bases, and capital improvements, over half of which was spent in California. The money provided more jobs, and the jobs lured newcomers to the region. In southern California alone, government orders created more than 250,000 new jobs in the aircraft and shipbuilding industries. More than one million people moved to California, and most settled in the southern part of the state. Before the war, San Diego was a small city of 60,000 people; during the war, it grew to more than 250,000.

Defense industries spurred the growth and industrial expansion of the West. Probably more than any other person, industrialist **Henry J. Kaiser** epitomized the driving concern for defense and dollars. A central player in the development of the western infrastructure of roads, dams, bridges, and pipelines, Kaiser went into the shipbuilding business at the outbreak of war. He built steel works in Fontana, California, and shipyards in Richmond, Oakland, Sausalito, Vallejo, and San Pedro, California. Altogether, his industries employed close to 300,000 people, to whom they paid high wages and offered attractive medical and retirement benefits.

Others followed the trail Kaiser blazed. The Boeing plant in Seattle and the Douglas, Lockheed, North American, Northrop, and Hughes plants in southern California dominated the aircraft industry and provided several hundred thousand good-paying jobs. The growth of the aircraft industry even threatened to overshadow the motion picture industry in southern California. Almost as a symbol of the emergence of the new industry, Warner Brothers Studios, located near Lockheed and fearing an enemy attack, painted a 20-foot arrow on the roof of a sound stage with the message: LOCKHEED—THAT-AWAY. And Hollywood film stars complained that all the good chauffeurs, butlers, cooks, and maids had either enlisted or taken better-paying jobs in aircraft factories. One advertisement announced: "Maid wanted; will pay Lockheed wages."

The end result was the transformation of the West, and especially California, from a virtual colony of the East into the fastest growing, most economically booming section of the country. Once western-

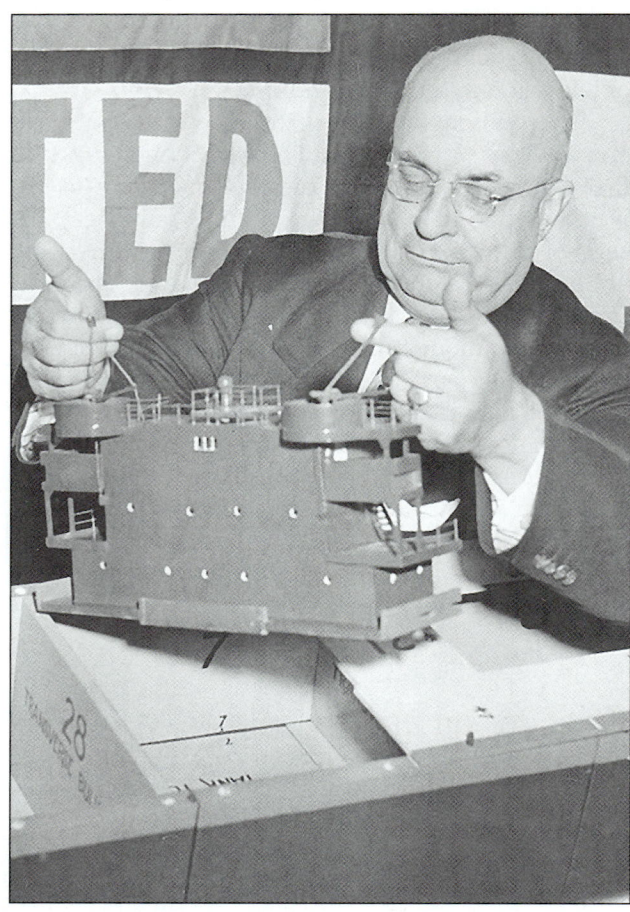

Henry Kaiser epitomized the close relationship between government and industry in the West. Government loans financed Kaiser's shipyards and cost-plus government contracts guaranteed his profits.

ers had complained about the East's near monopoly over banks and financial institutions. By the end of the war, the largest bank in the world was the Bank of America, the San Francisco–based bank run by the Giannini family which had financed not only much of the growth of the film industry but the expansion of Bendix, Chrysler, Westinghouse, North American Aviation, and Northrop Aircraft Corporation. As G. P. Giannini observed in 1945: "The West has all the money to finance whatever it wants to; we no longer have to go New York for financing, and we're not at its mercy. Wall Street used to give a western enterprise plenty of rope, and when it broke, it took over." Now the West owned the rope.

From Extraction to Diversification

Walter O'Malley was once described as having "a face even Dale Carnegie would want to punch." In the mid-1950s, O'Malley, the owner of the Brooklyn

Dodgers, was known for his penny-pinching concern for profits and his lack of humor. But in late 1957, many residents of Brooklyn added "traitor" to O'Malley's list of character flaws. In that year he announced his decision to move his Dodgers the following year from Brooklyn to Los Angeles, and for good measure, he convinced Horace Stoneham, owner of the New York Giants, to relocate his team to San Francisco. Dodger and Giant fans sent up a howl of betrayal. Journalist Arthur Daley wrote that some "teams were forced to move by apathy, or incompetence. The only word that fits the Dodgers is greed.... Baseball is a sport, eh?... the crass materialism of O'Malley and Horace Stoneham of the Giants presents the disillusioning fact that it's big business, just another way to make a buck."

Actually, the Dodgers' move west was more complicated than the "disillusioning fact" suggests. O'Malley was concerned about the deterioration of the Brooklyn neighborhood that was the home of Ebbets Field. The quaint structure was located in an increasingly unsafe section of the city, and it lacked parking facilities. O'Malley wanted to move to a new Brooklyn stadium, but his plans were blocked by New York power broker Robert Moses. In the end, O'Malley fled the labyrinthine politics and regulations of New York for the more generous political and cultural climate of Los Angeles.

The Dodgers' move west symbolized the new westward tilt of the country. Professional baseball teams were businesses, subject to the same market forces as other businesses. Chambers of Commerce throughout the country actively competed to bring new businesses to their communities. New businesses translated into more jobs and more money. Eager state and local governments used promises of low-interest loans, free land, cheap leases on city-built facilities, low property taxes or even property tax exemptions, and the building of county access roads to factory sites to attract new businesses. Certainly by the end of World War II, the West could boast that it was the land of sunshine and jobs.

In the half-century after World War II, the West completed the transition from being a land of extractive industries—mining, agriculture, ranching, oil, and logging—to being a region of vast economic diversification. By the 1970s, the newer electronic, aerospace, high-technology, and service industries had surpassed in financial importance the older economic staples of farming and ranching, coal and copper mining, and oil drilling and lumber operations. This economic leap led directly to millions of new jobs and accelerated the flow of emigrants into the West. Between 1945 and 1960, population west of the Mississippi River increased from 32 to 45 million people. The population of Arizona, one of the fastest growing states, grew by 163 percent. In 1960, California, which led the rest of the West in growth and prosperity, passed New York as the most populous American state. By the 1980s, the combined population of the West and the South for the first time exceeded the combined population of the Northeast and Midwest.

As it had during World War II, the federal government aided the growth of the West. Part of the reason lies in the fact that the federal government owned so much of the arid land of the West: more than 85 percent of Nevada, 63 percent of Idaho, 61 percent of Utah, and 50 percent of Wyoming. By 1960, close to one-third of all workers in the Los Angeles area worked for the defense industry, and that figure was well over two-thirds in San Diego. Up and down the West Coast it was more of the same. From the marine base at Camp Pendleton and the shipyards in San Diego to the nuclear complex at Hanford, Washington, and the shipyards in Seattle, the federal government's military spending helped to subsidize the boom in the West.

In the process, the West became the nuclear heartland of America, a development that rested uneasily on the minds of many people in the region. Offutt Air Force Base near Omaha, Nebraska, headquartered the country's Strategic Air Command; Colorado's Cheyenne Mountain housed the Combat Operations Center of the North American Air Defense Command; and New Mexico, where the first atomic bomb was tested, provided a home for various missile sites, military bases, and Sandia Laboratories, the Atomic Energy Commission's primary research facility. In addition, the federal government assembled nuclear bombs in plants at Rocky Flats, Colorado, and Pantex, Texas; conducted extensive nuclear testing in Utah and Nevada; and dumped—or hoped to dump—nuclear waste in unoccupied western desert land.

Defense activity bred new industries and new jobs. Billions of dollars in federal and state grants went to researchers in western universities, enlarging the reputations of such schools as California Institute of Technology, the University of California at Berkeley, and the University of Washington. Private companies such as Martin-Marietta and General Dynamics contributed to western economies in the form of skilled, high-paying jobs. The aerospace industry, which blossomed in the West during World War II, remained largely in the West after the war. From Wichita, Kansas's line of smaller aircraft such as Learjet, Beach, and Cessna; to Los Angeles's and Fort

Worth's line of larger jets such as Lockheed, Douglas, and North American; to Houston's Johnson Space Center—the skies belonged to the West.

The Problems and Benefits of Growth

Such development was not without troubles, however. As the West discovered, government money and government waste went hand-in-hand. Few people complained when the government paid too much for a lug nut or toilet seat, but waste and sloppiness in nuclear development had more dire consequences. Under the pressures of the Cold War, the government proceeded recklessly in the development of its nuclear capabilities. Test blasts probably showered many westerners with deadly radioactive fallout. In 1953, for instance, the Atomic Energy Commission detonated 11 atomic bombs in the dry lake bed of Yucca Flats, Nevada. Two of the bombs were especially "dirty" with strontium 90 and cesium 137 isotopes. The surrounding desert was covered with a fine gray ash, and an aberrant wind carried some of the fallout more than 150 miles to the east, blanketing St. George, Utah, and the Escalante Valley. In 1954, when the John Wayne movie *The Conqueror* was filmed in the area, the levels of radioactivity were still high. Over the next thirty-five years, 91 of the cast and crew of 220 people would develop cancer, a number three times higher than actuarial tables would predict. Similarly, cancer rates in and around St. George would be among the highest in the nation.

Dealing with the hundreds of thousands of gallons of nuclear waste compounded the problem. The simple truth was that the government gave far too little thought to the by-products of nuclear development, and it wasn't until the end of the Cold War that more attention was focused on the problem. While some nuclear waste experts suggested a Yucca Flats dumping ground, others argued that there was no safe way to bury "hot" material with isotopes that might remain active for a hundred thousand years. To a large degree, it is still a debate that is being conducted in the West by westerners.

Nuclear waste was not the only problem created by the rapid growth of the West. Led by the Bureau of Reclamation and the Corps of Engineers, who often worked at cross-purposes, government planners and wealthy westerners continued their helter-skel-

Damming Western Waters

ter dam building. "Every major river of the West came, to a greater or lesser extent, under the control of the dam builders and water pumpers," commented two authorities on the twentieth-century West. Never had any country created a more elaborate "hydraulic society." Water from the great western rivers—from the Columbia, the Snake, the Colorado, the South Platte, and the Rio Grande to the Red, the Missouri, and the Arkansas—was dammed, drained, and diverted to provide irrigation, electricity, shipping channels, and leisure activities.

The benefits of the damming of the West were many, though they were not equally distributed throughout western society. With the help of irrigation, the West became the new American breadbasket, and the billions of kilowatt-hours of electric power supported the needs of the region. But there were costs as well. Flood control was often illusionary; water accumulated salt and selenium; land suffered from siltation, erosion, and salt residues; dams threatened to collapse. Most of all, water supplies dwindled. By the 1980s, many Americans grew alarmed by the declining levels of the Ogallala Aquifer, which provided water for irrigation in Texas and the Great Plains states.

A final problem created by the economic growth of and emigration to the West was its dependence on the automobile. Unlike many eastern cities that developed before the advent of the internal combustion engine—indeed, before the development of any useful form of mass transportation—the West matured with automobiles. This mobility, coupled with the availability of inexpensive land for individual homes, resulted in the emergence of an extended society of suburbs, connected by miles of highways woven together by underpasses and overpasses. If Boston, New York, and Philadelphia were "walking cities," Los Angeles, Phoenix, Denver, Dallas, and Houston became "driving cities." This condition was made worse by the decline in railroads and urban mass transit. By the 1970s it became clear that western cities had developed twin dependencies: diverted water and gasoline.

The gasoline addiction had predictable, but long-ignored, results. In the 1930s the word **"smog"** had been coined to describe the chemical-laden fogs that fell like a blanket over Pittsburgh. By the 1940s smog had become a problem—albeit a small, acceptable one—in the land of sunshine. The winds—or, more precisely, the lack of winds—in the Los Angeles basin contributed to the problem. The smog was the residue of unburned hydrocarbons, the by-product of running automobile engines. To make matters even worse, smog was not just an aesthetic eyesore;

Bright lights and spectacular entertainments help lure millions of tourists to the gambling casinos in Las Vegas.

it was an actual eyesore and a serious health problem, capable of killing crops and trees and endangering the lives of humans and animals.

For most of the second half of the twentieth century, however, the benefits of western growth overshadowed the question of nuclear waste, the shrinking water supply, and the spread of smog. From 1945 to the early 1970s, almost every sector of the western economy leaped forward. With the development of the interstate highway system and less expensive commercial air travel, western tourism flourished. Millions of tourists visited the Badlands, the Grand Canyon, Monument Valley, Yellowstone National Park, or the other natural sites in the West. Millions more invaded the ski resorts at Vail, Aspen, Snowbird, Sundance, and Sun Valley. Las Vegas and Reno attracted tourists determined to have fun and make money. Disneyland and the beaches of southern California acted like a magnet for young people—and their parents—from all over the world. Increasingly, when Europeans and South Americans thought of the United States, their minds conjured visions of deep canyons and Mickey Mouse.

For a while, even the traditional western extractive industries—agriculture, ranching, mining, lumber, and petroleum—boomed. More than even before the war, farming and ranching became big businesses. Highly capitalized, heavily mechanized, often dependent on federal price supports, both were fabulously productive. The same was true for mining, lumbering, and petroleum industries. Western

Aids: A Modern Plague

AMERICANS have long debated what to do about sexually transmitted disease (STD). Health officials have insisted that STD is a medical problem that should be handled like any other communicable disease: through research, treatment, public education, and the vigorous application of modern techniques of epidemiology. Others have argued that STD is primarily a moral problem.

World War I brought the issue to a head. Army planners debated whether to concentrate on trying to prevent STD through educational propaganda against extramarital sex (accompanied by a crackdown on red-light districts), or whether to sanction the use of condoms and focus on medical treatment to cure infection. In the end, they elected to combine both approaches. Moreover, when the problem reappeared in World War II, the government promptly adopted the same solution: scary propaganda against extramarital sex, followed by condoms and treatment for soldiers who surrendered to temptation. Even the debate over treatment sounded like an echo. The discovery of penicillin precipitated another round of arguments over whether this new "wonder drug" should be given to soldiers who contracted STD. The dispute was settled exactly as it had been in World War I: Wayward souls received treatment.

Following World War II, public funding for STD work rose and the number of cases fell. The victory over STD, however, proved to be short-lived, for infection rates tripled between 1950 and 1975. What happened? In part, health officials were victims of their own success. Given the power of new antibiotics, doctors stopped worrying as much about the social behavior that led to transmission, and they became less vigilant in their efforts to track down the partners of infected patients. Yet the doctors were not solely to blame. The public's apathy was reflected in reduced health budgets for STD work.

The lull ended in the 1980s with the appearance of acquired immune deficiency syndrome (AIDS), the most terrifying disease of modern times. As early as 1980, physicians began reporting a strange medical phenomenon among gay men. These patients were falling prey to fatigue, a puzzling combination of infections, a rare skin cancer known as Kaposi's sarcoma, and eventual death. No one recovered from the disease.

After prolonged and ill-funded research, AIDS was finally linked to a retrovirus, which scientists named the "human immuno-deficiency virus," or HIV. Additional research soon revealed AIDS cases among heterosexuals, Haitians, hemophiliacs, and intravenous drug users, indicating that the disease was not limited to a single group; rather, it threatened everyone. But why did it take so long to mobilize research efforts and public awareness? The explanation lies in long-standing attitudes about STD.

First and foremost, AIDS was widely regarded at first as a "gay" disease, and homosexuals were a favorite target of the "new right" and the "moral majority," whose political clout had helped put Ronald Reagan in the White House. Patrick Buchanan, White House director of communications, proclaimed that homosexuals had "declared war on nature, and now nature is extracting an awful retribution." By the time the United States finally took notice of AIDS in 1987, more than 21,000 Americans had already died. Part of the reason lay in President Reagan's cutbacks in domestic programs: AIDS became another casualty of Reaganomics, another victim of the administration's hostility to social services. In the end, however, a series of shocking events forced the government to act: These included the discovery of AIDS-contaminated hospital blood supplies; the appearance of AIDS in heterosexuals; and the surprisingly bold anti-AIDS campaign of Surgeon General C. Everett Koop.

Koop recommended AIDS education for schoolchildren "at the earliest date possible," and he further advocated the promotion and use of condoms. Conservatives were outraged and charged the government with attempting to promote immorality. But Koop and other public health officials held firm. The government sponsored television and radio ads warning the public against "unsafe sex," and mailed an explicit brochure on AIDS to every household in America.

As public concern rose, various groups demanded that AIDS sufferers be quarantined. Though health authorities repeatedly stressed that casual contacts could not spread the disease, many people feared the worst. The objections of civil libertarians, who opposed quarantine, left most people cold, as did the arguments of those who rejected quarantine on practical grounds. (Where were tens of thousands of AIDS sufferers to be kept? Who was to pay for their care during this forced isolation?) While these arguments kept any serious movement for quarantine

from developing, the public remained edgy. Some parents withdrew their children from schools where AIDS patients were enrolled, and AIDS sufferers found that many of their co-workers wanted them removed from their jobs.

Yet some of the reactions to AIDS within the gay community were no less extreme. Granted, most gay leaders struggled from the outset to publicize AIDS and to promote safe sex and monogamous relationships. But other gays reacted with denial. Some initially believed (or chose to believe) that AIDS was a heterosexual propaganda tactic designed to crush the nascent gay movement or that it reflected a secretly planned biological warfare against gay men by the CIA or some secret government cabal. To many, gay liberation meant not merely toleration of homosexuality but a celebration of sexuality, a reordering of values with greater emphasis on the long-suppressed pleasure principle. Multiple and unprotected contacts were the final necessary step to political freedom. Others proclaimed that AIDS could never hit them. And still others became resigned and carried on as usual—in the gay community they became known as Doris Days, after the actress famous for singing *"Qué será, será" ("What Will Be, Will Be")*.

The end of the AIDS story is still to be written, for no one can predict the impact this deadly disease will have on American society. By 1995 more than 475,000 Americans had been diagnosed with the disease, more than 285,000 had died from it, and another 1 million are believed to be infected. With a cure nowhere in sight, medical authorities expect to be confronted by literally hundreds of thousands of AIDS patients by the turn of the century. Their care will be both protracted and expensive. Who will pay for it?

Despite such grim realities, sex researchers report few changes in the public's private behavior, especially in those groups that are at high risk for contracting the disease. Though hard data are lacking, the experts agree that "unsafe sex" remains a common practice among adolescents and young adults, and the same holds true for many like the progressives, many Americans today will no doubt continue to place their hopes on education and on the search for new medical advances with which to eradicate AIDS, debating all the while whether those who contract the disease should be pitied or condemned.

copper, uranium, wood, and oil were in constant demand. But in the late 1960s and early 1970s those industries began to face difficult times. Foreign competition plagued all of them. Chilean copper, Canadian lumber, and Arab oil often undersold Americans even in their own markets. In addition, environmentalists and government regulatory agencies made it more difficult, and more expensive, for lumber interests, miners, and oil drillers to practice business as usual. By the 1990s, there were signs that the oil industry might regain some of its former profitability, but the outlook for agriculture, lumber operations, and mining was less optimistic.

The post–World War II West was too diversified, however, for the decline in the extractive industries to mean a collapse of the western economy. Manufacturing, tourism, service, and high-tech industries ensured that the West would continue to grow economically. The emergence of high-tech manufacturing in California's Silicon Valley, Austin, Texas, and Seattle, Washington; the shipyards of Oakland and Long Beach in California; the banking and medical complex in Houston, Texas; and the defense-aerospace industries throughout the West prospered even while the national economy sagged. The age of the cowboy, the romantic man on horseback, had ended. Increasingly, Bill Gates, founder of Microsoft Corporation and America's wealthiest individual, sitting in front of his home computer screen in Seattle, Washington, symbolized the new West.

Politics Western Style

In the early 1960s, Arizona Senator **Barry Goldwater** seemed out of step with most of his colleagues in Washington. In both parties eastern liberalism and style seemed the order of the day. Democratic President John F. Kennedy talked confidently and eloquently about a more active role for government in the quest for social justice. Republican politicians such as Nelson Rockefeller of New York, Henry Cabot Lodge of Massachusetts, William Scranton of Pennsylvania, and George Romney of Michigan also advocated a more liberal domestic agenda, one more in accordance with Franklin D. Roosevelt's New Deal and Dwight Eisenhower's Modern Republicanism than the more conservative ideas of such former Republican leaders as Senator Robert Taft of Ohio. But Goldwater seemed unaffected by the charge toward liberalism.

Goldwater believed that the country's problem was not too little government activity but too much. In his 1960 book *The Conscience of a Conservative* Goldwater wrote that he was dedicated to "achieving the maximum amount of freedom for individuals that is consistent with the maintenance of social order." The enemy of individual freedom, he argued, was the federal government, which had become "a Leviathan, a vast national authority out of touch with the people, and out of control." He wanted to rein in the government, reduce its size, and restrict its activities to establishing order, maintaining defense, and administering justice.

In terms of concrete measures, Goldwater called for the end of all subsidies and price supports for farmers, the passage of right-to-work laws and the abolition of the closed shop, a new form of taxation (he called the federal income tax "confiscatory"), and a reduction of federal bureaucracy and spending. He opposed most forms of welfare and government spending on social, educational, public housing, and urban renewal programs. "I have little interest in streamlining government or making it more efficient, for I mean to reduce its size," he wrote. "I do not undertake to promote welfare, for I propose to extend freedom. My aim is not to pass laws, but to repeal them." As for foreign affairs, he called for a vigorous fight against communism and the defense of freedom throughout the world.

An Aberration or an Omen?

Who was this new conservative marksman? Barry Goldwater was a product of the twentieth-century West. "My life," he wrote, "parallels that of twentieth-century America—raw energy amid boundless land and unlimited horizons." He was born in Arizona when it was still a territory and raised on tales of the men and women who settled in the West. "My mother spoke a lot about our country when we were kids—our heritage of freedom, the history of Arizona, how individual initiative had made the desert bloom." But, as a westerner, he was quite aware that the federal government restricted his freedom. Only 17 percent of his home state, he noted, was "in private hands," and often the capital needed for western development was in the hands of eastern bankers. In his successful 1952 race for the U.S. Senate, he attacked "America's new super state—burgeoning federal spending and a bloated bureaucracy."

Once in the Senate, Goldwater continued his attack on eastern power bases and leaders. "For a century, the West had been a colony of big Eastern money—a boom when they had invested and a bust when they had pulled out of various mining and

THE PEOPLE SPEAK

The Conscience of a Conservative

Barry Goldwater's 1960 book *The Conscience of a Conservative* was small (only 123 pages, with large print) and ghostwritten (it was mostly culled from his past speeches and notes), but it sold 3.5 million copies in just four years. It also inspired a new generation of conservative thinkers. Patrick Buchanan called the volume "our new testament; it contained the core beliefs of our political faith, it told us why we had failed, what we must do. We read it, memorized it, quoted it. . . . For those of us wandering around in the arid desert of Eisenhower Republicanism, it hit like a rifle shot." Here Goldwater uses the notion of individual freedom to outline the theoretical foundations behind Conservatism.

> Surely the first obligation of a political thinker is to understand the nature of man. The Conservative does not claim special powers of perception on this point, but he does claim a familiarity with the accumulated wisdom and experience of history, and he is not too proud to learn from the great minds of the past.
>
> The first thing about man is that each member of the species is a unique creature. Man's most sacred possession is his individual soul—which has an immortal side, but also a mortal one. The mortal side establishes his absolute differentness from every other human being. *Only a philosophy that takes into account the essential differences between men, and, accordingly, makes provision for developing the different potentialities of each man can claim to be in accord with Nature.* We have heard much in our time about the "common man." It is a concept that pays little attention to the history of a nation that grew great through the initiative and ambition of uncommon men. The Conservative knows that to regard man as part of an undifferentiated mass is to consign him to slavery.
>
> Secondly, the Conservative has learned that the economic and spiritual aspects of man's nature are inextricably intertwined. He cannot be economically free, or even economically efficient, if he is enslaved politically; conversely, man's political freedom is illusory if he is dependent for his economic needs on the State.
>
> The Conservative realizes, thirdly, that man's development, in both its spiritual and material aspects, is not something that can be directed by outside forces. Every man, for his individual good and for the good of his society, is responsible for his *own* development. The choices that govern his life are choices that *he* must make: they cannot be made by any other human being, or by a collectivity of human beings. If the Conservative is less anxious than his Liberal brethren to increase Social Security "benefits," it is because he is more anxious than his Liberal brethren that people be free throughout their lives to spend their earnings when and as they see fit.

Source: Barry Goldwater, *The Conscience of a Conservative.* Copyright © 1960 Chariot-Victor Books.

---

other operations," he noted. "We had been left with ghost towns and holes in the ground where gold, silver, and mineral deposits had been discovered." Goldwater saw himself as an outsider and had no desire to become part of the inner circle of the Republican party. Instead, he articulated a political credo that aimed at taking power away from Washington and Wall Street and returning it to individual states. What he called for was a radical change in the Republican party that reflected the new realities of America, an "effort to move the party from the dominance of less than a dozen families and others in the East to hundred of thousands of small businessmen and others in the South, West, and elsewhere."

In 1964 Goldwater saw an opportunity. Attacking big government, deficit spending, high taxes, and social programs, he campaigned for the Republican nomination for president. "I will not change my beliefs to win a vote," he promised. "I will offer a choice, not an echo." Although the delivery of his speeches was often flat and his personal style wooden, his words were charged with outrage over a government that he believed had become too big, too fat, and too complacent. Throughout the winter and spring of 1964, he stumbled toward the nomination, eliminating one Republican rival after another. At times, the political struggles became bitter. Rockefeller branded Goldwater as a wild-eyed radical who might lead the country into a nuclear war. "WHO DO YOU WANT IN THE ROOM WITH THE H-BOMB BUTTON?" asked a Rockefeller campaign flyer. Other opponents also accused him of being trigger-happy and harboring racist beliefs; they even compared him to Adolph Hitler. But Goldwater won the battle. Reflecting the beliefs of their new candidate, the Republican platform called for spending cuts, reduced taxes, and a balanced budget; advocated stopping the flow of pornography through the mail and

In his campaign appearances during the 1964 presidential race, Barry Goldwater drew crowds of well-wishers as well as detractors, who were often concerned that his aggressive stance against Communists might lead to nuclear war.

restoring school prayers; and demanded a foreign policy that aggressively confronted Communists.

In the 1964 presidential election Goldwater faced Lyndon Johnson and his well-oiled Democratic machine. Johnson promised more government and more federal activity. Summarizing the Democratic agenda, Johnson said, "I just want to tell you this—we're in favor of a lot of things and we're against mighty few." On Johnson's side were prosperity and a substantial legislative record, which included the Civil Rights Act, the Wildlife Preservation Act, and the War on Poverty's Economic Opportunity Act. Looking toward the future, the Texas politician promised a **Great Society,** where want and suffering were eliminated. Medicare, Medicaid, regional redevelopment, urban renewal, and support for education—all were on Johnson's ambitious agenda. As several politicians suggested, criticizing Lyndon Johnson was like taking a shot at Santa Claus.

Not content just to say what they were for, Johnson and his campaign organizers made it clear what they were against. In two words: Barry Goldwater. In their public statements, television advertisements, and bumper stickers, they implied that if Goldwater was elected he might lead the nation into a nuclear war. "In your heart, you know he might" and "In your guts, you know he's nuts" were their constant refrains. In one television commercial, a young girl was shown picking the petals of a daisy in a sun-drenched field. As she plucked she counted, until her voice was drowned out by a stronger, military voice that commenced a military countdown, ending with the sight of a nuclear blast. The commercial ended with the voice of Lyndon Johnson: "These are the stakes. To make a world in which all of God's children can live, or go into the dark. We must either love each other, or we must die." To the end, the Democrats waged a bitter, effective campaign. Later in his life, Goldwater said, "I've often said that if I hadn't known Barry Goldwater in 1964 and I had to depend on the press and the cartoons, I'd have voted against the son of the bitch."

That is exactly what most Americans did. Goldwater lost big in 1964—43 million votes to 27 million votes. Johnson carried over 60 percent of the popular vote, something that few other presidential candidates had ever done. Newspaper and television commentators were quick to write off Goldwater and his conservative supporters as a political aberration. A *Time* magazine writer prophesied, "The conservative cause whose championship Goldwater assumed suffered a crippling setback. . . . The humiliation of their defeat was so complete that they will not have another shot at party domination for some time to come." Yet when conservatives began to study the returns, the defeat did not seem so absolute. Goldwater had run well in the Deep South, long considered sacred ground for the Democratic party. He had also attracted considerable support in the Southwest, the mountain states, southern California, and northeastern urban, ethnic-Catholic neighborhoods.

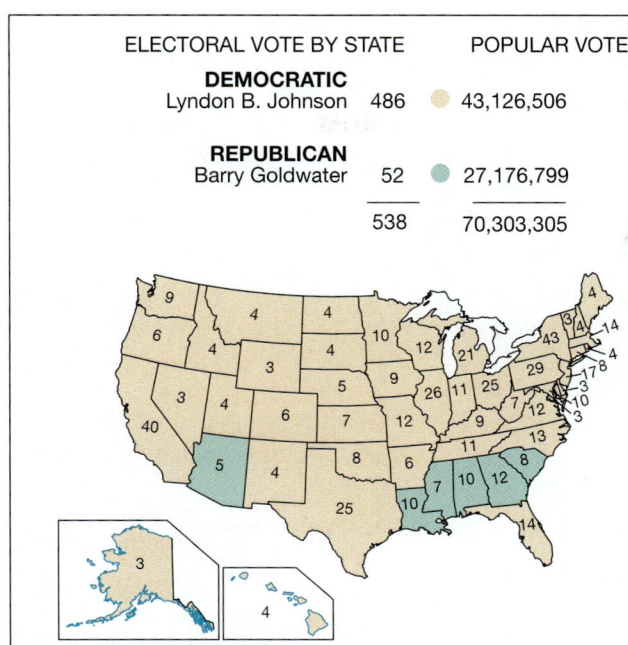

Election of 1964

Taken as a whole, Republican strategist Kevin Phillips believed that the 1964 returns contained good news for the future of the Republican party and the conservative movement. In his book *The Emerging Republican Party* (1969), Phillips argued that an important shift in power was taking place in American politics. New Deal liberalism and the northeastern intellectual and media elite no longer expressed the needs and met the demands of most Americans, especially westerners and southerners. Deep in the South, out on the range, on the Sunbelt golf courses, and in working-class Catholic neighborhoods, a new ethos was taking shape. The political revolt, Phillips noted, would be led by people like Goldwater, men and women who wanted less government, less special-interest reforms, and more of their own paychecks. As one conservative Texan later said, "The '64 campaign was the Alamo before San Jacinto.... 1964 would prove a pivotal election, a beginning rather than an end."

Shifting Party Loyalties

Ultimately, Phillips was right. There was a political earthquake taking place in the United States, and its rumblings would be felt for the rest of the century. In 1968 and 1972, presidential candidate Californian Richard Nixon, though more moderate than Goldwater on social issues, attacked liberal rulings by the Supreme Court, called for a return to "law and order," and appealed to the traditional values of hard work, religious faith, patriotism, and family. The South and West responded. In 1968, Nixon carried almost the entire West and most of the upper South (the Deep South went to American Independent candidate George Wallace). In his 1972 landslide victory, Nixon won every southern and western state. Eight years later, Ronald Reagan captured the presidency running on a platform that could have been written by Barry Goldwater. Reagan called upon American politicians to get tough on the Soviet Union, balance the federal budget, reduce the size of government, and support legislation to strengthen family values. Americans responded, sending him into office in 1980 and then overwhelmingly endorsing his first term in 1984. Texas Republican George Bush served two terms as vice president and then won the presidency in 1988, uniting the same coalition that Goldwater and Nixon had built and Reagan had satisfied.

The reasons for the shift in the center of political power from Northeast and Midwest to South and West and party alliances from Democrat to Republican had become clear by the 1990s. The power shift was largely the result of the movements of peoples. In the 1970s, for example, the decade in which the Republicans made their largest gains, millions of Americans relocated and immigrants moved to the South and West: the population of Florida increased by 3,124,000, California by 2,338,000, and Texas by 2,112,000; while New York's population declined by 1,582,000, Ohio by 649,000, and Illinois by 476,000.

Election of 1968

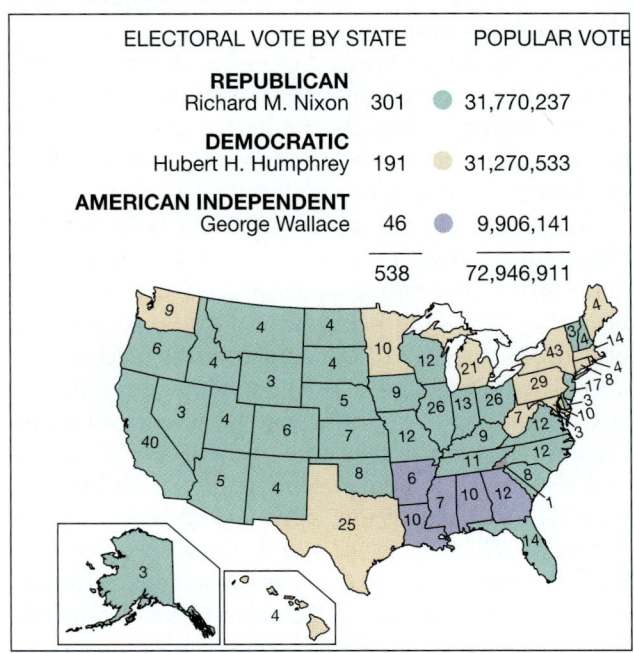

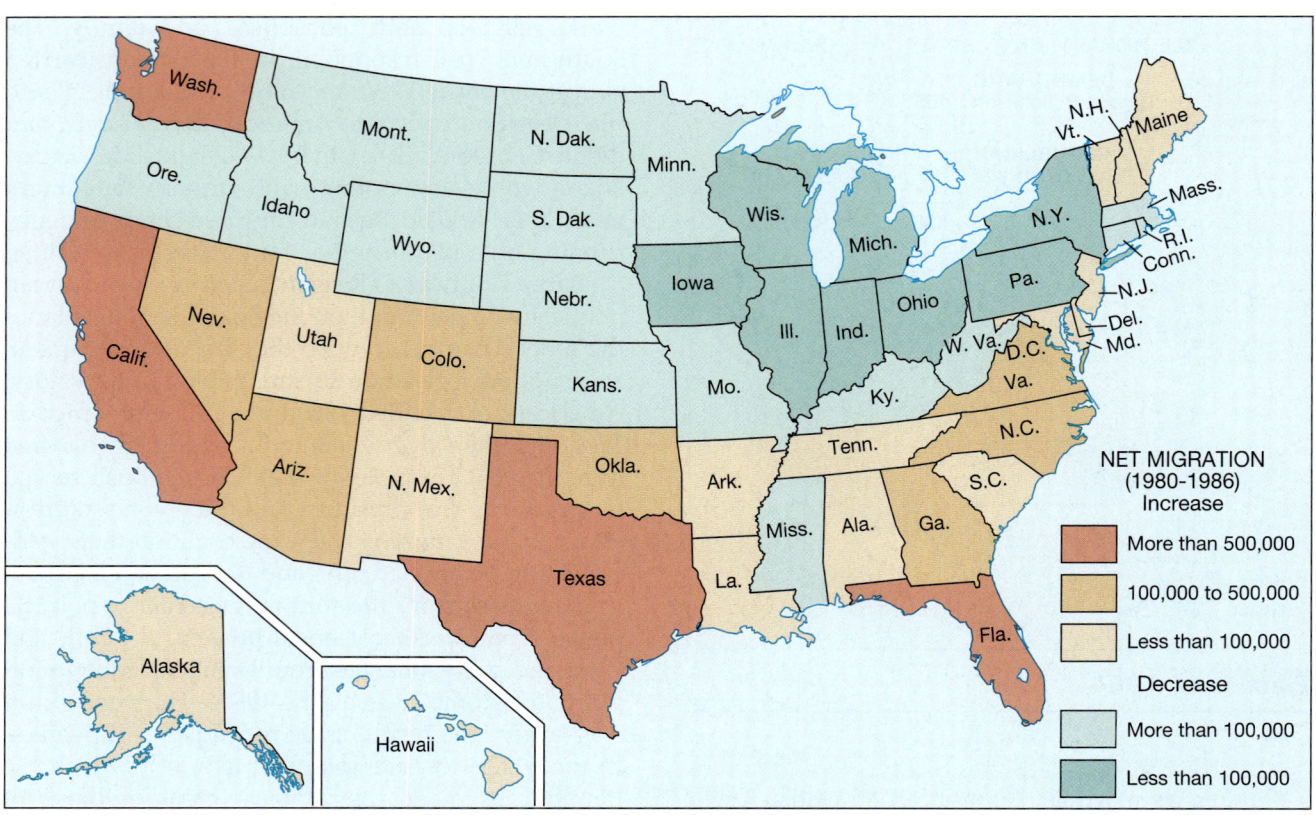

Population Shifts, 1980–1986

The same pattern was true for other states. Traditional industrial states—Massachusetts, Pennsylvania, Michigan, and Indiana—suffered sharp declines. Southern and western states—Virginia, North Carolina, Georgia, Arizona, Colorado, Oregon, and Washington—enjoyed equally sharp increases. By 1980, for the first time in American history, the majority of the population lived in the South and West. Such population shifts bolstered the political power of the South and West and reduced the political clout of the Northeast and the Midwest.

The same decade saw a shift in party loyalties in the South. For nearly a century white Southerners had voted Democrat, or, more precisely, non-Republican. For them, the Republican party was the party of Lincoln, the Civil War, and military Reconstruction. Their Democratic party stood for limiting the size and power of the federal government and for allowing the states to take care of their own problems and exploit their own resources. Barry Goldwater, and then Richard Nixon, appealed directly to these issues. In *The Conscience of a Conservative*, Goldwater's condemnation of the growth in federal power was as much a defense of the constitutional principle of states' rights. He particularly attacked the idea that the federal government could demand the integration of southern public schools. Goldwater wrote, "I am firmly convinced—not only that integrated schools are not required—but that the Constitution does not permit any interference whatsoever by the federal government in the field of education." Although Nixon did not go quite as far as Goldwater, he did succeed in limiting the role of the federal government in forcing desegregation of southern public schools. In addition, he argued that the Supreme Court had enlarged the power of the federal government; he appointed justices who were committed to reversing that trend. By the time Reagan ran for the presidency in 1980, the Republican party had become "the new Grand Old Party" for much of the white South.

Unlike the South, the West had never had a strong tradition of party loyalties. The seats of both parties, they argued, were in the East, and both parties were dominated by eastern interests. As a result the West never developed the machine politics of the East and was more sensitive to democratic political innovations. Initiative, referendum and recall, and woman suffrage, for instance, were more quickly accepted in the West than in other sections of the country. Similarly, the West was more receptive to left-wing and right-wing third-party movements. From the Populist movement in the 1890s and the Wobblies in the early part of the twentieth century to Francis Townsend's campaign in the 1930s and Barry Goldwater's revolt in the 1960s, the West had been more apt to swing toward political extremes.

The Politics of Liberation

The idea of individual freedom, as measured by less government and fewer restrictions, has characterized much of the political thinking of the post–1945 West. To be sure, individual freedom provided the core of the Goldwater and Reagan movements. It helps explain Goldwater's attack on the federal government and defense of a version of states' rights and Reagan's demands for deregulation. But the idea of individual freedom has also energized movements outside of Republican politics.

On the political left, the West Coast counterculture movement and such African-American liberation movements as the Black Panthers proclaimed a profound distrust of "government" solutions and federal bureaucracies. **Ken Kesey,** the novelist whose fictional heroes seemed to speak for many alienated youths, rejected the politics of party organizations and mass solutions. The heroes of his novels *One Flew Over the Cuckoo's Nest* (1962) and *Sometimes a Great Notion* (1964) are first and foremost individualists who battle more for individual dignity—the right to make individual decisions—than any sort of collective ideal. Similarly, Black Panther leaders struggled to gain control of their own communities and steered clear of traditional party politics.

Yet it was on the political right where individualism and antifederal sentiment made their most important political impact. Often the battle was over the control of land and natural resources. With the downturn in the economy in the 1970s, Western developers and businesspeople began to complain about federal environmental legislation. The debate over "beneficial use" became the flash point. Environmentalist groups such as the Sierra Club and the Friends of the Earth charged that developers were willing to destroy the land and the ecosystem in their pursuit of profits. Loggers, ranchers, miners, and other Westerners who depended on inexpensive access to government lands argued that the mass of federal regulations made it impossible for them to hold their own in competitive world markets.

The **Sagebrush Rebellion** was the most dramatic example of the battle between state and federal governments over control of state land. In the late 1970s and early 1980s, some conservative Western politicians began to clamor for the federal government to cede its control of western land to the individual states. The idea was to develop some of the land, sell much of the rest, and promote Western growth and prosperity. (Other Westerners, liberal and conservative, saw the rebellion as an attempted land grab by miners, ranchers, and loggers, a sort of return to the most exploitive methods of the nineteenth century.) Utah Senator Orrin Hatch introduced in 1979 legislation to return 544 million acres in 13 Western states from federal to state control; then-presidential-hopeful Ronald Reagan endorsed the proposal. But the rebellion failed. Arizona governor Bruce Babbitt summed it up as an attempt to "sell off the land into private ownership, lock the gates, post the no-trespassing sign, and proceed to use and abuse the land." In truth, though many Westerners had little faith in the wisdom of the federal government and resented federal regulation, they had even less faith in and more fear of their own developers. In the battle between developers and preservationists, most Westerners found themselves seeking middle ground.

The fight over Western lands, however, did not slow down the West's steady political drift to the right. Tax revolts were more successful than the Sagebrush Rebellion. If Westerners were content to allow the government to control a vast portion of their land, they steadfastly maintained that they should be able to control more of their own incomes. The tax rebellion was waged on state and federal fronts. In 1978 California passed Proposition 13, which demanded a 57 percent cut in state property taxes. The bill drained the state's treasury surplus and resulted in less services. In other states the rebellion was less extreme, but most Western state politicians had to move toward rigid fiscal conservatism to win election or to stay in office. In several cases, politicians—most notably Phil Gramm of Texas—even left the Democratic party and became Republicans.

CONCLUSION

The November 21, 1994, cover of *Time* magazine said it all without a word. A stampeding elephant, eyes fixed straight ahead in a pitiless stare, has trampled and killed a tiny donkey. The donkey is utterly flat-

Chronology of Key Events

1951	Inexpensive, efficient window air conditioner unit introduced	1972	Nixon is elected to second term, winning every southern and western state
1958	Dodgers and Giants professional baseball teams move from New York to California	1978	California voters approve Proposition 13, which calls for a 57 percent reduction in state property taxes
1960	The *Conscience of a Conservative*, in which politician Barry Goldwater outlines his beliefs, is published; sells 3.5 million copies in four years; California surpasses New York as the nation's most populous state	1980	Ronald Reagan is elected fortieth president
		1984	Reagan is reelected to second term
		1988	George Bush, Reagan's vice president, is elected forty-first president
1964	Barry Goldwater wins the Republican nomination for president; Democrat Lyndon Johnson defeats Goldwater in landslide victory	1992	Democrat Bill Clinton defeats Bush to become nation's forty-second president
1966	Braves professional baseball team moves from Milwaukee to Atlanta	1994	Democrats suffer overwhelming defeats in congressional and gubernatorial elections
1968	Richard Nixon is elected nation's thirty-seventh president		

tened, its eyes and tongue forced out of its head. The off-year elections, the cartoon indicated, had resulted in a complete and total Republican victory. Before the election the Democratic party had controlled the Senate 56 to 44, the House of Representative 256 to 178, and state governors' mansions 29 to 20. After the election, the Republican party controlled the Senate 53 to 47, the House 227 to 199, and governorships 30 to 17. It was a landslide rejection of President Bill Clinton's first two years in office and, according to many commentators, a generation of Democratic policy making. Putting the election into perspective, a *Newsweek* magazine writer noted, "Seventy-seven years ago, almost to the day, Bolsheviks in Petrograd raced into the Winter Palace in the name of communism. Last week in one of the most profound electoral routs in American history, Republicans won the right to occupy the Capitol and to mount what their more hyperbolic commanders think of as a counter-revolution: a full-scale attack on the notion that a central government should play a central role in the life of a nation."

The importance of the election, however, transcended party politics. It was not so much which party had won the election but which Republicans controlled the agenda that was crucial. The new Speaker of the House, and Republican lightning rod, was Newt Gingrich, a southern congressman who spoke the language of Barry Goldwater. Gingrich's "Contract With America" called for major budget cuts, tax cuts, and federal bureaucratic cuts. He promised to make the federal government cheaper and smaller, to return power to the states, and to reform government benefit programs. Sounding every bit a revolutionary, Gingrich said, "I will cooperate, but I won't compromise.... I may fail, we may fail. But this is real. I am who I seem to be."

Gingrich and his message underscored an important shift in American history. No longer were leaders from the biggest Eastern and Midwestern states. The new leaders in Washington came from the South and the West. Gingrich represented Georgia, Senate Majority Leader Robert Dole, Kansas; Phil Gramm, Texas. Their battle call was freedom. Criticizing President Clinton's comment that the election represented the wish by Americans for a government that "empowers" them, Gramm remarked, "He just doesn't get it. Government doesn't empower you. Freedom empowers you." It was a western credo he proclaimed, a doctrine that runs through a hundred John Wayne films. The question unanswered was: Is it a credo for the twenty-first century?

Suggestions for Further Reading

Carl Abbott, *New Urban America: Growth and Politics in the Sunbelt Cities of the South* (1981). A perceptive and knowledgeable analysis of regional demographics and politics.

Raymond Arsenault, *The End of the Long Hot Summer: The Air Conditioner and Southern Culture* (1984). Explores the social impact of air-conditioning in the South—a neglected but important aspect of the region's history.

William Cronon, George Miles, and Jay Gitlin, eds., *Under An Open Sky: Rethinking America's Western Past* (1992). Seeks to dislodge western history from its old moorings and point it in new directions.

Patricia Nelson Limerick, Clyde Millner II, and Charles Rankin, eds., *Trails: Toward a New Western History* (1991). Essays on the cutting edge of new historical interpretations of the West.

Richard Slotkin, *Gunfighter Nation: The Myth of the Frontier in Twentieth-Century America* (1992). Surveys the intersection between popular culture and the mythic American West.

Randy Roberts and James S. Olson, *John Wayne: American* (1995). Explores the life of an important Western icon, and examines his influence on national identity.

Richard White, *"It's Your Misfortune and None of My Own": A New History of the American West* (1991). A fresh perspective on the history of a region.

Donald Worster, *Rivers of Empire: Water, Aridity, and the Growth of the American West* (1985). How the West's most precious resource shaped regional identity.

Overviews and Surveys

Richard M. Bernard and Bradley R. Rice, eds., *Sunbelt Cities: Politics and Growth Since World War II* (1983); Mary C. Brennan, *Turning Right in the Sixties: The Conservative Capture of the GOP* (1995); Dan T. Carter, *The Politics of Rage: George Wallace, the Origins of the New Conservatism, and the Transformation of American Politics* (1995); Dan T. Carter, *From George Wallace to Newt Gingrich: Race in the Conservative Counterrevolution, 1963–1994* (1996); David R. Goldfield, *Cotton Fields and Skyscrapers, Southern City and Region, 1607–1980*, rev. ed. (1989); Roger Gottlieb and Peter Wiley, *Empires in the Sun: The Rise of the New American West* (1982); Bradford Luckingham, *The Urban Southwest* (1982); Michael P. Malone and Richard W. Etulain, *The American West: A Twentieth-Century History* (1989); Raymond A. Mohl, ed., *Searching for the Sunbelt: Historical Perspectives on a Region* (1990); Gerald Nash, *The American West in the Twentieth Century* (1973), *The American West Transformed: The Impact of the Second World War* (1985), and with Richard W. Etulain, eds., *The Twentieth-Century West: Historical Interpretations* (1989); David C. Perry and Alfred J. Watkins, eds., *The Rise of the Sunbelt Cities* (1977); Kirkpatrick Sale, *Power Shift: The Rise of the Southern Rim and Its Challenge to the Eastern Establishment* (1975); Bruce J. Schulman, *From Cotton Belt to Sunbelt: Federal Policy, Economic Development and the Transformation of the South, 1938–1980* (1991); Bernard L. Weinstein and Robert E. Firestine, *Regional Growth and Decline in the United States: The Rise of the Sunbelt and the Decline of the Northeast* (1978).

The Emergence of the Southern Rim

Shirley Abbott, *Womenfolks: Growing Up Down South* (1983); Jack Bass and Walter Devries, *The Transformation of Southern Politics* (1976); Earl Black and Merle Black, *The Vital South: How Presidents Are Elected* (1992); James Cobb, *Industrialization and Southern Society, 1877–1984* (1984), and *Selling of the South* (1982); Albert E. Cowdrey, *This Land, This South: An Environmental Hobby* (1983); Carl Degler, *Place Over Time: The Continuity of Southern Distinctiveness* (1977); John Egerton, *The Americanization of Dixie: The Southernization of America* (1974); Flora Gill, *Economics and Black Exodus: An Analysis of Negro Emigration from the Southern United States, 1910–1970* (1979); Barbara Griffith, *The Crisis of American Labor: Operation Dixie and the Defeat of the CIO* (1988); Elizabeth Jacoway and David R. Colburn, eds., *Southern Businessmen and Desegregation* (1982); F. Ray Marshall, *Labor in the South* (1967); Lucy Randolph Mason, *To Win These Rights: A Personal Story of the CIO in the South* (1952); Merl E. Reed, Leslie S. Hough, and Gary M. Fink, eds., *Southern Workers and Their Unions, 1880–1975* (1981); Charles P. Roland, *The Improbable Era: The South Since World War II* (1975); Nannie May Tilley, *The R. J. Reynolds Tobacco Company* (1985).

The Myth and Reality of the West

Susan Armitrage and Elizabeth Jameson, eds., *The Women's West* (1987); Leonard J. Arrington and Anthony Cluff, *Federally Financed Industrial Plants Constructed in Utah During World War II* (1969); Robert G. Athearn, *The Mythic West in Twentieth-Century America* (1986); Howard Ball, *Justice Downwind: America's Atomic Testing Program in the 1950's* (1986); Scott L. Bottles, *Los Angeles and the Automobile: The Making of a Modern City* (1987); Patricia Janis Broder, *The American West: The Modern Vision* (1984); Jeni Calder, *There Must Be a Lone Ranger: The American West in Film and in Reality* (1975); John G. Cawelti, *The Six-Gun Mystique*, 2d ed. (1984); Richard O. Davies, *The Age of Asphalt: The Automobile, the Freeway, and the Condition of Metropolitan America* (1975); John M. Findlay, *Magic Lands: Western Cityscapes and American Culture After 1940* (1992); William H. Goetzmann and William N. Goetzmann, *The West of the Imagination* (1986); Donald E. Green, *Land of the Underground Rain: Irrigation on the Texas High Plains, 1910–1970* (1973); Lynton

R. Hayes, *Energy, Economic Growth, and Regionalism in the West* (1980); Norris Hundley, Jr., *The Great Thirst: California and Water, 1770's–1990's* (1992); William Kahrl, *Water and Power: The Conflict over Los Angeles' Water Supply* (1982); Patricia Nelson Limerick, *The Legacy of Conquest: The Unbroken Past of the American West* (1987); Gerald D. Nash, *World War II and the West: Reshaping the Economy* (1990); Rita Parks, *The Western Hero in Film and Television: Mass Media Mythology* (1982); Donald J. Pisani, *From the Family Farm to Agribusiness: The Irrigation Crusade in California and the West* (1984); Earl Pomeroy, *The Pacific Slope* (1965); Marc Reisner, *Cadillac Desert: The American West and Its Disappearing Water* (1986); Elmo Richardson, *Dams, Parks, and Politics: Resource Development and Preservation in the Truman-Eisenhower Era* (1973); William W. Savage, Jr., *The Cowboy Hero: His Image in American History and Culture*, (1979); Richard Slotkin, *The Fatal Environment: The Myth of the Frontier in the Age of Industrialization* (1985); Duane Smith, *Mining America: The Industry and the Environment* (1987); Henry Nash Smith, *Virgin Land: The American West as Symbol and Myth* (1950); Jane Tompkins, *West of Everything: The Inner Life of Westerns* (1991); Jon Tuska, *The Filming of the West* (1976); Will Wright, *Six-guns and Society: A Structural Study of the Western* (1975); Daniel Yergin, *The Prize* (1991).

Politics Western Style

Daniel J. Elazar, *Cities of the Prairie: The Metropolitan Frontier and American Politics* (1970); Phillip O. Foss, *Politics and Grass: The Administration of Grazing on the Public Domain* (1960); Peter F. Galderisi, et al., eds, *The Politics of Realignment: Party Change in the Mountain West* (1987); William L. Graf, *Wilderness Preservation and the Sagebrush Rebellions* (1990); Samuel P. Hays, *Beauty, Health and Permanence: Environmental Politics in the United States, 1955–1985* (1987); Norris Hundley, *Water and the West: The Colorado River Compact and the Politics of Water in the American West* (1975); Frank H. Jonas, ed., *Western Politics* (1969); Robert L. Kelley, *Battling the Inland Sea: American Political Culture, Public Policy, and the Sacramento Valley, 1850–1986* (1989); Richard D. Lamm and Michael McCarthy, *The Angry West: A Vulnerable Land and Its Future* (1982); Gary D. Libecap, *Locking Up the Range: Federal Land Controls and Grazing* (1981); Roger W. Lotchin, *Fortress California, 1910–1961: From Warfare to Welfare* (1992); Carl J. Mayer and George A. Riley, *Public Domain, Private Domain: A History of Public Mineral Policy in America* (1985); Neil Morgan, *Westward Tilt: The American West Today* (1961); David F. Prindle, *Petroleum Politics and the Texas Railroad Commission* (1981); Roger Rapaport, *California Dreaming: The Political Odyssey of Pat and Jerry Brown* (1982); Clive S. Thomas, ed., *Politics and Public Policy in the Contemporary American West* (1991); A. Constandina Titus, *Bombs in the Backyard: Atomic Testing and American Politics* (1986).

Biographies

Robert A. Caro, *The Years of Lyndon Johnson: The Path to Power* (1982), and *Means of Ascent* (1990); Jimmy Carter, *Keeping Faith* (1982); Paul Conkin, *Big Daddy from the Pedernales: Lyndon Baines Johnson* (1986); Mark S. Foster, *Henry J. Kaiser: Builder in the Modern American West* (1989); Robert Alan Goldberg, *Barry Goldwater* (1995); Erwin Hargrove, *Jimmy Carter as President* (1989); John Keats, *Howard Hughes* (1966); Albert P. Heiner, *Henry J. Kaiser, American Empire Builder: An Insider's View* (1989); Gerald D. Nash, *A. P. Giannini and the Bank of America* (1992); Randy Shilts, *The Mayor of Castro Street: The Life and Times of Harvey Milk* (1982).

Internet Resources

Virtual Museum of Computing
http://www.cs.reading.ac.uk/museum/vlmp/computing.html
This University of Reading site says it is "an eclectic Collection of World Wide Web hyperlinks connected with the history of computing and on-line computer-based exhibits."

Lyndon B. Johnson
http://www.ipl.org/ref/POTUS/lbjohnson.html
This page contains basic factual data about his election and presidency, speeches, and on-line biographies.

Lyndon B. Johnson Library and Museum
http://www.lbjlib.utexas.edu/
This presidential library contains images and online exhibits.

A Giant Leap—America and Space
http://cnn.com/TECH/specials/apollo/
This CNN site commemorates the thirtieth anniversary of the 1969 moonwalk and tells the story of NASA and the ongoing space program.

National Aeronautics and Space Administration
http://www.hq.nasa.gov/office/pao/History/histsub.htm
NASA's Office of Policy and Plans History Office maintains this site about NASA and its history.

Information Age: People, Information and Technology Exhibit
http://photo2.si.edu/infoage.html
National Museum of American History hosts this site about how technology, particularly information technology, has shaped American's lives.

History of the Computer
http://www.tcm.org/html/history/index.html
Included are a timeline of the history of computers and computing as well as information about the people and inventions who made it possible.

Key Terms

Jimmy Carter (p. 823)

Hydraulic Society (p. 827)

Henry J. Kaiser (p. 828)

Walter O'Malley (p. 828)

Smog (p. 831)

Barry Goldwater (p. 834)

Great Society (p. 836)

Ken Kesey (p. 839)

The Sagebrush Rebellion (p. 839)

REVIEW QUESTIONS

1. What factors turned the idea of the "New South" into a reality in the post–World War II era?
2. How has the West developed such a booming, diverse economy?
3. What qualities define "Politics—Western Style"? How have these values influenced modern American politics?

29

VIETNAM AND THE CRISIS OF AUTHORITY

THE ILLUSION OF GREATNESS
Television's President
The "Macho" Presidency
Something Short of Camelot
Cuba Libre Revisited

VIETNAM: AMERICA'S LONGEST WAR
A Small Corner of a Bigger Picture
Kennedy's Testing Ground
Texas Tough in the Gulf of Tonkin
Lyndon's War
To Tet and Beyond
The Politics of a Divided Nation

THE TORTUOUS PATH TOWARD PEACE
Outsiders on the Inside
Vietnamization: The Idea and the Process
A "Decent Interval"
The Legacy of the War

"Uncle Ho"

Ho Chi Minh was born roughly 9000 miles from America, but he might as well have come from a different planet. Ho was a tiny, frail, thin splinter of a man. He was gentle, and in public always deferential. Even after he had come to sole power in North Vietnam, he steadfastly avoided all the trappings of authority. Instead of uniforms or the white sharkskin suit of the mandarin, Ho favored the simple shorts and sandals worn by the Vietnamese peasants. He was sure of who he was—certain of his place in Vietnamese history—and he had no desire to impress others with his position. To his followers, he was "Uncle Ho," the kind, bachelor relative who treated all Vietnamese citizens like the children he never had. But in the pursuit of Vietnamese independence and the realization of a Communist nation, Ho could be cold-blooded and ruthless.

Ho was born in 1890 in a village in a central province of the French colony of Vietnam and was originally named Nguyen Sinh Cung. In 1912 he left Vietnam and began a generation-long world odyssey. Signing on as a sailor aboard a French freighter, he moved from one port to the next. For a time he stayed in the United States, visiting Boston, New York City, and San Francisco. He was amazed not only by America's skyscrapers but also by the fact that immigrants in the United States enjoyed the same legal rights as American citizens. He was also struck by the impatience of the American people, their expectations of immediate results. (Later, during the Vietnam War, Ho would say to his military leaders, "Don't worry, Americans are an impatient people. When things begin to go wrong, they'll leave.")

After three years of almost constant travel, Ho settled in London, where he worked at the elegant Carlton Hotel. His living quarters were squalid, and he quickly learned that poverty existed even in the wealthiest, most powerful countries. Then it was on to Paris, where he came in contact with the French left. As he studied there, his nationalist ambitions became tinged with revolutionary teachings. He was still in Paris when World War I ended and the world leaders came to Versailles for the Peace Conference. Inspired by Woodrow Wilson's call for national self-determination, Ho wrote that "all subject peoples are filled with hope by the prospect that an era of right and justice is opening to them." Ho wanted to meet Wilson; he wanted to plead for independence for his country. Wilson ignored his request; Vietnam remained France's colony. Ho moved on—farther east and further left.

Disillusioned with France and socialism, Ho traveled to Moscow, where Lenin had declared war against imperialism; there Ho embraced communism. In Communist ideology he saw a road to his ultimate goal, the liberation of Vietnam. By the early 1920s he was actively organizing Vietnamese exiles into a revolutionary force. He continued to travel—to Western Europe, back to Russia, to China, back to Russia, to Thailand, back to the West. He lived a life of secrecy, moving from place to place, changing his name, renouncing anything even remotely resembling a personal life. No wife, no children, few friends—only a cause. As he advised one Vietnamese returning to the homeland, "The colonialists will be on your trail. Keep away from our friends' homes and don't hesitate to pose as a degenerate if it will help put the police off the scent."

In 1941 Ho returned to Vietnam. The time was right, he believed, to free Vietnam from colonial domination. During the early part of World War II, the Japanese had won control of the country from the French; now Ho and his followers would force out the Japanese. Ho allied himself with the United States. Working alongside American Office of Strategic Services (OSS) agents, he proved his mettle. He impressed the agents with his bravery, intelligence, and unflagging devotion to his cause. On September 2, 1945, borrowing passages from the American Declaration of Independence, Ho declared Vietnamese independence.

The French, who returned to Vietnam after the war, had different plans for Vietnam, so Ho's struggle continued. In candid moments he admitted that he didn't expect to live to see Vietnam fully independent. Yet he knew that the struggle of others would eventually secure independence. Ho had patience. It was a quality that the West found difficult to understand.

That was only one of the qualities of Ho and of the Vietnamese that the West did not understand. A deep intellectual chasm divided Vietnam and the West. The latter viewed history as a straight line in which

Ho Chi Minh was influenced as a young man by French socialism and Soviet communism in his goal to liberate Vietnam from the French.

progress was the governing principle. Emphasizing technological advancements and material improvements, Westerners glorified change and prized individualism.

The Vietnamese were products of different beliefs. Notions of competition, individualism, and technological change were anathema to tradition-bound Vietnamese. For a thousand years they had survived using the same rice-cultivating methods. Often, however, the margin between survival and death was a razor's edge. Unlike the United States, Vietnam did not have fertile frontiers to settle. To make do with the land they had, the Vietnamese organized life around villages and practiced a cooperative existence. Rich people were considered selfish because their wealth *had* to be gained at the direct expense of others. As one authority explained, "the idea remains with the Vietnamese that great wealth is antisocial, not a sign of success but a sign of selfishness."

Like wealth, individualism threatened the corporate nature of village life, which was based on duties and social harmony, not individual rights and individual justice. Even their language excluded the idea of individualism. Vietnamese has no personal pronoun equivalent to the Western *I, je, ich*. A person speaks of oneself in relationship to the person being addressed—for example, as "your teacher," "your brother," "your wife."

Nor did Vietnamese believe in intellectual freedom, which fostered debate and discord, rather than community stability. Americans considered Soviet communism evil because it discouraged the exchange of free ideas; Ho Chi Minh was drawn to the doctrine because it provided a set of answers not subject to questioning; he was the product of that closed world. America was the prophet of an open world. Motivated by the Cold War, during the period between 1954 and 1973, U.S. officials became convinced that they had to "save" Vietnam from Ho Chi Minh and his Communist brand of nationalism. Given Vietnamese leadership, traditions, and desire for independence, the American intervention in Vietnam was almost certain to fail.

THE ILLUSION OF GREATNESS

In the 1960 presidential race Kennedy challenged his Republican opponent, Richard M. Nixon, to a series of television debates. At the time, Kennedy faced an uphill battle. Young, handsome, and wealthy, Kennedy was considered by many too young, too handsome, and too wealthy to make an effective president. His undistinguished political record stood in stark contrast to Nixon's work in Congress and his eight years as Eisenhower's vice president. In addition, Kennedy was Catholic, and Americans had never elected a Catholic president. Behind in the polls, Kennedy needed a dramatic boost. Thus the challenge. Against the advice of his campaign manager, Nixon accepted.

Television's President

John Fitzgerald Kennedy was made for television. His tall, thin body gave him the strong vertical line that cameras love, and his weather-beaten good looks appealed to women without intimidating men. He had a full head of hair, and even in the winter he maintained a tan. Complementing his appearance was his attitude. He was always "cool" in public. This too was tailor-made for the "cool medium," television. Wit, irony, and understatement, all delivered with a studied nonchalance, translate well on television. Table-thumping, impassioned speech, and even earnest sincerity often just do not work on television.

The first debate was held in Chicago on September 26, 1960, only a little more than a month before the election. Nixon arrived looking ill and weak—during the previous six weeks he had banged his kneecap, which became infected, spent several weeks in the hospital, and then caught a bad chest cold that left him hoarse and weak. By the day of the debate he looked like a nervous corpse—pale, 20 pounds underweight, and haggard. Makeup experts offered to hide his heavy beard and soften his jowls, but Nixon accepted only a thin coat of Max Factor's "Lazy Shave," a pancake cosmetic.

During the Kennedy-Nixon debates, John F. Kennedy demonstrated that for television politics, style was as important as substance.

Kennedy looked better, very much better. He didn't need makeup to appear healthy, nor did he need special lighting to hide a weak profile. He did, however, change suits. He believed that a dark blue rather than a gray suit would look better under the bright lights. Kennedy was right, of course, as anyone who watches a nightly news program realizes.

When the debate started, Kennedy spoke first. Although he was nervous, he intentionally slowed down his delivery. His face was controlled and cool. He smiled with his eyes and perhaps the corners of his mouth, and his laugh was a mere suggestion of a laugh. His body language was perfect. As for what he said, Kennedy disregarded the prearranged ground rules and shifted what was supposed to be a debate on domestic issues to one on foreign policy.

Nixon fought back. He perspired, scored debating points, produced memorized facts, and struggled to win; but his efforts were "hot"—bad television. Instead of hearing a knowledgeable candidate, viewers saw a nervous, uncertain man, one whose clothes did not fit and whose face looked pasty and white. In contrast, what Kennedy said sounded statesmanlike, and he *looked* right. Kennedy was the clear winner. Only later did Nixon realize that the telecast had been a production, not a debate.

When the polls on the results came out, Kennedy inched ahead of Nixon in a Gallup poll for the first time during the campaign. Republicans realized the impact of the debate—Republican Senator Barry Goldwater called it "a disaster." Most of the people who were undecided before watching the debate ended up voting for Kennedy. That proved to be the margin of victory: only one-tenth of one percent separated the two candidates. Perhaps the most important result of the election, however, was not Kennedy's victory but the demonstration of the power of television. The medium came into its own in 1960.

The "Macho" Presidency

In his inaugural address Kennedy issued threats and challenges as well as making promises. Proud to be the first American president born in the twentieth century, determined to be the torch-bearer for "a new generation," Kennedy wanted the world to know where he stood: "Let every nation know, whether it wishes us well or ill, that we shall pay any price, bear any burden, meet any hardship, support any friend, oppose any foe to assure the survival and the success of liberty." And who would pay, bear, meet, support, and oppose? On this point too Kennedy was clear: "And so, my fellow Americans: ask not what your country can do for you—ask what you can do for your country."

After listening to the blandness and mangled syntax of Eisenhower's addresses, here was a speaker of rare ability, here were speeches beautifully phrased. Only years after his death did people begin to ask if he was serious or if he was more concerned with how he said something rather than with what he said. Indeed, he and his speech writers were attracted to verbal sleight-of-hand tricks: "If a free society cannot help the many who are poor, it cannot save the few who are rich. . . . Let us never negotiate out of fear, let us never fear to negotiate." Like the television debates, such statements emphasized style over substance.

Who was this speaker? Competition and an aggressively masculine view of the world ran through the life of John F. Kennedy. He was the son of a multimillionaire who demanded excellence of all his sons and who believed that as Boston Irish Catholics they had to try harder and be tougher than their Protestant neighbors. This was particularly difficult for John Kennedy, who suffered throughout his life from a series of illnesses and physical problems, including Addison's disease and chronic back trouble. His brother Bobby recalled, "At least one-half of the days that he spent on this earth were days of intense physical pain."

But he never used—and his father never accepted—pain as an excuse for inactivity. At Harvard University he played football, boxed, swam, and ran, and during vacations at the family home in Hyannisport he roughhoused with his brothers and sisters. Throughout his life, Kennedy maintained this physical view of life. To impress the Kennedys, one associate remembered, you had to "show raw guts, fall on your face now and then. Smash into the house once in a while going after a pass. Laugh off twisted ankles or a big hole torn in your best suit."

Kennedy's macho ethos extended to his attitude toward women. Like his father, he regarded sexual conquests as a sign of manhood. During his Washington years as a U.S. senator, he moved from one affair to the next. He did not even bother to learn the names of his one-night-stands, referring to them by such generic names as "Kiddo" or "Sweetie." Nor did Kennedy's affairs end after he was married and elected president. When he wanted companionship and conversation he turned to his male friends.

In his speeches Kennedy stressed the theme that America was entering a period of crisis: "In the long history of the world, only a few generations have been granted the role of defending freedom in its maximum danger. I do not shrink from this responsibility—I welcome it." Without crisis, Kennedy believed, no person could achieve greatness, and he desired greatness. As was expressed in his Pulitzer-Prize-winning *Profiles in Courage*, "Great crises produce great men, and great deeds of courage."

Something Short of Camelot

From the very first, journalists associated the Kennedy administration with Camelot. According to the popular legend, King Arthur and his Knights of the Round Table established in the realm of Camelot a period of unparalleled peace and prosperity. Although Kennedy himself enjoyed the Camelot comparisons, the record of his administration and personal behavior fell short of the ideal.

Several factors worked to limit the success of Kennedy's domestic programs. To begin with, Kennedy lacked both political support in Congress and a firm commitment to push for liberal reforms. Ideologically, he was a centrist Democrat. In addition, although his party held a solid majority in the House, 101 of 261 Democratic representatives came from southern and border states, and they normally voted with conservative Republicans. Added to this problem was Kennedy's distaste for legislative infighting and his poor working relations with many senators. He limited his domestic agenda to such traditional Democratic proposals as a higher minimum wage, increased Social Security benefits, and modest housing and educational programs. In his inaugural address he did not even mention poverty or race. In the final analysis, Kennedy was so concerned with the "crises abroad" that he did not want to risk any of his political capital on unpopular domestic reforms.

There were small successes. Congress raised the minimum wage, expanded Social Security, and appropriated a few billion dollars for public housing and aid to economically depressed areas. But such legislation hardly amounted to the "new frontier" Kennedy promised. Congress defeated the president's plan for federal aid to education, a health insurance plan for the aged, and programs to help migrant workers, unemployed youths, and urban commuters.

African Americans were especially disappointed with Kennedy's performance. They had, after all, supplied Kennedy's margin of victory in the 1960 election. But once elected JFK was slow in using his office to further the cause of civil rights.

For African Americans, the early 1960s were difficult, violent years that tested their resolve. White segregationists confronted nonviolent desegregation efforts with unprovoked ferocity. Violence erupted in city after city. NAACP organizer Medgar Evers was shot down outside his home in Jackson, Mississippi. Four young African-American girls were killed when a Birmingham church was bombed. Police authorities sprayed civil rights protesters, including children, with high-pressure fire hoses and unleashed attack dogs on them. (See Chapter 30 for a fuller treatment of the fight for civil rights.)

Through his first two years in office, Kennedy remained largely silent. To win southern congressional support he even backed the nomination of a Mississippi jurist—who had once referred to African Americans as "chimpanzees"—for a seat on the federal bench. Although Attorney General Robert Kennedy aided protesters when federal laws were violated, JFK and the FBI did virtually nothing.

In 1963 Kennedy changed his position. In part this about-face was the result of Robert Kennedy's prodding; in part it was the result of television, which daily showed shocking examples of brutality in the South and accelerated the demand for change. In late May 1963, Kennedy eloquently announced his new position. It should be possible, he said, "for American students of any color to attend any public institution without having to be backed up by troops.... But this is not the case.... We preach freedom around the world ... but are we to say to the world ... that we have no second-class citizens except Negroes, that we have no class or caste system, no ghettos, no master race except with respect to Negroes?"

Perhaps Kennedy was convinced that the time had come for "the nation to fulfill its promise." Perhaps, as his supporters claim, in 1963 Kennedy was beginning to fulfill his own promise. His death in late 1963 left questions unanswered, potential unrealized. Judged by his accomplishments, however, Kennedy's Camelot, like King Arthur's, existed largely in the realm of myth. Although he could inspire people to follow, too often on domestic issues he chose not to lead.

Cuba Libre Revisited

Foreign affairs consumed Kennedy's interest. Unlike domestic politics, international conflicts were more clear-cut, and the divisions between "us" and "them" more certain. Foreign affairs also allowed Kennedy to express his masculine view of the world. He could employ the Kennedy approach to difficult decisions, which he once described as: calculate the odds, make your choice, and "grab [your] balls and go."

In his approach to the world, Kennedy generally continued the essentially Cold War policies of Truman and Eisenhower. He accepted the strategy of containment and the notion that the Soviet Union would take advantage of any sign of weakness by the United States. He was also suspicious of conventional diplomatic channels, preferring to listen to his young advisers rather than seasoned State Department officials.

Kennedy's handling of Cuban relations revealed his bellicose tendencies. Like Eisenhower, Kennedy was dismayed by the success of Fidel Castro. Just as Americans during the 1890s had cried *"Cuba Libre,"* on taking office Kennedy began to search for a way to "free" Cuba, this time from Castro's communism rather than Spain's colonialism. His desire to strike a blow against communism led him to embrace a CIA plan to overthrow Castro. If the CIA had successfully planned coups in Guatemala, Iran, and Laos, Kennedy reasoned, then perhaps it could do the job in Cuba.

The CIA plan, hatched during the Eisenhower administration, entailed both the assassination of Castro and the training and transporting of a force of Cuban exiles to Cuba, where they would launch a counterrevolution. It was a plan that even the joint chiefs of staff believed would probably fail. Even worse, the plan was one of the worst-kept secrets in the Western Hemisphere. As one historian noted, "Washington knew because the CIA had to drum up broad support in the government for it. Miami knew because the CIA had done everything but take out classified ads to get volunteers. Guatemala knew because the exile brigade was training there, as a local newspaper pointed out. And Castro knew because everyone else did—except the American people." Pierre Salinger, Kennedy's press secretary, later called the plan "the least covert military operation in history."

The invasion on April 17, 1961, at the Bay of Pigs was an unmitigated disaster. Several attempts to assassinate Castro failed, and the Cuban people did not rise up to join the invaders, who were trapped on the beaches. Nor would Kennedy authorize U.S. air support for the exile forces. As a result, all but 300 of the 1500 invaders were killed or captured. If anything, the **Bay of Pigs fiasco** strengthened Castro's position in Cuba.

The Bay of Pigs invasion, however, did not end Kennedy's problems with Cuba. In the fall of 1962 a more serious crisis arose when the Soviet Union began to install intermediate-range ballistic missiles (IRBMs) in Cuba. Instead of trying to work through proper diplomatic avenues—a process that would have taken time and might have hurt the Democrats in the upcoming election—Kennedy announced the alarming news to an anxious television audience. After showing the public the American cities that the missiles could destroy, Kennedy said he would not permit Soviet ships transporting the weapons to enter Cuban waters. "The people were assured," a scholar commented, "that he would run any risk, including thermonuclear war, on their behalf." Such assurances created a genuine mood of crisis in the country.

Behind the scenes, Kennedy and Soviet Premier Nikita Khrushchev searched for a way to defuse the crisis. During the entire affair Bobby Kennedy counseled level-headed restraint and Khrushchev eschewed any shoe-pounding antics. In the end, the world leaders achieved a solution. Khrushchev agreed to remove the missiles under United Nations inspection in return for an American pledge not to invade Cuba. The Kennedy administration interpreted the result as a victory. "We're eyeball to eyeball and I think the other fellow just blinked," Secretary of State Dean Rusk observed during the episode. And, indeed, the Soviet Union could hardly disagree. The **Cuban missile crisis** provided the ammunition to force Khrushchev out of power.

The two "superpowers" had stood at the brink, gazed into the abyss, and stepped back. And for what? "When all is said and done," observed one historian, "it seems that President Kennedy had risked ultimate disaster in service to a crisis that was more illusory than real, at least in military terms."

Again, the unsatisfactory "perhaps" reappeared. Perhaps Kennedy learned more from the Cuban missile crisis than he had from the Bay of Pigs invasion. Friends of Kennedy claimed that he

Shocked and saddened Americans everywhere shared the loss felt by President Kennedy's widow and two young children.

reached maturity during the crisis and that it motivated him to move toward détente—an easing of tensions—with the Soviet Union. In several 1963 speeches he called for "not merely peace in our time but peace for all time" and a "world safe for diversity." And he did support a treaty banning all atmospheric testing of nuclear weapons. Perhaps Kennedy had come to a new maturity.

The tragedy is that nobody can ever know. On November 22, 1963, Lee Harvey Oswald assassinated President Kennedy in Dallas, Texas. (Later investigations questioned whether Oswald acted alone, although the most thorough study of the assassination concluded that he did.) The event moved the nation. Newsman Walter Cronkite cried on television, and millions of Americans cried in their homes. Once again, television gave the event a mythical quality—showing his grieving wife, his barely understanding children, his solemn funeral. Americans mourned together, eyes fixed on their television sets. And immediately commentators began to evaluate Kennedy's presidency in terms of not what had been but what might have been.

VIETNAM: AMERICA'S LONGEST WAR

How did it start? And when? Even while the war in Vietnam tore at the heart of America in the 1960s most Americans, including some foreign policy experts, were not exactly sure of the answers to such basic questions. Johnson said he was continuing Kennedy's policy, who had continued Eisenhower's, who had continued Truman's, who had acted as he believed Roosevelt would have acted. The answers stretch back into time.

A Small Corner of a Bigger Picture

Struggle, like a mighty river, runs through the history of the small country of Vietnam. For almost 2000 years agriculturally fertile Vietnam battled against the invading Chinese for its independence. Next came the French. During the seventeenth, eighteenth, and nineteenth centuries, French traders and missionaries penetrated Vietnam, establishing their control over the country in the name of *la mission civilisatrice*. This "civilizing mission," however, robbed the Vietnamese of the wealth of their land and their independence. France's rules of governing Vietnam—described as "a lot of subjugation, very little autonomy, a dash of assimilation"—created discontent among the Vietnamese, some of whom welcomed the next invader, Japanese, who took over the country during World War II.

Vietnam and Southeast Asia

The Vietnamese declared their independence in 1945, but that same year the French returned, bent on the resubjugation of the country. The struggle continued, with the Communist Vietminh under Ho Chi Minh controlling the north of the country and the French in the south. Between 1945 and 1954 both sides suffered terrible losses in the bitter guerrilla struggle.

The United States faced a difficult decision over this struggle. During World War II, Franklin Roosevelt had favored Vietnamese independence and had aided Ho's fight against the Japanese. He recognized that the age of colonialism was doomed, and he wanted the United States identified with anticolonialism. At the same time, however, Roosevelt believed that a strong postwar Western Europe was essential to American security, and he did not want to alienate Britain or France by pressing too hard for an end to empires.

On Roosevelt's death, Harry Truman inherited FDR's problems. Even more than his former boss, he advocated a strong Western Europe, even if that strength had to be based on the continuation of empires. It was a Cold War decision. The United States, Truman maintained, "had no interest" in "championing schemes of international trusteeship" that would weaken the "European states whose help we need to balance Soviet power in Europe."

Vietnam became a pawn in the game of Cold War politics. Truman wanted French support against the Soviet Union. France wanted Vietnam. Truman willingly agreed to aid France's ambitions in exchange for that country's support. The success of Mao Zedong's Communist revolution in China strengthened America's support of the French in Vietnam. Obsessed with the idea of an international Communist conspiracy, Truman and his advisers contended that Stalin, Mao, and Ho were united by the single ambition of world domination. They overlooked the historical rivalries that pulled Russia, China, and Vietnam apart. As Ho Chi Minh once told his people, "It is better to sniff French dung for a while than eat China's all our life."

By the late 1940s, the United States had assumed a large part of the cost of France's effort to regain its control over Vietnam, and the price escalated during the early 1950s. By 1952 the United States was shouldering roughly one-third of the cost of the war, and between 1950 and 1954 America contributed $2.6 billion to France's war effort. But it was not enough—France could not defeat Ho's Vietminh.

In 1954 the war reached a crisis stage. In an effort to lure the Vietminh into a major engagement, the leading French commander moved more than 13,000 soldiers to **Dien Bien Phu,** a remote outpost in a river valley in northwest Vietnam. The Vietminh surrounded the fort and moved artillery pieces to the hills above the French airstrip. From there they mounted a siege of the outpost. As the months passed, French manpower and prestige suffered punishing blows. Inside Dien Bien Phu, latrines overflowed, food supplies ran out, water spoiled, and unburied bodies fouled the air. Finally, on May 7, 1954, the last French commander surrendered.

During the siege the French continually asked President Eisenhower for military support, but he refused to act without the consent of Congress and Britain. Neither favored American military intervention. Senator Lyndon Johnson of Texas expressed the majority view in Congress when he opposed "sending American G.I.s into the mud and muck of Indochina on a blood-letting spree to perpetuate colonialism and white man's exploitation in Asia." As a result, France gave up its attempt to recolonize Vietnam. At the peace talks in Geneva, the countries involved agreed to temporarily divide Vietnam at the 17th parallel into two countries and hold elections in the summer of 1956 to reunify Vietnam.

Eisenhower would not militarily aid France, but he quickly supported the independent government established in South Vietnam under the leadership of **Ngo Dinh Diem**. In America, where he spent several years in a Catholic seminary, Diem was known as an anti-Communist and a nationalist. In Vietnam, where he had not been for 20 years, he was hardly known at all. As a popular leader, he had no appeal. Imperious, often paranoid, overly reliant on his own family, Diem, a Catholic in an overwhelmingly Buddhist nation, successfully alienated almost everyone who came into contact with him. Even United States intelligence sources rated his chances of establishing order in South Vietnam as "poor."

Diem, nevertheless, was America's man. Why? Because he was an anti-Communist and a nationalist, and, as John Foster Dulles said, "because we know of no one better." Lyndon Johnson put it more bluntly in 1961: "Diem's the only boy we got out there." Even Eisenhower supported Diem militarily and politically. Vietnam became a test case, an opportunity for the United States to battle communism in Asia with dollars instead of Americans. When the time came to hold the unification election, Diem, with American backing, refused. Instead, to show his popularity he held "free" elections in South Vietnam, where he received an improbable 98.2 percent of the popular vote. The dishonesty of the elections was underscored by the Saigon returns where Diem received 605,000 votes, although there were only 405,000 registered voters.

Diem's absolutist policies created problems. By the end of 1957, Vietminh guerrillas in South Vietnam—often called the Vietcong—were in open revolt. Two years later, North and South Vietnam resumed hostilities. The United States increased its aid, most of which went to improving the South Vietnamese military or into the pockets of corrupt officials. The United States spent little money on improving the quality of life of the peasants. Nor did the United States object strongly to Diem's dictatorial methods. Diem once said that the sovereign was "the mediator between the people and heaven," and he demanded absolute obedience.

By the end of Eisenhower's second term America had become fully committed to Diem and South Vietnam. To be sure, problems in Vietnam were not America's major concern. In fact, most Americans were unaware of their country's involvement there. More than anything, Vietnam was a small corner of a bigger picture. U.S. policy there was determined by larger Cold War concerns. America's presence in Vietnam, however, would soon be expanded.

Kennedy's Testing Ground

On taking office, John Kennedy reaffirmed his country's commitment to Diem and South Vietnam. He announced his intention to be even more aggressive than Truman or Eisenhower. In Vietnam Kennedy saw an opportunity to "prove" his nation's resolve and strength. Ultimately, however, South Vietnam as a country was less important to Kennedy than the challenge it presented.

Kennedy believed that the United States needed a fresh military approach. Eisenhower's "massive retaliation" was too limited. It was of no use in a guerrilla war like Vietnam. Kennedy labeled his approach **"flexible response,"** and it entailed the development of conventional and counterinsurgency (antiguerrilla) forces as well as a nuclear response. Vietnam rapidly became the laboratory for counterinsurgency activities, a place for Special Forces (Green Berets) units to develop their own tactics. To achieve this end, Kennedy expanded the Special Forces from 2500 to 10,000 men.

To "win" in Vietnam, Kennedy realized that he would have to strengthen America's presence there. In November of 1961 he decided to deploy American troops to South Vietnam. By the end of 1961, 3205 American "advisers" were in Vietnam. Kennedy increased this force to 11,300 in 1962 and 16,300 in

1963. Although several of his advisers questioned this military escalation, arguing that once the United States committed troops it would be more difficult to pull out of the conflict, Kennedy remained firm in his desire to "save" South Vietnam.

As American involvement deepened, Diem's control over South Vietnam declined. He alienated peasants by refusing to enact meaningful land reforms and Buddhists by passing laws to restrict their activities. Responding to Diem's pro-Catholic policies, Buddhists began organized protests. They conducted hunger strikes and nonviolent protests. Several Buddhist monks engaged in self-immolation. In full view of American reporters and cameras, one burned himself to death on a busy, downtown Saigon intersection. Although the gruesome sight shocked Americans, Diem's sister-in-law, Madame Nhu, laughed at the "barbecues," offering gasoline and matches for more fiery deaths.

More deaths followed, and protests mounted. Diem exerted little influence outside of Saigon. Insightful American reporters such as David Halberstam, Neil Sheehan, Peter Arnett, and Stanley Karnow argued that the Diem regime was isolated and paranoid, that a stable democracy would never develop as long as Diem held power. Rather than talk with reporters, Diem would deliver bizarre five-, six-, even ten-hour monologues.

The Kennedy administration soon reached the conclusion that without Diem South Vietnam had serious problems, with Diem the country was doomed. In sum, Diem had to go. Behind the scenes, Kennedy encouraged Vietnamese generals to overthrow Diem. On November 1, 1963, Vietnamese army officers arrested and murdered Diem and his brother. Although Kennedy did not approve of the assassination, the United States quickly aided the new government.

Three weeks later Kennedy was assassinated in Dallas. Several of his friends have suggested that he had begun to reevaluate his Vietnam policy and that after the 1964 election he would have started the process of American disengagement. In a moment of insight, Kennedy himself had observed, "The troops will march in; the bands will play; the crowds will cheer; and in four days everyone will have forgotten. Then we will be told we have to send more troops. It's like taking a drink. The effect wears off, and you have to take another." But whatever Kennedy's future plans or insights, he still had increased U.S. involvement in Vietnam.

Unfortunately for Kennedy's successor, the prospects for South Vietnam's survival were less than they had been in 1961. By 1963 South Vietnam had lost the fertile Mekong Delta to the Vietcong and with it most of the country's rural population.

From the peasants' perspective, the Saigon government stood for heavy taxes, no services, and military destruction; and increasingly they identified the United States with Saigon. Such was the situation Lyndon Johnson inherited.

Texas Tough in the Gulf of Tonkin

Lyndon Baines Johnson (LBJ) was a complex man—shrewd, arrogant, intelligent, sensitive, vulgar, vain, and occasionally cruel. He loved power, and he knew where it was, how to get it, and how to use it. "I'm a powerful sonofabitch," he told two Texas congressmen in 1958 when he was the most powerful legislator on Capitol Hill. Everything about Johnson seemed to emphasize or enhance his power. He was physically large and seemed even bigger, and he used his size to persuade people. The "Johnson treatment" involved "pressing the flesh"—a back-slapping, hugging sort of camaraderie. He also used symbols of power adroitly, especially the telephone, which had replaced the sword and pen as the symbol of power. "No gunman," remarked one historian, "ever held a Colt .44 so easily" as Johnson handled a telephone.

A legislative genius, Johnson had little experience in foreign affairs. Reared in the poverty of the Texas hill country, educated at a small teachers' college, and concerned politically with domestic issues, before becoming president LBJ had expressed little interest in foreign affairs. "Foreigners are not like the folks I am used to," he often said, and whether it was a joke or not he meant it. He was particularly uncomfortable around foreign dignitaries and ambassadors, often receiving them in groups and scarcely paying attention to them. "Why do I have to see them?" he once asked. "They're [Secretary of State] Dean Rusk's clients, not mine."

Yet to say Johnson had little experience in foreign affairs is not to suggest that he did not have strong opinions on the subject. Like most politicians of the period, Johnson was an unquestioning Cold Warrior. In addition, along with accepting the domino theory—the idea that if Vietnam fell, other nations would also fall to communism—and a monolithic view of communism, Johnson cherished a traditionally southern notion of honor and masculinity. It was his duty, he maintained, to honor commitments made by earlier presidents. "We are [in Vietnam] because . . . we remain fixed on the pursuit of freedom, a deep and moral obligation *that will not let us go.*" Leaving Vietnam, Johnson believed, would be a dishonorable act, dangerous for the nation's future. Raised in an area where the frontier was still visible, Johnson approached foreign policy like a Texas Ranger. To show weakness and back down was worse than cowardly—it was unmanly. As he often said, "If you let a bully come into your front yard one day, the next day he will be up on your porch and the day after that he will rape your wife in your own bed."

Furthermore, Johnson believed that any retreat from Vietnam would destroy him politically. Soon after becoming president, he told America's ambassador to Vietnam, "I am not going to be the President who saw Southeast Asia go the way China went." No, he would not "lose" Vietnam and allow Republican critics to attack him as they had Truman. "I knew," LBJ later noted, "that Harry Truman and Dean Acheson had lost their effectiveness from the day the communists took over China." Johnson was determined to win the war, to "nail the coonskin to the wall."

Before winning in Vietnam, however, he had to win in the United States. The presidential election in 1964 was his top priority. He was pitted against Barry Goldwater, the powerful Arizona senator from the Republican Right. "Extremism in the defense of liberty is no vice," Goldwater said, and if elected he promised to defend South Vietnam at any cost. He also preached against the welfare state, Social Security, the Nuclear Test Ban Treaty of 1963, and any rapprochement with the Soviet Union or China. Democrats transformed his campaign slogan "In Your Heart, You Know He's Right," to "In Your Heart, You Know He Might," by which they meant that Goldwater might start a nuclear war. Goldwater did little to discourage such thinking. In his campaign he labored to make "nukes" socially acceptable, even coining the uncomfortably comforting phrase "conventional nuclear weapon."

Johnson's campaign strategy was to appear as the thoughtful, strong moderate. He would not lose Vietnam, he told voters, but neither would he use nuclear weapons or "send American boys nine or ten thousand miles from home to do what Asian boys ought to be doing themselves." Johnson promised that if elected he would create a "Great Society" at home and honor American commitments abroad. As usual, he knew what the voters wanted to hear, and they rewarded him with a landslide victory in the November election.

Behind the scenes, however, the Johnson administration was maneuvering to obtain a free hand for conducting a more aggressive war in Vietnam. He did not want a formal declaration of war, which might frighten voters. Rather he desired a quietly passed resolution giving him the authority to deploy American forces. Such a resolution would allow him to act without the consent of Congress. Johnson and his advisers were planning to escalate American involvement in the Vietnam War, but they hoped it would go unnoticed.

Johnson used two reported North Vietnamese attacks on the American destroyer *Maddox* as a pretext for going before Congress to ask for the resolution. Actually, he was less than truthful about the circumstances of the attack. The first incident occurred in the Gulf of Tonkin in early August 1964 when the North Vietnamese suspected the *Maddox* of aiding a South Vietnamese commando raid into North Vietnam, a violation of that country's sovereignty. When North Vietnamese patrol boats approached the *Maddox,* the American ship and supporting navy jets opened fire, sinking one of the

One of the most skilled politicians to serve as president, Lyndon Johnson was far more successful with domestic programs than in foreign affairs. Among the accomplishments of his "Great Society" agenda was passage of the 1965 Voting Rights Act.

North Vietnamese ships and crippling two others. Although the North Vietnamese ships had launched several torpedoes, the *Maddox* was not hit and suffered only superficial machine-gun damage and a loss of ammunition. The second of the Gulf of Tonkin incidents probably never occurred. Assaulted by high waves, thunderstorms, and freak atmospheric conditions, the *Maddox*'s sonar equipment apparently malfunctioned registering 22 invisible enemy torpedoes. No enemy ships were visually sighted, and none of the electronically sighted torpedoes hit the *Maddox* or its accompanying ship the *C. Turner Joy*. Soon after the incident the commander of the *Maddox* reached the conclusion that no attack had ever taken place.

Johnson realized the dubious nature of the second attack. He told an aide, "Hell, those dumb stupid soldiers were just shooting at flying fish." Nevertheless, he went on national television and announced, "Aggression by terror against peaceful villages of South Vietnam has now been joined by open aggression on the high seas against the United States of America." Reassuring the country, he continued, "We know, although others appear to forget, the risks of spreading conflict. We seek no wider war." A few days later he pressed Congress for a resolution. American ships, he emphasized, had been repeatedly attacked, and he wanted authorization to "take all necessary measures" to repel attacks, prevent aggression, and protect American security. It was a broad resolution; Johnson said that it was "like Grandma's nightshirt—it covered everything." Almost without debate, the Senate passed the resolution on August 7 with only two dissenting votes, and the House of Representatives endorsed it unanimously. You "will live to regret it," Wayne Morse, who voted against it in the Senate, told the resolution's supporters. In the years that followed, as Johnson used his new powers to escalate the war, Morse's vote and prediction were vindicated, for the **Gulf of Tonkin Resolution** allowed Johnson to act in an imperial fashion.

Lyndon's War

Lyndon Johnson liked to personalize things. He did not start the Vietnam War, but once reelected he quickly made it "his war." One authority on the war described Johnson's role:

> He made appointments, approved promotions, reviewed troop requests, determined deployments, selected bombing targets, and restricted aircraft sorties. Night after night, wearing a dressing gown and carrying a flashlight, he would descend into the White House basement "situation room" to monitor the conduct of the conflict . . . often, too, he would doze by his bedside telephone, waiting to hear the outcome of a mission to rescue one of "my pilots" shot down over Haiphong or Vinh or Thai Nguyen. It was his war.

When he became president it was still a relatively obscure conflict for most Americans. Public opinion polls showed that 70 percent of the American public paid little attention to U.S. activities in Vietnam. At the end of 1963 only 16,300 U.S. military personnel were in Vietnam, with the number rising to 23,300 by the end of 1964. Most of the soldiers there, however, were volunteers. Only a few people strongly opposed America's involvement. All this would change dramatically over the next four years.

With the election behind him, Johnson started in early 1965 to reevaluate the position of the United States. In Saigon crisis followed crisis as one unpopular government gave way to the next. Something had to be done, and Johnson's advisers suggested two courses. The military and most of LBJ's foreign policy experts called for a more aggressive military presence in Vietnam, including bombing raids into North Vietnam and more ground troops. Other advisers, notably Under Secretary of State George Ball, believed the United States was making the same mistakes as the French. Ball believed that a land war in Indochina was not in America's best strategic interests and that bombing North Vietnam would only stiffen the resolve of the Communists. "Once on the tiger's back," Ball warned, "we cannot be sure of picking the place to dismount."

Johnson chose the first course, claiming it would be dishonorable not to come to South Vietnam's aid. In February 1965 Vietcong troops attacked the American base in Pleiku, killing several soldiers. Johnson used the assault as a pretext to commence air raids into the North. Code-named ROLLING THUNDER, the operation was designed to use American technological superiority to defeat North Vietnam. At first, Johnson limited U.S. air strikes to enemy radar and bridges below the 20th parallel. But as the war dragged on, he ordered "his pilots" to hit military targets in metropolitan areas. Between 1965 and 1973, American pilots flew more than 526,000 sorties and dropped 6,162,000 tons of bombs on enemy targets. (As a point of contrast, the total tonnage of explosives dropped in World War II by *all* belligerent countries was 2,150,000 tons.) Some of the landscape of South and North Vietnam began taking on a lunar look.

But the bombs did not lead to victory. Ironically, as Ball had predicted, the bombing missions actually strengthened the Communist government in North Vietnam. As a U.S. intelligence report noted, the bombing of North Vietnam "had no significantly harmful effects on popular morale. In fact, the

Vietnam Conflict, 1964–1975

use of rangers and special forces and marines." Between 1965 and 1968 the escalation of American forces was dramatic. When George Ball warned in 1965 that 500,000 American troops in Vietnam might not be able to win the war, other members of the Johnson administration laughed. By 1968 no one was laughing. Ball's prediction was painfully accurate. Escalation of American troops and deaths went hand in hand. The year-end totals for the United States between 1965 and 1968 were:

1965:	184,300 troops	636 killed.
1966:	385,300 troops	6644 killed.
1967:	485,600 troops	16,021 killed.
1968:	536,000 troops	30,610 killed.

But still there was no victory.

To Tet and Beyond

Throughout the escalation Johnson was less than candid with the American people. He argued that there had been no real change in American policy and that victory was in sight. Any reporter who said otherwise was roundly criticized. Increasingly he demanded unquestioning loyalty from his close advisers. Such demands led to an administration "party line." As the war ground on, the "party line" bore less and less similarity to reality.

In late 1967, General William Westmoreland returned to America briefly to assure the public that he could now see the "light at the end of the tunnel." In his annual report Westmoreland commented, "The year ended with the enemy increasingly resorting to desperation tactics; ... and he has experienced only failure in these attempts." Westmoreland assured everyone that victory there was certain.

Then with a suddenness that caught all America by surprise, North Vietnam struck into the very heart of South Vietnam. On the morning of January 30, 1968, North Vietnam launched the **Tet offensive.** "Tet," the Vietnamese holiday that celebrates the lunar new year, traditionally is supposed to determine family fortunes for the rest of the year. Certainly the Tet offensive boded well for North Vietnam. A Vietcong suicide squad broke into the U.S. embassy in Saigon, and Vietnamese Communists mounted offensives against every major target in South Vietnam, including 5 cities, 64 district capitals, 36 provincial capitals, and 50 hamlets.

For what it was worth, the United States repelled the Tet offensive. For a few days the fighting was ferocious and bloody, as the rivals fought in highly populated cities and almost evacuated hamlets. In order to retake Hue, the ancient cultural center close

regime has apparently been able to increase its control of the populace and perhaps even to break through the political apathy and indifference which have characterized the outlook of the average North Vietnamese in recent years."

The massive use of air power also undermined U.S. counterinsurgency efforts. Colonel John Paul Vann, an American expert on counterinsurgency warfare noted, "The best weapon 'for this type of war' ... would be a knife.... The worst is an airplane. The next worst is artillery. Barring a knife, the best is a rifle—you know who you're killing." By using bombing raids against the enemy in both the North and South, U.S. forces inevitably killed large numbers of civilians, the very people they were there to help. For peasants everywhere in Vietnam, U.S. jets, helicopters, and artillery "meant more bombing, more death, and more suffering."

A larger air war also led to more ground troops. As Johnson informed Ambassador Maxwell Taylor, "I have never felt that this war will be won from the air, and it seems to me what is much more needed and will be more effective is a larger and stronger

to the border between North and South Vietnam where the fighting lasted for several weeks, allied U.S. and South Vietnamese troops had to destroy part of the city. One observer recorded that the city was left a "shattered, stinking hulk, its streets choked with rubble and rotting bodies." When the allied troops finally recaptured Hue, they discovered that North Vietnamese and Vietcong soldiers had killed several thousand political leaders, teachers, and other civilians, many of whom had been buried alive in one mass grave. Both sides suffered terribly. But after the allies cleared the cities of enemy troops, General Westmoreland judged the episode a great allied victory. In the end, American and South Vietnamese troops recaptured lost areas and South Vietnamese civilians did not rally to the Vietcong cause. Indeed the Vietcong was so decimated by the Tet offensive that it never regained its full fighting strength.

If, technically speaking, the Tet offensive was a military defeat for North Vietnam, it was also a profound psychological victory. Johnson, his advisers, and his generals had been proclaiming that the enemy was on the run, almost defeated, tired of war, ready to quit. Tet demonstrated that the contrary was true. Upset and confused, CBS anchorman Walter Cronkite, the national voice of reason, expressed that attitude on his nightly newscast: "What the hell is going on? I thought we were winning the war?" The Tet offensive, more than any other single event, turned the media against the war and exposed the widening "credibility gap" between official pronouncements and public beliefs. NBC anchorman Frank McGee reported that the time had come "when we must decide whether it is futile to destroy Vietnam in the effort to save it."

After Tet, Americans stopped thinking about victory and turned toward thoughts of how best to get out of Vietnam. "Lyndon's planes" and "Lyndon's boys" had been unable to achieve Lyndon's objectives. For Johnson this fact was politically disastrous. His popularity plummeted, and in the New Hampshire primary Democratic peace candidate Eugene McCarthy received surprisingly solid support. On CBS's the *Smothers Brothers Comedy Hour* folk singer Pete Seeger openly criticized Johnson in the song "Waist Deep in the Big Muddy" about a "Big Fool [who] Says To Push On." Too intelligent a politician not to realize what was happening, on the night of March 31, 1968, LBJ went on television and made two important announcements. First, he said that the United States would limit its bombing of North Vietnam and would enter into peace talks any time and at any place. And second, Johnson surprised the nation by saying, "I will not seek, and I will not accept, the nomination of my party for another term as your President." A major turning point had been reached. The gradual escalation of the war was over. The period of deescalation had started. Even in official government circles, peace had replaced victory as America's objective in Vietnam.

The Politics of a Divided Nation

If Johnson's fall seemed remarkably swift, and if it seemed as if he were surrendering power without a fight, it was because he knew that his policies had badly divided the nation. LBJ honestly believed he had pursued the only honorable course in Vietnam, that he had had America's best interests at heart. His problem, however, was *not* that his intentions were dishonorable but that his *modus operandi*—the style of his leadership—involved great duplicity. Instead of fully committing the United States by calling up the reserves and National Guardsmen and by pushing for higher taxes to pay for the war, Johnson gambled that a slow, steady escalation would be enough to force North Vietnam to accept a negotiated peace. All during the buildup, LBJ assured the American people that he was not drastically changing policy and, besides, victory was in sight. But he could not fool all the people, and after the Tet offensive he knew that he could not even fool most of the people any more.

Dissatisfaction with Johnson's policy surfaced first among the young, the very people who were being asked to fight and die for the cause. Most of the young men who were drafted did serve, and most served bravely. In the early years of "Lyndon's war," many soldiers sincerely believed that they were fighting—and dying—to preserve freedom and nourish democracy in Southeast Asia. One career soldier, who did his first tour in Vietnam in 1966, recalled the idealism of his experience. He talked enthusiastically about American contributions to the improvements in South Vietnamese village life. But by his last tour, in 1970, his idealism had died. As he told a friend, "I'm still ready to serve—any time. But as a killing machine, not a humanitarian."

As the war lengthened, an ever-growing number of soldiers shared in this disillusionment, which took different forms. Journalist Michael Herr has written eloquently about the horrors of the war: "Satchel charges and grenades blew up jeeps and movie houses, the VC (Vietcong) got work inside all the camps as shoeshine boys and laundresses, . . . they'd starch your fatigues . . . then go home and mortar your area. Saigon and Cholan and Danang held such hostile vibes that you felt that you were being dry sniped every time someone looked at you." Drugs and sex helped some soldiers—many just boys away from home for the first time—to cope with the nature of a guerrilla war. One GI recalled that R&R—the traditional rest and recreation leave—was really I&I—"intoxication and intercourse." A 1969 Pentagon study estimated that nearly two of every three American soldiers in Vietnam were using marijuana and that one of every three or four had tried heroin. In 1970 CBS News televised a "smoke-in," in which GIs smoked marijuana through the barrel of a combat rifle. In such an atmosphere boys became men, fast. "How do you feel," Herr asked, "when a nineteen-year-old kid tells you from the bottom of his heart that he has gotten too old for this kind of shit?"

Other soldiers reacted by viewing *all* Vietnamese as the enemy. The nature of the war against the Vietcong caused this attitude in part. In a village of "civilians" any man, woman, or child *might* be the enemy. "Vietnam was a dark room full of deadly objects," wrote Herr, "and the VC were everywhere all at once like spider cancer." Tension and anxiety were as ever-present as olive drab.

Empty government phrases, however, also contributed to the problem. How could soldiers win the "hearts and minds" of villagers one day and rain napalm on them the next? Reacting to the surface idealism of U.S. policy, one experienced soldier commented, "All that is just a *load,* man. We're here to kill gooks, period." The My Lai massacre, in which American soldiers killed more than 100 (the official figure was 122 but it was probably many more) South Vietnamese civilians, was the sad extension of this attitude.

The morale of American soldiers plummeted. Desertion and absent-without-leave (AWOL) rates skyrocketed. The army desertion rate in 1966 had been 14.9 men per thousand; by 1971 it had risen to 73.5. In 1966 there were 57.2 AWOL incidents per thousand; that figure leaped to 176.9 in 1971. Even worse, "fragging"—the assassination of overzealous officers and noncommissioned officers (NCOs) by their own troops—increased at an alarming rate. The army claimed that at least 1011 officers and NCOs were killed or wounded by their own men during the Vietnam War.

At home, university students, most of whom were draft-exempt, also reacted to the war and Johnson's policies. The earliest and most vocal critics of the Vietnam War, they may have lacked a coherent ideology, but they were strong in numbers and energy. Between 1946 and 1970 enrollments in institutions of higher education had climbed from 2 to 8 million. Although not all students protested against the war, the most politically active ones did. As politicians they formed a curious breed—segregated from society as a whole, freed from adult responsibilities, bound to no real constituency, and encour-

LOGISTICS IN A GUERRILLA WAR

The Longest War

The Vietnam War, fought 9000 miles from America's shores, was a logistical nightmare for the United States. It had to ship hundreds of tons of supplies daily from the United States to bases in the Pacific and finally to fortified positions along the coast of Vietnam. Once the supplies were in Vietnam, they had to be protected from Vietcong guerrillas, who blended into the civilian population and often obtained jobs on U.S. bases. As a result, although American forces established defense perimeters around their bases, the areas were never totally secure. Bombs in U.S. movie theaters or even mess halls were haunting reminders of the unpredictability of guerrilla warfare.

North Vietnam sent much of its supplies south along the Ho Chi Minh Trail. Following a traditional series of trails through mountains and jungles from North Vietnam into Laos and Cambodia, finally emptying into South Vietnam, the Ho Chi Minh Trail was widened into a road capable of handling heavy trucks and thousands of troops. Along the Trail, support facilities, often built underground to escape American detection and air strikes, included operating rooms, fuel storage tanks, and supply caches. Throughout the war, United States forces tried, but failed, to effectively disrupt the flow of supplies and soldiers south.

The Vietcong tunnel complex, another example of the unconventional war in Vietnam, created even more problems for American troops. The tunnels allowed Vietcong troops to appear and disappear almost by magic. The most famous tunnel complex was under Cu Chi, approximately 25 miles northeast of Saigon. It contained conference rooms, sleeping chambers, storage halls, and kitchens. U.S. forces bombed, gassed, and defoliated the Cu Chi area but failed to destroy the tunnels. "Tunnel rats"—South Vietnamese soldiers and short, wiry GI combat engineer SWAT teams—fought heroically in the tunnels, but they too were unable to destroy the complexes. In the end, it was the unconventional nature of the Vietnam War that guaranteed frustration and made it America's longest war.

Source: From *The Tunnels of Cu Chi* by Tom Mangold and John Penycate. Copyright © 1985 by Tom Mangold and John Penycate. Reprinted by permission of Random House, Inc. Map: Harold Ober Associates.

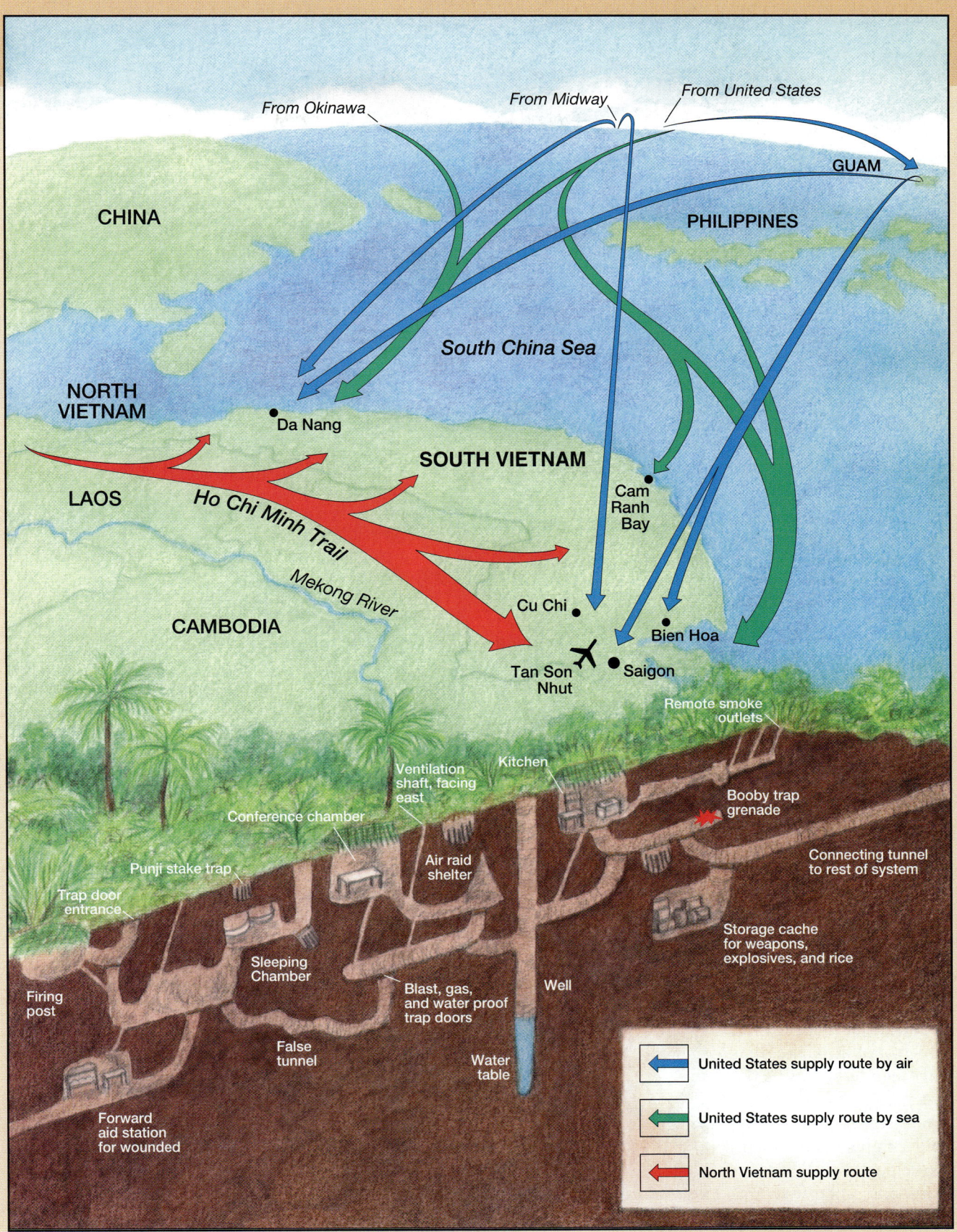

THE PEOPLE SPEAK

Bloods

Arthur E. Woodley "went to Vietnam as a basic naive young man of eighteen." By his nineteenth birthday, he described himself as an "animal." A proud black man from a poor, "hard-core" neighborhood in Baltimore, Woodley volunteered to serve as a Special Forces Ranger. He chose this difficult and dangerous path partly out of patriotism, and partly out of his own individual pride. His experience, however, hardly matched his ideals. Perhaps his most difficult experience came in the second week of February 1969, on a reconnaissance mission for a downed helicopter.

> We recon this area, and we came across this fella, a white guy, who was staked to the ground. His arms and legs tied down to stakes. And he had a leather band around his neck that's staked to the ground so he couldn't move his head to the left or right.
>
> He had numerous scars on his face where he might have been beaten and mutilated. And he had been peeled from his upper part of chest to down to his waist. Skinned. Like they slit your skin with a knife. And they take a pair of pliers or a instrument similar, and they just peel the skin off your body and expose it to the elements. . . .
>
> And he start to cryin', beggin' to die.
>
> He said, "I can't go back like this. I can't live like this. I'm dying. You can't leave me here like this dying."
>
> It was a situation where it had to be remove him from his bondage or remove him from his suffering. Movin' him from this bondage was unfeasible. It would have put him in more pain than he had ever endured. There was no use talkin' 'bout tryin' and takin' him back, because there was nothing left of him. It was that or kill the brother, and I use the term "brother" because in a war circumstance, we all brothers. . .
>
> It took me somewhere close to 20 minutes to get my mind together. Not because I was squeamish about killing someone, because I had at that time numerous body counts. Killing someone wasn't the issue. It was killing another American citizen, another GI. . . .
>
> The only thing that I could see that had to be done is that the man's sufferin' had to be ended.
>
> I put my M-16 next to his head. Next to his temple.
>
> I said, "You sure you want me to do this?"
>
> He said, "Man, kill me. Thank you."
>
> I stopped thinking. I just pulled the trigger. I cancelled his suffering.
>
> When the team came back, we talked nothing about it.
>
> We buried him. We buried him. Very deep.
>
> Then I cried.

Source: Wallace Terry, *Bloods: An Oral History of the Vietnam War by Black Veterans* (New York: Ballantine, 1984), pp. 241–243. Copyright © 1984 by Wallace Terry. Reprinted by permission of Random House.

---

aged by their teachers to think critically. Most student protesters were from upper middle-class families and could afford the intellectual luxury of being political idealists. (Youth culture as a whole will be discussed in greater detail in Chapter 30.)

Led by such leftist groups as Students for a Democratic Society (SDS), university students called for a more just society in which political life was governed by morality, not greed. During the early 1960s they focused on the civil rights movement, participating in freedom rides and voter registration drives. By the mid-1960s, however, they were increasingly shifting their attention to America's "unjust and immoral" war in Southeast Asia. With the shift their numbers swelled—only ten universities had SDS chapters in 1962, and each chapter had only a handful of members. By 1968 the organization could boast more than 100,000 members. By then, too, older voices had joined the student chorus of condemnation.

In 1968, Democrat Eugene McCarthy ran for his party's presidential nomination as a peace candidate.

It was the older voices, energized by the idealism of youth, that led to Johnson's decision not to seek reelection in 1968. For many, it seemed as if the future of American politics belonged to the proponents of peace and morality. Students flocked to presidential candidate Gene McCarthy's peace cause. They cut their long hair, shaved their beards ("be clean for Gene"), put on coats and ties, and worked for McCarthy's campaign. McCarthy's success encouraged **Robert Kennedy** (RFK) to throw his hat into the ring. Although McCarthy supporters saw him as a political opportunist, Kennedy spoke eloquently for the cause of humanity and peace. When students at a Catholic university called for more bombings, RFK asked, "Do you understand what that means? It means you are voting to send people, Americans and

Although he was slow to declare his candidacy, Robert Kennedy soon became the darling of the antiwar movement.

At the Democratic convention in Chicago, police attacked thousands of unarmed, middle-class, antiwar college students in what was later termed a "police riot."

Vietnamese, to die.... Don't you understand that what we are doing to the Vietnamese is not very different than what Hitler did to the Jews?" Kennedy, who enjoyed midnight bull sessions on the meaning of existence and looked at ease with his tie loosened and his shirt sleeves rolled above his elbows, spoke a language that radical students understood. He exhibited the passion and commitment that McCarthy lacked. By the conclusion of the campaign, Kennedy had become the foremost peace candidate, and representative of young liberals.

At the celebration party after his narrow victory in the California primary, Kennedy said, "We are a great country, an unselfish country, and a compassionate country. I intend to make that my basis for running." Moments later a fanatic Palestinian shot him in the head. Along with Kennedy died the dreams of many Americans for a moral society. Columnist Murray Kempton spoke for many people: "I have liked many public men immensely, but I guess [RFK] is the only one I have ever loved." Although RFK had started in political life as a committed, aggressive anti-Communist and Cold Warrior, by the time of his death he had radically reevaluated his earlier beliefs.

The Democratic party went to the Chicago convention without a candidate. There they battled among themselves—young and old; radical, liberal, and conservative. In the streets, outside the convention hall, police beat protesters in full view of television cameras. An official commission later termed it a "police riot." Inside the convention hall the fighting was largely verbal, but it was just as intense and bitter. Abraham Ribicoff, a senator from Connecticut, accused Chicago's mayor Richard Daley of allowing the police to use "Gestapo tactics" in the street; Daley accused Ribicoff of having unnatural relations with his mother. In the end, the Democratic party chose Hubert Humphrey, Johnson's liberal vice president, as their presidential candidate. Instead of change, the Democratic party chose a representative of the "old politics."

In a more tranquil convention in Miami, the Republican party endorsed Richard M. Nixon, who promised when elected to honorably end the Vietnam War, move against forced busing of black children to white schools, and restore "law and order." Calmer and more relaxed than ever before, the "new Nixon" claimed to speak for the great majority of Americans who obeyed the nation's laws, paid their taxes, regularly attended church, and loved their country. It was the same message Alabama's Governor **George Wallace** used as the foundation of his third-party candidacy. Running on the American Independent ticket, Wallace spoke for millions of working-class white Americans, young and old alike, who opposed forced integration of schools and neighborhoods, the activities of radical college students, and what they believed was the country's drift toward the left. Although Humphrey's finish in the campaign was strong, Nixon's and Wallace's appeal to traditional values had an undeniable attraction. And on election day, Nixon received 43.4 percent of the popular vote, Humphrey 42.7 percent, and Wallace 13.5 percent. Given the combined votes for Nixon and Wallace—57 percent—it was clear that the country was moving right rather than left.

THE TORTUOUS PATH TOWARD PEACE

During the presidential campaign of 1968, Richard Nixon expected the American voter to accept certain things on faith. First, he asked them to believe that he had a plan to honorably end the war in Vietnam. Second, he hoped that they would "buy" his new public image—the "new Nixon," experienced, statesmanlike, mature, secure, and ever so well adjusted. Most Americans probably did not believe either in the "new Nixon" or his pledge to "bring us together." On election day only 27 percent of eligible voters cast their ballot for him, but in 1968 that proved enough votes to win the election.

Outsiders on the Inside

If Nixon had developed "new" characteristics, those qualities had not forced out the "old." Richard Nixon still considered himself something of an outsider, a battler against an entrenched political establishment. Reared on the West Coast in humble circumstances, he had to overcome considerable obstacles in his rise to power. In the process certain character traits emerged. He was a hard worker—careful, studious, with a tendency toward perfectionism; no detail was too small for his consideration. He also did not shy away from an unpopular task. During his years as Eisenhower's vice president, Nixon had proved particularly adept as a political hatchet man. He was also a loner—shy, introverted, humorless, uncomfortable in social situations. He was essentially a man of action, one who for most of his career carried a list of things to do in the inside pocket of his suit coat. Journalist Tom Wicker noted that the new Nixon was not very different from the old. Wicker observed: "He is, if anything, more reserved and inward, as difficult as ever to know, driven still by deep inner compulsion toward power and personal vindication, painfully conscious of slights and failures, a man who had imposed upon himself a self-control so rigid as to be all but visible."

As a restless outsider, Nixon harbored a heightened suspicion of political insiders. Throughout his career he had been an outspoken critic of State Department officials and other establishment bureaucrats. On taking office he, therefore, surrounded himself with close advisers who held noncabinet titles. Cabinet appointees, and particularly his secretary of state, William Rogers, had almost no voice in key decisions. Personal aides H. R. Haldeman and John Ehrlichman—called the "Germans" by the White House press corps—advised Nixon on domestic political issues. Vice President Spiro Agnew assumed the role of the administration's hatchet man so well that he became known as "Nixon's Nixon." He attacked the establishment with the ferocity of a professional wrestler verbally abusing an archrival. The "sniveling, hand-wringing power structure," he said, "deserves the violent rebellion it encourages." As for foreign affairs, Nixon relied on his national security advisor, **Henry Kissinger.**

Most commentators regarded Kissinger as a strange ally for Nixon. Kissinger, after all, taught at Harvard, was a close associate of Nelson Rockefeller—Nixon's longtime Republican opponent—and had even offered to work for Nixon's Democratic opponent Hubert Humphrey. "Look," Kissinger said in 1968, "I've hated Nixon for years." Yet even while Kissinger was courting Humphrey, he was secretly working for Nixon's election. No matter who won in 1968, Kissinger would be on the victorious side. It was a piece of Machiavellian maneuvering that Nixon might have appreciated.

Beneath Kissinger's sophisticated exterior, he shared with Nixon fundamental characteristics and beliefs. Like Nixon, Kissinger's path to power was not a traditional one. A German Jew, he had lived for five years (between the ages of 10 and 15) in Nazi Germany; he had been verbally and physically abused by his Aryan classmates. He fled with the rest of his family to the United States during the late 1930s. After serving as an army translator-interrogator during World War II, he enrolled as a scholarship student at Harvard, from where he graduated *summa cum laude* in 1950 and earned his Ph.D. in 1954. During the late 1950s and 1960s, Kissinger wrote, taught, and emerged as a leading expert on foreign affairs. Kissinger viewed himself as a political realist, and he resisted rigid ideological or moral stands. Successful diplomacy, he believed, demanded flexible and creative leaders.

Vain, irreverent, articulate, and intellectual, Kissinger shared Nixon's desire to alter the very nature of the country's foreign relations and to make history. Neither particularly enjoyed being part of a committee process, and the diplomacy of secrecy and intrigue attracted both. For all their surface differences, the shy politician and the flamboyant scholar were kindred spirits who combined to form an impressive team. As one historian observed, "each filled a vital gap in the other's abilities. Kissinger had no gift for American politics; he needed to serve a president who could manipulate the electorate into supporting his policies. Nixon benefited from Kissinger's good press contacts since his own were disastrous."

Vietnamization: The Idea and the Process

During his campaign Nixon had promised "peace with honor." He suggested that he had a secret plan to achieve those ends, but controversy surrounded just what that plan entailed. Several historians have suggested that Nixon's plan was an updated version of Eisenhower's plan to end the Korean War: threatening to use nuclear weapons. Nixon told his White House aide H. R. Haldeman that his plan was similar to Eisenhower's. He wanted North Vietnam to believe that he was a "madman." "I want the North Vietnamese to believe I've reached the point where I might do anything to stop the war," Nixon told Haldeman. "We'll just slip the word to them that 'for God's sakes, you know Nixon is obsessed about communists. We can't restrain him when he's angry—and he has his hand on the nuclear button'— and Ho Chi Minh himself will be in Paris in two days begging for peace." The "madman theory" helps to explain Nixon's dramatic shifts during his first four years in office as he moved between the poles of peacefully concluding the war and violently expanding the conflict.

One thing was certain, however. Nixon knew that he could not continue Johnson's policy. "I'm not going to end up like LBJ," he remarked, "holed up in the White House afraid to show my face on the street." The country needed something new. Whatever else he did, Nixon realized that to ensure some semblance of domestic tranquility he would have to begin to remove American troops from Vietnam. In May 1969 he announced, "The time is approaching when the South Vietnamese forces will be able to take over some of the fighting fronts now being manned by Americans." That summer he drummed harder on the idea of the South Vietnamese fighting their own war. In what has become known as the **"Nixon Doctrine,"** the president insisted that Asian soldiers must carry more of the combat burden. Certainly the United States would continue to materially aid any anti-Communist struggle, but the aid would not include the wholesale use of American troops.

The Nixon Doctrine formed the foundation of Nixon's Vietnamization policy. Working from the questionable premise that the government of Nguyen Van Thieu was stable and prepared to assume greater responsibility for fighting the war, Nixon announced that he planned to gradually deescalate American military involvement. Increasingly, U.S. aid would be limited to war materiel, military advice, and air support. He coupled Vietnamization with a more strenuous effort to move along the peace talks.

Actually, the idea of Vietnamization was hardly new. In 1951 the French had called it *jaunissement,* or "yellowing." Advisers for Eisenhower, Kennedy, and Johnson had suggested one variation or another of the plan as the solution to the war. The major problem was that the South Vietnamese could not successfully fight the war—not in 1951, or 1961, or 1971. But faced with angry criticism at home, Nixon had no choice but to implement the policy.

At the same time as he extended the olive branch, he expanded the nature of the conflict. Hoping to slow down the flow of North Vietnamese supplies and soldiers into South Vietnam, Nixon ordered American B-52 pilots to bomb the Ho Chi Minh Trail both in Vietnam and in Cambodia. He kept this violation of Cambodian neutrality secret from the American public. It was a bold move, but not very productive. The bombs only reduced the flow of men and supplies by approximately 10 percent.

When both the increased bombing of North Vietnam and Kissinger's peace talks with North Vietnamese officials failed to end the war, Nixon resorted to harsher military efforts. After watching *Patton,* his favorite movie, on board the presidential yacht *Sequoia,* he decided to "go for all the marbles" and send American ground forces to Cambodia to destroy Communist supply bases. On the night of April 30, 1970, he went on television and told the American people of his plan. Ignoring previous American violations of Cambodian neutrality, he said that U.S. policy had been "to scrupulously respect the neutrality of the Cambodian people," while North Vietnam had used the border areas for "major base camps, training sites, logistics facilities, weapons and ammunition factories, airstrips and prisoner-of-war compounds," as well as their chief military headquarters. As a result, Nixon announced a joint American and South Vietnamese "incursion" into Cambodia's border regions, to be limited to 60 days.

Militarily the invasion fell far short of success. Although American forces captured large stockpiles of weapons and supplies, the operation did not force North Vietnam to end the war. But the "incursion" had dangerously enlarged the battlefield. More importantly, the invasion of Cambodia reignited the fires of the peace movement at home. Throughout the country, colleges and universities shut down in protest. Students raged at what they believed was an "immoral, imperialist policy." At Kent State University in Ohio a volley of gunshots fired by Ohio National Guardsmen broke up a peaceful demonstration. The shots killed 4 students and wounded 9 others. Less than two weeks later, policemen shot 2 more in-

In the spring of 1970, Ohio National Guardsmen fired into a group of protesting students at Kent State University, killing four students.

nocent students at Jackson State University in Mississippi. Instead of victory or even peace, Nixon's efforts had further divided America.

As an effective policy for ending the war, Vietnamization was a failure. To be sure, the policy allowed Nixon to bring home American combat troops. When Nixon took office 540,000 American troops were in Vietnam; four years later only 70,000 remained. But American reductions were not accompanied by a marked improvement in the South Vietnamese army. This was clearly illustrated by the unsuccessful 1971 South Vietnamese invasion into Laos. If anything, South Vietnam became more dependent on the United States during the years of Vietnamization. By 1972 South Vietnam's only product and export was war, and even this commodity was of inferior quality.

A "Decent Interval"

By 1972 Nixon simply wanted to end the war with as little embarrassment as possible. As a viable country, South Vietnam was hopeless. Without an active U.S. military presence, the country's demise was a foregone conclusion. Negotiations presented the only way out. Nixon and Kissinger hoped to arrange for a peace that would permit the United States and South Vietnam to save face and allow a "decent interval" of time to ensue between the American departure and the collapse of the government in Saigon. In the pursuit of the goal, Nixon changed the character of American foreign policy.

The Soviet Union and the People's Republic of China aided and advised North Vietnam. Yet the two large Communist nations were hardly allies themselves. In fact, the Sino-Soviet split demonstrated to American leaders the fallacy of the old Cold War theme of a monolithic Communist movement. Nixon and Kissinger were astute enough to use the Sino-Soviet rift to improve U.S. relations with both countries. Improved relations, they believed, would move the United States several steps closer to an "honorable" peace in Vietnam. Unfortunately, Nixon and Kissinger greatly overestimated the influence of the Soviet Union and China on North Vietnam.

From his first days in office, Nixon had his eyes on the People's Republic of China, a nation that the United States had refused to recognize. One Nixon aide reported in 1969, "You're not going to believe this, but Nixon wants to recognize China." It seemed remarkable, since Nixon's Cold War record—his opposition to any concession to the Communists—was well known. But Nixon understood that his very record would protect him from public cries of being soft on communism; Nixon knew that unlike Truman, Kennedy, and Johnson, he did not have a Nixon to worry about.

Nixon approached China like a man holding a vase from the Ming dynasty, mixing caution with slow careful movements. In fact, both China and the United States walked on eggshells. Mao Tse-tung (Zedong) told reporter Edgar Snow that he "would be happy to talk with [Nixon] either as a tourist or as President." And Mao ended China's athletic isolation in 1971 by sending a table tennis team to the world championships in Nagoya, Japan, and then inviting an American team to compete in Beijing. Capitalizing on the success of **Ping-Pong diplomacy,** in the summer of 1971 Kissinger made a very secret trip to China. Kissinger's mission paved the way for Nixon's

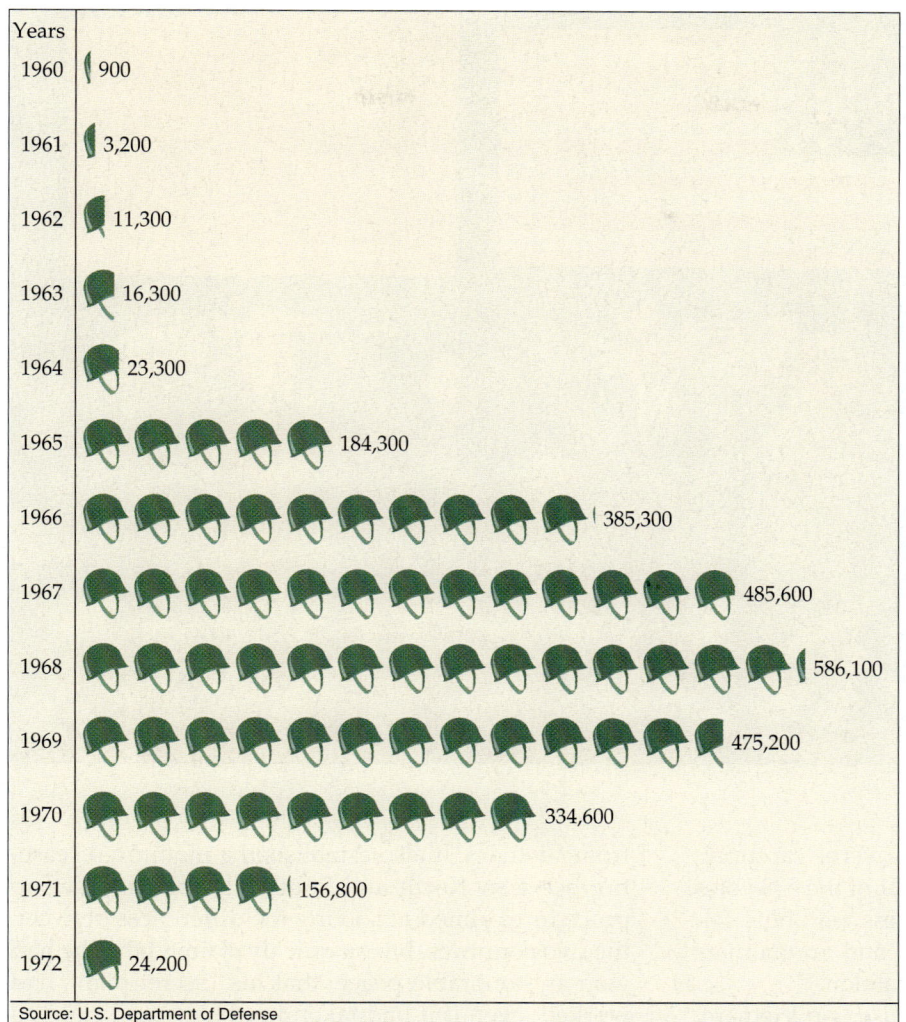

FIGURE 29.1
U.S. Troop Levels in Vietnam, 1960–1972

own very public trip to China in February 1972. American television cameras recorded Nixon's every move as he toured the Great Wall, the Imperial Palace, and the other sites of historic China. For the White House, one reporter noted, "It was the social event of the year." Constantly smiling and bubbling with excitement, Nixon thoroughly enjoyed the event, going so far as quoting Chairman Mao at an official toast and learning to eat with chopsticks. Although full diplomatic relations would not be established until 1979 under Jimmy Carter, Nixon's trip to China was the single most important event in the history of the relations between the United States and the People's Republic of China. It bridged, as Chinese foreign minister Chou En-lai remarked, "the vastest ocean in the world, twenty-five years of no communication."

Concerned about the growing rapprochement between China and America, the Soviet Union sought to move closer to the United States. Once again, Nixon and Kissinger were pleased to oblige.

In late May 1972, after many months of preparatory talks, Nixon traveled to Moscow to sign an arms control treaty with Soviet leader Leonid Brezhnev. The **Strategic Arms Limitation Treaty of 1972 (SALT I)** certainly did not preclude a future nuclear war between the superpowers. Although it froze intercontinental ballistic missile (ICBM) deployment, it did not alter the buildup of the more dangerous multiple independent reentry vehicles (MIRVs), which, according to one historian "was about as meaningful as freezing the cavalry of the European nations in 1938 but not the tanks." As so often has been the case during the Cold War, SALT I provided more of a warm breeze than the real heat wave necessary for a complete thaw of the Cold War.

Although Nixon had not been able to end the Vietnam War, his 1972 triumphs in the Soviet Union and China gave him more influence with North Vietnam's major allies. His visits to Beijing and Moscow also dazzled American voters. In 1972 Nixon easily defeated

In 1972 Richard Nixon visited China in an attempt to improve relations with that country. It was the first step toward achieving détente with the Soviet Union.

Democratic candidate George McGovern, capturing 61 percent of the popular vote and 521 of the 538 votes of the electoral college. Nixon's success with blue-collar workers, conservative Catholics, and Southerners signified the end of the New Deal coalition.

Once reelected, Nixon again focused on Vietnam. A month before the election, Kissinger had announced, "Peace is at hand," but no sooner was Nixon safely reelected than the peace talks broke down once again. Nixon's response was more and heavier bombing of North Vietnam. Starting on December 18 and continuing for the next ten days, the Christmas bombings—code-named Operation LINEBACKER II—attacked military targets in Hanoi and Haiphong and killed more than 1500 civilians, leveled a hospital, and destroyed large parts of Hanoi. Critics charged that Nixon was attempting to "wage war by tantrum" and that the bombings served no military purpose. Some even suggested that Nixon had become mentally unbalanced. Military authorities, however, maintained that the bombings quickened the pace of the peace process. When the bombings concluded, the warring nations resumed peace talks.

In a week North Vietnam and the United States had hammered out a peace, one that was strikingly similar to the October proposal. On January 27, 1973, America ended its active participation in the Vietnam War. The peace treaty provided for the release of all prisoners of war and America's military withdrawal from Vietnam. It also established a monitored cease-fire between North and South Vietnam and set up procedures aimed at solving the differences between the two countries. Nixon quickly claimed that he had won an honorable peace, that his "secret plan" had worked, even if it had taken four years and claimed the lives of 21,000 Americans, 107,000 South Vietnamese, and more than 500,000 North Vietnamese soldiers. And, of course, the lives of many thousands of Vietnamese civilians. Informing the American people of the peace, Nixon claimed, "South Vietnam has gained the right to determine its own future. . . . Let us be proud that America did not settle for a peace that would have betrayed our ally . . . that would have ended the war for us but continued the war for the fifty million people of Indochina." But as one historian commented, "In all likelihood, the peace accords that were finally signed in January 1973 could have been negotiated four years earlier. In the name of credibility, honor, and patriotism, hundreds of thousands of lives had been lost."

America left the war in 1973, but the war did not end then. All the peace provided for was a "decent interval" between America's withdrawal and North Vietnam's complete victory. When the South Vietnamese leader Nguyen Cao Ky heard Nixon's peace speech, he commented, "I could not stomach [it], so nauseating was its hypocrisy and self-delusion . . . there is no reason why they [the Communists] should stop now. . . . I give them a couple of years before they invade the South." He was right. Almost as soon as the ink on the "peace treaty" was dry, both North Vietnam and South Vietnam began to violate the treaty. Finally, in the spring of 1975 South Vietnamese forces collapsed. In March North Vietnam forces took Hue and Da Nang; by late April they were close to Saigon. On April 21 President Nguyen Van Thieu publicly lambasted the United States, resigned, and beat a hasty retreat from his country. On April 30 South Vietnam formally announced its unconditional surrender. Vietnam was finally unified. Free elections in 1956 might have accomplished the same results.

The Legacy of the War

Although America's active military participation in the Vietnam War ended in 1973, the controversy engendered by the war raged on long after the firing of the last shot. Much of the controversy centered on the returning veterans. Reports of drug use and fragging frightened many Americans who had come no closer to the war than their television sets. And veterans—most of whom had served their country faithfully and to the best of their abilities—were shocked by the cold, hostile reception they received when they returned to the United States. In *First Blood* (1982), John Rambo, played by Sylvester Stallone, captured the pain of the returning veterans: "Nothing is over. Nothing! You just don't turn it off. It wasn't my war—you asked me, I didn't ask you ... and I did what I had to do to win.... Then I came back to the world and I see all those maggots at the airport, protesting me, spitting on me, calling me a baby-killer and all kinds of vile crap.... Back there I could fly a gunship, I could drive a tank, I was in charge of million-dollar equipment. Back here I can't even hold down a job parking cars.... Back here there's nothing!"

During the 1970s and 1980s the returning Vietnam War veteran loomed large in American popular culture. He was first portrayed as a dangerous killer, a deranged ticking time bomb that could explode at any time and in any place. He was Travis Bickle in *Taxi Driver* (1976), a veteran wound so tight that he seemed perpetually on the verge of snapping. Travis Bickle, wrote one film historian, "is the prototypical movie vet: in ways we can only imagine, the horror of the war unhinged him. He's lost contact with other human beings.... He's edgy: he can't sleep at night." He waits to explode. Or he was Colonel Kurtz in *Apocalypse Now* (1979), who adjusted to a mad war by going mad himself.

Not until the late 1970s did popular culture begin to treat the Vietnam War veteran as a victim of the war rather than a madman produced by the war. *Coming Home* (1978) and *The Deer Hunter* (1978) be-

The Vietnam War inspired a number of movies dealing with the conflict veterans faced on their return home. Some movies portrayed the veterans as victims of a tragic war; others like *Rambo: First Blood II* (shown here) made the veteran a hero and transformed the conflict into a noble crusade.

gan the popular rehabilitation of the veteran, and such films as *First Blood* (1982), *Rambo: First Blood II* (1985), and *Missing in Action* (1984) transformed the veteran into a hero. On television, "Magnum, P.I.," "The A-Team," and "Air Wolf" also presented the veteran as a misunderstood hero.

The transformation of the veteran that took place in the late 1970s and 1980s indicated a fundamental shift in America's attitude toward the war. Millions of Americans began once again to see the war in terms of a noble crusade that could have been won. As John Rambo said in *Rambo: First Blood II*, "Do we get to win this time?" His former commander replied: "This time it's up to you." This message fit well with the political message of Ronald Reagan's America.

As American filmmakers "Ramboized" the conflict, Vietnam labored to reconstruct a viable nation out of the rubble of war. It was a difficult struggle. Roads and bridges, power plants and factories lay in ruins. Ports suffered from damage and neglect. Raw materials and investment capital were in short supply. If peace brought hope, it also brought the specter of economic ruin.

The recovery of the Socialist Republic of Vietnam was slow. One of the poorest countries in the world, it suffered from high inflation and unemployment, food shortages and starvation, and government inefficiency and corruption. In addition, military campaigns—such as the 1978 war against the Khmer Rouge in Kampuchea (formerly Cambodia)—siphoned off money needed to rebuild the country. Fi-

THE American Mosaic

My Lai and the Question of War Ethics

THAT terrible day began early on the morning of March 16, 1968, with the *whop-whop-whop-whop* sound of helicopters carrying the men of Charlie Company to their designated battle stations for the Pinkville operation. Their goal, along with the rest of Task Force Barker, was to utterly destroy the 48th Local Force Battalion of the National Liberation Front, the elusive and deadly Vietcong unit operating in Quang Ngai Province. Slightly more than 100 men comprised Charlie Company of the United States Army's 1st Battalion, 20th Infantry. Most were young, between 18 and 22 years old, and most were nervous. Each hoped that he would live though the day, but nobody had any guarantees and they all expected that some members of their company would not see the sun set.

There were sound reasons for the gloomier expectations. Although they had been in Vietnam for less than three months and had yet to have a major confrontation with a Vietcong unit, the company had been bloodied on several occasions. Trudging through Quang Ngai, a beautiful stretch of land between the Annamese mountains and the white sandy beaches of the South China Sea—a quiltwork province of rice paddies dotted with bamboo and banana trees—soldiers in Charlie Company had lost legs, arms, and lives to Vietcong boobytraps. February 25, 1968, had been a particularly bad day. Part of the unit had wandered into the middle of a minefield. Although the officer in charge screamed "Freeze!", a few men panicked, moved, and detonated more mines. "Anyone who moved to try to help someone just got blown up themselves," recalled one GI. One soldier was split open from his crotch to his chest cavity "as if someone had taken a cleaver" to him. Three GIs were killed, another 12 badly injured, and everyone was shaken. One GI remembered thinking, "This is war, this is what it is all about, this is what happens to you."

The men of Charlie Company regarded the Pinkville operation as a chance for revenge—revenge for their friends who had died or been wounded, revenge for their uncomfortable patrols though hostile country, revenge for the fear they felt and a land they hated and a people they did not understand. One sergeant recalled that the central message at the briefing on the eve of the operation was: "This was a time for us to get even. A time for us to settle the score. . . . The order we were given was to kill and destroy everything that was in the village. It was to kill the pigs, drop them in the wells; pollute the water supply; kill, cut down the banana trees; burn the village; burn the hootches as we went through it. It was clearly explained that there were to be no prisoners. The order that was given was to kill everything in the village. Someone asked if that meant women and children. And the order was: everyone in the village. Because those people that were in the village—the women, the kids, the old men—were VC. . . . It was quite clear that no one was to be spared in that village."

Thus when the men of Charlie Company climbed out of their helicopter transports near the tiny village designated My Lai 4, they expected to engage the enemy, and they expected to kill. The enemy, as so often had been the case, was gone. If they had been in Quang Ngai—and even that was doubtful—they had left. When the men moved into My Lai 4 and several subhamlets in the same general area, they encountered no enemy fire. The only people they met were villagers, mostly women, children, and old men. Unquestionably some were Vietcong supporters; Quang Ngai had long been regarded as VC country. But according to the rules of military engagement, the villagers were noncombatants, and U.S. soldiers were required to treat them accordingly.

On this day the rules of "civilized" warfare were not observed. From the very beginning, soldiers shot anything that moved, including unarmed villagers. Once the shooting began there was a chain reaction, as more and more soldiers discharged their weapons. They shot pigs, chickens, cows, ducks, and water buffalo in the fields. They shot old men sitting outside their homes, women holding babies, children searching for places to hide. A few soldiers raped women before they killed them. One group of children were shot as they reached their hands out toward a GI in the hope of receiving food or candy. At several points, scores of villagers were gathered into groups and executed. Altogether, the soldiers killed about 400 villagers.

Not every member of Charlie Company participated in the slaughter. Some only fired when they were given direct orders to fire, others simply refused to fire at all. Each man was presented with a difficult moral choice—follow what he believed were his orders or do what his conscience told him was right. At one

point helicopter pilot Hugh Thompson, Jr., shocked by what he saw from his Plexiglass "bubble ship," landed his chopper to protect a group of defenseless villagers. He told the American soldiers—his own countrymen—that if they shot the villagers he would turn his machine gun on them. He simply could not abide what he saw happening. And when he returned to base he reported what he had seen.

What had happened in those four hours the morning of March 16, 1968, was a spontaneous tragedy. Soldiers following orders, men out of control, the logical end result of a policy of free-fire zones and search and destroy missions and systematic body counts—all these explanations would later be employed to explain the massacre. There is no doubt that the GIs were given orders to shoot. Lieutenant William Calley, the ranking officer in My Lai, both ordered and participated in the worst executions, and he certainly believed that he was following the orders of his commander, Captain Ernest Medina. At one point, Calley told Medina that civilians were slowing the progress of Charlie Company; Medina "told Calley simply to get rid of them." In the mass confusion of the morning—in what one military strategist has called "the fog of war"—things happened that probably no one could have predicted.

But what happened after that morning was coldly calculated. A massacre, not a battle, had taken place—the signs of indiscriminate killing of civilians were apparent. Battles mean that your own men get killed and wounded; the only casualty in Charlie Company was one accidental, self-inflicted wound. Battles successfully waged mean the capture of enemy soldiers and weapons; the official account of the "battle" of My Lai listed 128 enemies killed but only 3 weapons recovered. Just looking at the numbers, any experienced officer could have guessed what had taken place. Thompson had reported the truth. But there was no serious investigation, only an unspoken coverup that reached up the chain of command from Captain Medina to Lieutenant Colonel Frank Barker to Colonel Oran Henderson to Major General Samuel Koster. As far as they were concerned, no infractions of the military code of engagement had occurred.

Later the world learned differently. On April 2, 1969, Ronald Ridenhour, a former soldier who had heard of the massacre while serving with several former members of Charlie Company, wrote letters to 31 leading United States senators and government officials, including President Richard Nixon and Secretary of Defense Melvin Laird, reporting what he had learned of the massacre. The letters led to several in-depth investigations, which ultimately resulted in charges against two generals, four full colonels, four lieutenant colonels, four majors, six captains, and eight lieutenants. Lieutenant General William Peers, head of the official military investigation, listed 224 serious violations of the military code. In the end, however, only one man, William Calley, was convicted of any wrongdoing, and he was pardoned three years after his conviction.

Chronology of Key Events

1954 The French garrison at Dien Bien Phu falls to Vietnamese nationalists led by Ho Chi Minh; Geneva conference divides Vietnam into two regions with the promise to hold elections to reunify the country in 1956; North Vietnam is led by the Communist government of Ho Chi Minh and South Vietnam by the government of Ngo Dinh Diem

1956 South Vietnam refuses to participate in elections to unify the two Vietnams

1961 John F. Kennedy is inaugurated thirty-fifth president; Alliance for Progress pledges $20 billion in U.S. aid to Latin America over a ten-year period; Cuban exiles stage abortive invasion of Cuba at Bay of Pigs; East Germans erect Berlin Wall; Soviet Union breaks a three-year moratorium on nuclear tests

1962 Cuban missile crisis: In response to Khrushchev's decision to build missile bases in Cuba, President Kennedy imposes a naval blockade of Cuba, and Khrushchev orders the bases dismantled; President Kennedy increases the number of American advisers in South Vietnam to approximately 16,000

1963 United States and Soviet Union agree to ban nuclear tests in atmosphere; South Vietnamese army officers arrest and murder President Diem; President Kennedy is assassinated; Lyndon Johnson becomes thirty-sixth president

1964 North Vietnamese torpedo boats attack the U.S. destroyers *Maddox* and *C. Turner Joy* in the Gulf of Tonkin off the North Vietnamese coast; Congress passes Gulf of Tonkin Resolution, which gives the president authority to retaliate against North Vietnamese aggression

1965 United States begins regular bombing missions over North Vietnam and sends first American ground combat troops into South Vietnam

1968 Tet offensive: During Tet, the Vietnamese lunar new year, the Vietcong stage attacks on major South Vietnamese cities; President Johnson suspends the bombing of North Vietnam and announces that he will not run for reelection; Democratic presidential candidate Robert F. Kennedy is assassinated; Richard M. Nixon is elected thirty-seventh president

1969 Nixon announces "Vietnamization" policy; South Vietnam to take increased responsibility for fighting the war

1970 32,000 U.S. troops join the South Vietnamese army in invading Cambodia; in antiwar protests, 4 students are killed and 9 injured at Kent State University in Ohio; and 2 students die and 12 are injured at Jackson State University in Mississippi; Congress repeals Gulf of Tonkin Resolution

1972 Nixon travels to China, ending 25 years of nonrecognition of the People's Republic of China; Strategic Arms Limitation Treaty with the Soviet Union freezes intercontinental ballistic missile deployment

1973 United States ends active participation in the Vietnam War

1975 North Vietnamese forces enter Saigon; North and South Vietnam are reunited; the former South Vietnamese capital is renamed Ho Chi Minh City

---

nally, the Soviet Union, Vietnam's closest ally, did not solve Vietnam's economic problems. "Americans without dollars," the Vietnamese have called the Soviets. One Vietnamese joke reflected the new relationship with the Soviet Union. After appealing to the Soviets for loans, Vietnam receives the cable: "Tighten your belts." Vietnam replies: "Send belts."

In 1986 Vietnam committed itself to radical change. A new generation of leaders turned to increased democracy and capitalism to solve their country's problems. They also turned to the West, and particularly the United States, for help. American leaders during the late 1980s and early 1990s, however, rejected Vietnam's pleas for aid. Although

Vietnam had weakened its ties to the Soviet Union, withdrawn from Kampuchea, and tried to resolve the prisoners of war—missing in action (POW-MIA)—issue, official American policy continued to regard the Socialist Republic of Vietnam as a country untouchable. Vietnam may have won the war, but it had not won peace. Finally, however, in the summer of 1995, President Bill Clinton's administration extended diplomatic recognition to Vietnam. Ironically, Clinton's decision was based partially on his belief that recognition would finally resolve the MIA issue.

Conclusion

The Vietnam War confused and divided the nation. Tim O'Brien captured something of this confusion in his acclaimed novel *Going After Cacciato* (1978). After fighting in the war, his protagonist "didn't know who was right, or what was right; he didn't know if it was a war of self-determination or self-destruction, outright aggression or national liberation; he didn't know which speeches to believe, which books, which politicians; he didn't know if nations would topple like dominos or stand separate like trees; he didn't know who started the war, or why, or when, or with what motives; he didn't know if it mattered."

Richard Nixon promised in 1968 that if he were elected president, he would end the war honorably and bring Americans together again. Instead, he enlarged the scope of the war before ending it and further divided the country. So, too, Johnson had divided the nation. His vision of a better, more just society—the Great Society (see Chapter 30)—was dashed on the rocks of Vietnam. There was in Johnson's position the essence of tragedy. As he later explained to biographer Doris Kearns, "I knew from the start that I was bound to be crucified either way I moved. If I left the woman I really loved—the Great Society—in order to get involved with the bitch of a war on the other side of the world, then I would lose everything at home . . . but if I left that war and let the communists take over South Vietnam, then I would be seen as a coward and my nation would be seen as an appeaser and we would both find it impossible to accomplish anything for anybody anywhere on the entire globe." In Johnson's view he was like a Puritan wrestling with the question of his own salvation:

> Damned if you do,
> Damned if you don't.
> Damned if you will
> Damned if you won't.

Of course, both Nixon and LBJ further injured their cause by being consciously deceptive in their dealings with the American people.

Vietnam, then, destroyed Johnson's presidency and it helped to undermine Nixon's. It was a war that left scars—on the people who fought in it and on the people who opposed and supported it; on Americans and on Vietnamese; and on U.S. foreign policy and its position in the world. For almost 35 years the United States had been actively involved in Indochina, but its influence in the region effectively ended in 1975. The Vietnam War, like the Communist victory in China in 1949, undercut America's position in Asia.

The most constructive outcome of the war was the lessons it taught. Congress learned that it had to take a more active role in foreign affairs. The War Powers Act (1973), which requires the president to account for his actions within 48 hours of committing troops in a foreign war, demonstrated that the Gulf of Tonkin Resolution had taught Congress a painful lesson. Ho Chi Minh's nationalism taught policymakers that communism was not a monolithic movement and that not all small nations are dominoes. Perhaps politicians, policy-makers, and citizens alike even learned that national policy should be based on the realities of individual situations and not Cold War stereotypes.

Suggestions for Further Reading

Carl Bernstein and Robert Woodward, *All the President's Men* (1974). The study of how two men, following a story, helped bring down a presidency.

Michael Beschloss, *The Crisis Years, Kennedy and Krushchev, 1960–1963* (1992). A readable popular narrative that presents a case study in misunderstanding.

Robert Caro, *The Years of Lyndon Johnson* and *The Path to Power* (1982), and *Means of Ascent* (1990). The first two volumes read like an indictment of Lyndon Johnson but are fascinating nonetheless.

David Halberstam, *The Making of a Quagmire: America and Vietnam During the Kennedy Era*, rev. ed. (1988). Sprawling study of the reasons for America's failure in Vietnam.

Robert S. McNamara, *In Retrospect: The Tragedy and Lessons of Vietnam* (1995). A recent attempt by one of Kennedy's advisers to explain why and how America became mired in Vietnam.

Allen Matusow, *The Unraveling of America: A History of Liberalism in the 1960's* (1984). A hard look at the few successes and many failures of the 1960s.

Neil Sheehan, *A Bright Shining Lie: John Paul Vann and America in Vietnam* (1988). Uses the career of John Paul Vann to provide an in-depth look at the war in Vietnam.

Overviews and Surveys

Stephen E. Ambrose, *Rise to Globalism: American Foreign Policy Since 1938*, 5th ed. (1988); H. W. Brands, *The Wages of Globalism: Lyndon Johnson and the Limits of American Power* (1994); William H. Chafe, *The Unfinished Journey*, 3d ed. (1995), and *The American Woman: Her Changing Social, Economic, and Political Roles, 1920–1970* (1972); Warren I. Cohen and Nancy Bernkopf, eds., *Lyndon Johnson Confronts the World: American Foreign Policy, 1963–1968* (1994); Mario T. García, *Mexican Americans: Leadership, Ideology, Identity, 1930–1960* (1989); Juan Gómez-Quiñones, *Chicano Politics: Reality and Promise, 1940–1990* (1990); Walter LaFeber, *America, Russia, and the Cold War*, 7th ed. (1993); Kim McQuaid, *The Anxious Years: America in the Vietnam-Watergate Era* (1989); Matt Meier and Feliciano Rivera, *The Chicanos: A History of Mexican-Americans* (1972); James S. Olson and Randy Roberts, *Where the Domino Fell: America in Vietnam, 1945–1990* (1991); Julian Samora, *Los Mojados: The Wetback Story* (1971); Robert D. Schulzinger, *A Time For War: The United States and Vietnam* (1997); Frederick F. Siegel, *A Troubled Journey* (1984); Ronald B. Taylor, *Chavez and the Farm Workers* (1975).

The Illusion of Greatness

Irving Bernstein, *Promises Kept: John F. Kennedy's New Frontier* (1991); James G. Blight and David A. Welch, *On the Brink: Americans and Soviets Reexamine the Cuban Missile Crisis* (1989); Carl M. Brauer, *John F. Kennedy and the Second Reconstruction* (1977); David Detzer, *The Brink: Cuban Missile Crisis, 1962* (1979); Herbert S. Dinerstein, *The Making of a Missile Crisis: October 1962* (1976); Louise FitzSimons, *The Kennedy Doctrine* (1972); John Hellmann, *The Kennedy Obsession: The American Myth of JFK* (1997); Trumbull Higgins, *The Perfect Failure: Kennedy, Eisenhower, and the C.I.A. at the Bay of Pigs* (1987); Richard D. Mahoney, *JFK: Ordeal in Africa* (1983); Ernest R. May and Philip D. Zelikow, eds., *The Kennedy Tapes: Inside the White House During the Cuban Missile Crisis* (1997); Bruce Miroff, *Pragmatic Illusions: The Presidential Politics of JFK* (1976); Victor Navasky, *Kennedy Justice* (1971); Thomas G. Patterson, *Contesting Castro: The United States and the Triumph of the Cuban Revolution* (1994); Jack M. Schick, *The Berlin Crisis, 1958–1962* (1971); Richard Walton, *Cold War and Counterrevolution: The Foreign Policy of John F. Kennedy* (1972); Pascaline Winand, *Eisenhower, Kennedy, and the United States of Europe* (1993); Peter Wyden, *Bay of Pigs* (1979).

Vietnam: America's Longest War

David L. Anderson, *Trapped by Success: The Eisenhower Administration and Vietnam, 1953–1961* (1991); Christian G. Appy, *Working-Class War: American Combat Soldiers and Vietnam* (1993); David M. Barret, *Uncertain Warriors: Lyndon Johnson and His Vietnam Advisors* (1993); Keith Beattie, *The Scar That Binds: American Culture and the Vietnam War* (1998); Larry Berman, *Planning a Tragedy: The Americanization of the War in Vietnam* (1982), and *Lyndon Johnson's War* (1989); Robert Buzzanco, *Masters of War: Military Dissent and Politics in the Vietnam Era* (1996); Larry E. Cable, *Conflict of Myths: The Development of American Counterinsurgency Doctrine and the Vietnam War* (1986), and *Unholy Grail: The United States and the Wars in Vietnam* (1991); Harry Caudill, *Night Comes to the Cumberlands* (1963); Warren I. Cohen and Nancy Bernkopf Tucker, eds., *Lyndon Johnson Confronts the World: American Foreign Policy, 1963–1968* (1994); Chester L. Cooper, *The Lost Crusade: America in Vietnam* (1970); Frances FitzGerald, *Fire in the Lake: The Vietnamese and the Americans in Vietnam* (1972); Todd Gitlin, *The Whole World Is Watching: Mass Media in the Making & Unmaking of the New Left* (1980); Sherry Gershon Gottlieb, *Hell No, We Won't Go: Evading the Draft During Vietnam* (1992); David Halberstam, *The Best and the Brightest* (1972); Michael Herr, *Dispatches* (1977); George C. Herring, *America's Longest War: The United States and Vietnam, 1950–1975*, 2d ed. (1986); Seymour Hersh, *My Lai 4: A Report on the Massacre and Its Aftermath* (1970); Stanley Karnow, *Vietnam, A History*, rev. ed. (1991); Christopher Lasch, *The Agony of the American Left* (1969); David Levy, *The Debate over Vietnam* (1991); Guenter Lewy, *America in Vietnam* (1978); Abraham Lowenthal, *The Dominican Intervention* (1972); H. R. McMaster, *Dereliction of Duty: Lyndon Johnson, Robert McNamara, The Joint Chiefs of Staff and the Lies that Led to Vietnam* (1998); Roger Morris, *Uncertain Greatness: Henry Kissinger and American Foreign Policy* (1977); Richard Moser, *The New Winter Soldiers: GI and Veteran Dissent During the Vietnam Era* (1996); Don Oberdorfer, *Tet!* (1971); James S. Olson and Randy Roberts, *My Lai: A Brief History with Documents* (1998); George Reedy, *The Twilight of the Presidency*, rev. ed. (1987); Ronald Spector, *After Tet: The Bloodiest War in Vietnam* (1992); Kathleen J. Turner, *Lyndon Johnson's Dual War: Vietnam and the Press* (1985); Brian VanDeMark, *Into the Quagmire: Lyndon Johnson and the Escalation of the Vietnam War* (1991); Clarence R. Wyatt, *Paper Soldiers: The American Press and the Vietnam War* (1993); Marilyn Young, *The Vietnam Wars: 1945–1990* (1991).

The Tortuous Path Toward Peace

William Bundy, *A Tangled Web: The Making of Foreign Policy in the Nixon Presidency* (1998); John Dean, *Blind Ambition: The White House Years* (1976); John Hart Ely, *War and Responsibility: Constitutional Lessons of Vietnam and Its Aftermath* (1993); Fred Emery, *Watergate: The Corruption of American Politics and the Fall of Richard Nixon* (1994); Stephen Graubard, *Kissinger: Portrait of a Mind* (1973); Robert T. Hartmann, *Palace Politics: An Inside Account of the Ford Years* (1980); Seymour Hersh, *The Price of Power: Kissinger in the Nixon White House* (1983); Leon Jaworski, *The Right and the Power: The Prosecution of Watergate* (1976); J. Anthony Lukas, *Nightmare: The Underside of the Nixon Years* (1976); Keith Nelson, *The Making of Detente: Soviet-American Relations in the Shadow of Vietnam* (1994); Richard Nixon, *RN: The Memoirs of Richard Nixon*, 2 vols. (1978); Thomas Powers, *The Man Who Kept the Secrets: Richard Helms & the CIA* (1979); William Shawcross, *Sideshow: Kissinger, Nixon, and the Destruction of Cambodia*, rev. ed. (1987); Edward R. F. Sheehan, *The Arabs, Israelis, and

Kissinger (1976); Terry Terriff, *The Nixon Administration and the Making of U.S. Nuclear Strategy* (1995); Richard C. Thornton, *The Nixon-Kissinger Years: Reshaping America's Foreign Policy* (1989); Theodore H. White, *Breach of Faith: The Fall of Richard Nixon* (1975).

Biographies

Anne E. Blair, *Lodge in Vietnam: A Patriot Abroad* (1995); Fawn M. Brodie, *Richard Nixon: The Shaping of His Character* (1981); David Burner, *John F. Kennedy and a New Generation* (1988); Warren Cohen, *Dean Rusk* (1980); Paul K. Conkin, *Big Daddy from the Pedernales: Lyndon Baines Johnson* (1986); Ronnie Dugger, *The Politician: The Life and Times of Lyndon Johnson* (1982); Henry Fairlie, *The Kennedy Promise: The Politics of Expectation* (1973); Lloyd C. Gardner, *Pay Any Price: Lyndon Johnson and the Wars for Vietnam* (1995); Eric Goldman, *The Tragedy of Lyndon Johnson* (1969); George C. Herring, *LBJ and Vietnam: A Different Kind of War* (1994); Joan Hoff, *Nixon Reconsidered* (1994); Doris Kearns, *Lyndon Johnson and the American Dream* (1976); Herbert S. Parmet, *Jack: The Struggles of John F. Kennedy* (1980), and *JFK: The Presidency of John F. Kennedy* (1983); Thomas C. Reeves, *A Question of Character: A Life of John F. Kennedy* (1991); Arthur Schlesinger, Jr., *A Thousand Days: John F. Kennedy in the White House* (1965); Tom Wicker, *One of Us: Richard Nixon and the American Dream* (1991).

INTERNET RESOURCES

May 4, 1970: 25 Years of Remembrance
http://www.library.kent.edu/exhibits/4may95/index.html
This site commemorates the 25th anniversary of the shootings at Kent State University with a detailed chronology and other information.

14 Days in October: The Cuban Missile Crisis
http://library.advanced.org/11046/
This clever site allows the viewer to interactively explore the Cuban Missile Crisis.

Investigating the Vietnam War
http://www.spartacus.schoolnet.co.uk/vietintro.htm
This site from Spartacus Educational Publishing, U.K. has an excellent list of annotated links to the best Vietnam-related sites.

Vitenam War Bibliography
http://hubcap.clemson.edu/~eemoise/bibliography.html
Edwin Moise of Clemson University maintains this extensive bibliography of print works about Vietnam and the Vietnam War.

Vietnam Online
http://www.pbs.org/wgbh/pages/amex/vietnam/index.html
From PBS and the American Experience, this site contains a detailed, interactive timeline of the war, interpretive essays, and autobiographical reflections.

My Lai Courts Martial (1970)
http://www.law.umkc.edu/faculty/projects/ftrials/mylai/mylai.htm
This site contains images, chronology, court and official documents maintained by Dr. Doug Linder at University of Missouri—Kansas City law School.

John F. Kennedy
http://www.ipl.org/ref/POTUS/jfkennedy.html
This page contains basic factual data about his election and presidency, speeches, and on-line biographies.

John F. Kennedy Library and Museum
http://www.cs.umb.edu/jfklibrary/
This site features exhibits about Robert Kennedy and Jacqueline Kennedy.

The Kennedy Assassination
http://mcadams.posc.mu.edu/home.htm
This well-organized site has images, essay, and photos.

JFK Assassination Web Page
http://ourworld.compuserve.com/homepages/MGriffith_2/jfk.htm
This is a personal but a very thorough page, which is a guide to the best Internet resources for the assassination.

KEY TERMS

Bay of Pigs Fiasco   (p. 850)
Cuban Missile Crisis   (p. 850)
Dien Bien Phu   (p. 852)
Ngo Dinh Diem   (p. 852)
Flexible Response   (p. 852)
Gulf of Tonkin Resolution   (p. 855)
Tet Offensive   (p. 856)
Robert Kennedy   (p. 860)
George Wallace   (p. 861)
Henry Kissinger   (p. 862)
The Nixon Doctrine   (p. 863)
Ping-Pong Diplomacy   (p. 864)
Strategic Arms Limitation Treaty of 1972 (SALT I)   (p. 865)

REVIEW QUESTIONS

1. Why do Americans continue to revere John F. Kennedy? What were his actual accomplishments as president?
2. How had America become involved in Vietnam before the presidency of Lyndon B. Johnson?
3. Why did Lyndon B. Johnson escalate American involvement in Vietnam? What effect did it have in Vietnam? In America?
4. What were Richard Nixon's strategies for ending the war in Vietnam? To what extent was he successful?
5. How has the American understanding of the Vietnam War changed in more recent times? Why?

30

THE STRUGGLE FOR A JUST SOCIETY

THE STRUGGLE FOR RACIAL JUSTICE
Freedom Now
To the Heart of Dixie
"Bombingham"
Kennedy Finally Acts
The March on Washington
The Civil Rights Act of 1964
Voting Rights
Black Nationalism and Black Power
The Civil Rights Movement Moves North
The Great Society and the Drive for Equality
White Backlash
The Struggle Continues

THE YOUTH REVOLT
The New Left
The Making and Unmaking of a Counterculture

LIBERATION MOVEMENTS
Women's Liberation
Sources of Discontent
Feminism Reborn
Radical Feminism
The Growth of Feminist Ideology
The Supreme Court and Sex Discrimination
The Equal Rights Amendment
Impact of the Women's Liberation Movement
¡Viva La Raza!
The Native-American Power Movement
Gay and Lesbian Liberation
The Earth First

875

The "endless discontents" of a "scold"

He has been called the nation's nag. He denounced soft drinks for containing excessive amounts of sugar (more than nine teaspoons a can). He warned Americans about the health hazards of red dyes used as food colorings and of nitrates used as preservatives in hot dogs. He even denounced high heels: "It is part of the whole tyranny of fashion, where women will inflict pain on themselves . . . for what, to please men." His name is Ralph Nader and since the mid-1960s he has been the nation's leading consumer advocate.

An extraordinarily frugal and committed crusader on behalf of the nation's consumers, Nader credits his parents, who came to the United States from Lebanon, with instilling the sense of justice and civic duty that has inspired his career.

Born in 1934, Nader received his bachelor's degree from Princeton and earned a law degree at Harvard, where he found his initial cause: automobile safety. After learning that auto accidents were the fourth leading cause of death (behind heart disease, cancer, and strokes), he launched a study of auto injury cases. His research convinced him that the law placed too much emphasis on driver mistakes and not enough on the unsafe design of cars.

In 1963, Nader decided to devote his life to consumer protection. Two years later he published the best-seller *Unsafe at Any Speed*, which charged that automakers stressed styling, comfort, speed, power, and a desire to cut costs at the expense of safety.

General Motors Corporation was so unhappy with the book that it hired a detective to investigate Nader's politics, religion, and sex life. GM's chairman was forced to apologize for this invasion of privacy before a Senate subcommittee, and eventually paid Nader a $425,000 settlement. Nader used the money to establish more than two dozen public interest groups. The people who work for these groups are known as "Nader's Raiders."

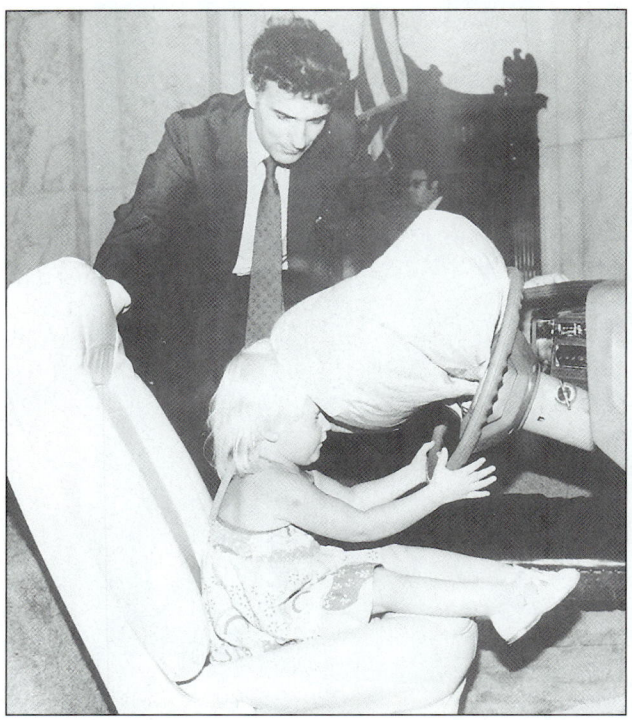

Ralph Nader is the best-known advocate of consumer protection laws in the United States. His group of attorneys, nicknamed "Nader's Raiders," have investigated such wide-ranging problems as automobile safety, the rights of the handicapped, tax reform, the environment, and public health. Here, Nader looks on during a demonstration showing the operation of an automobile airbag safety restraint.

During the 1960s and 1970s, Nader was the driving force behind the passage of more than two dozen landmark consumer protection laws, including the National Traffic and Motor Vehicle Safety Act (which set up a federal agency to establish auto-safety standards and order recalls of cars that failed to meet them), the Occupational Safety and Health Act (which established another agency to set standards for on-the-job safety), the Consumer Products Safety Act, and the Freedom of Information Act (which allows citizens to request and see government records). His efforts have been instrumental in attaining job protection for whistle-blowers (employees who expose corrupt or abusive business practices), federal financing of presidential elections, and the creation of the Environmental Protection Agency. Few other Americans have ever compiled such a long and impressive list of legislative accomplishment.

His ultimate goal, however, was not simply to protect consumers from shoddy or dangerous products. It was to reinvigorate the nation's ideal of democracy by encouraging active grassroots citizen participation in politics. The best answer to society's problems, he believed, was for ordinary citizens to campaign for safer consumer products, better schools, a cleaner environment, and safer workplaces.

During the late 1970s and 1980s, his influence seemed to wane. In 1978, Congress defeated his proposal for a Consumer Protection Agency. Critics dismissed him as a "scold." Said *Newsweek* magazine: "An optimistic society wearies of his endless discontents." In a decade of deregulation, Nader's call for greater regulations seemed out of step with the beat of the times.

During the 1990s, however, it was clear that Nader was still a major force in American politics. He played a central role in passing a California initiative that rolled back the cost of auto insurance. He led a bitter fight against a proposed 51 percent congressional pay raise. And in his long campaign for auto safety he achieved an important breakthrough when the major automobile manufacturers agreed to install air bags in most of their cars.

Ralph Nader illustrates in vivid terms the difference that one person's life can make. His life also epitomizes the idealism and activism of the 1960s—a decade when hundreds of thousands of ordinary Americans gave new life to the nation's democratic ideals. African Americans used sit-ins, freedom rides, and protest marches to fight segregation, poverty, and unemployment. Feminists demanded equal employment opportunities and an end to sexual discrimination. Mexican Americans protested discrimination in voting, education, and employment. Native Americans demanded that the government recognize their land rights and the right of tribes to govern themselves. Gays and lesbians fought for the end of discrimination according to sexual preference. Environmentalists demanded legislation that controlled the amount of pollution released into the atmosphere.

Although consumerists, environmentalists, civil rights workers, feminists, and other grassroots activists seemed to fade from public view during the 1980s and 1990s, they—like Ralph Nader—never abandoned their causes. Today they remain a powerful force in American life. Indeed, the very success of their efforts led to a conservative grassroots reaction, one in which equally committed Americans have denounced busing, affirmative action, quotas, and abortion.

THE STRUGGLE FOR RACIAL JUSTICE

For African Americans in 1960 statistics were grim. Their average life span was seven years less than that of white Americans. Their children had only half the chance of completing high school, only a third the chance of completing college, and a third the chance of entering a profession, when they grew up. On average, African Americans earned half as much as white Americans and were twice as likely to be unemployed.

Despite a string of court victories during the late 1950s, many African Americans remained second-class citizens. Six years after the landmark *Brown v. Board of Education* decision, just 1 percent of black schoolchildren in the 11 states of the old Confederacy attended public school with white classmates. Less than a quarter of the South's African-American voting-age population could vote, and in certain Southern counties African Americans could not vote, serve on grand juries and trial juries, or frequent all-white beaches, restaurants, and hotels.

In the North, too, African Americans suffered humiliation, insult, embarrassment, and discrimination. Many neighborhoods, businesses, and unions totally excluded them. Unemployment soared as labor-saving technology eliminated many semi-skilled and unskilled jobs that historically provided many African Americans with work. African-American families experienced severe strain; the proportion of families headed by women jumped from 8 percent in 1950 to 21 percent in 1960. "If you're white, you're right," a black folk saying went; "if you're brown stick around; if you're black, stay back."

During the 1960s, however, a growing hunger arose among African Americans for full equality. The Rev. Dr. Martin Luther King, Jr., gave voice to the new mood: "We're through with tokenism and grad-

TABLE 30.1
High School Graduates (Percentage of Population Ages 25–29)

	1960	1966	1970
African Americans			
Male	36	49	54
Female	41	47	58
Whites			
Male	63	73	79
Female	65	79	76

TABLE 30.2
Income Distribution of African Americans, Other Nonwhites, and Whites 1960, 1969

	African Americans and Other Nonwhites (Percentage)		Whites (Percentage)	
	1960	1969	1960	1969
Under $3000	38	20	14	~8
$3000–4999	22	19	14	10
$5000–6999	16	17	19	12
$7000–9999	14	20	26	22
$10,000 and over	~9	24	27	49

ualism and see-how-far-you've-comeism. We're through with we've-done-more-for-your-people-than-anyone-elseism. We can't wait any longer. Now is the time."

Freedom Now

"Now is the time." These words became the credo and rallying cry for a generation. On Monday, February 1, 1960, four African-American freshmen at North Carolina Agricultural and Technical College—Ezell Blair, Jr., Franklin McClain, Joseph McNeill, and David Richmond—walked into the F. W. Woolworth store in Greensboro, North Carolina, and sat down at the lunch counter. They asked for a cup of coffee. A waitress told them that she would only serve them if they stood.

Instead of walking away, the four college freshmen stayed in their seats until the lunch counter closed—giving birth to the **"sit-in."** The next morning, the four college students reappeared at Woolworth's, accompanied by 25 fellow students. By the end of the week protesters filled Woolworth's and other lunch counters in town. Although the student protesters subscribed to King's doctrine of nonviolence, their opponents did not—assaulting the students both verbally and physically. When the police finally arrived, they arrested African-American protesters, not the whites who tormented them.

By the end of February, lunch counter sit-ins had spread to 30 cities in seven southern states. In Charlotte, North Carolina, a storekeeper unscrewed the seats from his lunch counter. Alabama, Georgia, Mississippi, and Virginia hastily passed antitrespassing laws to stem the outbreak of sit-ins. Despite these efforts, the nonviolent student actions spread across the South as students protested segregated libraries, swimming pools, and other "public" facilities.

In April, 142 student sit-in leaders from 11 states met in Raleigh, North Carolina, and voted to set up a new group to coordinate the sit-ins, the Student Nonviolent Coordinating Committee (SNCC). The Rev. Dr. Martin Luther King, Jr., told the students that their willingness to go to jail would "be the thing to awaken the dozing conscience of many of our white brothers."

In the summer of 1960, sit-ins gave way to "wade-ins" at segregated public beaches. In Atlanta, Charlotte, Greensboro, and Nashville, African-American students lined up at white-only box offices of segregated movie theaters. Other students staged pray-ins (at all-white churches), study-ins (at segre-

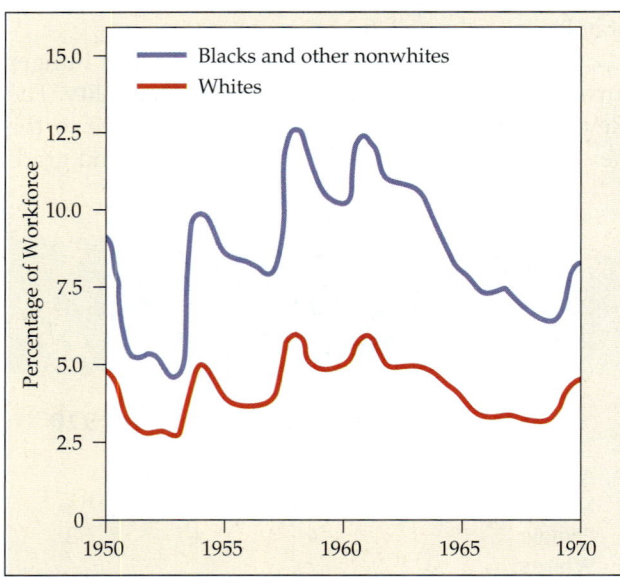

FIGURE 30.1
Unemployment, 1950–1970

Sit-ins were one example of the nonviolent direct action that characterized the civil rights movement in the early 1960s. Demonstrators endured the taunts and abuse of opponents, only to be arrested for "disturbing the peace" or "inciting a riot."

gated libraries), and apply-ins (at all-white businesses). By the end of 1960, 70,000 people had taken part in sit-ins in over 100 cities in 20 states. Police arrested and jailed more than 3600 protesters. But the new tactic worked. By August 1, lunch counters in 15 states had been integrated. By the end of the year, protesters had succeeded in integrating eating establishments in 108 cities.

The Greensboro sit-in initiated a new, activist phase in black America's struggle for equal rights. Fed up with the slow, legalistic approach that characterized the civil rights movement in the past, southern African-American college students began to attack Jim Crow directly. In the upper South, federal court orders and student sit-ins successfully desegregated lunch counters, theaters, hotels, public parks, churches, libraries, and beaches. But in three states—Alabama, Mississippi, and South Carolina—segregation in restaurants, hotels, and bus, train, and airplane terminals remained intact. In those states, young civil rights activists launched new assaults against segregation.

To the Heart of Dixie

In early May 1961 two busloads of men and women, African American and white, set out from Washington, D.C. They called themselves **"freedom riders,"** and they wanted to demonstrate that despite a federal ban on segregated travel on interstate buses, segregation prevailed throughout much of the South. The freedom riders' trip was sponsored by the Congress of Racial Equality (CORE), a civil rights group dedicated to breaking down racial barriers through nonviolent protest.

In Virginia and North Carolina, the freedom riders met little trouble. But in Winnsboro, South Carolina, police arrested two African-American freedom riders, and outside Anniston, Alabama, a white hurled a bomb through one of the bus's windows, setting the vehicle on fire. Waiting white thugs beat the freedom riders as they tried to escape the smoke and flames. Eight other whites boarded the second bus and assaulted the freedom riders before police restrained the attackers.

In Birmingham and Montgomery, Alabama, mobs attacked the freedom riders with clubs, blackjacks, and lengths of pipe. President Kennedy was appalled by the violence. He hastily deputized 400 federal marshals and Treasury agents and flew them

In a violent confrontation in Anniston, Alabama, angry whites set the Freedom Riders bus on fire, then beat the riders with blackjacks, iron bars, clubs, and tire chains as they tried to escape the smoke and flames. Local hospital workers refused to treat the injured riders.

to Alabama to protect the freedom riders' rights. The president publicly called for a "cooling-off period," but conflict continued. When freedom riders arrived in Jackson, Mississippi, 27 were arrested for entering a "white-only" washroom and were sentenced to 60 days on the state prison farm.

The threat of racial violence in the South led the Kennedy administration to pressure the Interstate Commerce Commission to desegregate air, bus, and train terminals. In more than 300 southern terminals, signs saying "white" and "colored" were taken down from waiting room entrances and lavatory doors.

Civil rights activists next aimed to open state universities to African-American students. Many Southern states integrated their universities without incident. Other states were stiff-backed in their opposition to integration, including Mississippi. In September 1962, a federal court ordered the state of Mississippi to admit **James Meredith**—a nine-year veteran of the air force—to the University of Mississippi in Oxford. Governor Ross Barnett vowed that he would "not surrender to the evil and illegal forces of tyranny" and would go to jail rather than permit Meredith to register for classes. Barnett flew into Oxford, named himself special registrar of the university, and ordered the arrest of federal officials who tried to enforce the court order.

James Meredith refused to back down. A "man with a mission and a nervous stomach," Meredith was determined to get a higher education. "I want to go to the university," he said. "This is the life I want. Just to live and breathe—that isn't life to me. There's got to be something more." He arrived at the Ole Miss campus in the company of police officers, federal marshals, and lawyers. Angry white students waited, chanting, "Two, four, six, eight—we don't want to integrate."

Four times James Meredith tried to register at Ole Miss. He finally succeeded on the fifth try, escorted by several hundred federal marshals. The ensuing riot left 2 people dead and 375 injured, including 166 marshals. Ultimately, President Kennedy sent 16,000 troops to put down the violence.

"Bombingham"

By the end of 1961, protests against segregation, job discrimination, and police brutality had erupted from Georgia to Mississippi and Tennessee to Alabama. Staunch segregationists responded by vowing to defend segregation. The symbol of unyielding resistance to integration was Alabama governor George C. Wallace. Elected on an extreme segregationist platform, Wallace declared at his inauguration in January 1963: "I draw the line in the dust and toss the gauntlet before the feet of tyranny, and I say segregation now, segregation tomorrow, segregation forever."

It was in Birmingham, Alabama, that civil rights activists faced the most determined resistance. A sprawling steel town of 340,000, Birmingham had a long history of racial acrimony. In open defiance of Supreme Court rulings, Birmingham had closed its 38 public playgrounds, 8 swimming pools, and 4 golf courses rather than integrate them. Calling Birmingham "the most thoroughly segregated city in the

Arrested during the Birmingham protests, Dr. King was held in the city jail for eight days, the first 24 hours of which were in solitary confinement.

THE PEOPLE SPEAK

Rev. Martin Luther King, Jr., Letter from Birmingham City Jail

In 1963, the Rev. Martin Luther King, Jr. came to Birmingham, Alabama to lead protests against segregation, job discrimination, and police brutality. After he was arrested for demonstrating without a permit, he wrote his "Letter from a Birmingham Jail," a scathing response to eight white Alabama clergymen who denounced King's protests and claimed that they were designed to provoke violence. Writing on scraps of toilet paper and newspaper margins, he explained why African Americans were unwilling to wait patiently for equal rights and why he defended his strategy of nonviolent direct action.

> We know through painful experience that freedom is never voluntarily given by the oppressor, it must be demanded by the oppressed. Frankly I have never yet engaged in a direct action movement that was "well timed," according to the timetable of those who have not suffered unduly from the disease of segregation. For years now I have heard the word "Wait!" It rings in the ear of every Negro with a piercing familiarity. This "wait" has almost always meant "never". . . . We have waited for more than 340 years for our constitutional and God-given rights. The nations of Asia and Africa are moving with jetlike speed toward the goal of political independence, and we still creep at horse and buggy pace toward the gaining of a cup of coffee at a lunch counter.
>
> I guess it is easy for those who have never felt the stinging darts of segregation to say wait. But when you have seen the vicious mobs lynch your mothers and fathers at will and drown your sisters and brothers at whim; when you have seen hate-filled policemen curse, kick, brutalize, and even kill your black brothers and sisters with impunity; when you see the vast majority of your 20 million Negro brothers smothering in an airtight cage of poverty in the midst of an affluent society; when you suddenly find your tongue twisted and your speech stammering as you seek to explain to your six-year-old daughter why she can't go to the public amusement park that has just been advertised on television, and see the tears welling up in her little eyes when she is told that Funtown is closed to colored children, and see the depressing clouds of inferiority begin to form in her little mental sky, and see her begin to distort her little personality by developing a bitterness toward white people; . . . when you are humiliated day in and day out by nagging signs reading "white" and "colored"; when your first name becomes "nigger," your middle name becomes "boy" (however old you are) and your last name becomes "John," and your wife and mother are never given the respected title "Mrs." . . .—then you will understand why we find it difficult to wait. There comes a time when the cup of endurance runs over, and men are no longer willing to be plunged into the abyss of despair. I hope, sirs, you can understand our legitimate and unavoidable impatience.
>
> You express a great deal of anxiety over our willingness to break laws. This is a legitimate concern. . . . I would be the first to advocate obeying just laws. . . . Conversely, one has a moral responsibility to disobey unjust laws. . . .
>
> One who breaks an unjust law must do so openly, lovingly, and with a willingness to accept the penalty. I submit that an individual who breaks a law that conscience tells him is unjust, and who willingly accepts the penalty of imprisonment in order to arouse the conscience of the community over its injustice, is in reality expressing the highest respect for law.

Source: "Letter from Birmingham Jail" and "Dr. King's Message to White Clergymen." Reprinted by arrangement with The Heirs to the Estate of Martin Luther King, Jr., c/o Writers House, Inc. as agent for the proprietor. Copyright © 1963 by Martin Luther King, Jr., copyright renewed 1991 by Coretta Scott King.

United States," the Rev. Dr. Martin Luther King, Jr., announced in early 1963 that he would lead demonstrations in the city until demands for fair hiring practices and desegregation were met.

Day after day, well-dressed and carefully groomed men, women, and children marched against segregation—only to be jailed for demonstrating without a permit. On April 12 King himself was arrested. While in jail he wrote his now-famous "Letter from Birmingham City Jail," a scathing response to a group of white clergymen who in a newspaper article had asked African Americans to wait patiently for equal rights. On pieces of toilet paper and newspaper margins, King wrote, "I am convinced that if your white brothers dismiss us as 'rabble rousers' and 'outside agitators'—those of us who are working through the channels of nonviolent direct action—and refuse to support our nonviolent efforts, millions of Negroes, out of frustration and despair, will seek solace and security in black nationalist ideologies, a development that will lead inevitably to a frightening racial nightmare."

For two weeks, all was quiet, but in early May demonstrations resumed with renewed vigor. On

May 2 and again on May 3, more than a thousand of Birmingham's African-American youth marched for equal rights. In response, Birmingham's police chief, Theophilus Eugene "Bull" Connor, unleashed police dogs on the protesters and sprayed them with high-pressure fire hoses. Watching the willful brutality on television, millions of Americans, white and African American, were shocked by this violent face of segregation.

Tension mounted as police arrested 2543 African Americans and whites between May 2 and May 7, 1963. Under intense pressure, the Birmingham Chamber of Commerce reached an agreement on May 9 with African-American leaders to desegregate public facilities, hire African Americans as clerks and salespersons, and release demonstrators without bail in return for an end to the protests.

King's goal was nonviolent social change, but the short-term result of protest was violence and confrontation. On May 11, white extremists firebombed an integrated motel. That same night, a bomb destroyed the home of King's brother. Shooting incidents and racial confrontations quickly spread across the South. In June, a gunman killed 37-year-old Medgar Evers, the NAACP field representative in Mississippi. In September, an explosion destroyed Birmingham's 50-year-old Sixteenth Street Baptist Church, killing 4 young African-American girls and injuring 14 others. All told, ten people died during civil rights protests in 1963, 35 African-American homes and churches were firebombed, and 20,000 people were arrested during civil rights protests.

Kennedy Finally Acts

The eruption of violence forced the Kennedy administration to introduce legislation guaranteeing civil rights. Twice before, in 1957 and 1960, the federal government had adopted weak civil rights acts designed to provide federal protection guaranteeing voting rights for African Americans. Now Kennedy responded to the racial violence by proposing a new, stronger civil rights bill that required the desegregation of public facilities, outlawed discrimination in employment and voting, and allowed the attorney general to initiate school desegregation suits.

Kennedy's record on civil rights inspired little confidence. He had voted against the 1957 Civil Rights Act, and in the 1960 campaign many African-American leaders, including former athlete and businessman Jackie Robinson, backed Richard Nixon even though Kennedy worked hard to court the African-American vote by promising new civil rights legislation and declaring that he would end housing discrimination with a "stroke of the pen." A few weeks before the 1960 election, Kennedy broadened his African-American support by helping to secure the release of Martin Luther King from an Atlanta jail, where he had been imprisoned for leading an antisegregation demonstration.

Once in office, however, Kennedy moved slowly on civil rights issues—both because he feared alienating white Southern Democrats and because he had no real commitment to the cause. Although Kennedy's administration filed 28 suits to protect

Police used dogs, clubs, bludgeons, electric cattle prods, and high-pressure water hoses to break up the nonviolent civil rights demonstration in Birmingham, Alabama, in May 1963. Scenes like this, televised to millions of viewers, aroused public indignation and sympathy for the civil rights movement.

African-American voting rights (compared to 10 suits filed during the Eisenhower years), it was not until November 1963 that Kennedy took steps to fulfill his campaign promise to end housing discrimination with a "stroke of the pen"—after he had received hundreds of pens from frustrated civil rights leaders.

The March on Washington

The violence that erupted in Birmingham and elsewhere alarmed many veteran civil rights leaders. In December 1962, two veteran fighters for civil rights—A. Philip Randolph and Bayard Rustin—met at the office of the Brotherhood of Sleeping Car Porters in Harlem. Both men were pacifists, eager to rededicate the civil rights movement to the principle of nonviolence. Both men decided that a massive march for civil rights and jobs might provide the necessary pressure to prompt Kennedy and Congress to act.

On August 28, 1963, over 200,000 people gathered around the Washington Monument and marched to the Lincoln Memorial. The marchers carried placards reading: "Effective Civil Rights Laws—Now! Integrated Schools—Now! Decent Housing—Now!" and sang the civil rights anthem, "We Shall Overcome." Ten speakers addressed the crowd, but the event's highlight was Rev. Dr. Martin Luther King, Jr.'s legendary "I have a dream" speech, which combined passion with an insistence on equal citizenship. "I have a dream," King declared, "that one day on the red hills of Georgia the sons of former slaves and the sons of former slaveowners will be able to sit down together at the table of brotherhood. . . . I have a dream that one day even the state of Mississippi, a state sweltering with people's injustices, sweltering with the heat of oppression, will be transformed into an oasis of freedom and justice." As his audience roared its approval, King continued: "I have a dream that one day this nation will rise up and live out the true meaning of its creed: 'We hold these truths to be self-evident; that all men are created equal.'"

The Civil Rights Act of 1964

For seven months, debate raged in the halls of Congress. In a futile effort to delay the Civil Rights Bill's passage, opponents proposed over 500 amendments and staged a protracted filibuster in the Senate. On July 2, 1964—a little over a year after President Kennedy had sent it to Congress—the Civil Rights Act was enacted into law. It had been skillfully pushed through Congress by President Lyndon Johnson. The act prohibited discrimination in voting, employment, and public facilities such as hotels and restaurants, and it established the Equal Employment Opportunity Commission to prevent discrimination in employment on the basis of race, religion, or gender.

In the first weeks after the act's passage, segregated restaurants and hotels across the South opened their doors to African-American patrons. Over the next ten years, the Justice Department brought legal suits against hundreds of school districts, hotels, restaurants, taverns, gas stations, and truck stops charged with racial discrimination.

Voting Rights

The **Civil Rights Act of 1964** prohibited discrimination in employment and public accommodations, but

On August 28, 1963, over 200,000 African Americans and whites gathered for a day-long rally at the Lincoln Memorial to demand an end to racial discrimination. The highlight of the event was Martin Luther King, Jr.'s inspiring "I Have a Dream" speech.

many African Americans were denied an equally fundamental constitutional right, the right to vote. The most effective barriers to voting were state laws requiring prospective voters to read and interpret sections of the state constitution. In Alabama, voters had to provide written answers to a 20-page test on the Constitution and state and local government. Questions included: "Where do presidential electors cast ballots for president?" "Name the rights a person has after he has been indicted by a grand jury."

In early 1965, in an effort to bring the issue of voting rights to national attention, Martin Luther King, Jr., launched a voter-registration drive in Selma, Alabama. Even though African Americans slightly outnumbered whites in the city of 29,500 people, Selma's voting rolls were 99 percent white and 1 percent African American. For seven weeks, King led hundreds of Selma's African-American residents to the county courthouse to register to vote. Nearly 2000 African American demonstrators, including King, were jailed by County Sheriff James Clark for contempt of court, juvenile delinquency, and parading without a permit. After a federal court ordered Clark not to interfere with orderly registration, the sheriff forced African-American applicants to stand in line for up to five hours before being permitted to take a "literacy" test. Not a single African-American was added to the registration rolls.

When a young African-American man was murdered in nearby Marion, King responded by calling for a march from Selma to the state capitol of Montgomery, 50 miles away. On March 7, 1965, voting-rights demonstrators began their march, but were attacked as they crossed a bridge spanning the Alabama River. The march was temporarily halted. It resumed on March 21 with federal protection. The demonstrators chanted: "Segregation's got to fall . . . you never can jail us all." On March 25, a crowd of 25,000 gathered at the state capitol to celebrate the march's completion. Martin Luther King, Jr., addressed the crowd and called for an end to segregated schools, poverty, and voting discrimination. "I know you are asking today, 'How long will it take?' . . . How long? Not long, because no lie can live forever."

Two measures adopted in 1965 helped safeguard the voting rights of all Americans. On January 23, the states completed ratification of the **Twenty-fourth Amendment** to the Constitution barring a poll tax in federal elections. At the time, five Southern states still had a poll tax. On August 6, President Johnson signed the **Voting Rights Act of 1965,** which prohibited literacy tests and sent federal examiners to seven Southern states to register voters. Within a year, 450,000 Southern African Americans had registered to vote.

Black Nationalism and Black Power

At the same time that such civil rights leaders as Dr. Martin Luther King, Jr., fought for racial integration, other African-American leaders emphasized sepa-

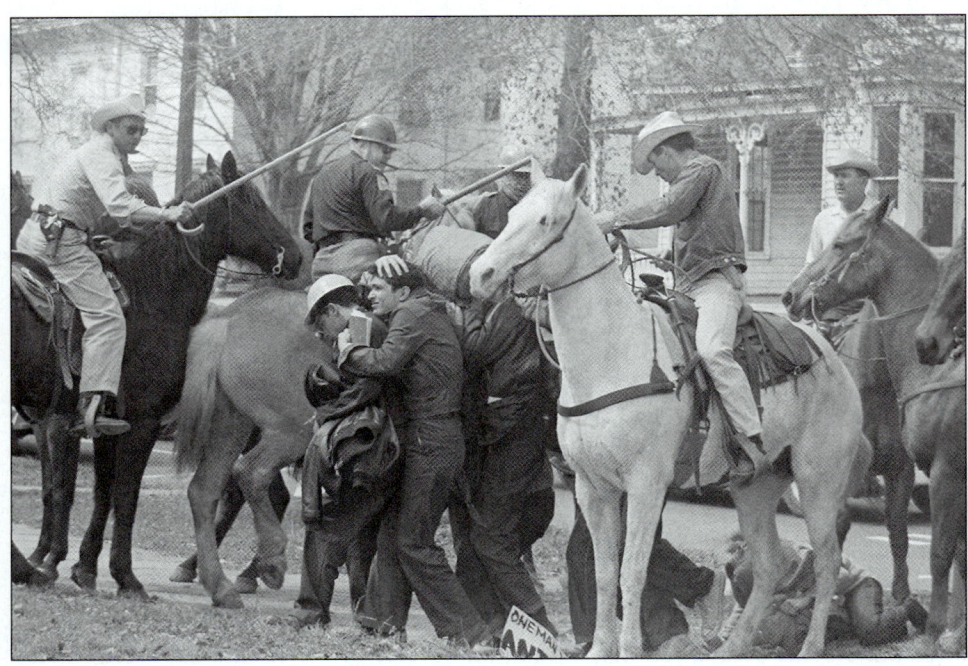

In March 1965, mounted state troopers met the 600 civil rights marchers en route from Selma, Alabama, to the state capital at Montgomery with nightsticks, clubs, tear gas, and bullwhips. The violence halted the march temporarily, but it resumed three weeks later, this time the marchers numbering nearly 3000.

ratism and identification with Africa. One of the most important expressions of the separatist impulse during the 1960s was the rise of the Nation of Islam, founded in 1931. The organization drew over 100,000 members, appealing to the growing numbers of urban African Americans living in poverty. The Black Muslims, led by Elijah Muhammad, emphasized racial separatism. "The white devil's day is over," Elijah Muhammad cried. "He was given six thousand years to rule.... He's already used up most trapping and murdering the black nations by the hundreds of thousands. Now he's worried, worried about the black man getting his revenge." Unless whites acceded to the Muslim demand for a separate territory for themselves, Muhammad said, "Your entire race will be destroyed and removed from this earth by Almighty God. And those black men who are still trying to integrate will inevitably be destroyed along with the whites."

The Black Muslims did more than vent anger and frustration. The organization was also a vehicle of African-American uplift and self-help. It called upon African Americans to "wake up, clean up, and stand up" in order to achieve true freedom and independence. To root out any behavior that conformed to racist stereotypes, the Muslims forbade eating pork and cornbread, drinking alcohol, and smoking cigarettes. Muslims also emphasized the creation of African-American businesses.

Malcolm X, frustrated with civil rights moderates, spoke sharply against racism and called for African Americans to defend themselves against white violence. In 1964, he founded the Organization of Afro-American Unity, which was socialist in its philosophy.

TABLE 30.3
Black Voter Registration Before and After the Voting Rights Act of 1965

State	1960	1966	Percent Increase
Alabama	66,000	250,000	278.8
Arkansas	73,000	115,000	57.5
Florida	183,000	303,000	65.6
Georgia	180,000	300,000	66.7
Louisiana	159,000	243,000	52.8
Mississippi	22,000	175,000	695.4
North Carolina	210,000	282,000	34.3
South Carolina	58,000	191,000	229.3
Tennessee	185,000	225,000	21.6
Texas	227,000	400,000	76.2
Virginia	100,000	205,000	105.0

Source: U.S. Bureau of the Census, *Statistical Abstract of the United States: 1982–83* (103d edition) Washington, D.C., 1982.

The most controversial exponent of black nationalism was **Malcolm X.** The son of a Baptist minister who had been an organizer for Marcus Garvey's Universal Negro Improvement Association, he was born Malcolm Little in Omaha, Nebraska. A reformed drug addict and criminal, Malcolm X learned about the Black Muslims in a maximum-security prison. After his release in 1952, he adopted the name Malcolm X to replace "the white slave-master name which had been imposed upon my paternal forebears by some blue-eyed devil." He quickly became one of the Black Muslims' most eloquent speakers, preaching a message of black nationalism and black pride.

His main message was that discrimination led many African Americans to despise themselves. Self-hatred, claimed Malcolm X, had caused many African Americans to lose their identity and become involved in crime, drug addiction, and alcoholism. Condemned by some whites as a demagogue for such statements as "If ballots won't work, bullets will," Malcolm X gained widespread public notoriety by attacking Dr. Martin Luther King, Jr., as a "chump" and an Uncle Tom, by advocating self-defense against white violence, and by emphasizing black political power.

In March 1964 Malcolm X withdrew from Elijah Muhammad's organization and set up his own Organization of Afro-Americans. Less than a year later, his life ended in bloodshed. On February 21, 1965, in front of 400 followers, he was shot and killed, apparently by followers of Black Muslim leader Elijah Muhammad.

Inspired by Malcolm X's example, young black activists increasingly challenged the traditional leadership of the civil rights movement and its philosophy of nonviolence. The single greatest contributor to the growth of militancy was the violence perpetrated by white racists. One of the most publicized incidents took place in June 1964, when three young civil rights workers—two whites, Andrew Goodman and Michael Schwerner, and one African American, James Chaney—disappeared near Philadelphia, Mississippi. Six weeks after they were reported missing, their bodies were found buried under a dam; all three had been beaten, then shot. In December, the sheriff and deputy sheriff of Neshoba County, Mississippi, along with 19 others, were arrested on charges of violating the three men's civil rights, but just six days later the charges were dropped. David Dennis, a civil rights worker, spoke at James Chaney's funeral. He angrily declared, "I'm sick and tired of going to the funerals of black men who have been murdered by white men. . . . I've got vengeance in my heart."

In 1966 two key civil rights organizations—SNCC and CORE—embraced black nationalism. Stokely Carmichael was elected chairman of SNCC in May and proceeded to transform SNCC from an interracial organization committed to nonviolence and integration into an all-black organization committed to **"black power."** "Integration is irrelevant," declared Carmichael. "Political and economic power is what the black people have to have." Although Carmichael initially denied that "black power" implied racial separatism, he eventually called on African Americans to form their own separate political organizations. In July 1966 CORE also endorsed black power and repudiated nonviolence.

Of all the groups advocating racial separatism and black power, the Black Panther party received the widest publicity. Formed in October 1966, in Oakland, California, the Black Panther party was an armed revolutionary socialist organization advocating self-determination for urban ghettoes. The Black Panthers gained public notoriety by entering the gallery of the California State Assembly brandishing guns and by following police to prevent police harassment and brutality toward African Americans.

A major achievement of the black power movement was an increase in educational opportunities for minorities in universities across the country; and it also spurred the creation of black studies programs in higher education.

Separatism and black nationalism attracted no more than a small minority of African Americans, and public opinion polls indicated that the overwhelming majority of blacks considered Martin Luther King, Jr. their favored spokesperson. The older civil rights organizations such as the NAACP rejected separatism and black power, viewing it as an abandonment of the goals of nonviolence and integration.

Yet despite their relatively small following, black power advocates exerted a powerful and positive influence upon the civil rights movement. In addition to giving birth to a host of community self-help organizations, supporters of black power spurred the creation of black studies programs in universities and encouraged African Americans to take pride in their racial background. A growing number of African Americans began to wear "Afro" hairstyles and take African or Islamic surnames. Singer James Brown captured the new spirit: "Say it loud—I'm black and I'm proud."

In an effort to maintain support among more militant African Americans, civil rights leaders began to address the problems of the lower classes who lived in the nation's cities. By the mid-1960s Martin Luther King, Jr., had begun to move toward the political left. He said it did no good to be allowed to eat in a restaurant if you had no money to pay for a hamburger. King denounced the Vietnam War as "an enemy of the poor" and urged a radical redistribution of wealth and political power in the United States in order to provide medical care, jobs, and education for all of the country's people.

The Civil Rights Movement Moves North

On August 11, 1965, five days after President Lyndon Johnson signed the Voting Rights Act, accusations of police brutality following the arrest of a 21-year-old for drunk driving ignited a riot in Watts, a predominantly black section of Los Angeles. The violence lasted five days and resulted in 34 deaths, 3900 arrests, and the destruction of over 744 buildings and 200 businesses in a 20-square-mile area. Rioters smashed windows, hurled bricks and bottles from rooftops, and stripped store shelves.

Over the next four summers, the nation's inner cities experienced a wave of violence and rioting. The worst violence occurred during the summer of 1967, when riots occurred in 127 cities. In Newark 26 persons lost their lives, over 1500 were injured, and 1397 were arrested. In Detroit 43 people died, $500 million in property was destroyed, and 14 square miles were gutted by fire. The last major wave occurred following the assassination of Martin Luther King, Jr., in Memphis, Tennessee, on April 4, 1968. Violence erupted in 168 cities, leaving 46 dead, 3500 injured, and $40 million worth of damage. In Washington, D.C., fires burned within three blocks of the White House. Joblessness, poverty, a lack of political power, decaying and dilapidated housing, police brutality, and poor schools bred a sense of frustration and rage that had exploded into violence.

In 1968 President Johnson appointed a commission to examine the causes of the race riots of the preceding three summers. The commission attributed racial violence to "white racism" and its heritage of discrimination and exclusion. The commission warned that unless major steps were taken, the United States would inevitably become "two societies, one black, one white—separate and unequal."

Until 1964 most white Northerners regarded race as a peculiarly Southern problem that could be solved by extending political and civil rights to Southern African Americans. Beginning in 1964 thousands of African Americans in the North staged demonstrations to protest school desegregation as well as job, housing, and employment discrimination. The nation learned that discrimination and racial prejudice were nationwide problems.

In the North, African Americans suffered from de facto discrimination in housing, schooling, and employment—discrimination that lacked the overt sanction of law. "De facto segregation," wrote James Baldwin, "means that Negroes are segregated but nobody did it." The most obvious example of de facto segregation was the fact that the overwhelming majority of northern black schoolchildren attended predominantly black inner-city schools while most white children attended schools with a majority of whites. In 1968—14 years after the *Brown* v. *Board of Education* decision—federal courts began to order busing as a way to deal with de facto segregation brought about by housing patterns. In April 1971 in the case of *Swann* v. *Charlotte-Mecklenburg Board of Education,* the Supreme Court upheld "bus transportation as a tool of school desegregation."

The Great Society and the Drive for Equality

Lyndon B. Johnson had a vision for America. Believing that problems of housing, income, employment, and health were ultimately a federal responsibility, Johnson used the weight of the presidency and his

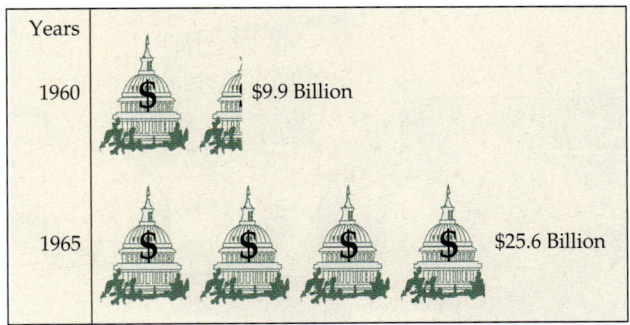

FIGURE 30.2
Federal Spending on Social Programs, Excluding Social Security

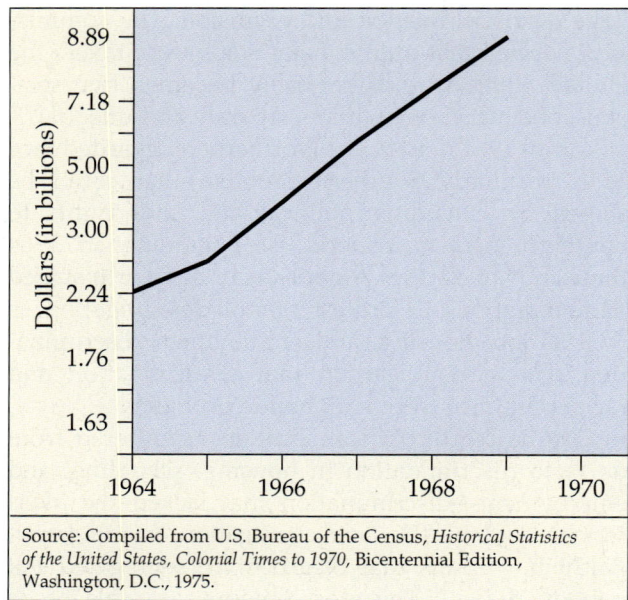

FIGURE 30.3
Federal Aid to Education, 1964–1970

formidable political skills to enact the most impressive array of reform legislation since the days of Franklin Roosevelt. He envisioned a society without poverty or discrimination, in which all Americans enjoyed equal educational and job opportunities. He called his vision the **"Great Society."**

A major feature of Johnson's Great Society was the "War on Poverty." The federal government raised the minimum wage and enacted programs to train poorer Americans for new and better jobs, including the 1964 Manpower Development and Training Act and the Economic Opportunity Act, which established such programs as the Job Corps and the Neighborhood Youth Corps. To assure adequate housing, in 1966 Congress adopted the Model Cities Act to attack urban decay, set up a cabinet-level Department of Housing and Urban Development, and began a program of rent supplements.

To promote education, Congress passed the Higher Education Act in 1965 providing student loans and scholarships, the Elementary and Secondary Schools Act of 1965 to pay for textbooks, and the Educational Opportunity Act of 1968 to help the poor finance college educations. To address the nation's health needs, the Child Health Improvement and Protection Act of 1968 provided for prenatal and postnatal care, the Medicaid Act of 1968 paid for the medical expenses of the poor, and Medicare, established in 1965, extended medical insurance to older Americans under the Social Security system.

Johnson also prodded Congress to pass a broad spectrum of civil rights laws, ranging from the Civil Rights Act of 1964 and the Voting Rights Act of 1965 to the 1968 Fair Housing Act barring discrimination in the sale or rental of housing. In 1965, LBJ issued an executive order requiring government contractors to ensure that job applicants and employees were not discriminated against. It required all contractors to prepare an "affirmative action plan" to achieve these goals.

Prior to being named the first black Supreme Court justice in 1967, Thurgood Marshall had presented the legal arguments against school segregation before the Supreme Court that resulted in the 1954 *Brown v. Board of Education of Topeka* decision.

Johnson broke many other color barriers. In 1966, he named the first black cabinet member and appointed the first black woman to the federal bench. In 1967 he appointed Thurgood Marshall to become the first African American to serve on the Supreme Court. The first southerner to reside in the White House in half a century, Johnson showed a stronger commitment to improving the position of African Americans than any previous president.

When President Johnson announced his Great Society program in 1964, he promised substantial reductions in the number of Americans living in poverty. When he left office, he could legitimately argue that he had delivered on his promise. In 1960, 40 million Americans, 20 percent of the population, were classified as poor. By 1969, their number had fallen to 24 million, 12 percent of the population. Johnson also pledged to qualify the poor for new and better jobs, to extend health insurance to the poor and elderly to cover hospital and doctor costs, and to provide better housing for low-income families. Here too Johnson delivered. Infant mortality among the poor, which had barely declined between 1950 and 1965, fell by one-third in the decade after 1965 as a result of expanded federal medical and nutritional programs. Before 1965, 20 percent of the poor had never seen a doctor; by 1970 the figure had been cut to 8 percent. The proportion of families living in houses lacking indoor plumbing also declined steeply, from 20 percent in 1960 to 11 percent a decade later.

Although critics argued that Johnson took a shotgun approach to reform and pushed poorly thought-out bills through Congress, supporters responded that at least Johnson tried to move toward a more compassionate society. For African Americans during the 1960s median family income rose 53 percent; employment in professional, technical, and clerical occupations doubled; and average educational attainment increased by four years. The proportion of African Americans below the poverty line fell from 55 percent in 1960 to 27 percent in 1968. The country had taken major strides toward extending equality of opportunity to both African Americans and whites below the poverty line.

White Backlash

Ghetto rioting, the rise of black militancy, and resentment over Great Society social legislation combined to produce a backlash among many whites. Commitment to granting African Americans full equality declined. In the wake of the riots, many whites fled the nation's cities. The Census Bureau estimated that 900,000 whites moved each year from central cities to the suburbs between 1965 and 1970.

The 1968 Republican candidate Richard Nixon promised to eliminate "wasteful" federal antipoverty programs and to name "strict constructionists" to the Supreme Court. As president, Nixon moved quickly to keep his commitments. In an effort to curb Great Society social programs, Nixon did away with the Model Cities program and the Office of Economic Opportunity. The administration urged Congress not to extend the Voting Rights Act of 1965 and to end a fair housing enforcement program.

During the 1960s, the Supreme Court greatly increased the ability of criminal defendants to defend themselves. In *Mapp* v. *Ohio* (1961), the high court ruled that evidence secured by the police through unreasonable searches must be excluded from trial. In *Gideon* v. *Wainwright* (1963), it declared that indigent defendants have a right to a court-appointed attorney. In *Escobedo* v. *Illinois* (1964), it ruled that suspects being interrogated by police have a right to legal counsel.

As president, Nixon made a series of Supreme Court appointments that brought to an end the liberal activist era of the Court. He selected Warren Burger, a moderate conservative, to replace Earl Warren as chief justice of the Supreme Court and eventually named four justices to the high court: Burger, Harry Blackmun, Lewis Powell, and William Rehnquist.

Under Chief Justice Burger and his successor William Rehnquist, the Supreme Court clarified the remedies that can be used to correct past racial discrimination. In 1974 the Court limited the use of school busing for purposes of racial desegregation by declaring that busing could not take place across school district lines. In the landmark 1978 case, *Bakke* v. *Regents of the University of California,* the Court held that educational institutions could take race into account when screening applicants but could not use rigid racial quotas.

The Struggle Continues

Over the past quarter-century, African Americans have made impressive social and economic gains, yet full equality remains an unrealized dream. State-sanctioned segregation in restaurants, hotels, courtrooms, libraries, drinking fountains, and public washrooms was eliminated and many barriers to equal opportunity were shattered. In political representation, educational attainment, and representation in white collar and professional occupations, African Americans have made striking gains.

African-American mayors have governed many of the nation's largest cities, including Chicago, Detroit, Los Angeles, New York, Philadelphia, and Washington, D.C.

Respect for African-American culture has also grown. The number of African-American performers on television and in film has increased, though most still appear in comedies and crime shows. African Americans also compose and perform much of the country's popular music, but one particular form of musical expression—rap—provoked calls for censorship from those who believed that its lyrics espoused violence.

Tom Bradley, the son of a sharecropper, became the first black mayor of Los Angeles in 1973, winning more than 56 percent of the total vote.

Nevertheless, millions of African Americans still do not share fully in the promise of American life. African Americans still suffer twice the unemployment rate of whites and earn only about half as much. The poverty rate among black families is three times that of whites, the same ratio as in the 1950s, and almost half of all African-American children are born into families earning less than the poverty level.

Although the United States has eliminated many obstacles to progress in civil rights, reformers maintain that much remains to be done before the country attains the equality that Martin Luther King and Lyndon Johnson envisioned.

THE YOUTH REVOLT

During the 1960s, one age group of Americans loomed larger than any other: youth. As a result of depressed birthrates during the 1930s and the postwar baby boom, there was a sudden explosion in the number of teenagers and young adults. Unlike their parents, whose values had been shaped by the Depression and World War II, young people of the 1960s grew up during a period of prosperity. This allowed them to seek personal fulfillment and to dismiss their parents' generation's success-oriented lives.

At no earlier time in American history had the gulf between generations seemed so wide. Blue jeans, long hair, psychedelic drugs, casual sex, hippie communes, campus demonstrations, and rock music all became symbols of the distance separating youth from the world of conventional adulthood.

The New Left

Late in the spring of 1962, five dozen college students gathered at a lakeside camp near Port Huron, Michigan, to discuss politics. For four days and nights the members of an obscure student group known as **Students for a Democratic Society (SDS)** talked passionately about such topics as civil rights, foreign policy, and the quality of American life. The gathering ended when the participants agreed on a political platform that expressed their sentiments. This manifesto, one of the pivotal political documents of the 1960s, became known as the Port Huron Statement.

The goal set forward in the Port Huron Statement was the creation of a radically democratic political movement in the United States that rejected hierarchy and bureaucracy. In its most important paragraphs, the document called for "participatory democracy"—direct individual involvement in the decisions that affected their lives. This notion would become the battle cry of the student movement of the 1960s—a movement that came to be known as the New Left.

During the 1960s, thousands of young college students became politically active. The first issue to spark student radicalism was the impersonality of the modern university, which many students criticized for being too bureaucratic and impersonal. Students questioned university requirements, restrictions on student political activities, and dormitory rules limiting the hours that male and female students could socialize with each other. Restrictions on students handing out political pamphlets on university property led to the first campus demonstrations that broke out at the University of California at Berkeley and soon spread to other campuses.

Involvement in the civil rights movement in the South initiated many students into radical politics. In the early 1960s, many white students from northern universities began to participate in voter registration drives, freedom schools, sit-ins, and freedom rides in order to help desegregate the South.

Student radicalism also drew inspiration from a literature of social criticism that flourished in the 1950s. During that decade, many of the most popular films, novels, and writings aimed at young people criticized conventional middle-class life. Popular films, like *Rebel Without a Cause,* and popular novels, like J. D. Salinger's *Catcher in the Rye,* celebrated sensitive, directionless, alienated youths unable to conform to the conventional

In late summer 1964 the first major student demonstrations took place at the University of California at Berkeley. Student protests against war, racism, and poverty continued throughout the country into the 1970s.

adult values of suburban and corporate America. Sophisticated works of social criticism by such maverick sociologists, psychologists, and economists as Herbert Marcuse, Norman O. Brown, Paul Goodman, Michael Harrington, and C. Wright Mills, documented the growing concentration of power in the hands of social elites, the persistence of poverty in a land of plenty, and the stresses and injustices in America's social order.

Above all, student radicalism owed its support to student opposition to the Vietnam War. In 1965 an SDS antiwar march attracted at least 15,000 protesters to Washington and commanded wide press attention. Over the next three years, opposition to the war brought thousands of new members to SDS. SDS also tried to organize a democratic "interracial movement of the poor" in northern city neighborhoods.

Many members of SDS quickly grew frustrated by the slow pace of social change and began to embrace violence as a tool to transform society. After 1968 SDS rapidly tore itself apart as an effective political force, and its final convention in 1969 degenerated into a shouting match between radicals and moderates. That same year the Weathermen, a surviving faction of SDS, attempted to launch a guerrilla war in the streets of Chicago—an incident known as the "Days of Rage"—to "tear pig city apart." Finally, in 1970 three members of the Weathermen blew themselves up in a Greenwich Village brownstone trying to make a bomb out of a stick of dynamite and an alarm clock.

Throughout the 1960s, the SDS and other radical student organizations claimed to speak for the nation's youth, and in thousands of editorials and magazine articles, journalists accepted this claim. In fact, the SDS represented only a small minority of college students, who themselves composed a minority of the country's youth. Far more young Americans voted for George Wallace in 1968 than joined SDS, and most college students during the decade spent far more time studying and enjoying the college experience than protesting. Nevertheless, radical students did help to draw the nation's attention to the problem of racism in American society and the moral issues involved in the Vietnam War. In that sense, their impact far exceeded their numbers.

The Making and Unmaking of a Counterculture

The New Left had a series of heroes—ranging from Marx, Lenin, Ho, and Mao to Fidel, Che, and other revolutionaries. It also had its own uniforms, rituals, and music. Faded blue work shirts and jeans, wire-rimmed glasses, and work shoes were de rigueur—so was the political protest music of Phil Ochs, Bob Dylan, and their ilk.

But the New Left was only one part of youth protest during the 1960s. While the New Left labored to change the world and remake American society, other youths attempted to alter themselves and reorder consciousness. Variously labeled the counterculture, hippies, or flower children, they had their own heroes, music, dress, and approach to life.

In theory, supporters of the counterculture rejected individualism, competition, and capitalism. Adopting rather unsystematically ideas from oriental religions, they sought to become one with the universe. Rejection of monogamy and the traditional nuclear family gave way to the tribal or communal ideal, where members renounced individualism and private property and shared food, work, and sex. In such a community, love was a general abstract ideal rather than a focused emotion.

The quest for oneness with the universe led many youths to experiment with hallucinogenic drugs. LSD had a particularly powerful allure. Under its influence, poets, musicians, politicians, and thousands of other Americans claimed to have tapped into an all-powerful spiritual force.

Although LSD was outlawed in 1966, use of the drug continued to spread. Perhaps some takers discovered profound truths, but by the late 1960s drugs had done more harm than good. The history of the Haight-Ashbury section of San Francisco illustrated the problems caused by drugs. In 1967 Haight was the center of the "counterculture," the home of the "flower children." In the "city of love" hippies ingested LSD, smoked pot, listened to "acid rock," and proclaimed the dawning of a new age. Yet the area was suffering from severe problems. High levels of racial violence, venereal disease, rape, drug overdoses, and poverty ensured more bad trips than good.

Even music, which along with drugs and sex formed the counterculture trinity, failed to alter human behavior. In 1969 journalists hailed the Woodstock Music Festival as a symbol of love. But a few months later a group of Hell's Angels violently interrupted the Altamont Raceway music festival. As Mick Jagger sang "Sympathy for the Devil" an Angel stabbed an African-American man to death.

Like the New Left, the counterculture fell victim to its own excesses. Sex, drugs, and rock and roll did not solve the problems facing the United States. And by the early 1970s the counterculture had lost its force.

Liberation Movements

The struggle of African Americans for racial justice inspired a host of other groups to seek full equality. Women, Mexican Americans, Native Americans, and many other deprived groups protested against discrimination and organized to promote social change.

Women's Liberation

One of the most popular daytime television shows of the 1950s was "Queen for a Day." Five times a week, three women, each with a hard-luck story, recited their tales of woe—diseases, difficult children, poverty—and the studio audience, with the aid of an applause meter, decided which woman was the most miserable. She became "Queen for a Day." Gifts for the queen included a year's supply of Helena Rubinstein cosmetics; a Clairol permanent and makeover by a Hollywood makeup artist; and the electric appliances thought to be necessary for female happiness—a toaster oven, automatic washer, automatic dryer, and an iron. Altogether, every-

The popular television show "Queen for a Day" reinforced established female sex roles by providing winners with everything they needed to be better housewives. Here, host Jack Bailey crowns a "Queen for a Day."

thing a woman needed to be a prettier and better housewife.

One woman in the television audience was **Betty Friedan.** A 1942 honors graduate of Smith College and former psychology Ph.D. candidate at the University of California at Berkeley, Friedan had quit graduate school, married, moved to the New York suburbs, and bore three children in rapid succession. American culture told her that husband, house, children, and electric appliances were true happiness. But Friedan was not happy. And she was not alone.

In 1957 Friedan sent out a questionnaire to fellow members of her college graduating class. The replies amazed her. Again and again, she found women suffering from "a sense of dissatisfaction." Over the next five years, Friedan interviewed hundreds of other women, and she repeatedly found an unexplainable sense of melancholy and incompleteness.

Friedan was not the only observer to detect a widespread sense of discontent among American women. Doctors identified a new female malady, the housewife's syndrome, characterized by a mixture of frustration and exhaustion. When *Redbook* magazine ran an article entitled "Why Young Mothers Feel Trapped," it received 24,000 replies.

Why, Friedan asked, were American women so discontented? In 1963 she published her answer in a book entitled *The Feminine Mystique.* Friedan analyzed and criticized the role of educators, psychologists, sociologists, and the mass media in conditioning women to believe that they could find fulfillment only as housewives and mothers. By requiring women to subordinate their own aspirations to the welfare of their husbands and children, the "feminine mystique" prevented women from achieving self-fulfillment and inevitably left women unhappy. One of the most influential books ever written by an American, *The Feminine Mystique* helped launch a new movement for women's liberation. The book touched a nerve, but the origins of the movement lay deeper, in the role of females in American society.

Sources of Discontent

During the 1950s, many American women reacted against the poverty of the Depression and the upheavals of World War II by placing renewed emphasis on family life. Young women married earlier than had their mothers, had more children, and bore them faster—producing a population growth rate approaching that of India. Growing numbers of women decided to forsake higher education or a career outside the home and achieve emotional fulfillment as wives and mothers.

Politicians, educators, psychologists, and the mass media all echoed the view that women would find their highest fulfillment managing a house and caring for children. Women's magazines pictured housewives as happy with their tasks and depicted career women as neurotic, unhappy, and dissatisfied.

Already underway, however, were dramatic social changes that would contribute to a rebirth of feminism. A dramatic upsurge took place during the 1950s in women's employment and education, as more and more married women entered the labor force. The number of women receiving college degrees also rose. Meanwhile, beginning in 1957 the birthrate began to drop as women elected to have fewer children. A growing discrepancy had begun to appear between the popular image of women as full-time housewives and mothers and the actual realities of many women's lives.

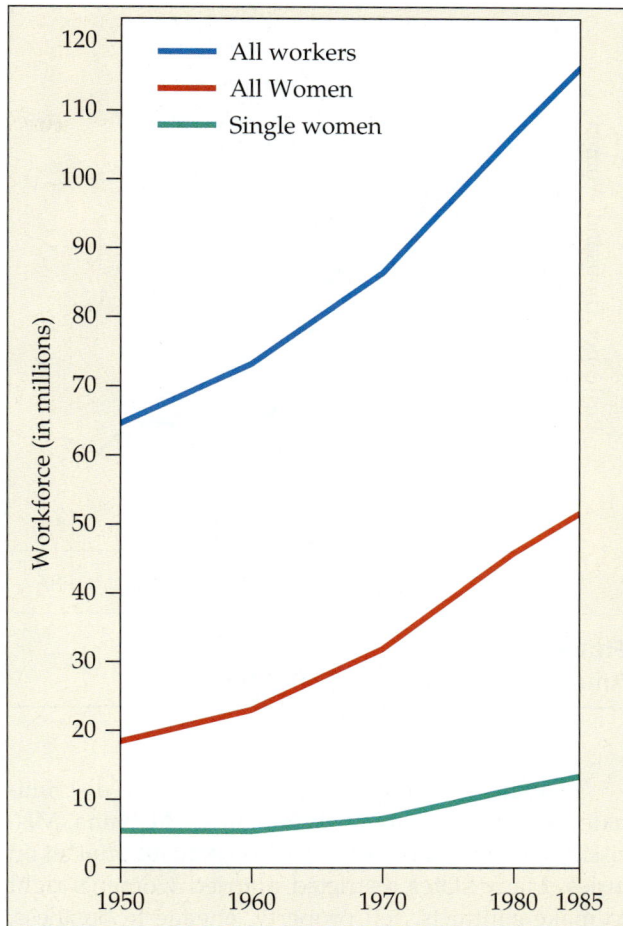

FIGURE 30.4
Women in the Workforce, 1950–1985

Feminism Reborn

In 1960 women played a limited role in American government. Although women comprised about half of the nation's voters, there were no female Supreme Court justices, federal appeals court justices, governors, cabinet officers, or ambassadors. Only 2 of 100 U.S. senators and 15 of 435 representatives were women.

Economically, women workers were concentrated in low-paying service and factory jobs. The overwhelming majority worked as secretaries, waitresses, beauticians, teachers, nurses, and librarians. Lower pay for women doing the same work as men was commonplace. One out of every three companies had separate pay scales for male and female workers. A female bank teller typically made $15 a week less than a man with the same amount of experience, and a female laundry worker made 49 cents an hour less than her male counterpart. Altogether, the earnings of women working full-time averaged only about 60 percent of those of men.

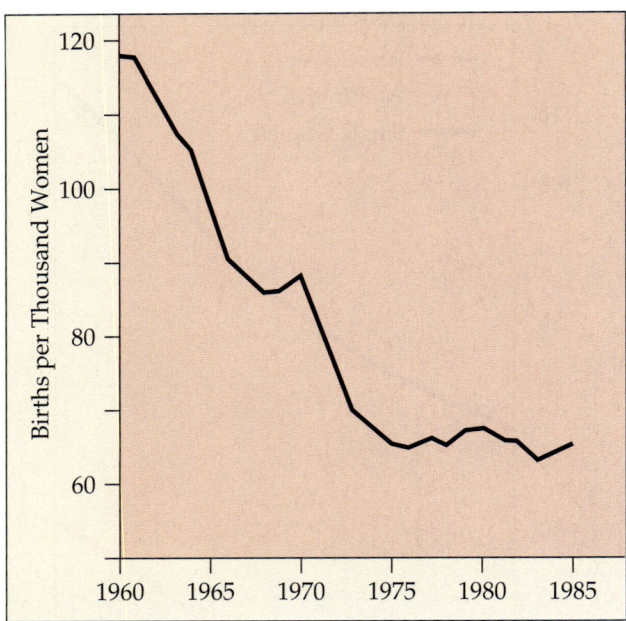

FIGURE 30.5
American Birthrate, 1960–1985

In many parts of the country, the law discriminated against women. In three states—Alabama, Mississippi, and South Carolina—women could not sit on juries. Many states restricted married women's right to make contracts, sell property, engage in business, control their own earnings, and make wills. In practically every state, men had a legal right to have intercourse with their wives whenever they chose to do so.

In December 1961 President John F. Kennedy placed the issue of women's rights on the national political agenda by establishing a President's Commission on the Status of Women. Chaired by Eleanor Roosevelt, the commission issued its report in 1963, the year that Betty Friedan published *The Feminine Mystique*. The report's recommendations included a call for an end to all legal restrictions on married women's right to own property, to enter into business, and to make contracts; equal opportunity in employment; and greater availability of child-care services.

The most important reform to grow out of the commission's investigations was the 1963 Equal Pay Act, which required equal pay for men and women who performed the same jobs under equal conditions. The Equal Pay Act was the first federal law to prohibit discrimination on the basis of gender.

The next year, Congress enacted a new weapon in the fight against gender discrimination. Title VII of the 1964 Civil Rights Act prohibited discrimination in hiring or promotion based on race, color, religion, national origin, or gender by private employers and unions. This act made it illegal for employers to discriminate against women in hiring and promotion unless the employer could show that gender was a "bona fide occupational qualification" (for example, hiring a man as an attendant for a men's restroom). To investigate complaints of employment discrimination, the act set up the Equal Employment Opportunity Commission (EEOC).

At first, the EEOC focused its enforcement efforts on racial discrimination and largely ignored gender discrimination. To pressure the EEOC to enforce the law prohibiting sex discrimination, Betty Friedan and 300 other women formed the National Organization for Women (NOW) in 1966. With Friedan as president, the organization filed suit against the EEOC "to force it to comply with its own government rules." It also sued the country's 1300 largest corporations for sex discrimination and lobbied President Johnson to issue an executive order that would include women within federal affirmative action requirements.

At its second national conference in November 1967, NOW drew up an eight-point bill of rights for women. It called for adoption of an Equal Rights Amendment (ERA) to the Constitution, prohibition of sex discrimination; provision for equal educational, job training, and housing opportunities for women; and repeal of laws limiting access to contraceptive devices and abortion.

Two proposals produced fierce dissension within the new organization. One source of disagreement was the Equal Rights Amendment, which stated "Equality of rights under the law shall not be denied or abridged by the United States or by any

Women have been involved in protest movements throughout the years. Here women march in support of the Equal Rights Amendment. Failure to achieve ratification by the required three-fourths of states sent the amendment to its final defeat in 1982.

state on account of sex." The other issue that generated controversy was the call for reform of abortion laws.

Despite internal disagreements, NOW's membership grew rapidly. The group broadened its attention to include such issues as the plight of poor and minority women, domestic violence, rape, sexual harassment, the role of women in sport, and the rights of lesbians. The organization also claimed a number of achievements. Two victories were particularly important. In 1967, NOW persuaded President Lyndon Johnson to issue Executive Order 11375, which prohibited government contractors from discriminating on the basis of sex and required them to take "affirmative action" to ensure that women are properly represented in their workforce. The next year, the EEOC ruled that separate want ads for men and women were a violation of Title VII of the 1964 Civil Rights Act.

Radical Feminism

Alongside NOW, other more radical feminist groups emerged during the 1960s. In cities across the country, independent women's groups sprouted up, establishing the first feminist bookstores, shelters for battered women, rape crisis centers, and abortion counseling centers. In 1971 Gloria Steinem and others published *Ms.*, the first national feminist magazine. The first 300,000 copies were sold out in eight days.

Meanwhile, radical new ideas began to fill the air and a host of new words and phrases entered the language, such as "consciousness raising," "bra burning," "sexism," "male chauvinist pig."

The Growth of Feminist Ideology

In the years following the publication of *The Feminine Mystique*, feminists developed a large body of literature analyzing the economic, psychological, and social roots of female subordination. It was not until 1970, however, that the more radical feminist writings reached the broader reading public in the form of the publication of Shulamith Firestone's *The Dialectic of Sex*, Germaine Greer's *The Female Eunuch,* and Kate Millett's *Sexual Politics.* These books argued that gender distinctions structure virtually every aspect of individual lives, not only in such areas as law and employment, but also in personal relationships, language, literature, religion, and an individual's self-perceptions. Even more controversially, these works attributed female oppression to men and an ideology of male supremacy. "Women have very little idea how much men hate them," declared Greer. As examples of misogyny these authors cited pornography, grotesque portrayals of women in literature, sexual harassment, wife abuse, and rape.

Since 1970 feminist theory has exploded in many different directions. Today, there are more than 30 national feminist news and opinion magazines along with an additional 20 academic journals dealing with women's issues. Historians, feminist literary and film critics, and physical and social scientists have begun to take insights derived from feminism and ask new questions about women's historical experience, the sex and status differences between women and men, gender role socialization, economic and legal discrimination, and the depiction of women in literature.

The Supreme Court and Sex Discrimination

Despite its conservative image, the Supreme Court under chief justices Warren Burger and William Rehnquist has been active in the area of sex discrimination and women's rights. The Burger Court issued its first important discrimination decision in 1971. In its landmark decision, *Griggs* v. *Duke Power Company*, the Court established the principle that regardless of an employer's intentions, any employment practice is illegal if it has a "disparate" impact on women or minorities and "if it cannot be shown to be related to job performance."

In 1975 the Burger Court reversed the Warren Court by striking down a Louisiana statute calling for all-male juries. In subsequent decisions, the high court ruled against a Utah law setting different ages at which men and women became adults, and overturned an Alabama law setting minimum height and weight requirements for prison guards, standards that disqualified almost all women.

The Court's most controversial decision involving women's rights was delivered in 1973 in the case of *Roe* v. *Wade.* A single, pregnant Texas waitress, assigned the pseudonym Jane Roe in order to protect her privacy, brought suit against Dallas district attorney Henry Wade, to prevent him from enforcing a nineteenth-century Texas statute prohibiting abortion. The Court ruled on the woman's behalf and struck down the Texas law and all similar laws in other states. In its ruling, the Court declared that the decision to have an abortion is a private matter of concern only to a woman and her physician, and that only in the last three months of pregnancy could the government limit the right to abortion.

Many Americans—including many Catholic lay and clerical organizations—bitterly opposed the Supreme Court's *Roe* v. *Wade* decision and banded

Right-to-life groups, backed by Protestant fundamentalists, conservatives, and the Catholic church, scored a victory with the Hyde Amendment. Prochoice groups, however, helped organize privately funded agencies and clinics to allow women a choice.

together to form the "right-to-life" movement. The major legislative success of the right-to-life movement was adoption by Congress of the so-called Hyde Amendment, which permitted states to refuse to fund abortions for indigent women.

The Equal Rights Amendment

In March 1972 Congress passed an **Equal Rights Amendment (ERA)** to the United States Constitution, prohibiting gender discrimination. Before the year was over, 22 state legislatures ratified the ERA. Ratification by 38 states was required before the amendment would be added to the Constitution. Over the next five years, only 13 more states ratified the amendment—and 5 states rescinded their ratification. In 1978, Congress gave proponents of the amendment 39 more months to complete ratification, but no other state gave its approval.

The ERA had been defeated in part by organized labor, which feared that the amendment would eliminate state "protective legislation," that established minimum wages and maximum hours for women workers. Increasingly, however, resistance to the amendment came from conservative activists such as Phyllis Schlafly, a Radcliffe-educated mother of six from Alton, Illinois. Schlafly argued that the ERA was unnecessary because women were already protected by the Equal Pay Act of 1963 and the Civil Rights Act of 1964, which barred sex discrimination, and that the amendment would outlaw separate public restrooms for men and women and deny wives the right to financial support. She also raised the "women in combat" issue by suggesting that the passage of the ERA would mean that women would have to fight alongside men during war.

Impact of the Women's Liberation Movement

Since 1960 women have made impressive social gains. Gains in employment have been particularly noteworthy. During the 1970s, the number of working women climbed 42 percent and much of the increase was in what traditionally was considered "men's" work and professional work—lawyers, professors, doctors, and administrators.

Striking gains have been made in undergraduate and graduate education. Today, for the first time in American history, women constitute a majority of the nation's college students and nearly as many women as men receive master's degrees. In addition,

Table 30.4
Percentage of Females in Selected Occupations

Occupation	1972 (Percentage)	1980 (Percentage)	1989 (Percentage)
Professional/technical	39.3	44.3	45.2
Accountants	21.7	36.2	48.6
Computer specialists	16.8	25.7	35.7
Engineers	0.8	4.0	7.6
Lawyers and judges	3.8	12.8	22.3
Life/physical scientists	10.0	20.3	26.9
Physicians/dentists	9.3	12.9	16.5
Professors	28.0	33.9	38.7
Engineering/science technicians	9.1	17.8	19.2
Writers/artists/entertainers	31.7	39.3	46.0
Sales	41.6	45.3	49.3
Real estate agents/brokers	36.7	50.7	51.0
Clerks, retail	68.9	71.1	81.8
Clerical	75.6	80.1	80.0
Bookkeepers	97.9	90.5	91.7
Clerical supervisors	57.8	70.5	58.2
Office machine operators	71.4	72.6	62.6
Secretaries	99.1	99.1	98.3
Crafts workers	3.6	6.0	8.6
Blue-collar supervisors	6.9	10.8	n/a*
Machinists and jobsetters	0.6	4.0	n/a*
Tool and die makers	0.5	2.8	n/a*
Mechanics (except automobile)	1.0	2.6	3.1

Source: U.S. Bureau of the Census, *Statistical Abstract of the United States: 1982–83* (103d edition), *1991* (111th edition), Washington, D.C., 1982, 1991.

*n/a = not available.

the number of women students receiving degrees from professional schools—including dentistry, law, and medicine—has shot upward, from just 1425 in 1966 to over 20,000 by the early 1990s. Women comprise nearly a third of the students attending law school and medical school.

Women have also made impressive political gains. More than two dozen women serve in Congress, and over 80 serve as mayors of large cities. In 1981 Sandra Day O'Connor became the first woman to sit on the U.S. Supreme Court, and in 1984 a major political party nominated a woman, Geraldine Ferraro, for the vice presidency.

In spite of all that has been achieved, however, problems remain. Most women today continue to work in a relatively small number of traditional "women's" jobs, and a full-time female worker earns only 68 cents for every $1 paid to men. Even more troubling is the fact that large numbers of women live in poverty. Today, nearly half of all marriages end in divorce and many others end in legal separation and desertion—and the economic plight of these women is often grave. Although female-headed families constitute only 15 percent of the U.S. population, they account for over 50 percent of the poor population.

¡Viva La Raza!

On election day, 1963, hundreds of Mexican Americans in Crystal City, Texas, the "spinach capital of the world," gathered near a statue of Popeye the Sailor to do something that most had never done before: vote. Although Mexican Americans outnumbered Anglos two to one, Anglos controlled all five

Table 30.5: Ratio of Divorces to Marriages, 1890–1987	
1890	1–17
1900	1–12
1910	1–11
1920	1–7
1930	1–5
1940	1–6
1950	1–4.3
1960	1–3.8
1970	1–3.5
1980	1–2
1987	1–2.1

seats on the Crystal City council. For three years, organizers struggled to register Mexican-American voters. When the election was over, Mexican Americans had won control of the city council. "We have done the impossible," declared Albert Fuentes, who led the voter-registration campaign. "If we can do it in Crystal City, we can do it all over Texas. We can awaken the sleeping giant."

As the 1960s began, Mexican Americans shared problems of poverty and discrimination with other minority groups. The median income of a Mexican-American family was just 62 percent of the median income of the general population, and over a third of Mexican-American families lived on less than $3000 a year. Unemployment was twice the rate among non-Hispanic whites, and four-fifths of employed Mexican Americans were concentrated in semi-skilled and unskilled jobs, a third in agriculture.

Educational attainment lagged behind other groups (Mexican Americans averaged less than nine years of schooling as recently as 1970), and Mexican-American pupils were concentrated in predominantly Mexican-American schools, less well staffed and supplied than non–Mexican-American schools, with few Hispanic or Spanish-speaking teachers. Gerrymandered election districts and restrictive voting legislation resulted in the political underrepresentation of Mexican Americans. In addition, they were underrepresented or excluded from juries by requirements that jurors be able to speak and understand English.

During the 1960s, a new Mexican-American militancy arose. In 1962 César Chávez began to organize California farmworkers, and three years later, in Delano, California, he led his first strike. At the same time that Chávez led the struggle for higher wages, enforcement of state labor laws, and recognition of the farmworker union, Reies Lopez Tijerina fought to restore the legal rights of heirs to Spanish and Mexican land grants that had been guaranteed under the treaty ending the Mexican War.

In Denver, Rodolfo ("Corky") Gonzales formed the Crusade for Justice in 1965 to protest school discrimination, provide legal, medical, and financial services and jobs for Chicanos; and foster the Mexican-American cultural heritage. La Raza Unida political parties arose in a number of small towns with large Mexican-American populations. On college campuses across the Southwest, Mexican Americans formed political organizations.

In 1968 Congress responded to the demand among Mexican Americans for equal educational opportunity by enacting legislation encouraging school districts to adopt bilingual education programs to instruct non–English speakers in both English and their native language. In a more recent action, Congress moved in 1986 to legalize the status of many immigrants, including many Mexicans, who entered the United States illegally. The Immigration Reform and Control Act of 1986 provided permanent legal residency to undocumented workers who had lived in the United States since before 1982, and prohibits employment of illegal aliens.

Since 1960 Mexican Americans have made important political gains. During the 1960s four Mexican Americans—Senator Joseph Montoya of New Mexico and representatives Eligio de la Garza and Henry B. Gonzales of Texas and Edward R. Roybal of California—were elected to Congress. In 1974 two

During his 1996 campaign for election to the U.S. Senate from Texas, candidate Victor Morales toured the state in his white pickup truck. He attracted many Hispanic voters but failed in his bid to unseat his opponent, Senator Phil Gramm.

Chicanos were elected governors—Jerry Apodaca in New Mexico and Raul Castro in Arizona—becoming the first Mexican-American governors since early in this century. In 1981 Henry Cisneros of San Antonio, Texas, became the first Mexican-American mayor of a large city. Today, 20 million Mexican Americans continue to struggle to expand their political influence, improve their economic condition, and preserve their distinctive culture.

The Native-American Power Movement

In November 1969, 200 Native Americans seized the abandoned federal penitentiary on Alcatraz Island in San Francisco Bay. For 19 months Indian activists occupied the island in order to draw attention to conditions on the nation's Indian reservations. Alcatraz, the Native Americans said, symbolized conditions on reservations: "It has no running water; it has inadequate sanitation facilities; there is no industry, and so unemployment is very great; there are no health care facilities; the soil is rocky and unproductive."

On Thanksgiving Day, 1970, 350 years after the Pilgrims' arrival, Wampanoag Indians, who had taken part at the first Thanksgiving, held a National Day of Mourning at Plymouth, Massachusetts. A tribal representative declared, "We forfeited our country. Our lands have fallen into the hands of the aggressor. We have allowed the white man to keep us on our knees." Meanwhile, another group of Native Americans established a settlement at Mount Rushmore, to demonstrate Indian claims to the Black Hills.

During the late 1960s and early 1970s, a new spirit of political militancy arose among the first Americans, just as it had among African Americans, women, and Mexican Americans. No other group, however, faced problems more severe than Native Americans. Throughout the 1960s, Native Americans were the nation's poorest minority group, worse off than any other group according to virtually every socioeconomic measure. In 1970 the Indian unemployment rate was ten times the national average, and 40 percent of the Native American population lived below the poverty line. In that year, Native-American life expectancy was just 44 years, a third less than that of the average American. Half a million Indian families lived in unsanitary dilapidated dwellings, many in shanties, huts, or even abandoned automobiles.

During World War II Native Americans began to revolt against such conditions. In 1944 Native Americans formed the National Congress of American Indians (NCAI), the first major intertribal association. Among the group's primary concerns were protection of Native-American land rights and improved educational opportunities for Native Americans. When Congress voted in 1953 to allow states to assert legal jurisdiction over Native-American reservations without tribal consent, and the federal government sought to transfer federal responsibilities for a dozen tribes to the states (a policy known as "termination") and to relocate Native Americans into urban areas, the NCAI led opposition to these measures.

By the late 1950s a new spirit of Native-American nationalism had arisen. In 1961 a militant new Native-American organization appeared, the National Indian Youth Council, which began to use the phrase "Red Power" and sponsored demonstrations, marches, and "fish-ins" to protest state efforts to abolish Native-American fishing rights guaranteed by federal treaties. Native Americans in the San Francisco Bay area in 1964 established the Indian Historical Society to present history from the Indian point of view, while the Native American Rights Fund brought legal suits against states that had taken Indian land and abolished Indian hunting, fishing, and water rights in violation of federal treaties. Many Indian nations also took legal action to prevent strip mining or spraying of pesticides on Native-American lands.

The best known of all Indian Power groups was AIM, the American Indian Movement, formed by a

In 1972 members of the American Indian Movement (AIM) occupied the Bureau of Indian Affairs—the federal government bureau charged with managing Indian reservations in the United States—building in Washington, D.C., to draw attention to the plight of Native Americans and to protest government policies toward them.

THE American Mosaic

César Chávez and La Causa

IN early April 1962, a 35-year-old community organizer named César Estrada Chávez set out to single-handedly organize impoverished migrant farm laborers in the California grape fields. He, his wife, and their eight children packed their belongings into a dilapidated 9-year-old station wagon, and moved to Delano, California, a town of 12,000 that was the center of the nation's table-grape industry. Over the next two years, Chávez spent his entire lifetime savings of $1200 creating a small social service organization for Delano's field laborers; it offered immigration counseling, citizenship classes, funeral benefits, credit to buy cars and homes, assistance with voter registration, and a cooperative to buy tires and gasoline. As the emblem of his new organization, the National Farm Workers Association, Chávez chose a black Aztec eagle inside a white circle on a red background.

Chávez's sympathy for the plight of migrant farmworkers came naturally. He was born in Yuma, Arizona, in 1927, one of five children of Mexican immigrants. When he was 10 years old, his parents lost their small farm; he, his brothers and sisters, and his parents hoed beets, picked grapes, and harvested peaches and figs in Arizona and California. There were times when the family had to sleep in its car or camp under bridges. When young César was able to attend school (he attended more than 30 schools as a child), he was often shunted into special classrooms set aside for Mexican-American children.

In 1944, when he was 17, Chávez joined the navy, and served for two years on a destroyer escort in the Pacific. After World War II ended, he married and spent two and a half years as a sharecropper raising strawberries. That was followed by work in apricot and prune orchards and in a lumber camp. Then in 1952 his life took a fateful turn. He joined the Community Service Organization (CSO), which wanted to educate and organize the poor so that they could solve their own social and economic problems. After founding CSO chapters in Madera, Bakersfield, and Hanford, California, Chávez became the organization's general director in 1958. Four years later, he broke with the organization when it rejected his proposal to establish a farmworkers union.

Most labor leaders considered Chávez's goal of creating the first successful union of farmworkers in U.S. history an impossible dream. Not only did farm laborers suffer from high rates of illiteracy and poverty (average family earnings were just $2000 in 1965), they also experienced persistently high rates of unemployment (traditionally around 19 percent) and were divided into a variety of ethnic groups (Mexican, Arab, Filipino, and Puerto Rican). Making unionization even more difficult were the facts that farmworkers rarely remained in one locality for very long, and they were easily replaced by inexpensive Mexican day laborers, known as *braceros*, who were trucked into California and the Southwest at harvest time.

Moreover, farmworkers were specifically excluded from the protection of the National Labor Relations Act of 1935. Unlike other American workers, farmworkers were not guaranteed the right to organize, had no guarantee of a minimum wage, and had no federally guaranteed standards of work in the fields. State laws requiring toilets, rest periods, and drinking water in the fields were largely ignored.

In September 1965, Chávez was drawn into his first important labor controversy. The Filipino grape pickers went on strike. "All right, Chávez," said one of the Filipino grape pickers' leaders, "are you going to stand beside us, or are you going to scab against us?" Despite his fear that the National Farm Workers Association was not sufficiently well organized to support a strike (it had less than $100 in its strike fund), he assured the Filipino workers that members of his association would not go into the field as strikebreakers. *¡Huelga!*—the Spanish word for strike—became the grape pickers' battle cry.

Within weeks, the labor strike began to attract national attention. Unions, church groups, and civil rights organizations offered financial support for *La Causa*, as the farm workers' movement became known. In March 1966, Chávez led a 250-mile Easter march from Delano to Sacramento to dramatize the plight of migrant farm laborers. That same year, Chávez's National Farm Workers Association merged with an AFL-CIO affiliate to form the United Farm Workers Organizing Committee.

A staunch apostle of nonviolence, Chávez was deeply troubled by violent incidents that marred the strike. Some growers raced tractors along the roadside, covering the strikers with dirt and dust. Others drove spraying machines along the edges of their fields, spraying insecticide and fertilizer on the picketers. Local police officers arrested a minister for reading Jack London's definition of a scab ("a two-legged animal with a corkscrew soul, a water-logged brain, and a combination backbone made of jelly

and glue"). Some strikers, in turn, intimidated strikebreakers by pelting them with marbles fired from slingshots and by setting fire to packing crates. One striker tried to drive a car into a group of growers.

In an effort to quell the escalating violence and to atone for the militancy of some union members, Chávez began to fast on February 14, 1968. For five days he kept the fast a secret. Then, in an hour-long speech to striking workers, he explained that continued violence would destroy everything the union stood for. He said that the "truest act of courage, the strongest act of manliness, is to sacrifice ourselves for others in a totally nonviolent struggle for justice." For 21 days he fasted; he lost 35 pounds and his doctor began to fear for his health. He finally agreed to take a small amount of bouillon and grapefruit juice and medication. On March 11, he ended his fast by taking communion and breaking bread with Senator Robert F. Kennedy.

The strike dragged on for three years. To heighten public awareness of the farmworkers' cause, Chávez in 1968 initiated a boycott of table grapes. It was the boycott that pressured many of the growers into settling the strike. An estimated 17 million American consumers went without grapes in support of the farmworkers' bargaining position. By mid-1970, two-thirds of California grapes were grown under contract with Chávez's union.

In the years following its 1970 victory, Chávez's union has been beset by problems from within and without. Union membership dwindled from a high of more than 60,000 in 1972 to a low of 5000 in 1974. (It has since climbed back to around 30,000). Meanwhile, public concern for the plight of migrant farmworkers declined.

Chávez died in 1993, at age 66. To commemorate his legacy, 25,000 people marched for more than two and a half hours to the spot where he had founded the United Farm Workers Union. As a result of Chávez's efforts, the most backbreaking tool used by farmworkers, the short hoe, was eliminated, and the use of many dangerous pesticides in the grape fields was prohibited. His efforts also brought about a 70 percent increase in real wages from 1964 to 1980, and establishment of health-care benefits, disability insurance, pension plans, and standardized grievance procedures for farmworkers. He helped secure passage of the nation's first agricultural labor relations act in California in 1975, which prohibited growers from firing striking workers or engaging in bad-faith bargaining. Thanks to his efforts, migrant farm laborers won a right held by all other American workers: the right to bargain collectively.

group of Chippewas in Minneapolis in 1966 to protest alleged police brutality. In the fall of 1972, AIM seized the offices of the Bureau of Indian Affairs and occupied them for a week in order to dramatize their grievances. In the spring of 1973, 200 heavily armed Native Americans took over the town of Wounded Knee, South Dakota, site of an 1890 massacre of 300 Sioux by the U.S. army cavalry. They occupied the town for 71 days.

Militant protests paid off. The 1972 Indian Education Act gave Indian parents greater control over their children's schools. The 1976 Indian Health Care Act sought to address deficiencies in health care, while the 1978 Indian Child Welfare Act gave tribes control over custody decisions involving Native-American children. A series of landmark Supreme Court decisions aided the cause of Native-American sovereignty and national self-government. The 1959 *Williams* v. *Lee* case upheld the authority of Native-American courts to make decisions involving non–Native Americans. The 1968 case of *Menominee Tribe* v. *United States* declared that states could not invalidate fishing and hunting rights Native Americans had acquired through treaty agreements.

Beginning in the 1970s, a number of nations initiated lawsuits to recover land illegally seized by whites. In 1980, the federal government agreed to pay $81.5 million to the Passamaquoddy and Penobscot of Maine, and $105 million to the Sioux in South Dakota. Court decisions also permitted tribal authorities to sell cigarettes, run gambling casinos, and levy taxes.

Native Americans are no longer a vanishing group of Americans. The 1990 census recorded a Native-American population of over 2 million, five times the number recorded in 1950. About half of these people live on reservations. The largest Native-American populations are located in Alaska, Arizona, California, New Mexico, and Oklahoma. As the Native-American population has grown in size, individual Indians have claimed many accomplishments, including receipt of the Pulitzer Prize for fiction by N. Scott Momaday, a Kiowa.

Although Native Americans continue to face severe problems of employment, income, and education, they have decisively demonstrated that they will not abandon their national identity and culture or be treated as dependent wards of the federal government.

Gay and Lesbian Liberation

On June 27, 1969, New York City police staged an early morning raid on the Stonewall Inn, a Greenwich Village bar catering primarily to transvestites, gay men, and lesbians. Raids on gay or cross-dressers' bars were common at the time. State law threatened bars with the loss of their liquor licenses if they tolerated same-sex dancing or employed or served men who wore women's clothing. Instead of acquiescing passively in the raid, the bar's patrons fought back, battling the police with bricks, bottles, and shards of broken glass. Three days of civil disobedience followed.

This incident ushered in a new era for gays and lesbians in the United States: an era of pride, openness, and activism. It led many gays and lesbians to "come out of the closet" and publicly assert their sexual identity and to organize politically. In Stonewall's wake, activist organizations like the Gay Liberation Front transformed sexual orientation into a political issue, attacking customs and laws that defined homosexuality as a sin, a crime, or a mental illness.

Hostility toward homosexuality had deep roots in American society. State sodomy laws criminalized homosexual acts. Federal immigration laws excluded homosexual aliens. The 1873 Comstock Act permitted postal authorities to exclude homosexual publications from the mail, while Hollywood's "Production Code," adopted in 1934, prohibited the depiction of gay characters or open discussion of homosexuality in film. The American Psychiatric Association's diagnostic manual defined homosexuality as a psychopathology. During the McCarthy era, the charge that homosexuals were "moral perverts" and security risks led the government to adopt rules explicitly excluding them from federal jobs or military service.

Although the emergence of the gay and lesbian liberation movement caught the general public by

Following the Stonewall Inn raid in 1969, many gays became more open in declaring and taking pride in their sexual identity. On the anniversary of the raid, some 10,000 marchers paraded down New York City's Sixth Avenue.

surprise, it did not emerge overnight. During the 1950s, a handful of advocacy groups, including the Mattachine Society and the Daughters of Bilitis, arose, opposing laws that prohibited and punished homosexuality. By the late 1960s, gay and lesbian subcultures and communities had grown in many of the nation's cities, complete with bars, cabarets, magazines, and restaurants.

At the same time, challenges to earlier legal and medical opinion about homosexuality appeared. Alfred Kinsey's studies of sexual behavior, published in 1948 and 1953, suggested that homosexual and lesbian behavior was far more prevalent than most Americans previously suspected. Kinsey estimated about 10 percent of men and 5 percent of women were sexually attracted primarily to members of their own sex. In 1961, Illinois became the first state to repeal its sodomy statutes. The next year the Supreme Court ruled that a magazine featuring photographs of male nudes was not obscene and therefore not subject to censorship. In 1973, the American Psychiatric Association removed homosexuality from its list of psychopathologies.

In recent years, homosexuality has become one of the most highly charged issues in American politics. In 1986 the Supreme Court upheld state sodomy laws, ruling that private acts of homosexuality were not protected by the Constitution. Gay advocacy groups responded to the decision by lobbying for passage of state and city civil rights acts that would ban discrimination on the basis of sexual orientation in employment and housing. As a result of the gay rights movement, two states—New York and Vermont—and several municipalities extended health and dental insurance to the gay and lesbian domestic partners of public employees. A number of municipalities and states, including Colorado, responded to these initiatives by passing referenda prohibiting government from extending special rights to homosexuals. But state courts found these to be unconstitutional infringements on the right of gay and lesbian citizens to petition government. In 1993, a major controversy erupted after President Bill Clinton proposed allowing gays and lesbians to serve openly in the military. The policy that eventually emerged—nicknamed "don't ask, don't tell"—satisfied few, and federal courts refused to permit the expulsion of gays from the military.

The Earth First

In 1962, Rachel Carson, a marine biologist, published a book that would do more to awaken environmental consciousness than any other single work. Entitled *Silent Spring*, it described how DDT and other chemical pesticides contaminated nature's food chain, killing large numbers of birds and fish and causing human illnesses.

The largest single-day demonstration of the activist 1960s era was the Earth Day celebration of April 22, 1970.

Modern environmentalism began at the end of the nineteenth century. In 1872, Congress created the first national park, Yellowstone. In 1891, the Forest Reserve Act gave the president the power to set up national forests. The next year saw the founding of the Sierra Club, the nation's first organization committed to protecting wilderness areas.

During the Progressive era, conflicting visions of the environment struggled for dominance. While some men, like Gifford Pinchot, the head of the U.S. Forest Service under Theodore Roosevelt, were primarily interested in using scarce natural resources more rationally and efficiently, others, like the naturalist John Muir, who was the Sierra Club's first president, were eager to preserve wilderness and wildlife for their own sake and prevent industrial development from despoiling nature's beauty.

Franklin Roosevelt's New Deal initiated a number of important conservation projects. The Civilian Conservation Corps put three million young men to work restoring national parks and forests. The Tennessee Valley Authority restored the region's forests by planting trees and controlling flooding, and provided cheap electricity by building dams. The Soil Conservation Service combatted the poor farming and ranching practices that contributed to the loss of topsoil during the Dust Bowl of the early 1930s.

It was during the 1960s, however, that environmentalism became a mass movement. A series of environmental horror stories broadened the environmentalist constituency from naturalists to include a majority of Americans. Cleveland's Cuyahoga River caught fire; toxic residues were discovered in mothers' breast milk; acid rain destroyed lakes and streams.

The establishment of new organizations, like the Environmental Defense Fund founded in 1967, and the heightened interest in "organic farming" and "natural foods"—foods produced without using synthetic chemicals—testified to the growing public interest in environmental protection. The National Environmental Policy Act, passed in 1969, required preparation of environmental impact statements for all federally funded highways, dams, pipelines, and power plants. But it was the celebration of the first "Earth Day" that underscored public concern for the environment. On April 22, 1970, 20 million Americans gathered in parks, planted trees, and staged demonstrations to observe Earth Day.

In Earth Day's wake, Congress combined 15 federal pollution programs to create the Environmental Protection Agency to set and enforce pollution standards; passed the Clean Air and Clean Water Acts; and enacted the Endangered Species Act in 1973, protecting threatened species of wildlife. Since these initial measures were adopted, environmental concern has surged and ebbed. During the mid-1970s, when the United States experienced severe oil shortages and economic productivity dipped, fewer Americans were willing to sacrifice economic growth or a high standard of living for environmental protection. But whenever news reports of environmental degradation appeared, public concern quickly resurfaced. In 1978 reports that dangerous chemicals had been buried beneath Love Canal in New York led Congress to create the "Superfund" to finance the clean-up of the nation's most dangerous toxic waste sites. Publicity over the dangers of "ozone depletion" led the United States and most other nations to negotiate a 1989 treaty cutting production of chlorofluorocarbons that destroy the atmosphere's protective ozone shield.

The report card on the nation's environmental record offers a mixed picture. Contamination levels of DDT, lead, and cancer-causing polychlorinated biphenyls have declined sharply. By 1995, environmental regulations had reduced sulfur dioxide emissions by 53 percent; carbon monoxide by 57 percent; smoke and soot by 59 percent; and smog by 39 percent; and had made America's water supply the cleanest in the industrial world. Strict federal rules curbed automobile and industrial emissions, while increasing automobile mileage and the efficiency of appliances. As a result, while the American economy grew by 50 percent between 1970 and 1995, energy usage increased by only 10 percent.

Yet in spite of the regulation of power-plant smokestacks, aquatic life in 4000 lakes remains threatened by acid rain, and while automobile tailpipe emissions have been sharply curtailed, half the population lives in counties that violate federal clean air standards. Despite efforts to clean the nation's rivers and lakes, many freshwater fish contain dangerous levels of toxic chemicals. And as some older environmental hazards have been addressed, new concerns have arisen, such as global warming—the greenhouse effect caused by the buildup of carbon dioxide and other gases in the stratosphere—and the depletion of the earth's protective ozone shield.

Public opinion polls indicate that Americans overwhelmingly support environmental protection and over three-quarters consider themselves environmentalists. But whether a fundamental change has taken place in America's relationship to nature remains uncertain. Despite limited efforts at recycling, America remains a "throwaway" society that produces twice as much garbage as Europe. With just 2 percent of the world's population, the United States uses 24 percent of the world's energy—twice as much as Japan and Western Europe. And the United States remains a growth-oriented society that continues to absorb millions of acres of cropland each year for highways, tract housing, and office buildings. Each year the federal government continues to add 35 to 50 species to the list of endangered species.

Conclusion

In the early 1960s, college students, impatient with the slow pace of legal change, staged sit-ins, freedom rides, and protest marches to challenge legal segregation in the South. Passionately committed to a philosophy of nonviolent direct action, these students suffered beatings and went to jail to achieve integration. Their efforts led the federal government to pass the Civil Rights Act of 1964, prohibiting discrimination in public facilities and employment, and the Twenty-fourth Amendment to the Constitution and the Voting Rights Act in 1965, guaranteeing voting rights.

Despite significant legal gains and the far-reaching effort of Lyndon Johnson's Great Society programs, many African Americans felt a growing sense of frustration and anger. The violence perpetrated by white racists and a growing white backlash against civil rights led black nationalists to downplay the goal of integration and instead emphasize black power and black pride. Frustration was particularly evident in urban ghettoes, where a disproportionate

Chronology of Key Events

1960 Four freshmen at North Carolina Agricultural and Technical College in Greensboro, North Carolina, stage the first sit-in to protest segregation; Student Nonviolent Coordinating Committee (SNCC) is founded

1961 Congress of Racial Equality (CORE) stages freedom rides to expose segregation in transportation; *Mapp* v. *Ohio* holds that evidence obtained by unreasonable searches must be excluded at trial

1962 James Meredith enrolls at the University of Mississippi; Students for a Democratic Society (SDS) issue Port Huron Statement; César Chávez begins to organize California farm workers

1963 George C. Wallace is inaugurated Alabama governor; Martin Luther King, Jr., leads demonstrations against segregation in Birmingham, Alabama; racial violence in the South leaves 10 people dead, 35 black homes and churches firebombed; Betty Friedan publishes *The Feminine Mystique*, helping launch a new feminist movement; Equal Pay Act, first federal law to prohibit sex discrimination, requires equal pay for identical work; *Gideon* v. *Wainwright* holds that indigent defendants have a right to a court-appointed attorney; March on Washington, D.C., for civil rights and jobs; John F. Kennedy is assassinated; Lyndon Johnson becomes thirty-sixth president

1964 President Johnson announces War on Poverty; Manpower Development and Training Act and Economic Opportunity Act establish the Job Corps and Neighborhood Youth Corps; in *Escobedo* v. *Illinois,* Supreme Court rules that suspects being interrogated by police have a right to legal counsel; Civil Rights Act prohibits discrimination in employment and public facilities; Twenty-fourth Amendment prohibits poll taxes in federal elections

1965 Malcolm X is assassinated; Martin Luther King, Jr., leads demonstrations in Selma, Alabama, to bring issue of voting rights to national attention; Voting Rights Act prohibits literacy tests and sends federal examiners to seven southern states to register black voters; riot in Watts, predominantly black section of Los Angeles, results in 34 deaths; Medicare extends medical insurance to older Americans; Executive Order 11246 requires government contractors to prepare affirmative action plans; Ralph Nader publishes *Unsafe at Any Speed*

1966 SNCC and CORE embrace black nationalism; Black Panther party is organized; National Organization for Women (NOW) is formed; Congress passes Model Cities Act to attack urban blight

1967 Riots take place in 127 cities

1968 Medicaid expanded to cover the medical expenses of the poor; assassination of Martin Luther King, Jr., in Memphis, Tennessee, is followed by riots in 168 cities

1969 Three days of civil disobedience follow a police raid on the Stonewall Inn in New York City, a gay and lesbian bar

1970 Twenty million Americans celebrate the first Earth Day; Congress creates the Environmental Protection Agency and passes the Clean Air and Clean Water Acts

1971 In *Swann* v. *Charlotte-Mecklenburg Board of Education,* U.S. Supreme Court upholds school busing as a tool of racial integration

1973 *Roe* v. *Wade* decision legalizes abortion; the American Psychiatric Association removes homosexuality from its list of psychopathologies; Congress enacts the Endangered Species Act

1986 Immigration Reform and Control Act provides permanent legal residency to undocumented workers who have lived in United States since 1982

1993 Gays and lesbians are permitted to serve in the military

number of African Americans faced problems of poverty, unemployment, and de facto segregation that were not addressed by civil rights legislation.

The example of the civil rights movement inspired other groups to press for equal opportunity. The women's movement fought for passage of antidiscrimination laws, equal educational and employment opportunities, and a transformation of traditional views about women's place in society. Mexican Americans battled for bilingual education programs in schools, unionization of farm workers, improved job opportunities, and increased political power. Native Americans pressed for control over their lands and resources, the preservation of native cultures, and tribal self-government. Gays and lesbians organized to end legal discrimination based on sexual orientation.

SUGGESTIONS FOR FURTHER READING

Rodolfo Acuña, *Occupied America*, 3rd ed. (1988). Discusses the Mexican-American struggle for equality.

Taylor Branch, *Parting the Waters: America in the King Years* (1988). Recounts the history of the Civil Rights movement.

William H. Chafe, *Unfinished Journey: America Since World War II*, 3d ed. (1995). Provides a comprehensive overview of the movements for gender and racial equality.

John D'Emilio, *Sexual Politics, Sexual Communities: The Making of a Homosexual Minority in the United States, 1940–1970* (1983). Traces the roots of the struggle for gay and lesbian liberation.

John Dittmer, *Local People: The Struggle for Civil Rights in Mississippi* (1994). Examines the Civil Rights movement in a specific state.

David G. Gutierrez, *Walls and Mirrors: Mexican Americans, Mexican Immigrants, and the Politics of Ethnicity* (1995). Analyzes the quest of Mexican Americans for equal rights.

Donald L. Parman, *Indians and the American West in the Twentieth Century* (1994). Examines the Native-American struggle to preserve tribal self-government and reassert control over resources.

Philip Shabecoff, *A Fierce Green Fire: The American Environmental Movement* (1993). Chronicles the growth of the American environmental movement.

Overviews And Surveys

David Burner, *Making Peace with the 60s* (1996); Robert Buzzanco, *Vietnam and the Transformation of American Life* (1999); William Chafe, *The Unfinished Journey* (1998); David Chalmers, *And the Crooked Places Made Straight: The Struggle for Social Change in the 1960s* (1996); David Farber, ed., *The Sixties: From Memory to History* (1994); Richard N. Goodwin, *Remembering America: A Voice from the Sixties* (1988); Godfrey Hodgson, *America in Our Time* (1976); Stephen Macedo, ed., *Reassessing the Sixties* (1997); Allen Matusow, *The Unraveling of America: A History of Liberalism in the 1960s* (1984); James S. Olson, *Historical Dictionary of the 1960s* (1998); William O'Neill, *Coming Apart: An Informal History of America in the 1960s* (1971); James Patterson, *Grand Expectations: Postwar America, 1945–1974* (1996); David Steigerwald, *The Sixties and the End of Modern America* (1995).

The Struggle for Racial Justice

Sally Belfrage, *Freedom Summer* (1965); Michael Belknap, *Federal Law and Southern Order: Racial Violence and Constitutional Conflict in the Post-Brown South* (1987); Derrick Bell, *And We Are Not Saved: The Elusive Quest for Racial Justice* (1987); Irving Bernstein, *Guns or Butter: The Presidency of Lyndon Johnson* (1996); Jack Bloom, *Class, Race, and the Civil Rights Movement* (1987); Taylor Branch, *Pillar of Fire: America in the King Years* (1998); Carl Brauer, *John F. Kennedy and the Second Reconstruction* (1977); Clayborne Carson, *In Struggle: SNCC and the Black Awakening of the 1960s* (1981); Sean Dennis Cashman, *African Americans and the Quest for Civil Rights* (1991); William H. Chafe, *Civilities and Civil Rights* (1980); David Chappell, *Inside Agitators: White Southerners in the Civil Rights Movement* (1994); Vicki L. Crawford et al., eds., *Women in the Civil Rights Movement* (1990); Chandler Davidson and Bernard Grofman, *Quiet Revolution: The Impact of the Voting Rights Act in the South* (1994); John Dittmer, *Local People: The Struggle for Civil Rights in Mississippi* (1994); Gary A. Donaldson, *The Second Reconstruction* (1999); Alan Draper, *Conflict of Interests: Organized Labor and the Civil Rights Movement in the South, 1954–1968* (1994); Michael Eric Dyson, *Making Malcolm: The Myth and Meaning of Malcolm X* (1995); Adam Fairclough, *Martin Luther King, Jr.* (1990); Ronald P. Formisano, *Boston Against Busing: Race, Class, and Ethnicity in the 1960s and 1970s* (1991); David Garrow, *Bearing the Cross: Martin Luther King, Jr. and the Southern Christian Leadership Conference* (1986), and *The FBI and Martin Luther King* (1981); David R. Goldfield, *Black, White, and Southern: Race Relations and Southern Culture* (1990); Hugh Davis Graham, *The Civil Rights Era: The Origins and Development of National Policy* (1990); Hugh Davis Graham, ed., *Civil Rights in the United States* (1994); Jack Greenberg, *Crusaders in the Courts: How a Dedicated Band of Lawyers Fought for the Civil Rights Revolution* (1994); Vincent Harding, *There is a River: The Black Struggle for Freedom in America* (1981); John Higham, ed., *Civil Rights and Social Wrongs: Black-White Relations Since World War II* (1997); Gerald Horne, *Fire This Time: The Watts Uprising and the 1960s* (1995); Morton J. Horowitz, *The Warren Court and the Pursuit of Justice* (1999); Walter A. Jackson, *Gunnar Myrdal and America's Conscience: Social Engineering and Racial Liberalism* (1990); Ben Keppel, *The Work of Democracy: Ralph Bunche, Kenneth B. Clark, Lorraine Hansberry, and the Cultural Politics of Race* (1995); Richard Kluger, *Simple Justice: The History of Brown v. Board of Education and Black America's Struggle for Equality* (1975); Steven Lawson, *Black Ballots: Voting Rights in the South, 1944–1969* (1976), and

Running for Freedom: Civil Rights and Black Politics (1991); Nicholas Lemann, *The Promised Land: The Great Black Migration and How It Changed America* (1991); Robert D. Loevy, ed., *The Civil Rights Act of 1964* (1997); Doug McAdam, *Freedom Summer* (1988); August Meier and Elliot Rudwick, *CORE: A Study in the Civil Rights Movement, 1942–1968* (1973); Robert J. Norrell, *Reaping the Whirlwind: The Civil Rights Movement in Tuskegee* (1998); Stephen Oates, *Let the Trumpet Sound: The Life and Times of Martin Luther King, Jr.* (1982); Frank R. Parker, *Black Votes Count: Political Empowerment in Mississippi* (1990); Thomas R. Peake, *Keeping the Dream Alive: A History of the Southern Christian Leadership Conference* (1987); James R. Ralph, Jr., *Northern Protest: Martin Luther King, Jr., Chicago, and the Civil Rights Movement* (1993); Armstead L. Robinson and Patricia Sullivan, eds., *New Directions in Civil Rights Studies* (1991); Belinda Robnett, *How Long? How Long? African-American Women in the Struggle for Civil Rights* (1997); John A. Salmond, *"My Mind Set on Freedom": A History of the Civil Rights Movement* (1997); Bernard Schwartz, *Inside the Warren Court* (1983); Harvard Sitkoff, *The Struggle for Black Equality* (1981); Mark V. Tushnet, *Making Civil Rights Law: Thurgood Marshall and the Supreme Court, 1936–1961* (1994); Melvin I. Urofsky, *A Conflict of Rights: The Supreme Court and Affirmative Action* (1991), and *The Continuity of Change: The Supreme Court and Individual Liberties, 1953–1986* (1990); William L. Van Deburg, *New Day in Babylon: The Black Power Movement and American Culture* (1992); Nancy J. Weiss, *Whitney M. Young, Jr., and the Struggle for Civil Rights* (1989); John White, *Black Leadership in America*, 2d ed. (1990); Eugene Wolfenstein, *The Victims of Democracy: Malcolm X and the Black Revolution* (1980); C. Vann Woodward, *Strange Career of Jim Crow*, 3d ed. (1974).

The Youth Revolt

Terry H. Anderson, *The Movement and the Sixties* (1995), and *The Sixties* (1999); Paul Buhle, *History and the New Left* (1990); William H. Chafe, *Never Stop Running: Allard Lowenstein and the Struggle to Save American Liberalism* (1993); Morris Dickstein, *Gates of Eden: American Culture in the Sixties* (1977); Donald A. Downs, *Cornell '69* (1999); Todd Gitlin, *The Sixties: Years of Hope, Days of Rage* (1993); Maurice Isserman, *. . . If I Had a Hammer: The Death of the Old Left and the Birth of the New Left* (1987); W. J. Rorabaugh, *Berkeley at War: The 1960s* (1989); Doug Rossinow, *The Politics of Authenticity: Liberalism, Christianity, and the New Left in America* (1998); Theodore Roszak, *The Making of a Counter Culture* (1969); Stanley Rothman and S. Robert Lichter, *Roots of Radicalism* (1982); Kirkpatrick Sale, *SDS* (1973); Melvin Small and William D. Hoover, eds., *Give Peace a Chance: Exploring the Vietnam Antiwar Movement* (1993); Jon Wiener, *Come Together: John Lennon in His Time* (1984).

Liberation Movements

Mary Jo Bane, *Here to Stay: American Families in the Twentieth Century* (1978); Mario Barrera, *Race and Class in the Southwest* (1979); Judith Barwick, *In Transition: How Feminism, Sexual Liberation, and the Search for Self-Fulfillment Have Altered America* (1979); Mary Frances Berry, *Why ERA Failed* (1986); Albert Camarillo, *Hispanics in a Changing Society* (1979); William H. Chafe, *Women and Equality* (1977); Andrew J. Cherlin, ed., *The Changing American Family and Public Policy* (1988); Margaret Cruikshank, *The Gay and Lesbian Liberation Movement* (1992); Sara Evans, *Personal Politics: The Roots of Women's Liberation in the Civil Rights Movement and the New Left* (1979); Amy Erdman Farrell, *Yours in Sisterhood: Ms. Magazine and the Promise of Popular Feminism* (1998); Victor R. Fuchs, *How We Live* (1983); Mario T. García, *Mexican Americans: Leadership, Ideology and Identity* (1989); David J. Garrow, *Liberty and Sexuality: The Right to Privacy and the Making of Roe v. Wade* (1994); Juan Gómez-Quiñones, *Chicano Politics* (1990), and *Mexican American Labor* (1994); Manuel G. Gonzales, *Mexicanos* (1999); Hazel W. Hertzberg, *The Search for an American Identity* (1971); Bill Ong Hing, *Making and Remaking Asian America Through Immigration Policy* (1993); Judith Hole and Ellen Levine, *Rebirth of Feminism* (1971); Peter Iverson, *The Navajo Nation* (1981); Virginia Sánchez Korrol, *From Colonia to Community* (1983); Sar A. Levitan et al., *What's Happening to the American Family? Tensions, Hopes, Realities* (1988); Matt S. Meier and Feliciano Ribera, ed., *Mexican Americans/American Mexicans* (1993); Neil Miller, *Out of the Past: Gay and Lesbian History* (1995); Steven Mintz and Susan Kellogg, *Domestic Revolutions: A Social History of American Family Life* (1988); Joan Moore and Harry Pachon, *Hispanics in the United States* (1985); Roger Nichols, *The American Indian: Past and Present*, 3d ed. (1985); David Popenoe, *Disturbing the Nest: Family Change and Decline in Modern Societies* (1988); Roslind Rosenberg, *Divided Lives: American Women in the Twentieth Century* (1992); Leila Rupp and Verta Taylor, *Survival in the Doldrums: The American Women's Rights Movement, 1945 to the 1960s* (1987); Kirkpatrick Sale, *The Green Revolution: The American Environmental Movement* (1993); George Sanchez, *Becoming Mexican American* (1993); Peter Skerry, *Mexican Americans: The Ambivalent Minority* (1993); William Wei, *The Asian American Movement* (1993).

Biographies

Jervis Anderson, *Bayard Rustin* (1997); John A. Andrew III, *Lyndon Johnson and the Great Society* (1998); Carl Brauer, *John F. Kennedy and the Second Reconstruction* (1977); Eric R. Burner, *And Gently He Shall Lead Them: Robert Parris Moses and Civil Rights in Mississippi* (1994); William H. Chafe, *Never Stop Running: Allard Lowenstein and the Struggle to Save American Liberalism* (1993); Robert Dallek, *Flawed Giant: Lyndon Johnson and His Times, 1961–1973* (1998); Adam Fairclough, *Martin Luther King, Jr.* (1990); David Garrow, *Bearing the Cross: Martin Luther King., Jr. and the Southern Christian Leadership Conference* (1986), and *The FBI and Martin Luther King* (1981); Richard Griswold del Castillo and Richard A. Garcia, *César Chávez* (1995); Judith Hennessee, *Betty Friedan* (1999); Daniel Horowitz, *Betty Friedan & the Making of the Feminine Mystique* (1998); Walter A. Jackson, *Gunnar Myrdal and America's Conscience: Social Engineering and Racial Liberalism* (1990); Kay Mills, *This Little Light of*

Mine: The Life of Fannie Lou Hamer (1993); Stephen Oates, Let the Trumpet Sound: The Life and Times of Martin Luther King, Jr. (1982); Nancy J. Weiss, Whitney M. Young, Jr., and the Struggle for Civil Rights (1989); Jon Wiener, Come Together: John Lennon In in His Time (1984); Juan Williams, Thurgood Marshall (1998); Eugene Wolfenstein, The Victims of Democracy: Malcolm X and the Black Revolution (1980).

INTERNET RESOURCES

Martin Luther King, Jr. Papers Project
http://www.stanford.edu/group/King/
This site at Stanford University has links and selected digital documents by and concerning Martin Luther King, Jr.

NAACP Online
http://www.naacp.org/about/history.html
The National Association for the Advancement of Colored People official Web site explains its mission and includes a primary document explaining the start of the NAACP.

Beyond the Playing Field: Jackie Robinson, Civil Rights Advocate
http://www.nara.gov/education/teaching/robinson/robmain.html
This National Archives and Records Administration teaching materials site contains images, essays, and documents about Robinson and Civil Rights.

National Civil Rights Museum
http://www.mecca.org/~crights/nc2.html
This site allows you to take a virtual tour of the museum with its interpretive exhibits.

American Identities
http://xroads.virginia.edu/~YP/ethnic.html
Find Resources for studying America's multiple ethnic identities on this site.

People with a History: An Online Guide to Lesbian, Gay, Bisexual and Trans History
http://pwh.base.org/
This site looks at its subject across all of history but has sections on America.

The Digger Archives
http://www.diggers.org/
This site provides information about The San Francisco Diggers who became one of the legendary groups in the Haight-Ashbury area during the years 1966 to 1968.

Free Speech Movement: Student Protest—U.C. Berkeley, 1964–1965
http://www.lib.berkeley.edu/BANC/FSM/
The Bancroft Library at U.C. Berkeley houses this exhibit with oral histories, a chronology, and documents.

Robert Kennedy
http://homepages.tcp.co.uk/~dlewis/
View photos and read interviews about the assassination of Robert Kennedy in 1968.

The Assassination of Martin Luther King
http://www.parascope.com/mx/luther1.htm
Six chapters about various aspects of the King assassination fill this Web site.

Voices of the Civil Rights Era
http://www.webcorp.com/civilrights/index.htm
Webcorp provides audio clips from prominent figures of the Civil Rights era, including Martin Luther King, Jr. and Malcolm X.

Martin Luther King, Jr.
http://www.seattletimes.com/mlk/
This site from the *Seattle Times* has several articles about King and the Civil Rights Movement.

The Sixties Project
http://lists.village.virginia.edu/sixties/
This University of Virginia site has extensive exhibits, documents, and personal narratives from the 1960s.

Civil Rights Oral History Bibliography
http://www.dept.usm.edu/~mcrohb/
This University of Southern Mississippi site includes complete transcripts of the selected oral resources.

National Civil Rights Museum in Memphis, Tennessee
http://www.midsouth.rr.com/civilrights/
This site houses images with annotation from the museum.

United States **v.** *Cecil Price et al.* **(The "Mississippi Burning" Trial) 1967**
http://www.law.umkc.edu/faculty/projects/ftrials/price&bowers/price&bowers.htm
This site contains images, chronology, and court and official documents maintained by Dr. Doug Linder at University of Missouri–Kansas City Law School.

KEY TERMS

Sit-In   (p. 878)

Freedom Riders   (p. 879)

James Meredith   (p. 880)

Civil Rights Act of 1964   (p. 883)

Twenty-Fourth Amendment   (p. 884)

Voting Rights Act of 1965   (p. 884)

Malcolm X   (p. 885)

Black Power   (p. 886)

The Great Society   (p. 888)

Students for a Democratic Society (SDS)   (p. 890)

Betty Friedan   (p. 892)

Equal Rights Amendment (ERA)   (p. 896)

REVIEW QUESTIONS

1. To what extent was the civil rights movement a grassroots movement shaped by ordinary Americans?
2. How did the political message of major civil rights leaders change by the late 1960s?

3. Was the New Left an important force in American politics? How did their ideas disseminate into the popular culture?
4. What does it mean to be a feminist? How did the feminist movement evolve in the 1960s and 1970s?
5. Why did so many social protest movements—including Mexican-American activism, Native American Power, gay liberation, and environmentalism—all begin to flourish in the late 1960s and early 1970s?

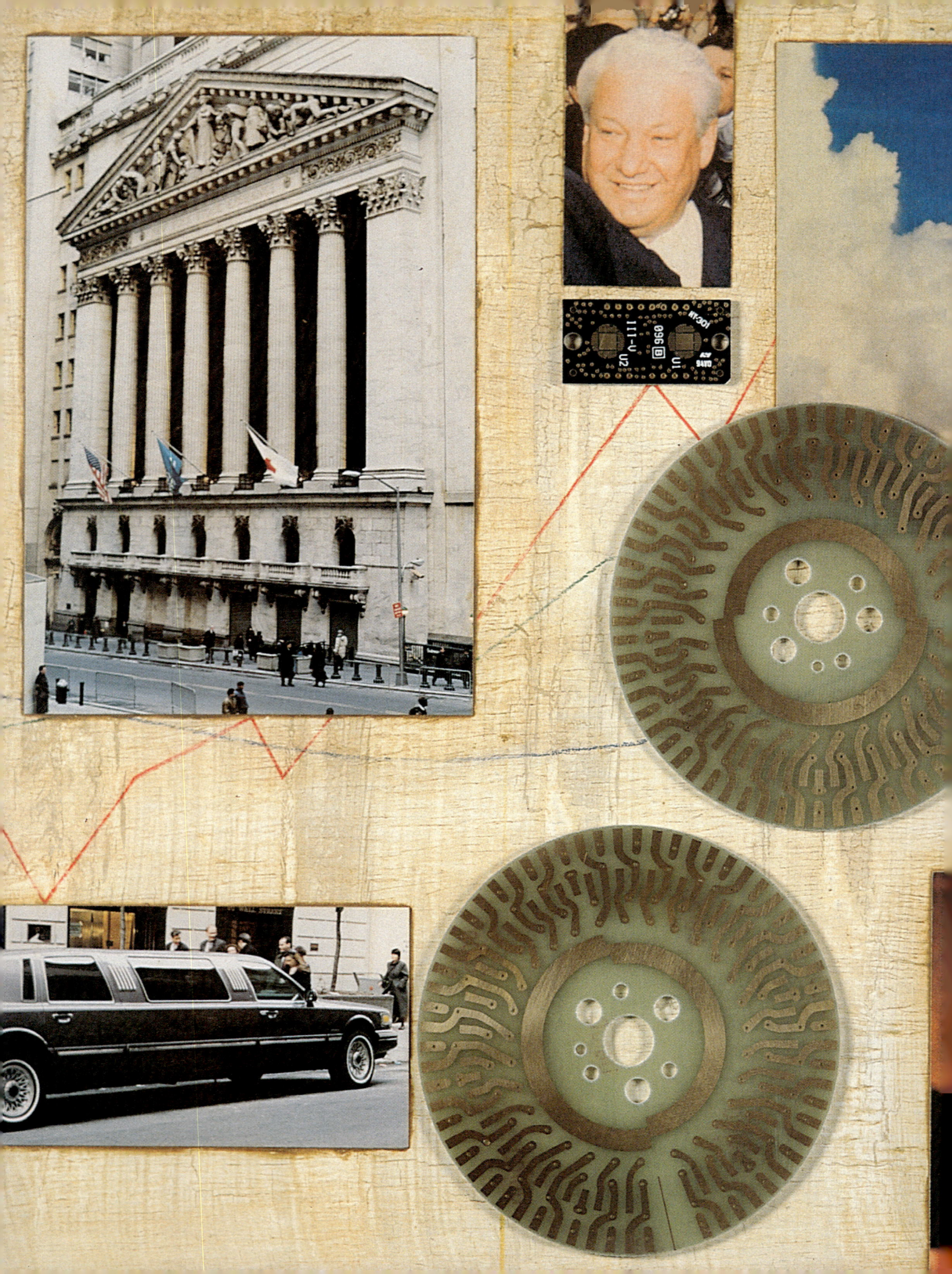

31

AMERICA IN OUR TIME

CRISIS OF POLITICAL LEADERSHIP
  Restraining the Imperial Presidency
  New-Style Presidents

WRENCHING ECONOMIC TRANSFORMATIONS
  The Age of Inflation
  Oil Embargo
  Foreign Competition and Deindustrialization
  Whipping Stagflation

A NEW AMERICAN ROLE IN THE WORLD
  Détente
  Foreign Policy Triumphs
  No Island of Stability

THE REAGAN REVOLUTION
  Reaganomics
  The Reagan Doctrine
  A Remarkable Ideological Turnaround
  The Reagan Revolution in Perspective

THE BUSH PRESIDENCY
  A Kinder, Gentler Nation
  Economic and Foreign Policy
  Collapse of Communism
  The Persian Gulf War
  Enter Bill Clinton

THE CLINTON PRESIDENCY
  "It's the Economy, Stupid"
  Foreign Policy

"Dirty tricks"

Shortly after 1 A.M. on the morning of June 17, 1972, a security guard at the Washington, D.C., Watergate office complex, spotted a strip of masking tape covering the lock of a basement door. He removed it. A short while later, he found the door taped open again. He called the police, who found two more taped locks, and a jammed door leading into the offices of the Democratic National Committee. Inside they discovered five men with cameras and electronic eavesdropping equipment.

At first, the **Watergate break-in** seemed like a minor incident. The identities of the burglars, however, suggested something more serious. One, James McCord, was chief security coordinator and electronics expert of the Committee for the Reelection of the President (CREEP). Others had links to the CIA.

Over the course of the next year, it became clear that the break-in was only one of a series of secret operations coordinated by the White House. Financed by illegal campaign contributions, these operations posed a threat to America's constitutional system of government and eventually forced Richard Nixon to resign the presidency.

The Watergate break-in had its roots in Richard Nixon's obsession with secrecy and political intelligence. To stop leaks of information to the press, in 1971 the Nixon White House assembled a team of "plumbers," consisting of former CIA operatives. This private police force, paid for in part by illegal campaign contributions, engaged in a wide range of criminal acts, including phone tapping and burglary, against those on its "enemies list."

In 1972 when President Nixon was running for reelection, his campaign committee authorized another series of illegal activities. It hired Donald Segretti to stage "dirty tricks" against potential Democratic candidates, which included mailing letters that falsely accused one candidate of homosexuality and fathering an illegitimate child. It considered a plan to use prostitutes to blackmail Democrats at their national convention and to kidnap anti-Nixon radical leaders. The committee also authorized $250,000 for intelligence-gathering operations. Four times the committee sent burglars to break into Democratic headquarters.

Precisely what the campaign committee hoped to learn from these intelligence-gathering activities remains a mystery. It seems likely that it was seeking

The Watergate Scandal led to the downfall of President Richard Nixon. Here the Senate Watergate Committee questions Nixon aide H. R. Halderman.

information about the Democratic party's campaign strategies and any information the Democrats had about illegal campaign contributions to the Republican party.

On June 23—six days after the botched break-in—President Nixon ordered aides to block an FBI investigation into White House involvement in the break-in on grounds that an investigation would endanger national security. He also counseled his aides to lie, under oath if necessary: "I don't give a [expletive deleted] what happens," he told his former attorney general, John Mitchell, who was then his campaign manager, "I want you all to stonewall it, let them plead the Fifth Amendment, cover-up, or anything else."

The Watergate break-in did not hurt Nixon's reelection campaign, since between the activities of the burglars and the president were layers of deception that had to be carefully peeled away. *Washington Post* reporters Bob Woodward and Carl Bernstein, sensing that the break-in was only part of a larger scandal, slowly pieced together part of the story. Facing long jail terms, some of the burglars began to tell the truth, and the truth illuminated a path leading to the White House.

If Nixon had few political friends, he had legions of enemies. Over the years he had offended or attacked many Democrats—and a number of prominent Republicans. His detractors latched onto the Watergate issue with the tenacity of bulldogs.

The Senate appointed a special committee to investigate the Watergate scandal. Most of Nixon's top aides continued the cover-up. John Dean, the president's counsel, did not. Throughout the episode he had kept careful notes, and in a quiet precise voice he told the Senate Watergate Committee that the president was deeply involved in the cover-up. The matter was still not solved. All the committee had was Dean's word against the other White House aides.

On July 16, 1973, a former White House employee dropped a bombshell by testifying that Nixon had recorded all Oval Office conversations. Whatever Nixon and his aides had said about Watergate in the Oval Office, therefore, was faithfully recorded on tape.

Nixon tried to keep the tapes from the committee by invoking executive privilege, insisting that a president had a right to keep confidential any White House communication, whether or not it involved sensitive diplomatic or national security matters. When Archibald Cox, a special prosecutor investigating the Watergate affair, persisted in demanding the tapes, Nixon ordered his attorney general, Elliot Richardson, to fire him; Richardson refused and resigned; Richardson's assistant, William Ruckelshaus also resigned. Ruckelshaus's assistant, Robert Bork, finally fired Cox, but Congress forced Nixon to name a new special prosecutor, Houston attorney Leon Jaworski.

In the midst of the Watergate investigations, another scandal broke. Federal prosecutors accused Vice President Spiro Agnew of extorting payoffs from engineers and road building contractors while he was Maryland's governor and Baltimore County executive. In a plea bargain, Agnew pleaded no contest to a relatively minor charge—that he had falsified his income tax in 1967—in exchange for a $10,000 fine. Agnew resigned and Nixon appointed Gerald Ford to succeed Agnew as vice president.

The Watergate scandal gradually came to encompass not just the cover-up but a wide range of presidential wrongdoings, including political favors to business groups in exchange for campaign contributions; misuse of public funds; deceiving Congress and the public about the secret bombing of Cambodia in 1969 and 1970; authorization of illegal domestic political surveillance and espionage against dissidents, political opponents, and journalists; and attempts to use FBI investigations and income tax

Faced with the release of his secret tapes and impending impeachment proceedings, Richard Nixon resigned the office of president on August 9, 1974. Here he signals his farewell as he prepares to leave the White House for the last time. The Watergate scandal and Nixon's role in it undermined public trust in and respect for the presidency.

audits by the Internal Revenue Service to harass political enemies.

On July 24, 1974, the House Judiciary Committee recommended that the House of Representatives impeach Nixon for obstruction of justice, abuse of power, and refusal to relinquish the tapes. On August 5 Nixon obeyed the Supreme Court ruling to release the tapes, which confirmed Dean's detailed testimony. Nixon had indeed been involved in a cover-up. On August 9, in a tearful farewell Nixon became the first American president to resign from office. The following day, Gerald Ford became the new president. "Our long national nightmare," he said, "is over."

Crisis of Political Leadership

The Vietnam War and the Watergate scandal had a profound effect on the presidency. The office suffered a dramatic decline in public respect, and Congress became increasingly unwilling to defer to presidential leadership. Congress enacted a series of reforms that would make future Watergate-type abuses of presidential authority less likely. In the process Congress recaptured constitutional powers that had been ceded to an increasingly dominant executive branch.

Restraining the Imperial Presidency

Over the course of the twentieth century, the presidency gradually supplanted Congress as the center of federal power. Presidential powers increased, presidential staff grew in size, and the executive branch gradually acquired a dominant relationship over Congress.

Beginning with Theodore Roosevelt, the president, and not Congress, established the nation's legislative agenda. Increasingly, Congress ceded its budget-making authority to the president. Presidents even found a way to make agreements with foreign nations without congressional approval. After World War II, presidents substituted executive agreements for treaties requiring Senate approval. Even more important, presidents gained the power to wage undeclared war, despite the fact that Congress is the sole branch of government empowered by the Constitution to declare war.

No president went further than Richard Nixon in concentrating powers in the presidency. He refused to spend funds that Congress had appropriated; he claimed executive privilege against disclosure of information on administration decisions; he refused to allow key decision makers to be questioned before congressional committees; he reorganized the executive branch and broadened the authority of new cabinet positions without congressional approval. And during the Vietnam War, he ordered harbors mined and bombing raids launched without consulting Congress.

Watergate brought an end to the "imperial presidency" and the growth of presidential power. Over the president's veto, Congress enacted the **War Powers Act** (1973), which required future presidents to win specific authorization from Congress to engage U.S. forces in foreign combat for more than 90 days. Under the law, a president who orders troops into action abroad must report the reason for this action to Congress within 48 hours.

In the wake of Watergate, Congress enacted a series of laws designed to reform the political process. Disclosures during the Watergate investigations of money laundering led Congress to provide for public financing of presidential elections, public disclosure of sources of funding, limits on private campaign contributions and spending, and enforcement of campaign finance laws by an independent Federal Election Commission.

To make it easier to investigate crimes in the executive branch, Congress required the attorney general to appoint a special prosecutor to investigate accusations of illegal activities. To reassert its budget-making authority, Congress created a Congressional Budget Office and specifically forbade a president to impound funds without its approval. To open government to public scrutiny, Congress opened more committee deliberations and enacted the **Freedom of Information Act,** which allows the public and press to request declassification of government documents.

The post-Watergate reforms have not been as effective as reformers anticipated. The War Powers Act has never been invoked and while various administrations have attempted to comply with the spirit of the law, no president has accepted its constitutional validity.

Campaign financing reform did not curb the power of special interests to curry favor with politicians or the ability of the very rich to outspend opponents. The Supreme Court struck down laws that forbade candidates to give more than $50,000 to their own presidential campaign and, more importantly, barred any limitations on unauthorized "independent expenditures" by individuals on behalf of a candidate.

On the other hand, Congress had somewhat more success in reining in the FBI and CIA. During the 1970s, congressional investigators discovered that the Federal Bureau of Investigation and the Central Intelligence Agency had, in defiance of their charters and federal law, broken into the homes, tapped the phones, and opened the mail of American citizens; illegally infiltrated antiwar groups and black radical organizations; and accumulated dossiers on dissidents. Investigators also found that the CIA had been involved in assassination plots against foreign leaders, among them Castro, and had tested the effects of radiation, electric shock, and drugs (such as LSD) on unsuspecting citizens.

In the wake of these investigations, the government severely limited CIA operations in the United States and laid down strict guidelines for FBI activities. To tighten congressional control over the CIA, Congress established a joint committee to supervise CIA operations.

New-Style Presidents

In contrast to Nixon's abuses of presidential powers, the next two presidents, Gerald Ford and Jimmy Carter, cultivated reputations as modest, honest, forthright leaders. Both were men of decency and integrity, but neither established reputations as strong, dynamic leaders. Although many Americans admired their honesty and sincerity, neither succeeded in winning the confidence of the American people. Moreover, neither administration had a clear sense of direction. Both Ford and Carter seemed to waffle on major issues of public policy. As a result, both came to be regarded as unsure, vacillating presidents.

A 13-term congressman from Grand Rapids, Michigan, Gerald Ford dismissed the possibility of pardoning Richard Nixon for his Watergate misdeeds, then changed his mind. In the realm of economic policy, he began by urging tax increases but later called for a large tax cut. Similar indecision crippled his energy policy. At first, he tried to raise prices by imposing import fees on imported oil and ending domestic price controls; then he abandoned that position in the face of severe political pressure.

Carter, too, suffered from the charge that he modified his stances in the face of political pressure. A two-term Democratic governor of Georgia who defeated Ford in the 1976 presidential election, Carter came to office determined to cut military spending, calling for the abolition of nuclear weapons and the withdrawal of American troops from South Korea. By the end of his term, however, Carter spoke of the need for sustained growth in defense spending, upgrading nuclear forces in Europe, and developing a new strategic bomber.

Both Ford and Carter were described as "passionless presidents" who failed to project a clear vision of where they wanted to lead the country. But in their defense, both faced serious problems, ranging from dealing with soaring oil prices to confronting third-world terrorists.

WRENCHING ECONOMIC TRANSFORMATIONS

At one time, the car makers in Detroit produced automobiles that mirrored America's strength and power. They were big, heavy, powerful cars, with such expensive options as power windows, power brakes, and power steering. So what if they weren't energy-efficient. So what if they only traveled 10 to 13 miles on a gallon of gas. Until 1973, gas was cheap; just 37 cents a gallon that year.

By the late 1970s, the rising costs of Middle Eastern oil forced the American automotive industry to rethink its strategy. Emerging Arab nationalism and the solidarity of the Organization of Petroleum Exporting Countries (OPEC) drove up the price of a gallon of gasoline toward the dollar mark. American drivers started purchasing smaller, better engineered, fuel-efficient cars manufactured by Japanese and European automakers. By 1982, Japanese-made cars had captured 30 percent of the U.S. market.

Since 1973, the American economy has undergone a series of wrenching economic transformations. Economic growth slowed; productivity flagged; inflation rose; and major industries faltered in the face of foreign competition. Despite a massive influx of women into the workforce, family wages stagnated. A quarter century of rapid post–World War II economic growth ended.

The Age of Inflation

In 1967, the average price of a three-bedroom house was $17,000. A brand-new Cadillac convertible went for $6700 and a new Volkswagen for $1497. A Hershey chocolate bar sold for a nickel, a pound of sirloin for 89 cents. Two decades later, the prices of these products had quadrupled.

The upsurge in inflation started when Lyndon Johnson decided to fight the Vietnam War without raising taxes enough to pay for it. By 1968 the war was costing the United States $3 billion dollars a month, and the federal budget skyrocketed to $179 billion. With hundreds of thousands of Americans in the military service and even more working in defense-related industries, unemployment fell, wages rose, demand mushroomed, and government deficits increased. Inflation was further fueled by a series of crop failures and sharp rises in commodities, especially oil.

High inflation had many negative effects on the American economy. It wiped out many families' savings. It encouraged speculation in tangible assets—like art, antiques, precious metals, and real estate—rather than productive investment in new factories and technology. Above all, certain organized interest groups were able to keep up with inflation, while other less powerful groups, such as welfare recipients, saw the value of their benefits decline significantly.

Inflation reduced the purchasing power of most Americans. For over a decade, family wages remained flat. Yet inflation raised the prices of virtually all goods and services. Health care and housing, in particular, experienced price rises far above the inflation rate. The consequences were a sharp increase in the number of Americans unable to afford health insurance, and a dramatic increase in the cost of housing, which resulted in a sharp increase in homelessness.

Oil Embargo

Political unrest in the oil-rich Middle East contributed significantly to America's economic troubles. After suffering a humiliating defeat at the hands of Israel in the 1973 "Yom Kippur" war, Arab leaders unsheathed a new political weapon: oil. In order to pressure Israel out of territory conquered in the 1967 and 1973 wars, Arab nations cut oil production 25 percent and embargoed all oil exports to the United States. Leading the way was OPEC, which had been founded by Iran, Saudi Arabia, and Venezuela in 1960 to fight a reduction in prices by oil companies.

Because Arab nations controlled 60 percent of the proven oil reserves in the non-Communist world, they had the western nations over a barrel. Production cutbacks produced an immediate global shortage. The United States imported a third of its oil from Arab nations; western Europe imported 72 percent from the Middle East; Japan, 82 percent. Gas prices rose, long lines formed at gas pumps, some factories shortened the workweek, and some shopping centers restricted business hours.

The **oil crisis** brought to an end an era of cheap and ample energy. Americans had to learn to live with smaller cars and less heating and air-conditioning. But the crisis did have a positive side-effect. It increased public consciousness about the environment and stimulated awareness of the importance of conservation. But for millions of Americans the lessons were painful.

Foreign Competition and Deindustrialization

In 1947, the United States was truly the world's factory. Half of all the world's manufacturing took place in the United States. Americans made 57 percent of the world's steel and 80 percent of the world's cars. It was inevitable that other countries would eventually challenge the dominance that American manufacturers had enjoyed in the aftermath of World War II. During the early 1960s, foreign manufacturers produced 6 percent of the cars purchased by Americans. That figure climbed to 20 percent in the late 1970s.

The foreign penetration extended far beyond the market for compact cars. Foreign countries began to dominate the highly profitable, technologically advanced fields, such as consumer electronics, luxury automobiles, and machine tools. Americans discovered that technologies their country had pioneered—such as semiconductors, color televisions, and videocassette recorders—were now produced almost exclusively by foreign manufacturers. The decline in the American share of the market meant fewer jobs in the American automobile, steel, rubber, and electronics industries. In addition, American and even Japanese companies shifted low-skill production work to such places as Hong Kong, Indonesia, Singapore, South Korea, and Taiwan, where goods could be produced more cheaply because of lower wage scales.

Few economic developments aroused as much public concern during the 1970s as the loss of American jobs in basic industry. According to one estimate, 30 million jobs disappeared during the 1970s as the direct result of plant, store, and office shutdowns. Displaced workers saw their savings depleted, mortgages foreclosed, and health and pension benefits lost. Even when they found new jobs, they typically had to settle for wages substantially below what they had earned before. Plant shutdowns and closings had profound effects on entire communities, which lost their tax bases at the time that they needed to fund health and welfare services.

Whipping Stagflation

During the 1960s, the primary goal of economic policy was to encourage growth and keep unemployment low. Inflationary pressures were successfully tamed through "jawboning" industry leaders and unions to keep prices and wages stable. But by the early 1970s the economy started to suffer from **stagflation**—high unemployment and inflation coupled with stagnant economic growth. This presented economic policy-makers with a new and perplexing problem since unemployment and inflation do not usually coexist.

The problem with stagflation was the pain of its options. To attack inflation by reducing consumer purchasing power only made unemployment worse. The other choice was no better. Stimulating purchasing power and creating jobs also drove prices higher.

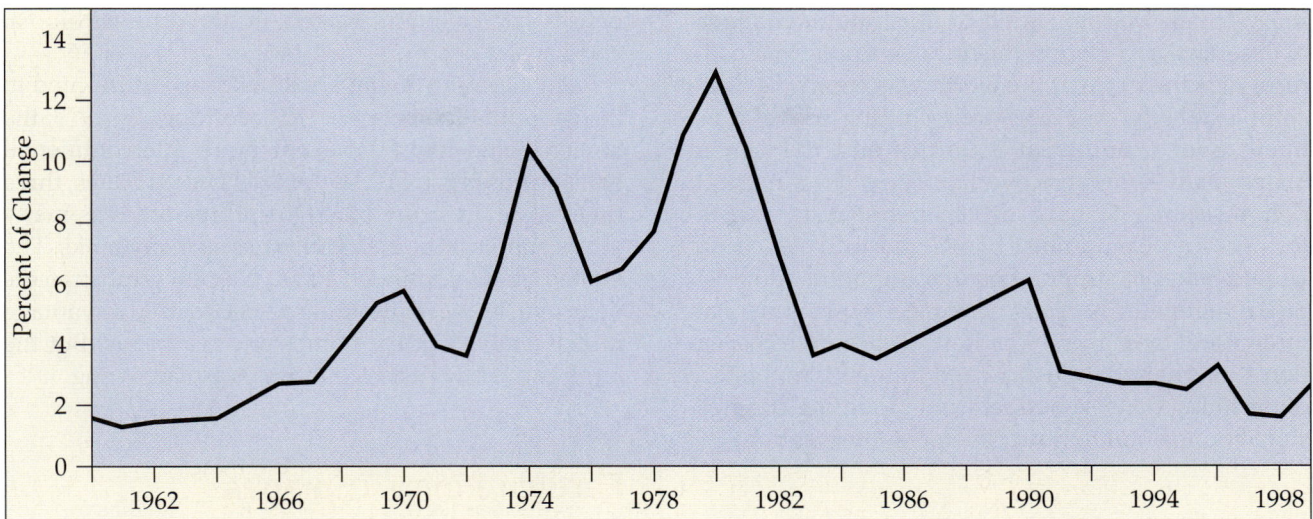

FIGURE 31.1
Consumer Price Index, 1960–1990

Not surprisingly, economic policy during the 1970s was a nightmare of confusion and contradiction.

By 1971, pressures produced by the Vietnam War and federal social spending pushed the inflation rate to 5 percent and unemployment to 6 percent. President Richard Nixon responded by increasing federal budget deficits and devaluing the dollar in an attempt to stimulate the economy and to make American goods more competitive overseas. Nixon also imposed a 90-day wage and price freeze, followed by a mandatory set of wage-price guidelines, and then by voluntary controls. Inflation stayed at about 4 percent during the freeze, but once controls were lifted, inflation resumed its upward climb.

In 1974 during the first oil embargo, inflation hit 12 percent. Gerald Ford, the new president, initially attacked the problem in a traditional Republican fashion, tightening the money supply by raising interest rates and limiting government spending. In the end, his economic policy proved to be no more than a series of ineffectual wage and price guidelines monitored by the federal government. In the subsequent recession, unemployment reached 9 percent.

When Jimmy Carter took office in January 1977, 7.4 percent of the workforce was unemployed. Carter responded with an ambitious spending program and called for the Federal Reserve (the Fed) to expand the money supply. Within two years, inflation had accelerated to 13.3 percent.

With inflation getting out of hand, the Federal Reserve Board announced in 1979 that it would fight inflation by restraining the growth of the money supply. Unemployment increased and interest rates moved to their highest levels in the nation's history. By November 1982, unemployment hit 10.8 percent, the highest since 1940. One out of every five American workers went some time without a job.

Along with high interest rates, the Carter administration adopted another weapon in the battle against stagflation: **deregulation**. Convinced that regulators too often protected the industries they were supposed to oversee, the Carter administration deregulated air and surface transportation and the savings and loan industry.

The effects of deregulation are hotly contested. Rural towns suffered cutbacks of bus, rail, and air service. Truckers and rail workers lost economic benefits of regulation. Travelers complained about rising airfares and congested airports. Cable TV viewers resented rising rates. Champions of deregulation argued that the policy increased competition, stimulated new investment, and forced inefficient firms either to become more efficient or shut down.

A NEW AMERICAN ROLE IN THE WORLD

In his inaugural address in 1961, John Kennedy stated that America would "pay any price, bear any burden, meet any hardship, support any friend or oppose any foe to assure the survival and the success of liberty." But by 1973, in the wake of the Vietnam War, American foreign-policy-makers regarded Kennedy's stirring pledge as unrealistic.

The Vietnam War offered a lesson about the limits of American power. It underscored the need to distinguish between vital national interests and peripheral interests, and to balance America's military commitments with its available resources. Above all, the Vietnam War appeared to illustrate the dangers of obsessive anti-Communism. Such a policy failed to recognize the fact that the world was becoming more complex, that power blocs were shifting, and that the interests of Communist countries and the United States could sometimes overlap. Too often, American policy seemed to have driven nationalists and reformers into Communist hands and to have led the United States to support corrupt, unpopular authoritarian regimes. The great challenge facing American foreign-policy-makers was how to preserve the nation's international prestige and influence in the face of declining defense budgets and mounting congressional opposition to direct overseas intervention.

Détente

As president, Richard Nixon radically redefined America's relationship with its two foremost adversaries, China and the Soviet Union. In a remarkable turnabout from his record of staunch anti-Communism, he opened relations with China and began strategic arms limitation talks with the Soviet Union. The goal of **détente** (the easing of tensions between nations) was to continue to resist and deter Soviet adventurism while striving for "more constructive relations" with the Communist world.

Nixon believed that it was necessary to curb the arms race, improve great power relationships, and learn to coexist with Communist regimes. The Nixon administration sought to use the Chinese and Soviet need for western trade and technology as a way to extract foreign policy concessions.

In 1972 Nixon took part in a summit meeting in Beijing, walked the Great Wall, and slowly expanded American trade with China (see Chapter 29 for further discussion of Nixon's foreign policy). Less dramatic, but no less important, was the beginning of a détente with the Soviet Union, culminating in a massive trade pact and strategic arms limitation talks. In a 1972 summit meeting in Moscow, the United States and Soviet Union vowed not to seek "unilateral advantages" against each other.

Recognizing that one of the legacies of Vietnam was a reluctance on the part of the American public to risk overseas interventions, Nixon also sought to build up regional powers that shared American strategic interests, most notably China, Iran, and Saudi Arabia.

By the late 1970s, an increasing number of Americans believed that Soviet hard-liners viewed détente as a mere tactic to lull the West into relaxing its vigilance. Soviet Communist party chief Leonid Brezhnev reinforced this view when he boasted of gains that his country had made at the United States' expense—in Vietnam, Angola, Cambodia, Ethiopia, and Laos.

An alarming Soviet arms build-up contributed to the sense that détente was not working. By 1975, the Soviet Union had 50 percent more intercontinental ballistic missiles (ICBMs) than the United States, three times as many army personnel, three times as many attack submarines, and four times as many tanks. The United States continued to have a powerful strategic deterrent, however, holding a 9000 to 3200 advantage in deliverable nuclear bombs and warheads. But the arms gap between the countries was narrowing.

Foreign Policy Triumphs

In the Middle East Jimmy Carter achieved a tremendous diplomatic success by negotiating peace between Egypt and Israel. Since the founding of Israel in 1948, Egypt's foreign policy had been built around destroying the Jewish state. In 1977, Anwar el-Sadat, the practical and farsighted leader of Egypt, decided to seek peace with Israel. It was an act of rare political courage, for Sadat risked alienating Egypt from the rest of the Arab world without a firm commitment for a peace treaty with Israel.

Jimmy Carter convinced Israel to return the Sinai to Egypt. In return, Egypt promised to recognize Israel, and as a result became a staunch American ally. For Carter it was a proud moment. Unfortunately, the **Camp David Accords** were denounced by the rest of the Arab Middle East, and in 1981 Sadat paid for his vision with his life when anti-Israeli Egyptian soldiers assassinated him.

In 1978 Carter also pushed the Panama Canal Treaty through the Senate, which provided for the return of the Canal Zone to Panama and improved the image of the United States in Latin America. One year later, he extended diplomatic recognition to the People's Republic of China. Carter's successes in the international arena, however, would soon be overshadowed by the greatest challenge of his presidency—the Iranian hostage crisis.

No Island of Stability

During Jimmy Carter's presidency, the United States began to show a growing regard for the human rights practices of its allies. Carter was convinced that American foreign policy should embody the country's basic moral beliefs. In 1977 Congress began to require reports on human rights conditions in countries receiving American aid.

Of the nations accused of practicing torture, one of the most frequently cited was Iran. Estimates of

Conflict in the Middle East and Europe

the number of political prisoners in Iran ranged from 25,000 to 100,000. It was widely believed that most of them had been tortured by SAVAK, the secret police. Tortures included electric shock, beatings, insertions of bottles in the rectum, hanging weights from the testicles, and rape. Writers, artists, and intellectuals were often targets of torture.

Since the end of World War II, Iran had been a valuable friend of the United States in the troubled Middle East. In 1953 the CIA had worked to ensure the power of the young Shah, Mohammad Reza Pahlavi. During the next 25 years, the Shah had often repaid the debt. He allowed the United States to establish electronic listening posts in northern Iran along the border of the Soviet Union, and during the 1973–1974 Arab oil embargo the Shah continued to sell oil to the United States. The Shah also bought arms from the United States, which helped ease the American balance-of-payments problem. Few world leaders were more loyal to the United States.

The Shah was popular among wealthy Iranians and Americans. In the slums of the southern section of Teheran and in the poverty-stricken villages of Iran, however, there was little respect, admiration, or love for his regime. Led by a fundamentalist Islamic clergy and emboldened by want, the masses of Iranians turned against the Shah and his westernization policy.

In the early fall of 1978 the revolutionary surge in Iran gained force. The Shah, who had once seemed so powerful and secure, was paralyzed by indecision, alternating between ruthless suppression and attempts to liberalize his regime. In Washington, Carter also vacillated, uncertain whether to stand firmly behind the Shah or to cut losses and prepare to deal with a new government in Iran.

In January 1979, the Shah fled to Egypt. Exiled religious leader Ayatollah Ruholla Khomeini returned to Iran, preaching the doctrine that the United States was the "Great Satan" behind the Shah. Relations between the United States and the new Iranian government were terrible, but Iranian officials warned that they would become infinitely worse if the Shah were granted asylum. Nevertheless, Carter permitted the Shah to come to the United States for treatment of lymphoma. The reaction in Iran was severe.

On November 4, 1979, Iranian supporters of Khomeini invaded the American embassy in Teheran and captured 66 Americans, 13 of whom were freed several weeks later. The rest were held

Jimmy Carter's greatest triumph as president came with the signing of the Camp David Accords between Egypt and Israel.

After 444 days the Iranian hostage crisis ended, but not before it had virtually paralyzed Carter's administration and destroyed his chances for reelection.

hostage for 444 days and were the objects of intense political interest and media coverage.

Carter was helpless. Because Iran was not a stable country in any recognizable sense, it was impossible to pressure. Iran's demands—the return of the Shah to Iran and admission of U.S. guilt in supporting the Shah—were unacceptable. Carter devoted far too much attention to the almost insoluble problem. The hostages stayed in the public spotlight in part because Carter kept them there.

Carter's foreign policy problems mounted in December 1979, when the Soviet Union sent tanks into Afghanistan. In response, the Carter administration imposed an embargo on grain and high-technology exports to the USSR and boycotted the 1980 Olympics in Moscow. The Soviet Union gradually withdrew its troops from Afghanistan a decade later.

As public disapproval of the president's handling of the Iran crisis increased, some Carter advisors advocated the use of force to free the hostages in Teheran. At first, Carter disagreed, but eventually he authorized a rescue attempt. It failed and his position became even worse. Negotiations finally brought the hostages' release, but in a final humiliation for Carter, the hostages were held until minutes after Ronald Reagan, Carter's successor, had taken the oath of office as president.

When Carter left office in January 1981 many Americans judged his presidency a failure. Instead of being remembered for the good he accomplished for the Middle East at Camp David, he was remembered for what he failed to accomplish. **The Iranian hostage crisis** had become emblematic of a perception that America's role in the world had declined.

THE REAGAN REVOLUTION

The traumatic events of the 1970s—Watergate, stagflation, the energy crisis, the defeat of South Vietnam, and the Iranian hostage crisis—produced a severe loss of confidence among the American people. Americans were deeply troubled by the relative decline of American strength in the world; the decline of the productivity and innovation in American industry; and the dramatic growth of lobbies and special-interest groups that seemed to have paralyzed the legislative process. Many worried that too much power had been stripped from the presidency, that political parties were so weakened and Congress so splintered that it was impossible to enact a coherent legislative program.

Republican Ronald Reagan capitalized on this frustration. In 1980 he won a landslide victory, carrying 43 states. A former movie actor and radio and television announcer, Reagan was catapulted into the national spotlight in 1964 when he gave an emotional television speech in support of Republican presidential nominee Barry Goldwater, denouncing big government, foreign aid, welfare, urban renewal, and high taxes. Two years later, Reagan successfully ran for governor of California, promising to cut state spending and crack down on student protesters.

In the 1980 presidential campaign, Reagan drew strong support from white Southerners, suburban

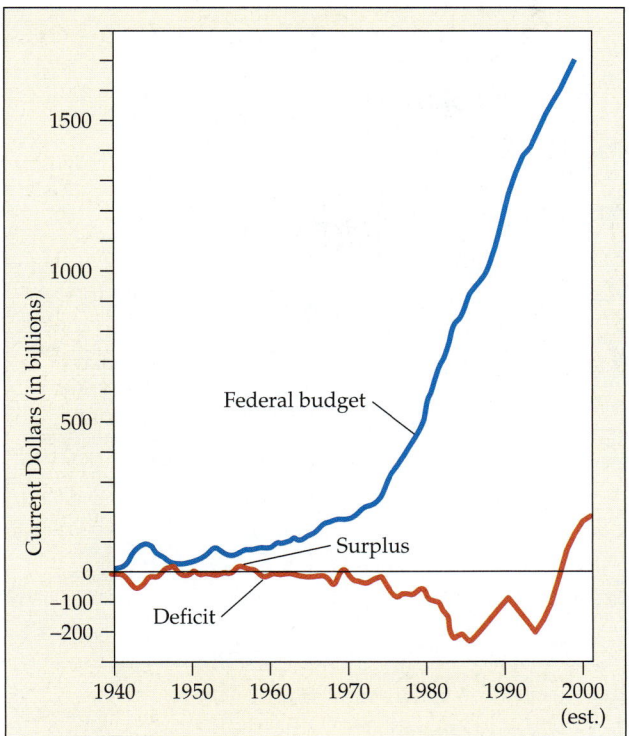

FIGURE 31.2
Budget Deficits, 1940–2000

Roman Catholics, evangelical Christians, and particularly the New Right, a confederation of disparate political and religious groups bound together by their concern over what they considered the erosion of values in America. In March 1981, when an assassin's bullet nearly killed Reagan, he captured the nation's imagination by responding to the shooting with remarkable courage. From his hospital bed, he sent a message to his wife Nancy, "Honey, I forgot to duck."

Reaganomics

When President Reagan took office he promised to rebuild the nation's defenses, cut inflation, restore economic growth, and trim the size of the federal government. He pledged to end exorbitant union contracts to make American goods competitive again, to cut taxes drastically to stimulate investment and purchasing power, and to decontrol business strangled by federal regulation in order to restore competition.

To strengthen the nation's defenses, the Reagan administration doubled the defense budget, to more than $330 billion in 1987. Reagan believed that a militarily strong United States would not have been humiliated by Iran and would have discouraged Soviet adventurism.

Reagan blamed the country's economic ills on declining capital investment and a tax structure biased against work and productive investment. To stimulate the economy, he persuaded Congress to slash tax rates. In August 1981, Reagan dealt a devastating blow to organized labor by dismissing 15,000 striking air traffic controllers.

Reagan expanded the Carter administration's efforts to decontrol and deregulate the economy. Congress deregulated the banking and natural gas industries and lifted ceilings on interest rates. Federal price controls on airfares were lifted as well. The Environmental Protection Agency relaxed its interpretation of the Clean Air Act; and the Department of the Interior opened up large areas of the federal domain, including offshore oil fields, to private development.

Reagan left office with the economy in the midst of its longest post–World War II expansion. The economy was growing faster, with less inflation, than any time since the mid-1960s. Adjusted for inflation, disposable personal income per person rose 20 percent after 1980. Inflation fell to less than 4 percent. Unemployment was down to around 5 percent. These figures compared favorably to January 1981, the month Reagan became president, when inflation was running at 13 percent a year and unemployment stood at 7.4 percent.

Reagan's critics, however, charged that Reagan had only created the illusion of prosperity. They denounced the massive federal budget deficit, which increased $1.5 trillion during the Reagan presidency, three times the debt accumulated by all 39 of Reagan's presidential predecessors. They decried the growing income gap between rich and poor, as well as the expensive consequences of reduced government regulation, such as cleaning up federal nuclear weapons facilities, and, especially, bailing out the nation's savings and loans industry.

The Reagan Doctrine

During the early years of the Reagan presidency, Cold War tensions between the Soviet Union and the United States intensified. Reagan entered office deeply suspicious of the Soviet Union. Reagan described the Soviet Union as "an evil empire" and called for a space-based missile defense system, derided by critics as "Star Wars."

In his 1985 state of the union address, President Reagan pledged his support for anti-Communist revolutions in what would become known as the

U.S. Involvement in Central America and the Caribbean

"Reagan Doctrine." In Afghanistan, the United States was already providing aid to anti-Soviet freedom fighters, ultimately helping to force Soviet troops to withdraw. It was in Nicaragua, however, that the Reagan doctrine received its most controversial application.

In 1979 Nicaraguans revolted against a corrupt Somoza regime, and a new junta took power, dominated by young Marxists known as Sandinistas. The Sandinistas insisted that they favored free elections, nonalignment, and a mixed economy, but once in power they postponed elections, forced opposition leaders into exile, and turned to the Soviet bloc for arms and advisers.

In his first months in office, President Reagan approved covert training of anti-Sandinista rebels (called "contras"). While the contras waged war on the Sandinistas from camps in Honduras, the CIA provided assistance, mining Nicaraguan harbors and issuing a manual offering ways of assassinating Sandinistas. In 1984 Congress ordered an end to all covert aid to the contras. The Reagan administration circumvented Congress by soliciting contributions for the contras from private individuals and from foreign governments seeking U.S. favor. The president also permitted the sale of arms to Iran, with profits diverted to the contras. Exposure of the Iran-contra affair in late 1986 provoked a major congressional investigation. The scandal seriously weakened the influence of the president. In national elections in 1990, the Nicaraguan opposition routed the Sandinistas, bringing an end to ten turbulent years of Sandinista rule.

A Remarkable Ideological Turnaround

In 1985, **Mikhail Gorbachev,** a 54-year-old agricultural specialist with little formal experience in foreign affairs, became leader of the Soviet Union. Within weeks, however, Gorbachev called for sweeping political liberalization—*glasnost*—and economic reform—*perestroika*. He allowed wider freedom of the press, assembly, travel, and religion. He persuaded the Communist party leadership to end its monopoly on power; created the Soviet Union's first working legislature; allowed the first nationwide competitive elections in 1989; and freed hundreds of political prisoners. In an effort to boost the sagging Soviet economy, he legalized small private business cooperatives, won parliamentary approval for the leasing of lands to individuals with the right of inheritance, and approved foreign investment within the Soviet Union.

In foreign affairs, Gorbachev completely reshaped world politics. He cut the Soviet defense

In order to stimulate the Soviet economy, Mikhail Gorbachev launched his program of *perestroika*, or economic restructuring, which welcomed foreign investment and encouraged joint ventures with foreign businesses. His policy of *glasnost*—or political liberalization—allowed the Soviet people greater political freedoms.

budget, withdrew Soviet troops from Afghanistan and eastern Europe, allowed a unified Germany to become a member of NATO, and agreed with the United States to destroy short-range and medium-range nuclear weapons. Most dramatically, Gorbachev actively promoted the democratization of former Soviet satellite nations in Eastern Europe. For his accomplishments in defusing Cold War tensions, he was awarded the 1990 Nobel Peace Prize.

The Reagan Revolution in Perspective

In the presidential election of 1984, Ronald Reagan and Vice President George Bush won in a landslide over Walter Mondale and Geraldine Ferraro, the first woman nominated for vice president on a major party ticket. Although Reagan's second term was plagued by the Iran-contra scandal, he left office after eight years more popular than he arrived. He could claim the distinction of being the first president to serve two full terms since Dwight Eisenhower.

Ronald Reagan could also point to an extraordinary string of accomplishments. He had dampened inflation, restored public confidence in government, and presided over the beginning of the end of the Cold War. He doubled the defense budget, named the first woman to the Supreme Court, launched a strong economic boom, and created a heightened sense of national unity. In addition, his supporters said that he restored vigor to the national economy and psyche, rebuilt America's military might, regained the nation's place as the world's preeminent power, restored American patriotism, and championed traditional family values.

On the other hand, his detractors criticized him for a reckless use of military power and for circumventing Congress in foreign affairs. They accused Reagan of fostering greed and intolerance, and they charged that his administration, in its zeal to cut waste from government, ripped the social safety net and skimped on the government's regulatory functions. The administration, they further charged, was insensitive on racial issues.

Reagan's detractors were particularly concerned about his economic legacy. During the Reagan years the national debt tripled, from $909 billion to almost $2.9 trillion (the interest alone amounted to 14 percent of the federal budget), soaking up savings, causing interest rates to rise, depressing local economies, and forcing the federal government to shift more and more responsibilities onto the states. Corporate and individual debt also soared. During the early 1990s, the American people consumed $1 trillion more goods and services than they produced. The United States also became the world's biggest debtor nation, as a result of a weak dollar, a low level of exports, and the need to borrow abroad to finance budget deficits.

THE BUSH PRESIDENCY

In the 1988 presidential campaign the Republican candidate, Vice President George Bush, was said to have the best resumé in Washington. Winning the Distinguished Service Cross during World War II, Bush had made a fortune in the Texas oil business, and then went to Washington where he served as a Congressman, ambassador to the United Nations, envoy to China, and director of the CIA. His Democratic opponent, Massachusetts governor Michael Dukakis, was a serious, hardworking son of Greek immigrants.

Mudslinging and personal invective are nothing new in American politics, but the 1988 campaign was unusually vacuous and cynical. Real differences between the candidates' positions—over health care, housing policy, foreign policy, and defense spending—were submerged in a battle over character, abortion, prison furloughs, school prayer, and patriotism. The campaign dramatized a development that had been reshaping American politics since the late 1960s: the growing power of media consultants and pollsters, who market candidates by emphasizing imagery and symbolism. At the end of a race that saw both candidates use negative campaigning, Bush was elected the forty-first president of the United States, with 56 percent of the popular vote.

A Kinder, Gentler Nation

In his inaugural address, Bush promised to be more of a "hands-on" administrator than his predecessor, and he committed his presidency to creating a "kinder, gentler" nation, more sensitive and caring to the poor and disadvantaged.

During his first years in office, President Bush and the Democratic-controlled Congress addressed many issues ignored during the Reagan years. For the first time in eight years, the federal government raised the minimum wage. For the first time in 13 years, Congress amended federal air pollution laws in order to reduce noxious emissions from smokestacks and tailpipes and reduce acid rain. For the first time since 1971, Congress considered child-care legislation and ultimately voted to provide subsidies to low-income families to defray the costs of child care. In other actions, Congress prohibited job discrimination against the disabled, required nutrition labeling on processed foods, and expanded immigration into the United States.

In two areas critics accused President Bush of reneging on his promise of a "kinder, gentler" nation. He vetoed a new civil rights bill bolstering protections for minorities and women against job discrimination, on the grounds that it would lead to quotas, and he also vetoed a bill that would have provided up to six months of unpaid family leave for workers with newly born or adopted children or emergencies. In November 1991, however, Bush signed a compromise Civil Rights Act, which made it easier for workers to win antidiscrimination lawsuits.

Economic and Foreign Policy

Many Americans believed that the end of the Cold War would bring a huge peace dividend, which could be used to reduce the federal budget deficit and fund domestic social programs. Soon after Bush took office, however, Americans learned that much of the peace dividend would have to be spent to clean up nuclear wastes produced at federal facilities and to bail out the nation's troubled savings and loan industry.

The roots of the savings and loan crisis were planted during the presidency of Jimmy Carter, when high inflation and high interest rates threatened to bankrupt savings institutions, which could not compete with other financial institutions permitted to pay high interest rates. A 1980 law lifted limits on the interest rates savings institutions could pay and allowed them to make a limited amount of investments in commercial real estate. In 1982 and 1983, Congress broadened the institution's capacity to make unsecured commercial loans and investments in commercial real estate.

The savings and loan industry's problems began in the mid-1980s, when falling oil prices led to a collapse of land values, especially in the Southwest, creating huge losses for savings institutions invested in real estate. By the end of the decade these institutions began to fail in large numbers. The mounting bills for the savings and loan bailout propelled President Bush in 1990 to violate his 1988 "no new taxes" campaign pledge.

The first important foreign policy act of the Bush administration was an invasion of Panama, which the Pentagon called **Operation JUST CAUSE**. The origins of the conflict stretched back to 1987 when a high Panamanian military official accused strongman General Manuel Antonio Noriega of committing fraud in the 1984 presidential election and of drug trafficking. Violent street demonstrations broke out in Panama. Angry Panamanians called for Noriega's overthrow. Noriega responded by declaring a state of emergency. The crisis escalated when two Florida grand juries indicted the general on charges that he protected and assisted the Colombian drug cartel.

U.S.-Panamanian relations deteriorated further when Noriega voided results of the 1989 presidential election and sent paramilitary forces into the streets of Panama City where they beat up opposition candidates. Conflict grew imminent when Noriega declared his country in a "state of war" against the United States. A day later Panamanian troops fired on four unarmed American military personnel at a roadblock, killing one. Bush dispatched a force of

United States troops patrol the streets of Panama City during the U.S. invasion of Panama in December 1989.

10,000 troops to safeguard the lives of Americans and protect the integrity of the Panama Canal treaties. It is estimated that between 300 and 800 Panamanian civilians and military personnel died during the invasion. There were 23 American casualties. In the end, however, Noriega was forced out of power and deported to the United States to stand trial for drug trafficking.

Collapse of Communism

For 40 years Communist party leaders in Eastern Europe had ruled confidently. Although each year their countries fell further behind the West, they remained secure in the knowledge that the Soviet Union, backed by the Red Army, would always send in the tanks when the forces for change became too great. But they had not bargained on a liberal Soviet leader like Mikhail Gorbachev.

As Gorbachev moved toward reform within the Soviet Union and détente with the West, he pushed the conservative regimes of Eastern Europe outside his protective umbrella. By the end of 1989 the Berlin

Lacking public and popular support, the attempted right-wing coup in the Soviet Union collapsed within days. Here, protesters cheer the soldiers who have withdrawn their tanks from the coup.

For nearly three decades the Berlin Wall was the most visible symbol of the Cold War and of the division between East and West. The most dramatic incident marking the end of the Cold War was the destruction of the Wall in November 1989.

Wall had been smashed and across Eastern Europe citizens took to the streets, overthrowing 40 years of Communist rule. Like a series of falling dominos, Communist parties in Poland, East Germany, Hungary, Czechoslovakia, and Bulgaria fell from power.

Gorbachev, who had wanted to reform communism, had not anticipated the swift swing toward democracy in Eastern Europe. Nor had he fully foreseen the impact that democracy in Eastern Europe would have on the Soviet Union. By 1990 leaders of several Soviet republics began to demand independence or greater autonomy within the Soviet Union.

In 1990, following the example of eastern Europe, the three Baltic states of Lithuania, Latvia, and Estonia announced their independence, and other Soviet republics demanded greater sovereignty. Nine of the 15 Soviet Republics agreed to sign a new union treaty, granting far greater freedom and autonomy to individual republics. But in August 1991, before the treaty could be signed, conservative communists tried to oust Gorbachev in a coup d'état. Boris Yeltsin, president of the Republic of Russia, and his supporters defeated the coup, which undermined support for the Communist party. Gorbachev fell from power. The Soviet Union ended its existence in December 1991, when Russia and most other republics formed the Commonwealth of Independent States.

In 1993, a new power struggle broke out, pitting Yeltsin against communists and nationalists in the Russian Parliament. In August, Yeltsin dissolved the Parliament, charging an "irreconcilable opposition" with blocking his reforms. Yeltsin ordered opposition legislators, holed up in the Parliament building,

THE American Mosaic

The End of Two Eras

THE dates on the obituary read 1922 to 1991. When the death was duly recorded in newspapers and magazines throughout the world, only a handful of bureaucrats mourned the corpse. That body—the Union of Soviet Socialist Republics (USSR)—was the light that failed. Born in the cold and ice of a late Russian December, the USSR promised equality and justice. Driven by the belief in communism, Vladimir Lenin, the leader of the Bolsheviks who came to power in Russia in 1917 and founded the USSR five years later, announced that Russia was only the first step. Eventually, he said, communism would free the entire world and introduce a new epoch of peace, prosperity, and happiness for all people. The epoch never arrived. It remained only in the minds of the true believers. Instead of liberating the world, Soviet leaders suppressed freedom inside the Soviet Union. As one journalist noted in his obituary of the Soviet Union, "There is no reason to mourn the death of a country that killed millions of its own citizens in the collectivization campaign, the purges and the famines that were used as an instrument of government policy."

Born in a brutal Russian winter, the USSR died in an equally severe winter. About the death there was a singular note of irony. The Soviet leader who had done the most to reform and humanize the country caused its death. Mikhail Gorbachev became the leader of the Soviet Union in 1985. He was relatively young—in 1980 he had become the youngest full member of the Politburo, the ruling body in the USSR—and very well educated. He knew that every year his country was falling further and further behind the West in every material sense. Determined to correct the slide, he introduced measures to restructure the Soviet economy (*perestroika*) and to create a new political openness (*glasnost*). His economic measures never worked, but his political initiatives worked all too well.

First, Eastern Europe used the new openness to break away from the Soviet orbit. Then, the USSR's Baltic republics of Lithuania, Latvia, and Estonia demanded and received independence. Finally, the remaining 12 republics of the Soviet Union decided that the union was unworkable and undesirable. Gorbachev attempted to hold the republics together but failed. On Christmas Day, 1991, he faced the reality that the Soviet Union no longer existed and resigned from office.

The Soviet newspaper *Izvestia* commented that Gorbachev "did all he could." Perhaps no leader could have kept the Soviet Union from breaking apart once liberalization had started. Political freedom was singularly out of step with Soviet political traditions. But Gorbachev did fail in several areas. A man who had risen through the Soviet bureaucracy, Gorbachev failed to significantly reform or abolish that bureaucracy even though it became clear that that very bureaucracy was the primary obstacle to *perestroika*. In addition, he never devised a plan to allow enough freedom in the individual republics, and he even tacitly permitted Soviet security forces to use tanks and guns to suppress the Baltic independence movements. But most importantly, Gorbachev's *perestroika* did not work because it did not bring a new era of prosperity to the Soviet Union. Gorbachev admitted that "the old system fell apart even before the new system began to work," but as one authority commented, "there was no new system." Like every Soviet leader since Lenin, Gorbachev had promised far more than he delivered.

The death of the Soviet Union posed immense problems both for the newly independent republics and the United States. Even before Gorbachev's resignation, 11 of the 12 remaining republics—only the republic of Georgia was excluded—joined together into a new confederation called the Commonwealth of Independent States. Led by the republics of Russia, Belorussia, and Ukraine, the new entity was more an alliance than a state. The republics agreed to cooperate in economic reforms aimed at moving them toward a free enterprise system and maintain at least temporarily the ruble as the common currency. Further, and without being very specific, they announced that the Commonwealth would coordinate economic, military, and foreign policies of its independent members. Central to the Commonwealth, however, was the idea that each member was and remained a sovereign nation. To underscore this idea, the Commonwealth located its capital in Minsk rather than Moscow, the seat of Soviet power, or St. Petersburg, the capital of czarist Russia.

From the first, the Commonwealth faced a difficult task. Disputes quickly arose over how to divide the military and economic resources of the old Soviet Union. The sovereign republics had to decide how to divide the forces and equipment of the Red Army and the Soviet Navy as well as the Soviet state treasury, central television network, space infrastructure, and the hundreds of other assets once controlled by the Soviet Union. As a symbol of the great change, in February 1992 the Commonwealth Olympic team competed in the Albertville Winter Games under the Olympic flag and their victories were

marked by the playing of the Olympic anthem.

Even more pressing than the decision on how to divide Soviet property was the conversion to a limited free-market system. In early 1992 the Commonwealth lifted most price controls and the cost of goods shot upward. The prices of such basic commodities as bread and gasoline, over which some controls still existed, tripled or quadrupled literally overnight. The prices of noncontrolled items increased much more. A kilo of kielbasa sausages was 2.20 rubles in January 1991; the price rose to 43.75 rubles (and as high as 200 rubles in particularly hard-pressed St. Petersburg) in January 1992. The ruble itself experienced the shock. The official exchange used to be 1.8 per dollar; in January 1992 the exchange rate rose to well over 100 rubles per dollar. The economic changes created severe hardships for people whose monthly income averaged 400 rubles. Many citizens of the Commonwealth considered the winter of 1992 as the worst in their lives.

The death of the Soviet Union also had a profound effect on the United States. On one level the United States had to redirect its foreign policy. The era of the Cold War was over. The Soviet Union, America's Cold War rival, no longer existed. President George Bush responded to the changes by announcing victory in the Cold War, recognizing the new independent republics, and sending aid to the beleaguered members of the Commonwealth. Although Americans continued to worry about who controlled the Commonwealth's nuclear weapons, there was no longer the fear of war between the Soviet Union and the United States.

On another level, the end of the Cold War undermined one of the organizing principles of American culture. American mass culture in particular revolved around the idea of "us" and "them." Throughout the Cold War era Hollywood made successful movies that played on this theme. From such movies as *I Was a Communist for the FBI*, *My Son John*, *Dr. Strangelove*, *Fail Safe*, *Red Alert*, and *On the Beach* to the James Bond action pictures and John Wayne westerns, Cold War issues provided the explicit or implicit basis for the films. Not to be outdone, popular writers capitalized on Cold War themes. John Le Carré, William F. Buckley, Jr., and Tom Clancy wrote best-sellers that centered on Cold War plots. Television also pitted "us" against "them" on numerous programs. During the 1960s *The Man from U.N.C.L.E.*, *Mission Impossible*, and *I Spy* were popular programs that featured Cold War storylines. Even sports were influenced by the Cold War. In particular, the Olympic Games reflected Cold War tension and anxieties. American cheers of "USA, USA" at Olympic events became ritualistic Cold War chants.

American education and science similarly were partial hostages to the Cold War. After the success of the Soviet *Sputnik* in 1957, Congress appropriated funds for the establishment of the National Aeronautics and Space Administration (NASA) and passed the National Defense Education Act. In the Cold War the space race and education became highly political issues. President John F. Kennedy's decision to push America's space program toward putting a person on the moon—a decision that many of America's leading scientists opposed—was more a response to the Cold War than the needs of science. And Neil Armstrong's July 21, 1969, moon walk was confirmation of America's victory in the space race.

The death of the Soviet Union, then, ended two eras. How citizens of both the United States and the Commonwealth of Independent States will respond to that death will be one of the most important issues in the twenty-first century.

927

to evacuate. Fierce street battles erupted between troops loyal to Yeltsin and thousands of armed communists and nationalists before the army crushed the uprising, attacked the building, and forced Yeltsin's opponents to surrender.

The struggles between reformers, nationalists, and communists persisted. The former Soviet Union remained beset by deep economic problems and severe ethnic and regional conflicts that showed little sign of abating.

The Persian Gulf War

At 2 A.M., August 2, 1990, 80,000 Iraqi troops invaded and occupied Kuwait, touching off the first major international crisis of the post–Cold War era. Iraqi's leader, Saddam Hussein, justified the invasion on the grounds that Kuwait, which he accused of intentionally depressing world oil prices, was historically a part of Iraq.

Iraq's invasion of Kuwait caught the United States off-guard. Hussein's regime was a brutal military dictatorship that ruled by secret police and used poison gas against Iranians, Kurds, and Shiite Muslims. During the 1970s and 1980s the United States—and Britain, France, the Soviet Union, and West Germany—sold Iraq an awesome arsenal of weapons, including missiles, tanks, and the equipment needed to produce biological, chemical, and nuclear weapons. During Baghdad's eight-year-long war with Iran, the United States, which opposed the growth of Muslim fundamentalist extremism, tilted toward Iraq.

On August 6, 1990, President Bush dramatically declared, "This aggression will not stand." He organized an international coalition against Iraq, convincing Turkey and Syria to close Iraqi pipelines, winning Soviet support for an arms embargo, and establishing a multinational army to protect Saudi Arabia. In the United Nations the administration persuaded the Security Council to adopt resolutions condemning the Iraqi invasion, demanding restoration of the Kuwaiti government, and imposing an economic blockade.

President Bush's decision to first resist and then to reverse Iraqi aggression reflected his assessment of vital national interests. The invasion had given Hussein direct control over a significant portion of the world's oil supply. It had also disrupted the balance of power in the Middle East and placed Saudi Arabia and the Persian Gulf emirates in jeopardy. Iraq's 545,000-man army threatened the security of such valuable U.S. allies as Egypt and Israel.

Bush's decision to liberate Kuwait was an enormous political and military gamble, and the allied

THE FIRST CRISIS OF THE POST–COLD WAR ERA

The Persian Gulf War

In August 1990, with Iraqi forces poised near the Saudi Arabian border, the Bush administration dispatched 180,000 troops to protect the Saudi kingdom. The crisis took a dramatic turn in November 1990 when Bush doubled the number of American troops deployed in the Persian Gulf. Iraqi forces in Kuwait had climbed to 430,000 and coalition forces had to increase if Iraq was to be ejected from Kuwait by force. The president went to the United Nations for a resolution permitting the use of force against Iraq if it did not withdraw by January 15, 1991. After a heated debate, Congress also gave the president authority to wage war.

The 545,000-strong Iraqi army, the world's fourth largest, was equipped with antiship Exocet missiles, top-of-the-line Soviet T-72 tanks, and long-range artillery capable of firing nerve gas. Hussein tried to bring Israel into the war by launching Scud missiles at Israeli cities, a strategy thwarted when the United States sent Patriot antimissile missiles to Israel. A month of allied bombing gave the coalition forces air supremacy and destroyed thousands of Iraqi tanks and artillery pieces, supply routes and communications lines, command-and-control bunkers, and limited Iraq's ability to produce nuclear, chemical, and biological weapons. Iraqi troop morale suffered so badly during the bombing that an estimated 30 percent of Baghdad's forces deserted before the ground campaign even started.

The allied ground campaign relied on deception, mobility, and overwhelming air superiority to defeat a larger Iraqi army. The allied strategy was to mislead the Iraqis into believing that the allied attack would occur along the Kuwaiti coastline and Kuwait's border with Saudi Arabia. Meanwhile, General H. Norman Schwarzkopf, U.S. commander of the coalition forces, shifted more than 300,000 U.S., British, and French troops into western Saudi Arabia, allowing them to strike deeply into Iraq and trap Iraqi forces deep in southern Iraq and Kuwait. Only 100 hours after the ground war started, the war ended.

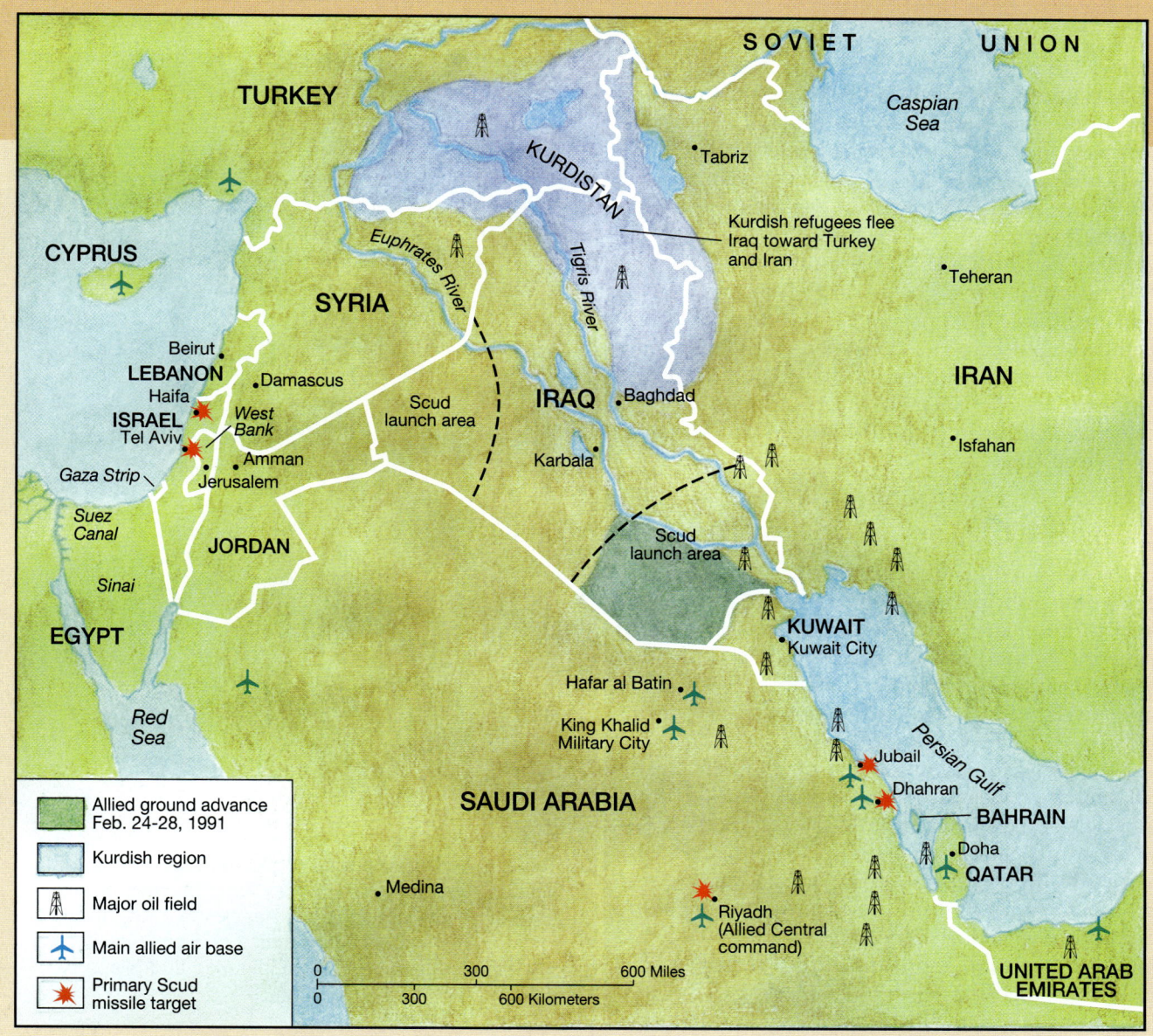

victory in the Persian Gulf War did not mean the end of hostilities. Saddam Hussein remained in power, and in the war's aftermath, he brutally suppressed independence movements by two minority groups—the Kurds and the Shiites—in his own country. Still, his ability to control events in the region was dramatically curtailed.

The Persian Gulf War was the most popular American war since World War II. It restored American confidence in its position as the world's sole superpower and helped exorcise the ghost of Vietnam that had haunted American foreign policy debates for nearly two decades. The doubt, drift, and demoralization that began with the Vietnam war appeared to have ended.

Enter Bill Clinton

In the Persian Gulf War, Bush acted from clear, unequivocal principles. Convinced that it was necessary to humiliate Saddam Hussein and prove that America would resist aggression, Bush demonstrated that a determined and skillful president has the power to move a reluctant nation to support his policies.

In domestic affairs, on the other hand, Bush's leadership was less decisive. On such issues as taxes, abortion, and civil rights, he adopted a flexible, pragmatic approach that led some critics to describe him as a political chameleon. Unlike Ronald Reagan, who brought a series of fixed philosophical principles to domestic issues, Bush appeared less interested in domestic affairs and more willing to renege on his pledge not to raise taxes.

Bush's failure to alter the downward slide of the American economy played the crucial role in the 1992 presidential election. In a bitter three-way contest, marked by intense assaults on both the candidates' records and their characters, Arkansas Governor Bill Clinton defeated George Bush and Texas businessman Ross Perot to become the first Democratic president in 12 years. President Bush, whose popularity soared to 90 percent after the Persian Gulf War, received 38 percent of the vote, to Clinton's 43 percent and Perot's 19 percent.

The central issue in the election was the nation's sluggish economy. During the Bush presidency, fewer new jobs were created than in any other presidential term since World War II. Indeed, fewer Americans were on private payrolls at the end of his term than when he took office. Unemployment reached the highest level in eight years; personal incomes stagnated; businesses failed in record numbers; the federal debt surpassed $4 trillion; and medical care absorbed 15 percent of the nation's output, while a quarter of the population lacked health in-

The acquittal of four white police officers, charged with beating black motorist Rodney King, touched off five days of deadly rioting in Los Angeles in 1992. In this most deadly and costly incidence of urban violence in the twentieth century, 50 people died and property damage exceeded $1 billion.

surance. Poverty rose to the highest rate in over two decades—a fact dramatically underscored by the outbreak of the deadliest riot in America's history, in Los Angeles in April 1992.

THE CLINTON PRESIDENCY

The youngest person elected to the presidency since John F. Kennedy, Bill Clinton had served nearly 12 years as governor of Arkansas before entering the White House. A self-described "new Democrat," Clinton promised a new approach to government between the unfettered free market championed by the Republicans and the welfare-state economics that the Democratic party had represented in the past.

As president, Clinton committed his administration to ending 12 years of "legislative gridlock" and "social neglect." During his first two years in office,

Bill Clinton focused much of his 1992 campaign for the presidency on health care reform. Though he won the 1992 election, he failed to win passage of his health care reform plan. A thriving economy helped Clinton win reelection in 1996. A low point of Clinton's second term was his impeachment by the House of Representatives on charges of perjury and obstruction of justice in connection with his sexual liaison with White House intern Monica Lewinsky (shown in photo at left embracing the president). The Senate impeachment trial began in early 1999, but Senate Republicans were unable to muster the two-thirds majority vote required for conviction and removal from office.

he had a string of legislative successes. To reduce the federal budget deficit, he persuaded Congress to raise taxes on the wealthiest Americans and on gasoline and to cut government spending. To create jobs, he persuaded the Senate to ratify the North American Free Trade Agreement (NAFTA), eliminating tariff barriers between Canada, Mexico, and the United States, and completed negotiations on the General Agreement on Trade and Tariffs (GATT), reducing global trading barriers. To aid working parents, he signed parental leave legislation, allowing parents to take unpaid leave during family emergencies. To combat violent crime, he convinced Congress to enact a waiting period for handgun purchases and a ban on the sale of assault weapons.

Two of his proposals, however, alienated many voters. In the face of vocal opposition, President Clinton backed away from a promise to end the ban on homosexuals in the military and instituted a compromise policy of "don't ask–don't tell," which satisfied no one. Meanwhile, the centerpiece of his legislative agenda—a program of universal health-care coverage—had to be withdrawn. His plan to provide medical care through local networks of insurers, hospitals, and doctors was criticized for its complexity and cost.

Clinton also suffered from allegations of financial and sexual misconduct before he became president. One controversy stemmed from investments he and his wife had made in the Whitewater Development Corporation, an Arkansas real estate development company. Another concerned charges of sexual harassment made by a former Arkansas government employee. Clinton eventually settled the sexual misconduct lawsuit for $850,000 and was ordered by a judge to pay an additional $90,000 for lying under oath.

In the midterm elections of 1994, Republicans won control of both houses of Congress. Campaigning on a 10-point "Contract with America," Republicans called for welfare reform; term limits for political office holders; a moratorium on environmental, health, and safety regulations; and a constitutional amendment requiring a balanced budget. Public support for President Clinton rebounded, however, after the Congressional Republicans temporarily shut down the federal government in an effort to force budget cuts and tax reductions, and antigovernment extremists blew up the Alfred P. Murrah Federal Office Building in Oklahoma City, killing 168 people—including 19 children—and injuring 624.

When he ran for office, Bill Clinton promised to cut the federal deficit in half, create millions of new jobs, and "end welfare as we know it." During his presidency he achieved many of his goals. Over Republican opposition in Congress, the Clinton ad-

THE PEOPLE SPEAK

The Starr Report and the White House Rebuttal

In 1999, the U.S. Senate held only the second impeachment trial of a president in American history. President Clinton was accused of lying in a deposition in a sexual harassment lawsuit about whether he had an affair with Monica Lewinsky, a 24-year-old White House intern. He was also accused of perjuring himself before a federal grand jury and of encouraging the former intern to lie. In a 453-page report, Independent Counsel Kenneth Starr accused the president of violating his oath of office. The President's attorneys responded by saying that while Clinton had engaged in an inappropriate relationship, he had not committed an impeachable offense.

The Starr Report

There is a substantial and credible information supporting the following eleven possible grounds for impeachment:

1. President Clinton lied under oath in his civil case when he denied a sexual affair, a sexual relationship, or sexual relations with Monica Lewinsky.
2. President Clinton lied under oath to the grand jury about his sexual relationship with Ms. Lewinsky.
3. In his civil deposition, to support his false statement about the sexual relationship, President Clinton also lied under oath about being alone with Ms. Lewinsky and about the many gifts exchanged between Ms. Lewinsky and him.
4. President Clinton lied under oath in his civil deposition about his discussions with Ms. Lewinsky concerning her involvement in the Jones case.
5. During the [Paula] Jones [sexual harassment] case, the President obstructed justice and had an understanding with Ms. Lewinsky to jointly conceal the truth about their relationship by concealing gifts subpoenaed by Ms. Jones's attorneys.
6. During the Jones case, the President obstructed justice and had an understanding with Ms. Lewinsky to jointly conceal the truth of their relationship from the judicial process by a scheme that included the following means: (i) Both the President and Ms. Lewinsky understood that they would lie under oath in the Jones case about their sexual relationship; (ii) the President suggested to Ms. Lewinsky that she prepare an affidavit that, for the President's purposes, would memorialize her testimony under oath and could be used to prevent questioning of both of them about their relationship; (iii) Ms. Lewinsky signed and filed the false affidavit; (iv) the President used Ms. Lewinsky's false affidavit at his deposition in an attempt to head off questions about Ms. Lewinsky; and (v) when that failed, the President lied under oath at his civil deposition about the relationship with Ms. Lewinsky.
7. President Clinton endeavored to obstruct justice by helping Ms. Lewinsky obtain a job in New York at a time when she would have been a witness harmful to him were she to tell the truth in the Jones case.
8. President Clinton lied under oath in his civil deposition about his discussions with [presidential advisor] Vernon Jordan concerning Miss Lewinsky's involvement in the Jones case.
9. The President improperly tampered with a potential witness by attempting to corruptly influence the testimony of his personal secretary, Betty Currie, in the days after his civil deposition.
10. President Clinton endeavored to obstruct justice during the grand jury investigation by refusing to testify for seven months and lying to senior White House aides with knowledge that they would relay the President's false statements to the grand jury—and did thereby deceive, obstruct, and impede the grand jury.
11. President Clinton abused his constitutional authority by (i) lying to the public and the Congress in January 1998 about his relationship with Ms. Lewinsky; (ii) promising at that time to cooperate fully with the grand jury investigation; (iii) later refusing six invitations to testify voluntarily to the grand jury; (iv) invoking Executive Privilege; (v) lying to the grand jury in August 1998; and (vi) lying again to the public and Congress on August 17, 1998—all as part of an effort to hinder, impede, and deflect possible inquiry by the Congress of the United States.

Source: Referral to the United States House of Representatives pursuant to Title 28, United States Code, Section 59(c), Submitted by The Office of the Independent Council, September 9, 1998.

---

ministration raised the minimum wage and the Earned Income Tax Credit (which provides financial assistance to the working poor). His administration also started "Americorp," a national service program; gave workers up to 12 weeks of unpaid leave to deal with family emergencies; and blocked efforts to restrict abortions. Working with Congressional Republicans, the administration reduced the size of the government work force, expanded international trade, and eliminated the federal budget deficit. Clinton and the Congressional Republicans also ended the 60-year-old welfare system. The welfare reform

The White House Rebuttal

The President has acknowledged a serious mistake—an inappropriate relationship with Monica Lewinsky. He has taken responsibility for his actions, and he has apologized to the country, to his friends, leaders of his party, the cabinet and most importantly, his family. . . .

This private mistake does not amount to an impeachable action. A relationship outside one's marriage is wrong—and the President admits that. It is not a high crime or misdemeanor. The Constitution specifically states that Congress shall impeach only for "treason, bribery or other high crimes and misdemeanors." These words in the Constitution were chosen with great care, and after extensive deliberations. . . .

"High crimes and misdemeanors" had a fixed meaning to the Framers of our Constitution—it meant wrongs committed against our system of government. The impeachment clause was designed to protect our country against a President who was using his official powers against the nation, against the American people, against our society. It was never designed to allow a political body to force a President from office for a very personal mistake. . . .

The law defines perjury very clearly. Perjury requires proof that an individual knowingly made a false statement while under oath. Answers to questions that are literally true are not perjury. Even if an answer doesn't directly answer the question asked, it is not perjury if it is true—no accused has an obligation to help his accuser. Answers to fundamentally ambiguous questions also can never be perjury. And nobody can be convicted of perjury based on only one other person's testimony. . . .

The President did not commit perjury. Most of the illegal leaks suggesting his testimony was perjurious falsely describe his testimony. First of all, the President never testified in the Jones deposition that he was not alone with Ms. Lewinsky. The President never testified that his relationship with Ms. Lewinsky was the same as with any other intern. To the contrary, he admitted exchanging gifts with her, knowing about her job search, receiving cards and notes from her, and knowing other details of her personal life that made it plain he had a special relationship with her. . . .

The President has admitted he had an improper sexual relationship with Ms. Lewinsky. In a civil deposition, he gave narrow answers to ambiguous questions. As a matter of law, those answers could not give rise to a criminal charge of perjury. In the face of the President's admission of his relationship, the disclosure of lurid and salacious allegations can only be intended to humiliate the President and force him out of office. . . .

There was no obstruction of justice. We believe Betty Currie testified that Ms. Lewinsky asked her to hold the gifts and that the President never talked to her about the gifts. The President admitted giving and receiving gifts from Ms. Lewinsky when he was asked about it. The President never asked Ms. Lewinsky to get rid of the gifts and he never asked Ms. Currie to get them. We believe that Ms. Currie's testimony supports the President's. . . .

The President never tried to get Ms. Lewinsky a job after she left the White House in order to influence her testimony in the Paula Jones case. The President knew Ms. Lewinsky was unhappy in her Pentagon job after she left the White House and did ask the White House personnel office to treat her fairly in her job search. He never instructed anyone to hire her, or even indicated that he very much wanted it to happen. Ms. Lewinsky was never offered a job at the White House after she left—and it's pretty apparent that if the President had ordered it, she would have been. . . .

There was no witness tampering. Betty Currie was not supposed to be a witness in the Paula Jones case. If she was not called or going to be called, it was impossible for any conversations the President had with her to be witness tampering. The President testified that he did not in any way attempt to influence her recollection. . . .

This means that the OIC [Office of Independent Counsel] report is left with nothing but the details of a private sexual relationship, told in graphic details with the intent to embarrass. Given the flimsy and unsubstantiated basis for the accusations, there is a complete lack of any credible evidence to initiate an impeachment inquiry concerning the President. And the principal purpose of this investigation, and the OIC's report, is to embarrass the President and titillate the public by producing a document that is little more than an unreliable, one-sided account of sexual behavior.

---

measures limited the time that people can spend on welfare rolls and required welfare recipients to work or receive training.

The low point in Clinton's presidency began when he was accused of encouraging a 24-year-old White House intern to lie to lawyers in a sexual harassment lawsuit about whether she had an affair with the president. For seven months the President denied that he had an inappropriate relationship with the intern but ultimately acknowledged the relationship and admitted that he had misled the American people about it. In December 1998, the

House Judiciary Committee, voting along straight party lines, approved four articles of impeachment, asserting that Clinton had committed perjury, obstructed justice, and abused his power. Later that month, the House of Representatives approved two articles of impeachment, making Clinton only the second American president to face an impeachment trial in the Senate. On the article charging the President with committing perjury before a grand jury, 45 Senators voted guilty and 55 not guilty. On the charge of obstruction of justice, 50 Senators voted guilty and 50 not guilty. A two-thirds vote was required for conviction and removal from office. While a majority of Americans told pollsters that they did not approve of President Clinton's behavior, they continued to support his policies, in part because of his success in handling the economy.

"It's the Economy, Stupid"

During the 1992 presidential campaign, Bill Clinton's campaign manager posted a sign on the wall: "It's the economy, stupid." As a candidate, Clinton promised to focus "like a laser beam" on economic issues, and the crowning achievement of his presidency was a booming economy. The stock market soared to record highs, inflation and unemployment fell to the lowest levels in decades, the federal budget was balanced, and millions of new jobs were created. The American economy achieved a preeminence unseen since the 1960s.

Economists attribute the economic boom to such factors as a sharp decline in the price of basic commodities such as oil and the restructuring of American businesses in the 1980s and early 1990s, which made them more productive and adaptable. America's leading competitors, Germany and Japan, became less competitive as their labor costs rose and their domestic economies slowed. Rising real incomes and declining interest rates made houses, cars, and other goods more affordable.

Perhaps the most important factor spurring America's economic resurgence was the growth of new computer and communication technologies dominated by American firms such as Microsoft and Intel. Global demand for information and entertainment soared during the 1990s, and American-owned companies dominated the information superhighway.

Still, despite the increases in the minimum wage and the earned income tax credit, declining interest rates, and low unemployment, average family incomes have improved only modestly. The median family income rose less than $300 in real terms between 1989 and 1999, while the average hours worked by a married couple with children increased by 256. Meanwhile, nearly 40 percent of full-time workers without a college degree lack health insurance.

Foreign Policy

In a famous article published in 1989, senior State Department official Francis Fukuyama announced the "end of history." With the collapse of authoritarian regimes of the right and the left, Fukuyama argued, the clash of political ideologies that had shaped the history of the twentieth century was over.

The Serbian campaign of "ethnic cleansing" forced the evacuation of many ethnic Albanians from the province of Kosovo. By the end of April 1999 nearly half of the two million residents of Kosovo had become refugees. The NATO bombing campaign, launched to halt Serbian aggression against the Kosovars, instead led to increased Serbian attacks.

Liberal democracy and free market capitalism, he proclaimed, had emerged triumphant. But in fact the end of the Cold War did not bring an end to international conflicts. To be sure, many hopeful developments occurred, such as the end of apartheid and the replacement of white rule with a multiracial democracy in South Africa and the Israeli transfer of control over the Gaza Strip and portions of the West Bank to the Palestinians. The conclusion of the Cold War, however, also unleashed violent ethnic turmoil in the Balkans, the Caucasus, and Africa.

As the twentieth century closed, two forces radically reshaped foreign affairs. One was a trend toward globalism. National borders became more porous, and domestic economies became increasingly interconnected as a result of the rapid movement of people, ideas, investment, and entertainment. Inexpensive air travel and the Internet tied the world together in new ways.

The other force for change was a resurgence of nationalism and ethnicity. Following the breakup of the Soviet Union, new nation-states proliferated at a rapid rate. In a decade, membership in the United Nations rose from 156 to 185 countries. During the Cold War, authoritarian governments had suppressed many ethnic conflicts. But when the superpower conflict between the United States and the Soviet Union ended, ethnic violence erupted in the Caucasus, East Timor, Liberia, Rwanda, Sierra Leone, Yugoslavia, and many other areas.

As a Rhodes scholar at Oxford University in England, Bill Clinton had avoided the military draft and demonstrated against the Vietnam War. During his two terms in office, President Clinton repeatedly faced a question posed by the Vietnam War: whether the United States should intervene to suppress conflict within sovereign nations. As president, he sent American forces into Haiti to oversee the transition from military to civilian rule and launched cruise missile attacks against terrorist targets in Afghanistan and Sudan. He also expanded NATO to include Poland, Hungary, and the Czech Republic, and led NATO air campaigns against Yugoslavia.

The major foreign policy crises of the Clinton presidency grew out of the breakup of Yugoslavia in southeastern Europe. In 1991 and 1992, Croatia broke away from Yugoslavia in bitter fighting. After a bloody three-year war, Bosnia gained independence from Yugoslavia. The United States helped negotiate a settlement in Bosnia that divided the country into areas dominated by Croats, Muslims, and Serbs.

To prevent the province of Kosovo from achieving independence, Yugoslavian authorities carried out a campaign of repression and abuse against the ethnic Albanians who made up 90 percent of the Kosovar population. When Yugoslavia rejected international pressure to grant autonomy to Kosovo, NATO launched a bombing campaign in 1999. Instead of quickly caving in, Yugoslavia's Communist dictator Sloboban Milosevic used his military and police forces to evict Kosovo's Albanian population. Ultimately, a casualty-free, two-month NATO air campaign forced Yugoslav forces to leave Kosovo. Nearly a million ethnic Albanian refugees returned to their homes under international protection.

CONCLUSION

As Americans enter the twenty-first century, America's ideals of democracy and personal freedom are ascendant across the world. From Tiananmen Square—where Chinese students erected a goddess of liberty modeled on the Statue of Liberty—to eastern Europe, popular protests and demonstrations called for "government of the people, by the people, and for the people." In eastern Europe, the former Soviet Union, Africa, and Latin America, people demand free speech, freedom of religion, freedom of the press, and free markets.

Yet paradoxically, as American ideals and values flourish abroad, Americans are anxious about their country's future. Many are angry, expressing cynical contempt toward their government. Others fear that while the economy booms, the society is experiencing a moral decline. Americans also worry about race relations, the state of the nation's central cities, and the quality of education. Even though crime rates have fallen in recent years, the United States continues to have the highest level of crime, violence, drug use, juvenile delinquency, teen pregnancy, and teen suicide in the industrialized world.

At the end of World War II, many commentators referred to the twentieth century as the "American century." Today, the United States remains the mightiest, most productive nation in the world, a model of freedom and pluralism that people across the globe strive to emulate. The great question to be asked as we enter a new century is whether Americans have the ingenuity and the will to solve the problems that confront our cities, our schools, and our physical environment.

SUGGESTIONS FOR FURTHER READING

William C. Berman, *America's Right Turn: From Nixon to Bush* (1998). Presents an incisive interpretation of recent American political history.

Chronology of Key Events

1971 A secret tape-recording system is installed in the White House; Nixon authorizes establishment of a plumbers unit to "stop security leaks and investigate other sensitive matters"

1972 Five burglars arrested breaking into Democratic national headquarters at Washington's Watergate office complex; President Nixon takes part in summit in China; President Nixon is reelected with 61 percent of the vote

1973 Televised Senate hearings on Watergate begin; Spiro Agnew pleads no contest to a charge of income tax evasion and resigns as vice president

1974 Federal grand jury indicts Nixon aides for perjury and obstruction of justice and names the president as an unindicted co-conspirator; House Judiciary Committee adopts three articles of impeachment against President Nixon; Nixon becomes the first president to resign from office; Ford becomes thirty-eighth president; Federal Campaign Reform Act sets limits on private campaign contributions and provides tax funds to presidential candidates

1976 Jimmy Carter is elected thirty-ninth president

1978 President Carter mediates Egyptian-Israeli peace settlement; Iranian revolution begins

1979 United States formally recognizes China; Iranian militants seize American hostages; Soviet Union invades Afghanistan; Somoza regime in Nicaragua is overthrown, Sandinistas take power

1980 Ronald Reagan is elected fortieth president

1981 American hostages are released from Iran; Reagan is shot in assassination attempt; Reagan approves covert training of anti-Sandinista contras; Reagan tax cuts are approved

1982 Congress deregulates banking industry and lifts controls on airfares

1983 Reagan proposes "Star Wars" missile defense system; United States topples Communist government on the Caribbean island of Grenada

1984 Congress orders an end to all covert aid to Nicaraguan contras

1985 United States begins secret arms-for-hostages negotiations with Iran; Mikhail Gorbachev becomes leader of the Soviet Union

1986 Profits from Iranian arms sales are diverted to Nicaraguan contras

1987 Iran-contra hearings; stock market plunges 508 points in a single session

1988 George Bush is elected forty-first president

1989 Opposition defeats Sandinistas in Nicaraguan elections; Communist regimes collapse in Eastern Europe

1990 Iraqi troops invade and occupy Kuwait

1991 U.S., Western, and Arab forces eject Iraq from Kuwait by force; failed coup in Soviet Union results in a shift in power to the Soviet republics and in independence for Lithuania, Latvia, and Estonia

1992 Bill Clinton is elected forty-second president

1993 Congress passes North American Free Trade Agreement (NAFTA), eliminating trade barriers between Canada, Mexico, and the United States; General Agreement on Trade and Tariffs (GATT) passed, reducing global trading barriers

1994 Congress defeats Clinton's health-care plan; Republicans win control of both the House and the Senate in the 1994 midterm elections.

1996 Clinton is reelected president

1998 The House of Representatives votes to impeach Clinton for perjury and abuse of power

1999 The Senate fails to convict Clinton; the United States leads the NATO bombing campaign of Yugoslavia

William H. Chafe, *The Unfinished Journey: America Since World War II*, 3d ed. (1995). Offers a concise synthesis of recent scholarship.

Paul Gottfried, *The Conservative Movement*, rev. ed. (1993). Gives acute analysis of the growth of political conservatism.

Stanley I. Kutler, *The Wars of Watergate: The Last Crisis of Richard Nixon* (1990), and Michael Schudson, *Watergate in American Memory* (1992). Dissect the historical legacy of the Watergate scandal.

Overviews and Surveys

Michael Barone, *Our Country: The Shaping of America from Roosevelt to Reagan* (1990); Peter N. Carroll, *It Seemed Like Nothing Happened: The Tragedy and Promise of the 1970s* (1990); Frederick F. Siegel, *Troubled Journey: From Pearl Harbor to Ronald Reagan* (1984).

Crisis of Political Leadership

Patrick Anderson, *Electing Jimmy Carter; The Campaign of 1976* (1994); Paul Berman, *A Tale of Two Utopias: The Political Journey of the Generation of 1968* (1996); Dan T. Carter, *From George Wallace to Newt Gingrich* (1996); Terry Deibel, *Presidents, Public Opinion, and Power: The Nixon, Carter, and Reagan Years* (1986); Lewis Gould, *1968: The Election That Changed America* (1993); John Robert Greene, *The Presidency of Gerald R. Ford* (1995); J. Anthony Lukas, *Nightmare: The Underside of the Nixon Years* (1976); Kim McQuaid, *The Anxious Years: America in the Vietnam-Watergate Era* (1989); Richard E. Neustadt, *Presidential Power and Modern Presidents*, rev. ed. (1990); James Reichley, *Conservatives in an Age of Change: The Nixon and Ford Administrations* (1981); Edward L. and Frederick H. Schapsmeier, *Gerald R. Ford's Date with Destiny: A Political Biography* (1989); Jonathan Schell, *The Time of Illusion* (1975); Arthur M. Schlesinger, Jr., *The Imperial Presidency* (1973).

Wrenching Economic Transformations

Michael A. Bernstein and David E. Adler, eds., *Understanding American Economic Decline* (1994); Barry Bluestone and Bennett Harrison, *The Deindustrialization of America* (1982); David Calleo, *The Imperious Economy* (1982); Emmett Dedmon, *Challenge and Response: A Modern History of the Standard Oil Company* (1984); Thomas Edsall, *The New Politics of Inequality* (1984); Michael Goldfield, *The Decline of Organized Labor in the United States* (1987); Frank Levy, *Dollars and Dreams: The Changing American Income Distribution* (1987); Allen J. Matusow, *Nixon's Economy* (1998); Martin V. Melosi, *Coping with Abundance: Energy and Environment in Industrial America* (1985); Norman E. Nordhauser, *The Quest for Stability: Domestic Oil Regulation* (1979); Bernard Nossiter, *Fat Years and Lean Years: The American Economy Since Roosevelt* (1990); Michael Piore, *The Second Industrial Divide* (1984); Stephen G. Rabe, *The Road to OPEC* (1982);

Herbert Stein, *Presidential Economics: The Making of Economic Policy from Roosevelt to Reagan*, 2d ed. (1988); Michael Stoff, *Oil, War, and Security* (1980); Daniel Yergin, *The Prize: The Epic Quest for Oil, Money, and Power* (1990).

A New American Role in the World

James A. Bill, *The Eagle and the Lion: The Tragedy of American-Iranian Relations* (1988); H. W. Brands, *The Wages of Globalism: Lyndon Johnson and the Limits of American Power* (1995); William Bundy, *A Tangled Web: The Making of Foreign Policy in the Nixon Presidency* (1999); Gordon H. Chang, *Friends and Enemies: The United States, China, and the Soviet Union* (1990); Mark Gasiorowski, *U.S. Foreign Policy and the Shah* (1991); J. Michael Hogan, *The Panama Canal in American Politics* (1986); Nikki R. Keddie, *Iran, the United States, and the Soviet Union* (1991); Walter LaFeber, *The Panama Canal*, rev. ed. (1989); Joseph Lepgold, *The Declining Hegemony: The United States and European Defense, 1960–1990* (1990); Richard A. Melanson, *Reconstructing Consensus: American Foreign Policy Since the Vietnam War* (1990); Keith L. Nelson, *The Making of Détente: Soviet-American Relations in the Shadow of Vietnam* (1995); Kuross A. Samii, *Involvement by Invitation: American Strategies of Containment in Iran* (1987); Robert D. Schulzinger, *Henry Kissinger* (1989); Melvin Small, *Democracy and Diplomacy: The Impact of Domestic Politics on U.S. Foreign Policy* (1995); Gaddis Smith, *Morality, Reason and Power: American Diplomacy in the Carter Years* (1986); Seth Tillman, *The United States in the Middle East* (1982); Marvin Zonis, *Majestic Failure: The Fall of the Shah* (1991).

The Reagan Revolution

Norman C. Amaker, *Civil Rights and the Reagan Administration* (1988); Cynthia J. Arnson, *Crossroads: Congress, the Reagan Administration, and Central America* (1989); Coral Bell, *The Reagan Paradox: American Foreign Policy in the 1980s* (1989); Sidney Blumenthal, *Our Long National Daydream: A Political Pageant of the Reagan Era* (1988); Paul Boyer, ed., *Reagan as President* (1990); Mary C. Brennan, *Turning Right in the Sixties: The Conservative Capture of the GOP* (1995); Lou Cannon, *President Reagan: The Role of a Lifetime* (1991); Joel A. Carpenter, *Revive Us Again: The Rewakening of American Fundamentalism* (1997); Robert Dallek, *Ronald Reagan: The Politics of Symbolism* (1984); Theodore Draper, *A Very Thin Line: The Iran-Contra Affair* (1991); Lee Edwards, *The Conservative Revolution* (1999); Thomas Ferguson and Joel Rogers, *Right Turn: The Decline of the Democrats and the Future of American Politics* (1986); Gary M. Fink and Hugh Davis Graham, eds., *The Carter Presidency* (1998); Beth A. Fischer, *The Reagan Reversal: Foreign Policy and the End of the Cold War* (1997); Steve Fraser and Gary Gerstle, *The Rise and Fall of the New Deal Order* (1990); Fred Halliday, *From Kabul to Managua: Soviet-American Relations in the 1980s* (1989); Kenneth J. Heineman, *God Is a Conservative: Religion, Politics, and Morality in Contemporary America* (1998); J. David Hoeveler, Jr., *Watch on the Right: Conservative Intellectuals in the Reagan Era* (1991); Haynes Johnson, *Sleepwalking

Through History: America in the Reagan Years (1991); David E. Kyvig, ed., *Reagan and the World* (1990); Jane Mayer and Doyle McManus, *Landslide: The Unmaking of the President, 1984–1988* (1988); John L. Palmer, ed., *Perspectives on the Reagan Years* (1986); Robert Pastor, *Condemned to Repetition: The United States and Nicaragua* (1987); Ronald Radosh, *Divided They Fell: The Demise of the Democratic Party, 1964–1996* (1996); Gregory L. Schneider, *Cadres for Conservatism: Young Americans for Freedom and the Rise of the Contemporary Right* (1999); Martin Wattenberg, *The Decline of American Political Parties, 1952–1988* (1990), and *The Rise of Candidate-Centered Politics: Presidential Elections of the 1980s* (1991); Garry Wills, *Reagan's America* (1987).

The Bush Presidency

Ryan J. Barilleaux and Mary E. Stuckey, eds., *Leadership and the Bush Presidency* (1992); Michael R. Beschloss and Strobe Talbott, *At the Highest Levels: The Inside Story of the End of the Cold War* (1993); Sidney Blumenthal, *Pledging Allegiance: The Last Campaign of the Cold War* (1990); Kevin Buckley, *Panama: The Whole Story* (1991); Colin Campbell and Bert A. Rockman, eds., *The Bush Presidency* (1991); Jill Crystal, *Oil and Politics in the Gulf* (1990); E. J. Dionne, Jr., *Why Americans Hate Politics* (1991); Alan Ehrenhalt, *The United States of Ambition: Politicians, Power, and the Pursuit of Office* (1991); Robert O. Freedman, *Moscow and the Middle East* (1991); Stephen Richards Graubard, *Mr. Bush's War* (1992); Majid Khadduri and Edmund Ghareeb, *War in the Gulf* (1997); Peter B. Levy, *Encyclopedia of the Reagan-Bush Years* (1996); Moshe Lewin, *The Gorbachev Phenomenon* (1991); Martin Mayer, *The Greatest Ever Bank Robbery: The Collapse of the Savings and Loan Industry* (1990); David Mervin, *George Bush and the Guardianship Presidency* (1996); Henry R. Nau, *The Myth of America's Decline* (1990); William Pfaff, *Barbarian Sentiments: How the American Century Ends* (1989); Stephen Pizzo, et al., *Inside Job: The Looting of America's Savings and Loans* (1989); Gail Sheehy, *The Man Who Changed the World: The Lives of Mikhail S. Gorbachev* (1990); Jean Edward Smith, *George Bush's War* (1992); Kenneth W. Thompson, *The Bush Presidency* (1998); Lawrence J. White, *The S&L Debacle* (1991); Garry Wills, *Under God: Religion and American Politics* (1990); Bob Woodward, *The Commanders* (1991).

The Clinton Presidency

Colin Campbell and Bert A. Rockman, eds., *The Clinton Presidency* (1996); Robert E. Denton, Jr. and Rachel L. Holloway, eds., *The Clinton Presidency* (1996); William G. Hyland, *Clinton's World: Remaking American Foreign Policy* (1999); David Hume Kennerly, *Back from the Dead: How Clinton Survived the Republican Revolution* (1997); Theodore J. Lowi, *Embattled Democracy: Politics and Policy in the Clinton Era* (1995); Richard A. Posner, *An Affair of State: The Investigation, Impeachment, and Trial of President Clinton* (1999); Stanley A. Renshon, ed., *The Clinton Presidency* (1995); James B. Stewart, *Blood Sport: The President and His Adversaries* (1997).

Biographies

Stephen E. Ambrose, *Nixon* (1987); Dan Carter, *The Politics of Rage: George Wallace, the Origins of the New Conservatism, and the Transformation of American Politics* (1995); Steven M. Gillon, *The Democrats' Dilemma: Walter F. Mondale and the Liberal Legacy* (1992); Burton Ira Kaufman, *The Presidency of James Earl Carter, Jr.* (1993); David Maraniss, *First in His Class: A Biography of Bill Clinton* (1995); Kenneth Morris, *Jimmy Carter* (1996); Roger Morris, *Richard Milhous Nixon: The Rise of an American Politician* (1990); Herbert S. Parmet, *Richard Nixon and His America* (1990), and *George Bush* (1997); Tom Wicker, *One of Us: Richard Nixon and the American Dream* (1991); Garry Wills, *Nixon Agonistes* (1970), and *Reagan's America* (1988).

INTERNET RESOURCES

Richard M. Nixon
http://www.ipl.org/ref/POTUS/rmnixon.html
This page contains basic factual data about his election and presidency, speeches, and on-line biographies.

Gerald R. Ford Library and Museum
http://www.ford.utexas.edu/
Several online exhibits accompany the images and primary texts on this site.

Jimmy Carter Library
http://carterlibrary.galileo.peachnet.edu/
This site has general information about the Carters as well as on-line images and documents.

Iran Hostage Crisis
http://magic.hofstra.edu/~cgordon1/iranhostage.htm
This site is an excellent essay with several images describing the crisis from its background to its conclusion.

Bibliography of the Iran Hostage Crisis
http://intellit.muskingum.edu/intellsite/
genpostwar70s_folder/postwar70siran.html
This site is a bibliography of printed works about the crisis and the aborted rescue attempt.

Watergate and the Washington Post
http://www.washingtonpost.com/wp-srv/national/
longterm/watergate/front.htm
This site features a chronology, images, searchable articles, and lots of background information.

Constitutional Issues: Watergate and the Constitution
http://www.nara.gov/education/teaching/watergate/
watergat.html
From the National Archives' teaching materials, this site has a good chronology of Watergate and a 1974 memorandum from the Watergate Special Prosecution Force weighing the pros and cons of seeking an indictment against former President Richard Nixon.

CNN 1970s Interactive Timeline
http://cnn.com/SPECIALS/1999/century/episodes/08/
CNN has a series of interactive timelines with several interesting sites. This one covers the years from 1970 to 1979.

The 80s Server
http://www.80s.com/
This site has a variety of sources of information about the 1980s, but the best parts are open to members only.

The Gulf War
http://www.pbs.org/pages/frontline/gulf/index.html
This Frontline and PBS site combines personal accounts with a chronology and general information about the war.

A Brief History of the Internet, Version 3.1
http://www.isoc.org/internet-history/
The Internet Society puts out this site that explores the development and impact of the internet.

Ronald Reagan Presidential Library
http://www.reagan.utexas.edu/
This site only has images and a thorough chronology so far, but it will be adding more data soon.

Los Angeles Riot
http://www.latimes.com/riots/
The *Los Angeles Times* site provides searchable information about the riot and its impact.

Religious Liberty
http://www.pfaw.org/issues/liberty/
With the so-called moral majority's rising voice in the 1980s, religious liberty issues became more important. This site discusses America and this pillar of the Constitution.

Desert Storm
http://www.desert-storm.com/
This site presents information about America's 1991 military action in Saudi Arabia, Kuwait, and Iraq.

George Bush
http://www.ipl.org/ref/POTUS/ghwbush.html
This page contains basic factual data about his election and presidency, speeches, and on-line biographies.

Iran-Contra Affair
http://www.umi.com/hp/Support/K12/GreatEvents/ContraHearings.html
This site draws on *New York Times* reporting to explore the 1985 scandal.

Bill Clinton
http://www.ipl.org/ref/POTUS/wjclinton.html
This page contains basic factual data about his election and presidency, speeches, and on-line biographies.

Kosovo
http://cgi.cnn.com/SPECIALS/1998/10/kosovo/
This in-depth site from CNN Interactive looks at the development and current resolutions of the turmoil in Kosovo.

Investigating President Clinton
http://www.cnn.com/ALLPOLITICS/resources/1998/lewinsky/
This site from CNN Interactive provides information about the scandals surrounding President Clinton and his impeachment.

The Microsoft Case
http://www.cnn.com/SPECIALS/1997/microsoft
CNN Interactive coverage of the Microsoft case with background, analysis, and some video make up this site.

KEY TERMS

Watergate Break-in (p. 912)
War Powers Act (p. 914)
Freedom of Information Act (p. 914)
Oil Crisis (p. 916)
Stagflation (p. 916)
Deregulation (p. 917)
Détente (p. 918)
Camp David Accords (p. 918)
Iranian Hostage Crisis (p. 920)
"Reagan Doctrine" (p. 922)
Mikhail Gorbachev (p. 922)
Operation Just Cause (p. 924)

REVIEW QUESTIONS

1. What was the "imperial presidecy"? How did it come to an end?
2. What problems did the American economy face in the 1970s? How did the federal government respond?
3. How did the "Reagan revolution" signal a change in domestic policies? In international relations? In American culture?
4. Was the Bush presidency an active and successful force in international affairs? In domestic affairs?
5. Why did the United States and its allies go to war against Iraq in 1991?
6. Describe President Bill Clinton's policies on (a) the economy, (b) welfare, (c) foreign affairs. How successful were his policies? Explain why the House of Representatives voted to impeach him and why the Senate failed to convict him. How would you have voted on impeachment and conviction? Why?

Appendix

The Declaration of Independence

The Constitution of the United States of America

Amendments to the Constitution

Presidential Elections

Vice Presidents and Cabinet Members by Administration

Supreme Court Justices

Admission of States to the Union

Territorial Expansion of the U.S.

U.S. Population, 1790–1990

Ethnic Diversity of the U.S., 1990

The Declaration of Independence

In Congress, July 4, 1776

The Unanimous Declaration of the Thirteen United States of America

When, in the course of human events, it becomes necessary for one people to dissolve the political bonds which have connected them with another, and to assume, among the powers of the earth, the separate and equal station to which the laws of nature and of nature's God entitle them, a decent respect to the opinions of mankind requires that they should declare the causes which impel them to the separation.

We hold these truths to be self-evident: That all men are created equal; that they are endowed by their Creator with certain unalienable rights; that among these are life, liberty, and the pursuit of happiness; that, to secure these rights, governments are instituted among men, deriving their just powers from the consent of the governed; that whenever any form of government becomes destructive of these ends, it is the right of the people to alter or to abolish it, and to institute new government, laying its foundation on such principles, and organizing its powers in such form, as to them shall seem most likely to effect their safety and happiness. Prudence, indeed, will dictate that governments long established should not be changed for light and transient causes; and accordingly all experience hath shown that mankind are more disposed to suffer, while evils are sufferable, than to right themselves by abolishing the forms to which they are accustomed. But when a long train of abuses and usurpations, pursuing invariably the same object, evinces a design to reduce them under absolute despotism, it is their right, it is their duty, to throw off such government, and to provide new guards for their future security. Such has been the patient sufferance of these colonies; and such is now the necessity which constrains them to alter their former systems of government. The history of the present King of Great Britain is a history of repeated injuries and usurpations, all having in direct object the establishment of an absolute tyranny over these states. To prove this, let facts be submitted to a candid world.

He has refused his assent to laws, the most wholesome and necessary for the public good.

He has forbidden his governors to pass laws of immediate and pressing importance, unless suspended in their operation till his assent should be obtained; and, when so suspended, he has utterly neglected to attend to them.

He has refused to pass other laws for the accommodation of large districts of people, unless those people would relinquish the right of representation in the legislature, a right inestimable to them, and formidable to tyrants only.

He has called together legislative bodies at places unusual, uncomfortable, and distant from the depository of their public records, for the sole purpose of fatiguing them into compliance with his measures.

He has dissolved representative houses repeatedly, for opposing, with manly firmness, his invasions on the rights of the people.

He has refused for a long time, after such dissolutions, to cause others to be elected; whereby the legislative powers, incapable of annihilation, have returned to the people at large for their exercise; the state remaining, in the mean time, exposed to all the dangers of invasions from without and convulsions within.

He has endeavored to prevent the population of these states; for that purpose obstructing the laws for naturalization of foreigners; refusing to pass others to encourage their migration hither, and raising the conditions of new appropriations of lands.

He has obstructed the administration of justice, by refusing his assent to laws for establishing judiciary powers.

He has made judges dependent on his will alone, for the tenure of their offices, and the amount and payment of their salaries.

He has erected a multitude of new offices, and sent hither swarms of officers to harass our people and eat out their substance.

He has kept among us, in times of peace, standing armies, without the consent of our legislatures.

He has affected to render the military independent of, and superior to, the civil power.

He has combined with others to subject us to a jurisdiction foreign to our constitution, and unacknowledged by our laws, giving his assent to their acts of pretended legislation:

For quartering large bodies of armed troops among us;

For protecting them, by a mock trial, from punishment for any murder which they should commit on the inhabitants of these states;

For cutting off our trade with all parts of the world;

For imposing taxes on us without our consent;

For depriving us, in many cases, of the benefits of trial by jury;

For transporting us beyond seas, to be tried for pretended offenses;

For abolishing the free system of English laws in a neighboring province, establishing therein an arbitrary government, and enlarging its boundaries, so as to render it at once an example and fit instrument for introducing the same absolute rule into these colonies;

For taking away our charters abolishing our most valuable laws, and altering fundamentally the forms of our governments;

For suspending our own legislatures, and declaring themselves invested with power to legislate for us in all cases whatsoever.

He has abdicated government here, by declaring us out of his protection and waging war against us.

He has plundered our seas, ravaged our coasts, burned our towns, and destroyed the lives of our people.

He is at this time transporting large armies of foreign mercenaries to complete the works of death, desolation, and tyranny already begun with circumstances of cruelty and perfidy scarcely paralleled in the most barbarous ages, and totally unworthy the head of a civilized nation.

He has constrained our fellow-citizens, taken captive on the high seas, to bear arms against their country, to become the executioners of their friends and brethren, or to fall themselves by their hands.

He has excited domestic insurrection among us, and has endeavored to bring on the inhabitants of our frontiers the merciless Indian savages, whose known rule of warfare is an undistinguished destruction of all ages, sexes, and conditions.

In every stage of these oppressions we have petitioned for redress in the most humble terms; our repeated petitions have been answered only by repeated injury. A prince, whose character is thus marked by every act which may define a tyrant, is unfit to be the ruler of a free people.

Nor have we been wanting in our attentions to our British brethren. We have warned them, from time to time, of attempts by their legislature to extend an unwarrantable jurisdiction over us. We have reminded them of the circumstances of our emigration and settlement here. We have appealed to their native justice and magnanimity; and we have conjured them, by the ties of our common kindred, to disavow these usurpations, which would inevitably interrupt our connections and correspondence. They, too, have been deaf to the voice of justice and of consanguinity. We must, therefore, acquiesce in the necessity which denounces our separation, and hold them, as we hold the rest of mankind, enemies in war, in peace friends.

We, therefore, the representatives of the United States of America, in General Congress assembled, appealing to the Supreme Judge of the world for the rectitude of our intentions, do, in the name and by the authority of the good people of these colonies, solemnly publish and declare, that these United Colonies are, and of right ought to be, FREE AND INDEPENDENT STATES; that they are absolved from all allegiance to the British crown, and that all political connection between them and the state of Great Britain is, and ought to be, totally dissolved; and that, as free and independent states, they have full power to levy war, conclude peace, contract alliances, establish commerce, and do all other acts and things which independent states may of right do. And for the support of this declaration, with a firm reliance on the protection of Divine Providence, we mutually pledge to each other our lives, our fortunes, and our sacred honor.

JOHN HANCOCK

BUTTON GWENNETT	THS. NELSON, JR.	RICHD. STOCKTON
LYMAN HALL	FRANCIS LIGHTFOOT LEE	JNO. WITHERSPOON
GEO. WALTON	CARTER BRAXTON	FRAS. HOPKINSON
WM. HOOPER	ROBT. MORRIS	JOHN HART
JOSEPH HEWES	BENJAMIN RUSH	ABRA. CLARK
JOHN PENN	BENJA. FRANKLIN	JOSIAH BARTLETT
EDWARD RUTLEDGE	JOHN MORTON	WM. WHIPPLE
THOS. HEYWARD, JUNR.	GEO. CLYMER	SAML. ADAMS
THOMAS LYNCH, JUNR.	JAS. SMITH	JOHN ADAMS
ARTHUR MIDDLETON	GEO. TAYLOR	ROBT. TREAT PAINE
SAMUEL CHASE	JAMES WILSON	ELBRIDGE GERRY
WM. PACA	GEO. ROSS	STEP. HOPKINS
THOS. STONE	CAESAR RODNEY	WILLIAM ELLERY
CHARLES CARROLL OF CARROLLTON	GEO. READ	ROGER SHERMAN
GEORGE WYTHE	THO. M'KEAN	SAM'EL. HUNTINGTON
RICHARD HENRY LEE	WM. FLOYD	WM. WILLIAMS
TH. JEFFERSON	PHIL. LIVINGSTON	OLIVER WOLCOTT
BENJA. HARRISON	FRANS. LEWIS	MATTHEW THORNTON
	LEWIS MORRIS	

The Constitution of the United States of America

PREAMBLE

We the People of the United States, in Order to form a more perfect Union, establish Justice, insure domestic Tranquility, provide for the common defence, promote the general Welfare, and secure the Blessings of Liberty to ourselves and our Posterity, do ordain and establish this Constitution for the United States of America.

ARTICLE I.

Section 1 All legislative Powers herein granted shall be vested in a Congress of the United States, which shall consist of a Senate and House of Representatives.

Section 2 The House of Representatives shall be composed of Members chosen every second Year by the People of the several States, and the Electors in each State shall have the Qualifications requisite for Electors of the most numerous Branch of the State Legislature.

No Person shall be a Representative who shall not have attained to the Age of twenty five Years, and been seven Years a Citizen of the United States, and who shall not, when elected, be an inhabitant of that State in which he shall be chosen.

Representatives and direct Taxes shall be apportioned among the several States which may be included within this Union, according to their respective Numbers, *which shall be determined by adding to the whole Number of free Persons, including those bound to Service for a Term of Years, and excluding Indians not taxed, three fifths of all other Persons.** The actual Enumeration shall be made within three Years after the first Meeting of the Congress of the United States, and within every subsequent Term of ten Years, in such Manner as they shall by Law direct. The Number of Representatives shall not exceed one for every thirty Thousand, but each State shall have at Least one Representative; *and until such enumeration shall be made, the State of New Hampshire shall be entitled to chuse three, Massachusetts eight, Rhode-Island and Providence Plantations one, Connecticut five, New York six, New Jersey four, Pennsylvania eight, Delaware one, Maryland six, Virginia ten, North Carolina five, South Carolina five, and Georgia three.*

When vacancies happen in the Representation from any State, the Executive Authority thereof shall issue Writs of Election to fill such Vacancies.

The House of Representatives shall choose their Speaker and other Officers; and shall have the sole Power of Impeachment.

*Passages no longer in effect are printed in italic type.

Section 3 The Senate of the United States shall be composed of two Senators from each State, *chosen by the Legislature thereof,* for six Years; and each Senator shall have one Vote.

Immediately after they shall be assembled in Consequence of the first Election, they shall be divided as equally as may be into three Classes. The Seats of the Senators of the first Class shall be vacated at the Expiration of the second Year, of the second Class at the Expiration of the fourth Year, and of the third Class at the Expiration of the sixth Year so that one third may be chosen every second Year; *and if Vacancies happen by Resignation, or otherwise, during the Recess of the Legislature of any state, the Executive thereof may make temporary Appointments until the next Meeting of the Legislature, which shall then fill such Vacancies.*

No Person shall be a Senator who shall not have attained to the Age of thirty Years, and been nine Years a Citizen of the United States, and who shall not, when elected, be an Inhabitant of that State for which he shall be chosen.

The Vice President of the United States shall be President of the Senate, but shall have no Vote, unless they be equally divided.

The Senate shall choose their other Officers, and also a President *pro tempore,* in the Absence of the Vice President, or when he shall exercise the Office of President of the United States.

The Senate shall have the sole Power to try all Impeachments. When sitting for that Purpose, they shall be on Oath or Affirmation. When the President of the United States is tried the Chief Justice shall preside: And no Person shall be convicted without the Concurrence of two thirds of the Members present.

Judgment in Cases of Impeachment shall not extend further than to removal from Office, and disqualification to hold and enjoy any Office of honor, Trust or Profit under the United States: but the Party convicted shall nevertheless be liable and subject to Indictment, Trial, Judgment and Punishment, according to Law.

Section 4 The Times, Places and Manner of holding Elections for Senators and Representatives, shall be prescribed in each State by the Legislature thereof; but the Congress may at any time by Law make or alter such Regulations, except as to the Places of choosing Senators.

The Congress shall assemble at least once in every Year, and such Meeting shall be on the first Monday in December, unless they shall by Law appoint a different Day.

Section 5 Each House shall be the Judge of the Elections, Returns and Qualifications of its own Members, and a Majority of each shall constitute a Quorum to do Business; but a smaller Number may adjourn from day to day, and may be authorized to compel the Attendance of absent Members, in such Manner, and under such Penalties as each House may provide.

Each House may determine the Rules of its Proceedings, punish its Members for disorderly Behaviour, and, with the Concurrence of two thirds, expel a Member.

Each House shall keep a Journal of its Proceedings, and from time to time publish the same, excepting such Parts as may in their Judgment require Secrecy; and the Yeas and Nays of the Members of either House on any question shall, at the Desire of one fifth of those Present, be entered on the Journal.

Neither House, during the Session of Congress, shall, without the Consent of the other, adjourn for more than three days, nor to any other Place than that in which the two Houses shall be sitting.

Section 6 The Senators and Representatives shall receive a Compensation for their Services, to be ascertained by Law, and paid out of the Treasury of the United States. They shall in all Cases, except Treason, Felony and Breach of the Peace, be privileged from Arrest during their Attendance at the Session of their respective Houses, and in going to and returning from the same; and for any Speech or Debate in either House, they shall not be questioned in any other Place.

No Senator or Representative shall, during the Time for which he was elected, be appointed to any civil Office under the Authority of the United States, which shall have been created, or the Emoluments whereof shall have been encreased during such time, and no Person holding any Office under the United States, shall be a Member of either House during his Continuance in Office.

Section 7 All Bills for raising Revenue shall originate in the House of Representatives; but the Senate may propose or concur with Amendments as on other Bills.

Every Bill which shall have passed the House of Representatives and the Senate, shall, before it become a Law, be presented to the President of the United States; If he approve he shall sign it, but if not he shall return it, with his Objections to the House in which it shall have originated, who shall enter the Objections at large on their Journal, and proceed to reconsider it. If after such Reconsideration two thirds of that House shall agree to pass the Bill, it shall be sent, together with the Objections, to the other House, by which it shall likewise be reconsidered, and if approved by two thirds of that House, it shall become a Law. But in all such Cases the Votes of both Houses shall be determined by Yeas and Nays, and the Names of the Persons voting for and against the Bill shall be entered on the Journal of each House respectively. If any Bill shall not be returned by the President within ten Days (Sundays excepted) after it shall have been presented to him, the Same shall be a Law, in like Manner as if he had signed it, unless the Congress by their Adjournment prevent its Return, in which Case it shall not be a Law.

Every Order, Resolution, or Vote to which the Concurrence of the Senate and House of Representatives may be necessary (except on a question of Adjournment) shall be presented to the President of the United States; and before the Same shall take Effect, shall be approved by him, or being disapproved by him, shall be repassed by two thirds of the Senate and House of Representatives, according to the Rules and Limitations prescribed in the Case of a Bill.

Section 8 The Congress shall have Power To lay and collect Taxes, Duties, Imposts and Excises, to pay the Debts and provide for the common Defence and general Welfare of the United States; but all Duties, Imposts and Excises shall be uniform throughout the United States;

To borrow Money on the credit of the United States;

To regulate Commerce with foreign Nations, and among the several States, and with the Indian Tribes;

To establish an uniform Rule of Naturalization, and uniform Laws on the subject of Bankruptcies throughout the United States;

To coin Money, regulate the Value thereof, and of foreign Coin, and fix the Standard of Weights and Measures;

To provide for the Punishment of counterfeiting the Securities and current Coin of the United States;

To establish Post Offices and post Roads;

To promote the Progress of Science and useful Arts, by securing for limited Times to Authors and Inventors the exclusive Right to their respective Writings and Discoveries;

To constitute Tribunals inferior to the supreme Court;

To define and punish Piracies and Felonies committed on the high Seas, and Offences against the Law of Nations;

To declare War, grant Letters of Marque and Reprisal, and make Rules concerning Captures on Land and Water;

To raise and support Armies, but no Appropriation of Money to that Use shall be for a longer Term than two Years;

To provide and maintain a Navy;

To make Rules for the Government and Regulation of the land and naval Forces;

To provide for calling forth the Militia to execute the Laws of the Union, suppress Insurrections and repel Invasions;

To provide for organizing, arming, and disciplining the Militia, and for governing such Part of them as may be employed in the Service of the United States, reserving to the States respectively, the Appointment of the Officers, and the Authority of training the Militia according to the discipline prescribed by Congress;

To exercise exclusive Legislation in all Cases whatsoever, over such District (not exceeding ten Miles square) as may, by Cession of particular States, and the Acceptance of Congress, become the Seat of the Government of the United States, and to exercise like Authority over all Places purchased by the Consent of the Legislature of the State in which the Same shall be, for the Erection of Forts, Magazines, Arsenals, dock-Yards, and other needful Buildings;—And

To make all Laws which shall be necessary and proper for carrying into Execution the foregoing Powers, and all other Powers vested by this Constitution in the Government of the United States, or in any Department of Officer thereof.

Section 9 The Migration or Importation of such Persons as any of the States now existing shall think proper to admit, shall not be prohibited by the Congress prior to the

Year one thousand eight hundred and eight, but a Tax or duty may be imposed on such Importation, not exceeding ten dollars for each Person.

The Privilege of the Writ of Habeas Corpus shall not be suspended, unless when in Cases of Rebellion or Invasion the public Safety may require it.

No Bill of Attainder or ex post facto Law shall be passed.

No Capitation, or other direct, Tax shall be laid, unless in Proportion to the Census or Enumeration herein before directed to be taken.

No Tax or Duty shall be laid on Articles exported from any State.

No Preference shall be given by any Regulation of Commerce or Revenue to the Ports of one State over those of another: nor shall Vessels bound to, or from, one State, be obliged to enter, clear, or pay Duties in another.

No Money shall be drawn from the Treasury, but in Consequence of Appropriations made by Law; and a regular Statement and Account of the Receipts and Expenditures of all public Money shall be published from time to time.

No Title of Nobility shall be granted by the United States: And no Person holding any Office of Profit or Trust under them, shall, without the Consent of the Congress, accept of any present, Emolument, Office, or Title, of any kind whatever, from any King, Prince, or foreign State.

Section 10 No State shall enter into any Treaty, Alliance, or Confederation; grant Letters of Marque and Reprisal; coin Money; emit Bills of Credit; make any Thing but gold and silver Coin a Tender in Payment of Debts; pass any Bill of Attainder, ex post facto Law, or Law impairing the obligation of Contracts, or grant any Title of Nobility.

No State shall, without the Consent of the Congress, lay any Imposts or Duties on Imports or Exports, except what may be absolutely necessary for executing its inspection Laws: and the net Produce of all Duties and Imposts, laid by any State on Imports or Exports, shall be for the Use of the Treasury of the United States; and all such Laws shall be subject to the Revision and Control of the Congress.

No State shall, without the Consent of Congress, lay any Duty of Tonnage, keep Troops, or Ships of War in time of Peace, enter into any Agreement or Compact with another State, or with a foreign Power, or engage in War, unless actually invaded, or in such imminent Danger as will not admit of delay.

Article II.

Section 1 The executive Power shall be vested in a President of the United States of America. He shall hold his Office during the Term of four Years, and, together with the Vice President, chosen for the same Term, be elected, as follows:

Each State shall appoint, in such Manner as the Legislature thereof may direct, a Number of Electors, equal to the whole Number of Senators and Representatives to which the State may be entitled in the Congress: but no Senator or Representative, or Person holding an Office of Trust or Profit under the United States, shall be appointed an Elector.

The Electors shall meet in their respective States, and vote by Ballot for two Persons, of whom one at least shall not be an Inhabitant of the same State with themselves. And they shall make a List of all the Persons voted for, and of the Number of Votes for each; which List they shall sign and certify, and transmit sealed to the Seat of the Government of the United States, directed to the President of the Senate. The President of the Senate shall, in the Presence of the Senate and House of Representatives, open all the Certificates, and the Votes shall then be counted. The Person having the greatest Number of Votes shall be the President, if such Number be a Majority of the whole number of Electors appointed; and if there be more than one who have such Majority, and have an equal Number of Votes, then the House of Representative shall immediately choose by Ballot one of them for President; and if no Person have a Majority, then from the five highest on the List the said House shall in like Manner choose the President. But in choosing the President, the Votes shall be taken by States, the Representation from each State having one Vote; A quorum for this Purpose shall consist of a Member or Members from two thirds of the States, and a Majority of all the States shall be necessary to a Choice. In every Case, after the Choice of the President, the Person having the greatest Number of Votes of the Electors shall be the Vice President. But if there should remain two or more who have equal Votes, the Senate shall choose from them by Ballot the Vice President.

The Congress may determine the time of choosing the Electors, and the Day on which they shall give their Votes; which Day shall be the same throughout the United States.

No person except a natural born Citizen, *or a Citizen of the United States, at the time of the Adoption of this Constitution,* shall be eligible to the Office of President; neither shall any Person be eligible to that Office who shall not have attained to the Age of thirty five Years, and been fourteen Years a Resident within the United States.

In Case of the Removal of the President from Office, or of his Death, Resignation, or Inability to discharge the Powers and Duties of the said Office, the Same shall devolve on the Vice President, and the Congress may by Law provide for the Case of Removal, Death, Resignation or Inability, both of the President and Vice President, declaring what Officer shall then act as President, and such Officer shall act accordingly, until the Disability be removed, or a President shall be elected.

The President shall, at stated Times, receive for his Services, a Compensation, which shall neither be encreased nor diminished during the Period for which he shall have been elected, and he shall not receive within that period any other Emolument from the United States, or any of them.

Before he enter on the Execution of his Office, he shall take the following Oath or Affirmation:—"I do solemnly swear (or affirm) that I will faithfully execute the Office of President of the United States, and will to the best of my Ability, preserve, protect and defend the Constitution of the United States."

Section 2 The President shall be Commander in Chief of the Army and Navy of the United States, and of the Militia of the several States, when called into the actual Service of the United States; he may require the Opinion, in writing, of the principal Officer in each of the executive Departments, upon any Subject relating to the Duties of their respective Offices, and he shall have Power to grant Reprieves and Pardons for Offences against the United States, except in Cases of Impeachment.

He shall have Power, by and with the Advice and Consent of the Senate, to make Treaties, provided two thirds of the Senators present concur; and he shall nominate, and by and with the Advice and Consent of the Senate, shall appoint Ambassadors, other public Ministers and Consuls, Judges of the supreme Court, and all other Officers of the United States, whose Appointments are not herein otherwise provided for, and which shall be established by Law: but the Congress may by Law vest the Appointment of such inferior Officers, as they think proper in the President alone, in the Courts of Law, or in the Heads of Departments.

The President shall have Power to fill up all Vacancies that may happen during the Recess of the Senate, by granting Commissions which shall expire at the End of their next Session.

Section 3 He shall from time to time give to the Congress Information of the State of the Union, and recommend to their Consideration such Measures as he shall judge necessary and expedient; he may, on extraordinary Occasions, convene both Houses, or either of them, and in Case of disagreement between them, with Respect to the Time of Adjournment, he may adjourn them to such Time as he shall think proper; he shall receive Ambassadors and other public Ministers; he shall take Care that the Laws be faithfully executed, and shall Commission all the officers of the United States.

Section 4 The President, Vice President and all civil Officers of the United States, shall be removed from Office on Impeachment for, and Conviction of, Treason, Bribery or other high Crimes and Misdemeanors.

Article III.

Section 1 The judicial Power of the United States, shall be vested in one supreme Court, and in such inferior Courts as the Congress may from time to time ordain and establish. The Judges, both of the supreme and inferior Courts, shall hold their offices during good Behaviour, and shall, at stated Times, receive for their Services, a Compensation, which shall not be diminished during their Continuance in Office.

Section 2 The judicial Power shall extend to all Cases, in Law and Equity, arising under this Constitution, the Laws of the United States, and Treaties made, or which shall be made, under their Authority;—to all Cases affecting Ambassadors, other public Ministers and Consuls;—to all Cases of admiralty and maritime Jurisdiction;—to Controversies to which the United States shall be a Party;—to Controversies between two or more States;—between a State and Citizens of another State;—between Citizens of different States,—between Citizens of the same State claiming Lands under Grants of different States, and between a State, or the Citizens thereof, and foreign States, Citizens or Subjects.

In all Cases affecting Ambassadors, other public Ministers and Consuls, and those in which a State shall be Party, the supreme Court shall have original Jurisdiction. In all the other Cases before mentioned, the supreme Court shall have appellate Jurisdiction, both as to Law and Fact, with such Exceptions, and under such Regulations as the Congress shall make.

The Trial of all Crimes, except in Cases of Impeachment, shall be by Jury; and such Trial shall be held in the State where the said Crimes shall have been committed, but when not committed within any State, the Trial shall be at such Place or Places as the Congress may by Law have directed.

Section 3 Treason against the United States, shall consist only in levying War against them, or in adhering to their Enemies, giving them Aid and Comfort. No person shall be convicted of Treason unless on the Testimony of two Witnesses to the same overt Act, or on Confession in open Court.

The Congress shall have Power to declare the Punishment of Treason, but no Attainder of Treason shall work Corruption of Blood, or Forfeiture except during the Life of the Person attainted.

Article IV.

Section 1 Full Faith and Credit shall be given in each State to the public Acts, Records, and judicial Proceedings of every other State. And the Congress may be general Laws prescribe the Manner in which such Acts, Records and Proceedings shall be proved, and the Effect thereof.

Section 2 The Citizens of each State shall be entitled to all Privileges and Immunities of Citizens in the several States.

A Person charged in any State with Treason, Felony, or other Crime, who shall flee from Justice, and be found in another State, shall on Demand of the executive Authority of the State from which he fled, be delivered up, to be removed to the State having Jurisdiction of the Crime.

No Person held to Service or Labour in one State, under the Laws thereof, escaping into another, shall, in Consequence of any Law or Regulation therein, be discharged from such Service or Labour, but shall be delivered up on Claim of the Party to whom such Service or Labour may be due.

Section 3 New States may be admitted by the Congress into this Union; but no new State shall be formed or erected within the Jurisdiction of any other State; nor any State be formed by the Junction of two or more States, or Parts of

States, without the Consent of the Legislatures of the States concerned as well as of the Congress.

The Congress shall have Power to dispose of and make all needful Rules and Regulations respecting the Territory or other Property belonging to the United States; and nothing in this Constitution shall be so construed as to Prejudice any Claims of the United States, or of any particular States.

Section 4 The United States shall guarantee to every State in this Union a Republican Form of Government, and shall protect each of them against Invasion; and on Application of the Legislature, or of the Executive (when the Legislature cannot be convened) against domestic violence.

ARTICLE V.

The Congress, whenever two thirds of both Houses shall deem it necessary, shall propose Amendments to this Constitution, or, on the Application of the Legislatures of two thirds of the several States, shall call a Convention for proposing Amendments, which, in either Case, shall be valid to all Intents and Purposes, as Part of this Constitution, when ratified by the Legislatures of three fourths of the several States, or by Conventions in three fourths thereof, as the one or the other Mode of Ratification may be proposed by the Congress; Provided *that no Amendment which may be made prior to the Year One thousand eight hundred and eight shall in any Manner affect the first and fourth Clauses in the Ninth Section of the first Article;* and that no State without its Consent, shall be deprived of its equal Suffrage in the Senate.

ARTICLE VI.

All Debts contracted and Engagements entered into, before the Adoption of this Constitution, shall be as valid against the United States under this Constitution, as under the Confederation.

This Constitution, and Laws of the United States which shall be made in Pursuance thereof; and all Treaties made, or which shall be made, under the Authority of the United States, shall be the supreme Law of the Land; and the Judges in every State shall be bound thereby, any Thing in the Constitution or Laws of any State to the Contrary notwithstanding.

The Senators and Representatives before mentioned, and the Members of the several State Legislatures, and all executive and Judicial Officers, both of the United States and of the several States, shall be bound by Oath or Affirmation, to support this Constitution; but no religious Test shall ever be required as a Qualification to any Office of public Trust under the United States.

ARTICLE VII.

The Ratification of the Conventions of nine States, shall be sufficient for the Establishment of this Constitution—between the States so ratifying the Same.

Done in Convention by the Unanimous Consent of the States present the Seventeenth Day of September in the Year of our Lord one thousand seven hundred and Eighty seven and of the Independence of the United States of America the Twelfth IN WITNESS whereof We have hereunto subscribed our Names,

GEORGE WASHINGTON,
President and Deputy from Virginia

New Hampshire
JOHN LANGDON
NICHOLAS GILMAN

Massachusetts
NATHANIEL GORHAM
RUFUS KING

Connecticut
WILLIAM S. JOHNSON
ROGER SHERMAN

New York
ALEXANDER HAMILTON

New Jersey
WILLIAM LIVINGSTON
DAVID BREARLEY
WILLIAM PATERSON
JONATHAN DAYTON

Pennsylvania
BENJAMIN FRANKLIN
THOMAS MIFFLIN
ROBERT MORRIS
GEORGE CLYMER
THOMAS FITZSIMONS
JARED INGERSOLL
JAMES WILSON
GOUVERNEUR MORRIS

Delaware
GEORGE READ
GUNNING BEDFORD, JR.
JOHN DICKINSON
RICHARD BASSETT
JACOB BROOM

Maryland
JAMES MCHENRY
DANIEL OF ST. THOMAS JENIFER
DANIEL CARROLL

Virginia
JOHN BLAIR
JAMES MADISON, JR.

North Carolina
WILLIAM BLOUNT
RICHARD DOBBS SPRAIGHT
HU WILLIAMSON

South Carolina
J. RUTLEDGE
CHARLES C. PINCKNEY
PIERCE BUTLER

Georgia
WILLIAM FEW
ABRAHAM BALDWIN

Amendments to the Constitution

The first ten amendments (the Bill of Rights) were adopted in 1791.

AMENDMENT I

Congress shall make no law respecting an establishment of religion, or prohibiting the free exercise thereof; or abridging the freedom of speech, or of the press; or the right of the people peaceably to assemble, and to petition the Government for a redress of grievances.

AMENDMENT II

A well regulated Militia being necessary to the security of a free State, the right of the people to keep and bear Arms, shall not be infringed.

AMENDMENT III

No Soldier shall, in time of peace be quartered in any house, without the consent of the Owner, nor in time of war, but in a manner to be prescribed by law.

AMENDMENT IV

The right of the people to be secure in their persons, houses, papers, and effects, against unreasonable searches and seizures, shall not be violated, and no Warrants shall issue, but upon probable cause, supported by Oath or affirmation, and particularly describing the place to be searched, and the persons or things to be seized.

AMENDMENT V

No person shall be held to answer for a capital, or otherwise infamous crime, unless on a presentment or indictment of a Grand Jury, except in cases arising in the land or naval forces, or in the Militia, when in actual service in time of War or public danger; nor shall any person be subject for the same offense to be twice put in jeopardy of life or limb; nor shall be compelled in any criminal case to be a witness against himself, nor be deprived of life, liberty, or property, without due process of law; nor shall private property be taken for public use, without just compensation.

AMENDMENT VI

In all criminal prosecutions, the accused shall enjoy the right to a speedy and public trial, by an impartial jury of the State and district wherein the crime shall have been committed, which district shall have been previously ascertained by law, and to be informed of the nature and cause of the accusation; to be confronted with the witnesses against him; to have compulsory process for obtaining witnesses in his favor, and to have the Assistance of Counsel for his defence.

AMENDMENT VII

In Suits at common law, where the value in controversy shall exceed twenty dollars, the right of trial by jury shall be preserved, and no fact trial by a jury, shall be otherwise re-examined in any Court of the United States, than according to the rules of the common law.

AMENDMENT VIII

Excessive bail shall not be required, nor excessive fines imposed, nor cruel and unusual punishments inflicted.

AMENDMENT IX

The enumeration in the Constitution, of certain rights, shall not be construed to deny or disparage others retained by the people.

AMENDMENT X

The powers not delegated to the United States by the Constitution, nor prohibited by it to the States, are reserved to the States respectively, or to the people.

AMENDMENT XI

[Adopted 1798]

The Judicial power of the United States shall not be construed to extend to any suit in law or equity, commenced or prosecuted against one of the United States by Citizens of another State, or by Citizens or Subjects of any Foreign State.

Amendment XII

[Adopted 1804]

The Electors shall meet in their respective states, and vote by ballot for President and Vice-President, one of whom, at least, shall not be an inhabitant of the same state with themselves; they shall name in their ballots the person voted for as President, and in distinct ballots the person voted for as Vice-President, and they shall make distinct lists of all persons voted for as President, and of all persons voted for as Vice-President, and of the number of votes for each, which lists they shall sign and certify, and transmit sealed to the seat of the government of the United States, directed to the President of the Senate;—The President of the Senate shall, in the presence of the Senate and House of Representatives, open all the certificates and the votes shall then be counted;—The person having the greatest number of votes for President, shall be the President, if such number be a majority of the whole number of Electors appointed; and if no person have such majority, then from the persons having the highest numbers not exceeding three on the list of those voted for as President, the House of Representatives shall choose immediately, by ballot, the President. But in choosing the President, the votes shall be taken by states, the representation from each state having one vote; a quorum for this purpose shall consist of a member or members from two-thirds of the states, and a majority of all the states shall be necessary to a choice. And if the House of Representatives shall not choose a President whenever the right of choice shall devolve upon them, before *the fourth day of March* next following, then the Vice-President shall act as President, as in the case of the death or other constitutional disability of the President.—The person having the greatest number of votes as Vice-President, shall be the Vice-President, if such number be a majority of the whole number of Electors appointed, and if no person have a majority, then from the two highest numbers on the list, the Senate shall choose the Vice-President; a quorum for the purpose shall consist of two-thirds of the whole number of Senators, and a majority of the whole number shall be necessary to a choice. But no person constitutionally ineligible to the office of President shall be eligible to that of Vice President of the United States.

Amendment XIII

[Adopted 1865]

Section 1 Neither slavery nor involuntary servitude, except as a punishment for crime whereof the party shall have been duly convicted, shall exist within the United States, or any place subject to their jurisdiction.

Section 2 Congress shall have power to enforce this article by appropriate legislation.

Amendment XIV

[Adopted 1868]

Section 1 All persons born or naturalized in the United States, and subject to the jurisdiction thereof, are citizens of the United States and of the State wherein they reside. No State shall make or enforce any law which shall abridge the privileges or immunities of citizens of the United States; nor shall any State deprive any person of life, liberty, or property, without due process of law; nor deny to any person within its jurisdiction the equal protection of the laws.

Section 2 Representatives shall be apportioned among the several States according to their respective numbers, counting the whole number of persons in each State, excluding Indians not taxed. But when the right to vote at any election for the choice of electors for President and Vice-President of the United States, Representatives in Congress, the Executive and Judicial officers of a State, or the members of the Legislature thereof, is denied to any of the male inhabitants of such State, being twenty-one years of age, and citizens of the United States, or in any way abridged, except for participation in rebellion, or other crime, the basis of representation therein shall be reduced in the proportion which the number of such male citizens shall bear to the whole number of male citizens twenty-one years of age in such State.

Section 3 No person shall be a Senator or Representative in Congress, or elector of President and Vice-President, or hold any office, civil or military, under the United States, or under any State, who, having previously taken an oath, as a member of Congress, or as an officer of the United States, or as a member of any State legislature, or as an executive or judicial officer of any State, to support the Constitution of the United States, shall have engaged in insurrection or rebellion against the same, or given aid or comfort to the enemies thereof. But Congress may by a vote of two-thirds of each House, remove such disability.

Section 4 The validity of the public debt of the United States, authorized by law, including debts incurred for payment of pensions and bounties for services in suppressing insurrection or rebellion, shall not be questioned. But neither the United States nor any State shall assume or pay any debt or obligation incurred in aid of insurrection or rebellion against the United States, or any claim for the loss or emancipation of any slave; but all such debts, obligations and claims shall be held illegal and void.

Section 5 The Congress shall have power to enforce, by appropriate legislation, the provisions of this article.

Amendment XV

[Adopted 1869]

Section 1 The right of citizens of the United States to vote shall not be denied or abridged by the United States or by any State on account of race, color, or previous condition of servitude.

Section 2 The Congress shall have power to enforce this article by appropriate legislation.

Amendment XVI

[Adopted 1913]

The Congress shall have power to lay and collect taxes on incomes, from whatever source derived, without apportionment among the several States, and without regard to any census or enumeration.

Amendment XVII

[Adopted 1913]

The Senate of the United States shall be composed of two Senators from each State, elected by the people thereof, for six years; and each Senator shall have one vote. The electors in each State shall have the qualifications requisite for electors of the most numerous branch of the State legislatures.

When vacancies happen in the representation of any State in the Senate, the executive authority of such State shall issue writs of election to fill such vacancies: *Provided,* That the legislature of any State may empower the executive thereof to make temporary appointments until the people fill the vacancies by election as the legislature may direct.

This amendment shall not be so construed as to affect the election or term of any Senator chosen before it becomes valid as part of the Constitution.

Amendment XVIII

[Adopted 1919, Repealed 1933]

Section 1 After one year from the ratification of this article the manufacture, sale, or transportation of intoxicating liquors within, the importation thereof into, or the exportation thereof from the United States and all territory subject to the jurisdiction thereof for beverage purposes is hereby prohibited.

Section 2 The Congress and the several States shall have concurrent power to enforce this article by appropriate legislation.

Section 3 This article shall be inoperative unless it shall have been ratified as an amendment to the Constitution by the legislatures of the several States, as provided in the Constitution, within seven years from the date of the submission hereof to the States by the Congress.

Amendment XIX

[Adopted 1920]

Section 1 The right of citizens of the United States to vote shall not be denied or abridged by the United States or by any State on account of sex.

Section 2 Congress shall have power to enforce this article by appropriate legislation.

Amendment XX

[Adopted 1933]

Section 1 The terms of the President and Vice-President shall end at noon on the 20th day of January, and the terms of Senators and Representatives at noon on the 3d day of January, of the years in which such terms would have ended if this article had not been ratified and the terms of their successors shall then begin.

Section 2 The Congress shall assemble at least once in every year, and such meeting shall begin at noon on the 3d day of January, unless they shall by law appoint a different day.

Section 3 If, at the time fixed for the beginning of the term of the President, the President elect shall have died, the Vice-President elect shall become President. If a President shall not have been chosen before the time fixed for the beginning of his term, or if the President elect shall have failed to qualify, then the Vice-President elect shall act as President until a President shall have qualified; and the Congress may by law provide for the case wherein neither a President elect nor a Vice-President elect shall have qualified, declaring who shall then act as President, or the manner in which one who is to act shall be selected, and such person shall act accordingly until a President or Vice-President shall have qualified.

Section 4 The Congress may by law provide for the case of the death of any of the persons from whom the House of Representatives may choose a President whenever the right of choice shall have devolved upon them, and for the case of the death of any of the persons from whom the Senate may choose a Vice-President whenever the right of choice shall have devolved upon them.

Section 5 Sections 1 and 2 shall take effect on the 15th day of October following the ratification of this article.

Section 6 This article shall be inoperative unless it shall have been ratified as an amendment to the Constitution by the legislatures of three fourths of the several States within seven years from the date of its submission.

Amendment XXI

[Adopted 1933]

Section 1 The eighteenth article of amendment to the Constitution of the United States is hereby repealed.

Section 2 The transportation or importation into any State, Territory, or possession of the United States for delivery or use therein of intoxicating liquors in violation of the laws thereof, is hereby prohibited.

Section 3 This article shall be inoperative unless it shall have been ratified as an amendment to the Constitution by conventions in the several States, as provided in the Constitution, within seven years from the date of the submission hereof to the States by the Congress.

Amendment XXII

[Adopted 1951]

Section 1 No person shall be elected to the office of the President more than twice, and no person who has held the office of President, or acted as President, for more than two years of a term to which some other person was elected President shall be elected to the office of the President more than once. But this Article shall not apply to any person holding the office of President when this Article was proposed by the Congress, and shall not prevent any person who may be holding the office of President, or acting as President, during the term within which this Article becomes operative from holding the office of President or acting as President during the remainder of such term.

Section 2 This article shall be inoperative unless it shall have been ratified as an amendment to the Constitution by the legislatures of three-fourths of the several States within several years from the date of its submission to the States within seven years from the date of its submission to the States by the Congress.

Amendment XXIII

[Adopted 1961]

Section 1 The District constituting the seat of Government of the United States shall appoint in such manner as the Congress shall direct:

A number of electors of President and Vice-President equal to the whole number of Senators and Representatives in Congress to which the District would be entitled if it were a State, but in no event more than the least populous State; they shall be in addition to those appointed by the States, but they shall be considered, for the purposes of the election of President and Vice-President, to be electors appointed by a State; and they shall meet in the District and perform such duties as provided by the twelfth article of amendment.

Section 2 The Congress shall have power to enforce this article by appropriate legislation.

Amendment XXIV

[Adopted 1944]

Section 1 The right of citizens of the United States to vote in any primary or other election for President or Vice-President, for electors for President or Vice-President, or for Senator or Representative in Congress, shall not be denied or abridged by the United States or any state by reason of failure to pay any poll tax or other tax.

Section 2 The Congress shall have the power to enforce this article by appropriate legislation.

Amendment XXV

[Adopted 1967]

Section 1 In case of the removal of the President from office or his death or resignation, the Vice-President shall become President.

Section 2 Whenever there is a vacancy in the office of the Vice-President, the President shall nominate a Vice President who shall take the office upon confirmation by a majority vote of both houses of Congress.

Section 3 Whenever the President transmits to the President pro tempore of the Senate and the Speaker of the House of Representatives his written declaration that he is unable to discharge the powers and duties of his office, and until he transmits to them a written declaration to the contrary, such powers and duties shall be discharged by the Vice-President as Acting President.

Section 4 Whenever the Vice-President and a majority of either the principal officers of the executive departments or of such other body as Congress may by law provide, transmit to the President pro tempore of the Senate and the Speaker of the House of Representatives their written declaration that the President is unable to discharge the powers and duties of his office, the Vice-President shall immediately assume the powers and duties of the office as Acting President.

Thereafter, when the President transmits to the President pro tempore of the Senate and the Speaker of the House of Representatives his written declaration that no inability exists, he shall resume the powers and duties of his office unless the Vice-President and a majority of either the principal officers of the executive department or of such other body as Congress may by law provide, transmit within four days to the President pro tempore of the Senate and the Speaker of the House of Representatives their written declaration that the President is unable to discharge the powers and duties of his office. Thereupon Congress shall decide the issue, assembling within 48 hours for that purpose if not in session. If the Congress, within 21 days after receipt of the latter written declaration, or, if Congress is not in session, within 21 days after Congress is required to assemble, determines by two-thirds vote of both houses that the President is unable to discharge the powers and duties of his office, the Vice-President shall continue to discharge the same as Acting President; otherwise, the President shall resume the powers and duties of his office.

Amendment XXVI

[Adopted 1971]

Section 1 The right of citizens of the United States, who are 18 years of age or older, to vote shall not be denied or abridged by the United States or any state on account of age.

Section 2 The Congress shall have the power to enforce this article by appropriate legislation.

Amendment XXVII

[Adopted 1992]

No law varying the compensation for the services of the Senators and Representatives shall take effect, until an election of Representatives shall have intervened.

Presidential Elections

Year	Candidates	Parties	Popular Vote	Electoral Vote	Voter Participation
1789	**GEORGE WASHINGTON**		*	69	
	John Adams			34	
	Others			35	
1792	**GEORGE WASHINGTON**		*	132	
	John Adams			77	
	George Clinton			50	
	Others			5	
1796	**JOHN ADAMS**	Federalist	*	71	
	Thomas Jefferson	Democratic-Republican		68	
	Thomas Pinckney	Federalist		59	
	Aaron Burr	Dem.-Rep.		30	
	Others			48	
1800	**THOMAS JEFFERSON**	Dem.-Rep.	*	73	
	Aaron Burr	Dem.-Rep.		73	
	John Adams	Federalist		65	
	C. C. Pinckney	Federalist		64	
	John Jay	Federalist		1	
1804	**THOMAS JEFFERSON**	Dem.-Rep.	*	162	
	C. C. Pinckney	Federalist		14	
1808	**JAMES MADISON**	Dem.-Rep.	*	122	
	C. C. Pinckney	Federalist		47	
	George Clinton	Dem.-Rep.		6	
1812	**JAMES MADISON**	Dem.-Rep.	*	128	
	De Witt Clinton	Federalist		89	
1816	**JAMES MONROE**	Dem.-Rep.	*	183	
	Rufus King	Federalist		34	
1820	**JAMES MONROE**	Dem.-Rep.	*	231	
	John Quincy Adams	Dem.-Rep.		1	
1824	**JOHN Q. ADAMS**	Dem.-Rep.	108,740 (30.5%)	84	26.9%
	Andrew Jackson	Dem.-Rep.	153,544 (43.1%)	99	
	William H. Crawford	Dem.-Rep.	46,618 (13.1%)	41	
	Henry Clay	Dem.-Rep.	47,136 (13.2%)	37	
1828	**ANDREW JACKSON**	Democratic	647,286 (56.0%)	178	57.6%
	John Quincy Adams	National Republican	508,064 (44.0%)	83	
1832	**ANDREW JACKSON**	Democratic	687,502 (55.0%)	219	55.4%
	Henry Clay	National Republican	530,189 (42.4%)	49	
	John Floyd	Independent		11	
	William Wirt	Anti-Mason	33,108 (2.6%)	7	
1836	**MARTIN VAN BUREN**	Democratic	765,483 (50.9%)	170	57.8%
	W. H. Harrison	Whig		73	
	Hugh L. White	Whig	739,795 (49.1%)	26	
	Daniel Webster	Whig		14	
	W. P. Magnum	Independent		11	
1840	**WILLIAM H. HARRISON**	Whig	1,274,624 (53.1%)	234	80.2%
	Martin Van Buren	Democratic	1,127,781 (46.9%)	60	
	J. G. Birney	Liberty	7069	—	
1844	**JAMES K. POLK**	Democratic	1,338,464 (49.6%)	170	78.9%
	Henry Clay	Whig	1,300,097 (48.1%)	105	
	J. G. Birney	Liberty	62,300 (2.3%)	—	

*Electors selected by state legislatures

14

Presidential Elections A-15

Year	Candidates	Parties	Popular Vote	Electoral Vote	Voter Participation
1848	ZACHARY TAYLOR	Whig	1,360,967 (47.4%)	163	72.7%
	Lewis Cass	Democratic	1,222,342 (42.5%)	127	
	Martin Van Buren	Free-Soil	291,263 (10.1%)	—	
1852	FRANKLIN PIERCE	Democratic	1,601,117 (50.9%)	254	69.6%
	Winfield Scott	Whig	1,385,453 (44.1%)	42	
	John P. Hale	Free-Soil	155,825 (5.0%)	—	
1856	JAMES BUCHANAN	Democratic	1,832,955 (45.3%)	174	78.9%
	John C. Frémont	Republican	1,339,932 (33.1%)	114	
	Millard Fillmore	American	871,731 (21.6%)	8	
1860	ABRAHAM LINCOLN	Republican	1,865,593 (39.8%)	180	81.2%
	Stephen A. Douglas	Democratic	1,382,713 (29.5%)	12	
	John C. Breckinridge	Democratic	848,356 (18.1%)	72	
	John Bell	Union	592,906 (12.6%)	39	
1864	ABRAHAM LINCOLN	Republican	2,213,655 (55.0%)	212	73.8%
	George B. McClellan	Democratic	1,805,237 (45.0%)	21	
1868	ULYSSES S. GRANT	Republican	3,012,833 (52.7%)	214	78.1%
	Horatio Seymour	Democratic	2,703,249 (47.3%)	80	
1872	ULYSSES S. GRANT	Republican	3,597,132 (55.6%)	286	71.3%
	Horace Greeley	Democratic	2,834,125 (43.9%)	66	
1876	RUTHERFORD B. HAYES	Republican	4,036,298 (48.0%)	185	81.8%
	Samuel J. Tilden	Democratic	4,300,590 (51.0%)	184	
1880	JAMES A. GARFIELD	Republican	4,454,416 (48.5%)	214	79.4%
	Winfield S. Hancock	Democratic	4,444,952 (48.1%)	155	
1884	GROVER CLEVELAND	Democratic	4,874,986 (48.5%)	219	77.5%
	James G. Blaine	Republican	4,851,981 (48.2%)	182	
1888	BENJAMIN HARRISON	Republican	5,439,853 (47.9%)	233	79.3%
	Grover Cleveland	Democratic	5,540,309 (48.6%)	168	
1892	GROVER CLEVELAND	Democratic	5,556,918 (46.1%)	277	74.7%
	Benjamin Harrison	Republican	5,176,108 (43.0%)	145	
	James B. Weaver	People's	1,041,028 (8.5%)	22	
1896	WILLIAM McKINLEY	Republican	7,104,779 (51.1%)	271	79.3%
	William J. Bryan	Democratic People's	6,502,925 (47.7%)	176	
1900	WILLIAM McKINLEY	Republican	7,207,923 (51.7%)	292	73.2%
	William J. Bryan	Dem.-Populist	6,358,133 (45.5%)	155	
1904	THEODORE ROOSEVELT	Republican	7,623,486 (57.9%)	336	65.2%
	Alton B. Parker	Democratic	5,077,911 (37.6%)	140	
	Eugene V. Debs	Socialist	402,283 (3.0%)	—	
1908	WILLIAM H. TAFT	Republican	7,678,908 (51.6%)	321	65.4%
	William J. Bryan	Democratic	6,409,104 (43.1%)	162	
	Eugene V. Debs	Socialist	420,793 (2.8%)	—	
1912	WOODROW WILSON	Democratic	6,293,454 (41.9%)	435	58.8%
	Theodore Roosevelt	Progressive	4,119,538 (27.4%)	88	
	William H. Taft	Republican	3,484,980 (23.2%)	8	
	Eugene V. Debs	Socialist	900,672 (6.0%)	—	
1916	WOODROW WILSON	Democratic	9,129,606 (49.4%)	277	61.6%
	Charles E. Hughes	Republican	8,538,221 (46.2%)	254	
	A. L. Benson	Socialist	585,113 (3.2%)	—	
1920	WARREN G. HARDING	Republican	16,152,200 (60.4%)	404	49.2%
	James M. Cox	Democratic	9,147,353 (34.2%)	127	
	Eugene V. Debs	Socialist	919,799 (3.4%)	—	
1924	CALVIN COOLIDGE	Republican	15,725,016 (54.0%)	382	48.9%
	John W. Davis	Democratic	8,386,503 (28.8%)	136	
	Robert M. La Follette	Progressive	4,822,856 (16.6%)	13	
1928	HERBERT HOOVER	Republican	21,391,381 (58.2%)	444	56.9%
	Alfred E. Smith	Democratic	15,016,443 (40.9%)	87	
	Norman Thomas	Socialist	267,835 (0.7%)	—	

Year	Candidates	Parties	Popular Vote	Electoral Vote	Voter Participation
1932	**FRANKLIN D. ROOSEVELT**	Democratic	22,821,857 (57.4%)	472	56.9%
	Herbert Hoover	Republican	15,761,841 (39.7%)	59	
	Norman Thomas	Socialist	881,951 (2.2%)	—	
1936	**FRANKLIN D. ROOSEVELT**	Democratic	27,751,597 (60.8%)	523	61.0%
	Alfred M. Landon	Republican	16,679,583 (36.5%)	8	
	William Lemke	Union	882,479 (1.9%)	—	
1940	**FRANKLIN D. ROOSEVELT**	Democratic	27,244,160 (54.8%)	449	62.5%
	Wendell L. Willkie	Republican	22,305,198 (44.8%)	82	
1944	**FRANKLIN D. ROOSEVELT**	Democratic	25,602,504 (53.5%)	432	55.9%
	Thomas E. Dewey	Republican	22,006,285 (46.0%)	99	
1948	**HARRY S TRUMAN**	Democratic	24,105,695 (49.5%)	304	53.0%
	Thomas E. Dewey	Republican	21,969,170 (45.1%)	189	
	J. Strom Thurmond	State-Rights Democratic	1,169,021 (2.4%)	38	
	Henry A. Wallace	Progressive	1,156,103 (2.4%)	—	
1952	**DWIGHT D. EISENHOWER**	Republican	33,936,252 (55.1%)	442	63.3%
	Adlai E. Stevenson	Democratic	27,314,992 (44.4%)	89	
1956	**DWIGHT D. EISENHOWER**	Republican	35,575,420 (57.6%)	457	60.6%
	Adlai E. Stevenson	Democratic	26,033,066 (42.1%)	73	
	Other	—	—	1	
1960	**JOHN F. KENNEDY**	Democratic	34,227,096 (49.9%)	303	62.8%
	Richard M. Nixon	Republican	34,108,546 (49.6%)	219	
	Other	—	—	15	
1964	**LYNDON B. JOHNSON**	Democratic	43,126,506 (61.1%)	486	61.7%
	Barry M. Goldwater	Republican	27,176,799 (38.5%)	52	
1968	**RICHARD M. NIXON**	Republican	31,770,237 (43.4%)	301	60.6%
	Hubert H. Humphrey	Democratic	31,270,533 (42.7%)	191	
	George Wallace	American Indep.	9,906,141 (13.5%)	46	
1972	**RICHARD M. NIXON**	Republican	47,169,911 (60.7%)	520	55.2%
	George S. McGovern	Democratic	29,170,383 (37.5%)	17	
	Other	—	—	1	
1976	**JIMMY CARTER**	Democratic	40,828,587 (50.0%)	297	53.5%
	Gerald R. Ford	Republican	39,147,613 (47.9%)	241	
	Other	—	1,575,459 (2.1%)	—	
1980	**RONALD REAGAN**	Republican	43,901,812 (50.7%)	489	52.6%
	Jimmy Carter	Democratic	35,483,820 (41.0%)	49	
	John B. Anderson	Independent	5,719,722 (6.6%)	—	
	Ed Clark	Libertarian	921,188 (1.1%)	—	
1984	**RONALD REAGAN**	Republican	54,455,075 (59.0%)	525	53.3%
	Walter Mondale	Democratic	37,577,185 (41.0%)	13	
1988	**GEORGE H. W. BUSH**	Republican	48,886,000 (53.4%)	426	57.4%
	Michael S. Dukakis	Democratic	41,809,000 (45.6%)	111	
1992	**BILL CLINTON**	Democratic	43,728,375 (43%)	370	55.0%
	George H. W. Bush	Republican	38,167,416 (38%)	168	
	H. Ross Perot	Independent	19,237,247 (19%)	—	
1996	**BILL CLINTON**	Democratic	47,402,357 (49%)	379	49.0%
	Robert Dole	Republican	39,198,755 (41%)	159	
	H. Ross Perot	Reform	8,085,402 (8%)	—	

Vice Presidents and Cabinet Members by Administration

The Washington Administration (1789-1797)

Vice President	John Adams	1789–1797
Secretary of State	Thomas Jefferson	1789–1793
	Edmund Randolph	1794–1795
	Timothy Pickering	1795–1797
Secretary of Treasury	Alexander Hamilton	1789–1795
	Oliver Wolcott	1795–1797
Secretary of War	Henry Knox	1789–1794
	Timothy Pickering	1795–1796
	James McHenry	1796–1797
Attorney General	Edmund Randolph	1789–1793
	William Bradford	1794–1795
	Charles Lee	1795–1797
Postmaster General	Samuel Osgood	1789–1791
	Timothy Pickering	1791–1794
	Joseph Habersham	1795–1797

The John Adams Administration (1797-1801)

Vice President	Thomas Jefferson	1797–1801
Secretary of State	Timothy Pickering	1797–1800
	John Marshall	1800–1801
Secretary of Treasury	Oliver Wolcott	1797–1800
	Samuel Dexter	1800–1801
Secretary of War	James McHenry	1797–1800
	Samuel Dexter	1800–1801
Attorney General	Charles Lee	1797–1801
Postmaster General	Joseph Habersham	1797–1801
Secretary of Navy	Benjamin Stoddert	1798–1801

The Jefferson Administration (1801-1809)

Vice President	Aaron Burr	1801–1805
	George Clinton	1805–1809
Secretary of State	James Madison	1801–1809
Secretary of Treasury	Samuel Dexter	1801
	Albert Gallatin	1801–1809
Secretary of War	Henry Dearborn	1801–1809
Attorney General	Levi Lincoln	1801–1805
	Robert Smith	1805
	John Breckinridge	1805–1806
	Caesar Rodney	1807–1809
Postmaster General	Joseph Habersham	1801
	Gideon Granger	1801–1809
Secretary of Navy	Robert Smith	1801–1809

The Madison Administration (1809-1817)

Vice President	George Clinton	1809–d. 1812
	Elbridge Gerry	1813–d. 1814
Secretary of State	Robert Smith	1809–1811
	James Monroe	1811–1817
Secretary of Treasury	Albert Gallatin	1809–1813
	George Campbell	1814
	Alexander Dallas	1814–1816
	William Crawford	1816–1817
Secretary of War	William Eustis	1809–1812
	John Armstrong	1813–1814
	James Monroe	1814–1815
	William Crawford	1815–1817
Attorney General	Caesar Rodney	1809–1811
	William Pinkney	1811–1814
	Richard Rush	1814–1817
Postmaster General	Gideon Granger	1809–1814
	Return Meigs	1814–1817
Secretary of Navy	Paul Hamilton	1809–1813
	William Jones	1813–1814
	Benjamin Crowninshield	1814–1817

The Monroe Administration (1817-1825)

Vice President	Daniel Tompkins	1817–1825
Secretary of State	John Quincy Adams	1817–1825
Secretary of Treasury	William Crawford	1817–1825
Secretary of War	George Graham	1817
	John C. Calhoun	1817–1825
Attorney General	Richard Rush	1817
	William Wirt	1817–1825
Postmaster General	Return Meigs	1817–1823
	John McLean	1823–1825
Secretary of Navy	Benjamin Crowninshield	1817–1818
	Smith Thompson	1818–1823
	Samuel Southard	1823–1825

The John Quincy Adams Administration (1825–1829)

Vice President	John C. Calhoun	1825–1829
Secretary of State	Henry Clay	1825–1829
Secretary of Treasury	Richard Rush	1825–1829
Secretary of War	James Barbour	1825–1829
	Peter Porter	1828–1829
Attorney General	William Wirt	1825–1829
Postmaster General	John McLean	1825–1829
Secretary of Navy	Samuel Southard	1825–1829

The Jackson Administration (1829–1837)

Vice President	John C. Calhoun	1829–1832
	Martin Van Buren	1833–1837
Secretary of State	Martin Van Buren	1829–1831
	Edward Livingston	1831–1833
	Louis McLane	1833–1834
	John Forsyth	1834–1837
Secretary of Treasury	Samuel Ingham	1829–1831
	Louis McLane	1831–1833
	William Duane	1833
	Roger B. Taney	1833–1834
	Levi Woodbury	1834–1837

Secretary of War	John H. Eaton	1829–1831
	Lewis Cass	1831–1837
	Benjamin Butler	1837
Attorney General	John M. Berrien	1829–1831
	Roger B. Taney	1831–1833
	Benjamin Butler	1833–1837
Postmaster General	William Barry	1829–1835
	Amos Kendall	1835–1837
Secretary of Navy	John Branch	1829–1831
	Levi Woodbury	1831–1834
	Mahlon Dickerson	1834–1837

The Van Buren Administration (1837–1841)

Vice President	Richard M. Johnson	1837–1841
Secretary of State	John Forsyth	1837–1841
Secretary of Treasury	Levi Woodbury	1837–1841
Secretary of War	Joel Poinsett	1837–1841
Attorney General	Benjamin Butler	1837–1838
	Felix Grundy	1838–1840
	Henry D. Gilpin	1840–1841
Postmaster General	Amos Kendall	1837–1840
	John M. Niles	1840–1841
Secretary of Navy	Mahlon Dickerson	1837–1838
	James Paulding	1838–1841

The William Harrison Administration (1841)

Vice President	John Tyler	1841
Secretary of State	Daniel Webster	1841
Secretary of Treasury	Thomas Ewing	1841
Secretary of War	John Bell	1841
Attorney General	John J. Crittenden	1841
Postmaster General	Francis Granger	1841
Secretary of Navy	George Badger	1841

The Tyler Administration (1841–1845)

Vice President	None	
Secretary of State	Daniel Webster	1841–1843
	Hugh S. Legaré	1843
	Abel P. Upshur	1843–1844
	John C. Calhoun	1844–1845
Secretary of Treasury	Thomas Ewing	1841
	Walter Forward	1841–1843
	John C. Spencer	1843–1844
	George Bibb	1844–1845
Secretary of War	John Bell	1841
	John C. Spencer	1841–1843
	James M. Porter	1843–1844
	William Wilkins	1844–1845
Attorney General	John J. Crittenden	1841
	Hugh S. Legaré	1841–1843
	John Nelson	1843–1845
Postmaster General	Francis Granger	1841
	Charles Wickliffe	1841
Secretary of Navy	George Badger	1841
	Abel P. Upshur	1841
	David Henshaw	1843–1844
	Thomas Gilmer	1844
	John Y. Mason	1844–1845

The Polk Administration (1845–1849)

Vice President	George M. Dallas	1845–1849
Secretary of State	James Buchanan	1845–1849
Secretary of Treasury	Robert J. Walker	1845–1849
Secretary of War	William L. Marcy	1845–1849
Attorney General	John Y. Mason	1845–1846
	Nathan Clifford	1846–1848
	Isaac Toucey	1848–1849
Postmaster General	Cave Johnson	1845–1849
Secretary of Navy	George Bancroft	1845–1846
	John Y. Mason	1846–1849

The Taylor Administration (1849–1850)

Vice President	Millard Fillmore	1849–1850
Secretary of State	John M. Clayton	1849–1850
Secretary of Treasury	William Meredith	1849–1850
Secretary of War	George Crawford	1849–1850
Attorney General	Reverdy Johnson	1849–1850
Postmaster General	Jacob Collamer	1849–1850
Secretary of Navy	William Preston	1849–1850
Secretary of Interior	Thomas Ewing	1849–1850

The Fillmore Administration (1850–1853)

Vice President	None	
Secretary of State	Daniel Webster	1850–1852
	Edward Everett	1852–1853
Secretary of Treasury	Thomas Corwin	1850–1853
Secretary of War	Charles Conrad	1850–1853
Attorney General	John J. Crittenden	1850–1853
Postmaster General	Nathan Hall	1850–1852
	Samuel D. Hubbard	1852–1853
Secretary of Navy	William A. Graham	1850–1852
	John P. Kennedy	1852–1853
Secretary of Interior	Thomas McKennan	1850
	Alexander Stuart	1850–1853

The Pierce Administration (1853–1857)

Vice President	William R. King	1853–d. 1853
Secretary of State	William L. Marcy	1853–1857
Secretary of Treasury	James Guthrie	1853–1857
Secretary of War	Jefferson Davis	1853–1857
Attorney General	Caleb Cushing	1853–1857
Postmaster General	James Campbell	1853–1857
Secretary of Navy	James C. Dobbin	1853–1857
Secretary of Interior	Robert McClelland	1853–1857

The Buchanan Administration (1857–1861)

Vice President	John C. Breckinridge	1857–1861
Secretary of State	Lewis Cass	1857–1860
	Jeremiah S. Black	1860–1861
Secretary of Treasury	Howell Cobb	1857–1860
	Philip Thomas	1860–1861
	John A. Dix	1861
Secretary of War	John B. Floyd	1857–1861
	Joseph Holt	1861
Attorney General	Jeremiah S. Black	1857–1860
	Edwin M. Stanton	1860–1861

Postmaster General	Aaron V. Brown	1857–1859
	Joseph Holt	1859–1861
	Horatio King	1861
Secretary of Navy	Isaac Toucey	1857–1861
Secretary of Interior	Jacob Thompson	1857–1861

The Lincoln Administration (1861–1865)

Vice President	Hannibal Hamlin	1861–1865
	Andrew Johnson	1865
Secretary of State	William H. Seward	1861–1865
Secretary of Treasury	Samuel P. Chase	1861–1864
	William P. Fessenden	1864–1865
	Hugh McCulloch	1865
Secretary of War	Simon Cameron	1861–1862
	Edwin M. Stanton	1862–1865
Attorney General	Edward Bates	1861–1864
	James Speed	1864–1865
Postmaster General	Horatio King	1861
	Montgomery Blair	1861–1864
	William Dennison	1864–1865
Secretary of Navy	Gideon Welles	1861–1865
Secretary of Interior	Caleb B. Smith	1861–1863
	John P. Usher	1863–1865

The Andrew Johnson Administration (1865–1869)

Vice President	None	
Secretary of State	William H. Seward	1865–1869
Secretary of Treasury	Hugh McCulloch	1865–1869
Secretary of War	Edwin M. Stanton	1865–1867
	Ulysses S. Grant	1867–1868
	Lorenzo Thomas	1868
	John M. Schofield	1868–1869
Attorney General	James Speed	1865–1866
	Henry Stanbery	1866–1868
	William M. Evarts	1868–1869
Postmaster General	William Dennison	1865–1866
	Alexander Randall	1866–1869
Secretary of Navy	Gideon Welles	1865–1869
Secretary of Interior	John P. Usher	1865
	James Harlan	1865–1866
	Ovrille H. Browning	1866–1869

The Grant Administration (1869–1877)

Vice President	Schuyler Colfax	1869–1873
	Henry Wilson	1873–d. 1875
Secretary of State	Elihu B. Washburne	1869
	Hamilton Fish	1869–1877
Secretary of Treasury	George S. Boutwell	1869–1873
	William Richardson	1873–1874
	Benjamin Bristow	1874–1876
	Lot M. Morrill	1876–1877
Secretary of War	John A. Rawlins	1869
	William T. Sherman	1869
	William W. Belknap	1869–1876
	Alphonso Taft	1876
	James D. Cameron	1876–1877
Attorney General	Ebenezer Hoar	1869–1870
	Amos T. Ackerman	1870–1871
	G. H. Williams	1871–1875
	Edwards Pierrepont	1875–1876
	Alphonso Taft	1876–1877
Postmaster General	John A. J. Creswell	1869–1874
	James W. Marshall	1874
	Marshall Jewell	1874–1876
	James N. Tyner	1876–1877
Secretary of Navy	Adolph E. Borie	1869
	George M. Robeson	1869–1877
Secretary of Interior	Jacob D. Cox	1869–1870
	Columbus Delano	1870–1875
	Zachariah Chandler	1875–1877

The Hayes Administration (1877–1881)

Vice President	William A. Wheeler	1877–1881
Secretary of State	William M. Evarts	1877–1881
Secretary of Treasury	John Sherman	1877–1881
Secretary of War	George W. McCrary	1877–1879
	Alex Ramsey	1879–1881
Attorney General	Charles Devens	1877–1881
Postmaster General	David M. Key	1877–1880
	Horace Maynard	1880–1881
Secretary of Navy	Richard W. Thompson	1877–1880
	Nathan Goff, Jr.	1881
Secretary of Interior	Carl Schurz	1877–1881

The Garfield Administration (1881)

Vice President	Chester A. Arthur	1881
Secretary of State	James G. Blaine	1881
Secretary of Treasury	William Windom	1881
Secretary of War	Robert T. Lincoln	1881
Attorney General	Wayne MacVeagh	1881
Postmaster General	Thomas L. James	1881
Secretary of Navy	William H. Hunt	1881
Secretary of Interior	Samuel J. Kirkwood	1881

The Arthur Administration (1881–1885)

Vice President	None	
Secretary of State	F. T. Frelinghuysen	1881–1885
Secretary of Treasury	Charles J. Folger	1881–1884
	Walter Q. Gresham	1884
	Hugh McCulloch	1884–1885
Secretary of War	Robert T. Lincoln	1881–1885
Attorney General	Benjamin H. Brewster	1881–1885
Postmaster General	Timothy O. Howe	1881–1883
	Walter Q. Gresham	1883–1884
	Frank Hatton	1884–1885
Secretary of Navy	William H. Hunt	1881–1882
	William E. Chandler	1882–1885
Secretary of Interior	Samuel J. Kirkwood	1881–1882
	Henry M. Teller	1882–1885

The Cleveland Administration (1885–1889)

Vice President	Thomas A. Hendricks	1885–d. 1885
Secretary of State	Thomas F. Bayard	1885–1889
Secretary of Treasury	Daniel Manning	1885–1887
	Charles S. Fairchild	1887–1889
Secretary of War	William C. Endicott	1885–1889
Attorney General	Augustus H. Garland	1885–1889

Postmaster General	William F. Vilas	1885–1888
	Don M. Dickinson	1888–1889
Secretary of Navy	William C. Whitney	1885–1889
Secretary of Interior	Lucius Q. C. Lamar	1885–1888
	William F. Vilas	1888–1889
Secretary of Agriculture	Norman J. Colman	1889

The Benjamin Harrison Administration (1889–1893)

Vice President	Levi P. Morton	1889–1893
Secretary of State	James G. Blaine	1889–1892
	John W. Foster	1892–1893
Secretary of Treasury	William Windom	1889–1891
	Charles Foster	1891–1893
Secretary of War	Redfield Proctor	1889–1891
	Stephen B. Elkins	1891–1893
Attorney General	William H. H. Miller	1889–1891
Postmaster General	John Wanamaker	1889–1893
Secretary of Navy	Benjamin F. Tracy	1889–1893
Secretary of Interior	John W. Noble	1889–1893
Secretary of Agriculture	Jeremiah M. Rusk	1889–1893

The Cleveland Administration (1893–1897)

Vice President	Adlai E. Stevenson	1893–1897
Secretary of State	Walter Q. Gresham	1893–1895
	Richard Olney	1895–1897
Secretary of Treasury	John G. Carlisle	1893–1897
Secretary of War	Daniel S. Lamont	1893–1897
Attorney General	Richard Olney	1893–1895
	James Harmon	1895–1897
Postmaster General	Wilson S. Bissell	1893–1895
	William L. Wilson	1895–1897
Secretary of Navy	Hilary A. Herbert	1893–1897
Secretary of Interior	Hoke Smith	1893–1896
	David R. Francis	1896–1897
Secretary of Agriculture	Julius S. Morton	1893–1897

The McKinley Administration (1897–1901)

Vice President	Garret A. Hobart	1897–d. 1899
	Theodore Roosevelt	1901
Secretary of State	John Sherman	1897–1898
	William R. Day	1898
	John Hay	1898–1901
Secretary of Treasury	Lyman J. Gage	1897–1901
Secretary of War	Russell A. Alger	1897–1899
	Elihu Root	1899–1901
Attorney General	Joseph McKenna	1897–1898
	John W. Griggs	1898–1901
	Philander C. Knox	1901
Postmaster General	James A. Gary	1897–1898
	Charles E. Smith	1898–1901
Secretary of Navy	John D. Long	1897–1901
Secretary of Interior	Cornelius N. Bliss	1897–1899
	Ethan A. Hitchcock	1899–1901
Secretary of Agriculture	James Wilson	1897–1901

The Theodore Roosevelt Administration (1901–1909)

Vice President	Charles Fairbanks	1905–1909
Secretary of State	John Hay	1901–1905
	Elihu Root	1905–1909
	Robert Bacon	1909
Secretary of Treasury	Lyman J. Gage	1901–1902
	Leslie M. Shaw	1902–1907
	George B. Cortelyou	1907–1909
Secretary of War	Elihu Root	1901–1904
	William H. Taft	1904–1908
	Luke E. Wright	1908–1909
Attorney General	Philander C. Knox	1901–1904
	William H. Moody	1904–1906
	Charles J. Bonaparte	1906–1909
Postmaster General	Charles E. Smith	1901–1902
	Henry C. Payne	1902–1904
	Robert J. Wynne	1904–1905
	George B. Cortelyou	1905–1907
	George von L. Meyer	1907–1909
Secretary of Navy	John D. Long	1901–1902
	William H. Moody	1902–1904
	Paul Morton	1904–1905
	Charles J. Bonaparte	1905–1906
	Victor H. Metcalf	1906–1908
	Truman H. Newberry	1908–1909
Secretary of Interior	Ethan A. Hitchcock	1901–1907
	James R. Garfield	1907–1909
Secretary of Agriculture	James Wilson	1901–1909
Secretary of Labor and Commerce	George B. Cortelyou	1903–1904
	Victor H. Metcalf	1904–1906
	Oscar S. Straus	1906–1909
	Charles Nagel	1909

The Taft Administration (1909–1913)

Vice President	James S. Sherman	1909–d. 1912
Secretary of State	Philander C. Knox	1909–1913
Secretary of Treasury	Franklin MacVeagh	1909–1913
Secretary of War	Jacob M. Dickinson	1909–1911
	Henry L. Stimson	1911–1913
Attorney General	George W. Wickersham	1909–1913
Postmaster General	Frank H. Hitchcock	1909–1913
Secretary of Navy	George von L. Meyer	1909–1913
Secretary of Interior	Richard A. Ballinger	1909–1911
	Walter L. Fisher	1911–1913
Secretary of Agriculture	James Wilson	1909–1913
Secretary of Labor and Commerce	Charles Nagel	1909–1913

The Wilson Administration (1913–1921)

Vice President	Thomas R. Marshall	1913–1921
Secretary of State	Williams J. Bryan	1913–1915
	Robert Lansing	1915–1920
	Bainbridge Colby	1920–1921
Secretary of Treasury	William G. McAdoo	1913–1918
	Carter Glass	1918–1920
	David F. Houston	1920–1921
Secretary of War	Lindley M. Garrison	1913–1916
	Newton D. Baker	1916–1921
Attorney General	James C. McReynolds	1913–1914
	Thomas W. Gregory	1914–1919
	A. Mitchell Palmer	1919–1921
Postmaster General	Albert S. Burleson	1913–1921

Secretary of Navy	Josephus Daniels	1913–1921
Secretary of Interior	Franklin K. Lane	1913–1920
	John B. Payne	1920–1921
Secretary of Agriculture	David F. Houston	1913–1920
	Edwin T. Meredith	1920–1921
Secretary of Commerce	William C. Redfield	1913–1919
	Joshua W. Alexander	1919–1921
Secretary of Labor	William B. Wilson	1913–1921

The Harding Administration (1921–1923)

Vice President	Calvin Coolidge	1921–1923
Secretary of State	Charles E. Hughes	1921–1923
Secretary of Treasury	Andrew Mellon	1921–1923
Secretary of War	John W. Weeks	1921–1923
Attorney General	Harry M. Daugherty	1921–1923
Postmaster General	Will H. Hays	1921–1922
	Hubert Work	1922–1923
	Harry S. New	1923
Secretary of Navy	Edwin Denby	1921–1923
Secretary of Interior	Albert B. Fall	1921–1923
	Hubert Work	1923
Secretary of Agriculture	Henry C. Wallace	1921–1923
Secretary of Commerce	Herbert C. Hoover	1921–1923
Secretary of Labor	James J. Davis	1921–1923

The Coolidge Administration (1923–1929)

Vice President	Charles G. Dawes	1925–1929
Secretary of State	Charles E. Hughes	1923–1925
	Frank B. Kellogg	1925–1929
Secretary of Treasury	Andrew Mellon	1923–1929
Secretary of War	John W. Weeks	1923–1925
	Dwight F. Davis	1925–1929
Attorney General	Henry M. Daugherty	1923–1924
	Harlan F. Stone	1924–1925
	John G. Sargent	1925–1929
Postmaster General	Harry S. New	1923–1929
Secretary of Navy	Edwin Derby	1923–1924
	Curtis D. Wilbur	1924–1929
Secretary of Interior	Hubert Work	1923–1928
	Roy O. West	1928–1929
Secretary of Agriculture	Henry C. Wallace	1923–1924
	Howard M. Gore	1924–1925
	William M. Jardine	1925–1929
Secretary of Commerce	Herbert C. Hoover	1923–1928
	William F. Whiting	1928–1929
Secretary of Labor	James J. Davis	1923–1929

The Hoover Administration (1929–1933)

Vice President	Charles Curtis	1929–1933
Secretary of State	Henry L. Stimson	1929–1933
Secretary of Treasury	Andrew Mellon	1929–1932
	Ogden L. Mills	1932–1933
Secretary of War	James W. Good	1929
	Patrick J. Hurley	1929–1933
Attorney General	William D. Mitchell	1929–1933
Postmaster General	Walter F. Brown	1929–1933
Secretary of Navy	Charles F. Adams	1929–1933
Secretary of Interior	Ray L. Wilbur	1929–1933
Secretary of Agriculture	Arthur M. Hyde	1929–1933
Secretary of Commerce	Robert P. Lamont	1929–1932
	Roy D. Chapin	1932–1933
Secretary of Labor	James J. Davis	1929–1930
	William N. Doak	1930–1933

The Franklin D. Roosevelt Administration (1933–1945)

Vice President	John Nance Garner	1933–1941
	Henry A. Wallace	1941–1945
	Harry S Truman	1945
Secretary of State	Cordell Hull	1933–1944
	Edward R. Stettinius, Jr.	1944–1945
Secretary of Treasury	William H. Woodin	1933–1934
	Henry Morgenthau, Jr.	1934–1945
Secretary of War	George H. Dern	1933–1936
	Henry A. Woodring	1936–1940
	Henry L. Stimson	1940–1945
Attorney General	Homer S. Cummings	1933–1939
	Frank Murphy	1939–1940
	Robert H. Jackson	1940–1941
	Francis Biddle	1941–1945
Postmaster General	James A. Farley	1933–1940
	Frank C. Walker	1940–1945
Secretary of Navy	Claude A. Swanson	1933–1940
	Charles Edison	1940
	Frank Knox	1940–1944
	James V. Forrestal	1944–1945
Secretary of Interior	Harold L. Ickes	1933–1945
Secretary of Agriculture	Henry A. Wallace	1933–1940
	Claude R. Wickard	1940–1945
Secretary of Commerce	Daniel C. Roper	1933–1939
	Harry L. Hopkins	1939–1940
	Jesse Jones	1940–1945
	Henry A. Wallace	1945
Secretary of Labor	Frances Perkins	1933–1945

The Truman Administration (1945–1953)

Vice President	Alben W. Barkley	1949–1953
Secretary of State	Edward R. Stettinius, Jr.	1945
	James F. Byrnes	1945–1947
	George C. Marshall	1947–1949
	Dean G. Acheson	1949–1953
Secretary of Treasury	Fred M. Vinson	1945–1946
	John W. Snyder	1946–1953
Secretary of War	Robert P. Patterson	1945–1947
	Kenneth C. Royall	1947
Attorney General	Tom C. Clark	1945–1949
	J. Howard McGrath	1949–1952
	James P. McGranery	1952–1953
Postmaster General	Frank C. Walker	1945
	Robert E. Hannegan	1945–1947
	Jesse M. Donaldson	1947–1953
Secretary of Navy	James V. Forrestal	1945–1947
Secretary of Interior	Harold L. Ickes	1945–1946
	Julius A. Krug	1946–1949
	Oscar L. Chapman	1949–1953

Secretary of Agriculture	Clinton P. Anderson	1945–1948
	Charles F. Brannan	1948–1953
Secretary of Commerce	Henry A. Wallace	1945–1946
	W. Averell Harriman	1946–1948
	Charles W. Sawyer	1948–1953
Secretary of Labor	Lewis B. Schwellenbach	1945–1948
	Maurice J. Tobin	1948–1953
Secretary of Defense	James V. Forrestal	1947–1949
	Louis A. Johnson	1949–1950
	George C. Marshall	1950–1951
	Robert A. Lovett	1951–1953

The Eisenhower Administration (1953–1961)

Vice President	Richard M. Nixon	1953–1961
Secretary of State	John Foster Dulles	1953–1959
	Christian A. Herter	1959–1961
Secretary of Treasury	George M. Humphrey	1953–1957
	Robert B. Anderson	1957–1961
Attorney General	Herbert Brownell, Jr.	1953–1958
	William P. Rogers	1958–1961
Postmaster General	Arthur E. Summerfield	1953–1961
Secretary of Interior	Douglas McKay	1953–1958
	Fred A. Seaton	1956–1961
Secretary of Agriculture	Ezra T. Benson	1953–1961
Secretary of Commerce	Sinclair Weeks	1953–1958
	Lewis L. Strauss	1958–1959
	Frederick H. Mueller	1959–1961
Secretary of Labor	Martin P. Durkin	1953
	James P. Mitchell	1953–1961
Secretary of Defense	Charles E. Wilson	1953–1957
	Neil H. McElroy	1957–1959
	Thomas S. Gates, Jr.	1959–1961
Secretary of Health, Education, and Welfare	Oveta Culp Hobby	1953–1955
	Marlon B. Folsom	1955–1958
	Arthur S. Flemming	1958–1961

The Kennedy Administration (1961–1963)

Vice President	Lyndon B. Johnson	1961–1963
Secretary of State	Dean Rusk	1961–1963
Secretary of Treasury	C. Douglas Dillon	1961–1963
Attorney General	Robert F. Kennedy	1961–1963
Postmaster General	J. Edward Day	1961–1963
	John A. Gronouski	1963
Secretary of Interior	Stewart L. Udall	1961–1963
Secretary of Agriculture	Orville L. Freeman	1961–1963
Secretary of Commerce	Luther H. Hodges	1961–1963
Secretary of Labor	Arthur J. Goldberg	1961–1962
	W. Willard Wirtz	1962–1963
Secretary of Defense	Robert S. McNamara	1961–1963
Secretary of Health, Education, and Welfare	Abraham A. Ribicoff	1961–1962
	Anthony J. Celebrezze	1962–1963

The Lyndon Johnson Administration (1963–1969)

Vice President	Hubert H. Humphrey	1965–1969
Secretary of State	Dean Rusk	1963–1969
Secretary of Treasury	C. Douglas Dillon	1963–1965
	Henry H. Fowler	1965–1969
Attorney General	Robert F. Kennedy	1963–1964
	Nicholas Katzenbach	1965–1966
	Ramsey Clark	1967–1969
Postmaster General	John A. Gronouski	1963–1965
	Lawrence F. O'Brien	1965–1968
	Marvin Watson	1968–1969
Secretary of Interior	Stewart L. Udall	1963–1969
Secretary of Agriculture	Orville L. Freeman	1963–1969
Secretary of Commerce	Luther H. Hodges	1963–1964
	John T. Connor	1964–1967
	Alexander B. Trowbridge	1967–1968
	Cyrus R. Smith	1968–1969
Secretary of Labor	W. Willard Wirtz	1963–1969
Secretary of Defense	Robert F. McNamara	1963–1968
	Clark Clifford	1968–1969
Secretary of Health, Education, and Welfare	Anthony J. Celebrezze	1963–1965
	John W. Gardner	1965–1968
	Wilbur J. Cohen	1968–1969
Secretary of Housing and Urban Development	Robert C. Weaver	1966–1969
	Robert C. Wood	1969
Secretary of Transportation	Alan S. Boyd	1967–1969

The Nixon Administration (1969–1974)

Vice President	Spiro T. Agnew	1969–1973
	Gerald R. Ford	1973–1974
Secretary of State	William P. Rogers	1969–1973
	Henry A. Kissinger	1973–1974
Secretary of Treasury	David M. Kennedy	1969–1970
	John B. Connally	1971–1972
	George P. Shultz	1972–1974
	William E. Simon	1974
Attorney General	John N. Mitchell	1969–1972
	Richard G. Kleindienst	1972–1973
	Elliot L. Richardson	1973
	William B. Saxbe	1973–1974
Postmaster General	Winton M. Blount	1969–1971
Secretary of Interior	Walter J. Hickel	1969–1970
	Rogers Morton	1971–1974
Secretary of Agriculture	Clifford M. Hardin	1969–1971
	Earl L. Butz	1971–1974
Secretary of Commerce	Maurice H. Stans	1969–1972
	Peter G. Peterson	1972–1973
	Frederick B. Dent	1973–1974
Secretary of Labor	George P. Shultz	1969–1970
	James D. Hodgson	1970–1973
	Peter J. Brennan	1973–1974
Secretary of Defense	Melvin R. Laird	1969–1973
	Elliot L. Richardson	1973
	James R. Schlesinger	1973–1974
Secretary of Health, Education, and Welfare	Robert H. Finch	1969–1970
	Elliot L. Richardson	1970–1973
	Caspar W. Weinberger	1973–1974

Secretary of Housing and Urban Development	George Romney	1969–1973
	James T. Lynn	1973–1974
Secretary of Transportation	John A. Volpe	1969–1973
	Claude S. Brinegar	1973–1974

The Ford Administration (1974–1977)

Vice President	Nelson A. Rockefeller	1974–1977
Secretary of State	Henry A. Kissinger	1974–1977
Secretary of Treasury	William E. Simon	1974–1977
Attorney General	William B. Saxbe	1974–1975
	Edward Levi	1975–1977
Secretary of Interior	Rogers Morton	1974–1975
	Stanley K. Hathaway	1975
	Thomas Kleppe	1975–1977
Secretary of Agriculture	Earl L. Butz	1974–1976
	John A. Knebel	1976–1977
Secretary of Commerce	Frederick B. Dent	1974–1975
	Rogers Morton	1975–1976
	Elliot L. Richardson	1976–1977
Secretary of Labor	Peter J. Brennan	1974–1975
	John T. Dunlop	1975–1976
	W. J. Usery	1976–1977
Secretary of Defense	James R. Schlesinger	1974–1975
	Donald Rumsfeld	1975–1977
Secretary of Health, Education, and Welfare	Caspar W. Weinberger	1974–1975
	Forrest D. Mathews	1975–1977
Secretary of Housing and Urban Development	James T. Lynn	1974–1975
	Carla A. Hills	1975–1977
Secretary of Transportation	Claude S. Brinegar	1974–1975
	William T. Coleman	1975–1977

The Carter Administration (1977–1981)

Vice President	Walter F. Mondale	1977–1981
Secretary of State	Cyrus R. Vance	1977–1980
	Edmund Muskie	1980–1981
Secretary of Treasury	W. Michael Blumenthal	1977–1979
	G. William Miller	1979–1981
Attorney General	Griffin Bell	1977–1979
	Benjamin R. Civiletti	1979–1981
Secretary of Interior	Cecil D. Andrus	1977–1981
Secretary of Agriculture	Robert Bergland	1977–1981
Secretary of Commerce	Juanita M. Kreps	1977–1979
	Philip M. Klutznick	1979–1981
Secretary of Labor	F. Ray Marshall	1977–1981
Secretary of Defense	Harold Brown	1977–1981
Secretary of Health Education, and Welfare	Joseph A. Califano	1977–1979
	Patricia R. Harris	1979
Secretary of Health and Human Services	Patricia R. Harris	1979–1981
Secretary of Education	Shirley M. Hufstedler	1979–1981
Secretary of Housing and Urban Development	Patricia R. Harris	1977–1979
	Moon Landrieu	1979–1981
Secretary of Transportation	Brock Adams	1977–1979
	Neil E. Goldschmidt	1979–1981
Secretary of Energy	James R. Schlesinger	1979–1979
	Charles W. Duncan	1979–1981

The Reagan Administration (1981–1989)

Vice President	George Bush	1981–1989
Secretary of State	Alexander M. Haig	1981–1982
	George P. Shultz	1982–1989
Secretary of Treasury	Donald Regan	1981–1985
	James A. Baker, III	1985–1988
	Nicholas Brady	1988–1989
Attorney General	William F. Smith	1981–1985
	Edwin A. Meese, III	1985–1988
	Richard Thornburgh	1988–1989
Secretary of Interior	James Watt	1981–1983
	William P. Clark, Jr.	1983–1985
	Donald P. Hodel	1985–1989
Secretary of Agriculture	John Block	1981–1986
	Richard E. Lyng	1986–1989
Secretary of Commerce	Malcolm Baldridge	1981–1987
	C. William Verity, Jr.	1987–1989
Secretary of Labor	Raymond Donovan	1981–1985
	William E. Brock	1985–1988
	Ann Dore McLaughlin	1988–1989
Secretary of Defense	Caspar W. Weinberger	1981–1988
	Frank Carlucci	1988–1989
Secretary of Health and Human Services	Richard Schweiker	1981–1983
	Margaret Heckler	1983–1985
	Otis R. Bowen	1985–1989
Secretary of Education	Terrel H. Bell	1981–1985
	William J. Bennett	1985–1988
	Lauro F. Cavazos	1988–1989
Secretary of Housing and Urban Development	Samuel Pierce	1981–1989
Secretary of Transportation	Drew Lewis	1981–1983
	Elizabeth Dole	1983–1987
	James L. Burnley, IV	1987–1989
Secretary of Energy	James Edwards	1981–1982
	Donald P. Hodel	1982–1985
	John S. Herrington	1985–1989

The Bush Administration (1989–1993)

Vice President	J. Danforth Quayle	1989–1993
Secretary of State	James A. Baker, III	1989–1992
	Lawrence Eagleburger	1992–1993
Secretary of Treasury	Nicholas F. Brady	1988–1993
Attorney General	Richard Thornburgh	1989–1991
	William Barr	1991–1992
Secretary of Interior	Manuel Lujan, Jr.	1989–1993
Secretary of Agriculture	Clayton K. Yeutter	1989–1991
	Edward Madigan	1991–1993

Secretary of Commerce	Robert A. Mosbacher	1989–1991
	Barbara Hackman Franklin	1992–1993
Secretary of Labor	Elizabeth H. Dole	1989–1990
	Lynn Morley Martin	1991–1993
Secretary of Defense	Richard Cheney	1989–1993
Secretary of Health and Human Services	Louis W. Sullivan	1989–1993
Secretary of Education	Lauro F. Cavazos	1989–1990
	Lamar Alexander	1991–1993
Secretary of Housing and Urban Development	Jack F. Kemp	1989–1993
Secretary of Transportation	Samuel K. Skinner	1989–1992
	Andrew H. Card, Jr.	1992–1993
Secretary of Energy	James D. Watkins	1989–1993
Secretary of Veterans Affairs	Edward J. Derwinski	1989–1992

The Clinton Administration (1993–2000)

Vice President	Albert Gore, Jr.	1993–
Secretary of State	Warren M. Christopher	1993–1997
	Madeleine K. Albright	1997–
Secretary of the Treasury	Lloyd M. Bentsen, Jr.	1993–1995
	Robert Rubin	1995–1999
	Lawrence H. Summers	1999–
Attorney General	Janet Reno	1993–
Secretary of the Interior	Bruce E. Babbitt	1993–
Secretary of Agriculture	Mike Espy	1993–1995
	Dan Glickman	1995–
Secretary of Commerce	Ronald H. Brown	1993–1995
	Mickey Kantor	1995–1996
	William M. Daley	1996–
Secretary of Labor	Robert B. Reich	1993–1997
	Alexis Herman	1997–
Secretary of Defense	Les Aspin	1993–1994
	William Perry	1994–1997
	William S. Cohen	1997–
Secretary of Health and Human Services	Donna E. Shalala	1993–
Secretary of Education	Richard W. Riley	1993–
Secretary of Housing and Urban Development	Henry G. Cisneros	1993–1997
	Andrew Cuomo	1997–
Secretary of Transportation	Frederico F. Peña	1993–1997
	Rodney Slater	1997–
Secretary of Energy	Hazel R. O'Leary	1993–1997
	Frederico F. Peña	1997–1998
	Bill Richardson	1998–
Secretary of Veteran's Affairs	Jesse Brown	1993–1998
	Togo West	1998–

Supreme Court Justices

Name	Terms of Service[1]	Appointed by	Name	Terms of Service	Appointed by
John Jay	1789–1795	Washington	Lucious Q. C. Lamar	1888–1893	Cleveland
James Wilson	1789–1798	Washington	**Melville W. Fuller**	1888–1910	Cleveland
John Rutledge	1790–1791	Washington	David J. Brewer	1890–1910	B. Harrison
William Cushing	1790–1810	Washington	Henry B. Brown	1891–1906	B. Harrison
John Blair	1790–1796	Washington	George Shiras, Jr.	1892–1903	B. Harrison
James Iredell	1790–1799	Washington	Howell E. Jackson	1893–1895	B. Harrison
Thomas Johnson	1792–1793	Washington	Edward D. White	1894–1910	Cleveland
William Paterson	1793–1806	Washington	Rufus W. Peckham	1896–1909	Cleveland
John Rutledge[2]	1795	Washington	Joseph McKenna	1898–1925	McKinley
Samuel Chase	1796–1811	Washington	Oliver W. Holmes	1902–1932	T. Roosevelt
Oliver Ellsworth	1796–1800	Washington	William R. Day	1903–1922	T. Roosevelt
Bushrod Washington	1799–1829	J. Adams	William H. Moody	1906–1910	T. Roosevelt
Alfred Moore	1800–1804	J. Adams	Horace H. Lurton	1910–1914	Taft
John Marshall	1801–1835	J. Adams	Charles E. Hughes	1910–1916	Taft
William Johnson	1804–1834	Jefferson	Willis Van Devanter	1911–1937	Taft
Brockholst Livingston	1807–1823	Jefferson	Joseph R. Lamar	1911–1916	Taft
Thomas Todd	1807–1826	Jefferson	**Edward D. White**	1910–1921	Taft
Gabriel Duvall	1811–1835	Madison	Mahlon Pitney	1912–1922	Taft
Joseph Story	1812–1845	Madison	James C. McReynolds	1914–1941	Wilson
Smith Thompson	1823–1843	Monroe	Louis D. Brandels	1916–1939	Wilson
Robert Trimble	1826–1828	J. Q. Adams	John H. Clarke	1916–1922	Wilson
John McLean	1830–1861	Jackson	**William H. Taft**	1921–1930	Harding
Henry Baldwin	1830–1844	Jackson	George Sutherland	1922–1938	Harding
James M. Wayne	1835–1867	Jackson	Pierce Butler	1923–1939	Harding
Roger B. Taney	1836–1864	Jackson	Edward T. Sanford	1923–1930	Harding
Philip P. Barbour	1836–1841	Jackson	Harlan F. Stone	1925–1941	Coolidge
John Cartron	1837–1865	Van Buren	**Charles E. Hughes**	1930–1941	Hoover
John McKinley	1838–1852	Van Buren	Owen J. Roberts	1930–1945	Hoover
Peter V. Daniel	1842–1860	Van Buren	Benjamin N. Cardozo	1932–1938	Hoover
Samuel Nelson	1845–1872	Tyler	Hugo L. Black	1937–1971	F. Roosevelt
Levi Woodbury	1845–1851	Polk	Stanley F. Reed	1938–1957	F. Roosevelt
Robert C. Grier	1846–1870	Polk	Felix Frankfurter	1939–1962	F. Roosevelt
Benjamin R. Curtis	1851–1857	Fillmore	William O. Douglas	1939–1975	F. Roosevelt
John A. Campbell	1853–1861	Pierce	Frank Murphy	1940–1949	F. Roosevelt
Nathan Clifford	1858–1881	Buchanan	**Harlan F. Stone**	1941–1946	F. Roosevelt
Noah H. Swayne	1862–1881	Lincoln	James F. Byrnes	1941–1942	F. Roosevelt
Samuel F. Miller	1862–1890	Lincoln	Robert H. Jackson	1941–1954	F. Roosevelt
David Davis	1862–1877	Lincoln	Wiley B. Rutledge	1943–1949	F. Roosevelt
Stephen J. Field	1863–1897	Lincoln	Harold H. Burton	1945–1958	Truman
Salmon P. Chase	1864–1873	Lincoln	**Frederick M. Vinson**	1946–1953	Truman
William Strong	1870–1880	Grant	Tom C. Clark	1949–1967	Truman
Joseph P. Bradley	1870–1892	Grant	Sherman Minton	1949–1956	Truman
Ward Hunt	1873–1882	Grant	**Earl Warren**	1953–1969	Eisenhower
Morrison R. Waite	1874–1888	Grant	John Marshall Harlan	1955–1971	Eisenhower
John M. Harlan	1877–1911	Hayes	William J. Brennan, Jr.	1956–1990	Eisenhower
William B. Woods	1881–1887	Hayes	Charles E. Whittaker	1957–1962	Eisenhower
Stanley Matthews	1881–1889	Garfield	Potter Stewart	1958–1981	Eisenhower
Horace Gray	1882–1902	Arthur	Byron R. White	1962–1993	Kennedy
Samuel Blatchford	1882–1893	Arthur	Arthur J. Goldberg	1962–1965	Kennedy

Name	Terms of Service	Appointed by	Name	Terms of Service	Appointed by
Abe Fortas	1965–1970	Johnson	**William H. Rehnquist**	1986–	Reagan
Thurgood Marshall	1967–1991	Johnson	Antonin Scalia	1986–	Reagan
Warren E. Burger	1969–1986	Nixon	Anthony M. Kennedy	1988–	Reagan
Harry A. Blackmun	1970–1994	Nixon	David H. Souter	1990–	Bush
Lewis F. Powell, Jr.	1971–1988	Nixon	Clarence Thomas	1991–	Bush
William H. Rehnquist	1971–1986	Nixon	Ruth Bader Ginsberg	1993–	Clinton
John Paul Stevens	1975–	Ford	Stephen G. Breyer	1994–	Clinton
Sandra Day O'Connor	1981–	Reagan			

Chief Justices in bold type

[1] The date on which the justice's took their judicial oath is here used as the date of the beginning of service, for until that oath is taken they are not vested with the prerogatives of their office. Justices, however, receive their commissions ("letters patent") before taking their oath—in some instances, in the preceding year.

[2] Acting Chief Justice; Senate refused to confirm appointment.

Admission of States to the Union

State	Date of Admission
1. Delaware	December 7, 1787
2. Pennsylvania	December 12, 1787
3. New Jersey	December 18, 1787
4. Georgia	January 2, 1788
5. Connecticut	January 9, 1788
6. Massachusetts	February 6, 1788
7. Maryland	April 28, 1788
8. South Carolina	May 23, 1788
9. New Hampshire	June 21, 1788
10. Virginia	June 25, 1788
11. New York	July 26, 1788
12. North Carolina	November 21, 1789
13. Rhode Island	May 29, 1790
14. Vermont	March 4, 1791
15. Kentucky	June 1, 1792
16. Tennessee	June 1, 1796
17. Ohio	March 1, 1803
18. Louisiana	April 30, 1812
19. Indiana	December 11, 1816
20. Mississippi	December 10, 1817
21. Illinois	December 3, 1818
22. Alabama	December 14, 1819
23. Maine	March 15, 1820
24. Missouri	August 10, 1821
25. Arkansas	June 15, 1836
26. Michigan	January 26, 1837
27. Florida	March 3, 1845
28. Texas	December 29, 1845
29. Iowa	December 28, 1846
30. Wisconsin	May 29, 1848
31. California	September 9, 1850
32. Minnesota	May 11, 1858
33. Oregon	February 14, 1859
34. Kansas	January 29, 1861
35. West Virginia	June 20, 1863
36. Nevada	October 31, 1864
37. Nebraska	March 1, 1867
38. Colorado	August 1, 1876
39. North Dakota	November 2, 1889
40. South Dakota	November 2, 1889
41. Montana	November 8, 1889
42. Washington	November 11, 1889
43. Idaho	July 3, 1890
44. Wyoming	July 10, 1890
45. Utah	January 4, 1896
46. Oklahoma	November 16, 1907
47. New Mexico	January 6, 1912
48. Arizona	February 14, 1912
49. Alaska	January 3, 1959
50. Hawaii	August 21, 1959

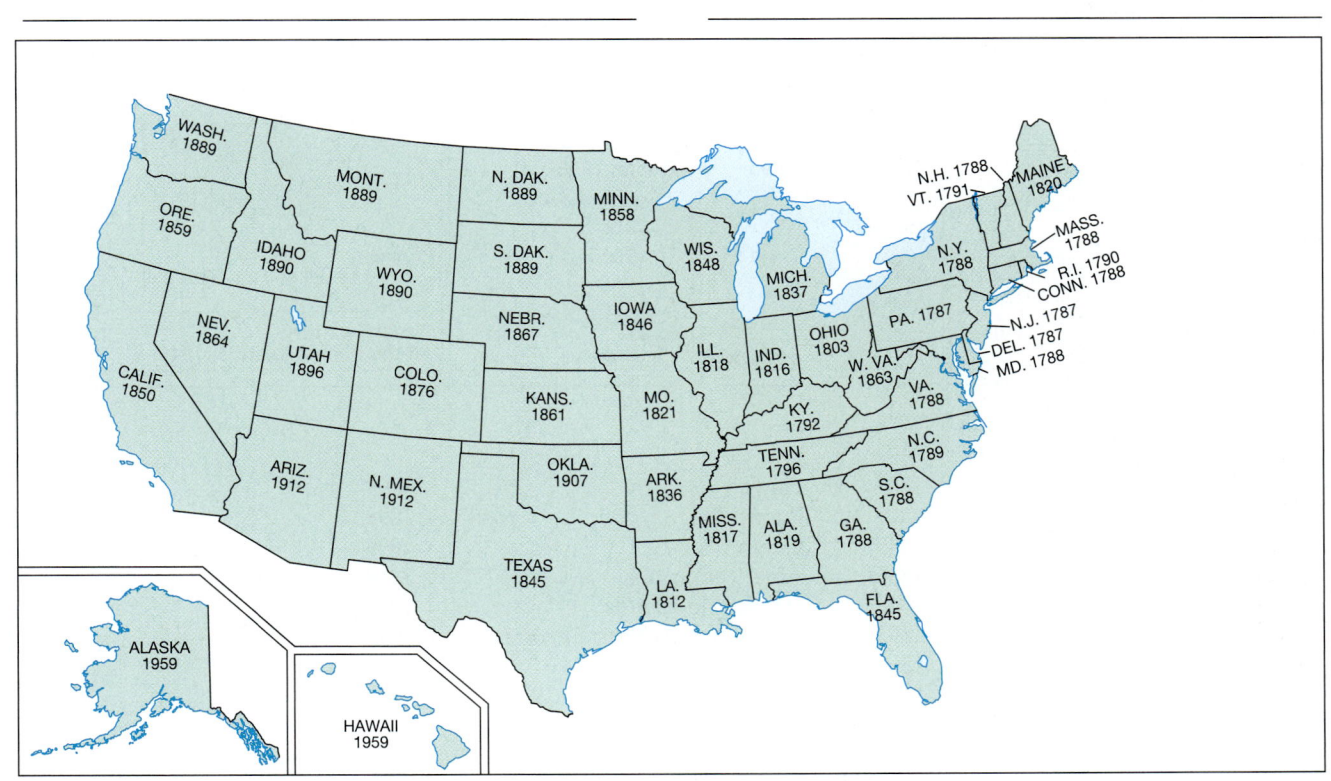

Territorial Expansion of the U.S.

Louisiana Purchase	1803	Hawaii	1898
Florida	1819	Puerto Rico	1898
Texas	1845	Guam	1898
Oregon	1846	American Samoa	1899
Mexican Cession	1848	U.S. Virgin Islands	1917
Gadsden Purchase	1853	Pacific Islands Trust Territory	1947
Alaska	1867		

U.S. Population, 1790–1990

Year	Population	Percent Increase	Population Per Square Mile	Sex (rounded to nearest million) Male	Female	Median Age
1790	3,929,214		4.5	NA	NA	NA
1800	5,308,483	35.1	6.1	NA	NA	NA
1810	7,239,881	36.4	4.3	NA	NA	NA
1820	9,638,453	33.1	5.5	5	5	16.7
1830	12,866,020	33.5	7.4	7	6	17.2
1840	17,069,453	32.7	9.8	9	8	17.8
1850	23,191,876	35.9	7.9	12	11	18.9
1860	31,443,321	35.6	10.6	16	15	19.4
1870	39,818,449	26.6	13.4	19	19	20.2
1880	50,155,783	26.0	16.9	26	25	20.9
1890	62,947,714	25.5	21.2	32	31	22.0
1900	75,994,575	20.7	25.6	39	37	22.9
1910	91,972,266	21.0	31.0	47	45	24.1
1920	105,710,620	14.9	35.6	54	52	25.3
1930	122,775,046	16.1	41.2	62	61	26.4
1940	131,669,275	7.2	44.2	66	66	29.0
1950	150,697,361	14.5	50.7	75	76	30.2
1960	179,323,175	18.5	50.6	88	91	29.5
1970	203,302,031	13.4	57.4	99	104	28.0
1980	226,545,805	11.4	64.0	110	116	30.0
1985	237,839,000	5.0	64.0	117	123	31.3
1990	249,975,000	1.1	70.3	121	127	32.6

NA = Not available.

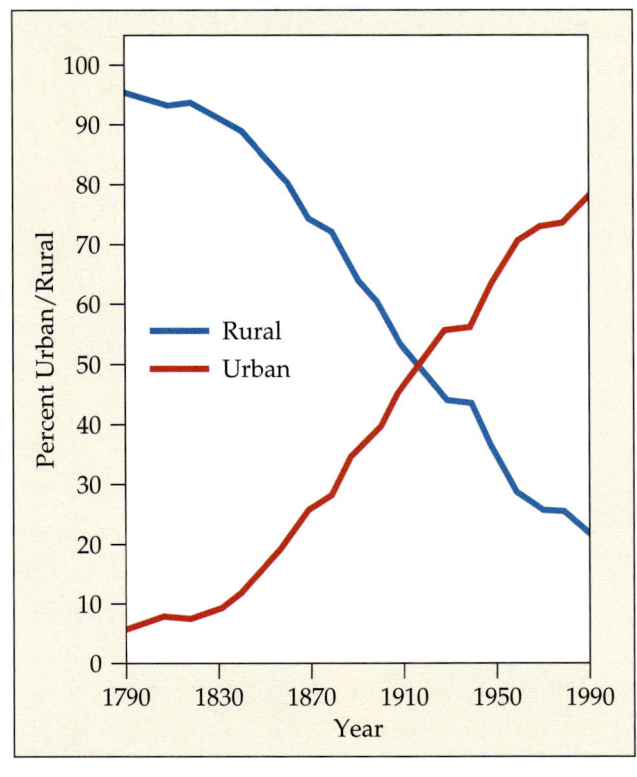

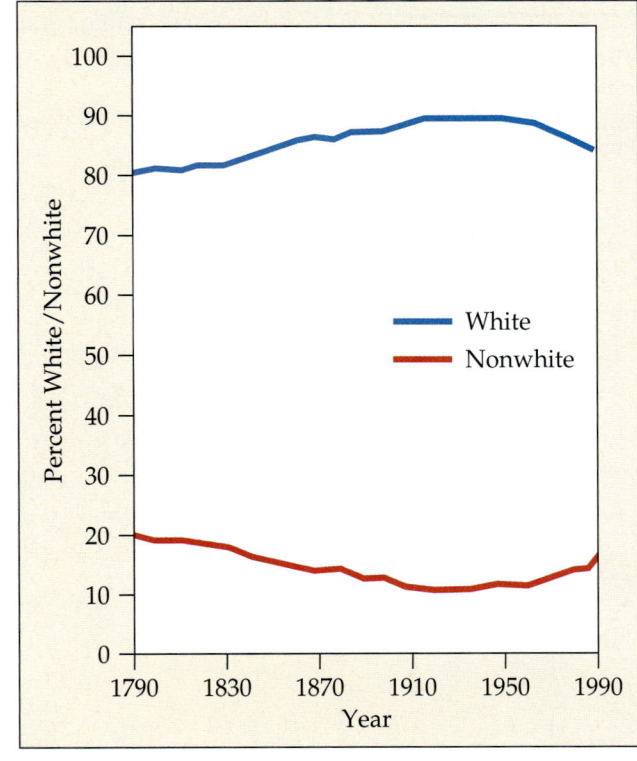

Ethnic Diversity of the U.S., 1990

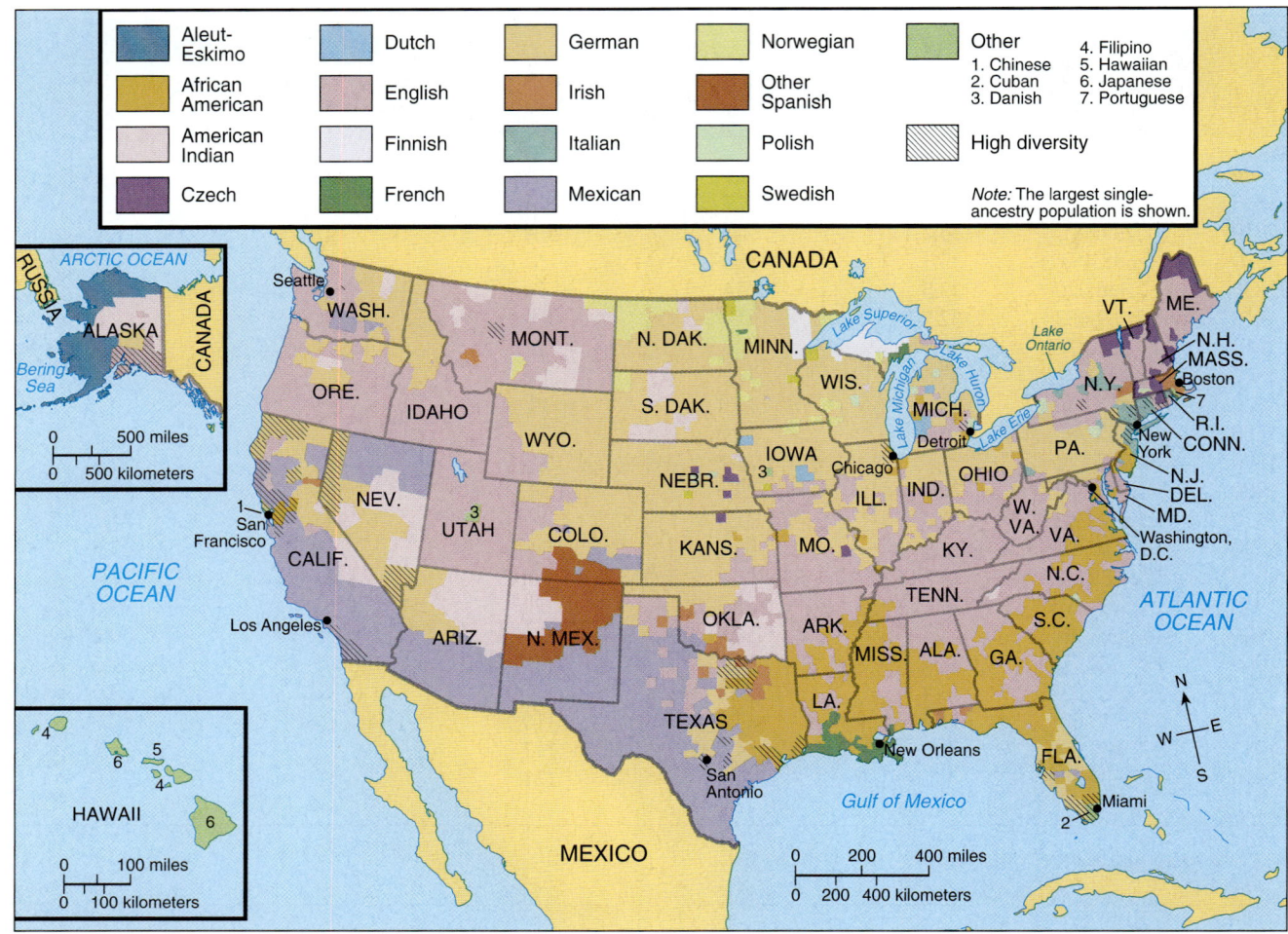

The classifications on this map suggest the pluralism of American society but fail to reflect completely the nation's ethnic diversity.

Data from U.S. Department of Commerce, Bureau of the Census, U.S. Summary Files, Population and Housing, 1990.

Glossary

Adams, John (p. 202) As the nation's second president, Adams had to deal with deteriorating relations between the United States and France. Conflicts between the two countries were evident in the XYZ Affair and the "Quasi-War" of 1798 to 1800.

Alien and Sedition Acts (p. 204) Four acts passed in 1798 designed to curb criticism of the federal government. Adopted during a period of conflict with France, the acts lengthened the period before an immigrant could obtain citizenship, gave the president power to deport dangerous aliens, and provided for the prosecution of those who wrote "false, scandalous and malicious" writings against the U.S. government.

Allies (p. 642) In World War I, the United States, Great Britain, France, and Russia, the alliance that opposed and defeated the Central Powers of Germany and Austria-Hungary and their allies; in World War II, primarily the United States, Great Britain, (free) France, and the Soviet Union that opposed and defeated the Axis powers of Germany, Italy, and Japan.

American Exceptionalism (p. 583) Notion that America houses biologically superior people and can spread democracy to the rest of the world. An intellectual foundation of expansion and racism in the late nineteenth and early twentieth centuries.

American Federation of Labor (p. 508) A confederation of labor unions founded in 1886, it was composed mainly of skilled craft unions and was the first national labor organization to survive and experience a degree of success, largely because of its conservative leadership that accepted industrial capitalism.

American System (of Henry Clay) (p. 265) Henry Clay's program for the national economy, which included a protective tariff to stimulate industry, a national bank to provide credit, and federally funded internal improvements to expand the market for farm products.

American System of Production (p. 245) The high cost of labor led to the establishment of a system of mass production through the manufacture of interchangeable parts.

Anaconda Plan (p. 419) General Winfield Scott designed this strategic plan in the early days of the Civil War to give direction to the Union war effort against the South. The plan advocated a full naval blockade of the South's coastline, a military campaign to gain control of the Mississippi River, and the placement of armies at key points in the South to squeeze—like the Anaconda snake—the life out of the Confederacy. In various ways, this plan helped inform overall Union strategy in militarily defeating the South.

Antifederalists (p. 181) These were opponents of the Constitution of 1787 who sought to continue the confederation of sovereign states and to keep power as close as possible to the people. In actuality, the Antifederalists were true federalists in seeking to balance powers among the states and the national government. Their confused identity may have cost them support in attempting to prevent ratification of the Constitution. See *Federalists*.

Antinomian (p. 47) Literally meaning against the laws of human governance. Antinomians believed that once they had earned saving grace, God would offer them direct revelation by which to order the steps of their lives. As such, human institutions, such as churches and government, were no longer necessary. Mainline Puritans believed Antinomianism would produce only social chaos and destroy the Bay Colony's mission, so they repudiated and even exiled prominent persons like Anne Hutchinson, who advocated such doctrines.

Axis Powers (p. 745) In World War II, the alliance of German and Italy, and later Japan.

Bank of the United States (p. 195) A central bank, chartered by the federal government in 1791. Proposed by Alexander Hamilton, the bank collected taxes, held government funds, and regulated state banks. The bank's charter expired in 1811. A second Bank of the United States was created in 1816. See *Second Bank of the United States*.

Bay of Pigs Fiasco (p. 850) A plan to assassinate Cuban leader Fidel Castro and liberate Cuba with a trained military force of political exiles. The limited 1961 invasion was an unmitigated military failure and actually strengthened Castro's position in Cuba.

Beat Generation (p. 814) A cultural style and artistic movement of the 1950s that rejected traditional American family life and material values and celebrated African-American culture. They tapped an underground dissatisfaction with mainstream American culture.

Big Stick Diplomacy (p. 629) The proclaimed foreign policy of Theodore Roosevelt, it was based on the proverb, "Speak softly and carry a big stick," and advocated the threat of force to achieve the United States' goals, especially in the Western Hemisphere.

Bill of Rights (p. 193) The first ten amendments to the U.S. Constitution, which protect the rights of individuals from the powers of the national government. Congress and the states adopted the ten amendments in 1791.

Billy Yank (p. 419) This appellation was used to refer to common soldiers serving in Union armies during the Civil War. See *Johnny Reb*.

Birds of Passage (p. 518) Immigrants who never intended to make the United States their home. Unable to make a living in their native countries, they came to America, worked and saved, and returned home. About 20 to 30 percent of immigrants returned home.

Black Codes (p. 453) Laws passed by Southern state legislatures during Reconstruction, while Congress was out of session. These laws limited the rights of former slaves and led Congress to ratify the Fourteenth Amendment.

Black Power (p. 886) A rallying cry for more militant blacks advocated by younger leaders like Stokely Carmichael and H. Rap Brown, beginning in the mid-1960s. It called for African Americans to form their own economic, political, and cultural institutions.

Black Tuesday (p. 692) October 29, 1929, the day of the stock market crash that initiated the Great Depression.

Bonus Army (p. 706) Group of unemployed World War I veterans who marched on Washington, D.C., in June 1932 to ask for immediate payment of their war pensions.

Brain Trust (p. 708) Close advisors to President Franklin Delano Roosevelt during the early days of his first term whose policy suggestions influenced much New Deal legislation.

Brown* v. *Board of Education of Topeka (p. 807) Supreme Court decision of 1954 that overturned the "separate but equal doctrine" that justified Jim Crow laws. Chief Justice Earl Warren argued that "separate educational facilities are inherently unequal."

Burr, Aaron (p. 206) Thomas Jefferson's first vice president, who killed Alexander Hamilton in a duel in 1804.

Cabinet (p. 173) This term refers to the heads of the executive departments.

Calhoun, John C. (p. 236) As vice president, Calhoun anonymously expounded the doctrine of nullification, which held that states could prevent the enforcement of a federal law within their boundaries.

Calvinism (p. 22) Broadly influential Protestant theology emanating from the French theologian John Calvin, who fled to Switzerland, where he reordered life in the community of Geneva according to his conception of the Bible. Calvinism emphasized the power and omnipotence of God and the importance of seeking to earn saving grace and salvation, even though God had already determined (the concept of predestination) who would be eternally saved or damned.

Camp David Accords (p. 918) An historic 1979 peace agreement negotiated between Egypt and Israel at the U.S. presidential retreat at Camp David, Maryland. Under the pact, Israel agreed to return captured territory to Egypt and to negotiate Palestinian autonomy in the West Bank and Gaza Strip.

Capital Punishment (p. 291) During the early nineteenth century, a movement arose to end the death penalty.

Carpetbaggers (p. 460) People who moved to the South during or following the Civil War and became active in politics, they helped to bring Republican control of southern state governments during Reconstruction and were bitterly resented by most white Southerners.

Carter, Jimmy (p. 823) Georgia governor in 1970, and president in 1976. His progressive racial views reflected an emergent South less concerned with racial distinctions and more concerned with economic development and political power.

Cautious Revolutionaries (p. 162) Sometimes called reluctant revolutionaries, these leaders lacked a strong trust in the people to rise above their own self-interest and provide for enlightened legislative policies (see *public virtue*). At the time of the American Revolution, they argued in favor of forms of government that could easily check the popular will. To assure political stability, they believed that political decision making should be in the hands of society's proven social and economic elite. John Dickinson, John Adams (very much an eager revolutionary), and Robert Morris might be described as cautious revolutionaries. See *radical revolutionaries.*

Central Powers (p. 646)   In World War I, Germany and Austria-Hungary and their allies.

Channing, William Ellery (p. 285)   America's leading exponent of religious liberalism, Channing was one of the founders of American Unitarianism.

The China Lobby (p. 773)   An informal group of media leaders and political pundits who criticized the communist takeover of China, claiming the United States could have prevented it.

City upon a Hill (p. 44)   Phrase from John Winthrop's sermon, "A Model of Christian Charity," in which he challenged his fellow Puritans to build a model, ideal community in America that would serve as an example of how the rest of the world should order its existence. Here was the beginning of the idea of America as a special, indeed exceptional society, therefore worthy of emulation by others. The concept of American exceptionalism has dominated American history and culture down to the present.

Civil Rights Act of 1964 (p. 883)   Landmark legislation that prohibited discrimination on the basis of race, sex, religion, or national origin in employment and public facilities such as hotels, restaurants, and playgrounds. It established the Equal Employment Opportunity Commission.

Clay, Henry (p. 236)   As Speaker of the House of Representatives, Senator, and unsuccessful candidate for the presidency, he was an advocate of the "American System," which called for a protective tariff, a national bank, and federally funded internal improvements. See *American system (of Henry Clay).*

Colonization (p. 294)   The effort to encourage masters to voluntarily emancipate their slaves and to resettle free blacks in Africa.

Columbian Exchange (p. 30)   The process of transferring plants, animals, foods, diseases, wealth, and culture between Europe and the Americas, beginning at the time of Christopher Columbus and continuing throughout the era of exploration and expansion. The exchange often resulted in the devastation of Native American peoples and cultures, so much so that the process is sometimes referred to as the "Columbian collision."

Committee on Public Information (CPI) (p. 653)   U.S. propaganda agency of World War I.

Committees of Correspondence (p. 119)   As American leaders became increasingly anxious about a perceived British imperial conspiracy to deprive them of their liberties, they set up networks of communication among the colonies. Beginning in 1773 colonial assemblies began to appoint committees of correspondence to warn each other about possible abuses. In some colonies, such as Massachusetts, local communities also organized such committees, all with the intention of being vigilant against arbitrary acts from British officials.

Common Sense (p. 138)   This best-selling pamphlet by Thomas Paine, first published in 1776, denounced the British monarchy, called for American independence, and encouraged the adoption of republican forms of government. Paine's bold words thus helped crack the power of reconciliationist leaders in the Second Continental Congress who did not believe the colonies could stand up to British arms and survive as an independent nation.

Compromise of 1877 (p. 473)   A bargain made between southern Democrats and Republican candidate Rutherford B. Hayes after the disputed presidential election of 1876. The southern Democrats pledged to let Hayes take office in return for his promise to withdraw the remaining federal troops from the southern states. The removal of the last troops in 1877 marked the end of Reconstruction.

Coney Island (p. 540)   Popular site of New York amusement parks opening in 1890s, attracting working class Americans with rides and games celebrating abandon and instant gratification.

Copperheads (p. 428)   Not every person living in the North during the Civil War favored making war against the Confederacy. Such persons came to be identified as Copperheads. Often affiliated with the Democratic party and residing in the Midwest, Copperheads favored a negotiated peace settlement that would allow the South to leave the Union. Some of them were arbitrarily thrown into jail without proper *habeas corpus* proceedings after publicly advocating their views.

Court Packing (p. 720)   President Franklin Delano Roosevelt's controversial plan to appoint Supreme Court justices who were sympathetic to his views, by offering retirement benefits to the sitting justices.

Coverture (p. 57)   Coverture is closely connected with patriarchy because this concept contends that the legal identity of women is subordinated first in their fathers and, then, in their husbands, as the sanctioned heads of households. See *patriarchal.*

Coxey's Army (p. 569)   A movement founded by Jacob S. Coxey to help the unemployed during the depression of the 1890s, it brought out-of-work people to Washington, D.C., to demand that the federal government provide jobs and inflate the currency.

Crandall, Prudence (p. 292)   A Quaker schoolteacher, Crandall sparked controversy when she opened a school for the education of free blacks.

Cuban Missile Crisis (p. 850)   The conflict in 1962 prompted by Soviet installation of missiles on Cuba and President Kennedy's announcement to the American Public. After days of genuine fear on both sides, the two sides negotiated an agreement whereby the Soviet Union removed the missiles and the United States pledged not to invade Cuba.

Cuffe, Paul (p. 294) An African-American sea captain, Cuffe led the first experiment in colonization when he transported 38 free blacks to Sierra Leone in 1815.

Dartmouth v. Woodward (p. 240) A landmark 1819 Supreme Court decision protecting contracts. In the case, Chief Justice John Marshall ruled that the charters of business corporations are contracts and thus protected under the U.S. Constitution.

Dawes Severalty Act (p. 471) Legislation passed in 1887 to authorize the president to divide tribal land and distribute it to individual Native Americans, it gave 160 acres to each head of the household in an attempt to assimilate Indians into citizenship.

D-Day (p. 747) June 6, 1944, the day Allied forces landed on the beaches of Normandy, in France, leading to the defeat of Germany.

Declension (p. 55) A term associated with the Massachusetts Bay Colony, referring to the declining zeal of later generations or movement away from the utopian ideals of those Puritan leaders, such as John Winthrop, who founded the colony. As an example of declension, see *half-way covenant*.

Deregulation (p. 917) An economic policy, begun during the administration of Jimmy Carter, which freed air and surface transportation, the savings and loan industry, natural gas, and other industries from many government economic controls.

Détente (p. 918) A relaxation of tensions between the United States and the Soviet Union that was begun by President Richard M. Nixon.

Diem, Ngo Dinh (p. 852) Although a Catholic in a Buddhist nation and a leader with no popular charm, the American government manufactured Diem's 1956 election because of his anticommunist views. The American government gradually realized Diem's lack of popular support and stood by when he was assassinated in 1963.

Dien Bien Phu (p. 852) Vietminh siege of 13,000 French soldiers in 1954 at a remote military outpost. The French surrender led to the 1956 elections designed to reunify Vietnam.

Divine Right Rule (p. 40) Long-held belief that monarchs were God's political stewards on earth. Because their authority to rule supposedly came directly from God, the decision making of monarchs was held to be infallible and thus could not be questioned. Some of England's Stuart kings in the seventeenth century viewed themselves as ruling by divine right, a position that numerous subjects rejected, even to the point of a civil war in the 1640s and the beheading of Charles I in 1649.

Dix, Dorothea (p. 293) The leader of efforts to reform the treatment of the mentally ill.

Douglass, Frederick (p. 296) The nation's most famous fugitive slave and African-American abolitionist, Douglass supported political action against slavery.

Dumbbell tenements (p. 528) Apartment buildings built to minimal codes and designed to cram the largest number of people into the smallest amount of space. The dumbbell indentation in the middle of the building, although unsightly, conformed to the Tenement Reform Law of 1879, which required all rooms to have access to light and air.

Dunmore's Ethiopian Regiment (p. 138) In November 1775 John Murray, Lord Dunmore (Virginia's last royal governor), issued an emancipation proclamation that freed all slaves and indentured servants living in Virginia who were willing to bear arms against their rebellious masters. As many as 2000 slaves fled to the British banner, and some became members of Dunmore's Ethiopian regiment. With little training in arms, this regiment fared poorly in a battle with Virginia militia in December 1775. An outbreak of smallpox later killed many of the ex-slaves who responded to Dunmore's proclamation.

Electric Trolley (p. 525) Public transportation for urban neighborhoods, using electric current from overhead wires. Between 1888 and 1902, 97 percent of urban transit mileage had been electrified.

Emancipation Proclamation (p. 426) President Abraham Lincoln issued a preliminary proclamation in September 1862 that all slaves would be declared free in those states that were still in rebellion against the Union at the beginning of 1863. Receiving no official response from the Confederacy, Lincoln announced the Emancipation Proclamation on January 1, 1863. All slaves in the rebellious Confederate states were to be forever free. However, slavery could continue to exist in border states that were not at war against the Union. Lincoln's Emancipation Proclamation represented the beginning of the end of chattel slavery in the United States.

Embargo of 1807 (p. 221) An attempt to stop British and French interference with American shipping by prohibiting foreign trade.

Emerson, Ralph Waldo (p. 303) A poet and essayist, Emerson espoused a philosophy called transcendentalism, which emphasized self-reliance and intuition.

Enclosure Movement (p. 23) As the demand for wool heightened in England during the sixteenth century because of the emerging textile industry, Parliament passed laws that allowed profit-seeking landowners to fence in their open fields to raise more sheep. Thousands of peasants who, as renters, had been farming these lands for generations were evicted and thrown into poverty. Many moved to the cities, where as "sturdy beggars" they too often found little work. In time, some migrated to English colonies in America, where work opportunities were far more abundant.

Encomienda **System** (p. 19)   The government in Spain gave away large tracts of conquered land in Spanish America, including whole villages of indigenous peoples, to court favorites, including many *conquistadores*. These new landlords, or *encomenderos*, were supposed to educate the natives and teach them the Roman Catholic faith. The system was rife with abuse, however. Landlords rarely offered much education, preferring instead to exploit the labor of the local inhabitants, whom they treated like slaves.

Enlightenment (p. 83, 285)   A broadly influential philosophical and intellectual movement that began in Europe during the eighteenth century. The Enlightenment unleashed a tidal wave of new learning, especially in the sciences and mathematics, that helped promote the notion that human beings, through the use of their reason, could solve society's problems. The Enlightenment era, as such, has also been called the "Age of Reason." Benjamin Franklin and Thomas Jefferson were leading proponents of Enlightenment thinking in America.

Enumerated Goods (p. 68)   Products grown or extracted from England's North American colonies that could be shipped only to England or other colonies within the empire. Goods on the first enumeration list included tobacco, indigo, and sugar. Later on furs, molasses, and rice would be added to a growing list of products that the English colonies could not sell directly to foreign nations.

Equal Rights Amendment (p. 684, 896)   Proposed Constitutional amendment that would prohibit discrimination on the basis of gender.

Era of Good Feelings (p. 234)   Phrase used to describe the years following the War of 1812, when one party, the Jeffersonian Republicans, dominated politics, and a spirit of nationalism characterized public policy.

Evangelical Revivalism (Revivals) (p. 288)   A current of Protestant Christianity emphasizing personal conversion, repentance of sin, and the authority of Scripture.

The Fair Deal (p. 778)   Failed 1948 legislative package proposed by President Truman. It included an expansion of Social Security, federal aid to education, a higher minimum wage, a national plan for medical insurance, and civil rights legislation for minorities.

Farewell Address (p. 202)   In this 1796 statement, in which he expresses his intention not to run for a third term as president, George Washington warns of the dangers of party divisions, sectionalism, and permanent alliances with foreign nations.

Federal Reserve System (p. 627)   The central banking system of the United States, established with passage of the Federal Reserve Act of 1913, charged with the responsibility of managing the country's money supply through such means as lowering or raising interest rates. A presidentially appointed board of seven members (the Federal Reserve Board) oversees the twelve regional banks of the Federal Reserve System.

Federalist Papers (p. 182)   These 85 newspaper essays, written in support of ratification of the Constitution of 1787 in New York by James Madison, Alexander Hamilton, and John Jay, described the proposed plan of national government as a sure foundation for long-term political stability and enlightened legislation. Although having little effect on the ratification debate in New York, the papers soon became classics of political philosophy about the Constitution as the framework of federal government for the American republic.

Federalists (p. 181, 196)   In the campaign to ratify the Constitution of 1787, nationalists started referring to themselves as federalists, which conveyed the meaning that they were in favor of splitting authority between their proposed strong national government and the states. The confusion in terminology may have helped win some support among citizens worried about a powerful—and potentially tyrannical—national government. Some leading nationalists of the 1780s became Federalists in the 1790s. See *Antifederalists*. The term also refers to a political party founded by Alexander Hamilton in the 1790s to support his economic program.

Finney, Charles Grandison (p. 288)   The "father of modern revivalism," Finney devised many techniques adopted by later revival preachers. He encouraged many women to participate actively in revival.

Fire-eaters (p. 411)   Radical leaders in the South during the years leading up to the Civil War, the fire-eaters were persons who took an extreme pro-slavery position. They repeatedly expressed their desire to see slavery spread throughout the United States, and they used states' rights arguments to support their uncompromising position.

Fireside Chats (p. 707)   Weekly radio addresses by President Franklin Delano Roosevelt in which he explained his actions directly to the American people.

First 100 Days (p. 707) President Franklin Delano Roosevelt's first 100 days in office, when he proposed and Congress passed fifteen major bills that reshaped the U.S. economy.

First Continental Congress (p. 121) This body was the most important expression of intercolonial protest activity up to 1774. Called in response to Parliament's Coercive Acts, the delegates met in Philadelphia for nearly two months. More radical delegates dominated the deliberations. Before dissolving itself, the Congress called for ongoing resistance, even military preparations to defend American communities, and a second congress, should King and Parliament not redress American grievances.

Flapper (p. 681) Term for a liberated woman who bucked conventional ideas of propriety in dress and manners during the 1920s.

Flexible Response (p. 856) Approach to foreign policy of the Kennedy administration based on developing and maintaining conventional, counterinsurgency (antiguerilla), and nuclear forces so that the United States would be able to choose from among these options in response to communist threat anywhere in the world.

Fourteen Points (p. 661) President Woodrow Wilson's formula for peace after World War I.

Free Soil Party (p. 296) An antislavery political party founded in 1848.

Freedmen's Bureau (Bureau of Refugees, Freedmen, and Abandoned Lands) (p. 450) An organization established by Congress on March 3, 1865 to deal with the dislocations of the Civil War. It provided relief, helped settle disputes, and founded schools and hospitals.

Freedom of Information Act (p. 914) This law allows the public and press to request declassification of government documents.

Freedom Riders (p. 879) Civil rights activists who in 1961 demonstrated that despite a federal ban on segregated travel on interstate buses, segregation prevailed in parts of the South.

Friedan, Betty (p. 892) Author of *The Feminine Mystique*, the 1963 book that articulated the discontent among white middle-class housewives in the "Baby Boom" era. She founded the National Organization for Women (NOW) in 1966.

Fugitive Slave Law (p. 389) The most controversial element of the Compromise of 1850, the Fugitive Slave Law provided for the return of runaway slaves to their masters.

Gabriel (p. 344) A Virginia slave and blacksmith who organized an attempted assault against Richmond in 1800.

Gallaudet, Thomas Hopkins (p. 293) Founder of the nation's first school to teach deaf mutes to read and write and communicate through hand signals.

Garrison, William Lloyd (p. 294) The leader of radical abolitionism, Garrison sought immediate freedom for slaves without compensation to their owners.

Goldwater, Barry (p. 831) Presidential candidate in 1964, Goldwater spearheaded an emergent conservative drive out of the South and West. Unhappy with the nation's path toward liberalism, Goldwater called for more limited taxes, a reduction in legislation aiding farmers and organized labor, and a reduction of federal spending.

Good Neighbor Policy (p. 730) During the administration of President Franklin D. Roosevelt, the U.S. policy of not interfering in the internal affairs of hemispheric neighbors.

Gorbachev, Mikhail (p. 925) The last leader of the Soviet Union, Gorbachev adopted policies of *glastnost* (political liberalization) and *perestroika* (economic reform).

Gospel of Wealth (p. 485) The belief that God ordains certain people to amass money and use it to further God's purposes, it justified the concentration of wealth as long as the rich used their money responsibly.

Grand Alliance (p. 745) In World War II, the alliance between the United States, Great Britain, and France.

Great Awakening (p. 86) Spilling over into the colonies from a wave of revivals in Europe, the Awakening placed renewed emphasis on vital religious faith, partially in reaction to more secular, rationalist thinking characterizing the Enlightenment. Beginning as scattered revivals in the 1720s, the Awakening grew into a fully developed outpouring of rejuvenated faith by the 1740s. Key figures included Jonathan Edwards and George Whitefield. The Awakening's legacy included more emphasis on personal choice, as opposed to state mandates about worship, in matters of religious faith.

Great Migration (p. 657) The mass movement of African Americans from the South to the North during World War I.

Great Society (p. 836) The liberal reform program of President Lyndon Johnson. The program included civil rights legislation, increased public spending to help the poor, Medicare and Medicaid programs, educational legislation, and liberalized immigration policies.

Greenback Party (p. 558) A political party founded in 1874 to promote the issuance of legal tender paper currency not backed by precious metals in order to inflate the money supply and relieve the suffering of people hurt by the era's deflation, most of its members merged with the Populist party.

Greenbacks (p. 425) To help fund the military forces used against the Confederacy during the Civil War, the federal Congress issued a paper currency known as greenbacks. Even though greenbacks had no backing in specie (hard currency), this currency held its value fairly well because of mounting confidence the Union would prevail in the war. See also *specie*.

Grimké, Angelina, and Sarah (p. 298) Born to a wealthy South Carolina slaveholding family, these sisters became leaders in the abolitionist and women's rights movements.

Gulf of Tonkin Resolution (p. 855) Following two reported attacks on the *U.S.S. Maddox* in 1964, American president Lyndon B. Johnson asked for and received this authorization from Congress to "take all necessary measures" to repel attacks, prevent aggression, and protect American security. It allowed Johnson to act without Congressional authorization on military matters in Vietnam.

Half-Way Covenant (p. 55) Realizing that many children of the Massachusetts Bay Colony's first generation were not actively seeking God's saving grace and full church membership, the question was how to keep the next generation of children active in church affairs. The solution, agreed to in 1662, was to permit the baptism of children and grandchildren of professing saints, thereby according them half-way membership. Full church membership still would come only after individuals testified to a conversion experience. This compromise on standards of membership was seen as a sign of declension. See *declension*.

Hamilton, Alexander (p. 194) The first secretary of the treasury and a leader of the Federalist party. As secretary of the treasury, he devised a plan for repaying the nation's debts and promoting economic growth. This plan included funding and assumption of the national and state debts at face value, establishment of the Bank of the United States, and tariffs on imported goods. Hamilton died following a duel with Aaron Burr in 1804.

Harlem Renaissance (p. 688) Self-conscious African American cultural, literary, and artistic movement centered in Harlem in New York City during the 1920s.

Hartford Convention (p. 227) Convention held in late 1814 and early 1815 by New Englanders opposed to the War of 1812, which recommended Constitutional amendments to weaken the power of the South and to restrict Congress's power to impose embargoes or declare war.

Haymarket Square riot (p. 507) A violent encounter between police and protestors in 1886 in Chicago, which led to the execution of four protest leaders, it scared the public with the specter of labor violence and demonstrated government's support of industrialists over workers.

Headright (p. 39) As an economic incentive to encourage English settlement in Virginia and other English colonies during the seventeenth century, sponsoring parties would offer 50 acres of land per person to those who migrated or who paid for the passage of others willing to migrate to America. Because of Virginia's high death rate and difficult living conditions, headrights functioned as an inducement to help bolster the colony's low settlement rate.

Helper, Hinton Rowan (p. 346) The North Carolina-born author of *The Impending Crisis of the South*, a book that argued that slavery was incompatible with economic progress.

Hessians (p. 140) Six German principalities provided 30,000 soldiers to Great Britain to fight against the American rebels during the War for Independence. More than half of these troops-for-hire came from Hesse-Cassel. Hessian thus would serve as the generic term for all German mercenaries fighting in the war, whether or not they came from Hesse-Cassel.

Holy Experiment (p. 71) Tolerance of religious diversity was at the core of William Penn's vision for a colony in America. As such, the colony of Pennsylvania represented a "holy experiment" for Penn. He encouraged people of all faiths to live together in harmony and to maintain harmonious relations with Native Americans in the region. The residents of early Pennsylvania never fully embraced Penn's vision, but the colony was open to religious dissenters and became a model for the diversity that later characterized America.

Hooverizing (p. 652) Herbert Hoover's program as director of the Food Administration to conserve food during World War I.

Hoovervilles (p. 701) Shanty-towns of the Great Depression, named after President Herbert Hoover.

House Un-American Activities Committee (HUAC) (p. 781) investigated subversive right- and left-wing movements. During the Cold War, it was best known for its two investigations of the American film industry.

Howe, Samuel Gridley (p. 293) Founder of the nation's first school for the blind.

Hudson Highlands Strategy (p. 147) The British tried to execute this strategy early in the War for American Independence but never successfully implemented it. The idea was to gain control of the Hudson River-Lake Champlain corridor running north from New York City and south from Montreal, Canada. Had the British done so, the effect would have been to cut off New England, the initial center of rebellion, from the rest of the colonies. New England could then have been reconquered in detail. The failure to coordinate the movements of British forces in 1776 and 1777 resulted in the capture of John Burgoyne's army at Saratoga, New York, in October 1777, which ended any attempt to snuff out the rebellion by retaking New England.

Hydraulic Society (p. 827) Defined by historian Donald Worster as "a social order based on the intensive manipulation of water and its products in an arid setting," it characterized the irrigated societies of the modern West, allowing for agricultural productivity and a massive demographic shift westward.

Implied Powers (p. 194) The view that the national government's powers are not limited to those stated explicitly in the U.S. Constitution.

Impressment (p. 221) The British practice of seizing seamen from American merchant ships and forcing them to serve in the British navy. Impressment was one of the causes of the War of 1812.

Imprisonment for Debt (p. 291) During the early nineteenth century, reformers succeeded in restricting imprisonment of debtors.

Indentured Servitude (p. 38) In an effort to entice English subjects to the colonies, parties would offer legal bonded contracts that would exchange the cost of passage across the Atlantic for up to seven years of labor in America. Indenture contracts also required masters to provide food, clothing, farm tools, and sometimes land when the term of bonded service had expired, thus allowing former servants the opportunity to gain full economic independence in America.

Indulgences (p. 21) Redemption certificates pardoning persons from punishment in the afterlife that were being sold by the Roman Catholic church. Martin Luther particularly condemned this practice in his Ninety-five Theses, bringing on the Protestant Reformation.

The Influence of Sea Power upon History (p. 586) 1890 book by Alfred Thayer Mahan that argued nations expand their world power through foreign commerce and a strong navy. Strongly influenced American politicians who advocated expansion.

Initiative and Referendum (p. 566) A procedure that allows citizens to propose legislation through petitions, it was passed by numerous states at the turn of the century but rarely used until the 1970s.

Insanity Defense (p. 291) The legal principle that a criminal act should only be punished if the offender was fully capable of distinguishing right from wrong.

Interstate Commerce Commission (ICC) (p. 560) The first federal regulatory agency, established by passage of the Interstate Commerce Act in 1887 to regulate the railroads. The ICC's powers were expanded to oversee other forms of transportation and communication.

Iranian Hostage Crisis (p. 920) In November 1979, Iranian students seized the U.S. embassy compound in Tehran and held 52 Americans inside hostage for 444 days.

Jackson, Andrew (p. 226) As major general during the War of 1812, he defeated the Creek Indians at the Battle of Horseshoe Bend and a British army at the Battle of New Orleans. In 1818, he led an American incursion into Spanish-held Florida. He served as seventh president of the United States from 1829 to 1837.

Jazz (p. 534) Musical style based on improvisation within a band format, combining African traditions of repetition, call and response, and strong beat with European structure.

Jefferson, Thomas (p. 205) The primary author of the Declaration of Independence, the first secretary of state, and the third president of the United States. As president, he was responsible for the Louisiana Purchase and the Embargo of 1807, which sought to end British and French interference with American shipping.

Johnny Reb (p. 419) This appellation was used to refer to common soldiers serving in Confederate armies during the Civil War. See *Billy Yank*.

Joint Stock Trading Companies (p. 25) These companies were given the right to develop trade between England and certain geographic regions, such as Russia or India. Investors would pool their capital, in return for shares of stock, to underwrite trading ventures. One such company, the Virginia Company, failed to secure profits for its investors but laid the basis for the first major English colony in the Americas.

Judicial Review (p. 216) The power of the courts to determine the constitutionality of acts of other branches of government and to declare unconstitutional acts null and void.

Judiciary Act of 1801 (p. 216) Passed by the Federalists after they had lost control of Congress in the election of 1800, the act reduced the size of the Supreme Court, created a new set of circuit courts, and increased the number of district court judges. The Jeffersonian Republicans repealed the act in 1801.

Kaiser, Henry J. (p. 828) Industrialist who epitomized the close relationship between government and industry in the West. His shipyards, financed by government loans and bolstered by cost-plus government contracts, employed close to 300,000 Californians.

Kansas-Nebraska Act (p. 396) Controversial legislation that opened Kansas and Nebraska to white settlement, repealed the Compromise of 1820, and led opponents to form the Republican party.

Kennedy, Robert (p. 860) After an early public life as a committed Cold Warrior, Kennedy ran for the Democratic nomination in 1968 as a peace candidate representative of young liberals. His assassination while on the campaign trail helped create the disenchantment of many young Americans with the political process.

Kesey, Ken (p. 839) Novelist at the forefront of the 1960s counterculture movement in the West. His *One Flew Over the Cuckoo's Nest* (1962) and *Sometimes a Great Notion* (1964) celebrated the right to make individual decisions rather than advocate a collective ideal.

Khrushchev, Nikita (p. 798) Personable Soviet premier during Eisenhower's presidential term. Khrushchev condemned Stalin's purges and welcomed a melting of the Cold War, although he crushed a 1956 democratic uprising in Hungary.

Kissinger, Henry (p. 862) The national security advisor to President Nixon, the Harvard-educated German Jewish immigrant was a staunch anti-Communist. He was Nixon's closest associate on matters of foreign policy.

Knights of Labor (p. 508) A labor organization founded in 1869, it called for the unity of all workers, rejected industrial capitalism, and favored cooperatively owned businesses but was discredited by such labor violence as the Haymarket Square riot and did not survive the depression of the 1890s.

Know Nothing Party (p. 394) An anti-foreign, anti-Catholic political party that arose following massive Irish and Catholic immigration during the late 1840s. The Know Nothing party replaced the Whigs as the second largest party in New England and some other states between 1853 and 1856.

Ku Klux Klan (p. 465, 687) A secret organization founded in the southern states during Reconstruction to terrorize and intimidate former slaves and prevent them from voting or holding public office. Officially disbanded in 1869, a second anti-black, anti-Catholic, and anti-Semitic Klan emerged in 1915 that aimed to preserve "Americanism."

Laissez-faire (p. 486) An economic theory based upon the ideas of Adam Smith, it contended that in a free economy self-interest would lead individuals to act in ways that benefited society as a whole and therefore government should not intervene.

Large Policy (p. 586) Bold foreign policy put forth by Henry Cabot Lodge and others, advocating a canal through the Central American isthmus and a strong American naval presence in the Caribbean and Pacific.

League of Nations (p. 661) Point Fourteen of Wilson's Fourteen Points, the proposal to establish an international organization to guarantee the territorial integrity of independent nations.

Lend-Lease Act (p. 736) The program by which the United States provided arms and supplies to the Allies in World War II before joining the fighting.

Liberty Party (p. 296) An antislavery political party founded in 1839.

Liluokalani, Queen (p. 588) Rising to power in Hawaii in 1891, she initiated a strong anti-American policy. Her overthrow in 1893 by white islanders paved the way for ultimate American annexation in 1897.

Little Rock Crisis (p. 808) Conflict in 1957 where governor Orval Faubus sent in the Arkansas National Guard to prevent the racial integration of Little Rock's Central High School. After a crucial delay, President Eisenhower federalized the National Guard troops and sent in 1000 paratroopers to foster the school's integration.

Loose Interpretation (p. 194) The view that the national government has the power to create agencies or enact statutes to fulfill the powers granted by the U.S. Constitution.

Louverture, Toussaint (p. 218) The leader of the Haitian Revolution.

Loyal Nine (p. 107) This informal group of pro-colonial rights leaders in Boston helped organize resistance against unwanted British policies, such as the Stamp Act. Working with more visible popular leaders like Samuel Adams and street leaders like Ebenezer Mackintosh, the Loyal Nine both planned and gave overall direction to controlled violent protests in defying the imperial will and protecting the community's interests in Boston during the 1760s.

Lusitania (p. 647) British ship carrying American passengers sunk by a German submarine on May 15, 1915.

MacArthur, General Douglas (p. 775) Bold, arrogant American general celebrated for his successful amphibious invasion at Inchon, on North Korean forces' rear. MacArthur's subsequent invasion into North Korea stalled, and President Truman removed him from command after his inflammatory, egomaniacal criticisms of America's containment policy.

Macon's Bill No. 2 (p. 221) An attempt to stop British and French interference with American trade.

Madison, James (p. 221) The Father of the Constitution and the Bill of Rights and a co-founder of the Jeffersonian Republican party, Madison served as president during the War of 1812.

Malcolm X (p. 885) Spokesman for the Nation of Islam, a black religious and political organization that advocated black-owned businesses and castigated "white devils." He achieved notoreity as a public speaker and recruiter of boxer Muhammad Ali to the organization. He left the Nation of Islam in 1964 to form the Organization of Afro-American Unity in 1964, and was assassinated in 1965.

Manhattan Project (p. 755) The secret government program to develop an atomic bomb during World War II.

Mann, Horace (p. 292) The early nineteenth century's leading educational reformer, Mann led the fight for government support for public schools in Massachusetts.

Manumission (p. 178) The freeing or emancipation of chattel slaves by their owners, which became more common in the upper South in the wake of so much talk during the American Revolution about human liberty. George Washington was among those planters who provided for the manumission of his slaves after the death of his wife Martha.

Marbury* v. *Madison (p. 216) This landmark 1803 Supreme Court decision, which established the principle of judicial review, marked the first time that the Court declared an act of Congress unconstitutional.

Maroons (p. 344) Escaped slaves who formed communities of runaways.

Marquis of Queensberry Rules (p. 536) Standardized boxing rules of the late nineteenth century, creating structured three minute rounds with one minute rest periods, outlawing wrestling throws and holds, and specifying the number of rounds.

Marshall Plan (p. 770) A massive foreign aid program to Western Europe of $17 billion over four years, beginning in 1948. Named after Secretary of State George Marshall, the program restored economic prosperity to the region and stabilized its system of democracy and capitalism.

Marshall, John (p. 215) Appointed Chief Justice in 1801, Marshall expanded the Supreme Court's power and prestige and established its power to determine the constitutionality of the acts of other branches of government and to declare unconstitutional acts null and void. He defended the supremacy of the federal government over state governments and held that the Constitution should be construed broadly and flexibly.

Matrilineal (p. 9) Unlike European nations that were male-based, or patrilineal, in organization, many Native American societies structured tribal and family power and authority through women. Quite often use rights to land and personal property passed from mother to daughter, and the eldest women chose male chiefs. Matrilineal societies thus placed great importance on the capacities of women to provide for the long-term welfare of their tribes.

McCullough* v. *Maryland (p. 239) A landmark 1819 Supreme Court decision establishing Congress's power to charter a national bank and declaring unconstitutional a tax imposed by Maryland on the bank's Baltimore branch.

Mercantilism (p. 67) An economic system built on the assumption that the world's supply of wealth is fixed and that nations must export more goods than they import to assure a steady supply of gold and silver into national coffers. Mercantile thinkers saw the inflow of such wealth as the key to maintaining and enhancing national power and self-sufficiency. Within this context, the accumulation and development of colonies was of great importance, since colonies could supply scarce raw materials to parent nations and serve as markets for finished goods.

Meredith, James (p. 880) Black student who courageously sought admission into all-white University of Mississippi in 1962. His enrollment sparked a riot instigated by a white mob that attacked federal marshals and national guard troops, leaving 2 dead and 375 injured. Meredith attended the university and eventually graduated.

Military Reconstruction Act (p. 456) A law passed after the South's refusal to accept the Fourteenth Amendment in 1867, it nullified existing state governments and divided the South into five military districts headed by military governors.

Modern Republicanism (p. 794) also called "dynamic conservatism," President Eisenhower's domestic agenda advocated conservative spending approaches without drastically cutting back New Deal social programs.

Monroe Doctrine (p. 241) In this 1823 statement of American foreign policy, President James Monroe declared that the United States would not allow European powers to create new colonies in the Western Hemisphere or to expand the boundaries of existing colonies.

Monroe, James (p. 235) The president of the United States during the Era of Good Feelings.

Muckrakers (p. 611) Investigative journalists during the Progressive Era, they wrote sensational exposés of social and political problems that helped spark the reform movements of their day.

Mugwumps (p. 554) A reform faction of the Republican party in the 1870s and 1880s, they crusaded for honest and effective government and sometimes supported Democratic reform candidates.

National American Woman Suffrage Association (NAWSA) (p. 556) An organization formed in

1890 from two factions of the suffrage movement, it sought a constitutional amendment to grant women the right to vote throughout the nation, eventually leading to the Nineteenth Amendment.

National Association for the Advancement of Colored People (NAACP) (p. 618, 687) Organization established in 1909 to fight for African-American civil rights through legal action.

National Origins Act of 1924 (p. 523, 686) Law that restricted immigration to 2 percent for any given nationality, based on the total amounts from the 1890 census. Use of the 1890 census effectively restricted immigrants from eastern and southern Europe.

National Recovery Administration (NRA) (p. 709) The federal government's plan to revive industry during the Great Depression through rational planning.

National Security Paper Number 68 (NSC-68) (p. 773) Influential National Security Council document arguing communism was a monolithic world movement directed from the Kremlin and advocating a massive military buildup to counteract the encroachment of communism.

National System of Interstate and Defense Highways Act (p. 795) 1956 legislation creating national highway system of 41,000 miles, costing $26 billion and taking 13 years to construct. It solidified the central role of the automobile in American culture.

Nationalists (p. 164) These revolutionary leaders favored a stronger national government than the one provided for in the Articles of Confederation. They believed that only a powerful national government, rather than self-serving states, could deal effectively with the many vexing problems besetting the new nation. George Washington, Alexander Hamilton, and James Madison were prominent nationalists.

Nativism (p. 521) A backlash against immigration by white native-born Protestants. Nativism could be based on racial prejudice (professors and scientists sometimes classified Eastern Europeans as innately inferior), religion (Protestants distrusted Catholics and Jews), politics (immigrants were often associated with radical political philosophies), and economics (labor leaders resented competition).

Naturalism (p. 531) Literary style of the late nineteenth and early twentieth century, where the individual was seen as a helpless victim in a world in which biological, social, and psychological forces determined his or her fate.

Navigation System (p. 68) To effect mercantilist goals, King and Parliament legislated a series of Navigation Acts (1651, 1660, 1663, 1673, 1696) that established England as the central hub of trade in its emerging empire. Various rules of trade, as embodied in the Navigation Acts, made it clear that England's colonies in the Americas existed first and foremost to serve the parent nation's economic interests, regardless of what was best for the colonists.

Neutrality (p. 643) U.S. policy of impartiality during World Wars I and II.

New Deal (p. 706) President Franklin Delano Roosevelt's program designed to bring about economic recovery and reform during the Great Depression.

New Lights (p. 87) As the Great Awakening spread during the 1730s and 1740s, various religious groups fractured into two camps, sometimes known as the New Lights and Old Lights. The New Lights placed emphasis on a "new birth" conversion experience—gaining God's saving grace. They also demanded ministers who had clearly experienced conversions themselves. See *Old Lights*.

The New Look (p. 798) President Eisenhower's adjustment to the doctrine of containment. He advocated saving money by emphasizing nuclear over conventional weapons, on the premise that the next major world conflict would be nuclear.

"New South" (p. 500) The ideology following Reconstruction that the South could be restored to its previous glory through a diversified economy, it was used to rally Southerners and convince outside investors to underwrite regional industrialization by extolling the resources, labor supply, and racial harmony of the South.

Nineteenth Amendment (p. 684) Passed in 1920, the Constitutional guarantee of women's right to vote.

Nixon Doctrine (p. 863) President Nixon argued for "Vietnamization," the notion that the South Vietnamese would carry more of the war's combat burden. This plan never reached full realization because of the South Vietnamese inability to carry on the war effort without American troops.

Non-Intercourse Act (p. 221) An 1809 statute which replaced the Embargo of 1807. It forbade trade with Britain, France, and their possessions, but reopened trade with other countries.

Nonseparatists (p. 42) Religious dissenters from England who wanted to purify, rather than separate from, what they viewed as the corrupted, state-supported Anglican church, or Church of England. By and large, the Puritans were nonseparatists, and some of them banded together to form a utopian community of believers in America. The Massachusetts Bay Colony was to be a model society that would show how godly societies and churches were to be properly organized. See *separatists*.

Northwest Passage (p. 20) During the Age of Exploration, adventurers from England, France, and the

Netherlands kept seeking an all-water route across North America. The goal was to gain access to Oriental material goods and riches while avoiding contact with the developing Spanish empire farther to the south in Central and South America.

Nullification (p. 266) The doctrine, devised by John C. Calhoun, that a state has the power to "nullify" federal legislation within its borders.

Oil Crisis (p. 916) Oil supply disruptions and soaring oil prices that the United States experienced in 1973 and 1979. In 1973, Middle Eastern nations imposed an embargo on oil shipments to punish the West for supporting Israel in that year's Arab-Israeli war. A second oil shock occurred when the Iranian Revolution disrupted oil shipments to the western nations.

Old Lights (p. 87) As the Great Awakening spread during the 1730s and 1740s, various religious groups fractured into two camps, sometimes known as the Old Lights and the New Lights. The Old Lights were not very enthusiastic about the Awakening, particularly in terms of what they viewed as popular excesses in seeking after God's grace. Old Light ministers emphasized formal schooling in theology as a source of their religious authority, and they emphasized good order in their churches. See *New Lights*.

O'Malley, Walter (p. 828) Penny-pinching owner of baseball's Dodgers who oversaw their 1958 move from Brooklyn to Los Angeles. Unhappy with the deterioration of Brooklyn's neighborhoods and lured by the economic promise of California, the Dodgers' move west illustrated the profound westward demographic shift in modern America.

Open Door Note (p. 600) Policy set forth in 1899 by Secretary of State John Hay preventing further partitioning of China by European powers, and protecting the principle of free trade.

Operation Just Cause (p. 924) An American military intervention in Panama in December 1989, which was launched after Panama's leader, Manuel Noriega, who was indicted on drug-related charges, invalidated civilian elections and declared a state of war with the United States.

Panic of 1837 (p. 276) A financial depression that lasted until the early 1840s.

Parks, Rosa (p. 808) African-American seamstress and active NAACP member arrested for refusing to give up her seat to a white patron in Montgomery, Alabama, prompting a huge bus boycott led by Martin Luther King, Jr.

Patriarchal (p. 51) Patriarchal social and political systems are denoted by power and authority residing in males, such as in the father of the family. Such authority then passes from father to son through the generations, and males, in general, control decision making. See *coverture*.

Patrons of Husbandry (p. 564) An organization founded in 1867 to aid farmers through its local granges, it was responsible for state laws regulating railroads, established cooperatives to help with marketing problems, and provided a social outlet for rural areas.

Pearl Harbor (p. 737) The main base of the U.S. Pacific fleet, which Japan attacked on December 7, 1941, forcing the United States to enter World War II.

Pendleton Act (p. 558) A law passed in 1883 to eliminate political corruption in the federal government, it outlawed political contributions by appointed officeholders and established the Civil Service Commission to administer competitive examinations for covered government jobs.

Permanent Immigrants (p. 519) Immigrants coming to America to settle permanently, often due to ethnic and religious persecution at home.

Perpetual Servitude (p. 56) Indentured servitude represented temporary service for a specified period, usually from four to seven years, to a legally designated owner. Perpetual servitude meant being owned by some other person for life—and ultimately, even through the generations. In the early days of Virginia, both English subjects and African Americans were indentured servants, but over time blacks would be subjected to perpetual servitude as chattels, defined as the movable property of their all-powerful masters and without legal rights of any kind.

Ping-Pong Diplomacy (p. 864) Communist China's chairman Mao Tse-tung sent a table tennis team to the world championships in Nagoya, Japan, and then invited an American team to compete in Japan in 1971. This small gesture paved the way for President Nixon's visit to China in February 1972.

Plantation Legend (p. 331) A stereotype, created by popular pre-Civil War writers, that depicted the South as a region of aristocratic planters, beautiful Southern belles, poor white trash, and faithful household slaves.

Platt Amendment (p. 595) 1901 amendment to the Army Appropriation Bill, limiting Cuban independence by giving the United States two naval bases on Cuba and the right to intervene in Cuban affairs if the American government felt Cuban independence was threatened.

Plessy v. Ferguson (p. 501) A Supreme Court decision in 1896 that ruled "separate but equal" facilities for African Americans were constitutional under the Fourteenth Amendment, it had the effect of legalizing segregation and led to the passage of much discriminatory legislation known as Jim Crow laws.

Political Slavery (p. 117) During the 1760s and 1770s many colonial leaders believed that if they did not keep resisting unwanted British policies, they would fall into a state of political slavery in which they had no liberties. As such, they would be akin to chattel slaves in their midst. Comprehending how potentially tyrannical chattel slavery was spurred on many colonists to defend American liberties, even to the point of open rebellion.

Polk, James K. (p. 365) As president of the United States during the Mexican War, Polk increased American territory by a third.

Popular Sovereignty (p. 388) The principle, incorporated into the Compromise of 1850 and the Kansas-Nebraska Act, that the people living in the western territories should decide whether or not to permit slavery.

Populist (People's) Party (p. 556) A political party established in 1892 primarily by remnants of the Farmers' Alliance and Greenback Party, it sought to inflate the currency with silver dollars and to establish an income tax; some of its platform was adopted by the Democrats in 1896 and it died out after the defeat of joint candidate William Jennings Bryan.

Pragmatism (p. 610) A distinctly American philosophy proposed by William James, it contends that any concept should be tested and its validity determined by its outcome and that the truth of an idea is found in the conduct it dictates or inspires.

Price Revolution (p. 23) The large influx of gold and silver into Europe from Spanish America during the sixteenth century, along with increased demand for limited supplies of goods, set off a threefold rise in prices (the "great inflation") that caused profound economic turmoil, social disruption, and political instability among European peoples and nations.

Progressive (Bull Moose) Party (p. 626) A political party established in 1912 by supporters of Theodore Roosevelt after William H. Taft won the Republican presidential nomination. The party proposed a broad program of reform but Bull Moose candidate Roosevelt and Republican nominee lost to the Democratic candidate, Woodrow Wilson.

Prohibition (p. 684) The ban of the production, sale, and consumption of alcoholic beverages. The Eighteenth Amendment to the U.S. Constitution, adopted in 1919, established prohibition. The amendment was repealed in 1933, with adoption of the Twenty-first Amendment.

Protestant Reformation (p. 21) A religious reform movement formally begun in 1517 when the German friar Martin Luther openly attacked abuses of Roman Catholic doctrine. Luther contended that the people could read scripture for themselves in seeking God's grace and that the Bible, not church doctrine, was the ultimate authority in human relationships. Luther's complaints helped foster a variety of dissenting religious groups, some of which would settle in America to get away from various forms of oppression in Europe.

Public Virtue (p. 162) A cornerstone of good citizenship in republican states, public virtue involved the subordination of individual self-interest to serving the greater good of the whole community. Revolutionary leaders believed that public virtue was essential for a republic to survive and thrive. If absent, governments would be torn apart by competing private interests and succumb to anarchy, at which point tyrants would emerge to offer political stability but with the loss of dearly won political liberties.

Radical Republicans (p. 451) A faction of the Republican party during Reconstruction, they favored forcing the South to make fundamental changes before readmission to the Union. Eventually they won control because of Southerners' refusal to accept more lenient plans for Reconstruction.

Radical Revolutionaries (p. 162) At the time of the American Revolution, they argued in favor of establishing more democratic forms of government. Radical revolutionaries had a strong trust in the people, viewed them as inherently virtuous (see *public virtue*), and believed that citizens could govern themselves. Samuel Adams, Thomas Jefferson, and Thomas Paine might be described as radical revolutionaries. See *cautious revolutionaries*.

Rage Militaire (p. 128) Meaning a passion for arms, the rage militaire characterized the attitudes of American colonists as the war with Great Britain began in 1775. When the ravages and deprivations of warfare became more self-evident, however, this early enthusiasm gave out. In 1776 Thomas Paine criticized the "summer soldiers and sunshine patriots" among the colonists who seemed so eager to fight at the beginning of the War for Independence but who so quickly dropped out as the dangers of engaging in warfare increased.

Rationalism (p. 83) A main tenet of the Enlightenment era, meaning a firm trust in the ability of the human mind to solve earthly problems, thereby lessening the role of—and reliance on—God as an active force in the ordering of human affairs.

Reagan Doctrine (p. 922) President Ronald Reagan's 1985 pledge of American aid to insurgent movements attempting to overthrow Soviet-backed regimes in the Third World.

Redemptioners (p. 79) The redemptioner labor system was similar to that of indentured servitude in providing a way for persons without financial means to get to America. Normally, the family had to locate someone to pay for its passage in return for a set number of years of labor. If no buyer could be found, then ships captains could sell the family's labor, most likely on less desirable terms for the family, to recoup the costs of passage. Thousands of Germans migrated to America as redemptioners in the eight-eenth century.

Referendum *See* Intiative and Referendum

Reform Darwinists (p. 610) Sociologists who rejected the determinism of the Social Darwinists, they accepted evolutionary theory but held that people could shape their environment rather than only be shaped by it and accepted human intervention in society.

Religious Liberalism (p. 285) A religious viewpoint that rejected the Calvinist doctrines of original sin and predestination and stressed the basic goodness of human nature.

Remember the *Maine*! (p. 593) A national catch phrase following the mysterious 1898 explosion of the U.S. battleship *Maine* in Havana harbor that inflamed public opinion, leading to the Spanish-American War.

Removal (Indian Removal Policy) (p. 269) A policy of resettling eastern Indian tribes on lands west of the Mississippi River.

Renaissance (p. 14) Beginning in the 1400s, the European Renaissance represented an intellectual and cultural flowering in the arts, literature, philosophy, and the sciences. One of the most important tenets of the Renaissance was the belief in human progress, or the betterment of society.

Republican Motherhood (p. 174) This definition of motherhood, emanating from the American Revolution, assigned mothers the task of raising dutiful children, especially sons, who would be prepared to serve the nation in disinterested fashion (see *public virtue*). Mothers thus acquired the special charge of assuring that future generations could uphold the tenets of republicanism. This expanded role for mothers meant that women, not men, would be responsible for the domestic sphere of life.

Republicanism (p. 162) At the time of the American Revolution, republicanism referred to the concept that sovereignty, or ultimate political authority, is vested in the people—the citizens of the nation. As such, republican governments not only derive their authority from the consent of the governed but also predicate themselves on the principles of rule by law and legislation by elected representatives.

Republicans (p. 196) A political party founded by James Madison and Thomas Jefferson to combat Alexander Hamilton's fiscal policies.

Rock and Roll (p. 813) Musical style new to the 1950s, combining black rhythm and blues with white country music. Listened to mostly by young Americans and embodied by Elvis Presley, the music softly challenged notions of sexual propriety and racial division.

Roderigue Hortalez & Cie. (p. 146) Prior to its formal involvement in the War for Independence, the French government supplied the American rebels with critically needed war goods through a bogus private trading firm known as Roderigue Hortalez & Cie. French officials did so because they hoped to see the power of Great Britain reduced but without becoming directly engaged in the war itself. Once the Franco-American alliance came into being in 1778, the French could abandon such ruses in favor of open support of their rebel allies.

Rosenberg, Julius and Ethel (p. 779) American radicals accused of passing atomic secrets to the Soviets during World War II. Although the death penalty was not mandatory for their crime, their 1953 execution reflected the national anti-communist hysteria.

Sagebrush Rebellion (p. 839) Failed movement led by conservative Western politicians to cede federal control of western land to individual states, promoting private ownership and commercial development.

Salisbury, Lord (p. 589) Imperious British prime minister who rejected American intervention in an 1895 border dispute between Venezuela and British Guiana, prompting an American threat of military involvement. Salisbury ultimately reversed his position and allowed a commission to arbitrate the dispute.

Salutary Neglect (p. 78) This term signifies England's relatively benign neglect of its American colonies from about 1690 to 1760. During these years King and Parliament rarely legislated constraints of any kind and allowed the colonists much autonomy in provincial and local matters. In turn, the colonists supported the parent nation's economic and political objectives. This harmonious period came to an end after the Seven Year's War when King and Parliament began asserting more control over the American colonists through taxes and trade regulations.

Santa Anna, General Antonio López de (p. 363) The Mexican general and president whose defeat at the Battle of San Jacinto in 1836 permitted Texas to gain its independence.

Scalawags (p. 461) Southern white Republicans during Reconstruction, they came from every class and had a variety of motives but were pictured by their opponents as ignorant and degraded.

Scopes Trial (p. 686)   Trial against John Scopes in 1925 for teaching Charles Darwin's theory of evolution in a Tennessee public school; also called the "Monkey Trial."

Scott, Dred (p. 400)   A Missouri slave, Scott sued for his freedom on the grounds that his master had taken him onto free soil. The Supreme Court ruled in 1857 that Scott was not a citizen and that Congress had no power to exclude slavery from the federal territories.

Second Bank of the United States (p. 274)   A national bank chartered in 1816 to hold government funds, ease the transfer of money across state lines, and regulate private banks. Its federal charter expired in 1836.

Second Continental Congress (p. 132)   This body gathered in Philadelphia during May 1775 after the shooting war with Great Britain had started. The second Congress functioned as a coordinating government for the colonies and states in providing overall direction for the patriot war effort. It continued as a central legislative body under the Articles of Confederation until 1789 when a new national legislature, the federal Congress as established under the Constitution of 1787, first convened.

Second Great Awakening (p. 285)   A wave of religious fervor and revivalism that swept the United States from the early nineteenth century through the Civil War.

Second New Deal (p. 713)   The second stage of President Franklin Delano Roosevelt's economic recovery and reform program, launched January 4, 1935.

Separatists (p. 42)   Religious dissenters from England who believed that the state-supported Anglican church, or Church of England, was too corrupt to be reformed. Thus, like the Pilgrims, they often migrated elsewhere to form their own religious communities. See *nonseparatists*.

Settlement House Movement (p. 615)   A reform movement growing out of Jane Addams' Hull House in the late nineteenth century, it led to the formation of community centers in which mainly middle-class women sought to meet the needs of recent immigrants to urban centers.

Seward, William Henry (p. 582)   Secretary of State for Abraham Lincoln and Andrew Johnson, and advocate of a vigorous expansionism. He is perhaps best known for the purchase of Alaska from Russia in 1867 for $7.2 million, an act labeled "Seward's Folly."

Sharecropping (p. 463)   A system of labor to replace slavery that allowed landless farmers to work the land of others for a share of the crops they produced. It was favored by freedpeople over gang labor but sometimes led to virtual peonage.

Shaysites (p. 169)   Beset by a hard-hitting economic depression after the War for American Independence, these farmers from western Massachusetts finally rose up in rebellion against their state government in 1786 because they had failed to obtain tax relief. One leader of the uprising was Daniel Shays, from whom the Shaysites derived their name.

Sherman Antitrust Act (p. 561)   A law passed in 1890 to break up trusts and monopolies, it was rarely enforced except against labor unions and most of its power was stripped away by the Supreme Court, but it began federal attempts to prevent unfair, anticompetitive business practices.

Sit-in (p. 878)   A form of nonviolent protest in which civil rights activists occupy seats in a segregated establishment.

Slave Codes (p. 339)   Legal codes that defined the slaveholders' power and the slaves' status as property.

Smith, Joseph, Jr. (p. 368)   The founder of the Mormon Church, Smith was murdered in Illinois in 1844.

Smog (p. 831)   The chemical-laden fog caused by automobile engines, a serious problem in southern California. Like nuclear waste and the shrinking water supply, it reflects the problems associated with the rapid demographic shift to the West in modern times.

Social Darwinism (p. 485)   An ideology based upon the evolutionary theories of Charles Darwin, it justified the concentration of wealth and lack of governmental protection of the weak through the ideas of natural selection and survival of the fittest.

Social Gospel (p. 610)   A movement among Christian theologians, it applied Christian doctrines to social problems and advocated creating living conditions conducive to saving souls by tackling the problems of the poor.

Social Security Act (p. 713)   New Deal legislation enacted in 1935 to provide monthly stipends for workers aged 65 or older and to provide assistance to the indigent elderly, blind and handicapped persons, and dependent children who did not have a wage-earning parent. The act also established the nation's first federally funded system of unemployment insurance.

Southern Strategy (p. 150)   Once France formally entered the War for Independence in 1778 on the American side, the British had to concern themselves with protecting such vital holdings as their sugar islands in the Caribbean region. Needing to disperse their troop strength, the idea of the Southern strategy was to tap into a perceived reservoir of loyalist numbers in the southern colonies. Reduced British forces could employ these loyalists as troops in subduing the rebels and as civil officials in reestablishing royal governments. The plan failed for many reasons, including a shortfall of loyalist support and an inability to hold ground once conquered in places like South Carolina.

Specie (p. 100)   A term for hard coin, such as gold or silver, that can also back and give a fixed point of valuation to paper currencies.

Spirituals (p. 343)   Religious songs composed by enslaved African Americans.

Spoils system (p. 268, 558)   The policy of awarding political or financial help with a government job. Abuses of the spoils system led to the passage in 1883 of the Pendleton Act, which created the Civil Service Commission to award government jobs on the basis of merit.

Sputnik (p. 800)   Russian satellite that successfully orbited the earth in 1957, prompting Americans to question their own values and educational system. The hysteria over Soviet technological superiority led to the 1958 National Defense Education Act.

Stagflation (p. 916)   The economic conditions of slow economic growth, rising inflation, and flagging productivity that characterized the American economy during the 1970s.

Stalin, Joseph (p. 745)   Soviet premier in the 1930s and 1940s, known for his violent purges of internal political enemies and his suspicion of Western leaders, an ideology guided by two major German invasions into Russia.

Stamp Act Congress (p. 109)   This intercolonial body of political leaders from nine colonies met for a few days in October 1765 to consider ways to protest the Stamp Act. The delegates drafted a petition declaring that Parliament should not tax Americans, since they were not represented in that legislative body. The Congress showed that the colonies, when aggrieved, could act in unity, an important precedent for further intercolonial resistance efforts in years to come.

Stanton, Elizabeth Cady (p. 299)   Organizer of the first women's rights convention in Seneca Falls, New York, in 1848, Stanton led the struggle for woman suffrage.

Strategic Arms Limitation Treaty of 1972 (SALT I) (p. 865)   Arms control treaty signed by President Nixon and Soviet premier Leonid Brezhnev. Although it only froze the deployment of relatively inconsequential intercontinental ballistic missiles, this first treaty would lead to more comprehensive arms reduction treaties in the future.

Strict Construction (p. 194)   The view that the powers of the national government are limited to those described in the U.S. Constitution.

Students for a Democratic Society (SDS) (p. 890)   Founded in Port Huron, Michigan in 1962, the radical organization aimed to rid American society of poverty, racism, and violence through an individually oriented approach called participatory democracy. By 1968, the organization had over 100,000 followers and was responsible for demonstrations at nearly 1000 colleges.

Taft-Hartley Act (p. 777)   Legislation in 1947 that reflected the conservative post-war mood. It outlawed the closed shop, gave presidential power to delay strikes with a "cooling-off" period, and curtailed the political and economic power of organized labor.

Tariff of Abominations (p. 265)   An 1828 protective tariff opposed by many Southerners.

Temperance (p. 290)   The pre-Civil War reform movement which sought to curb the drinking of hard liquor.

Tet Offensive (p. 856)   As American military and political leaders suggested victory in Vietnam was in sight, North Vietnam launched an offensive in January 1968 against every major South Vietnamese target. Although the United States repelled the Tet Offensive, it prompted waves of criticism from those who felt the government had been misleading the American people.

Thoreau, Henry David (p. 303)   A pencilmaker, poet, and author of the influential essay "Civil Disobedience," Thoreau sought to realize transcendentalist ideals in his personal life.

Tory (p. 139)   In England during the eighteenth century the Tory Party was closely identified with the king's interests and monarchism, or in the minds of many American patriots, with tyrannical government. As the Revolution dawned, tory became a term of derision applied to those colonists who sought to maintain their allegiance to the British crown. They preferred to think of themselves as loyalists, since they were not rebelling against but were still supporting British imperial authority in America.

Total War (p. 436)   As opposed to limited war, total war usually denotes a military conflict in which warfare ultimately affects the entire population, civilian as well as military. The American Civil War, at least in its latter stages, might serve as an example of total war because of the destruction of both military and civilian resources in the South by Union armies operating under General Grant and especially General Sherman during 1864 and 1865.

Transcendentalists (p. 303)   A group of New England intellectuals who glorified nature and believed that each person contains god-like potentialities.

Treaty of Guadalupe Hidalgo (p. 374)   The peace treaty ending the Mexican War gave the United States California, Nevada, New Mexico, Utah, and parts of Arizona, Colorado, Kansas, and Wyoming in exchange for $15 million and assumption of $3.25 million in debts owed to Americans by Mexico.

Treaty of Versailles (p. 664) The treaty that ended World War I.

Truman Doctrine (p. 769) A speech by President Truman in March 1947 that set the course of U.S. foreign policy for the next generation, painting international affairs as a struggle between free democratic governments and tyrannical communist governments, and advocating American intervention to protect democratic governments.

Trust (p. 490) A form of business organization that created a single board to trustees to oversee competing firms, the term came to apply when any single entity had the power to control competition within a given industry, such as oil production.

Truth, Sojourner (p. 284) A leading orator in the abolitionist and women's rights movements, Sojourner Truth was born into slavery in New York's Hudson River Valley and escaped in 1826.

Turner, Nat (p. 344) A black Baptist preacher who led a revolt against slavery in Southampton County in southern Virginia in 1831.

Twenty-Fourth Amendment (p. 884) This amendment, adopt-ed in 1964, barred a poll tax in federal elections.

Vertical Integration (p. 490) The practice of controlling every phase of production by owning the sources of raw materials and often the transportation facilities needed to distribute the product, it was a means of gaining a competitive edge over rival companies.

Vesey, Denmark (p. 344) A former West Indian slave who organized an attempted rebellion against slavery in Charleston, South Carolina, in 1822.

Vice-Admiralty Courts (p. 103) The English government established these courts in its North American colonies to deal with issues of maritime law, including smuggling. If judges condemned vessels for smuggling, they would share in profits from the sale of such craft and their cargoes. Judges made all rulings without juries and thus could clearly benefit from their own decisions, which caused many colonists to view these courts as centers of despotic imperial power. The Stamp Act of 1765 stated that colonists who did not pay stamp duties could be tried in vice-admiralty courts, which became another colonial grievance—in this case the prospect of being convicted and sent to jail without a jury trial, a violation of fundamental English liberties.

Virtual Representation (p. 105) King George III's chief minister, George Grenville, employed this concept in 1765 in relation to the Stamp Act. He insisted that all colonists were represented in Parliament by virtue of being English subjects, regardless of where they lived. Grenville was attempting to counter the colonists' position that King and Parliament had no authority to tax them, since the Americans had no duly elected representatives serving in Parliament.

Voting Rights Act of 1965 (p. 884) This law prohibited literacy tests and sent federal examiners to the South to register voters.

Wagner Act (National Labor Relations Act) (p. 712) New Deal legislation enacted in 1935 guaranteeing the right of workers to form unions and bargain collectively. The act established the National Labor Relations Board (NLRB) to settle union-management disputes over unfair labor practices.

Walker, David (p. 294) The free black author of *An Appeal to the Colored Citizens of the World*, which threatened violence if slavery was not abolished.

Wallace, George (p. 861) Alabama governor who ran for president in 1968 as a third-party candidate on the American Independent ticket. His message rejecting forced racial integration, the activities of radical college students, and the perceived national drift toward the left appealed to many working class Americans, and he received 13.5 percent of that election's vote.

War of 1812 (p. 227) War between Britain and the United States. Causes included British interference with American shipping, impressment of seamen, a desire to end British aid to Indians, and an American desire for expansion.

War Powers Act (p. 914) This 1973 law required presidents to win specific authorization from Congress to engage U.S. forces in foreign combat for more than 90 days.

War Production Board (p. 738) The board established in January 1942 to help mobilize the U.S. economy for war production.

Washington, George (p. 92) As the nation's first president, Washington helped define the powers of the presidency, demonstrated in the Whiskey Rebellion that the national government would enforce federal law, cleared the Ohio country of Indians, and attempted to preserve American neutrality during the war between Britain and France.

Watergate Break-In (p. 912) During the 1972 presidential campaign, burglars, tied to the Nixon White House, were caught installing eavesdropping devices in Democratic Party headquarters in the Watergate Complex in Washington, D.C. Revelations of White House efforts to obstruct the investigation of the break-in, of financial irregularities, and the use of government agencies for partisan purposes led President Nixon to resign in 1974.

Webster, Daniel (p. 236) A noted orator, Webster opposed the War of 1812 and the protectionist tariff of 1816 after his election to the House of Representatives. He later became a staunch nationalist and defender of tariff protection.

Whig Party, Whigs (p. 117, 277) During the eighteenth century in England the Whig Party was a loosely organized coalition of political leaders that opposed any hint of arbitrary authority that might emanate from the monarchy and royally appointed officials in government. Like the radical whig pamphleteers, they also viewed themselves as defenders of liberty, which is one reason why many American leaders, even though not organized as a political party, called themselves whigs. During the 1830s and 1840s in the United States, there was a Whig party that opposed the policies of Andrew Jackson, Martin Van Buren, and other members of the Democratic Party.

Whitney, Eli (p. 245, 320) The inventor of the cotton gin, Whitney pioneered a system of mass production of interchangeable parts. Whitney's cotton gin, which separated cotton from its seeds, met the growing demand for cotton from the textile industry and breathed new life into the institution of slavery.

Wilmot Proviso (p. 376) An amendment to an 1846 appropriations bill that would have forbade slavery from any territory acquired from Mexico. The amendment passed the House twice but was defeated in the Senate.

Woman's Christian Temperance Union (WCTU) (p. 614) An organization led by Frances Willard to stop the abuse of alcohol, it joined forces with other groups in the movement for the prohibition of alcohol to reduce such problems as wife abuse.

Women's Army Corps (WAC) (p. 741) The auxiliary women's unit to the U.S. army.

Workmen's Compensation Laws (p. 620) Legislation establishing mandatory insurance to be carried by employers to cover on-the-job injuries to their workers, it was a reform that provided protection to workers while also lowering the risk to employers.

Writs of Assistance (p. 107) Blanket search warrants used by English customs collectors in the colonies to try to catch suspected smugglers. These writs did not require any form of prior evidence to justify searches, which the colonies viewed as yet another imperial violation of fundamental English liberties.

Yalta Conference (p. 748) The meeting between President Franklin Roosevelt, British prime minister Winston Churchill, and Soviet premier Joseph Stalin at Yalta in the Russian Crimea in February 1945 to determine the post-World War II world order.

Yellow Journalism (p. 591) Sensationalistic press accounts of the volatile Cuban situation in the 1890s, led by William Randolph Hearst's *New York Journal* and Joseph Pulitzer's *New York World*. Helped mobilize pro-interventionist public opinion prior to the Spanish-American war.

Young, Brigham (p. 370) The leader of the Mormon church following Joseph Smith's murder, Young led the Mormon exodus from Illinois to the Great Salt Lake.

Zimmermann Telegram (p. 649) Telegram from German Foreign Minister Arnold Zimmermann to the German ambassador to Mexico pledging a Mexican-German alliance against the United States, which brought the United States into World War I.

CREDITS

Page abbreviations are as follows: (T)top, (C)center, (B)bottom, (L)left, (R)right.

Left page of title page spread: Suffragettes: Culver, Family photo: Collection of Michael Staats, FDR: Corbis/Bettmann, Nat Love: Library of Congress.
Right page of title page spread: Tom Torlino: Arizona Historical Society, Sojourner Truth: Sophia Smith Collection, Smith College, Northampton, MA, detail of Harrison campaign handkerchief: New York Historical Society.

CHAPTER OPENERS

Chapter 1 Spanish in New World and European War Dogs: Theodor deBry, *America,* 1617/ Laudonnnie with Indian Chief: Print Collection/Miriam & Ira D. Wallach Division of Arts, Prints & Photography/New York Public Library, Astor, Lenox & Tilden Foundations / Ad for Virginia Settlers: New York Public Library, Astor Lenox & Tilden **Chapter 2** Johnson Treaty with the Iroquois: New York Historical Society / View of New Amsterdam, Quaker Synod: New York Public Library, Astor, Lenox & Tilden Foundations / Photo: Ken Burris **Chapter 3** Braddock's defeat: The Granger Collection / Alexander de Batz, "Members of the Illinois Tribe": Peabody Museum/Harvard University / John Singleton Copley, "Head of a Negro": From the Collection of the Detroit Institute of Arts, Founders Society/Gibbs-Williams Fund / Benjamin West, "Penn's Treaty with the Indians": Pennsylvania Academy of the Fine Arts / Benjamin Franklin: Historical Society of Pennsylvania **Chapter 4** Act newspaper: *Pennsylvania Journal,* October 31, 1765 / Boston Long Wharf: Courtesy Henry Francis duPont Winterthur Museum / George Washington at Trenton: Library of Congress / Map of Fort Clinton: New York Historical Society / Philadelphia at time of revolution: North Wind Picture Archives **Chapter 5** Boston Long Wharf: Courtesy Henry Francis duPont Winterthur Museum / Navigation Treaty: New York Historical Society / James Madison portrait: Gilcrease Museum / Washington at Valley Forge: Courtesy Valley Forge Historical Society / George Washington: Metropolitan Museum of Art, Bequest of Grace Wilkes, 1922 / Joseph Brant: New York Public Library, Astor, Lenox & Tilden Foundation **Chapter 6** Continental currency: Smithsonian Institution / "Fairview Inn": Maryland Historical Society / *New Cleared Farm in the New World*: New York Public Library, Astor, Lenox & Tilden Foundations / Conestoga wagon: Shelburne Museum / Stagecoach: Library of Congress / "Signing of the Constitution": National Historical Park Collections, Eastern National Parks & Monuments Association **Chapter 7** Benjamin West, "Conference of the Treaty of Paris": Courtesy the Henry Francis du Pont Winterthur Museum / Alexander Hamilton: Copyright Yale University Art Gallery / John Quincy Adams: Historical Society of Pennsylvania **Chapter 8** "Burning of New York": Library of Congress / Dolly Madison: Pennsylvania Academy of the Fine Arts / Thomas Jefferson: Metropolitan Museum of Art, Bequest of Cornelia Crugar / Jefferson campaign broadside: New York Historical Society / James Madison: Gilcrease Museum / Tenskwatawa (the Prophet): Library of Congress **Chapter 9** Cotton gin: Corbis/Bettmann Archive / Robert Fulton: Collection of Michael Staats / Cotton mill: Library of Congress / "Mississippi River at St. Louis": St. Louis Museum of Art, Collection of Arthur Ziern, Jr. **Chapter 10** Harrison campaign handkerchief: New York Historical Society / Manchester factory: Library of Congress / Currier & Ives, "Preparing for Market": Copyright Yale University Art Gallery / Mabel Brady Garvan Collection / "Cherokee Phoenix": American Antiquarian Society / "Rafting Downstream": Indiana University Art Museum, Transfer from IU Collections to Museum **Chapter 11** Asher B. Durand, "In the Catskills": Walters Art Gallery / Edgar Allan Poe: Manuscripts Dept./Lilly Library, Indiana University, Bloomington, IN / Harriet Tubman: Library of Congress **Chapter 12** Steamboats on the Mississippi: Historic New Orleans Collection, Rochester, NY: George Eastman House, International Museum of Photography / Women working in cotton mill, Freed blacks in Richmond: Library of Congress / Middle-class livingroom: The Granger Collection / Immigrants aboard ship: Corbis / Lucretia Mott, Elizabeth Cady Stanton: Sophia Smith Collection, Smith College, Northampton **Chapter 13** Daguerreotype of two girls: Collection of Michael Staats / Illinois Central Railroad poster: Newberry Library / Miners: California State Library / Chief Joseph: Library of Congress / Mormons sitting in front of their covered wagons: Western History Department/Denver Public Library / William S. Jewett, "The Promised Land—The Grayson Family": Berry-Hill Galleries, NY **Chapter 14** Civil War soldier, Abraham Lincoln, Northern supplies: Library of Congress / The Lincoln–Douglas debates: AP/Wide World Photos / Anti-Slave-Catchers' poster: New York Public Library, Astor, Lenox & Tilden Foundations / "Monitor & Merrimac": Chicago Historical Society **Chapter 15** Robert E. Lee, Abraham Lincoln / "Storming of Fort Wagner": Library of Congress / Battery A, 2nd Colored Artillery: Chicago Historical Society **Chapter 16** Black Elk: Smithsonian Institution / Geronimo: National Archives / Carpetbagger: Culver Pictures Inc. / Black schoolroom, Ruins of Richmond **Chapter 17** Benjamin Reinhart, "Stopping for the Night": Corcoran Gallery of Art, gift of Mr. and Mrs. Landsell Christie / Geronimo and Buffalo Bill: Culver Pictures / Alexander Graham Bell: Brown Brothers / Cattle drive: Kansas State Historic Site/United States Department of the Interior / Classroom, Tuskegee: Corbis/Bettmann **Chapter 18** Department store: Corbis/Bettmann / King Oliver's Jazz Band: Hogan Jazz Archive/Tulane University / Trolley: Library of Congress / Aerial photo of New York City, Family photo: Collection of Michael Staats **Chapter 19** Granger Poster, Railroad crew: Library of Congress / Union Label, pamphlet: Collection of Michael Staats **Chapter 20** William Randolph Hearst: Corbis/Bettmann / Queen Liliuokalani: Hawaii State Archives / Map of Havana Harbor, 1901, Fern wallpaper: Collection of Michael Staats / "Sinking of the Maine": Chicago Historical Society / Theodore Roosevelt and Rough Riders: Library of Congress **Chapter 21** Theodore Roosevelt and Rough Riders, Suffragettes: Library of Congress / Women's Union march: Brown Brothers / College women in chemistry class: Corbis/Bettmann / Football game: Culver Pictures, / Linoleum: Collection of Michael Staats / Marines in Vera Cruz: Granger Collection / Child laborer in mill: George Eastman House, International Museum of Photography **Chapter 22** Franz Ferdinand and his wife: Corbis / Women welders: Granger Collection / Women repairing car: National Archives / 369th Infantry: Library of Congress /WWI medics: U.S. Signal Corps, The

National Archives, Office of the Chief Signal Officer / Traffic jam, Chicago: Chicago Historical Society **Chapter 23** Men and woman drinking champagne: The Granger Collection, New York / Coolidge: Corbis/UPI/Bettmann / Family on porch: Collection of Michael Staats / Breaker boys: Records of the Children's Bureau / KKK: Library of Congress / Marcus Garvery: Brown Brothers / Agents confiscating liquor during Prohibition: Culver Pictures **Chapter 24** Oklahoma family on the road, WPA workers, FDR: Corbis/Bettmann / Tractor, Roxy Movie Theater: Culver Pictures / Feed and Farm Supply receipt, Woman in car: Collection of Michael Staats / Farmer and son, Oklahoma: Library of Congress **Chapter 25** Mushroom cloud: United States Air Force photo / Children at relocation camp, Black family: Library of Congress / General MacArthur: Corbis/UPI/Bettmann / Cruise ship: Cunard Lines / Radio: Collection of Michael Staats **Chapter 26** Potsdam Conference, Berlin Airlift: Corbis/Bettmann / Soldiers in Korea, Joseph McCarthy: Corbis/UPI/Bettmann / Missiles: Cornell Capa/Magnum / Bomb shelter: AP/Wide World **Chapter 27** Nixon and Eisenhower: Corbis/Bettmann / Aerial photograph of housing subdivision: Eliott Erwitt/Magnum / Jackie Robinson: Corbis/UPI/Bettman / Jim Crow road sign: Costa Manos/Magnum Photos, Inc. / Highway traffic jam: Erich Hartmann/Magnum / Babe Ruth: National Baseball Library, Cooperstown, NY /Life Magazine Time Warner Inc., l957/NYT Pictures **Chapter 28** Oil Field, Bank of Atlanta: Culver Pictures, Robert Bechtle / " '58 Ramber": Sloan Collection, Valparaiso University Museum of Art, gift of Mrs. McCauley Conner in memory of her father Barklie McK. Henry / Air conditioning: Corbis **Chapter 29** LBJ and JFK: Culver Pictures / JFK and Jackie, Nikita Khrushchev and Fidel Castro: Corbis/UPI/Bettmann / Nixon in China: Sygma / U.S. soldiers in Vietnam: James Pickerell/Black Star **Chapter 30** César Chávez: Black Star / Troops at Little Rock High: Burt Glinn/Magnum / Lunch counter sit-in: Bruce Roberts/Photo Researchers / Astronaut on moon: NASA / Martin Luther King: Bob Henriques/Magnum / Black and Vietnamese Rights demonstration, Women's Movement demonstration: FPG / Confrontation on Selma-Montgomery march: Corbis / Malcolm X: Hulton Getty/Liaison Agency, Inc. / Lesbian Rights demonstration: Reno Dakota / **Chapter 31** George Bush: J. David Ake/Corbis/UPI/Bettmann / Boris Yeltsin: Corbis/Reuters/Bettmann / Space shuttle launch: NASA / Bill Clinton: White House photo.

CHAPTER 1

4 The Granger Collection **7R** Courtesy of the Library of Congress **7** Hillel Burger/Peabody Museum, Harvard University **8** Tony Linck **9** North Wind Picture Archives **11** Corbis **13** Hulton Getty/Liaison Agency, Inc. **14** Copyright © The British Museum **16** The New York Public Library, Rare Book Division **18** The Granger Collection **19** The Granger Collection **21** Philadelphia Museum of Art **21** National Portrait Gallery, London **21** National Portrait Gallery, London **22** Musee Historique de la Reformation **24** National Portrait Gallery, London **25** The Granger Collection **27** Hulton Getty/Liaison Agency, Inc.

CHAPTER 2

36 North Wind Picture Archives **38** The Granger Collection **39** Copyright © The British Museum **41** Copyright © National Maritime Museum Picture Library, London, England **41** National Portrait Gallery, London **43** Colonial Williamsburg Foundation **44** Pilgrim Society **44** American Antiquarian Society **46** Courtesy Massachusetts Historical Society, Boston **47** The Granger Collection **48** Brown County Library **49** The New York Public Library, Rare Book Division **49** The Huntington Library **50** Peabody Essex Museum **53** Abby Aldrich Rockefeller Folk Art Center **54** Brown Brothers **56** Ellett Tazewell **57** The Granger Collection **59** Abby Aldrich Rockefeller Folk Art Center

CHAPTER 3

66 Bernard Gallagher **68** Courtesy of the Library of Congress **72** Pennsylvania Academy of the Fine Arts **72** Abby Aldrich Rockefeller Folk Art Center **76** Peabody Essex Museum **83** The Granger Collection **85** The Granger Collection **86** Courtesy of Mr. and Mrs. Wharton Sinkler Collection/Philadelphia Museum of Art **87** Courtesy of the Library of Congress **87** National Portrait Gallery, London **88** Brown University **89** Paul Mellon Collection/National Gallery of Art, Washington, D.C. **92** Courtesy of the Library of Congress **93** The Granger Collection

CHAPTER 4

100 Spencer Collection/New York Public Library, Astor, Lenox & Tilden Foundations **102** Royal Academy of Arts **103** Anderson, Elmer G. (American, active c. 1935). Pa. German Painted Wooden Box, c. 1937, watercolor and graphite on paper, . 463 x . 369 (18 1/4 x 14 1/2). Index of American Design, Copyright © 2000 Board of Trustees, National Gallery of Art, Washington, D.C. **106** Courtesy of the Library of Congress **107** Courtesy Massachusetts Historical Society, Boston **108** Courtesy of the Library of Congress **109** Shelburne Museum **110** Courtesy of the Library of Congress **115** I. N. Phelps Stokes Collection/Miriam & Ira D. Wallach Division of Art, Prints & Photographs Division/New York Public Library, Astor, Lenox, and Tilden Foundations **116** Revere, Paul, Boston Massacre, 1770. U.S., 1735–1818. Engraving after Henry Pelham, hand-colored by Christian Remick (1726-after 1783) Sight: 10-1/4 x 8-5/8 in. Gift of Watson Grant Cutter. Courtesy, Museum of Fine Arts, Boston **117** Rhode Island Historical Society **121** North Wind Picture Archives

CHAPTER 5

129 Valley Forge Historical Society **132** Concord Free Public Library **133** Metropolitan Museum of Art, Bequest of Grace Wilkes, 1922 **137** Yale University Art Gallery **138** Independence National Historical Park **138** Courtesy of the Library of Congress **139** Yale University Art Gallery **141** Courtesy of the Library of Congress **143(T)** Brown University, Anne S. K. Brown Military Collection **143(L)** Brown University, Anne S. K. Brown Military Collection **143(R)** Brown University, Anne S. K. Brown Military Collection **144(R)** Collection of Mrs. Preston Davie **144(L)** The New York Public Library at Lincoln Center **148** Courtesy of the Library of Congress **149** National Gallery of Canada **152** The South Carolina Historical Society **153** Virginia State Library

CHAPTER 6

151(L) The Historical Society of Pennsylvania **161(R)** Courtesy of the Library of Congress **164** The Granger Collection **167** Courtesy of the Museum of American Art of the Pennsylvania Academy of the Fine Arts, Philadelphia, Bequest of Richard Ashhurst **169** Copyright © Collection of The New-York Historical Society **170** The New York Public Library, Rare Book Division **174(T)** The Granger Collection **174(B)** Courtesy of the Library of Congress **177** The Granger Collection **178(T)** Delaware Art Museum, Gift of Absalom Jones School, Wilmington **178(B)** Courtesy of the Library of Congress **179** Bowdoin College Museum of Art **182** Virginia Museum of Fine Arts, Richmond, Gift of Edgar William and Bernice Chrysler Garbisch. Copyright ©Virginia Museum of Fine Arts

CHAPTER 7

190(L) The New York Public Library, Rare Book Division **190(R)** The White House Photo Office **191** Smithsonian Institution **192** The Historical Society of York County, Pa. **193** North Wind Picture Archives **195** The New York Public Library, Rare Book Division **197** Gift of Edgar William and Bernice Chrysler Garbisch, 1963, Metropolitan Museum of Arts **199** Corbis **201** Courtesy of the Library of Congress **203** Courtesy of the Harvard University Portrait Collection/Bequest of Ward Nicholas Boylston, 1828, to Harvard College **204** White House Historical Association **205** Courtesy of the Library of Congress **206** The White House Photo Office

CHAPTER 8

212 Archive Photos **213** Smithsonian Institution **215** Robert Llewellyn **216** Washington and Lee University **217** The Mariners' Museum **218(T)** Louisiana State Museum **218(B)** North Wind Picture Archives **220** Copyright © Collection of The New-York Historical Society **222** Courtesy of the Library of Congress **225(L)** Courtesy of the Library of Congress **225(R)** The Field Museum, Neg#A93851, Chicago **226** Brown University Library

Credits C-3

CHAPTER 9

234 Yale University Art Gallery, The Mabel Brady Garvan Collection **235** Stokes Collection/New York Public Library, Astor, Lenox and Tilden Foundations **237(L)** The Granger Collection **237(C)** National Portrait Gallery/Transfer from the National Gallery of Art, Washington, D.C./Gift of Andrew W. Mellon **237(R)** The Granger Collection **239** Shelburne Museum **240** Museum purchase, Gallery Fund in the Collection of the Corcoran Gallery of Art **242** Rogers Fund 2942, Metropolitan Museum of Art **243(T)** I. N. Phelps Stokes Collection/Miriam and Ira D. Wallach Division of Arts, Print and Photographs/New York Public Library, Astor, Lenox and Tilden Foundation **243(B)** Munson-Williams-Proctor Institute **245** Harper's Weekly **246** The Historical Society of Pennsylvania **247** Print Collection, Miriam and Ira D. Wallach Division of Art, prints and Photographs/Astor, Lenox & Tilden Foundations/New York Public Library **251** The South Carolina Historical Society

CHAPTER 10

258 Copyright © Collection of The New-York Historical Society, Harrison Kerchief Collection **261** The New York Public Library, Rare Book Division **263** *Harper's Weekly* **265** The Historical Society of Pennsylvania **268(T)** Courtesy of the Library of Congress **268(B)** Memphis Park Commission Purchase/Memphis Brooks Museum of Art, Memphis, Tenn. **269** American Antiquarian Society **273** Courtesy of the Boston Public Library, Print Department **275(T)** Chicago Historical Society **275(B)** The Granger Collection **277** The White House Photo Office

CHAPTER 11

284 Sophia Smith Collection, Smith College **287** American Antiquarian Society **288** New Bedford Whaling Museum **289** Courtesy of the Library of Congress **291(T)** Brown Brothers **291(B)** Archive Photos **292(T)** American Antiquarian Society **292(B)** Courtesy, Cornell University Library **295(L)** Gift of I. N. Phelps Stokes, Edward S. Hawes, Alice Mary Hawes, Marion Augusta Hawes, 1937. Metropolitan Museum of Art **295(R)** Sophia Smith Collection, Smith College **297(L)** Corbis **297(R)** Courtesy of the Library of Congress **299** H. Armstrong Roberts **301** Lossing Collection/Huntington Library & Art Gallery, San Marino, Calif. **302** The New York Public Library, Rare Book Division **303** Corbis **304(L)** Concord Free Public Library **304(R)** Concord Free Public Library **305** Edgar Allen Poe, Manuscripts Dept/Lilly Library, Indiana University, Bloomington, Ind. **306** The New York Public Library, Rare Book Division **308** Hinman B. Hurlbut Collection/Cleveland Museum of Art, 1996 **311** The Granger Collection

CHAPTER 12

320 Gift of George Hoadley/Yale University Art Gallery **322** The Granger Collection **324** North Wind Picture Archives **325** Courtesy of the Library of Congress **326** The New York Public Library, Rare Book Division **328** Corbis **330** North Wind Picture Archives **333** The Granger Collection **337** North Wind Picture Archives **339** *Harper's Weekly* **340** North Wind Picture Archives **342** The New York Public Library, Rare Book Division **343** Jan White Brantley/The Historic New Orleans Collection **346** Jay P. Altmayer

CHAPTER 13

354 The Bancroft Library **355** Thomas Gilcrease Institute of American History and Art **356(T)** The Bancroft Library **356(B)** The Bancroft Library **357** Smithsonian Institution **358** University of California, Berkeley **359** The Granger Collection **360** Courtesy of the Library of Congress **362(T)** National Archives **362(B)** Courtesy of the Library of Congress **363** San Jacinto Museum of History, Houston **364** The Granger Collection **367** Friends of the Governor's Mansion **369** Fine Arts Collection/Brigham Young University Museum of Art **371** National Academy of Design **372** North Wind Picture Archives **376** Archive Photos

CHAPTER 14

384 Indiana Historical Society **385** California State Library **388** Courtesy of the Library of Congress **390(T)** Copyright © Collection of The New-York Historical Society **390(B)** The New York Public Library, Rare Book Division **391** Gift of I. N. Phelps Stokes, Edward S. Hawes, Alice Mary Hawes, Marion Augusta Hawes/Metropolitan Museum of Art **393** National Museum of American Art, Smithsonian Institution, Gift of William T. Evans/Art Resource **394** The Historical Society of Pennsylvania **395(L)** Smithsonian Institution **395(R)** Courtesy of the Library of Congress **399(T)** Kansas State Historical Society **399(B)** The New York Public Library, Rare Book Division **400(L)** Courtesy of the Library of Congress **400(R)** National Archives **403(T)** AP/Wide World Photos **403(B)** Courtesy of the Library of Congress

CHAPTER 15

410(L) Georgia Department of Archives and History **410(R)** Courtesy of the Library of Congress **412** The New York Public Library, Rare Book Division **417** U.S. Army Photograph **418** Courtesy of the Library of Congress **419** M. & M. Karolik Collection/Museum of Fine Arts, Boston **421** Library of Congress **424** Courtesy of the Library of Congress **425** Chicago Historical Society **428** Courtesy of the Library of Congress **431 (T)** Chicago Historical Society **431(B)** The Granger Collection **433** Henry Groskinsky **437** Cook Collection/Valentine Museum, Richmond, VA

CHAPTER 16

447 Brown Brothers **449** The Granger Collection **450** Valentine Museum **452** Courtesy of the Library of Congress **453** Courtesy of the Library of Congress **454** Courtesy of the Library of Congress **457** Stock Montage, Inc./Historical Pictures Collection **459** Culver Pictures, Inc. **460** Culver Pictures, Inc. **461** Courtesy of the Library of Congress **462** Culver Pictures, Inc. **465** Culver Pictures, Inc. **468** Montana Historical Society, Helena **470** Braun Research Library/Southwest Museum **471** Nebraska State Historical Society **473** Culver Pictures, Inc.

CHAPTER 17

481 Carnegie Library of Pittsburgh **483(T)** Chicago Historical Society **483(B)** National Park Service, Edison National Historic Site **486(L)** Culver Pictures, Inc. **486(R)** Culver Pictures, Inc. **487** Culver Pictures, Inc. **489** Culver Pictures, Inc. **490** Brown Brothers **492** Courtesy of the Library of Congress **493(B)** Culver Pictures, Inc. **493(T)** Courtesy of the Library of Congress **495** Nebraska State Historical Society **497** Stock Montage, Inc./Historical Pictures Collection **498** Nebraska State Historical Society **500** Corbis **503** International Museum of Photography/George Eastman House **504** *Puck* **505** Brown Brothers **507** The Granger Collection

CHAPTER 18

516 Culver Pictures, Inc. **519** Brown Brothers **520** Courtesy of the Library of Congress **522** Culver Pictures, Inc. **524** The New York Public Library, Rare Book Division **525** Museum of the City of New York **527** International Museum of Photography, George Eastman House **531** Corbis **532** Brown Brothers **533** Addison Gallery of American Art, Phillips Academy, Andover, Mass., photo by Greg Herns **534** Hogan Jazz Archives, Tulane University **539** The Granger Collection **541** Stock Montage, Inc./Historical Pictures Collection **542** Courtesy of the Library of Congress

CHAPTER 19

551(L) Corbis **551(R)** American Antiquarian Society **555** Harry P. Lepman Collection/Smithsonian Insitution **556** Culver Pictures, Inc. **557** Culver Pictures, Inc. **559** The Granger Collection **560(L)** The New York Public Library, Rare Book Division **560(R)** *Harper's Weekly* **562** Culver Pictures, Inc. **564** Courtesy of the Library of Congress **565** Kansas State Historical Society **566** The Granger Collection **568** Courtesy of the Library of Congress **569(L)** Brown Brothers **569(R)** Courtesy of the Library of Congress **570(L)** Robert W. Woodruff Library **570(R)** Corbis **573** The New York Public Library, Rare Book Division

CHAPTER 20

580 Mattew Brady/Corbis **581** Corbis **584** Courtesy of the Library of Congress **587** *Puck* **588** Corbis **591** Culver Pictures, Inc. **592** Chicago Historical Society **597** Courtesy of the Library of Congress **599** Courtesy of the Library of Congress **600** Courtesy of the Library of Congress

CHAPTER 21

607(L) Courtesy of the Library of Congress **607(R)** Corbis **608(L)** George Eastman House **608(R)** Lewis W. Hine/George Eastman House **609** Corbis **610** Corbis **611** Lawrence Lee Pelletier Library **613(L)** The Granger Collection **613(R)** Centers for Disease Control and Prevention (CDC) **615** Chicago Historical Society **616(T)** Corbis **616(B)** AP/Wide World Photos **618** Courtesy of the Library of Congress **621** Courtesy of the Library of Congress **623** Courtesy of the Library of Congress **625(T)** Brown Brothers **625(L)** Corbis **625(R)** State Historical Society of Wisconsin **627** Brown Brothers **633** Courtesy of the Library of Congress

CHAPTER 22

640 The Granger Collection **641** Corbis **643** Imperial War Museum, London **645** Imperial War Museum, London **647** Imperial War Museum, London **652** Wayne State University Archives of Labor and Urban Affairs **654** The New York Public Library, Rare Book Division **655** Corbis **656** National Archives **657** National Archives **659** Corbis **663** Brown Brothers **665** *The Chicago Tribune* New York News Syndicate

CHAPTER 23

672 Culver Pictures, Inc. **679(L)** Brown Brothers **679(R)** National Baseball Hall of Fame & Museum, Inc. **680(L)** *Vanity Fair* photograph by Breaker/Copyright © 1928, 1956 by Conde Nast Publications, Inc. **680(R)** Brown Brothers **681** Culver Pictures, Inc. **683** The Granger Collection **685** Courtesy of the Library of Congress **686** Shahn, Ben. *Bartolomeo Vanzetti and Nicola Sacco*, The Museum of Art **687** Brown Brothers **688(T)** AP/Wide World Photos **688(B)** Archibald Motley Jr., *Black Belt*, 1934. Oil on canvas, 31-7/8" x 39-1/4", Hampton University Museum, Hampton, Va. **689** *Life* **691** U.S. Bureau of Engraving and Printing **692** *The New York Times*

CHAPTER 24

700 Culver Pictures, Inc. **704** Corbis **705** AP/Wide World Photos **706** Courtesy of the Library of Congress **710** AP/Wide World Photos **711(L)** AP/Wide World Photos **711(R)** Culver Pictures, Inc. **715** By permission of Esquire Magazine. Copyright ©The Hearst Corporation. Also, Esquire is a trademark of The Hearst Corporation. All Rights Reserved **716** Corbis **719** Courtesy of the Library of Congress

CHAPTER 25

729 Archive Photos **733** Corbis **734** Corbis **736** Corbis **737** Official U. S. Naval Photograph **739** AP/Wide World Photos **740** *Up Front* by Bill Mauldin, published by Henry Holt & Co. **741(L)** Courtesy of the Library of Congress **741(R)** Harvard Business School **744** National Archives **748** Franklin D. Roosevelt Library **751** Corbis **753** U.S. Air Force **756** U.S. Air Force

CHAPTER 26

764(L) Time *Life* Syndication **764(R)** Thomas D. McAvoy/Time *Life* Syndication **766** Corbis **771** Ferno Jacobs/Black Star **772** Sovfoto/Eastfoto **773** Corbis **778** Corbis **779(L)** Elliott Erwitt/Magnum Photos, Inc. **779(R)** Elliott Erwitt/Magnum Photos, Inc. **781** Corbis **783** Alfred Eisenstaedt/Time *Life* Syndication **784** The Museum of Modern Art/Film Stills Archive

CHAPTER 27

792 AP/Wide World Photos **798** Sovfoto/Eastfoto **800** Corbis **802** AP/Wide World Photos **803** Costa Manos/Magnum Photos, Inc. **805** Corbis **806** Ed Clark/Time *Life* Syndication **808** AP/Wide World Photos **809(L)** AP/Wide World Photos **809(R)** AP/Wide World Photos **810** Time *Life* Syndication **813** Don Wright/Time Life Syndication **814** Corbis

CHAPTER 28

820 Everett Collection, Inc. **821** Photofest **823** Hulton Getty/Liaison Agency, Inc. **826** Gaslight Advertising Archives, Inc. N.Y. **827** Courtesy of the Library of Congress **828** Culver Pictures, Inc. **833** Jeffrey Markowitz/Corbis Sygma **836** Corbis

CHAPTER 29

846 Corbis **847** Corbis **850** New York Daily News **854** Lyndon Baines Johnson Library Collection **860** David Falcone/Black Star **861(L)** Steve Shapiro/Black Star **861(R)** AP/Wide World Photos **864** Kent State University News Service **866** Magnum Photos, Inc. **867** Kobal Collection **869** Ron Haeberle/Life Picture Service

CHAPTER 30

876 AP/Wide World Photos **879(T)** Shel Hershorn, UT Austin/Archive Photos **879(B)** Corbis **880** Charles Moore/Black Star **882** Hulton Getty/Liaison Agency, Inc. **883** Fred Ward/Black Star **884** Corbis **885** Hulton Getty/Liaison Agency, Inc. **886** Constantine Manos/Magnum Photos, Inc. **888** Yoichi Okatomo/Photo Researchers, Inc. **890** Lisa Quinones/Black Star **891** Wayne Miller/Magnum Photos, Inc. **892** Photofest **894** Arthur Grace/Corbis Sygma **896(T)** Rick Friedman/Black Star **896(B)** Ira Wyman/Corbis Sygma **898** Andrew Lichtenstein/Corbis Sygma **899** Archive Photos **901** Bob Fitch/Black Star **902** Corbis Sygma **903** Gifford/Liaison Agency, Inc.

CHAPTER 31

912 Mark Godfrey/Archive Photos **913** J. P. Laffont/Corbis Sygma **920(L)** Bill Fitzpatrick/The White House Photo Office **920(R)** SIPA Press **923** Novosti/Liaison Agency, Inc. **924** Timothy Ross/JB Pictures Ltd. **925(B)** R. Bossu/Corbis Sygma **925(T)** Klaus Reisinger/Black Star **927** P. Le Segretain/Corbis Sygma **930** Simonpietri/Corbis Sygma **931 (L)** CNN/Corbis Sygma **931(R)** Cynthia Johnson/Liaison Agency, Inc. **934** Roger Lemoyne/Liaison Agency, Inc.

TEXT CREDITS

673 From Mayer & Wade, *Chicago: Growth of a Metropolis*. Copyright © The University of Chicago Press. Reprinted by permission.

814 "HOWL" (5 lines) from *Collected Poems 1947–1980* by Allen Ginsberg. Copyright © 1955 by Allen Ginsberg. Reprinted by permission of HarperCollins Publishers.

Index

Abenaki Indians, 66
Abolitionism, 273, 294–297; arguments of, 295, 346; and colonization movement, 294, 296; divisions within, 296–297; and Emancipation Proclamation, 429; public reaction to, 295, 332; in revolutionary period, 175–178; in South, 175–178, 320, 336–337; and violence, 404, 405; and women's rights movement, 298, 299
Abortion, 177, 894, 895–896
Abrams v. United States, 655
Acheson, Dean, 769, 773, 774, 775, 780
Adams, Abigail, 172, 173, 202, 203, 204
Adams, Charles Francis, 426
Adams, Henry, 567
Adams, John, 113, 132, 154; and Abigail, 172–173; appointment of judgeships, 215, 216; in Britain, 168; and Declaration of Independence, 139; presidency of, 202–205; and quasi war with France, 203–204
Adams, John Quincy, 235–236, 252–253, 261; and Adams-Onis Treaty, 241; election of 1828, 266; and Oregon country, 368; presidency of, 264–265; on slavery debates, 264; and Texas annexation, 365
Adams, Samuel, 100–101; and Boston massacre, 117, 118; and First Continental Congress, 121; in resistance to British, 106, 107–108, 111, 113, 114, 131; and Second Continental Congress, 132; views on government, 162, 183
Adams, Samuel (father), 100
Adams-Onis Treaty, 241
Adamson Act, 628, 633
Addams, Jane, 595, 610, 615
The Adder's Den (Dye), 384–385
Adler, Renata, 820
The Adventures of Huckleberry Finn (Twain), 531
Advertising, 492, 677, 826
Aero Club of America, 618
Affirmative action, 888–889, 895
Afghanistan, 920, 922, 923, 935
Africa, 15, 57, 58; colonization to, 294, 296; Garvey and, 688; slave trade in, 15, 57, 59
African Americans. *See also* Free blacks; Racial violence; Racism; Segregation; Slavery; Slaves: in abolitionist movement, 294, 296–297; in American Revolution, 134–138, 144; athletes, 804–805; Black Codes, 453–454; and black nationalism/black power, 884–887; in Civil War, 429–431, 436; co-opting of culture by whites, 813–814; in colonies, 36–37, 78, 79; and colonization movement, 294, 296; and Dominican annexation plan, 580; education, 179, 292–293, 450, 464, 561–562, 609, 877, 880, 887, 889; ghettos, 675; in government, 461, 462–463; in Great Depression, 703, 716; Harlem Renaissance, 688–689; Lyndon B. Johnson and, 888–889; labor system after Civil War, 446, 453, 454, 463–464; land ownership, 450, 453, 463; late twentieth-century, 889–890; legal status/rights, 451, 453–454, 455; literature, 307; medical care, 392–393, 718; migration from South, 524, 657, 674, 676, 742; music, 343, 533–534, 813; New Deal and, 716; New South and, 500, 501; in New Spain, 19–20; in 1960s, 877, 889; in 1920s, 687–689; in North, 877, 887; and Philippines independence struggle, 599; and poor whites, 464; population growth, 78, 79; Populism and, 567; poverty among, 718, 889, 890; in Progressive Era, 609, 615, 617–618, 620–621, 633, 635; after Reconstruction, 472, 473, 562; in Reconstruction, 440, 446, 447–450, 453–456, 458–466, 474; religion of, 89, 178, 179, 289, 337, 343, 464; Republican party and, 531, 561–562, 635, 716; resistance to discrimination, 572–573, 617–618, 687–688, 742–743 (*See also* Civil rights movement); in revolutionary era, 161, 175–179; Theodore Roosevelt and, 633, 635; sharecropping, 463–464, 716; in Spanish-American War, 593; and sports, 537; stereotypes, 312–313, 678, 804, 814; Tuskegee syphilis study, 718–719; unemployment among, 877, 878; veterans, 660, 687; voting rights (*See* Black suffrage); women, 615; after World War I, 660, 687–688; in World War I, 657, 687; in World War II, 742–743, 806
African Free School, 179
African Methodist Episcopal Church, 178, 179, 250, 289, 464
Agnew, Spiro, 862, 913
Agrarianism, 564–566, 575, 584; southern, 720
Agricultural Adjustment Act, 708, 709, 717
Agriculture: agrarian movements, 564–566, 575, 584; and Columbian exchange, 30; commercial, 323, 499–500; declining prices and, 557, 562, 563–564, 693, 708; early nineteenth-century, 242, 245, 323; in Great Depression, 708–709; late nineteenth-century, 498–500, 557; mechanization of, 499, 505; migrant workers, 716, 898, 900–901; Native-American, 5–6; and New Deal, 708–709, 716; progressive reforms, 627; in 1920s, 693; sharecropping, 463–464, 708, 709, 716; in South, 334, 335–336, 463–464, 498–499, 720, 824–825; tenant, 499, 708–709, 716; in West, 494–500, 831, 834; in World War I, 652; in World War II, 738
Aguinaldo, Emilio, 599, 600
AIDS (acquired immunodeficiency syndrome), 832–833
AIM (American Indian Movement), 899–902
Air-conditioning, 822–823
Aircraft/aerospace industry, 828, 829–830
Alabama: civil rights movement, 879–880, 880–882, 884; Montgomery bus boycott, 808–810; women's rights, 894
Alabama (ship), 425
Alamo, the, 364, 366
Alaska, purchase of, 582
Albany Plan of Union, 92, 122
Albert, King of Belgium, 642
Alcott, Abba, 305
Alcott, Bronson, 302, 305
Alcott, Louisa May, 305
Aldrich, Nelson W., 625
Alexander, Charles C., 797
Alexander II, Czar of Russia, 520
Alexander VI (pope), 16
Alien Act, 204
Alien and Sedition acts, 204–205
Alien Enemies Act, 204
Allan, Ethan, 133
Allen, Frederick Lewis, 694–695
Allen, Richard, 178, 179
Allerton, Mary Norris, 52
Alliance movement, 565, 566
Altgeld, John, 568
American Anti-Boycott Association, 632
American Anti-Slavery Society, 296, 299, 313
American Civil Liberties Union, 655
The American Commonwealth (Bryce), 552
American exceptionalism, 583–584
American Federation of Labor (AFL), 509–510, 684, 713; in World War I, 652, 653
American Grafitti (film), 810
American Historical Association, 614
American Indian Movement, 899–902
American Medical Association, 614

I-1

American Negro Academy, 688
American Party (Know Nothings), 391–395, 399, 400, 553
American Peace Commission, 661–662
American Philosophical Society, 86
American Plague, 528
American Psychiatric Association, 902, 903
American Revolution, 101; beginning of, 129–132; British military buildup, 140–141; Bunker Hill, 118, 133–134, 136–137; Continental army, 128, 129, 132, 142–146, 149, 150, 152, 155; Declaration of Independence and, 138–140; events leading to, 100–123, 129–132; expansion of, 133–138; French assistance in, 146–147; Lexington and Concord, 131, 132, 134–135; in North, 131, 132, 133–137, 140–144, 147–149; peace settlement, 154–155; Second Continental Congress and, 132–133; in South, 134–138, 138, 150–153; surrender at Yorktown, 153–154; Valley Forge, 128, 129, 149
"The American Scholar" (Emerson), 301
American Society for the Promotion of Temperance, 290
American system, 265
American system of production, 245
American Tobacco Company, 632
American Woman Suffrage Association, 458, 459, 556
American Women's Hospital Service, 656
Amherst, Jeffrey, 93
Amish, 79
"Amos 'n Andy" (radio show), 678
Amusement parks, 540–541
Anaconda Plan, 419–421
Anarchists, 660, 686
Anderson, Billy, 826
Anderson, Marian, 715
Anderson, Robert, 414, 439
Andros, Edmund, 74, 75
Anglican church. See Church of England
Annapolis (Maryland), 168, 179
Anniston (Alabama), 879
Anthony, Susan B., 429, 458, 459, 556, 616, 682; trial of, 617
Anti-Comintern Pact, 732–733
Anti-imperialists, 582, 595–598, 628
Anti-Mason movement, 260–261, 277
Anti-Saloon League, 614
Antietam, battle of, 410–411, 422–423, 429
Antifederalists, 181, 182–183
Antigovernment sentiment, 552, 839, 931
Antinomian crisis, 47–48
Antismoking campaign, in 1920s, 685
Antitrust legislation: Clayton Antitrust Act, 627, 632; Sherman Antitrust Act, 561, 622, 624
Antiwar movement(s): Civil War, 428, 436; Mexican-American War, 373, 374; Vietnam War, 858–861, 863–864, 891; World War I, 648, 654, 655; between world wars, 729, 730–731, 736
Antrobus, John, 343
Apache Indians, 357, 468
Apes, William, 307
Apocalypse Now (film), 867
Apodaca, Jerry, 899
Appeal to the Colored Citizens of the World (Walker), 295
Appliances, "labor-saving," 677

Appomattox, surrender at, 438
Arapaho Indians, 8, 469
Arawak Indians, 15–16
Arizona: American settlement of, 356–357; Mexican Americans in, 376; Phelps Dodge strike incident, 654–655; population growth, 829; Spanish, 355, 356
Arizona (ship), 737
Arizona Territory, 376
Arkansas, 451, 452, 808
Arms race, 768, 772; and détente, 866, 918; under Reagan, 921; SALT I treaty, 865
Armstrong, Louis, 678
Armstrong, Neil, 927
Army, U.S. *See also* Union army: Eisenhower and, 798; McCarthy's attacks on, 781; reductions, post–Civil War, 581, 582; segregation in, 657, 742, 806; in Spanish-American War, 593, 594; in World War I, 657, 658, 659
Army Corps of Nurses, 656
Arnett, Peter, 853
Arnold, Benedict, 112, 133, 148, 152, 153
Arnold, Thurman, 708
Arrillaga, Mariano Paredes y, 371
Art: early nineteenth-century, 301, 307–308; in Great Depression, 711; Harlem Renaissance, 688; late nineteenth–early twentieth-century, 532–533, 609; Pre-Raphaelite, 613; in 1920s, 680
Arthur, Chester, 558, 559, 585
Articles of Confederation, 164; financial problems under, 164, 165–169; plans to revise, 166–167, 168, 179, 180; ratification of, 165
Artisans, 323–324, 505; free black, 344, 346
As I Lay Dying (Faulkner), 721
Ashcan school, 532–533, 609
Associated Negro Press, 689
Association for the Study of Negro Life and History, 689
Associationism, 690, 708
Astor, John Jacob, 365
Astor, William, 493
Astor Place Riot, 310
Asylums, 293
Atahualpa, 18
Atkinson, Edwin, 510
Atlanta (Georgia), 436
Atlantic Charter, 736
Atomic weapons. *See* Nuclear weapons
Attlee, Clement, 766
Attucks, Crispus, 116
Augusta (ship), 736
Auschwitz, 728
Austin, Stephen F., 362, 363, 364, 367
Austria, 733, 798
Austria-Hungary, 641
Autobahnen, 795
Autobiographies, by minority authors, 307
Automobile industry: auto safety movement and, 876, 877; foreign competition in, 916; oil crisis and, 915; in 1920s, 676–677; in South, 824; in World War II, 738
Automobiles, impact of, 676, 795–796, 831
Autry, Gene, 826
Avilés, Pedro Menéndez de, 23
Axis powers, 745
Azores, 15
Aztecs, 6, 7, 17–18

Babbitt, Bruce, 839
Babbitt, Irving, 720
Babbitt (Lewis), 680
Baby and Child Care (Spock), 811
Baby boom, 742, 890
Bachelor subculture, 535
Backus, Isaac, 88
Bacon, Nathaniel, 73
Bacon's rebellion, 73–74
Baer, George F., 606
Baez, Buenaventura, 580
Bahamas, 15–16
Baker, Ray Stannard, 611, 620
Bakke v. Regents of the University of California, 889
Balboa, Vasco Nuñez de, 17
Baldwin, James, 887
Baldwin, Luther, 204–205
Ball, George, 855, 856
Ballard, Martha, 52
Ballinger, Richard A., 626
Baltic states, 748, 925, 926
Baltimore & Ohio Railroad, 506
Baltimore incident, 587–588
Baltimore (Maryland), 226, 248, 258, 344, 427
bandidos, 354
Bank of America, 828
Bank of the United States, 194–195, 215; second, 236, 237, 239–240, 274–275
Bankers, 491
Banking system: bank failures, in Great Depression, 707–708; Federal Reserve, 627, 632–633; under Jackson, 274–276; and National Banking acts, 426; in 1920s, 677; savings and loan crisis, 924
Banneker, Benjamin, 178
banzai charges, 752
Baptists, 88–89, 170, 171, 285, 288, 336, 338
Barbadians, in South Carolina, 42, 43, 344
Barbados, 58
Barbary pirates, 217–218, 240
Barbour, Charlie, 449
Barker, Frank, 869
Barnett, Ross, 823, 880
Barnum, P. T., 310
Barré, Isaac, 105
barrios, 376
Barrow, Bennet H., 341
Bartholdi, Frederic Auguste, 517
Bartolomeo Vanzetti and Nicola Sacco (Shahn), 686
Barton, Clara, 437
Bartram, John, 83
Baruch, Bernard M., 652
Baseball, 535–536, 537, 679, 829; integration of, 804–805
Batista, Fulgencio, 801
Batman comics, 785
Battle of Britain, 735
Bay Company charter, 46
Bay of Pigs invasion, 801, 850
Bayard, Thomas F., 587
Beadle, Erasmus, 309
Bear Flag Revolt, 372
Beard, Charles A., 640
Beat Generation, 814
Beaumarchais, Pierre-Augustin Caron de, 146, 147
Beauregard, P. G. T., 414, 419, 424
Becknell, William, 360
Beckwourth, Jim, 360
Beecher, Catharine, 298

Beecher, Henry Ward, 486
Beecher, Lyman, 332
Beer-Hall Putsch, 731
Behaim, Martin, 14
Beheading, 13
Beiderbecke, Bix, 534
Belgium, 642, 646, 652, 735
Bell, Alexander Graham, 483
Bell, John, 411–412
Bellamy, Edward, 609
Bellows, George, 532–533
Bemis, Edward W., 523
Benin (kingdom), 57
Bennett, James Gordon, 309
Bennett, Rolla, 250
Bentley, Eric, 820
Benton, Thomas Hart, 272
Berger, Victor, 661
Berkeley, John (Lord Berkeley), 70
Berkeley, William, 73, 74
Berkman, Alexander, 568
Berle, Adolph, 708
Berlin: airlift, 771–772; destruction of Wall, 925
Bermuda, 37
Bernard, Francis, 106, 107, 108, 114
Bernstein, Carl, 913
Bethune, Mary McLeod, 716
Beveridge, Albert J., 583–584, 586, 593
Bibb, Henry, 296, 342
Biddle, Nicholas, 274
Bidwell, John, 361
Bienville, Sieur de (Jean Baptiste le Moyne), 89
Bierstadt, Albert, 308
Big business. *See also* Industry: and antitrust legislation, 561; control of competition by, 489–491; and expansion of middle class, 492; government and, 486–487, 493, 553; and Harding administration, 689; managerial styles, 491–492; and mass marketing, 492; and mass production, 493; and New Deal, 710; and Progressive Era, 606, 608, 632, 633; rise of, 489–493; Theodore Roosevelt and, 606, 607, 622–623, 626; search for overseas markets, 584–585; and wealthy elite, 493; in World War II, 738
Big stick diplomacy, 628, 629
Bilbo, Theodore G., 806
Bill Haley and the Comets, 813–814
Bill(s) of rights: GI, 740; state, 171; U.S., 183, 193
Bird, Robert Montgomery, 309
Birds of passage, 518–519
Birmingham (Alabama), 880–882
Birney, James G., 296, 337
Birth control, 176–177, 682, 683; Sanger's campaign for, 672, 674–675
Bismarck, Otto von, 587
Bissell, George, 482
Black Bart (Charles E. Boles), 497
Black Belt (Motley), 688
Black Codes, 453–454
Black Death (plague), 11
Black Hawk, 271, 307
Black Hawk War, 270–271, 418
Black Legend, 20
Black Like Me (Griffin), 806
Black Muslims, 885–886
Black nationalism, 884–887
Black Panthers, 839, 886

Black power, 886–887
"Black Sox" scandal, 679
Black studies, 886, 887
Black suffrage: in 1960, 877; after Civil War, 451, 453, 455, 456, 458–459, 465; Fifteenth Amendment and, 455; free blacks, 260, 346; in 1890s, 561, 569–570; 1960s movement for, 883–884, 885
Black Tuesday, 692
Blackboard Jungle (film), 784
Blackmun, Harry, 889
Blackwell, Elizabeth, 298
Blaine, James G., 554, 556, 559, 585, 587
Blair, Ezell, Jr., 878
Blair Education Bill, 561–562
Blake (Delany), 307
Bland-Allison Act, 558, 561
Bleeding Kansas, 398, 399, 401
Blind people, 293, 713
Blitzkrieg, 734
Blount, James H., 589
Blues, 534, 678, 813, 825
Boas, Franz, 640
Bolden, Buddy, 534
Boles, Peter, 112
Boleyn, Anne, 22
Bon Homme Richard (ship), 154
Bonsel, Stephen, 599
Bonus Army, 706
Bonvouloir, Achard de, 146
Book of Mormon, 368, 369
Boone, Daniel, 171, 172
Boorstin, Daniel, 812
Booth, John Wilkes, 440
Booth, Sherman M., 390
Borden, Andrew, 516–517
Borden, Hannah, 325
Borden, Lizzie, 516–517
Border states, in Civil War, 417
Bork, Robert, 913
Bosnia, 935
Bostic, Joe, 804, 805
Boston: in American Revolution, 131, 133–134, 136–137; antiabolitionist riots, 295; colonial, 46, 55, 70, 75, 87; early nineteenth-century, 246; Monroe's tour through, 235–236; resistance to British, 106–109, 112–121, 123; strike of 1835, 326; Washington's funeral, 207
Boston Massacre, 113, 115–116, 117
Boston Tea Party, 119–120
Bourne, Randolph Silliman, 640–641, 648, 649, 651, 653, 654, 664, 666
Bowie, Jim, 364, 366
Boxer Rebellion, 601
Boxing, 536–537, 678
Boyce, John, 307
Braceland, Francis J., 813
bracero, 743, 900
Braddock, Edward, 92–93
Bradford, William, 5, 42, 44, 45, 47
Bradley, Mamie, 793
Bradley, Tom, 890
Bradstreet, Anne, 52, 54
"Brain trust," 708
Brand, Max, 826
Brandeis, Louis B., 610, 611, 622, 628
Brandywine Creek, battle of, 147
Brant, Joseph (Thayendanegea), 148, 149
Brazil, 16, 57
Breaker boys, 608
Breckinridge, John C., 411, 413
Brezhnev, Leonid, 918

Briand, Aristide, 729
Britain. *See also* American Revolution: admiration for, 586; battle of, 735; and Civil War, 424–425, 426; civil war in, 41, 44; colonial rule, 74, 76–78, 82–83, 102, 103–106; colonial rupture, 117–123; colonial taxes, 104, 105–106; and colonial trade, 67–68, 77–78, 102, 103; colonists' resistance to, 106–111; colonization by, 24–28, 30; decline of, postwar, 769; emigration from, motives for, 23–24, 30; Glorious Revolution, 74–75; imperial wars and, 90–94; impressment by, 221; interwar foreign policy, 729, 731; and Ireland, 24, 643; Jay's Treaty with, 200–201; Jeffersonian-era conflicts with, 220–222; and Monroe Doctrine, 241; as nation-state, 15; New World exploration, 20; in Old Northwest, 200, 201, 222; and Panic of 1837, 276; Protestant Reformation and, 21–22; Puritans in, 22, 41, 43–44, 55; Quakers in, 70; and Seven Years' War, 93, 94, 101, 102; and slave trade, 58; Suez crisis, 799–800; territorial issues, nineteenth-century, 241, 365, 589, 629; trade with, after Revolution, 168; and Treaty of Versailles, 662; War of 1812, 222–228; war with France, 220–221; war with Spain, 23; and World War I, 642–647, 649, 658; and World War II, 734–736, 748–749
British Guiana, 589
Brontë, Emily, 612
Brook Farm, 305
Brooks, Preston, 399
Brown, Henry "Box," 307
Brown, John, 399, 403–405
Brown, Morris, 250
Brown, Moses, 324
Brown, Norman O., 891
Brown, William Wells, 296, 307
Brown v. Board of Education of Topeka, 807, 888; reactions to, 792, 808
Brownson, Orestes, 302
Brownsville (Texas), 635
Bryan, William Jennings: election of 1896, 550, 551, 555, 571; election of 1900, 607; election of 1908, 623; and Florida land boom, 691; and Philippines annexation, 595; and Scopes trial, 686; on wealth, 544; and World War I, 643, 646, 647, 648
Bryant, Carolyn, 793
Bryant, Roy, 792–793
Bryce, James, 552, 554
Buchanan, James, 385, 395, 399, 400, 401
Buchanan, Patrick, 832
Buckley, William F., Jr., 927
Budget deficit, 921. *See also* National debt
Buell, Don Carlos, 420, 422
Buena Vista, battle of, 372
Bulge, battle of the, 747, 750
Bull Moose party (Progressive party), 626, 690
Bull Run: battle of, 419; Second, battle of, 422
Bullocke, James, 85
Bumppo, Natty, 302
Bunau-Varilla, Philippe, 629–630
Bunker Hill, battle of, 118, 133–133, 136–137, 308
Buntline, Ned, 309

Bunyan, John, 611
Burden, Janet, 613
Bureau of Corporations, 622, 627
Bureau of Indian Affairs, occupation of, 899, 902
Burger, Warren, 889, 895
Burgess, Guy, 779–780
Burgoyne, John, 131, 133, 136, 137, 147, 148, 149
Burke Act, 471–472
Burlingame Treaty, 522
Burns, Anthony, 390
Burnside, Ambrose E., 410, 422, 434
Burr, Aaron, 202, 206; conspiracies of, 219–220; duel with Hamilton, 212, 219
Burroughs, Edgar Rice, 679
Bush, George, 837, 923–930; and end of Cold War, 927; and Panama, 924–925; and Persian Gulf War, 928–930; social legislation under, 924, 930
Business. *See* Big business; Industry
Busing, 887, 889
Butler, Andrew, 399
Butler, Pierce, 180
Buttrick, John, 134
Byrd, Lucy Parke, 56
Byrd, William, II, 56
Byrne, Eugene, 538
Byrnes, James F., 772, 808

C. Turner Joy (ship), 855
Cabinet, 193
Cable car, 525
Cabot, John (Giovanni Caboto), 20
Cabral, Pedro Alvares, 16
Cabrillo, Juan Rodríguez, 18
Cahan, Abraham, 541
Calhoun, John C., 222, 236, 237, 261, 264; and Jackson, 241, 273–274; and Mexican American War, 374; and nullification, 266; and secession, 389, 413; in slave power conspiracy theory, 384, 385; and slavery issue, 336, 365; and transportation policy, 239
Calhoun, William J., 591
California: acquisition of, 374; admission as free state, 385–386, 389; American revolt in, 371, 372; American settlement of, 357, 361; Donner party, 358; gold rush, 375, 377–379; grape-pickers' strike, 900–901; industrialization in, 828; Mexican Americans in, 375, 376; Native Americans in, 356, 357, 496; population growth, 741, 829, 837; Spanish, 355, 356; tax revolt, 839
California (ship), 737
Call It Sleep (Roth), 721
Callender, James Thomson, 190–191, 201
Calley, William, 869
Calvert, Cecilius (second Lord Baltimore), 40–41
Calvert, George (first Lord Baltimore), 40
Calvert, Leonard, 55, 58
Calvert family, 76–77
Calvin, John, 22
Calvinism, 22, 42
Cambodia, 863, 867
Camden, battle of, 152
Camera, 483
Camille, or the Fate of a Coquette (Dumas), 612
Camp David Accords, 918, 920
Campaign finance laws, 914

Campanella, Roy, 805
Canada: in American Revolution, 133; border disputes, 365, 368; British in, 90; exploration of, 20; French in, 28, 29–30, 93; in War of 1812, 222–223
Canals, 242–243
Cane Ridge revival, 214, 285
Canning, George, 241
Cannon, "Uncle Joe," 625
Capital formation, 488, 501
Capital punishment, 291
Capitol, U.S., 203
Capone, Al, 685
Capra, Frank, 721
Cardoza, Francis, 461
Carey, Matthew, 323
Caribbean. *See also* New Spain; *specific countries*: and American Revolution, 150; slavery in, 42, 57, 58, 344; trade with, 78; U.S. interwar policy in, 730
Caribs, 16
Carmichael, Stokely, 886
Carnegie, Andrew, 427, 480, 481, 485–486, 490, 553; as anti-imperialist, 595, 598, 600; and Homestead strike, 567–568; income, 608
Carnegie Steel Company, 480, 481
Carney, William H., 431
Carolinas. *See also* North Carolina; South Carolina: settlement of, 41–42
Caroline (ship), 365
Carpetbaggers, 460–462
Carranza, Venustiano, 630–631
Carson, "Fiddlin' John," 678
Carson, Rachel, 903
Carter, Jimmy, 821, 915; foreign policy, 865, 918–920; Iranian hostage crisis and, 918–920; race relations and, 823–824
Carter, Landon, 393
Carteret, George, 70
Cartier, Jacques, 12, 20
Cartwright, Alexander J., Jr., 535
Cartwright, Peter, 214
Cartwright, Samuel W., 393
Carver, George Washington, 500
Casablanca, 746
Cass, Lewis, 388
Castro, Fidel, 801, 850, 915
Castro, Raul, 899
Catcher in the Rye (Salinger), 890
Cather, Willa, 307
Catherine of Aragon, 21, 22
Catholics/Catholicism: Father Coughlin, 712, 715; Glorious Revolution, 74–75; hostility toward, 107, 391–394, 521, 559; and Know Nothings, 391–394; in Maryland colony, 40–41, 75, 76–77; in New Spain, 19, 20; in pre–Civil War era, 288–289; and progressivism, 611; and Protestant Reformation, 21–22; schools, 293
Catlin, George, 357
Cato's Letters (Trenchard and Gordon), 117
Catt, Carrie Chapman, 616, 656
Cattle barons, 496
Cattle ranching, 494, 495
Cayuga Indians, 148
Cemeteries, 308
Census, first, 191–192
Central Intelligence Agency (CIA), 798, 801, 919, 922; Castro assassination plot, 801, 850; congressional oversight of, 914–915

Central Park (New York), 540
Central Valley Project, 827
Chain stores, 677
Chamberlain, Neville, 733, 735
Chambers, Whittaker, 764–765
Champlain, Samuel de, 4, 29
Chancellorsville, battle of, 431, 434
Chandler, Raymond, 720
Chaney, James, 886
Channing, William Ellery, 285
Chapultepec, battle of, 372
Charities, 704
Charles, Robert, 572, 573
Charles I, King of England, 41, 44
Charles II, King of England, 41, 48, 67–70, 73, 74
Charles River Bridge v. Warren Bridge, 276
Charleston (South Carolina): African Americans in, 344, 703; in American Revolution, 114, 151; Barbadians in, 42, 43, 344; in Civil War, 414, 439–440; emancipation in, 448; and Jay's Treaty, 201; in Queen Anne's War, 90; and Tariff of Abominations, 266; Vesey conspiracy, 250–251, 344
Charlotte Temple (Rowson), 309–310
Chase, Salmon P., 398, 426
Chase, Samuel, 216–217
Chattanooga, battle of, 435
Chávez, César Estrada, 898, 900–901
Cherokee Indians, 8, 93, 94–95, 172, 197, 307; in American Revolution, 150–151; in Jacksonian era, 268, 269; removal of, 270, 271
Cherokee Nation v. Georgia, 269
Cherokee War, 94
Chesapeake colonies. *See also* Maryland colony; Virginia colony: family life, 51, 56; Great Awakening in, 89; indentured servitude in, 51, 54–55, 58; life expectancies, 50–51, 56; tobacco glut and, 68; women in, 51, 54, 55
Chesapeake (ship), 221
Chestnut, Charles, 688
Chew, Lee, 522
Cheyenne Indians, 357, 468, 469–470
Chiang Kai-shek (Jiang Jieshi), 772–773, 797
Chicago (Illinois): African-American population, 674; Columbian Exposition of 1893, 483, 540; Democratic convention of 1968, 861; growth of, 673; and jazz, 678; murder of Eugene Williams, 660; Pullman strike, 568; Republic mill shooting, 713; in 1890s, 526; skyscrapers, 526; Weathermen in, 891; worker housing and neighborhoods, 526, 608
Chickamauga, battle of, 435
Chickasaw Indians, 8, 93, 94, 150, 172, 197, 238, 268
Child labor, 324, 325, 327, 608; legislation, 615, 620, 628, 632, 710, 721; writing on, 611
Childbirth, 52–53
Children: African-American, and segregation, 807; colonial, 52, 55; slave, 341, 342
Chile, 587–588
China: civil war, 772–773; Cold War policy toward, 773; détente with, 866, 918; Japanese aggression in, 732, 737; and Korean War, 776; Nixon's trip to,

864–865, 866; Open Door Policy, 600–601; recognition of, 864–865, 918; Truman's "loss of," 773, 854; and Vietnam, 851, 864
China Lobby, 773
Chinese Exclusion Act, 522–523, 562
Chinese immigrants/Chinese Americans, 496, 503, 519, 522–523, 562
Chinook Indians, 8, 218
Chippewa Indians, 102, 200, 902
Chivington, J. M., 469–470
Choctaw Indians, 7, 8, 93, 150, 227, 268; removal of, 270
Choiseul, Duc de, 146
Cholera, 262–263
Chou En-lai (Zhou Enlai), 772, 865
Christian, Archer, 538
Christianity. *See also* Religion: and slaves, 89, 337, 343
Church, Frederick, 308
Church, Robb, 596, 597
Church bombings, 882
Church of England, 22, 42, 43, 171, 337
Churchill, Winston, 731, 732, 735, 736, 738, 745, 746, 768, 770; and Yalta Conference, 747–748
CIA. *See* Central Intelligence Agency
Cigarette industry, 500–501, 685, 826
Cincinnati (Ohio), 238, 246, 373
Cincinnati Red Stockings, 535
Circular Letter, 111–114
Cisneros, Henry, 899
Cities. *See also* Urbanization: African American migration to, 524, 657, 674; beautification campaigns, 308; central, 527, 673; before Civil War, 332; colonial, 82, 114; crime and violence in, 332–333, 527; culture of, 530–534; Democratic party machines in, 554; drug problems, 542–543; flight from, 795, 810, 889; free blacks in, 179–180; housing, 526–529, 703–704; immigrants in, 328, 524; late nineteenth-century, 524–544; mid-nineteenth-century, 523–524; parks, 540–541; police forces, 332–333, 527; popular entertainments, 534–543; poverty, 82, 248, 263, 285, 291, 330, 528, 529; "private" *vs.* "public," 528; progressive reforms in, 618–619, 631–632; prostitution in, 682; race riots of 1960s, 887; racial composition, 810–811; Renaissance, 14; residential segregation in, 526–527, 534, 674–675; sanitation problems, 247–248, 262, 528–529; skyscrapers, 526, 673; southern, 335, 824; transportation in, 526; urban planning, 528–529, 675; western, 831
Citizen Genêt Affair, 197
Citizenship. *See* Political rights
Civil Rights Act of 1866, 455
Civil Rights Act of 1875, 472
Civil Rights Act of 1957, 882
Civil Rights Act of 1964, 883, 888; Title VII, 894, 895
Civil Rights Act of 1991, 924
Civil rights movement, 806–810, 877–890, 905–906; and black nationalism/black power, 884–887; Civil Rights Act of 1964, 883; court decisions, 806–807; Eisenhower and, 807–808; freedom riders, 879–880; integration of Ole Miss, 880; Kennedy and, 849, 879–880,

882–883; Little Rock crisis, 808; march on Washington, 883; Montgomery bus boycott, 808–810; murder of Emmett Till, 793–794; in North, 887; sit-ins, 878–879; violence in, 810, 878, 879–880, 882, 886; and voting rights, 883–884, 885; white backlash, 889; white students in, 890; in World War II, 743
Civil service: investigation of, 780; reform of, 558–559; and spoils system, 268, 558
Civil War, 414–440; 1863-1865, 431–438; aftermath of, 446–450; Antietam, 410–411, 422–423, 429; beginning of, 414–417, 418–419; blockade of South, 419–420, 424–425; casualties, 438; causes, 411; demobilization after, 582; disease and medical care, 411, 437; early enthusiasm for, 415–417, 418; Emancipation Proclamation, 428–431; end of, 438–440; events leading to, 385–391, 396–406, 411–415, 416; Gettysburg, 432–433, 434–435; Grant's eastern campaign, 435–436, 438; leaders, 417–418; Native Americans and, 469; northern war effort, 426–428, 431–434; Peninsula campaign, 421–422; resources, North *vs.* South, 415–418, 424, 425, 436; Sherman's campaign, 436, 437–438; southern home front, 424–426, 436–437; and Theodore Roosevelt, 596; troop strength, North *vs.* South, 419; Union strategies, 419–421, 435–436; victory parades, 582; warfare, 432, 433, 436–438; western theater, 422–424, 435
Civil Works Administration, 710
Civilian Conservation Corps, 710, 716, 717, 739, 903
Clancy, Tom, 927
Clanton brothers, 497
Clark, James, 884
Clark, Kenneth, 807
Clark, Reuben, 730
Clark, William, 218, 359
Clark Memorandum, 730
Clarke, Edward Young, 687
Clay, Henry, 222, 236, 237, 241, 249, 264, 265, 272, 273, 274, 296; and Compromise of 1850, 388–389
Clayton Antitrust Act, 627, 632
Clemenceau, Georges, 662, 663
Clement VII (pope), 22
Clermont (steamboat), 242
Cleveland, Grover, 517, 523, 552, 585; election of 1884, 554, 559, 560; election of 1896, 550; foreign policy, 586–589, 591; presidencies of, 559–561, 567
Cleveland (Ohio), 619, 674, 903–904
Cliff Dwellers (Bellows), 532–533
Clifton, Nat "Sweetwater," 805
Clinton, Bill, 930–935; economic issues, 934; and elections of 1994, 840; foreign policy, 871, 934–935; and gays in military, 903, 931; impeachment of, 931, 934; scandals, 931, 932–934; social legislation, 930–933; and Vietnam, 871
Clinton, DeWitt, 243
Clinton, Henry, 131, 133, 134, 136, 137, 150, 151, 153
Clotel (Brown), 307
Coal industry, 482, 491, 506, 652; strike of 1902, 606, 607, 622, 632
Cobb, Ty, 679

Coca-Cola, 738
Cocaine, 542–543
Cockfighting, 84
Coercive Acts, 120–121, 123
Coinage Act, 558
Coin's Financial School (Harvey), 571
Cold Harbor, battle of, 436
Cold War, 765; arms race, 768, 772, 865, 918, 921; Berlin airlift, 771–772; containment policy, 770–776, 786, 797–798, 802; Cuban missile crisis, 850–851; détente, 866, 918; Eisenhower and, 797–802; end of, 927, 935; espionage, 779–780, 799, 802; inside U.S., 764–765, 776, 778–785; Johnson and, 853–854; Kennedy and, 849–851; Marshall Plan, 770; Nixon and, 864–865; NSC-68 and, 774–775; origins of, 766–768; paranoid style in, 781, 785; Reagan Doctrine, 921–922; rhetoric of, 768–770, 773, 779; space program and, 800–801, 927; thaws in, 785–786, 798–799, 864–865; Truman and, 767–776; Truman Doctrine, 769–770, 773–774; U-2 spy plane incident, 802; and Vietnam War, 847, 851, 871
The Cold War: A Study in U.S. Foreign Policy (Lippmann), 771
Cole, Thomas, 308, 532
Colfax, Schuyler, 467
College football, 538–539, 678–679
Collier, John, 717
Collier's, 611
Colombia, and Panama Canal, 629, 630
colonias, 376
Colonization, of African Americans, 294, 296, 398, 428
Colorado-Big Thompson Project, 827
Colorado Territory, 376
Columbian exchange, 30
Columbian Exposition of 1893, 483, 540
Columbus, Christopher, 15–16
Comanche Chasing Buffalo with Bows and Lances (Catlin), 357
Comanche Indians, 357
Comic books, 785
Coming Home (film), 867
Command of the Army Act, 456, 457
Committee of Industrial Organizations (CIO), 713
Committee on Public Information, 653–654
Committees of correspondence, 119
Commodity Credit Corporation, 709
Common Sense (Paine), 138
Commonwealth of Independent States, 926–927
Commonwealth v. Hunt, 326
Communications: early nineteenth-century, 244; late nineteenth-century, 482–483
Communism. *See also* Cold War: in China, 772–773; collapse of, 925–928, 926–927; Alger Hiss case, 764–765; Ho Chi Minh and, 846, 847; in Hollywood, 784; and Korean War, 774–776; McCarthyism, 780–781; Red scares, 660–661, 776–777, 778–784; in Soviet Union, 701, 922–923, 926; in U.S., 764, 765, 779, 780, 784; in Vietnam, 855–856
Community Chest, 694
Community Service Organization, 900
Compromise of 1850, 388–389, 397; and Fugitive Slave Law, 389–391

Compromise of 1877, 473
Comstock, Anthony, 683
Comstock Act, 902
Conestoga wagon, 239
Coney Island, 540–541
Confederate army, 414–417. *See also specific battles;* conscription, 425, 436; disease in, 437; soldier occupations, 427; troop strength, 419, 436
Confederate States of America, 414
Confiscation Act, 428
Congress. *See also* Continental Congress: and abolitionism, 295; African Americans in, 461; in Civil War, 428, 429; Clinton administration and, 931–932, 934; in Cold War, 777, 778, 780–781, 784; and Compromise of 1850, 386–389; conservative political revolt in, 840; in Constitution, 180, 181, 182; and Dominican annexation treaty, 580–581; establishment of national government by, 192–195; and expansionism, 581, 582, 585; impeachment of Andrew Johnson, 457–458; isolationism in, 581, 734, 736; Jefferson and, 214–215; and Kansas-Nebraska Act, 396–398; Kennedy and, 849; in late nineteenth century, 552; military reductions by, 581–582; and Missouri Compromise, 249–252; and navy, 581–582, 585; and New Deal, 707, 711, 712, 720, 739–740; and Reconstruction, 452, 453, 454–460, 473–474; and Red Scare of 1919-20, 660–661; resistance to presidential power, 871, 914–915; and Spanish-American War, 593; State Department reduction by, 581; and Treaty of Paris (1899), 598; and Treaty of Versailles, 661–662, 664–665; and War of 1812, 222; and Watergate scandal, 913, 914; and World War I, 649–650, 654; in World War II, 739, 743
Congress of Racial Equality (CORE), 743, 879, 886
Congressional Budget Office, 914
Congressional reconstruction, 454–460, 473–474
Conkling, Roscoe, 459, 554
Connecticut: colony, 48–49, 74, 109; constitution, 163
Connor, Theophilus Eugene "Bull," 882
The Conqueror (film), 830
Conquistadores, 16–18
The Conscience of a Conservative (Goldwater), 834, 835, 838
Conscription: in Confederacy, 425, 436; in North (Union), 434; in World War I, 658
Conscription Act, 434
Conservation, 622, 626, 633; disputes in West, 839; and environmental movement, 903–904
Conservatism: conservative political revolt, 821, 837–841; critique of liberalism, 820–821; "dynamic," 794–795; Goldwater and, 834–836; and individual freedom, 821, 822, 839
Constitution, U.S., 179–183. *See also specific amendments;* and Bill of Rights, 183, 193; framers, 179–180; framing of, 180–181; implementation of, 192–195; loose interpretation of, 194, 240; and national bank debate, 194; ratification of, 181–183; strict construction of, 194; voting rights legislation and, 458
Constitutional Unionist party, 411–412
Constitutions, state: first, 162–163; in Reconstruction, 456, 457
Consumer industries, in World War II, 738
Consumer Products Safety Act, 876
Consumerism: and environment, 904; late nineteenth-century, 530, 544; Ralph Nader and, 876–877; Progressive Era legislation, 623, 633; in 1920s, 673, 675–677; in 1950s, 811–812
Consumption (disease), 612–613
Containment policy, 770–776, 786; Eisenhower and, 797–798, 802
Continental army, 128, 129, 132, 142–143, 149, 150, 152, 155; composition of, 144–146; and Newburgh conspiracy, 167–168; payment of, 165, 167–168; western lands for soldiers, 171, 172
Continental Association, 121–122
Continental Congress: and Articles of Confederation, 164–169; and Constitutional Convention, 179–183; and Declaration of Independence, 138–140; First, 121–123; Second, 123, 132, 138–140, 141, 144
"Contract With America," 840, 931
Conwell, Russell, 485
Coode, John, 75
Coolidge, Calvin, 690, 729
Cooper, Anthony Ashley, 41
Cooper, Chuck, 805
Cooper, James Fenimore, 302
Cooperatives, agricultural, 564
Copley, John Singleton, 308
Copperheads, 428
Corbett, James J. ("Gentleman Jim"), 536
Corbin, Margaret ("Dirty Kate"), 144–146
CORE (Congress of Racial Equality), 743, 879, 886
Cornwallis, Charles (Lord Cornwallis), 142, 151–153
Coronado, Francisco Vásquez de, 18
Corporations. *See also* Big business; Industry: law favoring, 276, 487–488; taxation of, 620
Corruption: in election of 1876, 473; in Harding administration, 689, 690; late nineteenth-century (Gilded Age), 554, 555–556, 558–559; and organized crime, in 1950s, 782–783; Reconstruction-era, 463, 467; in sports, 785; Watergate scandal, 912–914
Cortés, Hernán, 17–18
Cortina, Juan Nepomuceno, 354, 375
Corwin, Thomas, 374
Cós, Martin Perfecto de, 366
Costello, Frank, 782
Costilla, Miguel Hidalgo y, 356
Cotton, 245–246, 325, 334, 341, 387, 424, 499
Cotton, John, 46
Cotton gin, 245–246, 320
Coughlin, Charles, 711, 712, 715
Council for the Indies, 18
Council of Economic Advisors, 777
Counterculture of 1960s, 839, 891–892
Country music, 678, 813, 825
Courts. *See* Judicial branch; Supreme Court
Coverture, 51, 55

Cowboys, 355, 364, 495
Cowtowns, 495
Cox, Archibald, 913
Cox, James M., 665, 705
Coxey, Jacob S., 569
Coxey's Army, 569
Craft, Ellen, 307
Craft, William, 307
Crandall, Prudence, 292–293
Crane, Stephen, 532
Crawford, William, 264
"Crazy Blues" (recording), 678
Credit, consumer, 677
Credit Mobilier scandal, 467
Creek Indians, 7, 8, 93, 226, 238, 265, 268; in American Revolution, 150, 151; removal of, 270
Creel, George W., 653
Creoles, 344
Crime: before American Revolution, 290; before Civil War, 284–285, 332–333; corporate, 488; defendants' rights, 889; late nineteenth-century, 527; organized, 782–783; and policing, 332–333, 527; and reform movements, 290–292; in 1990s, 935; after World War II, 782
criollos, 19
Crisis I (Paine), 144, 145
The Crisis (journal), 618
Crittenden, John J., 414
Crittenden Compromise, 414
Croatoan Indians, 25, 26
Crockett, Davy, 310, 364, 366
Cromwell, Oliver, 41, 67, 69
Cronkite, Walter, 851, 857
Crusade for Justice, 898
Crusades, 11
Cruz, Antonio, 366
Crystal City (Texas), 897–898
Cu Chi tunnel complex, 858–859
Cuba, 16; Bay of Pigs invasion, 801, 850; Castro's revolution in, 801; missile crisis, 850–851; revolution, 590–593; and Spanish-American War, 593–597; U.S. expansionism in, 395, 586, 595, 628, 730
Cuffe, Paul, 294
Cullen, Countee, 680, 689
Culley, Johnston, 354
cummings, e. e., 680
Cummins, Maria, 310
Currency Act, 104–105
Curtis Act, 471
Custer, George A., 470
Cuyahoga River fire, 903–904
Czolgosz, Leon, 522, 621

D-Day, 747, 748–749
da Gama, Vasco, 15
Dachau, 728
Daladier, Edouard, 733
Dale, Thomas, 38
Daley, Arthur, 829
Daley, Richard, 861
Dallin, Cyrus E., 44
Dams, 827, 830, 831
Dana, Richard Henry, Jr., 309
Daniels, Josephus, 708
Dare, Virginia, 25
Darrow, Clarence, 686
Dartmouth College, 240, 293
Dartmouth (ship), 119–12
Dartmouth v. Woodward, 240

Darwin, Charles, 583, 685
Daugherty, Harry, 690
Daughters of Bilitis, 903
Daughters of the American Revolution, 715
Davenport, John, 48
David Copperfield (Dickens), 612
Davis, David, 473
Davis, Jefferson, 339, 411, 449, 459; as Confederate president, 414, 418, 421, 424, 425, 434, 436
Davis, John W., 690
Davis, Joseph, 339
Davis, Richard Harding, 594, 597
Dawes, Charles, 731
Dawes, William, 131
Dawes Plan, 731
Dawes Severalty Act, 471, 562, 717
Day, Benjamin H., 309
Day of Jubilo, 448
Dayton (Ohio), 618
de Gaulle, Charles, 745
de Kooning, Willem, 711
de la Garza, Eligio, 898
De La Warr, Lord, 38
de Lôme, Enrique Dupuy, 592
De Mille, Cecil B., 678
de Soto, Hernando, 12, 18
de Vaca, Cabeza, 18
Dead Indian Act, 471
Deaf people, 293
Dean, John, 913, 914
Deane, Silas, 146
Death Comes to the Archbishop (Cather), 307
Debs, Eugene V., 568–569, 626; and election of 1920, 665; imprisonment of, 654, 655; and World War I, 648
Debt: colonial, 105; consumer, 693, 923; farm, 498, 499, 557; imprisonment for, 291; and "money question," 557–558; national (*See* National debt)
Decatur, Stephen, Jr., 217, 240
Declaration of Independence, 138–140, 170; events leading to, 138–139
Declaratory Act, 111
Declension, 55–56
The Deer Hunter (film), 867
Defense industries: discrimination in, 742; and growth of West, 828, 829–830; in World War II, 738, 741, 742, 828
Defense spending: 1940-64, 769; 1945-90, 797; Eisenhower's reduction of, 798; and growth of West, 828, 829; and NSC-68, 774; under Reagan, 921
Deindustrialization, 916
Deism, 86, 288
Delano (California), 900
Delany, Martin R., 296, 307
Delaware, 71, 138, 178
Delaware Indians, 71, 102, 172, 200
DeLeon, Daniel, 568
Delmonico, Lorenzo, 530
Democratic party. *See also specific elections*: African-American shift to, 716; after Civil War, 451; conservative-liberal split in 1930s, 720; conservative political revolt and, 839–840; convention of 1968, 861; Jacksonian, 265, 278, 332; and Know Nothings, 391, 394; late nineteenth-century, 552–556, 559, 560–561; and national Reconstruction policies, 451–458, 465, 467; New Deal coalition, 706, 707, 715, 759, 778, 866;
Nixon's "dirty tricks" against, 912–913; North-South split in, 411, 451; Peace Democrats, 428, 436; progressivism and, 619; in Reconstruction South, 461–465; in 1920s, 690; and slavery expansion issue, 386, 387, 389, 396; southern, 451, 567, 569, 574, 706, 707, 715, 716, 778, 806, 838, 882; and Whigs, 277; after World War I, 665–666
Democratic republicanism, 267
Demographic transition, 176
Dempsey, Jack, 678
Demuth, Charles, 680
Denmark, 734
Dennis, David, 886
Department of Commerce and Labor, 623
Department stores, 530, 544
Depression(s). *See also* Great Depression: of 1937, 720; after American Revolution, 168; late nineteenth-century, 584; Panic of 1819, 248, 261–264; Panic of 1837, 275–276; Panic of 1873, 467, 557; of 1890s, 567, 569; of 1970s, 917
Deregulation, 917, 921
Dermer, Thomas, 4
Desegregation. *See also* Civil rights movement: busing and, 887, 889; and Civil Rights Act of 1964, 883; of education, 792, 806–807, 808, 880, 882, 887, 889; Eisenhower and, 807–808; of lunch counters, 878–879; of military, 806; of public transportation, 572–573, 808–810, 880; Republican party and, 838; of sports, 804–805; violence in, 879–880
Desert Land Act, 495
Deslondes, Charles, 344
Détente, 866, 918
Detroit (Michigan): African-American population, 674; growth, in World War II, 738, 741; race riots, 742, 806, 887; in War of 1812, 222, 223
Dewey, George, 593–594
Dewey, John, 609, 610, 620, 640, 651
Dewey, Thomas E., 740, 772, 778
Dewson, Molly, 715
The Dialectic of Sex (Firestone), 895
Dias, Bartholomeu, 15
Díaz, Porfirio, 629–630
Dickens, Charles, 242, 309, 612
Dickinson, John, 111, 114, 132, 133, 138, 164, 179, 180
Dickson, William K. L., 541
Diem (Ngo Dinh Diem), 852
Dien Bien Phu, siege of, 852
Diet, of slaves, 341
Digger Indians massacre, 496
Diggs, Charles, 793
Dime novels, 309, 826
Dingley Tariff, 574–575
Dinwiddie, Robert, 92
Dirt, Andrew, 340
Discourse of Western Planting (Hakluyt), 23–24
Disease(s). *See also* Medical care: of African Americans, 341, 392, 393, 437, 718; AIDS, 832–833; cholera, 262–263; in cities, 528; in Civil War, 411, 437; in colonies, 37; in Europe, 11, 18; influenza, 640; inoculation for, 86; and Native Americans, 4, 5, 10, 16, 18, 30, 224; nineteenth- *vs.* twentieth-century view of, 612–613; on Oregon Trail, 362;
sexually transmitted, 832; of slaves, 341, 392, 393; tuberculosis, 612–613; yellow fever, 198–199
Disney, Walt, 784
Dissenters. *See* Baptists; Pilgrims; Puritans; Quakers
Divine right, 40
Dix, Dorothea, 293, 437
"Dixie" (song), 331
Dixiecrats (States' Rights Democratic party), 778
Dixon, George, 537
Dodgers, move to Los Angeles, 829
Dole, Robert, 840
Dole, Sanford B., 589
Dollar diplomacy, 629
Domestic novels, 309–310
Dominican Republic: Grant's annexation plan, 580–581; U.S. involvement in, 629
Doniphan, A. W., 372
Donner party, 358
"Don't ask, don't tell" policy, 903, 931
Dorais, Charles, 539
Dos Passos, John, 721
"Double V" campaign, 742
Doubleday, Abner, 535
Douglas, Stephen A., 388, 389, 396, 399, 401; on Brown's raid, 405; debates with Lincoln, 402–403; and election of 1860, 411, 413
Douglas, William, 768
Douglass, Frederick, 251, 284, 296, 297, 299, 307, 345; and black suffrage, 458; and Brown's raid, 403–404; call to arms, 430; and Emancipation Proclamation, 429, 430; on freedmen, 450; life of, 296
Dover (Delaware), 803
Dr. Jekyll and Mr. Hyde (Stevenson), 543
Dragging Canoe (Chincohacina), 150
Drake, Edwin L., 482
Drake, Francis, 23, 25
Dred Scott decision, 400–401, 402–403, 451
Dreiser, Theodore, 531–532, 536, 640
Dresden, firebombing of, 746
Drinking, in 1830s-40s, 285, 289–290
Driven from Jackson County, Missouri (Christensen), 369
Drug legislation, 627, 633
Drug use: late nineteenth-century, 542–543; in 1960s counterculture, 891–892; in Vietnam War, 857–858
Dry farming, 498, 499
Du Bois, W. E. B., 461, 617–618, 635, 657, 688
Duchamp, Marcel, 533
Dudingston, William, 118
Dueling, 285
Dukakis, Michael, 923
Duke, James B., 500–501
Dulles, John Foster, 770, 796–797, 799, 800, 852
Dumas, Alexander, 612
Dumbbell tenements, 528
Dunbar, Paul Lawrence, 688
Dunkirk, 735
Dunmore, Lord (John Murray), 134–138
Dunne, Finley Peter, 625
Dust Bowl, 709
Dustan, Hannah, 66–67
Dutch: in American Revolution, 150; in New World, 28, 69, 73, 75; in slave trade, 36; trade, 28, 69, 74, 150, 168

Dutch West India Company, 28, 69
Dwight, Timothy, 206
Dye, John Smith, 384, 385
Dyer, Mary, 70
"Dynamic conservatism," 794–795
Dynamic Sociology (Ward), 610

E. C. Knight ruling, 561, 622
Eakins, Thomas, 532
Earp brothers, 497
Earth Day, 903, 904
East: population decline, 837–838; westerners' view of, 821, 822, 827
East India Company, 119
Eastern Europe: collapse of communism in, 925; Soviet Union and, 746, 748, 750, 766–767, 768, 799, 800, 923, 925; in U.S. policy, 799
Eastland, James, 792
Eastman, George, 483
Eaton, Peggy, 272–273
Economic growth. *See also* Industrialization: American system and, 265; Civil War and, 426–427; Hamilton's financial program for, 193–195; late nineteenth-century, 481, 494–500, 509–510; late twentieth-century, 915, 921, 930, 934; in 1790s, 192; in 1950s, 795, 811–812; South and, 334–336, 338, 426–427, 500–502, 824–825; Taney Court and, 276; after War of 1812, 234, 236, 241–248; in West, 494–500, 828, 829–834; in World War II, 738
Economic recession. *See also* Depression(s): of 1970s, 917
Economic stratification: after American Revolution, 171; in colonies, 81–82; ideological justifications for, 485–486; Jacksonian view of, 268; late nineteenth-early twentieth centuries, 485–486, 493, 608; in 1920s, 693; in North, pre–Civil War, 329–330; by race, 1960-69, 878; in South, pre–Civil War, 335–336; in World War II, 743
Economics, progressive (institutional) *vs.* classical, 609–610
Edison, Thomas, 483–484, 530, 541, 607
Education. *See also* Universities: of African Americans, 179, 292–293, 450, 463, 464, 561–562, 609, 877, 880, 887, 889; Bronson Alcott and, 305; compulsory, 620, 632; desegregation of, 792, 806–807, 808, 880, 882, 887, 889; Dewey and, 609, 610, 620; federal spending on, 1964-70, 888; late eighteenth-century, 192; in Massachusetts Bay Colony, 46–47; medical, 614; of Mexican Americans, 898; of Native Americans, 471, 717, 902; in Progressive Era, 609, 610, 620, 632; public, 46–47, 292, 463; reforms, pre–Civil War, 292–293; in Republican platform, late nineteenth-century, 562; segregation of, 463, 792, 806, 807, 838, 887, 889; in South, 335, 338, 450, 463; space race and, 801; of women, 174–175, 293, 609, 896–897
Edwards, Jonathan, 86–87
Egypt, 918, 920; Suez crisis, 799–800
Ehrlichman, John, 862
Eighteenth Amendment, 655–656
Einstein, Albert, 752, 754
Eisenhower, Dwight D., 794; and civil rights, 807–808; foreign policy, 796–803; on "military-industrial complex," 803; presidency of, 794–803, 814–815; second term, 800–803; and Soviet Union, 798–799, 800, 802; and Vietnam, 852; in World War II, 746, 747, 748, 794
El Salvador, 730
Election(s): of 1796, 202; of 1800, 205–206; of 1804, 220; of 1824, 264; of 1828, and Jackson's campaign, 266; of 1832, 274; of 1836, 277; of 1840, and Harrison's campaign, 258–259, 277; of 1844, 365, 368; of 1846, 374; of 1848, 278–279; of 1852, 278, 279; of 1854, 397, 398; of 1856, 394, 399–400; of 1858, and Lincoln-Douglas debates, 402–403; of 1860, 411–413, 412–413, 486–487; of 1862, 429; of 1864, 436; of 1866, 455–456; of 1868, 458; of 1872, 467; of 1876, 472–473, 557; of 1880, 558; of 1884, 554, 559, 560; of 1888, 561; of 1892, 567; of 1896, 550–551, 555, 571; of 1900, 607, 621; of 1904, 623; of 1908, 623; of 1912, 626; of 1916, 627, 648; of 1920, 665–666; of 1924, 690; of 1928, 690–691; of 1932, 705–706; of 1936, 713–715; of 1940, 736; of 1944, 740; of 1948, 778; of 1952, 794; of 1960, and Kennedy-Nixon debates, 847–848; of 1964, anti-Goldwater campaign, 836–837, 854; of 1968, 837, 860–861, 861–862; of 1972, 837, 865–866, 912; of 1980, 837, 920–921; of 1984, 837; of 1988, Bush and Dukakis campaigns, 837, 923–924; of 1992, 930; of 1994, 839–840, 931; and campaign finance laws, 914; early nineteenth-century, 259, 332; late nineteenth-century, 554, 555; violence related to, 332, 465, 861
Electoral system: agrarian reform agenda, 566; campaign finance reform, 914; in election of 1824, 264; electoral college, 181, 206; initiatives and referendums, 566, 619; in Progressive Era, 619, 631–632; in western states, 619, 838–839
Electric trolley, 525–526
Electricity, 483–484, 530, 677; in rural areas, 709
Eleventh Amendment, 216
Eliot, Charles W., 595
Eliot, John, 49
Eliot, T. S., 680
Elites. *See also* Gentleman-planters; Industrialists: and attacks on privilege, in 1820s, 260–261; colonial, 81–83, 85; and Constitution, 182–183; consumption by, 530; flight from cities, 526; Jacksonians and, 267–268; late nineteenth-century, 493; and New Deal, 713; revolutionary-era, 162, 163; sports of, 537
Elizabeth I, Queen of England, 21, 23, 24, 25
Elkins Act, 623
Ellington, Duke, 678
Ellis, Edith, 683
Ellis, Havelock, 683
Ellison, William, 344–345
Ely, Richard T., 610
Emancipation proclamation (Dunmore's), 134–138
Emancipation Proclamation (Lincoln's), 411, 428–429; impact of, 429–431
Emergency Quota Act, 523
Emergency Relief Appropriation Act, 710

The Emerging Republican Party (Phillips), 837
Emerson, Ralph Waldo, 301, 302, 306, 311, 335, 376, 405, 612
Emmanuel (slave), 37
Emmett, Dan D., 331
Empire State Building, 673
Employment Act, 777
Enclosure movement, 23
encomienda system, 19
Endo case, 745
Enemy aliens, in World War II, 743–744
Enforcement Acts, 465
England. *See* Britain
English colonies, 37–60. *See also specific colonies*; Enlightenment in, 83–86; Glorious Revolution in, 74–75; government by England, 74, 76–78, 82–83, 102, 103–106; immigration to, 78–79, 82, 83; imperial wars in, 89–95; motives for immigration to, 23–24, 30; pastimes, 84–85; population growth, 78–80; resistance to British, 106–123; social stratification, 80–83; trade, 28–29, 37, 67–68, 73, 77–78
Enlightenment, the, 83–86, 176, 285
Enola Gay (plane), 753, 755–756; exhibit on, 757–759
Entertainment: colonial, 84–85; commercialization of, 534; mass, 677–678; politics as, 555; in 1920s, 677–680
Enumerated goods, 68, 73
Environmental Defense Fund, 904
Environmental Protection Agency, 876, 904, 921
Environmentalism, 903–904; disputes in West, 839; early conservation, 622, 626, 633, 903
Equal Opportunity Employment Commission, 894
Equal Pay Act, 894
Equal Rights Amendment, 684, 894–895, 896
Equiano, Olaudah, 57, 80–81
Era of Good Feelings, 234–253
Eratosthenes, 14
Eric the Red, 10
Ericson, Leif, 10, 11
Erie Canal, 242–243
Escobedo v. Illinois, 889
Esparza, Gregorio, 366
Espionage, Cold War, 779–780, 799, 802
Espionage Act, 654, 655
Essay Concerning Human Understanding (Locke), 83
Ether, 245
Ethiopian regiment, 138
Ethnic cleansing, 728, 934, 935
Ethnocide, of Native Americans, 471
Eugenics, 301
Europe. *See also* Eastern Europe; Western Europe: Axis takeovers in, 1936-39, 733; Black Death in, 11; and China policy, 600–601; and Civil War, 425, 426; claims in North America, 1750-1763, 90, 102; emigration from, 83; Middle Ages, 10–11; and Monroe Doctrine, 241; nation-states in, 15; population growth, 10–11, 517; postwar, 746; Price Revolution in, 23; Protestant Reformation in, 21–22; Renaissance, 14; trade with Orient, 11–14; after World War I, 663, 664; in World War I, 642; after World War II, 768; in World War II, 734–735, 745–750

European Economic Community (Common Market), 770
Europeans: and Columbian exchange, 30; exploration by, 14–17; fighting style, 12–13; in Middle Ages, 10–11; in slave trade, 57; social stratification, 80; view of Native Americans, 9–10, 12–13
Evangelical revivalism, 214, 285–288
Evans, Oliver, 244
Evarts, William, 585
Evers, Medgar, 849, 882
Evolutionary theory, religious objection to, 685–686
Executive Order 8802, 806
Executive Order 9835, 780
Executive privilege, 201
Existentialism, 681
Expansionism. *See also* Westward expansion: American exceptionalism and, 583–584; of Axis powers, 732–733; and "large policy," 586; late nineteenth-century, 580, 581, 582–601; and naval buildup, 585–586; and progressivism, 628; religious justifications for, 584; and search for markets, 584–585; southern, 338–339; Soviet, 771; Young America program (1850s), 395
Exploration: Dutch, 28; English, 20; European, 14–17; French, 20, 89; of Ohio river regions, 172; Portuguese, 15, 16; Spanish, 15, 16–18, 20; Viking, 10; of West, 359–360

Fair Deal, 778
Fair Employment Practices Commission, 742
Fair Housing Act, 888
Fair Labor Standards Act, 721
Falaba (ship), 647
Fall, Albert B., 690
Fallen Timbers, battle of, 197, 200, 224
Families: in Chesapeake colonies, 51, 54, 55, 56; elite, 81–83; and fall in birth rate, 176; in Great Depression, 701–703; industrialization and, 502, 503; Puritan, 51–54; slave, 342–343
Fannin, James, 364
A Farewell to Arms (Hemingway), 681
Farm Credit Administration, 709
Farm Security Administration, 711, 716
Farragut, David G., 420
Farrell, James T., 721
Fascism, 701, 732
Father Knows Best (TV show), 810
Faubus, Orval, 808
Faulkner, William, 680, 721
Federal Bureau of Investigation (FBI), 914–915
Federal Council of Churches of Christ in America, 614
Federal Deposit Insurance Corporation, 708
Federal Emergency Relief Act, 708
Federal Farm Loan Act, 627
Federal Highway Act, 675
Federal Home Loan Bank System, 705
Federal Housing Authority, 716
Federal Reserve Act, 627
Federal Reserve Board, 633, 917
Federal Reserve System, 627, 632–633; in Great Depression, 708; in 1920s, 693
Federal Trade Commission, 627, 632
Federal Writers Project, 711

Federalist Papers, 182
Federalists, 181–182, 183, 196; and election of 1796, 202; and election of 1800, 205–206; and Jeffersonian judicial conflicts, 215–216, 218; and Louisiana Purchase, 219–220; and Northern Confederacy scheme, 219; and quasi war with France, 204; and War of 1812, 222, 227, 235; and yellow fever epidemic of 1793, 198, 199
The Female Eunuch (Greer), 895
The Feminine Mystique (Friedan), 893
Feminism. *See also* Women's movement: in domestic novels, 310; early, 297–298, 310; as ideology, 895; in Progressive Era, 615–616; radical, 895; in 1920s, 684; in 1960s, 893–895
Ferdinand of Aragon, 15, 16
Ferebee, Thomas, 753
Ferguson, Patrick, 152
Fermi, Enrico, 752, 755
Ferraro, Geraldine, 897, 923
Field, James G., 566
Field, Marshall, 530, 543–544
Fields, W. C., 721
Fifteenth Amendment, 447, 455, 459, 473; laws skirting, 569–570
Fighting: backcountry, 286; boxing, 536–537, 678
Fillmore, Millard, 384, 389, 394, 399, 400
Film industry, 654, 678, 740, 828; origin of, 541–542; search for Communists in, 784
Films: anticommunist, 784, 927; John Wayne, 820, 821, 927; of 1920s, 678; of 1930s, 721; on Vietnam veterans, 867; westerns, 826–827; in World War I, 654; in World War II, 740; on 1950s youth, 784
Finney, Charles Grandison, 288, 293, 301
Fire-eaters, 406, 411
Fireside chats, 707
Firestone, Shulamith, 895
First Amendment, and World War I, 655
First Blood (film), 867
First Manassas, battle of, 419
Fish, Hamilton, 584, 585, 707
"Fish-ins," 899
Fiske, John, 583
Fitch, Samuel, 244
Fithian, Philip Vickers, 286
Fitzgerald, F. Scott, 679
Fitzhugh, George, 322
Five-Power Naval Treaty, 732
Flapper, 681, 683
Flathead Indians, 357
Fletcher v. Peck, 239
"Flexible response," 852
Flint, Alvin, Jr., 410
Flint, Alvin, Sr., 410–411
Florida: acquisition of, 241; American interest in, 220; in American Revolution, 154; Huguenots in, 23; land boom, 691; maroons in, 344; Seminole resistance in, 271; Spanish in, 17, 18, 23, 241; in War of 1812, 226–227
Florida (ship), 425
Foch, Ferdinand, 658–659
Folktales, slave, 343
Folliard, Edward T., 764
Following the Color Line (Baker), 611
Food Administration, 652
Food industry, 492–493, 677; regulation of, 623, 633

Football: college, 538–539, 678–679; integration in, 805; professional, 679; West Point scandal, 785
Foote, Andrew H., 424
Force Act, 273
Ford, Gerald, 913, 914, 915, 917
Ford, Henry, 675–676
Ford, Sarah, 448
Fordney-McCumber Tariff, 693
Foreign aid: in Cold War, 767, 769–770; Marshall Plan, 770; post-Cold War, 927; to Soviet Union, 767
Foreign Miners' Tax, 375
Foreign policy. *See also* Cold War; *specific wars*: under Bush, 924–925, 927, 928–930; under Carter, 865, 918–920; under Clinton, 871, 934–935; after Cold War, 934–935; under Eisenhower, 796–803; expansionist, 395, 580, 581, 582–601; good neighbor policy, 730; isolationism and, 581, 665, 666, 729, 730–731, 734, 736; under Lyndon B. Johnson, 853–854; under Kennedy, 849–851, 917; "large policy," 586; under Nixon, 864–865, 918; Open Door, 600–601; Reagan Doctrine, 921–922; under Theodore Roosevelt (Big stick diplomacy), 628–629; under Taft (Dollar diplomacy), 629; under Truman, 767–776, 797–798; after Vietnam War, 871, 917–918; under Wilson, 629–631, 643–651, 661–665; after World War II, 759; between world wars, 729–732, 734–737
Forest Reserve Act, 903
Formalism, revolt against, 609–610
Fort Duquesne, 92
Fort Lee, 142
Fort McHenry, 226
Fort Necessity, 92
Fort Pickens, 414
Fort Pickering, 454
Fort Schuyler, 147–148
Fort Sumter, 414, 415, 439–440
Fort Ticonderoga, 133, 147
Fort Wagner, battle of, 430–431
Forts Henry and Donelson, battle of, 422–424
Foster, Stephen, 311–312
Four-Party Treaty, 729
Fourier, Charles, 300
Fourteen Points, 661–662
Fourteenth Amendment, 447, 455, 458, 459, 473, 488, 552; and *Plessy v. Ferguson*, 501; ratification struggle, 455–456
Fox, George, 70
Fox Indians, 200, 270–271
"Fragging," 858
France: in American Revolution, 146–147, 149–150, 154; Citizen Genêt Affair, 197; exploration by, 20, 89; French Revolution, 196, 197; in imperial wars, 89–94; interwar foreign policy, 729, 731; and Louisiana Purchase, 218; as nation-state, 15; in New World, 22–23, 28, 29–30, 89, 93; quasi war with, 203–204; Suez crisis, 799–800; trade with, post-Revolution, 168; and Treaty of Versailles, 662, 663; and Vietnam, 846, 851–852; and World War I, 641–645, 647, 658–659; and World War II, 735, 745–749
Francis I, King of France, 20
Franciscans, 357

Franco, Francisco, 732
Frank, Leo, 521–522
Frankfurter, Felix, 764
Franklin, Benjamin, 86, 111, 176; and abolitionism, 175; and Albany Plan, 92; on British-American relations, 67; and Constitutional Convention, 180, 181; in France, 146–147, 154; on Germans, 79; and Great Awakening, 87; and Paine's *Crisis I*, 145; and Quebec Act, 120
Franz Ferdinand (Austrian archduke), 641
Fredericksburg, battle of, 434
Free blacks, 344–346; in abolitionist movement, 294, 296–297; in Civil War, 429–431; and colonization movement, 294, 296; education of, 292–293; and Fugitive Slave Law, 389, 390; legal status/rights, 260, 400, 402; in North, 178–179, 345–346; reenslavement of, 346; in revolutionary era, 138, 161, 178–179; in South, 338, 344–345, 346, 461; and Vesey conspiracy, 250
Free enterprise system: and laissez-faire policy, 486; and rise of big business, 489–491; Taney Court and, 276
Free Soilers, 296, 377, 387; and Kansas, 398, 401; Lincoln-Douglas debates and, 402, 403
Freedmen's Bureau, 450, 455, 459, 464
Freedom of Information Act, 876, 914
Freedom riders, 879–880
Freemasons, 260–261
Frelinghuysen, Frederick T., 585
Frelinghuysen, Theodorus, 86
Frémont, John C., 360, 372, 400, 428
French and Indian War, 75, 93, 94. *See also* Seven Years' War
French immigrants, 22–23, 198
French Revolution, 196, 197
Freud, Sigmund, 681
Frick, Henry Clay, 568
Friedan, Betty, 812, 892–893, 894
Fries, John, 205
Fries Rebellion, 205
Frontier violence, 496–497
Fruitlands, 305
Fuchs, Klaus, 779
Fuel Administration, 652
Fuentes, Albert, 898
Fugitive slaves, 296, 298; and Dred Scott decision, 400–401; Fugitive Slave Law, 389–391
Fukuyama, Francis, 934–935
Fulk, Joseph R., 541
Fuller, Margaret, 302, 304–305
Fulton, Robert, 242, 243, 245
Fur trade, 28–29, 30, 69, 73, 91, 172; in Pacific Northwest, 365; western, 360

Gabriel's rebellion, 344
Gadsden, Christopher, 114
Gadsden, James, 395
Gage, Thomas, 120, 129, 131, 133, 134, 136, 137, 140–141
Gall, Franz, 313
Gallatin, Albert, 215, 239, 554
Gallaudet, Thomas Hopkins, 293
Galloway, Joseph, 121, 122–123
Galveston hurricane, 618
Gálvez, Bernardo de, 154
Gandhi, Mohandas (Mahatma), 809
Garages, 795
Garbo, Greta, 678

Garden, Alexander, 83
Gardoqui, Diego de, 169
Garfield, James A., 552, 558, 559, 585
The Garies and Their Friends (Webb), 307
Garrison, William Lloyd, 285, 294–295, 296, 313, 373, 404, 405, 682
Garter, Robert, 392–393
Garvey, Marcus, 688
Gary, Elbert, 480
Gaspée (ship), 117–118
Gast, John, 362
Gates, Bill, 834
Gates, Horatio, 148, 149, 152, 167–168
Gates, Thomas, 38
Gatling, Richard J., 644
Gatling gun, 644
GATT (General Agreement on Trade and Tariffs), 931
Gay rights movement, 902–903; and AIDS, 833; and gays in military, 903, 931
Gell, Monday, 250, 251
General Agreement on Trade and Tariffs (GATT), 931
General Federation of Women's Clubs, 614
General Motors, 676, 691, 713, 876
Generals, Civil War, 417–418
Genêt, Edmond Charles, 197
Gentleman-planters: in American Revolution, 134; in Civil War, 425, 429, 436; in colonies, 56, 74, 82–83, 85; in Reconstruction, 464–465
George, A. J., 616
George, Henry, 609
George, Milton, 565
George II, King of England, 90, 93
George III, King of England, 101, 102, 103, 110, 116, 120, 129, 131, 133, 140, 240
Georgia: in American Revolution, 150; Cherokees and, 269; Civil War in, 435, 436, 437; Savannah streetcar boycott, 572–573; settlement of, 90–91; slavery in, 175–178
Germain, George, 140–141
German immigrants/German Americans: and drinking, 290; Fries Rebellion, 205; immigration of, 78, 79, 328–329, 391; in Pennsylvania, 71, 79, 205; in World War I, 654, 655; in World War II, 743
Germans, 140, 740
Germany: atomic bomb research, 752, 754, 755; *Autobahnen*, 795; Berlin airlift, 771–772; destruction of Berlin Wall, 925; expansionism in 1930s, 732–733; fascist rule in, 701, 731–732; Holocaust in, 728, 744; partition of, 767, 768; and Samoa, 586–587; and Treaty of Versailles, 662, 663–664; in Venezuela boundary dispute, 629; and World War I, 641–647, 649, 650, 658–659; and World War II, 734–735, 736, 746, 748, 750; and Yalta Conference, 747–748
Gerrish, Abigail, 50
Gershwin, George, 680
Gettysburg, battle of, 432–433, 434–435
Gettysburg address, 435
Ghana (kingdom), 57
Ghost Dance, 471
GI Bill of Rights, 740
Gianninni, G. P., 828
Gibbons v. Ogden, 240
Gibson, Hoot, 826
Gideon v. Wainwright, 889

Gilbert, Humphrey, 24
Gilded Age, 551–575
Gillespie, Archibald H., 371
Gingrich, Newt, 840
Ginsberg, Allen, 814
glasnost, 922, 923, 926
Glass, Patrick, 359
Glass-Steagall Act, 708
Glidden, Joseph A., 495
Globalism, 935
Glorious Revolution, 74–75, 77
Glover, Joshua, 390
Godkin, L. Edwin, 538, 558, 588, 598
Godwin, William, 176
Going After Cacciato (O'Brien), 871
Gold, Harry, 779
Gold rush, 375, 377–379
Gold standard, 550, 575, 708
The Golden Orange (Wambaugh), 821
Goldman, Emma, 648
Goldwater, Barry, 821, 834–836, 838, 839, 848, 854, 920
Goldwyn, Samuel, 542
Golf, 537
Goliad, battle of, 364, 367
Gompers, Samuel, 509–510, 522, 574, 595–598
Gomulka, Wladyslaw, 799
Gonzales, Henry B., 898
Gonzales, Rodolfo ("Corky"), 898
Good neighbor policy, 730
Goodman, Andrew, 886
Goodman, Benny, 678
Goodman, Paul, 891
Goodyear, Charles, 177
Goold, Margerie, 54
Gorbachev, Mikhail, 922–923, 925, 926
Gordon, Thomas, 117
Gore, Thomas, 648
Gosiute Indians, 357
Gospel of wealth, 485–486
Gouging matches, 286–287
Gouzenko, Igor, 779
Government. *See also* State governments; *specific presidents and programs*: John Quincy Adams' ideas for, 265; Samuel Adams' view of, 162, 183; agriculture and, 487, 499, 564, 565–566, 627, 709, 711, 716; after American Revolution, 161–164; and Articles of Confederation, 164–169, 179, 180; city, in Progressive Era, 618–619; colonial, 43, 46, 74, 76–78, 82–83, 102, 103–106; Confederate, 425; and Constitution, U.S., 179–183, 184; Coolidge's view of, 690; educational aid, in 1960s, 888; federalist-antifederalist debate, 181–183; first U.S. establishment of, 192–195; in Gilded Age, 552–562; Goldwater's view of, 834–836, 839; Great Depression's impact on, 701; hostility toward, 552, 839, 931; Jackson's view of, 268, 276; Jefferson's view of, 214–215, 265; Kennedy's view of, 834; New Deal and, 708, 710, 713, 722–723; and nullification, 272, 273; progressive view of, 608, 633; Reagan's view of, 839; Theodore Roosevelt's view of, 622, 626; in 1920s, 689; spoils system, 268, 558; and states rights (*See* States rights); strengthening after War of 1812, 239–240; Taft's view of, 624; Truman's view of, 778; Union war ef-

fort and, 426–428; and West, 495, 827–828, 829; Wilson's view of, 626, 627; women in, 893; in World War I, 640–641, 653
Government-business relationship. *See also* Government regulation: late nineteenth-century, 486–487, 493, 553; "military-industrial complex," 803; in Progressive Era, 606, 632; in 1920s, 689, 690; in 1930s, 704, 708, 710
Government regulation: and deregulation, 917, 921; Federal Trade Commission and, 632; food and drug, 623, 627; of interstate commerce, 560, 623–625, 632, 717; laissez-faire and, 486; Ralph Nader and, 876–877; in Progressive Era, 632–633; of railroads, 559–560, 619–620, 622, 623, 632; of trusts, 561, 622, 624, 627, 632; of utilities, 619, 620
Governors, progressive, 619
Grady, Henry W., 500
Graham, Martha, 721
Gramm, Phil, 839, 840
Grand Alliance, 745
Grand Coulee Dam, 827
Grandfather clauses, 570
Grange, Harold "Red," 679
Grange movement, 564, 584
Grant, Madison, 521
Grant, Ulysses S., 370, 467; in Civil War, 418, 422–424, 435–436, 438; election of 1868, 458; election of 1880, 558; foreign policy, 580–581, 584, 585; and Ku Klux Klan, 465
Grapes of Wrath (Steinbeck), 721
Grassroots activism, 877
Gray, John, 113, 115
Gray, Samuel, 116
Gray, Simon, 340
Great Awakening, 78, 86–89; Second, 285–288
Great Bridge, battle of, 138
Great Depression, 694, 700–705, 721; causes of, 692–694; Hoover and, 702, 704–705; human toll of, 701–704; international responses to, 700–701; New Deal and, 706–720, 721–723; popular culture during, 720–721; prices during, 703
Great Migration, 657
Great Plains: exploration of, 359; Indians of, 357, 468–472
Great Purge, 701
Great Society, 836, 854, 871, 887–889
Great Strike of 1877, 506
The Great Train Robbery (film), 541, 826
Greece, aid to, 769–770
Greek immigrants, 518
Greeley, Horace, 327, 414, 429, 459, 467
The Green Berets (film), 820
Greenback party, 557, 558
Greenbacks, 426
Greene, Catharine, 320
Greene, Nathanael, 142, 153, 320
Greenglass, David, 779
Greensboro sit-ins, 878, 879
Greer, Germaine, 895
Grenville, George, 103–106, 110
Grey, Edward, 646
Grey, Zane, 826
Gridley, Richard, 136
Griffin, John Howard, 806
Griggs v. Duke Power Company, 895
Grimké, Angelina, 298

Grimké, Sarah, 298
Griswold, Roger, 205
Guam, 595, 750, 751
Guatemala, 801
Guide to Geography (Ptolemy), 14
Guilford Courthouse, battle of, 153
Guiteau, Charles, 558, 559
Gulf of Tonkin incident/Resolution, 854–855
Gullah, 59
Gutenberg, Johannes, 14
Guthrie, Woodrow Wilson ("Woody"), 700
Gwynn, Nell, 69

haciendas, 19, 20
Haight-Ashbury (San Francisco), 892
Haiti: slave rebellion, 218, 250, 251, 344; U.S. involvement in, 629, 730, 935
Hakluyt, Richard, 23–24
Halberstam, David, 853
Haldeman, H. R., 862, 863
Hale, Eugene, 585
Hale, Sarah J., 298
Half-Breeds, 554, 558
Half-Way Covenant, 55
Halleck, Henry W., 418, 420, 422, 424, 434
Halley, Rudolph, 782
Hamilton, Alexander: on Articles of Confederation, 166, 167; and Constitution, 179, 180, 182; duel with Burr, 212, 219; and election of 1796, 202; and election of 1800, 206; and Federalist party, 196; financial program, 193–195, 197; and Florida, 220; industrial aid program, 195, 486; and Jay's Treaty, 200, 201; and Jefferson, 194–197; and quasi war with France, 204; and Whigs, 277; and yellow fever epidemic of 1793, 199
Hammett, Dashiell, 720
Hammond, William, 542
Hancock, John, 114, 131
Hancock, Winfield Scott, 433, 558
Handsome Lake, 197
Hanna, Mark, 571, 621
Hannah's Cowpens, battle of, 153
Happy Days (TV show), 810
Hardin, John Wesley, 497
Harding, Warren G., 665, 666, 685; presidency of, 689–690
Harlem Globetrotters, 804
Harlem (New York), 675
Harlem Renaissance, 688–689
Harper's Ferry (Virginia; West Virginia), 422; Brown's raid on, 403–405
Harrington, Michael, 891
Harris, George Washington, 310
Harris, Sarah, 292
Harrison, Benjamin, 496, 552, 554–555, 561, 567, 796; foreign policy, 585, 586, 587–588
Harrison, William Henry: as Indian fighter, 222, 223, 224–225, 227; presidential campaign, 258–259, 277; and slave power conspiracy theory, 384, 385
Harrison Anti-Narcotic Act, 543–544, 627
Harte, Bret, 310, 531, 596
Hartford Convention, 227
Harvard, 100, 244, 293, 303, 304, 617, 622, 689, 848, 862; football at, 538; founding of, 47

Harvey, John, 40
Harvey, William H., 571
Hat Act, 77
Hatch, Orrin, 839
Hatch Act of 1887, 499
Hawaii, 585; annexation of, 588–589, 595; Japanese Americans in, 744
Hawkins, Connie, 804
Hawkins, John, 23
Hawley-Smoot Tariff, 693
Hawthorne, Nathaniel, 302, 305, 306, 309
Hay, John, 586, 595, 600–601, 629
Hay-Bunau-Varilla Treaty, 629
Hay-Herrán Treaty, 629
Haycox, Ernest, 826
Hayes, Rutherford B., 473, 506, 552, 558; election of, 472–473, 557; foreign policy, 585; presidency of, 557
Haymarket riot, 507, 623
Hayne, Robert Y., 272, 273
Haynes, Marques, 804
Haywood, "Big Bill," 648
Headrights, 39
Health. *See also* Medical care: in English colonies, 50–51, 56, 80; of slaves, 341
Hearst, William Randolph, 591, 592, 713
Heenan, James C., 536
Hell's Angels, 892
Helper, Hinton Rowan, 346
Hemings, Sally, 190
Hemingway, Ernest, 680, 681
Henderson, Fletcher, 678
Henderson, Oran, 869
Hennessy, David, 520
Hennessy case, 520–521
Henry, Patrick, 121, 175, 183
Henry, Prince of Portugal ("the Navigator"), 15
Henry VII, King of England (Henry Tudor), 15, 20
Henry VIII, King of England, 21–22
Henson, Josiah, 307, 341–342
Hepburn Act, 623, 632
Herkimer, Nicholas, 148
Herr, Michael, 857, 858
Herrera, José, 371
Herschel, John, 309
Hessians, 140, 143, 149
Hester Street (Luks), 533
Heth, Joice, 310
Hickock, Wild Bill, 497
Higgins, Margaret, 672
Higgins, Michael, 672
Higginson, Thomas Wentworth, 429
Highways, 795–796
Hill, James J., 622
Hill, Lucille Eaton, 540
"Hillbilly" music, 678, 825
Hillsborough, Wills Hill, Lord, 114
Himmler, Heinrich, 728
Hiroshima, bombing of, 753, 754–755
Hispaniola, 16
Hiss, Alger, 764–765
History of Plymouth Plantation (Bradford), 43, 45
History of the Standard Oil Company (Tarbell), 611
Hitler, Adolf, 701, 728, 731, 732–733, 750
Ho Chi Minh (Nguyen Sinh Cung), 846, 847, 851
Ho Chi Minh Trail, 858, 863
Hoar, George Frisbie, 595
Hobbes, Thomas, 286

Hofstadter, Richard, 781
Hogan, James J., 538
Holbrook, Josiah, 310–311
Holliday, Doc, 497
Hollywood. *See* Film industry
"Hollywood Ten," 784
Holmes, Oliver Wendell, Jr., 610, 655, 660, 764
Holocaust, 728, 744
Homeowners Loan Act, 708
Homer, Winslow, 532
Homespun, 114
Homestead Act, 426, 495
Homestead steel strike, 567–568
Homosexuality: AIDS and, 832, 833; attitudes toward, 902, 903; comic books and, 785
Hong Kong, 750, 751
Honor, 286
Hood, James Walker, 461
Hood, Zachariah, 109
Hooker, Joseph ("Fighting Joe"), 418, 431, 434
Hooker, Thomas, 48
Hoover, Herbert: and Bonus Army, 706; election of, 691; foreign policy, 730; and Great Depression, 702, 704–705; as secretary of commerce, 689; and stock market crash, 692, 704; in World War I, 652
Hoover, J. Edgar, 661, 785
Hoover (Boulder) Dam, 827
Hoovervilles, 701, 704
Hope, John, 572
Hopi Indians, 8, 357, 468
Hopkins, Elizabeth, 52
Hopkins, Harry, 710, 711, 721
Hopkins, Oceanus, 52
Hopkins, Stephen, 106
Horatio Alger stories, 486
Horse racing, 85
Horsecar, 525
Horses, 30
Horseshoe Bend, battle of, 226
House, Edward, 646
House of Burgesses, 38–39, 74, 109
House of Representatives, 180, 181, 182. *See also* Congress
House Un-American Activities Committee (HUAC), 765, 784
Household industries, 322–323
Housewives, 811, 892–893
Housing: early twentieth-century, 608; of free blacks, 346; in Great Depression, 703–704; Great Society programs for, 888; in 1920s, 693; racial segregation in, 803; rising cost of, 916; of slaves, 340, 341–342; suburban, 795, 803, 810; urban, 321–322, 526–529
Houston, Charles, 807
Houston, Sam, 363–366
How the Other Half Lives (Riis), 521, 528
Howard, Oliver O., 450
Howe, David, 191
Howe, Frederick, 659–660
Howe, Julia Ward, 293
Howe, Richard, 141
Howe, Samuel Gridley, 293
Howe, William, 128, 131, 141, 143, 149, 150; in battle of Bunker Hill, 133, 134, 136, 137
Howells, William Dean, 528, 531, 595
"Howl" (Ginsberg), 814

HUAC (House Un-American Activities Committee), 765, 784
Hudson, Henry, 28
Hudson River school, 308
Hue (Vietnam), 856–857, 867
Huerta, Victoriano, 630–631
Hughes, Charles Evans, 628, 648, 729
Hughes, Langston, 680, 689
Huguenots, 22–23
Huitzilopochtli, 6
Hulbert, William A., 535
Hull, Cordell, 730, 732, 736
Hull House, 610, 615
Human rights, 170, 918
Humorists, 310
Humphrey, George, 795
Humphrey, Hubert, 861, 862
Hungarian uprising, 799, 800
Hunt, Henry J., 432, 433
Hunt, Thomas, 4
Huron Indians, 102
Hutchinson, Anne, 47–48, 301
Hutchinson, Thomas, 92, 100, 101, 106–107, 108, 113, 119, 120
Hyde Amendment, 896
Hydrogen bomb, 772

Ickes, Harold, 710, 716
I'll Take My Stand, 720
Illinois, Mormons in, 369
The Image (Boorstin), 812
Immigrants. *See also specific groups*: and Democratic party, 553; enemy alien, in World War II, 743–744; and film industry, 541, 542; hostility toward, 391–394, 520–522; migrant workers (birds of passage), 518–519; neighborhoods of, 526; permanent, 519–520; progressivism and, 615; and urbanization, 524; voting rights, 259
Immigration: Chinese, 519, 522–523; to colonies, 78–79, 82, 83; German, 78, 79, 328–328; Irish Catholic, 328; Italian, 518–519; of Jewish refugees, in World War II, 728, 743–744; late nineteenth-early twentieth centuries, 517–523; Mexican, 743, 898; to New Spain, 19; in 1920s, 674; old *vs.* new, 517–518; party positions on, 553; pre–Civil War, 328–329, 332, 391; restriction of, 522–523, 562, 686, 693; Russian Jewish, 519–520; Scots-Irish, 78–79
Immigration Reform and Control Act, 898
Impeachment: of Clinton, 931; of Andrew Johnson, 457–458
The Impending Crisis of the South (Helper), 346
Imperialism. *See* Expansionism
Implied powers, 194
Impost Plan of 1781, 166
Impost Plan of 1783, 168
Impressment, 221
Incas, 6, 7
Inchon, attack on, 776
Incidents in the Life of a Slave Girl (Jacobs), 307
Income: in 1890, 493; in Great Depression, 701–702; in World War II, 738; in 1950s, 795; in 1980s, 921; in 1990s, 934
Income tax, 627, 633, 653
Indentured servitude, 36, 38, 39, 51, 54–55, 58, 144; and slavery, 37, 58
Indian Appropriations Act, 271

Indian Child Welfare Act, 902
Indian Education Act, 902
Indian Emergency Conservation Program, 717
Indian Health Care Act, 902
Indian Reorganization Act, 717
Indiana, 225
Indianapolis Clowns, 804
Indigo, 67, 78
Individualism: in Vietnam, 847; and West, 820, 821, 839
Indulgences, 21
Industrial Workers of the World ("Wobblies"), 648, 652, 653, 655, 660–661
Industrialists, 480, 493, 506–507, 553
Industrialization: capital formation, 488; Civil War and, 426–427, 447; consolidation of industry, 489–493, 506–507; corporations, 487–488; early nineteenth-century, 234, 235, 237–238, 242, 245–247; government's role in, 486–487; Hamilton's program, 195, 486; ideological justifications, 484–486; immigrants and, 523; Jefferson's view of, 195; late nineteenth-century, 481–493; pre–Civil War, 321–331, 417; and social mobility, 330, 510; in South, 334, 335, 417, 500–501, 502, 823, 824–825; in West, 828–834
Industry. *See also* Big business; Industrialization; *specific industries*: consolidation of, 489–493, 506–507; deindustrialization, 916; foreign competition, in 1970s, 916; government and, 486–487, 493, 553, 606, 632, 689, 690, 704, 708, 710, 803; in Great Depression, 704, 705; and Great Migration, 657; household, 322–323; and New Deal, 709–710, 713; regulation of (*See* Government regulation); in 1920s, 675–677, 693; in 1990s, 934; work in, 234, 235, 324–326, 502–505, 608; and workmen's compensation, 620; in World War I, 652, 656; World War II and, 738, 739, 916
Inflation: and "money question," 557–558; in post-Communist Russia, 927; in 1960s-70s, 915–917; in sixteenth-century Europe, 23; stagflation, 916–917; after War of 1812, 237; after World War II, 777; in World War II, 738–739
The Influence of Sea Power upon History (Mahan), 586
Influenza epidemic of 1918, 640
Informers, colonial, 112–113
Ingersoll, Jared, 109
Initiatives, 566, 619
Inquisition, 15
Insanity defense, 291
The Instinct of Workmanship (Veblen), 610
Intellectuals: Enlightenment, 83–86, 176, 285; pragmatic, 610; Progressive Era, 609–610; of 1930s, 720; transcendentalist, 302–305
Interstate commerce regulation, 560, 623, 624–625, 632, 717
Invasion of the Body Snatchers (film), 812
Investment: late nineteenth-century, 488; in New South, 501; overseas, and dollar diplomacy, 629; in 1920s, 693; in West, 827
Iran, 801, 918–919, 922, 928; hostage crisis, 918, 919–920
Iran-contra affair, 922

Iraq, 800; and Persian Gulf War, 928–930
Ireland: Easter uprising (1916), 643; English in, 24; potato blight, 327–328; Scots-Irish and, 78
Irish immigrants/Irish Americans, 328; and boxing, 536; and cities, 328, 524; and drinking, 290; and factory work, 326, 328; hostility toward, 391–394; literature of, 307; in New York draft riots, 434; in Pennsylvania coal wars, 506; and World War I, 646
Iron Act, 77
Iron production, 1870-1900, 491
Iroquois, 9, 28, 69, 73, 92, 172, 197; in American Revolution, 147, 148, 149
Irving, Washington, 301–302
Isabella of Castile (Queen of Spain), 15, 16
Isolationism: late nineteenth-century, 581; between world wars, 665, 666, 729, 730–731, 734, 736
Israel, 799–800, 918, 920, 928
Italian immigrants/Italian Americans, 518–519, 521, 524, 526; media stereotypes, 678; and organized crime, 783; Sacco and Vanzetti case, 686–687; violence against, 520–521; in World War II, 743
Italy: emigration from, motives for, 518–519; fascist rule in, 701, 731, 732; Renaissance, 14; and Treaty of Versailles, 662; in World War II, 746

Jackson, Andrew, 265; assassination attempt, 384, 385; banking system and, 274–276; and Calhoun, 273–274; election of 1824, 264; election of 1828, 266; and Florida, 241; Indian policy, 268–272; legacy of, 276–277; and nullification, 272, 273; presidency of, 244, 266–277, 279; and Supreme Court, 276; and Texas, 365; in War of 1812, 226–227
Jackson, Rachel, 273
Jackson, Thomas J. "Stonewall," 370, 419, 421–422; battle of Chancellorsville, 431, 434
Jackson State shootings, 864
Jacob, Kathryn Allamong, 517
Jacobs, Harriet, 307
Jagger, Mick, 892
Jalapa, battle of, 372
Jamaica, 69, 344
James, Frank, 497
James, Henry, 526, 613
James, Jesse, 497
James, William, 610
James I, King of England, 26, 37, 40, 43–44
James II, King of England (Duke of York), 69–70, 74
Jamestown, 26–28, 73. See also Virginia colony
Japan: aggression by, 701, 732, 733, 736–737; atomic bombing of, 752–759; and international diplomacy, 628, 662, 729; opening of, 395; and World War II, 737, 745–746, 748, 752–759
Japanese, racism toward, 740, 752
Japanese Americans, in World War II, 743, 744–745
Jaworski, Leon, 913
Jay, John, 121, 154, 169, 182, 193, 200–201
Jay's Treaty, 200–201, 203
Jazz, 533–534, 678

"Jazz Age," 678, 679, 695
Jefferson, Thomas: and Alien and Sedition acts, 205; and Barbary pirates, 217–218; beliefs of, 213–214; and central government, 213, 214–215, 265; Declaration of Independence, 139, 140, 170; disunionist conspiracies under, 219–220; on doctors, 392; on education, 292; election of 1796, 202; election of 1800, 205–206; embargo under, 221; and federal officeholders, 215; and Hamilton, 194–197; and Sally Hemings, 190; and Jackson, 264, 277; and judicial branch, 215–217; Lewis and Clark expedition, 359; Louisiana Purchase, 218–219; on manufacturing, 195; and national bank, 194; and national debt plan, 194; on Native Americans, 269; nephews of, 339; on North and South, 331; novel about, 307; on political parties, 196, 215; presidency of, 213–221; and republicanism, 213, 214–215; on separation of church and state, 171; slavery and, 172, 178, 248; talents of, 213, 215; and Virginia legal code, 171; in Washington's administration, 193; on westward expansion, 238; on Whiskey Rebellion, 197
Jeffersonian era, 212–229
Jeffersonian Republicans. See Republican party (Jeffersonian)
Jenkins, Robert, 91
Jenney, William LeBaron, 526
Jet magazine, 793
Jews: in film industry, 542; in Germany, 731–732; Holocaust and, 728, 744; in Italy, 732; media stereotypes, 678; in New York City, 520, 526, 528; in pre–Civil War era, 289; prejudice against, 521–522, 731, 732, 743–744; Russian, 519–520, 521, 523; in Spain, 15; World War II refugees, 728, 743–744, 755
Jim Crow laws, 570, 803, 809. See also Black suffrage; Segregation
Joffre, Joseph, 645
John I, King of Portugal, 15
John II, King of Portugal, 15
Johnson, Andrew, 436, 452–453; and congressional Reconstruction, 454–458; foreign policy, 584–585; impeachment of, 457–458; Reconstruction plan of, 453
Johnson, Guy, 147
Johnson, James Weldon, 688
Johnson, Lyndon B., 853; and civil rights, 883, 884, 887, 888–889; election of 1964, 836; and foreign affairs, 853–854; Great Society, 836, 854, 871, 887–889; and Vietnam War, 853–857, 860, 871, 915; and women's rights, 895
Johnson, Tom L., 619
Johnson County war, 496
Johnston, Albert Sidney, 418, 422
Johnston, Augustus, 109
Johnston, Joseph E., 418, 421, 436
Joint-stock trading companies, 25
Jones, Absalom, 178
Jones, Buck, 826
Jones, John Paul, 154
Jones, Samuel "Golden Rule," 619
Joplin, Scott, 534
Jordan, David Starr, 595
Joseph, Chief, 468

Joseph, William, 75
Journalism: James Thompson Callender, 190–191; Margaret Fuller, 304; in Mexican-American War, 371, 373, 374; muckraking, 190–191, 611; penny press, 309; in Vietnam War, 853, 857; yellow, and Spain's war in Cuba, 591
Journals (Polo), 14–15
Journeymen, 323, 324, 326
Jubilee Singers, 688
Judicial branch: election of judges, 260; establishment of powers, 215–217; late nineteenth-century, 552–553
Judicial review, 216
Judiciary Act of 1789, 193
Judiciary Act of 1801, 216
Julian, George, 459
The Jungle (Sinclair), 611, 623

Kaiser, Henry J., 828
Kamikaze, 752
Kansas, civil war in, 398, 399, 401
Kansas-Nebraska Act, 396, 397, 399
Karankawa Indians, 357
Karnow, Stanley, 853
Kaufman, Irving R., 780
Kearns, Doris, 871
Kearny, Stephen, 372
Keating-Owen Child Labor Act, 628
Keats, John, 612
Kefauver, Estes, 782
Kefauver committee hearings, 782–783
Kelley, Oliver, 564
Kellogg, Frank B., 729
Kellogg, Will K., 615
Kellogg-Briand Pact, 729
Kelly, Florence, 615
Kempton, Murray, 861
Kendall, Amos, 266
Kennan, George, 769, 770, 771
Kennedy, John F., 848–851; assassination of, 851; and civil rights movement, 849, 879–880, 882–883; debates with Nixon, 847–848; domestic policy, 849; foreign policy, 849–851, 917; on government, 834; macho ethos of, 848–849; and space program, 927; and Vietnam War, 852–853; and women's rights, 894
Kennedy, Joseph, 736, 848
Kennedy, Robert F., 848, 849, 850, 860–861, 901
Kent State shooting, 863
Kenton, Simon, 172
Kentucky: and Alien and Sedition acts, 205; antislavery sentiment in, 336, 337; Indian wars in, 197; industry in, 246; settlement of, 171, 172, 192
Kerouac, Jack, 814
Kesey, Ken, 839
Key, Ellen, 683
Key, Francis Scott, 226
Khomeini, Ruholla (Ayatollah), 919
Khrushchev, Nikita, 772, 798–799, 802, 850
Kickapoo Indians, 200, 238
Kilrain, Jake, 536
Kilroy, Mathew, 115, 116
Kim Il Sung, 774, 775
King, Martin Luther, Jr., 809–810, 877–878, 880–887; assassination of, 887; "I have a dream" speech, 883; "Letter from Birmingham City Jail," 881; Montgomery bus boycott, 809–810; Selma campaign, 884

King, Rufus, 250
King George's War, 91
King Oliver's Creole Jazz Band, 533, 534
King Philip's War, 49–50
King William's War, 89
Kings Mountain, battle of, 152
Kinsey, Alfred C., 681, 903
Kissinger, Henry, 862–863, 864
Knights of Labor, 508
Knights of the Golden Circle, 338
Know Nothings (American party), 391–395, 399, 400, 553
Knox, Henry, 193
Knox, John, 22, 44
Knox, Philander C., 606
Koch, Robert, 262, 612
Koop, C. Everett, 832
Korean War, 773, 774–775, 785, 797; POWs, 785
Korechika, Anami, 753
Korematsu v. United States, 745
Kosovo, 934, 935
Koster, Samuel, 869
Kristallnacht, 731–732
Ku Klux Klan, 465, 466, 687
Kuwait, invasion of, 928

La Causa, 900–901
La Follette, Robert, 619, 620, 625, 690, 736
La Raza Unida, 898
La Salle, Sieur de (René-Robert Cavelier), 89
Labor. *See also* Child labor; Work: African American, after Civil War, 446, 453, 454, 463–464; artisan system, 323–324; division and specialization of, 324; early nineteenth-century, 234, 235, 323–327, 328, 330–331; indentured, 36, 38, 39, 51, 54–55, 58, 144; industrial, 234, 235, 325–326, 502–505, 608; late nineteenth-century, 502–509; migrant (birds of passage), 518–519; migrant farmworkers, 716, 898, 900–901; New Deal and, 710; sharecropping, 463–464, 708, 709, 716; slave, 340–341; southern view of northern, 336; tenant farmers, 708–709, 716; unskilled, 326, 327, 330–331, 522, 655; in World War II, 739, 741
Labor law: in Cold War, 777; in Progressive Era, 610, 620, 624, 627–628, 632, 633; in 1920s, 689; in 1930s, 710, 712–713, 721
Labor-Management Relations Act of 1947, 777
Labor protest: coal strike of 1902, 606, 607, 622, 632; in Cold War, 777; early nineteenth-century, 326–327, 505; grape-pickers' strike, 900–901; in Great Depression, 710, 712, 713; late nineteenth-century, 505–508, 567–569, 584; in Progressive Era, 606; ten-hour day movement, 326–327; after World War I, 660–661; in World War I, 652, 653, 654–655; in World War II, 739
Labor unions. *See also* Labor protest: and antitrust legislation, 632; early, 326, 507–509; in Great Depression, 704, 712; and Mexican Americans, 743; New Deal and, 710, 712–713; in Progressive Era, 606, 632; Reagan and, 921; Taft-Hartley Act and, 777; and women's rights, 656, 896; after World War I, 660; in World War I, 652–653; in World War II, 739

LaFarge, John, 532
Lafayette, Marquis de, 128
Laird, Melvin, 869
Laissez-faire, 486, 610, 633, 708
Lake Erie, battle of, 223
L'Amour, Louis, 826
Land banks, 100
Land cessions: to 1853, 377; Indian, 1750-1810, 227; Louisiana Purchase, 218–219; in Mexican-American War, 373, 374; in Pacific Northwest, 365–368; in Spanish-American War, 595, 598; after War of 1812, 227, 241
Land ordinances, Old Northwest, 172, 181
Land rights/distribution: after American Revolution, 155, 165, 171–172; in colonies, 39, 41, 46, 55, 69, 71, 72; and conservation movement, 622, 626, 839; labor demands for, 326; of Mexican Americans, 376; of Native Americans, 471, 472, 717; Plains Indian attitudes toward, 468; public land, 272, 326, 426, 487, 494, 495, 622, 625–626, 839, 921; and railroads, 487, 495; in South, after Civil War, 450, 453, 459, 463; in Spanish West, 357; after War of 1812, 238–239; in West, 494, 495, 829; and westward expansion, 272
Landon, Alfred M., 713–715
Lane, Ralph, 24, 25
Lansing, Robert, 646, 796
Larcom, Lucy, 235
Lardner, Ring, Jr., 784
"Large policy," 586
Las Casas, Bartolomé de, 19, 20
Las Vegas (Nevada), 831
Latin America: good neighbor policy, 730; southern schemes to conquer, 338–339; trade with, 584, 585; U.S. involvement in, early twentieth-century, 628–630
Latrobe, Benjamin, 203
Laud, William, 44, 47
Laulewasika (Tenskwatawa), 222, 224–225
Laurie, Walter, 134
Lawes Divine, Moral, and Martiall (Gates and Dale), 38
Lawrence, Richard, 384
Lawrence, T. E., 643
Lawrence, William, 486
Lawrence (Kansas), 398
Lawrence (ship), 223
Le Carré, John, 927
Le May, Alan, 826
League of Nations, 661, 663, 664, 666, 729, 732, 733
Lease, Mary E., 562, 565
Leather apron gangs, 107
Leaves of Grass (Whitman), 306–307
Lebanon, 800, 801
Lecompton constitution, 401
Lee, Arthur, 146–147
Lee, "Mother" Ann, 299
Lee, Richard Henry, 138, 183, 207
Lee, Robert E., 370, 417; and Brown's raid on Harper's Ferry, 403, 404; in Civil War, 418, 421, 422, 432, 434, 436, 438
Leighton, Alexander, 754
Leisler, Jacob, 75, 76
Lemon, Meadowlark, 804
Lend-lease bill, 736
Lenin, Vladimir I., 643, 663, 926
Lenorson, Samuel, 66
Leopard (ship), 221
Lesbians, 902–903

Letters on the Condition of Women and the Equality of the Sexes (Grimké), 298
Letters from a Farmer in Pennsylvania (Dickinson), 111
Levitt, William, 803
Lewelling, Lorenzo Dow, 563
Lewinsky, Monica, 931, 932
Lewis, Isham, 339
Lewis, John L., 777
Lewis, Lilburne, 339
Lewis, Meriwether, 218, 359
Lewis, Sinclair, 680
Lewis and Clark expedition, 218, 219, 359, 360
Lexington and Concord, battle of, 131, 132, 134–135
Leyte Gulf, battle of, 751
Liberal Republicans, 467
Liberalism, 834; conservative critique of, 820–821; religious, 285
The Liberator (newspaper), 294–295, 313, 373
Liberia, 294
Liberty party, 296
The Life and Adventures of Joaquin Murieta (Ridge), 307
Life expectancies: in colonies, 50–52, 56, 79; of slaves, 341
Life of Ma-Ka-Tai-Me-she-kia-Kiak or Black Hawk (Black Hawk), 307
Liliuokalani (Queen of Hawaii), 588, 589
Lincoln, Abraham, 214, 418; assassination of, 440; on Brown's raid, 405; and Civil War, 391, 414–415, 417–422, 427–430, 434, 435, 436; debates with Douglas, 402–403; and Dred Scott decision, 401; election of 1860, 411, 412; election of 1864, 436; Emancipation Proclamation, 411, 428–429; expansion of presidential powers, 427–428; and generals, 421, 429, 434, 435; Gettysburg address, 435; inaugural addresses, 414, 452; on Know Nothings, 394; as leader, 418; on Mexican-American War, 374; on mob violence, 332; Reconstruction plan, 440, 451–452; and Republican party, 398; on secession, 413, 414; on slavery, 398, 402–403, 428–429
Lincoln, Benjamin, 151, 169
Lindbergh, Charles, 678
Lippard, George, 309
Lippmann, Walter, 767, 771
List, Friedrich, 244–245
Literature: beat, 814; ethnic, 307; feminist, 895; Harlem Renaissance, 688; late nineteenth-early twentieth century, 531–532, 609; pre–Civil War, 301–302, 305–307, 309–310; Romantic, death in, 612–613; of 1920s, 679–681; of 1930s, 720, 721; southern, 338; on West, 826
Little Bighorn, battle of, 470
Little Richard, 813
Little Rock crisis, 808
Little Turtle, 197
Living standards: of free blacks, 346; late nineteenth-century, 502–503, 510, 526, 528–529; of Native Americans, 899; in North, pre–Civil War, 321–322; in 1950s, 795; in 1960s, 889; of slaves, 341–342; urban, 526, 528–529; working-class, 502–503
Livingston, Robert, 218
Lloyd George, David, 662, 663
Lochner v. New York, 610

Locke, John, 41, 83
Lockheed, 828
Lodge, Henry Cabot (1850-1924), 523, 561, 586, 598, 607; and Treaty of Versailles, 662, 664
Lodge, Henry Cabot (1960s), 834
Lodge Election Bill, 561
Logan, James, 83
London (England), 114, 333, 735
The Lonely Crowd (Riesman), 812
Long, Breckinridge, 743–744
Long, Crawford, 245
Long, Huey, 711–712, 715
Long, Stephen H., 359
Longfellow, Henry Wadsworth, 302, 306
Longstreet, James, 432
Looking Backward (Bellamy), 609
Loose interpretation, 194
Los Angeles (California): race riots, 743, 887, 930; smog, 831
Lost Generation, 680–681
Louis XI, King of France, 15
Louis XIV, King of France, 89–90
Louis XVI, King of France, 146, 147, 149, 196
Louisbourg, capture of, 91
Louisiana: Long and, 711; pre–Civil War, 336, 344; Reconstruction in, 451, 452, 463
Louisiana Purchase, 218–219
Love Canal, 904
Lovejoy, Elijah, 295
Lowell, Francis Cabot, 234
Lowell, James Russell, 372
Lowell (Massachusetts), 235, 327
Loyal Nine, 107–108
Loyalists, 122, 138, 140, 143–144, 150, 152, 155, 171
LSD, 891–892
Lucas, Eliza (Eliza Pinckney), 66, 67, 78
Lucas, George, 67
Lucas, James, 449
Luce, Henry, 773
Luks, George, 532, 533
Lumber industry, 495, 501–502, 831, 834
Lusitania (ship), sinking of, 647
Luther, Martin, 21
Luxembourg, 735
Lynching: of Communists, 660; of German Americans, 654; in pre–Civil War era, 285; progressive defense of, 621; in South, 465, 466, 569, 570, 571; after World War I, 660
Lyon, Mary, 293
Lyon, Matthew, 205

MacArthur, Douglas, 706, 753, 794; and Korean War, 775–776; in World War II, 745, 751, 756
Macaulay, Thomas Babington, 84
Macdonough, Thomas, 226
Machine gun, 643, 644
Mackintosh, Ebenezer, 107, 108, 116, 119
Maclean, Donald, 779–780
MacLeish, Archibald, 740
Macon County (Alabama), 718
Macon's Bill No. 2, 221
Macy, Rowland H., 530, 544
Maddox, Lester, 823
Maddox (ship), 854–855
Madero, Francisco, 630
Madison, Dolley, 226
Madison, James, 221; and Alien and Sedition acts, 205; and Articles of Confederation, 166; and Constitution, 179, 180, 182, 458; and Hamilton's national debt plan, 194; and *Marbury v. Madison*, 216; and political parties, 196; transportation policy, 239; and War of 1812, 221–222, 226
Mafia, 520, 783
Magazines, 309, 611, 680
Magdalene societies, 289
Magellan, Ferdinand, 20
Maggie: A Girl of the Streets (Crane), 532
Mahan, Alfred Thayer, 586
Mahicans, 8
Main Street (Lewis), 680
Maine, 48, 249, 290, 365
Maine laws, 290
Maine (ship), sinking of, 592–593
Makino, Nobuaki, 662
Malaeska, The Indian Wife (Beadle), 309
Malcolm X, 885–886
Malenkov, Georgi, 785
Mali (empire), 57
Malthus, Thomas Robert, 176
The Man from U.N.C.L.E. (TV show), 927
Manassas: First (battle), 419; Second (battle), 422
Manchuria, 732
Manhattan Project, 752, 755–756
Manifest destiny, 362–363
manitou, 8, 12
Mann Act, 625, 683
Mann-Elkins Act, 624
Manumission, 178, 338
Mao Tse-tung (Mao Zedong), 772, 773, 864
Mapp v. Ohio, 889
Marbury, William, 216
Marbury v. Madison, 216, 239
March on Washington, 883
Marcuse, Herbert, 891
Marcy, William, 268
Marian exiles, 22
Mariani, Vin, 542
Marin, John, 533
Marion, Francis ("Swamp Fox"), 152
Marlboro Man, 826
Marne, first battle of the, 642
Maroons, 344
Marquis of Queensberry Rules, 536
Marriage: in Chesapeake colonies, 55; "complex," 301; experimental, in 1920s, 683; in Great Depression, 702; Mormon, 369; Puritan, 51–54; ratio of divorce to, 1890-1987, 898; Sanger on, 674–675; slave, 58, 59, 342–343; in World War II, 741–742
Marshall, George C., 769, 770, 794
Marshall, James W., 377, 379
Marshall, John, 215, 216, 220, 239–240, 269, 276
Marshall, Thurgood, 888, 889
Marshall Plan, 770
Martin, Bradley, ball given by, 493
Martin, Joseph Plumb, 128, 144, 155
Martin v. Hunter's Lessee, 239
Martínez, Antonio José, 307
Marx Brothers, 721
Mary, Queen of Scots (Mary Stuart), 23
Mary I, Queen of England ("Bloody Mary"), 22
Mary II, Queen of England, 75, 76
Maryland, 165, 178; in Civil War, 417, 427; constitution of, 163; slavery in, 178

Maryland colony, 36, 58. *See also* Chesapeake colonies; in American Revolution, 138, 144; Catholics in, 40–41, 75, 76–77; family life, 56; Glorious Revolution in, 75; life expectancies, 50–51; settlement of, 40–41; slavery in, 36; Stamp Act resistance, 109; women in, 54
Mason, George, 170
Mason, James M., 426
Mass production, 245, 493, 676
Mass transit, 795–796
Massachusetts. *See also* Boston: abolition in, 175; Plymouth Colony, 4–5, 26, 42–43, 45, 47; public education in, 174; Shays's rebellion, 169–170; textile mills, 234, 235, 325, 326, 327
Massachusetts Bay Colony, 44–48, 55. *See also* Boston; in American Revolution, 131, 138, 144; Coercive Acts and, 120; English government of, 74, 75, 76, 100–101; Great Awakening in, 86–88; pastimes, 84; resistance to British, 106–109, 111–116, 121; witchcraft hysteria, 75–76
Massachusetts Bay Company, 44
Massachusetts 54th Infantry, 430–431
Massasoit, 49
Masterson, Bat, 497, 536
Matamoros (Mexico), 372, 374
Mather, Cotton, 66–67, 84, 86
Mather, Increase, 84
Mathews, Shailer, 539
Mattachine Society, 903
Maudlin, Bill, 740
Maverick, Samuel, 116
Maxim, Hiram, 644
May, Alan Munn, 779
Mayas, 6, 7
Mayflower Compact, 42
Mayflower voyage, 42, 52
Mayors: African American, 890; Mexican American, 899; progressive, 619
McCallum, Daniel, 491
McCarthy, Eugene, 857, 860
McCarthy, Joseph, 780–781
McCarthyism, 780–781, 902
McCauly, Mary Ludwig Hays, 173–174
McClain, Franklin, 878
McClellan, George, 370, 436; in Civil War, 410, 418, 421–422, 429
McClure's, 611
McCord, James, 912
McCormick, Anne O'Hare, 770
McCoy, Joseph G., 494
McCrea, Jane, 148
McCulloch v. Maryland, 239–240
McDowell, Irvin, 419, 421
McFeaing, John, 327
McGee, Frank, 857
McGilvray, Alexander, 197
McGovern, George, 866
McGuffey Readers, 486
McKay, Claude, 689
McKinley, William: assassination of, 522, 621; and Cuban Revolution, 591, 592, 593; election of 1896, 550–551, 571; election of 1900, 607; and Philippines independence struggle, 599, 600; and Spanish-American War, 593, 594, 595
McKinley Tariff Act, 561, 588
McLaurin v. Board of Regents, 806–807
McLemore, Jeff, 648
McNeill, Joseph, 878
McParlan, James, 506

McPartland, Jimmy, 678
Meade, George G., 374, 418, 434–435, 436, 582
Means, Gardiner, 708
Meany, George, 795
Meat Inspection Act, 623, 633
Meat-packing industry, 492–493, 505, 526, 611; regulation of, 623, 633
Mechaca, José Antonio, 307
Medical care. *See also* Disease(s): of African Americans, 392–393, 718, 719; AIDS, 832–833; birth control, 176–177, 672, 682, 683; cholera epidemics, 263; in Civil War, 437; Great Society programs for, 888; inoculations, 86; late nineteenth-century, 528, 542; pregnancy and childbirth, 52–53; in Progressive Era, 614; rising cost of, 916; and sexual behavior, 682; sexually transmitted disease, 832; of slaves, 392–393; training requirements, early nineteenth-century, 260; and Tuskegee syphilis study, 718–719; in World War II, 738; in yellow fever epidemic of 1793, 198, 199
Medina, Ernest, 869
Mein Kampf (Hitler), 731
Melodramas, 310
Melville, Herman, 305, 306, 373
Memphis (Tennessee), 454, 528
Men, in Great Depression, 702
Mencken, H.L., 84, 680
Mengele, Josef, 728
Mennonites, 79
Menominee Tribe v. United States, 902
Mentally ill, 293
Mercantilism, 67, 77
Merchandising, 676
Merchants of Death, 730
Meredith, James, 880
Merrimack (ship), 425
Merryman, Ex parte, 427
Merryman, John, 427
Mesmerism, 313
mestizo class, 19
Metacomet (King Philip), 49, 50
Methodists, 285, 288, 338
Mexican-American War, 370–374; causes of, 370–372; lands ceded in, 373, 374; Mexican Americans after, 374–376; public opinion in, 373–374; significance of, 376; warfare, 433
Mexican Americans: *bandidos*, 354; deportation of, in Great Depression, 704; discrimination against, 375–376; education of, 898; literature, 307; after Mexican-American War, 374–376; migrant farmworkers, 898, 900–901; and New Deal, 716; poverty among, 693, 898; racism toward, 367; since 1960s, 897–899; in Texas, 364, 366–367, 375, 376; and World War II, 743; and zoot suit riots, 743
Mexico: early Native Americans in, 6, 7; independence of, and West, 356–357; interwar relations with, 730; 1914 invasion of, 631; and Mexican-American War, 370–373, 374; revolution, 629–631; southern invasion of, 338; Spanish conquest of, 17–18; and Texas, 363–364, 370, 371; and Zimmermann telegram, 649
Miami Indians, 172, 197, 238

Micmac Indians, 8, 12
Middle Ages, 10–11
Middle class: colonial, 82; consumption by, 530; and fall in birth rate, 176; flight to suburbs, 526, 675; and industrialization, late nineteenth-century, 492; in North, pre–Civil War, 321–322, 330; and progressivism, 606–607, 608, 614, 615, 618, 619, 633
Middle East conflicts, 919
Midway, battle of, 751
Midway Islands, 582, 750, 751
Midwives, 52–53
Migrant farmworkers, 716, 898, 900–901
Migrant workers (birds of passage), 518–519
Milam, J. W., 792, 793
Miles, Nelson A., 595
Militarism, Japanese, 701
Military. *See also* Army, U.S.; Defense spending; Navy, U.S.; Union army: African Americans in, 742; desegregation of, 806; gays in, 903, 931; strength of, 1945-90, 797; in Vietnam War, 857–858; women in, 741
"Military-industrial complex," 803
Military Reconstruction Act, 456
Mill towns, southern, 501
Millay, Edna St. Vincent, 680
Millett, Kate, 895
Milligan, Ex parte, 457
Millin, Margrett, 449
Mills, C. Wright, 891
Milosevic, Slobodan, 935
Miners, 502
Mingoe Indians, 102
Mining industry, 482. *See also* Coal industry; child labor in, 608; in West, 831–834
Minorities. *See also specific groups*: control of, in Progressive Era, 614, 620
Minstrel shows, 311–313
Minutemen, 131
Mission to Moscow (film), 765
Missionaries, 357, 368, 584, 588, 595
Missionary diplomacy, 629–631
Missions, Spanish, 356
Mississippi: civil rights movement in, 879, 880, 886; Civil War in, 424, 435; Jackson State shootings, 864; murder of Emmett Till, 793–794; prevention of black voting in, 465, 570; women's rights in, 894
Mississippi River, 201–202, 218
Mississippian peoples, 7
Missouri, 369, 398, 417, 428
Missouri Compromise, 249–252, 388, 396; and Dred Scott decision, 400–401
Missouri ex rel Gaines, 806–807
Mitchell, John (attorney general), 913
Mitchell, John (labor leader), 606, 607
Mix, Tom, 826
Mob violence, 285, 332. *See also* Lynching; Racial violence; Riots; Vigilantism; Violence
Moby Dick (Melville), 306
"Modern Republicanism," 794, 796
Modern Woman: The Lost Sex, 811
Modernism, 533
Mohawk Indians, 28, 148
Molasses Act, 78, 104
Molly Maguires, 506
Molotov, V. M., 767, 772

Momaday, N. Scott, 902
Mondale, Walter, 923
Money (Mississippi), 793–794
Money policy: after American Revolution, 165; in Civil War, 425, 426; colonial, 100, 104–105; gold standard, 550, 575, 708; under Jackson, 274; late nineteenth-century, 550, 557–558, 561; in New Deal, 708; and Panic of 1819, 248; in 1920s, 693; in 1970s, 917; after War of 1812, 237
"Money question," 557, 561
Monitor (ship), 425
Monmouth Court House, battle of, 174
Monroe, James, 218; foreign policy, 240–241; on Native Americans, 269; political parties and, 259, 261; presidency of, 235–236, 261
Monroe Doctrine, 241, 589; Roosevelt Corollary to, 629, 730
Montezuma II, 18
Montgomery, Bernard, 746
Montgomery, Richard, 133
Montgomery (Alabama): bus boycott, 572, 573, 808–810; march on, 884
Montgomery Ward, 692
Montoya, Joseph, 898
Montreal, 93, 133, 223
Monuments, patriotic, 308
Moore's Creek Bridge, battle of, 139
Moral reform: early twentieth-century, 614–615, 625, 633, 682–683; mid-nineteenth-century, 285, 289–290; and New Deal, 708
Morales, Victor, 898
Morality: of adolescents, in 1950s, 784–785; and AIDS crisis, 832–833; Republican party and, 553–554, 557; rock and roll and, 813–814; in 1920s, 672, 673, 681, 683
Moravians, 79, 337
More, Paul Elmer, 720
Morgan, Daniel, 153
Morgan, J. P., 480, 483, 489, 491, 567, 606, 622; and Theodore Roosevelt, 622, 623, 626
Morgan, J. P., Jr., 660
Morgan, William, 261
Morgenthau, Henry, 720, 744
Mormons, 368–370
Morrill Land Grant Act, 426, 499
Morris, Gouverneur, 165–166, 167, 180
Morris, Robert, 165, 167, 180
Morrissey, John, 536
Morrow, Dwight, 730
Morse, Samuel F. B., 240, 244, 245
Morse, Wayne, 855
Morton, Ferdinand "Jelly Roll," 534
Morton, Thomas, 43
Mosby, John S., 538
Moses, Robert, 829
Mosinee (Wisconsin), 776
Mothers: child care responsibilities, 176; in republicanism, 174, 175
Motley, Archibald, Jr., 688
Mott, Lucretia, 299
Mound Builders, 6–7, 8
Mount Holyoke College, 293
Mountain men, 360
Ms. (magazine), 895
Muckrakers, 611
Mugwumps, 554, 558, 559
Muhammad, Elijah, 885, 886

Muir, John, 622, 903
mulatto class, 19
Muller v. Oregon, 610
Mumford, Lewis, 720, 811
Munich Conference, 769
Munich Pact, 733
Munn v. Illinois, 560
Murieta, Joaquín, 307, 354
Murphy, Edgar Gardner, 615
Murphy, Frank, 745
Murphy, Isaac, 537
Murray, Judith Sargent, 175
Muscovy Company, 25
Museums, 540
Music: African American, 343, 533–534, 813; blues, 534, 678, 813, 825; classical, 680; country/"hillbilly," 678, 813, 825; Guthrie's, 700; jazz, 533–534, 678; late nineteenth-century, 533–534; minstrel show, 311–312; ragtime, 534; rap, 890; rock and roll, 813–814; of 1920s, 678, 680; of 1960s, 892; spirituals, 343; of World War I, 648, 654
Muslims: and the Crusades, 11; scientific knowledge of, 14; in Spain, 15
Mussolini, Benito, 701, 732, 733
My Lai massacre, 858, 868–869

NAACP. *See* National Association for the Advancement of Colored People
Nader, Ralph, 876–877
NAFTA (North American Free Trade Agreement), 931
Nagasaki, bombing of, 753, 756
Nagy, Imre, 799
Napoleon, 218, 219, 220, 227; craze for, 590
Narragansett Indians, 47, 49
Narváez, Pánfilo de, 18
NASA (National Aeronautics and Space Administration), 927
Nashoba Colony, 301
Nashville (ship), 629
Nasser, Gamal Abdel, 799
Natchez Indians, 7
Nation of Islam, 885–886
Nation-states, emergence of, 15
National Aeronautics and Space Administration (NASA), 927
National American Woman Suffrage Association, 556, 616
National Association for the Advancement of Colored People (NAACP), 618, 635, 687, 793, 886; court cases, 806–807; founding of, 618; in World War I, 657; in World War II, 742, 743
National Association of Colored Women, 615
National Association Opposed to Woman Suffrage, 616
National bank. *See* Bank of the United States
National Banking acts, 426
National Child Labor Committee, 615, 620
National Congress of American Indians, 899
National Consumers League, 615
National debt: after American Revolution, 165; British, after Seven Years' War, 101; Hamilton's plan for, 193–194; and national bank, 194–195; under Reagan, 921, 923
National Defense Education Act, 801, 927
National Environmental Policy Act, 904

National Farm Workers Association, 900
National Indian Youth Council, 899
National Industrial Recovery Act, 708, 709, 710
National Labor Relations Act. *See* Wagner Act
National Labor Relations Board, 713
National Labor Union, 508
National League (baseball), 535
National Organization for Women (NOW), 894, 895
National Origins Act, 523, 686
National Recovery Administration, 709–710
National Republicans, 265, 277
National Resources and Planning Board, 739
National Security Council Paper Number 68 (NSC-68), 774–775
National System of Interstate and Defense Highways Act, 795
National Temperance Society, 621
National Trades' Union, 326
National Traffic and Motor Vehicle Safety Act, 876
National Union for Social Justice, 712
National Union party, 436
National Urban League, 687
National War Labor Board, 653
National Woman Suffrage Association, 458, 556, 616
National Woman's party, 616, 655, 656
National Women's Trade Union League, 615–616
National Youth Administration, 716, 717, 739
Nationalism: black, 884–887; Native American, 899; post-Cold War, 935; radical southern, 338–339; in 1890s, 589, 590; southern, 336, 338; after War of 1812, 234–237, 239, 240, 248
Nationalists, 164–168, 179–184
Native Americans, 4–10; John Quincy Adams' policy on, 180, 181; American Revolution and, 147, 148, 150, 155; assimilation of, 269, 469, 471–472, 717; in Bacon's rebellion, 73; beliefs and values of, 8–9, 12, 20; Black Hawk War, 270–271; in California, 356, 357, 496; Civil War and, 469; and Columbian exchange, 30; Columbus and, 15–16; complex societies, 6–7; cultural differences with whites, 468–469; and Dawes Severalty Act, 471, 562, 717; diseases and, 4, 5, 10, 16, 18, 30, 224; and Hannah Dustan, 66; Eastern Woodland, 8–10, 12, 13; education of, 471, 717, 902; European view of, 9–10, 12–13, 24; in Florida, 241; and French, 29–30, 89, 91; and fur trade, 28, 30, 91; imperial wars and, 66–67, 91, 92, 93–95; Indian power movement, 899–902; and Jamestown colony, 26, 27; and King Philip's War, 49–50; legal status, 471, 472; literature of, 307; loss of land, responses to, 197–200; New Deal for, 716–717; in Old Northwest (Ohio country), 197–200, 222, 223, 224–225, 227, 238; in Pacific Northwest, 357, 368; Paleo-Indians, 5, 6; and Pennsylvania-Delaware colony, 71, 72; Plains, 357, 468–472; and Plymouth Colony, 4–5, 43; Pontiac's rebellion,
102; population growth, 5, 8; poverty among, 693, 899; Proclamation line and, 103–104; Puritans and, 49–50; racism toward, 468; removal under Jackson, 268–272; reservations, 469, 470, 471, 899; and Roanoke colony, 24–25; and scalping, 12, 13; after Seven Years' War, 102; as slaves, 19, 42, 357; and Spanish, 16–20; in Spanish West, 356, 357; Tecumseh's alliance, 223, 224–225; termination policy, 899; and Tippecanoe, 222; and Virginia colony, 26, 27, 39–40; in War of 1812, 222, 223, 225, 227; warfare, 12, 13; western, 357–358, 360, 468–472; and westward expansion, 357–358, 468–472, 494; Roger Williams and, 47
Native Son (Wright), 721
Nativism, 391, 521–522, 686
NATO (North Atlantic Treaty Organization), 772, 935
Naturalism, 531, 609
Naturalization Act, 204
Nauvoo (Illinois), 369
Navajo Indians, 357, 468
Navigation Acts, 68, 73, 74, 77
Navigation System, 68, 69, 73
Navy, U.S.: African Americans in, 431, 742; buildup, late nineteenth-century, 585–586; in Civil War, 420, 425; reductions, post–Civil War, 581–582; in Spanish-American War, 593; in World War I, 658
Nazi party, 731
Nebraska territory, 396
Needham, Henry Beach, 538
Neff, Mary, 66
Neolin, 102
Netherlands, 735
Neutrality policy: in World War I, 643–651; in World War II, 735
New Amsterdam, 69
New Deal, 706–723; and African Americans, 716; and agriculture, 708–709; attacks on, 1940s, 739–740; "brain trust," 708; coalition, 706, 707, 715, 723, 759, 778; conservation programs, 903; critics of, 711–712, 713; decline of, 717–720; first, 706, 707–712; First Hundred Days, 707–708; impact of, 721–723; and industry, 709–710, 713; jobs programs, 710–711; and labor, 710, 712–713; and Mexican Americans, 716; and Native Americans, 716–717; Second Hundred Days, 712–713; Social Security, 713, 714; Supreme Court and, 717–720; in West, 827; and women, 715–716
New Deal coalition, 706, 707, 715, 759, 778, 866
New England colonies. *see also specific colonies*: in American Revolution (*See* North); commercial values in, 55–56, 60; as Dominion, 74, 75; family life, 51–54; founding of, 42–49; Great Awakening in, 86–88; and King Philip's War, 49–50; life expectancies, 50, 51; Navigation Acts and, 68; slavery in, 55, 58; witchcraft hysteria, 75–76
New France, 29–30, 89, 93
"New Freedom," 626, 627, 632
New Guinea, 751

New Hampshire, 138, 327
New Harmony, 300
New Haven (Connecticut), 112
New Humanists, 720
New Jersey: in American Revolution, 142–143, 144, 150; colonial, 70; constitution of, 163, 164
New Jersey Plan, 180
New Left, 890–891
"New Look" program, 798
New Mexico, 371, 374; American settlement of, 356–357; Mexican Americans in, 374, 375–376, 743; Spanish, 355, 356
"New Nationalism," 626
"New Negro," 687
New Netherland, 28, 69
New Orleans (Louisiana): in Civil War, 420; free blacks in, 344; Hennessy case, 520; and jazz, 533–534; murder of Robert Charles, 573; Reconstruction in, 453, 454; sanitation problems, 528; in War of 1812, 227
New Panama Canal Company, 628
"New South," 500–502, 822–825
New Spain, 16, 18–20, 23, 69, 241; conquest of, 16–18; slavery in, 19, 20, 57, 58
New York: in American Revolution, 138, 141–142, 147–148; colonial, 69–70, 73, 75, 76; and Constitution, 183; and election of 1800, 206; Leisler revolt, 75, 76; Native Americans in, 197; prisons, 291; religious ferment in, 368; resistance to British, 110, 114, 120; transportation in, early nineteenth-century, 242–243; voting rights, 259
New York City: after American Revolution, 168; in American Revolution, 140, 141, 143, 150; Central Park, 540; cholera epidemic of 1832, 262–263; Civil War draft riots, 434; Coney Island, 540–541; crime in, 284–285, 332–333; culture in, 530, 532–533; Dodgers' move from, 829; early nineteenth-century, 246, 247, 248, 284–285; Empire State Building, 673; ethnic neighborhoods, 526; Harlem, 675; Harrison campaign in, 258; Jewish immigrants in, 520, 526; late nineteenth-century, 520, 525–528, 530, 532–533; Panic of 1837, 275–276; police force, first, 333; poor relief in, 610; poverty in, 248, 291; prohibition in, 685; riots in 1830s, 332; Tammany Hall machine, 618–619; tenements in, 527, 528, 529
New York Federal Reserve bank, 633
New York Journal, 591, 592
New York Moral Reform Society, 289
New York *Morning Post*, 309
New York *Sun*, 309, 587–588
New York Times, 530, 648
New York *Tribune*, 304, 327, 401, 402, 414, 427, 429, 586
New York World, 591, 648
New York World's Fair, 721
Newark (New Jersey), 205
Newbold, Charles, 246
Newburgh conspiracy, 167–168
Newlands Reclamation Act, 622
Newport, Christopher, 26
Newspapers. *See also* Journalism: early, 309
Newton, Isaac, 83

Nez Percé Indians, 357, 468
Ngo Dinh Diem, 852
Nguyen Cao Ky, 866
Nguyen Van Thieu, 863, 867
Nhu, Madame, 853
Niagara Movement, 618
Nicaragua: and canal plan, 628; contra war in, 922; U.S. involvements in, 339, 629, 730
Nicholas II, Czar of Russia, 643
Nicholson, Francis, 75
Nickelodeons, 541, 542
Nicolls, Richard, 69, 70
Nimitz, Chester, 751
Nineteenth Amendment, 616, 656, 684
Nitze, Paul, 773
Nixon, Richard M., 837, 838; and African Americans, 882; character traits, 862; and China, 864–865; on communist conspiracy, 780; debates with Kennedy, 847–848; economic policies, 917; election of 1968, 861, 862; election of 1972, 865–866; foreign policy, 918; and Alger Hiss case, 765; and SALT I, 865; social programs and, 889; Supreme Court appointments, 889; and Vietnam War, 863–864, 866, 869, 871; Watergate scandal, 912–914
"Nixon Doctrine," 863
Non-Intercourse Act, 221
Nonseparatists, 42, 43
Noriega, Manuel Antonio, 924, 925
Norris, Frank, 484, 530–531
Norris, George, 625
North. *see also specific colonies and states; specific states*: African Americans in, 178–179, 345–346, 657, 674, 676, 742, 877, 887; after American Revolution, 168; American Revolution in, 131, 132, 133–137, 140–144, 147–149; Brown's raid and, 405; civil rights movement in, 887; and Civil War, 415, 417, 418, 426–428, 429, 431–434; before Civil War, 321–331; and Compromise of 1850, 387, 389; differences from South, 320–321, 331, 346–347; economic growth in, 246, 321–331; free blacks in, 178–179, 345–346; and Fugitive Slave Law, 390–391; in Great Depression, 703; industrialization in, 321–331; and Kansas-Nebraska Act, 396; and Missouri crisis, 248–249; population decline in, 837–838; racism in, 459; and Reconstruction, 459, 467, 472; religious freedom in, 171; segregation in, 803; slavery in, 55, 58, 175, 294, 320; and slavery in Constitution, 180–181; southern view of, 336; split with South, 346–347; tensions with South, 248–252, 346–347, 385–391, 396–406
North, Frederick (Lord), 116–117, 119, 123, 140, 154
North Africa, 746
North American Free Trade Agreement (NAFTA), 931
North Atlantic Treaty Organization (NATO), 772, 935
North Carolina: in American Revolution, 138, 153; Greensboro sit-ins, 878, 879; Reconstruction in, 453; settlement of, 42
Northern Confederacy, 219
Northern Securities Company, 622

Northrup, Solomon, 340
Northwest Ordinances, 172, 181
Northwest Passage, search for, 20–21
Norway, 734
Notre Dame football team, 539, 679
Novels. *See also* Literature: dime, 309, 826; domestic, 309–310; westerns, 826
NOW (National Organization for Women), 894, 895
Noyes, John Humphrey, 301
NSC-68 (National Security Council Paper Number 68), 774–775
Nuclear industry, 829, 830
Nuclear weapons: arms race, 768, 772, 865, 918, 921; bombing of Japan, 752–759; in 1964 campaign, 836, 854; development of, 752, 755–756, 772; Eisenhower's policy, 797, 798; Manhattan Project, 752, 755–756; postwar policy on, 767; and U.S.-Soviet relations, 767–768
Nude Descending a Staircase (Duchamp), 533
Nullification, 266, 272, 273–274
Nye, Gerald, 730

Oak Ridge (Tennessee), 824
Oberlin College, 293
Obregón, Alvaro, 630, 730
O'Brien, Tim, 871
Occupational Health and Safety Act, 876
O'Connor, Sandra Day, 897
Office of Price Administration, 739, 777
Office of Scientific Research and Development, 738
Oglethorpe, James, 90
O'Hara, Maureen, 821
O'Hare, Kate Richards, 654
Ohio, 197. *See also* Old Northwest
Ohio Company, 92
Ohio Gang, 690
Ohio River valley: early peoples, 6–7, 8; French-English conflicts in, 91–92
Oil crisis, 915, 916
Oil industry, 482, 690, 831–834
OK Corral shootout, 497
O'Keeffe, Georgia, 680
Okinawa, battle of, 751, 752
Oklahoma, Indian removal to, 269–272
Oklahoma City bombing, 931
Oklahoma (ship), 737
Old-age relief, 712, 713
Old Northwest (Ohio country): British in, 200, 201, 222; Indians in, 197–200, 222, 223, 224–225, 227; settlement of, 171, 172, 238–239
Old Republicans, 264
Olive Branch petition, 133
Oliver, Andrew, 106, 107, 108, 123
Oliver, Peter, 106, 108
Olmsted, Frederick Law, 540
Olney, Richard S., 560, 568, 589
Olympic Games, 537, 800, 926–927
O'Malley, Walter, 828–829
One Flew Over the Cuckoo's Nest (Kesey), 839
Oneida Community, 301
Oneida Indians, 148
O'Neill, Bucky, 596, 597
O'Neill, Eugene, 680
Only Yesterday (Allen), 695
OPEC (Organization of Petroleum Exporting Countries), 915, 916
Opechancanough, 39–40; massacre by, 13, 39

Open Door Policy, 600–601
Opiates, 542
Oppenheimer, J. Robert, 752
Oratory, 310–311
Oregon country, 361, 365–368, 368
Oregon Trail, 361
Organization of Afro-Americans, 886
Organization of Petroleum Exporting Countries (OPEC), 915, 916
Oriskany, battle of, 148
Orlando, Vittorio, 662, 663
Osceola, 271
Osgood, Samuel, 193
Ostend Manifesto, 395
O'Sullivan, John L., 362
Oswald, Lee Harvey, 851
Otis, James, Jr., 107, 109
Ottawa Indians, 200
Our Country: Its Possible Future and Present Crisis (Strong), 584
Outlaws, western, 497
Owen, Robert, 300, 339

Pacific Northwest: acquisition of, 365–368; Native Americans of, 357, 368; settlement of, 361, 368
Pacific Railway Act, 426
Page, Walter Hines, 646
Pahlavi, Mohammed Reza (Shah of Iran), 801, 919
Paine, Thomas, 138, 144, 145
Paiute Indians, 357
Pale of Settlement, 520
Paleo-Indians, 5, 6
Palmer, A. Mitchell, 661
Palmer, Phoebe, 298
Panama, 17, 91, 730; U.S. invasion of, 924–925
Panama Canal, 628–629, 918
Panay incident, 732
Panic of 1819, 248, 261–264
Panic of 1837, 275–276
Panic of 1873, 467, 557
Panic of 1893, 567
Paris (France), 528
Parker, Alton B., 623
Parker, Dorothy, 681
Parker, John, 131
Parkman, Francis, 309
Parks: city, 540; national, 903
Parks, Rosa, 808–809
Parsons, Lawrence, 134
Passamaquoddy, 902
Pastorius, Francis Daniel, 71
Paterson, William, 180
Paterson (New Jersey), 327
Patriarchalism, Puritan, 51, 54
Patronage, political, 268, 558–559
Patrons of Husbandry, 564
Patroonships, 69
Patton, George, 747
Patton (film), 863
Patuxet Indians, 4
Paul, Alice, 616, 655, 656
Paulding, James Kirk, 310
Pawnee Indians, 8, 468
Pawtucket (Rhode Island), 324
Payne-Aldrich Tariff, 625
Peabody, Elizabeth, 302
Peace Democrats, 428, 436
Peale, Charles Wilson, 308
Pearl Harbor attack, 737
Peck, Everard, 324

Peers, William, 869
Pemberton, John C., 435
Pendleton Act, 558–559
peninsulares, 19
Penitentiaries, 291
Penn, William, 70–72
Pennsylvania: abolition in, 175; Civil War in, 434–435; coal wars in, 506; colonial, 71–72, 79, 81–82; constitution, 163; economic stratification in, 81–82; and election of 1800, 206; Germans in, 71, 79; penitentiaries, 291; ten-hour day law, 327; transportation, 242, 243; Whiskey Rebellion, 197, 200
Pennsylvania Evening Post, 309
Pennsylvania State football, 538
Penobscot, 902
Pensacola (Florida), 154, 226–227
Pentecostalism, 685–686
Pepperell, William, 91
Pequot Indians, 13, 49, 307
Perceval, Prime Minister, 221
Percy, Lord (Hugh, Lord Percy), 134
perestroika, 922, 923, 926
Perkins, Frances, 714, 715
Perot, Ross, 930
Perry, Matthew, 395
Perry, Oliver Hazard, 223
Pershing, John J. "Black Jack," 631, 658
Persian Gulf War, 928–930
Pet banks, 274
Peters, John, 161
Petersburg, battle of, 436, 438
Phagan, Mary, 521
Phalanxes (Fourier communities), 300–301
Philadelphia (Pennsylvania): British seizure of, 147; Continental army march on, 168; founding of, 71; immigrants and, 79; Mexican-American war and, 373; resistance to British, 114, 120; riots in, 295, 332, 391, 394; strike in, 326–327; Washington's funeral in, 207; water supply, 528; yellow fever epidemic, 198–199
Philadelphia (ship), 217
Philby, Kim, 779–780
Philip II, King of Spain, 23
Philip Morris, 826
Philip of Anjou, 90
Philippines: annexation of, 595–598; independence struggle, 599–600; Spanish-American War and, 593–594, 595; in World War II, 745, 750, 751
Phillips, David Graham, 611
Phillips, Kevin, 837
Phillips, Sam, 813
Phips, William, wife of, 76
Phonograph, 678
Phrenology, 313
Pickering, John, 216
Pickett, George E., 432, 433, 434
Pickett's Charge, 432–433, 434
Picou, Alphonse, 534
Pierce, Franklin, 306, 384–385, 395; and slavery in Kansas, 396, 398, 399
Pigot, Robert, 136
Pike, Zebulon, 359
Pilgrims, 4–5, 42–43, 45, 47, 49, 52
The Pilgrim's Progress (Bunyan), 611
Pinchback, P. B. S., 461, 689
Pinchot, Gifford, 622, 625–626, 903
Pinckney, Charles, 67, 220
Pinckney, Charles Cotesworth, 67

Pinckney, Eliza (Eliza Lucas), 66, 67, 78
Pinckney, Thomas, 67, 202, 446
Pinckney's Treaty, 202
Ping-pong diplomacy, 864
Pioneers, 358, 361–362, 495–498; Mormon, 368–370
Pitcher, Molly, 174
Pitt, William, 93, 102, 103, 110–111
Pittsburgh Landing, battle of, 424
Pittsburgh (Pennsylvania): growth of, 247–248; Homestead strike, 567–568; pollution in, 527, 528
Pizarro, Francisco, 18
Plague, 11
Plains Indians, 357, 468–472
Plan of Union (Galloway's), 122
Plantation Burial (Antrobus), 343
Plantation legend, 331
Plantations, 331, 340–341, 448
Platt Amendment, 595, 628, 730
Players' League (baseball), 535–536
Pleiku, battle of, 855
Plessy v. Ferguson, 501, 570, 803
Plymouth Colony, 4–5, 26, 42–43, 45, 47
Pocahantas, 39
Poe, Edgar Allan, 304–306
Poems on Various Subjects, Religious and Moral (Wheatley), 160
Poets, 680, 814
Poland: German invasion of, 734; immigrants from, 519, 524, 526, 742; liberalization in, 799; Soviet Union and, 748, 766, 767
Police forces, 332–333, 527, 861
Political bosses, 260
Political dissent: and Alien and Sedition acts, 190, 204–205, 215; in Civil War, 427; of New Left, 890–891; after World War I, 660–661; in World War I, 654–655
Political machines, 554, 618–619, 631–632
Political participation: early nineteenth-century, 259–260, 266; late nineteenth-century, 554, 555; mid-nineteenth-century, 266; in Progressive Era, 631–632
Political parties. *See also specific parties*: early nineteenth-century, 236, 259, 261–264, 277–279; formation of system of, 184, 195–201; Jefferson's view of, 196, 215; late nineteenth-century, 552–556; machines, 554, 618–619, 631–632; realignments, 391–395, 396–398, 706, 707, 837–839; and Reconstruction, 451; and South, 451, 838; and West, 838–839; Working Men's parties, 326
Political rights. *See also* Black suffrage; Voting rights: of African Americans, 339–340, 400, 402, 451, 453–454, 455, 877; after American Revolution, 161–162, 163; in colonies, 42, 46, 55, 82–83, 105; of free blacks, 400, 402; of Native Americans, 471, 472; of slaves, 339–340; of women, 55, 894
Polk, James K., 365, 368; and Mexican-American War, 370, 371, 374; and slavery debates in Congress, 376–377
Polk, Leonidas L., 563
Pollock, Jackson, 711
Pollock v. The Farmer's Loan and Trust Co., 567
Pollution, 831, 903–904
Polo, Marco, 14–15

Ponce de León, Juan, 17
Pontiac's rebellion, 102–103
Ponzi, Charles, 691
Ponzi scheme, 691
Poor whites, in South, 388, 462, 463, 464, 501
Popé, 20
Pope, John, 422
Popular culture: in Great Depression, 720–721; on hard work and wealth, 486; modern, African Americans in, 890; pre–Civil War, 308–313; in 1920s, 677–681; in 1950s, 784–785, 810, 812–814, 890–891; urban, late nineteenth-century, 534–543; Vietnam veteran in, 867; West in, 826–827; westward expansion in, 354–355; in World War I, 654
Popular sovereignty, 163, 182, 190–191; in expansion of slavery question, 388, 396, 401
Population growth/decline: 1960-85, 894; in colonies, 78–80; in England, 23; in Europe, 10–11; in Great Depression, 702; late eighteenth-century, 176; Malthusian, 176; Native Americans, 5, 8, 902; in New England, 50; in 1950s, 795, 811, 890; slaves, 59, 294, 320; in South and West, 741, 824, 825, 828, 829, 837–838; in World War II, 741–742
Populism, 562–567, 569, 571–574, 584
Pornography, 683
Port Hudson (Louisiana), 435
Port Huron Statement, 890
Porter, Cole, 732
Porter, Edwin S., 541
Portsmouth (Rhode Island), 48
Portugal, 15, 16, 57
Potawatomi Indians, 102, 200
Potsdam conference, 752, 754, 755, 766
Pottawatomie Creek (Kansas), 399
Potter, David, 450–451
Pound, Roscoe, 610
Poverty: African American, 718, 889, 890; in Bush presidency, 930; and cholera, 262–263; civil rights movement and, 887; in colonies, 82; of Continental soldiers, 144, 146; in England, 23; Lyndon B. Johnson's "War on," 888–889; late nineteenth-century view of, 485–486; Mexican American, 693, 898; Native American, 693, 899; and progressivism, 615; in revolutionary era, 171; in 1920s, 693; in South, 501–502, 718, 822; of unskilled workers, pre–Civil War, 327; urban, 82, 248, 263, 285, 291, 330, 528, 529; women's, 897; and World War II, 743
Powderly, Terence V., 508
Powell, Lewis, 889
Powers, Francis Gary, 802
Powhatan, 27, 28, 39
Powhatan's Confederacy, 26, 27, 39–40
Poyas, Ned, 250
Poyas, Peter, 250
Praeger, Robert Paul, 654
Pragmatism, 610
Pratt, Richard, 471
Pre-Raphaelites, 613
Pregnancy, 52, 177
Presbyterians, 22, 44, 78, 88, 289, 336, 338
Prescott, William, 136, 137
Presidency: in Civil War, 427–428; establishment of, 181, 193; Jackson and, 267–268; Jefferson and, 214–215; in late nineteenth century, 552; Nixon and, 914; Franklin Roosevelt and, 722; selection of candidates, 264; Washington and, 193; Watergate and, 913, 914; Wilson and, 627; World War II and, 759
Presley, Elvis, 813, 814
Preston, Thomas, 116
Price, George M., 520
Price Revolution, 23
Princeton, battle of, 143, 144
Princeton University, 88
Princip, Gavrilo, 641
Prioleau, George W., 593
Prisoners-of-war, in Korean War, 785
Prisons: debtor, 292; pre–Civil War, 291
Pritchard, Gullah Jack, 250–251
Proclamation of 1763, 103–104
Proclamation of Amnesty and Reconstruction, 451
Proctor, Jenny, 449
Proctor, Renfield, 590–591
Profiles in Courage (Kennedy), 849
Progress and Poverty (George), 609
Progressive party, 626, 690, 778
Progressivism, 606–635, 690; in cities, 618–619, 631–632; factors leading to, 607–614; impact of, 631–635; in international arena, 628–631; at national level, 621–628; *vs.* New Deal, 708; organizing drive, 614–618; at state level, 619–621; twilight of, 690; and World War I, 631, 651
Prohibition, 627, 655–656, 684–685; in Maine, 290; movement for, 614, 620, 621, 655; in states, 620
Propaganda: in World War I, 653–654; in World War II, 740
Property rights: conflicts with human rights, 170; and voting rights, 73
Proposition 13 (California), 839
Prostitution, 285, 289, 614–615, 625, 682, 683
Protestant Reformation, 21–22
Provenzano, Joe, 520
Provenzano, Pete, 520
Providence (Rhode Island), 47
Pseudosciences, 313
Psychological testing, in World War I, 658
Psychology: and advertising, 677; of black children, in segregation, 807; Freudian, 681
Ptolemy, 14
Public Health Service, and Tuskegee syphilis study, 718–719
Public virtue, 162, 164, 165, 182
Public Works Administration, 710, 717
Pueblo Indians, 20, 357, 374
pueblos, 8
Puerto Rico, U.S. invasion of, 595
Pulitzer, Joseph, 591
Pullman strike, 568
Punch, John, 36
Pure Food and Drug Act, 623, 633
Puritans, 42, 43–49; commercial values and, 55–56; in England, 22, 41, 43–44, 55; family life, 51–54; and Glorious Revolution, 74, 75; and King Philip's War, 49–50; life expectancies, 50, 51; on Long Island, 69, 70, 75; and Massachusetts Bay Colony, 44–48; and Native Americans, 49–50; pastimes, 84; public schools of, 46–47, 292; Quakers and, 70, 71; religious controversies, 47–48; and witchcraft hysteria, 75–76
Purity crusaders, 615, 625, 682–683
Pusan perimeter, 775
Pushmataha, 270
Putney (Vermont), 301

Quakers (Society of Friends), 70, 71, 72, 175, 197, 336, 337
Quartering Act, 120
Quay, Matt, 555, 561
Quebec Act, 120
Quebec (Canada), 29, 93, 133
Queen Anne's War, 90
"Queen for a Day" (TV show), 892
Quetzalcoatl, 18
Quigley, Hugh, 307
Quinn, John, 533
Quivers, Emanuel, 340

Racial violence: anti-immigrant, 520–522; in cities, in 1960s, 887; in civil rights movement, 810, 878, 879–880, 882, 886; murder of Emmett Till, 792–793; in Reconstruction, 454, 465, 466; Rodney King riots, 930; in 1890s, 569–571, 573; in West, 496; after World War I, 660; in World War I, 657; in World War II, 742
Racism: advances against, in South, 823–824; toward African American soldiers, 593; of anti-imperialists, 598; and black pride, 885; toward Japanese, 740, 752; toward Jews, 728, 744; and medical care, 393, 718, 719; toward Mexican Americans, 367; in minstrel shows, 312; toward Native Americans, 468; in New Deal programs, 716; in Progressive Era, 620–621, 635; on radio, 678; and Reconstruction, 459, 464–465, 467–468, 472, 474; in response to Emancipation Proclamation, 429; in revolutionary era, 178; in 1950s, 803; as slavery rationale, 336; in sports, 537, 804; in World War II, 742
Radical Reconstruction, 455–458, 459
Radical reform, 293–203
Radical Republicans, 451–454, 458
Radicalism: African American, 687–688; early twentieth-century attacks on, 660–661, 686; feminist, 895; southern, 338–339; student, 890–891
Radio, 677–678
rage militaire, 128, 131, 144
Ragtime, 534
Railroads: and agriculture, 499; as big business, 487, 489, 490; commuter, 525, 526; construction of, 417, 484, 487; early, 243, 335, 338; Great Strike of 1877, 506; land and, 487, 495; in North *vs.* South, 417; regulation of, 559–560, 564, 619–620, 622, 623, 632, 652; in World War I, 652
Rainey, Ma, 678
Raleigh, Walter, 24, 25
Rall, Johann, 143
Rambo: First Blood II (film), 867
rancheros, 356, 357
Ranching, 494, 495
ranchos, 357
Randolph, A. Philip, 687, 742, 806, 883
Randolph, Edmund, 180, 193
Randolph, Edward, 74
Randolph, John, 265–266

Range wars, 495
Rankin, Jeannette, 619
Rap, 890
Raskob, John Jacob, 692
Rationalism, 83
Rauschenbusch, Walter, 610
Reagan, Ronald, 821, 837, 839, 921–923; and AIDS, 832; economic policies, 921; foreign policy, 921–922; legacy of, 923
Reagan Doctrine, 921–922
Realism, 531, 609
Rebel Without a Cause (film), 784, 890
Rebellions. *See also* Slave rebellions: of 1689 (Glorious Revolution), 75; Bacon's, 73–74; Bear Flag Revolt, 372; Boxer, 601; Fries, 205; Pontiac's, 102–103; Sagebrush, 839; Shays's, 169–170, 179; Whiskey, 197, 200
Reconstruction, 446–468, 472–474; Black Codes and, 453–454; and black suffrage, 451, 453, 455, 456, 458–459, 465; congressional, 454–460, 473–474; constitutional amendments, 455, 458, 459; economic and social adaptation in, 463–464; Johnson's plan, 452–453; Lincoln's plan, 440, 451–452; northern attitudes and, 459, 467; postwar conditions and issues, 447–451; presidential, 451–454, 473; racism and, 459, 464–465, 467–468, 472, 474; Radical, 455–458, 459; Republican rule under, 462–463, 473; retreat from, 472–473; in South, 460–467; white resistance to, 465
Reconstruction Finance Corporation, 704–705, 795
Red Cross, 437, 656, 694, 742
Red River (film), 820
Red Scare: of 1919-1920, 660–661, 684; in Cold War, 776–777, 780–784
Redemption, 456, 465
Redemptioners, 79
Reed, Esther DeBerdt, 173
Reed, Margaret, 358
Reed, Walter, 528
Referendums, 566, 619
Reform. *See also* Social reforms: agrarian, 564–566, 584; civil service, 558–559; electoral, 566, 619, 631–632, 838–839, 914; moral, 285, 289–290; pre–Civil War, 284–301; radical, 293–203; of slavery, from within, 337–338
Reform Darwinistst, 610
Refugees: Alien and Sedition acts and, 204; French, and yellow fever epidemic of 1793, 198; Jewish, in World War II, 728, 743–744
Rehnquist, William, 889, 895
Reid, Whitelaw, 586
Religion: African-American, 89, 178, 179, 250, 289, 337, 343, 464; Calvinist, 22; early nineteenth-century, 285–288; evangelical revivalism, 214, 285–288; evolutionary theory and, 685–686; expansionism and, 584; gospel of wealth, 485–486; Great Awakening, 78, 86–89; in Jeffersonian era, 214; liberal, 285; Mormon, 368–369; Native-American, 8–9, 12, 20, 197–200, 468–469; North-South split in, 338; and party affiliation, 553; Pilgrim, 42; and progressivism, 610–611, 614; Protestant Reformation and, 21–22; Puritan, 43, 44, 55, 56; Quaker, 70; separation of church and state, 171
Religious liberalism, 285
Religious tolerance: after American Revolution, 170–171; Great Awakening and, 89; in Maryland colony, 40–41; in Rhode Island, 47, 48
Remington, Frederic, 591, 826
Removal policy, 269–272
Renaissance, 14
"Rendezvous" system, 360
Republic mill shooting, 713
Republican motherhood, 174, 175
Republican party. *See also specific elections*: and African Americans, 531, 561–562, 635, 716; in Cold War, 780; conservative political revolt and, 837, 838, 839–840; "Contract With America," 840, 931; and Dred Scott decision, 401; and Fair Deal, 778; Goldwater and, 835–836, 837; industrialization platform, 486–487; late nineteenth-century, 552, 553–554, 560, 561–562; morality and, 553–554, 557; National, 265; origin of, 394, 396–398; progressivism and, 619; and Reconstruction, 451–458, 467; in Reconstruction South, 460, 461, 462–463, 465, 467; in 1920s, 689, 690; shift from, 1928-32, 707; shift to, 1960s-80s, 837–841; split during Progressive Era, 625–626; and Treaty of Versailles, 661–662, 664; after World War I, 665–666
Republican party (Jeffersonian), 196, 198, 200–201, 202, 204, 205, 206, 264; in Jefferson administration, 215–217; splintering of, 261, 264, 265; after War of 1812, 236, 261; and War of 1812, 222
Republicanism, 161–162, 174; in Constitution, 182, 184; democratic, 267; under Jefferson, 213, 214–215; "modern," 794, 796
Resumption Act, 558
Revels, Hiram, 461
Revenue Act, 739
Revere, Paul, 100, 121, 131
Reynolds, Maria, 190
Rhee, Syngman, 774, 797
Rhineland, 733
Rhode Island: in American Revolution, 138, 144; and Articles of Confederation, 167; colonial, 47, 48, 74, 109; constitution of, 163; and Constitutional Convention, 179; *Gaspée* incident, 117–118
Ribicoff, Abraham, 861
Rice, 60, 341
Richardson, Ebenezer, 112–113
Richardson, Elliot, 913
Richmond, David, 878
Richmond (Virginia), 335, 338; in Civil War, 418–419, 425, 434, 436, 437, 438; electric trolleys, 525; emancipation in, 448
Ridenhour, Ronald, 869
Ridge, John Rollin, 307
Ridgway, Matthew B., 776
Riesman, David, 812
Right-to-life movement, 896
Rights. *See also* Bill(s) of rights; Civil rights movement; Land rights/distribution; Political rights; Voting rights: human vs. property, 170

The Rights of the Colonies Examined (Hopkins), 106
Riis, Jacob, 521, 528
Riots. *See also* Racial violence; Vigilantism; Violence: anti-Catholic, 391, 394; antiabolitionist, 295; Astor Place, 310; in Confederacy, 425; Democratic convention of 1968, 861; in 1830s-40s, 285, 332; Haymarket, 507, 623; New York draft, 434; in Reconstruction, 454
"Rip It Up" (song), 813
Ripley, George, 302, 305
Ritchie, Thomas, 266
Road construction, 239, 242; interstate highway system, 795–7966; in 1920s, 676; urban, early twentieth-century, 675
Roanoke colony, 24–25
Robber barons, 507
Robinson, Jackie, 537, 804–805, 882
Robinson, Rachel, 805
Rochambeau, Comte de, 152
Rochester (New York), 324
Rock and roll, 813–814
Rockefeller, John D., 427, 485, 487, 489, 490, 660
Rockefeller, Nelson, 834, 835, 862
Rockingham, Marquis of, 110
Rockne, Knute, 539, 678–679
Rocky Mountain Fur Company, 360
Rodney King riots, 930
Roe v. Wade, 895–896
Rogers, Mary, 333
Rogers, Will, 553, 732
Rogers, William, 862
Rogue River Indians, 357
Rolfe, John, 28, 36, 37, 39
Romanticism, death in, 612–613
Rommel, Erwin, 746
Romney, George, 834
Roosevelt, Eleanor, 715, 716, 743, 894
Roosevelt, Franklin D., 705–706. *See also* New Deal; critics of, 711–712, 713, 715; election of 1920, 665; election of 1932, 705, 706; election of 1936, 715; election of 1940, 736; election of 1944, 740; European policy, 734, 735–736; impact of programs, 721–723; and Japan, 732, 736–737; Latin America policy, 730; and minorities, 716, 742, 743; and Supreme Court, 717–720; and Vietnam, 851; and West, 827; and World War II, 735–736, 745, 746, 759; and Yalta Conference, 747–750
Roosevelt, Theodore, 621–622, 914; and African Americans, 626, 633, 635; and big business, 606, 607, 622–623, 626; book by, 354–355; and Chilean crisis, 588; on cowardice, 590; and expansionism, 586; and football, 539; foreign policy, 628–629; on government, 622, 626; on muckrakers, 611; presidency of, 621–623, 914; and Progressive party, 626; and progressivism, 606, 607, 610; in Spanish-American War, 593, 596–597; and Taft, 625–626; on war, 589; on war preparedness, 586; on westward expansion, 469; on Wilson, 648; and World War I, 658
Roosevelt Corollary, 629, 730
Rosenberg, Ethel, 779, 780
Rosenberg, Julius, 779, 780
Ross, Edward Alsworth, 521

Rossetti, Gabriel, 613
Roth, Henry, 721
Rough Riders, 596–597
Rowson, Susanna, 309–310
Royal African Company, 58
Royalists, 114
Roybal, Edward R., 898
Ruckelshaus, William, 913
Rum industry, 78
Rural Electrification Administration, 709
Rural-urban split, in 1920s, 681–684
Rush, Benjamin, 198, 199
Rush-Bagot Agreement, 241
Rushin, Joel, 410
Rushin, Thomas Jefferson, 410
Rusk, Dean, 850
Russell, Charles, 826
Russell, John, 426
Russia. *See also* Soviet Union: emigration from, 519–520; Pacific claims, 241, 365; post-Communist, 925–928; revolution in, 643, 650, 663; Russo-Japanese War, 628; and World War I, 642, 643, 658; and World War I peace settlement, 662, 663
Russian immigrants, 519, 524
Russian Jews, 519–520, 521, 523
Russo-Japanese War, 628
Rustin, Bayard, 883
Ruth, George Herman ("Babe"), 679
Ryan, John A., 611

Sacajewea, 359
Sacco, Nicola, 686–687
Sacco and Vanzetti case, 686–687
sachems, 9
Sadat, Anwar el-, 918
Saddam Hussein, 928, 930
Sadlier, Mary Anne, 307
Sagebrush Rebellion, 839
St. George (Utah), 830
St. Augustine (Florida), 23, 90
St. Leger, Barry, 147–148
Saipan, battle of, 751
Salem witchcraft trials, 74–75
Salinger, J. D., 890
Salinger, Pierre, 850
Salisbury, Lord, 589
Salisbury Cotton Mills, 501
SALT I (Strategic Arms Limitation Treaty), 865
Saltworks, 246
Salutary neglect, 78
Samoa, 585, 586–587, 595
Samoset, 4
Sampson, Deborah, 144
San Antonio (Texas), 355, 364, 366, 367
San Diego (California), 828, 829
San Francisco (California), 356, 378, 892
San Jacinto, battle of, 364, 366
San Jacinto (ship), 426
San Juan Hill, battle of, 597
Sand Creek massacre, 469–470
Sandys, Edwin, 38
Sanger, Margaret, 672, 674–675
Sanger, William, 672
Sanitation, urban, 247–248, 262, 528–529
Santa Anna, Antonio López de, 363–364
Santa Clara County v. The Southern Pacific Railroad, 488
Santa Fe (New Mexico), 355, 372
Santa Fe Trail, 360–361

Saperstein, Abraham, 804, 805
Saratoga, battle of, 146, 149
Sargent, Dudley A., 540
Sauk Indians, 200, 270–271, 307
Savannah streetcar boycott, 572–573
Savings and loan crisis, 924
Scalawags, 460, 461, 462
Scalping, 12, 13
Schechter Poultry Corporation v. United States, 717
Schenck v. United States, 655
Schlafly, Phyllis, 896
Schurz, Carl, 447
Schuyler, Philip, 148
Schwab, Charles, 480
Schwarzkopf, H. Norman, 928
Schwerner, Michael, 886
Scientific agriculture, 499
Scopes, John, 685, 686
Scopes trial, 685, 686
Scots-Irish, 78–79
Scott, Winfield, 279; in Civil War, 418–421; in Mexican-American War, 372, 373, 374
Scranton, William, 834
Screwball comedy, 721
Scriven, Abream, 342
SDS (Students for a Democratic Society), 860
Sea dogs, 22
Secession, 411, 413–414, 417; growth of sentiment for, 387, 389, 406
Second Bull Run, battle of, 422
Second Great Awakening, 285–288
Sedgwick, Catharine, 310
Sedition Act of 1798, 190, 204–205, 215
Sedition Act of 1918, 654
Seduction of the Innocent (Wertham), 785
Seeger, Pete, 857
Segeretti, Donald, 912
Segregation. *See also* Desegregation: de facto, 887; educational, 463, 792, 806, 807, 838, 887; impacts of, 501, 807; in military, 430, 431, 657, 742, 806; in North, 803; *Plessy v. Ferguson* and, 501, 570; progressive defense of, 620, 635; residential, 526–527, 534, 674–675, 803; resistance to, 572–573, 806–810, 878–883, 887; in revolutionary era, 178–179; in 1950s, 803–807; in 1960s, 877, 887; in South, 463, 464, 501, 570, 803, 807, 809, 877; in sports, 537, 804; in Union army, 430, 431; in World War II, 742
Séguin, Erasmo, 366
Séguin, Juan, 307, 366, 367
Seider, Christopher, 113
Selective Service Act (1917), 658
Selma demonstrations, 884
Seminole Indians, 8, 241, 271, 344
Senate, 180, 181. *See also* Congress
Seneca Falls Declaration and Resolutions, 299, 300
Seneca Indians, 148, 197–200
Separatism, black, 885–886
Separatists, 42
Sequoyah, 269
Serapis (ship), 154
Serbia, 641, 934, 935
Settlement house movement, 610, 611, 615–616, 620
Seven Days, battle of the, 422
Seven Pines, battle of, 421

Seven Years' War, 93, 94. *See also* French and Indian War; aftermath of, 101, 102
Seventeenth Amendment, 619, 625
Sewall, Samuel, daughter of, 52
Seward, William H., 389, 398, 401, 412, 414, 426, 460, 468; and foreign expansionism, 582, 584–585
Sex discrimination, 893–894; Supreme Court on, 895–896
Sexual abuse, of slaves, 342
Sexual Politics (Millett), 895
Sexuality: attitudes toward homosexuality, 902–903; sexual revolution of 1920s, 681, 682–683
Sexually transmitted disease, 832
Shafter, William R., 594–595
Shahn, Ben, 686, 711
"Shake, Rattle and Roll" (song), 813–814
Shakers, 299–300, 301
Shakespeare, Joseph, 520
shamans, 9
The Shame of the Cities (Steffens), 611
Sharecropping, 463–464, 708, 709, 716
Sharpsburg, battle of, 410–411, 422–423, 429
Shasta Dam and Reservoir, 827
Shasta Indians, 357
Shaw, Anna Howard, 656
Shaw, Anne, 616
Shaw, Robert Gould, 430–431
Shawnee Indians, 102, 172, 197, 200, 222, 224–225
Shays, Daniel, 169
Shays's rebellion, 169–170, 179
Sheehan, Neil, 853
Shelley v. Kraemer, 803
Sheppard, Horatio David, 309
Sheridan, Philip, 447
Sherman, William Tecumseh, 370, 418, 446, 582; march through South, 436, 437–438, 447, 450
Sherman Antitrust Act, 561, 622, 624
Sherman Silver Purchase Act, 561, 567
Shiloh, battle of, 424
Shipbuilding, 68
Shippen, Nancy, 160–161
Shippen, William, 160
Sicilians, 520
Sierra Club, 622, 839, 903
Sierra Leone, 294
Sigourney, Lydia, 309
Silent Spring (Carson), 903
Silver, 550, 558, 561, 571
Simmons, William Joseph, 687
Simms, William Gilmore, 309, 338
Simpson, "Sockless" Jerry, 563
Sinclair, Upton, 611, 623
"Sinners in the Hands of an Angry God" (Edwards), 87
Sioux Indians, 200, 357, 468, 469, 470–471
Sister Carrie (Dreiser), 532
Sit-ins, 878–879
Sitting Bull, 470, 471
Sixteenth Amendment, 624–625, 627
Skelly, Jack, 537
Skyscrapers, 526, 673
Slader, Matthew, 85
Slater, Samuel, 324
Slave codes, 339; reform of, 337–338
Slave narratives, 307
Slave power conspiracy, 384–385

Slave rebellions, 60, 338, 344; in Haiti, 218, 250, 251, 344; Vesey conspiracy, 250–251, 274, 344

Slave trade, 15, 36, 56–58, 59, 178, 388, 389; end of, 294; growth of, 78, 79; in New Spain, 19; passage in, 57, 80–81

Slavery, 36–37, 56–60, 339–344, 386, 387–388. *See also* Slaves; in American Revolution, 134–138, 144; and California statehood, 385–386; in Caribbean, 42, 57, 58, 344; in colonies, 36, 37, 41–42, 58, 90; and Compromise of 1850, 385–389; congressional debates on, 249–252, 264, 376–377; and Constitution, 180–181; and Dred Scott decision, 400–401; and Emancipation Proclamation, 429; expansion bans, 172, 181, 249–252, 376–377; expansion in South, 320, 386, 387; expansion schemes, radical southern, 338–339; expansion westward, 376–377, 385–389, 396–398, 400–401, 412; and Fugitive Slave Law, 389–391; Hamilton's economic plans and, 195; Jefferson and, 172, 178; and Kansas, 396, 398–399, 401; manumission from, 178, 338; and Mexican-American War, 376; and Missouri crisis, 248–252; Native American, 19, 42, 357; in New Spain, 19, 20, 57, 58; in North, 55, 58, 175, 294; and nullification debate, 273–274; opposition to, 70 (*See also* Abolitionism); origins of, 56–58; reenslavement, 346; reform of, 337–338; revitalization, 1790s-1810, 320; and revolutionary ideology, 175; in 1700s, 78, 79; 1750s-1830s, 294; slave codes and, 337–338, 339–340; slave ownership, 331, 334, 336, 388; slave power conspiracy theory, 384–385; in South, 58–60, 294, 320, 339–344; and southern economy, 334–336; southern views of, 336; and Texas annexation, 364–365; and Wilmot Proviso, 376–377

Slaves. *See also* Slavery: in American Revolution, 134–138, 144; conscription of, 436; cultural expression, 343; emancipation of, 447–450; family life, 342–343; fugitive, 296, 298, 389–391, 400–401; legal status of, 339–340; lives of, 58–60, 339, 340–344; material conditions of, 341–342; medical care, 392–393; population growth, 59, 294, 320; punishments and tortures of, 337, 339–340, 341; religion of, 89, 337, 343; resistance of, 60, 343–344, 345; work of, 340–341

Slidell, John, 371, 426
Sloan, Alfred, 675, 676
Sloan, John, 533
Sloat, John D., 372
Sloughter, Henry, 76
Smallpox, 528
Smith, Adam, 486
Smith, Alfred E., 611, 619, 690, 691
Smith, Andrew, 538
Smith, Bessie, 678
Smith, Daniel E., 466
Smith, Francis, 131, 132, 134
Smith, Hoke, 572, 619
Smith, Jacob H., 600
Smith, James L., 392
Smith, Jedediah, 360
Smith, John, 4, 27, 28

Smith, Joseph, Jr., 368, 369
Smith, Lucy Wilmot, 615
Smith, Mamie, 678
Smith, Russell, 246
Smith, Wendell, 804
Smith-Connally Act, 739
Smithsonian Institution, 757–759
Smog, 831
Smothers Brothers Comedy Hour (TV show), 857
Smythe, Thomas, 37, 38
Snake Indians, 357
SNCC (Student Nonviolent Coordinating Committee), 878, 886
Snyder Act, 472
Sobell, Morton, 779
Social class: in Civil War, 425–426, 427; in colonies, 80–83; in North, pre–Civil War, 329–331; in Reconstruction, 464; and social mobility, 330–331, 510; in South, 85; and sport, 537; and urban neighborhoods, 526–527
Social control, in progressivism, 615, 620
Social criticism, in 1950s, 811–813, 814, 890–891
Social Darwinism, 485, 552, 583; rejection of, 610, 614
Social Gospel movement, 610–611
Social mobility, 330–331, 510
Social organization. *See also* Social class: colonial, 51–54, 80–83; Native American, 6, 9; in Spanish colonies, 19–20; urban, in 1830s, 332; of white South, 334
Social reforms: pre–Civil War, 290–293; in Progressive Era, 608–628, 631–635, 655–656; in 1920s, 690; in World War I, 655–656
Social sciences, 609–610
Social Security, 713, 714, 716, 721, 778
Social service programs. *See also* New Deal: Fair Deal (Truman), 778; in Great Depression, 704–705; Great Society (Lyndon B. Johnson), 836, 854, 871, 887–889; welfare, in 1920s, 690
Socialist Labor party, 568
Socialist party, 569, 619, 626, 665; repression of, 654, 655
Sociology, 610; Christian, 610–611
Soil Conservation Service, 709, 903
Soldiers. *See also* Veterans: African-American, 429–431, 436, 593, 599, 635, 657, 687, 742; Civil War, occupations of, 427; Continental, 144, 146, 171, 172; Japanese American, 744–745; Mexican American, 743; in Vietnam War, 857–858, 860, 868
Solomon Islands, battle of, 751
Sometimes a Great Notion (Kesey), 839
Somme offensive, 644–645, 658–659
Somohalla, Chief, 468
Sonntag, W. Louis, Jr., 525, 526
Sons of Liberty, 108, 109
The Souls of Black Folks (Du Bois), 617
"The Sources of Soviet Conduct" (Kennan), 770–771
Sousa, John Philip, 590
South. *See also* Black suffrage; Civil rights movement; Segregation; Slavery; *specific states and colonies*: abolitionism in, 175–178, 320, 336–337; agriculture in, 498–501, 562–567, 564–566, 824–825; air-conditioning and, 822–823; after American Revolution, 168; in American Revolution, 134–138, 144, 150–153; backcountry fighting, 286–287; Black Codes, 453–454; black emigration from, 657; Brown's raid and, 405, 406; after Civil War, 426–427, 447–451, 494, 498–502 (*See also* Reconstruction); before Civil War, 331–339; in Civil War, 415–421, 424–426, 429, 436–438, 447, 450; distinctive identity of, 320–321, 331–339, 346–347, 500, 825; economy of, 334–336, 338, 425, 426–427, 447, 494, 500–502, 822–825, 823; election of 1860 in, 412–413; free blacks in, 338, 344–345, 346; in Great Depression, 703, 718; improved race relations in, 823–824; industrialization, 334, 335, 417, 500–501, 502, 823; late nineteenth-century, 500–502, 561, 562–567; migration to, 823, 824, 825, 837, 838; nationalism of, 336, 338–339; "New South," 500–502, 822–825; northern view of, 320–321, 322, 331; party loyalties in, 838; pastimes, 84–85; plantation legend, 331; political power of, 451, 822, 837–839; poor whites, 388, 462, 463, 464, 501; Populism in, 566–567; poverty in, 501–502, 718, 822; in Progressive Era, 617, 619, 620; Reconstruction in, 453–454, 460–467, 473 (*See also* Reconstruction); religion in, 88–89, 171; secession of, 411, 413–414, 417; tariff opposition in, 265–266; tensions with North, 248–252, 346–347, 385–391, 396–406; urbanization in, 824–825; War of 1812 in, 226–227; after World War I, 660, 687, 822–825; after World War II, 822–825

South Carolina. *See also* Charleston: in American Revolution, 138, 151, 152; civil rights movement in, 879; Civil War and, 414, 429, 430–431, 438; free blacks in, 344, 345, 346; and nullification crisis, 273–274; Reconstruction in, 461, 463, 465; resistance to British, 120; secesssion of, 413–414; settlement of, 42, 43; slaves and slavery in, 42, 59, 60, 175–178, 273, 346; and Tariff of Abominations, 266; women's rights in, 894

Southern Agrarians, 720

Southwest: exploration of, 359; Mexican Americans in, 374–376; Native Americans of, 357; and Santa Fe Trail, 360–361; Spanish, 355–356

Soviet Union, 926. *See also* Cold War; in Afghanistan, 920, 922, 923; and American communism, 764, 765; and bombing of Japan, 752, 753, 754; collapse of communism in, 925, 926–927; détente with, 918; and Eastern Europe, 746, 748, 750, 766–767, 768, 799, 800, 923, 925; and Germany, in 1930s, 733; under Gorbachev, 922–923, 925, 926; in Great Depression, 701; under Khrushchev, 798–799; Reagan and, 921–922; recognition of, 734; SALT I and, 865; space program, 800, 801; after Stalin, 785–786; under Stalin, 701, 764, 765, 766; U-2 spy plane crash, 802; U.S. view of, 769, 779; and Vietnam, 870; and World War II, 735, 736, 745–748, 750, 756, 766

Space program, 800–801, 927

Spain: in American Revolution, 146, 150, 154; and Burr's conspiracy, 219–220; civil war, 732; conflicts with French and English, 22–23; and Cuba, 395, 590–591, 592; in imperial wars, 90, 91; Inquisition in, 218; and Louisiana territory, 218; and Mississippi River boundary, 201–202; as nation-state, 15; and New Spain, 16, 18, 19, 23, 241; New World exploration, 15, 16–18, 20; and Pacific Northwest, 365; in slave trade, 57; and Spanish-American War, 593–595, 597, 600; trade with, 169; and War of 1812, 226–227; western territories, 355–356

Spanish-American War, 586, 593–595; events leading to, 590–593; Rough Riders in, 596–597; settlement following, 595, 598, 600

Spanish Armada, defeat of, 23
Spargo, John, 611
Special Field Order 15, 450
Spencer, Herbert, 485, 583
Spies, August, 507
Spiritualism, 313
Spirituals, 343
Spock, Benjamin, 811
Spoils system, 268, 558
Sports: as anticommunist measure, 785; exclusion in, 537–540; integration of, 804–805; late nineteenth-century, 534–540; Native American, 9; Puritan, 84; in 1920s, 678–679; scandals of 1950s in, 785; in South, 84–85
Spotsylvania Courthouse, battle of, 436
Sprague, Frank, 525
Sputnik, 800, 801, 927
Squanto (Tisquantum), 4–5
"Square Deal," 623
Stag at Starkey's (Bellows), 532
Stagecoach (film), 827
Stagecoaches, 242
Stagflation, 916–917
Stalin, Joseph, 701, 765; and atomic bomb, 767–768; and Berlin airlift, 772; and bombing of Japan, 752, 754; death of, 785, 798; and Germany, 765, 767; mentality of, 766, 769, 771; and Poland, 767; U.S. image of, 765, 769; and World War II, 745, 746, 747; and Yalta Conference, 747–750
Stalwarts, 554, 558
Stamp Act, 105–106, 111; resistance to, 106–111
Stamp Act Congress, 109–110
Standard Oil Company, 490, 632
Standish, Miles, 13, 43
Stanton, Edwin M., 429, 457, 458
Stanton, Elizabeth Cady, 285, 299, 345, 429, 458, 459, 556
"The Star-Spangled Banner" (Key), 226
Stark, John, 149
Starr, Kenneth, 932
Starr Report, 932; White House rebuttal to, 933
"Stars and Stripes Forever" (Sousa), 590
State Department, U.S.: and expansionist policy, 584–585; McCarthy's attacks on, 780; trimming of, 581
State governments: and Bill of Rights, 455; first, 162–163; in Gilded Age, 556; in Progressive Era, 619–621; in Reconstruction, 451, 452, 453, 456, 457, 461–463, 465, 473; western land claims, 165; and women's suffrage, 556

States rights: and Alien and Sedition acts, 205; after American Revolution, 163; in Articles of Confederation, 164, 166; Calhoun and, 236, 237; after Civil War, 451; and Confederacy, 414, 425, 426; *McCulloch v. Maryland* and, 239, 240; nullification and, 266, 272, 273–274

States' Rights Democratic party (Dixiecrats), 778
Statue of Liberty, 517
Steam power, 242–245
Steaming Streets (Bellows), 533
Steel industry, 480, 481, 490, 491, 713
Steffens, Lincoln, 595, 611
Stein, Gertrude, 680–681
Steinbeck, John, 721
Steinem, Gloria, 895
Stella, Frank, 680
Stephens, Alexander H., 453
Sterns, Charles, 459
Stevens, Edward, 199
Stevens, John L., 588
Stevens, Thaddeus, 428, 451, 452, 472, 582
Stevens, Wallace, 680
Stevenson, Adlai, 794
Stevenson, Robert Louis, 543
Stewart, A. T., 544
Stieglitz, Alfred, 533
Stimson, Henry L., 767
Stock market crash of 1929, 691–694, 704; boom preceding, 692–693
Stockton, Robert F., 372
Stoddard, Solomon, 86
Stone, Lucy, 458
Stoneham, Horace, 829
Stonewall Inn raid, 902
Stono uprising, 60
Storyville (New Orleans), 534
Stowe, Harriet Beecher, 176, 305, 307, 341–342, 390–391
Strategic Arms Limitation Treaty (SALT I), 865
Strict construction, 194
Strikes. *See* Labor protest
Strode, Woody, 805
Strong, Josiah, 584
Stroyer, Jacob, 342
Stuart, Gilbert, 308
Stuart, John, 150
Stuart monarchy, 40, 41
Student Nonviolent Coordinating Committee (SNCC), 878, 886
Students, in 1960s, 858–861, 863–864, 890–891
Students for a Democratic Society (SDS), 860, 890, 891
Studs Lonigan trilogy (Farrell), 721
Stuyvesant, Peter, 69
Suburbs, 803, 810–812; flight to, 526, 675, 795, 810
Sudan, 935
Suez crisis, 799–800
Suffolk Resolves, 121
Sugar Act (Revenue Act), 104, 106
Sullivan, Bridget, 516
Sullivan, John, 148
Sullivan, John L., 536–537, 590
Sumner, Charles, 398–399, 428, 452, 458, 472; and anti-expansionism, 580–581, 582
Sumner, William Graham, 485, 552

The Sun Also Rises (Hemingway), 681
Sunbelt migration, 823, 824, 825, 829, 837–838
Sunday, Women Drying Their Hair (Sloan), 533
Supreme Court, U.S. *See also* Judicial branch: black suffrage and, 473, 570; business and, 488, 560, 561, 622; campaign finance and, 914; civil liberties and, 427, 457, 473, 655, 889; court-packing scheme, 717, 720; expansion of powers, 215, 216, 239–240; gay rights and, 903; Jackson and, 276; and judicial review, 216; labor and, 610, 689; Native American sovereignty and, 902; New Deal and, 717–720; in Progressive Era, 622, 628; railroad regulation and, 560, 564, 622; and Reconstruction, 457, 473; in 1960s and '70s, 889; segregation and, 501, 570, 806–807, 887, 889; sex discrimination and, 895–896; slavery and, 400–401
Sussex (ship), 647
Sutter, John A., 377, 379
Swann v. Charlotte-Mecklenburg Board of Education, 887
Sweatt v. Painter, 806–807
Swift, Gustavus, 492–493
Swift, Henry, 107
Syphilis, 718–719

Taft, Robert A., 794, 834
Taft, William Howard, 523, 536, 635; as Chief Justice, 689; foreign policy, 629, 630; presidency of, 623–626
Taft-Hartley Act, 777
Taiwan, 773
Talleyrand, Charles Maurice de, 203
Tallmadge, James, 249
Talmadge, Eugene, 806
Tammany Hall machine, 618–619
Taney, Roger B., 276, 400, 427
Taos (New Mexico), 374
Tappan, Arthur, 296
Tappan, Lewis, 296
Tarbell, Ida, 611
Tariff(s): of Abominations, 265; in John Quincy Adams' administration, 265–266; Civil War-era, 426; and Cleveland administration, 560–561; Dingley, 574–575; Fordney-McCumber, 693; and Great Depression, 693–694, 701; Hamilton's plan for, 195; Hawley-Smoot, 693; and Jacksonian nullification disputes, 272, 273–274; late nineteenth-century, 487, 561, 575, 588; McKinley, 561, 588; and Panic of 1819, 248; Payne-Aldrich, 625; Underwood, 627, 632; after War of 1812, 238; Wilson-Gorman, 567
Tarzan of the Apes (Burroughs), 679–680
Tatum, Goose, 804
Tax revolts, 839
Taxation. *See also* Tariff(s): under Articles of Confederation, 164, 166–167; in colonies, 104, 105–111; corporate, 619, 739; Hamilton's plan for, 194, 197; income, 627, 633, 653; Jefferson's policy of, 215; Reagan and, 921; Stamp Act, 104, 105–111; on tea, 117, 119; Townshend Duties, 111–117, 119; and Whiskey Rebellion, 197; in World War II, 739

Taxi Driver (film), 867
Taylor, Frederick, 505
Taylor, Marshall W. ("Major"), 537
Taylor, Maxwell, 856
Taylor, William Graham, 610
Taylor, Zachary, 278–279, 296, 377; in Mexican-American War, 371, 372; and slave power conspiracy theory, 384; and slavery expansion question, 389
Tea Act, 119
Teapot Dome scandal, 690
Technics and Civilization (Mumford), 720
Technology: agricultural, 246, 499; early American, 244–245, 246; late nineteenth-century, 482–484, 499, 524–526; naval, and European exploration, 14; urban, 524–526
Tecumseh, 223, 224–225
Teheran Conference, 746
Tejanos, 364, 366–367, 375, 376
Telegraph, 245
Telephones, 483
Television: civil rights movement and, 808, 810; Cold War and, 927; Kefauver committee hearings and, 782; Kennedy assassination and, 851; Kennedy-Nixon debates, 847–848; in 1950s, 810, 812, 892
Teller Amendment, 593
Temperance movement. *See also* Prohibition: nineteenth-century, 289, 290, 562; twentieth-century, 614, 620, 621, 655
Temperance Society of the Methodist Episcopal Church, 614
Temple Mound Builders, 7
Ten Commandments (film), 678
10 percent plan, 451–452
Ten Years' War, 590
Tenant farmers, 499, 708–709, 716
Tenements, 527, 529; dumbbell, 528
Tennent, Gilbert, 86, 87–88
Tennessee: Civil War in, 422–424, 435; Indian wars in, 197; Andrew Jackson and, 267; Mexican-American War and, 373; Reconstruction in, 451, 452, 456; settlement of, 171, 172, 192; slavery and, 336
Tennessee Valley Authority, 708, 709, 903
Tenochtitlán, 6, 17–18
Tenskwatawa (Laulewasika), 222, 224–225
Tenure of Office Act, 456–457, 458
Terán, Manuel de Mier y, 363
Tesla, Nikola, 484
Test Act, 78
Tet offensive, 856–857
Texas: American claims to, 241; American settlement of, 357, 362, 363, 364; annexation of, 364–365; border dispute, 371, 374; Mexicans in, 364, 366–367, 375, 376; under Mexico, 363–364; Spanish, 355, 363
Texas Revolution, 364, 366–367; and the Alamo, 364, 366
Texas (ship), 594
Texas v. White, 457
Textile industry: growth of, 324–325; mills, 234, 235, 324–326, 327, 501, 608; in 1920s, 677; in South, 501
Thames River, battle of, 223, 225
Theater, pre–Civil War, 310
Theory of the Leisure Class (Veblen), 610
Third World, Eisenhower's policies in, 801
Thirteenth Amendment, 447, 453, 455, 458

"This land is your land, this land is my land" ("God Blessed America") (Guthrie), 700
Thomas, Lorenzo, 457
Thompson, Hugh, Jr., 869
Thompson, Hugh Miller, 528
Thomson, Charles, 121, 123
Thoreau, Henry David, 302–303, 612, 809
Thorpe, Jim, 537
Thurmond, J. Strom, 778
Tibbets, Paul, 753
Tijerina, Reies Lopez, 898
Tilden, Samuel J., 472–473, 557
Till, Emmett, murder of, 793–794, 808
Tillman, "Pitchfork Ben," 565, 595
Timber, 68
Timber and Stone Act, 495
Timber Culture Act, 495
Time, changing concepts of, 503–504
Tinian, 751
Tippecanoe, battle of, 222
Tisquantum (Squanto), 4–5
Tituba, 76
Tlaloc, 7
Tobacco, 30, 37, 38; antismoking campaigns, 685; cigarette industry, 500–501, 685, 826; glut, trade policy and, 68, 73; and Jamestown colony, 28
Tocqueville, Alexis de, 244
Tojo, Hideki, 737
Toledo, progressive government in, 619
Toltecs, 6
Tompkins, Sally L., 437
Toombs, Robert, 387
Toomer, Jean, 689
Topeka (Kansas), 685
Tory, 122
Total war, in Civil War, 436–438
Tourism: in Sunbelt, 823; in West, 823, 831
Toussaint Louverture, 218
Townsend, Francis, 711, 712, 715
Townshend, Charles, 111, 116
Townshend Duties, 111, 116–117; resistance to, 111–117; on tea, 117, 119
Tracy, Benjamin F., 585
Trade. *See also* Fur trade; Slave trade; Tariff(s): after American Revolution, 168–169; colonial, 28–29, 37, 67–68, 73, 77–78, 101–102, 103, 112; colonial boycotts, 110, 114–115, 121–122; Dutch, 28, 69, 74; embargo, Jeffersonian era, 221; Europe-Africa, 57; Europe-Orient, 11–14; and expansionism, 584–585; and Great Depression, 693–694, 701; interstate, federal power over, 240; and Jamestown colony, 28; and mercantilism, 67–68, 77–78; Navigation Acts and, 68, 73, 77; on Santa Fe Trail, 360–361; smuggling, 101–102, 103, 112; Townshend Duties and, 111–117
Trade associations, 690
Traders, 360
Transcendentalism, 302–305
Transportation: desegregation of, 572–573, 808–810; early nineteenth-century, 239, 242–244, 335; interstate highway system, 795–796; urban, late nineteenth-century, 525–526
Trappers, 360
Travis, Joseph, 344

Travis, William Barrett, 364, 366
Treason, 220
Treaty of Aix-la-Chapelle, 91
Treaty of Alliance, 149
Treaty of Amity and Commerce, 149
Treaty of Ghent, 227
Treaty of Greenville, 197
Treaty of Guadalupe Hidalgo, 374, 375, 376
Treaty of Kanagawa, 395
Treaty of Paris of 1763, 101, 102
Treaty of Paris of 1899, 595, 598, 600
Treaty of Ryswick, 89
Treaty of San Lorenzo, 202
Treaty of Tordesillas, 16, 20
Treaty of Utrecht, 90
Treaty of Versailles, 661–664; ratification struggle, 664–665
Trenchard, John, 117
Trent (ship), 426
Trenton, battle of, 143, 144
Trevelyan, Charles Philips, 527
Triangle fire, 620
Trist, Nicholas, 374
Trotter, William Monroe, 618
True Grit (film), 821
Truman, Harry S, 740, 751–754; and atomic bombing of Japan, 752–756; atomic policy, postwar, 767, 772; and China, 773, 854; Cold War rhetoric of, 768–770, 773, 779; and Eastern Europe, 750; economy under, 777; Fair Deal, 778; foreign policy, 766, 767–776, 797–798; and Korean War, 775, 776; and labor, 777; and organized crime, 782; racial reforms, 806; and Stalin, 766, 767–768; and Vietnam, 851
Truman Doctrine, 769–770, 773–774
Trumbull, John, 308
Trusts, 490, 492, 622–623. *See also* Antitrust legislation; Big business
Truth, Sojourner, 284, 742
Tuberculosis, 612–613
Tubman, Harriet, 296, 297
Tucker, Nathaniel Beverly, 338
Tudor monarchy, 21
Tugwell, Rexford, 708
Turkey, aid to, 769–770
Turner, Joe, 813
Turner, Nat, 344
Tuscarora Indians, 148
Tuskegee Airmen, 742
Tuskegee Institute, 500, 617, 718
Tuskegee syphilis study, 718–719
Twain, Mark (Samuel Langhorne Clemens), 286, 310, 535, 551, 558; as anti-imperialist, 595, 598, 599
Twelfth Amendment, 206, 264
Twenty-fourth Amendment, 884
Twining, David, 72
Tyler, Elizabeth, 687
Tyler, John, 277, 365

U-2 spy plane, 802
U-boats, 647
Uncle Tom's Cabin (Stowe), 307, 341, 390, 391
Underground railroad, routes, 387
Underwood Tariff, 627, 632
Uneeda Biscuits, 677
Unemployment: African-American, 877, 878; in Great Depression, 701; relief programs, 569, 694, 710–711, 713; in 1950s, 795; in 1970s, 916–917

Union army. *See also specific battles*: African Americans in, 429–431; conscription, 434; disease in, 411, 437; soldier occupations, 427; troop strength, 419, 421
Unitarianism, 285, 336
United Auto Workers, 713
United Farm Workers Union, 901
United Mine Workers, 606, 607, 632, 660, 777
United Nations, 775, 796, 928, 935
United States v. E. C. Knight Co., 561, 622
Universal Negro Improvement Association, 688
Universities, 293; African Americans in, 464; anti-Vietnam War movement in, 858–860, 863–864; black studies in, 886, 887; desegregation of, 880; in early twentieth century, 609; founding of, 88, 338; revolt against formalism, in 1920s, 609–610; in 1960s, 890; women in, 609, 896–897
University of California at Berkeley, 890, 891
University of Mississippi, 880
Unsafe at Any Speed (Nader), 876
Unskilled workers, 326, 327, 330–331, 522, 655
Urban planning, 528–529, 675
Urbanization: early nineteenth-century, 246–248, 323, 330, 332, 335; early twentieth-century, 673–675; late nineteenth-century, 524–530; in South, 335, 336, 824–825; in World War II, 741
U.S. Steel Corporation, 626, 692, 713; formation of, 480, 481, 491
U.S. v. Debs, 655
U.S.A. (Dos Passos), 721
Utah, 370, 374
Utilities, 619, 620, 677, 709, 713
Utopian communities, 299–301, 305

Valentino, Rudolph, 678
Vallandigham, Clement L., 428
Valley Forge, 128, 129, 149
Van Buren, Martin, 258, 260, 264, 266, 277, 377; and Panic of 1837, 275, 276
Van Devanter, Willis, 720
van Twiller, Wouter, 69
Vandenberg, Arthur, 736, 769
Vanderbilt, Cornelius, 490, 510
Vanguard (satellite), 800, 801
Vann, John Paul, 856
Vanzetti, Bartolomeo, 686–687
vaqueros, 355, 495
Vardaman, James K., 619, 620–621
Vassar College, 298
Vause, Agatha, 55
Veblen, Thorstein, 610
Venezuela boundary dispute, 589, 629
Veracruz, siege of, 631
Verdun, battle of, 643
Vergennes, Comte de, 146, 147, 149
Vermont, 320
Verrazzano, Giovanni da, 20
Vertical integration, 490
Vesey, Denmark, conspiracy of, 250–251, 274, 344
Vesey, Joseph, 250
Vespucci, Amerigo, 16
Veterans: African-American, violence against, 660, 687; Bonus Army, 706; Continental army, 165, 167–168, 171, 172; GI Bill of Rights, 740; 1935 peace march, 730; of Vietnam War, 867; of World War II, and *Enola Gay* exhibit, 757–759
Vickers, George, 458
Vicksburg (Mississippi), siege of, 424, 435
Vietnam: cultural beliefs, 846–847; history of, 851; postwar, 867–871
Vietnam War, 847, 851–871; end of, 866–867; financial costs/financing of, 915; foreign policy impact of, 917–918; Gulf of Tonkin incident, 854–855; Johnson and, 853–857, 871; Kennedy's escalation of, 852–853; legacy of, 867–871; My Lai massacre, 858, 868–869; national division over, 857–862, 863–864; Nixon and, 862–864, 866, 869, 871; presidential powers and, 914; start of, 851–852; student opposition to, 891; Tet offensive, 856–857; U.S. troop levels, 865; Vietnamization policy, 863–864
Vietnamization, 863–864
Vigilantism. *See also* Violence: colonial, 112–113; in South, 569–570; in West, 496–497; after World War I, 660–661
Vikings, 10
Villa, Pancho, 631
Vinland, 10, 11
Vinson, Fred M., 807
Violence. *See also* Racial violence; Riots: as antislavery strategy, 296–297, 404, 405; against Communists, 660; in early nineteenth century, 284–285, 286–287, 332–333; in 1890s, 589–590; election, 332, 465, 861; in football, 538–539; frontier, 496–497; against German Americans, 654; against informers, in American Revolution, 112–113; labor, 506–507, 567–569, 713, 900–901; lynching, 285, 465, 466, 569, 570, 571, 621, 654, 660; as tool to transform society, in 1960s, 891; in Vietnam antiwar protests, 863–864; after World War I, 660–661
Virgin Islands, 582
Virginia: in American Revolution, 134–138, 138, 144, 153; in Civil War, 421–422, 436, 438; constitution of, 163; and Constitution (U.S.), 183; in early republic, 170–171, 205, 206; Roanoke colony, 24–25; slavery in, 134–138, 178, 336–337; Stamp Act resistance, 109; Turner rebellion, 344; western land claims, 165
Virginia colony, 26–28, 37–40. *See also* Chesapeake colonies; Bacon's rebellion, 73–74; conflict with French, 91–92; family life, 51; life expectancies, 50–51; slavery in, 36, 37, 58
Virginia Company, 25–28, 37, 38, 40, 42
Virginia Declaration of Rights, 170–171
Virginia Plan, 180
Virginia Resolutions, 109
Virginia (ship), 425
Virtual representation, 105
Volstead Act, 656
von Braun, Wernher, 801
von Steuben, Friedrich, 149
Voting rights: African American (*See* Black suffrage); in Constitution, 181; expansion of, early nineteenth-century, 259; and Fifteenth Amendment, 455, 459; in first state constitutions, 163, 164; in Plymouth colony, 42; and property ownership, 73, 259; for women, 163, 164, 259–260, 299, 458–459, 462–463, 556, 616, 617, 619, 655, 656, 684
Voting Rights Act of 1965, 884, 885, 888, 889

Wabash, St. Louis & Pacific Railway Company v. Illinois, 560, 564
Wade, Benjamin, 428, 452
Wade-Davis Bill, 452
Wages: at Ford, 676; late nineteenth-century, 502, 503, 506; male *vs.* female, 893; pre–Civil War era, 325, 326, 327; in World War II, 739
Wagner, Robert F., 611
Wagner Act (National Labor Relations Act), 712–713, 720, 721, 900
Walden Pond, 303–304
Walker, David, 294
Walker, Freeman, 249
Walker, Patrick, 115
Walker, Quok, 175
Walker, William, 338
Wallace, George, 861–862
Wallace, George C., 823, 837, 880, 891
Wallace, Henry, 709
Wambaugh, Joseph, 821
Wampanoag Indians, 49, 899
Wanamaker, John, 530, 544
War(s). *See also specific wars*: European, in Americas, 66–67, 89–95; glorification of, 590, 596; preparedness for, 585, 586, 647–648
War dogs, 13
War Hawks, 222, 236
War Industries Board, 652
War Labor Board, 739
War of 1812, 222–228; financial issues after, 237; significance of, 227–228
War of the Austrian Succession, 91
War of Jenkins's Ear, 91
War of the League of Augsburg, 89
War of the Spanish Succession, 90
"War on Poverty," 888–889
War Powers Act, 871, 914
The War Prayer (Twain), 599
War Production Board, 738
War Refugee Board, 744
War Relocation Authority, 744
Ward, Artemus, 310
Ward, John Montgomery, 535–536
Ward, Lester Frank, 610
Warfare: in American Revolution, 136–137; in Civil War, 432, 433, 436–438; Native American *vs.* European, 12–13; in Philippines independence struggle, 599–600; in Vietnam War, 858–859, 860, 868–869; in World War I, 642–643, 644–645
Warmouth, Henry C., 463
Warner, Charles Dudley, 551, 558
Warner, Susan, 309, 310
Warren, Earl, 807, 889
Warren, Fuller, 782
Warren, Joseph, 118, 121, 134, 137
Warren, William, 115, 116
Wars of the Roses, 15
Washington, Booker T., 500, 570, 572, 617, 618, 633, 635, 687
Washington, D.C., 194, 202–203; burning of, 223, 226; growth of, 741; 1963

march on, 883; race riots of 1960s, 887; slavery question in, 388, 389
Washington, George: in American Revolution, 141–142, 147, 153; and Citizen Genêt Affair, 197; and Constitutional Convention, 180, 181, 182; and Continental army, 128, 129, 132, 133, 144, 149, 150, 152; death of, 206–207; Farewell Address, 202; First Continental Congress and, 121; at forts Necessity and Duquesne, 92–93, 95; French Revolution and, 196, 197; and Jay's Treaty, 201; and Newburgh conspiracy, 167, 168; presidency of, 193, 195–202; and presidential powers, 193; and quasi war with France, 204; and Quebec Act, 120; on Shays's rebellion, 170; and Phillis Wheatley, 160; and Whiskey Rebellion, 197, 200
Washington, Kenny, 805
Washingtonian movement, 290
Water supplies: urban, 528, 529; in West, 622, 827, 830, 831
Watergate scandal, 912–914
Watson, Elkanah, 84
Watson, Tom, 522, 567, 569, 571, 574
Watts riots, 887
Wayles, John, 190
Wayne, Anthony, 197, 200, 224
Wayne, John (Marion Michael Morrison), 820–821, 826, 827, 830
Wealth. *See also* Economic stratification: of governing elites, pre-/post-Revolution, 162, 163
The Wealth of Nations (Smith), 486
Weathermen, 891
Weaver, James B., 558, 566, 567
Webb, Frank, 307
Webb-Kenyon Act, 627
Webster, Daniel, 237–238, 272, 273, 274, 277, 311, 374, 389
Webster-Ashburton Treaty, 365
Weed, Thurlow, 260
Weeks, Sinclair, 795
Welch, Joseph, 781
Weld, Theodore, 295
Welfare capitalism, 701
Welles, Gideon, 420
Wells, H. G., 526
Wells, Ida B. (Ida Wells-Barnett), 570, 571, 615, 618
Wertham, Frederic, 785
West: agrarian movements in, 564–566; agriculture in, 494–500, 562–567; conservative political revolt in, 837–838; early images of, 359–360; economic growth in, 494–500, 828, 829–834; exploration of, 359–360; federal government and, 495, 827–828, 829; frontier violence in, 496–497; mythical image of, 821, 825–827; and political parties, 838–839; political power shift to, 822, 837–839; population growth, 825, 837, 838; Populism in, 566–567; problems and benefits of growth in, 830–831; Spanish, 355–356; tourism in, 823; view of easterners, 821, 822, 827; women's suffrage in, 619
West, Mae, 721
West Point scandal, 785
West Virginia, creation of, 421
West Virginia (ship), 737
Western Europe, Marshall Plan, 770

Westerns, 826–827
Westinghouse, George, 483, 484
Westmoreland, William, 856, 857
Weston, Thomas, 42
Westward expansion: in Far West, 358–362, 494–500; gold rush and, 377–379; Kansas and Nebraska, 396, 398; manifest destiny and, 362–363; and Mexican-American War, 372; by Mormons, 368–370; mountain men, 360; and Native Americans, 357–358, 468–472, 494; in Old Northwest (Ohio country), 172, 224–225, 238–239; and Plains Indians, 357, 468–472; in popular culture, 354–355; and Proclamation of 1763, 103–104; and public land policy, 272; after Revolution, 165, 169, 171–172, 197; and slavery question, 172, 181, 249–252, 376–377, 386–389, 396–398, 400–401, 412; Texas, 362–365; trail life, 361–362; trails in, 360–361; after War of 1812, 224–225, 238–239
Weyler y Nicolau, Valeriano, 590, 591
Wheatley, Phillis, 160, 161, 175
Wheeling (West Virginia), 258
Wheelwright, John, 48
Whigs, 117, 258, 261, 277–279, 296, 332; decline of, 391, 394, 396; election of 1856, 399, 400; in England, 141; and slavery expansion issue, 386, 387, 389
Whipper, William, 462–463
Whiskey Rebellion, 197, 200
White, Hugh Lawson, 277
White, John, 25
White, Peregrine, 52
White, Richard, 828
White, Susanna, 52
White, William Allen, 611, 619
White Cap movement, 497
White House, 203, 204
White Plague, 612–613
"White slavery," 683
White Squadron, 585
Whitefield, George, 87
Whitman, Marcus, 368
Whitman, Narcissa Prentiss, 368
Whitman, Walt, 305, 306–307, 481
Whitney, Eli, 245, 320
Whitney, William, 585
Whitten, John C., 793
Wicker, Tom, 862
The Wide, Wide World (Warner), 309
Wild, Elizabeth, 54
The Wild One (film), 784
Wilde, Oscar, 585
Wilderness, battle of the, 436
Wiley, Harvey W., 623
Wilkins, Roy, 793
Wilkinson, James, 219, 220
Willard, Emma Hart, 293
Willard, Frances, 614
Willard, Samuel, 51
William of Orange, 75, 76
Williams, Eugene, 660
Williams, Roger, 47, 48
Williams v. Mississippi, 570
Willis, Albert S., 589
Willkie, Wendell, 736
Wilmot, David, 376
Wilmot Proviso, 376–377
Wilson, Edith Bolling, 665
Wilson, Sloan, 811

Wilson, Woodrow, 215, 626–627; and African Americans, 635; cabinet of, 796; declaration of war, 650–651; and domestic war effort, 652–653, 656; election of 1912, 626; election of 1916, 648; on government, 626, 627; Ho Chi Minh and, 846; immigration policy, 523; and labor, 652, 653, 660; Latin American policies, 629–631; and neutrality policy, 643–651; progressive reform under, 626–628; and Russia, 663; and Treaty of Versailles, 661–665; and women's suffrage, 656; and Woolworth Building, 526; and World War I, 641, 643, 646, 647, 650–651, 658
Wilson-Gorman Tariff, 567
Wingina, 25
The Winning of the West (Roosevelt), 354–355
Winthrop, John, 44, 47–48, 49
Wisconsin, La Follette and, 619, 620
Witchcraft hysteria, 75–76
Wolfe, James, 93, 95
Wolfe, Thomas, 680
Woman in the Nineteenth Century (Fuller), 304
Women: African American, 615; and birth control, 176–177, 672, 674–675; and childbirth, 52; in Civil War, 437; in colonies, 39, 51, 54, 55, 66–67, 70; discrimination against, 893–894, 895; dissatisfaction with domestic role, 811, 812, 892–893; early nineteenth-century, 297–298, 327; education of, 174–175, 293, 609, 896–897; employment of, 54, 234, 235, 325–326, 327, 503, 615, 620, 632, 656, 702, 741, 812, 893, 894, 896, 897; farmers, 564; in feminist theory, 895; in Great Depression, 702; household work, 327, 504, 677, 741; Italian immigrant, 519; legal status/rights, 55, 894; Native American, 9; New Deal and, 715–716; in 1920s, 681, 683, 684; in 1950s, 811, 812; novels by, 309–310; pioneer, 362; poverty among, 897; in Progressive Era, 614, 615–616, 620, 632; and prostitution, 285, 289, 614–615, 625, 683; revolutionary-era, 115, 144–146, 160–161, 163, 172–175; and sexual mores, 681, 682–683; slave, 342, 343; in South, 334, 425; in sports, 537–540; today, 896–897; Victorian ideals for, 517, 682; voting rights, 163, 164, 259–260, 299, 458, 459, 462–463, 556, 616, 617, 619, 655, 656, 684; and World War I, 656; in World War II, 741–742
Women's Army Corps, 741
Women's Christian Temperance Union, 614
Women's Committe of the Council of National Defense, 656
Women's movement: early, 297–299, 300, 304; and Equal Rights Amendment, 684, 894–895, 896; of 1960s, 892–897; and Seneca Falls Declaration and Resolutions, 300; against sex discrimination, 893–896; split in 1920s, 684; for suffrage, 458–459, 556, 616, 617, 619, 655, 656
Wood, Jethro, 246
Wood, Leonard, 595, 648
Woodley, Arthur E., 860
Woodmason, Charles, 286

Woodruff, Robert W., 738
Woodson, Carter, 689
Woodward, Bob, 913
Woolen Act, 77
Woolworth, Frank, 526
Woolworth Building, 526
Worcester v. Georgia, 269
Work. *See also* Labor: electricity's impact on, 530; Ford assembly line and, 676; household, 327, 504, 677, 741; industrial, 234, 235, 324–326, 502–505, 504–505, 620; late nineteenth-early twentieth century, 482, 502–505, 608; preindustrial, 323–324, 503; progressive reform of, 615, 620, 632; of slaves, 340–341
Working class, 327, 502–505, 526, 608, 619, 635. *See also* Poverty; Unskilled workers
Working Men's parties, 326
Workingmen's Benevolent Association, 506
Workmen's compensation, 620, 628, 632
Works Progress Administration, 710, 716, 717, 739
World War I, 640, 641–659, 666; Allied neutrality violations in, 646; casualties, 641, 643; economic policies during, 651–653; and immigration, 523; legacy of, 641, 730; neutrality of U.S. in, 643–651; political repression during, 654–655; preparedness controversy, 647–648; and progressivism, 631, 651; propaganda in, 653–654; reforms during, 655–656; social unrest following, 659–661; submarine warfare, 646–647, 649, 650; Treaty of Versailles, 661–666; U.S. in, 645, 650–651, 658–659; warfare in, 642–643, 644–645
World War II, 728–729, 731–759, 757; African Americans and, 742–743, 806; aid to Allies in, 735–746; beginning of, 734–735; casualties, 728–729, 759; consequences of, 759; D-Day, 747, 748–749; in Europe, 734–735, 745–750; events leading to, 731–734; mobilization for, 737–740; in Pacific, 736–737, 750–759; social changes during, 740–745, 759; and West, 827–828; Yalta Conference, 747–750
Wounded Knee (South Dakota): massacre, 471; seizure of, 902
Wright, Carroll D., 502
Wright, Frances, 298, 301
Wright, Harry, 535
Wright, Mose, 792, 793
Wright, Richard, 721
Writs of assistance, 107
Wyandot Indians, 238
Wyoming, 496, 556

XYZ Affair, 203

Yale, 538
Yalta Conference, 747–750, 752
Yancey, William L., 411, 426
Yellow fever, 198–199, 528
Yellow journalism, 591
Yeltsin, Boris, 925–928
Yerkes, Robert M., 658
Yorktown, battle of, 153–154
Yost, Fielding H., 538
Young, Brigham, 370
Young America program, 395
Younger brothers, 497
Youth: in 1950s, 784–785, 812–813; in 1960s, 858–860, 863–864, 890–892
Yucatan (ship), 596
Yucca Flats (Nevada), 830
Yugoslavia, 935

Zeg, Stephen, 775
Zimmermann, Arthur, 649
Zimmermann telegram, 649
Zoot suit riots, 743
Zorro, 354
Zuni Indians, 8, 357, 468